THE ROUGH GUIDE TO

Italy

We'resure you'll find it very useful for your trips all around Italy Fracesco Marta

written and researched by

**Robert Andrews, Ros Belford, Jonathan Buckley,
Martin Dunford, Natasha Foges, Tim Jepson,
Lucy Ratcliffe and Celia Woolfrey**

with additional contributions by

Gillian Arthur, Marc Di Duca, Charles Hebbert and Jo-Ann Titmarsh

roughguides.com

Contents

Introduction to
Italy

Ask an Italian where in the world they would most like to live, and the odds are that they will say "right here". Indeed, most people – not just Italians – have raved about Italy since tourism began, and to be honest the country really does have it all: one of the most diverse and beautiful landscapes in Europe; the world's greatest hoard of art treasures (many on display in fittingly spectacular cities and buildings); a climate that is on the whole benign; and, most important of all for many, a delicious and authentic national cuisine. The country is not perfect – its historic cities have often been marred by development, and beyond the showpiece sights the infrastructure is visibly straining – but as a visitor many of the old clichés still ring true; once you've visited, you may never want to travel anywhere else.

Italy might be the world's most celebrated tourist destination, but it only became a unified state in 1861, and as a result Italians often feel more loyalty to their region than to the nation as a whole – something manifest in its different cuisines, dialects, landscapes and often varying standards of living. However, if there is a single national Italian characteristic, it's to embrace life to the full – in the hundreds of local festivals taking place across the country on any given day to celebrate a saint or the local harvest; in the importance placed on good food; in the obsession with clothes and image; and in the daily ritual of the collective evening stroll or *passeggiata* – a sociable affair celebrated by young and old alike in every town and village across the country.

There is also the country's enormous **cultural legacy**: Tuscany alone has more classified historical monuments than any country in the world; there are considerable remnants of the Roman Empire all over the country, notably in Rome itself; and every region retains its own relics of an artistic tradition generally acknowledged to be among the world's richest. Yet if all you want to do is chill out, there's no reason to be put off. There are any number of places to just lie on a beach, from the resorts filled with regimented rows of sunbeds and umbrellas favoured by the Italians themselves, to

ABOVE PARMIGIANO REGGIANO CHEESE ON SHELVES, PARMA **RIGHT** CANAL GRANDE, VENICE secluded and less developed spots. And if you're looking for an active holiday, there's no better place: mountains run the country's length – from the Alps and Dolomites in the north right along the Apennines, which form the spine of the peninsula; skiing and other winter sports are practised avidly; and wildlife of all sorts thrives in the country's national parks.

Where to go

Rome, Italy's capital and the one city in the country that owes allegiance neither to the north or south, is a tremendous city quite unlike any other, and in terms of historical sights outstrips everywhere else in the country by some way. It's the focal point of **Lazio**, in part a poor and sometimes desolate region whose often rugged landscapes, particularly south of Rome, contrast with the more manicured beauty of the other central regions. The regions of **Piemonte** and **Lombardy**, in the northwest, make up the country's richest and most cosmopolitan region, and the two main centres, Turin and Milan, are its wealthiest cities. In their southern reaches, these regions are flat and scenically dull, especially Lombardy, but in the north the presence of the Alps shapes the character of each: skiing and hiking are prime activities, and the lakes and mountains of Lombardy are time-honoured tourist territory. **Liguria**, the small coastal province to the south, has long been known as the "Italian Riviera" and is accordingly crowded with sun-seekers for much of the summer. Nonetheless, it's a beautiful stretch of coast, and its capital, Genoa, is a vibrant, bustling port town with a long seafaring tradition.

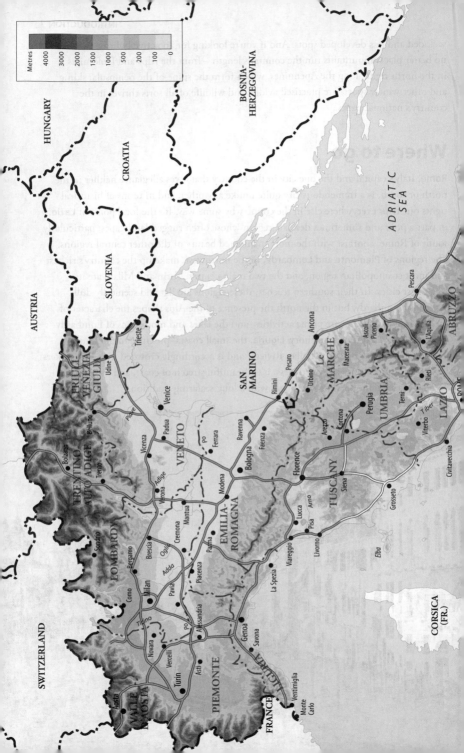

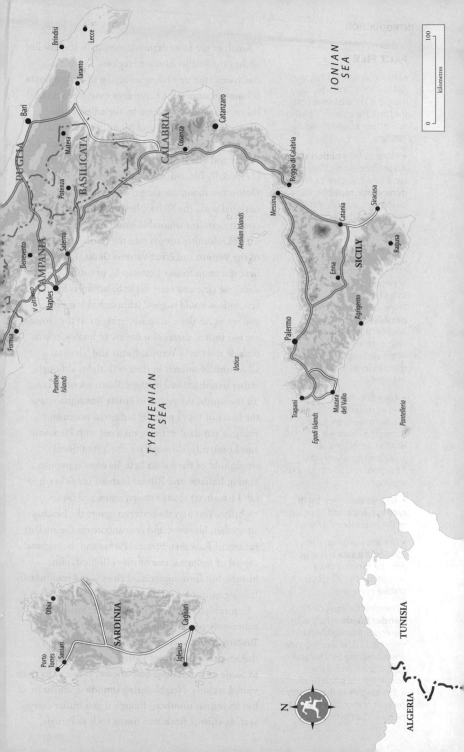

FACT FILE

- Napoleon claimed Italy was just "too long", and who can disagree? The **distance** from the tip of the country's "toe" to its northern border is about 1380km.

- Italy became a **nation state** in 1861, under King Vittorio Emanuele II, and has been a **democratic republic** since 1946, when the monarchy was abolished by popular referendum.

- The **parliament** consists of two houses, the Senate (315 seats) and the Chamber of Deputies (630 seats); both sit for five-year terms of office. The country has an elected **president**, but real power lies with the **prime minister**, who is generally the leader of the party with the biggest majority in the Chamber of Deputies.

- Italy's population is just over 61 million, over 4 million of whom live in the capital, Rome. The country is divided geographically and administratively into 15 regions and 5 autonomous regions.

- Italy has the lowest **birth rate** in Europe, and 20 percent of the population is over 65.

- The average Italian eats 25 kilos of **pasta** annually, and the nation drinks a staggering 14 billion cups of **coffee** every year.

- There's still a significant **gender divide** in Italy, with the country ranked 74th in the world in the recent gender equality survey (just behind Kazakhstan). And in the country of the *pizzaiolo*, it's a shocking thing that seventy percent of men claim never to have used an oven.

Much of the most dramatic mountain scenery lies within the smaller northern regions. In the far northwest, the tiny bilingual region of **Valle d'Aosta** is home to some of the country's most frequented ski resorts, and is bordered by the tallest of the Alps – the Matterhorn and Mont Blanc. In the northeast, **Trentino-Alto Adige**, another bilingual region and one in which the national boundary is especially blurred, marks the beginning of the Dolomites mountain range, where Italy's largest national park, the Stelvio, lies amid some of the country's most memorable landscapes.

The Dolomites stretch into the northeastern regions of the **Veneto** and **Friuli-Venezia Giulia**. However, here the main focus of interest is, of course, Venice: a unique city, and every bit as beautiful as its reputation would suggest (although this means you won't be alone in appreciating it). If the crowds are too much, there's also the arc of historic towns outside the city – Verona, Padua and Vicenza, all centres of interest in their own right, although rather overshadowed by their illustrious neighbour. To the south, the region of **Emilia-Romagna** was at the heart of Italy's postwar industrial boom and enjoys a standard of living on a par with Piemonte and Lombardy, although it's also a traditional stronghold of the Italian Left. Its coast is popular among Italians, and Rimini is about Italy's brashest (and trendiest) seaside resort, renowned for its nightlife. You may do better to ignore the beaches altogether, however, and concentrate on the ancient centres of Ravenna, Ferrara, Parma and the regional capital of Bologna, one of Italy's liveliest, most historic but least appreciated cities – and traditionally Italy's gastronomic and academic capital.

Central Italy represents perhaps the most commonly perceived image of the country, and **Tuscany**, with its classic rolling countryside and the art-packed towns of Florence, Pisa and Siena, to name only the three best-known, is one of its most visited regions. Neighbouring **Umbria** is similar in all but its tourist numbers, though it gets busier every year, as visitors flock into towns such as Perugia,

Author picks

We've spent loads of time in Italy over the years, but there are certain things we like to do, or places we have to visit, every time we return. Our favourite ways to spend time are below. For our definitive list of the highlights you really shouldn't miss, see pp.14–23.

Best beaches With 7600km of coastline, Italy is a great place to hang out on the beach, and although you have to put up with miles of parasols along the best stretches, we love the surfy vibe at Levanto, Liguria (p.208), and the diving and wildlife at Torre Guaceto in Puglia (p.829).

Ancient places Nowhere in Europe are there so many towns and villages where time seems to have stood still. Our favourites? The palaces and porticoes of Ferrara, Emilia-Romagna (p.490), the perfectly preserved village of Pienza, Tuscany (p.606), or the amazing sassi of Matera in Basilicata (p.845).

Hot, hot, hot? Italy lies at the centre of the most volcanic regions in Europe, something you can experience first-hand by climbing Vesuvius (p.767), Etna (p.906) or Stromboli (p.900), or, more easily, by just visiting the Solfatara just outside Naples (p.763).

Road trips There's nothing quite so Italian as cruising along a scenic coast road or through a mountain pass in a stylish convertible, so what are you waiting for? There are any number of great routes to do just that, and not just the obvious Amalfi Coast road in Campania (p.786), though that is as spectacular as you might expect, but also the Alghero to Bosa coast road in Sardinia (p.959) and the Great Dolomites Road, Trentino-Alto Adige (p.332).

Underground Italy Italy is full of subterranean wonders, like the amazing Toirano caves, Liguria (p.197) or the Grotta Gigante, Friuli-Venezia Giulia, the world's largest accessible cave (p.444).

> Our author recommendations don't end here. We've flagged up our favourite places – a perfectly sited hotel, an atmospheric café, a special restaurant – throughout the guide, highlighted with the ★ symbol.

FROM TOP AMALFI COAST ROAD; FERRARA, EMILIA-ROMAGNA

Spoleto and Assisi. Further east still, **Le Marche** has gone the same way, with old stone cottages being turned into foreign-owned holiday homes; the highlights of the region are the ancient towns of Urbino and Ascoli Piceno. South of Le Marche, the hills begin to pucker into mountains in the twin regions of **Abruzzo** and **Molise**, one of Italy's remotest areas, centring on one of the country's highest peaks – the Gran Sasso d'Italia.

The south proper begins with the region of **Campania**. Its capital, Naples, is a unique, unforgettable city, the spiritual heart of the Italian south, and close to some of Italy's finest ancient sites in Pompeii and Herculaneum, not to mention the country's most spectacular stretch of coast around Amalfi. **Basilicata** and **Calabria**, which make up the instep and toe of Italy's boot, are harder territory but still rewarding, the emphasis less on art, more on the landscape and quiet, relatively unspoilt coastlines. **Puglia**, the "heel" of Italy, has underrated pleasures, too, notably the landscape of its Gargano peninsula,

ICE CREAM

The taste of real Italian ice cream, eaten in Italy, is absolutely unbeatable. **Gelato**, as it's known, is the country's favourite dessert, and there's no better way to end a day, as Italians do, than with a stroll through the streets sampling a *gelato* while enjoying the cool of the evening. Italian ice cream really is better than any other, and like most Italian food this is down to the local insistence on using whole milk and eggs, and adding only naturally derived flavours. Everywhere but the tiniest village will have at least one *gelateria*, and many cafés serve ice cream as well. If you want to sample the very best, look for the signs saying "*artigianale*", which means that the ice cream is produced according to strictly traditional methods, or "*produzione propria*", which means it's home-made. There's usually a veritable cornucopia of flavours (*gusti*) to choose from, from those regarded as the classics – like lemon (*limone*) and hazelnut (*nocciola*) – through staples including vanilla with chocolate chips (*stracciatella*) and strawberry (*fragola*), to house specialities that might include cinnamon (*canella*), chocolate with chilli pepper (*cioccolato con peperoncino*) or even pumpkin (*zucca*).

ABOVE GELATERIA, SAN GIMIGNANO, TUSCANY **RIGHT** SCOPELLO, SICILY

CALCIO

Calcio – football, or soccer – is Italy's national sport, and enjoys a big following across the country. It's usually possible to get tickets to see one of the top sides – as long as they're not playing each other – and it's one of the best introductions to modern Italian culture you'll find.

Since World War II, Italian football has been dominated by **Internazionale** and **AC Milan** (of Milan) and **Juventus** (Turin), who have between them won the *scudetto* or **Serie A** (Italy's premier division) 54 times. It's a testament to the English origins of the game that AC Milan, as well as another big club, Genoa, continue to use anglicized names, and to sport the cross of St George in their insignia. Unfortunately, the other thing that has been copied from the English is **hooliganism**, which remains a problem in Italian football, along with a latent degree of racism, and, perhaps most notoriously, corruption – the country still hasn't forgotten the match-fixing scandal of 2006 ("Calciopoli"), and allegations regularly resurface at the highest levels. Juventus, AC Milan and Inter remain the top three teams, although the two Rome clubs, **AS Roma** and to a lesser extent **SS Lazio**, regularly do well, although Lazio's star has faded in recent years and their fans are perceived as among the worst examples of Italy's right-wing lunatic fringe. In Tuscany, **Fiorentina** reckon themselves a big club, while in the south **Napoli** are beginning to relive their Eighties "glory days", when they were led by Diego Maradona, although they still struggle to fill their giant 80,000 capacity stadium. We've given details of the big city clubs in the Guide, but wherever you are, grab one of Italy's three sports papers – *Gazzetta dello Sport, Corriere dello Sport* and *Tuttosport* – to see what's on.

the souk-like qualities of its capital, Bari, and the Baroque glories of Lecce in the far south. As for **Sicily**, the island is really a place apart, with a wide mixture of attractions ranging from some of the finest preserved Hellenistic treasures in Europe, to a couple of Italy's most appealing beach resorts in Taormina and Cefalu, not to mention some gorgeous upland scenery. Come this far south and you're closer to Africa than Milan, and it shows in the climate, the architecture and the cooking, with couscous featuring on many menus in the west of the island. **Sardinia**, too, feels far removed from the Italian mainland, especially in its relatively undiscovered interior, although you may be content just to laze on its fine beaches, which are among Italy's best.

When to go

If you're planning to visit popular areas, especially beach resorts, avoid July and especially August, when the weather can be too hot and the crowds at their most congested. In August, when most Italians are on holiday, you can expect the crush to be especially bad in the resorts, and the scene in the major historic cities – Rome, Florence, Venice – to be slightly artificial, as the only people around are fellow tourists. The nicest time to visit, in terms of the weather and lack of crowds, is April to late June, and September or October. If you're planning to swim, however, bear in mind that only the south of the country is likely to be warm enough outside the May to September period. For more information and a temperature chart, see Basics (p.44).

LEFT ITALIAN FOOTBALL FANS **ABOVE** COUNTRYSIDE NEAR SAN QUIRICO D'ORCIA, SOUTHERN TUSCANY

24

things not to miss

It's not possible to see everything that Italy has to offer in one trip – and we don't suggest you try. What follows is a selective taste, in no particular order, of the country's highlights: outstanding buildings and ancient sites, spectacular natural wonders, great food and idyllic beaches. All entries have a page reference to take you straight into the Guide, where you can find out more.

1

1 CENTRO STORICO, ROME

Page 55

There's so much to see in Rome that aimlessly wandering the city's fantastic old centre can yield a surprise at every turn, whether it's an ancient statue, a marvellous Baroque fountain or a bustling piazza.

2 LECCE

Page 830

This exuberant city of Baroque architecture and opulent churches is one of the must-sees of the Italian south.

3 SICILY'S GREEK RUINS

Pages 904, 917 & 925

The ancient theatres at Siracusa and Taormina are magnificent summer stages for Greek drama, while the temple complex at nearby Agrigento is one of the finest such sites outside Greece itself.

4 WINE BARS

Page 38

Italian wine is undergoing a resurgence, and there's nothing like sampling local varieties in an *enoteca* or wine bar, accompanied by a plate of regional cheese and cold meats.

10

11

12

19

20

21 AGRITURISMI
Page 35

Farmstays and rural retreats are one of Italy's lesser-known specialities and can be among the country's most spectacular and bucolic places to stay.

22 HIKING IN THE DOLOMITES
Page 309

The spiky landscape of the Dolomites is perfect hiking country, covered in dramatic long-distance trails.

23 BASILICA DI SAN FRANCESCO, ASSISI
Page 642

The burial place of St Francis and one of Italy's greatest church buildings, with frescoes by Giotto and Simone Martini.

24 VATICAN MUSEUMS, ROME
Page 94

The largest and richest collection of art and culture in the world. You'd be mad to miss it.

23

24

Itineraries

Italy is a large and complex destination and you can't hope to savour it all on one visit; indeed, experiencing and appreciating the country properly, in all its aspects, is arguably a lifetime's work. Nonetheless sooner or later you are going to need to decide on where to go; we've put together a few itineraries to help you out.

FOODIES' ITALY

Think of Italy and you think of food, and with so many regional variations you can try something different everywhere you go. Here's our rundown of the best places to stop off if you want to enjoy a foodie tour.

❶ **Truffles and wine in Alba** If you're here at the right time of year you may be able to sample the town's extraordinary white truffles; and at any time you can taste the excellent local wine. **See p.160**

❷ **Genoa, Liguria** The food of Liguria and in particular Genoa is among the country's most distinctive and best, the home of pesto, foccacia, *farinata* and everywhere great fish and seafood. **See p.180**

❸ **Bologna, Emilia-Romagna** Regarded as the culinary capital of Italy and much the best place to do a course in mastering Italian cuisine. **See p.465**

❹ **Norcia, Umbria** Famous nationwide for all kinds of pork products, from *guanciale* to pancetta, and – in season – superb black truffles too. **See p.661**

❺ **Rome** The "cucina povera" of Rome isn't the country's most well-known regional cuisine, but we think it's maybe the best, with gutsy pasta dishes and a focus on offal and the poorer cuts of meat – perfect for the more adventurous foodie. **See p.55**

❻ **Naples, Campania** Perhaps one of the most fun and enduring experiences you can have in Italy is to learn how to make pizza and pasta in their true home just outside Naples. **See p.773**

ITALY OUTDOORS: MOUNTAINS AND WATER

Italy has a wonderful mix of high mountains, lakes and sea, making it the ideal country for an outdoors holiday that takes in a variety of activities.

❶ **Gran Paradiso, Valle d'Aosta** Some of the most beautiful and best-organized high-altitude trekking in the country. **See p.169**

❷ **Hiking the Alta Via, Liguria** This long-distance high-level trail takes you the length of Liguria, and offers a very different view of the region than the resorts on the coast. **See p.201**

❸ **Windsurfing, Riva del Garda, Lombardy** There's no better place in the country for quality windsurfing and sailing. **See p.297**

❹ **Vie Ferrate, Trentino-Alto Adige** High-altitude climbing the Italian way, using the fixed ladders and pegs of the northern Dolomites. **See p.316**

❺ **Gran Sasso** The Gran Sasso national park holds the highest peaks of the Apennines, including the 3000m Corno Grande. **See p.716**

ABOVE GRAN SASSO; BAPTISTRY DOOR, FLORENCE

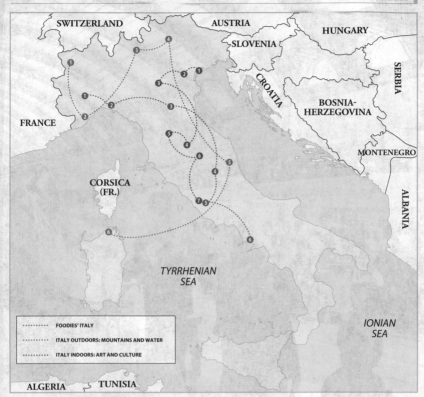

⑥ Kitesurfing, Porto Pollo, Sardinia Sardinia's northern Costa Smeralda is the home of all manner of waterborne activities, not least fab opportunities for kitesurfing. **See p.970**

ITALY INDOORS: ART AND CULTURE

No country in the world boasts the same volume of cultural artefacts, and you can stumble across great art displayed in fine historic buildings just about anywhere, but if that's your interest you may want to follow the itinerary below.

❶ Venice Italy's greatest maritime state, ossified in stone and oils. **See p.348**

❷ Padua, Veneto The amazingly preserved Giotto frescoes of Padua's Scrovegni chapel, dating back to the fourteenth century, are one of the absolute highlights of western European art. **See p.400**

❸ Mantua, Lombardy Two palaces, plastered with the work of two very different artists – Mantegna's beautiful refined frescoes in the Palazzo Ducale and Giulio Romano's later Mannerist experiment in the Palazzo Te. **See p.252**

❹ Arezzo, Tuscany Home to a hugely famous fresco cycle by Piero della Francesca, and to other works by the fifteenth-century painter. **See p.612**

❺ Florence Birthplace of the Italian Renaissance, with Ghiberti's famous bronze door, Brunelleschi's dome, and, er, the Uffizi too. **See p.513**

❻ Assisi One of the greatest works of art you can see in a church, Assisi's basilica is covered top to toe with fourteenth-century frescoes. **See p.642**

❼ Rome Where to start, but one of the great things about Rome is the chance to see some of the world's greatest paintings in the places they were meant for, best of all the many works of Caravaggio that remain in the city. **See p.55**

PASSENGERS AT MILAN'S STAZIONE CENTRALE

Basics

Getting there

The easiest way to get to Italy is to fly. Price-comparison sites such as ⓦ**sky scanner.com** and ⓦ**edreams.com** are invaluable for bargain-hunting, though it is usually cheaper to make bookings direct through an operator's website. Rail connections with the rest of Europe are also good and link well into the comprehensive national network.

Flights from the UK and Ireland

Of the scheduled **airlines** flying the Italian routes, British Airways (ⓦba.com) and Alitalia (ⓦalitalia .com) regularly serve most of the country including Turin, Milan, Rome, Bologna, Cagliari, Pisa, Verona, Venice, Naples and Catania. The majority of the routes are from London but they also fly from Edinburgh, Manchester, Birmingham and Bristol. Aer Lingus (ⓦaerlingus.com) has direct flights from Dublin to Milan, Bologna, Rome, Catania, Venice and Naples, as well as Cork and Belfast to Rome. Of the **low-cost carriers**, easyJet (ⓦeasyjet.com), Thomson (ⓦhttp://flights.thomson.co.uk), Jet2 (ⓦjet2.com), flybe (ⓦflybe.com) and Ryanair (ⓦryanair.com) fly from London and numerous smaller airports to bases throughout Italy and its islands.

Prices depend on how far in advance you book and the popularity of the destination, although **season** is also a factor: unless you book very well in advance, a ticket to anywhere between June and September will cost more than in the depths of winter (excluding Christmas and New Year). Note also that it is generally more expensive to fly at weekends. Book far enough in advance with one of the low-cost airlines and you can pick up a ticket for under £60 return, even in summer; book anything less than three weeks in advance and this could triple in price. Scheduled airline fares, booked within a month of travel, will cost around £120 out of season, and at least £250 in summer.

Flights from the US and Canada

Between them, Delta (ⓦdelta.com), Alitalia (ⓦalitalia .com) and American Airlines (ⓦaa.com) offer daily flights from New York, Atlanta, Los Angeles, Miami and Chicago to Rome and Milan; one short layover greatly extends the network. In addition, many European carriers fly to Italy (via their capitals) from all major US and Canadian cities – for example British Airways (ⓦba.com) via London, Lufthansa (ⓦlufthansa.com) via Frankfurt, KLM (ⓦklm.com) via Amsterdam, and so on.

The **direct scheduled fares** don't vary as much as you might think, and you'll more often than not be basing your choice around things like flight timings, routes and gateway cities, ticket restrictions, and even the airline's reputation for comfort and service. The cheapest **round-trip fares** to Rome or Milan, travelling midweek in low season, start at around US$450 from New York or Boston, and can rise to around US$1200 during the summer, though you can make considerable savings by combining flights from two carriers. Add another US$100–200 for flights from LA, Miami and Chicago. Note that these prices do not include taxes.

Air Canada (ⓦaircanada.com) has flights from Toronto to Rome for around Can$1000.

Flights from Australia, New Zealand and South Africa

Return fares to Rome and Milan from the main cities in Australia go for around Aus$1700 in low season, and around Aus$2000 in high season. You are likely to get most flexibility by travelling with Malaysian (ⓦmalaysia-airlines.com), Thai (ⓦthaiair .com), British Airways (ⓦba.com) or Qantas (ⓦqantas .com), though the cheapest fares are with Air China (ⓦairchina.com).

There are no direct flights to Italy from New Zealand. Return fares to Rome cost from NZ$2000– 2500, with operators including Air New Zealand (ⓦairnz.co.nz) and JAL (ⓦjal.com).

A BETTER KIND OF TRAVEL

At Rough Guides we are passionately committed to travel. We feel strongly that only through travelling do we truly come to understand the world we live in and the people we share it with – plus tourism has brought a great deal of **benefit** to developing economies around the world over the last few decades. But the growth in tourism has also damaged some places irreparably, and of course **climate change** is exacerbated by most forms of transport, especially flying. All Rough Guide flights are offset, and every year we donate money to a variety of charities devoted to combating the effects of climate change.

Various carriers serve **South Africa**, usually with a stop in their European or Middle Eastern hub. Return fares start at around ZAR5000.

Trains

Travelling by **train** to Italy from the UK can be an enjoyable and environmentally friendly way of getting to the country, and you can stop off in other parts of Europe on the way. Trains pass through Paris and head down through France towards Milan. A standard-class return **fare** from London to Paris using Eurostar (2hr 15min) starts at £70; travelling by high-speed TGV from Paris to Milan (7hr 25min) costs from £95. Fares from Paris to both Rome (15hr) and Venice (13hr) start at £100 return per person in a six-berth couchette.

The Franco-Italian Thello **sleeper** runs every evening from Paris to Venice via Milan, Padua, Verona and Vicenza; it departs from Paris Gare de Lyon at 7.45pm, and arrives in Venice thirteen hours later. Those heading straight to Rome (11hr 30min) need to change trains in Milan. Accommodation is in four- and six-berth couchettes, and one-, two- and three-berth cabins – the more you pay, the fewer people you share with; women can opt to share with other women if they are travelling alone. All services have a restaurant car and a steward who looks after each carriage. Prices vary hugely depending on the time of year and demand. The standard fare from Paris to Milan is £70, but purchasing tickets online in advance, you can pay as little as £31 (the so-called Smart fare).

If you really want to push the boat out, the **Orient Express** still runs from London to Venice, offering around thirty hours of pampered luxury starting from £2370, including all meals.

Advance booking on trains is essential (and can often save you quite a lot of money); there are also discounts for children and rail-pass holders. Take into account also that if you travel via Paris on Eurostar you will have to change stations, so you should give yourself a good hour (more like 1hr 30min if you have to queue for metro tickets) to travel on the metro from the Gare du Nord to the Gare de Lyon (for daytime services) or the Gare de Bercy (for sleeper trains). Allow more time for the return journey across Paris, as there is a minimum thirty-minute check-in for Eurostar departures. Note that there are no left-luggage lockers at the Gare de Bercy.

The **Man in Seat 61** website (Ⓦ seat61.com) offers exhaustive information on travelling by train, with details of routes, times and fares.

Rail passes

InterRail and **Eurail** passes offer unlimited rail travel throughout Italy and other European countries, but must be bought before leaving home. For details of Italy-only passes, see p.30.

InterRail

InterRail passes are only available to those who have been resident in Europe for six months or more and are not valid in the country of residence. They come in first- and second-class over-26 and (cheaper) under-26 versions. The passes are available to a combination of countries for five days within a ten-day period (£235 second class, £154 under-26), ten days within a 22-day period (£336 second class, £227 under-26), 22 consecutive days (£435 second class, £290 under-26) or one month unlimited (£562 second class, £372 under-26).

InterRail passes do not include travel between Britain and the Continent, although pass-holders are eligible for discounts on rail travel in Britain and Northern Ireland and cross-Channel ferries, as well as free travel on the Brindisi–Patras ferry between Italy and Greece, and the Villa San Giovanni–Messina crossing to Sicily.

Eurail

A **Eurail Pass** is for non-European residents and comes in a variety of forms: Italy only, Italy with France, Greece or Spain, Italy with bordering countries or with twenty other European countries. The pass, which must be purchased before arrival in Europe, allows unlimited free first-class train travel in combinations from ten days to three months. A one-month over-26 pass costs €853 (under-26 €556). There are numerous small-group, youth and saver versions, and passes can be purchased online or from the agents listed below.

RAIL CONTACTS

Eurail Ⓦ eurail.com.
European Rail UK Ⓣ 020 7619 1083, Ⓦ europeanrail.com.
Eurostar UK Ⓣ 0843 218 6186, Ⓦ eurostar.com
International Rail Ⓣ 0871 231 0790, Ⓦ international-rail.com.
InterRail Ⓦ interrailnet.com.
Rail Europe UK Ⓣ 0844 848 4064, Ⓦ raileurope.co.uk; US Ⓣ 1 800 622 8600, Canada Ⓣ 1 800 361 7245, Ⓦ raileurope.com.
Rail Plus Australia Ⓣ 1300 555 003, Ⓦ railplus.com.au; New Zealand Ⓣ 64 9 377 5415, Ⓦ railplus.co.nz.

Buses

It's difficult to see why anyone would want to travel to Italy by **bus**. National Express Eurolines do, however, have occasional bargain offers, and tickets cost from £62 one-way from London to Milan. The Milan service departs daily and takes around

24 hours. On Monday, Wednesday, Friday and Saturday it continues to Parma, Bologna, Florence, Rome and Naples, this last taking a gruelling 36 hours. There are also departures four times a week from London to Venice, taking around 29 hours.

Busabout Explorer is a popular option with backpackers. There are various Italian tours available as well as Europe-wide hop-on, hop-off services for around €490 per person.

BUS CONTACTS

Busabout UK ☎ 0845 026 7514, ⓦ busabout.com.
Eurolines UK ☎ 0871 781 8181, ⓦ eurolines.com.

Package and special interest holidays

As well as the travel agents offering **flight-and-accommodation package** deals, an increasing number of operators organize **specialist holidays** to Italy – covering walking, art and archeology, food and wine, short breaks to coincide with opera festivals or even football matches. If you want to rent a car in Italy, it's well worth checking **fly-drive** deals with tour operators (and flight agents) before you leave.

TOUR OPERATORS

North South Travel UK ☎ 01245 608291, ⓦ northsouthtravel .co.uk. Friendly, competitive travel agency offering discounted fares worldwide. Profits are used to support projects in the developing world, especially the promotion of sustainable tourism.
STA Travel UK ☎ 0871 230 0040, US ☎ 1 800 781 4040, Australia ☎ 134 782, New Zealand ☎ 0800 474 400, South Africa ☎ 0861 781 781; ⓦ statravel.co.uk. Worldwide specialists in independent travel; also student IDs, travel insurance, car rental, rail passes, and more. Good discounts for students and under-26s.
Trailfinders UK ☎ 0845 058 5858, Ireland ☎ 01 677 7888, Australia ☎ 1300 780 212; ⓦ trailfinders.com. One of the best-informed and most efficient agents for independent travellers.
Travel CUTS Canada ☎ 1 866 246 9762, US ☎ 1 800 592 2887; ⓦ travelcuts.com. Canadian youth and student travel firm.
USIT Ireland ☎ 01/602 1906, Northern Ireland ☎ 028 9032 7111, ⓦ usit.ie. Ireland's main student and youth travel specialists.

ITALY SPECIALISTS

Abercrombie and Kent UK ☎ 0845 485 1520, ⓦ abercrombiekent .co.uk. Luxury cultural holidays.
Alternative Travel Group UK ☎ 01865 315 678, ⓦ atg-oxford .co.uk. Walking and cycling holidays.
Backroads US ☎ 1 800 462 2848, ⓦ backroads.com. Cooking, cycling and hiking holidays, including family trips.
Central Holidays US ☎ 1 800 539 7098, ⓦ centralholidays.com. Independent and escorted tours plus city breaks.

CIT US & Canada ☎ 1 800 387 0711, ⓦ cittours.ca. Huge range of well-organized themed holidays and tours, plus advice for independent travellers on hotels.
Context Travel ⓦ contexttravel.com. Thematic walking tours for the "intellectually curious" in Rome, Florence, Venice and Naples, either in small groups of up to six or privately.
Long Travel UK ☎ 01694 722 193, ⓦ long-travel.co.uk. Well-established family company specializing in southern Italy, Sicily and Sardinia.
Martin Randall Travel UK ☎ 020 8742 3355, ⓦ martinrandall.com. Cultural tours focusing on art, architecture, music, archeology, gastronomy and history.
Mountain Travel–Sobek US ☎ 1 888 831 7526, ⓦ mtsobek.com. Hiking and special interest tours around Italy.
Walkabout Gourmet Adventures Australia ☎ 02 9871 5526, ⓦ walkaboutgourmet.com. Classy food, wine and walking tours.

Getting around

Italy is a big country and unless you opt for a one-base holiday you will probably find yourself travelling around a fair bit. Both rail and bus services are good value and relatively efficient while regular ferries service the islands and local buses link more out-of-the-way areas. Internal flights can be worthwhile for some of the longer journeys – and may even work out cheaper than travelling by train. Naturally, you'll have most flexibility with your own transport.

We've detailed train, bus and ferry frequencies in the "Arrival and departure" sections within the Guide; note that these refer to regular working-day schedules (Mon–Sat); services can be much reduced or even nonexistent on Sundays and in August.

By rail

The Italian train system is one of the least expensive in Europe, reasonably comprehensive and, in the north of the country at least, pretty efficient. Italian trains are run by **Ferrovie dello Stato** (**FS**; ⓦ ferrovie dellostato.it), under the brand name **Trenitalia** (☎ 89 20 21), operating a comprehensive network across the country with numerous types of train. Most are pretty basic, with no refreshments. **Eurocity** (**EC**) and **Euronight** (**EN**) trains connect the major Italian cities with cities such as Paris, Vienna, Hamburg and Barcelona. A new high-speed line (Turin, Milan, Bologna, Florence, Rome, Naples, Salerno) **forms** part of the Eurostar network, served by the swish, super-comfortable 300km/hr **Frecciarossa**. Two other luxury trains, **Frecciabianca** and **Frecciargento,** are

STAMP IT

All stations have yellow validating machines in which passengers must stamp their ticket before embarking on their journey. However, if your ticket is booked for a specific train, validation is not necessary. If in doubt, ask. Look out for them as you come onto the platform: if you fail to **validate your ticket** you'll be given a hefty on-the-spot fine.

also capable of high speeds, but currently also run on conventional tracks. The Frecciargento runs on routes between Rome and the following stations: Venice, Verona and Bolzano, Bari and Lecce, Lamezia Terme and Reggio Calabria. The Frecciabianca runs on the following routes: Turin/Milan to Venice, Udine and Trieste; Milan and Genova to Pisa and Rome; and from Venice, Turin, Milan, Bologna down the Adriatic coast to Bari, Lecce and Taranto. Reservations are required before you board for all of these services, and even if you have a rail pass (see p.28) you will need to pay a small supplement. However, tickets are best purchased in advance online.

Diretto (**D**) and **Interregionale** (**IR**) trains are the common long-distance expresses, calling only at larger stations. Although reservations are not required for these trains, it's worth **reserving** seats if you're making a long journey, especially in summer, when they can get very crowded. Note that even if all seats have been sold, you may be able to travel – as long as you are prepared to stand or squat for most of the journey. Reservations can be made at any major train station or travel agent, or via Trenitalia agents (see p.28). Lastly, there are the **Regionale** (**R**) services, which stop at every place with a population higher than zero.

In addition to the routes operated by FS, there are a number of **privately run** lines, using separate stations but charging similar fares. Where they're worth using, these are detailed in the Guide.

Timetables and fares

Timings and route information are posted up at train stations. If you're travelling extensively invest in the *In Treno In Tutt'Italia* timetable (available as a book or a CD, €5 for either), which covers the main routes and is sold at train-station newspaper stands. Digital versions of the *Tutt'Italia* (€3.90) and regional timetables (€1.50) are sold online (Ⓦtrenitalia.express.it).

Basic fares are calculated by the kilometre, with supplements added depending on the type of train. There are huge savings to be had by booking in advance online. As a rough guide, a second-class one-way fare from Rome to Milan can cost between €19 and €73.50 for the six-hour journey on the Intercity or Frecciabianca, and between €29 and €86 for the three-hour journey on the Frecciarossa.

Sleepers (*cuccetta*) are available on many long-distance services, and prices vary according to the length of journey and whether or not you're sharing. **Children** aged 4–12 pay half-price; under-4s (not occupying a seat) travel free. Return tickets are valid within two months of the outward journey, but as two one-way tickets cost the same it's hardly worth bothering.

Rail passes

A **rail pass** is unlikely to be worth your while for an Italy-only trip. Prices are low and as you need to have a reservation for the faster trains, the convenience of a pass is outweighed by the extra queues and booking fees.

Europe-wide **InterRail** and **Eurail** passes (see p.28) are accepted on the Trenitalia network, though you will still have to book for certain trains and pay a supplement for travel on the Freccia trains; children's, youth (under-26) and group tickets are available.

TIMETABLE READING

On **timetables** — and parking signs too — *lavorativo* or *feriale* is the word for the Monday-to-Saturday service, represented by two crossed hammers; and *festivo* means that a train runs only on Sundays and holidays, symbolized by a Christian cross.

Some other common terms on timetables are:

escluso sabato	not including Saturdays
si effettua fino al …	running until …
si effettua dal …	starting from …
giornalmente	daily
prenotazione obbligatoria	reservation obligatory
estivo	summer
invernale	winter

By bus

Trains don't go everywhere and sooner or later you'll probably have to use **regional buses** (*autobus*). Nearly all places are connected by some kind of bus service, but in out-of-the-way towns and villages schedules can be sketchy and are drastically reduced – sometimes nonexistent – on weekends, especially on Sundays. Bear in mind also that in rural areas schedules are often designed with the working and/or school day in mind – meaning a frighteningly early start if you want to catch that day's one bus out of town, and occasionally a complete absence of services during school holidays.

There's no national **bus company**, though a few regional ones do operate beyond their own immediate area. **Bus terminals** or *autostazione*, are often conveniently located next to the train station; wherever possible we've detailed their whereabouts in the text. In smaller towns and villages, most buses pull in at the central piazza; timetables are widely available. Buy **tickets** immediately before you travel from the bus station ticket office, or on the bus itself; on longer hauls you can try to buy them in advance online direct from the bus company, but seat reservations are not normally possible. If you want to get off, ask *Posso scendere?*; "the next stop" is *la prossima fermata*.

City buses are always cheap, usually costing a flat fare of around €1. **Tickets** are commonly available from newsagents and tobacconists, but also from anywhere displaying a sticker saying "tickets" or "*biglietti*", including many campsite shops and hotel front desks. Once on board, you must validate your ticket in the machine at the front or back of the bus. The whole system is based on trust, though in most cities checks for fare-dodging are regularly made, and hefty spot-fines are levied against offenders. Several cities, including Rome, now allow you to buy tickets on board – usually for a supplement of 50c. A useful site is **ⓦ** busstation.net/main/busita .htm, which has links to websites of hundreds of Italian bus companies.

WALK/DON'T WALK

It's worth bearing in mind that cars do not automatically stop at **pedestrian crossings** in Italy. Even on crossings with traffic lights you can be subjected to some close calls. Note that when there's a green light for pedestrians to go, it may be green for one of the lines of traffic too.

By car

Travelling **by car** in Italy is relatively painless, though cities and their ring roads can be hard work. The roads are good, the motorway network very comprehensive, and the notorious Italian drivers rather less erratic than their reputation suggests – except in Sicily and the south. The best plan is to avoid driving in cities as much as possible; the congestion, proliferation of complex one-way systems and confusing signage can make it a nightmare.

Bear in mind that **traffic** can be heavy on main roads (particularly over public holiday weekends and the first and last weekends of August) and appalling in city centres. Rush hour during the week usually runs from 7.30am to 9am and from 5pm to 9pm, when roads in and around the major cities can be gridlocked.

Although Italians are by no means the world's worst drivers they don't win any **safety** prizes either. The secret is to make it very clear what you're going to do – and then do it. A particular danger for unaccustomed drivers is the large number of scooters that can appear suddenly from the blind spot or dash across junctions and red lights with alarming recklessness.

Most **petrol stations** give you the choice of self-service (*Fai da te*) or, for a few centesimi more per litre, someone will fill the tank and usually wipe down the windscreen while they're at it. Petrol stations often have the same working hours as shops, which means they'll be closed for a couple of hours at noon, shut up shop at around 7pm and are likely to be closed on Sundays. Outside these times many have a self-service facility payable into a machine between the pumps by bank note or, more rarely, credit card; these are often not well advertised so you might need to go onto the forecourt to check.

Rules of the road

Rules of the road are straightforward: drive on the right; at junctions, where there's any ambiguity, give precedence to vehicles coming from the right; observe the speed limits – 50kph in built-up areas, 110kph on dual carriageways and 130kph on autostradas (for camper vans, these limits are 50kph, 80kph and 100kph respectively); and don't drink and drive. Drivers need to have their dipped headlights on while using any road outside a built-up area.

The centres of many Italian towns and villages have **Zona Traffico Limitato** (ZTL; restricted traffic areas) where vehicle access is for residents only. These zones are marked by a red-rimmed circular road sign giving the hours and days of the limitation and are vigorously enforced, often by police on the ground as well as by cameras. Note that car-rental companies invariably pass the fine on. If your hotel is within one of these areas make sure the reception arranges a provisional transit permit with the local police.

If you're bringing your own car, as well as current insurance, you need a valid driving licence and an international driving permit if you're a non-EU licence holder. If you hold a UK pre-1991 driving licence you'll need an international driving permit or to update your licence to a photocard version. It's compulsory to carry your car documents and passport while you're driving, and you can be fined on the spot if you cannot present them when stopped by the police. It's also obligatory to carry a warning triangle and a fluorescent jacket in case of breakdown. For more information, consult ⓦ theaa.com.

Motorway driving

All **motorways** (*autostrade*) are toll roads. Take a ticket as you join the motorway and pay on exit; the amount due is flashed up on a screen in front of you. Paying by cash is the most straightforward option – booths are marked "cash/*contanti*" and colour-coded white. To pay by credit card follow the Viacard sign (colour-coded blue). Avoid the Telepass lane (colour-coded yellow), which is for drivers holding post-paid electronic cards. Be alert as you get into lane as traffic zigzags in and out at high speed to get pole position at the shortest-looking queue. Rates aren't especially high but they can mount up on a long journey. Since other roads can be frustratingly slow, tolls are well worth it over long distances, but be prepared for queues at exits at peak times.

Parking

Parking can be a problem. Don't be surprised to see cars parked just about anywhere, notably on pavements, seemingly working tram lines and bus stops – it would be unwise to follow suit. Parking attendants are especially active in tourist areas and if you get fed up with driving around and settle for a space in a *zona di rimozione* (tow-away zone), don't expect your car to be there when you get back.

Most towns and villages have pay-and-display areas just outside the centre, but they can get very full during high season. An increasing number of towns operate a colour-coded parking scheme: **blue-zone** parking spaces (delineated by a blue line) usually have a maximum stay of one or two hours; they cost around €0.70–1.50 per hour (pay at meters, to attendants wearing authorizing badges or buy scratch-cards from local tobacconists) but are sometimes free at lunch-times, after 8pm and on Sundays. Meters can usually be fed the night before to allow a lie-in in the morning. Much coveted **white-zone** spaces (white lines) are

free; **yellow-zone** areas (yellow lines) are reserved for residents. In smaller towns, to use the designated areas, it's handy to have a mini clock-like dial which you set and display in the windscreen, to indicate when you parked and that you're still within the allowed limit. Rental cars generally come equipped with these, and some tourist offices have them too.

Car parks, usually small, enclosed garages, are universally expensive, costing up to €20 a day in big cities; it's not unknown for hotels to state that they have parking and then direct you to the nearest paying garage. Parking at night is easier than during the day, but make sure you're not parked in a street that turns into a market in the morning or on the one day of the week when it's cleaned in the small hours, otherwise you're likely to be towed.

Never leave anything visible in the car when you're not using it, including the radio. Certain cities have appalling reputations for theft – in Naples, some rental agencies won't insure a car left anywhere except in a locked garage. A patrolled car park is probably the safest option for during the night, especially if you have foreign plates.

Breakdown

If you **break down**, dial ☎ 116 and tell the operator where you are, the type of car you're in, and your registration number: the nearest office of the Automobile Club d'Italia (ACI) will send someone out to fix your car – however, it's not a free service and can work out very expensive if you need a tow. For this reason you might consider arranging cover with a motoring organization in your home country before you leave. Any ACI office in Italy can tell you where to get **spare parts** for your particular car.

Car rental

Car rental in Italy is pricey, especially in high season, at around €200–300 per week for a small hatchback, with unlimited mileage, if booked in advance. The major chains have offices in all the larger cities and at airports and train stations; addresses are detailed where relevant throughout the Guide. Local firms can be less expensive and often have an office at the airport, but generally the best deals are to be had by arranging things in advance, through one of the agents listed opposite or with specialist tour operators when you book your flight or holiday. You need to be over 21 to rent a car in Italy and will need a credit card to act as a deposit when picking up your vehicle. If booking with a small local company, be sure to check whether CDW is included in the price before booking.

Sat nav systems are available to rent with cars from many outlets; reserve in advance.

CAR RENTAL AGENCIES

Avis Ⓦ avis.com.

Budget Ⓦ budget.com.

Europcar Ⓦ europcar.com.

Hertz Ⓦ hertz.com.

Maggiore Ⓦ maggiore.com.

National Ⓦ nationalcar.com.

SIXT Ⓦ sixt.com.

Thrifty Ⓦ thrifty.com.

Camper van rental

Camper van or mobile home holidays are becoming increasingly popular in Italy and the rental market is opening up to meet the demand. To add to the obvious convenience of this type of holiday, facilities in campsites are usually dependable (see p.36), and more and more resorts have created free camper-van parking areas (*sosta camper*). Blurent (Ⓦ blurent.com), Comocaravan (Ⓦ comocaravan.it) and Magicamper (Ⓦ magicamper.com) are among the companies offering new (or newish) quality vehicles for rent. Prices are usually around €900 for a four-berth vehicle for a week in high season, with unlimited mileage.

By plane

In line with the rest of European airspace, internal airfares in Italy have been revolutionized in the last couple of years. Small companies have taken on the ailing state airline and what used to be a form of business transport has become a good-value, convenient way of getting around the country. **Budget airlines** open and close every season and there are often special deals being advertised; it pays to shop around and, as always, book as far in advance as you can.

DOMESTIC AIRLINES

Air Italy Ⓦ airitaly.com.

Airone Ⓦ flyairone.it.

Alitalia Ⓦ alitalia.it.

Blu Express Ⓦ blu-express.com

Meridiana Ⓦ meridiana.it.

By ferry and hydrofoil

Italy has a well-developed network of **ferries** and **hydrofoils** operated by a number of different private companies. Large car-ferries connect the major islands of Sardinia and Sicily with the mainland ports of Genoa, Livorno, La Spezia, Civitavecchia, Fiumicino and Naples, while the smaller island groupings – the Bay of Naples islands, the Pontine islands, the Aeolian islands – are usually linked to a number of nearby mainland towns. The larger lakes in the north of the country are also well served with regular ferries in season, although these are drastically reduced in winter.

Fares are quite expensive, with hydrofoils costing around twice as much as ferries, and on some of the more popular services – to Sardinia, for example – you should book well in advance in summer, especially if you're taking a vehicle across. Remember, too, that sailings are cut outside the summer months, and some services stop altogether. You'll find a broad guide to journey times and frequencies in the "Arrival and departure" sections within the Guide; for full schedules and prices, check the Italian website Ⓦ traghetti.com.

By bike and motorbike

Cycling is a very popular sport and mode of transport in much of Italy. Italians in small towns and villages are welcoming to cyclists, and hotels and hostels will take your bike in overnight for safekeeping. On the islands, in the mountains, in major resorts and larger cities, it's usually possible to **rent** a bike, but in rural areas rental facilities are few and far between.

Serious cyclists might consider staying at one of a chain of hotels that cater specifically for cycling enthusiasts. Each hotel has a secure room for your bike, a maintenance workshop, overnight laundry facilities, suggested itineraries and group-tour possibilities, a doctor on hand and even dietary consultation. Contact ☎ 39 0541 307 531, Ⓦ italybikehotels.it for further information. Bikes can be taken on local and slower inter-regional trains if you buy a *supplemento bici* (bike supplement) for €3.50, or for free in a bike bag; on faster Eurostar or equivalent trains cycles must be placed in bike bags.

An alternative is to tour by **motorbike**, though again there are relatively few rental places. **Mopeds** and **scooters** are comparatively easy to find: everyone in Italy, from kids to grannies, rides one and although they're not really built for long-distance travel, for shooting around towns and islands they're ideal; we've detailed outlets in the Guide. Crash helmets are compulsory.

Accommodation

There is an infinite variety of accommodation in Italy: mountain monasteries, boutique hotels, youth hostels, self-catering villas, family-run B&Bs and rural farmhouses. While rarely particularly cheap, standards are fairly reliable and accommodation is strictly regulated.

In popular resorts and the major cities **booking ahead** is advisable, particularly during July or August, while for Venice, Rome and Florence it's pretty much essential to book ahead from Easter until late September and over Christmas and New Year. The phrases on p.1020 should help you get over the language barrier.

Hotels

Italy has some of the most memorable hotels in Europe, ranging from grand hotels oozing *belle-époque* glamour to boutique hotels on the cutting edge of contemporary design. As is commonplace throughout Europe, Italian hotels are given an official rating of between one and five stars based on facilities and services, such as the number of rooms with en-suite bathroom or telephone, whether there is a restaurant on site, and whether there is 24-hour service. This means that the star rating is no guide to a hotel's subtler, more subjective charms, such as the style of decor or the friendliness or helpfulness of staff.

In very busy places at peak times of the year it's not unusual to have to stay for a minimum of three nights, and many proprietors will add the price of **breakfast** to your bill whether you want it or not; try to ask for accommodation only – you can always eat more cheaply in a bar. Be warned, too, that in major resorts you will often be obliged to take **half- or full board** in high season. Note that people travelling alone may sometimes have to pay for the price of a double room even when they only need a single, though it can also work the other way round – if all their **single rooms** are taken, a hotelier may well put you in a double room but only charge the single rate.

Bed and breakfasts

Bed and breakfast schemes are becoming a very popular alternative form of accommodation. The best ones offer a real flavour of Italian home life,

though they're not necessarily cheaper than an inexpensive hotel, and they rarely accept credit cards. Some places going under the name are actually little different from private rooms, with the owners not living on the premises, but you'll invariably find them clean and well maintained. The most recent trend is for boutique B&Bs, often in stylishly revamped old *palazzi*. Check out ⓦbbitalia .it, ⓦbbplanet.it and ⓦbed-and-breakfast-in-italy .com.

Hostels

There is a good network of private and HI **hostels** throughout the country – from family-friendly institutions on the edge of large cities to sociable town-centre backpacker-focused options. **Rates** at official HI hostels in Italy are around €18 per night for a dorm bed, while private city-centre establish-ments are usually closer to €25. You can easily base a tour of the country around them, although for two people travelling together they don't always represent a massive saving on the cheapest double hotel room. If you're travelling on your own, on the other hand, hostels are usually more sociable and can work out a lot cheaper; many have facilities such as inexpensive restaurants and self-catering kitchens that enable you to cut costs further.

HI hostels are members of the official Inter-national Youth Hostel Federation, and you'll need to be a member of the organization in order to use them – you can join through your home country's youth hostelling organization (see opposite) or often at the hostel on arrival. You need to reserve well ahead in the summer, most conveniently by using ⓦhostelbookers.com or ⓦhostelworld.com.

In some cities, it's also possible to stay in **student accommodation** vacated by Italian students for the summer. This is usually confined to July and August, but accommodation is generally in individual rooms and can work out a lot cheaper than a straight hotel room. Again you'll need to book in advance.

PRICES

An increasing number of hotels are beginning to base room prices on demand, rather than simply on season, particularly those that have booking facilities online. Many hotels no longer even publish rack rates. In addition **rates** vary greatly between the south and north of Italy, as well as between tourist hotspots and more rural areas. Although we have given a price reflective of the cheapest standard high-season double booked a couple of months in advance, readers should be aware that there are increasingly huge fluctuations in price. As a rule, substantial discounts are to be had by booking online, well in advance, or by looking for last-minute hotel bargains online on sites such as ⓦlastminute.com, ⓦbooking.com or ⓦlaterooms.com.

AGRITURISMO

The **agriturismo** scheme, which allows the owners of country estates, vineyards and farms to rent out converted barns and farm buildings to tourists, has boomed in recent years. Usually these comprise a self-contained flat or building, though a few places just rent rooms on a bed-and-breakfast basis. While some rooms are still annexed to working farms or vineyards, many are smart, self-contained rural vacation properties; attractions may include home-grown food, swimming pools and a range of outdoor activities. Many agriturismi have a minimum-stay requirement of one week in busy periods.

Rates start at around €120 per night for self-contained places with two bedrooms. Tourist offices keep lists of local properties; alternatively, you can search one of the growing number of agriturismo websites – try Ⓦ agriturismo.it, Ⓦ agriturismo.com, Ⓦ agriitalia.it and Ⓦ agriturist.it.

YOUTH HOSTEL ASSOCIATIONS

Australia ☎ 02 9261 1111, Ⓦ yha.org.au.
Canada ☎ 613 237 7884, Ⓦ hihostels.ca.
Ireland ☎ 01 830 4555, Ⓦ irelandyha.org.
New Zealand ☎ 0800 278 299, Ⓦ yha.co.nz.
Northern Ireland ☎ 028 9032 4733, Ⓦ hini.org.uk.
Scotland ☎ 0845 293 7373, Ⓦ syha.org.uk.
South Africa ☎ 021 424 2511, Ⓦ hisa.org.za.
UK ☎ 01629 592 700, Ⓦ yha.org.uk.
US ☎ 301 495 1240, Ⓦ hiayh.org.

Monasteries and convents

You will also come across accommodation operated by **religious organizations** – convents (normally for women only), welcome houses and the like, again with a mixture of dormitory and individual rooms, which can sometimes be a way of cutting costs as well as meeting like-minded people. Most operate a curfew of some sort, and you should bear in mind that they don't always work out a great deal cheaper than a bottom-line one-star hotel. Information can be found in the local tourist offices.

An online agency, Monastery Stays (Ⓦ monasterystays.com), offers a centralized booking service for over 250 convents and monasteries around Italy. There are no restrictions on age, sex or faith, all rooms have private bathrooms and few places have early curfews.

Self-catering

Self-catering is becoming an increasingly feasible option for visitors to Italy's cities. High prices mean that renting rooms or an **apartment** can be an attractive, cost-effective choice. Usually in well-located positions in city centres, and available for a couple of nights to a month or so, they come equipped with bedding and kitchen utensils, and there's nothing like shopping for supplies in a local market to make you feel part of Italian daily life.

If you don't intend to travel around a lot it might be worth renting a **villa** or farmhouse for a week or two. Most tend to be located in the affluent northern areas of Italy, especially Tuscany and Umbria, although attractive options are also available on Sicily and Sardinia and other rural locations too. They don't come cheap, but are of a high standard and often enjoy marvellous locations.

VILLA AND APARTMENT COMPANIES

Bridgewater UK ☎ 0161 787 8587, Ⓦ bridgewater-travel.co.uk. A company with over 25 years' experience sourcing apartments, agriturismi and country hotels.
Friendly Rentals UK ☎ 0800 520 0373, Ⓦ friendlyrentals.com. Well-run company offering stylish properties in Milan, Florence, Venice and Rome to suit most budgets.
Holiday Rentals UK Ⓦ holiday-rentals.co.uk. This site puts you in touch directly with the owners of over a thousand Italian properties.
Ilios Travel UK ☎ 0845 675 2601, Ⓦ iliostravel.com. High-quality selection of country mansions and villas, in various parts of the country.
Italian Breaks UK ☎ 020 8666 0407, Ⓦ italianbreaks.com. Accommodation for a range of budgets.
Italian Connection UK ☎ 01424 728900, Ⓦ italian-connection .co.uk. Major upmarket operator with an array of villas and smart apartments throughout the country.
Italian Homes UK ☎ 020 3178 4180, Ⓦ Italian-homes.com. Apartments in Rome, Florence and Umbria.
Livingitalia Italy ☎ 39 06 3211 0998, Ⓦ livingitalia.com. Apartments in Florence and Rome.
Owners Direct UK ☎ 020 8827 1998, Ⓦ ownersdirect.co.uk. User-friendly website advertising thousands of villas and apartments across Italy, booked direct through the owner.

Mountain refuges

If you're planning on hiking and climbing, check out the **rifugi** network, consisting of about five hundred mountain huts owned by the Club Alpino Italiano (**CAI**; ☎ 02 205 7231, Ⓦ cai.it). Non-members can use them for around €10 a night, though you should book at least ten days in advance. There are also private *rifugi* that charge around double this. Most are fairly spartan, with bunks in unheated dorms, but their settings can be magnificent and usually leave you well placed to continue your hike the next day. Note that the word *rifugio* can be used for anything from a smart chalet-hotel to a snack bar at the top of a cable-car line. We've indicated where this is the case.

Camping

Camping is popular in Italy and there are plenty of sites, mostly on the coast and in the mountains, and generally open April to September (though winter "camping" – in caravans and camper vans – is common in ski areas). The majority are well equipped and often have bungalows, mainly with four to six beds. On the coast in high season you can expect to pay a daily rate of around €12 per person plus €10–15 per tent or caravan and €8 per vehicle prices in the Guide are for two people. Local tourist offices have details of nearby sites, or visit Ⓦcamping.it.

Food and drink

The importance Italians attach to food and drink makes any holiday in the country a treat. The southern Italian diet especially, with its emphasis on olive oil, fresh and plentiful fruit, vegetables and fish, is one of the healthiest in Europe, and there are few national cuisines that can boast so much variety in both ingredients and cooking methods. Italy's wines, too, are among the finest and most diverse in Europe.

Italian food remains determinedly regional. Northern Italian cuisine includes the butter-, cream- and truffle-rich cooking of the French-influenced northwest, the Tyrolean ham, sausage and dumplings of the northeast, and the light basil, fish and pinenut dishes of Liguria. Food in central Italy is characterized by the hearty wood-roasted steaks of rural Tuscany and the black truffles, hams and salamis of Umbria, while in traditional trattorias of Rome, offal reigns supreme. Continuing south, the classic vegetables of the Mediterranean take over, and the predominant meat is lamb (spit-roast and scented with wild herbs) while traditional dishes based around pulses and wild greens belie the recent poverty of the region. Finally, across the Messina Straits to Sicily, history is enshrined in rich, fragrant dishes such as aubergine *caponata*, fish couscous, and almond-milk- and jasmine-scented granitas, the abiding legacy of Arab rule.

For more on the regional variety in cooking, see the boxes at the beginning of each chapter.

Restaurants

Traditionally, a trattoria is a cheaper and more basic purveyor of home-style cooking (*cucina casalinga*), while a *ristorante* is more upmarket, though the two are often interchangeable. *Osterie* are common too, basically an old-fashioned restaurant or pub-like place specializing in home cooking, though some upmarket places with pretensions to established antiquity borrow the name. A pizzeria is always best with a *forno a legna* (wood-burning oven) rather than an electric one. In mid-range establishments, pasta dishes go for €6–12, while the main fish or meat courses will normally cost between €8 and €16.

The menu

Traditionally, lunch (*pranzo*) and dinner (*cena*) start with **antipasto** (literally "before the meal"), a course consisting of various cold cuts of meat, seafood and vegetable dishes, generally costing €5–12. Some places offer self-service antipasto buffets. The next course, the **primo**, involves soup, risotto or pasta, and is followed by the **secondo** – the meat or fish course, usually served alone, except for perhaps a wedge of lemon or tomato. Fish will often be served whole or by weight – 250g is usually plenty for one person – or ask to have a look at the fish before it's cooked. Note that by law, any ingredients that have been frozen need to be marked (usually with an asterix and "*surgelato*") on the menu. Vegetables or salads – **contorni** – are ordered and served separately, and there often won't be much choice: potatoes will usually come as fries (*patate fritte*), but you can also find boiled (*lesse*) or roast (*arrostite*) potatoes, while salads are either green (*verde*) or mixed (*mista*) and vegetables (*verdure*) usually come very well boiled. Afterwards, you nearly always get a choice of fresh local fruit (*frutta*) and a selection of **desserts** (*dolci*) – sometimes just ice

> There's a detailed **menu reader** of Italian terms on pp.1022–1024.

cream or *macedonia* (fresh fruit salad), but often home-made items, like apple or pear cake (*torta di mela/pera*), *tiramisù*, or *zuppa inglese* (trifle). **Cheeses** (*formaggi*) are always worth a shot if you have any room left; ask to try a selection of local varieties.

You will need quite an appetite to tackle all these courses and if your stomach — or wallet — isn't up to it, it's perfectly acceptable to have less. If you're not sure of the size of the portions, start with a pasta or rice dish and ask to order the *secondo* when you've finished the first course. And, although it's not a very Italian thing to do, don't feel shy about just having an antipasto and a *primo*; they're probably the best way of trying local specialities anyway.

At the end of the meal ask for the **bill** (*il conto*); bear in mind that almost everywhere you'll pay a **cover charge** (*coperto*) of €1.50–3 a head. In many trattorias the bill amounts to little more than an illegible scrap of paper; if you want to check it, ask for a **receipt** (*ricevuta*). In more expensive places, service (*servizio*) will often be added on top of the cover charge, generally about ten percent; if it isn't, leave what you feel is appropriate for the service you received – up to ten percent.

Breakfast

Most Italians start their day in a bar, their **breakfast** (*prima colazione*) consisting of a coffee and a *brioche* or *cornetto* – a croissant often filled with jam, custard or chocolate, which you usually help yourself to from the counter and eat standing at the bar. It will cost between €1.30 and €1.60; note that it will cost more if you sit down (see "Where to drink", p.38). Breakfast in a hotel is all too often a limp affair of watery coffee, bread and processed meats, often not worth the price.

Pizza and snacks

Pizza is a worldwide phenomenon, but Italy remains the best place to eat it. Here pizza usually comes thin and flat, not deep-pan, and the choice of toppings is fairly limited, with none of the dubious pineapple and sweetcorn variations. For a quality pizza opt for somewhere with a wood-fired oven (*forno a legna*) rather than a squeaky-clean electric one, so that the pizzas arrive blasted and bubbling on the surface and with a distinctive charcoal taste. This adherence to tradition means that it's unusual to find a good pizzeria open at lunchtime; it takes hours for a wood-fired oven to heat up to the necessary temperature.

Pizzerias range from a stand-up counter selling slices (pizza *al taglio*) to a fully fledged sit-down restaurant, and on the whole they don't sell much else besides pizza, soft drinks and beer. A basic cheese and tomato *margherita* can cost from €3.50 to €6, depending on how fancy the pizzeria is. More elaborate pizzas will cost from around €6–10, and it's quite acceptable to cut it into slices and eat it with your fingers. Consult our food glossary (see pp.1022–1024) for the different varieties.

For a lunchtime snack **sandwiches** (*panini*) can be pretty substantial, a bread stick or roll packed with any number of fillings. A sandwich bar (*paninoteca*) in larger towns and cities, and in smaller places a grocer's shop (*alimentari*), will normally make you up whatever you want. Bars, particularly in the north, may also offer *tramezzini*, ready-made sliced white bread with mixed fillings.

Other sources of quick snacks are **markets**, where fresh, flavoursome produce is sold, often including cheese, cold meats, warm spit-roast chicken, and *arancini*, deep-fried balls of rice with meat (*rosso*) or butter and cheese (*bianco*) filling. **Bread shops** (*panetteria*) often serve slices of pizza or *focaccia* (bread with oil and salt topped with rosemary, olives or tomato). **Supermarkets**, also, are an obvious stop for a picnic lunch: larger branches are on the outskirts of cities, while smaller super-markets can be found in town centres.

Vegetarians and vegans

The quality of fruit and vegetables in Italy is excellent, with local, seasonal produce available throughout the country. There are numerous pasta sauces without meat, some superb vegetable antipasti and, if you eat fish and seafood, you should have no problem at all. Salads, too, are fresh and good. Outside the cities and resorts, you might be wise to check if a dish has meat in it (*C'è carne dentro?*) or ask for it "*senza carne e pesce*" to make sure it doesn't contain poultry or *prosciutto*.

Vegans will have a much harder time, though pizzas without cheese (*marinara* – nothing to do with fish – is a common option) are a good stand-by and vegetable soup (*minestrone*) is usually just that.

Drinks

Although *un mezzo* (half-litre carafe of house wine) is a standard accompaniment to a meal, there's not a great emphasis on dedicated **drinking** in Italy.

Public drunkenness is rare, young people don't devote their nights to getting wasted, and women especially are frowned on if they're seen to be overindulging. Nonetheless there's a wide choice of alcoholic drinks available, often at low prices. Soft drinks, crushed-ice drinks and, of course, mineral water are widely available.

Where to drink

Traditional **bars** are less social centres than functional places and are all very similar to each other – brightly lit places, with a counter, a Gaggia coffee machine and a picture of the local football team on the wall. This is the place to come for a coffee in the morning, a quick beer or a cup of tea – people don't generally idle away evenings in bars. Indeed in some more rural areas it's difficult to find a bar open much after 8pm.

It's cheapest to drink standing at the counter, in which case you pay first at the cash desk (*la cassa*), present your receipt (*scontrino*) to the barperson and give your order. There's always a list of prices (*listino prezzi*) behind the bar and it's customary to leave a small coin on the counter as a tip. If there's waiter service, just sit where you like, though bear in mind that to do this will cost you up to twice as much as positioning yourself at the bar, especially if you sit outside (*fuori*) – the difference is shown on the price list as *tavola* (table) or *terrazzo* (any outside seating area). Late-night bars and pubs rarely operate on the *scontrino* system; you may be asked to pay up front, in the British manner, or be presented with a bill. If not, head for the counter when you leave – the barperson will have kept a surprisingly accurate tally.

An **osteria** can be a more congenial setting, often a traditional place where you can try local specialities with a glass of wine. Real enthusiasts of the grape should head for an **enoteca**, though many of these are more oriented towards selling wine by the case than by the glass. Cities offer a much greater variety of places to sit and drink in the evening, sometimes with live music or DJs. The more energetic or late-opening of these have taken to calling themselves **pubs**, a spill-over from the success of Irish pubs, at least one of which you'll find, packed to the rafters, in almost every city.

Coffee and tea

Always excellent, **coffee** can be taken small and black (espresso, or just *caffè*), which costs around €1 a cup, or white and frothy (cappuccino, for about €1.30), but there are scores of variations. If you want your espresso watered down, ask for a *caffè lungo* or,

for something more like a filter coffee, an *Americano*; with a drop of milk is *caffè macchiato*; very milky is *caffè latte* or (in the South) *latte macchiato* (ordering just a "*latte*", New York café style, will get you a glass of milk). Coffee with a shot of alcohol – and you can ask for just about anything – is *caffè corretto*. Many places also serve decaffeinated coffee; in summer you might want to have your coffee cold (*caffè freddo*).

If you're not up for a coffee, there's always **tea**. In summer you can drink this cold, too (*tè freddo*) – excellent for taking the heat off. Hot tea (*tè caldo*) comes with lemon (*con limone*) unless you ask for milk (*con latte*). A small selection of herbal teas (*infusioni*) are generally available: camomile (*camomilla*) and peppermint (*menta*) are the most common.

Soft drinks and water

There are various **soft drinks** (*analcolichi*) to choose from. Slightly fizzy, bitter drinks like San Bittèr or Crodino are common, especially at *aperitivo* time. A **spremuta** is a fresh fruit juice, squeezed at the bar, usually orange, but sometimes lemon or grapefruit. There are also crushed-ice **granitas**, big in Sicily and offered in several flavours, available with or without whipped cream (*panna*) on top. Otherwise you'll find the usual range of fizzy drinks and concentrated juices: the home-grown Italian version of Coke, Chinotto, is less sweet and good with a slice of lemon. **Tap water** (*acqua del rubinetto*) is quite palatable in some places, undrinkable in others, though few Italians would dream of imbibing it. **Mineral water** (*acqua minerale*) is ubiquitous.

Beer and spirits

Beer (*birra*) usually comes in one-third or two-third litre bottles, or on tap (*alla spina*), measure for measure more expensive than the bottled variety. A small beer is a *piccola* (20cl or 25cl), a larger one (usually 40cl) a *media*. The cheapest and most common brands are the Italian Moretti, Peroni and Dreher, all of which are very drinkable; if this is what you want, either state the brand name or ask for *birra nazionale* or *birra chiara* – otherwise you could end up with a more expensive imported beer. You may also come across darker beers (*birra nera* or *birra rossa*), which have a sweeter, maltier taste and in appearance resemble stout or bitter.

All the usual **spirits** are on sale and known mostly by their generic names. There are also Italian brands of the main varieties: the best Italian brandies are Stock and Vecchia Romagna. A generous shot costs about €1.50, imported stuff much more.

You'll also find **fortified wines** like Martini, Cinzano and Campari; ask for a Campari-soda and you'll get a ready-mixed version from a little bottle; a slice of lemon is a *spicchio di limone*, ice is *ghiaccio*. You might also try Cynar – an artichoke-based sherry often drunk as an aperitif with water.

There's also a daunting selection of **liqueurs**. Amaro is a bitter after-dinner drink or *digestivo*; Amaretto much sweeter with a strong taste of almond; Sambuca a sticky-sweet aniseed concoction, traditionally served with a coffee bean in it and set on fire (though, increasingly, this is something put on to impress tourists). A shot of clear grappa is a common accompaniment to a coffee and can range from a warming palate-cleanser to throat-burning firewater, while another sweet alternative, originally from Sorrento, is *limoncello* or *limoncino*, a lemon-based liqueur best drunk in a frozen vase-shaped glass. *Strega* is another drink you'll see behind every bar, yellow, herb-and-saffron-based stuff in tall, elongated bottles: about as sweet as it looks but not unpleasant.

Wine

From sparkling Prosecco to deep-red Chianti, Italy is renowned for its wines. However, it's rare to find the snobbery often associated with "serious" wine drinking. Light **reds** such as those made from the *dolcetto* grape are hauled out of the fridge in hot weather, while some full-bodied **whites** are drunk at near room temperature. In restaurants you'll invariably be offered red (*rosso*) or white (*bianco*) – though rosé (*rosato*) is slowly becoming more available. The local stuff (*vino sfuso*) can be great or awful – there's no way of telling without trying – but it is inexpensive at an average of around €5 a litre, and you can always order just a glass or a quarter-litre (*un quarto*) to see what it's like. Bottled wine is pricier but still very good value; expect to pay €9–20 a bottle in a mid-priced restaurant, and less than half that from a shop or supermarket. In bars you can buy a decent glass of wine for about €3.

The media

Italy's decentralized press serves to emphasize the strength of regionalism in the country. Local TV is popular, too, in the light of little competition from the national channels. If you know where to look, journalistic standards can be high but you might find yourself turning to foreign TV channels or papers if you want an international outlook on events.

Newspapers

The **Italian press** is largely regionally based, with just a few newspapers available across the country. The centre-left *La Repubblica* (Ⓦ repubblica.it) and authoritative right-slanted *Corriere della Sera* (Ⓦ corriere.it) are the two most widely read, published nationwide with local supplements, but originating in Milan. Provincial newspapers include *La Stampa* (Ⓦ lastampa.it), the daily of Turin, and *Il Messaggero* (Ⓦ ilmessaggero.it) of Rome – both rather stuffy, establishment sheets. *Il Mattino* (Ⓦ ilmattino.it) is the more readable publication of Naples and the Campania area, while other southern editions include the *Giornale di Sicilia* and *La Gazzetta del Sud*. Many of the imprints you see on newsstands are the official mouthpieces for political parties: *L'Unità* (Ⓦ unita.it) is the party organ of the former Communist Party, while *La Padania* is the press of the right-wing, regionalist Lega Nord party. The traditionally radical *Il Manifesto* has always been regarded as one of the most serious and influential sources of Italian journalism. Perhaps the most avidly read newspapers of all, however, are the specialist sports papers, most notably the *Corriere dello Sport* (Ⓦ corrieredellosport.it) and the pink *Gazzetta dello Sport* (Ⓦ gazzetta.it) – both essential reading if you want an insight into the Italian football scene.

English-language newspapers can be found for around three times their home cover-price in all the larger cities and most resorts, usually a day late, though in Milan and Rome you can sometimes find papers on the day of publication. In remoter parts of the country it's not unusual for foreign papers to be delayed by several days.

To keep up with Italian news in English, go to Ⓦ lifeinitaly.com.

TV and radio

Italian **TV** is appalling, with mindless quiz shows, variety programmes and chat shows squeezed in between countless advertisements. There are three state-owned channels – RAI 1, 2 and 3 – along with the channels of Berlusconi's Mediaset Empire – Italia 1, Rete 4, Canale 5 – and a seventh channel, Canale 7. **Satellite television** is fairly widely distributed, and three-star hotels and above usually offer a mix of BBC World, CNN and French-, German- and Spanish-language news channels, as well as MTV and Eurosport.

As for **radio**, the most serious RAI channel is RAI 3, while the most listened-to pop radio stations are RTL (102.5 FM) and Radio Deejay (frequency depends on where you are listening – find them on Ⓦ radiodeejay.it).

Festivals

Whether for religious, traditional or cultural reasons, there are literally thousands of festivals in Italy and sometimes the best ones are those that you come across unexpectedly in the smaller towns.

Perhaps the most widespread local event in Italy is the **religious procession**, which can be a very dramatic affair. **Good Friday** is celebrated in places – particularly in the south – by parading models of Christ through the streets accompanied by white-robed, hooded figures singing penitential hymns. Many processions have strong pagan roots, marking important dates on the calendar and only relatively recently sanctified by the Church.

Despite the dwindling number of practising Catholics in Italy, there has been a revival of **pilgrimages** over the last couple of decades. These are as much social occasions as spiritual journeys with, for example, as many as a million pilgrims travelling through the night, mostly on foot, to the **Shrine of the Madonna di Polsi** in the inhospitable Aspromonte mountains in Calabria. Sardinia's biggest festival, the **Festa di Sant'Efisio**, sees a four-day march from Cagliari to Pula and back, to commemorate the saint's martyrdom.

Recently there's been a revival of the **carnival** (*carnevale*), the last fling before Lent, although the anarchic fun of the past has generally been replaced by elegant, self-conscious affairs, with ingenious costumes and handmade masks. The main places are Venice, Viareggio in Tuscany and Acireale in Sicily.

Many festivals evoke local pride in **tradition**. Medieval contests like the **Palio** horse race in Siena perpetuate allegiances to certain competing clans, while other towns put on crossbow, jousting and flag-twirling contests, accompanied by marching bands in full costume. These festivals are highly significant to those involved, with fierce rivalry between participants.

Food-inspired *feste* are lower-key, but no less enjoyable, usually celebrating the regional speciality with dancing, brass bands and noisy fireworks. There are literally hundreds of food festivals, sometimes advertised as **sagre**, and every region has them – look in the local papers or ask at the tourist office during summer and autumn.

This same home-town pride also expresses itself in some of Italy's **arts festivals**, particularly in the central part of the country – based in ancient amphitheatres or within medieval walls and occasionally marking the work of a native composer. Major concerts and opera are usually well advertised and extremely popular, so book well in advance.

One other type of festival to keep an eye out for is the summer **political** shindig, like the Festa de l'Unità. Begun initially to recruit members to the different political parties, they have become something akin to a village fete but with a healthy Italian twist. Taking place mainly in the evenings, there's usually bingo, the sort of dancing that will make teenagers crimson with embarrassment and the odd coconut shy, while the food tents are a great way to try tasty local dishes for a couple of euros, washed down by a cup of wine. In larger towns these have become more sophisticated affairs, with big-name national bands playing.

A festival calendar

Some of the highlights are listed here – more appear in the Guide. Note that dates change from year to year, so contact the local tourist office for specifics.

JANUARY

Milan Epifania (Jan 6). Costumed parade of the Three Kings from the Duomo to Sant'Eustorgio, the resting place of the bones of the Magi.

Rome Epifania (Jan 6). Toy and sweet fair in Piazza Navona, to celebrate the Befana, the good witch who brings toys and sweets to children who've been good, and coal to those who haven't.

FEBRUARY

Sicily Festa di Sant'Agata (Feb 3–5). Riotous religious procession in Catania.

Carnevale (weekend before Lent). Carnival festivities in Venice (ⓦ venicecarnival.com), Viareggio (ⓦ ilcarnevale.com), Foiano della Chiana (Arezzo), Cento (Ferrara), plus many towns throughout Italy.

Ivrea Battle of the Oranges (Carnival Sun–Shrove Tues). A messy couple of days when processions through the streets are an excuse to pelt each other with orange pulp; ⓦ carnevalediivrea.it.

Agrigento Almond Blossom Festival (last two weeks). Colourful celebration of spring with folk music from around the world.

MARCH

Milan Salone Internazionale del Mobile (third week). The city becomes a showcase for the world's best furniture and industrial design.

APRIL

Nocera Tirinese Rito dei Battienti (Easter Sat). Macabre parade of flagellants whipping themselves with shards of glass.

Florence Lo Scoppio del Carro (Easter Day). A symbolic firework display outside the Duomo after Mass.

Alba Truffle Festival (April 24–May 2). An opportunity to sample local delicacies as well as parades and a donkey *palio*.

MAY

Cocullo (L'Aquila) Festival of snakes (first week of May). One of the most ancient festivals celebrating the patron saint, San Domenico Abate, in which his statue is draped with live snakes and paraded through town.

Naples Festival of San Gennaro (first Sat). Naples waits with bated breath to see if the blood of San Gennaro liquefies. (See also Sept).

Gubbio Corsa dei Ceri (first Sun). Three 20ft-high wooden figures, representing three patron saints, are raced through the old town by *ceraioli* in medieval costume.

Countrywide International Museum Day (mid-May). Museums throughout the country put on events and stay open all night to celebrate the international initiative.

Siracusa Greek Drama festival (mid-May to mid-June). Classic plays performed by international companies in the spectacular ruins of the ancient Greek theatre.

Countrywide Cantine Aperte (last Sun). Wine estates all over Italy open their cellars to the public.

JUNE

Florence Calcio Storico Fiorentino (June 24). Medieval-style football and other festivities to celebrate San Giovanni, the city's patron saint.

Verona Verona opera season (from late June); Ⓦ arena.it.

Ravello (from late June). Amalfi Coast opera and chamber music festival.

Amalfi, Genoa, Pisa, Venice Regatta of the Maritime Republics (first Sat in June). Costumed procession and a race in replica Renaissance boats. Venue alternates yearly; 2013 is Amalfi's turn.

JULY

Siena Palio (July 2). Medieval bareback horse race in the Campo.

Palermo Festino di Santa Rosalia (second week). A five-day street party to celebrate the city's patron saint.

Perugia Umbria Jazz Festival (second week). Italy's foremost jazz event, attracting top names from all over the world; Ⓦ umbriajazz.com.

Lucca Summer Festival (throughout July). International rock and pop artists perform all month.

Venice Festa del Redentore (second Sat, third Sun). Venice's main religious festival, marked with a fireworks display.

AUGUST

Countrywide Ferragosto (Aug 15). National holiday with local festivals, water fights and fireworks all over Italy.

Siena (Aug 16). Second Palio horse race; Ⓦ rossinioperafestival.it.

Pesaro Rossini Opera Festival (mid-month).

Ferrara Ferrara Buskers Festival (end Aug). Gathering of some of the world's best street performers; Ⓦ ferrarabuskers.com.

Venice (end Aug). Start of the world's oldest International Film Festival; Ⓦ labiennale.org.

SEPTEMBER

Venice La Regata di Venezia (first Sun). The annual trial of strength for the city's gondoliers and other expert rowers; it starts with a procession of historic craft along the Canal Grande.

Verona (Sept 12). Street entertainment and general partying to celebrate the birthday of the town's most famous lover, Juliet.

Naples Festa di San Gennaro (Sept 19). Festival for the city's patron

saint with crowds gathering in the cathedral to witness the liquefaction of San Gennaro's blood.

San Giovanni Rotondo, Foggia (Sept 23). Thousands of followers commemorate the death of Padre Pio.

OCTOBER

Marino, Rome Sagra del Vino (first weekend). One of the country's most famous wine festivals, with fountains literally flowing with wine.

Perugia Eurochocolate (third and fourth weekend). Italy's chocolate city celebrates.

NOVEMBER

Countrywide Olive oil festivals all over Italy.

DECEMBER

Milan Oh Bej, Oh Bej! (Dec 7). The city's patron saint, Sant'Ambrogio, is celebrated with a huge street market around his church and a day off work and school for all.

Santa Lucia (Dec 13). Milan opera season starts with an all-star opening night at La Scala.

Orvieto Umbria Jazz Winter (end of month); Ⓦ umbriajazz.com.

Sports and outdoor pursuits

Spectator sports are popular in Italy, especially the hallowed *calcio* (football), and there is undying national passion for frenetic motor and cycle races. For visitors to Italy, the most accessible activities are centred on the mountains – where you can climb, ski, paraglide, raft, canoe or simply explore on foot or cycle – and the lake and coastal regions, with plenty of opportunities for swimming, sailing and windsurfing; Campania, Calabria and Sicily are particularly popular for scuba diving and snorkelling.

Football

Football – or **calcio** – is the national sport, followed fanatically by millions of Italians, and if you're at all interested in the game it would be a shame to leave the country without attending a *partita* or football match. The **season** starts around the middle of August, and finishes in June. **Il campionato** (the championship) is split into four principal divisions, with the twenty teams in the Serie A being the most prestigious. Matches are normally played on Sunday afternoons, although Saturday, Sunday-evening and Monday games are becoming more common. See

Ⓦ lega-calcio.it for results, a calendar of events and English links to the official team websites. English-language Italian football sites are also worth a look – Ⓦ football-italia.net or Ⓦ footballitaliano.co.uk.

Tickets

Inevitably, **tickets** for Serie A matches are not cheap, starting at about €25 for "*Curva*" seats where the *tifosi* or hard-core fans go, rising to €30–50 for for more widely available *distinti* tickets in the corners of the stadium, €30–75 for "*Tribuna*" seats along the side of the pitch, and anything up to €150 for the more comfortable "*Poltroncina*", cushioned seats in the centre of the *Tribuna*. Once at the football match, get into the atmosphere of the occasion by knocking back *borghetti* – little vials of cold coffee with a drop of spirit added.

You can get tickets from sites like Ⓦ listicket.it or Ⓦ seatwave.com, which will either sell you a ticket or give you details of the nearest outlet. You must carry photo ID when you purchase a ticket and when you go to a game.

Other spectator sports

Italy's chosen sport after football is **basketball**, introduced from the United States after World War II. Most cities have a team, and Italy is now ranked among the foremost in the world. The teams vying for the top spot are Montepaschi Siena, Cimberio Varese, Emporio Armani Milano, Banco di Sardegna Sassari, Scavolini Siviglia Pesaro, Bennet Cantu, Umana Venezia and CS Bologna. For more details on fixtures and the leagues, see Ⓦ eurobasket.com/italy/basketball.as.

In a country that has produced Ferrari, Maserati, Alfa Romeo and Fiat, it should come as no surprise that **motor racing** gives Italians such a buzz. There are grand prix tracks at Monza near Milan (home of the Italian Grand Prix) and at Imola, where the San Marino Grand Prix is held.

The other sport popular with participants and crowds of spectators alike is **cycling**. At weekends especially, you'll often see a club group out, dressed in bright team kit, whirring along on their slender machines. The annual Giro d'Italia (Ⓦ ilgiroditalia.it) in the second half of May is a prestigious event that attracts scores of international participants each year, closing down roads and creating great excitement.

Outdoor pursuits

With the Alps right on the doorstep, it's easy to spend a weekend **skiing** or **snowboarding** from Milan, Turin or Venice. Some of the most popular ski resorts

are Sestriere and Bardonecchia in Piemonte, Cervinia and Courmayeur in Valle d'Aosta, the Val Gardena and Val di Fassa in the stunning Dolomite mountains of Trentino-Alto Adige and the Veneto – home to one of Italy's best-known and most exclusive resorts, Cortina d'Ampezzo. Further south you can ski at the small resorts of Abetone and Amiata in Tuscany, Monte Vettore in Le Marche, Gran Sasso and Maiella in Abruzzo, Aspromonte in Calabria and on Mount Etna in Sicily. Contact the regional tourist offices for information about accommodation, ski schools and prices of lift passes.

All of these mountain resorts are equally ideal as bases for summer **hiking** and **climbing**, and most areas have detailed maps with itineraries and marked paths. For less strenuous treks, the rolling hills of Tuscany and Umbria make perfect walking and **mountain-bike** country and numerous tour operators offer independent or escorted tours. Many tourist offices also publish booklets suggesting itineraries.

The extensive Italian coast offers all the usual seaside resort activity and plenty of opportunities for **sailing** and **windsurfing**. **Scuba diving** is popular in Sicily and off most of the smaller islands – you can either join a diving school or rent equipment from one if you're an experienced diver. You can get a guide and map suggesting **sailing itineraries** round the coast of southern Italy from the Italian State Tourist Office (see p.48).

Watersports aren't just restricted to the coast and can be found in places such as lakes Como and Garda in the north, and Trasimeno and Bolsena further south towards Rome. River **canoeing**, **canyoning** and **rafting** are popular in the mountain areas of the north of the country.

Horseriding is becoming increasingly popular in rural areas and most tourist offices have lists of local stables (*maneggio*). Many agriturismi (see p.35) also have riding facilities and sometimes offer daily or weekly treks and night rides. Note that Italians rarely wear or provide riding hats.

Shopping

There is no shortage of temptation for shoppers and souvenir-hunters in Italy. Visitors can take advantage of Italy's traditional expertise in textiles, ceramics, leather and glassware in all price ranges.

There are factory outlets across the country, particularly for clothes and other textiles but also for pottery and glass; local tourist offices will be able to point you in the right direction. Rural areas will usually have good basketware, local terracotta or ceramic items as well a veritable banquet of locally produced wine, olive oils, cheeses, hams and salamis. It's always worth rooting out the local speciality, even in urban centres: Turin is known for its chocolate, Milan famous for designer clothes and furniture, Venice for glassware and lace, Florence for leather goods, Sicily and Perugia for ceramics.

Every large village and town has at least one weekly **market** (detailed in the Guide), and though these are usually geared towards household goods, they can be useful for picking up cheap clothing, basketware, ceramics and picnic ingredients.

Prices are mainly in line with most of Western Europe and are always a little higher in the north of the country and urban areas. **Credit/debit cards** have become increasingly acceptable, with swipe-and-pin machines the norm – though some small shops may still accept only cash. **Haggling** is also uncommon in most of Italy but in markets you might like to try your luck; ask for *uno sconto* (a discount) and see where it gets you. Bargaining is not practised when buying food, however, or in shops.

If you're resident outside the EU you are entitled to a rebate for the **VAT** (or *IVA*) paid on items over €155. You need to ask for a special receipt at the time of purchase and allow your goods to be checked at the airport and the receipt stamped when you leave the country. For more, see ⓦglobalrefund.com.

Work and study

All EU citizens are eligible to work and study in Italy. Work permits are pretty impossible for non-EU citizens to obtain: you must have the firm promise of a job that no Italian could do before you can even apply to the Italian embassy in your home country.

Red tape

The main bureaucratic requirements to stay legally in Italy are a Permesso di Soggiorno and a codice fiscale, respectively a piece of paper proving your right to be in the country and a tax number. Available from the *questura* (police station), a **Permesso di Soggiorno** requires you to produce a letter from your employer or place of study, or prove you have funds to maintain yourself. In reality, EU citizens can simply apply on the grounds of looking for work (*attesa di lavoro*), for which you'll need a passport and a photocopy, four passport photos, and a lot of patience. A **codice fiscale** is essential for most things in Italy including buying a transport season-pass, a SIM card, opening a bank account or renting a flat. It can be obtained from the local Ufficio delle Entrate although you can start the process online at ⓦagenziaentrate.gov.it.

Work options

One obvious work option is to **teach English**, for which the demand has expanded enormously in recent years. You can do this in two ways: freelance private lessons, or through a language school. For the less reputable places, you can get away without any qualifications, but you'll need to show a TEFL (Teaching of English as a Foreign Language) certificate for the more professional – and better-paid – establishments. For the main language schools, it's best to apply in writing before you leave (look for the ads in British newspapers *The Guardian* and *The Times Education Supplement*), preferably before the summer. If you're looking on the spot, sift through the local English-language press and phone books and do the rounds on foot, but don't bother to try in August when everything is closed. The best teaching jobs of all are with a university as a *lettore*, a job requiring fewer hours than the language schools and generally providing a fuller pay-packet. Universities require English-language teachers in most faculties, and you can write to the individual faculties. Strictly speaking you could get by without any knowledge of Italian while teaching, though it obviously helps, especially when setting up private classes.

If teaching's not up your street, there's the possibility of **holiday rep work** in the summer, especially around the seaside resorts. These are good places for finding **bar or restaurant work**, too. You'll have to ask around for both types of work, and some knowledge of Italian is essential. **Au pairing** is another option: again sift through the ads in locally produced English-language publications in the big cities or *The Lady* magazine to find openings.

Study programmes

One way of spending time in Italy is to combine a visit with **learning the language**, either as part of an overseas study scheme or by applying directly to a language school when you arrive.

AFS Intercultural Programs US ⓣ 1 800 AFS INFO or ⓣ 212 299 9000, ⓦ afs.org/usa. Runs two-semester student exchange programmes.

American Institute for Foreign Study US ☎ 1 800 727 2437, ⓦ aifs.com. Language study and cultural immersion for the summer or school year.

Australians Studying Abroad Australia ☎ 1800 645 755 or ☎ 03 9822 6899, ⓦ asatravinfo.com.au. Study tours focusing on art and culture.

British Council UK ☎ 0161 957 7755, ⓦ britishcouncil.org. Produces a free leaflet detailing study opportunities abroad. The Council's Central Management Direct Teaching (☎ 020 7389 4931) recruits TEFL teachers for posts worldwide.

Erasmus ⓦ http://ec.europa.eu/education. Europe-wide university-level initiative enabling students to study abroad for one year.

International House UK ☎ 020 7611 2400, ⓦ ihlondon.com. Head office for reputable English-teaching organization which offers TEFL training and recruits for teaching positions in Italy.

Italian Cultural Institute UK ☎ 020 7235 1461, ⓦ italcultur .org.uk. The official Italian government agency for the promotion of cultural exchanges between Britain and Italy. A number of scholarships are available to British students wishing to study at Italian universities.

Road Scholar US ☎ 1 800 454 5768, ⓦ roadscholar.org. Runs activity programmes in Italy for over-60s.

Travel essentials

Climate

Italy's **climate** is one of the most hospitable in the world, with a general pattern of warm, dry summers and mild winters. There are, however, marked regional variations, ranging from the more temperate northern part of the country to the firmly Mediterranean south. Summers are hot and dry along the coastal areas, especially as you move south, cool in the major mountain areas – the Alps and Apennines. Winters are mild in the south of the country, Rome and below, but in the north they can be at least as cold as anywhere in the northern hemisphere, sometimes worse, especially across the plains of Lombardy and Emilia-Romagna.

Costs

In general you'll find the south much less expensive than the north. As a broad guide, expect to pay most in Venice, Milan, Florence and Bologna, less in Rome, while in Naples and Sicily prices drop quite a lot.

As an indication you should be able to survive on a **budget** of about €50–60 per day if you stay in a hostel, have lunchtime snacks and a cheap evening meal. If you stay in a mid-range hotel and eat out twice a day, you'll spend closer to €130–140 per day.

Some **basics** are reasonably inexpensive, such as transport and, most notably, food, although drinking can be pricey unless you stick to wine. **Room rates** are in line with much of the rest of Europe, at least in the major cities and resorts. Bear in mind, too, that the **time of year** can make a big difference. During the height of summer, in July and August when the Italians take their holidays, hotel

AVERAGE DAILY TEMPERATURES AND RAINFALL

	Jan	Feb	Mar	Apr	May	Jun	Jul	Aug	Sep	Oct	Nov	Dec
FLORENCE												
Max/min (°C)	11/3	13/3	16/6	18/8	24/12	27/17	32/18	32/19	27/15	21/12	15/7	11/4
Rainfall (mm)	51	55	74	78	76	72	44	48	82	102	80	76
MILAN												
Max/min (°C)	7/-3	9/-2	14/2	17/5	23/10	27/14	28/17	28/17	23/12	18/7	12/2	3/-2
Rainfall (mm)	63	62	78	78	85	65	67	86	98	98	96	96
NAPLES												
Max/min (°C)	12/4	13/5	16/7	19/9	25/14	27/17	29/18	29/18	27/17	24/13	18/19	13/7
Rainfall (mm)	92	83	75	68	45	48	18	22	68	130	110	138
PALERMO												
Max/min (°C)	14/7	14/7	17/8	20/12	25/15	28/19	29/21	30/22	27/18	25/15	20/12	17/10
Rainfall (mm)	70	45	50	50	20	10	5	20	42	75	70	60
ROME												
Max/min (°C)	13/4	14/4	16/6	18/8	24/13	27/16	28/18	29/18	26/17	23/13	18/8	13/5
Rainfall (mm)	103	98	68	65	48	34	23	33	68	94	128	110

prices can escalate; outside the season, however, you can often negotiate much lower rates.

There are a few **reductions** and discounts for ISIC members, under-18s and over-65s, but only in the major cities and for entry into state museums and sites.

Crime and personal safety

Despite what you hear about the Mafia, most of the **crime** you'll come across as a visitor to Italy is of the small-time variety, prevalent in the major cities and the south of the country, where pickpockets and gangs of *scippatori* or "snatchers" operate. Crowded streets or markets and packed tourist sights are the places to be wary of; *scippatori* work on foot or on scooters, disappearing before you've had time to react. As well as handbags, they whip wallets, tear off visible jewellery and, if they're really adroit, unstrap watches. You can minimize the risk of this happening by being discreet: don't flash anything of value, keep a firm hand on your camera, and carry shoulderbags slung across your body. Never leave anything valuable in your car, and try to park in car parks on well-lit, well-used streets. On the whole it's a good idea to avoid badly lit areas completely at night and deserted inner-city areas by day.

Carabinieri, with their military-style uniforms and white shoulder-belts, deal with general crime, public order and drug control, while the **Vigili Urbani** are mainly concerned with directing traffic and issuing parking fines; the **Polizia Stradale** patrol the motorways. The **Polizia Statale**, the other general crime-fighting force, enjoy a fierce rivalry with the **Carabinieri**. You'll find the address of the Carabinieri barracks, *questura* or police station in the local telephone directory (in smaller places it may be just a local *commissariato*).

Electricity

The supply is 220V, though anything requiring 240V will work. Plugs either have two or three round pins: a multi-plug adapter is very useful.

EMERGENCY NUMBERS

- ☎**112** police (Carabinieri).
- ☎**113** any emergency service, including ambulance (Soccorso Pubblico di Emergenza).
- ☎**115** the fire brigade (Vigili del Fuoco).
- ☎**116** road assistance (Soccorso Stradale).
- ☎**118** ambulance (Ambulanza).

Entry requirements

British, Irish and other EU citizens can enter Italy and stay as long as they like on production of a valid **passport**. Citizens of the United States, Canada, Australia and New Zealand need only a valid passport, too, but are limited to stays of three months. All other nationals should consult the relevant embassy about visa requirements. Legally, you're required to register with the police within three days of entering Italy, though if you're staying at a hotel this will be done for you. Although the police in some towns have become more punctilious about this, most would still be amazed at any attempt to register yourself down at the local police station while on holiday. However, if you're going to be living here for a while, you'd be advised to do it.

Gay and lesbian Italy

Homosexuality is legal in Italy, and the age of consent is 16. Attitudes are most tolerant in the northern cities: Bologna is generally regarded as the gay capital, and Milan, Turin and Rome all have well-developed gay scenes; there are also a few *spiagge gay* (gay beaches) dotted along the coast: the more popular gay resorts include Taormina and Rimini. Away from the big cities and resorts, though, activity is more covert. You'll notice, in the south especially, that overt displays of affection between (all) men – linking arms during the *passeggiata*, kissing in greeting and so on – are common. The line determining what's acceptable, however, is finely drawn. The **national gay organization**, ARCI-Gay (☎051 649 3055, ⓦarcigay.it) is based in Bologna but has branches in most big towns. The ⓦgay.it website has a wealth of information for gays and lesbians in Italy.

Health

As a member of the European Union, Italy has free reciprocal health agreements with other member states. EU citizens are entitled to free treatment within Italy's public healthcare system on production of a **European Health Insurance Card** (EHIC), which British citizens can obtain by picking up a form at the post office, calling ☎0845 606 2030, or applying online at ⓦnhs.uk. The Australian Medicare system also has a reciprocal healthcare arrangement with Italy. **Vaccinations** are not required, and Italy doesn't present any more health worries than anywhere else in Europe; the worst that's likely to happen to you is suffering from the extreme heat in summer or from an upset stomach. The **water** is perfectly safe to drink and you'll find public fountains in squares and city streets everywhere, though look out for *acqua non potabile* signs, indicating that the water is unsafe to drink. It's worth taking **insect repellent**, as even inland towns, most notoriously Milan, suffer from a persistent mosquito problem, especially in summer.

An Italian **pharmacist** (*farmacia*) is well qualified to give you advice on minor ailments and to dispense prescriptions; pharmacies are generally open all night in the bigger towns and cities. A rota system operates, and you should find the address of the one currently open on any *farmacia* door or listed in the local paper. If you need to see a **doctor** (*medico*), take your EHIC with you to enable you to get free treatment and prescriptions for medicines at the local rate – about ten percent of the price of the medicine.

In an **emergency**, go straight to the Pronto Soccorso (casualty) of the nearest hospital (*ospedale*), or phone ❼118 and ask for an *ambulanza*. Throughout the Guide, you'll find listings for pharmacies, hospitals and emergency services in the big cities. Major train stations and airports also often have first-aid stations with doctors on hand.

Incidentally, try to avoid going to the **dentist** (*dentista*) while you're in Italy. These aren't covered by your EHIC or the health service, and for the smallest problem you'll pay through the teeth. Take local advice, or consult the local *Yellow Pages*. If you don't have a spare pair of **glasses**, it's worth taking a copy of your prescription so that an optician (*ottico*) can make you up a new pair should you lose or damage them.

Insurance

Even though EU healthcare privileges apply in Italy, you'd do well to take out an **insurance policy** before travelling to cover against theft, loss, illness or injury. A typical policy usually provides cover for the loss of baggage, tickets and – up to a certain limit – cash or cheques, as well as cancellation or curtailment of your journey. Most policies exclude so-called dangerous sports unless an extra premium is paid; in Italy this can mean scuba diving, windsurfing and trekking. Many policies can be chopped and changed to exclude coverage you don't need – for example, sickness and accident benefits can often be excluded or included at will. If you do take medical coverage, ascertain whether benefits will be paid as treatment proceeds or only after your return home, and whether there is a 24-hour medical emergency number. When securing baggage cover, make sure that the per-article limit – typically under £500 – will cover your most valuable possession. If you need to make a claim, you should keep receipts for medicines and medical treatment, and in the event you have anything stolen, you must obtain an official statement from the police (*polizia* or *carabinieri*).

Internet

Internet access is pretty standard in hostels and mid-range and luxury hotels. According to Italian law, all three-star hotels and above are now required to offer **wi-fi**, though not necessarily for free. In towns there will always be several **internet cafés** where you go online for around €2.50 for half an hour; the area around the station is always a good place to start looking. Cities often have several wi-fi zones, usually run by the local council. Access is generally via a card with a username and pin number. Details of how to access wi-fi zones are usually posted on signs or stickers around town.

Laundries

Coin-operated laundries, sometimes known as *tintorie*, are rare outside large cities, and even there, numbers are sparse; see the "Directory" sections of the main city accounts for addresses. More common is a *lavanderia*, a service-wash laundry, but this will be more expensive. Although you can usually get away with it, beware of washing clothes in your hotel room – the plumbing often can't cope with all the water.

Mail

Post office opening hours are usually Monday to Saturday 8.30am to 7.30pm, though branches in smaller towns tend to close at 1pm. Note too that offices close an hour earlier on the last working day of the month. **Stamps** (*francobolli*) are sold in *tabacchi*, too, as well as in some gift shops in the tourist resorts; they will often also weigh your letter. The Italian postal system is one of the slowest in Europe so if your letter is urgent make sure you send it "*posta prioritaria*", which has varying rates according to weight and destination. Letters can be sent *poste restante* to any Italian post office by addressing them "*Fermo Posta*" followed by the name of the town. When picking something up take your passport, and make sure they check under middle names and initials – and every other letter when all else fails – as filing is often diabolical.

Maps

The **town plans** throughout the Guide should be fine for most purposes, and practically all tourist offices give out maps of their local area for free. The clearest and best-value large-scale commercial **road map** of Italy is the Rough Guide 1:900,000 map, which covers the whole country including Sicily and Sardinia. There are also the 1:800,000 and 1:400,000 maps produced by the Touring Club Italiano, covering north, south and central Italy, and TCI also produces excellent 1:200,000 maps of the individual regions, which are indispensable if you are touring a specific area in depth.

For **hiking** you'll need at least a scale of 1:50,000. Studio FMB and the TCI cover the major mountain areas of northern Italy to this scale, but for more detailed, down-to-scale 1:25,000 maps, both the Istituto Geografico Centrale and Kompass series cover central and northwest Italy and the Alps. The Apennines and Tuscany are covered by Multigraphic (Firenze), easiest bought in Italy, while Tabacco produces a good series detailing the Dolomites and the northeast of the country. In Italy, the Club Alpino Italiano (Ⓦcai.it) is a good source of hiking maps; we've supplied details of branches throughout the Guide.

Money

Italy's currency is the **euro** (€; note that Italians pronounce it "eh-uro"), which is split into 100 cents (*centesimi*). You can check the current exchange rate at Ⓦxe.com. In Italy, you'll get the best rate of exchange (*cambio*) at a bank. **Banking hours** are normally Monday to Friday mornings from 8.30am until 1.30pm, and for an hour in the afternoon (usually 2.30–4pm). There are local variations on this and banks are usually open only in the morning on the day before a public holiday. Outside banking hours, the larger **hotels** will change money or travellers' cheques, although if you're staying in a reasonably large city the rate is invariably better at the train station **exchange bureaux** – normally open evenings and weekends. **ATMs** are common: most towns and even villages have at least one, although, as in most countries, you won't be able to withdraw more than €250 per day. Check with your bank before you leave home to make sure your card is authorized for transactions abroad and it's a good idea to let them know the dates you'll be away so that anti-fraud blocks can be lifted.

Opening hours and public holidays

Traditionally most **shops and businesses** open Monday to Saturday from around 8am until 1pm, and from about 4pm until 7pm, with additional closures on Saturday afternoons and Monday mornings, though these days an increasing number of shops are remaining open all day, on the Northern European model. Traditionally, everything except bars and restaurants closes on Sunday, though most towns have a *pasticceria* open in the mornings, while in large cities and tourist areas, Sunday shopping is becoming more common.

Most **churches** open in the early morning, around 7 or 8am for Mass, and close around noon, opening up again at 4pm and closing at 7 or 8pm. In more remote places, some will only open for early morning and evening services, while others are closed at all times except Sundays and on religious holidays; if you're determined to take a look, you may have to ask around for the key. Another problem is that lots of churches, monasteries,

> ### CLOSED MONDAYS
> Most museums, galleries and archeological sites throughout the country are **closed on Mondays**.

convents and oratories are **closed for restoration** (*chiuso per restauro*), though you might still be able to persuade someone to show you around.

Opening hours for state-run **museums**, and most private ones, are generally Tuesday to Saturday from 9am until any time from 2pm until 7pm, and Sunday from 9am until 1pm. Many large museums also run late-night openings in summer (till 10pm or later Tues–Sat, or 8pm Sun). The opening times of **archeological sites** are more flexible: most sites open every day, often including Sunday, from 9am until late evening – frequently specified as one hour before sunset, and thus changing according to the time of year. In winter, times are drastically cut, principally because of the darker evenings; 4pm is a common closing time.

Public holidays

Whereas it can be fun to stumble across a local festival, it's best to know when the national holidays are as almost everything will shut down. In **August**, particularly during the weeks either side of Ferragosto (Aug 15), when most of the country flees to the coast and mountains, many towns are left half-deserted, with shops, bars and restaurants closed and a reduced public transport service. Local religious holidays don't necessarily close down shops and businesses, but they do mean that accommodation space may be tight. The country's official **national holidays**, on the other hand, close everything down except bars and restaurants. A recent initiative has been to open national museums and monuments on public holidays to encourage Italians to make the most of their national heritage, although it's still best to

---

PUBLIC HOLIDAYS

January 1 *Primo dell'anno*, New Year's Day.
January 6 *Epifania*, Epiphany.
Pasquetta Easter Monday.
April 25 *Giorno della Liberazione*, Liberation Day.
May 1 *Festa dei Lavoratori*, Labour Day.
June 2 *Festa della Repubblica*, Republic Day.
August 15 *Ferragosto*, Assumption of the Blessed Virgin Mary.
November 1 *Ognissanti*, All Souls' Day.
December 8 *Immacolata*, Immaculate Conception of the Blessed Virgin Mary.
December 25 *Natale*, Christmas.
December 26 *Santo Stefano*, St Stephen's Day.

---

check beforehand if you are planning a trip around one particular sight.

Phones

Mobile (cell) phones in Italy work on the GSM European standard, usually compatible with phones from the UK, the rest of Europe, Australia and New Zealand, but not the US and Canada, which use a different system. Make sure you have made the necessary "roaming" arrangements with your provider before you leave home and note that you're likely to be charged for incoming calls in Italy and you may need a new international access code to retrieve your messages.

If you're going to be in the country for any length of time, it might be worth getting an **Italian SIM card**. You can do this before you leave home (sites like Ⓦ0044.co.uk and Ⓦtelestial.com/sim_cards .php are popular) or in Italy, but you'll need to present your passport on purchase and, depending on the provider, register the details over the phone.

Public telephones, run by Telecom Italia, come in various forms, usually with clear instructions in English. Coin-operated machines are increasingly hard to find in some areas of the country so you will probably have to buy a **telephone card** (*carta* or *scheda telefonica*), available from *tabacchi* and newsstands. Codes are an integral part of the number and always need to be dialled, regardless of whether or not you are in the zone you are telephoning. All telephone numbers listed in the Guide include the relevant code. Numbers beginning ☏800 are free, ☏170 will get you through to an English-speaking operator, ☏176 to international directory enquiries.

Phone **tariffs** are among the most expensive in Europe, especially if you're calling long-distance or internationally.

Time

Italy is always one hour ahead of Britain, seven hours ahead of US Eastern Standard Time and ten hours ahead of Pacific Time.

Tourist information

Before you leave home, it may be worth contacting the Italian State Tourist Office (ENIT; Ⓦenit.it) for a selection of maps and brochures, though you can usually pick up much the same information from tourist offices in Italy. Most towns, major train stations and airports in Italy have a **tourist office**,

CALLING HOME FROM ITALY

If you don't have a Skype account, the cheapest way of calling home is to buy a phonecard. The most reliable are those issued by Telecom Italia and Edicard. Edicards are the best value for money and are available for €5, €10 or €20 from tobacconists and newsagents. They work by calling a freephone number from a landline, Italian mobile number or phone box, and then inserting a pin number.

To **call abroad from Italy**, dial ❶00 followed by the required country code, then the area code (without its first 0) and the number.

"APT" (Azienda Promozione Turistica) or "IAT" (Ufficio Informazioni Accoglienza Turistica), all of which vary in usefulness (and helpfulness) but usually provide at least a town plan and local listings guide. In smaller villages there is sometimes a "Pro Loco" office that has much the same kind of information, but with more limited opening times, and the staff are less likely to speak English.

Opening hours vary: larger city and resort offices are likely to be open Monday to Saturday 9am to 1pm and 4 to 7pm (sometimes without the lunch-break in peak season), and sometimes for a short period on Sunday mornings. Smaller offices may open weekdays only, while Pro Loco times are notoriously erratic – some open for only a couple of hours a day, even in summer.

Travelling with children

Children are adored in Italy and will be made a fuss of in the street, and welcomed and catered for in bars and restaurants. Hotels normally charge around thirty percent extra to put a bed or cot in your room, though kids pay less on trains and can generally expect discounts for museum entry: prices vary, but 11–18-year-olds are usually admitted at half-price on production of some form of ID (although sometimes this applies only to EU citizens). Under-11s – or sometimes only under-6s – have free entry.

Supplies for **babies** and small children are pricey: nappies and milk formula can cost up to three times as much as in other parts of Europe. Discreet breastfeeding is widely accepted – even smiled on – but nappy changing facilities are few. Branches of the children's clothes and accessories chain, Prenatal, have changing facilities and a feeding area,

but otherwise you may have to be creative. High-chairs are unusual too, although establishments in tourist areas tend to be better equipped.

Check out ⓦ**italyfamilyhotels.it**, an organization of hotels across Italy with facilities from cots and bottle warmers in rooms to baby sitters, play areas and special menus. New hotels are constantly joining.

Travellers with disabilities

Public transport can be challenging, although low-level buses are gradually being introduced and most trains and stations have disabled facilities. Hotels and restaurants are required by law to provide facilites for the disabled. The cobbled streets in old town and village centres can present their own problems, but access to sights is improving all the time.

CONTACTS AND RESOURCES

Access-Able ⓦ access-able.com. Online resource for travellers with disabilities.

Accessible Italy Italy ❶ 378 994 1111, ⓦ accessibleitaly.com. Italian operation offering organized tours or tailor-made trips.

Accessible Journeys US ❶ 800 846 4537, ⓦ disabilitytravel.com. Travel tips and programmes for groups or individuals.

Irish Wheelchair Association Ireland ❶ 01 818 6400, ⓦ iwa.ie. Information and listings for wheelchair users travelling abroad.

Society for the Advancement of Travellers with Handicaps (SATH) US ❶ 212 447 7284, ⓦ sath.org. Information on the accessibility of specific airlines and advice on travelling with certain conditions.

Tourism for All UK ❶ 0845 124 9971, ⓦ tourismforall.org.uk. Free lists of accessible accommodation abroad and information on financial help for holidays.

Rome and Lazio

THE PANTHEON

1

Rome and Lazio

Rome is the most fascinating city in Italy, which makes it arguably the most fascinating city in the world. An ancient place packed with the relics of over two thousand years of inhabitation, you could spend a month here and still only scratch the surface. Yet it's so much more than an open-air museum: its culture, its food, its people make up a modern, vibrant city that would be worthy of a visit irrespective of its past. As a historic centre, it is special enough; as a contemporary European capital, it is utterly unique.

The former heart of the mighty Roman Empire, and still the home of the papacy, the city is made up of layers of history. There are Rome's classical features, most visibly the Colosseum, and the Forum and Palatine Hill; but beyond these there's an almost uninterrupted sequence of monuments – from early Christian basilicas and Romanesque churches to Renaissance palaces and the fountains and churches of the Baroque period, which perhaps more than any other era has determined the look of the city today. There is the modern epoch, too, from the ponderous Neoclassical architecture of the post-Unification period to prestige projects like Zaha Hadid's MAXXI exhibition space. And these various eras crowd in on one another to an almost overwhelming degree, with medieval churches atop ancient basilicas above Roman palaces; houses and apartment blocks that incorporate fragments of eroded Roman columns, carvings and inscriptions; roads and piazzas which follow the lines of ancient amphitheatres and stadiums.

REGIONAL FOOD AND WINE

Roman cooking is traditionally dominated by the earthy cuisine of the working classes, with a little influence from the city's centuries-old Jewish population thrown in. Although you'll find all sorts of **pasta** served in Roman restaurants, spaghetti is common, as is the local speciality of *bucatini* or thick-cut hollow spaghetti (sometimes called *tonarelli*), served *cacio e pepe* (with pecorino and ground black pepper), *alla carbonara* (with beaten eggs, cubes of pan-fried bacon, and pecorino or parmesan), *alla gricia* (with pecorino and bacon), *all'amatriciana* (with tomato and bacon) and *alle vongole* (with baby clams).

Fish features most frequently in Rome as salt cod – *baccalà* – best eaten Jewish-style, deep-fried. **Offal** is also key, and although it has been ousted from many of the more refined city-centre restaurants, you'll still find it on the menus of more traditional places, especially those in Testaccio. Most favoured is *pajata*, the intestines of an unweaned calf. Look out, too, for *coda alla vaccinara*, oxtail stewed in a rich sauce of tomato and celery; *abbacchio*, milk-fed lamb roasted to melting tenderness with rosemary, sage and garlic; *abbacchio scottadito*, grilled lamb chops eaten with the fingers; and *saltimbocca alla romana*, thin slices of veal cooked with a slice of prosciutto and sage on top. **Artichokes** (*carciofi*) are the quintessential Roman vegetable, served *alla romana* (stuffed with garlic and mint and stewed) and in all their unadulterated glory as *alla giudea* – flattened and deep-fried in olive oil. Another not-to-be-missed side dish is *fiori di zucca* – batter-fried courgette blossom, stuffed with mozzarella and a sliver of marinated anchovy. Roman **pizza** has a thin crust and is best when baked in a wood-fired oven (*forno a legna*), but you can also find lots of great pizza by the slice (*pizza al taglio*). Lazio's **wine** is enjoying a bit of a resurgence and is often better than most people think. Nonetheless you'll still mostly find wines from the Castelli Romani (most famously Frascati) to the south, and from around Montefiascone (Est! Est! Est!) in the north – both excellent, straightforward whites, great for sunny lunchtimes or as an evening *aperitivo* – but in the city's better and more contemporary restaurants you'll find wines from other regions and newer producers.

CEILING OF THE RAPHAEL ROOMS, VATICAN MUSEUMS

Highlights

❶ Pantheon The most complete ancient Roman structure in the city. **See p.61**

❷ Capitoline Museums The august and impressive home of some of Rome's finest ancient sculpture and paintings. **See p.69**

❸ Galleria Borghese One of the city's finest art galleries – and home to the cream of the work of the city's favourite sculptor, Bernini. **See p.76**

❹ Vatican Museums Quite simply the largest and richest collection of art in the world. **See p.94**

❺ Ostia Antica The old port of Rome is one of the best-preserved and most intriguing ancient sites in the country. **See p.114**

❻ Tivoli The site of Hadrian's villa, as well as the splendid landscaped gardens of Villa d'Este. **See p.114**

❼ Subiaco St Benedict's two monasteries are among Italy's most spiritual and peaceful locations, and you can stay overnight. **See p.128**

HIGHLIGHTS ARE MARKED ON THE MAPS ON P.54 AND PP.56–57

1

Beyond Rome, the region of **Lazio** inevitably pales in comparison, but there is plenty to draw you there, not least the landscape, which varies from the green hills and lakes of the northern reaches to the drier, more mountainous south. It's a relatively poor region, its lack of identity the butt of a number of Italian jokes, but it's the closest you'll get to the feel of the Italian South without catching the train to Naples. Much of the area can be easily seen on a day-trip from the capital, primarily the ancient sites of **Ostia Antica** and the various attractions of **Tivoli**. Further afield, in northern Lazio, the Etruscan sites of **Tarquinia** and **Cerveteri** provide the most obvious tourist focus, as does the pleasant provincial town of **Viterbo** and the gentle beauty of lakes **Bracciano**, **Vico** and **Bolsena**. The south arguably holds Lazio's most appealing enclaves, not least unpretentious resorts like **Terracina** and **Sperlonga**, and the island of **Ponza** – one of the most alluring spots on the entire western seaboard.

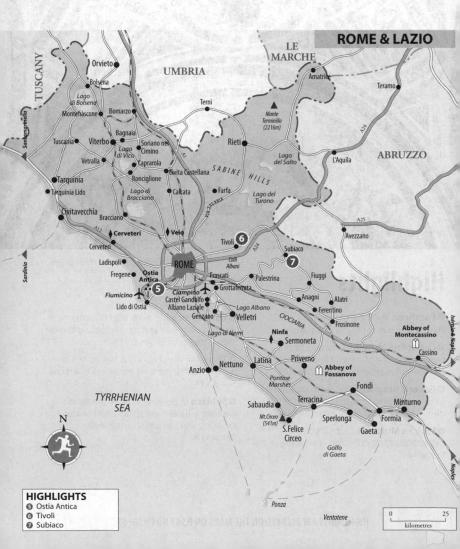

HIGHLIGHTS
⑤ Ostia Antica
⑥ Tivoli
⑦ Subiaco

Rome

You won't enjoy Rome if you spend your time trying to tick off sights. However, there are some places that it would be a pity to leave the city without seeing. The **Vatican** is perhaps the most obvious one, most notably **St Peter's** and the amazing stock of loot in the Vatican Museums; and the star attractions of the ancient city – the **Forum** and **Palatine**, the **Colosseum** – are worth a day or two in their own right. There are also the churches, fountains and works of art from the period that can be said to most define Rome, the Baroque, and in particular the works of Borromini and Bernini, whose efforts compete for space and attention throughout the city. Bernini was responsible for the Fountain of the Four Rivers in the city's most famous square, **Piazza Navona**, among other things; but arguably his best sculptural work is in the **Galleria Borghese**, or in various churches, like his statue of St Theresa in Santa Maria della Vittoria. Borromini, his great rival at the time, built the churches of San Carlo alle Quattro Fontane and Sant'Ivo, both buildings intricately squeezed into small sites – Borromini's trademark. Other great palaces are themselves treasure-troves of great art, like the **Doria Pamphilj** and **Palazzo Barberini**; and there are some unmissable museums, like the galleries of the **Capitoline**, and the main collections of the **Museo Nazionale Romano** in the Palazzo Altemps and Palazzo Massimo, all of which hold staggering collections of the cream of the city's ancient art and sculpture. And finally there's the city itself: stroll through the *centro storico* in the early morning, through Trastevere at sunset, or gaze down at the roofs and domes from the Janiculum Hill on a clear day, and you'll quickly realize that there's no place in Italy like it.

The **city centre** is divided neatly into distinct blocks. The warren of streets that makes up the **centro storico** occupies the hook of land on the left bank of the River Tiber, bordered to the east by Via del Corso and to the north and south by water. From here Rome's central core spreads south and east: down towards Campo de' Fiori; across Via del Corso to the major shopping streets and alleys around the **Spanish Steps**; to the major sites of the **ancient city** to the south; and to the expanse of the **Villa Borghese** park to the north. The left bank of the river is a little more distanced from the main hum of the city centre, home to the Vatican and St Peter's, and, to the south of these, **Trastevere** – even in ancient times a distinct entity from the city proper, although nowadays as much of a focus for tourists as anywhere, especially at night.

The centro storico

Immediately north of Piazza Venezia is the real heart of Rome – the **centro storico** or historic centre, which makes up most of the triangular knob of land that bulges into a bend in the Tiber. This area, known in ancient Roman times as the Campus Martius, was outside the city centre, a low-lying area that was mostly given over to barracks and sporting arenas, together with several temples, including the Pantheon. Later it became the heart of the Renaissance city, and nowadays it's the part of the town that is densest

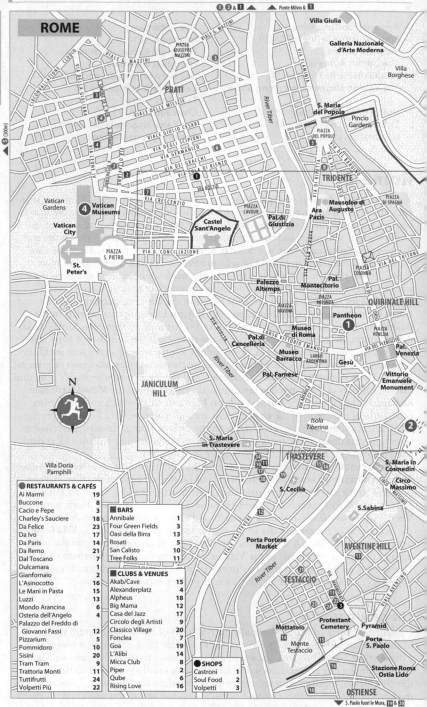

ROME

S (300m)

Villa Giulia

Galleria Nazionale
d'Arte Moderna

Villa
Borghese

PRATI

S. Maria
del Popolo

PIAZZA
DEL POPOLO

Pincio
Gardens

TRIDENTE

PIAZZA
DI SPAGNA

Vatican
Gardens

Vatican
Museums

Mausoleo di
Augusto

Ara
Pacis

PIAZZA
CAVOUR

Castel
Sant'Angelo

Pal. di
Giustizia

Vatican
City

St.
Peter's

PIAZZA
S. PIETRO

VIA D. CONCILIAZIONE

PIAZZA
COLONNA

PIAZZA
DEL TRITONE

Palazzo
Altemps

Pal.
Montecitorio

QUIRINALE HILL

Museo
di Roma

PIAZZA
ROTONDA

Pantheon

PIAZZA
VENEZIA

Pal. di
Cancelleria

Museo
Barracco

LARGO
ARGENTINA

Gesù

Pal.
Venezia

JANICULUM
HILL

Pal. Farnese

Vittorio
Emanuele
Monument

Isola
Tiberina

S. Maria
in Trastevere

TRASTEVERE

S. Maria in
Cosmedin

Villa Doria
Pamphili

S. Cecilia

Circo
Massimo

S.Sabina

AVENTINE HILL

Porta Portese
Market

TESTACCIO

Mattatoio

Monte
Testaccio

Protestant
Cemetery

Pyramid

Porta
S. Paolo

Stazione Roma
Ostia Lido

OSTIENSE

S. Paolo fuori le Mura, **19** & **20**

● RESTAURANTS & CAFÉS

Ai Marmi	19
Buccone	8
Cacio e Pepe	3
Charley's Sauciere	18
Da Felice	23
Da Ivo	17
Da Paris	14
Da Remo	21
Dal Toscano	7
Dulcamara	1
Gianfornaio	2
L'Asinocotto	16
Le Mani in Pasta	15
Luzzi	13
Mondo Arancina	6
Osteria dell'Angelo	4
Palazzo del Freddo di Giovanni Fassi	12
Pizzarium	5
Pommidoro	10
Sisini	20
Tram Tram	9
Trattoria Monti	11
Tuttifrutti	24
Volpetti Più	22

■ BARS

Annibale	1
Four Green Fields	3
Oasi della Birra	13
Rosati	5
San Calisto	10
Tree Folks	11

■ CLUBS & VENUES

Akab/Cave	15
Alexanderplatz	4
Alpheus	18
Big Mama	12
Casa del Jazz	17
Circolo degli Artisti	9
Classico Village	20
Fonclea	7
Goa	19
L'Alibi	14
Micca Club	8
Piper	2
Qube	6
Rising Love	16

● SHOPS

Castroni	1
Soul Food	2
Volpetti	3

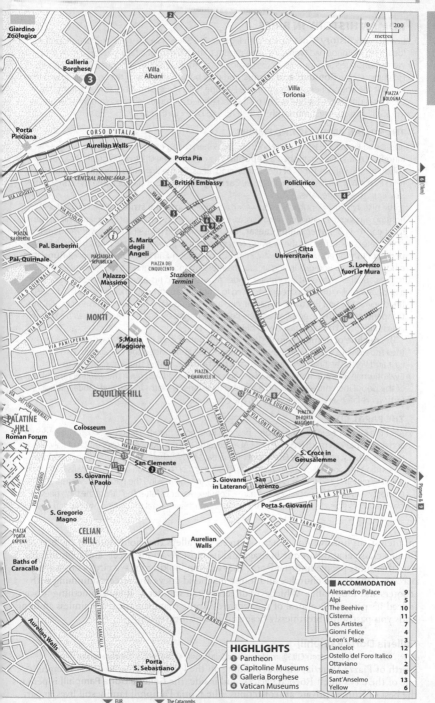

HIGHLIGHTS
1. Pantheon
2. Capitoline Museums
3. Galleria Borghese
4. Vatican Museums

■ ACCOMMODATION
Alessandro Palace	9
Alpi	5
The Beehive	10
Cisterna	11
Des Artistes	7
Giorni Felice	4
Leon's Place	3
Lancelot	12
Ostello del Foro Italico	1
Ottaviano	2
Romae	8
Sant'Anselmo	13
Yellow	6

1

ROMAN HISTORY IN BRIEF

Rome's early **history** is interwoven with legend. Rea Silvia, a vestal virgin and daughter of a local king, Numitor, had twin sons – the product, she alleged, of a rape by Mars. The two boys were abandoned and found by a wolf, who nursed them until their adoption by a shepherd. He named them **Romulus and Remus**, and they became leaders of the community and later laid out the boundaries of the city on the Palatine Hill. Before long it became apparent that there was only room for one ruler, and they quarrelled, Romulus killing Remus and becoming in 753 BC the city's first **monarch**, to be followed by six further kings.

THE ROMAN REPUBLIC AND EMPIRE

Rome as a kingdom lasted until about 507 BC, when the people rose up against the tyrannical King Tarquinius and established a **Republic**. The city prospered, growing greatly in size and subduing the various tribes of the surrounding areas. By the time it had fought and won the third Punic War against its principal rival, **Carthage**, in 146 BC, it had become the dominant power in the Mediterranean.

The history of the Republic was, however, also one of **internal strife**, marked by factional fighting among the patrician ruling classes, and the ordinary people, or plebeians. This all came to a head in 44 BC, when **Julius Caesar**, having proclaimed himself dictator, was murdered by conspirators concerned at the growing concentration of power into one man's hands. A brief period of turmoil ensued, giving way, in 27 BC, to the founding of the **Empire** under **Augustus**, who transformed Rome, building arches, theatres and monuments of a magnificence suited to the capital of an expanding empire. Under Augustus, and his successors, the city swelled to a population of a million, its people housed in cramped apartment blocks or *insulae*; crime in the city was rife, and the traffic apparently on a par with today's. But it was a time of peace and prosperity too, with the empire's borders being ever more extended, reaching their maximum limits under the Emperor Trajan, who died in 117 AD.

The **decline of Rome** is hard to date precisely, but it could be said to have started with the Emperor Diocletian, who assumed power in 284 and divided the empire into two parts, East and West. The first Christian emperor, **Constantine**, shifted the seat of power to Byzantium in 330, and Rome's period as capital of the world was over; the wealthier members of the population moved east and a series of invasions by Goths in 410 and Vandals about forty years later served only to quicken the city's ruin.

THE PAPAL CITY

After the fall of the empire, the **pope** – based in Rome owing to the fact that St Peter (the Apostle and first pope) was martyred here in 64 AD – became the temporal ruler over much of Italy, and it was the papacy, under **Pope Gregory I** ("the Great") in 590, that rescued Rome from its demise. By sending missions all over Europe to spread the word of the Church and publicize its holy relics, he drew pilgrims, and their money, back to the city, in time making the papacy the natural authority in Rome. The pope took the name "Pontifex Maximus" after the title of the high priest of classical times (literally "the keeper of the bridges", which were vital to the city's well-being).

in interest, an unruly knot of narrow streets and alleys that holds some of the best of Rome's classical and Baroque heritage and its most vivacious street- and nightlife. It's here that most people find the Rome they've been looking for – a city of crumbling piazzas, Renaissance churches and fountains, blind alleys and streets humming with scooters and foot-traffic. Whichever direction you wander in there's something to see; indeed it's part of the appeal of the centre of Rome that even the most aimless ambling leads you past some breathlessly beautiful and historic spots.

Galleria Doria Pamphilj

Via del Corso 305 • Daily 10am–5pm • €10.50, including audioguide in English • ☏ 06 679 7323, ⓦ doriapamphilj.it

North of Piazza Venezia, the first building on the left is the Palazzo Doria Pamphilj, one of the city's finest Rococo palaces, and inside, the **Galleria Doria Pamphilj** is perhaps the best of Rome's private art collections. The Doria Pamphilj family still lives in part

As time went on, power gradually became concentrated in a handful of **families**, who swapped the top jobs, including the papacy itself, between them. Under the burgeoning power of the pope, churches were built, the city's pagan monuments rediscovered and preserved, and artists began to arrive in Rome to work on commissions for the latest pope, who would invariably try to outdo his predecessor's efforts with ever more glorious buildings and works of art. This process reached a head during the Renaissance; Bramante, Raphael and Michelangelo all worked in the city throughout their careers, and the reigns of **Pope Julius II** and his successor, **Leo X**, were something of a golden age. However, in 1527 all this was brought abruptly to an end, when the armies of the Habsburg monarch Charles V swept into the city, occupying it for a year, while **Pope Clement VII** cowered in the Castel Sant'Angelo.

The ensuing years were ones of yet more restoration, and perhaps because of this it's the **seventeenth century** that has left the most tangible impression on Rome, the vigour of the **Counter-Reformation** throwing up huge sensational monuments like the Gesù church that were designed to confound the scepticism of the new Protestant thinking. This period also saw the completion of St Peter's under **Paul V**, and the ascendancy of Gian Lorenzo Bernini as the city's principal architect and sculptor. The **eighteenth century** witnessed the decline of the papacy as a political force, a phenomenon marked by the seventeen-year occupation of the city starting in 1798 by Napoleon, after which papal rule was restored.

THE POST-UNIFICATION CITY

Thirty-four years later a pro-Unification caucus under **Mazzini** declared the city a republic but was soon chased out, and Rome had to wait until troops stormed the walls in 1870 to join the unified country – symbolically the most important part of the Italian peninsula to do so. **Garibaldi** wasted no time in declaring the city the capital of the new kingdom – under **Vittorio Emanuele II** – and confining the by now quite powerless pontiff, **Pius IX**, to the Vatican. The Piemontese rulers of the new kingdom set about building a city fit to govern from, cutting new streets through Rome's central core (Via Nazionale, Via del Tritone) and constructing grandiose buildings like the Altar of the Nation. In 1929 **Mussolini** signed the **Lateran Pact** with **Pope Pius XI**, a compromise which forced the Vatican to accept the new Italian state and in return recognized the Vatican City as sovereign territory, independent of Italy, together with the key basilicas and papal palaces in Rome which remain technically independent of Italy to this day.

THE CONTEMPORARY CITY

During **World War II**, Mussolini famously made Rome his centre of operations until his resignation as leader in July 1943. The city was liberated by Allied forces in June 1944. The Italian republic since then has been a mixed affair, regularly changing its government (if not its leaders) every few months until a series of scandals forced the old guard from office. Since then things have continued in much the same vein, with the city symbolizing, to the rest of the country at least, the inertia of their nation's government. However, the city is looking sprucer, and more vibrant, than it has done for some time, and there are even plans afoot to deal with the city centre's chronic traffic problem, with the construction of a third metro line well under way.

of the building, and you're guided through the gallery and the state apartments beyond by way of a free audio-tour narrated by the urbane Jonathan Pamphilj.

The **picture gallery** extends around the main courtyard, the paintings displayed in old-fashioned style, crammed in frame-to-frame, floor-to-ceiling. It has perhaps Rome's best concentration of Dutch and Flemish paintings, with a rare Italian work by Brueghel the Elder showing a naval battle being fought outside Naples, a highly realistic portrait of two old men by Quinten Metsys and a Hans Memling *Deposition*, in the furthest rooms off the main gallery, as well as a further Metsys painting – the fabulously ugly *Moneylenders and their Clients* – in the main gallery, close by Annibale Carracci's bucolic *Flight into Egypt*. Also in the rooms off the courtyard are three paintings by Caravaggio – *Repentant Magdalene* and *John the Baptist*, and his wonderful *Rest on the Flight into Egypt* – hanging near *Salome with the head of St John*, by Titian. The gallery's most prized treasures, however, are in a small room on their own – a Bernini bust of the Pamphilj pope Innocent X and

1

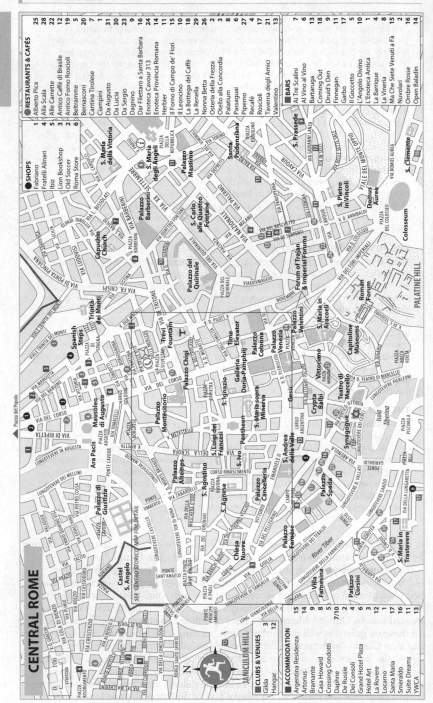

CENTRAL ROME

● RESTAURANTS & CAFÉS

Alberto Pica	25
Alla Scala	28
Alle Carrette	22
Antico Caffè di Brasile	12
Antico Forno Roscioli	19
Beltramme	5
Bernasconi	20
Cantina Tirolese	7
Ciampini	1
Da Augusto	31
Da Lucia	30
Da Sergio	23
Dagnino	9
Dar Filettaro a Santa Barbara	16
Enoteca Cavour 313	24
Enoteca Provincia Romana	14
Herbier	11
Il Forno di Campo de' Fiori	15
Il Leoncino	10
La Bottega del Caffè	8
La Renella	29
Nonna Betta	26
Osteria della Frezza	3
Otello alla Concordia	6
Palatium	2
Passaguai	27
Piperno	4
Recafé	17
Roscioli	21
Taverna degli Amici	13

● SHOPS

Fabriano	1
Fratelli Alinari	4
Ibiz	5
Lion Bookshop	3
Old Soccer	2
Roma Store	6

■ BARS

Ai Tre Scalini	7
Al Vino al Vino	6
Bartaruga	13
Coming Out	18
Druid's Den	9
Finnegan	11
Garbo	17
Il Goccetto	5
L'Angolo Divino	10
L'Enoteca Antica	1
La Barrique	4
La Vineria	8
Ma Che Siete Venuti a Fà	15
Nuvolari	3
Ombre Rosse	16
Open Baladin	14

■ CLUBS & VENUES

Gilda	3
Hangar	12

■ ACCOMMODATION

Argentina Residenza	15
Artorius	14
Bramante	8
Casa Howard	9
Crossing Condotti	7/10
Daphne	2
De Russie	5
Dei Consoli	6
Grand Hotel Plaza	3
Hotel Art	4
La Rovere	12
Locarno	1
Santa Maria	16
Smeraldo	11
Suite Dreams	17
YWCA	13

Velazquez's famous, penetrating painting of the same man. All in all it's a marvellous collection of work, displayed in a wonderfully appropriate setting.

Sant'Ignazio

Piazza di Sant'Ignazio • Mon–Sat 7.30am–7pm, Sun 9am–7pm • Free

Just off Via del Corso, **Piazza Sant'Ignazio** is a lovely little square, laid out like a theatre set and dominated by the facade of the Jesuit church of **Sant'Ignazio**. The saint isn't actually buried here; appropriately, for the founder of the Jesuit order, he's in the Gesù church a little way south. It's a spacious structure, built during the late seventeenth century, and worth visiting for the marvellous Baroque ceiling by Andrea Pozzo showing the entry of St Ignatius into paradise, a spectacular work that employs sledgehammer trompe l'oeil effects, notably in the mock cupola painted into the dome of the crossing. Stand on the disc in the centre of the nave, the focal point for the ingenious rendering of perspective: figures in various states of action and repose, conversation and silence, fix you with stares from their classical pediment.

The Pantheon

Piazza della Rotonda • Mon–Sat 8.30am–7.30pm, Sun 9am–6pm • Free

From Sant'Ignazio, Via del Seminario leads down to Piazza della Rotonda, where the main focus of interest is the **Pantheon**, easily the most complete ancient Roman structure in the city and, along with the Colosseum, visually the most impressive. Though originally a temple that formed part of Marcus Agrippa's redesign of the Campus Martius in around 27 BC – hence the inscription – it's since been proved that the building was entirely rebuilt by the Emperor Hadrian and finished around the year 125 AD. It's a formidable architectural achievement even now: the diameter is precisely equal to its height (43m), the hole in the centre of the dome – from which shafts of sunlight descend to illuminate the musty interior – a full 9m across. Most impressively, there are no visible arches or vaults to hold the whole thing up; instead they're sunk into the concrete of the walls of the building. It would have been richly decorated, the coffered ceiling heavily stuccoed and the niches filled with the statues of gods, but now, apart from its sheer size, the main things of interest are the tombs of two Italian kings, and the tomb of Raphael, between the second and third chapel on the left, with an inscription by the humanist bishop Pietro Bembo: "Living, great Nature feared he might outvie Her works, and dying, fears herself may die." The same kind of sentiments might well have been reserved for the Pantheon itself.

Santa Maria sopra Minerva

Piazza S. Maria della Minerva 42 • Mon–Fri 7am–7pm, Sat & Sun 8am–12.30pm & 3–7pm • ⓦ basilicaminerva.it • Free

There's more artistic splendour on view behind the Pantheon, though Bernini's **Elephant Statue** doesn't really prepare you for the church of Santa Maria sopra Minerva beyond. The statue is Bernini's most endearing piece of work, if not his most characteristic: a cheery elephant trumpeting under the weight of the obelisk he carries on his back – a reference to Pope Alexander VII's reign and supposed to illustrate the

---

MUSEUM PASSES

The **Roma Pass** (❶ 06 06 08, ⓦ romapass.it) costs €23 and is valid for three days. Available from major sights and tourist information kiosks, it entitles you to travel for free on buses, trams and the metro, gives you free admission to two and reduced entry to quite a few of the city's major sights and museums, and, perhaps most importantly, the opportunity not to queue at the first two sights you visit – quite a lifesaver at the Colosseum and one or two others.

You can visit the four museums that make up the **Museo Nazionale Romano** on one ticket, valid for seven days, which costs €7 and is available from each location – Palazzo Altemps, Palazzo Massimo, Crypta Balbi and the Museo delle Terme di Diocleziano.

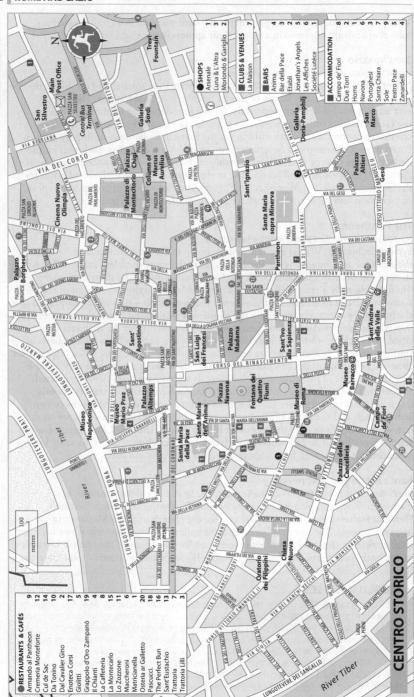

CENTRO STORICO

● SHOPS
Arsenale 1
Luna & L'Altra 3
Moriondo & Gariglio 2

■ CLUBS & VENUES
La Maison 7

■ BARS
Anima 4
Bar della Pace 3
Etablì 2
Jonathan's Angels 5
Les Affiches 6
Société Lutèce 1

■ ACCOMMODATION
Campo de' Fiori 8
Due Torri 2
Hotis 1
Navona 6
Portoghesi 3
Santa Chiara 7
Sole 5
Teatro Pace 9
Zanardelli 4

● RESTAURANTS & CAFÉS
Armando al Pantheon 9
Cremeria Monteforte 12
Cul de Sac 14
Da Tonino 10
Dal Cavalier Gino 2
Enoteca Corsi 17
Giolitti 8
Grappolo d'Oro Zampanò ... 19
Il Chianti 4
La Caffetteria 8
La Montecarlo 15
Lo Zozzone 11
Maccheroni 6
Matricianella 20
Osteria ar Galletto 18
Pascucci 8
The Perfect Bun 16
Sant'Eustachio 13
Trattoria 7
Trattoria Lilli 3

fact that strength should support wisdom. **Santa Maria sopra Minerva** is Rome's only Gothic church, and worth a look just for that. Built in the late thirteenth century on the ruins of a temple to Minerva, it's also one of Rome's art-treasure churches, crammed with the tombs and self-indulgences of wealthy Roman families. Of these, the Carafa chapel, in the south transept, is the best known, holding Filippino Lippi's fresco of the *Assumption*, below which one painting shows a hopeful Carafa (the religious zealot, Pope Paul IV) being presented to the Virgin Mary by Thomas Aquinas; another depicts Aquinas confounding the heretics in the sight of two beautiful young boys – the future Medici popes Leo X and Clement VII. The lives of Leo and Clement come full circle in the church, where they are both buried and remembered by two very grand tombs either side of the high altar – Leo on the left, Clement on the right, close by which is the figure of *Christ Bearing the Cross*, a serene work that Michelangelo completed for the church in 1521.

Sant'Ivo

Corso del Rinascimento 40 • Sun 9am–noon; closed July & Aug • Free

A few steps west of the Pantheon, on Corso del Rinascimento, the rather blank facade of the **Palazzo della Sapienza** cradles the church of **Sant'Ivo** – from the outside at least, one of Rome's most impressive churches, with a playful facade designed by Borromini. Though originally built for the Barberini pope, Urban VIII, the building actually spans the reign of three pontiffs. Each of the two small towers is topped with the weird pyramidal groupings that are the symbol of the Chigi family (representing the hills of Monti di Paschi di Siena), and the central cupola spirals helter-skelter to its zenith, crowned with flames that are supposed to represent the sting of the Barberini bee, their family symbol. The inside, too, is very cleverly designed, light and spacious given the small space the church is squeezed into, rising to the tall parabolic cupola.

San Luigi dei Francesi

Piazza S. Luigi dei Francesi 5 • Daily except Thurs afternoon 10am–12.30pm & 4–7pm • Free • ⓦ saintlouis-rome.net

A short walk from Piazza Navona, the French national church of **San Luigi dei Francesi** is worth a look, mainly for its works by Caravaggio. In the last chapel on the left are three paintings: *The Calling of St Matthew*, in which Christ points to Matthew, who is illuminated by a shaft of sunlight; *The Inspiration of St Matthew*, where Matthew is visited by an angel as he writes the Gospel; and *The Martyrdom of St Matthew*. Caravaggio's first public commission, these paintings were actually rejected at first, partly on grounds of indecorum, and it took considerable reworking by the artist before they were finally accepted.

Piazza Navona

Just west of San Luigi dei Francesi lies **Piazza Navona**, Rome's most famous square. Lined with cafés and restaurants, and often thronged with tourists, street artists and pigeons, it is as picturesque – and as vibrant, day and night – as any piazza in Italy. It takes its shape from the first-century-AD Stadium of Domitian, the principal venue of the athletic events and later chariot races that took place in the Campus Martius. Until the mid-fifteenth century the ruins of the arena were still here, overgrown and disused, but the square was given a facelift in the mid-seventeenth century by Pope Innocent X, who built most of the grandiose palaces that surround it and commissioned Borromini to design the facade of the church of **Sant'Agnese in Agone** on the piazza's western side (Tues–Sun 9.30am–12.30pm & 4–7pm; ⓦsantagneseinagone.org). The story goes that the 13-year-old St Agnes was stripped naked before the crowds in the stadium as punishment for refusing to marry, whereupon she miraculously grew hair to cover herself. The church, typically squeezed into the tightest of spaces by Borromini, is supposedly built on the spot where it all happened.Opposite, the **Fontana dei Quattro Fiumi**, one of three that punctuate the square, is a masterpiece by Bernini, Borromini's arch-rival, and it's said that all the figures are shielding their eyes in horror from Borromini's church facade (Bernini

1

was disdainful of the less successful Borromini, and their rivalry is well documented), but the fountain had actually been completed before the facade was begun. The grand complexity of rock, which represents the four great rivers of the world, is topped with an Egyptian obelisk, brought here by Pope Innocent X from the Circus of Maxentius.

Museo di Roma

Piazza S. Pantaleo 10 • Tues–Sun 10am–8pm; €9, €11.50 with Museo Barracco • ☎ 60 608, ⊛ en.museodiroma.it

Overlooking the south side of Piazza Navona, the eighteenth-century Palazzo Braschi is the home of the **Museo di Roma**, which has a permanent collection relating to the history of the city from the Middle Ages to the present day. The building itself is probably the main attraction – particularly the magnificent Sala Nobile where you enter, the main staircase, and one or two of the renovated rooms – but some of the paintings are of interest, showing views of the city during different eras, and frescoes from demolished palaces provide decent enough highlights.

Museo Barracco

Corso Vittorio Emanuele 16/A • Tues–Sun 9am–7pm • €5.50, €11.50 with Museo di Roma • ☎ 60 608 • ⊛ en.museobarracco.it

Across the street from the Museo di Roma, the **Museo Barracco**, housed in another palace, the so-called Piccola Farnesina, holds a small but high-quality collection of ancient sculpture that was donated to the city at the turn of the century by one Baron Barracco. There are some fine ancient-Egyptian pieces and ceramics and statuary from classical Greece and Rome. Highlights include a head of the young Rameses II, next to a bust of an Egyptian priest, a Roman figure of an athlete from an ancient Greek original, and a highly realistic depiction of a bitch washing herself, from the fourth century BC.

Piazza Pasquino and Via del Governo Vecchio

The triangular space of **Piazza Pasquino** is named after the small battered torso that still stands in the corner. Pasquino is perhaps the best known of Rome's "talking statues" of the Middle Ages and Renaissance times, on which anonymous comments on the affairs of the day would be attached – comments that had a serious as well as a humorous intent, and gave us our word "pasquinade". **Via del Governo Vecchio** leads west from here, and is home – along with the narrow streets around – to some of the *centro storico*'s liveliest restaurants and bars.

Palazzo Altemps

Piazza Sant'Apollinare 46 • Tues–Sun 9am–7.45pm • €7 with Museo Nazionale Romano pass • ☎ 06 3996 7700 • ⊛ archeoroma .beniculturali.it/

Just across the street from the north end of Piazza Navona, Piazza Sant'Apollinare is home to the beautifully restored **Palazzo Altemps**, part of the Museo Nazionale Romano (see box, p.61), and the cream of its collections of Roman statuary.

Ground floor

On the ground floor at the far end of the courtyard's loggia is a statue of the Emperor Antoninus Pius, and, around the corner, a couple of heads of Zeus and Pluto, and a bust of Julia, the daughter of the Emperor Augustus. There are two almost identical statues of Apollo the Lyrist, a magnificent statue of Athena taming a serpent, pieced together from fragments found near the church of Santa Maria sopra Minerva, and, in the far corner of the courtyard, a Dionysus with a satyr and panther, found on the Quirinale Hill.

First floor

Upstairs you get a slightly better sense of the original building – some of the frescoes remain and the north loggia retains its original, late sixteenth-century decoration, simulating a vine-laden pergola. Among the objects on display there's a fine statue of Hermes, a wonderful statue of a warrior at rest, and a charmingly sensitive portrayal of

Orestes and Electra from the first century AD by a sculptor called Menelaus – his name is carved at the base of one of the figures. In a later room stands a colossal head of Hera, and – what some consider the highlight of the entire collection – the famous **Ludovisi throne**, embellished with a delicate relief portraying the birth of Aphrodite. Further on, the Fireplace Salon – whose huge fireplace is embellished with caryatids and lurking ibex, the symbol of the Altemps family – has the so-called *Suicide of Galatian*, apparently commissioned by Julius Caesar to adorn his Quirinal estate. At the other end of the room, an incredible sarcophagus depicts a battle between the Romans and barbarians in graphic, almost viscerally sculptural detail.

Via dei Coronari

West of Palazzo Altemps, narrow **Via dei Coronari**, and some of the streets around, are the fulcrum of Rome's **antiques** trade, and, although the prices are as high as you might expect in such a location, there's a huge number of shops (Via dei Coronari consists of virtually nothing else) selling a tremendous variety of stuff, and a browse along here makes for an absorbing bit of sightseeing.

Sant'Agostino

Piazza Sant'Agostino • Daily 7.45am–noon & 4–7.30pm • Free

Just east of Palazzo Altemps, the Renaissance facade of the church of **Sant'Agostino** takes up one side of a drab piazza of the same name. It's not much to look at from the outside, but a handful of art treasures might draw you in. Just inside the door, the serene statue of the *Madonna del Parto*, by Sansovino, is traditionally invoked during pregnancy, and is accordingly surrounded by photos of newborn babes and their blissful parents. Further into the church, take a look at Raphael's vibrant fresco of Isaiah, on the third pillar on the left, beneath which is another work by Sansovino, a craggy *St Ann, Virgin and Child*. But the biggest crowds gather around the first chapel on the left, where the *Madonna and Pilgrims* by Caravaggio – a characteristic work of what was at the time almost revolutionary realism – shows two peasants with dirty clothes praying at the feet of a sensuous Mary and Child.

Piazza Montecitorio and around

A short walk east from Sant'Agostino, **Piazza Montecitorio** takes its name from the bulky **Palazzo di Montecitorio** on its northern side, home since 1871 to the Italian parliament. Just beyond, off Via del Corso, the **Palazzo Chigi** flanks the north side of **Piazza Colonna**, official residence of the prime minister. The **Column of Marcus Aurelius** in the centre of the piazza was erected between 180 and 190 AD to commemorate military victories in northern Europe, and, like the column of Trajan that inspired it, is decorated with reliefs depicting scenes from the campaigns.

Campo de' Fiori and the Ghetto

Just south of the *centro storico* proper, this is Rome's old centre part two, a similar neighbourhood of cramped, wanderable streets opening out into small squares flanked by churches. However, it's less monumental and more of a working quarter, as evidenced by its main focus, **Campo de' Fiori**, whose fruit and veg stalls are a marked contrast to the pavement artists of Piazza Navona. Close by are the dark alleys of the old **Jewish Ghetto**, and the busy traffic junction of Largo di Torre Argentina.

Campo de' Fiori

Campo de' Fiori is in many ways Rome's most appealing square, home to a lively fruit and vegetable market (Mon–Sat 8am–1pm), and flanked by restaurants and cafés. No one really knows how the square came by its name, which means "field of flowers", but one theory holds that it was derived from the Roman Campus Martius, which used to cover most of this part of town; another claims it is after Flora, the mistress of Pompey, whose theatre used to stand on what is now the square's northeast corner – a huge complex by all accounts, which was the supposed location of Julius Caesar's assassination. Later, Campo de' Fiori was an important point on papal processions between the Vatican and the major basilicas of Rome and a site of public executions. The most notorious killing was of Giordano Bruno, a late sixteenth-century freethinker who was denounced to the Inquisition; his trial lasted for years and he is commemorated by a statue in the middle of the square.

Palazzo Farnese

Piazza Farnese • Mon, Wed & Fri visits (45min) in French, Italian or English at 3pm, 4pm & 5pm • €5 • Book online at Ⓦ inventerrome.com

Just south of Campo de' Fiori, **Piazza Farnese** is a quite different square, with great fountains spurting out of lilies – the Farnese emblem – into marble tubs brought from the Baths of Caracalla, and the sober bulk of the **Palazzo Farnese** itself, begun in 1514 by Antonio da Sangallo the Younger and finished off after the architect's death by Michelangelo, who added the top tier of windows and cornice. The building now houses the **French Embassy** but is open to those organized enough to make an appointment, worth doing to see the amazing Baroque ceiling frescoes of Annibale Carracci in one of the rear reception rooms.

Galleria Spada

Piazza di Capo di Ferro 3 • Tues–Sun 8.30am–7.30pm • €5 • Guided tour every 45 min • ☎06 683 2409, Ⓦ galleriaborghese/spada/it/default.htm

If you can't make it to the Palazzo Farnese, make do instead with the Palazzo Spada, back towards Via Arenula, and the **Galleria Spada** inside; walk right through the courtyard to the back of the building. Its four rooms, decorated in the manner of a Roman noble family's home, have two portraits of Cardinal Bernardino Spada by Reni and Guercino, and the building itself is a treat, its facade frilled with stucco adornments. Left off the small courtyard, there's a crafty trompe l'oeil by Borromini – a tunnel whose actual length is multiplied about four times through the architect's tricks with perspective – though to get a proper look you have to wait for one of the guided tours.

Via Giulia

Via Giulia runs parallel to the Tiber from the Ponte Sisto, and was laid out by Julius II to connect the bridge with the Vatican. The street was conceived as the centre of papal Rome, and Julius commissioned Bramante to line it with imposing palaces. Bramante didn't get very far with the plan, as Julius was soon succeeded by Leo X, but the street quickly became a popular residence for wealthier Roman families, and is still packed full with stylish *palazzi* and antique shops.

Largo di Torre Argentina and around

Largo di Torre Argentina is a large square, frantic with traffic circling around the ruins of four Republican-era temples, home to a thriving cat sanctuary and shop that you can visit (daily noon–6pm; ☎06 4542 5240, Ⓦ romancats.com). On the far side of the square, the **Teatro Argentina** was in 1816 the venue for the first performance of Rossini's *Barber of Seville*, not a success on the night: Rossini was apparently booed into taking refuge in the Bernasconi pastry shop which used to be next door.

The Gesù

Via degli Astalli 16 • Daily 6.45am–12.45pm & 4–7.30pm • Free • Ⓦ chiesadelgesu.org

A short walk east of Largo di Torre Argentina, the church of **Gesù** is a huge structure. The headquarters of the Jesuits, it was ideal for the large and fervent congregations the order wanted to attract – indeed, high and wide, with a single-aisled nave and short transepts edging out under a huge dome, it has since served as the model for Jesuit churches everywhere. The facade is by Giacomo della Porta, the interior the work of Vignola.

The glitzy tomb of the order's founder, St Ignatius, is topped by a huge globe of lapis lazuli – the largest piece in existence. Opposite, the tomb of the sixteenth-century Jesuit missionary St Francis Xavier holds a reliquary containing the saint's arm, severed from the rest of his (incorruptible) body, which remains a focus of pilgrimage in Goa. Otherwise it's the staggering richness of the church's interior that you remember, especially the paintings by the Genoese painter Baciccia in the dome and the nave, the *Triumph in the Name of Jesus*, which oozes out of its frame in a tangle of writhing bodies, flowing drapery and stucco angels clinging on like limpets.

Rooms of St Ignatius

Via degli Astalli 16 • Mon–Sat 4–6pm, Sun 10am–noon • Free • Ⓦ ignatianspirituality.com/7187/the-rooms-of-st-ignatius

Next door to the Gesù, the **Rooms of St Ignatius** occupy part of the first floor of the Jesuit headquarters, and are basically the rooms – recently restored – where St Ignatius lived from 1544 until his death in 1556. There are bits and pieces of furniture and memorabilia relating to the saint, but the true draw is the decorative corridor just outside, designed by Andrea Pozzo in 1680 – a superb exercise in perspective on a minimized scale, giving an illusion of a grand hall in what is a relatively small space.

Via Portico d'Ottavia and around

Cross over to the far side of Via Arenula and you're in what was once the city's **Jewish Ghetto**, a crumbling area of narrow, switchback streets and alleys, easy to lose your way in. There was a Jewish population in Rome as far back as the second century BC, and although much depleted now, it still numbers 16,000 (around half Italy's total), and the quarter is thriving, with a few kosher restaurants, bakers and butchers on and around the main artery of the Jewish area, **Via Portico d'Ottavia**. This leads down to the **Portico d'Ottavia**, a not terribly well preserved second-century-BC gate, rebuilt by Augustus and dedicated to his sister in 23 BC, which was the entranceway to the adjacent amphitheatre of the **Teatro di Marcello** (daily: summer 9am–7pm; winter 9am–6pm; free). Begun by Julius Caesar, finished by Augustus, this was pillaged in the fourth century and not properly restored until the Middle Ages, after which it became a formidable fortified palace for a succession of different rulers, including the Orsini family. Crossing to the other side of Via Portico d'Ottavia, narrow Via della Reginella leads to **Piazza Mattei**, whose **Fontana delle Tartarughe**, or "turtle fountain", is a delightful, late sixteenth-century creation, perhaps restored by Bernini.

The Synagogue

Lungotevere Cenci X • Mid-June to mid-Sept Mon–Thurs & Sun 10am–4.15pm, Fri 9am–1.15pm; mid-Sept to mid-June Sun–Thurs 10am–6.15pm, Fri 10am–3.15pm; closed Sat & Jewish hols • €10, guided 50min tours of the Ghetto €8 • ☎ 06 6840 0661, Ⓦ museoebraico.roma.it

The Ghetto's principal Jewish sight is the huge **Synagogue** by the river, built in 1904 and very much dominating all around with its bulk – not to mention the *carabinieri* who stand guard 24 hours a day. The only way to see the building is on one of the free, regular guided tours it runs in English, afterwards taking in the Synagogue's **museum**. The interior of the building is impressive, rising to a high, rainbow-hued dome; the tours are excellent, giving good background on the building and Rome's Jewish community in general, and the recently revamped museum underneath holds one of the most important collections of Judaica in Europe.

Isola Tiberina

Almost opposite the Synagogue, the **Ponte Fabricio** crosses the river to **Isola Tiberina**. Built in 62 BC, it's the only classical bridge to remain intact without help from the restorers (the Ponte Cestio, on the other side of the island, was partially rebuilt in the nineteenth century). As for the island, it's a calm respite from the city centre proper, with its originally tenth-century church of **San Bartolomeo**, worth a peep inside for its ancient columns and an equally ancient wellhead on the altar steps, carved with figures

1

relating to the founding of the church; the figures include St Bartholomew himself, who also features in the painting above the altar, hands tied above his head, on the point of being skinned alive – his famous and gruesome mode of martyrdom. Beyond the island, you can see the **Ponte Rotto** (Broken Bridge) – all that remains of the first stone bridge to span the Tiber, originally built between 179 and 142 BC.

Piazza Venezia and around

Piazza Venezia is not so much a square as a road junction, and a busy one at that. But it's a good central place to start your wanderings, close to both the medieval and Renaissance centre of Rome and the bulk of the ruins of the ancient city. Flanked on all sides by imposing buildings, it's a dignified focal point for the city in spite of the traffic, and a spot you'll find yourself returning to time and again.

Palazzo Valentini

Via IV Novembre116/A • €7.50, booking and tours obligatory • ☎ 06 32 810, ⊛ palazzovalentini.it

Just off Piazza Venezia, solid, late sixteenth century **Palazzo Valentini** is the home of Rome's regional government but is also the location of a recently excavated, ancient Roman baths and residential complex, and these have in part been opened up to the public. You have to take a tour to see them, but they succeed pretty well in bringing the excavations to life, with glass floors and catwalks taking you through the site and technology that re-creates the rooms as they might have looked in ancient times.

Palazzo Venezia

Via del Plebiscito 118 • Tues–Sun 8.30am–7.30pm • €4 • ☎ 06 32 810, ⊛ galleriaborghese.it/nuove/evenezia.htm

Forming the western side of the piazza, **Palazzo Venezia** was the first large Renaissance palace in the city, built for the Venetian Pope Paul II in the mid-fifteenth century and for a long time the embassy of the Venetian Republic. More famously, **Mussolini** moved in here while in power, occupying the vast Sala del Mappamondo and making his declamatory speeches to the huge crowds below from the small balcony facing onto the piazza. Nowadays it's a venue for great exhibitions and home to the **Museo Nazionale di Palazzo Venezia**, a museum of Renaissance arts and crafts, with a number of fifteenth-century devotional paintings, bronzes and sculpture.

San Marco

Piazza S. Marco 52 • Tues–Sat 8.30am–noon & 4–6.30pm, Sun 9am–1pm & 4–8pm • Free

Adjacent to the Palazzo Venezia on its southern side, the church of **San Marco**, accessible from Piazza San Marco, is the Venetian church in Rome – and one of its most ancient basilicas. Standing on the spot where the apostle is supposed to have lived while in the city, it was rebuilt in 833 and added to by various Renaissance and eighteenth-century popes. Look out for the apse mosaic dating from the ninth century, which shows Pope Gregory offering his church to Christ.

The Vittoriano

Piazza Venezia • Daily 9.30am–6pm • Free • **Lifts** Summer Mon–Thurs 9am–7.30pm, Fri & Sat 9.30am–11.30pm, Sun 9.30am–8.30pm; winter Mon–Thurs 9.30am–6.30pm, Fri–Sun 9.30am–7.30pm • €7

Piazza Venezia is dominated by the Vittorio Emanuele Monument or **Vittoriano**, erected at the beginning of the twentieth century as the "Altar of the Nation" to commemorate Italian Unification. It has been variously likened in the past to a typewriter (because of its shape), and, by American GIs, to a wedding cake. It's great fun clambering up and down the sweeping terraces and flights of steps, cutting through eventually to the Capitoline Museums behind. There are things to see inside (principally a large Unification museum), but the main interest is on the outside: the Tomb of the Unknown Soldier at the top of the first flight of steps; the equestrian statue of Vittorio Emanuele II, one of the world's largest, on the next level, the terraces above this; and finally the **lifts** which whisk you to the terrace at the top – not cheap, but the views are all-encompassing, and of course this is the one place from which you can't see the Vittoriano.

The Capitoline Hill

The real pity about the Vittoriano is that it obscures views of the **Capitoline Hill** behind – once the spiritual and political centre of the Roman Empire. Apart from anything else, this hill has contributed key words to the English language, including, of course, "capitol", and "money", which comes from the temple to Juno Moneta that once stood up here and housed the Roman mint. The Capitoline also played a significant role in medieval and Renaissance times: the flamboyant fourteenth-century dictator Cola di Rienzo stood here in triumph in 1347, and was murdered here by an angry mob seven years later – a humble statue marks the spot.

Santa Maria in Aracoeli
Daily 9am–12.30pm & 2.30–5.30pm • Free

The church of **Santa Maria in Aracoeli** crowns the highest point on the Capitoline Hill, built on the site of a temple where, according to legend, the Tiburtine Sybil foretold the birth of Christ. Reached by a steep flight of steps erected by Cola di Rienzo in 1348, or more easily by cutting through from the Vittoriano or Campidoglio, it's one of Rome's most ancient basilicas, with, in the first chapel on the right, some fine frescoes by Pinturicchio recording the life of San Bernardino. The church is also known for its role as keeper of the "Bambino", a small statue of the infant Christ, carved from the wood of a Gethsemane olive tree. It's said to have healing powers and was traditionally called out to the sickbeds of the ill and dying all over the city, its coach commanding instant right-of-way through the heavy Rome traffic. The statue was stolen in 1994, however, and a copy now stands in its place, in a small chapel to the left of the high altar.

Piazza del Campidoglio

Next to the steps up to Santa Maria is the **cordonata**, an elegant, gently rising ramp, topped with two Roman statues of Castor and Pollux, leading to **Piazza del Campidoglio**, one of Rome's most elegant squares. Designed by Michelangelo in the last years of his life for Pope Paul III, the square wasn't in fact completed until the late seventeenth century. Michelangelo balanced the piazza, redesigning the facade of what is now the **Palazzo dei Conservatori** and projecting an identical building across the way, known as the **Palazzo Nuovo**. Both are angled slightly to focus on **Palazzo Senatorio**, Rome's town hall. In the centre of the square Michelangelo placed an equestrian statue of Emperor Marcus Aurelius, which had previously stood for years outside San Giovanni in Laterano; early Christians had refrained from melting it down because they believed it to be of the Emperor Constantine. After careful restoration, the original is now behind a glass wall in the Palazzo Nuovo, and a copy has taken its place at the centre of the piazza.

The Capitoline Museums
Tues–Sun 9am–8pm • €6.50, €8.50 7-day joint ticket with Centrale Montemartini – see p.89 • ⓦ museicapitolini.org

The Palazzo dei Conservatori and Palazzo Nuovo together make up the **Capitoline Museums**, containing some of the city's most important ancient sculpture and art.

Palazzo dei Conservatori

The **Palazzo dei Conservatori** holds the larger, more varied collection. Among its many treasures are the so-called *Spinario*, a Roman statue of a boy picking a thorn out of his foot; the Etruscan bronze she-wolf nursing the mythic founders of the city; and the Hannibal Room, covered in wonderfully vivid fifteenth-century paintings recording

1

Rome's wars with Carthage, and so named for a rendering of Hannibal seated impressively on an elephant.

The wonderfully airy **new wing** holds the original of Marcus Aurelius, formerly in the square outside, alongside a giant bronze statue of Constantine, or at least its head, hand and orb. Nearby stands the rippling bronze of Hercules, behind which are part of the foundations and a retaining wall from the original temple of Jupiter here, discovered when the work for the new wing was undertaken. And when museum fatigue sets in you can climb up to the floor above to the second-floor **café**, whose terrace commands one of the best views in Rome. The second-floor **pinacoteca** holds Renaissance painting from the fourteenth century to the late seventeenth century. Highlights include a couple of portraits by Van Dyck, a penetrating *Portrait of a Crossbowman* by Lorenzo Lotto, a pair of paintings from 1590 by Tintoretto, and a very fine early work by Lodovico Carracci, *Head of a Boy*. In one of the two large main galleries, there's a vast picture by Guercino, depicting the *Burial of Santa Petronilla* (an early Roman martyr who was the supposed daughter of St Peter), and two paintings by Caravaggio, one a replica of the young John the Baptist which hangs in the Palazzo Doria Pamphilj, the other an early work known as *The Fortune-Teller*.

Palazzo Nuovo

The **Palazzo Nuovo** across the square – also accessible by way of an underground walkway that takes in good views of the Roman Forum just below – is the more manageable of the two museums, with some of the best of the city's Roman sculpture crammed into half a dozen or so rooms. Among them is the remarkable statue *Dying Gaul*, as well as a *Satyr Resting* that was the inspiration for Nathaniel Hawthorne's book *The Marble Faun*; and the red marble *Laughing Silenus*. There are also busts and statues of Roman emperors and other famous names: a young Augustus, a cruel Caracalla and, the centrepiece, a life-size portrait of Helena, the mother of Constantine, reclining gracefully. Don't miss the coy, delicate *Capitoline Venus*, housed in a room on its own.

San Pietro in Carcere

Clivo Argentario 1 • Daily 9am–7.30pm • €10 • ☎ 06 8881 6186, ☒ operaromanapellegrinaggi.org

On the left side of the Palazzo Senatorio (as you face it from the Campidoglio) steps lead down to the little church of **San Pietro in Carcere**, built above the ancient **Mamertine Prison**, where spies, vanquished soldiers and other enemies of the Roman state were incarcerated, and where St Peter himself was held. The church and prison, together with some recent excavations of stretches of city wall, are now part of a multimedia tour, taking in the murky depths of the jail, in which you can see the column to which St Peter was chained, along with the spring the saint is said to have used to baptize his guards and other prisoners.

Piazza Bocca della Verità

On the other side of the Capitoline Hill, down towards the Tiber, Via di Teatro di Marcello meets the riverside main drag at the **Piazza Bocca della Verità**, home to two of the city's better-preserved Roman temples, the **Temple of Portunus** and the **Temple of Hercules Victor** – the oldest surviving marble structure in Rome and long known as the Temple of Vesta because, like all vestal temples, it's circular. Both date from the end of the second century BC, and although you can't get inside, they're worth a look as fine examples of Republican-era places of worship.

Santa Maria in Cosmedin

Daily 10am–5pm • Free

More interesting is the church of **Santa Maria in Cosmedin** on the far side of the square, a typically Roman medieval basilica with a huge marble altar and a colourful and ingenious Cosmati-work marble mosaic floor – one of the city's finest. Outside in the portico, and giving the square its name, is the **Bocca della Verità** (Mouth of Truth), an ancient Roman drain cover in the shape of an enormous face that in medieval times would apparently swallow the hand of anyone who hadn't told the truth. It was particularly popular with husbands anxious to test the faithfulness of their wives; now it is one of the city's biggest tour-bus attractions.

Ancient Rome

There are remnants of the ancient Roman era all over the city, but the most concentrated and central grouping – which for simplicity's sake we've called **Ancient Rome** – is the area that stretches southeast from the Capitoline Hill. It's a reasonably traffic-free and self-contained part of the city, but it wasn't always like this. Mussolini ploughed Via dei Fori Imperiali through here in the 1930s, with the intention of turning it into one giant archeological park, and this to some extent is what it is. You could spend a good day or so picking your way through the rubble of what was once the heart of the ancient world.

INFORMATION AND TOURS

Opening hours The Forum, Palatine Hill and Colosseum are visitable on the same ticket and are open daily at the following times: Jan to mid-Feb 8.30am–3.30pm; mid-Feb to mid-March 8.30am–4pm; mid- to end March 8.30am–4.30pm; April–Aug 8.30am–6.15pm; Sept 8.30am–6pm; Oct 8.30am–5.30pm; Nov & Dec 8.30am–3.30pm. Trajan's Market and the Imperial Forums have their own, separate opening times and admission prices (see below).

Admission Tickets cost €12 and include admission to the Forum, Palatine Hill and Colosseum, and any temporary exhibitions; they are valid for two days; EU citizens aged 18–24 €7.50; under-18s and over-65s free.

Access The only entrance to the Forum is halfway down Via dei Fori Imperiali on the right, although there are exits by the church of San Pietro in Carcere (see opposite) – from where you can walk up to the Capitoline Hill (p.69) or across the road to the Imperial Forums and Trajan's Markets – or at the opposite end, beyond the Arch of Titus, which leave you opposite the entrance to the Colosseum. You can also leave the Forum by way of the main entrance to the Palatine Hill, and there is a separate entrance to the Palatine on Via San Gregorio. Everywhere is about as wheelchair-accessible as it can be, with very few un-navigable steps, except the

upper levels of the Colosseum, where you can avoid the steps by taking the lift in the northeastern corner – just keep walking beyond the ticket office.

Queues These can be a problem, particularly at the Colosseum, and while they do move quickly, during summer they're rarely less than 100m long and often stretch into the scrum of touts outside the arena. To avoid them, try turning up before the Colosseum opens or right at the end of the day, or buy an Archeocard or RomaPass (see p.61), which allow you to use a different queue. You could also join a guided tour (see below), buy your ticket at the Palatine or Forum entrances which are usually quieter, and jump the queue that way, or book tickets in advance; go to ⓦ ticketclic.it or phone ☏ 06 3996 7700 (there's a charge of €1.50 per ticket).

Tours There are guided tours of the Colosseum roughly every 30min from 9.15am (€4), and of the Forum every day at 1pm (€4); audioguides for each site cost €4.50.

Further information There is no official site for the Forum and Palatine and the best place to go for up-to-date practical details is ⓦ 060608.it. See also ⓦ cvrlab.org, which has digital reconstructions of the buildings of the Forum and parts of the Colosseum – helpful if you're trying to make sense of all the rubble.

The Imperial Forums and Trajan's Markets

Via IV Novembre 94 • Tues–Sun 9am–7pm • €11, audioguide €3.50 • ☏ 060 608, ⓦ mercatiditraiano.it. The Imperial Forums visitor centre (daily 9.30am–6.30pm) just beyond Via Cavour, opposite the church of Santi Cosma e Damiano, has information, a bookshop, toilets and a café

One of the major victims of Mussolini's plan was the **Imperial Forums**, which were built as ancient Rome grew in power and the Forum proper became too small. The ruins of forums built by Caesar, Augustus and Trajan, among others, litter either side of the Via dei Fori Imperiali, and are still being excavated. But you can visit the largest and latest of these, the **Forum of Trajan**, which was constructed at what was probably the very pinnacle of Roman power and prestige and incorporates the crescent of shops and arcades known as **Trajan's Markets**. Accessible from Via IV Novembre, the Great Hall here is an impressive two-storey space, and incorporates a number of finds from the Imperial

1

Forums, including a colossal head of Constantine, a torso of a warrior, part of the temple of the Forum of Augustus and a bit of the frieze from Caesar's temple of Venus Genetrix – three columns of which still stand in the Forum of Caesar across the road, and are viewable from the terrace upstairs. Afterwards descend to the Via Biberatica, whose shops and taverns wind around the bottom of the arcade before climbing to the belvedere for a better view over the Forum proper, the most notable remains of which are the column stumps of the massive **Basilica Ulpia**, and the enormous **Column of Trajan** next to it – erected to celebrate the emperor's victories in Dacia (modern Romania) in 112 AD, and covered from top to bottom with reliefs commemorating the highlights of the campaign.

The Roman Forum

The five or so acres that make up the **Roman Forum** were once the heart of the Mediterranean world, and, although the glories of ancient Rome are hard to glimpse here now, there's a symbolic allure to the place, and at certain times of day a desolate drama, that make it one of the most compelling sets of ruins anywhere in the world.

Via Sacra to the Curia

You need some imagination and a little history to really appreciate the place but the public spaces are easy enough to discern, especially the spinal **Via Sacra**, the best-known street of ancient Rome, along which victorious emperors and generals would ride in procession to give thanks at the Capitoline's Temple of Juno. Towards the Capitoline Hill end of the Via Sacra, the large cube-shaped building is the **Curia**, built on the orders of Julius Caesar as part of his programme for expanding the Forum, although what you see now is a third-century-AD reconstruction. The Senate met here, and inside three wide stairs rise left and right, on which about three hundred senators could be accommodated with their folding chairs.

Arch of Septimius Severus and around

Nearby, the **Arch of Septimius Severus** was constructed in the early third century AD by his sons Caracalla and Galba to mark their father's victories in what is now Iran. Next to the arch, the low brown wall is the **Rostra**, from which important speeches were made (it was from here that Mark Anthony most likely spoke about Caesar after his death), to the left of which are the long stairs of the **Basilica Julia**, built by Julius Caesar in the 50s BC after he returned from the Gallic wars. A bit further along, on the right, rails mark the site of the **Lacus Curtius**, the spot where, according to legend, a chasm opened during the earliest days of the city and the soothsayers determined that it would only be closed once Rome had sacrificed its most valuable possession into it. Marcus Curtius, a Roman soldier who declared that Rome's most valuable possession was a loyal citizen, hurled himself and his horse into the void and it duly closed.

Basilica Julia and House of the Vestal Virgins

Next to the Basilica Julia, the enormous pile of rubble topped by three graceful Corinthian columns is the **Temple of Castor and Pollux**, dedicated in 484 BC to the divine twins or Dioscuri, who appeared miraculously to ensure victory for the Romans in a key battle. Beyond here, the **House of the Vestal Virgins** is a second-century-AD reconstruction of a building originally built by Nero: four storeys of rooms around a central courtyard, fringed by the statues or inscribed pedestals of the women themselves, with the round Temple of Vesta at the near end.

The Basilica of Maxentius and the Arch of Titus

Almost opposite, a shady walkway to the left leads to the **Basilica of Maxentius**, in terms of size and ingenuity probably the Forum's most impressive remains. Begun by Maxentius, it was continued by his co-emperor and rival, Constantine, after he had defeated him at the Battle of the Milvian Bridge in 312 AD. From here the Via Sacra climbs more steeply to the **Arch of Titus**, built by Titus's brother, Domitian, after the emperor's death in 81 AD, to commemorate his victories in Judea in 70 AD, and his triumphal return from that campaign.

The Palatine Hill
Rising above the Roman Forum, the **Palatine Hill** (for opening hours, see p.71) is supposedly where the city of Rome was founded, and is home to some of its most ancient remains. In a way it's a greener, more pleasant site to tour than the Forum. In the days of the Republic, the Palatine was the most desirable address in Rome (the word "palace" is derived from Palatine), and big names continued to colonize it during the imperial era, trying to outdo each other with ever larger and more magnificent dwellings.

The site
Along the main path up from the Forum, the **Domus Flavia** was once one of the most splendid residences, and, to the left, the top level of the gargantuan **Domus Augustana** spreads to the far brink of the hill. You can look down from here on its vast central courtyard with fountain and wander to the brink of the deep trench of the **Stadium**. On the far side of the Stadium, the ruins of the Domus and **Baths of Septimius Severus** cling to the side of the hill, while the large grey building nearby houses the **Museo Palatino**, which contains an assortment of statuary, pottery and architectural fragments that have been excavated on the Palatine during the last 150 years. In the opposite direction from the Domus Flavia is the **Cryptoporticus**, a long passage built by Nero to link the vestibule of his Domus Aurea (see p.83) with the Palatine palaces, and decorated with well-preserved Roman stuccowork at the far end, towards the **House of Livia** – originally believed to have been the residence of Livia, the wife of Augustus, though now identified as simply part of the **House of Augustus** – the set of ruins beyond, open only at certain times. Climb up the steps by the entrance to the Cryptoporticus and you're in the bottom corner of the **Farnese Gardens**, among the first botanical gardens in Europe, laid out by Cardinal Alessandro Farnese in the mid-sixteenth century and now a tidily planted retreat from the exposed heat of the ruins. At the far end of the gardens are the traces of an **Iron Age village** that perhaps marks the real centre of Rome's ancient beginnings.

The Arch of Constantine
Outside the Colosseum exit of the Forum, the huge **Arch of Constantine** on your right was placed here in the early decades of the fourth century AD after Constantine had consolidated his power as sole emperor. The arch demonstrates the deterioration of the arts during the late stages of the Roman Empire – most of the sculptural decoration here had to be removed from other monuments, and the builders were probably quite ignorant of the significance of the pieces they borrowed: the round medallions are taken from a temple dedicated to the Emperor Hadrian's lover, Antinous, and show Antinous and Hadrian engaged in a hunt. The other pieces, taken from the Forum of Trajan, show Dacian prisoners captured in Trajan's war.

The Colosseum
The **Colosseum** (for opening hours, see p.71) is perhaps Rome's most awe-inspiring ancient monument, an enormous structure that despite the depredations of nearly two thousand years of earthquakes, fires, riots, wars and, not least, plundering for its seemingly inexhaustible supply of ready-cut travertine blocks, still stands relatively intact – a recognizable symbol not just of the city of Rome, but of the entire ancient world. It's not much more than a shell now, eaten away by pollution and cracked by the vibrations of cars and the metro, but the basic structure is easy to see, and has served as a model for stadiums around the world ever since. You'll not be alone in appreciating it and during summer the combination of people and scaffolding can make a visit more like touring a contemporary building-site than an ancient monument. But visit late in the evening or

1

early morning before the tour buses have arrived, and the arena can seem more like the marvel it really is.

Originally known as the Flavian Amphitheatre (the name Colosseum is a much later invention), it was begun around 72 AD by the Emperor Vespasian. Inside, there was room for a total of around 60,000 people seated and 10,000 or so standing. Seating was allocated according to social status, with the emperor and his attendants naturally occupying the best seats in the house, and the social class of the spectators diminishing as you got nearer the top. There was a labyrinth below that was covered with a wooden floor and punctuated at various places for trap doors that could be opened as required, and lifts to raise and lower the animals that were to take part in the games. The floor was covered with canvas to make it waterproof and the canvas was covered with several centimetres of sand to absorb blood; in fact, our word "arena" is derived from the Latin word for sand.

The Tridente

The northern part of Rome's centre is sometimes known as the **Tridente** on account of the trident shape of the roads leading down from the apex of Piazza del Popolo – **Via di Ripetta**, **Via del Corso** and **Via del Babuino**. The area east of Via del Corso, focusing on **Piazza di Spagna**, was historically the artistic quarter of the city, and eighteenth- and nineteenth-century Grand Tourists would come here in search of the colourful and exotic; institutions like *Caffè Greco* and *Babington's Tea Rooms* were the meeting-places of the local expat community for close on a couple of centuries. Today these institutions have given ground to more latter-day traps for the tourist dollar, and the area around Via dei Condotti is these days strictly international designer territory. But the air of a Rome being discovered – even colonized – by foreigners persists, even if most of those hanging out on the Spanish Steps are flying-visit teenagers.

Via del Corso

The central prong of the Tridente and the boundary of the historic centre to the east, **Via del Corso** is Rome's main thoroughfare, leading all the way from Piazza Venezia at its southern end up to Piazza del Popolo to the north. On its eastern side, it gives onto the swish shopping streets that lead up to Piazza di Spagna; on the western side the web of streets tangles its way right down to the Tiber. It is Rome's principal shopping street, home to a mixture of upmarket boutiques and chain stores that make it a busy stretch during the day, full of hurrying pedestrians and crammed buses, but a relatively dead one after dark. The good news is that the top end, beyond Piazza Colonna, where the bulk of the shops are, is pedestrianized, so shopping and strolling is much easier and more enjoyable.

Piazza di Spagna

Via del Babuino leads down from Piazza del Popolo to **Piazza di Spagna**, a long straggle of a square almost entirely enclosed by buildings and centring on the distinctive boat-shaped **Barcaccia** fountain, the last work of Bernini's father. It apparently remembers the great flood of Christmas Day 1598, when a barge from the Tiber was washed up on the slopes of Pincio Hill here.

The Keats-Shelley House

Piazza di Spagna 26 • Mon–Fri 10am–1pm & 2–6pm, Sat 11am–2pm & 3–6pm • €4.50 • ☎ 06 678 4235, ⓦ keats-shelley-house.org • To rent the building's third-floor apartment, contact Landmark Trust ☎ 01628 825925, ⓦ landmarktrust.org.uk

Fronting Piazza di Spagna, opposite the fountain, is the house where the poet John Keats died in 1821. It now serves as the **Keats-Shelley House**, an archive of English-language literary and historical works and a museum of manuscripts and literary memorabilia relating to the Keats circle of the early nineteenth century – namely the poet himself, Shelley and Mary Shelley, and Byron (who at one time lived across the square). Among many bits of manuscript, letters and the like, there's a silver scallop-shell reliquary containing locks of Milton's and Elizabeth Barrett Browning's hair, while Keats's death mask, stored in the room where he died, captures a resigned grimace. Keats didn't really enjoy his time in Rome, referring to it as his "posthumous life": he was tormented by his love for Fanny Brawne, and spent months in pain before he died, confined to the rooming house with his artist friend Joseph Severn, to whom he remarked that he could already feel "the flowers growing over him".

The Spanish Steps

The only Spanish feature of the **Spanish Steps** (Scalinata di Spagna) is the fact that they lead down to the Spanish Embassy, which also gave the piazza its name. Sweeping down in a cascade of balustrades and balconies, in the nineteenth century the steps were the hangout of young hopefuls waiting to be chosen as artists' models. Nowadays the scene is not much changed, with the steps providing the venue for international posing and flirting late into the summer nights. At the top is the **Trinità dei Monti**, a largely sixteenth-century church designed by Carlo Maderno and paid for by the French king. Its rose-coloured Baroque facade overlooks the rest of Rome from its hilltop site, and it's worth clambering up just for the views, but do look inside for a couple of works by Daniele da Volterra, notably a soft, flowing fresco of the *Assumption* in the third chapel on the right, which includes a portrait of his teacher Michelangelo, and a *Deposition* across the nave.

Piazza del Popolo

The oval-shaped expanse of **Piazza del Popolo** is a dignified meeting of roads, now pedestrianized, laid out in 1538 by Pope Paul III (Alessandro Farnese) to make an impressive entrance to the city. The monumental **Porta del Popolo** went up in 1655, and was the work of Bernini, whose patron Alexander VII's Chigi family symbol – the heap of hills surmounted by a star – can clearly be seen above the main gateway. During summer, the steps around the obelisk and fountain, and the cafés on either side of the square, are popular hangouts. But the square's real attraction is the unbroken view it gives all the way down Via del Corso, to the central columns of the Vittoriano. If you get to choose your first view of the centre of Rome, make it this one.

Santa Maria del Popolo

Piazza del Popolo • Mon–Sat 7am–noon & 4–7pm, Sun 8am–1.30pm & 4.30–7.30pm • Free

On the far side of the piazza, hard against the city walls, **Santa Maria del Popolo** holds some of the best Renaissance art of any Roman church. It was originally erected here in 1099 over the supposed burial place of Nero, in order to sanctify what was believed to be an evil place. Inside, the Chigi chapel, second on the left, was designed by Raphael for Agostino Chigi in 1516. Michelangelo's protégé, Sebastiano del Piombo, was responsible for the altarpiece, and two of the sculptures in the corner niches, of Daniel and Habakkuk, are by Bernini. But it's two pictures by Caravaggio in the left-hand chapel of the north transept that attract the most attention. These are typically dramatic works – one, the *Conversion of St Paul*, showing Paul and horse bathed in a beatific radiance; the other, the *Crucifixion of St Peter*, depicting Peter as an aged but strong figure, dominated by the muscular figures hoisting him up.

Ara Pacis Augustae

Lungotevere in Augusta • Tues–Sun 9am–7pm • €9, audioguide €3.50 • ☎ 06 0608 • ⓦ arapacis.it

Via Ripetta runs southwest from Piazza del Popolo into **Piazza del Augusta Imperatore**, an odd square of largely Mussolini-era buildings, dominated by the massive **Mausoleum of Augustus**, burial place of the emperor and his family and now under long-term restoration.

On the far side of the square, the **Ara Pacis Augustae** or "Altar of Augustan Peace" is now enclosed in a controversial purpose-built structure designed by the New York-based architect Richard Meier, its angular lines and sheer white surfaces dominating the Tiber side of the square. The altar is a more substantially recognizable Roman remain than the mausoleum, a marble block enclosed by sculpted walls built in 13 BC, probably to celebrate Augustus's victory over Spain and Gaul and the peace it heralded. It's a superb example of Roman sculpture, with a frieze on one side showing the imperial family at the height of its power: Augustus, his great general Marcus Agrippa, and Augustus's wife Livia, followed by a victory procession containing her son – and Augustus's eventual successor – Tiberius and niece Antonia, the latter caught simply and realistically turning to her husband, Drusus. On the opposite side the veiled figure is believed to be Julia, Augustus's daughter.

The Villa Borghese and north

Immediately above Piazza del Popolo, the **Pincio Gardens** were laid out by Valadier in the early nineteenth century, and, fringed with dilapidated busts of classical and Italian heroes, give fine **views** over the roofs, domes and TV antennae of central Rome, right across to St Peter's and the Janiculum Hill. It's also a good place to rent bikes and and trikes to tour Rome's largest central open space, the **Villa Borghese**, which lies just beyond, and whose woods, lakes and lawns offer respite from the bustle of the city centre, and any number of attractions – including some of the city's finest museums – for those who want to do more than just stroll or sunbathe.

Galleria Borghese

Piazzale del Museo Borghese • Tues–Sun 8.30am–7.30pm • €10.50 • Pre-booked visits obligatory at ☏ 06 32 810 or online at Ⓦ ticketeria.it • Ⓦ galleriaborghese.it

On the far eastern edge of the Villa Borghese park, the wonderful **Galleria Borghese** was built in the early seventeenth century by Cardinal Scipione Borghese, and turned over to the state in 1902. Today it's one of Rome's great treasure-houses of art and should not be missed.

The ground floor

The **ground floor** contains mainly **sculpture**: a mixture of ancient Roman items and seventeenth-century works, roughly linked together with late eighteenth-century ceiling paintings showing scenes from the Trojan War. Highlights include, in the first room off the entrance hall, Canova's famously erotic statue *Paolina Borghese* – sister of Napoleon and married (reluctantly) to the reigning Prince Borghese – posed as Venus. Next door, there's a marvellous statue of *David* by **Bernini**, the face of which is a self-portrait of the sculptor, and, further on, a dramatic, poised statue of *Apollo and Daphne* that captures the split second when Daphne is transformed into a laurel tree, with her fingers becoming leaves and her legs tree-trunks. Next door, the Room of the Emperors has another Bernini sculpture, *The Rape of Persephone*, dating from 1622, a coolly virtuosic work that shows in melodramatic form the story of the abduction to the underworld of the beautiful nymph Persephone. Finally, the so-called Room of Silenus contains a variety of paintings by Cardinal Scipione's protégé **Caravaggio**, notably the *Madonna of the Grooms* from 1605, a painting that at the time was considered to have depicted Christ far too realistically to hang in a central Rome church. Look also at *St Jerome*, captured writing at a table lit only by a source of light that streams in from the upper left of the picture, and his *David holding the head of Goliath*, sent by Caravaggio to Cardinal Scipione from exile in Malta, where he had fled to escape capital punishment for various crimes, and perhaps the last painting he ever did.

The first floor

The **upstairs gallery** is one of the richest small collections of **paintings** in the world. In the first room are several important paintings by Raphael, including his *Deposition*, painted in 1507 for a noble of Perugia in memory of her son. Look out also for *Lady with a Unicorn* and *Portrait of a Man* by Perugino, and a copy of the artist's tired-out *Julius II*, painted in the last year of the pope's life, 1513. In further rooms there are more early sixteenth-century paintings; prominent works include Cranach's *Venus and Cupid with a Honeycomb*, Lorenzo Lotto's touching *Portrait of a Man*, and in the opposite direction a series of self-portraits by Bernini at various stages of his long life. Next to these are a lifelike bust of *Cardinal Scipione* executed by Bernini in 1632, and a smaller bust of *Pope Paul V*, also by Bernini. Beyond here, in a further room, is a painting of *Diana* by Domechino, depicting the goddess and her attendants doing a bit of target practice, and Titian's *Sacred and Profane Love*, painted in 1514 when he was about 25 years old, to celebrate the marriage of the Venetian noble Niccolò Aurelio.

Galleria Nazionale d'Arte Moderna

Viale delle Belli Arti 131 • Tues–Sun 8.30am–7.30pm • €10 • ☎ 06 3229 8221, ⓦ gnam.arti.beniculturali.it

The Villa Borghese has two other major museums and of them, the **Galleria Nazionale d'Arte Moderna** is probably the less compulsory – a lumbering, Neoclassical building housing a collection of nineteenth- and twentieth-century Italian paintings and a few foreign artists. There are paintings by Courbet, Cézanne and Van Gogh, and a twentieth-century collection upstairs including work by Modigliani, De Chirico, Boccioni and the Futurists, and postwar canvases by the likes of Mark Rothko, Jackson Pollock and Cy Twombly, who lived in Rome for much of his life.

Museo Nazionale Etrusco di Villa Giulia

Piazzale di Villa Giulia 9 • Tues–Sun 8.30am–7.30pm • €8 • ☎ 06 322 6751, ⓦ villagiulia.beniculturali.it

A harmonious collection of courtyards, loggias, gardens and temples put together in a playful Mannerist style for Pope Julius III in the mid-sixteenth century, the Villa Giulia now houses the **Museo Nazionale Etrusco di Villa Giulia**, the world's primary collection of Etruscan treasures (along with the Etruscan collection in the Vatican). Not much is known about the Etruscans, but they were a creative and civilized people, evidenced here by a wealth of sensual sculpture, jewellery and art. The most famous exhibit, in the octagonal room in the east wing, is the remarkable **Sarcophagus of the Married Couple** (dating from the sixth century BC) from Cerveteri – a touchingly lifelike portrayal of a husband and wife lying on a couch. Look also at the delicate and beautiful *cistae*, drum-like objects, engraved and adorned with figures, which were supposed to hold all the things needed for the care of the body after death. In the same room are marvellously intricate pieces of gold jewellery, delicately worked into tiny horses, birds, camels and other animals, as well as mirrors, candelabra, religious statues and tools used in everyday life, including a realistic bronze statuette of a ploughman at work. Further on you'll find a drinking horn in the shape of a dog's head that is so lifelike you almost expect it to bark; a *holmos*, or small table, to which the maker attached 24 little pendants around the edge; and a bronze disc breastplate from the seventh century BC decorated with a weird, almost modern abstract pattern of galloping creatures.

MAXXI

Via Guido Reni 4/A • Tues, Wed, Fri & Sun 11am–7pm, Thurs & Sat 11am–10pm • €11; guided tours €4, at Sat 1130am, noon, 5pm, 5.30pm, 6.30pm, 7pm, Sun 11.30am, noon, 5pm, 5.30pm; tours last 90min • ☎ 06 3996 7350, ⓦ fondazionemaxxi.it • Tram #2 from Piazzale Flaminio

A ten-minute tram journey north of Piazza del Popolo, **MAXXI** opened to much fanfare in 2010 in a landmark building by the Anglo-Iraqi architect Zaha Hadid – a great modern accompaniment to Renzo Piano's nearby Auditorium complex (see p.78). Built around a former military barracks, it's primarily a venue for temporary exhibitions of contemporary art and architecture (though it does have small collections of its own), but the building, a simultaneously jagged and curvy affair, is worth a visit in its own right, with its long, unravelling galleries and a towering lobby encompassing the inevitable café and bookstore.

1

The Auditorium

Viale Pietro de Coubertin 30 • Daily 10am–8pm • Free; guided tours €9 Sat & Sun every hour from 11.30am till 4.30pm, bookable on ☎ 06 8024 1281 • ☎ 06 80 242, ⊕ auditorium.com • Bus #M from Termini

Five minutes' walk from MAXXI, Rome's **Auditorium** is a complex of three concert halls, designed by everyone's favourite Italian architect, Renzo Piano. Each concert hall is conceived and designed for a different kind of musical performance: the smallest, the Sala Petrassi on the right side, accommodates 700 people and is designed for chamber concerts, the middle Sala Sinopoli holds 1200, while the largest of the three, the eastern Sala Santa Cecilia, can seat 2700 listening to big symphonic works, and is home to Rome's flagship Orchestra dell'Accademia di Santa Cecilia. You can walk right round the building outside, exploring the Parco della Musica, as it's known. The main entrance is on Via Pietro de Coubertin, where there's a great book and CD shop and decent café, or you can cut through to the complex from Viale Maresciallo Pilsudski, where there's a children's playground.

The Trevi Fountain and around

Across Via del Tritone from the area around Piazza di Spagna and the heart of the Tridente area, the web of streets around the famous **Trevi Fountain** is well worth exploring, and provides a relatively quiet route down to Piazza Venezia, avoiding what is perhaps Via del Corso's least interesting and most traffic-congested stretch.

The Trevi Fountain

The **Trevi Fountain** or Fontana di Trevi is one of Rome's more surprising sights, and easy to stumble on by accident – a huge, very Baroque gush of water over statues and rocks built onto the backside of a Renaissance palace and fed by the same source that surfaces at the Barcaccia fountain in Piazza di Spagna. There was a previous Trevi fountain, designed by Alberti, around the corner in Via dei Crociferi, a smaller, more modest affair by all accounts, but Urban VIII decided to upgrade it in line with his other grandiose schemes of the time and employed Bernini, among others, to design an alternative. Work didn't begin, however, until 1732, when Niccolò Salvi won a competition held by Clement XII to design the fountain, and even then it took thirty years to finish the project. Salvi died in the process, his lungs destroyed by the time spent in the dank waterworks of his construction. The fountain is now a popular hangout and, of course, the place you come to chuck in a coin if you want to guarantee your return to Rome. You might also remember Anita Ekberg frolicking in the fountain in *La Dolce Vita*, though any attempt at re-creating the scene would be met with an immediate reaction by the police here.

Galleria Colonna

Via della Pilotta 17 • Sat 9am–1.15pm, closed Aug • €7; free guided tours in English at 11.45am • ☎ 06 678 4350, ⊕ galleriacolonna.it

A short stroll south from the Trevi Fountain brings you to the **Galleria Colonna**, part of the Palazzo Colonna complex and home to one of the city's best collections of fine art still in private hands. The building itself is worth visiting for the massive chandelier-decked Great Hall, but the paintings, too, are worthy of attention, not least the two lascivious depictions of *Venus* and *Cupid* (one by Bronzino, the other Ghirlandaio) that eye each other across the room – once considered so risqué that clothes were painted on them and have only recently been removed. Through the Great Hall is the gallery's collection of landscapes by Dughet (Poussin's brother-in-law), and beyond that a small group of other high-quality works: Carracci's early and unusually spontaneous *Bean Eater*, Tintoretto's *Portrait of an Old Man* and a *Portrait of a Gentleman* caught in supremely confident pose by Veronese. Not a bad way to spend a Saturday morning in Rome.

FROM TOP SPERLONGA (P.133); COURTYARD, PALAZZO DEI CONSERVATORI (P.69) >

1

The Time Elevator

Via dei SS. Apostoli 20 • Adults €12, 5–12s €9; not suitable for children under 5 • ☎ 06 6992 1823, ⓦ timeelevator.it

Not far from the Galleria Colonna, the **Time Elevator** is a multimedia film show of the history of Rome from its founding to the present day, with visitors strapped into a chair that moves around a bit like a flight simulator – a half-hour or so the kids might enjoy.

The Quirinale and around

Of the hills that rise up on the eastern side of the centre of Rome, the **Quirinale** is perhaps the most appealing, home to some of the city's finest palaces, but also to some of Rome's greatest art collections, not least in the **Palazzo Barberini**.

Piazza Barberini

Piazza Barberini, a frenetic traffic junction at the top end of the busy shopping street of Via del Tritone, was named after Bernini's **Fontana del Tritone**, which gushes a high jet of water in the centre of the square. Traditionally, this was the Barberini family's quarter of the city; they were the greatest patrons of Gian Lorenzo Bernini, and the sculptor's works in their honour are thick on the ground around here. He finished the Tritone fountain in 1644, going on shortly after to design the **Fontana delle Api** ("Fountain of the Bees") at the bottom end of Via Veneto. Unlike the Tritone fountain you could walk right past this; it's a smaller, quirkier work, with a broad scallop shell studded with the bees that were the symbol of the Barberini.

Via Veneto

Via Veneto bends north from Piazza Barberini up to the southern edge of the Borghese gardens, its pricey bars and restaurants lining a street that was once the haunt of Rome's beautiful people, made famous by Fellini's *La Dolce Vita*. They left a long time ago, however, and Via Veneto isn't really any different from other busy streets in central Rome – a pretty, tree-lined road, but with a fair share of high-class tack trying to cash in on departed glory.

The Capuchin cemetery

Via Veneto 27 • Daily 9am–noon & 3–6pm • Minimum €1 donation expected

A little way up Via Veneto on the right, the Capuchin church of **Santa Maria della Concezione** was another sponsored creation of the Barberini, though it's not a particularly significant building in itself and most people come to see its **Capuchin cemetery**, one of Rome's more macabre and bizarre sights. Here, the bones of four thousand monks are set into the walls of a series of chapels, a monument to "Our Sister of Bodily Death" in the words of St Francis, which was erected in 1793. The bones appear in abstract or Christian patterns or as fully clothed skeletons, their faces peering out of their cowls in various twisted expressions of agony.

Palazzo Barberini: the Galleria Nazionale d'Arte Antica

Via dell Quattro Fontane 13 • Tues–Sun 9am–7pm • €5; audioguides €2.50 • Apartment tours can be booked in advance on ☎ 06 481 4591 • ☎ 06 32810, ⓦ galleriaborghese.it/barberini/it/default.htm

On the southern side of Piazza Barberini, the **Palazzo Barberini** houses the **Galleria Nazionale d'Arte Antica**, a rich patchwork of mainly Italian art from the early Renaissance to late Baroque periods, now better displayed than ever in a set of recently renovated galleries. Perhaps the most impressive feature of the gallery is the building itself, worked on at different times by the most favoured architects of the day – Bernini, Borromini, Maderno – and the epitome of Baroque grandeur. In an impressive show of balanced commissioning, there are two main staircases, one by Bernini and a second by his rival Borromini, and the two couldn't be more different – the former an ordered rectangle of ascending grandeur, the latter a more playful and more organic spiral staircase. But the palace's first-floor **Gran Salone** is its artistic high-spot, with a ceiling frescoed by Pietro da Cortona that is one of the best examples of exuberant Baroque trompe l'oeil you'll ever see, a manic rendering of *The Triumph of Divine Providence* that almost crawls down the walls to meet you. Note the bees – the Barberini family symbol – flying towards the figure of Providence.

Ground floor

The collection is divided into three sections, the first of which, on the ground floor, covers the **early Renaissance** period, with a couple of *Pietàs* by Giacomo Francia, Piero di Cosimo's *St Mary Magdalene*, with lovely colour and detail, along with numerous Madonnas, including Fra' Filippo Lippi's warmly maternal *Madonna and Child*, painted in 1437 and introducing background details, notably architecture, into Italian religious painting for the first time.

First floor

The second section, on the first floor, is the core of the collection, with works taking you through the **Renaissance** and **Baroque** eras, and including Raphael's beguiling *Fornarina*, a painting of a Trasteveran baker's daughter thought to have been the artist's mistress (Raphael's name appears clearly on the woman's bracelet), although some experts claim the painting to be the work of a pupil. Later rooms have works by Tintoretto and Titian, and an impressive array of **portraiture**: Bronzino's rendering of the marvellously erect *Stefano Colonna*, a portrait of *Henry VIII* by Hans Holbein and another of *Erasmus of Rotterdam* by Quentin Matsys. Next door are two unusually small paintings by El Greco, *The Baptism of Christ* and *Adoration of the Shepherds*, and then, further on, a couple of rooms of work by Caravaggio – notably *Judith and Holofernes* – and his followers, for example the seventeenth-century Neapolitan Ribera, and the Dutch Terbrugghen and Jan van Bronckhorst.

Top floor

The new galleries on the top floor finish off the collection by taking you from the **late Baroque era**, starting with works by more Neapolitan Baroque painters and their acolytes, most significantly Luca Giordano and the Calabrian Matia Preti, whose dark, dramatic canvases again owe a huge debt to Caravaggio. Next door, Bernini's portrait of *Urban VIII* has been rightfully reinstated in the pope's own palace, while the final rooms cover the late seventeenth and eighteenth centuries, with a number of cityscapes of Rome by Gaspar van Wittel and classic Venetian scenes by Guardi and Canaletto.

San Carlo alle Quattro Fontane

Via del Quirinale 23 • Mon–Fri 10am–1pm & 3–6pm, Sat 10am–1pm, Sun noon–1pm • Free

Heading southeast of Palazzo Barberini, along Via delle Quattro Fontane, brings you to a seventeenth-century landmark, the church of **San Carlo alle Quattro Fontane**. This was Borromini's first real design commission, and in it he displays all the ingenuity he later became famous for, cramming the church elegantly into a tiny and awkwardly shaped site. Outside the church are the four **fountains** that give the street and church their name, each cut into a niche in a corner of the crossroads that marks this, the highest point on the Quirinal Hill.

Sant'Andrea al Quirinale

Via del Quirinale 29 • Mon–Sat 8.30am–noon & 3.30–7pm, Sun 9am–noon & 4–7pm • Free

There's another piece of design ingenuity, on Via del Quirinale: the domed church of **Sant'Andrea al Quirinale**, which Bernini planned as a kind of flat oval shape to fit into its wide but shallow site. It's unusual and ingenious inside, and upstairs rooms where

1

the Polish saint, St Stanislaus Kostka, lived (and died) in 1568 focus on a disturbingly lifelike painted statue of Stanislaus lying on his deathbed.

The Palazzo del Quirinale

Piazza del Quirinale • Sun 8.30am–noon • €5 • ☏ 06 46 991, ⓦ quirinale.it

Opposite the church is the featureless wall of the **Palazzo del Quirinale**, a sixteenth-century structure that was the official summer residence of the popes until Unification, when it became the royal palace. It's now the home of Italy's president, and it's worth braving the security for a glimpse of the style in which popes, despots, kings and now presidents like to live, with a fine set of state rooms and works of art. You can appreciate its exceptional siting from the **Piazza del Quirinale**, from which views stretch right across the centre of Rome. The main feature of the piazza is the huge statue of the Dioscuri, or Castor and Pollux – massive 5m-high Roman copies of classical Greek statues, showing the two godlike twins, sons of Jupiter, who according to legend won victory for the Romans in an important battle.

Scuderie del Quirinale

Via XXIV Maggio 16 • Opening times vary • Exhibition admission usually around €10, or €18 including Palazzo dello Esposizioni • ☏ 06 3996 7500, ⓦ scuderiequirinale.it

The eighteenth-century papal stables, or **Scuderie del Quirinale**, face the Quirinale palace from across the square. Imaginatively restored as display space for major exhibitions, they feature an impressive equestrian spiral staircase winding up to the exhibition rooms. The modern glass staircase on the side of the building offers the best view over Rome from the Quirinale by far.

Via XX Settembre

Via XX Settembre spears out towards the Aurelian Wall from Via del Quirinale – not Rome's most appealing thoroughfare by any means, flanked by the deliberately faceless bureaucracies of the national government, erected after Unification in anticipation of Rome's ascension as a new world capital. It was, however, the route by which Italian troops entered the city on September 20, 1870; the place where they breached the wall is marked with a column.

Santa Maria della Vittoria

Via XX Settembre 17 • Daily 6.30–noon & 4.30–6pm • Free

The church of **Santa Maria della Vittoria** here was built by the Baroque-era architect Carlo Maderno and its interior is one of the most elaborate examples of Baroque decoration in Rome: its ceiling and walls are pitted with carving, and statues are crammed into remote corners as in an over-stuffed attic. The church's best-known feature, Bernini's carving *The Ecstasy of St Theresa*, the centrepiece of the sepulchral chapel of Cardinal Cornaro, is a deliberately melodramatic work featuring a theatrically posed St Theresa, who lays back in groaning submission beneath a mass of dishevelled garments in front of the murmuring cardinals.

The Esquiline, Monti and Termini

Immediately north of the Colosseum, the **Esquiline Hill** is the highest and largest of the city's seven hills. Formerly one of the most fashionable residential quarters of ancient Rome, it's nowadays a mixed area that together with the adjacent Viminale Hill make up the district known as **Monti**, an appealing and up-and-coming quarter of cobbled streets and neighbourhood bars and restaurants. It's also an area that most travellers to Rome encounter at some point – not just because of key sights like the basilica of Santa Maria Maggiore, but also because of its proximity to **Termini**, whose environs shelter many of Rome's budget hotels.

THE DOMUS AUREA

One of the Esquiline Hill's most intriguing sights is without doubt Nero's **Domus Aurea**, or Golden House, though unfortunately this is currently closed indefinitely due to flooding and conservation problems. Once covering a vast area between the Palatine and Esquiline, it was built by the Emperor Nero to glorify himself in typical excessive fashion. Rome was accustomed to Nero's excesses, but it had never seen anything like the Golden House before; the facade was supposed to have been coated in solid gold, there was hot and cold running water in the baths, and the grounds held vineyards and game. Nero didn't get to enjoy it for long: he died a couple of years after it was finished, and later emperors were determined to erase it from Rome's cityscape. Vespasian built the Colosseum over the lake and Trajan built his baths on top of the rest of the complex. But if and when it reopens you can view some of the paintings that so captivated artists when it was rediscovered during the Renaissance.

San Pietro in Vincoli

Piazza S. Pietro in Vincoli 4/A • Daily 7am–12.30pm & 3–7pm • Free

San Pietro in Vincoli is one of Rome's most delightfully plain churches. It was built to house an important relic, the **chains** (*vincoli*) that bound St Peter when imprisoned in Jerusalem and those that held him in the Mamertine Prison, which miraculously fused together when they were brought into contact with each other. The chains can still be seen beneath the high altar, but most people come to see the **tomb of Pope Julius II** at the far end of the southern aisle, which occupied Michelangelo on and off for much of his career. The artist eventually gave it up to paint the Sistine Chapel – the only statues that he managed to complete are the *Moses, Leah* and *Rachel*, which remain here, and two *Dying Slaves* (now in the Louvre). The figures are among the artist's most captivating works, especially *Moses*: because of a medieval mistranslation of scripture, he is depicted with satyr's horns instead of the "radiance of the Lord" that Exodus tells us shone around his head. Nonetheless this powerful statue is so lifelike that Michelangelo is alleged to have struck its knee with his hammer and shouted "Speak, damn you!"

Monti

Steps lead down from San Pietro in Vincoli to **Via Cavour**, a busy central thoroughfare slashed through the **Monti** neighbourhood in the 1890s to connect the station district to the river – although the last part was never completed. As you walk north towards Santa Maria Maggiore, the streets off to the left are worth a wander and form Monti's most atmospheric quarter, focusing on **Via dei Serpenti** and **Via del Boschetto**, and the narrow streets between them.

Santa Maria Maggiore

Via Liberiana 27 • Daily 7am–7pm • ☎ 06 6988 6802, ⓦ vatican.va/various/basiliche/sm_maggiore/index_en.html

Via Cavour opens out at Piazza Esquilino to reveal **Santa Maria Maggiore**, one of the city's greatest basilicas, and with one of Rome's best-preserved Byzantine interiors – a fact belied by its dull eighteenth-century exterior.

The interior

The present structure dates from about 420 AD, and was completed during the reign of Sixtus III, and survives remarkably intact, the broad nave fringed on both sides with strikingly well kept mosaics. The chapel in the right transept holds the elaborate tomb of Sixtus V – another, less famous, Sistine Chapel, decorated with frescoes and stucco reliefs portraying events from his reign. Outside this is the tomb of the Bernini family, including Gian Lorenzo himself, while opposite, the Pauline Chapel is home to the tombs of the Borghese pope Paul V and his immediate predecessor Clement VIII. The high altar contains the relics of St Matthew, among other Christian martyrs, but it's the mosaics of the arch that really dazzle, a vivid representation of scenes from the life of Christ.

1

The museum and loggia

Daily 9am–6.30pm • €4 • **Loggia** tours daily at 9am & 1pm, obligatory to book in advance • €5

There's a **museum** underneath the basilica that sports what even by Roman standards is a wide variety of relics, and a **loggia** above the main entrance whose thirteenth-century mosaics of the "legend of the snow" are worth seeing.

Santa Prassede

Via S. Prassede 9/A • Daily 7am–noon & 4–6.30pm • Free

South of Santa Maria Maggiore, off Via Merulana, the ninth-century church of **Santa Prassede** occupies an ancient site, where it's claimed St Prassede harboured Christians on the run from the Roman persecutions. She apparently collected the blood and remains of the martyrs and placed them in a well where she herself was later buried; a red marble disc in the floor of the nave marks the spot. In the southern aisle, the Chapel of St Zeno was built by Pope Paschal I as a mausoleum for his mother, Theodora, and is decorated with marvellous ninth-century mosaics that make it glitter like a jewel-encrusted bowl. The chapel also contains a fragment of a column supposed to be the one to which Christ was tied when he was scourged.

Via Nazionale

A couple of minutes' walk from Via XX Settembre, **Via Nazionale** connects Piazza Venezia and the centre of town with the area around Termini and the eastern districts beyond. A focus for much development after Unification, its heavy, overbearing buildings were constructed to give Rome some semblance of modern sophistication when it became capital, but most are now occupied by hotels and mainstream shops and boutiques.

Palazzo delle Esposizioni

Via Nazionale 194 • Tues–Thurs & Sun 10am–8pm, Fri & Sat 10am–10.30pm; limited opening hours in Aug • Admission varies, but usually €7–10, or €18 for a joint ticket with the Scuderie del Quirinale • ☎ 06 3996 7500, ⓦ palazzoesposizioni.it

About halfway down Via Nazionale, the imposing **Palazzo delle Esposizioni** was designed in 1883 by Pio Piacentini (father of the more famous Marcello, favourite architect of Mussolini), and reopened with much fanfare in 2008 after a five-year revamp. It now hosts regular large-scale exhibitions and houses a cinema, an excellent art and design bookshop and café in its basement, and the fancy *Open Colonna* restaurant up above.

Piazza della Repubblica

At the top of Via Nazionale, **Piazza della Repubblica** is typical of Rome's nineteenth-century regeneration, a stern and dignified semicircle of buildings that was until recently rather dilapidated but is now – with the help of the very stylish *Hotel Exedra* – resurgent, centring on a fountain surrounded by languishing nymphs and sea monsters.

Santa Maria degli Angeli

Piazza della Repubblica/Via Cernaia 9 • Mon–Sat 7am–6.30pm, Sun 7am–7.30pm • Free • ⓦ santamariadegliangeliroma.it

Piazza della Repubblica actually follows the outlines of the Baths of Diocletian, the remains of which lie across the piazza and are partially contained in the church of **Santa Maria degli Angeli**, one of Rome's least welcoming churches but giving the best impression of the size and grandeur of Diocletian's baths complex. It's a huge, open building, with an interior standardized by Vanvitelli into a rich eighteenth-century confection. The pink granite pillars, at nine feet in diameter the largest in Rome, are original, and the main transept formed the main hall of the baths. The meridian that strikes diagonally across the floor here was until 1846 the regulator of time for Romans (now a cannon shot is fired daily at noon from the Janiculum Hill).

Museo delle Terme di Diocleziano

Via Enrico di Nicola • Tues–Sun 9am–7.45pm • €7 with Museo Nazionale Romano pass • ☎06 3996 7700, ⓦhttp://archeoroma.beniculturali.it/en

Behind Santa Maria degli Angeli, the huge halls and courtyards of the **Museo delle Terme di Diocleziano**, or **Diocletian's baths**, have been renovated and they and an attached Carthusian monastery now hold what is probably the least interesting part of the **Museo Nazionale Romano** (see box, p.61). The museum's most evocative part is the large cloister of the church whose sides are crammed with statuary, funerary monuments and sarcophagi and fragments from all over Rome. The galleries that wrap around the cloister hold a reasonable if rather academically presented collection of pre-Roman and Roman finds.

Palazzo Massimo

Largo di Villa Peretti • Tues–Sun 9am–7.45pm • €7 with Museo Nazionale Romano pass • ☎ 06 3996 7700, ⓦ archeoroma
.beniculturali.it/

Across from Santa Maria degli Angeli, the **Palazzo Massimo** is one of the great museums of Rome, with something worth seeing on every floor.

The basement and ground floors

Start at the **basement** where there are displays of exquisite gold jewellery from the second century AD, and the mummified remains of an eight-year-old girl, along with a fantastic coin collection. The **ground floor** is devoted to statuary of the early empire, including a gallery with an unparalleled selection of unidentified busts found all over Rome – amazing pieces of portraiture, and as vivid a representation of patrician Roman life as you'll find. There are also identifiable faces – a bronze of Germanicus, a marvellous small bust of Caligula, several representations of Livia and a hooded statue of Augustus. Note the superb examples of Roman copies of Greek statuary – an altar found on Via Nomentana stands out, decorated with figures relating to the cult of Bacchus, as well as statues of Aphrodite and Melponome.

The first floor

The **first floor** has sculpted portraits of the various imperial dynasties in roughly chronological order, starting with the Flavian emperors – the craggy determination of Vespasian, the pinched nobility of Nerva – and leading on to Trajan, who appears with his wife Plotina as Hercules, next to a bust of his cousin Hadrian. The collection continues with the Antonine emperors – Antoninus Pius in a heroic nude pose and in several busts, flanked by likenesses of his daughter Faustina Minor. Faustina was the wife of Antoninus's successor, Marcus Aurelius, who appears in the next room. Further on are the Severans, with the fierce-looking Caracalla looking across past his father Septimius Severus to his brother Geta, whom he later murdered.

The second floor

The **second floor** takes in some of the finest Roman frescoes and mosaics ever found. There's a stunning set of frescoes from the **Villa di Livia**, depicting an orchard dense with fruit and flowers and patrolled by partridges and doves, wall paintings rescued from what was perhaps the riverside villa of Augustus's daughter Julia and Marcus Agrippa, and mosaics showing four chariot drivers and their horses, so finely crafted that from a distance they look as if they've been painted.

Termini station

The low white facade of **Termini station** (so named for its proximity to the Baths or "Terme" of Diocletian), and the vast, bus-crammed hubbub that is Piazza dei Cinquecento in front, is many people's first experience of Rome. The station is an ambitious piece of modern architectural design that was completed in 1950 and still entirely dominates the streets around with its low-slung, futuristic lines. As for

1

Piazza dei Cinquecento, it's a good place to find buses and taxis, but otherwise it and the areas around are not places you'd want to hang around for long.

San Lorenzo fuori le Mura

Piazzale del Verano 3 • Daily 8am–noon & 4–6.30pm • Free

A short walk from Termini, the studenty neighbourhood of San Lorenzo takes its name from the basilica of **San Lorenzo fuori le Mura** – one of the great pilgrimage churches of Rome, fronted by a columned portico and with a lovely twelfth-century cloister to its side. The original church here was built over the site of St Lawrence's martyrdom by Constantine. It is actually a combination of three churches built at different periods – one a sixth-century reconstruction of Constantine's church, which now forms the chancel, another a fifth-century church from the time of Sixtus III, both joined by a basilica from the thirteenth century. The church was bombed heavily during World War II, but it has been rebuilt with sensitivity, and inside there are features from all periods: a Cosmati floor, thirteenth-century pulpits and a Paschal candlestick, and a mosaic on the inside of the triumphal arch that is a sixth-century depiction of Pelagius offering his church to Christ; below stairs, catacombs – where St Lawrence was apparently buried – sit among pillars from Constantine's original structure.

The Celian Hill and San Giovanni

Some of the animals that were to die in the Colosseum were kept in a zoo up on the Celian Hill, just behind the arena, the furthest south of Rome's seven hills and probably still its most peaceful, with the **Villa Celimontana** park at its heart.

Santi Giovanni e Paolo

Piazza dei Santi Giovanni e Paolo 13 • Daily 8.30am–noon & 3.30–6.30pm • Free

At the summit of the Celian Hill, the church of **Santi Giovanni e Paolo**, marked by its colourful campanile, is dedicated to two government officials who were beheaded here in 316 AD after refusing military service; a railed-off tablet in mid-nave marks the shrine where the saints were martyred and buried.

The Case Romane

Clivo di Scauro • Daily except Tues & Wed 10am–1pm & 3–6pm • €6 • ☎ 06 7045 4544, ⓦ caseromane.it/en

The remains of what is believed to be their house, the **Case Romane**, are around the corner on Clivo di Scauro. Around twenty rooms are open in all, patchily frescoed with pagan and Christian subjects, including the Casa dei Genii, with winged youths and cupids, and the courtyard or nymphaeum, which has a marvellous fresco of a goddess being attended on.

San Gregorio Magno

Piazza di S. Gregorio 1 • Daily 8.30am–12.30pm & 3–6.30pm; ring the bell marked "portinare" to gain admission • Free

The road descends from the church and Roman house to the church of **San Gregorio Magno**, founded by St Gregory, who was a monk here before becoming pope in 590 AD. Gregory was an important pope, stabilizing the city after the fall of the empire and effectively establishing the powerful papal role that would endure for the best part of the following 1500 years. Today's rather ordinary interior doesn't really do justice to the historical importance of the church, but the lovely Cosmati floor remains intact, and the chapel at the end of the south aisle has a beautifully carved bath showing scenes from St Gregory's life along with his marble throne, a beaten-up specimen that actually predates the saint by five hundred years. Outside there are three frescoed chapels that are worth a look if they're open, and it's worth ringing the bell at the adjacent **Missionario della Carità**, the Rome heaquarters of the order founded by Mother Theresa of Calcutta, and home to her perfectly preserved bedroom.

San Clemente

Via Labicana 95 • **Church** Daily 9am–7pm • Free • **Lower church and temple** Mon–Sat 9am–12.30pm & 3–6pm, Sun noon–6pm • €5 •
Ⓦ basilicasanclemente.com

Down below the Celian Hill, five minutes' walk from the Colosseum, the church of **San Clemente** is one of the most visited sights of Rome, a cream-coloured twelfth-century basilica that's a conglomeration of three places of worship, encapsulating perhaps better than any other the continuity of history in the city. The ground-floor church is a superb example of a medieval basilica: its facade and courtyard face east in the archaic fashion, there are some fine, warm mosaics in the apse and – perhaps the highlight of the main church – a chapel with frescoes by Masolino, showing scenes from the life of St Catherine. Downstairs there's the nave of an earlier church, dating to 392 AD, and on a third level a dank Mithraic temple of the late second century where you can see a statue of Mithras slaying the bull and the seats on which the worshippers sat during their ceremonies.

San Giovanni in Laterano

Piazza San Giovanni in Laterano 4 • Daily 7am–6.30pm • Free • Ⓣ 06 6988 6392 for guided tours, Ⓦ vatican.va/various/basiliche
/san_giovanni/index_it.htm

At the far end of Via San Giovanni in Laterano, a ten-minute walk from the Colosseum, the basilica of **San Giovanni in Laterano** is officially Rome's cathedral, the seat of the pope as bishop of Rome, and was for centuries the main papal residence. There has been a church on this site since the fourth century, the first established by Constantine, and the present building, reworked by Borromini in the mid-seventeenth century, evokes Rome's staggering wealth of history, with a host of features from different periods. The **doors** to the church were taken from the Curia of the Roman Forum, while much of the **interior** dates from 1600, when Clement VIII had the church remodelled for that Holy Year. The first pillar on the left of the right-hand aisle shows a fragment of Giotto's fresco of Boniface VIII, proclaiming the first Holy Year in 1300. Further on, a more recent monument commemorates Sylvester I – "the magician pope", bishop of Rome during much of Constantine's reign – and incorporates part of his original tomb, said to sweat and rattle its bones when a pope is about to die. Outside, the **cloisters** (daily 9am–6pm; €2) are one of the most pleasing parts of the complex, decorated with early thirteenth-century Cosmati work and with fragments of the original basilica arranged around in no particular order.

The Lateran Palace

Daily visits on the hour 9am–noon • €5

Adjoining the basilica of San Giovanni in Laterano is the **Lateran Palace**, part of which is given over to the **Museo Storico Vaticano**. Largely the work of Sixtus V, this is home to the Lateran Treaty, which ceded control of Rome and the papal territories to the Italian state and was signed on February 11, 1929, at the large writing-desk in the well-named Sala della Conciliazione.

The Baptistry

Daily 7.30am–12.30pm & 4–6.30pm • Free

Next to the Lateran Palace, the **Baptistry** is the oldest surviving baptistry in the Christian world, a mosaic-lined, octagonal structure built during the fifth century that has been the model for many such buildings since.

The Scala Santa and Sancta Sanctorum

Daily: April–Sept 6.15am–noon & 3.30–6.45pm; Oct–March 6.15am–noon & 3–6.15pm • Free

There are more ancient remains on the other side of the church, on Piazza di Porta San Giovanni, foremost of which is the **Scala Santa**, said to be the staircase from Pontius Pilate's house down which Christ walked after his trial. The 28 steps are protected by boards, and the only way you're allowed to climb them is on your knees, which pilgrims do regularly – although there is also a staircase to the side for the less penitent.

1

At the top, the **Sancta Sanctorum** or chapel of San Lorenzo holds an ancient (sixth- or seventh-century) painting of Christ said to be the work of an angel, hence its name – *acheiropoeton*, or "not done by human hands".

Museo Storico della Liberazione

Via Tasso 145 • Wed, Sat & Sun 9.30am–12.30pm, Tues, Thurs & Fri 9.30am–12.30pm & 3.30–7.30pm • Free • ☎06 700 3866, ⒲viatasso.eu

Five minutes' walk from the San Giovanni basilica, the **Museo Storico della Liberazione** is a very different sort of attraction, occupying two floors of the building in which Nazi prisoners were held and interrogated during the wartime Occupation. It's a moving place and deliberately low key, with the original cells left as they were, including two isolation cells marked with the desperate notes and messages from the people held here, and other rooms displaying artefacts pertaining to the years of occupation, including one dedicated to the 335 victims of the Fosse Ardeatine massacre, a mass execution carried out by the Germans in 1944. One of the best of Rome's often overlooked sights.

The Aventine, Testaccio and south

The area south of the Forum and Palatine has some of the city's most compelling Christian and ancient sights, from the relatively central **Circo Massimo** and **Baths of Caracalla** to the famous **catacombs** on the fringe of the city on Via Appia Antica. It also has one of Rome's leafiest and most peaceful corners in the **Aventine Hill**, along with its funkiest neighbourhoods in **Testaccio** and up-and-coming **Ostiense**.

The Circus Maximus and Aventine Hill

On its southern side, the Palatine Hill drops down to the **Circus Maximus**, a long, thin, green expanse bordered by heavily trafficked roads that was the ancient city's main venue for chariot races; at one time this arena had a capacity of up to 400,000 spectators.

On the far side of the Circus Maximus is the **Aventine Hill**, the southernmost of the city's seven hills and the heart of plebeian Rome in ancient times. These days the working-class quarters of the city are further south, and the Aventine is in fact one of the city's more upmarket residential areas, covered with villas and gardens and one of the few places in the city where you can escape the traffic.

Santa Sabina

Piazza Pietro d'Illiria 1 • Daily 7.30am–12.30pm & 3.30–6.30pm • Free

A short way up Via Santa Sabina, the church of **Santa Sabina** is a strong contender for Rome's most beautiful basilica: high and wide, its nave and portico were restored back to their fifth-century appearance in the 1930s. Look especially at the main doors, which boast eighteen panels carved with Christian scenes, forming a complete illustrated Bible that includes one of the oldest representations of the Crucifixion in existence. Santa Sabina is also the principal church of the Dominicans, and it's claimed that the orange trees in the garden outside, which you can glimpse on your way to the restrained cloister, are descendants of those planted by St Dominic himself. Whatever the truth of this, the **views** from the gardens are splendid – right across the Tiber to the centre of Rome and St Peter's.

The Baths of Caracalla

Viale delle Terme di Caracalla 52 • Mon 9am–2pm, Tues–Sun 9am–1hr before sunset • €7.50, includes the Tomb of Cecilia Metella and the Villa dei Quintili • ☎06 3996 7700

Across the far side of Piazza di Porta Capena, the **Baths of Caracalla** are much better preserved and give a far better sense of the scale and monumentality of Roman architecture than most of the extant ruins in the city. The baths are no more than a shell now, but the walls still rise to very nearly their original height. There are many fragments of mosaics – none spectacular, but quite a few bright and well preserved – and it's easy to discern a floor plan. As for Caracalla, he was one of Rome's worst rulers, and it's no wonder there's nothing else in the city built by him. The baths are used as the venue for the **Teatro dell'Opera**'s summer season – one of Mussolini's better ideas – and attending an opera performance here allows you to see the baths at their most atmospheric.

Testaccio

Across the Aventine Hill, the solid working-class neighbourhood of **Testaccio** groups around a couple of main squares, a tight-knit community with a market and a number of bars and small trattorias that was for many years synonymous with the slaughterhouse that sprawls down to the Tiber just beyond. In recent years the area has become trendy, property prices have soared, and some unlikely juxtapositions have emerged, with vegetarian restaurants opening their doors in an area still known for the offal dishes served in its traditional trattorias, and gay and alternative clubs standing cheek-by-jowl with the car-repair shops gouged into Monte Testaccio.

The slaughterhouse, or **Mattatoio**, once the area's main employer, is used for concerts and exhibitions now, along with a branch of the Museum of Contemporary Art of Rome, **MACRO Future**. Opposite, **Monte Testaccio** gives the area its name, a 35m-high mound created out of the shards of Roman amphorae that were dumped here. It's an odd sight, the ceramic curls visible through the tufts of grass that crown its higher reaches, with bars and restaurants hollowed out of the slopes below.

The Protestant Cemetery

Via Caio Cestio 6 • Mon–Sat 9am–5pm, Sun 9am–1pm • Donation expected • ☎ 06 574 1900, ⓦ protestantcemetery.it

Via Zabaglia leads from Monte Testaccio to Via Caio Cestio, a left turn up which takes you to the entrance of the **Protestant Cemetery**, one of the shrines to the English in Rome and a fitting conclusion to a visit to the Keats-Shelley House (see p.74), since it is here that both poets are buried, along with a handful of other well-known names. In fact, the cemetery's title is a misnomer – the cemetery is reserved for non-Roman Catholics so you'll also find famous Italian atheists, Christians of the Orthodox persuasion, and the odd Jew or Muslim buried here.

Most visitors come here to see the **grave of Keats**, who lies next to the painter Joseph Severn, in the furthest corner of the less crowded, older part of the cemetery, his stone inscribed as he wished with the words "Here lies one whose name was writ in water." Severn died much later than Keats but asked to be laid here nonetheless, together with his brushes and palette. Shelley's ashes were brought here at Mary Shelley's request and interred in the newer part of the cemetery. Among other famous internees, Edward Trelawny, friend and literary associate of Byron and Shelley, lies next to him, the political writer and activist, Gramsci, on the far right-hand side in the middle, to name just two – though if you're at all interested in star-spotting you should ask to have a look at the English booklet at the entrance.

The Pyramid of Caius Cestius

The most distinctive landmark in this part of town is the mossy pyramidal tomb of one **Caius Cestius**, who died in 12 BC. Cestius had spent some time in Egypt, and part of his will decreed that all his slaves should be freed – the white pyramid you see today was thrown up by them in only 330 days of what must have been joyful building. It's open to the public on the second and fourth Saturday of each month, though you can visit the cats who live here, and the volunteers who care for them, any afternoon between 2.30 and 4.30pm.

Centrale Montemartini

Via Ostiense 106 • Tues–Sun 9am–7pm • €4.50, €14 for joint ticket with Capitoline Museums • ☎ 06 0608

It's a ten-minute walk south down Via Ostiense to the **Centrale Montemartini**, a former electricity generating station which was requisitioned to display the cream of the Capitoline Museums' sculpture while the main buildings were being renovated. It became

1

so popular that it's now a permanent outpost, attracting visitors to the formerly industrial area of Ostiense. The huge rooms of the power station are ideally suited to showing ancient sculpture, although the massive turbines and furnaces have a fascination of their own. Among many compelling objects are the head, feet and an arm from a colossal statue, once 8m high, found in Largo Argentina; a large Roman copy of *Athena*; a fragmented mosaic of hunting scenes; and an amazingly naturalistic statue of a girl seated on a stool with her legs crossed, from the third century BC. There's also a figure of *Hercules* and, next to it, the soft *Muse Polymnia*, the former braced for activity, the latter leaning on a rock and staring thoughtfully into the distance.

San Paolo fuori le Mura

Via Ostiense 186 • Daily 7am–6pm • Free • ⓦ abbaziasanpaolo.net

Some 2km south of the Porta San Paolo, the basilica of **San Paolo fuori le Mura**, accessible on metro line B, is one of the four patriarchal basilicas of Rome, occupying the supposed site of St Paul's tomb, where he was laid to rest after being beheaded nearby. A devastating fire in 1823 means that the church you see now is largely a nineteenth-century reconstruction but it's a very successful rehash, and it's impossible not to be awed by the space of the building inside. Some parts of the building did survive the fire. In the south transept, the paschal candlestick is a remarkable piece of Romanesque carving, supported by half-human beasts and rising through entwined tendrils and strangely human limbs and bodies to scenes from Christ's life. The bronze aisle doors date from 1070 and were also rescued from the old basilica, as was the thirteenth-century tabernacle by Arnolfo di Cambio. The arch across the apse is original, too, embellished with mosaics donated by the Byzantine queen Galla Placidia in the sixth century. There's also the cloister, just behind here – probably Rome's finest piece of Cosmatesque work, its spiralling, mosaic-encrusted columns enclosing a peaceful rose garden.

Via Appia Antica and the catacombs

The best way to get to Via Appia Antica is by bus – take #118 from Piazzale Ostiense, #218 from Piazza Porta San Giovanni or #660 from Colli Albani metro station (on line A). Alternatively, take the private Archeobus service (see p.99)

Starting at the Porta San Sebastiano, the **Via Appia Antica** (or Appian Way) is the most famous of Rome's consular roads that used to strike out in every direction from the ancient city. It was built by one Appio Claudio in 312 BC, and is the only Roman landmark mentioned in the Bible. During classical times it was the most important of all the Roman trade routes, carrying supplies through Campania to the port of Brindisi, and it remains an important part of early Christian Rome, its verges lined with numerous pagan and Christian sites, including most famously the underground burial cemeteries or catacombs of the first Christians.

Catacombs of San Callisto

Via Appia Antica 110/126 • Daily except Wed 9am–noon & 2–5pm • Tours last 45min • €8 • ☏ 06 513 0151, ⓦ catacombe.roma.it

Continuing on for 1km or so, the **Catacombs of San Callisto** are the largest of Rome's catacombs, founded in the second century AD; many of the early popes (of whom St Callisto was one) are buried here. The site also features some well-preserved seventh- and eighth-century frescoes, and the crypt of Santa Cecilia, who was buried here after her martyrdom, before being shifted to the church dedicated to her in Trastevere.

Catacombs of San Sebastiano

Via Appia Antica 136 • Mon–Sat 9am–noon & 2–5pm • €8 • ☏ 06 785 0350, ⓦ catacombe.org

The **Catacombs of San Sebastiano**, 500m further on, are situated under a basilica that was originally built by Constantine on the spot where the bodies of the apostles Peter and Paul are said to have been laid for a time. Tours take in paintings of doves and fish, a contemporary, carved oil lamp and inscriptions dating the tombs themselves. The most striking features, however, are not Christian at all, but three pagan tombs (one painted, two stuccoed) discovered when archeologists were burrowing beneath the floor of the basilica upstairs.

Trastevere and the Janiculum Hill

Across the river from the centre of town, on the right bank of the Tiber, the district of **Trastevere** was the artisan area of the city in classical times, neatly placed for the trade that came upriver from Ostia to be unloaded nearby. Outside the city walls, Trastevere (the name means "across the Tiber") was for centuries heavily populated by immigrants, and this separation lent the neighbourhood a strong identity that lasted well into the twentieth century. Nowadays it's a long way from the working-class quarter it used to be, often thronged with tourists, lured by the charm of its narrow streets and closeted squares. However, it is among the most pleasant places to stroll in Rome, particularly peaceful in the morning, lively come the evening, as dozens of trattorias set tables out along the cobbled streets, and still buzzing late at night when its **bars and clubs** provide a focus for one of Rome's most dynamic night-time scenes.

Santa Maria in Trastevere

Piazza Santa Maria in Trastevere • Daily 7am–9pm • Free

The heart of Trastevere is **Piazza Santa Maria in Trastevere**, a large square that takes its name from the **church** in its northwest corner. This is thought to have been the first Christian place of worship in Rome, built on a site where a fountain of oil is said to have sprung on the day of Christ's birth. The church's mosaics are among the city's most impressive, Byzantine-inspired works in the apse depicting a solemn yet sensitive parade of saints thronged around Christ and Mary, while underneath a series of panels shows scenes from the life of the Virgin by the painter Pietro Cavallini. Beneath the high altar on the right, an inscription – "FONS OLEI" – marks the spot where the oil is supposed to have sprung up.

Galleria Nazionale di Palazzo Corsini

Via della Lungara 10 • Tues–Sun 8.30am–7.30pm • €4 • ☎ 06 6880 2323, ⓦ galleriaborghese.it/ corsini/it/default.htm

Cutting north from Piazza Santa Maria in Trastevere, you come to the **Galleria Nazionale d'Arte di Palazzo Corsini**, an unexpected cultural attraction on this side of the river. It's a relatively small collection, and only takes up a few rooms of the giant palace, which was a fitting final home for Queen Christina of Sweden, who renounced Protestantism and with it the Swedish throne in 1655, bringing her library and fortune to Rome, to the delight of the Chigi pope, Alexander VII. Among the highlights are works by Rubens, Van Dyck, Guido Reni and Caravaggio, and the curious Corsini Throne, thought to be a Roman copy of an Etruscan throne of the second or first century. Cut out of marble, its back is carved with warriors in armour and helmets, below which is a boar hunt, with wild boars the size of horses pursued by hunters.

Villa Farnesina

Via della Lungara 230 • Mon–Sat & second Sun of the month 9am–1pm • €5 • ☎ 06 6802 7397, ⓦ villafarnesina.it

Across the road from the Palazzo Corsini is the **Villa Farnesina**, built during the early sixteenth century for the banker Agostino Chigi, and one of the earliest Renaissance villas, with opulent rooms decorated with frescoes by some of the masters of the period. Most people come to view the Raphael-designed painting **Cupid and Psyche** in the now glassed-in loggia, completed in 1517 by the artist's assistants. The painter and art historian Vasari claims Raphael didn't complete the work because his infatuation with his mistress – "La Fornarina", whose father's bakery was situated nearby – was making it difficult to concentrate. Nonetheless it's mightily impressive: a flowing, animated work bursting with muscular men and bare-bosomed women. He did, however, apparently manage to finish the **Galatea** in the room next door, whose bucolic country

1

PORTA PORTESE FLEA MARKET

Trastevere at its most disreputable but also most characteristic can be witnessed on Sunday, when the **Porta Portese flea market** stretches down from the Porta Portese gate down Via Portuense to Trastevere train station in a congested medley of antiques, old motor spares, cheap clothing, household goods, bric-a-brac, antiques and assorted junk. It starts around 7am, and you should come early if you want to buy, or even move – most of the bargains, not to mention the stolen goods, have gone by 10am, by which time the crush of people can be intense. It's pretty much all over by lunch time.

scenes are interspersed with Galatea on her scallop-shell chariot and a giant head said to have been painted by Michelangelo in one of the lunettes. The ceiling illustrates Chigi's horoscope constellations, frescoed by the architect of the building, Peruzzi, who also decorated the upstairs Salone delle Prospettive, where trompe l'oeil balconies give views onto contemporary Rome – one of the earliest examples of the technique.

Santa Cecilia in Trastevere

Piazza di Santa Cecilia 22 • **Church** Daily 9.30am–1pm & 4–7.15pm • Excavations €3 • **Singing gallery** Mon–Sat 10am–12.30pm • €2.50 • Ring the bell to the left of the church door to get in

One of Trastevere's most intriguing attractions is the church of **Santa Cecilia in Trastevere**, whose antiseptic eighteenth-century appearance belies its historical associations. A church was originally built here over the site of the second-century home of St Cecilia, whose husband Valerian was executed for refusing to worship Roman gods and who herself was subsequently persecuted for Christian beliefs. The story has it that Cecilia was locked in the caldarium of her own baths for several days but refused to die, singing her way through the ordeal (Cecilia is patron saint of music). Her head was finally half hacked off with an axe, though it took several blows before she finally succumbed. Below the high altar, Stefano Maderno's limp statue of the saint shows her incorruptible body as it was found when exhumed in 1599, with three deep cuts in her neck. Downstairs, excavations of the baths and the rest of the Roman house are on view in the crypt, but more alluring by far is the **singing gallery** above the nave, where Pietro Cavallini's late thirteenth-century fresco of the *Last Judgement* – all that remains of the decoration that once covered the entire church – is a powerful, amazingly naturalistic piece of work for its time.

The Janiculum Hill

It's about a fifteen-minute walk up Via Garibaldi from the centre of Trastevere to the summit of the **Janiculum Hill** – not one of the original seven hills of Rome, but the one with the best and most accessible views of the centre. Follow Vicolo del Cedro from Via della Scala and take the steps up from the end, cross the main road, and continue on the steps that lead up the hill to the Passeggiata del Gianicolo and then to **Piazzale Garibaldi**. Just below here is the spot from which a cannon is fired at noon each day for Romans to check their watches, and spread out before you are some of the best **views** in Rome, taking in pretty much the whole of the city.

The Vatican

Situated on the west bank of the Tiber, just across from the city centre, the **Vatican City** was established as a sovereign state in 1929, a tiny territory surrounded by high walls on its far western side and on the near side opening its doors to the rest of the city and its pilgrims in the form of **St Peter's** and its colonnaded piazza. The city-state's one thousand inhabitants have their own radio station, daily newspaper, postal service, and indeed security service in the colourfully dressed Swiss Guards. It's believed that St Peter was buried in a pagan cemetery on the Vatican hill, giving rise to the building of a basilica to venerate his name and the siting of the headquarters of the Catholic

Church here. St Peter's is obviously one of the highlights, but the only part of the Vatican Palace itself that you can visit independently is the **Vatican Museums** – quite simply, the largest, richest, most compelling and perhaps most exhausting museum complex in the world.

Castel Sant'Angelo

Lungotevere Castello 50 • Tues–Sun 9am–7.30pm • €8.50 • ☎ 06 681 9111, ⓦ castelsantangelo.com

The great circular hulk of the **Castel Sant'Angelo** marks the edge of the Vatican, designed and built by Hadrian as his own mausoleum. Renamed in the sixth century, when Pope Gregory the Great witnessed a vision of St Michael here that ended a terrible plague, the papal authorities converted the building for use as a fortress and built a passageway to link it with the Vatican as a refuge in times of siege or invasion.

Inside, a spiral ramp leads up into the centre of the mausoleum, over a drawbridge, to the main level at the top, where a small palace was built to house the papal residents in appropriate splendour. Pope Paul III had some especially fine renovations made, including the beautiful Sala Paolina, whose gilded ceiling displays the Farnese family arms. Elsewhere, the rooms hold swords, armour, guns and the like, while others are lavishly decorated with grotesques and paintings (don't miss the bathroom of Clement VII on the second floor, with its prototype hot and cold water taps and mildly erotic frescoes). Below are dungeons and storerooms that can be glimpsed from the spiralling ramp, testament to the castle's grisly past as the city's most notorious Renaissance prison. The quiet **café** upstairs offers one of the best views of Rome.

Piazza San Pietro

Perhaps the most famous of Rome's many piazzas, Bernini's **Piazza San Pietro** doesn't disappoint, although its size isn't really apparent until you're right on top of it, its colonnade arms symbolically welcoming the world into the lap of the Catholic Church. The obelisk in the centre was brought to Rome by Caligula in 36 AD, and was moved here in 1586, when Sixtus V ordered that it be erected in front of the basilica, a task that took four months and was apparently done in silence, on pain of death. The matching fountains on either side are the work of Carlo Maderno (on the right) and Bernini (on the left). In between the obelisk and each fountain, a circular stone set into the pavement marks the focal points of an ellipse, from which the four rows of columns on the perimeter of the piazza line up perfectly, making the colonnade appear to be supported by a single line of columns.

St Peter's

Daily: April–Sept 7am–7pm; Oct–March 7am–6pm • ⓦ stpetersbasilica.org

The Basilica di San Pietro, better known to many as **St Peter's**, is the principal shrine of the Catholic Church, built on the site of St Peter's tomb, and worked on by the greatest Italian architects of the sixteenth and seventeenth centuries. One of the channels on the right side of the piazza funnels you into the basilica (the other two lead to the underground grottoes or the ascent to the dome – see p.94). Bear in mind that whichever you opt for first, you need to be **properly dressed** to enter, which means no bare knees or shoulders – a rule that is very strictly enforced.

The interior

Going straight into the church, the first thing you see is Michelangelo's graceful **Pietà** on the right, completed when he was just 24. Following an attack by a vandal, it sits behind glass, strangely remote from the life of the rest of the building. Further into the church, the **dome** is breathtakingly imposing, rising high above the supposed site of St Peter's tomb. With a diameter of 41.5m it is Rome's largest dome, supported by four enormous piers, decorated with reliefs depicting the basilica's "major relics": St Veronica's handkerchief, which was used to wipe the face of Christ; the lance of St Longinus, which pierced

1

Christ's side; and a piece of the True Cross. On the right side of the nave, the bronze **statue of St Peter** is another of the most venerated monuments in the basilica, its right foot polished smooth by the attentions of pilgrims. Bronze was also the material used in Bernini's wild, spiralling **baldacchino**, a massive 26m high, cast out of 927 tonnes of metal removed from the Pantheon roof in 1633. Bernini's feverish sculpting decorates the apse, too, his bronze *Cattedra* enclosing the chair of St Peter, though more interesting is his **monument to Alexander VII** in the south transept, with its winged skeleton struggling underneath the heavy marble drapes, upon which the Chigi pope is kneeling in prayer.

The treasury and grottoes

An entrance off the aisle leads to the **treasury** (daily: April–Sept 9am–6.15pm; Oct–March 9am–5.15pm; €5), which has among many riches the late fifteenth-century bronze tomb of Pope Sixtus IV by Pollaiuolo. You can opt to visit the **grottoes** (daily: April–Sept 8am–6pm; Oct–March 7am–5pm), emerging in the basilica at the central crossing. They are not the legendary burial spot of St Peter himself (that's something different) but are in fact where a good number of later popes are buried, including the last one, John Paul II.

The roof and dome

Daily: April–Sept 8am–5.45pm; Oct–March 8am–4.45pm • €7 via lift, €4 using the stairs

Also accessible by one of three main outside entrances, the ascent to the **roof and dome** is well worth making. The views from the gallery around the interior of the dome give you a sense of the enormity of the church, and from there you can make the (challenging) ascent to the lantern at the top of the dome, from which the **views** over the city are as glorious as you'd expect.

The Vatican Museums

Viale Vaticano 13 • Mon–Sat 9am–6pm, last entrance at 4pm; last Sun of each month 9am–2pm, last entrance at 12.30pm; closed public and religious holidays; €15, €8 under-18s and under-26s with student ID, €4 extra for all tickets pre-booked online, last Sun of the month free; audioguides €6; Ⓦ vatican.va; book tickets online at Ⓦ http://biglietteriamusei.vatican.va

However much you may have enjoyed Rome's other museums, nothing else in the city quite measures up to the **Vatican Museums**, on Viale Vaticano, a fifteen-minute walk from St Peter's out of the north side of Piazza San Pietro. So much booty from the city's history has ended up here, from both classical and later times, and so many of the Renaissance's finest artists were in the employ of the pope, that not surprisingly the result is a set of museums stuffed with enough exhibits to put most other European collections to shame.

Museo Pio-Clementino

To the left of the entrance, the **Museo Pio-Clementino** is home to some of the best of the Vatican's classical statuary, including two statues that influenced Renaissance artists more than any others: the serene *Apollo Belvedere*, a Roman copy of a fourth-century-BC original, and the first-century-BC *Laocoön*, which shows a Trojan priest being crushed

---

THE VATICAN MUSEUMS: PLANNING A VISIT

As its name suggests, the complex actually holds a series of museums on very diverse subjects – displays of classical statuary, Renaissance painting, Etruscan relics, Egyptian artefacts, not to mention the furnishings and decoration of the building itself. There's no point in trying to see everything, at least not on one visit, and the only features you really shouldn't miss are the Raphael Rooms and the Sistine Chapel. Above all, decide how long you want to spend here, and what you want to see, before you start; you could spend anything from an hour to a whole day here, and it's easy to collapse from museum fatigue before you've even got to your most important target of interest. Also, bear in mind that the collections are in a constant state of restoration, and are often closed and shifted around with little or no notice – so check Ⓦ vatican.va for the current situation.

by serpents for warning of the danger of the Trojan horse – perhaps the most famous classical statue ever. There are also busts and statues of the Roman emperors, fantastic Roman floor mosaics, and the so-called *Venus of Cnidos*, the first known representation of the goddess.

Museo Gregoriano Egizio

The **Museo Gregoriano Egizio** isn't one of the Vatican's main highlights, but it has a distinguished collection of ancient Egyptian artefacts, including some vividly painted mummy cases (and two mummies), along with *canopi*, the alabaster vessels into which the entrails of the deceased were placed. There's also a partial reconstruction of the Temple of Serapis from Hadrian's villa near Tivoli, along with another statue of his lover, Antinous, who drowned close to the original temple in Egypt and so inspired Hadrian to build his replica.

Museo Gregoriano Etrusco

The **Museo Gregoriano Etrusco** holds sculpture, funerary art and applied art from the sites of southern Etruria – a good complement to Rome's specialist Etruscan collection in the Villa Giulia. Especially worth seeing are the finds from the Regolini-Galassi tomb, from the seventh century BC, discovered near Cerveteri, which contained the remains of three Etruscan nobles, two men and a woman; the breastplate of the woman and her huge *fibia* (clasp) are of gold. There's also armour, a bronze bedstead, a funeral chariot and a wagon, as well as a great number of enormous storage jars, in which food, oil and wine were stored for use in the afterlife.

Galleria dei Candelabri and Galleria degli Arazzi

Outside the Etruscan museum, a large monumental staircase leads back down to the **Galleria dei Candelabri**, the niches of which are adorned with huge candelabra taken from imperial Roman villas, and the **Galleria degli Arazzi** (Gallery of Tapestries), with Belgian tapestries to designs by the school of Raphael.

Galleria delle Carte Geografiche

Next, the **Galleria delle Carte Geografiche** (Gallery of Maps), which is as long as the previous two galleries put together, was decorated in the late sixteenth century at the behest of Pope Gregory XIII to show all of Italy, the major islands in the Mediterranean and the papal possessions in France, as well as large-scale maps of the maritime republics of Venice and Genoa.

The Raphael Rooms

The **Raphael Rooms** formed the private apartments of Pope Julius II, and when he moved in here he commissioned Raphael to redecorate them in a style more in tune with the times. Raphael died in 1520 before the scheme was complete, but the two rooms that were painted by him, as well as others completed by pupils, stand as one of the highlights of the Renaissance. The **Stanza di Eliodoro**, the first room you come to, was painted by three of Raphael's students five years after his death, and is best known for its painting the *Mass of Bolsena*, which relates a miracle that occurred in the town in northern Lazio in the 1260s, and, on the window wall opposite, the *Deliverance of St Peter*, showing the saint being assisted in a jail-break by the Angel of the Lord.

The other main room, the **Stanza della Segnatura** or Pope's Study, was painted in the years 1508–11, when Raphael first came to Rome, and comes close to the peak of the painter's art. The *School of Athens*, on the near wall as you come in, steals the show, a representation of the triumph of scientific truth in which all the great minds from antiquity are represented. It pairs with the *Disputation of the Sacrament* opposite, which is a reassertion of religious dogma – an allegorical mass of popes, cardinals, bishops, doctors and even the poet Dante.

1

The Appartamento Borgia

Outside the Raphael Rooms, the **Appartamento Borgia** was inhabited by Julius II's hated predecessor, Alexander VI, and is nowadays host to a large collection of modern religious art, although its ceiling frescoes, the work of Pinturicchio in the years 1492–95, are really the main reason to visit.

The Sistine Chapel

Steps lead from the Raphael Rooms to the **Sistine Chapel**, a huge barn-like structure that serves as the pope's official private chapel and the scene of the conclaves of cardinals for the election of each new pontiff. The ceiling frescoes here, and painting of the *Last Judgement* on the altar wall, are probably the most viewed paintings in the world: it's estimated that on an average day about 15,000 people trudge through here to take a look. It's useful to carry a pair of binoculars with you to view the ceiling, but bear in mind that photography is strictly prohibited and it's also officially forbidden to speak – a rule that is rampantly ignored.

The walls of the chapel were decorated by several prominent painters of the Renaissance – Pinturicchio, Perugino, Botticelli and Ghirlandaio. Recently restored, they would be a massive highlight anywhere else. As it is, they are entirely overshadowed by Michelangelo's more famous **ceiling frescoes**, commissioned by Pope Julius II in 1508. They depict scenes from the Old Testament, from the *Creation of Light* at the altar end to the *Drunkenness of Noah* over the door. Look at the pagan sibyls and biblical prophets which Michelangelo also incorporated in his scheme, including the figure of the prophet Jeremiah – a brooding self-portrait of an exhausted-looking Michelangelo.

On the altar wall of the chapel, the **Last Judgement** was painted by the artist more than twenty years later. It took four years, again single-handed, and is probably the most inspired and homogeneous large-scale painting you're ever likely to see, the technical virtuosity of Michelangelo taking a back seat to the sheer exuberance of the work. The centre is occupied by Christ, turning angrily as he gestures the condemned to the underworld. Below, a group of angels blast their trumpets to summon the dead from their sleep: on the left, they awaken from their tombs and are either levitated to heaven or pulled by angels who take them before Christ. At the bottom right, Charon, keeper of the underworld, swings his oar at the damned souls as they fall off the boat into the waiting gates of hell.

The Braccio Nuovo and Museo Chiaramonti

The **Braccio Nuovo** and **Museo Chiaramonti** both hold classical sculpture, although be warned that they are the Vatican at its most overwhelming – close on a thousand statues crammed into two long galleries. The **Braccio Nuovo** was built in the early 1800s to display classical statuary that was particularly prized, and it contains, among other things, probably the most famous extant image of Augustus, and a bizarre-looking statue depicting the Nile, whose yearly flooding was essential to the fertility of the Egyptian soil. The 300m-long **Chiaramonti gallery** is especially unnerving, lined as it is with the chill marble busts of hundreds of nameless, blank-eyed ancient Romans, along with the odd deity. It pays to have a leisurely wander, for there are some real characters here: sour, thin-lipped matrons; kids, caught in a sulk or mid-chortle; and ancient old men with flesh sagging and wrinkling.

The Pinacoteca

The **Pinacoteca** is housed in a separate building on the far side of the Vatican Museums' main spine and ranks highly among Rome's picture galleries, with works from the early to High Renaissance right up to the nineteenth century. Among early works is the stunning Simoneschi triptych by Giotto, the *Martyrdom of Sts Peter and Paul*, painted in the early 1300s for the old St Peter's, works by Masolino, Fra' Angelico and Fra' Filippo Lippi, and Melozzo da Forlì's musical angels – fragments of a fresco commissioned for the church has a room to himself, where you'll find his *Transfiguration*, [...] [...]leted when he died in 1520, the *Coronation of the Virgin*, [...] 19 years old, and, on the left, the *Madonna of Foglino*, showing [...]cis of Assisi and Jerome. Take a look also at the most gruesome [...] Poussin's *Martyrdom of St Erasmus*, which shows the saint being [...]ng".

[...]RE

[...]da Vinci, better known as [...]ority of scheduled flights, [...]o, where you'll arrive if you're travelling with Ryanair. Information on both airports is available at ☎ 06 65 951 and ⓦ adr.it.

Fiumicino The aiport is linked to the centre of Rome by direct trains, which take 30min to get to Termini and cost €15; services begin at 6.38am, leaving every 30min until 11.38pm. Alternatively, there are buses, run by COTRAL, which has around 6 services a day from 1.15am to 3.30pm (7pm at weekends) to Termini's Piazza dei Cinquecento (€4.50 one way, no return tickets; ⓦ cotralspa.it); SIT, which runs every half-hour from 5am to 8.30pm to Via Marsala (€5 one way, €10 return; ⓦ sitbusshuttle.it); and Terravision, which also runs every half-hour between 5.30am and 10.55pm (€4 one way, €8 return; ⓦ terravision.eu). All buses take about 45min. There are also slower trains to Ostiense and Tiburtina stations (tickets €5.50), on the edge of the city centre, which are also stops on Rome's metro. As for taxis to the city centre, you'll pay a fixed price of €40 for the 30–40min journey.

Ciampino From Ciampino, Terravision and SIT Bus run buses roughly every half-hour to Termini, where they pull up on Via Marsala; tickets cost €4 (€6 in the opposite direction), €8 return. All services take 30–45 min. If you don't want to go to Termini, and are staying near a metro stop on the A line (near the Spanish Steps or Via Veneto areas, for example), you could alternatively take a bus from the airport to Anagnina metro station at the end of metro Line A, and take a metro from there to your destination (20min; around €3), or a bus to Ciampino station and a train to Termini from there (around €3.50). The fixed price for taxis into the city centre is €30 (30–40min).

BY TRAIN

Travelling by train from most places in Italy, or indeed Europe, you arrive at Termini station, centrally placed for all parts of the city and meeting-point of the two metro lines and many city-bus routes. There are left-luggage facilities here, on the lower level by platform 24 (daily 6am–midnight; €3.80/5hr, then €0.60/hr). As for other train stations in Rome, Tiburtina is a stop for some north–south intercity trains; selected routes around Lazio are handled by the Regionali platforms of Termini station (a 5min walk beyond the end of the regular platforms); and there's also the Roma-Nord line station on Piazzale Flaminio, which runs to Viterbo.

ROME

Destinations Rome (Termini) to: Ancona (hourly; 4hr); Anzio/Nettuno (hourly; 1hr); Bologna (at least 2/hr; 2hr); Civitavecchia* (at least 2/hr; 1hr 10min); Florence (at least 2/hr; 1hr 30min); Formia (at least 2/hr; 1hr 25min); Latina (at least 2/hr; 35min); Milan (at least hourly; 3hr 30min); Naples (at least 2/hr; 2hr); Pescara (6 daily; 4hr); Tarquinia* (12 daily; 1hr 20min). Rome (Ostiense) to: Bracciano (every 30min; 1hr); Viterbo* (hourly; 1hr 40min). Rome (Roma-Nord line from Piazzale Flaminio) to: Viterbo (5 daily; 2hr 45min). * Trains also run from Rome Trastevere and Roma San Pietro.

BY BUS

Arriving by bus can leave you in any one of a number of places around the city. The main station for buses from outside the Rome area is Tiburtina. Others include Ponte Mammolo (trains from Tivoli and Subiaco); Lepanto (Cerveteri, Civitavecchia, Bracciano area); EUR Fermi (Nettuno, Anzio, southern Lazio coast); Anagnina (Castelli Romani); Saxa Rubra (Viterbo and around). All of these stations are on a metro line, except Saxa Rubra, which is on the Roma-Nord train line, connected every fifteen minutes with Piazzale Flaminio.

Destinations Rome (Anagnina) to: Palestrina (every 45min; 1hr). Rome (Laurentina) to: Sabaudia (10 daily; 1hr 40min); San Felice (10 daily; 2hr); Terracina (10 daily; 2hr 15min). Rome (Ponte Mammolo) to: Palestrina (12 daily; 55min); Subiaco (hourly; 1hr 15min); Tivoli (every 15min; 50min). Rome (Saxa Rubra) to: Viterbo (every 30min; 1hr 30min). Rome (Cornelia) to: Cerveteri (every 40min; 1hr 10min); Civitavecchia (every 30min; 1hr 35min).

BY CAR

Coming into the city by car can be confusing and isn't advisable unless you're used to driving in Italy and know where you are going to park. If you are coming from the north on the A1 highway take the exit "Roma Nord"; from the south, take the "Roma Est" exit. Both lead you to the Grande Raccordo Anulare (GRA), which circles the city and is connected with all of the major arteries into the city centre – Via Cassia from the north, Via Salaria from the northeast, Via Tiburtina or Via Nomentana from the east, Via Appia Nuova and the Pontina from the south, Via Prenestina and Via Casilina or Via Cristoforo Colombo from the southeast, and Via Aurelia from the northwest.

1

USEFUL TRANSPORT ROUTES

BUSES

#23 Piazzale Clodio–Piazza Risorgimento–Ponte Vittorio Emanuele–Ponte Garibaldi–Via Marmorata–Piazzale Ostiense–Centrale Montemartini–Basilica di S. Paolo.

#30 Express (Mon–Sat only) Piazzale Clodio–Piazza Mazzini–Piazza Cavour–Corso Rinascimento–Largo Argentina–Piazza Venezia–Lungotevere Aventino–Via Marmorata–Piramide–Via C. Colombo–EUR.

#40 Express Termini–Via Nazionale–Piazza Venezia–Largo Argentina–Piazza Pia.

#60 Express Via Nomentana–Porta Pia–Via XX Settembre–Piazza della Repubblica–Via Nazionale–Piazza Venezia–Imperial Forums–Colosseum–Circus Maximus–Piramide.

#62 Piazza Bologna–Via Nomentana–Porta Pia–Piazza Barberini–Piazza S. Silvestro–Via del Corso–Piazza Venezia–Corso V. Emanuele–Borgo Angelico– Piazza Pia.

#64 Termini–Piazza della Repubblica–Via Nazionale–Piazza Venezia–Largo Argentina–Corso V. Emanuele–Stazione S. Pietro.

#75 Via Poerio (Monteverde)–Via Induno–Porta Portese–Testaccio–Piramide–Circus Maximus–Colosseum–Via Cavour–Termini–Piazza Indipendenza.

#175 Termini–Piazza Barberini–Via del Corso–Piazza Venezia–Colosseum–Circus Maximus–Aventine–Stazione Ostiense.

#271 S. Paolo–Via Ostiense–Piramide–Viale Aventino–Circus Maximus–Colosseum–Piazza Venezia–Ponte Sisto–Castel Sant'Angelo–Via Vitelleschi–Piazza Risorgimento–Ottaviano–Foro Italico.

#492 Stazione Tiburtina–Piazzale Verano–Termini–Piazza Barberini–Via del Corso–Piazza Venezia–Largo Argentina–Corso del Rinascimento–Piazza Cavour–Piazza Risorgimento–Cipro (Vatican Museums).

#590 Same route as metro line A but with access for disabled; runs every 90 minutes.

#660 Largo Colli Albani–Via Appia Nuova–Via Appia Antica.

#714 Termini–Santa Maria Maggiore–Via Merulana–San Giovanni in Laterano–Terme di Caracalla–EUR.

#910 Termini–Piazza della Repubblica–Via Pinciana (Villa Borghese)–Piazza Euclide–Palazzetto dello Sport–Piazza Mancini.

MINIBUSES

These **small buses** negotiate circular routes through the narrow streets of Rome's centre.

#116 Porta Pinciana–Via Veneto–Via del Tritone–Piazza di Spagna–Piazza S. Silvestro–Corso Rinascimento–Campo de' Fiori–Piazza Farnese–Lungotevere Sangallo–Terminal Gianicolo.

#117 San Giovanni in Laterano–Piazza Celimontana–Via dei Due Macelli–Via del Babuino–Piazza del Popolo–Via del Corso–Piazza Venezia–Via Nazionale–Via dei Serpenti–Colosseum–Via Labicana.

GETTING AROUND

The best way to get around the centre of Rome is to walk. However, its ATAC-run public transport system, incorporating buses, metros and trams – is cheap, reliable and as quick as the clogged streets allow. There's an information office in the centre of Piazza dei Cinquecento outside Termini station; Ⓦ atac.roma.it has information in English and a route planner.

By bus Buses run till around midnight, when a network of nightbuses comes into service, accessing most parts of the city and operating until about 5am.

By metro The metro operates from 5.30am to 11.30pm (till 12.30am on Sat). Its two lines, crossing at Termini, only have a handful of stops in the city centre; a third line,

TICKETS AND TRAVEL CARDS

Flat-fare **tickets** (known as BIT) on all forms of transport currently cost €1.50 each and are good for any number of bus and tram rides and one metro ride within 75 minutes of validating them – bus tickets should be stamped in machines on board the bus. You can buy tickets from *tabacchi*, newsstands and ticket machines located in all metro stations and at major bus stops. If you're using transport extensively it's worth getting a **day-pass** (BIG) for €6, a **three-day pass** (BTI) for €16.50, or a **seven-day pass** (CIS) for €24. There are hefty fines for fare-dodging.

#119 Piazza del Popolo–Via del Corso–Piazza Venezia–Largo Argentina–Via del Tritone–Piazza Barberini–Via Veneto–Porta Pinciana–Piazza Barberini–Piazza di Spagna–Via del Babuino–Piazza del Popolo.

TRAMS

#2 Piazzale Flaminio–Via Flaminia–Viale Tiziano–MAXXI–Piazza Mancini.

#3 Stazione Trastevere–Via Marmorata–Piramide–Circus Maximus–Colosseum–San Giovanni–San Lorenzo–Via Nomentana–Parioli–Viale Belle Arti.

#8 Casaletto–Stazione Trastevere–Piazza Mastai–Viale Trastevere–Largo Argentina.

#14 Termini–Piazza Vittorio Emanuele–Porta Maggiore–Via Prenestina (Pigneto).

#19 Porta Maggiore–San Lorenzo–Piazzale Verano–Viale Regina Margherita–Viale Belle Arti–Via Flaminia–Ottaviano–Piazza Risorgimento.

NIGHTBUSES

#N1 Same route as metro line A.

#N2 Same route as metro line B.

#N7 Piazzale Clodio–Piazzale Flaminio–Piazza Cavour–Largo Argentina–Piazza Venezia–Via Nazionale–Termini.

#N8 Viale Trastevere–Piazza Venezia–Via Nazionale–Termini.

#N10 Piazzale Ostiense–Lungotevere De' Cenci–Via Crescenzio–Viale Belle Arte–Viale Regina Margherita–Via Labicana.

TOURIST BUSES

There are several operators offering circuits of the city with guided commentary, but the ATAC-run **#110 bus** is the best and most frequent (☎ 800 281 281, ⊕ trambusopen.com). It leaves from Termini station and stops at all the major sights, including Piazza di Spagna, Castel Sant'Angelo and the Vatican. The whole round-trip takes about two hours. In summer, departures are every twenty minutes from 8.30am until 8.30pm daily, including holidays and Sundays. Tickets cost €20 and are valid for 48 hours, allowing you to get on wherever you like and hop on and off throughout the day. Family tickets are available for €50; combined tickets for the #110 and Archeobus (see below) cost €25 and are valid for 72 hours. Tickets can be bought on board, before you get on at Piazza dei Cinquecento or online; discounts are available on entrance fees at a number of attractions on presentation of your ticket. Consider also the **Archeobus** (same contact details), which links some of the most compelling ancient sights, including the monuments on and around the Via Appia Antica. Buses start at Piazza dei Cinquecento and operate daily every half-hour from 9am until 4.30pm and tickets cost €12 and are valid 48 hours. You can also buy a combined ticket with bus #110 for €25, or family tickets for €40.

Line C, is scheduled for completion by 2015.

By taxi The easiest way to get a taxi is to find the nearest taxi stand (*fermata dei taxi*) – central ones include Termini, Piazza Venezia, Largo Argentina, Piazza San Silvestro, Piazza di Spagna, Piazza del Popolo and Piazza Barberini. Alternatively, you can simply call a taxi (☎ 06 3570, ☎ 06 4157, ☎ 06 6645, ☎ 06 4994 or ☎ 06 5551), but bear in mind that these usually cost more, as the meter starts ticking the moment the taxi is dispatched to collect you. A journey from one side of the city centre to the other should cost no more than €10, or around €15 on Sunday or at night. All taxis carry a rate card in English giving the current tariff.

By bike You can tour the city by bike using the city's bike-sharing scheme (⊕ roma-n-bike.com). Purchase a prepaid card at metro stops Termini, Spagna, Ottaviano or any of the end-of-the-line stops for €10 – €5 for the card, and €5 to get you started; after that it costs €0.50 an hour and there are enough drop-off points around town to make it convenient. Or you could just rent a bike or scooter: Barberini, Via della Purificazione 84 (daily 9am–7pm; ☎ 06 488 5485, ⊕ rentscooter.it), rents bicycles (€10/day), mopeds and scooters (from €30/day); Bici e Baci, Via del Viminale 5 (daily 8am–7pm; ☎ 06 482 8443, ⊕ bicibaci .com), has bicycles for €4/hr, €11/day; mopeds from €6/hr, €19/day, scooters €10/hr, €40/day.

INFORMATION

Tourist office There's an official tourist office at Fiumicino Terminal 2 (daily 9am–6.30pm; ☎ 060 608), a tourist desk at Termini, on the Via Giolitti side (daily 8am–7.30pm; same number) and information kiosks in key locations

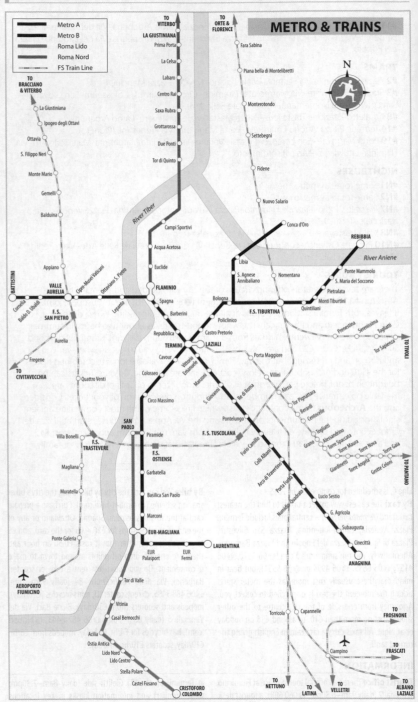

METRO & TRAINS

Metro A
Metro B
Roma Lido
Roma Nord
FS Train Line

INFORMATION KIOSKS

Castel Sant'Angelo (Piazza Pia); Piazza Navona (Piazza delle Cinque Lune); Santa Maria Maggiore (Via dell'Olmata); Termini station (Piazza dei Cinquecento); Trastevere (Piazza Sonnino); Trevi Fountain (Via Minghetti); Via Nazionale (Palazzo delle Esposizioni).

around the city centre (daily 9.30am–7.30pm; see box above).

Enjoy Rome You could also try the privately run Enjoy Rome, Via Marghera 8/A (Mon–Fri 9am–5.30pm, Sat 8.30am–2pm; ☎ 06 445 1843, ⓦ enjoyrome.com), whose friendly English-speaking staff hand out lots of free information; they also operate a free room-finding service, organize tours, have a left-luggage service for customers, and run shuttle buses to Fiumicino and Ciampino.

Magazines, newspapers and websites The city's best source of listings is the weekly *Romacè* (€1), which has a

helpful section in English giving information on tours, clubs, restaurants, services and weekly events and a decent website – ⓦ romace.it. The twice-monthly English expat magazine, *Wanted in Rome* (€0.75) – ⓦ wantedinrome.com – is also a useful source, especially if you're looking for an apartment or work. Both are available at most newsstands. Those with a bit of Italian should pick up a copy of the Thursday edition of *La Repubblica*, which includes the "Trova Roma" supplement, another handy guide to current offerings. And ⓦ inromenow.com and ⓦ eternallycool.net are both informative Rome-focused websites.

ACCOMMODATION

There's plenty of accommodation in Rome, and overall the choice of hotels in the city centre has improved a lot over recent years, with lots of new boutique hotels and contemporary B&Bs opening up. But it's always worth booking in advance, especially when the city is at its busiest – from Easter to the end of October, and over Christmas – and also because you can score much better rates online, sometimes as much as half the published rate.

HOTELS AND B&BS

Many of the city's cheapest places are located close to Termini station, but this isn't the nicest part of town and there are plenty of moderately priced places in the *centro storico* or around Campo de' Fiori. However, you'll need to book well in advance to be sure of a room. The Tridente, Trevi and the Quirinale Hill, towards Via Veneto and around the Spanish Steps, are home to more upscale accommodation, although there are a few affordable options here too. Consider also staying across the river in Prati, a pleasant neighbourhood, nicely distanced from the hubbub of the city centre proper, and handy for the Vatican, or in lively Trastevere, also on the west side of the river but an easy walk into the centre.

CENTRO STORICO AND CAMPO DE' FIORI

Argentina Residenza Via di Torre Argentina 47 ☎ 06 6813 5794, ⓦ argentinaresidenza.com; map p.60. This former noble carriage-house has been converted to a six-room hotel by the people who run the *Navona* (see below), and it's an elegant affair, with antique ceilings combining well with the well-chosen modern furnishings and amenities. **€120**

Campo de' Fiori Via del Biscione 6 ☎ 06 6880 6865, ⓦ hotelcampodefiori.com; map p.62. A friendly place in a nice location with 23 individually designed rooms. The sixth-floor roof terrace has great views, and the hotel also owns a number of small apartments nearby. **€190**

Due Torri Vicolo del Leonetto 23 ☎ 06 6880 6956, ⓦ hotelduetorriroma.com; map p.62. This little hotel was once a residence for cardinals, and later served as a brothel. Completely remodelled, it retains a homely feel and some of its rooms have lovely rooftop views. A good location just north of Piazza Navona. **€140**

★ **Navona** Via dei Sediari 8 ☎ 06 686 4203, ⓦ hotelnavona.com; map p.62. Completely renovated *pensione*-turned-hotel housed in a building built on the remains of the ancient Roman baths of Agrippa. It's pretty welcoming, run by a friendly Italian-Australian, and the rooms are decent; plus it's in a good position close to Piazza Navona. **€120**

Portoghesi Via dei Portoghesi 1 ☎ 06 686 4231, ⓦ hotelportoghesiroma.it; map p.62. Decent, well-equipped if slightly characterless modern rooms, a stone's throw from most *centro storico* attractions. Breakfast is served on the roof terrace. **€160**

Santa Chiara Via S. Chiara 21 ☎ 06 687 979, ⓦ albergosantachiara.com; map p.62. A friendly hotel in a great location, on a quiet piazza behind the Pantheon. The rooms are nicer than the bland lobby, and some overlook the church of Santa Maria sopra Minerva. **€200**

Smeraldo Vicolo dei Chiodaroli 9 ☎ 06 687 5929, ⓦ smeraldoroma.com; map p.60. Clean and comfortable hotel with a modern if rather bland interior and rooms with shiny new baths, televisions and a/c. The terrace and some rooms have lovely views over Rome's rooftops. Breakfast not included. **€100**

1

Sole Via del Biscione 76 ☎06 6880 6873, ⊛sole albiscione.it; map p.62. This place enjoys one of the best locations in the centre, and has been in the same family for generations. The rooms are simple but decent enough; it's worth splashing out on one of the ones with the spectacular view of the nearby domes from the top-floor terrace. **€100**

Teatro Pace Via del Teatro Pace 33 ☎06 687 9075, ⊛hotelteatropace.com; map p.62. This beautifully restored *palazzo*, a few paces from Piazza Navona, has an impressive Baroque spiral staircase (no lift) and four floors of elegant rooms with original wood beams, floor-sweeping drapes and luxurious bathrooms. **€210**

Zanardelli Via G. Zanardelli 7 ☎06 6821 1392, ⊛hotel navona.com; map p.62. Run by the same people as the *Navona*, this is the slightly more lavish alternative, just north of Piazza Navona, in a building which used to be a papal residence and has many original features. The rooms are quite elegant, with antique iron beds, silk-lined walls and modern amenities, but still decently priced. **€140**

THE TRIDENTE, TREVI AND THE QUIRINALE

★ **Casa Howard** Via Capo le Case 18 & Via Sistina 149 ☎06 69922 4555, ⊛casahoward.com; map p.60. Halfway between a boutique hotel and an upmarket *pensione*, the individually furnished if sometimes small rooms here are among Rome's most stylish. The location is good too, between Piazza Barberini and the Spanish Steps. **€200**

Crossing Condotti Via Mario de' Fiori 28 ☎06 6992 0633, ⊛crossingcondotti.com; map p.60. Classy modern suites and apartments in a great location close to Piazza di Spagna, furnished with antiques and painted in elegant, neutral tones. Free wi-fi and snacks. **€250**

Daphne Via di S. Basilio 55 & Via degli Avignonesi 20 ☎06 8745 0087, ⊛daphne-rome.com; map p.60. A welcoming *pensione* run by an American woman and her Roman husband. Bright, nicely renovated modern rooms in two good locations either side of Piazza Barberini, and as much advice as you need on how to spend your time in Rome. Some rooms are en suite. **€160**

De Russie Via del Babuino 9 ☎06 328 881, ⊛hotel derussie.it; map p.60. Coolly elegant and understated, this is the abode of choice for visiting movie stars and hip travellers spending someone else's money. **€500**

★ **Grand Hotel Plaza** Via del Corso 126 ☎06 6992 1111, ⊛grandhotelplaza.com; map p.60. One of Rome's most sumptuous hotels and sometime backdrop to films like *Angels and Demons* and *Ocean's 12*. The fantastic lobby, with plush velvets, sumptuous brocades, chandeliers and stained-glass ceiling give you some idea of what to expect in the rooms, and they don't disappoint: huge, well-renovated and well-appointed, all with wi-fi. **€330**

Homs Via della Vite 71–72 ☎06 679 2976, ⊛hotel homs.it; map p.62. In the heart of the Spanish Steps neighbourhood, this small four-star boasts a roof terrace with marvellous views, cosy rooms and a very friendly atmosphere – something that's not always guaranteed in the hotels of this ritzy neighbourhood. **€130**

Hotel Art Via Margutta 56 ☎06 328 711, ⊛hotelart.it; map p.60. Ingeniously converted from a convent, and with an impressive bar and lobby fashioned out of a vaulted chapel, the *Hotel Art* ticks most of the right boxes: it's in a great location, tucked away on Via Margutta, and its design theme is for the most part well-realized and luxurious. **€310**

Locarno Via della Penna 22 ☎06 361 0841, ⊛hotel locarno.com; map pp.56–57. No two rooms are alike at the *Locarno*, filled with antiques of various periods, and the atmospheric bar on some nights can attract a cast of hundreds. Literati, the film world, artists and those who could afford to pay much more relish the hotel's quirkiness and genteel charm. **€270**

THE ESQUILINE, MONTI AND TERMINI

Alpi Via Castelfidardo 84 ☎06 444 1235, ⊛hotelalpi .com; map pp.56–57. One of the more peaceful yet convenient options close to Termini, recently renovated, and within easy walking distance of the station. Pleasant, if somewhat small, rooms with bathrooms, and a great buffet breakfast – better than you would normally expect in a hotel of this category. **€120**

Artorius Via del Boschetto 13 ☎06 482 1196, ⊛hotel artorius.com; map p.60. A great choice if you want to stay in the heart of Monti, with just ten rooms decorated in classic style. There's also a pleasant courtyard for breakfast, or for drinks after dark. **€180**

The Beehive Via Marghera 8 ☎06 4470 4553, ⊛the -beehive.com; map pp.56–57. Linda and Steve set a new standard for Termini-area budget accommodation when they opened a dozen years ago, and their hotel-cum-hostel still delivers, with a choice of multi-bedded and private rooms with spotless shared bathrooms, along with a handful of en-suites in an annexe around the corner. Free wi-fi, a lovely outdoor bar area and basement breakfast room. One of the nicest places to stay close to the station. **€80**

Des Artistes Via Villafranca 20 ☎06 445 4365, ⊛hotel desartistes.com; map pp.56–57. One of the better hotels in the Termini area. Exceptionally good value, spotlessly clean, and with a wide range of rooms both with and without en-suite facilities, plus dorm beds for around €25. Eat breakfast or recover from a long day of sightseeing on the breezy roof terrace. **€100**

Giorni Felici Viale Ippocrate 116 ☎335 838 4927, ⊛bbgiornifelici.it; map pp.56–57. Feel like a proper Roman in this beautifully furnished apartment with two lovely, excellent-value double rooms, each with its own bathroom. You're not far from Termini, and in any case the Bologna neighbourhood is great, as are the couple who run the place. **€80**

Leon's Place Via XX Settembre 90/94 ☏ 06 890 871, ⓦ leonsplace.it; map pp.56–57. Near Termini, but on the edge of an upscale residential area with good shops and dining. The rooms are on the small side, but are sleekly modern, all black and white with splashes of colour and trendy design touches. €240

Romae Via Palestro 49 ☏ 06 446 3554, ⓦ hotelromae .com; map pp.56–57. Rome's self-styled "groovy" hotel is thoroughly welcoming and extremely comfortable, with thirty contemporary rooms that offer some of the best value in the Termini area, or indeed the city, all presided over by friendly Australian-Italian owners. They also run the *Yellow* hostel across the road (see below). Free wi-fi and iPads for rent. €130

Suite Dreams Via Modena 5 ☏ 06 4891 3907, ⓦ suite dreams.it; map p.60. Simple yet stylish rooms with good-sized bathrooms, and nice details like a DVD library for guests' use. Good value. €180

THE CELIAN HILL, SAN GIOVANNI AND THE AVENTINE

★ **Lancelot** Via Capo d'Africa 47 ☏ 06 7045 0615, ⓦ lancelothotel.com; map pp.56–57. Just 2min from the Colosseum, this friendly family-run hotel has rooms with oriental carpets and an attractive bar. Wi-fi is free, as is the lobby internet point. Dinner is good too, served at intimate round tables with other guests for €25 a head. They also have (limited) parking for €10. €150

Sant'Anselmo Piazza Sant'Anselmo 2 ☏ 06 570 057, ⓦ aventinohotels.com; map pp.56–57. One of the most peaceful places you could choose, this is one of a chain of Aventine Hill hotels. The rooms are beautifully furnished (each with a different theme) and have been fairly recently renovated. Parking is free. €160

TRASTEVERE AND PRATI

Bramante Vicolo delle Palline 24 ☏ 06 6880 6426, ⓦ hotelbramante.com; map p.60. Small and welcoming hotel that has a great location on this peaceful Borgo street and nicely furnished en-suite rooms with large bathrooms. €230

Cisterna Via della Cisterna 7–9 ☏ 06 581 7212, ⓦ cisternahotel.it; map pp.56–57. A friendly three-star bang in the middle of Trastevere. Nineteen rooms, some with colourful tiled floors and wood-beamed ceilings, and all with private bathrooms. €90

Dei Consoli Via Varrone 2D ☏ 06 6889 2972, ⓦ hotel deiconsoli.com; map p.60. Right in the heart of Prati, this is one of the best choices in the Vatican area, with thoughtfully designed rooms, a lovely roof terrace and excellent, friendly service. Parking available – €20 a night. €260

La Rovere Vicolo San Onofrio 4–5 ☏ 06 6880 6739, ⓦ hotellarovere.com; map p.60. Just across the bridge from Piazza Navona, this small hotel is tucked quietly away

FIVE HOTEL BARS
The Beehive p.102
De Russie p.102
Grand Hotel Plaza p.102
Hotel Art p.102
Locarno p.102

from all the bustle and offers a terrace garden and antique-filled setting for its guests to relax in. €140

Santa Maria Vicolo del Piede 2 ☏ 06 589 4626, ⓦ hotel santamaria.info; map p.60. Just steps from Piazza Santa Maria in the heart of Trastevere, the rooms of this small three-star surround an orange-tree-filled garden, giving the feel of a place far removed from the city. €120

HOSTELS

Alessandro Palace Via Vicenza 42 ☏ 06 446 1958, ⓦ hostelsalessandro.com; map pp.56–57. This place has been voted one of the top hostels in Europe, and it sparkles with creative style. Pluses include no lock-out or curfew, a good bar with free pizza every night, internet access and satellite TV. Dorms €15, doubles €115, with bath €130. They have another branch, *Alessandro Downtown* Via C. Cattaneo 23 (☏ 06 4434 0147), close by but on the city-centre side of Termini. Dorms €25, doubles €95

Ostello del Foro Italico Viale delle Olimpiadi 61 ☏ 06 323 6267, ⓦ ostellodiroma.it; map pp.56–57. Rome's official HI hostel (non-members can join here), though not particularly central or easy to get to from Termini – take bus #32, #224 or #280 and ask the driver for the "*ostello*". You can call ahead to check out availability, but they won't take phone bookings. Dorms €19

Ottaviano Via Ottaviano 6 ☏ 06 3973 8138, ⓦ pensione ottaviano.com; map pp.56–57. This simple hostel near the Vatican is very popular with backpackers; book well in advance. Facilities are a bit sparse: no wi-fi, one internet connection and no TV in the rooms, though the communal TV does play DVDs. Dorms €28, twin rooms €50

Yellow Via Palestro 44 ☏ 06 4938 2682, ⓦ yellowhostel .com; map pp.56–57. Friendly, youthful hostel over the road from grown-up sister hotel, the *Romae*, and equally well run and welcoming. It's self-consciously cool, and encourages a lively scene in the downstairs bar, so if you're after somewhere quiet it's probably not for you. Free wi-fi though. Dorms €26, en-suite doubles €55

YWCA Via C. Balbo 4 ☏ 06 488 0460, ⓦ ywca-ucdg.it; map p.60. Opera, ballet and music fans on a budget can stay right by the Teatro dell'Opera. Open to women and men, and just a 10min walk from Termini, although the market outside may wake you up earlier than you might want. Midnight curfew. There's a common room with TV. No wi-fi, but an internet point. Singles €50, doubles €80, triples and quads €28 per person

1

CAMPING

Camping Flaminio Via Flaminia Nuova 821 ☎ 06 333 2604, ⓦ villageflaminio.it; Roma-Nord train from Piazzale Flaminio to Due Ponti, or bus #910 to Piazza Mancini and then bus #200 (ask the driver to drop you at the "fermata più vicino al campeggio"). The closest site to the city, 8km north of the centre at where you can camp for €10 a head, plus €6 for a tent. It also has bungalows (doubles or for 5) and a swimming pool and restaurant. March–Oct. Pitches €26, bungalows €52/€155

Camping Tiber Via Tiberina Km1400 ☎ 06 3361 0733, ⓦ campingtiber.com; Roma-Nord train from Piazzale Flaminio (about 20min), then a free shuttle bus (8am–11pm every 30min) from the nearby Prima Porta station. Right beside the Tiber, quiet, spacious and friendly, with a supermarket, bar/pizzeria, swimming pool and really hot showers; and it has some 100 bungalows (with bath) as well as three camping areas. March–Oct. Pitches €27, bungalows €42

EATING

Rome is a great place to eat: its denizens know a good deal about freshness and authenticity, and can be very demanding when it comes to the quality of the dishes they are served. Most city-centre restaurants offer standard Italian menus, with the emphasis on traditional Roman dishes, although a few more adventurous places have been popping up of late; plus there are numerous establishments dedicated to a variety of regional cuisines. The city is also blessed with an abundance of good pizzerias, churning out thin, crispy-baked Roman pizza from wood-fired ovens.

COFFEE, SNACKS AND LUNCH

Rome has plenty of places in which to refuel during a long day's sightseeing, and it's easy to find places that aren't just targeted at tourists. Most bars sell panini and sandwiches (tramezzini), and there are plenty of stand-up rosticerrie for roast chicken and the like. The following are some of our favourite places for a good-quality, unpretentious lunch or snack.

CENTRO STORICO

Enoteca Corsi Via del Gesù 87–88 ☎ 06 679 0821; map p.62. An old-fashioned Roman trattoria and wine shop where you eat what they happen to have cooked that morning. The menu changes each day, and it gets very busy at lunchtimes – you may have to wait for a table. €9 for a primo and €13 for a main course. Mon–Sat noon–3pm; closed Aug.

La Caffeteria Piazza di Pietra 65 ☎ 06 679 8147; map p.62. Great Neapolitan café that imports its pastries daily from Naples. The coffee is among Rome's best. Daily 7.30am–10pm.

Lo Zozzone Via del Teatro Pace 32 ☎ 06 6880 8575; map p.62. This Rome legend, just around the corner from Piazza Navona and with outside seating, serves the best pizza bianca in town, by general consent – as well as lots of delicious pizza al taglio choices. Mon–Fri 9am–9pm, Sat 10am–11pm.

ICE CREAM

Alberto Pica Via della Seggiola 12; map p.60. Long-running and award-winning Campo de' Fiori area favourite with lots of unusual flavours. The place to try rice-pudding ice cream if you've ever fancied it. Mon–Sat 8.30am–2pm, Sun 4.30pm–2am.

Alla Scala Via della Scala 51; map p.60. This Sicilian-owned Trastevere joint has some of the very best ice cream in town, with unusual flavours such as cinnamon and cassata. The amarena (black cherry) and coconut are also great. Daily 1pm–midnight, until 1am on Sat & Sun.

Cremeria Monteforte Via della Rotonda 22 ☎ 06 686 7720; map p.62. There's no better place to eat ice cream than sitting on one of the walls that surround the Pantheon, and this award-winning gelateria has lots of flavours, including the intriguing rose petal – like cold Turkish Delight. Sicilian in origin and good if you like your ice cream on the sweet side. Tues–Sun 11am–11pm.

Giolitti Via Uffici del Vicario 40; map p.62. An Italian institution that once had a reputation – now lost – for the country's top ice cream. Still pretty good, however, with a choice of seventy flavours. Always very busy. Tues–Sun 7am–2am.

Palazzo del Freddo di Giovanni Fassi Via Principe Eugenio 65/67A ☎ 06 446 4740, ⓦ palazzodelfreddo .it; map pp.56–57. Known as "Fassi", this wonderful, huge and airy ice-cream parlour has been doing brilliant fruit ice creams and milk shakes since 1880. Tues–Sat noon–midnight, Sun 10am–midnight.

San Crispino Via della Panetteria 42; map p.62. Not far from the Trevi Fountain, this is considered by many to make the best ice cream in Rome. Other branches in the centro storico at Piazza Maddalena 3, by the Pantheon, and at Via Acaia 56 in San Giovanni. Daily noon–12.30am, Fri & Sat until 1.30am; closed Tues in autumn and winter.

FIVE GREAT ROMAN RESTAURANTS
Dal Cavalier Gino p.106
Da Paris p.108
Nonna Betta p.106
Pommidoro p.107
Trattoria Lilli p.106

Pascucci Via di Torre Argentina 20 ☎06 686 4816; map p.62. This tiny stand-up *centro storico* bar is *frullati* central. Your choice of fresh fruit whipped up with ice and milk – the ultimate Roman refreshment on a hot day. Mon–Fri 6.30am–midnight, Sat 6.30am–12.30am, Sun 10am–midnight.

Sant'Eustachio Piazza Sant'Eustachio 82 ☎06 6880 2048; map p.62. The home of what many consider to be Rome's best coffee, roasted on the premises and perennially popular. Nice coffee-based sweets and cakes too. Daily 8am–1am.

CAMPO DE' FIORI AND THE GHETTO
Antico Forno Roscioli Via dei Chiavari 34 ☎06 686 4045, ⊛salumeriaroscioli.com; map p.60. Old bakery that's associated with the swanky restaurant and deli around the corner and does great bread, lots of different kinds of pizza and other savoury and sweet delights. Mon–Sat 7am–8pm; closed Sat evening in summer.

Bernasconi Piazza Cairoli 16 ☎06 6880 6264; map p.60. Great, long-established Jewish *pasticceria* and café with *sfogiatelle* (flaky, custard-filled pastries) to die for, as well as a host of other goodies. Tues–Sun 7am–8.30pm.

Il Forno di Campo de' Fiori Campo de' Fiori 22 ☎06 6880 6662; map p.62. This bakery on the corner of Campo de' Fiori does all sorts of goodies, including fantastic *pizza al taglio*. Mon–Sat 7.30am–2.30pm & 4.30–8pm.

THE TRIDENTE
Buccone Via di Ripetta 19 ☎06 361 2154; map pp.56–57. This wine shop is one of the best places for lunch in the Tridente/Piazza del Popolo area, with tables laid out amid its bottle-lined shelves and a menu that changes daily, with salads and cold cut platters (€8–10), as well as a few hot daily specials – pasta and meat courses for €7–10. Mon–Fri noon–2pm.

Herbier Via San Claudio 87 ☎06 678 5847; map p.60. Well-located bar, just off Piazza San Silvestro in a small arcade and thus a real oasis of calm away from the hectic and fumy traffic. Offers snacks or even a full lunch. Mon–Sat 8am–8pm.

THE ESQUILINE, MONTI AND TERMINI
Antico Caffé di Brasile Via dei Serpenti 23 ☎06 488 2319; map p.60. Reliable old Monti stand-by that has been selling great coffee, sandwiches, snacks and cakes for over a century. Mon–Sat 6am–8.30pm, Sun 7am–7pm.

Dagnino Galleria Esedra Via E. Orlando 75 ☎06 481 8660; map p.60. Good for both a coffee and snack or light lunch, this long-established Sicilian bakery is a peaceful retreat in the Termini area, with tables outside on a small shopping arcade. Daily 7.30am–10.30pm.

La Bottega del Caffè Piazza Madonna dei Monti 5 ☎06 474 1578; map p.60. Bang in the heart of Monti, this is a good place for breakfast or a lunchtime snack, with tables outside on this peaceful square. Daily 8am–2am.

TESTACCIO
Volpetti Più Via A. Volta 8; map pp.56–57. This Testaccio *tavola calda* is attached to the famous deli of the same name, around the corner at Via Marmorata 47. It serves pizza, chicken, *supplì* (breaded rice balls) – all the usual classics. Mon–Sat 10.30am–3.30pm & 5.30–9.30pm.

TRASTEVERE
La Renella Via del Moro 15 ☎06 581 7265; map p.60. Arguably the best bakery in Rome, right in the heart of Trastevere, with great focaccia and superb *pizza al taglio*. Takeaway or eat on the premises at its long counter. Daily 7am–10pm.

Sisini Via San Francesco a Ripa 137 ☎06 589 7110; map pp.56–57. Hole-in-the-wall pizzeria that does great slices, as well as roast chicken and potatoes, *supplì* and all the usual *rosticceria* fare. Mon–Sat 9am–10.30pm.

VILLA BORGHESE AND NORTH
Gianfornaio Piazzale Ponte Milvio 35/37; map pp.56–57. Just across the ancient Ponte Milvio, this is the place for a snack lunch if you're visiting the Auditorium or MAXXI, with great *pizza al taglio* and lots of other goodies. Mon–Sat noon–11pm.

THE VATICAN AND PRATI
Mondo Arancina Via Marcantonio Colonna 38 ☎06 9761 214; map pp.56–57. Great *pizza al taglio*, but the real treats here are the *arancini* – deep-fried rice balls – which come in lots of varieties, all delicious and just €2 each. Daily 10am–midnight.

Pizzarium Via della Meloria 43; map pp.56–57. Undoubtedly Rome's best pizza-by-the-slice joint with creatively topped pizzas you won't find anywhere else. Standing-room-only inside and only a few benches for dining outside. Mon–Sat 11am–10pm & Sun 1–10pm.

RESTAURANTS AND PIZZERIAS
There are lots of good restaurants in the *centro storico*, and it's surprisingly easy to find places that are not tourist traps – prices in all but the really swanky restaurants remain pretty uniform throughout the city. The area around

Via Cavour and Termini is packed with inexpensive places, although some of them are of dubious cleanliness; if you're not in a hurry, you might do better heading to the nearby student area of San Lorenzo, where you can often eat far better for the same money. South of the centre, the Testaccio neighbourhood is also well endowed with good, inexpensive trattorias, as is Trastevere, across the river, Rome's traditional restaurant enclave.

CENTRO STORICO

Armando al Pantheon Salita de' Crescenzi 30 ☎ 06 6880 3034; map p.62. Surprisingly unpretentious surroundings and moderately priced, hearty food in this long-standing staple close by the Pantheon (open since 1961). Mon–Fri 12.30–3pm & 7–11pm, Sat 12.30–3pm.

★ **Da Tonino** Via del Governo Vecchio 18–19 ☎ 06 687 7002; map p.62. Basic but delicious Roman food is the order of the day at this unmarked *centro storico* favourite. The simple pasta dishes start at €6, while the *straccetti* (strips of beef with rocket) are a steal at €7. The few tables fill up quickly, so come early or be prepared to queue. No credit cards. Mon–Sat 12.30–3.30pm & 7–11pm.

Dal Cavalier Gino Vicolo Rosini 4 ☎ 06 687 3434; map p.62. Down a small alley by the parliament building, Gino presides over his bustling restaurant with unhurried authority, serving a determinedly trad Roman menu at keen prices – pastas €5–8, mains €9–10. It's been very much discovered by tourists, but at heart it remains a locals' joint. Mon–Sat 1–3pm & 8–10.30pm.

La Montecarlo Vicolo Savelli 12 ☎ 06 686 1877, ⓦ lamontecarlo.it; map p.62. This hectic pizzeria serves crisp, blistered pizza, along with heaped dishes of pasta. Tables outside in summer, but be prepared to queue. Tues–Sun noon–3pm & 7pm–1am.

Maccheroni Piazza delle Coppelle 44 ☎ 06 6830 7895; map p.62. Spartan yet comfortable restaurant that enjoys a perfect location on this quiet *centro storico* square. It serves good, basic Italian food at affordable prices. Mon–Sat 12.30–3pm & 8pm–midnight.

The Perfect Bun Largo del Teatro Valle 4 ☎ 06 4547 6337, ⓦ perfectbun.it; map p.62. Sometimes you just have to have a burger, and this by Rome standards is burger heaven, a big vaulted room with a long high table down the middle and tables round the side and upstairs, that serves burgers, steaks, grilled chicken and other Tex-Mexish delights for €13–17. Daily 12.45pm–3pm & 6pm–2am, Sun brunch 11.45am–3pm.

★ **Trattoria** Via Pozzo delle Cornacchie 25 ☎ 06 6830 1247; map p.62. The inside of this cool upstairs restaurant feels a million miles away from the streets of the *centro storico* outside, and the food makes a change too – inventive modern takes on Sicilian classics. Not cheap, but one of the better food experiences of central Rome. Mon–Fri 12.30–3.30pm & 7.30–11.30pm, Sat 7.30–11.30pm.

Trattoria Lilli Via di Tor di Nona 23 ☎ 06 686 1916; map p.62. One of the city centre's best and most untouristed old-style trattorias, with a great selection of classic Roman staples, well prepared and served with gritty Roman directness. Mon–Sat 1–3pm & 8–11pm.

CAMPO DE' FIORI AND THE GHETTO

Da Sergio Via delle Grotte 27 ☎ 06 686 4293; map p.60. An out-of-the-way, cosy trattoria with a traditional, limited menu and the deeply authentic feel of old Rome. Outdoor seating in summer. Mon–Sat 12.30–3.30pm & 6.30pm–midnight.

Dar Filettaro a Santa Barbara Largo dei Librari 88; map p.60. A fish-and-chip shop without the chips. Paper-covered Formica tables (outdoors in summer), cheap wine, beer and fried cod, a timeless Roman speciality. Mon–Sat 5–10.30pm; closed Aug.

Grappolo d'Oro Zampanò Piazza della Cancelleria 80 ☎ 06 686 4118; map p.62. This place has had a bit of a facelift but still remains relatively untouched by the hordes in nearby Campo de' Fiori, and serves imaginative Roman cuisine in a traditional trattoria atmosphere at moderate prices – pasta dishes for €9–12, mains, including Roman-style lamb, €15–17. Mon & Wed–Sat 12.30–2.30pm & 7.30–11pm, Tues & Sun 7.30–11pm.

★ **Nonna Betta** Via del Portico d'Ottavia 16 ☎ 06 6880 6263, ⓦ nonnabetta.it; map p.60. The best kosher restaurant in the Ghetto serves all the classics of Jewish Roman cuisine – deep-fried artichokes, anchovies with curly endive as well as a selection of Middle Eastern dishes like falafel and couscous. Mon–Thurs & Sun 12.30–3pm & 7.30–10pm, Fri 12.30–3pm, Sat 7.30–10.30pm.

Osteria ar Galletto Piazza Farnese 102 ☎ 06 686 1714, ⓦ ristoranteargallettoroma.com; map p.62. This long-running Campo favourite has shifted locations ever so slightly and no longer quite has the provincial trattoria feel that made it so special but it still serves good, wholesome Roman food at pretty decent prices. Mon–Sat 12.15–3pm & 7.15–11pm.

Piperno Monte de' Cenci 9 ☎ 06 6880 6629; map p.60. This stalwart of the Jewish Ghetto is not the cheapest but is perhaps the best place for a real Roman blowout, either in its elegant dining room or on the square outside. A great place to try classics like *baccalà*, Roman *fritti* and some of the classic pasta dishes. Tues–Sat 12.45–2.20pm & 7.45–11.20pm, Sun 12.45–2.20pm.

★ **Roscioli** Via dei Giubbonari 21/22 ☎ 06 687 5287; map p.60. Is it a deli, a wine bar, or fully fledged restaurant? Actually it's all three, and you can either just have a glass of wine and some cheese or go for the full menu, which has great pasta dishes and *secondi* at lunch and dinner. Nothing is cheap, but the *carbonara* is great. Mon–Sat 12.30–4pm & 6pm–midnight.

Taverna degli Amici Piazza Margana 37 ☎ 06 6992 0637, ⓦ latavernadegliamici.com; map p.60. Lots of tables outside at this long-established restaurant on the fringes of the Ghetto – a great place for lunch after the rigours of the Forum and an atmospheric spot for dinner too. The menu is unadventurous, with lots of Roman classics, and prices are moderate – pasta dishes €12, mains €15–20. Tues–Sun 12.30–3pm & 7.30–11pm.

THE TRIDENTE AND QUIRINALE

Beltramme Via della Croce 39; map p.60. This very old-fashioned *fiaschetteria* (originally it sold only wine, by the *fiasco* or flask) is always packed and fairly pricey, but if you want authentic Roman food, atmosphere and service the way it used to be, this is the place. No credit cards. Daily noon–3pm & 7–11pm.

Ciampini Viale Trinità dei Monti; map p.60. Across the road from the French Academy, this is a café, good for coffee and snacks in the morning and at lunchtime, but a restaurant too, with a great setting in an enclosed garden overlooking the roofs and domes below. There are pasta dishes and salads for €10–12, as well as fish, steaks and chicken from the grill. A good place for kids, who can watch the turtles playing in the fountain between courses. Daily 8am–midnight.

Il Chianti Via del Lavatore 81–82/A ☎ 06 678 7550; map p.62. This Tuscan restaurant and wine bar is quite a find, with good spreads of cold meats and cheeses, and full meals of pasta, pizza and beef dishes. Mon–Sat noon–2am.

Il Leoncino Via del Leoncino 28 ☎ 06 687 6306; map p.60. Cheap, hectic and genuine pizzeria, little known to out-of-towners, and one of the very best for lovers of crispy Roman-style pizza, and quite a boon in this neighbourhood. No credit cards. Mon–Fri 1–2.30pm & 7pm–midnight, Sat 7pm–midnight; closed Aug.

★ **Matricianella** Via del Leone 4 ☎ 06 683 2100; map p.62. Handily placed just off Via del Corso, this old favourite serves classic Roman food, either in the bustling main dining-room or on the outdoor terrace. A great city-centre choice. Mon–Sat 12.30–3pm & 7.30–11pm.

Osteria della Frezza Via della Frezza 16 ☎ 06 322 6273; map p.60. Part of the ultra-successful 'Gusto Empire, this place is good for snacks such as cheese or salami plates or for full meals (great pasta). Both the food and service are excellent. Daily noon–3.30pm & 7pm–12.30am.

Otello alla Concordia Via della Croce 81 ☎ 06 678 1454; map p.60. This place used to be one of Fellini's favourites – he lived just a few blocks away on Via Margutta – and remains an elegant, yet affordable choice in the heart of Rome. Mon–Sat 12.30–3pm & 7.30–11pm.

★ **Palatium** Via Frattina 94 ☎ 06 6920 2132; map p.60. Cool and sleek, this wine-bar-cum-restaurant celebrates the produce of the Lazio region and Rome, with a short menu of regional specialities and a long list of Lazio wines. You can settle for just a plate of salami and cheese for €5–7 or go for mains using rabbit and sausage from the hills outside the city. Very good value. Mon–Sat 11am–11pm.

Recafé Piazza Augusto Imperatore 9 ☎ 06 6813 4730; map p.60. The entrance on Via del Corso is a Neapolitan café, while on the square you can enjoy proper Neapolitan pizzas, good pasta and salad dishes and excellent grilled *secondi* at moderate prices. Neapolitan sweets and *fritti* too. Daily 12.45pm–1am.

THE ESQUILINE, MONTI AND TERMINI

Alle Carrette Via Madonna dei Monti 95 ☎ 06 679 2770; map p.60. This long-standing Monti pizza joint serves great thin and crispy Roman pizzas and deep-fried *baccalà*, and also does great desserts. It's cheap too. Daily 8pm–midnight.

Enoteca Cavour 313 Via Cavour 313; map p.60. This lovely old wine bar makes a handy retreat after seeing the ancient sites. Lots of wines and delicious (though not cheap) snacks and salads. Mon–Sat 12.45–2.45pm & 7.30pm–12.30am.

Enoteca Provincia Romana Largo di Foro di Traiano 84 ☎ 06 6766 2424; map p.60. Billed as "a wine bar in the heart of Rome", this place really couldn't be more central – or more welcome, situated as it is just off Piazza Venezia right by the ruins of Trajan's Forum – a relative restaurant desert. It's more of a restaurant than a wine bar though, serving up classic Roman and Lazio dishes in a bright comtemporary interior. Main courses go for €12–18 and include things like *polpo e patate*, *saltimbocca*, *cacio e pepe* or just plates of cold cuts and cheese for €15. Mon–Sat 1–3.30pm & 6–11pm.

★ **Pommidoro** Piazza dei Sanniti 44 ☎ 06 445 2692; map pp.56–57. Family-run Roman trattoria on San Lorenzo that's been around forever and serves great Roman home-cooking, very seasonal, with an emphasis on grilled lamb and game, cooked on a big open grill. All the pasta classics too, with a great *carbonara* among other things. Mon–Sat 12.30–3pm & 7.30–11pm.

Tram Tram Via dei Reti 44–46 ☎ 06 490 416; map pp.56–57. In a grungy location but cosy inside, this cool and animated San Lorenzo restaurant serves good Pugliese pasta dishes, fish and seafood and unusual salads. Tues–Sun noon–3pm & 7.30pm–midnight.

★ **Trattoria Monti** Via di San Vito 13/A ☎ 06 446 6573; map pp.56–57. Small, family-run restaurant that specializes in the cuisine of the Marche region – which means great pasta, interesting cabbage-wrapped starters and mainly meaty *secondi*. Very much a neighbourhood place, and moderately priced too. Tues–Sun noon–3pm & 7–11pm.

Valentino Via del Boschetto 37 ☎ 06 488 0643; map p.60. With only a faded Peroni sign above the door, this trattoria is easy to miss. Inside, it's always buzzing, with waiters zipping between the closely packed tables. You'll find lots of grilled meat options, plus a *scamorza* (grilled cheese) menu. Mon–Sat 12.45–2.45pm & 7.30–11.30pm.

1

THE CELIAN HILL AND SAN GIOVANNI

Charley's Sauciere Via San Giovanni in Laterano 270 ☎ 06 7049 5666; map pp.56–57. If the background *chansons* don't make you think you're in France – albeit a mythical one from the 1930s – the menu certainly will, with lots of French classics. Moderate prices – soups and starters €8–10, mains €18 – and it's just a 5min walk from the Colosseum. Mon–Sat 12.30–3pm & 7.30–11pm.

Luzzi Via San Giovanni in Laterano 88 ☎ 06 709 6332; map pp.56–57. Midway between San Giovanni in Laterano and the Colosseum, this bustling restaurant is a good choice amid the tourist joints of the neighbourhood. The food is hearty and well cooked and it's extremely cheap – *secondi* go for €6–9. There are pizzas, too, but only at dinner. Noon–3pm & 7pm–midnight; closed Wed.

THE AVENTINE AND TESTACCIO

Da Felice Via Mastro Giorgio 29 ☎ 06 574 6800, ⓦ feliceatestaccio.it; map pp.56–57. Always crowded, this isn't quite the rough-and-ready establishment it was, but it still serves honest, seasonal Roman cooking – *bucatini cacio e pepe*, lamb, and artichokes in winter: all the classics, well cooked and well served. *Primi* €8–10, *secondi* €12–15. Daily 12.30–2.45pm & 8–11.30pm.

Da Remo Piazza Santa Maria in Liberatrice 44 ☎ 06 574 6270; map pp.56–57. No-nonsense Testaccio pizzeria serving some of the crispiest thin-crust Roman pizzas you'll find. Mon–Sat 7pm–1am.

★ **Tuttifrutti** Via Luca della Robbia 3/A ☎ 06 575 7902; map pp.56–57. This Testaccio favourite is pretty much the perfect restaurant – family run, with good food, decent prices and lots of customers. The menu changes daily, and offers interesting variations on traditional Roman dishes. Tues–Sun 7.30–11.30pm.

TRASTEVERE

Ai Marmi Viale Trastevere 53–59 ☎ 06 580 0919; map pp.56–57. Nicknamed "the mortuary" because of its stark interior and marble tables, this place serves unique "*supplì al telefono*" (deep-fried rice balls, so named because of the string of mozzarella it forms when you take a bite), fresh *baccalà* and the best pizza in Trastevere. A lively slice of the real Rome. 6.30pm–2am; closed Wed.

Da Augusto Piazza de Renzi 15 ☎ 06 580 3798; map p.60. Diner-style neighbourhood staple serving Roman basics in an unpretentious, bustling atmosphere. Good pasta and soup starters and daily meat and fish specials. Daily 12.30–3pm & 8–11pm.

Da Ivo Via di San Francesco a Ripa 158 ☎ 06 581 7082; map pp.56–57. The archetypal Trastevere pizzeria, almost in danger of becoming a caricature, but still good. Arrive early to avoid a chaotic queue. 6pm–midnight; closed Tues.

Da Lucia Vicolo del Mattonato 2 ☎ 06 580 3601; map p.60. Outdoor Trastevere dining in summer is at its

traditional best at this wonderful old Roman trattoria. *Spaghetti cacio e pepe* is the speciality. Get here early for a table outside. Tues–Sun noon–3pm & 7.30–11.30pm.

★ **Da Paris** Piazza San Callisto 7/A ☎ 06 581 5378; map pp.56–57. Fine Roman-Jewish cookery and other traditional dishes in one of Trastevere's most atmospheric piazzas. Tues–Sat noon–3pm & 7.30–11.30pm, Sun 12.30–3pm.

★ **Le Mani in Pasta** Via dei Genovesi 37 ☎ 06 581 6017; map pp.56–57. This small and very relaxed restaurant with an open kitchen cooks up fantastic pasta and fish dishes for moderate-to-expensive prices. It's often very crowded, and it's worth reserving to be sure of getting in. Tues–Sat 12.20–3pm & 7.30–11pm.

VILLA BORGHESE AND NORTH

Dulcamara Via Flaminia Vecchia 449 ☎ 06 333 2108; map pp.56–57. Busy place in the increasingly hip neighbourhood around Ponte Milvio. A varied menu with great soups, pasta and inventive mains. Tues–Sat 12.15pm–2am.

THE VATICAN AND PRATI

Cacio e Pepe Via Avezzana 11 ☎ 06 321 7268; map pp.56–57. This rough-and-ready Prati cheapie is always busy. The menu taped to the wall offers great pasta staples like *cacio e pepe*, *carbonara*, and one of the best pastas *alla gricia* in town for around €7; mains go for €9–10 and are equally good. Mostly outside tables with a small inside room. No credit cards. Mon–Fri 12.30–3.30pm & 7.30–10.30pm, Sat 12.30–3.30pm.

Cantina Tirolese Via G. Vitelleschi 23 ☎ 06 6813 5297; map p.60. This rustic restaurant was reputedly the current pope's favourite lunch spot while he was still a cardinal, and no wonder – the hearty and wholesome Austrian and German fare served here is excellent. The lunchtime buffet served between noon and 3pm is good value at €9.50. Tues–Fri noon–3pm & 7.30–11pm, Sat & Sun noon–3pm & 7.30pm–midnight.

Dal Toscano Via Germanico 58–60 ☎ 06 3972 5717; map pp.56–57. This Tuscan restaurant specializes in *fiorentine* (the famous thick Tuscan T-bone steaks), perfectly grilled on charcoal, delicious *pici* (thick home-made spaghetti) and *ribollita* (veg and bread soup) – all at honest prices: *primi* around €10, mains for €12–15. Tues–Sun 12.30–3pm & 8–11.15pm.

Osteria dell'Angelo Via G. Bettolo 24 ☎ 06 372 9470; map pp.56–57. Above-average and reasonably priced Roman cooking, from a highly popular restaurant run by an ex-rugby player. A la carte at lunch, set menus only at dinner (€25 for three courses). Mon–Sat 8–11.15pm, plus Tues & Fri 12.45–2.30pm.

Passaguai Via Pomponio Leto 1 ☎ 06 8745 1358, ⓦ passaguai.it; map p.60. Basement wine bar that serves great platters of cheese, cold cuts, salads and various other snacks to go with its excellent choice of wine. Always busy,

with a great vibe and an emphasis on freshness, quality and seasonality. Mon–Fri 10.30am–2am, Sat & Sun 6pm–2am.

DRINKING

There are plenty of bars in Rome, and an Irish pub practically on every corner. There's also been a recent upsurge in wine bars (*enoteche* or *vinerie*); the old ones have gained new cachet, and newer ones are springing up too, often with accompanying gourmet menus, or just plates of salami and cheese. Bear in mind that there is sometimes considerable crossover between Rome's bars, restaurants and clubs. For the most part, the places we have listed are drinking spots, but you can eat, sometimes quite substantially, at many of them, and several could be classed just as easily as clubs, with loud music and occasionally even an entrance charge. Campo de' Fiori, Monti, Trastevere and Testaccio are the densest and most happening parts of town.

CENTRO STORICO

Anima Via Santa Maria dell' Anima 57 ☎ 347 850 9256; map p.62. At present one of the city's most popular bars, tricked out in postmodern *Flintstones* chic and offering an assortment of elegant snacks to go with your cocktails. Music tends towards chill-out, lounge and softer soul stuff. Tues–Sun 10pm–3am.

Bar della Pace Via della Pace 5 ☎ 06 686 1216; map p.62. Just off Piazza Navona, this is a long-established bar with a cosy interior and outside tables that are often thronged at night. Daily 10am–2am.

Cul de Sac Piazza Pasquino 73 ☎ 06 6880 1094; map p.62. Busy, long-running wine bar and restaurant with an excellent wine list, a great city-centre location with outside seating, and decent wine-bar food – cold meats, cheeses, salads, soups and pasta and main courses too. Daily noon–4pm & 7pm–12.30am.

Etabli Vicolo delle Vacche 9/A ☎ 06 9761 6694; map p.62. Lounge-style bar and restaurant in the heart of the *centro storico*. Comfy sofas, free wi-fi, and a pleasant, not-too-cool vibe. Daily 12.30–3pm & 7pm–2am.

Jonathan's Angels Via della Fossa 18 ☎ 06 689 3426; map p.62. This quirky bar, just behind Piazza Navona, certainly wins the "most decorated" award. Every inch (even the toilet, which is worth a visit in its own right) is plastered, painted or tricked out in outlandish style by the artist-proprietor. Daily 1pm–2am.

Les Affiches Via di Santa Maria dell'Anima 52 ☎ 06 686 8986; map p.62. Cool, slightly scruffy bar bang in the centre of the town that trades on boho chic rather than the vogueish posery more common in these parts. There's sometimes live music later on, and a laidback vibe early evening, with a rudimentary happy-hour buffet too. Mon–Sat 10am–2am.

Société Lutèce Piazza di Montevecchio 17 ☎ 06 6830 1472; map p.62. Tucked away on a tiny piazza 5min from Piazza Navona, this is one of the centre's coolest choices, with good cocktails and a free antipasto buffet early evening. Daily 6pm–2am.

CAMPO DE' FIORI AND THE GHETTO

Bartaruga Piazza Mattei 7 ☎ 06 689 2299; map p.60. Wonderfully camp bar furnished with all sorts of

eighteenth-century bits and pieces that, not surprisingly, make it a favourite with the thespian set. Mon–Thurs & Sun 6pm–midnight, Fri & Sat 6pm–2am.

Il Goccetto Via dei Banchi Vecchi 14 ☎ 06 686 4268, ⓦ ilgoccetto.com; map p.60. A short walk from Campo de' Fiori, this is one of the city centre's nicest wine bars, with lots of options by the glass and good plates of cheese and salami to go with it. Mon 6.30pm–midnight, Tues–Sat 11.30am–2pm & 6.30pm–midnight.

L'Angolo Divino Via dei Balestri 12 ☎ 06 686 4413; map p.60. A peaceful haven after the furore of Campo de' Fiori, this wine bar has a large selection of wine, and simple wine-bar food – bread, cheese, cold cuts, soups and the like. Tues–Sat 10.30am–2pm & 5.30pm–2am, Sun & Mon 5.30pm–2am.

La Vineria Campo de' Fiori 15 ☎ 06 6880 3268; map p.62. This long-established bar right on the Campo is patronized by devoted regulars, and also offers light meals. Mon–Sat 8.30am–2am.

Open Baladin Via degli Specchi ☎ 06 683 8989; map p.60. Central Rome's ultimate *birreria*, opened by the Baladin brewing company in 2009, and with a stark, modern interior and literally hundreds of mainly artisanal Italian beers to choose from. Daily noon–2am.

THE TRIDENTE AND QUIRINALE

L'Antica Enoteca Via della Croce 76/B ☎ 06 679 0896; map p.60. An old Spanish Steps-area wine bar, recently refurbished, with a selection of hot and cold dishes, including soups and attractive desserts. Intriguing trompe l'oeil decorations inside, majolica-topped tables outside. Daily 11am–11pm.

Rosati Piazza del Popolo 5 ☎ 06 322 5859; map pp.56–57. This bar hosted left-wingers, bohemians and writers in years gone by, and although that's no longer

---

FIVE GREAT WINE BARS

Cul de Sac p.109
Il Goccetto p.109
La Barrique p.110
L'Angolo Divino p.109
Passaguai p.108

1

really the case its cocktails and food still draw the crowds. A nice place from which to watch the action on Piazza del Popolo. Daily 8am–midnight.

THE ESQUILINE, MONTI AND TERMINI

Ai Tre Scalini Via Panisperna 251 ☎06 4890 7495; map p.60. Great, easy-to-miss little Monti bar, cosy and comfortable, with a good wine list, but beer on tap too, and food – cheese and salami plates, pasta basics, a good *melanzane parmigiana* and lots of snacks and salads. Mon–Fri noon–3pm & 6pm–midnight, Sat & Sun 6pm–midnight.

Al Vino al Vino Via dei Serpenti 19 ☎06 485 803; map p.60. Seriously good wine-bar situated on the Monti district's most happening street. Snacks too – generally Sicilian specialities. Daily 11.30am–1.30pm & 5.30pm–12.30am.

Druid's Den Via San Martino ai Monti 28 ☎06 4890 4781, ☻druidsdenrome.com; map p.60. Appealing Irish pub near Santa Maria Maggiore with a genuine Celtic feel (and owners). It has a mixed expat/Italian clientele, and is not just for the homesick. Daily 5pm–2am.

Finnegan Via Leonina 66 ☎06 474 7026, ☻finnegan pub.com; map p.60. Another of the area's crop of Irish pubs, with live football on TV, pool, and a friendly expat crowd. There's seating outside, too, on this bustling Monti street. Mon–Fri 5pm–2am, Sat & Sun 3pm–2am.

La Barrique Via del Boschetto 41/B ☎06 4782 5953; map p.60. Revamped wine bar in the heart of Monti is a great spot for an *aperitivo*, and platters of meats and cheeses keep pre-dinner hunger pangs at bay. Mon–Fri 1–3pm & 6pm–2am, Sat 6pm–2am.

THE CELIAN HILL AND SAN GIOVANNI

Tree Folks Via Capo d'Africa 29; map pp.56–57. Lots of Belgian and German brews in this popular Celio bar. Food too – plates of cold cuts, burgers and chips, salads – and their other speciality is whisky, with a selection of single malts that must be one of the city's best. Daily 6pm–2am.

THE AVENTINE AND TESTACCIO

Oasi della Birra Piazza Testaccio 41; map pp.56–57. Subterranean Testaccio bar with a beer selection that would rival anywhere in the world and plenty of wine to choose from as well, plus generous plates of cheese and salami. Mon–Sat 5pm–midnight, Sun 7pm–midnight.

TRASTEVERE

Ma Che Siete Venuti a Fà Via Benedetta 25 ☎06 9727 5218; map p.60. You'll find an amazing choice of artisanal beers from all over the world in this tiny Trastevere bar. Most of them you won't find anywhere else in the city, or even Italy, and this is a cosy place to work your way through them. Daily 3pm–2am.

★ **Ombre Rosse** Piazza Sant'Egidio 12/13 ☎06 588 4155; map p.60. A people-watching spot that has become a Trastevere institution, especially for a morning cappuccino, but also for light meals and evening drinks. Mon–Sat 7.30am–2am, Sun 10am–2am.

★ **San Calisto** Piazza S. Calisto 4; map pp.56–57. This bar attracts a huge crowd on late summer nights; the booze is cheap, and you can sit at outside tables for no extra cost. During the day it's simply a great spot to sip a cappuccino in the sunshine. Mon–Sat 5.30pm–1.30am.

VILLA BORGHESE AND NORTH

Annibale Piazza dei Carracci 4 ☎06 322 3835; map pp.56–57. Right around the corner from MAXXI, and not far from the Auditorium, this wine bar looks set to benefit from the resurgence of the area, and deservedly so. Its cool, white interior is a nice place to sip a glass of wine, and there's an outdoor terrace in summer. Mon–Fri noon–3pm & 6pm–1am, Sat 6pm–1am.

THE VATICAN AND PRATI

Nuvolari Via degli Ombrellari 10 ☎06 6880 3018; map p.60. This welcoming Borgo bar serves a full menu next door but also has a free early-evening buffet during the week. A good choice of wines, and a pleasant local vibe – not at all what you expect in this part of town. Mon–Sat 6.30pm–2am.

NIGHTLIFE

Roman nightlife is a lot cooler and more varied than it used to be. There are a few smart clubs, principally in the centre of town, but also quite a few smaller and more alternative clubs and live music venues, mainly confined to the neighbourhoods of Testaccio and Ostiense, and in up-and-coming Pigneto and Prenestino to the east of Termini – though bear in mind that some clubs close during August or move to summer premises in Ostia or Fregene.

CLUBS

Akab/Cave Via di Monte Testaccio 69 ☎06 5725 0585, ☻akabcave.com; map pp.56–57. Two venues in one: *Akab* is at ground level and usually plays house music; *Cave* is below-ground and features r'n'b. Concerts are generally once or twice a week. Tues–Sat 10pm–4am.

Classico Village Via Libetta 3 ☎06 5728 8857, ☻classico .it; map pp.56–57. Industrial Ostiense location with a big dancefloor, a venue for live music, and a restaurant. Mon–Thurs 9pm–1.30am, Fri & Sat 9pm–4am.

Gilda Via Mario de' Fiori 97 ☎06 678 4838, ☻gildabar .it; map p.60. A few blocks from the Spanish Steps,

GAY BARS, RESTAURANTS AND CLUBS

Asinocotto Via dei Vascellari 48 ☎ 06 589 8985, ⓦ asinocotto.com; map pp.56–57. One of the first restaurants to hang the rainbow flag above its door, this Trastevere joint is run by a gay couple and has a great, Proust-inspired menu of moderately priced pasta, meat and fish dishes. Worth a visit whatever your non-culinary preferences. Mon–Fri noon–2.30pm & 7.30–11pm, Sat & Sun 7.30–11pm.

Coming Out Via di San Giovanni in Laterano 8 ☎ 06 700 9871; map p.60. If any area has developed as Rome's gay zone, it is the stretch between the Colosseum and San Clemente. This little pub is the epicentre of the scene, frequented mostly by a younger clientele. Daily 10am–2am.

Garbo Vicolo di S. Margherita 1/A ☎ 06 5832 0782; map p.60. Friendly Trastevere bar, just behind Piazza di Santa Maria in Trastevere, with a relaxed atmosphere and a nice setting. Tues–Sun 10pm–3am.

Hangar Via in Selci 69 ☎ 06 488 1397, ⓦ hangar online.it; map p.60. About halfway between Termini and the Roman Forum, just off Via Cavour, this is one of Rome's oldest and least expensive gay spots, always crammed with young people. No charge with an ARCI-Gay card; without a card, you have to pay for at least one drink. Wed–Sun 10.30pm–2.30am.

L'Alibi Via Monte Testaccio 44 ☎ 06 574 3448, ⓦ lalibi.it; map pp.56–57. This predominantly but by no means exclusively male venue is one of Rome's oldest gay clubs, situated in the heart of the city's alternative night scene in Testaccio. It's no longer quite cutting edge, but is a good, all-round hangout, with a multi-room cellar disco and an upstairs open-air bar and big terrace to enjoy in the warm months. Thurs–Sun midnight–5am.

Qube Via di Portonaccio 212 ☎ 06 438 5445, ⓦ qubedisco.com; map pp.56–57. This club plays host to the extremely successful Muccassassina ("Killer Cow") gay night every Fri. Thurs–Sat 10.30pm–4am.

---

this slick club is the focus for the city's minor celebs and wannabes. Dress smart to get in. Thurs–Sun 11pm–5am.

Goa Via Libetta 13 ☎ 06 574 8277; map pp.56–57. Ostiense club that was opened by famous local DJ Giancarlino and is still playing techno, house and jungle; *Goa* also has sofas to help you recover after high-energy dancing. This is where all the biggest DJs who come to Rome spin. Tues–Sat 11pm–4am.

La Maison Vicolo dei Granari 4 ☎ 06 683 3312, ⓦ lamaisonroma.it; map p.62. Ritzy club whose chandeliers and glossy decor attract Rome's gilded youth. Wed–Sun 11pm–3am, until 5am on Fri & Sat.

Micca Club Via Pietro Micca 7A ☎ 06 8744 0079, ⓦ miccaclub.com; map pp.56–57. This cavernous underground club has a hugely varied programme, with popular themed nights – from swing to funk to burlesque. Admission €15 after 10pm. Mon, Tues & Thurs–Sat 10pm–4am, Sun 6pm–2am; closed late May to mid-Sept.

Piper Via Tagliamento 9 ☎ 06 855 5398, ⓦ piperclub.it; map pp.56–57. Established back in the 1970s, but still going strong, *Piper* has nightly events and a wide range of music.

LIVE MUSIC VENUES

Alexanderplatz Via Ostia 9 ☎ 06 5833 5781, ⓦ alexanderplatz.it; map pp.56–57. Rome's top live jazz club/restaurant with reasonable membership (€15 a month) and free entry, except when there's star billing. Reservations recommended. Doors open at 8pm, concerts at 9.45pm Mon–Thurs & Sun, 10.30pm Fri & Sat.

Alpheus Via del Commercio 36 ☎ 06 574 7826, ⓦ alpheus.it; map pp.56–57. Housed in an ex-factory off Via Ostiense, a little way beyond Testaccio, this has space for three simultaneous events – usually a concert, DJ, exhibition or piece of theatre. Fri–Sun 11am–4am.

★ **Big Mama** Vicolo S. Francesco a Ripa 18 ☎ 06 581 2551, ⓦ bigmama.it; map pp.56–57. Trastevere-based jazz/blues club of long standing, hosting nightly acts. Monthly membership costs €8, and then entry is free except for star attractions (when it's important to book ahead). Daily 9pm–1.30am, concerts begin at 10.30pm.

Casa del Jazz Viale di Porta Ardeatina 55 ☎ 06 704 731, ⓦ casajazz.it; Metro B Piramide, or bus #714 from Termini; map pp.56–57. This converted villa in leafy surroundings is the ultimate jazz-lovers' complex, with a book and CD store and restaurant, recording studios and a 150-seat auditorium that hosts jazz names most nights of the week. Admission €10–15. Most acts start at either 7pm or 9pm; closed Tues & Sun evening.

Circolo degli Artisti Via Casilina Vecchia 42 ☎ 06 7030 5684, ⓦ circoloartisti.it; bus #105 from Termini, or #810 from Piazza Venezia; map pp.56–57. A very large venue, located beyond Porta Maggiore, that was one of the first of the city's co-called *centri sociali*. A good range of bands, with frequent themed nights, from hip-hop to ska. Friday is Omogenic – gay night. Daily 9pm–3am.

Fonclea Via Crescenzio 82/A ☎ 06 689 6302, ⓦ fonclea .it; map p.60. Busy and happening basement bar in the Vatican area that hosts regular live music – usually jazz, soul and funk. Happy hour 7–8pm. Free Mon–Fri and Sun. Daily 7pm–2am.

1

Rising Love Via delle Conce 14 ☎333 308 2245, ⓦrisinglove.it; Metro Piramide, or bus #30 or #60 from Piazza Venezia, #75 from Termini, or #95 from Metro A Barberini; map pp.56–57. This Ostiense club's Thurs "I Love Rock" nights host indie bands and DJs. Other evenings see reggae, funk, hip-hop and jam sessions. Thurs–Sun 10am–3am.

ENTERTAINMENT

Even locals would admit that Rome is a bit of a backwater for the performing arts. Relatively few international-class performers put in an appearance here, and the current mayor has made significant cutbacks to the city's cultural funds, playing down the film festival and eliminating some of his predecessor's initiatives altogether. Nevertheless, the city does have a cultural life, and what the arts scene may lack in quality is made up for by the charm of the city's settings. Rome's summer festival, for example – ⓦestateromana.comune.roma.it – ensures a good range of classical music, opera, theatre and cinema throughout the warmer months, often in picturesque locations, and the summer opera performances at the Baths of Caracalla are resounding occasions – worth prolonging a stay for if you can.

CLASSICAL MUSIC AND OPERA

Oratorio del Gonfalone Via del Gonfalone 32/A ☎06 687 5952. This lovely theatre stages performances of chamber music, with an emphasis on the Baroque every Thurs at 9pm, with the season running from Nov to early June. Tickets cost €15; reservations are strongly recommended.

Parco della Musica Via P. de Coubertin 15 ☎199 109 783, ⓦauditorium.com. This landmark musical complex is Rome's most prestigious venue. It is home to the city's premier orchestra, the Accademia Nazionale di Santa Cecilia, who are resident part of the year in its largest hall, while two smaller venues host smaller chamber, choral, recital and experimental works. Daily 11am–8pm to visit; guided tours €9. Box office daily 11am–8pm.

Teatro dell'Opera di Roma Piazza Beniamino Gigli 1 ☎06 4816 0255, ⓦoperaroma.it. Nobody compares it to La Scala, but cheap tickets are a lot easier to come by at Rome's opera and ballet venue – they start at €24 for opera, less for ballet – and important artists do sometimes perform here. If you buy the very cheapest tickets, bring some high-powered binoculars, as you'll need them in order to see anything at all. Don't miss the summer opera season, set in the Baths of Caracalla. Box office Tues–Sat 9am–5pm, Sun 9am–1.30pm.

FILM

Alcazar Via Merry del Val 14 ☎06 588 0099. Trastevere cinema featuring mainstream American and English films, with the occasional weird one slipping in, on Mondays.

Casa del Cinema Largo Marcello Mastroianni 1 ☎06 423 601, ⓦcasadelcinema.it. Right by the Porta Pinciana entrance to the Villa Borghese, this building epitomizes Rome's cultural renaissance under former mayor Walter Veltroni, opened in 2004 as a venue for reruns and retrospectives and dedicated to Italy's most famous international film actor, Marcello Mastroianni.

Nuovo Olimpia Via in Lucina 16 ☎06 686 1068. Very central, just off Via del Corso, with two screens, and regularly featuring films in their original language.

Nuovo Sacher Largo Ascianghi 1 ☎06 581 8116. This Trastevere film theatre shows current films in their original version on Mon. Choices tend toward independent, Left-leaning works from around the world – as you might expect from film director and owner Nanni Moretti.

SHOPPING

At first glance, you may wonder where to start when it comes to **shopping** in a big, chaotic city like Rome. In fact the city promises a more appealing shopping experience than you might think, abounding with colourful shopping streets. There are some vibrant **markets** too: Porta Portese (see p.92) is chaotic but fun, while the market near Piazza Vittorio Emanuele (between Via Lamarmora and Via Ricasoli; Mon–Sat mornings) is great for foodie souvenirs. **Fashion** straight from the catwalk is well represented on the streets close to the Spanish Steps, where you'll find all the major A-list designers; more mainstream and chain fashion stores cluster on Via del Corso, Via Cola di Rienzo, near the Vatican, and Via Nazionale; while the streets of the Monti district are home to an increasing number of stylish independent boutiques, as is Via del Governo Vecchio in the *centro storico*. Or just follow your nose – in Rome you're almost bound to stumble across something interesting.

BOOKS, MUSIC AND STATIONERY

Fabriano Via del Babuino 172; map p.60. This long-running chain sells bright and contemporary stationery, wallets and briefcases. Mon–Sat 10am–7.30pm.

Lion Bookshop Via dei Greci 33; map p.60. Veteran English bookshop with a lounge area where you can enjoy a coffee or tea. Mon 3.30–7.30pm, Tues–Sun 10am–7.30pm.

Soul Food Via di S. Giovanni in Laterano 192–194; map pp.56–57. This vinyl junkie's paradise – a CD-free zone – has lots of stuff from the 1960s and 1970s, and genuinely enthusiastic staff too. Tues–Sat 10.30am–1.30pm & 3.30–8pm.

CLOTHES AND ACCESSORIES

Arsenale Via del Governo Vecchio 64; map p.62. One of the largest boutiques along this funky stretch, with great dresses by the owner Patrizia Pieroni and lots of other stuff by independent designers. Mon 3.30–7.30pm, Tues–Sat 10am–7.30pm.

Ibiz Via dei Chiavari 39; map p.60. Great leather bags, purses and rucksacks in exciting contemporary designs made on the premises. Mon–Sat 10am–7.30pm.

Luna & L'Altra Piazza Pasquino 76 ☎06 6880 4995; map p.62. Contemporary but not faddish store that stocks clothes by all kinds of designers. Mon 3.30–7.30pm, Tues–Sat 10am–2pm & 3.30–7.30pm.

FOOD AND WINE

Castroni Via Cola di Rienzo 196; map pp.56–57. Huge, labyrinthine food store that's a great place to stock up a large selection of Italian treats including chocolates, pastas, sauces, and olive oils – plus a café. Other branches at Via Ottaviano 55 and Via delle Quattro Fontane. Mon–Sat 8am–8pm.

Moriondo & Gariglio Via del Pie' di Marmo 21–22;

map p.62. The city centre's most sumptuous and refined handmade-chocolate shop – great for exquisitely wrapped gifts. Mon–Sat 9.30am–1pm & 3.30–7.30pm.

Volpetti Via Marmorata 47; map pp.56–57. It's worth seeking out this Testaccio deli, which is truly one of Rome's very best. If you're lucky, one of the staff will let you sample their truly incredible *mozzarella di bufala*. Mon–Sat 8am–2pm & 5–8pm.

GIFTS

Fratelli Alinari Via Alibert 16/A; map p.60. A fine selection of black-and-white photographs of Rome from over a hundred years ago. Prices start at around €40. Mon–Sat 3.30–7.30pm.

Old Soccer Via di Ripetta 30; map p.60. Old-fashioned Italian football shirts from around €70 – ironically enough, made in England. Daily 10am–8pm.

Roma Store Via della Lungaretta 63; map p.60. Not a football merchandise store but a shop selling classic perfumes, scented soaps, lotions and candles. Only the very finest from Italy, France and England. Mon 4–8pm, Tues–Sat 9.30am–1.30pm & 4–8pm.

DIRECTORY

Dentist Absolute Dentistry at Via G. Pisanelli 1/3 (☎06 3600 3837, ⓦabsolutedentistry.it) is English-speaking and has a 24hr emergency service on ☎339 250 701.

Embassies Australia, Via Bosio 5 ☎06 852 21; Britain, Via XX Settembre 80/A ☎06 4220 0001; Canada, Via Zara 30 ☎06 85 441; Ireland, Piazza Campitelli 3 ☎06 697 9121; New Zealand, Via Clitunno 44 ☎06 853 7501; US, Via Veneto 119 ☎06 46 741.

Emergencies Police ☎113; *Carabinieri* ☎112; Fire ☎115; Ambulance ☎118. Both the police and the *carabinieri* have offices in Termini. Otherwise the most central police office is off Via del Corso in Piazza del Collegio Romano 3 (☎06 46 86), and there's a *carabinieri* office in Piazza Venezia.

Exchange American Express, Piazza di Spagna 38 (Mon–Fri 9.30am–5.30pm, Sat 9am–12.30pm); Thomas Cook, Piazza Barberini 21/A (Mon–Sat 9am–8pm, Sun 9.30am–5pm) and Via della Conciliazione 23 (Mon–Sat 8.30am–7.30pm, Sun 9.30am–5pm). Post offices will exchange American Express travellers' cheques and cash commission-free.

Football Rome's two big football teams, AS Roma and SS Lazio, play on alternate Sundays between September and May at the Stadio Olimpico, northwest of the city centre. You can buy tickets through booking agencies such as ⓦlisticket.it and ⓦticketone.it which will either sell to you online or point you to a recognized sales outlet, at the stadium, or at the AS Roma store in the city centre. Bear in mind though that due to crowd trouble you must carry photo ID when you purchase a ticket and when you go to the game. To get to the stadium on public transport, you

can take tram #2 from Piazzale Flaminio to Piazza Mancini or bus #910 from Termini and then walk across the river; alternatively, take bus #32 from Piazza Risorgimento or #271 from Piazza Venezia direct.

Hospitals If you are seriously ill or involved in an accident, go straight to the **Pronto Soccorso** (casualty) of the nearest **hospital**, or phone ☎113 and ask for *ospedale* or *ambulanza*. The most central hospitals with emergency facilities are Fatebenefratelli on the Isola Tiberina (☎06 683 7299), San Giovanni at Via A. Aradam 8 (☎06 49 971) and Santo Spirito, near the Vatican at Lungotevere in Sassia 1 (☎06 68 351).

Internet and wi-fi Bibli Via dei Fienaroli 28 (Mon 5.30pm–midnight, Tues–Sun 11am–midnight); Il Mastello, Via S. Francesco a Ripa 62 (daily 7am–10.30pm); Internet Café, Via dei Marrucini 12 (Mon–Fri 9.30am–1am, Sat 10am–1am, Sun 2pm–midnight); Yex, Piazza Sant'Andrea delle Valle 1 (Mon–Fri 10am–11pm, Sat 10am–8pm, Sun noon–8pm).

Lost property For property lost on a train call ☎06 4730 6682 (daily 7am–11pm); on a bus ☎06 581 6040 (Mon & Fri 8.30am–1pm, Tues–Thurs 2.30–6pm); on the metro ☎06 487 4309.

Pharmacies The following pharmacies are open 24hr: Farmacia del Senato, Corso Rinascimento 50 (☎06 6880 3835); Farmacia della Stazione, Piazza dei Cinquecento (☎06 488 0019); Internazionale, Piazza Barberini 49 (☎06 487 1195); Piram, Via Nazionale 228 (☎06 488 0754).

Post office The main post office is on Piazza S. Silvestro (Mon–Fri 8am–7pm, Sat 8am–1.15pm).

1

Out from the city: Ostia Antica and Tivoli

You may find there's quite enough in Rome to keep you occupied during your stay, but it can be a hot, oppressive city and if you're around long enough you shouldn't feel badly about getting out to see something of the countryside; and in fact two of the main attractions visitable on a day-trip from Rome are the equal of anything you can see in the city. **Tivoli**, about an hour by bus east of Rome, is a small town famous for the travertine quarries nearby, the landscaped gardens and parks of its Renaissance villas, and a fine ancient Roman villa just outside. **Ostia**, in the opposite direction near the sea, and similarly easy to reach on public transport, was home to the port of Rome in classical times, and the well-preserved site is worth seeing.

Ostia Antica

April–Oct Tues–Sun 8.30am–6pm; March 8.30am–5pm; Nov–Feb 8.30am–4pm • €6.50 • Metro B to Piramide and then 25min train journey from Porta San Paolo of the Lido di Ostia line

There are two Ostias: one a rather over-visited seaside resort, **Lido di Ostia**; the other, one of the finest ancient Roman sites – the excavations of **OSTIA ANTICA** – which are on a par with anything you'll see in Rome itself (or indeed elsewhere in Italy) and easily merit the half-day journey out.

The site of Ostia Antica marked the coastline in classical times, and the town which grew up here was the port of ancient Rome, a thriving place whose commercial activities were vital to the city further upstream. The **excavations** are relatively free of tourists, and it's much easier to reconstruct a Roman town from these than from any amount of pottering around the Roman Forum. It's also very spread out, so be prepared for a fair amount of walking.

The site

The main street, the **Decumanus Maximus**, leads west from the entrance, past the **Baths of Neptune** on the right (where there's an interesting mosaic) to the town's commercial centre, otherwise known as the **Piazzale delle Corporazioni**, for the remains of shops and trading offices that still fringe the central square. These represented commercial enterprises from all over the ancient world, and the mosaics just in front denote their trade – grain merchants, ship-fitters, rope makers and the like. Flanking one side of the square, the **theatre** has been much restored but is nonetheless impressive, enlarged by Septimius Severus in the second century AD to hold up to four thousand people. On the left of the square, the **House of Apulius** preserves mosaic floors and, beyond, a dark-aisled *mithraeum* has more mosaics illustrating the cult's practices. Behind here – past the substantial remains of the *horrea* or warehouses that once stood all over the city – the **Casa di Diana** is probably the best-preserved private house in Ostia, with a dark, mysterious set of rooms around a central courtyard, again with a *mithraeum* at the back. You can climb up to its roof for a fine view of the rest of the site, afterwards crossing the road to the **Thermopolium** – an ancient Roman café, complete with seats outside, a high counter, display shelves and even wall paintings of parts of the menu. North of the Casa di Diana, the **Museo Ostiense** holds a variety of articles from the site, including a statue of Mithras killing a bull, wall paintings depicting domestic life in Ostia, and some fine sarcophagi and statuary from the imperial period. Left from here, the **Forum** centres on the **Capitol** building, reached by a wide flight of steps, and is fringed by the remains of baths and a basilica. Further on down the main street, more **horrea**, superbly preserved and complete with pediment and names inscribed on the marble, merit a detour off to the right; although you can't enter, you can peer into the courtyard. Beyond, the **House of Cupid and Psyche** has a courtyard you can walk into, its rooms clearly discernible on one side, a colourful marbled floor on the other.

Tivoli

Perched high on a hill just 40km from Rome, **TIVOLI** has always been something of a retreat from the city. In classical days it was a retirement town for wealthy Romans;

later, during Renaissance times, it again became the playground of the moneyed classes, attracting some of the city's most well-to-do families, who built their country villas out here. Nowadays the leisured classes have mostly gone, but Tivoli does very nicely on the fruits of its still-thriving travertine business, exporting the precious stone worldwide (the quarries line the main road into town from Rome), and supports a small centre that preserves a number of relics from its ritzier days. To do justice to the gardens and villas – especially if Villa Adriana is on your list, as indeed it should be – you'll need time, so it's worth setting out early.

Villa d'Este

Piazza Trento 5 • Daily: May–Aug 8.30am–6.45pm, Sept 8.30am–6.15pm, Oct 8.30am–5.30pm, Jan, Nov & Dec 8.30am–4pm, Feb 8.30am–4.30pm, March 8.30am–5.15pm, April 8.30am–6.30pm • €8 • ☎ 0774 320 920, ⓦ www.villadestetivoli.info

Tivoli's major sight is the **Villa d'Este**, across the main square of Largo Garibaldi, the country villa of Cardinal Ippolito d'Este, and now often thronged with visitors even outside peak season. The **villa** has been restored to its original state, with beautiful Mannerist frescoes in its seven ground-floor rooms showing scenes from the history of the d'Este family in Tivoli. But most people come here to see the **garden**, which peels away down the hill in a succession of terraces dotted with **fountains**. Among the highlights are the Fontana dell'Ovato on the right, topped with statues on a curved terrace around artificial mountains, behind which is a rather dank arcade. Beyond are the dark, gushing Grottoes of the Sibyls and behind them the Fontana dell'Organo, a giant and very elaborate water-organ which plays every couple of hours; right in front, the similarly large Fontana del Nettuno ejects a massive torrent down into a set of central fish ponds. Finish up on the far side of the garden, where the Rometta or "Little Rome" has reproductions of the city's major buildings and a boat holding an obelisk.

Villa Gregoriana

Piazza Tempio di Vesta • April to mid-Oct Tues–Sun 10am–6.30pm; March & mid-Oct to end Nov Tues–Sat 10am–2.30pm, Sun 10am–4pm • €5 • ☎ 0774 382733, ⓦ villagregoriana.it

Tivoli's second main attraction, the **Villa Gregoriana**, isn't actually a villa at all, but an impressively wild set of landscaped **gardens**, created when Pope Gregory XVI diverted the flow of the river here in 1831 to ease the periodic flooding of the town. At least as interesting and beautiful as the d'Este estate, it remains less well known and less visited, and has none of the latter's conceits – its vegetation is lush and overgrown, descending into a gorge over 60m deep.

There are two main **waterfalls** – the larger Grande Cascata on the far side, and a small Bernini-designed one at the neck of the gorge. The best thing to do is walk the main path in reverse, starting at the back entrance, over the river, and winding down to the bottom of the canyon. The ruins of a Republican-era villa cling to the far side of the gorge, and you can peek into them and then catch your breath down by the so-called Grotto of the Mermaid, before scaling the other side to the Grotto of Neptune, reached by a tunnelled-out passage through the rock, where you can sit right by the roaring falls, the dark, torn shapes of the rock glowering overhead. The path leads up from here to an exit and the substantial remains of an ancient **Temple of Vesta**, which marks the main entrance to the villa. You can take a breather at the small **café** here, and the view is probably Tivoli's best – down into the chasm and across to the high green hills that ring the town.

Villa Adriana

Via Imperatore Adriano • Daily 9am–1hr before sunset • €12 • The Auditorium in Rome organizes a series of open-air music and dance events here from mid-June to mid-July; see ⓦ auditorium.com/villaadriana for details • ☎ 06 3996 7900 • Ask the Rome–Tivoli bus to drop you off, or take the CAT #4 bus from Tivoli's Piazza Garibaldi; it's a 10min walk from the main road

Just outside town, at the bottom of the hill, fifteen minutes' walk off the main road, the **Villa Adriana** casts the invention of the Tivoli popes and cardinals very much into

1

the shade. This was probably the largest and most sumptuous villa in the Roman Empire, the retirement home of the Emperor Hadrian for a short while between 135 AD and his death three years later, and it occupies an enormous site. There's no point in doing it at a gallop and, taken with the rest of Tivoli, it makes for a long day's sightseeing.

The site is one of the most soothing spots around Rome, its stones almost the epitome of romantic, civilized ruins. The imperial palace buildings proper are in fact one of the least well preserved parts of the complex, but much else is clearly recognizable. Hadrian was a great traveller and a keen architect, and parts of the villa were inspired by buildings he had seen throughout the empire. The massive **Pecile**, for instance, through which you enter, is a reproduction of a building in Athens; and the **Canopus**, on the opposite side of the site, is a liberal copy of the sanctuary of Serapis near Alexandria, its long, elegant channel of water fringed by sporadic columns and statues leading up to a **Temple of Serapis** at the far end. Nearby, a **museum** displays the latest finds from the ongoing excavations, though most of the extensive original discoveries have found their way back to Rome. Walking back towards the entrance, make your way across the upper storey of the so-called Pretorio, a former warehouse, and down to the remains of two bath complexes. Beyond is a fishpond with a **cryptoporticus** (underground passageway) winding around underneath, and behind that the relics of the emperor's imperial apartments. The **Teatro Marittimo**, adjacent, with its island in the middle of a circular pond, is the place to which it's believed Hadrian would retire at siesta time to be sure of being alone.

ARRIVAL AND INFORMATION   TIVOLI

By bus Buses leave Rome for Tivoli every 10min from outside Ponte Mammolo metro station (line B; journey time 30–45min) and drop off on Tivoli's main square,

Piazza Garibaldi, 2min walk from the Villa d'Este.
Tourist office Largo Garibaldi (Mon & Sat 9am–3pm, Tues–Fri 9am–6.30pm; ☎ 0774 334 522).

EATING AND DRINKING

I Portici Piazza Garibaldi 5 ☎ 338 702 8165. Right in the centre of town, this is a good place for *baccalà* or pizza for lunch and has tables outside. Just 2min from the Villa d'Este so handy for a break between sights. Mon–Sat 10am–10pm.
Sibilla Via Sibilla 50 ☎ 0774 335 281, ✪ ristorante

sibilla.com. Overlooking the Villa Gregoriana, right by the entrance, this is one of the best restaurants in Tivoli. Roman cuisine, and great pasta in particular, including a decent *cacio e pepe*, and a fantastic setting if you can bag an outside table. Service is pretty good too. Daily noon–3pm & 7.30–10.30pm.

Northern Lazio

Northern Lazio, or "Alto Lazio", is quite a different entity from the region south of the capital and is well worth a visit. Green and wooded in the centre, its steadily more undulating hills hint at the landscapes of Tuscany and Umbria further north. Few large towns exist, however, and, with determination (and, ideally, a car), you can see much of it on day-trips from Rome.

Foremost among the area's attractions is the legacy of the **Etruscans**, a sophisticated pre-Roman people swathed in mystery. To the west, some of their most important sites are readily accessible by road or rail – principally the necropolises at **Cerveteri** and **Tarquinia**. Alternatively there's the town and lake at **Bracciano**, and places to swim from Tarquinia up to **Civitavecchia** – playgrounds for hot and bothered Romans on summer weekends. **Viterbo**, the medieval "city of popes", can serve as a base if you're thinking of a two- or three-day visit, particularly if you're touring without a car. It's close to some fine examples of the region's Mannerist villas and gardens at **Caprarola** and **Bagnaia** – and the amazing monster park at **Bomarzo**.

CLOCKWISE FROM TOP LEFT VIEW OF TIVOLI FROM THE VILLA D'ESTE (P.115); BASILICA DI SAN PIETRI, VATICAN CITY (P.93); SWISS GUARDS AT THE VATICAN CITY (P.92); PIAZZA DI SPAGNA (P.74) >

1

LAZIO PUBLIC TRANSPORT

The Lazio transport system, run by **COTRAL**, is divided into seven zones, which spread out concentrically from Rome. It's possible to buy season tickets – by the day, week, or month – to travel within them. The **BIRG** (Biglietto Integrato Regionale Giornaliero) is valid all day for unlimited travel on the state railway, COTRAL buses and the Rome metro, and prices range from €3.30 to €14 depending on the number of zones. A €9.30 ticket, covering four zones, for example, will get you from Rome to Viterbo. You can also buy three-day passes (BTR) for €8.90–39.20 and weekly passes (the **CIRS**; Carta Integrata Regionale Settimanale) – for €13.50–61.50. Vendors – train and bus ticket offices, newspaper stands and tobacconists – can advise you on the required zone, or go to ⓦatac.roma.it or ⓦcotralspa.it. Note that **COTRAL** buses often follow the school-day schedule during the week and run much less frequently on weekends, especially Sundays. In smaller towns, ticket offices close in the afternoon, so be sure to buy your ticket ahead of time.

Etruria and the coast

D.H. Lawrence had pretty much the last word on the plain, low hills stretching **north from Rome** towards the Tuscan border, describing the landscape as "lifeless looking … as if it had given up its last gasp and was now forever inert." His *Etruscan Places*, published in 1932, is one of the best introductions to this pre-Roman civilization and its cities, which, one or two beaches excepted (see box opposite), are the main reasons for venturing out here.

Cerveteri

CERVETERI provides the most accessible Etruscan taster. The settlement here dates back to the tenth century BC. Once known as Caere, it ranked among the top three cities in the twelve-strong Etruscan federation, its wealth derived largely from the mineral-rich **Tolfa hills** to the northeast – a gentle range that gives the plain a much-needed touch of scenic colour. In its heyday, the town spread over 150 hectares (something like thirty times its present size), controlling territory 50km up the coast. By the third century BC, Caere was under Roman control, leading to the decline of Etruscan culture in the region.

The Etruscan Necropolis

Tues–Sun: May–Sept 8.30am–7pm; Oct–April 8.30am–4pm • €6

The present town is a thirteenth-century creation, dismissed by D.H. Lawrence as "forlorn beyond words" – and you really can't blame him, so on arrival, make straight for the Etruscan **Necropolis**, just 1km from the town centre and signposted from the central piazza. From the seventh to second centuries BC, some fifty thousand Etruscans were buried in this literal city of the dead, weird and fantastically well preserved with complete streets and homes. The Etruscan elite did not practise cremation, preferring to have their remains laid on beds or in sarcophagi carved directly out of the rock. The tombs were kitted out like homes, complete with beds, furniture and wall decorations. There are twelve or so show-tombs, lying between the two main roads, the best of which are the **Tomba dei Rilievi** (Tomb of the Bas-Reliefs), **Tomba delle Cornici** (Tomb of the Frames) and the **Tomba dei Capitelli** (Tomb of the Column Capitals).

Museo Nazionale Cerite

Piazza S. Maria • Tues–Sun 8.30am–7pm • €6, €8 including the necropolis

You could spend several hours wandering about, but you might be better off heading back into town to the **Museo Nazionale Cerite** at the top of the old quarter in the sixteenth-century Castello Ruspoli. This has two large rooms containing a fraction of the huge wealth that was buried with the Etruscan dead – vases, terracottas and a run of miscellaneous day-to-day objects; most of the best stuff, though, has been whisked away to Villa Giulia in Rome (see p.77).

ARRIVAL AND DEPARTURE

CERVETERI

By bus and train You can get to Cerveteri from Rome's Cornelia station on line A by COTRAL bus (every 30min; 1hr); buses drop off in Piazza Aldo Moro. The same Rome–Cerverteri bus also links to the train station 7km away at Ladispoli, which you can reach from Termini station in about 45min (2 trains an hour). The site is just over 1km away in Banditaccia and is well signposted from the town.

EATING AND DRINKING

Tuchulcha Via delle Necropoli Etrusche 28 ☎ 338 203 5860. Named after an Etruscan demon, this little trattoria on the necropolis road serves hearty country-style food and crisp Cerveteri white wines. No credit cards. 1–3pm & 8–11pm; closed Mon.

Tarquinia

Second only to Cerveteri among northern Lazio's Etruscan sites, **TARQUINIA** is both an evocative site and pleasant town, its partial walls and crop of medieval towers making it a good place to pass an afternoon after seeing the ruins. Its museum is also the region's finest outside Rome.

Necropolis of Monterozzi

Via Monterozzi Marina • Tues–Sun: summer 8.30am–1hr before sunset; winter 8.30am–2pm • €6, €8 including museum • Take one of the regular buses from the central Barriera S. Giusto, or a 20min walk: follow Via Umberto I from Piazza Cavour, pass through the Porta Romana, cross Piazza Europa, follow Via IV Novembre/Via delle Croci up the hill, and the site is on the left

Once the artistic, cultural and probably political capital of Etruria, the wooden city has now all but vanished and all that is left is the **Necropolis of Monterozzi**. Founded in the tenth century BC, the city's population peaked around 100,000, but the Roman juggernaut triggered its decline six hundred years later and only a warren of graves remains. Since the eighteenth century, six thousand tombs have been uncovered, but grave-robbing is common (thieves are known as *tombaroli*). Fresh air and humidity have also damaged the wall paintings and attempts at conservation mean tombs are open on a rotating basis.

In the **tombs**, some of the frescoes depict the inhabitants' expectations of the afterlife: scenes of banqueting, hunting and even a ménage à trois. The famed Tomba dei Caronti makes a darker prediction, with demons greeting the deceased. The earliest paintings emphasize mythical and ritualistic scenes, but the sixth- to fourth-century works – in the dell'Orco, degli Auguri and della Caccia e Pesca tombs – show greater social realism. This style is a mixture of Greek, indigenous Etruscan and eastern influences: the ease and fluidity points to a civilization at its peak. Later efforts grow increasingly morbid with purely necromantic drawings – enough to discourage picnic lunches on the pleasant, grassy site.

Museo Nazionale Tarquiniense

Piazza Cavour • Tues–Sun 8.30am–7.30pm • €6, €8 including necropolis

In town, the **Museo Nazionale Tarquiniense** on Piazza Cavour has a choice collection of Etruscan finds, sensitively housed in an attractive Gothic-Renaissance *palazzo*. The ground floor exhibits superb sculpted sarcophagi, many decorated with warm and human portraits of the deceased. Upstairs are displays of exquisite Etruscan gold jewellery, painted ceramics, bronzes, candlesticks, heads and figures. The impressive top floor houses the collection's finest piece – the renowned **winged horses** (fourth century BC), probably from a temple frieze. The Sala delle Armi boasts panoramic views of the countryside and sea.

TARQUINIA LIDO

Reachable by bus from the train station, or the Barriera San Giusto, **Tarquinia Lido** is a fairly developed stretch of coast, with lots of bars, restaurants and hotels lining its sandy beaches, some of which are free, and it might just hit the spot after a dose of the Etruscans – as might the adjacent nature reserve and bird sanctuary, adapted from the nearby salt marshes.

1

CIVITAVECCHIA

The only reason to break a journey in **Civitavecchia**, 30km north of Cerveteri, is to catch a **ferry** to Sardinia (there are two daily crossings to Olbia, which take 8–10hr, and one daily to Calgiari, a much longer trip at around 14hr). The **docks** are in the city centre at the end of Viale Garibaldi beside the Forte Michelangelo, 10min walk from the **train station**. Beware of taxis (both legal and otherwise) lurking at the port and station: they charge outrageous prices to shuttle you and your luggage around town. If you're planning on staying the night, it's best to arrange a pick-up with your hotel; note also that the port has a left-luggage office (Piers 18–20).

There is a **tourist office** inside the Forte Michelangelo (Mon–Sat 9am–1pm; ☎ 0766 20 299). Just above the fortress in Piazza Vittorio, COTRAL buses depart for Cerveteri, Tarquinia and Viterbo. Free regular shuttles whisk passengers from the tourist office to the departure piers. Ferry tickets are sold at Piers 18–20; travel agents in town can make reservations (essential in the summer months) for a fee.

ARRIVAL AND DEPARTURE   TARQUINIA

By train Trains run roughly hourly to Tarquinia from Rome's Termini and Ostiense stations; journey time is around 1hr 20min from Termini, just under an hour from Ostiense. The train station is 2km below the town centre,

connected with the central Barriera San Giusto by regular local shuttles.

By bus There are around eight buses a day from Rome's Lepanto station on metro line A, and they take around 2hr.

EATING AND DRNKING

La Cantina dell'Etrusco Via Menotti Garibaldi 13 ☎ 0766 858 418. Rustic local fare in a converted fourteenth-century *cantina*, with great pasta, a short menu of meat

dishes and plates of cheese with honey and other usual wine-bar goodies. 12.30–2.30pm & 7.30–9.30pm; closed Thurs.

Lago di Bracciano

The closest of northern Lazio's lakes to Rome, **Lago di Bracciano** fills an enormous volcanic crater, a smooth, roughly circular expanse of water that's popular – but not too popular – with Romans keen to escape the city's summer heat. It's nothing spectacular, with few real sights and a landscape of rather plain, rolling countryside, but its shores are fairly peaceful even on summer Sundays, and you can eat excellent lake fish in its restaurants. The lake's main settlement is **BRACCIANO** on the western shore, a small town that was catapulted into the news when Tom Cruise and Katie Holmes got married here in 2006.

The best place to **swim** in the lake is from the beach at Lungolago Argenti, a ten-minute walk along Via del Lago from Bracciano Town. You can rent a boat and picnic on the beach – or eat in one of the nearby restaurants.

Castello Odescalchi

Piazza Mazzini 14 • April–Sept Tues–Sat 10am–12.30pm & 3–6pm, Sun 9am–12.30pm & 3–6.30pm; Oct–March Tues–Sat 10am–noon & 3–5pm, Sun 9am–noon & 3–5.30pm; tours every 30min; 1hr • €7 • ⊚ odescalchi.it

Tom and Katie tied the knot at the imposing **Castello Odescalchi**, which dominates the town, a late fifteenth-century structure privately owned by the Odescalchi family. The outer walls, now mostly disappeared, contained the rectangular piazza of the medieval town; the view from the ramparts is worth the admission price alone.

ARRIVAL AND DEPARTURE   LAGO DI BRACCIANO

By train Trains run to Bracciano from Roma Ostiense every 30min (direction Viterbo), and take just over 1hr (less from Trastevere and San Pietro, where they also stop).

By bus There are hourly buses from Saxa Rubra station on the Roma Nord line, which also take around 1hr. Bracciano's

train station is reasonably central, just a 10min walk from the castle and centre of town. Trains run on from Bracciano to Anguillara, from where there are regular buses to Trevignano.

EATING AND DRINKING

Da Tonino Lungolago Argenti 18 ☎ 06 9980 5580.
Decent, long-established restaurant that serves great pasta and fish dishes right on the water's edge. Not expensive either. Daily 12.30–2.30pm & 7.30–10pm.

Trattoria Castello Piazza Mazzini 1 ☎ 06 9980 4339.
Perhaps the town's best restaurant, with lovely pasta, an upscale place with prices to match; try the delicious *tonnarelli cacio e pepe*. Daily 12.30–2.30pm & 7.30–10pm.

Calcata

Around 15km northeast of Lake Bracciano, the small fortified village of **CALCATA** enjoys a spectacular location perched among the wooden hills of central Lazio, and a reputation far greater than its diminutive size might suggest. It was remote and inaccessible enough to be abandoned by its few remaining inhabitants not long after World War II, and in the 1960s was re-colonized by hippies from the city, who took over its crumbling buildings and turned the village into an artists' colony of some repute. You can drive to the edge of the village, and walk up through the thick walls into the main square, on and off which there are several workshops, and one or two new-agey cafés and restaurants. There's nothing special to do, but the views are splendid, and the people who live here welcoming and eager to tell you Calcata's story. Interestingly, the village's other claim to fame is that it was the final resting-place of the foreskin of the circumcized baby Jesus, and was as such (until depopulation) a place of pilgrimage, with a procession parading the so-called holy "precupe" annually. The relic disappeared in mysterious circumstances during the 1980s – something of a relief to the Church, who had attempted to ban all mention of it a century earlier.

Lago di Vico

The smallest of northern Lazio's lakes is the only one deemed worthy of nature-reserve status. **LAGO DI VICO** is a former volcanic crater ringed by mountains, the highest of which, Monte Fogliano, rises to 963m on the western shore. The **Via Cimina** traverses the summit ridges and is a popular scenic drive, dotted with restaurants, but there's a quieter road (closed to cars) near the shoreline, and lovely spots to swim from, with small beaches.

Caprarola

A few kilometres east of Lago di Vico, the small town of **CAPRAROLA** is home to the **Palazzo Farnese**, which, like the villas at Bagnaia and Bomarzo, ranks among the high points of sixteenth-century Italian Mannerism.

The Palazzo Farnese

Via Antonio di Sangallo 1 · Daily: mid-April to mid-Sept 8.30am–7pm · €5, guided visits 4 times daily €2.50 · ☎ 0761 646 6157

The **Palazzo Farnese** stands huge and imposing at the top of the town's steep main street, Via Nicolai. Begun by Antonio da Sangallo the Younger for Pierluigi Farnese in the early 1520s, it was originally more a castle than a palace, situated at the centre of the Farnese family lands. Later, Cardinal Alessandro Farnese took up residence here, in 1559 hiring Vignola to modify the building while retaining its peculiar pentagonal floor-plan. Vignola was among the most accomplished architects of the late Renaissance, and his creation here exemplifies the Mannerist style at its best.

Of the palace's five floors only the first is open to the public, accessed by a magnificently decorated spiral staircase that opens onto a circular courtyard. The first and last rooms are perhaps the best. The former has a super-embellished grotto-like fountain and pictures of local communities like Caprarola itself (the central scene is an imaginary one). The latter, the Sala del Mappamondo, boasts huge painted maps of the known world and a wonderful ceiling fresco of the constellations. Outside there are

1

gardens, divided into summer and winter sections. Look out for the artificial grotto and the stalactites in the lower gardens.

ARRIVAL AND DEPARTURE | CAPRAROLA

By bus Without your own car, it's best to use Viterbo as a base and take one of the regular buses (Mon–Sat) from here to Caprarola. This entails a very pleasant 45min ride through the wooded hills of the Monti Cimini that leaves you at the foot of the main street, from where it's a 10min walk to the palace at the top.

ACCOMMODATION AND EATING

Bella Gioia Via Antonio Tempesta 3 ☎ 0761 646 963. This simple and inexpensive trattoria is very conveniently located off to the left of Piazza Romei in front of the palace. Nice service too. 12.30–2.30pm & 7.30–9.30pm; closed Tues.

La Rocca Piazza Romeo Romei 7 ☎ 0761 646 411, ⓦ bblarocca.it. Not far from the *palazzo*, this cosy B&B with two en-suite double rooms and one twin, is your best bet in a town with few hotels if you decide to stay over. **€60**

Viterbo

The capital of its province, and indeed of northern Lazio as a whole, **VITERBO** is easily the region's most historic centre, a medieval town which, during the thirteenth century, was once something of a rival to Rome. It was, for a time, the residence of popes, a succession of whom relocated here after friction in the capital, and today there are some vestiges of its vanquished prestige – a handful of grand palaces and medieval churches, enclosed by an intact set of walls. The town is a well-kept place and refreshingly untouched by much tourist traffic; buses and trains run frequently to Rome and you can comfortably see the town in a day, but it makes the best base for seeing the rest of northern Lazio – see p.124.

Piazza del Plebiscito

If there is a centre to Viterbo, it's **Piazza del Plebiscito**, girdled almost entirely by fifteenth- and sixteenth-century buildings. The lions and palm trees that reflect each other across the square are the city's symbols, repeated, with grandiose echoes of Venice, all over town. You can peek into the fine Renaissance courtyard of the main, arcaded building of the **Palazzo dei Priori**. The council chamber is decorated with a series of murals depicting Viterbo's history right back to Etruscan times in a weird mixture of pagan and Christian motifs – a melange continued across the square in the church of **Sant'Angelo**.

Via San Lorenzo and the Quartiere San Pellegrino

Roads fork in many directions from Piazza del Plebiscito. Most interesting is **Via San Lorenzo**, which sweeps past the pretty Piazza di Gesù to the macabrely named **Piazza della Morte** – the "Square of Death", after the paupers and abandoned corpses that were buried here by the monks. A left from here leads to Viterbo's oldest district, the **Quartiere San Pellegrino**, a tight mess of hilly streets, home to a number of art and antique shops.

Palazzo dei Papi and the Duomo

Piazza San Lorenzo is flanked by the town's most historic buildings, chief among which is the **Palazzo dei Papi**, a thirteenth-century structure with impressive views from its loggia looking over the green gorge that cuts into central Viterbo. Most of the palace is closed to the public but you can visit the Aula del Conclave, venue of the election of half a dozen or so popes. Opposite, the **Duomo** is a plain Romanesque church that has an elegant striped floor and an understated beauty unusual among Italian churches. Some of its treasure is held in the **Museo del Colle del Duomo** next door (summer Tues–Sun 10am–1pm & 3–8pm; winter Tues–Sun 10am–1pm & 3–6pm; €3 for the museum, €7 incuding the Palazzo).

Corso Italia and Santa Rosa

Via Roma leads off Piazza del Plebiscito to become Viterbo's main commercial street, Corso Italia, scene of a busy *passeggiata* early evening. At its far end, steps lead up from the right side of Piazza Verdi to the church of **Santa Rosa**, where the dessicated corpse of the town's patron saint can be seen in the second chapel on the right – a slightly grotesque, doll-like figure dressed up in a nun's habit. On September 3 each year an icon of the saint is paraded through town to the accompaniment of much revelry and fireworks.

Museo Nazionale Etrusco

Tues–Sun 8.30am–7.30pm • €6

From Piazza Verdi, Via Matteotti leads up to Piazza della Rocca, a large square dominated by the fierce-looking **Rocca Albornoz**, home of the small **Museo Nazionale Etrusco**, whose archeological collection includes displays of locally unearthed Roman and Etruscan artefacts. Just off the opposite side of the square, the church of **San Francesco** is also worth a quick look. The high, unusually plain, Gothic church is the burial place of two of Viterbo's popes – Clement IV and Adrian V – both laid in now heavily restored, but impressive, Cosmatesque tombs on either side of the main altar.

ARRIVAL AND INFORMATION   VITERBO

By train Unusually for a small town, Viterbo has three train stations: the Porta Romana station south of the centre and Porta Fiorentina station to the north are both on the Roma–Viterbo line from Ostiense, Trastevere and San Pietro; of these, Porta Fiorentina on Viale Trento is handier for hotels. The third station is the terminus for the Roma-Nord line from Piazza Flaminia.

By bus The main bus depot (served by the COTRAL network) is a 10min walk from the centre, out past Porta Fiorentina on the Tangenziale Ovest.

Destinations Bagnaia (hourly; 20min); Bomarzo (6 daily; 30min); Caprarola (6 daily; 40min); Civitavecchia (5 daily; 1hr 25min); Tarquinia (almost hourly; 1hr).

Tourist office A 2min walk from Piazza Plebiscito at Via Ascenzi 4 (Tues–Sun 10am–1pm & 3–6pm; ☎0761 325 992.

ACCOMMODATION

Al Melograno Strada S. Caterina ☎347 828 3753, ⓦalmelograno.net. Just outside Viterbo, this is a lovely B&B with simple but nicely furnished rooms just a short walk from the Terme dei Papi and the *terme pubbliche*. **€70**

B&B dei Papi Via del Ginnasio ☎0761 309 039, ⓦbbdeipapi.it. Modern design in a fairy-tale setting. This lovely old vine-clad mansion is right in the town centre and has beautiful rooms furnished with flair and filled with antiques. There's also a suite with a canopy bed. **€100**

Casa Sabina ⓦcasa-sabina.com. Owned by an English-Italian family, this lovely apartment is located a 20min drive from Viterbo in the hill-town of Soriano del Cimino. It has two double bedrooms and is the perfect spot from which to explore northern Lazio if you're self-catering. **€600** a week

Tuscia Via Cairoli 41 ☎0761 344 400, ⓦtusciahotel .com. Large and central hotel with clean, fairly recently revamped rooms, a bright roof terrace that's a pleasant spot for breakfast, and private parking. **€82**

EATING AND DRINKING

Enopizzeria Da Lucio Via S. Pellegrino 21 ☎0761 340 626. This modern wine-bar/pizzeria/restaurant set in a fourteenth-century building does excellent wood-oven pizzas and *fritti*. Daily 7–11pm.

Enoteca la Torre Via la Torre 5 ☎0761 226 467, ⓦenotecalatorrevt.com. This long-running city-centre restaurant has always taken itself rather seriously, but with good reason – the food, in taste and presentation, is superb, and is accompanied by a great selection of local wines. Mon & Thurs–Sat 1–3pm & 8–11pm, Sun 1–3pm only.

Schenardi Corso Italia 11. With its regilded Art Nouveau interior, this historic café is one of the nicest places for a lunchtime snack or tea; and it has a small menu of hot food too. 8am–8pm; closed Wed.

Tre Re Via M. Gattesco 3 ☎0761 304 619, ⓦristorantetrere.com. This cosy place popular with locals is a good venue for trying regional specialities – the chickpea and chestnut soup is a must when in season. Good specials – try the *gnocchetti* with *taleggio* and chicory. *Primi* around €8, *secondi* around €10. Noon–3pm & 7–11pm; closed Thurs.

1

Around Viterbo

Viterbo makes an appealing and practical base for seeing the rest of northern Lazio, especially the places that aren't really feasible on a day-trip from the capital. The Mannerist villa of **Bagnaia** is a short distance away and easily reached on public transport, as are – from the same era – the bizarre gardens of **Bomarzo** and the shores of **Lago di Bolsena**.

Villa Lante

Via Jacopo Barozzi Bagnaia 71 • Gardens: Tues–Sun 8.30am–1hr before sunset • €5 • ☎ 0761 288 088 • Easily reached from Viterbo on the hourly bus #6 from Piazza Martiri d'Ungheria or from the stop at the beginning of Viale Trento, or on the less frequent trains of the Roma-Nord line

About 5km east of Viterbo, **BAGNAIA** isn't much of a town, but like Caprarola further south (see p.121) it's completely dominated by a sixteenth-century palace, the **Villa Lante**, whose small but superb estate is considered Vignola's masterpiece and a supreme creation of Mannerist garden art. Sacheverell Sitwell pronounced it "the most lovely place of the physical beauty of nature in all Italy or in all the world". A short walk uphill from the main square, the **villa** is actually two buildings, built twenty years apart for different cardinals, but symmetrically aligned as part of the same architectural plan. They are closed to the public, save for one loggia, but there's nothing much to write home about inside anyway, and the **gardens** are the main draw, some of the period's best preserved, and a summing-up of Mannerist aspirations, ranged over five gently sloping terraces. The route takes in various watery adventures – waterfalls, lakes and the like – and among numerous fountains and low hedges surface plenty of humorous or symbolic touches. Look for the ubiquitous shrimp motif, symbol of the villa's first patron Cardinal Gambara, allegories of the four elements, and a cascade designed as an elongated crayfish. The adjoining **park** (same hours; free), through which you can wander at will, is a popular spot for locals.

Parco dei Mostri

Località Giardino Bomarzo • Daily 8am–1hr before sunset • €10, children €8, under-4s free • ⓦ parcodeimostri.com • Eight buses a day run from Viterbo and 6 daily from Orte to Bomarzo's Piazza Matteotti, from where it's a signposted 10min walk downhill

Some 12km northeast of Bagnaia, the village of **BOMARZO** is home to another Mannerist creation, the **Parco dei Mostri**, and a greater contrast to the Villa Lante's restrained elegance would be hard to find. The "Monster Park" was built in 1552 by the hunchbacked Duke of Orsini, who set out to parody Mannerist self-glorification by deliberate vulgarity. The result was like a sixteenth-century theme park of fantasy and horror, today one of northern Lazio's primary tourist attractions. Throughout the park, there are dank, mossy sculptures of tortoises, elephants, a whale, a mad laughing mask, dragons, nymphs, butterflies and plenty more. Highlights include a perfect octagonal temple, dedicated to Orsini's wife, and a crooked, slanting house that makes your head spin. Numerous cryptic inscriptions dot the park and add to the mystery.

The site has a self-service **café**, bar, and ample picnic tables and spaces in the trees.

Lago di Bolsena

North along the Via Cassia from Viterbo, **LAGO DI BOLSENA** is a popular destination, though rarely overcrowded; its western shore is better for camping rough, and more picturesque into the bargain. On the northern shore of the lake, **BOLSENA** is the main focus, a relaxed and likeable place that's worth a brief stop. The town itself is set back from the water, around the main square, Piazza Matteotti, off which run medieval nooks and alleyways to the deconsecrated thirteenth-century church of **San Francesco**, which occasionally hosts concerts and exhibitions. The adjacent sixteenth-century portal is the entrance to the medieval *borgo*, with the well-preserved thirteenth-century Monaldeschi **castle** perched over its western end. Inside is the local **museum** (summer Tues–Sun 10am–1pm & 4–8pm; winter Tues–Fri 10am–1pm & 3–6pm; €3.50), with modest displays on underwater archeology and Villanovan and Etruscan finds, plus stunning views from the ramparts. East of Piazza Matteotti, the twelfth-century basilica of **Santa Cristina** conceals a good Romanesque interior behind a wide Renaissance facade added in 1494. Cristina, daughter of the town's third-century Roman prefect, was tortured by her father for her Christian beliefs, eventually being thrown into the lake with a stone round her neck. Miraculously the rock floated, though Cristina was martyred soon after. Adjoining the chapel is the Grotta di Santa Cristina, once part of early Christian **catacombs** (daily: summer 9.30am–noon & 3–6.30pm; winter 9.30am–noon & 3–5.30pm; €4).

There's a nice stretch of free **beach** by the *Naiardi* hotel, about 750m north of the main town.

ACCOMMODATION AND EATING | BOLSENA

Campeggio Internazionale il Lago Viale Cadorna 6 ☎0761 799 191, ⓦcampingillago.it. The closest of the campsites, a short walk out of town, is this waterside location, 500m from Bolsena and with its own little stretch of beach. April–Sept. Pitches **€22.50**

La Pineta Viale Diaz 48 ☎0761 799 801, ⓦlapineta bolsena.it. Lovely restaurant with a terrace and garden that serves an exquisite lake-fish fixed-price tasting menu for €39. Mon–Wed 1–3pm, Fri–Sun 1–3pm & 8–11pm; closed Thurs, and lunchtimes July & Aug.

Osteria del Borgo Dentro Corso Cavour 5 ☎0761 797 167, ⓦosteriaborgodentro.it. Best of the town centre's few restaurants, specializing in lake fish and with an impressive selection of locally produced cheeses. Eat under brick arches on the restaurant's lovely covered terrace. Tues–Sun noon–2.20pm & 7.30–10pm.

Pensione Italia Corso Cavour 53 ☎0761 799 193, ⓦpensioneitalia.it. Right in the middle of Bolsena, this is a no-frills hotel with pin-neat old-fashioned rooms. **€52**

Southern Lazio

The saying goes that the Italian South begins with the first petrol station below Rome, and certainly there's a radically different feel here. Green wooded hills give way to flat marshy land and harsh unyielding mountains that possess a poor, almost desperate, look in places – most travellers skate straight through en route to Naples. But the **coast** merits a more unhurried route south – its resorts, especially **Terracina** and **Sperlonga**, are fine places to take it easy after the rigours of the capital. And the **Pontine islands**, a couple of hours offshore, are – out of high season, at least – among Italy's undiscovered treasures. **Inland**, too, there are rewarding points to head for: the day-trip towns of the **Castelli Romani**; the peaceful retreat of **Subiaco**, set amid glorious scenery; and Cassino and its nearby abbey of **Montecassino**, where some of the fiercest fighting of World War II took place.

The Castelli Romani

Just free of the sprawling southern suburbs of Rome, the sixteen towns that make up the **Castelli Romani** date back to pre-Roman times. These hills – the **Colli Albani** – have long cooled rich and powerful urbanites, who also treasure the area's extraordinary white **wines**, inspired by the rich volcanic soil, and the spectacular views of Lago Albano. The region is now pretty heavily built up, with most of the historic centres ringed by unprepossessing suburbs, and summer weekends see traffic jams of Romans trooping out to local trattorias. But off-peak, it's worth the journey, either as an excursion from Rome or a stop on the way south.

Frascati

At just 20km from Rome, **FRASCATI** is the nearest of the Castelli towns and also the most striking, with a nice old centre and some great places to eat and drink. Its main square, **Piazza Marconi**, is dominated by the majestic **Villa Aldobrandini**, designed by Giacomo della Porta at the turn of the sixteenth century. The Baroque *palazzo* is off-limits, but the **gardens** are open (Mon–Fri: summer 9am–1pm & 3–6pm; winter

9am–1pm & 3–5pm; free). Sadly the elaborate water theatre, where statues once played flutes, is not in top form, but the view from the front terrace is superb, with Rome visible on a clear day. You can also visit the rough-hewn **Scuderie Aldobrandini** or Stables of the Villa, at Piazza Marconi 6 (Tues–Fri 10am–6pm, Sat & Sun 10am–7pm; €5.50; ☎06 941 7195), where they've assembled a collection of Roman finds from the nearby site of Tusculum and added an extra storey for local art exibitions.

Just beyond here is the pedestrianized old centre, which revolves around the two squares of **Piazza San Pietro** and **Piazza del Mercato**. Frascati is also about the most famous of the Colli Albani **wine** towns: ask at the tourist office for details of winery tours and tastings.

Abbazia San Nilo, Grottaferrata

Corso del Popolo 128 • **Church** Daily 9am–12.30pm & 3.30pm–1hr before sunset • **Monastery** Sat & Sun: May–Sept tours at 5pm, Oct–April tours at 4pm • Free

Some 3km south of Frascati, **GROTTAFERRATA** is also known for its wine and for its eleventh-century **Abbazia San Nilo**, at the bottom of the main Corso del Popolo – a Greek Orthodox monastery surrounded by high defensive walls and a now-empty moat. The monastery itself is only open briefly at weekends, but you can visit the little church of Santa Maria any time, which has a very ancient and atmospheric Byzantine-style interior decorated with thirteenth-century mosaics above the high altar, and, in the chapel of St Nilo off to the right, some big, busy frescoes by Domenichino. Look in also on the so-called **Cripta Ferrata**, a first-century-AD edifice where Mary appeared to saints Bartholomew and Nilo and they resolved to build a church here.

Castel Gandolfo

Leaving Marino, the road joins up with the ancient Roman Via Appia, which travels straight as an arrow down the west side of Lago Albano. **CASTEL GANDOLFO** is the first significant stop, best known as the **Pope's summer retreat** – between July and September he gives sporadic midday addresses on Sundays. Four hundred metres above the lake, it's a pleasantly airy place, and enjoys great views over Lago Albano from its terraces close by the main Piazza della Libertà, a pleasant oblong of cafés and papal souvenir shops, at the end of which is the imposing bulk of the Papal Palace itself. Below the town, there's a pleasant lido along the lakeshore with lots of restaurants and pizzerias and a small stretch of grey **beach** from where you could stroll the whole shoreline in about two hours. The road leads down from the main highway, just north of Castel Gandolfo's old centre.

Ariccia

ARICCIA enjoys a spectacular location on the ancient Via Appia, poised between two gorges, and with spectacular views on all sides. The main road crosses the town's central piazza, a well-proportioned square that owes its appearance to Baroque master Bernini. His Pantheon-inspired church of **Santa Maria dell'Assunzione** sits across the Piazza della Repubblica from the massive **Palazzo Chigi** (guided tours Tues–Fri at 11am, 4pm, 5.30pm, Sat & Sun hourly 10.30am–12.30pm & 4–7pm, 3–6pm in winter; €7; ⓦpalazzochigiariccia.it), built for Pope Alexander VII. Locally, Bernini's fame here is eclipsed by the town's most famous food, **porchetta** – roast pork, which is served from 10am to midnight in *fraschette*, rustic taverns, clustered on Via Borgo San Rocco.

Museo delle Navi, Nemi

Via Tempio di Diana 13 • Daily 9am–6.30pm • Free guided tours every Sun at 10.30am & 11.15am • €3 • ☎06 939 8040

The town of **NEMI**, built high above the tiny crater lake, isn't much to write home about, but it's famous for its strawberries and its local **Museo delle Navi** below the town on the lake's northern shore, a vast hangar-like building purpose-built by Mussolini in the 1930s which contains two ancient Roman pleasure boats, floating villas built by

Caligula. In the last days of the German occupation in 1944 they were set on fire, so apart from a few plans and wooden shutters that survived, what you see today are modern reconstructions of the imperial ships. The building itself is worth the trip, and also holds finds from the ships (though the best are in the Palazzo Massimo in Rome) and stretches of a Roman road that passes right through the site.

ARRIVAL & INFORMATION

THE CASTELLI ROMANI

By bus and train COTRAL buses serve the area (every 30min; 35min) from Rome's Anagnina metro station (line A) and regular trains depart from Termini station for Frascati, Albano, Marino and Velletri.

Tourist office Frascati's tourist office is the best for the region and very convenient at Piazza Marconi 5 (daily 10am–8pm; ☎ 06 942 0331).

ACCOMMODATION

FRASCATI

Colonna Piazza del Gesù 12 ☎ 06 9401 8088, ⓦ hotel colonna.it. The twenty rooms of this small hotel have all been fairly recently refubished and are a decent size with large bathrooms; there's a friendly welcome and you couldn't be more central. Free wi-fi and parking too. **€85**

Pinocchio Piazza del Mercato 21 ☎ 06 941 7883, ⓦ hotelpinocchio.it. A smaller hotel, with more simply and more characterfully furnished rooms than its close rival, the *Colonna*. Rooms are large, with big bathrooms, and all have free wi-fi. Good restaurant downstairs too, though the noisier location might be a drawback. **€70**

EATING AND DRINKING

FRASCATI

Amici di Pizza Corso Matteotti 30 ☎ 06 932 2908. Small restaurant with a simple and pretty interior dominated by a large pizza oven and a few tables on the street. Pizzas from €6.50, pasta dishes €7–8. 12.30–2.30pm & 7.30–10.30pm; closed Wed.

Grappolo d'Oro Piazza Filzi ☎ 06 942 2014. One of many *enoteche* in town, with tables outside or long tables inside under stone arches, and with a nice, easy-going vibe and really good pasta for €6 – *alla gricia, cacio e pepe, carbonara* – along with *porchetta, coppiette* and lovely plates of prosciutto and buffalo mozzarella. Daily 12.30–2.30pm & 7.30–10.30pm.

Osteria al 25 Via Regina Margherita 25 ☎ 338 420 1421. One of several *osterie* that make the most of the wide-ranging views across the countryside south of Rome from this street on the far edge of the old town, and serving a well-priced menu featuring lots of local specialities – all the Roman classic pasta dishes for €7–8, plus mains like *tripe alla Romana, abbachio* (baked lamb) and *coda alla vaccinara* (oxtail stew) for €8–10. Daily 12.30–2.30pm &

7.30–10.30pm.

Pinocchio Piazza del Mercato 21 ☎ 06 941 6694. A much more extensive menu than most of the other more basic Frascati offerings, with lots of *bruschette*, good, ultra-thin Roman pizzas from €6.50, a large array of pasta dishes from €7.50, both traditional and a bit more inventive, and meat and fish mains for around €16. Cosy inside, or with a biggish outside terrace. Daily noon–3pm & 7–11pm.

ARICCIA

L'Ariccarola Via Borgo S. Rocco 9 ☎ 06 933 4103, ⓦ osterialariccarola.it. One of a number of restaurants on this street, just outside Ariccia's old centre, with tables outside and a traditional and affordable menu featuring *primi* for €5–7 and main courses for €10. They do great *amatriciana* and *cacio e pepe*, or you could try the excellent *pappardelle allo sugo cinghiale* (with wild boar sauce) for €7 following it with grilled steak or local pork, all washed down with a litre of local wine for €4. Or just order cheese and cold cuts from the amazing spread at the counter. Tues–Sun noon–2.30pm & 7.30–10pm.

Palestrina

PALESTRINA was built on the site of the ancient Praeneste, originally an Etruscan settlement and later a favoured resort for patrician Romans. "Cool Praeneste", as Horace called it, was the site of an enormous Temple of Fortune whose foundations more or less determine the modern centre, which steps up the hillside in a series of terraces.

Palazzo Barberini and the Museo Nazionale Archeologico Prenestino

Piazza della Cortina • Daily 9am–1hr before sunset • €5, tickets also give access to the sanctuary in front of the site • ☎ 06 953 8100

The stepped streets of Palestrina encourage casual strolling, but you need to save your energy for Palestrina's real attraction, the **Palazzo Barberini**, right on top of the hill, which houses the **Museo Nazionale Archeologico Prenestino**, originally built in the eleventh century and greatly modified in 1640. The palace and the terraces below were carved out of a Republican temple which previously stood on this site, and the views are magnificent from the top, surveying the countryside around as far as the eye can see. Among the collection's highlights are a number of ancient Roman pieces found locally: a torso of *Fortune* in slate-grey marble; the *Triade Capitolina*, showing Juno, Jupiter and Minerva, illegally excavated in the early 1990s and narrowly apprehended in the Stelvio Pass on its way out of the country; Etruscan funerary *cistae*; and, the museum's prize possession, a marvellous first-century-BC *Mosaic of the Nile* housed at the very top of the building, which traces the flooding river from source to delta, chronicling everyday Egyptian life in amazing detail.

ARRIVAL AND INFORMATION
PALESTRINA

By bus The bus trip from Rome takes 65min (frequent departures from Ponte Mammolo on metro B), terminating at Via degli Arcioni, from where the trudge up to the town is a steep one.

Tourist office Piazza S. Maria degli Angeli 2 (Mon–Sat 8am–7pm; ☎ 06 957 3176).

ACCOMMODATION AND EATING

A Modo Via Anicia 11 ☎ 06 9531 0035. Tucked away down an alley off the old town's main artery, for fresh fish and grilled meat head to this inviting restaurant. Daily except Wed noon–3pm & 6–11pm.

Bottiglieria del Gallo Via Anicia 6 ☎ 06 9531 2012. Just off the main square, this *enoteca* is a nice place for a glass of wine and also does food, with lots of salads, pasta and grills. A wide choice of wine by the glass for €3, and a good selection of artisanal Italian beers. Excellent value and very friendly too. Tues–Sun 10am–2pm &

5–9.30pm.

Stella Piazzale della Liberazione 3 ☎ 06 953 8172, ⓦ hotelstella.it. Just past the cathedral, this hotel is central and is good enough for a night or two, with 30 sparsely but quite tastefully furnished en-suite rooms with satellite TV. It also has a lovely big and airy traditional restaurant serving wonderful Roman pasta classics – €7–9 – and various grilled meat and fish mains for €9. Restaurant daily 1–3pm & 8–10pm. **€70**

Subiaco

Around 15km northeast of Palestrina, **SUBIACO** is beautifully set around a hill topped by the Rocca Abbazia castle, and close to Monte Liviato – one of Lazio's premier ski resorts. Purpose-built for workmen on Nero's grand villa (very meagre traces of which survive), Subiaco became the contemplative base of St Benedict in the fifth century. The hermit dwelt in a mountain cave here for three years, before leaving to found the monastery at Montecassino (see opposite), but his legacy continues today in the shape of two monastic complexes just outside town. There's nothing much to the town centre – the bets bit is arguably the riverside, where there's a crumbling medieval bridge over the fast-flowing Aniene, footpaths, and even the chance to go canoeing.

Monastero di Santa Scolastica

Guided tours only daily 9.30am–12.30pm & 3.30–6.30pm • Free, though you should tip the guide • ⓦ benedettini-subiaco.it

The **Monastero di Santa Scolastica** is the closer (and larger) complex, the home of St Benedict's first foundation and home to around twenty monks; you can also stay here (see opposite). It was where the first book to be printed in Italy came off the press in 1465 and is a pleasant 3km walk along the Jenne road from the main bus stop – follow the signs left before the bridge. Dedicated to Benedict's sister, the monastery's most notable features are its three delightful cloisters. The first is from the Renaissance period; the second, one of the oldest Gothic works in Italy, dating from the thirteenth century, lushly planted and fragrant; and the third a Cosmati work with lovely arcades of pillars taken from a nearby ancient Roman villa (said to have belonged to Nero) – just like the large pillars in the plain church next door, a Neoclassical edifice inside the shell of the original Gothic church – the facade of which can be seen off the second cloister. The church also has the embalmed body of a local saint, Chelidonia, who inhabited a cave in the vicinity in the eleventh century.

Monastero di San Benedetto

Daily 9am–12.30pm & 3.30–6.30pm • Free • ⓦ benedettini-subiaco.it

Fifteen minutes up the road from the Monastero di Santa Scolastica, the landscape grows more dramatic as it approaches the craggy **Monastero di San Benedetto**, nicknamed the "swallow's nest", founded in the Middle Ages and home to five resident monks. This is perhaps the more interesting monastery of the two, and certainly the more dramatically sited, in the middle of craggy, tree-clad hills that radiate utter tranquillity. Its church, too, is a wonderful collage of religious paintings: its upper level has frescoes of the fourteenth-century Sienese school and fifteenth-century Perugian school, while the lower levels incorporate Benedict's cave, all raw authentic rock except for a serene statue by Raggi, a disciple of Bernini. From here a spiral staircase leads up to the chapel of San Gregorio, containing a 1224 picture of St Francis – pre-stigmata – that's reckoned to be the first portrait of the saint painted from life. In the other direction, the so-called Scala Santa, flanked by various images of death, descend to the chapel where Benedict preached to shepherds, and a terrace and garden overlooking the lush valley that used to be the burial place of the monastery's monks.

ARRIVAL AND DEPARTURE	SUBIACO

By bus Subiaco and its monasteries are a reasonable day-trip from Rome's Ponte Mammolo station (2hr; last bus Mon–Sat 8.30pm, Sun 7.30pm). Four daily buses also service Frosinone, a transport hub, if you're heading south to Campania.

ACCOMMODATION AND EATING

Aniene Via Cavour 21 ☎ 0774 85 565. A large restaurant right in the centre of Subiaco, with a back room overlooking the river valley. A simple trattoria, basically – Subiaco is not over-stuffed with quality restaurants – with a decent but unambitious menu, featuring pizzas from €5, pasta dishes from €6, mains from €8. Try the *ciocaria* pasta, with peas, mushrooms and pancetta, for €7, or the *abbachio al forno* (€12). They also have six basic, simply furnished rooms upstairs. Daily 12.30–2.30pm & 7.30–9.30pm. €55

Foresteria di Monastero di Santa Scolastica ☎ 0774 85 569, ⓦ benedettini-subiaco.it. If Subiaco's location makes you want to linger, and it should, you can book a room at the monastery, whose rooms, situated in separate chalet blocks in front of the main complex, are open to pilgrims and tourists alike. They're not exactly monkish cells but are pretty simply furnished, with twin beds, and small en-suite bathrooms with showers, and no TV or wi-fi. But then in a location like this, who needs those distractions? They also serve fixed-price menus in the main building. €50

Cassino and the Abbey of Montecassino

Abbey open daily: 9am–12.30pm & 3.30–5.30pm, closes 6.30pm in summer • Free

The town of **CASSINO** in the southeast corner of Lazio was fairly comprehensively destroyed during the last war, and has very little appeal (except for Fiat enthusiasts, who coo over the factory here), but it's the site of an important monastery, the **Abbazia di Montecassino** – itself the scene of fierce fighting during one of the seminal battles of the same conflict. Three ravens guided St Benedict to this spot, after he left Subiaco in 529. He founded one of the most important and influential Christian complexes in the world. Its monks spread the word as far away as Britain and Scandinavia, while developing the tradition of culture and learning that was at the core of the Benedictine order. Ironically, its strategically vital position, perched high on a mountaintop between Rome and Naples, was the abbey's downfall. A succession of invaders coveted and fought over this vantage point, and the buildings were repeatedly destroyed.

During World War II, the abbey came to be the lynchpin of the German presence in this part of Italy. After a battle that lasted almost six months, the Allies – a mixture of Poles, New Zealanders and Indian troops – eventually bombed it to ruins in May 1944, sacrificing several thousand lives in the process. The austere medieval architecture

1

has been faithfully re-created, but it's really more impressive for its position. Much is not open to the public, and its sterile white central courtyard is engaging only for the views of the surrounding hills and the Polish war cemetery below. The hideously ornate Baroque church has a small **museum** (€2) containing old manuscripts and the like. Yet you can't help but feel that Montecassino's glory days ended with the war.

ARRIVAL AND INFORMATION CASSINO

By train Cassino is connected by train from Rome and Frosinone, and buses leave the train station for the abbey three times daily at 9.45am, 11.45am and 3.35pm.

Tourist office Via di Biasio 54 (Mon 8am–2pm, Tues–Fri 8am–2pm & 3–6pm, Sat 9am–1pm; ☎ 0776 21 292).

The Pontine Marshes

South of the Castelli Romani lie the **Pontine Marshes**, until seventy-odd years ago a boggy plain prone to malaria and populated by only a few inhabitants and water buffalo. Julius Caesar hoped to drain the area, but was assassinated before he could carry out the plan. Instead Mussolini reclaimed the region in 1928 – building a series of spanking-new towns and exposing fertile, fresh farmland.

Sermoneta

The crumbling medieval hill-town of **SERMONETA**, linked with Latina by half a dozen buses daily (50min), is a bit of a gem, with views right over the plains and beyond to the sea, and remarkable for its walls erected to safeguard against the Saracens and later struggles between the papacy and other kingdoms, which raged throughout the Middle Ages. It has a magical, other-worldly air, and its well-preserved **Castello Caetani** is well worth the detour to see (guided tours hourly Mon–Wed & Fri–Sun: April–Oct Mon–Fri 10am–noon & 3–6pm, Sat & Sun 10am–6.30pm; Nov–March Sat & Sun 10am–noon & 2–4pm; €5; ☻fondazionecaetani.org). Erected in the 1200s by the feudal Caetani family, it's a near-perfect example of the medieval system of moats, portcullises, drawbridges and tunnels designed to render the place practically impregnable. Inside, there is a huge display of arms, armour, catapults and ancient cannons, plus the vast siege cisterns and silos.

Ninfa

April–June first Sat & Sun of each month 9am–noon & 2.30–6pm; July–Sept 9am–noon & 3–6.30pm; Oct & Nov 9am–noon & 2.30–4pm; Guided tours only, every 15min • €10 • ☻fondazionecaetani.org

Tucked away in the hills, the ruined towers of **NINFA**, another Caetani stronghold, represent a remarkable spectacle – a set of enchanting **gardens** huddled at the base of the cliff. It's a tranquil nook whose temples inspired the poetry of Pliny the Elder and grew into a thriving fortified village in the twelfth century. Bandits, mercenaries and malaria destroyed Ninfa, dubbed the "Pompeii of the Middle Ages". The citizens fled to Sermoneta and their ruins became the backdrop of spectacular landscaping in the early twentieth century. Wild and domestic flowers, shrubs and trees flourish among charming rivulets, waterfalls and ponds: the design is spontaneous, whimsical and entirely enchanting.

ACCOMMODATION AND EATING PONTINE MARSHES

Il Simposio al Corso Corso Garibaldi 33 ☎ 3392 846 905, ☻simposio.it. This restaurant specializes in hearty pasta dishes and grilled meats; try their *pasta al trombolotto*, in a sauce that combines porcini mushrooms with lemon oil and 14 herbs. From May to Sept, you can eat in their pergola-covered garden restaurant, *Enoteca Simposio*, the other side of the triangular main square

at Via della Condutture. Tues–Sun noon–2pm & 7.30–9.30pm.
Ostello San Nicola Via G. Matteotti 1 ☎ 0773 30 381, ☻sannicola-hostel.com. A thirteenth-century convent complete with Gothic church and fading frescoes, and a mixture of dorm beds and private rooms, plus a communal kitchen. Dorms €11

THE PARCO NAZIONALE DEL CIRCEO

Sabaudia's pine groves, beachfront and lake, together with Monte Circeo and the offshore Zannone island, form the **Parco Nazionale del Circeo**. Created in 1934, this preserves something of the marshes' wildlife and natural beauty (information at the Sabaudia and San Felice Circeo tourist offices, or at ⓦ parcocirceo.it). It's a fine spot for appreciating **flora and fauna** as well as **archeological ruins**: there are over a hundred sites in varying states of preservation. The park's office in San Felice Circeo (see p.132) can supply information and suggest **hikes**.

The southern Lazio coast

The **Lazio coast to the south** of Rome is a more attractive proposition than the northern stretches. Its towns have a bit more charm, the water is cleaner, and in the further reaches, beyond the flats of the Pontine Marshes and Monte Circeo, the shoreline begins to pucker into cliffs and coves that hint gently at the glories of Campania – all good either for day-trips and overnight outings from the city, or for a pleasingly wayward route to Naples.

Anzio

About 40km south of Rome, and fairly free of the pull of the capital, **Anzio** is worth visiting both for its **beaches** and its history – much of the town was damaged during a difficult Allied landing here on January 22, 1944, to which two military **cemeteries** (one British, another, at nearby Nettuno, American), as well as a small museum, bear testimony. It was also a favoured spot of the Roman emperor Nero, the ruins of whose villa spread along the cliffs above and even down onto the beach, which stretches north from the town centre.

ARRIVAL AND DEPARTURE ANZIO

By train Trains run to Anzio from Rome every hour and take about 1hr. The station is 10min from the centre of town and the waterfront.

By ferry There are regular ferries and hydrofoils between Anzio and Ponza and they take between 1hr and 1hr 45min. You can also reach Ventotene on two ferries daily (55min).

EATING AND DRINKING

Fraschetta del Mare Corso del Popolo 38 ☏06 984 6240. Anzio hosts a thriving fishing fleet and has some great restaurants in the harbour, such as this place, where they will bring you an endless supply of fishy specialities depending on the day's catch, for a fixed price of €16 a head. Tues–Sun 12.30–2.30pm & 7.30–10pm.

Pierino Piazza C. Battisti 3 ☏06 984 5683. Opposite the Municipio, a block back from Piazza Garibaldi and the waterfront, this is one of central Anzio's better restaurants, with great fish and pasta. Daily 1–3pm & 8–10.30pm.

San Felice Circeo

About 7km from the Torre Paola, the inland paved road rounds the mountain to emerge at **SAN FELICE CIRCEO**, a picturesque village of pretty stone houses bleached yellow by the sun that is split between the busy lower town and picuresque upper town. In summer, the lower town's marina can be unpleasantly crowded, bursting with fancy motor launches and yachts, its sandy beaches crowded with bodies and roads clogged with flashy cars. To escape the overpopulated sand, rent a boat at Circeo Mare, Via Ammiraglio Bergamini 124 (☏0773 549 335, ⓦcirceomare.it), to visit the famous **Grotta della Maga Circe**. Or explore on foot: take a left at the lighthouse (Faro di Torre Cervia) for the **Grotto delle Capre** or continue straight a few kilometres to a secluded and rocky swimming spot, also great for snorkelling. The town's main road winds up past the upper town, eventually arriving at the summit of Monte Circeo, where there's an ancient **temple** with marvellous views; there's a large car park at the top, with a summer bar.

ARRIVAL AND INFORMATION

SAN FELICE CIRCEO

By bus Buses arrive in the lower town from Via Domenichelli and depart for Rome Laurentina, Latina, Sabaudia and Terracina. A local minibus service connects the lower town to the historical centre above.

Tourist office Just off the town's main Piazza Vittorio Veneto, on Piazza Lanzuisi (daily: summer 9am–1pm; 0773 549 038); also serves as an office for the Monte Circeo park (see box, p.131).

ACCOMMODATION AND EATING

Claro de Lua Strada del Sole 9 0773 548 425, hotelcirceo.it. Smart and stylish, with lovely rooms looking across the sea to the Pontine Islands and candlelit barbecues in a panoramic gazebo. **€150**

Giardino degli Ulivi Via XXIV Maggio 13 0773 548 034, giardinodegliulivi.eu. Lovely B&B run by a hospitable lady just outside San Felice's upper town. Some of the simply furnished rooms have trerraces and either have splendid panoramas of the coast below or look out over the peaceful gardens behind. There's an on-site restaurant in July and Aug, when you may have to opt for

half-board – no great hardship. **€80**

Il Grottino Piazza Vittorio Veneto 3 0773 548 446. Backing onto the upper town's Piazza Vittorio Veneto and serving excellent seafood – try their *gnochetti alla pescatora*, which are delicious. 12.30–2.30pm & 7.30–10pm; closed Tues.

La Torre Piazza Vittorio Veneto 0773 547 962. You can eat outside on the main square of San Felice's old walled centre at this simple restaurant which does decent fish and pasta dishes. Starters €12, mains €15. Dailky noon–3pm & 7.30–10.30pm.

Terracina

A further 15km down the coast from San Felice, **TERRACINA** is an immediately likeable little town, divided between a tumbledown old quarter high on the hill and a lively newer area by the sea. During classical times, it was an important staging-post on the Appian Way, which meets the ocean here; nowadays it's primarily a seaside resort with good, ample beaches and frequent connections with the other points of interest, including daily ferries and hydrofoils to Ponza (see p.134). Apart from the scrubby oval of sand fringing the centre, Terracina's **beaches** stretch west pretty much indefinitely from the main harbour and are large enough to be uncrowded.

Piazza Municipio

The centre of the old quarter is **Piazza Municipio**, which occupies the site of the Roman forum – complete with the original steps and slabs – and now focuses on the colonnade of the town's **Duomo**, with its elegant campanile. An endearing church with a fine mosaic floor and a beautiful tile-studded pulpit and twisted mosaic candlestick, it was built within the shell of a Roman temple dedicated to the gods Augustus and Roma. Also on the square, the **Museo Civico Pio Capponi** (Tues–Sat 9am–1.30pm & 3–8pm, Sun 10am–1pm & 5–9pm; €1.55) has finds from the Roman town.

Temple of Jupiter Anxur

Take the steps up from Piazza Municipio onto Via Anxur and follow this for 200m, from where a road winds to the top (30min). You can also take the hourly bus #L from Via Roma or Piazzale Marconi

Terracina's main attraction is the **Temple of Jupiter Anxur**, which crowns the hill. The temple may date back to the first century BC and was connected to Terracina by some lengthy walls; these days it's an impressive if rather ruinous complex, with tremendous views both ways up the coast. You can walk right through the vaulted arches of the temple and scramble around among the remains of the acropolis, finishing off with a coffee in the temple's **café**.

ARRIVAL AND INFORMATION

TERRACINA

By bus There are hourly buses to Terracina from San Felice (15min) and Sabaudia (30min), regular buses from Rome and onto Sperlonga (40min) and Formia (1hr).

By ferry There are 1–3 ferries daily to Ponza Terracina (50min).

Tourist office A 5min walk from the sea in the new part of town, just off Via G. Leopardi, in the park behind Piazza Mazzini (Mon–Sat 9am–1pm & 5–8pm, Sun 9am–1pm; 0773 727 759).

ACCOMMODATION AND EATING

Centosedici Lungomare Circe 116 ☎0773 764 110, ⓦcentosedici.it. Bright, white minimalist rooms with lots of seaside motifs in a revamped villa on the seafront. They have a popular restaurant too, busy with chic locals who are attracted by a menu that constantly changes depending on the day's catch. Restaurant daily 12.30–2.30pm & 7.30–9.30pm. **€100**

Da Pino Piazza della Repubblica 42/43 ☎0773 702 352. This lower-town option is fairly basic but serves up superb Neapolitan-style pizzas. Noon–2pm & 8–10pm; closed Thurs.

Enoteca St Patrick Corso Anita Garibaldi 56 ☎0773 703 170, ⓦst-patrick.it. No it's not an Irish bar but a great little *enoteca* in Terracina's upper town that serves delicious plates of cheese and cold cuts, as well as pasta and other hot dishes, washed down with great local wines, under wooden beams in a relaxed and buzzy atmosphere. Daily 8pm–midnight.

Sperlonga and around

The coast south of Terracina is probably Lazio's prettiest stretch, the cliff punctured by tiny beaches signposted enticingly from the road. **SPERLONGA**, built high on a rocky promontory, is a fashionable spot for Roman and Neapolitan families, its whitewashed houses, arched alleys and stepped narrow streets almost Moorish in feel. Both the old upper town and modern lower district are almost given over entirely to tourists during summer, but it's still a pleasant place, and cars are not allowed into the old centre. There are **beaches** either side of Sperlonga's headland, and although a lot of space is private, it's never too difficult to find a decent spot.

Villa of Tiberius

Daily 8.30am–7.30pm • €4

A couple of kilometres south of Sperlonga, the remains of the **Villa of Tiberius** are the only real sight of note but are well worth the walk along the beach – head south from the town and turn off at the stone path after Lido Le Chiuse beach club. There's a small and extremely engaging **museum** with finds from the villa and its attached grotto, the setting for imperial banquets. The villa is right by the beach, and you can stroll around the excavations, as well as walking into the cave where fish still dart about Tiberius's fishpond.

ARRIVAL AND INFORMATION   SPERLONGA

By train The nearest train station is Fondi-Sperlonga, 8km away, where there are infrequent buses into town. Certified taxis which cost €6.50 per person (illegal drivers will negotiate) wait in front of the station.

By bus COTRAL buses run from Formia, Gaeta and Terracina with stops along Via Cristoforo Colombo in the lower town.

Tourist offices Via del Porto, the road that winds round the headland to the left of the main beach (daily 8am–8pm; ☎0771 557 341), and Via del Corso 25 (same hours).

ACCOMMODATION

Corallo Corso S. Leone 3 ☎0771 548 060, ⓦcorallo hotel.net. Great choice if you want to be up in the old town, just off Piazza della Repubblica, with beautifully and individually furnished rooms, some with large and panoramic balconies. **€160**

Grazia Via M.A. Colonna 8 ☎0771 548 223, ⓦhotel grazia.com. A block from the beach at the northern end of the beachfront strip (it has its own private stretch, included in room rates), this family-run hotel is a good choice with modern rooms, revamped only a few years ago, with satellite TV and a/c. **€125**

EATING AND DRINKING

Da Rocco Laocoonte Via C. Colombo 4 ☎0771 548 122. The best restaurant in the lower town, right by the beach and serving excellent fish dishes on a patio overlooking the sea. Tues–Sat 1–3pm & 8–11pm.

L'Angolo Via Tiberio ☎0771 548 808, ⓦlangolo sperlonga.it. On the sandy southern beach, this large restaurant does down-to-earth pasta with seafood and Neapolitan-style pizzas. Daily except Tues 12.30–2.30pm & 7.30–10.30pm; closed Tues.

Tropical Via C. Colombo 19 ☎0771 549 621, ⓦtropical .it. Lively bar and restaurant that does decent pizzas, right on the beachside road in the lower town. Daily 10am–midnight.

1

The Pontine islands

Scattered across the sea between Rome and Naples, the Pontine islands are relatively unknown to foreign travellers. Volcanic in origin, only two are inhabited – the small island of Ventotene and its larger neighbour **Ponza**. The latter bustles with Italian tourists, especially Romans, between mid-June and the end of August, but at any other time, it's yours for the asking.

Ponza

The group's main island, **PONZA**, is only 8km long and 2km across at its widest point. Beautiful **Ponza Town** is heaped around the bay in a series of neat, pastel-coloured pyramids, its flat-roofed houses radiating out from the pink semicircle that curls around the fishing harbour. It makes a marvellous place to rest up for a few days, having so far escaped the clutches of designer boutiques and souvenir shops. Although the island lacks specific sights, Ponza is great for aimless wanderings; in the early evening, locals parade along the yellow-painted **Municipio** arcade of shops and cafés. For lazing and swimming, there's a small, clean **cove** in the town.

Chiaia di Luna beach

A ten-minute walk across the island from Ponza Town, the **Chiaia di Luna beach** is a slender rim of sand edging a sheer sickle cliff – though be warned that the waves here are much choppier than on the sheltered side facing the mainland, and the beach is intermittently closed for safety reasons.

Le Forna and the Piscina Naturale

The only other real settlement on Ponza is **Le Forna**, a wide, green bay dotted with huddles of houses. The beach here is small and grubby, so follow the path down from the road, around the bay to the rocks: the water of the so-called **Piscina Naturale** is lovely and clear, perfect for sheltered swimming when the fishing boats have finished for the day. The settlement straggles on from Le Forna towards the sharp northern end of the island, where the road ends abruptly and a steep stony path (to the right) leads down to more rocks where you can swim.

ARRIVAL AND INFORMATION   PONZA

By ferry Formia has year-round services to Ponza, with two ferry crossings daily (2hr) and 1–3 hydrofoils (1hr 10min). There are also connections from Terracina (see p.132), and summer connections from Anzio (see p.131) and Naples (Naples to Ponza takes 2hr 50min, to Ventotene 1 hr 50min). There are also daily crossings between Ponza and Ventotene.

There is at least one ferry service daily between Ponza and Ventotene and the journey takes just under 1hr. Buses connect the port with other points on the island roughly hourly.

Tourist office Via Molo Musco in Ponza Town (daily 9am–1pm & 3–7pm; ☎0771 80 031) has maps and accommodation lists.

ACCOMMODATION

Casa Simonetta Via Calacaparra ☎0771 808 512, ⓦcasasimonetta.com. A reasonable choice with tidy rooms in the northern part of the island. €80

Gennarino al Mare Via Dante 64 ☎0771 80 071, ⓦgennarinoamare.com. Next to the town beach, this sky-blue hotel nestles on a dock. All the rooms have elegant decor, private wrought-iron balconies and great seascape views. €135

EXPLORING PONZA BY BOAT

For really secluded sea frolicking, rent a **boat** for the day from the **Spiaggia di Sant'Antonio** in Ponza Town (€60–100) and take your time circumnavigating the island and exploring its remote coves. The Cooperativa Barcaioli Ponzesi (☎0771 809 929, ⓦbarcaioliponza.it) offers trips around the island and excursions to uninhabited Palmarola and Zannone from €22 per person.

Ortensia Via Piscine Naturali ☎0771 808 922, ⓦhotel ortensia.it. The best and most convenient option in Le Forna is perhaps the best option on the entire island – a serene and chic hotel, with lovely en-suite rooms with private balconies, free wi-fi, and its own restaurant with a nice terrace overlooking the sea. <u>€160</u>

Pensione Silvia Via Marina ☎0771 80 075, ⓦpensione silvia.it. One of the cheapest places to stay in town, this *pensione* is 200m through the spooky Roman tunnel on the Santa Maria waterfront – a cheerful golden structure presiding over row-boat-strewn sands. Closed Oct–April. <u>€140</u>

EATING AND DRINKING

Ippocampo Piazzale Pisacane 7 ☎0771 809 852. One of quite a few restaurants in Ponza's main harbour, and doing good pasta and fish – great fresh tuna pasta with *vongole*. Daily noon–2pm & 8–10pm; closed Nov–Easter.

Orestorante Via Dietro la Chiesa 3 ☎0711 80 338, ⓦorestorante.it. Overlooking the harbour in Ponza Town, this is a cut above, with a menu of exquisite fish dishes like chickpeas with prawns and crayfish with sea urchins. A treat. Daily 7.30–10.30pm; closed Nov–Easter.

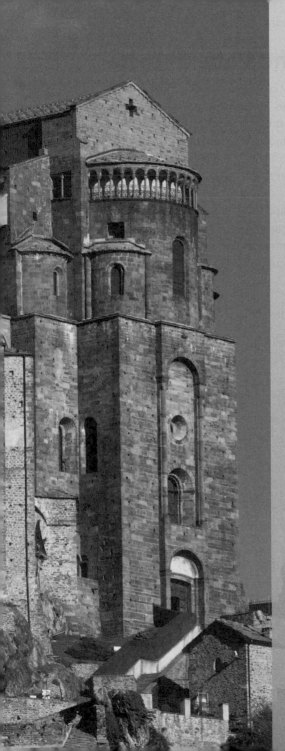

Piemonte and Valle d'Aosta

SACRA DI SAN MICHELE

Piemonte and Valle d'Aosta

In the extreme northwest of Italy, fringed by the French and Swiss Alps and grooved with deep valleys, Piemonte and Valle d'Aosta are among the least "Italian" regions in the country. Piemontesi spoke French until the end of the nineteenth century and Piemontese dialects reflect Provençal influence; Valle d'Aosta is bilingual and in some valleys the locals, whose ancestors emigrated from Switzerland, still speak a dialect based on German. Piemonte (literally "at the foot of the mountains") is one of Italy's wealthiest regions, known for its fine wines and food, and for being home to huge Italian corporations such as Fiat and Olivetti. Italy's longest river, the mighty Po, begins here, and the towns of its vast plain have grown rich on both manufacturing and rice, cultivated in sweeping paddy fields.

Turin, on the main rail and road route from France to Milan, is the obvious first stop and retains a freshly restored Baroque core, with a cornucopia of galleries and museums. South of Turin, **Alba** is a good base for visiting the region's wine cantinas. **Asti**, to the southeast, comes to life during its famous medieval Palio, or horse race. For the rest of the region, winter sports and walking are the main activities; Sestriere is the main skiing centre, while the ascent of Monviso in the far west appeals to the climbing fraternity.

Bordered by Europe's highest mountains, Mont Blanc, Monte Rosa and the Matterhorn, veined with valleys and studded with castles, the **Valle d'Aosta** region is picturesque. The Aosta Valley cuts across it, following the River Dora to the foot of Mont Blanc. It's in the more scenic tributary valleys that you'll want to linger, and **Aosta**, the regional capital, makes an excellent staging post on the way to the smaller mountain resorts.

Straddling the two provinces is the protected zone of Italy's oldest and largest national park, the **Gran Paradiso**. The mountain *rifugi* and hotels here become packed in summer but development is purposely restrained to preserve pristine conditions.

Although the western shore of **Lago Maggiore** is actually in Piemonte, we've treated all the lakes as a region and covered them in the "Lombardy and the Lakes" chapter; the Maggiore account starts on p.259.

GETTING AROUND

PIEMONTE

Piemonte is fairly easy. The network of trains and buses is comprehensive, and your own transport is only necessary for the out-of-the-way places. You can get to most places from Turin; Alba makes a good base for Le Langhe, Saluzzo for the western valleys. If you are planning to visit Le Langhe a sat nav is highly recommended.

VALLE D'AOSTA

Using public transport to explore the Valle d'Aosta is a bit trickier: buses run from Piemonte along the main valley past most of the castles, but services connecting the tributary valleys are infrequent, while trains are less regular and run only as far as Pré-St-Didier. For serious exploration, your own vehicle is a definite advantage.

MONT BLANC

Highlights

❶ White truffles This very costly speciality is shaved onto pasta and washed down with the excellent local Barolo or Barbaresco wine. **See p.141**

❷ The Museo Egizio, Turin A dazzling collection of Egyptian antiquities in a city rich in museums. **See p.145**

❸ Sacra di San Michele The views of the surrounding valley from this fortified abbey are more than worth making your way up. **See p.157**

❹ Pollenzo This medieval hamlet boasts a wine bank, a university of gastronomy and great hospitality. **See p.161**

❺ Parco Nazionale del Gran Paradiso Italy's first national park preserves Alpine valleys and peaks that are home to ibex, chamois and golden eagles. **See p.169**

❻ Mont Blanc Enjoy excellent views of this awe-inspiring mountain from the Testa d'Arpy. **See p.173**

HIGHLIGHTS ARE MARKED ON THE MAP ON P.140

Turin (Torino)

TURIN's renovated, gracious Baroque avenues and squares, opulent palaces and splendid collections of Egyptian antiquities and Northern European paintings, as well as spanking-new pedestrian-only areas, make it a pleasant surprise to those who might have been expecting satanic factories and little else. Ever since the major spruce-up for the 2006 Winter Olympics, Turin's emphasis has been on promoting its historic urban charms,

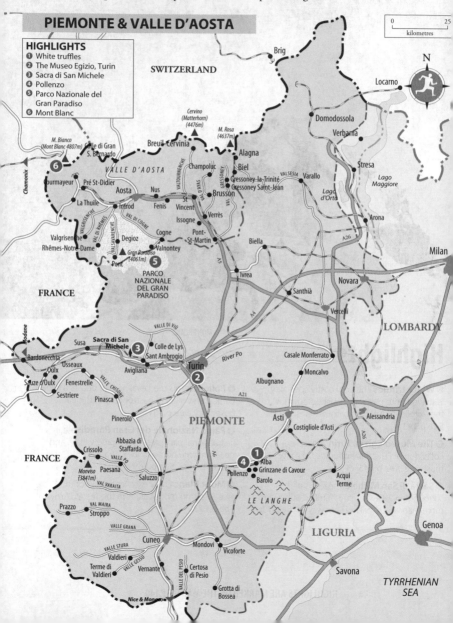

PIEMONTE & VALLE D'AOSTA

HIGHLIGHTS
① White truffles
② The Museo Egizio, Turin
③ Sacra di San Michele
④ Pollenzo
⑤ Parco Nazionale del Gran Paradiso
⑥ Mont Blanc

REGIONAL FOOD AND WINE

Piemonte and Valle d'Aosta are a paradise for gastronomes and connoisseurs of vintage wines. Rich Piemontese cuisine betrays close links with France through dishes like *fonduta* (fondue) and its preference for using **butter** and **cream** in cooking. Piemonte is perhaps most famous for its **white truffles**, the most exquisite of which come from around the town of Alba and are ferociously expensive. They are most often used in the form of shavings to subtly perfume a dish of pasta or a risotto. Watch out too for porcini mushrooms, chestnuts, and **bagna caöda** – a sauce of oil, anchovies, garlic, butter and cream, also served as a fondue. *Agnolotti* (pasta filled with meat or possibly with mushrooms or other vegetables) is the best-known dish, followed by meat *buji* (boiled) or braised in wine. Cheeses to look out for are *tomini, robiole* and *tume*. The sweets, too, are marvellous: *spumone piemontese*, a mousse of mascarpone cheese with rum; *panna cotta*, smooth cooked cream; and light pastries like *lingue di gatto* (cats' tongues) and *baci di dama* (lady's kisses).

The best known is the *bonet*, a confection of chocolate and *amaretti*. Turin is also credited as the home of *zabaglione*, an egg yolk, sugar and Marsala mixture used to fill pastries.

The hills of Le Langhe and Monferrato produce traditional **wines** such as Barolo, Barbera and Nebbiolo. These fine reds need ageing, and Barolo in particular can be very expensive. Everyday wines are made from the *dolcetto* grape, notably Dolcetto d'Alba. Probably the most famous is the sweet sparkling wine, Asti (wine makers dropped the "spumante" from the name in 1994 in a bid for a new image) – there has been a trend in recent years to make dry *spumante* too. Martini & Rossi and Cinzano vermouths are also produced in and around Turin, a fusion of the region's wines with at least thirteen of the wild herbs that grow on its mountains. The traditional version, now a brand name, is Punt e Mes ("point and a half") – one part bitter to half-a-part sweet.

such as its genteel *belle époque* cafés and traditional chocolate treats – not to mention an array of walking tours that explore the city's extraordinary, vivid heritage (see box, p.151).

The grid street-plan of Turin's Baroque centre makes it easy to find your way around. **Via Roma** is the central spine of the city, lined with designer shops and ritzy cafés. It's punctuated by the city's most elegant piazzas: at one end Piazza Carlo Felice, boasting a small park; in the middle Piazza San Carlo, close to which are some of the more prestigious museums; and at the other end is Piazza del Castello, with its royal palaces. On either side are pedestrianized shopping streets, more relaxed than Via Roma. North is **Piazza della Repubblica**, a huge square with the largest open-air market in Europe. To the east the porticoes of Via Po lead to Piazza Vittorio Veneto, slanting down to the **River Po**, along which a stroll southward brings you to the extensive Parco del Valentino, and some of the city's best nightlife just downriver at Murazzi. Beyond is the **Museo Nazionale dell'Automobile** and the **Lingotto Centre**, which houses the Pinacoteca Giovanni e Marella Agnelli, displaying the Fiat magnates' superb private art collection, while the hills across the river are crowned by the **Basilica di Superga**. Further south, beyond the city limits, lies the royal **Stupinigi Hunting Lodge**. Outside the city limits to the northwest stands the jewel in Turin's crown: the magnificent **Venaria Reale** palace and gardens.

Brief history

Although originally a Roman settlement, it was the Savoy dynasty that left the largest impression on Turin: from 1563 the city was the seat of the **Savoy dukes**, who persecuted Piemonte's Protestants and Jews, censored the press and placed education of the nobles in the fanatical hands of the Jesuits. The Savoys gained a royal title in 1713. After more than a century of military and diplomatic wrangling with foreign powers, Duke Carlo Alberto di Savoia teamed up with the liberal politician of the Risorgimento, Cavour, who used the royal family to lend credibility to the Italian Unification movement. In 1860, Sicily and southern Italy were handed over to Vittorio Emanuele, successor to Carlo Alberto, thereby elevating him to sovereign of all Italy. Turin became the new country's **capital**, but only two years later, political turmoil moved the court to Florence, and then finally in 1870, to Rome. Turin fell into the hands of the petty Piemontese nobility and quickly became a provincial backwater. Nevertheless, it retained its regal centre: its cafés lavishly encumbered with chandeliers, carved wood, frescoes and gilt – only slightly less ostentatious than the rooms of the **Savoy palaces**, fourteen in all, and now all listed as UNESCO World Heritage sites.

World War I brought plenty of work to the city, but also food shortages, and, in 1917, street riots erupted, establishing Turin as a focus of labour activism. Gramsci led occupations of the **Fiat factory**, going on to found the Communist Party. By the 1950s,

TURIN

■ ACCOMMODATION

All'Orso Poeta	13
Alpi Resort	10
Bologna	9
Boston	16
Chelsea	2
Conte Biancamano	7
Des Artistes	5
Foresteria degli Artisti	4
Genio	11
Grand Hotel Sitea	6
Liberty	14
Montevecchio	12
Open 011	1
Piemontese	15
Roma e Rocca Cavour	8
Terres d'aventure suites	3

● CAFÉS, PASTICCERIE & GELATERIE

Al Bicerin	1
Baratti & Milano	10
Brek	7
Exki	24
Fiorio	11
Gobino	17
Grom	25
Mood	8
Mulassano	9
Pepino	15
Platti	23
San Carlo	16
San Tommaso	5
Stratta	18
Torino	19

● RESTAURANTS

Alba	26
Caffè Vini Emilio Ranzini	3
Consorzio	6
Da Michele	22
Del Cambio	12
Kirkuk Kaffé	20
La Monachella	21
M**Bun	4
Sfashioncafé	14
Tabernalibraria	13
Tre Galline	2

Turin's population had soared to 700,000, mainly migrant workers from the poor south housed in shanty towns and shunned by the Torinesi. By the 1960s Fiat's workforce had grown to 130,000, with a further half million dependent on the company. Today there are fewer people involved in the industry, and Fiat's famous Lingotto factory is now a shopping centre and conference space; the gap left behind has been filled by some of the biggest names from other industries – Pininfarina, Einaudi, Ferrero, Martini & Rossi, Lavazza and many others – ensuring a continuation of Turin's economic prosperity.

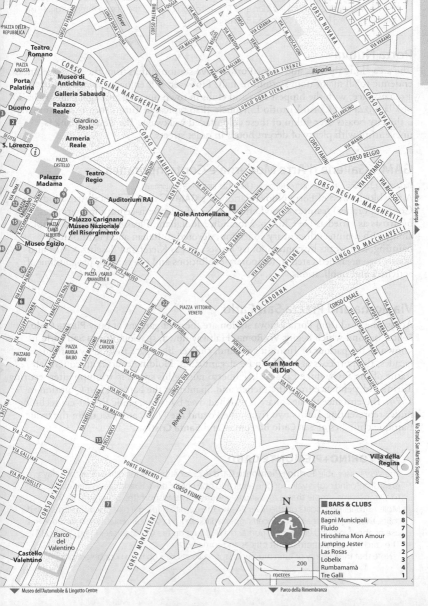

■ BARS & CLUBS	
Astoria	6
Bagni Municipali	8
Fluido	7
Hiroshima Mon Amour	9
Jumping Jester	5
Las Rosas	2
Lobelix	3
Rumbamamà	4
Tre Galli	1

2

LITERARY TURIN

Turin has been home to many major literary figures. Rousseau and Ruskin, Nietzsche, Flaubert and Twain all enjoyed sojourns here. Casanova wrote: "In Turin, the fair sex is most delightful, but the police regulations are troublesome to a degree." Melville wondered at the architecture, commenting that even the poor breakfasted in elegant coffee shops. But perhaps Turin's most famous literary resident is **Primo Levi**. Born at 75 Corso Re Umberto in 1919, Levi graduated in Chemistry from Turin University in 1941 before joining the Partisans. Captured by the Nazis in 1944, he spent the rest of the war In Auschwitz. Returning to Turin, he wrote his two masterpieces, *If This Is a Man* and *The Truce*. You can visit the Centro Internazionale di Studi Primo Levi in Via del Carmine 13 (primolevi.lt).

Porta Nuova

The area along the east side of the **Porta Nuova** station suffers from the usual seediness endemic to all major train stations in Italy. However, it is enjoying something of a renaissance, with the hippest bars and clubs in town opening among arcades (*portici*) of Via Nizza and Corso Vittorio Emanuele II so typical of Turin's measured symmetry – the city boasts over 40km of these colonnaded walkways. The western flank is uneventful, with plenty of decent hotels in quiet streets.

GAM – Galleria d'Arte Moderna e Contemporanea

Via Magenta 31 • Tues–Sun 10am–6pm • €10, free first Tues of the month • gamtorino.it

A few blocks west of Porta Nuova station, the **GAM** (Galleria Civica d'Arte Moderna e Contemporanea) features a good cross-section of twentieth-century masterpieces by artists as varied as De Chirico, Morandi, Modigliani, Picasso, Klee and Warhol, along with a ninteenth-century collection, devoted to Italian and Piedmontese painting, and works by contemporary artists such as Kiefer and Baselitz. GAM also boasts two areas dedicated to temporary exhibitions and offers a rich programme of activities and publications.

Via Roma and Piazza San Carlo

Across the road from Porta Nuova station are the neat gardens of busy **Piazza Carlo Felice**, beyond which begins **Via Roma**. Halfway down, spacious **Piazza San Carlo** is known as the parlour of Turin; it's a grand, cloister-like space fronted by Baroque facades, the porticoes of which house elegant cafés. Holding court is an equestrian statue of the Savoy duke Emanuele Filiberto raising his sword in triumph after securing Turin's independence from the French and Spanish at the battle of San Quintino in 1574. The entrance to the square is watched over by two gigantic Fascist-era reclining nudes representing Turin's two rivers, the Po and the Dora, and past them the twin Baroque churches of **San Carlo Borromeo** and **Santa Cristina**.

THE TORINO+PIEMONTE CARD

The very reasonable **Torino+Piemonte Card** (€25 for 48hr, €29 for 72hr or €34 for 5 days; turismotorino.org) is valid for one adult and one child under 12 and allows free entrance to all museums – more than 170 – and free tourist city transport (the panoramic lift in the Mole Antonelliana, boats on the River Po and the tram to Superga) plus discounts on guided tours, theatre performances, concerts, opera, parking and even car rental. It also includes free use of above-ground urban transport and a discount on the City Sightseeing bus (see p.151). The card is available from tourist offices and some hotels.

Note that the majority of Turin museums stop selling tickets up to an hour before closing time.

The Museo Egizio

Via Accademia delle Scienze 6 • Tues–Sun 8.30am–7.30pm • €7.50 • Ⓦ museoegizio.it

Around the corner from Piazza San Carlo, the **Museo Egizio** holds a superb collection of Egyptian antiquities, begun under Carlo Emanuele III in the mid-eighteenth century and added to over the ensuing centuries. A large space on the ground floor, designed by Oscar-winning set designer Dante Ferretti, evokes a vast temple with massive granite sphinxes, gods and pharaohs looming out of the subdued lighting. Upstairs, you'll find decorated mummy cases and an intriguing assortment of everyday objects and even food – eggs, pomegranates and grain, recognizable despite their shrivelled, darkened state. The collection's highlights are a **statue of Ramses II** and the **Tomb of Kha and Mirit**. The tomb, discovered in 1906 at Deir-el-Medina, is that of a 1400 BC architect, Kha, and his wife Mirit. Kha's burial chamber contains after-life supplies, including a board game to while away the posthumous hours, as well as his own personal illustrated copy of the Egyptian Book of the Dead. And to ensure that Mirit kept up appearances, she was provided with a cosmetic case, wig, comb and tweezers.

Museo Nazionale del Risorgimento Italiano

Piazza Carlo Alberto 8 • Tues–Sun 9am–7pm • €9 • Ⓦ museorisorgimentotorino.it

Via Roma heads north through the heart of Turin, passing near some of the significant monuments of the Savoys and Italian Unification. The **Museo Nazionale del Risorgimento Italiano**, housed in **Palazzo Carignano**, is worth a visit. The first meetings of the Italian parliament were held in the palace's circular Chamber of the Subalpine Parliament, and the building was the power base of leaders like Cavour, who ousted the more radical Garibaldi. It's ironic, then, that the most interesting sections of the museum are those dedicated to Garibaldi: portraits showing him as a scruffy, long-haired revolutionary wearing an embroidered fez, long stripy scarf and one of the famous red shirts adopted during his exile in South America. These shirts became the uniform of his army of a thousand volunteers.

The Palazzo Reale

Piazzetta Reale 1 • Tues–Sun 9am–7.30pm; occasional visits to the royal kitchen included • €6.50, €8 with Armeria Reale • Ⓦ piemonte.beniculturali.it

What Vittorio Emanuele II made of the eccentrically dressed revolutionary who secured half the kingdom for him is undocumented, but you feel sure that his residence, the sixteenth-century **Palazzo Reale**, at the head of the sprawling **Piazza del Castello**, wouldn't have impressed Garibaldi. Designed by Castellamonte, this nouveau-riche palace houses glitzy, semi-furnished rooms gilded virtually top-to-bottom and decorated with bombastic allegorical paintings.

Galleria Sabauda

Via XX Settembre 88 • Tues–Sun 9am–6.30pm • €8 • Ⓦ artito.arti.beniculturali.it

Recently ensconced in its new home within the Palazzo Reale complex, the **Galleria Sabauda** was built around the Savoys' private collection and is still firmly stamped with their taste: a crowded miscellany of Italian, Dutch and Flemish paintings punctuated by some real masterpieces. Of the Italian paintings, the most arresting is perhaps Botticelli's *Venus*. The fifteenth-century *Archangel Raphael and Tobias* by Antonio and Piero Pollaiuolo is another of the gallery's signature works, while the Dutch and Flemish section contains Van Eyck's *Stigmatization of St Francis*, a warmly human piece and the only panel by this artist in Italy. It's also worth seeking out Van Dyck's *The Children of Charles I of England*.

Armeria Reale

Piazza del Castello 191 • Tues–Sun 8.30am–7.30pm • €4, €8 with Palazzo Reale • ⓦ artito.arti.beniculturali.it

On the right-hand side of the Palazzo Reale is the **Armeria Reale**, a collection of armour and weapons spanning seven centuries and several continents started by King Carlo Alberto in 1837. Pride of place is given to his stuffed horse, and there's also an exotic, and rather chilling, collection of oriental arms, including gorgeously jewelled Turkish dagger sheaths and intimidating Japanese masks. The magnificent eighteenth-century Beaumont Gallery houses works of European Romanticism.

Biblioteca Reale

Piazza del Castello 191 • Thurs & Fri 2–6.30pm • Free, varying fees for temporary exhibitions

The Palazzo Real also houses the **Biblioteca Reale**, founded by Carlo Alberto in 1837. It is part of the Palazzo Reale project designed by Carlo Amedeo di Castellamonte. Home to the Savoy family until 1865, its collections include manuscripts, miniatures, engravings and over 2000 drawings by artists including Bellini, Raphael, Tiepolo and Rembrandt. The library also contains Carlo Alberto's acquisition of drawings by Leonardo da Vinci.

Palazzo Madama

Piazza del Castello • **Medieval Court and Juvarra Staircase** Tues–Sun 9am–7pm • Free • **Museo Civico d'Arte Antica** Tues–Sat 10am–6pm, Sun 10am–8pm • €10, free first Tues of the month • ⓦ palazzomadamatorino.it

Across the square from the Palazzo Reale, the **Palazzo Madama** has an ornate Baroque facade by the early eighteenth-century architect Juvarra, who also redesigned the piazza and many of the streets leading off it. Inside, the originally fifteenth-century palace incorporates parts of a thirteenth-century castle and some Roman portal foundations – in effect it's an architectural cross-section of the city's history. The most noteworthy architectural pieces are **Juvarra's Great Staircase** and the archeological excavations of the **Medieval Court**. The building houses the **Museo Civico d'Arte Antica**, containing over 70,000 works dating from the Middle Ages to the Baroque. Paintings, illuminated manuscripts, jewellery and royal furniture such as an inlaid Gothic commode illustrate the wealth of a millennium of European art.

The Duomo

Piazza S. Giovanni • Daily 7am–12.30pm & 3–7pm • Free

Behind the Palazzo Reale – and reached through a small passage – is the fifteenth-century **Duomo**. The only example of Renaissance architecture in Turin, it was severely damaged in a fire in 1997. It is most famous as the home of the **Turin Shroud** (see box below), but the

---

SHROUDED IN MYSTERY

During the devastating Duomo fire of 1997, a quick-thinking fireman rescued from a blazing chapel what has been called "the most remarkable forgery in history", the **Turin Shroud** – a linen sheet bearing the image of a man's body – claimed to be the shroud in which Christ was wrapped after his crucifixion. One of the most famous medieval relics, it made world headlines in 1988 after carbon-dating tests carried out by three universities each concluded it was a fake, made between 1260 and 1390. Since 1988, the Shroud has continued to be a tissue of contention between true believers and true scientists. Most recently, in 2005, an American chemist posited that somehow all three carbon tests were mistakenly conducted on a medieval patch and that the oldest parts of the fabric were in the target age range. But even if the cloth itself were proven of biblical vintage, that's just the starting point. Unless the Vatican gives full access (supremely unlikely) to a whole army of impartial experts to test the fragile fabric – including DNA tests of the supposed bloodstains – the Shroud's authenticity will always remain a simple matter of faith.

reconstruction of the fantastic Holy Shroud Chapel, designed by Guarini in 1668, has yet to be completed. Most of the time you can't see the Shroud; it is locked away and officially only on display once every 25 years (the last time was April–May of 2010). However, it is sometimes brought out for special occasions (it's worth checking at the tourist office). There's a photographic reproduction, on which the face of a bearded man, crowned with thorns, is clearly visible, together with marks supposed to have been left by a double-thonged whip, spear wounds, and bruises that could have been caused carrying a cross.

Relics of Turin's days as a small Roman colony are visible from outside the Duomo: the scant remains of a **theatre** and the impressive **Porta Palatina** – two sixteen-sided towers flanking an arched passageway. Smaller archeological finds can be seen in the **Museo di Antichità** (Tues–Sun 8.30am–7.30pm; €4; ⓦ museoarcheologico.piemonte .beniculturali.it), behind the Duomo at Via XX Settembre 88/C, in what were the Palazzo Reale's orangeries.

Museo della Sindone

Via S. Domenico 28 • Daily 9am–noon & 3–7pm • €6 • ⓦ sindone.it/museo.asp

For those whose interest in the Shroud is still not satiated, there is a dedicated museum that covers its history and science: the **Museo della Sindone**. Housed in the crypt of the Church of SS. Sudario, it exhibits documents and photographic reproductions regarding the history and veneration of, and scientific research on this sacred cloth.

Porta Palazzo Mercato

Northwest of the Duomo, the huge **Piazza della Repubblica**, otherwise known as the Porta Palazzo, hosts Europe's largest **outdoor market** (Mon–Fri 8.30am–1.30pm, Sun 8.30am–6.30pm) selling mainly fruit and vegetables, but also clothes and, in the indoor market hall, cheeses, bread and *salumi*. Behind the Porta Palazzo is the Saturday-morning Balôn, or **flea market**. On the second Sunday of each month there's a Gran Balôn on the same spot, with opportunities to buy collectables including lace, toys, secondhand furniture and books. The indoor food market is housed in the Tettoia dell'Orologio, a metal structure looking like a railway building, built in 1916.

Santuario della Consolata

Piazza della Consolata • Daily 6am–approx 8.30pm • Free • ⓦ laconsolata.org

West of Piazza della Repubblica stands the royal **Santuario della Consolata**, built to house an ancient statue of the Madonna, Maria Consolatrice, the protector of the city. Designed by Guarini, its Neoclassical facade is pink and white, while the interior has an impressive decorative altar by Juvarra. Don't miss the vast array of votive objects devout Torinesi have offered to the statue, housed in an ancient crypt. Not to be missed either is the series of paintings in the church, featuring people being "saved" from such disasters as being gored by a bull, cutting overhead electricity cables with garden shears and exploding frying pans.

After all this, head across the piazza to the beautiful old café, *Al Bicerin* (see p.152), for a pick-me-up. In nineteenth-century post-Unification Turin, it was the only café women could frequent without causing a scandal.

Museo d'Arte Orientale (MAO)

Via S. Domenico 11 • Tues–Sun 10am–6pm • €10 • ⓦ maotorino.it

Southwest of Piazza della Repubblica is the newest addition to world culture in the city, the **Museo d'Arte Orientale (MAO)**, with an extraordinary range of Asian collections, the highlights including a trove of second- to fourth-century Gandharan sculpture, millennia-old Chinese pieces and an impressive number of ninth- to seventeenth-century Islamic artworks.

The Mole Antonelliana

The porticoes of Via Po lead down to the river from Piazza del Castello, ending just before the bridge in the vast, arcaded Piazza Vittorio Veneto. Halfway down, a left onto Via Montebello brings you to the huge **Mole Antonelliana**, whose bishop's-hat dome, topped by a pagoda-like spire balancing on a mini-Greek temple, is a distinctive landmark. Designed as a synagogue in the nineteenth century by the eccentric architect Antonelli, the building was ceded to the local council by Turin's Jewish community while still under construction because of escalating costs.

Museo Nazionale del Cinema

Tues–Fri & Sun 9am–8pm, Sat 9am–11pm • €9, or €12 including the lift to the top, €6 for lift only • ⓦ museocinema.it

The decision to house the modern **Museo Nazionale del Cinema** in this rather unusual building seems a suitable way to celebrate the sheer spectacle of the place. Turin's involvement with cinema goes back to the early years of the twentieth century, when it was one of the first Italian cities to import and experiment with the new medium. The museum covers the early days of the magic lantern and experimental moving pictures, the development of the cinema as a global phenomenon, and twenty-first-century special effects.

Parco del Valentino

South along the river from Piazza Vittorio Veneto, the riverside **Parco del Valentino** borders the site of a cluster of Turin's nightclubs – known as the **Murazzi** area (see p.154). In the daytime the grounds make a pleasant place to wind down after the hum of the city centre. There are two **castles** here, though only one is the genuine article. The ornate **Castello Valentino** was another Savoy residence and is nowadays the seat of the university's faculty of architecture.

Borgo e Rocca Medievale

Daily: April–Oct 9am–8pm; Nov–March 9am–7pm • Free • ⓦ borgomedievaletorino.it

The **Borgo e Rocca Medievale** dates from an industrial exhibition held in 1884. The Borgo is a reconstructed medieval village whose houses are a true synthesis of Piemonte and Valle d'Aosta medieval dwellings, built with the same materials as the originals and using the same construction techniques. The centrepiece of the village, the **Rocca** (Tues–Sun 10am–6pm; €6, free first Tues of the month) is a fifteenth-century castle, which, although bogus, actually conjures up a picture of life in a medieval castle far better than many of the originals.

MAUTO (Museo Nazionale dell'Automobile)

Corso Unità d'Italia 40 • Mon 10am–2pm, Tues 2–7pm, Wed, Thurs & Sun 10am–7pm, Fri & Sat 10am–9pm • €8 • ⓦ museoauto.it

Three kilometres south along the river from Parco del Valentino takes you to the revamped **Museo Nazionale dell'Automobile** – or **MAUTO**, Italy's only motor museum. You'll discover strange vehicles from motoring's formative days and others familiar from classic films, as the museum traces the development from early cars, handcrafted for a privileged minority, to the mass-produced family version. One of the favourite luxury models is the gleaming Isotta Fraschini driven by Gloria Swanson in the film *Sunset Blvd.*, still with the initials of Norma Desmond, the character she played, on the side. The pride of the collection is the 1907 Itala, which won the Peking-to-Paris race in the same year; you can read of its adventures in Luigi Barzini's book *Peking to Paris*.

The Lingotto Centre

Via Nizza 250 • Pinacoteca Giovanni e Marella Agnelli open Tues–Sun 10am–7pm • €4, €3 surcharge for special exhibitions • ⓦ pinacoteca-agnelli.it • Tram #1 or #18 from Piazza del Castello or take the metro to Lingotto

Walking 200m further on and turning right down Via Garessio takes you to what was the original Fiat factory, the **Lingotto Centre**. Fiat's headquarters are still here but the main part of the building, redesigned by Renzo Piano, houses a conference and exhibition space, an auditorium and a shopping centre, as well as the **Pinacoteca Giovanni e Marella Agnelli** at no. 230, a priceless collection of artworks donated by the head of the Fiat dynasty and his wife. The paintings are housed in a glass-and-metal gallery called the *scrigno* (jewellery case), which overlooks the test track on top of the former Fiat car works. The collection consists of mainly nineteenth- and twentieth-century masterpieces, including a number of Matisses and a couple of Picassos. The eighteenth century is represented by six Canalettos and Tiepolo's *Halberdier in a Landscape*.

Parco della Rimembranza

Bus #70 from Piazza Vittorio Veneto

Southeast of the river, Turin fades into decrepit suburbs, beyond which lie the wooded hills concealing the fancy villas, originally the homes of the city's industrialists. The bus meanders up the hillside, offering a taste of the views enjoyed by Turin's mega-rich. The **Parco della Rimembranza** itself features ten thousand trees planted in honour of the Torinese victims of World War I and crowned with an enormous light-flashing statue of Victory.

The Sassi-Superga tram

Tram #15 from Piazza Castello to Sassi station from where the Sassi-Superga tram runs hourly on the hour every day (except Tues) 9am–noon & 2–8pm, Sat, Sun & hols 9am–8pm • €4 single, €6 return, weekends & holidays €6 single, €9 return • ⓦ gtt.to.it

The **Sassi-Superga tram**, complete with its original 1884 carriages, runs up to the grandiose Baroque **Basilica di Superga** (see below). The track is over 3km long and climbs over 400m. At the foot of the hill is a bar and restaurant, while at the top you can take in panoramic views of the city and the Alps.

Basilica di Superga

Strada Basilica di Superga 75 • **Apartments and tombs** March–Oct daily 9.30am–7pm; Nov–Feb Sat & Sun 9.30am–6.30pm; Dec 26–Jan 6 daily 9.30am 6.30pm • **Dome** March Mon & Wed–Fri 10am–5pm, Sat 9.30am–6pm, Sun & hols 12.45–6pm; April–Oct Mon–Fri 10am–6pm, Sat 9.30am–7pm, Sun & hols 12.45–7pm; Nov–Feb Sat 9.30am–5pm, Sun 12.45–5pm; Dec 26–Jan 6 daily 10am–5pm • Basilica free, dome €3, Savoy tombs and royal apartments €4

The **Basilica di Superga**, a Filippo Juvarra creation, stands high on a hill above the city. In 1706 Duke Vittorio Amedeo climbed the hill in order to study the positions of the French and Spanish armies who had been besieging the city, and vowed that he would erect a temple to the Madonna on this site if she were to aid him in the coming battle. Turin was spared, and the duke immediately set Juvarra to work, producing over the next 25 years the circular basilica you see today. The elegant dome, pierced by windows and supported on pairs of white columns, is flanked by delicately scalloped onion-domed towers and rises above a Greek temple entrance. Many Torinesi come here to visit the tomb of the 1949 Torino football team, all of whom were killed when their plane crashed into the side of the hill.

The Stupinigi Palace

Piazza Principe Amedeo 7 • Closed for restoration at the time of writing; check ⓦ piemonteitalia.eu • Bus #63 from Porta Nuova (bus stop #3492 "Porta Nuova FS" in Via Sacchi) then change at the stop after Piazza Caio Mario (bus stop #1080 "Imperia") to bus #41; get off at stop #1085 "Stupinigi"

A nearby attraction is the Savoy dynasty's luxurious hunting lodge, the **Palazzina di Caccia di Stupinigi**. Another Juvarra design, it was built in the 1730s and is perhaps his finest work. The exterior of the palace has been restored, while the interior is as luxurious as it ever was, also incorporating the **Museo d'Arte e Ammobiliamento**, a collection of art and furniture from other Savoy palaces. The oval Salone Centrale is a dizzying triumph of optical illusion that merges fake features with real in a superb trompe l'oeil. Other rooms are decorated with hunting motifs: even the chapel is dedicated to Sant'Uberto, patron saint of hunting.

Castello di Rivoli – Museo d'Arte Contemporanea

Piazza Mafalda di Savoia • Tues–Fri 10am–5pm, Sat & Sun 10am–7pm • €6.50 • ⊚ castellodirivoli.org • Take the metro service from Stazione Porta Susa to Collegno (🚇 Fermi)

Another rewarding trip is west to Rivoli and its **Museo d'Arte Contemporanea**, housed in the Baroque **Castello di Rivoli**, one-time residence of the Savoy family. It's the most important collection of postwar art in Italy, ranging from works by Jeff Koons, Carl Andre and Claes Oldenburg to Arte Povera artists such as Mario Merz and Alighiero Boetti.

The Venaria Reale

Piazza della Repubblica 4 • Tues–Fri 9am–5pm (ticket office closes 3.30pm), Sat & Sun 9am–8pm (ticket office closes 6.30pm) • €15 (€5 gardens only) • Shuttle bus from Turin city centre €5 return (free with Torino+Piemonte Card); for bus stops and timetable go to ⊚ comune.torino.it/gtt/turismo/reggia_venaria.shtml

Popularly known as the "Versailles of Italy", the magnificent **Venaria Reale** was originally used as a hunting lodge and thus dedicated to the goddess Diana. Begun in 1659 for Carlo Emanuele II, the palace was completed in the 1700s, and includes the Great Gallery, the Stables, the Orangery and the Clock Tower. The palace contains masterpieces from the Savoy collections housed in the sumptuous Baroque rooms. The outside is no less impressive, with a hazel grove, rose garden and kitchen garden, not to mention the Great Pond with its own gondolas (gondola rides May 19–Sept 9; €3.50).

ARRIVAL AND DEPARTURE   TURIN

By plane Turin's airport, Caselle (☎ 011 567 6361 or ☎ 011 567 6362, ⊚ aeroportoditorino.it), is 15km north of the city and is used by domestic and international traffic. It is connected by buses every 30–45min (less frequent on Sun) with Porta Susa and Porta Nuova train stations (40min; €6.50, or €7 on the bus) or by train to Dora-GTT Station (19min; €3.70 – also valid for 70min on Turin public transport). The flat-rate taxi service to or from the airport costs €35.

By train Turin's main train station, Porta Nuova, on Corso Vittorio Emanuele II at the southern end of Via Roma, is convenient for the city centre and hotels. Some trains also stop at Porta Susa on Corso Inghilterra (Piazza XVIII Dicembre), west of the centre and heralded as the city's primary hub in the near future. See ⊚ trenitalia.com for timetables.

Destinations Alba (hourly; 1hr 10min–1hr 40min); Aosta (hourly; 2–3hr); Asti (hourly; 30min–1hr); Milan (Milano Centrale; hourly; 50min–2hr); Novara (hourly; 1hr 5min–1hr 50min).

By bus The main bus station is at Corso Vittorio Emanuele II, 131/H (⊚ autostazionetorino.it), the arrival and departure point for most intercity and all international buses; however, local buses to Saluzzo arrive at, and leave from, the top of Corso Marconi, near the junction with Via Nizza. The bus station is linked to Via Nizza (near Porta Nuova) and Porta Susa by bus #9 or #68. See ⊚ comune.torino.it/gtt for timetables.

Destinations Aosta (8 daily; 2–3hr); Cervinia (1 Sun; 2hr 15min); Courmayeur (7 daily; 4hr); Ivrea (12 daily; 1hr 15min); Saluzzo (10 daily; 1hr 20min).

By car All the international companies have car-rental offices at the airport including Avis (☎ 011 470 1528), Europcar (☎ 011 567 8048), Hertz (☎ 011 577 8166) and Maggiore (☎ 011 470 1929). Parking spaces are marked with blue lines on the road and cost €1.30–2.50/hr. More expensive parking lots lie under some main piazzas. Beware of Turin's one-way systems as you enter and leave the city, and note that you cannot enter or drive through the centre between 7.30 and 10.30am.

GETTING AROUND

On foot The best way to see Turin is by walking. Almost all of the major sights can be reached from Porta Nuova station, and the mainly pedestrian centre means that walking is stress-free.

By metro Turin's metro service is limited but fast, efficient, safe and clean. Single tickets cost €1.50 and are valid for 90min, but 24hr, 48hr and 72hr options are available (€5, €7.50 and €10 respectively); ⓦ gtt.to.it.

By tram and bus If you're pushed for time you should take advantage of the city's fast and efficient overground network (ⓦ gtt.to.it). Tickets, valid for 90min, must be bought before you board – they cost €1.50 each or €17.50 for a carnet of fifteen from *tabacchi* and newsstands. Useful routes include tram #4, which heads north through the city from Porta Nuova along Via XX Settembre close to Piazza della Repubblica; bus #1 between Porta Nuova and the Lingotto Centre; tram #11 from Porta Nuova close to Piazza del Castello; bus #61 from Porta Nuova across the river to the Sassi-Superga tramway.

City Sightseeing Torino This red double-decker plies a hop-on-hop-off circular route (daily on the hour 10am–8pm, Jan & Feb weekends only; €15, valid 24hr; ⓦ torino.city -sightseeing.it) that takes in the major sights. There are two lines: "Torino Centre" and "Unexpected Torino", which heads a little further afield. You can pick it up at Piazza del Castello

and nine other points along the route; buy tickets on the bus.

By car Driving your own car in the city is best avoided: much of the centre is pedestrianized and the complicated one-way system means you risk getting lost or getting a ticket. There is also restricted access in the city centre (for details, see ⓦ comune.torino.it/ztlpermessi/ztl.htm). If you do want to drive, rental outlets in town include Avis, 37 Via Giusti 1 (☎ 011 205 3547); Europcar, Via Madama Cristina 72 (☎ 011 650 3603); and Hertz, Corso Turati 37A (☎ 011 502 080).

By taxi Taxi ranks are found on most of the main squares in the centre of Turin, as well as at the bus and train stations and the airport, or call ☎ 011 5730 or ☎ 011 5737. Most hotels can organize a taxi service for you.

By bike With its wide avenues, relatively car-free centre, grid system and some 40km of bicycle paths, many along the picturesque rivers, Turin is ideal for cyclists. A bike-sharing system, with over a hundred drop-off points, makes this a great way to see the city; a weekly pass costs €8 (ⓦ tobike.it). The council also rents bikes in summer at all major parks from €1/hr to €18/week; see ⓦ comune .torino.it/ambiente/bici for opening times.

INFORMATION

Tourist offices The main tourist office is in Piazza del Castello at Via Garibaldi (daily 9am–6pm; ☎ 011 535 181, ⓦ turismotorino.org). There are also branches at the Porta

Nuova train station (daily 9am–6pm) and the airport (daily 9am–5pm); as well as a good range of information they can supply you with the Torino+Piemonte Card (see box, p.144).

ACCOMMODATION

Turin has attractive **hotels** in every quarter. Demand is usually high, especially during the skiing season and trade fairs (when prices also rise), so it's a good idea to phone in advance. Be aware that some places offer special weekend packages – and that a few hotels close in August, which is low season for Turin.

HOTELS

Alpi Resort Via A. Bonafous 5 ☎ 011 812 9677, ⓦ hotelalpiresort.it. An elegant entrance on a busy street near the river leads to somewhat cramped but attractive soundproofed rooms. A great central location. Services include parking, laundry and internet. Breakfast extra. **€74**

Bologna Corso Vittorio Emanuele II 60 ☎ 011 562 0191, ⓦ hotelbolognasrl.it. Ideally located for transport, opposite Porta Nuova train station, in a period building offering 45 recently remodelled rooms, which are clean

and modern. Amenities include fridges, satellite TV and parking. **€80**

★ **Boston** Via Massena 70 ☎ 011 500 359, ⓦ hotel bostontorino.it. A stunning "art hotel", celebrating Turin as Italy's burgeoning capital of contemporary art. The collections adorning both common rooms and in the stylish guestrooms are of the highest gallery calibre, and there's even an audio guide available. Every comfort has been seen to. **€110**

Chelsea Via Cappel Verde 1/D ☎ 011 436 0100, ⓦ hotelchelsea.it. Rooms here are well appointed and

---

WALKING TOURS

Pedestrian-friendly Turin is a fine place to take a **walking tour**, with several different themes on offer. Perhaps the most intriguing tour is based on the city's age-old reputation as one of the three great European centres of the occult (along with London and Prague). To visit some of the noted esoteric sites, relating to both black and white magic, check out ⓦ somewhere.it (☎ 011 668 0580) for its Magic Turin evening walking tour (Thurs & Sat; 9pm at Piazza Statuto 15; 2hr 30min; €20). If the arcane is not your thing, it also offers at least eleven other tours, including Subterranean Turin (Fri; 8.30pm from Piazza Vittorio Veneto 5; 3hr; €25). Make reservations through the website or go to the tourist office site for further tour options (ⓦ turismotorino.org/en/guidedtours).

2

soundproof, with a/c, minibars and other quality touches. The hotel also has its own restaurant, *La Campana*, featuring Pugliese specialities. Breakfast not included. €160

★ **Conte Biancamano** Corso Vittorio Emanuele II 73 ☎011 562 3281, ⊛hotelcontebiancamano.it. If you feel like staying in a rather grandiose setting, go for this hotel. Set in a nineteenth-century palace, it has retained many of its original panelled ceilings and stuccos, and has large, elegant rooms. €130

Des Artistes Via Principe Amedeo 21 ☎011 812 4416, ⊛desartisteshotel.it. This comfortable hotel has simple, smart rooms with a/c and nearby parking. The hotel is bright and modern, and its location is ideal for attractions in the city centre. €95

Genio Corso Vittorio Emanuele II 47 ☎011 650 5771, ⊛hotelgenio.it. Very large, three-star Best Western, occupying a historic building. Rooms are elegant and diverse, some even boasting ceiling frescoes. Impressive buffet breakfast included. Great for transport and local nightlife. €145

★ **Grand Hotel Sitea** Via Carlo Alberto 35 ☎011 517 071, ⊛grandhotelsitea.it. Charming hotel on a pedestrianized street in the heart of town. Facilities include a reading room and piano bar. Rooms are comfortable and spacious, and the breakfast buffet generous. The friendly staff will help you navigate the city. €200

Liberty Via Gioberti 37 ☎011 1978 1101, ⊛hotel liberty-torino.it. A well-appointed and very welcoming find, with Art Nouveau (Liberty) architectural touches and a staff who take the hotel motto – Passion Lives Here – to heart. It's recently been renovated for maximum comfort and even boasts a small spa in the basement. €115

Montevecchio Via Montevecchio 13 bis ☎011 562 0023, ⊛hotelmontevecchio.com. Though rather spartan, this hotel does have TV and telephone in all rooms. Situated in a residential neighbourhood behind the train station, it is clean and quiet. €65

Piemontese Via Berthollet 21 ☎011 669 8101, ⊛hotelpiemontese.it. Handy location on the colourful,

commercial side of the train station. The well-appointed rooms range from suites with jacuzzi to comfortable singles, and there are family rooms available. Though breakfast is included, note that the afternoon aperitif and parking are extra. €99

Roma e Rocca Cavour Piazza Carlo Felice 60 ☎011 561 2772, ⊛romarocca.it. Large, old-style, family-run hotel in front of the Porta Nuova station, overlooking a lively square with park and fountain. Good value and classically attractive, with the choice of a very substantial buffet breakfast at €8 per person. All rooms have free wi-fi. €101

B&B

All'Orso Poeta Corso Vittorio Emanuele II 10 ☎011 517 8996, ⊛orsopoeta-bed-and-breakfast.it. Set in charming surroundings just steps away from the River Po and the Parco Valentino, the apartment is in a prestigious nineteenth-century building. It has spacious, elegantly furnished rooms with lovely views of the park and city. €110

★ **Foresteria degli Artisti** Via degli Artisti 15 ☎011 837 785, ⊛foresteriadegliartisti.it. Tucked in the east of the centre, a short walk from the river and the Mole Antonelliana (which you can see from the skylight), this bright and charming B&B is a friendly home from home. €90

★ **Terres d'aventure suites** Via Santa Maria 1 ☎389 434 2699, ⊛suitestorino.it. Parquet floors, smooth clean lines and minimalist design are predominant here in one of the most glamorous B&Bs in town. Options go from one-night stays to lengthier sojourns. €100

HOSTEL

Open 011 Corso Venezia 11 ☎011 250 535, ⊛openzero11.it. A little bit out of town but easy to reach from Turin's airport. Downright spartan but colourful and comfortable enough, serving also as a youth centre. Half- and full board also offered. Dorms €19.50, doubles €23.50

EATING AND DRINKING

It's worth taking your time over a drink, snack, pastry or ice cream in one of the fin-de-siècle **cafés** that are a Turin institution: prices are steep, but the elegant *belle époque* interiors – often with touches of Art Nouveau (known as "Liberty" style in Italy) – more than compensate. The city also has plenty of good **restaurants** in which to sample local cuisine.

CAFÉS, PASTICCERIE AND GELATERIE

★ **Al Bicerin** Piazza della Consolata 5 ☎011 436 9325, ⊛bicerin.it. This tiny, beautiful café is the place to try a *bicerin* – a Piemontese speciality of coffee fortified with brandy, cream and chocolate. It's been here since 1763 and age has not withered it. 8.30am–7.30pm; closed Wed & Aug.

★ **Baratti & Milano** Piazza del Castello 29 ☎011 440 7138, ⊛barattiemilano.it. Established in 1873

and preserving its nineteenth-century interior of mirrors, chandeliers and carved wood, where genteel Torinese ladies sip tea. Great hot chocolate and ice cream. If you have an espresso at the bar, you'll only pay €1. Tues–Sun 8am–9pm.

Brek Piazza Carlo Felice 22 (☎011 534 556) and Via Santa Teresa 23 (Piazza Solferino; ☎011 545 424); ⊛brek.com. Part of a national chain of efficient, high-quality, self-service spots with tables outside. Popular with

TURIN'S CHOCOLATE

Make sure you leave some room to sample one of Turin's signature products – **chocolate**, brought to the city by the Savoy family in 1559. Best known is the hazelnut milk chocolate Gianduiotto, which dates back to the nineteenth century. Some even claim that it was the Torinesi who introduced chocolate to France when chocolate making for export began in 1678.

You can taste samples of the finest chocolate products in all of Turin's historic establishments, confectionery shops and chocolate factories: Gianduiotti, pralines, various cakes, hot chocolate, and the distinctive *bicerin*, which is a bit like a cappuccino but fortified with brandy. The supreme Torinese spot to buy chocolate is *Gobino*; see below).

local workers and tourists alike. Main courses start at €5. Daily 11.30am–3pm & 6.30–10pm.

Exki Via Corso Vittorio Emanuele II 98 ☎011 086 8973, ⓦexki.it. Natural, fresh and organic is the philosophy of this snack-bar chain with six branches around the city. Sandwiches, soups and smoothies to eat in or take away. A great place to stock up on picnic items. Free wi-fi available. Mon–Fri 8am–7pm, Sat 7.30am–8pm (9pm July & Aug).

Fiorio Via Po 8 ☎011 817 3225, ⓦfioriocaffegelateria .com. Turin's most historic café, once patronized by Nietzsche, presumably for its legendary *gelato* and its signature cappuccino (€3). Mon–Fri 8am–1am, Sat & Sun 8am–2am.

★ **Gobino** Via Lagrange 1 ☎011 566 0707, ⓦguidogobino.it. Maestro Gobino is definitely in the running for producing the most delicious chocolates in the world. A sampling, at the very least, is not to be missed. There's also a boutique at Via Cagliari 15/B. Mon 3–8pm, Tues–Sun 10am–8pm.

Grom Via Accademia delle Scienze 4 ☎011 557 9095, ⓦgrom.it. This Torinese *gelateria* has conquered the market with its vibrant all-natural flavours that are simply unforgettable. Look for the queue out into the square. Go for the unique *crema di Grom*, with cornmeal biscuit bits and dark chocolate chips, or check out the flavours of the month. A single scoop is €2.50. There are now five parlours throughout Turin. Tues–Thurs 11am–midnight, Sat & Sun 11am–1am.

Mood Via Battisti 3 ☎011 518 8657, ⓦmoodlibri.it. Books, coffee and aperitifs in the cosy Turin tradition. Not part of Turin history, like the others, but very attractive. Events include art exhibitions, concerts and book signings. Daily 9am–9pm.

Mulassano Piazza del Castello ☎011 547 990. This inviting café first opened in 1900; it has marble fittings and a striking ceiling. Traditionally the favoured spot of actors and singers from the nearby Teatro Regio. Mon–Thurs & Sun 8am–midnight, Fri & Sat until 1am.

Pepino Piazza Carignano 8 ☎011 936 7615, ⓦgelatipepino.it. Ritzy café on the piazza, famed for its ice creams. Try the violet-flavoured *pinguino* or the outrageously rich cream-and-chocolate concoction of *pezzo duro*. Also offers an excellent Sunday-brunch buffet

menu for about €19. Tues–Sun 8am–11pm.

Platti Corso Vittorio Emanuele II 72 ☎011 506 9048, ⓦplatti.it. This Art Nouveau-furnished café dating from 1870 also hosts art exhibitions. Good place for lunch, or just a quick snack, with delicious *tramezzini* sandwiches going for about €3 each. The tuna with artichoke hearts is a classic. Daily 7.30am–9pm.

San Carlo Piazza S. Carlo 156 ☎011 532 586, ⓦcaffesancarlo.it. Heroes of the Risorgimento once met in this café/restaurant/ice-cream parlour, now regally restored with gilt pilasters and an immense chandelier. An incredibly smooth cappuccino will cost you €1.40 at the bar. Daily: Easter–Sept Mon 8am–9pm, Tues–Fri & Sun 8am–midnight, Sat until 1am; Oct–Easter Mon–Thurs & Sun 8am–9pm, Fri & Sat 8am–midnight.

San Tommaso Via S. Tommaso 10 ☎011 534 201, ⓦsantommaso10.it. A Torinese institution, the original home of Lavazza coffee has been transformed into a sleek, upbeat café where coffee in all its many guises is king, including, of course, that Torinese favourite, the *bicerin*. Mon–Sat 8am–10pm; restaurant 12.30–2.30pm & 8–11pm.

★ **Stratta** Piazza S. Carlo 191 ☎011 547 920, ⓦstratta1836.it. One of the oldest and most beautiful shops in the city, *Stratta* has been making sweet delights since 1836 and its window displays are worthy of Willy Wonka. Do not leave town without visiting for a hot chocolate or to load up on sugary treats. Mon–Fri 8am–8pm, Sat 9am–8pm, Sun 10am–7pm.

Torino Piazza S. Carlo 204 ☎011 545 118, ⓦcaffe -torino.it. Another plush place for a leisurely aperitif or cocktail, of which the most popular is the Torinese "Elvira", made with Martini, vodka and various secret ingredients. Illustrious regulars have included writer Cesare Pavese and Luigi Einaudi (a Torinese economist who became the second president of the Italian Republic). Mon–Thurs 7.30am–midnight, Sat & Sun 8am–midnight.

RESTAURANTS

Alba Via S. Pio V 8 ☎011 669 2054. A classic trattoria, near Porta Nuova station, where everything is home-made and prices and staff are very friendly. Full meals run to about €15. Noon–2.30pm & 7–11pm; closed Fri.

2

★ **Caffè Vini Emilio Ranzini** Via Porta Palatina 9/G ☎ 011 765 0477. Time has stopped in this most authentic of traditional Turin eateries, known as a *piola*, catering for workers, artists and students. Fare includes panini made with delicacies such as anchovies and sun-dried tomatoes, or salami and cheese; you can suggest your own combinations. Don't forget to sample the wines; €15–20 for a meal. Mon–Fri 9.30am–8.30pm, Sat 10am–7pm.

Consorzio Via Monte di Pietà 23 ☎ 011 276 7661, ⊛ ristoranteconsorzio.it. Pleasantly trendy Slow Food spot, where everything is organic, as well as lovingly and expertly prepared. The menu varies according to market finds. Expect to pay around €35 for a full meal, including a sampling of dry, fruity Ruché wine. 12.30–2.30pm & 7.30–11pm; closed Sat lunch & Sun.

Da Michele Piazza Vittorio Veneto 4 ☎ 011 888 836. Offering a commanding view of the long square from under the portico, this place is locally renowned for its superb fresh pastas and strictly seasonal specialities, as well as wood oven-fired pizzas. Full meals €20–40. 12.30–2.30pm & 7.30–11pm; closed Tues Nov–March.

Del Cambio Piazza Carignano 2 ☎ 011 546 690, ⊛ ristorantedelcambio.it. Historic, lavish shrine to Piemontese food, much frequented by expense-account types. A great opportunity to feast on traditional dishes such as Cavour's favourite of *fianziera* (veal, sweetbreads and porcini, cooked with butter and wine). Prices are suitably extravagant – starting around €25 for a main – and booking is advisable. Mon–Sat 12.30–2pm & 8–10pm; closed three weeks in Aug.

Kirkuk Kaffé Via Carlo Alberto 16/B ☎ 011 530 657, ⊛ kirkukkaffe.com. If the meaty Piemontese dishes are beginning to pall, try this cute Turkish restaurant on a leafy pedestrian street. Authentic cuisine, including vegetarian options, at decent prices (around €15 a head). Mon & Sat 7pm–midnight, Tues–Fri noon–3pm & 7pm–midnight.

★ **La Monachella** Via S. Croce 2 (Piazza Carlina) ☎ 011 813 8127, ⊛ lamonachella.it. A fantastic spot in a pretty square with tables outside in summer, this classy, fun pizzeria is the younger, cheaper sister of nearby *La Badessa*, housed in a seventeenth-century building with dining room in the basement. Try the pizza-and-champagne combination for €14. Tues–Sun noon–2.30pm & 6.30pm–12.30am.

M**bun Corso Siccardi 8/A ☎ 011 561 097, ⊛ mbun.it. A great alternative to *McDonald's*, *M**Bun* (*bun* means "good" in Torinese dialect) is a fast-food member of the Slow Food revolution, focusing on locally sourced meat, biodegradable utensils and organic produce. Though steak tartare (€6) is on the menu, you'll find plenty of gluten-free and vegetarian options too (from €3). Daily noon–midnight.

Sfashioncafé Via Cesare Battisti 13 (Piazza Carlo Alberto) ☎ 011 516 0085, ⊛ foodandcompany.com. Owned by famous Torinese comedian Piero Chiambretti. Enormous portions and great pizzas. Lunchtime bargains start at €8 and include a main course, a great house salad, drink and coffee or dessert. Colourful, friendly interior, plus sunny seating on the piazza. Daily 12.15–3pm & 7.30pm–midnight.

★ **Tabernalibraria** Via Bogino 5 ☎ 011 812 8028, ⊛ tabernalibraria.to.it. Great-value, friendly restaurant popular with students and businesspeople. Events include literary evenings and performances. The menu has vegetarian options and the wine list is extensive and excellent. A hearty lunch will set you back €10. Mon–Sat 10am–11pm.

Tre Galline Via Bellezia 37 ☎ 011 436 6553, ⊛ 3galline.it. The oldest restaurant in Turin, with a lovely panelled interior. The *agrodolce* (sweet-and-sour) rabbit is a house speciality. Reckon on €35 a head; booking advisable. Mon 7.45–11pm, Tues–Sat 12.30–2pm & 7.45–11pm; closed Aug.

NIGHTLIFE

Turin's **nightlife** is a reasonably varied mix of clubs and bars, with the liveliest spot down on the embankment bordered by the Parco del Valentino, known locally as the **Murazzi**. Its clubs are packed with a lively crowd, and if you go, you should keep an eye on your belongings. Note that some **clubs** require membership cards, purchased when you enter (€5–10) with your first drink usually included. After that, although drink prices can be inflated measures are relatively generous. Aside from the Murazzi, a good place to wander for a drink is the more tranquil medieval area, known as the **Quadrilatero Romano**, around Piazza Emanuele Filiberto and Via Santa Chiara. The latest place to be is the San Salvario neighbourhood near the train station, with bars and clubs serving up live music and killer cocktails. Many of the *vinerie* – wine bars – offer a substantial snack at aperitif time (known as a *marenda sinoira*).

BARS AND CLUBS

Astoria Via Berthollet 13 ☎ 011 026 8452. Although a pleasant daytime spot, the *Astoria* comes to life at night, with some of the best DJ sets in the city. A beer will set you back €5. Tues, Wed & Sun 10am–2am, Thurs–Sat 10am–4am.

★ **Bagni municipali** Via Oddino Morgari 14 ☎ 393 459 1027, ⊛ bagnimunicipali.org. Once the municipal baths, this hip bar is the newish kid on the block in the new place to be: the rough-and-ready neighbourhood of San Salvario. Cocktails are €5–6; in summer, the watermelon one is a must. Tuck into the giant buffet that comes free with your aperitif. Mon–Thurs 9pm–midnight, Fri & Sat 9pm–2am.

FROM TOP THE VENARIA REALE, TURIN (P.150); ALBA (P.160) >

TURIN'S FESTIVALS

For most of September a major festival called **MITO** (☎011 442 4703, ⊛mitosettembremusica. it) mixes jazz, world music, classical music and performance art at various venues in Turin and Milan. In July, **Traffic**, Turin's free rock festival, takes place in Parco Doria (⊛trafficfestival.com). There are also three annual international **film festivals**, including the Torino Film Festival (⊛torinofilmfest.org) and the Torino GLBT Film Festival, "Da Sodoma a Hollywood", (⊛tglff.com), plus the Salone del Libro **book** fair (⊛saleonedellibro.it) and a **food** event (⊛salonedelgusto).

2

Fluido Viale Cagni 7, Parco del Valentino ☎011 669 4557, ⊛fluido.to. You can spend all day sunbathing and all night partying at this riverside pleasure establishment. Breakfast is served from 10am. The disco action starts at about 10.30pm and goes till dawn. Tues & Wed 10am–2am, Thurs 10am–3am, Fri & Sat 10am–4am, Sun 10am–1.30am.

Hiroshima Mon Amour Via Bossoli 83 ☎011 317 6636, ⊛hiroshimamonamour.org. Live music, alternative theatre and cabaret in a converted school near the Lingotto Centre. Cover charge depending on the event. Thurs–Sun 10.30pm–4am.

Jumping Jester Via Mazzini 2 ☎011 517 1293. Old-fashioned wooden interior with huge TV screen on which football matches are shown live. Serves a great pint of cold Caffreys or Tennants. Mon–Sat 7pm–3am.

Las Rosas Via Bellezia 15 ☎011 290 485. Trendy *cantina*-style *taqueria*. Drinks and tacos served to the sounds of world music, though obviously the focus is on all things Mexican. Daily 7pm–2am.

Lobelix Via Corte d'Appello 15 (Piazza Savoia) ☎011 436 7206. *Simpatico* wine and cocktail bar with techno music, named for the obelisk that adorns the piazza, out into which the tables spill in summer. Daily 6.30pm–3am.

Rumbamamà Lungo Po Diaz 4 ☎347 864 9961. Popular with the local kids who fill the place almost every night, probably because of the cheap drinks during happy hour (two beers for €5, two shots for €6). A good starting place for an all-nighter down at the Murazzi. Daily 9pm–2.30am.

Tre Galli Via Sant'Agostino 25 ☎011 521 6027. Busy *vineria* that used to be an Agnelli (Fiat founder) hangout, with a list of some 400 local and Italian wines by the bottle or glass (for the latter, ask for a *mescita a calice*) as well as plates of cheeses, ham, salami and home-made *grissini* (breadsticks). Laidback atmosphere and tables outside on the piazza in summer. Mon–Wed 12.30–2.30pm & 6.30pm–midnight, Thurs–Sat 12.30–2.30pm & 7.30pm–2am.

ENTERTAINMENT

Turin's cultural life is suitably comprehensive for a place of this size. For what's-on listings and opening hours, check the pages of the Turin daily, *La Stampa*, particularly its Friday supplements. Alternatively, look out for free listings magazines and promo leaflets in bars and restaurants around town. Torino Cultura in Piazza del Castello at Via Garibaldi (⊛torinocultura.it) has a free ticket reservation service.

RAI National Symphony Orchestra Arturo Toscanini Auditorium, Piazza Rossaro ☎011 810 4653, ⊛orchestrasinfonica.rai.it. One of the most prestigious orchestras in Italy, offering a rich programme of classical music concerts and events throughout the year. Ticket office Tues–Fri 10am–6pm.

Teatro Regio Piazza del Castello 215 ☎011 881 5241, ⊛teatroregio.torino.it. The city's opera house is one of the best in the country and is recognizable from its pod-like Seventies architecture. Ticket office Tues–Fri 10.30am–6pm, Sat 10.30am–4pm and 1hr before performances.

Teatro Stabile Piazza Carignano 6 ☎011 517 6246, ⊛teatrostabiletorino.it. One of Italy's principal publicly funded theatre companies, the Stabile is acclaimed for its productions of major works by nineteenth- and twentieth-century European playwrights; performances are normally at the sumptuous Carignano Theatre, though it is one of at least half a dozen theatres in the city. Ticket office Tues–Sat 1–7pm and 1hr before performances.

DIRECTORY

Books and newspapers Libreria Luxembourg, Via Cesare Battisti 7, has an excellent range of British and American paperbacks and magazines. English-language newspapers can be bought from most newsagents in the city centre, in particular the one at the Porta Nuova station.

Exchange Outside normal banking hours you can exchange money at Porta Nuova station (Mon, Wed, Thurs & Fri 8am–7pm, Tues & Sat 9am–6pm, Sun 10am–6pm).

Football Turin's two teams, Juventus and Torino, play on Sat and Sun afternoons at respectively the Juventus Stadium, Strada Comunale di Altessano 131, and the Stadio Olimpico, Via Filadelfia 88. You can get to the Juventus Stadium on the metro Bernini stop and then bus #9; the Stadio Olimpico on Line #4 from Porta Nuova station or #10 from Porta Susa. Although Juventus has been voted the most popular team in Italy, most locals support the underdogs, Torino.

Hospital Ospedale Molinette, Corso Bramante 88–90 ☎ 011 633 1633; for 24hr emergency medical attention call ☎ 5747, ☎ 118 or ☎ 113.

Internet access Bu.Net, Via S. Quintino 13/F (daily 9am–1am; from €0.06/min).

Laundries Lav@sciuga, Via S. Massimo 4 and Piazza della Repubblica 5.

Markets In addition to Porta Palazzo/Piazza della Repubblica, and the weekly Balôn and monthly Gran Balôn markets behind Porta Palazzo, there's often heavily discounted designer fashion (the genuine thing, from end-of-line clearances) at the Crocetta market around Via Cassini and Via Marco Polo (Mon–Fri mornings & all day Sat) – not exactly street-market prices, but still much cheaper than in the shops.

Pharmacist Boniscontro, Corso Vittorio Emanuele II 66, is open all night.

Police City police station at Corso XI Febbraio 22; ☎ 113.

Post office The central post office is at Via Alfieri 10 (Mon–Fri 8.30am–7pm, Sat 8.30am–1pm).

The Susa and Chisone valleys

The main route to France from Turin runs through the **Susa Valley**, passing near the region's main ski resorts. The one real sight to spot is the **Sacra di San Michele**, a forbidding fortified abbey anchored atop a rocky hill; it's an easy day-trip from Turin. **Susa** itself, reached by a minor branch of the rail line, was once a modest Roman town and is now a modest provincial town – a pleasant stopover but with little else to lure you.

Sacra di San Michele

Via alla Sacra 14 • Mid-March to mid-Oct Tues–Sat 9.30am–12.30pm & 2.30–6pm, Sun & public hols 9.30am–noon & 2.40–6.30pm; July–Sept also open Mon, same hours; mid-Oct to mid-March 9.30am–12.30pm & 2.30–5pm, Sun & public hols 9.30am–noon & 2.30–5pm • €5 • ☎ 011 939 130, ⓦ sacradisanmichele.com

One of the closest towns to the **Sacra di San Michele** is **SANT'AMBROGIO**, a small town at the foot of San Michele's hill. It's thirty minutes by train from Turin and connected with the abbey by a very steep ninety-minute hike; with your own car, however, you can drive up to the abbey from the town of **AVIGLIANA**. The walk is worth it, both for the views and for the opportunity to soak up the eerie atmosphere. Climbing up to the abbey and hewn into the rock, a long flight of stairs – the Scalone dei Morti (Stairs of the Dead) – sets a morbid tone, for it was here that the skeletons of the monks used to be laid out for local peasants to come and pay their respects and to remind them of human frailty. The Romanesque entrance arch is carved with signs of the zodiac to the Gothic-Romanesque abbey church.

Susa

Some 25km up the valley from Sant'Ambrogio, **SUSA** is a likeable, rather scruffy old town. When the Romans ruled most of Italy, Susa and western Piemonte remained in the hands of the Celts. The best-known Celtic leader, Cottius, was much admired by the Romans and a handful of mainly Roman remains cluster around the town centre, notably in **Piazza San Giusto**, where there's a redoubtable defensive gate. The adjacent **cattedrale** – originally Romanesque but with Gothic and Baroque accretions – has a fine campanile, but its most interesting features are the external frescoes – a *Crucifixion* and an *Entry into Jerusalem*. Just above the piazza, Cottius erected the **Arco di Augusto** in honour of the Roman emperor, its top decorated with a processional frieze. Look through its broad arched opening frames for views of the Susa Valley's highest mountain – the Rocciamelone (3538m).

ACCOMMODATION	SUSA

Du Parc Via Rocchetta 15 ☎ 0122 622 273, ⓦ hotel duparcsusa.com. Though a little on the shabby side, the rooms are clean and offer spectacular views of the Alps. Popular with bikers and cyclists touring the region, the hotel has a garage for two-wheeled transport. **€80**

Napoleon Via Mazzini 44 ☎ 0122 622 855, ⓦ hotel napoleon.it. A friendly hotel in the centre of town. Though the rooms are somewhat lacking in charm, the hotel boasts a fitness centre and tiny spa and makes an ideal base for exploring the area. **€64**

2

PIEMONTE'S SKI RESORTS

Piemonte's main, purpose-built ski areas – Claviere, Cesana, Sestriere, Sansicario, Sauze d'Oulx and Bardonecchia – are well used by British tour operators and, as hosts of the alpine events of the Winter Olympics 2006, have all had their facilities recently upgraded. They collectively constitute some 400km of interconnected runs, more than 200 in all, known as **La Vialattea** (The Milky Way; Ⓦ vialattea.it). You can gain access from Pragelato, thanks to the cableway Pattemouche-Anfiteatro. One daily lift-pass for all five resorts is €34; a weekly pass will set you back €218.

Sestriere was the dream resort of Fiat baron, Gianni Agnelli, who conceived it as an aristocratic mountain retreat. Nowadays, the reality is a bland resort dominated by two cylindrical towers. The mountain is impeccable: the choice for World Cup and Olympic ski races. Modern **Bardonecchia** – unlike the others, not directly connected to the Vialattea, and run by another company, BardonecchiaSki (Ⓦ bardonecchiaski.com) – is a weekenders' haunt, with small chalet-style hotels and over 100km of runs. **Sauze d'Oulx**, a little way south, is generally known as the "Benidorm of the Alps", attracting hordes of youngsters – though it isn't so bad that it doesn't also attract its share of families.

The Chisone Valley

Taking the parallel **Chisone Valley** to the south back towards Turin, you will encounter a much more bucolic and less-developed area, dotted along the way with small towns. The picturesque slate-roofed hamlet of **USSEAUX**, whose weather-worn old walls are decorated with colourful murals, is well worth discovering and makes an agreeable spot for lunch.

Forte di Fenestrelle

July & Aug daily 10am–noon & 2.30–6pm; Sept–June Mon & Thurs–Sun 10am–noon & 2.30–6pm • €2 (though prices vary depending what type of visit you choose) • ☎ 0121 83 600 for tour reservations, Ⓦ fortedifenestrelle.com

Not far away, at an altitude of nearly 2000m, the impressive **Forte di Fenestrelle**, known as "The Great Wall of Piemonte", has been restored and is now a significant regional attraction. It constitutes a gigantic fortified castle and dependent buildings, along with an adjoining massive 3km rampart marching over the mountain. Built by the Savoys from 1728, it took some 122 years to complete. Simply put, it's the largest defensive structure ever built in Europe. Much of the wall's length can now be visited, and the longest guided tour (€12) takes you up all of the four thousand steps and back, a strenuous seven-hour trek.

ACCOMMODATION AND EATING   THE CHISONE VALLEY

★ **Bella Baita** Borgata Serre Marchetto, 1 Pinasca ☎ 339 750 3940, Ⓦ bellabaita.com. An accommodating inn nestled amid a panoramic mountain forest high above the valley's villages. The hosts are very welcoming and knowledgeable about the area, and they are trained professional chefs; a hearty breakfast is included, and half-board is also available. €55

Trattoria La Placette Via della Chiesa 5, Usseaux ☎ 0121 83 073, Ⓦ trattorialaplacette.com. Behind the church and on the village's edge overlooking the valley, this charming alpine chalet is equipped with a sunny porch on which you can partake of hearty pastas, game, and mountain cheeses. Rooms also available (€30). 12.30–2.30pm & 7.30–9.30pm; closed Thurs.

Saluzzo and the Po Valley

A flourishing medieval town, and later the seat of one of Piemonte's few Renaissance courts, **SALUZZO**, 57km south of Turin, retains much of its period appeal. Flaking ochre-washed terraces and Renaissance houses line cobbled streets that climb up to a castle, from where you can enjoy views of the town. A pleasant place to stay, the town is a great base for visiting the Po, Varaita and Maira valleys, which cut through the foothills of the Monviso mountain towards France.

Central Saluzzo

Just below the castle, the **Torre Civica** (March–Oct weekends & public hols 10.30am–12.30pm & 2.30–6.30pm; €2, combined ticket with Museo Civico €6) gives great views over the town and surrounding areas. The Gothic church of **San Giovanni** has a number of thirteenth- and fourteenth-century frescoes and the tomb of the leading light of Renaissance Saluzzo, Marchese Ludovico II, anachronistically depicted as a medieval knight beneath a fancily carved canopy. Close by, the Renaissance **Casa Cavassa**, Via San Giovanni 5, is a fifteenth-century palace with an arcaded courtyard that now houses the town's **Museo Civico** (March–Oct Tues & Wed 10am–1pm & 3–5pm; Thurs–Sun 10am–1pm & 3–7pm; at time of writing Oct–March hours unavailable; €5, combined ticket with Torre Civica €6). Inside are period furniture and paintings, including the gorgeously gilded *Madonna della Misericordia*, with the Madonna sheltering Ludovico, his wife and the population of Saluzzo in the folds of her cloak.

Castello della Manta

Tues–Sun 10am–5/6pm • ☎ 0175 87 822 • €56, including audioguide

Just to the south of Saluzzo, a five-minute bus ride from outside the train station, is the **Castello della Manta** – a medieval fortress transformed into a refined residence in the fifteenth century. Though from the outside it's as plain and austere as Saluzzo's castle, it houses evocative late-Gothic frescoes in the Baronial Hall. One of these illustrates the myth of the Fountain of Youth, elderly people processing towards the magical waters while others impatiently rip off their clothes to plunge in.

ARRIVAL AND INFORMATION   SALUZZO

By bus Saluzzo has an excellent bus service and you can reach the town by bus from Turin (line #91). There are also regular services into the Po, Varaita and Maira valleys. For timetables, see ⓦ atibus.it.
Destinations Paesana (Valle Po; Mon–Sat 11 daily, 3 Sun; 2hr); Val Varaita (3 daily; 1hr 15min).

Tourist office Piazza Risorgimento 1 (April–Sept Tues–Sun 10am–1pm & 3–6.30pm; Oct–March Tues–Sun 10am–12.30pm & 3–6pm; ☎ 0175 46 710, ⓦ saluzzo turistica.it). Saluzzo's tourist office can provide information on the whole of the western valleys region.

ACCOMMODATION AND EATING

★ **Agriturismo Camisassi** Via Torino 75 ☎ 0175 479 091, ⓦ agriturismocamisassi.it. This bucolic farmhouse hotel just outside Saluzzo has been owned by the same family for three generations. The rooms are spacious and tastefully decorated while the farm buildings have undergone careful restoration. **€70**

Griselda Corso XXVII Aprile 13 ☎ 0175 47 484, ⓦ hotelgriselda.it. This modern, three-star hotel provides comfortable, smart accommodation, albeit more suited to business travellers than tourists. All rooms have a/c and wi-fi service. The hotel also boasts a restaurant with local dishes on the menu. **€90**

Persico Vicolo Mercati 10 ☎ 0175 41 213, ⓦ albergo persico.net. One of the cheapest hotels in town, with rooms that are a little utilitarian but clean and a very

good restaurant serving traditional cuisine (noon–2pm & 7–10pm; closed Mon). Special offers are available for half- or full board. **€77**

★ **San Giovanni Resort** Via S. Giovanni 9/A ☎ 0175 45 420, ⓦ sangiovanniresort.it. Simply the loveliest hotel in town, it is part of the fifteenth-century monastery complex, with rooms overlooking the cloisters. It boasts a café in the cloisters and a great restaurant in the basement taverna. **€145**

Taverna dei Porti Scur Via Volta 14 ☎ 0175 219 483. This atmospheric tavern has a beautiful bare-brick vaulted ceiling and modern features. The menu contains regional dishes, but there are contemporary takes on traditional meals (€25). Tues–Fri 7.30–10pm, Sat & Sun noon–2pm & 7.30–10pm; closed last two weeks of Aug.

The Po Valley

West of Saluzzo lies the source of the River Po, Pian del Re, which lies in an uncontaminated environment within the Po River Natural Park. Towards the end of the valley is the alpine-style resort of **CRISSOLO**. From here you can hike 5km (or take a minibus in summer) to the **Pian del Re**, a plain around the source of the Po, for a view of one of the passes legend claims Hannibal and his elephants used.

Crissolo is also a good base for climbing **Monviso** (3841m), one of Piemonte's highest mountains; it's a long (about 6hr) rocky scramble from the *Quintino Sella rifugio*, two to three hours beyond the Pian del Re. The walk to the *rifugio* is lovely, passing a series of **mountain lakes**; or you can do a **circuit of the lakes**, turning off the main trail just before Lago Chiaretto, from where a path leads past Lago Superiore and back to Pian del Re.

2

Alba and Le Langhe

The town of **Alba** and the surrounding **Langhe** hills have come to signify two things: **white truffles** and **red wine**. The exquisite truffles are more delicate and aromatic than the black variety found further south, whereas most of the area's very different wines all come from the same grape, the Nebbiolo. The final taste is dependent on the soil: tuff-rich soil produces the grapes for the light red **Nebbiolo**; calcium and mineral-rich soil for the more robust **Barolo**, the "King of wines and the wine of Kings". In the hill-villages around Alba, there are a few wine museums and cantinas, the best being those at Barolo and Pollenzo. Ask at the tourist office for one of the excellent free maps and suggestions for wine tours. Buses from Alba don't reach all the hill-villages, so your own transport is best.

Alba

Whether or not you want to taste the extraordinary wines, **ALBA** is worth the visit for its alluring mix of red-brick medieval towers, Baroque and Renaissance palaces and cobbled streets. And if you come in early October, you might catch the town's hilarious annual donkey race – a skit on nearby Asti's prestigious Palio.

The town's only sight as such is its late-Gothic **Duomo**, standing confectionery-pink on the central Piazza Risorgimento. But Alba is primarily a place to stroll and eat. Leading up to the centre from Piazza Savona, the main drag of **Via Vittorio Emanuele** is a fine, bustling street, with Alba's local produce on display – wines, truffles, cheeses, weird and wonderful mushroom varieties, and the wickedly sticky *nocciola*, a nutty, chocolatey cake. Via Cavour is a pleasant medieval street, behind which the **donkey race** and displays of medieval pageantry attract the crowds during the October festival. There's also an annual **truffle festival** later in the month, when you could blow your whole budget on a knobbly truffle or a meal in one of the many swanky restaurants. At the end of April/beginning of May, the **Vinum wine festival** gives you the chance to taste five hundred local wines.

ARRIVAL AND INFORMATION

ALBA

By train There's a regular service from Turin to Alba, though you have to change at Asti or Bra; the whole journey takes 1hr 45min. There's an hourly service from Alba to Asti (50min).

By bus There are two daily services to Barolo (Mon–Sat; 30min). Buses leave from outside the train station.

Tourist office Piazza Risorgimento 2 (April–Sept Mon–Fri 9am–6.30pm, Sat & Sun 10am–6.30pm; Oct to mid-Nov Mon–Fri 9am–6.30pm, Sat & Sun 9am–8pm; mid-Nov to March Mon–Fri 9am–6pm, Sat & Sun 10am–6pm; 0173 35 833, langheroero.it). The tourist office has a free reservation service.

ACCOMMODATION

★ **Casa Scaparone** Località Scaparone 8 0173 33 946, casascaparone.it. A wonderful agriturismo in beautiful surroundings just outside Alba. Breakfast includes home-made jams and bread, and the restaurant uses many of its home-grown organic ingredients. Music and cultural events often take place in the evenings. The

rooms are spacious with many of the original beams and floorboards restored: the feel is rustic chic. **€85**

Cortiletto d'Alba Corso M. Coppino 27 0173 366 005, cortilettodalba.com. Very close to the centre and convenient for the train station, the *Cortiletto* offers comfortable a/c rooms and its restaurant serves full meals:

lunch special €9, dinner tasting menu €15. **€95**

Mammanella Località Biglini ☎339 272 7610, ⓦmammanella.it. Immaculate rooms, including family options, on a farm just outside Alba. Though there isn't a restaurant, meals can be prepared on request. The garden has a children's play area. **€65**

Savona Via Roma 1 ☎0173 440 440, ⓦhotelsavona .com. You'll need to plan ahead to be sure of a room at this four-star establishment, especially during the October festivals. It provides traditional comforts and an excellent breakfast, and has some junior suites. Adjacent parking is available for €6 per night. **€90**, suites **€140**

EATING AND DRINKING

Caffè Umberto Piazza Savona 4 ☎0173 33 994, ⓦcaffeumberto.it. More modestly priced than *Enoclub*, its sister restaurant downstairs, but just as stylish: upstairs it's all about light and airiness with seating on the piazza. The same attention to detail in both the menu and the wine list make this a viable alternative. €25–30 for a two-course meal. Tues–Sun noon–2.30pm & 7–11.30pm.

★ **Enoclub** Piazza Savona 4 ☎0173 33 994, ⓦcaffe umberto.it. To sample the finest of Albese cooking, book a table at this atmospheric and expensive place, which offers Slow Food perfection and flawless service.

Its underground setting, in a bare-brick cellar with an impressive river-stone curtain wall, add to the pleasure. A tasting menu will set you back €40. Tues–Sun noon–2.30pm & 7–11.30pm.

Vincafe Via Vittorio Emanuele 12 ☎0173 364 603, ⓦvincafe.com. For wine by the glass as well as excellent local dishes, try this place, which also offers a lavish complimentary buffet at *aperitivo* time: great value. The decor is a good mix of traditional and contemporary touches, and there are rooms (**€110**) should you wish to prolong your stay. You'll pay €30 for a meal. Daily noon–midnight.

Barolo

The entire picturesque area is dotted with attractive hill-towns, castles and wineries. A few kilometres south of Alba, in the heart of **Le Langhe**, perhaps the most famous spot is **BAROLO**, which gives its name to one of the premier Italian wines. It's a small village with peach- and ochre-washed houses set among extensive vineyards. A steady stream of wealthy gastronomes and wine connoisseurs come here for the **Enoteca Regionale del Barolo** (daily except Thurs: April to mid-Nov 10am–6.30pm; mid-Nov to March 10am–5pm; ☎0173 56 277, ⓦbaroloworld.it) and the **WiMu Wine Museum** (daily except Thurs: April to mid-Nov 10am–7pm; mid-Nov to March 10.30am–6.30pm; ☎0173 386 697, ⓦwimubarolo.it) housed in a turreted castle on Piazza Falletti 1.

ACCOMMODATION AND EATING   BAROLO

★ **Hotel Barolo** Via Lomondo 2 ☎0173 56 354, ⓦhotelbarolo.it. If you want to indulge yourself and stay a while, consider this great establishment featuring

rooms with views and a renowned family-run restaurant, *Brezza*, offering the very finest local cuisine. Relax by the pool and soak up the atmosphere. **€120**

Pollenzo

Though not as famous as Barolo, the pretty village of **POLLENZO**, situated just south of the Alba–Bra road, merits a visit. The buildings at Piazza Vittorio Emanuele 13 are of particular note: once home to the Agenzia di Pollenzo, King Carlo Alberto's headquarters for viticultural trials, they have been acquired by the Slow Food association and now contain the University of Gastronomic Sciences and the **Banca del Vino** (Tues–Sun 10.30am–1pm & 3.30–7.30pm; €2 entry or €8–20 for guided tours and tasting; ⓦbancadelvino.it), as well as a hotel and restaurant. Stored in the Savoy wine cellars, the Wine Bank is precisely what you'd imagine: it stores wines from all over Italy, a vault of the best vintages, as many producers do not keep reserves of their more age-worthy wine. Professional sommeliers guide you through the wine-tasting sessions, which are not solely focused on local produce. It's an essential stopping-point for all wine lovers.

INFORMATION

Tourist office Via della Piana 37 (10am–1pm & 3–6pm, closed Tues; ☎ 0172 422 180, ✉ pollenzo@langheroero.it).

ACCOMMODATION AND EATING

Carpe Noctem et Diem Via Amedeo di Savoia 5 ☎ 0172 458 282, ⓦ carpenoctemetdiem.it. Charming and set in the old royal stables, this family-run hotel has just five rooms, each tastefully furnished and en suite. The owners are excellent hosts. There's a fabulous restaurant downstairs. **€80**

La Corte Albertina Via Amedeo di Savoia 8 ☎ 0172 458 410, ⓦ albergocortealbertina.it. In lush surroundings, this hotel offers a peaceful haven and its rooms have been furnished in keeping with the philosophy of calm. A/c and wi-fi in all rooms. As you would expect from a hotel owned by

Slow Food, its restaurant is exemplary, as is the wine list. **€110**

★ **Ristorante Da Guido** Via Fossano 19 ☎ 0172 458 422, ⓦ guidoristorante.it. Chef Ugo Alciati takes inspiration from traditional recipes learned from his mother and international contemporary culinary techniques. The setting is all bare brick and modern furnishings, with a wonderful huge image of a hand: that of Ugo's mother, Lidia. The duck liver and black truffle tortelli (€25) and guinea fowl in Marsala sauce (€27) are just some of the treats on the menu. €75 for an average meal. Tues–Sun noon–2pm & 7–11pm.

Asti

Some 30km northeast of Alba, the wine continues to flow in **ASTI**, one of the most important towns in medieval times whose province is capital of Italy's sparkling-wine industry and the most famous producer of **Asti Spumante**. Each September, this small town becomes the focus of attention as it gears up for its **Palio**, the oldest in Italy. On the day of the race, the third Sunday in September, there's a thousand-strong **procession** of citizens dressed as their fourteenth-century ancestors, before the frenetic bare-backed horse race around Piazza Alfieri – followed by the awarding of the *palio* (banner) to the winner and all-night partying.

The rest of the year, the piazza and the former Palio site, the Piazza del Palio, together host the region's largest open-air market (Wed & Sat). On the second weekend of September the piazza houses the **Festival delle Sagre** during which producers sell traditional dishes and wines in a reconstructed medieval village. Hundreds of people dress in costume to evoke agricultural life in the Middle Ages.

Collegiata di San Secondo

Mon–Fri 10.45am–5pm, Sat & Sun 12.30–5pm • Free

Behind Piazza Alfieri is the **Collegiata di San Secondo**, a brick basilica with origins in the ninth century, dedicated to the city's patron saint and built on the site of the saint's martyrdom in the second century. Secondo, a Roman officer of the patrician class, who converted to Christianity, was beheaded on March 29 in 119 AD, during the reign of Emperor Hadrian.

Corso Alfieri

The main street, **Corso Alfieri** slices through the town from Piazza Alfieri, to the east of which lies the medieval complex of **San Pietro in Consavia** at Corso Alfieri 2 (Sat & Sun 4–7pm). At the other end of the Corso is the **Torre Rossa**, a medieval tower with a red-and-white chequered brick top, built on the remains of the sixteen-sided Roman tower in which San Secondo was imprisoned and tortured before his martyrdom. The **Duomo** (daily 8.30am–noon & 3–5.30pm; free) is one of the most beautiful examples of Gothic architecture in Piedmont. A fine example of eighteenth-century architecture is the Civic Museum inPalazzo Mazzetti, Corso Alfieri 357 (Tues–Sun 10.30am–6.30pm; €5; ⓦ palazzomazzetti.it). The museum has a fine collection of paintings and frescoes from the seventeenth to the twentieth centuries, and also hosts temporary exhibitions.

INFORMATION

ASTI

Tourist office Piazza Alfieri 29 (Mon–Sat 9am–1pm & 2.30–6.30pm, Sun 9am–1pm; ☎ 0141 530 357, ⓦ astiturismo.it).

ACCOMMODATION

Cavour Piazza Marconi 18 ☎ 0141 530 222, ⓦ hotel cavour-asti.com. The best of the town's affordable options is this conveniently sited hotel. The rooms are pretty spartan and the decor in general is not great, but all rooms are en suite, it is pristine and the staff are friendly. **€80**

Genova Corso Alessandria 26 ☎ 0141 593 197, ⓦ hotel genova.at.it. Slightly cheaper than the *Cavour* is the cheerful though slightly basic *Genova*. Not all rooms have en-suite bathrooms. Larger rooms are available for families and small groups. **€67**

EATING AND DRINKING

If you're into Asti Spumante or want to sample other wines from the region, come during the **wine festival**, the Douja d'Or, held from the second Friday to the third Sunday in September, with tastings in the Palazzo del Collegio.

Gener Neuv Lungo Tanaro dei Pescatori 4 ☎ 0141 557 270, ⓦ generneuv.it. This excellent and rather pricey restaurant serves delicious local cuisine (€45). A popular haunt with the locals, in autumn tourists can taste the wonderful truffles. Tues–Sat noon–2.30pm & 7–10.30pm, Sun (Sept–Dec) noon–2.30pm; closed Aug.

Monna Laura Via Cavour 30 ☎ 0141 594 159. This no-frills pizzeria is centrally located underneath the colonnade of Via Cavour, and boasts speedy service and an informal atmosphere. €15 for pizza, drink and dessert. Tues–Sun noon–2pm & 7–11pm.

Tre Bicchieri Piazza Statuto 37 ☎ 0141 324 137. This fashionable wine bar has an extremely well-stocked cellar, focusing predominantly on locally produced wines. Simple meals available. Tues–Thurs & Sun 7.30am–9.30pm, Fri & Sat 7.30am–1am.

Northern Piemonte

The main attraction of northern Piemonte is the mountains, especially the dramatic Alpine **Valsesia**, which winds up to the foot of Monte Rosa on the Swiss border. On the way is one of the region's most visited sanctuaries, the **Santuario di Oropa** near **Biella**. From here you're well poised for either Piemonte's mountains or those of Valle d'Aosta, a few kilometres west. Worth a slight detour is the magical train ride that starts at **Domodossola**, conveniently en route if you're heading for Switzerland.

Biella and the Santuario di Oropa

To the northeast of Turin lies the provincial capital of **BIELLA**, known for its wool industry, its periphery studded with nineteenth-century industrial chimneys and the hilltop upper town with the mansions and villas of wool barons. Its small medieval quarter, reached by funicular, is worth a visit – and it gives access to the **Santuario di Oropa**, about 11km northwest.

Santuario di Oropa

Daily 8am–noon & 2–7pm • Free, €3 for the museum • Bus #2 from Biella's train station; 40min; see ⓦ atapspa.it for timetables

The **Santuario di Oropa** is the most important Marian sanctuary of the Alps. According to tradition, it was founded in the fourth century by St Eusebio, the first Bishop of Vercelli, to house a black statue of the Madonna and Child. It's the most venerated of Piemonte's shrines, the old basilica being its spiritual centre. However, if you are expecting a secluded mountain hideaway, think again. This sanctuary has developed into a self-sufficient village, with a **museum** containing archeological finds, jewels and liturgical fittings. There are also shops, restaurants and various accommodation options (see p.164).

Walks around the sanctuary

The sanctuary is a good starting-point for walks into the surrounding mountains, and a cable car runs regularly up Monte Mucrone from here as far as the mountain refuge by a small mountain lake, **Lago Mucrone**. A network of marked **trails** begins here: one of the nicest and easiest is the Passeggiata dei Preti, a level path offering good views of the sanctuary. More energetic is the hike up to the summit of Monte Mucrone itself – a two-hour trek.

ARRIVAL AND INFORMATION

By train Trains from Turin run regularly (usually changing at Santhià) and take about 1hr 30min. Biella has two train stations (the main one is San Paolo).

By bus There are five buses a day between Biella and Ivrea (1hr 12min) and eight daily buses to the Santuario

BIELLA AND THE SANTUARIO DI OROPA

(bus #2 from the train station; 40min). See ⓦ atapspa.it for timetables.

Tourist office Piazza Vittorio Veneto 3 (Mon–Fri 8.30am–1pm & 2.30–6pm, Sat 9am–12.30pm & 2.30–5.30pm; ☎ 015 351 128, ⓦ atl.biella.it).

ACCOMMODATION

Albergo Savoia Biella Oropa ☎ 015 849 5131, ⓦ rifugiosavoia.it. A typical mountain hostel which offers traditional food and basic accommodation. Though rather characterless, it's an ideal base for exploring. If you're feeling active, the walk from the sanctuary takes about 1hr 30min. Lazier guests can take the cable car. Closed mid-Sept to May. Dorms €26

Bugella Via Cottolengo 65 ☎ 015 406 607, ⓦ hotel bugella.it. This clean and attractive hotel on the edge of

town has a/c rooms, all en suite. The communal areas are comfortable and homely, and include a bar and reading room. €85

Santuario di Oropa Via Santuario di Oropa 480 ☎ 015 255 51200, ⓦ santuariodioropa.it. The sanctuary has around 350 refurbished rooms, ranging from singles to large rooms for groups and families, to suites. All the beds have iron bedposts and the rooms contain slightly old-fashioned furniture. €52

EATING

La Baracca Via S. Eusebio 12 ☎ 015 21 941, ⓦ baracca ristorante.it. A bar in a converted nineteenth-century factory building that serves authentic Piemonte meals (€20); try the cholesterol-inducing risotto with Borlotti beans, salami and *lardo*. Mon–Fri noon–2.30pm & 7–10pm; closed mid-June to mid-July.

La Civetta Piazza Cucco 10/B ☎ 015 26 342, ⓦ lacivettadibiella.it. This charming husband-and-wife team turns out simple regional and Italian fare (€20–25) in an equally simple setting. On warm evenings sit under the cobbled colonnade. 7–10.30pm; closed Tues & Wed.

Ivrea

IVREA, to the north of Turin, is well worth a visit in the week leading up to Shrove Tuesday, when there's a **carnival** – featuring piping, drumming, masked balls, historic processions and fireworks – that culminates in a bizarre three-day "Battle of the Oranges" when the whole town and hundreds of spectators turn out to pelt each other with oranges – you have to wear a red hat if you don't want to be a target. Each morning there's a traditional handing-out of polenta and cod.

ACCOMMODATION AND EATING

Aquila Nera Corso Nigra 56 ☎ 0125 641 416, ⓦ aquilanera.it. Close to the train station and the Turin–Aosta A4 road, this is a handy base for travellers. The sixteen rooms have options for singles and families. Downstairs is the hotel's pizzeria and restaurant. Half-and full board available. €70

★ **Castello San Giuseppe** Chiaverano di Ivrea ☎ 0125 424 370, ⓦ castellosangiuseppe.it. Set in a converted Carmelite monastery, this fabulous four-star Hotels Relais accommodation is an ideal romantic getaway with four-poster beds, a spa centre and a panoramic pool overlooking the river and countryside. In summer, the hotel restaurant moves outside to the garden gazebo. €156

IVREA

★ **La Mugnaia** Via Arduino 53 ☎ 0125 40 530, ⓦ mugnaia.com. This modern restaurant, with warm colours and friendly service, bases its philosophy in local produce, from the flour for the home-made pasta to the wines from locally sourced vineyards. Gluten-free options available. Try the fettuccine with zucchini flowers, bacon and Taggiasche olives. Meals €35–40. Tues–Sun 11am–2pm & 7.30–11pm.

Spazio Bianco Via Patrioti 17 ☎ 0125 435 857, ⓦ spaziobiancoivrea.it. Set in the heart of the historic centre, this B&B has six rooms, each with a different local theme and colour. Singles, twins and doubles available. Art exhibitions are held here. €110

Valsesia

Heading on into the northern heights, the main road follows the River Sesia to the foot of multi-peaked Monte Rosa, whose massive bulk dominates five Italian valleys and spreads north into Switzerland. **VALSESIA**, the easternmost valley, is also the most dramatic and has been dubbed "Italy's Greenest Valley" – it's worth going for the ride even if you don't want to launch a hiking or skiing assault on the mountains. Flanked by dark pine-wooded slopes topped with a toothed ridge of rock, the road winds up the valley, the perspective changing at every turn.

Alagna

ALAGNA, at the head of the valley, right below Monte Rosa, is the most convenient place to stay. Predominantly modern, it has a cluster of traditional dwellings of the age-old Swiss religious sect known as the Walsers, who have maintained their unique language and culture here for at least seven centuries. Some of the houses still function as farms, while others are holiday homes, with geraniums tumbling from window boxes.

INFORMATION ALAGNA

Tourist office Piazza Grober 1 (Jan–April, June–Sept & Dec Mon & Wed–Fri 9am–noon & 3–6pm, Sat & Sun 9am–1pm & 2.30–6.30pm; May, Oct & Nov Sat & Sun only; ☏0163 922 988, ⊛atlvalsesiavercelli.it).

ACCOMMODATION

Genzianella Via per Casa Prati 2 ☏0163 923 205, ⊛pensionegenzianella.com. Alagna's cheapest three-star hotel is a towering chalet with a wonderful view. There are fourteen rooms, half with a private balcony. A great spot for trekking in summer and skiing in winter. The restaurant offers regional specialities and Italian fare. Half-board available. **€112**

Monte Rosa

There are lots of **walks** among the foothills near Alagna. However, the toughest and most spectacular hikes are those on **Monte Rosa** itself. It's possible to take the cable car up to the Indren glaciers (3275m), from where you can walk to one of the many *rifugi*; most of these are open from June to September and some are open all year, but check at the tourist office in Alagna before setting out. All these walks involve a good deal of scree-crossing and some sobering drops, and none is to be taken lightly – you'll need a good **map** (the IGC map of the four Monte Rosa valleys shows all paths, *rifugi* and pistes, as does the Kompass Monte Rosa map) and you should monitor the weather carefully. There's an ambitious long-distance circuit of Monte Rosa, starting at Alagna and taking in Zermatt across the Swiss border: reckon on five days if you make use of ski lifts and cable cars, and a good deal longer if you don't.

Skiing is organized by Monterosa Ski (☏0125 303 111, ⊛monterosa-ski.com), which has an office in Alagna, and equipment is available for rent in the village. The valleys are also popular for canoeing and rafting, and several centres organize classes and excursions – try Hidronica (☏0163 735 301, ⊛hidronica.com).

Domodossola and over the border

At the foot of the Simplon Pass, and on the main train-line between Milan and Bern, in Switzerland (15 trains daily from Novara), is the little town of **DOMODOSSOLA**. With its arcaded medieval centre and market square, it warrants a visit in its own right, but is more famous as the starting point of a scenic **train ride**, La Vigezzina–Centovalli, which connects Domodossola with **Locarno**, in Switzerland, taking in the vineyards and chestnut forests of the Val Vigezzo and Centovalli along the way. Although the ride is pricier than the regular train (one way €17), it's well worth it; InterRail passes are valid. The journey takes an hour and a half, but you can get off at any of the pretty flower-strewn stations en route; when you want the next train to stop, raise the red-and-white signal on the platform.

The road to Aosta and the eastern valleys

The tributary valleys in **eastern Valle d'Aosta** (ⓦ regione.vda.it) have suffered most from the skiing industry since they are the easiest to access from Turin and Milan. However, hiking is good here, and experienced mountaineers may be lured by the challenge of climbing Monte Rosa and the Matterhorn from **Valtournenche**. In the main Aosta Valley you'll find one of the region's more interesting castles, **Fenis**.

Valtournenche and the Matterhorn (Cervino)

VALTOURNENCHE, headed by the **Matterhorn** (4478m) at the north end and by the town of Chatillon at the southern-central valley end, should be one of the most spectacular of Italy's mountain valleys, but unfortunately the main towns are overdeveloped and hydroelectric works ruin the views on the plains. If you want to climb the Matterhorn you should consider approaching from Zermatt in Switzerland; the Italian route is strictly for experts.

Breuil-Cervinia

Breuil-Cervinia is reached by bus from Chatillon (6 daily; 1hr–1hr 30min; see ⓦ savda.it for timetable)

BREUIL-CERVINIA was one of Italy's first ski resorts, built as part of Mussolini's drive for a healthy nation. In its heyday the ski lifts, soaring to 3500m, broke all records, and its grand hotels ensured the patronage of Europe's wealthy. Today the wealthy are in modern buildings outside the resort, leaving the town for packaged hordes attracted by a large skiing area with lots of easy runs.

Castello di Fenis

Daily: March–June & Sept 9am–7pm; July & Aug 9am–8pm; Oct–Feb Tues–Sat 10am–12.30pm & 1.30–5pm, Sun & public hols 10am–12.30pm & 1.30–6pm • €5, guided tours only • ☏ 0165 764 044

Further up the main valley from Chatillon and overlooked by a ruined castle, the small, pretty village of **NUS** makes a good base for the **Castello di Fenis** 2km away. Backed by wooded hills and encircled by two rows of turreted walls, the castle is a fairy-tale cluster of towers decorated with scalloped arcades. Meanwhile, the Fenis branch of the Challant counts concentrated on refining their living quarters with fine Gothic frescoes; the best of these is in the courtyard, above the elaborate twin staircase that leads to the upper storeys. A courtly St George rescues a damsel in distress from the clutches of a tremendous dragon, overlooked by a tribe of protective saints brandishing moral maxims on curling scrolls.

ARRIVAL AND DEPARTURE — CASTELLO DI FENIS

By train The nearest train station is Nus, 1km from Fenis. Trains run almost hourly to Nus from Ivrea (1hr approx); from Aosta there is a regular service which takes about 10min.

By bus From Nus, there are six buses a day to Fenis, and a more regular direct service from Aosta (see ⓦ savda.it for timetables).

ACCOMMODATION

Agriturismo Le Bonheur Frazione Chez-Croiset ☏ 0165 764 117, ⓦ agriturismo-lebonheur.com. Lying between Nus and Fenis, this farmhouse hotel offers the pleasures of countryside living, with horseriding excursions and lessons available. The rooms are tastefully furnished in rustic style. The restaurant offers hearty fare, including local cheeses and game. Half-board available. €27

La Chatelaine Località Chez Sapin ☏ 0165 764 264, ✉ lachatelaine@mediavallee.it. Open year-round, this charming establishment looks more like a family chalet than a hotel. Standing in the centre of Fenis with the castle looming in the background, it's in a great location. The friendly staff speak English and there is also a restaurant. €70

Aosta and around

AOSTA, the attractive mountain-valley capital of Valle d'Aosta province, is an ideal base for exploring the northwest of the region. Surrounded by the Alps, the town's key attraction is its position, with access to the lovely valleys of the **Parco Nazionale del Gran Paradiso**, the ski resorts of **Mont Blanc** and a sprinkling of castles in between. Founded by the Romans in 25 BC Aosta was primarily an imperial military camp, vestiges of which can be seen in the extensive ruins of some towers and city walls.

2

Piazza E. Chanoux, Porta Praetoria and Teatro Romano

The large, elegant **Piazza E. Chanoux** forms the centre of town, from where Via Porta Praetoria and Via Sant'Anselmo lead east. Separating these two roads, the **Porta Praetoria** is one of the town's most impressive sights: two parallel triple-arched gateways that served as the main entrance into the Roman town. North of the gate is the **Teatro Romano** (daily: April–Aug 9am–8pm; Nov–Jan 9am–5pm; March & Sept 9am–7pm; Oct & Feb 9am–6.30pm; free); an elegant section of the four-storey facade remains, 22m high and pierced with arched windows. Evidence suggests that this Roman theatre was one of the few that was originally roofed.

Sant'Orso

Daily: March–Sept 9.30am–12.30pm & 2–5.45pm; Oct–Feb Mon–Sat 10am–12.30pm & 1.30–5pm, Sun open until 6pm • Free

To the east of the town centre, outside the main town walls off Via Sant'Anselmo, the church of **Sant'Orso** houses a number of eleventh-century frescoes. They're hidden up in the roof where you can examine them at close quarters from specially constructed walkways

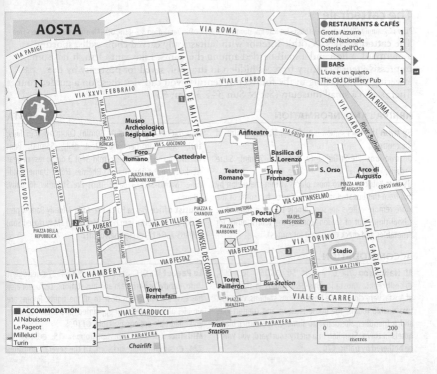

– though you'll need to find the sacristan to get up there (or call him on ☎349 642 9216). The fifteenth-century choir stalls, are carved with a menagerie of holy men and animals, ranging from bats and monkeys to a tonsured monk. There are even better carvings on the capitals of the Romanesque **cloisters** – mostly scenes from the story of Christ.

The Arco di Augusto and Roman bridge

At the far end of Via Sant'Anselmo, the **Arco di Augusto** was erected in 25 BC to honour the Emperor Augustus, after whom the town was named Augusta Praetoria (Aosta is a corruption of Augusta). Though the arch loses something in being stranded in a sea of traffic and topped by a rustic eighteenth-century slate roof, it's a dignified-looking monument. Beyond is a well-preserved **Roman bridge**, its single arch spanning the now-dried-up bed of the River Buthier.

Foro Romano and the Museo Archeologico Regionale

The **Foro Romano** (daily: March–Sept 10.30am–12.30pm & 1.30–6.30pm; Oct–Feb 11am–5pm) on Piazza Giovanni XXIII is now represented mostly by a vaulted passage (cryptoporticus) built under the forum area; such constructions were common enough in Roman forums, probably serving as protected walkways. Bear in mind that the site is not accessible to people with disabilities.

Nearby, the **Museo Archeologico Regionale** (daily 9am–7pm; open Dec 25 & Jan 1 3–7pm; free) has interesting exhibits on the settlements in and around Aosta since Neolithic times. Displays include artefacts of the Celtic Salassi tribe who ended up being sold as slaves by the Romans.

The cattedrale

Piazza Giovanni XXIII • Easter–Sept Mon–Sat 6.30am–noon & 2–7.30pm, Sun 7am–noon & 2–8pm; Oct–March closes 1hr earlier • Free

The **cattedrale** has a Gothic interior with fantastically carved choir stalls, sporting a mermaid, a lion and a snail nestled among the saints. Like Sant'Orso, it has some impressive tenth-century frescoes hidden in the roof, saved for posterity by the lowering of the ceiling in the fourteenth century; you can visit these on a guided tour. There's also a small **museum** (Sat & Sun 3–5.30pm; €3).

ARRIVAL AND INFORMATION

AOSTA

By train The train station is on Piazza Manzetti, south of the centre.

Destinations Pré-St-Didier (9 daily; 40–50min); Sarre (9 daily; 10min).

By bus You can get to most places within the region by bus from the bus station on Via G. Carrel, but some of the more remote valleys are served only by buses running at school times out of season (contact the tourist office for timetables and check ⓦsavda.it for routes).

Destinations Cogne (7 daily; 50min); Courmayeur (6 daily; 1hr); Gran San Bernardo (2–4 daily; 55min); Pont Valsavarenche (mid-June to mid-Sept 3 daily; rest of year weekdays only; 1hr 10min); Rhêmes Notre Dame (mid-June to mid-Sept 3 daily; 1hr); Pré-St-Didier (6 daily; 50min).

Tourist office Piazza Porta Praetoria 3 (daily 9am–7pm; out of season 9am–1pm & 3–7pm; April–May closed Sun; ☎0165 236 627, ⓦregione.vda.it).

ACCOMMODATION

Al Nabuisson Via E. Aubert 50 ☎0165 363 006, ⓦbedbreakfastaosta.it. This B&B stands in the centre of Aosta, very close to the train and bus stations. With just two double rooms, the house is clean and comfortable, and a friendlier alternative to some of the rather bland hotels in town. Standing in a pretty courtyard, you won't be bothered by traffic. **€70**

Le Pageot Via G. Carrel 31 ☎0165 32 433, ⓦlepageot .info. Handy for both train and bus stations, *Le Pageot* also has easy parking and is close to all the sights. Rooms are simple, pleasant and well appointed, and there are triple and quadruple options available. **€110**

Milleluci Località Porossan-Roppoz 15 ☎0165 44 274, ⓦcampingmilleluci.com. Of the several campsites nearby, this is the nearest, just 1km from the historic centre. Set amid mountain views and greenery, with a charming alpine lodge offering meals, bar snacks and services, it has just undergone extensive restoration. **€10pp**

Turin Via Torino 14 ☎ 0165 44 593, ⓦ hotelturin.it. Most centrally located, but starkly modern outside in an almost pre-fab style, and the rooms tend to be quite spartan. Nevertheless, the views of the encircling mountains can be spectacular, so ask for one on an upper storey. **€96**

EATING AND DRINKING

Caffè Nazionale Piazza Chanoux 9 ☎ 0165 262 158. Located under the arcades, part of which constituted a former convent; the main room, round and vaulted, was the chapel. Come for the all-you-can-eat lunchtime buffet (€20) in this most fascinating café. Tues–Sun noon–3pm.

Grotta Azzurra Via Croix de Ville 97 ☎ 0165 262 474. Pizza, pasta and good Italian side dishes keep this place filled to the brim with animated diners. For a pizzeria it has an excellent wine list. Expect to pay €15 a head. Noon–2.30pm & 7–10.30pm; closed Wed.

★ **L'uva e un quarto** Corso Père Laurent 21 ☎ 0165 548 986, ⓦ luvaeunquarto.it. This wonderful winery has recently and deservedly won the "Saveurs du Val d'Aoste" award. It also houses a wide selection of beers, grappas and vinegar, and hosts regular art exhibitions

and champagne evenings. Mon–Fri 4–8.30pm, Sat 10am–1pm & 4-8.30pm.

The Old Distillery Pub Via Près Fosses 7. Tucked away down a narrow side-alley, this place offers a very welcoming and energetic after-dark scene, especially for, but not limited to, the Anglophone crowd. Pub food available. Daily 6pm–2am.

★ **Osteria dell'Oca** Via E. Aubert 15/A ☎ 0165 231 419, ⓦ ristoranteosteriadelloca.com. On a quiet little square with cobblestones, local cuisine here includes pizzas, all topped with fresh ingredients, though a hearty porcini mushroom and chestnut soup is €8. Very atmospheric downstairs in the beautifully restored cellars. It's about €25 for a full meal. Tues–Sun noon–2pm & 7–10.30pm.

West of Aosta: Castello di Sarre

July & Aug daily 9am–8pm; March–June & Sept daily 9am–7pm; Oct–Feb Tues–Sat 10am–12.30pm & 1.30–5pm, Sun till 6pm • €5 • From Aosta there are regular trains (10 daily; 10min; the castle is a 10min walk uphill from the station), and buses on the urban line (ⓦ svap.it) or the regional service (line #7; ⓦ savda.it); walk from the bus stop up the main road and take the unmarked turning just before the tollbooth

West from Aosta are a number of **castles**, the best of which is the thirteenth-century **Castello di Sarre**, the former hunting lodge of **Vittorio Emanuele II**, who, the story goes, actually bought the castle by mistake. He had set his sights on the property of Aymaville opposite, but the agent got confused and ended up buying Sarre instead. The king stamped the halls of the castle with his astounding taste in interior decor, pushing the hunting-lodge motif to its limits, with horns of wild ibex lining the main gallery and thousands of white chamois skulls studding the stuccoed festoons. Pride of place is given to the first ibex slain by the king.

North of Aosta: Colle di Gran San Bernardo

The **Colle di Gran San Bernardo** (2473m) leads the way into Switzerland. Named after the famous monastery that for centuries provided shelter to travellers on the main pilgrim route from Northern Europe to Rome, it was the home of the eponymous big brown-and-white dogs which rescued Alpine travellers in distress. The history of the mountain pass is well documented in the **museum** (June–Sept daily 9am–6pm; €5) housed in the monastery-hospice, although you'll need your passport to visit as it's situated over the border in Switzerland. The pass is open only during summer, but the border is open year-round by way of a tunnel.

The Gran Paradiso National Park

For some of the area's most beautiful mountains and valleys, make for the south, down to the **Gran Paradiso National Park** (ⓦ pngp.it; from Piemonte access is through the village of Ceresole Reale) – Italy's first national park, spread around the valleys at the foot of 4061m-high Monte Gran Paradiso. The park's three valleys – **Cogne**, **Valsavarenche** and **Val di Rhêmes** – are popular, but tourist development has been cautious and well organized. The hotels are good and the campsites not too vast. There are a few mountain *rifugi* and *bivacchi* (unoccupied shelters) between which run well-marked footpaths. Though it's primarily a summer resort for walkers, the cross-country skiing is also good, and every winter a 45km **Gran Paradiso trek** is organized at Cogne (contact the tourist office in Cogne for details). The starting-point for the ascent of Gran Paradiso itself is **Pont** in the Valsavarenche, while Cogne gives access to the Alta Via 2, a long, high-level mountain trail.

GETTING AROUND   THE NATIONAL PARK

Regular **buses** run throughout the year from Aosta to Cogne and Valsavarenche, and along the Val di Rhêmes from mid-June to mid-September (see p.172). If you're using your own transport, access to either of these valleys is easiest from the village of Introd, about 2km from Villeneuve, which is on the main bus route. There's a frequent Cogne–Valnontey service (June 25–July 22 & Aug 29–Sept 11 10 daily; 23 July–28 Aug 22 23 daily; 15min; ⓦ savda.it).

Val di Cogne

Val di Cogne is the principal, most popular and most dramatic section of the park. Its lower reaches are narrow, the road running above the fast-flowing Grand Eyvia River overlooked by sheer mountains. The valley broadens out around the main village, **COGNE**, surrounded by gentle green meadows and glacier-covered mountains.

The tourist office (see below) has maps with descriptions in English of walks, one of which is an easy, scenic stroll that follows the river. It's worth visiting the **Maison de Gerard Dayné** (July & Aug 6 tours daily 10.40am–6.30pm; Sept–June Sat & Sun only; ask at the tourist office or call ☎0165 749 264; €3), a typical nineteenth-century Valdaostan house evocative of the traditional rustic lifestyle.

The small village of **VALNONTEY**, 2.5km southwest of Cogne, is the starting-point for a steep, three-hour walk up to the *Rifugio V. Sella* (☎0165 74 310, ⓦrifugiosella.com; Easter–Sept; 3hr 30min one way), a demanding hike that's incredibly popular in summer. The path passes a **botanical garden** (mid-June to mid-Sept daily 10am–6.30pm; €2.70), with rare alpine flora, then zigzags up through a forest and onto exposed mountainside before reaching the *rifugio*. At the mountain tarn of Lago Loson, a fifteen-minute walk from the *rifugio*, you may well spot ibex or more timid chamois. Hardened hikers who can cope with a stretch of climbing (difficulty "E") can press on over the **Colle de Lauson** to the Val di Rhêmes.

INFORMATION   VAL DI COGNE

Tourist office In the centre of Cogne at Via Bourgeois 34 (daily 9am–1pm & 3–6pm; ☎0165 74 040, ⓦ cogne.org).

ACCOMMODATION

Park accommodation is largely of the mountain-lodge variety and places are regularly monitored to maintain high standards of service. Some close part of the year, and all quickly get booked solid during peak seasons. Most will require half- or full board. There are several campsites, closed from about mid-September to about mid-May, so check exact dates. Many hotels here have restaurants open to non-guests.

★ **Bellevue** Rue Grand Paradis 22, Cogne ☎0165 74 825, ⓦhotelbellevue.it. Alpine ambiance, but with absolute luxury as the keynote. This is a Relais & Chateau property and boasts a world-class health and beauty spa among its many amenities. Three nights minimum. **€280**

Herbetet Frazione Valnontey 52 ☎0165 74 180, ⓦhotelherbetet.com. Swiss-style chalet with rustic mountain decor, including wood-beamed ceilings and cosy comforters. The restaurant features mostly Italian dishes, with a mix of country game and French cuisine. After a hard day's walking, treat yourself to a massage in the wellness centre. Closed mid-Sept to mid-May. B&B, half- or full board available. **€128**

La Barme Frazione Valnontey 8 ☎0165 74 158, ⓦhotellabarme.com. This very rustic stone complex with a small spa is set up for both summer and winter sports,

WILDLIFE IN GRAN PARADISO NATIONAL PARK

Gran Paradiso National Park owes its foundation to King Vittorio Emanuele II, who donated his extensive hunting park to the state in 1922, ensuring that the population of **ibex** that he and his hunters had managed to reduce to near extinction, would after all survive. There are now around 3500 ibex here and about 6000 **chamois**, living most of the year above the tree line but descending to the valleys in winter and spring. The most dramatic sightings are during the mating season in November and December, when you may see pairs of males fighting it out for possession of a female. You might also spy **golden eagles** nesting, and there are a number of rare **alpine flowers**, most of which can be seen in the botanical garden in the Val di Cogne.

2

including horseriding and skiing. The restaurant offers set menus for non-guests, starting at €15. Though the rooms could do with a revamp, the views are stunning. Closed Oct & Nov. €148

Paradisia Frazione Valnontey 36 ☎0165 74 158, ⓦ hotelparadisia.com. Converted mountain chalet offering homely comforts. The decor is a little bland but there is plenty of colour in the well-maintained hotel garden and the mountains beyond. Restaurant services for non-guests, featuring northern Italian and Swiss-style cookery. At breakfast, the home-baked pies are a treat. Closed Oct–Easter. €100

Stambecco Rue des Clementines 21, Cogne ☎0165 74

068, ⓦ hotelstambecco.netcom.com. Alpine chalet in style, very welcoming, with rooms featuring natural wood and warm colours. The bedrooms are cosy but spacious and the views are spectacular. The generous buffet breakfast with home-made cakes will put you in good stead for your day's activities. €98

CAMPING

Gran Paradiso Frazione Valnontey 59 ☎0165 749 204, ⓦ campinggranparadiso.it. Set in shady pines beside the Savara with 120 pitches; bungalows accommodating four people are available if you've forgotten to pack the tent. You can rent trekking and climbing equipment here. Closed mid-Sept to mid-May. Tents €4.50, bungalows €45

EATING

Brasserie du Bon Bec Rue Bourgeois 72, Cogne ☎0165 749 288. Rustic mountain food served by staff in traditional costume in an impressive wood-panelled "hut". Expect lots of local mountain cheese and meat on the menu, which you can wash down with a bottle from the extensive wine list; €25–30 per person. Tues–Sun noon–2pm & 7–10pm.

★ **Lou Ressignon** Rue Mines de Cogne 22, Cogne

☎0165 74 034, ⓦ louressignon.it. This place has been going since 1966, serving hearty soups and stews, with the likes of mountain goat ragout with pappardelle and deer carpaccio also on the menu (€25–30). There's a good wine list too. Attractive rooms are available should you wish to stay over. 12.15–2.15pm & 7.15–9.15pm; closed Mon eve & Tues.

Valsavarenche

Valsavarenche, the next valley west of Val di Cogne, has its own kind of beauty, attracting seasoned walkers. The most popular route is the ascent of **Gran Paradiso**, from Pont. Though considered the easiest of the higher Alps, it is a climb rather than a hike, with no path marked beyond the *Rifugio Vittorio Emanuele II* (☎0165 95 920, ⓦ rifugiovittorioemanuele.com; mid-March to mid-Sept), two and a half hours from Pont. If you feel safer along footpaths, the best hikes are from **Degioz**, a locality of Valsavarenche, up to the *Rifugio Orvielles* (2hr 30min; ☎0165 905 816) and then on to a series of high mountain lakes. This takes seven hours, but you can shorten it by taking path #3a down to Pont. Less taxing is the two-hour walk from Pont towards the glacier **Grand Etret** at the head of the valley.

ACCOMMODATION AND EATING   VALSAVARENCHE

Genzianella Località Pont 1 ☎0165 95 393, ⓦ genzianella.aosta.it. This chalet-style establishment stands in the heart of the Gran Paradiso. The rooms are modest but comfortable, the large restaurant offers typical local dishes, and the terrace has wonderful mountain views. Half- and full board possible. Closed

Oct–May. €84

Parco Nazionale Località Degioz ☎0165 905 706. This is the only hotel in Degioz and has 28 en-suite rooms. Unusually for this category, there are rooms for wheelchair users available. There's also a restaurant, reading room and lovely views. Closed Oct–March. €90

2

Pont Breuil Località Pont ☎0165 95 458, ⓦcamping pontbreuil.com. This campsite has a well-stocked site shop (there's no other for kilometres around); ibex come down to graze on the grassy meadow around the tents. The views are spectacular and you are in the very midst of nature. There are also some chalet rooms. Closed Oct–May. Tents **€5.50**, chalet rooms **€55**

Pub Brasserie l'Abro de la Leunna Frazione Degioz 93 ☎0165 905 732. One of the few places to eat out in the area. The interior is bright and welcoming and makes a nice change from the usual "rustic" theme. Rustic, however, is on the menu, with plenty of meat dishes and hearty soups (€15–20). Summer 11am–1am; winter 11am–5pm, Fri & Sat closes midnight; closed Tues.

Val di Rhêmes

The least touristed of the valleys, **Val di Rhêmes**, is also headed by glaciers. The best place to stay is **BRUIL**, a hamlet at the end of the valley, from where most of the walks start.

There's a fairly easy path along the river to a waterfall, the Cascata di Goletta, and from here you can continue to the mountain lake of Goletta and the *Rifugio Gian Federico Benevolo* (☎0165 936 143, ⓦrifugiobenevolo.com; March–Sept, closed first half of June), taking in some splendid views on the way.

ACCOMMODATION — VAL DI RHÊMES

Chez Lydia Località Bruil 59 ☎0165 936 103, ⓦhotelchezlidia.it. This delightful stone-built hotel has just seven rooms, all en suite and with standard services. The bar is renowned among true connoisseurs for the array of beers on offer. It also has a restaurant serving delicious local dishes. Open year-round. **€76**

Galisia Località Bruil 55 ☎165 936 100, ✉albergo galisia@gmail.com. This two-star establishment has 27 rooms and is a great base for walking and ski excursions. The hotel restaurant (closed Mon in low season) provides typical local fare, such as deer stew and polenta. **€80**

The northwest: around Mont Blanc

Dominated by the snowy peaks of **Mont Blanc** (Monte Bianco to the Italians), the northern reaches of Valle d'Aosta are spectacular and very popular. The most sensational views are from the cable cars that glide and swoop across the mountain to Chamonix in France. The trip is expensive (€55 return, €46 one way), even if you take a bus back to Italy through the 11km-long Mont Blanc tunnel, and the service is often suspended because of bad weather.

La Thuile

You can walk up to the **Testa d'Arpy** – a natural balcony with a bird's-eye view towards Mont Blanc – from **LA THUILE**, on the road to the Petit-St-Bernard Pass into France: from the resort it's just over two hours' walk by path or road to the top of the Colle San Carlo. From here a path leads through woods to Testa d'Arpy in around ten minutes. It's well worth having a good map (IGC *Monte Bianco*) so as to identify the peaks and glaciers spread out before you.

La Thuile itself is a rather overdeveloped resort but it's worth popping into the **tourist office** for maps. Of the mountain walks starting from above the town, the most interesting is the 45-minute hike to **Lago d'Arpy**.

ARRIVAL AND INFORMATION — LA THUILE

By bus There are eleven daily buses from Pré-St-Didier, the first town you reach from Aosta, to La Thuile (25min).

Tourist office Via M. Collomb 36 (daily 9am–12.30pm & 3–6pm; ☎0165 883 049, ⓦlathuile.it).

ACCOMMODATION

Du Glacier Petite Golette 14 ☎0165 884 137, ⓦhotelduglacier.it. Though the rooms are somewhat

anonymous and lacking in charm, they are en suite, spotless, and have wide balconies overlooking the mountain landscape. In high season they may require a stay of between three and seven days. Closed Oct & May–June. **€100**

★ **La Genzianella** Località Colle S. Carlo ☎0165 841 689, ⊛hotelgenzianella.net. At the top of the Colle San Carlo, this hotel is well worth the effort it takes to get here – it's a 2hr walk by path or road from La Thuile. Family run, the rooms are roomy and welcoming. The restaurant serves local cuisine in a warm setting. A great base for walks and treks. **€40**

Courmayeur and Mont Blanc

COURMAYEUR (⊛courmayeur.com) is the smartest and most popular of Valle d'Aosta's ski resorts – the skiing is good and the scenery is magnificent. There are two ski schools here: Monte Bianco Ski and Snowboard School (⊛scuolascimontebianco.com) and the Snowboard and Ski School Courmayeur (⊛scuolascicourmayeur.it). Lift passes start at about €200 for six days. If you've come to hike or take the cable cars across to Chamonix, the most convenient place to stay is **LA PALUD**, 5km outside Courmayeur (3 buses a day; ⊛savda.it).

The **cable car** runs from La Palud to Punta Helbronner all year round, but continues to Chamonix only between July and September (Punta Hellbronner–Chamonix €70 return). There are between ten and twelve departures a day, depending on the time of year, roughly hourly starting at 8.30am – although regularity depends on the weather. Set out early since it's usually cloudy by midday. Even if it's blazing hot in the valley, the temperature plunges to near freezing at the top, so come prepared.

There are good **walks** along the two valleys at the foot of the Mont Blanc glaciers, both of which have seasonal campsites accessible by bus from Courmayeur. In Val Ferret you can walk from Frebouze over Monte de la Saxe, with some incredible views of Mont Blanc en route.

ACCOMMODATION AND EATING — COURMAYEUR AND LA PALUD

Chalet Joli Frazione La Palud ☎0165 869 722, ⊛chaletjoli.com. This charming hotel has various types of room, including a large family room. A homely drawing room means that guests can relax together. Furnishings are tasteful and many of the rooms retain the original stone walls. The on-site restaurant is superb: try the deer meat ragout with tagliatelle. Half-board is available. **€110**

Crampon Via delle Villette 8, Courmayeur ☎0165 842 385, ⊛crampon.it. A lovely chalet hotel, just a few minutes' walk from the town centre. The communal areas are spacious and welcoming: sip your hot chocolate in front of the open fire or enjoy a drink at the bar. The rooms are more functional but still pleasant. Closed May–June & mid-Sept to Dec (open for Christmas). **€130**

Vallée Blanche Località La Palud ☎0165 897 002, ⊛hotelvalleeblanche.com. The Perona family has run this place since 1969 and they are passionate about the mountains and their hotel. This is a great choice for families, with connecting rooms and apartments available. There's free mountain-bike use in summer and a free shuttle bus to the slopes in winter. **€140**

Venezia Via delle Villette 2, Courmayeur ☎0165 842 461. One of the cheapest places to stay is the one-star mountain chalet situated close to the cable lifts in a quiet part of town. Though fairly basic, with no en-suite rooms, the family-run hotel boasts magnificent views and has cosy communal areas. **€51**

Liguria

PIAZZA DE FERRARI, GENOA

Liguria

Sheltering on the seaward side of the mountains that divide Piemonte from the coast, Liguria is the classic introduction to Italy for travellers journeying overland through France. There's an unexpected change as you cross the border: the Italian Riviera, as Liguria's commercially developed strip of coast is known, has more variety of landscape and architecture than its French counterpart, and is generally less frenetic. And if you want to escape the crowds, the mountains, which in places drop sheer to the sea, can offer respite from the standard format of beach, beach and more beach. Teetering on slopes carpeted with olives and vines are isolated mountain villages that retain their own rural culture and cuisine.

The chief city of the region is **Genoa**, an ancient, sprawling port often acclaimed as the most atmospheric of all Italian cities. It has a dense and fascinating old quarter that is complemented by a vibrant social and ethnic mix and a newly energized dockside district. Genoa stands more or less in the middle of Liguria, between two distinct stretches of coast.

REGIONAL FOOD AND WINE

Liguria may lie in the north of Italy, but its benign Mediterranean climate, and to some extent its cooking, belong further south. Traditionally, the recipes from this region make something out of nothing, and the best-known Ligurian speciality is *pesto*, the simplest of dishes, invented by the Genoese to help their long-term sailors fight off scurvy, and made with chopped basil, garlic, pine nuts and grated sharp cheese (pecorino or parmesan) ground up together in olive oil. It's used as a sauce for pasta (often flat *trenette* noodles, or knobbly little potato-flour shapes known as **trofie**), and often served with a few boiled potatoes and green beans, or stirred into soup to make *minestrone alla genovese*. Look out also for pasta, usually *pansotti*, served with a creamy hazelnut sauce – *salsa di noci*; and other typical dishes like **cima alla genovese** (cold, stuffed veal); *tomaxelle* (veal meatballs); *cappon magro* (basically a seafood and vegetable salad served over hard, ship's biscuits); **torta pasqualina** (a spinach-and-cheese pie with eggs); **sardenaira** (a Ligurian pizza made with tomatoes, onions and garlic); and, of course, the ubiquitous golden focaccia bread, often flavoured with olives, sage or rosemary, or covered with toppings. There are lots of things with chickpeas too, which grow abundantly along the coast and crop up most regularly in *farinata*, a kind of chickpea pancake displayed in broad, round baking trays that you'll see everywhere, and in *zuppa di ceci*.

Otherwise, **fish** dominates – not surprising in a region where more than two-thirds of the population lives on the coast. Local **anchovies** are a common antipasto, while pasta with a variety of fish and seafood sauces appears everywhere (mussels, scampi, octopus and clams are all excellent); you'll find delicious *polpo* (octopus), usually served cold with potatoes, good swordfish, and dishes like *ciuppin* or fish soup, *burrida di seppie* (cuttlefish stew), fish *in carpione* (marinated in vinegar and herbs), or just a good *fritto del Golfo* (mixed fish fry-up). Salt cod (*baccalà*) and wind-dried cod (*stoccofisso*) are also big local favourites. Many restaurants in Rapallo and along the Tigullio coast serve *bagnun*, a dish based on anchovies, tomato, garlic, onion and white wine, and in Cinque Terre and Levanto you'll often see **gattafin** – a delicious deep-fried vegetable pasty. Liguria's soil and aspect aren't well suited to vine-growing, although plenty of local **wine** – mainly white – is quite drinkable. The steep, terraced slopes of the Cinque Terre are home to some decent eponymous white wine and a sweet, expensive dessert wine called Sciacchetrà, made from partially dried grapes. From the Riviera di Ponente, look out for the crisp whites of Pigato (from Albenga) and Vermentino (from Imperia), as well as the acclaimed Rossese di Dolceacqua, Liguria's best red.

THE CASINO, SAN REMO

Highlights

❶ **Genoa** With its rabbit warren of medieval streets, revamped port area and clutch of first-rate museums and churches, Genoa could easily justify a week of your time. **See p.180**

❷ **Finale Ligure** If you just want somewhere to relax and spend time swimming and beach-lounging, look no further – this is the classic Ligurian family resort. **See p.196**

❸ **San Remo** With its famous Art Nouveau casino, elegant palm-tree-lined seafront and unique old quarter, San Remo affords a glimpse of old-style Riviera glamour. **See p.198**

❹ **Levanto** In a way it's nothing special, but its large beach, popular with surfers, and its family-friendly, unpretentious centre, make Levanto perhaps the nicest resort on the coast – and a great authentically Italian base for the Cinque Terre. **See p.208**

❺ **Cinque Terre** Five picturesque villages shoehorned into one of the most rugged parts of Liguria's coastline and linked by a highly scenic, coastal walking path. **See p.209**

HIGHLIGHTS ARE MARKED ON THE MAP ON PP.178–179

To the west, the **Riviera di Ponente** is the more developed, a long ribbon of hotels and resorts packed in summer with Italian families. Picking your route carefully means you can avoid the most crowded places, and in any case there's nowhere really overcrowded as long as you avoid August. **San Remo**, the *grande dame* of Riviera resorts, is flanked by hillsides covered with glasshouses, and is a major centre for the worldwide export of flowers; **Albenga** and **Noli** are attractive medieval centres that have also retained a good deal of

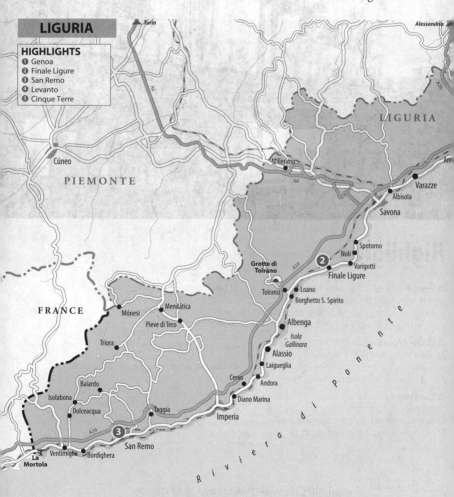

LIGURIA

HIGHLIGHTS
1. Genoa
2. Finale Ligure
3. San Remo
4. Levanto
5. Cinque Terre

character; and **Finale Ligure** is a thoroughly pleasant Mediterranean seaside town. On Genoa's eastern side is the more rugged **Riviera di Levante**, a mix of mountains and fishing villages, some formerly accessible only by boat, which appealed to the early nineteenth-century Romantics who "discovered" the Riviera, preparing the way for other artists and poets and the first package tourists. It's still wild and extremely beautiful in places, although any sense of remoteness has long gone, and again you'd do best to visit outside peak season. Resorts like **Portofino** are among the most expensive in the country, although nearby **Santa Margherita Ligure** makes a great base for exploring the surrounding coastline by train or car, as does the pretty fishing village of **Camogli**. Walks on **Monte di Portofino** and through the dramatic coastal scenery of the **Cinque Terre** take you through scrubland and vineyards for memorable views over broad gulfs and jutting headlands.

In a **car**, the shore road is for the most part a disappointment: the coast is extremely built up, and you get a much better sense of the beauty of the region by taking the east–west autostrada which cuts through the mountains a few kilometres inland by means of a mixture of tunnels and viaducts. Fleeting bursts of daylight between tunnels

give glimpses of the string of resorts along the coast, silvery olive groves and a brilliant sea. It's ten times quicker, too. However, the real plus of Liguria is that so many of the coastal resorts are easily accessible by **train**, with regular services stopping just about everywhere, and, because the track is forced to squeeze along the narrow coastal strip, stations are invariably centrally located.

Genoa

GENOA (**Genova** in Italian) is "the most winding, incoherent of cities, the most entangled topographical ravel in the world". So said Henry James, and the city – Italy's sixth largest, and its biggest port – is still marvellously eclectic, vibrant and full of rough-edged style; indeed "La Superba", as it was known at the height of its powers, boasts more zest and intrigue than all the surrounding coastal resorts put together. Its **old town** is a dense and fascinating warren of medieval alleyways home to large *palazzi* built in the sixteenth and seventeenth centuries by Genoa's wealthy mercantile families and now transformed into museums and art galleries. The tidying-up hasn't sanitized the **old town**, however; the core of the city, between the two stations and the waterfront, is dark and slightly menacing, but the overriding impression is of a buzzing hive of activity – food shops nestled in the portals of former palaces, carpenters' workshops sandwiched between designer furniture outlets, everything surrounded by a crush of people and the squashed vowels of the impenetrable Genoese dialect that has, over the centuries, absorbed elements of Neapolitan, Calabrese and Portuguese. Aside from the cosmopolitan street life, you should seek out the **Cattedrale di San Lorenzo**, the **Palazzo Ducale**, and the Renaissance palaces of **Via Garibaldi** which contain the cream of Genoa's art collections, as well as furniture and decor from the grandest days of the city's past.

Brief history

Genoa made its money at sea, through trade, colonial exploitation and piracy. It was one of the four major Italian maritime republics (the others being Venice, Pisa and Amalfi), and a local superpower with its own well-developed system of government that lasted several hundred years. By the thirteenth century, after playing a major part in the **Crusades**, the Genoese were roaming the Mediterranean, bringing back ideas as well as goods: the city's architects were using Arab pointed arches a century before the rest of Italy. The San Giorgio banking syndicate effectively controlled the city for much of the fifteenth century, and cold-shouldered **Columbus** (who had grown up in Genoa) when he sought funding for his voyages. With Spanish backing, he opened up new Atlantic trade routes that ironically would later reduce Genoa to a backwater. Following foreign invasion, in 1768 the Banco di San Giorgio was forced to sell the Genoese colony of Corsica to the French, and a century later, the city became a hotbed of radicalism: **Mazzini**, one of the main protagonists of the Risorgimento, was born here, and in 1860 **Garibaldi** set sail for Sicily with his "Thousand" from the city's harbour. Around the same time, Italy's industrial revolution began in Genoa, with steelworks and shipyards spreading along the coast. These suffered heavy **bombing** in World War II, and the subsequent economic decline hobbled Genoa for decades. Things started to look up in the 1990s: state funding to celebrate the 500th anniversary

---

THE CARD MUSEI

If you're planning to visit a number of museums, it might be worth investing in the city's **museum card**, or Card Musei, which costs €12 for 24hr (including public transport €13.50), or €16 for 48hr (including public transport €20). It's valid for most of Genoa's museums and gives discounts at others. You can buy the card at the tourist office or from the museums themselves.

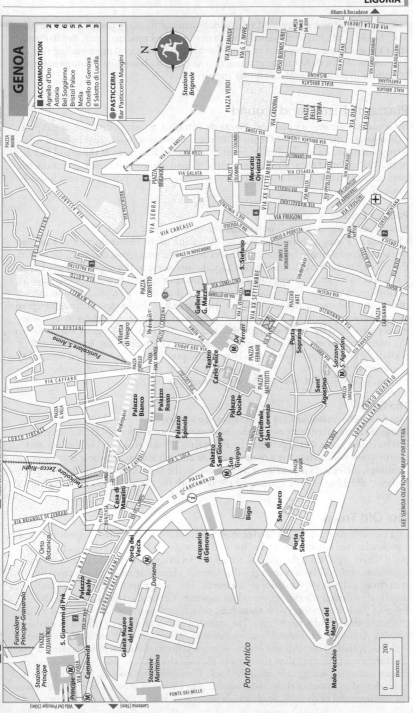

of Columbus's 1492 voyage paid to renovate many of the city's late-Renaissance palaces and the old port area, with Genoa's most famous son of modern times, **Renzo Piano** (best known as the co-designer of Paris's Pompidou Centre), taking a leading role. The results of a twelve-year programme that saw Genoa becoming a **European Capital of Culture** in 2004 are evident all over the city.

Piazza de Ferrari and around

If Genoa has a centre it's probably **Piazza de Ferrari**, a mainly pedestrian, open space that separates the old part of Genoa from the nineteenth-century city. Focused on a large fountain, it's overlooked by a statue of Garibaldi in front of the grand facade of the **Teatro Carlo Felice**, a rather war-torn, messed-about-with building that doesn't have much to recommend it architecturally, but as the city's principal opera house hosts some fine performances.

Palazzo Ducale

Piazza Matteotti 19 • Daily 9am–7pm • Free • ☎ 010 557 4000, ⓦ palazzoducale.genova.it

One side of Piazza de Ferrari is taken up by a flank of the sixteenth-century **Palazzo Ducale** (its main facade faces nearby Piazza Matteotti which you can reach by way of the palace's main arcade). The Palazzo Ducale was home to the doge of Genoa between 1384 and 1515, and its huge vaulted atrium makes a splendid venue for regular exhibitions. During summer, parts of the rest of the building are also open to the public for exhibitions, and you can visit the vast hall of the Maggior Consiglio upstairs, where massive chandeliers hang above the space once occupied by the 400 Genoese nobles who ruled the maritime republic. You can also view the Doge's Chapel, perhaps the most frescoed room of all time, and from there climb up to the **Torre Grimaldi** (early July to Sept Tues–Sun 10am–1pm & 3–6pm; €5) for the views and some of the grimmest dungeons you'll ever see: home for a while to Garibaldi and another Italian patriot, Jacopo Ruffini, who cut his own throat here in 1833.

The Gesù

Piazza Matteotti • Mon–Sat 7am–1pm & 3.30–7.30pm, Sun 8am–1pm & 4–10pm • Free

Piazza de Ferrari feeds through to the more regular open space of Piazza Matteotti. On its corner is the **Gesù**, designed by Pellegrino Tibaldi at the end of the sixteenth century, and which contains a mass of marble and gilt stucco and some fine Baroque paintings, including Guido Reni's *Assumption* in the right aisle and two works by Rubens: *The Miracles of St Ignatius* on the left and *The Circumcision* on the high altar.

The Old Town

Old Genoa's main artery, **Via San Lorenzo**, leads from Piazza Matteotti down to the port, a pedestrianized stretch that makes for a busy evening *passeggiata*, and a handy reference point when negotiating the old city, which it effectively splits in two, an atmospheric confusion of tiny alleyways (*caruggi*) that spreads either side and upwards from the waterfront as far as **Via Garibaldi** to the north. The *caruggi* are lined with high buildings, usually six or seven storeys, set very close together. Grocers, textile workshops and bakeries jostle for position with boutiques, design outlets and goldsmiths amid a flurry of shouts, smells and scrawny cats. The cramped layout of the area reflects its medieval politics. Around the thirteenth and fourteenth centuries, the city's principal families – Doria, Spinola, Grimaldi and Fieschi – marked out certain streets and squares as their territory, even extending their domains to include churches: to pray in someone else's chapel was to risk being stabbed in the back. New buildings on each family's patch had to be slotted in wherever they could, resulting in a maze of crooked alleyways that was the battleground of dynastic feuds which lasted well into the eighteenth century.

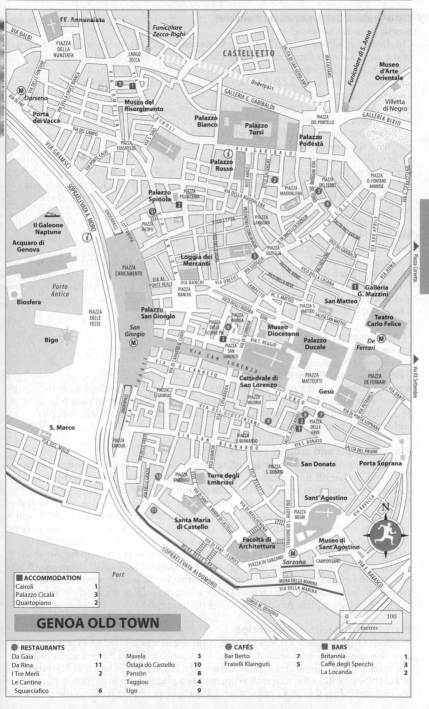

GENOA OLD TOWN

3

▶ Piazza Corvetto

▶ Via XX Settembre

ACCOMMODATION

Cairoli	1
Palazzo Cicala	3
Quartopiano	2

● RESTAURANTS			
Da Gaia	1	Maxela	3
Da Rina	11	Östaja dö Castello	10
I Tre Merli	2	Pansön	8
Le Cantine		Taggiou	4
Squarciafico	6	Ugo	9

● CAFÉS		■ BARS	
Bar Berto	7	Britannia	1
Fratelli Klainguti	5	Caffè degli Specchi	3
		La Locanda	2

Cattedrale di San Lorenzo and around

Piazza San Lorenzo • Daily 9am–noon & 3–6pm • Free

On the eastern side of Via San Lorenzo, the **Cattedrale di San Lorenzo** anchors the square of the same name, its facade an elaborate confection of twisting, fluted columns and black-and-white striped stone that was added by Gothic craftsmen from France in the early thirteenth century. The stripes here, like other examples throughout the city, were a sign of prestige: families could use them only if they had a permit, awarded for "some illustrious deed to the advantage of their native city". While the rest of Genoa's churches were portioned out between the ruling dynasties, the cathedral remained open to all.

The **interior** has some well-preserved Byzantine frescoes of the *Last Judgement* above the main entrance, and is home, off the left aisle, to the large Renaissance chapel of St John the Baptist, whose ashes – legend has it – once rested in the thirteenth-century sarcophagus. After a particularly bad storm in medieval times, priests carried his casket through the city down to the port to placate the sea, and a procession still takes place each June 24 in honour of the saint. Note the central figures of the saint and the Madonna by Sansovino on either side of the sarcophagus.

Museo del Tesoro

Mon–Sat 9am–noon & 3–6pm • €4.50, €6 including Museo Diocesano

Just past the chapel of St John the Baptist and housed in an atmospheric crypt, the **Museo del Tesoro** holds a polished quartz plate on which, legend says, Salome received John the Baptist's severed head, a green bowl brought to Genoa in the eleventh century and believed once to have been the Holy Grail, and a reliquary believed to contain a lock of the Virgin Mary's hair.

Museo Diocesano

Via Tommaso Reggio 20 • Mon–Sat 9am–noon & 3–6pm • €2, €6 including Museo del Tesoro • ☎ 010 254 1250, ⓦ diocesi.genova.it/museodiocesano

Take a look at the **Museo Diocesano**, behind the cathedral, which occupies a partially frescoed cloister and the medieval buildings that surround it, and displays more religious art and sculpture, including paintings by Luca Cambiaso among others, and a dozen or so dyed blue cloths from the early sixteenth century which depict various scenes from the Passion of Christ.

Piazza Soziglia and around

The busiest and more obviously appealing part of old Genoa lies to the north of Via San Lorenzo. Just off the cathedral's square, tiny **Piazza Invrea** gives on to the shopping square of the **Campetto** and adjacent **Via degli Orefici**, "Street of the Goldsmiths". Much of the jewellery here is still made by hand at upper-storey workshops around the Campetto, which links to the genteel sliver of **Piazza Soziglia**, crowded with stalls and café tables. From here **Via Luccoli** heads north, with glitzy boutiques and design outlets galore, while a few streets to the east is the city's prettiest small square, **Piazza San Matteo**. This lay in the territory of the Doria family, who went one step further than merely striping the twelfth-century church of **San Matteo** (Mon–Sat 7.30am–noon & 4–5.30pm; free) and ordered elaborate testimonials to the family's worthiness to be carved on the facade of the church and their adjoining palaces; inside, the tomb of the patriarch and sea captain Andrew Doria lies in the crypt.

Piazza Banchi to Stazione Principe

Via degli Orefici leads down to a thriving commercial area centred on **Piazza Banchi**, a small enclosed square of secondhand books, records, fruit and flowers which was once the heart of the medieval city. Up the steps to the left, the little church of **San Pietro in Banchi** was built in the sixteenth century after a plague; with little money to spare, the city authorities sold plots of commercial space in arcades underneath the church in order to fund construction of the main building. From Piazza Banchi, the animated **Via San Luca** heads north, lined with shops selling counterfeit designer clothes and accessories. The street was in Spinola family territory, and their grand, former residence is now the Galleria Nazionale di Palazzo Spinola (see below). Beyond here lies a kasbah-like quarter that centres on the street of **Via di Pre**, which leads towards the port and the **Stazione Principe**, while to the north the old town is a fair bit seedier, centred on busy **Via della Maddalena**, which skirts the city's thriving red-light trade. Steep lanes rise north of Via della Maddalena, lifting you out of the melee and into the ordered calm of **Via Garibaldi** (see p.186).

Galleria Nazionale di Palazzo Spinola

Piazza Pellicceria 1 • Tues–Sat 8.30am–7.30pm, Sun 1.30–7.30pm • €4, joint ticket with Palazzo Reale €6.50 • ☎ 010 270 5300, ⓦ palazzospinola.it

Just off Via San Luca, is the tucked-away but excellent **Galleria Nazionale di Palazzo Spinola**, whose first two floors are perhaps Genoa's best example of a grand family palace, with original furniture and rooms crammed with high-quality paintings. There are Van Dyck portraits of Matthew, Mark, Luke and John as men of books, a portrait of Paolo Spinola by the Rome-based German painter Angelika Kaufmann, and upstairs an intensely mournful *Ecce Homo* by the Sicilian master Antonello da Messina and the splendid *Adoration of the Magi* by Joos van Cleve, sawn into planks when stolen from the church of San Donato in the 1970s. Don't miss the little terrace, way up on the spine of the roof and shaded with orange and lemon trees.

Museo del Risorgimento

Via Lomellini 11 • Tues–Fri 9am–7pm, Sat 10am–7pm • €4 • ☎ 010 246 5843, ⓦ museidigenova.it

A short walk from the Palazzo Spinola is the **Museo del Risorgimento**, birthplace of one of the most influential activists of Italian Unification, Giuseppe Mazzini, in 1805. As you might expect, this is quite a shrine to the great man and indeed to the Risorgimento in general, with documents and relics from Mazzini's life, lots of paintings and other artworks relating to the Unification struggle, and personal effects from other local heroes, including Mazzini's fellow Genoese, Goffredo Mameli and Nino Bixio.

The Palazzo Reale

Via Balbi 10 • Tues & Wed 9am–1.30pm, Thurs–Sun 9am–7pm • €4, joint ticket with Palazzo Spinola €6.50 • ⓦ palazzorealegenova.it

The vast **Palazzo Reale** was built by the Balbi family in the early seventeenth century and later occupied by the Durazzo dynasty and the Savoyard royals. A large atrium overlooks an elegant courtyard garden, while a grand staircase leads to the ballroom, with gilt stucco ceiling, and several rooms to the left, one of which is a stunning hall of mirrors; Joseph II, Emperor of Austria, is said to have remarked in 1784 that the palace appeared more of a royal residence than his own simple pad back in Vienna. Beyond here are the private quarters of the Duke of Genoa, with the duke's bedchamber featuring a sumptuous Baroque ceiling fresco and an en-suite bathroom holding elegant furniture carved in England in the 1820s. On the other side of the palace are the royal quarters: a chapel gallery behind the ballroom, covered in trompe-l'oeil frescoes from the seventeenth and eighteenth centuries; the adjacent throne room, dotted with dozens of "C.A." monograms in honour of Carlo Alberto, King of Savoy, and two large and dramatic paintings by the Neapolitan master Luca Giordano; and a lavish audience room with a grand portrait of a tight-lipped Caterina Durazzo Balbi painted by Van Dyck in 1624 during his six-year stay in Genoa. Alongside, the king's bedchamber has Van Dyck's first canvas of the *Crucifixion*, also dating from 1624 (though this is occasionally displayed elsewhere), and on the seaward side of the palace, the queen's quarters feature a hyper-naturalistic *St Lawrence* by Bernardo Strozzi and a ghostly pale *Crucifixion* by Luca Giordano. Don't miss also the grand terrace which gives airy views over the port.

Museo delle Culture del Mondo

Corso Dogali 18 • April–Sept Tues–Fri 10am–6pm, Sat & Sun 10am–7pm; Oct–March Tues–Fri 10am–5pm, Sat & Sun 10am–6pm • €6, €14 including Museo del Mare • ☏ 010 272 3820, Ⓦ museidigenova.it

Via Balbi leads eventually to Piazza Acquaverde and the Stazione Principe, but in the heights above the station (and reachable by *ascensore* from the piazza), is one of the city's more overlooked sights, the **Museo delle Culture del Mondo**, housed in the grand neo-Gothic home of the nineteenth-century adventurer Captain D'Albertis, who spent much of his later life filling its rooms with masks, musical instruments, pottery, paintings, stuffed animals and more picked up during voyages to the Americas, Africa and Oceania.

Via San Bernardo to Piazza Sarzano

The section of the old town south of Via San Lorenzo is less visited than the districts to the north, and more residential. Many of Genoa's students and young professionals live in the upper storeys of the old buildings lining Via dei Giustiniani and Via San Bernardo, generating a lively bar culture in the surrounding alleys. From the cathedral and Piazza Matteotti, narrow **Salita Pollaiuoli** plunges you into the gloom between high buildings down to a crossroads with **Via San Bernardo**, one of Genoa's most vibrant old-town streets, with grocers and bakers trading behind the portals of palaces decorated in the fifteenth and sixteenth centuries. On the south side of the crossroads tiny **Piazza San Donato** is overlooked by San Donato, a crumbling, bare Romanesque church with a Roman architrave surviving over its door and an octagonal Byzantine-style campanile, while beyond, Stradone Sant'Agostino was laid out in the eighteenth century and is now home to a quirky array of bars and workshops. At the top, the long, narrow bulge of **Piazza Sarzano** was originally home to Genoa's many rope-making workshops and, owing to its enormous length, is still the scene for medieval-style jousting tournaments. Beyond, Via Ravecca, lined with a collection of cool bars and clubs, leads up to the **Porta Soprana**, a twin-towered stone gateway featuring impressive Gothic arches – beyond which lies the nineteenth-century city.

Museo di Sant'Agostino

Piazza Sarzano • Tues–Fri 9am–7pm, Sat & Sun 10am–7pm • €4 • ☏ 010 251 1263, Ⓦ museidigenova.it

On the left of Piazza Sarzano is the (rebuilt) thirteenth-century church of **Sant'Agostino**, whose unique triangular cloister houses the **Museo di Sant'Agostino**, which displays fragments of sculpture through Genoa's long history. Among the highlights is a fragment of the tomb of Margherita of Brabant, sculpted in 1312 by Giovanni Pisano, the tomb of the first doge of Genoa, Simone Boccanegra, from 1363, and a collection of fifteenth-century paintings by northern-Italian artists.

The Musei di Strada Nuova

When newly made fortunes encouraged Genoa's merchant bankers to move out of the cramped old town in the mid-sixteenth century, artisans' houses were pulled down to make way for the Strada Nuova, later named **Via Garibaldi**. To walk along the surprisingly narrow street is to stroll through a Renaissance architect's drawing pad – sculpted facades, stuccowork and medallions decorate the exteriors of the three-storey *palazzi*, while some of the large courtyards are almost like private squares. Three of the street's finest *palazzi* – Bianco, Rosso and Tursi – have been re-branded the **Musei di Strada Nuova** and together they hold the city's finest collection of old-master paintings. Tickets are available from the office on the ground floor of the Palazzo Tursi.

Palazzo Bianco

Via Garibaldi 11 • Tues–Thurs 9am–7pm, Fri 9am–11pm, Sat & Sun 10am–7pm • €8 combined ticket • Ⓦ museidigenova.it.

The first of the Via Garibaldi palaces that is open to the public, the **Palazzo Bianco** was built between 1530 and 1540 for the important Genoese family, the Grimaldis.

Its gallery houses the largest collection of Genoese and Ligurian painting – including work by Cambiaso, Piola, Castiglione and Castello – alongside works by Flemish and Dutch masters such as Gerard David and Hans Memling.

Palazzo Tursi

Via Garibaldi 9 • Tues–Fri 9am–7pm, Sat & Sun 10am–7pm • €8 combined ticket • ⓦ museidigenova.it.

The Palazzo Bianco provides access to the next-door **Palazzo Tursi**, the largest of Genoa's palaces, with an imposing main courtyard. It's the site of the town hall and as such much of it is closed to the public, but you can see more paintings, ceramics and furniture, and look in on the **Sala Paganiniana**, on the first floor – a couple of rooms dedicated to the great Italian violinist Niccolò Paganini, who was born in Genoa in 1782. The prime exhibits are his two violins – the *cannone*, the great man's Guarneri violin made in 1743, along with a copy of it made in Paris in 1834, which he is said to have preferred.

Palazzo Rosso

Via Garibaldi 18 • Tues–Fri 9am–7pm, Sat & Sun 10am–7pm • €8 combined ticket • ⓦ museidigenova.it.

Across the road from the Palazzo Tursi, the **Palazzo Rosso** has a splendid first-floor picture gallery, with paintings by mainly fifteenth- and sixteenth-century Italian artists – Andrea del Sarto, Mattia Preti, Guercino and a whole room of works by local Bernardo Strozzi – along with a choice few northern-European works by the likes of Roger van der Weyden, Dürer and Gerard David. The rooms on the floor above have been restored to their original Baroque grandeur, bedecked with chandeliers, mirrors, frescoed ceilings and an excess of gilding, and there's a series of splendid portraits by Van Dyck of the Brignole-Sale family, who built the palace in 1671. On the floor above this is a mock-up of the refined twentieth-century apartment of the former director of Genoa's museums, an odd mixture of classic and modern furniture and old masters, and above this a rooftop terrace that offers fantastic views of the city centre.

The Porto Antico

It's a short stroll from Piazza Banchi out into the open spaces of Genoa's old port or **Porto Antico** – more integrated now with the city than it has perhaps ever been, and indeed to some extent totally revitalized over the past two decades, its old warehouses converted into exhibition spaces, concert halls, museums and waterfront cafés and restaurants. The sea once came up to the vaulted arcades of Via Sottoripa, which runs alongside the large pedestrianized space of **Piazza Caricamento**, above which the *sopraelevata*, or elevated highway, shoots along the waterfront above.

Palazzo di San Giorgio

The **Palazzo di San Giorgio** is a brightly painted, fortified palace built in 1260 from the stones of a captured Venetian fortress. After the great sea-battle of Curzola in 1298, the Genoese used the building to keep their Venetian prisoners under lock and key; among them was one Marco Polo, who met a Pisan writer named Rustichello inside and spun tales of adventure to him of worlds beyond the seas. After their release,

---

TICKETS FOR THE PORT ATTRACTIONS

There are lots of **tickets** that combine the Aquarium with the other museums of the Porto Antico, available in various combinations, such as the Aquarium and Galata Museo del Mare for €29 (children €19). You can also buy an **Acquario Village** ticket that covers pretty much everything at the port: the Aquarium, Biosfera, Bigo and Galata Museo del Mare, and gives discounts at restaurants and other attractions, plus free rides on the mini-train that tours the port. This costs €39 (children €27).

Rustichello published the stories in a single volume that became *The Travels of Marco Polo*. These days, the building is home to the harbour authorities, but you can ask the guardian on the door to let you in to see the medieval Sala dei Protettori and beautiful Sala Manica Lunga, whose decor was restored to its thirteenth-century grandeur following bomb damage in World War II.

The Bigo

Elevator March, April, Sept & Oct Mon 2–6pm, Tues–Sun 10am–6pm; June–Aug Mon 4–11pm, Tues–Sun 10am–11pm; Jan, Feb, Nov & Dec Sat & Sun 10am–5pm • €4, children €3, €20/€13 including Aquarium

Beyond the Palazzo di San Giorgio, the visual centrepiece of the resurgent waterfront is the **Bigo** – a curious multi-armed contraption designed by Renzo Piano, intended to recall the harbourside cranes of old. It consists of a tent-roofed exhibition/concert space where waterside performances are given in summer and an ice-skating rink is set up in winter, next to which stands a circular **elevator** that ascends 60m in the air to let visitors see Genoa "as it is seen by the seagulls".

The Acquario di Genova

Ponte Spinola • March–June, Sept & Oct Mon–Fri 9am–7.30pm, Sat & Sun 8.45am–8.30pm; July & Aug daily 8.30am–10pm; Nov–Feb Mon–Fri 9.30am–7.30pm, Sat & Sun 9.30am–8.30pm; last entry 1hr 30min before closing • €19, children (4–12yr) €13 • ☎ 010 23 451, Ⓦ acquariodigenova.it

North of the Bigo, the **Acquario di Genova** is the city's pride and joy, parked like a giant ocean liner on the waterfront, with seventy tanks housing sea creatures from all the world's major habitats, including the world's biggest reconstruction of a Caribbean coral reef, complete with moray eels, turtles and angelfish, and lots of larger beasts too – sharks, dolphins, seals, an enclosure of penguins, and the usual rays in their petting pools. It's a great aquarium by any standards, the second largest in Europe by capacity, and boasts a fashionably ecology-conscious slant and excellent background information in Italian and English.

Biosfera

Ponte Spinola • Daily 10am–5pm, April–Oct open till 7pm • €5 • ☎ 010 234 5659, Ⓦ biosferagenova.it

Alongside the aquarium there's the futuristic-looking **Biosfera**, a steel-and-glass Renzo Piano-designed sphere – a hothouse, basically – housing a small tropical ecosystem, complete with trees, flowers, insects and the odd tropical bird. It's crammed with vegetation inside, warm and atmospheric, and well worth a quick tour – though you can see it all in ten minutes.

Il Galeone Neptune

Porto Antico • Daily 10am–6pm • €5

Moored at the next pier along from the Biosfera, **Il Galeone Neptune** is a kitschy, full-size replica of a seventeenth-century galleon with a huge, colourful Neptune figurehead, and several decks to explore. It's fun to stumble around the low-beamed interior, convincingly dark and cannon-crammed, and then emerge onto the open deck, which is similarly kitted out with cannons, ropes and rigging – and a poop deck to declaim from.

Galata Museo del Mare

Calata de Mari 1 • March–Oct daily except Tues 10am–7.30pm; Nov–Feb Tues–Fri 10am–6pm, Sat & Sun 10am–7.30pm • €12, children €7, €17/€12 including submarine, €29/€19 including aquarium, €14/€9 including Castello di Albertis • ☎ 010 234 5655, Ⓦ galatamuseodelmare.it

About five minutes' walk from the Aquarium, a giant glass building holds the wonderful **Galata Museo del Mare**, one of the best museums in the city, detailing on four floors the history of Genoa and its relationship with the sea. The ground floor covers the age of Christopher Colombus, with portraits of, and even letters by the great mariner, and the age of the Genoese galleys, with lots of background on the oarsmen who powered them and a full-sized replica of one. There are also displays on the silver trade and one of the greatest galley commanders of them all, Andrea Doria. One floor up, there are models of later sailing ships, from the last days of the Genoese republic to the brigantines of the nineteenth century (including another full-size example). However, perhaps the most involving part of the museum is the top-floor exhibition on the **steamship era**, in particular Italian immigration to the US, with authentic and affecting mock-ups of a typical crossing, complete with squalid dorms, first-class cabins and dining quarters, with the ocean rushing past the portholes. Outside, it's worth spending the extra to don a hard hat and climb aboard the moored submarine, whose interior is described in detail with an English audioguide. It's pretty much what you would expect – claustrophobic and tricky to negotiate; you will be glad of the hard hat.

The Stazione Maríttima and Ponte dei Mille

Beyond the redeveloped part of the port lies the fin-de-siècle **Stazione Maríttima**, the ferry terminal for services to Corsica, Sardinia, Sicily and Tunisia (see p.191). Just in front, the **Ponte dei Mille** (Jetty of the Thousand) is so called for **Giuseppe Garibaldi**, ex-mercenary and spaghetti salesman, who persuaded his thousand Red Shirts to set off for Sicily in two clapped-out paddle steamers, armed with just a few rifles and no ammunition. Their mission, to support a Sicilian uprising and unite the island with the mainland states, greatly annoyed some northern politicians, who didn't want anything to do with the undeveloped south.

Villa del Principe

Piazza del Principe 4 • March– Sept Wed–Sun 10am–5pm • €9 • ☎ 010 255 509, ⓦ dopart.it/genova/en

Between the port and the station, and with oddly peaceful, contained gardens, (despite the views over the cranes and containers of the port and the buzzing activity of the *sopraelavata*), the **Villa del Principe** was built in the early 1530s by the sea commander and doge of Genoa Andrea Doria, who made his reputation and fortune attacking Turkish fleets and Barbary pirates and liberating the Genoese republic from the French and Spanish, and whose family was perhaps the republic's most glorious. It's a grand old palace, and often overlooked, which is a pity because it has plenty to recommend it, not least the central **Loggia of the Heroes**, whose walls depict the twelve naval warriors of the illustrious Doria family, bearded heroes in Roman dress who fought and won key naval battles between the thirteenth and fifteenth centuries. Next door the **Hall of the Giants** is decorated with a ceiling fresco showing Jupiter striking the rebellious giants with thunderbolts, an enormous decorative marble chimneypiece, two amazing Belgian tapestries depicting the deeds of Alexander the Great and a picture of an aged, red-eyed Doria that's quite at odds with Bronzino's portrait next door which shows him as a musclebound sea god. The magnificent Golden Gallery beyond has seen better days, but it continues the Roman theme with its Roman generals in each lunette, culminating with Doria himself at the far end, his foot on the head of a beaten Turk. In the opposite wing, Sebastiano del Piombo's striking portrait of Doria is perhaps the best-known representation of the great sea captain, painted in 1526 when he became commander of the papal fleet. Hanging alongside is a portrait of his heir Giamentino, who cuts an elegant and successful figure, although he died while Andrea was still alive. His son Giovanni Andrea inherited the palace and his commands; he's pictured with a dog, a gift of the Spanish king.

The Promenade and Lanterna

Via Milano 134 • Sat & Sun 10am–7pm • €2 • ☎ 010 910 001, ⓦ liguri.org/lanterna

There's a promenade walk you can follow further round the port from the Stazione Maríttima (daily 8am–sunset; free) to Genoa's sixteenth-century lighthouse, the **Lanterna**, which has been restored as a museum. It takes around twenty minutes and once there you can climb the 172 steps to the first terrace, and compare the building with the nearby **Matitone**, a postmodern polygonal tower housing municipal offices whose pointed roof has given it its sardonic nickname, "The Big Pencil".

Modern Genoa

In the nineteenth century, Genoa began to expand beyond its old-town constraints. The newer districts begin with the large, central **Piazza de Ferrari**, from where **Via XX Settembre** runs a straight course east through the commercial centre of the city towards Stazione Brignole. This grand boulevard features big department stores, clothes shops and pavement cafés beneath its arcades, prized delicatessens in the side streets around Stazione Brignole and Piazza Colombo, and a bustling covered **Mercato Orientale** partway along, in the cloisters of an old Augustinian monastery. At the eastern end of Via XX Settembre, the park outside the Stazione Brignole extends south into **Piazza della Vittoria**, a huge and dazzling white square built during the Fascist period that now serves as the long-distance bus station. Walking north from Piazza de Ferrari takes you up to **Piazza Corvetto** – built by the Austrians in the nineteenth century and now a major confluence of traffic and people.

The Villetta di Negro and Museo d'Arte Orientale Edoardo Chiossone

Museum Tues–Fri 9am–7pm, Sat & Sun 10am–7pm • €4 • ⓦ museidigenova.it

On the far side of busy Piazza Corvetto, a thoughtful-looking statue of Giuseppe Mazzini marks the entrance to the **Villetta di Negro**, a lushly landscaped park whose artificial waterfalls and grottoes scale the hill. At the top, the **Museo d'Arte Orientale Edoardo Chiossone** holds a collection of oriental art that includes eighteenth-century sculpture and paintings and samurai armour. Chiossone was a printer and engraver for the Italian mint, and, on the strength of his banknote-engraving skills, he was invited by the Meiji dynasty to establish the Japanese Imperial Mint. He lived in Japan from 1875 until his death in Tokyo in 1898, building up a fascinating and extensive collection.

The funiculars

If you're not satisfied with the view from the Villetta di Negro, you can take the Art Nouveau-style public lift from **Piazza del Portello** up to the **Castelletto**, which offers a great panorama over the port and the roofs of the old town; a **funicular** also leaves from the same place up to the residential **Sant'Anna** district, although the views from here aren't as good (ordinary bus tickets are valid for both). When Genoa ran out of building space, plots for houses were hewn out of the hillside behind, like the steps of an amphitheatre, and the funicular enables you to see these at close quarters, as the carriages edge past people's front windows. Another funicular runs from Largo Zecca, further west, to the suburb of **Righi**, where you can admire vistas of the city below and wander off on any of a number of paths, although locals generally come here to sit in the various panoramic restaurants for extended sessions of family dining.

ARRIVAL AND DEPARTURE   **GENOA**

By plane The Aeroporto Cristoforo Colombo (☏ 010 60151, ⓦ aeroportodigenova.com) is 6km west of the city centre and is connected to it by the Volabus, which runs to Stazione Principe, Piazza de Ferrari and Stazione Brignole roughly every 40min throughout the day; tickets cost €6 and it's about half an hour to Stazione Brignole. Taxis pull up outside the Arrivals building and charge a fixed price of €7 per person to Stazione Principe, €8 to Brignole (minimum 3 people); otherwise a taxi will cost you €20–25 to the city centre.

By train Genoa has two main train stations: Stazione Principe, on Piazza Acquaverde, just north of the port and west of the centre, and Stazione Brignole on Piazza Verdi, east of the old town. Most trains stop at both stations so just use the one that's most convenient, and in any case they're well connected: buses #30, #33 and #37, among others, ply

BOAT TRIPS

There are lots of trips you can do from Genoa's harbour. Consorzio Liguria Viamare (☎010 256 775, ⓦ liguriaviamare.it) operates 45min boat trips around Genoa's port, departing from the quayside by the Aquarium (May–Aug Mon–Fri 7 daily 7.40am–6.40pm, Sat 4 daily 2–6.30pm; €6), and summer excursions east along the Riviera, including San Fruttuoso and Portofino (€20) and the Cinque Terre and Portovenere (€33–35). It also runs regular summer whale-watching trips on Saturdays at 1.15pm (€33 per person). Golfo Paradiso (☎0185 772 091, ⓦ golfoparadiso .it) also runs regular services east along the coast to Recco, Camogli, San Fruttuoso, Portofino and the Cinque Terre.

between the two, and they are also linked by regular trains (and will be one day by metro). Train information is available on ☎06 3000. As for connections, Genoa is on the fast line between Milan and Rome, meaning that you can reach each city in 1hr 30min and 4hr respectively, and La Spezia and Pisa in 1hr and 1hr 40min. Regular, slower trains also ply the coastal routes in both directions.

Destinations Camogli (every 30min; 20–30min); Finale Ligure (every 30min; 45min–1hr); La Spezia (every 30min; 1hr); Levanto (every 30min; 1hr 30min); Milan (hourly; 1hr 30min); Pisa (14 daily; 1hr 40min); Rapallo (every 30min; 30–40min); Rome (every 1–2hr; 4hr); San Remo (every 30min; 2hr); Sestri Levante (every 30min; 1hr); Ventimiglia (every 30min; 2hr 15min–3hr).

By bus Buses heading to the city outskirts, the Riviera and inland arrive on Piazza della Vittoria, a few minutes' walk south of Brignole, though for most places you're better off taking the train.

By ferry Genoa is one of Italy's biggest passenger ports, not just for cruise ships but also serving a range of ferry routes. See ⓦ moby.it, ⓦ gnv.it and ⓦ tirrenia.it for up-to-date schedules.

Destinations Arbatax, Sardinia (2 weekly; 14hr); Barcelona (2 weekly; 18hr); Bastia (1–2 daily; 10hr); Olbia (1–2 daily; 10hr); Palermo (1 weekly; 39hr); Porto Torres (1–2 daily; 13hr); Tunis (3 weekly; 25hr).

GETTING AROUND

By public transport The best way to get around the city is to walk, but you may want to use the city's public transport network at some point. It's mostly made up of buses but there's also a short metro line connecting Piazza de Ferrari to Stazione Principe that can be useful for crossing the city centre – even more so when its planned extension to Stazione Brignole is completed. Tickets cost €1.50 and are valid for 90min. AMT also run the lifts and funiculars that scale the city's many hills; tickets to use these cost €0.80. You can also buy 24hr transport tickets for €4.50 (4 people €9 for 24hr), or a museum card that includes public transport (see p.180). More information is available at ⓦ amt.genova.it.

By car There are a dozen or so central car parks, all of which cost around €1.80/hr, €15/day; the largest is

beneath Piazza della Vittoria (open 24hr); there are several others in and around the Porto Antico. The old quarter is barred to traffic.

Car rental Europcar, Via Cararegis 42 (☎010 595 5428, airport ☎010 650 4881); Hertz, Via E. Ruspoli 78 (☎010 592 101, airport ☎010 651 2422); Maggiore, Corso Sardegna 275 (☎010 839 2153, airport ☎010 651 2467); Sixt, Piazza Giuccardini Rosso (☎010 651 2716, airport ☎010 651 2111).

By taxi Taxi fares start at €5 plus 0.90c per km within the city, although prices from the airport are fixed for groups (see opposite). There are taxi stands all over the city centre, principally outside Stazione Brignole and Stazione Principe, Piazza de Ferrari, Piazza Dante, Piazza Caricamento and Piazza Nunziata, among others. Or call ☎010 5966.

INFORMATION

Tourist offices The most central tourist office is at Via Garibaldi 12 (daily 9am––6.30pm; ☎010 557 2903,

ⓦ genova-turismo.it). There's also a kiosk on Piazza Caricamento (daily 9.30am–6.30pm; ☎010 557 4200).

CITY TOURS

Various operators offer tours of Genoa, all starting from Piazza Caricamento. Pippo run a **mini-train** around the city centre (40min; Mon–Fri 10am–5pm, Sat & Sun 10am–8pm; adults €7, children €3.50; ⓦ treninopippo.it); **Citysightseeing Genova** organize hour-long **open-top bus** tours with commentary (March–Nov daily 9.30am–5pm every 30min; €15, children €8; ⓦ city-sightseeing.com); and at weekends the tourist office runs walking tours around the old town (€12, 12–18yr €8, under-12s free; ⓦ genova-turismo.it).

ACCOMMODATION

Genoa's not the greatest place to find somewhere to stay, with a choice of characterless chain hotels and characterful but dowdy budget choices and not much in between. The area just west of Stazione Brignole (Piazza Colombo and Via XX Settembre) is preferable to anything around Stazione Principe, and there's a handful of quality hotels in the old quarter; though you should steer clear of the one-star places down by the port (mostly on and beyond Via di Prè).

Agnello d'Oro Vico Monachette 6 ☎010 246 2084, ⓦhotelagnellodoro.it; map p.181. Not a bad location just off Via Balbi, close to Stazione Principe and only 10min or so from the heart of Genoa's old town, this place has spacious, modernized rooms – some with balconies – and free wi-fi throughout. €70

Astoria Piazza Brignole 4 ☎010 873 316, ⓦhotel astoriagenova.it; map p.181. A reliable and convenient choice, a short walk from Stazione Brignole, with large, plainly furnished rooms and big, comfy public spaces. A little bit tired in places, but with a bit more character than most, and a decent location. Free wi-fi throughout. €80

Bel Soggiorno Via XX Settembre 19/2 ☎010 542 880, ⓦbelsoggiornohotel.com; map p.181. Run by a gregarious German woman (who speaks English), this first-floor B&B is a welcoming place, with a cosy lobby and breakfast room, and although the rooms are a little lacking in character, the warm welcome more than makes up for it. Not a bad location either. €74

Bristol Palace Via XX Settembre 35 ☎010 592 541, ⓦhotelbristolpalace.it; map p.181. Formerly one of the city's posher options, this is still a decent hotel, although its slightly tired air means it's often possible to pick up decent bargains. Rooms are spacious and well equipped, bathrooms have baths and wi-fi is free throughout – and the lovely elliptical staircase that stretches up to its nineteenth-century roof is worth looking in for alone. The location, too, handy for both old town and new, is excellent. €139

Cairoli Via Cairoli 14/4 ☎010 246 1454, ⓦhotelcairoli genova.com; map p.183. A superior three-star, with a choice of doubles, triples and family rooms, all brightly furnished, modern, en-suite and soundproof. The location, on the edge of the old town but handyish for Principe station, is excellent, and there's also a roof terrace and two apartments for rent. One of the city's best options. €70

Il Salotto di Lucilla Passo Palestro 3/5 ☎010 882 391, ⓦilsalottodilucilla.com; map p.181. A quiet, elegant B&B with a lovely sitting room and great breakfasts, right in the heart of town. There are three rooms, two doubles and a twin, with private bathrooms and TV, free wi-fi access

and a comfy drawing room. Very popular so be sure to book in advance. €85

Melia Via Corsica 5 ☎010 531 5111, ⓦmelia-hotels .com; map p.181. Housed in a grand, black Fascist-era building in the leafy Carignano neighbourhood, the sleek lines of this large (99 rooms), contemporary hotel are spot-on. Choose from standard or much larger deluxe doubles, both of which have flat-screen TV, wi-fi (with line connection) and slick bathrooms with TV screens that project onto the mirrors at the touch of a remote. There's a comfy bar, a restaurant, a gym and a pool. Good if you want somewhere slightly apart from Genoa's hubbub, yet only a 5min walk from Piazza de Ferrari. €173

Ostello di Genova Via Giovanni Costanzi ☎010 242 2457, ⓦostellogenova.it; from Stazione Principe take bus #35, then switch at the first stop on Via Napoli to bus #40 or #640, or from Stazione Brignole take bus #40 or #640 all the way; map p.181. Genoa's HI hostel is clean and well-run, and has free wi-fi, although its out-of-town location means you will be heavily reliant on buses. It's up in the hills of Righi, north of the centre. Check-in is from 2.30pm–midnight. Dorms €17, doubles €50

Palazzo Cicala Piazza San Lorenzo ☎010 251 8824, ⓦpalazzocicala.it; map p.183. You couldn't be more central at this boutiquey option, tucked away on the first floor of a *palazzo* in the corner of the cathedral's square. The public areas are self-consciously contemporary, and so are the rooms, which are nicely done if slightly spartan. The nice thing is you always have the feeling you're staying in an old palace, with big old rooms with high ceilings and fancy stuccowork – with only the free wi-fi to bring you back to reality. €149

Quartopiano Piazza di Pellicceria 2/4 ☎010 928 9738, ⓦquarto-piano.it; map p.183. In a great location bang in the heart of the old town, yet an oasis of peace and elegance, with ultra-stylish, almost minimalist rooms with bang-on bathrooms and a lovely contemporary sitting room to coolly make the most of the free wi-fi connection. There's an outside terrace too. It's a bit of a hike, but this is one of the best choices in this part of town. €90

GENOA ADDRESSES

Genoa is one of the handful of Italian cities with a double system of street-numbering: commercial establishments, such as bars and restaurants, have **red** numbers (*rosso*), while all other buildings have **black** numbers (*nero*) – and the two systems don't run in tandem. This means, for example, that Via Banchi 35/R might be next door to Via Banchi 89/N, but several hundred metres from Via Banchi 33/N.

EATING AND DRINKING

Most Italian cities are great places to eat, but Genoa is one of the best, with a fantastic range of cheap trattorias and upscale restaurants. You can eat *farinata* and focaccia from street outlets all over, though perhaps more readily in the old town, where there is a good choice of places to enjoy *pasta al pesto, pansotti alle noce* and any number of great fish and seafood dishes.

CAFÉS AND PASTICCERIE

Bar Berto Piazza delle Erbe 6/R ☎010 275 8157; map p.183. Narrow little stand-up café-bar founded in 1904 by Signor Berto who walked some 15km west to the ceramics centre of Albisola in order to collect colourful bits of broken tile to decorate the walls. There's lots of seating outside on the pedestrianized square, and it's a busy, vaguely trendy spot for coffee, beer or a reasonably priced light meal, with decent pizzas from €6 and pasta dishes from about €8. Mon–Thurs 9am–1am, Fri–Sun 9am–2am.

Bar Pasticceria Mangini Piazza Corvetto 3 ☎010 564 013; map p.181. One of Genoa's most venerable *pasticcerie*, in business since the early 1800s and still top-notch today, with a fantastic array of pastries and seats outside at which to enjoy them. Daily 8am–7.30pm.

Caffè degli Specchi Salita Pollaiuoli 43/R ☎010 246 8193; map p.183. This has been a prime spot since 1917 for Genoese artists, writers and intellectuals to take coffee while admiring themselves in the mirrors (*specchi*) that cover the magnificent tiled interior. It's both a bar, with a few seats downstairs, at which you can get a panino or focaccia, and an upstairs restaurant which serves a changing chalkboard of hot dishes from about €8. Great for lunch, and very popular. Mon–Fri 7am–9pm, Sat 8am–9pm.

Fratelli Klainguti Piazza Soziglia 98–100/R ☎010 860 2628; map p.183. An Austrian-style café dating from 1828, with cakes, coffee and ice cream under chandeliers and tables on the square outside. A good spot for lunch – it serves sandwiches, pasta dishes and salads – and breakfast: they still produce the hazelnut croissant known as a Falstaff, much esteemed by Giuseppe Verdi, who spent forty winters in Genoa ("Thanks for the Falstaff, much better than mine," he wrote to the bakers). Daily 8am–8pm.

RESTAURANTS

★ **Da Gaia** Vicolo dell'Argento 13 ☎010 246 1629; map p.183. Tucked away down a slender alley, this is a classic, brightly lit neighbourhood trattoria, and a good place to try authentic Ligurian food, with starters and antipasti for €10–12 and main courses for €10–18. They do a generous and powerful *trofie al pesto*, Ligurian-style rabbit and great *tomaxelle* (veal rolls). It's everything an Italian restaurant should be: homely, child-friendly, and with good, properly regional cooking. Mon–Fri 12.30–2.30pm & 7–10.30pm, Sat 7–10.30pm only.

Da Rina Mura delle Grazie 3/R ☎010 246 6475, ⓦristorantedarina.it; map p.183. Family-run and expertly so, *Da Rina* has been going for sixty years and is what passes

for posh in Genoa, serving simple, high-quality Genoese cooking down near the waterfront. There's nothing like tucking into their fish soup or *pansotti alle noce* in the wonderfully serene dining room while glimpsing the rushing traffic outside. Prices are high to moderate, the clientele ever-so-slightly middle-aged, but the food can't be faulted. Mostly fish, though with a few meat dishes – steak, rabbit – too. Tues–Sun 12.30–2.30pm & 7–10.30pm; closed Aug.

I Tre Merli Via Dietro il Coro della Maddalena 26/R ☎010 247 4095, ⓦitremerli.it; map p.183. Despite its location in the heart of the red-light district, this is one of the city's best choices, serving Ligurian cuisine with an innovative twist in a cool, contemporary conversion of an ancient wine shop and stable. They do great *cappon magro* (€14), rabbit (€16), fish soup (€22) and octopus salad (€12), with lots of different focaccie to start (including the cheesy Recco variety). A huge wine list, too, plus excellent artisanal Italian beers by Via dei Birrai. Also with branches down on the seafront (*I Tre Merli al Porto Antico*; ☎010 246 4416), in nearby Camogli, and, er, New York City. Mon–Fri 12.30–3pm & 7.30–11pm, Sat 7.30–11pm.

Le Cantine Squarciafico Piazza Invrea 3/R ☎010 247 0823, ⓦsquarciafico.it; map p.183. Atmospheric *cantina* in the basement wine cellar of a fifteenth-century mansion just off Piazza San Lorenzo. Innovative, carefully prepared food and a great wine list complement each other perfectly, though it is on the expensive side. Daily 12.30–2.30pm & 7.30–11pm; often closed for part of Aug.

Maxela Vico Inferiore del Ferro 9 ☎010 247 4209, ⓦmaxela.it; map p.183. There's been a restaurant in this building since 1790. The latest, *Maxela*, is part of a small chain, and specializes in meat dishes, with big steaks, odd bun-less burgers and various offal dishes, served under a stripped-down old vaulting. There are a few pasta dishes on the menu too. Moderately priced, with mains around €12–18. Mon–Sat 12.30–2.30pm & 7–10.30pm.

Östaja dö Castello Salita S. Maria di Castello 32/R ☎010 246 8980; map p.183. This is a great old-town, family-run trattoria serving good, inexpensive fish and seafood specialities, such as octopus with potatoes and grilled prawns. Pasta dishes €9–12, mains €10–12. Mon–Sat noon–3pm & 7–10pm.

Pansön Piazza delle Erbe 5/R ☎010 246 8903, ⓦristorantepanson.com; map p.183. Venerable Genoese institution, in the same family since 1790, with an attractive location on this tucked-away yet lively piazza. The food is excellent, if highly traditional. Mon–Sat 12.30–2.30pm & 7–10.30pm, Sun 12.30–2.30pm only.

3

Taggiou Via Superiore del Ferroi 8 ☎010 275 9225, ⓦtaggiou.it; map p.183. More of a wine bar than a restaurant, but very popular, drawing crowds at lunch and dinner for its great choice of Italian wine, plates of cold cuts and cheese and blackboard of hot dishes – typically various pastas, *polpettone* or *involtini*. A good old-town choice, for lunch especially when its €6.50 specials (main dish plus water or wine and a coffee) are excellent value. Mon–Sat noon–3pm & 6pm–midnight.

Ugo Via Giustiniani 86/R ☎010 246 9302; map p.183. Convivial, reasonably priced trattoria in the heart of the old town just off Via San Lorenzo, with a boisterous, friendly group of regulars who pack in at shared tables to wolf down the Genoese and Ligurian dishes – heavy on pesto, pasta with *salsa di noci* and seafood – try the *frittura del Golfo*.

Simple pricing – *primi* are €10, *secondi* €12; or get two courses for €16. Tues–Sat noon–3pm & 7.30–11pm.

BARS

Britannia Vico Casana 76 ☎010 247 4532; map p.183. Right across from the opera house, this long-standing Genova watering-hole is a cosy, reasonably authentic approximation of an English pub, serving sandwiches and toasties from €3.50, mains like spaghetti and burgers, fish and chips and omelettes, from €8.50. Mon–Sat 11am–1am.

La Locanda Salita Pollaiuoli 13 ☎348 135 1367; map p.183. Buzzy bar with lots of seats in the back, though most people tend to congregate in the front bar or outside on the street. Beers and cocktails for €5, and focaccia to soak up the drinks, in a lively old-town hot spot. Daily 4pm–2am.

DIRECTORY

Bookshops Feltrinelli, Via Ceccardi 16 (Mon–9am–8pm, Sun 10am–1pm & 3–8pm; ☎010 573 331), has English-language paperbacks and other books.

Consulates UK Piazza Verdi 6/A ☎010 574 0071; US, Via Dante 2 ☎010 584 492.

Football Genoa has two major teams – Genoa, the oldest team in Italy, founded in 1893 as the Genoa Cricket and Athletic Club, originally for British expats only, and marginally less popular Sampdoria, formerly a top-flight club but now languishing in Serie B. Both teams play at the 36,000-capacity Luigi Ferraris stadium, behind Stazione Brignole. Bus #12 from Piazza Caricamento, bus #14 from Piazza de Ferrari, or bus #480 or #482 from

Stazione Principe pass near the stadium, or you can walk it in 15–20min from Brignole.

Hospitals Ospedale Galliera, Via Volta Alessandro 8 (☎010 56 321), is the city's most central hospital, situated just south of Piazza Vittoria. In an emergency, call ☎118.

Pharmacies Farmacia Pescetto, close to Stazione Principe at Via Balbi 185/R (☎010 261 609), is open 24hr.

Police Carabinieri ☎112; Polizia ☎113; coastguard police ☎010 27 771. Genoa's police HQ is at Via Armando Diaz 2 (☎010 53 661).

Post office Via Dante 4B/R (Mon–Fri 8.25am–7.10pm, Sat 8.25am–12.35pm; two desks with English-speaking staff). Sub-post offices are at both train stations, open same hours.

The Riviera di Ponente

The coast west of Genoa, the **Riviera di Ponente**, is Liguria's most built-up stretch, home to practical, unpretentious resorts, functional towns and the occasional attractive medieval quarter. In some ways it's the ideal location for the perfect family holiday – the beaches are sandy and the prices low – and thousands of Italians come here every year for just that. Almost every settlement along the stretch of coast from Genoa to San Remo is a resort of some kind, and extremely busy during July and especially August, when prices are at their highest. But there are some gems among the run-of-the-mill holiday towns, not least the likeable resort of **Finale Ligure**, nearby **Noli**, with its alley-laden old centre, the medieval centre of **Albenga** and the grand old resort of **San Remo**, which can also make a good base for exploring sections of the **Alta Via dei Monti Liguri** (see box, p.201).

THE TRAIN RIDE TO CASELLA

There's no better way to get into inland Liguria than by taking the narrow-gauge **trains** which leave roughly every 90 minutes from Genoa's Piazza Manin (reachable by bus #34 from Stazione Principe). They start off climbing through the Val Bisagno and coil northwards up to **Casella**, in a wooded dell at the foot of Monte Maggio, just over an hour from Genoa. Return fares to Casella are €2.30 (☎010 837 321, ⓦferroviagenovacasella.it). Casella is the trailhead for a number of hiking routes in the picturesque **Valle Scrivia** (ⓦaltavallescrivia.it) and has a couple of hotels and half a dozen restaurants.

Savona

Some 50km along the coast from Genoa, **SAVONA** is the Ligurian coast at its most functional, a port city that was substantially rebuilt after a hammering in World War II. However, its ugly outskirts hide a picturesque if small medieval centre, and although you're unlikely to want to stay the night, it is worth a look, especially when it's taken over on summer Saturdays by a huge antiques and bric-a-brac market. The town's main claim to fame is as the "Città dei Papi" (City of Popes), after local boy Francesco Della Rovere, who became Pope Sixtus IV in 1471, and his nephew Giuliano, who became Pope Julius II in 1503. Both men left a huge legacy, not least in the Vatican's Sistine Chapel, which Sixtus IV built and Julius II famously commissioned Michelangelo to decorate.

The Duomo

Piazza del Duomo • Daily 10am–12.30pm & 4–6pm • Free

Savona's atmospheric old quarter lies to the right of the main, arcaded Via Paleocapa, and focuses on the **Duomo**, a huge building that was constructed in the early seventeenth century to replace an earlier church destroyed by the Genoese. It was a Franciscan convent, and is the city's main memorial to the powerful Delle Rovere family – in the church itself and also in its own Sistine Chapel, off the cloister, which was built as a funerary monument by Pope Sixtus IV for his parents. Their simple Renaissance memorials survive, along with some fragments of fresco, though the rest has since been dolled up in a flashy Rococo style that's quite at odds with the cathedral. Inside, which there's a column from the original church frescoed with a Madonna and Child in a side chapel, although the major remnant is the well-preserved inlaid wood choir, an early sixteenth-century gift of Sixtus IV's nephew Julius II, which shows the Apostles and other saints with Christ at the centre flanked on either side by Sixtus IV and Julius II.

Fortezza di Priamàr

Corso Giuseppe Mazzini 1 • Daily 9am–6.30pm • ☎ 019 831 0325, ⓦ museoarcheosavona.it

Across the road from the old town, right by the sea, the huge **Fortezza di Priamàr** was built in 1528 by the Genoese as a sign of their superiority over the defeated Savonese. It's a sprawling complex, with grassy turrets, keeps and courtyards, the ruins of a cathedral at the top and of a monastery in front, although the main things to see are two museums: the second-floor **Museo d'Arte Sandro Pertini** (Mon 9.30am–12.30pm; €2.50), displaying modern Italian art collected by the one-time president of Italy, and the **Museo Storico Archeologico** (summer Tues–Sat 10am–noon & 3–5pm, Sun 3–5pm; winter Wed–Fri 9.30am–12.30pm & 2.30–4.30pm, Sat & Sun 10.30am–3pm; €2.50), which has Greek and Etruscan bits and bobs along with some Islamic and Byzantine ceramics. Just below and to the right of the fortress there's a small town beach.

ARRIVAL AND INFORMATION

By train Savona's train station is a 10min walk from the old quarter, across the River Letimbro: go left out of the station and follow the road across the river and turn right just past the large car park to get to the end of Via Paleocapa.

Tourist office Via Paleocapa 76 (Mon–Sat 9am–12.30pm & 3–7pm, closed Tues & Wed Sept–June; ☎ 019 840 2321, ⓦ turismo.provincia.savona.it).

ACCOMMODATION AND EATING

Café Due Merli Piazza della Maddalena 1/R ☎ 019 833 5010. Good place for a coffee or a drink, with outside tables on this triangular piazza. Daily 8am–10pm.

Hotel Riviera Suisse Via Paleocapa 24 ☎ 019 850 853, ⓦ rivierasuissehotel.it. It's probably not the best hotel in town, but it's maybe the most convenient, situated at the end of Savona's main street and just a 5–10min walk from the train station. Rooms are decent enough, as is the service. €70

Vino e Farinata Via Pia 15/R. Great *farinata* place, with a takeaway counter and a few seats inside and dining room out the back serving a more extensive menu – *frittura del Golfo*, squid, fish soup, among other things. Service can be a bit hit-and-miss, but the food is pretty good – and you'll pay less than €20 even if you have a couple of courses. Tues–Sat noon–3pm & 6–9.30pm; closed Sept.

3

Finale Ligure

FINALE LIGURE, half an hour from Savona, is a full-on Italian resort, in summer crowded with Italian families who pack the outdoor restaurants, seafront fairground and open-air cinema, or take an extended *passeggiata* along the promenade and through the old alleys. It's a thoroughly enjoyable place for all that, with a long sandy beach that stretches the entire length of the town and a busy, buzzy vibe that lasts long into the evening.

The main part of town is **Finalmarina**, with a promenade lined with palms, and a small quarter of narrow shopping streets set back from the seafront, focused on the arcaded Piazza Vittorio Emanuele II in the middle. At the eastern end of town, **Finalpia** is a small district on the other side of the River Sciusa, with the twelfth-century church of Santa Maria di Pia (rebuilt in florid, early eighteenth-century style) and the adjacent sixteenth-century cloistered abbey at its centre; while **Finalborgo**, perhaps the most attractive part of Finale, is a medieval walled quarter 2km inland, overlooked by bare rock-faces that are a favourite with free climbers who gather at *Bar Centrale* in Finalborgo's Piazza Garibaldi at weekends. Finalborgo has quite a chi-chi air these days, and is a nice place to eat and shop – there are free buses from Finalpia (opposite the *Hotel Boncardo*) and the bottom of Via Brunenghi (near the station) every forty minutes in summer. Once there you can just wander its old streets, or take a look at the array of prehistoric remains and other artefacts unearthed locally at the **Museo Archeologico di Finale** in the cloisters of the convent of Santa Caterina (Tues–Sun: July & Aug 10am–noon & 4–7pm; Sept–June 9am–noon & 2.30–5pm; €4).

ARRIVAL AND INFORMATION

By train Finale Ligure's train station is at the western end of Finalmarina, the main part of town, just a 5min walk from the main street and the seafront.

By bus Buses leave Finalmarina every 15min for Finalborgo

and you can pick them up at the train station.

Tourist office On the seafront boulevard at Via S. Pietro 14 (Mon–Sat 9am–12.30pm & 3–7pm; ☎ 019 681 019).

ACCOMMODATION

★**Castello Vuillermin** Via Caviglia 46 ☎019 690 515, @finaleligurehostel@libero.it. This HI hostel occupies an old castle high above the train station and has marvellous views out to sea. Downside if you're backpacking is the hike to get up here, and there are no cooking facilities, but otherwise the place is a cut above most hostels. Closed mid-Oct to mid-March. Dorms €13

Giardino Via Pertico 49 ☎019 692 815, @giardinofi @libero.it. This seafront hotel is a good budget choice considering its central location, with a wide choice of rooms, some of which have shared bathrooms. €60

Medusa Vico Bricchieri 7 ☎019 692 545, ⓦmedusa hotel.it. A good option if you want slightly more comfort and to be right on the beach, with a friendly welcome and recently renovated rooms – though the best ones with sea views are of course more expensive. Free wi-fi. €100

Villa Gina Via Brunenghi 6 ☎019 691 297, ⓦvillagina .it. Just 2min from the station on the other side of the

railway tracks, *Villa Gina* has well-kept rooms with a/c and wi-fi and comfy public areas downstairs, looked after by a nice elderly lady. €90

CAMPING

Camping del Mulino Via Castello, Finalpia ☎019 601 669, ⓦcampingmulino.it. A 10min walk inland from the centre of Finalpia, up winding Via Castello, this site has shady pitches, great views and well-priced bungalows (sleeping 2–4) too. Pitches €24, bungalows €70

Eurocamping Via Calvisio 37, Finalpia ☎019 601 240, ⓦeurocampingcalvisio.it. This well-run riverside site, about 1500m inland from the seafront at Finalpia, has pitches for tents and caravans and a holiday "village" with a selection of apartments. Facilities include two pools, a decent restaurant, shops and wi-fi. There's also a shuttle bus service into town. Great for kids. April–Sept. Pitches around €27

EATING AND DRINKING

Ai Torchi Via dell'Annunziata 12, Finalborgo ☎019 690 531, ⓦristoranteaitorchi.com. This refined restaurant occupies an ancient olive-oil factory in Finalborgo and serves expensive pasta and fish dishes with care and some style. 12.30–2.30pm & 7–10.30pm; closed Tues & Aug.

Alla Vecchia Maniera Via Roma 25, Finalmarina ☎019 692 562. A central and unpretentious place to eat local fish and seafood, but it's popular – book in advance if you can, especially if you want to sit outside. Tues–Sun 12.30–2pm & 7.30–9pm; closed Mon–Wed Oct–June.

Chiesa Vico Gandolino 12, Finalmarina ☎ 018 692 516. A small, canteen-like place with a different menu every day – good food, and cheap at €5 for a *primo* and €7–9 for a main. Popular with locals, it serves up good pasta basics and roasts, good fish dishes, rabbit and *baccalà*. Check out also its *salumeria*, around the corner on the main street at Via Pertica 13, which is the best central option for picking up delicious picnic supplies. Mon–Sat 9am–1pm & 4–7pm.

Patrick Via Roma 45, Finalmarina ☎ 019 680 007, ⓦ ristorantepatrick.com. Good seafood pasta dishes and other local specialities. It's more expensive than some of the other places along here, but prices are moderate – *trofie* for €9, seafood ravioli €12, swordfish €14 – and its outside terrace is lovely. Mon & Tues 7.30–10.30pm, Wed–Sun 12.30–2.30pm & 7.30–10.30pm.

Albenga

The small market town of **ALBENGA** is one of the most attractive places along this part of the Ligurian coast, an ex-port whose estuary silted up long ago but left a wanderable old quarter, still within medieval walls and following the grid-pattern of its ancient Roman predecessor, Albingaunum.

The centre of town is **Piazza San Michele**, where you'll find the elegant **cathedral**, the main part of which was built in the eleventh century and enlarged in the early fourteenth, and, just beyond, in the Torre Comunale, the **Museo Civico Ingauno** (Tues–Sun 9.30am–12.30pm & 3.30–7.30pm; €3.50), home to an array of Roman masonry and fragments, including a patch of original mosaic floor, and, off to the right, the fifth-century **baptistry**. This ingenious building was built in the fifth century, and combines a ten-sided exterior with an octagonal interior. Inside are fragmentary mosaics showing the Apostles represented by twelve doves. Behind the baptistry to the north, the archbishop's palace houses the diverting **Museo Diocesano**, Via Episcopio 5 (Tues–Thurs 10am–noon & 3–5pm, Fri & Sat 10am–12.30pm & 2.30–5pm; €3), where there are paintings by Lanfranco and Guido Reni. The archbishop's partially frescoed bedchamber, next door to his private chapel, is also decorated with fifteenth-century frescoes. A few metres from here, at the junction of Via Medaglie d'Oro and Via Ricci, the thirteenth-century **Loggia dei Quattro Canti** marks the centre of the Roman town, while some 500m further north, beyond Piazza Garibaldi and along Viale Pontelungo, is the elegant, arcaded **Pontelungo bridge**. Built in the twelfth century to cross the river, which shifted course soon afterwards, it now makes an odd sight.

In the opposite direction, five minutes' walk beyond the train station, lies Albenga's seafront and **beaches** – mostly sandy and with a couple of reasonable free sections.

ARRIVAL AND INFORMATION   ALBENGA

By train Albenga's train station is 800m east of the old town; turn left outside the station and cross the road to follow Viale Martiri della Libertà to the modern centre's Piazza del Popolo.

Tourist office Piazza del Popolo 11 (Mon–Sat 9am–12.30pm & 4–7.30pm, Sun 9am–12.30pm; ☎ 0182 558 444).

ACCOMMODATION AND EATING

Da Puppo Via Torlaro 20 ☎ 0182 98 062, ⓦ dapuppo .it. Just off Via Medaglie d'Oro, this is a basic canteen-like trattoria with a great menu of cheap grilled staples – swordfish, prawns and even Argentinian steaks. Mid-June to mid-Sept Tues–Sun 6.30–10pm; mid-Sept to mid-June Tues–Sat 12.30–2pm & 6.30–10pm.

Sole Mare Lungomare Colombo 15 ☎ 0182 51 817, ⓦ albergosolemare.it. Down on Albenga's seafront, right opposite the beaches, this small hotel has fourteen cosy rooms, all nicely furnished with satellite TV and about half with sea views. There's wi-fi, but you have to pay. **€85**

The Caves of Toirano

Via alle Grotte Toirano • Daily: July & Aug 9.30am–12.30pm & 2–5.30pm; Sept–June 9.30am–12.30pm & 2–5pm • €12 • Tours leave every 30min and last 1hr • ☎ 0182 98 062, ⓦ toiranogrotte.it

The resort of **Borghetto Santo Spirito** is the transfer point for buses to the spectacular **caves** just outside the village of **Toirano** a few kilometres inland. The **caves** are up a track a kilometre or so beyond the main part of the village, and are quite well developed as an attraction, with plenty of parking and a café and shop. They are well worth seeing, made up of two accessible complexes, connected by a man-made tunnel. The first, the so-called **Grotta della Bàsura**, or "Witch's Cave", was inhabited some 12,000 years ago, and you can see well-marked foot- and handprints to prove it, as well as the well-preserved bones of bears who lived here around 20,000 years earlier. Beyond, the **Grotta di Santa Lucia Inferiore** has some remarkable stalagmite and stalactite formations, including stone flowers and rare, rounded stalactites; while outside and above, the grotto and church of **Santa Lucia Superiore** holds a natural spring that was dedicated in the Middle Ages to St Lucy, patron saint of eyesight, after several miraculous cures were effected here. You too can have a drink – bottles are left out for the purpose. If you need more, *Da Malin*, on Toirano's central Piazza della Libertà, is good for lunch.

3 Imperia

Some 30km west of Albenga is the provincial capital of **IMPERIA**, a sprawling settlement formed in 1923 when Mussolini linked twin townships on either side of the River Impero. Imposing **Porto Maurizio**, on the western bank, is the more likeable of the two, ascending the hillside in a series of zigzags from a marina and small beach, with its stepped old quarter dominated by a massive, late eighteenth-century cathedral and a series of Baroque churches and elegant villas. Quieter **Oneglia**, 2km east, is a more workaday place, devoted to fishing and the local olive industry, most manifest in local producer Fratelli Carli's **Museo dell'Olivo** behind the train station at Via Garessio 11 (Mon–Sat 9am–12.30pm & 3–6.30pm; €5; ☎0183 295 762, ⓦmuseodellolivo.com), which houses modern displays devoted to the history of the olive hereabouts and in particular the green nectar it produces.

ACCOMMODATION AND EATING   IMPERIA

Corallo Corso Garibaldi 29 ☎0183 666 264, ⓦcorallo imperia.it. Light, airy rooms all with sea views, overlooking the beach. **€130**

Croce di Malta Via Scarincio 148 ☎0183 667 020, ⓦhotelcrocedimalta.com. Overlooking the old harbour, the rooms are a bit old-fashioned at this long-established hotel, but decent enough. **€130**

Osteria dai Pippi Via dei Pellegrini 9 ☎0183 652 122. Small restaurant close to the water in Porto Maurizio, serving a small menu of mainly regional goodies but also a few surprises, including slow-cooked rabbit, great gnocchi and excellent desserts. It's pretty popular so you may have to book. Daily 12.30–2.30pm & 7–10.30pm.

San Remo

Set on a broad, sweeping bay between twin headlands, **SAN REMO** had its heyday as a classy resort in the sixty years or so up to the outbreak of World War II, when the Empress Maria Alexandrovna headed a substantial Russian community in the town (Tchaikovsky completed *Eugene Onegin* and wrote his Fourth Symphony in San Remo in 1878). Some of the grand hotels overlooking the sea, especially those near the train station, are now grimy and crumbling, but others in the ritzier, western parts of town are still in pristine condition, opening their doors to Europe's remaining aristocrats season after season. San Remo is blessed with the Italian Riviera's most famous **casino**, and remains a showy and attractive town, with a good beach and a labyrinthine old town standing guard over the palm-laden walkways below.

Corso Matteotti

San Remo's main artery is the largely pedestrianized **Corso Matteotti**, lined with cocktail bars, *gelaterie*, cinemas and clothes stores, which runs through the commercial

CORNIGLIA, CINQUE TERRE (P.210) >

centre of town. At no. 143, the Renaissance Palazzo Borea d'Olmo houses the **Museo Civico** (Tues–Sat 9am–7pm; free), with the usual array of local archeological finds, paintings and items relating to the Risorgimento (Garibaldi spent quite a bit of time in San Remo).

The Casino

Corso degli Inglesi 18 • Mon–Thurs & Sun 2.30pm–2.30am, Fri & Sat 3pm–3.30am, slots from 10am–2.30am • Free • ☎ 0184 59 51, ⓦ casinosanremo.it

At the far end of Corso Matteotti is the town's landmark **Casino**, an ornate white palace with grand staircases and distinctive turrets which epitomizes the town's old-fashioned fin-de-siècle charm. It's a theatre too, and hosts San Remo's long-running festival of popular song every March. Anyone can visit, as long as you have your passport (you don't even need to dress up); or you can see the gaming rooms, roof garden and theatre on regular guided tours throughout the summer (July & Aug Sat 9.30am; €3); entrance is from the side entrance to the theatre on the left.

The Cathedral and La Pigna

The streets just above San Remo's main street and Casino are probably its most atmospheric, where busy Via Palazzo gives way to a warren of narrow streets and eventually the mainly Romanesque **Cattedrale di San Siro** (Mon–Sat 8–11.45am & 3–5.45pm, Sun 7.30am–12.15pm & 3.30–7pm; free), decorated with unusual twelfth-century bas reliefs above each of its side doors and with a very ancient feel within; note the fifteenth-century processional black crucifix in the right aisle.

Above here is **La Pigna** or "The Pine Cone", perhaps San Remo's most fascinating quarter, accessible up steep lanes north of Piazza Eroi Sanremesi and Piazza Cassini. Known for its kasbah-like arched passageways and alleys, it is remarkably ungentrified – and a stark contrast to the crisp and bustling modern streets down below. It's fascinating to wander through its quiet streets and the views from the top are great.

The seafront

Beyond the Casino, the palm-lined boulevard of **Corso Imperatrice** stretches along the **seafront** west of the centre, just back from which the impressive onion-domed **Russian Orthodox church**, built in the 1920s, is a manifestation of San Remo's former Russian community (Tues–Sun 9.30am–12.30pm & 3–6.30pm; free), though it's more impressive outside than in. Opposite there are some small stretches of **beach**, while in the other direction, Corso Mombello takes you down to the **Porto Vecchio**, full of high-end boats and lined with restaurants and cafés, just east of which, not far from the train station, there is another, larger stretch of beach.

ARRIVAL AND INFORMATION   SAN REMO

By train San Remo's modern underground train station is east of the town centre on Corso Cavallotti. It's a 5min walk east from here along Corso Garibaldi to the end of Corso Matteotti.

By bus The main bus station is on Piazza Colombo, right in the centre of town at the eastern end of Corso Matteotti.

Tourist office On the opposite side of the town centre to the train and bus station, not far from the Casino, at Largo Nuvoloni 1 (Mon–Sat 8.30am–7pm, Sun 9am–1pm; ☎ 0184 59 059, ⓦ visitrivieradeifiori.it).

ACCOMMODATION

Al Dom Corso Mombello 13 ☎ 0184 501 460. This third-floor family-run hotel has large and airy rooms and is in a great location, but it can be a bit noisy. You also need to like dogs. **€70**

Alexander Corso Garibaldi 123 ☎ 0184 504 591, ⓦ hotelalexandersanremo.com. A 5min walk from the train station, the rooms here don't quite live up to the

beautiful *belle époque* building, but they're nice enough, the welcome is friendly, and there's a pleasant garden out the front and parking at the rear. **€90**

Paradiso Via Roccasterone 12 ☎ 0184 571 211, ⓦ paradisohotel.it. If you want a quiet location above the town's bustle, this is the place, a family-run hotel with sunny, modern rooms, a secluded garden and pool, and wi-fi. **€190**

Royal Hotel Corso Imperatrice 80 ☎0184 5391, ⓦ royalhotelsanremo.com. A grand white presence above San Remo's western seafront, this is how they did things in times gone by, and is really the place to stay if you're dressing for dinner and gambling at the Casino down below. Great facilities – three restaurants and a vast, heated, salt-water swimming pool set in a tropical garden – and lovely,

large, renovated rooms. €350

Villaggio dei Fiori Via Tiro a Volo 3 ☎0184 660 635, ⓦ villaggiodeifiori.it. Facility-laden campsite about 2km west of town with space for tents and caravans, plus chalets and bungalows for rent. Open all year but best to book in advance in high season. Pitches around €60, chalets €180

EATING AND DRINKING

Café Permare Corso N. Sauro 42/44 ☎0184 503 755, ⓦ cafepermare.it. Cool, modern café-restaurant, good for lunch and dinner, with daily specials for €9–14, pizzas in the evening and relaxed terrace overlooking the port from which to enjoy them. There's a trendy bar out back, too. Daily noon–2am.

Cantine Sanremesi Via Palazzo 7 ☎0184 572 063. Informal wine bar with a few tables outside that make a good lunch stop, with great focaccia, and lots of pasta

dishes and Ligurian specialities like potato and octopus salad and *sardenaira*. Most options €10 or less. Tues–Sun noon–3pm & 6–midnight.

Nuovo Piccolo Mondo Via Piave 7 ☎0184 509 012. Charming trattoria in an alley off Corso Matteotti, with tables outside and serving delicious Ligurian specialities such as stuffed anchovies and pasta with home-made pesto, beans and courgettes (€10.50). The owner speaks good English. No credit cards. Tues–Sat 12.30–2pm & 7.30–9.30pm.

Mortola Inferiore: the Giardini Botanici Hanbury

Corso Montecarlo 42 • March to mid-June & mid-Sept to mid-Oct daily 9.30am–6pm; mid-June to mid-Sept daily 9am–7pm; mid-Oct to Feb Tues–Sun 9.30am–5pm; • €7.50 low season, €9 high season • ☎0184 229 292 • Hourly bus #1a from Via Cavour or Ventimiglia train station; no service 3–4pm

Some 11km west of San Remo, just near the French border, the village of **Mortola Inferiore** is famed for the spectacular hillside **Giardini Botanici Hanbury**. The gardens were laid out in 1867 by Sir Thomas Hanbury, a London spice merchant who set up home here, and are highly atmospheric, with hidden corners and pergola-covered walks tumbling down to the sea. A thirty-minute walk further west along the coast road – or a few minutes on bus #1a – is the frontier post.

THE ALTA VIA DEI MONTI LIGURI

The **Alta Via dei Monti Liguri** is a long-distance high-level trail covering the length of Liguria, from Ventimiglia in the west all across the ridge-tops to Ceparana on the Tuscan border above La Spezia in the east – a total distance of some 440km. The mountains, which form the connection between the Alps and the Apennines, aren't high – rarely more than 1500m – meaning that the scenic route, which makes full use of the many passes between peaks, is correspondingly easy going. The whole thing would take weeks to complete in full, but has been divided up into 43 stages of between 2 and 4 hours each, making it easy to dip in and out of. Trail support and maintenance is good, with *rifugi* dotted along the path and distinctive waymarks (red-white-red "AV" signs).

Unfortunately, **access** from the main coastal towns to most other parts of the *Alta Via* can be tricky, and requires juggling with route itineraries and bus timetables. A sample walk starts from point 26 – **Crocetta d'Orero**, on the Genoa–Casella train line: heading east from Crocetta, an easy route covers 7.8km to point 27, **Colle di Creto** (2hr 30min, and served by Genoa buses), with a diversion along the way to a lovely flower-strewn path in and around the deserted hamlet of **Ciatti**.

For information on the *Alta Via*, your best bet is the **Associazione Alta Via dei Monti Liguri**, which produces a full-colour wall-map of the route, along with detailed English descriptions and timings of all 43 stages (plus hotels and restaurants along the way). Books and an eight-pamphlet guide to the trail are on sale in bookshops. The same information is at ⓦ parks.it. **Club Alpino Italiano** offices in the major towns have information on *rifugi*, and the **Federazione Italiano Escursionismo (FIE)** publishes detailed guides to all the inland paths of Liguria.

The Riviera di Levante

The coast **east of Genoa**, dubbed the **Riviera di Levante**, is perhaps more varied and beautiful than its counterpart to the west, but also not the place to come for a get-away-from-it-all holiday, with a series of towns and villages that once eked a living from fishing and coral diving but have been transformed by thirty years of tourism. That said, it's a glorious and rugged stretch of coast, its cliffs and bays covered with pine and olive trees, and with a number of very appealing resorts. The footpaths that crisscross the headland of **Monte di Portofino** are a great way to get off the beaten tourist track, and the harbour towns each side – **Camogli** towards Genoa and **Santa Margherita** in the Golfo di Tigullio – are well worth a visit; and of course **Portofino** itself is an upscale resort of some renown. Other highlights include big, feisty resorts like **Rapallo**, and smaller, quieter places like **Sestri Levante**, while further east, the main road (though not the railway) heads inland, bypassing the laidback beach town of **Levanto** and the spectacular **Cinque Terre** coast (now a national park and great, organized walking country). The road joins the train line again at the naval port of **La Spezia**, at the head of the Golfo dei Poeti, on either side of which **Portovenere** and **Lerici** (the latter almost in Tuscany) are very enticing spots.

Camogli

CAMOGLI was the "saltiest, roughest, most piratical little place", according to Dickens when he visited the town. Though it still has the "smell of fish, and seaweed, and old rope" that the author relished, it's had its rough edges knocked off since his day, and is now one of the most attractive small resorts along this stretch of the coast. The town's name, a contraction of *Casa Mogli* (House of Wives), comes from the days when voyages lasted for years and the women ran the port while the men were away. Camogli supported a huge fleet of seven hundred vessels in its day, which once saw off Napoleon. The town declined in the age of steam, but has been reborn as a classy getaway without the exaggerated prices found further round the coast.

Camogli's serried towers of nineteenth-century apartment blocks line up above the waterfront and a small promontory topped with the medieval **Castello Dragone**,

---

COASTAL FERRIES

FERRIES FROM GENOA, CAMOGLI AND PORTOFINO

In summer, dozens of **boats** serve points along the Tigullio coast and beyond. There are shuttles between Genoa's Porto Antico and Camogli, San Fruttuoso and Portofino, several times a day (see p.191). **Golfo Paradiso** (Via Scalo 3, Camogli ☎0185 77 209, ⓦgolfoparadiso .it) run regular ferries connecting Camogli with tranquil **Punta Chiappa**, ideal for a spot of swimming and basking in the sun, and to **San Fruttuoso** – ditto (May–Sept at least hourly; Oct–April Mon–Fri 3 daily, Sat & Sun hourly; €9 return to Punta Chiappa, €12 return to San Fruttuoso). There are also connections from Camogli to Portofino (€17 return) and to the **Cinque Terre** and **Portovenere** (€28 return).

OTHER SERVICES

Another line – **Servizio Maríttimo Tigullio** (Piazza Mazzini 33, Santa Margherita Ligure ☎0185 284 670, ⓦtraghettiportofino.it) – shuttles hourly in summer between **Rapallo**, **Santa Margherita**, **Portofino** and **San Fruttuoso**, taking around fifteen minutes between each town and half an hour between Portofino and San Fruttuoso (Rapallo to San Fruttuoso costs €15.50 return). There are also lovely **night excursions** on the same route (July Sat only & Aug Fri & Sat), and the same company also runs services down the coast to Sestri Levante, and to the Cinque Terre (€24.50 return); its Super Cinque Terre trip (13 times a week during summer) lets you stop off at Riomaggiore, Monterosso (for lunch) and Vernazza, for €32 from Santa Margherita.

OPEN OR WRAPPED?

If you're visiting Camogli on the second Sunday in May, you won't be able to miss the **Sagra del Pesce**, preceded on the Saturday night by fireworks and a huge bonfire. This generous – and smelly – event has its origins in celebrating the munificence of the sea and retains its ancient resonance for Camogli's fisherfolk even today. Thousands of fish are plucked fresh from the waves, flipped into a giant frying-pan set up on the harbourfront and distributed free of charge to all and sundry as a demonstration of the sea's abundance. In recent years the event has been beset by quibbles: bureaucrats have suggested that the frying pan – some 4m across – is a health hazard, and there have even been allegations that frozen fish is defrosted out at sea and then passed off as fresh. For all that, local enthusiasm for the festival hasn't waned one bit.

on one side of which there's a busy **harbour**, crammed with fishing boats, and on the other a section of pebble **beach**, backed by a long promenade of bars and restaurants.

ARRIVAL AND INFORMATION   CAMOGLI

By train The train station is just inland and uphill from the centre of Camogli, a 5min walk.

Tourist office Not far from the train station at Via XX Settembre 33 (Mon–Sat 9am–12.30pm & 3–7pm, Sun 9am–12.30pm; ☎ 0185 771 066, ⓦ prolococamogli.it).

ACCOMMODATION

Augusta Via Piero Schiaffino 100 ☎ 0185 770 592, ⓦ htlaugusta.com. Just above the harbour, this is a good-value family-run hotel with attractive a/c rooms, all en suite, and wi-fi. **€100**

Casmona Salita Pineto 13 ☎ 0185 770 015, ⓦ casmona .com. Up towards the train station from the town centre, this hotel is housed in a seafront nineteenth-century villa and has light, airy rooms with sea views and balconies, wi-fi and satellite TV. **€105**

Cenobio dei Dogi Via Cuneo 34 ☎ 0185 72 41, ⓦ cenobio .it. Camogli's most traditional upmarket alternative, a lavish

hotel that was once the summer palace of Genoa's doges, with its own park, beach, pool, tennis courts and restaurants. Its location is perfect, within easy reach of the town yet set apart with great views over the bay. You can stay here much more cheaply if you're prepared to forego the sea view. **€330**

Villa Rosmarino Via Figari 38 ☎ 0185 771 580, ⓦ villa rosmarino.com. Just out of town, Camogli's best choice is a 5min walk from the train station – a boutique hotel in a nineteenth-century *palazzo* with six cool white rooms hung with contemporary art, lush grounds and a pool. **€220**

EATING

La Camogliese Via Garibaldi 78 ☎ 0185 771 086. Right on the seafront, with one of the best views in town, and one of the most reliable menus, with great *vongole* and mussels with pasta and without, *focaccia di Recco, pansotti alle noce* and *trofie al pesto* – at decent prices too. The service can depend on how busy they are. Daily 12.30–2.30pm & 7.30–10.30pm.

Nonna Nina Viale F. Molfino 126, San Rocco ☎ 0185 773 835, ⓦ nonnanina.it. Perhaps Camogli's best choice, about a 10min walk from the seafront up on the Portofino headland, and serving wonderful fresh fish and great Ligurian food cooked with local ingredients in a gorgeous old house with garden overlooking the sea. Menus change with the seasons. 12.30–2.30pm & 7.30–10pm; closed Wed.

Portofino

Situated at the end of a narrow and treacherously winding road just 5km south of Santa Margherita, there's no denying the appeal of **PORTOFINO**, tucked into a protected inlet surrounded by lush cypress- and olive-clad slopes. It's an A-list resort that has been attracting high-flying bankers, celebs and their hangers-on for years, as evidenced by the flotillas of giant yachts usually anchored just outside. It's a tiny place that manages to be both attractive and off-putting at the same time, with a quota of fancy shops, bars and restaurants that would suit a place twice its size. For those wanting to stay, accommodation is unsurprisingly expensive: luxury is really the point of Portofino.

Northwest from the village, steeply stepped paths head through vineyards and orchards to Olmi and on to **San Fruttuoso** (see p.205), while the best sandy **beach** is the sparkling cove at **Paraggi**, 2km back towards Santa Margherita on the coast road (buses will stop on request) – not exactly remote, but less formal than Portofino and with a small stretch of pebbly sand and a couple of bars set back from the water.

To get a sense of Portofino's idyllic setting follow the footpath which heads south from the harbour up onto the headland. Five minutes from the village is the church of **San Giorgio**, said to contain relics of St George, and a further ten minutes up is the spectacularly located **Castello Brown** (daily: summer 10am–7pm; winter 10am–5pm; €4; ⓦcastellobrown.it), from whose terrace there are breathtaking views of a pint-sized Portofino. The castle, which dates back to the Roman period and now frequently hosts art and photography exhibitions, is named after its former owner, British Consul Montague Yeats Brown, who bought it in 1867 and set about transforming it. In 1870 he planted two pines on the main terrace for his wedding – one for him and one for his wife, Agnes Bellingham – and they are still a prominent feature today. The scenic path continues for a kilometre or so, down to the **Faro** (lighthouse) on the very tip of the promontory. The only way back is up the same path.

ARRIVAL AND INFORMATION
PORTOFINO

By bus and ferry There are regular buses to Portofino from nearby Santa Margherita (every 15–20min); they're supposed to take 15min but can take longer and indeed it can be quicker and easier to jump on one of the boats that shuttle regularly from Santa Margherita in summer.

You can also reach Portofino easily from Camogli, though it takes slightly longer.

Tourist office Via Roma 35 (summer daily 10am–1pm & 3–7pm; winter Tues–Sun 10.30am–1.30pm & 2.30–4.30pm; ☎0185 269 024).

ACCOMMODATION

Eden Vico Dritto 8 ☎0185 269 091, ⓦhoteleden portofino.com. Probably Portofino's cheapest option, set within its own delightful gardens in the centre of town, and very nice it is too, with simply furnished rooms with balconies looking onto the garden. Rates drop drastically midweek, out of season. **€290**

Splendido Viale Baratta 16 ☎0185 269 551, ⓦhotel

splendido.com. High above the village, this is the place to stay if money is no object, with its fabulously lush grounds and stupendous views, and although it is a little way out, the pool, tennis courts, views and two restaurants may mean you won't want to leave anyway. For those who prefer to be in the thick of things there is another, smaller location – the *Splendido Mare* – down in the port. **€1000**

WALKS AROUND PORTOFINO

The Portofino headland – protected as the Parco Naturale Regionale di Portofino (ⓦparks.it) and encircled by cliffs and small coves – is one of the most rewarding areas for **walking** on the Riviera coast. At 612m, **Monte di Portofino** is high enough to be interesting but not so high as to demand any specialist hiking prowess. The trails cross slopes of wild thyme, pine and holm oak, enveloped in summer in the constant whirring of cicadas. From the summit, the view over successive headlands is breathtaking. Not many people walk these marked paths, maybe because their early stages are fairly steep – but they aren't particularly strenuous, levelling off later and with plenty of places to stop. One of the best trails skirts the whole headland, beginning in **Camogli**, on the western side of the promontory. The path rises gently for 1km south to **San Rocco** (221m), then follows the coast south to a viewpoint above Punta Chiappa, before swinging east to the scenic **Passo del Bacio** (200m), rising to a ridge-top and then descending gently through the olive trees and palms to **San Fruttuoso** (3hr from Camogli). It continues east over a little headland and onto the wild and beautiful cliff-tops above **Punta Carega**, before passing through the hamlets of Prato, Olmi and Cappelletta and down steps to Portofino (4hr 30min from Camogli). There are plenty of alternative routes. About 1km south of San Rocco, an easier path forks inland up to **Portofino Vetta** and **Pietre Strette** (452m), before leading down again through the foliage to San Fruttuoso (2hr 30min from Camogli). **Ruta** is a small village 250m up on the north side of Monte di Portofino, served by buses from Camogli, Santa Margherita and Rapallo; a peaceful, little-trod trail from Ruta heads up to the summit of the mountain (2hr), or diverts partway along to take you across country to Olmi and on to Portofino (2hr 30min from Ruta).

EATING AND DRINKING

Chuflay Via Roma 2 ☎ 0185 269 020. Right on the harbour, the *Splendido*'s waterfront restaurant has a relatively small, fairly international menu at lunchtime, and more exciting, more Ligurian choices in the evening. The food is great, especially the fish and seafood, and the location can't be bettered, but prices are not surprisingly on the high side. Summer daily 12.30–3.30pm & 7.30–11pm.

Il Pitosforo Molo Umberto I 9 ☎ 0185 269 020, ⓦ pitosforo-portofino.it. One of the best of Portofino's waterfront choices, and very well established, serving excellent food. Fish especially is great but be prepared – it's not cheap. You may need to book. Wed–Sun 12.30–2.30pm & 7–10.30pm.

San Fruttuoso

The enchanting thousand-year-old abbey of **SAN FRUTTUOSO** is one of the principal draws along this stretch of the Riviera, occupying a picturesque little bay at the southern foot of Monte di Portofino. The only way to get there is on foot or by boat, dozens of which shuttle backwards and forwards from practically every harbour along the coast during peak season. On summer weekends, the tiny pebble beach and church may be uncomfortably crowded, but out of season (or at twilight, courtesy of the occasional night cruise), San Fruttuoso is a peaceful, excellent place for doing very little. There are a handful of simple restaurants on the beach serving sandwiches, pasta and steamed mussels, the largest of which – *Da Giovanni* (☎ 0185 770 047) – offers simple rooms, but you'll need to book ahead.

Abbazia di San Fruttuoso

Daily: June to mid-Sept 10am–5.45pm; April, May & late Sept 10am–4.45pm; Jan–March & Oct–Dec 10am–3.45pm • €5 • ☎ 0185 772 703, ⓦ sanfruttuoso.eu

The **Abbazia di San Fruttuoso** was originally built to house the relics of the third-century martyr St Fructuosus, which were brought here from Spain after the Moorish invasion in 711. It was rebuilt in 984 with an unusual Byzantine-style cupola and distinctive waterside arches and later became a Benedictine abbey that exerted a sizeable degree of control over the surrounding countryside. The Doria family took over in the sixteenth century, adding the defensive **Torre dei Doria** nearby, and the small, elegant church, with its compact little cloister and half-dozen Doria tombs.

Cristo degli Abissi

Off the headland, a 1954 bronze statue known as the **Cristo degli Abissi** (Christ of the Depths) rests eight fathoms down on the sea bed, to honour the memory of divers who have lost their lives at sea and to protect those still working beneath the waves. Taxi boats queue up to take you there.

Santa Margherita Ligure

SANTA MARGHERITA LIGURE is a small, thoroughly attractive, palm-laden resort, tucked into an inlet and replete with grand hotels, garden villas and views of the glittering bay. In the daytime, trendy young Italians cruise the streets or whizz around the harbour on jet skis, while the rest of the family sunbathes or crams the *gelaterie*. Santa Margherita is far cheaper to stay in than Portofino and less crowded than Rapallo, and makes a good base both for taking boats and trains up and down the coast and for exploring the countryside on foot.

The town is in two parts: one set around a harbour and gardens and a small town beach, and a second, more commercial harbour around the headland. In between there's a small **castle**, and behind this the shady gardens of the sixteenth-century **Villa Durazzo** (Jan–March 9am–5pm; April & Oct 9am–6pm; May, June & Sept 9am–7pm; July & Aug 9am–8pm; free), which is host to art exhibitions and the like. There's a decent if small town **beach**, but the best beaches are out of town, accessible by bus:

south towards Portofino is Paraggi (see p.204), while to the north the road drops down to a patch of beach in the bay of **San Michele di Pagana**. In addition to its beach bars and crystal-clear water, a *Crucifixion* by Van Dyck in the church of San Michele may prove an added incentive for a visit.

ARRIVAL AND INFORMATION
SANTA MARGHERITA LIGURE

By train Santa Margherita's train station overlooks the harbour, a 5min walk from the centre of town and the seafront.

By bus Buses for Portofino, San Michele and Rapallo stop right outside the tourist office in the centre of town.

Tourist office Right in the centre on the waterfront Piazza Vittorio Veneto (daily 9.30am–12.30pm & 1–8pm; ☎ 0185 287 485).

ACCOMMODATION

Albergo Fasce Via L. Bozzo 3 ☎ 0185 286 435, ⓦ hotel fasce.eu. A good mid-priced hotel nicely located on a quiet side-street, with good-sized rooms and a panoramic roof-terrace. Free bikes for guests' use. **€125**

Continental Via Pagana 8 ☎ 0185 286 512, ⓦ hotel -continental.it. One of a group of hotels just above Santa Margherita, a 5min walk from the centre, this has spacious rooms with balconies and sea views, a lovely terrace and gardens which lead down to private bathing facilities. A treat for the price. **€220**

Lido Palace Via Doria 3 ☎ 0185 285 821, ⓦ lidopalace hotel.com. This impressive seafront hotel is right by Santa Margherita's small beach and has spacious, modern rooms, with a choice of hill or sea view. There's a restaurant, bar and fitness centre, although its major asset is the fact that it's the most central of the town's upmarket hotels. **€200**

EATING AND DRINKING

Dei Pescatori Via Bottaro 43 ☎ 0185 286 747, ⓦ navicello.it/trattoriapescatori. Santa Margherita's oldest restaurant, this is a nice place on the waterfront in the old port for traditional fish dishes such as fish baked with potatoes, olives and pine nuts (€16.50), plus great *trenette alle pesto* and *pasta alle noce*, made with home-made pasta. 12.30–2.30pm & 7–10.30pm; closed Tues.

L'Ancora Via A. Maragliano 7 ☎ 0185 280 559. This excellent-value, mid-priced, traditional fish restaurant a block back from the waterfront in the old port is a great place to try baked fish with potatoes. Very simple but delicious cooking. No outside seating. 12.30–2.30pm & 7–10.30pm; closed Tues.

★ **Trattoria Baicin** Via Algeria 5 ☎ 0185 286 763. A very good and reasonably priced family-run seafood restaurant, right in the centre of town, just back from the waterfront park, offering great Ligurian specialities such as swordfish with tomato sauce and olives, a great *fritto misto* and home-made pasta with pesto. Starters around €5, main courses €10–15. Tues–Sun noon–3pm & 7–10pm.

Rapallo

RAPALLO is larger and has a more urban feel than anywhere else along the coast, a highly developed resort with an expanse of glass-fronted restaurants and plush hotels crowding around a south-facing bay. In the early part of the twentieth century it was a backwater, and writers in particular came for the bay's extraordinary beauty, of which you now get an inkling only early in the morning or at dusk. Max Beerbohm lived in Rapallo for the second half of his life, and attracted a literary circle to the town; Ezra Pound wrote the first thirty of his *Cantos* here between 1925 and 1930; D.H. Lawrence stayed for a while and Hemingway also dropped by (but came away muttering that the sea was flat and boring). There's a pleasant **old town** tucked away behind the seafront hotels, but otherwise the town's landmarks are the large **marina** and the **castle**, now converted into an exhibition space, at the end of a small causeway. Despite the beauty of the bay, there's not much to Rapallo's **beaches**: there's a free patch of shingle right by the castle, and some pay-beaches on the other side of the bay close to the Riviera.

ARRIVAL AND INFORMATION
RAPALLO

By train Rapallo's train station is a 5min walk from the sea on Piazza Molfino – just follow Corso Italia from the station and turn left at Piazza Cavour for the old town and seafront.

By bus Buses stop at the Santa Margherita end of the seafront and at the train station. Bus is much the easiest way to get here from Santa Margherita, with services every 20min.

Tourist office Lungomare V. Veneto 7 (Mon–Sat 9.30am–12.30pm & 3.30–6.30pm; ☎ 0185 230 346).

ACCOMMODATION

Bandoni Via Marsala 24 ☎0185 50 423, ⓦalbergo bandonirapallo.com. Housed in a fine old *palazzo* next door to the more expensive *Miramare*, this is the best bargain in town, with a mix of en-suite and shared-bath rooms. It's old-fashioned and a bit tatty in places, but clean and simple, and has a great location right on the waterfront. **€90**

Excelsior Palace Via S. Michele di Pagana 8 ☎0185 230 666, ⓦexcelsiorpalace.it. Rapallo's flagship five-star hotel, at the western edge of town high above the shore, has splendidly lavish rooms, a state-of-the-art spa, and two refined, romantic restaurants. **€200**

Miramare Lungomare V. Veneto 27 ☎0185 230 261, ⓦmiramare-hotel.it. Pleasant hotel with spacious, spotless rooms overlooking the sea and a nice, old-fashioned feel, good service and often bargain rates, even in season. **€170**

Riviera Piazza IV Novembre 2 ☎0185 50 248, ⓦhotel rivierarapallo.com. Hemingway wrote his short story *Cat in the Rain* while staying in this *belle époque* family-owned hotel overlooking the sea in 1923. Service is good and the rooms are nice with balconies and sea views, but the sense of history has been lost in their renovation. **€120**

Stella Via Aurelia Ponente 6 ☎0185 50 367, ⓦhotel stella-riviera.com. An affordable and welcoming place, with a roof terrace and decent rooms, a couple of which have small balconies, though the busy main road outside can be noisy. **€130**

EATING AND DRINKING

★ **Antica Cucina Genovese** Via S. M. del Campo 133–139 ☎0185 206 036, ⓦanticacucinagenovese.it. A couple of kilometres outside town, this place gives you the chance not only to sample some of the region's best cuisine, but to learn how to cook it as well. There's an emphasis on the vegetables and local produce of the area, with lots of vegetarian options, and the chefs give demonstrations on cooking everything from ravioli to cheese focaccia. Tues–Sun 12.30–2.30pm & 7.30–9.30pm.

Da Mario Piazza Garibaldi 23 ☎0185 51 736, ⓦtrattoriadamario.com. Moderate prices, and great seafood served on tables outside under Rapallo's medieval arcades. Pasta dishes €7–11, mains €15–20. Popular so you may need to book, or wait for a table. 12.30–2.30pm & 7–10.30pm; closed Wed.

O Bansin Via Venezia 105 ☎0185 231 119, ⓦtrattoria bansin.it. Affordable old-town restaurant; try the signature pasta dish with pesto, tomatoes and cream. Mon–Sat noon–2.30pm & 7.30–10pm, Sun 7.30–10pm.

Sestri Levante

Some 20km east of Rapallo, **SESTRI LEVANTE** is another large resort, though with a quite different feel to its brasher neighbours, its centre set on a narrow isthmus between two bays – the Bay of Fables, with a broad sandy beach decked with umbrellas, and the quieter Bay of Silence, a picturesque curve of sand overlooked by bobbing fishing boats. A former fishing village, the town has a relaxed feel, and is one of the nicer places to stay along this stretch of coast, with a number of decent hotels in its old quarter and within easy walking distance of the town's beaches.

ARRIVAL AND INFORMATION

By train The train station is a 10min walk from the beach at the end of Viale Roma in the modern part of town, on Piazza Caduti di Via Fani.

SESTRI LEVANTE

Tourist office In a kiosk between the old centre and the train station at Piazza Sant'Antonio 10 (daily 9.30am–1pm & 2–5.30pm; ☎0185 457 011).

ACCOMMODATION

Due Mari Vico del Coro 18 ☎0185 42 695, ⓦduemari hotel.it. Appropriately named for its location overlooking both bays of Sestri, and with gardens and a pool, as well as fairly large and palatial rooms and parking. It's a bit of a hike from the station if you're on foot, but worth it for the location. **€125**

San Pietro Via Palesto 13 ☎0185 41 279, ⓦalbergo ristorantesanpietro.com. A simple hotel but in a great location just steps from the sands of the Bay of Silence, and with a homely restaurant downstairs too. **€70**

Villa Jolanda Vico Pozzetto 15 ☎0185 41 354, ⓦvilla iolanda.it. On the far side of the bay and with nice rooms with balconies, a shady terrace and garden for alfresco breakfasts. Parking too. **€85**

EATING AND DRINKING

Cantina del Polpo Piazza Cavour 2 ☎0185 485 296. Cosy, dark-wood restaurant with covered terrace that does a good line in seafood and fish, mostly for €10–15, and has lots of daily specials marked up on a blackboard. Nice, friendly service on the whole, too. Daily 12.30–2.30pm & 7–10.30pm.

L'Osteria Mattana Via XXV Aprile 34 ☎ 0185 457 633, ⓦ osteriamattana.com. Canteen-like restaurant with long tables and serving Ligurian specialities that are chalked up on blackboards – great *farinata*, seafood spaghetti, stewed octopus with potatoes and the like – all good simple

stuff that is sometimes accompanied by live jazz. Cash only. Tues–Thurs 7.30–11pm, Fri–Sun 12.30–2.30pm & 7.30–11pm.

Millelire Via XXV Aprile 149/153 ☎ 0185 41 191, ⓦ millelire.it. Lively bar that's a good spot for focaccia and snacks at lunchtime, cocktails and occasional live music later on. Mon–Sat 11am–midnight.

Levanto

Anchoring the westernmost point of the Cinque Terre, the unpretentious small resort of **LEVANTO** feels quite cut off by Ligurian standards, but it has a nice sandy **beach** (attracting a surfy crowd), inexpensive hotels and good transport links that make it perhaps the best base for exploring the area. There are no real sights – only the **Loggia Comunale** on the central Piazza del Popolo, the black-and-white-striped church of **Sant'Andrea** across the road from here in the old part of town, and the odd surviving stretch of medieval wall – but the town is a pleasant and, for the most part, thoroughly Italian seaside resort.

ARRIVAL AND INFORMATION

By train The train station is a 10min walk inland from the seafront.

Tourist office Right by the beach Piazza Mazzini 3

(Mon–Sat 9am–1pm & 3–6pm, Sun 9am–1pm; ☎ 0187 808 125).

ACCOMMODATION

Acqua Dolce Via Semenza 5 ☎ 0187 808 465, ⓦ camping acquadolce.com. Right by the medieval walls of the old town, this is the most central of several decent campsites in and around the town. Closed mid-Nov to mid-Dec & mid-Jan to Feb. Pitches around €29

Europa Via Dante Alighieri 41 ☎ 0187 808 126, ⓦ europa levanto.com. This charmingly old-fashioned hotel is one of the nicest places to stay in the centre of Levanto. It's not high on mod cons, but does the simple things well, with pleasant, clean rooms and a warm welcome. €116

Maremesco Via Vecchia Mesco 10 ☎ 0187 808 154, ⓦ maremesco.it. A secluded and relaxing B&B on the footpath leading towards Monterosso; driftwood sculptures and beach-glass mosaics decorate the rooms and terraces,

and the 10min walk up from town is rewarded by spectacular views – and, when it's hot, a dip in Enrico's hand-built plunge pool. €70

Ospitalia del Mare Via S. Nicolò ☎ 0187 802 562, ⓦ ospitaliadelmare.it. A clean, modern and central hostel, with a choice of accommodation, ranging from beds in 4-, 6- and 9-bed dormitories to private doubles and singles. Free wi-fi, and scooter, bike and surfboard rental too. Dorms €22.50, doubles €60

Stella Maris Via Marconi 4 ☎ 0187 808 258, ⓦ hotel stellamaris.it. Perhaps the nicest of Levanto's hotels, with a handful of opulent rooms in the nineteenth-century Palazzo Vannoni, plus some others in a more modern annexe. €150

EATING AND DRINKING

Antica Trattoria Centro Corso Italia 4 ☎ 0187 808 157. Plenty of room here, inside and out, at one of Levanto's longest-established restaurants. Excellent food and the best service in town. 12.30–2.30pm & 7–10.30pm; closed Tues.

Bruna Piazza Staglieno 42 ☎ 0187 807 796. With a few tables outside and a fairly bare interior, there's nothing immediately alluring about this place, but the pizzas are absolutely top-notch and reasonably priced. Not surprisingly, you can't book, and you may have to wait for a table. Daily 12.30–2.30pm & 7–10.30pm.

Da Rino Via Garibaldi 10 ☎ 0187 813 475. In the heart of old Levanto, this place has outside tables and another room across the street to take the overflow. Its menu is not especially adventurous but consistently hits the mark with great seafood pasta. Daily 12.30–2.30pm & 7–10.30pm.

Da Tapulin Corso Italia 10 ☎ 0187 808 671. One of the cheapest and best places in town, with great pasta and mains, and pizzas too, but it's ever-popular – you may have to book to be sure of a table, particularly if you want to sit outside. Daily 12.30–2.30pm & 7–10.30pm.

The Cinque Terre

The breathtaking folded coastline of the **Cinque Terre** (Five Lands) stretches between the beach resort of Levanto and the port of La Spezia. It's named for five tiny villages – **Monterosso**, **Vernazza**, **Corniglia**, **Manarola** and **Riomaggiore** – wedged into a series of coves between sheer cliffs, and their comparative remoteness, and the dramatic nature of their positions, makes the region the principal scenic highlight of the whole Riviera. The scenery, certainly, is lovely, but bear in mind that it's also the convenience which makes the Cinque Terre so popular: the main clifftop route is not particularly arduous – it's pretty flat most of the way, the villages are not that far apart and all of them have plenty of amenities and places to stay; and if you get fed up with walking you can always jump on a train (or a boat). No surprise, then, that the area is teeming with travellers during summer, and the villages have lost some of their character to the tide of kitschy souvenir shops and overpriced, under-quality restaurants. But outside of August you should try to take in at least part of the area – it's worth it, especially if you use quieter and more authentic Levanto (see opposite) or even La Spezia as a base (p.212).

3

Monterosso

Tucked into a bay on the east side of the jutting headland of Punta Mesco, **MONTEROSSO** is the chief village of the Cinque Terre. It's the largest of the five – population 1800 – and perhaps the most developed, conjoined with the modern beach resort of **Fegina** whose shingle beach strings along the shore by Monterosso's station; there's a free section right by the station. Beyond the rocky outcrop at the end, atop which is the seventeenth-century **Convento dei Cappuccini**, the old village is a pleasant tangle of streets around the striped thirteenth-century church of **San Giovanni Battista**. One of Monterosso's most recent claims to fame is as the home town of the Nobel Prize-winning poet Eugenio Montale; his *Ossi di Seppia* (Cuttlefish Bones) is a collection of early poems about his youth in the village. The other is that along with neighbouring Vernazza the village suffered a massive landslide in late 2011 and has only just recovered. The coastal ferries stop in the little harbour, and there's another, smaller stretch of shingle beach, again with a small free section.

WALKING IN THE CINQUE TERRE

Most people come to the Cinque Terre to **walk**, and these days it's crammed mainly with Americans and Australians in full hiking gear. The national park's most popular route is the coastal **Blue Route** from Riomaggiore to Monterosso (Sentiero Azzurro), and to walk that you have to invest in a **Cinque Terre Card**, which gives access to the path for one (€5), two (€9), three (€12) or seven days (€20). You can also get a version which includes the train for €10 (1 day)/€19 (2 days). Children pay less (under-4s are free), and you can also buy a family Cinque Terre pass for €12.50 (€26 including the train). All of the park's other marked routes, including the inland **Red Routes** (Sentieri Rossi), are free and are mostly much, much steeper – proper hiking.

The most challenging is Path no. 1, which runs 25km all the way from Portovenere to Levanto – a great walk to do over a couple of days with an overnight stop. Despite its popularity, the Blue Route – Path no. 2 – is well worth doing, out of season at least (11km; around 5hr); it hugs the shoreline between all five villages, offering spectacular scenery along the way. However, before you set out do check to make sure that all sections are open; they have been prone to closure due to floods and landslides over recent years, and it's likely that the Corniglia–Manarola stretch will be closed for some time. Another rewarding walk is **Path no. 10**, which leads from Monterosso station up through pine woods and onto a flight of steps that emerge at the Sant'Antonio church on the high point of the Punta Mesco headland (1hr), giving a spectacular panorama along the length of the Cinque Terre coastline.

Note that most of the paths are **unshaded** and can be blisteringly hot in summer – make sure you wear a hat and carry a water bottle for even a short stroll. Walking shoes are advisable as paths are rocky and uneven at the best of times. Also, take note of weather forecasts in spring and autumn, as rainstorms can brew up rapidly and make paths treacherously slippery.

Vernazza

A few headlands east of Monterosso, **VERNAZZA**, loveliest of the five villages, sits behind the only natural harbour on this rocky coast. The narrow lanes with their tall, colourful houses are typical of the area, and the cramped village is overlooked by stout medieval bastions and a watchtower, built by the Genoese after they'd destroyed the previous castle in 1182 to punish the locals for piracy. Like nearby Monterosso, Vernazza was hit by a massive mudslide in October 2011, which wiped out the beach and many houses and caused three deaths. It's recovered well since then and is very much open for business, but there are still signs of damage on the outskirts of town. See ⓦsavevernazza.com for more.

The village's main street, Via Roma, leads down from the station to Piazza Marconi and the small harbour, where the Gothic church of **Santa Margherita di Antiochia**, with its elegant octagonal campanile, overlooks the small town beach.

Corniglia

CORNIGLIA is the smallest and remotest of the Cinque Terre villages, clinging to a high cliff 90m above the sea, its only access to the water (and the train station) via a long flight of steps. Floral-decorated squares fill the village, and the little Gothic church of **San Pietro** boasts an exquisite, marble rose window. Oddly for a hilltop village, Corniglia stands out for its **beach**: on the southern side of the village's rocky promontory is the **Spiaggone di Corniglia**, a narrow stretch of pebbles that has relatively easy access from the footpath towards Manarola.

Manarola

MANAROLA is almost as pretty as Vernazza, its pastel-shaded houses either squeezed into a cleft in the cliffs or crowded impossibly up the sides of the prominent headland of dark rock. The station is on the other side of the headland, connected to the main part of the village by a tunnel, from where you can either turn left up the hill, past a small **museum** devoted to the local white dessert wine, Sciacchetrà, and eventually to the fourteenth-century church of San Lorenzo, or left around the main square down the main street to Manarola's pretty **harbour**. You can swim from the rocks or the slipway down into the harbour – the water is lovely – but there's no beach. Bear in mind also that a lot of people walk from Manarola to Riomaggiore on the paved **Via dell'Amore** (Lovers' Path) – a twenty-minute jaunt that's perhaps the least demanding trail in the national park; the path starts at the train station and you will almost certainly be asked for your Cinque Terre pass (see box, p.209) if you decide to take it. Look out for the padlocks attached to the fences and just about everything else along the way – left here by couples to seal their love forever.

Riomaggiore

Lively **RIOMAGGIORE** is the easternmost of the Cinque Terre, and its relatively easy road link to the outside world makes it also the most crowded of the five. Nonetheless, its vividly multicoloured houses piling up the steep slopes above the romantic little harbour give the place a charm untempered by the café crowds, especially the higher you climb. Like Manarola, the train station is connected to the main part of the village by a tunnel (and to its upper town by a lift), which brings you out at the bottom of the main street. From here you can either go right under the rail track down to the harbour – where you can hire snorkels and kayaks, plus there's a small stony beach just around the headland to the left – or left up the main street, which is home to the bulk of Riomaggiore's rooms and restaurants.

GETTING AROUND   THE CINQUE TERRE

By train There are regular slow trains between Levanto and La Spezia that stop at every village.

By boat Boats from every company on the Riviera shuttle along this bit of coast all summer long. Be sure to confirm which of the four waterside villages you'll be stopping at (Corniglia has no harbour), and specify if you want a one-way ticket, rather than the more usual round-trip.

On foot The most satisfactory way to get around is on foot:

there's a network of trails (see box, p.209) linking the villages along the coast or up on the ridge-tops, which offer spectacular views. However, the coastal path in particular can get uncomfortably crowded throughout the summer months.

By car Trying to tour the area by car or motorbike truly isn't worth the effort. All five villages have road access, although the streets are narrow and exceptionally steep. There's also very little public parking. You'd do better to leave your vehicle in Levanto or La Spezia.

INFORMATION

Tourist offices Much of the area is now officially protected as the Parco Nazionale delle Cinque Terre and there are information offices for the park – called Cinque Terre Points – in each of the five villages' train stations as well as Levanto and La Spezia. They sell Cinque Terre cards and can provide maps and information, and advise on itineraries.

Website The national park's website – w cinqueterre.com – is a good source of information.

Accommodation booking The national park website operates a hotel booking service, or you can also book apartments and hotels through Arbaspaa (☎ 0187 920 783, w arbaspaa.com), based in Manarola.

ACCOMMODATION

MONTEROSSO

Amici Via Buranco 36 ☎ 0187 817 544, w hotelamici.it. In the old part of Monterosso and maybe the town's cheapest option, with a garden with views of the sea, as well as a good restaurant. **€120**

Porto Roca Via Corone 1 ☎ 0187 817 502, w portoroca .it. Atop the rocks above Monterosso's beach, this is the top hotel in town. The public areas are decorated in rather dingy style, with suits of armour and huge drab pictures, but the bedrooms are imaginatively and beautifully decorated and come with gorgeous sea views, terraces and sun loungers. There's a lovely large public terrace too. **€195**

Villa Adriana Via IV Novembre 23 ☎ 0187 818 109, w villaadriana.info. At the far end of town in Fegina, two blocks from the beach, nicely furnished rooms in a large villa in a pleasant garden. Parking too. **€160**

VERNAZZA

Antonio e Ingrid Via Carattino 2 ☎ 0187 812 183. Just off Via Roma, this charming B&B has lovely rooms and Antonio and Ingrid are wonderful hosts. Some rooms have balconies and there's a top-floor apartment too. **€80**

Barbara Piazza Marconi 30 ☎ 0187 812 398, w albergo barbara.it. This simple hotel has a great position right by the harbour in Vernazza, and seven rooms, a couple with great views over the harbour. Prices vary quite a lot, with the most expensive rooms naturally being the large ones with sea views – nab one of these if you can. **€110**

CORNIGLIA

Ostello di Corniglia Via alla Stazione 3 ☎ 0187 812 559, w ostellocorniglia.com. One of few places to stay in Corniglia, with a choice of two dormitories with eight beds

in each and four private doubles. Reception daily 7am–1pm & 3pm–1.30am. Dorms **€24**, doubles **€60**

MANAROLA

Ca' d'Andrean Via Discovolo 101 ☎ 0187 920 040, w cadandrean.it. Just below the church, this place takes pride in its service and airy rooms (some with balcony); breakfast is taken in the garden in summer. **€100**

Marina Piccola Via Birolli 120 ☎ 0187 762 065, w hotel marinapiccola.com. Down near the harbour, this has thirteen cosy rooms, half with lovely sea views. The restaurant offers a raft of reasonably priced fish dishes – good *fritto misto* – and has a terrace right on the harbour. **€120**

Ostello Cinque Terre Via Riccobaldi 21 ☎ 0187 920 215, w hostel5terre.com. A great hostel, clean, friendly and well situated up the hill by the church of San Lorenzo at the top end of Manarola. Very popular though – book well in advance in summer. Reception daily 7am–1pm & 4pm– midnight. Dorms **€23**, doubles **€65**

RIOMAGGIORE

Il Boma Via C. Colombo 99 ☎ 0187 920 395, w ilboma .com. Three simple rooms in a great position right in the heart of Riomaggiore – very handy for the station so a good and affordable Cinque Terre base. The rooms are nothing fancy but are beautifully kept, wi-fi is available and breakfast is served in your room. **€90**

Villa Argentina Via De Gasperi 170 ☎ 0187 920 213, w villargentina.com. In a lovely spot in the upper part of town, with well-furnished rooms, parking and free wi-fi – though it's a bit of a hike from the old part of town. There are also apartments for rent. **€135**

EATING AND DRINKING

MONTEROSSO

Il Moretto Piazza Colombo 13 ☎ 0187 817 483. A fairly typical Ligurian menu but also branching out into more

adventurous territory with swordfish and Tuscan steaks. Consistently good cooking and service. Daily 12.30– 2.30pm & 7–10.30pm.

3

VERNAZZA

Gianni Franzi Piazza Marconi 5 ☎0187 823 1003. Decent food, right on the harbour. Often full of worn-out hikers, but its pasta and seafood dishes do really hit the spot. Daily 12.30–2.30pm & 7–10.30pm.

Osteria Il Baretto Via Roma 31 ☎0187 812 381, ⓦil -baretto.it. This place is halfway up the main street towards the station, and as such lacks a sea view, but the seafood pasta, fish baked in the oven, pesto and other mostly Ligurian dishes are excellent, and there are lots of tables outside at which to enjoy them. Daily noon–3pm & 7–10pm.

MANAROLA

La Scogliera Via Birolli 103 ☎0187 921 029. Right on the main street down to the harbour, this serves a fine signature seafood spaghetti on its outside terrace, along with great lobster pasta and tuna *carpaccio*. Pizzas too. Mon–Sat noon–3pm & 8–11pm.

RIOMAGGIORE

La Lanterna Via San Giacomo 46 ☎0187 24 581, ⓦlalanterna.org. A good, moderately priced pasta and seafood menu, and a great location at the harbour, housed in what was once a fishery. Lovely *zuppa di ceccie e seppie* (cuttlefish and chickpeas) for €10, great pasta (try the *ricci*, sea urchins), and lots of fresh fish. Daily 12.30–2.30pm & 7–10.30pm.

Ripa del Sole Via De Gasperi 4 ☎0187 920 143. Old-fashioned restaurant in the upper town serving unusual specialities such as pasta with rabbit *ragù* or lobster ravioli at very reasonable prices. Great anchovies and mussels, too. Tues–Sun 12.30–2.30pm & 8–11pm.

The Golfo dei Poeti

After the beauty of the Golfo Paradiso and Golfo del Tigullio, and the drama of the Cinque Terre, Liguria still has a final flourish. Hard up against the Tuscan border is the majestic Golfo di La Spezia, an impressively sweeping panorama of islands and rough headlands renamed the **Golfo dei Poeti** in 1919 by Italian playwright Sem Benelli for the succession of romantic souls who fell in love with the place. Petrarch was the first; Shelley lived and died on these shores; Byron was another regular; and D.H. Lawrence passed the pre-World War I years here. The town at the head of the gulf is workaday **La Spezia**, a major naval and shipbuilding centre with a fine art gallery. Small resorts line the fringes of the bay, linked by buses that hug the twisting roads or boats that shuttle across the glittering blue water – **Portovenere**, sitting astride a spit of land to the southwest, and **Lerici**, on the southeastern shore, are both highly picturesque stopovers.

La Spezia

Most travellers pass by **LA SPEZIA** or just use it to change trains. Its large mercantile port and the largest naval base in the country aren't particular draws for tourists, and the city doesn't have a great many other tangible attractions. But it's not a bad place by any means, and in the Museo Amedeo Lia, probably the finest collection of medieval and Renaissance art in Liguria, it has a genuinely compelling sight.

The town centre and seafront

Sandwiched between the hills and the sea, La Spezia proved an early attraction to conquerors, but it took Napoleon to capitalize on what is one of Europe's finest natural harbours and construct a naval complex at La Spezia early in the nineteenth century. Later the town was a prime target in World War II and much of the centre was rebuilt following Allied bombing. It is now a largely pedestrianized grid of streets behind the palm-fringed harbourfront promenade of **Viale Mazzini** and busy **Via Chiodo**, focused around the main pedestrian spine of Via del Prione and the central market square of **Piazza Cavour**, where there is a great selection of fish and other stalls.

Museo Amedeo Lia

Via del Prione 234 • Tues–Sun 10am–6pm • €7

Right in the heart of town, the **Museo Amedeo Lia** has a large and surprisingly interesting collection, including bronzes, illuminated manuscripts and a wide array of paintings, including lots of fourteenth- and fifteenth-century Italian works, in a restored seventeenth-century Franciscan convent. Among the highlights are Pontormo's sharp-eyed *Self-Portrait*, a supremely self-assured *Portrait of a Gentleman* by Titian, and Bellini's *Portrait of an Attorney*, as well as bronzes by Giambologna and Ammanati. Upstairs, be sure to search out one of the museum's most celebrated items – the *Madonna Dolente*, a half-statue in polychrome terracotta of a sorrowful Madonna by Benedetto da Maiano.

Museo Tecnico Navale

Viale Giovanni Amendola 1 • Daily 8am–7.30pm • €1.55 • ☎ 0187 770 750

At the western end of the seafront is the vast naval **Arsenale**. There's no public admittance to the complex itself, but just to the left of the entrance the engaging **Museo Tecnico Navale** contains lots of wonderful figureheads, models of ships, submersibles and other nautical artefacts.

ARRIVAL AND DEPARTURE   LA SPEZIA

By train The train station is a 10min walk from the town centre and a 5min walk north from the pedestrianized artery of Via del Prione.

By bus Buses stop at various points around town – on Via Chiodo at the end of Via del Prione, on Piazza Chiodo in front of the naval arsenal, at the train station and also on Piazza Cavour. Bus #L runs to Lerici every 10min and takes around 20–30min; bus #P runs to Portovenere from either the train-station forecourt or Via Chiodo every half-hour and takes 20min.

INFORMATION

Tourist offices There's a branch of the tourist office on the right side of the forecourt of the train station that's erratically open and a larger office on the seafront at Viale Italia 5 (Mon–Sat 9.30am–12.30pm & 2.30–6pm, Sun 9am–2pm; ☎ 0187 770 900, ⓦ turismoprovincia .laspezia.it).

ACCOMMODATION

Mary Via Fiume 177 ☎ 0187 743 254, ⓦ hotelmary.it. Probably the nicest of the hotels grouped around the train station, with simply but decently furnished rooms with wi-fi and flat-screen TV. Very friendly, with a pleasant downstairs lounge and breakfast room. They have a few smaller doubles for €75. **€90**

My One Hotel Via XX Settembre 81 ☎ 0187 738 848, ⓦ myonehotel.it. Very central, accessible from Via del Prione, and with functional, modern, if slightly character-less rooms, with large bathrooms and free wi-fi. Probably the nicest choice in the city centre. **€85**

EATING AND DRINKING

Kandinsky 1900 Via Calatafimi 23 ☎ 338 933 9532. Good bar just off Via del Prione with lots of tables outside and decent plates of goodies during *aperitivo* hour. Daily 4pm–1am.

La Pia Via Magenta 12 ☎ 0187 739 999, ⓦ lapia.it. Just off Via del Prione, this place does great focaccia, pizza and delicious *farinata* to eat in or take away. Mon–Sat 10am–10pm.

Osteria della Corte Via Napoli 86 ☎ 0187 715 210, ⓦ osteriadellacorte.com. Not far from the station, this is perhaps the town's best restaurant, offering a fairly high-end dining experience for which you'd be well advised to book. The service can be irritatingly snooty, but the food is pretty good and, considering the quality, moderately priced, with pasta *primi* for around €10 and meat and fish *secondi* for €16–20 – plus the odd themed menu for around €30. Tues–Sun 12.30–2.30pm & 8–10pm.

FERRIES FROM LA SPEZIA

Dozens of boats make excursions throughout the summer – and on certain days in winter too – between La Spezia and just about every port along this coast, leaving from the waterfront Passeggiata Morin, at the far end of Via del Prione. The most popular line is the one to **Portovenere and the Cinque Terre**, which operates daily in season, taking 45min to Portovenere and reaching Monterosso in just under 2hr. Return prices range from €7 to Portovenere to €25 for the whole Cinque Terre; a one-way ticket to the Cinque Terre is €12. The principal operator is **Consorzio Maríttimo Turistico**, "5 Terre–Golfo dei Poeti", Via Don Minzoni 13, La Spezia (☎ 0187 732 987, ⓦ navigazionegolfodeipoeti.it). The same line also operates services across the Golfo dei Poeti and to the island of Palmaria (€7 return).

Toa degli Arancio Via Daniele Manin 23 ☎ 0187 826 416. Great place where you can eat as much or as little as you want, with a fantastic array of *bruschette* (€3–4.50), generous €10 plates of cheese and/or *salumi*, along with *trofie* and other pasta; also various *secondi* for €10–12 that vary from day to day, though there are always steaks. Great service, and a lovely outdoor terrace hung with fairy lights.

Mon–Thurs 7.30pm–midnight, Fri & Sat 7.30pm–1am.
Trittico Via Cavalotti 64–66 ☎ 0187 735 509. This place serves a huge choice of pizzas – and very good they are too, enjoyed either in the cosy interior or at the plentiful tables outside on this peaceful side-street just off Via del Prione, not far from the seafront. Most pizzas €5–8. Mon–Sat noon–3pm & 7–11pm.

Portovenere

The ancient, narrow-laned town of **PORTOVENERE** sits astride a spit of land on the very tip of the southwestern arm of the Golfo dei Poeti, blessed with breathtaking views, a memorably tranquil atmosphere and a string of three islets just offshore, each smaller and rockier than the last (see box opposite).

The town's characteristic rose- and yellow-painted tower-houses form a defensive wall along the photogenic harbourfront, Calata Doria, a busy waterside strip lined with cafés and restaurants and known as the **Palazzata**. Up above, the town's main street, **Via Capellini**, runs parallel, and both continue to the end of the promontory to join at the thirteenth-century church of **San Pietro**, which was built over the ruins of a Roman temple to Venus, goddess of love (hence the town's name), and occupies a fantastic location overlooking the sea. You can wander in and enjoy the view from the attached loggia, and afterwards head through the gate in the nearby stretch of wall down to the rocky cove of the **Grotto Arpaia**, a favoured spot of Lord Byron, who swam across the bay from here to visit Shelley at San Terenzo. To this day, the gulf has the nickname of the "Baia di Byron".

Back in the main part of town, steps lead up from Via Capellini to the bare twelfth-century church of **San Lorenzo**, and above here to the remains of the sixteenth-century **Castello Doria** (daily 10.30am–1.30pm & 2.30–6.30pm; €2.20), where you can amble around the ramparts enjoying yet more great views. The tiny but clean **beach**, right in the centre, is good for paddling, though not much else. Otherwise most people swim from the rocks off the Calata Doria, the rocky cove of Grotto Arpaia, or a couple of crowded shingle beaches one or two kilometres back towards La Spezia.

ARRIVAL AND INFORMATION

PORTOVENERE

By bus Bus #P runs from the train station and Via Chiodo to Portovenere every 30min and takes about half an hour, dropping off a block back from the seafront.

By ferry There are 3–4 ferries daily between Portovenere and Lerici (€10 return).

By water-taxi A more flexible way of getting between

Portovenere and Lerici (€10 one way, €15 return; min €40 per trip).

Tourist office Right in the centre of town, just back from the beach at Piazza Bastreri 7 (daily 10am–noon & 4–8pm; ☎ 0187 790 691, ⓦ portovenere.it).

ACCOMMODATION

Genio Piazza Bastreri 8 ☎ 0187 790 611, ⓦ hotelgenio portovenere.com. Next door to the tourist office, this is Portovenere's least expensive and most convenient hotel, with nice if undistinguished rooms and free parking – a boon in a town where parking spaces are at a premium. **€100**

Locanda La Lucciola Via dell'Olivo 101 ☎ 0187 790 145, ⓦ locandalalucciola.com. A 5min walk along the waterfront towards La Spezia, this has lovely, bright, contemporary rooms with sea views and balconies, and a terrace restaurant and pizzeria too. **€125**

Locanda Lorena Via Cavour 4, Isola Palmaria ☎ 0187

792 370, ⓦ locandalorena.com. A small *pensione* on the Isola Palmaria that has half a dozen bright, simply but beautifully furnished rooms. Not cheap, but it's a lovely place, and you're also paying for its unique location. It also has a restaurant so you don't even have to go to the mainland to eat. Closed Oct–March. **€150**

Royal Sporting Via dell'Olivo 345 ☎ 0187 790 326, ⓦ royalsporting.it. Its rooms are nice, if unspectacular, but it also has pleasant, cool interior courtyards, spectacular views and a huge saltwater swimming pool, among other amenities, and is close to Portovenere's shingly beaches. **€180**

THE ISLANDS

Of the three islands that lie south of the peninsula, all but the nearest are in a military zone and so can only be viewed from the water. **Isola Palmaria** is the largest, just across the water, and regular boats shuttle back and forth for a cost of €2.50 one way, €4 return. Its star attraction is the Grotta Azzurra, which you can reach by boat, and a couple of beaches and places to stay (see opposite). Next is the **Isola del Tino**, a rocky islet marked with a lighthouse and the remains of a Romanesque abbey. Finally comes the even tinier **Isola del Tinetto**, also home to a monastic community in centuries gone by.

EATING AND DRINKING

Antica Osteria del Carugio Via Capellini 66 ☎0187 790 617, ⓦanticaosteriadelcarugio.com. This atmospheric, century-old place right in the heart of the old town has affordable specialities – anchovies, sheep's cheese and great mussels (which are cultivated on poles in Portovenere's harbour). 12.30–2.30pm & 7.30–10.30pm; closed Thurs.

La Pizzacia Via Capellini 96 ☎0187 792 722, ⓦlapizzaccia.com. Perfect if all you want is pizza or focaccia – mainly a takeaway but it has a few tables on the street outside. Daily noon–8pm.

Le Bocche Calata Doria 102 ☎0187 900 622, ⓦlebocche.it. Slick restaurant at the far end of the waterfront that's famous for its warm seafood salad, dressed with a pesto of anchovies, capers, pistachios and pine nuts, and has lots of fish and seafood dishes for €15–20 – not to mention a great location overlooking the channel between Portovenere and Palmaria. 12.30–2.30pm & 7–10.30pm; closed Tues in winter.

Lerici

On the other side of La Spezia's bay there is a string of small resorts, the largest and best known of which is **LERICI**, with its garden villas, seafront bars, trattorias and gift shops, grouped around the circular main square of Piazza Garibaldi, and busy quaysides whose outdoor restaurants provide an attractive setting as the sun goes down. Steps lead up from the harbour (you can also take an elevator) to the **Castello di San Giorgio** at the top of the town (summer Tues–Sun 10.30am–1pm & 2.30–6pm, stays open later in July & Aug; winter Tues–Fri 10.30am–12.30pm, Sat & Sun 10.30am–12.30pm & 2.30–5.30pm; €6, family tickets €12; ⓦcastellodilerici.it), which has fabulous views across to Portovenere and back to La Spezia. Inside there's a small Gothic chapel, but most of the rest of the interior is given over to a museum documenting prehistoric dinosaur life in the area. Finally, there are **beaches** five minutes' walk north of town towards San Terenzo.

ARRIVAL AND DEPARTURE   LERICI

By bus Bus #L runs from the train station and Via Chiodo to Lerici every 15min and takes about 20min, dropping close to the seafront. Leaving Lerici, wait at the stop on the corner of the central Piazza Garibaldi.

By ferry There are 3–4 ferries daily between Portovenere and Lerici, leaving Lerici at 9.30am, 10.30am and 2.30pm (€10 return).

By water-taxi The other way of getting to Portovenere is by water-taxi (€10 one way, €15 return; min €40 per trip).

ACCOMMODATION AND EATING

Byron Via Biaggini 19 ☎0187 967 104, ⓦbyronhotel.com. Overlooking Lerici's beach, 5min from the centre of town, this Sixties-era purpose-built hotel has large if slightly dowdy rooms, all with balconies except those on the first floor. Free wi-fi throughout. **€100**

Jeri Via Mazzini 20 ☎0187 967 605, ⓦristorantejeri.it. Above the fish market, right by the steps to the castle, it's no surprise that this place concentrates on cooking the freshest fish and seafood, and serves it up from great-value fixed-priced menus (€35–40) on its scenic terrace. Daily 12.30–2.30pm & 7–10.30pm.

Shelley & delle Palme Via Biaggini 5 ☎0187 968 204, ⓦhotelshelley.it. Smallish rooms, quite plain, but with nice balconies and great views over to Palmaria and Portovenere, with just the lazy clinking of the rigging in the boats below to lull you to sleep. Free wi-fi, and the Superior rooms are much larger and better furnished, with bigger balconies and baths. **€160**

3

Lombardy and the Lakes

SHOPPING IN THE GALLERIA EMANUEL VITTORIO, MILAN

Lombardy and the Lakes

Lombardy, Italy's richest region, often seems to have more in common with its northern European neighbours than with the rest of Italy. Given its history, this is hardly surprising: it was ruled for almost two centuries by the French and Austrians and takes its name from the northern Lombards, who ousted the Romans. As a border region, Lombardy has always been vulnerable to invasion, just as it has always profited by being a commercial crossroads. Emperors from Charlemagne to Napoleon came to Lombardy to be crowned king – and big business continues to take Lombardy's capital, Milan, more seriously than Rome.

The region's people, ranging from Milanese workaholics to cosseted provincial urbanites, hardly fit the popular image of Italians – and, in truth, they have little time for most of their compatriots. This led to the rise of the **Lega Nord** over the last fifteen years, a political party nominally demanding independence from Rome, although working in the government there in coalition with Berlusconi, and successfully exploiting the popular sentiment that northern taxes sustain the inefficient, workshy south.

Sadly all this economic success has taken its toll on the landscape: industry chokes the peripheries of towns, sprawls across the Po plain and even spreads its polluting tentacles into the Alpine valleys. Traffic, too, is bad, with many roads – autostradas and lakeside lanes alike – gridlocked at peak times. Nonetheless, Lombardy's towns and cities retain medieval cores boasting world-class art and architecture, and the stunning scenery of the so-called **Italian Lakes** – notably **lakes Maggiore**, **Como** and **Garda** – never fails to seduce.

Milan's lowland neighbours – **Cremona** and **Mantua** – flourished during the Middle Ages and Renaissance and retain much character. To the north, Lombardy is quite different, the lakes and valleys sheltering fewer historic towns, the cities of **Bergamo** and **Brescia** excepted. Reaching into the high Alps, lakes Maggiore, Como, Garda and their lesser-celebrated siblings have long been popular tourist territory with both Italians and foreigners.

Although the western shore of Lake Maggiore and the northern and eastern shores of Lake Garda fall outside Lombardy (in Piemonte, Trentino and Veneto respectively), the **Lakes region** and its resorts are all covered in this chapter.

THE ROOF OF THE DUOMO, MILAN

Highlights

❶ Roof of Milan's Duomo Wander around the roof of the world's largest Gothic cathedral with the best views of the city and the mountains beyond. **See p.227**

❷ The Last Supper Leonardo da Vinci's mural for the refectory wall of Santa Maria delle Grazie is one of the world's most resonant images. **See p.235**

❸ Shopping in Milan Steel yourself for the ultimate shopping trip in the fashion and design capital of the world. **See p.245**

❹ Certosa di Pavia This Carthusian monastery is a fantastic construction rising out of the rice fields near Pavia. **See p.248**

❺ Cycling around Mantua Rent a bike and explore elegant Mantua and the surrounding waterways. **See p.257**

❻ Tortelli alla zucca Tuck into a plate of delicious pumpkin ravioli topped with sage butter; find it on the menu in Mantua. **See p.258**

❼ Lake Como Explore the most romantic of the Lakes by ferry. **See p.267**

❽ Città Alta, Bergamo Bergamo's medieval upper town is an enchanting spot to spend an evening. **See p.277**

HIGHLIGHTS ARE MARKED ON THE MAP ON P.220

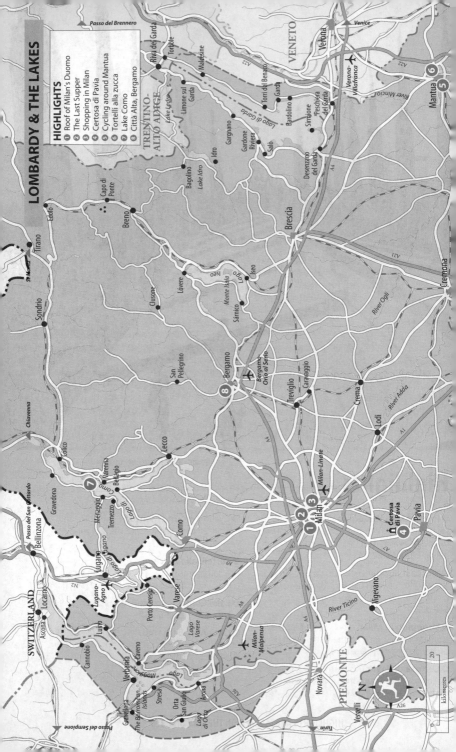

THE LAKES AND THEIR FEATURES

Although they share many things – dreamy vistas, quality local cooking and sheer romance, to name but a few – the Italian Lakes each have a very different character and it's worth thinking about the type of holiday you're looking for before you book.

Activity holidays The mountainous regions behind all the Lakes provide great hiking and mountain-biking opportunities but the combined winds to its north and the presence of Monte Baldo make Lake Garda the destination for on- and off-water thrill seekers.

Incurable romantics Watch the sun set behind Isola San Guilio on Lake Orta or from the Lake Como waterfront at Varenna or, alternatively, hole up in Gargnano on Lake Garda for a winter like D.H. Lawrence and his mistress did in 1912.

Visiting lakeside villas Lake Como offers the best selection of romantic waterfront residences with dreamy gardens to visit, although *belle époque* villas and sumptuous *palazzi* are dotted around the shore lines of all the lakes.

Wine tasting With Franciacorta and the various DOC regions to the south and southeast of Lake Garda – including Bardolino, Valpolicella and Lugana – you're never far from somewhere to try a local vintage or two.

Botanic gardens The microclimate of this corner of Lake Maggiore make the Isole Borromee and gardens in Verbania some of the most glorious gardens on the lakes, although competition is steep.

Travelling by public transport A quick train ride from Milan, Varenna is at the heart of the most spectacular part of Lake Como from where an excellent boat service will ferry you around to explore further.

Holidaying with kids With older children you can't beat the activities available on and around Lake Garda – from windsurfing or castle climbing to the theme and water parks in the southeast of the lake. Younger children might enjoy the shorter distances around the centre of Lake Como more, the family-friendly resort of Cannobio on Lake Maggiore, or the dragon stories linked with Lake Orta.

Milan

The dynamo behind the country's "economic miracle" in the 1950s, **MILAN** is an Italian city like no other. It's foggy in winter, muggy and mosquito-ridden in summer, and is closer in outlook, as well as distance, to London than to Palermo. It's a historic city, with a spectacular cathedral and enough ancient churches and galleries to keep you busy for a week, but there are also bars and cafés to relax in, and the contemporary aspects of the place represent the cutting edge of Italy's fashion and design industry. Milan wears its history on its well-tailored sleeve: medieval buildings nestle next to nineteenth-century splendour, rickety trams trundle past overgrown bombsites left from World War II and Fascist-era bombastic facades. But the Milanese keep the best for themselves: peep through a doorway into one of Milan's fabulous courtyards and you will be smitten.

The obvious focal point of central Milan is Piazza del Duomo, which, as well as being home to the city's iconic **Duomo**, leads on to the elegant **Galleria Vittorio Emanuele** and Piazza della Scala, home to the world-famous **opera house**. Heading northwest from Piazza del Duomo along the shopping street of Via Dante takes you to the imperious **Castello Sforzesco** and the extensive **Parco Sempione** beyond. North, the well-heeled neighbourhoods of **Brera** and **Moscova** are the haunt of Milan's most style-conscious citizens. Here you'll find the fine-art collection of the **Pinacoteca di Brera** and, nearby, the so-called **Quadrilatero d'Oro** (Golden Quadrangle), a concentration of top designer fashion boutiques. Slightly further north is Milan's most pleasant park, the **Giardini Pubblici**. Southwest of the Duomo, the shopping streets of Via Torino take you to the **Ticinese** district, a focal point at *aperitivo* time, and home to a couple of the city's most beautiful ancient churches. Continuing south to the **Navigli** leads to the bar and restaurant area around the city's remaining canals. West of the cathedral, the **Museo Archeologico** gives a taste of Roman Milan, while the basilica of Milan's Christian

MILAN

4

Campsite Autodromo

SHOPS
10 Corso Como	1
Il Salvagente	2

ACCOMMODATION
Città di Milano	3
Kennedy	2
La Cordata	5
La Dolce Vita	4
Nhow	6
Valley	1

BARS, CLUBS & LIVE-MUSIC VENUES
ATM	5
Atomic	8
Blue Note	1
Corso Como 10	7
Gasoline	6
Hollywood	4
L'Atlantique	11
Le Biciclette	10
Loolapaloosa	6
Magazzini Generali	14
Radetzky Café	9
Rita	12
Roialto	3
Scimmie	13
Tunnel	2

RESTAURANTS, CAFÉS & GELATERIE
Al Pont De Ferr	8
Anema e Cozze	6
Antica Trattoria della Pesa	1
California Bakery	4
Il Coniglio Bianco	5
L'Osteria del Treno	2
Pizza OK	3
Osteria di Porta Cicca	8
Tradizionale	7

0 200 metres

REGIONAL FOOD AND DRINK

Lombardy is distinctive in its variations in culinary habits. For example, the sophisticated recipes of the Milanese contrast sharply with the more rustic dishes of the Alpine foothills and lakes. The latter are sometimes known as *piatti poveri* (poor food): devised over centuries, these employ imagination and often time-consuming techniques to make up for the lack of expensive ingredients. *Risotto alla Milanese*, on the other hand, golden yellow with saffron, is Milan's most renowned culinary invention – and, it is said, only truly Milanese if cooked with the juices of roast veal flavoured with sage and rosemary. *Ossobuco* (shin of veal) is another Milanese favourite, as is *panettone*, the soft, eggy cake with sultanas eaten at Christmas time.

The short-grain rice used for **risotto** is grown in the paddy fields of the Ticino and Po valleys; other staples include green pasta and **polenta**. The latter – made from maize meal which is boiled and patiently stirred for around forty minutes, all the time watched with an eagle eye so it doesn't go lumpy – is found all over northern Italy. It can be eaten straightaway, or else left to cool and then sliced and grilled and served as an accompaniment to meat.

From Cremona comes *mostarda di frutta* (pickled fruit with mustard), the traditional condiment to serve with *bollito misto* (boiled meats). Stuffed pastas come in various guises – for example, around the Po Valley *tortelli alla zucca* (ravioli filled with pumpkin) or around Bergamo and Brescia *casoncei* (ravioli stuffed with sausage meat). Veal is eaten hot or cold in dishes like *vitello tonnato* (thin slices of cold veal covered with tuna mayonnaise) and wild *funghi* (mushrooms) are everywhere in autumn.

Lombardy is also one of the largest **cheese-making** regions in the country. As well as Gorgonzola there are numerous other local cheeses: among the best known are parmesan-like Grana Padano, smooth, creamy Mascarpone (used in sweet dishes) and the tangy, soft Taleggio.

Although Lombardy is not renowned internationally for its **wines**, supermarket shelves bulge with decent reds from the Oltrepò Pavese, and "Inferno" from the northern areas of Valtellina; while around Brescia, the Franciacorta area has earned plaudits for its excellent sparkling whites.

father, **Sant'Ambrogio**, is a couple of blocks away. A little further west stands the church of **Santa Maria delle Grazie** and the adjacent refectory building, holding Leonardo da Vinci's *The Last Supper*.

Some history

Milan first stepped into the historical limelight in 313 AD when Emperor Constantine issued the **Edict of Milan**, granting Christians throughout the Roman Empire the freedom to worship for the first time. The city, under its charismatic bishop, **Ambrogio** (Ambrose), swiftly became a major centre of Christianity; many of today's churches stand on the sites, or even retain parts, of fourth-century predecessors.

Medieval Milan rose to prominence under the **Visconti** dynasty, who founded the florid late-Gothic **Duomo**, and built the nucleus of the **Castello** – which, under their successors, the **Sforza**, was extended to house what became one of the most luxurious courts of the Renaissance. The last Sforza, Lodovico, commissioned **Leonardo da Vinci** in 1495 to paint *The Last Supper*.

Milan fell to the French in 1499, marking the beginning of almost four centuries of foreign rule, which included the Spanish, Napoleon and the Austrian Habsburgs. **Mussolini** made his mark on the city, too: arrive by train and you emerge into the massive white Stazione Centrale, built on the dictator's orders. And it was on the innocuous roundabout of Piazzale Loreto that the dictator's corpse was strung up for display in April 1945 as proof of his demise.

Milan's postwar development was characterized by the boom periods of the 1950s and 1980s: the city's wealth also comes from banking and its position at the top of the world's **fashion** and **design** industries. Politically, too, Milan has been key to Italy's postwar history. A bomb in Piazza Fontana in 1969 that killed sixteen people signalled the beginning of the dark and bloody period known as the **Anni di piombo**, when secret-service machinations led to over a hundred deaths from bomb attacks. In the 1980s, corruption and political scandal once again focused attention on Milan, which gained the nickname **Tangentopoli** ("Bribesville"). The self-promoting media magnate **Silvio Berlusconi** – Italy's longest serving prime minister since World War II – is also Milan born and bred. And despite having lost his political weight he maintains his power base in the city's media conglomerates as well as owning the football club AC Milan.

Piazza del Duomo and around

The hub of the city is **Piazza del Duomo**, a large, mostly pedestrianized square lorded over by the exaggerated spires of the **Duomo**, Milan's cathedral. The piazza was given its present form in 1860 when medieval buildings were demolished to allow grander, unobstructed views of the cathedral, and the **Galleria Vittorio Emanuele II** was constructed to link the piazza with the showy new opera theatre, **La Scala**. Facing the Duomo, Mussolini's **Palazzo dell'Arengario** houses a collection of nineteenth-century art, while south of medieval **Piazza dei Mercanti** nearby, the **Pinacoteca Ambrosiana** boasts a collection including Leonardo da Vinci, Caravaggio and Raphael.

The Duomo

Piazza del Duomo • Daily 7am–7pm • Free • Ⓦ duomomilano.it • Ⓜ Duomo

Milan's vast **Duomo** was begun in 1386 under the Viscontis, but not completed until the finishing touches to the facade were added in 1813. It is characterized by a hotchpotch of styles that range from Gothic to Neoclassical. From the **outside** at least it's incredible, notable as much for its strange confection of Baroque and Gothic decoration as its sheer size. The marble, chosen by the Viscontis in preference to the usual material of brick, was brought on specially built canals from the quarries of Candoglia, near Lake Maggiore, and continues to be used in renovation today.

The interior

The **interior** is striking for its dimension and atmosphere. The five aisles are separated by 52 towering piers, while an almost subterranean half-light filters through the stained-glass windows, lending the marble columns a bone-like hue that led the French writer Suarés to compare the interior to "the hollow of a colossal beast".

By the entrance, the narrow brass strip embedded in the pavement with the signs of the zodiac alongside is Europe's largest **sundial**, laid out in 1786. A beam of light still falls on it through a hole in the ceiling, though changes in the Earth's axis mean that it's no longer accurate. To the left of the entrance a door leads down to the remains of a fourth-century **Battistero Paleocristiano** (daily 9.30am–5.15pm; €4) where the city's patron saint, Ambrogio, baptized St Augustine in 387 AD.

At the far end of the church, the large crucifix suspended high above the chancel contains the most important of the Duomo's holy relics – **a nail from Christ's cross**, which was also crafted into the bit for the bridle of Emperor Constantine's horse. The cross is lowered once a year, on September 14, the Feast of the Cross, by a device invented by Leonardo da Vinci.

Close by, beneath the presbytery, the **treasury** (daily 9am–noon & 2.30–6pm; €3) features extravagant silverwork, Byzantine ivory carvings and heavily embroidered vestments. Here, too, is the Duomo's most surprising exhibit: British artist Mark Wallinger's haunting video installation *Via Dolorosa*. Commissioned by the diocese of Milan in a bold attempt to resurrect the role of the Church as a patron of the arts, it comprises a large screen showing the last eighteen minutes of Zeffirelli's *Jesus of Nazareth*, with ninety percent of the image blacked out, leaving just a narrow frame visible round the sides. Beside here is the **crypt** housing the remains of San Carlo Borromeo, the zealous sixteenth-century cardinal who was canonized for his work

4

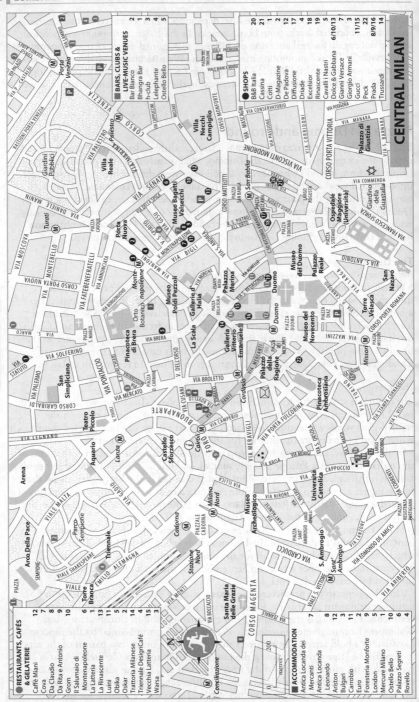

CENTRAL MILAN

■ **BARS, CLUBS & LIVE-MUSIC VENUES**

Bar Blanco	2
Bhangra Bar	1
h-club	3
Lelephante	4
Ostello Bello	5

● **SHOPS**

B&B Italia	20
Cassina	21
Cotti	1
D-Magazine	12
De Padova	17
Diffusione	4
Driade	18
Rinascente	19
Cavalli Nastri	5
Dolce & Gabbana	6/10/13
Gianni Versace	7
Giorgio Armani	3
Gucci	11/15
Peck	22
Prada	8/9/16
Trussardi	14

● **RESTAURANTS, CAFÉS & GELATERIE**

Caffè Miani	12
Cova	8
Da Claudio	9
Da Rita e Antonio	10
Grom	6
Il Salumaio di Montenapoleone	7
La Latteria	13
La Rinascente	11
Luini	5
Obika	2
Oskar	14
Trattoria Milanese	15
Triennale DesignCafé	3
Vecchia Latteria	
Warsa	

■ **ACCOMMODATION**

Antica Locanda dei Mercanti	7
Antica Locanda Leonardo	8
Ariston	12
Bulgari	3
Carrobio	11
Euro	2
Foresteria Monforte	9
London	1
Mercure Milano	10
Ostello Bello	5
Palazzo Segreti	6
Rovello	4

among the poor of the city, especially during the Plague of 1630. He lies here in a glass coffin, clothed, bejewelled, masked and gloved, wearing a gold crown attributed to Cellini. Borromeo was also responsible for the large altar in the north transept, erected to close off a door that was used by locals as a shortcut to the market.

To the right of the chancel, by the door to the Palazzo Reale, the sixteenth-century statue of **St Bartholomew**, with his flayed skin thrown like a toga over his shoulder, is one of the church's more gruesome statues, its veins, muscles and bones sculpted with anatomical accuracy and the draped skin retaining the form of knee, foot, toes and toenails.

The roof

Daily 9am–6.15pm • €7 to walk, €12 for the elevator • Collect tickets reserved online or buy from Duomo Point, Via Arcivescovado, at the eastern end of the cathedral (9am–12pm & 1–6pm)

Outside again, from the northeast end of the cathedral you can access the **cathedral roof**, where you can stroll around the forest of tracery, pinnacles and statues while enjoying fine views of the city and, on clear days, even the Alps. The highlight is the central spire, its lacy marble crowned by a gilded statue of the Madonna – the *Madonnina*, the city's guardian – in summer looking out over the rooftop sunbathers.

Museo del Novecento

Palazzo dell'Arengario, Piazza del Duomo 12 • Mon 2.30–7.30pm, Tues, Wed & Fri 9.30am–7.30pm, Thurs & Sat 9.30am–10.30pm • €5, free Fri 3.30pm onwards or under 25 • ⓦ museodelnovecento.org • Ⓜ Duomo

The city's collection of twentieth-century art is collected together in a gallery built around the monumental, Fascist, Palazzo dell'Arengario from where Mussolini used to address the Milan crowds. It's a confusing, labyrinthine gallery, but worth a wander to see works by the masters of the Futurist movement like Umberto Boccioni and Mario Sironi, and De Chirico. There are also several beautiful subdued works by Morandi, and Milan's *Arte povera* movement is repesented by works by Piero Manzoni and Jannis Kounellis, among others. Linked by a glass bridge, the gallery spaces spill into the adjacent Palazzo Reale and there are great views of Piazza del Duomo from the top floor, which houses Lucio Fontana's neon spiral. The smart, pricey, but quality restaurant here, *Giacomo Arengario* (☎02 7209 3824, ⓦgiacomoarengario.com), also offers lovely views of the Duomo.

Biblioteca Pinacoteca Ambrosiana

Piazza Pio XI 2 • Tues–Sun 10am–6pm • €15, €10 Codice Atlantico only, plus obligatory booking fee • ⓦ ambrosiana.it • Ⓜ Duomo

Five minutes' walk southwest of the Piazza, just off Via Torino, lies the **Biblioteca Pinacoteca Ambrosiana**, founded by Cardinal Federico Borromeo in the early seventeenth century. In the face of Protestant reforms, the Cardinal was concerned to defend Catholic traditions not only through doctrine and liturgy, but also by educating the faithful about their Catholic origins. To this end he set about collecting paintings and ancient manuscripts, assembling one of the largest libraries in Europe. You can visit the original reading room and other rooms, but the main attraction is the world's largest bound collection of Leonardo da Vinci's drawings and writings, known as the **Codice Atlantico Leonardo**.

The extensive **art collection** is stamped with Borromeo's taste for Jan Brueghel, sixteenth-century Venetians and some of the more kitsch followers of Leonardo. Among many mediocre works, there is a rare painting by Leonardo da Vinci, *Portrait of a Musician*, a cartoon by Raphael for the School of Athens, and a Caravaggio considered to be Italy's first still life. The prize for the quirkiest exhibit is shared between a pair of white gloves that Napoleon reputedly wore at Waterloo, and a lock of Lucrezia Borgia's hair – displayed for safe-keeping in a glass phial ever since Byron (having decided that her hair was the most beautiful he had ever seen) extracted a strand as a keepsake from the library downstairs, where it used to be kept unprotected.

4

Piazza dei Mercanti

Northwest out of Piazza del Duomo, at the start of pedestrianized Via Dante which leads to the Castello Sforzesco (see opposite), lies **Piazza dei Mercanti**, the commercial centre of medieval Milan. The square is dominated by the thirteenth-century **Palazzo della Ragione**, where council meetings and tribunals were held on the upper floor, with markets under the porticoes below. The stone relief on the facade above the arcade shows the rather forlorn-looking Oldrado di Tressano, the mayor who commissioned the building in 1228, astride his horse. Opposite, the striped black-and-white marble **Loggia degli Orsi**, built in 1316, was where council proclamations were made and sentences announced. The coats of arms of the various districts of Milan are just about visible beneath the grime left by Milanese smog.

Galleria Vittorio Emanuele II

Leading off to the north of Piazza del Duomo is the gaudily opulent **Galleria Vittorio Emanuele II**, a cruciform glass-domed gallery designed in 1865 by Giuseppe Mengoni, who was killed when he fell from the roof a few days before the inaugural ceremony. The circular mosaic beneath the glass cupola is composed of the symbols that made up the cities of the newly unified Italy: Romulus and Remus for Rome, a *fleur-de-lys* for Florence, a white shield with a red cross for Milan and a bull for Turin – it's considered good luck to spin round three times on the bull's testicles, hence the indentation in the floor.

The *galleria* was designed as a covered walkway between the Piazza del Duomo and Piazza della Scala to the north; nicknamed the "*salotto*" – or drawing room – of Milan, it used to be the focal point for the parading Milanese on their *passeggiata*. These days, visitors rather than locals are more likely to swallow the extortionate prices at the gallery's cafés, which include the historic *Zucca*, with its glorious 1920s tiled interior at one end, and the newer, stylish *Gucci Café* at the other. Shops, too, are aimed at visitors to the city, with top designer labels sitting next to pricey souvenir outlets. Somehow, however, the *galleria* still manages to retain most of its original dignity, helped along by quietly elegant boutiques including the handsome 80-year-old Prada shop in the centre.

La Scala

Museum daily 9am–12.30pm & 1.30–5pm • €6 • ⓦ teatroallascala.org • Ⓜ Duomo

The main branch of Galleria Vittorio Emanuele leads through to **Piazza della Scala**, fronted by the rather plain Neoclassical facade of the world-famous Teatro alla Scala opera house, popularly known as **La Scala**. The theatre was commissioned by Empress Maria Theresa of Austria from the architect Piermarini and many of the leading names in Italian opera had their major works premiered here, including Bellini, Donizetti and Rossini. But it is **Giuseppe Verdi** who is most closely associated with the opera house and whose fame was consolidated here in 1842 with the first performance of *Nabucco*, with its perfectly timed patriotic sentiments. The post-World War II period saw another breathtaking roll call of top composers and musical performers – among them Schoenberg, Lucio Berio, Rudolf Nureyev and Maria Callas – while Toscanini, perhaps the most influential conductor of all time, devoted more than fifty years to the theatre. These days, however, La Scala is a bit at sea: no quality Italian composers have emerged for a generation and the repertoire has become a touch predictable.

Tickets can be hard to come by, but if you want to experience one of the world's most famous opera houses in action, there are numerous avenues; see p.245 for ticket information.

Tucked into one corner of the theatre, a small **museum** features costumes, sets, composers' death masks, plaster casts of conductors' hands and a rugged statue of Puccini in a capacious overcoat. A visit to the auditorium is included in the ticket, providing there is no rehearsal taking place; times when the auditorium is empty are listed daily outside the entrance to the museum.

Piazza Castello and around

At the far end of the pedestrianized Via Dante, the Castello Sforzesco rises imperiously from Foro Buonaparte, a road laid out by Napoleon in self-tribute. He had a vision of a grand new centre for his Italian capital, designed along Roman lines, but he only got as far as constructing an arena, a triumphal arch and these two semicircular roads before he lost Milan to the Austrians. The arena and triumphal arch still stand half-forgotten behind the castle on the edges of the **Parco Sempione**, the city centre's largest patch of green and once the castle's garden and hunting grounds.

Castello Sforzesco

Piazza Castello • Daily 7am–7pm, closes 1hr earlier in winter • ⓦ milanocastello.it • ⓜ Cairoli

With its crenellated towers and fortified walls, the red-brick **Castello Sforzesco** is one of Milan's most striking landmarks. The result of numerous rebuildings, it was begun by the Viscontis, destroyed by mobs rebelling against their regime in 1447, and rebuilt by their successors, the Sforzas. Under Lodovico Sforza the court became one of the most powerful, luxurious and cultured of the Renaissance, renowned for its ostentatious wealth and court artists like Leonardo and Bramante. Lodovico's days of glory came to an end when Milan was invaded by the French in 1499, and from then until the end of the nineteenth century the castle was used as a barracks by successive occupying armies. Just over a century ago it was converted into a series of museums. Ongoing restoration means that parts of the complex may be closed when you visit.

The *castello*'s buildings are grouped around three courtyards: through the **Filarete Tower** (rebuilt in 1905, having been destroyed in the sixteenth century by an explosion of gunpowder) you enter the larger of the three, the dusty-looking parade ground. It's not until you're through the gateway opposite that you begin to sense a Renaissance castle: this is the **Corte Ducale**, which formed the centre of the residential quarters and is now the home of the castle's museums. The **Rocchetta**, to your left, was the most secure part of the fortress and is now used for temporary exhibitions. The gateway ahead leads to the Parco Sempione.

The museums

Tues–Sun 9am–5.30pm • Combined ticket €3, free after 2pm on Fri, after 4.30pm other days

The ticket office, on your right as you enter the Corte Ducale, gives access to the **Museo d'Arte Antica**, a succession of rooms containing an extensive collection of ancient artefacts saved from the city's churches and archeological excavations. More interesting, however, are the castle rooms themselves, especially the **Sala delle Asse**, designed by Leonardo da Vinci; his black-and-white preparatory sketches were discovered in the 1950s. After some rather dull armoury you reach the museum's star exhibit: Michelangelo's **Rondanini Pietà**, which the artist worked on for the last nine years of his life. It's an unfinished but oddly powerful work; much of the marble is unpolished and a third arm, indicating a change of position for Christ's body, hangs limply from a block of stone to his right.

Upstairs, the **Museo delle Arti Decorative** exhibits furniture and decorative arts through the ages, including fascinating early works by the great twentieth-century Milanese designer, Gio Ponte. The Torre Falconiere (Falconry Tower) next door holds the castle's **art collection** containing numerous paintings by Lombard artists such as Foppa and Bramantino, as well as minor Venetian works, including some Canalettos. The best are all grouped together in Room XIII and include Antonello da Messina's *St Benedict*, originally part of a five-piece polyptych, of which two panels are in the Uffizi in Florence.

Across the courtyard, in the castle cellars, are the smaller **Egyptian collection**, with displays of mummies, sarcophagi and papyrus fragments from *The Book of the Dead*, and the deftly lit **prehistoric collection** – an assortment of finds from the Iron Age burial grounds of the Golasecca civilization.

The Parco Sempione

Park Dawn to dusk • Free **Aquario Civico** Tues–Sun 9am–1pm & 2–5.30pm • Free • Ⓦ verdeacqua.eu • **Torre Branca** Wed 10.30am–12.30pm & 4–6.30pm, Sat 10.30am–1pm, 3–6.30pm & 8.30pm–midnight, Sun 10.30am–2pm & 2.30–7pm, also May–Sept Tues–Sun 9.30pm–midnight • €4, free Wed for over 65s • Ⓜ Cairoli or Cadorna or Lanza

The **Parco Sempione**, the city centre's largest area of greenery, was laid out in the castle's old hunting grounds and orchards. It can make a refreshing break from the city's traffic-choked roads, with a playground for younger kids, grass to sprawl or kick a football on and a café or two. On the eastern edge of the park by the **Arena Civica**, a Colosseum-inspired area where mock chariot races and naval battles were held to entertain Napoleon's generals, stands the **Aquario Civico**, in a pretty Liberty building with a small collection of tanks that will keep children entertained for a spell. Opposite, on the western edge the **Torre Branca**, designed by Gio Ponte on the occasion of the fifth Triennale in 1933, offers a birds'-eye view of the city.

Triennale

Viale Emilio Alemagna 6 • Tues, Wed, Sat & Sun 10.30am–8.30pm, Thurs & Fri 10.30am–11pm • Exhibitions €8 • Ⓦ triennale.it • Ⓜ Cadorna or Cairoli

The Palazzo dell'Arte or **Triennale**, on the western reaches of the park, makes a refreshing diversion from the greenery. Designed by Giovanni Muzio in 1931, the building played a pivotal role in the development of Milan's importance in the world of design, providing a permanent home to the triannual design exhibition held here since the 1930s. The majestic lines of the building and its light airy interior are reason enough for a visit, but the *palazzo* also holds the **Triennale Design Museum** and other good-quality temporary exhibitions of design, architecture and contemporary art. There's a great café-bar, *DesignCafé* (see p.241), which overflows downstairs into the park in the summer.

Studio Museo Achille Castiglioni

Piazza Castello 27 • Tues–Sat guided tours 10am, 11am & noon • €8 • Ⓦ achillecastiglioni.it • Ⓜ Cadorna or Cairoli

The highlight of a trip to Milan for many design buffs is one of the city's little-visited gems, the **Studio Museo Achille Castiglioni**, just outside the park gates. The utterly beguiling studio of one of Milan's best-known industrial designers is stuffed with found objects, plans and sketches, as well as prototypes of some of his most famous works.

Brera and Moscova

Due north of La Scala, **Via Brera** sets the tone for Milan's arty quarter: small galleries nestle in the lanes surrounding the Accademia di Belle Arti and Pinacoteca di Brera. As you'll notice from the café prices and designer styles of those who can afford to sit outside them, these cobbled streets are the terrain of the urban rich.

Across Via Fatebenefratelli, the stylish bars and traditional trattorias continue north through the neighbourhood of **Moscova**, home to the offices of the *Corriere della Sera* newspaper. A good area for shopping and browsing, Corso Garibaldi, Via Solferino and Via San Marco lead up to the bastion in Piazza XXV Aprile, which marks the beginning of **Corso Como**, a trendy street full of bars, clubs and boutiques, which in turn leads up to the train and bus station of Porta Garibaldi.

Pinacoteca di Brera

Via Brera 28 • Tues–Sun 8.30am–7.15pm • €6 • Ⓦ brera.beniculturali.it • Ⓜ Lanza or Montenapoleone

Milan's most prestigious art gallery, the **Pinacoteca di Brera** was opened to the public in 1809 by Napoleon, who filled the building with works looted from the churches and aristocratic collections of French-occupied Italy. It's big: your visit will probably be more enjoyable if you're selective, dipping into the collection guided by your own personal tastes. There's a good **audioguide** available (€5), although it does rather gallop through the highlights.

Room VI

Exiting the three rooms of early medieval works brings you face to face with the stunningly powerful *The Dead Christ*, a painting by Andrea Mantegna, the court artist in fifteenth-century Mantova responsible for the Camera degli Sposi (see p.255). One of Mantegna's sons had died around the time he was working on this painting and the desolation in the women's faces and the powerful sense of bereavement emanating from the work seem autobiographical. In the same room, the *Pietà* by Mantegna's brother-in-law, Giovanni Gentile, is another beautifully balanced work of grief and pain that has been deemed "one of the most moving paintings in the history of art".

Room VIII

Next door in Room VIII, the impressive *St Mark Preaching in St Euphemia Square* introduces an exotic note, the square bustling with turbaned men, veiled women, camels and even a giraffe. Gentile Bellini, who had lived and worked in Constantinople for several years, died before the painting was complete, so it was finished off by his brother Giovanni for the Scuola Grande di San Marco in Venice.

Room IX

Another theatrical work hanging nearby is Paolo Veronese's depiction of *Supper in the House of Simon*; it got him into trouble with the Inquisition, who considered the introduction of frolicking animals and unruly kids unsuitable subject matter for a religious painting. Tintoretto's *Pietà* was more starkly in tune with requirements of the time, a scene of intense concentration and grief over Christ's body, painted in the 1560s. Nearby in the same room is another Tintoretto, *The Finding of the Body of Saint Mark in Alexandria*: the dramatic use of perspective coupled with mystical use of light and shadow create a truly operatic ensemble.

Room XXIV

The pride of the Brera collection, room XXIV contains three paintings ranked among the highest expression of Renaissance culture in art: Piero della Francesca's haunting *Madonna and Child with Saints*, and *Federigo da Montefeltro* which is the most arresting, with its stylized composition and geometric harmony. On the wall opposite, *Christ at the Column* is the only known painting by the architect Bramante. Take a look, too, at Raphael's altarpiece, the *Marriage of the Virgin*, whose lucid, languid Renaissance mood stands in sharp contrast to the grim realism of Caravaggio's deeply human *Supper at Emmaus* (Room XXIX), set in a dark tavern.

The rest of the gallery

Less well known but equally naturalistic are the paintings of Lombardy's brilliant eighteenth-century realist, Ceruti – known as Il Pitochetto (The Little Beggar) for his unfashionable sympathy with the poor, who stare out with reproachful dignity from his canvases (Room XXXVI).

There is also a small collection of modern work from the Jesi donation on display in Room X, which is particularly strong on the Futurists and also includes paintings by Morandi, Modigliani, De Chirico and Carrà, as well as abstract sculpture by Marino Marini and Medardo Rosso.

Quadrilatero d'Oro

The Roman thoroughfare **Via Manzoni** leads north from La Scala to Porta Nuova, one of the medieval entrances to the city forming one side of the **Quadrilatero d'Oro**. Comprising a few hundred square metres bordered by Via Montenapoleone, Via Sant'Andrea, Via della Spiga and Via Manzoni, the quarter is home to shops of all the big international and Italian fashion names, along with design studios and contemporary art galleries. This is

Milan in its element and the area is well worth a wander if only to see the city's better-heeled residents in their natural habitat. For more on shopping in Milan, see p.245.

Museo Bagatti Valsecchi

Via Santo Spirito 10/Via Gesù 5 • Tues–Sun 1–5.45pm • €8, or €15 with the Casamuseocard including entrance to Museo Poldi Pezzoli & Casa Necchi Campiglio • ⓦ museobagattivalsecchi.org • ⓜ Montenapoleone or San Babila

In a house linking Via Santo Spirito with Via Gesù 5, just off Via Montenapoleone, is the **Museo Bagatti Valsecchi**, an absorbing private museum affording an intriguing insight into the tastes of the Bagatti Valsecchi brothers, Giuseppe and Fausto. Taking the nineteenth-century fashion for collecting to an extreme, in 1883 they built a Renaissance-style home, inspired by the Palazzo Ducale in Mantova, in which to house their Renaissance collections, as well as a home for their families. All the rooms are richly decorated with carved fireplaces, painted ceilings and heavy wall-hangings and paintings. The fireplace in the drawing room perfectly illustrates the brothers' eclectic approach to decoration: the main surround is sixteenth-century Venetian, the frescoes in the middle are from Cremona, while the whole ensemble is topped off with the Bagatti Valsecchi coat of arms. Modern conveniences were incorporated into the house but not allowed to ruin the harmony, so the shower in the bathroom is disguised in a niche, and the piano, which was not realized as an instrument until the eighteenth century, is incorporated within a cabinet. Look out also for touching domestic items, such as the nursery furniture for Giuseppe's children.

Museo Poldi Pezzoli

Via Manzoni 12 • 10am–6pm; closed Tues • €8, or €15 with the Casamuseocard including entrance to Museo Bagatti Valsecchi & Villa Necchi Campiglio • ⓦ museopoldipezzoli.it • ⓜ Montenapoleone

Halfway between La Scala and Porta Nuova, the eclectic **Museo Poldi Pezzoli** comprises pieces assembled by the nineteenth-century collector Gian Giacomo Poldi Pezzoli. Much of this is made up of rather dull rooms of clocks, watches, cutlery and jewellery, but the Salone Dorato upstairs contains a number of intriguing paintings, including a portrait of a portly *San Nicola da Tolentino* by Piero della Francesca, part of an altarpiece on which he worked intermittently for fifteen years. St Nicholas looks across at two works by Botticelli; one a gentle *Madonna del Libro*, among the many variations of the Madonna and Child theme which he produced at the end of the fifteenth century, and the other a mesmerizing *Deposition*, painted towards the end of his life in response to the monk Savonarola's crusade against his earlier, more humanistic canvases. Also in the room is the museum's best-known portrait, *Portrait of a Young Woman* by Antonio Pollaiuolo, whose anatomical studies are evidenced in the subtle suggestion of bone structure beneath skin.

Galleria d'Italia

Via Manzoni 10 • Tues–Sun 9.30am–7.30pm • €5 • ⓦ gallerieditalia.com • ⓜ Duomo or Montenapoleone

The Neoclassical Palazzo Anguissola and Palazzo Bretani together hold the **Galleria d'Italia**, a decent collection of mainly Romantic and Naturalistic nineteenth-century paintings that also touches on Symbolism and early Futurism. Highlights include atmospheric depictions of Lombard and Milanese life, on the top floor, including Carlo Canella's *Porta Tusa* and *Santa Maria dell Pace* as well as scenes of the insurrections against French rule known as the *5 Giornate*. The decorative interiors of the *palazzi* have been restored to their original Neoclassical splendour of gilded, framed frescoes and mosaic floors.

Around the Giardini Pubblici

At the top of Piazza Cavour, on the northern side of Porta Nuova, are the **Giardini Pubblici** (open dawn until dusk; ⓜPalestro, ⓜTurati or ⓜPorta Venezia), stretching over to Porta Venezia. Milan's most attractive green space, it was designed by Piermarini shortly after he completed La Scala. Re-landscaped in the nineteenth century to give a more rustic look, the park, with its shady avenues, children's play areas and small lake, is ideal for a break from the busy streets. Across the road, the **Giardini della Villa Reale** is an urban oasis reserved for those with children under 13. With a small area of swings, lawns, shady trees and a little pond with ducks, turtles and giant carp, it makes a perfect bolthole.

Corso Venezia, which leads back down from here to San Babila and the centre, is lined with nineteenth-century palaces. Hereabouts are the city homes of many of Milan's most moneyed residents, including the rooftop apartments of Dominco Dolce and Stefano Gabbana.

Villa Necchi Campiglio

Via Mozart 14 • Wed–Sun 10am–6pm • €8, €15 Casamuseocard including entrance to Museo Bagatti Valsecchi & Museo Poldi Pezzoli, free for National Trust members • Ⓦ casemuseo.it • Ⓜ Palestra or Porta Venezia

A refreshing addition to Milan's collection of museum houses, **Necchi Campiglio Villa** wonderfully showcases the tastes and way of life of the privileged Milan bourgeoisie in the heady days of the twentieth century. Built in the 1930s by the Milanese architect Piero Portaluppi for an industrialist who had made his fortune from sewing machines, the villa, complete with a lovely garden, swimming pool and tennis court, will perhaps be familiar from the film *I Am Love* where it starred alongside Tilda Swinton. It is an Art Deco beauty, beautifully preserved with a sweeping walnut stairway, marble bathrooms, brass radiator covers and the original kitchen and pantry.

The Ticinese district

Leading southwest away from the Duomo, past the chain stores of Via Torino, the city takes on a different, slightly more alternative air. The main thoroughfare of the **Ticinese** district, the Corso di Porta Ticinese, has become a focus for street fashion and is lined with small boutiques and bars. The area really comes into its own at *aperitivo* time, especially during summer when people spill on to the pedestrian streets from the numerous bars and cafés. The neighbourhood also boasts two of Milan's most important churches – and most rewarding sights – **San Lorenzo Maggiore** and **Sant'Eustorgio**.

San Lorenzo Maggiore

Corso di Porto Ticinese 12 • Daily 7.30am–12.30pm & 2.30–6.45pm • **Cappella di San Aquilino** Daily 7.30am–6pm • €4; combined ticket with Cappella Portinari & Museo Diocesano €12 • Ⓦ sanlorenzomaggiore.com • Tram #3

Towards the northern end of Corso Ticinese stands **San Lorenzo Maggiore**, considered by Leonardo da Vinci to be the most beautiful church in Milan. It is indeed a graceful building with a quiet dignity, somewhat at odds with the skateboarding and partying that goes on in the piazza outside. One of the four churches founded by Sant'Ambrogio in the city in the fourth century, it was built with masonry salvaged from various Roman buildings. The sixteen Corinthian columns outside – the **Colonne di San Lorenzo** – were placed here in the fourth century as a portico to the church. To the right of the altar, the **Cappella di San Aquilino** was probably built as an imperial mausoleum. The lunettes in the Roman octagonal room hold beautiful fourth-century mosaics, which would originally have covered all the walls, while beneath the relics of Sant'Aquilino steps lead down to what is left of the original foundations, a jigsaw of fragments of Roman architecture.

Sant'Eustorgio

Piazza Sant'Eustorgio 1 • Daily 7.30am–5pm • Tram #3

Heading south down Corso Ticinese, you come to **Sant'Eustorgio**, another fourth-century church, built to house the bones of the Magi, said to have been brought here by Sant'Ambrogio. It was rebuilt in the eleventh century, and in the twelfth century was virtually destroyed by Barbarossa, who seized the Magi's bones and deposited them in Cologne's cathedral. Some of the bones were returned in 1903 and are kept in a Roman sarcophagus tucked away in the right transept.

4

Cappella Portinari

Cappella Portinari Tues–Sun 10am–6pm • €6, combined ticket with Cappella di San Aquilino & Museo Diocesano €12

A must-see while here is the **Capella Portinari** or chapel, accessed round to the left of the main entrance. The beautiful chapel consciously recalls Brunelleschi's San Lorenzo in Florence, with two domed rooms, the smaller one housing the altar. It has been credited with being Milan's first true Renaissance building because of its simple geometric design; the mixture of Lombard terracotta sculpture and Florentine monochromatic simplicity makes an enchanting stylistic fusion. It was commissioned from the Florentine architect Michelozzi in the 1460s by one Pigello Portinari, an agent of the Medici bank, to house the remains of St Peter the Martyr, an unattractive saint who was excommunicated for entertaining women in his cell, then cleared and given a job as an Inquisitor.

The Navigli

The southern end of Corso di Porta Ticinese is guarded by the nineteenth-century **Arco di Porta Ticinese**, marking the beginning of Milan's canal – or **Navigli** – neighbourhood, once a bustling industrial area and these days a focus for the city's nightlife, although it is scruffy and often disappointing in the harsh light of day. The best time to visit is in the evening when the quarter's many restaurants and bars come alive, although the monthly Sunday **antiques street-market** (last Sun of month; closed July and Aug) also brings a vivacious focus to the waterways.

Naviglio Grande and Naviglio Pavese

South from the Darsena (the main goods dock), the **Naviglio Grande** and the **Naviglio Pavese**, respectively the first and last of the city's canals to be completed, lead into the plains of Lombardy. This was once Milan at its grittiest. Some of the warehouses and traditional tenement blocks, or *case di ringhiera*, have been refurbished and become prime real-estate but you'll still find plenty of unreconstructed corners. Craftsmen and

---

MILAN'S CANALS

Improbable though it may seem, less than fifty years ago Milan was still a viable port – and less than a hundred years ago several of its main arteries – including Via Senato and Via San Marco – were busy waterways.

In the twelfth century, the first **canals** linked irrigation channels and the various defensive moats of the city. Later, in 1386, the **Naviglio Grande** was opened, linking the city to the River Ticino and thus Lake Maggiore. It was Gian Galeazzo Visconti, however, who was really responsible for the development of the system, in the fourteenth century to transport the building materials for the Duomo, especially marble from Lake Maggiore.

Travellers were also seen on the canals: the ruling families of the North used them to visit one another, Prospero and Miranda escaped along the Navigli in *The Tempest*, and they were still plied by the Grand Tourists in the eighteenth century; Goethe, for example, describes the hazards of journeying by canal.

A number of rivers and canals were added to the system over the centuries; the Spanish developed the **Darsena** to the south in 1603 and under Napoleon's regime the **Naviglio Pavese** was made navigable all the way to Pavia and down to the River Po, and so to the Adriatic. During the Industrial Revolution, raw materials like coal, iron and silk were brought into the city, and handmade products transported out with an efficiency that ensured Milan's commercial and economic dominance of the region. The process of covering over the canals began in the 1930s, to make way for the city's trams and trolley buses. In the 1950s, desperately needed materials were floated in for reconstructing the badly bombed city but by the mid-1970s, only a handful of canals were left uncovered; the last working boat plied the waters in 1977.

The best way to explore Milan's waterways is on a relaxing **boat trip**, which run between April and mid-September when the canals are not being dredged or cleaned; for more information ask at the tourist office, call the information line on ☎ 02 3322 7336 or check ⊛ naviglilombardi.it.

artists have moved in and although the overpriced craft and antique shops won't hold your attention for long, a wander round the streets, popping into open courtyards, will give you a feel of the neighbourhood. Take a look at the prettified Vicolo dei Lavandai (Washerwomen's Alley), near the beginning of the Naviglio Grande, where washerwomen scrubbed smalls in the murky canal waters.

Porta Genova

Five minutes' walk west from the Naviglio Grande is **Porta Genova**, the train station for Milan's southern outskirts. It is also the name given to one of Milan's up-and-coming areas. Across the tracks from the train station, bars and restaurants have moved in and disused warehouses and factories are being reclaimed by photographers, fashion houses and designers. Giorgio Armani has an exhibition space and workshops here, as does Prada.

Santa Maria delle Grazie and around

Due west from the Duomo, on Corso Magenta, stands the attraction that brings most visitors to Milan – the beautiful terracotta-and-brick church of **Santa Maria delle Grazie**, famous for its mural of **The Last Supper** by Leonardo da Vinci. More ancient exhibits are on display at the nearby **Museo Archeologico**.

Santa Maria delle Grazie

Piazza Santa Maria delle Grazia, Via Magenta • Ⓜ Cadorna or Conciliazione

The beautiful terracotta-and-brick church of **Santa Maria delle Grazie** was first built in Gothic style by the fifteenth-century architect Guiniforte Solari. It was part of the Dominican monastery that headed the Inquisition for over one hundred years in the late fifteenth and sixteenth centuries. Soon after its completion, Lodovico Sforza commissioned Bramante to rework and model the Gothic structure into a grand dynastic mausoleum. Bramante promptly tore down the existing chancel and replaced it with a massive dome supported by an airy Renaissance cube. Lodovico also intended to replace the nave and facade, but was unable to do so before Milan fell to the French, leaving an odd combination of styles – Gothic vaults, decorated in powdery blues, reds and ochre, illuminated by the light that floods through the windows of Bramante's dome. A side door leads into Bramante's cool and tranquil cloisters, from which there's a good view of the sixteen-sided drum the architect placed around his dome.

The Last Supper

Leonardo's *The Last Supper* – signposted **Cenacolo Vinciano** – is one of the world's great paintings and most resonant images. However, getting to see art of this magnitude doesn't come easily (see box, p.236).

Henry James likened the painting to an "illustrious invalid" that people visited with "leave-taking sighs and almost death-bed or tip-toe precautions"; certainly it's hard, when you visit the fragile painting, not to feel that it's the last time you'll see it. A twenty-year restoration has re-established the original colours using contemporary descriptions and copies, but that the work survived at all is something of a miracle. Leonardo's decision to use oil paint rather than the more usual faster-drying – and

---

EVIL PERSONIFIED

Leonardo spent two years on the mural, wandering the streets of Milan searching for and sketching models. When the monks complained that the face of Judas was still unfinished, Leonardo replied that he had been searching for over a year among the city's criminals for a sufficiently evil visage, and that if he didn't find one he would use the face of the prior. Whether or not Judas is modelled on the prior is unrecorded, but Leonardo's Judas does seem, as Vasari wrote, "the very embodiment of treachery and inhumanity".

THE LAST SUPPER: BOOKING INFORMATION AND TOURS

Visiting one of the world's great paintings and most resonant images doesn't come easily: visits must be booked at least a week in advance, more like a month or three in summer and for weekends. If it's fully booked when you ring, try asking about cancellations on the day: people don't always turn up for the early-morning slots so it might be worth chancing your luck and enquiring at the desk. At your allotted hour, once you've passed through a series of air-filtering systems along the rebuilt sides of what was the monastery's largest courtyard, your fifteen-minute slot face-to-face with the masterpiece begins.

Viewing times Tues–Sun 8.15am–6.45pm
Reservations Mon–Sat 8am–6.30pm on ☎ 02 9280 0360 or via the website ⓦ cenacolovinciano.net

Admission €6.50, plus €1.50 obligatory booking fee
Tours Alternatively, try the city tours (see p.239), where entrance to view the painting can be included.

longer-lasting – fresco technique with watercolours led to the painting disintegrating within five years of its completion. A couple of centuries later Napoleonic troops billeted here used the wall for target practice. And, in 1943, an Allied bomb destroyed the building, amazingly leaving only *The Last Supper*'s wall standing.

A Last Supper was a conventional theme for refectory walls, but Leonardo's decision to capture the moment when Christ announces that one of his disciples will betray him imbues the work with an unprecedented sense of drama.

Goethe commented on how very Italian the painting was in that so much is conveyed through the expressions of the characters' hands; the group of Matthew, Thaddaeus and Simon on the far right of the mural could be discussing a football match or the latest government scandal in any bar in Italy today. The only disciple not gesticulating or protesting in some way is the recoiling Judas who has one hand clenched while a bread roll has just dropped dramatically out of the other. Christ is calmly reaching out to share his bread with him while his other hand falls open in a gesture of sacrifice.

If you feel you need any confirmation of the emotional tenor or accomplishment of the painting, take a look at the contemporary *Crucifixion* by Montorfano on the wall at other end of the refectory: not a bad fresco in itself, but destined always to pale in comparison with Leonardo's masterpiece.

Museo Archeologico

Corso Magenta 15 • Tues–Sun 9am–1pm & 2–5.30pm • €2; free on Fri after 2pm • Ⓜ Cadorna

Bits and pieces of Roman buildings can be found across the city centre but the **Museo Archeologico** presents more domestic examples of the heritage. Housed in the former Monastero Maggiore, the museum is worth a quick visit if you wish to delve deeper into the city's Roman heritage. The displays of glass phials, kitchen utensils and jewellery from Roman Milan are compelling, and though there's a scarcity of larger objects, you can see a colossal stone head of Jove, found near the castle, a carved torso of Hercules and a smattering of mosaic pavements unearthed around the city.

Leading away from the museum, **Via Brisa** runs alongside the ruins of the imperial palace of the Roman emperor Maximian, unearthed after World War II bombing. South of here towards Via Torino, the medieval plan of the streets belies the Roman origins of the neighbourhood. Here stood a bath complex, the arena and the huge circus, the only traces of which are the rather forlorn looking foundations at the corner of Via Circo and Via Cappuccio.

Sant'Ambrogio

Piazza Sant'Ambrogio 15 • Mon–Sat 9.30am–noon & 2.30–6pm, Sun 3–7pm • Free • ⓦ basilicasantambrogio.it • Ⓜ Sant'Ambrogio

The church of **Sant'Ambrogio** was founded in the fourth century by Milan's patron saint, St Ambrose. The saint's remains still lie in the church's crypt, but there's nothing left of the original church in which his most famous convert, St Augustine, first heard him preach. The present twelfth-century church, the blueprint for many of Lombardy's Romanesque basilicas is, however, one of the city's loveliest, reached through a colonnaded quadrangle with column capitals carved with rearing horses, contorted dragons and an assortment of bizarre predators. Inside, to the left of the nave, a freestanding Byzantine pillar is topped with a "magic" bronze serpent, flicked into a loop and symbolizing Aaron's rod – an ancient tradition held that on the Day of Judgement it would crawl back to the Valley of Josaphat. Look, too, at the pulpit, a superb piece of Romanesque carving decorated with reliefs of wild animals and the occasional human, most of whom are intent upon devouring one another. There are older relics further down the nave, notably the ciborium, reliefed with the figures of saints Gervasius and Protasius – martyred Roman soldiers whose clothed bodies flank that of St Ambrose in the crypt. A nineteenth-century autopsy revealed that they had been killed by having their throats cut. Similar investigations into St Ambrose's remains restored the reputation of the anonymous fifth-century artist responsible for the mosaic portrait of the saint in the Cappella di San Vittorio in Ciel d'Oro (to the right of the sacristy). Until then it was assumed that Ambrose owed his crooked face to a slip of the artist's hand, but the examination of his skull revealed an abnormally deep-set tooth, suggesting that his face would indeed have been slightly deformed.

ARRIVAL AND DEPARTURE
MILAN

BY PLANE

Milan has two main airports – Malpensa and Linate – both used by domestic and international traffic (enquiries for both on ☎ 02 7485 2200; daily 7am–11pm). Bergamo-Orio al Serio (see p.281) is also touted as Milan, though it's a comfortable 45min away.

Malpensa (⦿ sea-aeroportimilano.it), 50km northwest of the city near Lake Maggiore, is connected by direct bus with the Stazione Centrale, Milan's main train station (every 20min 4.25am–midnight; 1hr; €7), and by a fast train, the Malpensa Express, with Milano Nord (also called Cadorna; every 30min 4.20am–11.27pm; 50min; ☎ 199 151 152, ⦿ malpensaexpress.it; early morning and evening services are replaced by a bus from Via Leopardi, just to the left of the station as you face it). Tickets cost €11 if bought beforehand, more if purchased on the train; €25 family tickets include two adults and two children. Both the Stazione Centrale and Milano Nord are connected with the city's metro system: the stations are called Centrale F.S. and Cadorna respectively. A taxi from Malpensa to the centre takes about 40min and costs €120; you can book a taxi at ⦿ taximilano.it.

Linate (⦿ sea-aeroportimilano.it), Milan's other airport, is just 7km east of the city centre; airport buses connect it with the Piazza Luigi di Savoia, on the east side of Stazione Centrale (every 20min 5.40am–9.30pm; 20min; €2; buy ticket on board). Ordinary ATM urban transport buses (#73 or #X73) also run every 10min from 5.30am until around midnight between Linate and the city centre, just south of Piazza San Babila (M1) on Corso Europa, and take around 30min; tickets cost the usual €1.50 and should be bought before you get on the bus from the airport newsagent, or, if you have change, from the ticket machine at the bus stop. A taxi to the centre from the rank outside will cost around €35.

BY TRAIN

Most international and domestic trains pull in at the monumental Stazione Centrale, northeast of the city centre on Piazza Duca d'Aosta, at the hub of the metro network on lines M2 and M3. Other services, especially those from stations in the Milan region – Bergamo, Pavia, Como and the other western lakes – terminate at smaller stations around the city: Garibaldi, Lambrate, Porta Genova and Milano Nord, all on M2 (the metro stop for Milano Nord is "Cadorna"), although these often also stop at Stazione Centrale. There are separate train enquiries lines for Ferrovie dello Stato (☎ 848 888 088, ⦿ trenitalia.com; daily 7am–9pm) and for Ferrovie Milano Nord (☎ 02 20 222; daily 9am–6pm).

MILANO STAZIONE CENTRALE

Destinations Bergamo (hourly; 50min); Brescia (every 45min; 1hr 15min); Certosa di Pavia (every 2hr; 30min); Chiasso (hourly; 50min); Como (hourly; 40min); Cremona (7 daily; 1hr 40min); Desenzano (every 30min; 1hr 10min); Lecco (every 2hr; 50min); Pavia (every 30min; 25min); Peschiera (hourly; 1hr 17min); Stresa (9 daily; 1hr 10min); Varenna (every 2hr; 1hr 10min); Verbania-Pallanza (9 daily; 1hr 20min); Verona (hourly; 1hr 35min).

MILANO LAMBRATE

Destinations Bergamo (hourly; 45min); Brescia (hourly; 1hr 20min); Certosa di Pavia (9 daily; 20min); Cremona (3 daily; 1hr 25min); Desenzano (2 daily; 1hr); Pavia (every 25min; 25min); Peschiera (2 daily; 1hr 10min); Verona (hourly; 1hr 35min).

MILANO NORD CADORNA

Destinations Como (every 30min; 1hr 5min); Varese (every 30min; 1hr).

4

MILANO PORTA GARIBALDI

Destinations Bergamo (every 40min; 55min); Chiasso (hourly; 1hr 15min); Como (7 daily; 30min); Cremona (3 daily; 1hr 30min); Lecco (hourly; 1hr); Luino (4 daily; 1hr 40min); Stresa (9 daily; 1hr 30min); Verbania-Pallanza (9 daily; 1hr 35min).

BY BUS

All international and long-distance buses, and many regional **buses**, arrive at and depart from the bus station in front of the Porta Garibaldi train station (M2), where you can get information and buy tickets from the Autostradale/Eurolines bus office (☎02 3391 0794; Mon–Fri 9am–6.30pm).

BY CAR

If you're driving, try to time your arrival to avoid the morning and evening rush hours (approximately 7.30–10am & 4.30–7pm) when Milan's ring road, the infamous Tangenziale, is often gridlocked. Signage is copious, if not always very clear, and the ring road links onto the autostradas for Bergamo, Brescia, Verona and Lake Garda (A4), Varese and Lake Maggiore (A8), Lake Como (A9) and the "Autostrada del Sole" (A1) for Cremona and Mantova. Information about the Ecopass zone, car rental and advice on parking in Milan is provided below (p.239).

GETTING AROUND

Milan's street-plan resembles a spider's web, with roads radiating out from the central Piazza del Duomo. The bulk of the city is encircled by two concentric ring-roads following the medieval and Spanish walls of the city, while the suburbs and industrial estates spill out towards a third ring, the Tangenziale, which links the main motorways. The city centre is just about compact enough to explore on foot and you'll probably only want to use the easy-to-master **public transport** system when you're flagging or going out of the way.

BY PUBLIC TRANSPORT

Metro The metro is made up of four lines: the red M1, green M2, yellow M3, and blue *passante ferroviario*; the four main intersections are Stazione Centrale, Duomo, Cadorna (Milano Nord) and Loreto (see map below). The front of each metro train shows the station at the end of the line. Services run from around 6am to midnight.

Buses and trams Most bus and tram stops display the route and direction of travel. Services run from around 6am to midnight, after which nightbuses take over, following the metro routes until 1am.

Enquiries For all public transport enquiries (🌐atm-mi.it) the information offices at the Duomo or Stazione Centrale metro stations are helpful, and have English-speaking staff.

Tickets are valid for 75min, cost €1.50 and can be used for one metro trip and as many bus and tram rides as you want. They are on sale at tobacconists, bars and at the metro station newsagents; most outlets close at 8pm, so it's best to buy a few tickets in advance if you intend to use public transport after this time, or get a carnet of ten for €13.80. Some stations have automatic ticket machines, although only the newer ones give change. You can also buy a one-day (€4.50) or two-day pass (€8.25) from the Stazione Centrale or Duomo metro stations. Remember to validate your ticket in the orange machines when you enter the metro and board buses and trams, as inspections are common.

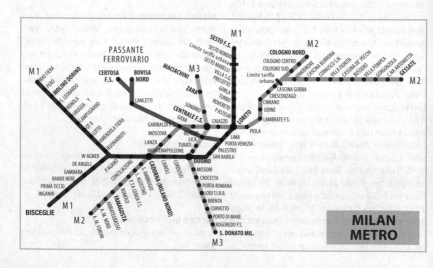

BY TAXI

Taxis don't cruise the streets, so don't bother trying to flag one down. Your best bet is to phone one of the following numbers (operators speak English): ☎ 02 6767, ☎ 02 4040 or ☎ 02 8585, say where you are and the operator will check how long before a cab can get to you (usually under 5min) and then give you a code to quote to the driver. Alternatively, there are a number of taxi ranks around town – including in Piazza del Duomo, Largo Cairoli, Piazza San Babila and Stazione Centrale. All cabs are metered and prices are reasonable, although in the daytime Milan's traffic-logged streets can quickly start to push fares up.

BY CAR

Driving your own car in the city is best avoided: the streets are congested and street parking nigh on impossible in the evenings and on Saturdays. If you do bring a car, you need to know that the Ecopass – an initiative to cut pollution and congestion in the city centre – is in force (Mon–Fri 7am–7pm) in the area within the Cerchia de Bastione (see map, p.226). The pass must be bought on the day of entry or up to midnight of the day afterwards and the fee is worked out on a sliding scale depending on your engine type. Payments can be made at authorized newsagents and tobacconists, through Intesa-SanPaolo ATMs, or, in English, by freephone (☎ 800 437 437) or online (ⓦ comune.milano.it/ecopass). If your hotel is within the Ecopass area, ask reception if they have any special provision for guests.

Parking Head for one of the numerous central car parks, costing around €2.50 per hour, less if you stay longer than four hours. Central options include Autosilo Diaz, Piazza Diaz 6, just south of Piazza del Duomo; Garage Traversi, on Via Bagutta, close to Piazza San Babila; Parking Majno, on Viale Majno and Garage Venezia, Corso Venezia 11, both near Porta Venezia. Parking in prohibited zones is not worth it; you'll be fined if caught and have your car impounded by the police.

Car rental All the international companies have car rental offices at the airports and Stazione Centrale including Avis (☎ 02 670 11654), Europcar (☎ 02 6698 7826), Hertz (☎ 02 669 0061) and Maggiore (☎ 02 669 0934).

BY BIKE

Cycling is a very pleasant way of exploring Milan: the terrain is flat, there is little of the aggression that you see on the streets of London or New York, and it is easy to head off down a quiet side-road and get away from it all. Do be careful with the tram lines though.

Bike Mi ☎ 800 808 181, ⓦ bikemi.com. To use the city's bike-sharing service, BikeMi, register for a temporary subscription by phone, online or at ATM points like Duomo, Stazione Centrale and Cadorna. Payment can only be by credit card. Rental is for a maximum of 2hr at a time and it's €2.50 for 24hr, €6 for a week.

INFORMATION

Tourist office Piazza Castello 1 ☎ 02 7740 4343, ⓦ visitamilano.it. Mon–Fri 9am–6pm, Sat & Sun 9am–1.30pm 2–5pm. Information and tickets on tours.

Tourist booths Tourist booths provide useful leaflets and city maps and can be found at Linate and Malpensa airports and on the main concourse in the Stazione Centrale. Linate & Malpensa daily 9am–4pm; Stazione Centrale Mon–Fri 9am–6pm, Sat & Sun 9am–1pm & 2–5pm.

ACCOMMODATION

Much of Milan's accommodation is geared towards business travellers and, as a result, prices are high, rooms can be characterless and many hotels are booked up all year round. You'd be wise to reserve ahead, especially during the spring (mid-Feb) and autumn (end Sept) fashion weeks and during the Salone del Mobile in April. Hotel prices can more than double during these periods. In August, on the other hand, visitors are so scarce that some hotels shut up shop for the month and those that don't might be prepared to negotiate over prices.

MILAN TOURS

The central tourist office has information and sells tickets for various English-speaking tours.

Gran Tour di Milano ⓦ zaniviaggi.it. The Gran Tour di Milano is a coach and walking tour that includes entrance to the castle, La Scala museum and *The Last Supper*. Advance booking highly recommended. €60. Daily 9.30am & 2.30pm.

City Sightseeing Milano ⓦ milano.city -sightseeing.it. The double-decker bus CitySightseeing Milano offers a hop-on,

hop-off bus tour with two different routes around the centre of town. Daily every 45min 9.30am–5.30pm; €20 for 48hr, multi-language headphone commentaries included.

Canal boat cruises along the Navigli are organized periodically in summer (see p.234).

San Siro tour For information on how to visit the home of AC Milan and InterMilan, see p.247.

HOTELS

The hotels below have been divided into three areas – the Station area, covering places within a 20min walk of the Stazione Centrale, and districts north and south of Piazza del Duomo, all within a half-hour stroll of the cathedral. The area around Stazione Centrale and across to Corso Buenos Aires is home to many of the city's cheaper hotels, which often cater to the area's considerable red-light trade; you should be fine at any of the places we recommend.

STAZIONE CENTRALE AND AROUND

★ **Euro** Via Sirtori 24 ☎02 3040 4010, ⓦeuro hotelmilano.it; ⓜPta Venezia; map p.226. Very good value a/c rooms with parquet floors are offered in this well-located hotel. There's also a small gym, a patio for alfresco breakfast and cheaper – but still pleasant – rooms available without a/c if your budget is tighter. €110

Kennedy Viale Tunisia 6, sixth floor ☎02 2940 0934, ⓦkennedyhotel.it; ⓜRepubblica or Pta Venezia; map pp.222–223. A well-organized, friendly one-star with bright, plain rooms, some of which are en suite. Some rooms even have their own balconies overlooking the rooftops. €65

Mercure Milano Porta Venezia 1 ☎02 2940 0937, ⓦmercure.com; ⓜPta Venezia; map p.226. One of the city's several branches of this French hotel chain offering very pleasant, comfortable rooms in a convenient location right on Porta Venezia. €150

Valley Via Soperga 19 ☎02 669 2777, ⓦhotelvalley.it; ⓜCentrale; map pp.222–223. A 2min walk north of the Stazione Centrale, this basic spot is a good budget choice if you're catching an early train or arriving late at night. Most rooms are en suite and those at the back are pleasant and airy. €50

NORTH OF PIAZZA DUOMO

Antica Locanda Leonardo Corso Magenta 78 ☎02 4801 4197, ⓦanticalocandaleonardo.com; ⓜCadorna; map p.226. Just steps away from *The Last Supper*, this discreet three-star offers light airy rooms, some overlooking a pretty internal garden. €170

★ **Antica Locanda dei Mercanti** Via San Tomaso 6 ☎02 805 4080, ⓦlocanda.it; ⓜCairoli; map p.226. Tucked away near the castle, this quietly elegant *locanda* offers individually decorated rooms; two even have their own roof terraces. Breakfast (not included) is served in the rooms. The *Alle Meraviglie* (ⓦallemeraviglie.it) next door, at no. 8, is run by the same people with similarly bright, tastefully decorated rooms. €255

Bulgari Via Fratelli Gabba 7/B ☎02 058 051, ⓦbulgari hotels.com; ⓜMontenapoleone; map p.226. In a hidden corner of Brera, the city's top hotel has all the style you could wish for on a trip to Milan and none of the attitude you might expect. Staff are charming, facilities

impeccable, and the bar terrace and garden are an absolute treat. Look out for the special offers. €600

London Via Rovello 3 ☎02 7202 0166, ⓦhotellondon milano.com; ⓜCairoli; map p.226. A plain, family-run hotel in a good central position. There's a choice of singles and doubles with or without en-suite shower; the decor is unexciting but all rooms have a/c. €130

Palazzo Segreti Via San Tomaso 8 ☎02 4952 9250, ⓦpalazzosegreti.com; ⓜCairoli; map p.226. As if the central location on a quiet pedestrian street wasn't enough, each one of the eighteen rooms is individually designed – all chic and stylish – many furnished with designer pieces. The bathrooms are often part of the bedrooms themselves. Downstairs the hip bar is part of an art gallery. €270

Rovello Via Rovello 18/A ☎02 8646 4654, ⓦhotel -rovello.it; ⓜCairoli; map p.226. Close to Castello Sforzesco, the spacious rooms at this well-located two-star hotel are en suite and a/c. You're paying for the location but rates may be negotiable in summer. Breakfast included. €155

SOUTH OF PIAZZA DEL DUOMO

Ariston Largo Carobbio 2 ☎02 7200 0556, ⓦariston hotel.com; ⓜDuomo, then tram #2, #3 or #14; map p.226. The best thing about this pleasant modern hotel is its position – within walking distance of the Duomo and the Navigli – and the free bicycles. Rooms are a little cramped, but all are en suite and there's a decent breakfast included. €135

Carrobio Via Medici 3 ☎02 890 10740, ⓦhotel carrobiomilano.com; map p.226. This family-run hotel aims to combine a homely feel with comfortable contemporary bedrooms. The hotchpotch of communal areas includes a small outside terrace and the generous breakfast offers a selection of home-made cakes and pastries. It's in a great location too, halfway between the Duomo and Sant'Ambrogio. €135

Nhow Via Tortona 35 ☎02 489 8861, ⓦnhow-hotels .com; ⓜPta Genova; map pp.222–223. A 246-room hotel to the south of the centre in the up-and-coming Porta Genova district. This spacious design-fest is aimed at those coming to town on business – albeit the design business – but the weekend offers can be worthwhile and the colours, textures and contemporary feel are streets away from Milan's usual unimaginative offerings. €150

B&BS AND APARTMENTS

As many of the mid-range hotels are rather dingy you may want to look into the range of bed and breakfast accommodation that's opened in recent years. The English-speaking agency Friendly Rentals (☎0800 520 0373, ⓦfriendlyrentals.com) has an excellent selection of attractive apartments throughout the city which make an economical alternative for a small group or family (min 3 nights from €420). Check out the websites ⓦbed-and -beakfast.it and ⓦairbnb.com for more options.

★ **Foresteria Monforto** Piazza Tricolore 2 ☎ 340 237 0272, ⓦforesteriamonforte.it; ⓜSan Babilia; map p.226. These good-value stylish rooms get booked up quickly so reserve in advance. **€160**

La Dolce Vita Via Cola di Rienzo ☎347 377 3044, ⓦladolcevite.net; ⓜSan Agostino; map pp.222–223. An attractive choice to the south of the centre in a leafy home boasting bright en-suite rooms and a garden. **€130**

HOSTELS AND CAMPING

Città di Milano Via G. Airaghi 61 ☎02 4820 7017, ⓦcampingmilano.it; ⓜM1 to De Angeli, then bus #72; map pp.222–223. Next to an aquapark and the nearest campsite to the centre, but still a metro trip and a bus ride away. Open all year. Pitches **€25**

La Cordata Via Burigozzo 11, off Corso Italia ☎02 5831 4675, ⓦostellolacordata.com; ⓜMissori, or four stops on tram #15 from Piazza Fontana by the Duomo; map

pp.222–223. Clean, basic and in a good central location with large kitchen, internet access and a communal TV room for residents' use. Bunks are in single-sex dorms; each dorm has its own shower room. Alternatively, there are spacious twin rooms plus singles, triples and quads. Dorms **€21**, doubles/twins **€70**

Ostello Bello Via Medici 4 ☎02 365 82720, ⓦostellobello.com; ⓜMissori; map p.226. The best budget accommodation in town if you're looking for a sociable meeting-point, *Ostello Bello* was recently voted the second-best new hostel in the world. This cool spot is very well located with all mod cons like free wi-fi, a/c and a bathroom in each room, but also has special touches like a roof terrace complete with its own veg patch (the produce used as ingredients in the kitchen), breakfast included whenever you get up and a happening bar downstairs with live music and other events (see p.242). Dorms **€28**, doubles **€80**

EATING AND DRINKING

Whether you're looking for a neighbourhood trattoria, want to watch models pick at their salads or crave a bit of well-priced ethnic food, Milan has it all – usually within easy reach of wherever you're staying. If you don't fancy a sit-down meal, make the most of the Milanese custom of **aperitivo** (see box, p.242) to curb your hunger. To the south of the centre, the area around the **Ticinese** and **Navigli** is full of restaurants and cafés but you should choose carefully as this is a touristy area and quality is not always a priority. The districts of **Brera** and **Moscova** are also popular in the evening, so we've included a few of the better establishments there, as well as several bargain places around the budget hotels near the **Stazione Centrale** and **Porta Venezia**.

LUNCH AND SNACKS

★ **Da Claudio** Via Cusani 1 ☎02 805 6857, ⓦpescheriadaclaudio.it; ⓜCairoli/Lanza; map p.226. Mouthwateringly fresh *carpaccio* and shellfish served in this sleek designer incarnation of the neighbourhood's traditional fishmonger on the edge of Brera. There's a smart restaurant upstairs these days too. Mon–Sat 12.30–3pm & 7–11pm.

La Rinascente Food Hall, Top floor, Via San Raffaele 2; ⓜDuomo; map p.226. Enjoy one of the best views in town with a plate of nibbles or a full-blown meal to match, although the service is not always of the same quality. The space is divided between the city's best breadmakers, mozzarella specialists, sushi chefs, experts in Milanese cooking and chocolatiers to provide a gourmet pick-and-mix to please all tastes. Choose a table on the terrace outside and you can almost reach over and feed the gargoyles on the Duomo roof. Daily 10am–midnight.

Luini Via S. Radegonda 16 ⓦluini.it; ⓜDuomo; map p.226. A city institution that's been serving *panzerotti* (deep-fried mini-*calzone*) round the corner from the Duomo for over 150 years; be prepared to queue. There are a couple of benches in nearby Piazza San Fedele if you want to eat sitting down. Mon 10am–3pm, Tues–Sat 10am–8pm; closed Aug.

Obika Via Mercato (cnr Via Fiori Chiari) ☎02 8645 0568, ⓦobika.it; ⓜLanza; map p.226. Stylish mozarella

bar serving simple top-quality food. Great-value *aperitivo* 6–8pm daily. Mon–Fri noon–3.30pm & 6.30pm to midnight, Sat & Sun noon–2am.

★ **Triennale DesignCafé** Viale Alemagne 6 ☎02 875 441, ⓦtriennale.org; ⓜCadorna; map p.226. Many of the chairs are design classics in this bright, spacious café, with huge picture windows overlooking the Parco Sempione. There's a good lunchtime menu (noon–2.30pm) and snacks throughout the day. In summer, the café overflows outside into the garden with a bar and relaxed terrace. 10.30am–7pm; closed Mon.

★ **Vecchia Latteria** Via dell'Unione 6; ⓜDuomo/Missori; map p.226. Delicious vegetarian dishes in a tiny neighbourhood café just off Via Torino. Mon–Sat 11.30am–5pm.

CAFÉS AND GELATERIE

Caffè Miani Piazza Duomo 21 ☎02 8646 4435; ⓜDuomo; map p.226. Opened with the *Galleria* in 1867, *Caffè Miani*, also known as *Zucca in Galleria* and *Camparino*, was where David Campari invented Milan's famous sticky red drink. These days it's both expensive and touristy, but the price of a coffee standing at the tiled bar is easier to swallow. Tues–Sun 7.30am–8.30pm.

Cova Via Montenapoleone 8 ☎02 7600 0578, ⓦpasticceriacova.it; ⓜMontenapoleone; map p.226.

4

UN APERITIVO

An Italian custom that has been honed to a fine art in Milan is the **aperitivo**, or pre-dinner drink. Between 6 and 9pm the city unwinds over a drink and a bite to eat. As well as another opportunity to preen and pose, *aperitivo* time – or happy hour as it is also called – is a boon for budget travellers: counters often groan under the weight of hot and cold food, all of which is included in the price of your drink (somewhere between €3 and €10, depending on the establishment). Take a plate and help yourself, although if you're really planning to fill up, it'll go down better if you go back several times rather than piling your plate high. If you choose your venue wisely you won't need to spend another penny on food all night. Most *aperitivo* bars evolve as the evening goes on: the lights dim, the volume of the music increases and you can settle in for the night.

Some of the top bars in town for an *aperitivo* include:

h-club Diana Garden Sheraton Majestic, Viale Piave 42 ⓦsheratondianamajestic.com/en/hclubdiana _milan; ⓜPta Venezia; map p.226. Still one of the venues for Milan's beautiful people with prices to match: the garden and bars at this hotel continue to draw those out on the town and dressed to kill for *aperitivo* (7.30–10pm), cocktails (10pm–12.30am) and Saturday & Sunday brunch (12.30–2.30pm).

★ **Ostello Bello** Via Medici 4 ⓣ02 3658 2720, ⓦostellobello.com; ⓜDuomo or tram #14 or #2; map p.226. A stone's throw from the epicentre of Milan's *aperitivo* time for 20-/30-somethings around the Colonne di San Lorenzo, this funky bar/café under the hostel of the same name offers good prices in a relaxed atmosphere with tasty home-made snacks. There's often live music or other things going on too.

Daily 10am–9pm; times vary according to what's happening.

★ **Le Biciclette** Conca del Naviglio 10 ⓣ02 839 4177, ⓦlebiciclette.eu; ⓜS. Ambrogio, bus #94 or tram #14 or #2; map pp.222–223. Smart young things prop up the bar in this swish modern joint in a leafy street near the Navigli. The definitive *aperitivo* bar that keeps going once the food has been put away. Mon–Sat 6pm–2am & Sun 12.30–2pm.

Bhangra Bar Corso Sempione 1 ⓣ02 3493 4469, ⓦbhangrabar.it; tram #1, 29 or 30; map p.226. Corso Sempione is another popular area to head for in the early evenings and this India-themed bar has one of the best views of the Arco delle Pace as well as tasty samosas, bhajis and other Indian specialities, live DJs and a buzzy atmosphere. Daily 9am–3pm & 6.30–2pm.

Fin-de-siècle surroundings set the scene for this elegant tearoom dating from the Napoleonic era. Discreet service and starched linen accompany the mouthwatering chocolate delicacies, although naturally they don't come cheap. Mon–Sat 7.45am–8.30pm.

★ **Grom** Via S. Margherita 16 ⓣ02 8058 1041, ⓦgrom.it; ⓜDuomo; map p.226. Practically opposite La Scala the central branch of this specialist ice-cream chain serves up traditional flavours using top-quality organic ingredients. Also at Corso di Porta Ticinese 51 and Corso Buenos Aires 13. Mon–Sat noon–11pm, Sun 11am–11pm.

RESTAURANTS
NORTH OF PIAZZA DEL DUOMO
Antica Trattoria della Pesa Viale Pasubio 10 ⓣ02 6566 741; ⓜMoscova/Pta Garibaldi; map pp.222–223. Just west of Corso Como, this elegant trattoria serves up well-presented Lombard classics in a very friendly atmosphere. Step in from Milan's inclement weather and choose home-made pasta, creamy risotto, or a filling *casoela*. The bistro round the corner (Via Maroncelli 1 ⓣ02 65 92 880) run by the owner's son is definitely worth a try too. Mon–Sat 12.30–2.30pm & 7.30–11pm.

Da Rita e Antonio Via Puccini 2; ⓜCairoli; map p.226. In a very handy location near the castle and Via Dante, this Milanese classic is a 1970s pizzeria serving authentic Neapolitan pizzas as well as home-made bread and good mains, the fish in particular. No reservations taken but brusque, no-nonsense service sees you to a table quickly. Tues–Sun noon–2.30pm & 7–10.30pm; closed Aug.

Il Salumaio di Montenapoleone Via Santo Spirito 10/Via Gesù 5 ⓣ02 760 01123, ⓦilsalumaiodi montenapoleone.com; ⓜSan Babila or Montenapoleone; map p.226. Set in the lovely courtyard of the Palazzo Bagatti Valsecchi, this chic, relaxed corner of Milan has a well-heeled clientele. Pop in just for coffee, an *aperitivo* or for a full lunch or dinner. The menu is a simple list of Milanese/Italian staples sourced from the delicatessen of the same name. This being the Golden Quadrangle, prices are a little steep but the food is good and the atmosphere suits. Daily 8am–midnight.

La Latteria Via S. Marco 24 ⓣ02 659 7653; ⓜMoscova; map p.226. This former dairy shop has been converted into a cosy trattoria that's a favourite with the designer folk of the area. Delicious home-made pastas and roast meats are served up by the owner; reckon on around €15 for a main course. Mon–Fri 12.30–2.30pm & 7.30–10pm; closed Aug.

★ **l'Osteria del Treno** Via S. Gregorio 46–48 📞 02 670 0479, ⓦ osteriadeltreno.it; ⓜ Repubblica; map pp.222–223. The welcome couldn't be friendlier in the attractive Art Nouveau rooms of this converted railworkers' canteen. Many diners opt for the delicious house platters of cold meats or cheese (€14), although the pasta dishes are recommended, too. Mon–Fri 12.30–3pm & 7.30–11pm, Sun 12.30–3pm.

Oskar Via Palazzi 4; ⓜ Pta Venezia; map p.226. A popular restaurant with bags of local atmosphere, serving fantastic-value pasta dishes (€8 a plate) in huge portions. Don't be put off by the voluble owner or the Mussolini memorabilia in the corners. Mon–Sat 12.30–2.30pm & 7.30–11pm.

Pizza OK Via Lambro 15; ⓜ Pta Venezia; map pp.222–223. Very busy pizzeria that serves some of the best – and biggest – pizzas in town in plain surroundings. Huge choice of toppings and good prices that start at €5 for a margherita. Noon–3pm & 7pm–12.30am; closed Sun lunch.

Warsa Via Melzo 16 📞 02 201 607, ⓦ ristorantewarsa.it; ⓜ Pta Venezia; map p.226. An Eritrean restaurant in among the shops and bars of Milan's African community, serving very tasty bargain-priced food; good variety of vegetarian dishes, as well as various meat options. Count on around €20 for a full meal. Noon–3pm & 7–10.30pm; closed Wed.

SOUTH OF PIAZZA DEL DUOMO

Al Pont De Ferr Ripa di Porta Ticinese 55 📞 02 8940 6277; ⓜ Pta Genova FS; map pp.222–223. An intimate restaurant right by the canal that offers an unusual take on local classics – try the delicious pumpkin risotto with pistachio (€15). There's also an excellent cheese selection to accompany the impressive wine list. Daily 12.30–2.30pm & 8pm–midnight; closed Aug.

Anema e Cozze Via Casale 7 📞 02 837 5459, ⓦ anemaecozze.com; ⓜ Pta Genova FS; map pp.222–223. This bright, lively spot sitting plump on a corner of the Naviglio Grande is a good choice for tasty, informal meals. The pizzas are crispy, the seafood fresh and the salads make a pleasant change from pasta; around €35 a head. Sister

restaurants at Via Palermo 15 (📞 02 8646 1646) and Via Orseolo 1 (📞 02 3657 6140) are equally recommended. Daily 12.30–3pm & 7.30pm–midnight.

California Bakery Piazza Sant'Eustorgio 4 📞 02 3981 1517, ⓦ californiabakery.it; tram #3; map pp.222–223. The leafy terrace tucked in beside Sant'Eustorgio church is a good spot to enjoy delicious savouries and mouthwatering cakes. More San Fran than Milan but pleasant outside eating is tricky to find in this city. Tues–Sat 8am–midnight, Sun 9am–midnight.

★ **Il Coniglio Bianco** Alzaia Naviglio Grande 12 📞 02 5810 0910, ⓦ alconigliobianco.it; ⓜ Pta Genova FS; map pp.222–223. A great choice if you're looking for quality cooking in a relaxed but stylish Milanese atmosphere; there are even a handful of tables outside in the shade by the canalside in summer. The selection of well-judged traditional dishes mixes well with the odd inspired newcomer and costs around €35 for a two-course meal before wine. Mon & Wed–Sun 7.15–11pm, Sat & Sun also 12.30–3pm.

Osteria di Porta Cicca Ripa di Porta Ticinese 51 📞 02 8372 763; ⓜ Pta Genova FS; map pp.222–223. Pretty, romantic bistro on the canalside offering the freshest fish and other seasonal ingredients in its stylish pan-Italian dishes with a creative twist. Expect around €35 without drinks, but do make the most of the good-value wine list. Daily 12.30–2.30 & 8pm–midnight.

Tradizionale Ripa de Porta Ticinese 7 📞 02 839 5133; ⓜ Pta Genova FS; map pp.222–223. Tasty pizzas and yummy fish dishes are on offer in the rustic atmosphere of this popular canal-side joint. There's another branch at Via de Amicis 26 📞 02 4952 3729. Noon–3pm & 7.30pm–1am; closed Wed.

Trattoria Milanese Via S. Marta 11 📞 02 8645 1991, ⓦ trattoriamilanese.it; ⓜ Duomo; map p.226. An elegant, well-priced restaurant in the labyrinth of ancient streets a 10min walk west of the Duomo. Understandably, risotto and *ossobuco* take pride of place among all that's best of Milanese cooking (main courses weigh in at €15–20). Mon–Wed noon–2.30pm, Thurs–Sat 8–10.30pm; closed Aug.

NIGHTLIFE

Milan's **nightlife** traditionally centres on two main areas: the designer-label streets around Corso Como and Via Brera and the canal-side Navigli and the adjacent Ticinese quarter, south of the city, where a more mixed clientele enjoys the lively bars, restaurants and nightclubs, some hosting regular live bands. But there are numerous other pockets – including the area around Porta Venezia, Le Colonne di San Lorenzo, Corso Sempione and Porta Romana – and Milan's relatively small size and car-and-scooter culture mean that people are happy to drive to places out of the centre, so some of the more popular bars and clubs we recommend below may require a bus, a bike or a quick taxi ride.

BARS

ATM Bastione di Porta Volta 15 📞 02 8945 4988; ⓜ Moscova; map pp.222–223. A former tram station is reincarnated as this stylish bar with roof terrace that's popular with a laidback 30-something crowd, especially at

aperitivo time during the week. Mon–Fri 6pm–2am, Sat 10pm–3am.

Atomic Via Felice Casati 24 📞 02 8905 9169; ⓜ Pta Venezia/Republicca; map pp.222–223. Refreshing spot just north of Porta Venezia where you can have an

4

after-dinner drink and a dance in a cool but relaxed atmosphere – most un-Milanese. Tues–Sun 7pm–1am; closed Aug.

Bar Bianco Parco Sempione ☎02 8699 2026; bus #61, tram #30 or ⓂMoscova; map p.226. Right in the heart of the park, this unassuming café becomes a very popular spot on summer nights when it turns into a late-night bar with thumping music. Tues–Sun 9am–11.30pm, June–Aug Thurs–Sun closes 2am.

★ **Corso Como 10** Corso Como 10 ☎02 653 531, ⓦ10corsocomo.com; ⓂPta Garibaldi FS; map pp.222–223. The bar is the best bit of this chi-chi setup of exhibition space, boutiques, a restaurant and a courtyard café-bar. Prices are extortionate but the atmosphere is very chic and exclusive. Mon 3pm–1am, Tues–Sun 10am–1am.

Lelephante Via Melzo 22 ☎02 2951 8768; ⓂPta Venezia; map p.226. Cocktails are the speciality at this good-time bar popular with a mixed crowd. Hardly a poseur in sight. Tues–Sun 6.30pm–2am.

★ **Radetzky Café** Largo La Foppa 5 ☎02 657 2645; ⓂMoscova; map pp.222–223. Particularly popular for long lazy Sunday brunches, this place has become a bit of an institution with a laidback stylish set. Tables out on the pavement add to the appeal. Daily 8–1.30am.

Rita Via Angelo Fumagalli 1 ☎02 837 2865; ⓂPta Genova FS; map pp.222–223. One of the city's best cocktail bars: it's a small friendly place in the Navigli area with a local-bar vibe, excellent bar staff and a good soundtrack. The *aperitivi* can be a bit scarce but it's a good bet for a laidback late-night drink. Daily 7pm–1am.

Roialto Via Piero della Francesca 55 ☎02 3493 6616, ⓦroialtogroup.it/roialto; bus #43 & #57; map pp.222–223. This huge converted garage on various levels is done out in every conceivable style from 1930s colonial to chill-out lounge. Tues–Sun 6pm–2am; closed mid-July to mid-Sept.

LIVE-MUSIC VENUES AND CLUBS

The city's clubs are at their hippest midweek, particularly Thursdays – at weekends out-of-towners flood in and any self-respecting Milanese trendy either stays at home or hits a bar. For clubs, there are a number of lively places for a good dance in a central location around Corso Como, otherwise you might need to grab a cab to some of the more out of the way places. In summer some clubs move out to waterside venues at the Idroscalo, by Linate airport. Many have obscure door policies, often dependent on the whim of the bouncer; assuming you get in, you can expect to pay €15–30 entry, which usually includes your first drink. As for live music, Milan scores high on jazz and there are regular gigs by local bands.

★ **Blue Note** Via Borsieri 37 ☎02 6901 6888, ⓦbluenotemilano.com; ⓂGaribaldi FS; map pp.222–223. Top-name jazz club located in the alternative neighbourhood of Isola, just north of Stazione Garibaldi. Quality bookings and a relaxed atmosphere make this place a top venue. There's a small restaurant, as well as the bar. 7.30pm–late, first show at 9pm.

Gasoline Via Bonnet 11/A ☎02 6901 6888; ⓂGaribaldi FS; map pp.222–223. Small, dark, funky club handy for the bars of Brera and Corso Como. On Sun afternoons it hosts a popular gay club called *Bus Stop*. Wed–Sun 11pm–5am; closed July & Aug.

Hollywood Corso Como 15 ☎02 655 5318, ⓦdiscoteca hollywood.com; ⓂGaribaldi FS; map pp.222–223. Long established as the place to go if you want to be surrounded by beautiful people. Very Milanese but certainly no mould-breaker. Wed–Sun 10.30pm–4am; closed June–Aug.

L'Atlantique Viale Umbria 42 ☎02 202 322, ⓦcafe atlantique.it; bus #92; map pp.222–223. The spot where the slickest of Milan's slick meet. Top DJs regularly spin their stuff. Tues–Sun 11pm–4am; closed Aug.

Loolapaloosa Corso Como 15 ☎02 655 5693, ⓦloolapaloosa.com; ⓂGaribaldi FS; map pp.222–223. Renowned for its riotous Thurs nights with dancing on the bar and other entertainment, this is a fun, lively option in the Corso Como area; Sun nights are distinctly more chilled. *Aperitivo* every night from 7–10.30pm to start you off on the right foot. Daily 7pm–3am; closed July & Aug.

Magazzini Generali Via Pietrasanta 14 ☎02 5521 1313, ⓦmagazzinigenerali.it; bus #91 or #24; map pp.222–223. Ex-warehouse that's become a Milan institution with a mixture of popular club nights and live music. Wed–Sat 11.30pm–5am; closed June–Aug.

CENTRI SOCIALI

If you need an antidote to the expensive designer side of Milan's nightlife, check out the very healthy alternative scene, which revolves around the city's many **Centri Sociali**. Born out of the student protests of the late 1960s, these centres are essentially legally squatted buildings, where committees organize cheap, sometimes free, entertainment, such as concerts and film showings. They also contain bars and – often good – restaurants. Check out the flagship *Leoncavallo*, at Via Watteau 7 (☎02 3651 0287, ⓦleoncavallo.org); the newer, family-friendly *Cascina Cuccagna* in a very central seventeenth-century farmhouse, with a lovely good-value restaurant (☎02 545 7785, ⓦcuccagna.org); or look in the listings section of the newspaper *Il Manifesto* for other *centri*.

LESBIAN AND GAY MILAN

Milan is one of the country's most gay-friendly cities and while many of the city's nightspots welcome a mixed crowd, they often hold specific gay nights, too (see opposite). Naturally, see-and-be-seen venues are Milan's forte, though there is also a choice of more relaxed, as well as more hardcore establishments, as well. The gay bookshop, La Babele, at Regina Giovanna 24/B (ⓦlibreriababele.it; ⓜ Cadorna; closed Mon), with a gallery alongside a good selection of books and videos, is the place to pick up a copy of the *Gay Milan* map, detailing the city's saunas, clubs and cruising areas. In May, the city hosts an international gay and lesbian film festival (ⓦcinemagaylesbico.com), which often has fringe activities organized around the same time.

Scimmie Via Ascanio Sforza 49 ☏02 8940 2874, ⓦscimmie.it; ⓜ Pta Genova FS; map pp.222–223. This Ticinese club is one of Milan's most popular venues, with a different band every night and jazz-fusion predominating. Small and intimate, with a restaurant – and a barge on the canal in summer. Mon–Sat 7pm–3am.

Tunnel Via Sammartini 30 ☏02 6671 1370, ⓦtunnel-milano.it; ⓜ Centrale FS; map pp.222–223. With its eye firmly on what's happening abroad, this large club and venue located in a warehouse near the Stazione Centrale is as close as Milan gets to having its finger on the pulse. Wed–Sun 11pm–5am; closed July & Aug.

OPERA

LA SCALA

Many of Milan's tourists are in the city for just one reason – La Scala, at Via dei Filodrammatici 2 (info ☏02 7200 3744, ⓦteatroallascala.org), one of the world's most prestigious opera houses. The opera season runs from 7 December through to July, and there are usually also classical concerts and ballet performances between September and November. The average price of a ticket is about €90 and seats often sell out months in advance.

Advance tickets can be bought on the phone or online (☏02 860 775, ⓦteatroallascala.org; the website has a useful seating plan with a twenty-percent advance booking fee; plan at least two months before the performance), or in person at the Central Box Office, Galleria del Sagrato, underground in the corridors of the Duomo metro station, opposite the ATM office (Sept–July daily noon–6pm), a month before.

Ticket collection for reservations is possible from two hours before the start of the performance at the opera house.

Same-day sales Some tickets for each performance are set aside for sale on the day; 140 tickets are available for operas and ballets and eighty for concerts, with a maximum purchase of one ticket per person. The system changes frequently, but currently, a list of names is compiled at the box office at 1pm, with tickets to be collected and paid for at 5pm: check the website or ask at the box office for the latest information.

SHOPPING

Milan is synonymous with shopping. If your pockets are not deep enough to tackle the big-name designer boutiques you could always rummage through last season's leftovers at the many factory outlets around town, or check out the city's wide range of medium- and budget-range clothes shops. Milan also excels in furniture and design, with showrooms from the world's top companies, plus a handful of shops offering a selection of brands and labels under one roof.

DEPARTMENT STORES

10 Corso Como Corso Como 10 ⓦcorsocomo10.com; ⓜ Moscova or Garibaldi FS; map pp.222–223. A Milan institution selling a small range of perfectly selected design and fashion items, as well as books and music, with a café and art gallery, too. Outlet store round the corner at Via Tazzoli 3. Mon 3.30–7.30pm, Tues & Fri–Sun 10.30am–7.30pm, Wed & Thurs 10.30am–9pm.

Excelsior Milano Galleria del Corso 4 ⓦexcelsiormilano.com; ⓜ Duomo; map p.226. The very latest in luxury, this seven-storey department store in an old cinema building reworked by Jean Nouvel offers a multi-brand pick and mix representing the very latest in high-end fashion and design, and rounded off by a tempting foodie floor including café, bistro and bar.

Mon–Sat 9am–10pm, Sun 10am–9pm.

Rinascente Piazza del Duomo 14 ⓦrinascente.it; ⓜ Duomo; map p.226. Milan's best one-stop shop: each department is divided up into boutiques so browsing among the designer goods, from bed linen to bridal wear, toasters to top-quality togs is a joy. The top-floor food hall is a great refuelling stop (see p.241). Daily 10am–9pm.

FASHION

Milan's top-name fashion stores are mainly concentrated in three areas. The Quadrilatero d'Oro – Via Montenapoleone, Via della Spiga and around – is the place for Versace, Prada et al. Corso di Porta Ticinese houses funkier, more youth-oriented shops – independents as well as global names like Diesel, Carhartt and Stussy. Head to Corso Vittorio

4

Emanuele or Via Torino for mid-range chains, including Max Mara, Benetton and Stefanel, plus H&M and Zara.

DESIGNER

Cavalli i Nastri Via Brera 2 ☎02 7200 0449, ⦿ cavallinastri.com; ⓜ montenapoleone; map p.226. The ultimate in vintage chic offer exquisite pieces to complement any wardrobe or home from their Brera showroom. Mon 3–7.30pm & Tues–Sat 10.30am–7.30pm.

Dolce & Gabbana Menswear, Corso Venezia 15 ☎02 7602 8485, ⦿ dolcegabbana.com; Womenswear and shoes, Via della Spiga 26 ☎02 7600 1155; D&G trendy line including D&G junior at Corso Venezia 7 ☎02 7600 4091; ⓜ San Babila; map p.226. Go through to the courtyard on the ground floor of the eighteenth-century palace for the menswear collection to find a space dedicated to enhancing your shopping experience. There's an old-fashioned barber's, a small grooming centre and the *Bar Martini*, popular with beautiful people of all nationalities. All Mon–Sat 10am–7pm.

Gianni Versace Via Montenapoleone 11 ☎02 7600 8528, ⦿ versace.com; ⓜ Montenapoleone or ⓜ San Babila; map p.226. Unusually for Versace, this store, spread over five storeys, is nothing if not understated. The clean lines provide a perfect backdrop for the luxurious ostentation of the clothes, shoes and accessories in glinting gold and swirling colours. Mon–Sat 10am–7pm.

Giorgio Armani Via Manzoni 31 ☎02 7231 8600, ⦿ armani.com; ⓜ Montenapoleone; map p.226. This temple to all things Giorgio is more a mini-shopping centre than a shop. There are boutiques for all his ranges – womens- and menswear, furnishings and houseware – accompanied by *Armani Café*, a relaxed pavement café, and *Nobu*, a pricey, high-tech Japanese restaurant that's been one of the places in town to be seen for years. With a hotel, chic bar, book corner selling design and coffee-table books, a florists' and a chocolate counter offering monogrammed sugary confections, you really won't need to spend your money anywhere else in town. Mon–Sat 10.30am–7.30pm.

Gucci Via Montenapoleone 5–7 & Galleria Vittorio Emanuele II ☎02 771 1271, ⦿ gucci.com; ⓜ Montenapoleone or ⓜ San Babila; map p.226. Every desirable fashion item imaginable is available in the warren of sleek showrooms in Montenapoleone, while the newer store in the Galleria Vittorio Emanuele II has the *Gucci café*, where you can get a freshly squeezed fruit juice or a coffee accompanied by an exquisite chocolate – sporting the famous GG symbol, of course – all in an atmosphere of elegant minimalism. Mon–Sat 10am–7pm.

Prada Galleria Vittorio Emanuele II ☎02 876 979, ⦿ prada.com; ⓜ Duomo; map p.226. The original Prada store, complete with walnut display cabinets and swirling staircase, dating from 1913, stands on a side corner in the centre of the Galleria Vittorio Emanuele II.

Menswear: Via Montenapoleone 6 ☎02 7602 0273; Women: Via Montenapoleone 8 ☎02 777 1771. All Mon–Sat 10am–7.30pm.

Trussardi Piazza della Scala 5 ☎02 806 8821, ⦿ trussardi.com; ⓜ Duomo; map p.226. A spacious boutique spread across three floors. The uber-chic *Trussardi-Marino Alla Scala* café occupies the ground floor, serving some of the best cocktails in town. On the floor above the soft leather bags and crisp home lines is the formal Michelin-starred restaurant, and one floor higher still is a gallery space that's worth checking out for contemporary art and fashion exhibitions. Mon–Sat 10am–7pm.

FACTORY STORES

D-Magazine Via Manzoni 44 ⦿ dmagazine.it; ⓜ montenapoleone; map p.226. Rails of different designer labels squished next to the golden rectangle. Daily 9.30am–7.45pm.

Diffusione Tessile Galleria S. Carlo 6 ⦿ diffusionetessile.it; ⓜ San Babila; map p.226. Good discounts on the range of Max Mara brands. Mon 3–7pm, Tues–Sat 10am–7pm.

Il Salvagente Via Bronzetti 16, 15min east of San Babila by bus ⦿ salvagentemilano.it; bus #54 or #61; map pp.222–223. The *grande dame* of Milan's outlet stores where, with a little rummaging, you can bag a designer label for around a third of its original price. Mon 3–7pm, Tues–Sat 10am–12.30pm & 3–7pm.

DESIGN AND FURNITURE

B&B Italia Via Durini 14 ⦿ bebitalia.it; ⓜ San Babila; map p.226. International name that specializes in stylish contemporary furniture by big names in Italian modern design. Mon 3–7pm, Tues–Sat 10am–7pm.

Cassina Via Durini 16 ⦿ cassina.it; ⓜ San Babila; map p.226. The showroom of this legendary Milanese company, which worked with all the greats in Italian design in the 1950s, is always worth a visit for both new designs and its range of twentieth-century design classics including Eames, De Stijl and Rennie Mackintosh chairs. Mon 2.30–7pm, Tues–Sat 10am–7pm.

De Padova Corso Venezia 14 ⦿ depadova.it; ⓜ San Babila; map p.226. Two floors of elegant own-brand furniture and houseware artfully displayed in a stylish showroom including collections by Vico Magestretti and Patricia Urquiola. Mon 2.30–7pm, Tues–Sat 10am–7pm.

Driade Via Manzoni 30 ⦿ driade.com; ⓜ Montenapoleone; map p.226. A wonderful multi-brand store with its own designs, as well as work by designers like Ron Arad and Philippe Starck. The collection includes furniture, tableware, kitchen and bathroom accessories, but the real treat here is the showroom housed in an elegant nineteenth-century *palazzo*. Mon 3–7pm, Tues–Sat 10am–7pm.

CALCIO CRAZY

Milan has two rival football teams – **Inter Milan** and **AC Milan** – which share the G. Meazza or San Siro stadium, playing on alternate Sundays. In 1899 AC (Associazione Calcio or Football Association) Milan was founded by players from the Milan Cricket and Football Club. Eight years later, a splinter group broke away to form Inter in reaction to a ruling banning foreigners playing in the championships. Inter – or the Internationals – were traditionally supported by the middle classes, while AC Milan, with its socialist red stripe, claimed the loyalty of the city's working class. This distinction was blown apart in the mid-1980s when the ardent capitalist Silvio Berlusconi bought the ailing AC and revived its fortunes, leaving many an AC fan with a moral quandary. Their twice-yearly derbies are a highlight of the city's calendar and well worth experiencing live.

Tours There are hourly guided tours around the G. Meazza stadium, at Via Piccolomini 5 (☎ 02 404 2432, ⓦ sansiro.net; Ⓜ Lotto, then a longish walk; Mon–Sat 10am–5pm from Gate 14; €13), including a visit to the clubs' museum. Match tickets can be bought here.

Tickets Other ticket outlets are New Milan Point, in Piazza San Fedele (☎ 02 4548 6224) for AC Milan games (ⓦ acmilan.it); and for Inter games (ⓦ inter.it) Feltrinelli Books and Music, Piazza Piemonte 2 (Mon–Sat 11am–2.30pm & 3.30–7pm), and at Banca Popolare di Milano branches or online (☎ 800 001 908).

FOOD AND DRINK

Cotti Via Solferino 42 ⓦ enotecacotti.it; Ⓜ Moscova; map p.226. A treasure-trove of wines and liqueurs from across the country is accompanied by an array of gourmet treats – both sweet and savoury. Tues–Sat 9am–1pm & 3–7.30pm.

Peck Via Spadari 7–9 ⓦ peck.it; Ⓜ Duomo; map p.226.

Three storeys of top-priced Italian delicacies, from olive oil and home-made chocolate to mouthwatering prosciutto, cheeses, and an impressive wine cellar. There's also a café on the first floor and a swish cocktail bar and restaurant round the corner at Via Cantù 3. Mon 3.30–7.30pm, Tues–Sat 9.15am–7.30pm.

DIRECTORY

Consulates Australia, Via Borgogna 2 ☎ 02 776 741, ⓦ italy.embassy.gov.au; Canada, Via V. Pisani 19 ☎ 02 6758 3900, ⓦ voyage.gc.ca; Ireland, Piazza San Pietro in Gessate 2 ☎ 02 5518 8848, ⓦ ambasciata-irlanda.it; New Zealand, Via Terraggio 17 ☎ 02 721 70001, ⓦ nzembassy .com/italy; South Africa, Vicolo San Giovanni sul Muro 4 ☎ 02 885 8581, ⓦ sudafrica.it; UK, Via S. Paolo 7 ☎ 02 723 001, ⓦ ukinitaly.fco.gov.uk/en; US, Via Principe Amedeo 2/10 ⓦ italy.usembassy.gov.

Doctors English-speaking doctors are available at the private International Health Center (☎ 02 7634 0720, ⓦ ihc.it) and The Milan Clinic (☎ 02 7601 6047, ⓦ milanclinic.com).

Exchange Banks usually offer the best rates, but out of normal banking hours you can change money and travellers' cheques at the Stazione Centrale office (daily 7am–11pm). The airports all have exchange facilities.

Hospital There is a 24hr casualty service at the Ospedale

Maggiore Policlinico, Via Francesco Sforza 35 (☎ 02 55 031), a short walk from Piazza del Duomo. Emergency ☎ 118.

Internet There are internet cafés all over town, generally charging around €2/hr. There are various places along Via Giuseppe Ferrari, the main road immediately to the west of the main station.

Left luggage Stazione Centrale (daily 6am–midnight; €4.10 for 5hr, then small increments up to a max of five days). Stazione Nord (Cadorna) has no left luggage service.

Pharmacy The Stazione Centrale (☎ 02 669 0735), which has English-speaking assistants, and Carlo Erba, on Piazza del Duomo (☎ 02 8646 4832); both have 24hr services.

Police ☎ 113. Headquarters at Via Fatebenefratelli 11 (☎ 02 62 261), near the Pinacoteca di Brera.

Post office Via Cordusio 4, off Piazza Cordusio – not the building marked "Poste", but around the corner (Mon–Fri 8am–7pm, Sat 8.30am–noon).

Southern Lombardy

Strung across the broad plain of the River Po in southern Lombardy, a belt of well-preserved ancient towns offers a handful of spectacular masterpieces of art and architecture against the backdrop of comfortable provincial life.

Just outside the ancient town of **Pavia**, the fabulous **Certosa monastery complex** makes an attractive introduction to this part of Lombardy. To the east, **Cremona**, birthplace of the violin, has a neat, well-preserved centre that's worth popping in to visit. **Mantua**, on the eastern edge of the region, is Lombardy's most visually appealing city: the powerful Gonzaga family ruled for three hundred years from an extravagant ducal palace and later the Palazzo Te, on the outskirts of the city, which contains some of the finest (and most steamily erotic) fresco-painting of the entire Renaissance.

Certosa di Pavia

Tues–Sun: April–Sept 9–11.30am & 2.30–5.30pm; Oct–March closes 4.30pm • Free

Among the rice fields around 40km south of Milan, one of the most extravagant monasteries in Europe, the **Certosa di Pavia** (Charterhouse of Pavia), was commissioned by the Duke of Milan, Galeazzo II Visconti in 1396 as the family mausoleum. Visconti intended the church here to resemble Milan's late-Gothic cathedral and the same architects and craftsmen worked on the construction. It took a century to build; by the time it was finished tastes had changed (and the Viscontis had been replaced by the Sforzas). As a work of art the monastery is one of the most important testimonies to the transformation from late-Gothic to Renaissance and Mannerist styles, but it also affords a wonderful insight into the lives and beliefs of the Carthusian monks.

You can see the church unaccompanied, but to visit the rest of the monastery you need to join a **guided tour** of just under an hour (free but contributions welcomed), led by one of the monks released from the strict vow of silence. Tours run regularly – basically when enough people have gathered. They're in Italian, but well worth doing – even if you don't understand a word – as it allows you to visit the best parts of the monastery complex.

The church

The monastery lies at the end of a tree-lined avenue, part of a former Visconti hunting range that stretched all the way from Pavia's *castello*. Encircled by a high wall, the complex is entered through a central gateway bearing a motif that recurs throughout the monastery – "GRA-CAR" or "Gratiarum Carthusiae", a reference to the fact that the Carthusian monastery is dedicated to Santa Maria delle Grazie, who appears in numerous works of art in the church. Beyond the gateway is a gracious courtyard, with the seventeenth-century Ducal Palace on the right-hand side and outbuildings along the left. Rising up before you is the fantastical **facade** of the church, festooned with inlaid marble, twisted columns, statues and friezes. Despite more than a century's work by leading architects, the facade remains unfinished: the tympanum was never added, giving the church its stocky, truncated look.

The interior

Inside, the Gothic design of the **church** was a deliberate reference to Milan's Duomo, but it has a lighter, more joyous feel, with its painted ceiling, and light streaming in through the one hundred windows high up in the walls. The elaborate seventeenth-century gates to the transept and highly decorated altar, at the far end, are opened when a tour is about to start.

The sculptural highlights of the church lie in the two wings of the transept. In the centre of the north transept lies the stone **funerary monument** of the greatest of the dukes of Milan, Ludovico il Moro, and his wife Beatrice d'Este, neither of whom is actually buried here. The exquisite detail of the statue is an important document of sixteenth-century fashions with its tasselled latticework dress and glam-rock platform shoes. The south transept contains the magnificent **mausoleum** of the founder of the monastery, Gian Galeazzo Visconti, by Cristoforo Romano, including a carving of Gian Galeazzo presenting a model of the Certosa to the Virgin. Both he and his wife, Isabella di Valois, are buried here.

The monastery

Opposite the mausoleum is the door to the delightful **small cloister**, with fine terracotta decoration and a geometric garden around a fountain where monks shared the communal part of their lives, meeting here to pace the courtyard during their weekly ration of talking time. In the adjacent **refectory**, the monks would eat together in silence on Sundays and holy days; the Bible was read throughout the meal from the pulpit (with a hidden entrance in the panelling). The dining room is divided by a blind wall, which allowed the monastery to feed lay workers and guest pilgrims without compromising the rules of their closed order. Further on, the **great cloister** is stunning for its size and tranquillity. It is surrounded on three sides by the **monks' houses**, each consisting of two rooms, a chapel, a garden and a loggia, with a bedroom above. The hatches to the side of the entrances were designed to enable food to be passed through without any communication. The final call is the Certosa **shop**, stocked with honey, chocolate, souvenirs and the famous Chartreuse liqueur.

ARRIVAL AND DEPARTURE	CERTOSA DI PAVIA
By train Arriving by train, turn left out of the station and walk around the Certosa walls until you reach the entrance – a 15min walk. Direct trains leave Milan Centrale, Milan Lambrate, Milan Rigoredo and Pavia stations regularly. Destinations Milan Centrale (7 daily; 35min); Milan	Lambrate (hourly; 25min); Milan Rigoredo (hourly; 20min); Pavia (14 daily; 10min). **By bus** Buses are hourly from Famagosta station (M3) in Milan or from Pavia's bus station, dropping you a 15min walk from the Certosa.

Cremona

A cosy provincial town in the middle of the Po plain, **CREMONA** is renowned for its **violins**. Ever since Andrea Amati established the first violin workshop here in 1566, followed by his son, grandson (Nicolò) and pupils Guarneri and – most famously – **Antonio Stradivari** (1644–1737), Cremona has been a focus for the instrument. Today the city hosts an internationally famous school of violin making, as well as frequent classical concerts.

Cremona has some fine Renaissance and medieval buildings, and its cobbled streets make for some pleasant wandering, but it's a modest sort of place: target it as a half-day trip from Bergamo or Milan, en route towards the richer pickings of Mantua.

Piazza del Comune

At the centre of Cremona is the splendid **Piazza del Comune**, a narrow space dominated by monumental architecture.

In the northeast corner looms the gawky Romanesque **Torrazzo** (Tues–Sun 10am–1pm & 2.30–6pm; €4, joint ticket with Baptistry €5), at 112m one of Italy's tallest medieval towers. Built in the mid-thirteenth century and bearing a fine Renaissance clock dating from 1583, its 502 steps can be climbed for excellent views.

Adjacent to the Torrazzo stands the **Duomo** (Mon–Sat 8am–noon & 3.30–7pm, Sun 10.30–11am & 3.30–5.30pm; free), connected to it by way of a Renaissance loggia. The Duomo's huge facade, made up of classical, Romanesque and fancy Gothic elements, focuses on a rose window from 1274. The interior is rather oppressive – lofty and dim, marked by the dark stone of its piers, and covered by naïve frescoes done in the sixteenth century, including a trompe l'oeil by Pordenone on the west wall showing the *Crucifixion* and *Deposition*. Also of note are the fifteenth-century pulpits, decorated with finely tortured reliefs.

The south side of Piazza del Comune features the octagonal **Baptistry** (Tues–Sun 10am–1pm & 2.30–6pm; €2, joint ticket with Torrazzo €5) dating from the late twelfth century. Its vast bare-brick interior is rather severe, though lightened by the twin columns in each bay and a series of upper balconies.

Directly opposite the Duomo, the **Palazzo del Comune** (Tues–Sat 9am–6pm, Sun 10am–6pm; €6, joint ticket with Museo Civico €10) has a small exhibition of nine

---

LUTHIERS IN ACTION

Cremona is a natural magnet for **violin makers** of all nationalities. There are workshops across the city, many of which can be visited. The tourist office has details of open studios including Gaspar Borchardt at Piazza Zaccaria 11 (☎0372 319 69), just off the main square.

---

historic violins in its upstairs **Sala dei Violini**, including a very early example made by Andrea Amati in 1566, as well as later instruments by Amati's pupils, Guarneri and Stradivari. There are recordings of the different instruments and at certain times of the day on weekdays you can hear one of them being played live (check times with the tourist office).

Museo Civico: the Museo Stradivario

Via Ugolani Dati 4 • Tues–Sat 9am–6pm, Sun 10am–6pm • €7, joint ticket with Collezione di Violini €10

The pilastered Palazzo Affaitati – a pleasant ten-minute stroll north of Piazza del Comune – holds the **Museo Civico "Ala Ponzone"**, displaying a pedestrian collection of mainly Cremonese art. Head upstairs to a suite of eighteenth-century rooms – filled with the sound of recorded violin music – which hold the **Museo Stradivario**, displaying models, paper patterns, tools and acoustic diagrams from Stradivari's workshop. An informative video helps to unravel the mysteries of the violin-maker's art.

The rest of town

Southwest of Piazza del Comune, on Via Tibaldi, the church of **San Pietro al Po** has better frescoes than the Duomo; look for Bernadino Gatti's hearty *Feeding of the Five Thousand* in the refectory next door. If you like that, you'll love **San Sigismondo** in the eastern outskirts (bus #2 from Piazza Cavour). Built in 1441, its Mannerist decor is among Italy's best, ranging from Camillo Boccaccino's soaring apse fresco to Giulio Campi's *Annunciation*, in which Gabriel floats in mid-air.

ARRIVAL AND DEPARTURE | CREMONA

By train Cremona's train station is on Via Dante, a 10min walk north of the main Piazza del Comune, linked to Piazza Cavour in the centre by bus #1.

Destinations Mantua (8 daily; 1hr); Milan (every 2hr; 1hr 10min).

INFORMATION AND GETTING AROUND

Tourist office Piazza del Comune 5, opposite the Torrazzo (Mon–Sat 9.30am–1pm & 2–5pm; Sun, July & Aug 9.30am–1pm only; ☎0372 406 391, ⑩provincia.cremona .it). Has details of classical concerts around town as well

as violin-makers' workshops that can be visited.

By bike To explore the narrow lanes of Cremona or perhaps head down to the river for a picnic, rent a bicycle from Mata Store on Via San Tommaso (☎0373 457 483).

ACCOMMODATION

Cascina Nuova Via Boschetto 51 ☎0372 460 433, ⑩cascinanuova.it. In the countryside, a comfortable 30min stroll from the centre of town, this old farmhouse offers handsome rooms, some apartments, a garden and lovely home-cooking in the attached restaurant. **€80**

Dellearti Design Hotel Via Bonomelli 8 ☎0372 23 131, ⑩dellearti.com. Slightly incongruous in provincial Cremona, the contemporary styling of this self-fashioned

art hotel offers comfortable, über-designed rooms, a small spa and courtyard café. Good discounts available online. **€190**

Duomo Via Gonfalonieri 13, down the side of the Palazzo del Comune ☎0372 35 242, ⑩hotelduomo cremona.com. Simple three-star with a/c and en-suite rooms, just off the main square; also has a decent restaurant (see p.252). **€70**

EATING AND DRINKING

Numerous cosy *osterie* serve Cremona's specialities: *bollito misto* – a mixture of boiled meats, served with *mostarda di frutta* (also known as *mostarda di Cremona*), fruit suspended in a sweet mustard syrup. The excellent *gastronomie* that cluster around Corso Garibaldi and Corso Campi make good places to put together a picnic.

Duomo Via Gonfalonieri 13, down the side of the Palazzo del Comune ☎0372 35 296. The tables outside this popular restaurant/pizzeria make a fine, sunny spot to tuck into a crispy pizza. Mon–Sat 12.30–2.30pm & 7–10pm.

La Piadineria Via Platina 20. Flat-bread wraps at this central branch of a quality chain make a filling, fast snack. Tucked behind the cathedral on the central square. Tues–Sun noon–2pm & 6–9pm.

La Sosta Via Sicardo 9 ☎0372 456 656. By the main piazza, this attractive *osteria* does a great line in Cremonese specialities at reasonable prices. Tues–Sun noon–2.30pm & 7–10pm.

Porta Mosa Via S. Maria Betlem 11 ☎0372 411 803. This simple *osteria*, a 10min walk east of Piazza del Comune, serves delicious local dishes, washed down with well-chosen wines. Mon–Sat 12.15–2.30pm & 7.15–10pm.

Mantua (Mantova) and around

Aldous Huxley called it the most romantic city in the world. With a skyline of domes and towers rising above its three encircling lakes, **MANTUA** (Mantova) is undeniably evocative. This was where Romeo heard of Juliet's supposed death, and where Verdi set *Rigoletto*. Its history is one of equally operatic plots, most of them acted out by the **Gonzaga**, one of Renaissance Italy's richest and most powerful families, who ruled the town for three centuries. Its cobbled squares retain a medieval aspect, and there are two splendid palaces: the **Palazzo Ducale**, containing Mantegna's stunning fresco of the Gonzaga family and court, and **Palazzo Te**, whose frescoes by the flashy Mannerist Giulio Romano encompass steamy erotica and illusionistic fantasy. Mantua's lakes, and the flat surrounding plain, offer numerous boat cruises and cycling routes.

The centre of Mantua is made up of four attractive squares, each connected to the next. Lively Piazza Mantegna is overlooked by the massive **Sant'Andrea** church. Beside it is the lovely Piazza delle Erbe, with fine arcades facing the medieval **Rotonda** church. To the north, through medieval passageways and across Piazza Broletto, the long, cobbled slope of Piazza Sordello is dominated by the **Palazzo Ducale**, the fortress and residence of the Gonzaga, packed with Renaissance art.

Mantua's other great palace stands in its own gardens 1.5km south of the historic centre – **Palazzo Te**, adorned with sensational frescoes.

Sant'Andrea

Piazza Mantegna • Daily 8am–noon & 3–7pm • ⓦ santandreainmantova.it

Dominating **Piazza Mantegna** – a wedge-shaped open space at the end of the arcaded shopping thoroughfares of Corso Umberto and Via Roma – is the facade of Leon Battista Alberti's church of **Sant'Andrea**, an unfinished basilica that says a lot about the ego of Lodovico II Gonzaga, who commissioned it in 1470. He felt that the existing medieval church was neither impressive enough to represent the splendour of his state nor large enough to hold the droves of people who packed in every Ascension Day to see the holy relic of Christ's blood which had been found on the site. Lodovico brought in the court architect, Luca Fancelli, to oversee Alberti's plans. There was a bitchy rivalry between the two, and when, on one of his many visits, Alberti fell and hurt a testicle, Fancelli gleefully told him: "God lets men punish themselves in the place where they sin." Work started in earnest after Alberti's death in 1472, and took more than two decades to complete.

TUMBLING TOWERS AND SHAKING FRESCOES

In May 2012 earthquakes reaching 5.9 on the Richter scale shook this part of Italy. No one was killed in Mantua, unlike nearby Parma (see p.483) but ancient buildings and frescoes around town, including the Palazzo Ducale and the Palazzo Te, were badly damaged. When you visit there is a possibility that some rooms or even entire buildings will be closed for restoration; check ahead with the tourist office.

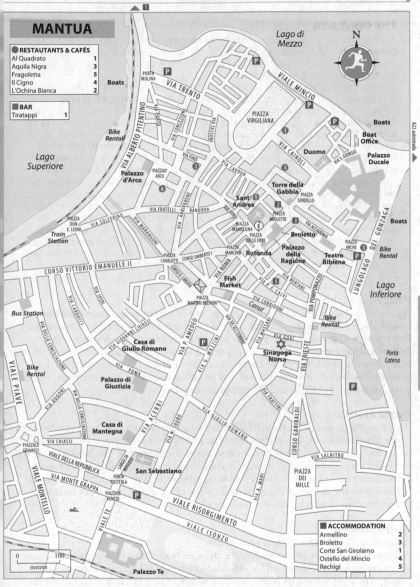

MANTUA

● RESTAUTANTS & CAFÉS

Al Quadrato	1
Aquila Nigra	3
Fragoletta	5
Il Cigno	4
L'Ochina Bianca	2

■ BAR

Tiratappi	1

■ ACCOMMODATION

Armellino	2
Broletto	3
Corte San Girolamo	1
Ostello del Mincio	4
Rechigi	5

The Classical **facade** is focused on an immense triumphal arch supported on giant pilasters. **Inside**, the vast, column-free space is roofed with one large barrel-vault, echoing the facade. The octagonal balustrade at the crossing stands above the crypt where the holy relic is kept in two vases, copies of originals designed by Cellini and stolen by the Austrians in 1846; to see them, ask the sacristan. The painter Mantegna is buried in the first chapel on the left, his tomb topped with a bust of the artist that is said to be a self-portrait. The wall-paintings in the chapel were designed by Mantegna and executed by students, Correggio being one.

THE GONZAGA

At the time of the coup of 1328, when **Luigi Gonzaga** seized Mantua from the Bonacolsi, the **Gonzaga** family were wealthy local landowners living outside Mantua on vast estates with an army of retainers. Luigi nominated himself Captain of the People, a role which quickly became hereditary, eventually growing to that of marquis.

Mantua's renaissance began in 1459, when a visiting pope complained that the city was muddy, marshy and riddled with fever. This spurred his host, **Lodovico II Gonzaga**, to give the city a facelift, ranging from paving the squares and repainting the shops to engaging **Andrea Mantegna** as court artist and calling in the prestigious architectural theorist **Leon Battista Alberti** to design the monumental church of Sant'Andrea, one of the most influential buildings of the early Renaissance. Later, Lodovico's grandson, **Francesco II** (1466–1519), swelled the family coffers by hiring himself out as a mercenary – money his wife, **Isabella d'Este**, spent amassing a prestigious collection of paintings, sculpture and objets d'art.

Under Isabella's son, **Federico II**, Gonzaga fortunes reached their height; his marriage in 1531 to the heiress of the duchy of Monferrato procured a ducal title for the family, while he continued the policy of self-glorification by commissioning an out-of-town villa – the **Palazzo Te** – for himself and his mistress. Federico's descendants were for the most part less colourful characters, one notable exception being **Vincenzo I**, whose debauchery and corruption provided the inspiration for Verdi's licentious duke in *Rigoletto*. After Vincenzo's death in 1612, the then-bankrupt court was forced to sell many of the family treasures to Charles I of England (many are still in London's Victoria and Albert Museum), just three years before the arrival of the Habsburgs.

Piazza delle Erbe

Beside Sant'Andrea, Piazza Mantegna gives way to atmospheric **Piazza delle Erbe**, with a small daily market and cafés sheltering in the arcades below the thirteenth-century **Palazzo della Ragione**. Sunk below the present street level is the eleventh-century **Rotonda di San Lorenzo** (daily 10am–1pm & 3–6pm, Sat & Sun 10am–6pm), which was partially demolished in the sixteenth century and used as a courtyard by the surrounding houses. Rebuilt in 1908 and beautifully restored in recent years, it still contains traces of twelfth- and thirteenth-century frescoes.

Piazza Broletto

At the northern end of Piazza delle Erbe, a passage leads under the red-brick **Broletto**, or medieval town hall, into the smaller **Piazza Broletto**, where you can view two reminders of how "criminals" were treated under the Gonzagas. The bridge to the right has metal rings embedded in its vault, to which victims were chained by the wrists, before being hauled up by a pulley and suspended in mid-air; while on your far left – actually on the corner of Piazza Sordello – the tall, medieval **Torre della Gabbia** has a cage attached in which prisoners were displayed.

Teatro Bibiena

Via Accademia 47 • Tues–Sun 9.30am–12.30pm & 3–6pm • €2

A diversion up Via Accademia leads to the Baroque **Teatro Bibiena**, a splendid, intimate theatre, its curved walls lined with boxes. Mozart gave the inaugural concert here on January 16, 1770, a few days before his fourteenth birthday. His father was fulsome in his praise for the building, calling it "the most beautiful thing in its genre that I have ever seen".

The Duomo

Piazza Sordello • Daily 7am–noon & 3–7pm • Free

Northeast of Piazza Broletto, **Piazza Sordello** is a large, sombre, rectangular square, headed by the Baroque facade of the **Duomo**. Flanked by touristy pavement cafés and grim crenellated palaces built by the Bonacolsi (the Gonzagas' predecessors) the Duomo conceals a rich interior, designed by Giulio Romano after the church had been gutted by fire in 1545.

Palazzo Ducale

Piazza Sordello • Tues–Sun 8.15am–7.15pm, last entry 6.20pm • €6.50, audioguides €4, or €5.50 for two • Nov–March guided tour essential
(1hr 30min; free); these start every 15min, or when twenty people have gathered • ☏ 041 241 1897, ⓦ mantovaducale.beniculturali.it

Across the square, the Palazzo del Capitano and Magna Domus form the core of the **Palazzo Ducale**, an enormous complex that was once the largest palace in Europe. In its heyday it covered 34,000 square metres and had a population of over a thousand; when it was sacked by the Habsburgs in 1630 eighty carriages were needed to carry away the two thousand works of art contained in its five hundred rooms.

Rooms 1–14

The tour starts in the Corte Vecchia, the oldest wing of the palace. In the **Sala del Morone** (room 1) hangs a painting from 1494 by Domenico Morone showing the *Expulsion of the Bonacolsi* from Piazza Sordello, with the Duomo sporting its old, Gothic facade (replaced in the eighteenth century). In the **Sala del Pisanello** (room 3) are the fragments of a half-finished fresco by Pisanello, discovered in 1969 behind two layers of plaster.

The splendid Neoclassical **Sala degli Specchi** (Hall of Mirrors; room 6) was originally an open loggia, bricked up in 1773; the barrel-vaulted ceiling holds a fresco depicting teams of horses being driven from Night to Day. In the **Sala degli Arcieri** (Hall of Archers; room 7), a huge canvas by Rubens shows the Gonzaga family of 1604 seated comfortably in the presence of the Holy Trinity; look out for Vincenzo with his handlebar moustache. The picture was originally part of a huge triptych, but Napoleonic troops carried off two-thirds of it in 1797 (one part is now in Antwerp, the other in Nancy) and chopped the remaining third into saleable chunks of portraiture; some gaps remain. Around the room is a curious frieze of horses, glimpsed behind curtains. Beyond the **Sala del Labirinto** (room 9), named for the maze on its painted and gilded wooden ceiling, the **Sala di Amore e Psiche** (room 11) is an intimate space with a wooden floor and an eighteenth-century *tondo* of Cupid and Psyche in the ceiling.

Rooms 15–17: Camera degli Sposi

From here follow signs along corridors, down stairs and over a moat into the fourteenth-century **Castello di San Giorgio**, which contains the palace's principal treasure: Mantegna's frescoes of the Gonzaga family in the **Camera degli Sposi** (room 17). Painted between 1465–74, they're naturalistic pieces of work, giving a vivid impression of the Marquis Lodovico, his wife Barbara and their family, and of the relationships between them. In the main fresco Lodovico discusses a letter with a courtier while his wife looks on; their youngest daughter leans on her mother's lap, about to bite into an apple, while an older son and daughter look towards the door, where an ambassador from another court is being welcomed. The other fresco, divided into three sections, shows Lodovico welcoming his son Francesco back from Rome. In the background are the Holy Roman Emperor Frederick III and the king of Denmark. Don't forget to look up: the ceiling features another nice piece of trompe l'oeil, in which two women, peering down from a balustrade, have balanced a tub of plants on a pole and appear to be on the verge of letting it tumble into the room.

Rooms 18–36: Corte Nuova and Corte Vecchia

Next comes the sixteenth-century Corte Nuova wing, designed by Giulio Romano for Federico II Gonzaga. After several formal audience rooms you come to the **Sala di Troia**

VISITING CAMERA DEGLI SPOSI

For conservation reasons, only 1500 people a day are allowed to visit the **Camera degli Sposi** (also called the **Camera Picta**). In the peak season for school trips (mid-March to mid-June and Sept to mid-Oct), individuals must book in advance for a timed slot for admission to this room, on ☏ 041 241 1897 (press 1 for English-speaking operators; Mon–Fri 9am–6pm, Sat 9am–2pm). Booking costs €1 extra, payable on arrival.

4

(room 22), decorated with Romano's brilliantly colourful scenes from the *Iliad* and *Aeneid*. The adjacent **Galleria dei Marmi** (room 23), with delicate floral and wildlife motifs, looks out over the Cortile della Cavallerizza (Courtyard of the Riding School). Along the courtyard's long side runs the immense **Galleria della Mostra** (room 24), once hung with paintings by Titian, Caravaggio, Breughel and others, all now dispersed; in their place are 64 Roman marble busts. Push on through the smaller rooms and up more stairs to the stunning **Sala dello Zodiaco** (room 33), whose late sixteenth-century ceiling is spangled with stars and constellations. The adjoining Rococo **Sala dei Fiumi** (room 34) features an elaborate painted allegory of Mantua's six rivers, flanked by two over-the-top stucco-and-mosaic fountains.

Save some wonder for rooms 35–37, beside the Sala dello Zodiaco. These comprise the **Stanze degli Arazzi**, three rooms (and a small chapel) altered in the eighteenth century to house nine sixteenth-century Flemish tapestries of exceptional virtuosity, depicting stories from the Acts of the Apostles, made from Raphael's cartoons for the Sistine Chapel (now in London's Victoria and Albert Museum).

South of the centre

South of the central squares, Giulio Romano's **Fish Market** – to the left off Piazza Martiri Belfiori – a short covered bridge over the river, is still used as a market building. Following Via Principe Amedeo south, the **Casa di Giulio Romano**, off to the right at Via Poma 18 – overshadowed by the monster-studded Palazzo di Giustizia – was meant to impress the sophisticated, who would have found the licence taken with the Classical rules of architecture witty. A five-minute walk away on busy Via Acerbi stands the austere brick **Casa del Mantegna**, now used as a contemporary art space (hours and admission vary).

San Sebastiano

Mid-March to mid-Nov Tues–Sun 10.30am–12.30pm & 3–5pm • €1.50

The church of **San Sebastiano**, the work of Alberti, is famous as the first Renaissance church to be built on a central Greek-cross plan, described as "curiously pagan" by Nikolaus Pevsner. Lodovico II's son was less polite: "I could not understand whether it was meant to turn out as a church, a mosque or a synagogue." The bare interior – now deconsecrated – is dedicated to Mantua's war dead.

Palazzo Te

Southern end of Via Acerbi • Mon 1–6pm, Tues–Sun 9am–6pm, last entry 5.30pm • €8 • ⓦ palazzote.it

A twenty-minute walk from the centre of Mantua, at the end of the long spine of Via Principe Amedeo and Via Acerbi, the **Palazzo Te** is the later of the city's two Gonzaga palaces, and equally compelling. Set in its own grounds, the *palazzo* was designed by Giulio Romano in the 1520s for playboy Federico Gonzaga and his mistress, Isabella Boschetta. It's the artist's greatest work and a renowned Renaissance pleasure dome – originally an island connected to the mainland by bridge, an ideal location for an amorous retreat away from Federico's wife and the restrictions of life in the Palazzo Ducale. Although the upstairs rooms display paintings and antiquities, the main reason for visiting is to see Giulio's amazing decorative scheme on the ground floor.

Camera del Sole and Sala dei Cavalli

A tour of the palace is like a voyage around Giulio's imagination, a sumptuous world where very little is what it seems. In the **Camera del Sole**, the sun and the moon are represented by a pair of horse-drawn chariots viewed from below, giving a fine array of human and equine bottoms on the ceiling. The **Sala dei Cavalli** holds portraits of prime specimens from the Gonzaga stud-farm (which was also on the island), standing before an illusionistic background in which simulated marble, fake pilasters and mock reliefs surround views of painted landscapes through nonexistent windows.

Sala di Amore e Psiche

The function of the **Sala di Amore e Psiche**, further on, is undocumented, but the graphically erotic frescoes, and the proximity to Federico's private quarters, are powerful clues. The ceiling paintings tell the story of Cupid and Psyche with more dizzying *sotto in su* ("from the bottom up") works by Giulio, while the walls are covered with orgiastic wedding-feast scenes, at which drunken gods in various states of undress are attended by a menagerie of real and mythical beasts. On one wall, Mars and Venus are climbing out of the bath together, their cave watered by a river-god lounging above who is gushing with deliberately ambiguous liquid, flowing from his beard, a vessel he's holding and his genitals. Other scenes show Olympia about to be raped by a half-serpentine Jupiter, and Pasiphae disguising herself as a cow in order to seduce a bull – all watched over by the giant Polyphemus, perched above the fireplace, clutching the pan-pipes with which he sang of his love for Galatea before murdering her lover.

Sala dei Giganti

Polyphemus and his fellow giants are revenged in the extraordinary **Sala dei Giganti** beyond – "the most fantastic and frightening creation of the whole Renaissance", according to the critic Frederick Hartt – showing the destruction of the giants by the gods. As if at some kind of advanced disaster movie, the destruction appears to be all around: cracking pillars, toppling brickwork and screaming giants, mangled and crushed by great chunks of architecture, appearing to crash down into the room. Stamp your feet and you'll discover another parallel to modern cinema – the sound effects that Giulio created by turning the room into an echo chamber.

4

ARRIVAL AND INFORMATION   MANTUA

By train The train station is a 10min walk west of the centre (buses from Verona drop off first in the more convenient Piazza Sordello).
Destinations Bologna (2 daily; 1hr 35min); Milan (9 daily; 1hr 50min); Modena (hourly; 45min); Verona (hourly; 50min).
By bus Alongside the train station, although note that buses from Verona drop off first in the more convenient Piazza Sordello.
Destinations Brescia (every 2hr; 1hr 40min); Milan (1 daily; 2hr 15min); Peschiera (hourly; 1hr 10min).
Tourist office Piazza Mantegna 6 (daily 9am–6pm; ☎ 0376 432 432, ⊛ turismo.mantova.it).

GETTING AROUND

On foot or by bike The city is small enough to cover on foot: even the walk south to Palazzo Te is only 20min. The best bets for bike rental are Mantua Bike, Viale Piave 22/B (☎ 0376 220 909), and La Rigola at Via Trieste 7 (☎ 0376 366 677). For longer rides, see box below.
By bus Bus #1 follows a circular route linking the train station, the central squares and Palazzo Te.

EXPLORING MANTUA: BIKES AND BOATS

Several companies offer **cruises** on Mantua's lakes – bulges in the course of the River Mincio – and on the river itself down to its confluence with the Po, ranging from one-hour jaunts (around €8) up to full-day voyages as far as Ferrara and Venice (around €90/140). All run daily but must be **booked in advance**: usually a day ahead, but sometimes an hour or so will do. The leading company is Motonavi Andes Negrini, whose ticket office is at Via San Giorgio 2 (☎ 0376 322 875, ⊛ motonaviandes.it), three minutes' walk from its jetty on Lago Inferiore. Navi Andes (☎ 0376 324 506, ⊛ naviandes.com) is a separate concern, based at its jetty on Lago di Mezzo. Alternatives include the Barcaioli del Mincio (☎ 0376 349 292, ⊛ fiumemincio.it), local boatmen operating small craft upstream from Mantua.

Many of the boats accept bikes, so you can make a great day-trip – a morning on the boat, a picnic lunch at, say, Rivalta, then a gentle cycle-ride back in the afternoon. The tourist office has a good map (also on its website) detailing cycle routes, plus information on bus, boat and train combinations. For bike rental, see above.

ACCOMMODATION

★ **Armellino** Via Cavour 67 ☎ 0346 314 8060, ⓦ bebarmellino.it. Four large, beautifully furnished double rooms in an eighteenth-century palace right in the heart of town. There's a pretty garden for drinks and breakfast is served in the period dining-room. No credit cards. **€95**

Broletto Via Accademia 1 ☎ 0376 326 784, ⓦ hotel broletto.com. A comfortable, welcoming boutique hotel in the very heart of the old town. Service is cheery and the smart en-suite rooms are attractive if a little small. **€120**

Corte San Girolamo Via S. Girolamo 1, Gambarara ☎ 0376 391 018, ⓦ agriturismo-sangirolamo.it. Occupying a renovated watermill 3km north of town on the cycle route from Mantua to Lake Garda, this serene agriturismo has en-suite doubles, plus a four-person apartment. Bicycles available. **€80**

Ostello del Mincio Via Porto 23, Rivalta ☎ 0376 653 924, ⓦ ostellodelmincio.org. Fine hostel 10km west of town, in a sleepy village on the River Mincio, with canoes and bicycles available for rent and boat trips. It stands 5km from Castellucchio train station (on the Cremona–Mantua line), and the hourly bus #13 (Mantua–Asola; ⓦ apam.it) stops outside. There are double and family rooms as well as dorms. Dorms **€15**, doubles **€40**

Rechigi Via Calvi 30 ☎ 0376 320 781, ⓦ rechigi.com. Professional four-star hotel in the historic centre. The lobby is all gleaming marble and contemporary art; the rooms are calmer, while still being modern and functional. Private parking. **€160**

EATING AND DRINKING

Mantua has plenty of excellent, reasonably priced restaurants, many serving local specialities like *spezzatino di Mantova* (donkey stew), *agnoli in brodo* (pasta stuffed with cheese and sausage in broth) or the delicious *tortelli di zucca* (sweet pumpkin-filled pasta). If you're in town on a Saturday, head for the tempting goodies at the farmers' market in Lungorio IV Novembre (8am–1pm).

Al Quadrato Piazza Virgiliana 49 ☎ 0376 368 896. A tranquil spot away from the fray, overlooking the Piazza Virgiliana park north of the centre. Serves good pizzas (€7–8) and tasty fish dishes. Expect to pay around €25. Tues–Sun 12.30am–2pm & 7–11pm.

Aquila Nigra Vicolo Bonacolsi 4 ☎ 0376 327 180, ⓦ aquilanigra.it. A formal restaurant housed in an elegant *palazzo* just off Piazza Sordello, serving delicious seasonal dishes complemented by an impressive wine list. The fish and, especially, seafood are highly regarded. Menus are €70/80. There's also a contemporary bistro next door with a briefer menu at lower prices. Tues–Sat 12.30–2.30pm & 7–11pm; closed Aug.

Fragoletta Piazza Arche 5/A ☎ 0376 323 300, ⓦ fragoletta.it. Over towards the Lago Inferiore, this is a lively *osteria* shoehorned into a cramped little building. It's been around since 1748 and remains popular with locals for its well-priced regional cuisine (meals for around €30 a head). Tues–Sun noon–3pm & 8–11pm.

Il Cigno (Trattoria dei Martini) Piazza d'Arco 1 ☎ 0376 327 101. Wonderful restaurant occupying a sixteenth-century mansion in a quiet corner away from the centre, overlooking a beautiful private garden. Choose from the seasonal menu, which includes delectable *tortelli di zucca* with amaretti and the signature roast guinea-fowl. Service is discreet yet welcoming. Expect to pay around €80 per head. Wed–Sun 12.130–2pm & 7.30–11.30pm; closed Aug.

★ **L'Ochina Bianca** Via Finzi 2 ☎ 0376 323 700. Cosy *osteria* a 5min walk west from Piazza delle Erbe, where friendly staff serve tasty Mantuan dishes – this is a mainstay of the Italian Slow Food movement, dedicated to promoting quality and conviviality. Daily 12.30–2.30pm & 7.45–10pm; closed Mon lunch.

Tiratappi Piazza Alberti 30 ☎ 0376 322 366. Atmospheric old wine-bar on this little-visited square, down a concealed passageway beside the Sant'Andrea church. Its terrace tables are a sun-trap – perfect for sampling Mantuan vintages on a slow afternoon. The welcome is genuine and the cuisine is local mid-priced specialities served with care. Daily noon–2.30pm & 6–11pm; closed lunch Tues & Thurs.

Northern Lombardy: lakes and mountains

"One can't describe the beauty of the **Italian lakes**, nor would one try if one could." Henry James's sentiment hasn't stopped generations of writers producing reams of purple prose in the attempt. Yet, in truth, the Lakes just about deserve it: their beauty is extravagant, and it's not surprising that the most romantic and melodramatic of Italy's opera composers – Verdi, Rossini and Bellini – rented villas here in which to work. British and German Romantic poets also enthused about the Lakes, and in doing so planted them firmly in northern-European imaginations. The result is an influx

GETTING AROUND THE LAKES

Lakes Garda, Como and Maggiore are all well served by ferries and hydrofoils, which dock at jetties that are usually conveniently positioned on the main lakeside piazzas: travelling by water makes a lot more sense than struggling through lakeside traffic. All three also have useful **car ferry** routes across the centre of the lakes.

For **timetables and fares** covering all three lakes, check Ⓦnavigazionelaghi.it or consult the posters displayed at every lakeside jetty (and local tourist offices). Prices aren't expensive – the two-hour voyage from Como to Bellagio is €10.40, for example, while it costs €17 to take a small car plus two people across Lake Garda – and there are good-value day-passes available, with some discounts for children and EU citizens over 65.

Trains serve several points on all three lakes, and **buses** also run regularly up and down the shores. Tourist offices can advise about routes and timings, or check Ⓦvcoinbus.it for transport around the western shore of Lake Maggiore (in Piemonte), Ⓦaptv.it for buses along the eastern shore of Lake Garda (in the Veneto), and Ⓦtrasporti.regione.lombardia.it for everything in between.

Public transport between the lakes is not very good and you're probably better off using Milan as a hub rather than fiddling around with lots of local changes.

every summer of tourists from cooler climes, come to savour the Italian dream and to take gulps at what Keats called "the beaker of the warm south".

Garda is the largest lake, and one of the best centres in Europe for windsurfing and sailing. It is also visually stunning, especially in its mountainous northern stretches – yet **Como** matches (or, some say, betters) it, with forested slopes rising directly from the water's edge. On both lakes, the luxuriance of the waterfront vegetation is equalled by the opulence of the local villas and *palazzi*; both also offer good hiking in the mountainous hinterland.

Further west, **Maggiore** is less popular yet just as beautiful, with several sedate *fin-de-siècle* resorts. There are, however, some good walks, and superb formal gardens adorning Isola Bella and other grand villas. Nearby, the picture-postcard charms of Orta San Giulio, the main village on **Lake Orta** – with its steepled offshore islet – ensure that it is a popular spot, yet this too can be a wonderfully romantic place to hole up.

The hilly terrain between the lakes is sliced up by **mountain valleys** – largely residential and industrial in their lower reaches though mostly untouched further up, hosting lots of modest ski resorts in winter (none worth making a special trip for). The nearby city of **Brescia** is a treat as a day-trip, while its neighbour **Bergamo** is a lovely place to stay, with an old walled hilltop quarter that ranks as one of the most alluring in Italy.

Lake Maggiore

For generations of overland travellers, weary of journeying over the Alps, **LAKE MAGGIORE** (Lago Maggiore) has been a first taste of Italy: the sight of limpid blue waters, green hills and exotic vegetation is evidence of arrival in the warm south. With palms and oleanders lining the lakeside promenades and a peaceful, serene air, Maggiore – at 66km, Italy's longest lake – may not be somewhere for thrill-seekers, but it is seductively relaxing.

The majority of tourists head for the western shore, from where the sumptuous gardens and villas of the **Borromean islands** are within easy reach. The area retains much of its charm: the genteel old resort of **Stresa** is still a convenient base, linked by high-speed train to Milan (1hr) and by bus and boat to all points around the lake. Across the bay, pretty **Verbania** is also well connected by train, bus and ferry, while further north, enchanting **Cannobio** – the last stop before Switzerland – is popular with families and a good place from which to explore Maggiore's hilly hinterland. Note that in winter (Nov–Easter) many hotels close down and attractions may be shut. For tourist information, check Ⓦdistrettolaghi.it.

Stresa

The Maggiore of the tourist brochures begins at **STRESA**, whose popularity as a resort started in 1906, when the Simplon Tunnel opened, the final link in a chain of railways connecting Lake Geneva to Milan, and thus northern Europe to the Mediterranean. International trains, including the *Orient Express*, were routed through Stresa, which quickly became a holiday retreat for Europe's high society.

Today, Stresa is a bustling little place, but its greatest days have passed. Stroll the floral promenade, take in the lake views – which are worth coming for – head out to the islands, then retire to a waterside bench with an ice cream.

Mottarone

Cable cars to the top daily every 20min 9.30am–5.30pm • €10.50 one way, €17.50 return • ⓦ stresa-mottarone.it

Separating Stresa from Lake Orta (see p.265) is the **Mottarone** mountain, rising to 1491m. From the top – accessed by **cable car** (*funivia*), rising from the Carciano ferry stop, 750m north of Stresa – the views are impressive, stretching to Monte Rosa on the Swiss border. Its wooded western slopes are a favourite destination for rambles and family outings. You can rent **mountain bikes** at the base station (€25/day including cable-car ticket; ⓦ bicico.it). The easy walk up, signposted as path 1, takes four hours.

Aquadventure Park

Strada Cavali • ☎ 0323 919 7999 • €12 pools, other activities extra, family tickets also available • ⓦ aquadventurepark.com

Six kilometres north of Stresa, just after Baveno, this combination of adventure park and swimming pools with water slides also offers climbing, mountain biking and other sporty options for kids and adults alike. Prices depend on the activities selected.

ARRIVAL AND INFORMATION
STRESA

By train Stresa is an hour from Milano Centrale on the fast trains heading for Switzerland; slower trains also run from Milano Centrale and Milano Porta Garibaldi. Taxis wait outside the station or walk right to the crossroads, then left on Via Duchessa di Genova for 200m down to the lakefront.

By bus Buses from Milan Malpensa airport (Terminal 1 stop 22, Terminal 2 stop 12) run along the western shore of Lake Maggiore between April and October (€9; booking essential 48hr in advance; ☎ 0323 552 17, ⓦ safduemila .com). There's also a year-round service from Malpensa to Gravellona Toce (€9; ⓦ comazzibus.com) 9km away. Tickets can be bought on the bus.

Destinations Malpensa (Terminals 1 & 2; April–Oct 6 daily); Orta San Giulio (3 daily mid-June to early Sept; 1hr).

By boat Stresa is at the centre of the network of boats serving the Borromean islands as well as ferries heading up and down the lake. Private boat-taxis also head from Stresa for trips to the islands. The imbarcadero is on Piazza Marconi, across the main road from the village centre.

Destinations Arona (approx hourly; 1hr); Intra (every 30min; 55min); Isola Bella (every 30min; 10min); Isola Madre (every 30min; 30min); Pallanza (every 30min; 35min); Santa Caterina (hourly; 15min); Villa Taranto (every 30min; 45min).

Tourist office Piazza Marconi 16, on the lakefront, beside the imbarcadero (daily 10am–12.30pm & 3–6.30pm; Nov–Feb closed Sat & Sun; ☎ 0323 31 308, ⓦ stresaturismo .it or ⓦ distrettolaghi.it).

LAGO MAGGIORE EXPRESS

A highlight of any Lake Maggiore holiday, the Lago Maggiore Express (ⓦ lagomaggioreexpress .com; one day €32, two days €40) is a triangular combination of rail and ferry travel to explore the lake and mountains while dipping into Switzerland too. Don't forget your passport.

Take Itinerary 7 on the advertised route heading up to the mountain village of Domodossola by train from Stresa and then catch the spectacular narrow-gauge railway to Locarno in Switzerland. Here you have time to wander and have lunch before boarding the ferry for a relaxed three-hour cruise back to Stresa. The route can be reversed – taking lunch on board the ferry – spread over two days or put together from other points on the lake.

ACCOMMODATION

Fiorentino Via Am Bolongaro 9 ☎ 0323 30 254, ⓦ hotelfiorentino.com. House-proud two-star hotel tucked away in the town centre with fourteen plain, comfortable rooms. €90

Flora Via Sempione Nord 26 ☎ 0323 30524, ⓦ hotel florastresa.com. An attractive three-star hotel about 10min walk along the waterfront promenade from the centre of Stresa. Rooms are comfortable, some with lovely lake views and there's a little garden and swimming pool. €125

Grand Hotel Bristol Corso Umberto I 73 ☎ 0323 32 601, ⓦ zaccherahotels.com. One of Stresa's landmarks, located in splendid lakeside grounds. Interiors are plush with marble, carpets and Tiffany glass but this is a four-star

property, so prices are slightly less than the *Grand Hotel* competition. €225

Grand Hotel de Iles Borromées Corso Umberto I 67 ☎ 0323 938 938, ⓦ borromees.it. Stresa's grandest hotel, a lakeside palace dating from 1861 that has hosted international royalty, celebrities and high society. Hemingway was a regular and the hotel features in *A Farewell to Arms*. Today the traditionally styled luxury continues to address every comfort. €275

La Luna nel Porto Corso Italia 60 ☎ 0323 934 466, ⓦ lalunanelporto.it. Bright spotless rooms perched above the lakefront road right next to the imbarcadero, with good-value suites all with their own water-facing balcony or terrace. €160

EATING

Fiorentino Via A.M. Bolongato 9 ☎ 0323 30 254. Simple home-cooking in a welcoming atmosphere in this family-run place. The €15 set menu is great value. Choose to sit in the large dining room or on the sunny terrace out the back. Daily noon–2.15pm & 7–10.30pm.

Il Vicoletto Vicolo del Poncivo 3 ☎ 0323 93 2102. This is a stylish little newcomer serving well-judged pan-Italian dishes like stuffed *calamari* (€13) or Piemontese roast lamb with rosemary (€18). There are some tables on a tiny terrace in summer. 12.30–2.30pm & 7.15–11pm; closed Thurs out of season.

La Botte Via Mazzini 6 ☎ 0323 30 462. The friendly host at this snug restaurant serves up Piemontese game,

polenta and pasta dishes. The generous plates of pasta and risotto cost €8–10. Noon–2.30pm & 7–10.15pm; closed Thurs.

Osteria degli Amici Via A.M. Bolongaro 31 ☎ 0323 30 453. This simple *osteria* serves tasty risotto and fish on an attractive vine-covered terrace. There is also a long list of crispy pizzas. Noon–2.15pm & 6.30–10.30pm; closed Wed.

Taverna del Pappagallo Via Principessa Margherita 46 ☎ 0323 30 411. A very popular pizzeria serving pizzas bubbling from the wood-fired oven as well as good-quality local fare. There's a courtyard outside for warmer weather. Noon–2.30pm & 7–10.30pm; closed Wed.

The Borromean islands

Lake Maggiore's leading attractions are three lush islands rising from the bay between Stresa and Pallanza. All three are often dubbed the **Borromean islands** (Isole Borromee), though strictly speaking only two are property of the Borromeo family (originally bankers, raised to nobility in the 1450s and still prominent locally).

Isola Bella

Mid-March to mid-Oct daily 9am–5.30pm • €13, €3 extra for the galleries; same-day joint ticket with Isola Madre €18; entrance free to members of the Royal Horticultural Society • Audioguide €3 • Book at least one day in advance for a 35min guided tour of the palace in English (€45) • ☎ 0323 30 556, ⓦ borromeoturismo.it

Romantics – if they can bear the crowds and the sheer hyperbole – will be knocked for six: the short voyage from Stresa to **Isola Bella** is Italian Lakes fantasy brought to life. In 1630, Carlo III Borromeo began a redesign of this modest rock: soil was brought across from the mainland, a villa, fountains and statues were built, white peacocks imported, and terraces of orange and lemon trees, camellias, magnolias, box trees, laurels and cypresses carved out. Carlo's son Vitaliano died in 1690 with most of the work completed. As well as roaming the sumptuous Baroque gardens, complete with obelisks and classical statuary, dip into the island's opulent *palazzo*, which boasts a banqueting hall, ballroom, throne room and a three-storey domed *salone*, as well as mirror- and shell-encrusted grottoes down at water level. It's definitely worth seeing.

Isola Madre

Mid-March to mid-Oct daily 9am–5.30pm • €11, free to members of the Royal Horticultural Society; same-day joint ticket with Isola Bella €18 • ☎ 0323 30 556, ⓦ borromeoturismo.it

Larger but less visited than its neighbour, **Isola Madre** has an extensive garden – home to carob, hibiscus and banana plants, a colony of parrots and Europe's largest Kashmir cypress – alongside a small, tasteful *palazzo* housing a collection of eighteenth-century puppets.

Isola dei Superiore

Closest to shore, Hemingway's favourite island, **Isola Superiore**, is also known as **Isola dei Pescatori**, as it was once populated by fishermen. Despite the trinket shops, the island retains a certain charm which is best enjoyed after the crowds have left in the evening. There are no sights bar a cluster of attractive old houses, but it has some decent restaurants and is a good spot for a picnic.

ARRIVAL AND DEPARTURE   THE BORROMEAN ISLANDS

By ferry Public ferries (ⓦ navigazionelaghi.it) shuttle frequently between the islands in both directions connecting to Stresa, Carciano, Baveno and Pallanza. Private boat-taxis also offer excursions for negotiable rates.

ACCOMMODATION AND EATING

Belvedere Via di Mezzo ☎ 0323 32 292, ⓦ belvedere isolapescatori.it. Eight simple rooms above the recommended restaurant of the same name at the western end of the island offer a chance to make the most of the island after the last ferry has departed. **€250**

Verbano Via Ugo Ara 2 ☎ 0323 30 408, ⓦ hotelverbano

.it. For an unforgettable night on Hemingway's favourite island, book in and enjoy this enchanting corner of the lake once the crowds have gone. Handsome furniture and lake vistas from each of the twelve rooms are coupled with a charming, moderately priced restaurant below. **€170**

Verbania

Across the bay from Stresa lies **VERBANIA** (a conglomerate town including neighbouring villages Suna, Intra and Pallanza), whose title recalls *Lacus Verbanus*, the Roman name for verbena-fringed Lake Maggiore. Car ferries shuttle between Intra and Laveno on the eastern shore. Pallanza is a relaxed, pretty little corner with a ferry jetty and views across to the Borromean islands, while behind its manicured flower-beds, busier Intra's cobbled centre has local shops and boutiques for all pockets.

Villa Taranto

Via Vittorio Veneto 111 • Mid-March to Oct daily 8.30am–6.30pm (Oct closes 5pm) • €9.50 • ⓦ villataranto.it

Verbania's balmy climate prompted Captain Neil McEacharn, scion of a Scottish industrial family, to buy the lakeside **Villa Taranto** in 1931; the botanical garden he created – a thirty-minute walk northeast of Pallanza towards Intra, also served by regular boats – remains exceptional, taking in giant Amazonian lilies, lotus blossoms, Japanese maples and more, laid out with geometric precision. You need a couple of hours to do the place justice; there is also a pleasant **café**.

ARRIVAL AND INFORMATION   VERBANIA

By boat From Intra, just north of Pallanza, a car ferry shuttles frequently over to Laveno (every 20min; 20min), from where trains run direct to Milan, and roads connect to Varese and the A8 autostrada. Verbania has several landing stages – Suna, Intra, Villa Taranto and Pallanza – served by lake ferries

heading to the Borromean islands, Stresa and beyond.

By train Verbania-Pallanza train station is on the Stresa–Domodossola main line with trains from Milan (Centrale and Porta Garibaldi). Bus #2 or taxis cover the 8km into the town centre.

LAGO MAGGIORE EXPRESS

For a great day out combining ferry and train services, see p.260.

Tourist offices The main tourist office is at Corso Zanitello 8 in Pallanza (April–Sept daily 9am–1pm & 3–6pm; Oct–March Mon, Tues & Thurs 9am–1pm & 3–5.30pm, Wed & Fri 9am–1pm; ☎ 0323 503 249), with a branch by the Pallanza landing-stage (Mon–Sat 8.30–11am & 2.30am & 3–6pm; ☎ 0323 557 676, ⓦ verbania-turismo.it).

ACCOMMODATION

★ **Grand Hotel Majestic** Via V. Veneto 21, Pallanza ☎ 03223 504 305, ⓦ grandhotelmajestic.it. This is a grand hotel with a difference: certainly it has all the trappings with a magnificent waterfront location, impressive history and state-of-the art facilities but there is nothing stuffy here. The touch is genuinely personal, the staff are friendly and helpful, and the atmosphere is relaxed. The location is unbeatable too. It's a top spot to sit back and hear the lake waters lapping and the parquet floors creaking. Closed Oct–March. **€220**

Ostello Villa Congreve Via delle Rose 7, Pallanza ☎ 0323 501 648, ⓦ aighostels.com. Lake Maggiore's only hostel is a friendly place set in an attractive hillside villa with small dorms, en-suite doubles and resourceful staff. It's a 10min walk uphill from the bus terminal at Piazza Gramsci and the tourist office. Closed Oct–March. Dorms **€21**, doubles **€56**

Pesce d'Oro Via Troubetzkoy 136, Suna ☎ 0323 504 445, ⓦ hotelpescedoro.it. A bright, pleasant option on the waterfront in Suna, a 10min walk west of Pallanza. Run by the same family for over thirty years this is a warm, friendly mid-range option. They also offer three attractive self-catering apartments in the lanes behind the hotel. **€100**

EATING

Dei Cigni Via delle Magnolie, Suna ☎ 0323 558 842. Excellent-quality fish-biased meals at under €30 per head; reserve a table on the terrace looking over the trees to the Borromean islands or in the informal dining rooms. Noon–2.45pm & 7–10.45; closed Tues.

Il Torchio Via Manzoni 29, Pallanza ☎ 0323 503 352, ⓦ ristoranteiltorchioverbania.it. This is a wonderful corner in which to enjoy seasonal-based local ingredients creatively mixed with herbs and flavours in pretty spacious dining rooms. Expect to pay around €35 a head for two courses and wine. 7.30–10.30pm, Sun also 12.30–2.30pm; closed Wed.

Milano Corso Zantiello 2, Pallanza ☎ 0323 556 816, ⓦ ristorantemilanolagomaggiore.it. An elegant restaurant serving a small selection of carefully chosen traditional dishes in an attractive formal dining room and terrace over the lake. The set menu is €30 per head, the à la carte significantly more. Mon 7.45–10.30pm, Wed–Sun noon–2.30pm & 7.45–10.30pm; closed Tues.

Cannobio

CANNOBIO, 25km north of Pallanza (and 5km from the Swiss border), is one of Lake Maggiore's most appealing places to stay and a good base for exploring the lake. The village leads back from the water, its lakefront piazza of pastel-washed houses giving onto a tightly tangled web of stepped alleyways and stone houses. On Sunday mornings the local **market** takes over the waterfront selling everything from fresh produce to leather goods. The town's only sight is the **Santuario della Pietà**, a Bramante-inspired church beside the landing stage with a curious openwork cupola, built to house a painting of the pietà which supposedly bled in 1522. On the northern edge of the village is a blue-flag **beach**, backed by pleasant lawns with trees and picnic tables.

Inland along the Val Cannobina

Extending behind Cannobio, the wooded **Val Cannobina** offers beautiful views and little-visited stone-built hamlets. An easy **riverside cycle path** heads off into the valley to the **Orrido di Sant'Anna**, an impressive rocky gorge surrounded by wooded slopes that is a popular picnic spot. Beside the Roman bridge and the chapel is a small river beach and restaurant (see p.264). The Orrido is also accessible on the summer miniature train and by car off the Val Cannobina road.

ARRIVAL AND INFORMATION   CANNOBIO

By bus Buses run approximately hourly to and from Verbania (35 min). See timetables at ⓦ vcoinbus.it.

By boat Cannobio has regular ferry links up and down the lake as well a good service across to Luino (see p.264).

Tourist office Via A. Giovanola 25, behind San Vittore church (Mon–Sat 9am–noon & 4.30–7pm, Sun 9am–noon; ☎ 0323 71 212, ⓦ cannobio4you.it).

4

GETTING AROUND

By bus From early June to early September an evening shuttle bus (June–Aug 6.30pm–1am; €1) runs a 15min circular tour around town and up to the Orrido every half-hour.

By bike Intra's Living Lake (☎ 349 544 6819, ⓦ livinglake .it) delivers rental bikes to Cannobio (€16/day).

ACCOMMODATION

Antica Stallera Via P. Zacchero 7 ☎ 0323 71 595, ⓦ anticastallera.com. This family-run three-star hotel in the village has a vine-shaded garden restaurant overlooked by simple, modern en-suite rooms. **€110**

Hotel Cannobio Piazza Vittorio Emanuele III 6 ☎ 0323 739 639, ⓦ hotelcannobio.com. This historic hotel is on the lakefront piazza so many rooms have lovely views. It has decent four-star standards and attentive staff. **€210**

Hotel Pironi Via Marconi 35 ☎ 0323 70 624, ⓦ pironi hotel.it. Cannobio's loveliest hotel is a real charmer, edged into a narrow fifteenth-century ex-convent on a cobbled lane in the village centre. Rooms are light, bright and attractive. Closed Dec–Feb. **€145**

Residenzia Patrizia Via Veneto ☎ 0323 739 713, ⓦ residenzapatrizia.com. A brand-new building divided up into self-catering apartments and eight hotel rooms all done out with wooden floors and designer bathrooms. Many rooms have balconies and there's a shared pool. **€140**

EATING AND DRINKING

Antica Stallera Via P. Zaccheo 3 ☎ 0323 71 595. Pleasant, vine-covered terrace restaurant where the home cooking and local specialities are good value at around €25 a head. Daily 12.30–2.30pm & 7–10.30pm in season.

★ **La Streccia** Via Merzagora 5 ☎ 0323 70 575. Up a narrow alley behind the lakefront, this is the top choice in town for very good Piemontese food – including home-made breads and pasta – in a rustic, low-ceilinged dining room. Expect around €25 before wine for a three-course meal. Noon–3pm & 6–10pm; closed Tues.

Lo Scalo Piazza Vittorio Emanuele III 32 ☎ 0323 71 480, ⓦ loscalo.com. In a prime site on the lakefront piazza in a fourteenth-century *palazzo* this elegant restaurant serves classic Piemontese specialities in formal surroundings; around €50 a head for the taster menu. Tues 7–11pm, Wed–Sun 12.30–2.30pm & 7–11pm.

Sant'Anna Via Sant'Anna 30 ☎ 0323 70 682. With stone tables perched outside right above the gushing water of the gorge this little country restaurant serves surprisingly creative pan-Italian food including very fancy desserts. Portions are small but you're paying for the unbeatable location (around €45 per head). Tues–Sun noon–1.45pm & 7–8.45pm.

The eastern shore

The highlight of Maggiore's eastern shore is **Santa Caterina del Sasso**, the tiny monastery hewn out of the rock face, although there's good **hiking** into the hills behind the more northern villages.

Luino

The commercial town and rail hub of **LUINO** – with a strollable *centro storico* and frescoes by Bernardino Luini, a follower of Leonardo, at the oratory of **SS Pietro e Paolo** – is besieged every Wednesday by people pouring in for what is, purportedly, the largest weekly **market** in Europe; dodge the fake-label handbag and novelty stalls to seek out the tasty food section, piled high with salami and cheeses from all over Italy and Switzerland. Roads are jam-packed from 7am onwards and extra boats and buses serve Luino all day long.

ARRIVAL AND INFORMATION

By bus Buses connect Luino with towns up and down the eastern shoreline. For more details see ⓦ trasporti.regione .lombardia.it (click "orari").

By boat Boats from Luino head across to Cannobio as well as to other Italian towns and across the border to Locarno and Ascona in Switzerland. On Wednesdays there are extra sailings to service the market.

Tourist office Via Piero Chiara 1, across the road from the imbarcadero (daily 9am–noon & 2.30–6pm; Nov–March closed Sun; ☎ 0332 530 019, ⓦ vareselandoftourism.it).

ACCOMMODATION

Camin Hotel Colmegna Via Palazzi 1, 3km north of Luino ☎ 0332 510 855, ⓦ caminhotel.com. One of the best accommodation options on this side of the lake, this eighteenth-century building is tucked into the rock just where the shoreline road enters a tunnel, so the lakeside gardens are wonderfully tranquil and the swimming areas are difficult to beat. It's a friendly, family-orientated place, with light, bright and comfortable rooms and a moderately priced restaurant. **€175**

Laveno

Roughly 25km south of Luino, **LAVENO** is a significant transport hub with car-ferries shuttling across between the western shore at Verbania-Intra and various rail links with Milan. There's a pleasant little centre around Piazza Fontana which is worth a wander while you wait for your ferry.

In a fine sixteenth-century porticoed monastery, just south of the centre on the lakefront in the neighbourhood of Cerro, the **Museo Internazionale Design Ceramico** at Via Lungolago Perabò 5 (Tues 10am–noon, Wed–Sun 10am–noon & 2.30–5.30pm; free; Ⓦ midec.org) holds a strong collection of mainly twentieth-century ceramics.

ARRIVAL AND INFORMATION   LAVENO

By train Laveno-Mombello Nord station is a terminus for trains from Milan Nord/Cadorna. The town's other station, Laveno-Mombello, 1km south of the centre, is served by trains from Luino to Milan Porta Garibaldi (change at Gallarate).

By boat Car ferries shuttle between Laveno and Intra (see p.262) docking directly in front of the Laveno-Mombello Nord train station.

Tourist office Piazza Italia 2 (11am–5.30pm, closed Wed; ☏ 0332 669 820, Ⓦ vareselandoftourism.it).

Santa Caterina del Sasso

Via Santa Caterina 13, off the main SP69 between Cellina and Reno • April–Oct daily 8.30am–noon & 2.30–6pm; March daily 9am–noon & 2–5pm; Nov–Feb Sat & Sun 9am–noon & 2–5pm • Free • Ⓦ santacaterinadelsasso.com

One of the most popular sights on the lake, the hermitage of **Santa Caterina del Sasso** is a beautiful little cliffside **monastery** – visible only from the water – that is well worth a visit, though it can get crowded. It is most atmospherically reached by one of the many ferries from around the lake. The site dates back to 1170, when a local sailor was caught in a storm, invoked the help of St Catherine of Alexandria and survived; he withdrew to a cave, where local people began construction of a votive chapel. By 1620 fourteen monks lived here; today, it is still home to a small community of Benedictine monks.

The complex is tiny: you could walk from one end to the other in three minutes. Steep steps and a sparkling new lift take you down from the upper entrance or up from the jetty to the lovely entrance gallery (1624), with arches looking out over the lake, which leads to the South Convent. Inside is the Gothic Chapterhouse, decorated with a pristine fresco from 1439 of St Eligius healing a horse. Ahead, beneath the four Gothic arches of the Small Convent (1315) is the church, with its stubby Romanesque belltower and graceful Renaissance porch; a fresco of *God the Father*, dated 1610, adorns the Baroque vault above the high altar.

Lake Orta

The locals call **LAKE ORTA** (Lago d'Orta) "Cinderella", capturing perfectly the reticent beauty of this small lake, with its deep blue waters and intriguing island. Lying west of Lake Maggiore, wholly within Piemonte, it is unmissable for **Orta San Giulio**, the most captivating medieval village on this – or, perhaps, any – Italian lake, with narrow, cobbled lanes snaking between the wrought-iron balconies of tall, pastel-washed *palazzi*. The village is unforgettably romantic, but consequently popular: on summer Sundays the approach roads are jammed with traffic (though the charm returns after dark). If you can, visit midweek or out of season.

Orta San Giulio

Occupying the tip of a peninsula on the lake's eastern shore, **ORTA SAN GIULIO** is a seductive little bolthole with charm and character in spades. The pace of life is slow, with everything revolving around the main waterside square, **Piazza Motta**, which is lined on three sides by faded butterscotch facades and open on the fourth to the lake and island. *Gelaterie*, terrace cafés and restaurants share space under the arcades with traditional shops and boutiques. Opposite the lake, Salità della Motta steps steeply upward towards the fifteenth-century Baroque church **Santa Maria Assunta** and the **Sacro Monte** (see below) along a lovely wide lane where the Renaissance Palazzo Gemelli vies for your attention with Orta's oldest house, **Casa dei Nani**, named for its tiny windows. Back on the Piazza Motta, head northward on the main street, Via Olina – cobbled, and barely 3m wide – through the village and out for a stroll or a sunbathe on the lakeside promenade.

Isola San Giulio

Basilica: April–Sept Mon noon–6.45pm, Tues–Sun 9.30am–6.45pm; Oct–March Mon 2–5pm, Tues–Sun 9.30am–noon & 2–5pm

Motorboats do the five-minute run more or less on demand out to the **Isola San Giulio**, dominated by a white convent and the Romanesque tower of its basilica. According to legend, the island was the realm of dragons until 390 AD, when Julius, a Christian from Greece, crossed the lake using his staff as a rudder and his cloak as a sail, banished the monsters, founded a sanctuary and thus earned himself sainthood. The resulting **Basilica di San Giulio** has an impressively lofty interior. Much of its decoration, including the vaulting, dates from a Baroque eighteenth-century refit, but frescoes from as early as the fourteenth century survive. The fine **pulpit** was carved from local stone in the early twelfth century with symbols of the Four Evangelists and images of good winning over evil: note the crocodile locked in battle with the phoenix.

From the church, it takes twenty minutes to walk round the island on its one cobbled lane, past a couple of shops, a restaurant and some enticingly scenic picnic-spots.

Sacro Monte di San Francesco

Via al Sacro Monte • Daily 9.30am–6.30pm • ⓦ sacromonteorta.it

Above Orta, the **Sacro Monte di San Francesco** – 21 chapels containing life-size, painted terracotta statues acting out scenes from the Bible and the life of San Francesco – winds around the wooded hillsides, making up a devotional route still followed by pilgrims, though as many visitors come simply to admire the views and inhale the pine-scented air.

ARRIVAL AND INFORMATION
ORTA SAN GIULIO

By train Orta-Miasino train station – on the little-used Novara–Domodossola branch line (change at Novara from/ to Milano Centrale) – is around 3km east: turn left out of the station and walk downhill for about 20min to reach Orta San Giulio.

By bus Three buses a day link Stresa (1hr; mid-June to early Sept only) with Piazzale Prarondo just outside the pedestrianized part of the village.

By car The village and the island of San Giulio are traffic-free: follow signs to the big car parks on the hillside above

town. From here take the *trenino* (see below) or pick any of the footpaths heading downhill to take you into the pedestrianized centre within a few minutes.

Tourist office Main office in the hut in the car park on Via Panoramica (Wed–Sun 9am–1pm & 2–6pm; ☎ 0322 905 163, ⓦ distreetolaghi.it). Small local office in the town hall on the main street in the village centre (Via Bossi 11; Mon & Wed–Fri 11am–1pm & 2–6pm, Sat & Sun 10am–1pm & 2–6pm; ☎ 0322 911 972, ⓦ comune.ortasanguilio.no.it) with more limited information.

GETTING AROUND

By boat Moored at the foot of Piazza Motta, small motor launches are the official "ferries" to the island. They depart when they're more or less full and a journey costs €4. There are also boat-taxis on which you can negotiate rates and excursions; for example, a jaunt around the lake and a stop on the island for €8.

By trenino The village's tourist train, the *trenino*, is a good

way to take the puff out of some of the steps and slopes in Orta San Guilio. It plies between the tourist office at the top of town to Piazza Motta and sometimes on to the Sacro Monte at peak times (May–Sept daily 9am–7pm; March, April & Oct daily 9am–5.30pm; Nov–Feb Sat & Sun 9.30am–5.30pm; ⓦ treninodorta.it; €2.50).

ACCOMMODATION

Aracoeli Piazza Motta 34 ☎ 0322 905 173, ⓦ ortainfo .com. Eye-popping design hotel (pronounced *ara-chaylee*)

on the main square; check-in is at *Hotel Olina* down the street. There are only seven rooms, each stylishly presented with plain white walls, designer furniture, a/c and walk-in showers. Breakfast is gourmet. **€135**

Contrada dei Monti Via dei Monti 10 ☏ 0322 905 114, ⓦ lacontradadeimonti.it. Comfortable, well-kept little hotel in an eighteenth-century house – better value than its neighbours as it's away from the lake. Many of the stylish rooms overlook a little internal courtyard where breakfast is served in summer. Closed Jan. **€110**

Leon d'Oro Piazza Motta 42 ☏ 0322 911 991, ⓦ albergo leondoro.it. Long-standing old *albergo* directly on the waterfront behind the main square, with comfortable

three-star rooms offering some great lake views. **€140**

Piccolo Hotel Olina Via Olina 40 ☏ 0322 905 532, ⓦ ortainfo.com. Little hotel alongside the *Olina* restaurant in the historic centre, with twelve modern rooms of varying sizes – very clean and attractive. Also has an annexe nearby on Via Poli. Closed Nov to mid-Dec. **€110**

San Rocco Via Gippini 11 ☏ 0322 911 977, ⓦ hotel sanrocco.it. In an unbeatable location on the edge of the village right on the water, this five-star hotel offers tasteful, recently refurbished rooms and a lakeside swimming pool to die for. **€245**

EATING AND DRINKING

You're spoilt for choice for wonderful views in San Giulio. Grab a slice of pizza or ask at the ★ unnamed *gastronomia* at Piazza Motta 15 and they'll make you up a huge tasty *panino* for just €3 or €4; dip down any of the alleyways leading to the water and settle down on a jetty to tuck in. The shady benches in the garden behind the town hall at Via Bossi 11 are another dreamy location for a picnic.

★ **Il Boeuc** Via Bersani 28 ☏ 0322 915 854. Tucked away from the bustle of the main square, this cosy *enoteca* has a handful of tables outside in the cobbled lane. Tasty platters of cold meats and local cheeses can be washed down by an excellent range of Piemontese wines. 12.15–2.30pm & 7–11pm; closed Tues.

Olina Via Olina 40 ☏ 0322 905 656. In a relaxed, elegant setting, tasty local specialities are served, along with thoughtful extras like aperitifs on the house. Main dishes around €14. 12.30–3pm & 7.30–11pm; closed Wed.

San Giulio Isola San Giulio ☏ 0322 90 234. Although the cooking is no great shakes, the waterside panorama from this restaurant – the only one on the island – make it

simply unbeatable. Expect to pay around €30 per head. Advance booking essential; ferry ride included in your bill. 12.30–2.30pm & 7.30–10.30pm; closed Tues, Nov & Mon–Fri Dec–Feb.

Villa Crespi Via Fava 18 ☏ 0322 911 902, ⓦ villacrespi .it. The Michelin-starred restaurant in this exclusive hotel in a turreted Moorish villa at the top of town is the place to head for a splurge. Dating from 1879 the decoration of this ornate villa is as singular as the creative cooking. Expect to pay at least €80 per head or €140 plus wine for the chef's ten-course taster menu. Tues 7.30–11pm, Wed–Sat 12.30–2.30pm & 7.30–11pm; closed early Jan.

Lake Como

Of all the Italian Lakes, it's the forked **LAKE COMO** (Lago di Como) that comes most heavily praised: Wordsworth thought it "a treasure which the earth keeps to itself". Today, despite huge visitor numbers, the lake is still surrounded by abundant vegetation: zigzagging slowly between shores by boat can seem impossibly romantic. As well as lakeside villas to visit, there is also some great walking to be done in the mountainous hinterland hereabouts. The principal towns – **Como** and **Lecco** – are at the southernmost tips of their own branches of the lake – Ramo di Como and Ramo di Lecco – while narrow winding roads follow the shoreline above and through erstwhile fishermen's villages past *belle époque* houses and Neoclassical villas up to the Centro Lago or centre of the lake. Here three small towns stand out as the highlight of the lakes: **Varenna** and **Bellagio** for unrepentant romantics, and **Menaggio** if you want a pleasant, affordable base for walking, swimming or cycling. To the north, the Ramo di Colico is less spectacular and much of the shoreline is marshy or occupied by campsites.

GETTING AROUND   LAKE COMO

Boats stop at many villages on the lake, supplemented by car ferries shuttling from Cadenabbia and Menaggio across to Bellagio and Varenna. The #C10 bus (ⓦ sptlinea.it) runs northwards from Como, stopping everywhere on the shoreline to Colico, from where the train takes you back to Lecco and the #C40 bus to Como. The #C30 links Como and Bellagio. The lakeside roads are busy and narrow, and there are pay and display car parks on the edge of all the villages.

Como

Standing astride main routes to and from Switzerland, **COMO** is a comfortable, ancient town, much of its wealth coming from the factories dotted around the outskirts which produce luxury silk items for the fashion houses of Milan, Paris and New York. The town reaches around a small bay at the southernmost tip of the western fork of the lake, but Como gets on with life relatively regardless of the lake and the visitors passing through.

At the centre of the bay, lakeside **Piazza Cavour** is bounded by hotels, the tourist office and the main ferry jetty. To the northwest the lakeside promenade curls through a pleasant park to Villa Olmo, while to the northeast the road curves round to the funicular station up to Brunate and on to Villa Geno. Via Plinio leads back from Piazza Cavour to the eminently wanderable once-walled quarter: the criss-cross of pedestrianized cobbled lanes reflect their Roman origins and offer the town's main sight – the Duomo – plus plenty of window shopping and shady pavement cafés.

The Duomo

Piazza del Duomo • Daily 7am–noon & 3–7pm • Free

Work began on Como's splendid **Duomo** in the 1390s, when Gothic held sway, but wasn't completed until 1744, with the addition of a Baroque cupola. The church is reckoned to be Italy's best example of Gothic-Renaissance fusion: the fairytale pinnacles, rose windows and buffoonish gargoyles are all Gothic, while the rounded portals and statues of Classical figures such as Pliny the Elder and Younger flanking the main door exemplify the Renaissance spirit. Inside, the Gothic aisles are hung with rich Renaissance tapestries, some woven with perspective scenes.

4

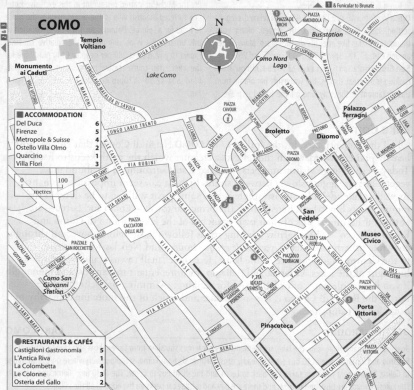

COMO

ACCOMMODATION

Del Duca	6
Firenze	5
Metropole & Suisse	4
Ostello Villa Olmo	2
Quarcino	1
Villa Flori	3

RESTAURANTS & CAFÉS

Castiglioni Gastronomia	5
L'Antica Riva	1
La Colombetta	4
Le Colonne	3
Osteria del Gallo	2

Casa del Fascio (Palazzo Terragni)

Piazza del Popolo • No public access: guided tours mid-April to Oct 5pm, 5.20pm & 5.40pm; 20min • €5

In striking contrast to the town's medieval buildings, across the train tracks behind the Duomo stands the definitive example of Rationalist architecture by Como-born Giuseppe Terragni. Built as the headquarters for the local Fascist party in the 1930s, this light, deftly functional building is now dubbed **Palazzo Terragni** and houses the Guardia di Finanza. From a distance the angular building is almost transparent: you can see right through its loggia to the wooden hills behind.

The waterside park

Northwest of Piazza Cavour, a lakeside park curves along the water; it's currently being refurbished (and has been for several years) but it's worthwhile persevering past the hoardings and getting in. Inside the **Tempio Voltiano** (Tues–Sun: April–Sept 10am–noon & 3–6pm; Oct–March 10am–noon & 2–4pm; €3), dedicated to Alessandro Volta, a Como man and pioneer in electricity who gave his name to the volt, there's a small museum displaying some of his instruments. Next door, the stark **Monumento ai Caduti**, a memorial to the dead of World War I, was built by Terragni to the design of the Futurist architect Antonio Sant'Elia, who was killed in 1916 aged 28. Ten minutes' walk beyond, past the Seaplane hangar and compellingly illuminated at night, is the **Villa Olmo**, a Neoclassical pile which hosts conferences and temporary exhibitions; whatever is on, its **gardens** (Mon–Sat: summer 8am–11pm; winter 9am–7pm; free) are the biggest draw and, in summer, Como's largest **lido** with two swimming pools, sunbeds and lake swimming (pools May–Sept 10am–6pm, bar 10m–9pm; ⓦlidovillaolmo.it).

Brunate

Funicular: Piazza Alcide de Gaspari • Daily 6am–10.30pm, every 15–30min; June–Aug until midnight • €5.10 return • ⓦfunicolarecomo.it

From the base-station of the **funicular** northwest from Piazza Cavour, it takes seven minutes to creep up the hillside past the gardens of wonderful nineteenth-century villas to **Brunate**, a small hilltop resort that has a few bars and restaurants and great views of the lake. It is also a good starting-point for hikes – from a couple of hours to a two-day trip along mule paths to Bellagio; the tourist office has details of routes.

ARRIVAL AND DEPARTURE   COMO

By plane From Milan-Malpensa airport, take the Malpensa Express train towards Milan and change at Saronno for the train to Como Lago.

By train The main train station is Como San Giovanni (Como S.G.), on the fast line from Milano Centrale to Chiasso and also served by several trains from Lecco and Milano Garibaldi. The station lies about a 10min walk west of the centre. Como Nord Lago station – the terminus of a slower line from Milano Nord/Cadorna – stands on the lakefront Piazza Matteotti, alongside the old quarter and the bus station.

By bus The bus station is right on the water on Piazza Matteoti. Services link Como with the lake's western shore (#C10); with Bellagio (#C30); with Lecco (#C40/#D41);

and with Bergamo (#C46/#D46). See timetables at ⓦasfautolinee.it.

Destinations Bellagio (hourly; 1hr 10min); Bergamo (6 daily; 2hr); Lecco (daily; 1hr 10min); Menaggio (every 20min; 1hr 10min).

By ferry Boats dock at the jetties on Piazza Cavour, where you also buy tickets. There are regular services to all points along the lake as well as fast *aliscafi* services. In summer there are evening cruises and private companies offer hour-long trips around the southern end of the lake.

Destinations Bellagio (6 daily; 45min–2hr 10min); Cernobbio (every 20min; 15min); Colico (5 daily; 1hr 50min–4hr); Menaggio (6 daily; 50min–2hr 25min); Varenna (6 daily; 1hr–2hr 40min).

INFORMATION

Tourist office The very helpful tourist office is at Piazza Cavour 17 (Mon–Sat 9am–1pm & 2.30–6pm; ☎031 269 712, ⓦlakecomo.org). There are also information points

on Via Comacino beside the Duomo, in the bus station and the main train station.

4

ACCOMMODATION

Del Duca Piazza Mazzini 12 ☎031 264 859, ⓦalbergodelduca.it. Great little three-star hotel on a picturesque old-town square, a short walk from the lake and the Duomo. Rooms are small, but windows onto the piazza – as well as nice touches like window boxes and some two-person showers – make it special. €100

Firenze Piazza Volta 16 ☎031 300 333, ⓦcentro hotelslagocomo.it. Pleasant mid-range option just back from the lakefront, with comfortable, modernized rooms set mainly around a quiet internal courtyard. Some have balconies over the square. €120

Metropole & Suisse Piazza Cavour 19 ☎031 269 444, ⓦhotelmetropolesuisse.com. Right on the waterfront Piazza Cavour, this historic old hotel has decent three-star rooms (some refurbished), a good breakfast and particularly helpful front-desk staff. €200

Ostello Villa Olmo Via Bellinzona 2 ☎031 573 800, ⓦaighostels.com; bus #1 or #6 from San Giovanni station, or take the long flight of steps in front of the station and turn left for about 1.5km along Via Borgo Vico. Decent HI hostel located within the Villa Olmo grounds. Serves evening meals, has laundry facilities, rents bikes and provides a discount on the funicular. March–Nov. Dorms €18

Quarcino Salita Quarcino 4 ☎031 303 934, ⓦhotel quarcino.it. A family-run hotel on the northeast side of the old town, near the funicular, with simple, quiet rooms, some with their own balconies overlooking the hillside. The family rooms and suites are particularly good value (€120) and there is parking included. €85

Villa Flori Via Cernobbio 12 ☎031 33 820, ⓦhotel villaflori.com. Beautiful lakeside villa 2km north of the city centre on the western shore with lovely gardens shaded by citrus trees. The house dates from the nineteenth century and has recently been luxuriously redecorated; many rooms have balconies over the water. €220

EATING AND DRINKING

Castiglioni Gastronomia Via Cantù 9 ☎031 263 388. Put together a lunch from a mouthwatering selection of home-made pasta, salamis and cheeses at the counter of this wonderful delicatessen or from a very reasonably priced menu, served outside in the pretty courtyard. Mon–Sat: shop 8am–3pm & 4–7.30pm; café noon–2.30pm.

L'Antica Riva Via Lungo Lario Trieste 50 ☎031 305 221, ⓦanticariva.it. Close to the base of the funicular station, this smart, relaxed restaurant has excellent fish dishes as well as plentiful plates of pasta. The dining rooms inside are comfortable and cosy and there are tables outside to enjoy the views of the bay in summer. Expect to pay around €40 a head with wine. Noon–2am; closed Tues.

La Colombetta Via Diaz 40 ☎031 262 703. Light, creative, Sardinian-inspired cooking served in handsome dining rooms in this very stylish restaurant in the centre of the old town. Expect to pay around €60 per head. Mon–Sat 12.30–3pm & 7.45–11pm.

Le Colonne Piazza Mazzini 12 ☎031 264 859. This pleasant, family-run restaurant on an attractive square has a friendly buzz and serves tasty pasta and crispy pizza for around €9. Daily 12.15–3pm & 7–10.30pm.

Osteria del Gallo Via Vitani 16 ☎031 270 279. Atmospheric little spot in a lane near the cathedral – one of several wine bars around here offering tasty nibbles with a fine selection of wines. Mon noon–3pm & Tues–Sat 12.15–8.30pm.

Ramo di Como

The scenic **Ramo di Como** – the Como branch of the lake – is the stuff of tourist brochures: wooded mountain slopes protect the villages crammed onto the narrow shoreline from extremes of temperature, and lush gardens abound. Many of the opulent villas that line this stretch are still privately owned by industrialists and celebrities – George Clooney is a much-fêted resident of Laglio.

Western shore: Cernobbio to Isola Comacina

A stone's throw outside Como Town, the village of **CERNOBBIO** comprises a compact quarter of old houses, loomed over by Monte Bisbino (1325m). The broad lakeside piazza is bordered by glitzy boutiques and the upmarket hotels that characterize the village, including the famous, palatial **Villa d'Este** hotel (ⓦvilladeste.it) beloved of celebrities and the super-rich.

The old road leaving Cernobbio, the **SP71 Vecchia Regina**, is what this part of Lake Como is all about. The narrow road weaves by lush gardens and celebrity-owned villas, through the little hamlets of Urio, Carate and Laglio and along the waterside to Brienno and Argegno.

From Sala Comacino or nearby Ossucio drop in at the eleventh-century church and Antiquarium, while you're there (Via Somalvico; Tues, Wed & Fri–Sun 10am & 3–5pm; free to see the small museum and visitor centre) – catch a row boat (€5) over to **Isola Comacina** (daily: mid-March to Oct 10am–5pm; July & Aug until 6.30pm; ⓦ isola-comacina.it), Lake Como's only island – wild, unkempt and dotted with the ruins of nine abandoned churches. Occupied by the Romans, it later attracted an eclectic mix of dethroned monarchs, artists, future saints and the pirate Federico Barbarossa. Wander the island at will, or book for dinner at its famous **restaurant** (see below).

The eastern shore

The rugged cliffs of the eastern shore, north of Como, are stepped into terraces where small village communities cling on to the rock. The boats that zigzag their way up the lake are as good a way as any of sampling the landscapes. Tiny Torno's tranquil lakeside plaza belies its medieval importance as a rival of Como and the string of visiting celebrities – from Byron and Shelly to Stendhal and Rossini – at Villa Pliniana. In spring, water pours down through gorges in tiny Nesso, fed by the mountains behind. The road continues on to Bellagio (see p.273).

ACCOMMODATION	RAMO DI COMO

Crotto di Misto Crotto 10, Lezzeno ☎031 914 541, ⓦ crottodelmisto.com. On the eastern shore of the Como branch, this ten-room hotel offers pleasant rooms with a good restaurant under the vines with lovely lake views. It's a popular choice for families for the swimming pool, garden and attached water-ski school. **€95**

Orso Bruno Via Regina Vecchia 45, Urio ☎031 400 136, ⓦ hotelorsobruno.com. This pleasant little family-run three star has ten bright, fresh rooms offering peace, quiet and – in some – balconies over the water. **€110**

Vapore Via Plinio 20, Torno ☎031 419 311, ⓦ hotel vapore.it. The twelve bedrooms in this family-run hotel are very plain and simple but there is a good restaurant with full lake views, a wonderful location and something special about the welcoming atmosphere in this quiet corner of the lake. **€115**

Villa Aurora Via Sossana 2, Lezzeno ☎031 914 645, ⓦ hotelauroralezzeno.com. Boutique hotel with some great-value family rooms and a pair of rather stylish self-catering apartments. The lakeside terrace and restaurant have dreamy views across to Villa Balbianello. **€115**

EATING

Gatto Nero Via Monte Santo 69 ☎031 512 042, ⓦ gattonerocernobbio.com. A hillside trattoria with a difference: the terrace views are stunning, but with footballers and fashionistas as regulars, this place is just as much about who's at the next table. The simple but top-quality, stylish food matches the elegant ambience. First courses start at around €15. Wed–Sun 12.30–3pm & 7.30–11pm.

Locanda dell'Isola Comacina ☎0344 55 083, ⓦ comacina.it. The same six-course set menu (€65; no credit cards) has been served by father and son at this island's famous restaurant since 1948. The highlight is the elaborate "exorcism by fire" at the end of every meal to ward off a curse laid on the island in 1169 by the Bishop of Como. Decent food and an infectious atmosphere make this less gimmicky and more enjoyable than it sounds. June–Aug daily noon–2pm & 7–9.30pm; March–May, Sept & Oct closed Tues; closed Nov–Feb.

Centro Lago: western shore

Halfway up the lake where the Como, Lecco and Colico branches meet, is the **Centro Lago**, the most scenically attractive part of the lake, hosting its three most sought-after destinations. If you have just one day to spend on Lake Como spend it here.

The western side north of the sheltered shore around Tremezzo boasts two of the lake's most famous villas – **Villa Balbianello** and **Villa Carlotta**, while just north lies the busy village resort of **Menaggio** with some great hiking in the surrounding hills. Opposite on the eastern shore, trapped between towering cliffs, stands the alluring waterfront village of **Varenna** (see p.275). Midway between the two, occupying a headland jutting into the lake, nestles **Bellagio** (see p.273), a picture-perfect village of steps and cobbled alleys.

Villa del Balbianello

Via Comoedia 5 · Mid-March to mid-Nov Tues & Thurs–Sun 10am–6pm · Villa €12, or €3 to UK National Trust cardholders, gardens only €6/free · **⊕** fondoambiente.it

Access to the **Villa del Balbianello** is chiefly by boat from Lenno and Sala Comacina, but on Tuesdays, Saturdays and Sundays you can walk through the grounds (roughly 800m from Lenno). The house is a classic eighteenth-century set piece, but it's the romantic **gardens** that inspire, with gravel paths between lush foliage, and stone urns framing spectacular views. Parts of *Star Wars: Episode II* and the 2006 version of the James Bond classic *Casino Royale* were filmed here.

Mezzegra

Euphemistic signposts in the pretty village of **Mezzegra** direct you to the gateway of a house where on April 28, 1945, Mussolini and his mistress Clara Petacci were shot dead by partisans, having been arrested the night before as they tried to escape to Switzerland. Their bodies were taken to Milan and hung upside down outside a petrol station as proof the Fascist leader was dead. Local rumours and rivalries continue about what happened to the fortune in cash and jewellery they were carrying.

Villa Carlotta

Via Regina 2, Tremezzo · Daily: April–Sept 9am–6pm; March & Oct 10am–5pm · €9 · **⊕** villacarlotta.it

Tremezzo became a popular resort in the nineteenth century and is best known for **Villa Carlotta**, located on the lakefront road but best glimpsed from the water (it has its own ferry stop). Pink, white and exceptionally photogenic this grand house – built in 1690 – was given by a Prussian princess to her daughter Carlotta as a wedding present. It now houses a collection of pompous eighteenth-century statuary, including Canova's romantic *Cupid & Psyche*, and boasts beautifully ordered fourteen-acre **gardens**, rich with camellias, rhododendrons and azaleas.

ACCOMMODATION AND EATING　　　　　　　　　　　**TREMEZZO AND AROUND**

La Darsena Via Regina 3 **☎**0344 43 166, **⊕**hotel ladarsena.it. A small, pretty, comfortable hotel and restaurant on the lakeside of the road near Tremezzo's landing stage with spacious, elegant rooms (many with balconies). This hotel is a good bet: refreshingly different from many of the fading grand hotels nearby. **€150**

La Marianna Via Regina 57 **☎**0344 43 095, **⊕**la-marianna.com. Wonderful old hotel-restaurant just north of Cadenabbia on the lakefront road run by a welcoming husband-and-wife team. The balconied rooms look over the road to the water and a good, informal restaurant serving traditional Lakes cuisine. Restaurant Tues–Fri noon–2.30pm & 7–10.30pm. **€95**

Menaggio

MENAGGIO, 37km north of Como, a lively and bustling village resort, is a good base for hiking and cycling in the mountains as well as sunbathing and swimming. **Hiking possibilities** range from a two-and-a-half-hour walk to the pretty village of Codogna, to the Sentiero delle Quattro Valli, which leads for 50km through four valleys to Lugano in Switzerland. There's a beach and vast pool at the **Lido** (end June to mid-Sept daily 9am–7pm), as well as boat rental and **waterskiing** and other activities at Centro Lago Service on the waterfront.

THE GREENWAY

The Greenway is an enchanting 10km trail of paths and waterside lanes that link Colonno with Cadenabbia, passing through unspoilt countryside past ancient churches, Roman relics and lakeside villas. The route can be broken down into forty-minute sections and combined with the ferry service, or the whole walk takes three and a half hours. Maps are available in English from tourist offices (**⊕** greenwaydellago.it).

ARRIVAL AND INFORMATION

By ferry Ferries dock about a 5min walk from the main lakefront square, Piazza Garibaldi. The car ferry across to Bellagio leaves from just south of Menaggio at Cadenabbia.

By bus Bus #C10 links Menaggio with Como and the other villages and towns on the western shore of the lake.

Tourist office Piazza Garibaldi 3 (Mon–Sat 9am–12.30pm & 2.30–6pm, Sun 10am–4pm; Nov–March closed Wed & Sun; ☎ 0344 32 924, ⓦ menaggio.com). A very well organized office, with English-language information on everything, including Menaggio's numerous hiking possibilities.

ACCOMMODATION

Garni Corona Largo Cavour 3 ☎ 0344 32 006, ⓦ hotel garnicorona.com. A comfortable, family-run hotel on the waterfront Piazza Garibaldi at the heart of the village, so ideal if you're travelling around by public transport. Rooms are good-sized and simple and ten boast lake views. Closed Dec–Feb. **€110**

Grand Hotel Menaggio Via IV Novembre 69 ☎ 0344 30 640, ⓦ grandhotelmenaggio.com. The better of the grand hotels in Menaggio because of its lakeside swimming pool but you are paying for location. The anonymous, carpeted rooms are comfortable without being special. Closed Nov–Feb. **€220**

Lauro Rezzonico, 7km north of Menaggio ☎ 348 264

6726, ⓦ hotellauro.com. In a tumbledown hamlet north of Menaggio (you'll need your own transport as there's no ferry service to Rezzonico), eight simple rooms and a family-run restaurant offer a wonderful bolt-hole. Relax on the shingle beach and drink in the peace and quiet of this corner of the lake. **€55**

Ostello La Primula Via IV Novembre 86 ☎ 0344 32 356, ⓦ menaggiohostel.com. Menaggio's excellent HI hostel is just outside the village, with small, clean dorms and a couple of en-suite family rooms: reservations are essential. It has its own small beach, bikes for rent and discounts on boat rental. Closed Dec–Feb. Dorms **€18**, four-person room **€78**

EATING AND DRINKING

Il Pozzo Piazza Garibaldi ☎ 0344 32 333. An attractive small terrace restaurant squished into an alley just off the main square, serving good local produce from salamis and cheeses to home-made pasta. Expect around €30 per head. Noon–2.30 & 7–10.30pm; closed Wed.

★ **Il Ristorante di Paolo** Largo Cavour 5 ☎ 0344 32 133. Under the *Corona*, with lots of outside tables and cosy dining rooms inside, this relaxed but elegant wine bar serves very well-judged cuisine using fresh local ingredients. Ask the staff to recommend one of their excellent, good-value wines to accompany your meal. Noon–2.30pm & 7–11pm; closed Tues.

Red Bay Piazzale Vittorio Emanuele 7 ☎ 347 197 8605. If you want to be on the waterfront, *Red Bay*, a 5min stroll along the lake north of the village centre, is perfect for a drink or a decent meal while enjoying the lake views. 10am–midnight; closed Thurs out of season.

Pizzeria Lugano Via Como 26 ☎ 0344 31 664. Bag one of the best pizzas on the lake for around €10 at this unreconstructed family-run pizzeria serving crispy, delicious wood-fired versions. Take one down to the lakeside or sit in under the strip lights among local families. Tues–Sun 11.30am–2.45pm & 6.30–11pm.

Centro Lago: Bellagio

Cradled by cypress-spiked hills on the tip of the Triangolo Lariano – the triangle of mountainous land between the Como and Lecco branches of the lake – **BELLAGIO** has been called the most beautiful town in Italy. With a promenade planted with oleanders and limes, *fin-de-siècle* hotels painted shades of butterscotch, peach and cream, and a hilly old quarter of steep cobbled streets and alleyways – to say nothing of its spectacular mid-lake location – it's easy to see why Bellagio has become so popular. These days, the alleys are lined with upmarket boutiques and souvenir shops; town life plays second fiddle to tourism, but this is still a charming, attractive resort.

The waterfront

Bellagio's first hotel, the *Genazzini*, opened in 1825; its second, the *Florence*, opened in 1852. The two flank Bellagio's scenic **waterfront** to this day, and passenger boats dock midway between them (the *Genazzini* is now the *Metropole*). The **views** from here westwards to the mountains above Cadenabbia are simply lovely; spending an afternoon watching the shadows lengthen, as the ferries parade to and fro, is pure Bellagio.

The village centre

The old quarter at the heart of the village is tiny, with three streets parallel to the waterfront connected by seven steep, perpendicular, stepped alleyways. At the top is a piazza with the eleventh-century Romanesque church of **San Giacomo**, alongside a tower which is all that's left of Bellagio's medieval defences.

Punta Spartivento

A stroll along the road 350m north of the village brings you to the **Punta Spartivento**, the "Point Which Divides the Winds", at the very tip of Bellagio's promontory. There's a tiny harbour here, a handkerchief-sized park where you could enjoy a picnic and a pleasant restaurant from which to drink in the unique panorama.

Pescallo

Ten minutes' walk east of Bellagio on an attractive footpath through vineyards, the enchanting little harbour of **Pescallo**, a fishing port since Roman times, offers a tremendous view of the Grigne mountains looming over the Lecco branch of the lake. There's nothing here but a small hotel and restaurant (see opposite) and a handful of fishing boats.

Villa Serbelloni

April–Oct Tues–Sun 11am & 3.30pm • €8.50; buy tickets 15min in advance from the Promo Bellagio office on Piazza della Chiesa

Bellagio is blessed with luxuriant flora; it's worth booking for a guided **tour** of the gorgeous formal gardens of the **Villa Serbelloni**. The villa, now owned by the Rockefeller Foundation and maintained as a study centre, is splendidly sited on a hill above the town.

Villa Melzi

April–Oct daily 9.30am–6.30pm • €6 • ⓦ giardinidivillamelzi.it

South of town, the lake promenade continues for about 500m to the gardens of the **Villa Melzi**, a luxuriant affair crammed with azaleas, rhododendrons, ornamental lemon trees, cypresses, palms, camellias and even a sequoia. The gardens extend to the fishing hamlet of **Loppia**, a picturesque retreat.

The lido and the beach

The refurbished Art Deco **lido** on Lungo Lario Marconi (April–Sept 9am–6.30pm; €8; ⓣ 031 951 195, ⓦlidodibellagio.com) is a good spot for a sunbathe and a dip in the lake; evening drinks and summer discos add to the appeal. Alternatively, head for the shingle **beach** with a pontoon for swimming, signposted off the main road along Via alla Spaggia halfway between Loppia and San Giovanni. There is also a summertime beach bar serving light meals in the daytime and cocktails in the evening (summer only noon–late).

ARRIVAL AND INFORMATION   BELLAGIO

By boat Boats arrive frequently from Tremezzo, Cadenabbia, Menaggio and Varenna. Passenger ships and hydrofoils dock at the main Piazza Mazzini; car ferries dock 150m south by the car parks. Tickets are available from the jetties.

By bus or car By road, Bellagio is 30km from Como (served by bus #C30) on a narrow, scenic road coiling along

the rocky cliffs. Bellagio is mainly car free and pay-and-display car parks line the approach road.

Tourist office Piazza Mazzini (Mon–Sat 9am–12.30pm & 1–6pm, Sun 10am–2pm; ⓣ 031 950 204, ⓦ bellagio lakecomo.com). Has information on activities including hiking, horseriding, mountain biking and watersports.

ACCOMMODATION

Bellagio Salita Grandi 6 ⓣ 031 950 424, ⓦhotel bellagio.it. An appealing modern hotel in one of Bellagio's tallest buildings, with huge picture windows in many rooms. Go for the rooftop vistas from the fourth floor (especially the corner rooms 401 and 404). Use of the outdoor pools and sports facilities at Bellagio Sporting Club

is included. **€140**

Belvedere Via Valassina 31 ⓣ 031 950 410, ⓦ belvederebellagio.com. A very comfortable four-star hotel in its own attractive grounds at the top of the town, with a swimming pool and wonderful views over the Lecco arm of the lake. Closed Dec–March. **€295**

Giardinetto Via Roncati 12 ☏031 950 168. ✉giardinetto@aol.it. Basic one-star place at the very top of Bellagio: some of the rooms have lake views and there's a garden where you can picnic. Best of the budget options. No credit cards. Closed Nov–Feb. €70

★ **La Pergola** Piazza del Porto 4, Pescallo ☏031 950 263, ⊛lapergolabellagio.it. Stylish, en-suite rooms with balconies overlooking the lake and the vine-covered restaurant below in this enchanting fishing hamlet. It's a good 15min walk over the hill from Bellagio, so you'll probably need your own transport (or taxi). Closed Dec–March. €150

Silvio Via Carcano 12 ☏031 950 322, ⊛bellagiosilvio .com. Just out of town, this bright two-star has rooms with lake views, and an excellent restaurant serving home-made dishes featuring fish freshly caught by the friendly owner. Closed Nov–March. €120

EATING AND DRINKING

Alle Darsene di Loppia Loppia ☏031 952 069, ⊛alledarsenediloppia.com. A quiet, attractive fish restaurant on Loppia harbour, a little south of Bellagio where you'll spend around €45 for a two-course meal. Call ahead to bag one of the few outside tables by the fishing boats. Tues–Sun noon–2.30pm & 7–9.30pm.

Forma & Gusto Salita Mella 13 ☏031 951 030. More informal sister restaurant downstairs from *La Barchetta* and with tables out on the cobbled lanes, serving quality local ingredients, including wood-fired pizzas, from under €30 a head. Be guided by the affable maître d'. Noon–10.30pm; closed Tues.

La Barchetta Salita Mella 13 ☏031 951 389. The place in town to head for a romantic treat on the rooftop under vines. The excellent pan-Italian dishes specialize in fish and seafood but the locally sourced lamb is also delicious. Noon–3pm & 7–10pm; closed Tues.

La Grotta Salita Cernaia 14 ☏031 951 152. There's decent wood-fired pizza at this cosy place which serves meals till 1am. Credit cards accepted over €25. Tues–Sun noon–2.30pm & 7–10.30pm.

La Pergola Piazza del Porto 4, Pescallo ☏031 950 263. Family-run restaurant in this enchanting hamlet over the hill from Bellagio. Although the service is rather dour, the position is simply unbeatable with tables on the terrace out over the water. The cooking is decent Lake cuisine with a focus on local ingredients and traditions. Tues–Sun noon–2.30pm & 7–10pm.

La Punta Punta Spartivento ☏031 951 888. A 5min walk north of town, this place serves excellent food – especially lake fish – at good prices (expect around €40 for a meal plus wine), and offers lovely views over the Punta Spartivento. 12.30–2.30pm & 7–10pm; closed Sun eve.

Silvio Via Carcano 12, Loppia ☏031 950 322, ⊛bellagiosilvio.com. One of Bellagio's most attractive dining spots, located just above nearby Loppia. This is an excellent restaurant and hotel; the views are beautiful, and the fish – freshly caught by Silvio himself – is superbly prepared (mains from around €17). Daily 12.30–3pm & 7.30–11pm in season.

Centro Lago: Varenna

Gazing back at Bellagio's Punta Spartivento from the eastern shore of the lake, **VARENNA** is perhaps the loveliest spot on Lake Como. Free of through traffic, shaded by pines and planes and almost completely free of souvenir shops, the village oozes character. This is the quiet side of the lake, less visited and with fewer places to stay, and the highlight of the eastern shore, if not the region.

The village

As well as the thirteenth-century **San Giorgio** on the main piazza, Varenna also hosts one of the oldest churches on the lake, the eleventh-century **San Giovanni Battista** opposite, with well-preserved, fragmentary frescoes depicting St John the Baptist. Varenna's other main sights are botanical: the nineteenth-century **Villa Cipressi** (March to mid-Nov daily 9am–8pm; €4; ⊛hotelvillacipressi.it), on the southern fringe of the village, has terraced gardens tumbling down to the lake that make a perfect spot to relax. The adjacent **Villa Monastero** gardens (April–Oct daily 9am–6pm, June–Sept until 7pm; €3; ⊛villamonastero.eu) are even more lavish. The splendid house, built over a convent dissolved in 1569, is now used as a conference centre and hotel.

Castello di Vezio

April–Oct daily 10am–sunset • €4 • ⊛castellodivezio.it

A very steep twenty-minute walk up the steps opposite Villa Monastero leads to spectacular views from the landscaped ruins of the **Castello di Vezio**, allegedly founded by the Lombard Queen Theodolinda in the seventh century. There are falconry displays at weekends and a good outside restaurant-café serving local specialities.

ARRIVAL AND DEPARTURE
VARENNA

Thanks to its rocky shoreline, Varenna is split into two fragments. Boats dock to the north, above which stands the train station. Some 300m south via the main road – or the *passarella*, a scenic walkway which clings to the rocks – is the main village.

By train Regular trains from Milano Centrale and Lecco pull in at Varenna-Esino station, a steep 5min walk uphill from the boat landing stage. The station is unstaffed; if you haven't got a return ticket you'll need to buy one from the office next to *Hotel Beretta* just below the station (Mon–Fri 8.30am–7pm & Sat 9am–noon; don't forget to stamp your ticket in the machine at the station before you board).

Destinations Bergamo (6 daily, changing at Lecco; 1hr 40min); Milano Centrale (10 daily; 45min); Lecco (every 20min; 20min).
By bus The #D20 Lecco–Colico bus stops on the central square.
By boat Ferries shuttle between Varenna, Bellagio, Menaggio and other points. Car ferries cross to Bellagio and Menaggio.

INFORMATION

Tourist office Piazza San Giorgio (April–Sept Tues–Sat 10am–12.30pm & 3–6.30pm, Sun 10am–12.30pm; Oct– March Sat 10am–5pm; ☎0341 830 367, ⊛varenna italy.com).

ACCOMMODATION

Albergo del Sole Piazza S. Giorgio 21 ☎0341 815 218, ⊛albergodelsole.lc.it. Excellent three-star hotel on the main piazza. Rooms are light, airy and modern – some with lake views – and there's a pizzeria too (see below). €120

★ **Albergo Milano** Via XX Settembre 29 ☎0341 830 298, ⊛varenna.net. One of Lake Como's friendliest, most stylish small hotels lies in the narrow lanes behind the waterfront. Well run by a charming couple, it has great views and a romantic air. There are also a couple of self-catering apartments and a family room (sleeping four).

Great food too. Closed Dec–Feb. €160, family room €250
Beretta Via per Esino 1 ☎0341 830 132, ⊛hotel beretta.it. Welcoming place near the train station with a B&B atmosphere that is the best of the cheaper options. €70
Du Lac Via del Prestino 11 ☎0341 830 238, ⊛albergodulac.com. Spacious, comfortable rooms, most with lovely lake views in this relaxed, good-value hotel right on the water. Sit on the vine-shaded terrace and drink in the views. €190

EATING AND DRINKING

Albergo del Sole Piazza S. Giorgio 21 ☎0341 815 218. Fine, inexpensive pizzeria on the main square, with an attractive summer garden out the back. Noon–2.30pm & 7–10pm; closed Tues.
Il Cavatappi Via XX Settembre ☎0341 815 349, ⊛ilcavatappiwine-food.it. Tiny restaurant with just six tables, tucked away in the thicket of lanes off the main square. The owner/manager/chef takes the time to discuss the menu with you before turning out simple, well-cooked dishes with first-class ingredients. Meals around €35 a head. 12.30–2.30pm & 7.30–9.45pm; closed Wed.
La Vista Via XX Settembre 35 ☎0341 830 298. Hide away on this beautiful lake-view terrace for a romantic dinner of light, tasty Mediterranean cuisine. Expect to pay around €40 and reserve in advance. 7–10pm; closed Tues.
Vecchia Varenna Contrada Scoscesa ☎0341 830 793, ⊛vecchiavarenna.it. In an unbeatable location, beneath

the arcades on the lakeside promenade (book for a terrace table), with food that is good, though not outstanding. Tues–Sun 12.30–2pm & 7.30–9.30pm.
Nuova Isola 1169 Via del Prato 6 ☎0341 830 125, ⊛nuovaisola1169.it. On a lovely piazzetta away from the lake in the shade of a huge pine tree, the jasmine-scented terrace of this restaurant is the place for balmy evenings. The food is good and well priced – home-made spaghetti with *missoltini* (Lake Como's signature dried fish) and tomatoes is just €9. 9.30am–2.30pm & 7–9.30pm; closed Tues.
Quatro Pass Via XX Settembre 20 ☎0341 815 091, ⊛quattropass.com. Set back away from the lake in a vaulted cellar, this welcoming *osteria* serves authentic, seasonal cuisine at modest prices. There's a good wine list that the staff are happy to advise on. 12.30–2.30pm & 7.30–9.30pm; closed Mon–Wed in winter.

Ramo di Colico

The northern reach of Lake Como – the **Ramo di Colico** or Alto Lario – is something of a letdown. The jagged cliffs that characterize the lower two thirds of the lake retreat from the water's edge and the shore comprises marshy plains and reedy inlets. None of the towns have the charm of those further south, and campsites and holiday camps line the shores.

Abbazia di Piona

Daily 9am–12.30pm & 1.30–6.30pm • Free • ⓦ abbaziadipiona.it

About 16km north of Varenna on the eastern shore, a minor road branches down to the tranquil Romanesque **Abbazia di Piona**, dating from the twelfth century, perched on a headland. A shop by the gates sells bottles of the monks' fiery herb liqueur.

Ramo di Lecco

The Lecco branch of the lake to the southeast is often dubbed "Lago di Lecco", even though it is an integral part of the whole: it's austere and fjord-like, at its most atmospheric in the morning mists. At its foot is the workaday town of **Lecco**, 30km east of Como, with the brooding Grigne mountain range above. It's a commercial centre with few attractions; literary types might appreciate **Villa Manzoni**, Via Guanella 7 (Tues–Sun 9.30am–5.30pm; €4), the childhood home of Alessandro Manzoni, author of the great nineteenth-century Italian novel *I Promessi Sposi* ("The Betrothed"); otherwise, pop into the lakefront **Basilica** to see its fourteenth-century Giottesque frescoes.

ARRIVAL AND INFORMATION **LECCO**

By train Lecco is directly linked with Milan and is the hub for changing trains if you're connecting between Lake Como and Bergamo.
Destinations Bergamo (hourly; 45min); Como (6 daily; 1hr 5min); Milano Centrale (10 daily; 45min); Varenna (every 20min; 20min).
By bus #C40/#D41 bus links Lecco with Como, #D10 serves Bellagio and #D20 shuttles between Lecco and Colico.
Destinations Bellagio (every 2hr; 50min); Como (every 2hr;

1hr 10min); Varenna (daily; 1hr 10min); ⓦ asfautolinee.it.
By boat Boats from Bellagio to Lecco every day in summer and on Sundays in spring and autumn; there is no service in winter.
Tourist office Via Nazario Sauro 6, off lakefront Piazza Garibaldi (daily 9am–1pm & 2.30–6.30pm; ☏ 0341 295 720, ⓦ turismo.provincia.lecco.it). Has information on mountain hikes in the isolated Valsassina.

Bergamo

Just 50km northeast of Milan, yet much closer to the mountains in look and feel, **BERGAMO** comprises two distinct parts – **Bergamo Bassa**, the city centre on the plain, and medieval **Bergamo Alta**, 100m above. Bergamo Bassa is a harmonious mixture of medieval cobbled quarters blending into late nineteenth- and early twentieth-century town planning, while Bergamo Alta is one of northern Italy's loveliest urban centres, with wanderable lanes and a lively, easygoing pace of life.

Bergamo owes much of its magic to the Venetians, who ruled the town for over 350 years, adorning facades and open spaces with the Venetian lion, symbol of the Republic, and leaving a ring of gated walls. Now worn, mellow and overgrown with creepers, these kept armies out until the French invaded in 1796.

Bergamo Alta: the upper town

With its steep, narrow streets, flanked by high facades and encircled by sixteenth-century walls, **Bergamo Alta** – the upper town – remains in appearance largely as it was in the Middle Ages. The main public spaces – **Piazza Vecchia** and adjacent **Piazza del Duomo** – combine medieval austerity with the grace of later, Renaissance design. The funicular railway from the lower town arrives at the tiny station on Piazza Mercato delle Scarpe from where the main street, beginning as Via Gombito and continuing as Via Colleoni after Piazza Vecchia, follows the line of the Roman *decumanus maximus*, topped and tailed by evidence of Bergamo's military past – the **Rocca** to the east, the **Cittadella** to the west. Just beyond the Cittadella, through Porta Sant Alessandro, another funicular ride whisks you up to the highest point of town, San Vigilio.

BERGAMO

ACCOMMODATION

Agnello d'Oro	6
Central Hostel BG	3
Gombit	7
La Valletta Relais	4
Mercure Palazzo Dolci	2
Nuovo Ostello di Bergamo	1
Piazza Vecchia	5

RESTAURANTS & CAFÉS

Baretto di San Vigilio	1
Cooperativa Città Alta	5
Donizetti	7
La Colombina	4
La Mariana	3
San Vigilio	2
Vineria Cozzi	6

SEE 'BERGAMO ALTA' MAP FOR DETAILS

BERGAMO ALTA
(SEE MAP BELOW)

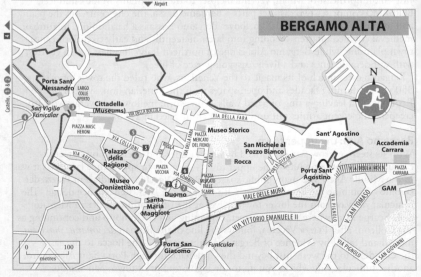

BERGAMO ALTA

Piazza Vecchia

Bergamo's magnificent **Piazza Vecchia** is enclosed by a harmonious miscellany of buildings, ranging from wrought-iron-balconied houses containing cafés and restaurants to the opulent Palladian-style civic library. Le Corbusier proclaimed this "the most beautiful square in Europe", and it's certainly a striking space. The piazza was the scene of joyous celebrations in 1797, when the French formed the Republic of Bergamo: the square was carpeted with tapestries and transformed into an open-air ballroom in which – as a symbol of the new democracy – dances were led by an aristocrat partnered by a butcher.

Palazzo della Ragione

Piazza Vecchia • June–Sept Tues–Fri & Sun 10am–9pm, Sat 10am–11pm; Oct–May Tues–Fri 9.30am–5.30pm, Sat & Sun 10am–6pm • €5 • Ⓦ accademiacarrara.bergamo.it

The most imposing presence on the Piazza Vecchia is the medieval **Palazzo della Ragione**, a Venetian-Gothic building stretching right across the piazza opposite the library. Court cases used to be heard under the open arcades that form the ground floor. A grand covered stairway, dating from 1453, rises from alongside up to the large hall which often holds temporary exhibitions and displays.

While Bergamo's prestigious Accademia Carrara gallery is closed for renovation, the *palazzo* is housing around a hundred of its masterpieces. At the time of writing the layout had not been determined; it seems likely, though, that you will be able to view **Titian**'s remarkable *Virgin and Child*, painted at the age of 27, a touchingly effeminate *St Sebastian* by the young **Raphael** and **Botticelli**'s startlingly modern *Portrait of Giuliano de' Medici* – among many other works.

Torre Civica

Piazza Vecchia • April–Oct Tues–Fri 9.30am–7pm, Sat & Sun 9.30am–9.30pm; Nov–March Sat & Sun 9.30am–4.30pm • €3

To the right of the *palazzo* looms the massive **Torre Civica**, or **Campanone**, which you can ascend by lift. Its seventeenth-century bell, which narrowly escaped being melted down by the Germans during World War II, still tolls every half-hour and there are magnificent views across the rooftops of Bergamo to the mountains.

Santa Maria Maggiore

Piazza del Duomo • Mon–Sat 9.30am–12.30pm & 2.30–6pm • Free

Walk beneath the Palazzo della Ragione's arcades to enter **Piazza del Duomo** – a small, cramped space where the **Duomo** is of less interest than **Santa Maria Maggiore** alongside, a rambling Romanesque church with a scalloped Gothic porch. Inside, it is a perfect example of high Baroque, its ceiling marzipanned with ornament, encrusted with gilded stucco, painted vignettes and languishing statues. Look for the kitsch nineteenth-century monument to Donizetti, the Bergamo-born composer of comic opera: bas-relief putti stamp their feet and smash their lyres in misery at his death. More subtly, the intarsia biblical scenes on the choir stalls – designed by Lorenzo Lotto, and executed by a local craftsman – are remarkable not only for their intricacy but also for the incredible colour-range of the natural wood.

Cappella Colleoni

Piazza del Duomo • Tues–Sun 9am–12.30pm & 2–6pm • Free

Even the glitziness of Santa Maria is overshadowed by the Renaissance decoration of the **Cappella Colleoni** next door. Commissioned by Bartolomeo Colleoni, a Bergamo mercenary in the pay of Venice, and built onto the church in the 1470s, the chapel is an extravagant confection of pastel-coloured marble carved into an abundance of miniature arcades, balustrades and twisted columns, capped with a mosque-like dome. The opulent interior, with its frescoed ceiling, shelters Colleoni's sarcophagus, topped with a gilded equestrian statue; the tomb of his 15-year-old daughter, Medea, is more modest. Note Colleoni's coat of arms on the gate as you enter; the smoothness of the decorative third "testicle" (supposedly biologically accurate) bears witness to the local tradition that rubbing it will bring you luck.

Museo Donizettiano

Via Arena 9 • Tues–Sun 9.30am–1pm & 2–5.30pm; Oct–March mornings only Tues–Fri • €5, combined ticket with Torre Civica, Museo Storico (Rocca) and Museo Storico (Convento di San Francesco) • <i>W</i> bergamoestoria.org

From the south door of Santa Maria Maggiore, **Via Arena** climbs towards the west end of the Città Alta. Partway up at no. 9, a frescoed doorway opens into the grounds of the Santa Grata monastery, also home to the **Museo Donizettiano**. One of the masters of the "bel canto" opera style (along with Bellini and Rossini), Gaetano Donizetti (1797–1848), who was born and died in Bergamo, is celebrated for his melodramatic lyricism, which reached a peak in *Lucia di Lammermoor*. The museum contains portraits of the maestro, original letters and scores, as well as his imperial-style bed and his patron's fortepiano.

Museo Storico

San Francesco, Piazza Mercato del Fieno 6/A and other locations • June–Sept Tues–Fri 9.30am–1pm & 2–5.30pm, Sat & Sun 9am–7pm; Oct–May Tues–Sun 9.30am–1pm & 2–5.30pm • €5; combined ticket with Campanone, Museo Donizettiano and all of Museo Storico (Rocca) €8 • <i>W</i> bergamoestoria.org

East of Piazza Vecchia, Via San Lorenzo heads north from the Torre Gombito to the **Museo Storico**. Housed in the ex-convent of San Francesco, with a beautiful thirteenth-century cloister, it spans the history of the city from the eighteenth century to 1945.

The rest of the museum is divided chronologically and among different locations around town including the **Rocca** on Piazzalle Brigata Legnano. Following Via Solata east from the convent leads after a short, steep haul along Via Rocca to what was probably the site of the Roman Capitol, rebuilt in the 1330s. The memorial gardens are a great spot for a picnic with spectacular views across eastern Bergamo and cannons and numerous armoured vehicles that kids can clamber over. Inside the castle or Rocca itself, the nineteenth-century section of the Museo Storico focuses on the Italian Wars of Unification, the Risorgimento, in which Bergamo had a very proud role and earned itself the name the "Città dei Mille" after the thousand volunteers from the city who went to join Garibaldi's army.

Towards the Cittadella

Leading northwest out of Piazza Vecchia, the narrow, pedestrianized **Via Colleoni** is lined with boutiques, delicatessens and pastry shops selling sweet polenta cakes topped with chocolate birds. At the top of the street, Piazza Mascheroni lies at the entrance to the **Cittadella**, a military stronghold built by Barnabo Visconti, now housing a small theatre and two didactic (Italian labelling only) museums of archeology and natural history.

The Colle Aperto and San Vigilio

Beyond the Cittadella lies the **Colle Aperto**, an open hillside beyond the city walls. Just through the Porta Sant'Alessandro, leading off Colle Aperto, a funicular trundles up the short track to the hamlet of **San Vigilio** – it's also a pleasant but very steep walk up a cobbled lane overlooking villas and gardens. At the top perches San Viglio, with a couple of lovely restaurants, castle ruins and more wonderful vistas across the ornate gardens of Bergamo's most prestigious summer retreats.

Returning to Colle Aperto, you can follow the old **walls** around its circumference – the whole circuit takes a couple of hours, with the most picturesque stretch lying between the Colle Aperto and Porta San Giacomo (from where a long flight of steps leads down into Bergamo Bassa alongside the vegetable patches and orchards growing in the shade of the walls.

Bergamo Bassa: the lower town

Bergamo Bassa spreads north from the train station in a comfortable blend of Neoclassical ostentation, Fascist severity and tree-lined elegance. At the heart of the busy streets, midway along the main Viale Papa Giovanni XXIII, the mock-Doric temples of the **Porta Nuova** mark the **Sentierone**, a favourite spot for Bergamo's citizens to meet and stroll. Frowning down on the square is the **Palazzo di Giustizia**, built in the bombastic rectangular style of the Mussolini era. Via XX Settembre to the west is the main focus for Bergamo's shoppers, with a selection of quality mainstream stores.

From the Sentierone, Via Tasso leads east into the oldest part of the Città Bassa, formed in the Middle Ages as overspill from the upper town; shady **Via Pignolo** has a largely unchanged appearance, with many architectural features – balconies, mullioned windows – surviving. Follow it up to the attractive **Piazzetta del Delfino**, occupied by a dolphin fountain built here in 1526. From here, Via Pignolo continues to the Porta Sant'Agostino, at the bottom of Bergamo Alta, while Via San Tomaso, lined with galleries, antiques shops and cafés, heads right towards the Accademia Carrara – Bergamo's finest art gallery, currently closed for renovation– and its neighbour, the **Galleria d'Arte Moderna e Contemporanea (GAM)**, Via San Tomaso 53 (⊕gamec.it; opening hours and admission varies with the temporary exhibitions but at least Tues–Sun 10am–1pm & 3–7pm), with world-class temporary exhibitions and a small permanent collection including works by Kandinsky and a moody *Still Life With Fruit* by Giorgio de Chirico.

ARRIVAL AND DEPARTURE BERGAMO

BY PLANE

Bergamo's Orio al Serio airport (⊕035 326 323, ⊕orioaeroporto.it) – also called "Milan-Bergamo" – is 4km southeast of Bergamo city centre. To reach **the centre**, take city bus #1 (daily every 30min 6am–midnight; 15min; ordinary ticket €2, day-pass €4.50, three-day pass €7; ⊕atb.bergamo .it). All stop at the train station, with most continuing to the funicular base station and into the Città Alta. A taxi (⊕035 451 9090) is around €30 into Bergamo, over €120 to Milan.

Connections to Milan Direct buses leave for Milano Centrale station from outside Arrivals at Orio al Serio. The different companies offer very similar services and rates; look out for the three-for-two deals on the tickets which can be bought from the different booths – Orioshuttle (⊕035 330 706, ⊕orioshuttle.com; €10) or Autostradale (⊕035 339 10794, ⊕autostradale.it; €10). Both run daily (approx every 30min 3/4am–11.15pm) and journey time is about an hour.

Connections to Brescia Autostradale also operates to Brescia bus station (8 daily; 1hr; €10).

BY TRAIN

Bergamo's train station is at the southernmost end of the Città Bassa's central avenue, Viale Papa Giovanni XXIII, a long walk from the Città Alta but well linked by bus (#1) with the airport, the upper town and the funicular station. Left-luggage facilities are a 2min walk away just outside the bus station (below). There are fast trains from Milan (Centrale and Lambrate) and Brescia, and slower ones from Como, Cremona and Lecco.

Destinations Brescia (hourly; 50min); Lecco (hourly; 40min); Milano Centrale or Porta Garibaldi (every 40min; 50min).

BY BUS

Bergamo bus station is behind the lower town tourist office, opposite the train station and has a secure, automated left-luggage facility just outside (€4/24hr). There are six daily services to Como (2hr).

GETTING AROUND

By bus Bus #1 runs frequently between the airport, the train station, the base station of the funicular (from where you can make the ascent to Bergamo Alta for no extra charge as long as you show your bus ticket; otherwise €1) and on to Colle Aperto at the top of the town; check timetables carefully as some services stop short.

By funicular A funicular (daily 7am–12.30am) runs every few minutes on the steep route between Viale Vittorio Emanuele II in the Città Bassa (the extension of Viale Papa

Giovanni) and Piazza Mercato delle Scarpe in the Città Alta. A separate funicular also runs from just behind Colle Aperto in the upper town up to San Vigilio.

By tourist train The tourist train Gulliberg links the upper and lower towns on Sundays and holidays (€2; 2–7pm).

By bike, scooter and micro-car Electric bikes, scooters and micro-cars take the puff out of the city's hills. Available for good-value rents from Eco-rent (⊕035 529 388, ⊕eco-rent.it) by the bus station in the lower town.

INFORMATION AND GUIDED WALKS

Tourist information Offices can be found in the Orio al Serio airport arrivals hall (daily 8am–11pm; ⊕035 320

402, ⊕turismo.bergamo.it), in the Urban Center, Piazzale Marconi, opposite the train station in Città Bassa (daily

9am–12.30pm & 2–5.30pm; Oct–May closed Sat & Sun; ☎035 210 204, ⓦprovincia.bergamo.it/turismo) and at Via Gombito 13 at the base of the Torre Gombito in Città Alta (daily 9am–12.30pm & 2–5.30pm; ☎035 242 226). **Guided walks** A guided walk in English starts from Piazza Mercato delle Scarpe (April–Oct Wed & Sun 3pm; 2hr; €10).

ACCOMMODATION

Bergamo is not somewhere to arrive without a reservation, even out of season: **accommodation** is pricey and, in the centre, fairly limited. There are a handful of atmospheric hotels in the Città Alta, with mostly business hotels in the Città Bassa. As always B&Bs provide a good, low-key alternative – there are several located in attractive buildings in Bergamo Alta; consult ⓦbedandbergamo.it and ⓦbebilmondoincasa.com.

UPPER TOWN

Agnello d'Oro Via Gombito 22 ☎035 249 883, ⓦagnellodoro.it. In the heart of the upper town, this family-run two-star offers small, plain en-suite rooms, some with balconies onto the tiny square below. Breakfast not included. **€120**

★ **Gombit Hotel** Via Mario Lupo 6 ☎035 247 009, ⓦgombithotel.it. Housed in a medieval tower just off the main pedestrian drag, this is one of Bergamo's best accommodation options. Nothing is too much trouble for the friendly staff at this stylish boutique hotel. **€180**

La Valletta Relais Via Castagneta 19 ☎035 242 746, ⓦlavallettabergamo.it. A perfect place to kick back, this atmospheric hotel is on a hillside a 10min walk from the upper town with lovely views from the terrace and garden. The pretty rooms are en suite and the owners can suggest country walks and bike rides if you're interested. **€120**

Piazza Vecchia Via Colleoni 3 ☎035 253 179, ⓦhotel piazzavecchia.it. This fourteenth-century building has a wonderful location on the main, pedestrian street. Comfortable rooms are fresh with great shower rooms and little balconies with views of the hills, but service can be less than forthcoming. Private parking. **€170**

LOWER TOWN

Central Hostel BG Via Ghislanzoni 30 ☎035 211 359, ⓦcentralhostelbg.com. Right in the centre of the lower town and handy for the train station, this bright, new hostel has single, twin, triple and quad rooms as well as dorms. Breakfast is included and there's also a small bar and TV room plus useful extras like free international phone calls, wi-fi, room safes and parking. Dorms **€25**, doubles **€56**

Mercure Palazzo Dolci Viale Papa Giovanni XXIII 100 ☎035 227 411, ⓦmercure.com. This four-star chain hotel is in a good location in the lower town, conveniently just a short walk from the station and with discounted car parking. With stylish, if slightly anonymous, swish contemporary interiors and good soundproofing, it's excellent value. **€110**

Nuovo Ostello di Bergamo Via Galileo Ferraris 1 ☎035 361 724, ⓦostellodibergamo.it; bus #3 from Piazza Mercato delle Scarpe in the Città Alta. This award-winning, institutional-feeling HI hostel has bathrooms in every room, bicycles for rent and a rooftop terrace with great views. There are doubles, triple and quads as well as dorms. It's a fair way from the centre: bus #3 runs to the door. Dorms **€18**, doubles **€50**

EATING AND DRINKING

One of the pleasures of Bergamo is its food and drink, whether you're assembling picnics from the many *salumerie* and bakeries in the upper town – most lining the main streets of Via Gombito and Via Colleoni – or grazing around the city's *osterie*. The town's signature dish is **polenta**, often served with veal or local game although polenta *taragna* is a creamy cheese and butter combination. *Casoncelli* – ravioli stuffed with sausage meat and served with sage and melted butter – is another justified favourite. With Bergamo's popularity it's always worth **booking ahead** – essential at weekends. All the places listed below are in the upper town.

Baretto di San Vigilio Via Castello 1 ☎035 252 845, ⓦbaretto.it. A stylish, classic restaurant opposite the top station of the San Vigilio funicular. The shaded terrace is an unbeatable spot for a long, lazy summer lunch or for a balmy evening with wonderful views and lovely food. Prices reflect the location: expect around €60 per head. Tues–Sun 11am–12.30am.

Cooperativa Città Alta Vicolo Sant'Agata, signposted off Via Colleoni. This informal co-operative serves up large portions of excellent low-priced local dishes in the huge shady garden. Perfect for a leisurely coffee, an evening beer or a full meal. 11am–2am, Sun 9am–2am; closed Wed.

Donizetti Via Gombito 17/A ☎035 242 661, ⓦdonizetti .it. Excellent place for a slap-up meal or a *degustazione* platter of local meats and cheeses washed down with fine wine. Inside is warm and welcoming; in summer tables are laid out in the covered market space. Daily 11am–midnight.

La Colombina Via Borgo Canale 12 ☎035 261 402. A wonderful, old-fashioned trattoria with tasty, good-value Bergamasco food and glorious views (ask for a table by the window when you book). A plate of home-made pasta costs around €12. Wed–Sun 12.15–2.30pm & 7.45–11pm.

FRANCIACORTA WINERIES

Between Bergamo and Brescia is **FRANCIACORTA**, a hilly wine-producing district rising from the built-up plain. It got its name from the religious communities that lived here from the eleventh century onwards: they were exempt from tax and known as the Corti Franche, or free courts. This small area of Lombardy is best known for the **Franciacorta DOCG** (Denominazione di Origine Controllata e Garantita), Italy's most refined sparkling wine, produced according to Champagne methods. It was first produced in the 1960s and the secret lies in the second fermentation in the bottle which can last from eighteen to sixty months. Usually a blend of Chardonnay and Pinot Noir or Blanc grapes, the sparkling wine comes in various types: Not Dosed/Pas Dosé (extremely dry), Extra Brut, Brut Satèn (a light silky-smooth mixture), Sec, Demisec and Rosé.

Some of the best known **Franciacorta sparkling wine producers** are Bellavista (Ⓦterramoretti.it), Belucchi (Ⓦberlucchi.it), Ca'del Bosco (Ⓦcadelbosco.com) and Majolini (Ⓦmajolini.it) but all of the vineyards – and there are over one hundred of them – have their own story and often lovely headquarters in ancient farmhouses or villas. Most guided tours end with a tasting and very competitive prices are offered in the *cantina* shops, where they can usually arrange shipping back home for you too.

The Consortium Franciacorta (Via G. Verdi 53, Erbusco ☎030 776 0477, Ⓦfranciacorta.net) has a list and can give advice on vineyards to visit or be guided by local suggestions from B&B owners.

In mid-September on even years, the **Festival Franciacorta** sees wineries open for special tasting sessions and local restaurants offering themed seasonal menus.

THE STRADA DEL VINO FRANCIACORTA

Tourist offices and hotels stock a map of the **Strada del Vino Franciacorta** (Ⓦstradadelfranciacorta.it), a route which winds for 80km through the area, passing visitable vineyards, hotels and restaurants. There are well-thought-out routes for cars, cyclists or walkers lasting for a couple of hours to a day or two. Contact details are given for wineries along the route, most of which offer tours and tastings; advance booking is preferred.

★ **La Marianna** Largo Colle Aperto 2/4, Ⓦlamarianna.it. Bergamo's oldest *pasticceria*, under balconies dripping with geraniums in the upper town, serves the best ice cream in town. They even claim to have invented the flavour *stracciatella*. Mon–Sat 7.30am–11pm, Sun 8am–11pm.

San Vigilio Via San Vigilio 35 ☎035 253 188, Ⓦristorantepizzeriasanvigilio.it. Informal restaurant with tasty pizzas from a wood-burning oven plus well-judged, creative dishes. Reserve a table by the window for views across the nearby villas with their splendid gardens to the plains. Noon–2.30pm & 7pm–midnight; closed Wed.

Vineria Cozzi Via Colleoni 22/A ☎035 238 836, Ⓦvineriacozzi.it. A historic wine-bar on the main thoroughfare in the upper town with a great selection of quality local wines, grappas and excellent cooking too. There's a network of pretty dining rooms behind the bar where well-judged takes on traditional dishes are served. Prices are around €55 per head in the evening. 10.30am–5pm & 6.30–midnight; closed Wed.

Brescia

Surrounded by vine-covered hills, the ancient settlement of **BRESCIA** is a wealthy city, boasting Roman remains, Renaissance squares and a medieval city centre with the outstanding museum complex of Santa Guilia. Yet for all this, it lacks the elegance and charm of other northern-Italian cities and is best visited as a day-trip or to break a journey elsewhere – easy, as the town is well connected by road, rail and bus.

Piazza della Loggia

Brescia's centre comprises a compact cluster of piazzas linked by cobbled streets. The main square, **Piazza della Loggia**, is also the prettiest, dating from 1433, when the city invited Venice to protect it from Milan's power-hungry Viscontis. The Venetian influence is clearest in the fancy **Loggia**, in which both Palladio and Titian had a hand,

and the **Torre dell'Orologio**, modelled on the campanile in Venice's Piazza San Marco. Below it, a monument commemorates the Fascist bombing, in 1974, of a trade-union rally here, in which eight people were killed and over a hundred injured: you can still see the blast damage on the pillar. Alongside is the **Porta Bruciata**, a defensive medieval tower-gate. Streets connect south into the austere, Fascist-built **Piazza della Vittoria**, under the stern gaze of the monumental post-office building.

Piazza Paolo VI and the duomos

Passages from Piazza della Loggia and Piazza della Vittoria lead east across galleried Via X Giornate through to **Piazza Paolo VI**, one of the few squares in Italy to have two cathedrals – though, frankly, it would have been better off without the chilly **Duomo Nuovo** (Mon–Sat 7.30am–noon & 4–7pm, Sun 8am–1pm & 4–7pm), its grim Neoclassical facade concealing a tall cupola. Much more appealing is the adjacent twelfth-century **Duomo Vecchio**, or **Rotonda** (Tues–Sun: April–Oct 9am–noon & 3–7pm; Nov–March 10am–noon & 3–6pm), a circular church of local stone, sunk below the current level of the piazza. Inside, glass set into the transept pavement reveals the remains of Roman baths (a wall and geometrical mosaics) and the apse of an eighth-century basilica, which burned down in 1097. The crypt is supported on a random array of reused Roman columns.

Piazza del Foro and the Tempio Capitolino

From the top end of the square, Via dei Musei marks the *decumanus maximus* (east–west road) of the Roman settlement of Brixia; a short walk east brings you to **Piazza del Foro**, built over the ancient forum (which was substantially larger than the current square). Dominating the area are the tall columns of the **Tempio Capitolino**, a Roman temple built in 73 AD, now partly reconstructed with red brick. Adjacent to the east is a part-excavated Roman **theatre**. The complexes are currently closed to visitors while work continues, but they are still visible from the road.

Santa Giulia

Via dei Musei 81 • Tues–Sun: June–Sept 10am–6pm; Oct–May 9.30am–5.30pm • €8 • ⓦ bresciamusei.com

A short walk further along Via dei Musei is Brescia's fabulous civic museum of **Santa Giulia**, housed in an ex-Benedictine convent built over what was a Roman quarter of frescoed villas. The layers of history on show make this a fascinating place to spend a couple of hours. Inside are three churches: twelfth-century **San Salvatore**, which includes the remains of a crypt built in 762; **Santa Maria in Solario**, covered in frescoes painted mainly by the Renaissance artist Floriano Ferramola; and the late sixteenth-century church of **Santa Giulia**, with further frescoes by Ferramola. The museum holds a collection of artefacts chronicling the city's history, including a life-sized Roman *Winged Victory* in bronze; beautiful Roman mosaic floors and frescoed walls preserved in situ; and the eighth-century wooden cross of Desiderius, first-century King of the Lombards, studded with more than two hundred gemstones. The complex also stages major art exhibitions (ⓦlineadombra.it).

Up to the Castello

Behind the museum, Via Piamarta climbs the **Cydnean Hill**, the core of early Roman Brixia (though remains are scanty), topped by the **Castello** (daily 8am–8pm; free), begun in the fifteenth century by Luchino Visconti and added to by the Venetians, French and Austrians, now housing two small museums, the **Museo delle Armi** and **Museo del Risorgimento** (both Tues–Sun: June–Sept 10.30am–6pm; Oct–May 9.30am–5pm; €5) with low-key displays of weapons and Unification memorabilia. The resulting confusion of towers, ramparts, halls and courtyards makes a good place for an atmospheric picnic.

Pinacoteca Tosio Martinengo

Piazza Moretto 4 • ⓦ bresciamusei.com • Closed at the time of writing

A short walk south of Santa Giulia, Brescia's main art gallery, the **Pinacoteca Tosio Martinengo**, was closed at the time of writing but during restoration works highlights will be on show at the Santa Giulia complex. These will no doubt include two masterpieces by Raphael – an *Angel* and a *Risen Christ* – and Moretto's chilling *Passion* (c.1550), depicting a reproachful Christ slouched before an angry, tearful angel.

ARRIVAL AND DEPARTURE	BRESCIA

By train The town is served by main-line trains from Milano Centrale, Verona and Desenzano/Sirmione, as well as slower trains from Lecco, Bergamo and Cremona. The train station is a dull 15min walk southwest from the centre with a large underground car park next door.

Destinations Bergamo (hourly; 50min); Cremona (hourly; 55min); Desenzano/Sirmione (hourly; 20min); Iseo (approx hourly; 40min); Lecco (hourly; 1hr 55min); Milano Centrale (every 30min; 1hr); Verona (every 30min; 35min).

By bus Flanking the train station are two bus stations – the main Stazione Autolinee, with buses from Verona, Mantua, Iseo, Bergamo-Orio al Serio airport and Brescia-Montichiari airport, and the SIA bus station, with buses from Desenzano, Salò, Riva, Idro and Val Trompia.

Destinations Cremona (hourly; 1hr 15min); Desenzano (at least hourly; 1hr); Gargnano (every 30min; 1hr 25min); Iseo (8 daily; 40min–1hr); Mantua (hourly; 1hr 25min); Riva del Garda (3 daily; 2hr 5min); Salò (at least every 30min; 55min); Verona (hourly; 2hr 20min).

GETTING AROUND

By bus To skip the dull 15min walk to the centre from the train station, hop on one of the buses from the stop opposite (#1 direction Mompiano or #10 direction Marconi; tickets from the driver or from the shop by the bus stop; €1.20). Full details at ⓦ bresciamobilita.it.

On foot Central Brescia is compact and mainly pedestrianized, making it safe and pleasant to wander on foot.

By bike The city's bike-sharing initiative, *bicimia*, that you'll see around town is aimed at residents and takes over a month to register but bike rental from the station makes a good alternative to walking (Mon–Sat 7.30am–7.30pm; €1 for up to 5hr; ☎ 030 306 1224).

Trenino storico At weekends and in summer, a miniature train, the *trenino storico* (€5; tickets and hours available on board or from the tourist office), leaves from outside the tourist office and scuttles along the main thoroughfares of the old town.

INFORMATION

Tourist office Piazza della Loggia 13/B (Mon–Sat 9.30am–6.30pm, Sun 10am–6pm; ☎ 030 240 0357). Very well organized office with helpful staff, buckets of information, leaflets and free self-guided audio tours (passport or ID needed as deposit).

Provincial tourist office Via dei Musei 32 (Mon–Thurs 9am–noon & 2.30–4.30pm, Fri 9am–noon; ☎ 030 374 9916, ⓦ bresciatourism.it). A good place for info on Brescia Province, which stretches over to the western shore of Lake Garda.

ACCOMMODATION

Brescia's **hotels** are a fairly undistinguished bunch, almost universally aimed at business travellers. At the lower end of the market, there's a cluster of rather nasty cheap hotels around the station and adjacent main roads that are best avoided. Book ahead if you're coming in May, when the Mille Miglia vintage car rally attracts thousands to the city.

Orologio Via Beccaria 17 ☎ 030 375 5411, ⓦ albergo orologio.it. Attractive boutique three-star in an old building beside the Broletto and Piazza Paolo VI. Rooms have been carefully renovated and updated with a good deal of taste, matching the warm welcome and genial service. €125

Vittoria Via X Giornate 20 ☎ 030 280 061, ⓦ hotel vittoria.com. Brescia's central five-star option, built in 1933 in Fascist style, has had a makeover and is a good-value, luxurious, contemporary hotel in an excellent location. €160

EATING AND DRINKING

Central Brescia has plenty of reasonably priced places to eat, specializing in local dishes such as *casoncei* (large meat-filled ravioli) and *brasato d'asino* (donkey stew). Many menus feature pasta stuffed with (or polenta smothered in) *bagòss*, a local cheese – rich, spicy and flavourful. Piazzale Arnaldo to the east of the centre has a clutch of café-bars that fill up quickly after work and stay buzzing into the small hours.

Al Bianchi Via Gasparo da Salò 30 ☎ 030 292 328, ⓦ osteriaalbianchi.it. Historic restaurant in a quiet central location. A popular spot, serving a variety of tasty, well-priced local dishes, specializing in Brescian meaty mains. A good place to head for an *aperitivo* on a Saturday morning. Noon–2pm & 7–11pm; closed Tues & Wed.

Al Granaio Piazzale Arnaldo ☎ 030 375 9345. A fine *osteria* under the arcades of the old city granary. The covered terrace is an atmospheric place for lunch, and is candlelit after dark. The food is moderately priced local fare, with a broad choice of wines. Tues–Sun 12.30–2.30pm & 7.30–10.30pm.

Buonissimo Corso Mameli 23 ☎ 030 280 8245, ⓦ buonissimo-store.it If you're feeling indecisive head to this four-storey food hall with an informal, well-priced restaurant, wine bar and bookshop café where you can eat, relax and shop for take-home goodies from across Italy all under one roof. Tues–Sun 9.30am–8pm.

Osteria dell'Elfo Piazza Vescovato 1/B ☎ 030 377 4858. Decent little restaurant on this central square, with terrace tables catering to the pre- and post-theatre crowd – think salads and light meals of pasta and fish. 12.15–2.30pm & 7.15–10.30pm; closed Tues.

Osteria La Grotta Vicolo del Prezzemolo 10 ☎ 030 44 068, ⓦ osterialagrotta.it. Charming spot with an atmospheric interior and a menu centred on its own, high-quality *salumi* and other local specialities. Expect to pay around €35. 12.30–2.30pm & 7–11pm; closed Wed.

Lake Garda

LAKE GARDA (Lago di Garda) is the largest lake in Italy (52km long by 17km wide): it's so big that it alters the local climate, which is milder and – thanks to a complex pattern

LEMON HOUSES

The western shore is dubbed the **Riviera del Limone** for the citrus orchards that once flourished here. The crop, introduced by the Franciscans in the fourteenth century, was cultivated in the *limonaie*, or "lemon houses" that are still in evidence, although many of the stone-pillared constructions were abandoned last century when Sicilian lemons became cheaper to produce. Several structures around the lake are open to visitors; head for Gargnano (see p.293), Limone (see p.295) or Torri del Benaco (see p.299).

of lake breezes – sunnier than might be expected. It's also the most popular of the lakes, attracting around seven percent of all tourists to Italy and acting as a bridge between the Alps and the rest of the country. The narrow north of the lake is tightly enclosed by mountains that drop sheer into the water with villages wedged into gaps in the cliffs. Further south, the lake spreads out comfortably, flanked by gentle hills and lined by placid holiday resorts.

In the south, **Desenzano** is a cheery spot with the advantage of good transport links, plus proximity to the very popular and scenically impressive **Sirmione**. On the western shore are the old Venetian town of **Salò** and **Gargnano**, the lake's best destination, a small village that remains largely unspoilt. The mountainous scenery is spectacular on the approach to the genteel resort of **Riva del Garda** at the head of the lake. It's a handsome town with a long history and is a focal point for sports and water activities.

Overlooked by the ridges of Monte Baldo, which tops 2100m, the main resorts of Lake Garda's **eastern shore** struggle to match the charm of the villages opposite. Aim for **Torbole** if you're an outdoors enthusiast. To the south, the very popular resort of **Malcesine** has direct access up to Monte Baldo, as does **Brenzone**, comprising a string of attractive little harbours and a good base for walks and mountain-bike rides into Monte Baldo behind. **Torri del Benaco**, a little to the south, is an attractive corner that has avoided the worst of the crowds.

GETTING AROUND — LAKE GARDA

By bus Regular buses ply the main road along both shores: #80 leads from Desenzano to Riva and back on the western shore (transportibrescia.it), while on the eastern shore bus #62-64 heads from Riva to Verona and back stopping everywhere in between (aptv.it).

By boat The water offers the most relaxing form of transport, with at least hourly boat services between the main resorts plus several sightseeing and evening cruise services in summer. Two car ferries cross the lake (Maderno–Torri del Benaco, and Limone–Malcesine). Services are significantly reduced in winter; navigazionelaghi.it has all the details.

By car On summer weekends you should expect heavy traffic on the scenic lakeshore road, which has one lane in each direction (often squeezing round villages and through dimly lit tunnels). There is pay and display parking outside all the villages but there can be queues in summer.

INFORMATION

For information on resorts and activities all round the lake – which fall into three different regions and therefore tourism authorities, consult visitgarda.com. Each tourist office on the northern and western shore has a **hotel-booking service** with a display board showing which hotels have vacancies (also available out of hours).

Sirmione

At the bottom of the lake, the long narrow promontory of **SIRMIONE** is lined with hotels leading up to the very pretty village accessed through ancient castle walls. It's in a striking location, although the narrow cobbled lanes creak under the weight of ice-cream parlours and the strain of a million overnight visitors a year. Your best best is to press on through the crowded lanes of the village, past the ferry dock on Piazza Carducci and out to the grassy park and cypress-clad hills at the head of the peninsula. Sirmione is one of northern Italy's top spa destinations and many come to take the waters or enjoy a day in the health and beauty centre (termedisirmione.com).

THEME PARKS: GARDALAND AND CANEVAWORLD

The **theme parks** around the southeast corner of the lake are a good day out for all ages. **GARDALAND** is the biggest theme park in the area (daily: mid-March to end Sept 10am–6pm; mid-June to early Sept until 11pm; also weekends in Oct & Dec; €37.50, children under 10 €31, children less than 1m tall free; discounts for part-day and multi-day tickets; ☎045 644 9777, ⓦgardaland.it), and includes the small but well-planned **SeaLife aquarium** nearby. It's pricey but well thought out with lots of shade, water games and rides for all ages from around 3 upwards. Parking costs an extra €5, or take the free shuttle-bus which runs from Peschiera train station, 2km away.

Gardaland Hotel Via Palù 11, Castelnuovo ☎045 640 4407, ⓦgardalandhotel.it. If you're in the market for giant friendly dragons and face-painting, the New England-style *Gardaland Hotel* offers very comfortable family-orientated accommodation with gardens and pool area and a free shuttle-bus to the park five minutes away. Online special offers available. Closed Nov– March. **€150**

A little north is **CANEVAWORLD** (☎045 696 9900, ⓦcanevaworld.it), comprising two adjacent parks: **Movieland** (mid-April to mid-Sept daily 10am–6pm, later opening at weekends and in July & Aug; also weekends in Oct), with fake movie-sets and shows revealing the secrets of special effects; and **AquaParadise** (mid-May to mid-Sept daily 10am–6pm; July & Aug until 7pm), with slides, flumes, pools and a pirate island. One day's admission is €24 for one park (€19 for kids under 1.40m high), or special deals for both parks or more days. Children under 1m go free. Free buses shuttle every 30min (mornings only) to Canevaworld from Peschiera station.

Rocca Scaligera

Tues–Sun 8.30am–7pm • €4

Sirmione's picture-postcard looks owe much to the fairytale castle at its entrance. Built when the Della Scala/Scaligeri family of Verona expanded and fortified their territory in the thirteenth century, the **Rocca Scaligera**, with boxy towers, is almost entirely surrounded by water. It dates from the thirteenth century. You're free to roam around the walls – the enclosed harbour is especially photogenic – and climb the towers: 77 steps lead up to the keep, followed by another 92 to the top of the highest tower, from where views over the rooftops of Sirmione are gorgeous.

Grotte di Catullo

Tues–Sat 8.30am–7pm, Sun until 5pm; Nov–Feb closes 5pm • €4

At the far end of the promontory, a pleasant fifteen-minute stroll from the castle, stand the remains of a first century BC/AD Roman villa, purportedly belonging to Roman poet Catullus, though the evidence is scant. The ruins, scattered among ancient olive trees, are lovely, and offer superb views across the lake.

Lido delle Bionde

May–Oct daily 8am–midnight • €8

Partway along the route to the Roman ruins, a path heads down to water level to a shingle beach where you can eat, drink, swim in the lake or sunbathe on the pontoon or nearby rocks. Alternatively turn right when you reach the water and follow the walkway along to the free public beach by the village, where there is also room to paddle.

ARRIVAL AND INFORMATION   SIRMIONE

By bus The bus station is at the end of Viale Marconi by the tourist office and the entrance to the walled village.
Destinations Brescia (hourly; 1hr 10min); Desenzano (at least hourly; 20min); Verona (hourly; 1hr).

By boat The *imbarcadero* is on Piazza Carducci, and regular boats link the resorts at the southern end of the lake while a reduced number of boats also head to the towns to the north of the lake (see p.259).

By car Sirmione is closed to traffic; there is plenty of pay and display parking at the end of the approach road, Viale Marconi.

Tourist office Viale Marconi 2 (Easter–Nov daily 9am–8pm; Nov–Easter Mon–Fri 9am–12.30pm & 3–6pm, Sat 9am–12.30pm; ☎ 030 916 114, ⓦ sirmionehotel.com).

EATING AND DRINKING

L'Oficina Vicolo Strentelle 5. Grab a slice of pizza, an *arancini* or a sandwich and head down to the nearby public beach to savour the views while you eat. Daily 9am–7pm; closed Nov–March.

La Rucola Vicolo Strentelle 5 ☎ 030 916 326, ⓦ ristorantelarucola.it. A sophisticated little spot near the castle, this is the top gourmet restaurant in town. Prices are high: expect more than €80 per head. 12.30–2.30pm & 7–11pm; closed Thurs & Nov–Feb.

★ **Selva Capuzza** San Martino della Battaglia ☎ 030

991 0279, ⓦ selvacapuzza.it. This popular local secret is wonderfully set among olive groves in ivy-covered farm buildings 5km south of the lake (follow the signs from the Sirmione exit of the A4 motorway). Go for the four-course meal washed down with their award-winning wines (also available by the crate). The atmosphere is informal, the food hearty made with local ingredients and presented with pride. Also lovely self-catering accommodation with a pool. Mon–Wed 7–10.30pm, Thurs–Sun 12.30–2.30pm & 7–10.30pm.

Desenzano del Garda

At its southwest extremity, **DESENZANO** is a good access point to the lake. Its attractive waterfront squares – Piazza Malvezzi and Piazza Matteotti, are lined with bars and restaurants, while nearby the **Roman villa** on Via Crocifisso (Tues–Sun 8.30am–7pm; Nov–Feb closes 4.30pm; €2) displays some good mosaics. Looming over the town, the **castle** offers spectacular views.

ARRIVAL AND INFORMATION   DESENZANO

By train The town has a good train service on the fast Milan–Brescia–Verona line.
Destinations Brescia (hourly; 20min); Milano Centrale (hourly; 1hr 10min); Venice (approx hourly; 1hr 40min); Verona (approx twice hourly; 30min).
By bus Regular buses service the western shore of the lake as well as linking the town with Brescia and Sirmione to the east.
Destinations Brescia (every 30min; 35min); Riva (hourly;

1hr 50min); Salò (9 daily; 40min); Sirmione (at least hourly; 20min).
By boat Regular ferries zip between Sirmione and the towns on the lower eastern shore while fast services leave several times a day for Riva at the top of the lake, calling at most larger villages on both shores along the way.
Tourist office Via Porto Vecchio 34, just off the main square on the old harbour (Mon–Fri 9am–12.30pm & 3–6pm, Sat 9am–12.30pm; ☎ 030 914 1510, ⓦ visitgarda.com).

Isola del Garda

Guided tours only June–Sept • €25–30 depending on starting point • ⓦ isoladelgarda.com

Off the Valtenesi shore north of Desenzano, the elongated **ISOLA DEL GARDA** is the lake's largest island, formerly the site of an ancient monastery once visited by St Francis. The old buildings were replaced around 1900 by a fanciful **villa** in Venetian neo-Gothic style. Lush Italianate terraced **gardens** lead down to the lake, alongside Mediterranean shrubs, cypresses, cedars, bay trees and more.

The Cavazza family own and live on the island and it is visitable only on a **guided tour** in summer. Trips run from several points, most frequently from Salò (6 weekly), but also with direct service from Garda, Desenzano, Sirmione and elsewhere (all 2–3 weekly). The fare covers return boat transport and a two-hour guided tour, including a tasting of local products.

Salò

SALÒ, splendidly sited on its own bay, is one of Garda's more handsome towns. Capital of the Magnifica Patria – a grouping of lake communes – for more than four hundred years until the fall of the Venetian Republic in 1797, it retains something of its old-fashioned hauteur, exemplified by the grand seventeenth-century town hall, directly on the lakefront by the ferry dock, and the unfinished Renaissance facade of the Duomo, which holds paintings by Romanino. From 1943 to 1945, Salò was the nominal capital of Italy, as the Nazis installed Mussolini here at the head of a puppet regime in a failed attempt to hold off the Allied advance. It's now something of a yachties' town, with a less touristy profile than its neighbours, offering everything you'd want – long, quiet waterfront promenade, great views, alluring old quarter – but without the crowds.

ARRIVAL AND INFORMATION SALÒ

By bus Buses stop on Largo Dante Alighieri. Destinations Brescia (every 30min; 1hr); Desenzano (9 daily; 50min); Gargnano (every 30min; 25min); Milan (3 daily; 2hr 40min); Riva (9 daily; 1hr 15min).
By boat The imbarcadero stands at one end of Piazza della

Vittoria. Regular ferries and cruises leave for destinations around the lake.
Tourist office Behind the town hall on Piazza Sant'Antonio (Mon–Sat 10am–12.30pm & 3–6pm, Sun 10am–1pm & 3.30–6.30pm; ☎0365 21 423, ⊕visitgarda.com).

ACCOMMODATION

Bellerive Via Pietro da Salò 11 ☎0365 520 410, ⊕hotelbellerive.it. On the edge of the centre, this four-star offers pleasant, fresh rooms, many with lake views. Service is exceptional and the restaurant, *Ristorante 100km* (see below), outstanding. An annexe holds apartments for

rent (min three-night stay). Closed Dec & Jan. **€195**
Benaco Lungolago Zanardelli 44 ☎0365 20 308, ⊕benacohotel.com. A small family-run boutique hotel in the historic centre with a fine restaurant. **€120**

EATING AND DRINKING

La Casa del Dolce Piazza Duomo 1. Salò's best ice cream is served at this little hole in the wall by the Duomo. Only seasonal produce is used so the flavours are constantly changing. Daily 11am–11pm; closed Nov–March.
Pizzeria Papillon Via Lungolago Zanardelli 69 ☎0365 41 429. Pizzas are served bubbling from the wood-fired oven here but the pasta and fish options are good too. In summer reserve a table outside next to the lake. Tues–Sun 12.30–2.30pm & 7.30–11pm.

Ristorante 100km In *Hotel Bellerive*, Via Pietro da Salò 11 ☎0365 520 410, ⊕hotelbellerive.it. This is a classy, contemporary restaurant, where everything – ingredients, recipes, wines – are sourced from within a 100km radius of Salò. The menu focuses on classic Brescian cuisine, including exquisite *coregone* (white lake fish), served with flair and innovation (around €50). Daily 12.30–2.45pm & 7.45–10.30pm.

Gardone Riviera

Just 2km east of Salò, **GARDONE RIVIERA** was once the most fashionable of Lake Garda's resorts and still retains its symbols of sophistication, though the lush gardens, opulent villas and ritzy hotels now have to compete with more recent tourist paraphernalia. **Gardone Sotto**, the old village on the lakeside, comprises a cobbled street and a couple of piazzas sandwiched between the busy Corso Zanardelli road and the lake. **Gardone Sopra** spreads across the hillside above, with a tiny centre at the chapel and piazza just by the entrance to Il Vittoriale.

Giardino Botanico André Heller

Via Roma 2, Gardone Sopra • March–Oct daily 9am–7pm • €9 • ⊕hellergarden.com

Gardone's success as a health retreat and winter resort was in great part due to its famously consistent climate which has also encouraged the exotic **Giardino Botanico André Heller**, laid out just above Gardone Sotto in 1912 by Arturo Hruska, dentist to the Russian tsar, and now owned by Heller, an artist. Bamboo, water-lilies, camphor trees, banana plants and more, set amid artificial cliffs and streams, are interspersed with sculptures and modern artworks.

Il Vittoriale

Via Vittoriale 12, Gardone Sopra • Tues–Sun 8.30am–8pm; Oct–March 9am–1pm & 2–5pm • €16 or €8 for gardens only; extra €4 to see the adjoining Museo della Guerra (War Museum; closed Wed), which isn't worth it • Tickets can be restricted at peak times (Sun, national holidays, some days in July & Aug), when you should arrive an hour or more before the opening time to be sure of entry • ⊕vittoriale.it

On the hillside above Gardone, **Il Vittoriale** was the home of Italy's most notorious twentieth-century writer, Gabriele D'Annunzio (see box, p.292). A deeply idiosyncratic

GABRIELE D'ANNUNZIO

Born in 1863, Gaetano Rapagnetta – who took the name **Gabriele D'Annunzio** (Gabriel of the Annunciation) – is often acclaimed as one of Italy's greatest poets, though he became better known as a soldier and socialite, leading his own private army and indulging in much-publicized affairs with numerous women, including the actress Eleonora Duse (when berated by his friends for treating her cruelly, he simply replied, "I gave her everything, even suffering.") He was a fervent supporter of Mussolini, providing the Fascist Party with their (meaningless) war cry *"eia! eia! alalà!"* – though Mussolini eventually found his excessive exhibitionism an embarrassment and in 1921 presented D'Annunzio with the Vittoriale villa, ostensibly to reward his patriotism, in reality to shut him up. D'Annunzio died in the house in 1938, suffering a brain haemorrhage while sitting at his desk in the Zambracca room, which remains untouched.

complex, it gives an insight into the poet's eccentric character, and is a hugely popular destination with Italians.

D'Annunzio's personality makes itself felt from the start in the Prioria's two reception rooms – one a chilly and formal room for guests he didn't like, the other warm and inviting for those he did. Mussolini was apparently shown to the former, where the mirror has an inscription reputedly aimed at him: "Remember that you are made of glass and I of steel." Dining with D'Annunzio was never a reassuring experience: in the glitzy dining room, as a warning to greedy guests, pride of place was given to a gilded tortoise that had died of overeating. The rest of the house is no less bizarre: the bathroom has a bathtub hemmed in by hundreds of objects, ranging from Persian ceramic tiles and Buddhas to toy animals; and the Sala del Mappamondo, as well as the huge globe for which it is named, contains an Austrian machine gun and an oversized edition of *The Divine Comedy*. Suspended from the ceiling of the auditorium adjoining the house is the biplane that D'Annunzio used in a daring flight over Vienna in World War I.

Outside amid the cypress trees is the prow of the battleship *Puglia* used in D'Annunzio's so-called "Fiume adventure". Fiume (now Rijeka), on the North Adriatic, had been promised to Italy before they entered World War I, but was handed to Yugoslavia instead. Incensed, D'Annunzio gathered an army, occupied Fiume and returned home a hero. Amid the gardens above stands D'Annunzio's mausoleum, a Fascistic array of angular travertine stonework.

ARRIVAL AND INFORMATION
GARDONE RIVIERA

By bus Regular services connect Gardone with villages and towns along the western shore of the lake. Buses stop at several points along the main road; ask at the tourist office. Destinations Brescia (every 30min; 1hr 5min); Limone (3 daily; 1hr); Riva del Garda (5 daily; 1hr 15min).
By boat The *imbarcadero* is just by Piazza Wimmer in

Gardone Sotto. Services leave for around the lake with a reduced service in winter.
Tourist office Corso Repubblica in Gardone Sotto (July & Aug Mon–Sat 9am–12.30pm & 3.30–6.30pm, Sun 9am–12.30pm; Sept–June Mon–Sat 9am–12.30pm & 3–6pm; ☎0365 20 347, ⓦvisitgarda.com).

ACCOMMODATION

Gardone Riviera – once Lake Garda's ritziest resort – specializes in opulent **luxury hotels**, many of which occupy grandiose Art Nouveau villas that went up, often in spacious park-like grounds, in the early years of the last century.

Colombér Via Val di Sur 111 ☎0365 21 108, ⓦcolomber .com. In the village of San Michele just outside Gardone, *Hotel Colombér* has comfortable en-suite rooms (some with balconies), a pool and a decent restaurant serving local specialities and well-chosen wine. Makes a good base for walks. Closed mid-Dec to mid-March. **€100**

★ **Florida Residence** Corso Zanardelli 113 ☎0365 21 836, ⓦhotelfloridaresidence.com. Thoughtfully run

by a charming family, who are a fascinating wealth of information on the history of the area. The attractive rooms are good-sized suites with kitchen corners and balconies offering lovely lake views. Large pool and pretty grounds. **€150**

Grand Hotel Fasano Corso Zanardelli 190 ☎0365 290 220, ⓦghf.it. Perhaps the finest of Gardone's luxury hotels occupying Art Nouveau villas. Built in the nineteenth century as a hunting lodge for the Austrian imperial family and converted into a hotel around 1900, the spacious interiors are characterized by a classic, traditionally styled comfort. Closed Nov–Feb. **€220**

Locanda Agli Angeli Piazza Garibaldi 2 ☎ 0365 20 832, ⓦ agliangeli.com. Small, family-run place with airy rooms, a veranda, and the peace and quiet of Gardone Sopra in the evening, just by Il Vittoriale. **€150**

EATING AND DRINKING

The lakeside cafés in Gardone Sotto are the perfect place to enjoy a coffee or an ice cream with dreamy views across the water. For a full meal, the quality is often better in the trattorias dotted around Gardone Sopra although prices always reflect their popularity. It's best to book ahead in summer.

Agli Angeli Piazza Garibaldi 2 ☎ 0365 20 832, ⓦ agliangeli.com. A good choice up near Il Vittoriale and part of the family-run hotel of the same name (see above) serves quality lake fish and platters of home-cured meats. Wed–Sun 12.30–2.30pm & 7–10.30pm.

La Taverna Corso Repubblica 34 ☎ 0365 20 412. A decent wine-bar tucked into the lanes down near the lakeside with inexpensive plates of typical local fare

including tasty home-made pasta. 12.30–2.30pm & 7.30–11pm; closed Tues.

Trattoria Riolet Via Fasano Sopra 75 ☎ 0365 20545. Hidden away at the top of a steep climb, this popular family-run trattoria offers pasta starters and a mixed-grill for mains. The service can be brusque but the setting outside under the vines is lovely. 12.30–2.30pm & 7–10.30pm; closed Nov–Feb.

Toscalano Maderno

Barely 3km east of Gardone, the road passes through the twin *comune* of **TOSCOLANO MADERNO**, which straddles the delta of the Toscolano river. A car ferry crosses to Torri del Benaco on the western shore of the lake from here. There's a decent beach and the valley behind has a tradition of paper-making going back to the fourth century. Following the riverside road up into the beautiful, wooded valley brings you past many disused **paper mills** to the **Fondazione Valle delle Cartierie**, with a well-presented **museum** offering an insight into the processes and importance of the industry (mid-June to Sept daily 10.30am–6pm; April, May & Oct Sat & Sun only, same hours; €5). This is also a lovely area for shady walks or picnics.

ARRIVAL AND DEPARTURE	TOSCOLANO MADERNO

By bus Local and longer distance buses stop at various points along the main road.
Destinations Brescia (9 daily; 1hr 10min); Gargnano (9 daily; 10min); Riva del Garda (5 daily; 1hr).

By boat The *imbarcadero* is just off the main road on Lungolago Zanardelli. Services run to villages round the lake (p.259) and regular car ferries cross throughout the year to Torri del Benaco (p.299).

Gargnano

Some 15km north of Salò is **GARGNANO**, the prettiest village on Lake Garda. Traffic runs above and slightly inland here, leaving the old village itself noise-free. In addition, the narrow, difficult road north of town means tour buses don't bother trying to reach Gargnano. Still more a working village than a resort, it's the perfect spot to unwind for a day or two and wander around the abandoned olive factory or the lakefront villas with their boathouses, or just to relax by one of the tiny ports in a waterfront café. D.H. Lawrence stayed here while writing *Twilight in Italy*, a work which is beautifully evocative of Lake Garda's attractions.

San Francesco

Church daily 8am–noon & 4–7pm; cloister closed to the public

Aside from the harbourside, former **Palazzo Comunale**, which has two cannonballs wedged in the wall facing the lake – dating from the naval bombings suffered in 1866 during the war of independence from the Austrians – the main sight in Gargnano is the simple Romanesque church of **San Francesco**, built in 1289. The attached monastery became a citrus-fruit warehouse at the end of the nineteenth century. Its cloister has columns carved with citrus fruits, a reference to the Franciscans' introduction of the crop to Europe, but it is currently a point of contention over developer's plans to turn the complex into luxury apartments.

San Giacomo di Calino
Via San Giacomo

A stroll along the road which leads north out of Gargnano from the harbour takes you for 3km past the beach and through olive and lemon groves, past the *Villa Feltrinelli* (see below), to the tiny eleventh-century chapel of **San Giacomo di Calino**. On the side facing the lake, under the portico where the fishermen keep their equipment, is a thirteenth-century fresco of St Christopher, patron saint of travellers.

ARRIVAL AND DEPARTURE
GARGNANO

By bus Buses stop at Piazza Boldini on the main road, by the multistorey car park opposite the tourist office.
Destinations Brescia (3 daily; 1hr 10min); Desenzano (9 daily; 1hr); Riva (9 daily; 50 min); Salò (9 daily; 30min).

By boat Ferries for regular services round the lake pull in to the *imbarcadero* by the little harbour lined with orange trees on Piazza Feltrinelli.

INFORMATION AND ACTIVITIES

Tourist office Piazza Boldini, on the main road by the multistorey car park (Mon, Tues, Thurs–Sat 3.30–6.30pm) & Pro Locco at Piazza Feltrinelli 2 by the main port (Mon–Sat 10am–noon & 5–7pm, closed Tues & Sun pm; ☎0365 791 243, ⓦ visitgarda.com). Has details of various walks and hikes in the area.
Website There's information on Gargnano and around at ⓦ gargnanosulgarda.com. Descriptions of the area's walks and hikes are on ⓦ gargnanosulgarda.com/Sport-Leisure /Walking-and-Hiking.html.

Bikes and surfing OKSurf, Parco Fontanella (☎328 471 7777, ⓦ oksurf.it), rents mountain and electric bikes (€21/ day) and also runs windsurfing and kitesurfing courses for adults and children.
Sailing Every September hundreds of boats take to the waters off Gargnano for the round-Garda yacht race, the Centomiglia (ⓦ centomiglia.it). It's been celebrated for over sixty years and attracts top international sailors and locals alike. The village celebrates with open-air concerts and markets.

ACCOMMODATION

Du Lac Via Colletta 21, Villa di Gargnano ☎0365 71 107, ⓦ hotel-dulac.it. Run by the same family as the *Gardenia* – standards are high, the welcome is warm and the rooms are comfortable and unfussy. Six of them look over the lake, with a balcony or terrace. Antique furniture, en-suite bathrooms and a/c come as standard. Closed Dec–Feb. **€110**
Gardenia Via Colletta 53, Villa di Gargnano ☎0365 71 195, ⓦ hotel-gardenia.it. A lovely family-run hotel in a nineteenth-century lakeside villa. The public areas feature beautifully maintained 1950s decor and fittings while the guest rooms have been completely renovated with big comfy beds, well-appointed bathrooms and airy lake views. Excellent garden restaurant too. Closed Nov–March. **€130**
Riviera Via Roma 1 ☎0365 72 292, ⓦ garniriviera.it. Comfortable, good-value en-suite rooms in an enviable lakeside position in the village centre. Breakfast is served on the lovely waterside terrace. **€85**
Tiziana Via Dosso 51 ☎0365 71 342, ⓦ albergotiziana

.com. Small, friendly, no-frills two-star, located slightly off the main road above the village. Rooms are comfortable, in modern style, most with lake views. Closed Nov–March. **€65**
Villa Feltrinelli Via Rimembranza 38 ☎0365 798 000, ⓦ villafeltrinelli.com. Built by local lumber magnates in 1892, this grand lakeside house is set in its own sizeable grounds – an elegant eleven-roomed villa with an enviable lakeside position just north of the village. Home to Mussolini and his family during the Republic of Salò (see p.290), this is now one of the world's top hotels where every detail has been stylishly considered. Min two-night stay. Closed Nov–March. **€900**
★ **Villa Sostaga** Via Sostaga 19, Navazzo ☎0365 791218, ⓦ villasostaga.com. On the hillside above Gargnano, this handsome villa is a wonderful bolthole with lovely rooms, spacious grounds and a pool. The views are breathtaking, the welcome genuine and the seasonal cooking excellent (restaurant open to non-residents). **€220**

EATING AND DRINKING

Bar Vittorio Piazza Villa 1/2. An unbeatable place for a drink or simple snack right on the tiny harbour in the Villa neighbourhood. Mon, Tues & Thurs 8am–9pm, Fri–Sun 8am–11pm.

La Tortuga Via XXIV Maggio 5 ☎0365 71 251. Small, intimate dining room serving top-rate creative cuisine in a formal setting. Helpful staff take you through the good-value gourmet set-menus showcasing local produce (€80 per head). Book well in advance. Mon–Sat 7.30 10.30pm, Sun 12.30–2.30pm.

Miralago Via Zanardelli 5 ☎0365 71 209. A relaxed waterfront restaurant serving excellent food at fair prices. Sit back with a glass of wine and a seafood pasta, and enjoy the view – life doesn't get much better. Daily 12.30–2.30pm & 7–10.30pm.

Osteria del Restauro Piazza Villa 19. Good, inexpensive

local cuisine by the tiny harbour in this atmospheric part of the village. 12.30–2.15pm & 7.30–10.30pm; closed Wed.

★ **Villa Sostaga** Via Sostaga 19, Navazzo ☎0365 791218, ⓦvillasostaga.com. The restaurant in this hillside hotel serves very well-judged local cuisine with flair. Reserve one of the tables by the window for stunning views. Daily 12.30–2.30pm & 7.30–11pm.

The SP38 road to Tremosine

North of Gargnano the lake road skirts the water, passing through treacherously narrow road tunnels. Just after the windsurfing destination Campione del Garda there's a turning to the village of Pieve on the high plateau of the Tremosine (signposted Tremosine and Via Benaco). Not for the faint hearted or large vehicles, the breathtakingly narrow **SP38** road, described by Winston Churchill as "the eighth wonder of the world", switchbacks its way up the mountain through the scenic Brasa gorge to the Alpine plains above.

Limone sul Garda

The last town in Lombardy, 20km from Gargnano on a tongue of land surrounded by rugged mountains, is **LIMONE SUL GARDA** (ⓦvisitlimonesulgarda.com). Although famous for its lemon cultivation – a commercial concern until the 1920s – the name derives from its location at what was the frontier (*limen* in Latin) of Roman control. Limone is undeniably pretty, a stone-built village jammed onto a slender slope between the mountains and the lake, and with some one million overnight visitors a year, can feel overrun.

ACCOMMODATION
LIMONE SUL GARDA

Park Hotel Imperial Via Tamas ☎0365 954 591, ⓦparkhotelimperial.com. A five-star hotel on the hill above the village offers lovely lake views from the room

balconies. An extensive spa, tennis court, children's play area and outside landscaped pool area are only some of the luxurious facilities. **€360**

Riva del Garda

Dramatically located beneath sheer cliffs at the northwest tip of the lake, **RIVA DEL GARDA** is unmistakeably a holiday town, but it has a long history and the pedestrianized old quarter is still full of character. Windsurfing and sailing on the lake are major preoccupations. Cheaper than many other lake resorts, Riva is a good base for a budget holiday.

Piazza III Novembre

Riva's showpiece main square, **Piazza III Novembre** (named to celebrate the arrival of Italian forces in 1918), is an attractive, cobbled space, its medieval Lombard and Venetian facades lined up on three sides below the rugged face of Monte Rocchetta, the fourth side open to the lake.

Dominating Piazza III Novembre is the thirteenth-century **Torre Apponale**, 34m high and climbable inside for sensational lake views (March–Oct Tues–Sun 10am–6pm; June–Aug also Mon; €1). In the middle of the square are the Veronese **Palazzo Pretorio**, dating from 1375, and the Venetian **Casa del Comune**, completed in 1482, while to one side, behind the *imbarcadero* looms a 1920s-era hydroelectric **power station**, designed to exploit the 500m drop in water level from Lake Ledro to this point; today, the generators are hidden within the mountain, and these buildings and pipes are only for show.

The Rocca

Museo: March–Oct Tues–Sun 10am–12.30pm & 1.30–6pm, June–Aug also Mon • €2

The stout **Rocca** was originally built in 1124 but has been much altered since, not least by the Austrians, who lopped some height off the main tower in 1852 and turned the fortress into a barracks. It now houses the **Museo Civico**, with temporary exhibits on the ground floor, a modest *pinacoteca* upstairs and displays of archeology and local history upstairs again.

Parco Grotta Cascata Varone

May–Aug daily 9am–7pm; April & Sept daily 9am–6pm; March & Oct daily 9am–5pm; Nov–Feb Sun 10am–5pm • €5.50 • ⓦcascata-varone .com • About 45min on foot from Riva waterfront, along Via Ardaro/Marone or slow bus #862 from Riva bus station (40min)

Three kilometres north of Riva, the **Parco Grotta Cascata Varone** is a gorge and waterfall system where you penetrate the canyon on a series of catwalks, as the waters of the River Magnone thunder down from almost 100m above. There's a small bar and picnic area on site.

ARRIVAL AND INFORMATION

RIVA DEL GARDA

By bus Riva's bus station is about 1km north of the lakefront, on Viale Trento, but all intercity buses drop off at the *imbarcadero* (if approaching from Limone) or Viale Carducci (if approaching from Torbole).

Destinations Brescia (3 daily; 2hr 5min); Desenzano (9 daily; 1hr 50min); Malcesine (approx hourly; 25min); Salò (9 daily; 1hr 15min); Torbole (approx every 30min; 5min); Torri del Benaco (approx hourly; 1hr); Verona (hourly; 2hr 20min).

By boat The *imbarcadero* stands beside Piazza III Novembre. Riva is one of the hubs for lake ferries with fast services heading for the larger villages and resorts around the lake.

Tourist information The tourist office is at Largo Medaglie d'Oro (daily 9am–7pm; ☎0464 554 444, ⓦgardatrentino.it) and there's an information kiosk at the *imbarcadero* (May–Sept 10am–1pm & 2–5.30pm, closed Wed; ☎0464 550 776).

ACCOMMODATION

Fiore d'Ulivo Via Ballino 13/C ☎348 853 5245, ⓦagriturismofioredulivo.it. Set among vines and olive groves just outside Riva this simple, contemporary styled B&B makes a peaceful base. Well linked by cycle routes. **€75**
Hotel Antico Borgo Via A. Diaz 15 ☎0464 552 277, ⓦbluhotels.it/hotel/lago-di-garda/riva-del-garda/hotel -antico-borgo. Stylish contemporary hotel with fresh rooms,

splashes of colour and a lovely roof terrace with lake views. **€120**
Ostello Benacus (HI hostel) Piazza Cavour 10 ☎0464 554 911, ⓦostelloriva.com. Very central hostel, well run, with renovated two-, four- and multi-bed rooms. Parking €3 for 24hr. Closed Nov–Feb. Dorms **€18**, doubles/ twins **€44**

EATING AND DRINKING

Bella Napoli Via A. Diaz 29 ☎0464 552 139. With a cosy interior and outside seating for good weather, it's difficult to beat the wood-fired pizzas at this convivial pizzeria in the centre of the old town. There's a good selection for around €8 each. 11.30am–2.30pm & 5.30pm–midnight; closed Wed.
La Colombera Via Rovigo 30 ☎0464 556 033, ⓦlacolombera.it. Among the vineyards on the edge of Riva this excellent, mid-priced country restaurant is crowded nightly with locals and others in the know. The

menu comprises hearty, straightforward fare served with gusto in a cheery, unpretentious setting. 7–9.30pm, Sun also 12.30–2.30pm; closed Wed.
★ **Osteria Il Gallo** Piazza S. Rocco 12 ☎0464 556 200, ⓦosteriailgallo.com. A great little place under the porticoes just off the main square. There's a short menu of simple local mountain staples and the owner will reel off many more dishes. The good wine list of Trento wines and the relaxed atmosphere make this a fine spot to settle down for the evening. Noon–2.30pm & 6–10pm; Nov–Feb closed Mon.

Torbole

TORBOLE, 4km east of Riva, played an important role in the fifteenth-century war between Milan and Venice, when a fleet of warships was dragged overland here and launched into the lake. Nowadays the water still dominates, since Torbole's main diversions are sailing and windsurfing; enthusiasts come here from all over Europe, attracted by ideal wind conditions (see box opposite).

INFORMATION

TORBOLE

Tourist office Lungolago Conca d'Oro 25, on the lakefront between the town centre and the landing stage (May–Sept Mon–Sat 9am–1pm & 3–7pm; April Tues–Sun 9.30am–12.40pm & 2.30–6.30pm; Oct–March Mon–Sat

9.30am–12.40pm & 2.30–6pm; ☎0464 505 177, ⓦgardatrentino.it). The tourist office and its website have a good list of the many self-catering apartments and *residences* nearby.

SPORTS AND ACTIVITIES

All around Lake Garda – as well as lakes Idro and Ledro – there are horseriding stables and you can rent out canoes, mountain bikes and often windsurfing equipment at reasonable prices; tourist offices and their websites have details. The northern shore around **Riva**, **Arco** and **Torbole**, however, is the real hub for sporting activity. All prices below are approximate; check details directly or with local tourist offices.

WATERSPORTS

Top of the list is watersports, with a clutch of local outfits offering **windsurfing**: first-timers can get individual tuition (€45/hr) or there are group lessons at various grades (€70/3hr). If you're already proficient, you can rent for €60 a day. **Sailing** is also popular, with beginners' courses in a dinghy or catamaran (€70/2hr) and rental (€90/half-day, depending on the size of boat). Shop around: local operators include ⓦpierwindsurf.it, ⓦvascorenna.com, ⓦsailingdulac.com, ⓦsurfsegnana.it, ⓦsurflb.com and ⓦgscharter.com. You can **rent canoes** (€35/day for two people) at the Sabbioni beach in Riva.

CLIMBING, TREKKING AND CANYONING

With over a dozen good locations within easy reach of the lake, **canyoning** is a good bet (April–Oct only; half-day €40–65, full day €75–110; ⓦcanyonadv.com or ⓦcanyonadv.com). Several companies offer more traditional **Alpine activities** – free-climbing, ice-climbing, *via ferrata*, trekking and so on; check ⓦfriendsofarco.it, ⓦalpinguide.com and ⓦguidealpinearco .com for details.

PARAGLIDING

Paragliding – notably off Monte Baldo above Malcesine – is a spectacular way to get an eagle's-eye view of the lake. Check out ⓦtimetofly.net and ⓦparaglidingmalcesine.it.

4

ACCOMMODATION

Lido Blu Via Foci del Sarca 1 ☎0464 505 180, ⓦlidoblu .com. On an elongated spit of land at the mouth of the River Sarca, away from the traffic, this four-star hotel has some great beaches and the bright, fresh rooms are popular with families on holiday. Has its own windsurf school. Cut-price deals in the low season (open year-round). **€180**

Villa Verde Via Sarca Vecchio 15 ☎0464 505 274, ⓦhotel-villaverde.it. Decent, modern three-star in a peaceful setting also near the river, with its own pool and garden. No credit cards. **€90**

Malcesine

Occupying a headland backed by the slopes of Monte Baldo, the small lakefront village of **MALCESINE**, 14km south of Torbole, boasts a pretty, historic core overlooked by the battlements of a medieval castle: it is a picture-perfect backdrop for an Italian Lakes holiday – but hardly undiscovered. In season the lanes are packed with holiday-makers and it's a very popular choice for northern-European weddings.

Castello Scaligera

Via Castello • Daily 9.30am–7.30pm; Nov–March Sat & Sun 11am–4pm • €6

Malcesine's main sight is the thirteenth-century **Castello Scaligera**, built, like Sirmione's (see p.289), by the Della Scala family of Verona. Goethe was imprisoned here briefly in 1786, having been arrested on suspicion of being a spy: he'd been caught making sketches of the castle's towers, which still loom over the old village.

Monte Baldo

Cable car: March–Oct daily every 30min 8am–7pm • €19 return • ⓦfuniviadelbaldo.it

For a change of perspective and a breath of mountain air, head up **Monte Baldo**. There are well-marked trails up the mountain, or you can take the **cable car** (*funivia*), which rises more than 1600m in ten minutes. The trip alone is well worthwhile, with slowly revolving cable cars giving splendid views of the lake and mountains. At the top, footpaths let you explore the summit ridge.

There are several special trips a day for cyclists to transport their bikes to the top; you can **rent a mountain bike** at Bikexxxtreme, next to the cable car (☎045 740 0105) and make a panoramic descent down easy trails to the shore. Be prepared for queues in summer for walkers, and in winter for skiers.

ARRIVAL AND INFORMATION

MALCESINE

By bus The bus station is on the main lakeside road: the old village spreads out below.
Destinations Riva (approx hourly; 30min); Torri del Benaco (approx hourly; 35min); Verona (approx hourly; 1hr 45min).
By boat From the central square Piazza Statuto, stepped lanes head down to the old port and the *imbarcadero*. Car ferries cross to Limone and regular ferries leave for destinations all around the lake.

Tourist information The main tourist office is beside the bus station on the main road Via Gardesana 238 (Mon–Sat 10am–1pm & 2–6pm, Sun 10am–4pm; ☎045 740 0044, ⓦvisitgarda.com or ⓦtourism.verona.it), with a branch near the *imbarcadero* at Via Capitanato 8 (Mon–Sat 9am–1pm & 3–7pm; May–Oct also Sun 9am–1pm; ☎045 740 0837, ⓦmalcesinepiu.it).

ACCOMMODATION

Many hotels in Malcesine are block-booked by tour operators; many others insist on half-board and a three-night minimum stay in peak season around Easter and in summer. Most hotels close in winter from mid-October until Easter.

Aurora Piazza Matteotti 10 ☎045 740 0114, ⓦaurora -malcesine.com. Good, flexible budget option in the heart of the old lanes, with a/c. **€70**
Europa Via Gardesana 173 ☎045 740 0022, ⓦeuropa

-hotel.net. Sleek, contemporary interiors herald this chic four-star hotel just north of town on the lake side of the main road. It has its own gravel beach, pool, parking, spa and an excellent restaurant. Closed Nov–Feb. **€180**

EATING AND DRINKING

Most of central Malcesine's restaurants are pretty poor with slapdash service and spag bol the norm, although locations are often lovely. But choose carefully, or head out of the village centre, and you'll find some great cooking, service and atmosphere.

Al Corsaro Via Paina 17 ☎045 658 4064, ⓦalcorsaro.it. Contemporary styled restaurant concealed at the base of the castle walls, directly on its own patch of beach and out of sight from anywhere but the water. The cooking is based on freshly caught lake fish, done a thousand different ways: this is a charming, relaxed, modern setting in which to enjoy a refined meal to remember. Prices around €40 a head. Mon– Fri 7–10.30pm, Sat & Sun 12.30–3pm & 7–10.30pm.
La Pace Via Castello 1, Port Vecchio ☎045 740 0057, ⓦvecchiamalcesine.com. A pretty spot at the foot of

the castle by the old port, good for a cosy meal on cooler days and with lots of tables outside for the summer. A plate of tasty pasta will set you back around €10. Daily 10am–10.30pm; closed Nov & Dec.
Speck Stube Via Navene Vecchia 139 ☎045 740 1177. In a lovely rustic setting among olive groves, hearty portions of spit roast meat are served at wooden trestle tables and washed down by beer. Unusually the kitchen is open daily from noon to midnight. Daily noon–11pm; closed Nov–Feb.

Brenzone

South of Malcesine, the elongated community of **BRENZONE** encompasses several lakeside villages dotted along 5km of shoreline, as well as a clutch of hamlets clinging to the mountainsides above. The tourist office in the waterfront hamlet of Porto has maps and information about **walking and mountain biking** in the hills – including Path 33, which climbs (in about 2hr 15min) from just above Porto on a steep, scenic forest trail to **Prada Alta**, a village at 1000m. Other paths lead to the ruins of a Roman villa, a pair of eleventh-century churches and the wonderfully atmospheric abandoned medieval hamlet of Campo.

A short way south of Porto lies the centre of Brenzone, **Magugnano**, in reality no more than a little cluster of alleyways by the water. It's a perfect spot for a quiet meal: gaze across the lake and watch as the ferries glide into the lake barely 10m away. A kilometre or more south, you come to **Castelletto**, with two more recommended restaurants.

Hotel Brenzone Directly opposite the imbarcadero ☎045 742 0388, ⓦhotelbrenzone.com. Built in 1911 and still with an appealingly old-fashioned atmosphere to its public rooms; the bedrooms have been modernized and there's a genuine welcome from the Brighenti family who run it. Closed mid-Oct to mid-April. **€110**
Locanda San Marco Piazza S. Marco 22, Pai di Sopra ☎045 726 0004, ⓦlocandasanmarco.it. In this little village

above the lake, among hiking and cycling trails, this decent family-run inn has recently renovated all its simple rooms. There's a small pool and restaurant serving local fare too. **€80**
Santa Maria Via Benaco 14 ☎045 742 0555, ⓦbertoncellihotels.it. Lovely lakeside position for this simple family-run three-star. Rooms are standard but comfortable, many with balconies, and there's a covered pool and small garden. **€100**

EATING AND DRINKING

Al Fassa Via Nascimbeni 13, Castelletto ☎045 743 0319. Highly recommended restaurant with a delightful lakeside terrace serving very tasty lake fish combinations. The home-made gnocchi is served with creative combinations of fish and seasonal vegetables. There's a good wine list too. Around €35 a head. 12.30–2pm & 7–11pm; closed Tues in winter.

Al Sole Via Imbarcadero, Castelletto ☎045 659 9035. These waterside tables overlooking the little port and sheltered from the road noise are the perfect place to enjoy crispy pizzas (around €10) straight from the wood-fired oven. 12.30–2.30pm & 7.30–11pm; closed Wed in winter.

Torri del Benaco

TORRI DEL BENACO, 13km south of Brenzone, is one of the prettiest of the villages on this side of the lake. Part of its tenth-century walls still stand, notably the West Tower of the lakefront castle, which was overhauled in 1383 by the Della Scala of Verona. During the following centuries, Torri was a financial centre, controlling trade and imposing customs duties.

Torri's old centre – which consists of one long cobbled street, **Corso Dante**, crisscrossed with tunnelling alleyways and lined with mellow stone *palazzi* – is quiet and appealing. The swallowtail battlements of the **Castello Scaligero** stand guard over the quaint harbour at one end of the village, while there's a green park and shingle beach at the northern end.

Castello Scaligero

Daily 9.30am–12.30pm & 2.30–6pm • €5 • ⓦmuseodelcastelloditorridelbenaco.it

These days the castle buildings are home to an engaging display of local fishing and olive-oil making traditions as well as information on prehistoric rock carvings in the area (see box below).

The castle also boasts one of the oldest working *limonaie*, or glasshouses on the lake, dating from 1760, built to protect the lemon trees inside during cold weather (see box, p.288).

ARRIVAL AND INFORMATION **TORRI DEL BENACO**

By bus Buses pull in at the bus stop on the main road, Via Gardesana, near the tourist office.
Destinations Malcesine (approx hourly; 35min); Riva (approx hourly; 1hr); Verona (approx hourly; 1hr 15min).

By car If you're driving, park in the pay-and-display (free in winter) by the castle walls: the old centre is off-limits to cars.
By boat Regular services cover points across the lake and

ANCIENT ROCK CARVINGS

In 1964, **rock carvings** dating back to the Bronze Age around 1500 BC were discovered in the hills between Torri and San Vigilio. Since then 250 rocks with over 3000 figures have been discovered, with more being unearthed all the time. The carvings often represent warriors, sometimes on horseback, as well as fishermen, boats and religious worship.

A 7km walk from Torri del Benaco (or slightly longer from Garda) takes you through oak woods on the slopes of hills behind the lake to see some of the carvings in situ. Ask at the tourist office for details.

car ferries cross to Toscalano-Maderno throughout the year (see box, p.259).

Tourist office Via F.lli Lavanda 3 – the wooden building on the main road by the main car park south of the village

(June–Aug daily 9am–1pm & 3–7pm; otherwise restricted hours; ☏ 045 722 5120, ⊛ infotorri.it). Has information on walks into the hills behind including to Bronze Age rock carvings 7km away.

ACCOMMODATION

Del Porto Lungolago Barbarani ☏ 045 722 5051, ⊛ hoteldelportotorri.com. Stylish waterfront rooms with parquet flooring and swish bathrooms in the heart of the village. Also four attractive apartments in a villa with garden and pool away from the water. **€270**

Gardesana Piazza Calderini 20 ☏ 045 722 5411, ⊛ hotel-gardesana.com. In an unbeatable location, the harbourside classic *Gardesana* has hosted the likes of Churchill, Maria Callas, Laurence Olivier and Vivien Leigh.

The three-star rooms are comfortable and you can choose between a view of the harbour and castle or the lake (with or without a balcony). **€140**

★ **Garni Onda** Via per Albisano 28 ☏ 045 722 5895, ⊛ garnionda.com. Budget hotel 100m up from the centre. Each simple but spotlessly clean room has its own balcony or terrace and the friendly owners provide a first-rate breakfast and lots of local knowledge on hikes, bike rides and local restaurants. Closed Nov–Feb. **€78**

EATING AND DRINKING

Gardesana Piazza Calderini 20 ☏ 045 722 5411. You could hardly invent a more romantic setting for a meal (book for a table at the railing). Lake fish specials are served in a refined but not stuffy ambience, with care taken over presentation and service. Daily 12.30–2.30pm & 7–10.30pm.

★ **Trattoria agli Olivi** Via Valmagra 7 ☏ 045 722 5483, ⊛ agliolivi.com. Some of the tastiest food in the area is served at bargain prices in this lovely restaurant

with a splendid lake-view terrace among the olive groves on the hillside above town. Daily 12.30–2.30pm & 7–10.30pm.

Trattoria Bell'Arrivo Piazza Calderini 10 ☏ 045 629 9028. A small, cosy restaurant with unusually good food at very reasonable prices. There are tables outside under vines for when the weather is good. Tues–Sun 12.30–2.30pm & 7–10.30pm.

Punta San Vigilio

Four kilometres south of Torri, **PUNTA SAN VIGILIO** is a private promontory set back from the main road. There is an attractive, well-equipped pay beach, the **Parco Baia delle Sirene** (April Sat & Sun 10am–7pm, €5; May to mid-June daily 10am–8pm, €8, or €5 after 3pm; mid-June to mid-Sept daily 9.30am–8pm, €11, or €8 after 2.30pm, or €5 after 4.30pm; ⊛ parcobaiadellesirene.it) plus a historic **hotel** in a sixteenth-century villa and **taverna** (see below) surrounded by olive and citrus groves.

ACCOMMODATION AND EATING   PUNTA SAN VIGILIO

Locanda San Vigilio Punta San Vigilio ☏ 045 725 6688, ⊛ locanda-sanvigilio.it. An impossibly romantic hotel, a favourite with Churchill and various other heads of state, with just seven doubles and a handful of suites in a beautiful lakeside location amid olive groves and cyprus trees. **€550**

Taverna San Vigilio Punta San Vigilio ☏ 045 725

6688, ⊛ locanda-sanvigilio.it. This tiny horseshoe harbour beside the hotel is the stuff holiday memories are made of. Prices are high for the day-long snacks but a sundowner prosecco or a morning coffee is worth every penny. On summer evenings there is a buffet laid out in the olive groves by the side. Open to the public. 9am–10pm; closed Sun eve & Dec–Feb.

Bardolino

About 4km south of Punta San Vigilio is the spruce resort of **BARDOLINO**, home of light, red Bardolino wine. The town is at its most animated in mid-September during the bibulous **Festa dell'Uva**; otherwise, strolling the lush palm- and pine-shaded promenade is the main activity. On Thursdays the promenade is taken over by the weekly market.

If you have your own transport, grab a map from the tourist office and head off along the **Strada del Bardolino** (⊛ stradadelbardolino.com) to enjoy the inland countryside, taking in wineries and olive-oil producers on the way.

ARRIVAL AND INFORMATION

By boat Bardolino is well linked with towns and villages up and down the lake with both regular and fast ferry services (see p.259).

By bus The #62/#64 bus runs from Verona to Riva del Garda throughout the year stopping at Bardolino en route.

Destinations Malcesine (hourly; 50min); Peschiera (hourly; 25min); Riva (6 daily;1hr 15min); Torri del Benaco (hourly; 15min); Verona (6 daily; 1hr 5min).

Tourist office Piazzale Aldo Moro (9am–1pm & 3–7pm; ☎045 721 0078, ⓦ tourism.verona.it).

ACCOMMODATION AND EATING

Biri Via Solferino 13 ☎045 721 0873. Good-value local specialities are served in this little backstreet restaurant, washed down with quality local wines. Try the *tagliata di manzo al rosmarino* (roast fillet of beef in rosemary) for a change from lake fish. Tues–Sun 12.30–2.30pm & 7–10.30pm.

Cà Castellani Strada Galeazzo 1 ☎045 721 1698, ⓦ agriturismocastellani.com. Among vineyards 2km from the lake, this attractive agriturismo has a handful of double rooms and bright modern apartments (sleeping 2–7) with a large garden and pool. €80

Lazise

A further 5km south of Bardolino, the walled village of **LAZISE** was once a major port and retains a photogenic **castle** and, on the harbour, an arcaded medieval **customs house**. Nowadays the village is lined with cafés, pizzerias and holiday-makers, but retains an appealing character, with some picturesque corners. Wednesday sees the main piazzas bustling with the weekly market. Out of season, when it reverts to being a sleepy lakeside village, the allure is stronger still.

ARRIVAL AND INFORMATION

By boat The *imbarcadero* is just by the little harbour at the pedestrianized centre of the walled village. Boats head for other resorts around the southern part of the lake; the service is greatly reduced in winter (see p.259).

By bus Lazise is on the main bus route from Verona to Riva del Garda, which runs throughout the year.

Destinations Malcesine (hourly; 1hr); Peschiera (hourly; 15min); Riva (6 daily; 1hr 25min); Torri del Benaco (hourly; 25min); Verona (6 daily; 55min).

Tourist office Via Francesco Fontana 14 (daily 9am–1pm & 3–7pm; ☎045 758 0114, ⓦ tourism.verona.it).

Trentino-Alto Adige

ALPE DI SIUSI

5

Trentino-Alto Adige

Draped across the high Alps, where Italy, Austria and Switzerland collide and their cultures blur, Italy's northernmost region is a major draw for holiday-makers who mostly come for winter skiing, summer hiking and tranquil year-round vistas. However, in past times this region was far from today's peaceful vacation paradise; a string of castles along the Adige (Etsch) valley bear witness to the cut and thrust of medieval politics, and World War I saw prolonged and ferocious fighting, with Italian and Austrian troops battling it out in the harsh conditions of the alpine ridges. Armies of brightly attired skiers and sturdily booted hikers have long since replaced the troops, invading the sunny slopes on ski and board or marching along one of the hundreds of dramatic trails that crisscross the landscape.

As its double-barrelled name suggests, the region is made up of two areas: **Trentino**, the southern part, is 98 percent Italian-speaking and the cuisine and architecture belong predominantly to the south rather than the Alps. By contrast, the mountainous terrain around Bolzano – known both as the Südtirol (South Tyrol) and **Alto Adige** – was only incorporated into Italy at the end of the First World War (see box, p.325). Here, onion-domed churches dot vineyards and forests, street signs are in German and Italian and the landscape is redolent of illustrations from the Brothers Grimm. German is the dominant tongue though immigrants from Italy's south rarely speak anything other than Italian. Both Trentino and Alto Adige enjoy autonomy from central government, along with one of the highest standards of living in Italy.

The region is dominated by the barren, jagged rock walls of the **Dolomites**. Some of the most eye-catching peaks in Europe, these vast massifs abound in myths and legends and have been eroded over the last 200 million years into a weird and wonderful array of needles, towers and pinnacles. In 2009 the range was added to the UNESCO World Natural Heritage List for their unique geology – they began life around 250 million years ago as a giant coral reef beneath the ancient Tethys Ocean – and for their diverse ecosystem abundant in rare flora and fauna. Numerous cable cars rising from the small resorts dotted around the region enable you to hike at 2000–3000m without needing anything beyond average fitness or expertise. The web of well-marked trails and detailed, locally sourced maps mean you can easily fashion a trip of any length from a gentle day-hike to a two-week trek.

If hiking gear and ski sticks make you shudder, views of this spectacular landscape can also be savoured from the comfort of luxurious spa hotels, offering first-rate regional cuisine and a unique selection of treatments from bathing in thermal water to elaborate "dry baths" involving lying swaddled in sheep's wool or mountain hay. Down

SKIING IN CANAZEI

Highlights

❶ Mountain refuges Bunk down in some of Central Europe's most isolated and vista-rich locations. **See p.309**

❷ MART Rovereto's museum of contemporary art is one of Italy's best, with an unmissable permanent collection and expertly curated temporary shows. **See p.315**

❸ Hiking in the Pale di San Martino One of the most spectacular areas in the Dolomites with a great choice of high-altitude trails. **See p.320**

❹ Skiing in Canazei A vast choice of slopes for intermediates – you could spend a week there and barely ski the same piste twice. **See p.324**

❺ Ice Man The star exhibit at Bolzano's Museo Archeologico is the incredibly well preserved "Ice Man", discovered in the Ötzaler Alps in 1991. **See p.327**

❻ Wine tasting along the Strada del Vino Follow the "Wine Road" through the Adige valley, sampling some of the region's best food and wine as you go. **See p.331**

❼ Messner Mountain Museum Learn about the colourful cultures of mountainous areas around the globe at the four branches of this intriguing and unique museum. **See p.335**

HIGHLIGHTS ARE MARKED ON THE MAP ON PP.306–307

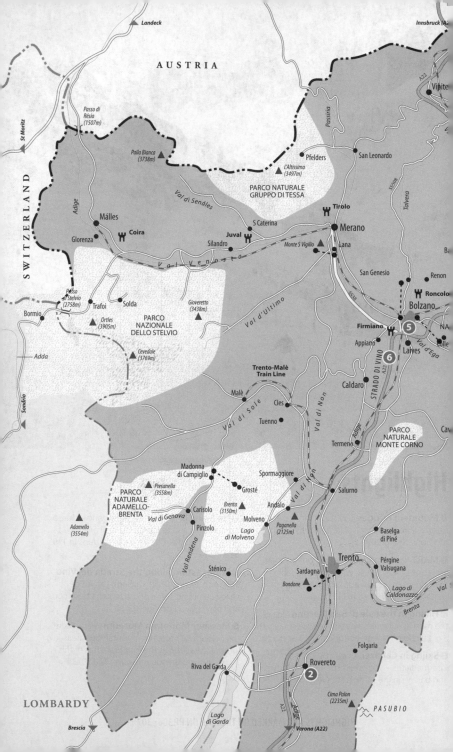

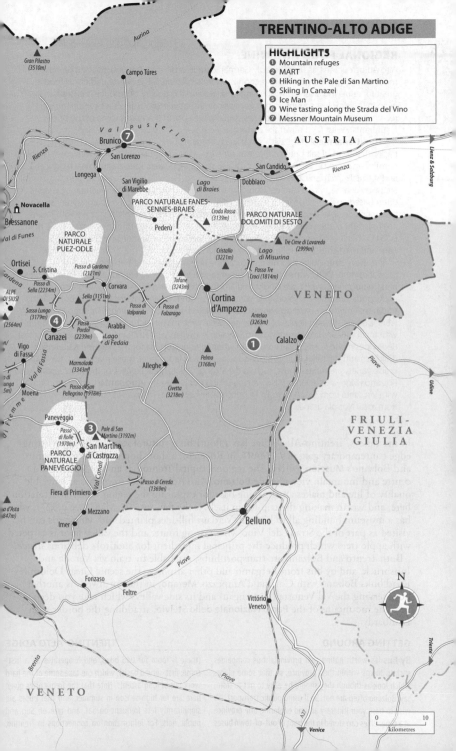

5

REGIONAL FOOD AND WINE

Alto Adige cuisine has unreservedly Germanic traditions, while Trentino cooking blends mountain influences with more recognizably Italian flavours. The hearty traditional food is great for refuelling after a day of hiking or skiing and the quality of produce is exceptional, even in the simplest mountain hut. For finer dining, adventurous chefs are reworking old recipes to fashion much lighter dishes, and it is well worth trying out some of the pricier restaurants we list for a new take on local specialities.

A **traditional meal** starts with some kind of salami (*lucanicche* in local dialect), often paper-thin slices of salt beef, or Tyrolean *canederli* – bread dumplings spiked with *speck* (smoked ham) often served in broth (*brodo*). You'll also see *strangolapreti* (bread and spinach gnocchi) and *schlutzkrapfen* (spinach-filled pasta) on the menu. Fresh lake and river fish, game and rabbit are popular as *secondi*, as are venison goulash or boiled cured pork with sauerkraut. Desserts are often based on apples, pears or plums, readily available from the local orchards. Other sweet treats include *apfel strudel*, *sachertorte* and *kaiserschmarren*, a scrambled pancake with raisins.

A highlight of the year for food- and wine-lovers is the autumn Törggelen season (see box, p.331), when everyone heads for the hills to sample the new vintage and snack on mountain ham and roast chestnuts, followed by a walk to work it all off.

Vines have been cultivated here since before Roman times, and Trentino-Alto Adige produces more **DOC wines** than any other region in Italy. Most famous are the Pinot Grigios and Chardonnays, which are bright and aromatic from being grown at high altitudes and in cool conditions. These also provide wine makers with the raw material for some outstanding traditional-method sparkling wines, often marketed under the spumante Trentino Classico label. Despite the excellence of the whites, local wine makers actually make more reds often with local varieties like Teroldego and Schiava (known as Vernatsch in German-speaking areas). Red wines made from Schiava are good when young: look out for the pale-red Kalterersee (Caldaro) and the fuller, fruitier St Magdalene (Santa Maddalena); those made from the Lagrein grape variety are more robust, such as the strong, dark Lagrein Dunkel, or the Kretzer rosé from Bolzano's vineyards at Gries. Also worth seeking out is the rare **vino santo** (not to be confused with *vin santo* from Tuscany) from Trentino's Valle dei Laghi – a luscious dessert wine made from local Nosiola grapes.

in the valleys, Trentino-Alto Adige has a flourishing **cultural scene**, with two cutting-edge contemporary galleries – **MART**, in Rovereto, a short hop by train from Trento, and Bolzano's **Museion** gallery. The regional capital **Trento** has an atmospheric old centre and mountain views, while **Bolzano**, Alto Adige's chief town, has an enviable quality of life and makes an engaging base for exploring the region. The star attraction here, and worth making the trip for in itself, is the famous "Ice Man" (see p.327), who has a museum building all to himself. Verdant hillsides planted with **vineyards** can be visited as part of the Strada del Vino wine-tasting route, and the valley floor is carpeted with apple trees which produce the principal ingredient for Südtirol's delicious *strudel*.

Both Trento and Bolzano are transport hubs, reachable by train via Verona and Innsbruck, and by bus from Bergamo and other airports. The scenic Great Dolomites Road links Bolzano with Cortina d'Ampezzo. **Merano**, in the northwest, is another hub, serving the Val Venosta (Vinschgau) and its side valleys which take you deep into the mountains of the **Parco Nazionale dello Stelvio**, straddling the border with Lombardy.

GETTING AROUND

By bus It's worth noting that provincial bus companies stick to towns within their province, so that some places which look as though they should be easy to get to from, say, Bolzano often are not. So if using public transport, it's wise to base your itinerary around exploring one province at a time. Bikes can stored in the boot of out-of-town buses (there is room for two bikes, and it operates on a first-come, first-served basis), which can take some of the hard work out of long ascents. Note that the frequencies given here are for high season in summer, and that buses are significantly less frequent on Sat, and rare on Sun and public hols. For information on connections in Trentino, visit ⓦ ttesercizio.it; in Alto Adige ⓦ sii.bz.it. Information on buses through the Dolomites around Cortina is available at ⓦ dolomitibus.it.

By train As throughout Italy, if there's a train, take it – this is definitely the way to go between Bolzano and Trento, served by frequent fast services, and to larger towns north of Bolzano. Cyclists can stow bikes on certain trains on the private Trento–Malè line (see p.313). For online timetables, go to ⓦ fsitaliane.it.

By car Scenic drives can be a great way of touring the region, but with steep ascents to high passes, erratic Italian drivers and slow-moving tour buses, life behind the wheel can be nerve-racking and frustrating. The switch backs and bucking stretches of tarmac are also very popular with motorbikers from across Europe, so watch those mirrors. If you're driving outside the summer months, be aware that many passes can remain closed until well after Easter. Approach roads all have signs indicating whether the pass is open, or you can call ☎0471 200 198 for information on road conditions. The Südtirol's official website, ⓦ south-tirol.com, also has winter road reports. Finally, note that the motorway between the Brenner Pass and Rovereto is a toll road.

ACTIVITIES

HIKING

This section of the Italian Alps offers some exhilarating hiking, often subject to snow, ice and scorching sun in the same day. There are plenty of opportunities for day-walks: routes are well established and well signposted, and there are suggestions in this chapter for walks in some stunning scenery that are within average capabilities. For more ambitious walking over a number of days, you might consider tackling one of the longer trails, known as *alte vie* (literally "high ways"). Four of these run north–south between the Val Pusteria (Pustertal) and the Veneto; four from the Val d'Isarco (Eisacktal) south; and two from Bolzano, with plenty of mountain huts along the way for meals and overnight accommodation. Some of the initial ascents are strenuous, but once you are up on the ridges the paths level out and afford stupendous views across the valleys and glaciers. Parts of the trails are exposed, or have snowfields across them, but there are usually detours you can take to avoid these.

RIFUGI

A network of mountain huts – *rifugi* (refuges) – allows you to stay at high altitude without having to dip down to the valley for meals or accommodation. Solidly constructed, usually two- or three-storey buildings, they provide dormitory accommodation (and often double or quad rooms if you book well ahead), meals and a bar. These days, most have hot showers. Blankets are provided, but you must bring your own sheet sleeping bag – if you don't have one, you can usually buy one at the hut for around €10. Run by enthusiastic and dedicated staff, *rifugi* are open from 20 June until late September, and many also operate in the skiing season; we've given opening periods as a guide, but these are still subject to weather conditions. If you're planning a long trek that relies on *rifugi* for accommodation, you should definitely call ahead; at the same time, you can check that the place isn't likely to be packed out by a large party – nobody is ever turned away, but overflow accommodation is either on a mattress in the bar or, *in extremis*, the hen house. If you are a member of the Club Alpino Italiano (ⓦ cai.it) the overnight rate at CAI-run *rifugi* is around €12; if not, expect to pay around €25, but unless you want to carry food with you, count on paying €40–50 for a bunk, breakfast and dinner – good value for the hearty home-cooking and local wine that are rustled up in some pretty remote locations. Emergency calls can be made from most *rifugi*; to call Soccorso Alpino (Alpine Rescue), dial ☎118. A directory of refuges is available at ⓦ trentinorifugi.com and ⓦ suedtirol-ferien.it.

FESTIVALS AND EVENTS

Wine-related festivities abound across the region with almost every village celebrating its vintages, harvest or related traditions – ask local tourist offices for details. However, the biggest wine bash, the **Festa in Vino** takes place in the sixteen towns along the South Tyrolean Wine Road from mid-May to mid-June, with tours, music, tastings and myriad other events. The month of events comes to a climax with the **Night of the Cellars** when wine producers throw open their doors on the final night. See ⓦ suedtiroler-weinstrasse.it for further details.

There are plenty of summer concerts, but possibly the best event is the **Suoni delle Dolomiti** series of jazz, folk and world music concerts by artists from all over the world: the concept is an original one – you hike (sometimes with the artists) to the chosen location – a wood, perhaps, or a rocky gully – and then listen to the concert. Performances are in the evenings and sometimes at dawn. Visit ⓦ isuonidelledolomiti.it for details of concerts, local accommodation, and walking times to venues. On a yuletide note, vast **Christmas markets** in the best Central European tradition take over the historic centres of Trento and Bolzano, attracting visitors from miles around.

5

> ### THE SALEWA CUBE
>
> Without doubt the Dolomites are prime climbing territory, but if you fancy a bit of practice beforehand, head to the mammoth **Salewa Cube** (Waltraud-Gebert-Deeg-Strasse ☎0471 188 6867, ⓦsalewa-cube.com) in Bolzano, Italy's largest climbing hall with 1850 square metres of indoor climbing walls, plus outdoor climbing and bouldering areas. A ticket valid all day costs €12 and buses #10A or #10B from Piazza Walther will get you near.

INFORMATION

Guides Gillian Price's *Trekking in the Dolomites* covers Alte Vie 1 and 2; her *Shorter Walks in the Dolomites* outlines forty day-walks of varying levels of difficulty. Italian or German speakers should get hold of a copy of Alpina Verlag's *Dolomite Alte Vie/Dolomiten Hohenwegel 1–10*, an extremely thorough companion to each of the trails available from larger tourist offices.

Maps To plan your own routes through the Dolomites, you'll need to invest in the Kompass 1:50,000 maps that are on sale in every bookshop and tourist office throughout the region. You can check which sheets you'll need at ⓦkompass.de before you leave. Paths are numbered and easy to follow – just look out for the red-and-white blaze on rocks and trees by the side of the path along the way. When figuring out how long hikes will take, bear in mind that an averagely fit person takes around three hours to ascend 1000m.

Websites Online, ⓦdolomiti.it is a good source of general information on the area.

SKIING

Trentino-Alto Adige is home to many of Italy's top ski resorts. Popular with families, and with a fairly laidback atmosphere, skiing is often not top priority – it's more a case of long lunches on a sunny terrace after a morning of piste-bashing. Italian tourist offices overseas, and the regional offices in Italy, have details of Settimane Bianche (White Weeks). These are bargain package deals offering full or half-board and a ski-pass, although be wary of deals very late in the season – the downside of all those south-facing slopes is that the snow deteriorates fast in the warmer spring weather. January and February are the best months to come; March can also be good, although by mid-April the winter season is over.

SELLA RONDA

The big attraction of skiing in the eastern Dolomites is that twelve different ski areas are linked, creating long circuits including the famous "**Sella Ronda**" which takes you around **Marmolada** (3342m). You can access all areas with the Dolomiti Superski pass (€215–269 for 7 days, depending on the season) giving use of 1220km of runs and 450 cable cars and chair lifts (log on to ⓦdolomitisuperski.com for details and to buy online). Corvara is the main resort on the Sella Ronda; it is popular with foodies and families; the slopes will appeal mainly to intermediates, but there are steeper runs at Arabba to challenge advanced skiers. To help decide which resort to choose, check out details of chair lifts, altitude and length of runs on the regional tourist office websites ⓦsouth-tirol.com and ⓦtrentino.to.

has a huge ski area ideal for intermediates. The resorts of the Val Gardena (Ortisei, Santa Cristina and Selva) also offer plenty of variety in terms of places to eat, stay and ski. Beginners and intermediates can cruise the slopes in beautiful surroundings at the fashionable resort of Cortina d'Ampezzo, although the ski area is fragmented and much of it only accessible by bus from town.

SUMMER SKIING

Note that there's also summer skiing from June to November on glaciers accessible from the Val Senales, the Stelvio Pass, and the inexpensive resort at the Passo Tonale (which links Trentino with Lombardy), although in these days of climate change this is dependent on the state of the glaciers and there being a good dump of snow the winter before.

OTHER RESORTS

Madonna di Campiglio is popular with wealthy Italian families as it has a good sun and snow record (it's a relatively high resort for Italy) and a lively nightlife. Canazei

WEATHER INFORMATION

From December onwards, get the latest on snow conditions in Trentino at ⓦmeteotrentino.it. Otherwise check the national winter weather website ⓦmeteomont.net.

Trento and around

Just three hours from Venice by train, and a short hop from Verona, **TRENTO** makes a good base for exploring the southern reaches of the region, not least because of its bus services into the Dolomites. Overshadowed by Monte Bedone just 13km away, the town is beautifully situated, encircled by mountains and exuding an easy-going pace of life. Visitors inevitably gravitate to the central, café-lined Piazza del Duomo, all fading frescoes and cobblestones, with fashionable shops, boutiques and restaurants occupying the narrow streets that lead off it. Mammoth, moss-covered city walls lurk beyond.

Brief history

Trento was known as Tridentum to the Romans, a name celebrated by the eighteenth-century Neptune fountain in the central **Piazza del Duomo**. From the tenth to the eighteenth centuries, the city was a powerful bishopric ruled by a dynasty of princes; it was the venue of the Council of Trent between 1545 and 1563, when the Catholic Church, threatened by the Reformation in northern Europe, met to plan its counterattack. Later, throughout the nineteenth century, ownership of the city, which remained in Austrian hands, was hotly contested, and it only became properly part of Italy in 1919, following World War I.

The Duomo

Piazza del Duomo • Daily 6.30am–noon & 2.30–8pm • Free **Crypt** Mon–Sat 10am–noon, 2.30–5.30pm • €1.50

The three most significant meetings of the Council of Trent – convened to confront the growth of Protestantism and to establish the so-called Counter-Reformation – took

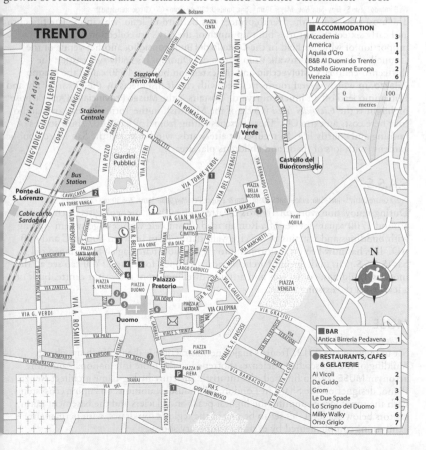

5

place in the **Duomo** between 1545 and 1563. The building itself was begun in the thirteenth century, but wasn't completed until the sixteenth. Inside, an enormous, carved marble *baldachino*, held over the altar by four chunky Baroque barley-twist columns, is a replica of the one in St Peter's, Rome. However, by far the most interesting part of the building lies beneath the cathedral, where a **medieval crypt** and foundations of an early Christian basilica built over the tomb of St Vigilio, the third bishop of Trento, were discovered in 1977.

Museo Diocesano Tridentino

Piazza del Duomo 18 • Daily except Tues: June–Sept 9.30am–12.30pm & 2.30–6pm; Oct–May 9.30am–12.30pm & 2–5.30pm • €4 • ⓦ museodiocesanotridentino.it

Next to the Duomo, the **Museo Diocesano Tridentino**, housed in the Palazzo Pretorio, includes large annotated paintings of the sessions of the Council of Trent and some carved altarpieces from the church of San Zeno in the Val di Non. The building is appealing in itself, too, with its fishtail battlements, heavy studded doors and a view from the upper storey of the frescoed palaces around the square.

Castello del Buonconsiglio

Via Bernardo Clesio 5 • Tues–Sun: Nov–May 9.30am–5pm; June–Oct 10am–6pm • €8 • ⓦ buonconsiglio.it

The most powerful of the Trento princes was Bernardo Clesio, who in the late fifteenth and early sixteenth centuries built up much of the city's art collection, a good proportion of which is held in the **Castello del Buonconsiglio**, another venue of the Council of Trent, a short walk from Piazza del Duomo. It's really two castles: the thirteenth-century **Castelvecchio** and the extension built in 1530 called the **Magno Palazzo**, in which several rooms frescoed with classical subjects by the Dossi family and Romanino lead off an inner courtyard. Upstairs is the **Museo Provinciale d'Arte**, whose highlight is the *Ciclo dei Mesi* (Cycle of the Months), in the Torre d'Aquila (the audio tour here costs an extra €1). These frescoes dating from 1391 to 1407 show scenes of farming and courtly life. To recuperate afterwards, wind down in the San Marco public gardens (with lots of shade and children's play areas).

S.A.S.S.

Piazza Cesare Battisti • Tues–Sun: June–Sept 9.30am–1pm & 2–6pm; Oct–May 9am–1pm & 2–5.30pm • €2.50

During renovation work on Trento's theatre in the 1990s, archeologists discovered around 1700 square metres of a Roman road – complete with sewage system – along with buildings and remains of the city walls dating from between 1000 BC and 400 AD. This has now been transformed into the Spazio Archeologico Sotterraneo del Sas (**S.A.S.S.**), an underground archeological area open for visitors. You can see all the mosaics, buildings, courtyards and artisans' dwellings from the visitor centre, built on a level with the existing road.

MUSE

Via Calepina 14 • ☎ 0461 270 311

Set to open in late 2012, Trento's major new attraction is the unflinchingly brash building of the Museo delle Scienze, shortened to the more international-sounding acronym **MUSE**. When finished, the futuristic structure by big-name architect Renzo Piano, designer of The Shard in London, will house exhibitions on Alpine ecosystems, with the top floors examining the highest peaks and glaciers and the basement taking visitors below sea level. It's set to be one of the region's top draws, with permanent exhibitions complemented by exciting temporary shows.

ARRIVAL AND DEPARTURE

By train Trento's main train station is at Piazza Dante and Via Pozzo. The separate station belonging to the privately run Trento–Malè railway for the Val di Non is on Via Dogana 2, just beyond the train station (follow platform 1 for 100m heading north).

Destinations Bologna (8 daily; 2hr–3hr); Bolzano (every 20–30min; 30–50min); Bressanone (8 daily; 1hr 10min, or change in Bolzano); Malè (at least hourly; 1hr 30min); Rovereto (at least hourly; 15min); Venice (at least hourly; 2hr 30min–3hr); Verona (2 hourly; 1hr 20min).

By bus The bus station is almost next door to the train station.

Destinations Canazei (4 daily; 2hr 45min); Madonna di Campiglio (4 daily, more in winter; 2hr 8min); Molveno (4 daily, train and bus; change at Mezzolombardo; 1hr 30min); Predazzo (7 daily; 1hr 51min); San Martino di Castrozza (4 daily, bus and train connection; 3hr); Vigo di Fassa (4 daily; 2hr 20min).

INFORMATION AND GETTING AROUND

By bike Trento's cycle path network is excellent, and with free bike rental if you purchase a Trento Card, it's well worth exploring as an alternative to crowded buses and cable cars.

Taxis Radiotaxi, Via Degasperi 27 ☎ 0461 930 002.

Tourist office The tourist office, close to the main train station at Via Manci 2 (daily 9am–7pm; ☎ 0461 216 000,

ⓦ apt.trento.it), stocks *Trentino Mese* (€2), the city's monthly listings guide and sells the extremely useful Trento Card (€10 for 24hr, €15 for 48hr) offering free city transport and admission to many museums.

Websites The regional information website (ⓦ visittrentino .it) has details on mountain refuges, transport, hiking, skiing and agriturismo accommodation.

ACCOMMODATION

Albergo Accademia Vicolo Colico 4 ☎ 0461 233 600, ⓦ accademiahotel.it. A short walk from the train station, this professionally run hotel in a fifteenth-century building enjoys a quiet location. The forty well-maintained rooms have simple, uncluttered design, small bathrooms and wi-fi (€3/day); breakfast is taken in the wonderfully arching dining room. Guests also have access to a relaxing lounge, a secluded garden and a library with free wi-fi. **€152**

Aquila d'Oro Via Belenzani 76 ☎ 0461 986 282, ⓦ aquiladoro.it. Contemporary rooms each featuring a wall-to-ceiling photo, occupying the six storeys of an old pink townhouse a stone's throw from the Duomo. Every storey has a Junior Suite (each with a huge bathroom and romantic sauna lit with a constellation of tiny star-like lights), a standard room (small bathroom with *bisazza*-mosaic-walled showers) and a generously proportioned single with a double bed. **€170**

B&B Al Duomo di Trento Via Belenzani 47 ☎ 0461 261 524, ⓦ bebalduomoditrento.it. The three generously cut doubles at this small B&B, a few paces from the cathedral, are quite stylishly fitted out and all en suite. There's also a convivial

lounge and a library, and wi-fi is free throughout. **€100**

Hotel America Via Torre Verde 52 ☎ 0461 983 010, ⓦ hotelamerica.it. The personal, attentive service, enthusiastic staff and lively bar make this one of Trento's better options. All recently renovated, the 67 pastel-hued rooms here are very comfortable, and around half come with baths. The hotel also has sixteen mini serviced apartments (from €385/wk) in a separate annexe with cooking facilities. Free wi-fi in rooms but parking is €5/day. **€112**

Ostello Giovane Europa Via Torre Vanga 9 ☎ 0461 263 484. Busy hostel near the train station popular with students in term time (facilities include a study as well as a laundry and TV room). Four- to six-bed rooms, plus singles, doubles and triples attract an eclectic mix of solo travellers, young workers, families and budget-minded couples. Dorms **€18.50**, doubles **€40**

Venezia Piazza del Duomo 45 ☎ 0461 234 559, ⓦ hotelveneziatn.it. Spread over two buildings, rooms are whitewashed and spartan but who cares when some have views of the cathedral and you're in such a central location. Staff are friendly and there's free wi-fi. **€78**

EATING, DRINKING AND NIGHTLIFE

You'll eat well in Trento and the surrounding area, as the unfussy local specialities abound in flavour. Foodies might consider a winter visit as, from late November until Christmas, hundreds of food and craft stalls fill the streets to celebrate the feast of St Lucy. If you're up for a bit of local wine tasting, head out to the *cantine* in the suburbs and villages around Trento, all marked on the tourist office map.

Ai Vicoli Piazza S. Verzeri 1 ☎ 0461 260 673. A lovely setting on a tiny piazza close to the Duomo, this distinctive place serves up dishes that skilfully combine tradition and innovation. The menu, divided into fish and meat, changes with the seasons but if they're on, try the beef fillet with

black truffles (€22) or *sformatino* (like a smooth mousse) of corn and fontina cheese with local black truffles (€15). Delectable gnocchi served with black truffles and butter (€13), and the typical mountain dish of *carne salada* (cured beef) sliced thin and tossed in a pan, with beans and onions are other dishes to look out for. Mon–Sat 11.30am–2pm & 7–10.30pm.

Antica Birreria Pedavena Piazza Fiera 13 ☎ 0461 986 255, ⓦ birreriapedavena.com. The most tourist-friendly place in town, this mammoth *birreria*, built around two oversize brewing vats in polished copper, pipes three kinds of house-brewed beer (dark, light and *weiss*) as well as offering huge portions of hearty food. The *piatto pedavena* with goulash, pork, *wurstel*, *canederli*, sauerkraut and polenta (€11.50) is a good way to sample the most famous Trento dishes, or you could try the filling goulash with polenta (€8). Budget-minded diners have simple pasta dishes (€6) and pizzas (from €5) to choose from. Mon, Wed & Thurs 9am–12.30am, Fri & Sat 9am–1am, Sun 9am–midnight.

Da Guido Via Marchetti 9 ☎ 0461 262 418, ⓦ osteria daguido.com. Post modern styling (violet, lime and magenta suede upholstery, a blue neon bar, and state-of-the-art flower arrangements) in a seventeenth-century *palazzo* marvellously set in the San Marco gardens near the Palazzo Buonconsiglio. The menu is seasonal and pretty traditional, with Trento-style *strangolapreti* (€10), *canederli* with goulash (€8) and *zander* in lemon batter (€16). Outdoor eating in summer – ideal if you have kids as they can run free and play between courses. Tues–Sun noon–2.30pm & 7–10.30pm.

★ **Grom** Piazza del Duomo 27. The queues are long at this branch of the northern-Italian ice-cream chain, committed to using seasonal and often organic ingredients. The ice cream is "turned" before every serving and flavours change from month to month. Daily 11am–11pm.

Le Due Spade Via Don Arcangelo Rizzi 11 ☎ 0461 234 343, ⓦ leduespade.com. The atmospheric wood-panelled interior of this first-rate *osteria* is almost as much a reason to come as the Michelin-starred food. The €25 lunch menu is a real bargain for this standard;

otherwise the menu is divided into "sea" and "mountains" and obviously it's the Alpine victuals most come for. Imaginative dishes include cocoa-bean-coated loin of lamb in foie gras sauce (€22) and loin of deer cooked in white spruce buds (€18). Mon 7–10pm, Tues–Sat noon–2.30pm & 7–10pm.

Lo Scrigno del Duomo Piazza del Duomo 29 ☎ 0461 220 030, ⓦ scrignodelduomo.com. Elegant wine bar (and Michelin-starred restaurant) right opposite the Duomo, serving up some highly creative, delicious and pretty expensive dishes in a gorgeous *palazzo* with frescoed beams. The restaurant has two menus which change every three weeks – meat, *Terra* (€65), and fish, *Mare* (€75). You can either go for the full menus, select a couple of courses, or mix and match between the two. In the wine bar food is more simple and prices are more reasonable, but the quality still high. 12.30–2pm & 7.30–10pm, closed Mon & Sat dinner.

Milky Walky Via Garibaldi 27 ☎ 0461 233 160, ⓦ milkywalky.com. Just steps from the Duomo, this tunnel-shaped café serves up salads, soups, milkshakes, pastas and couscous dishes in a trendy space daubed in retro shades of orange, lime green and brown. No dish is over €7 and organic ingredients are used wherever possible. Mon–Wed 11.30am–7.30pm, Thurs–Sat 11.30am–11pm.

Orso Grigio Via degli Orti 19 ☎ 0461 984 400, ⓦ orsogrigiotrento.com. Relaxed, welcoming place where you can eat inside or out under a canopy. Feast on fabulous vegetables *sott'olio* (€3) or a *carpaccio di carne salada* (cured beef, €8) followed by local specialities such as *rufioi* (€9), a kind of handmade ravioli stuffed with Savoy cabbage and served with melted butter and parmesan, or, in season, a soup of porcini mushrooms (€10). *Secondi* include polenta with local *finferli* mushrooms and cheese (€15) or, for the unsentimental, a grilled *filleto di puledro* (€15) – young horse. Mon–Sat noon–2.30pm & 7.30–10.30pm.

DIRECTORY

Doctor Guardia Medica, Via Malta 4 (☎ 0461 915 809), offers out-of-hours (Mon–Fri 8pm–8am, and all weekend) medical service.

Hospitals In an emergency, call ☎ 118. Casualty ☎ 0461 903 111 at the Ospedale Santa Chiara, Largo Medaglie d'Oro 9.

Internet Olimpia, Via Belenzani 33 (€5/hr).

Markets Mon–Sat mornings, food in Piazza Vittoria; Thurs

mornings, weekly market in the historic centre; second Sat of month (except Jan & Aug), flea market in Piazza Garzetti.

Pharmacies Dall'Armi, Piazza del Duomo 10; Madonna, Via Manci 42; S. Chiara, Via S. Croce 57.

Police Via Maccani 148 ☎ 0461 889 111.

Post office Piazza A. Vittoria 20 ☎ 0461 275 311. Mon–Fri 8.30am–6.30pm, Sat 8am–12.30pm.

Public toilets Via Belenzani; €0.50.

Around Trento

The city is linked via the grander Valle dell Adige cycle path to Bolzano to the north and Verona to the south, with many charming towns and villages along either route.

A cable car runs from the San Lorenzo bridge, near Trento's bus station (every 15–30min until 10pm; €9), to the lower slopes of the towering Monte Bondone, from where you get a wonderful view.

Museo degli Usi e Costumi della Gente Trentina (MUCGT)

Via Mach 2, San Michelle all'Adige • Tues–Sat 9am–12.30pm & 2.30–6pm • €5 • ⓦ museosanmichele.it• Easily reachable by train from
Trento (heading north and alighting at Mezzocorona) or via the Adige cycle path

An enjoyable half-day trip from the city, the **Museo degli Usi e Costumi della Gente Trentina** – or **MUCGT** – at **SAN MICHELE ALL'ADIGE**, 15km northeast of Trento, is one of the largest of its kind in Europe. Exhibits range from re-creations of village houses (complete with muddy boots drying by the stove) to displays on hunting, grazing and wine making; the museum gives a real flavour of what life in Trentino was like until the twentieth century.

Rovereto

Some 20km to the south of Trento and a mere 13km from Lago di Garda, **ROVERETO** is a small town with one stellar attraction – the Museo di Arte Moderna e Contemporanea (MART). This outstanding gallery with world-class exhibitions is one of Trentino's unmissable experiences, but Rovereto itself, with its stylish *palazzi* containing university faculties and a young feel on the streets, is worth the other half of the day that's left after a visit.

Easily accessible from Verona, Trento and Bolzano, Rovereto is best tackled as a day-trip.

MART

Corso Bettini 43 • Tues–Sun 10am–6pm, Fri late opening until 9pm • €11 • ⓦ mart.trento.it

Italy's largest modern-art museum, the **Museo di Arte Moderna e Contemporanea (MART)** was designed by Mario Botta and opened in December 2002. The spectacular building, with spacious galleries wrapping themselves around a central circular atrium flooded with light, is impressive enough before you view the art inside. Skilfully curated, themed exhibitions use works loaned from institutions and individuals around the world as well as drawing on the gallery's collection of 30,000 paintings, design pieces and sculptures by big-hitting names including Lichtenstein, Rauschenberg and Warhol (as well as lesser-known locals such as Italian Futurist Fortunato Depero, Giorgio de Chirico and Giorgio Morandi). At least four large shows run at any one time and previous installations have covered Postmodernism, futuristic car design, Schiele, Klimt and Kokoschka, and *Alice in Wonderland* in art and design. Allow at least three hours to see everything.

Casa d'Arte Futurista Depero

Via della Terra 53 • Tues–Sun 10am–6pm • €7

Laid out by Depero himself a year before his death in 1960 this small branch of MART is a worthwhile add-on to the main building. The space shows off his large cloth collages, tapestries, furniture and other design pieces to great effect as well as hosting themed exhibitions.

ARRIVAL AND INFORMATION

ROVERETO

By train Rovereto's train station is located at the southern end of Corso Rosmini, with MART and the tourist office at the northern end. Buses #1, #2, #3, #4 and #6 make the run.

Destinations Trento (at least hourly; 15min); Bolzano (at least hourly; 1hr); Venice (at least hourly; 2–3hr, change in Verona); Verona (2 hourly; 1hr).

Tourist office Corso Rosmini 6 (daily 9am–1pm and 2–6pm Mon–Sat; ☏ 0464 430 363, ⓦ visitrovereto.it).

5

The Dolomiti di Brenta

Northwest of Trento lies a mountain range with a separate identity from the more famous Dolomitic peaks to the east. With their saw-toothed peaks and glaciers, the **Dolomiti di Brenta** have a rougher character than, say, the Catinaccio/Rosengarten range in the main Dolomites – and their trails are far less well-trodden. While they are steep, few peaks rise above 3000m, and the paths are easy to follow. It should be said, though, that the walking is strenuous. Climbers come here for the towers of **Cima Tosa** and **Cima Brenta**, accessible by *vie ferrate* – iron "ladders" knocked into the rock (see below). If you are looking for easier strolls, **Val Genova** has a gentler beauty, with a woodland path taking you past a number of waterfalls cascading down the mountainside.

The range is circled by a good but slow and winding road, the southern half of which passes through the quiet lake resort of **Molveno**. The Trento-to-Madonna di Campiglio road takes you past the frescoed churches and wooded valleys of the Valle Rendena before arriving at **Campiglio** itself, the best base for skiing in the area, and a transport hub for walkers and climbers. The northern half of the Brenta mountains is bounded by the Val di Non and the Val di Sole, both served by the privately run Trento–Malè railway.

Pinzolo and the Val Genova

Buses from Trento to Madonna di Campiglio skirt Monte Bondone and wind their way past a series of patchy hills and villages, passing Lago di Toblino. From here, the road continues west, turning into the Valle Rendena at Tione di Trento, where a more remote landscape of pasture and forest begins. Two settlements worth jumping off the bus for are the ski village of **PINZOLO** and **CARISOLO**, which lie just a couple of kilometres apart on the main road, for their well-preserved sixteenth-century frescoes of the *danse macabre*.

VIE FERRATE

Vie ferrate (literally "iron ways") are an Italian phenomenon, consisting of fixed metal ladders, pegs and cables that climbers clip onto with karabiners, making otherwise difficult (or downright impossible) routes accessible. Many *vie ferrate* began life as far back as the late nineteenth century as mountaineering took off as a sport in Europe; Alpini troops put others in place during World War I to assist the climbs that were a matter of survival for the soldiers fighting in the mountains. In the decades since then, volunteers from local Club Alpino Italiano groups have created many more.

Kompass maps show *vie ferrate* as a line of little black dots or crosses, so you can easily avoid them – they are definitely not for beginners or vertigo-sufferers. To use them, you need to be confident belaying and have the proper equipment (including helmet, ropes, two self-locking karabiners and a chest- or seat-harness). Incidentally, it's not advisable to climb a *via ferrata* in a **thunderstorm** either, as it might just become one long lightning conductor.

Once you've done a few straightforward paths up in the mountains you may be inspired to tackle some *ferrate*, and there are plenty of specialist guides around who can show you the ropes. Individual guides charge by the hour, so save money by getting a small group together. Many of the *rifugi* are run by mountain guides, or you could enrol on a mountain skills course: both Trentino and Alto Adige provincial tourist offices keep lists of guides and mountaineering schools, but you'll need to book well in advance. For more in-depth information, contact the Collegio Guide Alpine del Trentino, Vicolo Galasso 19, Trento (☎0461 981 207, ⓦguidealpinetrentino.it), an organization for Alpine guides in the province of Trentino. If you want a private guide, book at least a week ahead in high season. For Alto Adige, contact Verband der Südtiroler Berg- und Skiführer, Weintraubengasse 9, Bolzano (☎0471 976 357, ⓦguidealpine-altoadige.it).

5

Chiesa di San Vigilio

Pinzolo • Tues–Sat 9.30–11.30am & 2.30–5.30pm, Sun 2.30–5.30pm; longer hours in summer • Free

Simone Baschenis was one of a family of itinerant artists who decorated several small churches in Trentino in the 1500s. Among them was Pinzolo's Romanesque **church of San Vigilio**. On the south facade, a band of skeletons playing trumpets and bag-pipes accompanies a procession representing the social order of the day – from emperors, cardinals and finely dressed ladies to soldiers, beggars and even a cherubic toddler who has a mini skeleton friend to remind him of his own mortality. Inside is a fine *Annunciation* from the thirteenth century, attributed to the Tuscan school, and other works by Simone Baschenis, among them the *Life of San Vigilio*, the young Bishop of Trento.

Chiesa di Santo Stefano

2km west of Carisolo • Tues–Sat 10.30–11.30am & 3.30–5pm; July–Sept also Sun 3.30–5pm • Free

Decorated by the same artists as the Chiesa di San Vigilio, the modest **Chiesa di Santo Stefano** perches on a huge chunk of granite just off the road into the beautiful **Val Genova**. Near the start of the valley you'll see a sign pointing down a track to the church which has more frescoes of the *danse macabre* by the Baschenis on an outside wall, and others inside the spare, atmospheric interior depicting the legend of Charlemagne's passage through the Val di Campiglio on the way to his coronation in Rome.

Ponte Verde and the Cascata di Nardis

Following the Val Genova road out of Carisolo, your route follows a cascading river up through woods to an information point at **Ponte Verde** (4km from Carisolo) where you can rent bikes or take a footpath that passes several waterfalls, spectacular in the spring melt and after rain, or in winter when they are frozen solid and a glacial turquoise inside. Most impressive is the **Cascata di Nardis**, a five-minute walk from Ponte Verde, where several channels spill down the granite rock walls of the mountainside.

Ponte Maria, Malga Bedole and the Adamello glaciers

A 4.5km walk or bike ride from Cascata di Nardis will bring you to **Ponte Maria** (no cars are allowed beyond this point) from where a shuttle bus runs (July & Aug daily, every 30min) another 8.5km to **Malga Bedole** (1584m), a settlement used by shepherds in summer. A two- to three-hour hike from there along trail 212 is *Rifugio Città di Trento* (☎0465 501 193; mid-June to mid-Sept & April; access in snowy weather is from Passo Tonale by cable car and then chair lift) at 2480m, within reach of the **Adamello glaciers**.

Madonna di Campiglio

The major village in the Val Rendena is **MADONNA DI CAMPIGLIO**, an upmarket ski resort 70km from Trento known as "Campiglio" for short. This is where the Austro-Hungarian aristocracy holidayed in the nineteenth century, although not much of that era remains – what you see now is a very twentieth century resort, hotel balconies groaning under the weight of geraniums. Winter sports and a quiet summer hiking season are Campiglio's reason for existence, and the climbing and walking in the Dolomiti di Brenta are superb.

Reaching the trailheads

The best way to approach the trailheads is by cable car from **Carlo Magno**, 3km north of the village centre, to Groste (daily: mid-June to mid-Sept 8.30am–12.30pm & 2–5pm; €5). If you're not into hard trekking, an alternative is to take the **Cinque Laghi** cable car (late June to late Aug daily 8.30am–12.50pm & 2–5.20pm; €11 one way, €16 return) from the centre of the village west into the Presanella group. A scenic two-and-a-half-hour route will take you via **Lago Ritorto** back down to the valley.

5

WALKING IN THE BRENTA MASSIF

From the village of **GROSTE** (2437m) planning your own routes is easy enough if you have a decent hiking map. *Rifugio Graffer* (☎0465 441 358, ⊚graffer.com; June 20–Sept 20 & Dec–April) is conveniently next to the cable-car terminus, at 2261m. Head out along trail 316 nearby, which crosses the boulder-strewn slopes towards the *Sella* and *Tuckett rifugi* at 2272m (both ☎0465 441 226, ⊚sat.tn.it; June 20–Sept 20). The latter is named after the most prodigious of nineteenth-century climbers, Francis Fox Tuckett, who wrote that he "roamed amongst toppling rocks, and spires of white and brown and bronze coloured stone" when he climbed in this range, and succeeded in opening up a difficult new route called the Bochetta di Tuckett. As ice axes hadn't been invented, he negotiated snowfields with a ladder and alpenstock (long staff), and carried joints of meat and bottles of wine for mountaintop breakfasts.

Trail 328 (becoming 318) starts just past the *Sella* and *Tuckett* refuges, bringing you (in about 4hr from Groste) to *Rifugio Brentei* (☎0465 441 244, ⊚rifugiobrentei.it; mid-June to early Oct), set at 2489m, midway between the Cima Brenta and Cima Tosa mountain peaks. If you stay overnight here, next day, if you can cope with snowfields, you can extend your walk by trekking up to the Bocca di Brenta and crossing over the ridge to meet trail 319 down to Molveno, or simply return to Campiglio via trails 318 and 316 (3hr 30min).

Molveno and Andalo

On the other side of the Brenta mountain range from Campiglio is the lakeside village of **MOLVENO**, and 4km away by road or beautiful wooded trail is the slightly smaller town of **ANDALO**. Both are known for the quality of their wild **mushrooms**, and many Italians come here to pick them, getting hold of a mushrooming licence (€5/day, €20/week) from the local *comune* or the tourist office at Andalo (see below). Each year 40,000 or so Italians suffer mushroom poisoning, so obviously only pick them if you know what you are doing.

Brown Bear Area

Mid-June to mid-Sept daily 9.30am–6.30pm • €7, €6 for under 14, free for under 6 • ☎0461 653 622, ⊚parcofaunistico.tn.it

In Spormaggiore, about 14km northeast of Molveno and accessible by bus from there, you'll find the Parco Faunistico's **Brown Bear Area**. The Life Ursus project has created a "natural habitat" for a declining bear population, with animals taken from Italian zoos to prepare them for reintroduction into the wild. The enclosed outdoor area (follow the signs for the *area orsi*) lets you observe the bears – although the stars of the show spend a lot of time asleep. A **visitor centre** back in the village (same hours; combined ticket with Brown Bear Area; ⊚pnab.it) tells the story of the project.

ARRIVAL AND INFORMATION

By bus Two express bus services run from Madonna di Campiglio, and from Pinzolo and Carisolo, to Bedole once a day in the morning, returning late afternoon. A dozen buses a day run from Trento to Madonna di Campiglio's main square, and there are handily timed services that coincide with arrivals and departures of the train (approx hourly) to Malè, 23km north.

DOLOMITI DI BRENTA

Tourist offices There are tourist offices at Madonna di Campiglio (Via Pradalago 4; Mon–Sat 9am–12.30pm & 2–6pm, Sun 9am–12.30pm; ☎0465 447 501, ⊚campiglio .to) and Andalo (Piazza Dolomiti 1; July & Aug Mon–Sat 9am–12.30pm & 3.30–7pm, Sun 9.30am–12.30pm; Sept–June Mon–Sat 9am–12.30pm & 3–6.30pm, Sun 9.30am–12.30pm; ☎0461 585 836).

ACCOMMODATION

PINZOLO

Faè della Val Rendena Near Sant'Antonio di Mavignola ☎0465 801 669, ⊚campingvalrendena .com. Of the small campsites around Pinzolo, this one with its comfortable huts and good facilities is possibly the best. Pitches €33

Salvaterra Via Marconi 44 ☎0465 501 171, ⊚salvaterra

.biz. This friendly and charming B&B has spacious doubles with modernized bathrooms and mountain views. Min stay three nights in summer. €40

MADONNA DI CAMPIGLIO

Hotel Fontanella Via Dolomiti di Brenta 125 ☎0465 443 399, ⊚hotelfontanella.it. Lodgings in Campiglio tend to be on the pricier side, but this renovated Alpine tower-hotel represents good value. Rooms are pristine affairs in carved wood, and striking fabrics, but it's the panoramic mountainscape views that provide the wow factor. **€100**

East of Trento

If soaring peaks get your pulse racing, a trip **east of Trento** to a group of stunningly bare peaks called the **Pale di San Martino** is unmissable. Now 2000m above sea level, the range was formed as a coral reef sixty million years ago – white shells crunch underfoot as you walk, and the pale rock reflects light, even at dawn. The Pale are part of the **Parco Naturale Paneveggio**, an area of gently rolling woods and summer pastures with many walks, trails and campsites. The nearest resort is **San Martino di Castrozza**, the terminus for buses travelling from Trento along the **Valsugana** and the **Val di Fiemme**.

Imer and Mezzano

On the way from Trento to San Martino you pass through the archetypal tourist villages of **IMER** and, a couple of kilometres east, **MEZZANO**. The valley they're located in is wide, with hay meadows spreading either side, and makes a good place to walk or cycle, with cycle tracks linking the villages and easy paths running into the foothills.

Fiera di Primiero

Around 4km from Imer, **FIERA DI PRIMIERO** is a large resort and market town. It's a major crossroads in the area, from where buses run up to the beginning of the Val Canali and to Passo Cereda (1369m). The mountains around Fiera were worked for silver, iron and copper from the thirteenth century, and miners' guilds paid for the town's late-Gothic **parish church** near the fortified Palazzo delle Miniere (where the precious metals were guarded before being sent to the mint). Inside the church is a beautiful painting of *The Hunt of the Mystic Unicorn* and a fine fifteenth-century carved altar showing scenes from the Virgin Mary's life. Recent excavations have brought to light the remains of a **paleo-Christian basilica** dating from the fifth to sixth centuries. It's well worth a stroll round the village – paintings made in the sixteenth century on the outside of some of the older houses have survived the elements.

San Martino di Castrozza

The road into **SAN MARTINO DI CASTROZZA** twists and turns, and you feel like you're in the middle of nowhere until the resort's new hotels appear around the corner. One of the smarter Dolomite resorts, tourism took off here in the nineteenth century, but as far back as the Middle Ages, travellers and pilgrims stopped here for the night, staying at the monastery, of which only traces remain. Visitors come here now for skiing and hiking – hourly buses south to Fiera di Primiero and Imer, and cable-car routes into the mountains make San Martino one of the best walking bases in the area.

Parco Naturale Paneveggio

🕿 0439 64 854 • 🌐 parcopan.org

Beyond the village of San Martino, traffic files up to **Passo di Rolle**, a beautiful stretch of high moorland dotted with avalanche breaks and a few sheep. There are only two buses a day, so a car really helps here. The Passo di Rolle falls within the **Parco Naturale Paneveggio**, which protects a vast area of ancient woodland as well as the high peaks of the Pale di San Martino, prime hiking country. Crisscrossed by nature trails and ancient paved paths called *reversi*, the park gives you a sense of rural life on the summer

HIKING IN THE PALE DI SAN MARTINO

The most dramatic part of the Paneveggio national park is the **Pale di San Martino** – a large plateau surrounded by razor-sharp peaks. Ranging from 2600m to 3200m in altitude, you should be prepared for snow, wind and rain, even in the summer, as well as scorching sunlight and the most stupendous views. There are two main entry points – the **Val Canali** (accessed from Fiera di Primiero) and the **cable car** from San Martino di Castrozza.

The **Val Canali** was described by Amelia Edwards in the nineteenth century as the most "lonely, desolate and tremendous scene to be found this side of the Andes". Things have changed slightly since then with the arrival of the Alta Via 2 walking route which runs through here, but the valley retains a feeling of isolation. Buses from Fiera di Primiero run to the trailheads of the valley via the Passo Cereda. *Rifugio Treviso* (☎0439 62 311; late June to mid-Sept) is a possible overnight stop, while the more luxurious *Cant del Gal* (☎0439 62 997), further down the valley, has ten rooms and a good restaurant.

A stiff ascent from *Rifugio Treviso* brings you onto the **Altopiano delle Pale** at Passo di Pradidali, where eagles circle above the barren plateau and the silence is broken every so often by a trickle of falling stones. Once you are at this altitude, there are many possibilities for linking up with other trails across the stark upland. *Rifugio Pedrotti alla Rosetta* (☎03470 498 929, ⊕rifugiorosetta.it; mid-June–Sept 20), at 2581m, is the nearest place with accommodation (a 2hr 30min hike north; also reachable by cable car – see below). The fastest route into the Pale di San Martino is via **cable car** from San Martino. The Colverde funicular (June 14–Sept 20 daily 8am–4.45pm; ☎0439 68 204) from the village runs to the foot of the Pale, from where the Rosetta chair lift takes you up to the *Rifugio Pedrotti alla Rosetta* perched on the edge of the Altopiano. From the Rosetta chair-lift terminus, you can make for *Rifugio Pradidali* at 2278m (☎0439 64 180, ⊕rifugiopradidali.com; June 20–Sept 20), a walk and descent of three hours. A more ambitious walk would be to continue on from the refuge over the **Passo di Ball**, returning from there to San Martino or descending over into Val Canali at *the Cant del Gal*.

pastures and in the forest, and makes an atmospheric venue for some of the open-air concerts in the Suoni delle Dolomiti series (see p.309). The main Paneveggio visitor centre is located outside Predazzo on the road up to the Passo di Rolle.

Predazzo

Out of the confines of the Parco Naturale Paneveggio, **PREDAZZO** is the first town you come to in the **Val di Fiemme**, which lies between two immense mountain massifs: the Latemar and the Catena di Lagorai. Predazzo has become something of a pilgrimage site for geologists, owing to the extensive collection of local rocks and fossils in the **Museo Civico di Geologia** next to the church at Piazza Santi Filippo e Giacomo 1 (July–Sept Mon–Sat 10am–noon & 5–7pm; ☎0462 500 366). Surprisingly accessible to non-experts, the displays include samples of the Dolomitic calcite rock first identified by the elaborately named French mineralogist Dieudonné Sylvain Guy Tancrède de Gratet de Dolomieu.

Tesero

Between Predazzo and Cavalese, the only reason to stop at the village of **TESERO** is to view the small but intriguing chapel next to the parish church. This is decorated with a fresco called the *Cristo della Domenica* (Christ of the Sabbath) – around the Christ figure are depictions of activities you mustn't do on a Sunday and tools you mustn't use. Crossbow shooting, music playing and wood chopping are on the list and the fresco also shows a couple in bed; apparently you aren't supposed to do that on the Sabbath either. If you just want to stop to view the fresco, there's free parking outside the church.

HIKING IN THE DOLOMITES (P.309) >

5

Cavalese

Built around its colourful church tower and still sporting a cobbled main street, **CAVALESE**, the chief town of the Val di Fiemme, makes for an engaging afternoon halt.

Long and painstaking restoration was completed in summer 2012 on the **Palazzo della Magnifica Comunità**, a fabulously frescoed medieval palace in the centre of Cavalese. This was the Bishop of Trento's grand summer palace, and now houses a small **museum and gallery** (€5; ☎0462 340 365, ⬤magnificacomunitafiemme.it) containing the original valley statutes, carefully kept in wood-panelled rooms, with fine wooden ceilings and painted friezes. The building's lack of fortifications indicates that Trento's bishop felt safe from the armed rebellions that had plagued him in the city, and its exterior is covered in frescoes depicting St Vigilio (Trento's patron saint).

INFORMATION

CAVALESE

Tourist office A short way beyond the town centre at Via Fratelli Bronzetti 60 (Mon–Sat 9am–noon & 3.30–7pm; mid-July & Aug also Sun 9am–noon; ☎0462 241 111, ⬤visitfiemme.it).

FIERA DI PRIMIERO

Tourist office Via Dante 6 (July & Aug Mon–Sat 9am–12.30pm & 3.30–7pm, Sun 9.30am–12.30pm; Sept–June Mon–Sat 8.30am–12.30pm & 3.30–6pm, Sun 9.30am–noon; ☎0439 62 407).

PARCO NATURALE PANEVEGGIO

Visitor centres The park has three visitor centres: San Martino (late June to early Sept daily 9am–12.30pm & 3.30–7pm; ☎0439 768 859), Villa Welsperg in the Val

EAST OF TRENTO

Canali (June–Sept daily 9am–12.30pm & 3–6pm; Oct–Dec Mon–Fri 9.30am–12.30pm & 2–5pm; Jan–May Mon–Sat 10am–12.30pm & 3–6pm; ☎0439 64 854) and Paneveggio (9am–12.30pm & 2–5.30pm: early June to mid-Sept daily; Christmas to March Tues & Fri; mid-April to early June Sun only; ☎0462 576 283).

SAN MARTINO DI CASTROZZA

Tourist office Next to the bus stop at Via Passo Rolle 165 (mid-June to Sept Mon–Sat 9am–12.30pm & 3.40–7pm; Sun July & Aug 9.30am–12.30pm & 4–7pm, June & Sept 9.30am–12.30pm; Oct to mid-June Mon–Sat 9am–12.30pm & 2.20–5.30pm, Sun 9.30am–noon; ☎0439 768 867, ⬤sanmartino.com). Provides a detailed walking map of the area, giving information about *rifugi*, difficulty levels, estimated hiking times etc.

ACCOMMODATION

CAVALESE

★ **Laurino** Via Antoniazzi 14 ☎0462 340 151, ⬤hotelgarnilaurino.com. Just off the main road through town (turn off at the church and head downhill) the fifteen rooms in this cosy seventeenth-century mini-palace are decorated in Tyrolean style with Alpine antiques, local artwork and almost shamanistic little charms, made by the owner. Breakfast is taken in a beautifully panelled dining room and the hotel strives to be as ecofriendly as possible. **€110**

IMER AND MEZZANO

Camping Calavise 1km from Imer ☎0439 67 468, ⬤campingcalavise.it. Well signposted from Imer, this enjoyable campsite boasts a bar and swimming pool nearby as well as a wi-fi zone and jazz concerts in summer. Pitches **€10**, plus **€7.50** per adult

Rifugio Fonteghi ☎0439 67 043, ⬤rifugiofonteghi.com. The 45min walk along the path on the south side of the Val Noana reservoir will help you build up an appetite for the home-made pasta, home-grown veg and game dishes served here. Half-board per person **€50**

PARCO NATURALE

Bellamonte Via Cece 16 ☎0462 576 119, ⬤camping bellamonte.it. Located in the tranquil Alpine village of Bellamonte, 4km along the Passo Rolle road from Predazzo, this well-run campsite is surrounded by meadows and hay lofts. Pitches **€6**, plus **€8** per adult

SAN MARTINO DI CASTROZZA

Ostello Dolomiti Via Laghetti 4 ☎0439 769 166, ⬤ostellodolomiti.com. For a low-cost place to stay without a tent, try this hostel with six-bed dorms and private rooms for smaller groups and families. Located 1km from the town centre near the Malga Ces lifts and Sass Maòr campsite. Dorms **€33**, doubles **€72**

Sass Maòr Via Laghetti 48 ☎0439 68 347, ⬤camping sassmaor.it. Dramatically located below jagged peaks, this campsite has a bar, pizzeria, laundry facilities and a mini-market. Booking ahead is essential here in high season. Pitches **€10**, plus **€8** per adult

The Catinaccio and Gruppo di Sella

The **Catinaccio** (or **Rosengarten**) range is one of the best-known sights in the Dolomites, its unmistakeable bare-rock pinnacles appearing on brochures, guides and myriad souvenirs. This immense wall of stone along the edge of the 3000m-high massif takes on a famously rosy glow at sunset, and the mountain plays lead role in the area's best-known myths and legends. Trails across this mountain are popular with mainly Italian and German walkers and, although the zigzag paths to the peaks can be crowded in August, once you're above the cable-car line, there's plenty of wilderness to lose yourself in.

Access is simple enough from **Vigo di Fassa**, the main place to stay in the Val di Fassa, which splits off from the Val di Fiemme north of Predazzo at Moena. If you travel these roads and trails, you pass through one of the heartlands of **Ladino** culture (see box below).

At the head of the Val di Fassa, **Canazei** makes a good springboard for the high plateaux of the **Gruppo di Sella**, and the gentler trail of the **Viel del Pan**, which leads down to the tiny resort of **Arabba**. On the northern side of the Sella group, **Corvara** is a much larger resort with a sizeable Ladino population.

Catinaccio

The **Catinaccio** range was described by nineteenth-century writer Theodor Christomannos as a "gigantic fortification… the gate into the kingdom of immortal ghosts, of high-flying giants". The area's German name, **Rosengarten** (rose garden), derives from the legend of Laurin, king of the dwarves, who used to grow roses here. The king, angered when he was prevented from being with his beloved princess Similde, put a spell on the roses so that no one would see them again by day or night, but forgot to include dawn and dusk, which is when the low sun gives the rock its fiery glow.

The **trails** across the range cater for all levels of hiking ability; however, the going does get tough on the ridges, from where you can see as far as the Stubaier Alps, on the border with Austria, but if you buy a Kompass map and plan your route carefully, you can keep walks well within your capabilities.

The most popular approach to Catinaccio is from the hamlet of Vigo di Fassa, served by buses on the Trento–Canazei route. Once you're up above the tree line,

---

LADIN COUNTRY

The **Ladins** (*Ladini* in Italian, *Ladinisch* in German) are a community of around 30,000 people living in the Gardena, Badia, Fassa, Livinallongo and Ampezzo valleys around the Sella massif. They're united by their ancient language – Ladin – which was once spoken over a wide area, from Austria down to the River Po (in what's now Emilia-Romagna). The Dolomitic Ladin language, preserved by the relative remoteness of the territory, is linked to Swiss Romansch (there are 40,000 speakers in the Swiss Engadine) and Friulano (more than 700,000 speakers in the Friuli region of Italy).

The history of the Ladins is recorded in their epics, which recount tales of battles, treachery and reversals of fortune. Around 400 AD, the Ladins were constantly threatened with invasion by Germanic tribes from the north and others from the Po valley. Christianity later emerged as a major threat, but the Ladins absorbed and transformed the new religion, investing the new saints with the powers of more ancient female divinities.

The **Museo Ladin de Fascia** (early June to early Sept daily 10am–12.30pm & 3–7pm; rest of the year Tues–Sat 3–7pm; €5; ⊛ istladin.net), between San Giovanni and Vigo di Fassa, is devoted to traditional Ladin working life and provides a fascinating introduction to Ladin culture, with intriguing exhibits on the language and history. It also has exhibits scattered throughout the territory, including a restored nineteenth-century cooperage (Botega da Pinter) at Via Dolomiti 3, in **Moena**; a restored watermill (Molin de Pezol) at Via Jumela 6 in **Pera di Fassa**; and a working, antique sawmill (La Sia) at Via Pian Trevisan in **Penia**, just outside Canazei. Tourist offices throughout the area have details of festivals, exhibitions and events.

5

rifugi abound, serving the hordes of summer walkers who file along the trails. If you're looking for wilderness trekking in the Dolomites, you may want to go elsewhere.

Canazei and around

CANAZEI, a buzzing summer and winter resort at the head of the Val di Fassa (wfassa.com) is a stepping stone to the stupendous high road passes between here and Cortina d'Ampezzo. You may also find yourself staying here before or after walking in the Gruppo di Sella or strolling along a much easier trail – the **Viel del Pan** opposite glacier-topped Marmolada.

The road to the Passo Pordoi

With your own vehicle, it's well worth driving the **switchback road** of 27 bends that climbs for 12km out of Canazei towards the **Passo Pordoi**. Although it's often busy with busloads of tourists heading for the scenic Great Dolomites Road and determined cyclists making the thousand-metre ascent, the view when you get there is unforgettable.

Halfway along the road, the cable car at Pradel leads to **Passo di Sella** (2240m), one of the most impressive of the Dolomite passes. Paths climb from here onto the jagged peaks of the **Sasso Lungo** (Langkofel) and follow the ridges down onto the Alpe di Siusi. Just past Pradel the road forks. Straight ahead is the **Gruppo di Sella** – an arid lunar plateau surrounded by pink, dolomitic peaks. A right-hand turning takes you up to the **Passo Pordoi** (2242m), an astonishing vantage point between the Gruppo di Sella and Marmolada, from where mountains radiate in every direction, giving you a chance to identify the distinctive shapes of each of the main Dolomite ranges. In the foreground, the Sasso Lungo look like a jagged, gloved hand, flanked by two prominent peaks; the Gruppo di Sella is squat and chunky; and Sciliar (Schlern), just visible in the distance, comprises a flat rocky tabletop, culminating in two peaks. A small road winds downwards to Passo Falzarego, and ultimately Cortina d'Ampezzo.

From the Passo Pordoi you can join Alta Via 2, or if you simply want to stretch your legs, walk a short section of it known as the Viel del Pan (see box below). Most tourist buses and plenty of bikers stop at the collection of cafés and stalls at the pass.

Corvara and around

The central town of the Ladin ethnic group, CORVARA is primarily a ski resort, and it also makes a good base for the excellent trails of the nearby Fanes Park (see p.336), a bus ride away, where most of the Ladin legends are based.

A WALK ALONG THE VIEL DEL PAN

If you're not a great walker, this easy twenty-minute stroll from the Passo Pordoi affords terrific Dolomite vistas – far better than the views from the road. Pick up the Alta Via 2 trail just past the Albergo Savoia. A narrow path cut into the turf traverses the mountainside opposite the glaciers of Marmolada, which was right on the front during World War I. Entire Austrian battalions managed to overwinter inside Marmolada by blasting 8km of tunnel tens of metres deep under the ice and rock.

From the seventeenth century this path was on the grain-smuggling route called the Viel del Pan ("trail of bread" in Venetian dialect), and it remained busy enough in the nineteenth century for the Guardia di Finanza to set up armed patrols along it. The contrast between the glacier on Marmolada and the peaks of the Sella group – 360 degrees of mountain – is superb. When you've had enough of walking, the easiest option is to return the same way to the Passo Pordoi. Or you can keep going on the same path until you reach Lago Fedaia, from where there are irregular buses in summer back to Canazei.

Some 4.5km north of Corvara is **La Villa**, a small village with a fairy-tale sixteenth-century castle.

ARRIVAL AND INFORMATION

By bus Between mid-June and mid-Sept there are just two buses daily from Canazei to Passo Pordoi, both in the afternoon (35min). Corvara is on the summer bus route from Canazei (1hr 20min); buses also leave hourly for

CATINACCIO AND GRUPPO DI SELLA

Brunico (1hr), which is on the rail line into Austria.
Tourist office Strada Col Alt 36, Corvara (Mon–Fri 8am–noon & 3–7pm, Sat 8.30am–12.30pm & 3–6pm, Sun 10am–noon & 4–6pm; ☏ 0471 836 176, ⓦ altabadia.org).

ACCOMMODATION

CANAZEI

Giardino delle Rose Via Dolomiti 116 ☏ 0462 602 221, ⓦ giardinodellerosecanazei.com. The ten rooms above a popular après-ski pub are functional and fairly comfortable as well as providing a great no-frills base for hikers and skiers in the village centre. **€50**

La Zondra Strada de Ciampac 25 ☏ 0462 601 233, ⓦ lazondra.com. Basic balconied rooms at this easy-going Alpine chalet tick all the boxes and are priced just right. Ski rental and wi-fi available. **€70**

CORVARA

Monti Pallidi Via Col Alt 75 ☏ 0471 836 081, ⓦ montipallidi.net. This chalet-style B&B offers excellent-value, contemporary rooms and mini-apartments, most with kitchenette. There's paid wi-fi and free parking on the premises. **€64**

Rosa Alpina Strada Micura de Rü 20, San Cassiano

☏ 0471 849 500, ⓦ rosalpina.it. The luxurious "Alpine Rose" is a cool, luscious and extremely hip spa-hotel with a celebrated restaurant. Taking a dip in the pool, indulging in the various spa treatments on offer and dining in the *St Hubertus* restaurant, you could easily part with €800 a day. **€350**

VIGO DI FASSA

Piccolo Hotel Strada Neva 70 ☏ 0462 764 217, ⓦ piccolohotel.net. Vigo has lots of three-star hotels but the *Piccolo* (the irony of the name is lost on no one – it's big) has been around for fifty years and is a cut above the rest. In addition to the wood-rich rooms, extra services include a games room, a wellness area and a large restaurant. **€90**

Rifugio Roda di Vael Sella del Ciampaz ☏ 0462 764 450, ⓦ rodadivael.it. This mountain chalet occupies a spectacular position a 90min walk from the village along trails 547 and 545. Half-board per person **€46**

Bolzano (Bozen)

The gently historic capital of Alto Adige, **BOLZANO** (largely known by its German name, Bozen) straddles the junction of the jade-hued Alpine waters of the Talvera (Talfer) and Isarco (Eisack) rivers. Winter and summer see the town's 100,000

THE ITALIANIZATION OF THE TYROL

The **South Tyrol** (Südtirol) was Italy's reward for cooperating with the Allies during World War I. But when Mussolini's Fascists came to power in 1923 the region was renamed Alto Adige after the upper reaches of the Adige River, and despite the fact that German speakers outnumbered Italian speakers by around ten to one, a process of sometimes brutal Italianization was imposed on the area. Cartographers remade maps, substituting Italian place names (often made up) for German; people were forced to adopt Italian names; the teaching of German in schools was banned and stonemasons were even brought in to chip away German inscriptions from tombstones. World War II then intervened, and by 1946, Austria and Italy came to an agreement ratified under the Paris Peace Treaty that Austria would give up its claim to the region on condition that Italy took steps to redress some of the cultural damage perpetrated under Fascism.

Successive governments have channelled funds into the area allowing both more independence than ever before and much greater say in local law. Over the last few years, Italy has moved closer into the European Union, and its central and regional governments have become more tolerant of ethnic diversity and, increasingly, German is the language of preference in Südtirol.

population swell with tourists, although it manages to maintain a relaxed pace of life and is possibly the best jumping-off point for flits into the surrounding mountainscape. Away from the high trails and slopes, Bolzano's centre provides enough distraction for at least a day of exploration, the highlight of which for most is "Ötzi" the iceman and the museum dedicated to this prehistoric phenomenon. The local **wine** isn't bad either, with Bolzano located at the head of the Wine Road (Strada del Vino/Südtiroler Weinstrasse), which runs south to the border with Trentino.

Brief history

Located in a predominantly sunny, sheltered bowl, for centuries Bolzano was a valley market town and way-station whose fortunes in the Middle Ages swayed as the counts of Tyrol and the bishops of Trento competed for power. The town passed to the Habsburgs in the fourteenth century, then at the beginning of the nineteenth century Bavaria took control, opposed by Tyrolese patriot and military leader Andreas Hofer. His battle in 1809 to keep the Tyrol under Austrian rule was only temporarily successful, as in the same year the Austrian emperor ceded the Tyrol to the Napoleonic kingdom of Italy. More changes followed, as Bolzano was handed back to Austria until World War I, whereupon it passed, like the rest of the province, to Italy.

Piazza Walther and the Duomo

5

Bolzano's heart is **Piazza Walther**, whose pavement cafés, around its statue of the *Minnesänger* (troubadour) Walther von der Vogelweide, are the town's favoured meeting places. The southern flank is dominated by the **Duomo**, a church converted into a cathedral as recently as 1964. Built in the fourteenth and fifteenth centuries, and restored following bomb damage during World War II, it sports a strikingly multi-coloured ceramic roof and elaborately carved spire.

Chiesa dei Domenicani and the Cappella di San Giovanni

A couple of streets west of Piazza Walther, on Via Cappuccini, the **Chiesa dei Domenicani** has frescoes of fifteenth-century courtly life painted on the walls of the decaying cloisters, framed by a growth of stone tracery. The **Cappella di San Giovanni**, built at the beginning of the fourteenth century, resembles a Byzantine church, retaining frescoes by painters of the Giotto school, including a *Triumph of Death*, underneath a star-spangled vault.

Museo Archeologico

Via Museo (Museumstrasse) 43 • Tues–Sun 10am–6pm; also open Mon in July & Aug • €9 • ⓦ archaeologiemuseum.it

Bolzano's top attraction by far is the **Museo Archeologico**, a superb and informative exhibition built around the **Ice Man**, a frozen, mummified body discovered in the ice of the Ötzaler Alps in 1991, just 92m from the border with Austria. At first a policeman estimated the body – nicknamed "Ötzi" – to be around 100 years old – he was out by around 5200 years, as later experts dated the corpse to around 3300 BC. Visitors queue up to peer into the €200,000-per-year, temperature-controlled cell where the surprisingly diminutive Ötzi lies dry-frozen, his complexion that of dry-cured ham and glistening with tiny ice crystals, but it's the rest of the exhibits that really hold interest for most. These include possessions found on or around the body – his still serviceable bearskin cap, his longbow and arrows, firelighting gear, a shamanic first-aid kit – as well as an incredibly realistic, life-size silicon model showing what experts think Ötzi would have looked like and numerous displays and films explaining how he came to be preserved on the mountainside. The Ötzi story is one of the most fascinating archeology has ever produced and arguments about who he was and how he died rage on in academia.

Museion

Via Dante 6 • Daily 10am–6pm, Thurs closes 10pm • €6 • ⓦ museion.it

Bolzano's museum of contemporary art, **Museion**, is housed in a strikingly contemporary building, opened in 2008. Appropriately for a bilingual area (or trilingual if you include the Ladin tongue) the theme "art and language" is central to the works in the permanent collection, with two thousand pieces in the area of art that lies between images and words.

THE ÖTZI CULT

Since Europe's most famous ice man was discovered on a lonely Alpine mountainside in 1991, an entire culture has sprouted around this anonymous Ladin forebear. Conspiracy theories have come thick and fast with some "revealing" Ötzi to be a Peruvian mummy transported to the Alps for publicity purposes. Others have claimed to be his direct descendants, while the "Ötzi diaries", which appeared in the wake of the infamous "Hitler diaries" were quickly dismissed as a bit of tomfoolery. Perhaps more seriously, the "Ötzi curse" stems from the fact that he was found on a palindromic date (19.9.1991), and indeed some people linked with the discovery have since died. But the most bizarre episode concerning the icy corpse came when a woman offered to bear a child using Ötzi's 5000-year-old sperm. The offer was politely rejected.

5

Piazza della Vittoria

Across the River Talvera (Talfer) a riverside walk upstream brings you to the older Ponte Talvera where Bolzano's German and Gothic quarter ends and **Piazza della Vittoria** signals the beginning of the 1930s Functionalist quarter, much of it laid out by Mussolini's favourite architect, Marcello Piacentini. The Fascist-period triumphal arch (1928) on the square is something of a controversial monument, not least due to its inscription: "Here is the border of the Motherland. Set the banners down. From this point on we educated others with language, law and culture." It was bombed by German-speaking separatists in the late 1980s and, until a clean-up a few years ago, was covered with graffiti. Today it is surrounded by railings and seems to be permanently under renovation – possibly to keep protestors at arm's length.

ARRIVAL AND DEPARTURE   BOLZANO

By plane Bolzano's tiny airport, Aeroporto Bolzano Dolomiti (☎ 0471 255 255, ⊛ abd-airport.it), only handles seasonal charters and three scheduled flights a day to/from Rome. It's a €10 taxi ride, or take bus #10A or #10B which stop nearby.

By train The train station is a few minutes' walk southeast of Piazza Walther through a scruffy park on Via Stazione. Destinations Bressanone (every 30min; 30min); Merano (every 30min; 40min); Trento (every 30min; 30–50min);

Vipiteno (every 30min; 1hr).

By bus Bolzano's bus station, centrally placed at Via Perathoner 4, serves most (but not all) of the small villages and resorts in the province.

Destinations Cavalese (hourly; 1hr 25min; first train to Auer then bus); Corvara (6 daily; 2hr 30min; via Plan/ Wolkenstein or Ortisei); Merano (hourly; 50min); Ortisei (at least hourly; 1hr); Predazzo (every 2 hr; 1hr 45min); Siusi (every 30min; 40min); Vigo di Fassa (6 daily; 1hr 10min).

INFORMATION AND GETTING AROUND

Tourist office Piazza Walther 8 (Mon–Fri 9am–7pm, Sat 9.30am–6pm; ☎ 0471 307 000, ⊛ bolzano-bozen.it).

By bike Bikes are available to rent from the tourist office for €10/day.

By car Hertz has branches at the airport (☎ 0471 254 266)

and at Via Garibaldi 34, Maggiore (☎ 0471 971 531). You can park at Parcheggio Piazza Walther; Central Parking, Piazza Stazione; Bolzano Centro, Via Mayr-Nusser. All charge €1.70/hr.

By taxi Radio Taxi is your best bet (☎ 0471 981 111).

ACCOMMODATION

Located on the historic route south from other parts of Europe, Bolzano has a long tradition of hospitality and offers some special places to stay that are well worth splashing out on. If you're on a budget, there are plenty of affordable beds in town, plus two excellent campsites just a short city bus-ride away.

Figl Piazza del Grano 9 ☎ 0471 978 412, ⊛ figl.net. This shuttered guesthouse occupying the Corn Market has been serving guests for a century so must be doing something right. Rooms are simple, cheerful, business-standard affairs with stock-issue bathrooms and free wi-fi. Breakfast can be taken in the wood-panelled restaurant or out on the piazza. Parking is €15 a night. **€125**

★ **Hotel Greif** Piazza Walther (enter from Raingasse) ☎ 0471 318 000, ⊛ greif.it. This boutique hotel just off the main square has 33 spacious rooms styled with contemporary chic but far from soulless. Blond wood, sturdy timber floors and weird and wonderful artwork

blend with dark-green marble bathrooms. Every room is different so ask to see what you're getting. Guests have use of the park and pool at *Grief*'s sister hotel, the *Parkhotel Laurin*, there's free bike rental and the *Cosmo* cocktail bar is one of the coolest in town. **€176**

Hotel Regina Via Renon 1 ☎ 0471 972 195, ⊛ hotelreginabz.it. A handy location opposite the train station, and friendly staff make this comfortable, if not exactly inspiring, hotel a good deal. Rooms at the back are quietest though effective soundproofing keeps most traffic noise out at the front. Free wi-fi and parking. **€100**

Ostello Bolzano/Jugendherberge Bozen Via Renon 23

THE MUSEUMOBIL CARD

The **Museumobil card** gives free unlimited use of public transport (buses, regional trains and certain *funivie*) in the region, and free access to over eighty museums (almost all museums in the Alto Adige): a three-day card costs €23 and a seven-day card €28 (€14 and €16 for 6- to 14-year-olds). It's available from every tourist office across the Alto Adige.

☎0471 300 865, ⊚ostello.bz. Cheerful and fresh, this hostel is one of a chain in the South Tyrol offering good-quality, low-cost accommodation to young people and families with children. Facilities include internet access, board games, table tennis and the use of laundry facilities. **€21.50**

★ **Parkhotel Laurin** Via Laurin 4 ☎0471 311 000, ⊚laurin.it. Südtirol's grandest hotel was built in 1910, and is set in a verdant garden oasis with a small summer swimming pool, children's play area, bar, gourmet restaurant and several commissioned works of contemporary sculpture. The Art Deco-styled rooms are restful and understated, some have terraces, others balconies, and one (no. 522) has its own roof terrace. The food in the secluded open-air restaurant is first rate and the same menu is available in the lounge bar, with its *King Laurin* fresco (1911) by Jugendstil artist Bruno Goldschmitt (worth stopping by to see even if you're not staying here). Bikes for guest use (with child seats available too) and free wi-fi. **€151**

Pension Röllhof Kampenn, Kohlern ☎0471 329 958, ⊚roellhof.com. Set 930m above sea level, this is an appealing, chalet-style *pensione* a 10min drive up a steep, switchback road from the centre of Bolzano. Closed Dec–

Easter. **€70**

Post Gries Corso Libertà 117 ☎0471 279 000, ⊚hotel-post-gries.com; bus #10A gets you near. Located at the opposite end of Corso Libertà (Freiheitsstrasse) to the Talfer Bridge, this comfortable inn with business-standard rooms and a decent restaurant is a sound option away from the city centre. **€110**

CAMPING

Moosbauer Via Merano 101, 5km from the city centre on the main Bolzano–Merano road ☎0471 918 492, ⊚moosbauer.com. This eco-campsite dedicates its efforts to helping guests understand all aspects of the Alto Adige. Pitches **€16**, plus **€9** per adult.

Steiner Kennedystrasse 32, Leifers (Laives) ☎0471 950 105, ⊚campingsteiner.com; bus #2 from Bolzano stops outside as do trains from Bolzano, Trento and Rovereto. Located in the busy valley town of Leifers (Laives) 8km from Bolzano, this very well equipped and professionally run campsite fills with German camper vans but has a camping meadow for tents as well as a swimming pool, minimarket and restaurant. Pitches **€12**, plus **€8** per adult.

EATING, DRINKING AND NIGHTLIFE

Piazza delle Erbe is the place to go for a quick eat, packed as it is with stalls selling *wurstel*, *apfel strudel*, local cheeses, hams, breads, and fabulous fruit and salads, with no shortage of exuberant bars and cafés offering beer and inexpensive fare. As for **nightlife** there are pubs aplenty, with Friday- and Saturday-night crowds spilling out onto the street; for a local aperitif, ask for a Veneziana (Aperol, champagne or prosecco, ice and a slice of lemon).

CAFÉS

Café Lintner Via Leonardo da Vinci 8/A ☎0471 973 052. If it's a quick coffee and cake halt you need, but don't fancy the tourist crowds on Piazza Walther, retreat to this traditional café, fragrant with newly milled beans and freshly baked goodies. Wedges of *strudel* and blocks of cream cake tempt from the window, and the interior is soothingly well dressed. 7.30am–7.30pm; closed Tues.

★ **Stadt Café** Piazza Walther. Far southern Italy meets the Alps at this alluring, grand café. The owner's southern origins are evident in the artisanal fizzy drinks such as the Lurisia brand of *gazzosa* (made with Amalfi lemons) and *chinotto* (made with real *chinotto*, a rare citrus fruit), along with organic Sicilian honeys. Compare this with the magnificently heavy cakes, such as *sachertorte*, *apfel strudel*, and a cake made with buckwheat flour and berries plus local sausages and *Bauerntoast*. Good for breakfast or an inexpensive lunch, with seating outside on Piazza Walther. Daily 10am–10pm.

RESTAURANTS

Cavallino Bianco (Weisses Rössl) Via dei Bottai/Bindergasse 6 ☎0471 973 267. This popular wood-panelled *bierkeller* features a menu strong on meat-rich Tyrolean specialities with hearty rustic mains going for

€6.50–18. Mon–Fri 9am–1am, Sat 9am–3pm.

Hopfen & Co Piazza delle Erbe/Obstplatz 17 ☎0471 300 788. Two pot-bellied brewing kettles let you know this is Bozen's favourite brewpub, where timber-clad dining rooms set the perfect scene for nights on the house suds as well as some fine soak-up material such as leek and potato soup (€5.70), goulash (€5.90), *Südtiroler Rostbraten* (South Tirolese roast beef, €7.50) and, to finish off, *apfel strudel* swimming in vanilla sauce. Mon–Sat 9.30am–1am, Sun 9.30am–midnight.

★ **Humus** Via Argentieri/Silbergasse 18 ☎0471 971 961. Newly opened Franco-Israeli bistro serving organic salads, veggie dishes, cakes, breakfasts, daily changing lunch menus and, of course, humus (mains around €7.50) in a pleasingly jumbled and tightly packed dining space. Service is rapid fire and friendly, the vibe easy-going. Mon–Fri 8am–8pm, Sat 8am–3.30pm.

Oca Bianca Piazza delle Erbe 24 ☎0471 300 054. Seasonally changing local delicacies such as horse carpaccio with wild mushrooms, and ravioli with duck-prosciutto are served in the simple, bench-lined dining room here. The pasta is all home-made, and there is great fish and seafood and a good choice of regional Italian wines. Expect to pay around €30 a head. Mon–Sat noon–2.30pm & 7–11pm.

5

Vögele Goethestrasse 3 ☎0471 923 938. *Vögele's* outdoor tables under a portico, and big oak candle-lit tables in the wood-clad interior make it a popular place to sample local wines and delicacies, along with fresh fish and dishes from further afield. A mixed fish antipasti of scallops, mussels and smoked fish (€13), makes for a decent light lunch, or go for something heartier such as *canederli* in broth (€5) or grilled *scamorza* cheese with stir-fried veg and chilli sauce (€10.50). Mon–Sat 8.30am–1am.

Zur Kaiserkron Piazza di Mostra/Musterplatz 1 ☎0471 980 214. Fine dining with refined regional and international food in a Baroque, former merchant's palace, or outside on the quiet, elegant piazza. The menu changes with the seasons but mains remain between €12 and €24 whatever the time of year. Mon–Sat noon–2.30pm & 7–9.30pm.

BARS

Fischbanke Via D. Streiter 26/A ☎0471 971 714. Laidback wine bar where you sip your Chardonnay at marble counters that once made up the city's fish market – hence the name. The enthusiastic owner creates a relaxed ambience, and you can snack on salads and bruschettas stacked high with local produce. Mon–Fri 9am–7pm, Sat 12.30–2.30pm.

Nadamas Piazza Erbe 44 ☎0471 980 684. Hip bar-restaurant serving up a wide range of dishes from sausage and chips and Thai rice to asparagus risotto and pizzas (mains €6–13). The walls are lined with posters advertising music and theatre events in Bolzano and there's a lively vibe. Daily 9am–1am.

Paulaner Stuben Via Argentieri/Silbergasse 16 ☎0471 980 407. Occupying an ancient frescoed town-house, this traditional beer hall is more Munich than Italy with Paulaner beer on tap and a small beer garden. All kinds of dishes, from pizza and pasta (€10) to steaks (€15) and seasonal fare populate the English-language menu. Daily 10am–1am.

DIRECTORY

Hospital Krankenhaus Bozen, Via Lorenz Böhler 5 ☎0471 908 111. In emergency call ☎118.

Internet Multikulti, Via Doctor Streiter 9. Web access on new machines Mon–Sat 9am–11pm.

Pharmacies Madonna, Via Portici 17 ☎0471 976 749; Communale Domenicani, Piazza Domenicani 24 ☎0471 971 452.

Police station Largo Palatucci 1 ☎0471 947 611.

Post office Piazza Parrocchia/Pfarrplatz 13 ☎0471 322 211.

Around Bolzano

If you like castles, it's worth leaving Bolzano city centre for a few easy half-day trips to strongholds and fortresses that almost ring the city, and the region's Wine Road is another worthwhile attraction.

Castello Roncolo

Tues–Sun 10am–6pm • €8 • ⓦ roncolo.info • Free shuttle bus from Piazza Walther (every 30min Tues–Sun, from 10am–6pm) or bus #12 from the bus station

Just 5km from Bolzano, the thirteenth-century **Castello Roncolo** (Schloss Runkelstein) contains probably the best secular frescoes in Europe, showing people hunting and dancing, and other scenes from courtly life. In the Sala del Torneo, look out for a fresco showing a fishing party: in the background a noble is offering a fish to a lady – the medieval equivalent of an indecent proposal. Pier Paolo Pasolini filmed some of his *Decameron* (1971) here.

BOLZANO'S CABLE CARS

A trip up in any of Bolzano's three cable cars gives a small taste of the high peaks that surround the city. The first ascends from Via Renòn (Rittnerstrasse), a ten-minute walk from the train station, to Soprabolzano (Oberbozen). It's the longest cable-car journey in Europe, with the largest change in height. Alternatively the San Genesio/Jenesien cable-car ride offers stupendous views of the Catinaccio/Rosengarten massif – the station is at Via Sarentino, 1.5km north of the town centre along the river (bus #12). On the high Alpine pastures at the top, you'll see blond-maned Haflinger horses grazing. The third cable-car goes to Colle/Kohlern from the station across the river south of the train station at Ponte Campiglio. The oldest cable-car ride in the world, it celebrated its centenary in 2008. For fares and times, see ⓦsii.bz.it.

Castello Appiano

Hocheppanerweg • April–Oct 10am–6pm; closed Wed • €4 • ☏ 0471 936 081, ⓦ hocheppan.com

Around 8km southwest of Bolzano, high above the village of **APPIANO** (Eppan), a clutch of thirty or so fortresses and castles can be seen from the ruined battlements of **Castello Appiano** (Schloss Hocheppan). In the castle chapel, secular frescoes show women flirting at the altar and one of the earliest representations of the South Tyrolean *knödel*, or dumpling.

Firmiano/Sigmundskron

Sigmundskronerstrasse 53 • From first Sun in March till third Sun in Nov 10am–6pm; closed Thurs • €9 • ☏ 0471 631 264, ⓦ messner-mountain-museum.it; bus #9 from Bolzano bus station

One of the most imposing fortresses in the area is **Firmiano/Sigmundskron**, perched on an outcrop of porphyry rock which made it a strategic base for the Bishop of Trento in the tenth century before falling into ruin in the sixteenth. The site was brought back from the dead in 2003 by mountaineer Reinhold Messner, who transformed it into the flagship of his group of mountain museums. A trail leads up and through the castle towers that contain a vast collection of paintings, sculptures – and objects such as a huge prayer wheel – celebrating the Himalayas, the Alps and the world's other lofty locations.

The Wine Road

Fans of the grape are certainly well catered for around Bolzano, with a **Wine Road** (*Strada del Vino;* ⓦ weinstrasse.com) enabling visitors to indulge in a happy combination of sightseeing and tastings. The 30km route proper begins at **Terlano** (Terlan) just north of Bolzano, but you can also join it at **Appiano** (Eppan) and wend your way through sunny vineyards to **Salerno** (Salurn) halfway between Bolzano and Trento. This is one of the oldest wine-growing areas of all German-speaking regions – some claim the tradition goes back to the Iron Age – and it's also one of the smallest in Italy. Certainly, the wine industry was well established in Roman times, with the colonists from down south finding that locally made barrels with metal hoops were much better for transporting wine back to Rome than their clay amphorae. The vines in the region are often strung on wide pergolas, the traditional method of viticulture here, which allows the Ora breeze blowing from Lake Garda to circulate around the grapes, giving a beneficial cooling effect. Others are on hillsides too steep for machinery, so all work still has to be done by hand.

The route's main halt is **CALDARO** (Kaltern), home to many sixteenth-century buildings in Uberetsch style, combining northern Gothic and southern Renaissance architectural details. Wines from the vineyards around this small village have won numerous awards; one of the best places to taste them is *Punkt* (ⓦ wein.kaltern.com), a wine bar/information point on the main square. Alternatively, three **cellars** close to the village centre also offer wine tasting – Kellerei Kaltern, Erste Kellerei Kaltern and Neue Kellerei Kaltern (ⓦ erste -neue.it). Within walking distance, too, on the Wine Road on the way to Lake Caldaro, the producer Manincor (ⓦ manincor.com) is well worth a visit for its combination of modern architecture and traditional estate buildings, as well as its fine vintages.

TÖRGGELEN SEASON

A good time to sample Alto Adige's wine is in the autumn during the **Törggelen season**. This roughly coincides with the arrival of the *Neuien* – the first bottles of new, young wine – from about the end of September to the beginning of December. It traditionally marks the passage of the year, celebrating a golden time of clear autumnal weather before winter really sets in. Farmers and innkeepers lay on a spread of *speck* (smoked ham), a bread called *schüttelbrot* and roast chestnuts, accompanied by wines from the surrounding hills. As well as the village taverns and *enotecas* along the wine road (see above) try visiting *Loosmannhof* (☏ 0471 365 551), Località Signato/Signat.

5

Another centre to head for is the village of **TERMENO** (Tramin), from which the varietal Gewürztraminer gets its name.

Alpe di Siusi (Seiser Alm)

The grasslands of the **Alpe di Siusi** (Seiser Alm), to the east of Bolzano, are Europe's largest Alpine plateau, extending over sixty square kilometres above the rest of the valley bordered by **Sciliar** (Schlern), a flat-topped, sheer mountain which splits off at one end into two peaks. The lush summer pastures 2000m above sea level are superb for mountain biking and hiking, especially now that the area, protected by the **Parco Naturale dello Sciliar**, is closed to road traffic (except for guests of hotels on the Alpe) between 9am and 5pm.

If you are travelling by bus to **Siusi** (Seis) from Bolzano you can stash mountain bikes in the luggage compartment of the bus. The service passes through **FIÈ AM SCILIAR** (Völs am Schlern), famous for inventing the curative "hay bath", presumably only beneficial if you don't suffer from hayfever.

Compaccio and Saltria

From Siusi you can ascend to **COMPACCIO** (Compatsch) on the plateau by a connecting bus service or by cable car (mid-May to mid-Sept 8am–7pm; mid-Sept to early Nov 8am–6pm). Compaccio is the starting point for many excellent day-hikes, such as the two-and-a-half-hour trek to *Tierser Alpl* or a climb of similar length to *Rifugio Bolzano al Monte Pez*. You can get the views the easier way by taking the chair lift to *Restaurant Bullaccia/Puflatsch*, enjoying a coffee and *buchweizentorte* (buckwheat and redcurrant cake) when you get there.

A shuttle bus from Compaccio runs to **SALTRIA** (Saltner), 2km to the west, where a smattering of **hotels** are more or less the only buildings. Here, horses graze on the tough grass, picking their way between the bogs and streams, and the main evidence of human activity is dairy farming and some logging in the woods.

Val Gardena (Grödnertal)

Trails and chair lifts connect the Alpe di Suisi with the **Val Gardena** (Grödnertal), a valley with plenty of squeaky-clean guesthouses linked by a continuous stream of tourist buses making their way along the Great Dolomites Road to Cortina d'Ampezzo. The main village in the valley, **Ortisei** (Sankt Ulrich), has for centuries been a big producer of religious sculpture and, more recently, hand-carved wooden toys, with several families each keeping their own particular design going. Almost three thousand woodcarvers in the valley still make furniture and religious statues, but Ortisei, like the neighbouring villages of **Santa Cristina** (Sankt Christina) and **Selva** (Wolkenstein), is now mainly a ski resort, within easy reach of the **Sella Ronda**, a route of ski-runs and lifts encircling the Sella mountain range that takes a whole day to complete.

ARRIVAL AND INFORMATION

ALPE DI SIUSI

By bus There are connections from Bolzano to Siusi (every 30min; 40min) and Ortisei (hourly; 1hr 15min), and from Siusi to Ortisei (hourly; 30min).

Tourist office Compaccio (Mon–Fri 8.15am–12.30pm, Sat 8.15am–noon; ☎ 0471 727 904, ⚑ seiseralm.net). This office handles information requests for the entire area.

ACCOMMODATION

COMPACCIO AND SALTRIA

Almgasthof Tirler Saltria 59 ☎ 0471 727 927, ⚑ tirler .it. Four-star ecohotel and one of the better deals in Saltria,

with huge and wonderfully woody rooms and friendly service. There's also a sauna, a pool and an in-house wellness area. **€200**

Anemone Seiseralm Compaccio 56 ☎0471 727 963, ⓦanemone-seiseralm.com. A simple chalet-style guesthouse with en-suite rooms and vista-rich balconies. Minimum stay of three nights in summer. **€70**

Schlernhaus ☎0471 612 024, ⓦschlernhaus.it; accessible by cable car then on foot from Sius. One of the original Alpine huts from the 1880s with 120 beds and hearty meals. Half board per person **€50**

Seiser Alm Urthaler Compaccio ☎0471 727 919, ⓦseiseralm.com. A beautiful hotel constructed in 2002 using sustainable building methods and boasting a long list of luxurious amenities. Half-board only. **€110**

Tierser Alpl ☎0471 707 460, ⓦtierseralpl.com. Located at a trail intersection at 2440m, this cute, red-roofed *rifugio* has gobsmacking views. Bed only, B&B and half-board options. Half-board per person **€50.50**

VAL GARDENA

Pension Briol Tre Chiese (Dreikirchen) ☎0471 650 125, ⓦbriol.it. Not in the Val Gardena itself, but across the Isarco River from Ponte Gardena, the gateway to the valley, above the village of Barbiano (Barbian), this guesthouse is a rare example of Bauhaus style in the Alps – nothing much has changed since 1928, when it was designed by artist Hubert Lanzinger. Although there are few mod cons, the simplicity and unspoilt location in flower-filled meadows are unbeatable. **€89.50**

Northeast of Bolzano

The route northeast from Bolzano along the **Isarco** (Eisacktal) valley is one of the main routes between Italy and northern Europe, crossing the border into Austria at the famous Brenner Pass (1375m), the lowest in the Alps. Protestant reformer Martin Luther was one of many travellers to have walked over the Brenner Pass on his epic journey to Rome in 1510. A motorway and high-speed train line to Innsbruck now make light work of the distance, and the ancient towns of **Bressanone** (Brixen) and **Vipiteno** (Sterzing) are engaging places on the way to stretch the legs. Nearby is the wild protected area called the **Parco Naturale Fanes-Sennes-Braies** accessible via the **Val Pusteria** (Pustertal), a side valley off the Isarco. If you are planning to walk any of the long-distance walking trails known as **alte vie** (literally "high ways") you will almost certainly visit the Val Pusteria, as most of the trails launch from there. Train is the best way to reach it with a line branching off the main Bolzano–Innsbruck tracks at **Fortezza** (Franzenfeste) and serving the drowsy settlements of the Val Pusteria, the market town of **Brunico** (Bruneck) and **Dobbiaco** (Toblach; from where there are buses to Cortina d'Ampezzo).

Bressanone (Brixen)

Wonderfully medieval **BRESSANONE** (Brixen), the principal settlement in the Val d'Isarco, is well worth a halt or even a couple of days for its atmospheric old town and some fine places to stay. This entirely German-speaking town was an independent state for a thousand years, its bishops in a constant state of rivalry with the neighbouring Counts of Tyrol based in Merano. The bishops' palace, next to the Duomo, still serves as the town's epicentre.

Duomo

Piazza del Duomo (Domplatz) • Daily 9am–6pm • Free

Destroyed by fire in the eleventh century and rebuilt in its current Baroque style in the eighteenth, the **Duomo** is Bressanone's most imposing building. The single-nave building has an interior decorated in faux marble, glass chandeliers and lots of gilding, but the really interesting part lies to the side, in the fantastically ornate **cloisters**, which were frescoed in the fourteenth century.

Museo Diocesano

Piazza Palazzo Vescovile (Hofburgplatz) 2 • Mid-March to Oct & late Nov to early Jan Tues–Sun 10am–5pm • €7 • ⓦdioezesanmuseum.bz.it

Trinkets and baubles assembled by the diocese over the centuries are safely stored in the **Museo Diocesano** next to the cathedral. Here you can see vestments belonging to

5

Bressanone's bishop-princes, their strong influence in the region evident from the gift given by Emperor Henry II to Bishop Albuino: a tenth-century Byzantine silk cloak, spread with the stylized eagle that was the bishop's personal emblem.

Pharmaziemuseum

Via Ponte Aquila (Adlerbrückengasse) 4 • July & Aug Mon–Fri 2–6pm, Sat 11am–4pm; Sept–June Tues & Wed 2–6pm, Sat 11am–4pm • €3.50 • ☎ 0472 209 112, ⓦ pharmazie.it

This unexpected gem in the town's old pharmacy, the **Pharmaziemuseum** boasts a weird and wonderful selection of antique vials and pillboxes, pharmaceutical apparatus, and sumptuously illustrated medical manuals from the late sixteenth century. The pharmacy was known for its exotic charms which bedecked the shop, items such as a crocodile, snakes, coconuts, an armadillo and an (obviously fake) unicorn, all of which can now be found in the museum's Wunderkammer (Room of Wonders).

Neustift (Novacella) Monastery

Guided tours Mon–Sat: summer hourly 10am–4pm; winter 11am & 3pm • €6 • ☎ 0472 836 189, ⓦ kloster-neustift.it

Just 3km from the town centre and reachable by bus (at least hourly), the **Neustift Monastery** is the most important in the Südtirol. It's known for its beautiful Baroque library, art collection and museum, as well for the well-regarded wine produced here and sold direct to the public. The medieval cloisters are also well worth viewing.

ARRIVAL AND INFORMATION   BRESSANONE

By train The train station is 500m southwest of the historical centre along Via Stazione.
Destinations Bolzano (at least hourly; 35min), Brennero (every 30min; 50min; change here for Innsbruck).
By bus The bus station is on the southeastern edge of the historical centre.

Destinations Bolzano (5 daily; 50min); Brunico (every 30min; 1hr); Ortisei (8 daily; 1hr); Siusi (hourly; 1hr).
Tourist office Opposite the bus station (Mon–Fri 8.30am–12.30pm & 2.30–6pm, Sat 9am–12.30pm; July & Aug Mon–Fri 8.30am–6pm, Sat 9am–12.30pm; ☎ 0472 836 401, ⓦ brixen.org).

ACCOMMODATION

Elephant Via Rio Bianco 4 ☎ 0472 832 750, ⓦ hotel elephant.com. Bressanone's top sleep is one of the longest-established and grandest hotels in the Dolomites (with an elephant statue above a pond in its grounds). Rooms are studies in elegance and furnished in understated Tyrolean style. **€96**

Goldene Krone Stadelgasse 4 ☎ 0472 835 154, ⓦ goldenekrone.com. The focus at this clean-cut hotel is firmly on wellness and motorbikers (and cyclists) with a wide range of spa treatments available, including the local "hay bath", and lots of amenities and extras for two-wheelers. Though seemingly new, the building is fairly old meaning all the light-filled doubles are different sizes. Some have balconies with mountain views. **€170**

Löwenhof Via Lago di Varna 60 ☎ 0472 836 216,

ⓦ loewenhof.it. Hotel and campsite complex, with a large outdoor swimming pool, in meadowland 2km north of Bressanone in Varna (Vahrn); several buses travel here on weekdays, fewer at weekends. Campsite closed Nov–March. Doubles **€92**, pitches **€6** plus **€8.50** per person

Mayrhofer Via Tratten 17 ☎ 0472 836 327, ⓦ mayrhofer .it. Friendly, family-run guesthouse with twelve rooms in a 500-year-old Altstadt townhouse. Breakfast can be taken on request in the secluded suntrap garden. There's paid wi-fi and half-board costs €15 extra. **€92**

Tallero Via Mercato Vecchio 35 ☎ 0472 830 577, ⓦ tallero.it. This modern, three-star hotel in the old town has nineteen comfy, clean but carbon-copy rooms, a sunny roof space and free parking at the Aquarena opposite. The building dates from 1659, though you'd never know it. **€110**

BRIXEN CARD

This gratis discount pass gives free access to public transport, the Acquarena pool, all of Südtirol's museums and much more. However it's only available to those staying at registered accommodation facilities in the Brixen and around. See ⓦ brixencard.info for details.

EATING AND DRINKING

Elephant Via Rio Bianco 4 ☏0472 836 579. The restaurant of the *Elephant* hotel dishes up expertly prepared regional cuisine, with menus changing on a daily basis. Mains €13–27. Daily noon–2.30pm & 7–11pm.

Finsterwirt Domgasse 3 ☏0472 835 343. This elegantly old-fashioned restaurant, with old prints, oils and photographs on the walls, serves excellent local specialities such as venison cutlet with cranberry sauce (€25), and Südtirol bio beef steak with balsamic vinegar sauce, radicchio and buckwheat polenta (€25). The wine list is the best in town. Worth splashing out on. 11.30am–2.15pm & 6.30–9.15pm; closed Sun evening & Mon.

Goldene Rose Portici Maggiori 7/A ☏0472 835 067. No-nonsense, old-school bar-café banging down unfussy lunches of panini, *strudel*, *weisswurst*, goulash and *tirtlan*, a round flat pastry filled with spinach or sauerkraut, the local speciality. Mon–Fri 9am–8pm, Sat 9am–4pm.

Val Pusteria (Pusertal)

The entrance to the **Val Pusteria** (Pusertal), a wide, sleepy valley of corn fields and hay meadows skirting the northern edge of the Dolomites, lies 4km north of Bressanone. This is a rural area where in the side valleys dippers dart in and out of the streams and the sawing of timber cuts through the air. Higher up, you're likely to see marmots – timid creatures similar to guinea pigs – or more likely hear them, as they give out a piercing whistle as a warning before speeding off to their burrows; on the scree-covered slopes, chamois betray their presence with a tumbling of stones.

Many of the long-distance *alte vie* footpaths start in the Val Pusteria: Alta Via 1 starts from Lago di Braies (Pragser Wildsee), Alta Via 3 from Villabassa (Niederdorf), Alta Via 4 from San Candido (Innichen) and Alta Via 5 from Sesto (Sexten).

The valley is served by bus from **Brunico** (Bruneck), and by train from **Fortezza** (Franzensfeste).

Brunico (Bruneck)

An influx of people from the surrounding villages arrives daily in the otherwise quiet market town of **BRUNICO** (Bruneck), which is also the transport centre of the region. Brunico was the home of the painter and sculptor Michael Pacher (c.1435–98); his *Vine Madonna* can be found in the parish church of the village of San Lorenzo, 4km to the southwest. Pacher is probably the most famous Tyrolean painter and woodcarver, straddling German Gothic and the more spare Italian styles; there's something vaguely unsavoury about this particular Madonna and her pudgy child, gripping a bunch of black grapes, but it's refreshing to see work in its original setting rather than in a museum.

Brunico Castle, on Schlossweg 2, is home to a branch of the **Messner Mountain Museum** (mid-May to Oct & Dec–March 10am–6pm, closed Tues; €8; see box below) focusing exclusively on the Sherpas of Nepal.

THE MESSNER MOUNTAIN MUSEUM

Bressanone-born climber and explorer Reinhold Messner is renowned primarily for having made the first ascent of Everest without oxygen in 1978 and for being the first human to climb all fourteen of the world's peaks over 8000m. Having retired from the Earth's high places, Messner has set up an inspiring and engaging museum in his home region dedicated to the world's mountain ranges and the cultures of the people who inhabit them. The museum is spread over five branches – Firmian at Schloss Sigmundskron, Ortles near Solda, the Dolomites branch south of Cortina d'Ampezzo, Juval in the Val Venosta and Ripa at Brunico Castle – occupying some pretty spectacular and sometimes remote real estate. Log onto ⓦmessner-mountain-museum.it to find out more.

5

Schloss Taufers
Daily 10am–5pm • €5 • ☎ 0474 678 053

North of Brunico extends the remote Val di Tures where the main attraction is medieval **Schloss Taufers**, located in the valley's main settlement, **CAMPO TURES** (Sand in Taufers). The dungeons boast a gruesome array of torture instruments, and there are frescoes by Pacher, but the most appealing aspect of the castle is its setting: stark grey walls, bristling with towers, stand in contrast to the glistening backdrop of the Zillertal glaciers.

ARRIVAL AND INFORMATION   BRUNICO

By train The train station is a short walk southeast of the town centre. There's a service to Dobbiaco (at least hourly; 35min).
By bus Buses leave from near the train station.
Destinations Bressanone (every 30min; 1hr); Campo Tures (every 30min; 35min); Corvara (hourly; 1hr); Dobbiaco (at least 2 per hour; 1hr).

Tourist office Rathausplatz 7 (July & Aug Mon–Fri 9am–7pm, Sat 9.30am–12.30pm & 3–6pm; Sept–June Mon–Fri 9am–12.30pm & 3–6pm, Sat 9.30am–12.30pm; ☎ 0474 555 722, ⓦ bruneck.com).

ACCOMMODATION

Andreas Hofer Via Campo Tures 1 ☎ 0474 551 469, ⓦ andreashofer.it. This very comfortable, traditionally minded four-star hotel offers immaculate rooms boasting lots of chunky wood, big-print black-and-white photos of bygone days in the Dolomites and 21st-century bathrooms. **€110**
Camping Schiesstand Via Dobbiaco 4 ☎ 0474 401 326. Well-equipped campsite around 1km west of the town centre as the crow flies. May–Sept. Pitches **€8**, plus **€6** per adult

Parco Naturale Fanes-Sannes-Braies

For dramatic mountain vistas and not-too-crowded paths – plus an insight into some of the Ladin legends – head for the awkwardly named **Parco Naturale Fanes-Sannes-Braies**, southeast of Brunico. If you have a limited amount of time to spend in this beautiful protected area, you should aim for the upper slopes of **Alpe di Fanes**, where you pick up some of the best ridgeway paths.

Footpaths cross the grassy plateaus, passing the rocks of **Castel de Fanes**, home of Dolasilla, the mythical princess of the Ladini, and an area called the Marmot Parliament. The lakes are fed by underground streams, which you can sometimes hear, burbling deep beneath your feet.

Another way to see the park is to walk the (often busy) section of Alta Via 1 that runs through it, a hike that takes three to four days, with overnight stops at refuges. The trail starts at **Lago di Braies** (Pragser Wildsee), a deep-green lake surrounded by pines, 8km off the main road through the Val Pusteria – an extraordinary place (according to legend, the lake is a gateway to an underground kingdom). Several buses go to the lake from Dobbiaco.

Also accessible from Brunico by cable car is the **Plan de Corones**, surrounded by jagged peaks. Here, legend has it, Dolasilla was crowned a warrior princess at the top of the mountain with the *raïeta* – a crystal that harnessed powerful forces.

Vipiteno (Sterzing)

Straddling the busy road north over the Brenner Pass to Innsbruck, **VIPITENO** (Sterzing) is typically Tyrolean, with geranium-filled balconies and wood-panelled old inns. The porticoed main street, however, **Via Città Nuova** (Neustadtstrasse), is more reminiscent of locations further south, lined with elegant, battlemented *palazzi* erected in Renaissance times by a locally based Florentine bank. At one end, the **Zwölferturm clock tower** divides the old town from the new: the roof was rebuilt in 1867 after fire destroyed the fifteenth-century original. The town is especially pretty on summer nights when it's lit by lanterns and there's often a local festival, with live music and foodie specialities.

ARRIVAL AND INFORMATION

By train The train station is in Via Stazione, a short walk east of the town centre.
Destinations Bolzano (hourly; 1hr); Brennero (at least hourly; 20min; change here for Innsbruck).

Tourist office Piazza Città 3 (Mon–Sat 8.30am–noon & 2.30–6pm, open Sun in high season; ☎ 0472 765 325, ⓦ vipiteno.com).

Cortina d'Ampezzo

Dubbed the "Pearl of the Dolomites", **CORTINA D'AMPEZZO** is well and truly part of the mountains of Trentino-Alto Adige, even though it officially belongs to the Veneto region next door. An upmarket ski resort – think an Italian St Moritz – Cortina boasts a gorgeous setting, surrounded by a great circle of mountains, and it's had a starring role in many films, including *The Pink Panther* and *For Your Eyes Only*.

After hosting the **Winter Olympics** in 1956, Cortina swiftly became *the* resort to be seen in and in the 1960s you were just as likely to spot movie stars such as Brigitte Bardot and Sophia Loren sauntering down the Corso Italia as people in ski boots. Nowadays, the VIPs it attracts tend to be titans of Italian industry – the Agnellis, Benettons, Barillas and the president of Ferrari all frequent the resort – and the population swells from 7000 to around 40,000 during the ski season (roughly Christmas to Easter).

ARRIVAL AND INFORMATION

By train The nearest train station is Calalzo di Cadore, 32km southeast; buses to Cortina are timed to coincide with trains.
By bus Express bus services run by Cortina Express (ⓦ cortinaexpress.it) run to Cortina from Venezia airport and Mestre train station, as well as Bologna train station during

CORTINA D'AMPEZZO

the ski season. The bus station is on Via Marconi, above town.
Destinations Dobbiaco (every 2hr; 45min); Calalzo (17 daily; 1hr).
Tourist office Piazzetta San Francesco 8 (daily 9am–12.30pm & 3.30–6.30pm; ☎ 0436 3231, ⓦ infodolomiti.it).

ACCOMMODATION

Things aren't easy for budget travellers in Cortina and prices climb exponentially during the peak ski season and in August. The tourist office has a list of rooms to rent, and in summer there's the option of camping at one of several well-equipped sites.

Hotel de La Poste Piazza Roma 14 ☎ 0436 4271, ⓦ delaposte.it. Rooms at this, one of Cortina's classic hotels with a great central location, are plush, chintzy and beautifully composed. One of the hotel's highlights is the bar – barman Antonio di Franco is a legend who has been shaking cocktails at *La Poste* for 46 years, and has invented cocktails for many of the famous people who stay here. **€171**
★ **Menardi** Via Majon 110 ☎ 0436 2400, ⓦ hotel menardi.it. An old country house, this family-run hotel is 1km from town, set in gorgeous – and extensive – grounds. There are rooms in a modern annexe as well as in the original house, and facilities include a jacuzzi, sauna and Turkish baths, and an elegant restaurant. **€110**

Montana Corso Italia 94 ☎ 0436 862 126, ⓦ cortina -hotel.com. This small Alpine hotel dating from 1927 is situated in the pedestrianized heart of Cortina, and offers no-frills rooms, some of which are definitely on the miniature side. **€100**
Olympia 5km north at Flames ☎ 0436 5057, ⓦ campingolympiacortina.it. Year-round campsite with a pool, 314 pitches, two eating places and a shuttle bus to get you to the action in town. Pitches **€7**, plus **€6** per adult
Pontejel Largo della Poste 11 ☎ 0436 2525. This recently refurbished, two-star B&B is one of the cheapest deals in town, especially in the madly expensive summer and winter seasons. Also has a much-praised restaurant. **€80**

EATING AND DRINKING

There are plenty of places to eat in Cortina and prices aren't as high as you might expect. However if your euros don't stretch to sit-down meals, there's always the Cooperativa supermarket on Corso Italia in the centre of town, as well as a few takeaway pizza places.

Baita Fraina Via Fraina 2 ☎ 0436 3634. Ten minutes from the centre in the hamlet of Fraina to the east of town, this place has been in the same family for over forty years and

serves typical, quality Ampezzana fare, backed up by a huge wine list. There are excellent soups all at €9 – barley and spelt, artichoke, leek and potato, lettuce, mushroom or pumpkin,

5

depending on the season – while pasta dishes include ricotta gnocchi with vegetables (€11), and *tagliolini* with a venison *ragù* (€11). Also has six simple rooms. Daily mid-June to Sept & Dec to mid-April noon–2.30pm & 7–10pm.

Bar Dolomiti Via Roma 50 ☎ 0436 868 344. A perfect café for wannabe-watching on the main pedestrian high-street, while you indulge in some genuine *cornetti alla crema*. Daily 8am–8pm.

Lago Ghedina Via Lago Ghedina 2, 3km west of the village ☎ 0436 860 876. A restaurant in a magical setting next to a lake that reflects the Dolomite mountains, surrounded by tall firs. It is owned by Romans, so the food differs a bit from most other places hereabouts – grilled meats and fresh river trout (€18). Daily 11.30am–2pm & 7–11pm.

★ **Leone e Anna** Localita Alverà 112, 2km out of town ☎ 0436 2768. Perfectly executed Sardinian cuisine in a great chalet atmosphere. Try *malloreddus* (home-made dumplings with tomato and Sardinian salami sauce), spaghetti with *bottarga* (salted tuna roe) or *puligioni* (ravioli stuffed with ricotta and orange peel, served with butter and basil). Also great Sardinian desserts. Mains around €11. Noon–2pm & 7–10.30pm; closed Tues in low season.

Prosciutteria LP26 Largo delle Poste 26 ☎ 0436 862 284. A café by day and wine bar/restaurant with a good buzz at night. As the name suggests, *prosciutto* is its speciality – a plate of mixed pig, wild boar and venison hams (€9.50) is a good way to sample them – but there are also tasty pasta dishes, notably *tortellini* filled with *prosciutto* and aged parmesan (€8). Tues–Sun 11am–2am.

Merano and around

An hour north by train from Bolzano **MERANO** (Meran) lies in an attractive, broad stretch of the Adige (Etsch) valley. Neatly tended apple orchards and vineyards cover almost every square inch of the lower slopes and valley floor, but when you look upwards the scale changes due to the two great mountain ranges – the Ortles (Ortler) and the Giogaia di Tessa (Texelgruppe) encircling the town. Closer geographically and in looks to the Swiss and Austrian Alps than the Dolomites, the grandeur of the landscape turns up a notch here – and a simple event like a summer storm becomes a drama, with the whole valley reverberating to the rumble of thunder.

A well-heeled **spa town**, relaxed, stylish and often packed with affluent shoppers and spa-goers, Merano has a mild climate that attracted Central Europeans at the beginning of the last century after Empress Elizabeth of Austria – known as Sissi – chose the town for her winter cure. The *époque* bequeathed a resort of fin-de-siècle hotels, neat gardens and elegant promenades.

Therme Meran

Daily 9am–10pm • €18.50 for a day-ticket for the inside and outdoor pools, €24.50 for pools plus sauna; supplement of €2 or €3 winter weekends • ☎ 0473 252 000 • ⓦ thermemeran.it

Sitting impressively on the river's south bank is Merano's sparkling **spa complex** Therme Meran, with no less than thirteen indoor pools and a raft of wellness, spa and fitness facilities, all contained inside a huge steel-and-glass cube designed by architect Matteo Thun. Treatments often utilize local South Tyrolean produce such as apples, grapes, wool, hay and chestnuts, and the list of procedures is pretty comprehensive. If all that pummelling and pampering sounds like too much hard work, just take a dip in the outdoor pools, open all year round.

Trauttmansdorff botanical gardens, castle and Touriseum

Via Valentino 51/A • April–Oct daily 9am–7pm • €10.80 • ⓦ trauttmansdorff.it or ⓦ touriseum.it; take bus #4 or #1B to the Botanischer Garten stop

Trauttmansdorff Castle, set amid the town's **botanical gardens**, is home to the fascinatingly fun **Touriseum** (Museum of Tourism; same hours as gardens). This delves into the relationship between political events, social change and the rise of tourism in the South Tyrol over the past couple of centuries using some highly entertaining and often hands-on displays.

5

Duomo

Piazza del Duomo • Daily 9am–7pm • Free

At the eastern end of the fabulously arcaded Laubengasse/Via Portici you'll find the town's **cathedral**, dedicated to St Nicholas. Pure Gothic in and out, it was one of the first churches to be built in the style in Tyrol. The most notable features are its intricate stained-glass windows, attractive ceramic floor and the 83m-high clock tower, South Tyrol's tallest.

ARRIVAL AND INFORMATION   MERANO

By train Merano's train station is on Piazza Stazione, a 10min walk from the centre of town along Corso Libertà.
Destinations Bolzano (at least hourly; 40min); Mals (at least hourly; 1hr 10min); Silandro (at least hourly; 50min).
By bus Buses arrive and depart directly outside the train station.
Destinations Bolzano (hourly; 45min); Lana (approx every

15min; 17min); Silandro (at least 2 per hour; 1hr).
Tourist office Corso Libertà 45 (Mon–Fri 9am–6pm, Sat 10am–4pm, Sun 10am–12.30pm; ☎0473 272 000, ⓦmeran.eu). Merano's tourist office produces an annual *City Guide*, a commendably comprehensive publication containing details of sights, shopping, activities and places to eat as well as bus and train timetables.

ACCOMMODATION

★ **Castel Fragsburg** ☎0473 244 071, ⓦfragsburg .com. Hugging a mountainside above the city, this former hunting lodge has dramatically styled rooms, Michelin-starred food, a spa and tremendous views – especially from the outdoor pool. Prices for the standard doubles are surprisingly low. Sadly it's only open April–Nov. **€150**
Gasthof Rainer Via Portici/Laubengasse 266 ☎0473 236 149, ⓦgasthof-rainer.it. Thick-of-the-action guest-house above a busy arcade tavern with contemporary, comfortable, but space-miserly rooms. There's no more central place to sleep with the best of Merano's shopping on the doorstep. Half-board is a mere €13 extra. **€90**

Ostello della Gioventù Carduccistrasse 77 ☎0473 201 475, ⓦjugendherberge.it. Merano's youth hostel is a 10min walk from the station. There are some en-suite rooms, a laundry and TV room, a workshop for bicycle repairs, skis and bikes to rent and baby-changing facilities. Rates include breakfast. **€22**
Westend Speckbacherstrasse 9 ☎0473 447 654, ⓦwestend.it. Strong on charm, this spa hotel is set in gardens right on the river promenade; most of the rooms have balconies and the Art Nouveau dining room is worth a peek, even if you're not eating. **€122**

EATING AND DRINKING

Forsterbräu Freiheitsstrasse/Corsa Libertà 90 ☎0473 236 535. Tuck into hearty platters of roast lamb, beef goulash, mountain mushroom risotto and *wiener schnitzel* in a variety of dining spaces at the showcase tavern of the Forst Brewery. The delicious Forst beer is made with the purest mountain spring water around. Daily 10am–midnight.
Onkel Taa's Bahnhofstrasse 17, Töll ☎0473 967342; take bus #5613. This unmissable place around 6km northwest of Merano, is located in the privately owned Bad Egart Habsburg museum, though the colourful restaurant, bedecked in thousands of rural knick-knacks of yesteryear, resembles a museum itself. Onkel Taa cooks up some scrumptious Alpine fare (mains around €15), most of which

is made with local ingredients. Tues–Sun noon–3pm & 6.30–11pm.
Sissi Galileistrasse 44 ☎0473 231 062. The best place to dine out in town is the pricey *Sissi* where renowned Italian chef Andrea Fenoglio puts a sophisticated twist on traditional Alpine and Mediterranean dishes. The best way to experience what Fenoglio has to offer is to opt for the "8 piatti" menu (€90) – eight courses, selected by the chef daily to capitalize on the best of the day's ingredients. Tues–Sun 12.15–2.30pm & 7–10pm.
Weinstube Haisrainer Via Portici/Laubengasse 100 ☎0473 237 944. Traditional inn serving gutsy Italian and Tyrolean dishes such as smoked pork, *strudel* and goulash with dumplings. Mains €12.50–15.50. Daily 9am–11pm.

Around Merano

Merano is a good base for exploring some seriously remote mountainscapes as well as discovering one of the most significant castles in the region, **Tirolo**, and **San Leonardo**, birthplace of local nineteenth-century hero, Andreas Hofer.

5

Castel Tirolo

Schlossweg 24, Tirol • Mid-March to early Dec Tues–Sun 10am–5pm, Aug until 6pm • €7 • ☎ 0473 220 221, ⓦ schlosstirol.it

On the northern outskirts of Merano you'll discover twelfth-century **Castel Tirolo**. Such was the influence of its owners, the Counts of Tirol, that the whole Tyrol region takes its name from here. The castle itself is worth visiting for its museum on daily life in the Middle Ages. Below it is **Brunnenburg**, a neo-Gothic pile that's all fishtail battlements and conical towers, where American poet Ezra Pound spent the last years of his life.

San Leonardo

San Leonardo (Sankt Leonhard), some 20km to the north of Merano, is the birthplace of Andreas Hofer. Originally an innkeeper, wine merchant and cattle dealer, Hofer fought for the Tyrol's return to Austria after it had been ceded to Bavaria in 1805, becoming a hero of the people after successful uprisings against occupying Bavarian and Napoleonic troops. However, larger political forces overtook him and Hofer was arrested in 1810 and executed under Napoleon's orders in Mantua. There's a small Hofer **museum** (March–Nov Tues–Sun 10am–6pm; €7; ⓦmuseum.passeier.it) at Passeierstrasse 72, his birthplace. Four buses an hour make the trip from Merano.

Val d'Ultimo (Ultental)

A traditional place of hiding in an area renowned for mountain warfare, the **Val d'Ultimo** (Ultental) to the southwest of Merano remained relatively isolated and closed to outsiders until the early twentieth century. The road into the valley begins its ascent just south of Merano at **LANA** and ends at the remote village of **SANTA GERTRUDE** (Sankt Gertraud), the terminus for buses along the valley. From here trails (3hr) lead over rock-strewn moorland to *Rifugio Canziani* aka *Höchster Hütte* (☎0473 798 120; mid-June to mid-Oct), surrounded by the glaciers and peaks of **Gioveretto** (Zufrittspitze). If you're feeling less energetic, the valley is still a good place for some shorter walks, using the village as base. Buses from Merano and Lana make the trip along the valley.

Parco Nazionale dello Stelvio

The **Parco Nazionale dello Stelvio** (or the Stilfser National Park) is one of Italy's major national parks: it extends north to the Swiss Engadine and southwest into Lombardy and covers the whole **Ortles** (Ortler) mountain range. The park is topped by one of Europe's largest glaciers (the Ghiacciaio dei Forni) and crossed by the **Passo dello Stelvio** (2758m), which misses being the highest pass in the Alps by just 12m.

Ski tourism has made its mark, and the park is as crisscrossed by lifts as anywhere in the Alps, but it's still a remarkable place. People come here for the high trails and glacier skiing in summer, or for the chance of seeing **wildlife** such as the red and roe deer, elk, chamois, golden eagle and ibex. A railway line running from Merano to Malles and connecting buses from stations along the way into the side valleys makes all places of interest below easily accessible.

The Val Venosta (Vinschgau)

Extending west from Merano, the **Val Venosta** is the main approach to the Stelvio park, and while it's often busy with traffic a rural feel remains away from the road. Every weekend during July and August, one or other of the villages holds a summer **street festival**, with live music, beer gardens and fresh produce. One of the best is the Marmor e Marillen (Marble and Apricots) in early August in the tiny village of **Laas** which offers the chance to sample *marillenknödel* – sweet potato dumplings filled with whole apricots and rolled in sugar and breadcrumbs.

CROSSING THE PASSO DELLO STELVIO

The journey across the Ortles mountains over the **Passo dello Stelvio** (Stelvio Pass) to Bormio in Lombardy makes for a white-knuckle drive. This amazingly convoluted route consists of 48 switchbacks and turns but is well worth it for both the thrill and the view. Motorbikers love it and cyclists view the climb as the ultimate challenge – it's often an important stage of the Girò d'Italia. Beware that this is one of the last Alpine passes to open to traffic each year, and it's not unknown for the road to stay closed until July if there's been a late fall of snow. If you're travelling by **public transport** you can access the pass by bus from Malles, one early morning, the other mid-afternoon.

The end point of the route, **Bormio**, is a rather snooty resort with a sprawl of hotels in its cobblestoned core. There's a visitor centre at Via Roma 131/B (Mon–Sat 9am–12.30pm & 3–6pm, July & Aug daily 9am—7pm; ⓣ0342 903 300, ⓦbookbormio.com) which can advise on accommodation as well as nature trails in the southern reaches of the Stelvio national park.

Forest

At the beginning of the valley the village of **Forest** (Forst) is dominated by the Forst brewery (ⓦforst.it), whose hop-scented brews you can knock back throughout South Tyrol. Guided tours of the brewery run every Thursday from June through to September at 2pm but only in Italian. Call ahead (ⓣ0473 260 111) to book a place.

Castello Juval

April–June & Sept to first Sun in Nov Thurs–Tues 10am–4pm • €8 • ⓦmessner-mountain-museum.it

At the Vinschgau village of Kastelbell, the dramatic **Castello Juval**, dating from the thirteenth century, houses another branch of the Messner Mountain Museum and doubles up as the famous mountaineer Reinhold Messner's home. Inside you'll discover a superb collection of Tibetica, an assembly of paintings depicting the world's holy peaks and an Expedition Cellar packed with old climbing gear that's been to some pretty lonely places, as well as a reasonable *osteria*.

Glorenza

The ancient walled village of **GLORENZA** (Glurns), 2.5km before the railway ends at Malles, has a population of less than nine hundred, but still enjoys special privileges conferred in 1294 when it was a salt-trading centre. An architectural gem, the settlement boasts numerous porticoes and merchants' houses dating back to the sixteenth century, as well as well-preserved defences.

Churburg

Visits are by one-hour guided tour only: mid-March to Oct Tues–Sun 10am–noon & 2–4.30pm • €8 • ⓦchurburg.com

End of the line for the railway comes at Malles (Mals) where the castle at **Coira**, more frequently known by its German name of **Churburg**, was owned by the lords of Matsch at the beginning of the thirteenth century. Back then, it was just one castle in a whole chain stretching from Bavaria to just north of Milan and was battled over by various knights – their suits of armour, some weighing nearly 25kg, can be seen in the **armoury**.

The side valleys

Three main **side valleys** thread their way from the Val Venosta into the foothills of the Ortles range: the Val Martello (Martelltal), the Val di Trafoi (Trafoiertal) and the Val di Solda (Suldental).

Val Martello

Buses run regularly from Goldrain into the stunning **VAL MARTELLO** (Martelltal), passing silver birch woods, the ruins of Castel Montani and an aviary for falcons at Morter along

5

the way. At the head of the valley, **Paradiso del Cevedale** (2088m) is one of the busiest bases for climbers and cross-country skiers, lying close to Monte Cevedale (Zufallspitze; 3769m); other trails lead across high passes to Val d'Ultimo and Val di Solda.

Val di Trafoi

TRAFOI is a beautifully situated hamlet perched at 1543m by the side of the road towards the beginning of the main climb up to the Stelvio Pass. The uninterrupted views of the mighty **Ortles** are stupendous, and the slopes remarkably unsullied by tourism. A cable car makes the ascent from Trafoi to *Rifugio Forcola* (no accommodation) at 2250m, from where a fine path (4hr) continues up and round to the pass which until 1918 marked the frontier between Italy, Switzerland and Austria. On your way, you pass the **Pizzo Garibaldi** (Dreisprachenspitze), a spur of rock that's the symbolic meeting place for the three main languages of the area.

Val di Solda

The isolated Val di Solda is a tributary valley off the Val di Trafoi. At its head lies the hamlet of **SOLDA** (Sulden), a major climbing and skiing centre since the nineteenth century. If you have time, it's worth checking out the tiny, eccentric **museum** (daily 9am–7pm; free) celebrating Solda's existence as a mountain resort as well as the **MMM Ortles** ice museum (June to mid-Oct & mid-Dec to April 2–6pm, closed Tues; ☎0473 613 577, ⍵messner-mountain-museum.it; €6), a branch of Reinhold Messner's network of mountain museums. As well as exhibits on the nearby glaciers of the Ortles, the highlight is the jagged skylight giving the impression you're at the bottom of a crevasse, looking up.

Although Solda attracts fairly serious climbers and skiers, you don't have to be experienced to attempt some of the trails. There are easy paths (2hr) up to *Rifugio-Albergo Città di Milano* (*Schaubachhütte*; ☎0473 613 024; late June to early Oct & Dec–May) at 2581m, or more difficult trails (3.5hr) to *Rifugio Payer* (*Payerhütte*; ☎0473 613 010; mid-June to Sept) at 3029m, a fantastic viewpoint and base for the ascent of **Ortles** (Ortler). At 3905m high, it was the tallest mountain of the old Austrian Empire before the border changed, and was once marked on local maps as "The End of the World".

ARRIVAL AND DEPARTURE	**PARCO NAZIONALE DELLO STELVIO**

If you don't have your own vehicle, train is the easiest way to travel along the Val Venosta from where you can access the park. Bus services run from the railway line into the side valleys of Martello, Trafoi and Solda.

By train The privately operated Vinschgaubahn/Ferrovia della Val Venosta runs every 30min between Merano and Malles (Mals) and gives access to several villages along the valley, connecting with local bus services. Trains carry bicycles free of charge.

By bus There are services from Merano to Kastelbell (hourly; 50min) and Silandro (every 30min; 1hr); from Mals to Glurns (hourly; 4min); from Spondinig to Trafoi (3 daily; 40min) and Solda (3 daily; 50min); from Goldrain to Martello (hourly; 20min).

INFORMATION

Tourist offices There are offices at Solda, Via Principale 72 (Mon–Fri 9am–noon & 3–6pm, Sat 9am–noon; ☎0473 613 015, ⍵ortlergebiet.it); Silandro, Kapuzinerstrasse 10 (Mon–Fri 8am–noon & 1–5pm, Sat 9am–12.30pm; ☎0473 620 480, ⍵vinschgau.net); and Malles, Via S.

Benedetto 1 (Mon–Fri 8am–noon & 3–6pm, Sat 9am–noon; ☎0473 831 190, ⍵ferienregion-obervinschgau.it), which serves the far western end of the Val Venosta.
Websites For general information on the area, visit ⍵stelviopark.it or ⍵vinschgau.net.

ACCOMMODATION

GLORENZA

Hotel Gasthof Grüner Baum Piazza Città/Stadtplatz 7 ☎0473 831 206, ⍵gasthofgruenerbaum.it. If you fancy

an overnight stop in enchanting Glorenza, you can't do better than this traditional inn which has been sensitively reinvented in austere, minimalist style. Free wi-fi. **€103**

5

SOLDA

Garni des Alpes Hauptstrasse 93 ☎0473 613 062, ⓦgarnidesalpes.com. A 10min walk away from the village centre, in the upper part of town, this guesthouse offers modern rooms and the services of a resident climbing/skiing guide. €58

Ortlerhof ☎0473 613 052, ⓦortlerhof-sulden.com. The first hotel on the way into Solda provides B&B accommodation in en-suite rooms with window-boxed balconies; May–Sept; minimum stay three days. €50

Paulmichl Hauptstrasse 20 ☎0473 613 064, ⓦpension paulmichl.com. A modest guesthouse, right next to the tourist office in Solda's lower town, and best located for restaurants and services. €60

TRAFOI

Hotel Bella Vista ☎0473 611 716, ⓦbella-vista.it. On the road up to the Stelvio Pass, this stylish hotel is the home of Olympic gold-medal-winning skier Gustav Thöni. The hotel has large, Scandinavian-style rooms, most with balconies, as well as a sauna and Turkish bath. €144

Tuckett ☎0473 611 722, ⓦgasthof-tuckett.com. This family-run, chalet-style guesthouse on the main road in Trafoi offers traditionally simple accommodation in reasonably priced rooms with balconies. €64

Venice and the Veneto

BASILICA DI SAN MARCO, VENICE

Venice and the Veneto

6

The first-time visitor to Venice arrives full of expectations, most of which turn out to be well founded. All the photographs you've seen of the Palazzo Ducale, of the Basilica di San Marco, of the palaces along the Canal Grande – they've simply been recording the extraordinary truth. All the bad things you've heard about the city turn out to be right as well. Economically and socially ossified, it is losing hundreds of residents by the year and plays virtually no part in the life of modern Italy. It's deluged with tourists and occasionally things get so bad that entry into the city is barred to those who haven't already booked a room. And it's expensive – the price of a good meal almost anywhere else in Italy will get you a lousy one in Venice, and its hoteliers make the most of a situation where demand will always far outstrip supply.

As soon as you begin to explore Venice, though, every day will bring its surprises, for this is an urban landscape so rich that you can't walk for a minute without coming across something that's worth a stop. And although it's true that the city can be unbearably crowded, things aren't so bad beyond the magnetic field of San Marco, and in the off-season (Nov to Christmas; Jan to Easter, excluding Carnevale) it's possible to have parts of the centre virtually to yourself. As for keeping your costs down, Venice does have some good-value eating places, and you can, with planning, find a bed without spending a fortune.

Tourism is far from being the only strand to the economy of the **Veneto**, the surrounding region of which Venice is capital. The rich, flat land around the Po supports some of Italy's most productive farms and vineyards, and industrial development around the main towns rivals even the better-known areas around Milan, making the region one of the richest in Europe. At Marghera, just over the lagoon from Venice, the Veneto has the largest industrial complex in the country, albeit one that is now in decline. **Padua** and **Verona** are the main tourist attractions after Venice, thanks to their masterpieces by Giotto, Donatello and Mantegna. None of the other towns of the Veneto can match the cultural wealth of these two, but there are nonetheless plenty of places that justify a detour – the Palladian city of **Vicenza**, for instance, the fortified settlements of **Castelfranco** and **Cittadella**, and the idyllic upland town of **Asolo**.

For outdoor types, the interesting terrain lies in the northern part of the Veneto, where the wooded slopes of the foothills soon give way to the savage precipices of the eastern Dolomites. Because most of the high peaks of the Dolomites lie within Trentino-Alto Adige, and the eastern Dolomites are most easily explored as part of a tour of the range as a whole, the area of the Veneto north of **Belluno** is covered in Chapter Five. Similarly, the eastern shore of Lake Garda is covered as part of the Lakes region in Chapter Four.

PIAZZA DELLE ERBE, VERONA

Highlights

❶ **Basilica di San Marco, Venice** San Marco is an amazing sight with its 4000 square metres of golden mosaics. **See p.352**

❷ **The Accademia, Venice** Masterpieces by Titian, Bellini, Veronese and Tintoretto feature strongly in the world's best collection of Venetian painting. **See p.361**

❸ **Punta della Dogana, Venice** If you have even the slightest interest in contemporary art, make time for the Dogana – the best collection of its kind in Europe. **See p.363**

❹ **Carnevale** Venice's carnival is the most famous, but if you want a less touristic event, head for Verona, where the whole town turns out for a procession of more than eighty floats. **See p.396**

❺ **Giotto frescoes, Padua** Giotto's frescoes in the Cappella degli Scrovegni constitute one of the pivotal works in the history of European art. **See p.401**

❻ **Vicenza** The well-heeled city of Vicenza is renowned above all for the buildings of Palladio, perhaps the most influential architect ever. **See p.408**

❼ **Verona** Cradled in a tight curve of the Adige river, Verona is a fabulously handsome city. **See p.414**

HIGHLIGHTS ARE MARKED ON THE MAPS ON P.348 AND PP.354–355

Venice (Venezia)

The monuments that draw the largest crowds in Venice are the **Basilica di San Marco** – the mausoleum of the city's patron saint – and the **Palazzo Ducale** – the home of the doge and all the governing councils. Certainly these are the most dramatic structures in the city: the first a mosaic-clad emblem of Venice's Byzantine origins, the second perhaps the finest of all secular Gothic buildings. But every parish rewards exploration, and a roll-call of the churches worth visiting would feature over fifty names, and a list of the important paintings and sculptures they contain would be twice as long. Two of the distinctively Venetian institutions known as the **scuole** retain some of the outstanding examples of Italian Renaissance art – the **Scuola di San Rocco**, with its sequence of pictures by Tintoretto, and the **Scuola di San Giorgio degli Schiavoni**, decorated with a gorgeous sequence by Carpaccio.

Although many of the city's treasures remain in the buildings for which they were created, a sizeable number have been removed to Venice's **museums**. The one that should not be missed is the **Accademia**, an assembly of Venetian painting that consists of virtually nothing but masterpieces; other prominent collections include the museum of eighteenth-century art in the **Ca' Rezzonico**, the **Museo Correr** (the civic museum of Venice), and the city's superb showcase for contemporary art, the **Punta della Dogana**.

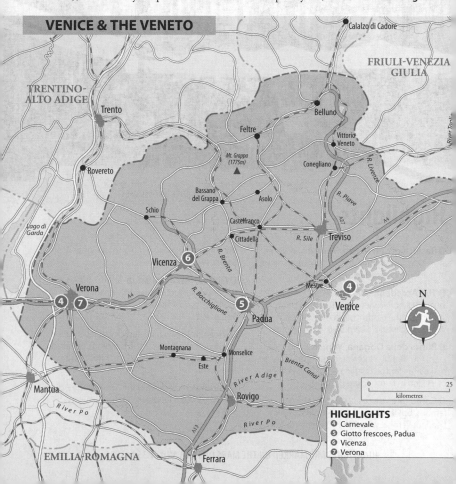

VENICE & THE VENETO

HIGHLIGHTS
- ❹ Carnevale
- ❺ Giotto frescoes, Padua
- ❻ Vicenza
- ❼ Verona

REGIONAL FOOD AND WINE

Venice specializes in fish and **seafood**, together with exotic ingredients like pomegranates, pine nuts and raisins, harking back to its days as a port and merchant city. The surrounding Veneto vies with Lombardy for the risotto-making crown – the end product tending to be more liquid than those to the west, usually with a seafood base although peas (*bisi* in the local dialect) are also common, as are other seasonal vegetables including spinach, asparagus and pumpkin. The red salad-leaf radicchio also has its home in the Veneto, as does the renowned Italian dessert, **tiramisù**. Polenta is eaten, too, while **pork** in all forms features strongly, together with heavy **soups** of beans, rice and root vegetables.

Pastries and **sweets** are also an area of Venetian expertise. Look out for the thin oval biscuits called *baicoli*, the ring-shaped cinnamon-flavoured *bussolai* (a speciality of the Venetian island of Burano) and *mandorlato*, a cross between nougat and toffee, made with almonds.

The Veneto has been very successful at developing **wines** with French and German grape varieties, notably Merlot, Cabernet, Pinot Bianco, Pinot Grigio, Müller-Thurgau, Riesling, Chardonnay and Gewürztraminer. The quintessentially Italian Bardolino, Valpolicella and Soave are all from the Verona area and, like so many Italian wines, taste better near their region of origin. This is also true of **Prosecco**, a light champagne-like wine from the area around Conegliano. **Grappa**, the local firewater, is associated particularly with the upland town of Bassano di Grappa, where every *alimentari* stocks a dozen varieties. Made from grape husks, juniper berries or plums, grappa is very much an acquired taste.

6

Venice's cultural heritage is a source of endless fascination, but you should also allow time just to wander – the anonymous parts of the city reveal as much of the city's essence as the highlighted attractions. And equally indispensable for a full understanding of Venice's way of life and development are expeditions to the outer **islands** of the lagoon.

Brief history

Small groups of fishermen and hunters were living on the mudbanks of the Venetian lagoon at the start of the Christian era, but the first mass migration was provoked by the arrival in the Veneto of **Attila the Hun**'s hordes in 453, and the rate of settlement accelerated when the **Lombards** swept into northern Italy in 568. The loose confederation of island communes that developed owed political allegiance to **Byzantium**. But with the steep increase in the population of the islands the ties with the empire grew weaker, and in 726 the settlers chose their own leader of the provincial government – the first **doge**.

The control of Byzantium soon became no more than nominal, and the inhabitants of the lagoon signalled their independence through one great symbolic act – the theft of the body of **St Mark** from Alexandria in 828. St Mark displaced Byzantium's St Theodore as the city's patron, and a basilica was built alongside the doge's castle to accommodate the relics. These two buildings – the **Basilica di San Marco** and the **Palazzo Ducale** – were to remain the emblems of the Venetian state and the repository of power within the city for almost one thousand years.

Before the close of the tenth century the Venetian **trading networks** were well established through concessions granted by Byzantium in the markets of the East. By the early twelfth century Venetian merchants had won exemption from all tolls within the eastern empire and were profiting from the chaos that followed the **First Crusade**, launched in 1095. Prosperity found expression in the fabric of the city: the basilica and many of its mosaics are from this period. The **Fourth Crusade**, diverted to Constantinople by the Venetians, set the seal on their maritime empire. They brought back shiploads of treasure (including the horses of San Marco) from the **Sack of Constantinople** in 1204, but more significant was the division of the territorial spoils, which left "one quarter and half a quarter" of the Roman Empire under Venice's sway and gave it a chain of ports that stretched to the Black Sea.

After the **Sack of Rome** in 1527 the whole Italian peninsula, with the exception of Venice, came under the domination of Emperor Charles V. Hemmed in at home, Venice saw its overseas territory further whittled away by the Turks as the century progressed: by 1529 the

6

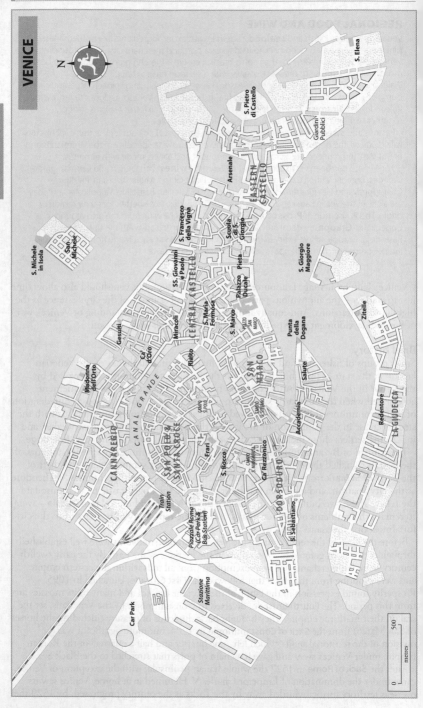

VENICE

N

S. Michele in Isola

San Michele

Madonna dell'Orto

CANNAREGIO

Gesuiti

Ca' d'Oro

Miracoli

SS. Giovanni e Paolo

S. Francesco della Vigna

EASTERN CASTELLO

S. Pietro di Castello

Arsenale

Giardini Pubblici

S. Elena

CENTRAL CASTELLO

S. Maria Formosa

Scuola di S. Giorgio

Rialto

CANAL GRANDE

SAN POLO & SANTA CROCE

S. Rocco

Frari

Ca' Mocenigo

Ca' Rezzonico

DORSODURO

S. Sebastiano

Train Station

Piazzale Roma (Car Park) & Bus Station

Stazione Marittima

Car Park

S. Marco

CAMPO S. STEFANO

SAN MARCO

PALAZZO SAN MARCO

Palazzo Ducale

Pietà

Punta della Dogana

Salute

Accademia

S. Giorgio Maggiore

Zitelle

Redentore

LA GIUDECCA

0   500
metres

6

THE *SESTIERI* OF VENICE

The 121 islands of central Venice are divided into six districts known as **sestieri**, and the houses within each *sestiere* are numbered in a sequence that makes sense solely to the functionaries of the post office – this explains how buildings facing each other across an alleyway can have numbers that are separated by hundreds.

Venice's main thoroughfare, the **Canal Grande**, divides the city in half – three *sestieri* to the west and three to the east. On the east side of the Canal Grande is the *sestiere* of **San Marco**, the area where the majority of the essential sights are clustered, and accordingly the most expensive and most crowded district of the city. East of San Marco is **Castello**, and to the north is **Cannaregio** – both of which become more residential, and quieter, the further you get from the centre. On the other side of the Canal Grande, the largest of the *sestieri* is **Dorsoduro**, stretching from the fashionable quarter at the southern tip of the canal to the docks in the west. **Santa Croce**, named after a now-demolished church, roughly follows the curve of the Canal Grande from Piazzale Roma to a point just short of the Rialto, where it joins the smartest and commercially most active of the districts on this bank – **San Polo**.

Ottoman Empire extended right along the southern Mediterranean to Morocco, and even the great naval success at **Lepanto** in 1571 was followed by the surrender of Cyprus.

The decline continued throughout the 1600s and by the eighteenth century Venice had become a political nonentity: the playground of Europe, a city of casinos and perpetual festivals. **Napoleon** finally brought the show to an end: on May 12, 1797, the Maggior Consiglio met for the last time, voting to accede to his demand that it dismantle the machinery of government. After Waterloo, Venice fell to the Austrians and remained a Habsburg province until united with the Kingdom of Italy in 1866.

The need for a more substantial economic base led, in the wake of World War I, to the construction of the industrial centre across the lagoon at **Marghera**, adjacent to Mestre, which in 1933 was connected to Venice by a road link. After World War II Mestre-Marghera's growth accelerated greatly, and the mainland conurbation has continued to expand, to the detriment of the *centro storico*. The factories of Mestre-Marghera are essential to the economy of the province, but have caused problems too: apart from polluting the lagoon, they have siphoned many people out of Venice and into the cheaper housing of Mestre, making Mestre-Marghera today more than three times larger than the historic centre of Venice, where the population has dropped since World War II from around 170,000 to under 60,000. No city has suffered more from the tourist industry than Venice – around twenty million people visit the city each year – though without them Venice would barely survive.

San Marco

The section of Venice enclosed by the lower loop of the Canal Grande – a rectangle smaller than 1000m by 500m – is, in essence, the Venice of the travel brochures. The plush hotels are concentrated here, in the *sestiere* of **San Marco**, as are the swankier shops and the best-known cultural attractions of the city.

"The finest drawing-room in Europe" was how Napoleon described its focal point, the **Piazza San Marco** – the only piazza in Venice, all other squares being *campi* or *campielli*. Less genteel phrases might seem appropriate on a suffocating summer afternoon, but the Piazza has been congested for centuries. Its parades, festivities and markets have always drawn visitors, the biggest attraction being the trade fair known as the **Fiera della Sensa**, which kept the Piazza buzzing for the fortnight following the Ascension Day ceremony of the Marriage of Venice to the Sea; nowadays the Piazza is the focal point of the Carnevale shenanigans. The coffee shops of the Piazza were a vital component of eighteenth-century high society, and the two survivors from that period – **Florian** and **Quadri** – are still the most expensive in town.

6

MUSEUM AND CHURCH PASSES

There are two **museum cards** for the city's civic museums (ⓦvisitmuve.it). The **Musei di Piazza San Marco card** costs €16.50 (€8.50 for ages 6–14, students under 30, EU citizens over 65 & Rolling Venice Card holders), and gets you into the Palazzo Ducale, Museo Correr, Museo Archeologico and the Biblioteca Marciana; it's valid for three months. The **Museum Pass**, costing €20.50/14.50, covers these four, plus all the other civic museums: Ca' Rezzonico, Casa Goldoni, Palazzo Mocenigo, Museo di Storia Naturale, Ca' Pesaro (the modern art and oriental museums), the Museo del Merletto (Burano) and the Museo del Vetro (Murano). It's valid for six months. Both passes allow one visit to each attraction and are available from any of the participating museums. The Palazzo Ducale and Museo Correr can be visited only with a museum card; at the other places you have the option of paying an entry charge just for that attraction. Accompanied disabled people have free access to all the civic museums.

For tourists who intend to do some intensive sightseeing, the city has introduced the ludicrously complicated **Venice Connected** scheme (ⓦveniceconnected.com), in which you choose a menu of services online (museum passes, transport, wi-fi networks, public toilets), and are then quoted a price that varies not just with the time of year but also with the days of the week. You get discounts if you order your card at least fifteen days in advance, but the discounts aren't great and the period of validity of any Venice Connected card begins when you collect it, whereas ACTV Travel Cards (see p.385) are valid from the moment you first use them.

You can also buy a thing called the **Venice Card** (€39.90/€29.90), in effect a combined Museum Pass and Chorus Pass (see below), with a few small discounts thrown in, plus a map for which the tourist offices would otherwise charge you €2, and two free uses of the public toilets each day. It's poor value, and is valid for only seven days, a far shorter period than the Museum and Chorus passes.

If you're aged between 14 and 29, you are eligible for a **Rolling Venice Card**, which entitles you to discounts at some shops, restaurants, hostels, campsites, museums, concerts and exhibitions, plus a big discount on the 72-hour ACTV travel pass. The card costs €4, is valid until the end of the year in which it's bought, and is worth buying if you're in town for at least a week and aim to make the most of every minute. The Rolling Venice Card is available from the tourist offices, on production of a passport or similar ID.

Sixteen churches are part of the **Chorus Pass** scheme (ⓦchorusvenezia.org), whereby a €10 ticket allows one visit to each of the churches over a one-year period; the individual entrance fee at each of the participating churches is €3. The churches involved are: the Frari; the Gesuati; Madonna dell'Orto; the Redentore; San Giacomo dell'Orio; San Giobbe; San Giovanni Elemosinario; San Pietro di Castello; San Polo; San Sebastiano; San Stae; Sant'Alvise; Santa Maria dei Miracoli; Santa Maria del Giglio; Santa Maria Formosa; and Santo Stefano. The Chorus Pass is available at each of these churches and the tourist offices.

The Basilica di San Marco

San Marco is open to tourists Mon–Sat 9.45am–5pm, Sun 2–5pm (4pm from Nov to Easter); one part of the church, the Loggia dei Cavalli, is open daily 9.45am–4.45pm • Entrance to the main body of the church is free, but the Loggia dei Cavalli costs €4, the sanctuary €2 and the treasury €3

The **Basilica di San Marco** is the most exotic of Europe's cathedrals, and no visitor can remain dispassionate when confronted by it. Herbert Spencer loathed it – "a fine sample of barbaric architecture", but to John Ruskin it was a "treasure-heap … a confusion of delight". It's certainly confusing, increasingly so as you come nearer and the details emerge; some knowledge of the history of the building helps bring a little order out of chaos.

A brief history of the Basilica

According to the **legend of St Mark's annunciation**, the Evangelist was moored in the lagoon, on his way to Rome, when an angel appeared and told him that his body would rest there. (The angel's salute – *Pax tibi, Marce evangelista meus* – is the text cut into the book that the Lion of St Mark is always shown holding.) The founders of Venice, having persuaded themselves of the sacred ordination of their city, duly went about fulfilling the angelic prophecy, and in 828 the body of St Mark was stolen from Alexandria and brought here.

Modelled on Constantinople's Church of the Twelve Apostles, the shrine of St Mark was consecrated in 832, but in 976 both the church and the Palazzo Ducale were burnt down. The present basilica was finished in 1094 and embellished over the succeeding centuries. Every trophy that the doge stuck onto his church (this church was not the cathedral of Venice but the doge's own chapel) was proof of Venice's secular might and so of the spiritual power of St Mark.

The exterior

Of the exterior features that can be seen easily from the ground, the **Romanesque carvings** of the **central door** demand the closest attention – especially the middle arch's figures of the months and seasons and outer arch's series of the trades of Venice. The carvings were begun around 1225 and finished in the early fourteenth century. Take a look also at the mosaic above the doorway on the far left – *The Arrival of the Body of St Mark* – which was made around 1260 (the only early mosaic left on the main facade) and includes the oldest known image of the basilica.

The narthex

From the Piazza you pass into the vestibule known as the **narthex**, which is decorated with thirteenth-century **mosaics** of Old Testament scenes on the domes and arches; *The Madonna with Apostles and Evangelists*, in the niches flanking the main door, date from the 1060s and are the oldest mosaics in San Marco.

The Loggia dei Cavalli

A steep staircase goes from the church's main door up to the **Museo di San Marco** and the Loggia dei Cavalli. Apart from giving you an all-round view, the loggia is also the best place from which to inspect the Gothic carvings along the apex of the facade. The **horses** outside are replicas, the genuine articles having been removed inside. Thieved from the Hippodrome of Constantinople in 1204 during the Fourth Crusade, the horses are probably Roman works of the second century – the only such ancient group, or *quadriga*, to have survived.

The interior's mosaics

With its undulating floor of twelfth-century patterned marble, its plates of eastern stone on the lower walls, and its four thousand square metres of **mosaics** covering every other inch of wall and vaulting, the interior of San Marco is the most opulent of any cathedral. One visit is not enough – there's too much to take in at one go, and the shifting light reveals and hides parts of the decoration as the day progresses; try calling in for half an hour at the beginning and end of a couple of days.

The majority of the mosaics were in position by the middle of the thirteenth century; some date from the fourteenth and fifteenth centuries, and others were created as recently as the eighteenth century to replace damaged early sections. Some of the best are the following: on the west wall, above the door, *Christ, the Virgin and St Mark*; in the west dome, *Pentecost*; on the arch between the west and central domes, the *Crucifixion* and *Resurrection*; in the central dome, *Ascension*; and in the east dome, *Religion of Christ Foretold by the Prophets*.

The Sanctuary

From the south transept you can enter the **Sanctuary** where, behind the altar, you'll find the most precious of San Marco's treasures – the **Pala d'Oro** (Golden Altar Panel). Commissioned in 976 in Constantinople, the Pala was enlarged, enriched and rearranged by Byzantine goldsmiths in 1105, then by Venetians in 1209 (to incorporate some less-cumbersome loot from the Fourth Crusade) and again (finally) in 1345.

6

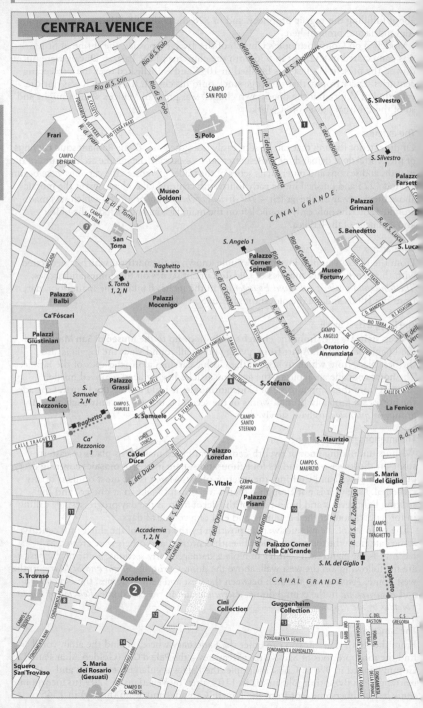

CENTRAL VENICE

HIGHLIGHTS
❶ Basilica di San Marco
❷ The Accademia
❸ Punta della Dogana

⬤RESTAURANTS	
Alla Madonna	3
Al Testiere	6
Antico Dolo	1
Da Carla	11
Rosticceria Gislon	4

⬤CAFÉS, PASTICCERIE & GELATERIE	
Caffè del Doge	2
Cioccolateria VizioVirtù	7
Florian	10
La Boutique del Gelato	5
Marchini	9
Marchini Time	8

⬛BARS	
Al Portego	2
Al Volto	6
Bácaro Jazz	3
Cantina del Vino già Schiavi	8
Do Mori	1
Enoteca Mascareta	5
I Rusteghi	4
Torino	7

⬛ACCOMMODATION	
Accademia Villa Maravege	11
Agli Alboretti	12
Ai Do Mori	4
Al Gambero	3
Art Deco	8
Ca' Arco Antico	1
Ca' Maria Adele	15
Ca' Pisani	14
Casa Petrarca	5
Casa Verardo	13
DD 724	13
Fiorita	7
Locanda San Barnaba	9
Novecento	10
Orseolo	6

6

VENICE IN FLOOD

Called the *acqua alta*, the **winter flooding** of Venice is caused by a combination of seasonal tides, fluctuations in atmospheric pressure in the Adriatic and persistent southeasterly winds, and has always been a feature of Venetian life. In recent years, however, it has been getting worse, with more than a hundred floods a year – though most of these are minor. If the siren sounds, you can expect a serious flood in three to four hours' time. A system of plank walkways is immediately set up in the low-lying parts of the city – most boat stops have maps of where those walkways run. The usual high-tide season is September to April, with the worst flooding between November and February.

A grand plan is being implemented to protect the city, involving building a **tidal barrier** across the three entrances to the lagoon. Nicknamed Moisè (Moses), the barrier aroused considerable opposition, both to its cost and to its potential environmental impact. However, mounting concern about global warming gave the matter more urgency and has led to widespread acceptance. More than twenty years after the first plan was submitted, work finally began on the barrier in 2003 and is due to be completed in 2014.

The completed screen holds 83 enamel plaques, 74 enamelled roundels, 38 chiselled figures, 300 sapphires, 300 emeralds, 400 garnets, 15 rubies, 1300 pearls and a couple of hundred other stones.

The treasury

Tucked into the corner of the south transept is the door of the **treasury**, installed in a thick-walled chamber which is perhaps a vestige of the first Palazzo Ducale. This dazzling warehouse of chalices, icons, reliquaries, candelabra and other ecclesiastical appurtenances is an unsurpassed collection of Byzantine work in silver, gold and semiprecious stones. Particularly splendid are a twelfth-century Byzantine incense burner in the shape of a domed church, and a gilded silver Gospel cover from Aquileia, also made in the twelfth century.

The rest of the Basilica

Back in the main body of the church, there's still more to see on the lower levels of the building. Don't overlook the **rood screen**'s marble figures of The Virgin, St Mark and the Apostles, carved in 1394 by the dominant sculptors in Venice at that time, Jacobello and Pietro Paolo Dalle Masegne. The **pulpits** on each side of the screen were assembled in the early fourteenth century from miscellaneous panels (some from Constantinople); the new doge was presented to the people from the right-hand one. The tenth-century **Icon of the Madonna of Nicopeia** (in the chapel on the east side of the north transept) is the most revered religious image in Venice; it used to be one of the most revered in Constantinople.

The Palazzo Ducale

Daily: April–Oct 8.30am–7pm; Nov–March 9am–5.30pm • Entrance with Museum Pass • ⓦ palazzoducale.visitmuve.it

Architecturally, the **Palazzo Ducale** is a unique mixture: the style of its exterior, with its geometrically patterned stonework and continuous tracery walls, can only be called Islamicized Gothic, whereas the courtyards and much of the interior are based on Classical forms – a blending of influences that led Ruskin to declare it "the central building of the world". Unquestionably, it is the finest secular building of its era in Europe, and the central building of Venice. The Palazzo Ducale was far more than the residence of the doge – it was the home of all of Venice's governing councils, its law courts, a sizeable number of its civil servants and even its prisons. All power in the Venetian Republic and its domains was controlled within this one building.

At the head of the network was the **doge**, the one politician to sit on all the major councils of state and the only one elected for life; he could be immensely influential in policy and appointments, and restrictions were accordingly imposed on his actions to

---

THE ITINERARI SEGRETI

Go behind the scenes at the palace on one of the **Itinerari Segreti del Palazzo Ducale**, an intriguing guided tour through the warren of offices and passageways that interlocks with the public rooms of the building. It's not cheap (€20, or €14 with Museum Card; includes admission to the rest of the Palazzo Ducale), but well worth the price. Tickets can be booked up to 48hr in advance on ☎848 0820 00 or online through Ⓦvisitmuve.it; for visits on the next or same day go in person to the Palazzo Ducale ticket desk to check availability; the tour is held in English every day at 9.55am, 10.45am and 11.35am.

---

reduce the possibility of his abusing that power – his letters were read by censors and he wasn't permitted to receive foreign delegations alone. The privileges of the job far outweighed the inconveniences though, and men campaigned for years to increase their chances of election.

The Porta della Carta and courtyard

Like the Basilica, the Palazzo Ducale has been rebuilt many times since its foundation in the first years of the ninth century. The principal entrance to the *palazzo* – the **Porta della Carta** – is one of the most ornate Gothic works in the city. It was commissioned in 1438 by Doge Francesco Fóscari from Bartolomeo and Giovanni Bon, but the figures of Fóscari and his lion are replicas – the originals were pulverized in 1797 as a favour to Napoleon. Fóscari's head survived the hammering, however, and is on display inside.

Tourists no longer enter the building by the Porta della Carta, but instead are herded through a doorway on the lagoon side. Once through the ticket hall you emerge in the **courtyard**, opposite the other end of the passageway into the Palazzo – the **Arco Fóscari**. The itinerary begins on the left side of the courtyard, where the finest of the capitals from the Palazzo's exterior arcade are displayed in the **Museo dell'Opera**.

The Anticollegio

Upstairs, the route takes you through the doge's private apartments, then on to the **Anticollegio**, the room in which embassies had to wait before being admitted to the presence of the doge and his cabinet. This is one of the richest rooms in the Palazzo Ducale for paintings: four pictures by Tintoretto hang on the door walls, and facing the windows is Veronese's *Rape of Europa*.

The Sala del Collegio and Sala del Maggior Consiglio

The cycle of paintings on the ceiling of the adjoining **Sala del Collegio** is also by Veronese, and he features strongly again in the most stupendous room in the building – the **Sala del Maggior Consiglio**. Veronese's ceiling panel of *The Apotheosis of Venice* is suspended over the dais from which the doge oversaw the sessions of the city's general assembly; the backdrop is **Tintoretto**'s immense *Paradiso*, painted towards the end of his life, with the aid of his son, Domenico. At the opposite end there's a curiosity: the frieze of portraits of the first 76 doges (the series continues in the Sala dello Scrutinio – through the door at the far end) is interrupted by a painted black veil, marking the place where **Doge Marin Falier** would have been honoured had he not been beheaded for conspiring against the state in 1355.

Bridge of Sighs and the prisons

A couple of rooms later you descend to the underbelly of the Venetian state, crossing the **Ponte dei Sospiri**, or **Bridge of Sighs**, to the prisons. Before the construction of these cells in the early seventeenth century all prisoners were kept in the Piombi (the Leads), under the roof of the Palazzo Ducale, or in the Pozzi (the Wells) in the bottom two storeys; the new block was occupied mainly by petty criminals. The route finishes with a detour through the Pozzi, but if you want to see the Piombi, and the rooms in which the day-to-day administration of Venice took place, you have to go on one of the "secret" tours.

The Campanile

Daily: April–June & Oct 9am–7pm; July–Sept 9am–9pm; Nov–Easter 9am–3.45pm; usually closed for 20 days after Christmas • €8

Most of the landscape of the Piazza dates from the great period of urban renewal that began at the end of the fifteenth century and went on for much of the following century. The one exception – excluding San Marco itself – is the **Campanile**, which began life as a lighthouse in the ninth century and was modified frequently up to the early sixteenth. The present structure is a reconstruction: the original tower collapsed on July 14, 1902 – a catastrophe that injured nobody, except a cat. The collapse reduced to rubble the **Loggetta** at the base of the Campanile, but somehow it was pieced together again; built between 1537 and 1549 by Sansovino, it has served as a meeting-room for the nobility, a guardhouse and the place at which the state lottery was drawn. At 99m, the Campanile is the tallest structure in the city, and from the top (there is a lift) you can make out virtually every building, but not a single canal.

The Torre dell'Orologio

Guided tours daily 10am–5pm; tours in English Mon–Wed 10am & 11am, Thurs–Sun 2pm & 3pm • €12, or €7 for holders of I Musei di Piazza San Marco card or Museum Pass • tours must be pre-booked, either on ☎ 848 082 000 or at ⓦ torreorologio.visitmuve.it

The other tower in the Piazza, the **Torre dell'Orologio** (Clock Tower), is ornately decorated, with an astronomical clock filling much of the facade and two bronze figures – popularly known as the Moors – striking the bell on the roof. The tower was built between 1496 and 1506, while the clock mechanism dates from 1753. If you're in Venice for Epiphany or Ascension Day, you'll witness the clock's star turn – on the hour the Magi, led by an angel, troop out and bow to the figure of the Madonna. After a long restoration, the tower is now open to the public; fascinating hour-long **tours** take you up the steep narrow staircase, stopping on each of the five floors to admire the clock's complex workings.

The Procuratie

Away to the left of the Torre dell'Orologio stretches the **Procuratie Vecchie**; begun around 1500 by Codussi, this block housed the offices of the **Procurators of St Mark**, a committee of nine men whose responsibilities included the upkeep of the Basilica and other public buildings. A century or so after taking possession, the procurators were moved to the opposite side of the Piazza, into the **Procuratie Nuove**. Napoleon converted these apartments and offices into a royal palace and then, having realized that the building lacked a ballroom, remedied the deficiency by smashing down the church of San Geminiano to connect the two *procuratie* with a new wing for dancing.

The Museo Correr, Museo Archeologico and Libreria Sansoviniana

Daily: April–Oct 10am–7pm; Nov–March 10am–5pm • Entrance with Museum Pass • ⓦ correr.visitmuve.it

Generally known as the **Ala Napoleonica**, this short side of the Piazza is partly occupied by the **Museo Correr**, an immense triple-decker museum with a vast **historical collection** of coins, weapons, regalia, prints, paintings and miscellanea. Much of this is heavy going unless you have an intense interest in Venetian history, though there's an appealing exhibition of Venetian applied arts, and one show-stopping item in the form of the original blocks and a print of Jacopo de' Barbari's astonishing aerial view of Venice, engraved in 1500. The **Quadreria** on the second floor is no rival for the Accademia's collection, but it does set out clearly the evolution of painting in Venice from the thirteenth century to around 1500, and it contains some gems – the most famous being the **Carpaccio** picture usually known as *The Courtesans*, although its subjects are really a couple of bored-looking bourgeois ladies. The section of the Correr devoted to the **Museo del Risorgimento** is largely given over to the 1848 rebellion against the Austrians; it's often closed.

The archeological museum

Accessed from within the Correr, the **Museo Archeologico** is a somewhat scrappy museum, with cases of Roman coins and gems, fragments of sarcophagi and inscriptions, headless statues and bodiless heads interspersed with the odd Bronze Age, Egyptian or Assyrian relic.

The library

From the archeological museum you pass into the hall of the **Libreria Sansoviniana**, described by Palladio as "perhaps the richest and most ornate building to be created since the times of ancient Greece and Rome". Paintings by Veronese, Tintoretto, Andrea Schiavone and others cover the walls and ceiling, gazing down on selected volumes from the library's immense collection; Titian's *Allegory of Wisdom* occupies the central panel of the ceiling of the anteroom, beyond which lies the intended approach to the library, a magnificent staircase encrusted with stuccowork by Vittoria.

The Piazzetta

The **Piazzetta** – the open space between San Marco and the waterfront pavement known as the Molo – was the area where the politicians used to gather before meetings. Facing the Palazzo Ducale is Sansovino's masterpiece, the **Libreria Sansoviniana** (see above), which is attached to his first major building in Venice, the **Zecca** (Mint), built between 1537 and 1545 on the site of the thirteenth-century mint. By the beginning of the fifteenth century the city's prosperity was such that the Venetian coinage was in use in every European exchange, and the doge could with some justification call Venice "the mistress of all the gold in Christendom".

The Piazzetta's two **columns** were brought here from the Levant at the end of the twelfth century, in company with a third, which fell off the barge and still lies somewhere just off the Molo. The figures perched on top are St Theodore (the original is in the Palazzo Ducale), patron saint of Venice when it was dependent on Byzantium, and a Chimera, customized to look like the Lion of St Mark. Public executions were carried out between the columns, the techniques employed ranging from straightforward hanging to burial alive, head downwards. Superstitious Venetians avoid passing between them.

North of the Piazza

The **Mercerie**, a chain of streets that starts under the Torre dell'Orologio and finishes at the Campo San Bartolomeo, is the most direct route between San Marco and the Rialto Bridge, and has always been the main land thoroughfare of the city and a prime site for its shopkeepers. For those immune to the charms of window-shopping there's little reason to linger until you reach the church of **San Salvador**.

San Salvador

Campo San Salvador • June–Aug Mon–Sat 9am–noon & 4–7pm, Sun 4–7pm; Sept–May Mon–Sat 9am–noon & 3–7.15pm, Sun 3–7.15pm • Free

At its northern end, the Mercerie veers right at the church of **San Salvador** or Salvatore, which was consecrated in 1177. The facade, applied in 1663, is less interesting than the sixteenth-century interior, cleverly planned in the form of three Greek crosses placed end to end. It has a couple of late Titian paintings – an altarpiece of the *Transfiguration* (1560) and an *Annunciation* (1566), whose awkward angel is often blamed on the great man's assistants. The end of the south transept is filled by the tomb of Caterina Cornaro (see p.427).

Campo San Bartolomeo

Campo San Bartolomeo, terminus of the Mercerie, is at its best in the evening, when it's often as packed as any bar in town. To show off their new wardrobes the Venetians take themselves off to the Piazza, but Campo San Bartolomeo is one of the favoured spots to just meet friends and talk. The **church of San Bartolomeo** (Tues, Thurs & Sat 10am–noon) has a landmark campanile, but its interior isn't thrilling: its organ panels, beautifully painted by Sebastiano del Piombo, are now housed in the Accademia.

6

Campo San Luca and Campo Manin

To the west of San Salvador lies **Campo San Luca**, another focus of after-work gatherings but not as much of a pressure-cooker as San Bartolomeo. Beyond Campo San Luca is **Campo Manin**, on the south side of which is a sign for the spiral staircase known as the **Scala del Bovolo** (*bovolo* means "snail shell" in Venetian dialect), a piece of flamboyant engineering dating from around 1500. It's been under restoration for many years; when the work is finished it should be possible to go up the staircase – for a fee, of course.

Museo Fortuny

Campiello San Beneto • 10am–6pm; closed Tues • Entry charge varies according to what's on – usually about €10 • ⓦ fortuny.visitmuve.it

The **Museo Fortuny** is also close at hand, similarly tucked away in a spot you'd never accidentally pass. In addition to making his famous silk dresses, which were said to be fine enough to be threaded through a wedding ring, Mariano Fortuny (1871–1949) was a painter, architect, engraver, photographer and sculptor. Design and photography exhibitions are held pretty much constantly in the Museo Fortuny, and how much of the building you get to see depends on how extensive the show is – often only a couple of rooms are used. And in high season you'll have to queue, as the *palazzo* is so fragile that only 75 people are allowed in at a time.

West of the Piazza

Leaving the Piazza **by the west side**, through the colonnade of the Ala Napoleonica, you enter another major shopping district, but one that presents a contrast to the frenetic Mercerie: here the big Italian fashion houses rule the roost. Most visitors hurry through this part of the city **en route to the Accademia**, but it does have a handful of things worth stopping for.

San Moisè

Campo San Moisè • Mon–Sat 9.30am–12.30pm • Free

In naming the church of **San Moisè** ("Saint Moses") the Venetians were following the Byzantine custom of canonizing Old Testament figures, while simultaneously honouring Moisè Venier, who paid for a rebuilding in the tenth century – the church was founded back in the eighth. Its facade, featuring a species of camel unknown to zoology, was designed in 1668 by Alessandro Tremignon and sculpted largely by **Heinrich Meyring**, a follower of Bernini. And if you think this is in questionable taste, wait till you see the miniature mountain that Tremignon and Meyring created as the main altarpiece, representing *Mount Sinai with Moses Receiving the Tablets*.

Campo San Fantin and La Fenice

Halfway along the Calle Larga XXII Marzo, on the right, is the Calle del Sartor da Veste, which takes you over a canal and into the Campo San Fantin, where the Renaissance church of **San Fantin** has a graceful domed apse by Sansovino. Across the *campo* is Venice's largest and oldest theatre, **La Fenice**, opened in December 1792, rebuilt in 1836 after the place had been wrecked by fire, and rebuilt yet again after another blaze on the night of January 29, 1996. Tours of the magnificently restored interior with an audioguide cost €7.

Santa Maria del Giglio

Campo Santa Maria del Giglio • Mon–Sat 10am–5pm • €3, or Chorus Pass

Back on the main road to the Accademia, another very odd church awaits – **Santa Maria del Giglio**, otherwise known as Santa Maria Zobenigo. You can stare at this all day and still not find a single Christian image: the statues are of the five Barbaro brothers who financed the rebuilding of the church in 1678; Virtue, Honour, Fame and Wisdom hover respectfully around them; and the maps in relief depict the towns the brothers graced during their military and diplomatic careers. The interior, full to bursting with devotional sculptures and pictures (notably *The Evangelists* by **Tintoretto**), overcompensates for the impiety of the exterior.

Santo Stefano

Campo Santo Stefano • Mon–Sat 10am–5pm • Admission to sacristy €3, or Chorus Pass

The tilting campanile that soon looms into view over the vapid church of San Maurizio belongs to Santo Stefano, which stands at the end of the next *campo* – the spacious **Campo Santo Stefano**. The church of **Santo Stefano** dates from the thirteenth century, but was rebuilt in the fourteenth and altered again in the first half of the fifteenth; the Gothic doorway and the ship's-keel roof both belong to this last phase. The best paintings are in the sacristy: *The Agony in the Garden*, *The Last Supper* and *The Washing of the Disciples' Feet*, all late works by Tintoretto.

Palazzo Grassi

Campo San Samuele 3231 • €15, or €20 with the Punta della Dogana • ⓦ palazzograssi.it

A short distance to the north of Campo Santo Stefano lies the gigantic **Palazzo Grassi**, which in 2005 was acquired by a consortium headed by **François Pinault**, France's pre-eminent collector of modern art. A couple of years later, Pinault acquired the Dogana di Mare (see p.363), which has become the main showcase for his vast collection, while the Grassi stages immense art shows that also draw heavily on works owned by him.

Dorsoduro

Some of the finest architecture in Venice, both domestic and public, is to be found in the *sestiere* of **Dorsoduro**, a situation partly attributable to the stability of its sandbanks – Dorsoduro means "hard back". Yet for all its attractions, not many visitors wander off the strip that runs between the main sights of the area – Ca' Rezzonico, the Accademia, the Salute and the Punta della Dogana.

The Accademia

Campo della Carità • Mon 8.15am–2pm, Tues–Sun 8.15am–7.15pm • €6.50, but ticket price is higher whenever a special exhibition is on • ⓦ gallerieaccademia.org

The **Galleria dell'Accademia** is one of the finest specialist collections of European art, following the history of Venetian painting from the fourteenth to the eighteenth centuries. With San Marco and the Palazzo Ducale, the Accademia completes the triad of obligatory tourist sights in Venice, but admissions are presently restricted to batches of 300 people at a time, so queues can be huge in high season. This situation will change when the gallery takes over the renovated ground-floor and basement rooms of the convent buildings, an expansion which has entailed moving the art college to the nearby Casa degli Incurabili. When this huge rebuilding project is completed, the Accademia will have space not just for the scores of paintings currently held in storage, but also for large-scale one-off exhibitions. The upper-storey galleries of the new Accademia will also have a somewhat different layout than the one given below.

The early Renaissance

The gallery is laid out in a roughly chronological succession of rooms going anticlockwise. The first room at the top of the stairs is the fifteenth-century assembly room of the Scuola della Carità, whose church and convent the gallery now occupies. This has works by the earliest known Venetian painters, of whom **Paolo Veneziano** (from the first half of the fourteenth century) and his follower **Lorenzo Veneziano** are the most absorbing.

Room 2 moves on to works from the late fifteenth and early sixteenth centuries, with large altarpieces that are contemplative even when the scenes are far from calm.

Carpaccio's strange and gruesome *Crucifixion and Glorification of the Ten Thousand Martyrs of Mount Ararat* (painted around 1512) and his *Presentation of Jesus in the Temple* accompany works by **Giovanni Bellini** and **Cima da Conegliano**.

In the next room you can observe the emergence of the characteristically Venetian treatment of colour, but there's nothing here as exciting as the small paintings in rooms 4 and 5, a high point of the collection. As well as an exquisite *St George* by **Mantegna** and a series of **Giovanni Bellini** Madonnas, this section contains **Giorgione**'s enigmatic *Tempest*.

6

The High Renaissance

Rooms 6 to 8 introduce some of the heavyweights of High-Renaissance Venetian painting: **Tintoretto**, **Titian** and **Lorenzo Lotto**. Room 10 is dominated by epic productions, and an entire wall is filled by **Paolo Veronese**'s *Christ in the House of Levi*. Originally called *The Last Supper*, this picture provoked a stern reaction from the Court of the Holy Office: "Does it appear to you fitting that at our Lord's last supper you should paint buffoons, drunkards, Germans, dwarfs, and similar indecencies?" Veronese responded simply by changing the title, which made the work acceptable. The pieces by **Tintoretto** in here include three legends of St Mark: *St Mark Rescues a Slave* (1548), which was the painting that made his reputation, *The Theft of the Body of St Mark* and *St Mark Saves a Saracen* (both 1560s). Tintoretto's love of physical and psychological drama, the energy of his brushstrokes, and the sometimes uncomfortable originality of his colours and poses, are all displayed in this group. Opposite is **Titian's last painting**, a *Pietà* intended for his own tomb in the Frari.

The eighteenth century

Room 11 contains a number of works by **Giambattista Tiepolo**, the most prominent painter of eighteenth-century Venice, including two shaped fragments rescued from the Scalzi (1743–45) and *The Translation of the Holy House of Loreto* (1743), a sketch for the same ceiling. There's also more from **Tintoretto**; the *Madonna dei Tesorieri* (1566) shows facial types still found in Venice today.

The following stretch of seventeenth- and eighteenth-century paintings isn't too enthralling – the highlights are a trio of small Canalettos, accompanied by **Guardi**'s impressionistic views of Venice, **Pietro Longhi**'s documentary interiors and a series of portraits by **Rosalba Carriera**, all in room 17.

The Vivarinis, the Bellinis and Carpaccio

The top part of the Carità church now forms **room 23**, which houses works mainly from the fifteenth and early sixteenth centuries, the era of two of Venice's most significant artistic dynasties, the **Vivarini** and **Bellini** families. The extraordinary *Blessed Lorenzo Giustinian* by **Gentile Bellini** is one of the oldest surviving Venetian canvases, and was possibly used as a standard in processions, which would account for its state.

There's more from Gentile over in **room 20**, which is entirely filled by the cycle of *The Miracles of the Relic of the Cross*, a cycle of pictures painted around 1500 for the Scuola di San Giovanni Evangelista. All of the paintings are replete with fascinating local details, but particularly rich are **Gentile Bellini**'s *Recovery of the Relic from the Canale di San Lorenzo* and *Procession of the Relic in the Piazza*, and **Carpaccio**'s *Cure of a Lunatic*. The next room contains a complete cycle of pictures by **Carpaccio** illustrating the *Story of St Ursula*, painted for the Scuola di Sant'Orsola at San Zanipolo (1490–94). The sequence depicts the legend of Ursula, a Breton princess, who undertook a pilgrimage with a company of 11,000 virgins, which ended with their massacre by the Huns.

Finally, in room 24 (the former hostel of the Scuola), there's **Titian**'s *Presentation of the Virgin* (dating from 1539). It was painted for the place where it hangs, as was the triptych by **Antonio Vivarini** and **Giovanni d'Alemagna** (1446).

The Guggenheim Collection

Calle San Cristoforo 701 • 10am–6pm; closed Tues • €12 • ⓦ guggenheim-venice.it

Within five minutes' walk of the Accademia, east beyond the Campo San Vio, is the unfinished Palazzo Venier dei Leoni, home of Peggy Guggenheim for thirty years until her death in 1979 and now the base for the **Guggenheim Collection**. Her private collection is a quirky choice of mainly excellent pieces from her favourite modernist movements and artists. Prime pieces include Brancusi's *Bird in Space* and *Maestra*, De Chirico's *Red Tower* and *Nostalgia of the Poet*, Max Ernst's *Robing of the Bride*, sculpture by Laurens and Lipchitz, and paintings by Malevich.

Santa Maria della Salute

Campo della Salute • Daily 9am–noon & 3–5.30pm • Admission to sacristy €3

The massive Santa Maria della Salute, better known simply as the **Salute**, was built to fulfil a Senate decree of October 22, 1630, that a new church would be dedicated to Mary if the city were delivered from the plague that was ravaging it – an outbreak that killed about a third of the population. Work began in 1631 on **Baldassare Longhena**'s design and the church was consecrated in 1687. On November 21, for the Festa della Salute (*salute* meaning "health"), a pontoon bridge is built across the Canal Grande to the steps of the church, where people pray for, or give thanks for, good health.

In 1656, a hoard of **Titian** paintings from the suppressed church of Santo Spirito was moved here and is now housed in the sacristy. The most prominent of these is the altarpiece *St Mark Enthroned with Saints Cosmas, Damian, Sebastian and Rocco* (the plague saints). *The Marriage at Cana*, with its dramatic lighting and perspective, is by **Tintoretto** (1561), and features likenesses of a number of the artist's friends.

The Punta della Dogana

Fondamenta della Dogana alla Salute • Mon & Wed–Sun 10am–7pm • €15, or €20 with Palazzo Grassi • ⓦ palazzograssi.it

On the point where the Canal Grande and the Giudecca canal merge stands the huge **Dogana di Mare** (Customs House), another late seventeenth-century building, which in 2009 reopened as the **Punta della Dogana** exhibition space. Financed by François Pinault, the co-owner of Palazzo Grassi, the Dogana – like the Grassi – has been beautifully renovated to designs by Tadao Ando, and is unquestionably one of the world's great showcases for contemporary art. The entry charge is savage, but well over one hundred works from Pinault's collection are usually on display here at any one time, and he has invested in most of the really big names of the current art scene, so you can expect to see pieces by the likes of Cindy Sherman, Luc Tuymans, Cy Twombly, Thomas Schütte, Maurizio Cattelan, Jeff Koons and Marlene Dumas, to name but a few.

The Záttere and San Sebastiano

Known collectively as the **Záttere**, the sequence of waterfront pavements between the Punta della Dogana and the Stazione Marittima is now a popular place for a stroll or an alfresco meal, but was formerly the place where most of the bulky goods coming into Venice were unloaded onto floating rafts called *záttere*.

The Gesuati

Fondamenta delle Záttere ai Gesuati • Mon–Sat 10am–5pm • €3, or Chorus Pass • ⓦ chorusvenezia.org

The principal monument on the Záttere is the church of Santa Maria del Rosario, invariably known as the **Gesuati**; rebuilt in 1726–43, about half a century after the church was taken over from the order of the Gesuati by the Dominicans, it was designed by **Giorgio Massari** and is notable mainly for its paintings by **Giambattista Tiepolo**, who created the first altarpiece on the right, *The Virgin with SS. Catherine of Siena, Rose and Agnes* (c.1740), and the three magnificent ceiling panels of *Scenes from the Life of St Dominic* (1737–39).

6

San Trovaso

Campo San Trovaso • Mon–Sat 2.30–5.30pm • Free

A diversion to the right after the Gesuati takes you past the **squero di San Trovaso**, one of only two gondola workshops left in Venice, and on to the church of **San Trovaso**. Its paintings include a fine pair by Tintoretto (*The Temptation of St Anthony* and *The Last Supper*), and two large scenes that were begun by Tintoretto and completed by his son and other assistants: *The Adoration of the Magi* and *The Expulsion from the Temple*.

San Sebastiano

Campo San Sebastiano • Mon–Sat 10am–5pm • €3, or Chorus Pass • ⓦ chorusvenezia.org

At the end of the Záttere the barred gates of the Stazione Marittima deflect you away from the waterfront and towards the church of **San Sebastiano**. Built between 1505 and 1545, this was the parish church of **Paolo Veronese**, who provided most of its paintings and is buried here. He was first brought in to paint the ceiling of the sacristy with a *Coronation of the Virgin* and the *Four Evangelists*, followed by the *Scenes from the Life of St Esther* on the ceiling of the church. He then painted the dome of the chancel (since destroyed), and with the help of his brother, Benedetto, moved on to the walls of the church and the nuns' choir. The paintings around the high altar and the organ came last, being painted in the 1560s.

Campo Santa Margherita and around

Campo di Santa Margherita is the social heart of Dorsoduro, and is one of the most appealing squares in the whole city. Piazza San Marco is overrun with tourists, but Campo di Santa Margherita – the largest square on this side of the Canal Grande – belongs to the Venetians and retains a spirit of authenticity. Ringed by houses that date back as far as the fourteenth century, it's spacious and at the same time modest, taking its tone not from any grandiose architecture but from its cluster of market stalls and its plethora of bars and cafés, which draw a lot of their custom from the university.

The Scuola Grande dei Carmini

Campo Santa Margherita 2617 • Daily 10am–5pm • €5 • ⓦ scuolagrandecarmini.it

In Campo Santa Margherita's southwest extremity stands the **Scuola Grande dei Carmini**, once the Venetian base of the Carmelite order. Originating in Palestine towards the close of the twelfth century, the Carmelites blossomed during the Counter-Reformation, when they became the shock-troops through whom the cult of the Virgin was disseminated, as a response to the inroads of Protestantism. As happened elsewhere in Europe, the Venetian Carmelites became immensely wealthy, and in the 1660s they called in an architect – probably Longhena – to redesign the property they had acquired. The core of this complex, which in 1767 was raised to the status of a *scuola grande*, is now effectively a showcase for the art of **Giambattista Tiepolo**, who in the 1740s painted the wonderful ceiling of the upstairs hall.

Santa Maria del Carmelo

Campo dei Carmini • Mon–Sat 2.30–5.30pm • Free

The adjacent Santa Maria del Carmelo – usually known simply as the **Carmini** – is identifiable from a long way off, thanks to the statue of the Virgin atop the campanile. A dull series of Baroque paintings illustrating the history of the Carmelite order covers a lot of space inside, but the second altar on the right has a fine *Nativity* by Cima da Conegliano (before 1510), and Lorenzo Lotto's *SS. Nicholas of Bari, John the Baptist and Lucy* (1529) – featuring what Bernard Berenson ranked as one of the most beautiful landscapes in all Italian art – hangs on the opposite side of the nave.

San Pantalon

Campo San Pantalon • Mon–Sat 10am–noon & 1–3pm • Free • Ⓦ sanpantalon.it

A short distance to the north of Campo Santa Margherita rises the raw brick hulk of **San Pantalon**, which possesses a *Coronation of the Virgin* by Antonio Vivarini and Giovanni d'Alemagna (in the chapel to the left of the chancel) and Veronese's last painting, *San Pantaleone Healing a Boy* (second chapel on right). The church also boasts the most melodramatic ceiling in the city: *The Martyrdom and Apotheosis of San Pantaleone*, which kept Gian Antonio Fumiani busy from 1680 to 1704.

Ca' Rezzonico

Fondamenta Rezzonico 3136 • Daily except Tues: April–Oct 10am–6pm; Nov–March 10am–5pm • €8.50, or Museum Pass • Ⓦ carezzonico.visitmuve.it

The eighteenth century, the period of Venice's political senility, was also the period of its grand flourish in the visual and decorative arts. The main showcase for the art of that era, the **Museo del Settecento Veneziano** spreads through most of the enormous **Ca' Rezzonico**, which the city authorities bought in 1934 specifically as a home for the museum. Recently restored, it's a spectacular building, furnished and decorated mostly with genuine eighteenth-century items and fabrics: where originals weren't available, the eighteenth-century ambience has been preserved by using almost indistinguishable modern reproductions. The applied arts of the eighteenth century are not to everyone's taste, but even if you find most of the museum's contents frivolous or grotesque, the frescoes by the Tiepolo family and Pietro Longhi's affectionate Venetian scenes should justify the entrance fee.

6

San Polo and Santa Croce

Two *sestieri* are covered in this section: **San Polo**, which extends from the Rialto market to the Frari area; and **Santa Croce**, a far less sight-heavy district which lies to the north of San Polo and reaches right across to Piazzale Roma. There are two main routes through the district – one runs between the Rialto and the Scalzi Bridge, the other takes you in the opposite direction from the Rialto, down towards the Accademia. Virtually all the essential sights lie around these two routes.

The Rialto Bridge

The famous **Ponte di Rialto** (Rialto Bridge), the perpetually thronged link between San Marco and San Polo, superseded a succession of wooden structures – one of Carpaccio's *Miracles of the True Cross*, in the Accademia, shows what one of the old drawbridges looked like. The decision to construct a stone bridge was taken in 1524, and the job was awarded to the aptly named **Antonio da Ponte**, whose top-heavy design was described by Edward Gibbon as "a fine bridge, spoilt by two rows of houses upon it". Until 1854, when the first Accademia Bridge was built, this was the only point at which the Canal Grande could be crossed on foot.

The Rialto district

West of the Rialto Bridge, the relatively stable building land drew some of the earliest lagoon settlers to the high bank (*rivo alto*) that was to develop into the **Rialto** district. While the political centre of the new city grew up around San Marco, the Rialto became the commercial zone. It was through the markets of the Rialto that Venice earned its reputation as the bazaar of Europe. Virtually anything could be bought or sold here: Italian fabrics, precious stones, silver plate and gold jewellery, and spices and dyes from the Orient. After a fire destroyed everything in the area except the church in 1514, work began on the **Fabbriche Vecchie** (the arcaded buildings along the Ruga degli Orefici and around the Campo San Giacomo); Sansovino's **Fabbriche Nuove** (running along the Canal Grande from Campo Cesare Battisti) followed about thirty years later.

6

The market

Today's Rialto market may be tamer than that of Venice at its peak, but it's still one of the liveliest spots in the city, and one of the few places where it's possible to stand in a crowd and hear nothing but Italian spoken. There's a shoal of memento-sellers by the church and along the Ruga degli Orefici; the market proper lies between them and the Canal Grande – mainly fruit stalls around the **Campo San Giacomo**, vegetable stalls and butchers' shops as you go through to the Campo Battisti, after which you come to the fish market.

San Giacomo di Rialto

Campo San Giacomo • Mon–Sat 9.30am–noon & 4–6pm • Free

A popular Venetian legend asserts that the city was founded on Friday, March 25, 421 AD at exactly midday; from the same legend derives the claim that the church of **San Giacomo di Rialto** was founded in that year, and is thus the oldest church in Venice. Whether it is or not, what is not disputed is that the church was rebuilt in 1071 and that parts of the present structure date from then.

San Cassiano

Campo San Cassiano • Daily 9am–noon & 5–7pm • Free

The church of **San Cassiano** is a building you're bound to pass as you wander west from the Rialto. Don't be put off by its barn-like appearance: it contains three paintings by **Tintoretto**: *The Resurrection*, *The Descent into Limbo* and *The Crucifixion*. The last of these is one of the most arresting pictures in Venice, a startling composition dominated not by the Cross but by the ladder on which the executioners stand.

Ca' Pésaro

Calle Pésaro 2076 • Tues–Sun: April–Oct 10am–6pm; Nov–March 10am–5pm • €8 for both museums, or Museum Pass • ⓦ capesaro.visitmuve.it

The immense **Ca' Pésaro** was bequeathed to the city at the end of the nineteenth century by the Duchessa Felicità Bevilacqua La Masa, an energetic patron of the arts who stipulated in her will that the *palazzo* should provide studio and exhibition space for impoverished young artists. Although exhibitions were later held at Ca' Pésaro, and the Bevilacqua La Masa foundation still promotes progressive art, the Duchess's plans were never fully realized, and in place of the intended living arts centre the *palazzo* became home to the city's modern art gallery.

The Galleria Internazionale d'Arte Moderna

The **Galleria d'Arte Moderna** has a smattering of work by such heavyweights as Klimt, Kandinsky, Matisse, Klee, Nolde, Giacometti, Morandi, Ernst and Miró, but many of the pieces here are modern only in the chronological sense of the word. A room is devoted to the portentously intense sculpture of Adolfo Wildt, and others are dedicated to the exhibitions held here from 1908 to 1924, when Ca' Pésaro had a reputation for being a more daring venue than the Biennale. In the later sections of the museum, covering the years in which the Biennale established its avant-garde credentials, the Venetian artist Emilio Vedova is the outstanding figure among a broad showing of Italian work from the 1950s.

The Museo Orientale

In the creaky top-storey rooms of Ca' Pésaro you'll find the **Museo Orientale**, which is built around a hoard of artefacts amassed by the Conte di Bardi (a Bourbon prince) during a long Far Eastern voyage in the nineteenth century. Until recently, this was a notoriously dowdy and ramshackle museum, but the labelling and general presentation are now exemplary. It's a tightly packed array of porcelain, ceremonial armour, netsuke, musical instruments, clothing, paintings, and enough swords, daggers and lances to equip a private army. Many of the pieces are exquisite – look out for an incredibly intricate ivory-and-coral chess set, and a room full of marvellous lacquerwork.

The Museo di Storia Naturale

Salizzada del Fontego dei Turchi 1730 • June–Oct Tues–Sun 10am–6pm; Nov–May Tues–Fri 9am–5pm, Sat & Sun 10am–6pm • €8, or Museum Pass • Ⓦ msn.visitmuve.it

In 2012 the **Museo di Storia Naturale**, which occupies the **Fondaco dei Turchi**, at last reopened after many years of restoration, and it has re-emerged as a superb museum. The opening sequence of rooms takes you through the fossil collection, which has been laid out in such a way as to trace the process of evolution – the fossilized animal tracks set into the floor are a typically imaginative touch. Beyond, there are rooms devoted to locomotion (with separate sections for land, water and air), an extraordinary miscellany of items gathered by Giovanni Miani during his 1859–60 expedition to trace the source of the Nile, a hideous array of African hunting trophies harvested by Giuseppe de Reali and – in the long room overlooking the Canal Grande – a splendid sequence of cabinets illustrating the development of the study of natural history in Venice, with some exquisitely grisly specimens of dissected animals.

San Polo

Mon–Sat 10am–5pm • €3, or Chorus Pass • Ⓦ chorusvenezia.org

The largest square in Venice after the Piazza, the **Campo San Polo** used to be the city's favourite bullfighting arena as well as the site of weekly markets and occasional fairs. **San Polo** church should be visited for *The Last Supper* by **Tintoretto** and **Giandomenico Tiepolo**'s *The Stations of the Cross*, a series painted when the artist was only 20. The sober piety of these pictures will come as a surprise if you've been to the Ca' Rezzonico, though it often seems that his interest was less in the central drama than in the portraits that occupy the edges of the stage.

The Frari

Campo dei Frari • Mon–Sat 9am–6pm, Sun 1–6pm • €3, or Chorus Pass

The Franciscans were granted a large plot of land near San Polo in about 1250, not long after the death of St Francis. Replacement of their first church by the present Santa Maria Gloriosa dei Frari – more generally known simply as the **Frari** – began in the mid-fourteenth century and took over a hundred years. This mountain of brick is not an immediately attractive building but its collection of paintings, sculptures and monuments makes it a guaranteed highlight of anyone's visit to Venice.

Wherever you stand in the Frari, you'll be facing something that rewards your attention. Apart from the Salute and the Accademia, the Frari is the only building in Venice with more than a single significant work by **Titian**. One of these – *The Assumption*, painted in 1518 – you will see almost immediately as you look towards the altar, a swirling, dazzling piece of compositional bravura for which there was no precedent in Venetian art. The other Titian masterpiece here, the *Madonna di Ca' Pésaro*, was equally innovative in its displacement of the figure of the Virgin from the centre of the picture.

Two funerary monuments embodying the emergence in Venice of Renaissance sculptural technique flank the Titian *Assumption*: on the left is the tomb of Doge Niccolò Tron, by **Antonio Rizzo** and assistants, dating from 1476; on the right, the more chaotic tomb of Doge Francesco Fóscari, carved by **Antonio and Paolo Bregno** shortly after Fóscari's death in 1457. Head through the door in the right transept for the sacristy, where on the altar stands a picture that alone would justify a visit to the Frari – the *Madonna and Child with Saints Nicholas of Bari, Peter, Mark and Benedict*, painted in 1488 by **Giovanni Bellini**.

Two massive tombs take up much of the nave. One is the bombastic monument to Titian, built in the mid-nineteenth century on the supposed site of his grave. Opposite is a tomb of similarly pompous dimensions but of redeeming peculiarity: the mausoleum of Canova, erected in 1827 by his pupils, following a design he had made for the tomb of Titian.

6

THE CANAL GRANDE

Below is a selection of the most impressive buildings to be seen on the **Canal Grande**. To see both banks at once, make sure you get a seat at the front or the back of the *vaporetto*; and don't miss the experience of a nocturnal boat ride.

1. Calatrava Bridge The newest feature of Venice's cityscape is officially known as the Ponte della Costituzione, but Venetians generally use the name of its designer, Santiago Calatrava. The elegant arc of steel, stone and glass is modelled on a gondola's hull.

2. Scalzi Bridge The successor of an iron structure put up by the Austrians in 1858–60, which had to be replaced in the early 1930s to give the new steamboats sufficient clearance.

3. Fondaco dei Turchi A private house from the early thirteenth century until 1621, the Fondaco dei Turchi was then turned over to Turkish traders, who stayed here until 1838. Though over-restored, the building's towers and arcade give a reasonably precise picture of what a Veneto-Byzantine palace would have looked like. It's now the natural history museum.

4. Palazzo Vendramin-Calergi Begun by Mauro Codussi at the very end of the fifteenth century, this was the first Venetian palace built on Renaissance lines. The *palazzo*'s most famous resident was Richard Wagner, who died here in February 1883. It's now the casino.

5. Ca' Pésaro The thickly ornamented Ca' Pésaro, bristling with diamond-shaped spikes and grotesque heads, took half a century to build – work finished in 1703, long after the death of the architect, Baldassare Longhena. See also p.366.

6. Palazzo Corner della Regina This *palazzo* was built in 1724 on the site of the home of Caterina Cornaro, Queen of Cyprus, from whom the palace takes its name.

7. Ca' d'Oro Incorporating fragments of a thirteenth-century palace that once stood on the site, the gorgeous Ca' d'Oro was built in the 1420s and 30s, and acquired its nickname – "The Golden House" – from the gilding that used to accentuate its carving.

8. Ca' da Mosto The arches of the first storey of the Ca' da Mosto and the carved panels above them are remnants of a thirteenth-century Veneto-Byzantine building, and are thus among the oldest structures on the canal.

9. Rialto market See p.366.

10. Fondaco dei Tedeschi The *fondaco* was once headquarters of the city's German merchants, who as early as 1228 were leasing a building here. In 1505 the Fondaco burned down; Giorgione and Titian were commissioned to paint the exterior of its replacement. The remnants of their contribution are now in the Ca' d'Oro.

11. Rialto Bridge See p.365.

12. Palazzo Loredan and Palazzo Farsetti These neighbouring *palazzi* are heavily restored Veneto-Byzantine palaces of the thirteenth century; now the town hall.

13. Palazzo Grimani Work began on the immense Palazzo Grimani in 1559, to designs by Sanmicheli, but was not completed until 1575, sixteen years after his death.

14. The Mocenigo palaces Four houses that once belonged to the Mocenigo family stand side by side on the Canal Grande's sharpest turn: the **Palazzo Mocenigo-Nero**, a late sixteenth-century building, once home to Byron; the double **Palazzo Mocenigo**, built in the eighteenth century; and the **Palazzo Mocenigo Vecchio**, a Gothic palace remodelled in the seventeenth century.

15. Ca' Fóscari The largest private house in Venice at the time of its construction (c.1435), Ca' Fóscari was the home of Doge Francesco Fóscari, whose extraordinarily long term of office (34 years) came to an end with his forced resignation.

16. The Palazzi Giustinian These twinned palaces were built in the mid-fifteenth century for two brothers who wanted attached but self-contained houses.

17. Ca' Rezzonico Longhena's gargantuan Ca' Rezzonico was begun in 1667 as a commission from the Bon family, but they were obliged to sell the still unfinished palace to the Rezzonico, a family of stupendously wealthy Genoese bankers. Among its subsequent owners was Pen Browning, whose father Robert died here in 1889.

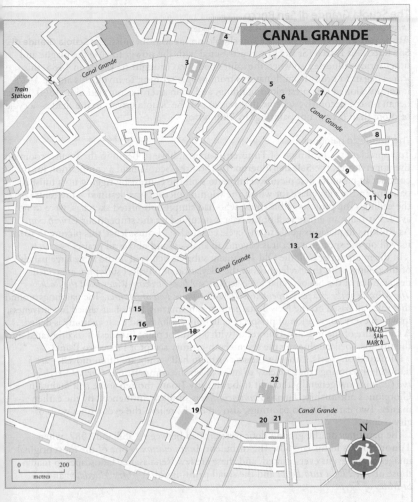

CANAL GRANDE

18. Palazzo Grassi This vast *palazzo* was built in 1748–72 by Massari, and was the last great house to be raised on the Canal Grande.

19. Accademia Bridge As the larger *vaporetti* couldn't get under the iron Ponte dell'Accademia built by the Austrians in 1854, it was replaced in 1932 by a wooden structure, later reinforced with steel.

20. Palazzo Venier dei Leoni In 1759 the Venier family, one of Venice's richest dynasties, began rebuilding their home, but this *palazzo*, which would have been the largest palace on the canal, never progressed further than the first storey. The stump of the building is occupied by the Guggenheim Collection.

21. Palazzo Dario This exquisite little *palazzo* was built in the late 1480s, and the multicoloured marbles of the facade are characteristic of the work of the Lombardo family.

22. Palazzo Corner della Ca' Grande The palace that used to stand here was destroyed when a fire lit to dry out a stock of sugar ran out of control. Sansovino's design – built from 1545 – is notable for its rugged lower-storey stonework, which makes it the prototype for the Ca' Pésaro and Ca' Rezzonico.

6

The Scuola Grande di San Rocco

Campo San Rocco • Daily 9.30am–5.30pm • €8 • ⓦ scuolagrandesanrocco.it

At the rear of the Frari is a place you should on no account miss: the **Scuola Grande di San Rocco**. St Rocco (St Roch) was attributed with the power to cure the plague and other serious illnesses, so when the saint's body was brought to Venice in 1485, this *scuola* began to profit from donations from people wishing to invoke his aid. In 1515 it commissioned this prestigious building, and soon after its completion in 1560, work began on the decorative scheme that was to put the Scuola's rivals in the shade – a cycle of more than fifty major paintings by **Tintoretto**.

The Tintoretto paintings

To appreciate the evolution of Tintoretto's art you have to begin in the smaller room on the upper storey, the **Sala dell'Albergo**. In 1564 the Scuola held a competition for the contract to paint its first picture. Tintoretto won the contest by rigging up a finished painting in the very place for which the winning picture was destined – the centre of the ceiling. The protests of his rivals, who had simply submitted sketches, were to no avail. Virtually an entire wall of the Sala is occupied by the stupendous *Crucifixion*. As Ruskin's loquacious guide to the cycle concludes: "I must leave this picture to work its will on the spectator; for it is beyond all analysis, and above all praise."

In the main upper hall, the Old Testament subjects depicted in the three large panels of the **ceiling**, with their references to the alleviation of physical suffering, are coded declarations of the Scuola's charitable activities: *Moses Striking Water from the Rock*, *The Miracle of the Brazen Serpent* and *The Miraculous Fall of Manna*. The paintings around the walls, all based on the New Testament, are an amazing feat of sustained inventiveness, in which every convention of perspective, lighting, colour and even anatomy is defied. A caricature of the irascible Tintoretto (with a jarful of paint brushes) is incorporated into the trompe-l'oeil carvings by the seventeenth-century sculptor Francesco Pianta.

Displayed on easels, either in the *sala* or main hall – they are often moved – are a handful of paintings that are easy to miss, given the competition. *Christ Carrying the Cross* is now generally thought to be an early **Titian**, though some still maintain Giorgione's authorship; Titian's *Annunciation* is similarly influenced by the earlier master. Two early **Tiepolo** paintings, also on easels, relieve the eyes with a wash of airy colour.

The paintings on the ground floor were created between 1583 and 1587, when Tintoretto was in his late 60s. The turbulent *Annunciation* is one of the most original images of the event ever painted, and there are few Renaissance landscapes to match those of *The Flight into Egypt* and the small paintings of *St Mary Magdalen* and *St Mary of Egypt*.

San Rocco

Campo San Rocco • Daily 9.30am–5.30pm • Free

Yet more paintings by Tintoretto adorn the church of **San Rocco**. On the south wall of the nave you'll find *St Roch Taken to Prison*, and below it *The Pool of Bethesda* – though only the latter is definitely by Tintoretto. In the chancel are four large works, all of them difficult to see properly: the best are *St Roch Curing the Plague Victims* (lower right) and *St Roch in Prison* (lower left).

Cannaregio

In the northernmost section of Venice, **CANNAREGIO**, you can go from the bustle of the train station and the tawdry Lista di Spagna to areas which, although no longer rural (Cannaregio comes from *canna*, meaning "reed") are still among the quietest and prettiest parts of the whole city. The district also has the dubious distinction of containing the world's original ghetto.

The Scalzi

Fondamenta dei Scalzi • Daily 7am–noon & 4–7pm • Free

Right next to the station stands the **Scalzi**, or Santa Maria di Nazareth. Built by Baldassare Longhena in the 1670s for the barefoot (*scalzi*) order of Carmelites, the church has frescoes by Giambattista Tiepolo in the first chapel on the left and the second on the right, but his major work on the ceiling was destroyed in 1915 by an Austrian bomb. A couple of fragments, now in the Accademia, were all that was salvaged. The second chapel on the left is the resting place of **Lodovico Manin** (d.1802), Venice's last doge. The bare inscription set into the floor – "Manini Cineres" (the ashes of Manin) – is a fair reflection of the low esteem in which he was held.

San Geremia

Campo San Geremia e Lucia • Mon–Sat 8am–noon & 3.30–6.30pm, Sun 9.15am–12.15pm & 5.30–6.30pm • Free

The church of **San Geremia** at the end of the street is chiefly notable for being the present home of **St Lucy**, martyred in Syracuse in 304. In one version of her legend, Lucy's response to an unwanted suitor who praised her beautiful eyes was to pluck out the offending organs and hand them to him, saying "Now let me live for God"; in another version, she was blinded by her executioner. She is the patron saint of the blind and those afflicted with ocular ailments, and is usually depicted holding her eyes on a dish. The glass case on the high altar contains her desiccated body. Architecturally, the church's main point of interest is the twelfth-century campanile, one of the oldest in the city.

Palazzo Labia

The ballroom of the **Palazzo Labia**, next door to San Geremia, contains frescoes by Giambattista Tiepolo and his assistants (1745–50), illustrating the story of *Antony and Cleopatra*. The present owners, RAI (the state radio and TV service), usually allow public access for a few hours each week, but the *palazzo* is currently *in restauro*. Its facade overlooks the **Canale di Cannaregio**, once the main entrance to Venice.

The Ghetto

The Venetian **Ghetto** was, in a sense, the first in the world: the word comes from the Venetian dialect *getar* (to found), or *geto* (foundry), which is what this area was until 1390. In 1516 all the city's Jews were ordered to move to the island of the Ghetto Nuovo. Distinctive badges or caps had to be worn by all Jews, and there were various economic and social restraints on the community, although oppression was lighter in Venice than in most other parts of Europe. When Jews were expelled en masse from Spain in 1492 and Portugal in 1497, many came here.

The Jewish population grew to about five thousand and, even though they were allowed to spread into the **Ghetto Vecchio** (called the "old ghetto" because that's where the foundries used to be) and the **Ghetto Nuovissimo**, there was gross overcrowding. As the Ghetto buildings were not allowed to be more than a third higher than the surrounding houses, the result was a stack of low-ceilinged storeys – seven is the usual number. Napoleon removed the gates of the Ghetto in 1797 but Venice's Jews didn't achieve equal rights with other Venetians until Unification with Italy in 1866. In a corner of the *campo* a series of reliefs by **Arbit Blatas** commemorates the two hundred Venetian Jews deported to the death camps during World War II – their names and ages are inscribed on a separate memorial entitled *The Last Train*. Today Venice's Jewish population of around six hundred is spread all over the city, but the Ghetto remains the centre of the community.

The Jewish Museum

Daily except Sat & Jewish hols: June–Sept 10am–7pm; Oct–May 10am–5.30pm • €3, or €8.50 with Ghetto tour • Ghetto tours in English on the half-hour; last tour June–Sept 5.30pm, Oct–May 4.30pm

Each wave of Jewish immigrants established its own **synagogue** and four of the most significant – the ornate Scola Levantina (founded in 1538), the Scola Spagnola, the

6

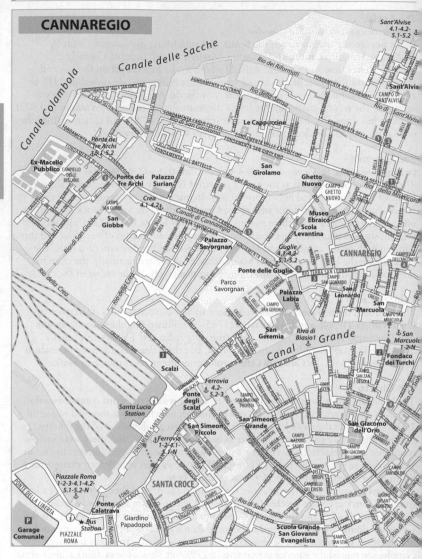

beautiful Scola al Canton and the Scola Italiana – can be viewed in a fascinating hourly tour of the area organized by the **Jewish Museum** in Campo Ghetto Nuovo; the collection in the museum itself consists mainly of silverware, embroidery and other liturgical objects.

Sant'Alvise

Campo Sant'Alvise • Mon–Sat 10am–5pm • €3, or Chorus Pass • ⓦ chorusvenezia.org

A few minutes north of the Ghetto stands the church of **Sant'Alvise**. Commissioned by Antonia Venier, daughter of Doge Antonio Venier, after the saint appeared to her in a vision in 1388, the church has one outstanding picture, *The Road to Calvary* by Tiepolo, painted in 1743. His *Crown of Thorns* and *Flagellation*, slightly earlier works, are on the right-hand wall of the nave.

ACCOMMODATION

Abbazia	3
Al Ponte Antico	9
Bernardi Semenzato	6
Ca' Favretto-San Cassiano	7
Ca' San Giorgio	2
Giorgione	5
Locanda Leon Bianco	8
Ostello Santa Fosca	1
Palazzo Abadessa	4

RESTAURANTS

Ai Promessi Sposi	10
Ai 40 Ladroni	1
Alla Fontana	3
Alla Madonna	17
Alla Vedova	8
Anice Stellato	2
Antico Dolo	15
Bancogiro	13
La Zucca	9
Naranzaria	14
Pontini	5
Vecio Fritolin	12
Vini da Gigio	7

CAFÉS & GELATERIE

Caffè del Doge	16
Gelateria Ca' d'Oro	11
Il Gelatone	6
Pasticceria Nobile	4

BARS & SNACKS

All'Arco	9
Al Ponte	6
Al Timon	1
Da Luca e Fred	3
Do Mori	8
La Cantina	4
Marcà	7
Paradiso Perduto	2
Un Mondo diVino	5

Madonna dell'Orto

Campiello Madonna dell'Orto • Mon–Sat 10am–5pm • €3, or Chorus Pass • ⓦ chorusvenezia.org

A circuitous stroll eastward from Sant'Alvise brings you to the Gothic church of
Madonna dell'Orto. Dedicated to St Christopher in about 1350, the church was
renamed after a large stone Madonna by Giovanni de' Santi, found discarded in a local
vegetable garden (*orto*), began to work miracles. Brought inside the church in 1377,
the figure can still be seen (now heavily restored) in the Cappella di San Mauro
through a door at the front end of the right aisle. This was Tintoretto's parish church
– he's buried in the chapel to the right of the high altar – and there are a number of his
paintings here, notably the colossal *Making of the Golden Calf* and *The Last Judgement*,
which flank the main altar.

Ca' d'Oro

Calle Ca' d'Oro • Mon 8.15am–2pm, Tues–Sat 8.15am–7.15pm • €6 • ⓦ polomuseale.venezia.beniculturali.it

The **Strada Nova** – the main thoroughfare of Cannaregio – was carved through the houses in 1871–72 and is now a bustling shopping street. Nearly halfway along is the inconspicuous *calle* named after, and leading to, the **Ca' d'Oro**, a spectacular Gothic palace that now houses the **Galleria Giorgio Franchetti**. Its main attraction is the *St Sebastian* painted by **Mantegna** shortly before his death in 1506, although the collection of sculpture has more outstanding items, notably **Tullio Lombardo**'s beautifully carved *Young Couple*, and superb portrait busts by Bernini and Alessandro Vittoria.

San Giovanni Crisostomo

Campo San Giovanni Crisostomo • Mon–Sat 8.30am–noon & 3.30–7pm, Sun 3.30–7pm • Free

Tucked into the southernmost corner of Cannaregio stands **San Giovanni Crisostomo** (John the Golden-Mouthed), named after the famously eloquent Archbishop of Constantinople. An intimate church with a compact Greek-cross plan, it was possibly the last project of Mauro Codussi, and was built between 1497 and 1504. It possesses two outstanding altarpieces: in the chapel to the right hangs one of the last works by **Giovanni Bellini**, *SS Jerome, Christopher and Louis of Toulouse*, painted in 1513 when the artist was in his 80s; and on the high altar, **Sebastiano del Piombo**'s *St John Chrysostom with SS John the Baptist, Liberale, Mary Magdalen, Agnes and Catherine*, painted in 1509–11. On the left side is a marble panel of the *Coronation of the Virgin* by Tullio Lombardo, a contrast with his more playful stuff in the nearby Miracoli.

The Miracoli

Campiello dei Miracoli • Mon–Sat 10am–5pm • €3, or Chorus Pass • ⓦ chorusvenezia.org

The exquisite marble-clad church of Santa Maria dei Miracoli, known simply as the **Miracoli**, sits on the lip of a canal on the very edge of Cannaregio. Thought to have been designed by Pietro Lombardo, it was built in the 1480s to house a painting of the Madonna (still the altarpiece) that was believed to have performed a number of miracles, such as reviving a man who'd spent half an hour lying at the bottom of the Giudecca canal. Typically for Renaissance architecture in Venice, richness of effect takes precedence over classical correctness, and the interior contains some of the most intricate decorative sculpture to be seen in the city.

The Gesuiti

Salizzada dei Spechieri • Daily 10am–noon & 4–6pm • Free

The major monument in the northeastern corner of Cannaregio is **Santa Maria Assunta**, commonly known simply as the **Gesuiti**. Built for the Jesuits in 1714–29, it has a disproportionately huge facade, which makes quite an impact, but not as much as the **interior**, where the walls are clad in green and white marble carved to resemble swags of damask. The stonework is astonishing, and also very heavy – a factor in the subsidence which is a constant problem. Unless you're a devotee of Palma il Giovane (in which case make for the sacristy, where the walls and ceiling are covered with paintings by him), the only painting to seek out is the *Martyrdom of St Lawrence* (first altar on the left), a broodingly intense night-scene painted by **Titian** in 1558.

Castello

Bordering both San Marco and Cannaregio, and spreading right across the city to the housing estates of Sant'Elena in the east, Castello is the largest of the *sestieri*. In terms of its tourist appeal, centre stage is occupied by the huge **Santi Giovanni e Paolo**. Within a few minutes' walk of here are two other fascinating churches, **Santa Maria Formosa** and **San Zaccaria**, as well as the beguiling Carpaccio paintings in the Scuola di San Giorgio degli Schiavoni.

Much of the eastern section of the Castello *sestiere* is given over to the **Arsenale**, once the industrial hub of the city and now a large naval base. Beyond it lies a predominantly residential quarter that has little to offer of cultural significance, except when the Biennale art and architecture shows are on, though its open spaces – the **Giardini Garibaldi**, **Giardini Pubblici** and **Parco della Rimembranza** – offer a little green relief.

Santi Giovanni e Paolo

Campo Santi Giovanni e Paolo • Mon–Sat 8am–6.30pm, Sun noon–6.30pm • €2.50 • ⓦ basilicasantigiovanniepaolo.it

The church of **Santi Giovanni e Paolo** – known locally as Zanipolo – is the Dominicans' equivalent of the Frari, founded in 1246, rebuilt and enlarged from 1333, and finally consecrated in 1430. The sarcophagus of Doge Giacomo Tiepolo, who gave the site to the Dominicans, is on the left of the door outside.

Approximately 90m long, 38m wide at the transepts and 33m high in the centre, the **interior** is stunning for its sheer size, and is more spacious than it would have been up to 1682, when the wooden choir was demolished. The simplicity of the design, a nave with two aisles and gracefully soaring arches, is offset by the huge number of tombs and monuments around the walls, including those of 25 doges.

The south aisle and south transept

In the **south aisle** you'll find Giovanni Bellini's superb polyptych *St Vincent Ferrer, with Saints Christopher and Sebastian*, with an *Annunciation* and pietà above. At the far end of this aisle, before you turn into the transept, you'll see a small shrine with the **foot of St Catherine of Siena**: most of her body is in Rome, her head is in her house in Siena and other relics are scattered about Italy.

The **south transept** has a painting by Alvise Vivarini, *Christ Carrying the Cross* (1474), and Lorenzo Lotto's *St Antonine* (1542), painted in return for nothing more than his expenses and permission to be buried in the church. Sadly, Lotto was eventually driven from his home town by the jealousies and plots of other artists (including Titian), and died in a monastery at Loreto.

The chancel and the rest of the church

On the right of the **chancel** is the tomb of Doge Michele Morosini, selected by Ruskin as "the richest monument of the Gothic period in Venice". The Renaissance tomb of Doge Andrea Vendramin, opposite, was singled out as its antithesis – only the half of the effigy's head that would be visible from below was completed by the artist, a short cut denounced by Ruskin as indicative of "an extreme of intellectual and moral degradation". Tullio Lombardo is thought to have been the sculptor.

In 1867 a fire wrecked the **Cappella del Rosario**, at the end of the north transept, destroying paintings by Tintoretto, Palma il Giovane and others; of their replacements, the best are **Veronese**'s ceiling panels and *Adoration*. Funerary sculpture is the main attraction of the north aisle. To the left of the sacristy door is the monument to Doge Pasquale Malipiero by Pietro Lombardo, one of the earliest in Renaissance style in Venice.

Campo Santi Giovanni e Paolo

The spectacular building on the north side of **Campo Santi Giovanni e Paolo** is the **Scuola Grande di San Marco**, which has provided a sumptuous facade and foyer for the Ospedale Civile since its suppression in the early nineteenth century. The facade was started by Pietro Lombardo and Giovanni Buora in 1487, and finished in 1495 by Mauro Codussi.

When the *condottiere* **Bartolomeo Colleoni** died, he left a handsome legacy to the republic on condition that a monument should be erected to him in the square in front of San Marco, an impossible proposition to Venice's rulers, with their cult of anonymous service to the state. They got around this dilemma by interpreting the will in a way that allowed them to raise the monument in front of the Scuola Grande di San Marco, rather than the Basilica, and still claim the money. In 1481 the commission for the monument was won by **Andrea Verrocchio**, who was working on the piece when he died at the end of June 1488. **Alessandro Leopardi** was called in to finish the work and produce the plinth for it, which he gladly did – even adding his signature on the horse's girth and appending *del Cavallo* to his name.

San Francesco della Vigna

Campo San Francesco • Mon–Sat 8am–12.30pm & 3–6.30pm, Sun 3–6.30pm • Free

The church of **San Francesco della Vigna**, to the east of Zanipolo, takes its name from the vineyard that was here when the Franciscans were given the site in 1253. The present church building was begun in 1534, designed and supervised by Sansovino, but the design was modified during construction, and Palladio was later brought in to provide the facade. Some fine works of art are to be seen inside, including Giambattista Tiepolo's frescoes in the **Cappella Sagredo**, a *Sacra Conversazione* by Veronese, sculptures of Prophets and Evangelists by the Lombardo family and their assistants (in the chapel to the left of the chancel), and a large *Madonna and Child Enthroned* by **Antonio da Negroponte**. And don't overlook the tranquil fifteenth-century cloisters.

Santa Maria Formosa

Campo Santa Maria Formosa • Mon–Sat 10am–5pm • €3, or Chorus Pass • ⊕ chorusvenezia.org

South of San Zanipolo lies the atmospheric Campo Santa Maria Formosa. The eponymous church was founded by St Magnus, Bishop of Oderzo, in the seventh century, having been inspired by a dream in which he saw a buxom (*formosa*) figure of the Madonna. The present building is another Codussi design, dating from 1492. Palma il Vecchio's altarpiece *St Barbara*, the church's outstanding picture, was admired by George Eliot as "an almost unique presentation of a hero-woman".

Pinacoteca Querini-Stampalia

Campo Santa Maria Formosa 5252 • Tues–Sun 10am–6pm • €10 • ⊕ querinistampalia.it

The Palazzo Querini-Stampalia, just round the corner from Santa Maria Formosa, houses the **Pinacoteca Querini-Stampalia**. Although there is a batch of Renaissance pieces – such as Palma il Vecchio's marriage portraits of Francesco Querini and Paola Priuli Querini (for whom the palace was built), and **Giovanni Bellini**'s *Presentation in the Temple* – the general tone of the collection is set by the culture of eighteenth-century Venice, a period to which much of the palace's decor belongs. The winningly inept pieces by **Gabriel Bella** form a comprehensive record of Venetian social life in that century, and the more accomplished genre paintings of **Pietro and Alessandro Longhi** feature prominently as well. Another attraction of the Querini-Stampalia is that visitors are treated to a free chamber-music concert inside the museum at 5pm every Saturday.

Palazzo Grimani

Ramo Grimani 4858 • Mon 9am–2pm, Tues–Sun 9am–7.15pm • €4 • ⊕ palazzogrimani.org

One of the most impressive palaces in the city stands on the island immediately to the south of Santa Maria Formosa. Turn first left off Ruga Giuffa and you'll be confronted by the land entrance of the gargantuan sixteenth-century **Palazzo Grimani**, once owned by the branch of the Grimani family whose collection of antiquities became the basis of the Museo Archeologico. The neo-Roman interior, featuring some of the most spectacular rooms in the city (the tribune, with its huge skylight, is especially dramatic), has been beautifully restored and furnished with a miscellany of objets d'art.

San Zaccaria

Campo San Zaccaria • Mon–Sat 10am–noon & 4–6pm, Sun 4–6pm • Free

The towering church of **San Zaccaria**, a pleasing mixture of Gothic and Renaissance, was started by Antonio Gambello and finished after his death in 1481 by Mauro Codussi, who was responsible for the facade from the first storey upwards. Inside is one of the city's most stunning altarpieces, a *Madonna and Four Saints* by Giovanni Bellini. A fee of €1 gets you into the rebuilt remnants of the old church, the Cappella di Sant'Atanasio and Cappella di San Tarasio, where you'll find an early Tintoretto, *The Birth of John the Baptist*, and three wonderful altarpieces by Antonio Vivarini and Giovanni d'Alemagna.

The Pietà

Riva degli Schiavoni • Tues–Fri 10am–noon & 3–5pm, Sat & Sun 10am–noon • Free

The principal promenade of Castello, the **Riva degli Schiavoni**, has one outstanding monument: the **Pietà**, or Santa Maria della Visitazione. **Vivaldi** wrote many of his finest pieces for the orphanage attached to the church, where he worked as violin-master (1704–18) and later as choirmaster (1735–38). Giorgio Massari won a competition to redesign the church in 1736, and it's possible that Vivaldi advised him on its acoustics; building didn't actually begin until 1745, and the facade was finished only in 1906. The interior, which looks like a wedding cake turned inside out, has one of Venice's most ostentatious ceiling paintings, Giambattista Tiepolo's *The Glory of Paradise*.

San Giorgio dei Greci

Campiello dei Greci • Mon & Wed–Sat 9.30am–12.30pm & 2.30–4.30pm, Sun 9am–1pm • Free

Stroll north along the flank of the Pietà and you'll come to **San Giorgio dei Greci**, focal point of the city's Greek community. The Greek presence was strong in Venice from the eleventh century, and grew stronger after Constantinople's capture by the Turks in 1453; by the close of the fifteenth century they had founded their own church, college and school here. The **church** contains icons dating back to the twelfth century and a lot of work by Michael Danaskinàs, a sixteenth-century Cretan artist.

Museo Dipinti Sacri Bizantini

Daily 9am–5pm • €4

The *scuola* adjoining the church is home to the **Museo Dipinti Sacri Bizantini**. Although many of the most beautiful of the exhibited works (mainly fifteenth to eighteenth century) maintain the traditions of icon painting in terms of composition and use of symbolic figures rather than attempts at realism, it's fascinating to see how some of the artists absorbed Western influences.

The Scuola di San Giorgio degli Schiavoni

Calle dei Furlani 3259/A • Tues–Sat 10am–12.30pm & 3–6pm, Sun 10am–12.30pm • €4

The ground-floor hall of the **Scuola di San Giorgio degli Schiavoni** is one of the most beautiful rooms in Europe. Venice's resident Slavs (*Schiavoni*), most of whom were traders, set up a *scuola* to look after their interests in 1451; the present building dates from the early sixteenth century, and the whole interior looks more or less as it would have then. Entering it, you step straight from the street into the lower hall, the walls of which are decorated with a superb cycle of pictures created by Vittore Carpaccio between 1502 and 1509. Outstanding among them is *The Vision of St Augustine*, depicting the moment that Augustine, while writing to St Jerome, had a vision of Jerome's death.

The Arsenale

The dockyards and factories of the **Arsenale** were the foundations on which Venice's mercantile and military supremacy rested. A corruption of the Arabic *darsin'a* (house of industry), its very name is indicative of the strength of the city's trading links with the eastern Mediterranean. Construction of the Arsenale began in the early years of the twelfth century, and by the third decade of the fifteenth century it had become the base for some 300 shipping companies, operating around 3000 vessels in excess of 200 tonnes.

Expansion of the Arsenale continued into the sixteenth century – Sanmicheli's covered dock for the state barge (the *Bucintoro*) was built in the 1540s, for example, and da Ponte's gigantic rope-factory (the Tana) in 1579. By then, though, the maritime strength of Venice

6

was past its peak; militarily, too, despite the conspicuous success at Lepanto in 1571, Venice was on the wane. When Napoleon took over the city in 1797 he burned down the wharves, sank the last *Bucintoro* and confiscated the remnant of the Venetian navy.

There's no public access to the Arsenale complex except during the Biennale, but you can get a look at part of it from the bridge connecting the Campo Arsenale and the Fondamenta dell'Arsenale. The main **gateway**, built by Antonio Gambello in 1460, was the first structure in Venice to employ the classical vocabulary of Renaissance architecture. The four **lions** to the side of the gateway must be the most photographed in the city: the two on the right were probably taken from Delos (at an unknown date); the larger pair were brought back from Piraeus in 1687 by Francesco Morosini after the reconquest of the Morea.

Museo Storico Navale

Campo San Biagio 2148 • Mon–Fri 8.45am–1.30pm, Sat 8.45am–1pm • €3

Occupying a vast old granary at the mouth of the Arsenale canal, the **Museo Storico Navale** is a somewhat rambling museum, but it's an essential supplement to a walk round the Arsenale district. Chiefly of interest for its models of Venetian craft from gondolas to the state barge known as the *Bucintoro* (these models were the equivalents of blueprints), the museum gives a comprehensive picture of the working life of the Arsenale and the smaller boatyards of Venice.

San Pietro di Castello

Campo San Pietro • Mon–Sat 10am–5pm • €3, or Chorus Pass • ⓦ chorusvenezia.org

In 1808 the greater part of the canal connecting the Bacino di San Marco to the broad inlet of the Canale di San Pietro was filled in to form what is now **Via Garibaldi**, the widest street in the city and the busiest commercial area in the eastern district. Head along the right-hand side of the street and you'll soon cross the Ponte di Quintavalle onto the island of **San Pietro**, a slightly down-at-heel area where the chief activity is the repairing of boats. **San Pietro di Castello**, the city's cathedral throughout the life of the Venetian Republic (San Marco was regarded as the doge's church), is the successor of a church that was raised here as early as the seventh century; the present building was raised nearly a millennium later, with a facade designed in the mid-sixteenth century by **Palladio**. Inside, the body of Lorenzo Giustiniani, the first Patriarch of Venice, who died in 1456, lies in the glass case within the elaborate high altar; otherwise there's little of interest.

Sant'Elena

Campo della Chiesa • Mon–Sat 5–7pm • Free

Located at the eastern limit of the city, the island of **Sant'Elena** was enlarged tenfold during the Austrian administration, partly to form exercise grounds for the troops. It's now largely occupied by apartment buildings, but the **church of Sant'Elena** – next to the city's ramshackle football stadium – is worth a visit, chiefly for the facade sculpture created in the 1470s by Antonio Rizzo, showing Vittore Cappello (captain-general of the republic's navy) kneeling before St Helena, Constantine's mother. Inside, a chapel on the right enshrines the alleged remains of Helena, whose body is more generally believed to lie in Rome's church of Santa Maria in Aracoeli.

The northern islands

The islands lying to the north of Venice – **San Michele**, **Murano**, **Burano** and **Torcello** – are the places to visit when the throng of tourists in the main part of the city becomes too oppressive; Murano has been a glass-producing centre for hundreds of years, while Burano was once renowned for its lace work.

To get to the northern islands, the main *vaporetto* stop is **Fondamente Nove** (or Nuove): all of the island services start here or call here.

San Michele

A church was founded on **San Michele**, the innermost of the northern islands, in the tenth century, and a monastery was established in the thirteenth. Its best-known resident was Fra Mauro (d.1459), whose map of the world – the most accurate of its time – is now a precious possession of the Libreria Sansoviniana. The monastery was suppressed in the early nineteenth century, but in 1829, after a spell as an Austrian prison for political offenders, it was handed back to the Franciscans, who look after the church and the cemetery to this day.

San Michele in Isola

Daily: April–Sept 7.30am–6pm; Oct–March 7.30am–4pm • Free

The high brick wall around the cemetery gives way by the landing stage to the elegant white facade of **San Michele in Isola**, designed by Mauro Codussi in 1469. With this building, Codussi not only helped introduce Renaissance architecture to Venice, but also promoted the use of Istrian stone. Easy to carve yet resistant to water, it had been used as damp-proofing at ground level, but never before for a complete facade; it was to be used on the facades of most major buildings in Venice from the Renaissance onwards. Attached on the left, and entered from within the church, is the dainty **Cappella Emiliana**, built around 1530 by **Guglielmo dei Grigi**.

The cemetery

Daily: April–Sept 7.30am–6pm; Oct–March 7.30am–4pm

The main part of the island, through the cloisters, is the city **cemetery**, which was established by Napoleonic decree. The majority of Venetians lie here for just ten years or so, when their bones are dug up and removed to an ossuary: only those who can afford it stay longer. The cemetery is laid out in sections, the most dilapidated of which is for the Protestants (no. XV), **Ezra Pound**'s final resting place; Nobel laureate Joseph Brodsky is buried here too. In section XIV are the Greek and Russian Orthodox graves, including the restrained memorial stones of **Igor and Vera Stravinsky** and the more elaborate tomb of **Serge Diaghilev**.

Even with the grave-rotation system, the island is reaching full capacity, so in 1998 a competition was held for the **redevelopment** of San Michele. The winning entry, from English architect David Chipperfield, places a sequence of formal courtyards alongside a new funerary chapel and crematorium. It promises to be an austerely beautiful place, resembling a cross between a necropolis and a philosopher's retreat.

Murano

The **glass-blowing industry** is what made Murano famous all over Europe, and today its furnaces constitute Venice's sole surviving manufacturing zone. The main *fondamente* of Murano are given over almost entirely to shops selling glasswork, and it's difficult to walk more than a few metres on this island without being invited to step inside a showroom – and once inside, you're likely to be pressured into forking out for some piece of kitsch which may not even have been made here. However, some of the showrooms have furnaces attached, and you shouldn't pass up the chance to see these astoundingly skilful craftsmen in action, even if they're only churning out little glass ponies and other knick-knacks.

The glass furnaces were moved to here from Venice as a safety measure in 1291, and so jealously did the Muranese guard their industrial secrets that for a long while they had the European monopoly on glass mirror-making. The glass-blowers of Murano were accorded various privileges not allowed to other artisans, such as being able to wear swords. From 1376 the offspring of a marriage between a Venetian nobleman and the daughter of a glass-worker were allowed to be entered into the *Libro d'Oro*, unlike the children of other cross-class matches.

San Pietro Martire

Fondamenta dei Vetrai • Mon–Sat 9am–noon & 3–6pm, Sun 3–6pm • Free

When the Venetian Republic fell to Napoleon in 1797, there were seventeen churches on Murano; today only two are open. The Dominican church of **San Pietro Martire**, which was begun in 1363 and largely rebuilt after a fire in 1474, contains a handful of fine paintings, notably **Giovanni Bellini**'s large *Madonna and Child with St Mark, St Augustine and Doge Barbarigo*, and, on the opposite side of the church, two pieces by Veronese – *St Agatha in Prison* and *St Jerome in the Desert*.

The Museo del Vetro

Fondamenta Giustinian 8 • Daily: April–Oct 10am–6pm; Nov–March 10am–5pm • €8, or Museum Pass • Ⓦ museovetro.visitmuve.it

The seventeenth-century Palazzo Giustinian is now home to the **Museo del Vetro** (Glass Museum), where perhaps the finest single item is the dark-blue Barovier marriage cup, dating from around 1470 – it's on show in room 1 on the first floor, along with some splendid Renaissance enamelled and painted glass. But every room contains some amazing creations: glass beakers that look as if they are made from veined stone; sixteenth-century platters that look like discs of crackled ice; stupendously ugly nineteenth-century decorative pieces, with fat little birds enmeshed in trellises of glass. A separate room contains a fascinating exhibition on the history of Murano glass techniques.

Santi Maria e Donato

Calle San Donato • Mon–Sat 9am–noon & 3.30–7pm, Sun 3.30–7pm • Free

Murano's finest building is the Veneto-Byzantine church of **Santi Maria e Donato**, which was founded in the seventh century and rebuilt in the twelfth. Its beautiful **mosaic floor**, dated 1141 in the nave, mingles abstract patterns with images of beasts and birds – an eagle carries off a deer; two roosters carry off a fox slung from a pole. The church was originally dedicated to Mary, but in 1125 was rededicated when the relics of St Donatus were brought here from the Greek island, Kefalonia. Four splendid bones from an unfortunate dragon that was slain by the holy spit of Donatus are now hanging behind the altar. Above these, in the apse, is a twelfth-century **mosaic of the Madonna** and fifteenth-century frescoes of the Evangelists.

Burano

After the peeling plaster and eroded stonework of the other lagoon settlements, the small, brightly painted houses of **Burano** come as something of a surprise. Local tradition says that the colours once enabled each fisherman to identify his house from out at sea, but nowadays the colours are used simply for decorative effect.

This is still largely a fishing community, the lagoon's main yield being shellfish of various kinds, such as *vongole* (tiny clams) and small crabs. (The catch can be bought either here, on the Fondamenta Pescheria, or at the Rialto.) The lives of the women of Burano used to be dominated by the **lace** industry, but the production of handmade lace is no longer a large-scale enterprise, and much of the stuff sold in the shops lining the narrow street leading from the *vaporetto* stop is produced by machine, outside Italy.

Scuola del Merletto

Piazza Galuppi • Tues–Sun: April–Oct 10am–5pm; Nov–March 10am–4pm • €5, or Museum Pass • Ⓦ museomerletto.visitmuve.it

The **Scuola del Merletto** is simply a school rather than a confraternity-cum-guild – unlike all other craftspeople in Venice, the lacemakers had no guild to represent them, perhaps because the workforce was exclusively female. It was opened in 1872, when the indigenous crafting of lace had declined so far that it was left to one woman, Francesca Memo, to transmit the necessary skills to a younger generation of women.

CLOCKWISE FROM TOP LEFT GONDOLAS, VENICE (P.386); BURANO (ABOVE); GROCERY BARGE, SAN BARNABA, VENICE (P.391); THE CLOCK TOWER OF THE BASILICA, VICENZA (P.408) >

6

Although the *scuola* has not operated as a full-time school since the late 1960s and is now almost moribund, a few courses are still held here.

Reopened in 2011 after a major restoration, the *scuola*'s museum showcases around 150 examples of exquisite Murano lacework, along with paintings and a profusion of other documentation. The most engrossing, and poignant, display is the live demonstration by master lacemakers – these women are almost certainly the last practitioners of this highly specialized and exacting art.

Torcello

Torcello was settled as early as the fifth century, became the seat of the Bishop of Altinum from 638, and the home of about twenty thousand people by the fourteenth century, before being eclipsed by Venice – by the end of the fifteenth century Torcello was largely deserted and today only about thirty people remain in residence.

Santa Maria dell'Assunta

Piazza di Torcello • Daily: March–Oct 10.30am–6pm; Nov–Feb 10am–5pm • €5

The main reason people come to Torcello today is to visit Venice's first cathedral, **Santa Maria dell'Assunta**, a Veneto-Byzantine building that evolved from the original seventh-century church.

A stunning twelfth-century **mosaic** of the Madonna and Child, on a pure gold background, covers the semi-dome of the apse, resting on an eleventh-century mosaic frieze of the Apostles. In the centre of the frieze, below the window, is St Heliodorus, the first Bishop of Altinum, whose remains were brought here by the first settlers. It's interesting to compare this image with the gold-plated face mask given to his remains in a Roman sarcophagus in front of the original seventh-century altar. Ruskin described the view from the **campanile** as "one of the most notable scenes in this wide world", a verdict you can't test for yourself at the moment, as the campanile is currently being restored.

Santa Fosca

Piazza di Torcello • Daily: March–Oct 10.30am–5.30pm; Nov–Feb 10am–4.30pm • Free

The church of **Santa Fosca** was built in the eleventh and twelfth centuries to house the body of the eponymous saint, brought to Torcello from Libya some time before 1011 and now resting under the altar. In the square outside sits the curious **chair of Attila**. Local legend has it that if you sit in it you will be wed within a year. Behind it, in two buildings round the square, is the **Museo di Torcello** (same hours as cathedral; €3, or joint ticket), which includes nicely displayed thirteenth-century beaten gold figures, sections of mosaic heads, and jewellery.

The southern islands

The islands in the section of the lagoon to the south of the city, enclosed by the **Lido** and **Pellestrina**, are scattered over a larger expanse of water than the northern lagoon, but the nearer islands – notably **San Giorgio Maggiore**, **La Giudecca** and **San Lazzaro** – are the more interesting ones. The farther-flung settlements of the southern lagoon have played a significant role in the history of Venice, but nowadays they have little going for them other than the pleasure of the trip.

San Giorgio Maggiore

Daily: May–Sept 9.30am–12.30pm & 2–5.30pm; Oct–April 9.30am–12.30pm & 2.30–4.30pm • Free

Palladio's church of **San Giorgio Maggiore**, facing the Palazzo Ducale across the Bacino di San Marco, is one of the most prominent and familiar of all Venetian landmarks. It is a startling building, with an impact that's enhanced by its isolation on an island of its own. The Venetians were the first to cover church interiors with white stucco, and the technique is used to dazzling effect in San Giorgio Maggiore – "Of all the colours, none is more proper for churches than white; since the purity of colour, as of the life, is particularly gratifying to God," wrote Palladio. Of its paintings, two stand out: Tintoretto's *The Fall of Manna* and *The Last Supper*, which hang in the chancel and were painted as a pair in 1592–94, the last years of the artist's life. On the left of the choir a corridor leads to the lift that takes you up the **campanile** (€5), perhaps the best vantage point in the city.

The monastery

Guided tours Sat & Sun 10am–4.30pm, in Italian and English • €10

Since the early ninth century there's been a church on this island, and at the end of the tenth century the lagoon's most important Benedictine monastery was established here. Now the home of the **Fondazione Giorgio Cini**, a cultural institute that hosts conferences and courses here, the monastery is one of the architectural wonders of the city. Two adjoining cloisters form the heart of the complex: the **Cloister of the Bay Trees**, planned by Giovanni Buora and built by his son Andrea in the two decades up to 1540; and the **Cloister of the Cypresses**, designed in 1579 by Palladio. Inside, there's a 128m-long **dormitory** by Giovanni Buora (c.1494), a **double staircase** (1641–43) and **library** (1641–53) by Longhena and, approached by an ascent through two anterooms, a magnificent **refectory** by Palladio (1560–62). A dazzlingly accurate computer-generated reproduction of Veronese's great *Marriage at Cana* fills the end wall of the refectory; the original, stolen by Napoleon's army, is now in the Louvre.

La Giudecca

In the earliest records of Venice, the island of **La Giudecca** was known as Spina Longa, a name clearly derived from its shape; the modern name might refer to the Jews (*Giudei*) who were based here from the late thirteenth century until their removal to the Ghetto, or to the disruptive noble families who, from the ninth century, were shoved onto this chain of islets to keep them out of mischief (*giudicati* meaning "judged"). Before the banks of the Brenta became prestigious, the Giudecca was where the wealthiest aristocrats of early Renaissance Venice built their villas, and in places you can still see traces of their gardens. Wealth is still present, in the form of the luxury *Cipriani* and *Hilton* hotels at either end of the island; the latter occupies the immense Mulino Stucky, once a flour mill. In between are the workshops, boatyards and housing estates that make Giudecca one of the few places in Venice where tourism doesn't prevail.

The Redentore

Campo del Santissimo Redentore • Mon–Sat 10am–5pm • €3, or Chorus Pass • ⓦ chorusvenezia.org

The Franciscan church of the **Redentore**, designed by Palladio in 1577, is the Giudecca's main monument. In 1575–76 Venice suffered an outbreak of bubonic plague that killed nearly fifty thousand people – virtually a third of the city's population. The Redentore was built in thanks for Venice's deliverance, and every year the doge and his senators attended a Mass in the church on the Feast of the Redentore. The procession walked to the church over a pontoon bridge from the Záttere, a ceremony perpetuated by the people of Venice on the third Sunday in July.

As in San Giorgio, the complex white surfaces of the Redentore modulate the natural light to draw the eye – and the mind – inward and upward. In the side chapels you'll find a couple of pictures by Francesco Bassano and an *Ascension* by Tintoretto and his assistants, but the best paintings – including a *John the Baptist* by **Jacopo Bassano**, a *Baptism of Christ* by **Paolo Veronese** and *Madonna with Child and Angels* by **Alvise Vivarini** – are in the sacristy, which is rarely opened.

San Lazzaro degli Armeni

No foreign community has a longer pedigree in Venice than the Armenians: they were established by the end of the thirteenth century, and for around five hundred years have had a church within a few yards of the Piazza (in Calle degli Armeni). They are far less numerous now, and the most conspicuous sign of their presence is the island by the Lido, **San Lazzaro degli Armeni**, identifiable from the city by the onion-shaped top of its campanile.

The monastery

Guided tours daily June–Sept 3pm, Oct–May 3.25pm • €6 • The #20 boat leaves San Zaccaria 15min before the tour starts and returns within 10min of the end

The Roman Catholic Armenian monastery here was founded in 1717 by Manug di Pietro (known as Mechitar, "The Consoler"), and derived its name from the island's past function as a leper colony – Lazarus being the patron saint of lepers. The Armenian monks have always had a reputation as scholars and linguists, and the monastery's collection of precious books and manuscripts, some going back to the fifth century, is a highlight of the tour, along with a Tiepolo ceiling panel and the room in which Byron stayed while lending a hand with the preparation of an Armenian–English dictionary.

The Lido

For about eight centuries, the **Lido** was the focus of the annual hullaballoo of Venice's "Marriage to the Sea", when the doge went out to the Porto di Lido to drop a gold ring into the brine and then disembarked for Mass at San Nicolò al Lido. It was then an unspoilt strip of land, and remained so into the nineteenth century. By the twentieth century, however, it had become the smartest bathing resort in Italy, and although it's no longer as chic as it was when Thomas Mann set *Death in Venice* here, there's less room on its beaches now than ever before. Unless you're staying at one of the hotels that stand shoulder to shoulder along the seafront, you won't be made welcome on the prime stretch of Lido sand. The ungroomed public beaches are at the northern and southern ends of the island.

ARRIVAL AND DEPARTURE VENICE

BY PLANE

MARCO POLO AIRPORT

Venice's **Marco Polo** airport is a little over 7km north of the *centro storico*, on the edge of the lagoon.

Buses into the city The most inexpensive way of getting into the city is to take one of the bus services to the terminal at Piazzale Roma: the ATVO (Azienda Trasporti Veneto Orientale; ⓦatvo.it) coach, which departs every half-hour and takes around 20min (€5), or the ACTV (Azienda del Consorzio Trasporti Veneziano; ⓦactv.it) bus #5, which is equally frequent but usually takes a few minutes longer (it's a local bus service, so it picks up and puts down passengers between the airport and Piazzale Roma), and also costs €5. For €10 you can buy an ACTV bus+boat ticket, which gets you to Piazzale Roma then gives you one *vaporetto* journey of up to 90min. (Note that you can buy an ACTV travel pass at the airport, but you have to pay a supplement if you want to use it for the airport bus; see opposite for more.)

Water-buses into the city If you'd prefer to approach the city by water, you could take one of the Alilaguna water-buses, which operate on three routes from the airport: the fare is €15 to any stop in central Venice, and €8 to Murano. All services are hourly, and the journey time to San Marco is usually a little over an hour. Ticket offices for Alilaguna, ATVO and ACTV buses are in the arrivals hall; in addition to single tickets, you can also get ACTV passes here (see opposite) – a wise investment for most visitors. ACTV passes

are not valid on the Alilaguna service nor on the ATVO bus.

Taxis into the city Water-taxi drivers tout for business in and around the arrivals hall. This is the most luxurious means of getting into the city, but it's expensive: you'll pay in the region of €100 to San Marco, for up to six people. Ordinary car-taxis cost about €35 to Piazzale Roma.

TREVISO AIRPORT

Treviso, 30km to the north of Venice, is a very small airport used chiefly by **charter** companies, some of which provide a bus link from the airport into Venice. An ATVO bus service to Venice's Piazzale Roma meets the incoming Ryanair flights; the fare is €7 single and the journey takes 1hr 10min. Much quicker are the Barzi buses that run 10–15 times from Treviso airport to Piazzale Roma – also costing €7, they take just 40min.

BY TRAIN OR BUS

Arriving by train or long-distance bus, you simply get off at the end of the line. The Piazzale Roma bus station and Santa Lucia train station are just a 5min walk from each other, linked by the Ponte della Costituzione, at the top of the Canal Grande, and both are well served by *vaporetto* services to the core of the city. Buses run from Piazzale Roma to various parts of the Veneto, but trains are generally quicker, more frequent, and no more expensive. Main Veneto train services from Venice are as follows: Destinations Bassano (hourly; 1hr 15min–1hr 40min);

Belluno (4 daily; 1hr 50min–2hr 20min); Conegliano (every 30min; 50min–1hr 10min); Padua (every 15min; 25–50min); Treviso (every 20min; 30–40min); Verona (every 30min; 1hr 10min–2hr 25min); Vicenza (every 30min; 30min–1hr 15min); Vittorio Veneto (6 daily; 1hr 10min–1hr 20min).

BY CAR

Visitors arriving by car must leave their vehicle either on the mainland or in one of the city's car parks – at Piazzale Roma

of the ever expanding Tronchetto, Europe's largest car park. Prices at these two vary according to the time of year, the length of stay and the size of car, but it's never cheap, and in summer the tailbacks can be horrendous. It's better to use either the less expensive open-air San Giuliano car park at **Mestre** (open summer, Easter and during Carnevale), linked by ACTV buses with central Venice, or the terminal at **Fusina**, just south of Mestre, open year-round and connected by water-buses with Piazza San Marco (ACTV passes not valid).

GETTING AROUND

Venice has two interlocking street systems – the canals and the pavements. The #1, #2, the "Vaporetto dell'Arte" and the night service all shuttle along the Canal Grande, but most water-buses skirt the city centre, connecting points on the periphery and the outer islands. Taking a water-bus is usually the quickest way of getting between far-flung points, but in many cases the speediest way of getting from A to B is **on foot** – you don't have to run, for instance, to cover the distance from the Piazza to the Rialto Bridge quicker than the #1.

WATER-BUSES

There are two basic types of boat: *vaporetti*, which are the lumbering workhorses used on the Canal Grande and other heavily used routes, and *motoscafi*, smaller vessels employed on routes where the volume of traffic isn't as great.

Fares The standard fare is an exorbitant €7 for a single journey; the ticket is valid for an hour, and for any number of changes of water-bus, as long as you're travelling from point A to point B – it cannot, in other words, be used as a return ticket. Should you have more than one piece of large luggage, you're supposed to pay €7 per additional item. Children under 4 travel free.

Tickets Tickets are available from most landing stages, from *tabacchi*, from shops displaying the ACTV sign, from the tourist offices and the ACTV office at Piazzale Roma (daily: summer 6am–11.30pm; winter 6am–8pm). Tickets can also be bought on board at the standard price, as long as you ask the attendant as soon as you get on board; if you delay, you could be liable for a spot-fine of €52. Note that all tickets and travel cards have to be swiped before each journey at the meter-like machines which are at every stop.

TRAGHETTI

There are just four bridges spanning the Canal Grande – the Ponte Calatrava (at Piazzale Roma), Ponte dei Scalzi (at the train station), Ponte di Rialto and Ponte dell'Accademia – so the *traghetti* (gondola ferries) that cross it can be useful

time-savers. Costing just 50 cents, they are also the only cheap way of getting a ride on a gondola, albeit a stripped-down version, with none of the trimmings and no padded seats: most locals stand rather than sit. There used to be almost thirty gondola *traghetti* across the Canal Grande, but today there are just seven, listed here from the San Marco end to the station end: Dogana–San Marco Vallaresso (daily 9am–2pm); Santa Maria del Giglio–Salute (daily 9am–6pm); Ca' Rezzonico–San Samuele (Mon–Sat 8.30am–1.30pm); San Tomà–Sant'Angelo (Mon–Sat 7.30am–8pm, Sun 8.30am–7.30pm); Riva del Carbon–Fondamenta del Vin (Mon–Sat 8am–1pm); Santa Sofia–Rialto (Mon–Sat 7.30am–8pm, Sun 8.45am–7pm); San Marcuola–Fondaco dei Turchi (Mon–Sat 9am–1pm). In the winter months it's common for *traghetti* to cease operating considerably earlier than the times indicated above, or even to be suspended altogether.

WATER-TAXIS

Venice's **water-taxis** are sleek and speedy vehicles that can penetrate most of the city's canals. Unfortunately their use is confined to all but the owners of the deepest pockets, for they are possibly the most expensive form of taxi in western Europe: the clock starts at €15 and goes up €2 every minute. All sorts of surcharges are levied as well: €5 for each extra person if there are more than two people in the party; €3 for each piece of luggage other than the first

TRAVEL CARDS

ACTV produces Tourist Travel Cards valid for **12 hours** (€18), **24 hours** (€20), **36 hours** (€25), **48 hours** (€30), **72 hours** (€35), and **seven days** (€50), which can be used on all ACTV services within Venice, except the "Vaporetto dell'Arte" (see p.387). Holders of a Rolling Venice Card (see p.352) can get a 72-hr ACTV card for €18. A supplement of €3 per journey is payable if you want to use an ACTV pass for the airport buses. Travel cards are available from the tourist offices, at Piazzale Roma, the train station and the airport, and at the Ca' d'Oro, Rialto, Accademia, San Marco, San Zaccaria, Arsenale, Zàttere, Fondamenta Nove and Tronchetto *vaporetto* stops.

6

WATER-BUS ROUTES

What follows is a run-through of the **routes** that visitors are most likely to find useful. Be warned that so many services call at San Marco, San Zaccaria, Rialto, Piazzale Roma and the train station that the stops at these points are spread out over a long stretch of waterfront, so you might have to walk past several stops before finding the one you need. Note also that the San Marco stop has two sections, San Marco Vallaresso and San Marco Giardinetti, which are just yards from each other, and that the San Zaccaria stop is as close to the Piazza as are the San Marco stops.

#1: The #1 is the slowest of the water-buses, and the one you're likely to use most often. It starts at Piazzale Roma, calls at every stop on the Canal Grande except San Samuele, works its way along the San Marco waterfront to Sant'Elena, then goes over to the Lido. The #1 runs every 20min between 5 and 6.30am, every 10min between 6.30am and 10pm, and every 20min between 10 and 11.40pm.

#2: The #2 is in part a speeded-up version of the #1, as it makes far fewer stops on the Canal Grande. Its clockwise route takes it from San Zaccaria to San Giorgio Maggiore, Giudecca (Zitelle, Redentore and Palanca), Záttere, San Basilio, Sacca Fisola, Tronchetto, Piazzale Roma, the train station, then down the Canal Grande (calling at Rialto, San Tomà, San Samuele and Accademia; from around 4–8pm it also calls at San Marcuola) to San Marco; the anticlockwise version calls at the same stops. Its timetable is complicated, but basically from Monday to Friday the #2 runs along the upper part of the Canal Grande every 10min from about 6.30am to 8.30pm, then every 20min until about 11.30pm, but for the section between Rialto and San Marco it runs every 20min from around 9am to 8.30pm – in other words, many more #2s run between Piazzale Roma and Rialto than between Piazzale Roma and San Marco. At weekends the #2 runs every 20min for its whole route. In summer the #2 is extended from San Zaccaria to the Lido.

#4.1/4.2: The circular service, running right round the core of Venice, with a short detour at the northern end to San Michele and Murano. The #4.1 travels anticlockwise, the #4.2 clockwise and both run every 20min from about 7am to 8.30pm; before and after that, the #4.1/4.2 together act as a shuttle service between Murano and Fondamente Nove, running every 20min from 4.30am until around 11.30pm.

#5.1/5.2: Similar to the #4.1/4.2, this route also circles Venice, but heads out to the Lido (rather than Murano) at the easternmost end of the loop. The #5.1 runs anticlockwise, the #5.2 clockwise, and both run fast through the Giudecca canal, stopping only at Záttere and Santa Marta between San Zaccaria and Piazzale Roma. Both run every 20min for most of the day. In the early morning and late evening (4.30–6.20am & 8.30–11.20pm) the #5.1 doesn't do a complete lap of the city – instead it departs every 20min from Fondamenta Nove and proceeds via the train station and Záttere to the Lido, where it terminates; similarly, from about 8–11pm the #5.2 (which starts operating at 6am) shuttles between the Lido and Fondamente Nove in the opposite direction, and from 11pm to around 12.20am goes no farther than the train station.

#12: For most of the day, from 4.30am, the #12 runs every half-hour from Fondamente Nove (approximately hourly from 7.40pm to 11pm), calling first at Murano-Faro before heading on to Mazzorbo, Burano (from where there is a connecting half-hourly shuttle to Torcello) and Treporti; it runs with the same frequency in the opposite direction.

#N: The main night service (11.30pm–4.15am) is a selective fusion of the #1 and #2 routes, running from the Lido to Giardini, San Zaccaria, San Marco (Vallaresso), Accademia, San Samuele, San Tomà, Rialto, Ca'd'Oro, San Stae, San Marcuola, train station, Piazzale Roma, Tronchetto, Sacca Fisola, San Basilio, Záttere, Giudecca (Palanca, Redentore and Zitelle), San Giorgio and San Zaccaria – and vice versa. It runs along the whole of the route in both directions every 40min, and along the Rialto-to-Tronchetto part every 20min. Another night service connects Venice with Murano and Burano, running to and from Fondamente Nove every hour between 11.30pm and 3am.

item; €10 for a ride between 10pm and 6am. There are three ways of getting a taxi: go to one of the main stands (at Piazzale Roma, the train station, Rialto and San Marco Vallaresso), find one in the process of disgorging its passengers, or call one by phone (☎ 041 522 2303). If you phone for one, you'll pay a surcharge, of course.

GONDOLAS

The gondola is no longer a form of transport but rather an adjunct of the tourist industry. But however much the gondola's image has become tarnished, it is an astonishingly graceful craft, perfectly designed for negotiating the tortuous and shallow waterways: a gondola displaces so

THE VAPORETTO DELL'ARTE

Some days in high season the number of tourists coming into Venice is greater than the city's population, and these crowds put a terrible strain on the Canal Grande *vaporetto* services. The latest scheme to tackle the congestion is the "Vaporetto dell'Arte" (Ⓦ vaporettoarte.com), a tourists' service that departs from the train station every 30min from 9am to 8pm, calling at the stops that are closest to the main museums and exhibition spaces: San Stae, Ca' d'Oro, San Samuele, Accademia, Salute, San Marco, San Giorgio Maggiore and then, in Biennale years, the Arsenale and Giardini. The €22 ticket is valid for a calendar day, but only for this service, which means a standard ACTV travel pass is better value, even though the Vaporetto dell'Arte ticket gives small discounts at some of the museums.

little water, and the gondoliers are so dexterous, that there's hardly a canal in the city they can't negotiate. To hire one costs €80 per 40min for up to six passengers, rising to €100 between 8pm and 8am; you pay an extra €40 for every additional 20min, or €50 from 8pm to 8am. Further hefty surcharges will be levied should you require the services of an on-board accordionist or tenor. Even though the tariff is set by the local authorities, it's been known for gondoliers to extort even higher rates than these – if you do decide to go for a ride, establish the charge before setting off. To minimize the chances of being ripped off, only take a boat from one of the following official gondola stands: west of Piazza San Marco at Calle Vallaresso, Campo San Moisè or Campo Santa Maria del Giglio; immediately north of the Piazza at Bacino Orseolo; on the Molo, in front of the Palazzo Ducale; outside the *Danieli* hotel on Riva degli Schiavoni; at the train station; at Piazzale Roma; at Campo Santa Sofia, near the Ca' d'Oro; at San Tomà; or by the Rialto Bridge on Riva Carbon.

INFORMATION

Tourist office Venice's main tourist office – known as the Venice Pavilion – occupies the Palazzina del Santi, the waterfront building on the west side of the Giardinetti Reali, within a minute of the Piazza (daily 9am–2.30pm; ☎ 041 529 8711, Ⓦ turismovenezia.it); other offices operate at Calle dell'Ascensione 71/F, in the corner of the Piazza's arcades (daily 1.30–7pm), the train station (daily 8am–9pm, or 7pm in winter), in the airport arrivals area (Mon–Sat 9am–8pm), and at the Piazzale Roma car park (daily 9am–2.30pm; ☎ 041 529 8711). The Calle dell'Ascensione office is also the city's main outlet for information on the rest of the Veneto.

Listings magazines The English–Italian magazine *Un Ospite di Venezia* (Ⓦ unospitedivenezia.it), which is produced fortnightly in summer and monthly in winter, gives information on exhibitions and events, plus extras such as *vaporetto* timetables; it's free from the reception desks of many four- and five-star hotels. The fullest source of information, though, is *VENews* (€2.50; Ⓦ venezianews .it), published on the first day of each month and sold at newsstands all over the city.

ACCOMMODATION

Limitless demand for holiday accommodation has made this city the most expensive in western Europe, and the **high season** here is longer than anywhere else in the country – it officially runs from March 15 to November 15 and then from December 21 to January 6, but many places don't recognize the existence of a low season any more. Several hotels, on the other hand, lower their prices in August, the month in which many Italians – including Venetian restaurateurs and bar owners – decamp to the beaches and the mountains. It's wisest to book your place at least three months in advance, but should you bowl into town with nowhere to stay, you could call in at one of the VeneziaSi **booking offices**: at the **train station** (daily: summer 8am–9pm; winter 8am–7pm); on the **Tronchetto** (daily: 9am–8pm); in the multistorey car park at **Piazzale Roma** (daily: 9am–9pm); and at **Marco Polo airport** (daily: summer 9am–7pm; winter noon–7pm). They only deal with hotels, and take a deposit that's deductible from your first night's bill. Finally, the tourist office's website (Ⓦ turismovenezia.it) gives details of accommodation of all types.

HOTELS AND LOCANDE

Venice has well in excess of two hundred hotels, ranging from spartan one-star joints to five-star *lusso* establishments charging over €1500 per night for the best double room in high season. Bear in mind that you pay through the nose for your proximity to **Piazza San Marco**, so if you want maximum comfort for your money, decide how much you can afford and then look for a place outside the San Marco *sestiere* – after all, it's not far to walk, wherever you're staying. If you are looking for a small family-run establishment, a *locanda* – guesthouse – might fit the bill: Venice's best *locande* offer a standard of accommodation equivalent to three- or even four-star hotels (24hr room service is just about the only facility they don't provide), but often at a lower cost.

6

SAN MARCO

★ **Ai Do Mori** Calle Larga S. Marzo 658 ☎ 041 520 4817, ⓦ hotelaidomori.com. Very friendly, and situated a few paces off the Piazza, this is a top recommendation for budget travellers. The top-floor room has a private terrace looking over the roofs of the Basilica and the Torre dell'Orologio, and is one of the most attractive (and, of course, expensive) one-star rooms in the city. All rooms have their own bathroom. **€150**

Al Gambero Calle dei Fabbri 4687 ☎ 041 522 4384, ⓦ locandaalgambero.com. Twenty-six-room three-star hotel in an excellent position a short distance off the north side of the Piazza; many of the rooms overlook a canal that's on the standard gondola route from the Bacino Orseolo. There's a busy restaurant on the ground floor. **€200**

Art Deco Calle delle Botteghe 2966 ☎ 041 277 0558, ⓦ locandaartdeco.com. This cosy *locanda* has a seventeenth-century *palazzo* setting, but the interior is strewn with 1930s and '40s objects, and the pristinely white bedrooms have modern wrought-iron furniture. **€150**

★ **Casa Petrarca** Calle delle Schiavini 4386 ☎ 041 520 0430, ⓦ casapetrarca.com. A very hospitable one-star, one of the cheapest hotels within a stone's throw of the Piazza – but make sure you contact them first, as it only has seven rooms. **€135**

Fiorita Campiello Nuovo 3457 ☎ 041 523 4754, ⓦ locandafiorita.com. Welcoming *locanda* with just ten rooms, so it's crucial to book well in advance. Rooms are all en suite and decorated in eighteenth-century style, and many are spacious. **€150**

★ **Novecento** Calle del Dose 2683 ☎ 041 241 3765, ⓦ locandanovecento.it. Beautiful, intimate and very welcoming *locanda* with nine individually decorated doubles and luxurious bathrooms. Styling is ethnic/eclectic (furnishings from Morocco, China, Japan and Egypt), and there's a small courtyard for breakfast. **€250**

★ **Orseolo** Corte Zorzi 1083 ☎ 041 520 4827, ⓦ locandaorseolo.com. Superb family-run *locanda* overlooking the Orseolo canal, 50m north of Piazza S. Marco. Rooms are spacious and light, breakfasts substantial, and the staff extremely hospitable. Entrance is through a gate in Campo S. Gallo. **€200**

DORSODURO

Accademia Villa Maravege Fondamenta Bollani 1058 ☎ 041 521 0188, ⓦ pensioneaccademia.it. Once the Russian embassy, this three-star seventeenth-century villa has a devoted following, not least on account of its garden, which occupies a promontory at the convergence of two canals, with a view of a small section of the Canal Grande. To be sure of a room, get your booking in at least three months ahead. **€200**

Agli Alboretti Rio Terrà Foscarini 884 ☎ 041 523 0058, ⓦ aglialboretti.com. Friendly and popular family-run

three-star, well situated right next to the Accademia. The rooms are quite plain, but all have a/c and TV, and its high-season prices compare very favourably with those of most others in this category. **€120**

★ **Ca' Maria Adele** Rio Terrà dei Catecumeni 111 ☎ 041 520 3078, ⓦ camariaadele.it. Five of the twelve rooms in this very upmarket *locanda* are so-called "theme rooms", with every item designed to enhance a particular atmosphere – the Sala Noir, for example, is a "voluptuous and hot" creation in cocoa and spice tones. Others include the "Oriental" and the "Moorish" rooms. The non-themed accommodation is less artfully conceived (and a lot cheaper), but spacious and very comfortable. The standard tariffs are steep, but online discounts can bring the price down by more than fifty percent. **€300**

★ **Ca' Pisani** Rio Terà Foscarini 979A ☎ 041 240 1411, ⓦ capisanihotel.it. This glamorous 29-room four-star, just a few metres from the Accademia, created quite a stir when it opened in 2000, partly because of its location, on the opposite side of the Canal Grande from its top-echelon peers, but chiefly because of its high-class retro look. Taking its cue from the style of the 1930s and '40s, the *Ca' Pisani* makes heavy use of dark wood and chrome, a refreshing break from the Renaissance and Rococo flourishes that tend to prevail in Venice's upmarket establishments. **€200**

DD 724 Ramo da Mula 724 ☎ 041 277 0262, ⓦ thecharminghouse.com. In a city awash with nostalgia, the cool high-grade modernist style of this *locanda*, right by the Guggenheim, comes as a refreshing change. It has just seven rooms, each of them impeccably cool and luxurious – and not a Murano chandelier in sight. As you'll see on the website, the same team runs a couple of other similarly sleek properties: a *palazzo* by Santa Maria Formosa, containing four suites; and a single apartment close to *DD 724*. **€270**

★ **La Calcina** Zàttere ai Gesuati 780 ☎ 041 520 6466, ⓦ lacalcina.com. Charismatic three-star hotel in the house where Ruskin wrote much of *The Stones of Venice*. From the more expensive rooms you can gaze across to the Redentore, a church that gave him apoplexy. All rooms have parquet floors (unusual in Venice), and antique wooden furniture. Its restaurant (see p.392) is good too. **€160**

★ **Locanda San Barnaba** Calle del Traghetto 2785 ☎ 041 241 1233, ⓦ locanda-sanbarnaba.com. Exceptionally pleasant and nicely priced *locanda* right by the Ca' Rezzonico. The "superior double" rooms have eighteenth-century frescoes on the ceilings, and one has a really enormous bath. **€180**

Montin Fondamenta di Borgo 1147 ☎ 041 522 7151, ⓦ locandamontin.com. The *Montin* is known principally for its upmarket and once-fashionable restaurant; few people realize that it offers some of Venice's best budget accommodation. Only eleven rooms, three of them without private bathroom; the best rooms are spacious and balconied. **€130**

SAN POLO AND SANTA CROCE

Ca' Arco Antico Calle del Forno, San Polo 1451 ☎ 041 241 1227, ⓦ arcoanticovenice.com. Owners Gianfranco and Marco have done a fine job of making this eight-room *locanda* an attractive mix of traditional and modern. With big rooms, great location and excellent breakfasts (a rarity in itself), *Ca' Arco Antico* offers some of the best budget-range accommodation in the city. **€150**

★ **Ca' Favretto-San Cassiano** Calle della Rosa, Santa Croce 2232 ☎ 041 524 1768, ⓦ sancassiano.it. Beautiful 35-room four-star with some rooms looking across the Canal Grande towards the Ca' d'Oro. Has very helpful staff, a nice courtyard garden and a grand entrance hall. It was once the home of the nineteenth-century painter Giacomo Favretto, and is fitted out in the style of the period. Discounts for stays of three days or more. **€180**

★ **Ca' San Giorgio** Salizada del Fontego dei Turchi 1725, Santa Croce ☎ 041 275 9177, ⓦ casangiorgio .com. Exposed timber beams and walls of raw brick advertise the age of the Gothic *palazzo* that's occupied by this fine little *locanda*, while the bedrooms are tastefully and very comfortably furnished in quasi-antique style. The gorgeous top-floor suite has its own rooftop terrace. **€140**

CANNAREGIO

Abbazia Calle Priuli 68 ☎ 041 717 333, ⓦ abbaziahotel .com. One of Cannaregio's most restful hotels, the light-filled *Abbazia* occupies a former Carmelite monastery (the monks attached to the Scalzi still live in a building adjoining the hotel), and provides three-star amenities without losing its air of quasi-monastic austerity. There's a delightful garden too, and the staff are exceptionally helpful. **€170**

★ **Al Ponte Antico** Calle dell'Aseo 5768 ☎ 041 241 1944, ⓦ alponteantico.com. This plush four-star *residenza*, a few metres upstream of the Rialto Bridge, is one of the best small hotels in the city. Decorated throughout in eighteenth-century style, with lashings of gold and blue satin in the bedrooms, it has four grades of accommodation – the best rooms, the "Deluxe", have huge windows that open onto the Canal Grande. Exceptionally nice staff, too. **€290**

★ **Bernardi Semenzato** Calle dell'Oca 4366 ☎ 041 522 7257, ⓦ hotelbernardi.com. Very well priced two-star hidden in a tiny alleyway close to Campo S. Apostoli, with bright and good-sized rooms, and immensely helpful owners who speak excellent English. **€90**

Giorgione Calle Larga dei Proverbi 4587 ☎ 041 522 5810, ⓦ hotelgiorgione.com. This plush but very reasonably priced four-star, not far from the Rialto Bridge, has a more personal touch than many of the city's upmarket hotels – it has been run by the same family for many generations. Amenities include a quiet garden and a pool table, and some of the 76 well-equipped rooms have a

small private terrace. Free tea and coffee served in the lounge in the afternoon. **€170**

Locanda Leon Bianco Corte Leon Bianco 5629 ☎ 041 523 3572, ⓦ leonbianco.it. Friendly and charming three-star in a superb location not far from the Rialto Bridge, tucked away beside the decaying Ca' da Mosto. Only eight rooms, but three of them overlook the Canal Grande (for which there's a premium, of course) and most of the others are spacious and tastefully furnished in eighteenth-century style – one room even has a huge fresco copied from a Tiepolo ceiling. **€150**

★ **Palazzo Abadessa** Calle Priuli 4011 ☎ 041 241 3784, ⓦ abadessa.com. This gorgeous *residenza d'epoca* is a meticulously restored *palazzo* behind the church of Santa Sofia; all eight of its bedrooms (some of them huge) are nicely furnished with genuine antiques, and there's a lovely secluded garden as well. **€225**

CASTELLO

Casa Verardo Calle della Chiesa 4765 ☎ 041 528 6127, ⓦ casaverardo.it. A fine three-star hotel occupying a nicely refurbished sixteenth-century *palazzo* between San Marco and Campo Santa Maria Formosa. Twenty-three well-equipped rooms with a breakfast terrace downstairs, a small garden, a sun lounge at the top and another terrace attached to the priciest of the rooms. **€140**

Gabrielli Riva degli Schiavoni 4110 ☎ 041 523 1580, ⓦ hotelgabrielli.it. Occupying a beautifully converted Gothic palace, the 103-room *Gabrielli* offers four-star comforts and *Danieli*-style views across the Bacino di San Marco for a fraction of the price of the *Danieli*. It also has an attractive little courtyard and a lovely small garden. The website regularly has excellent special offers. **€180**

★ **La Residenza** Campo Bandiera e Moro 3608 ☎ 041 528 5315, ⓦ venicelaresidenza.com. This fourteenth-century *palazzo* is a mid-budget gem (in Venetian terms), occupying much of one side of a tranquil square just off the main waterfront. It's pricier than many two-stars, but the recently refurbished rooms are very spacious (rare at this price) and elegant, and the management extremely *simpatico*. Payment by cash is preferred for short stays. **€150**

HOSTELS

Venice has a large HI hostel and a few other hostel-like establishments – most run by religious foundations – offering basic accommodation. Some of the latter are more expensive than one-star hotels and B&Bs; we've listed only the low-cost options.

Domus Civica Calle Campazzo, San Polo 3082 ☎ 041 721 103, ⓦ domuscivica.com. This Catholic women's student hostel is open to tourists from mid-June to mid-Sept. Most rooms are double with running water; showers free; no breakfast; 11.30pm curfew. Big reductions if you're staying for a week or more. Dorms **€25**

6

B&BS AND SELF-CATERING

As you may expect in a city in which demand is such that someone could get away with charging €100 for the privilege of sleeping on a mattress in the attic, much of Venice's accommodation is not terribly attractive, but many B&Bs are excellent, offering accommodation that compares favourably with budget hotels – and some are in effect small-scale *locande*, with rooms of three-star standard or better. Full listings can be found at ⓦturismovenezia.it.

If you're staying in Venice for at least a week, it can be worth looking at a **self-catering apartment**. The best sources are ⓦvenice-rentals.com, ⓦveniceapartment.com, ⓦviewsonvenice.com, ⓦvisitvenice.co.uk and ⓦholiday-rentals.com.

Foresteria Valdese S. Maria Formosa, Castello 5170 ☎041 528 6797, ⓦforesteriavenezia.it. Run by Waldensians, this hostel is installed in a wonderful *palazzo* at the end of Calle Lunga S. Maria Formosa, with flaking frescoes in the rooms and a large communal salon. It has several large dorms, plus bedrooms that can accommodate up to nine people. Dorm beds cannot be booked in advance, except by groups. Registration 9am–1pm & 6–8pm. Dorms €30, doubles €105

Ostello Santa Fosca S. Maria dei Servi, Cannaregio 2372 ☎041 715 775, ⓦsantafosca.com. Student-run hostel in an atmospheric former Servite convent in a quiet part of Cannaregio, with bedrooms sleeping 2–6 people, nearly all of them with shared bathrooms. 12.30pm curfew. Dorms €25

Ostello Venezia Fondamenta delle Zitelle, Giudecca 86 ☎041 523 8211, ⓦostellovenezia.it. The city's 260-bed, eighteen-room HI hostel is a briskly run operation, occupying a superb location looking over the water to San Marco. Breakfast and sheets included in the price – but remember to add the expense of the boat. No kitchen, but no curfew either. HI card necessary, but you can join on the spot. Dorms €23

CAMPING

There are some unlovely campsites near the airport – better to head out to the outer edge of the lagoon, to the **Litorale del Cavallino**, which stretches from Punta Sabbioni to Jesolo and has around 60,000 pitches, many quite luxurious; from Punta Sabbioni the #14 *vaporetto* goes to San Zaccaria via the Lido. Alternatively, you could

camp on the mainland at Fusina; a Linea Fusina water-bus links Fusina to the Záttere in central Venice (ACTV tickets not valid), taking 15min, with an hourly service from 8am until around 10.30pm (late May–Sept), and till around 6.30pm in winter.

LITORALE DEL CAVALLINO

Marina di Venezia Via Montello 6 ☎041 966 146, ⓦmarinadivenezia.it. This big and well-equipped four-star site is a couple of kilometres from the Punta Sabbioni *vaporetto* stop, on the seaward side of the Litorale del Cavallino, adjoining the beach and the huge AquaMarina waterpark. It has a big range of accommodation, with seven-berth a/c chalets at the top. Open late April to end Sept. Pitches €21–52; chalets and bungalows €50–170

Miramare Lungomare Dante Alighieri 29 ☎041 966 150, ⓦcamping-miramare.it. A three-star site, located at the mouth of the lagoon, very near the *vaporetto* stop, with bungalows and maxi caravans. Open April–Oct. Pitches €21–37; bungalows €32–46

FUSINA

Camping Fusina Via Moranzani 93 ☎041 547 0055, ⓦcampingfusina.com. Situated at the mouth of the Brenta River, this is the closest campsite to central Venice. Marketing itself as a "tourist village", it has cabins as well as pitches for tents and campervans, plus a pizzeria, bar, beer garden, internet café and 24hr laundry. The boat stop for Venice is only 100m from the front gate, and there's a bus service too. Open all year. Pitches €29; cabins €30

EATING AND DRINKING

Venice has fewer good moderately priced **restaurants** than any other major Italian city, but things have been improving in recent years, due in part to the efforts of the Ristorante della Buona Accoglienza, an association of restaurateurs determined to present the best of genuine Venetian cuisine at sensible prices – which in the Venetian context means in the region of €35–40 per person. A distinctive aspect of the Venetian social scene is the **bácaro**, which in its purest form is a bar that offers a range of snacks called **cicheti** (sometimes spelled *ciccheti*); the array will typically include *polpette* (small beef and garlic meatballs), *carciofini* (artichoke hearts), eggs, anchovies, *polipi* (baby octopus or squid) and tomatoes, peppers and courgettes cooked in oil. Some *bácari* also produce one or two more substantial dishes each day, such as risotto or seafood pasta. Excellent food is also served at many of Venice's **osterie** (or *ostarie*), the simplest of which are indistinguishable from *bácari*, while others have sizeable dining areas. We've classified our bars and restaurants according to which aspect of the business draws most of the customers, but if you're looking for a simple meal in a particular area of the city, be sure to check both listings.

CAFES, PASTICCERIE AND GELATERIE

As in every Italian city, Venice's **cafés** are central to its social life, and you'll never be more than a couple of minutes from a decent one. In addition to their marvellous local confections, many *pasticcerie* also serve coffee, but will have at most a few bar stools. Calorie control is further jeopardized by Venice's terrific *gelaterie*.

SAN MARCO

Florian Piazza S. Marco 56–59 ☎041 520 5641, ⓦ caffeflorian.com. The most famous café in Venice began life in 1720, when Florian Francesconi's Venezia Trionfante (Venice Triumphant) opened for business here, and the place is still redolent of the eighteenth century, though the gorgeous interior – a frothy confection of mirrors, stucco and frescoes – is a nineteenth-century pastiche. Its prices match its pedigree: a simple cappuccino at an outside table will set you back around €10, and you'll have to take out a mortgage for a cocktail; if the "orchestra" is playing, you'll be taxed another €6 for the privilege of hearing them. (*Quadri* and *Lavena* levy a similar surcharge.) 10am–midnight; closed Wed in winter.

★ **Marchini** Calle Spadaria 676 ☎041 241 3087. The oldest, most delicious and most expensive of Venetian *pasticcerie*, which on Sunday mornings is thronged with Venetians buying family treats. The cakes are wonderful, as are the *Marchini* chocolate and the coffee. June–Sept Mon & Wed–Sat 9am–8pm; Oct–May daily 9am–10pm.

Marchini Time Campo S. Luca 4589 ☎041 241 3087. Sample the succulent *Marchini* pastries with a cup of top-grade coffee at this sleek café. Mon–Sat 7am–8.30pm.

DORSODURO

Il Caffè Campo S. Margherita 2963 ☎041 528 7998. Known as *Caffè Rosso* for its big red sign, this small,

atmospheric, old fashioned café-bar is another student favourite. Good sandwiches, and lots of seats outside in the *campo*. Mon–Sat 7am–1am.

★ **Il Doge** Campo S. Margherita 3058 ☎041 523 4607. Well-established, very friendly and extremely good hole-in-the-wall *gelateria*, which also does a superb *granita*, made in the traditional Sicilian way. Daily 10am–midnight, but often closes earlier; closed Nov & Dec.

Nico Zàttere ai Gesuati 922 ☎041 522 5293. This café-*gelateria*, which has been in existence for more than seventy years, is celebrated for an artery-clogging creation called a *gianduiotto da passeggio* – a paper cup with a block of praline ice cream drowned in whipped cream. 6.45am–10pm; closed Thurs.

SAN POLO AND SANTA CROCE

Caffè del Doge Calle dei Cinque 609 ☎041 522 7787, ⓦ caffedeldoge.com. Fantastically good coffee (they supply many of the city's bars and restaurants), served in a chic minimalist setup very close to the Rialto Bridge. Mon–Sat 7am–7pm, Sun 7am–1pm.

★ **Cioccolateria VizioVirtù** Calle del Campaniel 2898/A ☎041 275 0149, ⓦ viziovirtu.com. Venice's best chocolates, and the most expensive *gelati* in town. A few yards away, on Campiello S. Tomà, there's now *VizioVirtù e altro*, selling spectacular pastries and other sweet stuff. Daily 10am–7.30pm; closed Aug.

CANNAREGIO

Gelateria Ca' d'Oro Strada Nova 4273 ☎041 522 8982. A wide range of wonderfully smooth ice creams is served at Andrea Busolin's long-established shop. Daily 10am–11pm.

Il Gelatone Rio Terà Maddalena 2063 ☎041 720 631. Despite the recent arrival of *Grom*, this place or the *Ca' d'Oro*

PICNICKING IN VENICE

The price of restaurants in Venice makes **picnicking** an attractive option, but you can't just spread your lunch wherever you like: bylaws forbid picnicking on the Piazza and other busy tourist spots, and it's illegal to sit down on a bridge. To be on the safe side always use a bench, not the pavement.

The best places to buy food – especially fruit and veg – are the markets that are held in various squares every day except Sunday: the biggest and best is of course the **Rialto**, but you'll also find stalls on **Campo Santa Maria Formosa (Castello)**, **Campo Santa Margherita (Dorsoduro)**, and between **Ponte delle Guglie and Campiello dell'Anconeta** in Cannaregio. Fresh produce is also sold from barges moored by **Campo San Barnaba (Dorsoduro)** and at the top end of **Via Garibaldi (Castello)**. Virtually every parish has its **alimentari**, and Venice has several well-hidden **supermarkets**, the most central of which is Coop, on the corner of Salizzada San Lio and Calle Mondo Nuovo (Castello). Others are: Punto Sma, tucked between houses 3019 and 3112 on Campo Santa Margherita (Dorsoduro); Billa at Zàttere Ponte Lungo 1491, by the San Basilio *vaporetto* stop (Dorsoduro); the large Coop by the Piazzale Roma *vaporetto* stop for services to Murano; Billa at Strada Nova 3660, near San Felice (Cannaregio); and Prix, at Fondamenta San Giacomo 203/A (Giudecca). Most are open daily 8.30am–8/8.30pm, though some of the smaller ones close for a couple of hours in the middle of the day, and on Sunday.

6

would still win a local vote for the title Best Gelateria in Cannaregio. Daily: mid-Jan to April & Oct to mid-Dec 11am–8pm; May–Sept 11am–10.30pm.

Pasticceria Nobile Calle del Pistor 1818 ☎041 720 731. Established back in the 1930s, this is still the classiest café in Cannaregio, and is always thronged with locals at breakfast and after work; the pastries are excellent, and they also turn out some interesting novelties, such as a chocolate toolkit. Tues–Sun 7am–8.30pm; closed July & two weeks in Feb.

CASTELLO

La Boutique del Gelato Salizzada S. Lio 5727 ☎041 522 3283. Top-grade ice creams – as good as any in Venice – are created at this tiny outlet. Daily: June–Sept 10am–11.30pm; Oct, Nov & Feb–May 10.30am–10.30pm.

Rosa Salva Campo SS. Giovanni e Paolo 6779 ☎041 522 7949. With its marble-topped bar and outside tables facing Zanipolo, this is the most characterful of the three *Rosa Salva* branches in the city. (The others are at Calle Fiubera 951 and Merceria S. Salvador 5020, both a short way north of the Piazza.) The coffee and ice cream are superb. 7.30am–8.30pm; closed Wed.

RESTAURANTS

Value for money tends to increase with distance from San Marco; plenty of restaurants within a short radius of the Piazza offer menus that seem to be reasonable, but you'll find the food unappetizing and the portions tiny. As a rule of thumb, avoid anywhere that advertises a "menù turistico". There are three notable concentrations of good-value restaurants: around Rialto market; around San Barnaba in Dorsoduro, especially Calle Lunga San Barnaba; and the western part of Cannaregio, around the Ghetto. In most cases, booking is advisable in high season, and you should also be aware that Venetians tend to eat early and that restaurateurs close early if trade is slack, so if you're in town at a quiet time, don't turn up later than 8.30pm, unless you're dining at one of the more expensive restaurants, which tend to keep longer hours.

SAN MARCO

Da Carla Sottoportego Corte Contarina 1535/A ☎041 523 7855. Hidden down a *sottoportego* off the west side of Frezzeria, *Da Carla* has a battered old sign that's rather misleading, as this place has been refashioned as a slick modern *osteria*. The menu is short but the food is well prepared, and the prices (main courses €15–20) make this one of the best places for a simple meal close to the Piazza. The service – polite and attentive – is better than average for this part of town. Mon–Sat 8.30am–10.30pm.

Rosticceria Gislon Calle della Bissa 5424/A. Downstairs it's a sort of glorified snack-bar, serving pizzas and set meals starting at around €12 – the trick is to first grab a

place at the tables along the windows, then order from the counter. Good if you need to refuel quickly and cheaply but can't face a pizza. There's a slightly less rudimentary restaurant upstairs, where prices are considerably higher for no great increase in quality. Daily 9.30am–9.30pm.

DORSODURO

Ai Quattro Ferri Calle Lunga S. Barnaba 2754/A ☎041 520 6978. A very popular *osteria* just off Campo S. Barnaba, with a small menu that changes daily but often consists entirely of fish and seafood, with *secondi* at around the €20 mark. Limited seating (some might find the place a bit too cramped), so booking essential at all times. No credit cards. Mon–Sat 12.30–3.30pm & 7–10.30pm.

★ **La Bitta** Calle Lunga S. Barnaba 2753/A ☎041 523 0531. Innovative fare at a welcoming little *osteria* that's remarkable for featuring hardly anything aquatic. Marcellino runs the kitchen while his wife Debora serves and cajoles the guests, offering expert guidance on the impressive wine and grappa list. Delicious cheese platter, served with honey and fruit chutney. Expect to pay about €40–50 per person for three courses. Tiny dining room (and garden), so booking is essential. No credit cards. Mon–Sat 6.30–11pm.

La Piscina Záttere ai Gesuati 780 ☎041 520 6466. Stretching onto the waterfront outside the *Calcina* hotel, to which it's attached, this is one of the most pleasant restaurants in Dorsoduro. The service is excellent, the menu has a far wider range of vegetarian options than the vast majority of restaurants in Venice, and the view of Giudecca from the terrace is wonderful. Tues–Sun 12.30–2.30pm & 7–10.30pm.

Pane, Vino e San Daniele Campo Angelo Raffaele 1722 ☎041 523 7456, ⓦpanevinoesandaniele.net. Founded in 1998 in the Friuli region, *Pane, Vino e San Daniele* is a rapidly growing chain of nouveau-*osteries*, in which the menu is dominated by San Daniele *prosciutto*, the finest of all Italian hams. The house speciality is a wooden platter loaded with *prosciutto* and a variety of other uncooked goodies, and it's a prominent ingredient in cooked dishes such as San Daniele gnocchi. The front-of-house bar is also excellent for a snack and a glass of Friulian wine, and there's ample seating on the secluded *campo*. Venice now has two other branches: one is nearby, at Calle Lunga S. Barnaba 2861, and the other is in the Rialto district at Calle dei Botteri 1544. 9am–2pm & 4pm–midnight; closed Wed.

SAN POLO AND SANTA CROCE

Alla Madonna Calle della Madonna 594 ☎041 522 3824, ⓦristoranteallamadonna.com. Roomy, loud and bustling seafood restaurant that's been going strong for nearly six decades and is now run by the founder's son. Little finesse (the atmosphere is rather refectory-like), and service can be brisk, but many locals still rate its kitchen as one of the city's best. Quite good value for money, even if prices have gone up noticeably of late – reckon on around €45 per person. Daily noon–3pm & 7–10pm.

★ **Antico Dolo** Ruga Vecchia S. Giovanni 778 ☎ 041 522 6546, ⓦ anticodolo.it. You can pop into this excellent and long-established *osteria* for a few *cicheti* and a glass of Merlot and come away just a few euros poorer; or you can take a table and eat an excellent meal for something in the region of €40. Either way, you're almost certain to think it was money well spent. Mon–Sat noon–10pm.

Bancogiro Sottoportego del Banco Giro 122 ☎ 041 523 2061. This very successful and smart *osteria*, in a splendid location in the midst of the Rialto market, was instrumental in making this zone a fashionable one. Come here to nurse a glass of fine wine beside the Canal Grande, or nip upstairs to the dining room for a well-prepared meal from the tight, imaginative and not inexpensive menu (around €20–25 for main courses). Tues–Sun noon–2am.

La Zucca Ponte del Megio 1762 ☎ 041 524 1570, ⓦ lazucca.it. Long a well-respected restaurant, *La Zucca* was once a vegetarian establishment (its name means "pumpkin") but now goes against the Venetian grain by featuring a lot of meat – chicken, lamb, beef – alongside the Eastern-inflected vegetable dishes. The quality remains high, prices are moderate (most mains are under €20) and the canalside setting is nice. Mon–Sat 12.30–2.30pm & 7–10.30pm.

Naranzaria Sottoportego del Banco Giro 130 ☎ 041 724 1035, ⓦ naranzaria.it. The canalside buildings of the Rialto market have lately become colonized by smart bars and *osterie*, and this is one of the most impressive new arrivals. Like neighbouring *Bancogiro*, *Naranzaria* has a bar downstairs and a restaurant crammed into the brick-vaulted room upstairs, plus a few seats by the water, but it's distinctive in having a hybrid Venetian–Japanese menu, with main courses up to €20. Daily noon–1am.

Vecio Fritolin Calle della Regina 2262 ☎ 041 522 2881, ⓦ veciofritolin.it. The name translates as "the old frying-place", and one of its signature dishes is a succulent fry-up of estuary fish; but the *Vecio Fritolin* has come a very long way since its time as a purveyor of Venetian fast food – it's esteemed nowadays for its distinctive take on Venetian fishy classics, making imaginative use of seasonal herbs and vegetables. You'll pay around €60 per person, with wine. Tues–Sun noon–2.30pm & 7–10.30pm.

CANNAREGIO

Ai 40 Ladroni Fondamenta della Sensa 3253 ☎ 041 715 736. This busy *osteria* serves high-quality *cicheti* at the bar, and good Venetian standards at the tables. Generally big helpings too – something of a rarity in Venice. Tues–Sun 10am–midnight.

Ai Promessi Sposi Calle dell'Oca 4367 ☎ 041 241 2747. Now run by former employees of *Alla Vedova* (see below), this

moderately priced (mains around €15) and cosy little *osteria* specializes in *baccalà* and other traditional fish recipes. Excellent range of *cicheti* at the bar. Tues & Thurs–Sun 11.30am–3pm & 6.30–11.30pm, Wed 6.30–11.30pm.

★ **Alla Fontana** Fondamenta Cannaregio 1102 ☎ 041 715 077. Once primarily a bar, *Alla Fontana* has transformed itself into a great little trattoria, offering a small menu of classic Venetian maritime dishes, which changes daily according to what the boats have brought in; tables beside the canal are an added attraction in summer. Portions are generous (especially the pasta dishes) and prices good – you'll pay about €40 per person for two courses with house wine. Tues–Sun 6.30–10pm.

Alla Vedova Calle del Pistor 3912 ☎ 041 528 5324. Located in an alley directly opposite the one leading to the Ca' d'Oro, this long-established little restaurant – formally called the *Ca' d'Oro*, but known to all as *Alla Vedova* – is fronted by a bar offering a mouthwatering selection of *cicheti* and a good range of wines. It's known as one of the best-value places in town (antipasti and main courses from just €10), so reservations are always a good idea. No credit cards. Mon–Wed, Fri & Sat 11.30am–2.30pm & 6.30–10.30pm, Sun 6.30–10.30pm.

★ **Anice Stellato** Fondamenta della Sensa 3272 ☎ 041 720 744. Hugely popular with Venetians for the superb, reasonably priced meals and unfussy atmosphere. Situated by one of the northernmost Cannaregio canals, it's a little too remote for many tourists. If you can't get a table – it's frequently booked solid – at least drop by for the excellent *cicheti* at the bar. Wed–Sun 12.30–3pm & 7pm–midnight.

★ **Pontini** Fondamenta Pescheria 1268 ☎ 041 714 123. From outside, this looks like any number of ordinary Venetian trattoria-bars, but it's very far from ordinary: the menu consists of classic Venetian *osteria* fare, and the quality is excellent. Not only that, the portions are generous and the prices unbeatable, with some delicious set meals for less than €30. And the staff are perhaps the most welcoming in Venice. Mon–Sat 7am–10.30pm.

Vini da Gigio Fondamenta S. Felice 3628/A ☎ 041 528 5140, ⓦ vinidagigio.com. Until a few years ago most of the customers at this popular, family-run trattoria were locals; it's now firmly on the tourist map yet it retains its authenticity and is still good value by local standards, with main courses at around €20, even if prices have crept up in recent years. It has two short but excellent menus – one for meat dishes, one for fish and seafood – and, as the name suggests, the wine list is remarkable. Reservations essential. Wed–Sun noon–2.30pm & 7–10.30pm.

CASTELLO

★ **Alle Testiere** Calle Mondo Nuovo 5801 ☎ 041 522 7220, ⓦ osterialletestiere.it. Very small, expensive (mains €25–30) but very special fish and seafood restaurant in the alley on the other side of the canal from

6

6

the front of Santa Maria Formosa, with ever-changing menu and a superb wine selection. In the evening there are sittings at 7pm and 9pm, to handle the demand – booking is essential. Tues–Sat noon–3pm & 7pm–midnight; closed mid-July to mid-Aug.

★ **Corte Sconta** Calle del Pestrin 3886 ☎041 522 7024. Secreted in a lane to the east of San Giovanni in Bragora, this restaurant is one of Venice's finest. The exceptionally pleasant staff tend to make it difficult to resist ordering the day's specials, which could easily result in a bill in the region of €80-plus each – and it would be just about the best meal you could get in Venice for that price. If expenditure is an issue, check the menu in the window carefully before going in (often the waiters will simply recite what's on offer rather than give you anything printed). Booking several days in advance is essential for most of the year. Tues–Sat 12.30–2pm & 7.15–10pm.

Da Remigio Salizzada dei Greci 3416 ☎041 523 0089. Superb trattoria, serving straightforwardly excellent fish dishes and gorgeous home-made gnocchi. The wine list is outstanding too. Be sure to book – the locals (and ever-increasing numbers of tourists) pack this place every night. While many other restaurants have ramped up their prices in recent years, it remains good value for the quality – mains are mostly €15–20. Mon 12.30–2.30pm, Wed–Sun 1–3pm & 7.30–10pm.

MURANO

Busa alla Torre Campo S. Stefano 3 ☎041 739 662. This trattoria is the finest restaurant on Murano – unfortunately, though, the kitchen is open for lunch only (noon–3pm). The set menu, at around €20, is a real bargain. For the rest of the day it functions as a café-bar. Tues–Sun 9am–5pm.

MAZZORBO

Venissa Fondamenta S. Caterina 3 ☎041 52 72 281, ⓦvenissa.it. The decade that Gianluca Bisol spent restoring this farmhouse was time well spent – as soon as it opened, in 2010, *Venissa* become one of Venice's foodie havens. Chef Paola Budel, who trained with Michel Roux, uses the resources of the lagoon and the restaurant's garden to create a menu that mixes the traditional and the innovative to brilliant effect, with traditional Italian favourites remade and updated. The dining room is stylish and intimate (booking is essential), and there are tables outside in good weather. Budget for €100 per person, with wine; if you want to push the boat out, there's a fabulous six-course tasting menu. March–Nov Tues–Sun 12.30–3pm & 7–9.30pm.

BURANO

Al Gatto Nero Fondamenta Giudecca 88 ☎041 730 120, ⓦgattonero.com/it. Founded way back in 1946, this is an outstanding trattoria, located just a minute's walk

from the busy Via Galuppi, opposite the Pescheria. It's been run since the 1960s by Ruggero Bovo and his wife Lucia, who are now helped by their son Massimiliano, and what this family doesn't know about the edible delicacies of the lagoon, and the wines of the region, isn't worth knowing. Tues–Sun lunch & dinner; closed Nov.

LA GIUDECCA

Mistrà ai Tre Scalini Calle Michelangelo 53/C ☎041 520 0119. Recently relocated from its original site amid the Giudecca boatyards, the *Mistrà osteria* retains a canteen-like atmosphere and solid local following, though most of the regulars use it as a bar rather than a restaurant; the menu is of course strong on fish and seafood, but there's a lot of beef here too, with mains around €20. For the cost-conscious, they do pizzas too, and the new location has a small garden. Tues–Sun 10am–3pm & 6–11pm.

BARS

Most bars serve some kind of **food**, their counters usually bearing trays of the characteristically Venetian, fat little crustless sandwiches called *tramezzini*, which are stuffed with fillings such as egg and mushroom, egg and anchovy, or Parma ham and artichoke. Many bars will have a selection of *cicheti* as well, and even two or three more substantial dishes. Venice is notoriously somnolent after dark, but are three areas in which you'll find a good concentration of lively **bars**: in and around Campo Santa Margherita; the Rialto market area; and in northern Cannaregio, along the canals to the north of the Ghetto.

SAN MARCO

Al Volto Calle Cavalli 4081 ☎041 522 8945, ⓦalvoltoenoteca.it. This dark little bar is an *enoteca* in the true sense of the word – 1300 wines from Italy and elsewhere, 100 of them served by the glass, some cheap, many not; good snacks, too, plus more substantial fare. Mon–Sat 10am–3pm & 6.30–11pm.

Bácaro Jazz Salizzada Fondaco dei Tedeschi 5546 ☎041 528 5249, ⓦbacarojazz.com. A jazz-themed bar-restaurant that's proved a big hit with young Venetians, mainly on account of its late hours; there's food, but it's far from the best quality. Daily 1pm–2am.

★ **I Rusteghi** Corte del Tintor 5513 ☎041 523 2205. A small *osteria*, secreted away in a tiny courtyard close to

---

TOP 5 PLACES FOR OUTDOOR DRINKING

Al Timon p.395
Florian p.391
Il Caffè p.391
La Cantina p.395
Nico p.391

Campo San Bartolomeo, with great *cicheti*, nice wine and a congenial host – plus a few outside tables. The perfect place for a quiet snack in the San Marco area. Mon–Sat 10.30am–3pm & 6–9pm.

Torino Campo S. Luca 4591 ☎ 041 520 7634. During the daytime this is an unremarkable bar-café, but at night it becomes the loud and lively *Torino@Notte*, with DJs and/or live music on Wed. Tues–Sun 8am–1am.

DORSODURO

Ai do Draghi Campo S. Margherita 3665 ☎ 041 528 9731. Taking its name from the two dragons on the wall opposite, this is a tiny, friendly café-bar, with a good range of wines. The back room exhibits the work of local photographers and artists. April–Oct 8am–2am; Nov–March 8am–11pm; closed Thurs.

Café Noir Crosera S. Pantalon 3805 ☎ 041 710 227. A favourite student bar, often with live music on Tues. Mon–Fri 11am–2am, Sat & Sun 7pm–2am.

★ **Cantina del Vino già Schiavi** Fondamenta Nani 992 ☎ 041 523 0034. Known to Venetians as the *Cantinone* or *Al Bottegon*, this is a great bar and wine shop opposite San Trovaso. Excellent *cicheti* and generously filled panini too. Mon–Sat 8.30am–8.30pm; Sun 9am–1pm.

Margaret DuChamp Campo S. Margherita 3019 ☎ 041 528 6255. Despite the challenge from the neighbouring *Orange*, *DuChamp* is still the first-choice Santa Margherita bar for the style-conscious. 8am–2am; closed Tues.

Osteria alla Bifora Campo S. Margherita 2930 ☎ 041 523 6119. A candlelit wood-beamed and brick interior, friendly service, good wine, excellent *cicheti*, and large plates of meat and cheese if you need more calories – the *Bifora* is one of several fine places for a pit-stop on Campo Santa Margherita. Mon–Sat noon–3pm & 7–11pm.

SAN POLO AND SANTA CROCE

All'Arco Calle del'Ochialer 436 ☎ 041 520 5666. A great stand-up Rialto bar, which does superb *sarde in saor* and other snacks. Mon–Sat 7am–5pm.

Da Lele Campo dei Tolentini 183. As you can tell by the opening hours, this tiny and utterly authentic micro-bar attracts a lot of custom from workers en route to or from Piazzale Roma. Sandwiches and rolls made freshly to order, and wine by the glass from just 60c. Mon–Sat 6am–8pm.

Do Mori Calle Do Mori 429 ☎ 041 522 5401. Hidden just off Ruga Vecchia S. Giovanni, this single narrow room, with no seating, is packed every evening with home-bound shopworkers, Rialto porters, and locals just out for a stroll. Delicious snacks, great range of wines, nice atmosphere. Mon–Sat 8.30am–8pm.

Marcà Campo Cesare Battisti 213 ☎ 347 100 2583. Another minuscule stand-up Rialto bar, perfect for a quick panino and glass of *prosecco*. Mon–Sat 7am–3pm & 6–9pm, Sun 6–9pm.

CANNAREGIO

Al Ponte Calle Larga G. Gallina 6378 ☎ 041 528 6157, ⓦ ostariaalponte.com. Superb *osteria* between the Miracoli and Santi Giovanni e Paolo: one of the best places in Venice for a glass of wine and a light meal or snack. Mon–Sat 8am–8.30pm.

Al Timon Fondamenta degli Ormesini 2754 ☎ 041 524 6066. This newish *osteria*, with its attractively spartan neo-traditional decor, has been a big hit with Venice's students and 20-somethings – most nights, the crowd spills out onto the canalside. The meals are generally good, but this is really a place for a snack and a drink or two with your mates. Daily 11–1am.

Da Luca e Fred Rio Terrà S. Leonardo 1518 ☎ 041 716 170. Terrific gritty old *cichetteria*, serving excellent snacks and simple meals to a regular clientele, a few of whom are usually to be found sitting outside, watching the world go by. Very few tables inside, so if you want to eat here in winter, be prepared to wait for a space. 9am–10pm; closed Tues.

La Cantina Strada Nova 3689 ☎ 041 522 8258. Welcoming *enoteca* with a good range of wines, substantial and excellent (but not inexpensive) snacks, and its own custom-brewed beer. Mon–Sat 10am–10pm.

Paradiso Perduto Fondamenta della Misericordia 2540 ☎ 041 720 581, ⓦ http://ilparadisoperduto .wordpress.com. A real fixture on the Venice scene, *Paradiso Perduto* is packed to the rafters most nights, with a predominantly young crowd. The restaurant section is like a boho refectory and the atmosphere at the tables is usually terrific, though there are many better kitchens in the neighbourhood. Go for the drinks, the *cicheti* and the buzz. Tues–Thurs 7pm–1am, Fri–Sun 11am–2am.

★ **Un Mondo diVino** Salizzada S. Canciano 5984/A ☎ 041 521 1093. Occupying a marble-fronted and wood-beamed old butcher's shop, this little *bácaro* has rapidly built up a great reputation, for its fantastic array of *cicheti*, its choice selection of wines, and the warmth of its staff. Prices are quite steep, though. 10am–midnight; closed Tues.

CASTELLO

Al Portego Calle Malvasia 6015 ☎ 041 522 9038. In the middle of the day this bar is crammed with customers eating *cicheti* and in the evening there's often a queue for a place at one of the tiny tables, where some well-prepared basics (pasta, risotto, *fegato alla veneziana* etc) are served. No reservations are taken. Mon–Sat 10.30am–3pm & 5.30–10pm, Sun 5.30–10pm.

Enoteca Mascareta Calle Lunga S. Maria Formosa 5183 ☎ 041 523 0744. First-rate and perpetually busy wine bar with delicious *cicheti* and a small menu of more substantial fare. Daily 7am–1am.

ENTERTAINMENT

Venice does not have a single club, and though there's a number of late-opening bars with DJs or live music, strict bylaws against late-night noise mean that the gig often entails nothing wilder than an aspiring singer-songwriter on acoustic guitar. The Teatro Malibran stages concerts by Italian rock outfits from time to time, but bands rarely come nearer than Padua, and the biggest names tend to favour Verona. Music in Venice, to all intents and purposes, means classical music.

OPERA AND CLASSICAL MUSIC

Classical concerts, with a very strong bias towards the eighteenth century (and Vivaldi in particular – barely a day goes by without a fancy-dress performance of the *Four Seasons*), are given at various venues, such as the Palazzo Prigione Vecchie, the Scuola Grande di San Giovanni Evangelista, the Scuola di San Teodoro, Palazzo Albrizzi and the churches of Santo Stefano, the Frari, San Stae, San Samuele, San Vidal, San Giacomo di Rialto, the Ospedaletto and the Pietà (the most regularly used). Tickets for concerts at these venues are usually €25–30, with reductions for students and children. The two big venues are as follows:

La Fenice Campo S. Fantin ☎041 786 511, ⊛teatro lafenice.it. The third-ranking Italian opera house after Milan's La Scala and Naples' San Carlo, La Fenice is more

affordable than you might think – the cheapest seats (from a mere €10) may give no view of the stage, but very good seats can be had for a reasonable €50–60 on most nights. You'll pay around twice as much for the opening night of a production as you would for the same seat later in the run (midweek prices are the lowest). The opera season runs from late November to the end of June, punctuated by ballet performances; classical concerts are held in the Fenice's Sale Apollinee. Tickets can be bought at the Fenice box office and the Hellovenezia offices at Piazzale Roma and the train station.

Teatro Malibran Campiello del Teatro Malibran ⊛teatrolafenice.it. The Malibran and Sale Apollinee share top billing as the city's prime venues for classical recitals; the Malibran also has occasional opera, jazz and

---

FESTIVALS AND EVENTS

CARNEVALE

Venice's **Carnevale** (⊛carnivalofvenice.com) occupies the ten days leading up to Lent, finishing on Shrove Tuesday with a masked ball for the glitterati and dancing in the Piazza for the plebs. After falling out of fashion for many years, it was revived in 1979 and is now supported by the city authorities who organize various pageants and performances, beginning with the "Flight of the Angel" from the Campanile. Apart from these events, Carnevale is an endless parade: during the day people don costumes and go to the Piazza to be photographed, while business types do their shopping in the classic white mask, black cloak and tricorn hat. In the evening some congregate in the remoter squares, while those who have spent hundreds of pounds on their costumes install themselves in the windows of *Florian* and pose. Masks are on sale throughout the year, but special mask and costume shops magically appear during Carnevale, and Campo San Maurizio sprouts a marquee with mask-making demonstrations and a variety of designs for sale.

LA SENSA AND THE VOGALONGA

From the twelfth century until the fall of the Republic, Ascension Day was marked by the ceremony of The Marriage of Venice to the Sea, a ritual which was followed by a huge trade-fair called the Fiera della Sensa (*Sensa* being dialect for Ascension). Today the feast of **La Sensa** happens on the Sunday after Ascension Day, and features a feeble modern version of the ceremony, plus a gondola regatta. Far more spectacular is the **Vogalonga** or "long row", held a week later. Established in 1974, the Vogalonga is open to any crew in any class of rowing boat, and covers a 32km course from the Bacino di San Marco out to Burano and back, with the competitors setting off from in front of the Palazzo Ducale around 9am.

THE BIENNALE

The **Venice Biennale** (⊛labiennale.org), set up in 1895 as a showpiece for international contemporary art, is held from June to November of every odd-numbered year. Its permanent site in the Giardini Pubblici has pavilions for about forty countries (the largest for Italy's representatives), plus a thematic international exhibition. Supplementing this central part are events at venues all over the city: the salt warehouses on the Záttere, for instance, or the Corderie in the Arsenale. In even-numbered years the city hosts an architecture Biennale, a smaller-scale event which usually runs from September to November; this overlaps with a short music Biennale, and is preceded by a two-week dance Biennale (usually in June).

rock shows. Tickets for the Malibran can be bought from the same places as for the Fenice; its own box office sells tickets only on the night of the concert, from around one hour before the start.

FILM

The old Rossini cinema, close to Campo Manin, is due to reopen soon as a three-screener, and there is a film club by San Stae church, but at the moment the only cinemas in Venice are the two listed below. From around mid-July to the end of August an open-air screen in Campo San Polo shows dubbed or Italian-language films each night at around 9pm.

Giorgione Rio Terrà dei Franceschi 4612A, Cannaregio ☎041 522 6298. A small two-screen cinema: Sala B is used for less-mainstream films than those shown in Sala A, and non-dubbed English-language films are shown on Tues from Oct to May.

Multisala Astra Via Corfu 12, Lido ☎041 526 5736. Another two-screener, running the same programmes as the Giorgione, but slightly out of synch.

DIRECTORY

Banks Banks are concentrated along a chain of squares and alleyways between Campo San Bartolomeo and Campo Manin.

Consulates and embassies There's a British consulate in Mestre at Piazzale Donatori di Sangue 2–5 (☎041 505 5990); this office is staffed by an honorary consul – the closest full consulate is in Milan. The nearest US consulate is also in Milan, but there's a consular agency at Marco Polo airport (☎041 541 5944). Travellers from Ireland, Australia, New Zealand and Canada should contact their Rome embassies.

Hospital Ospedale Civile, Campo SS. Giovanni e Paolo ☎041 529 4111.

Lost property If you lose anything on the train or at the station, call ☎041 785 531; at the airport call ☎041 260 9222; on ACTV water- or land buses call ☎041 272 2179; and anywhere in the city itself call ☎041 274 8225.

Internet Many hotels, hostels and bars now offer free internet access, and internet points (usually charging €6–8/hr) are all over the city, especially in the area around

THE FILM FESTIVAL

The **Venice Film Festival** (🌐labiennale.org) – the world's oldest, founded in 1932 – takes place on the Lido every year in late August and/or early September. Tickets are available to the general public on the day before the performance, at the Palazzo del Cinemà and PalaBiennale ticket offices. Any remaining tickets are sold off at PalaGalileo one hour before the screening, but nearly all seats are taken well before then.

THE REGATA STORICA

Held on the first Sunday in September, the **Regata Storica** is the annual trial of strength and skill for the city's gondoliers and other expert rowers. It starts with a procession of historic craft along the Canal Grande course, their crews all decked out in period dress, followed by a series of races up the canal. The opening parade is a spectacular affair, and is followed by a race for young rowers in two-oared *pupparini*; the women come next (in boats called *mascarete*), followed by a race for canoe-like *caorline*; and then it's the men's race, in specialized two-man racing gondolas called *gondolini*.

LA FESTA DEL REDENTORE

For Venetians it's not Carnevale that's Venice's quintessential festival – it's the **Festa del Redentore**, which marks the end of the plague of 1576. Celebrated on the **third Sunday in July and the preceding Saturday**, the *festa* is centred on Palladio's church of the Redentore, which was built in thanksgiving for the city's deliverance from that terrible epidemic. On the Saturday the bishop of Venice marks the commencement of the festive weekend by leading a procession to the church, crossing the Giudecca canal on a bridge that's supported by dozens of boats that are strung across the waterway from the Záttere. By the evening the Bacino di San Marco is clogged with boats, as people row out for a picnic on the lagoon, then at midnight there's the mother of all firework displays, after which it's traditional to row to the Lido for the sunrise.

LA FESTA DELLA SALUTE

Named after the church of the Salute, the **Festa della Salute** is a reminder of the plague of 1630–31, which killed one third of the city's population. The church was built after the outbreak, and every **November 21** people process to it over a pontoon bridge across the Canal Grande, to give thanks for good health, or to pray for it.

6

SHOPPING IN VENICE

With every passing year the population of Venice falls, while commercial rents increase. The result: small-scale family-run shops are an endangered species here. Venice has two major shopping districts – the Mercerie, connecting the Piazza to the area around the Rialto Bridge; and Calle Larga XXII Marzo, running west from the Piazza – and these zones are almost monopolized by Italian mega-brands such as Gucci, Dolce e Gabbana and Prada, which you'll find in every other major tourist destination in Italy. On the island of Murano you'll find a lot of showrooms selling local glass, but much of the cheaper stuff is mass-produced outside Italy – look for the "Vetro Artistico Murano" trademark, the sign of authenticity. Likewise, most Carnival masks – the quintessential Venetian souvenirs – are manufactured abroad; for a terrific selection of handmade Venetian masks, go to **Ca' Macana**, Calle delle Botteghe 3172, Dorsoduro (☎041 277 6142, Ⓦcamacana.com) – it's very near San Barnaba church. With Burano lace, the situation is much the same: if it's inexpensive, it's fake. In central Venice, one of the best outlets for real Burano lace is Kerer, Calle Canonica 4328/A, Castello (☎041 523 5485, Ⓦkerer.it) – it's in the Palazzo Trevisan-Cappello, across the Ponte Cappello at the rear of the Basilica di San Marco.

Campo Santa Margherita and Campo San Barnaba.
San Marco: Venetian Navigator, Calle dei Stagneri 5239 (daily: summer 10am–1pm; winter 10am–8.30pm).
Dorsoduro: Teleradiofuga, Crosera S. Pantalon 3812 (Mon–Sat 10.30am–7.30pm); San Barnaba, Campo S. Barnaba 2759 (Mon–Sat 7am–7pm).
Cannaregio: Planet Internet, Rio Terà S. Leonardo 1519 (daily 9am–11pm); ABColor, Lista di Spagna 220 (daily: summer 10am–10pm; winter 10am–8pm).
Castello: Venetian Navigator, Calle Casselleria 5300 (daily: summer 10am–10pm; winter 10am–8.30pm).
Laundries Venice's self-service laundries are now virtually extinct; one survivor is to be found to the south of Campo Santa Maria Formosa, at Ruga Giuffa 4826 (daily 8.30am–8pm).

Police To notify police of a theft or lost passport, report to the *questura* at Rampa S. Chiara 500, on the north side of Piazzale Roma (☎041 271 5511); in an emergency, ring ☎113. There's a small police station on the Piazza, at no. 63.
Post offices Venice's central post office is at Calle delle Acque 5016, close to San Salvador, and is open Mon–Fri 8.25am–7.10pm, Sat 8.25am–12.35pm. The principal branch offices are at Calle dell'Ascensione 1241, off the west side of the Piazza (Tues–Fri 8.25am–1.35pm, Sat 8.25am–12.35pm); Calle del Spezier 233, Dorsoduro (same hours); Zàttere 1507, Dorsoduro (same hours); Campo S. Polo 2012, San Polo (same hours); Barbaria delle Tole 6674, Castello (Tues–Fri 8.15am–1.45pm, Sat 8.15am–12.45pm); and Via Garibaldi 1641, Castello (same hours).

The Veneto

Virtually every acre of the Veneto bears the imprint of Venetian rule – Venice dominated this region for centuries and is still the capital of the province today. In **Belluno**, right under the crags of the Dolomites, the style of the buildings declares the town's former allegiance, while the Lion of St Mark looks over the market square of **Verona**, on the Veneto's western edge. On the flatlands of the Po basin (the southern border of the region) and on farming estates all over the Veneto, the elegant **villas** of the Venetian nobility are still standing.

Yet the Veneto is as diverse culturally as it is geographically. The aspects of Verona that make the city so attractive were created long before the expansion of Venice's terra firma empire, and in **Padua** – a university seat since the thirteenth century – the civilization of the Renaissance displays a character quite distinct from that which evolved in Venice. Even in **Vicenza**, which reached its present form mainly during its long period of subservience, the very appearance of the streets is proof of a fundamental independence.

Nowadays this is one of Italy's wealthiest regions. Verona, Padua, Vicenza and **Treviso**, 30km north of Venice, are all major industrial and commercial centres, while intensive dairies, fruit farms and vineyards (around Conegliano, for example) have made the Veneto a leading agricultural producer too.

The Veneto's densest concentration of industry is at **Mestre** and **Marghera**, the grim conurbation through which road and rail lines from Venice pass before spreading out over

the mainland. It's less a city than an economic life-support system for Venice, and the
negative impression you get on your way through is entirely valid. Some people trim their
holiday expenses by staying in Mestre's cheaper hotels (Venice's tourist offices will supply
addresses), but venturing further inland is a more pleasurable cost-cutting exercise.

The Brenta

The southernmost of the three main rivers that empty into the Venetian lagoon, the
Brenta caused no end of trouble for the earliest settlers in the area, with its frequent
flooding and its deposits of silt. By the sixteenth century, though, the canalization of
the river had brought it under control, and it became a favoured building site for the
Venetian aristocracy. Some villas were built as a combination of summer residence and
farmhouse – many, however, were intended solely for the former function.

Around one hundred **villas** are left on the river between Padua and Venice, though
only a handful are open to the public. Of this last category, two are outstanding – the
Villa Fóscari and the **Villa Pisani** – both of which are accessible by bus from Venice: four
ACTV services go to the former, while the hourly buses between Padua and Venice (the
ACTV bus going via Dolo, not the SITA bus that goes on the autostrada) go past both.

Villa Fóscari

Mira • May–Oct Tues & Sat 9am–noon • €10

The **Villa Fóscari** at Malcontenta was designed in 1559 by Palladio (see box, p.407) and
is the nearest of his villas to Venice. Most of Palladio's villas fall into two broad groups:
those built on cohesive farming estates, with a central low block for living quarters and
wings for storage and associated uses, such as the Villa Barbaro at Maser (see p.428);
and the single-block villas built for landowners whose fields were dispersed or unsuitable
for the construction of a major building. The Villa Fóscari is the masterpiece of this
second group, evoking the architecture of ancient Rome with its rusticated exterior,
massive Ionic portico and two-storey main hall.

The frescoes in the living rooms include what is said to be a portrait of a woman of
the Fóscari family who was exiled here as punishment for an amorous escapade, and
whose subsequent misery was the source of the name Malcontenta. The reality is more
prosaic – the area has long been known by that name, either because of some local
discontent over the development of the land or because of the political *malcontenti* who
hid in the nearby salt marshes.

Villa Pisani

Stra • Tues–Sun: April–Sept 9am–7pm; Oct–March 9am–4pm • €10 house and garden, €7.50 garden only

The **Villa Pisani** (or Nazionale) at Stra, virtually on the outskirts of Padua (ask the bus
driver where to get off), looks more like a product of the *ancien régime* than a house for
the Venetian gentry. Commissioned when Alvise Pisani was elected Doge of Venice in
1735, it was the biggest such residence to be built in Venetian territory during that
century. It has appealed to megalomaniacs ever since: Napoleon bought it off the Pisani
in 1807 and handed it over to Eugène Beauharnais, his stepson and Viceroy of Italy;
and in 1934 it was chosen for the first meeting of Mussolini and Hitler.

Most of what you see is unexciting and sparsely furnished, but stick with it for the
ballroom, its ceiling covered with a dazzling fresco, *The Apotheosis of the Pisani Family*,
painted by **Tiepolo** at the age of 66. And if you're trying to puzzle out what's going on
– the Pisani family, accompanied by Venice, are being courted by the Arts, Sciences and
Spirits of Peace, while Fame plays a fanfare in praise of the Pisani while the Madonna
looks on with appropriate pride.

In the **grounds**, the long fish-pond ends in front of a stable-block which from
a distance might be mistaken for another grand house. Off to the right there's an
impressive maze, which is closed in winter.

Padua (Padova)

Hemmed in by the sprawl that has accompanied its development as the most important economic centre of the Veneto, **PADUA** (Padova) is not immediately the most alluring city in northern Italy. It is, however, one of the most ancient, and plentiful evidence remains of its impressive lineage. A large student population creates a young, vibrant atmosphere, and yet in spite of having two big attractions – the **Giotto frescoes** and the **Basilica of St Antony** – Padua has the feel of a town that is just getting on with its own business.

6

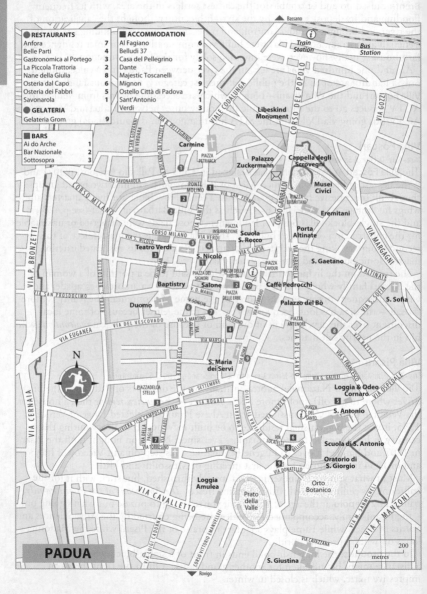

● RESTAURANTS	
Anfora	7
Belle Parti	4
Gastronomica al Portego	3
La Piccola Trattoria	2
Nane della Giulia	8
Osteria dal Capo	6
Osteria dei Fabbri	5
Savonarola	1

● GELATERIA	
Gelateria Grom	9

■ ACCOMMODATION	
Al Fagiano	6
Belludi 37	8
Casa del Pellegrino	5
Dante	2
Majestic Toscanelli	4
Mignon	1
Ostello Città di Padova	7
Sant'Antonio	
Verdi	3

■ BARS	
Ai do Arche	1
Bar Nazionale	2
Sottosopra	3

PADUA

PADOVACARD

Costing €16 for 48 hours or €21 for 72 hours, the **PadovaCard** (⑩ padovacard.it) allows one visit for one adult and one child under 14 to twelve sites in the city and environs, including the Musei Civici degli Eremitani, Scrovegni Chapel and Palazzo della Ragione. There are further discounts on the other main attractions, as well as free parking in the Piazza Rabin car park by Prato della Valle, free travel on the APS buses, free bicycle rental and discounts at some bed and breakfasts. It's available from the tourist office and participating museums and monuments. Note that advance booking is required for the Scrovegni Chapel, for which an extra €1 booking fee is payable.

6

Brief history

A Roman municipium from 45 BC, the city thrived until the barbarian onslaughts and the subsequent Lombard invasion at the start of the seventh century. Recovery was slow, but by the middle of the twelfth century, when it became a free commune, Padua was prosperous once again. Italy's second oldest **university** was founded here in 1221, and a decade later the city became a place of pilgrimage following the death here of **St Antony**.

In 1337 the **Da Carrara** family established control. Under their domination, Padua's cultural eminence was secured – Giotto, Dante and Petrarch were among those attracted here – but Carraresi territorial ambitions led to conflict with Venice, and in 1405 the city's independence ended with its conquest by the neighbouring republic. Though politically nullified, Padua remained an artistic and intellectual centre: Donatello and Mantegna both worked here, and in the seventeenth century Galileo researched at the university, where the medical faculty was one of the most ambitious in Europe. With the fall of the Venetian Republic the city passed to Napoleon and then to the Austrians, who ruled until Padua was annexed to Italy in 1866. Bombed several times by the Allies in World War II, the city has been extensively restored.

Corso Garibaldi

Corso del Popolo and its extension **Corso Garibaldi** lead south from the railway station, passing the 17m-tall structure of glass and steel designed by the architect **Daniel Libeskind** as a memorial to the victims of the September 11 attacks. Named *Memory and Light*, it contains part of a girder salvaged from the World Trade Center. A couple of minutes' walk further on are two of the city's biggest draws, the **Cappella degli Scrovegni** and **Musei Civici degli Eremitani**.

The Cappella degli Scrovegni

Entry through the gates of the Musei Civici, Piazza Eremitani 8 • Mon 9am–7pm, Tues–Sun 9am–10pm • For prices, see box, p.402 • ⑩ cappelladegliscrovegni.it

The **Cappella degli Scrovegni** was commissioned in 1303 by Enrico Scrovegni in atonement for his father's usury, which was so vicious that he was denied a Christian burial. **Giotto** was commissioned to cover the walls with illustrations of the life of Mary, the life of Jesus and the story of the Passion, and the finished cycle is one of the high points in the development of European art. The frescoes are a marvellous demonstration of Giotto's innovative attention to the inner nature of his subjects. In terms of sheer physical presence and the relationships between the figures and their environment, Giotto's work takes the first important strides towards realism and humanism.

The Joachim series on the top row of the north wall (facing you as you walk in) is particularly powerful – note the exchange of looks between the two shepherds in the *Arrival of Joachim*. Beneath the main pictures are shown the Vices and Virtues in human (usually female) form, while on the wall above the door is a *Last Judgement* – in rather poor condition and thought to be only partly by Giotto. At the bottom is a

6

TICKETS FOR THE CAPPELLA DEGLI SCROVEGNI

Tickets for the Cappella are €13, which includes entry to the Musei Civici Eremitani, or €8 when the museum is closed (on Mon and after 7pm); the PadovaCard also gets you in free, but you still have to pay a €1 booking fee. After 7pm (when you get 20min inside) you can also book a double slot ("*doppia turno*"), which gives you forty minutes inside the chapel for €12. The number of visitors permitted each day is strictly limited, so it's usually advisable to book tickets in advance – at least three or four days in advance in summer, though in winter you may find there is no need to wait. Reservations can be made at the museum ticket desk, or by phoning ☏049 201 0020 (Mon–Fri 9am–7pm, Sat 9am–6pm), or online at ⊕cappelladegliscrovegni.it. Tickets must be picked up from the ticket desk an hour before your timed entry; you have to be at the chapel waiting-room five minutes before your allotted time. Groups of 25 are admitted every fifteen minutes (every 20min after 7pm), and if you miss your slot you have to book and pay again. Once inside, the air humidity of the waiting room is adjusted down to that of the chapel, while you watch a video about the frescoes, with just a meagre fifteen to twenty minutes allowed inside the chapel itself.

---

portrait of Scrovegni presenting the chapel; his tomb is at the far end, behind the altar with its statues by **Giovanni Pisano**.

The Musei Civici degli Eremitani

Piazza Eremitani 8 • Tues–Sun 9am–7pm • €10 combined with the Palazzo Zuckermann, or €13 including the Cappella; free with PadovaCard

Next to the chapel, the **Musei Civici degli Eremitani**, formerly the monastery of the Eremitani, is a well-presented museum complex that holds the Museo Archeologico and the Museo d'Arte Medioevale e Moderna. The **archeological collection**, on the ground floor, has an array of pre-Roman, Roman and paleo-Christian objects. Upstairs, the vast **Museo d'Arte** houses an assembly of fourteenth- to nineteenth-century art from the Veneto and further afield. The collection is arranged in chronological order, and it's a long walk through tracts of workaday stuff, but works by names such as Titian, Tintoretto and Tiepolo leaven the mix. Highlights are the Giotto *Crucifixion* that was once in the Scrovegni chapel, and a fine *Portrait of a Young Senator* by Bellini. The Capodilista collection, an offshoot of the main gallery, has four mysterious Titian and Giorgione landscapes, and some good Luca Giordano grotesques.

The Chiesa degli Eremitani

Piazza Eremitani • Mon–Sat 9am–1pm & 3.30–7pm, Sun 9.30am–12.30pm & 4–7pm • Free

Next door to the Musei Civici the church of the **Eremitani**, built at the turn of the fourteenth century, was wrecked by an Allied bombing raid in 1944 but has been fastidiously rebuilt. The worst aspect of the bombardment was the damage to **Mantegna**'s frescoes of the lives of St James and St Christopher; some 80,000 fresco fragments were meticulously pieced together in 2008, creating the jigsaw puzzle-like reconstruction that is preserved in the chapel to the right of the high altar.

Palazzo Zuckermann

Corso Garibaldi 33 • Tues–Sun 10am–7pm • €10 combined with the Musei Civici, or €13 including the Cappella; free with PadovaCard

Across Corso Garibaldi, the recently restored **Palazzo Zuckermann** houses two small museums of specialist interest: the new **Museo di Arti Applicate e Decorative** displays pottery, jewellery, textiles and furniture; while upstairs, the **Museo Bottacin** contains over 100,000 coins, medals and seals, making it one of the most important museums of its type in the world.

The central squares

Continuing down the Corso Garibaldi from the Palazzo Zuckermann and turning right leads you past the **Caffè Pedrocchi**, once the city's main intellectual salon; it's no longer that, but it does have a multiplicity of functions — chic café, concert hall, local history museum and conference centre. Just beyond, the **Piazza della Frutta** and **Piazza delle Erbe**, the sites of Padua's daily markets, are lined with bars, restaurants and shops.

The Palazzo della Ragione

Tues–Sun 9am–7pm; €4, or more if there is an exhibition in the hall; free with PadovaCard

Separating the **Piazza della Frutta** and **Piazza delle Erbe** is the extraordinary **Palazzo della Ragione** or **Il Salone**, which you enter by the stairs at the eastern end of Piazza delle Erbe. When it was built in the 1210s, this vast hall was the largest room to have been built on top of another storey. Its decoration would once have been as astounding as its size, but the original frescoes by Giotto and his assistants were destroyed by fire in 1420, though some by Giusto de' Menabuoi have survived. Most of the extant frescoes are by Nicolò Miretto, depicting an astrological calendar distinctively medieval in its complexity. Mainly used as the city council's assembly hall, it was also a place where Padua's citizens could plead for justice – hence the appellation *della Ragione*, meaning "of reason". The large wooden horse with disproportionately gigantic gonads is modelled on Donatello's *Gattamelata*, and was made for a joust in 1466. There's a useful information screen about the frescoes and the horse in one corner of the hall.

The Duomo and baptistry

Duomo Mon–Sat 7.30am–noon & 4–7.30pm, Sun 8am–1pm & 4–8pm • Free **Baptistry** Daily 10am–6pm • €2.80, or free with PadovaCard

Padua's **Duomo** is an unlovely church whose architect took his design from drawings by Michelangelo. The adjacent Romanesque **baptistry**, however, is one of the unproclaimed delights of the city. Built by the Da Carraras in the thirteenth century, and still in use today, it's lined with fourteenth-century frescoes by Giusto de' Menabuoi, a cycle which makes a fascinating comparison with the Cappella degli Scrovegni. In striving for greater realism Giusto has lost Giotto's monumentality and made some of his figures unconvincing, yet many of the scenes are delightful, and the vibrancy of their colours, coupled with the relative quiet of the building, make for a memorable visit.

The university

Tours March–Oct Mon, Wed & Fri 3.15pm, 4.15pm & 5.15pm, Tues, Thurs & Sat 9.15am, 10.15am & 11.15am; Nov–Feb the 9.15am and 5.15pm tours do not run • €5 • Tickets (no reservations) are on sale 15min beforehand – the ticket office is by the bar in the more modern of the two courtyards and is well signposted

The area just southeast of the *Caffè Pedrocchi* is dominated by the main block of the university, the Palazzo del Bò ("the Ox", named after an inn that used to stand here). Established in September 1221, the University of Padua is older than any other in Italy except that of Bologna. The first permanent anatomy theatre was built on this site in 1594, a facility that doubtless greatly helped William Harvey, who went on to develop the theory of blood circulation after taking his degree here in 1602. Galileo taught physics at the university from 1592 to 1610, declaiming from a lectern that is still on show. And in 1678 Elena Lucrezia Corner Piscopia became the first woman in the world to collect a university degree – her statue is in the courtyard. The Bò is only open for guided tours.

The Prato della Valle and Santa Giustina

Past the *palazzo*, Via VIII Febbraio turns into Via Roma and then Via Umberto I, before opening up into the sprawling **Prato della Valle**, claimed to be the largest town square in Italy. It's a generally cheerless area, ringed by very wide roads, but the vast Saturday market and the summer funfair do a lot to make it jollier. It's also a favourite place for the *passeggiata* on summer evenings, and the location of an antiques fair on the third Sunday of each month.

Basilica di Santa Giustina

Mon–Sat 8am–noon & 3–6pm, Sun 6.30am–1pm & 3–8pm • Free

One side of the Prato della Valle is fronted by the sixteenth-century Basilica di Santa Giustina. A pair of fifteenth-century griffins, one holding a knight and the other a lion, are the only notable adornments to the unclad brick facade; the interior has little of interest except a huge *Martyrdom of St Justina* by Paolo Veronese (in the apse), some highly proficient carving on the choir stalls, and the sarcophagus which once contained the relics of Luke the Evangelist (apse of right transept).

Piazza del Santo and the Gattamelata monument

Walking up Via Belludi from the Prato delle Valle, an increasing density of shops selling garishly decorated candles and outsize souvenir rosaries will prepare you for the pilgrim-ensnaring stalls of the **Piazza del Santo**. The main sight on the piazza – apart from the mighty basilica – is Donatello's **Monument to Gattamelata** (which translates literally as "The Honeyed Cat"), as the *condottiere* Erasmo da Narni was known. He died in 1443 and this monument was raised ten years later, the first large bronze sculpture of the Renaissance.

The Basilica di Sant'Antonio

Piazza del Santo • Daily 6.20am–7.45pm, closes 7pm Mon–Fri Oct–March • Free

At the far end of Via Belludi the **Basilica di Sant'Antonio**, or **Il Santo**, towers over Piazza del Santo. Within eighteen months of his death in 1231, St Antony had been canonized and his tomb was attracting enough pilgrims to warrant the building of the basilica. It was not until the start of the fourteenth century that the church reached a state that enabled the saint's body to be placed in the **Cappella del Santo** (in the left transept). Plastered with such votive offerings as photographs of healed limbs and car crashes survived with the saint's intervention, the shrine has an uneasy, irresistible pull. The chapel's more formal decoration includes the most important series of relief sculpture created in sixteenth-century Italy, a sequence of nine marble panels showing scenes from the life of St Antony. Carved between 1505 and 1577, most have the names of their sculptors incised into the base, Antonio Lombardo, Tullio Lombardo and Jacopo Sansovino being among the most famous.

The smaller chapels

Adjoining the chapel is the **Cappella della Madonna Mora** (named after its fourteenth-century French altar statue), which in turn gives on to the **Cappella del Beato Luca**, whose fourteenth-century frescoes include a lovely image of St James lifting a prison tower to free a prisoner. Back in the aisle, just outside the Cappella del Santo, is Padua's finest work by Pietro Lombardo, the monument to Antonio Roselli (1467). More impressive still are the high altar's bronze sculptures and reliefs by Donatello (1444–45), the works that introduced Renaissance classicism to Padua. There are more fine frescoes across the aisle from the Cappella del Santo in the **Cappella di San Giacomo**, where Altichiero da Zevio depicted a masterly Crucifixion and scenes from the life of St James. Built onto the farthest point of the ambulatory, the **Cappella del Tesoro** houses the tongue and vocal chords of St Antony, as well as a host of lesser relics.

The Museo Antoniano and Museo della Devozione Populare

April–Oct 9am–1pm & 2.30–6.30pm; Nov–March Tues–Sun 9am–1pm & 2–6pm • Museo Antoniano €2.50; Museo della Devozione Populare free

Parts of the cloisters, on the south side of the basilica, are occupied by the **Museo Antoniano** and the **Museo della Devozione Populare**. The former, on the first floor, is a collection of paintings (including a fresco of *SS. Anthony and Bernardine* by **Mantegna**), ornate incense-holders, ceremonial robes and other paraphernalia linked to the basilica; the latter, on the ground floor, is a history of votive gifts, with copious examples of the genre.

Oratorio di San Giorgio

Piazza del Santo • Daily 9am–12.30pm & 2.30–7pm, but closes 5pm Nov–March • €3, or €5 joint ticket with Scuola del Santo

To the left as you leave the basilica is the **Oratorio di San Giorgio**. The oratory was founded in 1377 as a mortuary chapel; its frescoes, by Altichiero da Zevio and Jacopo Avanzi, were completed soon after and have been recently restored. One wall is adorned by the wonderfully titled *St Lucy Remains Immovable at an Attempt to Drag Her with the Help of Oxen to a House of Ill Repute.*

Scuola del Santo

Piazza del Santo • Daily 9am–12.30pm & 2.30–7pm, but closes 5pm Nov–March • €3, or €5 joint ticket with Oratorio di San Giorgio

The **Scuola del Santo** was founded soon after Antony's canonization, though this building only goes back as far as the early fifteenth century. The ground floor is still used for religious purposes, while upstairs is maintained to look pretty much as it would have in the sixteenth century, with its fine ceiling and paintings dating mainly from 1509–15, three or four of which are thought to be by Titian.

Orto Botanico

Via dell'Orto Botanico • April–Oct daily 9am–1pm & 3–7pm; Nov–March Mon–Sat 9am–1pm • €4, free with PadovaCard

A good place to relax after a visit to the basilica is the **Orto Botanico**, the oldest botanic gardens in Europe. Planted in 1545 by the university's medical faculty as a collection of medicinal herbs, the gardens have mainly kept their original layout, and the specimens on show haven't changed too much either. Goethe came here in 1786 to see a palm tree that had been planted in 1585; the selfsame tree still stands, the oldest in the garden.

Loggia e Odeo Cornaro

Via Cesarotti 37 • Summer Tues–Fri 10am–1pm, Sat & Sun 10am–1pm & 4–7pm; winter Tues–Fri 10am–1pm, Sat & Sun 10am–1pm & 3–6pm • Visitors allowed in on the hour and 30min past the hour • €3, or free with PadovaCard

Just northeast of the basilica is the **Loggia e Odeo Cornaro**, the remains of a set of buildings and gardens commissioned in 1524–30 by Alvise Cornaro, a local landowner, architectural theoretician and patron of the arts. The main attraction here is the **Odeo**, where Cornaro held concerts and literary gatherings; the vault of its octagonal chamber has Roman-style decorations with a series of grotesque figures, while the walls of the shell-hooded niches are painted with watery landscapes. You can admire the ceiling of the adjoining loggia, but the theatre above is closed.

ARRIVAL AND DEPARTURE   PADUA

By train Trains arrive in the north of the town, just a few minutes' walk up Corso del Popolo from the old city walls. Destinations Bassano (16 daily; 1hr 5min); Belluno (13 daily; 2hr); Milan (24 daily; 2hr 30min); Venice (every 20min; 25–50min) Verona (every 30min; 45min–1hr 15min); Vicenza (every 20min; 15–30min).

Buses The main bus station is next to the railway station at Piazzale della Stazione; local buses for the city and nearby towns such as Abano and Montegrotto leave from outside the railway station.
Destination Bassano (every 30min; 1hr 10min).

GETTING AROUND

On foot It's a 10min walk from the station into town, and from the centre everything is in walking distance – though you might want to resort to the tram if you are going from the station straight to the basilica or the youth hostel.
By bus Local buses for the city and nearby towns such as

Abano and Montegrotto leave from outside the train station.
By tram A system of electric trams (Metrobus) is slowly being introduced to the city; the first line runs between the station and Prato della Valle and is the simplest way of getting around town quickly. Details are on ⓦ trampadova.it.

INFORMATION

Tourist offices There are tourist offices at the train station (Mon–Sat 9.15am–7pm, Sun 9am–noon; ☎ 049 875 2077, ⓦ turismopadova.it); in the town centre at Piazzetta

Pedrocchi (Mon–Sat 9am–1.30pm & 3–7pm; ☎ 049 876 7927) and in season (April–Oct) on Piazza del Santo (Mon–Sat 9am–1pm & 3–6pm, Sun 9am–noon; ☎ 049 875 3087).

6

ACCOMMODATION

Though rooms are cheaper in Padua than Venice, availability can be a problem, especially during high season or during festivals. Don't despair, however – Padua has plenty of reasonably priced hotels and a growing number of bed and breakfasts; the tourist office has a full list of both. Many of the B&Bs are out in the suburbs, but they usually have good links to the centre; some places offer a small reduction on stays of more than two nights with the PadovaCard (see box, p.401).

★ **Al Fagiano** Via Locatelli 45 ☎049 875 0073, ⓦalfagiano.com. A friendly two-star, with forty rooms, each floor decorated in a different colour and with a bizarre selection of art. The rooms vary in size; ask for no. 72, with its own large terrace. **€100**

Belludi 37 Via Luca Belludi 37 ☎049 665 633, ⓦbelludi37.it. This slickly renovated *palazzo* near the Basilica di Sant'Antonio has fifteen tasteful rooms decorated in neutral tones. All rooms are spacious, with high ceilings, luxurious bathrooms and DVD players, but it's worth paying the extra for views of the basilica; the best is no. 107, with its own balcony. **€150**

Casa del Pellegrino Via M. Cesarotti 21 ☎049 823 9711, ⓦcasadelpellegrino.com. The "Pilgrim's House", popular with groups coming to pay their respects to St Antony across the road, is somewhat reminiscent of student accommodation, though the rooms are comfortable and most have en-suite bathrooms. It's worth paying an extra €5 for the more spacious "superior" rooms in the annexe. **€80**

Dante Via S. Polo 5 ☎049 876 0408, ⓦhoteldante.eu. Clean and central one-star near the Ponte Molino, run by a friendly signora who speaks little English. Just eight rooms, some with en-suite bathrooms. Wi-fi but no breakfast. **€60**

Majestic Toscanelli Via dell'Arco 2 ☎049 663 244, ⓦtoscanelli.com. The most appealing of the city's four-stars, with elegant, well-appointed rooms; it's located in the

old Jewish quarter, just south of Piazza delle Erbe. **€200**

Mignon Via Luca Belludi 22 ☎049 661 722, ⓦhotelmignonpadova.it. Lying between the Prato della Valle and the botanic garden, this simple but comfortable two-star has 23 rooms with a/c and TV. Most rooms overlook the street; those at the back are quieter. **€74**

Ostello Città di Padova Via Aleardo Aleardi 30 ☎049 875 2219, ⓦostellopadova.it; reservations via ⓦhostelbookers.com or ⓦhostelsclub.com. Padua's friendly HI hostel is in a quiet street in the south of the city, a half-hour walk from the station but the tram goes to nearby Prato della Valle. Wi-fi and laundry facilities. Check-in 7–9.30am & 3.30–11pm; reception is closed between these times; 11.30pm curfew. Six-bed dorms, with some four-bed rooms for families. Prices include breakfast. Dorms **€19**

Sant'Antonio Via S. Fermo 118 ☎049 875 1393, ⓦhotelsantantonio.it. Large rooms with unfussy decor; those at the back have views over the Ponte Molino. The nicest rooms are nos. 311 and 312, on two levels, with a small sitting area upstairs. **€100**

Verdi Via Dondi dell'Orologio 7 ☎049 836 4163, ⓦalbergoverdipadova.it. Light and airy, this friendly three-star lies on a quiet street between the university buildings and the Teatro Verdi. Its fourteen rooms are fully modernized. Special offers bring price of a double room down to as low as €40. **€150**

EATING AND DRINKING

Catering for the midday stampede of ravenous students, Padua's bars generally produce weightier **snacks** than the routine *tramezzini* – slabs of pizza and sandwiches vast enough to satisfy a glutton are standard; you'll find several amid the food stalls underneath the Palazzo della Ragione. For a *passeggiata* and a place to sit and watch the world go by, the main areas to head for are Piazza delle Erbe, Piazza del Duomo, Via Roma and Prato della Valle. For **nightlife**, the real action takes place in the lively student bars in the old Jewish Ghetto area around the central piazzas and the university, although it tends to fluctuate in synch with term time; and note that on Sunday many restaurants and bars are closed.

RESTAURANTS AND GELATERIE

★ **Anfora** Via dei Soncin 13 ☎049 656 629. Boisterous restaurant that doubles as a bar between sittings, with delicious snacks. The pasta dishes range around the €8–10 mark. Get there early or book in advance. Mon–Sat 12.30–3.15pm & 8–11.30pm.

Belle Parti Via Belle Parti 11 ☎049 875 1822, ⓦristorantebelleparti.it. Relaxed but very elegant restaurant just off Via Verdi where the food is superb. With mains at €22–35, it is not cheap, but the *degustazione* menu (around €50) is good value. A highlight is the *gran crudità di mare* – a local raw fish speciality (€25 for a starter). Booking advisable. Mon–Sat noon–3pm & 7–11pm.

Gastronomica al Portego Via Dante 9. High-quality yet inexpensive self-service restaurant with dishes – they have a wide range of pastas – sold by weight. A good spot for a quick lunch. Tues–Sat 8.30am–2.30pm & 5–8.30pm, Sun 8.30am–1.30pm; closed Aug.

Gelateria Grom Via Roma 101. The most exquisite ice cream in the city is made here, by the chain that started in Turin and is set to conquer the world. The lemon, vanilla and coffee flavours have won awards. Mon–Fri noon–midnight, Sat & Sun 11.30am–midnight.

La Piccola Trattoria Via R. Da Piazzola 21 ☎049 656 163, ⓦpiccolatrattoria.it. Friendly place full of locals; it serves Sardinian specialities, all superbly presented.

Secondi are around €15, but there are also cheap lunchtime specials. Mon 8–11pm, Tues–Sat noon–2.30pm & 8–11pm.

★ **Nane della Giulia** Via S. Sofia 1 ☎049 660 742. There has been an *osteria* in this former church hospital since 1820; the present incarnation is a trendy and unpretentious place that serves reasonably priced Veneto and vegetarian specialities – *secondi* are €8–14 – all made from locally sourced and seasonal products, with regional wines to boot. The summer garden is lovely, too. Booking advisable at weekends. Tues 7pm–midnight and Wed–Sun 12.30–2.30pm & 7pm–midnight.

★ **Osteria dal Capo** Via degli Obizzi 2 ☎049 663 105. Small restaurant celebrated for its fish, rabbit and liver dishes, and home-made pasta. The chef comes round the tables to chat to guests after their meal, and diners are offered a grappa in the best Italian tradition. Booking advised for dinner. Mon 7.30–10pm, Tues–Sat 12.30–2.30pm & 7.30–10.30pm.

★ **Osteria dei Fabbri** Via dei Fabbri 13 ☎049 650 336, ⊚osteriadeifabbri.it. Excellent trattoria in a street running off Piazza delle Erbe; you'll be lucky to get a seat if you haven't booked. Moderate prices – pasta dishes are less than €10. Mon–Sat noon–3pm & 7–11pm.

Savonarola Via Savonarola 38 ☎049 875 9128.

Busy pizzeria just outside the city walls with a good atmosphere and moderate prices – pizzas start at €3.50. Popular with students – you'll need to book at weekends. Mon–Fri 12.30–2.30pm & 7.30pm–midnight, Sat & Sun 7pm–midnight.

BARS

★ **Ai do Arche** Via Nazario Sauro 23 ☎380 316 0317. Small wine bar off Piazza Signori with a very lively vibe. Good music and a great atmosphere, together with tasty bruschetta and crostini to accompany your drinks. Daily 6pm–midnight.

★ **Bar Nazionale** Piazza delle Erbe 40. This unmarked bar by the steps leading up to the Palazzo della Ragione is the ideal place to sit with an aperitif and look out over the square, the fruit market and the *passeggiata*. Mon–Sat 8am–11.30pm; winter closes 9.30pm.

★ **Sottosopra** Via XX Settembre 77 ☎049 664 898. The "Upside down" bar has been serving its teas (fifty of them), wines and snacks for more than twenty years. Run by a very friendly couple, it attracts an unusually varied clientele, from retired couples to students. It's in a quiet part of town and has outdoor tables in summer. Tues–Sat noon–3pm & 7pm–1am, Sun 7pm–1am; opens 5pm in winter.

ENTERTAINMENT

Of the local newspapers, the most comprehensive for listings is *Il Mattino*, but for more offbeat events check out the posters up around the city.

Teatro Verdi Corso Milano ☎049 8777 0213, ⊚teatro stabileveneto.it. Padua's main theatre is the Teatro Verdi, hosting opera and big-name dramatists; details of the season's events can be obtained from the tourist office or in

the bilingual information booklet *Padova Today*, distributed in tourist offices and most hotels. Closed in summer; tickets €10–27, discounts with PadovaCard.

PALLADIO

Born in Padua in 1508, Andrea di Pietro (or della Gondola) began his career as an apprentice stonemason in Vicenza. At 30 he became the protégé of a local nobleman, Count Giangiorgio Trissino, who gave the architect his classicized name, **Palladio**. Tressino directed Palladio's training and, perhaps most crucially, took him to Rome – the first of many trips he made sketching imperial Roman remains.

Between 1540 and his death in 1580, Palladio created around a dozen palaces and public buildings in Vicenza, nearly twenty villas in the countryside of the Veneto, and the churches of the Redentore and San Giorgio Maggiore in Venice. But unlike the pioneers of Renaissance Classicism – architects such as Alberti, Brunelleschi and Bramante – Palladio's reputation does not rest on a particular transformation of architectural style. Instead, his fame – and he is arguably the most influential architect in the world – rests on the way he perfected existing values of harmony and proportion.

In particular, his lasting influence stems from **I Quattro Libri dell'Architettura** or "The Four Books of Architecture", a treatise he published in 1570, towards the end of his career. Other architects had written important works of theory, but Palladio's is unique in its practical applicability, serving almost as a textbook for Classical architecture. As the style spread into the rest of Europe and beyond, it was to Palladio's book that architects like Inigo Jones (and later, Thomas Jefferson) turned, finding both inspiration and guidance in his examples.

Vicenza

Europe's largest producer of textiles and the focus of Italy's "Silicon Valley", **VICENZA** is a very sleek city, where it can seem that every second car is a BMW. Prosperity hasn't ruined the look of the city though, and the centre, still partly enclosed by medieval walls, today looks much as it did at the close of the eighteenth century. In 1404 Vicenza was absorbed by Venice, and the city's numerous Gothic palaces reflect its status as a Venetian satellite. But in the latter half of the sixteenth century the city was transformed by the work of an architect who owed nothing to Venice and was to influence every succeeding generation – Andrea di Pietro, alias **Palladio**. The historic core is compact enough to be explored in a day, but the city and its environs really require a short stay to do them justice.

Corso Andrea Palladio

The main street of Vicenza, **Corso Andrea Palladio**, cuts right through the old centre from Piazza del Castello down to Piazza Matteotti, and is lined with *palazzi*, all of them now occupied by shops, offices and banks. Palladio's last palace, the fragmentary **Palazzo Porto-Breganze**, stands on the southern side of Piazza Castello; no. 163 on the Corso, the **Casa Cogollo**, is confusingly known as the Casa del Palladio, though he never lived here and few people think he designed it.

The Museo Civico

Piazza Matteotti 37/39 • Tues–Sun 9am–5pm • Entry with Card Musei only

The Corso ends with one of Palladio's most imperious buildings, the Palazzo Chiericati (begun in 1551), now home of the **Museo Civico**, also known as the Pinacoteca. The core of the picture collection is made up of Vicentine artists, none of whose work will knock you flat on your back; it's left to a few more celebrated names – Memling, Tintoretto, Veronese, Tiepolo – and some fine fifteenth-century painting to make the visit memorable.

Teatro Olimpico

Piazza Matteotti 11 • Tues–Sun: July & Aug 9am–7pm; Sept–June 9am–5pm • Entry with Card Musei only • ⓦ olimpicovicenza.it

Across the Piazza Matteotti is the one building in Vicenza you shouldn't fail to go into – the **Teatro Olimpico**, the oldest indoor theatre in Europe. Approached in 1579 by the members of the Olympic Academy (a society dedicated to the study of the humanities) to produce a design for a permanent theatre, Palladio devised a covered amphitheatre based on his studies of Roman works. He died soon after work commenced, and the scheme was overseen by Scamozzi, who added the backstage perspective of a classical city, creating the illusion of long urban vistas by tilting the "streets" at an alarming angle. The theatre opened on March 3, 1585, and is still used for concerts and plays.

The basilica and around

At the hub of the city, the **Piazza dei Signori**, stands the most portentous of Palladio's creations – the **basilica**. Designed in the late 1540s (but not finished until almost seventy years later), this was Palladio's first public project and the one that secured his reputation. The monumental regularity of the basilica disguises the fact that the Palladian building is effectively a stupendous piece of buttressing – the Doric and Ionic colonnades enclose the fifteenth-century hall of the city council, an unstable

---

THE CARD MUSEI

To visit the Museo Civico, Teatro Olimpico and Museo Naturalistico-Archeologico you'll need to buy the €8.50 **Card Musei** (€12 for a family card), which also gives admission to the Palazzo Leoni Montanari, the Museo Diocesano and the Museo del Risorgimento. The Card Musei can be bought at the Teatro Olimpico and the Museo del Risorgimento and is valid for three days.

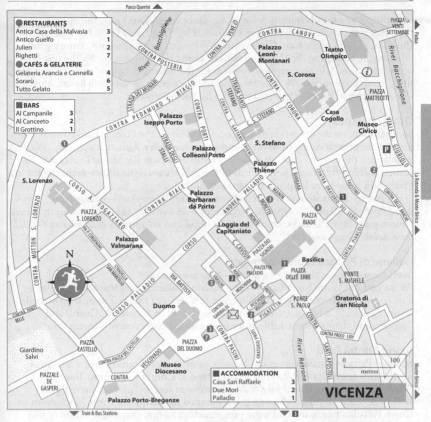

● RESTAURANTS

Antica Casa della Malvasia	3
Antico Guelfo	1
Julien	2
Righetti	7

● CAFÉS & GELATERIE

Gelateria Arancia e Cannella	4
Sorarù	6
Tutto Gelato	5

■ BARS

Al Campanile	3
Al Canceeto	2
Il Grottino	1

■ ACCOMMODATION

Casa San Raffaele	3
Due Mori	2
Palladio	1

VICENZA

▼ Train & Bus Stations

structure that had defied all previous attempts to prop it up. The vast Gothic hall is often used for contemporary exhibitions. On Tuesdays a huge **market** fills the streets between the basilica and the Duomo, while on Thursdays a fruit and vegetable market occupies Piazza delle Erbe, behind the basilica; though if you're shopping for picnic food, you'll save money by going down the slope and over the river, where the shops are a good bit cheaper.

A late Palladian building, the unfinished **Loggia del Capitaniato**, faces the basilica across the Piazza dei Signori. Built as accommodation for the Venetian military commander of the city, it's decorated with reliefs in celebration of the Venetian victory over the Turks at Lepanto in 1571.

The Duomo

Piazza del Duomo • Mon–Sat 10.30–11.45am & 3.30–6pm, Sun 3.30–5.15pm & 6–7.15pm • Free

Vicenza's **Duomo** was bombed flat in 1944 and, though carefully reconstructed after the war, it's a rather gloomy place. A polyptych by **Lorenzo Veneziano** (fifth chapel on right) and a *Madonna* by **Montagna** (fourth chapel on left) are the best of its paintings.

Museo Diocesano

Piazza del Duomo 2 • Tues–Sun 10am–1pm & 2–6pm • €5, or Card Musei

Aside from the usual collection of church vestments and silverware, the **Museo Diocesano** has an excellent display of stone fragments from Roman times onwards, including a fine fourth-century relief of the Three Magi. Don't miss the magnificent cape that was donated to the Bishop of Vicenza by King Louis IX in 1259, or the thorn that's supposedly from Christ's crown – housed in a fourteenth-century gold reliquary, it belongs to the church of Santa Corona but is on display on the first floor of the museum. Also on temporary show from the Santa Corona are two of Vicenza's finest church paintings: *The Baptism of Christ*, a late work by **Giovanni Bellini**, and *The Adoration of the Magi*, painted in 1573 by **Paolo Veronese**.

Other churches

Santa Corona, on the other side of the Corso Palladio (at the Piazza Matteotti end), is a Dominican church dating from the mid-thirteenth century. Although currently closed for restoration, the church's main attractions can still be seen at the Museo Diocesano. The cloisters behind the church house a run-of-the-mill **Museo Naturalistico-Archeologico** (Tues–Sun 9am–5pm; for prices see box, p.408).

The nearby **Santo Stefano** (Piazzetta Santo Stefano; Mon–Sat 9–10.30am & 3–6.30pm, Sun 9am–12.30pm & 3–6.30pm; free) contains the third of the city's fine church paintings: Palma Vecchio's typically stolid and voluptuous *Madonna and Child with Saints George and Lucy*.

Gallerie di Palazzo Leoni Montanari

Contrà S. Corona 25 • Tues–Sun 10am–6pm • €5, or Card Musei • ⓦ palazzomontanari.com

At the end of Contrà Santa Corona, the Baroque **Palazzo Leoni Montanari** houses a collection of art from the Veneto, displayed in a series of frescoed rooms. Eighteenth-century painting is best represented, including works by Canaletto, Guardi and Tiepolo, and there's a remarkable and well-presented collection of Russian icons.

Along Contrà Porti

More of Palladio's masterpieces can be seen on or around Contrà Porti, which runs northwards from Corso Palladio. **Palazzo Thiene** at Contrà S. Gaetano Thiene 11 (Wed–Fri 9am–5pm; closed July & Aug; admission free, by advance booking on ☎0444 339 989, ⓦpalazzothiene.it), was planned to occupy the entire block down to Corso Palladio, but in the end work progressed no further than the addition of this wing to the existing fifteenth-century house.

Facing Palazzo Thiene on the Contrà Porti side is the **Palazzo Barbaran da Porto** (opening hours and entrance fees vary according to exhibition schedules; ⓦcisapalladio.org), which houses a research institute for Palladian architecture and often has excellent exhibitions on Classical architects.

Outstanding buildings on Contrà Porti are the fourteenth-century **Palazzo Colleoni Porto** (no. 19) and Palladio's neighbouring **Palazzo Iseppo da Porto**, designed a few years after the Thiene palace. The parallel Corso A. Fogazzaro completes the itinerary of major Palladian buildings with the Palazzo Valmarana (no. 16), perhaps the most eccentric of his projects – note the gigantic stucco figures at the sides of the facade, where you'd expect columns to be.

Contrà Porti takes you towards the Pusteria Bridge and the **Parco Querini** (daily 8am–sunset), the biggest expanse of green in the city, enlivened by a decorative hillock populated by ducks, rabbits and peacocks.

The outskirts – Monte Bérico and the villas

In 1426 Vicenza was struck by bubonic plague, during the course of which outbreak the Virgin is said to have appeared twice at the summit of Monte Bérico – the hill on the southern edge of the city – to announce the city's deliverance. The chapel raised on the site of her appearance became a place of pilgrimage, and at the end of the seventeenth century it was replaced by the present **Basilica di Monte Bérico**.

Basilica di Monte Bérico

Viale X Giugno • Daily 8am–12.30pm & 2.30–6pm • Free • Around 30min on foot from the centre of town, less than 10min by taxi. FTV bus #6 runs up the hill from the bus station roughly hourly; on Sun only, bus #18 goes more frequently from Viale Roma, the road leading into the centre from the station

Pilgrims regularly arrive here by the busload, and the glossy interior of the basilica is immaculately maintained to receive them. Those in search of artistic fulfilment should venture into the church for Montagna's *Pietà* (in the chapel to the right of the apse) and *The Supper of St Gregory the Great* by Veronese (in the refectory). The latter, the prototype of *The Feast in the House of Levi* in Venice's Accademia, was used for bayonet practice by Austrian troops in 1848 – the small reproduction nearby shows what a thorough job the vandals and subsequent restorers did.

Museo del Risorgimento e della Resistenza

Viale X Giugno 87 • Tues–Sun 9am–1pm & 2.15–5pm • €3, or Card Musei

Carry on towards the summit of the hill and you come to the **Museo del Risorgimento e della Resistenza**, some ten minutes' walk beyond the basilica. The museum houses an impressive display, paying particular attention to Vicenza's resistance to the Austrians in the mid-nineteenth century and to the efforts of the anti-fascist Alpine fighters a century later; but for many visitors the big attraction will be the extensive wooded **parkland** (Tues–Sun: Oct–March 9am–5.30pm; April–Sept 9am–7.30pm; free) laid out on the slopes below the Villa Guiccioli, the main building.

Villa Valmarana

Stradella dei Nani 87 • Mid-March to early Nov Tues–Sun 10am–12.30pm & 3–6pm • €9

Ten minutes' walk from the basilica is the **Villa Valmarana "ai Nani"** – go back down the hill, head along Via M. D'Azeglio for 100m, then turn right into the cobbled Via S. Bastiano, which ends at the villa. This is an undistinguished house made extraordinary by the decorations of Giambattista and Giandomenico Tiepolo. *Nani*, by the way, means "dwarfs", the significance of which becomes clear when you see the garden wall.

There are two parts to the house: the **Palazzina**, containing six rooms frescoed with typical virtuosity by Giambattista (you're handed a brief guide to the paintings at the entrance); and the **Foresteria**, one room of which is frescoed by Giambattista and six by Giandomenico, whose predilections are a little less heroic than his father's.

You can fortify yourself at the old coach house to the left of the entrance, which has been turned into a **café** (Tues–Sun 11am–2pm & 4–6pm).

La Rotonda

Via della Rotonda 45 • Villa open mid-March to early Nov Wed & Sat 10am–noon & 3–6pm; grounds also open Tues–Sun same hours, all year round • €10 for both villa and grounds, €5 for grounds only

From Villa Valmarana the narrow Strada Valmarana descends the slope to one of Europe's most imitated buildings – Palladio's Villa Capra, known as **La Rotonda**. La Rotonda is unique among Palladio's villas in that it was designed not as the main building of a farm but as a pavilion in which entertainments could be held and the landscape enjoyed. Only a walk round the lavishly decorated rooms will fully reveal the subtleties of the Rotonda's design, which gives a strong impression of being as symmetrical as a square while in fact having a definite main axis. Unless you're an architecture student and really want to scrutinize the walls from point-blank range, the garden can be given a miss, as it's just a narrow belt of grass and gravel.

ARRIVAL AND INFORMATION | VICENZA

By train The station is a 10min walk southwest of the historic centre.

Destinations Castelfranco Veneto (16 daily; 30–40min); Cittadella (15 daily; 25min); Milan (25 daily; 1hr 50min–2hr 40min); Padua (every 20min; 15–30min); Thiene (20 daily; 25min); Treviso (hourly; 45min–1hr 15min); Venice (every 30min; 45min–1hr 20min); Verona (every 30min; 25–60min).

By bus The bus terminus is next to the railway station.

Destinations Bassano (hourly; 1hr); Padua (every 30min; 30min–1hr).

Tourist offices The main tourist office is by the entrance to the Teatro Olimpico, at Piazza Matteotti 12 (daily 9am–1pm & 2–6pm; ☎ 0444 320 854); there's another office at Piazza dei Signori 8 (daily 10am–2pm & 2.30–6.30pm).

ACCOMMODATION

Vicenza is a big conference destination, and many of its **hotels** are stuck out in characterless suburbs, so it pays to be careful where you book. If you want to stay in the centre, book ahead, especially during the conference periods – January, May and September. Note also that some places close in August.

Casa San Raffaele Viale X Giugno 10 ☎ 0444 545 767, ⊛ albergosanraffaele.it. This pleasant two-star is the cheapest hotel within reach of the centre, but it's half an hour's walk out from it, lying just below the basilica on Monte Bérico. Some rooms have superb views northwards across to the mountains. **€65**

★ **Due Mori** Contrà Do Rode 26 ☎ 0444 321 886, ⊛ hotelduemori.com. Friendly hotel by the Piazza dei Signori – it's only a two-star but feels better than that. Rooms are capacious (especially those in the annexe, across the road),

and have pleasant Art Nouveau-style furniture. Rooms in the main hotel have no television and are €15 cheaper; the three without en-suite bathrooms are cheaper still. **€125**

Palladio Contrà Oratorio dei Servi 27 ☎ 0444 325 347, ⊛ hotel-palladio.it. Friendly, sleek four-star hotel in a quiet street just off the central square. Its 23 rooms have minimalist modern furnishings, including comfortable Japanese mattresses and wall radiators that look like abstract paintings. Room 302 at the top has the largest balcony. **€170**

EATING AND DRINKING

Vicenza is not the liveliest of the Veneto's towns, but it has a pleasant buzz in the evening, as the populace gathers in the Piazza dei Signori or just saunters up and down the Corso Palladio, where there are plenty of **bars** and **cafés**. While there are few **restaurants** in the centre, standards are high, which means you'll need to book or get there early. You should also remember that many places close their kitchens by 11pm – and many shut up shop altogether in August. Popular specialities include *baccalà alla Vicentina* (dried cod in milk and oil) and *sopressa*, a kind of salami, generally eaten with a slice of grilled polenta.

CAFÉS AND GELATERIE

★ **Gelateria Arancia e Cannella** Piazza delle Biade 18. Possibly the best ice creams in town: winning combinations include cinnamon and orange, of course, given the shop's name. Daily 10am–10pm.

Sorarù Piazzetta Andrea Palladio 17. Picturesque old-world *pasticceria-café* in the shadow of the basilica. You can have a coffee and cake inside at the bar or at its outdoor tables, next to the statue of Palladio. 7.30am–12.30pm & 4–7.30pm; closed Wed.

Tutto Gelato Contrà Frasche del Gambero 26 ☎ 0444 545 378. A highly rated *gelateria* with an enormous selection. It's renowned for its mascarpone-and-hazelnut flavour. Tues–Sun: mid-April to Oct 10am–11.30pm; Nov to mid-April 10am–8.30pm.

RESTAURANTS

Antica Casa della Malvasia Contrà delle Morette 5 ☎ 0444 543 704. This bustling, roomy inn just off Piazza dei Signori is a popular budget choice, with a cheap lunchtime menu (*primi* €4, *secondi* €5.50) and a lively *enoteca* next door. Tues–Sun noon–2.30pm & 7–11pm.

★ **Antico Guelfo** Contrà Pedemuro S. Biagio 92 ☎ 0444 547 897, ⊛ anticoguelfo.it. Superb gourmet fare: Francesco, the chef, is an expert in gluten-free cuisine and uses a variety of grains in his inventive dishes,

such as the buckwheat pancakes with cheese and honey (a heavenly starter). Mon–Sat 7–11pm.

Julien Contrà Jacopo Cabianca 13 ☎ 0444 326 168. A lively modern restaurant-bar, located off Piazza Matteotti. The menu has interesting combinations such as black ravioli with fish and ginger, and the clientele ranges from cool young *aperitivi*-sippers to families having a meal with their children. Live music on Thurs. Mon–Sat 10.30am–3pm & 5pm–1/2am (kitchen opens 7.30pm).

Righetti Piazza Duomo 3 ☎ 0444 543 135. Cosier than your average self-service restaurant and a firm favourite with locals, *Righetti* is a model of honest pricing – a substantial meal here will set you back just €10–15. Mon–Fri noon–2.30pm & 7pm–midnight, Fri closes 1am.

BARS

Al Campanile Contrà Fontana 2. This traditional *enoteca* occupies a locale that's been a bar for three hundred years; it serves a wide range of wines, and sandwiches to mop up the alcohol. Daily 8am–10pm.

★ **Al Canceeto** Stradella dei Tre Scalini 5. The barrels outside are the only clue to the presence of this popular *osteria* with an unpretentious retro feel. The music is good and it serves *pizzette* and sandwiches. Mon–Thurs 7am–2.30pm & 4–9pm, till midnight Fri & Sat.

FROM TOP VIEW OF SAN MARCO VENICE (P.351); SANTI GIOVANNI E PAOLO, VENICE (P.375) >

★ **Il Grottino** Piazza dell'Erbe 2. Atmospheric, dimly lit cellar bar beneath the basilica, with tables spilling out on to the pavement. It is the bar of choice at *aperitivo* hour, with an extensive Spritz menu, a good range of wines and some snacks – but no coffee; there's also music. 5pm–1.30am; closed Tues.

Verona

With its wealth of Roman sites and streets of pink-hued medieval buildings, the easy-going city of **VERONA** has more in the way of sights than any other place in the Veneto except Venice itself. It is Shakespeare who brings most people here: the city was the setting for *Romeo and Juliet*, and many people come to see the scene of their great, but fictional, romance. It also hosts one of the major cultural events in the region, when the Roman Arena becomes a magical setting for an outdoor opera festival (see p.421). Unlike Venice, though, Verona is not dependent on the tourist industry, and its economic success is largely due to its position at the crossing of the major routes from Germany and Austria to central Italy and from the west to Venice and Trieste. The spending power of its citizens contributes to a vivacious street-life – one of Verona's most appealing assets.

Brief history

Verona's initial development as a **Roman** settlement was similarly due to its straddling the main lines of communication. A period of decline after the disintegration of the Roman Empire was followed by revival under the Ostrogoths, who in turn were succeeded by the Franks. By the twelfth century Verona had become a city-state, and in the following century approached the zenith of its independent existence with the rise of the Scaligers. The ruthless Scaligers were at the same time energetic patrons of the arts, and many of Verona's finest buildings date from their rule.

With the fall of their dynasty a time of upheaval ensued, Gian Galeazzo Visconti of Milan emerging in control of the city. Absorption into the Venetian Empire came in 1405, and Verona was governed from Venice until the arrival of Napoleon. Verona's history thereafter shadowed that of Venice.

The old centre

Coming from the train station, you pass Verona's south gate, the **Porta Nuova**, and come onto the long Corso Porta Nuova, which ends at the battlemented arches that precede the **Piazza Brà**. Here stands the mightiest of Verona's Roman monuments, the **Arena**, marking the edge of the old city that nestles in the bend of the River Adige and is crisscrossed by a neat grid of streets around the old Roman forum.

The Arena

Piazza Brà · Mon 1.30–7.30pm, Tues–Sun 9am–7.30pm, but closes 3.30pm during the opera season in July & Aug · €6, or Verona Card; €1 on first Sun of the month Oct–May

Dating from the first century AD, the **Arena** has survived in remarkable condition, despite the twelfth-century earthquake that destroyed all but four of the arches of the

---

THE *BIGLIETTO UNICO* AND VERONACARD

A **biglietto unico**, costing €5, allows one visit each to San Zeno, the Duomo, Sant'Anastasia and San Fermo. The ticket can be bought at any of these churches, which individually charge €2.50 for admission (ⓦ chieseverona.it). If you're planning to be very busy, it might be worth getting the **VeronaCard** (ⓦ veronacard.it), which gives access to all the sights listed above, plus the Arena, the Torre dei Lamberti, the Castelvecchio, the Casa di Giulietta, the Tomba di Giulietta, the Roman Theatre and the Museo Archeologico, as well as free travel on city buses. The two-day ticket costs €15, the five-day €20. You can buy it at *tabacchi*, tourist offices and at the museums and monuments, too, though sometimes they run out of stock. Note that many museums are closed on Monday mornings, and most ticket offices shut 30–45 minutes before the official closing time.

outer wall. The interior was scarcely damaged by the tremor, and where once crowds of around 20,000 packed the benches for gladiatorial contests, nowadays audiences come to watch gargantuan opera productions (see p.421). Originally measuring 152m by 123m overall, and thus the third largest of all Roman amphitheatres, the Arena remains an incredible sight – and offers a tremendous urban panorama from the topmost of the 44 pink-marble tiers.

The Casa di Giulietta

Via Cappello 23 • Mon 1.30–7.30pm, Tues–Sun 9am–7.30pm • €6, or €1 on first Sun of the month Oct–May

North of the Arena, **Via Mazzini** is a narrow traffic-free street lined with clothes, shoe and jewellery shops. A left turn at the end leads to the Piazza delle Erbe, while a right takes you into **Via Cappello**, a street named after the family that Shakespeare turned into the Capulets – and on the left, at no. 23, is the **Casa di Giulietta**. In fact, although the "Capulets" and the "Montagues" (Montecchi) did exist, Romeo and Juliet were entirely fictional creations. The house itself, constructed at the start of the fourteenth century, is in a fine state of preservation, but is largely empty, save for the occasional exhibition. More compelling are the walls at the entrance to the courtyard, every inch graffitied with amorous messages and plastered with love notes.

San Fermo

March–Oct Mon–Sat 10am–6pm, Sun 1–6pm; Nov–Feb Tues–Sat 10am–1pm & 1.30–5pm, Sun 1–5pm • €2.50, or *biglietto unico*/VeronaCard – see box, p.414

Via Cappello leads into Via Leoni with its Roman gate, the **Porta Leona**, and a segment of excavated Roman street, exposed 3m below today's street level. At the end of Via Leoni rises the red-brick **San Fermo** church, whose inconsistent exterior betrays the fact that it consists of two churches combined. Flooding forced the Benedictines to superimpose a second church on the one founded in the eighth century. The Romanesque lower church, entered from the left of the choir, has impressive low vaulting, sometimes obscured by exhibitions.

Piazza delle Erbe

Originally a major Roman crossroads and the site of the forum, **Piazza delle Erbe**, at the northern end of Via Cappello, is still the heart of the city. As the name suggests, the market used to sell mainly vegetables, but nowadays it has been largely taken over by ugly, semi-permanent booths selling clothes, souvenirs, antiques and fast food. The rich variety of buildings framing the square is far more attractive. Most striking are the **Domus Mercatorum** (on the left as you come from Via Cappello), which was founded in 1301 as a merchants' warehouse and exchange, the fourteenth-century **Torre del Gardello** and, to the right of the tower, the **Casa Mazzanti**, whose sixteenth-century murals are best seen after dark, under enhancing spotlights.

Piazza dei Signori

The **Piazza dei Signori** used to be the chief public square of Verona. Facing you as you come into the square is the medieval **Palazzo degli Scaligeri**, residence of the Scaligers; extending from it at a right angle is the fifteenth-century **Loggia del Consiglio**, the former assembly hall of the city council and Verona's outstanding early-Renaissance building. The rank of Roman notables along the roof includes Verona's most illustrious native poet, Catullus. For a dizzying view of the city, take a sharp right as soon as you come into the square, and go up the twelfth-century **Torre dei Lamberti** (daily 8.30am–7.30pm; €6 or VeronaCard, plus €1 for the lift). There are 368 steps, but a lift whisks you two-thirds of the way to the top.

The Scaligeri tombs

Passing under the arch linking the Palazzo degli Scaligeri to the Palazzo del Capitano, you come to the little Romanesque church of Santa Maria Antica, in front of which are ranged the **Arche Scaligeri**, some of the most elaborate Gothic funerary monuments in Italy: the tombs are currently closed for restoration, but are partly visible from the street. Over the side entrance to the church, an equestrian statue of **Cangrande I** ("Big Dog"; died 1329) gawps down from his tomb's pyramidal roof; the statue is a copy, the original being displayed in the Castelvecchio. The canopied tombs of the rest of the clan are enclosed within a wrought-iron palisade decorated with ladder motifs, the emblem of the Scaligers.

Mastino I ("Mastiff"; died 1277), founder of the dynasty, is buried in the simple tomb against the wall of the church; Mastino II (died 1351) is to the left of the entrance, opposite the most florid of the tombs, that of **Cansignorio** ("Top Dog"; died 1375).

Sant'Anastasia

Piazza Sant'Anastasia • March–Oct Mon–Sat 9am–6pm, Sun 1–6pm; Nov–Feb Tues–Sat 10am–1pm & 1–5pm, Sun 1–5pm • €2.50, or biglietto unico/VeronaCard

Going on past the Arche Scaligeri, and turning left along Via San Pietro, you come to **Sant'Anastasia**, Verona's largest church. Started in 1290 and completed in 1481, it's mainly Gothic in style, with undertones of the Romanesque. The fourteenth-century carvings of New Testament scenes around the doors are the most arresting feature of its bare exterior; the interior's highlight is Pisanello's delicately coloured fresco *St George and the Princess* (high above the chapel to the right of the altar), a work in which the normally martial saint appears as something of a dandy.

San Pietro Martire

Piazza Sant'Anastasia • Wed–Fri 2–6pm, Sat & Sun 10am–noon & 2–6pm • Free

On one side of the little piazza fronting Sant'Anastasia stands **San Pietro Martire**, deconsecrated since its ransacking by Napoleon. The highlight of the small interior is the vast lunette fresco from the sixteenth century on the east wall. Easily the strangest picture in Verona, it's an allegorical account of the Virgin's Assumption, though the bizarre collection of animals appears to have little connection with a bemused-looking Madonna.

The Duomo

Piazza del Duomo • March–Oct Mon–Sat 10am–5.30pm, Sun 1.30–5.30pm; Nov–Feb Tues–Sat 10am–1pm & 1.30–4pm, Sun 1.30–5pm • €2.50, or biglietto unico/VeronaCard

Verona's red-and-white-striped **Duomo** lies just round the river's bend, past the Roman Ponte Pietra. Consecrated in 1187, it's Romanesque in its lower parts, developing into Gothic as it goes up; the two doorways are twelfth century – look for the story of Jonah and the whale on the south porch, and the statues of Roland and Oliver, two of Charlemagne's paladins, on the west. In the first chapel on the left, an *Assumption* by Titian occupies an architectural frame by Sansovino, who also designed the choir.

The Porta Borsari

After the Arena and the Teatro Romano, Verona's most impressive Roman remnant is the **Porta Borsari** (on the junction of Via Diaz and Corso Porta Borsari), a structure that was as great an influence on the city's Renaissance architects as the amphitheatre. This was Verona's largest Roman gate; the inscription dates it at 265 AD, but it's almost certainly older than that.

Corso Cavour

Heading on from Porta Borsari down the busy thoroughfare of **Corso Cavour** you pass the small twelfth-century **San Lorenzo** at no. 28 (Mon–Sat 9am–noon & 3–5pm, Sun 3–6pm; free) before coming to the **Arco dei Gavi**, a first-century Roman triumphal arch that was rebuilt in 1930 as Napoleon's troops tore down the original. This is your best vantage point from which to admire the **Ponte Scaligero**, built by Cangrande II between 1355 and 1375. The retreating German army blew up the bridge in 1945, but the salvaged material was used for its reconstruction.

The Castelvecchio

Corso Castelvecchio 2 • Mon 1.30–7.30pm, Tues–Sun 8.30am–7.30pm • €6, or VeronaCard; €1 on first Sun of the month Oct–May

The fortress from which the bridge springs, the **Castelvecchio**, was commissioned by Cangrande II at around the same time and became the stronghold for Verona's subsequent rulers. Opened as the city museum in 1925, it was damaged by bombing

6

during World War II. The equestrian figure Cangrande I, removed from his tomb, is strikingly displayed on an outdoor pedestal; his expression is disconcerting at close range, the simpleton's grin being difficult to reconcile with the image of the ruthless warlord. Outstanding among paintings are two works by Jacopo Bellini, two Madonnas by Giovanni Bellini, another Madonna by Pisanello, Veronese's *Descent from the Cross*, a Tintoretto *Nativity*, a Lotto portrait and works by Giambattista and Giandomenico Tiepolo. The real joy of the museum, however, is in wandering round the medieval pieces: beautiful sculpture and frescoes by the often nameless artists of the late Middle Ages.

San Zeno Maggiore

Piazza San Zeno • March–Oct Mon–Sat 8.30am–6pm, Sun 1–6pm; Nov–Feb Tues–Sat 10am–1pm & 1.30–5pm, Sun 1–5pm • €2.50, or *biglietto unico*/VeronaCard

A little over 1km northwest of the Castelvecchio is the **Basilica di San Zeno Maggiore**, one of the most significant Romanesque churches in northern Italy. A church was founded here, above the tomb of the city's patron saint, as early as the fifth century, but the present building and its campanile were put up in the first half of the twelfth century, with additions continuing up to the end of the fourteenth. Its large rose window, representing the Wheel of Fortune, dates from the early twelfth century, as does the magnificent portal, whose lintels bear relief sculptures representing the months – look also for St Zeno trampling the devil. Extraordinary bronze panels on the doors depict scenes from the Bible and the *Miracles of San Zeno*, their style influenced by Byzantine art; most of those on the left are from around 1100, and most of the right-hand panels date from a century or so later. Inside the lofty interior the most compelling image is the high altar's luminous *Madonna and Saints* by Mantegna.

Across the Adige

On the far side of the river, the Veronetta district has a more spacious feel, but it has its share of Verona's finest sights, including Roman remains, fascinating churches and the tranquillity of the Giardino Giusti.

San Giorgio in Braida

Lungadige San Giorgio 6 • Daily 7.30–11am & 5–7pm • Free

On the other side of Ponte Garibaldi, and right along the embankments or through the public gardens, is **San Giorgio in Braida**, in terms of its works of art the richest of Verona's churches. A *Baptism* by Tintoretto hangs over the door, while the main altar, designed by Sanmicheli, incorporates a marvellous piece by Paolo Veronese – *The Martyrdom of St George*.

Santo Stefano

Via Scaletta Santo Stefano 2 • Daily 9am–noon & 4–6pm, but closed Tues afternoon • Free

It's a short walk along the embankment from San Giorgio to the delightful Romanesque **Santo Stefano**. One of the city's oldest churches, it was founded in the fifth century but gained its present shape in the twelfth; later additions include sixteenth-century frescoes and incongruous Baroque chapels.

Teatro Romano and Museo Archeologico

Regaste Redentore 2 • Mon 1.30–7.30pm, Tues–Sun 8.30am–7.30pm • €4.50, or VeronaCard; €1 on first Sun of the month Oct–May

Walking along the river past the Ponte Pietra, you come to the first-century-BC **Teatro Romano**; much restored, the theatre is used for concerts and plays (see p.421). High above it, and reached by a lift, the **Museo Archeologico** occupies the buildings of an old convent. Its well-arranged collection features a number of Greek, Roman and Etruscan finds, including a magnificent Roman bronze head; from the old frescoed chapel at the top the views are magnificent.

Santa Maria in Organo

Piazzetta Santa Maria in Organo 1 • Daily 8am–noon & 2.30–6pm • Free

In the heart of the **Veronetta** district stands the church of **Santa Maria in Organo**, which possesses what Vasari praised as the finest choir stall in Italy. Dating from the 1490s, this marquetry was the work of a Benedictine monk, one Fra Giovanni, and is astonishing in its precision and use of perspective. There's more of his work in the sacristy, while in the crypt you can see reused upside-down Roman columns.

Giardino Giusti

Via Giardino Giusti 2 • Daily: April–Sept 9am–8pm; Oct–March 9am–sunset • €6

Close to Santa Maria in Organo you'll find one of the finest formal gardens in the country, the **Giardino Giusti**, entered from the street that bears its name. Created in the 1570s by Count Agostino Giusti,the garden has faced an uncertain future for the past few years, since ownership passed to no fewer than twenty different members of the Giusti family, following the death of the diplomat Justo Giusti. After feuding between some of the heirs, the whole estate – the grounds plus the splendid Palazzo Giusti (which is not open to the public) – has been put up for sale. Rumour has it that it will become a luxury hotel or even a casino, but for the time being the garden's fountains and shaded corners continue to provide the city's most pleasant refuge from the streets, as they have done for centuries – Goethe and Mozart both paid a visit, and were much impressed.

ARRIVAL AND GETTING AROUND   VERONA

By plane Verona's Valerio Catullo airport is at Villafranca, 12km away; regular ATV buses (every 20min 7am–11.30pm; €6) head to the Porta Nuova train station, near the city centre.

By train From the main train station (Verona Porta Nuova) it's a 15min walk to Piazza Brà.
Destinations Milan (every 30min; 1hr 20min–2hr); Padua (every 30min; 45min–1hr 20min); Venice (every 30min; 1hr 10min–2hr 20min); Vicenza (every 30min; 25–60min).

By bus Local buses leave from the stands outside the train station. Tickets can be bought before boarding for €1.10 from

the machines alongside bay A or from the *tabacchi* inside the train station ticket hall, or for €1.50 on board; alternatively, you can get ten rides for €10 or a day-pass for €3.50.

By car There are well-signed car parks just before Piazza Brà and at Piazza Isolo in Veronetta, or there is free parking across the river, beyond Santo Stefano.

By bike You can rent bikes from Zanchi, Corso Cavour 13/A, near the Porta Borsari (☎045 800 5681 ⓦciclizanchi .it; Mon 3.30–7.30pm, Tues–Sat 9am–12.30pm & 3.30–7.30pm; €5/hr, €1/hr thereafter).

INFORMATION

Tourist information The tourist office is by Piazza Brà, tucked into the old town walls at Via degli Alpini 6, just beyond the Palazzo del Municipale (Mon–Sat 9am–7pm, Sun

10am–4pm; ☎045 806 8680, ⓦtourism.verona.it). As well as providing information, it organizes walking tours, runs a hotel-booking service and can book tickets for the Arena.

ACCOMMODATION

Peak periods for Verona's hotel prices include the opera season (late June to early Sept) and the numerous trade fairs in the autumn. Whatever time of year you're coming, reserve your room well in advance. The tourist office also runs a hotel-booking service.

Antica Porta Leona Via Corticella Leoni 3 ☎045 595 499, ⓦanticaportaleona.com. This very elegant hotel offers tasteful standard rooms as well as five opera-themed suites, such as the dramatic Tosca, with floor-sweeping red drapes. There's also a swimming pool, spa and restaurant. **€350**

Arena Stradone Porta Palio 2 ☎045 803 2440, ⓦalbergoarena.it. Small one-star next to Castelvecchio (not as close to the Arena as its name might suggest), where the new management has carried out some much-needed improvements to the breakfast room, bathrooms and overall furnishings. **€110**

Aurora Piazza delle Erbe ☎045 594 717, ⓦhotelaurora .biz. A complete renovation in 2012 upgraded this hotel to a three-star: all nineteen rooms now have steam showers, for example. Many rooms have a view of the Piazza delle Erbe, and the staff are welcoming and knowledgeable. An excellent buffet breakfast is served on a terrace overlooking the square. **€200**

Ostello della Gioventù Salita Fontana del Ferro 15 ☎045 590 360, ⓦostelloverona.it; bus #73, or #91 after 7.45pm and on Sun, from the station to Piazza Isolo. The official HI hostel is in the lovely setting of sixteenth-century

6

Villa Francescatti. It has 241 beds, including some family rooms (bunk beds only); some rooms have frescoed ceilings, others a private terrace; many have splendid views over the rooftops. The midnight curfew is extended for guests with opera tickets. Dinner is available for €8. Dorms **€18**, family rooms **€20** per person

Palazzo Victoria Via Adua 8 ☎ 045 590 566, ⓦ palazzovictoria.com. Superb four-star by the Porta Borsari that has been transformed by its new owners. The hotel is made up of three old buildings linked by a modern foyer – but even here, Roman remains are on display. In the well-equipped rooms medieval reliefs, stones and frescoes abound – if you want to treat yourself, the junior suite, with its ceiling fresco and parquet flooring, is fabulous. Good special offers out of season. **€400**

Protezione della Giovane Via Pigna 7 ☎ 045 596 880, ⓦ protezionedellagiovane.it. Spartan but friendly convent-run hostel for women, with an 11pm curfew, although there is some flexibility for guests with opera tickets. Dorms **€22** doubles **€27** per person (**€30** in July & Aug)

★ **Torcolo** Vicolo Listone 3 ☎ 045 800 7512, ⓦ hotel torcolo.it. An extremely welcoming two-star hotel within 100m of the Arena, just off Piazza Brà. It's run by two sisters who have been in the business for more than thirty years, and is a favourite with the opera crowds, so book ahead. **€140**

CAMPING

Campeggio Castel San Pietro Via Castel S. Pietro 2 ☎ 045 592 037, ⓦ campingcastelsanpietro.com; bus #41 or #95 from the station to Via Marsala and then a steep walk up the hill. This pleasant shady site out by the old city walls, the only place to camp near the centre of Verona, offers marvellous views over the city. Open May–Sept. Pitches **€24**

EATING AND DRINKING

The Veronesi have a reputation for liking their food – one thirteenth-century story tells of the defenders of a castle opening their gates when they heard that the besiegers were cooking *baccalà*, dried cod. You can certainly eat well in the city: if the local speciality of horsemeat is not to your taste you can try the local salamis, pumpkin ravioli or *bigoli*, a handmade, thicker version of spaghetti. The best **restaurants** in Verona tend to be packed after 9pm, so book beforehand or go out early. In the week before and after the Arena season (July and Aug) you may find places close early or shut completely as the city takes a rest. For a **drink**, head to one of the city's numerous **osterie**, traditionally old-fashioned bars with wine served by the glass for as little as €1, accompanied by delicious *bocconcini* (savoury tartlets and panini). In recent years, the *osteria* label has been appropriated by smarter restaurants, and now just as often applies to more modern – and pricier – establishments.

CAFÉS AND GELATERIE

Caffè Coloniale Piazzetta Viviani 14/C. Good cakes, light meals and the best hot chocolate in the city, in a mock-colonial setting with an attractive outdoor terrace. Daily 7.45am–midnight.

Caffè Monte Baldo Via Rosa 12 ☎ 045 803 0579. Hugely popular in the early evening for drinks, and renowned for its delicious *bocconcini*, this bottle-lined *osteria* also has a small menu of simple pasta dishes and main courses for €5–9. Tues–Sun 10am–3pm & 5–10pm.

Gelateria Artigianale Ponte Pietra Via Ponte Pietra 23. The best ice cream in the city is served at this friendly *gelateria* by the Roman bridge. The orange-and-cinnamon and *Sachertorte* flavours are specialities. Daily 2–11pm, until 7.30pm in spring; closed Nov–Feb.

RESTAURANTS

★ **Alla Colonna** Largo Pescheria Vecchia 4 ☎ 045 596 718. This place is usually packed with savvy locals – the food is simple, superb, the portions large and the prices excellent (€14 menu). Mon–Sat noon–3.30pm (kitchen closes 2.30pm) & 7pm–2am (kitchen closes 11.30pm).

Bella Napoli Via Marconi 14. Serves the best pizza in Verona – and the largest, with half a metre of pizza for €14 – in a distinctly Neapolitan atmosphere. A second branch over the road at no. 11 is more modern, serving restaurant food.

Daily noon–2.30pm & 6.30pm–1am, Fri & Sat till 2.30am.

★ **Osteria a la Carega** Via Cadrega 8 ☎ 045 806 9248, ⓦ osterialacarega.com. Friendly, small *osteria* with a few outside tables in the side yard. A fine selection of wines, plus excellent *piadine* (flatbread), huge salads, light lunches and bar snacks. Has jazz and other live music on Thurs. Mon 10am–midnight, Tues–Sun 10am–2am.

★ **Osteria al Duomo** Via Duomo 7/A ☎ 045 800 7333. There has been a bar here for at least a century, and the current owners have made few concessions to modern fashion – it still serves old Veronese favourites such as *bigoli* with a donkey sauce (*sugo d'asino*; €8) and horse stew (*pastissada*; €15). The decor – a miscellany of musical instruments – is one of the quirkiest in the city, and the hosts, now well into their second decade here, are terrific. Mon–Sat 11am–3pm & 7pm–midnight (kitchen closes 10.30pm).

Osteria del Bugiardo Corso Porta Borsari 17/A ☎ 045 591 869. Small establishment with an excellent range of antipasti and *crostini*, as well as some *primi* and *secondi*. Its high tables are packed at lunchtime with locals grabbing a quick meal. Daily 11am–11pm.

★ **Osteria Sottoriva** Via Sottoriva 9. Verona's traditional *osterie* don't come much more authentic than this: it's rumbustious, full of locals, and serves delicious local specialities – on the bar you'll see horse *polpette* and

VERONA'S FESTIVALS AND EVENTS

Opera festival The city's opera festival, held in the Arena during July and August, has been a major draw since 1913, always featuring a no-expense-spared production of *Aida*. Tickets range from around €20 for a seat high up on the terraces to €200 for the best, and can be bought from the ticket office at Via Dietro Anfiteatro, at the tourist office, or by phone or online (☎045 800 5151, ⓦarena.it).

Carnevale One of the most enjoyable days in the calendar is Verona's Carnevale. On the Friday before Shrove Tuesday, a huge procession winds through the centre from Piazza Brà. This is a local event with none of the masks and posing of Venice – just lots of people dressing up, loud music and confetti – though mind the kids who get carried away spraying white foam everywhere. The procession is led by a large character called the Papa del Gnocco – most of the city's restaurants serve gnocchi on that Friday.

Vinitaly As the Veneto produces more DOC wine than any other region in Italy, it's not surprising that Italy's main wine fair, Vinitaly (ⓦvinitaly.com), is held in Verona. It takes place in April and offers abundant sampling opportunities; day-tickets cost about €50, less if you book online.

6

hicken wings (ask the staff to explain the Veronese slang name), all at very reasonable prices. In summer you can enjoy the atmosphere at the tables outside under the arches. No reservations. 10.30am–10.30pm; closed Wed.

Trattoria alla Pigna Via Pigna 4 ☎045 800 4080, ⓦosteriapigna.it. This elegant restaurant has a well-deserved reputation among locals and tourists alike, and serves traditional dishes such as stewed horsemeat in polenta (€12) and risotto *all'Amarone*, braised in the local wine (€12). Tues–Sun 12.30–2.30pm & 7pm–2am.

Tre Marchetti "Da Barca" Vicolo Tre Marchetti 19/B ☎045 803 0463. A couple of steps north of the Arena, this family-run place is perfect for a pre- or post-opera meal of Veronese specialities, such as *bigoli* pasta or veal braised in Amarone. It's very refined, and unsurprisingly pricey, given its location. Booking essential. Mon–Sat 9.30am–3pm & 5pm–midnight; July & Aug closed Mon.

BARS

Al Carro Armato Vicolo Gatto 2/A. One of the most atmospheric *osterie* in the city, with a counter full of delicious antipasti for you to choose from, such as *polpette* (meatballs) and *sfilacci* (fine slices of horse). Tues–Sun 11am–3pm & 6pm–1am (kitchen closes 10.30pm), till midnight Sun.

Cappa Café Piazzetta Brà Molinari 1/A. Lying just down from the Roman bridge, this bar's winning feature is its riverfront terrace, though it can get very crammed. July–Sept 9am–2am; Oct–June 7.30am–2am.

Osteria Le Vecete Via Pellicciai 32 ☎045 594 748. Atmospheric *osteria* with a delicious selection of *bocconcini*, and a good menu too (*secondi* €15–20). Its wine list is excellent, ranging from cheap to very expensive. Booking advised for dinner at weekends. Mon–Fri 10.30am–12.30am, Sat 10.30am–1.30am, Sun 11.30am–12.30am.

Rivamancina Vicolo Quadrelli 1, Veronetta ☎349 066 0174, ⓦrivamancina.com. New management has given a boost to this bar, near the Ponte Nuovo on the far side of the Adige. It is proud of its cocktails and it has live music on alternate Fridays. Tues–Sun 8pm–2am.

ENTERTAINMENT

Music and **theatre** are the dominant art forms in the cultural life of Verona. Verona's **club** scene is much livelier than in Venice, but most venues are outside the centre. The *Spettacoli* section of *L'Arena* (there's a copy in every bar) is a good source of information on what's happening (in Italian only). The city's major arts venues are listed below.

Arena Piazza Brà ⓦarena.it. The grand Roman venue is still busy two thousand years on: as well as the summer opera festival, big rock events also crop up on the Arena's calendar. If you are on the cheaper seats on the stone steps, it is worth taking a cushion with you, or renting one there. For booking details see box above.

Teatro Filarmonico Via Dei Mutilati 4 ⓦarena.it. When Verona's opera isn't at the Arena, it moves to this grand old theatre just outside the Porta Brà.

Teatro Nuovo Piazza Viviani 10 ⓦteatrostabileverona .it. Plays and classical music.

Teatro Ristori Via Teatro Ristori 7 ⓦteatroristori.org. This newly restored venue presents music and dance.

Teatro Romano Regaste Redentore 2. A season of ballet and of Shakespeare and other dramatists in Italian is the principal summer fare here. Some events are free; for the rest, if you don't mind inferior acoustics park yourself on the steps going up the hill alongside the theatre.

Treviso

One of the overlooked gems of the Veneto, **TREVISO** makes an ideal jumping-off point for the northern Veneto. Treviso was an important town long before its assimilation by Venice in 1389, and plenty of evidence of its early status survives in the form of Gothic churches, public buildings and, most dramatically of all, the paintings of **Tomaso da Modena** (1325–79), the major artist in northern Italy in the years immediately after Giotto's death. The general townscape within Treviso's sixteenth-century walls is appealing too – long porticoes and frescoed house facades give many of the streets an appearance quite distinct from that of other towns in the region – and wandering the maze of backstreets and meandering canals is a pleasant way to while away an hour or two. Treviso was pounded during both world wars and on Good Friday 1944 was half-destroyed in a single bombing raid, but enough survived or was rebuilt to restore the atmosphere of the old streets.

Piazza dei Signori

Piazza dei Signori is the town's focal point, and the scene of a lively evening *passeggiata*. On one side of the piazza stands the early thirteenth-century **Palazzo dei Trecento**, which was badly damaged in the 1944 bombing. It has recently been restored, though as the seat of the city council it's not open to the public. The adjoining **Palazzo del Podestà** is a nineteenth-century concoction. Of more interest are the two churches at the back of the block on Piazza San Vito: **San Vito** and **Santa Lucia** (daily 8am–noon; free). The tiny chapel of Santa Lucia has extensive frescoes by Tomaso da Modena and his followers; San Vito has even older paintings in the alcove through which you enter from Santa Lucia.

The Duomo

Piazza del Duomo • Mon–Sat 8am–noon & 3.30–6pm, Sun 8am–1pm & 3.30–8pm • Free

Stretching from Piazza dei Signori is the narrow main street of the city, **Calmaggiore**, lined with smart boutiques and thronged with window-shoppers throughout the day. It ends at the **Duomo** of Treviso, San Pietro, founded in the twelfth century and much altered in succeeding centuries; it was eventually rebuilt to rectify the damage of 1944. The interior is chiefly notable for its crypt – a thicket of twelfth-century columns with scraps of medieval mosaics – and the Cappella Malchiostro, with fragmentary frescoes by Pordenone and an *Annunciation* by Titian.

The canals

Crisscrossed with **canals**, Treviso markets itself as a "piccola Venezia", and although it can hardly compare with the attractions of its better-endowed neighbour, its tranquil waterways, edged with grassy slopes, weeping willows and waterwheels, have their own low-key charm. A short stroll east of Piazza dei Signori is **Buranelli**, the prettiest of the canals, lined with pastel *palazzi* and crossed with wrought-iron bridges. The nearby **Pescheria** (fish market), sitting on its own islet in the middle of the Canale Cagnan, is one of Treviso's liveliest corners, both day and night; close to the market at Via Palestro 33–35, the **Casa dei Carraresi** hosts big-name international art exhibitions.

Museo di Santa Caterina and around

Piazzetta Mario Botter • Tues–Sun 9am–12.30pm & 2.30–6pm • €3

East of the Pescheria, the deconsecrated church of **Santa Caterina**, now the city **museum**, harbours another brilliant fresco cycle by Tomaso da Modena, *The Story of the Life of Saint Ursula*. Painted for the now-extinct church of Santa Margherita sul Sile, the frescoes were detached from the walls in the late nineteenth century shortly before the church was destroyed and were badly damaged, but have recently been restored. The museum also houses two storeys of local archeological finds, as well as paintings by the likes of Titian and Lorenzo Lotto.

The Basilica di Santa Maria Maggiore

Piazza Santa Maria Maggiore • Daily 8am–noon & 3.30–6pm • Free

The district around Santa Caterina is pleasantly low-key, coming to life on Tuesday and Saturday mornings with the hubbub of the stalls around the **market**, stretching from Piazza Matteotti to Borgo Mazzini and along the city walls to Viale Burchiellati. To the south stands the **Basilica di Santa Maria Maggiore**, which houses the most venerated image in Treviso, a fresco of the Madonna originally painted by Tomaso but subsequently retouched.

San Nicolò

Mon–Fri 8am–noon & 3.30–6pm • Free

West of the centre, just over the River Sile from the railway station, is the severe Dominican church of **San Nicolò**, which has frescoes dating from the thirteenth to the sixteenth centuries. Some of the columns are decorated with paintings by Tomaso da Modena and his school, of which the best are *Sts Jerome and Agnes* (by Tomaso) on the first column on your right as you enter.

The Seminario

Piazzetta Benedetto XI 2 • Daily: summer 8am–6pm; winter 8am–5.30pm • Free

For a comprehensive demonstration of Tomaso da Modena's talents you have to visit the neighbouring **Seminario**, where the chapterhouse (*sala del capitolo*), to the left as you enter (you may need to ring the bell to get in), is decorated with forty *Portraits of Members of the Dominican Order*, painted in 1352. Each shows a friar at study in his cell, but there is never a hint of the formulaic: one man is shown sharpening a quill, another checks a text through a magnifier, a third blows the surplus ink from his nib, a fourth scowls as if you've interrupted his work.

ARRIVAL AND INFORMATION
TREVISO

By plane See p.384 for arriving at Treviso's airport.

By train Arriving at the train station on Piazza Duca d'Aosta, head straight across the bridge, bending slightly left at the first roundabout to reach the centre.
Destinations Castelfranco Veneto (15 daily; 25min); Cittadella (13 daily; 35min); Conegliano (every 30min; 15–25min); Udine (every 40min; 1hr 10min–1hr 40min); Venice (every 20min; 35min); Vicenza (13 daily; 1hr 10min).

By bus Treviso's bus station is on Lungosile Antonio Mattei, up the road towards the centre from the train station.

Destinations Asolo (10 daily; 1hr); Bassano (hourly; 1hr 30min); Castelfranco (every 30min; 50min); Conegliano (every 30min; 45min); Padua (every 30min, hourly at weekends; 1hr 10min); Venice (every 30min, hourly at weekends; 55min); Vittorio Veneto (every 30min; 1hr 15min).

Tourist office Across the road from the train station, on Piazza Duca d'Aosta (daily 9am–1pm & 2–6pm; **☏**0422 547 632, **w**visittreviso.it or **w**turismo.provincia.treviso.it). Dispenses useful leaflets on Treviso and its province and a full list of the growing number of B&Bs.

ACCOMMODATION

Il Focolare Piazza Ancilotto 4 **☏**0422 56601, **w**albergoilfocolare.net. Recently refurbished in chintzy, country-house style, three-star *Il Focolare* enjoys an excellent central location, just steps from Piazza dei Signori. No lift. **€150**

★ **Locanda San Tomaso** Viale Burchiellati 5 **☏**0422 541 550 or **☏**346 951 3652, **w**locandasantomaso.it. The six rooms of this charming, family-run B&B have been decorated with painstaking attention to detail. Some have stencilled walls, others hold family antiques or paintings by

the owner, an artist. Breakfast is taken in the family's trattoria downstairs. **€95**

★ **Maison Matilda** Via Jacopo Riccati 44 **☏**0422 582 212, **w**maisonmatilda.com. An ultra-luxurious bolt-hole just round the corner from the Duomo, with five elegantly furnished rooms and one suite. Roll-top baths, antique furnishings and floor-sweeping drapes give it an opulent feel, and the sumptuous breakfast can be served at any hour of the day. No lift. **€240**

EATING, DRINKING AND NIGHTLIFE

Treviso has some excellent **restaurants**, many of which feature radicchio, the bitter red lettuce, and *tiramisù*, which as every local knows was invented here in the 1970s. The **bars** and **cafés** around the Pescheria, particularly along

6

Via Palestro, are always buzzing, and those clustered beneath and around the Palazzo dei Trecento are good for people watching. With a growing university population, Treviso's **nightlife** is on the up, although the most popular places are still chic wine-bars rather than studenty hangouts.

★ **Dai Naneti** Vicolo Brolo 2. Round the corner from the Palazzo Trecento, Beppe and Fabio preside over a small bar that is packed with locals sampling the wine, food and congenial atmosphere. Mon–Fri 9am–2pm & 5–8pm, Sat 9am–1.30pm & 5–8.30pm.

★ **Due Mori** Via Bailo 9 ☎ 0422 540 383, ⓦ trattoria2 mori.com. There's been a hostelry on this site for more than six hundred years. Today's incarnation is a large, bright and friendly restaurant serving good Trevigian cooking at moderate prices; it specializes in fish, and does a superb risotto too. 11.30am–2.45pm & 6.30–11pm; closed Wed.

Due Torri Via Palestro 8 ☎ 0422 541 243. The *Antica Contrada delle Due Torri*, to give it its full name, offers a sophisticated and fresh take on local specialities: the *tagliolini* with courgette flowers and scallops, for example, is exceptional. The brick-lined interior is inviting, and the well-informed staff are attentive. The lunch menu is just €10; in the evening you'll spend closer to €30 a head.

Booking essential. Noon–3pm & 7–11pm; closed Tues.

Muscoli's Via Pescheria 23 ☎ 0422 583 390. A perennially popular *osteria*, where the customers spill out onto the fish market island opposite when the weather permits. The menu is traditional and mainly fishy, with *secondi* at around €10. 7am–3pm & 5pm–2am; closed Wed.

★ **Osteria da Arman** Via Manzoni 27 ☎ 0422 54? 747. Discerning Trevisans flock to this old family-run establishment north of Santa Caterina, near the city walls for its home cooking and convivial atmosphere. It sells its own Prosecco to accompany generous helpings of past (around €7). Mon–Sat 9am–3pm & 4pm–1am.

Toni del Spin Via Inferiore 7 ☎ 0422 543 829 ⓦ ristorantetonidelspin.com. This convivial place ha been winning plaudits for many years. The *garganelli* with rabbit and the lasagne with vegetables are both delicious and the *casatella*, a soft cheese served with rocket and polenta, is superb. Mon 7.30–10.30pm, Tues–Sur 12.30–2.30pm & 7.30–10.30pm.

Castelfranco

CASTELFRANCO VENETO once stood on the western edge of Treviso's territory, and battlemented brick walls the Trevisans threw round the town in 1199 to protect it against the Paduans still encircle most of the old centre (or *castello*). Of all the walled towns of the Veneto, few bear comparison with Castelfranco, and the place would merit a visit on the strength of this alone. But Castelfranco was also the birthplace of **Giorgione** and possesses a painting that single-handedly vindicates Vasari's judgement that Giorgione's place in Venetian art is equivalent to Leonardo da Vinci's in that of Florence.

The Duomo

Piazza San Liberale • Daily 9am–noon & 3.30–6pm • Free

Known simply as the **Castelfranco Madonna**, Giorgione's magnificent *Madonna and Child with Saints* hangs in the eighteenth-century Duomo, in a chapel to the right of the chancel. The left-hand saint is St Francis, but there are several possibilities for the right-hand figure, of which Nicasius and Liberale (patron saint of Castelfranco) are the leading contenders. Giorgione is the most elusive of all the great figures of the Renaissance: only six surviving paintings can indisputably be attributed to him, and so little is known about his life that legends have proliferated to fill the gaps. (There is also a frieze attributed to Giorgione in the neighbouring **Casa Giorgione**, but most of the rooms are strangely empty in this museum, so it's hardly worth the €2.50 entry fee.)

ARRIVAL AND INFORMATION

By train Castelfranco is the major crossroads of the Veneto rail network.
Destinations Belluno (12 daily; 1hr 20min–1hr 40min); Feltre (12 daily; 50min–1hr); Padua (19 daily; 35min); Treviso (10 daily; 25min); Venice (20 daily; 55min); Vicenza

(16 daily; 40min).
Tourist office Via F. M. Preti 66 (Wed & Thurs 9.30am–12.30pm, Fri & Sat 9.30am–12.30pm & 3–6pm; ☎ 0423 491 416).

EATING

★ **Alle Mura** Via Francesco Maria Preti 69 ☎ 0423 498 098, ⓦ ristoranteallemura.com. Seafood is the speciality at Castelfranco's top restaurant, which has a bizarre interior decorated with Polynesian artefacts. It's not a cheap place to eat in the evening, but the €15 lunch menu is excellent value. 12.30–3pm & 7–10.30pm; closed Thurs & 2–3 weeks in Aug.

Bistrò San Giustino Via Francesco Maria Preti 35 ☎ 0423 420 918, ⓦ bistrosangiustino.it. Located right next to the Duomo, this friendly bistro serves excellent pasta and salads, as well as sandwiches and pastries. Lunch menus from €8. Mon–Sat 7am–10pm.

Cittadella

When Treviso turned Castelfranco into a garrison, the Paduans promptly retaliated by reinforcing the defences of **CITTADELLA**, 15km to the west, on the train line to Vicenza. The fortified walls of Cittadella were built in the first quarter of the thirteenth century, and are even more impressive than those of its neighbour. You enter the town through one of four rugged brick gateways; if you're coming from the train station it'll be the Porta Padova, the most daunting of the four, flanked by the **Torre di Malta**. The tower was built as a prison and torture chamber by the monstrous Ezzelino da Romano, known to those he terrorized in this region in the mid-thirteenth century as "The Son of Satan". His atrocities earned him a place in the seventh circle of Dante's *Inferno*, where he's condemned to boil eternally in a river of blood.

Bassano del Grappa

Situated on the River Brenta, **BASSANO** has expanded rapidly over the last few decades, though its historic centre – the area between the Brenta and the train station – remains largely unspoiled. For centuries a major producer of ceramics and wrought iron, Bassano is also renowned for its **grappa** distilleries and its culinary delicacies such as porcini mushrooms, white asparagus and honey. Although it has few outstanding monuments or fine architecture, Bassano's airy situation on the edge of the mountains and the quiet charm of the old streets make it well worth the trip.

Piazza Garibaldi

Heading up from the station, you pass through the city walls on the far side of the orbital Viale delle Fosse and walk down to **Piazza Garibaldi**, one of the two main squares. The piazza is overlooked by the 42m **Torre Civica**, once a lookout tower for the twelfth-century inner walls, now a clock tower with spurious nineteenth-century battlements and windows.

Museo Civico

Piazza Garibaldi 34 · Tues–Sat 9am–6.30pm, Sun 10am–1pm & 3–6pm · €4, or €5 including Palazzo Sturm

On the other side of Piazza Garibaldi the cloister of the fourteenth-century church of San Francesco now houses the **Museo Civico**, devoted to Roman finds and paintings by the da Ponte family (better known as the Bassano family). Jacopo Bassano is the most famous, though his works can be sentimental and derivative; his son Francesco is better represented by some brooding portraits. Don't miss the tucked-away medieval rooms concealing a couple of typically luminous Bartolomeo Vivarini works. Other rooms are devoted to a number of plaster works by Canova and to the great baritone Tito Gobbi, who was born in Bassano.

The Ponte degli Alpini

Walking to the bottom of Piazza Garibaldi and through the adjacent Piazza Libertà, you come to Piazzetta Montevecchio. From here a little jumble of streets and stairways run down to the river and the **Ponte degli Alpini**, which takes its name from the Alpine soldiers who rebuilt the bridge in 1948. The present structure was designed by **Palladio**

6

in 1568, and built in wood to make the bridge as flexible as possible – torrential meltwater would demolish an unyielding stone version. Mined by the Resistance during World War II, and badly damaged by the retreating German army, it was restored in accordance with Palladio's design.

Palazzo Sturm

Via Schiavonetti 7 • Tues–Sat 9am–1pm & 3–6pm, Sun 10.30am–1pm & 3–6pm • €4, or €5 for joint ticket with Museo Civico

From the Ponte degli Alpini follow Via Ferracina downstream for a couple of minutes and you'll come to the eighteenth-century **Palazzo Sturm**, a showcase for the town's famed majolica ware, with a display on the Remondini printing works, founded in Bassano in the seventeenth century.

The Monte Grappa war memorial

Various streets and squares in Bassano commemorate the dead of the two world wars. In 1944 resistance fighters were rounded up and hanged from trees along the street now called Viale dei Martiri. The major **war memorial**, however, is out of town on **Monte Grappa**, an hour's drive away. From the top (1775m) the views are astounding; on a clear day you can see Venice.

ARRIVAL AND INFORMATION BASSANO DEL GRAPPA

By train Trains from Venice pull in fifteen times daily; the journey takes 90min.

By bus Bus services all run from in front of the train station, and connect with Asolo (6 daily) and Maser

(4 daily); services are much less frequent on Sun.

Tourist office Just through the walls at Largo Corona d'Italia 35 (daily 9am–1pm & 2–6pm; ☎0424 524 351, ⓦ vicenzae.org or ⓦ bassano.eu).

ACCOMMODATION

Al Castello Via Bonamigo 19 ☎0424 228 665, ⓦ hotelalcastello.it. The only hotel in the old centre, this three-star is right by the castle. The rooms are on the small side; ask for no. 10, which is larger, with its own balcony. Breakfast is not included but there's a bar downstairs. **€100**

Ostello Don Cremona Via Chini 6 ☎0424 219 137, Wostellobassanodelgrappa.it. For a low-budget stay, just south of the centre is the youth hostel with ninety beds, half of which are bunks. Check-in Mon–Fri 8.30am–12.30pm &

4–10pm, Sat 8.30am–noon & 7–10pm, Sun 7–10pm. Dorms **€18**, doubles **€48**

★ **Villa Brocchi Colonna** Contrà S. Giorgio 98 ☎0424 501 580, ⓦ villabrocchicolonna.it. Charming converted villa 2km from the centre on the western edge of town. The welcoming mother-and-daughter team offer very comfortable rooms and the breakfast – with pancakes and a fantastic array of jams made from produce in the orchard – is delectable. **€160**

EATING AND DRINKING

Bassano's central streets and squares come alive at the end of the siesta, and the bars and restaurants around the main square have a real buzz by early evening.

Al Caneseo Via Vendramini 20 ☎0424 228 524. Both the food and the atmosphere are very good in this small restaurant, which serves dishes from Abruzzo and the Veneto. Tues–Sun noon–2am & 7.30–10pm; closed Aug.

★ **Al Caneva** Via Matteotti 34. This cosy bar does delicious snacks as well as more substantial dishes, and has tables out in the street when the weather permits. 9.30am–3pm & 7pm–midnight; closed Tues.

Antica Osteria Via Matteotti 7. Old-fashioned bar just

GRAPPA IN BASSANO

Bassano del Grappa is naturally best known for its **grappa**, the Italian firewater. The two big names in grappa production can both be found by the old bridge: The Nardini grappa distillery, founded in 1779, is at the foot of the Ponte degli Alpini; these days the distilling process takes place elsewhere, but the original shop and bar are still functioning here (Tues–Sun 8am–8pm). You can also taste and buy the stuff in the **Museo della Grappa** across the road at Via Gamba 6 (daily 9am–7.30pm), which is really a glorified showcase for the Poli distillery.

in the road from the central squares that has a strong local following, and serves good snacks – it feels like it has been serving the same fare for years. Tues–Sun 7am–1.30pm & 3–9pm.

Osteria Terraglio Piazzale Terraglio 28 ☎ 0424 526

158, ⊚ osteriaterraglio.it. Relaxed restaurant with a large terrace in the middle of the square. Pasta dishes such as *bigoli* with rabbit or the *garganelli* with artichokes and blue cheese are recommended, and the pudding selection is excellent. Tues–Sat 10am–2am.

Asolo

6

East of Bassano, the medieval hilltop town of **ASOLO** presides over a tightly grouped range of 27 gentle peaks in the foothills of the Dolomites. Known as *la città dai cento orizzonti* ("the city with a hundred horizons"), the town was popular with writers and artists who found the atmosphere convivial: Robert Browning's last published work – *Asolando* – was written here.

Piazza Garibaldi and around

The narrow streets leading up through the town open up at the top into the hub of the town, **Piazza Garibaldi** (also known as Piazza Maggiore), where a big antiques market is held on the second Sunday of the month (except July & Aug).

Museo Civico

Via Regina Cornaro 74 • Sat & Sun 10am–noon, 3–7pm • €4

Off the piazza is the **Museo Civico**, whose most diverting exhibits are the memorabilia of Asolo's celebrated residents, including the portraits, photos and personal effects of **Eleonora Duse** (1858–1924). An actress in the Sarah Bernhardt mould, Duse was almost as well known for her tempestuous love life as for her roles in Shakespeare, Hugo and Ibsen, and she came to Asolo to seek refuge from gossip.

The Castello

Duse gave her name to the theatre that is now up the road from the museum in the **Castello**, which from 1489 to 1509 was home to Asolo's most celebrated resident, **Caterina Cornaro**. Born into one of Venice's most powerful families, Caterina was married to Jacques II, King of Cyprus. Within a year Jacques was dead, and Caterina was pressurized into ceding Cyprus to the Republic. She was given the region of Asolo as a sign of Venice's indebtedness. Eventually Asolo, too, was taken away from her by the Emperor Maximilian, and she sought asylum in Venice, where she died soon after, in 1510. The castle also contains a children's play area and a bar, and there are great views from its walls.

The Rocca

Sun 10am–sunset • Free

Asolo's ruined medieval fortress, the **Rocca**, is reached by taking Via Collegio up the hill from the back of Piazza Brugnoli (the car park next to Piazza Garibaldi) and going through the Porta Colmarian. Built on Roman foundations, the Rocca stands 350m above sea level, and the views are worth the effort of the climb.

Santa Caterina

May–Sept daily 9am–6.30pm; Oct–April Sat & Sun 9am–4.30pm • Free

Via Canova leads west away from the town centre past Eleonora Duse's house (no. 306), near the Porta Santa Caterina. The church of **Santa Caterina** next to the Carabinieri, is deconsecrated but open to allow visitors to see its fifteenth-century frescoes. A little further along Via di Santa Caterina, the cemetery of the church of **Sant'Anna** holds the graves of Eleonora Duse and the third of Asolo's famous female residents, the English writer and adventuress Freya Stark.

6

The Villa Barbaro at Maser

March, July & Aug Tues, Thurs & Sat 10.30am–6pm, Sun 11am–6pm; April–June, Sept & Oct Tues–Sat 10am–6pm, Sun 11am–6pm; Nov–Feb Sat & Sun 11am–5pm • €6 • ⓦ villadimaser.it • If you're reliant on public transport, a visit is best made by bus from Bassano via Asolo or from Treviso – services from Treviso to Asolo all pass through Maser

The **Villa Barbaro**, or the **Villa di Maser**, a few kilometres northeast of Asolo, is a masterpiece created in unison by **Palladio** and **Paolo Veronese**, whose careers crossed here and nowhere else. The villa was commissioned in the 1550s by Daniele and Marcantonio Barbaro, Venetian ambassadors and connoisseurs of the arts. Apart from its beautifully symmetrical architecture, the standout feature is the magnificent series of **frescoes** by Veronese, which make fantastic use of trompe l'oeil effects: servants peer round painted doors, a dog sniffs along the base of a flat balustrade, a huntsman (probably Veronese himself) steps into the house through an entrance that's a solid wall. In the grounds in front of the villa (now separated by a busy main road) stands Palladio's **Tempietto**, the only church by him outside Venice. Built in 1580, the year Palladio died, its interior is notable for its rich yet simple stucco decoration.

ARRIVAL AND INFORMATION

ASOLO

By public transport There are regular buses to Asolo from Bassano. From Venice, the quickest route is to take a train to Treviso, where you won't have to wait more than an hour for a bus to Asolo (some change at Montebelluna), though it can be longer on Sundays – in addition to the direct services, all buses to Bassano go through Asolo and Maser. The bus drops you at the foot of the hill, a connecting minibus (€1.30 day-ticket) taking you up into the town.

Tourist office Piazza D'Annunzio 2 (Tues & Wed 3–6pm, Thurs–Sun 9.30am–12.30pm; ☎ 0423 529 046, ⓦ asolo.it).

ACCOMMODATION

Asolo is an expensive little town, with two of the Veneto's flashiest hotels, the *Villa Cipriani* and *Al Sole*, but there are alterntives for those on more sensible budgets. Note that all accommodation is booked solid on the second Sunday of every month, during the antiques fair.

★ **Agriturismo Sant'Andrea** Via Cornuda 72, Maser ☎ 0423 565 358, ⓦ agrsantandrea.it. This friendly wine-making agriturismo, down the road from the Villa Barbaro, makes the perfect base for exploring the region. Eleven rooms, three with cooking facilites; ample buffet breakfast too. €75

Duse Via Browning 190 ☎ 0423 55 241, ⓦ hotelduse .com. The cheapest hotel in the centre, this three-star has 22 rooms, most of them spacious. €120

EATING

Antica Osteria Al Bacaro Via Browning 165 ☎ 0423 55150. Welcoming *osteria* with a very local feel. The food is unpretentious and well prepared, and prices are reasonable, with *secondi* for €8–15. Noon–2.30pm & 7–11pm; closed Wed.

★ **Locanda Baggio** Via Bassane 1, Casonetto ☎ 0423 529 648, ⓦ locandabaggio.it. Located 1km northeast of town in the hamlet of Casonetto, this restaurant offers superb and inventive cooking that is not too expensive, with *secondi* ranging from €18 to €25. It also has an excellent wine list, including vintages from the Villa Barbaro. Tues 7–11pm, Wed–Sun noon–2.30pm & 7–11pm.

Conegliano

The hills surrounding **CONEGLIANO** are patched with vineyards, and the production of wine (Prosecco in particular) is central to the economy of the town. Italy's first wine-growers' college was set up in Conegliano in 1876, and a couple of well-established **wine routes** meet here: the **Strada dei Vini del Piave**, which runs for 68km southeast to Oderzo and concentrates on the region's red wines (ⓦ stradavinidelpiave .com), and the more rewarding **Strada del Prosecco**, the first to be established in Italy, a 42km journey west to Valdobbiadene (ⓦ coneglianovaldobbiadene.it). The main square is given over to a medieval pageant in mid-June, the **Dama Castellana**, and the streets of Conegliano host a major **wine festival** on the last weekend in September.

The Duomo and around

Via XX Settembre • Daily 7am–noon & 3.15–7.30pm • Free

On the central street of the old town, Via XX Settembre, the most decorative feature is the unusual facade of the **Duomo**: a fourteenth-century portico, frescoed in the sixteenth century. The interior has been much rebuilt, but has a fine *Madonna and Child with Saints and Angels*, painted in 1493 by Giambattista Cima, the most famous native of Conegliano.

Cima's birthplace, at the rear of the Duomo, has been restored and converted into the **Casa Museo di G.B. Cima** (Sat & Sun: April–Oct 4–7pm; Nov–March 3–6pm; free). However, this consists mainly of reproductions of his paintings and archeological finds made during the restoration of the house.

Sala dei Battuti

Sat 10am–noon, Sun 3–6pm • Free

Alongside the Duomo, at the top of the steps facing the door off the right-hand aisle of the church, is the **Sala dei Battuti** or Hall of the Flagellants, the frescoed meeting-place of a local confraternity. The pictures are mostly sixteenth-century, incorporating the weirdest *Ascension* you'll ever see, with the ascendant Christ half out of the frame and a pair of footprints left behind at the point of lift-off.

Museo Civico

Piazza San Leonardo • Tues–Sun: April–Oct 10am–12.30pm & 3.30–7pm; Nov–March closes 6.30pm • €2.50

The **Museo Civico** is housed in the tower of the *castello* on top of the hill. It has some damaged frescoes by Pordenone and a small bronze horse by Giambologna, but the main reason to visit is the climb to the tower's roof from where there's a fine panorama of the vine-clad landscape.

ARRIVAL AND INFORMATION
CONEGLIANO

By train Access to Conegliano itself is straightforward, as nearly all the regular Venice–Udine trains stop here.
Destinations Belluno (8 daily; 55min); Udine (every 30min; 50min–1hr 15min); Venice (every 30min; 50min–1hr 20min); Vittorio Veneto (every 40min–1hr; 25min).
Tourist office Via XX Settembre 61, on the corner of

Piazza G.B. Cima (Wed–Fri 9.30am–12.30pm & 3–6pm, Sat & Sun closes 7pm; ☎ 0438 21 230, ⊚ turismo.provincia .treviso.it). Well-stocked with information, including the latest list of recommended Prosecco outlets, and details of the wine routes.

ACCOMMODATION AND EATING

Canon d'Oro Via XX Settembre 131 ☎ 0438 34 246, ⊚ hotelcanondoro.it. The first-choice hotel in town, this Best Western four-star is housed in one of the street's fine frescoed *palazzi*. It has a terraced garden to the rear, and whirlpool baths in the more expensive rooms. **€150**
Osteria La Bea Venezia Via XX Settembre 77–79 ☎ 0438 23 186. An excellent trattoria, specializing in fish and seafood. In summer the front terrace is a very nice

place to eat. Tues–Sat noon–3pm & 6.30pm–midnight, Sun noon–3pm.
★ **Trattoria Stella** Via Accademia 3 ☎ 0438 22 178. The fare is simple but tasty at this friendly small restaurant in the centre of the old town: spinach crespelle (pancakes) and ravioli are recommended. Mon–Wed, Fri & Sat noon–2.30pm & 7–10pm, Thurs noon–2.30pm.

Vittorio Veneto

Some 13km north of Conegliano, **VITTORIO VENETO** first appeared on the map in 1866 when the towns of Ceneda and Serravalle (not previously the best of friends) were knotted together and rechristened in honour of Italy's new king. A town hall was built midway between the two, with a new train station opposite, so that the visitor steps straight from the train into a sort of no-man's-land.

6

Ceneda

CENEDA is primarily worth a visit for the **Museo della Battaglia** (Tues–Sun: May–Sept 9.30am–12.30pm & 4–7pm; Oct–April 9.30am–12.30pm & 2–5pm; €3, or €5 joint ticket with the Museo del Cenedese) at Piazza G. Paolo 1, whose loggia was built by Sansovino. The museum is dedicated to the Battle of Vittorio, the final engagement of World War I for the Italian army.

Serravalle

SERRAVALLE, wedged up against the mouth of a gorge, is entirely different. Most of the buildings on the stage-like Piazza Marcantonio Flaminio and the neighbouring streets date from the fifteenth and sixteenth centuries – the handsomest being the shield-encrusted Loggia Serravallese. This is now home to the **Museo del Cenedese** (same times and price as Museo della Battaglia; see above), a jumble of sculptural and archeological bits, detached frescoes and minor paintings. Your time will be more profitably spent in the church of **San Lorenzo dei Battuti** (same ticket and opening time; an attendant takes you there), immediately inside the south gate, which is decorated with frescoes painted around 1450. Uncovered in 1953 and restored to rectify the damage done when Napoleon's soldiers used the chapel as a kitchen, this is one of the best-preserved fresco cycles in the Veneto.

ARRIVAL AND INFORMATION   VITTORIO VENETO

By train Plenty of services pull in at the town's central train station.
Destinations Belluno (8 daily; 30min); Conegliano (every 40min–1hr; 25min); Venice (6 direct trains daily; 1hr 10min).
By bus The bus station is across the main road from the train station, behind the post office. Bus #1 shuttles between the two towns every 30min.
Destinations Belluno (1 daily; 1hr); Conegliano (11 daily; 45min).
Tourist office Near the train station at Viale della Vittoria 110 (Tues–Sun 9.30am–12.30pm, Thurs–Sun also 3–6pm; ☎ 0438 57 243).

Belluno

BELLUNO was once a strategically important ally of Venice, and today is the capital of a province that extends mainly over the eastern Dolomites (covered in Chapter 5). Its position is Belluno's main attraction, but the old centre calls for an hour or two's exploration if you're passing through. The hub of the modern town, and where you'll find its most popular bars and cafés, is the wide **Piazza dei Martiri**.

Piazza del Duomo

Off the south side of **Piazza dei Martiri** a road leads to the **Piazza del Duomo**, the kernel of the old town. The sixteenth-century **Duomo**, an amalgam of the Gothic and Classical, was designed by Tullio Lombardo. There are a couple of good paintings inside: one by Andrea Schiavone (first altar on right) and one by Jacopo Bassano (third altar on right).

Occupying one complete side of the Piazza del Duomo is the residence of the Venetian administrators of the town, the **Palazzo dei Rettori**, a frilly, late fifteenth-century building dolled up with Baroque trimmings. A relic of more independent times stands on the right – the twelfth-century **Torre Civica**, all that's left of the medieval castle.

Museo Civico

Piazza del Duomo 16 • Mon–Fri 10am–1pm, plus Tues & Fri 3–6pm • €3

Along the side of the town hall, you'll find the **Museo Civico**. The collection is strong on the work of Belluno's three best-known artists – the painters Sebastiano and Marco Ricci and the sculptor-woodcarver **Andrea Brustolon** – all of whom were born here between 1659 and 1673.

Piazza del Mercato and Via Mezzaterra

Leading out of Piazza del Duomo, Via Duomo ends at the **Piazza del Mercato**, a tiny square hemmed in by porticoed Renaissance buildings. The principal street of the old town, **Via Mezzaterra**, goes down to the medieval **Porta Rugo** (veer left along the cobbled Via Santa Croce about 50m from the end), from where the view up into the mountains is magnificent.

ARRIVAL AND INFORMATION   BELLUNO

Belluno's focus of attention lies to the north – the network of the Dolomiti Bus company radiates out from here, trains run regularly up the Piave valley to Calalzo, and the tourist handouts are geared mostly to hikers and skiers.

By train Just four direct trains a day make the two-hour journey from Venice to Belluno, but it's almost as quick to change at Ponte nelle Alpi, Conegliano or Castelfranco Veneto; from Padua (directly or via Castelfranco) there are thirteen trains daily.

Destinations Conegliano (8 daily; 55min); Vittorio Veneto (8 daily; 30min).
Tourist office Piazza del Duomo 2 (daily 9am–12.30pm & 3.30–6.30pm; Oct, Nov & mid-March to mid-June closed Sun afternoon; ☎ 0437 940 083, ⓦ infodolomiti.it).

ACCOMMODATION AND EATING

Al Borgo Via Anconetta 8 ☎ 0437 926 755, ⓦ alborgo .to. The best restaurant in the Belluno area is a couple of kilometres from the centre (it's across the river, in the direction of Feltre), but it's well worth the excursion – it's a family-run place, offering fantastic food in a delightful setting. Mon noon–2.30pm, Wed–Sun noon–2.30pm & 7–10pm.

Cappello e Cadore Via Ricci 8 ☎ 0437 940 246, ⓦ albergocappello.com. This long-established three-star hotel, tucked away off the main square, is the best place to stay in the centre of Belluno. Its eighteen rooms are plain but comfortable and quiet, and some have whirlpool baths. **€95**

Terracotta Borgo Garibaldi 66 ☎ 0437 291 692, ⓦ ristoranteterracotta.it. Recently taken over by new owners, the friendly and elegantly plain *Terracotta* is now the best place to eat in central Belluno. The menu changes with the seasons, but you can expect to find some excellent fish dishes at any time of year, at around €18 for a main course. The set lunch menu, at €16 including a glass of wine, is a bargain. In summer, the garden is a lovely spot to eat. Mon & Thurs–Sun noon–2pm & 7.30–9.30pm, Wed 7.30–9.30pm.

6

Friuli-Venezia Giulia

PIAZZA UNITÀ D'ITALIA, TRIESTE

Friuli-Venezia Giulia

Established only in 1963 and given special status as one of Italy's five semi-autonomous regions, Friuli-Venezia Giulia is odd, even in its name (Friuli is a corruption of the ancient name for modern-day Cividale, Foro Iulii "Forum of Julius", while Venezia Giulia "Julian Venetia" also references the area's abiding association with Caesar). Bordering Austria to the north and Slovenia to the east, it has always been a major bone of contention among rival powers. Today, Slavic, Germanic and Italian populations all call it home and are fiercely proud of their local language, Friulano (a Romance language related to Swiss Romansch and Ladin). The area's landscapes are equally varied with one-half alps, about one-third limestone plateaux (carso) and the rest alluvial and gravel plains sloping down to the Adriatic.

The cities and towns here are as wildly dissimilar as one might expect. **Trieste**, the capital, is an urbanely elegant Habsburg creation, built by Austria to showcase the empire's only port. In spirit and appearance it is essentially Central European, a character it shares with **Gorizia**, to the north, though the latter has an even more Slavic flavour, and in fact straddles the border with Slovenia. Both cities benefit from castles looming on a central hilltop, affording memorable views, and provide access to walkabouts in the **Carso** – the windswept, limestone plateau that extends eastwards into Slovenia – while Trieste also boasts its very own **riviera**, complete with attractive beach resorts. A little further west, **Udine**'s architecture and art collections evoke Venice at its grandest, while UNESCO-listed **Cividale del Friuli** preserves a picturesque historic centre perched over the aquamarine Natisone River. The archeologically minded, however, head straight to **Aquileia** and the ruins of the Roman capital of Friuli, with its impressive basilica and huge paleo-Christian floor mosaic. From here it's south to the lagoon resort of **Grado**, which conceals a beautiful, early Christian centre surrounded by beach hotels.

Historically, what unites the region is its perennial role as a link between the Mediterranean and Central Europe. It has been repeatedly overrun from east and west and north, by the Romans, Huns, Goths, Lombards, Nazis and even the Cossacks. By turns, it has been lorded over by the Venetian Republic, Napoleonic France and the Austrian Empire. More recently, the area witnessed some of the most savage fighting of World War I, and World War II saw Fascism become especially virulent in Trieste, site of one of Italy's two death camps.

Today, right-wing and xenophobic tendencies are still strong. While most Friulani certainly want Italian nationality, the sociopolitical baggage of Rome and the south strike many as a drag. Currently, economic anxiety and general malaise about Italy's direction have resulted in something of a conservative resurgence.

THE BASILICA, AQUILEIA

Highlights

❶ Trieste From the castle atop the San Giusto, take in a panoramic view of this elegant and atmospheric maritime city. **See p.436**

❷ Grotta Gigante The world's largest accessible cave. **See p.444**

❸ Osmize An *osmiza* lunch is a taste of the Carso's Slovene culture. **See p.444**

❹ Aquileia The glorious fourth-century mosaic pavements rank among the most important monuments of early Christendom. **See p.449**

❺ Udine's Piazza della Libertà The central piazza of the provincial capital is a perfect

example of classic Venetian architecture. **See p.453**

❻ Cividale del Friuli This attractive small town has recently been granted UNESCO World Heritage status for its extraordinary medieval monuments and art treasures, including the splendid eighth-century Tempietto Longobardo. **See p.457**

❼ Valle del Natisone Follow a network of hiking trails to explore this area of outstanding natural beauty. **See p.459**

HIGHLIGHTS ARE MARKED ON THE MAP ON P.436

Trieste

Framed by green hills and white limestone cliffs **TRIESTE** looks out over the blue Adriatic, offering an idyllic panorama from its hilltop citadel, at least when the gale-force Bora winds aren't blasting you off the seafront. But in any weather, there's a distinct atmosphere of grandeur with a cosmopolitan twist. The city's main squares are adorned with spectacular Neoclassical buildings, and the much-photographed canal, clustered with open-air cafés, is a reminder that, just like Venice and its lagoon, this city has enjoyed a glorious seafaring past, too. Like so many ports in Europe, there is a certain seediness here, particularly evident in some areas around the train station, although in recent years the city has been spruced up. The heart of modern Trieste is in the grid-like streets of the **Borgo Teresiano**, but no visit would be complete without a climb to the top of its hill, San Giusto, named for its patron saint and with the best views for miles around.

Brief history

Trieste dates back as far as the third millennium BC, with Jason and the Argonauts alleged to have been among its earliest visitors. Roman ruins scattered around the city attest to its incorporation into the Roman Republic in 178 BC, when it was called Tergeste, from *terg* or market. However, with the exception of the castle and cathedral

FRIULI-VENEZIA GIULIA

HIGHLIGHTS
- ❶ Trieste
- ❷ Grotta Gigante
- ❸ Osmize
- ❹ Aquileia
- ❺ Udine's Piazza della Libertà
- ❻ Cividale del Friuli
- ❼ Valle del Natisone

REGIONAL FOOD AND WINE

Food in Friuli-Venezia Giulia reflects its cultural eclecticism, with the legacy of the Austro-Hungarian era always present. The food tends to be hearty and uncomplicated, from thick soups to warming stews, such as the ubiquitous goulash. This is the home of **prosciutto**, the best of which comes from San Daniele, and you will be offered plates of *affettati* or home-cured meats as part of a meal or to accompany a glass of wine. Pasta and gnocchi come with a Friulian twist, sweet and salty flavours combined; try *cialzons*, a pasta filled with spinach, chocolate, raisins and nutmeg. *Jota* is the local soup, a bean and sauerkraut combination with the possible addition of pork or sausage, good on a cold day. Friuli's signature dish is **frico**, a type of potato cake; potato and Montasio cheese grated together, fried until golden brown and served up with polenta. Another speciality is *brovada*, made from wine-fermented turnips and served with sausage. Desserts tend towards cakes and pastries, usually filled with nuts, dried fruit and alcohol – look out for *presnitz*, *strukliji* and *gubana*. The Austrian influence makes itself felt in the form of *strudel*, filled with fruit or ricotta cheese.

Friuli-Venezia Giulia is Italy's third most important quality **wine** region, after Piedmont and Tuscany, and has long been acclaimed for its fragrant, elegant whites. The two premium regions are the Collio and the Colli Orientali del Friuli, hilly zones sharing a border with Slovenia. Tocai or Sauvignon Vert is the most widely planted grape variety and the white wine you will generally be offered; pale in colour it is usually drunk young and makes a perfect aperitif. In 2007 Tocai underwent a name change, due to a long-running legal battle with Hungary, and is now simply called Friulano. Although the region is better known for its whites, the reputation of its red varietals and blends is catching up fast. Top reds include Cabernet Franc, Refosco or Terrano as it called around Trieste, and best of all, the obscure Schioppettino. Last but not least is the cult dessert wine Picolit, produced in very small quantities and commanding high prices.

7

of San Giusto, and the tiny medieval quarter below it, the city's whole pre-nineteenth-century history seems somewhat overwhelmed by the massive Neoclassical architecture of the **Borgo Teresiano** – named after the Empress Maria Theresa (1740–80), who poured money into the city. This was Trieste's golden age, as the Austrians spared no expense on embellishing what was to become the Habsburg Empire's only seaport. For a time, it even eclipsed Venice, but its heyday was short-lived and drew to an ignominious close after 1918, when the city was annexed to Italy. A grim period ensued under Mussolini as he rode roughshod over ethnic diversity.

Lying on the political and ethnic fault-line between the Latin and Slavic worlds, Trieste has long been a city of political turbulence. In the nineteenth century it was a hotbed of *irredentismo* – an Italian nationalist movement to "redeem" the Austrian lands of Trieste, Istria and Trentino. After 1918, tensions increased between the city's ethnic groups, with Slovenes suffering persecution at the hands of the rising Fascist regime. Trieste was annexed by the Germans in 1943 and then at the end of the war, the city and surrounding area became a "Free Territory" administered by the Allies before being divided between Italy and Yugoslavia in 1954. Trieste was awarded to Italy but lost its coastal hinterland, Istria, to Yugoslavia. It was a bitter settlement and the definitive **border settlement** was not reached until 1975. As Tito kept Istria, huge numbers of its fearful Italian population abandoned the peninsula: Fiume (Rijeka), for example, lost 58,000 of its 60,000 Italians. The Slovene population of the area around Trieste, previously in the majority, suddenly found itself treated as second-class citizens, with Italians dominant politically and culturally. In the last sixty years, the Slovene and Italian populations have mixed and intermarried and, along with other newer arrivals, have made Trieste one of the more multicultural cities in Italy.

The Castello

Tues–Sun 9am–7pm • €4

At the very summit of San Giusto, overlooking the remnants of the Roman forum, is the **Castello**, a fifteenth-century Venetian fortress. There's nothing much to see inside,

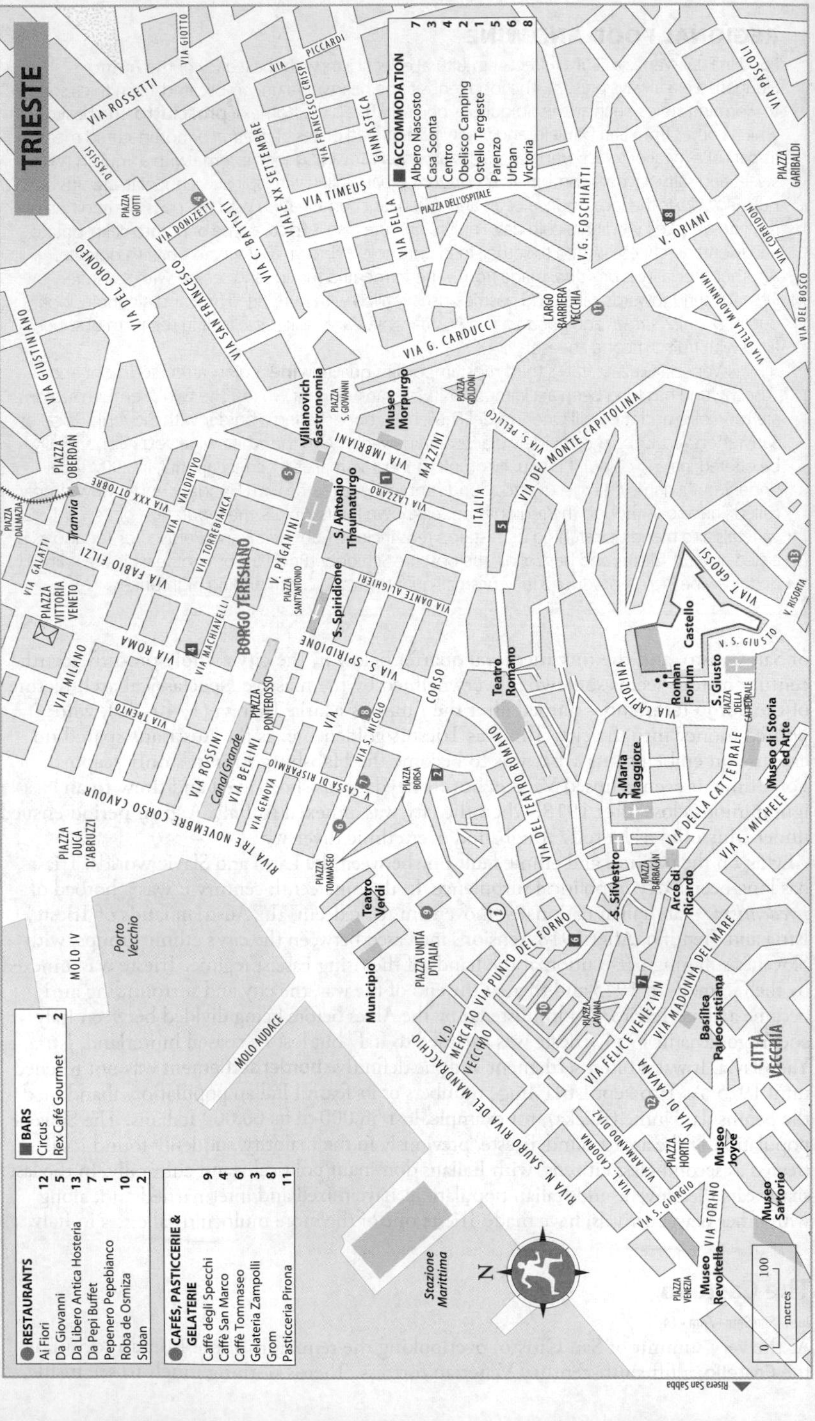

TRIESTE
ACCOMMODATION
Albero Nascosto 7
Casa Sconta 3
Centro 4
Obelisco Camping 2
Ostello Tergeste 1
Parenzo 5
Urban 6
Victoria 8
RESTAURANTS
Ai Fiori 12
Da Giovanni 5
Da Libero Antica Hosteria 13
Da Pepi Buffet 7
Pepenero Pepebianco 1
Roba de Osmiza 10
Suban 2
BARS
Circus 1
Rex Café Gourmet 2
CAFÉS, PASTICCERIE & GELATERIE
Caffè degli Specchi 9
Caffè San Marco 4
Caffè Tommaseo 6
Gelateria Zampolli 3
Grom 8
Pasticceria Pirona 11
1, 2, 3, Train & Bus Stations
1, 2, 3 & Opicina
Risiera San Sabba
Tranvia
BORGO TERESIANO
CITTÀ VECCHIA
Canal Grande
Porto Vecchio
Molo IV
Molo Audace
Stazione Marittima
Villanovich Gastronomia
Museo Morpurgo
S. Antonio Thaumaturgo
S. Spiridione
Teatro Romano
Teatro Verdi
Municipio
Roman Forum
Castello
S. Giusto
Museo di Storia ed Arte
S.Maria Maggiore
S. Silvestro
Arco di Ricardo
Basilica Paleocristiana
Museo Joyce
Museo Sartorio
Museo Revoltella
Piazza Oberdan
Piazza Dalmazia
Piazza Vittoria Veneto
Piazza Duca d'Abruzzi
Piazza Ponterosso
Piazza Sant'Antonio
Piazza S. Giovanni
Piazza Goldoni
Piazza Borsa
Piazza Tommaseo
Piazza Unità d'Italia
Piazza Cavana
Piazza Barbacan
Piazza della Cattedrale
Piazza Hortis
Piazza Venezia
Piazza Garibaldi
Piazza Giotti
Piazza dell'Ospitale
Largo Barriera Vecchia
Via Giustiniano
Via del Coroneo
Via San Francesco
Via C. Battisti
Viale XX Settembre
Via Timeus
Via Francesco Crispi
Via Rossetti
Via Giotto
Via Piccardi
Via Ginnastica
Via della
Via G. Carducci
V.G. Foschiatti
V. Oriani
Via Pascoli
Via Corridoni
Via della Madonnina
Via del Bosco
Via Galatti
Via XXX Ottobre
Via Valdirivo
Via Torrebianca
Via Fabio Filzi
Via Milano
Via Roma
Via Machiavelli
V. Paganini
Via Imbriani
Via Lazzaro
Mazzini
Italia
Via S. Pellico
Via del Monte Capitolina
Via Trento
Via Rossini
Via Bellini
Via Genova
V. Cassa di Risparmio
Via S. Nicolò
Via S. Spiridione
Via Dante Alighieri
Corso
Riva Tre Novembre
Corso Cavour
Via del Teatro Romano
Via Punto del Forno
Mercato Vecchio
V.D.
Riva N. Sauro
Riva del Mandracchio
Via Felice Venezian
Via Madonna del Mare
Via di Cavana
Via Armando Diaz
Via L. Cadorna
Via S. Giorgio
Via Torino
Via Capitolina
Via della Cattedrale
Via S. Michele
V. S. Giusto
Via T. Grossi
V. Risorta
N
0 100 metres

THE FVG CARD

The **FVG Card**, available at many hotels, travel agents and at all tourist offices (€15/48hr, €20/72hr and €29/week), allows access to over 200 services, listed in a pocket-sized tourist guide, at special prices. Among other things, it entitles you to discounts on sport and recreation facilities, some hotels and restaurants, as well as free admission to virtually all public museums, several guided tours and free use of some public transport, including the *tranvia* (see p.446).

---

but a walk round the ramparts offers panoramic views of the city and the busy port below, while beyond the city confines, the high escarpment of the Carso looms over the Adriatic. Its small **museum** houses archeological finds, and an extensive weapons and armoury collection.

Cattedrale di San Giusto

Mon–Sat 7.30am–noon & 2.30–6.30pm, Sun closes 7.30pm • Free, campanile €1.50

The **Cattedrale di San Giusto** is a fusion of two churches built on Roman ruins. Some ancient fragments remain: the base of the campanile has been chipped away to reveal the original pillars, the columns at the entrance are actually stelae from a Roman tomb and part of the Roman floor mosaic is incorporated in the present flooring. In around 1050 an earlier Christian chapel was replaced by two churches, the Basilica di Santa Maria Assunta and the Cappella di San Giusto. The site was further expanded in the early thirteenth century in an extraordinary stroke of pragmatic architectural genius: the two adjacent buildings were bridged by a high-beamed vault, forming the current cathedral nave and leaving a double aisle on each side. The complex history of the building becomes clearer if you study the arches in the interior, or look down on the apse from the castle wall behind. As it stands today, the cathedral is a typically Triestine synthesis of styles, with a serene, largely Romanesque interior marred only by an ugly modern choir. The Cappella di Santa Maria Assunta (north aisle) has fine Venetian-Ravennan mosaics of the *Coronation of the Virgin*, revealing the Byzantine roots of the style, while the Cappella di San Giusto (south aisle) has thirteenth-century frescoes of the life of the saint, framed between Byzantine pillars. The facade is predominantly Romanesque, but includes a Gothic rose window.

Museo di Storia ed Arte

Via della Cattedrale • Tues–Sun 9am–1pm • €4

Atop the hill, the **Museo di Storia ed Arte** houses a collection of cultural plunder that embraces Himalayan sculpture, Egyptian manuscripts and Roman glass. Part of the museum, the **Orto Lapidario**, is a pleasant environment in which fragments of classical statuary, pottery and inscriptions are arranged on benches and against walls, among cow-parsley and miniature palm trees. The little Corinthian temple on the upper level contains the remains of J.J. Winckelmann (1717–68), the German archeologist and theorist of Neoclassicism, who was murdered in Trieste by a man to whom he had shown off his collection of antique coins.

The Old Town

The tiny remnant of the **Città Vecchia** (Old Town) lies between the castle hill and the Stazione Maríttima below. It has been freshly restored – even at risk of over-restoration, as evidenced by the rather jarring presence of a design hotel (the *Urban*) inserted into its tilting medieval structures and cobbled lanes. Still, the area is delightful for a stroll, and farther down Via della Cattedrale, the tiny, early Romanesque **San Silvestro** (Thurs & Sat 10am–noon; free) is worth a look as the city's oldest extant church; it's now used by adherents of the rare Helvetic-Waldensian sect. A short way below are the heavily restored remains of the Roman theatre, where performances are sometimes staged during the city's spring–autumn festival season. There's little else of monumental note in the old city, but mosaic enthusiasts may want to stop off at the remains of the **Basilica Paleocristiana** (Wed 10am–noon, or by appointment; ☎040 43 631; free) under the building at Via Madonna del Mare 11. The evocative **Arco di Riccardo**, on the nearby Piazza Barbacan, comprises reassembled remnants of the Roman walls dating from 33 BC, while excavation works nearby are revealing more traces of the city's ancient imperial past and will eventually complete an archeological tourist trail from San Giusto down to Piazza Unità (see below).

The Borgo Teresiano

To the north of the old centre, Trieste's "new" town, the **Borgo Teresiano**, is imposingly laid out in a Neoclassical style imported from nineteenth-century Vienna, with wide boulevards and a vast piazza on the waterfront. The focus of the main grid of streets is the picturesque **Piazza Sant'Antonio Nuovo**, with its small yacht basin overlooked by cafés and dominated by two churches: the Neoclassical hulk of Sant'Antonio Thaumaturgo and the smaller, more appealing Serbian Orthodox San Spiridione. The bridge here is where you'll pass a strolling James Joyce lost in literary rumination (see box below). The real heart of town, however, is the grandiose **Piazza Unità d'Italia**, directly below the hill of San Giusto. Built mostly by Giuseppe Bruni in the late nineteenth century, the expanse of flagstones with one side open to the water is deliberately reminiscent of Venice's Piazza and Piazzetta – Trieste had commercially eclipsed the older city some years before. Projecting into the harbour nearby, the **Molo Audace**, named after the first boat of Italian soldiers to land here in 1918, is the venue for the evening *passeggiata*.

Revoltella

Via Armando Diaz 27 • 10am–7pm; closed Tues • €6.50, €7.50 for special exhibitions • ⓦ museorevoltella.it

Trieste's principal museum is the **Revoltella**, housed in a Viennese-style *palazzo* bequeathed to the city by the financier Baron Pasquale Revoltella in 1869. Its display of nineteenth-century stately home furnishings and Triestine paintings is well worth a look, and the adjacent palace, redesigned by the architect Carlo Scarpa, houses an extensive collection of modern art, including works by Fontana, Guttoso, Carrà and De Chirico.

Museo Sartorio

Largo Papa Giovanni XXIII 1 • Tues–Sun 9am–1pm • €5.50

The **Museo Sartorio** is set in an urban villa and has an interesting collection of ceramics, porcelain and pictures mainly from the nineteenth century; it gives you a good idea of

---

JOYCE IN TRIESTE

From 1905 to 1915, and again in 1919–20, **James Joyce** and his wife Nora lived in Trieste. After staying at Piazza Ponterosso 3 for a month, they moved to the third-floor flat at Via San Nicolò 30. He supported himself by teaching English at the Berlitz school where his most famous pupil was the Italian writer Italo Svevo. While living here he wrote *The Dubliners* and *A Portrait of the Artist as a Young Man* and started work on *Ulysses*. He lived a somewhat peripatetic life and you can visit his many homes and old haunts by picking up the walking-tour guide from the tourist office. There's a plaque in Via San Nicolò, and one at Via Bramante 4, quoting the postcard Joyce despatched in 1915 to his brother Stanislaus, whose Irredentist sympathies had landed him in an Austrian internment camp. The postcard announced that the first chapter of *Ulysses* was finished. Don't miss the wry bronze statue of the writer, strolling bemusedly across the little canal bridge of Via Roma.

how the well-to-do lived at that time. It is also home to an early fourteenth century Santa Chiara triptych and an important collection of drawings by Tiepolo. The museum hosts temporary exhibitions and concerts in the summer. Incidentally, the villa was used by the Allies as their headquarters after World War II when the city was partitioned and occupied.

Risiera di San Sabba

Via Palatucci 5 · Daily 9am–7pm · Free, guided tours upon request €2.70 · Located on the #8 (from the train station and from Piazza Unità) and #10 (from Piazza Tommaseo) bus routes

One of the darkest periods of modern European history is embodied by the **Risiera di San Sabba** on the outskirts of Trieste. This was one of only two concentration camps in Italy and now houses a museum which serves as a reminder of Fascist crimes in the region. At least five thousand prisoners were burned in the Risiera crematorium and many more passed through here before being transported to forced labour and concentration camps in other parts of Europe. Nazism had plenty of sympathizers in this part of Italy: in 1920 Mussolini extolled the zealots of Friuli-Venezia Giulia as model Fascists, and the commander of the camp was, in fact, a local man.

ARRIVAL AND DEPARTURE
TRIESTE

By plane The nearest airport is at Ronchi dei Legionari (📞 0481 773 224, 🌐 aeroporto.fvg.it), 31km northwest of the city, connected to the bus station by APT bus #51 (every 30min; 50min; €3.50 from the machine directly outside arrivals, €1 surcharge if ticket bought on bus; freephone 📞 800 955 957, 🌐 aptgorizia.it). A taxi should cost about €40; there's a booking desk in the airport. Avis, Europcar and Hertz all have desks at the airport.

By train The train station is a 10min walk from the town centre; international services from Austria and Slovenia arrive here.
Destinations Gorizia (every 30min; 45min); Udine (every 20min; 1hr); Venice (hourly; 2hr).

By bus Trieste's Piazza Libertà bus station is right by the train station.

Destinations Duino (hourly; 30min–1hr); Grado (14 daily; 1hr–1hr 30min); Monfalcone (for Aquileia and Grado; hourly; 45min); Udine (hourly; 1hr 15min).

By ferry This is an enjoyable way to travel to the coastal resorts, though most services are infrequent and summertime only. Agemar, Piazza Duca degli Abruzzi 1/A (📞 040 363 737, 🌐 agemar.it), is a travel agent selling ferry tickets to Grado and Ligano, Piran (Slovenia), Brijuni and Rovinj (Croatia).

Destinations Barcola, Grignano and Sistiana (July–Sept 3 daily; 1hr 45min); Grado (mid-June to Aug 3 daily; 1hr 30min–2hr); Muggia (daily every hour; 30min); Rovinj (June–Sept Tues–Sun 1 daily; 1hr 45min); Slovenia: Piran (June–Sept Tues–Sun 1 daily; 30min).

GETTING AROUND

By bus City buses (freephone 📞 800 016 675, 🌐 triestetrasporti.it) cost €1.15 for any journey of up to an hour; provincial buses cost a standard €1.35, except private APT services which depend on distance. Timetables and tickets can be bought from automatic machines at main stops or from newsagents, bars and *tabacchi*; a ten-ticket *blocchetto* is slightly cheaper and more convenient than buying individual tickets. Useful services include #30, which connects the train station with Via Roma and the waterfront; #24, which goes to/from Castello di San Giusto; and #36 which links Trieste bus station with Miramare.

By car There are very few places to park in Trieste and the streets are congested. If you come with a car leave it in your hotel parking or use the waterfront public parking. Pick up a rental car at Molo dei Bersaglieri 3: Avis 📞 040 300 820; Europcar 📞 040 322 0820; Hertz 📞 040 322 0098.

By taxi The best outfit is Radio Taxi 📞 040 307 730.

INFORMATION

Tourist office Piazza Unità d'Italia 4/B (Mon–Sat 9am–7pm, Sun 9am–1pm; 📞 040 347 8312, 🌐 turismofvg.it).

ACCOMMODATION

★ **Albero Nascosto** Via Felice Venezian 18 📞 040 300 188, 🌐 alberonascosto.it Stylish, small hotel, and part of the restoration project of the historical centre of Trieste. The building is beautifully renovated using the best-quality materials. Studio-apartments are bright, with fully equipped kitchen unit, satellite TV, refrigerator, a/c and wi-fi. Within walking distance of the city centre. €125

★ **Casa Sconta B & B** Via dei Moreri 86 ☎334 332 7148, ⓦcasasconta.it Attractive stone house in the hills, just a 15min walk from the centre, complete with garden and pool. Three recently renovated rooms, smart bathrooms, very friendly owners and an excellent breakfast. €95

Centro Via Roma 13 ☎040 347 8790, ⓦhotel centrotrieste.it. This moderately priced little two-star, close to the station, has 24 bright, spotless rooms, helpful staff and free wi-fi. Ask for one of the quieter rooms at the back. There's an equally excellent facility on the floor above, *Al Canal Grande*, run by the same family. Ten-percent discount for guests showing a copy of this book. €45 without bath, €60 with

Ostello Tergeste Viale Miramare 331 ☎0404 224 102, ⓦostellotrieste.135.it; bus #51 from the airport lets you off about 500m away, or take #36 from the station to Grignano and get off at Bivio al Miramare, from where it's a 5min walk. Basic facilities but this HI hostel boasts stunning sea views, and is just 500m from Castello

Miramare 5km out of the city. Two- and four-bed rooms with private facilities are also available. Dorms €17, two-bed rooms €46, four-bed rooms €84

Parenzo Via degli Artisti 8 ☎040 631 133, ⓦhotel parenzo.com. A well-positioned, welcoming three-star establishment with nice touches such as bathrobes and slippers. Rooms are spacious and comfortable if a little dated. Friendly staff and free wi-fi but no on-site parking. €110

Urban Androna Chiusa 4 ☎040 302 065, ⓦurbanhotel .it. An ultramodern boutique hotel in the backstreets of the recently renovated medieval quarter. The interiors are a study in contemporary design and cutting-edge luxury. Special pluses include valet parking and your own PC. Special prices available through the website. €117

Victoria Via Alfredo Oriani 2 ☎040 362 415, ⓦhotel victoriatrieste.com. This is one of Trieste's finest four-star hotels. The building was once home to James Joyce and you can book the suite of the same name. Rooms are well appointed and elegant, while staff are helpful and speak good English. Free wi-fi throughout. €115

CAMPING

Obelisco Strada Nuova per Opicina 37 ☎040 212 744, ⓦcampeggiobelisco.it; from Piazza Oberdan take either bus #4 or the tranvia (cable tramway), which runs until 8pm: get off at the obelisk (Obelisco), cross over the tracks and you'll see a sign to the campsite

which is 1min walk away. Shady, tranquil campsite set on a hillside 7km from the city, below Opicina, catering for tents and caravans. It has a bar, restaurant and children's playground, while you'll find shops and ice cream in Opicina. Open all year. Tents €14.50, caravans €18.50

EATING AND DRINKING

Trieste has a huge range of good-value **restaurants**, while coffee (see box opposite) and ice-cream lovers are also well catered for. The best area to head for is pedestrian-only **Viale XX Settembre**, known as the Acquedotto ("aqueduct"), where citizens stroll in the evening. Via C. Battisti, east of Sant'Antonio, is good for **food shops**. For late-night **drinking**, Via Madonna del Mare, below the castle, has a number of bars whose names, managements and popularity come and go each year.

CAFÉS, PASTICCERIE AND GELATERIE

★ **Caffè degli Specchi** Piazza Unità 7 ☎040 661 973, ⓦcaffèspecchi.it. Located in the centre of Trieste's main square, this historic café is a great place to indulge in an early evening *aperitivo*, afternoon tea or a spot of people-watching. Daily 7am–9.30pm.

Caffè San Marco Via C. Battisti 18/A ☎040 363 538. One of Trieste's favourite cafés, the *San Marco* has been here for some eighty years. It's a huge, relaxed place with a clientele of all ages chatting and playing chess in the mahogany-and-mirrored Art Nouveau-style interior. Tues–Sun 8.30am–11pm.

★ **Caffè Tommaseo** Piazza Tommaseo ☎040 362 666, ⓦcaffetommaseo.com. A rendezvous for Italian nationalists in the nineteenth century, this is the oldest café in Trieste and supposedly introduced *gelato* to the city. Convivial *belle époque* surroundings, fabulous pastries, a restaurant and live music. Daily 8am–12.30am.

★ **Gelateria Zampolli** Via Ghega 10 ☎040 364 868. If you are anywhere near the station don't miss this.

A favourite with locals, serving fabulous flavours including *tiramisù*, puffed rice and coffee. There's another branch at Viale XX Settembre 25A. 9.30am–midnight; closed Wed.

Grom Via S. Nicolò 18/B. Part of a national chain of all-natural *gelaterie* that have taken northern Italy by storm. Flavours vary according to season and availability of quality ingredients. Classics include *bacio*, Syrian pistachio and Madagascan vanilla. Mon–Thurs & Sun 11am–11pm, Fri & Sat 11am–midnight.

★ **Pasticceria Pirona** Largo Barriera Vecchia 12 ☎040 636 046. Since 1900 this shop has been the place for truly extraordinary pastries – James Joyce was a regular. Tues–Sat 7.30am–8pm, Sun 7.30am–1.30pm.

RESTAURANTS

Ai Fiori Piazza Hortis 7 ☎040 300 633, ⓦaifiori.com. Beautifully presented gourmet food, served up by a husband-and-wife team. Artful fish dishes with an Istrian twist are the focus, with a set menu including wine for €30. Tues–Sat noon–2.30pm & 7.30–10.30pm.

TRIESTE AND THE ROASTED BEAN

Trieste's love affair with **coffee** dates back to the mid-eighteenth century, when the port was given tax-free status by Habsburg Emperor Charles VI. The resultant boom in port trade coincided with the coffee craze hitting Europe, in particular Vienna, and coffee beans destined for Austrian cafés became one of Trieste's biggest imports. Even today it's the leading coffee port in the Mediterranean – forty percent of Italy's coffee arrives here – and Trieste's denizens imbibe twice as much on average as their fellow countrymen. One of the pleasures of walking around the city centre is the exotic scent of roasting beans emanating from choice establishments – known as *torrefazioni* – where experts toast beans to order. The city's most famous brand is Illy, founded in 1933 and producer of a world-renowned 100-percent Arabica blend. So supreme is the coffee culture in the city that Riccardo Illy, scion of the clan, has held the offices of mayor and regional president, among numerous other posts. Illy offers specialized courses in coffee appreciation at the Università del Caffè (Ⓦilly.com).

A word to the wise: coffee terminology in Trieste is a little different from other parts of Italy, and if you order a cappuccino you will end up with a *caffè macchiato* – instead you need to ask for a *latte macchiato* or a *caffè latte*.

7

Da Giovanni Via S. Lazzaro 14/B Ⓣ040 639 396, Ⓦtrattoriadagiovanni.com. Historic trattoria, with simple meals served at bench tables. Hams hanging from the ceiling and barrels of wine behind the bar lend a distinctly rustic air. Mixed fried fish and marinated sardines are a speciality, as well as various pork dishes, gammon and bowls of steaming *jota*, bean and sauerkraut soup. Great for a snack at the bar or a sit-down meal. Expect to pay €20–25. Mon–Sat 8am–3pm & 4.30–11pm; closed three weeks in Aug.

Da Libero Antica Hostaria Via Risorta 7/A Ⓣ040 301 113, Ⓦhostariadalibero.com. This old-fashioned establishment at the foot of the castle is virtually the last remaining genuine *osteria* in the city, full of quirky mementoes collected by the proprietor over the decades. The seasonal menu includes polenta with porcini and cheese, and guinea fowl with potato puree. Tourist menu from €19, with mainly meat options. Mon–Sat 12.30–2.30pm & 7.30–10.30pm.

★ **Da Pepi Buffet** Via Cassa di Risparmio 3 Ⓣ040 366 858, Ⓦbuffetdapepi.com. Traditional locale that's the perfect place for snacks and lunches. The speciality here is *bollito di maiale* – various cuts of pork, including sausages, cooked in broth and served up with mustard and horseradish, accompanied by *crauti*, fermented cabbage flavoured with cumin. Full meals €18. Mon–Sat noon–midnight.

Pepenero Pepebianco Via Rittmeyer 14/A Ⓣ040 760 0716, Ⓦpepeneropepebianco.it. This place is ultra-modern in atmosphere and food, and a convenient walk for

those staying in the Piazza della Libertà and central station area. The dishes are intensely fragrant and innovative – try monkfish tartare accompanied by sweet-and-sour red onions or a pumpkin and crab risotto. Expensive if you go à la carte, but there's an excellent-value €30 three-course menu. Tues–Sat 7pm–midnight.

Roba de Osmiza Via della Torretta 1 Ⓣ040 322 0262, Ⓦrobadeosmiza.com. Sample products straight from the Carso, including *prosciutto crudo*, olives, salami and boiled eggs. Local wines, including Terrano and Malvasia, are available by the glass. Very simple, inexpensive food, good for lunch or a snack. Daily 9.30am–midnight.

Suban Via Comici 2/D Ⓣ040 54 368, Ⓦsuban.it. Traditional dishes are perfectly prepared at this family-run restaurant. The food is very *mittel*-European with dishes such as cheese strudel accompanied by truffle sauce and roasted veal shank. The excellent wine list includes bottles from Slovenia. There's outdoor seating under the pergola in summer. A three-course meal without wine is €45. Mon 12.30–3pm, Wed–Sun 12.30–3pm & 7.30–11pm; closed Aug.

BARS

★ **Circus** Via S. Lazzaro 9 Ⓣ040 633 499. A trendy, buzzing wine-bar decorated in retro style with old movie posters, and with tables outside. Eclectic music, and drinks come with substantial snacks. Mon–Sat 8am–10.30pm.

TRIESTE FESTIVALS AND EVENTS

The second Sunday of October sees the **Barcolana** (Ⓦbarcolana.it), Italy's largest sailing regatta with over 2000 boats of all types skimming the bay; the race attracts thousands of spectators and there are ten days of festivities around the event. From spring to autumn, events abound, including at the Teatro Verdi (Ⓣ040 672 2111, Ⓦteatroverdi-trieste.com). For details, contact the tourist office or consult *Il Piccolo*, Trieste's daily paper; check for festivals in the surrounding villages, too, such as the **Nozze carsiche** in Monrupino (see p.446).

Rex Café Gourmet Galleria Protti 1 ☎ 040 773 411. Modern wine and music bar with a jazzy lounge setting and outdoor tables, too. Mon–Thurs 7am–midnight, Fri & Sat 7am–2am, Sun 9am–10pm.

DIRECTORY

Consulates UK, Via Dante Alighieri 7 (Tues 10am–noon, Fri 2.30–4.30pm; ☎ 040 347 8303); US Consular Agency, Via Roma 15 (Mon–Fri 10am–noon; ☎ 040 660 177).
Hospital Ospedale Maggiore, Piazza dell'Ospedale ☎ 040 399 1111; in an emergency dial ☎ 118.
Internet access KNULP, Via Madonna del Mare 7/A (with computer, €2.50/hr; wi-fi €1/hr; open till midnight,

closed Wed).
Laundry Lava & Suga, Via del Sale 1/A. Daily 7am–3am.
Police Via Tor Bandena 6 (☎ 040 379 0111). Otherwise call ☎ 113.
Post office Piazza Vittorio Veneto 1 (Mon–Sat 8.30am–7pm).

Around Trieste: the Carso

The **CARSO** is the Italian name for the strip of limestone uplands that rise from the Venetian plain south of Monfalcone and eventually merge into the Istrian plateau. The particular shape and look of the karst landscape is due to the weathering of the limestone bedrock by water and wind. Although within a thirty-minute bus ride of Trieste, it feels like an entirely different country, and is geologically, botanically and demographically distinct from anywhere else in Italy. Most of the Carso now lies within Slovenia (its Slovene name is Kras), and even the narrow strip inside Italy, though supporting a population of just 20,000, remains distinctively Slovene in culture, boasting places with names like Zagradec and Koludrovica. The thick-walled houses seem built to withstand the blasts of the *bora*, the fierce northeasterly wind which can reach gusts of 90mph. When it's at its worst ropes are strung along the steeper streets in Trieste and old folk stay indoors.

Like all limestone landscapes the environment is harsh: arid in summer and sometimes snowbound in winter. The surface of the plateau is studded with sink-holes left by streams which have formed vast caverns, underground lakes and rivers.

The distinctive landscape and unspoiled natural environment make for fine **walking**. If the scenery isn't as grand as the Dolomites, the pace is gentler, and you can stop for refreshments at an *osmiza* (see box below).

Grotta Gigante

Guided visits daily: April–Sept every 30min 10am–6pm; Oct–March hourly 10am–4pm • €11

The **Grotta Gigante** is the Carso's main tourist attraction, and with good reason: it's the world's largest accessible cave, and the second-largest natural chamber anywhere in the

---

OSMIZE

Perhaps the best way to experience the Slovene culture of the Carso is to find an **osmiza** (see p.443 for one in Trieste itself), a rustic eating place where farmers sell their own produce, such as cured meats, cheese, olives, hard-boiled eggs, bread and wine. The name comes from the Slovene word *osem*, "eight days", which was the period of time allowed by imperial edict for the peasants to sell their wares. The food is simple and cheap, and the locations often stunning. The problem with *osmize* is that they have limited opening times, vary hugely in quality, and are hard to find – which makes tracking down a good one all the more difficult. Ask the tourist office for a list or look at ⓦ interware.it/tsr/ambiente/carso/osmizze.htm (Italian only) or ⓦ osmize. Otherwise, as long as you don't mind taking a few detours, just take a #44 bus from outside the station in Trieste, get off at the villages Prosecco or Contovello, and start asking if there is an *osmiza* nearby. You'll know you're getting close when you see wooden signs and branches of ivy suspended from archways and lampposts.

CIVIDALE DEL FRIULI (P.457) >

world. As it's 98m high by 76m wide, the dome of St Peter's would fit comfortably inside. It's a steady 11°C inside, so bring warm clothes.

The cave is impressive in scale and, like most of the caves in the Carso, was created by the erosive action of a river, in this case the Timavo, which sank deeper and deeper underground before changing course (the cave is now dry). The fantastically shaped stalactites and stalagmites were formed by deposits of calcium carbonate and colourful metal oxides. Much more recently, ferns and moss have started to grow in what was previously a lifeless environment, thanks to photosynthesis triggered by electric lighting. The two long "pillars" in the centre of the cave are in fact wires sheathed in plastic. At the bottom end two super-accurate pendulums are suspended, used to measure seismic shifts in isolation from surface noise and air currents.

Rupingrande

7

Apart from the Grotta Gigante, the main sights to head for are in and around the village of **RUPINGRANDE** (aka Monrupino), just 3km northeast of the cave. A short walk east of the village is a fourteenth-century castle built to defend the area from Turkish incursions. In Rupingrande itself the **Carsica** (April–Nov Sun & hols 10am–11.30pm & 3–5pm, or by appointment; ☎040 327 124; free) is a typical rural home and hosts various cultural exhibitions throughout the year. The village hosts an important Slovene folk festival, the **Nozze carsiche** (Carsic Wedding; see box, p.443), in August in odd-numbered years.

ARRIVAL AND DEPARTURE
THE CARSO

By bus Several bus services run to the Carso from Piazza Oberdan in central Trieste, including the #42 and #44.

By tram The most picturesque way up into the Carso is to take the *tranvia* (cable tramway; 7.30am–8pm; every 20min; €1.10, same ticket as for buses) from Trieste's Piazza Oberdan to the village of Opicina, at the edge of the plateau. From the tram stop, cross the square and take bus #42.

WALKING IN AND AROUND TRIESTE: THE STRADA VICENTINA AND THE VAL ROSANDRA

The tourist office publishes a useful map of the network of numbered footpaths in the Carso; it shouldn't be used for serious navigation but is a useful guide. For serious hiking in the hills you need Tabacco's *Carso Triestino e Isontino Map #047*. Two walks near Trieste can be particularly recommended:

The Strada Vicentina Also known as the *Napoleonica*, the Strada Vicentina is some 3.7km long, contouring the hillside above the city, between the *Obelisco* campsite (see p.442) and the hamlet of Borgo Nazario (near Prosecco). It's a scenic, easy walk, partly shaded by trees and partly cut through almost sheer limestone cliffs; on a clear day the views are superb. Access to the Strada Vicentina couldn't be simpler: *Obelisco* is a stop on the *tranvia*, and the Borgo Nazario end is near Via San Nazario, where the #42 bus stops on its way back to Trieste station.

The Val Rosandra A miniature wilderness of limestone cliffs and sumac trees, the Val Rosandra is the local rock-climbing headquarters and is crisscrossed with walking paths. From the bus stop at Bagnoli Della Rosandra (bus #40 from Trieste), follow the road behind the square to Bagnoli Superiore where the marked hiking trails begin. Highlights include the remains of a Roman aqueduct, the little sanctuary church of Santa Maria in Siaris, and various pools and waterfalls. If you get as far as the tiny hamlet of Bottazzo – the last habitation before Slovenia – you'll see a sign indicating a friendship path linking communities on either side of the frontier.

EATING

Agriturismo Milic Lóc. Sagrado 2, Sgonico ⊕ 040 229 383, ⓦ agriturismomilic.it. Tasty and reasonably priced country cooking, with everything produced on the farm, including the excellent wine. Specialities include home-cured meats, gnocchi and the mixed grill. Tables in the garden for summer dining. Fri–Sun noon–9.30pm.

The Triestine Riviera

The thirty-odd kilometres of coastline either side of Trieste, from Muggia to the south and as far as Duino in the north, are optimistically known as the **TRIESTINE RIVIERA**. While beaches aren't as good as you'll find further down the Adriatic, or even at nearby Grado, some fine walks, historic sites and castles are worth a day-trip from Trieste.

Muggia

Directly south across the bay from Trieste, 11km away by road, **MUGGIA**, the last remnant of Venice's Istrian possessions, is now little more than a popular spot for lunch expeditions from Trieste, though the town comes into its own during carnival time. The ferry-trip across the bay from Trieste (summer only) can be a good enough reason in itself to visit, but there are also appealing signs of the past, particularly in the brightly painted buildings on the main square. On the east side of the piazza, the fifteenth-century **Duomo** reveals its origins in its Venetian-Gothic arches and a bas-relief of Christ Pantocrator in the lunette above the main door; the handsome **Palazzo dei Rettori**, on the north side of the square, displays the tell-tale *leone marciano*, the lion of St Mark, symbol of Venice's former hegemony here. The piazza is backed by a handful of narrow streets and tumbledown houses, many dating back to Venetian times.

On the seaward side of the piazza, the tiny *mandracchio* is now used as a basin for pleasure boats, while the working harbour just beyond is spoilt only by the unenviable view of Trieste's industrial backside.

Muggia Vecchia

It's worth visiting **Muggia Vecchia**, on the hilltop hard against the Slovene border and less than 20km from Croatia. It's a steep twenty-minute walk past Muggia's fourteenth-century castle and town walls, but bus #50 from outside the bus station, 100m inland from the main road, runs every hour or so.

Barcola

BARCOLA, 2km northwest of Trieste, is the nearest beach resort. Developed during Trieste's great days at the end of the nineteenth century, it is now really a suburb that comes to life in summer, when all Trieste seems to come here. Despite the cargo ships and tankers moored in the harbour, the water is moderately clean. Just short of the resort, perched on the slope of the limestone escarpment and offering stunning views along the coast, is the **Faro della Vittoria**, the third-tallest lighthouse in the world.

Miramare

Daily 9am–6.30pm • €6 • ⊕ 040 224 143, ⓦ castello-miramare.it

Standing at the tip of a rocky promontory 7km from Trieste, the fairytale castle of **MIRAMARE** is the area's prime tourist attraction. Archduke Maximilian of Habsburg, the younger brother of Emperor Franz Joseph of Austria, built his dream castle and laid out its grounds between 1856 and 1870, but never lived to see it completed. He was duped into accepting Napoleon III's offer to become the Emperor of Mexico, and was executed by firing squad by his Mexican opponents in 1867. His wife Carlotta went mad after his execution, and Archduke Franz Ferdinand stayed here on his way to his assassination in

Sarajevo in 1914. These events gave rise to the legend that anyone who spends a night in Miramare will come to a bad end; when the British general Freybourg chose the castle as his headquarters at the end of the war, he opted for caution and slept in the garden.

The park and gardens, which are free, make an excellent spot for a picnic, but the real draw is the castle's kitsch **interior**, a remarkable example of regal decadence and over-the-top furnishings. The Monarchs' Salon, for instance, is embellished with portraits of a King of Norway, the Emperor of Brazil, a Czar of Russia – anyone, no matter how fraudulent or despotic, as long as they're nominal monarchs. The bedroom is full of images chronicling the construction of the castle. Other rooms are panelled and furnished like ship's quarters, reflecting Maximilian's devotion to the Austrian Navy.

In July and August son et lumière productions are presented beside the sea, often with a regular version in English; check with Trieste's tourist office or the castle.

Duino

The village of **DUINO**, 14km northwest along the coast from Trieste, is dominated by its two castles, the **Castello Vecchio**, built around the tenth century and now just a ruined eyrie above the sea, and the early fifteenth-century **Castello Nuovo**, seat of the princes of Thurn und Taxis down to the present day.

Castello Nuovo

Daily except Tues: mid- to end March & mid-Oct to Nov 9.30am–4.30pm; April to mid-Oct 9.30am–5.30pm • €8, not included on FVG Card

The **Castello Nuovo** and its grounds opened to the public in 2003, allowing visitors to stroll through the lavishly decorated rooms, take a look at a massive doll's house given to the family by Napoleon III's widow and a history of the family's eighteenth-century pan-European postal service, and admire the fantastic coastal views from the beautiful gardens and the top of the third-century Roman tower.

Sentiero Rilke

Near the Castello Nuovo, the **Sentiero Rilke** is a panoramic coastal footpath, named after Rainer Maria Rilke who began the famous *Duino Elegies* while staying at the castle. Apparently, while walking along the castle bastions in a gale he heard a voice speaking the words, "Who, if I cried out, would hear me among the angelic orders?" and, so inspired, he started work on the Elegies. The path ends at Sistiana, where there's a large yacht harbour and a beach.

ARRIVAL AND INFORMATION

By train There's a train from Trieste to Miramare, Bivio d'Aurisina and Sistiano (hourly; 10–20 min).

By bus Frequent buses trace the coast road; #36 from Trieste's bus station (every 20min) runs to Miramare and Barcola, while #20 from Piazza Oberdan or the bus station (every 15min) connects with Muggia. Duino and Sistiana can be reached on the half-hourly service #44 from Piazza Oberdan.

THE TRIESTINE RIVIERA

By ferry In summer, ferries from the central dock call at all the coastal towns, including Muggia (10 daily; 30 min), Barcola and Sistiana (both 3 daily mid-June to mid-Sept; 20min & 1hr 20min respectively).

Tourist office Via Roma 20, Muggia (☎040 273 259; open daily Carnevale and July & Aug only 9am–7pm).

EATING

Trattoria al Castello Salita delle Mura 11/B ☎040 272 667, ⓦtrattoriaalcastello.net. The speciality is traditional fish cookery with a menu that changes daily depending on availability, but regular favourites include fish soup, gnocchi with crab and an excellent *fritto misto*. Book a table on the terrace in the summer. *Secondi* around €20. Tues–Sat noon–3pm & 7–10pm, Sun noon–3pm.

Trattoria Risorta Riva de Amicis 1/A ☎040 271 219, ⓦtrattoriarisorta.it. Talented chef Stefano Blasotti cooks up the freshest seafood dishes, both traditional Italian standards and modern creative combinations. Try the grilled octopus served up with mozzarella cream, tomatoes and basil oil, or foie gras topped with prawns. A full meal will set you back around €60. Tues–Sat 12.30–3pm & 7–10.30pm, Sun 12.30–3pm.

Aquileia

Bordered by the Tagliamento in the west and the Isonzo in the east, the triangle of flatlands west of Trieste and south of Udine seems unpromising territory for a visitor – mile upon mile of maize fields, streams, market gardens and newish villages. Yet **Aquileia** was once the Roman capital of Friuli and is the most important archeological site in northern Italy. These unremarkable fields have yielded a wealth of Roman remains, while the glorious basilica here ranks among the most important monuments of early Christendom.

Brief history

Some 45km west of Trieste, Aquileia was established as a **Roman colony** in 181 BC, its location at the eastern edge of the Venetian plain – on the bank of a navigable river a few kilometres from the sea – being ideal for defensive and trading purposes. It became the nexus for all Rome's dealings with points east and north, and by 10 BC, when the Emperor Augustus received Herod the Great here, Aquileia was the fourth most important city in Italy, after Rome, Milan and Capua. In 314 AD the Patriarchate of Aquileia was founded, and under the first patriarch, Theodore, a great basilica was built. Sacked by Attila in 452 and again by the Lombards in 568, Aquileia lost the patriarchate to Grado, which was protected from invasion by its lagoons. Aquileia regained its primacy in the early eleventh century under Patriarch Poppo, who rebuilt the basilica and erected the campanile, a landmark for miles around. But regional power inevitably passed to Venice, and in 1751 Aquileia lost its patriarchate for the last time, to Udine. The sea has long since retreated, the River Natissa reduced to a reed-clogged stream, and Aquileia is now a quiet little town of 3500 people.

The basilica

Summer daily 9am–7pm; winter Mon–Fri 9am–4.30 pm, Sat & Sun 9am–5pm • Free, access to the two crypts €3

A UNESCO World Heritage Site, Aquileia's rich history is made visible in the layers of the vast **basilica**, just east of the main road. The earliest part, Theodore's extraordinary **mosaic pavement**, was discovered below the nave floor at the beginning of the twentieth century and is thought to be the earliest surviving remnant of any Christian church. The mosaic undulates the full length of the nave in a riotous sequence of colours, patterns and images, many of which draw on Roman iconography. Look for the blond angel bearing the laurel wreath and palm frond – whether it represents the Pax Romana or Christian Victory, no one is sure. Beyond the red line extending across the aisle the Christian imagery begins with the story of Jonah, complete with waves, whale and fish everywhere – a motif not unconnected to the nearby Adriatic. Other mosaics from Theodore's original basilica, depicting a whole bestiary, have been discovered around the base of the campanile (access from inside the basilica). Next door, a climb up the **belltower** (March–Oct daily 9.30am–1pm & 2.30–6pm; €1.10) gives a new perspective on the basilica as well as views stretching from the mountains to the coast.

In 1348 an earthquake destroyed much of Poppo's work, but the building is still superb, the Gothic elements of the reconstruction – all points above the capitals – harmonizing perfectly with the Romanesque below. The fine nave ceiling, like the steeple of the campanile, dates from the early sixteenth century. The ninth-century **crypt** under the chancel has very faded twelfth-century frescoes telling the story of St Hermagora, the legendary first bishop of Aquileia, including a gory beheading scene and a moving descent from the cross.

7

The Museo Archeologico

Via Roma 1 • Tues–Sun 8.30am–7.30pm • €4

A couple of minutes' walk west from the basilica, on the other side of the main road, is the **Museo Archeologico**. Worked stone and everyday items litter the fields around Aquileia, but the finer pieces have been collected here, ranging from precise surgical needles, delicate coloured glass and precious stones to great piles of jumbled masonry. The two courtyards, in particular, resemble a junkyard of Roman stone, with hundreds of funerary monuments, including urns piled in neat pyramids; concerts are occasionally held here in summer. It's worth persevering up to the top floor of the museum where two extraordinary bronze heads are displayed side by side. One is a fantastical relief in the Hellenistic style, the other a naturalistic bust that may portray a dictator of the third century AD; the cruel expression certainly supports such speculation. On the ground floor rows of marble sculptures and busts mostly derive from the Roman tombs that once lined the roads into Aquileia.

7

ARRIVAL AND INFORMATION

AQUILEIA

By bus The hourly bus from Udine calls in here. From Trieste change at Monfalcone, and take the bus to Grado that stops at Aquileia. Details on ⓦ aptgorizia.it and ⓦ saf.ud.it.

By train Take the hourly train to Cervignano, on the Udine–Trieste line, and then bus #59 which coincides with train arrival time.

Tourist office In the Via Giulia Augusta bus-terminal car park at the northern edge of town (daily 9am–7pm; ☏ 0431 919 491, ⓦ turismofvg.it); the Pro Loco office beside the basilica does not provide tourist information.

ACCOMMODATION

B & B Casa di Giulia Via Giulia Augusta 21 ☏ 043 191 8742, ⓦ casadagiulia.it. Just three spacious rooms and a lovely garden. The building dates back to the 1400s and was renovated in 2011. A/c, flatscreen TVs, wooden floors and luxurious bathrooms complete the picture. €70

Camping Aquilei Via Gemina 10 ☏ 043 191 042, ⓦ campingaquileia.it. Also has bungalows. A fenced campsite in beautiful parklands, with plenty of shade. Facilities include swimming pool, bar and restaurant, playground, ping pong, laundry, minimarket, bike rental and internet point. Mid-May to mid-Sept. Tents €28, bungalows €55

HI hostel, Domus Augusta Via Roma 25 ☏ 043 191 024, ⓦ ostelloaquileia.it. This simple 92-bed youth hostel is relatively modern, clean and quiet although well connected for public transport. Services include bike rental, laundry facilities and internet point. Dorms €20, rooms €46

Hotel Patriarchi Via G. Augusta 12 ☏ 0431 919 595, ⓦ hotelpatriarchi.it. This three-star sits on the main road not far from the bus terminal and offers comfortable, attractively furnished rooms with wooden floors, many with views of the basilica and belltower. It also rents out bikes and has a good restaurant. €90

EATING AND DRINKING

Agriturismo La Pergola Via Beligna 4 ☏ 340 530 0162, ⓦ beligna.com. Set back off the main road with seating both indoors and out. Serves home-cured prosciutto and salami, excellent, good-value home-cooked pasta dishes and good wine produced at its own nearby winery. 9.30am–11pm; closed Tues & Jan.

Antica Pizzeria Via Bertrando de S. Genies 2 ☏ 0431 918 825, ⓦ anticaaquileia.it. This place serves decent pizzas cooked in a wood-fired oven, as well as tasty dishes such as seafood pasta, mixed grill and wild boar. Very good value for money. Daily 10.30am–2.30pm & 5.30–11pm.

Grado

Some 11km south of Aquileia, isolated among lagoons, is the ancient island-town of **GRADO**, through which Aquileia once traded with Syria, Cyprus, Arabia and Asia Minor. Grado enjoyed its heyday under the Austrians who developed it as a health resort due to the presence of curative waters – and you can still take a cure here. It's worth seeking out Grado's **historic centre**, for its three early-Christian buildings, grouped close together in the heart of a miniature network of old streets.

For relaxing on the **beach**, this is one of the best places in the northern Adriatic; the water is safe and warm as a bath, and almost as shallow – indeed, the name of the town comes from the gentle angle of its shore. The free beaches are at the eastern and western ends; if you want a locker, deckchair and shower facilities, you have to pay a few euros to one of the businesses on the Lungomare Adriatico.

The basilica

Daily 8am–7pm • Free

Grado's sixth-century **basilica** was heavily restored between the 1930s and 1950s, but preserves a bizarre parade of ill-matched nave pillars topped by an assortment of Corinthian capitals; it's thought that these were recycled from various Roman buildings in Aquileia. The pulpit is of similarly hybrid origins, perched on six slender Roman columns under a Venetian canopy that resembles an oriental tent. Venice's presence is also felt in the fourteenth-century silver *pala* on the high altar. The mosaic pavement, while not as impressive as Aquileia's, is beautiful, the pattern being formed by an endless knot.

7

The baptistry and Santa Maria delle Grazie

Adjacent to the basilica, the octagonal **baptistry** (erratic opening hours) also dates back to the fifth century and the arrival of the first Christians in the lagoon. The church of **Santa Maria delle Grazie** (daily 8.30am–6.15pm; free), on its far side, is from the same period and has another mongrel collection of columns and capitals. From the outside it's possible to see how the ground level has sunk over the centuries.

ARRIVAL AND INFORMATION

GRADO

By bus From Udine hourly buses depart for Grado, stopping at Palmanova and Aquileia. From Trieste, take the bus to Monfalcone, where you change onto the Aquileia and Grado service (hourly). From Gorizia take bus #22 (hourly; 1hr). There's also a service that meets the trains at Cervignano railway station (25min).

By ferry In summer there are three daily services from Trieste's Molo Pescheria to Grado's Molo Torpediniere.
Tourist office Viale Dante Alighieri 72 (daily: May–Sept 9am–7pm; Oct–March 9am–1pm & 2–6pm, Sun 9am–1pm; ☎ 0431 877 111, ⓦ turismofvg.it).

ACCOMMODATION

Camping Punta Spin Via Monfalcone 10 ☎ 0431 80 732, ⓦ puntaspin.it. Camping spots, caravans and chalets and a wide range of facilities, including restaurants, tennis courts and three swimming pools. April–Sept. Tents €39, caravans €41, chalets €100
Locanda Ambriabella Riva Sant'Andrea 36, Isola della Schiusa ☎ 0431 84 753, ⓦ ambriella.it. A charming small hotel in an idyllic position facing out over the lagoon, a 10min walk from the town centre. Just six spacious, light and airy rooms, with homely furnishings, and a good restaurant too. Good value for money. €90
Villa Marin Via dei Provveditori 20 ☎ 0431 80 789,

ⓦ villamarin.it. The rooms are somewhat dated and fairly small but the wonderful sea views compensate. Free wi-fi and a reasonably priced restaurant. Closed Dec–Feb. €100
Villa Romana Viale Dante Alighieri 20 ☎ 0431 82 604, ⓦ gradovillaromana.com. This small hotel is just east of the historic centre and one street back from the beach. Rooms are a little spartan but clean and spacious. Closed Oct–April. €94
Villaggio Turistico Europa Via Monfalcone 12 ☎ 0431 80 877, ⓦ villaggioeuropa.com. This place offers camping spots and smart chalets and features a sizeable aquatic park. Mid-April to mid-Sept. Tents €40, chalets €120

EATING AND DRINKING

Agli Artisti Campiello Grande 2 ☎ 0431 183 081, ⓦ agliartistigrado.com. Locally caught fish is the order of the day in this traditional seafood restaurant, where the menu changes according to market availability. Sardines, mussels and scallops all feature on the antipasto menu

plate and grilled fish makes an excellent main course. Home-made desserts include delicious chocolate cake. €38 for a full meal. Noon–2pm & 7–10.30pm; closed Tues.
Al Bon Vento Via Cittanova 17, Fossalon di Grado ☎ 0431 188 028. If you want a break from fish and fancy

a 15min drive into the country, try this organic farm restaurant featuring a seasonally changing menu with vegan, vegetarian and macrobiotic dishes created with fresh ingredients. There are Japanese influences at work here. Very good value. Sat & Sun noon–11pm.

Spaghetti House Via Gradenigo 33 ☎0431 82 687.

Don't be put off by the name, this is an elegant establishment; specialities include mixed seafood antipasto, fried sardines, pasta with squid and great mussels, plus good home-made desserts. There are tables outside in the summer. You'll pay €45 for a three-course meal excluding drinks. Noon–2pm & 7–10pm; closed Wed.

Gorizia and around

As with other towns in this region, the tranquillity of present-day **GORIZIA** – virtually midway along the Trieste–Udine rail line – belies the turbulence of its past. The castle that dominates the old centre was the power-base of the dukes of Gorizia, who ruled the area for four centuries. After their eclipse, Venice briefly ruled the town at the start of the sixteenth century, before the Habsburgs took over. It was controlled from Vienna until August 8, 1916, when the Italian army occupied it. The border settlement after World War II literally split houses in Gorizia down the middle. Italy kept the town proper, but lost its eastern perimeter to what was then Yugoslavia, where the new regime resolved to build its own Gorizia: **Nova Gorica** – New Gorizia – is the result.

The town's appearance, like that of Trieste, is distinctly Central European, stamped with the authority of Empress Maria Theresa. Numerous parks and gardens – thriving in the area's mild climate – further enhance the *fin-de-siècle* atmosphere. It's a major shopping town for Slovenes, which explains the large number of electrical, clothes and food shops, and the cafés and restaurants.

The Borgo Castello

The main sight in town is the **Borgo Castello**, the quarter built round the castle by the Venetians, mostly in the sixteenth century. It's a pleasant place to wander, but the view from the castle walls is more inspiring. The graceful rooms of the **castle** itself (Tues–Sun 9.30am–6pm; €3, more for exhibitions and special events) hold an unexceptional collection of musical instruments, weaponry, and paintings and models of the castle and town. One of the finest of Gorizia's Neoclassical buildings is the **Palazzo Attems** (Tues–Sun 9am–7pm; €6) in Piazza De Amicis, northwest of the castle, built by Nicolò Pacassi, Maria Theresa's favourite architect. Behind the *palazzo*, in what was once the Jewish quarter, the **Synagogue**, at Via Ascoli 19 (Tues & Thurs 5–7pm, second Sun of month only 10am–1pm; free), is also of Neoclassical design; the serene interior resembles those in Venice's Ghetto.

The monastery at Castagnavizza

Mon–Sat 9am–noon & 3–5pm, Sun 3–5pm • €1.50 donation expected • The easiest way to get to the monastery is to cross the border on Via San Gabriele, in the northeast part of town (take your passport as there's usually someone checking), cross the railway line and follow the signs uphill – it's about a 10min walk

Probably the strangest sight in Gorizia is the crypt in the Franciscan monastery at **Castagnavizza** – Kostanjevica, actually, because the **monastery** lies across the border in Slovenian Nova Gorica. This is the burial place of the last but one French king, Charles X. After being ousted by the bloodless revolution of July 1830 and sent into exile, the family eventually ended up in Gorizia in 1836, where the Habsburgs allowed them to stay, though Charles died of cholera just seventeen days after his arrival. The Bourbon Institute has asked for the return to France of the family's remains, but both the monks and the Slovenian government have refused, asserting that the royal relics now form part of Slovenia's history.

Central Market

Corso Verdi • Mon–Fri 7.30am–3pm & Sat 7.30am–6pm

Don't leave Gorizia without a visit to the **Central Market** on Corso Verdi. This food-lovers' market is divided into three areas, one for flowers, another for fruit and vegetables, and one for home-grown produce brought in by *contadini* from the surrounding countryside. It's fun to visit and a great place to buy picnic supplies.

ARRIVAL AND INFORMATION
GORIZIA

By train Gorizia's train station is at Piazzale Martiri on the southwestern edge of the city, about 1km from the centre. **Destinations** Trieste (every 30min; 50 min); Udine (every 30 min; 35min).

By bus The bus station is directly in front of the railway station. There are three daily services to Cividale (1hr). **Tourist office** Corso Italia 9 (Mon–Sat 9am–1pm & 2.30–6.30pm, Sun 9am–1pm; ☎ 0481 535 764, Ⱳ turismofvg.it).

ACCOMMODATION

Bed & Breakfast Flumen Via Brigata Cuneo 20 ☎ 0481 391 877, Ⱳ bbflumen.it. This place is a little out of town and has a beautiful location on the banks of the acquamarine river Isonzo. Gorgeous setting, excellent facilities and nice people. **€90**

Gorizia Palace Corso Italia 63 ☎ 0481 82 166, Ⱳ goriziapalace.com. This modern, well-equipped and well-located hotel is a reasonable option, handy to the main sights and the railway station. **€95**

Palazzo Lantieri Piazza Sant'Antonio 6 ☎ 0481 533 284, Ⱳ palazzo-lantieri.com. This atmospheric fourteenth-century city residence is a glorious place to stay, complete with frescoes, surrounded by its own park and right in the centre of Gorizia. You'll be in good company as both Goethe and Casanova stayed here. **€140**

EATING AND DRINKING

Ai Tre Soldi Goriziana Corso Italia 38 ☎ 0481 531 956. This place has garden seating in summer and serves up a wide range of well-cooked Friulian specialities, Gorizian goulash and local wines – try the *menù degustazione* for €25. Tues–Sun 11am–3pm & 7–11pm.

Alla Luna Trattoria Via Oberdan 13 ☎ 0481 530 374. This colourful *osteria*, close to the market, is popular and serves good local food. The handwritten menus feature specialities such as ham baked in a pastry crust, pancakes stuffed with cabbage and thick soups – all excellent value. Tues–Sat noon–3pm & 7–10.30pm, Sun noon–3pm.

Majda Wine Bar Via d'Aosta 71 ☎ 0481 30 871. An exotically decorated place that's good for pre- and post-dinner drinks, a full meal or just a glass of wine and a snack. The seasonal menu features classic dishes including chestnut and porcini soup, cheese dumplings with truffles and stuffed pasta. Mon–Fri 12.30–3pm & 7–11pm, Sat 7–11pm.

Udine and around

UDINE, 71km northwest of Trieste, is the provincial capital and radically different to its larger sister city. Framed by mountains and hemmed in by sombre suburbs, the oval-shaped historic centre retains much of its Venetian charm. In many ways Udine harks back to the Venetian Republic, for which it was one of the most important cities. Admittedly, its canals, called *roggie*, are little more than rivulets compared to those of Venice, but its gorgeous Piazza della Libertà could have been airlifted directly from *La Serenissima*. In addition to grand architecture, the churches and galleries here also boast scores of fine works by **Giambattista Tiepolo**, whose airy brilliance evokes the city's easygoing atmosphere on a fine day, when the watery light from the canals dances on nearby walls. Two relaxed days provide enough time to get a good taste of what Udine has to offer.

The place to start any exploration of Udine is at the foot of the hill, in the **Piazza della Libertà**, a square whose architectural ensemble is matched by few cities in Italy. The fifteenth-century **Palazzo del Comune** is a clear homage to the Palazzo Ducale in Venice, and the clock tower facing the *palazzo*, built in 1527, similarly has a Venetian model – the lion on the facade and the bronze Moors who strike the hours on top of the tower are explicit references to the Torre dell'Orologio in Piazza San Marco. The statue at the north end of the square is a bad allegory called *Peace*, donated to the town by

7

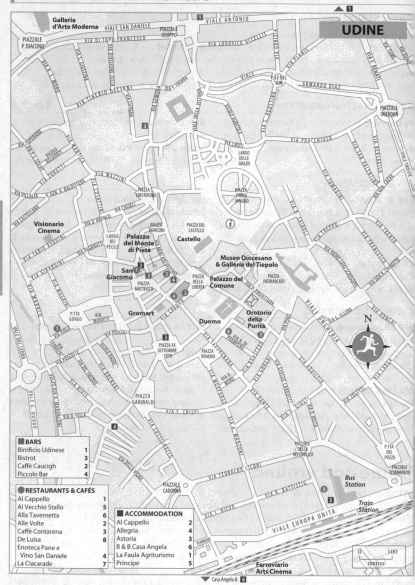

UDINE

BARS

Birrificio Udinese	1
Bistrot	3
Caffè Caucigh	2
Piccolo Bar	4

RESTAURANTS & CAFÉS

Al Cappello	1
Al Vecchio Stallo	5
Alla Tavernetta	6
Alle Volte	2
Caffè Contarena	3
De Luisa	8
Enoteca Pane e	
Vino San Daniele	4
La Ciacarade	7

ACCOMMODATION

Al Cappello	2
Allegria	4
Astoria	3
B & B Casa Angela	6
La Faula Agriturismo	1
Principe	5

Emperor Franz I to commemorate the Habsburg acquisition of Udine. All points of interest are about a fifteen-minute stroll from the piazza.

Brief history

Along with Cividale (see p.457), Udine was one of the frontier towns of imperial Rome but it was not until the thirteenth century that it started to become a regional centre. Patriarch **Bertoldo di Andechs** (1218–51) can be seen as the father of Udine – he established two markets (the old market in Via Mercatovecchio, and the new one in Piazza Matteotti, still a marketplace), moved the patriarchate from Cividale to the castle of Udine and set up a city council. In 1362 the dukes of Austria acquired the place by treaty, but not for long: Venice, now hungry for territory, captured Udine in 1420, after several assaults and sieges. The city was ruled by Venetian governors for almost four hundred years – until 1797, when the Venetian Republic surrendered to Napoleon. These days it's a centre of Friulian nationalism.

The castello

Tues–Sun 10.30am–7pm • €5

The sixteenth-century **castello**, decorated by local artists and once the seat of the Friulian parliament, now houses an excellent **Galleria d'Arte Antica**, containing works by Carpaccio, Bronzino and Tiepolo, as well as an indifferent Caravaggio and an interesting historical painting by Palma Il Giovanni showing St Mark putting the city under the patronage of St Hermagora, first bishop of Aquileia; Piazza della Libertà is clearly visible on the right. The best-known painting in its collection is Tiepolo's *Consilium in Arena*, showing a meeting of the Order of the Knights of Malta, said to be a faithful rendering, amazingly painted entirely on the basis of written accounts given to the artist.

Via Mercatovecchio

North from the Piazza della Libertà is **Via Mercatovecchio**, once the mercantile heart of the city and now the town's busiest shopping street. The little chapel of **Santa Maria**, incorporated into the Palazzo del Monte di Pietà here, is a beauty: viewed through the glass booth from the street, the interior, with its cloudy Baroque frescoes by Giulio Quaglio (1694), has a pristine, subaqueous appearance.

Piazza Matteotti

Due west of Via Mercatovecchio lies the **Piazza Matteotti**, with galleries on three sides and the fine Baroque facade of San Giacomo on the fourth. The square's importance as the centre of public life in Udine is proved by the outside altar on the first-floor balcony of **San Giacomo**; Mass was celebrated here on Saturdays so that selling and buying could go on uninterrupted in the market below. As well as being the town's main market, this was the setting for tournaments, plays and carnivals, and still sees summer festivals today. The fountain in the middle of the square was designed in 1543 by Giovanni da Udine, a pupil of Raphael, who also had a hand in building the castle.

The Duomo

Daily 9am–noon & 4–6pm • Free

Off the south side of Piazza della Libertà is the **Duomo**, a Romanesque construction that was given a Baroque refit in the eighteenth century. Altarpieces and frescoes by Giambattista Tiepolo are the main attraction – they decorate the first two chapels on the right and the Chapel of the Sacrament, a little way beyond. There's a series of frescoes painted by Tiepolo in collaboration with his son, Giandomenico, in the tiny **Oratorio della Purità** opposite – ask the sacristan in the Duomo to show you.

Gallerie del Tiepolo

Wed–Sun 10am–1pm & 3–6.pm • €7, including Museo Diocesano

Udine's outstanding works of art are the Giambattista Tiepolo frescoes in the **Gallerie del Tiepolo** in the beautifully furnished **Palazzo Arcivescoville**. Painted in the late 1720s, these luminous and consummately theatrical scenes add up to a sort of Rococo epic of the Old Testament. *Fall of the Rebel Angels* is the first work you see as you climb the staircase, while the finest room, the Gallery, is at the top, immediately on your right. Every surface is painted with either trompe-l'oeil architectural details or scenes from the story of Abraham, Isaac and Jacob. To the left is a sequence of rooms decorated in rich colours: watch for Tiepolo's *Judgement of Solomon* in the Red Room, and Bambini's wonderful *Triumph of Wisdom* in the serene Delfino library. Arranged around the Tiepolo galleries is the **Museo Diocesano**, with an assortment of sculpture and funerary monuments, as well as an exhibition of naive art – popular sculptures from Friuli's churches spanning the Gothic, Renaissance and Baroque periods.

Galleria d'Arte Moderna

Via Ampezzo 2 • Tues–Sat 9.30am–12.30pm & 3–6pm, Sun 9.30am–12.30pm • €3

The **Galleria d'Arte Moderna** (GAMUD), was founded in 1895 and aims to give an overview of Italian art in the twentieth century, with a few foreign greats thrown in for good measure. The gallery boasts a collection of over 4000 works of art including paintings, drawings and sculpture. Works include those by Martini, Guttuso, Fontana, de Chirico, Dufy and de Kooning.

7

ARRIVAL AND INFORMATION — UDINE

By plane The nearest airport is Ronchi dei Legionari, 43km away, connected to Udine by regular bus #51 (1hr).

By train Udine's train station is in the south of the town, at Viale Europa Unità 40.

Destinations Cividale (hourly; 20min); Gorizia (every 30min; 35min); Venice (hourly; 2hr).

By bus The bus station is close to the train station at Viale Europa Unità 31.

Destinations Aquileia (16 daily; 40min); Grado (12 daily; 1hr); Trieste (9 daily; 2hr).

Tourist office Piazza I (Primo) Maggio 7 (Mon–Sat 9am–6pm, Sun 9am–1pm; ☎ 0432 295 972, ⓦ turismofvg.it).

ACCOMMODATION

★ **Al Cappello** Via Sarpi 5 ☎ 0432 299 327, ⓦ osteriaalcappello.it. This traditional, welcoming *osteria* also offers a small *locanda* with six spacious, smartly designed rooms. The restaurant, too, is one of the most convivial and warmly attractive in town – and four-legged friends are welcome. **€120**

Allegria Via Grazzano 18 ☎ 0432 201 116, ⓦ hotelallegria.it. On a quiet pedestrianized street, this is the city's chicest design hotel. Recently refurbished in modern minimalist style, it boasts large rooms, cool colours, state-of-the-art bathrooms and an elevator to the underground garage, all in a beautifully restored medieval building. **€120**

Astoria Piazza XX Settembre 24 ☎ 0432 505 091, ⓦ hotelastoria.udine.it. Centrally located with clean, well-equipped rooms, albeit with slightly dated decor. Free wi-fi and off-site parking for a hefty fee. Weekend offers can see rates fall by almost half. **€150**

B&B Casa Angela Via Calatafimi 7 ☎ 337 532 623, ⓦ casaangela.it. Excellent option a 10min walk from the city centre in a recently renovated Art Nouveau building. Two attractive apartments, with three airy, bright bedrooms, all en suite. **€90**

La Faula Agriturismo Via Faula 5, Ravosa di Povoletto ☎ 334 399 6734, ⓦ faula.com. A 15min drive north of Udine, this working farm set in idyllic countryside provides nine rooms all bursting with character. The restaurant serves up farm-fresh produce accompanied by the estate's excellent wines. Two-night stay minimum; prices include dinner, bed and breakfast. Closed Sept–March. **€75**

Principe Viale Europa Unità 51 ☎ 0432 506 000, ⓦ principe-hotel.it. Ideally located for travellers by train or bus, this friendly, fresh and efficient choice is set back in its own courtyard to ensure quiet. There's free parking, too, and the choice of non-smoking rooms. Good value. **€90**

EATING, DRINKING AND ENTERTAINMENT

CAFÉS, PASTICCERIE AND RESTAURANTS

Al Cappello Via Sarpi 5 ☎ 0432 299 327, ⓦ osteriaalcappello.it. A trendy locale right in the centre with tables and benches outside. Lively atmosphere, popular with locals, best for a snack and a glass of wine rather than a meal. Tues–Sun 5–11pm.

Al Vecchio Stallo Via Viola 7 ☎ 0432 21 296. A traditional *osteria* serving typical Friulian dishes such as gnocchi with sausage sauce, *frico*, tripe and *frittata* – housed, as the name reveals, in a converted old stables. Service can be a bit slow. Expect to pay about €30 with wine – good value. 11am–3pm & 7–11pm; closed Wed.

FESTIVALS AND EVENTS IN UDINE

In summer there's a busy programme of cultural events in and around town: ask the tourist office for the fortnightly listings of events. Throughout the year the Visionario arts cinema at Via Asquini 33 (📞0432 299 545, 🌐visionario.info) holds cinematic events, jazz evenings and shows films in English on Mondays. The **Far East Film Festival**, one of the most exciting and comprehensive festivals of Asian film, is held here every year in April/May; details on 🌐fareastfilm.com.

The **Friuli DOC** wine festival, held over four days in mid-September, has been an annual event since1995; food and wine lovers come from all over Europe to drink wine, take master classes, sample the local food and enjoy the enogastronomic extravaganza (🌐movimentoturismo.it).

⭐ **Alla Tavernetta** Via Artico di Prampero 2 📞0432 501 066, 🌐allatavernettaudine.com. One of Udine's best establishments, serving regional dishes with a modern twist, such as barley and bean soup, stuffed gnocchi and roast goose. Top-quality ingredients and attentive service. You'll get a full meal for €35. Tues–Sat noon–3pm & 7pm–midnight.

⭐ **Alle Volte** Via Merceria 6 & Via Mercatovecchio 4 📞0432 502 800, 🌐osteriallevolte.it. Atmospheric restaurant set in a fifteenth-century stone building with vaulted ceilings and pillars – one floor is an *enoteca-osteria*, for wine tasting and traditional snacks, the other the main restaurant. Classic dishes include swordfish and *spaghetti alle vongole*, or try the fish-based tasting menu (€40 including wine). Mon–Sat 9am–3pm & 5pm–midnight.

⭐ **Caffè Contarena** Via Cavour 1 📞0432 512 741. Attractive *enoteca-caffè*, decorated with mosaics. Great for coffee and cake or to sample the huge range of wines available by the glass. Tues–Thurs 8am–midnight, Fri & Sat 8am–2am, Sun 9am–1 am.

De Luisa Via Palmanova 61 📞0432 521 429. For a sweet treat, cakes, ice cream and coffee, head to this little *pasticceria* which has been turning out delicious local treats, such as *gubana* (a yeasted fruit and nut cake), for three generations. Daily 5.30am–1.30pm & 3–8pm.

Enoteca Pane Vino e San Daniele Piazzetta Lionello 12 📞0432 299 934. A good place to sample a variety of hams, cheese and salami, washed down with a glass or two of excellent local wine. Mon–Sat 9am–midnight.

⭐ **La Ciacarade** Via S. Francesco 6/A 📞0432 510 250, 🌐laciacarade.it. This wood-beamed dining room has a handful of tables plus a long bar for drinking and dining. Enjoy smoked trout, cheese fritters with onion and *prosciutto cotto d'oca all'arancio* – orange-flavoured goose prosciutto. Pleasant courtyard and an excellent wine list. €30 for a full meal without drinks. Mon–Sat 9.30am–3pm & 4.30–9.30pm.

Trattoria alla Ghiacciaia Via Zanon 13/B 📞0432 502 471. Romantic little spot serving simple local dishes, mostly priced around €8–10. There's seating available on a terrace overlooking the canal, making this a good place for lunch. Tues–Sun 11am–3pm & 6pm–midnight.

BARS

Birrificio Udinese Via Caccia 5 📞0432 510988, 🌐bire.it. This microbrewery features a range of artisan beers and substantial snacks to match, from pizza to sauerkraut to crêpes. Maxi screens for watching televised matches. Service can be slow. Daily noon–midnight.

Bistrot Piazza Matteotti 18. One of the hottest spots in this happening square, at the centre of the city's nightlife. Tues–Fri 7.45pm–2am, Sat 9pm–2am.

Caffè Caucigh Via Gemona 36 📞0432 502719, 🌐caucigh.com. A comfy Irish pub, claiming to be the city's oldest café, with live jazz on Fridays from 10pm, with Italian and international artists. Tues–Sun 7am–1am.

Piccolo Bar Via Rialto 2. This stylish option is an intimate wine bar in the *centro storico*. Enjoy a drink at the tables arranged underneath the portico, just right for starting the evening off. Mon–Sat 5–9pm.

Cividale del Friuli and around

Lying only 17km east of Udine, **CIVIDALE DEL FRIULI** is a well-preserved medieval gem and one of the most beautiful towns in the area. Visitors are drawn to its dramatic setting, perched over the Natisone River, and to its art treasures. The town has ancient roots, founded in 50 BC by Julius Caesar at the picturesque point where the Natisone River valley opens into the plain. In the sixth century AD it became the capital of the first Lombard duchy. In the eighth century the Patriarch of Aquileia moved here, inaugurating Cividale's most prosperous period. Cividale has been the main market town in the Natisone valley for two hundred years, and today you'll hear Italian, Friulano and Slovene dialects spoken in the street. Just strolling around the town, within the oval ring bisected by Via Carlo Alberto and Corso Mazzini, is a pleasure, the pace of life leisurely and unhurried. The historic centre lies between the train and coach stations. Make sure you walk across the Ponte del Diavolo (Devil's Bridge) to take in the iconic view of the Natisone River.

Tempietto Longobardo

Piazza San Biagio • Oct–March Mon–Sat 10am–1pm & 3–5pm, Sun 10am–5pm; April–Sept Mon–Sat 9.30am–12.30pm & 3–6.30pm, Sun 9.30am–1pm & 3–7.30pm • €4

The tiny **Tempietto Longobardo**, poised above the Natisone, is a fine example of Lombard art. Constructed in the ninth century, largely from older fragments, much of the elaborate stuccowork inside the chapel was reduced to rubble in the terrible earthquake of 1222. The delicate interior preserves faded frescoes and carved stalls from its use as a convent chapel in the late fourteenth century, but the eye is drawn to the east wall where an exquisite stucco arch is flanked by six female figures. Whether they represent saints, queens or nuns is uncertain, but the luminous, smiling statues are among the most splendid surviving works of art from the ninth century.

Museo Cristiano

Via Candotti 1 • Wed–Sun 10am–1pm & 3–6pm • €4

Two beautiful Lombard pieces are in the **Museo Cristiano**, housed in the precincts of the fifteenth-century Duomo. The **Altar of Ratchis** was carved for Ratchis, Duke of Cividale and King of the Lombards at Pavia, who died as a Benedictine monk at Montecassino in 759; the reliefs of *Christ in Triumph* and the *Adoration of the Magi* are delicate and haunting.

The other highlight is the **Baptistry of Callisto**, named after Callisto de Treviso, the first Patriarch of Aquileia to move to Cividale. He lived here from 730 to 756 and initiated the building of the patriarchal palace, the cathedral and this octagonal baptistry, which used to stand beside the cathedral. It's constructed from older Lombard fragments, the columns and capitals dating from the fifth century.

The Duomo

Piazza del Duomo • Mon 9am–2pm, Tues–Sun 8.30am–7.30pm • Free

The **Duomo** itself houses a twelfth-century masterpiece of silversmithery: the *pala* (altarpiece) named after Pellegrino II, the patriarch who commissioned and donated it to the town; it depicts the Virgin seated between the archangels Michael and Gabriel, who are flanked by 25 saints and framed by more saints, prophets and the patron himself.

Museo Archeologico

Piazza del Duomo • Mon 9am–2pm, Tues–Sun 8.30am–7.30pm • €4

The **Museo Archeologico** houses an excellent exhibition on the Lombards on the first floor, incorporating local finds including some beautiful gold brooches. On the ground floor is a hotchpotch of late Roman and early Christian pieces, the highlight being a second-century mosaic of a wild-eyed Neptune.

The Ipogeo Celtico

East of the piazza, on Via Monastero Maggiore, is a cellar-like cavern called the **Ipogeo Celtico** (to visit, contact the bar *All'Ipogeo* next door; donation requested). The hypogeum was probably used as a tomb for Celtic leaders between the fifth and second centuries BC, but there is still some dispute as to whether it's artificial or was merely adapted by its users. Either way, the spectral faces carved on the walls make it a most unsettling place.

Ponte del Diavolo

Just beyond the Ipogeo, and spanning the Natisone, the **Ponte del Diavolo** (Devil's Bridge) is a reconstruction of the original fifteenth-century structure destroyed during World War I. Of many legends concerning the bridge's demonic name, a favourite involves the devil agreeing to aid the speedy construction of the bridge in return for the soul of the first living thing to cross it – Cividale's wily inhabitants sent a hapless dog.

ARRIVAL AND INFORMATION

CIVIDALE DEL FRIULI

By train Cividale is reached on an hourly service from Udine (20min; free with the FVG Card – see box, p.439). The train station is a 5min walk north of the city centre.
By bus Three daily buses from Gorizia (1hr) pull in at

Cividale's bus station, which is adjacent to the train station.
Tourist office Piazza Diacono 9 (daily 9.30am–noon & 3.30–6pm; ☎0432 710 460, ⓦ cividale.net); offers free internet access.

ACCOMMODATION

Casa dei Dolci B & B Via Alpi Giulie 5 ☎0432 734 385, ⓦ bedandbreakfastfvg.com. A 10min walk from the town centre, this newly renovated, stylish B&B and self-catering apartment is set in a beautiful garden. It offers genuine hospitality and wonderful breakfasts. **€70**
Locanda al Castello Via del Castello 12 ☎0432 733 242, ⓦ alcastello.net. This family-run hotel, a 20min walk from the *centro storico*, is a renovated nineteenth-century

castle formerly occupied by the Jesuits, with large, old-fashioned rooms and modern services. Facilities include an indoor pool, wellness centre and good restaurant. **€130**
Locanda al Pomo d'Oro Piazzetta S. Giovanni 20 ☎0432 731 489, ⓦ alpomodoro.com. Slap-bang in the centre of town, this modest hotel still serves its original purpose of providing travellers with shelter, tasty food and good wine. **€85**

EATING AND DRINKING

Al Cjant dal Rusignul Via Mernico 8, Mernico ☎0481 60 452, ⓦ ferrucciosgubin.it. Attractive country restaurant, a 10min drive from Cividale, set among the vines. The seasonal menu changes regularly, and the excellent wine list showcases the best of the Collio and beyond. Delicious home-made pasta, mushroom and game dishes are the stars here, and there are very good home-made desserts. The wine produced on the estate is top quality. Fri–Sun 12.30–2.30pm & 7.30–11pm.
Antica Osteria La Speranza Foro Giulio Cesare 15 ☎0432 731 131. Historic bar and *osteria* with a great atmosphere, serving up traditional dishes with a modern

twist. The blackboard menu changes frequently and is complemented by a good wine list including a large selection by the glass. Try fresh tagliatelle with *rucola* pesto. Great casual dining at fair prices. Daily 10am–2.30pm & 5–10pm.
gustobase Piazza Paolo Diacono 24 ☎0432 731 383, ⓦ gustobase.it. Attractive, recently opened *enoteca* in the centre of Cividale. Blackboard menu of traditional Friulian offerings plus other more exotic dishes, including plates of ham and salami or chicken cooked in soy sauce served with basmati rice, and a large range of international and Italian wines. Daily 10.30am–2pm & 5–9pm.

Valle del Natisone

Five kilometres east of Cividale lies the magical **Valle del Natisone**, an area of wild natural beauty dominated by the region's highest mountain, **Mount Matajur** (1643m). This is a landscape of rushing rivers and steep forested hills, dotted with tiny stone villages linked by a network of walking trails – indeed, the best way to explore is on foot. The area is completely cross border in character, neither Italian nor Slovenian but an intriguing mix of both. It's also a foodie heaven and holds its own food festival **Invito a Pranzo** –"Come for Lunch" – every autumn (details on ⓦ invitoapranzo.it).

FESTIVALS IN CIVIDALE DEL FRIULI

Cividale hosts many festivals including **Mittelfest** (ⓦ mittelfest.org), held each July, a celebration of Central European culture with concerts, theatre and dance. In August the **Palio di San Donato** (ⓦ paliodicividale.it) transforms the town centre into a medieval stage, complete with fourteenth-century costumes, food, jousts and archery. The town's **chamber music festival** (ⓦ perfezionamentomusicale.net) in August is a world-class event.

Emilia-Romagna

BOLOGNA

Emilia-Romagna

Emilia-Romagna doesn't attract nearly the same volume of tourists as its neighbouring provinces of Lombardy, the Veneto and Tuscany, which is strange because it offers just as fine a distillation of the region's charms: glorious countryside, plenty of historic architecture and local cuisine renowned across the rest of Italy. It's also pretty easy to get around, with most of its main sites located along the Via Emilia (or more prosaically the A1 and A14 roads), the dead-straight road first laid down by the Romans in 187 BC that splits the province in two along its east–west axis, dividing the Apennine mountains in the south from the flat fields of the northern plain, the Pianura Padana.

Dotted along this road are some proud, historic towns, filled with restored medieval and Renaissance *palazzi*, the legacy of a handful of feuding families – the **Este** in Ferrara and Modena, the **Farnese** in Parma, and lesser dynasties in Ravenna and Rimini – who used to control the area before the papacy took charge. The largest urban centre, and the main tourist draw, is **Bologna**, the site of Europe's first university – and today best known as the gastronomic capital of Italy. It's generally regarded as one of the country's most beautiful cities with a mazy network of porticoed, medieval streets housing a collection of restaurants that easily live up to the town's reputation.

To the west are the wealthy, provincial towns of **Modena**, **Parma** and **Reggio Emilia**, easily reached by train, and each with their own charming historic centres and gastronomic delights, while to the east lies **Ravenna**, once the capital of the Western Roman Empire and today home to the finest set of Byzantine mosaics in the world. The Adriatic coast south is an overdeveloped ribbon of settlements, although **Rimini**, at its southern end, provides a spark of interest, with its wild seaside nightlife and surprisingly historic town centre.

Away from the central artery, Emilia-Romagna's **countryside** comes in two topographical varieties: flat or hilly. To the north lies one of the largest areas of flat land in Italy, a primarily agricultural region where much of the produce for the region's famed kitchens is grown. It also boasts a good deal of wildlife, particularly around the **Po Delta** on the Adriatic (a soggy expanse of marshland and lagoons that has become a prime destination for birdwatchers) and in **Ferrara**, just thirty minutes north of Bologna, one of the most important Renaissance centres in Italy. To the south are the **Apennines**, an area best explored using your own transport, sampling local cuisine and joining in the festivals; although it's still possible to get a taste of this beautiful region, far removed from the functional plain to the north, by bus. If you're a keen hiker, you might be tempted by the Grande Escursione Appenninica, a 25-day-long trek following the backbone of the range from refuge to refuge, which can be accessed from the foothills south of Reggio Emilia.

ROCCA VISCONTEA

Highlights

❶ **Bologna's restaurants** A meal out in the gastronomic capital of Italy is a rite of passage for any true food-lover. **See p.474**

❷ **Duomo, Modena** One of the finest Romanesque buildings in Italy, with some magnificent decoration inside and out. **See p.478**

❸ **Gourmet Parma** Parma is inextricably linked to two great delicacies, Parma ham and Parmesan cheese, both of which can be sampled in the city or in the surrounding region. **See p.483**

❹ **Rocca Viscontea** Northern Emilia-Romagna's most majestic castle. **See p.488**

❺ **Brisighella festivals** This medieval village is known for its truffle, polenta and olive festivals in autumn. **See p.490**

❻ **Ravenna's mosaics** Unrivalled both in beauty and preservation, these mosaics are unmissable. **See p.496**

❼ **Rimini's nightlife** The hottest, loudest and wildest in the country. **See p.506**

HIGHLIGHTS ARE MARKED ON THE MAP ON P.464

EMILIA-ROMAGNA

ADRIATIC SEA

VENETO

LOMBARDY

TUSCANY

MEDITERRANEAN SEA

HIGHLIGHTS
1. Bologna's restaurants
2. Duomo, Modena
3. Gourmet Parma
4. Rocca Viscontea
5. Brisighella festivals
6. Ravenna's mosaics
7. Rimini's nightlife

REGIONAL FOOD AND WINE

Emilia-Romagna has a just reputation for producing the richest, most lavish food in Italy, with its famous specialities of **parmesan** cheese (*parmigiano-reggiano*), egg pasta, **Parma ham** (generically known as *prosciutto di Parma*) and balsamic vinegar. Despite its current foodie connotations, **balsamic vinegar** started off as a cottage industry, with many Emilian families distilling and then redistilling local wine to form a dark liquor that is then matured in wooden barrels for at least twelve years. Bologna is regarded as the gastronomic capital of Italy, and Emilia is the only true home of **pasta** in the North: often lovingly handmade, the dough is formed into *lasagne*, *tortellini* stuffed with ricotta cheese and spinach, pumpkin or pork, and other fresh pastas served with *ragù* (meat sauce), cream sauces or simply with butter and parmesan – *alla parmigiana* usually denotes something cooked with parmesan. Modena and Parma specialize in *bollito misto* – boiled **meats**, such as flank of beef, trotters, tongue and spicy sausage – while another Modenese dish is *zampone* – stuffed pig's trotter. The region is second only to Sicily for the amount of **fish** caught in its waters.

Regional **wines** are, like the landscapes and people, quite distinct. Emilia is synonymous with **Lambrusco**, but don't despair: buy only DOC Lambrusco and be amazed by the dark, often blackberry-coloured wine that foams into the glass and cuts through the fattiness of the typically meaty Emilian meal. There are four DOC zones for Lambrusco and you get a glimpse of three of them, all around Modena, from the Via Emilia, each supporting neat rows of high-trellised vines. The fourth zone extends across the plains and foothills of the Apennines, in the province of Reggio Emilia. Other wines to try, both whites, are Trebbianino Val Trebbia and Monterosso Val D'Arda, while the lively Malvasia (also white) from the Colli di Parma goes well with the celebrated local ham.

Heading east towards the Adriatic coast, you come to the Romagna, a flatter, drier province where the wines have less exuberance but more body and are dominated by Albana and Sangiovese. The sweeter versions of **Albana** are often more successful at bringing out the peachy, toasted-almond flavours of this white. The robust red of **Sangiovese**, from the hills around Imola and Rimini, comes in various "weights" – all around the heavy mark. Much lighter is Cagnina di Romagna, which is best drunk young (within six months of harvest).

8

Bologna and around

Emilia's capital, **BOLOGNA**, is a thriving city, whose light-engineering and high-tech industries have brought conspicuous wealth to the old brick palaces and porticoed streets. It's well known for its food – undeniably the richest in the country – and for its **politics**. "Red Bologna" became the Italian Left's stronghold and spiritual home, having evolved out of the resistance movement to German occupation during World War II. Consequently, Bologna's train station was singled out by Fascist groups in 1980 for a bomb attack in Italy's worst postwar terrorist atrocity – a glassed-in jagged gash in the station wall commemorates the tragedy in which 84 people died. In subsequent decades, the city's political leanings have been less predictable, although its "leftist" reputation continues to stick.

Bologna is certainly one of the best-looking cities in the country. The centre is startlingly medieval in plan, a jumble of red brick, tiled roofs and balconies radiating out from the great central square of Piazza Maggiore. There are enough monuments and curiosities for several days' leisured exploration, including plenty of small, quirky museums, some tremendously grand Gothic and Renaissance architecture and, most conspicuously, the **Due Torri**, the city's own "leaning towers". Thanks to the **university**, there's always something happening – be it theatre, music, the city's lively summer festival, or just the café and bar scene, which is among northern Italy's most convivial.

Piazza del Nettuno and Piazza Maggiore

Bologna's city centre is compact, with most sights within easy reach of the main ring road. Lined with shops and bars, **Via dell'Indipendenza** runs from the train station

THE 2012 EARTHQUAKES

On 20 May 2012, pressure caused by the slow movement of the Apennines through the Po valley caused a magnitude-6 **earthquake** to shake the Emilia-Romagna region. The first quake was followed in successive days by hundreds of aftershocks, leaving 26 people dead, 20,000 homeless and many historic structures damaged. The epicentre was in the province of Modena, and although the town itself was largely unaffected, the surroundings fared less well; many of the dead were workers in warehouses and factories which had not been constructed to withstand serious seismic movement. An important contributor to the local economy – the production of *grana padano* and *parmigiano-reggiano* cheeses – was affected when storage facilities collapsed, causing an estimated €200 million-worth of damage. In total, it is thought that the earthquake damage will exceed €4 billion, and experts believe that the spate of earthquakes will continue for years to come.

to the centre, finishing up at the linked central squares of **Piazza Maggiore** and **Piazza del Nettuno**.

The Neptune Fountain

At the centre of Piazza del Nettuno, the **Neptune Fountain**, one of the most celebrated symbols of the city, was created by Giambologna in the late sixteenth century. Its extravagant – and, when first unveiled, highly controversial – composition sees a trident-wielding Neptune sat atop a pile of *putti* and mermaids – who are themselves arranged rather indelicately astride dolphins shooting water from their breasts. Beside the fountain is a wall lined with photographs of partisans who died in World War II, near another memorial to those killed in the 1980 train station bombing.

Palazzo Re Enzo and Palazzo Podestà

Piazza del Nettuno • Both *palazzi* open occasionally for special exhibitions

Across the square from the fountain, the **Palazzo Re Enzo** takes its name from its time as the prison-home of Enzo, king of Sicily, confined here by papal supporters for two decades after the Battle of Fossalta in 1249. Next door to the Palazzo Re Enzo, **Palazzo Podestà** fills the northern side of Piazza Maggiore, built in the fifteenth century at the behest of the Bentivoglio clan.

Palazzo d'Accursio

Piazza del Nettuno 6

On the piazza's western edge, the **Palazzo Comunale** gives some indication of the political shifts in power, its facade adorned by a huge statue of Pope Gregory XIII as an affirmation of papal authority. Inside are two art collections.

Museo Morandi

Tues–Fri 11am–6pm, Sat & Sun 11am–8pm • €6 • ⓦ museomorandi.it

The first museum, the **Museo Morandi**, is devoted to the life and works of one of Italy's most important twentieth-century painters. Over two hundred works and a faithful reconstruction of Giorgio Morandi's studio offer a fascinating glimpse into the artist best known for his still lifes.

Collezioni Comunali d'Arte

Tues–Fri 9am–6.30pm, Sat & Sun 10am–6.30pm • €4, free first Sat of the month from 3pm

The **Collezioni Comunali d'Arte** forms one third of the city's Museo Civici d'Arte Antica, along with the Museo Davia Bargellini and the Museo Civico Medievale. Its galleries of ornate furniture and paintings include works by Vitale da Bologna, Simone dei Crocifissi and others of the Bolognese School.

San Petronio
Piazza Maggiore • Church daily: 7.45am–1.15pm & 3–6.30pm; museum Tues–Sat 10am–12.30pm & 3–5pm • Free

On the southern side of Piazza Maggiore stands the church of **San Petronio**, one of the finest Gothic brick buildings in Italy. This enormous structure was originally intended to have been larger than St Peter's in Rome, but money and land for the side aisle were diverted by the pope's man in Bologna towards a new university and plans had to be modified. The end result looks a little strange at first glance, with the beginnings of the planned aisles on both sides of the building clearly visible. There are models of what the church was supposed to look like in the **museum**. Note that you are not permitted to take large backpacks into the church, and there are no storage facilities provided.

Museo Civico Archeologico
Via dell'Archiginnasio 2 • Tues–Fri 9am–3pm, Sat & Sun 10am–6.30pm • €4, admission free on first Sat of the month from 3pm • Ⓦ comune.bologna.it/museoarcheologico

In the Palazzo Galvani, the **Museo Civico Archeologico** is rather stuffy but has good displays of Egyptian and Roman antiquities, and an Etruscan section that is one of the best outside Lazio, with finds drawn from the settlement of Felsina, which predated Bologna.

Via Clavature
Via Clavature – together with nearby Via Pescerie Vecchie and Via Draperie – is home to a grouping of **market stalls** and shops that makes for one of the city's most enticing sights. In autumn, especially, the market is a visual feast, with fat porcini mushrooms, truffles in baskets of rice, thick rolls of *mortadella*, hanging pheasants, ducks and hares, and skinned frogs by the kilo.

At no. 10, the church of **Santa Maria della Vita** (Mon–Sat 10am–6pm, Sun 4.30pm–6pm; free) holds an outstanding pietà by Niccolò dell'Arca – seven life-sized terracotta figures that are among the most dramatic examples of Renaissance sculpture you'll see.

The Archiginnasio
Bologna's old university – the **Archiginnasio** – was founded at more or less the same time as Piazza Maggiore was laid out, predating the rest of Europe's universities, although it didn't get a special building until 1565, when Antonio Morandi was commissioned to construct the present building on the site until then reserved for San Petronio. You can wander into the main courtyard, covered with the coats of arms of its more famous graduates, and visit the upstairs library, but the main attraction is the Teatro Anatomico.

Teatro Anatomico
Mon–Sat 9am–6.45pm, Sat 9am–1.45pm, reduced hours in Aug • Free

The Archiginnasio's most interesting feature is the **Teatro Anatomico**, the original medical faculty dissection theatre. Tiers of seats surround an extraordinary professor's chair, covered with a canopy supported by figures known as *gli spellati* – "the skinned ones". Not many dissections went on, owing to prohibitions of the Church, but when they did (usually around carnival time), artists and the general public used to turn up as much for the social occasion as for studying the body.

Piazza San Domenico
A few minutes south of the old university, down Via Garibaldi, is **Piazza San Domenico**, with its strange canopied tombs holding the bones of medieval law scholars. Bologna was instrumental in sorting out wrangles between the pope and the Holy Roman Emperor in the tenth and eleventh centuries, earning itself the title of *La Dotta* ("The Learned") and forming the basis for the university's prominent law faculties.

8

San Domenico

Piazza San Domenico 13 • Church Mon–Fri 9.30am–12.30pm & 3.30–6.30pm, Sat & Sun closes 5.30pm; museum Mon–Fri 9.30am–12.30pm & 3.30–6.30pm, Sat opens and closes 30min earlier • Free

The church of **San Domenico** was built in 1221 to house the relics of St Dominic, which were placed in the so-called *Arca di San Domenico*, the creation of Nicola Pisano, among other sculptors. The angel resting on St Dominic's tomb is the work of **Michelangelo**. While you're in the church, try also to see the **Museo di San Domenico**, displaying a very fine polychrome terracotta bust of St Dominic by Niccolò dell'Arca

● RESTAURANTS	
All'Osteria Bottega	16
Al Sangiovese	19
Canton de Fiori	6
Casa Monica	5
Clorofilla	13
È Cucina Bologna	17
Franco Rossi	3
Grassilli	10
Il Tarì	15
Osteria dell'Orsa	2
Osteria La Traviata	18
Scacco Matto	8
Trattoria Danio	4
Trattoria Da Gianni	12

■ BARS & CLUBS	
Caffè Zamboni	8
Cantina Bentivoglio	4
Cassero	1
Clauricane Irish Pub	7
Enoteca des Arts	6
La Scuderia	5
Le Stanze	3
MamBo Ex-Forno	2
Osteria del Sole	10
Soda Pops	9
Villa Serena	11
Zanarini	12

● CAFÉS, PASTICCERIE & GELATERIE	
A.F Tamburini	9
Altero	1
Cremeria Funivia	14
Il Gelatauro	7
La Baita Formaggi	11

■ ACCOMMODATION	
Accademia	1
Al Cappello Rosso	9
Antica Residenza d'Azeglio	12
Centrale	6
Corona d'Oro	3
Garisenda	7
Grand Hotel Majestic	2
Il Nosadillo	11
Orologio	8
Palazzo Trevi	10
Panorama	5
San Vitale	4

12 & 19

along with paintings, reliquaries and vestments, and, beyond, the intricately inlaid mid-sixteenth-century choir stalls.

The university district

Bordered by Via Oberdan to the west and Strada Maggiore to the south, the eastern section of Bologna's *centro storico* preserves many of the older **university** departments, housed for the most part in large seventeenth- and eighteenth-century palaces.

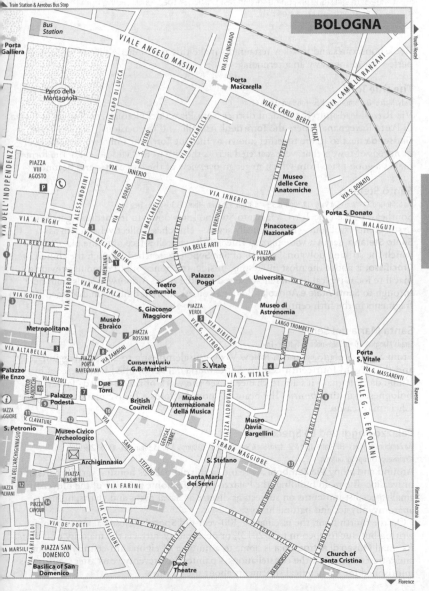

BOLOGNA

> ## BOLOGNA'S PORTICOES
>
> No other city has anything like the number of **porticoes** or covered walkways found in Bologna. In the city centre there are barely any stretches of pavement not topped by an ornate, arched covering. They make a vivid first impression, especially at night, while by day they provide an unofficial catwalk for Bologna's well-turned-out residents. The first porticoes were built out of wood, some thirteenth-century examples of which still stand. They proved so popular that by the fourteenth century construction of stone or brick porticoes, high enough to accommodate people on horseback, had become compulsory on all new streets. Today, some 38km still stand, including the longest portico in the world, leading from the city up to the Santuario di San Luca (see p.477).

Bookshops, cafés and low-key restaurants make this atmospheric slice of studentville perfect for idling away an afternoon.

The Due Torri

Daily: March–Oct 9am–6pm; Nov–Feb 9am–5pm • €3

Via Rizzoli leads into the student district from Piazza del Nettuno, ending up at Piazza di Porta Ravegnana, where the **Torre degli Asinelli**, and the perilously leaning **Torre Garisenda** next to it, are together known as the **Due Torri**, the only two remaining of hundreds of towers that were scattered across the city in the Middle Ages. The former makes a good place from which to get an overview of the city centre and beyond.

Santo Stefano

Via S. Stefano 24 • Mon–Sat 9am–12.30pm & 3.30–6.30pm, Sun 9am–1pm & 3.30–7pm • Free

Southeast of the Due Torri, Via Santo Stefano leads down to its medieval gateway, past a complex of four – but originally seven – churches, collectively known as **Santo Stefano**, set in a wide piazza. Three of the churches face onto the piazza, of which the striking polygonal church of **San Sepolcro**, reached through the church of **Crocifisso**, is about the most interesting. Inside, the bones of St Petronius provide a macabre focus typical of the relic-obsessed Middle Ages. A doorway leads from here through to **Santi Vitale e Agricola**, Bologna's oldest church, built from discarded Roman fragments in the fifth century.

Santa Maria dei Servi

Strada Maggiore • Daily 7am–noon & 4–8pm • Free

From Santo Stefano, you can follow Via Gerusalemme up to Strada Maggiore and the elegant fourteenth-century **Santa Maria dei Servi**, filled with frescoes by Vitale da Bologna – it's a rare chance to see the work of the so-called "father" of Bolognese painting *in situ*. The beautiful portico holds a festive market during the Christmas season.

Palazzo Poggi and La Specola

Via Zamboni 33 • Tues–Fri 10am–1pm & 2–4pm, Sat & Sun 10.30am–1.30pm & 2.30–5.30pm • €3 • ☎ 051 209 9398, ⓦ museopalazzopoggi.unibo.it

Around and along **Via Zamboni** are many of the old palaces housing various parts of the university. The main building, the **Palazzo Poggi**, is home to many of the university's small specialist museums on subjects as diverse as naval maps and charts, human anatomy, physics and natural history.

On the fourth floor, the fascinating 300-year-old **Specola** (closed at the time of writing but due to open in mid-2013), or observatory, attracts the majority of visitors. Its small **Museo di Astronomia** is home to a number of eighteenth-century instruments and a frescoed map of the constellations – painted just seventy years after Galileo was imprisoned for his heretical statements about the cosmos.

Museo delle Cere Anatomiche

Via Irnerio 48 • Mon–Thurs 9am–12.30pm & 2–4.30pm, Fri 9am–12.30pm • Free • ⓦ museocereanatomiche.it

The **Museo delle Cere Anatomiche "Luigi Cattaneo"** might seem an odd place to visit, but it would be a shame to leave Bologna without seeing its idiosyncratic (and beautiful) **waxworks**. These were used until the nineteenth century for medical demonstrations, and the lurid anatomical cutaways, plus models of such things as conjoined twins and deformed limbs, are as startling as any art or sculpture in the city.

Pinacoteca Nazionale

Via delle Belle Arti 56 • Tues–Sat 9am–7pm, Sun hours vary • €4 • ⓦ pinacotecabologna.beneculturali.it

The paintings in the **Pinacoteca Nazionale** concentrate mainly on the heavier religious works of Bolognese artists. There are early pieces, such as those by the fourteenth-century painter Vitale da Bologna, with later works by Francia and Tibaldi, as well as paintings from the city's most productive artistic period, the early seventeenth century.

San Giacomo Maggiore

Piazza Rossini • Mon–Fri 7.30am–12.30pm & 3.30–6.30pm, Sat & Sun 8.30am–12.30pm & 3.30–6.30pm • Free

Back towards the centre down Via Zamboni is the church of **San Giacomo Maggiore**, a Romanesque structure begun in 1267 and enlarged over the centuries. The target here is the Bentivoglio Chapel, decorated with funds provided by one Annibale Bentivoglio to celebrate the family's victory in a local feud in 1488. Lorenzo Costa painted frescoes called *The Triumph of Fame, The Triumph of Death* and *Madonna Enthroned* as well as some of the Bentivoglio family – a deceptively pious-looking lot, captured in what was a fairly innovative picture in its time for the careful characterizations of its patrons.

Adjoining the church is the **Oratorio di Santa Cecilia** (daily 10am–1pm & 2–6pm), its walls covered with exquisite frescoes commissioned by the Bentivoglio family in 1505, depicting ten scenes from the life of St Cecilia, patron saint of music. The oratory makes an atmospheric backdrop for free classical music concerts in summer.

Museo Internazionale della Musica

Palazzo Sanguinetti, Strada Maggiore 34 • Tues–Fri 9.30am–4pm, Sat & Sun 10am–6.30pm • €4, free first Sat of the month from 3pm • ⓦ museomusicabologna.it

The beautifully frescoed sixteenth-century **Palazzo Sanguinetti** is home to a museum displaying an impressive trove of musical instruments, original manuscripts and paintings, including a portrait of Vivaldi and one of J.C. Bach by Gainsborough.

Museo Ebraico

Via Valdonica 1/5 • Mon–Thurs & Sun 10am–6pm, Fri 10am–4pm • €4 • ⓦ museoebraicobo.it

Situated in the old Jewish ghetto, the **Museo Ebraico** presents the history and migratory patterns of the once-thriving Jewish community in Emilia-Romagna, through rather dry display panels; it also has temporary exhibitions by Jewish artists.

North and west of Piazza Maggiore

There are fewer sights as such to the north and west of Bologna's central squares, although the covered market off **Via Ugo Bassi** (see box, p.475) is worth a wander. This street and busy **Via dell'Indipendenza** are lined with shops, while further west, **Via del Pratello** is a lively spot after dark.

Metropolitana di San Pietro

Via dell'Indipendenza 9 • Daily 7.15am–6.45pm • Free

A couple of blocks north of Piazza del Nettuno, the city's cathedral, the **Metropolitana di San Pietro**, was originally a tenth-century building but has been rebuilt many times and is these days more enjoyable for its stately atmosphere than any particular features.

Museo Civico Medievale

Via Manzoni 4 • Tues–Fri 9am–3pm, Sat & Sun 10am–6.30pm • €4, free first Sat of the month from 3pm

The **Museo Civico Medievale** is housed in the Renaissance Palazzo Fava and decorated with frescoes by Carracci and members of the Bolognese School depicting the *History of Europa*, *Jason's Feats* and scenes from the *Aeneid*. The museum collection itself includes bits of armour, ceramics, numerous tombs and busts of various popes and other dignitaries, and a *Madonna and Saints* by Jacopo della Quercia.

Basilica di San Francesco

Piazza San Francesco • Daily 6.30am–noon & 3–7pm • Free

West of Piazza del Nettuno, the **Basilica di San Francesco** is a huge, Gothic brick pile supported by flying buttresses that was built in 1236, heavily restored in the 1920s and partly rebuilt after World War II. Inside there are a beautiful and very ornate altarpiece from 1392 and a pleasant cloister.

MAMbo – Museo d'Arte Moderna di Bologna

Via Don Minzoni 14 • Tues, Wed & Fri noon–6pm, Thurs, Sat & Sun noon–8pm • €6 • ⊛ mambo-bologna.org • Bus #33 or #35 from the station

Known, inevitably perhaps, by the acronym **MAMbo**, the **Museo d'Arte Moderna di Bologna** is Bologna's answer to Bilbao's Guggenheim or New York's MOMA. Opened in 2007, it now forms the centrepiece of a burgeoning new cultural complex occupying a former industrial estate in the northwest of the city. Housed in a former bakery, the gallery is as stark, white and Modernist-looking as you'd expect and has been given the mission of providing a complete overview of Italian art from the 1950s on. It's not quite there yet, although the permanent collection is a thought-provoking cross-section and there are also regular touring exhibitions. Part of a self-styled **Manifattura delle Arti** (Factory of Arts), the museum shares the complex with an art-house cinema and film archive, the **Cineteca** (see p.477), as well as various restaurants and bars.

ARRIVAL AND DEPARTURE   BOLOGNA

BY PLANE

Marconi airport (☏051 647 9615, ⊛ bologna-airport.it) lies northwest of town, linked to the centre and the train station by the Aerobus (BLQ; €6, buy tickets on board), which runs roughly every 15min and takes around 25min in light traffic. Taxis to the centre cost around €20. Ryanair passengers with check-in luggage need to go to the new Terminal Est to drop it off: it's the first airport stop on the Aerobus, or an 8min walk from the main terminal.

BY TRAIN

The station is at Piazza delle Medaglie d'Oro. Buses #A, #11, #25 or #27 run to Piazza Maggiore or Via Rizzoli, or it's a 15min walk. Destinations Ancona (every 30–45min; 1hr 45min–3hr 30min); Faenza (every 30min; 25–40min); Ferrara (every 30min; 20–55min); Florence (every 30min; 35min–1hr 20min); Forlì (hourly; 30min–1hr); Milan (every 30min; 1hr 5min–2hr 55min); Modena (every 30min; 20–30min); Parma (every 30min; 50min–1hr 20min); Ravenna (13 daily; 1hr–1hr 20min); Reggio Emilia (every 30min; 35–50min);

Rimini (every 30min; 55min–2hr 25min).

BY BUS

All long-distance buses terminate at the bus station, 300m from the train station at Piazza XX Settembre 6. Bus #A, #11 or #27 from the bus station take you to Piazza Maggiore. Otherwise it's a 15min walk.

BY CAR

Avoid bringing a car into central Bologna if possible: there are traffic restrictions all over town and the city centre is closed to private traffic between 7am and 8pm every day. If your hotel is in the historic centre you'll be allowed to bring your car in, but you'll need to inform your hotel first.
Car rental Try Avis, Via Marco Polo 91 (☏051 634 1632); Europcar, Via Cesare Boldrini 226 (☏051 415 8456); Maggiore, Via Cairoli 4 (☏051 252 525). All the major companies also have desks at the airport.
Parking There's parking on Piazza XX Settembre and Piazza VIII Agosto, adjacent to the bus station.

GETTING AROUND AND INFORMATION

On foot The best way to enjoy Bologna is on foot, strolling beneath some of the city's beautiful porticoes amid Italy's

most courteous drivers. Guided sightseeing tours of the city in English leave from the main tourist office Mon & Fri at

11am, Tues & Thurs at 4.30pm, Wed, Sat & Sun at 10.15am (times can change, so call to check; €13).

By bike Autorimessa Pincio at Via dell'Indipendenza 71/Z (Mon–Thurs & Sun 7am–midnight, Fri & Sat 7am–1am), near the station, rents bikes for €2/hr.

By bus Buses (ⓦ tper.it) are fast and frequent. Tickets cost €1.20 each from *tabacchi*, newsstands, ticket machines and bus info kiosks and are valid on as many buses as you like within one hour, or within 1hr 30min during the reduced service period in August. If you plan to make frequent use of them it might be worth buying a day-ticket for €4, or a Citypass (€11, valid for ten journeys).

By open-top bus The open-top, hop-on hop-off City redbus makes a tour of the city (C12, or C10 with San Luca Express; ⓣ 051 379 452, ⓦ cityredbus.com). There are ten departures daily between 10am and 4.30pm from Viale Pietramellara in front of the train station.

By taxi Cotabo (ⓣ 051 372 727); CAT (ⓣ 051 4590).

Tourist offices Bologna's main tourist office, Bologna Welcome, at Piazza Maggiore 1 (Mon–Sat 9am–7pm, Sun 10am–5pm; ⓣ 051 239 660, ⓦ bolognawelcome.it), is packed with information, including the excellent bilingual publication *L'ospite di/A Guest of Bologna*, plus details of gourmet tours and cookery courses. There's also detailed, up-to-date information on the website. There's a second office at the airport (Mon–Sat 9am–7pm, Sun 9am–4pm).

ACCOMMODATION

Bologna's **accommodation** mostly caters for business travellers with only a few inexpensive hotels. During the **trade-fair peak** (March to early May & Sept–Dec) prices can more than double. Many hotels prefer to take block bookings during these times and making an individual reservation can be tricky. In July and August prices are much lower. The tourist office has a helpful booking service (Piazza Maggiore ⓣ 051 658 3111, airport ⓣ 051 647 2201): they can book rooms for you at no charge, or you can do it yourself through ⓦ bolognawelcome.it. Note that Bologna has introduced a **hotel tax**: you'll be charged €1–4 per person, per night, depending on the type of accommodation.

Accademia Via Belle Arti 6 ⓣ 051 232 318, ⓦ hotel accademia.com. In the heart of the university quarter, this recently refurbished large three-star hotel has modestly sized and furnished en-suite doubles, some with balconies. Periodic art shows decorate the public areas. All rooms have a/c. **€120**

★ **Al Cappello Rosso** Via de' Fusari 9 ⓣ 051 261 891, ⓦ alcappellorosso.it. It may be one of the city's oldest hotels, with six centuries of service behind it, but the *Cappello Rosso* has certainly done its best to move with the times, now offering dedicated rooms for ladies, a pet-care service and even special allergy-proof rooms. Bedrooms are stylishly modern, large and comfortable – some have been individually decorated by artists, such as the Shock in Pink room, a homage to Italian fashion designer Elsa Schiaparelli. There's also a library-cum-book-swapping service, and free bikes for guests' use. **€140**

Antica Residenza d'Azeglio Via Massimo d'Azeglio 64 ⓣ 051 644 7389, ⓦ anticaresidenzadazeglio.it. This B&B's five rooms are large, comfortable and elegantly decorated, with thoughtful touches such as wine and fresh fruit. Ultra-helpful hosts Agostino and Roberto are on hand to answer questions and make restaurant recommendations. **€100**

Centrale Via della Zecca 2 ⓣ 051 225 114, ⓦ albergo centralebologna.it. Recently refurbished two-star in the heart of the city. All of the 25 spacious rooms come with bathrooms and a/c, and there are great views from the top floor. A generous breakfast is included. **€70**

Corona d'Oro Via Oberdan 12 ⓣ 051 745 7611, ⓦ coronaoro.bolognahotels.it. One of the city's "art" hotels offers four-star opulence in a plush *palazzo* graced with a lovely wooden portico, the city's oldest. **€125**

★ **Garisenda** Galleria del Leone 1/Via Rizzoli 9 ⓣ 051 224 369, ⓦ albergogarisenda.com. The seven rooms here are basic – only three have private bathrooms – but the location is great and the welcome very genuine; above the Via Rizzoli shops right opposite the two towers. Surprisingly quiet for its commercial location. Includes breakfast and wi-fi. **€65**

Grand Hotel Majestic Via dell'Indipendenza 8 ⓣ 051 225 445, ⓦ grandhotelmajestic.duetorrihotels .com. A luxurious five-star option in the heart of town, with rooms that go all-out for glamour and elegance, with fabric-covered walls, heavy drapery, ornate beds and marble bathrooms. **€270**

Il Nosadillo Via Nosadella 19 ⓦ hostels.com. Bologna's official HI hostel is 6km out of town; this small hostel in the historic centre makes a more convenient alternative (though rates are around €10 per night higher). As the staff aren't around all day, it feels more like a shared apartment than a hostel, with two mixed dorms (one sleeping four, one five) sharing two bathrooms, a kitchen and living room. Check-in 2–8pm. Dorms **€28.50**, doubles **€67**

Orologio Via IV Novembre 10 ⓣ 051 745 7411, ⓦ orologio.hotelsbologna.it. On a side street just south of Piazza Maggiore – look for the clock sign – this elegant, superior three-star is an "art" hotel, with an air of understated luxury and well-equipped rooms. **€105**

★ **Palazzo Trevi** Via Frassinago 31 ⓣ 051 580 230, ⓦ palazzotrevi.it. An impeccably run little six-room B&B a 5min walk from Piazza Maggiore. The rooms vary in size – some are very large – but all are comfortably furnished, with an attention to detail that goes beyond the usual B&B standard, from complimentary wine and snacks to fluffy dressing gown and slippers in the bathroom. Breakfast is

8

also excellent, taken on a pretty flower-filled terrace in summer. **€120**

★ **Panorama** Via Livraghi 1 ☎ 051 221 802, ⓦ hotel panoramabologna.it. Offering excellent value, this one-star hotel has three- and four-bed rooms as well as large doubles and singles, a little old-fashioned but spotlessly clean. Only one room comes with private bath; the rest share clean and

pleasant facilities down the corridor. Helpful owners. **€60**

★ **San Vitale** Via San Vitale 94 ☎ 051 225 966, ⓦ albergosanvitale.com. A little hotel in the heart of the city with a rare treat – its own lush garden. The rooms are basic but spotless and all have private bath. The friendly owners provide a very warm welcome. Breakfast costs an extra €3 and is taken in a bar nearby. **€70**

EATING

Eating is especially important to the Bolognese: the city is known as *La Grassa* ("The Fat One"), the result of a rich culinary tradition. Its **restaurants** are said to be the best in Italy, and even the simplest restaurants and the many *osterie* often serve dishes of a very high standard. The most convenient **supermarket** is the Co-op, at Via Garibaldi 1/D, next to Piazza Cavour (Mon–Sat 9am–8.30pm, Sun 9.30am–1.30pm & 4.30–7.30pm).

CAFÉS, GELATERIE AND PASTICCERIE

★ **A.F. Tamburini** Via Caprarie 1 ☎ 051 234 726. This fabulous, traditional delicatessen is a real gourmet's delight, its ceiling thick with hanging hams, and its counters bulging with giant cheeses. It's also got a great little café selling roasted meats and plates of filled pasta for around €5–7. Daily 8.30am–8pm, wine bar noon–12.30am.

Altero Via dell'Indipendenza 33 ☎ 051 234 758. Selling pizza by the slice till 1am – Margherita €1.30, mushroom €1.60, and for those with a sweet tooth, a slice of white pizza topped with Nutella for €1.20. Not quite the gastronomy for which Bologna is famed, but still. Mon–Fri 9am–1.30am, Sat 9am–2am, Sun 10am–1.30am.

Canton de Fiori Via dell'Indipendenza 1 ☎ 051 267 300. Enjoy a splendid coffee and cake under the porticoes at the "Corner of Flowers" just off Piazza del Nettuno, served to you with all due deference by smartly attired waiters. Mon–Fri & Sun 7.30am–8.30pm, Sat 8am–9pm.

★ **Cremeria Funivia** Piazza Cavour 1 ☎ 051 656 9365. More perfectly executed *gelato* would be impossible to find anywhere: incredibly silky and richly flavoured. You'll find the classics, such as *bacio* and *zabaione*, but also innovations like the toasted pine nut, dubbed "Leonardo", and the white chocolate with crunchy puffed rice, by the name of "San Luca". Tues–Sat noon–11.30pm, Sun 11am–11.30pm.

★ **Il Gelatauro** Via S. Vitale 98/B ☎ 051 230 049. A 10min walk east of the centre, this is a charming little place serving organic pastries, handmade chocolates, speciality wines and fantastic ice cream, in all manner of flavours, including green tea, pumpkin and cinnamon, and the "Principe di Calabria", with bergamot, jasmine and sponge cake. Mon 9am–8pm, Tues–Thurs 8.30am–11pm, Fri & Sat 8.30am–11.30pm, Sun 9.30am–10.30pm.

La Baita Formaggi Via Pescherie Vecchie 3 ☎ 051 223 940. A renowned cheese shop, stuffed with tempting gourmet goodies. You can stop by at lunch for a generous platter of cold cuts and cheeses for around €10, washed down with a glass of the local wine. Mon–Sat 8am–8pm.

RESTAURANTS

All'Osteria Bottega Via S. Caterina 51 ☎ 051 585 111. One of the city's top choices for top-notch dining, featuring a masterfully prepared, meat-centric menu that might include veal cheeks in Sangiovese wine (€16) or braised pigeon with chicory (€18). The place is low-lit, cosy and tiny, so booking is a must. Tues–Sat 12.30–2.30pm & 8pm–1am.

★ **Al Sangiovese** Vicolo del Falcone 2 ☎ 051 583 057, ⓦ alsangiovese.com. Tucked away on an unprepossessing backstreet, this traditional trattoria with outdoor seating serves excellent pasta dishes such as *strozzapreti* with porcini mushrooms, peas and ham (€8), as well as meaty mains (around €16), washed down with a fine Sangiovese red from the family vineyard. Mon–Sat noon–2.30pm & 7–10.30pm.

★ **Casa Monica** Via S. Rocco 16 ☎ 051 522 522. With its bright, Fellini-esque, high-ceilinged interior, this makes a fresh change from the traditional, rather dark and cramped, Bolognese restaurant norm. The menu varies daily, always something creative and light, such as carrot, ginger and almond soup or courgette flan with Gorgonzola cream; a full meal without wine will set you back around €30. Booking recommended. Daily 8–11.30pm.

★ **Clorofilla** Strada Maggiore 64/C ☎ 051 235 343. This warmly inviting vegetarian and fish place is just the spot if the "fat of Bologna" has been weighing you down, offering over a dozen types of salad (contadino, *greco*, couscous etc), all around €7, as well as tofu and seitan

---

BOLOGNA COOKERY SCHOOLS

If a visit to Bologna has inspired you to improve your culinary skills, you could sign up for a course at one of the city's many **cookery schools**. Il Salotto di Penelope (Via San Felice 116/G; ☎ 051 649 3627) is highly regarded, or the tourist office has a list.

FOODIE SOUVENIRS

Some of Bologna's most colourful sights are inside its many **food stores**, particularly those between Piazza Maggiore and the Due Torri, epitomized by Tamburini at Via Caprarie 1 (see opposite). All manner of goodies are on offer, but look out in particular for *tagliatelle* and *tortellini*, regarded with great affection by Bologna's inhabitants – the first *tortellini* are said to have been made by a Bolognese innkeeper trying to re-create the beauty of Venus's navel.

There's also a great **food market** in the city centre where you can pick up a tasty picnic or some gourmet souvenirs: the large and lively Mercato delle Erbe is at Via Ugo Bassi 2 (Mon–Sat 7am–1.15pm & 5.30–7.30pm, closed Thurs & Sat afternoon), while the Mercato di Mezzo is made up of a cluster of food shops along Via Pescherie Vecchie (Mon–Sat 7am–1pm & 4.15–7.30pm; closed Thurs morning).

dishes, along with fish specialities for €10. Mon–Sat noon–3pm & 7.30–11pm.

È Cucina Bologna Via Senzanome 42 ☎ 051 275 0069. Owned by hot young celebrity chef Cesare Marretti, this is a funky bistro with the graffitied names of satisfied diners scribbled over the walls and a menu of fresh, creative dishes. Three-course set menus at lunch cost €10–20; dinner mains start at €8. A bargain for cooking of this calibre. Tues–Sat 10am–5pm & 7pm–1am.

Franco Rossi Via Goito 3 ☎ 051 238 818. Run by two brothers, this cosy gourmet spot offers light, inventive interpretations of heavy Romagnan staples, with mains such as veal fillet in balsamic vinegar with cinnamon apples and pine nuts (€16), and a menu of fish dishes such as *paccheri* pasta with lobster, cherry tomatoes and basil (€23). Mon–Sat 12.30–3pm & 7.30–11pm.

Grassilli Via del Luzzo 3 ☎ 051 222 961. Emilian dishes adapted with flair to suit modern tastes, accompanied by good service. The restaurant was founded by opera singer Francesco Grassilli, and the walls are crammed with pictures of opera singers who dined here, adding to the glam ambiance. An experience to remember, though you'll need to book and it's above averagely priced (*primi* €11, *secondi* €16). 12.30–2.30pm & 7.30–10.30pm; closed Wed & Sun.

Il Tarì Via Collegio di Spagna 13 ☎ 051 226 046. A no-frills trattoria and pizzeria featuring fish dishes, such as delicious *spaghetti alle vongole* (with clams; €11) and pizzas at €7. Enormous servings of everything. Noon–3pm & 7pm–midnight; closed Thurs.

★ **Osteria dell'Orsa** Via Mentana 1/F ☎ 051 231 576. Bustling, friendly and cheap, this is where both students and locals go for good food. Panini, salads and main dishes

cost around €5–8. Share one of the big tables and join in the pub-like conviviality. Daily 12.30pm–1am.

Osteria La Traviata Via Urbana 5/C ☎ 051 331 298, ☷ ristorantelatraviata.it. A simple, homely *osteria* with plenty of outdoor tables and great pasta dishes: this is a good place to try local speciality *tortellini in brodo* (€12). The *secondi* are mainly meaty grills for €15–22. Mon–Sat noon–2.30pm & 8–10.30pm.

★ **Scacco Matto** Via Broccaindosso 63/B ☎ 051 263 404. A welcoming and elegant dining space adorned with framed tarot and playing cards, this venue offers some of the city's most unusual flavours, featuring gourmet variants on traditional Basilicata cuisine. Menu varies daily; superb wines. Expect €40–50 per person. Reservations a must. Mon–Sat 12.15–2.15pm & 8–10.45pm, Sun 8–10.45pm.

Trattoria Danio Via San Felice 50 ☎ 051 555 202. This rough-and-ready local secret is a great place for a budget meal, and its Seventies-style decor and TV blaring in the background are all part of its charm. The set menu costs just €11.50 for a huge and hearty two-course meal: a *primo* of spaghetti with *ragù* and *secondo* of grilled sausages with vegetables, plus house wine. Alternatively, €7.50 will get you the daily *primo*, *secondo* and side dish, all served without ceremony on the same plate. Mon–Fri noon–4pm & 7pm–1am, Sat & Sun noon–4.30pm & 7pm–1am.

Trattoria Da Gianni Via Clavature 18 ☎ 051 229 434. Hidden down a narrow side-alley, this is one of the top options in Bologna: try the ultra-traditional *bolliti*, a variety of meats boiled in the Emilian way, or the fantastic home-made *tortellini*. Moderate prices: you can eat very well for €25–30. Reservations recommended. Tues–Sat 12.30–2.30pm & 7.30–10.30pm, Sun 12.30–2.30pm.

DRINKING AND NIGHTLIFE

Bologna's **bar and club** culture thrives thanks to its huge student population, with most drinking places centred on and around Via Zamboni. Piazza Verdi, at the heart of the university district, pulls in the crowds on summer evenings with its open-air bars and live music, while Via del Pratello, west of the centre, is lined with bars and restaurants and draws more of a mixed (not exclusively studenty) crowd. The tourist office has a free pamphlet called *2night* (☷ 2night.it) with details of life in the city after dark. For listings there's the useful *Bologna Spettacolo* (☷ bolognaspettacolo.it) and for concerts and venues, you could try wading through the flyers at *La Scuderia* (see p.476).

8

BARS

Caffè Zamboni Via Zamboni 6 ☎051 273 102. The city's best place for a heaping *aperitivo* buffet (from 7pm; €8 for a drink, including free snacks), washed down with the ubiquitous Aperol Spritz. Daily 6.30am–1/2am.

Clauricaune Irish Pub Via Zamboni 18 ☎051 263 419. One of the largest bars in town, very popular with students from the university up the road, with punters spilling out onto the busy street on hot evenings. It also serves fast food such as burger and chips (€7) and screens big sports matches. Mon–Thurs & Sun noon–2am, Fri & Sat noon–2.30am.

★ **Enoteca des Arts** Via S. Felice 9 ☎051 236 422. This tiny, dark and atmospheric bar is a proper *enoteca* – all warm wood and dusty bottles – serving cheap local wine and preparing simple snacks (panini, cold meat platters) on request. Organizes regular tastings. Mon–Sat 5pm–3am.

La Scuderia Piazza Verdi 2 ☎051 656 9619. Occupying a former stable block, this huge bar is aimed squarely at students. Cheap drinks and seating on the square, where in the evening the sound of opera wafts across from the theatre opposite. Mon–Fri 8.15pm–3am, Sat 5pm–3am.

Le Stanze Via Borgo di San Pietro 1/A ☎051 228 767. Elegant place to unwind and sip wine and cocktails in the airy splendour of a converted Bentivoglio *palazzo*; there's a good *aperitivo* buffet 6.30–9pm. The sixteenth-century frescoed ceilings, romantic candles and occasional art exhibition produce an evocative atmosphere lapped up by the chic clientele. Mon 6pm–2am, Tues–Thurs & Sun 3.30pm–2am, Fri & Sat 3.30pm–4am.

MAMbo Ex Forno Via Don Minzoni 14 ☎051 649 3896, ⓦmambo-bologna.org/en/ristorante. Chic, dimly lit cocktail bar inside the modern art museum, attracting a cultured and arty crowd. There are sometimes DJs at weekends, both inside and in the park outside, but it's more about the chat and the fancy *aperitivo* buffet (from 7pm on), with tempura, platters of couscous and wholesome salads. Tues–Sun 10am–2am; closed three weeks in Aug.

★ **Osteria del Sole** Vicolo Ranocchi 1/D ☎347 968 0171. There's been an *osteria* on this spot since 1465, and it still retains a charmingly old-fashioned atmosphere. Turning the usual concept of BYO on its head, here you pick up a bite to eat in the nearby market and buy a glass of wine or two to wash it down with. Mon–Thurs 10.30am–10pm, Fri & Sat 10.30am–11pm.

Zanarini Piazza Galvani 1 ☎051 275 0041. On an elegant square, this is where well-heeled Bolognesi gather for their *aperitivi* and to soak up the last of the sun's rays. Suitably sleek and expensive – expect to pay €8 for a small *insalata di riso* or €6 for a beer. Mon–Fri 7am–9pm, Sat & Sun 8am–9pm.

CLUBS AND LIVE MUSIC

★ **Cantina Bentivoglio** Via Mascarella 4/B ☎051 265 416, ⓦcantinabentivoglio.it. As much a *ristorante* as a bar, this place has live jazz from around 10pm in the cellars of a sixteenth-century *palazzo*, and the food (snacks to full meals; mains €9–18) and wines are excellent. From the end of June to August (Wed, Thurs & Fri), concerts take place outside as part of the Salotto del Jazz festival (see box below). Daily 8pm–2am; closed Sun in summer.

★ **Cassero** Via Don Minzoni 18 ☎051 649 4416, ⓦcassero.it. Housed on the "garden floor" in historic La Salara, one of the old city fortifications, this is the best of Bologna's gay clubs, with bar and entertainment. Opens daily anywhere from 9pm to midnight.

Soda Pops Via Castel Tialto 6 ☎051 272 0279, ⓦsodapops.it. This *simpatico* disco-bar caters for the young, studenty crowd who make this area nonstop Party Central most evenings. There's a different theme every night, from Mon's Latin night to Sun's karaoke. Daily 8pm–3am.

Villa Serena Via della Barca 1 ☎051 615 6789, ⓦvillaserena.bo.it; take bus #14 or #21 (direction: Stadio) and get off at the Certosa stop. Spread over three floors, this buzzing live music and arts venue offers exhibitions and installations throughout the year, but from

BOLOGNA FESTIVALS AND EVENTS

Bologna has tried to curb the July and August exodus by mounting a summer arts festival, called **bè bolognaestate** (ⓦbolognaestate.it), with concerts, cinema screenings and dance performances every evening in the courtyards of the civic buildings and churches. June sees the annual **Gay Pride** celebrations (ⓦbolognapride.it) while from the end of June to August the **Salotto del Jazz** takes place in Via Mascarella, with live music under the stars on Wednesday, Thursday and Friday nights. In spring and autumn, classical concerts are staged under the aegis of the **Bologna Festival** (ⓦbolognafestival.it), for which the Auditorium Manzoni at Via de' Monari (ⓦauditoriumanzoni.it) is one of the main venues. Tickets cost from €15. The **Bologna Jazz Festival** in November sees concerts performed by international musicians in venues around town (ⓦfestivaljazzbologna.it).

mid May to July it really comes into its own with Latin and house night on Tues; electronica, hip-hop or reggae on Wed; cultural events on Thurs; live music on Fri and Sat; and open-air cinema on Sun. Tues–Thurs 8pm–3am, Fri & Sat 8pm–3.30am.

CINEMA

Cineteca Via Riva di Reno 72 ☎051 219 4826, ⓦcinetecadibologna.it. An art-house cinema and film archive in the city's northwest near MAMbo (see p.472); films screened in the original language with Italian subtitles. Tickets €6–7.

DIRECTORY

Books There's a huge selection of English books and magazines at Feltrinelli International, Via Zamboni 7 (Mon–Sat 9am–7.30pm).

Hospital In an emergency, dial ☎118; or go to the Pronto Soccorso (24hr casualty) at the Ospedale Sant'Orsola-Malpighi, Via Massarenti 9 (☎051 636 3111); bus #14 from Via Rizzoli.

Internet access Bar Planet at Via Portanova 16 (Mon–Sat 7am–7pm) has access for €2/hr, or free wi-fi.

Left luggage At the station (daily 6am–10pm; first 5hr €5, 6th–12th hour €0.70/hr).

Pharmacy Farmacia Comunale in Piazza Maggiore is open 24hr (☎051 239 690).

Police The *questura* is at Piazza Galileo 7 (☎051 640 1111).

Post office The main post office is on Piazza Minghetti (Mon–Fri 8.25am–7.10pm, Sat 8.25am–12.35pm).

Santuario di San Luca

Via di San Luca 36 • March–Oct Mon–Sat 6.30am–12.30pm & 2.30–7pm, Sun 7am–7pm; Nov–Feb same hours but closes 5pm • Free • Bus #20 from the centre, or #32 or #33 from the station drop you at the start of the route, by Porta Saragozza southwest of the centre; #20 takes you to the bottom of the hill, or take the San Luca Express

In the heat of the summer the hills that start almost as soon as you leave Bologna's gates take you high enough to catch some cooling breezes. The most obvious destination for a short trip is the eighteenth-century shrine of **Santuario di Madonna di San Luca**, close on 4km southwest of the city centre but connected by way of the world's longest portico, which meanders across the hillside in a series of 666 arches – a shelter for pilgrims on the trek to the top.

A tourist train, the **San Luca Express**, runs from Piazza Malpighi, a few minutes' walk west of Piazza Maggiore, to the Santuario di San Luca (mid-March to Oct Thurs–Sun 6 daily; first departure 9.30am, last at 4pm). The journey takes 45 minutes and costs €10, or €18 including the City redbus tour (see p.473).

Modena and around

Though only thirty minutes northwest by train, **MODENA** has a quite distinct identity from Bologna. It proclaims itself the "spiritual capital" of Emilia and has a number of claims to fame: great car names such as Ferrari, Lamborghini and Maserati are tied to the town (celebrated in Modena Terra di Motori every spring, when the piazzas are filled with classic models; ⓦmodenaterradimotori.com); the late Pavarotti was a native of Modena, his name commemorated in the Teatro Comunale Luciano Pavarotti; the area's balsamic vinegar has become a cult product in kitchens around the world, duly celebrated in nearby Carpi during the Balsamica festival in May; and the cathedral – a UNESCO World Heritage Site – is considered one of the finest Romanesque buildings in Italy. Of things to see, top of most people's lists are the rich collections of **paintings** and **manuscripts** built up by the Este family, who decamped here from Ferrara in 1598, after it was annexed by the Papal States, and who ruled the town until the nineteenth century. But really the appeal of Modena is in wandering its labyrinthine **old centre**, finishing off the day with some good food. The town's small, concentric medieval core is bisected by **Via Emilia**, which runs past the edge of **Piazza Grande**, the nominal centre of town, its stone buildings and arcades forming the focus of much of its life.

8

The Duomo

Piazza Grande • **Church** Daily 6.30am–12.30pm & 3.30–7pm • Free **Museums** Tues–Sun 9.30am–12.30pm & 3.30–6.30pm • €3
Torre Ghirlandina April–July, Sept & Oct Sat & Sun 9.30am–12.30pm & 3–7pm • €2 • ⓦ duomodimodena.it

Dominating Piazza Grande, the twelfth-century **Duomo** is one of the finest products of
the Romanesque period in Italy and is on the UNESCO World Heritage list. Its most
striking feature is the west facade whose portal is supported by two fierce-looking lions
and fringed with marvellous reliefs – the work of one **Wiligelmo**, who also did the
larger reliefs that run along the wall. Inside, under the choir is the plain stone coffin
of St Geminianus, the patron saint of Modena – on his feast day, January 31, crowds
come to visit his coffin, and a big market is held out in the main square.

There are two museums inside the Duomo: the **Musei del Duomo** holds the usual
ecclesiastical artefacts, while the **Museo Lapidario** displays Roman-age marbles from
the Duomo. On the other side of the church looms the 86m-high **Torre Ghirlandina**,
which provides a bird's-eye view of the city.

Palazzo dei Musei

Viale Vittorio Veneto 5 • **Biblioteca Estense** Mon, Fri & Sat 9am–1pm, Tues, Wed & Thurs 9am–1pm & 2.30–6.30pm • Free **Museo
Civico Archeologico Etnologico** Tues–Fri 9am–noon, Sat & Sun 10am–1pm & 3–7pm, Oct–May closes 6pm • Free **Galleria Estense**
Mon 8.30am–2pm, Tues–Sat 8.30am–7.30pm, Sun 2–7.30pm; closed last Sun of the month except June, Sept & Oct • €4

The other main focus for your wanderings is at the far, northwestern end of Via Emilia,
where the **Palazzo dei Musei** houses the city museums and art galleries. Through an
archway lined with Roman tombstones – nearby Piazza Matteotti was the site of a
necropolis – a staircase leads to the **Biblioteca Estense**, on the first floor, where you
can see letters sent by monarchs, popes and despots, with great wax seals, old maps,
and the prize treasure, Borso d'Este's Bible – the *Bibbia di Borso d'Este* – arguably the
most decorated book in the world. The **Museo Civico Archeologico Etnologico**, on the
second floor, has a large collection of artefacts of archeological and artistic significance,
while on the top floor, the **Galleria Estense** is the highlight. Made up of the picture

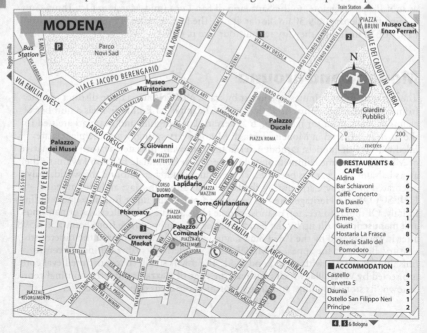

collection of the Este family, it contains paintings of the local schools, from the early Renaissance through to the works of the Carraccis, Guercino and Guido Reni.

Museo Casa Enzo Ferrari

Via Paolo Ferrari 85 • Daily: May–Sept 9.30am–7pm; Oct–April 9.30am–6pm • €13, or €22 joint ticket with the Museo Ferrari in Maranello • Bus #1, #3 or #9 from the station; a bus shuttle to the Museo Ferrari in Maranello runs hourly • ⓦ museocasaenzoferrari.it

Fans of motor racing won't want to miss the two local sights inspired by the king of the sport, Enzo Ferrari: the Museo Ferrari (see p.480), and the **Museo Casa Enzo Ferrari**, opened in 2012. Built on the spot where Ferrari was born in 1898, the museum preserves Ferrari's original house and workshop, alongside a gallery space encased within a futuristic aluminium "bonnet" the bright yellow of the famous prancing horse logo, designed by Jan Kaplický. Inside, gleaming ranks of supercars are exhibited like works of art.

ARRIVAL AND INFORMATION   MODENA

By plane There's a shuttle from Bologna airport (see p.472) to Modena (9 daily; 50min; €15); buy tickets on the bus.

By train Modena's centre, marked by the main Piazza Grande, is a 10min walk southwest from the train station on Piazza Dante Alighieri, down the wide Corso Vittorio Emanuele II. Buses #7 and #11 connect the station with the main street of Via Emilia.
Destinations Bologna (every 15min; 20–45min); Carpi (every 30min; 15min); Parma (every 15min; 25–40min).

By bus The bus station is on Via Bacchini, off Viale Monte Kosica, a 10min walk west from the train station and

northeast from the centre of town.
Destinations Carpi (20 daily; 50min); Maranello (hourly; 30min).

By car There's free parking inside the stadium at Parco Novi Sad and on Piazzale N. Bruni, though most hotels in the centre either have a garage or can give you free parking permits; driving in the centre's one-way system during weekdays can be something of a nightmare.

Tourist office Via Scudari 8 (Mon 3–6pm, Tues–Sat 9am–1pm & 3–6pm, Sun 9.30am–12.30pm; ☎ 059 203 2660, ⓦ turismo.comune.modena.it).

ACCOMMODATION

Modena makes a relaxing place to stay for a night or two. The few reasonably priced hotels in the centre fill up quickly, so you'll need to book ahead. Note that there's a hotel tax in Modena: €0.50–4 per person per night in addition to your room rate, depending on the type of accommodation.

Castello Via Pica 321 ☎ 059 36 10 33, ⓦ hotelcastello -mo.it. This hotel, 10min outside Modena, was once the country house of a noble Modena family. The spacious, comfortable rooms are spread across two buildings; those in the central historical part are the nicest. The pleasant, leafy grounds are equipped with gazebos in which to sit and enjoy the views. **€120**

★ **Cervetta 5** Via Cervetta 5 ☎ 059 238 447, ⓦ hotel cervetta5.com. A stylish, modern choice – all white walls and clean lines. Very helpful staff and breakfast is above average, though pricey at an extra €10. Free wi-fi access. **€120**

Daunia Via del Pozzo 158 ☎ 059 371 182, ⓦ hoteldaunia

.it. Despite its unpromising exterior, this basic hotel has large, comfortable rooms, and staff are friendly. Easy to find – it's the big red building with green shutters opposite the hospital. **€95**

Ostello San Filippo Neri Via Sant'Orsola 48/52 ☎ 059 234 598, ✉ modena@aighostels.com. Clean and pleasant HI hostel with two- and three-bed rooms: it's a touch austere with no kitchen but with a TV room. Lockout 10am–2pm, no curfew. No breakfast. Dorms **€18.50**

Principe Corso Vittorio Emanuele 94 ☎ 059 218 670, ⓦ hotelprincipe.mo.it. A small business hotel, with adequate but characterless rooms, conveniently located near the station. Very welcoming and helpful staff. **€118**

EATING AND DRINKING

Modena is packed with places to eat. Try to sample some of the local pork-based specialities, like *ciccioli* – flaky pork scratchings laid out in bars in the evening – or, in a restaurant, *zampone* (pig's trotters, boned and filled with minced meat) or *cotechino* – the same thing, but stuffed inside a pig's bladder. The covered Mercato Albinelli (Mon–Fri 6.30am–2.30pm, Sat 4.30–7.30pm), just south of Piazza Grande, has a fantastic array of fresh vegetables, fruit and meat, as well as balsamic vinegars (a 40-year-old vintage goes for around €20). You can even have blocks of parma ham and parmesan vacuum-packed to take home with you.

Aldina Via Albinelli 40 ☎ 059 236 106. This traditional, family-run restaurant is an example of what the Slow Food

movement is all about. The simple, delicious, home-made offerings of the day are recited, not written, and the pastas

8

HIT THE GOURMET TRAIL

If you want to see Modena's famous balsamic vinegar being created, contact the **Modenatur** office next door to the tourist office at Via Scudari 8/10 (☎059 220 022, ⦿ modenatur.it) for information on trips to *aceterie* (these are free but, being private establishments, visits depend on the owners' schedules). They also have information on tours to Lambrusco wineries, parmesan dairies and some of the region's renowned car manufacturers.

The tourist office can advise you on **gourmet itineraries** in the wooded foothills of the Apennines surrounding the town. However, they're not really necessary: restaurant signs by the side of the road invite you in to try cuisine "*alla tua nonna*" – "like grandma used to make" – usually involving *mortadella* (cold pork sausage, spotted with lumps of fat and often flavoured with nutmeg, coriander and myrtle), salami or *crescente* (a kind of pitta bread eaten with a mixture of oil, garlic, rosemary and parmesan). Higher in the mountains you can still find *ciacci* – chestnut-flour pancakes, filled with ricotta and sugar – and walnuts that go to make *nocino* liqueur.

are the crowning glory. About €15 for a full meal; no credit cards. Mon–Thurs 12.30–3pm, Fri & Sat 12.30–3pm & 8–10.30pm; closed July & Aug.

Bar Schiavoni Via Albinelli 13 ☎059 243 073. Good, popular choice for a great coffee, a glass of wine and delectable and inventive panini for around €4, as well as various fresh, gourmet creations. Daily 6am–3.30pm; summer Fri also 6–9pm, winter Sat also 6–8pm.

Caffè Concerto Piazza Grande 26 ☎059 222 232. Large, elegant place that operates a buffet service during the day (a plate of your choice, water and coffee for €15) and an à la carte restaurant at night (when prices are around double). Its main role, however, is as Modena's most celebrated meeting place and premier soiree spot. DJ Fri & Sat. Daily noon–3.30pm & 7.30–11pm.

★ **Da Danilo** Via Coltellini 51 ☎059 225 498. The archetypal Modena eating experience – regional specialities served in a cosy backstreet dining room. Be adventurous and try the mixed meat platter – including stuffed pig's trotters, cheek and tongue – for €16. Mon–Sat noon–3pm & 7–10.30pm.

Da Enzo Via Coltellini 17 ☎059 225 177. Pleasant, slightly old-fashioned place serving Modenese specialities – though not especially cheap. *Primi* €6–8, *secondi* €10–15. Tues–Sat noon–2.30pm & 7.15–10.30pm, Sun noon–2.30pm; closed Aug.

Ermes Via Ganaceto 89–91 ☎059 238 065. A tiny, archetypal workers' and students' eatery, as authentic as it gets. The oral menu changes daily according to market finds. Around €20 for a full meal; worth the queue. No credit cards. Mon–Sat noon–3pm; closed Aug.

★ **Hostaria La Frasca** Via San Paolo 51 ☎059 216 271. Eating at this rough-and-ready trattoria, a locals' favourite, is always an experience. There's no menu and the owner speaks no English, but making yourself understood is half the fun. It's a small place, so booking is a good idea; meals cost around €30 a head. 12.30–2.30pm & 8–10.30pm; closed Wed.

★ **Hosteria Giusti** Vicolo Squallore 46 ☎059 222 533. This marvellous family-run place, set at the back of a 400-year-old *salumeria*, serves hearty home-cooking at lunch only: try the traditional *tortellini in brodo* followed by pork slow-braised in white wine and herbs (*secondi* €10–18). There are only four tables, so be sure to book, and pick up a jar of the home-made black cherry jam in the shop before you leave. Mon–Sat 12.30–2pm.

Osteria Stallo del Pomodoro Largo Hannover 63 ☎059 214 664. Good for a relaxed dinner with friends – the high ceiling of this former stable can make it pretty noisy, so it's not the place for a romantic meal. Unusually, all of the dishes are available in gluten-free versions. The wine list is endless, and the waiters are very happy to advise on what best to pair with your ox cheek or roast lamb; a full meal will set you back around €30 without wine. Daily 12.30–2.30pm & 8–10.30pm.

Museo Ferrari

Via Dino Ferrari 43, Maranello • Daily: May–Sept 9.30am–7pm; Oct–April 9.30am–6pm • €13, joint ticket €22 • ⦿ ferrari.com • Trains run from Modena roughly hourly; a shuttle bus operates from Modena train station and from the Museo Casa Enzo Ferrari 6 times daily (35min; €10 if you're visiting both museums, or €11 if only one museum)

Around 20km south of Modena in **MARANELLO** is the **Museo Ferrari**, an exhibition centre dedicated to the racing dynasty. On display are the cups and trophies won by the Ferrari team over the years and an assortment of Ferrari engines, along with vintage and contemporary examples of the cars themselves. There's also a shop stocking all manner of merchandise, from baseball caps to surf boards.

MAUSOLEO DI GALLA PLACIDIA, RAVENNA (P.499) >

Reggio Emilia

About 25km northwest of Modena, up the Via Emilia, is **REGGIO EMILIA**, a pleasant, well-heeled place with a handsome historic core. Though nicknamed "the red town" – in 1960 five protestors were killed by police during demonstrations designed to prevent Fascists joining the government – you wouldn't credit such a revolutionary past wandering its quiet streets; these days, it's more associated with high-end fashion house MaxMara.

Piazza San Prospero

The town is built around two central squares, Piazza Prampolini and **Piazza San Prospero**, which come alive on market days (Tues and Fri). Stalls specialize in rather tacky clothes – the shops surrounding the market are far more alluring, crammed with a mighty range of local produce such as salami and *parmigiano-reggiano*. Around the square, the buildings squeeze up so close to the church of **San Prospero** that they seem to have pushed it off-balance so that it now lurches to one side. Built in the sixteenth century, it's guarded by six lions in rose-coloured Verona marble.

Piazza Prampolini

Via Broletto leads through from Piazza San Prospero into **Piazza Prampolini**, skirting the side of the **Duomo**, which displays an awkward amalgamation of styles. Underneath the marble tacked on in the sixteenth century, it's possible to see the church's Romanesque facade, with incongruously Mannerist statues of Adam and Eve lounging over the medieval portal.

At right angles to the Duomo is the sugar-pink **Palazzo del Capitano del Popolo**. The Italian tricolour of red, white and green was proclaimed here as the official national flag of Italy when Napoleon's Cispadane Republic was formed in 1797. North of here on the edge of Piazza della Vittoria are the **Musei Civici** (July & Aug Tues–Sat 9am–noon & 9pm–midnight, Sun 9pm–midnight; Sept–June Tues–Fri 9am–noon, Sat & Sun 10am–1pm & 4–7pm; free), containing an eighteenth-century private collection of archeological finds, fossils and paintings. In the corner of the square, the **Galleria Parmeggiani** (same hours; free) houses an important collection of Spanish, Flemish and Italian art, including sculptures and bronzes, as well as costumes and textiles. Nearby stands the **Basilica della Ghiara** (Sun 3.30–6pm; advance booking necessary on ☎0522 439 707; free), built in the seventeenth century and decorated with Bolognese School frescoes of scenes from the Old Testament and a *Crucifixion* by Guercino.

ARRIVAL AND INFORMATION   REGGIO EMILIA

By train Reggio is on the main rail-line between Bologna and Milan. The train station is on Piazza Marconi, just east of the old centre.

By bus The bus station is on Piazzale Europa, near the station.

Tourist information The tourist office is on the southern side of Piazza Prampolini at Via Farini 1/A (Mon–Sat 8.30am–1pm & 2.30–6pm, Sun 9am–noon; ☎0522 451 152, ⊛turismo.comune.re.it), while the helpful Club Alpino Italiano office at Viale dei Mille 32 (☎0522 436 685, ⊛caireggioemilia.it) has information on walking in the nearby hills (Wed, Thurs & Fri 6–7.30pm, Sat 5.30–7pm; closed most of Aug).

KING OF CHEESES

The foothills south of Reggio are **cheese country**. Signs along the roadside advertise the local *parmigiano-reggiano* while the village of **Casina**, 27km outside Reggio on the N63 to La Spezia, holds a popular Festa del Parmigiano in early August, when the vats of cheese mixture are stirred with enormous wooden paddles. Buses run to Casina from Reggio hourly and take around an hour.

ACCOMMODATION AND EATING

★ **B&B Cantarelli** Via Monzermone 3 ☎329 714 9847, ⓦcantarellibandb.com. A beautifully turned out, cosy retreat in the heart of town. Some rooms are up in the rafters (be prepared to duck), which adds to the character, and all are beautifully furnished. The extremely helpful owner will make restaurant reservations, drive you around town, even organize local Pecorino tastings. There's no breakfast room but coffee and pastries are served directly to your room. **€70**

Caffè Arti E Mestieri Via Emilia S. Pietro 14 ☎0522 432 202. A rather smart restaurant with a menu of stylishly updated classic dishes from the region (expect to pay upwards of €40 for two courses with wine). Mon–Fri 12.30–2.30pm & 8–10.30pm, Sat 8–10.30pm.

Canossa Via Roma 37 ☎0522 454 196. Specializing in antipasti and meaty grills, this ultra-traditional place is consistently popular with locals. A full meal costs around €30. 12.30–2pm & 7.30–10pm; closed Wed.

★ **Osteria del Macellaio** Via Anna Frank 100 ☎0522 394 096. There's no need to go to Tuscany for a prime *fiorentina* steak – this place serves up exceptional meat grills, with a hearty meal costing €30–35. It's justly popular, so booking is essential. Wed–Sat 12.40–2.30pm & 8.30–11pm, Sun 12.40–2.30pm.

Posta Piazza del Monte 2 ☎0522 432 944, ⓦhotel posta.re.it. This four-star in the historic Palazzo del Capitano del Popolo offers great service, comfortable rooms – some of which are sumptuously decorated – and plenty of character. Free bikes are available for guests' use, and the owner can arrange visits to his family farm, to see the making of the local *aceto di balsamico* up close. **€119**

Student's Hostel della Ghiara Via Guasco 6 ☎0522 452 323, ⓦostelloreggioemilia.it. A basic, 100-bed hostel, 1km from the station, with no curfew, and breakfast and internet included. The cloister and garden make a pleasant place to relax in summer. Dorms **€18**, doubles **€50**

Parma

Generally reckoned to have one of the highest standards of living in Italy, **PARMA**, 28km along the Via Emilia northwest of Reggio, is about as comfortable a town as you could wish for, distinguished by the measured pace of its streets and the general air of ease and affluence. There's plenty to keep you occupied here too – you could easily fill a day or two seeing the sights and sampling the delights of the city's many excellent **restaurants**. A visit to the **opera** can be an experience – the audience are considered one of the toughest outside Milan's La Scala and don't pull any punches if they consider a singer to be performing badly – and the city's **works of art** include the legacy of two great artists, Correggio and Parmigianino.

Santa Maria della Steccata

Piazza Steccata 9 • **Church** Daily 7.30am–noon & 3–6.30pm • Free **Museum** Entrance by guided tour (daily 10am, 11am, 4pm & 5pm • €5 • ☎0521 282 854

The Renaissance church of **Santa Maria della Steccata** was apparently built using Bramante's original plan for St Peter's as a model. Inside there are frescoes by a number of sixteenth-century painters, notably **Parmigianino**, who spent the last ten years of his life on this work, eventually being sacked for breach of contract by the disgruntled church authorities. Also inside the church, the **Museo Costantino** includes the sacristy, intricately carved in ebony in the seventeenth century, as well as precious silverware, paintings and textiles.

The Duomo

Piazza del Duomo • Daily 9am–12.30pm & 3–7pm • Free

Five minutes' walk from Piazza Garibaldi, the slightly gloomy **Piazza del Duomo** forms part of the old *centro episcopale*, away from the shopping streets of the commercial centre. The Lombard–Romanesque **Duomo**, dating from the eleventh century, holds earlier work by Parmigianino in its south transept, executed when the artist was a pupil of **Correggio** – who painted the fresco of the *Assumption* in the central cupola. Finished in 1534, this is among the most famous of Correggio's works, the Virgin Mary floating up through a sea of limbs, faces and swirling clouds, which attracted some bemused comments at the time. One contemporary compared it to a "hash of frogs' legs",

8

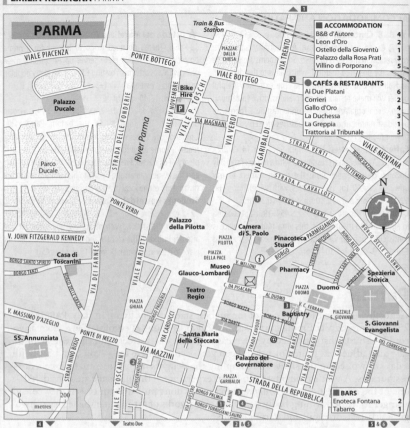

while Dickens thought it a sight that "no operative surgeon gone mad could imagine in his wildest delirium". Correggio was paid for the painting with a sackful of small change to annoy him, since he was known to be a miser. The story goes that he carried the sack of coins home in the heat, caught a fever and died at the age of 40.

The baptistry

Piazza del Duomo • Daily 9am–12.30pm & 3–6.45pm • €6

Just a few steps southwest of the Duomo is the beautiful twelfth-century octagonal **baptistry**, its sugary pink-and-white Verona marble rising four storeys high. Its three elaborately carved portals and frieze are the work of the architect Benedetto Antelami. Inside, sixteen arches frame thirteenth- and fourteenth-century frescoes under a beautifully painted dome.

San Giovanni Evangelista and the Spezieria di San Giovanni

There's more work by Correggio in the cupola of the church of **San Giovanni Evangelista** behind the Duomo, Piazzale San Giovanni 1 (church Mon–Sat 8.30–11.45am & 3–5.30pm, Sun 3–5.30pm; monastery Mon–Wed, Fri & Sat 9–11.45am & 3–5pm; free) – a fresco of the *Vision of St John at Patmos*. Next door, the **Spezieria di San Giovanni**, at Borgo Pipa 1 (Tues–Sun 8.30am–1.30pm; €2), is a thirteenth-century pharmacy with a medieval interior.

Camera di San Paolo

Via Melloni 3 • Tues–Sun 8.30am–1.30pm • €2

A short walk northwest from Piazza del Duomo, the **Camera di San Paolo** in the former Benedictine convent off Via Garibaldi houses more frescoes by Correggio executed in 1519; above the fireplace, the abbess who commissioned the work is portrayed by Correggio as the goddess Diana.

Pinacoteca Stuard

Borgo del Parmigianino 2 • Mon & Wed–Sun 9am–6.30pm • €4

Housed in a former convent, the **Pinacoteca Stuard** holds 270 paintings from the fourteenth to the nineteenth centuries that used to form the private collection of the nobleman Giuseppe Stuard. Upon his death in 1834, the collection was bequeathed to the congregation of San Filippo Neri, but has only recently gone on public display.

Museo Glauco-Lombardi

Via Garibaldi 15 • Tues–Sat 9.30am–3.30pm, Sun 9am–6.30pm; closes 1.30pm Sun in July & Aug • €5

The **Museo Glauco-Lombardi** has a display of memorabilia relating to Marie-Louise of Austria, who reigned here after the defeat of her husband Napoleon at Waterloo. She set herself up with another suitor (much to the chagrin of her exiled spouse) and expanded the Parma-violet perfume industry.

Palazzo della Pilotta

Piazza della Pilotta • Tues–Sun 8.30am–1.30pm • €6, including the Teatro Farnese; theatre only €2 • ⓦ galiannazionaleparma.it • **Museo Archeologico Nazionale** Tues–Fri 9am–5pm, Sat 9am–3pm, Sun 12.30–7.30pm • €4

It's hard to miss Parma's biggest monument, the **Palazzo della Pilotta**, surrounded by vast expanses of wonderfully green lawn. Begun for Alessandro Farnese – the wily Pope Paul III – in the sixteenth century, the building was reduced to a shell by World War II bombing, but has been rebuilt and now houses a number of Parma's museums.

Galleria Nazionale

On the second floor, the city's main art gallery, the **Galleria Nazionale** is a modern, high-tech display that includes more work by Correggio and Parmigianino, as well as El Greco, Fra Angelico and Da Vinci, plus the remarkable *Apostles at the Sepulchre* and *Funeral of the Virgin* by Carracci.

Teatro Farnese

The **Teatro Farnese**, which you pass through to get to the gallery, in the former arms room of the palace, was almost entirely destroyed by bombing in 1944. The restored theatre, still used occasionally, has an extended semicircle of seats three tiers high, made completely of wood, in a facsimile of Palladio's Teatro Olimpico at Vicenza, and also houses Italy's first revolving stage.

Museo Archeologico Nazionale

On the first floor, the **Museo Archeologico Nazionale** is a less essential stop but still worth a glance, with finds from the prehistoric lake villages around Parma, as well as the table top on which the Emperor Trajan notched up a record of his gifts to the poor.

Across the river

Behind the Palazzo della Pilotta, the Ponte Verdi crosses the River Parma, bringing you to the **Parco Ducale** (daily: April–Oct 6am–midnight; Nov–March 7am–8pm; free), a set of eighteenth-century formal gardens arranged to offset the sixteenth-century **Palazzo Ducale** (Mon–Sat 9am–noon; €3) built for Ottaviano Farnese and filled with frescoes by Carracci. Just south, the **Casa di Toscanini**, Via R. Tanzi 13 (Wed–Sat 9am–1pm & 2–6pm, Sun 2–6pm; €2), is the birthplace of the conductor who debuted in the Teatro Regio here (see p.487).

8

ARRIVAL AND DEPARTURE

By plane Ryanair flies three times weekly from London Stansted to Parma's airport (☎ 0521 9515, ⓦ parma-airport.it), 5km from the train station. Bus #6 (hourly) runs to the station; a taxi will cost around €10.

By train Parma's train station is a 15min walk from the central Piazza Garibaldi, or take bus #1, #8, #9 or #13.

By bus The bus station is next to the train station; take bus #2, #8, #9 or #13 to get to the centre.

Destinations Busseto/Le Roncole (6 daily; 1hr); Roncole Verdi (6 daily; 55min).

INFORMATION AND GETTING AROUND

Tourist office Via Melloni 1/A (Jan–March, July, Aug, Nov & Dec Mon 9am–1pm & 3–7pm, Tues–Sat 9am–7pm, Sun 9am–1pm; April–June, Sept & Oct Mon 1–7pm, Tues–Sat 9am–7pm, Sun 9am–1pm & 2–6pm; ☎ 0521 218 889, ⓦ turismo.comune.parma.it).

Bike rental Bikes can be rented from one of several agencies, including Parma Punto Bici at Viale Toschi 2, next to a large car park by the river (Jan & Feb Mon–Sat 9am–1pm & 3–7pm, Sun 10am–6pm; March–Dec Mon–Sat 9am–1pm & 3–7pm, Sun 10am–6pm; €0.70/hr; ☎ 0521 281 979).

ACCOMMODATION

If you're planning a trip during spring or the run-up to Christmas, be sure to book in advance as this is also trade-fair season in Parma. You really need to plan ahead for the town's cheaper hotels too, including the HI hostel.

B&B d'Autore Strada Nino Bixio 89 ☎ 348 898 2304, ⓦ bbdautore.it; bus #1, #6 or #20 from the station. A welcoming B&B in a quiet location on the western side of the river, impeccably run by Giacomo and Roberto, who are happy to make concert and restaurant bookings for their guests, and provide free bikes. The two cosy rooms are stylishly decorated. Breakfast €5. Cash only. **€75**

Leon d'Oro Viale A. Fratti 4/A ☎ 0521 773 182, ⓦ leon doroparma.com. Offering rooms above a traditional trattoria, the place has an old-fashioned feel but is comfortable enough, and quiet if you get a room at the back. Breakfast not offered. **€65**

Ostello della Gioventù Via S. Leonardo 86 ☎ 0521 191 7547, ⓦ ostelloparma.it; a 10min bus ride north of the centre (lines #2 & #13 from the train station). This hostel offers spick-and-span six-bed dorms, double and triple rooms with private bathrooms, plus a host of extra facilities including wi-fi, internet and bike rental (€5/day). Open 24hr. Breakfast €3 extra. Dorms **€20**, doubles **€44**

★ **Palazzo dalla Rosa Prati** Piazza Duomo 7 ☎ 0521 386 429, ⓦ palazzodallarosaprati.it. Luxurious conversion of an old *palazzo* in the heart of town, with some rooms looking out on the Duomo and baptistry. The suites are elegantly decorated and wonderfully roomy, with huge bathrooms, and the apartments (available even for single-night stays) offer even more space. Breakfast is served in your room or in a café nearby. **€280**

★ **Villino di Porporano** Strada Bodrio 26, Porporano, 4.5km from central Parma ☎ 0521 642 268, ⓦ villino diporporano.com. Surrounded by gardens and with a swimming pool and views of the Apennines, this lovely, airy B&B – converted from an old barn – makes a great base for exploring the region. Floating staircases lead to the five rustic-chic rooms, each different and beautifully decorated with antique finds and luxurious touches such as fine linens and complimentary chocolates. An excellent breakfast of home-made cakes and local jams completes the experience. **€120**

EATING AND DRINKING

Many restaurants in Parma – especially the ones in the centre – can be rather pricey, though less expensive options do exist, most noticeably on Via Garibaldi and Strada Farini. Local specialities include the obvious Parma ham (*prosciutto*) and *parmigiano-reggiano* – which are often served together as an antipasto – as well as *guancia di manzo*, cheek of beef. For snacks, *prosciutto* stuffed into pastries and other local delights are available for around €2 from the many bakeries, and picnic supplies can be bought at the market by the river on Piazza Ghiaia (Wed & Sat 7am–2pm).

★ **Ai Due Platani** Strada Budellungo 104/A, Località Coloreto, 7km from central Parma ☎ 0521 645 626. If you have a car, don't miss the chance to eat at this fantastic trattoria. You can't go wrong with any dish, but the rosemary and duck *pappardelle* (€9) and beef braised in wine with crunchy polenta (€13) are standouts. Save room for the home-made vanilla ice cream, freshly churned and served in a huge tower that's wheeled round the tables at 10pm nightly. The only

problem is in securing a table – it's packed with locals every night, so book ahead. Mon noon–2pm, Wed–Sun noon–2pm & 7.30–10pm.

Corrieri Via del Conservatorio 1 ☎ 0521 234 426. Good-value and charmingly traditional spot for enjoying classic Parmesan cookery. The pumpkin pastas are excellent (€8), and the greenery-draped terrace is a pleasant spot in fine weather. Expect to pay about €25 for a full meal without wine. Daily noon–2.30pm & 7.30–10pm.

⭐ **Enoteca Fontana** Strada Farini 24/A ☎0521 286 037. Authentic old bar, with long wooden tables, a huge choice of wines from all over the region, many by the glass, and great sandwiches such as *caprino* cheese with sun-dried tomatoes (€3). Tues–Thurs 9am–3pm & 5–10pm, Fri & Sat 9am–3pm & 5–10pm.

⭐ **Gallo d'Oro** Borgo della Salina 3 ☎0521 208 846. Atmospheric little trattoria on a quiet side-street. Excellent filled pastas such as pumpkin ravioli (€8) are the main attraction, while the *secondi* include a tasty rabbit with herbs (€9). Mon–Sat noon–2.30pm & 7.30–11pm, Sun noon–2.30pm.

La Duchessa Piazza Garibaldi 1 ☎0521 235 962. One of several restaurants with outdoor seating on the square, this offers the best food, with thirty types of pizza (€4.50–9), traditional *primi* and *secondi* (€8–17) and great people-watching opportunities. Tues–Sun noon–2.45pm & 6.30pm–midnight.

⭐ **La Greppia** Via Garibaldi 39/A ☎0521 233 686. Even by Parma's elegant, expensive standards, this is a cut above, offering antipasti such as parmesan foam with pears in wine (€12) and *primi* such as *tagliatelle* with artichokes and Parma ham (€12); mains go for €16–25. Wine buffs will be spoilt for choice with almost 600 labels available. Wed–Sun 12.30–2pm & 8–10.30pm.

⭐ **Tabarro** Strada Farini 5/B ☎0521 200 223. This cosy little wine bar with geometric-tiled floor, copper-topped bar and beer barrels as tables is a convivial spot for an *aperitivo*. It also serves gourmet panini stuffed with top-notch organic ingredients (€5). Tues–Thurs & Sun 5pm–midnight, Fri & Sat 5pm–1am.

Trattoria al Tribunale Vicolo Politi 5/B, up an alleyway off Strada Farini ☎0521 285 527. This old-fashioned, wood-beamed trattoria is an affordable gourmet option (count on about €25 a head for a full meal with wine) that serves large plates of creamy pink *prosciutto* and other antipasti delights. More adventurous diners might like to try the braised veal-cheek. Daily noon–3pm & 7–11pm.

ENTERTAINMENT

For nightlife in refined Parma, opera and theatre take precedence over clubs. In summer the city's entertainment options become more diverse – the piazzas host live jazz bands and during July and August locals flock to the garden behind Camera di San Paolo for a free season on Wednesday nights of old horror movies, dubbed into Italian (9.30pm; ⓦ ufficiocinema.it).

Teatro Due Next to the river at Viale Basetti 12/A ☎0521 208 088, ⓦteatrodue.org. The home of top theatre company L'Ensemble del Teatro Due, who perform between Oct and April.

Teatro Regio Via Garibaldi 16/A ☎0521 039 393, ⓦ teatroregioparma.org. Theatre buffs should head to this imposing nineteenth-century opera house, closely associated with Verdi, who was born in nearby Busseto. The season runs from Jan to April, with a Verdi festival taking place in Oct.

DIRECTORY

Internet access Corso S. Brigida 7 (Mon–Wed, Fri & Sat 9.30am–1.30pm & 2.30–8.30pm, Thurs 9.30am–1.30pm & 3–8.30pm; €1.50/hr).

Police The *questura* is at Borgo della Posta 14 (☎0521 2194).

Post office Via Melloni 4/C (Mon–Fri 8.30am–6.30pm).

Around Parma

The countryside **around Parma** is a strange mixture: some of the major roads follow bleak gorges, skirting the edge of blank rock walls for miles; others look as if they will lead precisely nowhere before emerging into meadows and orchards with rich farmland stretching into the distance.

Prime targets are any of the **medieval castles** strung out across the foothills to the south. There are around twenty, many built by the powerful Farnese dynasty. One of the best-situated is at **TORRECHIARA** (March–Oct Wed–Sat 8.30am–7.30pm, Tues & Sun 10.30am–7.30pm; Nov–Feb Tues–Fri 9am–4.30pm, Sat & Sun 10am–5pm; €3), about 18km south of Parma. The castle provides a superb vantage-point over the surrounding area and also has frescoes by Bembo in the **Camera d'Oro**. The website ⓦcastellidelducato.it has a useful map locating all the castles and can help you plan a tour. It's also worth buying a Castelli del Ducato card (€2) available from tourist offices or the castles themselves that will give you a €1 reduction on admission fees and is valid for a whole year.

CORNIGLIO is a centre for hiking and skiing. Buses squeeze themselves round the tight bends to the small villages of Monchio (16km), Trefiumi (20km) and Prato Spilla

(23km from Corniglio), leaving you on the lower slopes of **Monte Malpasso** (1716m) – glistening with small lakes and tarns. Buses also run to **Lagdei** (14km), a starting point for further walks.

Castell'Arquato

Some 35km west of Parma is the beautiful **CASTELL'ARQUATO**, a nicely restored medieval town set on a hillside overlooking the Arda valley. At the top of the town is Piazza del Municipio, lined with some stunning buildings. The thirteenth-century **Palazzo del Podestà** isn't open to the public, but you can visit the **Basilica**, a magnificently preserved Romanesque monument with an eighth-century baptismal font in the right-hand **apse** (April–Sept 9am–noon & 3–7pm; March–Oct 9.30am–noon & 2.30–5pm). The restored tower of the fourteenth-century **Rocca Viscontea** (March–Oct Tues–Fri 10am–1pm & 3–6pm, Sat & Sun 10am–1pm & 2–6.30pm; Nov–Feb Sat & Sun only 10am–5pm; €4) offers amazing views of the surrounding countryside.

ARRIVAL AND INFORMATION

By bus Take bus #61 from outside Parma's train station to get to Corniglio (hourly; 30min).

Tourist office On the ground floor of the castellated medieval Palazzo del Podestà, at Piazza Municipio 1 in Castell'Arquato (Tues–Sun 10am–1pm & 2.30–5.30pm; ☎0523 803 215, ⓦcastellarquatoturismo.it).

ACCOMMODATION AND EATING

8

CORNIGLIO

Ostello di Corniglio Largo Castello 1 ☎0521 881 012, ⓦostello-corniglio.it. One of the wings of Corniglio castle has been converted into this basic but comfortable hostel with eight dormitories, ten bathrooms and one kitchen. The countryside location next to the Cento Laghi park provides plenty of opportunities for hiking, cycling and horseriding. Dorms €13

CASTELL'ARQUATO

Casa del Pane Piazza Europa 1 ☎0523 806 084, ⓦlacasadelpanesrl.it. For snacks and pastries you can't beat this thriving bakery/café which has outside tables with a view of the castle. Arrive in the evening for an *aperitivo* served with home-made snacks. Daily 7am–1pm & 4.30–7.30pm.

Enoteca del Borgo Vicolo Riorzo 1/3 ☎0523 804 199, ⓦenotecadelborgo.it. A humble but welcoming trattoria

---

VERDI COUNTRY

About 30km northwest of Parma, the small village of **Le Roncole** marks the start of **Verdi** country. By the main road on Piazza Giovannino Guareschi – named after the author of the Don Camillo books who also lived here – you can visit the humble **house** where the great composer was born (March–Nov Tues–Sun 9.30am–1pm & 2.30–6pm, also open Mon in Oct; Dec & Jan Sat & Sun 9.30am–1pm & 2.30–5.30pm; €4, or with combined ticket for three Verdiana sites €8.50). Some 5km up the road is **Busseto**, the childhood home of Verdi and the centre of the industry that has grown up around the composer, with regular opera performances during summer. It's an appealing little battlemented town, but the main attractions are strictly for Verdi pilgrims. The **Casa Barezzi** (guided tours only Tues–Sun 10am–12.30pm & 3–6.30pm; Dec–Feb Sun only; €4, or included on combined ticket), Via Roma 119, now a Verdi museum, was the home of Antonio Barezzi, a wealthy merchant who spotted the young Verdi's talent and brought him in as a teacher for his daughter. Verdi lived here for a while and later married his pupil, Margherita. Now restored to its nineteenth-century state, the museum contains the piano that Verdi played on and memorabilia such as the baton that Toscanini used to conduct his Verdi memorial concert in 1926. The tourist office at Piazza Verdi 10 (☎0524 931 740, ⓦbussetolive.com) can give you information about the sights and about tickets for concerts in the **Verdi Theatre** (visit also included on combined ticket). You'll need private transport to get to the last of the Verdi sights, the composer's **villa**, a couple of kilometres west of Busseto at **Sant'Agata di Villanova**. The villa (ⓦvillaverdi.org), which contains a mock-up of the Milan hotel room where Verdi died, is open for 45min guided tours (March–Oct Tues–Sun 9.30–11.30am & 2.30–6.30pm; Nov–Feb Sat & Sun 9.30–11.30am & 2.30–6.30pm; €9).

which offers lunch and dinner as well as afternoon snacks and drink. The menu changes according to the season with pasta dishes such as *tagliatelle al ragù* costing around €8–10. Sat & Sun 12.30pm till late.

La Rocca da Franco Piazza del Municipio ☎0523 805 154, ⓦlarocca1964.it. This family-run restaurant has been serving typical Piacentine specialities in the town's main square since 1964. Try the four-course tasting menu (€35) to sample local dishes such as *pisarei e fasò* (gnocchi with tomato and beans). 12.30–3pm & 7–10.30pm; closed Wed.

Leon d'Oro Piazza Europa 6 ☎0523 805 319, ⓦleondorocastellarquato.it. A historic, recently refurbished *palazzo*, the friendly *Leon d'Oro* has comfortable, simply furnished doubles with free wi-fi. In summer guests have use of an outdoor swimming pool, garden and sun terrace. **€135**

East along the Via Emilia from Bologna

East of Bologna, the Via Emilia passes through a clutch of small towns – some of them industrialized and mostly postwar, like Forlì, the unappealing administrative capital of the region, others, like **Faenza**, with medieval piazzas surrounded by towers and battlements. Both started life as Roman way-stations and were under the rule of the Papal States for much of their subsequent history. The **lowlands** to the north are farmed intensively, while on the southern side lie hilly vineyards and pastures, narrow gorges that lead up into the mountains and a couple of ski resorts around Monte Fumaiolo (1407m).

Faenza

Travelling east, cypress trees and umbrella pines, gentler hills and vineyards signal the fact that you're leaving Emilia and entering the Romagna – although strictly speaking there's no distinct boundary between the two regions. **FAENZA**, 50km from Bologna, gives its name to the faïence-ware it has been producing for the last six hundred years. This style of decorated ceramic ware reached its zenith in the fifteenth and sixteenth centuries, and Faenza is still home to one of Italy's leading ceramics schools, teaching techniques of tin-glazing first introduced in the fourteenth century, as well as a major production centre, with small workshops down most of its side streets.

The town is worth a visit for the vast **Museo Internazionale delle Ceramiche** (April–Sept Tues–Sun 10am–7pm; Oct–March Tues–Fri 10am–1.30pm, Sat & Sun 10am–5.30pm; €8; ⓦmicfaenza.org) alone, one of the most important ceramic museums in the world. Housed at Viale Baccarini 19, this exhaustive collection includes early local work decorated in the characteristic blue and ochre, as well as pre-Columbian, Greco-Roman and Islamic pieces; although the highlight is perhaps the Sala Europa, featuring ceramic art by Picasso, Matisse and Chagall.

The rest of Faenza is an attractive town with buildings garnished with ceramic art and an appealing medieval centre formed by the long, crenellated **Palazzo del Podestà**, the **Piazza del Popolo** and the **Piazza della Libertà**, which is the scene of much activity on market days (Tues, Thurs and Sat). **Piazza Martiri della Libertà** – through an archway from Piazza del Popolo – is where you'll find more stalls selling cheese and other local foodstuffs. Each July the local *bambini* turn entrepreneur hosting their own colourful **children's market** on Thursday evenings in Piazza del Popolo until around 8pm, selling toys, books and bric-a-brac. Another good time to be in Faenza is for the **Palio del Niballo** (ⓦpaliodifaenza.it), which takes place on the fourth Sunday in June and sees the five neighbourhoods of the town compete in a medieval jousting tournament.

ARRIVAL AND INFORMATION

FAENZA

By train Trains run from Faenza to Brisighella (hourly; 10–20min), Ravenna (every 2hr; 30–45min) and Rimini (every 30min; 40–55min).

Tourist office Piazza del Popolo 1 (May–Sept Mon–Sat 9.30am–12.30pm & 3.30–6.30pm, Sun 9.30am–12.30pm; Oct–April Tues–Sat 9.30am–12.30pm & 3.30–5.30pm, closed Thurs pm; ☎0546 25 231, ⓦprolocofaenza.it).

8

ACCOMMODATION AND EATING

Osteria del Mercato Piazza Martiri della Libertà 13 ☎ 0546 680 797, ⓦ osteriadelmercato.it. This lively *osteria* is located in several interlinking underground cellars and offers an excellent-value, richly varied menu including authentic wood-fired pizzas (from €4) and a wide selection of pasta dishes (from €5). Daily 12.30–2.30pm & 7.30pm–midnight.

Osteria La Baita Via Naviglio 25/C ☎ 0546 21 584, ⓦ labaitaosteria.com. Developed from a small shop which sells local gastronomic specialities, *La Baita* is an inviting restaurant which serves high-quality traditional dishes and boasts an excellent selection of wines. The menu changes weekly but usually features the home-made pasta. Expect to pay €35–40 for a full meal. Tues–Sat 8.30am–3pm & 5–11pm.

Vittoria Corso Garibaldi 23 ☎ 0546 21 508, ⓦ hotel-vittoria.com. The best hotel in town, the four-star *Vittoria* is located a few blocks north of Piazza del Popolo and features nineteenth-century decor and a dining room with frescoed ceiling. Breakfast included. €125

Brisighella

South of Faenza, the medieval village of **BRISIGHELLA**, halfway up a hillside, is a real food-lover's delight, famed both for its restaurants (visited by people from as far afield as Milan) and its numerous **festivals of gastronomy**, which include the Sagra della Polenta (Oct), del Tartufo (truffle) and dell'Ulivo (both in Nov).

EATING

BRISIGHELLA

Cantina del Bonsignore Via Recuperati 4/A ☎ 0546 81 889, ⓦ cantinadelbonsignore.com. This romantic restaurant with friendly staff offers an interesting, varied menu and a good wine list. The menu changes weekly and includes dishes such as *ravioli gratinati ai pinoli e profumo di tartufo* (baked ravioli with pine nuts and truffle; €8). Mon–Sat 7pm–midnight, Sun noon–3pm & 7pm–midnight.

La Grotta Via Metelli 1 ☎ 0546 81 488, ⓦ ristorante-lagrotta.it. Set in an atmospheric underground cave, *La Grotta* serves creative Italian cuisine such as *strozzapreti* con carciofi e piselli (pasta with artichokes and peas; €7). There are also daily fixed-price menus based on both meat (€25) and fish (€30). Noon–2.30pm & 7.30–10.30pm; closed Wed.

La Rocca Via delle Volte 10 ☎ 0546 81 180, ⓦ albergo-larocca.it. This hotel restaurant prides itself on using the freshest, locally sourced ingredients for its menu of Romagnolo cuisine and offers home-made pasta dishes such as the *tagliatelle all romagnola* (with sausage ragù, €7) and meat courses from €13. 12.30–3pm & 7–10.30pm; closed Wed.

Ferrara

Thirty minutes' train ride north of Bologna, **FERRARA** was the residence of the Este dukes, an eccentric dynasty that ranked as a major political force throughout Renaissance times. The Este kept the main artists of the day in commissions and built a town which, despite a relatively small population, was – and still is – one of the most elegant urban creations of the period.

At the end of the sixteenth century, with no heir to inherit their lands, the Este were forced to hand over Ferrara to the papacy and leave for good. Life in the city effectively collapsed: eighteenth-century travellers found a ghost town of empty streets and clogged-up canals infested with mosquitoes. Since then Ferrara has picked itself up, dusted itself off, and is now a vibrant, provincial town that, with its grand squares, restored medieval palaces and portico-lined streets, looks a bit like a mini Bologna. It's a popular stop for tourists travelling up from Bologna to Venice, but they rarely stay, leaving the city centre enjoyably peaceful in the evenings.

Ferrara's main sights are clustered together in an area that's easily explored on foot. The castle is the main focus, but several other palaces and museums offer reminders of the town's more glorious past. Ferrara's **market days** are Monday and Friday, with most activity taking place on Piazza Travaglio. On the first weekend of the month (except Aug) a large antiques market takes place between the *castello* and the Duomo.

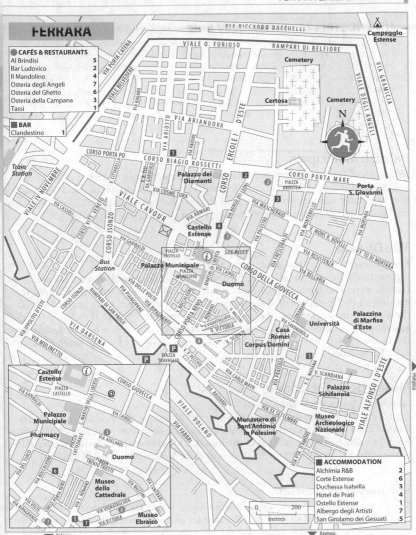

FERRARA

CAFÉS & RESTAURANTS
Al Brindisi	5
Bar Ludovico	2
Il Mandolino	4
Osteria degli Angeli	7
Osteria del Ghetto	6
Osteria della Campana	3
Tassi	1

BAR
Clandestino	1

ACCOMMODATION
Alchimia R&B	2
Corte Estense	6
Duchessa Isabella	3
Hotel de Prati	4
Ostello Estense	1
Albergo degli Artisti	7
San Girolamo dei Gesuati	5

Castello Estense

Tues–Sun 9.30am–5.30pm, last entry 4.45pm • €8 • ⓦ castelloestense.it

The bulky, moated **Castello Estense** dominates the centre of Ferrara, built in response to a late fourteenth-century uprising and generally held at the time to be a major feat of military engineering. Behind its impenetrable brick walls, the Este court thrived, supporting artists like Pisanello, Jacopo Bellini, Mantegna, and the poets Ariosto and Tasso. It's hard to credit all this as you walk through the castle now, much of which is used as offices and inaccessible to the public. The few rooms that you can see go some way to bringing back the days of Este magnificence, especially the *saletta* and Salone dei Giochi, or games rooms, decorated by Sebastiano Filippi with vigorous scenes of wrestling, discus throwing, ball tossing and chariot racing. There's also the less-innocent poison room which was apparently mainly used as a toxic pharmacy for the Este's political enemies.

HIT THE STREETS – FERRARA BY BIKE

Ferrara is famed as a *città della bicicletta*. Seemingly everyone in the city, from young to old, makes the majority of their journeys on two wheels. Outside the centre, the roads are bordered by cycle lanes. No such concessions are required in the traffic-free centre, although the largely cobbled streets do pose their own set of difficulties. You can **rent bicycles** at the station (to the left as you come out) from Pirani e Bagni (☎0532 772 190) or from Barlati at Via degli Adelardi 1/3/3A, just by the Duomo (☎0532 206 863), for around €2/hr (€7/day). The tourist office has details of routes both within the city and out into the Po Delta Park.

Palazzo Municipale

Just south of here, the crenellated **Palazzo Municipale**, built in 1243 but much altered and restored since, holds statues of Niccolò III and son, Borso, on its facade – though they're actually twentieth-century reproductions. Walk through the arch into the pretty, enclosed square of **Piazza del Municipio** for a view of the rest of the building.

The Duomo

Piazza della Cattedrale • Mon–Sat 7.30am–noon & 3–6.30pm, Sun 7.30am–12.30pm & 3.30–7.30pm • Free

Opposite the Palazzo Municipale, the **Duomo** is a mixture of Romanesque and Gothic styles and has a monumental facade, focused on a carved central portal that was begun in the mid-twelfth century and finished a century or so later. Much of the carving depicts the Last Judgement. Inside, the main part of the church has the grandeur of a ballroom, with sparkling chandeliers, but is much less intriguing than the exterior, with most of the best works having been moved to the nearby Museo della Cattedrale.

Museo della Cattedrale

Via San Romano • Tues–Sun 9.30am–1pm & 3–6pm • €6

Across the square from the cathedral, the former church of San Romano now houses most of the Duomo's treasures. The highlights of the collection include a set of intricate bas-reliefs illustrating the labours of the months, which formerly adorned the outside of the cathedral, and the beautiful *Madonna della Melagrana* by Della Quercia.

The medieval quarter

The long, arcaded south side of the Duomo flanks **Piazza Trento e Trieste**, whose rickety-looking rows of shops herald the arcades of the appealing **Via San Romano** that runs off the far side of the square past the museum. Beyond this lies the labyrinth of alleyways that make up Ferrara's **medieval quarter**; the arched **Via delle Volte**, a long street running east, parallel to Via Carlo Mayr, is one of the most characteristic. At Via Mazzini 95 a couple of **synagogues** and the **Museo Ebraico di Ferrara**, the town's small Jewish museum (visits by guided tour only Mon–Thurs & Sun 10am, 11am & noon; ⊛comune.fe.it/museoebraico; €4) recounts the story of the town's Jewish Ghetto. On the wider streets above the tangled medieval district are a number of the Renaissance palaces, most of them closed to the public. The **Casa Romei**, at Via Savonarola 30 (Tues–Sun 8.30am–7.30pm; €3), is a typical building of the time, with frescoes and graceful courtyards alongside artefacts rescued from various local churches. Just beyond is the house, at no. 19, where the monk Savonarola was born and lived for twenty years, while behind the palace, the monastery church of **Corpus Domini** at Via Pergolato 4 (Mon–Fri 9.30–11.30am & 3.30–5.30pm; free but contributions accepted) holds the tombs of Alfonso I and II d'Este and **Lucrezia Borgia**.

Palazzo Schifanoia

Via Scandiana 23 • Tues–Sun 9.30am–6pm • €6

The **Palazzo Schifanoia** – the "Palace of Joy" – is one of the grandest of Ferrara's palaces. It belonged to the Este family, and Cosimo Tura's frescoes inside transplanted their court to Arcadia. In the Salone dei Mesi (the "Room of the Months"), the blinds are kept closed to protect the colours, and the room seems silent and empty compared with what's happening on the walls, where three bands of frescoes depict Borso Este surrounded by friends and hunting dogs, along with groups of musicians, weavers and embroiderers with white rabbits nibbling the grass at their feet. Above, each section is topped with a sign of the zodiac and, above that, various mythological scenes.

Palazzina di Marfisa d'Este

Corso della Giovecca 170 • Tues–Sun 9.30am–1pm & 3–6pm • €4

The sixteenth-century **Palazzina di Marfisa d'Este** has more frescoes, this time by Filippi, and although its gloomy interior filled with heavy furniture and antiques is less impressive than the Schifanoia complex, in summer the loggia and orange grove are a welcome refuge from the heat.

Museo Archeologico Nazionale

Via XX Settembre 124 • Tues–Sun 9.30am–5pm • €5

The **Museo Archeologico Nazionale** holds the city's well-organized archeological collections, most of which are finds from Spina, the Greco-Etruscan seaport and trading colony near Comacchio. Highlights include red-figure vases from the fifth-century BC and many funerary objects from the ancient necropolis of Spina.

Monastero di Sant'Antonio in Polesine

Vicolo del Gambone • Mon–Fri 9.30–11.30am & 3.15–5pm, Sat 9.30–11.30am & 3–4.30pm • Donations expected

Down in the southeast corner of the town is a gem of a place: the **Monastero di Sant'Antonio in Polesine**, with exquisite frescoes. Knock at the door of the convent and the nuns shepherd you into a chapel covered with works by the school of Giotto, including a rare *Flight from Egypt* in which Joseph carries Jesus on his shoulders.

North of the castle

There are some more impressive palaces north of the *castello*, on and around **Corso Ercole I d'Este** – named after Ercole I, who succeeded to the throne in 1441 after his father Niccolò III died, probably poisoned, and who promptly disposed of anyone likely to pose a threat. His reputation for coldness earned him nicknames such as "North Wind" and "Diamond" and his huge ambition led him to order the extension of the northern quarter of the city, the so-called "Herculean Addition", on such a grand scale that Ferrara was doubled, incorporating a planning system that was considered at the time to be boldly avant-garde.

Palazzo dei Diamanti

Corso Ercole I d'Este 21 • Pinacoteca open Tues, Wed, Fri & Sat 9am–2pm, Thurs 9am–7pm, Sun 9am–1pm • €4

The **Palazzo dei Diamanti**, a little way down the Corso on the left, named after the 8500 pink-and-white marble ashlars in the form of pyramids (or diamonds) that stud its facade, was at the heart of Ercole's town plan and is nowadays used for modern art exhibitions as well as being home to the **Pinacoteca Nazionale**, holding works from the Ferrara and Bologna schools, notably paintings by Dossi, Garofalo and Guercino, and a spirited *St Christopher* by "Il Bastianino" (Sebastiano Filippi).

ARRIVAL AND DEPARTURE

By train Ferrara's train station is west of the city walls, a half-hour walk along Viale Cavour to the centre of town, or take bus #1, #2, #9 or #3C (#2 is the most direct).
Destinations Bologna (every 30min; 30–50min); Ravenna (hourly; 1hr–1hr 30min); Rimini (hourly; 1hr 50min–2hr 30min).

By bus The bus station lies just southwest of the main square, on Corso Isonzo.
Destinations Comacchio (10 daily; 1hr 10min).
By car Parking is available at the southern end of the city, by the city walls on the piazzas Kennedy and Travaglio for €2/hr.

INFORMATION AND SERVICES

Tourist office On the north side of the *castello* courtyard (Mon–Sat 9am–1pm & 2–6pm, Sun 9.30am–1pm & 2–5pm; ☎ 0532 209 370, ⓦ ferraraterraeacqua.it).

Internet Infopoint, Via degli Spadari 1/2 (Mon–Fri 8.30am–12.30pm & 2–4.30pm, Sat 9–11.30am; 30min a day free of charge).

ACCOMMODATION

Albergo degli Artisti Via Vittoria 66 ☎ 0532 761 038, ⓦ albergoartisti.it. Friendly, very unpretentious option in a modern block in the medieval quarter. Rooms are clean and quiet and are available with or without bathrooms; one has a private kitchen. No breakfast, no credit cards. **€60**
Alchimia R&B Via Borgo dei Leoni 122 ☎ 0532 186 4656, ⓦ alchimiaferrara.it. This recently renovated B&B offers carefully designed, modern rooms, a generous breakfast and courteous staff. The hotel also has a reading area, art exhibitions and free bicycle rental available to guests. Parking included. **€80**
Corte Estense Via Correggiari 4/A ☎ 0532 242 168, ⓦ corteestense.it. This historic *palazzo* is a rather grand option with its oriental carpets, elegant courtyard and spacious rooms. The hotel is all about total, inviting comfort and boasts a fantastic position in the heart of the historic centre. Breakfast included. **€140**
★ **Duchessa Isabella** Via Palestro 70 ☎ 0532 202 121, ⓦ duchessaisabella.it. A Relais & Chateaux-affiliated sixteenth-century palace filled with bright frescoes is the top choice for five-star luxury. The opulent rooms come replete with antique furniture, giant plasma-screen TVs and wi-fi. Parking and breakfast included. Closed Aug. **€299**
★ **Hotel de Prati** Via Padiglioni 5 ☎ 0532 241 905, ⓦ hoteldeprati.com. Very friendly and helpful family-run establishment draped with interesting modern paintings by local artists; it offers comfortable rooms with antique furniture and wi-fi. In a convenient location just a few minutes on foot from the town centre. Breakfast included. **€110**
Ostello Estense Corso Biagio Rossetti 24 ☎ 0532 201 158, ⓦ ostelloestense.com. HI hostel situated northwest of the centre with huge, bright, spotlessly clean rooms with grand, wooden ceiling beams and a calm but friendly atmosphere; internet and wi-fi are available; always open. Dorms **€16**
San Girolamo dei Gesuati Via Madama 40/A ☎ 0532 207 448, ⓦ sangirolamodeigesuati.com. This quiet, friendly and good-value hotel is a converted fourteenth-century convent complete with cloistered courtyard and gardens. The rooms are basic but comfortable and there is also a very good restaurant offering traditional dishes. Parking and breakfast included. **€90**

CAMPING

Campeggio Comunale Estense Via Gramicia 76 ☎ 0532 752 396, ⓦ campeggioestense.it; take bus #1 or #5 from the train station to Piazzale San Giovanni by the walls, from where it's a 10min walk north. Campsite for tents and caravans on the northeast edge of town with helpful staff and a tranquil, relaxing atmosphere. Closed Feb. Pitches **€13**

EATING AND DRINKING

Ferrara has a good range of restaurants and trattorias with prices to suit most pockets, plus a few bars in which to while away the evening with the locals. For self-caterers, try Antica Salumeria Marchetti (☎ 0532 204 800), a great traditional delicatessen on Via Cortevecchia 35, just south of the Palazzo Municipale, which does a particularly fine line in salamis.

FESTIVALS AND EVENTS IN FERRARA

One of the big annual events, held the last weekend in May, is the **Palio**, smaller than the famous Siena race, but still an exciting time to be here (ⓦ paliodiferrara.it). In August, the streets of the town ring to the annual **buskers' festival** (ⓦ ferrarabuskers.com), with musical offerings ranging from African drums to Dixieland bands, while the following month the skies are filled with giant blobs of colour as the **Ferrara Balloon Festival** (ⓦ ferrarafestival.it), one of the largest in Europe, gets under way.

★ **Al Bríndisi** Via dogli Adelardi 11 ☎0532 471 725, ⓦalbrindisi.net. The unprepossessing exterior conceals Ferrara's oldest (at least fifteenth-century) *osteria*, once frequented by the likes of Cellini and Titian. The food is good and reasonably priced, with set menus ranging between €13 and €50, while some of the vintages in the magnificent collection of port wines are among Italy's finest and priced accordingly. Tues–Sun 11am–midnight; closed Thurs eve.

Bar Ludovico Piazza Ariostea 7 ⓦludovicowinebar .com. Welcoming café-bar set beneath arcades overlooking a pretty, grassy park (site of the city's Palio) and seemingly always filled with gossiping locals, particularly for the early-evening *aperitivo*. Great inventive salads (€6) and jumbo panini (€4) take their place alongside a large drinks menu. Mon 4–9pm, Tues–Sun noon–midnight.

Clandestino Via Ragno 35 ☎0532 767 101. Down a narrow backstreet, this welcoming bar is a popular pre/ post film stopoff for people heading to the nearby Apollo cinema and also serves food, with a good selection of wines, cocktails and local craft beers (€5). Wi-fi, too. Daily 7pm–1.30am.

Il Mandolino Via del Volte 52 ☎0532 760 080, ⓦristoranteilmandolino.it. A homely little trattoria down a narrow, atmospheric back alley (look for the flower boxes outside), offering a great range of intensely flavoured rustic dishes, as well as a mouthwatering (and when you think about it, eye-watering) *agnello o castrato* (€9). 12.30–3.30pm & 7.30–11.30pm; closed Mon eve, Tues & mid-June until mid-Aug.

Osteria degli Angeli Via delle Volte 4 ☎0532 764 376. A bustling, welcoming place, with lots of different wines and a changing daily menu of good local dishes, with particular focus on pumpkin (*zucca*). Moderately priced with *primi* €7–8, *secondi* €10–14. Tues–Sun 7–10pm.

★ **Osteria del Ghetto** Via della Vittoria 26 ☎0532 764 936, ⓦosteriadelghetto.it. On a Ghetto backstreet, set – rather incongruously – next to a modern yoga centre, this friendly place serves up all manner of fish specialities, such as *spaghetti alle vongole* (€12), as well as pork, beef or lamb for €10–15. Tues–Sun noon–2.30pm & 7.30–10.30pm.

Osteria della Campana Via Borgo dei Leoni 26 ☎0532 241 256, ⓦosteriadellacampana.com. Romantic, spacious spot down a narrow alleyway with an interesting menu of traditional specialities, local cheeses and home-made desserts. Highlights include the typical Ferrarese pasta dish of *cappellacci con zucca* for €9. Tues–Sun noon–2pm & 7–10.30pm.

Tassi Viale Repubblica 23, Bondeno ☎0532 893 030. Some 20km west of Ferrara – accessible by the "Bondeno" bus from the bus station – this fourth-generation, family-run place is a food-lover's heaven. There's no menu; you just let Signor Tassi lead you through an amazing succession of fine Ferrarese dishes such as *bolliti* (mixed boiled meats; €20) or *salama del sugo* (a traditional minced pork dish; €15). It's not cheap but it is unforgettable. If you're wise, you'll book one of the large, comfortable rooms upstairs so you don't have too far to stagger to bed. Noon–2pm & 8–10pm; closed Sun eve & Mon.

The Po Delta

East of Ferrara lies the **Po Delta**, an expanse of marshland and lagoons where the River Po splits into several channels, trickling to the sea, and small fingers of land poke out into the Adriatic. Etruscan traders set up the port of Spina here between the fourth and third centuries BC, when the sea covered much of the land from Comacchio to Ravenna. Partly owing to drainage schemes, the briny waters have since retreated by 12km, and the area becomes a bit less marshy each year – an advantage for local farmers but a threat to the many varieties of sea and shore **birds** that inhabit the area. The two main lagoons of **Valli di Comacchio** and **Valle Bertuzzi** together form a major part of the Parco del Delta del Po (ⓦparcodeltapo.it), which with the surrounding

---

BOAT TRIPS AROUND THE PO DELTA

The most evocative way of seeing the delta is by **boat**. Every spring free birdwatching trips are organized by the tourist office in Comacchio as part of the annual International Po Delta Birdwatching Fair (ⓦpodeltabirdfair.it). And between April and October voluntary groups run free boat tours on a typical marshland boat called a *batane* from its mooring at the fish market of Trepponti in Comacchio. Two-hour boat trips also set off from the harbour of Stazione Foce, south of Comacchio (daily April–Oct at 9am, 11am, 3pm & 5pm; ☎340 253 4267, ⓦvallidicomacchio.info; €10), accessible by car only; follow signs for "Museo delle Valli". More information is available at the tourist office in Comacchio (see p.496).

wetlands now constitute one of Europe's most highly regarded birdwatching areas, providing a habitat for nesting and migrating birds, including heron, egret, curlew, avocet and tern.

Comacchio

The region's main centre, **COMACCHIO** is a small fishing town intersected by a network of canals, also accessible by boat tour, with a famous local attraction in its triple-bridge or **Trepponti**, built in 1634, which crosses three of the canals. Comacchio is an eel port and a good time to visit is in October when the Festival of the Eel sees wriggling masses of the creatures fished out of the canals on their way to the Sargasso Sea. Eel (*anguille*) unsurprisingly takes centre stage in many local restaurants with other regional dishes like fish risotto and *fritto misto* particularly recommended.

ARRIVAL AND INFORMATION COMACCHIO

By bus There is no train station in Comacchio so the only way to arrive is by bus from either Ferrara (10 daily; 1hr 10min) or Ravenna (6 daily; 1hr 10min).

Tourist office Piazza Mazzini 4 (June–Oct Mon–Sat 9.30am–12.30pm & 4–7pm, Sun 10am–12.30pm & 4–6.30pm; ☎ 0533 314 154, ⊛ turismocomacchio.it).

EATING

La Barcaccia Piazza XX Settembre 41 ☎ 0533 311 081, ⊛ trattorialabarcaccia.eu. Situated opposite Comacchio's cathedral, *La Barcaccia* serves typical cuisine of the lagoon area with some particular dishes such as *ravioli di branzino e olive* (ravioli with sea bass and olives; €12) as well as fresh grilled and fried fish from €13. Tues–Sun 12.30-2.30pm & 7.15–10.30pm.

Trattoria Vasco e Giulia Via Muratori 21 ☎ 0533 81 252, ⊛ vascoegiulia.it. Welcoming, unassuming restaurant run by a mother and two daughters and specializing in fish dishes. Aside from the local eel, which is served in different ways including the *risotto di anguilla* (€9.50), there's also a delicious *fritto misto di pesce* (mixed fried fish; €12). Tues–Sat 12.30–2.30pm & 7–10.30pm; closed Wed eve.

Ravenna and around

The main reason to visit **RAVENNA**, a few kilometres inland of the Adriatic coast, is simple – it holds a set of **mosaics** generally acknowledged to be the crowning achievement of Byzantine art. No fewer than eight of Ravenna's buildings have been designated UNESCO World Heritage sites. They date from a strange interlude in the city's history during the late Roman–early Byzantine period when this otherwise unremarkable provincial centre briefly became one of the most important cities in all of Europe (see opposite).

Tourism seems almost incidental and for a city that has such historic monuments, the centre feels surprisingly modern – a combination of Mussolini's building programme and Allied bombing that levelled much of the city during World War II. It's a pleasant enough place to spend a couple of days and, though it has some excellent bars and restaurants, it's the churches and mosaics that will monopolize your time. Nightlife is sparse, but a number of small **coastal resorts**, known as the lido towns, a dozen or so kilometres away provide some excitement in summer. And if you're looking for thrills and spills, the nearby **Mirabilandia** (☎ 0544 561 156, ⊛ mirabilandia.it), a Disneyesque theme park, helps bring in the crowds during summer.

Brief history

When Ravenna became capital of the **Western Roman Empire** sixteen hundred years ago, it was more by quirk of fate than design. The Emperor Honorius, alarmed by armies invading from the north, moved his court from Milan to this obscure town on the Romagna coast around 402; it was easy to defend, surrounded by marshland, and was situated close to the port of Classis – at the time the biggest Roman naval base on the Adriatic. After enjoying a period of great monumental adornment as chief city of the empire, Ravenna was conquered by the Goths in 476. However, the new conquerors were also Christians and continued to embellish the city lavishly, particularly the Ostrogoth Theodoric, making it one of the most sought-after towns in the Mediterranean. In the mid-sixth century Byzantine forces annexed the city to the Eastern Empire and made it into an exarchate (province), under the rule of Constantinople. The Byzantine rulers were responsible for Ravenna's most glorious era, keen to outdo rival cities with magnificent palaces, churches and art. By the end of the eighth century, however, the glory years had passed. The city was captured by the Lombards, after which the Adriatic shoreline receded – an 11km-long canal now links Ravenna's port to the sea – and Ravenna sank slowly back into obscurity.

Piazza del Popolo and around

The centre of Ravenna is the **Piazza del Popolo**, an elegant open space, arcaded on two sides, laid out by the Venetians in the fifteenth century and now bordered by cafés.

Tomba di Dante

Via Dante Alighieri • Daily 9.30am–6.30pm • Free

A few blocks south of Piazza del Popolo, across Piazza Garibaldi, the **Tomba di Dante** is a site of local pride, a small Neoclassical building which was put up in the eighteenth century to enclose the tomb of Dante. The poet had been chased out of Florence by the

> ### RAVENNA'S MUSEUM CARDS
>
> Ravenna has three **museum cards**: the Ravenna Visit Card covers the basilicas of San Vitale and Sant'Apollinare Nuovo, the Neonian Baptistry, the Mausoleo di Galla Placidia and the Museo Arcivescovile – all the church-controlled sites. The card is valid for seven days, costs €9.50 and can be purchased from any participating site. Note that tickets for these sites cannot be purchased individually. For the state sites you can get a joint ticket for the Museo Nazionale and the Mausoleo di Teodorico (€8), or one that covers these two and also the Basilica di Sant'Apollinare in Classe (€10); these can be purchased at the sites.

time he arrived in Ravenna, and he was sheltered here by the Da Polenta family – then in control of the city – while he finished his *Divine Comedy*.

San Francesco and the Museo Dantesco

Via Dante Alighieri 9 • Church 8am–noon & 3–6pm; museum Tues–Sun 9.30am–6.30pm • Free

Dante died in 1321 and was laid to rest in the church of **San Francesco**, a much-restored building dating back to the fourth century. File down the stairs towards the tenth-century waterlogged crypt complete with swimming goldfish and remnants of a mosaic floor. The **Museo Dantesco** is off San Francesco's cloister and contains memorabilia of the poet and his final resting place.

The Duomo

Piazza del Duomo • Daily 8am–noon & 3–6pm • Free

A couple of minutes' walk west of San Francesco, a group of buildings around **Piazza del Duomo** shelters the **Duomo** itself, with its cylindrical – and slightly tipsy – tower. Originally a fifth-century building, it was completely destroyed by an earthquake in 1733 and rebuilt in unexceptional style soon after.

Museo Arcivescovile

Piazza Arcivescovile • Daily: April–Sept 9.30am–7pm; Nov–Feb 10am–7pm; March & Oct 9.30am–5.30pm • Museum card (see box above)

More interesting is the **Museo Arcivescovile** in the Bishop's Palace behind, with fragments of mosaics from around the city and the palace's sixth-century Oratorio Sant'Andrea, which is adorned with mosaics of birds in a meadow above a Christ dressed in the armour, cloak and gilded leather skirt of a Roman centurion.

Neonian Baptistry

Piazza del Duomo • Daily: April–Sept 9.30am–7pm; Nov–Feb 10am–7pm; March & Oct 9.30am–5.30pm • Museum card (see box above)

The **Neonian Baptistry**, on the same side of the Duomo by the belltower, is a conversion from a Roman bathhouse. The original floor level has sunk into the marshy ground, and the remains of the previous building are now 3m below. The choice of building was a logical one as baptisms involved total immersion in those days.

Basilica di Sant'Apollinare Nuovo and around

Via di Roma • Daily: April–Sept 9.30am–7pm; Nov–Feb 10am–7pm; March & Oct 9.30am–5.30pm • Museum card (see box above)

Via di Roma, lined with bland, official-looking palaces, cuts right through the modern centre of Ravenna and sees much of its traffic. Halfway up stands the **Basilica di Sant'Apollinare Nuovo**. Built by Theodoric in the sixth century, it contains some of Ravenna's most impressive mosaics, running the length of both sides of the nave. Each shows a line of martyrs – one side male, the other female – processing through avenues of date palms and bearing gifts for Christ and the Virgin enthroned. As a Goth,

Theodoric belonged to the Arian branch of Christianity which didn't accept the absolute divinity of Christ, a heresy stamped out by Constantinople as much for political as theological reasons. When the Byzantines came along, they removed many of the mosaic figures that had been placed here under Theodoric's reign. When Theodoric built the church in the early 500s, he dedicated it to Jesus, but when the Byzantines took over it was rededicated to St Martin, who was known for his anti-heretic campaigns and is shown at the head of the line of male devotees. Still later, in the ninth century, it was rededicated yet again to the present eponymous saint.

Five minutes' walk away up Via di Roma, next door to the Basilica dello Santo Spirito, is the **Arian Baptistry** (daily 8.30am–7.30pm; free), also built by Theodoric, with a fine mosaic ceiling showing the twelve Apostles and the baptism of Christ.

San Vitale

Via Fiandrini Benedetto • Daily: April–Sept 9.30am–7pm; Nov–Feb 10am–7pm; March & Oct 9.30am–5.30pm • Museum card (see box opposite)

In terms of monuments, Ravenna's biggest draw is the area ten minutes' walk northwest of the city centre, around the Basilica di San Vitale, which holds the finest of the mosaics and is now gathered together into one big complex, including the mausoleum of Galla Placidia and the National Museum.

San Vitale, which was begun in 525 under the Roman Emperor Theodoric and finished in 548 under the Byzantine ruler Justinian, remains unique for an Italian building. Created to an Eastern-inspired arrangement of void and solid and dark and light, the design was the basis for the great church of Hagia Sofia in Istanbul, built fifteen years later.

The series of mosaics in the basilica starts with Old Testament scenes spread across the semicircular lunettes of the choir; the triumphal arch shows Christ, the Apostles and sons of St Vitalis. Further in, on the semi-dome of the apse, a beardless Christ stands between two angels, presenting a model of the church to St Vitalis and Bishop Ecclesius. Of the mosaics on the side walls of the apse, the two processional panels are the best surviving portraits of the Emperor Justinian and his wife Theodora – he's on the left and she's on the right – and a rich example of Byzantine mosaic technique. The minute glass *tesserae* are laid in sections, alternate rows set at slightly different angles to vary the reflection of light and give an impression of depth.

There were definite rules about who appeared where in **mosaics** – the higher up and further to the east, the more important or holy the subject. Colour is used emblematically, too, with gold backgrounds denoting either holiness or high status.

Mausoleo di Galla Placidia

Via Fiandrini Benedetto • Daily: April–Sept 9.30am–7pm; Nov–Feb 10am–7pm; March & Oct 9.30am–5.30pm • Museum card (see box opposite)

Across the grass from the basilica is the tiny **Mausoleo di Galla Placidia** named after the half-sister of Honorius. The emperor's frequent absences left Galla in charge of the city and she was responsible for much of the grandeur of Ravenna's early days. Despite the name and the three sarcophagi inside, it's unlikely that the building ever held her bones. Galla Placidia was taken hostage when the Goths sacked Rome, and caused a scandal by marrying one of her kidnappers, Ataulf. She went into battle with him as his army forged south, and later they reigned jointly over the Gothic kingdom. When Ataulf was assassinated the Romans took her back for a ransom of corn, after which she was obliged to marry a Roman general, Constantius. Their son formally became the Emperor Valentinian III at the age of 6, and as his regent, Galla Placidia assumed control of the Western Empire.

Inside the *mausoleo*, filtered through thin alabaster windows, the light falls on mosaics that glow with a deep blue lustre, most in an earlier style than those of San Vitale, full of Roman and naturalistic motifs.

Museo Nazionale

Via Fiandrini Benedetto • Tues–Sun 8.30am–7.30pm • €5

Adjacent to San Vitale on the southern side, housed in the former cloisters of the church, the **Museo Nazionale** contains various items from this and later periods – fifteenth-century icons, early Byzantine glass and embroidery from Florence. Among the most eye-catching exhibits is a sixth-century statue of Hercules capturing a stag, possibly a copy of a Greek original.

Domus dei Tappeti di Pietra

Via Gianbattista Barbiani • March–Oct 10am–6.30pm; Nov–Feb Tues–Fri 10am–5pm, Sat & Sun 10am–6pm • €4

Just a couple of hundred metres south of San Vitale, and accessed through the small church of Santa Eufemia, is one of the city's more recently discovered Byzantine treasures. Uncovered in the early 1990s, the **Domus dei Tappeti di Pietra**, which translates as the "House of Stone Carpets", is the remains of a palace from the late Roman–early Byzantine period. It comprises fourteen rooms, each adorned with intricately crafted floor and wall mosaics, the most striking of which shows figures representing the Four Seasons dancing hand in hand while another figure provides a musical accompaniment on a pan-flute.

Mausoleo di Teodorico

Via delle Industrie 14 • Daily 8.30am–7pm • €4

Still within Ravenna, but a bit of a hike north of the train station, lies one more early sixth-century monument that's worth visiting: the **Mausoleo di Teodorico**. This ten-sided curiosity is unique in Western architecture owing much to Syrian models of its day, and constructed of Istrian limestone. The 300-tonne cupola is a single, if cracked, chunk and no one knows exactly how it was manoeuvred into place. Inside the decagonal second storey sits an ancient porphyry bathtub, pressed into use as the royal sarcophagus.

ARRIVAL AND DEPARTURE

RAVENNA

By train From the train station on Piazza Farini in the east of town, it's a 5min walk along Viale Farini and Via Armando Diaz to Ravenna's central square, Piazza del Popolo. Destinations Bologna (hourly; 1hr 20min–2hr); Ferrara (hourly; 1hr 15min); Rimini (hourly; 1hr–1hr 10min).
By bus The bus station is across the tracks behind the train station, in Piazzale Aldo Moro.
Destinations Classe (every 30min; 10min); Marina di Ravenna (every 30min; 20min).
By car Parking is available – for around €1/hr – on various squares around the centre, including Piazza Barracca and Piazza Mameli.

INFORMATION AND GETTING AROUND

Tourist office Via Salara 8 (Mon–Sat 8.30am–7pm, Sun 10am–6pm; ☎ 0544 35 404, ✇ turismo.ravenna.it).
Bike rental With much of its centre pedestrianized, Ravenna is best explored by foot or on two wheels. Bikes can be rented from the Cooperativa San Vitale (Mon–Fri 7am–7pm; ☎ 0544 37 031), the green building next to the train station, for €1.50/hr or €12/day; it also gives out maps and holds left luggage.

RAVENNA'S FESTIVALS

The **Ravenna Festival** in June and July attracts big names in the classical music world (✇ ravennafestival.org) with performances taking place in different venues across town including churches, gardens and theatres, while the venerable **Jazz Festival** in July also draws international stars (✇ erjn.it/ravenna/). Every two years the city also hosts **RavennaMosaico** which celebrates contemporary mosaics and visual arts with exhibitions, workshops and concerts (✇ ravennamosaico.it).

ACCOMMODATION

Albergo Cappello Via IV Novembre 41 ☎0544 219 813, ⓦalbergocappello.it. Old *palazzo* right in the heart of town that's been turned into an extremely stylish small hotel with just seven chic rooms each decorated in its own colour and style. It also has an excellent restaurant. **€150**

Centrale Byron Via IV Novembre 14 ☎0544 212 225, ⓦhotelbyron.com. This great-value hotel offers comfortable, smart furnishings throughout and is located right in the heart of town. There's a friendly, family atmosphere and each of the well-appointed rooms has wi-fi, satellite TV and a/c in summer. Breakfast included. **€90**

La Reunion Via Corrado Ricci 29 ☎0544 212 949, ⓦlareunion.it. Opposite the Tomba di Dante, *La Residence* offers a range of bright mini-apartments for up to six people, each equipped with free wi-fi and a small but well-equipped kitchen corner, convenient for those wishing to eat in. Breakfast included. **€90**

M Club Piazza Francesco Baracca 26 ☎0544 37 538, ⓦm-club.it. A stylish B&B just a few minutes from San Vitale with six beautifully decorated rooms each with wood-beamed ceilings and carefully selected furnishings. Breakfast and bike rental is included in the price. **€80**

Ostello Galletti Abbiosi Via di Roma 140 ☎0544 31 313, ⓦgalletti.ra.it. Welcoming eighteenth-century palace, smartly refurbished with comfortable a/c singles and doubles. Three of the large rooms have fine painted ceilings and antique terracotta floors. Amenities include wi-fi, a gym, a garden and parking; very good value. Breakfast included. **€84**

Youth Hostel Dante Via Nicolodi 12 ☎0544 421 164, ⓦhostelravenna.com. HI hostel a 10min walk east of the station, handily opposite a large Co-op supermarket. An all-you-can-eat buffet breakfast is included in the price. Lock-out between noon & 2.30pm; 11.30pm curfew, or you can pay €1 for your own key. Dorms **€16**

CAMPING

Camping Adriano Via dei Campeggi 7 ☎0544 437 230, ⓦcampingadriano.com; bus #80 from in front of Ravenna train station. One of many campsites in the area, this one is in the coastal resort of Punta Marina Terme, 9km away, allowing easy access to the beach. There are a range of amenities and activities including a swimming pool, bike rental, entertainments and games, plus bungalows and mobile homes for rent. Pitches **€12**

EATING AND DRINKING

Central Ravenna is not exactly filled with places to eat, and you need to know where to go to avoid fruitless wandering. The covered market on Piazza A. Costa is open from 7am to 1.30pm and is a good source of picnic supplies.

Albergo Cappello Via IV Novembre 41 ☎0544 240 128, ⓦalbergocappello.it. The hotel's elegant restaurant and wine bar are both excellent and offer a delicious and creative menu of home-made pasta and local meats and seafood. Try the *strozzapreti con fiori di zucca e vongole veraci*, pasta with courgette flowers and clams €10). 12.30–2.30pm & 7.30–10.30pm; closed Sun eve & Mon.

Al Rustichello Via Maggiore 21 ☎0544 36 043. Consistently popular place where the excitable owner tells you the menu (in English too) and serves food that an Italian grandmother would be proud of – the *cappelletti* with asparagus, *proscuitto* and cream is recommended (€10). Booking advised. Mon–Fri noon–2.15pm & 7.30–10.15pm.

Bella Venezia Via IV Novembre 16 ☎0544 21 274, ⓦbellavenezia.it. Come here for simple meals, expertly prepared – handmade pumpkin *cappelletti* (€8), *asparagi alla Bismarck* (asparagus topped with parmesan and an egg), etc. Eat formally inside amid the starched tablecloths or informally outside watching the city pass by. Mon–Sat noon–3pm & 7–11pm.

★ **Bizantino** Piazza A. Costa ☎0544 32 073. Self-service (or "free-flow") place, just inside the market, dishing up excellent-value, fresh-from-the-market hot and cold dishes including some vegetarian options. Pick up

three courses here for under €10. Mon–Fri noon–3pm.

★ **Ca' De Ven** Via C. Ricci 24 ☎0544 30 163, ⓦcadeven.it. Stunning wood-panelled *enoteca* with painted ceilings and wine racks covering every available space. It offers a simple, changing menu of a few pizza and pasta dishes, as well as a selection of *piadine* for around €4.50. There's also a huge range of vintages to sample by the glass from €1.50 upwards. Tues–Sun 11am–2.30pm & 6–10.30pm.

Grand Italia Piazza del Popolo 9/10 ☎0544 217 529, ⓦgranditalia.ra.it. This extensive lounge, bar and restaurant offers everything from *gelato* sundaes to full meals, from elaborate buffets to casual drinks and people-watching on the piazza. For a light lunch expect about €15, with wine at €5 a glass. 7am–1am; closed Tues in winter.

La Gardela Via Ponte Marino 3 ☎0544 217 147, ⓦristorantegardela.it. Rather smart spot featuring a view of the Torre Civica (Ravenna's own leaning tower) with a varied menu of fish dishes and home-made pasta; classic *primi* are around €6–7, *secondi* €7–16; there is a four-course Romagnolo tasting menu for €25. Noon–2.30pm & 7–10pm; closed Thurs.

Osteria L'Acciuga Via Francesco Baracca 74 ☎0544 212 713, ⓦosterialacciuga.it. With the decor based on the interior of a submarine, it's no surprise that this lively restaurant sells fish. The menu changes every day depending on the day's catch, ensuring quality and freshness; the five-course tasting menu (€35) is a good way to try a variety of

dishes. Noon–3pm & 7.30pm–midnight; closed Sun eve & Mon.

Sant'Apollinare in Classe

Via Romea Sud • Mon–Sat 8.30am–7.30pm, Sun 1–7.30pm • €5 • Archeological site closed until 2014 • Train or bus #4 and #44 from Ravenna's station

About 6km south of Ravenna, the ruins of the old port of **Classe** are very thin indeed – the buildings have been looted for stone and the ancient harbour has now completely disappeared under the silt of the River Uniti. One building, however, does survive – the church of **Sant'Apollinare in Classe**, spared because it was the burial place of Ravenna's patron saint. It's a typical basilical church with further fine mosaics including a marvellous allegorical depiction of the Transfiguration in the apse, with Christ represented by a large cross in a star-spangled universe.

Ravenna's seaside resorts

Buses leave from outside Ravenna's station: #60 or #70 to Marina di Ravenna, #75 or #80 for Punta Marina and #90 to Porto Corsini

There's easy access by bus through Ravenna's heavy industry belt to the nine lido towns nearby totalling 35km of coast. **Marina di Ravenna** and **Punta Marina** are both crowded, lively places; or for something quieter head north to the beaches at **Porto Corsini**, **Casalborsetti** and **Marina Romea**. Just before Porto Corsini, you pass the **Capanno Garibaldi**, a reconstruction of the hut in which Garibaldi hid on his epic 800-kilometre march from Rome after the fall of the short-lived Roman republic in 1849. Garibaldi's life-long partner Anita, who often fought alongside him, died on the way and he was unable to stop for long enough to bury her.

Rimini

RIMINI, Italy's largest and most varied beach resort, has long been a traditional summer magnet for families, to which many Italians return year after year. But there is also an upmarket side to the town, with its boutique hotels, high-end restaurants and chi-chi clubs. And with that comes a less savoury aspect: Rimini is known throughout Italy for its fast-living and chancy nightlife, and there's a thriving hetero- and transsexual prostitution scene alongside the town's more wholesome attractions.

The resort is best avoided in August, unless you have a penchant for teeming crowds. Out of season, it's pleasant enough, though bear in mind that many hotels, restaurants and shops are closed and the atmosphere along the seafront is almost eerily quiet.

Given that Rimini was almost entirely destroyed in the last war, it's surprising to find that the town has a much-ignored **old centre** that is worth at least a morning of your time. Located inland, past the station, it is an often unseen part of Rimini, made up of old stone buildings clustered around the beautiful twin squares of Piazza Tre Martiri and Piazza Cavour, and bordered by the port-canal and town ramparts. Unlike the touristy side of town, this quiet, refined community stays in business throughout the winter, albeit in a low-key, backwater sort of way. But it's the beach, the crowds and the wild nights that you really come for: Rimini is still the country's best place to party.

The beach

The main attraction of Rimini is the long, clean, sandy **beach** which is lined by largely indistinguishable three- to five-star hotels, all of which have parcelled up their own particular stretches of beach and equipped them with beach bars, volleyball courts, watersports outfitters and other such holiday essentials. Running behind the front is

Viale Amerigo Vespucci, a brash drag crammed with souvenir shops, restaurants and video arcades.

Arco d'Augusto and Ponte Tiberio

Founded in 286 BC as Ariminum, Rimini was once an important Roman colony. On the southern and northern edges of the old centre respectively sit the **Arco d'Augusto** and **Ponte Tiberio**. The patched-up Arco was built at the beginning of the first century AD at the point where Via Emilia joined Via Flaminia. Rimini's other Roman remains consist of the **Anfiteatro**, of which there are sparse foundations off Via Roma.

Piazza Tre Martiri and Piazza Cavour

Just south of the Ponte Tiberio, **Piazza Tre Martiri**, which largely follows the layout of the original Roman square, and **Piazza Cavour** are the two main squares. Piazza Cavour boasts a statue of Pope Paul V and the Gothic **Palazzo del Podestà**; the square was rebuilt in the 1920s, and purists argue that it was ruined, although the fishtail battlements are still impressive enough. Opposite, beyond the sixteenth-century fountain incorporating Roman reliefs, the beautiful **old fish market** often shades antiques stalls worth a browse.

RIMINI

ACCOMMODATION
Camping Italia International	1
Card International	10
Duomo	11
Happy Camping Village	2
Il Grand Hotel Rimini	3
Jammin' Party Hostel	8
La Gradisca	6
Le Meridien	7
Sunflower City Hostel	4
Verudella	9
Villa Adriatica	5

CLUBS
Byblos	3
Carnaby	4
Coconuts	1
Le Cocorico	5
Nomi	2

CAFÉS & RESTAURANTS
Amerigo	4
Café Cavour	7
Casina del Bosco	1
Osteria de Börg	2
Osteria Tiresia	8
Pic-Nic	6
Rimini Key	5
Squilla Mantis	3

8

0   400
metres

Museo della Città

Via L. Tonini 1 • Mid-June to mid-Sept Tues–Sat 10.30am–12.30pm & 4.30–7.30pm, Sun 4.30–7.30pm; mid-Sept to mid-June Tues–Sat 8.30am–12.30pm & 5–7pm, Sun 10am–12.30pm & 3–7pm • €5 (Sun free) • ⓦ domusrimini.com

The **Museo della Città** has a collection of art dating from the fourteenth to the nineteenth centuries, the highlight of which is Giovanni Bellini's pietà. Also part of the museum, just a few metres west on Piazza Ferrari, is the **Domus del Chirurgo**, where a glass-sided structure sits above the remains of a third-century Roman surgeon's house. The site has yielded numerous fascinating finds, including coins and bronze surgeon's instruments (such as forceps and pliers), which are now on display in the archeology gallery on the ground floor of the museum. What remains here are the foundations and a set of mosaic pavements, including one showing Orpheus surrounded by animals.

Tempio Malatestiano

Via IV Novembre • Mon–Sat 8.30am–12.30pm & 3.30–7pm, Sun 9am–1pm & 3.30–7pm • Free

Just south of the Museo della Città is Rimini's best-known monument, the **Tempio Malatestiano**, which serves as the town's cathedral. Built by the Guelph family of Malatesta, it was originally a Franciscan Gothic church before being transformed in 1450 into a gorgeous monument to Sigismondo Malatesta, a notorious *condottiere* whose long list of alleged crimes included rape, incest and looting. Understandably, the pope of the time, Pius II, was less than impressed and publicly consigned an ambivalent Sigismondo to hell. Sigismondo was more concerned with his great love, Isotta degli Atti, and treated the *tempio* as a private memorial chapel to her. Their initials are linked in emblems all over the building, and the Malatesta family's favourite heraldic animal – a trumpeting elephant – appears almost as often. There are a number of fine artworks, now restored, to look out for, including a *Crucifix* attributed to Giotto, friezes and reliefs by Agostino di Duccio and a fresco by Piero della Francesca of Sigismondo himself.

Museo Fellini

Via Nigra 26 • Sat & Sun 10am–noon & 4–7pm • Free • ☎ 0541 50 303

There's plenty of homegrown hedonism on offer at the temporary site of the **Museo Fellini**, which celebrates the famous director's career with exhibits ranging from his drawings – the director began his career as a cartoon illustrator – to movie posters.

ARRIVAL AND DEPARTURE | RIMINI

By plane From Federico Fellini Airport (☎ 0541 715 711, ⓦ riminiairport.com), 8km south of Rimini, bus #9 goes to the train station every 30min; tickets cost €1.20, and can be bought at the airport bar and kiosks. A taxi costs around €20.

By train Rimini's train station is situated in the centre of town, on Piazzale Cesare Battisti, a 10min walk from both the sea and the old centre.

Destinations Bologna (every 20min; 1hr–1hr 30min); Ferrara (hourly; 1hr 30min–2hr 30min); Ravenna (hourly; 1hr–1hr 10min).

By bus The bus station is next to the train station in the centre of town.

Destinations Rome (2 daily in summer, 2 weekly in winter; 5hr 30min); San Marino (hourly; 45min); Santarcangelo (hourly; 30min).

GETTING AROUND AND INFORMATION

On foot Getting around is best done on foot, at least within the town centre.

By bus If you need to use the buses, buy a blue ticket from a tobacconist or newsstand; it gives 24 hours' unlimited travel in Rimini and the surrounding area (including Santarcangelo, Riccione and Bellaria) for €5. Nightbuses called Blue Lines (ⓦ tramservizi.it) act as

Rimini's club shuttles in weekends in July and all of August throughout the night (10.30pm–6am). There are five colour-coded lines with the main blue line trundling between Rimini's train station and the nearby town of Riccione every 20min, stopping at over fifteen clubs en route. Nightly bus passes cost €5; tickets available on board.

By bike Alternatively, you could rent your own mode of transport – anything from a bike (€6/day) to a quad bike (€40/day) – from one of about two dozen vendors, such as Tiraferri Aurelio, Viale Medaglie d'Oro 1 (☏ 0541 391 072).
By car For car rental, try Avis, Viale Trieste 16/D ☏ 0541 51256; Europcar, Via Ravegnani 18 ☏ 0541 54 746; Mondaini Massimo, Viale Tripoli 16 ☏ 0541 782 646.
By taxi Radiotaxi Cooperative (☏ 0541 50 020) has a 24hr rank outside the train station.

Tourist offices There's a tourist office right outside the train station to the left (March–Oct Mon–Sat 8.30am–6pm, Sun 9.30am–12.30pm; Nov–Feb Mon–Sat 10am–4pm; ☏ 0541 51 331). The main tourist office is at Piazza Federico Fellini 3, just back from the seafront (April–Sept Mon–Sat 8.30am–7pm, Sun 9.30am–12.30pm; Oct–March Mon–Sat 9.30am–12.30pm & 3.30–6.30pm; ☏ 0541 56902, ⊕ riminiturismo.it).

ACCOMMODATION

Despite its 1300 hotels, finding accommodation can be a problem in Rimini, and in summer especially you may have to take the expensive option of full board. Out of season those few hotels that do remain open will be mainly geared to business travellers or school groups. You can book accommodation through the tourist office or Rimini Reservation (June to early Sept daily 8.15am–2pm & 2.15–7.45pm; ☏ 0541 51 441, ⊕ riminireservation.it), next door.

Card International Via Dante Alighieri 50 ☏ 0541 26 412, ⊕ hotelcard.it. Conveniently situated close to the train station, this modern design hotel has standard and superior rooms as well as two luxury suites. The rooms are fresh, clean and spacious. A home-made breakfast is included. **€90**
★ **Duomo** Via G. Bruno 28 ☏ 0541 24 215, ⊕ duomo hotel.com. In the heart of the old town, this designer hotel is terribly swanky and self-consciously ultramodern. The reception desk is a giant neon-adorned, flying stainless-steel doughnut, while the huge bedrooms are truly space-age and extremely well equipped. Great breakfasts and very friendly staff. Breakfast included. **€179**
Il Grand Hotel Rimini Parco Federico Fellini ☏ 0541 56 000, ⊕ grandhotelrimini.com. A five-star vision of grand Fellini-esque luxury defines this historic property which has a quietly refined ambience. It's right on the sea, surrounded by elegant lush grounds, and the opulent rooms are graced by Venetian and French antiques. **€310**
Jammin' Party Hostel Viale Derna 22 ☏ 0541 390 800, ⊕ hosteljammin.com. Popular, friendly hostel in a convenient location near the beach which offers a great range of services as well as regular events both in the hostel and in the bars around town. There's 24hr reception and free wi-fi. Breakfast included. Closed Oct–March. Dorms **€18**
La Gradisca Viale Fiume 1 ☏ 0541 25 200, ⊕ hotellagradisca.it. Although part of the Best Western chain, this is a totally unique, luxurious four-star, where the whimsical decor inside and out echoes the over-the-top set of a Fellini dream sequence – in fact, the name itself comes from the maestro's unforgettable character in *Amarcord*. **€150**
Le Meridien Viale Lungomare Murri 13 ☏ 0541 396 600, ⊕ lemeridienrimini.com. This plush seafront hotel was designed by Paolo Portoghesi and boasts every facility imaginable, including a spa, a swimming pool, a good seafood restaurant and a beach club. It's worth paying

extra for the large, bright, sea-facing rooms, as the cheaper city-view rooms are rather small. **€130**
Sunflower City Hostel Viale Dardanelli 102 ☏ 0541 25 180, ⊕ sunflowerhostel.com. Non-HI hostel open year round and offering clean dorms, lockers, bike rental and free wi-fi access. It also operates a smaller beachside branch (Via Siracusa 25 ☏ 0541 373 432; March–Oct only). Dorms **€15**
★ **Verudella** Viale Tripoli 238 ☏ 0541 391 124, ⊕ hotelverudella.it. Attractively smart – with a touch of the ubiquitous Fellini fantasy – this is one of the town's best options, run by a friendly brother-and-sister team. The rooms are simple but comfortable. Open all year round. Half-board generally required. **€80**
Villa Adriatica Viale Vespucci 3 ☏ 0541 54 599, ⊕ villaadriatica.it. Part of the Ambient hotel group, this stylish choice is a refurbished Liberty villa, vintage 1880, set in a private park with a swimming pool. The pricier rooms come with wooden floors, larger beds and a/c. Breakfast included. **€162**

CAMPING
Camping Italia International Via Toscanelli 112 ☏ 0541 732 882, ⊕ campingitaliarimini.it; bus #4 from the station will drop you right outside at stop 14. Around 3km north of the city centre, right on the seafront, this campsite boasts its own beach, plus all the facilities you'd expect. Camping for small tents as well as bungalows and mobile homes for rent. Pitches **€26**
Happy Camping Village Via Panzini 228, Bellaria 112 ☏ 0541 346 102, ⊕ happycamping.it; bus #4 from the station will drop you right outside at stop 1. Some 12km north of Rimini, this spacious campsite has a wealth of facilities, including a private beach, swimming pool, restaurant and supermarket. In addition to pitches for tents it also offers a hotel, bungalows and apartments to rent. Pitches **€24**

8

8

EATING AND DRINKING

★ **Amerigo** Viale Amerigo Vespucci 137 ☎0541 391 338, ⓦristoranteamerigo.it. A welcoming, always bustling spot with a huge menu – and all of it delicious. Servings are generally enormous, too, everything from fresh *mozzarella di bufala* salads (€8) to seafood pastas (€12), as well as wood-fired pizzas and *piadine*. Daily noon–1am.

Caffè Cavour Piazza Cavour 13 ☎0541 785 123. Good choice for a leisurely drink or a light meal, this elegant café serves sandwiches, *piadine* (€5–6) and salads (€6–10). Sit outside and admire the location in one of the old town's finest medieval squares. Daily 7am–midnight.

Casina del Bosco Via Beccadelli 15 ☎0541 56 295, ⓦcasinadelbosco.it. In among a row of similar establishments, this place offers a large selection of generously filled *piadine* – tuna and carrot €4.50, roast beef, parmesan and rocket €6.50 – with seating under shady trees. There are also home-made desserts and local craft beers. Daily 11.30am–2am.

★ **Osteria de Börg** Via Forzieri 12 ☎0541 56 074, ⓦosteriadeborg.it. Friendly, busy and moderately priced restaurant serving innovative regional cooking, such as *galletto al tagame* (wine-cooked chicken in a skillet; €12), fire-roasted steak (€16) and a dozen different vegetable dishes. Antipasti €8–10, *primi* €7.50–10, *secondi* €10–16.

Booking strongly advised. Tues–Sun noon–midnight.

Osteria Tiresia Via XX Settembre 41 ☎0541 781 896, ⓦosteriatiresia.it. A busy, friendly restaurant located in the town centre. It's a great choice for meat-lovers, with delicious steaks (€20) and hamburgers (€18) as well as a good-value choice of wines. Tues–Sat 7pm–midnight; Sun noon–3pm & 7pm–midnight.

Pic-Nic Via Tempio Malatestiano 30 ☎0541 21 916, ⓦpicnicristorante.it. One of the old town's institutions, *Pic-Nic* has been serving great-value food since 1965 in its rather elegant interior and spacious garden. With reasonably priced pizzas (Margherita €5), calzones (€8–9) and classic pasta dishes. Daily noon–3pm & 7pm–midnight.

Rimini Key Piazzale B. Croce 7 ☎0541 381 445. Good-value set menus and pizzas, in a prime location for observing Rimini's evening *passeggiata* along the seafront. The house specialities include fish dishes such as *tortellini di pesce alle capesante* (tortellini with fish and scallops; €13). Daily noon–3pm & 6.30pm–midnight.

Squilla Mantis Viale Tiberio 11 ☎0541 53 577, ⓦsquillamantisrimini.it. A wine bar and restaurant in the old town which also does a great *aperitivo* in the late afternoon. The menu is mainly fish-based with *primi* such as pasta with clams and radicchio (€11). Tues–Sat 12.30–2.30pm & 7.30–10.30pm.

NIGHTLIFE

Rimini's nightlife is mainly concentrated on the seafront and in the fashionable enclave of Misano Monte above the town. Clubbing is a seasonal activity here, with full-on nightlife in summer, and few places open in winter. Even on a balmy July evening, things tend to start late with crowds cruising the bars from about 11pm onwards before heading off to the first club at around 1am. If you haven't got a car, or are drinking, use nightbuses (see p.504). For up-to-date **information** on the Rimini club scene, pick up the free Italian weekly listings magazine *Chiamami Città* from the tourist office, or check ⓦchiamamicitta.com or ⓦriminilive.com.

Byblos Via Pozzo Castello 24, Misano Monte ☎0541 697 745, ⓦbyblosclub.com. Summer-only club with several different bars and dance areas as well as a restaurant and an outdoor courtyard with a swimming pool all set in a beautiful Mediterranean villa. Music played includes house and Seventies/Eighties funk. Fri–Sun 9pm–5am.

Carnaby Via Brindisi 20 ☎0541 373 204, ⓦcarnaby.it. Wildly popular club spread over three floors, the lowest of which is subterranean and appropriately named "The Cave". The music gets lighter, and less intense the higher you go. Like its namesake, it swings. Free shuttle service. Daily 10pm–5am.

Coconuts Via Lungomare Tintori 5 ☎0541 52 325, ⓦcoconuts.it. Right on the beach, this bills itself as a "Miami-style" club, which translates as palm trees, neon,

salsa and podium dancers. As well as house music there are Latin nights with salsa and reggaeton. Attracts a slightly older crowd. Daily 6.30pm–4am.

Le Cocoricò Viale Chieti 44 ☎0541 605 183, ⓦcocorico.it. Located in nearby Riccione, this is one of Italy's most celebrated clubs. There are five rooms but the best DJs play under an enormous glass pyramid where thousands come to rave to the latest in Italian techno. Sat 11pm–7am.

Nomi Via G. Bruno 28 ☎0541 24 215, ⓦduomohotel .com. This fashionable disco club in the *Duomo* hotel is a place to pose charmingly, rather than dance too intently and risk dishevelling your carefully crafted look. Instead, perch on one of the spring-like chairs surrounding the mirrored-steel central bar, then watch and be watched. Mon–Thurs & Sat 8–11pm; Fri & Sun 8pm–2am.

DIRECTORY

Doctor ☎ 118, or ☎ 0541 787 461, or Infermi hospital ☎ 0541 705 111.

Internet Inside the Sala Giochi Central Park, Viale Vespucci 21 (daily 9am–2am; ☎ 0541 27 550).

Laundry Lavaservice del Mare, Via Misurata 5 (daily 7am–midnight, till 10pm in winter).

Pharmacy Farmacia Comunale, Via IV Novembre 39/41 (Mon–Fri 8.30am–12.30pm & 4–8pm; ☎ 0541 24 414).

Post office Main office at Largo Giulio Cesare 1 (Mon–Fri 8am–6.30pm, Sat 8am–12.30pm).

San Marino

Around 25km southwest of Rimini, the **REPUBLIC OF SAN MARINO** is an unashamed, though not entirely unpleasant, tourist destination that trades on its nearly two millennia of precariously maintained autonomy. Said to have been founded around 300 AD by a monk fleeing the persecutions of Diocletian – it claims to be the world's oldest constitutional republic – it has been bumbling along ever since in a quiet, unobtrusive fashion, away from the fierce battles and intrigues of mainstream Italian politics. Essentially too small and inconsequential to be worth conquering, the republic has – save for a brief Borgia episode in the sixteenth century – been left largely to its own devices. Culturally, it is essentially Italian – there's no San Marinese language – but in legal, constitutional terms, it remains **independent**, electing its own government, passing its own laws, minting its own money, producing its own postage stamps, and even maintaining its own, largely unused, army of around a thousand.

There's not a great deal to see. The ramparts and medieval-style buildings of the citadel above Borgomaggiore, restored in the last century, are mildly interesting; there's a **waxworks museum** in Via Lapicidi Marini 17 (daily: April–Sept 8.30am–6.30pm, July & Aug till 8pm; Oct–March 8.30am–12.30pm & 2–5.30pm; €6) as well as tacky souvenir shops and restaurants. And you can also get your passport stamped, for €5, by the border guards or at the information office (see below). All the touristy tawdriness aside, however, it's a good place just to stroll around; the walk up through town to the **rocce**, battlemented castles along the highest three ridges, is worth the effort for the all-round views. Below, in Borgomaggiore, is Giovanni Michelucci's "fearless and controversial" modernist church, built in the 1960s, with a roof that seems to cascade down in waves.

8

ARRIVAL AND INFORMATION

SAN MARINO

By bus The express bus from Rimini leaves from Piazza Marvelli via the station (hourly; 1hr). Tickets €4.

Tourist office Contrada del Collegio (daily 10am–5pm; ☎ 0549 882 914).

Tuscany

SANTA CROCE, FLORENCE

9

Tuscany

The tourist brochure view of Tuscany as an idyll of olive groves, vineyards, hill-towns and frescoed churches may be one-dimensional, but Tuscany is indeed the essence of Italy in many ways. The national language evolved from the Tuscan dialect, a supremacy ensured by Dante – who wrote the *Divine Comedy* in the vernacular of his birthplace, Florence – and Tuscan writers such as Petrarch and Boccaccio. And the era we know as the Renaissance, which played so large a role in forming the culture, not just of Italy but of Europe as a whole, is associated more strongly with this part of the country than with anywhere else. Florence was the most active centre of the Renaissance, flourishing principally through the all-powerful patronage of the Medici dynasty. Every eminent artistic figure from Giotto onwards – Masaccio, Brunelleschi, Alberti, Donatello, Botticelli, Leonardo da Vinci, Michelangelo – is represented here, in an unrivalled gathering of churches, galleries and museums.

The problem is, of course, that the whole world knows about the attractions of Florence, with the result that the city can be offputtingly busy in high season. **Siena** tends to provoke a less ambivalent response. One of the great medieval cities of Europe, it remains almost perfectly preserved, and holds superb works of art in its religious and secular buildings. In addition, its beautiful Campo – the central, scallop-shaped market square – is the scene of the **Palio**, when bareback horseriders career around the cobbles amid an extravagant display of pageantry. The cities of **Pisa** and **Lucca** have their own fair share of attractions and provide convenient entry points to the region, either by air (via Pisa's airport) or along the coastal rail route from Genoa. **Arezzo** and **Cortona** serve as fine introductions to Tuscany if you're approaching from the south (Rome) or east (Perugia).

Tucked away to the west and south of Siena, dozens of small **hill-towns** epitomize the region for many visitors. **San Gimignano**, the most famous, is worth visiting as much for its spectacular array of frescoes as for its bristle of medieval tower-houses, even if it

MOSAIC AT SAN FREDIANO, LUCCA

Highlights

❶ **The Duomo, Florence** Climbing Brunelleschi's dome is a must. **See p.518**

❷ **The Uffizi, Florence** The world's greatest collection of Italian Renaissance paintings. **See p.524**

❸ **Chianti** The country's most famous vineyards. **See p.550**

❹ **The Leaning Tower, Pisa** Still defying gravity and still continuing to amaze. **See p.555**

❺ **Lucca** A stunning array of Romanesque churches in this most urbane of Tuscan towns. **See p.559**

❻ **The Palio** Siena's historic horse race, run over three frenetic laps of the Campo. **See p.577**

❼ **Tuscan hill-towns** Tuscany's hill-towns epitomize the region for many visitors, with San Gimignano the most popular. **See p.589**

HIGHLIGHTS ARE MARKED ON THE MAP ON P.512

9

has become a little too popular for its own good. Both **Montepulciano** and **Pienza** are superbly located and dripping with atmosphere, but the best candidates for a Tuscan hill-town escape are places such as **Volterra**, **Massa Maríttima** or **Pitigliano**, where tourism has yet to undermine local character. You may find lesser-known sights even more memorable – remote monasteries like **Monte Oliveto Maggiore** and **San Galgano**, or the sulphur spa of **Bagno Vignoni**. The one area where Tuscany fails to impress is its over-developed **coast**, with horrible beach-umbrella compounds filling every last scrap of sand. **Elba**, the largest of several Tuscan islands, offers great beaches and good hiking, but is busy in summer.

Finding **accommodation** can be a major problem in the summer, so you should definitely reserve in advance; ⓦturismo.intoscana.it is a useful resource, and includes details of **agriturismi**, family-run places dotted around the countryside offering anything from budget rooms in a farmhouse to luxury apartments in restored castles.

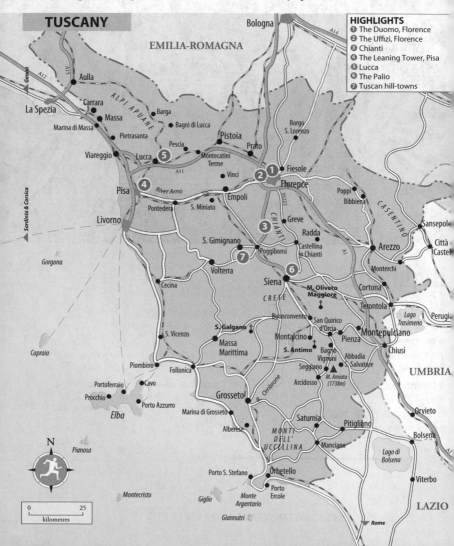

TUSCANY

HIGHLIGHTS
❶ The Duomo, Florence
❷ The Uffizi, Florence
❸ Chianti
❹ The Leaning Tower, Pisa
❺ Lucca
❻ The Palio
❼ Tuscan hill-towns

REGIONAL FOOD AND WINE

Tuscan cooking, with its emphasis on simple dishes using fresh, quality, local ingredients, has had a seminal influence on Italian cuisine. Classic Tuscan antipasti are peasant fare: bruschetta is stale bread, toasted and dressed with oil and garlic; *crostini* is toast and pâté. **Olive oil** is the essential flavouring, used as a dressing for salads, a medium for frying and to drizzle over bread or vegetables and into soups and stews just before serving.

Soups are very popular – Tuscan menus always include either *ribollita*, a hearty stew of vegetables, beans and chunks of bread, or *zuppa di farro*, a thick soup with spelt (a barley-like grain). *Pappa col pomodoro* (bread and tomato soup) is also good, while fish restaurants serve *cacciucco*, a spiced fish and seafood soup. White cannellini **beans** (*fagioli*) are another favourite, turning up in salads, with pasta (*tuoni e lampo*), with sausages in a stew (*fagioli all'uccelletto*), or just dressed with olive oil. Tuscany is not known for its **pasta**, but many towns in the south serve *pici*, thick, hand-rolled spaghetti with toasted breadcrumbs. **Meat** is kept plain, often grilled, and Florentines profess to liking nothing better than a good *bistecca alla fiorentina* (rare char-grilled steak), or the simple rustic dishes of *arista* (roast pork loin stuffed with rosemary and garlic) or *pollo alla diavola* (chicken flattened, marinated and then grilled with herbs). Hunters' fare such as *cinghiale* (wild boar) and *coniglio* (rabbit) often turns up in hill-town trattorias.

Spinach is often married with ricotta and gnocchi, used as a pasta filling, and in *crespoline* (pancakes) or between two chunks of *focaccia* and eaten as a snack. Sheep's milk *pecorino* is the most widespread Tuscan **cheese** (best in Pienza), but the most famous is the oval *marzolino* from the Chianti region, which is eaten either fresh or ripened. **Dessert** menus will often include *cantuccini*, hard, almond-flavoured biscuits to be dipped in a glass of Vinsanto (sweet dessert wine); Siena is the main source of sweet treats, including almond macaroons and *panforte*, a rich and very dense cake full of nuts and fruit.

Tuscany has some of Italy's finest **wines**. Three top names, which all bear the exclusive DOCG mark (and price tags to match), are Chianti Classico, Brunello di Montalcino and Vino Nobile di Montepulciano – not the sort of thing you'd knock back at a trattoria. There are dozens of other Chianti varieties, most of them excellent, but it can be difficult to find a bargain. Both Montalcino and Montepulciano produce *rosso* varieties that are more pocket-friendly, and other names to look for include Carmignano and Rosso delle Colline Lucchesi. Two notable whites are dry Vernaccia di San Gimignano and the fresh Galestro.

Florence (Firenze)

Since the early nineteenth century **FLORENCE** has been celebrated by many as the most beautiful city in Italy. Stendhal staggered around its streets in a perpetual stupor of delight; the Brownings sighed over its charms; and E.M. Forster's *Room with a View* portrayed it as the great southern antidote to the sterility of Anglo-Saxon life. The pinnacle of Brunelleschi's stupendous cathedral dome dominates the cityscape, and the close-up view is even more breathtaking, with the multicoloured **Duomo** rising beside the marble-clad **Baptistry**. Wander from here down towards the River Arno and the attraction still holds: beyond the broad Piazza della Signoria – site of the towering **Palazzo Vecchio** – the river is spanned by the medieval, shop-lined **Ponte Vecchio**, with the gorgeous church of **San Miniato al Monte** glistening on the hill behind it.

For art lovers, Florence has no equal in Europe. The development of the Renaissance can be plotted in the vast picture collection of the **Uffizi** and in the sculpture of the **Bargello** and the **Museo dell'Opera del Duomo**. Equally revelatory are the fabulously decorated chapels of **Santa Croce** and **Santa Maria Novella**, forerunners of such astonishing creations as Masaccio's superb frescoes in the **Cappella Brancacci**. The Renaissance emphasis on harmony and rational design is expressed with unrivalled eloquence in Brunelleschi's architecture, specifically in the churches of **San Lorenzo**, **Santo Spirito** and the **Cappella dei Pazzi**. While the full genius of Michelangelo, the dominant creative figure of sixteenth-century Italy, is on display in San Lorenzo's

9

FLORENCE

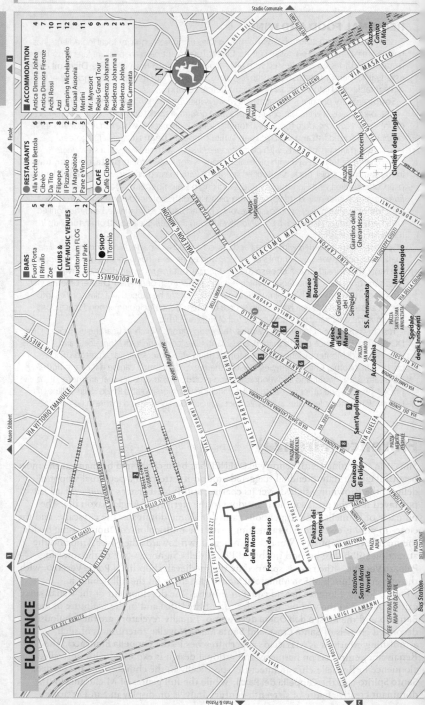

ACCOMMODATION
Antica Dimora Johlea	4
Antica Dimora Firenze	7
Archi Rossi	10
Azzi	11
Camping Michelangelo	12
Kursaal Ausonia	8
Merlini	11
Mr. Myresort	6
Relais Grand Tour	9
Residenza Johanna I	3
Residenza Johanna II	2
Residenza Johlea	5
Villa Camerata	1

RESTAURANTS
Alla Vecchia Bettola	6
Cibrèo	3
Da Tito	3
Filipepe	1
Il Pizzaiuolo	8
La Mangiatoia	2
Pane e Vino	7
	5

CAFÉ
Caffè Cibrèo	4

BARS
Fuori Porta	5
Il Rifrullo	4
Zoe	3

CLUBS & LIVE-MUSIC VENUES
Auditorium FLOG	1
Central Park	2

SHOP
Il Torchio	1

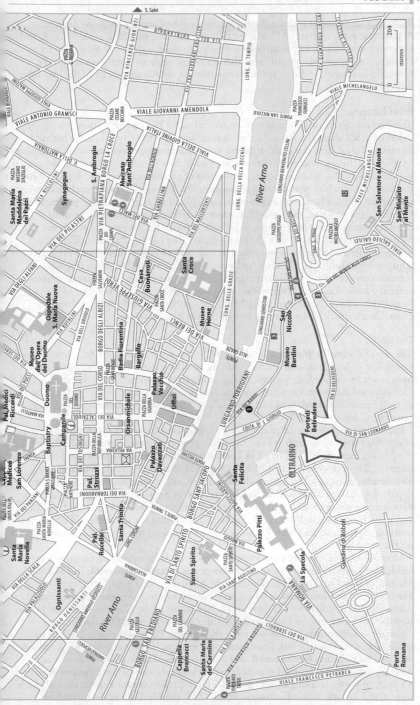

9

Biblioteca Laurenziana and the marble statuary of the **Cappelle Medicee** and the **Accademia**, every quarter of Florence can boast a church worth an extended call, and the enormous **Palazzo Pitti** south of the river constitutes a museum district on its own. If you're on a whistle-stop tour, note that it's not possible to simply stroll into the Cappella Brancacci, and that spontaneous visits to the Accademia and Uffizi are often difficult.

Brief history

The Roman colony of Florentia was established in 59 BC and expansion was rapid, based on trade along the Arno. In the sixth century AD the city fell to the barbarian hordes of Totila, then the Lombards and then Charlemagne's Franks. In 1078 Countess Mathilda of Tuscia supervised the construction of new fortifications, and in the year of her death – 1115 – granted Florence the status of an independent city. Around 1200, the first Arti (Guilds) were formed to promote the interests of traders and bankers in the face of conflict between the pro-imperial Ghibelline faction and the pro-papal Guelphs. The exclusion of the nobility from government in 1293 was the most dramatic measure in a programme of political reform that invested power in the Signoria, a council drawn from the major guilds. The mighty Palazzo della Signoria – now the Palazzo Vecchio – was raised as a visible demonstration of authority over a huge city: at this time, Florence had a population around 100,000, a thriving mercantile sector and a highly developed banking system (the florin was common currency across Europe). Strife within the Guelph camp marked the start of the fourteenth century, and then in the 1340s the two largest banks collapsed and the Black Death struck, destroying up to half the city's population.

The Medici

The rise of **Cosimo de' Medici**, later dubbed Cosimo il Vecchio ("the Old"), was to some extent due to his family's sympathies with the smaller guilds. The **Medici** fortune had been made by the banking prowess of Cosimo's father, Giovanni Bicci de' Medici, and Cosimo used the power conferred by wealth to great effect. Partly through his patronage of such figures as Brunelleschi and Donatello, Florence became the centre of artistic activity in Italy.

The ascendancy continued under Cosimo's grandson **Lorenzo il Magnifico**, who in effect ruled the city at the height of its artistic prowess. Before Lorenzo's death in 1492, the Medici bank failed, and in 1494 Lorenzo's son Piero was obliged to flee. Florentine hearts and minds were seized by the charismatic Dominican monk, **Girolamo Savonarola**, who preached against the decadence and corruption of the city. Artists departed in droves as Savonarola and his cohorts, in a symbolic demonstration of the new order, gathered books, paintings, tapestries, fancy furniture and other frivolities, and piled them high in Piazza della Signoria in a **Bonfire of the Vanities**. Within a year, however, Savonarola had been found guilty of heresy and treason, and was burned alive on the same spot.

After Savonarola, the city functioned peacefully under a republican constitution headed by Piero Soderini, whose chief adviser was **Niccolò Machiavelli**. In 1512 the Medici returned, and in 1516, Giovanni de' Medici became **Pope Leo X**, granting Michelangelo and Leonardo da Vinci major commissions. After the assassination of Alessandro de' Medici in 1537, power was handed to a new Cosimo, who seized the Republic of Siena and, in 1569, took the title **Cosimo I**, Grand Duke of Tuscany.

Florence's subsequent decline was slow and painful. Each of the later Medicis was more ridiculous than the last: **Francesco** spent most of his thirteen-year reign indoors, obsessed by alchemy; **Ferdinando II** sat back as harvests failed, plagues ran riot and banking and textiles slumped to nothing; the virulently anti-Semitic **Cosimo III** spent 53 years in power cracking down on dissidents; and **Gian Gastone** spent virtually all his time drunk in bed. When Gastone died, in 1737, the Medici line died with him.

Florence after the Medici

Under the terms of a treaty signed by Gian Gastone's sister, **Anna Maria Ludovica**, Florence – and the whole Grand Duchy of Tuscany – passed to Francesco of Lorraine, the future Francis I of Austria. Austrian rule lasted until the coming of the French in 1799; after a fifteen-year interval of French control, the Lorraine dynasty was brought back, remaining in residence until being overthrown in the Risorgimento upheavals of 1859. Absorbed into the united Italian state in the following year, Florence became the **capital** of the Kingdom of Italy in 1865, a position it held until 1870.

At the end of the nineteenth century, large areas of the medieval city were **demolished** by government officials and developers; buildings that had stood in the area of what is now Piazza della Repubblica since the early Middle Ages were pulled down to make way for undistinguished office blocks, and old quarters around Santa Croce and Santa Maria Novella were razed. In 1944, the retreating German army blew up all the city's bridges except the Ponte Vecchio and destroyed acres of medieval architecture. A disastrous **flood** in November 1966 drowned several people and wrecked buildings and works of art, and restoration of the damage is still going on. Indeed, monuments and paintings are the basis of Florence's survival, a state of affairs that gives rise to considerable disquiet. The development of new industrial parks on the northern outskirts is the latest and most ambitious attempt to break Florence's ever-increasing dependence on its tourists.

Piazza del Duomo and around

Traffic and people gravitate towards the square at the heart of Florence, **Piazza del Duomo**, beckoned by the pinnacle of Brunelleschi's extraordinary dome, which dominates the cityscape in a way unmatched by any architectural creation in any other

---

FLORENCE'S MUSEUMS: TICKETS AND INFORMATION

All of Florence's state-run museums belong to an association called **Firenze Musei**, which sets aside a daily quota of tickets that can be **reserved in advance**. The Uffizi, the Accademia and the Bargello belong to this group, as do the Palazzo Pitti museums (including the Bóboli gardens), the Medici chapels, the archeological museum and the San Marco museum. The best source of online info for all of these museums is ⓦ uffizi.firenze.it.

You can **reserve tickets** (booking fee of €4 for Uffizi and Accademia, €3 for the rest) by phoning ☏ 055 294 883 (Mon–Fri 8.30am–6.30pm, Sat 8.30am–12.30pm), online at ⓦ firenzemusei.it and ⓦ uffizi.firenze.it, at the Firenze Musei booth at Orsanmichele (Mon–Sat 10am–5.30pm), and at the museums themselves, in the case of the Uffizi and Pitti. If you book by phone, an English-speaking operator will allocate you a ticket for a specific hour, to be collected at the museum at a specific time, shortly before entry. Generally, the under-publicized Orsanmichele booth – which is set into the wall of the church on the Via Calzaiuoli side – is the easiest option. Pre-booking is strongly recommended at any time of year for the Uffizi and the Accademia, whose allocation of reservable tickets is often sold out many days ahead.

The **Firenze Card**, costing €50, is valid for 72 hours from the first time you use it, and gives access to more than 30 museums in greater Florence (including all the big ones), plus unlimited use of public transport. It also enables you to by-pass the queues, as the major museums have separate gates for card-holders. You do, though, have to pack a hell of a lot into each day to make it worth the investment. The card can be bought at the Via Cavour and Piazza Stazione tourist offices, from the Uffizi, Bargello, Palazzo Pitti, Museo Bardini and Museo di Santa Maria Novella, and at ⓦ firenzecard.it.

Admission to all state-run museums is free for EU citizens under 18 and over 65; 18–25s get a fifty-percent discount, as do teachers. Nearly all of Florence's major museums are routinely **closed on Monday**.

For Florence's **civic museums** – of which the main ones are the Museo Bardini, Museo Santa Maria Novella, Palazzo Vecchio and the Cappella Brancacci – the website is ⓦ museicivicifiorentini.it.

9

> ## TICKETS FOR THE PIAZZA DEL DUOMO SIGHTS
> In addition to tickets for single admission, you can buy an €11 ticket for the Dome plus the Museo dell'Opera, a €15 ticket for the Campanile, Santa Reparata, Baptistry and Museo, and a €23 ticket for all five. These tickets are valid for four days.

Italian city. Yet even though the magnitude of the **Duomo** is apparent from a distance, the first full sight of the church and the adjacent **Baptistry** still comes as a jolt, the colours of their patterned exteriors making a startling contrast with the dun-coloured buildings around them.

The Duomo (Santa Maria del Fiore)
Mon–Wed & Fri 10am–5pm, Thurs 10am–4.30pm (May & Oct 4pm, July–Sept 5pm), Sat 10am–4.45pm, Sun 1.30–4.45pm • Free • Ⓦ operaduomo.firenze.it

It was sometime in the seventh century when the seat of the Bishop of Florence was transferred from San Lorenzo to the ancient church that stood on the site of the **Duomo**. In the thirteenth century, it was decided that a new cathedral was required, to better reflect the wealth of the city and to put the Pisans and Sienese in their place. In 1294 **Arnolfo di Cambio** designed a vast basilica focused on a domed tribune; by 1418 this project was complete except for its crowning feature. The conception was magnificent: the dome was to span a distance of nearly 42m and rise from a base some 54m above the floor of the nave. It was to be the largest dome ever constructed – but nobody had yet worked out how to build it.

A committee of the masons' guild was set up to ponder the problem, and it was to them that **Filippo Brunelleschi** presented himself. Some seventeen years before, in 1401, Brunelleschi had been defeated by Ghiberti in the competition to design the Baptistry doors, and had spent the intervening time studying classical architecture and developing new theories of engineering. He won the commission on condition that he worked jointly with Ghiberti – a partnership that did not last long. The key to the dome's success was the construction of two shells: a light outer shell about one metre thick, and an inner shell four times thicker. On March 25, 1436 – Annunciation Day, and the Florentine New Year – the completion of the dome was marked by the papal consecration of the cathedral.

The exterior
The Duomo's overblown main **facade** is a nineteenth-century imitation of a Gothic front, its marble cladding quarried from the same sources as the first builders used – white stone from Carrara, red from the Maremma, green from Prato. The south side is the oldest part, but the most attractive adornment is the **Porta della Mandorla**, on the north side. This takes its name from the almond-shaped frame that contains the relief *The Assumption of the Virgin*, sculpted by Nanni di Banco around 1420.

The interior
The Duomo's **interior** is a vast enclosure of bare masonry that makes a stark contrast to the fussy exterior. Initially, the most conspicuous pieces of decoration are two memorials to *condottieri* (mercenary commanders) in the north aisle – Uccello's monument to **Sir John Hawkwood**, painted in 1436, and Castagno's monument to **Niccolò da Tolentino**, created twenty years later. Just beyond, Domenico do Michelino's *Dante Explaining the Divine Comedy* makes the dome only marginally less prominent than the mountain of Purgatory. Judged by mere size, the major work of art in the Duomo is the fresco of *The Last Judgement* inside the dome; painted by Vasari and Zuccari, it merely defaces Brunelleschi's masterpiece. Below the fresco are seven stained-glass roundels designed by Uccello, Ghiberti, Castagno and Donatello; they are best inspected from the gallery immediately below them, which forms part of the

route up **inside the dome** – the entrance is outside, on the north side (Mon–Fri 8.30am–7pm, Sat 8.30am–5.40pm; €8). The gallery is the queasiest part of the climb, most of which winds between the brick walls of the outer and inner shells of the dome, up to the very summit with its stunning views over the city.

In the 1960s remnants of the Duomo's predecessor, **Santa Reparata**, were uncovered beneath the west end of the **nave** (€3). A detailed model helps make sense of the jigsaw of Roman, early Christian and Romanesque remains, areas of mosaic and patches of fourteenth-century frescoes. Also down here is the **tomb of Brunelleschi**, one of the few Florentines honoured with burial inside the Duomo.

The Campanile

Daily 8.30am–7.30pm • €6 • ⓦ operaduomo.firenze.it

Alongside Italy's most impressive cathedral dome is perhaps its most elegant belltower. The **Campanile** was begun in 1334 by **Giotto**, who was no engineer: after his death in 1337 Andrea Pisano and Francesco Talenti took over the teetering, half-built edifice, and immediately doubled the thickness of the walls to stop it collapsing. The first storey is studded with two rows of remarkable bas-reliefs; the lower row, *The Creation of Man* and the *Arts and Industries*, was carved by Pisano himself, the upper by his pupils. The figures of *Prophets* and *Sibyls* in the second-storey niches were created by Donatello and others. (All the sculptures are copies – the originals are in the Museo dell'Opera del Duomo.)

The Baptistry

Mon–Sat 11.15am–7pm, Sun & first Sat of month 8.30am–2pm • €5 • ⓦ operaduomo.firenze.it

Generally thought to date from the sixth or seventh century, the **Baptistry** is the oldest building in Florence, and no building better illustrates the special relationship between Florence and the Roman world. Throughout the Middle Ages the Florentines chose to believe that the Baptistry was originally a Roman temple to Mars, a belief bolstered by the interior's inclusion of Roman granite columns. The pattern of its marble cladding, applied in the eleventh and twelfth centuries, is clearly classical in inspiration, and the Baptistry's most famous embellishments – its gilded bronze doors – mark the emergence of a self-conscious interest in the art of the ancient world.

The doors

After Andrea Pisano's success in 1336 with the **doors** that are now on the south side of the building, the merchants' guild held a competition in 1401 for the job of making a new set. The two finalists were Brunelleschi and **Lorenzo Ghiberti** – and the latter won the day. Ghiberti's **north doors** show a new naturalism and classical sense of harmony, but their innovation is timid in comparison with his sublime **east doors**, which are known as the "Gates of Paradise", supposedly because Michelangelo once remarked that they deserved to be the portals of heaven, though it's more likely that the name came about because the space between a cathedral and its baptistry was called the *paradiso*. Unprecedented in the subtlety of their modelling, these Old Testament scenes are a primer of early Renaissance art, using perspective, gesture and sophisticated grouping of their subjects to convey the human drama of each scene. Ghiberti has included a self-portrait in the frame of the left-hand door – his is the fourth head from the top of the right-hand band. All the panels now set in the door are replicas, with the originals on display in the Museo dell'Opera; the original competition entries are in the Bargello.

The interior

Inside, both the mosaic floor and the magnificent mosaic ceiling – including a fearsome platoon of demons at the feet of Christ in Judgement – were created in the thirteenth century. To the right of the altar is the **tomb of John XXIII**, the schismatic pope who died in Florence in 1419. The monument, draped by an illusionistic marble canopy, is the work of Donatello and his pupil Michelozzo.

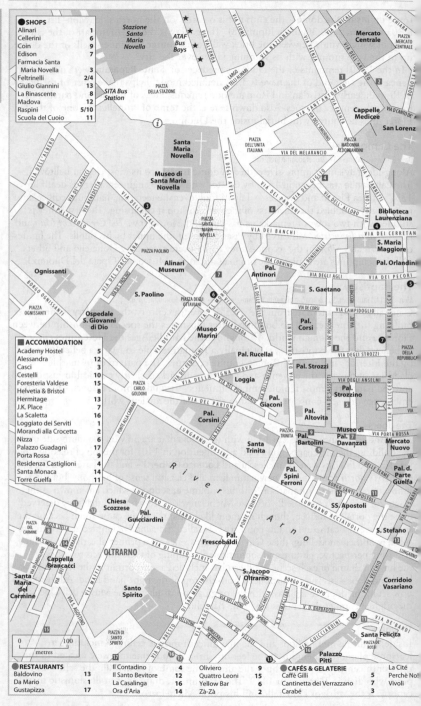

● SHOPS

Alinari	1
Cellerini	6
Coin	9
Edison	7
Farmacia Santa Maria Novella	3
Feltrinelli	2/4
Giulio Giannini	13
La Rinascente	8
Madova	12
Raspini	5/10
Scuola del Cuoio	11

■ ACCOMMODATION

Academy Hostel	5
Alessandra	12
Casci	3
Cestelli	10
Foresteria Valdese	15
Helvetia & Bristol	8
Hermitage	13
J.K. Place	7
La Scaletta	16
Loggiato dei Servi	1
Morandi alla Crocetta	2
Nizza	6
Palazzo Guadagni	17
Porta Rossa	9
Residenza Castiglioni	4
Santa Monaca	14
Torre Guelfa	11

● RESTAURANTS

Baldovino	13	Il Contadino	4	Oliviero	9
Da Mario	1	Il Santo Bevitore	12	Quattro Leoni	15
Gustapizza	17	La Casalinga	16	Yellow Bar	6
		Ora d'Aria	14	Zà-Zà	2

● CAFÉS & GELATERIE

Caffè Gilli	5	La Cité	
Cantinetta dei Verrazzano	7	Perchè No!	
Carabé	3	Vivoli	

9

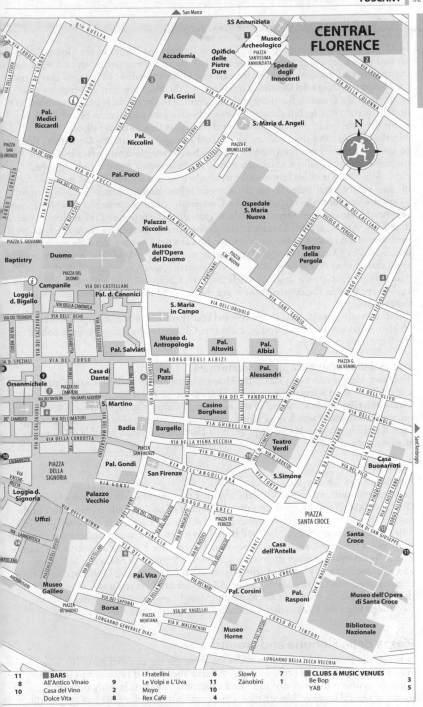

	BARS				
11	All'Antico Vinaio	9	I Fratellini	6	Slowly	7	**CLUBS & MUSIC VENUES**
8	Casa del Vino	2	Le Volpi e L'Uva	11	Zanobini	1	Be Bop	3
10	Dolce Vita	8	Moyo	10			YAB	5
			Rex Café	4			

9 The Museo dell'Opera del Duomo

Mon–Sat 9am–7.30pm, Sun 9am–1.40pm • €6 • ⓦ operaduomo.firenze.it

In 1296 a body called the Opera del Duomo, literally the "Work of the Duomo", was created to oversee the maintenance of the Duomo. In the early fifteenth century it took occupation of a building opposite the east end of the cathedral, which now also houses the **Museo dell'Opera del Duomo**, a repository of the most precious and fragile works of art from the Duomo, Baptistry and Campanile. The museum is being expanded to double its present size, but the work is not scheduled for completion before 2016, so for the time being the arrangement of the exhibits should be as follows.

In the large ground-floor hall are four seated *Evangelists* (including **Donatello**'s fine *St John*) wrenched from the Duomo's demolished sixteenth-century facade. On the mezzanine is the highlight of the museum – **Michelangelo**'s angular and anguished pietà. This was one of his last works, carved when he was almost 80 and intended for his own tomb: Vasari records that the face of the hooded Nicodemus is a self-portrait.

Upstairs are **Donatello**'s figures for the Campanile, the most powerful of which is the prophet *Habbakuk*, the intensity of whose gaze allegedly prompted the sculptor to seize it and yell "Speak, speak!" Donatello also created one of the ornate *cantorie* (choir-lofts) here; the other, created at the same time, is by **Luca della Robbia**. An adjacent room is dominated by Donatello's haggard wooden figure of *Mary Magdalene*, a wild presence amid cases full of rich vestments, jewelled reliquaries, and a huge silver-gilt **altar**. Also on this floor are the original reliefs from the Campanile and a corridor lined with equipment used in the construction of the dome – and look out for Brunelleschi's **death mask**.

You return to ground level into a covered **courtyard** where Michelangelo worked from 1501 to 1504 on his *David*. Today, it displays Ghiberti's original ten **bronze panels** for the Baptistry's east doors.

Piazza della Repubblica and Orsanmichele

The main route south from Piazza del Duomo is the arrow-straight **Via dei Calzaiuoli**, a catwalk for the Florentine *passeggiata*. Halfway down the street is the opening into **Piazza della Repubblica**, created in the nineteenth century by razing the old Jewish quarter and markets which once stood here in an attempt to give Florence – briefly the capital of Italy – a grand public square. It's a characterless place, notable solely for its size and upmarket cafés.

Orsanmichele

Via dei Calzaiuoli • Daily 10am–5pm • Free

Towards the southern end of Via dei Calzaiuoli rises the block-like church of **Orsanmichele**. From the ninth century, the church of San Michele ad Hortum ("at the garden") stood here, which was replaced in 1240 by a grain market and after a fire in 1304 by a merchants' loggia. In 1380 the loggia was walled in and dedicated exclusively to religious functions, while two upper storeys were added for use as emergency grain stores. Its **exterior** has some impressive sculpture, including *St Matthew*, *St Stephen* and *John the Baptist* by Ghiberti (the *Baptist* was the first life-size bronze statue of the Renaissance), and Donatello's *St George*. All these statues are replicas – nearly all of the originals are on display in the **museum** (Mon 10am–5pm; free), entered via the footbridge from the Palazzo dell'Arte della Lana, opposite the church entrance.

Piazza della Signoria and around

Whereas the Piazza del Duomo provides the focus for the city's religious life, the **Piazza della Signoria** – site of the mighty **Palazzo Vecchio** and forecourt to the **Uffizi** – has always been the centre of its secular existence. The most lavishly decorated rooms of the Palazzo Vecchio are now a museum, but the rest of the building is still the HQ of the city's councillors and bureaucrats, and the piazza in front of it provides the stage for major civic events and political rallies.

The piazza's array of **statuary** starts with Giambologna's equestrian statue of *Cosimo I* and continues with Ammanati's fatuous *Neptune Fountain* and copies of Donatello's *Marzocco* (the city's heraldic lion), his *Judith and Holofernes* and of Michelangelo's *David*. Conceived as a partner piece to *David*, Bandinelli's lumpen **Hercules and Cacus** was designed as a personal emblem of Cosimo I and a symbol of Florentine fortitude; Benvenuto Cellini described the musclebound Hercules as looking like "a sackful of melons". Near Ammanati's fountain is a plaque set into the pavement to mark the site of Savonarola's **Bonfire of the Vanities** and his execution. The square's **Loggia della Signoria** was built in the late fourteenth century as a dais for city officials during ceremonies; only in the late eighteenth century did it become a showcase for sculpture, the best of which are Giambologna's *Rape of the Sabine* and Cellini's superb *Perseus*.

The Palazzo Vecchio
April–Sept Mon–Wed & Fri–Sun 9am–midnight, Thurs 9am–2pm; Oct–March Mon–Wed & Fri–Sun 9am–7pm, Thurs 9am–2pm • €6.50 • W museicivicifiorentini.it

Probably designed by Arnolfo di Cambio, Florence's fortress-like town hall, the **Palazzo Vecchio**, was begun as the Palazzo dei Priori in the last year of the thirteenth century, to provide premises for the highest tier of the city's republican government. Changes in the Florentine constitution over the years entailed alterations to the layout of the palace, the most radical coming in 1540, when Cosimo I moved his retinue here from the Palazzo Medici and grafted a huge extension onto the rear. The Medici remained in residence for only nine years before moving to the Palazzo Pitti; the old (*vecchio*) palace – which they left to their son, Francesco – then acquired its present name.

The first floor
Giorgio Vasari, court architect from 1555 until his death in 1574, was responsible for much of the decor in the courtyard, and his limited talents were given full rein in the huge **Salone dei Cinquecento** at the top of the stairs, built at the end of the fifteenth century as a council assembly hall. This room might have become one of Italy's most extraordinary showcases of Renaissance art, when in 1503 Leonardo da Vinci and Michelangelo were commissioned to fresco opposite walls of the chamber. Unfortunately, Leonardo abandoned the project after his experimental fresco technique went wrong, and Michelangelo's work existed only on paper when he was summoned to Rome by Pope Julius II. (The discovery of a cavity behind *The Battle of Marciano* has raised the possibility that Vasari constructed a false wall over Leonardo's fresco, to preserve his great predecessor's painting. Investigations are proceeding.) A few decades later Vasari stepped in, and covered the room with drearily bombastic murals celebrating Cosimo's military prowess. Michelangelo's *Victory*, facing the entrance door, was sculpted for Julius's tomb but was donated to the Medici by the artist's nephew.

From the Salone del Cinquecento, a roped-off door allows a glimpse of the strangest room in the building, the Studiolo di Francesco I. Designed by Vasari towards the end of his career and decorated by no fewer than thirty Mannerist artists (1570–74), this windowless cell was created as a retreat for the introverted son of Cosimo and Eleanor.

The upper floor
Upstairs, you first enter the **Quartiere degli Elementi**, where all five salons are slavishly devoted to a different member of the Medici clan. More interesting are the private apartments of **Eleanor di Toledo**, Cosimo I's wife – especially the tiny and exquisite **chapel**, vividly decorated by Bronzino in the 1540s. Beyond the frescoed Sala dell'Udienza (originally the audience chamber of the Republic) you come to the **Sala dei Gigli**, which takes its name from the lilies (*gigli*) that adorn most of its surfaces. The room has frescoes by Domenico Ghirlandaio, but the highlight is **Donatello**'s original *Judith and Holofernes*.

9

Commissioned by Cosimo il Vecchio, it freezes the moment at which Judith's arm begins the scything stroke that is to cut off Holofernes' head, a dramatic conception that no other sculptor of the period would have attempted.

The two small side-rooms are the Cancelleria, **Machiavelli**'s office for fifteen years and now containing a bust and portrait of the much-maligned political thinker; and the lovely **Sala delle Carte**, decorated with 57 maps painted in 1563 by the Medici court astronomer Fra' Ignazio Danti, depicting what was then the entire known world.

The Uffizi

Piazzale degli Uffizi • Tues–Sun 8.15am–6.50pm, but in high summer and at festive periods it sometimes stays open until 10pm • €6.50, but more when special exhibitions are on, which is usually the case; see box, p.517, for booking details • ⓦ uffizi.firenze.it

The **Galleria degli Uffizi**, the finest picture gallery in Italy, is housed in what were once government offices (*uffizi*) built by Vasari for Cosimo I in 1560. After Vasari's death, work on the building was continued by Buontalenti, who was asked by Francesco I to glaze the upper storey so that it could house his art collection. Each of the succeeding Medici added to the family's trove of art treasures, which was preserved for public inspection by the last member of the family, Anna Maria Lodovica, whose will specified that it should be left to the people of Florence and never be allowed to leave the city. In the nineteenth century a large proportion of the statuary was transferred to the Bargello, while most of the antiquities went to the Museo Archeologico, leaving the Uffizi as essentially a gallery of paintings supplemented with some classical sculptures. The gallery is in the process of expansion, doubling the number of rooms open to the public in order to show some eight hundred pictures that have been kept in storage; accordingly, some paintings – especially those in the later sections – may not be on show precisely where they appear in the following account.

Pre-Renaissance

You can take a lift up to the galleries, but if you take the staircase instead, you'll pass the entrance to the Uffizi's prints and drawings section. The bulk of this vast collection is reserved for scholarly scrutiny but samples are often on public show.

The beginnings of the stylistic evolution of that period can be traced in the three altarpieces of the *Maestà* (Madonna Enthroned) that dominate **Room 2**: the *Madonna Rucellai*, *Maestà di Santa Trinità* and *Madonna d'Ognissanti*, by **Duccio**, **Cimabue** and **Giotto** respectively. These great works, which dwarf everything around them, show the softening of the hieratic Byzantine style into a more tactile form of representation.

Painters from fourteenth-century Siena fill **Room 3**, with several pieces by Ambrogio and Pietro Lorenzetti and **Simone Martini**'s glorious *Annunciation*. In **Room 5**, devoted to the last flowering of Gothic art, **Lorenzo Monaco** is represented by an *Adoration of the Magi* and his greatest masterpiece, *The Coronation of the Virgin*. Equally arresting is another *Adoration of the Magi* by **Gentile da Fabriano**, a picture spangled with gold and crammed with incidental detail. Opposite is the *Thebaid*, a beguiling little narrative that depicts monastic life in the Egyptian desert as a sort of holy fairy-tale; though labelled as being by the young Fra' Angelico, it's also been attributed to the now-obscure Gherardo di Jacopo Starnina.

Early Renaissance

Room 7 reveals the sheer diversity of early Renaissance painting. **Fra' Angelico**'s gorgeous *Coronation of the Virgin* takes place against a Gothic-like field of gold, but there's a very un-Gothic sensibility at work in its individualized depiction of the attendant throng. **Paolo Uccello**'s *The Battle of San Romano* once hung in Lorenzo il Magnifico's bedchamber, in company with its two companion pieces now in the Louvre and London's National Gallery. *The Madonna and Child with Sts Francis, John the Baptist, Zenobius and Lucy* is one of only twelve extant paintings by **Domenico Veneziano**, whose greatest pupil, **Piero della Francesca**, is represented in **Room 8** by the paired portraits of *Federico da Montefeltro and Battista Sforza*, the duke and duchess of Urbino. Much of this room is given over to **Fra' Filippo Lippi**, whose *Madonna and Child with Two Angels* is one of the gallery's most popular faces: the model was Lucrezia Buti, a convent novice who became the object of one of his more enduring sexual obsessions. Lucrezia puts in another appearance in Lippi's crowded *Coronation of the Virgin*, where she's the young woman gazing out in the right foreground; Filippo himself, hand on chin, makes eye contact on the left side of the picture. Their liaison produced a son, the aptly named **Filippino** "Little Philip" **Lippi**, whose *Otto Altarpiece* – one of several works by him here – is typical of the more melancholic cast of the younger Lippi's art.

The Pollaiuolo brothers and Botticelli

Lippi's great pupil, Botticelli, steals some of the thunder in **Room 9** – *Fortitude*, one of the series of cardinal and theological virtues, is a very early work by him. The rest of the series is by **Piero del Pollaiuolo**, whose brother Antonio (primarily a sculptor) assisted him in the creation of *Sts Vincent, James and Eustace*, their finest collaboration.

It's in the merged **rooms 10–14** that the finest of **Botticelli**'s productions are gathered. The identities of the characters in the **Primavera** are clear enough: on the right Zephyrus, god of the west wind, chases the nymph Cloris, who is then transfigured into Flora, the pregnant goddess of spring; Venus stands in the centre, to the side of the three Graces, who are targeted by Cupid; on the left Mercury wards off the clouds of winter. What this all means, however, has occupied scholars for decades, but the consensus seems to be that it shows the triumph of Venus, with the Graces as the physical embodiment of her beauty and Flora the symbol of her fruitfulness.

The **Birth of Venus** is less obscure: it takes as its source the myth that the goddess emerged from the sea after it had been impregnated by the castration of Uranus, an allegory for the creation of beauty through the mingling of the spirit (Uranus) and the physical world.

Botticelli's devotional paintings are equally stunning. *The Adoration of the Magi* is traditionally thought to contain a gallery of Medici portraits: Cosimo il Vecchio as the first king, his sons Giovanni and Piero as the other two kings, Lorenzo the Magnificent on the far left, and his brother Giuliano as the black-haired young man in profile on the right. Only the identification of Cosimo is reasonably certain, along with that of Botticelli himself, on the right in the yellow robe. In later life, influenced by Savonarola's teaching, Botticelli confined himself to religious subjects and moral fables, and his style became increasingly severe. The transformation is clear when comparing the easy grace of the *Madonna of the Magnificat* with the angularity and agitation of the *Calumny of Apelles*.

Not quite every masterpiece in this room is by Botticelli. Set away from the walls is the *Adoration of the Shepherds* by his Flemish contemporary **Hugo van der Goes**. Brought to Florence in 1483 by Tommaso Portinari, the Medici agent in Bruges, it provided the city's artists with their first large-scale demonstration of the realism of Northern European oil painting, and had a great influence on the way the medium was exploited here.

Leonardo to Mantegna

Works in **Room 15** trace the formative years of **Leonardo da Vinci**, whose distinctive touch appears first in the *Baptism of Christ* by his master Verrocchio: the wistful angel in profile is by the 18-year-old apprentice, as is the misty landscape in the background, and Leonardo also worked heavily on the figure of Christ. A similar terrain of soft-focus mountains and water occupies the far distance in Leonardo's slightly later *Annunciation*, in which a diffused light falls on a scene where everything is observed with a scientist's precision. In contrast to the poise of the *Annunciation*, the sketch of *The Adoration of the Magi* – abandoned when Leonardo left Florence for Milan in early 1482 – presents the infant Christ as the eye of a vortex of figures, all drawn into his

9

presence by a force as irresistible as a whirlpool. Most of the rest of the room is given over to Raphael's teacher, **Perugino**.

Room 18, the octagonal **Tribuna**, houses the most important of the Medici's collection of classical sculpture – in particular, the *Medici Venus* – but also some fascinating portraits by **Bronzino**, painted like figures of porcelain, and Andrea del Sarto's flirtatious *Portrait of a Young Woman*.

The last section of this wing throws together Renaissance paintings from outside Florence. **Signorelli**, **Perugino** and **Piero di Cosimo** are the principal artists in **Room 19**, and after them comes a room devoted to **Cranach**, **Dürer** and other German artists. A taste of the Uffizi's remarkable collection of Venetian painting follows, with an impenetrable *Sacred Allegory* by **Giovanni Bellini**, and three works attributed to **Giorgione**. In **Room 22**, a clutch of Northern European paintings includes some superb portraits by **Holbein** (notably *Sir Richard Southwell* and a self-portrait) and Hans Memling. The following room has a trio of **Correggio** pictures and a clutch of exquisite paintings by **Mantegna**, including the *Madonna delle Cave*, which takes its name from the minuscule quarry (cave) in the background.

Michelangelo, Mannerism and Titian

Beyond the stockpile of statues in the short corridor overlooking the Arno, the main attraction in **Room 25** is **Michelangelo**'s *Doni Tondo*, the only easel painting he came close to completing. The adjoining room contains **Andrea del Sarto**'s sultry *Madonna of the Harpies* and a number of compositions by **Raphael**, including his self-portrait, the lovely *Madonna of the Goldfinch* and *Pope Leo X with Cardinals Giulio de' Medici and Luigi de' Rossi*. The Michelangelo tondo's contorted gestures and virulent colours were greatly influential on the Mannerist painters of the sixteenth century, as can be gauged from *Moses Defending the Daughters of Jethro* by **Rosso Fiorentino**, one of the seminal figures of the movement, whose works hang in **Room 27**, along with major works by Bronzino and his adoptive father, Pontormo.

Room 28 is dominated by another of the titanic figures of sixteenth-century art, **Titian**, with ten of his paintings on show. His *Flora* and *A Knight of Malta* are stunning, but most eyes tend to swivel towards the *Urbino Venus*, the most provocative of all Renaissance nudes, described by Mark Twain as "the foulest, the vilest, the obscenest picture the world possesses". A brief diversion through the painters of the sixteenth-century Emilian school follows, centred on **Parmigianino**, whose *Madonna of the Long Neck* is one of the pivotal Mannerist creations. **Rooms 31 to 34** feature a miscellany of sixteenth-century artists (look out for the El Greco) and some masterpieces from Venice and the Veneto, including work by **Moroni**, **Tintoretto**, **Paolo Veronese** and **Lorenzo Lotto**.

The seventeenth and eighteenth centuries

The Uffizi's collection of seventeenth-century art is in rooms 41–45. **Room 41** features strong work from **Van Dyck** and **Rubens**, whose *Portrait of Isabella Brandt* is perhaps his finest painting here. The most overwhelming, however, are the huge *Henry IV at the Battle of Ivry* and *The Triumphal Entry of Henry IV into Paris* – Henry's marriage to Marie de' Medici is the connection with Florence. This pair are displayed in the majestic Neoclassical Niobe Room. In this section of the gallery you should also see some superb works by **Rembrandt**, **Goya**, **Guercino**, **Canaletto**, **Tiepolo** and **Chardin**, but the plan is to move the non-Italian artists to new rooms downstairs some time soon.

At the moment these new galleries are used for temporary exhibitions and as a showcase for Italian art of the seventeenth century. Dramatic images from Salvator Rosa, Luca Giordano and Artemisia Gentileschi make quite an impression, but the presiding genius is **Caravaggio**, with his bravura *Medusa* (painted on a shield), the smug little *Bacchus*, and the throat-grabbing *Sacrifice of Isaac*.

The Bargello

Via del Proconsolo 4 • Tues–Sat 8.15am–1.50pm, plus second & fourth Sun of month and first, third & fifth Mon of month, same hours • €4, but higher charge for special exhibitions • ⓦ uffizi.firenze.it

The **Museo Nazionale del Bargello**, which is both an outstanding museum of sculpture and a huge applied-art collection, is installed in the daunting Palazzo del Bargello on Via del Proconsolo, halfway between the Duomo and the Palazzo Vecchio. The *palazzo* was built in 1255, and soon became the seat of the Podestà, the chief magistrate. Numerous malefactors were tried, sentenced and executed here; the building acquired its present name in the sixteenth century, after the resident *bargello*, or police chief.

The courtyard and ground floor

From the ticket desk, you enter the beautiful Gothic **courtyard**, which is plastered with the coats of arms of the Podestà and contains, among many other pieces, six allegorical figures by **Ammanati**. At the foot of the courtyard steps is the **Michelangelo Room**, containing his first major sculpture, a tipsy, soft-bellied figure of *Bacchus*, carved at the age of 22 – a year before his great *Pietà* in Rome. Michelangelo's style soon evolved into something less ostentatiously virtuosic, as is shown by the tender *Tondo Pitti*, while the rugged expressivity of his late manner is exemplified by the square-jawed *Bust of Brutus*. Works by Michelangelo's followers and contemporaries are ranged in the immediate vicinity – **Cellini**'s *Bust of Cosimo I* and **Giambologna**'s famous *Mercury* are the best of them.

The upper floors

At the top of the courtyard staircase, the **loggia** has been turned into an aviary for Giambologna's bronze birds, brought here from the Medici villa at Castello. In the adjacent **Salone di Donatello**, vestiges of the artist's sinuous Gothic manner are evident in the drapery of his marble *David*, placed against the left wall, but there's nothing antiquated in the alert, tense *St George*, carved just eight years later for the tabernacle of the armourers' guild at Orsanmichele and installed here in a replica of its original niche. In front stands Donatello's sexually ambiguous bronze *David*, cast around 1435, as the first freestanding nude figure since classical times. His strange, jubilant figure known as *Amor/Attis* dates from around 1440, while his breathtakingly vivid bust of *Niccolò da Uzzano* shows that he was just as comfortable with portraiture. The less complex humanism of **Luca della Robbia** is embodied in the glazed terracotta Madonnas set round the walls, while Donatello's master, **Ghiberti**, is represented by his relief *The Sacrifice of Isaac*, his successful entry in the competition for the Baptistry doors. The treatment of the same theme submitted by **Brunelleschi** is displayed nearby. Most of the rest of this floor is occupied by a collection of **European and Islamic applied art**, of so high a standard that it would constitute an engrossing museum in its own right. Elsewhere on this floor is dazzling carved **ivory** from Byzantium and medieval France.

The sculptural display resumes on the next floor up, where you'll find superb work by the **della Robbia** family, Italy's best assembly of small Renaissance bronzes (with plentiful evidence of Giambologna's virtuosity at table-top scale) and two rooms devoted mainly to Renaissance busts, including magnificent portraits by Verrocchio, Francesco Laurana and Mino da Fiesole.

Museo Galileo

Piazza dei Giudici 1 • Mon & Wed–Sun 9.30am–6pm, Tues 9.30am–1pm • €9 • ⓦ museogalileo.it

Long after Florence had declined from its artistic apogee, the intellectual reputation of the city was maintained by its scientists. Grand Duke Ferdinando II and his brother Leopoldo, both of whom studied with **Galileo**, founded the Accademia del Cimento (Academy of Experiment) in 1657, and the instruments made and acquired by this academy form the core of the excellent **Museo Galileo**, close to the river, on Piazza dei Giudici. The **first floor** features timepieces and measuring instruments (such as beautiful

Arab astrolabes), as well as a massive armillary sphere made for Ferdinando I to prove the fallacy of Copernicus's heliocentric universe. Some of Galileo's original instruments are on show here, including the lens with which he discovered the four moons of Jupiter. On the floor above there are all kinds of exquisitely manufactured **scientific and mechanical equipment**, several of which were built to demonstrate the fundamental laws of physics. (A new interactive area, opened in 2012, explains the function of many of the museum's exhibits.) Dozens of clocks and timepieces are on show too, while the medical section is full of alarming surgical instruments and wax anatomical models for teaching obstetrics.

The western city centre

Several streets in central Florence retain their medieval character, especially in the district immediately to the west of Piazza della Signoria. Forming a gateway to this quarter is the **Mercato Nuovo**, whose souvenir stalls are the busiest in the city. Usually a small group is gathered round the bronze boar known as **Il Porcellino**, trying to gain some good luck by getting a coin to fall from the animal's mouth through the grill below his head.

Museo di Palazzo Davanzati

Via Porta Rossa 13 • Tues–Sun 8.15am–1.50pm, plus second & fourth Mon of month, same hours • €2 • Visitors have unrestricted access to the first floor; visits to the second and third floors are at 10am, 11am & noon, and must be pre-booked in person or by phone • ☎ 055 238 8610, ☺ uffizi.firenze.it

For more of an immersion in the world of medieval Florence you should visit the fourteenth-century **Palazzo Davanzati**, nowadays maintained as the **Museo Davanzati**. This huge house is decorated in predominantly medieval style, using furniture from the fourteenth to the nineteenth centuries gathered from various Florentine museums, most notably the Bargello.

The coat of arms of the wealthy Davanzati family, who occupied the house from 1578 until 1838, is still visible on the facade, and you can admire their impressive family tree in the entrance hall. Upstairs are several frescoed rooms – the **Sala dei Pappagalli** (Parrot Room) and the **Camera dei Pavoni** (Peacock Bedroom) are particularly splendid – as well as some interesting reconstructions of day-to-day life in the house, with chests full of linen in the bedrooms and a clutter of household utensils, tools, looms and spinning wheels in the third-floor kitchen. There are also fine collections of lace work and ceramics on the first floor.

Santa Trinità

Piazza Santa Trinità • Mon–Sat 8am–noon & 4–6pm, Sun 4–6pm • Free

Via Porta Rossa culminates at Piazza Santa Trinità, close to the city's most stylish bridge, the **Ponte Santa Trinità**, which was rebuilt stone by stone after the retreating Nazis had blown up the original in 1944. **Santa Trinità church** was founded in the eleventh century, but piecemeal additions have lent it a pleasantly hybrid air: the largely Gothic interior contrasts with Buontalenti's Mannerist facade of 1594.

The interior is notable above all for **Ghirlandaio**'s frescoes of the *Life of St Francis* in the **Cappella Sassetti** – as notable for their depiction of fifteenth-century Florence as for their ostensible subjects, they feature portraits of various Medici.

Via de' Tornabuoni and around

In recent years **Via de' Tornabuoni** and nearby Piazza Strozzi have come to be monopolized by high-end designer stores – Versace, Cartier, Armani, Prada, Cavalli, Pucci, Gucci and Ferragamo all have outlets here, to the dismay of those who lament the erosion of Florentine identity by the ever-burgeoning megabrands. (Though the last four in that list are at least Florentine in origin.) Conspicuous wealth is nothing new here, for looming above everything is the vast **Palazzo Strozzi**, the last, the largest and the least subtle of Florentine Renaissance palaces. Filippo Strozzi bought and demolished a dozen townhouses to make space for Giuliano da Sangallo's design (1536). Now administered by the Fondazione Palazzo Strozzi, the building has become a venue for outstanding art exhibitions; it has a nice café too.

Some of Florence's other plutocrats made an impression with a touch more subtlety than the Strozzi. In the 1440s Giovanni Rucellai, one of the richest businessmen in the city (and an esteemed scholar too), decided to commission a new house from Leon Battista Alberti. The resultant **Palazzo Rucellai**, two minutes' walk from the Strozzi house at Via della Vigna Nuova 18, was the first palace in Florence to follow the rules of classical architecture. The nearby church of San Pancrazio, on Via della Spada, has been converted into the slick **Museo Marino Marini** (Mon & Wed–Sat 10am–5pm; €4), a spacious showcase for the work of one of Italy's foremost twentieth-century sculptors.

Ognissanti

Borgo Ognissanti • **Church** Mon–Sat 7.30am–12.30pm & 4–8pm, Sun 9am–1pm & 4–8pm • **Refectory** Mon, Tues & Sat 9am–noon • Free

In medieval times a major area of cloth production – the foundation of the Florentine economy – lay in the west of the city, in the parish of **Ognissanti**, located on Borgo Ognissanti, five minutes' walk west of Via de' Tornabuoni. The Baroque facade is not very interesting, but the interior is a different matter. The young face squeezed between the Madonna and the dark-cloaked man in **Ghirlandaio**'s *Madonna della Misericordia* fresco, over the second altar on the right, is said to be that of Amerigo Vespucci – later to set sail on voyages that would give his name to America. Just beyond this, on opposite sides of the nave, are mounted **Botticelli**'s *St Augustine* and Ghirlandaio's *St Jerome*, both painted in 1480. In the same year Ghirlandaio painted the bucolic *Last Supper* that covers one wall of the **refectory**, reached through the cloister entered to the left of the church. And don't miss the dazzling Crucifix that hangs in the left transept: in 2010 it emerged from a seven-year restoration, and in the course of the cleaning it was established that it's almost certainly by **Giotto**.

Santa Maria Novella

Piazza Santa Maria Novella • Mon–Thurs 9am–5.30pm, Fri 11am–5.30pm, Sat 9am–5pm, Sun 1–5pm • €3.50

Presiding over the recently refurbished **Piazza Santa Maria Novella**, the marble facade designed by Alberti for the Dominican church of **Santa Maria Novella** is one of the most attractive in the city. The church's interior – designed to enable preachers to address their sermons to as large a congregation as possible – is filled with masterworks, not least **Masaccio's** extraordinary 1427 fresco of *The Trinity* (left aisle), one of the earliest works in which perspective and classical proportion were rigorously employed. Nearby, Giotto's *Crucifix*, a radically naturalistic and probably very early work (c.1288–90), hangs in what is thought to be its intended position, poised dramatically over the nave.

Filippino Lippi's frescoes for the **Cappella di Filippo Strozzi** (immediately to the right of the chancel) are a fantasy vision of classical ruins in which the narrative (on the life of St Philip the Apostle) often seems to take second place – before starting the project Filippino spent some time in Rome, and this work displays an archeologist's obsession with ancient Roman culture. As a chronicle of fifteenth-century life in Florence, no series of frescoes is more fascinating than **Domenico Ghirlandaio's** cycle in the Cappella Tornabuoni, behind the high altar; the cycle was commissioned by Giovanni Tornabuoni – which explains why certain ladies of the Tornabuoni family are present at the birth of John the Baptist and of the Virgin. **Brunelleschi**'s *Crucifix*, popularly supposed to have been carved as a response to Donatello's uncouth version at Santa Croce, hangs in the Cappella Gondi, left of the chancel. At the end of the left transept is the raised **Cappella Strozzi**, whose faded frescoes by Nardo di Cione (1350s) include an entire wall of visual commentary on Dante's *Inferno*. The magnificent altarpiece by Nardo's brother Andrea (better known as **Orcagna**) is a piece of propaganda for the

9

Dominicans – Christ is shown bestowing favour simultaneously on St Peter and St Thomas Aquinas, a figure second only to St Dominic in the order's hierarchy.

The Museo di Santa Maria Novella

Piazza Santa Maria Novella • Mon & Fri–Sun 10am–4pm • €3 • ⓦ museicivicifiorentini.it

More remarkable paintings are on display in the spacious Romanesque conventual buildings to the left of the church, now the **Museo di Santa Maria Novella**. You enter into the **Chiostro Verde**, which features *Stories from Genesis* by **Paolo Uccello** and his workshop. Leading off from this cloister is the **Cappellone degli Spagnuoli** (Spanish Chapel), which received its new name after Eleanor of Toledo reserved it for the use of her Spanish entourage. Its fresco cycle by Andrea di Firenze, an extended depiction of the triumph of the Catholic Church, was described by Ruskin as "the most noble piece of pictorial philosophy in Italy". The left wall depicts the *Triumph of Divine Wisdom*: Thomas Aquinas is enthroned below the Virgin and Apostles amid winged Virtues and biblical notables. The more spectacular right wall depicts the *Triumph of the Church*, and includes Florence's cathedral, imagined eighty years before its actual completion.

The northern city centre

The busy quarter north of the Duomo and east of the train station is focused on Florence's main food market, the vast **Mercato Centrale** (July & Aug Mon–Sat 7am–2am; Sept–June Mon–Fri 7am–2pm, Sat 7am–5pm). Butchers, *alimentari*, tripe sellers, greengrocers, pasta stalls and bars are all gathered under one roof, charging prices lower than you'll find elsewhere. All around is a hectic **street market** (daily 8.30am–7pm), thronged with stalls selling leather bags, belts, clothes and shoes.

San Lorenzo

Piazza San Lorenzo • Mon–Sat 10am–5.30pm, Sun 1.30–5.30pm (closed Sun Nov–Feb) • €3.50, or €6 with Biblioteca Laurenziana • ⓦ operamedicealaurenziana.it

Founded in the fourth century, **San Lorenzo** has a claim to be the oldest church in Florence – though the current building dates from the 1420s – and was the city's cathedral for almost three centuries. Although Michelangelo and several other architects laboured to produce a scheme for San Lorenzo's facade, the bare brick of the exterior has never been clad; it's a stark prelude to the powerful simplicity of Brunelleschi's interior, one of the earliest Renaissance church designs. Inside are two amazing **bronze pulpits** by **Donatello**. Covered in densely populated reliefs, chiefly of scenes preceding and following the Crucifixion, these are the artist's last works and were completed by his pupils. Close by, at the foot of the altar steps, a large disc of multicoloured marble marks the grave of Cosimo il Vecchio, the artist's main patron. Further pieces by Donatello (who is buried here) adorn the beautiful **Sagrestia Vecchia**, off the left transept.

The Biblioteca Medicea-Laurenziana

Piazza San Lorenzo • Mon, Wed Fri & Sat 9.30am–1.30pm, Tues & Thurs 9.30am–5.30pm • €3, or €6 with San Lorenzo • ⓦ operamedicealaurenziana.it

A gateway to the left of the church facade leads to the **Biblioteca Medicea-Laurenziana**. Wishing to create a suitably grandiose home for the precious manuscripts assembled by Cosimo and Lorenzo de' Medici, Pope Clement VII – Lorenzo's nephew – asked Michelangelo to design a new library in 1524. His Ricetto, or vestibule (1559–71), is a revolutionary showpiece of Mannerist architecture, delighting in paradoxical display: brackets that support nothing, columns that sink into the walls rather than stand out from them, and a flight of steps so large that it almost fills the room. From this eccentric space, you're sometimes allowed into the tranquil reading room; here, too, almost everything is the work of Michelangelo, even the inlaid desks.

The Cappelle Medicee

Tues–Sat 8.15am–4.50pm, plus first, third & fifth Sun of month and second & fourth Mon of month same hours • €6 •
Ⓦ operamedicealaurenziana.it

Some of Michelangelo's most celebrated works are in San Lorenzo's Sagrestia Nuova, part of the **Cappelle Medicee**. The entrance to the chapels is round the back of San Lorenzo, on Piazza Madonna degli Aldobrandini, and leads directly into the low-vaulted **crypt**, last resting-place of a clutch of minor Medici. After filing through the crypt, you climb into the **Cappella dei Principi** (Chapel of the Princes), a gloomy, stone-plated octagonal hall built as a mausoleum for Cosimo I and his ancestors. Morbid and dowdy, it was the most expensive building project ever financed by the family.

A corridor leads to the **Sagrestia Nuova**, begun by Michelangelo in 1520 and intended as a tribute to, and subversion of, Brunelleschi's Sagrestia Vecchia in San Lorenzo. Architectural connoisseurs go into raptures over the complex alcoves and other such sophistications, but you might be more drawn to the fabulous **Medici tombs**, carved by Michelangelo. To the left is the **tomb of Lorenzo**, Duke of Urbino, grandson of Lorenzo il Magnifico. Opposite is the **tomb of Giuliano**, Duke of Nemours, youngest son of Lorenzo il Magnifico. Their effigies were intended to face the equally grand tombs of Lorenzo il Magnifico and his brother Giuliano, two Medici who had genuine claims to fame and honour, but the only part of the project realized by Michelangelo is the serene **Madonna and Child**, the last image of the Madonna he ever sculpted and one of the most affecting, now flanked by *Cosmas* and *Damian*, patron saints of doctors (*medici*) and thus of the dynasty.

The Palazzo Medici-Riccardi

Via Cavour 1 • 9am–6pm; closed Wed • €7 • Ⓦ palazzo-medici.it

On the northeastern edge of Piazza San Lorenzo stands the **Palazzo Medici-Riccardi**, built by Michelozzo in the 1440s for Cosimo il Vecchio and for more than a century the principal seat of the Medici. With its heavily rusticated exterior, this mighty palace was the prototype for such houses as the Palazzo Pitti and Palazzo Strozzi, but was greatly altered in the seventeenth century by its new owners, the Riccardi family, who took over after Cosimo I moved out. Of Michelozzo's original scheme, only the courtyard and upstairs **chapel** remain intact. The chapel's interior is covered by brilliantly colourful and wonderfully detailed **frescoes** of *The Procession of the Magi*, painted around 1460 by Benozzo Gozzoli. Only ten people are allowed to view these paintings at any one time, with viewings every five minutes, so the queues can be long.

After the chapel, you visit the **Riccardi apartments**, including the sumptuous Sala di Carlo VIII and, further on, the Sala di Luca Giordano, a gilded and mirrored gallery notable for Luca Giordano's overblown ceiling fresco, *The Apotheosis of the Medici*, showing Cosimo III with his son, Gian Gastone (d. 1737), the last male Medici. In a nearby room is Fra' Filippo Lippi's *Madonna and Child*.

Off the courtyard, the **Museo dei Marmi** holds the Riccardi's sculpture collection, and a multimedia room explains the history of the chapel frescoes.

The Accademia

Via Ricasoli 66 • Tues–Sun 8.15am–6.50pm • €6.50, but more when special exhibitions are on • Ⓦ uffizi.firenze.it

Europe's first academy of drawing was founded northeast of San Lorenzo on Via Ricasoli in the mid-sixteenth century by Bronzino, Ammanati and Vasari. In 1784, Grand Duke Pietro Leopoldo opened the adjoining **Galleria dell'Accademia**, which has an impressive collection of paintings, especially of Florentine altarpieces from the fourteenth to the early sixteenth centuries. What pulls the crowds, however, is one of the most famous sculptures in the world: **Michelangelo's** *David*.

David

Commissioned by the Opera del Duomo in 1501, *David* was conceived to invoke parallels with Florence's freedom from outside domination (despite the superior force

9

of its enemies), and its recent liberation from Savonarola and the Medici. It's an incomparable show of technical bravura, all the more impressive given the difficulties posed by the marble from which it was carved. The four-metre block of stone – thin, shallow and riddled with cracks – had been quarried from Carrara forty years earlier. Several artists had already attempted to work with it, notably Agostino di Duccio, Andrea Sansovino and Leonardo da Vinci. Michelangelo succeeded where others had failed, completing the work in 1504 when he was still just 29.

When they gave Michelangelo his commission, the Opera del Duomo had in mind a large statue that would be placed high on the cathedral's facade. Perhaps because the finished *David* was even larger than had been envisaged, it was decided that it should be placed instead at ground level, in the Piazza della Signoria. The statue remained in its outdoor setting, exposed to the elements, until it was sent to the Accademia in 1873, by which time it had lost its gilded hair and the gilded band across its chest. *David* now occupies a specially built alcove, protected by a glass barrier that was built in 1991, after one of its toes was cracked by a hammer-wielding artist. With its massive head and gangling arms, *David* looks to some people like a monstrous adolescent, but its proportions would not have appeared so graceless in the setting for which it was first conceived, at a rather higher altitude and at a greater distance from the public than the position it occupies in this chapel-like space.

The Slaves

Michelangelo once described the process of sculpting as being the liberation of the form from within the stone, a notion that seems to be embodied by the unfinished **Slaves** that line the approach to *David*. His procedure, clearly demonstrated here, was to cut the figure as if it were a deep relief, and then to free the three-dimensional figure; often his assistants would perform the initial operation, working from the master's pencil marks, so it's possible that Michelangelo's own chisel never actually touched these stones. Carved in the 1520s and 1530s, these powerful creations were intended for the tomb of Pope Julius II, but in 1564 the artist's nephew gave them to the Medici, who installed them in the grotto of the Bóboli gardens.

The Museo di San Marco

Piazza San Marco • Mon–Fri 8.15am–1.50pm, Sat & Sun 8.15am–4.50pm, but closed second & fourth Mon of month and first, third & fifth Sun • €4 • ⓦ uffizi.firenze.it

A whole side of Piazza San Marco is taken up by the Dominican convent and church of San Marco, the first of which is now the **Museo di San Marco**. In the 1430s, the convent was the recipient of Cosimo il Vecchio's most lavish patronage: he financed Michelozzo's enlargement of the buildings, and went on to establish a vast public library here. Ironically, the convent became the centre of resistance to the Medici later in the century – Savonarola was prior of San Marco from 1491. Meanwhile, as Michelozzo was altering and expanding the convent, its walls were being decorated by one of its friars, **Fra' Angelico**, a painter in whom a medieval simplicity of faith was allied to a Renaissance sophistication of manner. The **Ospizio dei Pellegrini** (Pilgrims' Hospice) contains around twenty paintings by Fra' Angelico, most brought here from other churches in Florence, but the most celebrated work is the glorious **Annunciation** at the summit of the main staircase. All round this upper storey are ranged 44 tiny **dormitory cells**, each frescoed either by Angelico himself or by his assistants.

Spedale degli Innocenti

Piazza Santissima Annunziata • Daily 10am–7pm • €4 • ⓦ istitutodeglinnocenti.it

To the east of San Marco lies the handsome **Piazza Santissima Annunziata**, whose tone is set by Brunelleschi's **Spedale degli Innocenti**, which opened in 1445 as the first foundlings' hospital in Europe and still incorporates an orphanage – Luca della Robbia's ceramic tondi of swaddled babies advertise the building's function.

The convent, centred on two beautiful cloisters, now also contains a miscellany of Florentine Renaissance art including one of Luca della Robbia's most charming Madonnas and an incident-packed *Adoration of the Magi* by Ghirlandaio.

Santissima Annunziata

Piazza Santissima Annunziata • Daily 7am–12.30pm & 4–6.30pm, plus Sun 8.45–9.45pm • Free

The church of **Santissima Annunziata** is the mother church of the Servite order, which was founded by seven Florentine aristocrats in 1234. Its dedication took place in the fourteenth century, in recognition of a miraculous image of the Virgin which, left unfinished by the monastic artist, was purportedly completed by an angel. It attracted so many pilgrims that the Medici commissioned **Michelozzo** to rebuild the church in the second half of the fifteenth century in order to accommodate them. In the Chiostro dei Voti, the atrium that Michelozzo built onto the church, are some beautiful frescoes mainly painted in the 1510s, including a *Visitation* by **Pontormo** and a series by **Andrea del Sarto**. Inside the church, the miraculous painting is enshrined in a huge tabernacle to the left; in the second chapel along, there's a striking fresco by Andrea del Castagno, of the *Holy Trinity and St Jerome* (1454). The adjoining Chiostro dei Morti is worth visiting for Andrea del Sarto's *Madonna del Sacco*, painted over the door that connects the cloister to the left transept of the church.

The Museo Archeologico

Via della Colonna 36 • Tues–Fri 8.30am–7pm, Sat & Sun 8.30am–2pm • €4 • ⓦ firenzemusei.it/archeologico

On the other side of Via della Colonna from Santissima Annunziata, the **Museo Archeologico** houses the finest collection of its kind in northern Italy, but struggles to draw visitors for whom the Renaissance is the beginning and the end of Florence's appeal. Long-overdue renovation works are under way, so you can anticipate some disruption.

The museum's special strength is its **Etruscan** collection (much of it bequeathed by the Medici), which features two outstanding bronze sculptures – the *Arringatore* (Orator) and the *Chimera*, a triple-headed monster made in the fourth century BC. The **Egyptian collection** is mostly displayed in an uninspiring manner, but a recent renovation has vastly improved the top storey, where the primary focus is on the **Greek and Roman collections**. The star piece in the huge hoard of Greek vases is the large *François Vase*, a sixth-century-BC *krater* discovered in an Etruscan tomb near Chiusi in 1844. Other attention-grabbing items are the life-size bronze torso known as the *Torso di Livorno*, a large horse's head that was once a feature of the garden of the Palazzo Medici, two beautiful sixth-century-BC Greek *kouroi*, and the bronze statue of a young man known as the *Idilono di Pésaro*, generally thought to be a Roman replica of a Greek figure dating from around 100 BC.

The eastern city centre

The Santa Croce district – the hub of the eastern part of central Florence – was one of the city's more densely populated areas before November 4, 1966, when the Arno burst its banks, with catastrophic consequences for this low-lying zone, which was then packed with tenements and small workshops. Many residents moved out permanently in the following years, but now the more traditional businesses that survived the flood have been joined by a growing number of bars and restaurants. **Piazza Santa Croce**, one of the city's largest squares, has traditionally been used for ceremonies and festivities, and is still used for the **Calcio Storico**, a football tournament between the city's four *quartieri*. The contest is held in June, with the final on June 24, and is characterized by incomprehensible rules and an extraordinary degree of violence – the rules have recently been revised, but it used to be the case that virtually any method of tackling short of outright murder was permitted.

9

Santa Croce

Piazza Santa Croce • Mon–Sat 9.30am–5.30pm, Sun 2–5.30pm • €6, or €8.50 joint ticket with Casa Buonarroti • Ⓦ santacroceopera.it

Florence's two most lavish churches after the Duomo were the headquarters of two preaching orders: the Dominicans occupied Santa Maria Novella, while the Franciscans were based at **Santa Croce**, which also evolved into the mausoleum of Tuscany's most eminent citizens. More than 270 monuments are to be found here, commemorating the likes of Ghiberti, Michelangelo, Alberti, Machiavelli, Galileo and **Dante** – although Dante was actually buried in Ravenna, where he died.

The tombs are not the principal attraction of Santa Croce, however. Far more remarkable are the dazzling chapels at the east end, a compendium of Florentine fourteenth-century art, showing the extent of Giotto's influence and the full diversity of his followers. The two immediately to the right of the chancel are covered with frescoes by **Giotto**: beside the chancel is the **Cappella Bardi**, featuring scenes from the life of St Francis, while next to it is the **Cappella Peruzzi** with a cycle on the lives of St John the Baptist and John the Evangelist. On the south side of the right transept is the **Cappella Baroncelli**, featuring the first night-scene in Western painting, Taddeo Gaddi's *Annunciation to the Shepherds*. On the north side of the left transept, the second **Cappella Bardi** houses a wooden *Crucifix* by **Donatello** – supposedly criticized by Brunelleschi as resembling a "peasant on the Cross".

The Cappella dei Pazzi

The door in the south aisle opens onto the Primo Chiostro (First Cloister), at the head of which stands Brunelleschi's **Cappella dei Pazzi**. If one building could be said to typify the spirit of the early Renaissance, this is it: geometrically perfect without seeming pedantic, it's exemplary in the way its decorative detail harmonizes with the design. The polychrome lining of the portico's shallow cupola is by **Luca della Robbia**, as is the tondo of *St Andrew* over the door; inside, Della Robbia also produced the blue-and-white tondi of the *Apostles*.

Museo dell'Opera di Santa Croce

Santa Croce's spacious **Secondo Chiostro** was also designed by Brunelleschi, and is perhaps the most peaceful spot in the centre of Florence. The **Museo dell'Opera di Santa Croce**, between the two cloisters, houses a damaged *Crucifixion* by **Cimabue** on the right wall, which has become the emblem of the havoc caused by the 1966 flood – six metres of filthy water surged into the church, tearing the artwork from its mounting. Also in this room are Taddeo Gaddi's fresco of *The Last Supper*, Domenico Veneziano's *Sts John and Francis*, and **Donatello**'s enormous gilded *St Louis of Toulouse*, made for Orsanmichele.

Casa Buonarroti

Via Ghibellina 70 • Mon & Wed–Sun 10am–5pm • €6.50, or €8.50 joint ticket with Santa Croce • Ⓦ casabuonarroti.it

The **Casa Buonarroti** occupies a site where Michelangelo probably lived intermittently between 1516 and 1525, and contains a smart but low-key museum, mostly consisting of works created in homage to the great man. The two main treasures are to be found upstairs: the *Madonna della Scala* (c.1490–92) is Michelangelo's earliest known work, a delicate relief carved when he was no older than 16; the similarly unfinished *Battle of the Centaurs* was created shortly afterwards, when the boy was living in the Medici household. In an adjacent room you'll find the artist's wooden model (1517) for the facade of San Lorenzo. Close by is the largest of all the sculptural models on display, the torso of a *River God* (1524), a work in wood and wax probably intended for the Medici chapel in San Lorenzo.

South of the river – Oltrarno

Visitors to Florence might perceive the Arno as merely a brief interruption in the urban fabric, but Florentines talk as though a ravine divides their city. North of the river is

Arno di quà ("over here"), while the south side is *Arno di là* ("over there"), also known as the **Oltrarno**, literally "Beyond the Arno". Traditionally an artisans' quarter, Oltrarno is still home to plenty of small workshops (particularly furniture restorers and leather-workers), and Via Maggio remains the focus of Florence's thriving antiques trade. The ambience is distinctly less tourist-centred here than in the zone immediately across the water, which is not to say that Oltrarno doesn't have major sights – **Palazzo Pitti**, **Santa Maria del Carmine**, **San Miniato** and **Santo Spirito** are all essential visits.

The Ponte Vecchio

The direct route from the city centre to the heart of Oltrarno crosses the river on the **Ponte Vecchio**, the only bridge not mined by the retreating Nazis in 1944. Built in 1345 to replace an ancient wooden bridge, it has always been loaded with shops. Up until the sixteenth century, butchers, fishmongers and tanners occupied the bridge, but in 1593 Ferdinando I ejected these malodorous enterprises and installed goldsmiths instead. Today, still replete with jewellery firms, the bridge is crammed with sightseers and big-spending shoppers during the day, and remains busy after the shutters come down.

Santa Felicità

Piazza Santa Felicità • Mon–Sat 9.30am–12.30pm & 3.30–5.30pm • Free

Just over the bridge, off Via Guicciardini, **Santa Felicità** might well be the oldest church in Florence. It's thought to have been founded in the second century AD close to the Via Cassia, over an early Christian cemetery that's commemorated by the column outside. The interior demands a visit for the amazing paintings by Pontormo in the **Cappella Capponi**. Under the cupola are four tondi of the *Evangelists*, painted with the help of Bronzino (his adoptive son), while on opposite sides of the window on the right wall are the *Virgin* and the angel of Pontormo's delightfully simple *Annunciation*. The centrepiece is the **Deposition** (1525–28), one of the masterworks of Florentine Mannerism, in which there's no sign of the Cross, the thieves, soldiers, or any of the other scene-setting devices usual in paintings of this subject.

Palazzo Pitti

Piazza Pitti • ⊕ uffizi.firenze.it

Although the Medici later took possession of the largest palace in Florence – **Palazzo Pitti** – it still bears the name of the man for whom it was built. Luca Pitti was a prominent rival of Cosimo il Vecchio, and much of the impetus behind the building of his new house came from a desire to trump the Medici. No sooner was the palace completed, however, than the Pittis' fortunes began to decline and by 1549 they were forced to sell. The palace then became the Medici family pile, growing in bulk until the seventeenth century, when it achieved its present gargantuan dimensions.

Galleria Palatina

Tues–Sun 8.15am–6.50pm • €8.50, including admission to the Galleria d'Arte Moderna, but more if a special exhibition is on, which is usually the case

Today, the *palazzo* and the pavilions of the **Giardino di Bóboli** hold eight museums, of which the foremost is the huge art collection of the **Galleria Palatina**. **Andrea del Sarto** is represented by no fewer than seventeen paintings, but even more remarkable is the assembly of work by **Raphael**, including portraits of Angelo and Maddalena Doni, the celebrated *Madonna della Seggiola*, and the equally famous *Donna Velata*, for which the model was the painter's mistress, a Roman baker's daughter known to posterity as La Fornarina. An even larger contingent of supreme works by **Titian** includes a number of his most trenchant portraits – among them *Pietro Aretino*, *Cardinal Ippolito de' Medici*, and the *Portrait of an Englishman*, a picture that makes the viewer feel as closely scrutinized as was the subject. Elsewhere in the Palatina you'll find masterpieces by Rubens, Fra' Filippo Lippi and Caravaggio, to mention but a few.

9

Much of the rest of this floor comprises the **Appartamenti Reali** – the Pitti's state rooms, renovated by the dukes of Lorraine in the eighteenth century, and then again by King Vittorio Emanuele when Florence became Italy's capital.

Galleria d'Arte Moderna

Tues–Sat 8.15am–6.50pm • €8.50, including admission to the Galleria Palatina, but more if a special exhibition is on, which is usually the case

On the floor above is the **Galleria d'Arte Moderna**, which comprises a chronological survey of primarily Tuscan art from the mid-eighteenth century to 1945. Much space is devoted to the work of the Macchiaioli (the open-air painters who were in some respects the Italian equivalent of the Impressionists), but there's a lot of mediocre stuff here, with ranks of academically proficient portraits, bombastic history paintings and sentimental dross such as Rodolfo Morgari's *Raphael Dying* and Gabriele Castagnola's depiction of Fra' Filippo Lippi on the brink of kissing the lovely young novice, Lucrezia Buti.

Museo degli Argenti, Galleria del Costume and Museo delle Porcellane

All open daily at 8.15am; March closes 5.30pm; April, May, Sept & Oct closes 6.30pm; June–Aug closes 7.30pm; Nov–Feb closes 4.30pm; closed first & last Mon of month • €10 joint ticket for all three museums, plus Giardino di Bóboli & Giardino Bardini

Entered from the garden courtyard, the **Museo degli Argenti** is a massive collection of portable (and often hideous) luxury artefacts, including Lorenzo il Magnifico's trove of antique vases, displayed in one of the four splendidly frescoed reception rooms on the ground floor.

Visitors without a specialist interest are unlikely to be riveted by the other Pitti museums. In the Palazzina della Meridiana, the eighteenth-century southern wing of the Pitti, the **Galleria del Costume** provides the opportunity to see the dress that Eleonora di Toledo is wearing in Bronzino's famous portrait of her (in the Palazzo Vecchio). The well-presented if esoteric collection of porcelain, the **Museo delle Porcellane**, is located on the other side of the Bóboli garden.

The Giardino di Bóboli

Opens daily at 8.15am; March closes 5.30pm; April, May, Sept & Oct closes 6.30pm; June–Aug closes 7.30pm; Nov–Feb closes 4.30pm; closed 1st & last Mon of month • €10 joint ticket with Museo degli Argenti, Museo delle Porcellane, Galleria del Costume & Giardino Bardini

The delightful formal garden of the Palazzo Pitti, the **Giardino di Bóboli** takes its name from the Bóboli family, erstwhile owners of much of this area, which was once a quarry. When the Medici acquired the house in 1549 they set to work transforming their back yard into a 111-acre garden. Of all the garden's Mannerist embellishments, the most celebrated is the **Grotta del Buontalenti**, beyond the turtle-back figure of Cosimo I's court dwarf (as seen on a thousand postcards). In among the fake stalactites are shepherds and sheep that look like calcified sponges, while embedded in the corners are replicas of Michelangelo's *Slaves*, replacing the originals that were here until 1908. In the deepest recesses of the cave stands Giambologna's *Venus*, leered at by attendant imps.

La Specola

Via Romana 17 • Tues–Sun 9.30am–4.30pm • €6 • Ⓦ msn.unifi.it/CMpro-l-s-11.html

Within a stone's throw of the Pitti, on the third floor of one of the university buildings, you'll find what can reasonably claim to be the strangest museum in the city. Taking its name from the telescope (*specola*) on its roof, **La Specola** is a museum of zoology, housing ranks of shells, insects and crustaceans, and a veritable ark of animals stuffed, pickled and desiccated. The exhibits everyone comes to see, however, are the **Cere Anatomiche** (Anatomical Waxworks): wax arms, legs and internal organs cover the walls, arrayed around satin beds on which wax cadavers recline in progressive stages of deconstruction, each muscle fibre and nerve cluster moulded and dyed with scarcely believable precision. Most of the six hundred models – and nearly all of the amazing full-body mannequins – were made between 1775 and 1791 by one Clemente Susini and his team of assistants, and were intended as teaching aids.

Santo Spirito

Piazza di Santa Spirito • Mon, Tues & Thurs–Sat 9.30am–12.30pm & 4–5.30pm, Sun 4–5.30pm • Free

With its market stalls, cafés and restaurants, the lively **Piazza Santo Spirito** is the social hub of this quarter. Don't be deterred by the vacant facade of the church of **Santo Spirito** – the interior, one of Brunelleschi's last projects, prompted Bernini to describe it as "the most beautiful church in the world". It's so perfectly proportioned it seems artless, yet the plan is extremely sophisticated – a Latin cross with a continuous chain of 38 chapels round the outside and a line of columns running parallel to the chapels, right round the building. Unfortunately, a Baroque baldachin covers the high altar, but this is the sole disruption of Brunelleschi's arrangement. The best of the church's paintings, Filippino Lippi's **Nerli Altarpiece**, is in the south transept.

A door in the north aisle leads through to Giuliano da Sangallo's stunning vestibule and **sacristy** (1489–93), the latter designed in imitation of Brunelleschi's Pazzi chapel. Hanging above the altar is a delicate wooden crucifix, attributed to **Michelangelo**. It's known that the young Michelangelo was commissioned by the monks of Santo Spirito to make a crucifix for the church in the early 1490s, but many scholars think that this one was made half a century later, by Taddeo Curradi.

The Cappella Brancacci

Piazza del Carmine • Mon & Wed–Sat 10am–5pm, Sun 1–5pm • €6 • Tickets must be reserved on ☎ 055 276 8224 (daily 9am–5pm) at least a day in advance • ⊕ museicivicifiorentini.it

In 1771 fire wrecked the Carmelite convent and church of **Santa Maria del Carmine** some 300m west of Santo Spirito, but somehow the flames did not damage the frescoes of the church's **Cappella Brancacci**, a cycle of paintings that is one of the essential sights of Florence. The chapel is barricaded off from the rest of the Carmine, and visits are restricted to a maximum of thirty people at a time, for an inadequate fifteen minutes.

The decoration of the chapel was begun in 1424 by **Masolino** and **Masaccio**, when the former was aged 41 and the latter just 22. Within a short time the elder was taking lessons from the younger, whose grasp of the texture of the real world, of the principles of perspective, and of the dramatic potential of the biblical texts they were illustrating far exceeded that of his precursors. In 1428 Masolino was called away to Rome, where he was followed by Masaccio a few months later. Neither would return to the chapel. Masaccio died the same year, aged just 27, but, in the words of Vasari, "All the most celebrated sculptors and painters since Masaccio's day have become excellent and illustrious by studying their art in this chapel."

The Brancacci frescoes are as startling as the Sistine Chapel in Rome, the brightness and delicacy of their colours and the solidity of the figures exemplifying what Bernard Berenson singled out as the tactile quality of Florentine art. The small scene on the left of the entrance arch is the quintessence of Masaccio's art. Depictions of **The Expulsion of Adam and Eve** had never before captured the desolation of the sinners so graphically – Adam presses his hands to his face in bottomless despair, Eve raises her head and screams. In contrast to the emotional charge of Masaccio's couple, Masolino's dainty *Adam and Eve*, opposite, pose as if to have their portraits painted.

St Peter is chief protagonist of most of the remaining scenes, some of which were left unfinished in 1428 – work did not resume until 1480, when the frescoes were completed by **Filippino Lippi**. One of the scenes finished by Lippi is the *Raising of Theophilus's Son and St Peter Enthroned*, which depicts St Peter bringing the son of the Prefect of Antioch to life and then preaching to the people of the city from a throne. The three figures to the right of the throne are thought to be Masaccio, Alberti and Brunelleschi.

9

Giardino Bardini

Entrances at Costa di San Giorgio 2 and Via de' Bardi 1/R • Opens daily at 8.15am; March closes 5.30pm; April, May, Sept & Oct closes 6.30pm; June–Aug closes 7.30pm; Nov–Feb closes 4.30pm; closed 1st & last Mon of month • €10 joint ticket with Museo degli Argenti, Museo delle Porcellane, Galleria del Costume & Giardino di Bóboli • ⓦ bardinipeyron.it

The **Giardino Bardini** occupies the slope that was formerly the olive grove of the **Palazzo dei Mozzi**, a colossal house built in the late thirteenth century by the Mozzi family, at that time one of the richest families in Florence. After Stefano Bardini (see below) bought the property in 1913 he set about creating a semi-formal garden which has now been restored to its original appearance, with a neo-Baroque staircase and terraces dividing the fruit-growing section from the miniature woodland of the "*bosco inglese*". At the summit of the garden, reached by a lovely long pergola of wisteria and hortensia, a colonnaded belvedere gives a splendid view of the city.

Villa Bardini

Costa di San Giorgio 2 • Tues–Sun 10am–7pm • €6 • ⓦ bardinipeyron.it

At the top of the Giardino Bardini stands the **Villa Bardini**, which was built in the seventeenth century and extended by Stefano Bardini. Having been thoroughly restored, the villa is used as an exhibition space and also houses a museum dedicated to **Pietro Annigoni** (1910–88), a vehemently anti-Modernist painter who was best known for his portraits of luminaries such as Pope John XXIII and Queen Elizabeth II.

Museo Stefano Bardini

Piazza de' Mozzi 1 • Mon & Fri–Sun 11am–5pm • €6 • ⓦ museicivicifiorentini.it

The **Museo Stefano Bardini**, which stands at the end of the handsome Via de' Bardi, houses the collection of **Stefano Bardini** (1836–1922), once the most important art dealer in Italy, whose tireless activity laid the cornerstone of many important European and American museums. Determined that no visitor to his native city should remain unaware of his success, he bought the former monastery of San Gregorio alla Pace, and converted it into a vast house for himself and his collection. Sculpture, paintings, ceramics, armour, furniture, picture frames, carpets, wooden ceilings, tombstones – Bardini bought it all, and he bequeathed the whole lot to the city. Reopened in 2011 after a protracted restoration, the museum now looks much as it did when Bardini died, though a few pieces – notably Pietro Tacca's bronze boar and Giambologna's so-called *Diavolino* (Little Devil) – were added after his death.

The Bardini is more like a colossal showroom than a modern museum, with items strewn all about the place, many of them unlabelled: on the **ground floor**, for example, Tino da Camaino's *Charity* is one of the very few pieces to be individually identified. The most interesting items are **upstairs**, where you'll find two reliefs of the *Madonna and Child* that may be by Donatello (in a room that's stacked with similar reliefs), a beautiful terracotta *Virgin Annunciate* from fifteenth-century Siena, and some fine drawings by Giambattista Tiepolo and his son Lorenzo.

San Miniato al Monte

Via del Monte alle Croci • Daily: summer 8am–8pm; winter 8am–1pm & 3.30–7pm • Free

The brilliant, multicoloured facade of **San Miniato al Monte** lures hordes of visitors up the hill on which it sits, and it more than fulfils the promise of its appearance from a distance: this is the finest Romanesque church in Tuscany. The church's dedicatee, St Minias, belonged to a Christian community that settled in Florence in the third century; according to legend, after his martyrdom his corpse was seen to carry his severed head over the river and up the hill to this spot, where a shrine was subsequently erected to him. Construction of the present building began in 1013 with the foundation of a Cluniac monastery. The gorgeous marble facade – alluding to the Baptistry in its geometrical patterning – was added towards the end of that century, though the external mosaic *Christ between the Virgin and St Minias* dates from the thirteenth.

The interior

The **interior** is like no other in the city, with the choir raised on a platform above the large crypt. The main structural addition is the Cappella del Cardinale del Portogallo, a paragon of artistic collaboration: the basic design was by Antonio Manetti (a pupil of Brunelleschi), the tomb was carved by Antonio Rossellino, the terracotta decoration of the ceiling is by Luca della Robbia, and the paintings are by Alesso Baldovinetti, except for the altarpiece, which is a copy of a work by the Pollaiuolo brothers (the original is in the Uffizi). Be sure to also visit the sacristy, which is covered in *Scenes from the Life of St Benedict*, painted in the 1380s by Spinello Aretino.

ARRIVAL AND DEPARTURE — FLORENCE

By plane Pisa's Galileo Galilei airport (see box, p.558) is the main airport for Tuscany. A small number of international air services use Peretola (or Amerigo Vespucci) airport (T 055 306 1300, W aeroporto.firenze.it), 5km northwest of the city centre; the Volainbus service provides shuttles from here into Florence Santa Maria Novella station every 30min.

By train Nearly all trains arrive at Santa Maria Novella station (Firenze SMN), a few blocks west of the Duomo. A few trains use Campo di Marte, over in the east of the city, from where there are regular buses into the centre.

Destinations Arezzo (hourly; 1hr); Assisi (8 daily; 2hr–2hr 30min); Bologna (every 30min; 1hr–1hr 40min); Genoa (2 daily; 3hr 10min); Lucca (every 30min; 1hr 15min–1hr 45min); Milan (hourly; 2hr 45min–3hr 30min); Naples (hourly; 3hr 30min–5hr); Perugia (8 daily; 1hr 35min–2hr 10min); Pisa (every 30min; 60–1hr 20min); Pistoia (every 20–30min; 40–55min); Prato (every 20–30min; 20–30min); Rome (every 20min; 1hr 45min–3hr 40min); Siena (hourly, via Empoli; 1hr 30min–2hr); Venice (9 daily; 2hr 50min–3hr 45min); Verona (6 daily; 2hr 20min–2hr 45min).

By bus The state-owned SITA bus terminal is on Via di Santa Caterina da Siena, a few steps west of the station; private CAP, Rama, Lazzi and Copit buses operate from the east side of the train station. The main SITA services are listed below; in addition to these, the private bus companies operate services to most Tuscan towns, including Arezzo, Lucca and Pisa.

Destinations Castellina in Chianti (3 daily; 1hr 35min); Greve in Chianti (3 daily; 1hr 5min); Radda in Chianti (2–3 daily Mon–Sat; 1hr 35min); Siena (30 daily; 1hr 20min–3hr); Volterra (6 daily; 2hr 25min).

By car Only residents are allowed to park in the centre, so you have to leave your car in one of the main car parks, unless you're staying at a hotel with reserved spaces. North of the Arno, the car parks nearest the centre are underneath the train station, just off Piazza della Libertà, and at Piazza Annigoni, near Santa Croce; south of the river the best option is Piazza della Calza, at the southwest tip of the Bóboli garden. For free parking the best place is Piazzale Michelangelo, which is about a 20min walk from Piazza della Signoria, or a short ride on bus #12 or #13.

GETTING AROUND

Florence is a small city and walking is the most efficient way of getting around the centre; it's also much more pleasant than it used to be, now that most of the *centro storico*, all the way from the Palazzo Medici to the Palazzo Pitti, has been closed to inessential traffic.

Buses For cross-town journeys you might want to use ATAF buses (W ataf.net). Tickets are valid for unlimited journeys within 90min (€1.20), 24hr (€5) or 72hr (€12). A Biglietto Multiplo gives four 90min tickets for €4.50; better value is the ATAF electronic card called the Carnet Agile, which comes in two versions – the €10 one gives ten 90min tickets, while the €20 card is equivalent to 21.

The Tramvia The first line of the city's controversial Tramvia tram system was completed in 2010, but it's a commuter line that's of no use to tourists. Line #2, scheduled for completion in 2014, was originally planned to go from Peretola airport to Piazza della Libertà, via Piazza del Duomo, but its route is now being reassessed.

FLORENCE ADDRESSES

Florence has a complicated double system of street numbering: commercial establishments (such as bars and restaurants) have red numbers (*rosso*), while private buildings have black or blue numbers – and the two systems don't run in tandem. This means, for example, that no. 35/R might be next door to no. 89 and a hundred metres from no. 33.

9

INFORMATION

Tourist offices The main tourist office is at Via Cavour 1/R, a 5min walk north of the Duomo (Mon–Sat 8.30am–6.30pm, Sun 8.30am–1.30pm; ☎ 055 290 832, ⍵ firenzeturismo.it); this office provides information not just on the city but on the whole of Florence province. Smaller offices are to be found in the Loggia del Bigallo, by the Baptistry (March–Oct Mon–Sat 9am–7pm, Sun 9am–2pm; Nov–March Mon–Sat 9am–5pm, Sun 9am–2pm), and opposite the train station, at Piazza della

Stazione 4 (Mon–Sat 8.30am–7pm, Sun 8.30am–2pm).
Magazines A good source of information on events is *Firenze Spettacolo* (⍵ firenzespettacolo.it; €2), a monthly, partly bilingual listings magazine available from bookshops and larger newsstands. Also useful is *The Florentine*, a free bi-weekly English-language paper, available at the tourist office, most bookshops and various other spots (listed at ⍵ theflorentine.net).

ACCOMMODATION

Hotels are plentiful in Florence but demand is almost limitless, which means that prices are high and the tourist inundation has few slack spots: "low season" is defined by most hotels as meaning mid-July to the end of August (the weeks during which nearly all Italians head for the beaches or the mountains), and from mid-November to mid-March, except for the Christmas and New Year period; between March and October, booking ahead is strongly advised. In recent years, boutique hotels and B&Bs have sprung up all over the city, operating under several different labels: places calling themselves a *relais* or a *residenza d'epoca* are generally smart B&Bs, often located in historic *palazzi*. The Via Cavour tourist office has a full accommodation list, or see ⍵ firenzeturismo.it.

HOTELS, RESIDENZE AND B&BS

THE CITY CENTRE

★ **Alessandra** Borgo SS. Apostoli 17 ☎ 055 283 438, ⍵ hotelalessandra.com; map pp.520–521. One of the best and friendliest of the central two-stars, with 27 rooms occupying a sixteenth-century *palazzo* and furnished in a mixture of antique and modern styles. The more expensive en-suite doubles overlook the river; those with shared bathrooms are considerably cheaper. **€160**

Cestelli Borgo SS. Apostoli 25 ☎ 055 214 213, ⍵ hotel cestelli.com; map pp.520–521. Spotlessly maintained by its young Florentine–Japanese owners and offering excellent value for money, this eight-roomed one-star occupies part of a house that once belonged to a minor Medici. The rooms are a good size, and most are en suite. **€100**

★ **Helvetia & Bristol** Via dei Pescioni 2 ☎ 055 266 51, ⍵ royaldemeure.com; map pp.520–521. In business since 1894, this is a superb five-star hotel. The rooms mix antique furnishings and modern facilities – such as hydromassage baths – to create a style that evokes the *belle époque* without being suffocatingly nostalgic. The standard rooms are not huge, but have lovely marble bathrooms; the superior rooms and suites are worth the splurge. If you're going to treat yourself, this is a leading contender. **€300**

Hermitage Vicolo Marzio 1/Piazza del Pesce ☎ 055 287 216, ⍵ hermitagehotel.com; map pp.520–521. Pre-booking is recommended at any time of year to secure one of the 28 rooms in this superbly located three-star hotel, right next to the Ponte Vecchio. The service is friendly, the rooms are cosy, and there are unbeatable views from some rooms, as well as from the flower-filled roof garden. **€150**

Porta Rossa Via Porta Rossa 19 ☎ 055 271 0911, ⍵ nh-hotels.it; map pp.520–521. Florence's most venerable

four-star hotel, the 72-room *Porta Rossa* has been in business since the beginning of the nineteenth century and has hosted, among others, Byron and Stendhal. Recently reopened after a long renovation, it retains something of its old ambience while the rooms have been fitted out in crisp but luxuriously modern style, with red and white the dominant tones. **€180**

Torre Guelfa Borgo SS. Apostoli 8 ☎ 055 239 6338, ⍵ hoteltorreguelfa.com; map pp.520–521. There are twenty tastefully furnished rooms crammed into this ancient tower, the tallest private building in the city. Guests can enjoy the marvellous views all over the city from the tower's small roof terrace. Very charismatic and one of the most popular three-stars in Florence – book well ahead. **€130**

THE SANTA MARIA NOVELLA AREA

J.K. Place Piazza S. Maria Novella 7 ☎ 055 264 5181, ⍵ jkplace.com; map pp.520–521. One of the most appealing of Florence's designer hotels occupies a fine eighteenth-century building on Piazza Santa Maria Novella. The twenty rooms of this elegant townhouse have been designed by Michele Bönan in retro-modernist hybrid style, and have DVD players and flat-screen TVs. **€350**

Nizza Via del Giglio 5 ☎ 055 239 6897, ⍵ hotelnizza .com; map pp.520–521. A smart family-run two star, with helpful staff and a very central location. All rooms are en suite – the five out back are quieter – and are better furnished and decorated than many in this category. **€80**

NORTH OF THE CENTRE

Antica Dimora Firenze Via S. Gallo 72 ☎ 055 462 7296, ⍵ johanna.it; map pp.514–515. This plush *residenza*, run by the owners of the neighbouring *Antica Dimora Johlea* and *Residenza Johlea*, has six very comfortable double rooms, some with four-poster beds. **€160**

★ **Antica Dimora Johlea** Via S. Gallo 80 ☎ 055 461 185, ⊕ johanna.it; map pp.514–515. Slightly pricier and a little more luxurious than the *Antica Dimora Firenze*, this lovely *residenza* also has a nice roof terrace, giving a roofline view of the Duomo and the hills beyond. **€170**

Azzi Via Faenza 56 ☎ 055 213 806, ⊕ hotelazzi.com; map pp.514–515. This two-star has fifteen bedrooms decorated in a cosily rustic style, with antique furnishings and garden views from most rooms. The management also has two rooms and an apartment over the road. **€120**

Casci Via Cavour 13 ☎ 055 211 686, ⊕ hotelcasci.com; map pp.520–521. It would be hard to find a better two-star in central Florence than this 26-room hotel, which occupies part of a building in which Rossini once lived. Only two (sound-proofed) rooms face the busy street; the rest are very quiet, and all are clean and neat. The welcome is warm and the owners helpful. The big buffet breakfast under the frescoed ceiling of the reception area is a plus, as is free internet. **€120**

Kursaal Ausonia Via Nazionale 24 ☎ 055 496 324, ⊕ kursonia.com; map pp.514–515. Welcoming, recently refurbished three-star near the station, with accommodation ranging from spacious "superior" doubles, in faux-antique style, to rather more bland and functional "standard" rooms. **€120**

★ **Loggiato dei Serviti** Piazza Santissima Annunziata 3 ☎ 055 289 592, ⊕ loggiatodeiservitihotel .it; map pp.520–521. The 38 rooms of this elegant, extremely tasteful three-star hotel have been incorporated into a building designed in the sixteenth century to accommodate Servite priests. All the rooms are decorated with fine fabrics and antiques, and look out onto either the piazza, the peaceful gardens to the rear, or towards the Duomo. The five rooms in the annexe, at Via dei Servi 49, are similarly styled, but don't have the same charm. **€150**

Merlini Via Faenza 56 ☎ 055 212 848, ⊕ hotelmerlini .it; map pp.514–515. Several budget hotels are crammed into this address, but the family-run *Merlini*, on the third floor (no lift), is the best. Its ten rooms have marble bathrooms – an unexpected bonus in this price bracket – and six give views of the Duomo. **€110**

Morandi alla Crocetta Via Laura 50 ☎ 055 234 4747, ⊕ hotelmorandi.it; map pp.520–521. An intimate three-star gem, whose small size and friendly welcome ensure a home-from-home atmosphere. Rooms are tastefully decorated with antiques and old prints, and vivid carpets laid on parquet floors. Two rooms have balconies opening onto a modest garden; the best room – with fresco fragments and medieval nooks – was converted from a convent chapel. **€120**

Mr. Myresort Via delle Ruote 14/A ☎ 055 283 955, ⊕ mrflorence.it; map pp.514–515. Run by the same friendly family as *Relais Grand Tour* (see below), this luxury B&B has five bright, quirkily furnished rooms arranged around a tranquil garden, but the real draw is the private,

stone-walled spa in the basement, complete with Turkish bath and jacuzzi. **€160**

★ **Relais Grand Tour** Via S. Reparata 21 ☎ 055 283 955, ⊕ florencegrandtour.com; map pp.514–515. The very hospitable owners have done a great job of turning two floors of this old *palazzo* into a superb guesthouse, with three charming rooms on the second floor and three suites on the floor below. Each room is unique – the "mirrors suite" is much requested by honeymooners. **€140**

Residenza Castiglioni Via del Giglio 8 ☎ 055 239 6013, ⊕ residenzacastiglioni.com; map pp.520–521. This discreet and hugely stylish hideaway has just half a dozen spacious en-suite double rooms (three of them frescoed), on the second floor of a *palazzo* very close to San Lorenzo church. Room 22 is the one to go for, with wall-to-wall frescoes. **€130**

Residenza Johanna I Via Bonifacio Lupi 14 ☎ 055 481 896, ⊕ johanna.it; map pp.514–515. The longest-established of the *Johanna/Johlea* family of *residenze*, this genteel place is hidden away in an unmarked apartment building in a quiet, leafy corner of the city, a 5min walk north of San Marco. Rooms are cosy and well kept, and the management are as friendly and helpful as you could hope for. **€130**

Residenza Johanna II Via Cinque Giornate 12 ☎ 055 473 377, ⊕ johanna.it; map pp.514–515. The location of this *residenza* – to the north of the Fortezza da Basso – is a little less convenient than that of its siblings (see above and below), but the accommodation is of the same high standard, as is the hospitality. **€110**

Residenza Johlea Via S. Gallo 76 ☎ 055 463 3292, ⊕ johanna.it; map pp.514–515. Another venture from the owners of *Residenza Johanna*, offering the same low-cost, high-comfort package. **€130**

OLTRARNO

La Scaletta Via Guicciardini 13 ☎ 055 283 028, ⊕ lascaletta.com; map pp.520–521. Some of the rooms in this tidy and recently refurbished sixteen-room two-star give views across to the Bóboli garden; those on the Via Guiccardini side are double-glazed against the traffic. Drinks are served on the rooftop terraces, where you look across the Bóboli in one direction and the city in the other. All rooms are en suite and nicely decorated in creamy tones. **€125**

★ **Palazzo Guadagni** Piazza Santo Spirito 9 ☎ 055 265 8376, ⊕ palazzoguadagni.com; map pp.520–521. Beautifully refurbished in 2009, this three-star hotel has 15 rooms on three floors, furnished with family antiques. The middle floor is nicest, particularly room 10, with its frescoed ceiling. The lovely loggia gets the evening sun – the perfect place to wind down with an *aperitivo*. **€140**

HOSTELS

★ **Academy Hostel** Via Ricasoli 9 ☎ 055 239 8665, ⊕ academyhostel.eu; map pp.520–521. Since opening in

9

2008, this modern hostel has won awards for its service and excellent facilities: set in a seventeenth-century *palazzo*, it offers airy, high-ceilinged rooms and a common area with huge flat-screen TV, book and DVD library and lots of computer terminals, plus a sunny terrace. All this, and an unbeatable location – just steps from the Duomo. Breakfast and internet included. From €30 per person

Archi Rossi Via Faenza 94/R ☎055 290 804, ⓦ hostelarchirossi.com; map pp.514–515. A 5min walk from the train station, this privately owned hostel is spotlessly clean and decorated with guests' wall-paintings and graffiti. It's popular – the 140 beds fill up quickly – and has a pleasant garden and terrace. There are some basic en-suite doubles too (on the third floor; no lift), and a restaurant serving cheap meals. Breakfast and internet included. Dorms from €22, single rooms from €40

Foresteria Valdese Firenze–Istituto Gould Via dei Serragli 49 ☎055 212 576, ⓦ istitutogould.it; map pp.520–521. Run by the Waldensian Church, this hostel-cum-evangelical college occupies part of a seventeenth-century *palazzo* between Santo Spirito and the Carmine. The 99 beds (in 39 rooms) are extremely popular, so book in advance, especially during the academic year. Street-front rooms can be noisy (rear rooms cost a little more), but the old courtyard, terracotta floors and stone staircases provide atmosphere throughout. Check-in Mon–Fri 8.45am–1pm & 3–7.30pm, Sat 9am–1.30pm & 2.30–6pm; reception closed Sun. No curfew. Dorms from €22, single rooms from €45

Santa Monaca Via S. Monaca 6 ☎055 268 338, ⓦ ostello.it; a 10min walk from the station, or take bus #11, #36 or #37 to the second stop after the bridge; map pp.520–521. This privately owned hostel in Oltrarno has

112 beds (female-only and mixed), arranged in a dozen dorms with between two and twenty beds. Kitchen facilities, laundry and free internet; meals are available but are not included. Check-in 6am–2am; lock-out 10am–2pm. Curfew 2am. Dorms from €17

Villa Camerata Viale Augusto Righi 2–4 ☎055 601 451, ⓦ ostellofirenze.it; buses #17a and #17b from the station; map pp.514–515. This HI hostel in a beautiful park 5km northeast of the city is one of Europe's most attractive hostels, a sixteenth-century house with frescoed ceilings. There are 320 beds, and a few private rooms. Films in English are shown every night. Breakfast is included, but there are no kitchen facilities; dinner costs around €12. Check-in from 2pm. Dorms from €18

CAMPING

Camping Michelangelo Viale Michelangiolo 80 ☎055 681 1977, ⓦ ecvacanze.it; take bus #13 from the train station; map pp.514–515. A 240-pitch site that's always crowded, owing to its superb hillside location in an olive grove overlooking the city centre. It has kitchen facilities and a well-stocked, if expensive, shop nearby. Open all year. From €9.50 per adult; pitches from €11.50

Camping Panoramico Via Peramondo 1, Fiesole ☎055 559 069, ⓦ florencecamping.com. Located in Fiesole (see p.549), this 120-pitch three-star site has a bar, restaurant, pool and small supermarket. Mid-March to Dec. From €9 per adult and €6 per tent

Villa Camerata Viale Augusto Righi 2–4 ☎055 601 451, ⓦ ostellofirenze.it; buses #17a and #17b from the station; map pp.514–515. A basic, 55-pitch site in the grounds of the *Villa Camerata* HI hostel. Open all year.

EATING AND DRINKING

As you'd expect in a major tourist city, Florence has plenty of **restaurants**, but – unsurprisingly – a large number of them are aimed squarely at the outsiders, so standards are often patchy. But the situation is nowhere near as bad as some would have it – in fact it's been improving in recent years, with the appearance of several stylish and good-value restaurants. Bear in mind also that simple meals are served in many Florentine bars and cafés, so if you fancy a quick bite to eat rather than a full-blown restaurant meal, take a look at our listings for cafés and bars.

CAFÉS, BARS AND GELATERIE

As elsewhere in Italy, the distinction between Florentine bars and cafés can be tricky to the point of impossibility, as almost every café serves alcohol and almost every bar serves coffee. That said, there are some cafés in which the emphasis is on coffee, cakes and ice cream, just as there are some bars – *enoteche* – where the enjoyment of wine is

the chief point of the exercise. That said, almost all *enoteche* also serve food, and in some instances they've evolved into restaurants with huge wine lists – places like that have been listed under "Restaurants". Just to complicate things further, some of Florence's coolest bars are clubs in all but name – you'll find the best of them listed here. Devotees of Italian **ice cream** will find that Florence offers plenty of

---

PICNIC SUPPLIES

For **picnic supplies** an obvious place to shop is the Mercato Centrale by San Lorenzo church, where everything you could possibly need can be bought under one roof: bread, ham, cheese, fruit, wine, ready-made sandwiches. The Mercato Sant'Ambrogio over by Santa Croce is smaller but of comparable quality.

9

TOP 5 PLACES FOR OUTDOOR DRINKING

Caffè Gilli p.543
Dolce Vita p.543
Il Rifrullo p.544
Le Volpi e L'Uva p.544
Zoe p.544

opportunities to indulge: the city has several superb *gelaterie*, and many would claim that *Vivoli* is one of the top purveyors in the country.

CITY CENTRE

All'Antico Vinaio Via dei Neri 65/R ☏ 055 238 2723; map pp.520–521. Though recently revamped, this wine bar – located between the Uffizi and Santa Croce – preserves much of the rough-and-ready atmosphere that's made it one of Florence's most popular wine bars for the last hundred years. Also serves coffee, rolls and pasta. Mon–Sat 8am–10pm; closed three weeks late July & early Aug.

Caffè Gilli Piazza della Repubblica 36–39/R ☏ 055 213 896; map pp.520–521. Founded in 1733, *Gilli* is the most appealing of this square's expensive cafés. The lavish *belle époque* interior is a sight in itself, but most people choose to sit on the big outdoor terrace. Daily 8am–midnight.

Cantinetta dei Verrazzano Via dei Tavolini 18–20/R ☏ 055 268 590; map pp.520–521. Owned by a major Chianti vineyard, this wood-panelled place near Orsanmichele is part-bar, part-café and part-bakery, making its own excellent pizza, *focaccia* and cakes. Sept–June Mon–Sat 8am–9pm, Sun 10am–4.30pm; end July & Aug Mon–Sat 8am–4pm; closed first three weeks July.

I Fratellini Via dei Cimatori 38/R ☏ 055 239 6096; map pp.520–521. This minuscule stand-up bar – which attracts a melee most lunchtimes – has been in operation since the 1870s; Armando and Michele, the current proprietors, serve 29 varieties of panini, and local wines by the glass. Daily 9am–8pm.

Perchè No! Via de' Tavolini 19/R ☏ 055 239 8969; map pp.520–521. "Why Not!" is a superb *gelateria* that's been in business since 1939, with seasonal and daily specials: those in the know go for the pistachio and fruit flavours in summer and the *castagna* (chestnut) and *caco* (persimmon) in winter. Mon & Wed–Sat: March–Oct 11am–midnight; Nov–Feb noon–8pm.

Slowly Via Porta Rossa 63/R ☏ 055 264 5354; map pp.520–521. This extremely trendy bar, with its neat little banquettes and candle lanterns, tends to attract a showy, beautifully dressed young crowd, who while away the hours chatting over pricey cocktails and bar snacks (the *aperitivo* buffet is one of the best in Florence). The atmosphere is pretty laidback, even when the DJ gets to work. Mon–Sat 7pm–2am.

NORTH OF THE CENTRE

Carabé Via Ricasoli 60/R ☏ 055 289 476; map pp.520–521. Wonderful Sicilian ice cream. Try the *Spirito Siciliano* flavour – the most lemony lemon you'll ever taste. Also serves delicious *cannoli* (pastry stuffed with sweet ricotta and candied fruits). Daily: April–Oct daily 10am–1am; Nov–March 11am–8pm; closed mid-Dec to mid-Jan.

★ **Casa del Vino** Via dell'Ariento 16/R ☏ 055 215 609; map pp.520–521. Located a few yards south of the Mercato Centrale, the *Casa del Vino* is particularly busy in the middle of the day, when market traders pitch up for a drink, a quick bite, and a chat with owner Gianni Migliorini. Oct–May Mon–Sat 9.30am–5pm; June, July & Sept closed Sat; closed Aug.

Zanobini Via Sant'Antonino 47/R ☏ 055 239 6850; map pp.520–521. Like the nearby *Casa del Vino*, this is an authentic and long-established place, but here the emphasis is much more on the wine: few bars in Florence have a better selection. Mon–Sat 8am–2pm & 3.30–8pm.

EAST OF THE CENTRE

Caffè Cibrèo Via Andrea del Verrocchio 5/R ☏ 055 234 5853; map pp.514–515. Possibly the prettiest café in Florence, *Caffè Cibrèo* opened in 1989, but the wood-panelled interior gives it the look of a place that's at least two hundred years older. Cakes and desserts are great, and the light meals bear the stamp of the *Cibrèo* restaurant kitchens opposite (see p.545). Tues–Sat 8am–1am.

Moyo Via de' Benci 23/R ☏ 055 247 9738; map pp.520–521. A young crowd flocks to this bar every evening – the food's pretty good (come for the early-evening *aperitivo* buffet) and the free wi-fi access is a plus, but it's the buzz that really brings them in. Mon–Thurs & Sun 8am–2am, Fri & Sat 9am–3am.

Rex Café Via Fiesolana 25/R ☏ 055 248 0331; map pp.520–521. This friendly and extravagantly decorated place has been one of Florence's coolest bars for years. Lots of cosy seating around the central bar, and good cocktails and DJs (from 10.30pm) add to the appeal. The *aperitivi* session is 6–9.30pm. Daily 5pm–3am.

Vivoli Via Isola delle Stinche 7/R ☏ 055 292 334; map pp.520–521. Operating from deceptively unprepossessing premises in a side-street close to Santa Croce, this café has long been rated one of the best ice cream-makers in Florence – the very best, in the opinion of many. Tues–Sun: summer 7.30am–midnight; winter closes 9pm. Closed two weeks in Aug.

OLTRARNO

★ **Dolce Vita** Piazza del Carmine 6/R ☏ 055 284 595; map pp.520–521. This smart and extremely popular bar with a buzzy outdoor terrace has been going for more than 25 years and has stayed ahead of the game by constantly updating. Install yourself on one of the aluminium bar

9

stools and preen with Florence's beautiful young things. There's live music (Latin, rock or jazz) Tues from 7.30pm, a DJ other nights, a sushi buffet on Thurs and *aperitivi* every night 7.30–10pm. Daily 7.30pm–2am.

Fuori Porta Via del Monte alle Croci 10/R ☎ 055 234 2483; map pp.514–515. This famous *enoteca–osteria* has more than five hundred wines to choose from by the bottle, and an ever-changing selection of wines by the glass. Cheese and meat platters are available, together with a full menu of pasta dishes and tasty *secondi*, mainly around €10. Daily: April–Sept 12.30pm–12.30am; Oct–March 12.30–3.30pm & 7pm–12.30am.

Il Rifrullo Via S. Niccolò 53–57/R ☎ 055 234 2621, ✆ ilrifrullo.com; map pp.514–515. Lying to the east of the Ponte Vecchio–Pitti Palace route, this place attracts fewer tourists than many Oltrarno café-bars. Delicious snacks with the early-evening *aperitivi* (when the music gets turned up), as well as more substantial (and quite pricey) dishes in the restaurant section. There's a pleasant garden terrace, too. Daily 8am–2am; closed two weeks in Aug.

La Cité Borgo S. Frediano 20/R ☎ 055 210 387; map pp.520–521. With its huge windows, mezzanine balcony and shelves of books (to buy or just to browse), this café-bar-bookshop has an arty quasi-Parisian ambience. An area is set aside for live performances (usually music), and food-tastings are regular occurrences too. Mon & Sun 3.30pm–midnight, Tues–Sat 10.30am–midnight.

★ **Le Volpi e L'Uva** Piazza dei Rossi 1/R, off Piazza di Santa Felicità ☎ 055 239 8132; map pp.520–521. This discreet, friendly little *enoteca* does good business by concentrating on the wines of small producers and providing tasty cold meats and snacks to accompany them (the selection of cheeses is tremendous). In summer the shady terrace is a very pleasant refuge from the heat. Mon–Sat 11am–9pm.

Zoe Via dei Renai 13 ☎ 055 243 111; map pp.514–515. Like the neighbouring *Negroni*, *Zoe* is perennially popular for summer evening drinks, but also attracts lots of young Florentines right through the day: 8am–noon is breakfast time, lunch is noon–3pm, then it's "Aperitif" from 6–10pm, when the "American Bar" theme takes over (the Crimson Zoe cocktail is notorious). It also does good snacks and simple meals, there's a DJ in the back room, and it's something of an art venue too. Mon–Thurs 8am–1.30am, Fri & Sat 8am–3am, Sun 6pm–1am.

RESTAURANTS

Florence has scores of **restaurants**, but such is the volume of customers that in high season advance bookings are virtually compulsory – especially on Sundays, when many places are closed. And bear in mind that meals – not just snacks – are served in many Florentine bars, so if you're exploring a particular area of the city and fancy a quick bite to eat rather than a full-blown restaurant meal, take a look at the "Cafés and bars" listings.

THE CITY CENTRE

★ **Oliviero** Via delle Terme 51/R ☎ 055 287 643, ✆ ristorante-oliviero.it; map pp.520–521. *Oliviero* has a welcoming and old-fashioned feel – something like an Italian restaurant from the 1960s. There are two menus – one traditional meat-centric Tuscan, one modern Italian – and the quality is exceptional: five types of bread, plus pasta and ice cream are all made on site. Expect to pay around €25 for your *secondi*. Mon–Sat 11am–3pm & 7pm–1am; closed three weeks in Aug.

Ora d'Aria Via dei Georgofili 11/R ☎ 055 200 1699, ✆ oradariaristorante.com; map pp.520–521. Marco Stabile, the young boss of *Ora d'Aria*, has recently relocated his stylish restaurant to this more central location, but his winning formula remains unchanged: a high-quality mix of the traditional and the innovative, in a relaxed yet elegant setting. The tasting menus (€50–70) are very good value; à la carte, main courses are around €30. The lunch menu is more traditionally Tuscan, and less expensive. Mon 7.30–10pm, Tues–Sat 12.30–2.30pm & 7.30–10pm; closed two weeks in Aug.

Yellow Bar Via del Proconsolo 39/R ☎ 055 211 766; map pp.520–521. This place looks like a fast-food joint, but the queues of Florentines waiting for a table give you a clue that first impressions are misleading. Inside, the convivial atmosphere in the large dining room is matched by superlative pan-Italian food (including excellent pizzas) in large portions at very reasonable prices. You can often get a table in the mildly less appealing rooms downstairs when the main dining room is busy. Mon & Wed–Sun noon–3pm & 7pm–midnight, Tues noon–3pm.

WEST OF THE CENTRE

Il Contadino Via Palazzuolo 71/R ☎ 055 238 2673, ✆ trattoriailcontadino.com; map pp.520–521. Small, popular place with a simple black-and-white interior and fascinating large photos of old Florence on the walls. Fast and friendly service, shared tables (no booking), and very cheap but good food. Three-course menu costs a mere €13 in the evening, and even less at lunch. No reservations. Mon–Fri noon–9.30pm.

NORTH OF THE CENTRE

Da Mario Via Rosina 2/R ☎ 055 218 550, ✆ trattoria-mario.com; map pp.520–521. For earthy Florentine cooking at very low prices, there's nowhere better then *Da Mario*, which has been in operation right by the Mercato Centrale since 1953. It's just a pity it isn't open in the evenings. No credit cards; no booking. Mon–Sat noon–3.30pm; closed Aug.

Da Tito Via S. Gallo 112/R ☎ 055 472 475; map pp.514–515. Full of locals every night and offering excellent food at fair prices, a meal at *Da Tito* is well worth the extra few minutes' walk from the centre. Dishes are simple but elegant

– beef fillet with rocket pesto, for example – and *secondi* go for a reasonable €9–15. But if you don't like your meat the way Florentines like it, go elsewhere – the kitchen refuses to serve anything "well done". Mon–Sat 12.30–3pm & 7–11pm, Sun 7–11pm.

Zà-Zà Piazza del Mercato Centrale 26/R ☎ 055 210 756, ⊚ trattoriazaza.it; map pp.520–521. In business for more than thirty years, *Zà-Zà* is one of the best of several *trattorie* close to the Mercato Centrale. The interior is dark, stone-walled and brick-arched, with a handful of tables – though in summer there's plenty more space on the outside terraces. There's usually a set menu for around €15, with a choice of three or four pastas and mains; otherwise you'll pay around €30 per head. Booking is virtually obligatory in summer. Daily noon–3pm & 7pm–1am; closed Aug.

EAST OF THE CENTRE

★ **Baldovino** Via S. Giuseppe 22/R ☎ 055 241 773, ⊚ baldovino.com; map pp.520–521. This superb place is renowned above all for its pizzas (made in a wood-fired oven), but the main menu (which changes monthly) is full of good Tuscan and Italian dishes, with *secondi* at €12–20. Portions are generous. And the adjacent café-bar – *Baldobar* – is good for a quick snack. April–Oct Mon 11am–3pm, Tues–Sun 11am–3pm & 7–1pm; Nov–March closed Mon.

★ **Cibrèo** Via de' Macci 118/R ☎ 055 234 1100, ⊚ edizioniteatrodelsalecibreofirenze.it; map pp.514–515. Fabio Picchi's *Cibrèo* is the first Florentine port-of-call for foodies, known for its superb, creative cuisine and top-notch service. You'll need to book days in advance for a table in the main restaurant, but next door there's a small, spartan trattoria section (*Cibrèino*) where the food is similar (though the menu is smaller), no bookings are taken and prices are around €15 for *secondi*, as opposed to €35 in the restaurant. And across the street there's Fabio's *Teatro del Sale*, where, for €5 membership, you can enjoy generous breakfast, lunch and dinner buffets (€7/€20/€30) made by *Cibrèo* chefs, with film, theatre or music performance thrown in. Tues–Sun 12.30–2.30pm & 7–11.15pm; closed Aug.

Il Pizzaiuolo Via de' Macci 113/R ☎ 055 241 171, ⊚ ilpizzaiuolo.it; map pp.514–515. The Neapolitan pizzas here are among the best in the city. Wines and other dishes also have a Neapolitan touch, as does the atmosphere, which is friendly and high-spirited. Booking's a good idea, at least in the evening. Mon–Sat 12.30–3pm & 7.30pm–midnight; closed Aug.

OLTRARNO

★ **Alla Vecchia Bettola** Viale Lodovico Ariosto 32–34/R ☎ 055 224 158, ⊚ allavecchiabettola.com; map pp.514–515. Located on a major traffic intersection a couple of minutes' walk from the Carmine, this wonderfully old-fashioned place – with its marble-topped tables – has

something of the atmosphere of an old-style drinking den, which is what it once was; it boasts a good repertoire of Tuscan meat dishes, with main courses mostly €12–15. No credit cards. Tues–Sat noon–2.30pm & 7.30–10.30pm.

Filipepe Via S. Niccolò 39/R ☎ 055 200 1397, ⊚ filipepe .com; map pp.514–515. An imaginative place, with a menu that changes with the seasons and is markedly different from most of the competition – it markets itself as a "Mediterranean restaurant", and offers delicious food drawn from a variety of Italian regional cuisines. The wine list is similarly wide-ranging, and the decor offbeat and attractive. Most main courses are around €20. Daily 7.30–11.30pm; closed two weeks in Aug.

Gustapizza Via Maggio 46/R; map pp.520–521. The wood-fired Neapolitan pizzas served here are the best in Oltrarno – and pizzas are all they do, which is always a good thing. No reservations, and the dining room is not large, so be prepared to queue. Tues–Sun 11.30am–3pm & 7–11pm.

Il Santo Bevitore Via Santo Spirito 64–66/R ☎ 055 211 264, ⊚ ilsantobevitore.com; map pp.520–521. "The Holy Drinker" is an airy, stylish and hugely popular gastronomic *enoteca* with a small but classy menu (around €35 for a meal without drinks) to complement its enticing wine list. Two doors down, *Il Santino*, run by the same owners (daily 10am–10.30pm), is an excellent wine bar with good cheese and cold meat plates. Daily 12.30–2.30pm & 7.30–11.30pm, Sun 7.30–11.30pm; closed two weeks Aug.

La Casalinga Via del Michelozzo 9/R ☎ 055 218 624, ⊚ trattorialacasalinga.it; map pp.520–521. This long-established family-run trattoria serves up some of the best low-cost Tuscan dishes in town (from €7 for a *secondo*). Most nights it's filled with regulars and a good few outsiders – by 8pm there's invariably a queue. Mon–Sat noon–2.30pm & 7–10pm; closed three weeks in Aug.

La Mangiatoia Piazza S. Felice 8–9/R ☎ 055 224 060; map pp.514–515. Ideally placed for lunch before or after a visit to Palazzo Pitti, this *rosticceria* has a no-frills trattoria out back, where a full menu of Tuscan fare is served in a somewhat spartan interior, with most *secondi* less than €10. There are good pizzas too, cooked in a wood-fired oven. Tues–Sun noon–3pm & 7–10pm.

★ **Pane e Vino** Piazza di Cestello 3/R ☎ 055 247 6956, ⊚ ristorantepaneevino.it; map pp.514–515. The ambience of this place is stylish yet relaxed, and the menu small and consistently excellent (*secondi* €15–25), featuring a very enticing tasting-menu at €45. Small TV screens in the dining area show the chefs beavering away in the kitchen, producing some of the best food in town – the ravioli with asparagus in a lemon cream melts in your mouth. *Pane e Vino* began life as a bar, so it's no surprise that the wine list is excellent. Mon–Sat 7.30pm–1am; closed two weeks in Aug.

9

NIGHTLIFE AND ENTERTAINMENT

Florence is quite a sedate city, but like every university town it has some decent clubs and live music venues, and events such as the Maggio Musicale maintain Florence's standing as the hub of cultural life in Tuscany. The best clubs and music venues are listed below, but for a full picture of the Florence after-dark scene, check the "Bars" listings too – many of Florence's bars try to keep punters on the premises all night, by serving free snacks with the *aperitivi* (usually from about 7–9/10pm) before the music kicks in, either live or (more often) courtesy of the in-house DJ. For information about concerts and shows, get hold of the *Firenze Spettacolo* monthly listings magazine or drop in at the Box Office ticket agency, which is at Via delle Vecchie Carceri 1, near the Mercato di Sant'Ambrogio (☎055 210 804, ⓦboxol.it; Mon–Fri 9.30am–7pm, Sat 9.30am–2pm). Online, a great info source is ⓦnottefiorentina.it.

CLUBS AND LIVE MUSIC VENUES

Auditorium FLOG Via Michele Mercati 24/B ☎055 477 978, ⓦflog.it; map pp.514–515; take bus #4 or #28 from Santa Maria Novella. One of the city's best-known mid-sized venues, and a perennial student favourite for all forms of live music (and DJs), but particularly local indie-type bands. It's usually packed, despite a position way out in the northern suburbs.

Be Bop Via de' Servi 76/R ☎055 264 5756; map pp.520–521. This scruffy music bar, popular with students from 10pm on, is a good bet for a fun night out. There's always live music, from jazz to rock to tribute bands; for over a decade, Tuesday night has been Beatles night. Tues–Sun 7pm–3am.

Central Park Via Fosso Macinante 2, Parco delle Cascine ☎055 353 505; map pp.514–515. One of the city's biggest and most commercial clubs, with three dancefloors and DJs who know what they're doing – and have access to a superb sound system. The first drink is included in the admission – around €20–25 after midnight, usually free before. Summer Tues–Sat 11pm–4am; winter Fri & Sat same hours.

Tenax Via Pratese 46 ☎055 632 958, ⓦtenax.org; bus #29 or #30 from Santa Maria Novella. Florence's biggest club, pulling in the odd jet-setting DJ. Given its location in the northwest of town, near the airport, you'll escape the hordes of *internazionalisti* in the more central clubs. With two floors, it's a major venue for concerts as well. Admission €20–25. Thurs–Sat 10.30pm–4am; closed mid-May to mid-Sept.

YAB Via Sassetti 5/R ☎055 215 160, ⓦyab.it; map pp.520–521. This long-established basement club (full name: You Are Beautiful) has been popular for years, and is known throughout the country for Monday's Yabsmoove – Italy's longest-running hip-hop night. It doesn't have the most up-to-the-minute playlist in the world, but still offers probably the most relaxed and reliable night's clubbing in central Florence. Mon & Wed–Sat 9pm–4am; closed June–Sept.

FILM

The Odeon is the only cinema still in operation in the centre of Florence, apart from the Fulgor, near Ognissanti in

---

FLORENCE'S FESTIVALS

Scoppio del Carro The first major festival of the year is Easter Sunday's Scoppio del Carro (Explosion of the Cart), when a cartload of fireworks is hauled by six white oxen from the Porta a Prato to the Duomo; there, during midday Mass, the pile is ignited by a "dove" that whizzes down a wire from the high altar.

Festa del Grillo On the first Sunday after Ascension Day (forty days after Easter), the "Festival of the Cricket" is held in the Cascine park. In among the market stalls and the picnickers you'll find people selling tiny mechanical crickets – live crickets were sold until recently, a vestige of a ritual that may hark back to the days when farmers had to scour their land for locusts.

Maggio Musicale Fiorentino The highlight of Florence's cultural calendar and one of Europe's leading festivals of opera and classical music, a rich mix of opera and concert; confusingly, it isn't restricted to May (Maggio), but often starts in late April and runs into June. Information and tickets can be obtained

from the Teatro del Maggio Musicale Fiorentino (see opposite). ⓦmaggiofiorentino.com.

St John's Day and the Calcio Storico The saint's day of John the Baptist, Florence's patron, is June 24 – the occasion for a massive fireworks display on Piazzale Michelangelo, and for the final of the Calcio Storico on Piazza Santa Croce. Played in sixteenth-century costume to commemorate a game played at Santa Croce during the siege of 1530, this uniquely Florentine mayhem is a three-match series, with two games in early June preceding the bedlam of June 24.

Festa delle Rificolone The "Festival of the Lanterns" takes place on the Virgin's birthday, September 7, with a procession of children to Piazza Santissima Annunziata, where a small fair is held. Each child carries a coloured paper lantern with a candle inside it – a throwback to the days when people from the surrounding countryside would troop by lantern light into the city for the Feast of the Virgin. The procession is followed by a parade of floats and street parties.

Via Maso Finiquerra, which rarely has *versione originale* screenings. In summer there are often **open-air screens** at the Forte Belvedere and a few other spots – check *Firenze Spettacolo* for the latest screenings.

Odeon Original Sound Piazza Strozzi 2 ☎055 214 068. This cinema screens films in their original language (*versione originale*) once a week, generally on Mon, for most of the year, plus Tues and Thurs in summer.

CLASSICAL MUSIC, OPERA AND DANCE

The **Maggio Musicale** is the most conspicuous sign of the health of the city's classical music scene, though it should be said that the fare tends towards the conservative. In addition to this and the festival in Fiesole (see p.550), the **Amici della Musica** host a season of chamber concerts with top-name international performers from September to April, mostly in the Teatro della Pergola, and the **Orchestra da Camera Fiorentina** (Florence Chamber Orchestra; ℗orcafi.it) plays concerts from March to October, often in Orsanmichele.

CONCERT VENUES

Teatro del Maggio Musicale Fiorentino Corso Italia 16 ☎055 213 535, ℗maggiofiorentino.com. Florence's main municipal theatre, out to the west of Santa Maria Novella, hosts many of the city's major classical music, dance and theatre events. It has its own orchestra, chorus and dance company, attracting top-name international guest performers. The main season for dance and opera runs from Oct to Dec, with classical music concerts taking over from Jan until the start of the Maggio Musicale festival. Chamber music and other small-scale events are held in the theatre's Teatro Piccolo.

Teatro Goldoni Via Santa Maria 15 ☎055 210 804. This exquisite little eighteenth-century theatre, near the Palazzo Pitti, is used for chamber music, opera and dance productions.

Teatro della Pergola Via della Pergola 18 ☎055 226 4353, ℗teatrodellapergola.com. The beautiful little Pergola was built in 1656 and is Italy's oldest surviving theatre. From Oct to April it plays host to chamber concerts, small-scale operas, and some of the best-known Italian theatre companies.

Teatro Verdi Via Ghibellina 99–101 ☎055 212 320, ℗teatroverdionline.it. Home to the Orchestra della Toscana, which performs once or twice a month between Nov and May.

SHOPPING

Florence is known as a producer of **luxury items**, notably gold jewellery and top-quality leather goods. The whole Ponte Vecchio is crammed with goldsmiths, but the city's premier shopping thoroughfare is **Via de' Tornabuoni**, where you'll find not only an array of expensive jewellery and shoe shops but also the showrooms of Italy's top fashion designers. For cheap and cheerful stuff there's the plethora of street stalls around the San Lorenzo market, while if you want everything under one roof, there's also a handful of **department stores**. Marbled paper is another Florentine speciality, and, as you'd expect in this arty city, Florence is also one of the best places in the country to pick up **books** on Italian art, architecture and culture.

BOOKS AND MAPS

Edison Piazza della Repubblica 27/R ☎055 213 110; map pp.520–521. This US-style operation is arranged on four floors, with English-language books at the top; the stock is impressive, as are the opening hours. Mon–Sat 9am–midnight, Sun 10am–midnight.

Feltrinelli Via Cavour 12–20/R ☎055 219 524; map pp.520–521. Bright and well staffed, this has a good selection of English and other foreign-language books, plus newspapers, videos, posters, cards and magazines. There's another big branch in the city centre at Via de' Cerretani 30/R. Mon–Sat 9am–7.30pm.

CLOTHING

Raspini Via Por S. Maria 70/R & Via Roma 25–29/R ☎055 215 796, ℗raspini.com; map pp.520–521. Florence's biggest multi-label clothes shop, with a good stock of diffusion lines. These are the two main branches; the "vintage" outlets at Via de' Martelli 5–7/R and Via Calimaruzza 17/R sell the previous season's stock at reduced prices. Mon 2.30–7.30pm, Tues–Sat 10.30am–7.30pm, Sun 2.30–7.30pm.

DEPARTMENT STORES

Coin Via dei Calzaiuoli 56/R ☎055 280 531, ℗coin.it; map pp.520–521. Central, clothes-dominated chain store. Quality is generally high, though styles are conservative except for one or two youth-oriented franchises on the ground floor. Also a good place for linen and other household goods. Mon–Sat 10am–8pm, Sun 11am–8pm.

La Rinascente Piazza della Repubblica 1 ☎055 219 113, ℗rinascente.it; map pp.520–521. Like Coin, La Rinascente is part of a countrywide chain, though it's perhaps a touch more upmarket than its nearby rival. Sells clothing, linen, cosmetics, household goods and other staples. Mon–Sat 10am–9pm, Sun 10.30am–8pm.

PAPER AND STATIONERY

★ **Giulio Giannini e Figlio** Piazza Pitti 36/R ☎055 212 621, ℗giuliogiannini.it; map pp.520–521. Established in 1856, this paper-making and book-binding firm has been honoured with exhibitions dedicated to its work. Once the only place in Florence to make its own marbled papers, it now offers a wide variety of diaries, address books and so forth as well. Mon–Sat 10am–7.30pm, Sun 10.30am–6.30pm.

9

FASHION FACTORY OUTLETS

If you want to get hold of top-label clothing without breaking the bank, you'll need to take a trip into Florence's hinterland. Tuscany is the powerhouse of the country's textile industry, and the Arno valley is the home of many of the factories that manufacture clothes for the top labels. Several retail outlets within easy reach of Florence sell each season's leftovers at discounts as high as sixty percent. The best are below; ask at the tourist office for a full list.

Barberino Designer Outlet Via Meucci, Barberino di Mugello ☎055 842 161, ⊛mcarthurglen.it /barberino; SITA bus from Via Santa Caterina da Siena or shuttle bus from outside Santa Maria Novella station (2 daily). The biggest range, including D&G, Missoni and Prada, plus discounted high-street gear from labels such as Diesel and Furla. Mon 2–8pm (Jan, June–Sept & Dec), Tues–Fri 10am–8pm, Sat & Sun 10am–9pm.

Dolce & Gabbana Via Pian dell'Isola 49, Località Santa Maria Maddalena ☎055 833 1300; train to Rignano sull'Arno-Reggello, then taxi. This two-storey shed, a few kilometres north of Incisa Val d'Arno, is packed with clothes, accessories and household items from Dolce & Gabbana. Daily 10am–7.30pm.

The Mall Via Europa 8, Leccio Regello ☎055 865 7775, ⊛themall.it; SITA bus from Via Santa Caterina da Siena or shuttle bus from outside Santa Maria Novella station (2 daily). Outlets for Balenciaga, Bottega Veneta, Fendi, Marni, Salvatore Ferragamo, Sergio Rossi and Valentino, among others. Gucci is the dominant presence, with a huge range of bags, shoes and sunglasses. Daily 10am–7pm.

Space Levanella, Montevarchi ☎055 91 901; train to Montevarchi, then taxi. On a small industrial estate in the Levanella district (on the SS69), this outlet is stacked with Prada clothes, as well as a selection from the Miu Miu diffusion label. Mon–Fri & Sun 10.30am–8pm, Sat 9.30am–8pm.

Il Torchio Via de' Bardi 17 ☎055 234 2862, ⊛legatoriailtorchio.com; map pp.514–515. Now owned by young Sicilian-Canadian Erin Ciulla, Il Torchio produces marbled paper, desk accessories, diaries, albums and other items in paper and leather. Mon–Fri 9.30am–1.30pm & 2.30–7pm, Sat 9.30am–1pm.

PERFUME AND TOILETRIES

★ **Farmacia Santa Maria Novella** Via della Scala 16 ☎055 216 276, ⊛smnovella.it; map pp.520–521. Occupying the pharmacy of the Santa Maria Novella monastery, this sixteenth-century shop was founded by Dominican monks as an outlet for their herbal potions, ointments and remedies. Many of these are still in production, together with face-creams, shampoos, and more esoteric concoctions. Mon–Sat 9.30am–7.30pm, Sun 10.30am–6.30pm; closed Sun in Feb & Nov.

PRINTS AND PHOTOS

Alinari Largo Alinari 15 ☎055 23 951, ⊛alinari.com; map pp.520–521. Founded in 1852, this is the world's oldest photographic business. They sell books, calendars, posters and cards, and will print any image you choose from their huge catalogue, the largest archive of old

photographs in Italy. Mon–Fri 9am–1pm & 2–6pm; closed two weeks in mid-Aug.

SHOES AND ACCESSORIES

Cellerini Via del Sole 37/R ☎055 282 533, ⊛cellerini .it; map pp.520–521. Bags, bags and more bags. Everything is made on the premises under the supervision of the firm's founders, the city's premier exponents of the craft; bags don't come more elegant or durable. Summer Mon–Fri 9am–1pm & 3–7pm, Sat 9am–1pm; winter Mon 3–7pm, Tues–Sat 9am–1pm & 3–7pm.

★ **Madova** Via Guicciardini 1/R ☎055 239 6526, ⊛madova.com; map pp.520–521. The last word in gloves – every colour, every size, every style, lined with lambswool, silk, cashmere or nothing. Prices range from around €40 to €200. Mon–Sat 9.30am–7.30pm.

Scuola del Cuoio Via S. Giuseppe 5/R ☎055 244 533, ⊛scuoladelcuoio.com; map pp.520–521. This academy for leather-workers at the back of Santa Croce church sells bags, jackets, belts and other accessories at prices that compare very favourably with the shops. You won't find any startlingly original designs, but the quality is very high and the staff knowledgeable and helpful. Mon–Sat 9.30am–6pm, Sun 10am–6pm.

DIRECTORY

Banks and exchange Florence's main bank branches are on or around Piazza della Repubblica.

Consulates The UK consulate for northern Italy is in Milan (see p.247); the US has a consulate in Florence, at Lungarno

Amerigo Vespucci 38 ☎055 266 951.

Doctors The Tourist Medical Service is a private service with doctors on call 24hr a day (☎055 475 411, ⊛medical service.firenze.it), or you can visit its clinic at Via Lorenzo il

Magnifico 59 (Mon–Fri 11am–noon & 5–6pm, Sat 11am–noon). Note that you'll need insurance cover to recoup the cost of a consultation, which will be at least €50. Florence's central hospital is on Piazza Santa Maria Nuova.

Internet access Internet Train (ⓦinternettrain.it) has branches at Via de Benci 36/R, Via Porta Rossa 38/R, Via Guelfa 54–56/R, Borgo San Jacopo 30/R and Via dell'Oriuolo 40/R.

Laundry Wash & Dry has branches throughout the city, open 8am–10pm daily, including Via dei Servi 102/R, Via della Scala 52–54/R, Via Ghibellina 143/R and Borgo S. Frediano 29/R.

Lost property Lost property handed in at the city or railway police ends up at Via Veracini 5 (Mon, Wed & Fri 9am–12.30, Tues & Thurs 9am–12.30pm & 2.30–4.30pm;

☏ 055 334 802; bus #17, #29, #30 or #35)

Pharmacies The Farmacia Comunale, on the train station concourse, is open 24hr. All'Insegna del Moro, at Piazza San Giovanni 20/R, on the north side of the Baptistry, and Farmacia Molteni, at Via dei Calzaiuoli 7/R, alternate their 24hr service every two weeks.

Police To report a theft or other crime, go to the Carabinieri at Borgo Ognissanti 48, to the Questura at Via Duca d'Aosta 3 (both 24hr), or to the tourist police at Via Pietrapiana 50/R (Mon–Fri 8.30am–6.30pm, Sat closes 1pm) – you're more likely to find an English-speaker at the last of these.

Post office The main central post office is near Piazza della Repubblica at Via Pellicceria 3 (Mon–Fri 8.25am–7.10pm, Sat 8.25am–12.35pm).

Around Florence

The greater Florence area has a number of towns and attractions to entice you on a day-trip from the city or even act as a base for exploring the region. City buses run northeast to the hill-village of **Fiesole**, while inter-town services run south into the hills of **Chianti**, Italy's premier wine region.

Fiesole

A long-established Florentine retreat from the summer heat and crowds, **FIESOLE** spreads over a cluster of hilltops 8km northeast of the city. It predates Florence by several hundred years: the Etruscans held out so long up here that the Romans were forced to set up permanent camp in the valley below – thus creating the beginnings of the settlement that was to become Florence.

The Duomo

Piazza Mino da Fiesole • Daily: summer 7.30am–noon & 3–6pm; winter closes 5pm • Free

The slightly unkempt central square, **Piazza Mino**, is named after the fifteenth-century sculptor Mino da Fiesole, who has two fine pieces in the **Duomo** that dominates its north side. Nineteenth-century restoration ruined the Duomo's exterior, and the interior is something like a stripped-down version of Florence's San Miniato; the highlight is the Cappella Salutati, to the right of the choir, which contains Mino's panel of the *Madonna and Saints* and tomb of Bishop Salutati.

Museo Bandini

Via Dupré 1 • Wed–Sun March & Oct 10am–6pm; April–Sept 10am–7pm; Nov–Feb 10am–2pm • €5, or joint one-day ticket for all Fiesole's museums €12 • ⓦ museidifiesole.it

The **Museo Bandini** possesses a collection of glazed terracotta in the style of the della Robbias, the odd piece of Byzantine ivory work and a few thirteenth- and fourteenth-century Tuscan pictures, including pieces by Bernardo Daddi, Lorenzo Monaco and Taddeo Gaddi.

Teatro Romano and the Museo Archeologico

Via Portigiani 1 • Mon & Wed–Sun: March & Oct 10am–6pm; April–Sept 10am–7pm; Nov–Feb 10am–2pm • €10, or joint one-day ticket for all Fiesole's museums €12 • ⓦ museidifiesole.it

Across the road from the Bandini, the 3000-seat **Teatro Romano** was built in the first century BC and excavated towards the end of the nineteenth century. It's in such good repair that it's used for performances during the Estate Fiesolana festival, though parts of the site are sometimes closed for excavation work. Most of the exhibits in the site's small **Museo Archeologico** were excavated in this area, and encompass pieces from the Bronze Age to Roman occupation; the well-presented Etruscan section is the highlight.

9

ESTATE FIESOLANA

Slightly less exclusive than Florence's Maggio Musicale, Fiesole's cultural festival concentrates on chamber music, orchestral music and jazz. It's held every summer, usually from mid-June to late Aug or early Sept. Films and theatre are also featured, and most events are held in the Teatro Romano. The festival's website is ⓦ estatefiesolana.it.

Oratorio di San Jacopo, Sant'Alessandro and San Francesco

Fiesole's other major churches are reached by the narrow Via San Francesco, which rises steeply from Piazza Mino, past the **Oratorio di San Jacopo** (rarely open), a little chapel containing a fifteenth-century fresco and some ecclesiastical treasures. **Sant'Alessandro** (open for exhibitions only) was founded in the sixth century on the site of Etruscan and Roman temples and has beautiful *marmorino cipollino* (onion marble) columns adorning its basilical interior. The Gothic church of **San Francesco** (daily: April–Sept 7am–noon & 3–7pm; Oct–March 9am–noon & 3–5pm) occupies the site of the acropolis; across one of the tiny cloisters there's a chaotic museum of pieces brought back from Egypt and China by missionaries.

San Domenico

For a lovely walk, head southwest from Piazza Mino for 1.5km down the narrow, winding Via Vecchia Fiesolana to the hamlet of **San Domenico**. Fra' Angelico was once prior of the Dominican **monastery** here and the church retains a 1420 *Madonna and Angels* by him (first chapel on the left), while the chapterhouse also has the Fra' Angelico fresco *The Crucifixion*.

Badia Fiesolana

Mon–Fri 9am–5.30pm, Sat 9am–12.30pm • Free

Five minutes' walk northwest from San Domenico stands the **Badia Fiesolana**, Fiesole's cathedral from the ninth century to the eleventh. Cosimo il Vecchio had the church altered in the 1460s, a project which kept the magnificent Romanesque facade intact while transforming the interior into a superb Renaissance building.

ARRIVAL AND INFORMATION | FIESOLE

By bus Fiesole is an easy hop from central Florence: bus #7 makes the half-hour journey from Santa Maria Novella train station to Piazza Mino da Fiesole three times an hour.

Tourist office Via Portigiani 3/5, next to the entrance to the archeological site (March–Oct Mon–Sat 9.30am–6.30pm, Sun 10am–1pm & 2–6pm; Nov–Feb Mon–Sat 9am–5pm, Sun 10am–4pm; ⓣ 055 598 720).

EATING

La Reggia degli Etruschi Via S. Francesco 18 ⓣ 055 59 385. As you'd expect, Fiesole has plenty of restaurants to cater for the day-trippers, but none is better than this place – the food is fine (mains €15–20), and the views from its dining rooms and terraces are tremendous. Lunch & dinner; closed Tues.

Chianti

Ask a sample of middle-class Northern Europeans to define their idea of paradise and the odds are that a hefty percentage will come up with something that sounds a lot like Chianti, the territory of vineyards and hill-towns that stretches between Florence and Siena. Life in Chianti seems in perfect balance: the landscape is a softly varied terrain of hills and valleys; the climate for most of the year is sunny; and on top of all this there's the wine, the one Italian vintage that's familiar to just about everyone. Visitors from Britain and other similarly ill-favoured climes were long ago alerted to Chianti's charms, and the rate of immigration has been so rapid since the 1960s that the region is now wryly dubbed **Chiantishire**. Yet it would be an exaggeration to say that Chianti

9

> ### AGRITURISMI IN CHIANTI
>
> Hotels in Chianti are rarely inexpensive, but this is prime **agriturismo** territory, with scores of farms offering rooms or apartments (or even self-contained mini-villas), generally for a minimum period of one week, which for an extended stay can provide a good-value alternative to hotel accommodation. We've recommended a small selection in our listings – you'll find hundreds more properties at ⓦagriturismo.net and ⓦagriturismo.it.

has completely lost its character: the tone of certain parts has been altered, but concessions to tourism have been more or less successfully absorbed into the rhythm of local life.

If you're relying on **buses** from Florence, the best target is Greve in Chianti; from Siena, you can take a bus to Castellina in Chianti or Radda in Chianti. But the only realistic way to get to know the region is with **your own transport**, following the SS222 (or Chiantigiana), which snakes its way between Florence and Siena through the most beautiful parts of Chianti.

Greve in Chianti

The venue for Chianti's biggest wine fair (the Rassegna del Chianti Classico, usually held in early September), **GREVE** is a thriving mercantile town where there's wine for sale on every street. The funnel-shaped Piazza Matteotti – venue for the Saturday-morning market – is focused on a statue of Giovanni da Verrazzano, the first European to see what became Manhattan; he was born in the nearby Castello di Verrazzano. Greve's only real sight is the **Museo di San Francesco**, at Via San Francesco 14 (April–Oct Tues & Thurs–Sun 4–7pm, plus Sat & Sun 10am–1pm; Nov–March Tues & Thurs–Sun 3–6pm, plus Sat & Sun 10am–1pm; €3), where the chief exhibit is a painted terracotta *Lamentation*, created in the 1530s.

Castellina in Chianti

Well-heeled **CASTELLINA IN CHIANTI** formerly stood on the front line of the continual wars between Florence and Siena, and its walls and fortress bear testimony to an embattled past. Traces of a more distant era can be seen at the **Ipogeo Etrusco di Montecalvario** (daylight hours; free), a complex of subterranean sixth-century BC Etruscan burial chambers, carved into the summit of a small hill that's five minutes' walk north of the village.

The area's distant history is illuminated in the **Museo Archeologico del Chianti Senese** (Mon, Tues & Thurs–Sun 10am–1pm & 3.30–6.30pm; €3), which also gives you access to the town's tower, but neither the Etruscans nor Castellina's one sizeable church – the neo-Romanesque San Salvatore, which is notable mainly for the mummified remains of the obscure St Fausto – are what brings in the tourists. Wine is Castellina's primary attraction, as is evident from the power-station bulk of the **wine co-operative** on the main road; the local vintages (and olive oil) can be sampled at several places in town.

Radda in Chianti

The best of Chianti lies east of Castellina and the Chiantigiana, in the less domesticated terrain of the **Monti del Chianti** – the stronghold of the Lega di Chianti, whose power bases were Castellina itself and the two principal settlements of this craggy region, Radda and Gaiole. The nearer of these, the ancient Etruscan-founded town of **RADDA IN CHIANTI**, became the league's capital in 1384, and the imprint of the period is still strong here – though perhaps not quite as strong as the imprint of middle-class tourism, which has almost smothered the town's identity. The minuscule *centro storico* is focused on Piazza Ferrucci, where the frescoed and shield-studded Palazzo Comunale faces a church raised on a high platform.

INFORMATION

Tourist offices Greve: Via delle Capanne 11 (Mon–Fri 10.30am–2pm & 3–6pm; ☎ 055 854 5243); Castellina: Via Ferruccio 40 (daily 9am–1pm & 2.30–6.30pm; ☎ 0577 741 392); Radda: Hidden in a corner of the tiny Piazza del Castello, behind the church (Mon–Sat 10.15am–1pm & 3.15–6.30pm, Sun 10.30am–12.30pm).

ACCOMMODATION AND EATING

GREVE IN CHIANTI

Da Verrazzano 28 Piazza Matteotti ☎ 055 853 189, ⓦ albergoverrazzano.it. A plain but characterful three-star hotel which also has a good restaurant, with full meals at around €40; in summer you can eat on the terrace overlooking the piazza. Lunch & dinner Tues–Sat, plus lunch Sun; closed mid-Jan to mid-Feb. **€105**

Poggio Asciutto Via Montagliari 40 ☎ 055 852 835, ⓦ poggioasciutto.it. A wonderful agriturismo, offering very comfortable accommodation (plus a pool) in a beautifully restored building on an organic farm amid vineyards 2.5km southeast of Greve. **€100**

CASTELLINA IN CHIANTI

Fattoria Trégole Trégole 86 ☎ 0577 740 991, ⓦ fattoria-tregole.com. Located 4km south of Castellina, the *Fattoria Trégole* vineyard is the best rustic B&B in the area, with a couple of self-contained apartments in addition to the spacious doubles. The hosts are immensely welcoming, and provide delicious home-cooking in their restaurant. There's a small pool too. **€160**

★ **Palazzo Squarcialupi** Via Ferruccio 22 ☎ 0577 741 186, ⓦ palazzosquarcialupi.com. Pick of Castellina's hotels is the three-star *Palazzo Squarcialupi*, which occupies the upper storeys of a vast fifteenth-century *palazzo*. The rooms are large and well furnished, and there's a sauna in the basement and a pool in the garden, which commands a wonderful view. **€130**

RADDA IN CHIANTI

La Locanda Montanino di Volpaia ☎ 0577 738 832, ⓦ lalocanda.it. This three-star country house is located almost halfway between Radda and Greve, near the famous Castello di Volpaia, one of the area's great wine producers. Beautifully restored by affable owners Guido and Martina, it enjoys a scenic hilltop setting and has a swimming pool and a good restaurant (Mon, Wed & Fri). Closed Nov–March. **€230**

Palazzo Leopoldo Via Roma 33 ☎ 0577 735 603, ⓦ palazzoleopoldo.it. This place was founded as a pilgrims' hostel, then converted into a magnificent townhouse prior to becoming an extremely elegant four-star hotel, with a good restaurant, plus gym, sauna and pool. **€120**

Pisa, Lucca and the coast

Thanks to its Leaning Tower, **Pisa** is known by name to just about every visitor to Italy, though it remains an underrated place, seen by most people on a whistle-stop day-trip that takes in nothing of the city except the tower and its immediate environs. Genteel **Lucca** nearby, its walled old town crammed with Romanesque churches, is even less explored.

Tuscany's **coast** is a mixed bag, generally too overdeveloped to be consistently attractive. North of Pisa, the succession of beach resorts enjoys the backdrop of the mighty Alpi Apuane, which harbour the marble quarries of Carrara. South from Pisa, past the untouristed port of Livorno, are a hundred scrubby strips of hotels and campsites. The Tuscan shoreline is at its best in the **Maremma** region, where you'll find the protected **Monti dell'Uccellina** reserve and the wild, wooded peninsula of **Monte Argentario**. Tuscany's main island, **Elba**, also offers a breath of fresh air.

Pisa

For too many tourists, **PISA** means just one thing – the **Leaning Tower**, which serves around the world as a shorthand image for Italy. It is indeed a freakishly beautiful building, a sight whose impact no amount of prior knowledge can blunt. Yet it is just a single component of Pisa's breathtaking **Campo dei Miracoli**, or Field of Miracles, where the **Duomo**, **Baptistry** and **Camposanto** complete a dazzling architectural ensemble. These amazing buildings belong to Pisa's Golden Age, from the eleventh to the thirteenth centuries, when the city was one of the maritime powers of the Mediterranean. Decline set in with defeat by the Genoese in 1284, followed by the silting-up of Pisa's harbour, and

9

from 1406 the city was governed by Florence, whose rulers re-established the University of Pisa, one of the great intellectual establishments of the Renaissance – **Galileo** was a teacher here. Subsequent centuries saw Pisa fade into provinciality, though landmarks from its glory days now bring in hundreds of thousands of visitors a year, and the combination of tourism and a large student population give the contemporary city a lively feel.

It has to be said that visiting the Campo in high season is not a calming experience – the tourist maelstrom here can be fierce. Within a short radius of the Campo dei Miracoli, however, Pisa takes on a quite different character, because very few tourists bother to venture far from the shadow of the Leaning Tower. To the southeast of the Campo, on the river, you'll find the **Museo Nazionale di San Matteo**, a fine collection of ecclesiastical art and sculpture, while west along the Arno stands another good museum, the **Palazzo Reale**, which faces the exquisite little **Santa Maria della Spina**, on the opposite bank.

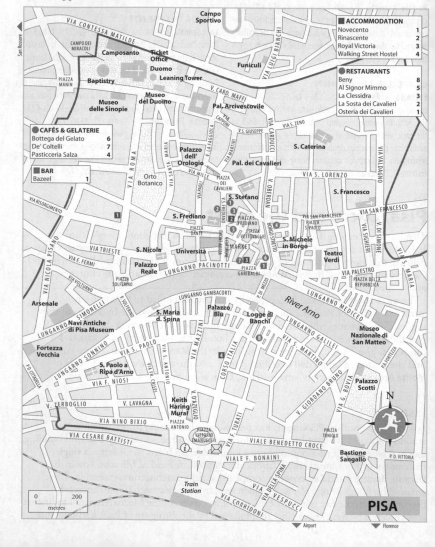

TICKETS FOR THE CAMPO DEI MIRACOLI

Tickets for all five museums and monuments of the Campo dei Miracoli – the Duomo, Baptistry, Museo dell'Opera, Camposanto and Museo delle Sinopie – can only be bought at two **ticket offices**: one on the north side of the Leaning Tower, the other inside the Museo delle Sinopie. **Prices** are as follows: the Duomo costs €2, except from November to February, when it's free. Single admission to the other sights costs €5. Admission to any two sights (including the Duomo) is €6, to any four is €8 and to all five is €10; these combined tickets are valid for the day of issue only. There's a separate ticket (€15) for the **Leaning Tower**; groups of thirty are allowed in for half an hour, and you should expect a long wait in high season. Note that the last entrance to all sights is thirty minutes before closing. For an extra €2 you can **pre-book** your visit online at ⓦopapisa.it, as long as you're making your reservation between 45 and 15 days in advance. Children under the age of 8 are not allowed into the tower.

The Leaning Tower

Daily: Jan & Dec 10am–4.30pm; Feb & Nov 9.30am–5pm; March 9am–5.30pm; April, May & Sept 8.30am–8pm; June–Aug 8.30am–10.30pm; Oct 9am–7pm • Tours in English given three times daily, April–Sept • For ticket details see box above

The **Leaning Tower** (Torre Pendente) has always tilted. Begun in 1173, it started to subside when it had reached just three of its eight storeys, but it leaned in the opposite direction to the present one. Odd-shaped stones were inserted to correct this deficiency, whereupon the tower lurched the other way. Over the next 180 years a succession of architects continued to extend the thing upwards, each one endeavouring to compensate for the angle, the end result being that the main part of the tower is slightly bent. Around 1350, Tommaso di Andrea da Pontedera completed the magnificent stack of marble and granite arcades by crowning it with a bell chamber, set closer to the perpendicular than the storeys below it, so that it looks like a hat set at a rakish angle.

By 1990 the tower was leaning 4.5m from the upright and nearing its limits. A huge rescue operation was then launched, which involved wrapping steel bands around the lowest section of the tower, placing 900 tonnes of lead ingots at its base to counterbalance the leaning stonework, removing water and silt from beneath the tower's foundations, and finally reinforcing the foundations and walls with steel bars. Eleven years and many millions of euros later, the tower was officially reopened to the public in November 2001.

The ascent to the bell chamber takes you up a narrow spiral staircase of 294 steps, at a fairly disorientating five-degree angle. It's not for the claustrophobic or those afraid of heights, but you might think the steep admission fee is worth it for the privilege of getting inside one of the world's most famous and uncanny buildings.

The Duomo

Daily: March 10am–6pm; April–Sept 10am–8pm; Oct 10am–7pm; Nov–Feb 10am–12.45pm & 2–5pm; no admittance to tourists before 1pm on Sun • For ticket details see box above

Pisa's breathtaking **Duomo** was begun in 1064 and completed around a century later. With its four levels of variegated colonnades and its subtle interplay of dark-grey marble and white stone, the building is the archetype of Pisan-Romanesque, a model often imitated in buildings across Tuscany, but never surpassed.

The vast interior is defined by the crisp black-and-white marble of the long arcades, which are suggestive of Moorish architecture. Much of the interior was redecorated, and some of the chapels remodelled, after a fire in 1595, but a notable survivor is the apse mosaic *Christ in Majesty*, completed by Cimabue in 1302. And don't miss the **pulpit**, which **Giovanni Pisano** began to sculpt in the same year. The last of the great series of three pulpits created in Tuscany by Giovanni and his father Nicola (the others are in Siena and Pistoia), it is a work of amazing virtuosity, its whole surface animated by figures almost wholly freed from the stone.

9

The Baptistry

Daily: Jan & Dec 9.30am–4.30pm; Feb & Nov 9am–5pm; March 9am–6pm; April & Sept 8am–8pm; Oct 8.30am–7pm • For ticket details see box, p.555

The **Baptistry**, the largest such building in Italy, was begun in 1152 by a certain Diotisalvi ("God Save You"), who left his name on a column to the left of the door; it was continued in the thirteenth century by Nicola and Giovanni Pisano, and completed late in the fourteenth century. Inside you're immediately struck by the plainness of the vast interior (the acoustics are astonishing, as the guard will demonstrate), but take time to look closely at Nicola Pisano's beautiful **pulpit**, sculpted in 1260, half a century before his son's work in the cathedral.

Camposanto

Daily: March 9am–6pm; April, May & Sept 8am–8pm; June–Aug 8am–11pm; Oct 9am–7pm; Nov–Feb 10am–5pm • For ticket details see box, p.555

The screen of sepulchral white marble running along the north edge of the Campo dei Miracoli is the perimeter wall of what has been called the most beautiful cemetery in the world – the **Camposanto**. According to legend, the Archbishop Ubaldo Lanfranchi had Pisan knights on the Fourth Crusade of 1203 bring a cargo of soil back to Pisa from the hill of Golgotha, in order that eminent Pisans might be buried in holy earth. The building enclosing this sanctified site was completed almost a century later and takes the form of an enormous Gothic cloister. However, when Ruskin described the Camposanto as one of the most precious buildings in Italy, it was the **frescoes** he was praising. Paintings once covered over two thousand square metres of cloister wall, but now the brickwork is mostly bare: incendiary bombs dropped by Allied planes on July 27, 1944, set the roofing on fire and drenched the frescoes in molten lead. The most important survivor is the remarkable *Triumph of Death* cycle, now displayed in a room attached to the cloister.

The museums of the Campo dei Miracoli

Both museums open daily: Jan & Dec 9.30am–4.30pm; Feb & Nov 9am–5pm; March 8.30am–5.30pm; April–Sept 8am–7.30pm; Oct 9am–7pm • For ticket details see box, p.555

The **Museo dell'Opera del Duomo** is a vast array of statuary from the Duomo and Baptistry, plus ecclesiastical finery, paintings and other miscellaneous pieces. Highlights include the extraordinary bronze doors made for the Duomo by **Bonanno Pisano** (first architect of the Leaning Tower) in 1180, and Giovanni Pisano's affecting *Madonna del Colloquio* (Madonna of the Conversation), so called because of the intensity of the gazes exchanged by the Madonna and Child. On the south side of the Campo, the only gap in the souvenir stalls is for the **Museo delle Sinopie**. After the damage wreaked on the Camposanto, restorers removed its *sinopie* (the sketches over which frescoes are painted) and these great plates of plaster now hang from the walls of this high-tech museum.

Piazza dei Cavalieri to Piazza Garibaldi

If you have time for a wider exploration of the city, head first for **Piazza dei Cavalieri**, the central civic square of medieval Pisa, which opens unexpectedly from the narrow backstreets to the southeast of the Campo. Covered in monochrome *sgraffiti* and topped with busts of the Medici, the **Palazzo dei Cavalieri** is next to the church of **Santo Stefano**, which still houses banners captured from Turkish ships by the Knights of St Stephen – a grand title for a gang of state-sponsored pirates. On the other side of the square is the Renaissance-adapted **Palazzo dell'Orologio**, in whose tower the military leader Ugolino della Gherardesca was starved to death with his sons and grandsons in 1208, as punishment for his alleged duplicity with the Genoese enemy – the grisly episode is described in Dante's *Inferno* and Shelley's *Tower of Famine*. From here Via Dini heads east to the arcaded **Borgo Stretto**, Pisa's smartest street; Pisa's market area is west of here, on **Piazza Vettovaglie** and the narrow streets that surround it. The Borgo meets the river at **Piazza Garibaldi**, at the foot of the Ponte di Mezzo.

Museo Nazionale di San Matteo

Piazza S. Matteo 1 • Tues–Sat 8.30am–7pm, Sun 9am–1.30pm • €5, €8 with Palazzo Reale

East of Piazza Garibaldi, on Lungarno Mediceo, is the **Museo Nazionale di San Matteo**, where most of the major works of art from Pisa's churches are now gathered. Best of the paintings are polyptychs by Simone Martini and Francesco Traini, a panel of *St Paul* by Masaccio, Gentile da Fabriano's *Madonna of Humility*, and a trio of works by Gozzoli; among the sculptures, two masterpieces stand out – Donatello's reliquary bust of the introspective *St Rossore*, and Andrea and Nino Pisano's *Madonna del Latte*, a touchingly crafted work showing Mary breastfeeding the baby Jesus. The museum also has a stash of fine Middle Eastern ceramics pilfered by Pisan adventurers.

Museo Nazionale di Palazzo Reale

Lungarno Pacinotti 46 • Mon & Wed–Fri 9am–2.30pm, Sat 9am–1.30pm • €5, €8 with Museo Nazionale di San Matteo

The **Museo Nazionale di Palazzo Reale** displays artefacts that once belonged to the Medici, Lorraine and Savoy rulers of the city, who successively occupied the house. Lavish sixteenth-century Flemish tapestries share space with antique weaponry, ivory miniatures, porcelain and a largely undistinguished picture collection; the best-known painting, a version of Bronzino's portrait of Eleanora di Toledo, is displayed alongside a dress that belonged to her.

The Arsenale Mediceo

Lungarno Ranieri Simonelli

West along the river from the Palazzo Reale lies the **Arsenale Mediceo**. Built by Cosimo I, it is being converted into the **Museo delle Navi Romane**, which will house the sixteen Roman ships that have been excavated since 1998 from the silt at nearby San Rossore. Almost perfectly preserved in mud for two millennia, the cargo-laden fleet includes what experts believe could be the oldest Roman warship ever found. The museum is scheduled to open in 2014; you can follow its progress at ⓦcantierenavipisa.it.

Palazzo Blu

Lungarno Gambacorti 9 • Tues–Fri 10am–7pm, Sat & Sun 10am–8pm • Free, except during special exhibitions • ⓦ palazzoblu.org

On the south bank of the river, west of the Ponte di Mezzo, the line of *palazzi* is enlivened by the brightly hued **Palazzo Blu**, which opened in 2009 after a lengthy restoration. It holds a permanent collection of regional art from the fourteenth to the twentieth centuries, as well as occasional big-name exhibitions on the ground floor.

Santa Maria della Spina

Lungarno Gambacorti • June & Aug Tues–Fri 10am–1pm & 3–6pm, Sat & Sun closes 7pm; rest of year Tues–Fri 11am–1pm & 2–5pm, Sat & Sun closes 6pm • €1.50

Further along the *lungarno*, just before the Ponte Solferino, is the oratory of **Santa Maria della Spina**. Founded in 1230 but rebuilt in the 1320s by a merchant who had acquired one of the thorns (*spine*) of Christ's crown, this effervescent little church is the finest flourish of Pisan-Gothic. Originally built closer to the water, it was moved here for fear of floods in 1871. The single-naved interior has lost most of its furnishings, but contains a trio of statues by Andrea and Nino Pisano.

ARRIVAL AND INFORMATION   **PISA**

By train Pisa Centrale train station is about 1km south of the River Arno; the Campo dei Miracoli is about a 30min walk north, or a 5min ride on bus #1, which leaves from outside the station.

Destinations Empoli (every 30min; 35min; change for Volterra and Siena), Florence (every 30min; 1hr–1hr 20min), Lucca (hourly; 20min); Pisa airport (every 30min; 5min).

9

PISA AIRPORT

Pisa's **Galileo Galilei airport** (☎050 849 300, ⓦpisa-airport.com) lies about 3km south of the city centre. The **drive** to Florence is straightforward (a slip road takes you directly onto the motorway), but the road into Pisa is so confusing that, without directions from the car-rental desk, you may well end up getting lost.

Trains from the airport to Florence's Santa Maria Novella station cost €7.10; there are only eight direct services daily (taking 60min, most stopping only at Pisa Centrale), but every thirty minutes a shuttle runs from the airport to Pisa Centrale (5min: €1.40), where you can change to one of the regular services to Florence. Train tickets can be bought from the machines on the station platform or at the office at the opposite end of the airport concourse; the office charges a commission on all tickets. The first train from the airport to Pisa Centrale is at 6.50am, and the last departs at 9pm; the last train from Pisa Centrale to Florence is at 10pm, with services resuming at around 6.40am. From Monday to Saturday there's also a LAM *rossa* bus (roughly every 10min; €1, or €1.75 on board), which goes from the airport to Piazza Arcivescovado (near the Campo dei Miracoli), via the Ponte di Mezzo.

Terravision **buses to Florence** are scheduled to synchronize with budget airline flights and leave from in front of the terminal; they take seventy minutes to reach Florence's Santa Maria Novella station, and tickets (€10 single) are sold at the stand right in front of you as you come out into the airport concourse.

By bus The main bus terminus is Piazza Sant'Antonio, in front of the train station.
Destinations Florence (hourly via Lucca; 2hr 30min, but a quicker service departs from airport – see above); Livorno (hourly; 40min); Lucca (hourly; 50min); Viareggio (hourly; 50min).

Tourist offices The main office is at Piazza Vittorio Emanuele 13, near the train station (daily 9am–6pm; ☎050 42 291, ⓦpisaunicaterra.it); there's usually an info desk at the Campo dei Miracoli too, but none was in operation as we went to press.

ACCOMMODATION

Novecento Via Roma 37 ☎050 500 323, ⓦhotel novecento.pisa.it. This three-star *residenza d'epoca* occupies a handsome old townhouse, but the rooms are immaculately modern in style. The rates are very reasonable (you can pay twice as much for similar accommodation closer to the Campo), the location convenient and quiet, and it has a pleasant garden as well. €140

Rinascente Via del Castelletto 28 ☎050 580 460, ⓦrinascentehotel.com. This very popular one-star occupies part of an old *palazzo* hidden away a short distance south of Piazza dei Cavalieri. Shared or private bathrooms. €65

★ **Royal Victoria** Lungarno Pacinotti 12 ☎050 940 111, ⓦroyalvictoria.it. Run by the same family since its foundation in 1837, this old-fashioned and appealingly

frayed three-star is the most characterful of central Pisa's hotels – and the best value. The public rooms, with their musty engravings and antique furniture, are redolent of the place's history, but if you're uncharmed by wobbly door-handles and patched-up ceiling frescoes, it's not the place for you. And there's no double-glazing, which might be a problem for light sleepers. €120

Walking Street Hostel Corso Italia 58 ☎393 064 8737, ⓦwalkingstreethostel.com. Opened in 2010, this hostel has an excellent location, on Pisa's busy main drag, as well as clean, bright dorms, a pool table, free internet access and a kitchen for guests' use, with free tea and coffee. Space is limited – twenty beds in six rooms – so book ahead. Dorms from €22

EATING AND DRINKING

Pisa's proximity to the coast means that seafood is served in most restaurants, with *baccalà alla Pisana* (dried cod in tomato sauce) and *pesce spada* (swordfish) featuring prominently; nearly all menus have two sections, typically labelled "mare" (for fish) and "terra" (for meat). Avoid the temptation to eat in the vicinity of the Campo dei Miracoli – aimed squarely at the tourist trade, these places are generally of poor quality. There are plenty of cheap eateries and studenty bars around Piazza Dante and Piazza delle Vettovaglie, and between Piazza Garibaldi and Piazza Cairoli.

CAFÉS, BARS AND GELATERIE

Bazeel Piazza Garibaldi 15 ☎340 288 1113. This bar has been one of Pisa's favourite hangouts for some time – the

interior is cool and spacious, but when the weather's good the punters prefer the outside tables. DJs on Fri & Sat, live music Thurs & Sun. Daily 5pm–2am.

THE GIOCO DEL PONTE AND OTHER FESTIVALS

Pisa's big traditional event is the **Gioco del Ponte**, held on the last Sunday of June, when twelve teams from the north and south banks of the city stage a series of "push-of-war" battles, shoving a seven-tonne carriage over the Ponte di Mezzo. First recorded in 1568, the contest and attendant parades are still held in Renaissance costume. Other celebrations – concerts, regattas, art events – are held throughout June as part of the **Giugno Pisano** (w giugnopisano.com), during which the city has a distinctly festive feel. The most spectacular event is the **Luminara di San Ranieri** (June 16), when buildings along both river banks are lit by 70,000 candles in honour of Pisa's patron saint, and there's a fireworks display at midnight. At 6.30pm the following evening, the various quarters of the city compete in the Palio di San Ranieri, a boat race along the Arno.

Italy's four great maritime republics (Amalfi, Pisa, Genoa and Venice) take turns to host the **Regata delle Antiche Repubbliche Marinare** at the end of May or beginning of June. Four eight-man crews from each of the cities race against each other, in between festivities and parades.

Bottega del Gelato Piazza Garibaldi 11 ☎050 575 467. In business for more than a quarter of a century, this ever-popular *gelateria* has a great range of flavours – the *Tuttobosco* (forest fruits) is gorgeous. Noon–1am; closed Wed in winter.

De' Coltelli Lungarno Pacinotti 23 ☎345 481 1903. The De' Coltelli family are credited with having devised the recipe for ice cream back in the seventeenth century, and the shop that bears their name is one of Italy's top-rank *gelaterie*, with a penchant for adventurous concoctions – anyone for seafood ice cream? Mon–Thurs & Sun noon–11pm, Fri & Sat noon–midnight; closed Jan.

Pasticceria Salza Borgo Stretto 46 ☎050 580 144. The best-known café-*pasticceria* in Pisa, and rightly so; it has a restaurant section at the back, but the coffee and cakes are the main reason to come. Try the Pisan speciality *torta coi bischeri*, a pastry tart made with dark chocolate, dried fruit and pine nuts. Tues–Sun 7.45am–8.30pm.

RESTAURANTS

Al Signor Mimmo Via Cavalca 44 ☎050 543 344. A relaxed spot for lunch, with a handful of outdoor tables at the foot of a medieval belltower. The menu changes daily and is cheaper at lunchtime, but even at dinner no mains are over €15. Summer: Mon–Fri noon–3pm & 7–11pm, Sat 7–11pm; winter: Mon & Tues noon–3pm, Wed–Fri noon–3pm & 7–11pm, Sat 7–11pm.

Beny Piazza Gambacorti 22 ☎050 25 067. This warm and elegant restaurant is a good place for an atmospheric dinner. Fish is the speciality, though the meat dishes are excellent too, with an emphasis on fresh local produce; even the ostrich which is always on the menu (grilled and flavoured with sage and rosemary) is locally reared. Expect to pay €20–30 for your main course. Mon–Fri 12.45–2.45pm & 7.45–11.45pm, Sat 7.45–11.45pm.

La Clessidra Via del Castelletto 26–30 ☎050 540 160. Tucked away in an obscure alley parallel to Via San Frediano, *La Clessidra* offers a small but elegant menu of classic Tuscan dishes, usually with three fish *secondi* and three meat (€12–25), plus tasting menus at around €35 for four courses. Mon–Sat 7.30pm–midnight.

La Sosta dei Cavalieri Via S. Frediano 3 ☎050 991 2410. This is the smaller, cosier and slightly more refined sibling of the *Osteria dei Cavalieri*, over the road. Mains are in the €17–25 range, on a menu that concentrates on classic Pisan meat and fish dishes; the set menus – €20 for the "sea", €25 for the "land" – are excellent value. Mon–Sat 12.30–2.30pm & 7.45–10.30pm.

★ **Osteria dei Cavalieri** Via S. Frediano 16 ☎050 580 858. The *Osteria dei Cavalieri* has built a solid reputation over the years for its straightforward local food and very reasonable prices, with main courses in the €12–16 range; reservations essential in high season. Mon–Fri 12.30–2pm & 7.45–10pm, Sat 7.45–10pm.

Lucca

The most graceful of Tuscany's provincial capitals, encircled by an imposing ring of Renaissance walls fronted by gardens and huge bastions, **LUCCA** stands 17km northeast of Pisa. Charming and quiet out of season, Lucca's narrow streets become busier in summer, without ever being as thronged as those of Florence or Siena.

The town is a delightful place in which to wander at random; while workaday and even scruffy in parts, it's consistently lovely, and full of life. Much of the centre is free from traffic, although you will have to keep an eye out for the many cyclists weaving

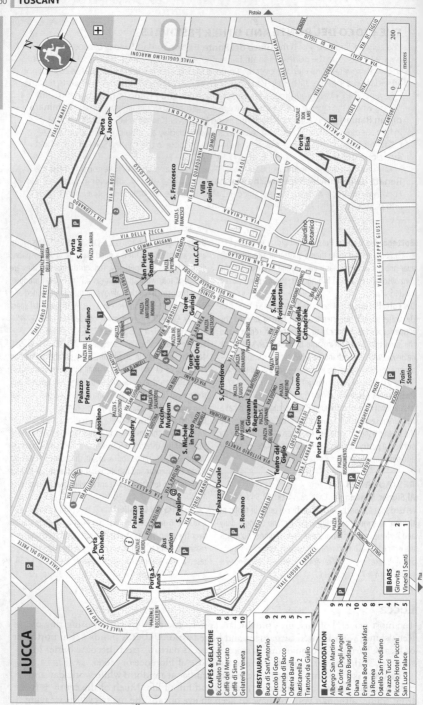

LUCCA

CAFÉS & GELATERIE

B.cellato Taddeucci	8
Caffè del Mercato	6
Caffè di Simo	4
Gelateria Veneta	10

RESTAURANTS

Buca di Sant'Antonio	9
Circolo Il Geco	3
Locanda di Bacco	2
Osteria Baralla	5
Rusticanella 2	7
Trattoria da Giulio	1

ACCOMMODATION

Albergo San Martino	9
Alba Corte Degli Angeli	3
A Palazzo Busdraghi	2
Diana	10
Evelina Bed and Breakfast	6
La Romea	8
Ostello San Frediano	1
Pa azzo Tucci	4
Piccolo Hotel Puccini	7
San Luca Palace	5

BARS

| Girovita | 2 |
| Vineria I Santi | 1 |

through the crowds (plenty of outlets rent bikes if you wish to join them). While the focus of Lucca's compact *centro storico* is the vast Piazza Napoleone, its social heart is **Piazza San Michele** just to the north. Once the site of the Roman forum, these days this lively square is fringed with shops and cafés; its daily **market** sells clothes, bags, sweets and tourist knick-knacks.

The "long thread", Via Fillungo, heads northeast, cutting through Lucca's shopping district to reach the extraordinary circular **Piazza Anfiteatro**, while further east, beyond the Fosso ("ditch"), lies San Francesco and Lucca's major art museum, housed in the **Villa Guinigi**. Whatever else you do, be sure to walk – or cycle – some or all of the city **walls**, which are crested by a broad, tree-lined promenade.

Brief history

Set at the heart of one of Italy's richest agricultural regions, Lucca has prospered since Roman times. Its heyday was the eleventh to fourteenth centuries, when the silk trade brought wealth and political power. Lucca first lost its independence to Pisa in 1314, then, under Castruccio Castracani, forged an empire in the west of Tuscany. Pisa and Pistoia both fell, and, but for Castracani's untimely death in 1325, Lucca might well have taken Florence. In subsequent centuries it remained largely independent until falling into the hands of Napoleon and then the Bourbons. Composer **Giacomo Puccini** was born here in 1858. Today Lucca is among the wealthiest and most conservative cities in Tuscany, its prosperity gained largely through **silk** and high-quality **olive oil**.

San Michele in Foro

Piazza San Michele • Daily 7.40am–noon & 3–6pm, closes 5pm in winter • Free

Dating mainly from the century following 1070, the church of **San Michele in Foro** boasts one of Tuscany's most exquisite facades. The church is unfinished, however, as the money ran out before the body of the building could be raised to the level of the facade; the effect is wonderful, the upper loggias and the windows fronting air. Its Pisan-inspired intricacy is a triumph of poetic eccentricity: each of its myriad columns is different – some twisted, others sculpted or candy-striped. The impressive **campanile** is Lucca's tallest. It would be hard to follow this act and the interior barely tries; the best work of art is a beautifully framed painting called *Saints Jerome, Sebastian, Roch and Helena* by Filippino Lippi in the right-hand nave.

Puccini Museum

Corte S. Lorenzo 9 • April–Oct 10am–6pm; Nov–March 11am–5pm; closed Tues • €7 • ⦿ puccinimuseum.it

The composer Giacomo Puccini was born on December 22, 1858, about a block from San Michele; his father and grandfather had both been organists at the church. Puccini lived here until 1880, when he moved to Milan to complete his studies. The family home has recently reopened after a lengthy restoration as the **Puccini Museum**, and opera buffs can now admire the maestro's original furniture, scores and letters; the splendid gown from a 1926 performance of *Turandot* is the highlight. The museum also organizes a varied programme of Puccini-related **events** (see box, p.565).

Museo Nazionale di Palazzo Mansi

Via Galli Tassi 43 • Tues–Sat 8.30am–7.30pm, last admission 7pm • €4, joint ticket with Museo Guinigi €6.50 • ⦿ luccamuseinazionali.it

A short way west of the Puccini Museum, the **Museo Nazionale di Palazzo Mansi**, set in a seventeenth-century *palazzo*, is worth seeing for its magnificent Rococo decor: from a vast, frescoed **music salon**, you pass through three drawing rooms hung with seventeenth-century Flemish **tapestries** to a gilded bridal suite, complete with lavish canopied bed. Rooms 11–14 in the far wing hold an eclectic **Pinacoteca**, the highlights of which are **Pontormo**'s portrait of Alessandro de' Medici, and Sienese Mannerist works by Domenico Beccafumi and Rutilio Manetti.

9

Duomo di San Martino

Piazza San Martino • Mid-March to Oct daily 7am–6pm; Nov to mid-March daily 7am–5pm • Free • **The Sacristy** Mid-March to Oct Mon–Sat 9.30am–5.45pm, Sat 9.30am–6.45pm, Sun 9.30–10.45am & noon–5pm; Nov to mid-March Mon–Fri 9.30am–4.45pm, Sat 9.30am–6.45pm, Sun 9.30–10.45am & noon–6pm • €4, or €6 with Museo della Cattedrale and church of San Giovanni • ⊛ museocattedralelucca.it

It needs a double-take before you realize why the **Duomo** (also known as the Cattedrale di San Martino) looks odd. A severely asymmetric facade fronts the building – its right-hand arch and loggias are squeezed by the belltower, which was already in place from an earlier building. Little however detracts from its overall grandeur, created by the repetition of tiny columns and loggias and by the stunning **atrium**, with its magnificent bas-reliefs. The carvings over the left-hand door – a *Deposition*, *Annunciation*, *Nativity* and *Adoration of the Magi* – are by **Nicola Pisano**. Other panels display a symbolic labyrinth, a *Tree of Life* (with Adam and Eve at the bottom and Christ at the top), a bestiary of grotesques and the months of the year.

The **interior** is best known for the work of sculptor **Matteo Civitali** (1435–1501). His most celebrated contribution is the *Tempietto*, a gilt-and-marble octagon halfway down the church. Acts of devotion are performed in front of it, directed at the **Volto Santo** (Holy Face) within, a cedarwood crucifix with bulging eyes and dark brown skin popularly said to be a true effigy of Christ carved by Nicodemus, an eyewitness to the Crucifixion. Legend has it that the *Volto Santo* came to Lucca of its own volition, first journeying by boat from the Holy Land, and then brought by oxen guided by divine will. The effigy attracted pilgrims from all over Europe, including kings – William II of England used to swear by it ("*Per sanctum vultum de Lucca!*").

The **Tomb of Ilaria del Carretto** (1410) in the sacristy is considered the masterpiece of Sienese sculptor **Jacopo della Quercia**. It consists of a raised dais and the sculpted body of Ilaria, second wife of Paolo Guinigi, one of Lucca's medieval big-shots. In a touching, almost sentimental gesture, the artist has carved the family dog at her feet. Also within the sacristy is a superb *Madonna Enthroned* by Ghirlandaio.

Museo della Cattedrale

Piazza Antelminelli • Mid-March to Oct daily 10am–6pm; Nov to mid-March Mon–Fri 10am–2pm, Sat & Sun 10am–5pm • €4, or €6 with the cathedral sacristy & San Giovanni • ⊛ museocattedralelucca.it

The **Museo della Cattedrale** occupies a converted twelfth-century building opposite the Duomo. As well as some unnerving Romanesque stone heads, human and equine, it holds, in Room II on the upper floor, a reliquary from Limoges decorated with stories from the life of St Thomas à Becket alongside the Croce dei Pisani, an ornate fifteenth-century gold crucifix.

Santi Giovanni e Reparata

Piazza San Giovanni • Mid-March to Oct daily 10am–6pm; Nov to mid-March Mon–Fri by appointment, Sat & Sun 10am–5pm • €2.50, combined ticket with Tomb of Ilaria & Museo della Cattedrale €6 • ⊛ museocattedralelucca.it

West of the Duomo, what was originally Lucca's cathedral until 715 is now the **church of San Giovanni**. Excavations here have unearthed a tangle of remains, from Roman villa mosaics to an eighth-century baptistry and traces of a ninth-century Carolingian church.

San Frediano

Piazza San Frediano • Mon–Sat 8.30am–noon & 3–5pm, Sun 10.30am–5pm • Free

San Frediano, between Via Fillungo and the northwest city walls, is Pisan-Romanesque, featuring the magnificent thirteenth-century exterior mosaic *Christ in Majesty*, with the Apostles gathered below. A delicately lit, hall-like basilica, the **interior** lives up to the promise of the facade. Facing the door, the **Fonta Lustrale** is a huge twelfth-century font executed by three unknown craftsmen. An *Annunciation* by Andrea della Robbia, behind the font, is festooned with trailing garlands of ceramic fruit. The left-hand of the two rear chapels houses the apparently incorrupt body of **St Zita** (died 1278), a Lucchese maidservant who achieved sainthood by means of a white lie: she used to give bread from her household to the poor, and when challenged one day by her boss as to the contents of her apron, she replied "only roses and flowers" – into which the bread was transformed. On April 27, a flower market outside the church commemorates her. Lucca's finest frescoes – **Amico Aspertini**'s sixteenth-century scenes of *The Arrival of the Volto Santo*, *The Life of St Augustine* and *The Miracle of St Frediano* – occupy the second chapel of the left aisle. Frediano, an Irish monk, is said to have brought Christianity to Lucca in the sixth century and is depicted here saving the city from flood.

Palazzo Pfanner

Via degli Asili 33 • April–Oct daily 10am–6pm; Nov Mon & Thurs –Sun 11am–4pm • Garden or palace €4.50, garden and palace €6, €0.50 reduction in April, Oct & Nov • ⓦ palazzopfanner.it

A short distance west of San Frediano, **Palazzo Pfanner** houses a collection of period furnishings as well as an exhibition of medical instruments belonging to one Pietro Pfanner, surgeon, philanthropist and mayor of Lucca in the 1920s. More interesting are the rear loggia and exquisite statued gardens with fountain. They can be seen to good effect from the city walls just nearby.

Piazza Anfiteatro

The remarkable **Piazza Anfiteatro**, east of San Frediano, is a ramshackle circuit of medieval buildings that was built on the foundations of a Roman amphitheatre – the original arches and columns can still be discerned – and is now ringed by cafés.

Torre Guinigi

Via Sant'Andrea • Daily: Jan & Feb 9.30am–4.30pm; March & Oct 9.30am–5.30pm; April & May 9.30am–6.30pm; June–Sept 9.30am–7.30pm • €3.50

The bizarre **Torre Guinigi**, a castellated tower that once belonged to Lucca's leading fifteenth-century family, is surmounted, 44m up, by a **holm oak** whose roots have grown into the room below. You can climb the tower's 230 steps for wonderful views.

Lu.C.C.A.

Via della Fratta 36 • Tues–Sun 10am–7pm; entry until 1hr before closing • €7 • ⓦ luccamuseum.com

Lucca's new contemporary arts centre, going by the snappy acronym **Lu.C.C.A.**, offers slickly presented exhibitions of sculpture, photography, painting and video art. The upper floor is dedicated to temporary exhibitions by established artists; downstairs, amid the remains of the town's medieval walls and some sixteenth-century frescoed columns, are works by emerging talents.

Museo Nazionale di Villa Guinigi

Via della Quarquonia • Tues–Sat 8.30am–7.30pm • €4, or €6.50 combined ticket with Palazzo Mansi • ⓦ luccamuseinazionali.it

Lucca's key collection of painting, sculpture, furniture and applied arts is housed in the Guinigi family's much-restored mansion, the **Museo Nazionale di Villa Guinigi**. Its lower floor holds mainly sculpture and archeological finds, with numerous Romanesque pieces and works by della Quercia and Matteo Civitali. Upstairs are paintings, with several enormous sixteenth-century canvases, and more impressive works by early Lucchese and Sienese masters, as well as fine Renaissance offerings from such as Fra' Bartolomeo.

ARRIVAL AND DEPARTURE   **LUCCA**

By train Lucca's train station is just south of the city walls, on Piazza Ricasoli.

Destinations Florence (every 30min; 1hr 20min–1hr 45min); Pisa (every 30min; 30min); Pistoia (every 30min; 40min–1hr); Rome (every 15–30min; 3hr 15min–5hr); Viareggio (every 30min–1hr; 20–30min).

By bus Buses stop in Piazzale Verdi; see ⓦ vaibus.com for full timetables.

Destinations Florence (30 daily; 1hr 15min); Pisa (every 30min–1hr; 45min); Pisa airport (every 30min–1hr; 1hr); Viareggio (hourly; 45min).

9

HIKING AND BIKING LUCCA'S CITY WALLS

Lucca's monumental **city walls** make a striking first impression: entirely enclosing the city, they're are an impressive reminder of Lucca's history as an independent city-state. The present-day structure is actually the fourth – after the Roman, medieval and fifteenth-century efforts – constructed between the mid-sixteenth and mid-seventeenth centuries, and extending further than the previous defences.

The walls harbour an attractive swathe of parkland – you can **walk or cycle** the 4.9km loop, taking in lovely views of the city on one side and surrounding countryside on the other. Pick up a picnic from Gastronomia da Sergio, Via dei Boschi 24, just off Piazza Santa Maria (Mon–Sat daily 7am–1.30pm & 3.30–8pm), and rent bikes from one of the outlets in the piazza, such as Poli (daily 8.30am–8pm; €3/hr); from Piazza Santa Maria there's direct access to the ramparts.

By car Virtually all of the centre that isn't pedestrianized is covered by a restricted traffic zone (ZTL), so park at one of the car parks just inside or outside the walls and walk in. There's parking on Piazzale Verdi and Piazza Santa Maria, among other places, but it's only free outside the walls. If you're heading for a hotel, ask the management for directions.

GETTING AROUND AND INFORMATION

By bike Try the outlets in Piazza Santa Maria (see box above); bikes are also available to rent at the tourist office in Piazzale Verdi (€3/hr).
On foot Walking tours are organized by the tourist office in Piazzale Verdi (Mon–Sat at 2pm, Sun at 9.30pm; €10).

By taxi There are ranks on Piazzale Verdi and Piazza Napoleone (☎0583 333 434).
Tourist office Piazzale Verdi (daily: April–Sept 9am–7pm; Oct–March 9am–5pm; ☎0583 583 150, ⓦluccaitinera.it).

ACCOMMODATION

Albergo San Martino Via della Dogana 9 ☎0583 469 181, ⓦalbergosanmartino.it. This cosy little hotel is tucked up an old-town alleyway not far from the Duomo. The spacious, wood-beamed rooms are decorated in soothing neutral tones, and some are painted with bucolic scenes. Exceptionally helpful staff and home-made pastries at breakfast are further draws. €130

★ **Alla Corte Degli Angeli** Via degli Angeli 23 ☎0583 469 204, ⓦallacortedegliangeli.it. Charming, romantic family-run hotel, within the walled town on its northern side; the ten comfortable rooms have delicately frescoed walls and exposed beams; those on the top floor are the nicest. €165

A Palazzo Busdraghi Via Fillungo 170 ☎0583 950 856, ⓦapalazzobusdraghi.it. Ravishing and very central little boutique hotel, overlooking Lucca's main shopping drag; each of its seven antique-furnished rooms has a luxurious bathroom with jacuzzi. Rooms can be on the small side, so it's worth paying extra for a "deluxe". €157

Diana Via del Molinetto 11 ☎0583 492 202, ⓦalbergo diana.com. A block west of the Duomo, this unfussy, somewhat austere place has seven double rooms with private bathroom and two singles without. Rooms in the annexe are more spacious (and cost a little more). No breakfast, but there are plenty of cafés nearby. Great value. €65

★ **Evelina Bed and Breakfast** Via Streghi 12 ☎0583 493 643, ⓦbedandbreakfastevelina.it. Tucked away on a tranquil alley off Via Fillungo, this five-room B&B makes a great base. Thoughtful hosts Simona and Giulio provide plenty of local information, and the comfortable and spacious bedrooms (which share three bathrooms) are a relaxing haven after a long day of pounding the pavements. A generous Tuscan breakfast is served on a terrace overlooking the rooftops. €75

La Romea Vicolo delle Ventaglie 2 ☎0583 464 175, ⓦlaromea.com. This friendly B&B, in a fourteenth-century *palazzo* just off Via Sant'Andrea, is one of Lucca's most sophisticated options. Five pretty, intimate rooms, and an excellent breakfast, served in the spacious hall. Note that the B&B is up several flights of steps (and there's no lift). €135

Ostello San Frediano Via della Cavallerizza 12 ☎0583 469 957, ⓦostellolucca.it. Lucca's HI hostel, conveniently located just inside the walls. Very simple rooms, with a nice garden and shared spaces. Breakfast costs an extra €3, and a full meal at lunch or dinner is €11. Dorms €20, doubles €65

★ **Palazzo Tucci** Via C. Battisti 13 ☎0583 464 279, ⓦpalazzotucci.com. For an opportunity to stay in a noble *palazzo* in the centre of town, look no further than the six-room *Palazzo Tucci*. From its grand entrance to its vast rooms – all ceiling mouldings, ornate wallpaper and family heirlooms – it has character in spades. It's very central too: everything is within easy walking distance. €170

Piccolo Hotel Puccini Via di Poggio 9 ☎0583 55 421, ⓦhotelpuccini.com. Very friendly, central three-star, just steps from the Puccini Museum and San Michele, with fourteen simple en-suite rooms. The high ceilings, large windows and ceiling fans come into their own in summer (though there's no a/c). €97

San Luca Palace Via S. Paolino 103 ☎ 0583 317 446, ⓦ sanlucapalace.com. Conveniently located just steps from Piazzale Verdi's bus stops, this smart four-star hotel offers large and comfortable if slightly characterless rooms, with swish modern bathrooms. Staff are extremely helpful, and the breakfast is ample. **€190**

EATING AND DRINKING

Lucca has a number of high-quality **restaurants**. Keep an eye out for local specialities such as *zuppa di farro*, a thick soup made with spelt (a type of grain); *torta di spinaci*, a sweet spinach tart; and robust pasta dishes such as *pappardelle alla lepre* (with hare). The town's **food shops** are equally good and make great places to stock up for a picnic, or just pick up some foodie souvenirs: Caniparoli at Via San Paolina 96 (daily: Easter–Nov 9.30am–7.30pm; Dec–Easter 9.30am–1pm & 3.30–7.30pm) is a standout chocolate shop. Countless **bars** buzz with drinkers come *aperitivo* time (around 7pm), when free snacks are laid on – just wander the streets and follow the crowds.

CAFÉS, SNACKS AND GELATERIE

Buccellato Taddeucci Piazza S. Michele 34 ☎ 0583 494 933. A stunning interior of wood panelling and mosaic tiles matches the great coffee and selection of cakey delights: try the local speciality *buccellato*, a sweet loaf made with aniseed and raisins. Daily 8.30am–8pm.

Caffè del Mercato Piazza S. Michele 17 ☎ 0583 494 127. Among the most alluring of the bars around the main piazza, kept nice and shady by the church at lunchtime. A handful of hot dishes – lasagne, risotto and the like – are available, as well as filling sandwiches such as Parma ham with olive pâté (€4). Daily 7am–midnight, Fri & Sat closes 1/2am.

★ **Caffè di Simo** Via Fillungo 58 ☎ 0583 496 234. Lucca's most famous café-bar was Puccini's favourite haunt and retains an appealing, late nineteenth-century ambience. It serves a decent array of cakes as well as a few simple meals: at lunch you can get a hot dish and a glass of wine for €9. Daily 8am–8pm; closed Mon in winter.

Gelateria Veneta Via Vittorio Veneto 74 ☎ 0583 493 727. Serving Lucca's finest ice cream since 1927, with several local outlets. The *gelato* here is made with fresh seasonal fruit; try the standout *pinolata* (with pine nuts) and cassata flavours. Daily 10.30am–1am, shorter hours out of season; closed Nov–Feb.

RESTAURANTS

Buca di Sant'Antonio Via della Cervia 3 ☎ 0583 55 881, ⓦ bucadisantantonio.it. Lucca's finest restaurant, in this spot since at least 1782, abounds in old-world charm. Excellent service, top-quality meat or fish menu and delicious house pasta and desserts such as *semifreddo Buccellato*. Lunch menu at €22, dinner can easily be double that. Booking essential. Tues–Sat noon–3pm & 7.30–10.30pm, Sun noon–3pm.

★ **Circolo Il Geco** Via M. Rosi 34 ☎ 0583 494 538. Don't be put off by the lack of signage outside – the dark entranceway leads to a warm, wood-beamed back room with a clutter of old photos and antique clocks, where a local culinary-cultural association runs this great little restaurant. The menu changes daily depending on what's available at market, but the pastas always include the local stuffed *tortelli*, perhaps with courgettes or cheese, as well as a handful of simple mains such as veal escalope cooked in wine (€7). There's a pretty garden for alfresco dining when the weather's fine. Daily 7–10.30pm; closed Mon in summer.

Locanda di Bacco Via S. Giorgio 36 ☎ 0583 495 692. Set in an elegant wood-panelled space, this local favourite serves quality meals to suit any palate, with the usual meat and fish but also vegetarian options such as chickpea

---

FESTIVALS AND EVENTS IN LUCCA

The **Lucchese Settembre** festival features plenty of activity throughout September, centred on a **candlelit procession** on the 13th, when the bejewelled Volto Santo (see p.562) is carried through the streets from San Frediano to the Duomo. Consult the tourist office for details of affiliated September events, such as **classical concerts** (including performances of a Puccini opera) at the intimate, four-tiered Teatro Comunale in Piazza del Giglio, as well as **jazz** gigs and **art** exhibitions. Another key musical event is July's **Summer Festival** (☎ 0584 46477, ⓦ summer-festival.com) in which big-name international stars perform, some for free, in Piazza Napoleone. The smaller-scale Amphitheatre Music Festival in August sees live concerts of various genres in Piazza Anfiteatro (tickets around €10).

The **Puccini e la sua Lucca** music festival sees concerts performed daily at 7pm from mid-March to mid-November at the church of San Giovanni (ⓦ puccinielasualucca.com; tickets €17), while the Puccini Museum (see p.561) organizes concerts of the composer's work in atmospheric venues around town, including the botanic gardens (Friday nights June–Aug).

Every third weekend of the month, an **antiques fair** takes over the central streets and squares, with hundreds of dealers selling everything from secondhand furniture to vintage stamps.

9

fritters with radicchio and *scamorza* cheese (€16). The weekday lunch menu is good value at €15. Daily noon–2.30pm & 7–11pm; closed Tues in winter.

Osteria Baralla Via dell'Anfiteatro 5 ☎ 0583 440 240, ⓦ osteriabaralla.it. This much-loved traditional *osteria* serves simple local food in a pair of vaulted dining rooms: come for hearty Tuscan fare such as *peposo* (beef stew in pepper and wine sauce; €14) and braised Chianina beef cooked in spelt beer (€15). Mon–Sat 12.30–2.20pm & 7–10.20pm.

Rusticanella 2 Via S. Paolino 32 ☎ 058 355 838, ⓦ rusticanella2.it. This wood-panelled restaurant with Italian flags hanging from the rafters and the TV blaring in the bustling back room makes a convivial spot for a cheap meal. Dishes (€8–22) are local and earthy, such as sausage with beans, or salt cod with chickpeas, and the pizzas (from €7) are good and crispy. Mon–Sat 11am–3pm & 6.45–11pm.

Trattoria Da Giulio Via della Conce 45 ☎ 0583 55 948. This classic trattoria is always packed in the evenings – the food is not exceptional, but the prices are very reasonable (*primi* from €6, *secondi* €7 and up) and the atmosphere makes it worth it. Mon–Sat noon–3pm & 6–10.30pm.

BARS

Girovita Piazza Antelminelli 2 ☎ 0583 469 412. With tables outside in the quiet piazza opposite the cathedral, trendy *Girovita* is the place to come for a lengthy afternoon coffee or an *aperitivo* in the early evening (free snack buffet when you buy a drink); it also has free wi-fi. Off the bar, a smarter restaurant space serves up *leccese* dishes for around €10. Tues–Sun 9am–midnight.

Vineria I Santi Via dell'Anfiteatro 29/A ☎ 0583 496 124. With tables outside on a small piazza behind the amphitheatre, this wine bar is a good spot for an evening drink and a spot of people-watching, and there's a simple menu of inventive, well-prepared dishes too (duck liver pâté with orange marmalade €15). 7.30–10.30pm, Sat & Sun also 12.30–2.30pm; closed Wed.

DIRECTORY

Hospital Ospedale Campo di Marte, Via dell'Ospedale (☎ 0583 9701).

Internet Copisteria Paolini, Via di San Paolino 63 (Mon–Fri 9am–1pm & 3.30–7.30pm, Sat 9am–1pm; €2/30min). There's also access at the tourist office (€1/30min).

Left luggage At the tourist office on Piazzale Verdi (€1.50/hr or €7.50/day).

Police Viale Cavour 38 (☎ 0583 4551).

Post office Via Vallisneri 2 (Mon–Fri 8.25am–7.10pm, Sat 8.25am–1.10pm).

North of Pisa

A solid strip of unattractive beach resorts stretches north along the coast from near Pisa to the Ligurian border. This **Riviera della Versilia** ought to be something more special, given the dramatic backdrop of the **Alpi Apuane**, but the beaches share the coastal plain with a railway, autostrada and clogged urban roads, while the sea itself is far from being the cleanest in Italy. The resort of **Viareggio** provides a lively diversion on a coastal journey north to the stunning Cinque Terre. Otherwise, the only real appeal lies inland, exploring the famed marble-quarrying centre of **Carrara**.

Viareggio

Tuscany's largest seaside resort, **VIAREGGIO**, 22km northwest of Pisa, may feature on few independent travellers' itineraries – everyone wants picturesque former fishing villages and converted farmhouses these days – but it does still cling to a certain stately elegance. The real problem is that the sheer demand keeps prices alarmingly high in summer, when many hotels insist on at least half-board. Apart from a free stretch south of town, most of the **beach** has been parcelled up into private strips, charging around €20 for a day's use of a sun lounger and parasol.

Life in Viareggio centres on the grand seafront boulevard, **Viale Regina Margherita**; locals and visitors alike promenade each night beneath the palm trees that line this 3km thoroughfare. Interspersed among its imposing old hotels are several fine **Art Nouveau frontages**, as well as a plentiful array of bars and restaurants. On a balmy summer evening, the ensemble has a strip-like neon-lit aesthetic more American in feel than Tuscan. To see Viareggio at its liveliest, come for its famously boisterous **Carnevale** in February, when for four consecutive Sundays it stages an amazing parade of floats, or *carri* – colossal, lavishly designed papier-mâché models of politicians and celebrities (ⓦ viareggio.ilcarnevale.com).

ARRIVAL AND INFORMATION

By train The train station is on Piazza Dante, a 10min walk inland from the seafront. Trains leave for Carrara every 30min (15–25min).

By bus Buses stop nearer the centre, on Piazza d'Azeglio and Piazza Mazzini, with services to Lucca (hourly; 45min) and Pisa airport (hourly; 1hr).

Tourist office The tourist office faces the sea about 100m north of Piazza Mazzini, at Viale Carducci 10 (Mon–Sat 9am–2pm & 3–7pm, Sun 9am–1pm; ☎0584 962 233, ⓦaptversilia.it); there's also an information point at the station (Mon 9am–2pm, Tues–Sat 9am–2pm & 3–7pm; ☎0584 46 382).

ACCOMMODATION AND EATING

Romano Via Mazzini 120 ☎0584 31 382, ⓦromano ristorante.it. The best local restaurant is the Michelin-starred *Romano*, which specializes in sublime fish and seafood: try the *calamaretti* stuffed with vegetables or the scampi with courgette flowers. A three-course meal will set you back around €70 per head, not including wine. Tues–Sun 12.30–3pm & 8–10.30pm; closed Tues lunch in July & Aug.

Tirrenia Via S. Martino 23 ☎0584 49 641, ⓦtirrenia hotel.com. Viareggio's best option in the heart of town is this gem of a hotel near the seafront. The rooms are spotless and cheerfully furnished, with bright pops of colour and modern art on the walls. The generous breakfast and helpful staff are further bonuses. **€100**

Carrara

CARRARA sits just inside the Ligurian border, 28km north of Viareggio, and enjoys a fame that far outstrips its modest size. Ever since the Roman era, the mountains here have been a principal source of **marble**; everyone from Michelangelo to Henry Moore has tramped up here in search of the perfect stone. Despite fierce modern competition from Brazil and India, Carrara still ranks among the world's largest producers and exporters of marble, shipping out a million tonnes a year from the container port in the middle of ugly **Marina di Carrara**. But quiet Carrara itself has a pleasant, rural feel and comes as a relief after the holiday coast.

From the central **Piazza Matteotti**, pedestrianized Via Roma heads north to the attractive Piazza Accademia, with steps down (west) to the old town and Carrara's Romanesque-Gothic **Duomo** (daily 7am–noon & 3.30–7pm), adorned with a lovely Pisan-style marble facade. Gracious **Piazza Alberica**, at the heart of the old town, is the focus for a biennial summer display of contemporary marble sculpture,

---

FERRIES FROM LIVORNO

The major, mostly modern port city of **Livorno**, 18km southwest of Pisa, holds little of interest for most casual visitors. However, dozens of **ferries** sail from here to **Corsica** (Bastia and Porto Vecchio), **Sardinia** (Olbia, Golfo Aranci or Cagliari), **Sicily** (Palermo) and the **Tuscan Islands**. Nearly all ferries to Corsica, Sicily and Sardinia leave from alongside the **Stazione Maríttima**, west of the centre behind the Fortezza Vecchia, although some depart from **Varco Galvani**, a long way north of town with no transport connections to the centre. Ferries to Capraia leave from the central **Porto Mediceo**. For times and prices, check the various companies' websites, or ask at the tourist office on Piazza Municipio (June–Sept Mon–Sat 8am–6pm, Sun 9am–6pm); **reserve** well ahead in summer.

There are **trains** to Livorno from Florence (12 daily; 1hr 20min), La Spezia (13 daily; 55min–1hr 15min), Pisa (every 20min; 15–25min) and Rome (12 daily; 2hr 35min–3hr 45min). Eight daily **buses** run from Piombino (2hr).

FERRY COMPANIES

Corsica Ferries/Sardinia Ferries Stazione Maríttima, Calata Carrara ☎0586 881 380, ⓦcorsicaferries.com. To Bastia (Corsica) and Golfo Aranci (Sardinia).

Grandi Navi Veloci (Grimaldi) Varco Galvani, Darsena 1 ☎0586 409 804, ⓦgrimaldi-lines.com. To Barcelona and Tangiers.

Moby Lines Stazione Maríttima, Calata Carrara ☎0586 899 950, ⓦmoby.it. To Bastia (Corsica) and Olbia (Sardinia).

Toremar Porto Mediceo ☎0586 896 113, ⓦtoremar .it. To Capraia.

9

Scolpire all'Aperto, when internationally renowned artists arrive to create new works in public. To get the full low-down on marble, call in at the impressive **Museo del Marmo** on Viale XX Settembre, 2km south of town (Mon–Sat: May–Sept 9.30am–1pm & 3.30–6pm; Oct–April 9am–12.30pm & 2.30–5pm; €4.50).

Colonnata and the marble quarries

There are nine daily buses to Colonnata from Via Minzoni in Carrara; get off when you see the Visita Cave signs

Any short trip into the interior brings you to the startling sight of the **marble quarries**. To get a closer view, head up the twisting road towards **Colonnata**, 8km northeast of Carrara. Once there, you're confronted by a huge, blindingly white marble basin, its floor and sides perfectly squared by the enormous wire saws used to cut the blocks that litter the surroundings.

ARRIVAL AND DEPARTURE CARRARA

By train Regular buses from Carrara-Avenza train station, close to the Marina di Carrara seafront, run 4km inland to Carrara's central Piazza Matteotti.

By bus Buses from Florence arrive in Piazza Menconi in Marina di Carrara; more local services stop in Via Don Minzoni.

By boat In summer, Navigazione Golfo dei Poeti runs boats to Portovenere and the Cinque Terre from Marina di Carrara (mid-June to mid-Sept daily; €25; w navigazionegolfodeipoeti.it).

ACCOMMODATION AND EATING

Galeria Ars Apua Via Antica Bergiola 19 ☎ 0585 70 496, w g-arsapua.com. This delightful rural B&B in the hills makes a perfect retreat if you have a car. Marble is everywhere to be seen here: not just in the bathrooms but in the sculptures that decorate the public spaces. The soothing bedrooms have wonderful views of the Alpi Apuane and the nearby quarries. **€65**

'L Purtunzin d'Ninan Via Bartolini 3 ☎ 0585 74741, w ristorantepurtunzin.com. The pick of the restaurants in Carrara is this cosy little place, with only a handful of tables and bags of charm. It's known for serving up the freshest fish and seafood in town. Expect to pay about €50 per person, excluding wine. Tues–Sun 12.30–3.30pm & 7.30–11pm.

Elba

Nearly 30km long by some 20km wide, **ELBA** is Italy's third-largest island. Ever since Napoleon was exiled here, it has been captivating visitors. It has exceptionally clear water, fine white-sand beaches, and a lush, wooded interior, superb for walking; almost everyone, including a surge of package tourists in July and August, comes for the beach resorts, so the inland villages remain largely quiet even in high season.

Historically, Elba has been well out of the mainstream. The principal industry until World War II was **mining**, especially of iron ore. The **Romans** wrote of "the island of good wines" – a reputation Elban wines retain to this day – while control in later centuries passed from Pisa to Genoa and on to the Medici, Spain, Turkey and finally France. That cosmopolitan mix has left its legacy on both architecture and cultivation. Most people know the island as the place of exile for **Napoleon**, who, after he was banished here in May 1814, revamped education and the legal system, built roads and modernized the economy before escaping back to France in February 1815.

Portoferraio and around

Elba's principal town, **PORTOFERRAIO**, makes a worthwhile day-trip destination from the mainland. If you head straight off to the beaches and resorts, however, you'll hardly see it; the long, unattractive, modern quayside used by the island ferries is well away from the town's atmospheric old quarter, with its stepped alleys and ancient churches.

Head to the right of the ferry dock for a few minutes, and you'll reach a short flight of steps that leads to the old quarter's "back entrance", the **Porta a Terra**. From here, steep alleys fan out on different levels; zigzag your way up to the first entrance of the **Fortezze Medicee** that loom over the town, where an *enoteca* (see p.573) allows you to enjoy the view with a glass of the local wine. A ten-minute walk east of here, along Via del Falcone, is the town's main sight: the Villa dei Mulini.

Villa dei Mulini

Via Napoleone • Mon & Wed–Sat 9am–7pm, Sun 9am–1pm • €7, or €13 joint three-day ticket with Villa di San Martino

At the highest point of the old quarter sits Napoleon's residence-in-exile, the **Villa dei Mulini**. Purpose-built on a well-chosen site with grand views of the bay, the villa is a fair-sized old building, albeit undoubtedly not what the emperor was used to. Inside, you'll find a gallery with empire-style furniture, a Baroque bedroom with an absurdly over-gilded bed, a library of two thousand books sent over from Fontainebleau, and various items of memorabilia. The peaceful rear garden looks down over the rocky headland.

Villa di San Martino

Via San Martino • Tues–Sat 9am–7pm, Sun 9am–1pm • €3, or €7.50 joint three-day ticket with Villa dei Mulini • From Portoferraio's bus station on Viale Elba take bus #1 (hourly)

The arrow-straight avenue leading up to the **Villa di San Martino** is designed to impress, even if the villa itself – bought by Napoleon's sister Elise just before the emperor left the island for good – is a rather chilly affair, with a drab Neoclassical facade enlivened with "N" motifs. The monograms were the idea of Prince Demidoff, husband of Napoleon's niece, and it was he who created the Napoleonic museum. The interior halls of the *palazzo* are devoted to temporary art exhibitions. To see Napoleon's modest

---

PARCO NAZIONALE DELL'ARCIPELAGO TOSCANO

All seven Tuscan Islands, and the seas around them, form the **Parco Nazionale dell'Arcipelago Toscano**, the largest protected marine park in Europe. You can take a ferry from Portoferraio or Porto Azzurro to various smaller islands, and from Marina di Campo in the south you can visit the beautiful island of **Pianosa**, an uninhabited former military base, with great beaches and abundant wildlife. See ⓦparks.it and ⓦislepark.it for further information.

9

summer retreat, head left of the facade to the ticket office, and then up flights of stairs to the back of the site. Of the handful of empire-style rooms, the best is the **Sala Egizio**, decorated with Nilotic scenes.

Eastern Elba

Eastern Elba comprises two tongues of land, each dominated by mountain ridges, and a coastline given over entirely to beach tourism. The main road east from Portoferraio heads through the former mining town of **Rio nell'Elba** to **Rio Marina**. Tourism and ferry links have replaced iron ore as the town's principal source of revenue. Some boats stop at picturesque **Cavo**, 9km north of Rio Marina, with a 1km-long sandy beach.

The busy resort of **PORTO AZZURRO** was heavily fortified by Philip III of Spain in 1603; today his fortress is the island's prison. The town's small, pretty, old quarter – closed to traffic – centres on bustling Via d'Alarcon, while broad Piazza Matteotti, lined with pavement cafés, fronts the marina. Plenty of places rent bikes, boats and scooters, while motorboats shuttle across the bay to the sandy beach at Naregno.

Some 3.5km southwest of Porto Azzurro and overlooked by Monte Calamita, **CAPOLIVERI** is the nicest town on Elba's eastern fringe, a prosperous inland centre whose close-knit lanes have made few concessions to tourism. In summer, minibuses run to the nearby beach towns.

Western Elba

The main road west from Portoferraio heads to prim **Marciana Marina**, whose traffic-filled promenade of bars, restaurants and trinket shops does little to lure you into staying. A winding road heads south for 5km into the hills to **Poggio**, a village renowned for its mineral water and medieval centre, with decorated doorways and a patchwork of cheerful gardens.

The high, isolated village of **Marciana**, up 4km of switchbacks from Poggio, is the oldest settlement and most alluring spot on Elba, perfectly located between great beaches and the mountainous interior. Its steep **old quarter** is a delight of narrow alleys, arches, belvederes and stone stairs festooned with flowers and climbing plants that culminate at the twelfth-century **Fortezza Pisano** (closed to the public, but with great views from its lofty location).

Monte Capanne

Cable car operates daily: 10am–1pm & 2.20–5.30pm • €18 return

The main draw of Marciana is 500m south of the village – the base-station of a **cable car** (*cabinovia*) that climbs 650m (15min) to the summit of 1019m **Monte Capanne**, Elba's highest point. Note that "cable car" is something of a misnomer: it's a series of small exposed cages, each big enough for two people to stand up in, hooked onto a continually running cable. At the top is a bar at which to soothe jangled nerves and a terrace from which to take in the stupendous panorama; hardy types can take trail #1 from here back down the mountain to Marciana (1hr 30min).

The western coast

The wild **western coast** harbours a handful of small towns, a clutch of stunning **beaches** and little else. The spread-out village of **Sant'Andrea**, 6km west of Marciana, just off the coast road, is the main focus, popular with divers lured by the crystal-clear seas. A little west, the road hugs the coast for a scenic drive that offers breathtaking views at every turn.

ARRIVAL AND GETTING AROUND   ELBA

By boat Most ferries (see box, p.572) arrive at Portoferraio, sliding past the old town to dock at the Calata Italia. Island buses leave from Viale Elba just inland of the dock. Boats are also much used to reach out-of-the-way beaches, and are well advertised at all ports (see opposite).

By bus or minibus ATL buses serve just about every

ELBA'S BEST BEACHES

No less than 156 **beaches** dot Elba's rocky coast, from little-visited shingly coves to broad white-sand stretches. The island's best-known beaches can get suffocatingly packed in high season, but if you don't mind negotiating the ranks of baking bodies on sunloungers, they offer all the facilities you could wish for, from snack bars to diving centres. The big five are fine-sand **Procchio**; **Fetovaia**, with its crystal-clear water; beautiful **Cavoli**, a sandy arc in a sheltered bay where you can swim well out of season; **Marina di Campo**, a full-blown resort; and **Biodola**, occupying an idyllic sweeping bay near Portoferraio. To avoid the worst of the crowds, however, head to one of the beaches below.

Acquavivetta Not far from Sansone, this shingly beach is backed by high rocks. The gently sloping seashore makes it a good spot for swimming, especially if you have kids in tow.

Cotoncello Reachable from the beach at Sant'Andrea, this small patch of sandy beach has a natural pool of clear, shallow water formed by two tongues of rock.

Forno In the bay of Biodola, sandy Forno is less busy than Biodola beach itself, set in a lovely little bay, surrounded by villas and dense vegetation. There's a restaurant here (though it's the island's most expensive), as well as snack bars.

La Guardia Also known as La Polveraia, this sheltered shingly beach on the island's western coast is always fairly quiet, even in high season. The dark rocks here plunge sheer to the transparent water below.

Sansone A dazzling stretch of shingle, enclosed by sheer white cliffs and lapped by clear water.

Sant'Andrea A lovely, fine-sand beach, well set up with sun loungers, parasols and beach bars. A natural rocky barrier keeps the water shallow, and you can rent boats, windsurf and dive here too.

---

settlement on the island (☎0565 914 783, timetables on ⓦ infoelba.com; no service after 8pm; single ticket €1.20–4 depending on distance, daily ticket €8.50). In addition, council minibuses run several times a day between town centres and their outlying beaches in the summer season; Marciana is connected with the western beaches and Capoliveri with the eastern beaches, for example.

By bike or scooter All the main agencies are near Portoferraio's ferry dock; TWN, Viale Elba 32 (April–Oct daily 9am–noon & 4–7pm; Nov–March Mon–Fri 9am–noon & 4–6pm; ☎0565 914 666, ⓦ twn-rent.it), is reliable. The per-day rate for a small car is around €45–65, a 50cc scooter €25, a mountain-bike €15, and an ordinary bike €10.

By car Car rental is not advisable in high season: roads to the beaches and around the resorts get nastily congested. Ouside of July and August, however, this can be a great way of exploring the island, particularly the wilder western coast, where the winding roads make for exhilarating driving. The car park opposite the bus station on Viale Elba in Portoferraio is free. Cars are banned from Portoferraio's old quarter during the summer.

By taxi In Portoferraio, taxis wait on Calata Italia (☎0565 915 112); in Porto Azzurro, Piazza Palestro (☎338 860 9896).

INFORMATION AND ACTIVITIES

TOURIST INFORMATION

The tourist office is at Viale Elba 4, Portoferraio (summer Mon–Sat 9am–7pm, Sun 10am–1pm & 3–6pm; winter Mon–Thurs 9am–5pm, Fri 9am–2pm; ☎0565 914 671, ⓦ isoleditoscana.it). Useful online resources include the websites ⓦ elbalink.it, ⓦ elba.org and ⓦ infoelba.com.

ACTIVITIES

Boating A 5m boat costs €65–115/day, not including fuel. Try Bartolini Yachting at Lungomare S. Giovanni 3, Portoferraio (☎0565 916 957, ⓦ bartoliniyachting.com). For boat tours with beach stops, the *Dollaro* II leaves twice daily from Porto Azzurro for a half-day trip (€15; ☎328 689 0227). Aquavision (☎0328 709 5470, ⓦ aquavision.it; €20.90 return) runs daily sea cruises to the Isola Pianosa.

Diving Part of the biggest marine park in Europe, the waters around Elba offer perfect diving conditions. The spots to head for are the islet of La Corbella, off Monte Calamita; the Formiche della Zanca rock formations near Sant'Andrea; the wreck of the *Elviscot* near Pomonte to the southwest; and the Scoglietto north of Portoferraio, with an underwater statue of Christ. Rio Diving at Via Scappini, Rio Marina (☎335 570 9947, ⓦ riodiving.it), offer excursions by boat around little-visited coves where you can snorkel or dive, from €25, while Diving in Elba (☎347 371 5788, ⓦ divinginelba.com) have diving schools in Procchio and Biodola, with courses at all levels.

Walking Elba is criss-crossed with walking routes for all abilities. Ask at the tourist office for the booklet on local walks (available in English), including a 20km hike round Monte Calamita, where wild orchids thrive, and the 7.6km Monserrato loop from Porto Azzurro, offering splendid views.

9

FERRIES TO ELBA

Most ferries to Elba depart from the port of **Piombino**, 75km south of Livorno – not a great place to spend any time, since it was flattened in World War II and these days makes its living from a giant steelworks. If you're arriving by **train**, you'll probably have to change at Campiglia Maríttima station, and catch a connecting train to Piombino Maríttima. There are two daily SITA **buses** from Florence to Piombino's port (2hr 30min). The ferry terminal at the port – the Stazione Maríttima – holds ticket outlets for all ferry companies; it also has ample parking, both paid and free.

ROUTES AND FREQUENCIES

Most ferries head to Portoferraio (1hr 10min), though there are also sailings to Rio Marina (45min) and Cavo (35min). Passenger-only hydrofoils arrive at Cavo (20min) and Portoferraio (35min). Toremar, Moby and Blu Navy ferries run every day of the year, and Corsica Ferries from mid-June to mid-September only, with the first departure at around 6am and the last around 10.30pm. In summer, there's a huge ferry every half-hour or so, but it's still best to book well in advance if you're taking a car; in low season the frequency drops to more like one every two to three hours.

FARES AND BOOKING

Precise **fares** vary according to the season and the day of the week, but the cheapest are on the Toremar line. In high summer, Toremar charges a typical one-way fare per passenger of €13, with a car costing from €40; return fares are double that. Toremar also runs slightly cheaper sailings to Rio Marina (passengers €8, car €30) and Cavo (passengers €9.60, car €18) on the island's east coast, though they're less appealing as day-trip destinations.

Either book online via ⓦ infoelba.it, direct through the ferry companies below, or, in Elba, at the Lari & Palombo travel agency at Calata Italia 22, Portoferraio (daily 9am–1pm & 3–8pm; ⓣ0565 914 648).

FERRY COMPANY OFFICES

Blu Navy Piombino ⓣ349 007 6956; Calata Italia 8, Portoferraio ⓣ349 007 1781, ⓦblunavytraghetti.com. **Corsica Ferries** ⓣ+33 4 95 32 95 95, ⓦcorsica-ferries .it. **Moby** Piombino ⓣ0565 221 212; Via Ninci 1, Portoferraio ⓣ0565 914 133, ⓦmoby.it. **Toremar** Piombino ⓣ0565 31 100, ⓦtoremar.it; Calata Italia 42, Portoferraio ⓣ0565 960 131; Calata Voltoni 20, Rio Marina ⓣ0565 962 073; or Via Michelangelo 54, Cavo ⓣ0565 949 871.

ACCOMMODATION

Portoferraio has a particularly poor range of **accommodation**, and visitors tend to disperse around the island. If you arrive without a reservation and are having trouble finding a room, try the Associazione Albergatori Elbani (ⓣ0565 915 555, ⓦelbapromotion.it), which has hotels, apartments and private homes on its books. Elba also has a good selection of **campsites**: see ⓦcampingelba.net for a full list. Most hotels and campsites are open April–Oct only.

AROUND PORTOFERRAIO

Biodola Biodola beach ⓣ0565 974 812, ⓦelba4star.it. In an enviable location perched above Biodola beach, this comfortable four-star has breezy, seaside-y decor, with gleaming blue tiles in the bedrooms and a light and airy feel throughout. There's a wealth of activities on offer on site, from swimming pool and tennis courts to a spa, and there's a good restaurant too; many guests stay on a half-board basis. €336

Lacona Via del Golfi 71, Lacona ⓣ0565 964 161, ⓦcamping-lacona.it. The key site in Lacona, Elba's camping hotspot on the coast 7km south of Portoferraio. It's set in pine woods a little away from the flat foreshore crowded with bars and discos, and also has apartments (min 3 nights, 10 nights in high season). Camping €13, apartments €120

★ **Le Stanze del Casale** Località S. Giovanni 99 ⓣ0565 944 340, ⓦlestanzedelcasale.com. Just a few kilometres from Portoferraio, this beautifully decorated B&B has several well-appointed en-suite rooms combining wood beams and antiques with modern touches. The generous breakfast is served on the shady veranda, which is lit by lantern in the evenings. €140

Relais delle Picchiaie La Picchiaie ⓣ0565 933 110, ⓦrelaisdellepicchiaie.it. A gorgeous, well-priced hillside retreat, 5km south of town, with plenty of attractions to keep you from the beaches, including a spa, pool and restaurant. The rooms are very comfortable and tastefully decked out in calming shades. €190

9

WESTERN ELBA

Arrighi Barbarossa ☎ 0565 95 568, ⓦ campingarrighi .it. This campsite 1km north of town gives straight onto the beach. There are also apartments, caravans and wooden bungalows (3–5 people) for rent. Tents €27, caravans €85, bungalows €95, apartments €100

Residence Gavila's Loc. Sassi Turchini 5 ☎ 0565 958 129, ⓦ gavilas.isoladelba.it. Perched on a hill overlooking Porto Azzurro bay and only 1km from the beach, this rose-pink villa is surrounded by lawns dotted with palm trees. The simply furnished apartments come complete with kitchenette and outdoor terrace, with lovely views. €88

Villa Capitorsola Loc. Colle del Lido di Capoliveri ☎ 0565 933 546, ⓦ villacapitorsola.it. Just outside Capoliveri, and a short walk from two lovely beaches, this immaculate B&B is in a wonderfully scenic spot with views over the gulf. Cool, simple rooms with tiled floors, a warm welcome and a generous breakfast are further pluses. €145

Villa Italia Viale Italia 41 ☎ 0565 59119, ⓦ villa italiahotel.it. This no-frills hotel, just outside the town centre and steps from the beach, offers old-fashioned but spotless rooms of a decent size (a/c costs extra). Staff are friendly and helpful, and there's free parking too. €99

EASTERN ELBA

Barsalini Sant'Andrea beach ☎ 0565 908 920, ⓦ hotel barsalini.com. At the foot of a lush, forested mountainside and just steps from Sant'Andrea beach, this family-run hotel makes an idyllic escape. The elegant rooms either overlook the sea or the flower-filled garden, and there's a swimming pool and a small spa too. €110

★ **Ilio** Via Sant'Andrea 5 ☎ 0565 908 018, ⓦ hotelilio .com. A boutique hotel just above the beach, the ecofriendly *Ilio* has breezy, comfortable rooms with wonderful views; some come with their own little patch of garden, complete with lemon trees. Delicious meals are served in the newly revamped restaurant (half-board available), and breakfast is a five-star feast. €160

EATING AND DRINKING

There are plenty of decent **restaurants** scattered across the island. There's a big Coop **supermarket** on Via Tesei at Portoferraio's dock (Mon–Sat 8am–8pm, Sun 8am–1.30pm). **Market day** in Portoferraio's harbour is Friday; Cavo's is on Wednesday, Capoliveri's on Thursday and Porto Azzurro's on Saturday.

PORTOFERRAIO

Enoteca della Fortezza Via Scoscesa ☎ 335 839 3722, ⓦ enotecadellafortezza.com. In an atmospheric location in the grotto of Portoferraio's sixteenth-century Medicean fortress, this is a serious *enoteca* with a comprehensive list of local and regional wines, as well as a Slow Food-dedicated menu. Sip a chilled Vermentino on the terrace as you tuck into a fresh octopus salad (*secondi* around €9). March–Oct Thurs & Fri 6–11pm, Sat & Sun noon–3pm & 6–11pm; Nov–Feb Sat & Sun 6–11pm.

★ **Osteria Libertaria** Calata Matteotti 12 ☎ 0565 914 978. A very welcome exception to Portoferraio's largely poor-value restaurants, with some outdoor tables on the Medici harbourfront. Wonderful seafood, including a fabulous gnocchi with swordfish (€9.50) and tuna fillet with pistachio (€14). Daily noon–2.30pm & 7–11pm.

Osteria Pepenero Via dell'Amore 48 ☎ 0565 916 240. This rustic little place with wood beams and hand-written menus offers *primi* for €8–13, and mains such as fish soup for €12. Tues–Sun noon–3pm & 7pm–midnight.

★ **Ristorante Pizzeria La Carretta** Loc. Magazzini 92 ☎ 0565 933 223, ⓦ ristorantelacarretta.it. In the little village of Magazzini not far from Portoferraio, this excellent pizzeria is well worth seeking out. It also serves home-cooked meals, chalked up on the blackboard daily, with an emphasis on fresh fish. Daily 7pm–midnight.

EASTERN ELBA

Osteria La Botte Gaia Viale Europa 5/7 ☎ 0565 95 607, ⓦ labottegaia.com. This attractive corner *osteria* is a 5min walk from the old centre and does tasty pastas such as *tonnarelli* with vegetable *caponata* and smoked ricotta (€11), as well as mains like fish soup (€22), served up in a glass bowl. Tues–Sun 7–11pm.

Ristorante Pizzeria Rendez Vous Lungomare C. Colombo 7 ☎ 0565 931 060. This informal local restaurant right on the harbour is perennially popular with locals, who crowd in for a taste of their speciality crêpes, both sweet and savoury; the *covacini* – pizza stuffed with an array of fillings – are good too. You can get a satisfying meal for well under €20 a head – a bargain. Daily 8am–midnight.

Tamata Via Cesare Battisti 3 ☎ 349 358 6956, ⓦ tamata winebar.it. A wine bar and restaurant with outside tables on an attractive piazza. The creative menu might include octopus served three ways with *pappa al pomodoro* soup (€12), or duck with smoked aubergine, *caprino* cheese and coffee (€16). More traditional cold-cuts are also available. Come at *aperitivo* time (6–9pm) for bite-sized tastings of fish dishes. Daily 12.30–2pm & 6–10pm.

WESTERN ELBA

Da Publius Piazza del Castagneto 11, Poggio ☎ 0565 99 208, ⓦ ristorantepublius.it. *Da Publius* enjoys fantastic views from its terrace; indoors is rustic but elegant. The steeply priced menu offers refined, beautifully presented dishes such as pink gnocchi with a seafood pesto, or chocolate ravioli with wild boar (*secondi* from €15). Mon 6–10.30pm, Tues–Sun 9am–2pm & 6–10.30pm.

9

★ **Osteria del Noce** Via della Madonna 14, Marciana ☎0565 901 284, ⚲osteriadelnoce.it. Book a table on the terrace for the spectacular views and excellent food. Fish is the main draw here, with *primi* such as spaghetti with fish roe and lemon (€10) and the always-delicious fish dish of the day chalked up on the blackboard. A full meal will come to around €30 a head, not including wine. Easter–Sept daily noon–3pm & 7–11pm.

DIRECTORY

Hospital The hospital is at Località Largo Torchiana, Portoferraio (☎0565 926 111).

Internet On the marina in Portoferraio at Calata Mazzini 22–23, the *tabacchi* shop (look for the T sign; daily 8am–2am) is also an internet café, with access for €3.50/hr, or €2.50 with own computer.

Laundry Via dell'Amore 9, Portoferraio (Mon–Sat 8.30am–6pm & 6.15–7.30pm).

Police Via Giuseppe Garibaldi 17, Portoferraio (☎0565 937 252).

Post office Via Rodolfo Manganaro 7 in Portoferraio (Mon–Fri 8.25am–7.10pm, Sat 8.25am–12.35pm).

The Maremma

The Tuscan shoreline is at its best in the **Maremma** region; the name derives from *maríttima*, referring to the coastal strip and inland hills of the Provincia di Grosseto, Tuscany's southernmost province. The northern heartland of the Etruscans, this became depopulated in the Middle Ages after wars disrupted the drainage schemes and allowed malarial swamps to build up behind the dunes. The area became almost synonymous with disease, and nineteenth-century guides advised strongly against a visit – even so, *butteri* cowboys roamed freely then, as now, taking care of the region's half-feral horses and its celebrated white cattle. Today, the provincial capital of Grosseto remains uninspiring, though there are some patches of fine scenery – notably the **Monti dell'Uccellina**, protected in the **Parco Naturale della Maremma**, and the wooded peninsula of **Monte Argentario**.

Monti dell'Uccellina

Admission to the park €6, payable at the visitor centre

Recognized as the last virgin coastal landscape to survive on the Italian peninsula, the hilly **Monti dell'Uccellina**, 12km south of Grosseto, is protected as the **Parco Regionale della Maremma**. This breathtaking piece of countryside combines cliffs, coastal marsh, *macchia*, forest-covered hills, pristine beaches and beautiful stands of umbrella pine. A microcosm of all that's best in the Maremma, it remains devoid of the bars, marinas, hotels and half-finished houses that have destroyed much of the Italian littoral. The best **beach** here (20min from Pratini, along the Strada degli Olivi) is a beautifully unspoilt, curved bay, backed by lush greenery.

The park authorities have defined half a dozen different **walking itineraries**; some set off from Alberese itself, with the remainder leaving from **Pratini**, 10km into the hills, reached via hourly shuttle bus from the visitor centre. Between mid-June and mid-September, you can only follow the most popular trails, like the circular **Trail A1** (San Rabano; 6km; 5hr), which climbs a ridge from Pratini and passes the eleventh-century ruined abbey of San Rabano, on a guided **walk** (no extra charge); for the rest of the year, you can explore at your own pace. Some trails close altogether in midsummer when the risk of fire is high.

ARRIVAL AND GETTING AROUND · MONTI DELL'UCCELLINA

By car There's no public road access – drivers should park in Alberese, near the visitor centre.

By bus Hourly buses run from Grosseto station to the visitor centre. Hourly shuttle buses from the visitor centre run to Pratini, where some of the walking itineraries start (last bus back at 5.30pm, earlier in winter).

INFORMATION AND ACTIVITIES

Tourist information The visitor centre is on Via del Bersagliere 7–9 in Alberese (daily 8.30am–5pm; ☎0564 407 098).

Activities ⓦparco-maremma.it has full details of riding, canoeing and mountain-biking opportunities, as well as night tours and birdwatching. Most tours cost €10–15.

Monte Argentario

The high, rocky terrain of **Monte Argentario**, 37km south of Grosseto, is as close to wilderness as southern Tuscany gets. The interior is mountainous, reaching 635m at its highest point, while the coast is sectioned dramatically into headlands, bays and shingle beaches. Much of the area is still uninhabited scrub and woodland, badly prone to forest fires but still excellent walking country.

Orbetello

Long ago, Monte Argentario was an island. Over several thousand years, inshore currents built up two narrow sand spits (*tomboli*) between the mountain and the mainland, creating a lagoon between them. The ancient town of **Orbetello** occupied a peninsula sticking out into the lagoon; then the Romans built a causeway to link Orbetello to the Argentario, forming a third spit of land and dividing the lagoon in two. Today, Orbetello's strange location is its most exciting feature.

Porto Ercole

On summer weekends the roads over the northern Tombolo della Giannella sand bar and through Orbetello become bottlenecks as tourists pile into resorts such as **PORTO ERCOLE**, which has an attractive old quarter and a fishing-village atmosphere. Though founded by the Romans, its chief historical monuments are two **Spanish fortresses**, facing each other across the harbour. At the entrance to the old town, a plaque on the stone gate commemorates the painter **Caravaggio**, who in 1610 keeled over with sunstroke on a beach nearby and died of a fever; he was buried in the parish church of Sant'Erasmo. From the village, you can easily **walk** across the Tombolo di Feniglia, barred to traffic and a prime spot for birdwatching over the lagoon.

ARRIVAL AND INFORMATION   PORTO ERCOLE

By bus Buses run to Orbetello (hourly; 30min), from where you can change for Grosseto and destinations further afield.

Tourist office Piazza Roma (Easter–June Sat & Sun

10.30am–12.30pm & 4–6pm; July & Aug daily 9am–1pm & 6–8pm; Sept daily 10am–1pm; ☎0564 811 979).

ACCOMMODATION AND EATING

Don Pedro Via Panoramica ☎0564 833 914, ⓦhoteldonpedro.it. Porto Ercole has a number of mid-range hotels, of which friendly *Don Pedro* is the best. Rooms are basic but have fantastic views of the harbour, and it's an easy walk down the hill into town. Though small and rocky, the hotel's private beach (a 15min walk away) is a bonus in the height of summer. Rates are reduced by a third in low season. Open Easter–Sept. €150

Osteria dei Nobili Santi Via dell'Ospizio 8 ☎0564 833 015. Wonderfully fresh seafood is the order of the day at this slightly kitsch but charming place that's a cut above the average trattoria; try the good-value tasting menu (€40 for four courses, including wine). Mon–Wed 7.30–11pm; Thurs–Sun 12.15–1.30pm & 7.30–11pm; closed Mon in winter.

Siena

Immediately ravishing yet endlessly mysterious, and all on a far less daunting scale than Florence, the glorious medieval city of **SIENA** cradles within its ancient walls a majestic Gothic ensemble that can be enjoyed without venturing into a single museum. Far too

9

many visitors breeze through Siena on a day-trip, but it's hard to feel you've even scraped the surface unless you stay at least one night here.

The physical and spiritual heart of the city, and arguably Italy's loveliest square, is the sloping, scallop-shaped piazza **Il Campo**, the setting for the thrilling **Palio** bareback horse race. Siena's **Duomo** and **Palazzo Pubblico** are two of the purest expressions of Italian Gothic architecture, and the best of the city's paintings – collected in the **Museo Civico** and **Pinacoteca Nazionale** – are in the same tradition. The finest example of Sienese Gothic is Duccio's *Maestà*, on show in the outstanding **Museo dell'Opera**, while splendid frescoes adorn the walls of **Santa Maria della Scala**.

Brief history

Established as a Roman colony by Augustus, Siena enjoyed its heyday in the twelfth and thirteenth centuries, when it became for a brief period one of the major cities of Europe. Almost as large as Paris, it controlled most of southern Tuscany and its wool industry, dominated the trade routes between France and Rome, and maintained Italy's richest pre-Medici banks. This era climaxed with the defeat of a far superior Florentine army at **Montaperti** in 1260. Although the result was reversed permanently nine years later, Siena embarked on an unrivalled urban development under its mercantile governors, the **Council of Nine**. Between 1287 and 1355, the city underwrote the completion first of its cathedral, and then the Campo and its exuberant Palazzo Pubblico. Prosperity came to an abrupt halt with the **Black Death**, which reached Siena in May 1348; by October, two-thirds of the 100,000 inhabitants had died. The city never fully recovered (the population today remains under 60,000) and its politics, always factional, descended into chaos. In 1557 Philip II gave up Siena to **Cosimo de' Medici** in lieu of war services, and it became part of Cosimo's Grand Duchy of Tuscany. The lack of subsequent development explains Siena's astonishing state of preservation: little was built and still less demolished.

Since World War II, Siena has again become prosperous, thanks partly to **tourism** and partly to the resurgence of the **Monte dei Paschi di Siena**. This bank, founded in Siena in 1472 and currently the city's largest employer, is a major player in Italian finance. It today sponsors much of Siena's cultural life, coexisting, apparently easily, with one of Italy's strongest left-wing councils.

Orientation

Everything is easily walkable from Siena's great central square, **Il Campo**, which is built at the intersection of three hills configured like an upside-down Y. Each arm of that Y counts as one of the city's *terzi*, or thirds, and each has its principal thoroughfare, leading out from the Campo on elevated ridges: humdrum **Banchi di Sotto** in the Terzo di San Martino on the southeast; bustling, commercial **Via di Città** in the Terzo di Città on the southwest; and elegant **Banchi di Sopra** in the Terzo di Camollia on the north. This central core – almost entirely medieval in plan and appearance, and closed to traffic – can get a little disorienting, but use the Campo as your guide and you can't go far wrong.

The Campo

The **Campo** is the centre of Siena in every sense: the main streets lead into it, the **Palio** (see box opposite) is held around its perimeter, and every evening visitors and residents alike are drawn to it. Be sure to soak up the atmosphere last thing at night, when the amphitheatre curve of the piazza throws the low hum of café conversation around in an invisible spiral of sound that's drowned out in the daytime. Four hundred years ago, Montaigne described this as the most beautiful square in the world; it's hard to disagree today.

THE SIENA PALIO

The **Siena Palio** is Italy's most spectacular festival event: a twice-yearly **bareback horse race** around the Campo, preceded by days of preparation, medieval pageantry and chicanery. Only ten of the seventeen *contrade*, chosen by lot, take part in any one race; horses and jockeys too are assigned at random. The seven that miss out are automatically entitled to run the next year. The only rule is that riders cannot interfere with each other's reins. Otherwise, anything goes: each *contrada* has a traditional rival, and ensuring that it loses is as important as winning oneself. Jockeys may be bribed to throw the race or whip a rival or a rival's horse; *contrade* have been known to drug horses and even to ambush a jockey on his way to the race.

Held since at least the thirteenth century, the race originally followed a circuit through the town. Since the sixteenth century it has consisted of three laps of the **Campo**, around a track covered with sand and padded with mattresses to minimize injury to riders and horses.

THE RACE

There are two Palios a year, on **July 2 and August 16**, each of which is preceded by all manner of trial races and processions. At around 5pm on the day of the Palio the Palazzo Pubblico's bell rings, and *comparse* – equerries, ensigns, pages and drummers in medieval costume – proceed to the Campo for a display of flag-twirling and pageantry. The **race** itself begins at 7.45pm on July 2, or 7pm on August 16, and lasts little more than ninety seconds. At the start all the horses except one are penned between two ropes; the free one charges the group from behind, when its rivals least expect it, and the race is on. It's a hectic and violent spectacle; a horse that throws its rider is still eligible to win. The jockeys don't stop at the finishing line but keep going at top speed out of the Campo, pursued by frenzied supporters. The **palio** – a silk banner – is subsequently presented to the winner.

PRACTICALITIES

While seating is available in viciously expensive stands (booked months ahead; try Palio Viaggi on ☏0577 280 828, ⓦpalioviaggi.it), most spectators crowd for free into the centre of the Campo. For the **best view**, find a position on the inner rail by 2pm (ideally at the start/finish line), then stand your ground; people keep pouring in until just before the race, and the swell of the crowd can be overwhelming. Toilets, shade and refreshments are minimal, and you won't be able to leave the Campo until at least 8.30pm. **Hotel rooms** are very hard to find; if you haven't booked, either visit for the day or stay up all night.

Brief history

When the Council of Nine were planning the piazza in 1293, this old marketplace, which lay at the convergence of the city quarters but was part of none, was the only possible site. Created in nine segments in honour of the council, the piazza became from the moment it was completed in 1349 the focus of city life, the scene of executions, bullfights, communal boxing matches, and, of course, the Palio. St Bernardino preached here, holding before him the monogram of Christ's name in Greek ("IHS"), which the council placed on the facade of the Palazzo Pubblico, alongside the city's she-wolf symbol – a reference to Siena's legendary foundation by Senius, son of Remus.

Fonte Gaia

On the uppermost slope of the Campo, the Renaissance makes a fleeting appearance with the **Fonte Gaia** (Gay Fountain), designed and carved by Jacopo della Quercia in the early fifteenth century but now replaced by a poor nineteenth-century reproduction.

The Palazzo Pubblico and the Museo Civico

Piazza del Campo • Museum daily: mid-March to Oct 10am–7pm; Nov to mid-March 10am–6pm • €8, €11 with Santa Maria della Scala, or €13 with Torre del Mangia

The **Palazzo Pubblico** (also known as Palazzo Comunale), topped by a 97m belltower, the **Torre del Mangia** (see p.581), is the focus of the Campo, occupying virtually the

9

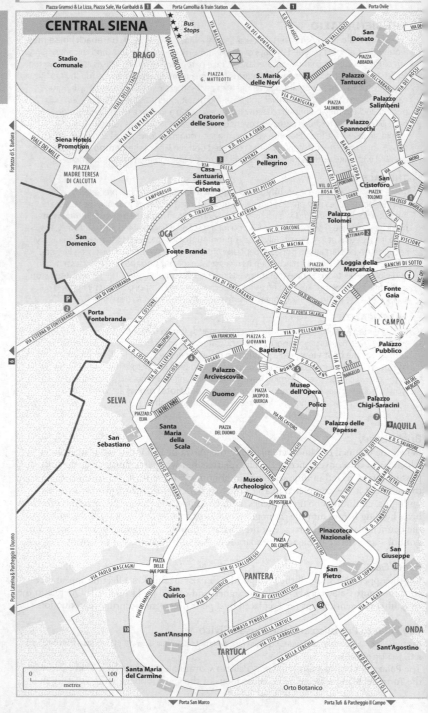

CENTRAL SIENA

Bus
Stops

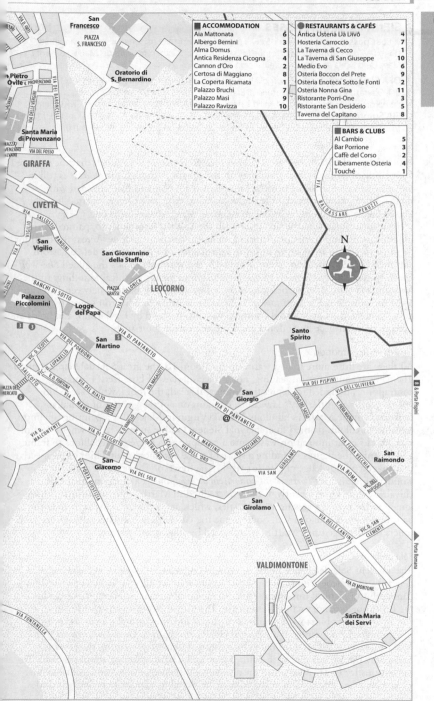

ACCOMMODATION

Aia Mattonata	6
Albergo Bernini	3
Alma Domus	5
Antica Residenza Cicogna	4
Cannon d'Oro	2
Certosa di Maggiano	8
La Coperta Ricamata	1
Palazzo Bruchi	7
Palazzo Masi	9
Palazzo Ravizza	10

RESTAURANTS & CAFÉS

Antica Osteria Dà Divò	4
Hosteria Carroccio	7
La Taverna di Cecco	1
La Taverna di San Giuseppe	10
Medio Evo	6
Osteria Boccon del Prete	9
Osteria Enoteca Sotto le Fonti	2
Osteria Nonna Gina	11
Ristorante Porri-One	3
Ristorante San Desiderio	5
Taverna del Capitano	8

BARS & CLUBS

Al Cambio	5
Bar Porrione	3
Caffè del Corso	2
Liberamente Osteria	4
Touché	1

9

SIENA MUSEUM PASSES

Various **passes** are available for Siena's museums – worth considering if you're planning to stay a few days. **Joint tickets** for the Museo Civico and either the Torre del Mangia or Santa Maria della Scala are also on offer (see p.577).

OPA SI pass Includes the Duomo, Museo dell'Opera, baptistry, crypt, Oratorio di San Bernardino (summer only): €14, valid 7 days.

SIA Summer Includes Museo Civico, Santa Maria della Scala, Museo dell'Opera, Oratorio di San Bernardino, Sant'Agostino: €17, valid 7 days; mid-March to Oct only.

SIA Winter Includes Museo Civico, Santa Maria della Scala, Museo dell'Opera: €14, valid 7 days; Nov to mid-March only.

entire south side. Its three-part windows pleased the council so much that they ordered their emulation on all other buildings on the square. Although the *palazzo* is still in use as Siena's town hall, its principal rooms, a series of grand halls frescoed with themes integral to the secular life of the medieval city, have been converted into the **Museo Civico**. If you only visit one museum in Siena, make it this one.

The museum starts on the first floor with the **Sala del Risorgimento**, painted with nineteenth-century scenes of Vittorio Emanuele, first king of Italy. Across the corridor lie three successive frescoed rooms: the **Sala di Balia**, the **Anticamera del Concistoro**, and the grand **Sala del Concistoro**. Room 13, the **Vestibolo**, holds the gilded *She-Wolf Suckling Romulus and Remus* (1429), an allusion to Siena's mythical founding. In the **Anticappella** alongside, decorations executed by Taddeo di Bartolo between 1407 and 1414 include a huge *St Christopher*. Behind a majestic wrought-iron screen by Jacopo della Quercia, the **Cappella del Consiglio** was also frescoed by Di Bartolo, and holds an exceptional altarpiece by Sodoma and exquisite inlaid choir-stalls.

Sala del Mappamondo

All these are little more than a warm-up for Room 16, the great **Sala del Mappamondo**. The name is somewhat misleading; not a trace survives of Lorenzetti's "rotating contraption", designed to depict the cosmos. Instead, the room, which served for several centuries as the city's law court, contains one of the greatest of all Italian frescoes. Simone Martini's fabulous *Maestà* (Virgin in Majesty) is a painting of almost translucent colour, painted in archetypal Sienese Gothic style in 1315, when Martini was 30. His great innovation was to use a canopy and a frieze of medallions to frame and organize the figures – lending a sense of space and more than a hint of perspective that suggest a knowledge of Giotto's work. The fresco on the opposite wall, the wonderful *Equestrian Portrait of Guidoriccio da Fogliano*, is a motif for medieval chivalric Siena. Until recently, it too was credited to Martini, but art historians have long puzzled over the anachronistic castles, which are of a much later style than the painting's signed date of 1328. Some argue the *Guidoriccio* is a sixteenth-century fake, others that it's a genuine Martini overpainted by subsequent restorers.

Sala della Pace

The adjacent **Sala della Pace** holds Ambrogio Lorenzetti's *Allegories of Good and Bad Government*, frescoes commissioned in 1338 to remind the councillors of their duties. Among Europe's most important cycles of medieval secular painting, this includes the first-known panorama in Western art. The walled city shown is clearly Siena, and the paintings burst with details of medieval life; their moral theme is expressed in a complex iconography of allegorical virtues and figures. *Good Government* (the better-preserved half) is dominated by a throned figure representing the *comune*, flanked by the Virtues and with Faith, Hope and Charity buzzing about his head. To the left, Justice (with Wisdom in the air above) dispenses rewards and punishments, while below her throne Concordia advises the Republic's councillors on their duties.

Bad Government is ruled by a horned demon, while over the city flies the figure of Fear, whose scroll reads: "Because he looks for his own good in the world, he places Justice beneath tyranny. So nobody walks this road without Fear: robbery thrives inside and outside the city gates." Some fine panel paintings by Lorenzetti's contemporaries are displayed in the **Sala dei Pilastri** to one side.

The loggia

Finally, climb the stairs to the rear **loggia** for clear views of quite how abruptly the town ends: buildings rise to the right and left for a few hundred metres along the ridges of the Terzo di San Martino and Terzo di Città, holding a rural valley in their embrace.

Torre del Mangia

Piazza del Campo • Daily: March to mid-Oct 10am–7pm; mid-Oct to Feb 10am–4pm • €8, or €13 with Museo Civico

Opposite the entrance to the Museo Civico, to the left of the Palazzo Pubblico's internal courtyard, a door leads to the 503 steps of the **Torre del Mangia**, which gives fabulous views across the town and surrounding countryside. The tower takes its name from its first watchman – a slothful glutton (*mangiaguadagni*) commemorated by a statue in the courtyard.

Loggia della Mercanzia and Banchi di Sotto

Behind the Fonte Gaia, assorted stairways and alleys between the buildings climb up to where the intersection of Siena's three main streets is marked by the fifteenth-century **Loggia della Mercanzia**. Reluctantly Renaissance, with its Gothic niches for the saints, it was designed as a tribune house for merchants to do their deals.

From the Loggia della Mercanzia, Banchi di Sopra heads north, while Via di Città curves west (see p.584). Follow **Banchi di Sotto** east, and you soon reach the **Logge del Papa** with, alongside it, the **Palazzo Piccolomini**, a committed Renaissance building by Bernardo Rossellino, the architect employed at Pienza by the Sienese Pope Pius II (Aeneas Sylvius Piccolomini).

The Duomo

Piazza del Duomo • March–Oct & early Jan Mon–Sat 10.30am–7pm, Sun 1.30–5.30pm; Nov–Feb Mon–Sat 10.30am–5.30pm, Sun 1.30–6pm • €3, €6 during the summer uncovering of the marble pavement; covered by OPA SI pass (see box opposite) • ⓦ operaduomo.siena.it

Siena's **Duomo** is an absolute delight, its exterior an amazing conglomeration of Romanesque and Gothic, delineated by bands of black and white marble. Few buildings can reveal so much of a city's history and aspirations; completed to virtually its present size around 1215, it was subjected to constant plans for expansion. Early in the fourteenth century, attempts were made to double its extent by building a baptistry on the slope below, to serve as a foundation for a rebuilt nave, but work ground to a halt when walls and joints gaped under the pressure. After the Black Death reduced the city's population by two thirds in 1348, funds were suddenly cut off, and the plan abandoned. The part-extension still stands at the north end of the square – a vast structure that would have created the largest church in Italy outside Rome. The **facade** of the Duomo was designed in 1284 by Giovanni Pisano who, with his workshop, created much of the statuary – philosophers, patriarchs and prophets, now replaced by copies. In the next century the **Campanile** and a Gothic **rose window** were added. The mosaics in the gables, however, had to wait until the nineteenth century.

The interior

The black-and-white motif continues in the sgraffito marble **pavement** that begins outside the church, and takes off into a startling sequence of 56 panels adorning the

9

interior. Depicting an eccentric mixture of Biblical themes, secular stories and allegories, the floor panels were completed between 1349 and 1547, with virtually every artist in the city trying his hand on a design. However, you may not see much of the pavement, which these days is only stripped of its protective boarding for a few unpredictable weeks in late summer; check the website for the latest schedule.

The zebra-striped interior is equally arresting above floor level, with its line of popes' heads set above the pillars, the same hollow-cheeked scowls cropping up repeatedly. The greatest individual artistic treasure is Nicola Pisano's **pulpit**, with its elaborate high-relief detail of the *Life of Jesus* and *Last Judgement*. In the north transept is a bronze statue by **Donatello**, the emaciated *St John the Baptist*, companion piece to his equally ragged *Mary Magdalene* in Florence (see p.522), and superb candelabra-carrying angels by Beccafumi flank the Renaissance high altar.

Libreria Piccolomini

Entered off the nave, halfway along on the left, the stunning **Libreria Piccolomini** was commissioned by Francesco Piccolomini (who for ten days was Pius III) as a library for the books of his uncle Aeneas (Pius II). A cycle of crystal-sharp, brilliantly colourful frescoes by **Pinturicchio** celebrates Aeneas's life. It starts to the right of the window, with Aeneas attending the Council of Basel as a secretary, then, in subsequent panels, presenting himself as envoy to James II of Scotland; being crowned poet laureate by Holy Roman Emperor, Frederick II; representing Frederick on a visit to Pope Eugenius IV; and then – as Bishop of Siena – presiding over the meeting of Frederick III and his bride-to-be Eleanora outside Siena's Porta Camollia. The next panels show Aeneas being made a cardinal in 1456; being elected pope two years later; and then launching a call for a crusade against the Turks, who had just seized Constantinople. His best-remembered action was the canonization of St Catherine, shown in the penultimate panel. The final fresco shows his death at Ancona.

The baptistry and crypt

Piazza San Giovanni • March–Oct & early Jan Mon–Sat 10.30am–7pm, Sun 1.30–5.30pm; Nov–Feb Mon–Sat 10.30am–5.30pm, Sun 1.30–6pm • Baptistry €3, crypt €8, included in OPA SI pass (see box, p.580)

Behind the Duomo, down some steep steps, is the **baptistry**, beautifully frescoed by Vecchietta and his school in the mid-fifteenth century, and restored in the nineteenth. The main focus is the hexagonal marble **font** (1417–30), with gilded brass panels by Ghiberti, Donatello and Jacopo della Quercia. Donatello's depiction of the *Feast of Herod* is perhaps the finest work: a dramatic scene in which John the Baptist's executioner kneels, carrying the head of the saint on a platter, as Herod recoils in horror.

Accessed through the baptistry, the **crypt** was only discovered in 1999 and is worth a visit for the remains of a marvellous, richly coloured fresco cycle of Old Testament stories (c.1270–80).

SIENA'S *CONTRADE*

Siena takes great pride in its division into neighbourhoods, or **contrade**, ancient self-governing wards that formed a patchwork of tribal identity within the fabric of the city and that still flourish today, helping to foster tight bonds of community and contributing to Siena's surprisingly low crime rate. Each of the seventeen *contrade* has its own church, social club and museum. Each, too, has a heraldic **motif**, from caterpillar to unicorn, displayed in a fountain-sculpture in its neighbourhood piazza. Allegiance to one's *contrada* – conferred by birth – remains a strong element of civic life, and identification with the *contrade* is integral to the competition of the Palio. You'll often see groups of *comparse* practising flag-waving and drum-playing around town.

Santa Maria della Scala

Piazza del Duomo • Daily 10.30am–6.30pm • €6, joint ticket with Museo Civico €11; included in SIA Summer and SIA Winter passes (see box, p.580) • ⓦ santamariadellascala.com

For nine hundred years until the 1980s, the vast **Santa Maria della Scala** complex, opposite the Duomo, served as Siena's main hospital. Today its wonderful interiors have been converted into a major centre for art and culture, revealing works that remained barely seen for centuries.

Santissima Annunziata

Beyond the ticket hall, the first room you enter is a small chapel adorned with fifteenth-century frescoes by Vecchietta. That leads in turn to the larger church of **Santissima Annunziata**, where the same artist's bronze statue of the *Risen Christ* is on the high altar – the figure is so gaunt that the veins show through the skin.

Cappella del Manto

Beyond that, the **Cappella del Manto** holds a strikingly beautiful fresco by Beccafumi, *St Anne and St Joachim* (1512). It shows the aged parents of the Virgin who, having failed to conceive in their twenty years of marriage, are told by an angel to meet at Jerusalem's Golden Gate and kiss – a moment that symbolizes the Immaculate Conception of their daughter.

Sala del Pellegrinaio

The real highlight here, however, is the vast **Sala del Pellegrinaio**. Formerly the main hospital ward, it's entirely frescoed with scenes from the hospital's history, intended to promote charity toward the sick and orphaned. Naturalistic and still vivid, their almost entirely secular content was extraordinary at the time they were painted (after 1440).

Oratorio di Santa Caterina della Notte

Stairs lead down to the **Oratorio di Santa Caterina della Notte**, an oratory that belonged to one of several medieval confraternities which maintained places of worship in the basement of the hospital. It's a dark and strangely spooky place, despite the plethora of decoration – you can easily imagine St Catherine passing nocturnal vigils down here.

Museo Archeologico

Much of the lowest level is given over to the remodelled **Museo Archeologico**. Walkways through the vaults lead past all sorts of Roman and pre-Roman treasures, largely gathered by private Sienese collectors during the nineteenth century.

Museo dell'Opera

Piazza del Duomo • March–Oct daily 10.30–7pm; Nov–Feb 10.30am–5.30pm • €6; included in various museum passes (see box, p.580) • ⓦ operaduomo.siena.it

Home to some superlative artworks from the cathedral's history, and also offering amazing if perilous views over the city, the impressive **Museo dell'Opera** is tucked into a corner of what was originally intended to be the Duomo's new nave.

As you enter on the ground floor, you're immediately confronted by the **Galleria delle Statue**. Donatello's delicate ochre *Madonna and Child* is poised above a doorway, while huge, elongated, twisting figures by Giovanni Pisano loom on all sides. The museum's greatest treasure, Duccio's vast and justly celebrated **Maestà**, dominates a dimly lit air-conditioned gallery upstairs. The Duomo's altarpiece from 1311 until 1505, it's a masterpiece of Sienese art. Its iconic, Byzantine spirituality is accentuated by Duccio's flowing composition, his realization of the space in which action takes place, and a new attention to narrative detail in the panels of the predella and the reverse of the altarpiece which are now displayed to its side.

9

Upstairs again, you can admire the Duomo's original altarpiece, a haunting Byzantine icon known as the **Madonna dagli Occhi Grossi** (of the Big Eyes). A small passageway leads to the open-air **Panorama dal Facciatone**, via steep spiral stairs that climb the walls of the abandoned nave. The sensational view is worth enjoying even if you choose not to venture onto the narrow, scarily exposed, topmost walkway.

Via di Città and around

Via di Città, the main thoroughfare linking the Duomo with the Campo, is lined with shops and plenty of explorable side-alleys, as well as being fronted by some of Siena's finest private *palazzi*. The **Palazzo Chigi-Saracini**, at no. 82, is a Gothic beauty, with its curved facade and rear courtyard.

Pinacoteca Nazionale

Via di S. Pietro 29 • Mon 9am–1pm, Tues–Sat 10am–6pm, Sun 9am–1pm • €4 • ⓦ pinacotecanazionale.siena.it

Via di Città continues to a small piazza from where Via di San Pietro leads south to the fourteenth-century Palazzo Buonsignori, now the home of the **Pinacoteca Nazionale**. A roll of honour of Sienese Gothic painting, the collection starts on the second floor with the first known Sienese work, an altar frontal from 1215. Romanesque and Byzantine influences dominate the early rooms, with the intricate gilded backgrounds that became so characteristic of Sienese style. Specific artists showcased thereafter include Duccio di Buoninsegna, who together with his school takes up two full rooms, and Simone Martini, whose masterpiece *Blessed Agostino Novello and Four of his Miracles* is in Room 5. On the next floor down you'll find Renaissance works by such as Sodoma, whose panel of the *Deposition* (Room 32) and frescoes from Sant'Agostino (Room 37) show his characteristic drama and delight in costume and landscape.

The gallery's topmost storey is devoted to the **Collezione Spannocchi**. This miscellany of Italian, German and Flemish works includes the only painting in the museum by a female artist – *Bernardo Campi Painting Sofonisba's Portrait* by Sofonisba Anguissola, a neat little joke in which the artist excels in her portrait of Campi, but depicts his portrait of her as a flat stereotype.

Sant'Agostino and around

South of the Pinacoteca Nazionale, the church of **Sant'Agostino** (erratic hours, but officially mid-June to Aug Mon–Wed, Fri & Sat 2.30–5.30pm; €2.50), in the square known as Prato di Sant'Agostino, holds outstanding paintings by Perugino and Sodoma. A nice walk loops southwest along Via della Cerchia into a student-dominated area around the church of **Santa Maria del Carmine** (which contains a hermaphrodite *St Michael and the Devil* by Beccafumi). Via del Fosso di San Ansano, north of the Carmine square, is a country lane above terraced vineyards that leads to the Selva (Rhinoceros) *contrada*'s square, from where the stepped Vicolo di San Girolamo leads up to the Duomo.

North of the Campo

Exploring beyond the touristed central alleys between the Campo and the Duomo reveals much more of the bustling everyday life of Siena. North of the Campo, the **Banchi di Sopra** leads through the commercial heart of town to **Piazza Matteotti**, home of the main post office; north again lies the workaday neighbourhood of the Terzo di Camollia. The city's northwest corner holds the gardens of **La Lizza**, site of Siena's busting town market on Wednesdays (8am–2pm). The gardens lead up to the bastions of the **Fortezza di Santa Barbara**, rebuilt by the Medici and now home to occasional summer concerts.

San Domenico

Piazza San Domenico • Daily 9am–6.30pm • Free • ⓦ basilicacateriniana.com

Until the start of the thirteenth century, monasteries were essentially rural, meditative retreats. Then in the space of a few decades, preaching orders of friars were established, and started to found monasteries on the periphery of the major Italian cities. In Siena the two greatest orders, the Dominicans and Franciscans, located themselves respectively to the west and east. Founded in 1125, west of Piazza Matteotti, the vast brick **San Domenico** church remains closely identified with St Catherine of Siena (see box below). Inside on the right, a raised chapel holds a contemporary portrait of the saint by her friend Andrea Vanni. Her own chapel, on the south side of the enormous, airy nave, has frescoes by Sodoma of her swooning (to the left of the altar) and in ecstasy (to the right), as well as a reliquary containing her head.

Casa Santuario di Santa Caterina

Via Santa Caterina • Daily 9am–6pm • Free

The **Casa Santuario di Santa Caterina** – St Catherine's family house, where she lived as a Dominican nun – is just south of the church, down the hill. The building has been much adapted, with a Renaissance loggia and a series of oratories – one on the site of her cell.

Fonte Branda

Down the road from the Casa Santuario di Santa Caterina, at the bottom of the hill, through the Oca (Goose) *contrada*, the **Fonte Branda** is the best preserved of Siena's medieval fountains. According to local folklore, it was the haunt of werewolves, who would throw themselves into the water at dawn to return in human form.

Oratorio di San Bernardino

Piazza di S. Francesco 9 • March–Oct & end Dec to early Jan daily 1.30–7pm; rest of year on request • €3; included in various museum passes (see box, p.580) • ☏ 0577 283 048

Born in 1380, the year of St Catherine's death, St Bernardino began his preaching life at the chill monastic church of **San Francesco**, across the city to the east. Alongside, the **Oratorio di San Bernardino** holds a beautifully wood-panelled upper chapel frescoed by Sodoma and Beccafumi. In the lower chapel are seventeenth-century scenes from the saint's life, which was taken up by incessant travel throughout Italy, preaching against usury and denouncing political strife; his sermons in the Campo frequently went on for the best part of a day. Canonized in 1444, he was made patron saint of advertising in the 1980s – thanks to his dictum on rhetoric, "Make it clear, short and to the point".

ST CATHERINE OF SIENA

St Catherine of Siena was born on March 25, 1347, the 24th child of Jacopo Benincasa, a dyer, and Lapa of Duccio de' Piacenti. Her path to beatification began early, with a vision aged 6 of Christ as pope, followed a year later by a vow of perpetual virginity. Her family tried to drill some sense into her by forcing her to work at household chores, but when her father discovered her at prayer one day with a dove fluttering above her head, he realized her holy destiny. Catherine took the Dominican habit aged 16, then began charitable works in post-plague Siena before turning her hand to politics. After preventing Siena and Pisa from joining Florence in rising against Pope Urban V (then absent in Avignon), she travelled herself to Avignon in 1376 to persuade Pope Gregory XI to return to Rome. It was a fulfilment of the ultimate Dominican ideal – a union of the practical and mystical life. Catherine returned to Siena to a life of contemplation, retaining a political role in her attempts to reconcile the 1378 schism between the Popes and Antipopes. She died in Rome in 1380, and was the first woman ever to be **canonized** – by Pius II in 1461. Pius IX made her **co-patron of Rome** in 1866; Pius XII raised her to be **co-patron of Italy** (alongside St Francis) in 1939; and then John Paul II declared her **co-patron of Europe** in 1999.

9

ARRIVAL AND DEPARTURE
SIENA

BY TRAIN

Siena's train station is 2km northwest of town. It has a counter selling city bus tickets, as well as tourist information. To get into town, you can either walk, which takes a good 20–25min, or cross the road and take bus #3, #8, #10, #17 or #77 into town. Tickets cost €1.10 (€2 on board).

Destinations Buonconvento (10 daily; 25min); Chiusi (hourly; 1hr 5min–1hr 30min); Florence (hourly; 1hr 10min–1hr 45min); Grosseto (9 daily; 1hr 30min); Pisa (via Empoli; every 30min–1hr; 1hr 45min).

BY BUS

Most intercity buses arrive on or near Viale Federico Tozzi, the road running alongside Piazza Gramsci–Piazza Matteotti, or at nearby La Lizza, but some terminate at the train station or at San Domenico instead. For San Gimignano, you may have to change at Poggibonsi, and for Montepulciano at Buonconvento. Ticket offices beneath Piazza Gramsci (daily 5.50am–8.30pm) have information on all routes.

Bus companies Siena's buses, as well as those in the local area, are run by Tiemme (☎ 0577 204111, ⓦ sienamobilita .it). SENA buses (☎ 0861 199 1900, ⓦ sena.it) are long-distance to Rome, Milan, Venice and other cities outside Tuscany, while SITA offer express services from Florence.

Take a "Rapido" rather than "Diretta" service, as these are much quicker.

Destinations Abbadia San Salvatore (3 daily; 1hr 40min–2hr); Arezzo (6 daily; 1hr 30min); Bologna (2 daily; 3hr); Buonconvento (8 daily; 40min); Florence (30 daily; 1hr 15min–3hr); Massa Maríttima (2 daily; 1hr 55min); Milan (5 daily; 5hr 40min); Montalcino (5 daily; 1hr 30min); Montepulciano (5 daily; 1hr 30min); Perugia (1 daily; 1hr 10min); Pisa airport (1 daily; 1hr 45min); Pienza (7 daily; 1hr 15min); Poggibonsi (every 30min; 30min–1hr); Rome (10 daily; 3hr); San Galgano (3 daily; 1hr 5min); San Gimignano (10 daily; 1hr 5min–1hr 15min); Turin (4 weekly; 6hr 45min); Venice (2 daily; 5hr 20min).

BY CAR

Car rental You can rent a car at Perozzi (see below), from €50/day.

Parking There's plentiful free parking outside the walls. The two biggest parking garages (€1.70/hr) are misleadingly named: "Parcheggio Il Campo" and "Parcheggio Il Duomo" are a long way south of either the Campo or the Duomo, just inside the Porta Tufi and Porta San Marco respectively (ⓦ sienaparcheggi.com). Visitors can drive through the old-town alleys only in order to check in at their hotels.

INFORMATION AND GETTING AROUND

By bike and scooter For bike rental, head to Perozzi at Via dei Gazzani 16 (Mon–Fri 8.30am–12.30pm & 3–7pm, Sat 8.30am–12.30pm & 4–6.30pm; ☎ 0577 288 387, ⓦ perozzi.it; bikes €2/day, scooters €26/day).

On foot See ⓦ terresiena.it for downloadable walking itineraries (or "urban trekking").

By taxi Call Radio Taxi (☎ 0577 49 222), or taxis wait in Piazza Matteotti and Piazza Indipendenza.

Tourist office Piazza del Campo 56 (Easter–Oct Mon–Sat 10am–6.30pm, Sun 10am–5pm; Nov–Easter daily 10am–5pm; ☎ 0577 280 551, ⓦ terresiena.it).

ACCOMMODATION

Siena is small enough that every hotel within the old walls is within fifteen minutes' walk of the main sights. Anyone visiting in summer should **reserve accommodation** as far in advance as possible; hotels are especially booked up at Palio time (early July & mid-Aug), when they charge higher prices. You'll also be glad of air conditioning in the summer heat. The official Siena Hotels Promotion agency (☎ 0577 288 084, ⓦ hotelsiena.com) offers free online reservations for all hotels, and runs a booth on Piazza Madre Teresa di Calcutta in front of San Domenico (Mon–Sat 9am–7pm), where you can make same-day bookings for €2. A Siena **hotel tax** has been introduced: depending on the type of accommodation, you will be charged €1–5 per person, per night, in addition to the room rate, for a maximum of six consecutive nights.

Aia Mattonata Strada del Ceraiolo 1, 4km south of the centre ☎ 0577 592 677, ⓦ aiamattonata.com. Ravishing little hotel in a converted hilltop farmhouse, with six very comfortable rooms and superb views over the city. Swimming pool, jacuzzi and Turkish bath, with massage available and use of mountain bikes. **€215**

Albergo Bernini Via della Sapienza 15 ☎ 0577 289 047, ⓦ albergobernini.com. Friendly, well-situated one-star hotel near San Domenico, with ten good-value rooms, some of which lack a/c and share bathrooms; the walls are very thin, so ear plugs are a good idea. The roof terrace with

a fantastic view over Siena is the main draw here. Breakfast costs an extra €3.50. No credit cards. **€65**

★ **Alma Domus** Via Camporegio 37 ☎ 0577 44 177, ⓦ hotelalmadomus.it. Originally a pilgrim hostel, this fourteenth-century building, reached via a stairway down from close to San Domenico church, offers great-value and remarkably peaceful accommodation; its en-suite doubles, triples and quads enjoy wonderful views. **€75**

★ **Antica Residenza Cicogna** Via delle Terme 75 ☎ 0577 285 613, ⓦ anticaresidenzacicogna.it. Charming B&B on the first floor of a medieval *palazzo* not far north of the Campo, with seven a/c, soundproof en-suite rooms, all beautifully decorated. Ask for the Liberty room, a hand-stencilled beauty with four-poster bed and antique furniture. The breakfast is delicious, there's free computer use and wi-fi, and free tea and biscuits add to the home-from-home feel. **€95**

Cannon d'Oro Via Montanini 28 ☎ 0577 44 321, ⓦ cannondoro.com. Simple, friendly hotel, tucked down an alleyway. Its thirty rooms show signs of age, but they're spacious, high-ceilinged and spotless, and some enjoy fine roofscape views. Breakfast is included but poor. **€70**

⭐ **Certosa di Maggiano** Via Certosa 82 ☎ 0577 288 180, ⓦ certosadimaggiano.com. This stunning former monastery, in a rural setting 1km southeast of the centre, offers large, elegant rooms surrounding the central cloister, beneath the (still functioning) belltower. There's also a library, a swimming pool and a swanky restaurant. Prices are equally fantastic. **€370**

La Coperta Ricamata Via Garibaldi 46 ☎ 0577 43 657, ⓦ lacopertaricamata.it. Quiet, clean and friendly B&B, not far north of the centre and within easy walking distance of the bus station, with six large and attractively decorated en-suite rooms. Friendly hostess Luciana is on hand to offer advice on seeing the city and its environs. **€80**

Palazzo Bruchi Via Pantaneto 105 ☎ 0577 287 342, ⓦ palazzobruchi.it. Housed in a seventeenth-century *palazzo*, this small B&B, run by a friendly mother-and-daughter team, is a real bargain. Ask for the Camera degli Affreschi, with lovely frescoed ceilings. **€100**

Palazzo Masi Casato di Sotto 29 ☎ 349 600 9155, ⓦ palazzomasi.it. In a medieval building, this family-run place is just steps from the Campo. It's worth paying a little more for one of the superior rooms, for extras such as beamed celings, tiled floors and antiques. The standard rooms upstairs are more basic and share a bathroom. Breakfast costs an extra €8. **€100**

⭐ **Palazzo Ravizza** Pian dei Mantellini 34 ☎ 0577 280 462, ⓦ palazzoravizza.it. Elegant, nicely restored hotel in the peaceful southwest corner of the old town, with very pleasant public areas, and a lovely garden with stunning views over the surrounding countryside. All rooms have a/c and tasteful furnishings, and many have frescoes; the best are upstairs at the back. Rates include a fine breakfast. Free parking. **€130**

EATING

Although Siena has no shortage of places where you can eat well, it can feel distinctly provincial after Florence. However, with several new, imaginative *osterie* having raised the general standard of Siena's **restaurants**, you'll have no trouble finding good places in all price ranges – though the over-priced Campo is to be avoided. Putting together a **picnic** in the Campo or elsewhere is easy: you can buy pizza by weight from many central hole-in-the-wall places, or gourmet supplies at two gorgeous old **groceries**: Miccoli, Via di Città 95 (daily 8am–8pm), for cheeses and cold meats, and nearby Manganelli, Via di Città 71 (Mon–Sat 9am–7.30pm), for wine, chocolates and biscuits. There's a Sma **supermarket** at Via di Città 152 (Mon–Sat 7.30am–8pm).

Antica Osteria Da Divo Via Franciosa 29 ☎ 0577 286 054, ⓦ osteriadadivo.it. Hearty, high-quality Tuscan food, aimed primarily at tourists, a few steps down from the Duomo. There's no pavement seating, but the attractive underground dining rooms incorporate Etruscan vaults, and the upstairs area is pleasant too. Starters at €8 or €10 include a fabulous risotto with courgettes and *pecorino*; mains €20 or €24. Mon & Wed–Sun noon–2.30pm & 7–10.30pm.

Hosteria Carroccio Via Casato di Sotto 32 ☎ 0577 41 165. Popular, good-value little *osteria*, with outdoor tables just a minute's walk from the Campo. Good Sienese dishes such as pasta with salami and broad beans (€8) and rabbit with sausage and olives (€18), and an extensive wine list.

No credit cards. 12.30–2.30pm & 7.30–9.30pm; closed Wed.

La Taverna di Cecco Via Cecco Angiolieri 19 ☎ 0577 288 518. Attentive service, moderate prices and heavenly truffle risotto (€10). Good pasta dishes too, including *pappardelle* with rabbit (€10). Mains cost €10–20. Daily noon–4pm & 7pm–1am.

⭐ **La Taverna di San Giuseppe** Via Giovanni Duprè 132 ☎ 0577 42 286, ⓦ latavernasangiuseppe.it. Booking is always a good idea for a table in this elegant, brick-vaulted restaurant, which serves up unusual antipasti such as *spiedini di scamorza fusa alle zucchine* (smoked cheese, sage, parsley and courgette skewers), and seasonal Tuscan specialities, including impressive *fiorentina* steaks. Have a

---

SWEET TREATS

Siena is famous for its **cakes**, including the trademark **panforte** – a dense and delicious wedge of nuts, fruit and honey – and biscuits like *cavallucci* (aniseed, nut and spice) and *ricciarelli* (almond). Buy them fresh, by the *etto* (100g), in the bakeries or *pasticcerie* along Banchi di Sopra; the gift-packaged boxes aren't as good.

9

peek at the Etruscan dwelling downstairs; discovered in 1998, it now helps to keep the wines and cheeses cool. Mon–Sat noon–2.30pm & 7–10pm.

Medio Evo Piazza del Mercato 34 ☎0577 280 315. Traditional rich Tuscan food, served in grand style beneath the splendid brick ceiling of its flag-festooned dining room, or outside on the square; the prices are reasonable, with a short menu of sumptuous mains, such as *ossobuco* with risotto, at €11–20. Noon–3pm & 7–10.30pm; closed Wed.

Osteria Boccon del Prete Via di S. Pietro 17 ☎0577 280 388. A cellar-like little restaurant, with a vaulted ceiling, close to the Pinacoteca. Starters such as *bruschette* and *crostini*, *primi* like gnocchi with sea bream (€6.50–8), and mains such as pork fillet with roast potatoes (€9–13), are tasty and well-priced, though service can be brusque. Mon–Sat 12.15–3pm & 7.15–10pm.

★ **Osteria Enoteca Sotto le Fonti** Via Esterna di Fontebranda 114 ☎0577 226 446, ⓦsottolefonti.it. This friendly *osteria* with a rustic, homespun feel (and only ten tables) offers Tuscan specialities such as *ribollita* (vegetable soup), *pappardelle* with wild boar (€6.50), and an array of meaty mains for €9.50–17: hearty fare that will set you up nicely for the 10min walk uphill back to town. It's also an *enoteca*, with over a hundred wines, many offered by the glass. Mon–Sat 12.30–2.30pm & 7.30–10pm.

Osteria Nonna Gina Piano del Mantellini ☎0577 287 247. No-nonsense, ultra-fresh, Italian home-cooking in a friendly family atmosphere at the southwest end of town, with some outdoor tables. Most dishes under €10 (it's renowned for its gnocchi), and the house wine is a real bargain at €6 per litre. Tues–Sun 12.30–2.30pm & 7.30–10.30pm.

Ristorante Porri-One Via del Porrione 28 ☎0577 221 442. This elegant restaurant with pavement seating in a pedestrian lane just off the Campo is a good option if you've had your fill of traditional Tuscan fare: the creative menu includes plenty of culinary curveballs, including artichoke in goose-liver sauce with black truffles (€14) and duck with onion and cinnamon (€22). A full meal without wine will set you back around €45. Noon–3pm & 7–11pm; closed Wed.

Ristorante San Desiderio Piazzetta L. Bonelli 2 ☎0577 286 091, ⓦristorantesandesiderio.com. This cavernous former church, just below the Duomo en route to the Campo, also has a handful of outdoor tables. *Primi* such as risotto with Vino Nobile, *radicchio* and *pecorino* cost €7–10; *secondi* like beef stew cooked in Chianti with chard €13–16. Noon–2.30pm & 7–10.30pm; closed Tues.

Taverna del Capitano Via del Capitano 8 ☎0577 288 094. Just down from the Duomo, with spacious outdoor seating and a serene medieval dining-room. Dependable local specialities include appetizers like *crostini Toscani* at €7.50, and main courses such as rabbit with herbs (€13) or pork with Vin Santo (€14). Daily noon–4pm & 7pm–midnight.

NIGHTLIFE

The main action of an evening is the **passeggiata** from Piazza Matteotti along Banchi di Sopra to the Campo – and there's not much in the way of nightlife after that. For most visitors, though, the Campo, the universal gathering place, provides diversion enough, while local students ensure a bit of life in the **bars**, which are scattered all over town. The bar in the garden of the *Palazzo Ravizza* hotel (see p.587) is a tranquil spot on a hot afternoon.

Al Cambio Via di Pantaneto 48 ☎339 817 7044, ⓦalcambio.net. This club-bar is pretty much the only central late-night spot. Tues is student night, while Wed is dedicated to dance music (a menu of cocktails at €2.50 ensures a lively crowd). Mon–Sat 11pm–3am.

Bar Porrione Via del Porrione 14. Just an ordinary bar off the Campo, but it's popular with a studenty crowd at weekends thanks to its late opening hours. Tues–Sun 9am–3am.

Caffè del Corso Banchi di Sopra 25 ☎0577 226 656. This diminutive bar serves up a decent *aperitivo* with snacks from 7 to 9pm, and gets lively later on with students thanks to its late hours, loud music and cheap cocktails (€3.50). It has a few tables on the tiny alley outside too. Tues–Sun 8am–3am.

SIENA MUSIC FESTIVALS

Siena hosts prestigious classical concerts throughout the year. The **Accademia Musicale Chigiana** (Via di Città 89 ☎0577 22 091, ⓦchigiana.it) is the driving force, staging the Estate Musicale Chigiana cycle all summer, and the Settimana Musicale Senese in July, often featuring a major opera production. Venues vary from the Teatro dei Rozzi and Sant'Agostino to out-of-town locations such as the atmospheric ruined abbey of Sant'Antimo. Tickets start at €8, bookable through ⓦchigiana.it from late May onwards, in person at the Accademia Musicale Chigiana (daily 3.30–6pm) or from the venue itself up to two hours before the performance. For jazz fans, **Siena Jazz** (☎0577 271 401, ⓦsienajazz.it) is a low-key festival in late July and early August, one of several summer events.

Liberamente Osteria Piazza del Campo 27. Of the terrace café-bars ringing the Campo, *Liberamente* is the nicest. With outdoor seating on the corner or the square, it offers a ringside seat for the evening *passeggiata*, and offers drinks (cocktails around €7), as well as breakfast and light meals (sandwiches €10). Daily: March–Oct 8am–2am; Nov–Feb 5pm–2am.

Touché Piazza del Sale 3/A ☎0577 43 314. North of the centre, this pubby place serves up cocktails and bottled beers (with a few on tap), and has plenty of tables and cosy corners in which to play board games (loaned for free), graze on snacks or take in the occasional DJ set. Wed & Fri there's an *aperitivo* snack buffet from 7pm on. Daily noon–3pm & 7pm–2am.

DIRECTORY

Hospital Loc. Le Scotte ☎0577 585 111.
Internet Le Quattro Stelle, Via S. Pietro 74 (Mon–Fri 9am–1.30pm & 3.30–7pm; €1/30min); Netrunner, Via Pantaneto 132 (Mon–Fri 10am–7.30pm, Sat 10am–7pm; €2/30min).
Laundry Lavanderia San Pietro, Via S. Pietro 70 (daily 8am–10pm); Ondablu, Casato di Sotto 17 (daily

8am–9.15pm).
Left luggage At the bus information centre below Piazza Gramsci (daily 7am–7pm; €5.50 per piece, same day only).
Police The Questura is at Via del Castoro 6 (☎0577 201 111).
Post office Piazza Matteotti 1 (Mon–Fri 8.25am–7.10pm, Sat 8.25am–12.35pm).

San Gimignano

SAN GIMIGNANO, 27km northwest of Siena, is perhaps the most visited small village in Italy. Its stunning hilltop skyline of towers, built in aristocratic rivalry by the feuding nobles of the twelfth and thirteenth centuries, evokes the appearance of medieval Tuscany more than any other sight. And the town is all that it's cracked up to be: quietly monumental, beautifully preserved, enticingly rural, and with a fine array of religious and secular frescoes. It takes around twenty minutes to walk from one end of town to the other, but it deserves at least a day, both for its frescoes and for its lovely surrounding countryside.

From Easter until October, San Gimignano has very little life of its own, with hordes of day-trippers traipsing up and down its narrow streets and filing in and out of its innumerable olive oil, wine and souvenir shops. If you want to reach beyond its facade of quaintness, try to come well out of season; if you can't, then aim to spend the night here – the town takes on a very different pace and atmosphere in the evenings.

Brief history

In the early Middle Ages, San Gimignano was a force to be reckoned with. It was controlled by two great families – the Ardinghelli and the Salvucci – and its 15,000 population (twice the present number) prospered on agricultural holdings and its position on the Lombardy-to-Rome pilgrim route. At its peak, the town's walls enclosed five monasteries, four hospitals, public baths and a brothel. **Feuds**, however, had long wrought havoc: the first Ardinghelli–Salvucci conflict erupted in 1246. Whenever the town itself was united, it picked fights with Volterra, Poggibonsi and other neighbours. These were halted only by the **Black Death**, which devastated first the population and then, as the pilgrim trade collapsed, the economy. Subjection to Florence broke the power of the nobles and so their tower-houses, symbolic in other towns of real control, were not torn down; today, fourteen of an original 72 survive.

Via San Giovanni

From the southern gate, **Porta San Giovanni**, the *palazzo*-lined **Via San Giovanni** leads to the interlocking main squares, the Piazza del Duomo and the Piazza della Cisterna. On the right of the street, about 100m up, is the former church of **San Francesco** – a Romanesque building converted, like many of the *palazzi*, to a wine shop specializing in the local Vernaccia.

9

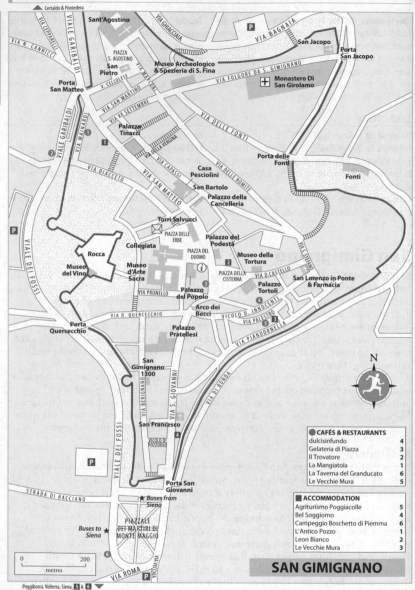

Piazza della Cisterna

You enter the **Piazza della Cisterna** through the **Arco dei Becci**, part of the original fortifications built before the town expanded in the twelfth century. The square itself is flanked by an anarchic cluster of towers and *palazzi*, and is named after the thirteenth-century public **cistern**, still functioning in the centre. Northwest of the square is one of the old Ardinghelli towers; a Salvucci rival rears up behind.

An arch leads from Piazza della Cisterna through to the more austere **Piazza del Duomo**, with further towers and civic *palazzi*.

The Collegiata

Piazza del Duomo • **Church** April–Oct Mon–Fri 10am–7.10pm, Sat 10am–5.10pm, Sun 12.30–7.10pm; Feb, March, first half of Nov & Dec to mid-Jan Mon–Sat 10am–4.40pm, Sun 12.30–4.40pm; mid- to end Nov & mid- to end Jan open for religious celebrations only; museum same hours, but closed mid- to end Nov & mid- to end Jan • Church €3.50, museum €3, church and museum €5.50

The plain facade of the Duomo, or more properly the **Collegiata**, since San Gimignano no longer has a bishop, could hardly provide a greater contrast with its interior. This is one of the most comprehensively frescoed churches in Tuscany, with cycles of paintings filling every available space, their brilliant colours set off by Pisan-Romanesque arcades of black-and-white-striped marble. Entrance is from the side courtyard, where you'll also find the small **Museo d'Arte Sacra**. While less spectacular, it's still worth a look for its rescued religious art.

The frescoes

The Collegiata's three principal **fresco cycles** fill the north and south walls, as well as two short side-walls that protrude from the east (exit) wall of the facade. The **Old Testament** scenes on the north wall, completed by Bartolo di Fredi around 1367, are full of medieval detail in the costumes, activities and interiors. They are also quirkily naturalistic: there are few odder frescoes than the depiction of Noah exposing himself in a drunken stupor. The cycle (read from left to right, top to bottom) follows the story of the **Flood** with those of **Abraham and Lot** (their trip to Canaan), **Joseph** (his dream; being let down the well; having his brothers arrested, and being recognized by them), **Moses** (changing a stick into a serpent before the Pharaoh; the Red Sea; Mount Sinai) and **Job** (temptation; the devil killing his herds; thanking God; being consoled). Above, note the beautiful fresco depicting the Creation of Eve, in which Eve emerges from the rib of the sleeping Adam. The **New Testament** scenes opposite (begun 1333), attributed to either Barna da Siena or Lippo Memmi, impress most by the intensity of their emotional expression. In the dramatic *Resurrection of Lazarus*, a dumbstruck crowd witnesses the removal of a door to reveal the living Lazarus in the winding bandages of burial. An altogether different vision pervades Taddeo di Bartolo's **Last Judgement** (1410), with paradise to the left and hell to the right. A gruesome depiction of what's always a lurid subject, it features no-holds-barred illustrations of the Seven Deadly Sins.

On the north side of the Collegiata, San Gimignano's most important Renaissance artwork is the superb fresco cycle made by Domenico Ghirlandaio for the small **Cappella di Santa Fina**. The subject, a local saint, born in 1238, was struck by an incurable disease at the age of 10. She gave herself immediately to God, repented her sins (the worst seems to have been accepting an orange from a boy), and insisted on spending the five agonizing years until her death lying on a plank on the floor. The fresco of the right-hand lunette shows Fina experiencing a vision of St Gregory. Opposite it, the *Funeral of St Fina* is an even more accomplished work – Raphael was especially impressed with it – showing the saint on her deathbed with the towers of San Gimignano in the background. Ghirlandaio left a self-portrait: he's the figure behind the bishop who is saying Mass.

Palazzo Comunale

Piazza del Duomo • April–Sept 9.30am–7pm; Oct–May 11am–5.30pm • €5 joint ticket with Torre Grossa, or €7.50 joint ticket with Museo Archeologico, Spezieria and Galleria d'Arte Moderna

The **Palazzo Comunale** is the other key component of Piazza del Duomo. Its lovely courtyard was built in 1323; a loggia opens on the right, from which judicial and public decrees were occasionally proclaimed (hence the subject matter of its frescoes). Stairs lead up to a picturesque little balcony, and the Pinacoteca.

The Pinacoteca

The first room of the **Pinacoteca**, frescoed with hunting scenes, is the **Sala di Dante** – the poet visited as Florence's ambassador to the town in 1299, to plead for Guelph

9

unity. Most of the paintings are Sienese in origin or inspiration, with the highlight being Lippo Memmi's *Maestà* (1317). Off the Sala di Dante are busts of a winsome *Santa Fina* (1496) and *San Gregorio* by Pietro Torrigiano. Highlights upstairs include two outstanding tondi by **Filippino Lippi**. Rooms off to the right hold a triptych by **Taddeo di Bartolo**, the *Scenes from the Life of St Gimignano* (1393) – with the saint holding the eponymous town on his lap – and **Lorenzo di Niccolò**'s *Scenes from the Life of St Bartholomew* (1401), which includes a graphic depiction of the saint being flayed alive. The most enjoyable paintings are hidden away in a small room off the stairs. Frescoes of wedding scenes completed in the 1320s by the Sienese painter Memmo di Filipuccio are unique in their subject matter: they show a tournament where the wife rides on her husband's back, followed by the couple taking a shared bath and then climbing into bed – the man managing to retain the same red hat throughout.

Torre Grossa

The entrance ticket also allows access to the **Torre Grossa**, the only one of San Gimignano's towers which you can climb; it's a stiff ascent – the top section involves scrambling up a ladder – but worth it for the great views of the Val d'Elsa, dotted with villages and olive groves.

San Lorenzo in Ponte

Via di Castello continues east past the Romanesque **San Lorenzo in Ponte** (with a dramatic fresco of the *Last Judgement*) to a rural lane that winds down between vineyards to the city walls; just beyond the public wellhouse, or **Fonti**, stretches open countryside.

The Rocca

A signposted lane leads from Piazza del Duomo up to the **Rocca**, the old fortress, with its one surviving tower and wonderful views. It was built, at local expense, by the Florentines "to remove every cause of evil thinking from the inhabitants" after their union with the *comune*. Later, its purpose presumably fulfilled, it was dismantled by Cosimo de' Medici. Nowadays it encloses an orchard-like public garden, with fig and olive trees, and the small **Museo del Vino Vernaccia** (April–Nov daily 11.30am–6.30pm; Dec–March open erratic hours), with a small display on the history of local wine production and a bar, the perfect place to sample the local Vernaccia while drinking in the views.

The Galleria d'Arte Moderna, Museo Archeologico and Spezieria

The grand, impressively preserved **Via San Matteo** runs north from Piazza del Duomo. Just before the main **Porta San Matteo** gate, Via XX Settembre heads east to the former convent of Santa Chiara, which houses both the **Galleria d'Arte Moderna**, with works by nineteenth- and twentieth-century Tuscan artists, and the dreary **Museo Archeologico** (both open daily 11am–6pm; €3.50 for the two museums, joint ticket with Pinacoteca and Torre Grossa €7.50). In the same complex, the fragrant halls of the **Spezieria di Santa Fina** (same hours and ticket) are filled with exhibits from the sixteenth-century spice and herb pharmacy of the Santa Fina hospital.

Sant'Agostino

Piazza Sant'Agostino 10 • Jan to mid-April Mon 4–6pm; Tues–Sun 10am–noon & 3–6pm; mid-April to Oct daily 7am–noon & 3–7pm; Nov & Dec daily 7am–noon & 3–6pm • Free

At the northern end of town is the large church of **Sant'Agostino**. Inside, an outstanding fresco cycle by Benozzo Gozzoli, the *Life of St Augustine* (1465), provides an amazing record of life in Renaissance Florence. Read from low down on the left, the panels depict the saint – born in what's now Tunisia in 354 – being taken to school and flogged by his teacher, studying grammar at Carthage university, crossing the sea to Italy, teaching in Rome and Milan, and being received by Emperor Theodosius. Then comes the turning point, when he hears St Ambrose preach and, while reading

St Paul, hears a child's voice extolling him "*Tolle, lege*" (take and read). After this, he was baptized and returned to Africa to found a monastic community.

San Gimignano del 1300
Via Berignano 23 · Daily 9am–7pm · €5

A must if you have kids in tow, **San Gimignano del 1300** presents a potted local history with its meticulously crafted ceramic reconstructions of the town as it was in the year 1300. There are bustling street scenes and views of country life outside the walls, as well as a cross-section of a grand *palazzo*, revealing the relatively privileged existence of the family living within.

ARRIVAL AND INFORMATION   SAN GIMIGNANO

By train Most visitors see San Gimignano on a day-trip from Siena. Take a train to Poggibonsi (40min) and change there for the 20min bus trip (every 15–30min) up to San Gimignano.

By bus Catch one of the direct buses from Siena (10 daily; 1hr 5min–1hr 15min), or take a bus to Poggibonsi station (hourly; 45min) and change there for the bus to San Gimignano. Buses from Florence to Poggibonsi run at least hourly (50min). The bus stop is just outside the walls, by Porta San Giovanni. Note that despite their proximity, getting a bus between San Gimignano and Volterra is not practical, as it involves an inconvenient change at Colle di Val d'Elsa – a 3hr 45min journey in all.

By car If you're driving, the easiest parking is in the three pay car-parks along the road that circles outside the walls; you can only enter the town itself if you have a permit from a hotel.

Tourist office On the south side of Piazza del Duomo (March–Oct 10am–1pm & 3–7pm; Nov–Feb daily 9am–1pm & 2–6pm; ☎ 0577 940 008, ⓦ sangimignano.com). Has information on local wine routes in the surrounding country-side, as well as tastings in cellars and wineries.

ACCOMMODATION

The tourist office can help with accommodation, or you can use the ⓦ hotelsiena.com website to compare prices online. The local hotel tax (€1.50–3 per person per night) will be added to your bill, in addition to the room rate.

★ **Agriturismo Poggiacolle** Strada di Montauto 58, a 5min drive south from San Gimignano ☎ 0577 941 537, ⓦ poggiacolle.com. In an eighteenth-century farmhouse set between an olive grove and a vineyard, this dream of an agriturismo has comfortable, spotless rooms with stunning countryside views, as well as apartments sleeping two to ten people. Lounge by the infinity pool soaking up the views of San Gimignano, tour the farm or have a jaunt through the surrounding countryside – bikes are available free of charge, and there are trekking paths through the estate. €95

Bel Soggiorno Via S. Giovanni 91 ☎ 0577 940 375, ⓦ hotelbelsoggiorno.it. Twenty-one smallish, no-frills rooms in a converted thirteenth-century townhouse on the main street; it's worth paying extra for a room with a view. There's a restaurant with panoramic terrace too. €95

L'Antico Pozzo Via S. Matteo 87 ☎ 0577 942 014, ⓦ anticopozzo.com. In a tastefully restored *palazzo*, part of which dates back to the Middle Ages, this three-star hotel has comfortable rooms; the "Dante" rooms are superior (and cost €40 more), with hand-painted walls, high ceilings and four-posters. The brick-vaulted bar downstairs makes a cosy spot for a drink, while the sumptuous breakfast is served in what was once the ballroom. €140

Leon Bianco Piazza Cisterna 13 ☎ 0577 941 294, ⓦ leonbianco.com. Tasteful three-star hotel, in a fourteenth-century mansion in the main square. Rooms without views are a little cheaper, but it would be a shame not to make the most of this prime people-watching spot. The roof terrace is a lovely spot for breakfast, drinks and lounging. €110

Le Vecchie Mura Via Piandornella 13 ☎ 0577 940 270, ⓦ vecchiemura.it. Three simply furnished, en-suite doubles above a restaurant (see p.594), with superb views over vine-yards and rolling Tuscan countryside. Friendly owners. €60

CAMPING

Campeggio Boschetto di Piemma 2km downhill from Porta San Giovanni at Santa Lucia, off the Volterra road ☎ 0577 940 352, ⓦ boschettodipiemma.it. The nearest campsite, with camping pitches and chalets as well as a bar, restaurant and pool. Closed Nov to mid-March. Pitches €20, chalets €110

EATING AND DRINKING

San Gimignano has too many visitors and too few locals to ensure high standards in its **restaurants**. However, the tables set out on the car-free squares and lanes, and the good local wines, make for pleasant dining. Good **bars** are similarly thin on the ground, though each of the main piazzas has one or two pleasant places to sit and watch the world go by.

9

Dulcisinfundo Vicolo degli Innocenti ☎ 0577 941 919, ⓦ fortezzacortesi.com. A great little restaurant with outdoor tables overlooking the rolling hills. Indoors is elegant, with a smooth jazz soundtrack and a menu of well-executed Tuscan dishes. Mains (€12.50–16) include roast chicken cooked in Vernaccia wine, rosemary and sage, and grilled beef with rocket and *scamorza* cheese. 12.30–2.30pm & 7.15–9.30pm; closed Wed.

★ **Gelateria di Piazza** Piazza della Cisterna 4 ☎ 0577 942 244, ⓦ gelateriadipiazza.com. This small but extraordinarily popular *gelateria* is renowned for making the best ice cream in Tuscany. Owner Sergio's incomparable pistachio flavour is made from the finest Sicilian nuts, and his trademark *crema di Santa Fina* is perfumed with saffron; but you'd be hard pushed to beat the trio of raspberry and rosemary, champagne with grapefruit, and Vernaccia – a fragrant sorbet made from the crisp local white wine. Daily: Easter to mid-Oct 8am–midnight; mid-Oct to end Nov 8am–8pm.

★ **Il Trovatore** Viale dei Fossi 17 ☎ 0577 942 240, ⓦ trovatoresangimignano.it. A cheerful, no-frills place just outside the walls serving deliciously crispy pizzas cooked in a wood-fired oven (€5.50–9.50). There are some

forty types to choose from, including the house special, with salami, Tabasco, mozzarella and olives. They also serve pastas and grilled-meat dishes. 6.30pm–midnight; closed Wed.

La Mangiatoia Via Mainardi 5 ☎ 0577 941 528. Classical music and stained glass compete for attention with some imaginative pasta dishes and wild boar stew. Pavement seating, plus a garden that's open for dinner only. Expect to spend about €35 per head including wine. 12.30–2.30pm & 7.30–9.30pm; closed Tues.

La Taverna del Granducato Piazza Martiri di Montemaggio 5 ☎ 0577 940 824. It may not offer the scenic charms of the restaurants inside the walls, but this cavernous place serves up good, old-fashioned pizzas at non-tourist prices (€7; evenings only), as well as a daily menu of two courses for €13. Tues–Sun 12.30–2.30pm & 7.30–11.30pm.

Le Vecchie Mura Via Piandornella 15 ☎ 0577 940 270, ⓦ vecchiemura.it. Housed in an old vaulted stable set into the city walls, this place serves good regional food (*primi* €9–11, *secondi* €11–19), but the real draw is the terrace across the road, offering the best views in town. 6–10pm; closed Tues.

Volterra

The dramatic location of **VOLTERRA** – built on a high plateau enclosed by volcanic hills midway between Siena and the sea – prompted D.H. Lawrence to write that "it gets all the wind and sees all the world – a sort of inland island", and indeed, you can often find seashells embedded in the paving of streets and squares. Busy but still atmospheric, the town's walled medieval core is made from the yellow-grey stone *panchino*. Tourism has boomed here recently thanks to an unlikely and incongruous source: its fictional role, in Stephenie Meyer's *Twilight* novels, as the home of a 3000-year-old vampire coven known as the Volturi; the tourist office proffers a walking trail of vampire-related sites.

Brief history

Volterra is one of the most ancient of all **Etruscan** communities, and still abounds in Etruscan artefacts. Thanks both to its impregnable position, and its alabaster mines, the Etruscan settlement of Velathri survived through the Roman era and beyond. In due course, however, its isolation proved to be its downfall. Under **Florentine** control from 1360, Volterra failed to keep pace with changing trade patterns, and the town itself began to subside, its walls and houses slipping away to the west over the **Balze** cliffs, which form a dramatic prospect from the Pisa road. Today, Volterra occupies less than a third of its ancient extent.

Palazzo dei Priori

Piazza dei Priori • Mid-March to Oct daily 10.30am–5.30pm; Nov to mid-March Sat & Sun 11am–5pm • €1.50

Dominating the almost totally medieval square of **Piazza dei Priori**, the **Palazzo dei Priori** is the oldest town hall in Tuscany. Constructed between 1208 and 1257, it may have been the model for Florence's Palazzo Vecchio. Visitors can enjoy great views from its tower, while the upstairs **Sala del Consiglio** has served as the town's council chamber without interruption since 1257. Its end wall is frescoed with a huge *Annunciation*, attributed to Jacopo di Cione.

> ## VOLTERRA'S ALABASTER
>
> A form of crystallized chalk that has a delicate, milky texture, **alabaster** lends itself to the sculpture of fine, flowing lines and close ornamental detail. Even in quite large blocks, it is translucent. The Etruscans and Romans extensively mined Volterra's alabaster for sculpting. Until the 1960s, large alabaster factories were scattered throughout the town centre, but – not least because of the quantity of dust they threw up – large-scale production was moved to outlying areas. These days, only about a dozen artisans are permitted to maintain workshops in the town centre, and Volterra's famous art school is the only one in Europe to train students to work alabaster.
>
> Most of the plentiful **alabaster shops** in the centre are outlets for factories that produce machined pieces from the tasteful to the tacky. Alab'Arte, whose workshop is down the alley alongside the Museo Guarnacci at Via Orti di Sant'Agostino 28 (☎0588 87 968, ⊛alabarte.com), is one of the few to stick to hand production; you can browse a selection of their wares at their shop at Via Don Minzoni 18.

Palazzo Pretorio

Among the other fine *palazzi* that loom over Piazza dei Priori, the **Palazzo Pretorio** is topped by the **Torre del Porcellino** (Piglet's Tower), named after the weathered carved boar perched on a bracket to the right of the top window.

Museo Diocesano di Arte Sacra

Via Roma 13 • Daily: mid-March to Oct 9am–1pm & 3–6pm; Nov to mid-March 9am–1pm • €10 joint ticket with Museo Etrusco and Pinacoteca

Be sure not to miss the small but exquisite **Museo d'Arte Sacra**, whose highlights include a painted terracotta bust of *St Linus* by Andrea della Robbia, and a wonderful stylized, gilded thirteenth-century *Crucifixion*. The museum is due to move to the church of Sant'Agostino some time in 2013; ask at the tourist office for an update.

The Duomo

Piazza del Duomo • April–Oct Mon–Thurs, Sat & Sun 8am–12.30pm & 3–6.30pm, Fri 8am–12.30pm & 4–6.30pm; Nov–March Mon–Thurs, Sat & Sun 8am–12.30pm & 3–6.30pm, Fri 8am–12.30pm & 4–6.30pm • Free

Via Roma leads into the slightly down-at-heel cathedral square, site of the Pisan-Romanesque **Duomo**, consecrated in 1120, and **baptistry** (late thirteenth century). The Duomo's greatest treasure is a sculpture of the *Deposition* (1228) in the south transept, disarmingly repainted in its original bright colours. Behind the baptistry is an old foundling's hospital decorated by della Robbia.

Pinacoteca e Museo Civico

Via dei Sarti 1 • Daily: mid-March to Oct 9am–7pm; Nov to mid-March 8.30am–1.45pm • €10 joint ticket with Museo Etrusco and Museo Diocesano

The beautiful Renaissance Palazzo Minucci-Solaini houses the **Pinacoteca e Museo Civico**, where, unusually, the exhibits are comprehensively captioned in English. Its key works are Florentine: Ghirlandaio's marvellous *Christ in Glory*, set in an imaginary landscape that's very reminiscent of Volterra's own Balze (see p.596); Luca Signorelli's stunning *Annunciation*; and, best of all, Rosso Fiorentino's extraordinary *Deposition*. An altarpiece, painted for the church of San Francesco in 1521, it's a true masterpiece of Mannerism, its figures, without any central focus, creating an agitated tension from sharp lines and blocks of discordant colour.

Ecomuseo dell'Alabastro

Torri Minucci, Piazzetta Minucci • Mid-March to Oct daily 11am–5pm; Nov to mid-March Sat & Sun 9am–1.30pm • €3.50

The Palazzo Minucci-Solaini also contains the **Ecomuseo dell'Alabastro**, which provides an overview of alabaster-working in the area from Etruscan times to the present day and has a replica sculptor's workshop. The most important pieces are two Etruscan *cinerari* (receptacles for ashes), two capitals that are the only known examples of

9

alabaster work in the Middle Ages, and a collection of sculpture from the eighteenth and nineteenth centuries.

Palazzo Incontri-Viti

Via dei Sarti 41 • April–Oct daily 10am–1pm & 2.30–6.30pm; Nov–March by appointment only • €5 • ☎ 0588 840 47, ⓦ www.comune .volterra.pi.it

Not far along from the Pinacoteca, the warm sandstone facade of the **Palazzo Viti** is attributed to Bartolomeo Ammanati. An extensively frescoed Renaissance mansion, the *palazzo* was bought in 1850 by alabaster salesman and traveller Benedetto Giuseppe Viti, who filled his home with beautiful objects in alabaster, everything from 2m-high candelabras to tiles laid in the floor of the ballroom.

Museo Etrusco Guarnacci

Via Don Minzoni 15 • Daily: mid-March to Oct 9am–7pm; Nov to mid-March 8.30am–1.45pm • €10 joint ticket with Pinacoteca and Museo Diocesano

Volterra's **Museo Etrusco Guarnacci**, 500m east of Piazza dei Priori, ranks among Italy's most important archeological museums, specializing in this region's rich **Etruscan** history and holding some truly remarkable treasures. The star piece is the so-called **Ombra della Sera** ("Evening Shadow"), an elongated nude figure of a young boy that looks like a proto-Giacometti. Archeologists feel that modern descriptions of this beautiful bronze statuette as being personalized, and depicting a specific individual, fail to reflect its original role as a votive offering. Also on the top floor, the **Urna degli Sposi** is a rare and artistically unique clay urn-lid which features a disturbing double portrait of a husband and wife, all piercing eyes and dreadful looks. The bulk of the museum's vast collection consists, however, of around six hundred Etruscan **funerary urns**. Carved in alabaster, terracotta or local sandstone or limestone, they date from the fourth to first centuries BC, and follow a standard pattern: below a reclining figure of the subject (always leaning on their left side), bas-reliefs depict domestic events, Greek myths or simply a symbolic flower – one for a young person, two for middle-aged, three for elderly.

Parco Archeologico and around

Via Marchesi heads south uphill from the Piazza dei Priori to a lush area of grass, trees and shade known as the **Parco Archeologico** (daily 8.30am–dusk; free). There's precious little archeology about the place – a few odd lumps of rock, said to be part of a Roman bathhouse – but it's a beautiful area to stroll around. Overlooking the park to the east is the Medicean **Fortezza**, with rounded bastions and a central tower; a fabulous specimen of Italian military architecture, it has for the last 150 years been a prison. West of the park is an Etruscan **acropolis** (mid-March to Oct daily 10.30am–5.30pm; Nov to mid-March Sat & Sun 10am–4pm; €3.50, includes the Roman Theatre to the west of town).

Nearby, the first turning off Via Marchesi, Via Porta dell'Arco, runs to the **Porta all'Arco**, an Etruscan gateway, third century BC in origin, built in cyclopean blocks of stone. The gate was narrowly saved from destruction in the last war during a ten-day battle between partisans and Nazis.

To the Balze

To reach the eroded **Balze** cliffs, head northwest from the Piazza dei Priori. Beyond the church of **San Francesco**, where fifteenth-century frescoes by Cenni di Francesco depict the *Legend of the True Cross*, you leave town through the Porta San Francesco. From here, follow Borgo Santo Stefano and its continuation, Borgo San Giusto, past the Baroque church and former abbey of **San Giusto**, its striking facade framed by an avenue of cypress trees. At the Balze (almost 2km west of Piazza dei Priori) you gain a real sense of the extent of Etruscan Volterra, whose old walls drop away into the chasms. Gashes in the slopes and the natural erosion of sand and clay are made more dramatic by alabaster mines, ancient and modern. Great tracts of the Etruscan and

Roman city lie buried below, and landslips continue – as evidenced by the ruined eleventh-century **Badia** monastery ebbing away over the precipice.

ARRIVAL AND INFORMATION   VOLTERRA

By bus All the various, mostly infrequent buses that climb up here arrive on the south side of the walls at Piazza Martiri, a 2min walk from the central square. Note that it takes around 1hr 50min to get here from Florence by bus, and you have to change at Colle Val d'Elsa; and due to the infrequency of buses, travelling between San Gimignano and Volterra (a 3hr 45min round trip) is not advisable.
Destinations Colle Val d'Elsa (for connections to Florence & Siena; 6 daily; 50min).

By car Driving up the spectacular road that twists and turns past endless green hills to reach Volterra from the south is an extraordinary experience. As ever, though, you'll have to park outside the walls, in the free car parks 5, 6 or 8 on the northern side, or the paying underground one to the south.
By taxi Call ☎ 0588 87 257.
Tourist office In the centre at Piazza dei Priori 20 (daily 9.30am–1pm & 2–6pm; ☎ 0588 87 257, ⓦ provolterra.it).

ACCOMMODATION

★ **Albergo Etruria** Via Matteotti 32 ☎ 0588 87 377, ⓦ albergoetruria.it. With a central location, wonderful views from its roof garden, and warm, friendly staff, the *Etruria* makes a great base. The bathrooms are on the small side and the furnishings a little tired, but it's still the best choice in town. Book ahead to secure the roof garden room. **€79**
Campeggio Le Balze 1km west of the centre at Via di Mandringa 15 ☎ 0588 87 880, ⓦ campinglebalze.com. The well-equipped *Le Balze* campsite has shady pitches, a pool and tennis courts. Late March to mid-Oct. Pitches **€17**
Chiosco delle Monache Via del Teatro 4, in the San Girolamo neighbourhood ☎ 0588 86 613, in winter ☎ 0588 80 050, ⓦ youthhostelvolterra.com. This youth

hostel is 1km (a 15min walk) east of town in yet another converted monastery, recently refurbished, with doubles as well as dorms; all rooms come with private bathroom, and are airy and spacious, with cool tiled floors. Breakfast costs an extra €6 per day for the dorms; it's included in private rooms. Half-board is available for €16 per day. Dorms **€18**, doubles **€69**
San Lino Via S. Lino 26 ☎ 0588 85 250, ⓦ hotelsanlino .com. A converted medieval monastery, just inside the walls at the northwest end of town, a 5min walk from the centre, offering comfortable rooms – some of which come with a terrace overlooking the surrounding countryside – plus a great swimming pool and a pretty courtyard for breakfast. **€90**

EATING AND DRINKING

Alla Vecchia Maniera Via Ricciarelli 38 ☎ 0588 88 819. This unassuming little place doesn't look much from the outside, but locals flock here at lunch for the delicious pizzas, with an array of creative toppings and served crispy from the wood-fired oven. The Primavera – loaded with bresaola, rocket and parmesan, and drizzled with olive oil – costs just €8. Tues–Sun 9am–2pm & 3pm–midnight.
★ **L'Incontro** Via Matteotti 18 ☎ 0588 80 500. A lovely nineteenth-century café, pastry shop and *gelateria*, with a tempting selection of gourmet chocolates and cakes: try the traditional *mandorlato volterrano* (with candied orange, almonds and honey). They also serve light lunches. Daily 6am–midnight; closed Wed in winter.

Ombra de la Sera Via Gramsci 70 ☎ 0588 86 663. One of only a few restaurants in Volterra to have outdoor seating, with tables nestling against a tiny chapel, or you can eat indoors in the wood-beamed dining rooms. Try the beef *tagliata* cooked in herbs and balsamic vinegar (€16), or the menu of soups (€7.50–8.50) provides a lighter alternative. Tues–Sun noon–3pm & 7–10pm.
Vecchia Lira Via Matteotti 19 ☎ 0588 86 180, ⓦ vecchialira.com. Particularly good value, this *rosticceria* serves take-out meals and cheap self-service lunches, but also offers excellent meals at dinner, with most dishes, like the delicious seafood spaghetti *mareggiata*, costing €10. 11.30am–2.30pm & 7–10.30pm; closed Thurs.

Southern Tuscany

The inland hills of **southern Tuscany** display the region at its best, an infinite gradation of trees and vineyards that encompasses the depopulated *crete* before climbing into the hills around Monte Amiata. Southwest of Siena towards the sea, the memorable but little-visited hill-town of **Massa Marittima** presides over a marshy coastal plain. Magnificent monastic architecture survives in the tranquil settings of **San Galgano** and, further east, **Monte Oliveto Maggiore**, which also boasts some marvellous frescoes.

9

The finest of the hill-towns to the south of Siena is **Montepulciano**, with its superb wines and an ensemble of Renaissance architecture that rivals neighbouring **Pienza**.

Further south, the tourist crush is noticeably eased in smaller towns and villages that are often overlooked by visitors gorged on Florentine art and Sienese countryside. Wild **Monte Amiata** offers scenic mountain walks, while the isolated, dramatic medieval town of **Pitigliano** nurtures the amazing story – and scant remains – of what was once Tuscany's strongest Jewish community.

Massa Marittima

The road south from Volterra over the mountains to **MASSA MARITTIMA** is scenically magnificent yet little explored: classic Tuscan countryside which is given an added surreal quality around **Larderello** by the presence of *soffioni* (hot steam geysers), huge silver pipes snaking across the fields, and sulphurous smoke rising from chimneys amid the foliage.

The outskirts of Massa have been marred by modern development, but the medieval town itself at the top of the hill, divided between two very distinct levels, remains a splendid ensemble. While visitor numbers are much lower than, say, San Gimignano, Massa is the closest hill-town to several coastal resorts, and on summer evenings it fills up with beach-based day-trippers.

Brief history

Like Volterra, Massa has been a wealthy **mining** town since Etruscan times. In 1225, it passed Europe's first-ever charter for the protection of miners; in the century afterwards, before Siena took over in 1335, its exquisite **Duomo** went up and the population doubled. The trend was reversed in the sixteenth century, and by 1737, after bouts of plague and malaria, it was a virtual ghost town. Massa gained its "Marittima" suffix in the Middle Ages when it became the leading hill-town of this coastal region, even though the sea is 20km distant across a silty plain. Its recovery began with the draining of coastal marshes in the 1830s. Today, it's a quiet but well-off town, where the effects of mining are less evident than agriculture and low-profile tourism.

Città Vecchia

Piazza Garibaldi, the main square of the older, lower part of town, is a perfect example of Tuscan town planning. Its thirteenth-century **Duomo** (daily 8am–noon & 3–7pm; free), set on broad steps at a dramatically oblique angle to the square, is dedicated to the sixth-century St Cerbone, whose claim to fame was to persuade a flock of geese to follow him when summoned to Rome on heresy charges. Behind the altar in its airy interior, the *Arca di San Cerbone* is a marble "ark" carved with bas-reliefs depicting the life of the saint. The Duomo makes a striking backdrop for the Lirica in Piazza **opera festival** in August (tickets €12–46; ⓦliricainpiazza.it).

The **Museo Archeologico**, divided into modest prehistory and Etruscan sections, occupies the Palazzo del Podestà opposite (Tues–Sun 10am–12.30pm & 3.30–7pm; Nov–March closes at 5pm; €3).

Città Nuova

A picturesque lane, Via Moncini, climbs steeply from the northern end of the square up to the quiet Gothic "new" town, known as the **Città Nuova**. Passing through a gateway, you emerge beneath a slender and very spectacular – albeit militarily useless – arch that connects the high town walls to the **Torre del Candeliere**. Set in the centre of **Piazza Matteotti**, and part of the thirteenth-century Fortezza Senese, the tower is open to visitors, who can enjoy a stupendous panorama from the top (April–Oct daily 10.30am–1.30pm & 4–7pm; Nov–March 11am–1pm & 2.30–4.30pm; €3).

9

Museo di Arte Sacra

Corso Díaz 36 • Tues–Sun: April–Oct 10am–1pm & 3–6pm; Nov–March 11am–1pm & 3–5pm • €5

Also in the Città Nuova is the **Museo di Arte Sacra**, containing sculptures of the facade of the Duomo by Pisano, as well as the town's undisputed masterpiece, a superb *Maestà* altarpiece by Ambrogio Lorenzetti, coloured in vivid pink, green and tangerine, with Cerbone and his geese lurking in the corner.

ARRIVAL AND INFORMATION

MASSA MARITTIMA

By bus Buses stop on Via Corridoni near Piazza Garibaldi and run to Piombino (2 daily; 25min) and Siena (2 daily; 1hr 55min).

Tourist office The tourist office is just below Piazza Garibaldi at Via Todini 3/5 (Tues–Sat 10am–1pm & 2–6pm; ☎0566 902 756, ⓦaltamaremmaturismo.it).

ACCOMMODATION AND EATING

A La Tana del Brillo Parlante Vicolo del Ciambellano 4 ☎0566 901 274. A lovely little place just off Massa's main drag, Via della Libertà, with a couple of outdoor tables. Dedicated to Slow Food, it serves tasty pasta and meat dishes such as *pici* pasta with *cacio* cheese and pepper (€9) and roast pork with apples and cannellini beans (€14). Noon–2.30pm & 7.30–10pm; closed Wed.

Duca del Mare Piazza Dante Alighieri 1 ☎0566 902 284, ⓦducadelmare.it. This pleasant, slightly motel-like place immediately below the old town has cheery rooms and a nice pool. €85

Il Girifalco Via Massetana Nord 25 ☎0566 902 177, ⓦilgirifalco.com. Thirty no-frills rooms in a lovely countryside setting, just a 10min walk from the centre.

A good choice for the summer months, thanks to its swimming pool surrounded by olive and fruit trees and its flower-filled veranda, where meals are served (half board €22). €95

Ostello Sant'Anna Via Gramsci 3 ☎0566 901 115, ⓦdigilander.libero.it/leclarisse. A simple hostel in the higher part of town, converted from a school. Breakfast costs €1.50. Reception 9am–noon & 5pm–midnight. Dorms €15

★ **Osteria da Tronca** Vicolo Porte 5 ☎0566 901 991. Tucked away on a backstreet, this atmospheric, grotto-like restaurant serves typical Tuscan pastas (€7–10), as well as mains such as artichoke *frittata* (€7) and wild boar stew (€11.50). 11.40am–3pm & 6pm–midnight; closed Wed.

The crete

The classic Tuscan countryside that stretches south of Siena is known as the **crete**. This tranquil, sparsely populated region of pale clay hillsides, dotted with sheep, cypresses and the odd monumental-looking farmhouse, was a heartland of medieval monasticism in Tuscany. The Vallombrosan order maintained their main house at Torri just south of Siena; the Benedictine order had theirs at Sant'Antimo near Montalcino (see p.607); and the Cistercians founded the convent and abbey of **San Galgano**. Now ruined, this is one of the most alluring sights in Tuscany, complete with its hilltop chapel housing a "sword in the stone". The finest monastery of all lies southeast of Siena, at **Monte Oliveto Maggiore**.

Abbazia di San Galgano

Chiusdino • **Abbey** April–Oct daily 9am–8pm; Nov–March Mon–Sat 9.30am–5.30pm, Sun 9.30am–6.30pm • €2 **Eremo di Montesiepi** Daily 9am–sunset • Free • ⓦsangalgano.org

The **Abbazia di San Galgano**, surrounded by majestic fields of sunflowers in a peaceful rural setting 26km northeast of Massa Marittima, is perhaps the most evocative Gothic building in all Italy – roofless, with grass for a floor in the nave, nebulous patches of fresco amid the vegetation, and panoramas of the sky, clouds and hills through a rose window.

Brief history

During the twelfth and thirteenth centuries, local **Cistercian** monks were the leading power in Tuscany. The abbots exercised powers of arbitration in city disputes, while the monks in Siena served as the city's accountants. Through them, the ideas of Gothic building were imported to Italy. The order began a hilltop **church** and monastic buildings here in 1218, but their project to build a grand abbey on the fertile land below was doomed to failure. Building work took seventy years up to 1288, but then famine struck in 1329, the Black Death in 1348, and mercenaries ran amok in subsequent decades. By 1500, all the monks had moved to the security of Siena. The buildings mouldered until 1786, when the belltower was struck by lightning and collapsed. Three years later, the church was deconsecrated, and the complex was abandoned for good.

The ruins

These days, the main appeal of the **abbey** is its general state of ruin, although the basic structure has been stabilized. In summer, it makes a wonderful open-air venue for **opera** performances, staged on various evenings between late June and the end of July; see ⓦsangalgano.org for schedules.

Eremo di Montesiepi

Atop the solitary hill nearby, the unusual, round, Romanesque **Eremo di Montesiepi** commemorates the spot where Galgano – a local twelfth-century knight – renounced his violent past by thrusting his sword into a stone. Amazingly enough, Galgano's **sword in the stone** has survived, protected under glass as an object of veneration. A side chapel preserves the decaying remains of a man's hands: local legend has it that two wolves – companions of Galgano – tore them from a robber who had broken into the saint's tomb.

ARRIVAL AND DEPARTURE | ABBAZIA DI SAN GALGANO

By car The easiest way to reach the abbey is to drive. From Florence, the quickest route is via Colle Val d'Elsa, but for a more picturesque route take the SP 73.

By bus Three daily buses from Siena drop passengers at the abbey (1hr).

ACCOMMODATION AND EATING

Fattoria le Planaie Località Pentolina, Chiusdino ☎0577 799 018. This very authentic little agriturismo a few kilometres from the abbey, surrounded by woodland, has comfortable en-suite rooms if you fancy spending a night or two in this isolated spot. Its restaurant offers huge portions of Tuscan cuisine such as wild boar stew (four-course menu with wine €23). **€75**

Abbazia di Monte Oliveto Maggiore

Asciano • Daily: summer 9am–noon & 3–6pm, winter 9.15am–noon & 3.15–5pm; Gregorian chants Mon–Sat 8am & 6.15pm, Sun 8.45am, 11am & 6.30pm • Free • ⓦ monteolivetomaggiore.it

Tuscany's grandest monastery – the **Abbazia di Monte Oliveto Maggiore**, renowned for its absorbing Renaissance **frescoes** – stands 26km southeast of Siena, or roughly 50km east of San Galgano, in a secluded but exceptionally beautiful tract of countryside.

Brief history

When Pius II visited in 1463, it was the overall scene that impressed him: the architecture, in honey-coloured Sienese brick, merging into the woods and gardens that the **Olivetan** or White Benedictine monks had created from the eroded hills of the *crete*. The pope recognized the order within six years, and over the following two centuries this, their principal house, was transformed into one of the most powerful monasteries in the land. Only in 1810, when the monastery was suppressed by Napoleon, did it fall from influence. Today it's maintained by a small group of Olivetan monks, who supplement their state income with a high-tech centre for the restoration of ancient books.

The abbey complex

From the **gatehouse**, an avenue of cypresses leads to the abbey. Signs at the bottom of the slope direct you along a walk to **Blessed Bernardo's grotto** – a chapel built on the site where the founder lived as a hermit.

9

The abbey is a huge complex, though much of it remains off-limits to visitors. The entrance leads to the **Chiostro Grande**, where the cloister walls are covered by frescoes that depict the *Life of St Benedict*, the founder of Christian monasticism. The fresco cycle, which begins on the east wall, immediately to the left of worshippers emerging from the church itself, was started in 1497 by Luca Signorelli, who painted nine panels in the middle of the series that start with the depiction of a collapsing house. The colourful Antonio Bazzi, known as **Il Sodoma**, painted the remaining 27 scenes between 1505 and 1508. He was by all accounts a lively presence, bringing with him part of his menagerie of pets, which included badgers, depicted at his feet in a self-portrait in the third panel. There's a sensuality in many of the secular figures, especially the young men – as befits the artist's nickname – but also the "evil women" (originally nudes, until the abbot protested).

The **church** was given a Baroque remodelling in the eighteenth century and some superb stained-glass in the twentieth. Its main treasure is the choir stalls, inlaid by Giovanni di Verona and others with architectural, landscape and domestic scenes (including a nod to Sodoma's pets with a cat in a window). Stairs lead from the cloister up to the **library**, again with carving by Giovanni; sadly, it has had to be viewed from the door since the theft of sixteen of its twenty codices in 1975.

ARRIVAL	ABBAZIA DI MONTE OLIVETO MAGGIORE
By train The closest train station is at Buonconvento, from where you can take a taxi (☎0577 806 094 or ☎333 358 4410). **By bus** One afternoon bus a day goes from Siena's train station to the village of Chiusure, 2km east of the abbey.	**By car** By car, you can approach from the crossroads town of Buonconvento, climbing quickly into forests of pine, oak and cypress, and then into the olive groves that enclose the monastery.

Montepulciano

Highest of all the major Tuscan hill-towns, at more than 600m, the ravishing, self-contained community of **MONTEPULCIANO** stretches atop a long, narrow ridge 65km southeast of Siena. Its main street, the **Corso**, coils its way between scores of crumbling Renaissance *palazzi* and churches, here clustered around perfect little squares, there towering over tiny alleyways. Wherever stairways or mysterious passages drop down the hillside, you get sudden, stunning glimpses of the quintessential wine-growing countryside rolling off to the horizon; occasionally terraced gardens allow you to contemplate the whole stunning prospect at leisure.

Henry James, who compared Montepulciano to a ship, spent most of his time here drinking – a sound policy, in view of the much-celebrated **Vino Nobile**, production of which dates back well over a thousand years. More recent visitors have been enticed by the drinking of **blood** rather than wine; Montepulciano's ancient squares made an ideal location for the 2009 teen vampire movie *New Moon*.

Brief history

Montepulciano's rise to eminence began in 1511, when the town finally threw in its lot with Florence rather than Siena. The Florentines thereupon sent **Antonio Sangallo the Elder** to rebuild the town's gates and walls, which he did so impressively that the council took him on to work on the town hall and a series of churches. The local nobles meanwhile hired Sangallo, his nephew Antonio Sangallo the Younger, and later the Modena-born **Vignola**, a founding figure of Baroque, to work on their own *palazzi*. Totally assured in conception and execution, this trio's work makes a fascinating comparison with Rossellino's Pienza.

The Corso

The town's bustling main street, the **Corso**, runs from north to south through town. The street begins inside Montepulciano's northern gate, the **Porta al Prato**, Sangallo's

first commission. At the first square,
Piazza Savonarola, a stone column
bears the heraldic lion (*marzocco*) of
Florence. The steep climb from this,
the lowest point in Montepulciano,
up to the highest, the main Piazza
Grande, takes around twenty minutes.
It's a delightful walk, passing a superb
and unusually consistent array of
Renaissance architectural treasures.

Sant'Agostino

Piazzale Pasquino da Montepulciano 6 • Daily 9am–noon
& 3–6pm

The church of **Sant'Agostino**, just
beyond the Porta al Prato, was
designed by the earlier Medici protégé,
Michelozzo, who also carved the relief
above the door. Its interior holds fine
Sienese paintings by Lorenzo di Credi
and Giovanni di Paolo, and the
Crucifix on the high altar is believed
to be the work of Donatello.

Santa Lucia and around

Piazza di Santa Lucia • Erratic opening hours

The street forks about 100m further
along from Sant'Agostino, where
the Renaissance **Loggia di Mercato**
overlooks Piazza dell'Erbe. Turning
right off the Corso will lead you
steeply up to a beautiful little piazza
fronting the church of **Santa Lucia**,
where a chapel on the right contains
a fabulous *Madonna* by Signorelli.

Museo Civico

Via Ricci 10 • Tues–Sun 10am–1pm & 3–6pm, closes 7pm in
summer • €5

The imposing Via Ricci leads up to the
Piazza Grande past the Sienese-Gothic
Palazzo Neri-Orselli, home to the
Museo Civico. Besides an extensive
collection of small-town Gothic and

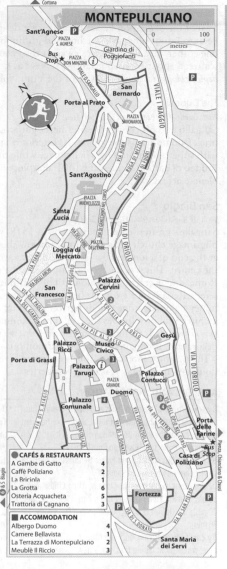

Renaissance works, including glazed terracottas by Andrea della Robbia, this hosts
substantial temporary exhibitions each year.

Piazza Grande

Piazza Grande, Montepulciano's theatrical flourish of a main square, is built on the
highest point of the ridge. Its most distinctive building is the **Palazzo Comunale**,
a thirteenth-century Gothic mansion that continues to serve as the town hall.
Michelozzo added its **clock tower** (April–Oct Mon–Sat 10am–6pm; €2) and rustication
in imitation of Florence's Palazzo Vecchio; the views across the countryside from here
are stunning.

9

Palazzo Tarugi and Palazzo Contucci

Two of the *palazzi* on Piazza Grande were designed by Sangallo. The highly innovative **Palazzo Tarugi**, alongside the lion and griffin fountain, has a public loggia cut through one corner. Headier pleasures await at the **Palazzo Contucci**, one of the many buildings scattered about Montepulciano that serve as *cantine* for the wine trade, offering free *degustazioni* (tastings) and sale of the Vino Nobile.

The Duomo

Piazza Grande • Daily 9am–1pm & 3.30–7pm • Free

Sangallo and his contemporaries never got around to building a facade for the plain brick **Duomo** across the square. Its interior is an elegant Renaissance design, scattered with superb sculptures by Michelozzo, while the finest of its paintings is the Sienese **Taddeo di Bartolo**'s iridescent 1401 altarpiece of the *Assumption*, a favourite subject for Sienese artists.

San Biagio

Via di San Biagio • Daily 9am–12.30pm & 3–6/7pm • Free

Sangallo's greatest commission came in 1518, when he was invited to design the pilgrimage church of **San Biagio** just below the town. Set amid lush, pristine lawns, at the end of a long rural avenue, it makes a wonderful fifteen-minute walk down from the centre. This was the second-largest church project of its time after St Peter's in Rome, and exercised Antonio until his death in 1534. The result is one of the most serene Renaissance creations in Italy, constructed from a porous travertine whose soft honey-coloured stone blends perfectly into its niche in the landscape. Its major architectural novelty was the use of freestanding towers to flank the facade (only one was completed). While the interior is somewhat spoiled by Baroque trompe l'oeil decoration, it remains supremely harmonious.

The nearby **Canonica** (rectory), endowed by Sangallo with a graceful portico and double-tiered loggia, is scarcely less perfect.

ARRIVAL AND INFORMATION   **MONTEPULCIANO**

By train The local train station is also on the Siena–Chiusi line, but it's 10km northeast of town, and more frequent services call at the main-line station of Chiusi itself, 22km southeast; connecting buses run from both.

By bus The bus station is on Piazza Nenni. Note that bus services are very patchy on Sundays.

Destinations Buonconvento (7 daily; 1hr); Chiusi (every 30min; 50min); Florence (1–2 daily; 2hr); Pienza (2 daily; 20min); San Quirico (2 daily; 40min); Siena (3–8 daily; 1hr 30 min).

By car If you're driving, only enter the town if you have a hotel reservation; failing that, you'll have to park outside the walls – try the free spaces to the east.

Tourist information The main tourist office is outside the walls at the lower end of town, at Piazza Don Minzoni 1 (Mon–Sat 9.30am–12.30pm & 3–6pm, Sun 9.30am–12.30pm; ☎ 0578 757 341, ⓦ prolocomontepulciano.it). It offers internet access at €1.80/30min and sells bus and train tickets. La Strada del Vino Nobile has an office at Piazza Grande 8 (Mon–Fri 10am–1pm & 3–6pm, Sat in summer 10am–1pm; ☎ 0578 717 484, ⓦ stradavinonobile .it), offering basic information and details on wine tours in vineyards around Montepulciano from €18 and cookery classes from €35 per person.

FESTIVALS AND EVENTS IN MONTEPULCIANO

From April to September, Palazzo Ricci on Via Ricci hosts a series of classical music concerts (☎ 0578 756 022, ⓦ palazzoricci.com). Montepulciano comes alive in July during the **Cantiere Internazionale d'Arte** (☎ 0578 757 007, ⓦ fondazionecantiere.it), which presents exhibitions and concerts around town. The last Sunday in August sees the **Bravìo delle Botti** (☎ 0578 757 575, ⓦ braviodellebotti.com), a barrel-race in medieval costume that's the culmination of a week of run-up events. In early September, the five-night, irresistibly named **Live Rock Festival of Beer** (ⓦ liverockfestivalofbeer.it) is celebrated in the tiny village of **Acquaviva**, 10km northeast near Montepulciano's train station.

ACCOMMODATION

Montepulciano doesn't hold nearly enough hotels to meet summer demand, though private rooms are also available. Reserve well ahead, and visit the website ⓦmontepulcianohotels.it. On summer nights, the town's cool hilltop breezes offer a welcome relief from the heat at lower elevations.

Albergo Duomo Via S. Donato 14 ☎0578 757 473, ⓦalbergoduomo.it. A short distance from Piazza Grande, the three-star *Duomo* has excellent facilities and smart, clean rooms, plus free private parking and generous breakfasts. **€110**

★ **Camere Bellavista** Via Ricci 25 ☎0578 757 348, ⓦcamerebellavista.it. Ten great-value rooms near the main square, all with en-suite bathrooms, and several with superb countryside views; ask for Room 6 (an extra €25), which comes with a beautiful terrace. Cash only; breakfast costs an extra €3 per person. **€75**

La Terrazza di Montepulciano Via Piè al Sasso 16 ☎0578 757 440, ⓦlaterrazzadimontepulciano.it. Peaceful, well-equipped little hotel, in an old house just below the Duomo; breakfast is served on the leafy roof terrace in summer. Owner Roberto is an enthusiastic host. **€90**

Meublè Il Riccio Via Talosa 21 ☎0578 757 713, ⓦilriccio.net. Lovely little B&B in a stunning medieval building just off Piazza Grande, with very comfortable rooms, and a mosaic-floored courtyard; it's popular, so book ahead. Next door, *Riccio Suite* is a sister B&B with five elegant, high-ceilinged and light-filled rooms, costing an extra €20–50 per night. **€110**

EATING AND DRINKING

Abundant restaurants line the streets and squares of Montepulciano, and you'll also find several small cafés, as well as plenty of places to sample the region's Vino Nobile (see box below).

★ **A Gambe di Gatto** Via dell'Oppio nel Corso 34 ☎0578 757 431. Tiny, hugely friendly bistro, with an emphasis on organic wine and olive oils, and a devotion to "Slow Food". Only come if you've plenty of time; if you do, you're in for a treat, with daily menus of simple but imaginative cuisine at very reasonable prices. You might find a platter of local cheeses with prickly pear jam (€12) or *mezze maniche* pasta with artichokes and olives (€9.50), but whatever you order, it'll be delicious. Noon–8.30pm, but opens later if you book; closed Wed & early Jan–Easter.

Caffè Poliziano Via di Voltaia nel Corso 27. This glorious wood-panelled 1868 tearoom, restored to a classic Art Nouveau design, serves tea, coffee and pastries, with free wi-fi, and offers great views from a small terrace at the back. Its adjoining restaurant, *Il Grifon d'Oro* (closed Sun dinner), has a panoramic terrace and serves three-course meals with wine for €30, including Tuscan specialities like *pici* pasta with wild boar *ragù*. Daily 7am–midnight.

La Briciola Via delle Cantine 23 ☎0578 716 903. Friendly restaurant with outdoor tables on a quiet alley just inside the Porta al Prato, with a well-stocked *enoteca* as well as a range of flavourful Tuscan *primi* (€8–12) and *secondi* (€10–18), such as grilled Pienza *pecorino* with spinach. Noon–2.30pm & 7–10.30pm; closed Wed.

La Grotta Via di S. Biagio ☎0578 757 607. Opposite San Biagio church, about 1km outside the city walls, this brick-vaulted sixteenth-century restaurant serves refined Tuscan dishes such as rabbit in bacon flavoured with thyme with a courgette flan (€20), and has its own garden. 12.30–2.15pm & 7.30–10pm; closed Wed.

★ **Osteria Acquacheta** Via del Teatro 22 ☎0578 717 086, ⓦacquacheta.eu. Small, traditional *osteria*, just down from the Duomo, that's always busy with locals. Lots of cheese and truffle, a changing menu of the day, and home-made pasta dishes from €5.50; you can get a truly memorable meal for under €20. 12.30–3pm & 7.30–10.30pm; closed Tues.

WINE TASTING IN MONTEPULCIANO

Acclaimed since the medieval era, **Vino Nobile di Montepulciano** today boasts a top-rated DOCG mark, something the townspeople have not been shy in exploiting. Wine shops along the streets of Montepulciano sell gift sets, while local vineyards often offer in-town tastings (usually free, but requiring advance notice). Every restaurant can provide a range of vintages, the very cheapest of which will still set you back at least €20. The tourist office can organize **wine-tasting** rambles for visitors. Among the many places to check out are the venerable *Contucci* at Via San Donato 15 and also in the Palazzo Contucci on the Piazza Grande (☎0578 757 006, ⓦcontucci.it) – the family line in Montepulciano goes back a thousand years – and *De' Ricci*, Via di Collazi 7 (☎0578 757 166, ⓦdericci.it).

9

Trattoria di Cagnano Via dell Opio nel Corso 30 ☎ 0578 758 757. Popular and bustling, this place offers a wide range of pizzas, from the simple €4.50 *margherita* to the €10 *Tartufo*, with mozzarella and fresh truffle, as well as the usual Tuscan *primi* and *secondi*. Outside seating available. Tues–Sun 12.30–3pm & 7.30–10.30pm.

Pienza

The tiny, perfectly preserved village of **PIENZA**, 11km west of Montepulciano, is as complete a Renaissance creation as any in Italy, established as a Utopian "New Town", in an act of considerable vanity, by **Pope Pius II**. A scion of the leading family of what was formerly Cortignano, he set about transforming his birthplace in 1459, under the architect **Bernardo Rossellino**. The cost was astronomical, but the cathedral, papal and bishop's palaces, and the core of a town (renamed in Pius's honour), were completed in just three years. Pius lived just two more years, and of his successors only his nephew paid Pienza any regard: intended to spread across the hill, the planned city remained village-sized. Today, despite the large number of visitors, it still has an air of emptiness and folly: a natural stage-set, where Zeffirelli filmed *Romeo and Juliet*.

Piazza Pio II

Traffic converges on **Piazza Dante**, just outside the main gate, Porta al Murello. From there the **Corso** leads straight to Rossellino's centrepiece, **Piazza Pio II**, which deliberately juxtaposes civic and religious buildings – the Duomo, Palazzo Piccolomini (papal palace), Bishop's Palace and Palazzo Pubblico – to underline the balance between Church and Town. While making the usual medieval nod to Florence in its town hall, the square is otherwise entirely Renaissance in conception.

The Duomo

Piazza Pio II • Daily 7am–1pm & 2–7/8pm • Free

The **Duomo** boasts one of the earliest Renaissance facades in Tuscany; the interior, on Pius's orders, took inspiration from the German hall-churches he had seen on his travels, and remains essentially Gothic. The chapels house an outstanding series of Sienese altarpieces, commissioned from the major painters of the age – Giovanni di Paolo, Matteo di Giovanni, Vecchietta and Sano di Pietro. How long the building itself will remain standing is uncertain though. Even before completion a crack appeared, and since an earthquake in the nineteenth century it has required much buttressing – the nave currently dips crazily towards the back of the church.

Palazzo Piccolomini

Piazza Pio II • Tues–Sun: mid-March to mid-Oct 10am–6.30pm; mid-Oct to mid-March 10am–4.30pm, but closed early Jan to mid-Feb and last two weeks of Nov; open Mon on public hols • €7 • ⓦ palazzopiccolominipienza.it

Pius's residence, the **Palazzo Piccolomini** sits alongside the Duomo. Visitors are free to walk into the courtyard and through to the original "hanging garden" behind to the left, where a triple-tiered loggia offers a superb view over the valley. To see the **apartments** above, however, which include Pius II's bedroom, library and other rooms filled with collections of weapons and medals, you have to join one of the frequent half-hour guided tours, for no extra charge.

Museo Diocesano

Corso Rossellino 30 • April to mid-Nov daily except Tues 10am–1pm & 3–6pm; mid-Nov to March Sat & Sun 10am–1pm & 2–5pm • €4.10

Further mementoes of the pope – notably his English-made embroidered cape – are cherished in the excellent **Museo Diocesano** across the piazza. The true highlights there, however, are some stunning tapestries and, especially, paintings, including a wonderful anonymous depiction of the life of Christ in 48 tiny panels, one of which shows Jesus meeting a black devil, complete with wings and horns.

By bus Buses between Montepulciano and Buonconvento stop at both Pienza and San Quirico d'Orcia (see below). Buses drop off by Piazza Dante, just outside the walls. Destinations Buonconvento (9 daily; 35min); Montepulciano (5 daily; 20min); San Quirico d'Orcia (10 daily; 15min); Siena (7 daily; 1hr 15min).

By car Drivers should park outside the city walls in one of the paid car parks.

Tourist office Corso 30 (April to mid-Nov daily except Tues 10am–1pm & 3–6pm; mid-Nov to March Sat & Sun 10am–1pm & 2–5pm; ☎ 0578 749 905).

ACCOMMODATION AND EATING

Arca di Pienza Via San Gregorio 19 ☎ 0578 749 426, ⓦarcadipienza.it. A 5min walk from the centre, this family-run place offers eight cosily decorated rooms, some with balcony overlooking the pretty courtyard garden. The generous breakfast is a further draw. €95

La Bandita Podere la Bandita ☎ 333 404 6704, ⓦla-bandita.com. A luxurious, rustic-chic B&B in a scenic location a 15–20min drive from Pienza with serene rooms, an infinity pool and a laidback feel throughout. If you're hankering after total privacy, book the stand-alone Pig-Sty Suite (an extra €200 per night), which comes with its own kitchen. The owners are due to open a similarly stylish property, La Bandita Townhouse, in central Pienza in 2013. €295

La Buca di Enea Via della Buca 10 ☎ 0578 748 653. This cosy, hole-in-the-wall *bruschetteria* makes an excellent lunch stop, with delicious toasted Tuscan sandwiches as well as salads and pasta dishes. Pienza is the centre of a region producing sheep's cheese, and this is a great place to sample the local *pecorino*: a plate of warm *pecorino* with chestnut honey, pine nuts and walnuts (€9.50) hits the spot. Daily 10am–10.30pm.

Latte di Luna Just inside the walls at Via S. Carlo 6 ☎ 0578 748 606. The pretty outside seating area is screened by flowers, and the menu offers some tempting Tuscan *primi* (€7.50–10) such as home-made *pici* pasta with wild boar. Be sure to leave room for the house speciality: *maialino arrosto*, roast suckling pig (€12). Noon–2pm & 7–9pm; closed Tues.

San Quirico d'Orcia

The rambling old village of **SAN QUIRICO D'ORCIA** stands at a crossroads 8km west of Pienza. Its old town is a quiet and appealing place, whose main attraction is an exceptionally pretty Romanesque **Collegiata** church, its portals sculpted with wild beasts.

ARRIVAL AND INFORMATION   **SAN QUIRICO D'ORCIA**

By bus Buses stop on Via Cassia, on the eastern side of the village. Destinations Montepulciano (7 daily; 30min); Pienza (7 daily; 10min); Siena (7 daily; 1hr 10min).

Tourist office Piazza Chigi 2 (June–Sept daily except Wed 10am–1pm & 3.30–6.30pm, Sat 10am–1pm; April, May, Oct & early Nov Sat & Sun 10am–1pm; ☎ 0577 897 211).

ACCOMMODATION AND EATING

★ **Agriturismo Il Rigo** Loc. Casabianca 10 ☎ 0577 897 291, ⓦagriturismoilrigo.com. In a wonderfully picturesque position on its own hilltop 5km from San Quirico d'Orcia, this family-run agriturismo has bags of charm, with fifteen rustic, antique-furnished rooms across two buildings (ask for a room in the main house to feel in the thick of things). The home-cooked dinners are a further draw; €23 gets you four courses (wine extra). €110

Castello Ripa d'Orcia ☎ 0577 897 376, ⓦcastello ripadorcia.com. For drivers, this stunning but inaccessible, isolated castle hotel-restaurant down a gravel road 5km southwest of town makes a wonderfully peaceful place to

stay. There are six bedrooms, eight self-catering apartments and a stupendously-sited swimming pool. Minimum stay two nights; closed Nov to mid-March. Doubles €145, apartments €165

Il Pozzo Via Dante Alighieri 24 ☎ 0577 899 085. With its beautiful flower-filled garden set around a sixteenth-century well, this makes an appealing spot for lunch. On the menu are tasty home-made pastas (€6–8) and meaty mains such as sausages with cannellini beans (€8) or pork steak (€12), and it's an *enoteca* and a tearoom too. 11am–3pm & 6pm–midnight; closed Tues.

Montalcino

Another classic Tuscan hill-town, **MONTALCINO**, perches 20km west of Pienza. Set within a full circuit of walls and watched over by a fortress, it looks tremendous from

9

TAKING THE WATERS AT BAGNO VIGNONI

The extraordinary ancient site of **Bagno Vignoni** is tucked away 6km southeast of San Quirico. Its central square is entirely taken up by an arcaded Roman *piscina*, or open pool; the springs still bubble up at a steamy 51°C, with a backdrop of the Tuscan hills and Renaissance **loggia** – built by the Medici, who, like St Catherine of Siena, took the sulphur cure here. Bathing in the *piscina* itself is forbidden, but you can still take the waters at the sulphur springs below the village (30°C), or wallow in the mineral-rich waters of one of the nearby spas (advance booking necessary).

Adler Thermae Strada di Bagno Vignoni 1 ☎ 0577 889 001, ⓦ adler-thermae.com. Most luxurious of the town's crop of spa hotels, the slick *Adler's* thermal pools bubble at a pleasant 36°C and overlook the rolling hills. The staggering array of treatments ranges from saunas with Tuscan herbs to steam baths in caves complete with stalactites and stalagmites to the "Bacchus Ritual", a Vino Nobile-enriched bath and grapeseed peel. The rooms are spacious and comfortable, or limited day-passes are available for €50 (includes access to pools and saunas), plus the cost of one treatment.

Albergo le Terme Piazza delle Sorgenti 13 ☎ 0577 887 150, ⓦ albergoleterme.it. Facing the *piscina*, Pius II's fifteenth-century summer retreat is now the family-run *Albergo Le Terme*. The modern spa in the

garden offers treatments such as horse-chestnut peels and lavender steam baths as well as Ayurvedic massages. Day-passes (including access to pools and sauna) cost €28–38.

Antiche Terme di Bagno Vignoni Piazza del Moretto 12 ☎ 0577 887 365. From March to October (Mon–Sat 8am–1pm), the town's thermal baths make a more affordable alternative to the spa hotels. Massages cost from €35, or a thermal bath and massage €65.

Hotel Posta Marcucci Via Arca Urcea 43 ☎ 0577 887 112, ⓦ hotelpostamarcucci.it. A friendly hotel with indoor and outdoor thermal pools, as well as a sauna and Turkish bath. Various treatments are available, most of which tend to be classic rather than cutting-edge. Entrance to the pool €15; treatments extra.

below – and from up in the town, the surrounding countryside strewn with vineyards, orchards and olive groves is equally impressive. A quiet place, affluent in an unshowy way from its tourist trade, Montalcino produces a top-notch DOCG **wine**, Brunello di Montalcino, that's reckoned by many to be the finest in Italy. For a spell during the fifteenth century, the town acquired great symbolic importance: this was the last of the Sienese *comuni* to hold out against the Medici, the French and the Spanish, after Siena itself had capitulated. That role is acknowledged at the Siena Palio, where the Montalcino contingent – under its medieval banner proclaiming "The Republic of Siena in Montalcino" – takes pride of place.

Piazza del Popolo

Montalcino's main street, Via Mazzini, leads from **Piazza Cavour** at the north end of town to the **Piazza del Popolo**, an odd little square set beneath the elongated tower of the town hall, based in all but its dimensions on that of Siena. An elegant double-loggia occupies another side with, opposite, a wonderful and rather Germanic nineteenth-century café, the *Fiaschetteria Italiana* (see p.610), which is very much the heart of town life.

Musei di Montalcino, Raccolta Archeologica, Medievale, Moderna

Via Ricasoli 31 • Tues–Sun 10am–1pm & 2–5.50pm • €4.50 or €6 joint ticket with the Rocca fortress

Steps (Scale di Via Bandi) near the café lead up to the excellent, thoroughly modernized **Musei di Montalcino, Raccolta Archeologica, Medievale, Moderna**. The quality of the art on show is out of all proportion to the size of the town, and takes in a wealth of Sienese painting and early sculpture, including a fabulous twelfth-century *Crucifixion*. Separate basement galleries cover the early archeological history of this site, with a Neolithic burial chamber and some Bronze Age artefacts. The neighbouring church of **Sant'Agostino**, recently incorporated into the complex, is slowly being restored.

Fortezza di Montalcino

Ramparts daily: April–Oct 9am–8pm; Nov–March 9am–6pm • €4, or €6 joint ticket with Musei di Montalcino

Following Via Ricasoli south brings you to the hilltop, fourteenth-century **Fortezza di Montalcino**. The open space enclosed within its impressively intact walls makes a great venue for summer concerts. At the foot of one of its towers, a spacious **enoteca** (see p.610) provides access to the **ramparts**. The panorama that unfolds from up here is said to have inspired Leonardo's drawing of a bird's-eye view of the earth; on a clear day you can even see Siena.

ARRIVAL AND INFORMATION   MONTALCINO

By bus Regular buses stop first at the fortress, then terminate in Piazza Cavour at the north end of town from Buonconvento and Siena; most pass first through Buonconvento and Torrenieri, from where connections head to San Quirico, Pienza and Montepulciano.
Destinations Buonconvento (hourly; 20–30min); Siena (7 daily; 1hr 10min).

By car For once, Montalcino's streets are not too narrow to admit cars; there's a car park below the fortress.
Tourist office Just up from the central Piazza del Popolo at Costa del Municipio 1 (summer daily 10am–1pm & 2–5.50pm; winter Tues–Sun 10am–1pm & 2–5.40pm; ☏ 0577 849 331, ⍟ prolocomontalcino.it). Organizes wine tastings and tours.

ACCOMMODATION

As accommodation is limited, it's wise to book ahead at any time of year. Besides a handful of hotels and private rooms, numerous agriturismi can be found in the countryside immediately around town. The tourist office has a free accommodation booking service.

★ **Albergo Il Giglio** Via Soccorso Saloni 5 ☏ 0577 848 167, ⍟ gigliohotel.com. Stylish and appealing hotel in a central, sixteenth-century townhouse, where the pleasant a/c rooms come with travertine walls, cast-iron beds and great views; some have frescoed ceilings and terraces, too. **€130**
Castello di Velona Località Castello di Velona, Castelnuovo dell'Abate, about 10km south of Montalcino ☏ 0577 800 101, ⍟ castellodivelona.it. Elegant, recently renovated four-star hotel, isolated in lovely open countryside on its own hill and ringed by cypress, close to Castelnuovo dell'Abate. There's a fine-dining restaurant and a swanky new spa too. Expensive, but rates drop in low season and there are often online deals. **€445**

★ **Palazzina Cesira** Via Soccorso Saloni 2 ☏ 0577 846 055, ⍟ montalcinoitaly.com. Set in a medieval building in the centre of town, this place has a home-from-home feel, with comfortable if old-fashioned rooms, some of which (the "mini-suites", worth the extra €20) are large and have original frescoes. Great breakfast, with fluffy omelettes, fresh pastries and home-made jams. Minimum two-night stay. **€95**
Vecchia Oliviera Via Landi 1 ☏ 0577 846 028, ⍟ vecchiaoliviera.com. Three-star hotel on the edge of town, where the thirteen fine rooms form part of a well-restored former olive-mill close to Porta Cerbaia and the walls, but do get some traffic noise. There's also a pool, and the patio has excellent views. **€190**

EATING AND DRINKING

Montalcino is filled with good **restaurants**, and also holds a row of fine **enotecas** along Via Matteotti, all of which sell local wines by the glass or bottle and have pavement seating on the town side with sweeping views from the back. There are also plenty of places to pick up a **picnic**: alimentari along Via Mazzini sell the usual cheeses and salamis, and pasticcerie sell cakes and biscuits made with the local wine.

Al Giardino Piazza Cavour 1 ☏ 0577 849 076, ⍟ ristorantealgiardino.it. Fine local cooking, just outside the walls, that has won the approval of the Slow Food movement, such as rack of lamb with fried artichokes and marjoram (€16). Pleasant interior, while the "garden" in the name refers to its tables in the square opposite. Mon–Sat 12.30–2.30pm & 7.30–9.30pm.
★ **Castello Banfi La Taverna** Castello di Poggio alle Mura ☏ 0577 877 524, ⍟ castellobanfi.com. Set in 7000 acres of cultivated land (it's the biggest

producer of Brunello di Montalcino), the formidable Banfi wine estate holds a predictably well-stocked enoteca, as well as an excellent gourmet restaurant whose all-Tuscan menu includes a stellar pici with wild boar ragù (€12) and an expertly cooked fiorentina steak (€60 for two people). Feb Mon–Sat 1–2.30pm; March–early April Mon–Sat 1–2.30pm & 7.30–10pm, Sun 7.30–10pm; early April to early Nov daily 1–2.30pm & 7.30–10pm; early Nov to early Dec Mon–Sat 1–2.30pm.

9

Enoteca La Fortezza Piazzale Fortezza ☎ 0577 849 211, ⓦ enotecalafortezza.it. The *enoteca* of the fortress organizes tastings, with 35 different Brunellos to choose from (two glasses €9), along with light lunches such as soups (€8) and wild boar gnocchi (€10). Daily: summer 9am–8pm; winter 10am–6pm.

Fiaschetteria Italiana Piazza del Popolo 6 ☎ 0577 849 043. In business since 1888, this café has a lovely mosaic-tiled and antique-mirrored interior, as well as outdoor tables perfect for people-watching. It serves simple panini as well as platters of cheeses and cold cuts (€8–12). 7.30am–midnight; closed Thurs in winter.

Osteria di Porte Al Cassero Via Ricasoli 32 ☎ 0577 847 196. Indoor and outdoor seating near the fortress, very reasonable prices, and top-notch food, from home-made pastas and soups to a delicious *tiramisù*. A full meal will set you back about €25 per head with wine. Noon–2.30pm & 7–9.30pm; closed Wed.

★ **Taverna Il Grappolo Blu** Via Scale di Moglio 1 ☎ 0577 847 150. Located in a little alley off Via Mazzini. The old stone-walled and wood-beamed interior is cool and appealing, and the pastas are excellent. Mains include a tasty rabbit in Brunello sauce with polenta (€13) and guinea fowl in lemon sauce (€12). Daily noon–3pm & 7–10pm.

Monte Amiata

At 1738m, the extinct volcano of **Monte Amiata** is the highest point in southern Tuscany. Rising in a succession of hills forested in chestnut and fir, it's visible for miles around. A circle of towns rings its lower slopes, of which **Abbadia San Salvatore** draws most visitors; old castles and bucolic countryside make the area a good detour. Towns such as Abbadia are refreshingly cool for summer walking, and in winter are the nearest ski resorts to Rome.

Abbadia San Salvatore

The village of **ABBADIA SAN SALVATORE** shelters at its heart a perfect, self-contained medieval quarter. The Benedictine **abbey** around which it developed was founded under the Lombards and rebuilt in 1036. A mere fraction now remains of the original, and most remnants date from the Middle Ages; the highlight is a large and beautiful eighth-century **crypt**, its 35 columns decorated with Lombard motifs. Summer visitors arrive in droves, lured by the landscape, cool breezes and some good, easy walking paths. The best, the 29km **Anello della Montagna**, circles the mountain between 900m and 1300m – a long day's walk, or easily manageable in sections round to Arcidosso.

ARRIVAL AND INFORMATION   MONTE AMIATA

By bus If you're visiting Abbadia San Salvatore, avoid the Monte Amiata train station – it's 45km away. Buses serve the village from Siena, Buonconvento, Chiusi and Montepulciano; those from Rome pass first through Arcidosso.
Destinations Bagno Vignoni (3 daily; 50min); Buonconvento (3 daily; 1hr); Chiusi (1 daily in summer; 1hr 25min);

Florence (2 weekly in winter; 2hr 30min); Montalcino (1 daily; 1hr 5min); Montepulciano (2 daily; 1hr); Rome (1 daily; 2hr 50min); San Quirico d'Orcia (5 daily; 1hr); Siena (3 daily; 1hr 30min).
Tourist office Via Adua 21 (Mon–Sat 8.30am–1pm & 3–6pm, Sun 10am–1pm; ☎ 0577 775 811). The tourist office is headquarters for the Amiata region.

ACCOMMODATION AND EATING

★ **Castello di Potentino** Seggiano ☎ 0564 950 014, ⓦ potentino.com. Run by a welcoming English family of wine producers, this hulking, honey-coloured castle is well off the tourist trail, a few kilometres outside the town of Seggiano. This is very much a family home and working farm rather than a hotel, and the family are happy for guests to join in with activities such as harvesting – or simply to relax and enjoy the breathtaking views with a glass of wine. The rooms are splendid: a mix of antiques, well-loved books and family mementoes makes for a cosy, home-from-home atmosphere, and features such as

canopy beds and freestanding tubs in some rooms add to the appeal. €130
Il Silene Località Pescina, near Seggiano ☎ 0564 950 805, ⓦ ilsilene.it. A great place for a leisurely meal, this restaurant serves up top-quality cuisine – somewhat unexpectedly considering its unprepossessing location. A typical meal might include poached egg with asparagus and truffle, followed by pigeon-stuffed ravioli and *secondo* of fried rabbit; a full meal will cost around €60. Cookery courses are also organized here. Tues–Sun 12.30–2pm & 7.30–9.30pm; closed Sun eve in winter.

Pitigliano

Tuscany's deep south, on the Lazio border, is its least visited corner. **PITIGLIANO**, the area's largest town, is best approached along the road from Manciano, 15km west. As you draw close, the town soars above you on a spectacular outcrop of tufa, its quarters linked by the arches of an immense aqueduct. **Etruscan** tombs honeycomb the cliffs, but the town was known for centuries for its flourishing **Jewish** community. Today it has a slightly grim grandeur, owing to its mighty **fortress** and the tall and largely unaltered alleys of the old Jewish ghetto.

The fortress and around

Immediately through the main city gate, **Piazza Garibaldi** is flanked by the **fortress** (1459–62) and aqueduct (1543), with views across houses wedged against the cliffside. Within the fortress, the lovely interiors of the Renaissance **Palazzo Orsini** (April–July & Sept Tues–Sun 10am–1pm & 3–7pm; Aug daily 10am–7pm; Oct–March Tues–Sun 10am–1pm & 3–5pm; €4) are filled with jewellery and ecclesiastical ephemera. Opposite, the **Museo Archeologico** (same hours; €3) holds an interesting collection of Etruscan vases and trinkets.

Piazza della Repubblica

The fortress backs onto **Piazza della Repubblica**, Pitigliano's elongated main square. From the balcony here you can take in the sweeping views of the surrounding countryside, with Monte Amiata to the north.

The Ghetto

Beyond Piazza della Repubblica lies the old town proper, a tight huddle of arches and medieval alleys. This is where you'll find the **old Jewish Ghetto**, centred on Via Zuccarelli, which has been turned into a sort of outdoor museum known as La Piccola Gerusalemme (Little Jerusalem).

The synagogue and La Piccola Gerusalemme

Daily except Sat: April–Sept 10am–12.30pm & 4–7pm; Oct–March 10am–12.30pm & 3–5.30pm • €3

Pitigliano's eighteenth-century **synagogue** part-collapsed in the 1960s, and lay derelict until renovation in 1995. Only the grand stone arch and the stairs leading up to the women's gallery survive from the old building, along with plaques commemorating visits made by grand dukes Ferdinand III in 1823 and Leopold II in 1829. There are virtually no Jewish residents remaining in the town, but a number of buildings bearing witness to the once-thriving community now form part of **La Piccola Gerusalemme**, including a wine cellar, butcher and baker. There's also a museum of Jewish culture and a cemetery.

ARRIVAL AND INFORMATION PITIGLIANO

By bus Three RAMA buses daily from Manciano and Grosseto (2hr), one from Orbetello (1hr 30min) and one from Siena (2hr 55min) drop off on Piazza Petruccioli just outside the city gate.

Tourist office Piazza Garibaldi 51 (Tues–Sat

10am–12.30pm & 3.30–6pm, Sun 10am–12.30pm; winter closes 5pm Tues–Sat; ☏0564 617 111, ⓦturismo inmaremma.it). Has maps of the Vie Cave, ancient Etruscan paths that weave between tombs (mostly free) and cliffside caves all around the town.

ACCOMMODATION AND EATING

Guastini Piazza Petruccioli 16 ☏0564 616 065, ⓦalbergoguastini.it. The main selling point of this hotel is its excellent location, right in the heart of town. Though somewhat old-fashioned and lacking in mod cons, it has plenty of charm and stunning views from the rooms. There's also a good restaurant, with outside tables in this attractive square. **€66**

★ **Tufo Allegro** Vicolo della Costituzione 5 ☏0564 616 192. A local favourite whose menu is divided into creative, fine-dining dishes and more standard, cheaper fare; of the former, try the roast suckling pig cooked in milk, or duck breast with pumpkin mash, or opt for one of the three bargain fixed-price menus (€15–20), which include hearty dishes such as *buglione di agnello* (a typical lamb

9

stew of the Maremma). Note that this is a Slow Food restaurant in every sense, so head elsewhere if you're in a hurry. Mon & Thurs–Sun 12.30–2.30pm & 7.30–9.30pm, Wed 7.30–9.30pm.

Eastern Tuscany

The Valdarno (Arno valley) upstream from Florence is a heavily industrialized tract, with no compelling stop before you reach the provincial capital, **Arezzo**, which is visited by foreigners in their thousands for its Piero della Francesca frescoes, and by Italians in even greater numbers for its antiques trade. South of Arezzo is the ancient hill-town of **Cortona**, whose picturesquely steep streets and sense of hilltop isolation make it an irresistible place for a stopover.

Arezzo

Piero della Francesca's frescoes – which belong in the same company as Masaccio's cycle in Florence and Michelangelo's in Rome – are what makes **AREZZO** a tourist destination, but in Italy the city is equally well known for its jewellers, its goldsmiths, and its trade in **antiques**: in the vicinity of the Piazza Grande there are shops filled with museum-quality furniture, and once a month the Fiera Antiquaria turns the piazza into a vast showroom.

AREZZO'S FESTIVALS AND EVENTS

Arezzo's premier folkloric event is the **Giostra del Saracino**, which was first recorded in 1535 and is nowadays held in the Piazza Grande on the first Sunday in September. The day starts off with various costumed parades; at 5pm the action switches to the jousting arena in the piazza, with a procession of some 350 participants leading the way. Each quarter of the city is represented by a pair of knights on horseback, who do battle with a wooden effigy of a Saracen king. In one hand it holds a shield marked with point scores; in the other it has a cat-o'-three-tails which swings round when the shield is hit, necessitating nifty evasive action from the rider. A golden lance is awarded to the highest-scoring rider. In the days immediately preceding the joust you'll see rehearsals taking place, and in recent years the event has become so popular that a reduced version of the show is now held on the penultimate Saturday of June, with parades at around 8pm, followed by the main event at 9pm; to book tickets, call ☎0575 377 462 or see ⓦ giostradelsaracino.arezzo.it (Italian only).

The musical tradition that began with Guido d'Arezzo (widely regarded as the inventor of modern notation) is kept alive chiefly through the international choral competition that bears his name: the **Concorso Polifonico Guido d'Arezzo**, held in the last week of August. The less ambitious **Pomeriggi Musicali** is a season of free concerts held in various churches, museums and libraries; on average there's one concert a week from mid-January to June.

The **antiques fair** (*fiera antiquaria*) takes over the Piazza Grande on the first Sunday of each month and the preceding Saturday. The most expensive stuff is laid out by the Vasari loggia, with cheaper pieces lower down the square and in the side streets.

Arezzo has been one of Tuscany's most prosperous towns for a very long time. Occupying a site that controls the major passes of the central Apennines, it was a key settlement of the Etruscan federation, and grew to be an independent republic in the Middle Ages. In 1289, however, its Ghibelline allegiances led to a catastrophic clash with the Guelph Florentines at Campaldino; though Arezzo temporarily recovered under the leadership of the bellicose Bishop Guido Tarlati, it finally came under the control of Florence in 1384. Nowadays, while Florence's economy has become over-reliant on tourist traffic, well-heeled Arezzo goes its own way, though in recent years it has started to market itself more seriously as a place to visit.

There are two distinct parts to Arezzo: the older quarter, at the top of the hill, and the businesslike lower town, much of which remains hidden from day-trippers, as it spreads behind the train station and the adjacent bus terminal. From the station forecourt, go straight ahead for Via Guido Monaco, the traffic axis between the upper and lower town. The parallel Corso Italia, now pedestrianized, is the route to walk up the hill.

The Basilica di San Francesco

Piazza San Francesco • Mon–Fri 9am–6.30pm, Sat 9am–5.30pm, Sun 1–5.30pm; Nov–March closes Mon–Fri 5.30pm, Sat & Sun 5pm • Frescoes €8 for 30min, or €12 combined ticket; visits are limited to 25 people at a time • Tickets can be bought in advance by phone (☎0575 352 727) or online (ⓦ apt.arezzo.it); they can also be reserved at the office beneath the church – in summer you may have to wait an hour or two for the next available slot, but for most of the year there's rarely any delay

Built in the 1320s, the plain **Basilica di San Francesco** earned its renown in the early 1450s, when the Bacci family commissioned Piero della Francesca to depict **The Legend of the True Cross**, a story in which the wood of the Cross forms the link in the cycle of

AREZZO'S JOINT TICKET

A €12 **joint ticket** (*biglietto unico*) gives you a single admission to the following monuments and museums in Arezzo: the Museo Archeologico, the Museo Medievale, the Casa Vasari and the Della Francesca frescoes in San Francesco. The ticket can be bought at any of these four locations, but bear in mind that immediate admission to San Francesco may not be possible.

9

redemption that begins with humanity's original sin. The frescoes are in the apse and are visible from the nave, but to see them properly you need to buy a ticket.

Starting with the *Death of Adam* on the right wall, Piero painted the series in narrative sequence, working continuously until about 1457. However, the episodes are not arranged in narrative sequence, as the artist preferred to paint them according to the precepts of symmetry: thus the two battle scenes face each other across the chapel, rather than coming where the story dictates.

The literary source for the cycle, the *Golden Legend* by Jacopo de Voragine, is a very convoluted story, but the outline of the tale is as follows: a sprig from the Tree of Knowledge is planted in Adam's mouth; Solomon orders a bridge to be built from wood taken from the tree that grew from Adam's grave (below the *Death of Adam*, to the left); the visiting Queen of Sheba kneels, sensing the holiness of the wood, and then later (to the right) tells Solomon of her prophecy that the same wood will be used to crucify a man; Solomon then orders the beam to be buried (back wall, middle right); the Emperor Constantine (back wall, lower right) has a vision of victory under the sign of the Cross; Constantine defeats his rival Maxentius (lower right wall); under torture, Judas the Levite (back wall, middle left) reveals to St Helena, mother of Constantine, the burial place of the crosses from Golgotha, which are then excavated (middle left wall); the True Cross is recognized when it brings about a man's resurrection; and the Persian king Chosroes, who had stolen the Cross, is defeated by Emperor Heraclius (lower left wall), who returns the Cross to Jerusalem (upper left wall).

The Pieve di Santa Maria

Corso Italia • Daily: May–Sept 9am–1pm & 3–7pm; Oct–April 9am–noon & 3–6pm

At the top of the Corso stands one of the finest Romanesque structures in Tuscany, the twelfth-century **Pieve di Santa Maria**. Its arcaded facade, elaborate yet severe, is unusual in presenting its front to a fairly narrow street rather than to the town's main square. Dating from the 1210s, the carvings of the months over the portal are an especially lively group. Known locally as "the tower of the hundred holes", the campanile was added in the fourteenth century. The oldest section of the chalky grey interior is the raised sanctuary, where the altarpiece is Pietro Lorenzetti's *Madonna and Saints* polyptych, painted in 1320. The unfamiliar saint on the far left, accompanying Matthew, the Baptist and John the Evangelist, is St Donatus, the second bishop of Arezzo, who was martyred in 304. His relics are in the crypt, encased in a beautiful gold and silver bust made in 1346.

The Piazza Grande

On the other side of the Pieve, the steeply sloping **Piazza Grande** has an unusual assortment of buildings, with the wooden balconied apartments on the east side facing the apse of the Pieve, the Baroque Palazzo dei Tribunali and the Palazzetto della Fraternità dei Laici, which has a Renaissance upper storey and a Gothic lower. The piazza's northern edge is formed by the arcades of the Loggia di Vasari, occupied by restaurants and shops that in some instances still retain their original sixteenth-century stone counters.

The Duomo

Piazza del Duomo • Daily 7am–12.30pm & 3–6.30pm • Free

At the highest point of town looms the large and unfussy **Duomo**. Inside, just beyond the organ, is the tomb of Bishop Guido Tarlati, head of the *comune* of Arezzo during its resurgence in the early fourteenth century; the monument, plated with reliefs showing scenes from the militaristic bishop's career, was possibly designed by Giotto. The small fresco nestled against the right side of the tomb is Piero della Francesca's *Magdalene*, his only work in Arezzo outside San Francesco.

San Domenico

Piazza San Domenico • Daily 8am–7pm • Free

A short distance north of the Duomo, the church of **San Domenico** was constructed mostly in the late thirteenth century but with a Gothic campanile. Inside there are tatters of fifteenth- and sixteenth-century frescoes on the walls, while above the high altar hangs a dolorous *Crucifix* by Cimabue (1260), painted when the artist would have been about 20.

Casa di Giorgio Vasari

Via XX Settembre 55 • Mon & Wed–Sat 9am–7pm, Sun 9am–1pm • €4 or €12 combined ticket

The **Casa di Giorgio Vasari** was designed by the eponymous biographer-architect-artist who was born in Arezzo in 1511, was taught to paint by his distant relative Luca Signorelli, and went on to become general artistic supremo to Cosimo I. The industrious Vasari frescoed much of his house with portraits and mythological characters, a decorative scheme that makes this one of the brashest domestic interiors in Tuscany. Portraits include his wife as the muse of conjugal love (in the Chamber of Apollo) and Michelangelo and Andrea del Sarto (in the Chamber of Fame). Work by other minor artists is strewn all over the place.

Museo d'Arte Medievale e Moderna

Via S. Lorentino 8 • Tues–Sun 8.30am–7.30pm • €4 or €12 combined ticket

The fifteenth-century Palazzo Bruni-Ciocchi houses the **Museo d'Arte Medievale e Moderna**, containing a collection of paintings by local artists and majolica pieces from the thirteenth to the eighteenth centuries, generously spread over three floors. Highlights are the first floor's medieval and Renaissance paintings by the likes of Spinello Aretino, Luca Signorelli and Bartolomeo della Gatta, and the five rooms filled with ceramics from Deruta, Gubbio, Faenza and other major Italian centres of production.

Museo Archeologico

Via Margaritone • Daily 8.30am–7.30pm • €4, or €12 combined ticket

All the principal sights are in the upper part of town, with two exceptions, one of which is the **Museo Archeologico**, which occupies part of a monastery built into the wall of the town's Roman amphitheatre. The collection is impressive chiefly for the marvellously coloured coralline vases produced here in the first century BC – the skill of Arezzo's glassblowers achieved a reputation throughout the Roman world.

Santa Maria delle Grazie

Viale Mecenate • Daily 8am–7pm

A ten-minute walk south of the city centre, at the end of Viale Mecenate, stands Arezzo's most exquisite church, **Santa Maria delle Grazie**. Built at the instigation of St Bernardino, the church is fronted by a tiny pine-ringed meadow that's flanked by a pair of arcades, and is entered through a delicate portico built by Benedetto da Maiano in the 1470s. The church is essentially a single room, containing little more than a few seats and an altarpiece by Parri Spinello, painted on the instructions of St Bernardino; the beautiful marble-and-terracotta altar that encases it was created by Andrea della Robbia.

ARRIVAL AND INFORMATION   **AREZZO**

By train Sitting on the main line between Florence and Rome, Arezzo is a major hub for train services.

Destinations Assisi (12 daily; 1hr 35min); Camucia-Cortona (hourly; 20min); Florence (hourly; 1hr); Orvieto (7 daily; 1hr 20min); Perugia (every 2hr; 1hr 15min).

By bus Buses into Arezzo all terminate by the train station.

Destinations Città di Castello (at least 12 daily; 1hr 30min);

Cortona (hourly; 1hr); Sansepolcro (17 daily, some via Monterchi, most via Anghiari; 1hr); Siena (5 daily Mon–Fri).

Tourist offices There are offices in the Palazzo Comunale, Piazza della Libertà 1 (Mon–Fri 11am–1pm & 2–4pm, Sat & Sun 11am–4pm; ☎ 0575 401 945, ⦿ apt.arezzo.it), and in front of the train station, on Piazza della Repubblica (same hours).

9

ACCOMMODATION

Accommodation can be hard to come by, especially when the antiques fair is on. In addition, the town is booked solid at the end of August and beginning of September, when the Concorso Polifonico Guido d'Arezzo and the Giostra del Saracino follow in quick succession.

Antiche Mura Piaggia di Murello 35 ☎0575 20 410, ⓦ antichemura.info. This cosy six-room B&B has an excellent location, just a 2min walk from the Duomo, with wood-beamed ceilings and stone walls giving it an appealingly rustic feel. The rooms overlooking the internal courtyard are quieter. Breakfast is taken in a nearby bar. **€95**

★ **Graziella Patio** Via Cavour 23 ☎0575 401 962, ⓦ hotelpatio.it. This small, welcoming four-star is located a minute's stroll from San Francesco. The decor is inspired by the journeys of Bruce Chatwin, and most of the

bedrooms are painted in bright, exotic colours; for a real treat, go for the "Rio Grande" or the "Utz" suite. **€180**

Vogue Hotel Via Guido Monaco 54 ☎0575 24 361, ⓦ voguehotel.it. The common areas of the four-star *Vogue* are looking a little tired, but its 26 rooms, all with a traditional feel, have been carefully refurbished, with a sleek, modern look that makes a refreshing change from the antique-clogged interiors favoured by many of Arezzo's hotels. Avoid the overpriced "Queen" and "Vogue" rooms; the "Trend" rooms are spacious and fairly priced. **€170**

EATING AND DRINKING

★ **Antica Osteria L'Agania** Via Mazzini 10 ☎0575 29 381. A very good and informal trattoria with welcoming atmosphere and local dishes (special emphasis on truffles and mushrooms in season) at around €25 per head; it draws much of its clientele from the antiques dealers. The *Antica Vineria* next door serves soups, salads, and cheese and meat plates at even lower prices in a bustling dining room. Tues–Sun noon–4pm & 6–11pm.

Bacco e Arianna Via Cesalpino 10 ☎0575 299 598. A terrific little *enoteca*, very close to San Francesco, with very good food (dishes around €12–15) – an ideal place for a quick lunch. Mon & Thurs–Sun 11am–3pm & 7–11pm, Wed 7–11pm.

Fiaschetteria de' Redi Via de' Redi 10 ☎0575 355 012. Busy little *osteria* with a superb range of vintages and decent simple meals. Daily 11.30am–3pm & 7pm– midnight; closed Mon in winter.

Il Gelato Via de' Cenci 24. This *gelateria* off Corso Italia serves Arezzo's best ice cream; the speciality is the *pane e nutella* flavour, a calorific concoction of hazelnut, chocolate and brioche. 11am–midnight, closes 8pm in winter; closed Wed, and all Jan & Dec.

Il Saraceno Via Mazzini 6 ☎0575 27 644. Family-run trattoria, founded in 1946, with a good wine cellar and traditional Aretine specialities (notably duck) at around €35 per head for three courses; good wood-oven pizzas too. Noon–3.30pm & 7–11pm; closed Wed & two weeks in Jan.

Miseria e Nobiltà Via Piaggia di S. Bartolomeo 2 ☎0575 21 245. With its enticing, creative Italian menu and medieval, vaulted dining room, this stylish (but not expensive) place is one of the best and busiest in town. Tues 6pm–12.30am, Wed–Sun 12.30–2.30pm & 6pm–12.30am.

East of Arezzo: the Piero trail

Arezzo is the springboard for one of Italy's most rewarding art itineraries: the **Piero della Francesca trail**, which extends east of the city to **Monterchi** and **Sansepolcro** (the artist's birthplace), and continues through Urbino to Rimini. There's no **train** link between Arezzo and Sansepolcro, but the SITA **bus** company runs nearly twenty services a day between the two towns. Most of these buses continue to Città di Castello for train connections to Perugia, and five stop at Monterchi at convenient times for a visit.

The Madonna del Parto

Daily: April–Oct 9am–1pm & 2–7pm; Nov–March closes 5pm • €3.50

MONTERCHI is famous as the home of the **Madonna del Parto**, which is now the focal point of a permanent **exhibition** recounting the technical details of the fresco's restoration, and that of the San Francesco cycle in Arezzo. Images of the pregnant Mary, exemplifying the mystery of the Incarnation, began to appear in Tuscan art some time in the 1330s – Piero's glorious fresco, created around 1467, was one of the last additions to the genre. The picture is still an object of veneration, and the museum is sometimes cleared when local pregnant women come to pray to the Virgin; pregnant tourists are also admitted free.

Sansepolcro's Museo Civico

Via Niccolò Aggiunti 65 • Daily: June 15–Sept 15 9.30am–1.30pm & 2.30–7pm; rest of year 9.30am–1pm & 2.30–6pm • €8

SANSEPOLCRO, 40km northeast of Arezzo, is where Piero della Francesca was born in the 1410s, and where he spent much of his life. The **Museo Civico** houses a sizeable collection of pictures, including work by Pontormo and Santi di Tito, but the primary focus of attention is Della Francesca's *Resurrection*. Painted for the adjoining town hall in the 1450s and moved here in the sixteenth century, it's one of the most overpowering images of the event ever created, with a muscular Christ stepping onto the edge of the tomb – banner in hand – as if it were the rampart of a conquered city. Elsewhere in the museum, an early Della Francesca masterpiece, the *Madonna della Misericordia* polyptych, epitomizes the graceful solemnity of his work.

ACCOMMODATION, EATING AND DRINKING   SANSEPOLCRO

Da Ventura Via Niccolò Aggiunti 30 ☎ 0575 742 560, ⓦ albergodaventura.it. A fine place to eat is the family-run *Da Ventura*, in the same price range as the *Fiorentino* (see below); it also has inexpensive accommodation upstairs, but the rooms aren't as nice as at *La Locanda del Giglio*. Restaurant closed Sun eve & Mon. **€70**

★ **La Locanda del Giglio** Via Pacioli 60 ☎ 0575

742 033, ⓦ ristorantefiorentino.it. This B&B is the best place to stay in Sansepolcro, with four simply furnished en-suite rooms, right in the heart of the town. In the same building there's an excellent and well-priced restaurant, the *Fiorentino* (closed Wed), run by the same people. (The adjoining *Fiorentino* hotel is an entirely separate operation.) **€85**

Cortona

Travelling south from Arezzo you enter the **Valdichiana**, reclaimed swampland that is now prosperous farming country. From the valley floor, a 5km road winds up through terraces of vines and olives to the ancient hill-town of **CORTONA**, whose heights survey a vast domain: the Valdichiana stretching westwards, with Lago Trasimeno visible over the low hills to the south. The steep streets of Cortona are more or less untouched by modern building: limitations of space have confined almost all later development to the lower suburb of Camucia, which is where the approach road begins.

Even without its monuments and art treasures, this would be a good place to rest up, with decent hotels and excellent restaurants. In recent years, though, Cortona's tourist traffic has increased markedly, in the wake of Frances Mayes' *Under the Tuscan Sun* and *Bella Tuscany*, books that continue to entice coachloads of her readers to the town. And in late July/early August the town is filled to capacity by audiences for the **Festival del Sole/Tuscan Sun Festival**, an arts jamboree (mainly classical music) that was founded in 2002, partly at Mayes' instigation; for its tenth anniversary the festival relocated to Florence, but it should return to its original home in future years.

MAEC

Piazza Signorelli • April–Oct daily 10am–7pm; Nov–March Tues–Sun 10am–5pm • €8, or €10 combined ticket with Museo Diocesano • ⓦ cortonamaec.org

From **Piazza Garibaldi** – where buses terminate – Via Nazionale, the only level street in town, connects to **Piazza della Repubblica**, which is overlooked by the grandstand staircase of the Palazzo del Comune. Behind the Palazzo del Comune is **Piazza Signorelli**, named after Luca Signorelli (1441–1523), Cortona's most famous son, and site of the Museo dell'Accademia Etrusca e della Città di Cortona – or **MAEC**, for short. On the lowest floor, which charts the development of Cortona from the earliest recorded settlements to Roman times, some spectacular specimens of Etruscan jewellery catch the eye. Upstairs there's a good deal more Etruscan material on show, most notably a bronze lamp from the fourth century BC, which is honoured with a room all to itself. Etruscan and later bronze figurines fill an avenue of cabinets in the middle of the main hall, surrounded by some fairly undistinguished pictures.

9

The Duomo

Piazza del Duomo • Daily 8am–12.30pm & 3–6.30pm

Piazza Signorelli links with Piazza del Duomo, where the **Duomo** sits hard up against the city walls. The interior is rather chilly, but there's a Pietro da Cortona *Nativity* on the third altar on the left, and a possible Andrea del Sarto (an *Assumption*) to the left of the high altar.

Museo Diocesano

Piazza del Duomo • April–Oct daily 10am–7pm; Nov–March Tues–Sun 10am–5pm • €5, or €10 combined ticket with MAEC

The church that used to face the Duomo now forms part of the **Museo Diocesano**, a tiny but high-quality collection of Renaissance art plus a fine Roman sarcophagus, carved with fighting centaurs. Predictably Luca Signorelli features strongly, though only two works – *Lamentation* (1502) and *The Communion of the Apostles* (1512) – are unequivocally his. Paintings from Sassetta, Bartolomeo della Gatta and Pietro Lorenzetti are also on show, but none measures up to Fra' Angelico, represented by a *Madonna, Child and Saints* and an exquisite *Annunciation*, painted when he was based at Cortona's monastery of San Domenico.

San Francesco

Via Berrettini • Daily 9am–6.45pm

To get the full taste of Cortona take Via Santucci from Piazza della Repubblica and then clamber along Via Berrettini, at the near end of which stands the crusty and ancient church of **San Francesco**. Designed by St Francis's disciple Brother Elias, this was the first Franciscan church to be built outside Assisi after Francis's death. The church houses a Byzantine ivory reliquary that is said to contain a piece of the True Cross – it's on the high altar, behind which Brother Elias is buried. To the left of the altar are displayed various items that are reputed to have belonged to St Francis, while on the third altar on the left of the nave hangs an *Annunciation* by the man the street is named after, Pietro Berrettini, otherwise known as Pietro da Cortona. (He was born at no. 33, further up the hill.)

San Niccolò

Piazza Pescaia • Fri 3.30–6.30pm, Sat & Sun 11am–1pm & 3.30–6.30pm • €1 minimum donation expected

A further work by Signorelli is to be found in the church of **San Niccolò**, a frail little building with a delicate portico and a fine wooden ceiling that's sagging with age. Signorelli's high altarpiece is a standard which he painted on both sides: a characteristically angular *Entombment* on the front and a *Madonna and Saints* on the back – revealed by a neat hydraulic system that swivels the picture away from the wall, as the sacristan will demonstrate.

Santa Margherita

Piazza Santa Margherita • Daily: summer 8am–noon & 3–7pm; winter 9am–noon & 3–6pm

Near the summit of the town stands **Santa Margherita**, resting place of St Margaret of Cortona, the town's patron saint. Her tomb, with marble angels lifting the lid of her sarcophagus, was created in the mid-fourteenth century, and is now mounted on the wall to the left of the chancel, while her remains are on display in a glass coffin directly behind the chancel.

ARRIVAL AND INFORMATION | CORTONA

By train Stopping trains from Arezzo call at Camucia-Cortona station, from where a shuttle (roughly every 30min) takes 10min to run up to the old town. Florence–Rome trains stop at Terontola, 10km south, which is also served by a shuttle roughly every hour (25min to Cortona's

Piazza Garibaldi); Terontola is the station to get off at if you are approaching from Umbria.

By bus There are hourly LFI buses between Cortona and Arezzo, taking 50min.

By car The centre is closed to all but essential traffic, so if you're driving you should use one of the free car parks on the periphery.

Tourist office Palazzo Casali, Piazza Signorelli 9 (Mon–Fri 9am–12.30pm, plus Tues & Thurs 3–5.30pm; ⊙ 0575 637 269, ⓦ cortonaweb.net). The tourist office occupies part of the building that houses MAEC, and has information on the whole Valdichiana as well as Cortona itself.

ACCOMMODATION

Italia Via Ghibellina 5 ⊙ 0575 630 254, ⓦ hotelitalia cortona.com. An inexpensive three-star, occupying a renovated fifteenth-century house very near Piazza della Repubblica, with 26 rooms and a panoramic breakfast terrace. **€130**

Ostello San Marco Via G. Maffei 57 ⊙ 0575 601 765, ⓦ cortonahostel.com. Clean and spacious eighty-bed HI hostel in an old monastery in the heart of town, with fantastic views from the dormitories. Open mid-March to mid-Oct; reception daily 7–10am & 3.30pm–midnight. Doubles and family rooms available (€25 per person). Dorms **€17**

San Michele Via Guelfa 15 ⊙ 0575 604 348, ⓦ hotel sanmichele.net. The most luxurious central choice, this handsome 43-room four-star has been converted from a rambling medieval townhouse. The rooms are a generous size, and the suites, though much pricier, are worth splashing out on, especially no. 214, which offers marvellous views from its private terrace. **€150**

★ **Villa Marsili** Via Cesare Battisti 13 ⊙ 0575 605 252, ⓦ villamarsili.net. Situated a short distance down the slope from Piazza Garibaldi, this friendly four-star – occupying an eighteenth-century villa – has airy rooms nicely furnished with antiques: most command photogenic views of the Valdichiana. The breakfast is excellent, and thoughtful touches such as free early-evening *aperitivi* and post-dinner *cantuccini* are a bonus. **€140**

EATING AND DRINKING

★ **Dardano** Via Dardano 24 ⊙ 0575 601 944. This excellent, unpretentious and inexpensive trattoria is full to bursting most nights. With its appealing menu of local dishes, it's a good place for a hearty meal, followed by the house *digestivo*, made from laurel leaves. Noon–2.45pm & 7–10pm; closed Wed.

Fufluns Via Ghibellina 1–3 ⊙ 0575 604 140. There's a full menu of Tuscan dishes on offer, but this spacious and bustling place is best known for its generous pizzas. Booking advised at weekends. Noon–2.30pm & 7.15–10.30pm; closed Tues.

La Bucaccia Via Ghibellina 17 ⊙ 0575 606 039, ⓦ labucaccia.it. Husband-and-wife team Romano and Agostina are at the helm of this refined restaurant, with an atmospheric stone-walled dining room and 500-bottle wine cellar. Jovial Romano is a certified cheese expert, Agostina is the chef and daughter Francesca is the sommelier. You can eat very well for €40. Summer daily noon–4pm & 7–11.30pm; closed Mon in winter.

Osteria del Teatro Via Maffei 5 ⊙ 0575 630 556, ⓦ osteria-del-teatro.it. Occupying the whole lower floor of a rambling old mansion, this is a good-naturedly busy (sometimes frantic) place, featuring delicious home-made pastas on a meat-heavy menu; portions are generous and the prices more than fair – the bill should be around €35 per person. Noon–2.30pm & 7–10pm; closed Wed & three weeks in Nov.

Route 66 Via Nazionale 78 ⊙ 0575 627 27. This self-styled "music bar" with DJs at weekends attracts the youngest crowd in town. It does food too, but it's not the nosh that makes it popular. 11am–2am; closed Mon in winter.

Umbria

THE PIANO GRANDE

Umbria

Often referred to as "the green heart of Italy", Umbria is a predominantly beautiful and – despite the many visitors –largely unspoiled region of rolling hills, woods, streams and valleys. Within its borders it also contains a dozen or so classic hill-towns, each resolutely individual and crammed with artistic and architectural treasures to rival bigger and more famous cities. To the east, pastoral countryside gives way to more rugged scenery, none better than the dramatic twists and turns of the Valnerina and the high mountain landscapes of the Parco Nazionale dei Monti Sibillini.

10

Umbria was named by the Romans after the mysterious **Umbrii**, a tribe cited by Pliny as the oldest in Italy, and one that controlled territory reaching into present-day Tuscany and Le Marche. Although there is scant archeological evidence about them, it seems that their influence was mainly confined to the east of the Tiber; the darker and more sombre towns to the west – such as Perugia and Orvieto – were founded by the **Etruscans**, whose rise forced the Umbrii to retreat into the eastern hills. Roman domination was eventually undermined by the so-called barbarian invasions, in the

---

REGIONAL FOOD AND WINE

The cuisine of landlocked, hilly Umbria relies heavily on rustic staples – pastas and roast meats – and in the past tended to be simple and homely. The region is also the only area outside Piemonte where **truffles** are found in any abundance, and their perfumed shavings, particularly in the east of the region, find their way onto eggs, pasta, fish and meat – but at a price that prohibits overindulgence.

Meat plays a leading role – especially **lamb** and **pork**, which is made into hams, sausage, salami and, most famously, **porchetta**, whole suckling pig stuffed with rosemary or sage, roasted on a spit. **Game** may also crop up on some menus, most often as pigeon, pheasant or guinea fowl. The range of **fish** is restricted by the lack of a coast, but trout can be caught from the Nera River and Clitunno springs, while the lakes of Piediluco and Trasimeno yield eel, pike, tench and grey mullet. **Vegetable** delicacies include tiny lentils from Castelluccio, beans from Trasimeno, and celery and cardoons from around Trevi. Umbrian **olive oil**, though less hyped than Tuscan oils, is of excellent quality – about 90 percent is extra virgin – particularly that from around Trevi and Spoleto.

As for desserts, Perugia is renowned for its **chocolate** and pastries. **Cheeses** tend to be standard issue, although some smaller producers survive in the mountains around Norcia and Gubbio.

Umbria used to be best known outside Italy for fresh, dry white **wines**. Orvieto, once predominantly a medium-sweet wine, has been revived in a dry style. The wine was beloved of the artists and architects of Orvieto's Duomo: Luca Signorelli requested a thousand litres per year by contract. In recent years the pre-eminence of Orvieto in the domestic market has been successfully challenged by Grechetto, an inexpensive and almost unfailingly good wine made by countless producers across the region. Umbria's quest for quality is also increasingly reflected in a growing number of small producers, many of whom have followed the lead of Giorgio Lungarotti, one of the pioneers of Umbrian viticulture (any wine with his name on is reliable), and in some outstanding reds, notably the Torgiano Rosso Riserva DOCG and the Sagrantino DOCG of Montefalco. The region has four **wine routes** (*strade del vino*): the Strada del Sagrantino, around Montefalco; the Strada dei Vini del Cantico between Todi, Perugia, Torgiano, Spello and Assisi; the Strada del Vino Colli del Trasimeno; and the Strada dei Vini Etrusco-Romano, in the province of Terni.

FACADE OF THE DUOMO, ORVIETO

Highlights

❶ Galleria Nazionale dell'Umbria The region's finest and largest collection of medieval and Renaissance Umbrian paintings. **See p.628**

❷ Gubbio Best looking of Umbria's medieval hill-towns, and without Assisi's crowds and commercialism. **See p.637**

❸ Basilica di San Francesco Burial place of St Francis and one of Italy's great buildings, with frescoes by Giotto and Simone Martini. See p.642

❹ Valle di Spoleto A swathe of country with four of the region's most compelling villages: Spello, Bevagna, Trevi and Montefalco. See pp.649–653

❺ San Francesco, Montefalco One of Umbria's best small galleries, with a major fresco cycle by Benozzo Gozzoli. **See p.652**

❻ Valnerina A verdant, mountain-edged valley dotted with hill-villages and spectacular views. See p.660

❼ Piano Grande A glorious upland plain, the centrepiece of the Monti Sibillini national park. **See p.662**

❽ Duomo, Orvieto On a par with the cathedrals in Milan and Siena, Orvieto's Duomo has a glorious facade and a majestic fresco cycle by Luca Signorelli. **See p.669**

HIGHLIGHTS ARE MARKED ON THE MAP ON P.624

face of which the Umbrians withdrew into fortified hill-towns, paving the way for a pattern of bloody rivalry between independent city-states that continued through the Middle Ages. Weakened by constant warfare, most towns eventually fell to the papacy, entering a period of economic and cultural stagnation that continued to the very recent past.

Historically, however, Umbria is best known as the birthplace of several saints, **St Benedict** and **St Francis of Assisi** being the most famous, and for a religious tradition that earned the region such names as *Umbra santa*, *Umbra mistica* and *la terra dei*

UMBRIA

HIGHLIGHTS
1. Galleria Nazionale dell'Umbria
2. Gubbio
3. Basilica di San Francesco
4. Valle di Spoleto
5. San Francesco, Montefalco
6. Valnerina
7. Piano Grande
8. Duomo, Orvieto

10

santi ("the land of saints"). The landscape itself has contributed much to this mystical reputation, and even on a fleeting trip it's impossible to miss the strange quality of the Umbrian light, an oddly luminous silver haze that hangs over the hills.

After years as an impoverished backwater, Umbria has capitalized on its charms. Foreign acquisition of rural property is now as rapid as it was in Tuscany thirty years ago, though outsiders have done nothing to curb the region's renewed sense of identity and youthful enthusiasm, nor to blunt the artistic initiatives that have turned Umbria into one of the most flourishing cultural centres in Italy.

Most visitors head for **Perugia**, **Assisi** – the latter with its extraordinary frescoes by Giotto in the Basilica di San Francesco – or **Orvieto**, whose Duomo is one of the greatest Gothic buildings in the country. For a taste of the region's more understated qualities, it's best to concentrate on lesser-known places such as **Todi**, **Gubbio**, ranked as the most perfect medieval centre in Italy, and **Spoleto**, for many people the outstanding Umbrian town. Although there are few unattractive parts of the Umbrian landscape (the factories of Terni and the Tiber valley being the largest blots), some districts are especially enticing: principally the mountainous **Valnerina**, **Piano Grande** and **Lago Trasimeno**, the last of which is the largest lake in the Italian peninsula, with plenty of opportunities for swimming and watersports.

GETTING AROUND   UMBRIA

Getting around the region by public transport presents no problems. Distances between the main sights are short, and there are excellent rail links both within the region and to Florence and Rome. For travel information, see ⓦ umbriamobilita.it.

Perugia

The provincial capital **PERUGIA** is the most obvious place to kick off a tour of Umbria. A bustling university town, known for its chocolate and its jazz festival, there's at least a day's worth of good sightseeing here, and it's not a bad place to base yourself if you want to explore the surrounding area: it has big-city amenities and trains run to all the

THE PERUGIA CITTÀ MUSEO CARD

A **museum pass** is available for all the major museums and sights in Perugia, including all those mentioned in this chapter. The Perugia Città Museo Card (€10 for 48hr; ⓦperugiacitta museo.it) is valid for five sights and includes admission for one adult and one child under the age of 18. Students are eligible for the U card, also valid for five sights (€6; 1 month). If you are staying in Perugia for any length of time, and intend to visit lots of museums, the C1 and C2 cards give access to all museums for a year; C1 is for individuals and costs €20, C2 for families and costs €35. Audio and video guides are supplied free of charge at the sights, plus there are discounts at several restaurants in town. Buy the card at participating sights – C1 and C2 are available only at the National Gallery of Umbria and the Museo Penna.

major highlights, complemented by fast new roads and an extensive bus network. The town hinges around a single street, the **Corso Vannucci**, named after the city's most celebrated artist, Pietro Vannucci (c1450–1523), better known as Perugino. Lined with bustling pavement cafés, this is one of Italy's greatest people-watching streets, packed from dawn through to the early hours with a parade of tourists, students and trendsetters.

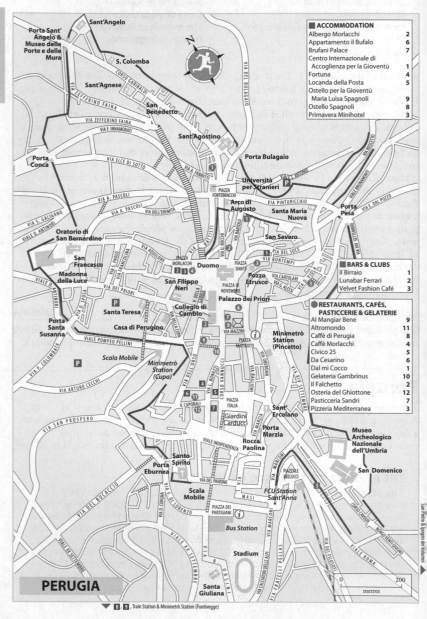

ACCOMMODATION

Albergo Morlacchi	2
Appartamento il Bufalo	6
Brufani Palace	7
Centro Internazionale di Accoglienza per la Gioventù	1
Fortuna	4
Locanda della Posta	5
Ostello per la Gioventù Maria Luisa Spagnoli	9
Ostello Spagnoli	8
Primavera Minihotel	3

BARS & CLUBS

Il Birraio	1
Lunabar Ferrari	2
Velvet Fashion Café	3

RESTAURANTS, CAFÉS, PASTICCERIE & GELATERIE

Al Mangiar Bene	9
Altromondo	11
Caffè di Perugia	8
Caffè Morlacchi	4
Civico 25	5
Da Cesarino	6
Dal mi Cocco	1
Gelateria Gambrinus	10
Il Falchetto	12
Osteria del Ghiottone	2
Pasticceria Sandri	7
Pizzeria Mediterranea	3

PERUGIA

0 — 200 metres

▼ 8 , 9 , Train Station & Minimetrò Station (Fontivegge)

The Giardini Carducci

Escalators up from the bus station emerge in **Piazza Italia**. Just south of here, the small but well-kept **Giardini Carducci**, full of smooching couples, is the best place to appreciate why Henry James called Perugia the "little city of the infinite views". When the usual cloak of haze lifts on crisp winter mornings, half of Umbria is laid out before you, with the mountains of Tuscany in the distance. An **antiques fair** takes place in the gardens and piazza on the last weekend of every month.

The Duomo

Piazza IV Novembre • Daily 7.30am–12.30pm & 4–7pm • Free

Austere and huge, **Piazza IV Novembre** – once a Roman reservoir – is backed by the unfinished ridged facade of the fifteenth-century **Duomo**. The intention was to cover it with pink and white scalloped lozenges, but this never happened – there is, however, a trial section around the door, along with the diminutive Cosmati pulpit from which San Bernardino di Siena preached to the Perugini in 1425.

While the cathedral's Baroque interior is big on size, it's pretty small on works of art and comes as a disappointment after the fifteenth-century facade, though the curious might like to see what is supposed to be the Virgin's "wedding ring", an unwieldy 2cm-diameter piece of agate that allegedly changes colour according to the character of the person wearing it. It is kept behind a heavy metal grille in the chapel almost immediately to your right as you enter, locked up in fifteen boxes fitted into one another like Russian dolls, each opened with a key held by a different person. It's brought out for general public edification once a year on July 30. In one of the transepts there's an urn holding the ashes of Pope Martin IV, who died in the city after eating too many eels. Urban IV's remains are here too – he was reputedly poisoned with *aquetta*, an imaginative brew made by rubbing white arsenic into pork fat and distilling the unpleasantness that oozes out.

Fontana Maggiore

Outside the Duomo in the piazza (which is the town's main hangout), the centrepiece is the **Fontana Maggiore**, designed in the thirteenth century to celebrate the completion of an aqueduct that brought fresh water to the city from a mountain spring five miles away. It was created by the father-and-son team, Nicola and Giovanni Pisano, with sculptures and bas-reliefs depicting episodes from the Old Testament, classical myth, Aesop's fables and the twelve months of the year – on the two polygonal basins. By some canny design work they never line up directly, encouraging you to walk round the fountain chasing a point of repose that never comes.

BLOODLUST IN MEDIEVAL PERUGIA

Medieval Perugia was evidently a hell of a place to be. "The most warlike of the people of Italy", wrote the historian Sismondi, "who always preferred Mars to the Muse." Male citizens played a game (and this was for pleasure) in which two teams, thickly padded in clothes stuffed with deer hair and wearing beaked helmets, stoned each other mercilessly until the majority of the other side were dead or wounded. Children were encouraged to join in for the first two hours to promote "application and aggression".

In 1265 Perugia was also the birthplace of the **Flagellants**, who had half of Europe whipping itself into a frenzy before the movement was declared heretical. In addition to some hearty scourging they took to the streets on moonlit nights, groaning and wailing, dancing in white sheets, singing dirges and clattering human bones together, all as expiation for sin and the wrongs of the world. Then there were the infamous **Baglioni**, the medieval family who misruled the city for several generations, their spellbinding history – full of vendetta, incest and mass slaughter – the stuff of great medieval soap opera.

The Palazzo dei Priori

Just opposite the cathedral on Piazza IV Novembre, and decidedly outdoing it in terms of architectural panache, rises the exquisite Gothic **Palazzo dei Priori**, often – and rightly – described as one of the greatest public palaces in Italy. Sheer bulk aside, it's certainly impressive – with rows of trefoil windows from which convicted criminals were once thrown to their deaths, majestic Gothic doorway, and business-like Guelph crenellations – though the overall effect is rather forbidding; its real beauty derives from the harmony set up by the medieval buildings around it.

Sala dei Notari

Daily 9am–1pm & 3–7pm; closed Mon Oct–June • Free

The lawyers' meeting hall, the **Sala dei Notari**, at the top of the fan-shaped steps, is noted for its frescoes portraying scenes from the Bible, Aesop's fables and the coats of arms of medieval civic worthies: lots of colour, fancy flags, swirls and no substance – but certainly worth a glance.

Collegio della Mercanzia

Corso Vannucci 15 • ☎ 075 573 0366 • March–Oct Tues–Sat 9am–1pm & 2.30–5.30pm, Sun 9am–1pm; Nov–Feb Tues, Thurs & Fri 8am–2pm, Wed & Sat 8am–4.30pm, Sun 9am–1pm • €1.50, or €5.50 with Collegio di Cambio

The small **Collegio della Mercanzia** lies farther down the Corso side of the palace, hidden behind an innocuous door. The seat of the Merchants' Guild, its walls and vaults are covered entirely with astonishingly intricate fifteenth-century inlaid wood panelling. The decision to have wooden walls instead of the more usual frescoes was not merely aesthetic – wood was far more expensive, and thus provided a subtle way for the Guild to flaunt their wealth and power.

Collegio di Cambio

Corso Vannucci 25 • ☎ 075 572 8599 • Mon–Sat 9am–12.30pm & 2.30–5.30pm, Sun 9am–1pm; Nov to mid-March closed Mon 2.30–5.30pm • €4.50, or €5.50, including Collegio della Mercanzia

A few doors down from Collegio della Mercanzia, the impressive **Collegio di Cambio** was the town's money exchange in medieval times. The superb frescoes on the walls were executed by Perugino at the height of his powers and are considered the artist's masterpiece; in true Renaissance fashion, they attempt to fuse ancient and Christian culture. Up on the door-side wall there's a famous but unremarkable self-portrait in which the artist looks like he had a bad lunch. Giannicola di Paolo frescoed the small chapel (1519) to the right of the Collegio, the last important Umbrian painter influenced by Perugino.

Galleria Nazionale dell'Umbria

Corso Vannucci 19 • ☎ 075 586 68410 • Tues–Sun 8.30am–7.30pm, ticket office closes 6.30pm; April–June open also Mon 9.30am–7.30pm • €6.50 • ⓦ www.gallerianazionaleumbria.it

The **Galleria Nazionale dell'Umbria** is on the upper floor of the palace complex (lift or stairs), with the entrance through its opulently carved **doorway**. One of central Italy's best and most charming galleries, this takes you on a romp through the history of Umbrian painting, with masterpieces by Perugino, Pinturicchio and many others, plus one or two stunning Tuscan masterpieces (Duccio, Fra' Angelico, Piero della Francesca) thrown in for good measure. The entrance is worth every cent if you're the slightest bit interested in early and mid-Renaissance art.

The Pozzo Etrusco

Piazza Danti 18 • April & Aug daily 10am–1.30pm & 2.30–6pm; May–July, Sept & Oct Tues–Sun 10am–1.30pm & 2.30–6pm; rest of year Tues–Sun 11am–1.30pm & 2.30–5pm • €3, includes admission to San Severo & Museo delle Porte e delle Mura Urbiche

Just east of Piazza Danti behind the cathedral lies the entrance to the **Pozzo Etrusco**, a massive cistern – 36m deep and with a capacity of 424,000 litres – that does more than hint at the dazzling engineering and technical skills of its Etruscan builders. It held water supplies for the entire Etruscan town, and if you look carefully you can see the steps descending right to its bottom – used by the Etrusan well-cleaners. Visiting is good fun – especially for kids – as you enter the cistern via an underground medieval tunnel, then cross it on a vertiginous bridge.

San Severo

Piazza Raffaello • April & Aug daily 10am–1.30pm & 2.30–6pm; May–July, Sept & Oct same hours but closed Mon; rest of year Tues–Sun 11am–1.30pm & 2.30–5pm • €3, includes admission to Pozzo Etrusco & Museo delle Porte e delle Mura Urbiche

A few minutes' walk farther east along Via del Sole brings you to the church of **San Severo** (same hours and ticket as Pozzo Etrusco) in Piazza Raffaello, known for its painting *Holy Trinity and Saints* by **Raphael**, who spent some five years in Umbria, studying with Perugino. According to Vasari, his mother wept when he was sent away to Perugia from his home in Urbino. She died in 1491, so if Vasari is correct, Raphael must have begun his apprenticeship when he was only 8 years old. *Holy Trinity and Saints* is a fascinating work, painted when he was around 23, its figures displaying the otherworldly pallor of the recently deceased Piero della Francesca, but with some of the same three-dimensional qualities Michelangelo would later demonstrate in the Sistine ceiling. It is the only painting by him still left in the region – Napoleon carted many of the artist's works off to France – except for a painted banner in the art gallery in Città di Castello (see p.636). Perugino, his erstwhile teacher, completed the lower third of the painting, *Six Saints*, in 1521 after Raphael's death.

Via dei Priori and around

The best streets to wander around for a feel of the old city are to the east and west of the Duomo, **Via dei Priori** being the most characteristic. Just behind the Palazzo dei Priori in Via della Gabbia there once hung a large iron cage used to imprison thieves and sometimes even clergy. You can still make out long spikes on some of the lower walls, used as hooks for the heads of executed criminals.

Madonna della Luce

Further down, Via dei Priori passes the rarely open **Madonna della Luce** on the north side after the medieval Torre degli Scirri, little more than a chapel dominated by an impressive altarpiece by G.B. Caporali, a follower of Perugino. The church takes its name from the story that in 1513 a young barber swore so profusely on losing at cards that a Madonna in a wayside shrine closed her eyes in horror and kept them closed for four days. The miracle prompted celebrations, processions and the building of a new church.

Oratorio di San Bernardino and the church of San Francesco

Some way beyond the Madonna della Luce, as the street bears right, is a nice patch of grass perfectly placed for relaxing with the crowd from the art school next door or for admiring Agostino di Duccio's colourful **Oratorio di San Bernardino**, whose richly embellished facade (1461) is far and away the best piece of sculpture in the city. To the north is what's left of **San Francesco**, once a colossal church, now ruined by centuries of earthquakes, but with a curiously jumbled and striking facade still just about standing.

The university and Arco di Augusto

The rather uninspiring Via A. Pascoli passes beneath the much-photographed Acquedotto (a raised walkway from the old centre to the north of the city – well worth taking for the views) and past the ugly university buildings, to the **Università Italiana per Stranieri** (☎075 57 461, ⓦunistrapg.it) in Piazza Fortebraccio. One of Italy's most prestigious centres of learning for foreigners, the university made international headlines in 2007 when 21-year-old British student Meredith Kercher was murdered.

The big patched-up gateway on one side of the piazza is the **Arco di Augusto**, its lowest section one of the few remaining monuments of Etruscan Perugia. The Romans added the upper remnant when they captured the city in 40 BC.

10

Sant'Agostino

Corso Garibaldi • Daily 9am–1pm & 4–7pm • Free

About a minute's walk north of the university is **Sant'Agostino**, once Romanesque, now botched Baroque and filled with wistful signs explaining what paintings used to hang in the church before they were spirited to France by light-fingered Napoleonic troops. The church, however, is not entirely ruined: there's a beautiful choir (probably based on a drawing by Perugino) and a couple of patches of fresco on the left-hand (north) wall, giving a tantalizing idea of what the place must once have been. Next door to the north side is the fifteenth-century **Oratorio di Sant'Agostino** (visits by advance booking only; ☎075 572 4815), its ludicrously ornate ceiling looking as if it's about to erupt in an explosion of gilt, stucco and chubby plaster cherubs.

Sant'Angelo

Corso Garibaldi • Daily 9am–1pm & 3.30–6.30pm • Free

Fifteen minutes' walk up the street from Sant'Agostino is the fifth-century church of **Sant'Angelo**, situated in a tranquil spot (with a pretty little patch of grass and trees – perfect for picnics and siestas) and based on a circular pagan temple; the 24 columns are from the earlier building.

Museo delle Porte e delle Mura Urbiche

Corso Garibaldi • April & Aug daily 10.30am–1.30pm & 3–6pm; May–July, Sept & Oct Tues–Sun 10.30am–1.30pm & 3–6pm; Nov–March Tues–Sun 11am–1pm & 3–5pm • Same ticket as Pozzo Etrusco and San Severo – see p.628 & 629 • ☎075 41 670

At the northern end of Corso Garibaldi, the city's largest medieval gate houses the **Museo delle Porte e delle Mura Urbiche**, a small museum which traces the development of the city through expansion of the city's three sections of wall: Etruscan, Medieval and Renaissance. Even if such things don't interest you, it is well worth a visit for the stunning views.

Rocca Paolina

Via Marzia • Nov–March Tues–Sun 11am–1.30pm & 2.30–5.30pm, May–July, Sept & Oct Tues–Sun 10am–1.30pm & 2.30–6pm; April & Aug daily 10am–1.30pm & 2.30–6pm • Free • ☎075 572 5778 • The site can also be accessed from the escalators to the bus station at Piazza dei Partigiani from the west side of Piazza Italia

During construction work on the escalator (*scala mobile*) linking Piazza Italia and the bus station on Piazza dei Partigiani, the ruins of **Rocca Paolina**, a once-enormous papal fortress destroyed by the Perugians at Unification, and a complex of medieval streets beneath it were unearthed below the Giardini Carducci. Now open to the public, the highlights of this amazing underground labyrinth are the medieval houses along the **Via Baglioni Sotterranea**, and the **Porta Marzia**, a gate that dates back to Etruscan times.

San Domenico

Piazza San Domenico, Corso Cavour • Daily 7am–noon & 4–7pm • Free

Heading southeast from the Rocca Paolina along Corso Cavour, you come to **San Domenico**, Umbria's biggest church. It has a desolate and unfinished air from the outside, but it's also appealing in a big and rather melancholy sort of way. The original Romanesque interior collapsed in the sixteenth century and the Baroque replacement is vast, cold and bare. Like Sant'Agostino, however, it's full of hints as to how beautiful it must have been – nowhere more so than in the fourth chapel on the right, where a superb **carved arch** by Agostino di Duccio is spoilt only by a doll-like Madonna. In the east transept, to the right of the altar, is the **tomb of Benedict XI** (1324), another pope who died in Perugia, this time from eating poisoned figs. It's an elegant and well-preserved piece by one of the period's three leading sculptors: Pisano, Lorenzo Maitani or Arnolfo di Cambio, no one knows which. There's also another good choir, together with some impressive **stained-glass** windows – the second biggest in Italy after those in Milan's Duomo.

Museo Archeologico Nazionale dell'Umbria

Convento di San Domenico • ☎ 075 572 7141 • Mon 10am–7.30pm, Tues–Sun 8.30am–7.30pm • €4

Housed in the church's cloisters is the **Museo Archeologico Nazionale dell'Umbria**. Before being hammered by Augustus, Perugia was a big shot in the twelve-strong Etruscan federation of cities, which is why the city has one of the most extensive Etruscan collections around. The place is definitely worth a visit, even if the Etruscans normally leave you cold, for there's far more here than the usual run of urns and funerary monuments. Particularly compelling are the Carri Etruschi di Castel San Marino, some exquisite sixth-century bronze chariots; a witty collection of eye-opening artefacts devoted to fashion and beauty in the Etruscan era; and the bewildering **Bellucci Collection**. The last is a private hoard of charms and amulets through the ages: everything from the obvious – lucky horseshoes – to strange and often sinister charms such as snake skins and dried animals.

San Pietro

Corso Cavour • Daily 8am–12.30pm & 3–6pm • Free

Beyond the archeological museum and San Domenico, advertised by a rocket-shaped belltower, is the tenth-century basilica of **San Pietro**, the most idiosyncratic of all the town's churches. Tangled up in a group of buildings belonging to the university's agriculture department, the none-too-obvious entrance is through a frescoed doorway in the far left-hand corner of the first courtyard off the road. Few churches can be so sumptuously decorated: every inch of available space is covered in gilt, paint or marble, though a guiding sense of taste seems to have prevailed, and in the candle-lit gloom it actually feels like the sacred place it's meant to be. All the woodwork is extraordinary; the **choir** has been called the best in Italy, and there is a host of works by Perugino, Fiorenzo di Lorenzo and others.

ARRIVAL AND DEPARTURE   PERUGIA

By plane Arriving by air (Ryanair flies from the UK) you'll land at the Aeroporto Regionale Umbro Sant'Egidio (☎ 075 592 141, ⌨ airport.umbria.it), 12km east of the centre. White minibus shuttles (€4; 15min) meet incoming flights and run to Piazza Italia, while APM run a service to Assisi (€8). A taxi should cost €25. Rome's Fiumicino airport (see p.97) is another option, with three direct buses to Perugia's bus station daily (2 on Sun; 3hr 45min; €14.50 one way).

By train Arriving on the state train network you'll find yourself southwest of the centre at Piazza Vittorio Veneto. Avoid walking into town from here – it's a steep haul on busy roads; the bus takes 15min (anything to Piazza Italia or Piazza Matteotti will do), while the Minimetrò light rail

system from the Stazione Fontivegge, 50m to the left of the station exit, has shuttles every 3min and takes 11min. The second stop, Cupa, drops you just west of the centre near Via dei Priori, while the last stop, Pincetto, is right in the centre, off Piazza Matteotti. If you're coming on the private FCU (Ferrovie Centrale Umbra) lines from Todi or Terni to the south, or from Città di Castello or Sansepolcro to the north, you'll arrive at the more central Stazione Sant'Anna, near the bus terminal at Piazza dei Partigiani.

Destinations Assisi (13 daily; 30min); Città di Castello (16 daily; 1hr 30min); Florence (8 daily; 2hr 15min); Foligno (13 daily; 45min); Sansepolcro (16 daily; 1hr 30min); Spello (18 daily; 30min); Terni (9 daily; 1hr 40min); Terontola (16 daily; 40min); Todi (10 daily; 1hr).

By bus Buses arrive at the terminal at Piazza dei Partigiani from where you can jump on a *scala mobile* (escalator) as it climbs through weird subterranean streets to Piazza Italia. Destinations Ascoli Piceno (1–4 daily; 3hr); Assisi (7 daily; 50min–1hr 20min); Castiglione del Lago (9 daily Mon–Sat; 1hr 20min); Chiusi (3 daily Mon–Sat; 1hr 35min); Florence (1 daily; 2hr–2hr 30min); Foligno (4 daily; 1hr 10min); Gubbio (10 daily; 1hr 10min); Milan (3 weekly; 6hr 50min); Norcia (1 daily; 2hr 50min); Orvieto (2 daily; 2hr 25min); Passignano (6 daily Mon–Sat; 1hr 15min); Rome (5 daily; 2hr 30min); Rome Fiumicino airport (1–3 daily; 3hr); Siena (3–7 daily; 1hr 30min); Spello (4 daily Mon–Sat; 55min); Spoleto (1–2 daily; 1hr 30min); Todi (6–8 daily; 1hr 15min).

10

By car As all the town's approaches are up steep hills and the centre is closed to traffic at peak times, you'll do best to leave your car at the main train station and take a bus. Alternatively head towards one of the big car parks – Piazza dei Partigiani is the largest and most central, or park in the free car park at Pian di Massiano just west of town and take the Minimetrò from there into the centre.

INFORMATION AND GETTING AROUND

City transport Tickets (valid on buses and Minimetrò) cost €1.50 for 70min and are available from the station newsagents and the booth outside the station; you can buy a ticket on the bus for a supplement of 50 cents. A 24hr ticket cost €5.40, while a 10-journey tickets is €12.90.

Tourist office Piazza Matteotti 18 (daily 9am–7pm; Ⓣ075 573 6458, Ⓦturismo.comune.perugia.it). The website is excellent, with downloadable maps and lots of interesting links.

ACCOMMODATION

Albergo Morlacchi Via L. Tiberi 2 Ⓣ075 572 0319, Ⓦhotelmorlacchi.it. This central, family-run hotel has comfortable rooms with parquet floors and an eclectic collection of art on the walls. Rooms vary in size, so ask to see a few. Breakfast is extra. **€80**

Appartamento il Bufalo Via del Bufalo Ⓣ349 661 3462, Ⓦtourinumbria.org. With vaulted ceilings, tasteful furnishings and luxuries such as CD and DVD players, not to mention a very central location, this two-bedroom apartment is great value if there are at least three of you. The owner prefers to let for at least three nights. **€50**

Brufani Palace Piazza Italia 12 Ⓣ075 573 2541, Ⓦbrufanipalace.com. Perugia's smartest and most luxurious option, with an equally elegant restaurant, is right in the centre of town. **€325**

Centro Internazionale di Accoglienza per la Gioventù Via Bontempi 13 Ⓣ075 572 2880, Ⓦostello.perugia.it. The town's original hostel is perfectly situated in a historic *palazzo* just 2min from the Duomo. It has frescoed common areas and a panoramic terrace that some of the rooms share. There are 100 beds in four-, six- and eight-bed dorms. Check-in 3.30pm–midnight; curfew 3.30am. Closed mid-Dec to mid-Jan. Dorms **€16**, plus €2 sheet rental.

Fortuna Via Bonazzi 19 Ⓣ075 572 2845, Ⓦumbriahotels.com. A central three-star in a historic fourteenth-century *palazzo* with frescoed ceilings in some rooms and a roof garden with good views of the old city. **€150**

Locanda della Posta Corso Vannucci 97 Ⓣ075 572 8925, Ⓦlocandadellaposta.com. Perugia's first choice if you want an upmarket treat: it's not as slick as the *Brufani* but just as central and in a historic building where the likes of Goethe and Hans Christian Andersen once stayed. **€170**

Ostello per la Gioventù Maria Luisa Spagnoli Via Cortonese 4, Località Pian di Massiano Ⓣ075 501 1366, Ⓦumbriahostels.org. Perugia's newer hostel is down near the main station with its own restaurant. It has 186 beds in 33 four- and six-bed dorms. Breakfast included. Open 7am to midnight year round. **€16**, single rooms **€22**, family rooms **€18** per person

★ **Primavera Minihotel** Via Vincioli 8 Ⓣ075 572 1657, Ⓦprimaveraminihotel.it. In a tranquil alley, this hotel has immaculate en-suite rooms, and the friendly staff are tirelessly helpful. **€100**

PERUGIA'S FESTIVALS

The town's main cultural draw in summer is **Umbria Jazz**, Italy's foremost jazz event. This ten-day extravaganza takes place in early to mid-July and features the top names in the jazz world, performing in atmospheric venues throughout town. Tickets for big names can be steep, but prices for many events start at €15 and there are free events in Piazza IV Novembre and the Giardini Carducci. Book well in advance on Ⓦumbriajazz.com. In mid-September, the town hosts the **Sagra Musicale Umbra** (Ⓦperugiamusicaclassica.com), one of Italy's oldest music festivals, with performances of religious orchestral and choir music. In October, **Eurochocolate** (Ⓦeurochocolate.perugia.it) is a large-scale celebration of the world's favourite confectionery – and Perugia's most famous export – with lessons, tasting sessions and exhibitions.

EATING AND DRINKING

Perugia's student population ensures that there is a plethora of reasonably priced places to eat out, from the many snack bars around the centre of town to simple trattorias serving traditional Umbrian cuisine. Local dishes feature wild mushrooms, truffles and game often succulently combined with home-made egg pasta. The city's liveliest cafés are clustered on Corso Vannucci.

CAFÉS, PASTICCERIE AND GELATERIE

Caffè di Perugia Via Mazzini 10 ☎075 573 1863. A pleasantly smart setting with superb vaulted ceiling from the thirteenth century, as well as lots of outdoor tables. All the café staples, plus a pricey restaurant with *secondi* at around €16, a pizzeria-grill and a wine bar, the last a good early-evening retreat. Daily 8am–8pm.

Caffè Morlacchi Piazza Morlacchi 8 ☎075 572 1760. Smart but student-oriented bar with occasional live music in the evenings. A nice place to hang out. Daily breakfast till late; opens at 4pm on Sun.

Gelateria Gambrinus Via Bonazzi 3. Queues from this ice-cream parlour off the Corso often stretch onto the nearby Piazza della Repubblica, especially at the height of the Sunday *passeggiata*. A great choice of flavours and very generous scoops. Daily: April–Oct 11am–1am; Nov–March 11am–8pm; closed Jan.

★ **Pasticceria Sandri** Corso Vannucci 32. Atmospheric, old-world café with a wonderful frescoed ceiling in a perfect position on the main street near the Palazzo dei Priori – a high spot for the sweet-toothed. Tues–Sun 8am–10pm.

RESTAURANTS

★ **Al Mangiar Bene** Via della Luna 21 ☎075 573 1047. Tucked away down a flight of steps off Corso Vannucci, this lovely, brick-vaulted space is a rare find: all-organic, with produce sourced from local farms. It's refreshingly laidback too: you can choose which pasta to pair with which sauce – a no-no in many fancier places. *Primi* cost €6–10 while a full and very tasty meal with wine will set you back around €35. Mon–Sat 12.30–2.45pm & 7.30–11.45pm.

Altromondo Via Caporali 11 ☎075 572 6157. Well-priced home cooking in a brick-vaulted, airy space. *Primi* cost from €7, mains €10–15. Try *pappardelle* with wild boar, risotto with radicchio, or the *straccetti di vitello* (veal strips) with rocket. Mon–Sat 12.30–2.30pm & 7.30–11pm.

Civico 25 Via della Viola 25 ☎075 571 6376. Wine bar with food close to the Università degli Stranieri, great for a glass of wine with a bruschetta of fava beans, chickpeas or chicken liver pâté, or for a full meal. Classics include gnocchi with goose *ragù* (or truffle in season), while in spring they do a great pasta with tiny fava beans, *guanciale* ham and pecorino. *Secondi* include a wonderful *ossobuco* braised in white wine. Around €25 for a full meal. Dinner Mon–Sat.

Da Cesarino Piazza IV Novembre 4–5 ☎075 572 8974. A great central restaurant and a Perugia tradition, with meals from around €28. Booking advised. Mon, Tues & Fri–Sun 12.30–3pm & 7.30–11pm, Thurs 7.30–11pm.

Dal mi Cocco Corso Garibaldi 12 ☎075 573 2511. Simple, good-value traditional dishes, including hand-made pasta, in a variety of set menus from €13. It's always busy, so book in advance. Tues–Sun 1–3pm & 8.30–10.30pm.

Il Falchetto Via Bartolo 20, just off Piazza Danti ☎075 573 1775. A reliably good and easy-going place with a medieval interior and traditional dishes such as wild boar and deer stew with polenta (€12.50). Tues–Sun 12.30–3pm & 7.30–11pm.

Osteria del Ghiottone Via Caporali 12 ☎075 572 7788. This tiny, no-frills *osteria*, dotted with antique odds and ends such as farm implements and a suitcase full of wine corks, makes an atmospheric place for a meal. The cuisine is rigorously Umbrian, using ancient recipes, with home-made pasta. Mains (€8–15) include wild boar stew with chicory, and dishes are prepared with olive oil made in the owner's farm near Trevi. Noon–3pm & 7–10.30pm; closed Tues.

Pizzeria Mediterranea Piazza Piccinino 11 ☎075 572 1322. Simple and tasteful pizzeria with small wood-fired oven and a couple of brick-vaulted rooms a few steps beyond the entrance to the Pozzo Etrusco. It makes 28 varieties (from €3.70), including the children's crowd-pleaser Nutella pizza. Daily 12.30–2.30pm & 7.30–11pm.

BARS AND CLUBS

Il Birraio Via delle Prome 18 ☎075 572 5932. There's no mistaking the beer bias of this odd, modern place, the entrance to which is lined with the copper tanks and vats of the in-house microbrewery. Tues–Sun 5pm–2am.

Lunabar Ferrari Via Scura 6 ☎075 572 2966. Just off Corso Vannucci, this stylish bar attracts an equally stylish crowd. There's moody lighting, a lively *aperitivo* hour (6–9pm), with drinks accompanied by good free snacks, and even a smoking room – a rarity in Italian bars. DJs Tues & Sat. Tues–Sun 7am–2am, daily in Aug.

Velvet Fashion Café Viale Roma 20 ☎075 572 1321, ⓦ velvetfashioncafe.com. Perugia's most central club. Offers smart dining, drinking and occasional live music. 9pm until late; closed Mon–Wed in winter and all summer.

10

Lago Trasimeno

The most tempting option around Perugia – whose surroundings are generally pretty bleak – is **LAGO TRASIMENO**, an ideal spot to hole up in for a few days, and particularly recommended if you want to get in some swimming, windsurfing or sailing. The lake is about 30km from Perugia and is easy to get to on public transport. It's the biggest inland stretch of water in mainland Italy, and, though you wouldn't think so to look at it, never deeper than 7m – hence bath-like warm water in summer.

A winning combination of tree-covered hills to the north, Umbria's subtle light, and placid lapping water produces some magical moments, but on overcast and squally days the mood can turn melancholy. Not all the reed-lined shore is uniformly pretty either; steer clear of the northern coast and head for the stretches south of Magione and Castiglione if you're after relative peace and quiet.

Passignano and Isola Polvese

Passignano is served by 6 daily buses and hourly trains from Perugia and Terontola. Boats to the island run once daily from here, 10 times daily from San Feliciano, on the lake's eastern shore

Strung out along the northern shore, **PASSIGNANO**, a newish town with a medieval heart, is the lake's most accessible point. In summer it can get a bit clogged with traffic, but in the evenings, the joint is jumping, with bars, discos and fish restaurants aplenty. The most compelling reason to come, however, is to take the daily boat to the largely uninhabited **Isola Polvese** and stay in its outstanding hostel.

ACCOMMODATION ISOLA POLVESE

Fattoria Il Poggio ☎075 965 9550, ⊛fattoria isolapolvese.com. An HI hostel with lovely views of the lake and recently refurbished accommodation in six- and four-bed dorms, rooms and mini-apartments. The restaurant uses produce from the garden, and has full meals for €12. It is popular with school groups – so weekdays in April and May are best avoided by those seeking peace and quiet. Check the website for details of weekends devoted to yoga, reiki and fishing with the lake's fishermen. Doubles **€56**, apartments **€80**

Castiglione del Lago

CASTIGLIONE DEL LAGO is the most appealing town on the lake and cuts a fine silhouette from other points around the shore, jutting out into the water on a fortified promontory. A friendly, unpretentious place, Castiglione has enough charm and action

---

ON THE TRAIL OF HANNIBAL

Somewhere along the lake shore towards the rambling village of Tuoro, probably at Sanguineto ("the Place of Blood") or Ossaia ("the Place of Bones"), is the spot where the Romans suffered their famous clobbering at the hands of **Hannibal** in 217 BC. Hannibal was headed for Rome, having just crossed the Alps, when he was met by a Roman force under the Consul Flaminius. Things might have gone better for Flaminius if he'd heeded the omens that piled up on the morning of battle. First he fell off his horse, next the legionary standards had to be dug out of the mud, then – and this really should have raised suspicions – the sacred chickens refused their breakfast. Poultry accompanied all Roman armies and, by some means presumably known to the legionnaire in charge of chickens, communicated the will of the gods to waiting commanders in the field. Hannibal lured Flaminius into a masterful ambush, with the only escape a muddy retreat into the lake. Sixteen thousand Romans, including the hapless commander, were killed. A hard-to-find drive and walkway have been laid out, starting and finishing just west of Tuoro on the road to Cortona, which take in salient features of the old battlefield; the information office on the lake shore can arrange guided tours.

ACTIVITIES ON LAGO TRASIMENO

There are plenty of activities on offer from operators based in Castiglione del Lago, including **windsurfing** (contact Club Velico at ☎075 953 035, ⓦcvcastiglionese.it), **canoeing**, **waterskiing** and **horseriding** (ask at the tourist office for recommended operators). You can **rent bikes** at Cicli Valentini (Via Firenze 68/B; Mon–Sat 9am–1pm & 4–8pm; ⓦciclivalentini.it).

The best of the little **beaches** is at the public lido on the southern side of Castiglione's promontory, with pedaloes for rent and boat trips, including regular excursions to the strangely rectangular island of **Isola Maggiore** (30min; €6.80 return), a fun ride if you don't mind the summer crowds. There's a pretty walk round the edge of the island, and one good, popular **hotel**, the three-star *Da Sauro*, Via Guglielmi 1 (☎075 826 168, ⓦdasauro.it; €70), which also doubles as a fine restaurant.

10

to hold anyone's interest for a couple of days – longer if all you want to do is crash out on the (albeit modest) beach.

ARRIVAL AND INFORMATION CASTIGLIONE DEL LAGO

By train Castiglione del Lago is served by slow train either from Chiusi or Terontola; the latter is more useful if you're coming from Arezzo or Perugia.
Destinations Florence (11 daily; 1hr 50min); Rome (9 daily; 2hr 5min).

By bus There are eight or nine buses daily from Perugia.
Tourist office Piazza Mazzini 10 (April–Sept Mon–Sat 8.30am–1pm & 3.30–7pm, Sun 9am–1pm & 4–7pm; Oct–March closed Sun; ☎075 965 2484, ⓦlagotrasimeno .net).

ACCOMMODATION

Aganoor Via Vittorio Emanuele 91 ☎075 953 837, whotelaganoor.it. Attached to *La Cantina* restaurant, this eight-room B&B has comfortable, traditionally styled rooms, as well as a rooftop solarium with lovely views. Ask for one of the four rooms with lake views. Half-board available for €50–56/person, excluding drinks. **€78**
Badiaccia Via Trasimeno I 91, Località Badiaccia ☎075 965 9097, ⓦbadiaccia.com. Most of the campsites are off the main road some way north or south of the town. This is the most highly rated, with excellent and very well maintained facilities, plus a large sandy beach.

Pitches **€18.50**
La Torre Via Vittorio Emanuele 50 ☎075 951 666, ⓦlatorretrasimeno.com. A friendly, family-run hotel right on the main street with comfortable, if rather dated, rooms. It also has a pleasant two-person apartment, *Bellavista*, across the street, with its own garden and lake views, for €100 a night. **€75**
Miralago Piazza Mazzini 6 ☎075 951 157 or ☎075 953 063, ⓦhotelmiralago.com. An atmospheric choice, with doubles, triples and family rooms right in the main square, with views of the lake behind. **€80**

EATING AND DRINKING

L'Acquario Via Vittorio Emanuele II 69 ☎075 965 2432, ⓦristorantelacquario.it. This is the place to eat game, fish fresh from the lake and other local dishes, on the old town's single main street. Try lake prawns with almonds and leeks or duck with figs and raspberry balsamic, and expect to pay around €35 a head for a full meal. Daily 12.30–2.30pm & 8–10.30pm; closed Wed eve, & Tues in winter.
Osteria Vinolento Via Vittorio Emanuele 112 ☎339 502

2178. A cheering little wine shop and *osteria*, where all the pasta is home-made, and all ingredients carefully sourced from friends, family and fair-trade producers. Try warm wild boar pâté with *crostini* (€8), aubergine ravioli with organic tomato, ricotta and pesto (€8.50) or roast pork with wild fennel (€12). June–Sept Tues–Sat 12.30–2.30pm & 8–10.30pm; Sept–June Tues–Fri 8–10.30pm, Sat & Sun 12.30–2.30pm & 8–10.30pm.

Città di Castello

CITTÀ DI CASTELLO is a charming and little-visited town some 56km to the north of Perugia in the Upper Tiber valley, with a sedate and ordered medieval centre that's well worth a few hours. It's also increasingly the focus for visitors staying in the many rented villas and farmhouses in hills to the east and west. In late August and early September the town becomes busier than usual during its renowned **Festival of**

Chamber Music (☎075 852 2823, ⓦfestivalnazioni.com), dedicated to a different country each year.

Once an important Roman centre – the grid-iron of streets is virtually the only legacy – today the plain-bound site preserves just a handful of fairly mediocre medieval monuments. The town's main attractions are a trio of museums and an art gallery, along with some quiet, pleasant medieval streets.

10 Pinacoteca

Via della Cannoniera 22 • Tues–Sun: April–Oct 10am–1pm & 2.30–6.30pm; Nov–March 10am–1pm & 3–6pm • €6 • ☎0758 554 202, ⓦdcnet.it

Foremost among the town's museums is the **Pinacoteca** at the southern edge of town, one of the region's best art galleries after Perugia's. The collection makes up in quality what it lacks in quantity, taking in works by **Raphael**, **Signorelli**, **Ghirlandaio** and **Lorenzetti**, plus a wondrous *Maestà* by the anonymous fourteenth-century Maestro di Città di Castello. There are also several sculptures, the most notable by Ghiberti, and a glittering reliquary of Florentine origin, dating from 1420.

The Museo del Duomo

Piazza Gabriotti • Oct–March Tues–Sun 10am–1pm & 2.30–6.30pm; April–Sept Tues–Sun 9.30am–1pm & 2.30–7pm • €5 • ⓦmuseoduomocdc.it

The banal, reworked **Duomo** warrants a call for its smart twelve-room museum, the **Museo del Duomo**, entered to the right of the church. It contains a completely unexpected collection of big-name paintings, including major works by Rosso Fiorentino, Giulio Romano and Pinturicchio. Even better is the **Treasure of Canoscio**, a precious hoard of sixth-century silver chalices dug up in 1932.

Signposted from the Duomo, the recently restored **Campanile Cilindrico** (Tues–Sun 10am–1pm & 3–6pm, open daily in Aug; €4) is a round belltower that's worth the climb for its fine views.

Collezione Tessile di Tela Umbra

Piazza A. Costa • Mon 9am–noon, Tues–Sun 10am–1pm & 3–6pm (workshop open Mon–Fri 8am–1pm & 3.30–6.30pm, Sat & Sun 10.30am–1pm & 3.30–6.30pm) • €3.50 • ☎0785 59 071, ⓦsistemamuseo.it

The third of the town's triumvirate of museums is the fascinating **Collezione Tessile di Tela Umbra**, just off the main square. The museum traces the history of textiles in the Upper Tiber valley, though in many ways the more interesting part of the concern is the original workshop, which continues to employ local women and still – almost uniquely in Italy – uses traditional hand-worked looms.

Palazzo Albizzini

Via degli Albizzini 1 • Tues–Sat 9.30am–12.30pm & 2.30–6pm, Sun 10.30am–12.30pm & 3–6pm; closes 1hr earlier in winter • €6, or joint ticket with the Ex Seccatoi €10 • ☎075 855 4649, ⓦfonazioneburri.org

Just north of the Collezione Tessile is the **Palazzo Albizzini**, off Piazza Garibaldi. It's home to the **Collezione Burri**, an extensive collection of large sculptural works by local-born artist Alberto Burri, one of the most significant figures of twentieth-century Italian art. If you have come to the town from the south you'll probably have seen the **Ex Seccatoi del Tobacco**, distinctive and colossal buildings on Via Pierucci that were once used to dry tobacco: today they house some of Burri's larger works (same ticket and hours).

Centro delle Tradizioni Popolari

Località Garavelle • Tues–Sun: April–Oct 8.30am–12.30pm & 3–7pm; Nov–March 8.30am–12.30pm & 2–6pm • €3.70 • Five daily buses from Piazza Garibaldi

A couple of kilometres south, in the hamlet of **GARAVELLE** is one of Umbria's best folk museums, the **Centro delle Tradizioni Popolari**. It's located in an eighteenth-century farmhouse, preserved with all the accoutrements of daily life – pots, pans, furniture and so forth, plus a range of exhibits covering rural activities such as wine making and weaving.

10

ARRIVAL AND DEPARTURE

By train The train station is east of the *centro storico*, outside the old walls. Città di Castello is on the FCU line. Destinations Perugia (12 daily; 1hr 20min); Sansepolcro (10 daily; 20min).

By bus Buses arrive at Piazza Garibaldi, inside the walls on the eastern side of town. There are regular connections with Arezzo, Florence, Urbino, Gubbio, Todi and Rome.

CITTÀ DI CASTELLO

By car There is a large, free car park just outside the walls to the west of town.

Tourist office In the Logge Bufalini just off Piazza Matteotti (Mon–Fri 9am–1pm & 3.30–6.30pm, Sat 9.30am–12.30pm & 3.30–6.30pm, Sun 9.30am–12.30pm; ☎075 855 4922, ⊛cittadicastello.regioneumbria.eu); deals with the whole Upper Tiber region.

ACCOMMODATION

Camping La Montesca 1km west of town on the minor road to Monte San Marina ☎075 855 8566, ⊛lamontesca.it. A pleasant, rural campsite, open May–Sept. Pitches **€22.50**

Residenza Antica Canonica Via S. Florido 23 ☎347 156 4910, ⊛umbriaholidays.net. Right next to the Museo del Duomo. Accommodation in recently restored

apartments in a Renaissance *palazzo*, tastefully furnished and with wood beams and frescoes in some rooms. **€100**

Tiferno Piazza Raffaello Sanzio 13 ☎075 855 0331, ⊛hoteltiferno.it. Centrally located four-star where the large, traditionally styled rooms have Burri prints on the walls. There are even some originals in the common areas. **€126**

EATING AND DRINKING

Caffetteria del Corso Corso Vittorio Emanuele 1 ☎075 855 4268. Just off the main piazza, this is the place for a great coffee, preferably accompanied by one of the scrumptious *cornetti* or brioche. Also a good choice for a glass of wine with local hams and cheeses, or an ice cream. Mon–Sat all day.

Il Cacciatore Via della Braccina 10 ☎075 852 0882. Downstairs in a medieval cellar, this is a traditionally styled *osteria* with a daily changing menu of simple regional dishes (*secondi* from €6). Wed–Sun 12.30–2.30pm.

L'Accademia Via del Modello 1 ☎075 852 3120. Come for a glass of wine and *aperitivo* snacks on the long counter in the front room, or for dinner upstairs. There are local

salami and heavenly unpasteurized cheeses, home-made bread with onion, fennel seeds or hazelnuts, and a great choice of handmade pasta – try it stuffed with pork and dressed with *pancetta* and lemon. A full meal will cost €25–30. Tues–Sun 8–10.30pm.

La Lea Via S. Florido 38/A ☎075 852 1678. A locals' favourite a short way south of the cathedral, with mains from €7–14.50 and a good selection of tasty *primi* from €5–12. Go for simple dishes like sausages or a *cotoletta* if you're on a budget; otherwise spend a bit more to have the grilled lamb, or, in season, a steak with porcini mushrooms. Tues–Sun 12.30–2.30pm & 8–10.30pm.

Gubbio

GUBBIO is the most thoroughly medieval of the Umbrian towns, an immediately likeable place that's hung on to its charm despite an ever-increasing influx of visitors. The streets are picture-book pretty, with houses of rosy-pink stone and seas of orange-tiled roofs; the setting is equally gorgeous with the forest-clad mountains of the Apennines rearing up behind. A broad and largely unspoilt plain stretches out in front of the town, and the whole ensemble – especially on grey, windswept days – maintains Gubbio's tough, mountain-outpost atmosphere.

A powerful medieval *comune*, and always important as the gateway to Ravenna and the Adriatic (it was a key point on the Roman Via Flaminia), these days it's a town apart, not really part of Umbria, Tuscany or Le Marche – one reason it's been spared the onslaught of modernity. Buses arrive in the **Piazza dei Quaranta Martiri** at the foot of town, named in memory of forty citizens shot by the Germans in 1944, a reprisal for partisan attacks in the surrounding hills. It's a ten-minute walk uphill from here to the central **Piazza Grande** and Gubbio's main sights.

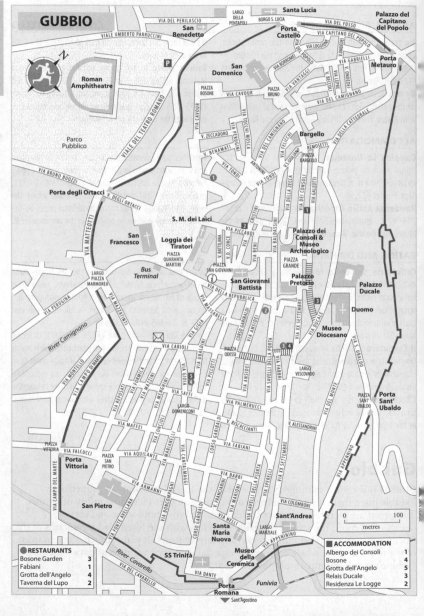

GUBBIO

RESTAURANTS
Bosone Garden	3
Fabiani	1
Grotta dell'Angelo	4
Taverna del Lupo	2

ACCOMMODATION
Albergo dei Consoli	1
Bosone	4
Grotta dell'Angelo	5
Relais Ducale	3
Residenza Le Logge	2

GUBBIO'S DOORS OF DEATH

Gubbio's **Porte della Morte**, the "doors of death", are as controversial as the *ceri*, as no one can quite agree on their origins. Almost unique to the town (there are a few others in Assisi and southern France), these are narrow, bricked-up doorways wedged into the facades of its medieval townhouses (with the best examples in Via dei Consoli). The party line is that they were used to carry a coffin out of a house, and then, having been tainted with death, were sealed up out of superstitious fear. Nice theory, and very Italian, but judging by the constricted stairways behind the doors, their purpose was probably defensive – the main door could be barricaded, leaving the more easily defended passageway as the only entrance.

10

Palazzo dei Consoli

Centre-stage is the immense and austere fourteenth-century **Palazzo dei Consoli**, whose crenellated outline and 98m campanile immediately grab your attention. Probably designed by Matteo Gattapone, who was also responsible for Spoleto's Ponte delle Torri, the palace took a couple of hundred years to build and required the levelling of vast tracts of the medieval town, mainly to accommodate the huge and windswept Piazza Grande.

Museo Archeologico

Piazza Grande • Daily: April–Oct 10am–1pm & 3–6pm; Nov–March 10am–1pm & 2.30–5.30pm • €5

Inside the *palazzo*, the **Museo Archeologico** houses a typical miscellany, unremarkable except for the famous **Eugubine Tablets**, Umbria's most important archeological find. Discovered in 1444 by an illiterate shepherd, later conned into swapping his priceless treasure-trove for a worthless piece of land, the seven bronze tablets are more or less the only extant record of the ancient Umbrian language, a vernacular tongue without written characters. The bastardized Etruscan and Latin of their religious texts were aimed at producing a phonetic translation of the dialect using the main languages of the day. Gubbio was close to the shrine of the so-called Apennine Jove, a major pagan deity visited by pilgrims from all over Italy, so the tablets were probably the work of Roman and Etruscan priests taking advantage of the established order to impose their religious cults in a region where their languages weren't understood. Most importantly, they suggest Romans, Etruscans and Umbrians achieved some sort of coexistence, refuting a long-held belief that succeeding civilizations wiped one another out.

Admission to the museum also gets you into the **Pinacoteca** at the top of the palace, worth a look for works by the Gubbian School – one of central Italy's earliest, and a collection of ponderous fourteenth-century furniture.

Palazzo Pretorio

The lesser **Palazzo Pretorio** was built to the same plan as the Palazzo dei Consoli. Deliberately dominating and humbling, it was what medieval civic pride was all about, an attempt to express power and supremacy in bricks and mortar. Behind a plain, square facade (there's a small hole top-right where criminals were hung in a cage called *la gogna* – from *vergogna* or "shame") is a cavernous baronial hall, the Salone dell'Arengo, where council officials and leading citizens met to discuss business. The word "harangue" derives from *arengo*, suggesting proceedings frequently boiled over.

The Duomo

Via Ducale • Daily 9.30am–5pm; closes earlier in winter • Free

To the north of the Piazza Grande lurks a not very inspiring thirteenth-century **Duomo**, partly redeemed by the odd fresco, twelfth-century stained glass, and some arches gracefully curved, apparently to emulate the meeting of hands in prayer. There are also a pair of carved **organ lofts** that for once don't look as if they'd be more at home in a fairground. The adjoining **Museo Diocesano** (June–Sept Tues–Sun 10.30am–6pm; Oct–May Thurs–Sun 10.30am–5pm; €5), to the right as you face the facade at the corner of Via Federico da Montefeltro, is well worth a few minutes, mainly for a florid Flemish cope, presented to the cathedral by Pope Marcellus II, who was born in Gubbio.

Palazzo Ducale

Via Federico da Montefeltro • Tues–Sun 8.30am–7.30pm, ticket office closes 30min earlier • €5

The plain-faced Gothic cathedral is overshadowed by the **Palazzo Ducale** in Via Federico da Montefeltro opposite, built over an earlier Lombard palace by the Dukes of Montefeltro as a scaled-down copy of their more famous palace in Urbino. The **courtyard** is particularly attractive, but the interior, stripped of most of its original furniture and other trappings, is a trifle dull, despite some fine views from the windows and the harmonious scale of the rooms.

Via dei Consoli

There are dozens of picturesque odds and ends around the streets, which are as wonderfully explorable as any in the region. The **Bargello**, the medieval police station, in Via dei Consoli – the main medieval street (and home to most of the ceramic shops) – is worth tracking down and gives you the chance to survey the adjacent **Fontana dei Matti** (the "fountain of the mad"), undistinguished but for the tradition that anyone walking round it three times will end up mad.

The Basilica di Sant'Ubaldo and around

Summer daily 10am–12.30pm & 2.30–5.30pm; winter same hours but closed Tues & Wed mornings • Free

On the hillside above the town stands the **Basilica di Sant'Ubaldo**, which has some great views (even better ones if you climb up to the **Rocca**). There's not much to see in the basilica itself, except the body of the town's patron saint, St Ubaldo, missing three fingers – they were hacked off by his manservant as a religious keepsake. You can't miss the big wooden pillars (*ceri*) featured in Gubbio's annual **Corsa dei Ceri** (see box below).

The cable car

March daily 10am–1.15pm & 2.30–5.30pm, Sun till 6pm; April & May 10am–1.15pm & 2.30–6.30pm, Sun till 7pm; June daily 9.30am–1.15pm & 2.30–7pm, Sun 9am–7.30pm; July to mid-Sept daily 9am–8pm; mid-Sept to end Sept daily 9.30am–1.15pm & 2.30–7pm, Sun 9am–7.30pm; Oct daily 10am–1.15pm & 2.30–6pm; Nov–Feb Thurs–Tues 10am–1.15pm & 2.30–5pm • €5 return

There are several ways up to the basilica, one being via the steep track that strikes off from behind the Duomo. However, it's quicker and far more fun – unless you have no head for heights – to take the **cable car** (*funivia*) from Porta Romana, over on the eastern side of town; you jump on small two-person cradles, which then dangle precariously over the woods and crags below as you shudder slowly upwards. From the

---

THE CORSA DEI CERI

Little known outside Italy but second only to Siena's Palio in terms of exuberance and bizarre pageantry, the **Corsa dei Ceri** (ⓦceri.it) takes place on May 15 every year. The rules and rigmarole of the 900-year-old ceremony are mind-boggling, but they boil down to three teams racing from Piazza della Signoria to the basilica, carrying the *ceri* (each representing a different saint) on wooden stretchers. By iron-clad tradition, the *cero* of St Ubaldo always wins, the other teams having to ensure they're in the basilica before the doors are shut by the leaders. The main event starts at 6pm.

FESTIVALS AND EVENTS IN GUBBIO

Gubbio has a lively calendar of festivals. Apart from the spectacular Corsa dei Ceri (see box opposite), the Summer Festival sees performances of classical music concerts in atmospheric venues around town (mid-July to mid-Aug; ask at the tourist office for a programme). The Torneo dei Quartieri is a few days of medieval fun and games in mid-August, culminating in a costumed parade in Piazza Grande. The medieval theme continues with the Palio delle Balestre on the last Sunday in May, with a crossbow contest against neighbouring Sansepolcro.

10

top there's a good view of the first-century-BC **Roman theatre** on the outskirts of town, which hosts events during the summer months; ask at the tourist office for details.

Near the cable-car exit at the bottom of the hill is the small **Museo della Ceramica** at Via Dante 24 (daily 9am–1pm & 3.30–7.30pm; free), which holds a collection of glazed ceramics from the sixteenth to the twentieth centuries.

ARRIVAL AND INFORMATION   GUBBIO

By train The nearest train station is at Fossato di Vico, 19km south on the Rome–Foligno–Ancona line; there are twelve connecting shuttle buses to Gubbio Mon–Sat, five on Sun.

By bus Gubbio is easiest approached by the regular bus from Perugia on the mostly pretty cross-country SS298 road. Destinations Città di Castello (change at Umbertide; 4

daily Mon–Sat; 1hr 10min); Rome (1 daily; 2hr 40min); Urbino (1 daily; 1hr 30min).

Tourist office Via della Repubblica 15 (March–Oct Mon–Fri 8.30am–1.45pm & 3.30–6.30pm, Sat 9am–1pm & 3–6.30pm, Sun 9.30am–1pm & 3–6pm; Oct–March closes 30min earlier Mon–Sat & closed Sun afternoon mid-Jan to Feb; ☎075 922 0693, ⓦcomune.gubbio.pg.it)).

ACCOMMODATION

Albergo dei Consoli Via dei Consoli 59 ☎075 922 0639, ⓦurbaniweb.com. Formerly a rather humble hotel that has been transformed into a four-star; has the advantage of a great position just a few steps down the hill from the Palazzo dei Consoli. **€130**

Bosone Via XX Settembre 22 ☎075 922 0688, ⓦhotelbosone.com. A long-established and traditional four-star hotel in a medieval palace with spectacular frescoed ceilings and lots of antiques. There's a good restaurant garden, too. **€140**

Grotta dell'Angelo Via Gioia 47 ☎075 927 1747,

ⓦgrottadellangelo.it. A reliable two-star option in a peaceful side-street; there's also an excellent and moderately priced restaurant. **€60**

Relais Ducale Via Galeotti 19 ☎075 922 0157, ⓦrelaisducale.com. A classy, intimate four-star just below the cathedral and entered from one of two tiny alleys – Via Ducale or Via Galleotti (signed off the east side of Piazza Grande). **€170**

Residenza Le Logge Via Piccardi 7–9 ☎075 927 7574. Pleasant wood-beamed rooms give this *residenza* a homely feel, plus there's a pretty garden. **€90**

EATING

Gubbio boasts a good selection of restaurants, with some high-quality, if rather expensive, options close to the Palazzo dei Consoli. Cheaper places for snacks, sandwiches or pizza *al taglio* are found in the grid of streets to the south, and towards the northern end of Via dei Consoli.

Bosone Garden Via XX Settembre 22 ☎075 922 1246. The restaurant of the *Bosone* hotel (see above) is open to non-patrons, and, thanks to its garden, is the nicest place to eat outdoors in the summer. Tasting menus from €25, with local dishes including pasta with goose *ragù*. Tues–Sun 12.30–2.30pm & 8–10.30pm.

Fabiani Piazza del Quaranta Martiri 26 ☎075 927 4639. Fine, friendly place, with several dining rooms set in part of the elegant Palazzo Fabiani; attractive terrace for summer alfresco dining. Good value (meals from around €30) given the quality of the cooking. Truffles are a speciality in season. Noon–3pm & 7–10.30pm; closed Tues.

Grotta dell'Angelo Via Gioia 47 ☎075 927 3438. Annexed to the *Grotta dell'Angelo* hotel (see above), offering very tasty and reasonably priced dishes such as triangles of pasta stuffed with ricotta and wild greens dressed with truffle (€8) in a wonderful dining room. 12.30–2pm & 7.30–9.30pm; closed Tues.

Taverna del Lupo Via Ansidei 21 ☎075 927 4368. A smart and long-established place in a medieval setting, popular for its classic Umbrian dishes and excellent truffle risotto. Tasting menus from €27.50, excluding drinks. Tues–Sun noon–3pm & 7–11pm, Aug & Sept open daily.

10

Assisi

ASSISI is already too well known for its own good, thanks to **St Francis**, Italy's premier saint and founder of the Franciscan order, which, with its various splinter groups, forms the world's biggest religious order. Had the man not been born here in 1182 the town wouldn't be thronged with visitors and pilgrims for ten months of the year, but then neither would it have the **Basilica of St Francis**, one of the greatest monuments to thirteenth- and fourteenth-century Italian art. You'll probably feel it's worth putting up with the crowds and increasingly overwhelming commercialism, but you may not want to hang around once you've seen all there is to see – something which can easily be done in a day. That said, Assisi quietens down in the evening, and it does retain considerable medieval hill-town charm.

The Basilica di San Francesco

Lower Church Mon–Sat 6am–6.45pm, closes 5.45pm in winter; **Upper Church** Mon–Sat 8.30am–7.45pm, closes 6.45pm in winter; entry may be restricted during services and on Sun morning • Free • ⓦ sanfrancescoassisi.org

Pilgrims and art lovers alike usually make straight for the **Basilica di San Francesco**, justifiably famed as Umbria's single greatest glory, and one of the most overwhelming collections of art outside a gallery anywhere in the world. Started in 1228, two years after the saint's death, and financed by donations that flooded in from all over Europe, it's not as grandiose as some religious shrines, though it still strikes you as being a long way from the embodiment of Franciscan principles. If you don't mind compromised ideals, the two churches making up the basilica – one built on top of the other – are a treat.

The Lower Church

The sombre **Lower Church** – down the steps to the left – comes earlier, both structurally and artistically. The complicated floor plan and claustrophobic low-lit vaults were

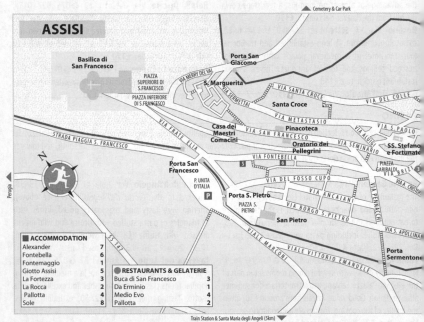

intended to create a mood of calm and meditative introspection – an effect added to by brown-robed monks, a ban on photography and a rule of silence. Francis lies under the floor in a **crypt** only brought to light in 1818 after 52 days of digging (entrance midway down the nave). He was hidden after his funeral for safekeeping, and nowadays endures almost continuous Masses in dozens of languages.

Frescoes cover almost every available space and span a century of continuous artistic development. Stilted early works by anonymous painters influenced by the Byzantines sit alongside Roman painters such as Cavallini, who with Cimabue pioneered the move from mosaic to naturalism and the "new" medium of fresco. They were followed by the best of the Sienese School, **Simone Martini** and **Pietro Lorenzetti**, whose paintings are the ones to make a real point of seeing.

Martini's frescoes are in the **Cappella di San Martino** (1322–26), the first chapel on the left as you enter the nave. He was given free rein in the chapel, and every detail, right down to the floor and stained glass, follows his drawings, adding up to a unified scheme unique in Italy. Lorenzetti's works, dominated by a powerful *Crucifixion*, are in the transept to the left of the main altar. Vaults above the altar itself contain four magnificent frescoes, complicated but colourful allegories of the virtues on which Francis founded his order: Poverty, Chastity and Obedience. Once thought to have been the work of Giotto, they're now attributed to one of the church's army of unknown artists. The big feature in the right transept is Cimabue's over-restored *Madonna, Child and Angels with St Francis*, a painting Ruskin described as "the noblest depiction of the Virgin in Christendom". Look out for the famous portrait of Francis and for the much-reproduced fresco of St Clare on the wall to its left.

If time allows check out the **cloisters**, accessible from the rear right-hand side of the Lower Church, and the Treasury, or **Museo del Tesoro e Collezione F.M. Perkins** (April–Oct Mon–Sat 9.30am–5pm; donation requested), reached via the apse of the Lower Church. The latter, often passed by, contains a rich collection of paintings – including works by Pietro Lorenzetti and Masolino da Panicale.

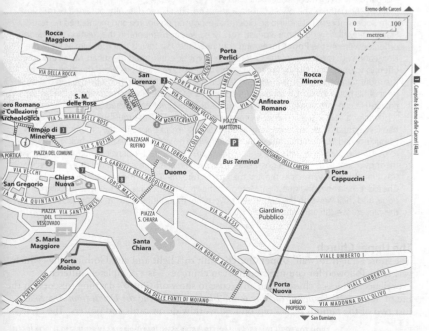

10

ST FRANCIS

The most extraordinary figure the Italian Church has produced, **St Francis** was a revolutionary figure who took Christianity back to basics. The impact he had on the evolution of the Catholic Church stands without parallel, and everything he accomplished in his short life was achieved by nothing more persuasive than the power of preaching and personal example. Dante placed him alongside another messianic figure, John the Baptist, and his appeal has remained undiminished – Mussolini called him "*il piu santo dei santi*" (the most saintly of the saints).

The events of his life, though doubtless embellished by myth, are well chronicled. He was born in Assisi in 1182, the son of a wealthy merchant and a Provençal woman – which is why he replaced his baptismal name, Giovanni, with Francesco (Little Frenchman). The Occitan literature of Provence, with its troubadour songs and courtly love poems, was later to be the making of Francis as a poet and speaker. One of the earliest writers in the vernacular, Francis laid the foundation of a great Franciscan literary tradition – his *Fioretti* and famous *Canticle to the Sun* ("brother sun … sister moon") stand comparison with the best of medieval verse.

In line with the early life of most male saints, his formative years were full of drinking and womanizing; he was, says one chronicler, "the first instigator of evil, and behind none in foolishness". Illness and imprisonment in a Perugian jail incubated the first seeds of contemplation. Abstinence and solitary wanderings soon followed. The call from God, the culmination of several visions, came in Assisi in 1209, when the crucifix in San Damiano bowed to him and told him to repair God's Church. Francis took the injunction literally, sold his father's stock of cloth and gave the money to Damiano's priest, who refused it.

Francis subsequently renounced his inheritance in the Piazza del Comune: before a large crowd and his outraged father, he stripped naked in a symbolic rejection of wealth and worldly shackles. Adopting the peasant's grey sackcloth (the brown Franciscan habit came later), he began to beg, preach and mix with lepers, a deliberate embodiment of Christ's invocation to the Apostles "to heal the sick, and carry neither purse, nor scrip [money], nor shoes". His message was disarmingly simple: throw out the materialistic trappings of daily life and return to a love of God rooted in poverty, chastity and obedience. Furthermore, learn to see in the beauty and profusion of the natural world the all-pervasive hand of the Divine – a keystone of humanist thought and a departure from the doom-laden strictures of the Dark Ages.

In time he gathered his own twelve apostles and, after some difficulty, obtained permission from Pope Innocent III to found an order that espoused no dogma and maintained no rule. Francis himself never became a priest. In 1212 he was instrumental in the creation of a second order for women, the **Poor Clares**, and continued the vast travels that took him as far as the Holy Land with the armies of the Crusades. In Egypt he confronted the sultan, Melek el-Kamel, offering to undergo a trial by fire to prove his faith. In 1224 Francis received the stigmata on the mountaintop at La Verna. Two years later, nursing his exhausted body, he died on the mud floor of his hovel in Assisi, having scorned the offer of grander accommodation at the bishop's palace. His canonization followed swiftly, in 1228, in a service conducted by Pope Gregory.

However, a split in the Franciscan Order was inevitable. Francis's message and movement had few sympathizers in the wealthy and morally bankrupt papacy of the time, and while his popularity had obliged the Vatican to applaud while he was alive, the papacy quickly moved in to quash the purist elements and encourage more "moderate" tendencies. Gradually it shaped the movement to its own designs, institutionalizing Francis's message in the process. Despite this, Francis's achievement as the first man to fracture the rigid orthodoxy of the hierarchical Church remains beyond question. Moreover, the Franciscans have not lost their ideological edge, and their views on the primacy of poverty are thought by many to be out of favour with the present Vatican administration.

The Upper Church

The more straightforward **Upper Church**, built to a light and airy Gothic plan – which was to be followed for countless Franciscan churches – is a completely different experience. It's less a church than an excuse to show off **Giotto**'s dazzling frescoes on the life of St Francis. *Francis Preaching to the Birds* and *Driving the Devils from Arezzo* are just two of the famous scenes reproduced worldwide on cards and posters. The cycle

FROM TOP PONTE DELLE TORRI, SPOLETO (P.658); ASSISI (P.642); PIAZZA SAN BENEDETTO, NORCIA (P.661) >

starts on the right-hand wall up by the main altar and continues clockwise. Giotto was still in his 20s when he accepted the commission, having been recommended for the job by Cimabue, whose own frescoes – almost ruined now by the oxidation of badly chosen pigments and further damaged in the 1997 earthquake – fill large parts of the apse and transepts. In the vaults, several harsh areas of bare plaster stand as graphic monuments to the collapse of that year.

10 The Pinacoteca

Via San Francesco • Daily: March–May, Sept & Oct 10am–1pm & 2–6pm; June–Aug 10am–1pm & 2–7pm; Nov–Feb 10am–1pm & 2–5pm • €3, or joint ticket with Foro Romano & Rocca Maggiore €8 • ☎ 075 815 5234

Via San Francesco leads back to the town centre from the basilica. Partway along the street on the left is the Palazzo Vallemani, the site of Assisi's excellent **Pinacoteca**. It would be easy to ignore this after the rich artistic pickings of the basilica, but the gallery is well worth the admission, not least for the many detached frescoes rescued from churches and other buildings around Assisi, among them important works by the Gubbian artist Ottaviano Nelli. The displays are enhanced by good English commentaries.

Oratorio dei Pellegrini

Via San Francesco • Mon–Sat 10am–noon & 4–6pm • Free

Beyond the Pinacoteca, a little further down Via San Francesco, are the remains of the fifteenth-century **Oratorio dei Pellegrini**, the hospice for pilgrims, frescoed inside and out by local painters Mezzastris and Matteo da Gualdo – appealing but modest offerings after the basilica (and often out of bounds because of praying nuns).

The Foro Romano and Tempio di Minerva

The **Foro Romano e Collezione Archeologica**, entered just off Piazza del Comune at Via Portica 2 (daily: March–May, Sept & Oct 10am–1pm & 2–6pm; June–Aug 10am–1pm & 2–7pm; Nov–Feb 10am–1pm & 2–5pm; €4, joint ticket with Pinacoteca & Rocca Maggiore €8), is housed in the crypt of the now defunct church of San Niccolò. The classical remains include an excavated street – probably part of the old Roman forum – buried under the Piazza del Comune. The piazza itself is dominated by the so-called **Tempio di Minerva**, an enticing and perfectly preserved classical facade from the first century, concealing a dull, if beautifully restored, seventeenth-century Baroque conversion; it was the only thing Goethe was bothered about seeing when he came to Assisi – the basilica he avoided, calling it a "Babylonian pile". Francis's birthplace lies just south of the piazza, marked by the Chiesa Nuova, a dreary church.

The Duomo

Piazza San Ruffino • Daily: summer 7am–12.30pm & 2.30–7pm, Aug 7am–7pm; winter 7am–1pm & 2.30–6pm

A short hike in the other direction up the steep Via di San Rufino brings you to the thirteenth-century **Duomo** with a typical and very lovely three-tiered Umbrian facade and sumptuously carved central doorway. The only point of interest in a boring interior is the font used to baptize St Francis, St Clare and – by a historical freak – the future Emperor Frederick II, born prematurely in a field outside the town. Off the right (south) nave, there's the small **Museo Diocesano** (mid-March to mid-Oct Thurs–Tues 10am–1pm & 3–6pm except Aug daily 10am–6pm; rest of year Thurs–Tues 10am–1pm & 2.30–5.30pm; €3.50), with a handful of good paintings, including a 1470 work by Niccolò Alunno, and an atmospheric crypt, the **Cripta di San Rufino** (same hours & ticket), entered outside down steps to the right of the facade.

Rocca Magglore

Via dell Rocca • Daily 10am–dusk; €5, €8 with Pinacoteca & Foro Romano

The cathedral makes a good point from which to strike off uphill for the **Rocca Maggiore**, one of the bigger and better preserved castles in the region, rising dramatically from the town walls, with some all-embracing views the reward after a stiff climb.

The Basilica di Santa Chiara

Piazza Santa Chiara • Daily 6.30am–noon & 2–7pm, closes 6pm in winter • Free

Below the Duomo, on the pedestrianized Piazza Santa Chiara, stands the **Basilica di Santa Chiara**, burial place of St Francis's devoted early companion, who at the age of 17 founded the Order of the Poor Clares, the female wing of the Franciscans. By some peculiar and not terribly dignified quirk she's also the patron saint of television. The church was consecrated in 1265 and is a virtual facsimile of the basilica up the road, down to the simple facade and opulent rose window. The scantily decorated interior has the body of St Clare herself and the Byzantine crucifix famous for having bowed to Francis and commanded him to embark on his sacred mission to repair God's Church (see box, p.644).

San Damiano

Daily 10am–noon & 2–6pm, closes 4.30pm in winter • Free

You're never long off the Francis trail in Assisi. **San Damiano**, a peaceful spot of genuine monastic charm, is one of its highlights, and is easily reached by taking the Via Borgo Aretino beyond the basilica and following signs from the Porta Nuova, a steep downhill walk of about fifteen minutes. Original home to the Poor Clares, and one of St Francis's favourite spots (he is thought to have written his well-known *Canticle to the Sun* here), the church, cloisters and rustic setting preserve – almost uniquely in Assisi – a sense of the original Franciscan ideals of humility and simplicity often absent in the rest of the town.

Santa Maria degli Angeli

Daily 6.15am–12.50pm & 2.30–7.30pm • Free

From the train station you can see the town's other major attraction, the vast but uninspiring **Santa Maria degli Angeli**, built in the seventeenth century and rebuilt after an earthquake in 1832. Somewhere in its Baroque bowels are the remains of the **Porziuncola**, a tiny chapel that was effectively the first Franciscan monastery. Francis lived here after founding the order in 1208, attracted by its then remote and wooded surroundings, and in time was joined by other monks and hermits who built a series of cells and mud huts in the vicinity. Today the church is crammed full of largely fourth-rate works of art and is a long way from the Franciscan ideal.

ARRIVAL AND DEPARTURE · ASSISI

By train There are very frequent (at least hourly) trains to Foligno (via Spello) and Terontola (via Perugia). Bus #C connects the station, which is 5km away to the southwest of the centre, with Piazza Matteotti every 30min.
Destinations Foligno (13 daily; 15min); Spello (17 daily; 9min); Terontola (12 daily; connections to Chiusi, Orvieto, Arezzo, Florence and Rome; 1hr 10min).

By bus Buses connect regularly with surrounding towns – especially Perugia – putting down and picking up in Piazza Matteotti, in the east of the town above the Duomo. In addition, two buses a day leave for Rome and one for Florence, from Piazza Unità d'Italia.

Destinations Florence (2 weekly Mon & Fri; 2hr 30min); Montefalco (from Santa Maria degli Angeli; 1 daily Mon–Sat; 40min); Naples (1 daily; 5hr 15min); Norcia and the Valnerina (from Santa Maria degli Angeli; 1 daily Mon–Sat; 2hr 10min); Rome (2 daily; 3hr 10min); Siena (from Santa Maria degli Angeli; 1–2 daily; 2hr 5min); Spello (2–5 daily Mon–Sat; 30min).

By car If you are driving, note that the centre of town is closed to traffic: your best bet is to park either in Piazza Matteotti at the top (eastern) end of the town, or below the basilica in Piazza Unità d'Italia.

INFORMATION

Tourist office Western end of Piazza del Comune (April–Oct Mon–Sat 8am–2pm & 3–6.30pm, Sun 10am–1pm & 3–6pm; Nov–March Mon–Fri 8am–2pm & 2–5pm, Sat 9am–1pm & 3–6pm, Sun 9am–1pm & 2–5pm; ☎ 075 813 8681, ⓦ assisi.regioneumbria.eu).

ACCOMMODATION

Assisi offers a wide range of accommodation, but the supply is often only just adequate for the number of visitors, so advance booking is highly advisable, and essential if you plan to visit over Easter or during the Festa di San Francesco (Oct 3–4) or Calendimaggio (early May). July and August are low season in Assisi, when hotels will often lower their rates. The tourist office has a full list of lodgings, including over thirty rooms for rent and can also supply details of B&Bs, agriturismi and pilgrim hostels. Spello is close enough to make seeing Assisi easy. Wherever you choose to stay, avoid the concentration of rooms and hotels in Santa Maria degli Angeli or the grim village of Bastia, 4km out of Assisi.

★ **Alexander** Piazza Chiesa Nuova 6 ☎075 816 190, ⓦhotelalexanderassisi.it. This nine-room hotel has an excellent position just off Piazza del Comune, but benefits from its location on a quiet piazza. The rooms are wood-beamed and decorated in neutral tones, with spotless en-suite bathrooms. Breakfast is taken in the nearby *Dei Priori* hotel. €100

Fontebella Via Fontebella 25 ☎075 812 883, ⓦfontebella.com. Though a little faded in places, this is still the town's most elegant and intimate choice. Ask for a room on one of the top floors for great panoramas. €260

Giotto Assisi Via Fontebella 41 ☎075 812 209, ⓦhotelgiottoassisi.it. In business since 1899, this four-star has recently been completely renovated. The rooms are very comfortable, if a little bland, and there are fine views from the terrace restaurant. It's the only hotel with parking in the *centro storico*. €140

La Fortezza Vicolo della Fortezza 19/B ☎075 812 418, ⓦlafortezzahotel.com. Friendly two-star with just seven rooms in a perfect position next to Piazza del Comune, with thoughtful touches such as free water and free tea and coffee in the afternoon; the co-owned restaurant is also excellent. €75

La Rocca Via di Porta Perlici 27 ☎075 812 284, ⓦhotelarocca.it. This one-star situated at the end of the street beyond the Duomo has been managed by the same family since the 1950s. Of the thirty rooms, book one of the five with views; all have private bathroom. Breakfast not included. €59

Pallotta Via San Rufino 6 ☎075 812 307, ⓦpallottaassisi.it. A two-star in a good location between the Duomo and Piazza del Comune; also has a first-rate co-owned trattoria just off Piazza del Comune (see opposite). €79

Sole Corso Mazzini 35 ☎075 812 373, ⓦassisihotelsole.com. This functional two-star 1min walk from the Basilica di Santa Chiara has outdated decor but at least the rooms are a decent size. Ask for one of the ones with a little balcony or terrace. Breakfast not included. €70

HOSTEL AND CAMPING

Fontemaggio 3km east of town on Via S. Rufino Campagna ☎075 813 636, ⓦfontemaggio.it. Hostel/hotel with a 244-pitch campsite. The fairly rural setting is better than the sites you may see advertised towards Baschi on the other side of Assisi; there's also a decent shop to save you the trek into town for supplies. Dorms €25 including breakfast, rooms €52, pitches €17.50

EATING AND DRINKING

Buca di San Francesco Via Brizzi 1 ☎075 812 204. The *Buca* has been around for ever, and is generally a reliable choice for a decent meal, with typical dishes including handmade spaghetti with roast mushroom, beef and herbs (€9), chickpea soup (€7) and lamb cooked with wild herbs (€11). Tues–Sun 12.30–2.30pm & 8–10.30pm.

Da Erminio Via Montecavallo 19 ☎075 812 506. Located above the Duomo in a quiet corner, this restaurant is very good value, with a hearty fixed menu of the day for €16. Eating à la carte, you can expect to pay €25–30 per head. Dishes worth trying include rabbit cooked with ten different herbs, and the Chianina steak spiked with juniper berries. Noon–2.30pm & 7–9pm; closed Tues (except in Aug for lunch), Feb & first half of July.

Medio Evo Via dell'Arco dei Priori 4/B ☎075 813 068. This place is highly recommended for its excellent, creative cuisine. Pasta stuffed with pheasant and black truffle (€18) is a speciality; tasting menus start at €30 without wine and €40 with. The dimly lit, stone-vaulted space, enlivened with background jazz and bossa nova, is atmospheric at dinner. Tues–Sun 12.30–3pm & 7.30–10.45pm; Nov–Feb open Fri–Sun only.

ASSISI'S FESTIVALS

Assisi's main festivals are the Festa di San Francesco (Oct 3–4), commemorating the death of the saint, and Calendimaggio, three days of lively games and contests between the two parts of the city, "Parte de Sopra" and "Parte di Sotto", which takes place in early May.

★ **Pallotta** Via Volta Piana 2 ☎ 075 812 649. An unpretentious and welcoming trattoria with a lovely wood-beamed dining room just south of Piazza del Comune – arrive early for a table at lunch, when it's usually packed. *Primi* (€7–10) include *stringozzi alla Pallotta*, handmade pasta (without egg) served with mushroom, chilli flakes and a generous swirl of good, local olive oil. *Secondi* (€7.50–16) include suckling pig, lamb chops and braised pigeon; if you are on a budget, go for the daily set three-course menu with wine, €16. Noon–3pm & 7–10.30pm; closed Tues.

Spello and around

10

Ranged on broad terraces above the Vale of Spoleto, medieval and pink-stoned **SPELLO** is the best place for a taste of small-town Umbria if you haven't time or means to explore farther, being easy to reach by road and rail from Assisi or Spoleto.

Emperor Augustus gave land in the adjacent valley to faithful legionnaires who had reached the end of their careers, turning the town (Hispellum) into a sort of Roman retirement home in the process, an ambience it still rather retains. The walls and three gateways are the most obvious Roman remnants. Don't bother walking out to the paltry and overgrown remains of the old amphitheatre hidden away beyond the main highway to Assisi: you can see all you need to from the top of the town.

Santa Maria Maggiore

Piazza Matteotti • Daily: April–Oct 8.30am–noon & 3–7pm; Nov–March 8.30am–noon & 3–6pm • Free

By far the most distinguished sight in Spello is **Pinturicchio's fresco cycle** in the thirteenth-century church of **Santa Maria Maggiore**, about a third of the way up the town's winding and steep main street on Piazza Matteotti. The number-two Umbrian painter after Perugino, he left other important works in Siena (the Duomo), Rome (the Sistine Chapel, Borgia apartments) and a host of churches scattered over central Italy. The frescoes themselves are fresh and glowing from restoration, with Pinturicchio's famous details and colouring brought out to stunning effect. Unfortunately they're behind glass, which also means you can't get a closer look at the chapel's praised but faded fifteenth-century **ceramic pavement**.

Pinacoteca Civica

Piazza Matteotti • Tues–Sun: April–Sept 10.30am–1pm & 3–6.30pm; Oct–March 10.30am–12.30pm & 3.30–5.30pm • €4 • ☎ 0742 301 497

Almost immediately to the north of the church stands an excellent little art gallery, the **Pinacoteca Civica**, which is currently expanding its exhibition space. It contains a handful of masterpieces by local Umbrian painters, notably Niccolò Alunno, as well as some rare pieces of sculpture. One of the works newly on display is the extremely rare figure of Christ with movable arms: during Holy Week the arms could be raised for ceremonies involving depictions of the Crucifixion and lowered for those depicting the Deposition and Resurrection.

Sant'Andrea

Daily 10.30am–12.30pm & 3–5pm • Free

Further up the busy, steep main street on the right stands **Sant'Andrea**, a striking Gothic church with another Pinturicchio painting in the right transept brightening up the gloomy interior. Also look out for the looming crucifix attributed to the School of Giotto.

SPELLO'S CARPETS OF FLOWERS

In early June, Spello is scene of an **Infiorate festival**, when the town's streets are carpeted with flower-petal representations of religious scenes. To find out more, visit ⓦ infioratespello.it.

10

ARRIVAL AND INFORMATION
SPELLO

By train If you're coming by train from the south, note that you may have to change trains at Foligno for Spello. The station is a 10min walk from the centre of town.

Tourist office Piazza Matteotti 3 (Daily 9.30am–12.30pm & 3–5pm, usually opens and closes a bit later in summer; ☎ 0742 301 009, ⓦ prospello.it).

ACCOMMODATION

Il Cacciatore Via Giulia 42 ☎ 0742 651 141, ⓦ ilcacciatorehotel.com. A good-value three-star hotel, with fine views from some rooms and potentially noisier rooms looking out over the street. **€85**

La Bastiglia Via dei Molini 17 ☎ 0742 651 277, ⓦ labastiglia.com. Smart, four-star place, where most of the rooms command a fine view. The standard rooms are on the small side – it's worth paying a bit more for a superior or deluxe room. The two suites come with vast hydromassage baths and there's a good restaurant too (see below). **€100**

Palazzo Bocci Via Cavour 17 ☎ 0742 301 021, ⓦ palazzo bocci.com. Right in the centre of town, this upmarket option has a tranquil garden – the perfect place for evening *aperitivi* – and is also cosy in winter, with a large fireplace in the communal lounge. Ask for one of the frescoed rooms. **€160**

EATING AND DRINKING

Bar Giardino Bonci Via Garibaldi 10–12 ☎ 0742 651 397. There appears nothing special about this small bar until you take your drink or ice cream out to the wonderful panoramic garden terrace at the back. Light meals also served, starting from around €6. Summer 7am–midnight, winter 7am–10pm; closed Mon.

Caffè Porta Consolare Piazza Kennedy 7 ☎ 075 803 9096. At the foot of the old town, this is a great place for a coffee and cornetto, plus the usual range of sandwiches, but is known for its ice cream – rich and creamy. Closed Sun eve and all day Mon, otherwise open all day.

Hostaria de Dadà Via Cavour 47 ☎ 0742 301 327. A tiny place with a handful of shared tables – good for cheap, light meals at lunch or dinner – look out for the great *bruschette*, a local soup of barley and chickpeas, *stringozzi* pasta with wild boar sauce, or roast duck breast with red peppers. Two-course menu €12 excluding drinks, or four courses for €18. Mon–Sat noon–3pm & 7–10pm, Sun noon–3pm.

Il Cacciatore Via Giulia 42 ☎ 0742 651 141. Attached to the hotel (see above), with middling food and lower prices (*primi* €8–14, mains €9–16) than nearby *La Bastiglia* but a tremendous terrace for alfresco dining. Tues–Sun 12.30–2.30pm & 7.30–10.30pm.

Il Molino Piazza Matteotti 6–7 ☎ 0742 651 305. Spello's most appealing restaurant, set in a vaulted medieval townhouse a few steps up from Santa Maria Maggiore; a fairly smart place (*primi* from €9, mains around €15) serving wonderful fresh pasta *taglierini* with crisp juliennes of *prosciutto crudo*, served with pistacchio, pecorino, toasted breadcrumbs and wild fennel (€11). 12.30–2.45pm & 7.45–10pm; closed Tues.

La Bastiglia Via Falnitraria 15 ☎ 0742 651 277. A Michelin-starred restaurant attached to the *La Bastiglia* hotel (see above), with stunning views, and a €35 menu focusing on local foods and traditions. Well worth a visit for a special meal. 12.30–2.30pm & 8–10.30pm; closed all day Wed & Thurs lunch.

Bevagna

The serene, attractive backwater of **BEVAGNA** is quieter and less visited than Spello, with a windswept **central square** of stark perfection. Flanked by two of Umbria's finest Romanesque churches – both untouched and creaking with age – the Piazza S. Silvestri dates from around the thirteenth century. The only exception is the fountain, which, while blending perfectly, was installed in 1889. Look out particularly for the surreal gargoyles over the doorway of the larger church, San Michele.

The Museo Civico

Corso Matteotti 70 • Jan–March Fri, Sat & Sun 10.30am–1pm & 2.30–5pm; April–Aug daily 10.30am–1pm & 3.30–6pm; Sept & Oct Tues–Sun 10.30am–1pm & 3–7.30pm; Nov Fri, Sat & Sun 10.30am–1pm & 2.30–5pm, Dec Tues–Sun 10.30am–1pm & 2.30–5pm • €5 joint ticket with Roman mosaic and Teatro Torti, or €7 including Circuito Culturale

The town's small **Museo Civico** is devoted to the history of the village and is divided into three sections: the archeological collection on the ground floor; maps, letters and other documents on the first floor; and the Pinacoteca on the second floor, with mainly seventeenth-century paintings.

While you're at the museum, find a guide to take you to see the town's **mosaic** on the north side of Via Porta Guelfa (same hours and ticket), an impressive relic of the town's Roman days that originally formed part of a bath complex.

Teatro Torti and the medieval workshops

The museum-and-mosaic joint ticket also gives access to the delightful little nineteenth-century **Teatro Torti**, just off the main square, and the **Circuito Culturale dei Mestieri Medievali** (April to mid-June & Sept same hours as museum). This involves visits to four re-created workshops connected with medieval trades, namely paper-maker, silk-weaver, a mint and a pharmacy.

10

ARRIVAL AND INFORMATION   BEVAGNA

By bus Buses from Montefalco, Foligno, Perugia and Spoleto (all Mon–Sat) arrive in Largo A. Gramsci, just behind the main square.
Destinations Foligno (4 daily Mon–Sat; 20min); Montefalco (12 daily; 35min).

Tourist office The Pro Loco tourist office is on Piazza Santa Maria Laurentia, off Corso Matteotti (daily: summer 9am–1pm & 3–7pm; winter 9am–1pm & 3.30–6pm; ☎ 074 236 1667).

ACCOMMODATION

Il Chiostro di Bevagna Corso Matteotti 107 ☎ 0742 361 987, ⊕ ilchiostrodibevagna.com. Simple hotel just off Piazza S. Silvestro, in an atmospheric renovated Dominican convent, with an original frescoed cloister and airy, pleasant rooms. **€80**

L'Orto degli Angeli Via dell'Anfiteatro ☎ 0742 360 130, ⊕ ortoangeli.it. Luxurious accommodation in two porticoed medieval *palazzi*, dripping effortlessly with once-upon-a-time atmosphere, that have been in the same family since 1788. There are gardens, and a fine gourmet restaurant, *Redibis*. **€300**

Palazzo Brunamonti Corso Matteotti 79 ☎ 0742 361 932, ⊕ brunamonti.com. A sumptuous place with a period setting, brocade soft furnishings, beamed ceilings and trompe l'oeil decorations. **€80**

EATING AND DRINKING

Enoteca di Piazza Onofri Just behind the Palazzo Comunale at Piazza Onofri 1 ☎ 0742 361 926. This *enoteca* is a great place to try local food – such as the *pappa al pomodoro* with grilled aubergine and goat cheese, or *taglierini* with a *ragù* of pigeon and truffle. In autumn there should be rabbit with *finferli* – chanterelle mushrooms. Prices are reasonable – around €35 for a full meal. Mon, Tues, Thurs & Fri 8–10.30pm, Sat & Sun 12.30–2.30pm & 8–10.30pm.

Miccheletto Largo Gramsci 1 ☎ 0742 360 999. Little café-bar with a few tables outside – nice for breakfast, a sandwich lunch, or an *aperitivo* with the chance to nibble at a good range of local cheeses and salami. Open all day, daily.

Redibis Via dell'Anfiteatro ☎ 0742 360 130, ⊕ redibis .it. Interesting restaurant, where the cuisine draws equally on family recipes and well-researched local traditions, as well as having some more inventive fare. Dishes you won't find anywhere else include a soup of spelt and black celery (which is grown only in Trevi), a frittata of cardoons and thyme, and artisanal Gragnano spaghetti served with fresh chilli, garlic and oil. There are tasting menus priced at €46 and €38, while eating à la carte, antipasti cost €10–14, *primi* €12–14, *secondi* €15–22 and desserts €10. 12.30–2.30pm & 8–10.30pm; closed Tues.

Montefalco

MONTEFALCO is a pleasing and intimate medieval village that's home to a superb collection of paintings. Its name, meaning Falcon's Mount, was glorified with the appendage *la ringhiera dell'Umbria* – "the balcony of Umbria" – a tribute to its wonderful views. It was also the birthplace of eight saints, good going even by Italian standards. Nowadays the town's sleepy rather than holy, with only a stupendously ugly water-tower and very slight urban sprawl to take the edge off its medieval appeal. The strong, blackberry-flavoured **local wine**, Sagrantino Passito, made from a grape variety found nowhere else in Europe, is well worth a try; it's available in many shops around town. Recommended producers are Adanti and Caprai, also makers of the excellent Rosso di Montefalco.

The town's lofty location was a godsend to Spoleto's papal governors, left high, dry and terrified by the fourteenth-century defection of the popes to Avignon. They took refuge here, and their cowering presence accounts for some of the rich decoration of Montefalco's churches, a richness out of all proportion to the town's size.

Museo di San Francesco

Via Ringhiera Umbra 6 • March–May, Sept & Oct daily 10.30am–1pm & 2–6pm; June & July daily 10.30am–1pm & 3–7pm; Aug daily 10.30am–1pm & 3–7.30pm; Nov–Feb Tues–Sun 10.30am–1pm & 2.30–5pm • €6 • ☎ 0742 379 598, ⓦ montefalcodoc.it

The cavernous ex-church of San Francesco, off the central Piazza del Comune, is now the **Museo di San Francesco**, housing the town's big feature, Benozzo Gozzoli's sumptuous **fresco cycle** on the life of St Francis. With Fra' Angelico, Gozzoli was one of the most prolific and influential Florentine painters to come south and show the backward Umbrians what the Renaissance was all about. Resplendent with colour and detail, the cycle copies many of the ideas and episodes from Giotto's Assisi cycle but, with two hundred years of artistic know-how to draw on, is more sophisticated and more immediately appealing.

Church and convent of St Clare

Probably the most bizarre sight in town is the mummified body of **St Clare** (St Chiara), which languishes in the otherwise dismal church of the same name, five minutes' walk from San Francesco in Via Verdi (this is a second St Clare, not to be confused with the one in Assisi). Ring the bell and, if the nuns aren't deep in prayer, they may show you round the adjoining convent – a fascinating behind-the-scenes look at monastic life, where you can see the remains of the saint's heart and the scissors used to hack it out. The story goes that Christ appeared to Clare, saying the burden of carrying the cross was becoming too heavy; Clare replied she would help by carrying it in her heart. When she was opened up after her death, a cross-shaped piece of tissue was duly found on her heart. Other strange exhibits include three of her kidney stones and a tree that miraculously grew from a staff planted in the garden here by Christ, during one of his appearances to Clare; the berries are used to make rosaries and are said to have powerful medicinal qualities.

ARRIVAL AND INFORMATION

MONTEFALCO

By bus You can get here by bus from most local towns and villages, including four services daily from Bevagna and three daily from Perugia (Mon–Sat). Buses drop off in the huge car park below town, from where it's a 5min walk uphill to the centre.

Tourist information The Strada del Sagrantino at Piazza del Comune 17 (Mon–Sat 9.30am–1pm & 4–6.30pm, Sun 10am–4pm; ☎ 0742 378 490, ⓦ stradadelsagrantino.it), a body promoting the wines of the region, has a free map of local *cantine*, perfect if you're planning a tour of the local wineries, and plenty of general background on places to stay, eat and visit, as well as local events, including the Agosto Montefalchese (mid-Aug) – two weeks of cultural events and open-air concerts culminating in the Fuga del Bove, a bull race that has taken place here for centuries.

ACCOMMODATION AND EATING

L'Alchemista Piazza del Comune 14 ☎ 0742 378 558. A family-run wine bar and restaurant, open from 9am for those who fancy breakfasting, Umbrian-peasant style, on a glass of wine with salami and cheese. At lunchtime and dinner there is more substantial fare on offer – try the *pasta alla carbonara* with local cheese and saffron or with shavings of summer truffle – while puddings are happily accompanied by a glass of local sweet wine, Passito di Sagrantino. Open daily, all day in summer; closed Tues in low season.

★ **Palazzo Bontadosi** Piazza del Comune 19 ☎ 0742 379 357, ⓦ hotelbontadosi.it. Right in the main square, with twelve sumptuously furnished rooms and a swanky spa in the basement. The vast junior suite, with frescoes and a bathtub in the bedroom, plus peerless views of the square, is worth a splurge. **€170**

Trevi

Road and rail south of Assisi and Spello run down the plain of Spoleto, past the light industrial sites that blight the whole stretch of the valley towards Terni and beyond. Not many people stop before Spoleto itself, giving **TREVI** and its towering position no more than an admiring glance. Its daunting inaccessibility is one of the reasons for its easy-going, old-fashioned charm; the feeling is of a pleasant, ordinary provincial town, unspoilt but beginning to feel the first effects of tourism. All around it are vast expanses of **olive groves**, renowned for producing central Italy's finest oil.

10

Museo di San Francesco

Largo Don Bosco • April, May & Sept Tues–Sun 10am–12.30pm & 2.30–6pm; June & July Tues–Sun 10am–12.30pm & 3.30–7pm; Aug daily 10.30am–12.30pm & 3–7.30pm; Oct–March Fri–Sun 10.30am–1pm & 2.30–5pm • €4 • ☎ 0742 381 021

The key sight in town is the superb **Museo di San Francesco** in the former Convento di San Francesco, reached by taking Via di San Francesco from the northern end of the main Piazza Mazzini. It houses a well-presented display of coins, ceramics and Roman fragments, several paintings by Umbrian masters and one outstanding work, a *Coronation of the Virgin* (1522) by Lo Spagna. Trevi's medieval governors commissioned this last painting as a copy of a more famous work by the Florentine Ghirlandaio, mainly because they couldn't afford the real thing. In the same complex, the **Museo della Civiltà dell'Ulivo** (same hours and ticket) is a smart museum devoted to history of the olive and olive oil production: it's packed with interesting information, in English and Italian.

ARRIVAL AND INFORMATION

TREVI

By train The medieval centre, looming high on its hill, is 4km from the train station, connected by just four buses daily, so check the timetable first on ⓦ umbriamobilita.it before deciding what time to arrive. There are trains approximately every hour from Trevi to Terni, a major junction, with services to Rome and north to Perugia and Città di Castello.

By bus Trevi is not very well connected by bus – there are five buses daily to Foligno.
Tourist office Piazza Garibaldi 4 (Tues–Sun daily 10am–1pm & 2.30–5.30pm; ☎ 0742 332 269, ⓦ trevi turismo.it). Has audioguides to the town as well as information on the local olive-oil route (ⓦ stradaoliodop umbria.it).

ACCOMMODATION AND EATING

Antica Dimora alla Rocca Piazza della Rocca ☎ 0742 38 541, ⓦ hotelallarocca.it. Centrally located, this smart hotel occupies part of a historic 1650 building with frescoed ceilings and other period features, all beautifully restored. For atmosphere, ask to be in the main building, rather than the less appealing ten-room annexe. **€75**
Il Terziere Località Costa 1 ☎ 0742 78 359, ⓦ ilterziere .com. A very appealingly styled hotel with restaurant whose gorgeous flower-filled garden, outdoor toys for children and swimming pool make it a great choice for families with young children. In addition, most of the rooms on the first floor have their own terrace-balconies.

It's about 3km outside town, and although the hotel will pick you up from the station, and organize bike rental, you really do need your own transport. **€100**
La Vecchia Posta Piazza Mazzini 14 ☎ 0742 381 690. A great little place that makes excellent use of local ingredients – Including truffles, and the town's rare black celery. The oil hereabouts is excellent as well – shown off to perfection in the very simple crostini with black celery pâté. Truffles turn up in pasta dishes and – most interestingly – encrusting a melting *scamorza* cheese. A full meal will cost around €25. 12.30–2.30pm & 8–10.30pm; closed Thurs.

Fonti del Clitunno

Via Flaminia 7, Località Fonti del Clitunno • Mon–Fri: March 9am–1pm & 2–6pm; April 9am–7.30pm; May–Aug 8.30am–8pm; Sept 9am–7pm; Oct 9am–1pm & 2–6pm; Nov–Feb 10am–1pm & 2–4.30pm; Sat & Sun same opening and closing hours year-round but remains open all day • €3 • ☎ 0743 521 141, ⓦ fontidelclitunno.com • Six buses (Mon–Sat; about 25 min) from Foligno and 4 daily from Spoleto (about 35 min). Timetables on ⓦ umbriamobilita.it

For a memorable break from hill-town-seeing, make the short hop north from Spoleto to the sacred **Fonti del Clitunno**, an unexpected beauty spot given the pockmarked surroundings. There's a certain amount of commercialized fuss and bother at the entrance, but the springs, streams and willow-shaded lake beyond – painted by Corot and an inspiration to poets from Virgil to Byron – are pure, languid romanticism. The spa waters have attracted people since Roman times – the likes of Caligula and Claudius came here to party – but their major curative effect is allegedly the dubious one of completely extinguishing any appetite for alcohol.

10 Tempietto del Clitunno

Daily: April–Oct 8.45am–7.45pm; Nov–March 8.45am–5.45pm • €3

A few hundred metres north of Fonti del Clitunno is the so-called **Tempietto del Clitunno**, looking for all the world like a miniature Greek temple but actually an eighth-century Christian church, cobbled together with a mixture of idiosyncrasy, wishful thinking and old Roman columns. It's only a small, one-off novelty, but still evocative, and with the bonus inside of some faded frescoes said to be the oldest in Umbria.

Spoleto

SPOLETO is among Umbria's most charming large towns, divided into the medieval and hilltop Upper Town, home to the Duomo and most of the key museums and galleries, and the predominantly modern Lower Town, which nonetheless preserves a handful of Romanesque churches and Roman ruins. Known these days mainly for its big **summer festival** (see box, p.658), it's also remarkable for its thorough-going medievalism, an extremely scenic setting, and several of Italy's most ancient Romanesque **churches**. Far more graceful and provincial a city than Perugia, nowadays it plays second fiddle politically to its long-time historical enemy, though for several centuries it was among the most influential of Italian towns.

Two kilometres of well-preserved walls stand as testament to the one-time grandeur of Spoleto's Roman colony, though its real importance dates from the sixth century when the Lombards made it the capital of one of their three Italian dukedoms. The autonomous **Duchy of Spoleto** eventually stretched to Rome, and by 890 its rulers had become powerful enough to lay claim to the imperial throne itself, making Spoleto, for a short time at least, the capital of the entire Holy Roman Empire. Barbarossa flattened the city in a fit of pique in 1155, and in 1499 Pope Alexander VI appointed his daughter, the 19-year-old Lucrezia Borgia, governor. After that it was one long decline until about fifty years ago and the arrival of the festival.

The Lower Town

The Lower Town was badly damaged by World War II bombing and its only real interest lies in the remains of a Roman amphitheatre and a couple of first-rate churches. Aficionados of Romanesque architecture – or anyone who fancies staying in a monastery – might also want to see **San Ponziano** just off Via Cimitero (ring the bell at the adjacent monastery to gain access), with a simple Romanesque facade and a beautiful tenth-century crypt supported on columns recycled from Roman buildings and with frescoes dating from the fourteenth century.

THE SPOLETO CARD

Available from April to September, the **Spoleto Card** (Ⓦ spoletocard.it) provides free entrance to the town's seven museums, as well as free local public transport. The card is valid for seven days and costs €9.50. You can buy it from any of the town's museums, or from the bookshop at the Duomo.

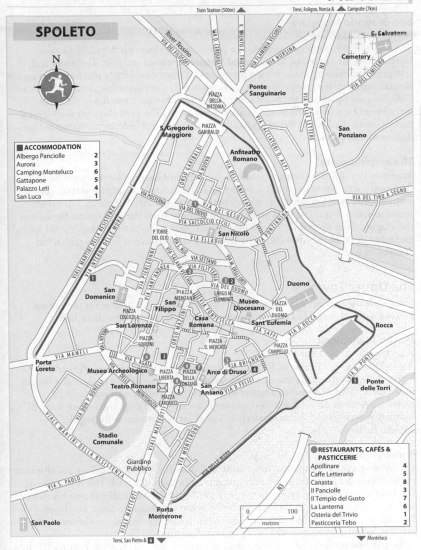

SPOLETO

N

ACCOMMODATION

Albergo Panciolle	2
Aurora	3
Camping Monteluco	6
Gattapone	5
Palazzo Leti	4
San Luca	1

RESTAURANTS, CAFÉS & PASTICCERIE

Apollinare	4
Caffe Letterario	5
Canasta	8
Il Panciolle	3
Il Tempio del Gusto	7
La Lanterna	6
Osteria del Trivio	1
Pasticceria Tebo	2

San Salvatore

Via del Cimitero • Daily: May–Aug 7am–7pm; April & Sept 7am–6pm; March & Oct 8am–6pm; Nov–Feb 8am–5pm • Free

The fourth-century paleo-Christian **San Salvatore**, built by Christian monks from the eastern Mediterranean in the fourth century, is one of Umbria's most remarkable buildings. Pretty much untampered with over the centuries, it was conceived at a time when the western world was still ruled by the Roman emperor, and the only models for religious buildings were Roman temples. This is pretty much what the monks came up with, the net result leaning more to paganism than Christianity. The walls inside are bare, the floors covered in fallen stone, and the dusty gloom is heavy with an almost eerie antiquity. Crumbling Corinthian columns from different ages are wedged awkwardly alongside one another, and at some point the arches in the nave were filled in to prevent total collapse.

San Gregorio Maggiore

Daily 8am–noon & 4–6pm • Free

The Lower Town's other attraction, in a prominent position on the main Piazza Garibaldi, is the church of **San Gregorio Maggiore**, started in 1069. The tower and intriguing portico are made from a patchwork of fragments clearly pinched from earlier Roman remains, but it's the interior that commands most attention. Stripped back to their Romanesque state, the walls are dotted with substantial patches of fresco and interrupted by a series of unusual stone confessionals. The presbytery is raised several metres above the level of the naves to allow for a masterful little crypt, supported by dozens of tiny pillars.

The amphitheatre

Tradition has it that somewhere under San Gregorio Maggiore lie the bones of ten thousand Christian martyrs killed by the Romans in Spoleto's **amphitheatre**. The amphitheatre now lies within a military barracks on Via dell'Anfiteatro, but no one seems to mind if you just walk straight in; bear right from the gateway for the best of the amphitheatre's remains. The ever-ingenious Romans apparently constructed special gutters to drain blood from the arena into the nearby Torrente Tessino, which ran crimson as a result.

The Upper Town

There's plenty to explore in the medieval **Upper Town**. Buses drop off at the central Piazza Carducci, and all of the sights are within a fifteen-minute walk of here.

Museo Archeologico

Via Sant'Agata • Daily 8.30am–7.30pm • €4

A good place to get a sense of Roman Spoleto, on the western edge of the central **Piazza della Libertà**, is the town's **Museo Archeologico**, evocatively housed in a former monastery, stylishly documenting the Roman presence in the city with artfully presented local finds; included in the ticket is a visit to the exquisite first-century-BC **Teatro Romano** behind the monastery, still used for performances during the Spoleto Festival.

Roman remains

Of the town's many Roman arches, the **Arco di Druso** (23 AD), straddling the entrance to the Piazza del Mercato, is the only one not embedded in a wall. This is because it was built as a triumphal, symbolic gateway to the old Forum, rather than a functional and defendable town gate, and was built to honour campaign victories on the part of Drusus, son of Tiberius, a heavy-drinking man, whose reputation for violence led to the sharpest of gladiator swords being named after him.

The patched-up walls behind it are the city's oldest, built in the sixth century BC by the Umbrians. To the right of the arch is what is described as a **Roman temple**, but unless you've a vivid imagination it's difficult to see it as anything other than a ditch. Pop into the adjacent church of **Sant'Ansano** (daily 8.30am–noon & 3.30–5.30pm, Nov–March closes 6.30pm) for a look at more of the temple and the wonderful fresco-covered crypt (down the stairs to the left of the high altar), originally the home of sixth-century monks.

Piazza del Mercato

Nowhere do you get a better sense of Spoleto's market-town roots than in the bustling **Piazza del Mercato** beyond Piazza della Fontana, whose two bars on the west side offer a fine opportunity to take in some streetlife. The *alimentari* on all sides are a cornucopia of goodies, with a definite bias towards truffles and sticky liqueurs.

The Duomo

Daily: April–Oct 8am–12.30pm & 3.30–7pm; Nov–March closes 5.30pm • Free

Leaving Piazza del Mercato to the north and turning right on Via A. Saffi brings you to the **Duomo**, whose facade of restrained elegance is one of the most memorable in the region. The careful balance of Romanesque and Renaissance elements is framed by a gently sloping piazza and lovely hanging gardens, but the broad background of sky and open countryside is what sets the seal on the whole thing. The church suffered like many in Italy from the desire of rich communities to make their wealth and power conspicuous, a desire usually realized by tearing the guts out of old churches and remodelling them in the latest style. This worked well on the thirteenth-century **facade**, which has an arched portico tacked on in 1491, but less well in the interior where Pope Urban VIII's architect, Luigi Arrigucci, applied great dollops of Baroque midway through the seventeenth century. His "improvements", luckily, are eclipsed by the apse's superlative **frescoes** by the great Florentine artist Fra' Filippo Lippi, dominated by his final masterpiece, a *Coronation of the Virgin* (1469).

10

You should also make a point of seeing the **Erioli Chapels** at the beginning of the right nave, primarily for a faded *Madonna and Child* (with Lago Trasimeno in the background) by Pinturicchio (1497). There's also a *Crucifix* of 1187, by Alberto Sotio, behind glass at the beginning of the left nave, which is reckoned to be the oldest painting in Umbria; a colourful chapel further down the left nave containing a framed letter written by St Francis (one of only two to survive); and the inevitable **icon**, which Federico Barbarossa gave to the town in 1185 to try to make amends for having flattened it thirty years earlier.

The Casa Romana and Palazzo Collicola

In a tiny sidestreet below the Palazzo Comunale is the **Casa Romana**, Via di Visiale (Mon–Thurs 11am–7pm; €3), a dark and atmospheric little corner that contains the impressive remains of a Roman house. The **Palazzo Collicola**, to the west across Corso Mazzini on Piazza Collicola (mid-March to mid-Oct Mon & Wed–Sun 10.30am–1pm & 3.30–7pm; closes earlier in winter; €6 for permament collection only, €9 with exhibition as well), holds the **Museo Carandente** devoted primarily to modern Italian artists, though it contains some works by foreigners who have been connected with the Spoleto Festival over the years, among them Alexander Calder, the man responsible for the large sculpture by the railway station, and American minimalist Sol LeWit. The top floor hosts some excellent temporary exhibitions.

Sant'Eufemia

Very close to the Palazzo Comunale's back entrance is the medieval town's most celebrated **church**, the eleventh-century **Sant'Eufemia** (seen with Museo Diocesano – see p.658), architecturally unique in Umbria for its *matronei*, high-arched galleries above the side-naves that segregated women from the men in the main body of the

---

THE DISAPPEARING CORPSE OF FRA' FILIPPO LIPPI

Fra' Filippo Lippi died shortly after completing the frescoes in Spoleto's Duomo, the rumour being that he was poisoned for seducing the daughter of a local noble family, his position as a monk having had no bearing on his sexual appetite. The Spoletans, not too perturbed by moral laxity, were delighted at having someone famous to put in their cathedral, being, as Vasari put it, "poorly provided with ornaments, above all with distinguished men", and so refused to send the dead artist back to Lorenzo de' Medici, his Florentine patron. Interred in a **tomb** designed by his son, Filippino Lippi (now in the right transept), the corpse disappeared during restoration two centuries later, the popular theory being that it was spirited away by descendants of the compromised girl – a sort of vendetta beyond the grave.

10

church. It was built over the site of the eighth-century Lombard ducal palace and appears to have been partly constructed from the remains of this and earlier Roman monuments; one or two of the completely mismatched columns are carved with distinctive Lombard motifs. The general dank solemnity of the place clearly points to an early foundation.

Museo Diocesano

Via A. Saffi • Wed–Sun 11am–1pm & 3–6pm, closes earlier in winter • €3 • ☎ 0743 231 022

Sant'Eufemia is visited in conjunction with the outstanding **Museo Diocesano**, located in the same courtyard as the church. The eight rooms contain several surprisingly good paintings, including a *Madonna* by Fra' Filippo Lippi and an early Domenico Beccafumi, a room of old wooden statues and some wonderfully graphic votive panels offering thanks for salvation from a host of vividly illustrated mishaps.

The Rocca

Piazza Campello • Daily 9.30am–7.30pm, earlier in winter; ticket office closes 45min before • €7.50 including the Museo Nazionale del Ducato • ☎ 0743 224 952

To the east of town, the **Rocca Albornoziana**, everyone's idea of a cartoon castle, with towers, crenellations and sheer walls, was another in the chain of fortresses with which the tireless Cardinal Albornoz hoped to re-establish Church domination in central Italy, a primacy lost during the fourteenth-century papal exile to Avignon. It served until 1982 as a high-security prison – testimony to the skill of its medieval builders – and was home to, among others, Pope John Paul II's would-be assassin and leading members of the Red Brigade. After years of restoration it now houses the sleek **Museo Nazionale del Ducato** (Tues–Sat 9.30am–7.30pm, Sun 9.30am–1.45pm; €7.50 for combined ticket with the Rocca) devoted to the Duchy of Spoleto, with paintings including a couple of big canvases by a follower of Perugino, Lo Spagna, one of several local Renaissance artists represented. Both the museum and fortress are well worth seeing, the Rocca in particular for its superb views, the imposing twin courtyards and the sheer scale of the building.

The Ponte delle Torri

If you do nothing else in Spoleto you should take the short walk out to the **Ponte delle Torri**, the town's picture-postcard favourite and an astonishing piece of medieval engineering. It's best taken in as part of a circular walk around the base of the Rocca or on the longer trek out to San Pietro (see opposite). Within a minute of leaving shady gardens in Piazza Campello you suddenly find yourself looking out over superb countryside, with a dramatic panorama across the Tessino gorge and south to the mountains of Castelmonte.

The bridge is genuinely impressive, with a 240m span supported by ten 80m arches that have been used as a launching pad by jilted lovers for six centuries. Designed by the Gubbian architect Gattapone, who was also responsible for Gubbio's Palazzo dei Consoli, it was initially planned as an aqueduct to bring water from Monteluco, replacing an earlier Roman causeway whose design Gattapone probably borrowed and enlarged upon. In time it also became used as an escape from the Rocca when Spoleto was under siege. The remains of what used to be a covered passageway connecting the two are still visible straggling down the hillside.

10

San Pietro

From the Ponte delle Torri, turn right on the road and make for the church of **San Pietro**, whose facade beckons from a not-too-distant hillside. Though the walk is a longish one (2km), it's pleasantly shady with some good glimpses of Spoleto, but on the country road (no pavements) beware drivers taking the bends too fast. The church would be undistinguished were it not for the splendid **sculptures** adorning its facade. Taken with Maitani's bas-reliefs in Orvieto, they are the best Romanesque carvings in Umbria, partly Lombard in their inspiration, and drawing variously on the Gospels and medieval legend for their complicated narrative and symbolic purpose. A particularly juicy scene to look out for includes the *Death of a Sinner* (left series, second from the top) where the Archangel Michael abandons the sinner to a couple of demons who bind and torture him before bringing in burning oil to finish the job. Fourth panel from the top (right series) shows a wolf disguised as a friar before a fleeing ram – a dig at dodgy monastic morals.

ARRIVAL AND DEPARTURE   SPOLETO

By train Spoleto is easily reached by train, with regular services on the main Rome–Ancona line, a daily train to Florence and local links with Foligno, Terni, Narni, Orte and elsewhere. The train station is just northwest of the Lower Town; shuttle buses (#A, #B, #C) to the centre (Piazza Carducci) depart from outside the station – buy tickets (€1, or €1.50 on board) from the station bar – as do services for Norcia; other buses leave from Piazza della Vittoria, just outside the walls to the north of the town.
Destinations Arezzo (12 daily; 2hr 10min–3hr 10min); Florence direct (1 daily; 2hr 50min); Foligno via Trevi (14 daily; connections for Assisi, Spello, Perugia, Terontola and

Florence; 20min); Fossato di Vico (8 daily; 50min–1hr 15min); Narni (9 daily; 30–40min); Perugia direct (7 daily; 55min–1hr 15min); Rome (14 daily; 1hr 20min–1hr 45min); Terni (17 daily; 25min).
By bus Buses stop at Piazza della Vittoria just outside the walls to the north of town.
Destinations Foligno (Mon–Sat 4–5 daily; 40min); Fonti del Clitunno (8 daily; 20min); Montefalco (3–4 daily Mon–Sat; 50min); Norcia (5–6 daily; 55min); Rome (1 daily; 2hr 20min); Scheggino (5 daily; 1hr 10min); Terni (6 daily; 45min); Trevi (7 daily; 25min).

INFORMATION

Tourist office Piazza Libertà 7 (April–Oct Mon–Fri 9am–1.30pm & 2–7pm, Sat 9am–1pm & 3–7pm, Sun 10am–1pm & 3.30–6.30pm; ☎0743 218 620, ⓦcomune

spoleto.gov.it – click on the La Città tab for tourist and cultural information).

ACCOMMODATION

Albergo Panciolle Via del Duomo 3 ☎0743 45 677, ⓦalbergopanciolle.it. Seven decent two-star rooms (two with a/c) – the best are nos. 3 and 4, with views over the rooftops. It's above the restaurant of the same name, and outdoor eating can make staying here a noisy option in summer. Half-board available for a €20 supplement. **€85**
Aurora Via dell'Apollinare 3 ☎0743 220 315, ⓦhotel auroraspoleto.it. A perfectly situated, 23-room three-star

in an alley off Piazza della Libertà, which is great value in low season. **€110**
★ **Gattapone** Via del Ponte 6 ☎0743 223 447, ⓦhotelgattapone.it. When this place opened in the 1960s, it rapidly became the hotel of choice for artists and performers at the festival – and its list of past guests is astonishing: Yehudi Menuhin, Leonard Bernstein, Pablo Neruda, Alan Ginsberg, Henry Moore, Audrey Hepburn,

10

Ingrid Bergman. It's a welcoming and beautifully styled family-run hotel with lovely views from most rooms, which are spectacularly situated above the gorge and almost alongside the Ponte delle Torri. €230

★ **Palazzo Leti** Via degli Eremiti 10 ☎ 0743 224 930, ⓦ palazzoleti.com. Set in the palatial residence of the noble Leti family, this gorgeously renovated hotel has elegantly decorated rooms with views of the valley; book one on the top floor for the best panorama. There's also a beautiful formal garden overlooking the valley. €140

San Luca Via Interna delle Mura 21 ☎ 0743 223 399,

ⓦ hotelsanluca.com. This very tastefully furnished four-star is efficiently run and has the bonus of a large, sunny garden and an internal furnished courtyard. €150

CAMPING

Camping Monteluco ☎ 0743 220 358, ⓦ campeggio monteluco.com. An attractively small pastoral site behind San Pietro, with several bungalows, 35 camping places and a bar/pizzeria, but quite an uphill trek to the Upper Town. April–Sept. Pitches €11.50

EATING AND DRINKING

★ **Apollinare** Via Sant'Agata 14 ☎ 0743 223 256, ⓦ ristoranteapollinare.it. The blue and gold upholstery is initially off-putting, but the medieval setting is good and the welcome friendly. *Secondi* are around €15, or go for the three-course "Surprise" tasting menu (€25, or €40 for 5 courses including wine) if you want to try something new. There's a vegetarian menu as well at €25. Don't miss the sublime *caramella* starter – a cheese-and-truffle delight. Daily noon–3.30pm & 7–11pm; closed Tues in winter.

Caffè Letterario Via Brignone ☎ 0743 46 691. Literary café in the *palazzo* that houses the town library, offering simple snacks and excellent coffees, along with books and magazines to leaf through. There are regular photo exhibitions and book presentations, and free wi-fi. Generally a jolly good place to hang out. Open daily, all day till around 9.30pm.

Canasta Piazza della Libertà 14 ☎ 0743 40 205. Historic café on the main square, which keeps the townspeople happy with tasty savouries and tempting pastries. A great place to start the day. Open all day; closed Wed.

Il Panciolle Largo Muzio Clemente–Via del Duomo 3 ☎ 0743 221 241. Below the hotel of the same name, this is a good choice for a reliable and reasonably priced meal of Umbrian specialities such as *stringozzi* and fire-grilled meats (*secondi* €9–17). Also known for its selection of cheeses. Has a great outside terrace – and the medieval interior with open fire is cosy in winter. Tues–Sun 12.30–3pm & 7.30pm–midnight.

Il Tempio del Gusto Via Arco del Druso 11 ☎ 0743 47 121. "The Temple of Taste'" was founded by Eros Patrizi, a former pupil of the legendary Vissani, patron of the eponymous restaurant near Baschi, in southern Umbria, that for years has rated as one of Italy's best, winning prizes for dishes such as a *risottina* of farro (spelt, cooked risotto-style) with scallops. Standards – and the often recherché cooking – are similar, and you'll be paying around €50 à la carte, but there are more reasonably charged tasting menus, plus cheaper menus at lunch. Noon–4pm & 7–11pm; closed Thurs.

La Lanterna Via della Trattoria 6 ☎ 0743 49 815. A convivial, central place and the best of the town's mid-price trattorias, on a side street left off the hill between Piazza della Libertà and Piazza Fontana. It serves huge helpings of delicious pasta for €7–11.50 and grilled meats from €7–14. 12.30–3pm & 7.30–10.30pm; closed Wed.

Osteria del Trivio Via del Trivio 16 ☎ 0743 44 349. A little away from the centre, and thus the crowds; nicely rustic, with photographs of the much-travelled owners and their family on the walls, and Spoletan classics on the menu; try the local *strangozzi* pasta with wild asparagus, fava beans and pecorino in spring, or with wild mushrooms in autumn. Reckon on around €30 for a full meal. 12.30–2.30pm & 7–11pm; closed Tues.

Pasticceria Tebo Via Minervia 1 ☎ 0743 45 400. Artisan pastries and ice cream in a historic café-*pasticceria*, well worth visits at breakfast, ice cream and *aperitivo* times. Be sure to try the silky espresso. Open all day, closed Tues.

The Valnerina

The **VALNERINA** is the most beautiful part of Umbria. Strictly translated as the "little valley of the Nera", it effectively refers to the whole eastern part of the region, a self-contained area of high mountains, poor communications, steep wooded valleys, upland villages and vast stretches of barren nothingness. Wolves still roam the summit ridges and the area is a genuine "forgotten corner", deserted farms everywhere bearing witness to a century of emigration.

Mountains nearby are 1500m high, with excellent walking, creeping up as you move east to about 2500m in the **Monti Sibillini**. It's difficult to explore with any sort of plan (unless you stick to the Nera), and the best approach is to follow your nose, poking into small valleys, tracing high country lanes to remote hamlets.

More deliberately, you could make for **Vallo di Nera**, the most archetypal of the **fortified villages** that pop up along the Lower Nera. Medieval **Triponzo** is a natural focus of communications, little more than a quaint staging-post and fortified tower (and a better target than modernish Cerreto nearby). **Monteleone** is the only place of any size for miles, with a fine church, and popular with trippers.

10

GETTING AROUND

The region is best explored with a car, as public transport is very limited. The easiest way to get to the region without a car is by bus from Spoleto: five to seven daily run from Spoleto station to Norcia (1hr 15min). A new road-tunnel links Spoleto to the valley, but for scenery stick to the old and tortuous N395 from Spoleto until you hit the "main" SS209 and the more pastoral run up the Nera valley towards Norcia.

Norcia

The very pleasant mountain retreat of **NORCIA** is the only place of any size or substance in the Valnerina. Noted on the one hand as the birthplace of **St Benedict** – founder of Western monasticism – and on the other as the producer of Italy's top salami, it has an air of charming dereliction, and its low, sturdy houses (built to be earthquake-resistant) are a world away from the pastoral, fairy-tale cities to the west. If transport allows, it could be the base for some good trips into neighbouring territory, particularly the famed Piano Grande (see p.662) and the mountains to the east and north. A big new road through the mountains into Le Marche has opened and brought in more visitors – good news for local employment, which is scarce, but a possible challenge to the environment. Hang-gliders and winter-sports enthusiasts have also discovered the area, another mixed blessing.

It doesn't take long to see the town, but you may want to stay on for the pleasant atmosphere and the surrounding scenery. Most of the action is in the central **Piazza San Benedetto**, site of the Roman forum and presided over by a statue of Benedict. Apart from its facade, you can largely forget about the **Duomo** – destroyed by several earthquakes (the last big one was in 1979), and patched up to look like nothing on earth. The **Castellina** is more captivating: a papal fortress full of gaunt medieval echoes, it contains a fine little **museum** (May–Sept Tues–Sun 10am–1pm & 4–7pm; usually closed Mon & Tues Oct–April; €4) with fascinating old wooden sculptures and several surprisingly accomplished paintings. The fortress makes a strange bedfellow for the labyrinthine church of **San Benedetto**, which supposedly was built over the saint's birthplace but was probably raised from the ruins of an earlier Roman temple. Inside there are a few paltry frescoes, nothing more, though the crypt contains the remains of a Roman-era house.

NORCIA FOR FOODIES

Meat-eaters would be daft not to try the deservedly famous local pork products. Anything that can be done to a pig, the Norcians apparently do – and supposedly better than anyone else. For this reason, *alimentari* throughout Italy who pride themselves on their hams and salamis will call themselves *norcineria*. If finances stretch, you could also indulge in the area's prized black truffle. The season runs from January to April (though you may come across the lesser-prized white summer truffles too). Plenty of shops, an attraction in themselves, are on hand to sell you all manner of local specialities, not just truffles, but also hams, the famed lentils of Castelluccio and lots of rare mountain cheeses.

ARRIVAL AND INFORMATION

By bus There are only a few services running to and from Norcia; check ⓦ umbriamobilita.it for timetables.
Destinations Castelluccio (1 daily Thurs only; 50min); Rome (2 daily Mon–Sat, 1 on Sun; 3hr); Terni (1 daily; 1hr).
Tourist offices The tourist office is inside the Palazzo Comunale on the main Piazza San Benedetto (Mon–Fri 9am–1pm, and possibly some afternoons in summer; ☎ 0743 828 173, ⓦ comune.norcia.pg.it). In summer there's also a branch of the Casa del Parco, with information on the Parco Nazionale dei Monti Sibillini, in the same building (July & Aug daily 9.30am–12.30pm & 3.30–6.30pm; ☎ 334 222 7698, ⓦ sibillini.net).

10

ACCOMMODATION

Norcia has always seen lots of pilgrims, in town for Benedict and trips to Assisi and Loreto in Le Marche for the house of the Virgin (see p.697). But these days its accommodation is under pressure from growing numbers of casual visitors, so it makes sense to book rooms well in advance, especially from June to August. Prices tend to go up at summer weekends. You should also book ahead during the truffle festival, between the last weekend in February and the first weekend in March.

Grotta Azzurra Via Alfieri 12 ☎ 0743 816 513, ⓦ hotel grottaazzurra.com. A rambling three-star with traditional decor and a very good restaurant – the *Granaro del Monte* (see below). **€80**

Ostello Il Capisterium Via Manzoni 2 ☎ 0743 817 487, ⓦ ilcapisterium.it. Hostel offering beds (in rooms sleeping 2, 4, 5 & 10), right in the centre of town in a beautiful ex-monastery. Dorms **€15**, doubles **€40**

★ **Palazzo Seneca** Via Cesare Battisti 12 ☎ 0743 817 434, ⓦ palazzoseneca.com. This sixteenth-century residence has recently been restored to create an elegant and supremely comfortable hotel. The rooms are tastefully furnished with antiques and four-poster beds, and the marble bathrooms are wonderfully luxurious. There's also a spa and gourmet restaurant, *Vespasia* (see below). **€215**

EATING AND DRINKING

Granaro del Monte Via Alfieri 12 ☎ 0743 816 513. A medieval dining-room complete with open fire and suits of armour is the setting for a meal at this long-established restaurant, with plenty of truffle-based dishes on the menu. *Primi* start at €7, though you can pay up to €26 for dishes involving the famed black truffle. There is also a full daily menu for €20. Daily 12.30–2.30pm & 8–10.30pm.

Trattoria dei Priori Via dei Priori 3 ☎ 0743 816 282. Well-prepared local dishes – such as *fettuccine al cinghiale* (with wild boar) – are served up in a simple, barrel-vaulted space. Fixed-price menu €22, truffle-tasting menu €31. Tues–Sun 12.30–2.30pm & 8–10.30pm.

★ **Trattoria del Francese** Via Riguardati 16 ☎ 0743 816 290. Don't be fooled by this trattoria's unassuming appearance: it's the town's most lauded restaurant, serving up top-notch local cuisine at very reasonable prices. *Primi* with truffles go for around €16, without €7–9. Not surprisingly, it's popular with locals, so be sure to book. 12.30–2.30pm & 8–10.30pm; closed Fri in low season.

Vespasia Via Cesare Battisti 12 ☎ 0743 817 434. Norcia's smartest hotel, *Palazzo Seneca*, has a suitably tasteful (and pricey) restaurant, serving up elegant versions of the local specialities such as *risotto alla crema d'ortica* (€12) – risotto with wild nettle. There are tasting menus from €55. Daily 12.30–2.30pm & 8–10.30pm.

The Piano Grande

The eerie, expansive **Piano Grande**, 20km east of Norcia, is an extraordinary prairie ringed by bare, whaleback mountains and stretching, uninterrupted by tree, hedge or habitation, for miles and miles. A decade or so ago, it was all but unknown: now, in summer at least, it can be disconcertingly busy. It's much photographed – especially in spring when it's ablaze with wild flowers of every description – and was used by Zeffirelli as a setting for his Franciscan film *Brother Sun, Sister Moon*. The desperately isolated village of **CASTELLUCCIO** hangs above it at around 1400m, and although no longer the sole preserve of shepherds, it remains an unspoilt base and the ideal starting point for any number of straightforward mountain walks. To plan routes, get hold of the 1:50,000 Kompass map no. 666 or the more detailed 1:25,000 CAI maps (the latter are often available in Norcia's or Castelluccio's bars).

Note that there's **no public transport** into the area (save for one bus in and out on a Thurs, market day in Norcia), though you might try your luck at catching lifts in high season.

ACCOMMODATION AND EATING THE PIANO GRANDE

La Sibilla Castelluccio ☎ 0743 821 113, ⓦ sibilla castelluccio.com. Simple but comfortable rooms (booking advised), an excellent restaurant and great views. There is also a shop selling local produce, a bar-*gelateria* and a tobacconist. **€70**

Terni and around

10

TERNI was the unlikely birthplace of one of the world's most famous saints, St Valentine, bishop of the town until his martyrdom in 273 and now entombed in his personal basilica at San Valentino, a village 2km to the southwest. A less romantic city, however, would be hard to imagine. Terni's important arms and steel industries made it a target for Allied bombing in 1944, and eighty percent of the town was reduced to rubble. Rebuilding replaced what was lost with a grey grid-iron; it also put the arms industry back on its feet – the gun used to assassinate Kennedy was made here. That said, a swathe of industrial wasteland on the outskirts is undergoing recovery, and an abandoned factory just east of the river at Viale Luigi Campofregoso 98 has been transformed into the **CAOS** complex (ⓦ caos.museum), a centre for contemporary art, and home to an archeological museum, a bookshop, theatre and bar.

ARRIVAL AND DEPARTURE TERNI

By train As might be expected of an industrial town, Terni has great train connections, and sits at the junction between the Ancona–Rome and L'Aquila–Todi–Perugia–Città di Castello–Sansepolcro lines. The station is a 5min walk from the town centre.

Destinations Città di Castello (FCU line 6 daily; 2hr 20min–4hr 50min); Foligno (every 30min–1hr; connections to Spello, Assisi, Gualdo Tadino, Fossato di Vico and Perugia; 35–50min); Narni (9 daily; 7min); Orte (11 daily; connections to Rome, Orvieto, Chiusi, Arezzo and Florence; 15–30min); Perugia (FCU line 7 daily; connections at FCU Sant'Anna station in Perugia for Città di Castello and Sansepolcro,

shared FCU and FS/Trenitalia station at Ponte San Giovanni for connections to Foligno and Terontola; 1hr 30min); Sansepolcro (FCU line; 10–16 daily via Perugia Sant'Anna; 2hr 40min–4hr 30min); Todi (FCU line; 7 daily; 45min).

By bus Buses also stop at the station, making it easy to move on from Terni without having to enter town, should you so wish.

Destinations Cascata delle Marmore (20 daily; 15min); Orvieto (13 daily Mon–Sat; 2hr–2hr 20min); Scheggino (8 daily; 55min); Todi (3 daily Mon–Sat; 1hr); also long-distance services to Bolsena (connection at Orvieto) and Rome (2 daily; 1hr 25min).

INFORMATION

Tourist office Via Cassian Bon 2–4 – take Viale della Stazione from the station, and it's 400m up, on the right, just beyond Piazza Cornelio Tacito (Mon–Sat 9am–1pm & 3–6pm; ☎ 0744 423 047, ⓦ marmore.it).

Schegginio and the Activo Park

Strada Valcasana, Scheggino • Late June to mid-Sept daily 10am–6.30pm; Easter to mid-June & mid-Sept–Oct weekends only 10am–6.30pm • €25 for all activities, €16 for one activity, €12 for children under 110cm, plus extra for certain activities • ☎ 074 361 8005, ⓦ activopark.com

By following the SS209 from Terni past the walled, medieval village of **SCHEGGINO** you can pick up the Spoleto road into the Valnerina, a route covered on p.660. If you have kids in tow, the **Activo Park**, signed from Scheggino, is worth seeking out. This adventure complex has activities galore, from tree-climbing to abseiling, and from whitewater rafting and archery to a donkey farm. There's a restaurant and pizzeria on site, as well as picnic areas.

ACCOMMODATION AND EATING SCHEGGINO

Albergo-Trattoria del Ponte Via del Borgo 11–17 ☎ 0743 61 253, ⓦ albergoristorantedelponte.com. Bright, simple bedrooms, perfect if you want to spend the weekend at the Activo Park. There is also an excellent restaurant – closed Mon except in Aug – the trout dishes with truffles, in particular, are superb. Half-board €50 per person. **€60**

10

Narni and around

NARNI claims to be the geographical centre of Italy, with a hilltop site jutting into the Nera valley on a majestic spur and crowned by another of Albornoz's formidable papal fortresses. Commanding one end of a steep gorge (about 10min of fairly spectacular train travel), it was once the gateway into Umbria, the last post before the Tiber valley and the undefended road to Rome. However, while the town retains a fine medieval character, the views from its heights are marred by steel and chemical works around **Narni Scalo**, the new town in the valley below.

The heart of the **old town** has all the standard fittings: the medieval piazzas, the warren of streets, a modest art gallery, the usual crop of Romanesque churches, and a huge *rocca*, open for occasional events. There's a **Roman bridge** on the outskirts, the subject of considerable local hype. Goethe arrived in Narni in the middle of the night and was peeved not to have seen it; he was only missing a solitary arch in the middle of the river – just as easily viewed from the train.

Museo della Città di Narni

Via Aurelio Saffi 1 • Tues–Sun 10.30am–6.30pm • €5 • ☎ 0744 717 117

The bulk of the town's paintings and other works of art are housed in the **Museo della Città di Narni** in the Palazzo Eroli. The highlight is a superlative and much-copied *Coronation of the Virgin* by Ghirlandaio, with a collection of good works by minor medieval Umbrian artists.

ARRIVAL, INFORMATION AND TOURS   NARNI

By train It's an easy 30min hop on the train from Terni to Narni, and there are buses roughly every hour to Piazza Garibaldi in the old town.

By bus Buses from out of town stop at the railway station and at Piazza Garibaldi in the old town; there are frequent services to Terni (11 daily; 30min).

Tourist office Piazza dei Priori 3 (Mon–Fri 9.30am–12.30pm & 4.30–7pm, Sat 9.30am–12.30pm, Sun 10am–noon & 5–7pm; ☎ 0744 715 362).

Guided tours Some of Narni's most captivating sights lie beneath the streets, parts of Roman cisterns, eighth-century chapels and more, all of which can be seen on 1hr guided tours led by Narni Sotterranea (usually at weekends only, but check the website for the latest programme; €6; ☎ 0744 722 292, ⓦ narnisotterranea.it), at Via S. Bernardo 12.

ACCOMMODATION AND EATING

Hotel Dei Priori Vicolo del Comune 4 ☎ 0744 726 843, ⓦ loggiadeipriori.it. Lovely family-run hotel in the heart of Narni, in a medieval building with loggia. Spick-and-span rooms, friendly service and a well-regarded restaurant. **€75**

Il Pincio Via XX Settembre 117 ☎ 0744 722 241. Occupying the cellar of a medieval *palazzo*, this little restaurant is an excellent place to come for game – you may even find thrush and lark on the menu. If that doesn't appeal, try the ravioli made of kamut flour, or handmade pasta with sausage and asparagus. You can eat very well for €25. 12.30–2.30pm & 8–10.30pm; closed Wed in low season.

Todi

TODI is one of the best-known Umbrian hill-towns, its central **Piazza del Popolo** widely held to be among the most perfect medieval piazzas in Italy, the town itself to be the country's most liveable. At heart a thriving and insular agricultural centre, Todi is also a favoured trendy retreat for foreign expats and Rome's arts and media types. In the way of these things the visitors haven't been far behind, but neither fact should deter you from making a day-trip: few places beat it for sheer location – its hilltop position is stunning – and fairy-tale medievalism.

The Duomo

Summer: Mon–Sat 8am–1pm & 3–6.30pm, Sun 8.30am–1pm & 3–7pm; winter Mon–Sat 8am–1pm & 1.30–5pm, Sun 8.30am–1pm & 3–6pm • Church free, museum €1.50

The **Duomo** at the far (northern) end of the central square, atop a broad flight of steps, is the main feature – a meeting point of the last of the Romanesque and the first of the Gothic forms filtering up from France in the early fourteenth century. The square, three-tiered **facade** is inspired simplicity; just a sumptuous rose window (1520) and ornately carved doorway to embellish the pinky weathered marble – the classic example of a form found all over Umbria. Inevitably the interior is less impressive. There's some delicate nineteenth-century stained glass in the arched nave on the right, and a good altarpiece by Giannicola di Paolo (a follower of Perugino), while a poor sixteenth-century *Last Judgement*, loosely derived from Michelangelo's, defaces the back wall. The strikingly carved **choir** (1530) – of incredible delicacy and precision – is the region's best, with panels at floor level near the front depicting the tools used to carve the piece. The crypt and small museum contains a rambling collection of ancient Roman – and possibly Etruscan – fragments and religious ephemera.

The palaces

The other key buildings in the piazza are the three **public palaces**, squared off near the Duomo in deliberately provocative fashion as an expression of medieval civic pride – definitely trying to put one over on the Church. The adjoining Palazzo del Capitano (1290) and adjacent Palazzo del Popolo (begun 1213) are most prominent, thanks mainly to the stone staircase that looks like the setting for a thousand B-movie sword fights.

The Museo-Pinacoteca di Todi

Piazza del Popolo • Tues–Sun: April–Oct 10am–1.30pm & 3–6pm; Nov–March 10.30am–1pm & 2.30–5pm • €5, or €7.50 for a combined ticket with the Cisterne Romane & Campanile di San Fortunato • ☎ 075 894 418, ⓦ sistemamuseo.it/museoid.php?uid=61

The Palazzo del Capitano houses a superb museum, the **Museo-Pinacoteca di Todi**, which brilliantly weaves an open-plan sequence of rooms into the existing medieval structure. The first section of the museum delves into Todi's history, followed by rooms devoted to archeology, coins and medallions, fabrics, ceramics and a picture gallery. In many cases the rooms are more alluring than their displays – particularly the lovely frescoed salon devoted to ceramics – but numerous individual exhibits merit a closer look, none more so than the museum's star painting: the sumptuous *Coronation of the Virgin* (1507) by Lo Spagna.

Palazzo dei Priori

The **Palazzo dei Priori** (1293–1337) is the southernmost building in the square, with all the various crenellations, battlements and mullioned windows of the other palaces but with the difference that they've been recently restored. It's been the seat of all the town's various rulers and today is still the town hall; if you can look as if you're on council business you should be able to peep inside.

Cisterne Romane

Via del Monte • April–Oct Tues–Sun 10.30am–1.30pm & 3–6pm; Nov–March Sat & Sun 10.30am–1pm & 2.30–5pm; €2, or €7.50 combined ticket with Museo della Città & Campanile di San Fortunato • ☎ 075 894 4148

A side street leads off the west side of Piazza del Popolo to the **Cisterne Romane**, a massive Roman cistern, which offers a graphic illustration of the Romans' prodigious engineering abilities. Though it is possible to visit only a fraction, the tunnels stretch for over 5km.

10

The Tempio di San Fortunato

Tues–Sun: April to mid-Oct 9am–1pm & 3–7pm; mid-Oct to March 10am–1pm & 2.30–5pm • Free

Streets to the right of the Duomo are quiet and dozy and worth a wander, though the single most celebrated sight in town after the piazza is the **Tempio di San Fortunato**, set above gardens a very short stroll from the centre. It's an enormous thing given the size of the town – testimony to Todi's medieval wealth and importance. The squat, messy and clearly unfinished facade, an amalgam of Romanesque and Gothic styles, reflects the time it took to build (1292–1462) and at first glance doesn't exactly raise expectations. A florid **Gothic doorway** of arched swirls and carved craziness, however, is the first of several surprises, second of which is the enormous light, airy interior, recently highlighted by cleaning and several dazzling coats of whitewash. It marks the pinnacle of the Umbrian tradition for large vaulted churches, a style based on the smaller and basic "barn churches" common in Tuscany, which were distinguished by a single, low-pitched roof, and naves and aisles of equal height. (San Domenico in Perugia, p.630, is another example.) It also marks a trend for side-chapels, a habit picked up from Catalonia and southern France in the thirteenth century and made necessary by the rising demand for daily Masses as the Franciscans became a more ministering order. There's another good **choir**, heavier and with more hints of the Baroque than the one in the Duomo, as well as a few scant patches of Sienese fresco. The fresco by **Masolino di Panicale** in the fourth chapel on the right is a good example of this painter's rare work, though a bit battered.

Some lovely **cloisters** to the rear round off a distinctive and worthwhile church. Climb the **campanile** (April–Oct Tues–Sun 10am–1pm & 3–6.30pm; Nov–March daily 10.30am–1pm & 2.30–5pm; €2, or €7.50 combined ticket with Museo della Città & Cisterne Romane) for sweeping views.

West of San Fortunato

The stony track to the right of San Fortunato leads to the rambling **Giardino Pubblico**, an ideal place for a siesta. Full of shady nooks and narrow pathways, it's a cut above the normal town plot. There's also a kids' playground and a very small **Rocca**, both less noteworthy than the views, which are extensive though usually hazy. A ten-minute walk west, **Santa Maria della Consolazione** (Wed–Mon: April–Oct 9am–12.30pm & 2.30–6.30pm; Nov–March 9.30am–12.30pm & 2.30–5pm), completed in 1607, was called the best Renaissance church in Italy by Victorian writers (pretty close to saying the best in the world). It's thought to have been based on an earlier Bramante draft for St Peter's in Rome; the alternating window types in the cupola are a Bramante trademark.

ARRIVAL AND INFORMATION | TODI

By train There are FCU trains from Terni and Perugia approximately hourly. Todi's train station, Ponte Rio, is in the middle of nowhere; bus #C runs to the centre roughly hourly. If you want to book a taxi, call ☎075 894 2375, ☎075 894 2525 or ☎347 774 8321 (€10–12).

By bus Buses are far less frequent, and stop below the town by the church of Santa Maria della Consolazione or higher up, just off the main square near San Fortunato.

Destinations Orvieto (1 daily; 1hr 30min); Perugia (4–7 daily; 1hr 15min); Terni (3 daily Mon–Sat; 1hr).

Tourist office Piazza del Popolo 36 (Mon–Sat 9.30am–1pm & 3–6pm, Sun 10am–1pm; ☎075 894 5416, ⓦcomune.todi.pg.it); has details on the many festivals and events held here throughout the year, including the increasingly popular Todi Festival (first 8 days of Sept; ⓦtodiartefestival.com).

ACCOMMODATION

★ **Entropia Country House** Via Loreto Grutti 6 ☎075 885 2249, ⓦprogettoentropia.it. Set in a nineteenth-century farmhouse surrounded by parkland just 6km from Todi, this agriturismo makes a wonderful retreat, with cosily furnished rooms and welcoming staff. There's a swimming pool and a very good restaurant too. €110

Fonte Cesia Via Lorenzo Leoni 3 ☎075 894 3737, ⓦfontecesia.it. Converted medieval townhouse at the heart of the historic core. Rooms vary in size and decoration, but all have period details, rich fabrics and up-to-the-minute facilities. €219

★ **San Lorenzo Tre** Via S. Lorenzo 3 ☎ 075 894 4555, ⓦ sanlorenzo3.it. If you don't mind lugging your suitcase up steep flights of steps, this elegantly furnished *residenza* inside a townhouse in the street parallel to Via del Duomo

is Todi's most appealing place to stay. Rooms vary in size (and in price); no. 5 is the nicest, beautifully furnished with antiques, and with stunning views of the surrounding countryside. What's more, there's a shady garden and a fabulous roof terrace. €110

EATING AND DRINKING

Cavour Corso Cavour 21 ☎ 075 894 3730. This unpretentious trattoria has stunning views from its outdoor terrace and several cosy rooms indoors. You can eat very well for €30, or more cheaply if you go for one of the generous pizzas (from €4.50) including asparagus and mushroom, and potato with gorgonzola. Daily noon–4pm & 7pm–2am; closed Thurs in winter.

La Mulinella Località Pontenaia 29 ☎ 075 894 4779. Wonderful place on the southern edge of town, where everything is home-made, from the bread (versions with sage, with chilli and with hazelnuts) to the pasta (€9). Great winter soups (€9) as well. Desserts, of course, are made at home as well, and include a marvellous *zuppa inglese*, or trifle. 12.30–2.30pm & 8–10.30pm; closed Wed.

Pane e Vino Via Ciuffelli 33 ☎ 075 894 5448. Just off the main square, this place is perfect for simple lunches and suppers (from €30 for three courses): there's a tremendous choice of antipasti. Try the house special: a sharing platter including smoked duck breast carpaccio and cheeses served with honey (€16). *Primi* include a risotto with pumpkin and saffron, and *taglierini* with tomato and lemon, as well as the usual game, mushroom and truffle dishes. 12.30–2.30pm & 5.30–8pm; closed Wed.

★ **Umbria** Via San Bonaventura ☎ 075 894 2737. The town's best-known restaurant. Prices are higher than average, but the panorama from the terrace is the thing; go for something simple, like the chargrilled meat (from around €14), and in season, book to be sure of an outside table. 12.30–2.30pm & 7.30–10.30pm; closed Tues.

10

Orvieto

Out on a limb from the rest of Umbria, **ORVIETO** is perfectly placed between Rome and Florence to serve as a historical picnic for tour operators. Visitors flood into the town in their millions, drawn by the **Duomo**, one of the greatest Gothic buildings in Italy. However, once its facade and Signorelli's frescoes have been admired, the town's not quite as exciting as guides and word of mouth make out. This is partly to do with the gloominess of the dark volcanic rock from which it's built, and, more poetically, because it harbours something of the characteristic brooding atmosphere of Etruscan towns (it was one of the twelve-strong federation of Etruscan cities). Two thousand years on, it's not difficult to detect a more laidback atmosphere in the cities east of the Tiber – founded by the Umbrians, a sunnier and easier-going people. All the same Orvieto is likeable, the setting superb, the Duomo unmissable, and the rest of the town good for a couple of hours' visit. And you could always indulge in its renowned white **wine** if you're stuck with time on your hands.

It is the first impressions of Orvieto from afar that tend to linger; its position is almost as remarkable and famous as its cathedral. The town, rising 300m sheer from the valley floor, sits on a tabletop plug of volcanic lava, one of four such remnants in the vicinity. It starts to look fairly average again from the dismal town around the train

CARTA ORVIETO UNICA

If you plan to visit all Orvieto's main sights, it would be worth buying the **Carta Orvieto Unica** (ⓦ cartaunica.it). Costing €18, it provides admission to the Signorelli frescoes in the cathedral (Cappella di San Brizio), tours of the caves and tunnels beneath the town (see box, p.672) the Museo Claudio Faina, Torre del Moro, Museo Emilio Greco, Museo Archeologico Nazionale, Etruscan tombs and the Pozzo di San Patrizio. It also allows you one trip on the funicular and one bus journey, or five hours' worth of parking at the Campo della Fiera car park. The ticket can be bought at the tourist office, the Piazza della Pace funicular car park, the Etruscan tombs, the Museo dell'Opera del Duomo or the Pozzo di San Patrizio.

10

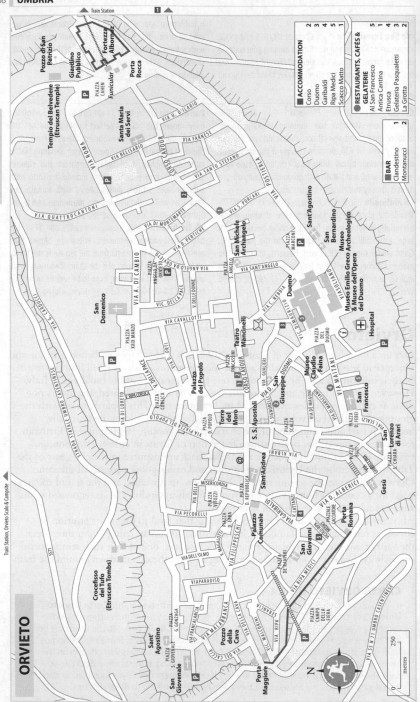

ORVIETO

Train Station

Train Station, Orvieto Scalo & Campsite

Viterbo

■ ACCOMMODATION	
Corso	2
Duomo	3
Garibaldi	4
Ripa Medici	5
Scacco Matto	1

● RESTAURANTS, CAFÉS & GELATERIE	
Al San Francesco	5
Antica Cantina	1
Etrusca	4
Gelateria Pasqualetti	3
La Grotta	2

■ BAR	
Clandestino	1
Montanucci	2

N

0   250
metres

station, but hit the twisting 3km road up to the old centre and you begin to get a sense of its drama and one-off weirdness. Orvieto's old centre is compact and walkable: all of the main sights are within a twenty-minute stroll of the Duomo.

The Duomo

Daily: April–Oct 9.30am–7.30pm; Nov–March 9.30am–1.30pm & 2.30–5.30pm • €2, €3 including Cappella di San Brizio, €5 including Museo dell'Opera del Duomo and Sant'Agostino

Burckhardt described Orvieto's Duomo as "the greatest and richest polychrome monument in the world", while Pope Leo XIII called it "the Golden Lily of Italian cathedrals", adding that on the Day of Judgement it would float up to heaven carried by its own beauty. According to a tradition fostered by the Church, it was built to celebrate the so-called **Miracle of Bolsena** of 1263 (see box below).

Brief history

It was miraculous that the Duomo was built at all. Medieval Orvieto was so violent that at times the population thought about giving up on it altogether. Dante wrote that its family feuds were worse than those between Verona's Montagues and Capulets. The building was also dogged by a committee approach to design – even the plans took thirty years to draw up. Yet though construction dragged on for three centuries and exhausted 33 architects, 152 sculptors, 68 painters and 90 mosaicists, the final product is a surprisingly unified example of the transitional Romanesque-Gothic style. Credit for guiding the work at its most important stage goes to the Sienese architect **Lorenzo Maitani** (c.1270–1330), with the initial plans probably drawn up by Arnolfo di Cambio, architect of Florence's Palazzo Vecchio.

The facade

The **facade** is the star turn, owing its undeniable impact to a decorative richness just the right side of overkill. It's a riot of columns, spires, bas-reliefs, sculptures, dazzling and almost overpowering use of colour, colossally emphasized doorways and hundreds of capricious details just about held together by four enormous fluted columns. Stunning from the dwarfed piazza, particularly at sunset or under floodlights, it's not all superficial gloss. The **four pillars** at the base, one of the highlights of fourteenth-century Italian sculpture, are well worth a close look. The work of Maitani and his pupils, they describe episodes from the Old and New Testaments in staggering detail: lashings of plague, famine, martyrdoms, grotesque mutilation, mad and emaciated figures, the Flagellation, the Massacre of the Innocents, strange visitations, Cain slaying Abel (particularly juicy), and only the occasional touch of light relief. In its day it was there to point an accusing finger at Orvieto's moral slackers, as the none-too-cheerful final panel makes clear, with the damned packed off to fire, brimstone and eternal misery.

THE MIRACLE OF BOLSENA

The story goes that a Bohemian priest was travelling to Rome to shake off a heretical disbelief in transubstantiation – the idea that the body and blood of Christ are physically present in the Eucharist. While he celebrated Mass in a church near Lago di Bolsena, blood started to drip from the host onto the *corporale*, the cloth underneath the chalice on the altar. The stained linen was whisked off to Pope Urban IV, who like many a pope was in Orvieto to escape the heat and political hassle of Rome. He immediately proclaimed a miracle, and a year later Thomas Aquinas, no less, drew up a papal bull instigating the feast of **Corpus Domini**. The Church at the time, however, was in retreat, and the Umbrian towns were at the height of their civic expansion. It's likely that the building of an awe-inspiring cathedral in one of the region's most powerful *comuni* was less an act to commemorate a miracle than a shrewd piece of political opportunism designed to remind errant citizens of the papacy's power.

10

10

Luca Signorelli and the Cappella di San Brizio

The **inside** is a disappointment at least at first glance, as if the facade either took all the enthusiasm or all the money and the church was tacked on merely to prop everything else up. Adorned with alternating stripes of coloured marble similar to those found in the cathedrals of Siena, Florence and Pisa, it's mainly distinguished by **Luca Signorelli**'s fresco cycle, *The Last Judgement* (1499–1504), in the **Cappella di San Brizio** at the end of the south nave (same hours, except Sun: April–June 1–5.30pm; July–Oct 1–6.30pm; Nov–March 2.30–5.30pm). Some claim it surpasses even Michelangelo's similar cycle in the Sistine Chapel, painted forty years later and obviously heavily influenced by Signorelli's earlier treatment.

Several painters, including Perugino and Fra' Angelico (who completed two ceiling panels), tackled the chapel before Signorelli – a free-thinking and singular artist from nearby Cortona – was commissioned to finish it off. All but the lower walls are crowded with the movement of passionate and beautifully observed muscular figures, creating an effect that's realistic and almost grotesquely fantastic at the same time. There are plenty of bizarre details to hold the narrative interest. A mass of monstrous lechery and naked writhing flesh fills the *Inferno* panel, including that of the painter's unfaithful mistress, immortalized in hell for all to see. In another an unfortunate is having his ear bitten off by a green-buttocked demon. Signorelli, suitably clad in black, has painted himself with Fra' Angelico in the lower left corner of *The Sermon of the Antichrist*, both calmly looking on as someone is garrotted at their feet.

The Cappella del Corporale

The twin **Cappella del Corporale** contains the sacred *corporale* itself, locked away in a massive, jewel-encrusted casket (designed as a deliberate copy of the facade), along with some appealing frescoes by local fourteenth-century painter Ugolino di Prete, describing events connected with the Miracle of Bolsena. The entire apse is covered in more frescoes by Ugolino, many of which were partly restored by Pinturicchio, who was eventually kicked off the job for "consuming too much gold, too much azure and too much wine". Also worth a mention are an easily missed *Madonna and Child* by Gentile da Fabriano and a beautifully delicate fifteenth-century font, both near the main doors.

Museo dell'Opera del Duomo (MODO)

Piazza del Duomo • March & Oct daily except Tues 10am–5pm; April–Sept daily 9.30am–7pm; Nov–Feb daily except Tues 10am–1pm & 2–5pm • €4, or €5 including admission to Signorelli frescoes in the Duomo & church of Sant'Agostino • ☏ 0763 342 477, ⓦ opsm.it

Next to the Duomo on the right as you look at it is the **Museo dell'Opera del Duomo** – or **MODO** for short. Highlights are paintings by Martini and Pastura (an artist from Viterbo influenced by Perugino), several important thirteenth-century sculptures by Arnolfo di Cambio and Andrea Pisano, and a lovely font filled with Escher-like carved fishes. The **Emilio Greco** section of the museum (same hours and ticket, or Orvieto Unica card – see box, p.667) comprises nearly a hundred works donated to the city by the artist who created the Duomo's bronze doors in the 1960s – peek through the door beyond the ground-floor ticket office and you'll see enough of the exhibits to know if you want a closer look.

Museo Claudio Faina and the Etruscan tombs

The wonderfully restored **Museo Claudio Faina** (incorporating the Museo Civico) at Piazza del Duomo 27 (April–Sept daily 9.30am–6pm; Nov–March Tues–Sun 10am–5pm; €4.50; ☏0763 341 216) has a superbly displayed collection of vases and fragments excavated from sixth-century-BC **tombs**. These tombs (daily: summer 8.30am–7pm; winter 8.30am–5pm; €3) are still visible just off the road that drops towards the station from Piazza Cahen and are worth tracking down for their rows of massive and sombre stone graves.

San Lorenzo di Arari

Piazza Santa Chiara • Daily 8.30am–1pm & 3–6pm • Free

As far as the town's **churches** go, they all naturally pale beside the Duomo, though most have something worthwhile to see. The tiny Romanesque **San Lorenzo di Arari** was built in 1291 on the site of a church destroyed by monks from nearby San Francesco because the sound of its bells got on their nerves. Four **frescoes** on the left of the nave depict typically traumatic scenes from the life of St Lawrence. There's also an Etruscan sacrificial slab, which rather oddly serves as the Christian altar (*arari* meaning "altar").

San Giovenale and around

Piazza San Giovenale • Daily 8.30am–1pm & 3–6pm • Free

From Piazzale Cacciatore there's a decent **walk** around the city's southern walls (Via Ripa Medici) with views over to a prominent outcrop of rock in the middle distance, part of the old volcanic crater. Ten minutes or so brings you to **San Giovenale**, whose rustic surroundings, on the very western tip of the *rupa*, Orvieto's volcanic plateau, are a far cry from the bustle of the Duomo. It's not much to look at from the outside, but the musty **medieval interior** is the best (and oldest) in the town. The thirteenth-century Gothic transept, with its two pointed arches, rather oddly stands a metre above the rounded Romanesque nave, making for a hybrid and distinctive church, all of it exhaustively decorated with thirteenth- and fifteenth-century **frescoes**. Check out the *Tree of Life* fresco right of the main door and the macabre *Calendar of Funeral Anniversaries* partly covered by the side entrance.

Pozzo di San Patrizio and Pozzo della Cava

Pozzo di San Patrizio Viale Sangallo • March, April, Sept & Oct 9am–6.45pm; May–Aug 9am–7.45pm; Nov–Feb 10am–4.45pm • €5, €3.50 if you have a ticket to the Pozzo della Cava • **Pozzo della Cava** Via della Cava 28 • Tues–Sun 9am–8pm, closed second half of Jan • €3, or €2 if you have a ticket to the Pozzo di San Patrizio • ☎ 0763 343 768, ⓦ pozzodellacava.it

The **Pozzo di San Patrizio**, just off Piazzale Cahen, is the town's novelty act, a huge cylindrical well commissioned in 1527 by Pope Clement VII to guarantee the town's water supply during an expected siege by the Imperial Army (which never came). Water was brought to the surface by donkeys on two broad staircases, cannily designed never to intersect. It's a striking piece of engineering, 13m wide and 62m deep, named after its supposed similarity to the Irish cave where St Patrick died in 493, aged 133.

Another well, the **Pozzo della Cava**, on the western side of town, was discovered in 1984 but only made fully accessible in 2004. You can explore the fascinating complex of nine caves, complete with archeological finds, on your own, or take one of the thematic guided tours (see website for details).

<table>
<tr><td>**ARRIVAL AND DEPARTURE**</td><td style="text-align:right">**ORVIETO**</td></tr>
</table>

By train If you arrive by train, take the restored nineteenth-century funicular (every 10–15min; €1; tickets from the funicular ticket office or station newsagent or bar, valid for 70min on city buses; €1.50 if bought on board a bus) from the station forecourt to Piazza Cahen: it's a pleasant walk from here along Corso Cavour to the centre of town (5–10min), or you can take the regular minibus #A that stops in Piazza Cahen every 10min for the run to Piazza del Duomo; bus #B stops in Piazza della Repubblica

before dropping off in Piazza del Duomo. Buses replace the funicular from 8.30pm till midnight. Orvieto has excellent train connections to Rome and into Tuscany, but is not well connected with the rest of Umbria.

Destinations Arezzo (12 daily; 45min–1hr 40min); Chiusi (hourly; 40min; connections to Siena, 1hr 45min–2hr 30min); Florence (17 daily; 1hr 30min–2hr 45min); Orte (17 daily; connections to Narni, Terni, Toto and Foligno; 35min); Rome (19 daily; 1hr 20min); Terontola (13 daily;

10

GOING UNDERGROUND

The fascinating **Orvieto Underground** tours explore the vast labyrinth of **tunnels**, caves and store rooms that riddle the soft volcanic rock on which Orvieto is built: most date back to medieval times, some to the Etruscan era. The ticket office is next to the tourist office at Piazza del Duomo 23. Tours leave daily (except Feb, when they run at weekends only) at 11am, 12.15pm, 4pm and 5.15pm (€5.50) and last about an hour. Call ☎0339 733 2764, or see ⓦorvietounderground.it for details and bookings.

connections to Perugia; 40min–1hr 15min).
By bus Inter-town buses take you directly to Piazza Cahen, Piazza XXIX Marzo, or Piazza della Repubblica, depending on the service.
Destinations Bolsena (2 daily Mon–Sat; 50min); Narni (6 daily Mon–Sat; 40min); Todi (1 daily Mon–Sat; 1hr 30min).

By car Without a doubt, the best approach is by car through the hills to the southwest (from Bolsena, see p.124). You can park at the Campo della Fiera car park, beneath the walls at the southwest corner of town; escalators (7am–9pm) and a lift (7am–midnight) run up to the centre from here.

INFORMATION

Tourist office Piazza del Duomo 24 (Mon–Fri 8.15am–1.50pm & 4–7pm, Sat & Sun 10am–1pm & 3–6pm; ☎0763 341 772, ⓦcomune.orvieto.tr.it). Ask here for information on events, including Umbria Jazz Winter: five days of marching bands and jazz performances over New Year. A second, summer-only tourist office is on Piazza Cahen, right next to the funicular (April–Sept daily 10am–6pm; ☎0763 340 168).

ACCOMMODATION

Most of the town's budget rooms – and nightlife – are in Orvieto Scalo, the unlovely district around the station, but this is very much a last resort; the hotels below are all in the upper old town.

Corso Corso Cavour 343 ☎0763 342 020, ⓦhotelcorso .net. A little way from the centre, and therefore relatively quiet, but still within easy walking distance of everything, with cosily decorated rooms. Breakfast is extra. **€108**
Duomo Via Vicolo di Maurizio 7 ☎0763 341 887, ⓦorvietohotelduomo.com. This 18-room hotel in a restructured medieval building has uninspired but comfortable rooms. It's extremely central and convenient for the Duomo, less than 1min walk away, and there's a garden too. The three rooms in the annexe 50m down the road are cheaper. **€130**
Garibaldi Vicolo dei Lattanzi 2 ☎339 812 7911,

ⓦvacanzetrusche.it. This B&B has large, spotless rooms and a helpful host who serves up a generous breakfast. There's parking too. **€150**
★ **Ripa Medici** Vicolo Ripa Medici 14 ☎0763 341 343, ⓦripamedici.it. This B&B's two bright, airy doubles have been decorated with real attention to detail by friendly owner Sabrina, and there are lovely views and a kitchen for guests' use too. **€65**
Scacco Matto 10km away on the SS448 near Lago di Corbora ☎0744 950 163, ⓦscaccomatto.net; bus to Baschi/Civitella. Orvieto's nearest campsite is on the Lake of Corbara and is open March–Oct. Pitches **€20**

EATING AND DRINKING

There are plenty of places to eat in Orvieto, though nowhere that stands out gastronomically. For a tourist town, though, many restaurants offer very good value and tasty Umbrian food. Restaurants are grouped together at the bottom (eastern end) of Corso Cavour. The wine bars around the Duomo are an expensive way of sampling the well-known Orvietan white.

Al San Francesco Via Bonaventura Cerretti 10 ☎076 334 3302. Deservedly popular for its excellent value and variety; a 450-seat canteen affair, with shady outdoor tables, offering a choice between restaurant and self-service pizzeria. *Primi* are around €8, *secondi* €9–14 and pizza kicks off at €4.40. Daily 12.30–2.30pm, and occasionally 8–10.30pm on Sat & Sun.
Antica Cantina Piazza Monaldeschi 18–19 ☎0763 344 746. Popular with locals, reasonably priced (€15 will buy a good, light meal) and succeeds in reproducing the old-fashioned trattoria atmosphere and simple, but well-cooked local seasonal staples. There are soups all year – try the chickpea and chestnut in winter – and the handmade pasta includes *ombrichelli* with sausage and freshly grated truffle, and fresh fusilli, made with cheese and black pepper and served with tomato and basil. Daily noon–4pm & 7–11pm; closed Mon.
Clandestino Corso Cavour 40 ☎328 972 7472. This bar is a good choice at aperitif time – with a great range of nibbles to accompany a glass of wine or a Campari spritz.

They also make good cappuccino, so you might want to consider it for breakfast too. Open daily all day.

Etrusca Via Maitani 10 ☎0763 344 016. A traditional and relaxed trattoria that takes its cooking seriously, with classic Umbrian dishes (rabbit and pigeon are specialities – both around €12) and an attractive, medieval vaulted dining-room. Check out the ancient wine cellars, carved from the solid rock. Daily 12.30–2.30pm & 8–10.30pm.

Gelateria Pasqualetti Piazza del Duomo 14. This ivy-covered *gelateria* in the main piazza is the town's best spot for ice cream. There's a second branch at Corso Cavour 56, open year-round. Daily 11.30am–midnight; closed Nov–March.

La Grotta Via Signorelli 5 ☎0763 341 348. Small, reliable trattoria that has been in business for over 40 years and is good value for central Orvieto (€25 and up for a meal); the staff are friendly too. Try *tagliatelle* with duck and follow with a hearty wild-boar stew. Noon–3pm & 7–10pm; closed Tues.

Montanucci Corso Cavour 21 ☎0763 341 261. Classic old-fashioned bar on the Corso that makes excellent coffee, and is a good place to sit outside for breakfast. Open all day; closed Wed.

10

Le Marche

DUCAL PALACE, URBINO

Le Marche

Wedged between the verdant Apennines and a turquoise Adriatic, Le Marche is a varied region, and one you could enjoy weeks of slow travel exploring. Sparsely populated inland areas are unspoilt and untouristed, particularly in the southwest, where stone hill-villages make atmospheric bases for hikes into the spectacular Monti Sibillini range. Ancona, the region's capital, is a gritty but engaging port town which gives way heading southwards to the dramatic Conero Riviera, with its natural white-pebble beaches backed by milky Dover-esque cliffs. In contrast north and south of the Ancona area the coastline is hemmed with boxy new-build resorts and mechanically pruned beaches of coarse sand.

11

Of Le Marche's old-fashioned and slightly forgotten seaside resorts, **Pesaro** is the largest, with a Renaissance centre maintaining its dignity behind the package-tour seafront, and lesser-known **Fano** to the south offers a similar experience. Away from the scorching seaside fun, most appealing – and best known – of Le Marche's sights are the small hilltop town of **Urbino**, with its spectacular Renaissance palace, and the dramatic fortress of **San Leo**, just across the border from San Marino. Further south, architecturally fascinating **Macerata** is a sleepy university town surrounded by lovely countryside, and, right on the regional border, the fascinating city of **Ascoli Piceno** is a worthy stopoff on the way into Abruzzo. **Loreto** just south of Ancona is one of Italy's top pilgrimage sites, the basilica providing shelter for what Catholics claim is Jesus' childhood house, air freighted to Le Marche by a band of angels.

REGIONAL FOOD AND WINE

Le Marche is very much a rural region, its food a mixture of **seafood** from the long coastline and **country cooking** from the interior, based on locally grown produce – tomatoes and fennel – and funghi, game, nuts and herbs gathered from the wild. The most distinctive dish, often served at summer festas, is a sweet-and-sour mix of olives stuffed with meat and fried, then served with crema fritta, little squares of fried cream. Rabbit and lamb are popular, as is pappardelle alla papera, wide, flat pasta with duck sauce, and, as in many other regions, truffles are considered a delicacy. Unfamiliar items on the antipasti menu include lonza (salt-cured pork) and ciauscolo (a pork-based spread). Meat grilled alla brace (over wood embers) is ubiquitous, and you may even come across porchetta, whole roast suckling pig, both in its original large-scale form and in a fast-food version used to fill crisp bread rolls. Don't confuse it with coniglio in porchetta though – this is rabbit cooked with fennel. Baked, stuffed dishes such as vincisgrassi, a rich layered dish of pasta, minced meat, mushrooms, giblets, brain, bechamel and truffles, are found everywhere. A typical seafood dish from Ancona is zuppa di pesce, a fish soup flavoured with saffron, though you'll find excellent fish broths – known simply as brodetto – all along the coast. Puddings include cicercchiata, balls of pasta fried and covered in honey, and frappe, fried leaves of filo-like pastry dusted with icing sugar.

Although it produces many drinkable **wines**, the region is best known for **Verdicchio**, a greeny-gold white, excellent with fish, which is instantly recognizable from its amphora-shaped bottle. This is in fact a hangover from a 1950s marketing ploy inspired by the ancient Greek custom of shipping wine from Ancona in clay amphorae and, reputedly, by the shape of the actress Gina Lollobrigida. Today, however, many producers sell their best Verdicchio in standard bottles – the one to look out for is Verdicchio dei Castelli di Jesi. Lesser-known **reds** include one of Italy's finest, Rosso Conero, a light wine based on the Montepulciano grape and full of fruit; more common is Rosso Piceno, based on the Sangiovese grape.

CONERO RIVIERA

Highlights

❶ Urbino "Ideal city" and art capital created by Federico da Montefeltro, the ultimate Renaissance man. **See p.678**

❷ San Leo This spectacular ancient town on a rocky outcrop is a landmark for miles around. **See p.685**

❸ Conero Riviera A coastline of white cliffs and turquoise seas ideal for walking, cycling and swimming or just working up a tan. **See p.695**

❹ Grotte di Frasassi Get under the region's skin at these impressive, publicly accessible caves bristling with outlandish stalactites and stalagmites. **See p.695**

❺ Loreto Experience religious fervour within the Santa Casa, allegedly Jesus' childhood abode, miraculously carried from Nazareth by angels. **See p.697**

❻ Macerata Catch some open-air opera in this attractive old university town surrounded by pretty countryside. **See p.699**

❼ Monti Sibillini Take to the hills in this hiker's mountain paradise. **See p.704**

❽ Ascoli Piceno A relatively undiscovered town of interesting food and architectural gems in southern Le Marche. **See p.706**

HIGHLIGHTS ARE MARKED ON THE MAP ON P.678

Getting around on public transport is relatively easy, though a car is useful in the more remote areas; ⓦ orari.trasporti .marche.it is a useful website with timetables covering the whole region (in Italian only). There are two main **rail routes**: along the coast on the Milan–Bari line or across Italy on the Ancona–Rome service. The provincial capitals – Urbino, Pesaro, Macerata, Ancona and Ascoli Piceno – are all well served by public transport, and Ancona is also a major port for **ferries** to Croatia, Greece and Turkey. For hiking in the Sibillini, **Amandola** has the best **bus** service; if you don't mind relying on fewer buses, **Montefortino** is a prettier base.

Urbino and around

Walled, austere and mostly built of brick, **URBINO** is a jumble of Renaissance and medieval houses, churches and *palazzi* atop a hill, dominated by the tremendous Palazzo Ducale. During the second half of the fifteenth century, it was one of the most prestigious courts in Europe, ruled by the remarkable Federico da Montefeltro, who employed some of the greatest artists and architects of the time to build and decorate his palace. Baldassarre Castiglione, whose sixteenth-century handbook of courtly behaviour, *Il Cortegiane* (The Courtier), is set in the palace, reckoned it to be the most beautiful in all Italy, and it does seem from contemporary accounts that

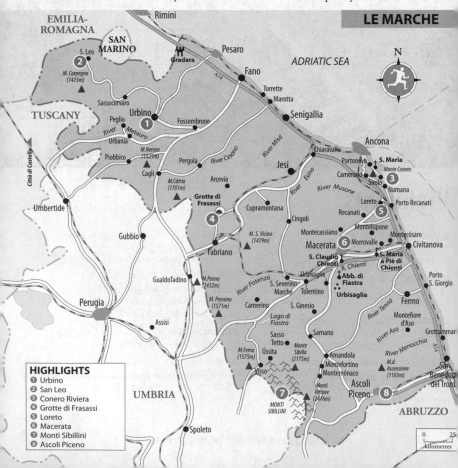

LE MARCHE

HIGHLIGHTS

① Urbino
② San Leo
③ Conero Riviera
④ Grotte di Frasassi
⑤ Loreto
⑥ Macerata
⑦ Monti Sibillini
⑧ Ascoli Piceno

fifteenth-century Urbino was an extraordinarily civilized place, a measured and urbane society in which life was lived without indulgence.

Nowadays Urbino is saved from an existence as an open-air museum by its lively university. In term-time at least, there's a refreshing, energetic feel to the town and plenty of places to eat and drink. Although a new town has grown up in the valley below, it seems to have been almost wilfully designed to be as ugly as possible, so as to better highlight the glories of the walled **upper town**, which, after all, is where you'll want to spend most of your time.

Outside the dour town walls, two places in northern Le Marche – the medieval strongholds of **Sassocorvaro** and **San Leo** – are well worth the effort it takes to reach them.

11

The Palazzo Ducale

Piazza Rinascimento 13 • Mon 8.30am–2pm, Tues–Sun 8.30am–7.15pm • Palace €5, temporary exhibitions €8

The **Palazzo Ducale**, rising above the town's uniform roofs, is a fitting monument to Federico, the urbane ruler of fifteenth-century Urbino. An elegant combination of the aesthetic and the practical, the facade comprises a triple-decked loggia in the form of a triumphal arch flanked by twin defensive towers. In contrast, the Palazzo's bare south side, forming one edge of the long central Piazza Rinascimento, looks rather bleak, and it's only inside that you begin to understand its reputation as one of the finest buildings of the Renaissance. The Palazzo houses the **Galleria Nazionale delle Marche**, but it's for the building itself most come for. Of the gallery's collections, the original Renaissance Urbino works justify most attention.

The courtyard

Just inside the entrance, the **Cortile d'Onore** is your first real taste of what Urbino is about. The courtyard is not immediately striking – the rest of Italy has a host of similar ones – but this is the prototype. Designed by Dalmatian-born Luciano Laurana, who was selected by Federico after he'd failed to find a suitably bold artist in Florence, it's both elegant and restrained.

The ground floor

Off the Cortile is the room that housed Federico's **library**, in its day one of the most comprehensive in Europe. He spent fourteen years and over thirty thousand ducats gathering books from across the continent, and employed forty scribes to make illuminated copies on kidskin, which were then covered in crimson and decorated with silver. They disappeared into the vaults of the Vatican after Urbino fell to the papacy in 1631 and now the rooms lie empty.

The first floor

A monumental staircase takes you up to the first floor where the tour starts in the austere, airy rooms of the **Appartamento della Jole**. Dotted with works of art, these rooms are an appetizer for what's to come, with huge fireplaces and wooden doors inlaid with everything from gyroscopes and mandolins to armour, representing the various facets of Federico's personality.

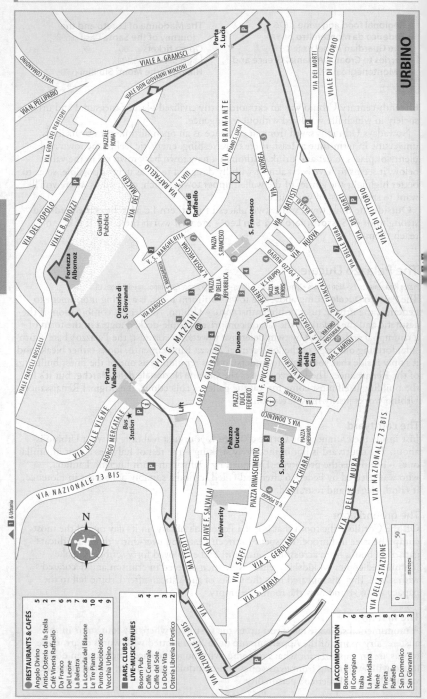

URBINO

Porta S. Lucia

VIALE A. GRAMSCI

VIALE DON GIOVANNI MINZONI

VIA COMMANDINO

VIA N. PELLIPARIO

PIAZZALE ROMA

VIA GIRO DEI DEBITORI

VIA T. V. RAFFAELLO

VIA DEI MACELLI

VIALE DI VITTORIO

VIA DEI MORTI

Casa di Raffaello

VIA BRAMANTE

VIA PIANO S. LUCIA

VIA S. ANDREA

S. Francesco

VIA C. BATTISTI

VIA VASARI

VIA VALERIO

VIALE DI VITTORIO

VIA DELLE MURA

VIA DEL MORTI

VIA DEL POPOLO

VIALE B. BUOZZI

Fortezza Albornoz

Giardini Pubblici

V. S. MARGHERITA

P. S. MARGHERITA

V. POSTA VECCHIA

PIAZZA S. FRANCESCO

VIA NUOVA

A. POZZO NUOVO

Oratorio di S. Giovanni

VIA BAROCCI

PIAZZA DELLA REPUBBLICA

V. S. FILIPPO

PIAZZA SAN FILIPPO

VIA V. VENETO

VIA DEL FIANCALE

VIA BUDASSI

OSTERIA DEL FIANCALE

VIALE FRATELLI ROSSELLI

Porta Valbona

VIA G. MAZZINI

@

Duomo

Museo della Città

VIA F. PUCCINOTTI

VIA S. BARTOLI

Bus Station

Lift

BORGO MERCATALE

CORSO GARIBALDI

PIAZZA DUCA FEDERICO

VIA F. PUCCINOTTI

VIA VETERANI

VIALE DELLE VIGNE

VIA NAZIONALE 73 BIS

Palazzo Ducale

S. Domenico

PIAZZA RINASCIMENTO

VIA S. DOMENICO

PIAZZA GHERARDI

VIA S. CHIARA

V. D. POGGIO

VIA DELLE MURA

VIA NAZIONALE 73 BIS

University

VIA PIAVE F. SALVALAI

VIA SAFFI

VIA S. GEROLAMO

VIA S. MARIA

VIA DELLA STAZIONE

MATTEOTTI

VIA NAZIONALE 73 BIS

N

B & Urbania

0   50
metres

RESTAURANTS & CAFÉS

Angolo Divino	5
Antica Osteria da la Stella	2
Café Vineria Raffaello	6
Da Franco	1
Del Leone	3
La Balestra	7
La Locanda del Blasone	8
Le Tre Piante	10
Punto Macrobiotico	4
Vecchia Urbino	9

BARS, CLUBS & LIVE-MUSIC VENUES

Bosom Pub	5
Caffè Centrale	4
Caffè del Sole	1
La Dolce Vita	3
Osteria Libreria Il Portico	2

ACCOMMODATION

Boncorte	7
Il Cortegiano	6
Italia	4
La Meridiana	9
Nenè	1
Pineta	8
Raffaello	2
San Domenico	5
San Giovanni	3

FEDERICO DA MONTEFELTRO

Federico da Montefeltro (1422–82) was a formidable soldier, a shrewd and humane ruler, and a genuine intellectual. As the elder but illegitimate son of the Montefeltro family, he only became ruler of Urbino after his tyrannical half-brother Oddantonio fell victim to an assassin during a popular rebellion. Federico promptly arrived on the scene – fuelling rumours that he'd engineered the uprising himself – and was elected to office after promising to cut taxes, to provide an education and health service, and to allow the people some say in the election of magistrates.

Urbino was a small state with few natural resources a long way from any major trading routes, so selling the military services of his army and himself was Federico's only way of keeping the city solvent. Federico's mercenary activities yielded a huge annual income, a substantial portion of which was used to keep taxes low, thus reducing the likelihood of social discontent during his long absences. When he was at home, he would leave his door open at mealtimes so that any member of his 500-strong court might speak to him between courses, and used to move around his state unarmed (unusual in a time when assassination was common), checking on the welfare of his people.

Between military and political commitments, Federico also found time to indulge his interest in the **arts**. Though he delighted in music, his first love was architecture, which he considered to be the highest form of intellectual and aesthetic activity. A friend of the leading architectural theorist Alberti, he commissioned buildings from Renaissance luminaries such as Francesco di Giorgio Martini and Piero della Francesca.

Passing through two more sets of similarly ornamented rooms, the most elaborately decorated part of the *palazzo* is the suite known as the **Appartamento del Duca**. On display here is a famous portrait of Federico by the Spanish artist **Pedro Berruguete**. Painted, as he always was, from the left, in profile (having lost his right eye in battle), Federico is shown as warrior, ruler, scholar and dynast; wearing an ermine-fringed gown over his armour, he sits reading a book, with his pasty and feeble-looking son, Guidobaldo, standing at his feet.

Sometimes on display in the Appartamento del Duca, but occasionally elsewhere, no painting better embodies the notion of perfection held by Urbino's elite than *The Ideal City*, long attributed to Piero but now thought to be by one of his followers. Probably intended as a design for a stage set, this famous display of perspective skill depicts a perfectly symmetrical, almost space-age cityscape, expressing the desire for a civic order that mirrors that of the heavens.

Continuing through the Duke's apartment, it's the next few rooms that give you the best insight into Federico's personality. A spiral staircase descends to two adjoining chapels, one dedicated to Apollo and the Muses, the other to the Christian God (no access from this floor when there is a special exhibition taking place below). This dualism typifies a strand of Renaissance thought in which mythology and Christianity were reconciled by positing a universe in which pagan deities were seen as aspects of the omnipotent Christian deity.

Back on the main floor you come to the most interesting and best-preserved of the palace's rooms, Federico's amazing **Studiolo**, a masterpiece of illusory perspective created not with paint but with intarsia (inlaid wood). Shelves laden with geometrical instruments appear to protrude from the walls and books seem about to tumble from cupboards, while doors creak ajar and a suit of armour sways on a wall peg. The upper half of the room is covered with 28 portraits of great men ranging from Homer and Petrarch to Solomon and St Ambrose – another example of Federico's eclecticism.

Beyond the Appartamento del Duca, the cavernous **Throne Room** was a huge roofed space for its time and is bedecked in mammoth Gobelin tapestries depicting the Acts of the Apostles. Some of the most interesting works of art are on show in the **Appartamento della Duchessa**, several by Renaissance Urbino artist Timoteo Viti. This includes a fascinating depiction of a red-robed and rather well fed St Thomas Becket of Canterbury kneeling before Bishop Giovan Pietro Arrivabene and Duke Guidobaldo.

The Duomo

Piazza Pascoli 1 • Museum: daily 9.30am–1pm & 2.30–6.30pm • €3.50

Next door to the Palazzo Ducale, the town's **Duomo** is a pompous Neoclassical replacement for Francesco di Giorgio Martini's Renaissance church, destroyed in an earthquake in 1789. There's a **museum** inside, but the only reason for going in would be to see Barocci's *Last Supper*, with Christ surrounded by the chaos of washers-up, dogs and angels.

Museo della Città

Via Valerio 1 • Mon–Fri 9.30am–1.30pm, Sat & Sun 10am–6pm • €1

Urbino's **Museo della Città** has displays on the city arranged around the central courtyard of the Renaissance Palazzo Odasi. An audioguide is available for €3 and, as the museum bills itself as a collection of ideas rather than objects, you'll probably need it to explain the thinking behind displays entitled "Desire" and "Memory". Look out for the collection of historic city signs and the scale model of Urbino.

Fortezza Albornoz and the Oratorio di San Giovanni

A trek up to the gardens dominated by the sixteenth-century fortress, **Fortezza Albornoz** (Fri 3.30–7.30pm, Sat & Sun 9.30am–12.30pm & 3.30–7.30pm; free) is rewarded with splendid views of the town and surrounding countryside. The fortress is a summer concert venue but is normally deserted. Close by is the **Oratorio di San Giovanni** (Mon–Sat 10am–12.30pm & 3–5.30pm, Sun 10am–12.30pm; €2.50), behind whose unfortunate modern facade is a stunning cycle of early fourteenth-century frescoes, depicting the life of St John the Baptist and the Crucifixion.

Casa Natale di Raffaello

Via Raffaello 57 • March–Oct Mon–Sat 9am–1pm & 3–7pm, Sun 10am–1pm; Nov–Feb Mon–Sat 9am–2pm, Sun 10am–1pm • €3.50

Possibly more interesting as a Renaissance house than anything else, the birthplace (in 1483) of Urbino's most famous son, the painter Raphael, proudly displays the "stone" where Raphael and his father Giovanni Santi mixed their pigments and sizes. There's one work which may be by Raphael, an early *Madonna and Child*, otherwise the walls are covered with reproductions and minor works by his contemporaries.

ARRIVAL AND DEPARTURE   URBINO

On arrival in Urbino by bus or by car (at the main Borgo Mercatale car park; €1.20/hr) take the lift (daily 8am–8pm; €0.50) to the old town, emerging outside the Palazzo Ducale. Outside these hours it's a 5min walk along Via Mazzini or a steep climb up ramps and steps next to the lift.

By bus The bus station is at Borgo Mercatale at the foot of the Palazzo Ducale.
Destinations Fano (at least hourly; 1hr 10min); Pesaro (every 30min; 45min–1hr).

By car Urbino's centre is car free and even if you are staying in a hotel here you'll still have to leave your car outside the old city walls. Park up at the Borgo Mercatale (€1.20/hr) or one of the other car parks that ring the old centre.

INFORMATION

Tourist offices The main tourist office is at Piazza Duca Federico 35, directly opposite the Palazzo Ducale (Mon 9am–1pm, Tues–Sat 9am–1pm & 3–6pm; July & Aug may also open Sun; ☎0722 2613, ⒲ urbinoculturaturismo.it)

but staff speak little English. More helpful is the small office at Borgo Mercatale by the entrance to the ramp and lift (Mon–Sat 9am–6pm, Sun 9am–1pm).

ACCOMMODATION

Urbino's accommodation ranges from comfortable and often characterful hotels to small, family-run B&Bs. With a car, and especially during the oppressive heat of summer, a hotel outside the city and camping are endorsable options.

11

CITY HOTELS AND B&BS

★ **Boncorte** Via delle Mura 28 ☎0722 2463, ⓦviphotels.it. Imaginatively renovated by enthusiastic owners, this is a real gem of a place to stay right on top of the town walls. Rooms are all travertine stone, chunky dark wood floors and sumptuous fabrics, oozing tradition but with all mod cons in place. However the icing on the cake is room 306, an exact replica of the Studiolo within the Palazzo Ducale, surely Le Marche's quirkiest hotel room. Shade-rich walled garden for breakfast and cosy lounge with real fireplace for the evenings. **€116**

Il Cortegiano Via Veterani 1 ☎340 844 1181, ⓦilcortegiano.it. Urbino's best-situated B&B, just across from the Palazzo Ducale above a bar/restaurant, has just six large sunny rooms, some with shared bathrooms. Free wi-fi and a ten-percent discount in the restaurant for guests. **€80**

Italia Corso Garibaldi 32 ☎0722 2701, ⓦalbergo-italia-urbino.it. Renovated hotel in a porticoed street, with terracotta floors and plain but attractive rooms. Breakfast is in the small private garden in summer. **€80**

Raffaello Via Santa Margherita 40 ☎0722 4896, ⓦalbergoraffaello.com. Filling out a typical red-brick, shuttered old-town edifice, this hotel offers fourteen simply furnished rooms with panoramic views over the pantiled roofs of Urbino. Changing art exhibitions in the communal areas and free wi-fi. **€110**

San Domenico Piazza Rinascimento 3 ☎0722 2626, ⓦviphotels.it. Located in a former convent across from the Palazzo Ducale, this hotel has been sumptuously decorated and offers 31 generously proportioned rooms, big beds, polished wood floors and breakfast tables under the porticoes. Despite its location opposite the Palazzo Ducale, there are no palace views. Paid wi-fi. **€127**

San Giovanni Via Barocci 13 ☎0722 2827, ⓦalbergo-sangiovanniurbino.it. Cheap, clean and central guest-house within a sixteenth-century patrician house, known as Palazzo della Spillara. No breakfast and some rooms share facilities. Closed late July. **€60**

OUTSIDE THE CITY

La Meridiana Via Urbinate 43 ☎0722 320 169, ⓦhotelmeridianaurbino.com. About 3km outside Urbino on the road to Pesaro. The interior decoration is bland but it has a swimming pool and a restaurant, friendly staff, and is an option of last resort if everything else is full. **€75**

Nenè Via Strada Rossa 30 ☎0722 2996, ⓦneneurbino.com. This restored stone house, 2km from Urbino, just off the "*strada rossa*" towards Fermignano, is visited as much for its great restaurant – with interesting vegetarian options – as for its simple rooms. There's an open-air pool too. **€60**

CAMPING

Pineta Via S. Donato Ca' Mignone ☎0722 4710, ⓦcamping-pineta-urbino.it; bus #7 drops you close by. The nearest campsite to Urbino, 2km east of town, has a large outdoor swimming pool and lots of soft, grassy pitches. Easter–Sept. Pitches **€40**

EATING, DRINKING AND NIGHTLIFE

There are plenty of reasonable places to eat in Urbino, with dozens of fast-food and inexpensive self-service places aimed at student budgets. There's also more refined cooking typical of the province in a selection of more formal restaurants. Self-caterers and picnickers have a convenient Conad supermarket at Via Raffaello 37 (Mon–Sat 7.30am–2pm & 4.30–8pm). During term-time, Urbino's late-night **bars** see a brisk trade, and there are reasonable dancing and live music options.

CAFÉS AND RESTAURANTS

Angolo Divino Via Sant'Andrea 14 ☎0722 327 559. Geranium-covered on the outside, and atmospheric within, this *osteria* is located in an ancient *palazzo* near the Botanical Gardens. It's well known for regional delicacies (including home-made pasta) and there are some good vegetarian choices as well. Various fixed menus, starting from €20. Tues–Sun noon–3pm & 7pm–midnight.

★ **Antica Osteria da la Stella** Via S. Margherita 1 ☎0722 320 228. This pretty restaurant offers a constantly changing seasonal menu reflecting chef-owner Giovanna Cecchetti's passion for authentic local produce. Savour dishes such as *tagliatelle* with local truffles and porcini mushrooms, and cocoa ravioli with parmesan sauce and black truffles. Some Le Marche restaurants let diners down with unimaginative desserts but here they're great – try the lavender cream with biscuit and sweet wine.

Primi €10–14, *secondi* €14–30. Tues–Sun noon–3pm & 7–11pm.

Café Vineria Raffaello Via Raffaello 41. Café-bar serving sit-down or takeaway *piadine* (flatbread with a variety of fillings, such as cheese and ham; €5–6) and *crescia sfogliata* (a bit like a pizza folded in half; €4.50). Mon–Sat 11am–11pm.

Da Franco Via del Poggio 1 ☎0722 2492. Studenty lunchtime hangout (self-service) with *primi* such as home-made *strozzapreti* – "strangled priests" (one can only assume that its twisted shape is supposed to be resonant of a strangled neck) – with vegetables, and *secondi* including rabbit cooked with fennel. A full meal will set you back around €20 including house wine. Mon–Sat noon–2.30pm.

★ **Del Leone** Via C. Battisti 5 ☎0722 329 894. This small, subterranean trattoria under the San Francesco church serves up some of the city's best food. Try the *menù di piatti tipici* featuring spinach and ricotta ravioli, roast pork, baked potatoes, biscuits and dessert wine for €20. Closed lunch Mon–Fri.

La Balestra Via Valerio 16 ☎0722 2942. Unpretentious restaurant with tables out on decking or in the brick-built dining room bedecked in rural and medieval knick-knacks. Game dishes, truffles and *strozzapreti* are the highlights of the English-language menu. *Primi* €7–9, *secondi* €7–18. Daily noon–3pm & 7pm–midnight.

La Locanda del Blasone Via Nuova 3 ☎0722 2528. At this recently revamped backstreet restaurant choose between the Pugliese menu (€30) or the more locally flavoured Tartufo menu (€45). Wallet-watching diners should plump for the generously laden pizzas, some with evocative names like "*bomba*" and "*atomica*". Tues–Sun 12.30–2.30pm & 7.30–11.30pm.

Le Tre Piante Via Voltaccia della Vecchia 1 ☎0722 4863. Rather hidden away, this restaurant is worth seeking out for its small terrace overlooking the hills. Pasta dishes such as *strozzapreti* with sausage, cream, mushrooms and peppers, and pizza are excellently crafted, or you could go for the signature beef steak. *Primi* €8, *secondi* €9–16. Daily noon–3pm & 7–11.30pm.

Punto Macrobiotico Via Pozzo Nuovo 6. Health-conscious students cram into this small almost refectory-like self-service joint for its bargain vegetarian dishes, made from home-grown cereals and vegetables. It also operates an on-site macrobiotic shop. Mon–Sat 12.30–2pm & 7.30–9pm.

★ **Vecchia Urbino** Via dei Vasari 3/5 ☎0722 4447. Upmarket but quite inconspicuous place with a traditional menu including *cappelletti con fegato grasso e tartufo*

(pasta filled with liver and truffles), marinated homemade sausage and olives as well as grilled meat and fish. The puddings are excellent too, and the wine list is good value. *Primi* €10.50, *secondi* €9–32. Daily noon–2pm & 7–11pm.

BARS, CLUBS AND LIVE MUSIC VENUES

Bosom Pub Via Budassi 24 ☎0722 4783. Stone-vaulted, if garishly lit, pub with a well-stocked bar, including Belgian beers, decent snacks and wi-fi. Plays mainstream Latin, house, pop and rock. Daily 7pm–3.30am.

Caffè Centrale Piazza della Repubblica. Epicentral and hence madly popular meeting-spot on a busy piazza. Order a *caffè lungo* and watch the trendoids filter in. Daily 6.30pm–2am.

Caffè del Sole Via Mazzini 34 ☎0722 2619. Up from the bus station, on the main drag into town, this café-bar is open from morning till the early hours. Expect a laidback atmosphere, comfy couches and lots of beer and aperitifs. Daily 8am–2am.

La Dolce Vita Corso Garibaldi 1 ☎0722 321 132. A new and cool design café where the theme is the golden years of Italian cinema. Black-and-white photos from various flicks revolve around the wall pulled on a bicycle chain and the decor is 1960s minimalist. Mostly invaded nighttimes by nonchalantly young and sun-glazed Italians but still fun. Daily 7.30am–2am.

Osteria Libreria Il Portico Via Mazzini 7 ☎0722 2722. An intriguing venue in an archway at the top of Via Mazzini that bills itself as a bookshop, pizzeria, pub and *osteria*. You can browse the shelves by day and at night it turns into a club open till 2am, but locals shun the food here. Daily noon–2am.

Sassocorvaro

Fortress April–Sept daily 9am–12.30pm & 3–7pm; Oct–March Sat & Sun 9am–12.30pm & 2.30–6pm • €4 • Reached by bus from Pesaro (6 daily; 1hr 30min)

Perched above an artificial lake some 30km northwest of Urbino by road, **SASSOCORVARO** is dominated by one of Francesco di Giorgio Martini's most ambitious **fortresses**. Built on the orders of Federico da Montefeltro for one of his *condottieri* (mercenary soldiers), Ottaviano degli Ubaldini, it was, like San Leo (see opposite), designed to withstand the onslaught of cannon. Unfortunately, the site lacked San Leo's natural advantages and Francesco was forced to seek a strictly architectural solution, doing away with straight walls and building a grim fortress bulging with hourglass towers. After the functional exterior, the inside comes as something of a surprise, with an elegant Renaissance courtyard and an intimate and frescoed theatre. It's a tribute to the strength of Francesco's architecture that the fortress was selected as a safe house for some of Italy's greatest works of art during World War II, including Piero della Francesca's *Flagellation* and Giorgione's *La Tempesta*, reproductions of which are on show.

There's also a **museum** of folk life (same hours and ticket), with displays of traditional weaving, wine-making equipment and a mock-up of an old kitchen.

San Leo

Fortress Daily 9am–6pm • €8

The menacing fortress of **SAN LEO**, clamped to the summit of a dizzying precipice in the northern tip of Le Marche, has staggered generations of visitors with its intimidating beauty. Machiavelli praised it, Dante modelled the terrain of his Purgatory on it, and Pietro Bembo considered it Italy's "most beautiful implement of war". In fact it's not as impregnable as it seems; one of the few invaders to have actually been repelled was Cesare Borgia, despite his having first persuaded a weak-willed retainer to give him the key.

Brief history

There's been a fortress at San Leo since the Romans founded a city on the rock. Later colonizers added to it until the fifteenth century, when Federico da Montefeltro realized that it was no match for the new gunpowder-charged weapons, and set his military architect, Francesco di Giorgio Martini, the task of creating a new one. The walls were built on a slight inward slope and backed with earth, thus reducing the impact of cannonballs. Three large squares were incorporated for the manoeuvring of heavy cannons, and every point was defended with firing posts.

From the eighteenth century San Leo was used as a prison for enemies of the Vatican, of whom the most notorious was the womanizing Count of Cagliostro, a self-proclaimed alchemist, miracle doctor and necromancer. At first the charismatic heretic was incarcerated in a regular prison, but on the insistence of his guards, who were terrified of his diabolic powers, he was moved to the so-called **Pozzetto di Cagliostro** (Cagliostro's Well), now the fortress's most memorable sight. The only entrance was through a trap door in the ceiling, so that food could be lowered to him without the warden running the risk of engaging Cagliostro's evil eye. There was one window, triple-barred and placed so that the prisoner couldn't avoid seeing San Leo's twin churches. Not that this had any effect – Cagliostro died of an apoplectic attack, unrepentant after four years of being virtually buried alive.

The village

As well as the fortress, there's the pleasant old **village** to explore. St Leo arrived in the third century and converted the local population to Christianity, and the two village churches, though they failed to impress Cagliostro, are worth a visit. The **Pieve** was built in the ninth century, with material salvaged from a Roman temple to Jupiter, by Byzantine-influenced architects from Ravenna. Sunk into the ground behind the church is a sixth-century chapel founded by and later dedicated to St Leo, whose body lay here until 1014 when Henry II, Emperor of Germany, calling in at the town on his way home from defeating the Greeks and Saracens in Rome, decided to remove it to Germany. His plans were thwarted by the horses bearing the saint's body – after a short distance they refused to go any further, so St Leo's body was left in the small village of Voghenza near Ferrara. The heavy lid of the sarcophagus remains in San Leo's twelfth-century **Duomo**, dedicated to the saint.

ARRIVAL AND INFORMATION

SAN LEO

By bus Getting to San Leo on public transport is a pain: you need to travel up the coast to Rimini, and take a bus from outside the train station to Pietracuta, from where buses connect with a service to San Leo.

Tourist office Piazza Dante 14 (daily 9am–6pm, open longer hours in summer; ☏ 0541 916 306, ⦿ san-leo.it).

Pesaro and around

The vast majority of tourists come to **PESARO**, an agreeably tranquil backwater, much of which dates from the 1920s and 1930s, for a lazy bake on the long stretch of sandy beach and little else. Though popular with Brits and Germans on cheap package holidays and

11

Italian families on annual getaways, this sometimes overlooked resort has gone slightly more upmarket in recent years with the bog-standard seasonal three-star hotels up against stiff competition from some world-class luxury establishments. Away from the bronzing masses, Pesaro's old town has an enjoyably off-the-beaten-track feel and makes for half a day's exploration. With regular transport connections to lesser-known towns like Gradara and Fano, it also makes a feasible base from which to explore northern Le Marche.

The centre of town is the dignified **Piazza del Popolo**, in which the rituals of the pavement café scene are played out against the sharp lines of Fascist-period buildings and the Renaissance restraint of the Palazzo Ducale. All of the main attractions are within a five-minute walk of here.

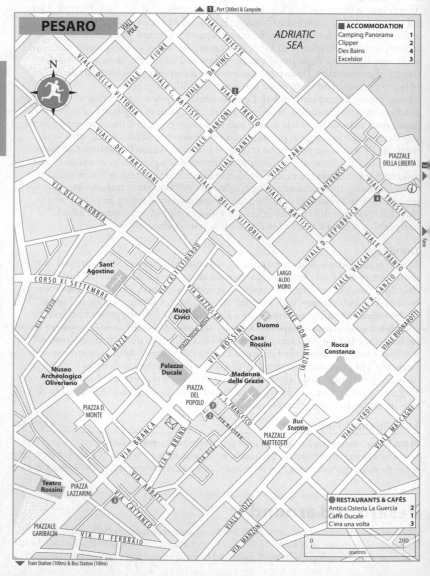

PESARO

ACCOMMODATION
Camping Panorama	1
Clipper	2
Des Bains	4
Excelsior	3

RESTAURANTS & CAFÉS
Antica Osteria La Guercia	2
Caffè Ducale	1
C'era una volta	3

The beach

Although the town has a clutch of museums, the main attraction is undoubtedly its **beach**. A tree-lined grid of rather bland and boxy looking apartments marks the long sandy beachfront, enlivened here and there by some rather marvellous Art Nouveau villas, including one on Piazzale della Libertà whose eaves are supported by white plaster lobsters.

Musei Civici

Piazza Toschi Mosca 29 • June–Sept Tues, Thurs & Fri–Sun 10am–1pm & 4–7.30pm, Wed 10am–1pm; winter hours vary • €4, €7 joint ticket with Casa Rossini • ⓦ museicivicipesaro.it

The most significant relic of Renaissance Pesaro is Giovanni Bellini's magnificent **Coronation of the Virgin** polyptych, housed in the Pinacoteca of the **Musei Civici**. Painted in the 1470s, the altarpiece situates the coronation not in some starry heaven but in the countryside around Pesaro, dominated by the castle of Gradara. Portraits of saints flank the central scene, ranging from the hesitant St Lawrence to the dreamy St Anthony, and below are a Nativity and scenes from the saints' lives.

The complex also contains the **Museo delle Ceramiche**. Renaissance Pesaro was famous for its ceramics, and the museum houses a fine collection – ranging from a *Madonna and Child* surrounded by pine cones, lemons and bilberries, from the workshop of Andrea della Robbia, to plates decorated with an Arabian bandit.

Casa Rossini

Via Rossini 34 • June–Sept Tues, Thurs & Fri–Sun 10am–1pm & 4–7.30pm, Wed 10am–1pm; winter hours vary • €4, €7 joint ticket with Musei Civici • ⓦ pesarocultura.it

The shuttered, four-storey **Casa Rossini** houses a growing shrine of memorabilia to the composer, who was born here in 1792, and has been a museum dedicated to his memory and work for over a century. Rossini fans might want to time a holiday in Pesaro with the **opera festival** (ⓦ rossinioperafestival.it) at the Teatro Rossini on Piazza Lazzarini which takes place every August.

Duomo

Via Rossini • Daily 9am–noon and 4–6pm • Free

Pesaro's **cathedral** has a Romanesque facade but most of the structure behind dates from a nineteenth-century rebuild. During the work a large mosaic on two levels showing incredibly intricate geometric Byzantine and medieval designs was discovered, the highlight of the building today.

Corso XI Settembre

Pesaro's most attractive street is porticoed **Corso XI Settembre**, scene of the evening *passeggiata*. If you want to do more than just browse in its shops, take a look inside the church of **Sant'Agostino** – the choir stalls are inlaid with landscapes, Renaissance cityscapes, and, displaying a wit to rival the *studiolo* in the Palazzo Ducale in Urbino, all half-open cupboards and protruding stacks of books.

Museo Archeologico Oliveriano

Via Mazza 97 • July & Aug Mon–Sat 4–7pm; Sept–June by request • ☎ 0721 33 344 • Free • ⓦ oliveriana.pu.it

Installed in the slightly inconspicuous Palazzo Almerici, the **Museo Archeologico Oliveriano** has a small but unusual collection of local finds. Among the relics from an Iron Age necropolis at nearby Novilara are a child's tomb filled with miniature domestic utensils and a tomb slab carved with pear-shaped figures rowing a square-sailed boat into battle. Even more intriguing is the collection of ex votos – breasts, feet, heads and even a dog – collected not from an early Catholic church but from a Roman sacred grove at San Veneranda (3km from Pesaro), consecrated in the second century BC.

ARRIVAL AND DEPARTURE

PESARO

By train The railway station is 1.5km inland from the sea along arrow-straight Via Montegrappa (which becomes Via Rossini).

Destinations Ancona (2 hourly; 30–50min); Fano (2 hourly; 8min); Rimini (at least 2 hourly; 20–30min).

By bus The bus station is next door to the train station.

Destinations Fano (up to 4 hourly; 18min); Gradara

(hourly; 50min); Sassocorvaro (6 daily; 1hr 30min); Urbino (approx every 30min; 1hr).

Tourist office On the seafront on Piazzale della Libertà (mid-June to mid-Sept daily 9am–1pm & 3–6pm; mid-Sept to mid-June Mon–Sat 9am–1pm, Tues & Fri 9am–1pm & 3–6pm; ☎0721 69 341, ⓦturismo .pesarourbino.it).

ACCOMMODATION

Camping Panorama 7km north of Pesaro on the Strada Brisighella ☎0721 20 8145, ⓦcamping panorama.it. This is the closest campsite to town and enjoys a tranquil setting perched on a clifftop above the sea (a path leads down to the beach below). May–Sept. Pitches **€30**

Clipper Viale Marconi 53 ☎0721 30 915, ⓦhotelclipper .it. Family-run since the 1950s, the *Clipper* lies a block back from the beach. Modernized rooms are crisp and well kept. The buffet breakfasts are served alfresco on the terrace and there's free wi-fi in the lobby. Closed Oct–April. **€80**

Des Bains Viale Trieste 221 ☎0721 34 957, ⓦinnitalia

.com. This friendly, smart and characterful hotel was built in 1905, and though modernized many times since then, still has something of the *belle époque* about it. **€104**

★ **Excelsior** Lungomare Nazario Sauro 30/34 ☎0721 630 011, ⓦexcelsiorpesaro.it. Pesaro's best hotel is this retro-styled new-build hugging the beach. Rates for the coolly 21st-century monochrome rooms include free bike rental, use of the pools and some spa facilities, access to the private beach and a humdinger of a continental breakfast. The entire seven-storey building, including the spa, restaurants and lobby, oozes clean-cut chic and staff are amazingly well regimented for Italy. Certainly worth a splurge. **€250**

EATING AND DRINKING

Antica Osteria La Guercia Via Baviera 33 ☎0721 33 463. One of the town's better choices, this beautifully beamed and frescoed restaurant does delicious pasta and fish dishes at affordable prices. Mains around €8. Daily noon–2.30pm & 7–10.30pm.

Caffè Ducale Piazza del Popolo 21 ☎0721 34 279. Indulge in a spot of people-watching while enjoying tasty coffees, sandwiches and cakes at this square-side café with

pretty views of the Palazzo Ducale. Just watch out for those rather insistent pigeons if you sit outside. Daily 8am–2am.

C'era Una Volta Via Cattaneo 26 ☎0721 30 911. Long regarded as the purveyor of the best pizza in town, this place certainly offers plenty of choice with around 100 different types of imaginatively named pizza on the menu, from simple "Ciclista" (€2.50) to "Billionaire" (€11). Other mains €6.50–18. Daily noon–midnight.

Gradara castle

Mon 8.30am–1pm, Tues–Sun 8.30am–6.30pm • €6 • ☎0541 964 115 • Buses from Pesaro bus station (hourly; 1hr)

Fifteen kilometres inland from Pesaro, the castle of **GRADARA** is a fairy-tale confection of mellow red brick and swallow-tail turrets, but not the place to go in season if you want to avoid crowds. The castle is said to have been the scene of a thirteenth-century scandal involving Francesca da Rimini, who committed adultery with Paolo da Malatesta, her husband's brother. The lovers were killed for their transgression and later consigned to hell by Dante – he meets their spirits in Canto V of the *Inferno*, where they are caught in a ceaseless whirlwind – though Francesca's unhappy spirit is said to wander the castle when the moon is full.

Inside the castle is a room decked out as the scene of the crime, with a sumptuously refurbished four-poster bed, fake wall hangings and an open book – Francesca tells Dante in hell that it was while reading the story of Lancelot and Guinevere that she and Paolo first succumbed to their passion. Further reminders of the story are found in two nineteenth-century paintings: one showing the lovers (either dead or in a state of post-coital collapse) watched by the crippled husband; the other, less ambiguous, of the naked couple. Other rooms are furnished as a torture chamber, complete with spiked iron ball, handcuffs and lances, and as the guards' room, a strange mixture of tavern and armoury. After touring the castle, it's well worth taking a walk round the walls for the fine views over the surrounding hills.

Fano

FANO is no longer quite the haven it was when Robert Browning washed up here in 1848, seeking respite from the heat and crowds of Florence. A large swathe of the seafront is dominated by an ugly industrial port, and although its beaches remain splendid, they now attract thousands of package tourists every year. Nevertheless, Fano is a pleasant enough place if a little humdrum, and comfortably combines its role as resort with that of small fishing port and minor historical town, the latter well worth the effort of leaving sand and sizzle for half a day's wander.

Fano's Roman precursor, named Fanum Fortunae after its Temple of Fortune, lay at the eastern terminus of the Via Flaminia, which traversed the Apennines to Rome. The town is still built around a **Roman crossroads** plan: Via Arco di Augusto and Corso Matteotti follow the routes of the *cardus* and *decumanus*, and their junction is marked with a copy of a Roman milestone stating its distance from the capital (195.4 Roman miles).

The Porta Maggiore and Arco di Augusto

Heading into Fano by bus, you could ask to be dropped off at the old town gate, the crenellated **Porta Maggiore**, to start your sightseeing with the remnants of the medieval defensive walls, on the southwestern side of the town centre. Behind them is a Roman gate, the **Arco di Augusto**, impressive despite having been truncated in the fifteenth century when Federico da Montefeltro blasted away its upper storey. You can see what it used to look like in a relief on the facade of the adjacent church of San Michele, which also houses a tiny – though rarely open – museum.

Corte Malatestiana

Piazza XX Settembre • Tues–Sat 9am–1pm & 5–8pm, extended hours in summer • €3

Overlooking the central Piazza XX Settembre are the reconstructed thirteenth-century Palazzo della Ragione and the fifteenth-century **Corte Malatestiana**, dating from the time Fano was ruled by the Malatesta family. The Corte is at its best nowadays on summer evenings, when its loggias, turrets and trefoil windows provide a backdrop for concerts. Inside there's a small **archeological museum and art gallery**, where the most sought out exhibit is Guercino's *The Guardian Angel*, which, thanks to Robert Browning's literary intervention, became one of Italy's most famous paintings in the nineteenth century (see box below).

> ## THE GUARDIAN ANGEL
>
> Not previously regarded as one of his finer works, *The Guardian Angel* by the Emilia-born Renaissance painter, **Guercino**, was quickly elevated to iconic status following a visit to Fano by the British poet, **Robert Browning**, in 1848. The picture, displayed in the Corte Malatestiana, shows a golden-haired child being shown how to pray by a rather chunky-looking angel, and so entranced Browning that he was inspired to write a poem of the same title. Expressing a wistful yearning to take the place of the child, the gushingly sentimental poem became incredibly popular, and Italy was flooded with reproductions of the painting for holidaying Browning fans. The keenest disciples set up a club, membership of which was gained by travelling to Fano and sending the founder a postcard.

11

ARRIVAL AND INFORMATION

By train The train station is a 10min walk from the seafront, at the end of Via Cavallotti.

Destinations Ancona (2 hourly; 30–40min); Pesaro (2 hourly; 8min); Rimini (hourly; 40min).

By bus Buses pull in next to the train station. There are regular services to Pesaro (up to 4 hourly; 18min).

Tourist office Just back from the seafront at Via C. Battisti 10 (June to mid-Sept Mon, Wed & Fri 9am–12.30pm, Tues & Thurs 9am–12.30pm & 4–7pm, Sat & Sun 9am–1pm; ☏ 0721 803 534, ⓦ turismo.pesarourbino.it).

ACCOMMODATION

Angela Viale Adriatico 13 ☏ 0721 801 239, ⓦ hotel angela.it. One of the most reasonably priced three-star hotels, right on the seafront near the tourist office, with 37 modestly equipped rooms, all with TV, and a garden. €114

Borgo della Luca Strada Madonna degli Angeli, Località Sant'Andrea in Villis 95/A ☏ 0721 885 763, ⓦ borgodellaluca.it. If you're on a low budget, go for this lovely country B&B in an old stone house around 5.5km inland from Fano towards Pesaro. €80

Pensione Sassenia Viale Adriatico 86 ☏ 0721 828 229, ⓦ pensionesassonia.it. Spanking new guesthouse near the port area with simple, uncluttered bedrooms, a small restaurant, a/c and free wi-fi and bike rental. Room rates plummet outside July and Aug. €102

★ **Relais Via di Villa Giulia** Località San Biagio ☏ 0721 823 159, ⓦ relaisvillagiulia.com. A good choice if you have your own transport is this country villa in extensive grounds with views to the sea, a short walk away. Capably run by its bohemian and cultured aristocratic owners, there are books and magazines everywhere, fires burning in winter and a large swimming pool in summer. The five rooms have frescoed walls, antique furniture and Turkish carpets, and there's an independent apartment to rent in the grounds. €170

EATING AND DRINKING

Caffè Centrale Corso Matteotti 102–104 ☏ 0721 801 417. With the Roman milestone embedded in its wall, there's no more central caffeine-and-cake halt in all Fano. Sit on the whitewashed outdoor decking or in the classy interior, where you can admire the bakery's miraculous wedding-cake creations. Daily 6.30am–midnight.

Da Giulio Viale Adriatico 100 ☏ 0721 805 680. Little antique touches, iron-fresh blue-striped table linens, friendly staff and Fano's best seafood make this a surefire choice come mealtimes. *Primi* €7–11.50, *secondi* €7.50–23.

Lunch & dinner; closed Tues.

Self Service Al Pesce Azzurro Viale Adriatico 48 ☏ 0721 803 165. Although it enjoys a pretty unprepossessing location at the wrong end of town (at the port), this huge, plasticky, almost industrial place, run by a cooperative of fishermen's wives, offers great-value three-course set meals of the freshest *pesce azzurro* – oily fish such as anchovies, sardines and mackerel – for just €10 a head. Tues–Sun noon–2pm & 7.30–10pm.

Ancona

War, earthquakes and that transient feel all large port cities possess conspire to make **ANCONA** an unlovable city. This busy ferry departure-point for Croatia, Albania, Greece and Turkey attracts an international fleet of fume-belching trucks that grumble through the port area night and day while lost *arrivés* clog up the station and insalubrious alleyways and derelict lots abound. But the centre does have a few historical saving-graces embedded in its tangle of commercial buildings and the authorities are making an effort to improve the visitor experience. This may have attracted the handful of cruise ships that now call in here, discharging their crews and guests for a day's wander through the tranquil old quarter and nineteenth-century shopping boulevards.

For many Ancona is a gateway to the Marche region thanks to Falconara airport, 10km away. There are also decent transport connections to much of Le Marche, though few would plump for the city as a base.

Duomo

Piazza del Duomo • Daily 8am–noon & 3–6pm • Free • Hourly bus #11 runs to the Duomo from Piazza Cavour if you don't fancy the climb

A stiff climb from the port area, passing Ancona's well-signposted Roman remains along the way, the pink-and-white **Duomo** is mostly built in a restrained Romanesque style, with an outburst of Gothic exuberance in the doorway's cluster of slender columns, some plain, others twisted and carved. The most memorable feature is a screen along the edge of the raised right transept, one section of which is carved with eagles, fantastic birds and storks entwined in a tree, the other with saints. However, it may be the views from here, the ferries lined up in the port and the coast fading into the haze, that remain longest in the memory.

Museo Archeologico Nazionale delle Marche

Via Ferretti 6 • Tues–Sun 8.30am–7.30pm • €4 • ⓦ archeomarche.it

Ancona's large, three-storey **Museo Archeologico** in the old quarter is not a bad place to while away an hour or two, its wacky moulded ceilings vaulting over a collection of finds ranging from red- and black-figure Greek *craters* to a stunning Celtic gold crown. A large section is devoted to the Piceni tribe, who occupied these parts in the seventh century BC.

Museo della Città

Piazza del Plebiscito • Mid-June to mid-Sept Tues–Fri 5–8pm, Sat & Sun 10am–1pm & 6–8pm; mid-Sept to mid-June Tues–Fri 10am–1pm, Thurs–Sun 10am–1pm & 4–7pm • Free

Tucked away at the foot of the flight of steps leading up to Ancona's austere Dominican church, this worthwhile museum displays models, paintings, sculptures and original documents showing key events in Ancona from 2000 BC to 2000 AD. Interestingly, the collections are housed in the former Hospital of St Thomas of Canterbury, dating from the eighteenth century.

Pinacoteca Comunale Francesco Podesti

Were it open to the public, the highlight of the **Pinacoteca Comunale Francesco Podesti** at Via Pizzecolli 17 would be Titian's *Apparition of the Virgin*, a sombre yet impassioned work, with the Virgin appearing to a rotund and fluffy-bearded bishop in a stormy sunset sky. However, the entire Palazzo Bosdari in which it is housed has been under heavy renovation for some years. The info board outside states that everything should have been completed by February 2011, so give it a few more years.

Santa Maria della Piazza

Piazzetta Santa Maria • Rarely open • Free

A block back from the ferry port, tiny Piazzetta Maria Santa is dominated by the delightfully decrepit Romanesque church of **Santa Maria della Piazza**, which dates from the thirteeth century. The building's facade is a fantasia of exquisitely carved blind loggias and its portal is decorated with incredibly well preserved floral and animal motifs. When open, visitors can admire some early Christian mosaics through glazed sections in the floor.

San Francesco delle Scale

Piazza San Francesco • Free

Towering over a small square off Via Pizzecolli, the church of **San Francesco delle Scale** is named for the steps leading up to it. Titian's *Apparition* was painted for this church, but today it houses works by Lotto, Tibaldi and Lilli.

ARRIVAL AND DEPARTURE	ANCONA

By plane Ryanair flies direct from the UK to Falconara airport. Buses (roughly hourly 6.30am–7.30pm; ⓦ coneronbus.it) run from here to the train station on Piazza Rosselli, taking around 30min. Buy your ticket (€1) before boarding from any bar or

11

FERRIES TO CROATIA, ALBANIA, GREECE AND MONTENEGRO

Ferries leave from the Stazione Maríttima, a couple of kilometres north of the train station (bus #1 or #4), close to the centre of town. For the best at-a-glance idea of timetables and routes, visit Ⓦdoricaportservices.it. Each of the main ferry lines has a ticket office (closed 1–3pm) and you can also buy tickets from the agencies all around the port, but booking online gets you the cheapest deals. Always aim to arrive at the Stazione Maríttima two hours before departure (3hr if you're taking a camper van).

Ferry companies operating out of Ancona include Superfast (Ⓦsuperfast.com), Minoan Lines (Ⓦminoan.it) and Anek (Ⓦanek.gr) to Igoumenitsa (15hr) and Patras (22hr) in Greece; Blue Line (Ⓦblueline-ferries.com), SNAV (Ⓦsnav.it), Amatori (Ⓦamatori.com) and Jadrolinija (Ⓦjadrolinija.hr) to Split in Croatia (8–9hr); Adria Ferries (Ⓦadriaferries.com) to Durazzo in Albania (11hr); and Montenegro Lines (Ⓦmontenegrolines.net) to Bar in Montenegro (8hr).

newspaper kiosk. A taxi will cost €35.

By bus The main bus terminus is dispersed around the edges of Piazza Cavour. From here, buses link up with the train station and the Stazione Maríttima, where ferries dock. Services to Sirolo, Numana and Loreto leave from Via Camerini just off the square.

Destinations Jesi (every 30min; 45min–1hr); Loreto (5 daily; 1hr 30min); Macerata (10 daily; 1hr 30min); Numana (16 daily; 40min); Portonovo (9 daily; 25–30min); Sirolo (16 daily; 35min).

By train The train station is 1.5km out of town.

Destinations Ascoli Piceno (via San Benedetto; 12 daily; 2–3hr); Bologna (at least hourly; 2–3hr); Fano (2 hourly; 30–40min); Jesi (up to 3 hourly; 20–30min); Loreto (every 30min; 15–20min); Pesaro (2 hourly; 30–50min); Rome (6 daily; 3–4hr).

INFORMATION

Tourist office Via Gramsci, next to the Teatro delle Muse (April–Dec Mon–Sat 10am–1pm & 3–7pm, Sun 10am–1pm; ☎071 222 6100, Ⓦcomune.ancona.it /turismo/it/).

ACCOMMODATION

Grand Hotel Passetto Via Thaon de Revel 1 ☎071 31 307, Ⓦhotelpassetto.it. Perched on a hill in a quiet part of town, this luxurious establishment offers excellent service, as well as an outdoor pool, a cocktail bar, health club and great views out over the Adriatic. **€175**

Jolly Hotel Ancona Rupi di Via XXIX Settembre 14 ☎071 201 171, Ⓦnh-hotels.com. Handily situated if you're catching the ferry, albeit a bit of a trek up the hill, this place provides reliable chain comfort and a sea-view restaurant. Discounts on the website. **€115**

Milano Via Montebello 1 ☎071 201 147, Ⓦhotel milanohm.it. This clean, appealing and centrally located hotel is possibly Ancona's best deal. It's understandably very popular, so book ahead. **€90**

Ostello Ancona Via Lamaticci 7 ☎071 42 257, Ⓦostelloancona.it. Ancona's clean and friendly hostel is centrally located 200m from the train station. Men and women are billeted on separate floors so you'll be split up if travelling as a couple. Dorms **€18**

★ **Roma e Pace** Via G. Leopardi 1 ☎071 202 007, Ⓦhotelromaepace.it. This super-central, time-warped 1930s hotel is by far the most interesting of Ancona's mid-range offerings and could easily serve as the backdrop to an Agatha Christie novel. Original fittings, polished wood and faded elegance abound throughout and there's a preposterously high-ceilinged breakfast room and an impressive lounge full of sofas. **€100**

EATING AND DRINKING

Ancona has some surprisingly good restaurants, especially family-run fish places. If you've been in Italy a while and are pining for a curry or just a change to the pizza-pasta routine, a sizeable non-Italian population means there's lots of ethnic food around, most notably from Turkey, Russia and Sri Lanka. Piazza Plebiscito is the place to head for a late-night tipple.

Alla Tazza D'Oro Corso Garibaldi 136 ☎071 203 368. Ancona has ample provision for fans of the bean but this open-all-hours coffee bar is special for its original, quirky interior, all Art Deco ceramics, blue-glass mirrors, coffee-quaffing Moors and African mosaic scenes. Daily 8am–2am.

Bar Duomo Via Giovanni XXIII 2 ☎071 207 4337. If you don't fancy schlepping it all the way back into town for lunch after visiting the cathedral, chew with a view at this simple place just below Piazza del Duomo. Tues–Fri 11am–midnight, Sat 11am–1.30am & Sun 10am–midnight.

FROM TOP GROTTE DI FRASASSI (P.695); ASCOLI PICENO (P.706) >

Clarice Via del Traffico 6 ☎071 202 926. An old-style, family place in a cobbled alleyway off Corso Garibaldi (on the right as you walk up from the sea). It serves traditional, very reasonably priced food, with local dishes such as *trippa alla parmegiana* (€8) and *tagliatelle con vongole* (€9). Closed Sat dinner & Sun.

★ **Enopolis** Corso Mazzini 7 ☎071 207 1505, ⓦenopolis.it. Wonderful, moderately priced restaurant-bar-cantina for lunch or dinner or just a glass of wine, set in a labyrinth of medieval, vaulted, art-filled cellars and musty tunnels that burrow their way underground to the sea. Dishes are simple but delicious and the fish and meat tasting menus a bargain at €25 and €30 respectively. Daily noon–2pm & 7pm–midnight.

La Cantineta Via Gramsci 1/C ☎071 201 107. Almost opposite the tourist office, this trattoria may look pretty unprepossessing but its speciality, *stoccafisso* (€14), a traditional recipe involving salt cod, is well worth sampling. Otherwise expect a lot of pasta and fish combinations and very welcoming proprietors. Daily noon–3pm & 7.30–11pm.

Osteria del Pozzo Via Bonda 2 ☎071 207 3996. This intimate but brightly decorated seafood restaurant on a narrow lane off the lower end of sloping Piazza del Plebiscito, is the place to tuck into some net-fresh fruits of the Adriatic. If you call in advance, cook can conjure up a *brodetto all'Anconetana* (fish soup; €20), or *padellata di crostacei* (pasta filled with shellfish; €18). Mon–Sat noon–2pm & 7–11pm.

Inland: the Esino valley

West of Ancona and cutting right across Le Marche, the **Esino valley** is broad and bland in the east, but narrows to a dramatic limestone gorge, the **Gola di Rossa**, just before the town of **Fabriano** and the border with Umbria. Famous for two things – paper-making and Gentile da Fabriano, the best of the International Gothic artists – Fabriano is now heavily industrialized and a pretty dismal town – one you're likely to pass straight through on your way to Umbria and Rome. Although Fabriano and **Jesi** are built up, most of the valley is given over to agriculture and is best known for **Verdicchio**, a dry white wine produced in the hilltop villages around Jesi. What most visitors come for, however, are the vast **Grotte di Frasassi** (Frasassi caves).

Jesi

Though its industrial development has led to **JESI** being known as "the little Milan of Le Marche", the historic centre of the town is well preserved. Clinging to a long ridge, it's fringed by medieval walls and retains a scattering of Renaissance and Baroque palaces. Encircling the town are the massive ramparts, restructured in the fourteenth century and built on top of the foundations of Roman walls – an escalator takes you through the ramparts, several metres thick, from the lower town to the upper town (with steps back down again).

Pinacoteca Civica

June–Aug Tues–Sun 10am–8pm; Sept to June Tues–Sat 10am–1pm & 4–7pm, Sun 10am–1pm & 5–8pm • €6

The Palazzo Pianetti houses the **Pinacoteca Civica**, where the highlight of the opulent interior is the magnificent 72m-long stuccoed, gilded and frescoed gallery – a Rococo fantasy of shells, flowers and festoons framing cloud-backed allegorical figures. The collection of paintings is best known for some late works by **Lorenzo Lotto**, including *The Annunciation* and *The Visitation* (both circa 1520); his use of colour and the expressive intensity of his portraits are exceptional.

Cupramontana

The village of **Cupramontana** in the hills above Jesi is known as the capital of Verdicchio country. The best time to visit is the first Sunday in October, when there's a parade and dancing, and the village streets are lined with stalls of wine and food for the **grape festival** marking the eve of the harvest. A *cantina aperta* ("open cellar") day at the end of May gives you the chance to sample the fruits of the wine-makers'

11

labours – if you're interested in knowing more about producers and vineyards, contact the local wine association, Assivip (☎0731 703 844, ⓦassivip.it). The regional *enoteca* at Via Federico Conti 5 (daily: April–Oct 11am–1pm & 5–9pm; rest of year 5–9pm; ☎0731 213 386) in Jesi's historic centre (near the top of the escalator) holds tasting sessions of local wines daily.

The Grotte di Frasassi

Guided tours only: March–Oct daily 10am, 11am, noon, 2.30pm, 4pm & 5pm; Jan & Feb Mon–Fri 11.30am & 3.30pm, Sat 11.30am, 2.30pm & 4.30pm • €15.50 • ☎ 800 166 250 • ⓦ frasassi.com • Shuttle buses run from Rimini and San Benedetto del Tronto; details on ⓦ frasassiexpress

Some 32km up the Esino valley from Jesi, just after the Gola di Rossa, a road leads up from Genga train station to the Frasassi gorge, carved by the River Sentino, which was also responsible for creating the 18km of caves beneath it. The largest of the **Grotte di Frasassi**, or Frasassi caves, was discovered only in 1971, and just over a kilometre of its caverns and tunnels is now open to the public on tours that last seventy minutes – note that the average temperature inside is 14ºC.

Inevitably, the most remarkable stalactite and stalagmite formations have been named: there's a petrified Niagara Falls, a giant's head with a wonderfully Roman profile, a cave whose floor is covered with candles complete with holders, and a set of organ pipes. The vast Cave of the Great Wind, at 240m high, is one of the biggest in Europe – large enough to contain Milan Cathedral – and has been used for a series of experiments, ranging from sensory deprivation (as a possible treatment for drug addicts) to a subterranean version of *Big Brother*.

11

The Conero Riviera

With its white cliffs, blanched pebble beaches, thick protected forests and easy-going resorts, the **Conero Riviera** to the south of Ancona is the northern Adriatic's most spectacular and enjoyable stretch of coastline. This tranquil holiday paradise is centred around **Monte Conero** which plunges straight into the sea. The area is easily accessible, with the seaside villages of **Portonovo**, **Sirolo** and **Numana** all linked by bus from Ancona. Sirolo and Numana are now as crowded in July and August as the rest of the Adriatic resorts, the main difference being that their cliff-backed beaches are more picturesque. The most stunning stretch of coast, a series of tiny coves at the base of Monte Conero between Portonovo and Sirolo, is best explored by boat – they leave from both bays. You can go just for the scenery or ask to be dropped off somewhere along the way and be picked up a few hours later.

This stretch of coast is the home of **Rosso Conero wine**, made from the same Montepulciano grape as Chianti, though less well known than its Tuscan counterpart. Rarely found outside Italy, there's a chance to sample it at the Rosso Conero **festival** at Camerano, 8km inland from Monte Conero, in the first week in September.

Portonovo

A short 11km bus ride from Ancona, **PORTONOVO**, nestling beneath Monte Conero, is a scattered resort made up of a couple of campsites and a clutch of expensive hotels, one of which is sited in the Napoleonic fort that dominates the bay. The main attraction is the unbeatable scenery and the transparent water, and though the main pebbly pay-beach gets very busy in summer, it's easy enough to escape by walking about 1km to Mezzavalle beach (free) just north of Portonovo bay or clambering over rocks to the few tiny beaches to the south. On the walk south, there's a lovely Romanesque church, **Santa Maria** (Tues–Sun 4.30–6.30pm), perched above the shore at the end of an oleander-lined path. There are lots of **trails** across Monte Conero of varying degrees of difficulty; the tourist office at Sirolo (see below) has hiking maps.

Sirolo

Cliff-top **SIROLO** has an old centre of terraced cottages divided by neat cobbled streets. The main square, **Piazza Veneto**, is on the cliff edge, with good views of the coast and Monte Conero. What used to be a quiet bolt-hole is now packed-out on weekends from June to September. In season, buses run roughly every thirty minutes to the two **beaches** below: Sassi Neri, a wide, long, black-pebbled strand, and San Michele, an attractive, narrow, sandy stretch.

Numana

The busiest of the three resorts, **NUMANA** is a small port with a large pebble beach. A windy headland just beyond the modern church provides some of the coast's most spectacular views and the town has an interesting archeology museum. From the port, boats run to the wonderfully secluded beach at **Due Sorelle** only reachable by water; Traghettatori del Conero (☎071 933 1795, ⊕traghettatoridelconero.it) has a daily service at 9.30am, with others at 10.30am, 11.30am and 2.30pm according to demand.

Antiquarium
Via La Fenice 4 • Daily 8.30am–7.30pm • €2

Away from the beach, Numana's main attraction is its small but unexpectedly intriguing archeology museum filled mostly with relics of the Piceni tribe, who occupied the area between Senigallia and Pescara from the seventh century BC. Explanations are in English and among the exhibits are burial finds from Sirolo and Numana, Bronze-Age helmets and lots of red-and-black pots decorated with scenes from Greek mythology, clearly illustrating the extent to which the Piceni were influenced by the Greeks, who set up a trading post nearby.

ARRIVAL AND INFORMATION   CONERO RIVIERA

By bus Portonovo is linked with Ancona by regular urban buses (mid-June to Aug; every 20min). Buses to Sirolo and Numana (16 daily; 35–40min) leave from a stop to the left of Ancona's train station (as you leave it) and just off Piazza Cavour.

Tourist offices The main tourist office for the area is in

Sirolo on Piazza Vittorio Veneto (Sat & Sun 9am–1pm & 4–8pm, longer (erratic) hours June–Aug; ☎071 933 0611); there's free internet access and staff speak some English. There's also a seasonal information office on Portonovo's main piazza in July and Aug, the opening hours varying from year to year.

ACCOMMODATION

There's somewhere to sleep on the Conero Riviera for every taste and budget, with everything from luxury hotels to B&Bs, campsites to traditional villa guesthouses lining the coast.

PORTONOVO
Camping Comunale La Torre ☎071 801 257. One of two large campsites in Portonovo, the *Torre* is sprinkled across woodland just back from the beach and has a bar-restaurant and games room. June to mid-Sept. Pitches **€21.50**

Fortino Napoleonico ☎071 801 450, ⊕hotelfortino .it. Just steps from the lapping sapphire waters, this luxury establishment was originally built by Napoleon to stop the English landing to take fresh water from Monte Conero's

springs. The hotel retains some military touches here and there but is generally rather chi-chi and grand. **€220**

SIROLO
Arturo Via Spiaggia 1 ☎071 933 0975, ⊕arturo residencesirolo.com. Beach lovers should head for this great place right on the white shingle strand of Spiaggia Urbani. The four rooms and two studio apartments have cooking facilities and open out onto small balconies and the sea. There's a restaurant with live music down on the beach,

and cars can be left in the public car park above. €100

Camping Internazionale ☎ 071 933 0884, ⓦ camping internazionale.com. The best campsite on the Conero Riviera is located on a terraced, wooded hillside below Sirolo, with easy access to two beaches. Facilities are kept spotless and there's free internet access at reception. Slightly tricky to access with large camper vans and caravans. April–Sept. Pitches €27

Stella Hotel Via Giulietti 9 ☎ 071 933 0704, ⓦ stella hotel.it. Right in the centre of Sirolo, this freshly refurbished three-star hotel has spacious rooms with balconies and far-reaching sea views. Buses from Ancona stop outside the door. €110

NUMANA

Scogliera Via del Golfo 21 ☎ 071 933 0622, ⓦ hotel scogliera.it. A modern, appealing place on a small

headland at the northern edge of the bay with a first-rate restaurant and art-covered walls. Some of the 36 rooms have Adriatic views. €90

Sorriso Via Flaminia 109 ☎ 071 933 0645, ⓦ hotel sorrisonumana.it. Just 50m from the beach this family-run hotel has 38 floral rooms, half of which enjoy dramatic bay views, and a palm-shaded garden where alfresco breakfast can be taken. Free wi-fi and discounts at some Numana restaurants. €112

Villa Sirena Via del Golfo 24 ☎ 071 933 0850, ⓦ villasirena.it. Once the only building on the seafront, this exotically red-hued hotel offers 23 freshly modernized rooms, all with balconies and sea views. A snazzy bar area, guest terrace, disabled facilities and its very own private beach area make these Numana's top lodgings. Closed Jan & Feb. €150

EATING

PORTONOVO

Il Clandestino ☎ 071 801 422; signposted from car parks. There's no better place to watch the sun go down than from this blue-hut beach bar and restaurant near the church, serving a menu of *susci italiano*: Italianized sushi described by the waiter as "raw fish, Italian style". It's better than it sounds and reservations are advised for dinner in July and Aug. Mains cost €18–25. Noon–2pm & 7.30pm–midnight; closed Nov–March.

SIROLO

La Taverna Piazza Veneto 10 ☎ 071 9331 382. Adriatic views, local wines, home-made fishy pasta dishes (€9–12) and main-course fish (€15–20) make this a madly popular

winner on Sirolo's main square. Daily noon–2.30pm & 7–11pm.

Trattoria Sara Via Corso Italia 9 ☎ 071 933 0716. Robust local dishes in a no-nonsense atmosphere; the seafood antipasti (€15) and risotto are especially recommended. Noon–2pm & 7–11pm; closed Wed.

NUMANA

La Torre Via La Torre 1 ☎ 071 933 0747. Numana's leading restaurant (with bay views) plates up top-notch gourmet fare with a modern twist. The *orecchiette con vongole* (€10) and sweet and sour *baccalà* (€18) are highly recommended. Daily 12.30–2.30pm & 7.30–10.30pm.

Loreto

The vast majority of people who visit **LORETO** are pilgrims, over four million of whom arrive every year to pay their respects at what they believe is the House of the Virgin Mary where Jesus spent his childhood. To find out how the house made its miraculous journey from Nazareth to Italy, see the box, p.698. The house is contained within a huge hilltop basilica visible from miles around. However, away from the religious frenzy, the town, it must be said, has little to offer.

The House of the Virgin Mary (Santa Casa)

Piazza della Madonna • Daily: April–Sept 6am–9.45pm; Oct–March 6.30am–7pm • Free

The primitive stone **House of the Virgin Mary (Santa Casa)** with only three walls, sits within a grand and very far from humble **basilica**, featuring works by such Renaissance luminaries as Bramante, Antonio da Sangallo, Sansovino, Lotto and Luca Signorelli, many of which depict scenes from the life of Mary. Inside the house, pride of place is given to a copy of the famous Black Madonna of Loreto; the medieval original, once crazily attributed to St Luke, was destroyed in a fire in 1921. For the non-believer the religious fervour can come as a surprise, with some pilgrims pressing their cheeks

THE MADONNA OF LORETO AND THE JOURNEY OF THE SANTA CASA

Loreto owes its existence to one of the Catholic Church's more surreal legends. The story goes that in 1292, when the Muslims kicked the Crusaders out of Palestine, a posse of angels flew the house of Mary from Nazareth, the Santa Casa, to Dalmatia, and then, a few years later, whisked it across the Adriatic to Loreto. In the face of growing scepticism, the Vatican came up with the more plausible story that the Holy House was transported to Loreto on board a Crusader ship. Not surprisingly, though, this new theory doesn't have the same hold on the Catholic imagination, and the Madonna of Loreto continues to be viewed as the patron saint of aviators: Lindbergh took an image of her on his landmark Atlantic flight in 1927, and a medallion inscribed with her image also accompanied the crew of Apollo 9. For centuries she was also credited with military victories – presumably she was thought to have power over projectiles.

During the Baroque period the Santa Casa was copied by pious architects across central Europe, most notably in Bohemia and Moravia where tens of replicas were built. The finest of these stands next to Prague Castle.

11

against the blackened, crumbling brick walls mumbling tearful prayers, others on their knees in a trance-like state in front of the Madonna. Talking in here is not a good idea as you will be unceremoniously shushed by the grim-faced nuns. Note that at peak times you may not be able to look around the Holy House as a service is usually being conducted for visiting pilgrims, and it is closed from 12.30pm to 2.30pm.

Over the centuries, Loreto built up a covetable collection of treasures donated by wealthy believers. One of the most costly and idiosyncratic was a golden baby bequeathed by Louis XIII of France, weighing exactly the same as his long-awaited heir, the future Louis XIV. The basilica was ransacked in 1798 by Napoleonic troops, most of the plunder ending up on the shelves of the Louvre in Paris. Following Napoleon's demise, subsequent popes managed to retrieve many of the valuables, but the majority were stolen again in 1974 in what became known as the "holy theft of the century".

The Antico Tesoro

Palazzo Apostolico, Piazza della Madonna • Tues–Fri 10am–1pm & 3–6pm, Sat & Sun 10am–1pm & 3–7pm • €4

The items left behind in the treasury after the 1974 burglary are now kept in the **Antico Tesoro**, well hidden and almost unmarked in the west wing of the Palazzo Apostolico (in the far right-hand corner of the square as you look from the basilica). It shouldn't be missed, principally for the eight paintings by Lorenzo Lotto that are held here, nearly all dated between 1549 and 1556, including his final work, *The Presentation in the Temple*. Plagued by neurosis and lack of money, Lotto finally joined the religious community at Loreto, painted some of the canvases on display, and died here in 1556. Looking at *The Presentation*, with its rotund, crumbling priest and frail, almost skeletal nun, it would appear that he never found much inner peace. *Christ and the Adulteress* is an even more powerful work, with Christ surrounded by maniacally intense men and a swooning adulteress.

ARRIVAL AND INFORMATION
LORETO

By train The town is easily accessible by train from Ancona (at least hourly; 15–20min); the station is some way out of town but connected with the centre by an almost hourly bus service.

By bus Buses stop near the tourist office.

Destinations Ancona (5 daily; 1hr 15min); Numana (5 daily; 30min); Sirolo (5 daily; 35min).

Tourist office Via Solari 3 (May–Sept Mon–Sat 9am–1pm & 3–6pm, Sun 9am–1pm; Oct–April Mon 9am–1pm, Tues–Fri 9am–1pm & 4–6pm; ☏ 071 970 276).

ACCOMMODATION

Finding accommodation in Loreto can be difficult, particularly during the main pilgrimage seasons of December 8–12 (the anniversary of the legendary flight), Aug 1–20, Sept 5–10, Easter, and from Christmas through to Jan 7. In any case, it's probably best tackled as a day-trip.

Hotel Giardinetto Corso Boccalini 10 ☎071 977 135, ⓦ hotelgiardinetto.it. Just inside the Porta Romana in a mellow stone building, this pleasingly old-fashioned place has sixty rooms with high ceilings, desks, big beds and cramped bathrooms. Parking costs €10 a night but the wi-fi is free. **€76**

Hotel Loreto Corso Boccalini 60 ☎071 750 0106, ⓦ loretohotel.it. I like most of the town's hotels the *Loreto* is dated and spartan, with rooms in shades of brown you never knew existed, but OK for a single night's sleepover. Pluses include a cheap restaurant, a/c, English-speaking staff and a location just a souvenir Black Madonna's throw from the basilica. **€64**

EATING

Garibaldi Via Vanvitelli 15 ☎071 977 690. Enjoy Loreto's best pizzas (€5–7) in a lovely vaulted dining room or out under twisted trees. Tues–Sun lunch & dinner.

Girarrosto Via Solari ☎071 970 173. In the *Centrale* hotel, this family-run place serves reasonably priced antipasti typical of the Conero peninsula, *vincisgrassi* and handmade pasta. Daily noon–2pm & 7–9pm.

Macerata and around

11

A hilltop gem built entirely of a soft-coloured brick, the little-known provincial capital of **MACERATA** is one of the region's most attractive and historically well-endowed towns. The comparisons with Urbino are inevitable but what Macerata lacks in Renaissance splendour it more than makes up for with its livelier atmosphere, especially on market day (Wed) when the streets and squares are clogged with stalls and punters. Easy paced and with a large student population, it's an ideal place to wind down in the evenings after exploring the province. For fans of **opera and ballet**, the annual Sferisterio Opera Festival from mid-July to mid-August, held in Italy's best open-air venue outside Verona, is a must (see box, p.700).

Piazza della Libertà

Piazza della Libertà is the heart of the old town, an odd square in which contrasting buildings vie for supremacy. The Renaissance **Loggia dei Mercanti** was supplied by Alessandro Farnese, better known as Pope Paul III, the instigator of many architectural improvements to sixteenth-century Rome. It's somewhat overshadowed by the bulky Palazzo del Comune and overlooked by the looming Torre del Comune. Perhaps the square's most striking feature, however, is the mournful brick facade of **San Paolo**, a deconsecrated seventeenth-century church now used as an exhibition space.

The Duomo

Piazza Strambi • Free

The town's **Duomo** is no architectural showpiece – a workaday chunk of Baroque, which might have looked slightly more appealing had its facade been finished. Inside there's a statue of Macerata's patron saint, Giuliano, whose path to sainthood sounds like something out of a Sunday tabloid. He arrived home to find two people in his bed and, thinking they were his wife and her lover, promptly killed them. Discovering he'd murdered his parents, he hacked one of his arms off in remorse – the severed limb is now kept in a church strongroom, encased in a sleeve of gold and silver. The relic is displayed on request, but a day's notice is required.

Palazzo Ricci

Via Domenico Ricci 1 • Visitable on free Italian-language guided tours • ☎ 0733 261 487, ⓦ palazzoricci.it

At the time of writing, Macerata was busy gathering all its impressive art collections into a single museum to be housed in the eighteenth-century **Palazzo Ricci**. When open, the extensive collection will range from Renaissance perfectionism to twentieth-century artworks. It's an ambitious project and one that may not be completed for many years.

Chiesa San Filippo

Corsa della Repubblica • Free

Architecturally Macerata's most interesting place of worship, the **Chiesa San Filippo**, is an eighteenth-century brick church with odd, blue onion domes and a small cupola and is the work of Roman architect Giovanni Battista Contini who was also responsible for the town's Palazzo Buonaccorsi. Two notable works of art adorn the interior: *The Crucifixion* by Francesco Mancini and *The Madonna and Saint Gaetano* by Ludovico Trasi.

ARRIVAL AND INFORMATION

By train The train station is a 10min walk south along Viale Don Bosco and connected to central Piazza della Libertà by frequent buses.

Destinations Civitanova (at least hourly; 30min; change here for Ancona); San Severino Marche (approx hourly; 30–40min); Tolentino (approx hourly; 15–25min).

By bus The bus station is just off Giardini Diaz, a short walk west of the town centre.

MACERATA

Destinations Abbazia di Fiastra (12 daily; 10min); Amandola (6 daily; 1hr 15–20min); Ancona (10 daily; 1hr 30min); Loreto (10 daily; 50min); San Severino (5 daily; 35min); Sarnano (12 daily; 55min–1hr 25min); Tolentino (12 daily; 30min); Urbisaglia (12 daily; 10min).

Tourist office Corso della Repubblica 32 (Mon–Fri 9am–1pm & 3–6pm, Sat 9–1pm; open Sun during the opera season; ☎ 0733 234 807).

ACCOMMODATION

Albergo Lauri Via Lauri 6 ☎ 0733 232 376, ⓦ albergo lauri.it. Basic, well-located guesthouse with 28 rooms and six apartments furnished mostly with cheap furniture of the flat-pack variety. A style-free zone but the cheapest deal in town. **€55**

Arena Vicolo Sferisterio 16 ☎ 0733 230 931, ⓦ albergo arena.com. Tucked away in a small courtyard behind the opera arena, the friendly *Arena* has an interior dotted with historic prints, antiques and intriguing knick-knacks. Rooms boast minibars, a/c, soundproofing and TVs hooked up to BBC/CNN. Free parking and wi-fi. **€70**

Claudiani Via Ulissi 8 ☎ 0733 261 400, ⓦ hotel claudiani.it. Macerata's principal four-star option is located just off Corso Matteotti in the historic centre. Its forty rooms are "hotel style" rather than "antique *palazzo*". Free wi-fi but parking €8 a night. **€105**

Il Vecchio Granaio Via Chiaravalle 49, Treia ☎ 0733 843 488, ⓦ ilvecchiogranaio.it; a 15min drive from Macerata along the SS361 at the km 40,400 marker (there are several buses a day from Macerata). This agriturismo complex is a pleasant out-of-town option. The large guest rooms are decorated with antiques and hunting prints, and there are exceptional hill views from the communal sun terrace, as well as a swimming pool. **€75**

EATING AND DRINKING

Lots of studenty budget eats as well as more upmarket establishments provide enough variety to keep most happy. Self-caterers should bail to the COAL supermarket at Via Armaroli 76.

Caffè Venanzetti Via Gramsci 21 ☎ 0733 236 055. The finest place to get your day's Arabica fix is this stylishly chandeliered, mirrored and marbled café, good for rich cakes and fresh pastries as well as your first and last cuppa of the day. Mon–Sat 7am–2am, Sun 2pm–2am.

Da Ezio Via Crescimbeni 65 ☎ 0733 232 366. A respectable, cheap trattoria, with daily specials: gnocchi

(€5) on Thurs, fish (€7) on Fri. *Vincisgrassi* (€6) is served every day and the family owners press their own olive oil. Mon–Sat noon–2pm & 7–11pm.

Da Rosa Via Armaroli 17 ☎ 0733 260 124. Serves beautiful home-made pasta (try the ravioli with ricotta and lemon) and, in season, *funghi porcini* and truffles. You can eat well for under €25 and house wine comes at €6 per

---

OPERA TICKETS

Book **tickets** for the Sferisterio Opera Festival at the Biglietteria dell'Arena Sferisterio, Piazza Mazzini 10 (Mon–Sat 10.30am–12.30pm & 5–7.30pm; ☎ 0733 230 735, ⓦ sferisterio.it). Prices from €10 in the balcony (not bookable) to €100 (plus ten-percent booking fee) in the front stalls.

half litre. Daily noon 3pm & 7–11pm.

★ **Da Secondo** Via Pescheria Vecchia ☎ 0733 260 912. It's obvious from the wall snaps of all the illustrious guests to have dined here since 1952 that you've landed in Macerata's most famous restaurant. They do a fabulous *vincisgrassi* (€9), along with excellent roast lamb or pigeon

with potatoes (€12–14), Tues–Sun noon–3.30pm & 7.30–11pm.

Il Pozzo Vicolo Costa 5 ☎ 0733 232 360. A popular, alternative pub-*birreria* dating back to the Seventies where you can eat simple local food and listen to live and recorded jazz. Lunch menu €10. Noon–3am; closed Tues.

Morrovalle

Rising above the **Chienti valley** which runs east from Macerata to the coast, the hill-village of **MORROVALLE** is worth a stop on the way to the sea. The settlement is skirted by a stepped street that disappears through arched gates and hemmed inside the main piazza at the top of the village is the squat Palazzo del Podestà, where Italy's first pawnshop was set up by St Bernard in 1428. The building next to it is the Palazzo Lazzarini, seat of the ruling family who survived their internecine battle for the privilege of ruling Morrovalle. The *palazzo*, though built in the fourteenth century, incorporates an earlier Romanesque-Gothic portal, possibly taken from a local church.

Santa Maria a Piè di Chienti

Daily 8am–8pm • Free • ⓦ santamariapiedichienti.it

The road and rail track along the Chienti valley pass the ex-monastery of **Santa Maria a Piè di Chienti** just after the fork for Montecosaro. It was built by Cluniac monks who came to the area in the tenth century, draining the flood-prone river into channels and creating fertile land out of what had been a fever-ridden marsh. Situated close to the coast, the monastery was vulnerable to Saracen invasion, so the monks encircled it with ditches, which could be flooded in the event of a raid. The monastery survived until the early nineteenth century, when it was destroyed by Napoleonic troops, and now all that remains is the church itself.

Basilica di San Nicola

Piazza Silveri 2, Tolentino • Daily 9am–noon & 3–6.30pm • Free • ⓦ sannicoladatolentino.it

Heading southwest of Macerata towards the Sibillini mountain range, you might stop off briefly at the little town of **TOLENTINO** to see the **Basilica di San Nicola**. Its west front is a real feast for the eyes – a curly Baroque facade with a grinning sun instead of a rose window and a fancily twisting Gothic portal topped by an oriental-style arch enclosing a dragon-slaying saint. Inside, the most intriguing feature is the **Cappellone di San Nicola**, a large chapel whose colourful frescoes were painted in 1310–25 under the supervision of Pietro da Rimini and are very much in the style of Giotto.

Castello della Rancia

Tues–Sun 9am–1pm & 3–7pm, slightly shorter hours in winter • €4

Some 7km east of Tolentino stands stately, fourteenth-century **Castello della Rancia**. This vast fort was the main grain store for the Cistercian abbey of Fiastra (see p.702) back in the twelfth century. Transformed into a castle in the fourteenth century, it became the focal point for a number of armed clashes, at one time harbouring the notorious Renaissance mercenary Sir John Hawkwood.

San Severino Marche

Some 12km northwest of Tolentino lies the ancient town of **SAN SEVERINO MARCHE**, a pretty little place whose modern centre converges on an unusual elliptical square,

11

Piazza del Popolo, surrounded by porticoes. There's enough to keep history, art and archeology fans busy for half a day here and the town makes for an interesting stopoff on the way to Umbria.

Pinacoteca Tacchi Venturi

Via Salimbeni • July & Aug Tues–Sun 9am–1pm & 4–7pm; Oct–June Tues–Sat 9am–1pm • €3, €4 with the Museo Civico Archeologico

The town's art gallery, named after a local historian, is as good a reason as any for a visit, with a memorable assembly of pieces, including works by Paolo Veneziano and Vittore Crivelli, as well as the Salimbeni brothers, the region's undervalued, early Renaissance painters who were born and worked in San Severino in the fifteenth century; they are represented by delicate and expressive frescoes detached from local churches, and the wooden polyptych *The Marriage of St Catherine*.

San Lorenzo in Dolìolo

Via Salimbeni • Free

The ancient-looking church of **San Lorenzo in Dolìolo**, at the top of Via Salimbeni, appears slightly odd thanks to a medieval brick tower standing on top of its stone portal. Inside, on the vault of the tenth-century crypt you'll find frescoes by the Salimbeni brothers illustrating the story of St Andrew. The back part of the crypt is thought to be a pagan temple dating back to the time of the refugees from Septempeda.

The Duomo Vecchio

Via Castello al Monte • Free

San Severino's cathedral lurks up in **Castello**, the upper part of town, a long and steep walk, although there are occasional buses from the main square. The **Duomo Vecchio** was founded in the tenth century but has a Romanesque-Gothic facade, simple Gothic cloisters, and a much rebuilt interior, featuring Salimbeni frescoes in the baptistry.

Museo Civico Archeologico

Via Castello al Monte • Sat & Sun 10am–1pm & 5–7pm • €3, €4 with the Pinacoteca Tacchi Venturi

Finds in the **Museo Civico Archeologico**, located near the cathedral, were excavated from the Roman valley town of Septempeda over the course of the twentieth century. Driven out by barbarian invasions in the sixth century the inhabitants escaped up to what is now the *castello*, thus establishing the town of San Severino.

South of Macerata: the road to Sarnano

With the Monti Sibillini on the horizon, snowcapped for most of the year, the route south from Macerata towards the spa town of Sarnano ranks as one of Le Marche's most beautiful.

Abbazia di Fiastra

June–Sept daily 10am–1pm & 3–7pm; Oct–May Sat, Sun & public hols 10am–1pm & 3–6pm • €5 for abbey and museum • ☏ 0733 202 942, ⓦ abbadiafiastra.net

Around 10km to the south of Macerata, on the edge of a dense wood, stands the Romanesque-Gothic complex of the **Abbazia di Fiastra**, a Cistercian abbey with a simple, pantiled brick cloister and monastic quarters adjoining a grandiose, aisled church.

The abbey complex is a popular day out, with a steady stream of visitors looking round the building and its grounds, now a nature reserve. The trails through the woods are a popular Sunday stroll, and you should take time to see the **Museo della Civiltà Contadina** (open summer only, same times as abbey), a folk museum filled with agricultural and weaving equipment laid out in the abbey's low-vaulted outhouses.

Urbs Salvia

Mid-June to mid-Sept daily 10am–12.30pm & 3–7pm; mid-Sept to mid-June Sat, Sun & public hols 10am–12.30pm & 3–5.30pm •
Guided tours €2 for a single monument, €5 for three and €7 for everything

A five-minute bus ride from the Abbazia di Fiastra you come to the site of **Urbs Salvia** near the modern-day town of Urbisaglia. This was one of Le Marche's most important Roman towns and home to 30,000 people until it was sacked by Alaric in 409 AD. The Lourdes of its day (Urbs Salvia means "city of health"), its fame continued into the Middle Ages, when Dante invoked it as an example of a city fallen from glory in his *Paradiso*. So far an amphitheatre, theatre, baths and parts of the walls have been excavated, and frescoes of hunting scenes have been discovered in a *cryptoportico* (underpassage). The theatre was one of the largest in Italy, and could seat 12,600 spectators. Up in modern Urbisaglia, there's also a small **archeological museum** (same hours), visitable on the same ticket, containing finds from the site.

San Ginesio

South of Urbisaglia, the hill-town health resort of **SAN GINESIO** is justifiably known as the balcony of the Sibillini: the panoramic view from the gardens of the Colle Ascarano, just outside the town walls, stretches from the Adriatic and Monte Conero to the Sibillini mountains and the highest of the Apennines, the Gran Sasso in Abruzzo. In the town itself, the central piazza is dominated by one of Le Marche's most unusual churches, the **Collegiata della Annunziata**, whose late-Gothic facade is decorated with filigree-like terracotta moulding. Rising above it are two campaniles, one capped by an onion dome and the other by what looks like a manicured cactus. Gothic frescoes adorn some of the chapels, and the crypt has frescoes by the Salimbeni brothers.

Sarnano

SARNANO, south of San Ginesio, was once a virtually abandoned, pretty down-at-heel village, but in the last couple of decades or so the authorities have woken up to the potential of its thermal springs – believed since Roman times to have wide-ranging curative properties – and have begun to develop the place into a spa resort and weekend day-trip destination. The medieval core, coiling in concentric circles around a gentle hill, has been subtly restored, and though it's now more of a showpiece than a living village, its narrow interconnecting cobbled streets and picturesque old houses make it an ideal place for an undemanding day's wander.

San Francesco

Just inside the **Porta Brunforte** gate of old Sarnano is the fourteenth-century church of **San Francesco**, decorated with Palestinian plates, thought to have been brought to Sarnano by souvenir-collecting Crusaders.

Santa Maria di Piazza

Piazza Alta • Free

The **Piazza Alta** lies at the town's summit and was once the political and religious centre, hemmed with fine medieval *palazzi*, as well as the thirteenth-century church of **Santa Maria di Piazza**. The fifteenth-century frescoes in this austere-looking church include a figure known as the *Madonna with Angels*, for the host of celestial musicians and choristers surrounding her. The wooden statue of Christ on the altar has been saddled with one of popular tradition's strangest myths – if it's about to rain, his beard is supposed to grow. On the second Sunday in August, Santa Maria is the starting-point for Sarnano's annual medieval knees-up, or **palio** – though apart from the costumes and processions, it has more in common with a kids' sports day, featuring a tug-of-war, pole climbing, and a race in which the competitors have to balance jugs of water on their heads.

Tourist office Largo Enrico Ricciardi 1 in the new town 657 144, ⓦsarnano.com).
(Mon–Sat 9am–1pm & 3–6pm, Sun 9am–1pm; ☎0733

Monti Sibillini National Park

With a mountain lake reddened by the blood of the devil, a narrow pass known as the gorge of hell and a cave reputed to have been the lair of an enchantress, the **Monti Sibillini** are not only the most beautiful section of the Apennines, but they teem with ancient legends too. Wolves, chamois and brown bear all have a home in the national park and even if you don't come across one of these, you may be lucky enough to see an equally rare golden eagle instead.

The best way to experience the park is by walking, cycling or horseriding, and if you're up for a challenge there's **Il Grande Anello dei Sibillini** (The Great Sibylline Ring), 120km of signposted footpaths that take nine days to walk, or four to five days to cover by mountain bike. Maps and accommodation details, including mountain refuges, are listed on ⓦsibillini.net. There are shorter trails too, through meadows filled with wild flowers, for which the most agreeable bases are the medieval hill-villages that crown the Sibillini foothills. Most villages are served by buses, but they're generally few and far between and it's definitely best to have your own transport.

Amandola

The small village of **AMANDOLA** is fairly easy to get to on public transport, making it a good base for seeing the region. As far as visitable sights go, the highlight here is the **Museo Antropogeografico** (July & Aug daily except Tues 9.30am–12.30pm & 4–7pm; Sept–June by appointment only, call ☎338 690 4069; €5), housed in the ex-convent of the church of San Francesco at Largo Leopardi 4 and chock-full of hands-on exhibits focusing on the wildlife and legends of the park. Amandola's other attraction is an excellent week-long international **theatre festival** (ⓦamandolateatro.it) in the first week of September. Low on pretension and high on participation, the festival overcomes language barriers with mime and movement performances and workshops – the atmosphere is irresistible, and it's well worth sticking around for the whole week. Otherwise, Amandola is just a great place to kick back after a day's hiking in the Sibillini.

Montefortino

Around 7km by road south of Amandola, the hill-village of **MONTEFORTINO** is a pretty base, though less well served by buses and invaded by tourists in season. Primarily a place to wander and admire the Sibillini views, the town also has a small **Pinacoteca**

LAGO DI PILATO

According to the legend surrounding the **Lago di Pilato**, Pontius Pilate's body was dispatched from Rome on a cart pulled by two wild oxen which climbed up into the Sibillini and ditched the corpse in the water here. In the Middle Ages it became a favourite haunt for **necromancers** seeking dialogues with the devil – stones inscribed with occult symbols have been found on its shores. Deciding they wanted to be rid of the magicians, one night the local lords put soldiers on guard around its shores. Nothing happened until the morning, when the soldiers discovered that the lake had turned red; assuming it was with the devil's blood, they fled. What in fact turned the water red was a mass of minuscule red *Chirocephalus marchesonii*, a species of fish indigenous to Asia; a shoal was stranded here millions of years ago when the sea receded, and its descendants still thrive.

(open on request; call ☎0736 859 491; free), whose chief attractions are a polyptych by Alemanno – a follower of the Crivelli who clearly took as much delight in painting embroidery as they did – and an arresting twelfth-century portrait of a man with a pipe and candle emerging from the darkness. Appropriately, given the necromantic traditions of this area, there's also an eighteenth-century painting of Circe with her occult apparatus.

Montemonaco and around

A short way south of Montefortino, **MONTEMONACO**, a walled medieval village of cobbled streets and yellow stone houses, is close to some of the Sibillini's most legendary sights. One, the **Grotta della Sibilla** (Sibyl's Cave), whose occupant gave her name to the mountain group, is a two-hour walk west from the village, though periodic rockfalls can block the way. The other, through the **Gola dell'Infernaccio** (Gorge of Hell), a few kilometres southwest of the village, is an easy and spectacular hike in summer. You can take a bus from Montefortino to the Infernaccio fork, from where it's a three-hour walk to the gorge along a well-defined path. The approach through a narrow valley is atmospheric: silent, except for the distant roar of the River Tenna, with memorial plaques on the cliffs at the entrance to commemorate climbers who've died scaling the walls. The path squeezes its way under jagged rocks, accompanied by the deafening sound of raging water. Once past a second bridge it forks, the lower path leading to the tranquil source of the Tenna while the upper brings you, in about thirty minutes, to the **Hermitage of San Leonardo**, until recently occupied by a solitary monk.

ARRIVAL AND DEPARTURE	**MONTI SIBILLINI NATIONAL PARK**
By bus Amandola is the main arrival and departure point for other places within the park. Destinations Ascoli Piceno (4 daily Mon–Sat; 1hr 10min);	Fermo (4 daily; 1hr); Montefortino (6 daily; 10min); Montemonaco (5 daily; 20–25min); Sarnano (6 daily; 30min).

ACCOMMODATION

AMANDOLA

Il Palazzo Via Indipendenza 59 ☎0736 847 082, ⓦpalazzopecci.com. This much-praised B&B occupies a fifteenth-century mansion a 2min walk from the main square. Original beams and tiled floors, as well as antiques throughout, add to the experience of staying in a piece of history but without the usual hefty price-tag. **€80**

★ **La Mela Rosa** Villa Caccianebbia 4 ☎0736 848 664, ⓦlamelarosa.net. Located in the hamlet of Caccianebbia, a short drive from Amandola, this Australian-owned luxury

B&B in a traditional stone farmhouse is the best in the Sibillini. Rooms are immaculate and stylish, there's a pool and the hosts could not be friendlier. Understandably popular, so book ahead. **€90**

MONTEMONACO

Agriturismo La Cittadella Loc. Cittadella ☎0736 856 361, ⓦcittadelladeisibillini.it. Some 2.5km down a dirt road from the northern end of Montemonaco, this rural spot is a peaceful place for an overnight stay with a decent

---

HIKING IN THE MONTI SIBILLINI

To tackle the best of the Sibillini treks, drive or take a taxi 8km east from Montemonaco to the quiet village of Foce. The hike up to Lago di Pilato (see box opposite) and Pizzo del Diavolo (Devil's Peak) is fairly tough; allow a whole day, take the Kompass *Monti Sibillini* map (the ominously, and rather aptly numbered, sheet no. 666), which can be bought locally, and only attempt it in good conditions during the high summer months as the snow doesn't melt until June. Here, guarding the entrance to Umbria, stands Monte Vettore (2476m), the highest of the Sibillini peaks.

If you're going to attempt a climb up Monte Sibilla, the *Rifugio Sibilla 1540* (June to mid-July & mid- to end Sept Sat & Sun; mid-July to mid-Sept daily; ☎0736 856 422, ☎338 429 2399 or ☎338 469 5073, ⓦrifugiosibilla1540.com) is the best base. It lies about 6km east of Montemonaco along the path that eventually leads to the cave of the sibyl Grotta della Sibilla (see above). The Kompass map is essential here, too, as the path is only barely visible.

restaurant to boot. A fitting base for flits into Sibillini backcountry. **€80**

MONTEFORTINO
Tabart Inn Via Papiri 24 ☎0736 859 054, ⓦtabart -inn.com. This wonderful French-owned, antique-filled B&B is housed in a sixteenth-century house within the walls of old Montefortino. The three light, spacious and elegantly beamed rooms have terraces overlooking the mountains. Cash only. **€80**

Ascoli Piceno

Located between the Monti Sibillini and the Adriatic, **ASCOLI PICENO** is Le Marche's greatest hidden gem and lies well off the tourist trail. This seems odd considering it has plenty of grand architecture and a lovely café-lined central square that's among the most pleasant in the region. At Mardi Gras it hosts Le Marche's most flamboyant carnival and in August its streets are given over to the Quintana, a medieval **festival** that incorporates a spectacular joust. If that wasn't enough, Ascoli's restaurants and food stalls are the proud purveyors of **olive all'ascolana** (deep-fried breadcrumb-crusted olives stuffed with veal), the closest Italy comes to the Scotch egg, but much tastier.

Ascoli has a compact centre, surrounded by largely intact walls. Piazza del Popolo is the place to get the feel of the town, while its small number of Roman remains and its churches and museums are scattered throughout the old centre.

ASCOLI PICENO

■ ACCOMMODATION	
100 Torri	3
Le Sorgenti	1
Ostello de' Longobardi	2
Palazzo Guiderocchi	4

● RESTAURANTS & CAFÉS	
Cantina dell'Arte	1
Meletti	3
Migliori	5
Osteria Nonna Nina	4
Rua dei Notari	2

Piazza del Popolo and around

Ascoli's historical centre is anchored by the centrepiece **Piazza del Popolo**, a pleasingly petite but beautiful Renaissance square hemmed by grand facades. The western flank is filled by the **Palazzo dei Capitani** which dates from the late twelfth century, when the free *comune* of Ascoli was at its height. That anything of the building has survived is something of a miracle, for in 1535 a certain Giambattista Quieti set it on fire with the intention of incinerating a rebel barricaded inside. The interior was gutted but enough remained of the facade for a swift facelift to suffice. Rectangular windows were slotted into medieval arches, and a grand portal affixed, on top of which sits a statue of Pope Paul III, who reintroduced peace by replacing Quieti with a neutral outsider.

When they weren't slaughtering each other, at least some of Ascoli's rulers found time to collect public money in order to finance city improvements. The sixteenth-century **loggias** that enclose the piazza are one of the results – each of a slightly different width, to correspond to the size of the contribution made by the various merchants and shopkeepers who worked here.

Chiesa di San Francesco

Piazza del Popolo • Free

Abutting Piazza del Popolo is the church of **San Francesco**, the construction of which was financed by the sale of a Franciscan convent outside the city, after Pope Alexander IV had given the Franciscans permission to move within its walls. The foundations were laid in 1258 but the building wasn't completed until 1549, when the low cupola was added. It's a somewhat restrained church, with little to seize the attention except for the intricate west portal on Via del Trivio, but a good place to take a break from the heat of Ascoli's narrow streets.

Adjoining the south side of the church and overlooking Corso Mazzini is the sixteenth-century **Loggia dei Mercanti**. Formerly the scene of commercial wheeling and dealing, there are still niches cut into the back wall in which bricks could be checked for size before being purchased. The cloister to the north of the church is now the site of a daily market.

Galleria d'Arte Contemporanea and Museo dell'Arte Ceramica

Corso Mazzini • Mid-March to Sept 10am–7pm • €6, or €8 with Pinacoteca Civica • Ⓦ ascolimusei.it

Following Corso Mazzini from Piazza del Popolo brings you to two of Ascoli's worthwhile museums: the **Galleria d'Arte Contemporanea**, where the beautifully displayed permanent collection includes works by Filippo de Pisis, Lucio Fontana, Hans Hartung and Gino Severini. It also offers a compelling introduction to the work of local artist Osvaldo Licini, a friend of Modigliani and Picasso, who once saved Picasso from being beaten up by turning on his attackers with the walking stick he had used since being injured in World War I. The **Museo dell'Arte Ceramica** (same hours and ticket) around the corner is of more limited appeal, though the setting, in the ex-convent of San Tommaso, is quite enchanting.

Chiesa dei Santi Vincenzo e Anastasio

Piazza Basso • Free

The **Chiesa dei Santi Vincenzo e Anastasio**, tucked away in the north of the historical centre is Ascoli's most distinctive church, with an austere fifteenth-century chessboard facade that was once filled in with frescoes. Beneath the mainly eleventh-century body of the building is a primitive crypt erected over a spring that was supposed to have leprosy-curing properties. Although the plunge bath is still there, the spring was diverted elsewhere in the last century.

Chiesa di San Pietro Martire

Piazza Basso • Free

Across the small square from the Chiesa dei Santi Vincenzo e Anastasio, the much larger **San Pietro Martire** is a far less appealing building, erected by Dominican monks in the thirteenth century in order not to be outdone by their Franciscan rivals down the road. It's as austere and intimidating as St Peter the Martyr himself, who, between founding Dominican communities like that at Ascoli, gained such a reputation as a persecutor of religious sects that he became the patron of inquisitors after his murder by a couple of so-called heretics.

Roman Ascoli

Little of Roman Ascoli survives, but beyond the thirteenth-century gate, the **Porta Solestà**, you'll find the Augustan-era **Roman bridge** – one of Italy's largest and most impressively preserved – spanning the River Tronto in a single, 25m-wide arch. Amazingly, it's still used by cars and trucks over 2000 years after it was erected.

The only other visitable sites are the sparse remains of a **Roman theatre**, on the southwest edge of town, which stands close to the Roman **Porta Gemina**, or Twin Gate, at the beginning of the road to Rome.

The Duomo

Piazza Arringo • Daily 8.30am–12.30pm & 4.30–7.30pm, may close earlier in winter • Free

Ascoli's Baroque **Duomo** is situated on the east side of Piazza Arringo. The interior is one of Italy's more colourful with panels of North African-style geometric patterns (like fake carpets) painted on the walls, huge shell alcoves, chandeliers suspended on strings of illuminated beads, a blue ceiling studded with gold stars and a cupola decorated with late nineteenth-century frescoes of obscure Ascolani saints. In the Cappella del Sacramento to the right of the altar you'll find a **polyptych** by Carlo Crivelli. The most arresting of the ten panels is the central pietà, in which the haggard expression of Mary, the torment that distorts Christ's face, and the Magdalene's horror as she examines the wound in his hand are given heightened impact by the strict semicircular composition. Held up by some hefty Romanesque pillars, the crypt contains the tomb of St Emidio, to whom the Duomo is dedicated, decorated with some fine mosaic-work.

Pinacoteca Civica

Palazzo Comunale, Piazza Arringo • Mid-March to Sept 10am–7pm • €6, or €8 with Galleria d'Arte Contemporanea & Museo dell'Arte Ceramica • ⓦ ascolimusei.it

As well as housing the tourist office, the Palazzo Comunale next to the Duomo also contains the **Pinacoteca Civica**. The highlights here are works by Crivelli who it is thought died in Ascoli around 1495. Many consider his finest work to be the polyptych, which can be found next door in the cathedral.

Chiesa di San Gregorio

Piazza San Gregorio • Free

A block behind the tourist office you'll discover this fourteenth-century church dedicated to **San Gregorio**. It was ingeniously built around the remains of a Roman temple and incorporated into the facade are two lofty Corinthian columns, originally imported by the Romans from Greece, and patches of *opus reticulatum* (diamond brickwork). In the adjoining convent is a tiny revolving door with the inscription *Qui si depositano gli innocenti* ("Here you deposit the innocent"), designed so that parents could remain anonymous when leaving unwanted children to the care of priests and nuns.

Museo Archeologico

Piazza Arringo 28 • Tues–Sun 8.30am–7.30pm • €2

If you want to know more about ancient Ascoli, visit the evocative **Museo Archeologico**, across the square from the Duomo. The collection includes Piceni projectiles inscribed with curses against their Roman enemies, jewellery, heavy bronze rings that were placed on the stomachs of dead women, and small test-tube-like containers used to assess the quality of grief by measuring the volume of tears.

ARRIVAL AND INFORMATION

ASCOLI PICENO

By train Ascoli's train station is just east of the town centre, a 10min walk along Viale Indipendenza and Corso Vittorio Emanuele. The only services from Ascoli are old-fashioned diesel trains to coastal San Benedetto del Tronto (15 daily; 40min–1hr) which straddles the north–south mainline.

By bus Buses stop outside the train station.

Destinations Amandola (4 daily Mon–Sat; 1hr 10min);

Montefortino (5 daily Mon–Sat; 1hr 20min); Montemonaco (5 daily Mon–Sat; 1hr 30min); San Benedetto del Tronto (every 30min; 1hr).

Tourist office Well hidden in the entrance to the Palazzo Comunale on Piazza Arringo (Mon–Sat 9am–6.30pm, Sun 10am–7pm; ☎ 0736 298 334, ⓦ comune.ascolipiceno.it). Italian-only office with a list of B&Bs.

ACCOMMODATION

★ **100 Torri** Via Mazzoni 6 ☎ 0736 255 123, ⓦ centotorri.com. If it's chic digs you're looking for, these nineteen cool, well-appointed rooms within a thirteenth-century building are aimed at affluent tourists and anyone with an appreciation of understated styling. Wi-fi, a ceramic-themed meeting room, a winter-garden breakfast room and extremely courteous service make the experience of staying here even more special. **€170**

Cantina dell'Arte Via Lupa 8 ☎ 0736 255 620, ⓦ cantinadellarte.it. Great-value, cheerful, well-kept hotel in the centre with eleven small rooms and five apartments in an annexe, along with a very reasonably priced, bustling restaurant. **€60**

Le Sorgenti Lago di Castel Trosino ☎ 0736 263 725, ⓦ agriturismolesorgenti.org. One of several good *agriturismi* within easy reach of town, this occupies a restored eighteenth-century villa set in rolling countryside

7km north of Ascoli. Rooms are simple and rustic, the food is made from fresh local ingredients (including home-pressed olive oil) and there are plenty of local walks to enjoy. **€65**

Ostello de' Longobardi Via Soderini 26 ☎ 0736 259 191, ⓦ aighostels.com. The town's most affordable option is this youth hostel located in a spooky medieval tower bang in the historic centre, open year-round. **€15**

★ **Palazzo Guiderocchi** Via Cesare Battisti 3 ☎ 0736 244 011, ⓦ palazzoguiderocchi.com. This *palazzo* hotel blends aristocratic style with rustic simplicity to create some of the best accommodation in Le Marche. The huge rooms are like medieval bedchambers with canopied beds, convincing replica antiques, full-on fabrics and the highest ceilings you're ever likely to see in a hotel. The hotel also has nine more modern rooms (€89) on Piazza del Popolo, five of them with kitchenette. **€120**

EATING AND DRINKING

Meletti Piazza del Popolo 20 ☎ 0736 259 626. Le Marche's best-situated piazza café is the classily preserved Art Nouveau *Meletti*, an Ascoli institution. The café makes its own superb *amaro* and anisette liqueur, and is lined with mahogany cases filled with obscure bottles, as well as serving up delightful sweets and pastries, brought pronto to your table by elegantly uniformed waiters. Daily 8am–7pm.

Migliori Piazza Arringo 2 ☎ 0736 250 042. A delightful three-in-one experience comprising a sit-down restaurant, where you can eat local specialities such as the *grande fritta* – deep-fried lamb cutlets, vegetables and *olive all'ascolana* for €12 – a well-stocked delicatessen and a small stall out front where you can purchase bags of eight hot stuffed

olives (almost a meal) for €4. Tues–Sat noon–11pm.

Osteria Nonna Nina Piazza della Viola 10 ☎ 0736 251 523. Simple, homely *osteria* in a typical Ascoli vaulted palace plating up dishes such as *fritto misto all'Ascolana* like *nonna* used to make. *Primi* €6–8, *secondi* €4.50–13. Tues–Sun 11am–4pm & 7pm–midnight.

Rua dei Notari Via Cesare Battisti 3 ☎ 0736 258 393. You'll find Ascoli's top dining-out spot within the *Palazzo Guiderocchi* hotel though it's not officially part of it. A recommended first course could be Campofilone pasta with Marchese *ragù* followed by any of the grilled meat *secondi*. Finish off with *crème brûlée* topped with Melletti anisette liqueur. *Primi* €7–10, *secondi* €10–18. Dinner only; closed Tues.

11

Abruzzo and Molise

CORNO GRANDE, PARK NAZIONALE DEL GRAN SASSO

Abruzzo and Molise

Abruzzo and Molise, one region until 1963, together make Italy's transition from north to south. Both are sparsely populated mountainous regions, and both have been outside the mainstream of Italian affairs since the Middle Ages. Bordered by the Apennines, Abruzzo holds some of Italy's wildest terrain: silent valleys, abandoned hill-villages and vast untamed mountain plains, once roamed by wolves, bears and chamois; sleepy Molise offers similar draws, but is even less visited. In recent years Abruzzo has come under international scrutiny, after a massive earthquake struck L'Aquila, the regional capital, in April 2009, virtually destroying the city, killing over 300 people and leaving 65,000 homeless. In spite of the widespread destruction, L'Aquila is slowly being pieced back together again, and these two little-visited regions continue to be among the few areas of Italy where there is still plenty to discover.

The Abruzzesi have done much to pull their region out of the poverty trap, developing resorts on the long, sandy Adriatic coastline and exploiting the tourist potential of a large, mountainous national park and some great historic towns. Following the earthquake, **Sulmona**, to the southeast, makes the most logical base. **L'Aquila**, at the foot of **Gran Sasso** – the Apennines' highest peak – is still worth a visit, though it's an unsettling experience wandering scaffolding-lined streets patrolled by the guards of the Protezione Civile.

The rising stars of Abruzzo are the **hill-villages** around L'Aquila, deeply rural places, where time seems to have stopped somewhere in the fifteenth century, whose traditions, cuisine and architecture are only now coming to be appreciated. South of Sulmona, in **Scanno** elderly women wear costumes that originated in Asia Minor, and make intricate lace on cylindrical cushions known as *tomboli*. Just down the road, the scruffy hill-village of **Cocullo** hosts one of Europe's most bizarre religious festivals (see box, p.721). The main resort on the Abruzzo coast is **Pescara**, with a good stretch of sandy beach. It makes a convenient base for excursions inland to **Chieti**, home to an excellent archeological museum. However the best spot for a sun-and-sand break is further south at **Vasto**, with its gently shelving, sandy beach and lively old centre.

Gentler, less rugged and somewhat poorer than Abruzzo, **Molise** has more in common with southern than central Italy. The cities, **Isernia** and **Campobasso**, are large and bland, with small historical centres, but Molise has its compensations: a scattering of low-key Roman ruins – most interestingly at **Saepinum**. Wandering among the ruins, and looking out over the green fields to the mountains beyond, you get some inkling of how Italy's first Grand Tourists must have felt. A less-refined but equally interesting attraction takes place in the village of **Ururi**, settled by Albanian refugees in the fifteenth century, where the annual chariot race is as barbaric as anything the Romans dreamed up (see box, p.733).

Finally, there's the sheer physical aspect of the place. Forty percent of Molise is covered by **mountains**, and although they are less dramatic than Abruzzo's, there are masses of

Highlights

❶ **Corno Grande** Hike in the wild and craggy Gran Sasso massif, out of which rises Italy's highest peak, the Corno Grande. **See p.716**

❷ **Driving from Sulmona to Scanno** A spectacular ride through the mountains up to the wonderfully unspoilt town of Scanno. **See p.722**

❸ **Parco Nazionale d'Abruzzo** Get back to nature in this lovely park, which has around one hundred indigenous species of fauna and flora. See p.723

❹ **Museo Archeologico, Chieti** Head here for the best and most comprehensive display of

Abruzzese antiquities, including the unique *Capestrano Warrior*. **See p.730**

❺ **Bull race at Ururi** The ordinary town of Ururi turns into a scene of frenetic activity once a year as horses, bulls and carts career through the streets. **See p.733**

❻ **Saepinum** This enchanting archeological site in rural Sepino is a throwback to the original Grand Tour, with overgrown Roman ruins dotted with inhabited dwellings. **See p.734**

HIGHLIGHTS ARE MARKED ON THE MAP ON P.714

possibilities for hiking. Visitors are also starting to explore the area's ancient sheep-droving routes, known as *tratturi*, which are gaining new life as mountain-bike or horseback-riding trails, served by occasional farmhouse guesthouses and riding stables along the way.

GETTING AROUND
ABRUZZO AND MOLISE

Don't expect to rush through Abruzzo and Molise if you're relying on public transport; in both regions, getting around on bus and train demands patience and the careful studying of timetables.

By car The regions are best explored by car and, rarely for Italy, driving here is usually a pleasure: the roads through the national parks are empty and driving through the towns is not as hair-raising an experience as elsewhere.
By bus If you're restricted to public transport, buses are

generally better than trains, and services are punctual and cheap. Check timetables on ⓦ arpaonline.it in Abruzzo; in Molise at ⓦ atm-molise.it.
By train Train lines run down the coast and into Molise; check timetables on ⓦ trenitalia.com.

Parco Nazionale del Gran Sasso and around

Whether you approach Abruzzo from Le Marche in the north or Rome in the west, your arrival will be signalled by the spectacular bulk of the **Gran Sasso** massif, containing by far the highest of the Apennine peaks as well as a **national park**

HIGHLIGHTS
❶ Corno Grande
❷ Driving from Sulmona to Scanno
❸ Parco Nazionale d'Abruzzo
❹ Museo Archeologico, Chieti
❺ Bull race at Ururi
❻ Saepinum

REGIONAL FOOD AND WINE

Abruzzo and Molise are mountainous regions where agriculture is difficult and sheep farming dominates. Consequently, **lamb** tends to feature strongly in the local cuisine. You'll come across *abbacchio*, unweaned baby lamb that is usually cut into chunks and roasted or grilled; *arrosticini*, tiny pieces of lamb skewered and flame grilled; and *intingolo di castrato*, lamb cooked as a casserole with tomatoes, wine, herbs, onion and celery.

In Abruzzo, a crucial ingredient is **olive oil**, a product that has gained international acclaim in recent years. Around Sulmona *aglio rosso* (red garlic) is believed by many locals to be a cure for ailments ranging from neuralgia to arthritis; around L'Aquila in particular saffron (*zafferano*) is also found widely in sweet and savoury dishes, grown in fields southeast of the city.

Probably Abruzzo's most famous dish is *maccheroni alla chitarra*, made by pressing a sheet of pasta over a wooden frame, and usually served with a tomato or lamb sauce. Cheese tends to be *pecorino* – either mature and grainy like parmesan, or still mild, soft and milky.

The **wines** of Molise are rarely found outside the region. The most interesting is the Biferno DOC, which can be red, white or *rosato*. The best-known wine of Abruzzo is Montepulciano d'Abruzzo, a heavy red made from the Montepulciano grape with up to 15 percent Sangiovese. Pecorino, a local varietal and DOC, produces a fresh and mineral white. One of Italy's most important wine events, **Cantine Aperte** (Open Cellars) was born in Abruzzo and takes place the last Sunday in May. Hundreds of producers open their doors to enthusiasts for free tastings and gastronomic events (ⓦmovimentoturismovino.it).

(ⓦgransassolagapark.it) with hiking trails. If you come by autostrada from Le Marche, you'll actually travel underneath the mountains, through a 10km tunnel, passing the entrance to a particle-physics research laboratory bored into the very heart of the mountain range. The massif itself consists of two parallel chains, flanking the **Campo Imperatore** plain that stretches for 27km at over 2000m above sea level.

12

Fonte Cerreto

FONTE CERRETO is the gateway to the Gran Sasso park. It consists of little more than a few hotels, a restaurant and a campsite clustered around a cable-car station (cable car Mon–Sat 8.30am–5pm, Sun 8am–5pm; every 30min; €11 return). Most of these were built in the 1930s as part of Mussolini's scheme to keep Italians fit by encouraging them to take exercise in the mountains. Ironically, he was imprisoned here in 1943, first at the *Villetta* inn (now the *Fior di Gigli*), and then at the *Campo Imperatore*, a hotel at the top of the cable-car route. Il Duce supposedly spent his days at the hotel on a diet of eggs, rice, boiled onions and grapes, contemplating suicide. Hitler came to his rescue, dispatching an ace pilot to airlift him out in a tiny plane.

ARRIVAL AND INFORMATION

By car Fonte Cerreto is just off the A24 motorway. The area is not well connected by public transport, so it's best to drive.
By bus Ama buses from L'Aquila to Funivia at Fonte Cerreto (every 2hr; 40min).

PARCO NAZIONALE DEL GRAN SASSO

Tourist information There's no tourist office, but local hotels are a good source of information on walks in the Gran Sasso park, and should be able to supply you with maps of trails and information on wildlife.

ACCOMMODATION AND EATING

Campo Imperatore At the top of the cable-car lift ☎0862 760 868, ⓦhotelcampoimperatore.it. Despite the somewhat forbidding exterior, this revamped four-star hotel has comfortable rooms, and the swimming pool and dining room (half-board €45 per person, full board €55) with spectacular views of the mountains are further draws. **€50**

Giampy SS17 bis, Km 18 ☎0862 606 225, ⓦhotel giampy.eu. A kilometre from the cable car, this friendly hotel with basic rooms is well placed for hitting both the ski slopes and the local walking trails. There's a decent restaurant too (half-board €60 per person), with a wood-fired pizza oven (evenings only). **€90**

GRAN SASSO TRAILS

Snow can continue to fall on the park's highest mountain, **Corno Grande** (2912m), until late May, and remain thick on the ground well into June, so outside July and August, **the ascent** should only be attempted by experienced and fully equipped climbers. At all times you should be prepared for some fairly strenuous scree-climbing and steep descents. If you are fit, but not experienced, it is probably wiser to take a guide: contact Mountain Evolution (☎347 817 9989, 🌐mountainevolution.com; €220 for 1–3 days; max two people). Perhaps the most challenging route is the tough trek from the *Campo Imperatore* (see p.715) right across the mountain range, taking in the Corno Grande, sleeping over at the *Rifugio Franchetti* (☎0861 959 634 or ☎333 232 4474, 🌐rifugiofranchetti.it; June–Sept; €20, or €43 for dinner, bed and breakfast). The website has several suggested itineraries (in Italian only), and the staff are also very knowledgeable. If you're going to do any of the Gran Sasso trails, you'll need the CAI *Gran Sasso d'Italia* **map** (on sale in newsagents around the region), and should check out **weather conditions** with your hotel or online at 🌐meteomont.org first.

The Campo Imperatore plain

The road continues from Fonte Cerreto across the vast **Campo Imperatore plain**, long the stomping ground of **nomadic shepherds**, who bring their flocks up here for summer grazing after wintering in the south – a practice that has endured since Roman times. The plain is fringed with hill-villages, many of them owing their existence to the medieval wool-trade.

Castel del Monte

Among the hill-villages in the Campo Imperatore is **Castel del Monte**, heavily fortified and crowned with a ruined castle and church, scene of a chilling episode at the beginning of the last century when workers discovered a series of caves containing hundreds of clothed skeletons sitting on cane chairs. The skeletons no longer exist, having been burnt as a health precaution, though their discovery perhaps lies behind the town's biggest event of the year, a **festival of witches** that takes place one night in mid-August (see 🌐lanottedellestreghe.org for the exact date), with locals acting out all manner of spooky scenarios.

Rocca Calascio and Santo Stefano di Sessanio

The pale-honey castle of **Rocca Calascio** sits crumbling above a village that is just beginning to be repopulated and restored after years of abandonment, as people revalue the potential of its medieval houses as holiday homes. Beyond is **Santo Stefano di Sessanio**, a bustling Medici stronghold in the fifteenth century, virtually abandoned, and seemingly destined for nothing, until visionary entrepreneur Daniele Kihlgren turned up there on his motorbike in 1999 (see box opposite).

L'Aquila

Until April 6, 2009, when an **earthquake** of 5.8 on the Richter scale struck the city (see box, p.718), **L'AQUILA** was Abruzzo's main cultural attraction. An ancient university town overlooked by the bulk of Gran Sasso, it was founded in 1242, when the Holy Roman Emperor Frederick II legendarily drew together the populations from 99 of Abruzzo's villages to form a new city. Each village built its own church, piazza and quarter, and one of the city's most-loved (and surviving) sights is a medieval fountain with 99 spouts. Post-earthquake, little progress has been made, and much of the town is still cordoned off and precariously propped up with scaffolding. You can still wander along the main Corso and into some of the surrounding sreets, but the emptiness of the place save for a few townspeople and the trucks of the Protezione Civile makes for a somewhat disquieting experience.

THE CULTURE OF POVERTY

The son of an Italian mother and Swedish father, **Daniele Kihlgren** was born heir to the vast fortune his mother's family had accrued by producing cement. Like many rich kids, he rebelled, getting himself expelled from school, then dabbling in hard drugs. A motorbike trip around Italy opened his eyes to the immense damage cement – and illegal development – had done to his country, especially in Sicily and the south, but in 1999, biking through Abruzzo, he discovered **Santo Stefano di Sessanio**, a hill-village that was so poor that no one had ever bothered to build anything new. In other similar villages around the south, those who wanted to make anything of their lives had emigrated, to America, Australia, Germany, Switzerland, often returning to build huge modern houses that had nothing to do with local traditions, materials or landscape. Returnees wanted to demonstrate their wealth and cosmopolitanism, and did so by constructing the horrendous Swiss-type chalets or American-style bungalows – most of them built with breezeblocks and cement but no planning permission – that make eyesores of so many small southern villages. Santo Stefano di Sessanio, it seemed, was so insignificant that no one who left bothered to return.

Kihlgren bought a house on the spot, then set about securing a deal with Santo Stefano's local authority. He promised to make a substantial investment in the village, in return for which the authority agreed to place a blanket ban on new building. Kihlgren bought eight more houses in Santo Stefano, and €4.5 million and eight years later opened **Sextantio** (Via Principe Umberto; ☎0862 899 112, ⊕sextantio.it; €200), an "albergo diffuso": a hotel whose rooms, restaurant and reception areas are spread among the medieval houses of the village.

The aesthetics and philosophy behind the restoration were radical. Kihlgren was sick of what he considers the over-valuation of planned cities, big-name architects, high art and culture, as opposed to the anonymous, organic, rural architecture of poverty and survival. And though not denying his guests the comfort of under-floor heating (and Philippe Starck bathtubs) he was determined that the spartan realities of rustic life were not papered over. Literally. Walls were stripped back to their ancient plaster and left bare, many preserving blackened patches where a fire once roared. Floors too were left bare, and original oak doors and locks lovingly restored – so that today guests are given iron keys to lug around, the size of a forearm. In the stone-vaulted restaurant, traditional dishes have been revived, and olive oil and pulses produced on the Sextantio's own land are served, along with local cheeses, salamis, home-made liqueurs and locally raised lamb.

Kihlgren has property in nine other villages around the south, but the highest-profile of his recent projects has been the restoration of cave-dwellings in Matera, Basilicata (see p.845).

Castello Cinquentesco

On the northeast edge of the historic centre, the **Castello Cinquentesco** was built by the Spanish in the sixteenth century to keep the locals under control, and until the earthquake was home to the Museo Nazionale d'Abruzzo. Although the interior was badly damaged – the museum won't reopen to the public until the end of 2013 at the earliest – you can still walk the circuit of the castle's four impressive bastions.

Santa Maria di Collemaggio

Piazzale Collemaggio • Daily 9.30am–1pm & 4–7pm • Free

East of the centre, outside the city walls, is **Santa Maria di Collemaggio**, its massive rectangular bulk faced with a geometric jigsaw of pink and white stone. The basilica was founded in the thirteenth century by Pietro of Morrone, a hermit unwillingly dragged from his mountain retreat to be made pope by power-hungry cardinals who reckoned he would be easy to manipulate. When he turned out to be too naive even for the uses of the cardinals, he was forced to resign and was posthumously compensated for the ordeal by being canonized.

While the basilica's beautiful facade remained intact after the earthquake, the interior fared less well, and much of it is still being renovated; a new plexiglass roof allows light to stream in and illuminate the space.

12

L'AQUILA AFTER THE QUAKE

At 3.32am on the morning of Monday, April 6, 2009, an **earthquake** of 5.8 on the Richter scale rocked central Italy. The shocks were felt as far as Rome and Campania, but the epicentre was **L'Aquila**, the regional capital of Abruzzo. Built on the bed of an ancient lake, the geological structure of the terrain amplified the seismic waves.

The city has a history of earthquakes, the worst being in 1703 when 5000 people were killed, and the city virtually flattened. This time, thousands of buildings in the city were badly damaged, and some surrounding villages were pretty much destroyed. However, nearby medieval hill-villages survived almost untouched, and it was clear in the aftermath that much of the damage and many of the deaths were due to shoddy building standards. In all, 308 people died, and over 65,000 were made homeless; 40,000 people were evacuated to tented camps, prompting Prime Minister Berlusconi to make his infamous comment that the earthquake victims should cheer up and consider themselves on a camping weekend.

Despite the funds that poured in after the earthquake to help with the reconstruction, the recovery project is at a standstill: much of L'Aquila's *centro storico* remains out of bounds to the public, many of its residents are still in temporary housing, and, according to a recent investigation by the newspaper *La Repubblica*, only five percent of the damage has been repaired. The townspeople haven't abandoned hope, however, setting in place a number of grass-roots initiatives that are perhaps L'Aquila's best chance of salvation.

Fontana delle 99 Cannelle

Close to the train station, L'Aquila's famous **Fontana delle 99 Cannelle** is set around three sides of a sunken piazza, each water spout a symbol of one of the villages that formed the city. This constant supply of fresh water sustained the Aquilani through plagues, earthquakes and sieges, and was used for washing clothes until after the war.

ARRIVAL AND INFORMATION
L'AQUILA

By train L'Aquila's train station is to the west of the centre, a 5- to 10min walk from the Fontana delle 99 Cannelle.
Destinations Rome via Terni (10 daily; 3hr–3hr 40min); Sulmona (9 daily; 1hr); Teramo (3 daily; 1hr–1hr 15min); Terni (8 daily; 2hr).
By bus Long-distance buses arrive at the Collemaggio terminal near Porta Bazzano, a short walk from Santa Maria di Collemaggio.
Destinations Bominaco (2 daily; 1hr); Pescara (8 daily; 1hr 30min–2hr 20min); Rome (hourly; 1hr 40min); Sulmona (4 daily; 1hr 35min–1hr 55min); Teramo (11 daily; 1hr–1hr 20min).

By car L'Aquila is a difficult place to negotiate by car; the best place to park to visit the centre is Viale Francesco Crispi, a 5min walk from the central Piazza del Duomo.
Tourist office The tourist office (Mon–Sat 9am–1pm & 3–6pm; ☎ 0862 410 808, ⌨ abruzzoturismo.it) is in a hut to the west of the city in the suburb of Acquasanta, at Parcheggio Stadio Rugby, a car park near the rugby stadium and the cemetery. Take bus #5 or #8 from the train station, or any bus going to the cemetery from the bus station. The staff are enthusiastic and efficient, and have up-to-date information on places to stay and restaurants, as well as accessible sights.

Bominaco

Off the SS17 • 3 buses daily from L'Aquila (1hr)

From L'Aquila, the SS17 follows the ancient route of the local shepherds across the saffron fields south to Sulmona. If you have your own transport, it's worth making a short detour on the way to **BOMINACO** (also accessible by bus from L'Aquila). The village itself is an inauspicious knot of grubby houses in a marvellous setting at the head of a valley, but it's worth a visit to admire two of Abruzzo's most beautiful churches.

Bominaco's churches

You can ask for admission to both churches from a local lady known as Signora Chiara (☎ 086 93 764; tip expected); bring change to illuminate the interiors (€2)

The endearingly askew and lichen-mottled facade of **San Pellegrino**, founded by Charlemagne, conceals floor-to-ceiling thirteenth-century frescoes in vivid hues reminiscent of a peacock's plume. The frescoes include pictures of the life of Christ, the Virgin and a huge St Christopher, as well as an intriguing calendar with signs of the zodiac. If you put your ear to the hole at the side of the altar, tradition says you'll hear the heartbeat of San Pellegrino buried below.

The church of **Santa Maria Assunta**, just beyond, stands on the foundations of a Roman temple to Venus. Beyond its coolly refined exterior, the creamy-white carvings are so exquisitely precise that it seems the mason has only just put down his chisel; in fact they're eight hundred years old.

Sulmona and around

Flanked by bleak mountains and bristling with legends about its most famous son, Ovid, **SULMONA** is a rich and comfortable provincial town owing its wealth to gold jewellery and sugared almonds. Although it sustained some damage during the 2009 earthquake, most of it was internal, and it remains an atmospheric little place, with a dark tangle of a historical centre lined with imposing palaces and overshadowed by the mountainous bulk of the Majella. Sulmona's sights can be seen in a morning, but the town makes a good base for exploring the surroundings – from ancient hermitages to towns with snake-infested festivals.

Corso Ovidio, Sulmona's main street, cuts through the centre from the park-side bus terminus, leading up to Piazza XX Settembre. From here, Sulmona's sights are within easy strolling distance.

The Annunziata

Tues–Sun 9am–1pm & 3.30–6.30pm • €3 joint ticket for all museums

The **Annunziata**, a Gothic-Renaissance *palazzo* adjoining a flamboyant Baroque church on Corso Ovidio, was established by a confraternity to take care of the citizens from birth until death, and its steps were once crowded with the ill and destitute. These days they are a hangout for the town's teenagers during the evening *passeggiata*, who naturally pay no attention whatsoever to the external decoration designed to remind onlookers of the cycles of life and death. The most intriguing statue, however, is just inside the entrance: Ovid, metamorphosed from pagan poet of love into an ascetic friar.

Inside the Annunziata are several **museums**, the most interesting of which is the **Museo del Costume Popolare Abruzzese-Molisano e della Transhumanza**, devoted to local costumes and transhumance – the practice of moving sheep to summer pastures – along with examples of work by Sulmona's Renaissance goldsmiths, a trade that continues here today, as evidenced by the number of jewellers' shops along the Corso; the **Museo Civico** has local sculpture and paintings from the sixteenth to seventeenth centuries; and a third, the **Museo "in situ"**, shows the excavations of a Roman villa inhabited from the first century BC to the second century AD, abandoned suddenly

---

SULMONA'S CONFETTI

As well as gold, the Corso's **shops** are full of Sulmona's other great product – *confetti* – a confection of sugared almonds or chocolate wired into elaborate flowers with the aid of coloured cellophane, crêpe paper and ribbons. Through ingenious marketing the Sulmonese *confetti* barons have made gifts of their intricate sculptures *de rigueur* at christenings, confirmations and weddings throughout Catholic Europe. You can learn more about *confetti* manufacture at the town's most famous conveyor of sugary confectionery, the **Fabbrica Confetti Pelino** at Via Stazione Introdacqua 55 at the southern end of Corso Ovidio (Mon–Sat 8.30am–12.30pm & 3–6.30pm; free). Here, the Museo d'Arte Confettiera holds an assortment of antique sweet-making machines and a sixteenth-century laboratory, complete with all manner of mills, toasters and polishing machines.

along with many other houses in the valley when a landslide or an earthquake struck. Among the fragments of fabulously coloured wall-painting are depictions of Pan, Eros, Dionysus and Ariadne, and there are several floor mosaics, all well labelled.

Piazza del Carmine

At the end of the Corso is **Piazza del Carmine**, where the weighty Romanesque portal of **San Francesco della Scarpa** was the only part of the church solid enough to withstand a 1703 earthquake. The church gets its name – della Scarpa (of the shoe) – from the fact that Franciscans wore shoes instead of the sandals worn by other monastic orders. Opposite, the impressive Gothic **aqueduct**, built to supply water to the town and power to its wool mills, ends at a small fifteenth-century fountain, the **Fontana del Vecchio**, named for the bust of a chubby-cheeked old man on top.

Piazza Garibaldi

On the other side of the aqueduct, and home to the town's market on Wednesday and Saturday, is **Piazza Garibaldi**, a vast square dominated by the austere slopes of **Monte Morrone**, on which the hermit Pietro Morrone lived until he was dragged away to be made Pope Celestine V. There's a former nunnery in the corner – take a look at the courtyard, where there's a tiny door at which unmarried mothers were permitted to abandon their babies. In the church and old refectory, the **Polo Museale di Santa Chiara** (Tues–Sun 9am–1pm & 3–7.30pm; €3) holds a collection of religious art, including a fresco cycle with episodes from the lives of Christ and St Francis, wooden sculptures of saints, and a collection of fifteenth-century gold items.

On the last weekend in July, Piazza Garibaldi sees the **Giostra Cavalleresca di Sulmona** (Ⓦ giostrasulmona.it), the re-enactment of a Renaissance joust with horses representing the town's seven *borghi* galloping round the square, as well as plenty of costumed pageantry and feasting.

ARRIVAL AND INFORMATION

SULMONA

By car There's covered parking underneath Piazza Garibaldi.

By train The train station is 1.5km outside the centre of town; bus #A runs from the station to the Villa Comunale next to the historic centre.

Destinations Avezzano (8 daily; 1hr–1hr 25min); Celano (7 daily; 50min–1hr 25min).

By bus Buses arrive at the Villa Comunale next to the *centro storico*.

Destinations Cocullo (1 daily; 40min); Scanno (6 daily; 1hr).

Tourist offices The main tourist office is at Corso Ovidio 208 (July–Sept Mon–Sat 9am–1pm & 4–7pm, Sun 9am–1pm; Oct–June Mon & Wed 9am–1pm, Tues, Thurs & Fri 9am–1pm & 3–6pm; Ⓣ 0864 53 276). There's a second office in the old pharmacy of the Palazzo Santissima Annunziata, with very helpful staff, maps and details of Sulmona's churches and palaces (daily 9am–12.30pm & 3.30–7pm; Ⓣ 0864 210 216).

ACCOMMODATION

Case Bonomini Via Quatrario Ⓣ 0864 52 308, Ⓦ bed andbreakfastcasebonomini.com. Comfortable apartments with views of the Majella scattered along Via Quatrario in the historic centre, run on a B&B basis. *Il Rustico* is the pick of the bunch, a rustic, brick-walled apartment on two floors that sleeps up to five. €60

★ **Rojan** Via degli Agghiacciati 15 Ⓣ 0864 950 126, Ⓦ hotelrojan.it. Rooms at this comfortable four-star hotel come with wood-beamed ceilings and are soothingly

decked out in a palette of neutrals. It's run by the ultra-friendly Casaccia family, whose attention to detail is second to none: breakfasts are home-made by Rosanna, while Gianluca helps guests plan their itineraries. €140

Stella Via Mazara 18 Ⓣ 0864 52 653, Ⓦ hasr.it. A relaxed, family-run establishment in a central location. The rooms are small and fairly basic but spotlessly clean. A simple breakfast is included. Doubles €70, apartments €80

EATING AND DRINKING

Cantina di Biffi Via Barbato 1, off Corso Ovidio Ⓣ 0864 32 025. A countrified place with a dedication to the Slow

Food movement and an excellent choice of wines. On the menu are handmade pasta dishes such as rigatoni with ricotta and *guanciale* (a type of bacon; €9), and home-made fruit tarts for dessert. Expect to spend around €35 a head for a full meal with wine. Noon–2.30pm & 6pm–1am; closed Wed.

Clemente Vico Quercia 20 📞 0864 210 679. A bright, family-run place in an old *palazzo* that's been serving home-produced *salumi* and dishes such as *agnello con aglio, rosmarino e pecorino* (pan-seared lamb with garlic, rosemary and *pecorino* cheese) for over fifty years. Be warned, though: the antipasti are a meal in themselves,

so go easy if you want to last till dessert. *Primi* cost €7, *secondi* €8–13. Mon–Wed, Fri & Sat 12.30–2.30pm & 7.30–10.30pm, Sun 12.30–2.30pm.

★ **Locanda di Gino** Piazza Plebiscito 12 📞 0864 5228, 🌐 lalocandadigino.it. Run by the Allega family since 1962 (mamma Lucia still reigns in the kitchen), this refined restaurant serves up some fantastic home-made pasta dishes including courgette-flower *carrati* with local saffron (€8), and traditional mains such as lamb casserole (€10), in a bright, buzzy dining room. Mon–Sat 12.30–2.45pm.

Parco Nazionale della Majella

The **Parco Nazionale della Majella**, 10km to the east of Sulmona, is named after the mountain – **Monte Majella** – that dominates the area. Dedicated to the Italic goddess Maja, the mountain was held sacred by the ancient people of Abruzzo, and the region around it was named Domus Christi by Petrarch, or the "House of God", for its proliferation of hermitages and abbeys. Over a hundred **hermits** made their retreat here in the Middle Ages; some reused cave dwellings, others built churches into the rock, haunting constructions to this day.

May is a particularly lovely month to visit because of the blossoming **wildflowers**, but its 500km of **walking trails and cycling paths** are a draw all year long. The southern part of the park harbours beautiful beechwood forests, with the possibility of spotting bears, deer and wolves; trails on the eastern side pass through dramatic rocky gorges; while the northern side is full of hermitages and shepherds' huts.

12

Pescocostanzo

Of the park's small towns, **Pescocostanzo** (🌐 pesconline.it) makes the nicest base, a picture-perfect medieval *borgo* on the slopes of Monte Calvario with a cobbled historic centre, a smattering of places to stay, and access to the ski resort of Vallefura.

ARRIVAL AND INFORMATION	**PARCO NAZIONALE DELLA MAJELLA**

By bus There are buses to the park's villages from Sulmona, Chieti and Pescara.

Tourist offices The park has various visitor centres, including one at Pescocostanzo, at Piazza Municipio 13 (March & Oct Sun 10–1pm; April Sat & Sun 9am–1pm &

3–6pm; May Sat & Sun 10am–1pm; June & Sept daily 10am–1pm & 4–7pm; July & Aug daily 9am–1pm & 4–8pm; Dec Fri–Sun 10am–1pm & 4–7pm; 📞 0864 641 311, 🌐 parcomajella.it), and at Pacentro, at Via Roma (same hours; 📞 0864 41 304).

COCULLO'S SNAKE FESTIVAL

A tatty hill-village west of Sulmona, **Cocullo** is neglected by outsiders for 364 days of the year. However, on the first Thursday in May it's invaded by what seems like half the population of central Italy, coming to celebrate the weird **festival of snakes**, an annual event held in memory of St Dominic, the patron saint of the village, who allegedly rid the area of venomous snakes back in the eleventh century.

The festival is an odd mixture of the modern and archaic. After Mass in the main square, a number of snake-charmers in the crowd drape a wooden statue of St Dominic with a writhing bunch of live but harmless snakes, which is then paraded through the streets in a bizarre celebration of the saint's unique powers (he was apparently good at curing snake-bites too). It's actually thought that Cocullo's preoccupation with serpents dates back to before the time of the saint when, in the pre-Christian era, local tribes worshipped their goddess Angitia with offerings of snakes.

Cocullo is connected by train (4 daily; 30–40min) and bus (1 daily; 40min) from Sulmona, though on festival day extra bus services are laid on. For further information on the festival, ask at Sulmona's tourist office (see opposite).

ACCOMMODATION AND EATING

★ **Al Piccolo Albergo "La Rua"** Via Rua Mozza 1/3, Pescocostanzo ☎0864 640 083, ⓦlarua.it. Just steps from the central Piazza Municipio, this friendly, family-run place welcomes guests in from the cold with a roaring fire in the entrance hall. The rooms are large and comfortable, with fantastic views, and breakfast is a feast of home-made cakes and jams. **€160**

Il Gatto Bianco Viale Appennini 3, Pescocostanzo ☎0864 641 466, ⓦilgattobianco.it. Luxuriously appointed rooms with chalet-luxe decor, big bathrooms-with-a-view, and generous breakfasts. The smart but relaxed restaurant serves good grilled-meat dishes. **€180**

Scanno and around

A popular tourist destination, **SCANNO** is reached by passing through the narrow and rocky **Gole del Sagittario**, a WWF reserve that makes a spectacular drive along galleries of rock and around blind hairpin bends that widen out at the glassy green **Lago di Scanno**. Perched over the lake is a church, the **Madonna del Lago**, with the cliff as its back wall, and nearby there are boats and pedaloes for rent in the summer.

A couple of kilometres beyond, Scanno itself is a well-preserved medieval village encircled by mountains. In 1951, Henri Cartier-Bresson photographed the village, in a series of atmospheric shots focusing on the **traditional dress** worn by Scanno's women. Some elderly women can still be seen wearing the long, dark, pleated skirts and bodices with a patterned apron that suggest a possible origin in Asia Minor; the annual Costume di Scanno festival in April sees the locals taking to the streets in their finery. Scannese **jewellery** also has something of the Orient about it – large, delicately filigreed earrings, and a charm in the form of a star, known as a *presuntosa*, given to fiancées to ward off other men. If you want to see the costume and jewellery at close quarters head for the shops on Strada Roma and Corso Centrale.

The old town

It's a pleasure strolling around the **old town**, built into the steep hillside, the squares and alleyways lined with solid stone houses built by wool barons when business was good. Though shepherding as a way of life is virtually extinct and the population has dwindled, it's still a living village.

The chair lift

Mid-June to mid-Sept & mid-Dec–April 9am–6pm • €9 return, winter €16 day-pass

A **chair lift**, signposted 300m from the centre, takes **skiers** up to a handful of runs on Monte Rotondo, operating also in the short summer season when it's worth going up just for the view of lake and mountains, especially at sunset.

ARRIVAL AND INFORMATION

SCANNO

By bus There are six daily buses from Sulmona (1hr) and four from Rome (3hr 35min).
Tourist office Piazza S. Maria della Valle 12 (summer Mon–Sat 9am–1pm & 4–7pm, Sun 9am–1pm, Aug open longer hours; winter Mon & Wed 9am–1pm, Tues, Thurs & Fri 9am–1pm & 3–6pm; ☎0864 74 317, ⓦabruzzoturismo.it).

ACCOMMODATION AND EATING

Al Peschio Pizzuto Località Le Prata, 3km from Scanno ☎346 720 9982, ⓦalpeschiopizzuto.it. This welcoming agriturismo has four no-frills but spotless and comfortable rooms, as well as a great rustic restaurant, serving up typical

SCANNO'S FESTIVALS

If you're around in August, you might catch Scanno's **summer festival**, with a series of cultural events and fireworks displays held throughout the month (contact the tourist office for details), and on January 17 there's a **lasagne festival** – the Festa di Sant'Antonio Abate – involving the cooking of a great cauldron of lasagne and beans outside the door of the church, which is then blessed and doled out with a somewhat unholy amount of pushing and shoving.

Abruzzese mountain cuisine, with many of the ingredients home-grown; a full meal with wine costs €25. Half-board is available for €50 per person. No credit cards. **€70**

★ **Gli Archetti** Via Silla 8 ✆ 0864 74 645. Inside the Porta della Croce entrance to the old town, this place cooks up imaginative variations on traditional Abruzzese cuisine – look out for dishes with wild vegetables, and save room

for the apple cake with ginger cream. 12.30–3pm & 7.30–10pm; closed Tues.

I Lupi 2km away outside the town of Villalago ✆ 0864 740 100, ⊛ campingilupi.it. A campsite on the shore of the lake; thanks to its picturesque location, it gets packed out in summer. Open all year. Pitches **€13.40**, bungalows **€44**

Parco Nazionale d'Abruzzo

At four hundred square kilometres, the **PARCO NAZIONALE D'ABRUZZO** is Italy's third-largest national park and holds some of its wildest mountain land, providing great walking and a hunter-free haven for wolves, brown bears, chamois, deer, lynx, wild boar, and three or four pairs of royal eagles.

Pescasseroli

The central village, **PESCASSEROLI**, is the main hub for visitors, surrounded by campsites, holiday apartments and hotels. The best way to strike out from here is to hike. Take advantage of the comprehensive information service, and get walking as quickly as possible: as soon as you get away from the vicinity of the tourist villages, the wild Apennine beauty really makes itself felt.

Museo Naturalistico
Via Colli dell'Oro • Daily 10am–1.30pm & 3–6.30pm • €6

In the same building as the park's visitor centre is the excellent **Museo Naturalistico**, which fills you in on the park's flora and fauna and acts as a clinic for sick animals. At the time of writing, the centre was caring for two Marsican brown bears and an Apennine wolf cub, among other animals. There's also a garden where the park's most typical plants and trees are cultivated, home to an array of local wildlife.

Opi

Perched on a hilltop some 6km from Pescasseroli, **Opi** is a charming, unspoilt little town. The centre holds the small **Centro Visita del Camoscio** (Chamois Museum; July & Aug daily 10am–1pm & 3–7pm; Sept–June Sat & Sun only); from a viewpoint near the museum you can observe the chamois in a nearby reserve. The tourist office houses a dusty **Museo dello Sci** (daily 9am–12.30pm & 4–7pm; free), with a collection of skis through the ages.

A good time to visit is during the Infiorata **flower festival**, on the festival of Corpus Domini in June, when since the seventeenth century locals have created vast pictures from flower petals all along the main street.

HIKING ROUTES

The tourist offices sell maps on which all **hiking routes** in the park are marked, along with an indication of the difficulty involved, the time needed, and the flora and fauna you're likely to see on the way. There are nearly 150 different routes, so making a choice can be difficult. Note that from July 15 to September 15, some of the most popular routes, including Val di Rosa and Monte Amara, are open by **reservation** only for a fee of €10–15. It's usually sufficient to book the day before. The rest of the year, these routes are open without restriction or fee, though guided tours can still be arranged. Hiking maps cost €12 from the Centro Visita at Pescasseroli.

12

PESCASSEROLI'S FESTIVALS

It's worth trying to coincide a trip with one of Pescasseroli's lively **festivals**. The **Sagra della Pecora** (early Sept) commemorates the work of local nomadic shepherds with a tasting of local products in the town's main square. The *Festa della Madonna*, on July 15 and 16, sees the Black Madonna carried 9km from her sanctuary on Monte Tranquillo to Pescasseroli and back to celebrate the town's miraculous escape from being bombed during World War II after prayers were offered to the Madonna.

ARRIVAL AND INFORMATION

PARCO NAZIONALE D'ABRUZZO

By train The nearest train station is Avezzano, a stop on the Pescara–Rome rail line. ARPA buses to Pescasseroli leave from outside Avezzano's train station.

By bus Pescasseroli is served by bus from Avezzano (4 daily; 1hr 30min), 30km west of Sulmona. There are also bus services from Castel di Sangro on the border with Molise (6–8 daily; 1hr 15min), which has connections with Naples. In summer (mid-June to mid-Sept) a daily service runs from Rome (3hr). There are five daily buses from Pescasseroli to Opi (10min).

Tourist offices The park's main visitor centre is in Pescasseroli at Via Colli dell'Oro (daily 10am–1.30pm & 3–6.30pm; ☎0863 911 3221, ⓦparcoabruzzo.it), while the tourist office in town is on Viale Principe di Napoli (summer: Mon–Sat 9am–1pm & 4–7pm, Sun 9am–1pm; winter Mon–Sat 9am–1pm & 3–6pm, Sun 9am–1pm; ☎0863 910 461). Opi's tourist office is on Via San Giovanni (daily except Wed: July & Aug, mid-Dec to mid-Jan 9.30am–1pm & 4–7pm; rest of year 9.30am–12.30pm & 3.30–6.30pm; ☎0863 910 622, ⓦopiabruzzo.com).

ACCOMMODATION

In high season, there's little chance of finding a room on arrival; you need to book at least a month in advance and be prepared for compulsory half-board in July & August. If you're coming here for a week or more, you might consider B&B accommodation in a private house or an apartment rental – the tourist offices can supply you with a list. Campers should manage to find space on one of the campsites, though be warned that temperatures are low even in summer.

La Pieja Via Salita la Croce 1, Opi ☎0863 910 772, ⓦlapieja.it. Overlooking picture-perfect Opi, this hotel makes a good base for exploring the park. The food is one of the big draws here; it's worth booking half-board (€68 per person) so that you can sample the delicious local dishes cooked up by chef Antonio. **€90**

WILDLIFE IN THE PARCO NAZIONALE D'ABRUZZO

The Abruzzo National Park (ⓦparcoabruzzo.it) is an area of exceptional biodiversity with around a hundred indigenous species.

One of the most important animals in the park is the **Marsican brown bear**. Until recently an endangered species, there are now thought to be around thirty to fifty in the park, but they are extremely shy, solitary and lazy, and difficult to spot – you're more likely to find traces of their presence than see an actual bear. The Centro Visita dell'Orso (April to mid-June Sat & Sun 9am–1pm & 2.30–6.30pm; mid-June to Sept Tues–Sun 9am–1pm & 2.30–6.30pm; Oct–March Sat & Sun 10.30am–1pm & 2.30–4pm; €3) at Villavallelonga has 3D displays on the evolution of bears in the park, as well as the opportunity to admire Yoga and Sandrino (from a distance), in the nearby reserve.

Another key park inhabitant is the **Apennine wolf**, of which there are around forty to fifty. As with the bears, the wolves offer no danger to humans, and they are also difficult to spot – the closest you're likely to get to either in the wild are footprints in mud or snow. Look out, too, for chamois, deer and roe deer, wildcats, martens, otters, badgers, polecats and the edible dormouse. Wolves can also be seen at the dedicated wolf museum at Civitella Alfadena (daily 10am–1.30pm & 3–6.30pm; €3); others can be seen close up at the fascinating clinic and natural history museum in Pescasseroli (see p.723).

Among **birds**, the park's species include the golden eagle, the peregrine hawk, the goshawk and the rare white-backed woodpecker. Higher up are snow finch, alpine accentor and rock partridge.

The park's **flora** includes many local orchids, among which the most important variety is Venus's little shoe or Our Lady's slipper, which thrives on the chalky soil in the park. There are also gentians, peonies, violets, irises and columbines, and black pine woods at Villetta Barrea and the Camosciara.

La Torre Via Castello 3, Civitella Alfedena ☎ 0864 890 121, ⓦ albergolatorre.com. In the medieval centre of Civitella Alfedena near Pescasseroli, this friendly hotel is set in an eighteenth-century palace and has simple, chalet-style rooms and a cosy restaurant. The owner is full of advice on local walking routes. **€60**

Paradiso Via Fonte Fracassi 4, Pescasseroli ☎ 0863 910 422, ⓦ albergo-paradiso.it. This delightful hotel, 1.5km from the centre of Pescasseroli, is run by Scottish Geraldine and her Italian husband Marco, with warm rustic decor, good country cooking and a pretty garden. Ask to see Geraldine's pub. Half-board (per person) **€60**

★ **Valle del Lupo** Via Collacchi, Pescasseroli ☎ 0863

910 534, ⓦ valledelupo.it. Run by two characterful sisters, this small hotel, 2km from the centre of Pescasseroli, on its own hilltop surrounded by stunning countryside, makes a great place to visit in every season. The ten rooms are simple and sparsely decorated, but spotlessly clean, and tasty local food is on offer in the restaurant (half-board available for €65 per person). **€70**

CAMPING

Le Foci Via Fonte dei Cementi, Opi ☎ 0863 912 233, ⓦ lefoci.it. Just outside Opi, this campsite is well set up with a restaurant, bar and supermarket. Pitches **€18**, caravans **€30**

EATING, DRINKING AND ENTERTAINMENT

★ **La Madonnina** SS83, Opi ☎ 0863 916 053. Signora Francesca has been serving up tasty home-cooking here for 27 years. On the menu is fresh local fare such as platters of cheeses and ravioli with butter and sage; you can watch your lamb cutlets or veal steaks being grilled on the open fire before you tuck in. A full meal with wine costs around €30. Tues–Sun 12.30–2.30pm & 7.30–9pm.

★ **Plistia** Via Principe di Napoli 28, Pescasseroli ☎ 0863 910 732. Great for local specialities: you can eat hearty mountain *primi* such as soup with local vegetables and pulses, or, in spring, gnocchi with asparagus and local saffron, for around €8; the €35 tasting menu is a good deal. Booking necessary. Tues–Sun 1–3pm & 8–9.30pm; open daily in summer.

12

Teramo and around

Rising from the Adriatic and rolling towards the eastern slopes of the Gran Sasso, the landscape of **northeast Abruzzo** is gentle, and its inland towns are usually ignored in favour of its long, sandy and highly popular coastline. **TERAMO**, capital of the province of the same name, is a modern town with an elegant centre, and if you're heading for the sea you may well pass through.

The Duomo and around

Piazza Orsini • Daily 7am–noon & 4–8pm • Free

Teramo's main attraction is the **Duomo** at the top of Corso San Giorgio, with its remarkable silver **altarfront** by the fifteenth-century Abruzzo silversmith Nicola da Guardiagrele. It has 35 panels with lively reliefs of religious scenes, starting with the Annunciation and moving through the New Testament, punctuating the narrative with portraits of various saints. The artist was famous enough to feature in a sumptuous polyptych by a Venetian artist, Jacobello del Fiore, in a Baroque chapel to the left. It features a model of Teramo, set against a gilded sky, with Nicola wearing a monk's habit on the left, Jacobello in the red gown on the right.

South of the Duomo, Via Irelli leads to the heart of Roman Teramo, with fragments of the **amphitheatre**, and the more substantial walls of the **theatre** (under restoration at the time of research), where two of the original twenty entrance arches remain.

The Pinacoteca

Viale Bovio 1 • Tues–Sun: July–Sept 10am–noon & 5–8pm; Oct–June 10am–1pm & 4–7pm • €5 with Museo Archeologico

Between Piazza Garibaldi and the Villa Comunale is the town's modest **Pinacoteca**. The collection of local art over the centuries is best represented by the *Madonna Enthroned with Saints* – a polyptych in which the colours are lucid and the forms almost sculpted, the work of local fifteenth-century artist Giacomo da Campli.

Museo Archeologico

Off Via Carducci at Via Delfico 30 • Tues–Sun: July–Sept 10am–noon & 5–8pm; Oct–June 10am–1pm & 4–7pm • €5 with Pinacoteca

On a parallel street to the main Corso, the **Museo Archeologico** is strong on Roman finds from excavations in Teramo and includes a reconstruction of the Roman theatre, as well as a first-century mosaic of a lion, among the forum columns and marble busts.

ARRIVAL AND INFORMATION   TERAMO

By train The train station is east of the centre on Via Crispi, linked with Piazza Garibaldi by regular #1 city buses.
By bus Buses stop at Piazza Garibaldi.
Destinations Atri (3 daily; 55min–1hr 10min); L'Aquila (9 daily; 1hr 30min); Pescara (via Giulianova; 15 daily; 2hr);

Rome (13 daily; 2hr 30min–2hr 55min).
Tourist office Via Oberdan 16, a cross-street off the main Corso (Mon–Sat 9am–1pm & 3–6pm; closed Sat afternoon in winter; ☎ 0861 244 222, ⊛ abruzzoturismo.it).

ACCOMMODATION, EATING AND DRINKING

Abruzzi Viale Mazzini 18 ☎ 0861 241 043, ⊛ hotel abruzziteramo.com. A modern hotel with smartly decorated, if slightly boxy, rooms. There's a restaurant on site, but it's mainly frequented by business travellers, so if you're after a place with atmosphere you're better off hitting the town. **€85**
★ **Cantina di Porta Romana** Corso Porta Romana 105 ☎ 0861 252 257. An atmospheric wine cellar plastered with photos and knick-knacks from the Fifties and Sixties, serving up dishes local to the Teramo area such as deep-fried courgettes (€10), platters of fried fish, and *mazzerelle alle Teramana* – parcels of finely chopped offal,

wrapped in lettuce leaves and cooked in white wine (€10). The set menu of three courses with wine costs €25. Mon–Sat noon–4pm & 7–11pm.
Enoteca Centrale Corso Cerulli 24 ☎ 0861 243 633. On a street leading off from the Duomo, this bustling place has a great wine list – 300 labels – backed up by excellent local dishes, such as the winter dish *scripelle*, thin crêpes filled with grated cheese and a sprinkle of cinnamon covered in chicken broth, while in summer much use is made of seasonal vegetables. All *primi* cost €7–12, *secondi* €7–15. Mon–Sat noon–2.30pm.

Atri

The pretty little town of **ATRI**, 24km southeast of Teramo, is well worth a visit for the pleasure of wandering the town and exploring the surrounding countryside, as well as for the fifteenth-century frescoes in its Duomo. Approaching the town from Teramo is like travelling through the background of a Renaissance painting, with gently undulating hills planted with orderly olive groves giving way to a surrealist landscape of sleek clay gullies known as *calanchi*, water-eroded into smooth ripples, wrinkles and folds.

The Duomo

Piazza del Duomo • Daily 9am–12.30pm & 3.30–6.30pm •

Atri's main piazza is dominated by the thirteenth-century **Duomo**. Its facade is understated, pierced by a rose window and perforated by the holes in which scaffolding beams were slotted during construction. The highlight is the cycle of **frescoes** in the apse by Andrea Delitio, known for his sophisticated and realistic portrayal of architecture and landscape. The most emotionally charged scene is the *Slaughter of the Innocents*, in which the horror is intensified by the refined Renaissance architectural setting and the fact that the massacre is coolly observed from a balcony by Herod's party of civic bigwigs.

Museo Capitolare

Summer daily 10am–noon & 4–7pm; winter daily except Wed 10am–noon & 3–5pm • €5, cloister and cistern only €2

Inside the Duomo, the **Museo Capitolare** holds a Benedictine cloister dating from the early thirteenth century, with a sixteenth-century well in the centre. Steps lead down to a **cistern** with mosaics from the third century BC, first used as a water supply for the city then as a baths complex. The ten-room **museum** holds various ecclesiastical objects, from reliquaries to paintings.

The Museo Archeologico and Museo Etnografico

Completing Atri's trio of historical museums are the **Museo Archeologico** (Oct–May Sat & Sun 10.30am–12.30pm & 4–6pm; June & Sept Tues–Sun 10.30am–12.30pm & 4.30–7.30pm; July & Aug Tues–Sun 4.30–7.30pm & 9–11pm; €2), with local prehistoric and Roman finds, and a huge folk museum, the **Museo Etnografico** (mid-June to mid-Sept Tues–Sun 4.30–7.30pm; mid-Sept to mid-June Tues–Sat 10am–12.30pm; €1.50), which conjures up traditional peasant life with replicas of a bedroom and kitchen, and over two thousand domestic and rustic objects.

ARRIVAL AND DEPARTURE	ATRI

By bus Buses from Pescara (12 daily; 40min–1hr) stop on Viale Gran Sasso, from where stairs lead up to the centre.

Buses from Teramo (3 daily; 55min–1hr 10min) stop on Via Ricciotti, a 5min walk from the centre.

ACCOMMODATION AND EATING

Arco di San Francesco Via San Francesco 8 ☏ 085 87 762, ⓦ arcodisanfrancesco.it. Located in the old town, this B&B has four prettily decorated rooms on the second floor of an early twentieth-century *palazzo*, as well as a garden. **€100**

Hostaria Zedi Piazza R. Tini ☏ 085 87 340. A good,

old-fashioned *osteria* in the historic centre, a few steps from the Museo Etnografico, with a menu of hearty Abruzzese fare such as gnocchi with sausage sauce (€6) and *cacao e uovo* (lamb stew with egg and cheese; €8), and a menu of strictly local wines. Mon, Tues & Thurs–Sat 12.20–2pm & 7.45–10pm, Sun 12.20–2pm.

Pescara and around

12

Abruzzo's **coastline** stretches for 125km from the border with the Marche region down to the seaside resort of Vasto. The main town and resort of the Abruzzo coast is **PESCARA**, a bustling, modern place that's the region's most commercial city, with a 16km stretch of beach. It's also the nearest town to Abruzzo's airport, where low-cost flights from the UK touch down.

Pescara was heavily bombed in World War II and architecturally there's little of distinction here, but the town makes a good base for excursions to the atmospheric medieval villages of Loreto Aprutino and Atri (see opposite). Next stop along the coast is **Chieti**, home to a superb archeological museum.

Corso Umberto to the beach

Opposite the train station, the main street, **Corso Umberto**, is lined with designer boutiques and packed with the label-conscious Pescaresi, who also hang out in the elegant cafés on **Piazza Rinascita**, known as Pescara's *salone*. The town's main attraction – its sandy **beach** – is at the end of the Corso.

Pescara's museums

In the little that remains of its historic streets, the town boasts an excellent and child-friendly museum at Via delle Caserme 22, the **Museo delle Genti d'Abruzzo** (Mon–Fri 9am–1.30pm, Sat 9am–1.30pm & 4–7pm, Sun 4–7pm; €6; ⓦ gentidabruzzo.it), dedicated to the life and popular traditions of the region. Perhaps the most enchanting room is one devoted to the nomadic shepherds, containing books of their poetry, carved objects and volumes of Ariosto's chivalric romance *Orlando Furioso*.

Admirers of eccentric poet **Gabriele d'Annunzio** (see box, p.292) may want to visit his birthplace, the **Casa Natale di Gabriele d'Annunzio**, at Corso Manthonè 116 (daily 9am–1.30pm, July & Aug hours vary; €2; ⓦ casadannunzio.beniculturali.it), while devotees of Art Nouveau and later twentieth-century art should head for the **Museo Civico Basilio Cascella** at Viale Marconi 45 (mid-June to mid-Sept Mon 9am–1pm,

Tues–Sat 9am–1pm & 5.30–10.30pm, Sun 5.30–10.30pm; mid-Sept to mid-June Mon 9am–1pm, Tues–Sat 9am–1pm & 3.30–7.30pm, Sun 3.30–7.30pm; €2.50), home to five hundred lithographic prints, paintings, ceramics and sculptures, including a stunning set of portraits (mounted on dinner plates) by the prolific Cascella family who lived and worked here.

ARRIVAL AND INFORMATION
PESCARA

By plane Ryanair flights from London Stansted land at Abruzzo airport (ⓦ abruzzo-airport.it), around 3km southwest of the city; from the airport, the #38 bus leaves for Piazza della Repubblica every 15min (€1.10).

By train Pescara has two train stations: Stazione Centrale, at Piazza della Repubblica, close to Corso Umberto and the beach, and Porta Nuova, convenient for the museums and restaurants clustered around Corso Manthonè.

Destinations Ancona (17 daily; 1–2hr); Chieti (16 daily; 15–20min); Rome (3 daily; 4hr); Sulmona (14 daily; 1hr–1hr 20min); Termoli (every 30min–1hr; 40min–1hr 25min); Vasto (20 daily; 35min–1hr).

By bus Buses to Rome (quicker than the train) and Naples, as well as regional buses, leave from outside Stazione Centrale, in Piazza della Repubbblica.

Destinations Atri (12 daily; 40min–1hr); Bologna (2 daily; 4hr); Chieti (7 daily; 30min); Florence (1 daily; 6hr 15min); L'Aquila (8 daily; 1hr 50min–2hr 20min); Naples (4 daily; 4hr); Perugia (1–2 daily; 4hr 15min); Rome (9 daily; 2hr 30min–2hr 50min); Salerno (2 daily; 5hr); Siena (1–2 daily; 5hr 25min); Sulmona (5 daily; 1hr–1h 30min).

By ferry SNAV's ferry service to Croatia was suspended at the time of writing, with Ancona the nearest port with Croatia connections; check ⓦ snav.it for updates.

Tourist office The tourist office is in Piazza della Rinascita (summer daily 9am–1pm & 2–6pm; winter hours vary; ☎ 085 422 6462, ⓦ abruzzoturismo.it). There's also tourist information at the airport (Mon–Fri 9am–1.30pm & 3.40–7.40pm, Sat 12.30–1.30pm; ☎ 085 50 168).

12 ACCOMMODATION

Alba Via M. Forti 14 ☎ 085 389 145, ⓦ hotelalba .pescara.it. A fairly upmarket choice a few minutes from the beach – the spacious rooms have a baroque, old-fashioned touch that takes them beyond the average business hotel, and there are often discounts at weekends. **€105**

★ **Dimora Novecento** Piazza Vittoria Colonna ☎ 085 693 447, ⓦ dimoranovecento.it. This luxurious B&B offers four large and stylishly decorated rooms in the heart of town, each one different: one has a glass-roofed bathroom, another a fireplace and a view of historic *palazzi*. There's also a kitchen for guests' use, and free snacks and drinks to help

yourself to during the day. Breakfast is a feast of home-made cakes and pastries. **€90**

Villa Maria d'Abruzzo Contrada Pretaro, Villafranca al Mare ☎ 085 450 051, ⓦ sportingvillamaria.it. A 10min drive from Pescara's airport, centre and the sea, and set in tranquil gardens with a swimming pool and a swanky spa, this place is unusually welcoming for a business hotel. It's a good deal if you get one of the newly revamped rooms; most guests are on a half-board basis (an extra €28 per person). Free shuttle to the hotel's private beach in summer. **€130**

EATING, DRINKING AND ENTERTAINMENT

For meals and nightlife, head for the little that remains of the old town of Pescara near the river. Along Corso Manthonè and Via delle Caserme there are scores of bars and restaurants. Frequent live concerts are organized during the summer on the seafront, many of them free. The town's main festival is Pescara Jazz (early July to early Aug), with big-name jazz artists performing in the Teatro Gabriele d'Annunzio (tickets from €15; ⓦ pescarajazz.com).

★ **Flaiano da Alfonso** Corso Manthonè 90–94 ☎ 085 62 388. This family-run restaurant is a reliable choice on busy Corso Manthonè. Tasty dishes such as handmade *orecchiette* pasta with salted ricotta and fresh tomatoes (€7.50), grilled beef with balsamic vinegar (€14), and pork with cherry tomatoes and wild herbs (€12), served up by smiling waiters. Mon–Fri 7pm–12.30am, Sat & Sun noon–3.30pm & 7pm–12.30am.

Pesci Corso Manthonè 39 ☎ 085 453 1183. An excellent fish restaurant with modern, unfussy decor and relaxed and

friendly service. Try the tasting platter of raw and cooked fishy starters for €25; *primi* cost €6–12, *secondi* such as the catch of the day cooked *all'acqua pazza* (in water, with olive oil and tomatoes) cost from €10, while the three-course tasting menu is good value at €30. Tues–Sat 8pm–midnight.

Taverna 58 Corso Manthonè 46 ☎ 085 690 724. Hearty Abruzzese dishes such as stew of Majella mountain lamb (€16) or crisp, honey-roasted chicken (€16), served up in a rowdy, atmospheric dining room. Mon–Thurs 12.30–2.30pm & 8–10.30pm, Sat 8–10.30pm.

Loreto Aprutino

LORETO APRUTINO is a quiet, medieval hilltop settlement 24km inland from Pescara. The labyrinthine old town is home to a dwindling number of artisans' workshops specializing in hand-crafted knives. There are also tiny *cantinas* in the old town selling **olive oil**, for which the area has been awarded a DOP (*denominazione di origine protetta*), the equivalent of the DOC designation for wine. Loreto heaves with people on **market day** (Thurs 7am–1pm) and in the evenings during the late-running *passeggiata*, when it's a pleasure to simply do nothing and soak up the atmosphere.

San Pietro Apostolo
Via del Baio 37 • Daily 9.30am–noon & 4.15–6.30pm • Free

At the top of the old town, on the end of a row of nineteenth-century *palazzi*, stands the church of **San Pietro Apostolo**, with medieval origins and an elegant Renaissance portico. Inside are the relics of the town's patron saint, San Zopito, who is venerated on the first Monday after Pentecost with a procession led by a child riding a white bull.

ARRIVAL AND INFORMATION | LORETO APRUTINO

By bus Regular buses make the trip from Pescara every 30min, dropping you on Via Roma, 150m from the tourist office.

Tourist office Piazza Garibaldi 1 (summer Mon–Fri 10am–noon, Tues & Thurs also 4.30–6.30pm; winter Mon–Fri 10am–noon, Tues & Thurs also 4–6pm; ☎ 085 829 0213).

ACCOMMODATION AND EATING

★ **B&B Lauretum** Via del Baio 3 ☎ 085 829 2000, ⓦ bedbreakfastlauretum.com. This B&B is fantastic value for money, with accommodation in a family house near the Castello. The huge, frescoed rooms come with antique furniture and there's a billiards room too. **€100**

Ristorante Carmine Contrada Re Martello 52 ☎ 085 820 8553. It might seem strange, but one of the best places to eat fresh fish hereabouts is not along Pescara's coast, but up in Loreto Aprutino. Just west of the *centro storico*, the freshest of fish is expertly prepared. The *coda di rospo con patate e rosmarino*, monkfish with potatoes and rosemary – a typical dish hereabouts – is sublime. A full meal will cost from around €40. Tues 7.30–10.30pm, Wed–Sun 12.30–2.30pm & 7.30–10.30pm.

Chieti

Half an hour by train or bus southwest of Pescara is the appealing town of **CHIETI**. Spread over a curving ridge, it offers great views of the Majella and Gran Sasso mountains and – on a clear day – out to sea. It also holds Abruzzo's best archeological museum.

From the chunky and much-reconstructed **cathedral**, the main **Corso Marrucino** cuts through the town centre to Piazza Trento e Trieste. Behind the post office, off Via Spaventa, are the remains of three little **Roman temples**.

Museo Archeologico Nazionale di Abruzzo
Via G. Costanzi • Tues–Fri 9am–8pm, Sat & Sun 9am–7pm • €4

The **Museo Archeologico Nazionale di Abruzzo**, laid out in the dignified Villa Comunale, holds finds from Abruzzo's major sites: a massive and muscular white-marble *Hercules* from his temple at Alba Fucens as well as a miniature bronze statue of him, one of several Roman copies of the Greek original by Lysippus. Most interesting is the *Capestrano Warrior*, a statue of a Bronze Age warrior-prince with strangely feminine hips and thighs.

La Civitella
Via G. Pianell • Tues–Sun 9am–7.30pm • €4

Further digs in Chieti have uncovered the core of **Teate** – the main town of the Marrucini, an Italic tribe – that became a Roman colony in the first century BC. The site lies on the edge of central Chieti west of the Villa Comunale at **La Civitella archeological park**, which comprises the amphitheatre, thermal baths and a museum with restored temple fragments and remains from Chieti and the nearby river basin.

ARRIVAL AND INFORMATION   CHIETI

By train Trains stop at Chieti Scalo down in the valley, from where it's 10min on bus #1 up to Chieti proper, 5km away. The #1 stops in the centre along Via Herio and at Largo Cavallerizza near the cathedral.
Destinations Pescara (16 daily; 15–20min); Rome (5 daily; 3hr 40min).
By bus Buses drop off by the station at Chieti Scalo, from

where it's a 10min journey on bus #1 up the hill to Chieti.
Destinations Pescara (7 daily; 30min); Rome (9 daily; 2hr 30min).
Tourist office Via Spaventa 47, just off Corso Marrucino (Mon–Sat 9am–1pm, Tues, Thurs & Fri also 3–6pm; ☏ 0871 63 640, ⓦ abruzzoturismo.it).

ACCOMMODATION AND EATING

Garibaldi Piazza Garibaldi 26 ☏ 0871 345 318, ⓦ albergogaribaldi.it. In the centre of town, this hotel has large and spotless rooms with a somewhat institutional feel. Breakfast (included) is served in the bar next door. €55
Trattoria Nino Via Principessa di Piemonte 7 ☏ 0871

63 781. Very good value meals can be had at this simple trattoria in central Chieti, near Piazza Trento e Trieste, where the service is slow but the family atmosphere and full meals of regional specialities for €20 compensate. Tues–Sun noon–3pm & 7–10pm.

The coast south of Pescara

South of Pescara, the coast becomes less developed, though the long ribbon of sand continues, followed by the train line and punctuated with small resorts. Here, hilltop **Vasto** and the seaside resort **Marina di Vasto** are attractive destinations for a beach holiday, while **Termoli** is a good jumping-off point for trips to the Tremiti islands.

12

Vasto

Some 75km southeast of Pescara and close to the border with Molise, **VASTO** is a fine old city, built on the site of the Roman town Histonium and overlooking the resort of **Marina di Vasto**. There are plenty of campsites, and some reasonable hotels along the broad sandy **beach** – palm-lined and beach-hutted in the centre, wilder and rockier to the north (the ever-shrinking free beach area is central), with devices known as *trabocchi* installed every so often. These are Heath Robinson-ish crane-like contraptions of wooden beams and nets, with a complex system of weights, designed for scooping up fish.

Vasto is all about the beach, though if you're here for a day or so you should definitely get a bus from the train station on the seafront to the **upper town**, whose rooftops and campaniles rise above palms and olive groves. The centre of town is **Piazza Rossetti**, dominated by the massive **Castello Caldoresco**.

Palazzo d'Avalos

Piazza Pudente • Mid-June to Aug daily 10.30am–12.30pm & 6pm–midnight; Sept daily 10.30am–12.30pm & 6–10pm; Jan to mid-June & Oct to mid-Dec Sat & Sun 10.30am–12.30pm & 4–7pm; mid- to end Dec daily 10.30am–12.30pm & 4–7pm • Museum and garden €5; garden only €1.50

Just off the piazza, next to the small Duomo, stands the Renaissance **Palazzo d'Avalos** and its enchanting Neapolitan garden, a courtyard with orange trees and pillars and gorgeous sea views. The *palazzo* was once the home of the poet and friend of Michelangelo, Vittoria Colonna, who was famous in her time for the bleak sonnets she wrote after her husband's death; nowadays it houses the town **museum**, a somewhat sparse collection of archeological objects and beautiful old costumes, as well as some paintings by the Palizzi brothers.

San Pietro's doorway

Next to the Palazzo d'Avalos, **Piazza del Popolo** opens onto a panoramic promenade that takes you to Vasto's most memorable sight, the **door** of the church of **San Pietro**, surrounded by Romanesque twists and zigzags, standing isolated against a backdrop of sky, sea and trees, the rest of the church having been destroyed in a landslide in 1956.

ARRIVAL AND INFORMATION

By train Trains arrive from Pescara (18 daily; 40min–1hr) and Termoli (16 daily; 10–20min). Buses run from the train station on the seafront to the upper town (#4 or #1 for the Marina and Vasto Centro; roughly every 30min, hourly on Sun, more frequent in summer; 10min; €1.50).

By bus The bus station is out of town, near the cemetery; bus #4 runs from here to the centre.

Destinations Chieti (9 daily Mon–Sat; 1hr 30min); L'Aquila (1 daily; 3hr); Pescara (3 daily Mon–Sat; 1hr 20min); Rome (5 daily; 3hr 20min).

Tourist office Piazza del Popolo 18 (June–Aug Mon–Sat 9am–1pm & 4–7pm, Sun 9am–1pm; Sept Mon–Sat 9am–1pm & 3–6pm; Oct–May Mon–Fri 9am–1pm, Tues, Thurs & Fri 3–6pm; ☎ 0873 367 312, ⊛ abruzzoturismo.it).

ACCOMMODATION AND EATING

Most of the action is down by the beach in Vasto Marina and further south in San Salvo, with no end of hotels, pizzerias and pubs. Note that hotels insist on half-board in July and August.

Da Ferri Località Punta Penna ☎ 0873 310 320. If you have a car, be sure to eat at this restaurant, above the old port 7km north of Vasto, where you can feast on fish caught from the nearby *trabocchi*; its *brodetto di pesce* (fish stew) is justly famous. A full meal will set you back about €35 a head. Tues–Sat 12.45–2.30pm & 7.50–9.30pm, Sun 12.45–2.30pm.

Il Pioppeto SS16 Sud 551 ☎ 0873 801 466, ⊛ ilpioppeto.it. There are numerous campsites along the

coast, most off the SS16 towards Foggia. *Il Pioppeto* is right on the beach and has pine trees for shade. Mid-May to mid-Sept. Pitches **€27.30**

Locanda dei Baroni Via San Francesco d'Assisi 68–70 ☎ 0873 370 737, ⊛ locandadeibaroni.it. Five minutes from the old town in a medieval *palazzo*, this B&B has bright rooms with four-poster beds and antique furniture and modern, spotless bathrooms. The brick-vaulted restaurant serves up well-priced local cuisine. **€110**

12

Termoli

Just 6km separate Vasto and the brief stretch of the **Molise coast**, which is less developed than Abruzzo's. Its only real town, **TERMOLI**, a fishing port and low-key resort, makes for a relaxing place to spend a day. The beach is long and sandy and the old town, walled and guarded by a castle, is a pretty *borgo* of pastel-painted houses. It's also a departure point for ferries to the Tremiti islands (see p.810) and in striking distance of the interior towns of **Portocannone** and **Ururi**.

Castello Svevo

The stark **Castello Svevo**, built above the beach in 1247 by Frederick II, lords it over the tiny old town. Outside there's a good viewpoint down to the coast below; beyond, the road follows the old walls around the headland.

The Duomo

Piazza del Duomo • Daily 7.45am–11.50am & 4.30–7.30pm • Free

The focus of the old town is the **Duomo**, most notable for its Romanesque exterior, decorated all the way round with a series of blind arcades and windows – a feature introduced by Frederick II's Norman-influenced architects. Inside are the relics of St Timothy, Termoli's patron saint, best known for the letters he received from St Paul, who advised him on how to go about converting the Greeks. That he ended up in Termoli is thanks to Termolese Crusaders, who brought his bones back from Constantinople as a souvenir. The Termolese hid them, fearing that if the Turks ever succeeded in penetrating the city they would seize and destroy them. In fact the relics were hidden so well they weren't discovered until 1945, during restoration work to repair bomb damage (the sacristan will show them to you).

ARRIVAL AND INFORMATION

By train The train station is in the new town, a 5min walk from the Castello and the start of the old town.

Destinations Campobasso (8 daily; 1hr 35min–1hr 50min);

Foggia (18 daily; 40min–1hr); Pescara (20 daily; 50min–1hr 20min); Vasto (14 daily; 15min).

By bus Long-distance buses pull up in Via Martiri della

CHARIOT-RACING IN THE ALBANIAN VILLAGES

Buses from Termoli run to the isolated villages of **Portocannone**, 12km south, and **Ururi**, another 15km beyond. Their remoteness is such that, six hundred years after their ancestors emigrated from Albania, the locals still speak an Albanian-Italian dialect incomprehensible to outsiders. The villages receive most visitors during their annual **carressi** – chariot races. Portocannone's takes place the Monday after Whit Sunday, while Ururi's is at the beginning of May. The *carresse* is a fierce and furious race through the village streets on gladiator-style carts, pulled by bulls and pushed by men on horseback with spiked poles. It's a ruthless business: the horses are fed beer before the race to excite them, and although the riders are supposed to push only the back of the carts, they are not averse to prodding the flanks of the bulls, who have already been given electric shocks to liven them up. The race itself is terrifying, but unforgettable, with bulls, carts and spikes hurtling past the frenzied crowds, nowadays protected by wire fences, though there are almost inevitably injuries. The *comuni* (☎0874 830 130, ⊛comune.ururi.cb.it and ☎0875 599 320, ⊛comune.portocannone.cb.it) have information.

Resistenza, 1km from Termoli's centre. A local bus service connects the bus station with the port and historical centre. Destinations Ancona (1 daily Mon–Sat; 3hr 10min); Campobasso (every 30min–1hr; 1hr 10min); Foggia (5 daily; 2hr 5min); Isernia (4 daily; 1hr 45min–2hr 5min); Naples (3 daily; 3hr 10min); Pescara (4 daily; 1hr 20min); Portocannone (10 daily; 20min); Rome (3 daily; 4hr 15min); Ururi (2 daily; 40min); Vasto (2 daily; 1hr 5min).

By ferry There are ferries to the Tremiti islands (1–3 ferries and hydrofoils daily in summer, 1 ferry daily in winter; 50min–1hr).

Tourist information The tourist office (July & Aug Mon & Wed 8am–2pm & 3–6pm, Tues, Thurs & Fri 8am–2pm & 4–6pm, Sat 9am–1pm; Sept–June Mon & Wed 8am–2pm & 3–6pm, Tues, Thurs & Fri 8am–2pm; ☎0875 703 913) is on Piazza M. Bega 42, near the train station. In the summer kiosks in main tourist-points around the old town promote local crafts and Molise in general.

ACCOMMODATION AND EATING

Locanda Alfieri Via Duomo 39 ☎0875 708 112, ⊛locandalfieri.com. This B&B has rooms scattered around the *borgo antico*. The comfortable rooms come with balconies and lovely sea views, and the more modern ones can even boast showers with soothing chromotherapy lighting. **€105**

Residenza Sveva Piazza del Duomo 11 ☎0875 706 803, ⊛residenzasveva.com. This self-styled "diffused hotel" offers individual rooms around town, rather than one central structure, but all share the same breezy decor, with gleaming tiled floors and a spacious feel throughout. The simple breakfast is taken on a sunny terrace. Rates include access to the hotel's private beach. **€129**

Ristorante Sveva Via Giudicato Vecchio 24 ☎0875 550 284, ⊛svevia.it. Termoli has its fair share of pizzerias, but if you're hankering after more refined cuisine, this handsome, brick-vaulted space with low lighting and a romantic atmosphere is the place. The menu might include local oysters, *linguine* with clams, and cod with cauliflower and sweet chilli; a five-course tasting menu costs €40. Tues–Sun 12.30–2.30pm & 8–10.30pm.

★ **Trattoria L'Opera** Via Adriatica 32 ☎0875 704 547. Traditional Molise cuisine with the odd creative twist, just off the main Corso Nazionale. From antipasto to *dolce*, every dish is prepared and presented with great care by Termoli-born chef Roberto, and the freshness and quality of the ingredients is superb. Try the home-made rigatoni with seafood (€10). Tues–Sun noon–2.30pm & 7.30–11pm.

Villaggio Azzurra About 5km from town along the SS16 ☎0875 52 404, ⊛villaggioazzurra.it. A seaside campsite with a bar, restaurant, mini-market and free beach. In the high season, there are buses every hour from the town centre. June–Sept. Pitches **€24**, apartments **€120**

Inland Molise

Much of Molise still seems to be struggling out of its past, its towns and villages victims of either economic neglect or hurried modern development. With few sights as such, the inland areas are little explored, but the unspoiled countryside and glimpses of an authentic, untouristed Italy to be found here are attractions in themselves. Inland from Termoli, while **Campobasso** and **Isernia** win no prizes for their looks, they do possess a certain gritty charm; from the former, you can reach the remarkable ruins at **Saepinum**.

12

Campobasso

CAMPOBASSO, Molise's regional capital, is a modern town whose most notable attraction is the **Museo Sannitico** (daily 9am–1.30pm & 2–5.30pm; free) at Via Chiarizia 12, with statues and a scattering of archeological finds from the area, most notably the haunting contents of a Longobard tomb, a warrior buried alongside his horse. Steep alleys of the old **upper town** lead up to a couple of Romanesque churches – **San Bartolomeo**, which has eerily contorted figures carved around its main door, and **San Giorgio**, whose entrance displays a dragon surrounded by stylized flowers. At the top of the hill are a monastery and sixteenth-century **castle** (Tues–Sun 9.30am–12.30pm & 3.30–6.30pm; free), from which there is a panorama over the environs and the historic centre's *borgo antico* below.

If you happen to be around sixty days after Easter, don't miss the town's spectacular Corpus Domini Sagra dei Misteri **procession**, in which citizens are dressed as saints, angels and devils, inserted into fantastic contraptions and transported, seemingly suspended in mid-air, through the streets.

ARRIVAL AND INFORMATION   CAMPOBASSO

By bus Campobasso is generally most easily reached by bus. Destinations Ancona (1 daily Mon–Sat; 4hr 10min); Foggia (2 daily Mon–Sat; 1hr 40min); Isernia (21 daily; 45min–1hr 20min); Naples (4 daily Mon–Sat; 2hr 45min); Pescara (5 daily; 2hr 40min); Termoli (every 30min–1hr; 1hr 10min–1hr 45min).

By train The train station is in the centre of town. Destinations Isernia (10 daily; 50min–1hr 5min); Naples (5 daily; 2hr 50min–3hr 10min); Rome (4 daily; 2hr 45min–3hr); Termoli (7 daily; 1hr 35min–2hr).
Tourist office Piazza della Vittoria 14 (Mon & Wed 8am–2pm & 3–6pm, Tues, Thurs & Fri 8am–2pm; ☎ 0874 415 662).

EATING

La Grotta Da Concetta Via Larino 7 ☎ 0874 311 378. Sate yourself on solid home-cooking for not much more than €20, with dishes such as meatballs in tomato sauce, and fried aubergines with *provola* cheese and cherry tomatoes. There's no menu but if you're lucky you'll get to try some of the family's home-produced salami. Mon–Fri 1–3pm & 8–10pm.

Saepinum

Site open access; museum Tues–Sun: April–Oct 9.30am–6.30pm; Nov–March 9am–5.30pm • Free; museum €2 • Take a bus from Campobasso – some stop right outside the site at Altilia (3 daily Mon–Sat; 35min), others at Sepino (6 daily Mon–Sat; ⓦ lariverabus.it) and walk the remaining 3km to Saepinum; by car, follow signs to Sepino

SAEPINUM, a ruined **Roman town** to the south, is arguably the most interesting sight in Molise. Surrounded by a lush plain fringed with the foothills of the Matese mountains, it's the best example in Italy of a provincial Roman town.

The main reason Saepinum is so intact is that it was never very important: nothing much happened here, and after the fall of the Roman Empire it carried on as the sleepy backwater it had always been – until the ninth century when it was sacked by Saracens. Over the centuries its inhabitants added only a handful of farms and cottages, incorporating the odd Roman column, and eventually moved south to the more secure hilltop site of present-day Sepino. Some have now moved back and rebuilt the farms and cottages on Saepinum's peripheries, contributing if anything to the site's appeal. Their sheep graze below an ancient mausoleum, chickens scratch around the walls, and the only sound is the tinkling of cowbells.

Depending on whether you arrive by bus or by car, the entrance to Saepinum is through the **Porta Terravecchia** or the **Porta Tammaro**, two of the town's four gates. The site is bisected by the *cardo maximus* (running north–south), still paved with the original stones and crossed by the *decumanus maximus*, once home to the public buildings and trading quarters.

On the left, grass spills through the cracks in the pavement of the **forum**, now used by the few local kids as a football pitch, bordered by the foundations of various municipal buildings: the *comitium* (assembly place), the *curia* (senate house), a temple, baths, and in the centre a fountain with a relief of a griffin. Beyond the forum, on the left of the *decumanus*, the **Casa Impluvio Sannitico** contains a vat to collect rainwater.

Back down the *decumanus* on the other side of the crossroads is the well-preserved **basilica** that served as the main courthouse. Beyond is the most interesting part of the town – the octagonal *macellum* (marketplace), with its small stone stalls and central rain-collecting dish, and a series of houses fronted by workshops, with small living quarters behind.

The *macellum* leads down to the best-preserved gate, the **Porta Boiano**, flanked by cylindrical towers with a relief showing two barbarians and chained prisoners. There is also a small **museum** with artefacts and artwork recovered during excavation.

Isernia

Though unbeguiling in itself, inland **ISERNIA** is a good starting point for exploring the rest of Molise, with good train connections from Rome and Naples. The first settlement dates back to the Samnites, yet very little of old Isernia survives. Earthquakes and wars have wreaked havoc on its historical monuments; much of the centre was destroyed in a bombing raid on September 10, 1943, and a monument to the four thousand who were killed – an anguished nude, ankle-deep in fractured tiles, bricks and gutters – is the centrepiece of the square called, understandably, Piazza X Settembre. In spite of it all, the city has rebuilt its commercial centre so that it's now comparatively busy and bustling.

Isernia's most iconic monument is the **Fontana Fraterna** in Piazza Celestino V, a Romanesque fountain built in the thirteenth century by the Rampini family from marble stripped from Roman tombs.

The city's main attraction is a prehistoric site called **La Pineta** (by reservation only Tues–Sun 9am–7pm; free; ☎0865 410 500), an easy 1.5km from the centre or a short ride on the #3 bus from the station. In 1978, road-builders unearthed traces of a Palaeolithic settlement at least 700,000 years old – the most ancient signs of human life yet found in Europe.

In the southern part of Isernia near the hospital (bus #2 from the station), the **Museo Nazionale Santa Maria delle Monache** (Mon–Fri 8.30am–7.30pm, Sat 8.30am–1pm; €2), on Corso Marcelli 48, displays finds from La Pineta. Contrary to the misleading publicity, there were no human remains found, just weapons, traps, traces of pigment thought to have been used as body paint, and animal bones, laid out to create a solid platform on the marshy land for the village.

ARRIVAL AND INFORMATION

By train The train station is on Piazza della Repubblica. Destinations Campobasso (11 daily; 55min–1hr 15min); Naples (4 daily; 1hr 50min); Rome (4 daily; 1hr 55min–2hr 15min).

By bus Local and longer-distance buses, including those to Rome and Naples, depart from outside the train station on Piazza della Repubblica.

Destinations Campobasso (22 daily; 45min–1hr 20min); Naples (9 daily; 1hr 45min); Pescara (3 daily Mon–Sat; 2hr 10min); Rome (8 daily; 2hr 25); Termoli (13 daily; 1hr 25min–1hr 55min).

Tourist office Via Farinacci 9 (Mon–Sat 8am–2pm; ☎086 53 992).

ACCOMMODATION AND EATING

★ **Antica Dimora 191** Corso Marcelli 191 ☎0865 410 547, ⊛anticadimora191.com. If you need to stay, head for this gem of a place, set in a historic *palazzo* in Isernia's old centre. Opulently decorated with paintings, antiques and frescoed ceilings, the rooms have plenty of character, and the owners are friendly and helpful. Breakfast is taken in the bar downstairs. **€70**

Osteria del Paradiso Via Occidentale 2 ☎0865 414 847. Near the cathedral, this is an old-style *osteria*, where you can eat good, cheap, local food such as *pasta e fagioli* (a thick soup with pasta and beans) or grilled *scamorza* cheese. You can eat very well for under €20. Daily 12.30–2.30pm & 7.30–11pm; closed Sun dinner.

Campania

RUINS AT PAESTUM

13

Campania

The region immediately south of Lazio, Campania, marks the real beginning of the Italian South or *mezzogiorno*. It's the part of the South too, perhaps inevitably, that most people see, as it's easily accessible from Rome and home to some of the area's (indeed Italy's) most notable features – Roman sites, spectacular stretches of coast, tiny islands. It's always been a sought-after region, first named by the Romans, who tagged it the *campania felix*, or "happy land" (to distinguish it from the rather dull *campagna* further north), and settled down here in villas and palatial estates that stretched right around the Bay of Naples. Later, when Naples became the final stop on northerners' Grand Tours, its bay became no less fabled, the relics of its heady Roman period only adding to the charm for most travellers.

Naples is the obvious focus, an utterly compelling city that dominates the region in every way. Taking one of the fastest trains, you can reach it now in a little over an hour from the capital, and there's no excuse for not seeing at least this part of Campania – though of course you need three or four days to absorb the city properly. The **Bay of Naples**, too, is dense enough in interest to occupy you for a good week: there are the ancient sites of **Pompeii** and **Herculaneum** just half an hour away – arguably Italy's best-preserved and most revealing Roman remains; there is the amazing, volcanic **Campi Flegrei** area to the northwest of the city; and of course there are the islands, **Capri**, **Ischia** and **Procida**. Capri swarms with visitors but is so beautiful that it's a shame to come to

REGIONAL FOOD AND WINE

The flavour of Naples dominates the whole of Campania. It's the true home of the **pizza**, rapidly baked in searingly hot wood-fired ovens and running with olive oil, as well as fantastic **street food**, served in numerous outlets known as *friggitorie* – sample delicacies such as fried pizzas (*pizzette* or *panzarotti*), heavenly *crocchè* (potato croquettes), *arancini* (rice balls) and *fiorilli* (courgette flowers in batter).

Naples is also the home of pasta and tomato sauce, made with fresh tomatoes and basil, and laced with garlic. Aubergines and courgettes turn up endlessly in pasta sauces, as does the tomato–mozzarella pairing (the regions to the north and east of Naples are the home of mozzarella), the latter particularly good with gnocchi. **Seafood** is excellent all along the coast: clams combine with garlic and oil for superb *spaghetti alle vongole*; mussels are often prepared as *zuppa di cozze* (with hot pepper sauce and croutons); fresh squid and octopus are ubiquitous.

There are loads of great pastries: not to be missed is the *sfogliatella*, a flaky triangular pastry-case stuffed with ricotta and candied peel, and the fragrant Easter cake, *pastiera*, made with ricotta and softened wheat grain. Further to the south, the marshy plains of the Cilento produce fabulous strawberries, artichokes and mozzarella cheese – much of the mozzarella that comes from here is made from pure buffalo milk, unmixed with cow's milk.

The volcanic slopes of Vesuvius are among the most ancient **wine-producing** areas in Italy, but despite that the region doesn't have a great reputation for wine. The best choices for a Campanian white are Greco di Tufo, Fiano di Avellino and Falanghina – all fruity yet dry. Ischia also produces good whites, notably Biancolella, while Lacryma Christi, from the slopes of Mount Vesuvius, is available in red and white varieties and is enjoying a resurgence after years of being considered cheap plonk. Among pure reds, there's the unusual but delicious Gragnano, a red sparkling wine that's best served slightly chilled, and Taurasi – like the best wines of the region made from the local Aglianico grape.

CASTELLO ARAGONESE, ISCHIA

Highlights

❶ Centro storico, Naples Still following the street plan of the original Greco-Roman settlement, Naples' ancient centre is unique both above and below ground. **See p.741**

❷ Museo Archeologico A superb museum with a wealth of Greek and Roman artefacts. **See p.751**

❸ Herculaneum and Pompeii These sites afford an unparalleled glimpse into ancient Roman daily life and architecture. **See p.766 & p.768**

❹ Capri A jewel of an island with stunning scenery and cliff walks. **See p.774**

❺ Ischia Larger than Capri and better able to absorb the visitors – as well as being no less alluring. **See p.779**

❻ Paestum Majestic Greek temples and colourful tomb paintings. **See p.795**

HIGHLIGHTS ARE MARKED ON THE MAP ON P.740

13

the area and miss it, while Ischia, which is the largest island and absorbs tourists more readily, is a lively and attractive place in which you could while away an entire holiday.

Inland Campania is, by contrast, a poor, unknown region for the most part, though the giant palace and gardens of **Caserta** are worth visiting, while **Benevento**, an old stop on the Roman route to Brindisi, has a flavour that's quite distinct from the coastal regions. The area **south of Naples** has more immediate appeal. **Sorrento**, at the far southeast end of the bay, is a major package-holiday destination, and as cheery and likeable a resort as you'll ever visit; and the **Amalfi Coast**, across the peninsula, is perhaps Europe's most dramatic stretch of coastline, whose enticing and sometimes exclusive resorts – Positano and Amalfi – need little introduction. Further south, the lively port of **Salerno** gives access to the Hellenistic site of **Paestum** and the relatively uncrowded coastline of the **Cilento** just beyond.

Naples

The capital of the Italian South, Naples is a city that comes laden with preconceptions, and most have some truth in them. It's huge, filthy, crime-ridden and falling apart;

HIGHLIGHTS
1 Centro storico, Naples
2 Museo Archeologico
3 Herculaneum and Pompeii
4 Capri
5 Ischia
6 Paestum

CAMPANIA

13

it's edgy and atmospheric, with a faint air of menace; and it is definitely like nowhere else in Italy. Yet Naples has bags of charm, making the noise and disorder easily endurable, even enjoyable, for most first-timers. It doesn't attract many visitors, and is refreshingly lacking in tourist gloss, but it's also a grand and beautiful place, with monumental squares, world-class museums, down-at-heel churches crammed with Baroque masterpieces and all manner of historic nooks and corners – plus innumerable places to enjoy arguably Italy's best and most delicious food.

Brief history

There was a settlement here, **Parthenope**, as early as the ninth century BC; this was superseded by a Greek colony in 750 BC, which they gave the name Neapolis. It prospered during Greek and later Roman times, and remained independent until the **Normans** took the city in 1139, after which it was passed from one dynasty to the next until Alfonso I of Aragon arrived in 1422, establishing a **Spanish** connection for the city for the next three hundred years.

Following the War of the Spanish Succession, Naples was briefly ceded to the Austrians, before being taken, to general rejoicing, by **Charles of Bourbon** in 1734. Charles was a cultivated and judicious monarch, but his dissolute son Ferdinand presided over a shambolic period in the city's history, abandoning it to the republican French. Their "Parthenopean Republic" here was short-lived, and the British re-installed the Bourbon monarch, carrying out vicious reprisals against the rebels. The instigator of these reprisals was Admiral Nelson – fresh from his victory at the Battle of the Nile. Under continuing Bourbon rule, the city became the second largest in Europe, and a requisite stop on the **Grand Tour**, a position it enjoyed not so much for its proximity to the major classical sites as for the ready availability of sex, giving new meaning (in the days when syphilis was rife) to the phrase "See Naples and die".

More recently, Naples and its surrounding area have been the recipient of much of the government and EU money that has poured into the Italian South. But the real power in the area is still in the hands of organized crime or the **Camorra**, with the result that there's been little real improvement in the living standards of the average Neapolitan: a very high percentage remain unemployed, and a large number still inhabit the typically Neapolitan one-room *bassi*, letting in no light and housing many in overcrowded conditions. **Antonio Bassolino**, mayor of the city from 1993 until 2000 and currently president of Campania, has done much to promote Naples and its attractions, and scores of neglected churches, museums and palaces have been restored and are now open to the public. There's also been a burst of creative activity from local filmmakers, songwriters and artists, with a thriving contemporary **art scene** manifest in two new, large galleries. However, the Camorra still cast a long shadow, as highlighted by Roberto Saviano's bestselling book and much-publicized film, *Gomorrah*.

The centro storico

Naples is a large, sprawling city, with a centre that has many different focuses. The area between Piazza Garibaldi and Via Toledo, roughly corresponding to the old Roman Neapolis (much of which is still unexcavated below the ground), makes up the old part of the city – the **centro storico** – the main streets of **Via dei Tribunali** and **Via San Biagio**

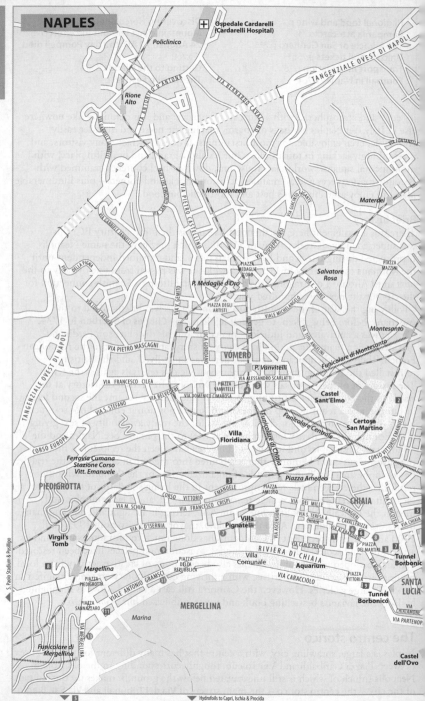

NAPLES

Ospedale Cardarelli
(Cardarelli Hospital)

Policlinico

VIA BERNARDO CAVALLINO

TANGENZIALE OVEST DI NAPOLI

Rione
Alto

VIA ANTONIO D'ANTONA

VIA GABRIELE ANNUNZIO

VIA FONTANELLE

VIA IMPERATORE DI MASSIMO

VIA PIETRO CASTELLINO

Montedonzelli

VIA GIACINTO GIGANTE

VIA GIUSEPPE ORSI

Materdei

PIAZZA
MAZZINI

VIA DELLA PIGNA

VIA LUIGI CALDIERI

VIA GABRIELE IANNELLI

VIA L. GEMITO

PIAZZA
MEDAGLIE
D'ORO

P. Medaglie d'Oro

PIAZZA DEGLI
ARTISTI

LUCA GIORDANO

VIA BERNINI

Salvatore
Rosa

VIA S. SUAREZ

Montesanto

VIA PIETRO MASCAGNI

Cilea

VIALE MICHELANGELO

VIA TITO ANGELINI

VÓMERO

Funicolare di Montesanto

2

VIA FRANCESCO CILEA

P. Vanvitelli

VIA ALESSANDRO SCARLATTI

PIAZZA
VANVITELLI

Castel
Sant'Elmo

VIA S. STEFANO

VIA BELVEDERE

VIA DOMENICO CIMAROSA

Funicolare Centrale

Certosa
San Martino

CORSO EUROPA

Villa
Floridiana

Funicolare di Chiaia

CORSO VITTORIO EMANUELE

Ferrovia Cumana
Stazione Corso
Vitt. Emanuele

3

Piazza Amedeo

PIEDIGROTTA

CORSO VITTORIO EMANUELE

PIAZZA
AMEDEO

CHIAIA

VIA DEI MILLE

VIA G. NICOTERA

VIA M. SCHIPA

VIA FRANCESCO CRISPI

4

V. FILANGIERI

VIA S. TERESA A
CHIAIA

V. CAVALLERIZZA

VIA CHIAIA

5

VIA A. D'ISERNIA

Villa
Pignatelli

VIA ASCENSIONE

VIA CARLO POERIO

1

VIA CALABRITTO

2 PIAZZA
DEI MARTIRI

6

7

Tunnel
Borbonico

Virgil's
Tomb

6

RIVIERA DI CHIAIA

S. Paolo Stadium & Posillipo

8

Mergellina

PIAZZA
PIEDIGROTTA

VIALE ANTONIO GRAMSCI

11

PIAZZA
DELLA
REPUBBLICA

Villa
Comunale

Aquarium

PIAZZA
VITTORIA

9

**SANTA
LUCIA**

Tunnel
Borbonico

VIA CARACCIOLO

VIA CHIATAMONE

PIAZZA
SANNAZZARO

11

VIA MERGELLINA

Marina

MERGELLINA

VIA PARTENOP.

Funicolare di
Mergellina

13

Castel
dell'Ovo

5

Hydrofoils to Capri, Ischia & Procida

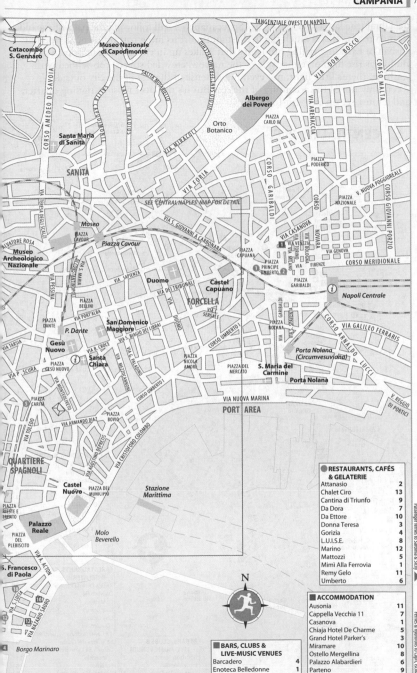

RESTAURANTS, CAFÉS & GELATERIE

Attanasio	2
Chalet Ciro	13
Cantina di Triunfo	9
Da Dora	7
Da Ettore	10
Donna Teresa	3
Gorizia	4
L.U.I.S.E.	8
Marino	12
Mattozzi	5
Mimì Alla Ferrovia	1
Remy Gelo	11
Umberto	6

ACCOMMODATION

Ausonia	11
Cappella Vecchia 11	7
Casanova	1
Chiaja Hotel De Charme	5
Grand Hotel Parker's	3
Miramare	10
Ostello Mergellina	8
Palazzo Alabardieri	6
Parteno	9
Pinto-Storey	4
Rex	12
San Francesco al Monte	2

BARS, CLUBS & LIVE-MUSIC VENUES

Barcadero	4
Enoteca Belledonne	1
Seventy	2
Vinarium	3
Virgilio Club	5

Passenger ferries to Sardinia & Sicily

Ferries & hydrofoils to Capri, Ischia & Procida

0   200
metres

N

13

dei Librai (the latter also known as "Spaccanapoli") still following the path of the old Roman roads. This is much the liveliest and most teeming part of town, an open-air kasbah of hawking, yelling humanity that makes up in energy what it lacks in grace. Buildings rise high on either side of the narrow, crowded streets, cobwebbed with washing; there's little light, not even much sense of the rest of the city outside – certainly not of the proximity of the sea. But it's the city's most intriguing quarter, and a must-see on any visit to the city.

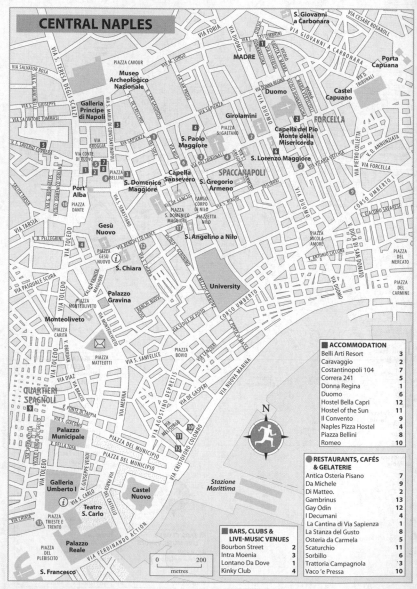

CENTRAL NAPLES

■ ACCOMMODATION	
Belli Arti Resort	3
Caravaggio	2
Costantinopoli 104	7
Correra 241	5
Donna Regina	1
Duomo	6
Hostel Bella Capri	12
Hostel of the Sun	11
Il Convento	9
Naples Pizza Hostel	4
Piazza Bellini	8
Romeo	10

● RESTAURANTS, CAFÉS & GELATERIE	
Antica Osteria Pisano	7
Da Michele	9
Di Matteo.	2
Gambrinus	13
Gay Odin	12
I Decumani	4
La Cantina di Via Sapienza	1
La Stanza del Gusto	8
Osteria da Carmela	5
Scaturchio	11
Sorbillo	6
Trattoria Campagnola	3
Vaco 'e Pressa	10

■ BARS, CLUBS & LIVE-MUSIC VENUES	
Bourbon Street	2
Intra Moenia	3
Lontano Da Dove	1
Kinky Club	4

0   200
metres

13

CAMPANIA ARTECARD

If you're considering visiting several museums and sights in Naples and around, it might be worth investing in a **Campania artecard**, which gives free admission to various sights and reductions on many others, as well as free travel on public transport. Most of the big attractions – in Naples and beyond – are included, and there are various combinations, ranging from a pass providing access to some key sights in the city centre (3 days; €12) to a pass for the entire region, including free transport, free admission to two sights and fifty percent off the others (€27). You can buy the cards at any of the participating museums or at tourist offices and Napoli Stazione Centrale. More details at ⓦcampaniartecard.it (☎800 600 601), or tourist offices have leaflets.

The Duomo

Via Duomo 147 • Mon–Sat 8am–1.30pm & 2.30–8pm, Sun 8 am–1.30pm & 4.30–7.30pm • Free • ☎ 081 449 097, ⓦ duomodinapoli.it

The **Duomo**, tucked away unassumingly from the main street, is a Gothic building from the early thirteenth century (though with a late nineteenth-century neo-Gothic facade) dedicated to the patron saint of the city, San Gennaro. The third chapel on the right as you walk into the cathedral is dedicated to San Gennaro. It's an eye-bogglingly ornate affair, practically a church in its own right, containing the precious phials of the saint's blood and his skull in a silver bust-reliquary from 1305 (stored behind the altar except for ceremonies).

On the other side of the cathedral, the basilica of **Santa Restituta** (Mon–Sat 8.30am–12.30pm & 4.30–6.30pm, Sun 8.30am–1pm; €3) is actually a separate church, officially the oldest structure in Naples, erected by Constantine in 324 and supported by columns that were taken from a temple to Apollo on this site. Off to the right of the main altar, you pay extra to visit the **baptistry**, which also contains relics from very early Christian times, including late fifth-century mosaics and a font believed to have been taken from a temple to Dionysus. The same ticket allows entry to the **excavations** below the church, which are open the same hours and also accessed from here – remains of a still earlier church basically, along with bits and pieces from the Roman and even Greek ancient cities. Finally be sure to also see the **crypt** of San Gennaro, founded by Cardinal Carafa and holding an altar dedicated to the saint, complete with his bones.

THE MIRACLE OF SAN GENNARO

Naples' cathedral and San Gennaro are key reference points for Neapolitans: San Gennaro was martyred at Pozzuoli, just outside Naples, in 305 AD under the purges of Diocletian. Tradition has it that, when his body was transferred here, two phials of his dried blood liquefied in the bishop's hands, since which time the "miracle" has continued to repeat itself no fewer than three times a year – on the first Saturday in May (when a procession leads from the church of Santa Chiara to the cathedral) and on September 19 and December 16. There is still a great deal of superstition surrounding this event: San Gennaro is seen as the saviour and protector of Naples, and if the blood refuses to liquefy – which luckily is rare – disaster is supposed to befall the city. Interestingly, one of the few occasions in recent times that Gennaro's blood hasn't turned was in 1944, an event followed by Vesuvius's last eruption. The last times were in 1980, the year of the earthquake, and in 1988, the day after which Naples lost an important football match to their rivals, Milan.

The miraculous liquefaction takes place during a special Mass in full view of the congregation – a service it's possible to attend, though the church authorities have yet to allow any close scientific examination of the blood or the "miraculous" process. Whatever the truth of the miracle, there's no question it's still a significant event in the Neapolitan calendar, and one of the more bizarre of the city's institutions.

13

MADRE

Via Settembrini 79 • Mon & Wed–Sat 10am–7.30pm, Sun 10.30am–11pm • €7, Mon free • ☎ 081 1931 3016, ⓦ museomadre.it

Just off the top end of Via Duomo, the Museo d'Arte Contemporaneo Donnaregina – **MADRE** for short – is emblematic of Naples' rebirth as a creative city. Opened in 2005, it hosts temporary exhibitions on its ground floor while the upper storeys house a high-quality collection of contemporary works by big-name international artists, some of which were specially commissioned for the museum. Highlights include a giant mural of the city by the Neapolitan-American artist Francesco Clemente, as well as work by Jeff Koons, Anish Kapoor, Damien Hirst, Gilbert & George, and others.

Via dei Tribunali

Via Duomo is crossed by **Via dei Tribunali**, one of the two main streets of old Naples, which leads straight through the heart of the old city to link to the modern centre around Via Toledo. It's richer in interest and sights than almost any other street in Naples, and you can spend many happy hours picking your way through its churches, palaces and underground caverns, stopping off for pizza at one of its numerous pizzerias before emerging at Piazza Bellini and strolling up to the archeological museum.

Quadreria e Cappella del Pio Monte della Misericordia

Via dei Tribunali 253 • Thurs–Tues 9am–2.30pm • €5 • ☎ 081 446 944, ⓦ piomontedellamisericordia.it

On the Forcella side of Via dei Tribunali, just around the corner from the Duomo, the **Quadreria e Cappella del Pio Monte della Misericordia** is worth stopping off at before diving into the old city proper – the church of the (still-functioning but originally seventeenth-century) charity of the same name, a beautiful octagonal structure, with paintings by Caravaggio and Luca Giordano. You can also visit the organization's picture gallery upstairs, which overlooks the church.

Napoli Sotterranea

Piazza S. Gaetano 68 • Mon–Wed & Fri tours at noon, 2pm & 4pm, Thurs noon, 2pm, 4pm & 9pm, Sat & Sun 10am, noon, 2pm, 4pm & 6pm • €9.30 • ☎ 081 296 944, ⓦ napolisotterranea.org

A short walk from Via Duomo, Via dei Tribunali opens out at **Piazza San Gaetano**, a spot which would have been the ancient agora or forum of the ancient Greek and Roman cities. Just beyond here is the entrance to **Napoli Sotterranea**, whose tours, many of which are in English, take you to look at the remnants of a nearby Roman theatre and through the aqueducts and cisterns 40m down below the old city – used from ancient times until the late nineteenth-century cholera outbreak, and then again as bomb shelters during World War II.

San Lorenzo Maggiore

Via dei Tribunali 316 • **Church** Daily 8am–1pm & 5.30–7.30pm • Free • **Museum and excavations** Mon–Sat 9.30am–5.30pm, Sun 9.30am–1pm • €9 • ☎ 081 211 0860, ⓦ sanlorenzomaggiorenapoli.it

Just off Piazza San Gaetano, **San Lorenzo Maggiore** is a light, spacious Gothic church, unspoiled by later additions and with a soaring apse – unusual in Italy, even more so in Naples. It's a mainly thirteenth- and fourteenth-century building, though with a much later facade, built during the reign of the Angevin king Robert the Wise on the site of a Roman basilica – remains of which are in the cloisters. You can look at bits and pieces from the church in the attached **museum** or descend to the **excavations** beneath the church to explore the remains of the Roman forum and, before that, the Greek agora – a rare chance to see exactly how the layers of the city were built up over the centuries, and to get some idea of how Naples must have looked back in the fifth century BC.

Via San Gregorio Armeno

Via San Gregorio Armeno leads down to the other main axis of the old centre from San Lorenzo, and is one of the old city's most picturesque streets, lined with places specializing in the making of *presepi* or Christmas cribs – a Neapolitan tradition kept up to this day, although the workshops along here turn them out more or less all year round. The often-inventive creations now incorporate modern figures into the huge crib scenes, which can contain moving water features, illuminated pizza ovens and tonnes of moss and bark.

San Gregorio Armeno

Via S. Gregorio Armeno 1 • Daily 9am–noon, Tues till 12.45pm, Sat & Sun till 12.30pm; cloister daily 9.30am–noon, Sun 9.30am–1pm • Free

The church of **San Gregorio Armeno** is a sumptuous Baroque edifice with frescoes above the entrance by the late seventeenth-century Neapolitan artist Luca Giordano, not to mention two stupendously ornate gilded organs, one on each side of the nave. Up above the south aisle, you'll notice a series of grilles through which the Benedictine nuns would view the services from the **Chiostro di San Gregorio Armeno** next door, a wonderfully peaceful haven from the noise outside, planted with limes and busy with nuns quietly going about their duties.

Santa Maria delle Anime del Purgatorio ad Arco

Via dei Tribunali 39 • Mon–Fri 9.30am–1pm, Sat 10am–5pm • €3 • ☎ 333 383 2561, ⓦ purgatorioadarco.com

Down the street from Piazza San Gaetano, the church of **Santa Maria delle Anime del Purgatorio ad Arco** is the site of a death cult that was outlawed in the 1960s by the Catholic authorities but still lives on in a semi-secret fashion in its downstairs **hypogeum**. Here, dusty chapels hold tiled shrines to the anonymous dead who are revered as intermediaries between the earthly and the divine, and given names that endeared the keepers of their graves to them – a peculiar place, yet still very much in use.

San Pietro a Maiella

Via S. Pietro a Maiella 35 • Daily 9am–noon & 5–7pm • Free

The fourteenth-century church of **San Pietro a Maiella** anchors the end of Via dei Tribunali at Piazza Miraglia, a Gothic building whose bare stone arches give way to its main decorative feature: a magnificent painted wooden ceiling by Matteo Preti dated 1657. Look too at the chapel to the left of the apse, which is covered with fragments of delicate frescoes done by the same Giotto follower who worked in San Lorenzo Maggiore.

Piazza Bellini

Just past the church of San Pietro a Maiella, **Piazza Bellini** is a rectangular open space which marks the end of the old city, and indeed always has: the ruins of the old Greco-Roman walls can still be seen at the bottom end of the square. It's a pleasant, leafy square lined with terraced cafés, a good spot for a coffee and a break from sightseeing. At night it's a major hub, with the cafés packed and the square full of cool folk hanging out and shooting the breeze.

Spaccanapoli

Running parallel to Via dei Tribunali, **Spaccanapoli** (literally, "Splitting Naples") cuts cleanly through the old city. It's a long street, and changes name several times: at the Via del Duomo end, it's **Via San Biagio dei Librai**, becoming **Via Benedetto Croce** at its western end, where it opens out at the large square of the Gesù Nuovo and the edge of old Naples.

Largo di Corpo di Nilo and around

Heading west down Via San Biagio leads to the **Largo di Corpo di Nilo**, where you'll find a Roman statue of a reclining old man, sculpted in Nero's time; it's a representation of the Nile and has a habit, it's claimed, of whispering to women as they walk by. The church opposite, on Piazzetta Nilo, **Sant'Angelo a Nilo**, is home to the city's earliest piece of Renaissance art – the funerary monument to Cardinal Rinaldo Brancaccio, made in Pisa in 1426 by Michelozzo and Donatello.

13 ## Guglia di San Domenico

Piazza S. Domenico Maggiore 8 • Mon–Sat 8.30am–noon & 4–7pm, Sun 9am–1pm & 4.30–7.15pm • Free

Piazza San Domenico Maggiore is marked by the **Guglia di San Domenico**, built in 1737 – one of the whimsical Baroque obelisks originally put up after times of plague or disease or to celebrate the Virgin. The **church** of the same name flanks the north side of the square, a Gothic building from 1289, one of whose chapels holds a miraculous painting of the Crucifixion which is said to have spoken to St Thomas Aquinas during his time at the adjacent monastery. Look also at the Brancaccio chapel, whose clear, bright frescoes by Pietro Cavallini date back to the early fourteenth century, and the sacristy, home to the velvet-clad coffins of the city's Aragonese rulers, who made this church the centre of their court in Naples.

Cappella Sansevero

Via Francesco di Sanctis 19/21 • Mon & Wed–Sat 10am–6pm, Sun 10am–1.30pm • €7 • ☎ 081 551 8470, ⓦ museosansevero.it

Off the top end of the Piazza San Domenico, Via de Sanctis leads off right to one of the city's odder monuments, the **Cappella Sansevero**, the tomb-chapel of the Di Sangro family, decorated by the sculptor Giuseppe Sammartino in the mid-eighteenth century. The decoration is extraordinary, the centrepiece a carving of a dead Christ, laid out flat and covered with a veil of stark and remarkable realism, not least because it was carved out of a single piece of marble. Even more accomplished is the veiled figure of *Modesty* on the left, and, on the right, its twin *Disillusionment*, in the form of a woeful figure struggling with marble netting. Look, too, at the effusive *Deposition* on the high altar and the memorial above the doorway, which shows one Cecco di Sangro climbing out of his tomb, sword in hand. You might also want to venture downstairs. The man responsible for the chapel, Prince Raimondo, was a well-known eighteenth-century alchemist, and down here are the results of some of his experiments: bodies of an upright man and woman, behind glass, their capillaries and most of their organs preserved by a mysterious liquid developed by the prince – who, incidentally, was excommunicated by the pope for such practices. Even now the black entanglements make for a gruesome sight.

Santa Chiara

Via S. Chiara 49 • **Church** Daily 7.30am–1pm & 4.30–8pm • Free • **Cloister** Mon–Sat 9.30am–5.30pm, Sun 10am–2.30pm • €5 • ⓦ monasterodisantachiara.eu

Dating from 1328, the church of **Santa Chiara** was completely destroyed by Allied bombs during the last war, then rebuilt in its original bare Gothic austerity. There's not very much to see inside, but the medieval tombs of the Angevin monarchs at the far end are very fine and include that of Robert the Wise at the altar, showing the king in a monk's habit. And the attached convent has a **cloister** that is truly one of the gems of the city, a shady haven planted with neatly clipped box hedges, and furnished with benches and low walls covered with colourful majolica tiles depicting bucolic scenes of life outside. There's also a giant *presepe* or Christmas crib, and in the far corner a well-put-together museum showing bits from the church before the bombing as well as the excavated remains of a Roman bath complex outside.

Gesù Nuovo

Piazza Gesù Nuovo • Daily 7am–12.30pm & 4–7pm • Free • ⓦ gesunuovo.it

Opposite Santa Chiara, the **Gesù Nuovo** church is most notable for its lava-stone facade, originally part of a fifteenth-century palace which stood here, prickled with pyramids that give it an impregnable, prison-like air. The inside is as over-sized and over-decorated as you might expect, and is worth a look for just that, although its most interesting feature is perhaps a quieter one: the simple chapel on the far right which is dedicated to San Guiseppe Moscati, a local doctor who died in 1927 and was reputed to perform medical miracles – as you can see from the votive plaques and thanks that plaster the walls.

Piazza Garibaldi and around

Naples' main transport hub is **Piazza Garibaldi**, a long, wide square crisscrossed by traffic lanes that cuts into the city centre from the modern train station. Most of the city buses leave from here, as do the Metropolitana and Circumvesuviana lines, and it's one of the city's most hectic junctions; indeed it's Piazza Garibaldi, perhaps more so than any other part of the city, that puts people off Naples. The entire piazza is currently a vast construction site due to work on the new metro; pedestrians are blocked by steel walls and challenged by traffic at every turn, especially when trying to reach the bus stops at the opposite side of the piazza. Of late, the area around here has also become a centre for Naples' growing African community, with a number of African restaurants and Moroccan groceries, and don't be surprised to hear Slavic accents too – many Ukrainians find their way here to work as housekeepers in the city.

Forcella

On the far side of Piazza Garibaldi is the city's **FORCELLA** quarter, which spreads down to Corso Umberto I and across as far as Via Duomo. It's an introduction to the old centre of Naples, an open-air **market**, stamping-ground of CD and sunglasses hawkers, contraband seafood sellers and a quantity of food stalls that make it one of the city's best places to wander. It's also one of the main city-centre strongholds of the Camorra and home to its most important families, and not an especially friendly place at night.

Corso Umberto I

Corso Umberto I spears off the far corner of the square, edging the old part of the city to the port. Known as the "*rettifilo*", it makes its long straight journey from the seedy gatherings of prostitutes and kerb crawlers at Piazza Garibaldi, past many of the city's more mainstream shops, to the symmetrical **Piazza Bovio** – currently disrupted by more metro-system workings. From here Via Duomo heads up the hill to the right, dividing Forcella from the *centro storico* on its left-hand side.

Via Toledo and the Quartieri Spagnoli

If you asked most people what they thought of as the centre of Naples, they'd say **Via Toledo**, sometimes known as Via Roma: the shop-lined thoroughfare that provides the modern city's spine. Its southern end is anchored by Piazza Trieste e Trento and the city's most monumental buildings: the Palazzo Reale, Galleria Umberto I and the Castel Nuovo. From here, Via Toledo leads north in a dead-straight line, climbing the hill towards the **Museo Archeologico Nazionale** and separating the city into two very distinct parts.

The streets to the left, scaling the footslopes of the Vomero, are some of the city's most narrow and crowded, a grid of alleys that was laid out to house Spanish troops during the seventeenth century and hence now known as the **Quartieri Spagnoli** – an enticing area, at least for visitors, although it's a poor part of town, too, and one you might want to avoid wandering too deeply into at night.

Piazza Trieste e Trento and around

Piazza Trieste e Trento is probably as close to central Naples as you can get, though it's more a roundabout than a piazza, whose life you can watch while sipping a pricey drink on the terrace of the sleekly historic **Caffè Gambrinus**. The **Galleria Umberto I** was erected in 1887, and after decades of neglect, is looking better than it has done for some time. Across the square, **Piazza del Plebiscito** is a decent attempt to create a grand and symmetrical city-centre space, with matching palaces on either side and a curve of columns modelled on Bernini's piazza for St Peter's in Rome. Its focal point, the church of **San Francesco di Paola**, is a copy of the Pantheon in Rome – obvious once you're standing under its enormous dome.

13

The Castel Nuovo

Piazza del Municipio • Mon–Sat 9am–7pm • €5

The brooding hulk of the **Castel Nuovo** – the "Maschio Angioino" – was erected in 1282 by the Angevins and later converted as the royal residence of the Aragon monarchs. The entrance incorporates a triumphal arch from 1454 that commemorates the taking of the city by Alfonso I, the first Aragon ruler, and shows details of his triumph topped by a rousing statue of St Michael. Inside incorporates the ground-floor Capella Palatina, with its fourteenth- to sixteenth-century frescoes, Renaissance sculptures and fifteenth-century marble portal and rose window, and a couple of floors of paintings and sculpture – take a look at the original bronze doors from 1468 which show scenes from Ferdinand of Aragon's struggle against the local barons. The cannonball wedged in the lower left-hand panel dates from a naval battle in 1495 between the French and the Genoese that took place while the former were pillaging the doors from the castle. On the upper floor are some nice nineteenth-century scenes of Naples, but it's probably the views over the port from the upper terrace that steal the show – that and the **Sala dei Baroni**, accessed from the courtyard, a huge room with magnificent umbrella-ribbed vaults that were once covered in frescoes by Giotto (sadly lost).

Teatro San Carlo

Via S. Carlo 98 • Tours Mon–Sat 10am–5.30pm, Sun 11am & 12.30pm • €5 Mon–Sat, €15 Sun, including a free *aperitivo* • ☎ 081 797 2468, ⓦ teatrosancarlo.it

Just beyond the castle, the **Teatro San Carlo** is an oddly unimpressive building from the outside. But inside you can see why this theatre was the envy of Europe when it opened in 1737 in time for Charles of Bourbon's birthday, for whom it was built. Destroyed by fire in 1816 and quickly rebuilt, it's one of the largest opera houses in Italy and one of the most distinguished in the world. Tours take in the auditorium itself, backstage areas and the dressing rooms of the principal singers.

The Palazzo Reale

Piazza del Plebiscito • Daily except Wed 9am–7.30pm • €4 • ⓦ palazzorealenapoli.it

The **Palazzo Reale** forms the fourth side of the Piazza del Plebiscito, and manages better than most of the buildings around here to retain some semblance of its former glories, though it's a bland, derivative building for the most part and even a bit of a fake, thrown up hurriedly in 1602 to accommodate Philip III on a visit here and never actually occupied by a monarch long term. Indeed it's more of a monument to monarchies than monarchs, with the various dynasties that ruled Naples by proxy for so long represented in the niches of the facade, from Roger the Norman to Vittorio Emanuele II, taking in among others Alfonso I and a slightly comic Murat on the way.

Upstairs, by way of an impressive white-marble double-staircase, the palace's first-floor rooms are decorated with fine Baroque excesses – gilded furniture, trompe l'oeil ceilings, great overbearing tapestries, impressive French Empire pieces and lots and lots of quite creditable seventeenth- and eighteenth-century paintings, including works by Guercino, Carracci and Titian, as well as Flemish old masters. The best bits are the little theatre – the first room on the right – which is refreshingly restrained after the rest of the palace; the vast ballroom; and the terrace, which gives good views over the port and the Castel Nuovo. Look in also on the chapel, on the far side of the central courtyard, which has one of the city's biggest *presepi*, filled with mainly eighteenth-century figures – 210 in all.

Montesanto, La Sanità and Capodimonte

Left of Via Toledo is the atmospheric district of **Montesanto**, focusing on the lively intersection of Piazza Pignasecca and the funicular station just beyond. On the right, **Piazza Dante** was designed by Luigi Vanvitelli during the eighteenth century and cuts an elegant semicircle around a graffitied statue of the poet. From here you can cut through the seventeenth-century **Port'Alba** into the old part of the city, or push straight on up to the **La Sanità** quarter, whose name literally means "health" due to its position outside the walls of the old city. However, the real interest lies in between: at the city's fantastic **archeological museum**, situated at one end of the busy nineteenth-century triangle of **Piazza Cavour**. If you see only one orthodox Naples sight, make it this, though the **Museo Nazionale di Capodimonte**, up on the hill beyond, is a close second.

The Museo Archeologico Nazionale

Piazza Museo 19 • Daily except Tues 9am–7.30pm • €6.50 • ☎ 081 442 2149, ⊛ museoarcheologiconazionale.campaniabeniculturali.it

Naples' **Museo Archeologico Nazionale** is home to the Farnese collection of antiquities from Lazio and Campania and the best of the finds from the nearby Roman sites of Pompeii and Herculaneum. It seems to be under almost constant reorganization, and to be honest the displays are tired and old-fashioned for the most part. But you'd be mad to miss it – it's truly one of the highlights of the city.

Ground floor

The ground floor of the museum has sculpture from the **Farnese collection**, displayed at its best in the mighty Great Hall, which holds imperial-era figures like the *Farnese Bull* and *Farnese Hercules* from the Baths of Caracalla in Rome – the former the largest piece of classical sculpture ever found. Don't miss *Ephesian Artemis*, an alabaster and bronze statue with rows of bulbous objects peeling off her chest – variously interpreted as breasts, eggs, bulls' scrota, dates or pollen sacs, and bees, mini-beasts and sphinxes adorning her lower half.

Campanian mosaics

The mezzanine floor holds the museum's collection of **mosaics** – remarkably preserved works that give a superb insight into ordinary Roman customs, beliefs and humour. All are worth looking at – images of fish, crustacea, wildlife on the banks of the Nile, a cheeky cat and quail with still-life beneath, masks and simple abstract decoration. But some highlights include a realistic *Battle Scene* (no. 10020); the *Three Musicians with Dwarf* (no. 9985); an urbane meeting of the Platonic Academy (no. 124545); and a marvellously captured scene from a comedy, *The Consultation of the Fattucchiera* (no. 9987), with a soothsayer giving a dour and doomy prediction. While at the far end the fascinating **Gabinetto Segreto** (Secret Room) contains erotic material taken from the brothels, baths, houses and taverns of Pompeii and Herculaneum – languidly sensual wall-paintings, preposterously phallic lamps and the like.

The Campanian wall paintings

Upstairs through the Salone della Meridiana, which contains a sparse but fine assortment of Roman figures, a series of rooms holds the **Campanian wall paintings**, lifted from the villas of Pompeii and Herculaneum, and rich in colour and invention. There are plenty here, and it's worth devoting some time to this section, which includes works from the Sacrarium – part of Pompeii's Egyptian temple of Isis, the most celebrated mystery cult of antiquity.

In the next series of rooms, some of the smallest and most easily missed works are among the most exquisite. Among those to look out for are a paternal *Achilles and Chirone* (no. 9109); the *Sacrifice of Iphiginia* (no. 9112) in the next room, one of the best preserved of all the murals; and a group of four small pictures, the best of which is a depiction of a woman gathering flowers entitled *Allegoria della Primavera* – a fluid, impressionistic piece of work capturing both the gentleness of Spring and the graceful beauty of the woman.

13

Other Campanian finds

Beyond the murals are the actual **finds from the Campanian cities** – everyday items like glass, silver, ceramics, charred pieces of rope, even foodstuffs (petrified cakes, figs, fruit and nuts), together with a model layout of Pompeii in cork. On the other side of the first floor, there are finds from the **Villa dei Papiri** in Herculaneum – sculptures in bronze mainly. The *Hermes at Rest* in the centre of the second room is perhaps the most arresting item, boyishly rapt and naked except for wings on his feet, while all around are other adept statues – a languid *Resting Satyr*, the convincingly woozy *Drunken Silenus*, and a pair of youthful *Runners*.

Santa Maria della Sanità and the Catacombe di San Gaudioso

Piazza Sanità 14 • Daily 10am–1pm, guided tours every hour • €8 • ☎ 081 744 3714, ⓦ catacombedinapoli.it

The church of **Santa Maria della Sanità**, on the piazza of the same name, is a Dominican church from the early seventeenth century whose design was based loosely on Bramante's for St Peter's in Rome. There are paintings by Giordano and other Neapolitan artists inside, although perhaps of more interest are the **Catacombe di San Gaudioso**, an intriguing, early Christian burial ground that's home to the fifth-century tomb of St Gaudioso, a bishop known as the "African", as he was from North Africa, and the final resting-places of the Dominicans themselves, who were decapitated and buried sitting down.

Catacombe di San Gennaro

Via Tondo di Capodimonte 11 • Mon–Sat 10am–5pm, Sun 10am–1pm, guided tours every hour • €8 • ☎ 081 744 3714, ⓦ catacombedinapoli.it • Bus #R4 from Via Toledo, or #178 from the Archeological Museum

Lifts link Sanità with Corso Amedeo up above, the main road up to Capodimonte, and you can walk up from here in ten minutes or so to another burial place, the **Catacombe di San Gennaro**, next door to the huge Madre del Buon Consiglio church, halfway up the hill to Capodimonte. This is a very different sort of catacomb, bigger and more open than San Gaudioso, and best known for being the final resting-place of San Gennaro, whose body was brought here in the fifth century. There are some amazing early Christian frescoes and mosaics, newly restored and amazingly bright.

Museo Nazionale di Capodimonte

Via Miano 2 • Daily except Wed 8.30am–7.30pm • €7.50, €6.50 after 2pm; audioguides €5 • ☎ 081 749 9111, ⓦ museodicapodimonte .campaniabeniculturali.it

At the top of the hill, the **Palazzo Reale di Capodimonte** was the royal residence of the Bourbon King Charles III. Built in 1738, it now houses the picture gallery of the Naples museum, the superb **Museo Nazionale di Capodimonte**, arguably one of the best collections of art in the country, with many important works by Campanian and other, mainly Italian artists, as well as curious objets d'art and fine pieces of Capodimonte porcelain.

First floor

The three-storey museum is organized roughly chronologically, but also by its various collections, which were built up by the Borgia, Farnese and Bourbon rulers of the city. The museum starts on the first floor with the Farnese collection, and a grouping of portraits of the Farnese pope, Paul III, by Titian, alongside the same artist's portrayal of Charles V and Philip II, which face his portratit of Alessandro Farnese and Andre del Sarto's glowering depiction of Leo X. Beyond are more works by Renaissance masters: Bellini's impressively coloured and composed *Transfiguration*; Lotto's odd *Madonna with St Peter*; Giulio Romano's dark and powerful *Madonna of the Cat*; Sebastiano del Piombo's haughty *Clement VII*; Marcello Venusti's small-scale 1549 copy of Michelangelo's *Last Judgement* – probably the only chance you'll get to see the painting this close up; and Titian's lascivious *Danaë*. There are also two rooms mainly devoted to the Carracci brothers, full of magnificent pieces like Annibale's *Mystical Marriage of St Catherine*.

13

If you have time to spare, take a walk around the **royal apartments** on this floor. They're kept much as they would have been in the eighteenth century, and high spots include the airy, mirrored ballroom, lined with portraits of various Bourbon monarchs and other European despots, and an entire room decked out entirely with dripping, colourful porcelain, sprouting three-dimensional Chinese scenes, monkeys, fruit and flowers.

Second floor

On the second floor are some outstanding Italian paintings from the fourteenth and fifteenth centuries, of which the most famous is *St Ludovic of Toulouse* by Simone Martini, a fascinating Gothic painting glowing with gold leaf. Elsewhere there are paintings that used to hang in Naples' churches: Niccolò Colantonio's *St Jerome in his Study* was painted for the altar of San Lorenzo Maggiore, and the same artist's *Deposition* used to hang in San Domenico Maggiore. Further on, Vasari's dramatic, almost snapshot-like *Presentation in the Temple* was done for the city's Monteoliveto church, and a series of smaller works by the same painter for the sacristry of San Giovanni Carbonara; while Titian's *Annunciation*, further on, was for the church of San Domenico Maggiore. The long series of rooms ends in fine style with one of Caravaggio's best-known works, his dark and brutal *Flagellation*, beyond which is the museum's collection of seventeenth- and eighteenth-century Neapolitan paintings, including a generally wonderful grouping of all the shining lights of the Neapolitan Baroque – Caracciolo, Ribera, the prolific Luca Giordano, and later work by Francesco de Mura and Solimena. Finally, upstairs is a smattering of **twentieth-century works**, of which the most notable is a painting of an erupting *Vesuvius* by Andy Warhol.

Chiaia, Santa Lucia and Mergellina

Lined with the city's fanciest shops, **Via Chiaia** leads west from Piazza Trieste e Trento to the elegant circle of **Piazza dei Martiri** – named after the nineteenth-century revolutionary martyrs commemorated by the column in its centre. This part of town, the **Chiaia** neighbourhood, displays a sense of order and classical elegance that is quite absent from the rest of the city centre, its buildings well preserved, the people noticeably better heeled. From Piazza dei Martiri, you can stroll down to the waterfront and **Villa Comunale**, Naples' most central city park, richly adorned with Classical sculpture and the best place to appreciate the city's maritime side with views stretching right around the bay to the distinctive silhouette of Vesuvius in the east.

Tunnel Borbonico

Vico del Grottone 4 • Fri–Sun tours at 10am, noon, 1.30pm & 3.30pm • ☎ 081 764 5808, ⓦ tunnelborbonico.info

Accessed through an old vet's surgery down an alley off Via Serra, the **Tunnel Borbonico** is really three sights in one: a tunnel built by the nervous king Ferdinand II in the 1850s as a means of escape from the Palazzo Reale; a series of cisterns used as the main water supply for this part of the city until the 1880s; and a series of bomb shelters from World War II which were fashioned out of the tunnel and a number of disused cisterns. You can enter from the Via Serra end or the Parcheggo Morelli end on Via Chiatamone, and tours last just over an hour. Among many things to see are a host of abandoned cars mainly from the 1940s and 1950s; the cisterns themselves, including the steps hollowed out of the rock that the "*pozzari*" or water attendants would use to get in and out; and the bomb shelters, full of affecting graffiti done by the folk who once sheltered here.

Castel dell'Ovo

Via Partenope • Mon–Sat 9am–6pm, Sun 9am–2pm • Free • ⓦ comune.napoli.it/casteldellovo

Down on the waterfront in the swanky **Santa Lucia** district, the grey mass of the **Castel dell'Ovo** or "egg-castle" takes its name from the whimsical legend that it was built over

13

an egg placed here by Virgil in Roman times: it is believed that if the egg breaks, Naples will fall. Actually it was built by the Hohenstaufen king Frederick II and extended by the Angevins. There's not much to see or do inside; it's just a series of terraces and views really. But the **views** are the best in town: a 360-degree panorama over the entire bay and back over Naples itself. When you're done you can go for drinks or dinner at one of the quayside restaurants in the **Borgo Marinaro** below.

Villa Comunale and around

The **Villa Comunale** park stretches around the bay for a good mile and is a nice way to walk to Mergellina, particularly in the early evening when the city lights enhance the views. On the way you might want to take in the Mediterranean marine life at the newly restored century-old **aquarium** (March–Oct Tues–Sat 9am–6pm, Sun 9.30am–7.30pm; Nov–Feb Tues–Sat 9am–5pm, Sun 9am–2pm; €1.50; ⊛szn.it), one large room basically, lined with tanks filled with impressive giant turtles, eels and rays as well as a couple of mock rock-pools. Across the other side of Riviera di Chiaia from the aquarium, the **Villa Pignatelli** (daily except Tues 8.30am–2pm; €2; ☎081 669 675, ⊛museopignatelli.campaniabeniculturali.it) is kept in much the same way as when it was the home of a prominent Naples family and a meeting place for the city's elite in the 1900s. It's tastefully furnished and by Naples standards low-key, its handful of rooms holding books, porcelain, the odd painting and a set of photos signed by various aristocrats and royal personages.

Mergellina

At the far end of the Villa Comunale lie the harbour and main square – **Piazza Sannazzaro** – of the **Mergellina** district, a good place to come and eat at night and a terminus for hydrofoils to the bay's islands. There's not a lot else here, though it's worth looking in on the little church of **Santa Maria in Piedigrotta** next door to the train station, home of the Madonna that gets carried through the streets every September in one of the city's most popular festivals, and the **Parco Virgiliano** just behind (daily 9am–6.30pm), where you can see the opening to a 700m-long Roman tunnel that was cut through the hillside here, and the supposed burial place of the Roman poet Virgil right by it, though this has long since been discredited.

Vomero

Vomero – the district topping the hill immediately above the old city – is one of Naples' relatively modern additions, a light, airy and relatively peaceful quarter connected most directly with the teeming morass below by funicular railway. It's a large area but mostly residential, and you're unlikely to want to stray beyond the streets that fan out from each of the three funicular stations, centring on the grand symmetry of **Piazza Vanvitelli**. Come up on the Montesanto funicular and you're well placed for a visit to two of the buildings that dominate Naples, way above the old city.

Castel Sant'Elmo

Via Tito Angelini 22 • Daily except Wed 8.30am–7.30pm • €3 • ☎ 081 229 4401, ⊛ polomusealenapoli.beniculturali.it/museo_se

Five minutes' walk from the funicular station, the **Castel Sant'Elmo** occupies Naples' highest point and is an impressive fortification, a fourteenth-century structure once used for incarcerating political prisoners and now lording it grandly over the streets below. Not surprisingly it has the very best views of Naples, and you can enjoy them from the top terrace of the castle before visiting the **Napoli Novecento** museum in the centre – a collection of painting and sculpture by Neapolitan artists from the early twentieth century to the 1980s.

Certosa San Martino

Largo S. Martino 5 • Daily except Wed 8.30am–7.30pm • €6 • ☎ 081 578 1769, ⓦ museosanmartino.campaniabeniculturali.it

Beyond Castel Sant'Elmo, the fourteenth-century **Certosa San Martino** has the next-best views over the bay and is home to the **Museo Nazionale di San Martino**. The views from its cunningly constructed terraced gardens are well worth the entrance fee alone but you also get to see the monastery's church, with a colourful pavement and an *Adoration of the Shepherds* by Reni above the altar, as well as works by some of the greats of Neaopolitan painters in most of the chapels and in the rooms off the high altar. In the museum proper, there are more paintings by Neapolitan masters – Ribera, Stanzione, Vaccaro – as well as sculpture by Pietro Bernini; the frescoed library and prior's apartments; and an unparalleled collection of *presepi* or Christmas cribs. The Baroque cloisters are lovely, too, though a little gone to seed, but they're surrounded by historical and maritime sections displaying models of ships, and documents, coins and costumes recording the era of the Kingdom of Naples. All in all, one of the city's better and more diverse museums, but with very little information in English.

Villa Floridiana

Via Cimarosa 77 • Daily except Tues 8am–2pm • €2.50 • ☎ 081 578 8418, ⓦ floridiana.spmn.campaniabeniculturali.it

One of Vomero's most popular sights is the Neoclassical **Villa Floridiana**, close to the Chiaia funicular, whose lush grounds make a good place for a picnic – though the **Museo Duca di Martina** is of fairly specialist interest, a porcelain collection varying from the beautifully simple to the outrageously kitsch – hideous teapots, ceramic asparagus sticks and the like. There are examples of Capodimonte and Meissen, and eighteenth-century English, French, German and Viennese work – as well as a handful of pieces of Qing-Dynasty Chinese porcelain and Murano glass, and exquisite non-ceramic items like inlaid ivory boxes and panels.

ARRIVAL AND DEPARTURE   NAPLES

By plane Naples' Capodichino airport (☎ 081 789 6111, ⓦ gesac.it) is only about 7km north of the city centre and very well connected. ANM bus #35 runs to Piazza Garibaldi (the stop is in front of the station at the *McDonald's* corner) every 30min, and the journey takes about 20min; buy tickets (€1.10) from the *tabacchi* in the departures hall. There's also an official airport bus, Alibus, also operated by ANM (☎ 081 763 2177), which runs to both Piazza Garibaldi and Piazza Municipio every 20min between 6.30am and midnight but it isn't very much quicker and tickets cost €3. Taxis tend to take about as long as buses to reach the centre, and cost €15.50 to the station. There are also about eight buses a day to Sorrento (1hr 30min; €10), and four services daily to Salerno (1hr; €7).

By train You're most likely to arrive at Napoli Centrale, situated on the edge of the city centre at one end of Piazza Garibaldi, at the main hub of city and suburban transport services; there's a left-luggage office here (open 24hr). Some trains also pull into Stazione Mergellina, on the opposite side of the city centre, which is connected with Piazza Garibaldi by the underground metropolitana.
Destinations Agropoli (8 daily; 1hr 30min); Benevento (12 daily; 1hr 20min–2hr 20min); Caserta (every 15min; 35–45min); Foggia (6 daily; via Caserta or Benevento 2hr 20min–4hr); Formia (hourly; 1hr–1hr 45min); Rome (every 30min; 1hr 10min–2hr); Salerno (every 30min; 30min–1hr 20min).

By bus City and suburban buses also stop on Piazza Garibaldi, though you'll need to check the stops carefully as they are not well signed and are subject to change while the square is undergoing construction of the new metro line. CTP (☎ 081 7000 1111, ⓦ ctpn.it) runs buses to Caserta, and SITA (☎ 081 552 2176, ⓦ sitabus.it) connects with Pompeii, Sorrento, the Amalfi Coast and Salerno.
Destinations Amalfi (4 daily; 1hr 55min); Bari (3 daily; 3hr); Benevento (6 daily; 1hr 30min); Caserta (every 20min; 45min); Pompeii (every 30min; 35min); Positano (2 daily Mon–Sat at 8.45am and 9.10am; 2hr 10min); Salerno (every 15–30min; 1hr 10min).

By ferry and hydrofoil Ferries – to the islands and other places in the Bay of Naples, including Sorrento, and along the Amalfi Coast – run from the Milo Beverello main ferry terminal, and there are also a few hydrofoils from Mergellina – see opposite for more details on these. There's also the Metro del Mare – ☎ 199 600 700, ⓦ metrodelmare .com – services which connect Pozzuoli, Naples, Sorrento, Positano, Amalfi, Minori, Salerno and several points in between. During high season they run down to the main towns of the Cilento too. Fares are cheap, and about the most you'll pay is for the trip from Naples to Salerno, which takes the best part of 3hr.
Destinations Aeolian islands (June–Aug daily at 2.30pm & also on Sat at 9am; 7hr); Cagliari (ferry: 1 weekly in high

13

season at 7.15pm; 16hr 15min); Catania (1 weekly in high season; 9hr); Milazzo, via Aeolian Islands (1 weekly in high season at 8pm; 16hr 30min); Palermo (2 daily; 10hr); Sorrento (6 daily; 35min).

INFORMATION AND TOURS

Tourist offices There is a Naples tourist-office desk (🖰inaples.it) at Capodichino airport (daily 8am–11pm), and two offices in the centre of the city, on Piazza del Gesù Nuovo (Mon–Sat 9.30am–1.30pm & 2.30–6.30pm, Sun 9am–1.30pm; 📞081 551 2701), and opposite the Teatro San Carlo at Via S. Carlo 9 (Mon–Sat 9.30am–1.30pm & 2.30–6.30pm, Sun 9am–1.30pm; 📞081 402 394). At each of them you can pick up a free city map, a decent free transport map and an English-language copy of the monthly *Qui Napoli* what's-on guide.

Tours CitySightseeing Napoli (📞081 551 7279, 🖰napoli.city-sightseeing.it) operates a hop-on, hop-off service taking in the sights on several routes around town (May and Oct; €22; tickets valid 24hr); tours leave from just in front of the Castel Nuovo. The same company also runs services to Vesuvius in summer.

GETTING AROUND

ON FOOT

The best way to **get around** central Naples and stay sane is to walk. Driving can be a nightmare, and to negotiate the narrow streets, hectic squares and racetrack boulevards on a moped or scooter takes years of training. In any case, not to walk would mean you'd miss a lot – Naples is the kind of place best appreciated at street level.

BY PUBLIC TRANSPORT

For longer journeys there are a number of alternatives, both for the city itself and the bay as a whole, and the system, most of which is run by ANM, is pretty well integrated.

City buses and the metropolitana City buses will get you almost everywhere, although they are crowded and slow. The bus system is supplemented by the metropolitana, a small-scale underground network that crosses the city centre, stopping at about four places between Piazza Garibaldi and Mergellina, and runs eventually out to Pozzuoli in about 30min; new stations – at Duomo, Piazza Municipio and Via Toledo – are in the pipeline, as evidenced by the construction chaos in these locations.

Funiculars In addition, three funiculars scale the hill of the Vomero: one, the Funicolare di Chiaia, from Piazza Amedeo; another, the Funicolare Centrale, from the Augusteo station, just off the bottom end of Via Toledo; and a third, the Funicolare di Montesanto, from the station on Piazza Montesanto. A fourth, the Funicolare di Mergellina, runs up the hill above Mergellina from Via Mergellina.

BY CAR

Only a crazy person, or someone picking up a rental car, would willingly drive in Naples. If you do have to do that, then at least try to avoid the city centre, which is always congested and anarchic, even by Italian standards, and made even worse by ongoing construction works for the metro. Car rental outfits include Avis (📞081 751 6052); Europcar (📞081 780 5643); Hertz (📞081 780 2971); Maggiore (📞199 151 120); Sixt (📞191 100 666).

BY TAXI

If you need to take a **taxi** make sure the driver switches on the meter when you start (they often don't), or request a flat fare at the beginning of the journey – which you can do (there are published rates to key locations that taxi drivers have to adhere to if requested); otherwise fares start at €3 for the initial journey, €5.50 after 10pm or on weekends. Note that certain journeys command a flat fare, for example to the airport (see p.755); or between the ferry terminal and station (€10.50) incur an extra charge of €2.60. There are taxi ranks at the train station, on Piazza Dante, Piazza del Gesù, Piazza Trieste e Trento, at Mergellina station, and other places. Reliable numbers are 📞081 5522 5252, 📞081 570 7070, 📞081 551 5151 and 📞081 556 4444.

BEYOND NAPLES

For solely out-of-town trips – around the bay in either direction – or sometimes to get from one side of the centre to another, there are three further rail systems. Unicanapoli **tickets** (see box below) are valid for all these suburban lines except the Circumvesuviana, for which tickets can be bought at any train station; tickets are cheap – €1.80 to Ercolano, Pompeii €2.40, and €3.40 to Sorrento.

The Circumvesuviana runs from Porta Nolana station, on Corso Garibaldi, just off Piazza Garibaldi, as well as Napoli

---

UNICONAPOLI TICKETS

Uniconapoli tickets for all ANM modes of transport cost a flat €1.20 for all journeys (valid 90min) and must be bought in advance from *tabacchi*, newsstands, stations, or the transport booth on Piazza Garibaldi. An all-day ticket costs €3.60 (€3 at the weekend), or you can buy a three-day tourist ticket for €20, which allows travel throughout Campania, including the airport bus, island buses and beyond.

13

TRANSPORT INFORMATION

Metropolitana/FS ☎ 800 568 866. City-centre stops include Piazza Garibaldi, Piazza Cavour, Montesanto, Piazza Amedeo, Vanvitelli, Mergellina, Museo, Dante – with stops at Duomo, Municipio and Toledo to come. Trains every 8min.

Circumvesuviana ☎ 081 772 2444. As its name suggests, this line runs all the way around Vesuvius, but the part most tourists use is the main section between Naples and Sorrento, with many stops around the southern part of the bay, including Ercolano and Pompeii. Trains every 30min.

Circumflegrea/Ferrovia Cumana ☎ 800 001 616. These two lines connect Naples Montesanto to Fuorigrotta, Agnano, Bagnoli, Pozzuoli, Baia, Fusaro, Cumae and Torregaveta. Trains every 20min.

Funiculars ☎ 800 568 866. There are four lines: Funicolare Centrale (Piazza Augusteo–Piazza Fuga; daily 6.30am–12.30am; every 10–15min); Funicolare di Montesanto (Montesanto FS–Via Morghen; daily 7am–10pm; every 10–15min); Funicolare di Chiaia Parco Margherita (Via Cimarosa–Parco Margherita; daily 6.30am–12.30am; every 10–15min; Funicolare di Mergellina (Mergellina–Manzoni; daily 7am–10pm; every 12–15min).

USEFUL BUS ROUTES

#R1 Piazza Medaglie d'Oro–Via Salvator Rosa–Piazza Dante–Via Toledo–Via Medina–Piazza Municipio–Via Monteoliveto–Piazza Dante–Piazza Museo–Via Salvator Rosa–Piazza Medaglie d'Oro.

#R2 Piazza Garibaldi–Corso Umberto I–Piazza Bovio–Via Depretis–Piazza Municipio–Via San Carlo–Piazza Trieste e Trento–Piazza Municipio–Via Medina–Via Sanfelice–Corso Umberto I–Piazza Garibaldi.

#R3 Mergellina Funicolare–Via Mergellina–Via Riviera di Chiaia–Piazza Municipio–Via Medina–Via Toledo–Piazza Municipio–Via San Carlo–Piazza Trieste e Trento–Piazza Municipio–Via Riviera di Chiaia–Mergellina Funicolare.

#R4 Via Cardarelli–Via Capodimonte–Piazza Dante–Via Depretis–Piazza Dante–Via Capodimonte–Via Cardarelli.

#E1 Piazza del Gesù–Via Mezzocannone–Via Santa Chiara–Via Duomo–Via Foria–Via Duomo–Via dei Tribunali–Corso Umberto I–Via Monteoliveto–Piazza del Gesù.

#140 Capo Posillipo–Via Posillipo–Via Mergellina–Via Caracciolo–Piazza Vittoria–Via Santa Lucia–Via Chiamatone–Piazza Vittoria–Via Riviera di Chiaia–Via Mergellina–Via Posillipo–Capo Posillipo.

#N1 (night bus) Piazzale Tecchio–Viale Augusto–Via Fuorigrotta–Via Riviera di Chiaia–Via Caracciolo–Piazza Vittoria–Via Partenope–Via Santa Lucia–Via Depretis–Via Medina–Corso Umberto I–Piazza Garibaldi–Corso Umberto I–Via Medina–Piazza Municipio–Via Santa Lucia–Via Chiatamone–Piazza Vittoria–Via Riviera di Chiaia–Via Piedigrotta–Viale Augusto–Piazzale Tecchio.

Centrale, right around Vesuvius and the southern part of the Bay of Naples every 30min, stopping everywhere as far south as Sorrento, which it reaches in about an hour; it's most useful for getting to Ercolano, Pompeii and, of course, Sorrento.

The Ferrovia Cumana and Circumflegrea In the opposite direction, the Ferrovia Cumana operates regularly from its terminus station in Piazza Montesanto west to Pozzuoli and beyond, as does the Circumflegrea, which follows a different route to the same terminal at Torregaveta.

ACCOMMODATION

Accommodation prices in Naples may come as a refreshing change after the north of Italy, but they're still not cheap, and you need to choose carefully from among the budget options around Piazza Garibaldi. A better bet is the lively and more atmospheric *centro storico*, where boutique hotels and small B&Bs are opening up all the time. For camping, see p.763 for the city's best option.

HOTELS AND B&BS

CENTRO STORICO AND PIAZZA GARIBALDI

Belle Arti Resort Via S. Maria di Costantinopoli 27 ☎ 081 557 1062, ⓦ belleartiresort.com; map p.744. Contemporary design meets historic elegance at this boutique

B&B near Piazza Bellini. Rooms are individually decorated with modern pieces and some have original seventeenth-century ceiling frescoes. Free internet access. **€90**

Caravaggio Piazza Riario Sforza 157 ☎ 081 211 0066, ⓦ caravaggiohotel.it; map p.744. Right in the thick of

13

things on the edge of Forcella, just around the corner from the Duomo, but quiet enough, on its own small square – which some of the nicer rooms in this elegant old *palazzo* overlook. **€190**

Casanova Via Venezia 2 ☎081 268 287, ⓦhotel casanova.com; map pp.742–743. Best of the station-area budget options, this creeper-clad hotel is quiet, run by an affable team, and has pleasant rooms (most of which are en suite) and a communal roof terrace. **€50**

Correra 241 Via Correra 241 ☎081 1956 2842, ⓦcorrera.it; map p.744. This well-located budget option has a deliberately contemporary feel, with bright primary colours and minimalist furnishings throughout. A good location too, 5min from Piazza Dante and the *centro storico*. **€140**

★ **Costantinopoli 104** Via S. Maria di Costantinopoli 104 ☎081 557 1035, ⓦcostantinopoli104.it; map p.744. A contemporary boutique hotel with its own garden and small swimming pool in a secluded location at the back of a Piazza Bellini *palazzo*. Some of the rooms open onto the garden, others on the upstairs terrace. Very peaceful, but also very convenient. **€200**

Donna Regina B&B Via L. Settembrini 80 ☎081 446 799, ⓦdiscovernaples.net; map p.744. Inside the former Donnaregina convent, each room of this lovely and welcoming B&B is spacious and uniquely decorated. The same owner has other B&Bs elsewhere in the city, as well as self-catering apartments to rent. **€100**

Duomo Via Duomo 228 ☎081 265 988, ⓦhotel duomonapoli.it; map p.744. Newly and stylishly done up, but prices are still among the lowest in town. Most rooms face onto a tranquil internal courtyard and all are en suite. Very welcoming, and in an ideal location for seeing all the major sights of the old centre. **€65**

Il Convento Via Speranzella 137/A ☎081 403 997, ⓦhotelilconvento.com; map p.744. Situated in the Quartieri Spagnoli, just two blocks off Via Toledo, this three-star has decent, cosy rooms, two of which have their own roof terraces. **€145**

Piazza Bellini Via S. Maria di Costantinopoli 101 ☎081 451 732, ⓦhotelpiazzabellini.com; map p.744. Stylish yet unpretentious and friendly contemporary hotel housed in a light-flooded high-ceilinged Renaissance *palazzo*, a short walk from both the archeological museum and Spaccanapoli. There's a secluded courtyard, and 48 spacious rooms with unfussy custom-designed furniture – the best have huge terraces looking over the city to Vesuvius. **€170**

Romeo Via Cristoforo Colombo 45 ☎081 017 5001, ⓦromeohotel.it; map p.744. Something of a standout building on this grungy stretch of the waterfront opposite the cruise-ship terminal, the *Romeo* is the ultimate Naples boutique hotel, complete with weird-looking furniture, sushi bar and a range of very well appointed rooms, the best with views over the bay. There's free and efficient wi-fi,

high standards of service and there's even a decent restaurant – though at these prices you might wish for a more simpatico location. That said, you can virtually fall out of bed into a ferry for one of the islands. **€430**

SANTA LUCIA, CHIAIA AND MERGELLINA

Ausonia Via Caracciolo 11 ☎081 682 278, ⓦhotel ausonianapoli.com; map pp.742–743. A two-star decorated to give the impression you're on a yacht, neatly placed in Mergellina, next to the stop for hydrofoils to Ischia and the Pontine islands. **€100**

Cappella Vecchia 11 Vicolo S. Maria a Cappella Vecchia 11 ☎081 240 5117, ⓦcappellavecchia11.it; map pp.742–743. Just off Piazza dei Martiri, this small B&B has six simple but brightly furnished en-suite rooms with free wi-fi. A warm welcome, too, from the young, friendly owners. **€80**

Chiaja Hotel De Charme Via Chiaia 216 ☎081 415 555, ⓦhotelchiaia.it; map pp.742–743. Lovely, old-fashioned hotel near Piazza del Plebiscito. The rooms have been fashioned from an eighteenth-century patrician home with all the antique furniture and old-world style to prove it. **€130**

Grand Hotel Parker's Corso Vittorio Emanuele 135 ☎081 761 2474, ⓦgrandhotelparkers.it; map pp.742–743. This upmarket and extremely comfortable hotel claims to be the oldest in Naples, and has hosted Oscar Wilde and Virginia Woolf, as well as King Vittorio Emanuele himself. It has an exalted vantage-point over the city – the views from the dining room across the bay and east to Vesuvius are unparalleled. **€350**

Miramare Via N. Sauro 24 ☎081 764 7589, ⓦhotel miramare.com; map pp.742–743. A great location on the waterfront a little way down from the Palazzo Reale, this Art Nouveau gem is the less obvious – and cheaper – alternative to the giant and more impersonal palaces nearby, with a more homely feel and a warmer welcome. **€200**

★ **Palazzo Alabardieri** Via Alabardieri 38 ☎081 415 278, ⓦpalazzoalabardieri.it; map pp.742–743. In the heart of Chiaia, this hotel is geared towards business travellers and discerning tourists looking for luxury and courteous service. The well-appointed rooms are decorated with parquet floors, marble and rich fabrics. **€220**

Parteno Via Partenope 1 ☎081 245 2095, ⓦparteno .it; map pp.742–743. Seven individually designed and beautifully furnished rooms in an eighteenth-century building near Villa Comunale. Great breakfasts and wonderful attention to detail from the owners. **€100**

Pinto-Storey Via Martucci 72 ☎081 681 260, ⓦpintostorey.it; map pp.742–743. An evocative Art Nouveau building in a pleasant part of Chiaia, near Naples' most elegant shopping area and close to the Villa Comunale and the sea. Rooms are attractively furnished and many have views of the bay. **€100**

★ **Rex** Via Palepoli 12 ☎081 764 9389, ⊕hotel rex.it; map pp.742–743. In a striking Art Nouveau-style building designed by the renowned Italian architect Coppedè, this family-run hotel in Santa Lucia has some of the friendliest staff around. There's a large sitting room in the reception area frequented by the owner's family and friends, and the rooms are simple and tidy. €118

★ **San Francesco al Monte** Corso Vittorio Emanuele 328 ☎081 423 9111, ⊕sanfrancescoalmonte.it; map pp.742–743. Occupying a commanding position on the slopes leading up to Vomero, this converted sixteenth-century monastery is an exceptional hotel, each of the 45 rooms beautifully decorated and offering panoramic views of the city. There's a pool, tranquil gardens and three restaurants in the grounds. €280

HOSTELS

Hostel Bella Capri Via Melisurgo 4 ☎081 552 9494, ⊕bellacapri.it; map p.744. This upper-floor hostel is virtually a neighbour of the swanky new *Romeo* a few doors down and enjoys an equally handy location right opposite the ferry terminal. It has a mixture of dorm beds and private rooms, internet access and a large, light and airy breakfast room. Ten-percent discount with this book. Dorms €15

Hostel of the Sun Via Melisurgo 15 ☎081 420 6393, ⊕hostelnapoli.com; map p.744. Almost opposite the *Bella Capri*, just off the main waterfront, this is perhaps the best and friendliest hostel in Naples – well placed for going out and with no curfew. Breakfast included, and it has a range of nicely furnished doubles, both en suite and with shared bathrooms, a couple of floors down. Dorms €15, doubles around €60

Naples Pizza Hostel Via S. Paolo ai Tribunali 44 ☎081 1932 3562, ⊕naplespizzahostel.com; map p.744. Run by the same owners as the *Bella Capri*, this new hostel is a bit cheaper and very well located right in the heart of the old centre. Er, they don't serve pizza. Dorms €18

Ostello Mergellina Salita della Grotta 23 ☎081 761 2346, ⊕ostellonapoli.com; map pp.742–743. A popular official youth hostel with a view of the bay, and conveniently located not far from the Mergellina metro station. Dorms are six-bed maximum and breakfast is included, though there's a three-day maximum stay in July & Aug. Dorms €13

EATING AND DRINKING

Neapolitan cuisine consists of simple dishes cooked with fresh, healthy ingredients (see box, p.738). As Naples is not primarily a tourist-geared city, most restaurants are family-run places used by locals and as such generally serve good food at very reasonable prices. There's no better place in Italy to eat pizza, at a solid core of almost obsessively unchanging places that still serve only the (very few) traditional varieties, and you're never far from a food stall for delectable snacks on the move at one of the city's many *friggitorie*.

CAFÉS, SNACKS AND GELATERIE

Attanasio Vico Ferrovia 2/4, off Via Milano; map pp.742–743. Bakery that specializes in delectable *sfogliatelle* (ricotta-stuffed pastries). Tues–Sun 7.30am–7.30pm.

Chalet Ciro Via Caracciolo 1–2; map pp.742–743. This Mergellina institution is known for its *babà* and other pastries as well as delicious ice cream. Its marathon opening hours make it a dependable early morning or after-dinner pit stop for sweets. Daily 6.30am–2am.

Gambrinus Via Chiaia 1–2; map p.744. The oldest and best-known of Neapolitan cafés, founded in 1861. Not cheap, but its aura of chandeliered gentility – and outside seating on Piazza Trieste e Trento – makes it worth at least one visit. Daily 7am–1am.

Gay Odin Via Benedetto Croce 61; map p.744. One of several locations around town, the Spaccanapoli branch of this long-established chocolatier also sells decadent ice cream. Daily 10am–8pm.

L.U.I.S.E. Via S. Caterina a Chiaia 68 ☎081 417 735, ⊕luisenapoli.it; map pp.742–743. Just off Piazza dei Martiri, this is the perfect place to drop after you've shopped, with *piazzette*, salads, *timballo di pasta* (baked pasta) and *peperoni imbottiti* (stuffed peppers), and rather good *arancini* and other deep-fried delights, plus a few tables in the back at which to enjoy them. Mon–Sat 8am–8pm, Sun 9am–2pm.

★ **Remy Gelo** Via F. Galiani 29/A; map pp.742–743. Off Via Caracciolo, near the hydrofoil terminal in Mergellina, this place does superb ice creams and *granite*. Mon–Fri 8am–midnight, Sat & Sun 8am–2am.

Scaturchio Piazza S. Domenico; map p.744. Another elegant old Naples standard, it's been serving coffee and pastries in the heart of Spaccanapoli for decades. Daily 7.30am–7pm.

Vaco 'e Pressa Piazza Dante 84 ☎081 549 9424; map p.744. True to its name ("I'm in a hurry"), this *friggitoria* on Via Toledo sells cheap, delicious Neapolitan street food like *zeppole* (fried doughballs) and *arancini* (rice balls) to a hungry university crowd. Mon–Sat 8am–8pm.

RESTAURANTS AND PIZZERIAS

CENTRO STORICO AND PIAZZA GARIBALDI

Antica Osteria Pisano Piazza Crocelle ai Mannesi 1–4 ☎081 554 8325; map p.744. Small and very traditional trattoria with a well-priced menu of much-loved local standards – a few pasta dishes, mainly with fish and seafood, and a short menu of meat mains for €5–8. Mon–Sat noon–3.30pm & 7.30–10.30pm; closed Aug.

13

Da Michele Via Cesare Sersale 1–3 ☎ 081 553 9204; map p.744. Tucked away off Corso Umberto I in the Forcella district, this is the most determinedly traditional of all the Naples pizzerias, offering just two varieties (allegedly the only two worth eating) – marinara and margherita – for about €3. Don't arrive late, as they sometimes run out of dough. Mon–Sat 7pm–midnight.

★ **Di Matteo** Via dei Tribunali 94 ☎ 081 294 203; map p.744. One of the best and most famous pizzerias in the city, a bit low on atmosphere, but the enormous and mouthwatering pizzas more than make up for it – after all, when Bill Clinton was in town, this is where he came to sample proper Neapolitan pizza. Mon–Sat 7pm–midnight.

★ **I Decumani** Via dei Tribunali 58–61 ☎ 081 557 1309; map p.744. One of several excellent pizzerias along this stretch and commonly recognized as among Naples' best. The *fritti misti* are a must, as are the huge, delicious pizzas, which average €4–5, although prices start at €2.50 for a marinara. It's one of the few places in the *centro storico* open on Sundays too. Tues–Sun 11.30am–11pm.

★ **La Cantina di Via Sapienza** Via Sapienza 40–41 ☎ 081 459 078; map p.744. Proprietor Gaetano's no-nonsense food and service draws a busy lunch crowd to feast on hearty home-cooked classics like *polpette* (meatballs) and a staggering array of seasonal vegetable side dishes. Two courses will cost you €10–12. Mon–Sat noon–3pm.

La Stanza del Gusto Via Santa Maria di Costantinopoli 100 ☎ 081 401 578; map p.744. This busy one-room restaurant is the brainchild of local culinary innovator Mario Avallone, and serves a lovely menu of locally sourced, southern regional specialities. Go for a snack – they do great Sicilian toasted sandwiches – or a full meal; try the *tagliata di bufala* or *baccalà*. Moderate prices too. Tues–Sat 10.30am–midnight, Sun 11am–3pm.

Mimì alla Ferrovia Via A. d'Aragona 21 ☎ 081 57 6883; map pp.742–743. A real old-fashioned bustling restaurant and something of a haven in the none-too-desirable streets off Piazza Garibaldi, with good traditional Neapolitan food at reasonable prices – pasta dishes for €6, and mains for €10. Two courses will cost you €10–12. Mon–Sat noon–3pm & 8–11pm; closed two weeks in Aug.

★ **Osteria da Carmela** Via Conte di Ruovo 11/12 ☎ 081 549 9738; map p.744. Right next door to the Teatro Bellini, this is just one room, serving variations on traditional Neapolitan cuisine – great fish, excellent antipasti and tasty pasta and meat too, in an intimate and friendly environment. Mon–Sat noon–3pm & 8pm–midnight.

Sorbillo Via dei Tribunali 32 ☎ 081 446 643, ⓦ accademiadellapizza.it; map p.744. In business since 1935, this place has a cult following that snubs the family's newer pizza joint a few doors down. It's a scrum most nights and you may have to give your name and wait for a

table. But the pizzas are great, and use the highest-quality ingredients – a novel idea in the pizza business. Pizzas from €4. Mon–Sat 7pm–midnight.

★ **Trattoria Campagnola** Via dei Tribunali 47 ☎ 081 459 034, ⓦ campagnolatribunali.com; map p.744. Small, busy, and serving excellent, cheap Neapolitan food, with great *spaghetti alle vongole* and *sautè di cozze*, and hearty mains like *salsiccia* and *friarielli*, *cotolette* and *scaloppine*. Nothing fancy, but full of people happily scoffing delicious, well-priced grub. Mon & Sun 7.30–11pm, Wed–Sat noon–3pm & 7.30–11pm.

CHIAIA, SANTA LUCIA, MERGELLINA AND VOMERO

★ **Cantina di Triunfo** Riviera di Chiaia 64 ☎ 081 668 101, ⓦ lacantinaditriunfo.it; map pp.742–743. A wine shop by day that transforms into an inventive and contemporary restaurant at night, serving imaginative local cuisine in a long white room decorated with sculptural modern paintings. There's no menu, and a different choice each night – listen carefully if you speak some Italian, or just let them choose for you. Mon–Sat: shop 10.30am–2pm & 5.30–8pm; restaurant 8.30–11.45pm.

★ **Da Dora** Via Palasciano 30 ☎ 081 680 519; map pp.742–743. Not cheap, but perhaps the best place in the city to eat seafood and fish. One room, more or less, tiled and decorated in nautical fashion, and presided over by the implacable Dora in her pink pinny, who serves up wonderful seafood *linguine* and mixed fried fish. Mon–Sat 12.30pm–4pm & 8pm–midnight; closed Aug.

Da Ettore Via S. Lucia 56 ☎ 081 764 0498; map pp.742–743. In the heart of Santa Lucia, this casual and lively neighbourhood restaurant is famous for its *pagnotelle* (*calzone* stuffed with mozzarella, ham and mushrooms), and there is a wide selection of pizza and traditional pasta dishes too. Mon–Sat noon–3pm & 7.30–11pm.

Donna Teresa Via Kerbaker 58 ☎ 081 556 7070; map pp.742–743. One of the few vestiges of simple dining left in Vomero, where the food and setting are authentic and the prices honest. Expect to pay €12–15 for a full meal. Mon–Sat 1–3pm & 8–11pm.

Gorizia Via Bernini 29 ☎ 081 578 2248; map pp.742–743. This unpretentious Vomero restaurant is close to the Centrale and Chiaia funicular and does some of Vomero's best pizza, as well as a decent full menu. Tues–Sun 12.30–3pm & 8–11pm.

★ **Marino** Via S. Lucia 118 ☎ 081 764 0280; map pp.742–743. A warm and welcoming family-style place in Santa Lucia with good pizzas and reliable Neapolitan dishes. Not at all expensive – pasta dishes from around €7, pizzas from €5. Mon–Sat 12.30–3.30pm & 7.30–11.30pm.

Mattozzi Via Filangieri 16 ☎ 081 416 378, ⓦ pizzeria mattozzi.it; map pp.742–743. Long-standing Chiaia pizzeria that does great *fritti*, big chewy-crusted pizzas (from

€6, so not the cheapest) alongside pasta and main courses (around €10). Mon–Sat noon–4pm & 8–midnight.

Umberto Via Alabardieri 30–31 ☎081 418 555; map pp.742–743. A longtime popular choice among the professional classes of the Chiaia district, serving marvellous food in somewhat old-fashioned surroundings. Choose between a simple pizzeria and more upmarket restaurant. Mon 7–10pm, Tues–Sun 12.30–2.30pm & 7–10pm.

NIGHTLIFE AND ENTERTAINMENT

Neapolitan **nightlife** is largely concentrated in two neighbourhoods – the *centro storico* and the Chiaia district, with the latter in particular a buzzing concentration of bars and clubs well into the small hours – though many clubs close down for the summer from June to September, when they move out around the bay to Posillipo, Bacoli, Fusaro or Pozzuoli. For **listings** of Naples nightlife, pick up *Zero* (⊛zero.eu) or *Urban*, free monthly publications available in bars, or for big events see ⊛angelsoflove.it, Italy's answer to the Ministry of Sound.

BARS AND CLUBS

Barcadero Banchina S. Lucia 2 ☎081 222 7023; map pp.742–743. The perfect place for an evening *aperitivo*, right on the harbour by the Castel dell'Ovo. There's quite a scene here early evening – take the steps down from the causeway to the castle. Daily 6pm–2am.

Bourbon Street Via Bellini 52/53 ☎338 825 3756, ⊛bourbonstreetjazzclub.com; map p.744. A premier venue for Italian and international jazz acts, bringing a slice of American jazz culture to the heart of Naples' *centro storico*. Tues–Sun 9pm–3am; closed June–Aug.

Enoteca Belledonne Vico Belledonne a Chiaia 18 ☎081 403 162, ⊛enotecabelledonne.com; map pp.742–743. Right in the heart of the Chiaia bar scene, this unpretentious *enoteca* serves an exhaustive collection of Italian wines and delicious selections of cheeses and *salumi* – and without the full-on noise of its nearby rivals. Daily 6pm–2am; closed Aug.

Intra Moenia Piazza Bellini 70; map p.744. One of several trendy haunts on Piazza Bellini, where tables spread across the square. A lovely place to sit and read under the wisteria on a sunny day, or for an early evening aperitif. Substantial snacks and fancy ice creams are served, and there's free wi-fi too. Daily 10am–2am.

Kinky Klub Via della Quercia 26 ☎335 547 7299, ⊛kinkyjam.com; map p.744. Contrary to what the name might suggest, this popular bar just off Via Toledo is Naples' home for reggae, rocksteady, dancehall and ska. Tues–Sun 9pm–4am; closed mid-June to mid-Sept.

Lontano Da Dove Via Bellini 3 ☎081 549 4304; map p.744. A bookstore, tearoom and literary café all rolled into one, with live performances of mostly jazz and blues, held three nights a week. Very comfy – lots of cushions and low-level tables. Mon, Tues & Thurs 10.30am–1pm & 5–8pm, Wed, Fri & Sat 10.30am–1pm & 5pm–1.30am; closed July & Aug.

Seventy Via Bisignano 19 ☎081 1956 6482; map pp.742–743. There's a decent early-evening buffet at this cool, white glitterball bar, playing thumping garage to a cool or just plain hungry clientele. Collapse onto a white leather sofa and try not to make a mess. Daily 6.30pm–2am.

Vinarium Vicolo S. Maria a Cappella Vecchia 7 ☎081 764 4114; map pp.742–743. Busy wine bar just off Piazza dei Martiri that has a good selection of wines and serves food from an ever-changing menu. Mon–Sat 11am–4pm & 7pm–1am.

Virgilio Club Via Tito Lucrezio Caro 6 ☎081 575 5261, ⊛virgilioclub.it; map pp.742–743. Immersed in the greenery of the Parco Virgiliano on the slopes of Posillipo, this place gets jam-packed on summer nights when they open a leafy terrace overlooking the bay. Entry from €20. June to mid-Oct Wed–Sun 10pm–4am; opening variable in winter.

DIRECTORY

Consulates Canada, Via Carducci 29 (☎081 401 338); South Africa, Via Stendhal 23 (☎081 552 5835); UK, Via dei Mille 40 (☎081 423 8911); US, Piazza della Repubblica 2 (☎081 583 8111).

FOOTBALL IN NAPLES

Football is something of a religion in Naples, and support for the local side, **Napoli**, reached its pinnacle in the 1987 season when they won the *scudetto* with Diego Maradona as their star player. Their following is not quite as fanatical as it was, and the team dropped down two divisions after going bankrupt. However, they have recently been rescued by the movie mogul Aurelio De Laurentiis and are thriving once more in the top flight. Napoli play at the **Stadio di San Paolo** in Fuorigrotta; take the Ferrovia Cumana from Montesanto to Mostra and the stadium is right in front of you. Tickets, available from the offices at the ground or from the club's outlets in town, cost from around €20 for seats in the end stands or "Curve", up to €60 in the side or "Tribuna" stands.

13

Hospital To call an ambulance, dial ☎118. The most central hospitals with A&E departments are Ascalesi, Via Egiziaca Forcella 31 (☎081 563 221); Cardarelli, Via Cardarelli 9 (☎081 747 1111); and Santa Maria di Loreto, Via Vespucci 86 (☎081 254 2711).

Internet *Intra Moenia* on Piazza Bellini (see p.761) has free wi-fi if your hotel doesn't.

Laundry Bolle Blu, Corso Novara 62–64, just up from the Stazione Centrale (Mon–Sat 8.30am–8pm).

Pharmacies The pharmacy at Napoli Centrale is open

24hr and there's a list of those open at night in the newspaper *Il Mattino*.

Police ☎112 or ☎113; you can speak to an operator in English. The main police station (*questura*) is at Via Medina 5 (☎081 794 1111); you can also report crimes at the small police station in the Stazione Centrale. To report the theft of a car, call ☎081 794 1435.

Post office The main post office is in the enormous building on Piazza Matteotti, just off Via Toledo (Mon–Sat 8.15am–7.20pm).

The Bay of Naples

Naples spreads right around its **bay** in an almost unbroken ribbon of docks, housing and development whose appeal is hard to discern, and only really becomes apparent the further away from the city you get. It's one of the most geologically unstable regions in the world, a fact that becomes obvious west of the city, where volcanic craters, hot springs and fumaroles make up the area known as the **Campi Flegrei**, the Phlegrean Fields of classical times, a mysterious place in turn mythologized by Homer and Virgil as the entrance to Hades. These days most of the mystery is gone – like most of the bay, the presence of Naples dominates in the form of new, mostly illegal, construction – and much of the volcanic activity is extinct, or at least dormant. But parts of the area still retain some of the doomy associations that first drew the ancients here, and there are some substantial remains of their presence at **Pozzuoli**, **Baia** and **Cumae**. In the opposite direction, the coast east from Naples is even more built up, the Circumvesuviana train edging out through derelict industrial buildings and dense housing that squeezes ever closer to the track. Most people come here for the ancient sights of **Herculaneum** and **Pompeii**, or to scale **Vesuvius** – or they skip the lot for the resort town of **Sorrento**. All are easy day-trips, and Sorrento, though overdeveloped, is worth a little more time and makes a good springboard for seeing some of the Amalfi Coast.

Pozzuoli

Heading west, the first town that can really be considered free of Naples' sprawl is **POZZUOLI**, which sits on a stout promontory jutting out from the slender crescent of volcanic hills behind. Despite achieving some glamour as the home town of Sophia Loren, it's an ordinary little place, nothing special but likeable enough, with ferry connections to the islands of Procida and Ischia. And although you wouldn't want to stay here (unless you're a camper; see "Accommodation", opposite), it's a good first stop before travelling on to the rest of the Campi Flegrei.

Pozzuoli has suffered more than most of the towns around here from the area's volcanic activity and subsidence is still a major – and carefully monitored – problem. In town there are a number of well-preserved relics of the Romans' liking for the place.

Temple of Serapide

Beyond the Cumana station, between Via Roma and Via Sacchini, just east of the port, the so-called **Temple of Serapide** sits enclosed within a small park, often flooded in winter, but otherwise accessible. Its name derives from the unearthing here of a statue of the Pluto-esque Egyptian god, *Serapis Enthroned* (now in the Naples archeological museum), but in fact the structure has since proved to be not a temple but a richly embellished produce-market from the first to the third centuries AD, one of the largest known to have been excavated.

13

Anfiteatro Flavio

Via Terracciano 75 • Mon & Wed–Sun 9am–1hr before sunset • €4 combined ticket with Cumae and the Parco Archeologico and Museo Archeologico in Baia (valid 48hr)

Pozzuoli's best-known sight is the **Antifeatro Flavio**, just north of the centre, which was at one time the third largest Roman amphitheatre in Italy, holding some 20,000 spectators. It's still reasonably intact, though visitors are not allowed on the seating area: the subterranean chambers for gladiators and wild beasts are especially complete, and lying around everywhere is an abundance of beautifully carved architectural fragments.

Solfatara

Via Solfatara 161 • Daily: 8.30am–1 hour before dusk • €6.50 • ⓦ solfatara.it • A 10min walk up the hill from the metropolitana/FS station; buses #152 and #M1 also stop outside

Just north of town, the **Solfatara** is further, and tangible, evidence of the volcanic nature of the Pozzuoli area, the exposed crater of a semi-extinct volcano – into which you can walk – that hasn't erupted for a couple of thousand years; in fact, it was a major tourist attraction in Roman times, too. Not surprisingly, it's a weird place: sulphur fumes rise from the rocks around and the grey-yellow ground is hot to the touch (and sounds hollow underfoot), emitting eerily silent jets or fumaroles that leave the air pungent with sulphurous fumes. In the 1800s some of the fumaroles were covered with brick, creating an almost unbearably warm, sauna-like environment into which you can bend if you can stand it, while others are just left open.

ARRIVAL AND INFORMATION

POZZUOLI

By train You can get to Pozzuoli from Naples on the metropolitana, or on the Ferrovia Cumana line from Montesanto station; both take about 20min; the Cumana station is in the centre of town, not far from the Temple of Serapis, so makes more sense if you're visiting the town only. The metropolitana/FS station is situated above the main part of Pozzuoli, off Via Solfatara, a 10min walk from the port, and so is better if you're just going to see the Solfatara.

By bus Buses #152 and #M1 also run direct to Pozzuoli from Piazza Garibaldi, stopping right outside the Solfatara before descending to the town centre.

Tourist office A little east of the port at Piazza Matteotti 1/A (Mon–Sat 9am–3.30pm; ☎081 526 6639, ⓦ info campiflegrei.it).

ACCOMMODATION

Hotel Solfatara Via Solfatara 163 ☎081 526 2666, ⓦ hotelsolfatara.it. Conveniently situated right by the bus stop on the corner of the street that leads to the volcano, this is a pleasant, modern place, with handsome, well-appointed guestrooms and good views of the bay. **€85**

Vulcano Solfatara Via Solfatara 161 ☎081 526 7413, ⓦsolfatara.i; from Naples take the metropolitana to Pozzuoli and walk 10min up the hill. Excellent campsite at the entrance to the Solfatara with tent pitches, double bungalows, a large swimming pool, grocery store and a snack bar/restaurant. Perhaps the best base for Naples if you're camping. Open all year. Pitches **€25**, bungalows **€48**

EATING AND DRINKING

Bobo Via Cristoforo Colombo 20 ☎081 526 2034. Moderate- to high-priced harbourside restaurant which does great fish and has an excellent wine list to go with it. Try the pasta with sea urchins or with mussels and broccoli. The perfect end to a morning at the market. 12.30–2.30pm & 7.30–10pm; closed Tues.

Don Antonio Via Magazzini ☎081 526 7941. Perhaps the best-value fish restaurant in Pozzuoli, an unpretentious place, with great *fritti misti* and seafood pasta dishes at very reasonable prices. Follow the quayside round the ferry dock and it's on the left, just past the Toscano *gelateria*. Tues–Sun noon–2pm & 7.30–9.30pm.

Baia

The next town along from Pozzuoli is **Baia**, a small port with a set of imperial-era Roman ruins piling up on the hill above. This was one of the bay's most favoured spots in Roman times, a trendy resort at which all the most fashionable of the city's patricians had villas: the Emperor Hadrian died here in 138 AD and Nero was rumoured to have murdered his mother in Baia.

13

Parco Archeologico

Tues–Sun 9am–1hr before sunset • €4 combined ticket with Cumae, the Museo Archeologico and the Anfiteatro Flavio di Pozzuoli • ☎ 081 868 7592, ⓦ archeobaia.sbanap.campaniabeniculturali.it

Baia's extensive **Parco Archeologico** lies at the top of a flight of steps off the main street. It's in fact a collection of different buildings from various eras – from the first century BC to the third century AD – but it's evocative for all that and quiet even in season, with plenty of shade and seats to rest on. Structured across several levels, it consists principally of a central villa with the remains of baths on either side. The villa has a series of rooms arched around a central fountain and what would have been a large courtyard below, around which you can see traces of frescoes and, beyond, a well-preserved stretch of mosaic floor. Beyond here is a small baths complex but the real treat lies on the other side, through an arched corridor – a wonderfully intact, domed frigidarium from the first century BC, water-filled and hauntingly atmospheric in the filtered sunlight.

Museo Archeologico

Via Castello 39 • Tues–Sun 9am–2.30pm • €4 combined ticket with Parco Archeologico, Cumae and Anfiteatro Flavio di Pozzuoli • ⓦ museoarcheologicocampiflegrei.campaniabeniculturali.it

Many of the finds from Baia and around are in the **Museo Archeologico**, housed in part of the town's mammoth fifteenth-century Aragon castle, a fifteen-minute walk up the main road towards Bacoli. Among the finds on display here is a *sacellum* – a shrine dedicated to the imperial cult – from the forum of ancient Misenum on Capo Miseno, rebuilt here on the ground floor, and a *nymphaeum* or monumental fountain, partially reconstructed on the top floor.

Cumae

Via Monte di Cuma 3, Località Cuma • Daily 9am–1hr before sunset • €4 combined ticket with the Parco Archeologico di Terme di Baia, Museo Archeologico and Anfiteatro Flavio di Pozzuoli • ☎ 081 804 0430

Further up the coast from Baia, the town of **Cumae** was the first Greek colony on the Italian mainland, a source of settlers for other colonies (Naples was originally settled by Greeks from Cumae) and a centre of Hellenistic civilization. Later it was home to the so-called Cumaean Sibyl, from whom Tarquinius purchased the Sibylline Books that laid down the laws for the Republic. The **site**, a short walk from the bus stop, is spread over a large area and not at all comprehensively excavated. But the only part you're likely to want to see forms a tight nucleus close to the entrance.

Grotto of the Sibyl

The best-known feature is the **Grotto of the Sibyl**, a long, dark corridor that was home to the most famous of the ancient oracles. The cave is rectangular in shape, with light admitted from a series of openings in the western wall; the Sibyl used to dispense her wisdom from the three large chambers at the far end of the 40ft passageway, the most famous occasion being when Aeneas came here to consult her – an event recorded by the lines of Virgil posted up either side of the entrance.

The acropolis and temple to Jupiter

Steps lead up from the Sibyl's cave to the main part of the site, where the Via Sacra winds past a belvedere on the left and the scanty remains of a temple of Apollo at the centre of Cumae's old **acropolis** on the right. Keep going and you'll find the remains of a **temple to Jupiter** at the summit of the hill, with tremendous views south across the shellfish-filled **Lago Fusaro** and the bottom corner of the coast; and, if you clamber down from the far side of the temple, north up the curving coast to the Gulf of Gaeta.

FROM TOP SORRENTO (P.770); PIZZA IN NAPLES (P.759); HERCULANEUM (P.766) >

13

Herculaneum

Daily: April–Oct 8.30am–7.30pm; Nov–March 8.30am–5pm • €11, combined ticket for 5 sites including Pompeii valid 3 days, €20 • ☎ 081 857 347, ⓦ pompeiisites.org

East of Naples the first real point of any interest is the town of **Ercolano**, the modern offshoot of the ancient site of **HERCULANEUM**, which was destroyed by the eruption of Vesuvius on August 24, 79 AD, and is situated at the seaward end of the town's main street.

The site

After the ticket office, but before you enter the city proper, there is a new pavilion housing the remains of a boat which archeologists have surmised was thrown onto the beach by the force of the earthquake and smashed against the ruins of houses. As well as the boat, and a serpent prow, finds include a coil of rope and a leather sheet (with signs of stitching) fused to scorched wooden planks.

Cardo III

Because Herculaneum wasn't a commercial town, there was no central open space or forum, just streets of villas and shops, cut as usual by two very straight main thoroughfares that cross in the centre. Start your tour just inside the entrance at the bottom end of **Cardo III**, where you'll see the **House of the Argus** (Casa d'Argo) on the left, a very grand building judging by its once-impressive courtyard – although upstaged by the so-called **Hotel** (Casa del Albergo) across the street, which covers a huge area, though you can only really get a true impression of its size from the rectangle of stumpy columns that made up its atrium.

Cardo IV

Further up, Cardo III joins the Decumanus Inferiore, just beyond which is the large **Thermae** or bath complex on the corner of Cardo IV – the domed frigidarium of its men's section decorated with a floor mosaic of dolphins, its caldarium containing a plunge bath and a scallop-shell apse. Still intact are the benches where people sat and the wooden, partitioned shelves for clothing. On the far side of the baths, the **House of Neptune and Amphitrite** (Casa di Nettuno ed Anfitrite) holds sparklingly preserved and richly ornamental wall mosaics. Adjacent is the **House of the Beautiful Courtyard** (Casa del Bel Cortile) where skeletons of bodies still lie in the positions they fell. From here you can stroll back down to the seaward end of Cardo IV, where the **House of the Wooden Partition** still has its original partition doors (now under glass).

DISCOVERING HERCULANEUM

The site of Herculaneum was discovered in 1709, when a well-digger accidentally struck the stage of the buried theatre. Excavations were undertaken throughout the eighteenth and nineteenth centuries, during which period much of the marble and bronze from the site was carted off to Naples to decorate the city's palaces, and it wasn't until 1927 that digging and preservation began in earnest. Herculaneum was a residential town, much smaller than Pompeii, and as such it makes a more manageable site, less architecturally impressive but better preserved and more easily taken in on a single visit. Archeologists held for a long time that unlike in Pompeii, on the other side of the volcano, most of the inhabitants of Herculaneum managed to escape. However, recent discoveries of entangled skeletons found at what was the shoreline of the town suggest otherwise, and it's now believed that most of the population was buried by huge avalanches of volcanic mud, which later hardened into the tufa-type rock that preserved much of the town so well. In early 2000 the remains of another 48 people were found; they were carrying coins, which suggests they were attempting to flee the disaster.

13

Cardo V

Turning right at the top of Cardo IV takes you around to **Cardo V** and most of the rest of the town's **shops** – including a baker's, complete with ovens and grinding mills, a weaver's, with loom and bones, and a dyer's, with a huge pot for dyes. Behind the ones on the left you can see the **Palestra**, where public games were held, opposite which there's a well-preserved **Taverna** with counters and, further down Cardo V on the right, another tavern, the **Taverna del Priapo**, with a priapic painting behind its counter.

Further down Cardo V, the **House of the Deer** (Casa dei Cervi) was another luxury villa, its two storeys built around a central courtyard and containing corridors decorated with richly coloured still-lifes. From here, the end of Cardo V, the path descends under a covered passageway down to the so-called **Suburban Baths** on the left: one of the most impressive – and intact – structures in Herculaneum, complete with extremely well-preserved stuccowork and a pretty much intact set of baths; it also has a complete original Roman door, the only one in Herculaneum that wasn't charred by fire.

Mount Vesuvius

Since its first eruption in 79 AD, when it buried the towns and inhabitants of Pompeii and Herculaneum, **Mount Vesuvius** (1281m) has dominated the lives of those who live on the Bay of Naples, its brooding bulk forming a stately backdrop to the ever-growing settlements that group around its lower slopes. It's still an active volcano, the only one on mainland Europe. There have been more than a hundred eruptions over the years, but only two others of real significance – one in December 1631 that engulfed many nearby towns and killed 3000 people; and the last, in March 1944, which caused widespread devastation in the towns around, though no one was actually killed. The people who live here still fear the reawakening of the volcano, and with good cause – scientists calculate it should erupt every thirty years or so, and it hasn't since 1944. It's carefully monitored, of course, and there is apparently no reason to expect any movement for some time. But the subsidence in towns like Ercolano below is a continuing reminder of the instability of the area, one of southern Italy's most densely populated: around half a million people would be immediately threatened by another eruption.

The ascent

Daily: Jan & Feb, Nov & Dec 9am–3pm; March & Oct 9am–4pm; April & May, June & Sept 9am–5pm; July & Aug 9am–6pm • €6.50 • ⓦ parks.it/parco.nazionale.vesuvio/Eindex.php or ⓦ vesuvioinrete.it

You have to pay to make the **ascent** to the crater from the car park, and it takes between twenty and thirty minutes depending on how fit you are. It's a stony and mildly strenuous stroll across reddened, barren gravel and rock along a marked-out path that nowadays is roped off to minimize the chance of stumbling and falling down the sheer drop to the right. At the top is a deep, wide, jagged ashtray of red rock swirled over by

---

MOUNTAIN VIEWS WITHOUT THE EFFORT

If you want to look down across the whole Bay of Naples but don't fancy sweating your way up Vesuvius, head a few kilometres further around the bay to Castellammare di Stabia. Here you can take a **funivia** or cable car up to the top of 1100m-high **Monte Faito** (daily every 20–30min: mid-June to Aug 7.25am–7.15pm; Sept to mid-June 9.35am–4.25pm; €7.60 return, children €2.90, July & Aug & Sun €8.20), only an eight-minute journey but even so definitely not for those of a delicate disposition, giving increasingly stupendous views of the bay and of the deepening gulf between you and the tree-filled hillside below. At the top, there are a couple of bars selling drinks and sandwiches, and if you really can't face the trip down, it's comforting to know that several roads meet here and there's a Circumvesuviana bus-stop nearby.

midges and emitting the odd plume of smoke, though since the last eruption effectively sealed up the main crevice, this is much less evident than it once was. There's also a small kiosk selling drinks and trinkets, and the path continues halfway around the crater so you can get a view from the other side – a further fifteen minutes or so on foot.

ARRIVAL AND DEPARTURE | VESUVIUS

From Ercolano There are three ways of getting to the crater from Ercolano: take a taxi from the train station (served by Circumvesuviana trains) – it's a drive of a little over 30min and the return journey (with waiting driver) will cost a highly negotiable €30–40; take a minibus taxi from the station, which charges a flat return fare of €15 per person – but you have to wait at either end until the bus is full; or pick up one of the buses from Pompeii that go via Ercolano station (see below).

From Pompeii EAVBus buses leave roughly hourly from Pompeii's main station and Piazza Anfiteatro between 8am and 3.30pm; the journey takes just over an hour and the last

bus back is at 4.40pm; tickets cost €10 return. Two of the buses go via Ercolano CS station, leaving there at 8.25am and 12.45pm; tickets from there cost €7.60. There are also excursions run by Busvia del Vesuvio – ⓦ busviadelvesuvio .com – which leave hourly between 9am and 3pm from Pompeii-Villa dei Misteri station or Boscoreale, from where you take a truck to within 600m of the summit.

From Naples There are two buses daily from Piazza Garibaldi (*Hotel Terminus*) – at 9.25am and 10.40am, taking 1hr 30min and returning at 12.30pm and 2pm respectively. The taxi fare from Naples city centre to Vesuvius is a fixed €90, which includes a 2hr wait.

Pompeii

The other Roman town to be destroyed by Vesuvius – **POMPEII** – was a much larger affair than Herculaneum and one of Campania's most important commercial centres – a moneyed resort for wealthy patricians and a trading town that exported wine and fish. In effect the eruption froze the town's way of life as it stood at the time; indeed the excavations have probably yielded more information about the ordinary life of Roman citizens during the imperial era than anywhere else: their social conventions, class structure, domestic arrangements and (very high) standard of living. Some of the buildings are even covered with ancient graffiti, either referring to contemporary political events or simply to the romantic entanglements of the inhabitants; and the full horror of their way of death is apparent in plaster casts made from the shapes their bodies left in the volcanic ash – with faces tortured with agony, or shielding themselves from the dust and ashes.

The first parts of ancient Pompeii were discovered in 1600, but it wasn't until 1748 that **excavations** began, continuing more or less without interruption until the present day. Indeed, exciting discoveries are still being made. A privately funded excavation some years ago revealed a covered heated swimming pool, whose erotic wall paintings have been deemed by the Vatican to be unsuitable for children. And, in a further development, a luxury "hotel" complex was uncovered in 2000 during the widening of a motorway, slabs of stacked cut marble suggesting it was still under construction when Vesuvius erupted. Recently, a flood of new funds is being used to excavate a further twenty hectares of the site; it is hoped to resolve whether or not the survivors attempted, vainly, to resettle Pompeii after the eruption.

24 AUGUST, 79 AD: THE DAY POMPEII DIED

Vesuvius had been spouting smoke and ash for several days before the eruption on 24 August. Fortunately most of Pompeii had already been evacuated when disaster struck: out of a total population of 20,000 it's thought that only 2000 actually perished, asphyxiated by the toxic fumes of the volcanic debris, their homes buried in several metres of volcanic ash and pumice. Pliny, the Roman naturalist, was one of the casualties – he died at nearby Stabiae (now Castellammare) of a heart attack. But his nephew, Pliny the Younger, described the full horror of the scene in two vivid letters to the historian Tacitus, who was compiling a history of the disaster, writing that the sky turned dark like "a room when it is shut up, and the lamp put out".

The site

Daily: April–Oct 8.30am–7.30pm, last entry 6pm; Nov–March 8.30am–5pm, last entry 3.30pm • €11, combined ticket for 5 sites including also Herculaneum, valid 3 days €20 • ☎ 081 857 5347, ⓦ pompeiisites.org

The **site** covers a wide area, and seeing it properly takes half a day at the very least; really you should devote most of a day to it and take plenty of breaks – unlike Herculaneum there's little shade, and the distances involved are quite large: flat, comfortable shoes are a must.

All of this makes Pompeii sound a bit of a chore – which it certainly isn't. But there is a lot to see, and you should be reasonably selective: many of the streets aren't lined by much more than foundations, and after a while one ruin begins to look much like another. Again, many of the most interesting structures are kept locked and only opened when a large group forms or a tip is handed over to one of the many custodians. It's worth studying the **site map**, which you'll find at every entrance – pins on the map indicate which areas are currently closed, as the site is in continuous restoration. To be sure of seeing as much as possible you could take a tour, although one of the pleasures of Pompeii is to escape the hordes and absorb the strangely still quality of the town, which, despite the large number of visitors, it is quite possible to do.

The western sector: from the Forum to the House of the Vettii

Entering the site from the Pompcii-Villa dei Misteri side, through the Porta Marina, the **Forum** is the first real feature of significance, a long, slim, open space surrounded by the ruins of what would have been some of the town's most important official buildings – a basilica, temples to Apollo and Jupiter, and a market hall. Walking north from here, up the so-called Via di Mercurio, takes you towards some of the town's more luxurious houses. On the left, the **House of the Tragic Poet** (Casa del Poetica Tragico) is named for its mosaics of a theatrical production and a poet inside, though the "Cave Canem" (Beware of the Dog) mosaic by the main entrance is more eye-catching. Close by, the residents of the **House of the Faun** (Casa del Fauno) must have been a friendlier lot, its "Ave" (Welcome) mosaic outside beckoning you in to view the atrium and the copy of a tiny, bronze, dancing faun (the original is in Naples) that gives the villa its name.

On the street behind, the **House of the Vettii** (Casa dei Vettii) is one of the most delightful houses in Pompeii and one of the best maintained, a merchant villa ranged around a lovely central peristyle that gives the best possible impression of the domestic environment of the city's upper middle classes. The first room on the right off the peristyle holds some of the best of Pompeii's murals: the one on the left shows the young Hercules struggling with serpents. There are more paintings beyond here, through the villa's kitchen in a small room that's normally kept locked – erotic works showing various techniques of lovemaking together with an absurdly potent-looking statue of Priapus from which women were supposed to drink to be fertile.

The eastern sector: the Grand Theatre to the Amphitheatre

Cross over to the other side of the site for the so-called **new excavations**, which began in 1911 and actually uncovered some of the town's most important quarters. The **Grand Theatre**, for one, is very well preserved and is still used for performances, overlooking the small, grassy, column-fringed square of the **Samnite Palestra** – a refectory and meeting-place for spectators from the theatre. Walk around to the far left side of the Grand Theatre, down the steps and up again, and you're in front of the **Little Theatre** – a smaller, more intimate venue also still used for summer performances and with a better-kept corridor behind the stage space. Walk up from here to rejoin the Via dell' Abbondanza, where there's lots of interest – the Lararium has a niche with a delicate relief showing scenes from the Trojan War; the **Fullonica Stephani** is a well-preserved laundry, with a large tiered tub for washing; the **House of the Venus in**

13

the **Shell** is named after the excellently preserved painting on its back wall; while next door, the **House of Octavius Quartio** is a gracious villa fronted by great bronze doors, with paintings of Narcissus gazing rapt at his reflection in the villa's lovely garden, which has been replanted with vines and shrubs.

Just beyond here is the town's **Amphitheatre** – one of Italy's most intact and accessible, and also its oldest, dating from 80 BC; it once had room for a crowd of some 12,000 – well over half the town's population. Next door, the **Palestra** is a vast parade ground that was used by Pompeii's youth for sport and exercise – still with its square of swimming pool in the centre. It must have been in use when the eruption struck Pompeii, since its southeast corner was found littered with the skeletons of young men trying to flee the disaster.

Villa dei Misteri

One last place you shouldn't miss at Pompeii is the **Villa dei Misteri**. This is probably the best preserved of all Pompeii's palatial houses, an originally third-century-BC structure with a warren of rooms and courtyards that derives its name from a series of paintings in one of its larger chambers: depictions of the initiation rites of a young woman into the Dionysiac Mysteries, an outlawed cult of the early imperial era. Not much is known about the cult itself, but the paintings are marvellously clear, remarkable for the surety of their execution and the brightness of their tones and colours.

ARRIVAL AND INFORMATION	POMPEII

By train The Circumvesuviana from Naples to Pompeii-Villa dei Misteri (40min) leaves you right outside the western, Porta Marina entrance to the site.

Tourist office Via Sacra 1, just off the modern town's main square (Mon–Sat 9am–6pm; ☎ 081 850 7255).

ACCOMMODATION

Camping Pompei Via Plinio 113, south of the main entrance ☎ 081 862 2882, ⓦ campingpompei.com. This site offers double bungalows as well as tent pitches. Open all year. Pitches around €22, bungalows around €45

Casa del Pellegrino Via Duca d'Aosta 4 ☎ 081 850 8644, ⓦ hostelspoint.com. Youth hostel situated in the centre of modern Pompeii, a 10min walk from the Piazza Anfiteatro entrance. Meals are available for €9. Dorms €19

Sorrento

Topping the rocky cliffs close to the end of its peninsula, 25km south of Pompeii, the last town of significance on this side of the bay, **SORRENTO** is solely and unashamedly a resort, its inspired location and mild climate drawing foreigners from all over Europe for close on two hundred years. Ibsen wrote part of *Peer Gynt* in Sorrento, Wagner and Nietzsche had a well-publicized row here, and Maxim Gorky lived for over a decade in the town. Nowadays it's strictly package-tour territory, but not too much the worse for it, with little of the brashness of its Spanish and Greek equivalents but all of their vigour, a bright, lively place that retains its southern-Italian roots. Cheap restaurants aren't too hard to find, nor – if you know where to look – is reasonably priced accommodation; and it's a handy place outside Naples itself from which to explore the rugged peninsula (even parts of the Amalfi Coast) and the islands of the bay.

Piazza Tasso

Sorrento's centre is **Piazza Tasso**, built astride the gorge that runs through the centre of town; it was named after the wayward sixteenth-century Italian poet to whom the town was home and has a statue of him in the far corner. There's nothing much to see in the town itself, but it's nice to wander through the streets that feed into the square, some of which are pedestrianized for the lively evening *passeggiata*. **Via San Cesareo** forms a backbone to the small grid of streets, most of them lined with shops selling tourist gear and *limoncello*.

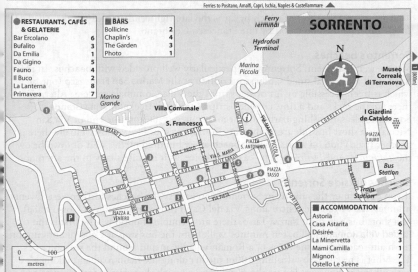

SORRENTO

● RESTAURANTS, CAFÉS	
& GELATERIE	
Bar Ercolano	6
Bufalito	3
Da Emilia	1
Da Gigino	5
Fauno	4
Il Buco	2
La Lanterna	8
Primavera	7

■ BARS	
Bollicine	2
Chaplin's	4
The Garden	3
Photo	1

■ ACCOMMODATION	
Astoria	4
Casa Astarita	6
Désirée	2
La Minervetta	3
Mami Camilla	1
Mignon	7
Ostello Le Sirene	5

Villa Comunale and San Francesco

It's worth strolling down from here to linger in the shady gardens of the **Villa Comunale**, whose terrace has lovely views out to sea. Off to the right, you can also peek into the small thirteenth-century cloister of the church of **San Francesco** just outside, planted with vines and bright bougainvillea – a peaceful escape from the bustle of the rest of Sorrento.

Corso Italia and the Cattedrale

Corso Italia 1 • Daily 8am–12.30pm & 4.30–8.30pm • Free

Skirting the northern edge of the old town, Sorrento's main artery is **Corso Italia**, and this is also pedestrianized every evening after 7pm for the lively evening *passeggiata*. A little way down on the left, Sorrento's **Cattedrale** has been much rebuilt, and the real challenge of its gaudy interior is how to tell the fake marble from the real. The bishop's throne, on the main aisle, is certainly authentic, dating from the late sixteenth century, as are the inlaid wood scenes on the main doors and choir stalls, which add a genuine Sorrentine touch. Take a look also at the large *presepe* just inside the main doors, and the chapel in the left aisle, which is dedicated to San Giuseppe Moscati – a Neapolitan doctor who died in 1927 and is venerated in Naples' Gesù church (see p.748).

Museo Bottega della Tarsialignea

Via San Nicola 28 • Daily 10am–6.30pm • €8

The **Museo Bottega della Tarsialignea**, housed in an ancient mansion in the artisanal quarter of the old town, is a shrine to Sorrento's craft speciality of inlaid woodwork – cheap and pretty awful examples of which you see all over town. Don't let the tourist tat put you off: the ground floor here has some clever and stylish examples of contemporary *intarsio* work (it's for sale, but not at all cheap), while upstairs displays the work of Sorrento's late nineteenth-century *intarsio* greats.

Museo Correale di Terranova

Via Correale 50 • Mon, Thurs, Fri & Sun 9.30am–1.30pm, Wed 9.30am–6pm, Sat 9.30am–1.30pm & 6–10pm • €6

On the western edge of town, the local **Museo Correale di Terranova**, housed in the airy former palace of a family of local counts at the far end of Via Correale, has more examples of *intarsio*, various Roman finds, along with a lot of badly lit paintings by

13

local artists upstairs, best of which by far is the late eighteenth-century roulette game, *Il Biri Bisso*, painted on wood by one Francesco Celebrano.

Sorrento's beaches

Strange as it may seem, Sorrento isn't particularly well provided with **beaches**. In the town itself are several small sandy strips of lido at the **Marina San Francesco** (one of which is free), accessible by lift or steps from the Villa Comunale gardens. Alternatively there are the rocks and a tiny, crowded strip of sand (all free) at **Marina Grande**, Sorrento's pleasant fishing harbour, fifteen minutes' walk from the end of Via San Nicola or a short bus ride (roughly every 30min) west of Piazza Tasso. Finally there is another (paid) lido on a small, stony **beach** a few hundred metres west of town below the *Tonnarella* and *Désirée* hotels – a good choice, as it is quite shady in the afternoon.

Beaches outside Sorrento

If you don't fancy the crowds in Sorrento, you can try the beaches further west. Twenty minutes' walk from the centre along Via del Capo (the continuation of Corso Italia), or a short bus ride from Piazza Tasso, there are a couple of options. The first is the **Ruderi Villa Romana Pollio**, ten minutes' walk from the bus stop at Capo di Sorrento on the main road, where the ruins of a Roman villa lie on and around the seashore rocks. The other is reachable by strolling 100m further along the main road and taking a path off to the right just before the *Hotel Dania*, which shortcuts in ten minutes or so to the **Marina di Puolo**, a short stretch of mainly sandy beach lined by fishing boats and a handful of trattorias, perhaps the best place to swim just outside Sorrento.

In the opposite direction, the adjacent-but-one town of **Meta** is home to **Alimuri** beach – two decent-sized stretches of grey sand that face away from each other on a small spit that sticks out from the high-sided cliffs of the bay here. A lift can deliver you there from the road above, or you can drive down to a small car park.

ARRIVAL AND DEPARTURE   SORRENTO

By train Sorrento's train station is in the centre of town, a 5min walk from the main Piazza Tasso along busy Corso Italia.

By bus The bus station – for buses to the Amalfi Coast and the airport – is just in front of the train station.

Destinations Amalfi (18 daily; 1hr 30min); Naples (1 daily at 6.40pm; 1hr 15min); Naples Capodichino airport (6 daily; 1hr); Positano (18 daily; 1hr 5min); Salerno (12 daily; 2hr 45min).

INFORMATION AND GETTING AROUND

By bus There are several (orange) bus routes around the town and surrounding area, including line #A between Meta, Piano, Sant'Agnello and Sorrento itself, line #B from the train station to Marine Piccola, via Piazza Tasso, and line #D between Marina Grande and Piazza Tasso.

Moped and scooter rental Jolly Service & Rent (Ⓦ jollyrent.eu) has outlets at both ends of town – Via degli Aranci 180 (Ⓣ 081 877 3450) and Corso Italia 3 (Ⓣ 081 878 2403); rates start at €32/day, €150/week.

Mini-train tours You can walk pretty much everywhere

in Sorrento, but if you want a bit of easy orientation, take one of the mini-train tours that leave every 35min from Piazza Tasso (daily 9am–midnight; €6, children €3); tours last about 30min.

Tourist office Just off Piazza Sant'Antonino in the large yellow Circolo dei Forestieri building, Via Luigi de Maio 35 (Mon–Sat 8.30am–4.15pm; Ⓣ 081 807 4033, Ⓦ sorrento tourism.com). During summer there are also staffed "info points" all around town, including one just off Piazza Tasso, another outside the train station and a third on Piazza Veniero.

ACCOMMODATION

★ **Astoria** Via S. Maria delle Grazie 24 Ⓣ 081 807 4030, Ⓦ hotelastoriasorrento.com. It's unusual to find a hotel right in the heart of old Sorrento, and this place is quite special, with reasonably sized doubles that have been nicely furnished and equipped, the best of which overlook a peaceful garden; prices include an excellent buffet breakfast. **€130**

Casa Astarita Corso Italia 69 Ⓣ 081 877 3991, Ⓦ casastarita.com. Six nice rooms overlooking the street, all with bathroom, flat-screen TV and fridge, and including internet access and a good breakfast round a communal table each morning. Cosy, friendly, and in a good position, it's one of Sorrento's best options at this price. **€110**

Désirée Via Capo 31/B ☎081 878 1563, ⓦ desiree
hotelsorrento.com. About 700m from the end of Corso
Italia, this is a nice, small hotel with very friendly
management and good-sized doubles with balconies
overlooking the sea (triples and quads also available) –
though they vary a bit in size. Breakfast is included. **€85**

La Minervetta Via Capo 25 ☎081 877 4455, ⓦ la
minervetta.com. Sorrento's only boutique hotel perches
on the cliff overlooking Marina Grande. There's a lovely
lounge terrace overlooking the sea, and below that a plunge
pool and steps leading down to Marina Grande's beaches
and restaurants. And the rooms are gorgeous – prices start at
around €300 for one of their deluxe rooms. **€280**

★ **Mami Camilla** Via Cocumella 4 ☎081 878 2067,
ⓦ mamicamilla.com. A great option, and one of the
cheapest in town, with simple but nicely furnished rooms in
a wonderfully peaceful villa in the suburb of Sant Agnello,
about a 15min walk from the centre of town. Owner and
chef Biagio cooks up a storm in the kitchen and they run
regular cooking courses if you want to get in on the act. **€80**

Mignon Via Sersale 9 ☎081 807 3824, ⓦ sorrento
hotelmignon.com. A really nice and well located two-star
with 24 very well appointed rooms, all with satellite TV,
a/c and free internet access. **€105**

Ostello Le Sirene Via degli Aranci 160 ☎081 807 2925,
ⓦ hostellesirene.com. A private youth hostel which is a bit
spartan but decent enough. Dorms **€18**, doubles from **€65**

CAMPING

Nube d'Argento Via del Capo 21 ☎081 878 1344,
ⓦ nubedargento.com. Scenic site on the western side
of the town centre, 100m from the end of Corso Italia.
March–Nov. Pitches around **€32**, bungalows **€85**

Santa Fortunata Via del Capo 41 ☎081 807 3579,
ⓦ santafortunata.com. Just over 1km out of Sorrento on
the way to Massa Lubrense, this site has a private beach and
superb sea views, as well as bungalows and cabins. April–
Oct. Pitches around **€32**, bungalows and cabins around **€90**

EATING AND DRINKING

CAFÉS AND GELATERIE

Bar Ercolano Piazza Tasso 28 ☎081 807 2951. The
friendlier and less self-important of the two main bars on
Piazza Tasso – with not such good views of the parading
crowds, but a lot shadier when it's hot. A good place to start
the day with a pastry. Daily 8am–midnight.

Fauno Piazza Tasso 13/15 ☎081 878 1135, ⓦ fauno
bar.it. The place to watch the crowds drift by during the
evening *passeggiata* – if you can bear the thinly disguised
contempt the waiters have for tourists. Food includes the
usual pasta dishes, burgers and omelettes. Daily 8am–1am.

Primavera Corso Italia 142 ☎081 807 3252, ⓦ primavera
sorrento.it. There's a great choice of flavours at this veteran
gelateria, just off Piazza Tasso. Check out the photos of the
famous and infamous who have stopped by for a quick *cono*.
Daily 10am–1am.

RESTAURANTS

Bufalito Vico Fuoro I 21 ☎081 365 6975. A great,
relaxed and busy restaurant specializing in buffalo dishes
– cheese, steaks, sausages and "slow" local and seasonal
produce. Good pasta dishes and inventive mains, big
baskets of country breads, cheese platters and delicious
antipasti misti. Daily noon–midnight.

Da Emilia Via Marina Grande 62 ☎081 807 2720. With
a menu as short as those in the upper town are long, this
restaurant serves simple food in perhaps Sorrento's best
location – on the waterfront at Marina Grande. Very good
for simple pasta dishes, with half a dozen great seafood and
tomato-based *primi*, and the same number of principally
fish *secondi*. No credit cards. Daily 1–3pm & 8–11pm.

Da Gigino Via degli Archi 15 ☎081 878 1927. A great,
no-nonsense choice, with a good menu of usual standards,
including decent pasta dishes from €7, main courses from
around €13 (good *saltimbocca*, *saute di cozze*) and excellent
pizzas from €6. Daily noon–11.45pm.

Il Buco Rampa Marina Piccola 11, Piazza San Antonino
☎081 878 2354. Housed in the wine cellar of a former
monastery, this is Sorrento at its gastronomic best, with a real
variety of antipasti and *primi* that focus on local ingredients
and a *secondi* menu that is mainly about fish. You can order
à la carte and pay around €18 for a pasta dish, €25 for a main
course, or choose from menus that start at €50 for three
courses to €85 for six. 1–3pm & 8–11pm; closed Wed.

La Lanterna Via S. Cesareo 23 ☎081 878 1355. Down
a dead end just off Piazza Tasso, this has long been one of
the better restaurants in the centre of town, with tables
outside and consistently good food – great fish, but much
else besides. It's moderately priced, and the service is
excellent. Noon–3pm & 7.30–10.30pm; closed Wed.

BARS

Bollicine Via Accademia 7. In the heart of the old town,
this small, wood-panelled wine bar has a wide range of
good Campanian wines, draught beer, a cosy atmosphere
– and tapas-style food too. Daily 7pm–late.

Chaplin's Corso Italia 18. Maybe the nicest of Sorrento's
English-style pubs, family-run with lovely, welcoming
owners and lots of live sport on their array of TVs. Check
out the wisdom behind the bar dispensed by the legions
of inebriated holiday-makers who have passed through
over the years. Daily 6pm–2am.

The Garden Corso Italia 50/52. This wine shop and wine
bar has a few tables inside and out and is a great place
for a drink, or to have a bite from an array of snacks. Daily
noon–2am.

Photo Via Correale 19/21. Just beyond Piazza Tasso, this is a deliberately cool bar-restaurant, though its studied boutiquey ambience means you could be pretty much anywhere. Daily noon–2am.

The islands

Guarding each prong of the Bay of Naples, the islands of Capri, Ischia and Procida between them make up the best-known group of Italian islands. Each is a very different creature, though. **Capri** is a place of legend, home to the mythical Sirens and a much-eulogized playground of the super-rich in the years since – though now settled down to a lucrative existence as a target for day-trippers from the mainland. Visit by all means, but bear in mind that you have to hunt hard these days to detect the origins of much of the purple prose. **Ischia** is a target for package tours (predominantly from Germany) and weekenders from Naples, but its size means that it doesn't feel as crowded as Capri, and plentiful hot springs, sandy beaches and a green volcanic interior make the island well worth a few days' visit. Pretty **Procida**, the smallest of the islands and the least interesting – though the best venue for fairly peaceful lazing – remains reasonably untouched by the high season.

Capri

Sheering out of the sea just off the far end of the Sorrentine peninsula, the island of **Capri** has long been the most sought-after part of the Bay of Naples. During Roman times Augustus retreated to the island's gorgeous cliffbound scenery to escape the cares

---

GETTING TO THE ISLANDS

There are regular **ferries, hydrofoils and catamarans** to all of the islands throughout the year, though they run more frequently and from more ports between April and October. The principal point of departure is Naples' main port, the **Molo Beverello** at the bottom of Piazza Municipio, but hydrofoils and catamarans also run from Naples **Mergellina** (for Procida and Ischia), **Pozzuoli** (for Procida and Ischia), **Castellammare** (Capri) and **Sorrento** (Capri and Ischia), and there are services operated by Metrò del Mare to Capri from the Cilento, south of Salerno; there are also connections between Capri and Ischia, and Ischia and Procida, although, curiously, the islands themselves are not that well connected. Whichever route you take, **day-trips** are feasible; usually the last connection delivers you back on the mainland in time for dinner. On foot, you can simply buy **tickets** when you turn up at the offices at the port; in general it's better to buy a single rather than a return ticket – it's no more expensive and you retain more flexibility on the time you come back, and the service you decide to use. Having said that, on summer Sundays (especially on Capri and Procida, and especially by hydrofoil), it's a good idea to buy your return ticket as soon as you arrive, to avoid the risk of finding the last service fully booked. Note that you can't take a car to Capri, nor, in summer months, to Ischia or Procida.

Ferry timings are published daily in newspaper *Il Mattino*, as well as being available from local tourist offices, and online at the island-specific websites as well as those belonging to the ferry lines themselves. There are quite a few companies competing for custom, all of which are listed below, along with the ports they serve; all offer online booking.

FERRY LINES

Alilauro ☏ 081 497 2222, **ⓦ** alilauro.it. Naples, Sorrento, Capri, Ischia Porto, Forio.

Caremar ☏ 081 244 4111, **ⓦ** caremar.it. Naples, Sorrento, Pozzuoli, Capri, Ischia Porto, Casamicciola, Procida.

Med Mar ☏ 081 333 4411, **ⓦ** medmargroup.it. Naples, Pozzuoli, Ischia Porto, Casamicciola, Procida.

Metrò del Mare ☏ 199 600 700, **ⓦ** metrodelmare .net. Naples, Sorrento, Capri, Amalfi Coast, Salerno, Cilento coast.

NLG ☏ 081 552 0763, **ⓦ** navlib.it. Naples, Castellammare, Sorrento, Capri.

SNAV ☏ 081 428 5555, **ⓦ** snav.it. Naples, Sorrento, Capri, Ischia Porto, Procida.

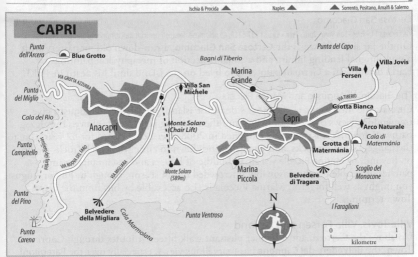

of office; later Tiberius moved the imperial capital here, indulging himself in legendarily debauched antics until his death in 37 AD. After the Romans left, Capri was rather neglected until the early nineteenth century, when the discovery of the Blue Grotto and the island's remarkable natural landscape coincided nicely with the rise of tourism. The English especially have always flocked here: D.H. Lawrence and George Bernard Shaw were among its more illustrious visitors; Graham Greene and Gracie Fields had houses here; and even Lenin visited for a time after the failure of the 1905 uprising.

Capri tends to get a mixed press these days, the consensus being that while it might have been an attractive place once, it's been pretty much ruined by the crowds and the prices. And Capri *is* crowded, to the degree that in July and August, and on *all* summer weekends, it's sensible to give it a miss, though the island does still have a unique charm, and it would be hard to find a place with more inspiring views. It is expensive, although prices aren't really any higher than at other major Italian resorts, and you can find very reasonably priced and attractive accommodation in Anacapri. Alternatively, just visit on a day-trip, which should give you time enough to see the major sights of the island.

Marina Grande

Marina Grande is almost certainly where you will arrive on Capri, a busy harbour that receives day-trippers on ferries and other vessels before dispatching them onward by bus, funicular or taxi. Beyond the port area and the bus terminal is a sand and shingle beach of mixed quality. It's often crowded but is possibly the easiest place to swim on the island. There are lots of free spots too, though you can pay for the usual facilities if you prefer.

Capri Town and around

CAPRI is the main town of the island, nestled between two mountains. Its houses are connected by winding, hilly alleyways that give onto the dinky main square of **Piazza Umberto I**, or "La Piazzetta", crowded with café tables and lit by twinkling fairy lights in the evenings. Don't neglect the maze of charming streets behind La Piazzetta, or the covered walkways up the steps to the right as you enter the square, past the Baroque dome of the seventeenth-century parish church of **Santo Stefano**, itself also worth a look for its marble floor, originally from the ancient Roman Villa Jovis and the ruins of other Tiberian villas.

13

Certosa San Giacomo

Via Certosa 11 • Tues–Sun 9am–2pm • Free • ☎ 081 837 6218, ⬤ polomusealenapoli.beniculturali.it/museo_sg/museo_sg.html

On the far side of town is the **Certosa San Giacomo**, a run-down old monastery with a multilingual lending library and a small collection of metaphysical paintings by Karl Diefenbach, a German painter who lived on the island until his death in 1913.

The Giardini di Augusto and Marina Piccola

On past the monastery, at the other side of the island, the **Giardini di Augusto** give tremendous views of the coast below and the towering jagged cliffs above. The zigzag pathway down, Via Krupp, was reopened in 2008 after being closed for 32 years due to the danger of falling rocks, and you can wind down to either the beach (rocks really), or, beyond, to **Marina Piccola** – a small huddle of houses and restaurants around patches of pebble beach: reasonably uncrowded out of season, though in July or August you might as well forget it. Marina Piccola is also accessible by bus from the Capri Town terminus.

Villa Jovis, Villa Fersen and beyond

Up above the Certosa, and a further pleasant walk fifteen minutes through Capri Town, the **Belvedere del Cannone** has marvellous views, especially over the **Faraglioni** rocks to the left and Marina Piccola to the right. Further out of Capri Town, there are two walks worth doing to the eastern edge of the island.

Villa Jovis

Via Tiberio • Daily: April–Oct 10am–5pm; Nov–March 10am–4pm • €2

It's a steep forty-minute hike up to the ruins of Tiberius's villa, the **Villa Jovis**; from Piazza Umberto follow Via Botteghe out of the square and then Via Tiberio up the hill – it's well signposted. It was here that Tiberius retired in 27 AD, reportedly to lead a life of vice and debauchery and to take revenge on his enemies, many of whom he apparently had thrown off the cliff face. You can see why he chose the site: it's among Capri's most exhilarating, with incredible vistas of the Sorrentine peninsula, including the Amalfi Coast, and the bay; on a clear day you can even see Salerno and beyond. There's not much left of the villa, but you can get a good sense of the shape and design of its various parts from the arched halls and narrow passageways that remain.

Villa Fersen

Via Lo Capo • April–Oct Mon–Sat 9am–1.30pm & 2.30–6.30pm • Free

A short detour on the way to the Villa Jovis (and an easier and shorter walk from Piazza Umberto), there's another villa, the more recent **Villa Lysis**, known to locals as **Villa Fersen** after Count Fersen-Adelsward, a somewhat dissolute, gay French-Swedish writer who built the house in the early 1900s. The building's empty now, but the location is amazing, and its echoing rooms and panoramic terraces retain a pungent atmosphere, with a handful of photos taken here of the count and his friends and lovers. You can look round the upstairs bedrooms with what would have been at the time state-of-the-art fitted bathrooms, one with a sunken bath, and a basement den where the count used to smoke opium. He passed away in style here in 1923 after overdoing it on a cocktail of champagne and cocaine – a somehow fitting end to a hedonistic life.

Arco Naturale and Grotta di Matermania

Another walk you can do is to the **Arco Naturale**, an impressive natural rock formation at the end of a high, lush valley, a 25-minute stroll from Capri Town, again following Via Botteghe out of the square but branching off up Via Matermania after ten minutes or so; just follow the signs. You can get quite close to the arch owing to the specially constructed viewing platforms. Just before the path descends towards the arch, steps lead down to the **Grotta di Matermania**, ten minutes away down quite a few steps – a dusty cutaway out of the rock that was converted to house a shrine to the goddess Cybele by the Romans. Steps lead on down from the cave, sheer through the trees, before flattening into a fine path that you can follow to the **Tragara Belvedere**, affording some of the island's best views along the way, and, eventually, back to Capri Town – reachable in about an hour.

Anacapri and around

The island's other main settlement, **ANACAPRI**, is more sprawling than Capri itself and less obviously picturesque, its main square, **Piazza della Vittoria**, flanked by souvenir shops, bland fashion boutiques and restaurants decked with tourist menus – Capri without the chic.

Church of San Michele

Piazza San Nicola • Daily: April–Oct 9am–7pm; Nov–March 9.30am–3pm • €2

A short walk away from Piazza della Vittoria down Via G. Orlandi, the church of **San Michele** is one of two principal sights, its tiled floor painted with an eighteenth-century depiction of the Fall that you view from an upstairs balcony – a lush work after a drawing by the Neapolitan painter **Solimena**, in rich blues and yellows, showing cats, unicorns and other creatures.

Villa San Michele

Via Axel Munthe 34 • Daily: March 9am–4.30pm; April & Oct 9am–5pm; May–Sept 9am–6pm; Nov–Feb 9am–3.30pm • €6 •
☏ 081 837 1401, ⓦ villasanmichele.eu

Anacapri's major sight is a short walk from Piazza della Vittoria, past a long gauntlet of souvenir stalls to Axel Munthe's **Villa San Michele**, a light, airy house with lush and fragrant gardens that is one of the real highlights of the island. A nineteenth-century Swedish writer and physician to the elite, Munthe lived here for a number of years, and the place is filled with his furniture and knick-knacks, as well as Roman artefacts and columns plundered from a ruined villa on the site. Busts and bronzes abound, Corinthian capitals are converted as coffee tables, other surfaces topped with intricate Cosmati mosaic-work. His book *The Story of San Michele* – more the story of his life – is well worth reading. There's also an attractive, small natural-history exhibition in the gardens, which fills you in on local flora and fauna.

Monte Solaro

Piazza della Vittoria • Daily: March–Oct 9.30am–6.30pm; Nov–Feb 10.30am–3pm • €7.50 one way, €10 return

A chair lift operates from Piazza della Vittoria up to **Monte Solaro**, the island's highest point (596m). The trip only takes thirteen minutes and there's not much at the top – a ruined castle and a café – but the ride and the location are very tranquil and the 360-degree views are marvellous – perhaps the bay's very best.

The Blue Grotto

Daily 9am–1hr before sunset, but closed in bad weather • Boat from Marina Grande €12, plus admission €12.50; or take a rowing boat direct from Anacapri, saving the price of the trip from Marina Grande

Continuing in the same direction, a good 45-minute hike away starting off down Via Lo Pozzo (or reachable by bus every twenty minutes from the bus station on Via di Tomasso), you come to the **Blue Grotto** or Grotta Azzurra, probably the island's best-known feature – though also its most exploitative, the boatmen here whisking visitors onto boats and in and out of the grotto in about five minutes flat. The grotto is quietly impressive, the blue of its innards caused by sunlight entering the cave through the water, but it's rather overrated. Technically, you can swim into the cave – it's not the exclusive preserve of the boatmen, though they'll try to persuade you otherwise – but the route through is so busy that unless you're a strong swimmer it's only advisable to try at the end of the day after the tours have finished.

13

ARRIVAL AND DEPARTURE

CAPRI

By boat All hydrofoils and ferries arrive at Marine Grande. It's a steep walk up 300 or so steps to Capri Town (20–45min depending on your stamina), or you can take the funicular (departures every 15min; April–Sept 6.30am–midnight, Oct–March 6.30am–10pm; €1.60 one way) or a bus.

GETTING AROUND

By bus The bus service runs from end to end and from side to side of the island, connecting all the main centres – Marina Grande, Capri Town, Marina Piccola, Anacapri – every 15min. Buses also run regularly down to the Blue Grotto from Anacapri, and also to Punta Carena. Tickets cost €1.60 for a single trip, €2.40 for an hour and €7.60 for a day, and they're available from ticket booths, newsstands and *tabacchi*, as well as upon boarding.

By boat Leomar, located to the right of Marina Grande near *Da Zio Ciccio* beach bar, rents boats for a minimum of 3hr (April–Oct 10am–6pm; ☎081 837 7181). There are also operators at Marina Grande offering boat excursions around the island, taking in the Blue Grotto, for €15; trips last 2hr 15min.

By scooter You can rent scooters in Marina Grande from Oasi, right by the path up to the town at Via Ruocco (☎081 837 713 or ☎334 353 2975; around €50/day).

By taxi Non-residents' cars are not allowed to disembark on Capri, and you can't rent a car, so the island's stylish – and very expensive – convertible taxis are the only private option. There are ranks on the right as you walk out of the port at Marina Grande (☎081 837 0543) and in Anacapri (☎081 837 1175).

INFORMATION

Tourist offices There are offices in Marina Grande (April–Oct Mon–Sat 9am–1pm & 4–7.15pm, Sun 9am–1pm; Nov–March Mon–Sat 9am–3pm; ☎081 837 0634, ⓦ capritourism.com); in Capri Town at Piazza Umberto I (April–Oct Mon–Sat 8.30am–8.30pm, Sun 9am–3pm; Nov–March Mon–Sat 9am–1pm & 3.30–6.45pm; ☎081 837 0686); and Anacapri, at Via G. Orlandi 59 (Mon–Sat 9am–3pm; ☎081 837 1524). All sell a handy map (€1) and have free promotional materials.

ACCOMMODATION

CAPRI TOWN, MARINA GRANDE AND MARINA PICCOLA

★ **A Paziella** Via Fuorlovado 36 ☎081 837 0044, ⓦ apaziella.com. Cool and breezy even on the hottest day, this place has a palpable serenity, yet it's located in the middle of town. The rooms are elegant and comfortable, many with private balconies and sea views, and there are lovely gardens and free use of the next-door *Sirene* hotel's pool. Closed mid-Oct to March. **€280**

Da Giorgio Via Roma 34 ☎081 837 5777, ⓦ dagiorgio capri.com. Gracious rooms with views of the bay, this is an excellent choice, not least because the same property also boasts one of the island's best restaurants. Closed Jan & Feb. **€110**

Italia Via Marina Grande 204 ☎081 837 0602, ⓦ hotel italiacapri.com. This elegant old mansion, surrounded by flower gardens and occupying its own corner on the road up to Capri Town is full of charm. All the airy rooms have private balconies and half of them sea-views; the others look out over the gardens. Breakfast €10 extra. Open year-round. **€120**

Quattro Stagioni Via Marina Piccola 1 ☎081 837 0041, ⓦ hotel4stagionicapri.com. In a pretty location, a little way out of Capri Town at the fork of the roads to Marina Piccola and Anacapri, this place offers a ten-percent discount to carriers of this book from mid-March to Oct. **€75**

Weber Ambassador Via Marina Piccola ☎081 837 0141, ⓦ hotelweber.com. This comfortable choice has great views from its multi-levelled terrace. Cosy and elegant inside, and steps leading directly down to the Marina Piccola beach. **€120**

ANACAPRI AND AROUND

La Bougainville Viale Tommaso de Tommaso 6 ☎081 837 3641, ⓦ hlb.it. A comfortable choice, set in a lush flower garden, which some rooms overlook, just a couple of minutes' walk down the main road from the centre of Anacapri. Rooms are comfortable and nicely furnished and amenities include a good restaurant, a solarium and guest pick-up/drop-off at Marina Grande. Closed mid-Nov to mid-March. **140**

★ **La Bussola** Traversa La Vigna 14 ☎081 838 2010, ⓦ bussolahermes.com. This boutiquey hotel is a true oasis of peace, 10min's walk from the centre of Anacapri. Cool, stylish rooms, all with balconies, and a friendly, welcoming vibe. Closed Nov–Feb. **€140**

★ **Villa Eva** Via La Fabbrica 8 ☎081 837 1549, ⓦ villaeva.com. For a long time now, *Villa Eva* has been the cult budget option of the island, and the legend only gets better. A wide choice of individually styled rooms to choose from, most of them spacious and light, as well as a grand-piano-shaped pool and a welcoming poolhouse/snack bar, where breakfast is served. Closed Nov–March. **€70**

EATING

CAPRI TOWN AND MARINA GRANDE

Buca di Bacco Via Longano 25 ☎081 837 0723. Just behind La Piazzetta, this old favourite is rated by locals and visitors alike as one of the best; try the *spaghetti alla pescatora* for €15, or fresh fish mains from around €10. Daily except Wed noon–3pm & 7.30–10.30pm; closed Jan.

★ **Da Gemma** Via Madre Serafina 6 ☎081 837 0461. Graham Greene's favourite restaurant, and still one of Capri's best choices, up the steps from La Piazzetta in a whitewashed arcade. The buffet spread is generally good, as is pretty much everything else, and they do decent wood-fired pizzas. Daily noon–3pm & 7.30–10.30pm July–Sept; closed Nov–April & Thurs May, June & Oct.

Da Giorgio Via Roma 34 ☎081 837 0898. This is a popular and very central choice in a picturesque location, and the food is excellent if not exactly cheap – try the *linguine ai frutti di mare* for €17. The place also offers good-value hotel rooms (see opposite). 12.30–2.30pm & 7.30–10.30pm; closed Tues, and Jan & Feb.

La Capannina Via le Botteghe 12bis ☎081 837 0732. Up to the left from La Piazzetta, this place is considered by many as the island's top restaurant, and it has colonized the area with its cosy wine bar around the corner and wine shop opposite. Prices are moderate-to-high even by Capri standards, with pasta dishes for €13–25 and fish mains €25. Noon–2.30pm & 7.30–11pm; mid-March–Nov closed Wed.

Sollievo Via Fuorlovado 36 ☎081 837 0665. Bright and airy restaurant a couple of minutes from La Piazzetta

that is pretty reasonably priced (for Capri), with pasta for €12–16 and mains from around €12. Excellent food and service too, and a lovely big terrace. Daily noon–3pm & 7.30–10.30pm.

ANACAPRI

★ **Il Solitario** Via G. Orlandi 96 ☎081 837 1382. Take the little walkway back from the street and discover an arboured garden patio setting decorated with appealingly kitsch painted statues and coloured fairy lights. A family-run restaurant, the food is excellent – they do a very generous *spaghetti alle vongole* with home-made pasta, and great pizzas too; the prices are moderate, and the service very friendly. Noon–3pm & 7.30–10.30pm; closed Tues, Nov & two weeks in Feb.

Lido del Faro ☎081 837 1798. This great restaurant is set above the dramatic rocky cove below Anacapri's lighthouse. Ladders lead down into the cove for sea-swimming, and there's a pool as well (no children after 3pm). Food is expensive but really good, and the setting is gorgeous. Easter to end Oct daily noon–sunset; June to end Sept Thurs–Sun open until 10pm.

Materita Via G. Orlandi 140/Piazza Diaz ☎081 837 3375. Attractive and well located, with cosy seating inside and terrace tables, too. The signature dish is the Neapolitan-style wood-fired pizza, served both lunch and dinner, but there's also a full menu. Lunch & dinner; closed Tues & Nov to mid-Dec.

Ischia

Largest of the islands in the Bay of Naples, **Ischia** (pronounced Iss-kee-ah) rises out of the sea in a cone-shaped series of pointy green hummocks. German, Scandinavian and British tourists flock here in large numbers during peak season, attracted by its charming beach resorts and thermal springs. Although its reputation has always been poorer than Capri's – it is perhaps not so dramatically beautiful – you can at least be sure of being alone in exploring parts of the mountainous interior, and **La Mortella**, the exotic garden cultivated by the British composer William Walton and his widow Susana, is an unmissable attraction. Indeed, if you're after some beach lounging, good walking and lively nightlife within striking distance of Naples and the rest of the bay, it might be just the place.

The island is fairly large and has some two-dozen towns, villages and hamlets, spread around in a ring, with the cone of the dormant volcano in the centre, and the more reasonable order for a visit is anticlockwise, given the way the towns are clustered.

Ischia Porto and Ponte

The main town of Ischia is **ISCHIA PORTO**, where the ferries dock, an appealing stretch of hotels, ritzy boutiques and beach shops planted with lemon trees and Indian figs fronted by golden sands: **Spiaggia San Pietro** is to the right of the port, accessible by following Via Buonocore off Via Roma. The inexplicably named **Spiaggia degli Inglesi**, on the other side, is reachable by way of the narrow path that leads over the headland from the end of Via Jasolino. Apart from the sunbathing the main thing to do is to window-shop and stroll along the main Corso Vittoria Colonna, either branching off to a further beach, the **Spiaggia dei Pescatori**, or following it all the way down to the

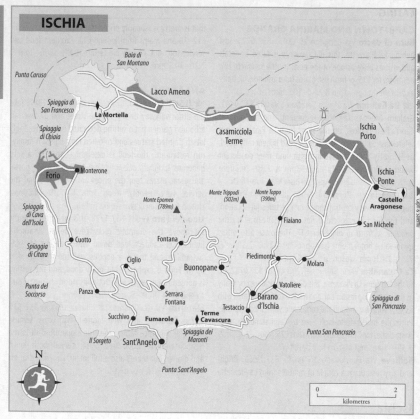

other part of Ischia's main town, **ISCHIA PONTE**, also reachable by bus #7, a quieter and less commercialized centre. Ischia Ponte is home to the island's **Museo del Mare** (daily except Mon: April–June, Sept & Oct 10.30am–12.30pm & 3–7pm; July & Aug 10.30am–12.30pm & 6.30–10pm; Nov–March 10.30am–12.30pm; closed Feb; €2.50), which traces the community's seafaring roots with ancient, barnacle-encrusted pottery retrieved from the sea and samples of marine fauna, as well as the full range of navigation instruments from sextants to sonar. But the main focus of this area is the Castello Aragonese (see below).

Castello Aragonese

Ischia Ponte • Daily 9.30am–6pm • €12 • ⓦ castelloaragonese.it

Accessible from Ischia Ponte via a short causeway, the stunningly distinctive pyramid of the **Castello Aragonese** was one of the backdrops in the film *The Talented Mr Ripley*. The citadel itself is rather tumbledown now and some of it is closed to the public, but below is a complex of buildings, almost a separate village really, around which you can stroll by way of olive-shaded paths and lush terraces. There's the weird open shell of a cathedral destroyed by the British in 1806, a prison that once held political prisoners during the Unification struggle, and the macabre remnants of a convent, in which a couple of dark rooms ringed with a set of commode-like seats served as a cemetery for the dead sisters – placed here to putrefy in front of the living members of the community. The rest of the convent has been converted to a rather nice hotel (see p.782).

Casamicciola Terme

The island is at its most developed along its northern and western shores – heading west from Ischia Porto. The first village you reach, **CASAMICCIOLA TERME**, is a spa centre with many hotels and a crowded central beach – though you can find a quieter one on the far side of the village. Ibsen spent a summer here, and the waters are said to be full of iodine (apparently beneficial for the skin and the nervous system).

Lacco Ameno

LACCO AMENO is a bright little town, with a beach and with spa waters that are said to be the most radioactive in Italy. It's known for the 10m-tall offshore tufa rock, affectionately nicknamed **Il Fungo**, and the **Museo Archeologico di Pithecusa**, housed in the eighteenth-century Villa Arbusto just above the centre of town on Corso Angelo Rizzoli (Tues–Sun: May–Oct 9.30am–1pm & 4–8pm; Nov–April 9.30am–1pm & 3–7pm; €5; ☎081 333 0288, ⓦpithecusae.it), whose most celebrated piece is the Coppa di Nestore, engraved with a light-hearted challenge to the cup mentioned in Homer's *Iliad*, while a shipwreck scene on a locally made bowl is thought to be the oldest example of figurative painting in Italy. You can also wander around the villa's gardens, which have lovely views over the town and are home to a couple of other galleries.

La Mortella

Via Francesco Calise 29 • Easter–Nov Tues, Thurs, Sat & Sun 9am–7pm • €12 • Bus #CD or taxis from Forio or Casamicciola cost about €10 • ☎ 081 986 220, ⓦ lamortella.org

The stunning garden of **La Mortella** is one of Ischia's highlights, created by the English composer William Walton and his Argentinian widow Susana, who lived here until her death in 2010. The Waltons moved to Ischia, then sparsely populated and little known to tourists, in 1949, forerunners of a coterie of writers and artists including Auden and Terence Rattigan. With the garden designer Russell Page, they created La Mortella from an unpromising volcanic stone quarry.

Paths wind up through the abundant site, which is home to some three hundred rare and exotic plants. Near the entrance is a glasshouse sheltering the world's largest water lily, while above the glasshouse is a charming terraced **tearoom**, where the strains of Walton's music can be heard. There's also a **museum**, which shows a video about the composer and features portraits by Cecil Beaton, a bust by Elizabeth Frink, and paintings and set-designs by John Piper. Paths loop through luxuriant foliage to the pyramid-shaped rock that holds Walton's ashes, a cascade guarded by a sculpted crocodile and a pretty **Thai pavilion** surrounded by heavy-headed purple agapanthus. At the garden's summit, a belvedere provides superb views across the island.

Forio

The growing resort of **FORIO** sprawls around its bay, and is quite pretty behind a seafront of bars and pizzerias, focusing around the busy main street of Corso Umberto. Out on the point on the far side of the old centre (turn right at the far end of Corso Umberto), the simple **Chiesa Soccorso** is a bold, whitewashed landmark from which to survey the town. There are good **beaches** either side of Forio: the **Spiaggia di Chiaia**, a short walk to the north; to the south **Cava del Isola**, which is popular with a young crowd; and the **Spiaggia di Citara**, a somewhat longer walk to the south along Via G. Mazzella.

Sant'Angelo and around

Ischia is most pleasant on its southern side, the landscape steeper and greener, with fewer people to enjoy it. **SANT'ANGELO** is probably its loveliest spot, a tiny fishing village crowded around a narrow isthmus linking with a humpy islet that's out of bounds to buses, which drop you right outside. It's inevitably quite developed, centring on a harbour and square crowded with café tables and surrounded by pricey boutiques, but if all you want to do is laze in the sun it's perhaps the island's most appealing spot

13

to do so. There's a reasonable **beach** lining one side of the isthmus that connects Sant'Angelo to its islet, as well as the nearby stretch of the **Spiaggia dei Maronti**, 1km east, which is accessible by plentiful taxi-boats from Sant'Angelo's harbour (around €5), or on foot in about 25 minutes – take the path from the top of the village.

Taxi-boats will drop you at one of a number of specific features: one, the **Fumarole**, is where steam emerges from under the rocks in a kind of outdoor sauna, popular on moonlit nights; further along, close by a couple of hotels, is a path that cuts inland through a mini-gorge to the **Terme Cavascura**, the most historic hot springs on the island, used since Roman times (mid-April to Oct daily 8.30am–6pm; swim and sauna €10, treatments €12–30; ⓦcavascura.it).

Fontana and Monte Epomeo

Up above Sant'Angelo looms the craggy summit of Ischia's now dormant volcano, **Monte Epomeo**. Both #CD and #CS buses regularly stop at **FONTANA**, a superb ride up, with wonderful views back over the coast, from where you can climb up to the summit of the volcano. Follow the signposted road off to the left from the centre of Fontana: after about five minutes it joins a larger road; after another ten to fifteen minutes take the left fork, a stony track off the road, and follow this up to the summit – when in doubt, always fork left and you can't go wrong. It's a steep climb of an hour or so, especially at the end when the path becomes no more than a channel cut out of the soft rock. However, there are a couple of scenically placed cafés in which to gather your energies at the top, where the views are stunning. Bear in mind, too, that you can drive to within about twenty minutes of the summit, leaving your vehicle by the signs for the military exclusion zone.

ARRIVAL AND DEPARTURE   ISCHIA

By boat Ferries and hydrofoils from various points around the bay (see box, p.774) arrive at three points: the main port, Ischia Porto (from Naples, Capri, Procida and Pozzuoli, and seasonally from the Amalfi Coast as well); at Casamicciola Terme (from Naples, Procida and Pozzuoli); and on the western end of the island at Forio (from Naples).

INFORMATION AND GETTING AROUND

You can rely on the efficient bus system to get to all of the major towns and some of the other popular spots, such as Maronti beach and the various points of departure for hikes. Outsiders are prohibited from bringing cars in peak months.

By bus The main buses, #CS (clockwise) and #CD (anticlockwise), circle the entire island at 30min intervals, while some sixteen lesser lines gain access to various byways and smaller settlements; the tourist office has timetables. Tickets cost €1.20 and are valid for 90min; day-tickets are available for €4, two-day tickets for €6.

Tourist offices Ischia Porto, right by the quayside ferry ticket offices in the old Terme Comunali building (Mon–Sat 9am–2pm & 3–8pm; ⓣ 081 507 4231, ⓦ infoischiaprocida .it); Ischia Ponte, the Museo del Mare building (daily 9.30am–1.30pm & 6–10pm).

ACCOMMODATION

ISCHIA PONTE AND ISCHIA PORTO

Continental Mare Via B. Cossa 25, Porto ⓣ 081 982 577, ⓦ continentalmare.it. A breezily elegant hotel in a splendid location above the port with its own stretch of beach. Rooms are spacious and contemporary in style, the best ones enjoying balconies with sea views. **€120**

Eurocamping dei Pini Via delle Ginestre 28, Porto ⓣ 081 982 069, ⓦ ischia.it/camping. A pleasant campsite with nice stands of trees a short walk from the port. To get there, follow Via Mazzella away from the sea and turn right several roads after the football fields. Open all year. Pitches **€30**, bungalows from **€55**

★ **Il Monastero** Castello Aragonese, Ponte ⓣ 081 992 433, ⓦ albergoilmonastero.it. Located on the upper floors of the Castello Aragonese, this is the place to stay in Ischia Ponte, with twenty-odd guestrooms in former nuns' cells, which are suitably spare but coolly and stylishly furnished. The hotel has a broad, sunny terrace overlooking the sea and a picturesque café and restaurant, *Il Terrazzo*. **€125**

Locanda sul Mare Via Jasolino 80, Porto ⓣ 081 981 470, ⓦ locandasulmare.it. Right on the waterfront just beyond the ferry terminal port, this tiny, idiosyncratically decorated and very pleasant hotel is a great bargain and has a decent restaurant. **€125**

Macrì Via Jasolino 78/A, Porto ☎ 081 992 603. Situated just behind its rival, *Locanda sul Mare*, this has simple, pleasantly furnished rooms, parking, and a very warm welcome. **€100**

FORIO

Punta del Sole Piazza Maltese ☎ 081 989 156, ⓦ casthotels.com. This charming and centrally located hotel has balconied rooms set in a beautiful garden close to Forio's sandy beaches; plus it offers full health and beauty services in its own recently created spa. Open all year. **€220**

★ **Ring Hostel** Via G. Morgera 72 ☎ 081 987 546, ⓦ ringhostels.com. In the centre of Forio is this fun-loving hostel, run by three outgoing local brothers who speak English, provide shuttle services free of charge and are full of ideas for making everyone's stay better. It's just a short walk from the beaches and other facilities. Open all year. Dorms **€18**, private doubles with bath from **€60**

SANT'ANGELO

Casa Giuseppina Via Gaetano D'Iorio 11 ☎ 081 907

771, ⓦ casagiuseppina.it. Up in Succhivo, a 10min walk back in the direction of Forio (the bus passes right by), this family-run, pleasantly rustic garden villa has a swimming pool and hot tub. Minimum stay three nights at weekends. Closed mid-Oct to April. **€130**

La Palma Via Conte Maddalena 15 ☎ 081 999 215, ⓦ lapalmatropical.it. Well placed in the centre of town, this recently renovated Moorish-style villa offers great views of Sant'Angelo and the bay and has plushly furnished rooms with tasteful decor, some with balcony, and an inviting garden terrace restaurant. Admission to their thermal complex, Terme Tropical, included in half-board price. Closed Nov to mid-March. Half-board **€240**

Villa Casa Bianca Maronti Beach ☎ 081 905 212, ⓦ casabiancaischia.it. Right on the beach, towards the eastern end, this is one of the area's best bargains: a gleaming Mediterranean villa with views of Capri from its sweeping terrace. Services include a swimming pool and sauna, plus beach facilities, and all rooms have either a balcony or terrace. Closed Nov–Feb. **€100**

EATING AND DRINKING

ISCHIA PONTE AND ISCHIA PORTO

Al Pontile Via Luigi Mazzella 15, Lungomare Aragonese 6, Ponte ☎ 081 983 492. On the waterfront directly opposite the Castello, this café and unassuming little restaurant serves anything from just drinks and light snacks and salads. Daily 10am–10pm; closed Nov–Feb.

Calise Caffè Piazza degli Eroi 69, Porto ☎ 081 991 270. An island institution in many locations, this branch is set in the midst of a veritable jungle oasis and is a truly all-purpose venue, serving up everything from excellent ice cream to scrumptious cakes and sandwiches, *tavola calda* dishes and pizzas. After hours, it becomes a lounge bar and music venue. 8am–2am; closed Wed Nov–March.

Da Coco' Piazzale Aragonese, Ponte ☎ 081 981 823. In an enviable position just below the Castello Aragonese, this bar-restaurant boasts lovely sea views and great seafood for around €10. 10am–9pm; closed Wed Sept–April.

Gennaro Via Porto 59, Porto ☎ 081 992 917. One of a string of restaurants on the harbourfront but one of the longest-established and best, with great seafood pasta and risottos for €9–12 and excellent fish and seafood mains as well – all presided over by the ever-attentive Gennaro himself. Wash it down with the local Ischia DOC wine made with white Biancolella grapes. Daily noon–3pm & 8–11pm; closed Nov to mid-March.

CASAMICCIOLA TERME

Il Focolare Via Cretajo al Crocefisso 3, Barano d'Ischia ☎ 081 902 944, ⓦ trattoriailfocolare.it. The Casamicciola area's most celebrated restaurant is worth the 5min taxi ride from the port, with a warm welcome and great views

of the port from its hilltop perch. The menu is refreshingly un-focused on the sea, with lots of produce from the hills like home-made *papardelle* with porcini mushrooms and their speciality *coniglio all'ischitana* (rabbit stew). Expect to pay about €30 per person. June–Oct daily 12.30–3pm & 8–11pm; Nov–May Mon, Tues, Thurs & Fri 8–11pm, Sat & Sun 12.30–3pm & 8–11pm.

FORIO

La Bussola Via Marina 36 ☎ 081 997 645. One of the best of the fish restaurants along this stretch, *La Bussola* also serves wood-fired pizzas for both lunch and dinner, starting at just €3 for the classic Neapolitan version. Pasta dishes start at about €6, fresh fish around €10, and there's ample terrace seating for people-watching. Daily noon–3pm & 7.30–10.30pm.

Umberto a Mare Via Soccorso 4 ☎ 081 997 171, ⓦ umbertoamare.it. Established in 1936, this restaurant sits atop a promontory, and the light changes over the water are dazzling. As for the food, the elegantly presented fish menu changes daily and is accompanied by a large wine selection. It's not cheap – reckon on about €65 a head for a meal with wine – but the food is excellent, and although the terrace has only ten tables, both dining rooms overlook the sea. They have rooms too, and moorings for small boats, if you plan to arrive that way. Daily 8–11pm; closed Jan–March.

SANT'ANGELO

Da Pasquale Via Sant'Angelo 79 ☎ 081 904 208, ⓦ dapasquale.it. Restaurants in Sant'Angelo don't come cheap, but you could do worse than stoke up on the fine

13

pizzas (from €5) they serve at this unpretentious pizzeria up in the old centre of the village. Daily 12.30–3pm & 7.30–10pm; closed Dec–March.

Neptunus Via Chiaia di Rose 1 ☎081 999 702. One of the most alluring places west of town, built on descending terraces and offering postcard-perfect views of Sant'Angelo. The food is delicious, with an emphasis on fresh seafood – the *linguine allo scoglio* is superb. Expect to pay about €35 per head for dinner. Daily noon–2.30pm & 7.30–10.30pm; closed Jan to mid-March.

Procida

A serrated hunk of volcanic rock that's the smallest (population 10,000) and nearest island to Naples, **Procida** has managed to fend off the kind of tourist numbers that have flooded into Capri and Ischia. It lacks the spectacle, or variety, of both islands, though it compensates with extra room and extra peace.

Marina Grande

The island's main town, **MARINA GRANDE**, where you arrive by ferry, is a slightly run-down but picturesque conglomeration of tall pastel-painted houses rising from the waterfront to a network of steep streets winding up to the fortified tip of the island – the so-called **Terra Murata**. Part of this was once given over to a rather forbidding prison, now abandoned, but it's worth walking up anyway to see the abbey church of **San Michele** (Mon–Sat 9.45am–12.45pm & 3–6pm, Sun 9.45am–12.45pm; €2 donation expected), whose domes are decorated with a stirring painting by Giordano of St Michael beating back the Turks from Procida's shore. The views, too, from the nearby belvedere are among the region's best, taking in the whole of the Bay of Naples.

For the rest, Procida's appeal lies in its opportunities to swim and eat in relative peace. There are **beaches** in Marina Grande itself, on the far side of the jetty, and, in the opposite direction, beyond the fishing harbour, though both are fairly grubby. Similarly, **Spiaggia Chiaia**, just beyond the fishing harbour of nearby Coricella, is a reasonable bathing beach but isn't very large and can get crowded. You can walk there, or the Chiaiolella bus stops nearby.

On the whole, if you want to swim you're better off making the fifteen-minute bus journey from Marina Grande to **CHIAIOLELLA**, where there's a handful of bars and **restaurants** around a pleasant, almost circular bay and a long stretch of sandy beach that is the island's best.

ARRIVAL AND INFORMATION   PROCIDA

By boat Ferries and hydrofoils from Naples and Ischia (see p.774) arrive in the port of Marina Grande; buses #L1 and #L2 (€1.10 single, tickets sold in *tabacchi* and newsstands and on board) coincide with all arrivals and connect Marina Grande with Chiaiolella roughly every 20min.

Tourist office Via Cavone 4 (daily 9.30am–1pm & 3–6pm; ☎081 896 9628) or Via V. Emanuele 173 (same hours; ☎081 810 1968, ⊛procida.it).

ACCOMMODATION

Crescenzo Via Marina Chiaiolella 33 ☎081 896 7255, ⊛hotelcrescenzo.it. Painted a beautiful sky-blue with white trim, this hotel with on-site restaurant-pizzeria near a sandy beach is a family-run, friendly place with plenty of repeat guests. Some of the ten rooms overlook Chiaiolella harbour. **€120**

La Casa sul Mare Via Salita Castello 13, Terra Murata ☎081 896 8799, ⊛lacasasulmare.it. One of the island's top choices, consisting of ten bright, elegant guestrooms with private balcony and views, in a pale pink seventeenth-century villa with gardens and terraces. Free shuttle to beaches. **€170**

EATING AND DRINKING

Fishbone Via Marina Chiaiolella 22 ☎081 896 7422. This place couldn't be better placed right in the Chiaiolella port, and it attracts its fair share of hungry yachtspeople passing through on flotillas. Food is good and hearty, with lots of good fish and seafood dishes for €10–15, pizzas from €3.50, and relaxed but attentive service both inside and at the restaurant's outside tables. Daily noon–2.30pm & 7.30–10.30pm.

La Medusa Via Roma 116, Marina Grande ☎081 896 7481. Opposite the ferry terminal this offers a house speciality of *pepata di cozze* for €8 and *spaghetti ai ricci di mare* (with sea urchins) for €12. The rest of the menu also draws on the day's catch. Noon–3pm & 7.30–10.30pm; closed Tues.

Inland Campania

As most people head to the coast, few visitors reach **inland Campania**. Indeed the territory immediately north of Naples, mostly a sprawl of unenticing suburbs, is irredeemably grim. Almost entirely dominated by the Camorra it's offputtingly sometimes known as the "**Triangle of Death**". It's not an area to linger, and you'd do well to pass right through and not stop until you reach **Caserta** just beyond, where the vast royal palace and its gardens is an obvious draw. Further inland, **Benevento** has a historic centre well worth exploring.

Caserta

A short train or bus ride direct from Naples, **CASERTA**, incongruously surrounded by a sprawl of industrial complexes and warehouses that stretches all the way back to Naples, is known as the "Versailles of Naples" for its vast eighteenth-century **Reggia di Caserta**, the only attraction in this otherwise completely nondescript modern town.

La Reggia di Caserta

Viale Giulio Douhet • Daily except Tues 8.30am–7.30pm, park closes between 2.30pm and 6pm, depending on time of year • €13 for apartments, €3 for the gardens • ☎ 0823 277 111, ⓦ reggiadicaserta.beniculturali.it

Begun in 1752 for the Bourbon king Charles III to plans drawn up by Vanvitelli, and completed a little over twenty years later, **La Reggia di Caserta** is an awesomely large complex, built around four courtyards, with a facade 245m long. However, it's a dull structure that generally substitutes size for inspiration.

Only the majestic central staircases up to the **royal apartments** hit exactly the right note. The apartments themselves are a grand parade of heavily painted and stuccoed rooms, sparsely furnished in French Empire style, with great, overbearing classical statues and smug portraits of the Bourbon dynasty – look out for the one of the podgy Francis I with his brat-like children.

The gardens

Daily except Tues: Jan, Feb, Nov & Dec 8.30am–2.30pm; March 8.30am–4pm; April 8.30am–5pm; May & Sept 8.30am–5.30pm; June–Aug 8.30am–6pm; Oct 8.30am–4.30pm • €3

Behind the palace, the **gardens** are on no less huge a scale, stretching out behind along one central 3km-long axis and punctured by myth-inspired fountains. The main promenade is longer than it looks from the palace (it's a good 30min walk or a short bicycle ride), and regular buses make the round trip, dropping you off at selected intervals along the way and turning round by the main cascade at the top, completed in 1779, which depicts Diana turning Actaeon into a stag. Walk to the top, look back at the palace, hop on a bus … and depart.

Benevento

Appealing **BENEVENTO**, reachable in about an hour and thirty minutes from Naples by bus or train (the private FBN line is quickest) was another important Roman settlement, a key point on the Via Appia between Rome and Brindisi and, as such, a thriving trading town. Founded in 278 BC, it was at the time the farthest point from Rome to be colonized, and even now it has a remote air about it, circled by hills and with a centre that was (pointlessly) bombed to smithereens in the last war and even now seems only half rebuilt. Its climate also ranks among southern Italy's most extreme.

13

Museo del Sannio
Corso Garibaldi 6 • Tues–Sun 9am–1pm • €4 • ☏ 0824 47 360

The excellent **Museo del Sannio**, in the cloister behind the eighth-century church of
Santa Sofia, holds a good selection of Roman finds from the local area, including
a number of artefacts from a temple of Isis – various sphinxes, bulls and a headless
statue of Isis herself. There are also terracotta votive figurines from the fifth century BC,
and the cloister itself has capitals carved with energetic scenes of animals, humans and
strange beasts, hunting, riding and attacking.

Arch of Trajan
Further along Corso Garibaldi, off to the right, the **Arch of Trajan** is the major remnant
of the Roman era, a marvellously preserved triumphal arch boasting much more
distinct images than Rome's arches, and you can get close enough to study its friezes.
Built to guard the entrance to Benevento from the Appian Way, it's actually as
heavy-handed a piece of self-acclaim as there ever was, showing the Emperor Trajan
in various scenes of triumph, power and generosity.

The Duomo
The city's star-crossed **Duomo** is an almost total reconstruction of a thirteenth-century
Romanesque original, but a few cobbled-together fragments of the original Lombard
structure now form the hotchpotch facade along with a celebrated set of twelfth-century
Byzantine bronze doors that have been recently restored. Take a look, too, at the
belltower, with its line-up of Roman busts scavenged from local funerary sites, and the
eighth-century crypt, which has thirteenth-century frescoes and hosts a small museum.

Teatro Romano
Piazza Ponzio Telesino • Daily 9am–sunset • €2 • ⊕ comune.benevento.it

Benevento has a shabby but picturesque medieval quarter, the **Triggio**, off to the left
of Corso Garibaldi beyond the cathedral, where there's a substantial but indifferently
maintained **Teatro Romano**, inaugurated in 126 AD. Built during the reign of Hadrian,
it seated 20,000 people in its heyday, and it's still an atmospheric sight, with views over
the rolling green countryside of the province.

ARRIVAL AND INFORMATION   **BENEVENTO**

By train There are trains from Naples about every hour;
most change at Caserta. The station is a 30min walk from
the centre, but there are frequent buses in.

By bus Six daily buses make the 90min trip from Naples,
dropping off in a car park below Benevento's centre, where

you can also park if you're driving.

Tourist office On the corner of Via Sandro Bertini (daily
9am–1pm & 3.30–7.30pm; ☏ 0824 28 180). Information
for the province is at Via Nicola Sala 31 (Mon–Fri 8am–2pm
& 3–6pm, Sat 9am–noon; ☏ 0824 319 911).

The Amalfi Coast

Occupying the southern side of Sorrento's peninsula, the **Amalfi Coast** (Costiera
Amalfitana) lays claim to being Europe's most beautiful stretch of coast, its corniche
road winding around the towering cliffs that slip almost sheer into the sea. By car
or bus it's an incredible ride (though it can get mighty congested in summer), with
some of the most spectacular stretches between Salerno and Amalfi. If you're staying
in Sorrento especially, it shouldn't be missed on any account; in any case the towns
along here hold the beaches that Sorrento lacks. The coast as a whole has become
rather developed, and these days it's in fact one of Italy's ritzier bits of shoreline, villas
atop its precarious slopes fetching a bomb in both cash and kudos. While it's home
to some stunning hotels, budget travellers should be aware that you certainly get what
you pay for here.

Positano

There's not much to **POSITANO**, only a couple of decent beaches and a great many boutiques; the town has long specialized in clothes made from linen, georgette and cotton, as well as handmade shoes and sandals. But its location, heaped up in a pyramid high above the water, has inspired a thousand postcards and helped to make it a moneyed resort that runs a close second to Capri in the celebrity stakes. Since John Steinbeck wrote up the place in glowing terms back in 1953, the town has enjoyed a fame quite out of proportion to its size. Franco Zefferelli is just one of many famous names who have villas nearby, and the people who come here to lie on the beach consider themselves a cut above your average sun-worshipper.

The beaches

Positano is, of course, expensive, but its beaches are nice enough and don't get too crowded. The main beach, the **Spiaggia Grande** right in front of the village, is reasonable, although you'll be sunbathing among the fishing boats unless you want to pay over the odds for the pleasanter bit on the far left. There's also another, larger stretch of beach, **Spiaggia del Fornillo**, around the headland to the west, accessible in five minutes by a pretty path that winds around from above the hydrofoil jetty – although its main section is also a pay area. Nonetheless the bar-terrace of the *Pupetto* hotel (see below), which runs along much of its length, is a cheaper place to eat and drink than anywhere in Positano proper.

ARRIVAL AND INFORMATION

By bus Buses stop at various points along the main coastal road, Via Marconi, which skirts the top of the old town of Positano. There's a stop on the Amalfi side of town, from where it's a steep walk or a short bus ride down to the little square at the bottom end of Via Cristoforo Colombo, a 5min walk from the seafront; or you could get off on the other side of the centre, by the *Bar Internazionale*, from where Viale Pasitea winds down to the Fornillo part of town.

By boat Ferries and hydrofoils from Capri, Naples, Amalfi and Salerno pull in at the jetty just to the right of the main beach, where there are also plenty of ticket booths.

By car Arriving by car, you'll shell out a lot on garage space as parking is very limited; reckon on at least €20 a day.

Tourist office Just back from the beach by the church steps at Via del Saracino 4 (June–Oct Tues–Sat 8.30am–7pm, Sun & Mon 8.30am–2pm; Nov–May Mon–Fri 8.30am–2pm; ☎ 089 875 067, ⊚ aziendaturismopositano.it).

ACCOMMODATION

Hostel Brikette Via G. Marconi 358 ☎ 089 875 857, ⊚ brikette.com. A couple of minutes' walk from the *Bar Internazionale* on the main coastal road, this is by far the cheapest accommodation in Positano. It's friendly and clean, with stunning Mediterranean views, bar and internet access, although the dorms (8- or 20-bed) can be a bit spartan and airless – private rooms are available too. Open late March–Nov. Dorms **€22/€25**, rooms **€65**

Maria Luisa Via Fornillo 42 ☎ 089 875 023, ⊚ pensione marialuisa.com. Perched high above Fornillo beach, and with great views, this is very friendly, and great value, though of course it's quite a climb down to the beach and back. Closed Jan & Dec. **€80**

Palazzo Murat Via dei Mulini 23 ☎ 089 875 177, ⊚ palazzomurat.it. Perhaps the nicest place to stay if you want to be right in the heart of things, just 2min from

the main beach, and with thirty good-sized and well-equipped rooms – though most of them are not in the old *palazzo* itself but in the newer extension. **€400**

Pupetto Via Fornillo 37 ☎ 089 875 087, ⊚ hotel pupetto.it. Right on Fornillo beach and with access for guests, this bright spot offers a huge terrace and pastel rooms with sea views. Full-range restaurant, from wood-fired pizza to catch of the day. **€170**

★ **Villa Verde** Viale Pasitea 338 ☎ 089 875 506, ⊚ pensionevillaverde.it. Just below the main road through town, a short walk from the *Bar Internazionale* bus stop. This place is friendly, very relaxed, and its fourteen good-sized rooms all have a/c and TV. And their balconies overlook central Positano from a wonderfully peaceful vantage-point. Excellent value. **€100**

EATING AND DRINKING

Bruno Via C. Colombo 157 ☎ 089 875 392. Some way from the more touristy places near the beach, both in

distance and in price. There are lovely views over the water at night (although you're basically sitting right on the

13

road), and the food is good and well priced; main courses – heavily weighted towards fish and seafood – start at around €16. Daily 12.30–2.30pm & 7.30–10.30pm.

Chez Black Spiaggia Grande ☎089 875 036, ⓦchezblack.it. A long-established seafood restaurant, maybe a bit over-branded these days, but the food is unfalteringly good, and the location probably Positano's best. Lots of great seafood options – try the *paccheri* with cuttlefish and octopus – but it also does pizza, from around

€7. Daily 12.30–3pm & 7.30–11pm; closed Jan.

★ **Lo Guarracino** Via Positanesi d'America 12 ☎089 875 794. Great food, relatively reasonably priced (pastas €10–16, mains €16–22), and wonderful views from a bright, flower-fringed terrace overlooking the sea and Fornillo beach. Try the *caponatina* – tuna, olives and cherry tomatoes on a slab of oily bread – or the *linguine ai ricci di mare* (with sea urchins). A 5min walk from the centre of Positano. Daily noon–2.30pm & 7.30–10pm.

Praiano and around

Around 6km east of Positano, **PRAIANO** is much smaller and very much quieter than its more renowned neighbour, and as such you might be tempted to stay here instead. It consists of two tiny centres: Vettica Maggiore, which is Praiano proper, scattered along the main road from Positano high above the sea; and Marina di Praia, squeezed into a cleft in the rock down at shore level, a couple of kilometres further along towards Amalfi.

There's not much to either bit of the village, but it does make a more peaceful and quite frankly more authentic place to stay than Positano. There's nothing whatsoever to see, but there are a few decent places to swim. The closest are the swimming spots off rocks down immediately below the village, most notably **Spiaggia Gavitella**, which you can reach from the main road by taking the path from the *San Gennaro* restaurant or from the *Smeraldo* hotel; there's also the small patch of shingly beach at **Marina di Praia**, surrounded by a couple of restaurants and places offering rooms. And there are some decent, properly sandy spots beyond Marina di Praia on the way to Amalfi.

The Grotta dello Smeraldo

Conca dei Marini • Daily: March–Oct 9am–5pm; Nov–Feb 10am–4pm • €5 • Taxi-boat from either Praiano or Amalfi €10 return, plus €5 entrance fee

About 4km out of Praiano, the **Grotta dello Smeraldo** is one of the most highly touted local natural features around here, a flooded cavern in which the sunlight turns the water a vivid shade of green. It's not unimpressive, but is basically one huge chamber and it doesn't take long for the boatman to whisk you around the main features, best of which is the intense colour of the water, and the stalagmites and stalactites that puncture, and drip from, every surface.

ACCOMMODATION · PRAIANO

Casa Angelina Via Capriglione 147 ☎089 813 1333, ⓦcasangelina.com. Newish boutique hotel that is the cool person's choice in Praiano, with a lobby full of contemporary art and a selection of rooms decorated with stark, modern white minimalism. **€325.**

★ **Costa Diva** Via Roma 12 ☎089 813 076, ⓦlocandacostadiva.it. Up above Marina di Praia, this

hotel spills down a lovely, leafy series of terraces from the road; all rooms have sea views and balconies. **€130**

Onda Verde Via Terramare 3 ☎089 874 143, ⓦondaverde.it. Extremely well placed, perched on the cliff edge at Marina di Praia, this lovely hotel has a great location, very nice rooms and even does cooking classes. **€200**

EATING AND DRINKING

La Brace Via Capriglione 146 ☎089 874 226, ⓦlabrace praiano.com. This restaurant on the main road is perhaps Praiano's best eating option, with pizzas straight from the wood-fired oven and excellent fresh fish from around €12, all of which you can enjoy on the covered terrace. Daily 12.30–2.30pm & 7.30–10.30pm; closed Nov–March.

Trattoria San Gennaro Via Capriglione 75 ☎089 874 293, ⓦsangennaro.it. Right next to the church, this is as central as you get in Vettica Maggiore, and serves huge portions of *antipasti di mare* and *primi* like *scialatielli con zucchine e gamberetti* for €8. Its outside terrace overlooks the church square and the sea, and has various amusements for kids. 12.30–2.30pm & 7.30–10.30pm; closed Thurs.

Amalfi and Atrani

13

Set in a wide cleft in the cliffs, **AMALFI**, a mere 4km or so further east, is the largest town and perhaps the highlight of the coast, and a good place to base yourself. It has been an established seaside resort since Edwardian times, when the British upper classes found the town a pleasant spot to spend their winters. Actually Amalfi's credentials go back much further: it was an independent republic during Byzantine times and one of the great naval powers, with a population of some 70,000; Webster's *Duchess of Malfi* was set here, and the city's traders established outposts all over the Mediterranean, setting up the Order of the Knights of St John of Jerusalem. Amalfi was finally vanquished by the Normans in 1131, and the town was devastated by an earthquake in 1343, but there is still the odd remnant of Amalfi's past glories around today, and the town has a crumbly attractiveness to its whitewashed courtyards and alleys that makes it fun to wander through. Plus there is a decent, mostly sandy beach to the left of the busy seafront, although once again the best bits are pay areas only, as well as a nice sandy beach in the attractive next-door resort, Atrani.

The Duomo

Piazza Duomo • Daily 10am–5pm • €3

The Duomo, at the top of a steep flight of steps, utterly dominates the town's main piazza, its tiered, almost gaudy facade topped by a glazed tiled cupola that's typical of the area. The bronze doors of the church came from Constantinople and date from 1066. Inside it's a mixture of Saracen and Romanesque styles, though now heavily restored, and the cloister – the so-called Chiostro del Paradiso – is the most appealing part of the building, oddly Arabic in feel with its whitewashed arches and palms. The adjacent museum, housed in an ancient, bare basilica, dates back to the sixth century and has various medieval and episcopal treasures, most intriguingly an eighteenth-century sedan chair from Macau, used by the bishop of Amalfi, a thirteenth-century mitre sewn with myriad seed pearls and a lovely fourteenth-century bone-and-ebony inlaid box, made by the renowned Embriarchi studio in Venice. Steps lead down from the museum to the heavily decorated crypt, where the remains of the apostle St Andrew lie under the altar, brought here (minus head) from Constantinople by the Knights of Malta in 1204.

The Arsenale

Largo Cesareo • Daily 10am–8.30pm • €2 • ☎ 089 871 170, ⓦ museoarsenaleamalfi.it

Facing the waterfront square, the town's ancient, vaulted **Arsenale** is another reminder of the former military might of Amalfi, used to build the maritime republic's fleet. Now it hosts temporary exhibitions and a small museum containing bits and pieces including the costumes worn by the great and the good of the town for the Regatta of the Maritime Republics, and the city banner, showing the emblems of Amalfi – the diagonal red strip and Maltese cross you see everywhere.

Museo della Carta

Via delle Cartiere 23 • Daily 10am–6.30pm • €4 • ☎ 089 830 4561, ⓦ museodellacarta.it

At the top of Via Genova, a fifteen-minute walk from the main square, the **Museo della Carta** is housed in a paper mill that dates back to 1350 and claims to be the oldest in Europe. The valley beyond the museum is still known as the **Valle dei Mulini** (Valley of Mills), from the fact that it was once the heart of Amalfi's paper industry, with around fifteen functioning mills. This is the only one to survive, and it makes all of the high-spec paper you see on sale around town. Tours take in the tools of the trade and the original paper-making process and equipment, including that in use when the mill shut down in 1969.

13

Atrani

A short walk around the headland (take the path off to the right just before the road tunnel and cut through the *Zaccaria* restaurant), **ATRANI** is to all extents and purposes an extension of Amalfi, and was indeed another part of the maritime republic, with a similarly styled church sporting another set of bronze doors from Constantinople, manufactured in 1086; it's here that the Regatta of the Maritime Republics (see p.41) begins every four years. It's a quiet place, with a pretty, almost entirely enclosed little square, Piazza Umberto, giving onto a smallish sandy beach – a little more developed than it once was, but still gloriously peaceful compared to Amalfi next door.

ARRIVAL AND INFORMATION   AMALFI AND ATRANI

By bus SITA buses from Positano, Ravello and Sorrento arrive at Piazza Flavio Gioia on the seafront.
By boat Ferries and hydrofoils from Salerno, Positano, Capri and Ischia arrive and leave at the landing stages in the harbour, right by the main bus terminal, as do the smaller boats to the Grotta dello Smeraldo and other points along the coast.

Tourist office In a courtyard on the seafront next door to the post office (Mon–Sat 9am–1pm & 2–6pm; ☎089 871 107, ⊛amalfitouristoffice.it); though not overburdened with information, it will provide a map of the town and answer basic questions.

ACCOMMODATION

A'Scalinatella Piazza Umberto 1, Atrani ☎089 871 492, ⊛hostelscalinatella.com. As good a reason as any for coming to Atrani is this hostel and hotel, one of the cheapest places to stay on the entire coast, a friendly, family-run establishment that offers excellent-value hostel beds and private en-suite rooms in various buildings around town. Open all year. Dorms €25, doubles €90
Aurora Piazzale dei Prontini 7 ☎089 871 209, ⊛aurora-hotel.it. Right in the corner of the harbour, a 5min walk from the centre of town, this hotel has bright rooms and large balconies, and a large lounge and terrace. Closed Nov–March. €149
Centrale Largo Piccolomini 1 ☎089 872 608, ⊛amalfi hotelcentrale.it. An excellent location, with good-sized and pleasantly furnished rooms, including TV, telephone, a/c and breakfast, eaten on the hotel's lovely roof terrace. €130
L'Argine Fiorito Via dei Dogi 45, Atrani ☎089 873 6309, ⊛larginefiorito.com. Up the road as far as you can go in Atrani is this peaceful B&B, with just five plain yet spacious rooms, a terrace and the soothing backdrop of the river as it tumbles down into the centre of Atrani. €105

Lidomare Via Piccolomini 9 ☎089 871 332, ⊛lidomare .it. Tucked away off to the left of Piazza del Duomo, this is perhaps the most characterful of Amalfi's central cheapies, a beautiful, family-run ex-ducal palace, nicely old-fashioned and full of antiques. Most of the rooms are lovely and large, and over half of them face the sea. €140
Palazzo Ferraioli Via Campo 16, Atrani ☎089 872 652, ⊛palazzoferraioli.it. Among the whitewashed steps and passages off to the left of Atrani's main square, the coolly contemporary rooms of this ingeniously converted *palazzo* are a wonderful escape, and have some good views over the town and bay. Each room is decorated differently, but each follows a determinedly stylish and modern theme. Closed Nov–March. €160
Residenza del Duca Via Mastalo del Duca 3 ☎089 873 6365, ⊛residencedelduca.it. Tiny *pensione* tucked away at the top of a building among the alleys and tiny courtyards off to the left of Amalfi's main street. All rooms have bathrooms with jacuzzi-style showers and flat-screen TVs, telephone and a/c, and breakfast is included in the price. €140

EATING AND DRINKING

A'Paranza Via Dragone 2, Atrani ☎089 871 840, ⊛ristoranteparanza.com. On the road that leads inland from the main square, a friendly seafood trattoria with fabulous home-made pasta and a speciality of *zuppa di pesce*. 1–3pm & 8–11pm; closed Tues.
Il Mulino Via della Cartiere 36, Amalfi ☎089 872 223. At the top of the main street, 10min walk from the Duomo, this is a cheery family-run place with an outside terrace that does good home-made seafood pasta for around €12, and decent pizzas too. Tues–Sun 12.30–3pm & 7.30–11pm.
La Caravella Via Mateo Camera 12 ☎089 871 029.

One of the town's posher options for a night out, or when you're tired of the same old offerings everywhere else. They serve great, individual takes on traditional dishes, all put together with fresh local ingredients, but it's a cut above the rest in price as well as tone, with most *primi* for around €20 and up, and fish and meat mains for €28–40. Noon–2.30pm & 7.15–10.30pm; closed Tues.
★ **Maccus** Largo S. Maria Maggiore 13 ☎089 873 6385. Good, reasonably priced food at a restaurant that makes the most of this atmospheric little square. *Totani e patate* €11, and pasta with zucchini €7. Daily noon–3pm & 7–10.30pm.

San Giuseppe Via Ruggiero 4. Left off the main street by *Trattoria da Gemma* and then right, this very simple restaurant puts a few tables out on a tiny courtyard and serves excellent pizzas and pretty much everything else at low prices – great value. Tues–Sun 12.30–2.30pm & 7.30–11pm.
Taverna degli Apostoli Supportivo Sant'Andrea 6 ✆ 089 872 991. Because of its location bang next to the cathedral steps, most people assume this is just another tourist joint. But its relatively small menu chalked on the blackboard outside is a good indication that it's not. Good food and a warm welcome. Daily noon–midnight.
Trattoria da Gemma Via Fra Gerardo Sasso 11 ✆ 089 871 345. A stalwart of the Amalfi restaurant scene, and still one of the best and most atmospheric places to eat in town, with a small, carefully considered menu, strong on fish and seafood, with pasta and *primi* for €16–18, mains at around €20–25, and a lovely terrace overlooking the main street. 12.30–3pm & 8–11pm; closed Wed.

Ravello

The best views of the coast can be had inland, high above Amalfi in **RAVELLO**: another renowned spot "closer to the sky than the seashore", wrote André Gide – with some justification. Ravello was also an independent republic for a while, and for a time an outpost of the Amalfi city-state. Now it's not much more than a large village, but its unrivalled location, spread across the top of one of the coast's mountains, makes it more than worth the thirty-minute bus ride through the steeply cultivated terraces up from Amalfi – although, like most of this coast, the charms of Ravello haven't been recently discovered. Wagner set part of *Parsifal*, one of his last operas, in the place; D.H. Lawrence wrote some of *Lady Chatterley's Lover* here; John Huston filmed his languid movie *Beat the Devil* in town; and more recently the writer and political polemicist Gore Vidal lived here for many years.

The Duomo

Everything in Ravello revolves around the main **Piazza del Duomo**, where the **Duomo**, a bright eleventh-century church, renovated in 1786, is dedicated to St Pantaleone, a fourth-century saint whose blood – kept in a chapel on the left-hand side – is supposed to liquefy (like Naples' San Gennaro and others) once a year on July 27. It's a richly decorated church, with a pair of twelfth-century bronze doors, cast with 54 scenes of the Passion; inside, there are two monumental thirteenth-century *ambones* (pulpits), both wonderfully adorned with intricate and glittering mosaics. The more elaborate one to the right of the altar, dated 1272, sports dragons and birds on spiral columns supported by six roaring lions, while the one on the left illustrates the story of Jonah and the whale. Downstairs in the crypt the **museo** (daily 9am–7pm; €2) holds the superb bust of Sigilgaita Rufolo and the silver reliquary of St Barbara, alongside a collection of highly decorative, fluid mosaic and marble reliefs from the same era.

Villa Rufolo

Piazza del Duomo • Daily April–Oct 9am–8pm; Nov–March 9am–4pm • €5, concerts €20 • ✆ 089 858 149, ⓦ villarufolo.it

The Rufolos figure again on the other side of the square, where various remains of their **Villa Rufolo** lie scattered among rich gardens overlooking the precipitous coastline; this is the spectacular main venue for the prestigious open-air chamber concerts held from March to October. If the crowds (best avoided by coming early in the morning) put you off, turn left by the entrance and walk up the steps over the tunnel for the best (free) view over the shore, from where it's a pleasant stroll through the back end of Ravello to the main square.

THE RAVELLO FESTIVAL

Ravello's **arts festival** (ⓦ ravellofestival.com) has grown into quite an annual event, and these days it dominates the summer months, with performances all over town stretching from the end of June to the end of October. Concentrating on classical music, dance, film and the visual arts, it makes the most of the town's settings and attracts an increasingly high level of international performers.

13

Villa Cimbrone

Via S. Chiara 26 • Daily 9am–sunset • €6 • ⓦ villacimbrone.com

It's just a ten-minute walk from the centre of Ravello to perhaps its most celebrated sight, the **Villa Cimbrone**, whose formal gardens spread across the furthest tip of Ravello's ridge. Most of the villa itself is now a luxury hotel but you can peep into the flower-hung cloister and crypt as you go in. The gardens are dotted with statues and little temples and lead down to what must be the most gorgeous spot in Ravello – a belvedere that looks over Atrani below and the sea beyond.

Ravello Auditorium

Via della Repubblica • ⓦ auditoriumoscarniemeyer.it

On the far side of Ravello's plateau, the **Ravello Auditorium** is an oddity in Ravello's otherwise mostly unchanged environment: a sleek, modern, white wave below the crown of the hill, designed by the prolific Brazilian architect Oscar Niemeyer, who was no less than 102 years old when it opened in 2009. It's not open for tours, but no one will stop you wandering down and peeking into its 400-seat main theatre space, which is the main venue for the Ravello Festival (see p.791) and more besides.

ARRIVAL AND INFORMATION
RAVELLO

By bus SITA buses run up to Ravello from Amalfi every half-hour from Piazza Flavio Gioia and drop off the other side of the tunnel from Piazza del Duomo, outside the *Garden* hotel at the top of Via della Repubblica. They take about 20min.

By car If you're driving, there's a useful car park that often has space just below the main square. Taxis stop just through the tunnel outside the *Garden* hotel, though be aware that taxis up here from Amalfi are around €30 one way.

Tourist office Off Via Roma, 2min from the main square (Mon–Sat: June–Aug 9.30am–8pm; Sept–May 9.30am–6pm; ☎ 089 857 096, ⓦ ravello.it).

ACCOMMODATION

Garden Via Boccaccio 4 ☎ 089 857 226, ⓦ garden ravello.com. Just the other side of the tunnel from central Ravello this small family-owned and -run hotel and restaurant occupies a prime spot looking up the coast, and makes the most of it with a large airy lobby and ten rooms that all have sea views. The rooms aren't huge, but they have small terraces and are well kept and well equipped – and the views, of course, are great. **€125**

Toro Via Roma 16 ☎ 089 857 211, ⓦ hoteltoro.it. In about as central a location as you can get in Ravello, just off the main piazza, the ten good-sized rooms here vary quite a bit in size but are tastefully furnished and, in any case, feel cool and peaceful compared to the touristy hubbub outside. Rooms include breakfast, and have TV and telephone but no a/c. **€118**

★ **Villa Amore** Via dei Fusco 5 ☎ 089 857 135, ⓦ villaamore.it. Down a short path off the main route between the centre of Ravello and the Villa Cimbrone, the rooms here are nothing special but some of them enjoy the best views in town – quite something by Ravello standards. There's a small and peaceful garden, and a restaurant that uses organic ingredients from the hotel's garden back on the main drag. The drawback is that you have to carry your luggage from the nearest parking 10min walk away back on the main piazza – or pay €5 per piece for the hotel to do it for you. **€100**

Villa Maria Via S. Chiara 2 ☎ 089 857 255, ⓦ villamaria .it. A lovely old-fashioned hotel situated 5min from the centre of Ravello on the way to Villa Cimbrone. It's not especially cheap, but the rooms have all facilities, including a/c and satellite TV, and rates include free parking and a pool at the nearby co-owned *Giordano* as well as the all-important luggage transportation. **€400**

EATING AND DRINKING

Cumpa Cosimo Via Roma 48 ☎ 089 857 988. Great local food, home-made pasta and wine at moderate prices in the heart of Ravello – though there are no views or outside seating. Tues–Sun noon–3pm & 7–11pm.

Da Salvatore Via della Repubblica 2 ☎ 089 857 227. In business for over fifty years, *Salvatore* has fantastic views from the restaurant and outside terrace, and an intriguing menu – tuna carbonara, gnocchi with cod, and rabbit doughnuts, to name just some of the more bizarre items. The food is excellent, and not all weird (you can order *spaghetti alle vongole* and steak if you want). *Primi* from €12 and mains around €15; there's a cheaper pizzeria downstairs, which does starters and pizzas only in the evenings. Daily noon–3pm & 8–11pm.

Villa Amore Via dei Fusco 5 ☎ 089 857 135, ⓦ villa amore.it. Tucked away halfway between Ravello's main square and the Villa Cimbrone, one of the most reasonably priced restaurants in Ravello also has one of the best views from its terrace. Its pasta dishes run around €8–9, but apart from a decent *spaghetti alle vongole* there's more of a focus on meat dishes, with lots of *scaloppini*, steaks and the like for €9–10. Daily 12.30–2.30pm & 7.30–10.30pm.

Salerno

Capital of Campania's southernmost province, the lively port of **SALERNO** is much less chaotic than Naples and is well off most travellers' itineraries, giving it a pleasant, relaxed air. It has a good supply of cheap accommodation, which makes it a reasonable base for some of the closer resorts of the Amalfi Coast and for the ancient site of Paestum to the south. During medieval times the town's medical school was the most eminent in Europe; more recently, it was the site of the Allied landing of September 9, 1943 – a landing that reduced much of the centre to rubble. The subsequent rebuilding has restored neither charm nor efficiency to the town centre, which is an odd mixture of wide, rather characterless boulevards and a small medieval core full of intriguingly dark corners and alleys. It is, however, a lively, sociable place, with a busy seafront boulevard and plenty of nightlife and shops.

Via dei Mercanti

There isn't a great deal to see in Salerno, but it's pleasant to wander through the vibrant streets of the centre, especially the ramshackle old medieval quarter, which starts at the far end of the pedestrianized main shopping drag of **Corso V. Emanuele**. The old quarter's main street is **Via dei Mercanti**, a narrow stretch which snakes through the heart of the centre and has been spruced up quite a lot over recent years.

Pinacoteca Provinciale di Salerno

Via dei Mercanti 63 • Tues–Sun 9am–7.45pm • Free

Part of Via dei Mercanti's makeover is the **Pinacoteca Provinciale di Salerno**, housed in the seventeenth-century Palazzo Pinto at Via dei Mercanti 63 – half a dozen rooms, basically, displaying one or two nice fifteenth-century altarpieces and a couple of works by Carlo Rosa and other Neapolitan Baroque artists.

The Duomo

Via del Duomo • Mon–Sat 10am–6.30pm, Sun 1–6.30pm • Free

Off to the right of Via dei Mercanti, up Via del Duomo, the **Duomo** is Salerno's highlight, an enormous church built in 1076 by Robert Guiscard and dedicated to St Matthew. Entrance is through a cool and shady courtyard, built with columns plundered from Paestum, and centring on a gently gurgling fountain set in an equally ancient bowl. In the heavily restored interior, the two elegant mosaic pulpits are the highlight, the one on the left dating from 1173, the other, with its matching paschal candlesticks, a century later. Immediately behind there's more sumptuous mosaic-work in the screens of the choir, as well as the quietly expressive fifteenth-century tomb of Margaret of Anjou, wife of Charles III of Durazzo, in the left aisle. To the left of the tomb, steps lead down to the polychrome marble crypt, which holds the body of St Matthew himself, brought here in the tenth century.

Museo Diocesano

Largo Plebiscito • Daily 9.30am–12.30pm & 3–6.30pm • Free

Next door to the cathedral, the main attraction at the **Museo Diocesano** is a set of 69 ivory panels depicting Biblical scenes from a large eleventh-century altar-front – said to be the largest work of its kind in the world. They're amazing, minutely crafted pieces, showing everything from Creation to the Expulsion from Paradise to the Last Supper – a sort of Biblical comic strip in ivory.

13

Museo Archeologico Provinciale

Via S. Benedetto 26 • Tues–Sun 9am–7.45pm • Free

Five minutes' walk from the cathedral, the **Museo Archeologico Provinciale** occupies two floors of a restored Romanesque palace. It's full of local finds, and has an array of terracotta heads and votive figurines, jewellery, lamps and household objects, from Etruscan as well as Roman times, but its most alluring piece is a sensual *Head of Apollo* upstairs, a Roman bronze fished from the Gulf of Salerno in the 1930s.

Giardini della Minerva

Via Ferrante Sanseverino 1 • Tues–Sun: April–Sept 10am–1pm & 5–8pm; Oct–March 9am–1pm • €2 • ⓦ giardinodellaminerva.it

After the cathedral, Salerno's most interesting attraction is the **Giardini della Minerva** on Via Ferrante Sanseverino, a medicinal garden laid out according to medieval medical principles and traversed by channels of tinkling water. It's a gloriously fragrant place, its shady terraces wonderfully soothing in summer, and there's even a café serving herbal tea to ensure you leave healthier than when you arrived.

ARRIVAL AND DEPARTURE

SALERNO

By train Salerno's train station lies at the southeastern end of the town centre on Piazza Vittorio Veneto, about a 10min walk from the old town.

Destinations Paestum/Agropoli (hourly; 35min); Sapri (every 30min; 2hr).

By bus City and local buses pull up here; those from Paestum and further south arrive and leave from Piazza della Concordia, down by the waterside nearby; buses from Naples use the SITA bus station at Corso Garibaldi 119.

Destinations Agropoli (hourly; 1hr 20min); Amalfi (hourly; 1hr 10min); Naples (every 15–30min; 1hr 5min); Padula (2 daily; 1hr 50min–2hr); Paestum (hourly; 1hr); Positano (every 1–2hr; 2hr); Sorrento (every 1–2hr; 2hr 45min).

By boat Ferries and hydrofoils from Amalfi Coast, Bay of Naples and elsewhere arrive in the harbour, 5min walk from the centre of town, and 10min from the train station.

Destinations Amalfi (April–Sept 6 daily hydrofoils; 35min); Positano (5 daily hydrofoils; 1hr 10min).

INFORMATION

Tourist office Corner of Piazza Vittorio Veneto and Corso Garibaldi, right outside the train station (Mon–Sat 9am–1pm & 3.15–7.15pm; ☎ 089 231 432).

ACCOMMODATION

Ave Gratia Plena Via dei Canali ☎ 089 234 776, ⓦ ostellodisalerno.it. Housed in a former church and cloister complex, Salerno's official HI youth hostel is right in the centre of town and is a clean and welcoming place with a mixture of dorms and private rooms. Its lovely central courtyard has wi-fi throughout. Dorms **€15**, doubles **€60**

Grand Hotel Salerno Via Lungomare Clemente Tafuri 1 ☎ 089 704 1111, ⓦ grandhotelsalerno.it. Grand in the sense of large rather than posh, a giant cruiseship of a place beached on the seafront a 5min walk south of the train station. Its rooms are functional rather than sumptuous, but they're nice enough and prices are keen; plus there's

plenty of facilities including wi-fi, a healthclub with pool and a large downstairs bar. **€100**

Plaza Piazza Vittorio Veneto 42 ☎ 089 224 477, ⓦ plazasalerno.it. Right opposite the train station, this is a decent, comfortable choice and handy for transport and the town centre. Its forty rooms are half a notch above the nearby *Santa Rosa*, but pricier. **€90**

Santa Rosa Corso Vittorio Emanuele 16 ☎ 089 225 346. This friendly, basic hotel has perfectly simple but perfectly pleasant double rooms with bathrooms, just around the corner from the train station. Prices are low, although you pay extra for a/c. **€60**

EATING AND DRINKING

Antica Pizzeria Vicolo della Neve Vicolo della Neve 24 ☎ 089 225 705, ⓦ vicolodellaneve.it. Take a left turn off Via Mercanti about 50m past Via Duomo to this attractively downbeat place serving great pizza and local specialities like *cotechino* sausage and broccoli, with a particularly good *calzone*. Pizzas go for €4 upwards, main courses for around €10. 7.30–11pm; closed Wed.

Caffè dei Mercanti Via dei Mercanti 114 ☎ 089 232

731. Cosy bar, good for both a quick coffee or a few drinks, with bar snacks and light lunch options if you're feeling peckish. Daily 8am–10pm.

Hostaria Il Brigante Via Fratelli Linguiti 4 ☎ 089 226 592. A great, old-fashioned *osteria* near the Duomo with mains at around €10 – try the *zuppa dell'aglio* (garlic soup) and dishes made with *calamarata* (tubular pasta). Tues–Sun 8–11pm.

Paestum

Via Magna Grecia • Daily 8.45am–1hr before sunset • Site €6, Museum €4, site and museum €11 including Velia further south •
ⓦ paestum.it

About an hour's bus ride south of Salerno, the ancient site of **Paestum** spreads across
a large area at the bottom end of the **Piana del Sele** – a wide, flat plain grazed by the
buffalo that produce a good quantity of southern Italy's mozzarella cheese. Paestum, or
Poseidonia as it was known, was founded by Greeks from Sybaris in the sixth century
BC, and later, in 273 BC, colonized by the Romans, who Latinized the name. But
by the ninth century a combination of malaria and Saracen raids had decimated the
population and left the buildings deserted and gradually overtaken by thick forest –
the site wasn't rediscovered until the eighteenth century during the building of a road
through here. It's a desolate, open place even now ("inexpressibly grand", Shelley called
it), mostly unrecognizable ruin but with three golden-stoned **temples** that are among
the best-preserved Doric temples in Europe. Of these, the Temple of Neptune, dating
from about 450 BC, is the most complete, with only its roof and parts of the inner
walls missing. The Basilica of Hera, built a century or so earlier, retains its double rows
of columns, while the Temple of Ceres at the northern end of the site was used as a
Christian church for a time. In between, the forum is little more than an open space,
and the buildings around are mere foundations.

The museum

Daily 9am–6.45pm; closed first and third Mon every month • €4, €6.50 including site

The splendid **museum**, across the road, holds Greek and Roman finds from the site
and around. Straight ahead of you as you enter are some stunning sixth-century bronze
vases (*hydriae*), decorated with rams, lions and sphinxes; behind them more bronze
– gleaming helmets, breastplates and greaves. Make a point of seeing the rare Greek
tomb paintings, the best of which are from the Tomb of the Diver, graceful and
expressively naturalistic pieces of work, including a diver in mid-plunge, said to
represent the passage from life to death, and male lovers banqueting. Attractive
fourth-century terracotta plates depict all sorts of comestibles – sweets, fruit and
cheese, and a set of weathered archaic-period Greek metopes from another temple
at the mouth of the Sele River, a few kilometres north, shows scenes of fighting and
hunting. On the first floor, which is devoted to Roman finds, highlights are a statue
of an abstracted-looking Pan with his pipes, a third-century relief showing a baby in
pointed hat and amulets, and a sarcophagus cover of a tenderly embracing couple.

ARRIVAL AND INFORMATION

PAESTUM

By bus It's easy to see Paestum on a day-trip from Salerno.
SCAT buses run from Piazza della Concordia on the seafront,
close to the Porto Turistico, about 4 times a day and take
about 45min. You can also reach Paestum by frequent bus
from Agropoli, about 15min away.

Tourist office Tucked away on a side street to the left of
the museum at Via Magna Grecia 887 (daily 9am–1pm &
2–5pm; ☎ 0828 811 016, ⓦ infopaestum.it).

The Cilento

Immediately south of Paestum, the coastline bulges out into a broad, mountainous
hump of territory known as the **Cilento** – one of the remotest parts of Campania.

Agropoli

AGROPOLI, the first town you reach, fifteen minutes out from Paestum and on the
main Salerno–Reggio railway line, is a good base for the ruins (buses every hour),
and its blend of the peaceful old quarter, heaped on a headland, and the new, modern
centre down below makes for a nice place to spend a few days, with a vivacious
main-street *passeggiata*. The beaches aren't great, but you can swim from the flat rocks
in the harbour and the water's perfectly clean.

13

Santa Maria di Castellabate

The next town, **SANTA MARIA DI CASTELLABATE**, is a pleasant and lively seaside town, with an animated waterfront which forms the start of a lovely crescent of sand that runs right round to the next town along, the less alluring **San Marco**. There's also the old town of Santa Maria which is also worth getting up to if you can, high on a hill a couple of kilometres inland, and with an intriguing little enclosed square, almost Moorish with its arches and passageways and tremendous views. In seaside Santa Maria the first stretches of beach are given over to beach bars and an excellent waterside hotel (see opposite), but there are other, free stretches beyond (and there's nothing wrong with the town patch).

Acciaroli and Marina d'Ascea

Buses run down to **ACCIAROLI**, about 25km south of Agropoli, one of the Cilento's larger resorts and a port for the hydrofoils plying the coast during summer. The railway joins the shoreline again at **MARINA D'ASCEA**, a fairly indifferent resort but surrounded by hotels and campsites, especially along the lengthy sand beach that stretches north to Marina del Casalvelino.

Velia

Piano di Velia Ascea • Daily 9am to 1hr before sunset • €2.50, €11 with Paestum

Some 20km on from Santa Maria, **MARINA DI VELIA** gives access to the site of **Velia** – comprising the ruins of the Hellenistic town of Elea, founded around 540 BC and an important port and cultural centre, home to its own school of philosophy. Later it became a favourite holiday resort for wealthy Romans, Horace being just one of many who came here on the advice of his doctor. The decline of Velia parallels that of Paestum – malarial swamp rendering much of the area uninhabitable – though the upper reaches were lived in until the fifteenth century. There, however, the comparison ends: the remains of Velia are considerably more decimated than those of Paestum and the town was never as crucial a centre, with nothing like as many temples. At the top of the site the "**Porta Rosa**", named after the wife of the archeologist who conducted the first investigations, is one of the earliest arches ever found – and the first indication to experts that the Greeks knew how to construct such things. Across from here, the **Acropolis** on the next peak has relics of an amphitheatre and a temple, together with a massive Norman tower – visible for some distance around.

Palinuro

The southernmost Cilento resort, cheerful **PALINURO** is worth a stop, named after the legendary pilot of the *Aeneid*, who is supposed to have drowned here. It's a much livelier place than anywhere else on the Cilento coast, and so can be packed out. But it's a relatively sprawling place, and a good alternative to Agropoli and Santa Maria, both as a base for the site of Velia and a beach-bumming spot – the sea here is one of the cleanest spots on the coast, and the sandy beach and harbour are lovely, if busy, with boats and people. From the harbour, you can explore the stunning craggy coast of the Capo Palinuro, studded with a series of caves, either by taking a guided **boat tour** (€8) or – more fun – by renting a **motorboat** (€25 for 2hr, plus around €10 for petrol).

ARRIVAL AND DEPARTURE
CILENTO COAST

By bus The towns of the Cilento coast are well linked by regular bus services, with around six buses daily between Agropoli to Acciaroli (1hr) and hourly buses to Paestum (15min) and Salerno (1hr 20min).

ACCOMMODATION

AGROPOLI

La Lanterna Via Lanterna 8 ☏ 0974 838 364, ⊚ cilento .it/lanterna. Great, independently owned youth hostel, about 1km from the station and conveniently close to the bus stop for Paestum. It has nice gardens and is a 2min walk from the beach; plus it does meals every evening and has a bar and TV and games room. Dorms are small (4–6 beds) – and there are private rooms too. Closed Nov to mid-March. Dorms €16, doubles €50

Serenella Lungomare S. Marco 140 ☏ 0974 823 333,

ⓦhotelserenella.it. A short walk north of Agropoli's old town, this hotel has clean and modern if rather characterless rooms and access to a private beach. **€120**

SANTA MARIA DI CASTELLABATE

Palazzo Belmonte Via Flavia Gioia 25 ☎0974 960 211, ⓦpalazzobelmonte.com. Maybe the nicest option along the coast, set in its own terraced gardens with well-equipped rooms either inside the original *palazzo* or in villas in the gardens themselves. It's also got a nice pool, and the food – served in the gardens each evening – is something special. **€275**

PALINURO

Hotel La Torre Via Porto 3 ☎0974 931 264, ⓦlatorre palinuro.it. The best hotel option in Palinuro, just 10m from the harbour; its rooms are comfortable and well kept, with cable wi-fi, and there's a sociable bar – a great place for a sundowner. **€120**

Villagio degli Olivi Corso Carlo Pisacane 171 ☎0974 938 501, ⓦvillaggiodegliolivi.it. Conveniently located in the heart of Palinuro, this complex of comfortable villas has access to a sandy beach, where steps from a series of rock pools take you straight into the sea. There's also a lovely pool, restaurant and bar on-site. Half-board only. **€200**

EATING AND DRINKING

SANTA MARIA DI CASTELLABATE

Taverna del Mare Via Landi 25 ☎0974 961 172. Right on the beach, this is a busy and reasonably priced restaurant that does good fish and seafood, though service can be patchy. Daily noon–3pm & 8–11pm.

PALINURO

Da Carmelo Strada Statale 562 ☎0974 931 138, ⓦdacarmelo.it. Blow your last few euros at *Da Carmelo*, 2km south of town at Località Isca, whose fish and seafood are said to be the best for miles around. Daily 8–11pm.

L'Ancora Via Indipendenza 115 ☎0974 931 373. Friendly, unpretentious restaurant whose speciality is *zuppa di pesce*, and the wood-fired oven turns out large and delicious pizzas. Daily noon–3pm & 7.30–11pm.

Taverna del Porto Via Porto 50 ☎0974 931 278. A good beachfront restaurant, which does great pizzas and excellent pasta and seafood. Daily noon–10pm.

Puglia

OSTUNI

Puglia

14

Puglia is the long strip of land, 400km from north to south, that makes up the heel of Italy. For centuries it was a strategic province, colonized, invaded and conquered by just about every major power of the day – from the Greeks through to the Spanish. These days clean seas and reliable sunshine are the draws for holiday-makers both Italian and foreign, and acres of campsite-and-bungalow-type tourist villages stud the shoreline, though there are still quiet spots to be found. Low-cost flights to Bari and Brindisi have opened up the area to British tourists, many of whom have been buying and doing up *trulli* (ancient storehouses; see p.821) and *masserie* (farm estates) as holiday accommodation. There's a brisk air of investment in many resorts, from the new top-of-the-range spa hotels in converted *masserie* to agriturismo places, where you can holiday among olive groves and orchards and go horseriding or mountain biking. B&Bs have been springing up everywhere, often in the historic centres of towns, some simple, some splendid, all of them better value for money than most hotels.

There's plenty of architectural interest in Puglia, as each ruling dynasty left its own distinctive mark on the landscape – the Romans their agricultural schemes and feudal lords their fortified medieval towns. Perhaps most distinctive are the kasbah-like quarters of many towns and cities, a vestige of the Saracen conquest of the ninth century – the one at **Bari** is the biggest and most atmospheric. The Normans endowed Puglia with splendidly ornate cathedrals, while the Baroque exuberance of towns like **Lecce** and **Martina Franca** are testament to the Spanish legacy. But if there's one symbol of Puglia that stands out, it's the imposing castles built by the Swabian Frederick II all over the province – foremost of which are the **Castel del Monte** (immortalized on the Italian five-cent euro coin) and the remnants of the palace at **Lucera**.

Puglia's cities, generally visited only as transport hubs, merit some exploration nevertheless. **Taranto** and its surroundings have fought a losing battle with the local steel industry, but **Lecce** is worth a visit of a day or two for its crazed confection of Baroque churches and laidback café life. Though **Bari** is not a traditional tourist destination, reinvestment in its maze-like old city is drawing visitors in-the-know for its ambience and excellent restaurants; while **Brindisi**, best known for its ferry connections with Greece, lies just 15km away from the beautiful **Torre Guaceto** nature reserve, a long stretch of uncontaminated sand dunes, *macchia* and clear water where you can cycle, walk or scuba dive.

Puglia is geographically diverse, though it has to be said that the **Tavoliere** (tableland) of the north with mile upon mile of wheatfields, is hardly the most exciting of landscapes. More alluring is the hilly, forested **Gargano promontory** jutting out to the east, fringed by gently shelving, sandy beaches, seaside hotels and campsite villages that make good places for a family holiday – though you'll need to catch a ferry to the **Tremiti islands** for the

NATURAL ARCH NEAR VIESTE

Highlights

❶ Vieste For sun and sea, head for this resort on the dramatic Gargano promontory, with the option in summer of travelling onwards to the Tremiti islands. **See p.807 & p.810**

❷ Trani This miniature medieval port is a jewel, with its eleventh-century cathedral impressively located on the waterfront. **See p.811**

❸ Castel del Monte Puglia's greatest Swabian castle is a testament to thirteenth-century engineering. **See p.816**

❹ Martina Franca This lively town with its Moorish feel makes a good base for exploring the surrounding area's *trulli* – Puglia's traditional conical whitewashed buildings. **See p.821**

❺ Ostuni One of the most stunning hilltop towns in southern Italy, with a sun-bleached old quarter and a sandy coastline 7km away. **See p.829**

❻ Lecce In the southern tip of Italy, Lecce is an exuberant city of Baroque architecture and opulent churches. **See p.830**

HIGHLIGHTS ARE MARKED ON THE MAP ON PP.802–803

clearest sea. The best escape is to the southernmost tip, the **Salentine peninsula** where the terrain is rocky and dry, more Greek than Italian, and there are some beautiful coves and sea caves to swim in.

GETTING AROUND   PUGLIA

Getting around Puglia by public transport is fairly easy, at least as far as the main towns and cities go. FS trains connect nearly all the major places, while small, private lines head into previously remote areas – in the Gargano and on the edges of Le Murge. Most other places can be reached by **bus**, although isolated village services can be infrequent or inconveniently early – a problem that can only really be solved by taking, or renting, your own **car**. In July and August buses connect coastal towns.

The Tavoliere

The province of Foggia, known also as the **Tavoliere** (tablelands), occupies a broad **plain** stretching from the foothills of the Apennines in the west and the Gargano massif in the east. **FOGGIA**, the capital and transport hub of the province, is not somewhere to linger – for more of an idea of what the Tavoliere is like, head for the walled town of **Lucera** or the little village of **Troia**.

Lucera and around

LUCERA (pronounced Loosh-airer) makes a wonderful introduction to Puglia. A charming small town with a bright, bustling centre and a lively *passeggiata* on summer evenings, it was once the capital of the Tavoliere – a thriving Saracen hub. Frederick II, having forced

Rijeka & Dubrovnik (Croatia)

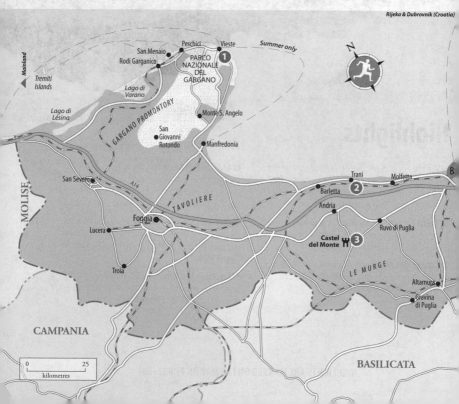

the Arabs out of Sicily, resettled 20,000 of them here, on the site of an abandoned Roman town, allowing them complete freedom in religious worship – an almost unheard of act of liberalism for the early thirteenth century.

The Duomo

Piazza del Duomo • Daily 8am–noon & 5–7pm • Free

Lucera's **Duomo** was built in the early fourteenth century after Frederick II's death, when the Angevins arrived and a conflict with the Saracens began. The Angevins won and built the cathedral on the site of a mosque; by the end of their rule, few of the town's original Arab-influenced buildings were left. However, the Arabic layout of Lucera survived and there's a powerful atmosphere here – best appreciated by wandering the narrow streets of the old town, peering into the courtyards and alleyways.

Museo Civico

Via De' Nicastri 74 • Tues–Sun 9am–1pm, Tues, Thurs & Sat also 5–8pm • Free

Behind the cathedral, on Via De' Nicastri, the **Museo Civico** has recently been restored, with an appealing collection ranging from Roman portrait busts, mosaics and a pair of muscly miniature gladiators tensed for battle, to moulds used by the town's medieval artisans to create terracotta Madonnas.

The Castello and the Roman amphitheatre

The main sights are outside the old centre, most notably the vast **Castello** (Tues–Sun: summer 9am–2pm & 3–8pm; winter 9am–2pm; free), built by Frederick and designed to house a lavish court that included a collection of exotic wild beasts. To get there

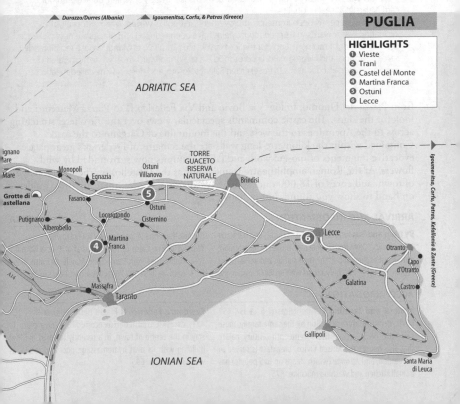

PUGLIA

HIGHLIGHTS
❶ Vieste
❷ Trani
❸ Castel del Monte
❹ Martina Franca
❺ Ostuni
❻ Lecce

14

REGIONAL FOOD AND WINE

Puglia is known as the breadbasket of Italy. It's the source of 80 percent of Europe's pasta and much of Italy's fish; it produces more wine than Germany and more olive oil than all the other regions of Italy combined. It's famous for olives (from Cerignola), almonds (from Ruvo di Puglia), dark juicy tomatoes (often sun-dried), *cime di rapa* (turnip tops), fava beans, figs (fresh and dried), *cotognata* (a moulded jam made from quince) and for its melons, grapes and green cauliflower. The influence of Puglia's former rulers is still evident in the region's food. Like the **Greeks**, Pugliesi eat lamb and goat spit-roast over herb-scented fires and deep-fried doughnut-like cakes steeped in honey; and like the **Spanish** they drink almond milk, *latte di mandorla*.

The most distinctive local **pasta** is *orecchiette*, ear-shaped pasta that you will still see women making in their doorways in the old part of Bari. Look out, too, for *panzarotti alla barese*, deep-fried pockets of dough stuffed with tomato or prosciutto and ricotta. Otherwise, there is a marked preference for short, stubby varieties of pasta, which you'll find served with peppers, cauliflower and *cime di rapa*. Not surprisingly, fish and shellfish dominate coastal menus. There are some good fish soups (*zuppe di pesce*) whose ingredients and style vary from place to place – the Brindisi version, for example, is dominated by eel. Vegetarians are well catered for with a range of meat-free antipasti, and combining pasta and vegetables is a typically Pugliese trait.

A local meat dish is *gnummerieddi*: resembling haggis, it's made by stuffing a lamb gut with minced offal, herbs and garlic – best grilled over an open fire. There is little beef or pork eaten in Puglia, poultry is uncommon, aside from small game birds in season; as a result, horsemeat is popular, especially in the Salento area. To confound your prejudices, go for *pezzetti di cavallo*, bits of horsemeat stewed in a rich tomato sauce.

Cheeses are a strong point, including ricotta, *caciocotta*, *canestrato* (sheep's-milk cheese formed in baskets) and *burrata* (cream encased in mozzarella, a speciality of Andria). Pair these products with the local durum-wheat breads, the most famous of which, *pane di Altamura*, carries the DOP seal of quality.

There have recently been immense improvements in Puglia's **wines**. While historically the inclination was towards mass production, yields have been reduced and grapes are now picked at precisely the right moment. Look for the formidable reds Primitivo di Manduria (aka red Zinfandel), Salice Salentino, and Negroamaro. Locorotondo is a straightforward, fresh white from Salento, a region known also for its *rosati* (rosé) called Salento Rosato, and dessert wine called Aleatico.

---

from Piazza del Duomo, follow Via Bovio and Via Federico II to Piazza Matteotti and look for the signs. The castle commands spectacular views over the Tavoliere, stretching across to the Apennines to the west and the mountains of Gargano to the east. Contained within the kilometre-long walls are the remains of Frederick's great palace, evocative fragments of mosaic-work and fallen columns now surrounded by wild flowers. At the Roman **amphitheatre** (same hours as the Castello) on the western edge of town, audiences of 18,000 once watched gladiatorial battles; there are (free) guides on hand to show you round, but in Italian only.

ARRIVAL AND INFORMATION

By train and bus Ferrovia del Gargano buses and trains run at least every 30min from Foggia East. Buses are slightly more convenient as they stop at the train station and in Piazza del Popolo, from where it's only a short walk up Via Gramsci to the Duomo, the centre of the medieval walled town.

Tourist office Close to the cathedral at Piazza Nocelli 6 (year-round Tues–Sun 9am–2pm; March–Oct also Tues–Fri 3–6pm; ☎ 0881 522 762, ⓦ comune.lucera.fg.it).

ACCOMMODATION

Mimosa and Jasmine Via De' Nicastri 6 ☎ 338 457 0070, ⓦ mimosalucera.it. Run by the same family, these two little B&Bs occupy the seventeenth-century palace that also houses the Museo Civico; breakfast is served in the garden, and *Jasmine* (which sleeps up to 5 people) has a small kitchen and washing machine. **€75**

Residenza Federico II Piazza del Popolo ☎ 0881 201 421, ⓦ residenzadifedericosecondo.it. A nice place to stay in the centre of town, in a recently restored medival building with its own hydromassage pool and sauna, as well as a pizzeria. **€95**

EATING AND DRINKING

Il Cortiletto Via De' Nicastri 26 ☎0881 542 554. A moderately priced place just behind the cathedral serving excellent local food, such as *orecchiette* with wild vegetables (€8.50), on a constantly changing menu and a *degustazione* menu (€27.50) that offers a great chance to sample whatever is in season – in spring, try the fillet of pork braised in local red wine. There is a vast array of Pugliese wines too. 12.30–2.30pm & 8–10.30pm; closed Sun eve.

Lupus in Fabula Via Mazzacarra 4 ☎0881 530 593. Pub-like place – restaurant/wine bar/jazz club – in the old town whose menu features typically Luceran dishes such as *orecchiette* with a local variety of tomato known as *prunillo*, sausage and rocket at moderate prices. From May to Sept it moves to Via Schiavone 7, a little alleyway where you can eat outside. Daily 12.30–2.30pm & 8pm–midnight.

14

Troia

Frequent buses from Lucera (and Foggia) make the short ride to **TROIA**, 18km due south. The locals seem curiously blasé as to the origin of their village's name; it means "slut" in Italian, but no one is able to offer a logical connection with the village. Whatever the reason, the Troiani atone for the name by having three patron saints, whose relics are paraded around town in a procession during the Gesta dei Santi Patroni every July 17.

The Duomo

Via Regina Margherita 77 • Daily 8.30am–noon & 3–7pm • Free

For most of the year Troia is a quiet, dusty village, its only sight the fine **Duomo**, an intriguing eleventh-century blend of Byzantine and Apulian-Romanesque styles, with a generous hint of Saracen. The great bronze doors are covered with reliefs of animals and biblical figures, while above, surrounded by a frenzy of carved lions frozen in stone, is an extraordinary rose window. Distinctly Saracen, the window resembles a finely worked piece of oriental ivory, composed of eleven stone panels, each one delicately carved. There's more exact detail inside, too, including a curiously decorated pulpit and some ornate capitals.

The Gargano promontory

The **Gargano promontory** rises like an island from the flat plains of the Tavoliere. It has a remarkably diverse landscape: beaches and lagoons to the north, a rocky, indented eastern coast and a mountainous, green heartland of oak and beech trees – reminiscent of a Germanic forest rather than a corner of southern Italy. For centuries the promontory was extremely isolated, visited only by pilgrims making their way along the valley to Monte Sant'Angelo and its shrine. Tourism has taken off in a big way, especially around the seaside resort of Vieste, but in 1991 the whole peninsula became a national park, helping to protect it from overbearing development and ensuring that much of the interior remains supremely unspoiled and quiet.

It may seem as though the promontory is one long strip of private beach, but bear in mind that by Italian law everyone has access to the actual seashore, as well as the 50m length between the reserved areas. Check with your hotel – often the price of a sunbed and umbrella at the nearest beach is included in the cost of an overnight stay.

ARRIVAL AND DEPARTURE

THE GARGANO PROMONTORY

Approaches to the promontory are pretty straightforward. FS trains run from Foggia to Manfredonia on the southeast side of Gargano, from where it's only 16km by **bus** to Monte Sant'Angelo. Alternatively, in the north of the region, Ferrovie del Gargano (☎0881 587 211, ⊛ferroviedelgargano.com) operates trains between Foggia and San Severo. You then change here for onward travel to Peschici–Calanelle, from where a bus connects with Peschici. Note that most FG stations are quite a distance from the towns and villages they serve, so always go for the connecting bus if there is one.

GETTING AROUND

Getting around the interior can be a little more tortuous. **Buses** are run by two companies: SITA (☎ 0881 352 011, ⊕ sitabus.it) which serves the inland towns and operates the inland route to Vieste; and Ferrovie del Gargano (see p.805), which runs the trains and connecting buses in northern Gargano, including a coastal bus route to Vieste, via Manfredonia, Mattinata and Pugnochiuso.

Monte Sant'Angelo

14

Perched almost 800m up in the hills, **MONTE SANT'ANGELO** is the highest – and coldest – settlement in the Gargano. Pilgrims have trudged up the switchback paths and roads for centuries to visit the spot where the archangel Michael is said to have made four separate appearances, mostly at the end of the fifth century – making the sanctuary here one of the earliest Christian shrines in Europe and one of the most important in Italy. Today, the pilgrims come by bus, and the village is a bit of a tourist trap. But the annual major **festivals** on May 8 and September 28, 29 and 30 attract locals from miles around, some of whom turn up in traditional dress.

Santuario di San Michele Arcangelo

Via Reale Basilica • Summer Mon–Sat 7.30am–12.30pm & 2.30–8pm; Sun 7.30am–8pm; winter Mon–Sat 7.30am–12.30pm & 2.30–5.30pm, Sun 7.30am–5.30pm • Free • ☎ 0884 561 150

From the central Piazza Duca d'Aosta the road runs uphill to the edge of the old town and the Via Reale Basilica, where you'll find the famous **Santuario di San Michele Arcangelo**. From the small courtyard on the right a flight of stone steps leads down to the crypts that form the entrance to the church, built on the site of the cave in which the archangel first appeared (in 490).

Tomba di Rotari and the Castello

Opposite the sanctuary, another set of steps leads down to the nearby ruins of the **Complesso di San Pietro**, behind which is the so-called **Tomba di Rotari** (daily 8.30am–12.30pm & 2.30–dusk; €1) – an imposing domed tower that contained a baptistry; the large baptismal font is just on the right as you enter the tower. Little remains of the church itself, wrecked by an earthquake, but the rose window – a Catherine wheel of entwined mermaids.

Back on Via Reale Basilica, it's an easy clamber up to the ruined Norman **Castello** (daily: July & Aug 8am–1pm & 2.30–7pm; Sept–June 9am–1pm & 2.30–6pm; €2; ☎ 0884 565444), whose views over the town and valley make a nice finale to a visit – especially at sunset.

ACCOMMODATION AND EATING   MONTE SANT'ANGELO

If you intend to stay overnight don't count on finding anywhere to sleep at the last minute during the main festival times. For snacks, ignore the touristy places in the lower town and head instead for the bakery outside the castle.

Casa del Pellegrino Via Carlo d'Angio ☎ 0884 561 150, ⊕ santuariosanmichele.it. A three-star hotel right next to the sanctuary run by a religious institution but open to everybody. The rooms are modern and well looked after, and there's a set lunch and dinner menu for €15. Only downside is the midnight curfew. **€65**

Hotel Sant'Angelo 1km out of town on the road to Pulsano ☎ 0884 562 146, ⊕ hotelsantangelo.com. Comfortable hotel with a swimming pool and its own restaurant and pizzeria, in a panoramic location. A good choice for families. **€75**

Medioevo Via Castello 21 ☎ 0884 565 356. One of

the best restaurants in town, serving excellent seasonal local dishes such as *pancotto con verza, patate e fave* (bread baked with cabbage, potatoes and fava beans) for €7.50 and delectable home-made desserts (€3–5). 12.30–2.30pm & 8–10.30pm; closed Mon in low season.

Taverna Li Jalantuùmene Piazza di Galganis ☎ 0884 565 484, ⊕ li-jalantuumene.it. The menu here is constantly changing to reflect seasonal produce and features both traditional and innovative recipes, with the *mucca podolica*, a rare-breed Pugliese cow, featuring prominently. You can eat à la carte, or choose one of the fixed menus: for example the vegetarian menu at €25 or a tasting menu at €38, both excluding wine. The owner also has four very competitively priced suites, furnished with

antiques. The unpronounceable name is dialect for *galant uomini* or "fine gentlemen". **€130**

The pilgrim route: San Giovanni Rotondo

The ancient **pilgrim route** weaved its way along the Stignano valley between San Severo in the west and Monte Sant'Angelo, and until comparatively recently was the only road that linked the villages of the Gargano interior. With your own transport, it's still a good route for exploring a couple of the region's most important religious centres. If you want to follow any part of the pilgrim route by bus, you'll have to plan your itinerary carefully and be prepared to travel in leisurely fashion.

Nestling under Monte Calvo, the highest peak hereabouts, **San Giovanni Rotondo** is a modern centre for pilgrimage on a massive scale: it's the burial place of Padre Pio, a local priest who died in 1968 and was canonized in 2002. Pio received the stigmata and won an immense following – especially among Italian Catholics – for his model piety and legendary ability to heal the sick. Proof of his divinity was announced in 2008 when his body was exhumed and pronounced to be in good condition and without signs of the stigmata, forty years after his burial.

Padre Pio is hugely popular in Italy, and you'll see his image – bearing an uncanny resemblance to the late John Peel – stuck on the walls of bars, shops and petrol stations throughout the south. A whole industry has grown up around him in San Giovanni Rotondo, fuelled by the seven million and more pilgrims who pass through every year, making it the most visited pilgrimage site in the world after Lourdes. In 2004, renowned architect Renzo Piano completed a striking new church, the shape of which resembles a large snail – its "shell" forming the roof and enveloping the pilgrims below. The town takes its name from the **Rotonda di San Giovanni**, a building of indeterminate origin on the edge of the old town – like the Tomba di Rotari (see opposite), it's thought to have been a baptistry, built on the site of an earlier pagan temple.

Vieste and around

The best base on the Gargano peninsula is **Vieste**, jutting out into the Adriatic on two promontories. Fifty years ago there wasn't even a proper road here, but today Vieste, with its excellent beaches, is the holiday capital of Gargano, and the streets and sands are packed in August. Despite the crowds, it is a lively and inviting town, with an interesting historic core and, in summer at least, a fairly lively nightlife.

The **old town** sits on the easternmost of the two promontories, at the tip of which stands the **Chiesa di San Francesco**, once a thriving monastery, and a *trabucco* – used by fishermen to catch mullet. Probably Phoenician in origin, these cantilevered arrangements of wooden beams, winches and ropes are found on the rocky Gargano coast, and further north around Vasto in Abruzzo (see p.731).

From the church, climb up Via Mafrolla, walking through the old town to Piazza Seggio. Straight ahead, Via Duomo is the site of the so-called **Chianca Amara**, the "bitter stone", where five thousand local people were beheaded when the Turks sacked the town in 1554. Further down, past the stone, the **Cattedrale**, eleventh century in origin but tampered with in the nineteenth, provides a cool retreat from the fierce glare of the sun in the whitewashed streets.

ARRIVAL AND INFORMATION   VIESTE

By bus All buses arrive at Piazzale Manzoni, to the west of the town centre. Vieste is a stop on the Pugliair service linking the Gargano peninsula with the airports of Bari, Brindisi and Foggia.

Destinations Foggia (5 daily; 2hr 45min); Rome (2 daily;

7hr 15min).

By ferry In summer (11 June–7 Sept) there is just one ferry daily from Vieste to the Tremiti islands, and just 3 a week (Tues, Thurs & Sun) from 24 April–10 June and 8–24 Sept. Tickets are available from ⓦ garganoviaggi.it or from

14

the Gargano Viaggi office at Via Roma 7 (☎0884 965 665). **Tourist office** Piazza Kennedy, on the seafront at the end of the main drag, Viale XXIV Maggio/Corso Lorenzo Fazzini (June to mid-Sept daily 8am–8pm; mid-Sept to June Mon–Sat 8am–2pm, Tues & Thurs also 3–7pm; ☎0884 707 495, ⊛viaggiareinpuglia.it).

ACCOMMODATION

Albergo Torrente Lungomare Mattei ☎0884 700 945, ⊛altorrente.it. Located 2.5km from the old town, this is an economic and atmospheric seaside choice. Closed Nov–March. **€94**

Albergo Vela Velo Lungomare Europa 55 ☎0884 706 303, ⊛velavelo.it. This small, friendly two-star is a good-value option, 1.5km north of the castle along the shore. Room rates include the use of a sunbed and umbrella at the San Lorenzo beach (except in high season) and it's an easy cycle into town on one of their mountain bikes (free to guests). They also run a windsurfing school. Closed Nov–March. **€110**

Casa Giulia Via Alarcon 9 ☎340 906 2046. New B&B

with five en-suite rooms – some with sea view – and a sea-facing terrace where breakfast is served. The owner speaks excellent English, and organizes boat tours (see below). **€120**

Punta San Francesco Via S. Francesco 2 ☎0884 701 422, ⊛hotelpuntasanfrancesco.it. Though showing its age, this hotel enjoys a quiet position in the old town with lovely views over the promontory. All rooms are en suite. Closed Nov–March. **€125**

Seggio Via Veste 7 ☎0884 708 123, ⊛hotelseggio.it. An upmarket option in the old town with vertiginous views down to its swimming pool, and with its own private sandy beach and lagoon. Closed Nov–March. **€160**

EATING AND DRINKING

There are plenty of fish restaurants to choose in and around the old town. If you're on a budget, try the pair of cheerful pizzerias in Piazza Vittorio Emanuele II. The terrace bar at *Hotel Seggio* (see above) is a perfect place to chill before dinner.

Al Dragone Via Duomo 8 ☎0884 701 212, ⊛aldragone .it. Located in a once-inhabited natural cave, *Al Dragone* is good for fish dishes, such as the antipasto of marinated grey mullet (€8), and twists on local dishes you won't find anywhere else, such as *orecchiette* with turnip greens, salted anchovies scattered with *bottarga* and shards of thin crispy bread spiked with capers, parsley, basil, garlic and chilli (€9). Unusual desserts too, such as *mostazzuoli* – made with almonds, wine must (the syrup made by boiling down what is left of the grapes after making wine) and

egg white. There are sometimes tasting menus for €30, including drinks. 12.30–2.30pm & 8–10.30pm; closed Nov to end March, plus Tues in April, May & Oct.

Osteria degli Archi Via Ripe 2 ☎0884 705 199. Occupying a restored stone building in the sea wall at the Punta di San Francesco end of the old town, it specializes in locally caught, grilled seafood. *Primi* for €8–11, including a fine dish of *troccoli* (local pasta) with stuffed squid, and fish mains from €12 – led by a good fish soup at €18. Daily 12.30–2.30pm & 8–10.30pm; closed Mon Oct–May, plus Dec–Feb.

DAY-TRIPS FROM VIESTE

Beaches The most obvious move is to the beaches: head for the small one between the promontories or to the north, San Lorenzo, with fine, soft, gently shelving sand, or finally, just south of town, Pizzomunno, which is also sandy. They all go in for the grill-pan variety of sunbathing with rows and rows of sunbeds. Slightly less crowded, if you're lucky, is the marvellous Scialmarino beach, 4.5km up the coast towards Peschici. Nicest of all is the small Baia di San Felice, squeezed between two headlands and backed by pine trees, just before you get to the Testa del Gargano, several kilometres south of town.

Boat trips If you want to swim away from the crowds, consider an organized boat trip to the grotto-ridden coastline around the headland of Testa del Gargano. Boats leave for the three-hour grotto excursion from next to San Francesco church at around 9am and 3.30pm; tickets cost €13 and are available from Terry at *Casa Giulia* (☎340 906 2046, ✉terry.bat @libero.it). If you really want to get away from it all, you could rent your own boat for the day, also from Terry.

The interior The interior of the Gargano promontory can make a cool break from its busy coast, and though there's not much public transport, apart from the odd bus from Vieste, San Menaio and Rodi Garganico, you can rent mountain bikes or fix up jeep safaris or pony trekking. The tourist office in Monte Sant'Angelo should be able to help you organize any of these. Terry at *Casa Giulia* (see above) also arranges tours and rents out cars and mountain bikes.

Peschici and northern Gargano

Atop its rocky vantage point overlooking a beautiful sandy bay, **PESCHICI** is a little smaller than Vieste and one of the most attractive village resorts in the Gargano. Though originally built in 970 AD as a buffer against Saracen incursions, its labyrinth of tiny streets and houses sporting domed roofs has a distinctly Arab flavour. Beach-lazing is the focus, although the town also makes a good base for exploring some of the caves and defensive medieval towers of the nearby coastline. The easiest trips are to the grotto at **San Nicola**, 3km east of town (some buses), or 5km west to the **Torre di Monte Pucci** for fine coastal views (and where there's a *trabucco* restaurant for refreshments in the summer months).

14

ARRIVAL AND DEPARTURE
PESCHICI

By train The FG train line ends at Calanelle, a few kilometres west of Peschici, but there's a bus connection to the town.

By bus All buses drop you in the newer, beach-resort part of Peschici, from where it's a short walk down to the main street – Corso Garibaldi – and the sea.

ACCOMMODATION

Baia San Nicola Località S. Nicola ☎0884 964 231, ⓦ baiasannicola.it. Along the coast at Punta San Nicola, 2km east of Peschici, this campsite features sandy beaches and shady pine groves. Mid-May to mid-Oct. Pitches **€34**

Hotel d'Amato Località Spiaggia ☎0884 963 415, ⓦ hoteldamato.it. Off the SS89 next to the beach, this hotel offers modern rooms, a restaurant, a bar and two swimming pools. Closed mid-Oct to March. **€140**

Locanda Al Castello Via Castello 29 ☎0884 964 038, ⓦ peschicialcastello.it. Up in the old town, down a narrow lane of whitewashed houses, *Al Castello* has nine simple rooms and a restaurant offering five or six daily specials. **€120**

Villa a Mare Località Marina di Peschici, Via Marina 1 ☎0884 963 414, ⓦ villaamare.it. Newly renovated and well-kept hotel next to the sea with a shady patio garden next to the car park. Closed mid-Oct to March. **€120**

EATING AND DRINKING

Fra Stefano Via Forno 8 ☎0884 964 141. An informal place serving moderately priced, delicious raw and cooked seafood antipasti (€20), *cavatelli* (home-made pasta with seafood (€10) and fish grilled over a wood fire (€16). If you order ahead you can try *ruoto* – baby goat or lamb roasted with onions and potatoes €15. 12.30–2.30pm & 8–10.30pm; closed mid-Jan to Feb.

Grotta delle Rondini Via al Porto 64 ☎0884 964 007. Built in a natural cave overlooking the port outside the old town, this restaurant specializes in fish and the antipasti are especially good. Try local dishes such as squid stuffed with breadcrumbs, cheese and herbs, or the unguent aubergines, in which the pulp of the vegetable is baked with local cheese, breadcrumbs and egg (€10). Choose carefully, and you can have a full meal for €25 including wine. 12.30–2.30pm & 8–10.30pm; closed Nov–Feb.

La Collinetta Località Madonna di Loreto ☎0884 964 151. This hotel-restaurant, on the coast road to Vieste, serves excellent fish dishes such as *gnocchi con scampi* (€12), *paccheri con frutti di mare* (€12), and, depending on the season, red mullet baked in foil, or monkfish or halibut baked with potato and tomato (€15). The restaurant also has rooms, and offers a good half-board deal (€50–80 per person). Daily 12.30–2.30pm & 8–10.30pm; closed Oct–Easter.

West along the coast and onwards

A string of white sandy beaches stretches from San Menaio to **RODI GARGANICO** – originally a Greek settlement ("Rodi" is derived from Rhodes) and now a highly popular summer resort. It's busy and expensive in August, but go a couple of months either side, and it can be delightful. **SAN MENAIO** is much quieter than Rodi – more compact and with fewer villas – and even in high season it's easy to get away from it all by walking a few hundred metres south along the strand.

From Rodi Garganico, both road and rail skirt the large **Lago di Varano**, a once-malarial swamp that swallowed the ancient Athenian town of Uria in the fourth century BC. The preserve of eel fishermen, it's the least-visited region on the Gargano promontory, and consequently attracts a great variety of birdlife, particularly curlew and warbler. Further west, the thin **Lago di Lesina** is a highly saline, shallow lagoon, cut off from the sea by a 27km stretch of sand dunes. It's still mercifully free from development – unlike the northern spit of Varano, which is slowly beginning to fill with campsites.

The Tremiti islands

A small group of islands 40km off the Gargano coast, the **Tremiti islands** – Isole Tremiti – are almost entirely given over to tourism in the summer, when the tiny population is swamped by visitors. Despite this, they remain relatively unspoilt and the sea crystal clear. The main Tremiti group consists of three islands: **San Nicola**, **San Domino** – the biggest – and **Capraia**, of which only the first two are inhabited.

14

Brief history

The islands were traditionally a place of exile and punishment. Augustus banished his granddaughter Julia to the islands, while Charlemagne packed his father-in-law off here (minus eyes and limbs) in the eighth century. Monks from Montecassino, on the mainland, first set about building a formidable fortress-abbey on one of the islands in the eleventh century, which managed to withstand frequent assault by the Turks. Later, during the eighteenth century, the islands returned to their old role as a place of confinement for political prisoners, though the Bourbons, concerned at the decline in the local population, shipped in two hundred single women from Naples to encourage a recovery.

San Nicola

Most **ferries** arrive at **SAN NICOLA**, where you can wander around the monastic fortress and the tiny church of **Santa Maria a Mare**, built by the monks in the eleventh century on the site of an earlier ninth-century hermitage. San Nicola is rugged and rocky with no beaches, although there is nude bathing on its east side and good swimming off the whole island.

San Domino

Ignore the offers of pricey boat-trips to the other islands and instead jump on the regular ferry that takes about a minute to cross to **SAN DOMINO**. It's a greener island than its neighbour, its pines offering welcome shade from the heat. Although there's a sandy **beach** – Cala delle Arene – right where the ferry lands on the northeast side of the island, it's packed in the summer. Your best bet is to follow the signs for the *Villaggio TCI* and make for the west of the island and the quieter coves, such as Cala dello Spido. If you're **walking**, head for the Punta di Diamante; maps are pinned up in some of the bars or can be bought from souvenir shops.

ARRIVAL AND DEPARTURE

THE TREMITI ISLANDS

By helicopter Year round, there is at least one helicopter daily to San Domino heliport from Foggia airport.

By ferry There is also a daily ferry service (mid-June to mid-Sept) to the Tremiti islands from Vieste (see p.807) and a service 3 times a week in mid-season. Ferries and fast ferries for foot passengers run throughout the year from Termoli (see p.732). There are also summer services from the Abruzzo ports of Vasto (see p.731) and Ortona.

You'll find plenty of tour boats in Vieste, Peschici and Rodi Garganico touting day-trips to the islands during the holiday season.

Destinations Ortona (end June to early Sept 1 daily; 2hr); Termoli (June–Sept 2–3 daily; 50min; ferries rest of year 2–3 weekly; 1hr 40min); Vasto (end June to early Sept 1 daily; 1hr); Vieste (June–Sept 1 daily; 1hr).

ACCOMMODATION

Accommodation on the islands is limited to San Domino and is largely full board in high season: count on paying €50–60 a night per person. The *municipio* on San Domino holds a list of B&Bs and private rooms – finding a place on spec in the slow season won't be a problem, but in high season you should book in advance. Bear in mind that mosquitoes can be a serious problem in the summer and that, as provisions have to be ferried across from the mainland, eating out can be a costly exercise – buy provisions on the mainland before you leave.

Albergo La Pineta Via della Cantina Sperimentale, San Domino ☎ 0882 463 202, ⓦ albergolapineta.info. The most appealing of the island's small hotels, this is a whitewashed villa surrounded by pine trees, near some peaceful rocky coves just outside the tiny village centre. Closed Nov–March. **€120**

Al Faro Via Aldo Moro 22 ☎ 0887 463 424, ⓦ alfarotremiti .it. With purple bougainvillaea outside and a brightly painted interior, this little place has four rooms as well as three 4-bed apartments with kitchen facilities, making it a great place to hole up for a while without spending a fortune in the island restaurants. Closed Nov–Feb. **€120**

Trani

The initial part of the coastal route south from Manfredonia is unremarkable, with flat lands given up to saline extraction. The first town of note down the coast is **TRANI**, a beautiful stone-built port and fishing village with an unusually cosmopolitan air. One of the most important medieval Italian ports, it was a prosperous trading centre with a large mercantile and Jewish community, and rivalled Bari as a commercial port. A wander through the streets around the harbour gives an impression of the medieval city, not least in the names that echo the town's mercantile and Jewish origins – Via Sinagoga, Via Doge Vecchia (the port had strong – not always amicable – links with Venice) and Via Cambio (Street of the Moneychangers).

The Duomo

Piazza del Duomo · Daily 8am–12.30pm & 3–7.30pm · Free

Centrepiece of the town is the cream-coloured, eleventh-century **Duomo**, right on the sea at the edge of the old town. Dedicated to San Nicola Pellegrino, it consists of no fewer than three churches, stacked on top of each other like an inverted wedding cake – the facade austere but lightened by a pretty rose window. The interior has been restored to its original Norman state, the stark nave displaying a timbered ceiling.

ARRIVAL AND DEPARTURE
TRANI

By train Trani is on the main train line between Bari and Foggia and well served by services from both cities.
By bus Buses arrive and depart from Piazza XX Settembre,

outside the train station, a 10–15min walk from the port. There are regular services to Bari and Foggia.

ACCOMMODATION AND EATING

BB60 Via La Giudea 60 ☎ 366 341 6550, ⓦ bbtrani60 .it. An outstanding B&B, a medieval house in the heart of the ghetto, with three contemporary styled rooms within its exposed stone walls. For an extra €10 per night, guests can have the use of a small kitchen. **€90**
Conteinfiore Via Ognissanti 18 ☎ 0883 508 402. Inspired contemporary fish dishes that change according to

the day's catch, in a tree-filled patio (heated in winter). A selection of five antipasti (€10) makes for a stunning lunch – there might be sea bass with a salsa of orange and courgette, swordfish rolled around ricotta, prawns steamed with fennel and orange for example – while a full meal should cost around €40 per head. 12.30–2.30pm & 8–10.30pm; closed Sun eve and all day Mon.

Bari

The commercial and administrative capital of Puglia, a university town and southern Italy's second city, **BARI** has its fair share of interest. But although it's an economically vibrant place, the town harbours no pretensions to being a major tourist attraction. People come here primarily for work or to leave for Greece, Croatia and Albania on its many ferries.

14

Brief history

Bari was already a thriving centre when the Romans arrived. Later, the city was the seat of the Byzantine governor of southern Italy, while, under the Normans, Bari rivalled Venice both as a maritime centre and, following the seizure of the remains of St Nicholas, as a place of pilgrimage. Since those heady days, Bari has declined considerably. Its fortunes revived briefly in 1813 when the king of Naples foisted a planned expansion on the city – giving the centre its contemporary gridded street pattern, wide avenues and piazzas. And Mussolini instituted a university and left a legacy of strident Fascist architecture. However, the city was heavily bombed during the last war, and today its compact and dynamic centre is a symbol of the south's zeal for commercial growth. Fortunately, heavy investment in redeveloping the old centre has given Bari a new lease on life.

The old town

Even if you're only in Bari to catch a ferry, try to make time for a wander around the **old city**, an entrancing jumble of streets that's possibly the most perplexing place to walk around in southern Italy. Situated at the far end of Corso Cavour, its labyrinth of seemingly endless passages weaving through courtyards and under arches was originally designed to spare the inhabitants from the wind and throw invaders into a state of confusion. This it still does admirably, and even with the best of maps you're going to get lost. Life is lived very much outdoors, and on summer evenings it's full of people sitting outside their kitchen doors.

Basilica di San Nicola

Largo Abate Elia • Daily 7.30am–7pm • Free

The **Basilica di San Nicola**, in the heart of the old city, was, as an inscription at the side of the main door testifies, consecrated in 1197 to house the relics of the saint plundered a century earlier from southern Turkey. The real beauty of the church lies in its stonework, with the twelfth-century altar canopy one of the finest in Italy. The motifs around the capitals are the work of stonemasons from Como, while the lovely twelfth-century carved doorway and simple, striking mosaic floor behind the altar are heavily influenced by the Saracens. Best of all is the twelfth-century episcopal throne behind the altar, a superb piece of work supported by small figures wheezing beneath its weight. Down in the crypt are the remains of the saint – patron of Bari, many surrounding towns, orphans, pawnbrokers, thieves, sailors, and of Russians.

Cattedrale di San Sabino

Piazza dell'Odegitria • Mon–Sat 8am–12.30pm & 4–7.30pm, Sun 8am–12.30pm & 5–8.30pm • Free

It's not far from the basilica to Bari's other important church, the **Cattedrale di San Sabino**, off Piazza dell'Odegitria, dedicated to the original patron saint of Bari, before he was usurped by Nicholas, and built at the end of the twelfth century. Come just for the contrast: uncluttered by arches, it retains its original medieval atmosphere and – unlike the basilica – a timbered roof. The cathedral houses an eighth-century icon known as the *Madonna Odegitria*, brought here for safety from Constantinople by Byzantine monks. It's said to be the most authentic likeness of the Madonna in

---

BARESI BAG-SNATCHERS

A word of warning: the Baresi take positive delight in portraying the old city as a den of thieves, and certainly strolling through the narrow alleys with your camera in full view isn't particularly wise. **Bag snatching** by young kids on mopeds (the *topini*, or "little mice") isn't as rife as it once was, but neither is it extinct, so it's best to keep your wits about you.

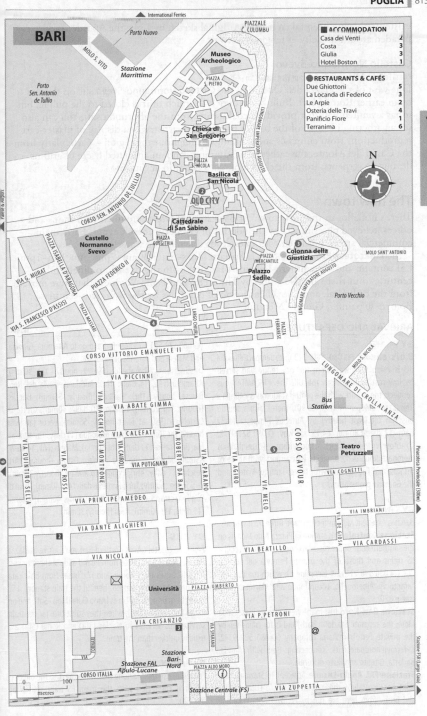

BARI

International Ferries

Porto Nuovo

PIAZZALE C. COLUMBU

MOLO S. VITO

Stazione
Marrittima

Porto
Sen. Antonio
de Tullio

Museo
Archeologico

PIAZZA S. PIETRO

Chiesa di
San Gregorio

PIAZZA S. NICOLA

Basilica di
San Nicola

OLD CITY

Cattedrale
di San Sabino

PIAZZA ODEGITRIA

Castello
Normanno-
Svevo

CORSO SEN. ANTONIO DE TULLIO

Colonna della
Giustizia

PIAZZA MERCANTILE

Palazzo
Sedile

MOLO SANT' ANTONIO

VIA G. MURAT

PIAZZA ISABELLA D'ARAGONA

VIA S. FRANCESCO D'ASSISI

PIAZZA FEDERICO II

PIAZZA MASSARI

LUNGOMARE IMPERATORE AUGUSTO

Porto Vecchio

LARGO CHIURLIA

PIAZZA FERRARESE

CORSO VITTORIO EMANUELE II

LUNGOMARE DI CROLLALANZA

MOLO S. NICOLA

VIA PICCINNI

VIA ABATE GIMMA

Bus
Station

VIA MARCHESE DI MONTRONE

VIA CALEFATI

VIA CAIROLI

VIA PUTIGNANI

VIA ROBERTO DA BARI

VIA SPARANO

VIA AGIRO

CORSO CAVOUR

Teatro
Petruzzelli

VIA COGNETTI

VIA QUINTINO SELLA

VIA DE ROSSI

VIA PRINCIPE AMEDEO

VIA MELO

VIA DANTE ALIGHIERI

VIA IMBRIANI

VIA DE GIOSA

VIA CARDASSI

VIA NICOLAI

VIA BEATILLO

Università

PIAZZA UMBERTO I

VIA CRISANZIO

VIA P. PETRONI

VIA SPARANO

Stazione FAL
Apulo-Lucane

Stazione
Bari-
Nord

PIAZZA ALDO MORO

CORSO ITALIA

Stazione Centrale (FS)

VIA ZUPPETTA

0   100
metres

Piazza & Airport

Pinacoteca Provinciale (300m)

Stazione FSB (Largo Casa)

N

14

existence, having been taken from an original sketch by Luke the Apostle, and is paraded around the city at religious festivals.

Castello Normanno-Svevo
Piazza Federico II di Svevia • Daily except Wed 9am–7pm • €3

Due west of the Piazza dell'Odegitria, the **Castello Normanno-Svevo** sits on the site of an earlier Roman fort. Built by Frederick II, much of it is closed to the public, but it has a vaulted hall that provides a cool escape from the afternoon sun. You can also see a gathering of some of the best of past Puglian artistry in a display of plaster-cast reproductions from churches and buildings throughout the region – particularly from the Castel del Monte, the cathedral at Altamura, and an animated frieze of griffins devouring serpents, from the church of San Leonardo at Siponto.

The new town

There's not a lot to the "new town" of Bari: straight streets are lined with shops and offices, relieved occasionally by the odd bit of greenery. **Corso Cavour**, Bari's main commercial street, bordered with trees, leads down to the waterfront.

The **Pinacoteca Provinciale** on Via Spalato (Tues–Sat 9.30am–7pm, Sun 9am–1pm; €3) contains mostly southern-Italian art ranging from the twelfth to nineteenth centuries, but there are also works by Tintoretto and Paolo Veronese that were moved from the cathedral, and a small collection of paintings by the twentieth-century Bolognese painter, Giorgio Morandi.

ARRIVAL AND DEPARTURE

BY PLANE

Bari's airport (☎080 580 0200, ⟨w⟩aeroportidipuglia .it) is 25km northwest from the city centre and served by low-cost airlines from the UK. The #16 AMTAB bus connects the airport with the central station every 40min– 1hr (5am–9.40pm; 40min; €0.90); there's also a shuttle bus run (at least hourly) by Autobus Tempesta (daily 6am–12.20am; 30min; €4.15 one way; ☎080 521 9172, ⟨w⟩autoservizitempesta.it). Pugliairbus (⟨w⟩pugliairbus .aeroportidipuglia.it) connects Bari airport with those of Brindisi and Foggia, and with Lecce, Taranto, Matera and the Gargano promontory.

BY TRAIN

Bari has excellent rail connections and three train stations.

Stazione Centrale This station in Piazza Aldo Moro is on the southern edge of the modern centre and serves regular FS trains and those of the private Ferrovia del Sud-Est line (☎080 546 2111, ⟨w⟩fseonline.it), which run down to Taranto via Alberobello, Locorotondo and Martina Franca (see p.820).

Stazione Bari-Nord Just to the west, also on Piazza Aldo Moro, the separate Stazione Bari-Nord is for trains run by the private FerroTramViaria company (☎080 529 9342, ⟨w⟩ferrovienordbarese.it), connecting Bari with Andria, Barletta, Bitonto and Ruvo di Puglia.

Stazione FAL Apulo-Lucane Adjacent to Stazione Bari-Nord, on Corso Italia, is the Stazione FAL Apulo-Lucane; trains and buses from here are run by Ferrovia Appulo-Lucane

(☎080 572 5211, ⟨w⟩fal-srl.it) and go to Altamura, Gravina, and Matera and Potenza in Basilicata.

Destinations Alberobello (FSE, 2 hourly; 1hr 30min); Altamura (FAL, 14 daily; 1hr); Andria (Ferrovia del Nord Barese, hourly; 1hr); Barletta (hourly; 55min); Brindisi (hourly; 1hr 20min); Fasano (10 daily; 40min); Grotte di Castellana (FSE, at least hourly; 55min); Lecce (at least hourly; 1hr 30min–2hr); Locorotondo (11 daily; 1hr 40min); Martina Franca (11 daily; 1hr 50min); Matera (FAL, 14 daily; 85min); Molfetta (hourly; 30min); Ostuni (hourly; 1hr); Peschici (1 daily; 4hr); Polignano a Mare (hourly; 30min); Putignano (hourly; 1hr); Rome (6 daily; 4hr 40min); Ruvo di Puglia (Ferrovia del Nord Barese, hourly; 40min); Taranto (19 daily; 1hr 30min); Trani (hourly; 30min).

BY BUS

From the coastal towns north of Bari you'll arrive at Piazza Eroi del Mare; SITA buses from inland and southern towns, Miccolis buses from Rome, and FAL buses from Basilicata pull up in Largo Sorrentino (behind the train station). FSE buses from Brindisi pull in at Largo Ciaia (Mon–Sat), and on Largo Sorrentino (Sun), when they substitute for the train service. Bus services to Naples (3hr) and Rome (5hr) are usually quicker than the train.

BY FERRY

Ferries all use the Stazione Maríttima, next to the old city, which is connected with the main FS train station by bus #20.

14

FERRIES FROM BARI

International ferry services run from Bari to Greece, Albania and Croatia; for information and timetables call ☎800 573 738 or visit ⓦaplevante.org, which also has an updated list of the day's arrivals and departures. Travel agents often have special offers on **tickets**, so it is worth comparing the prices they can offer with those you find on the websites. As a general rule, you will save twenty percent if you buy a return ticket. Once you've got your ticket, you must report to the relevant desk at the Stazione Maríttima at least two hours before departure. Prices given below are for travel in high season.

ALBANIA

ⓦVentouris (☎0805 217 609, ⓦventouris.gr), Azzurra (☎0805 928 400, ⓦazzurraline.com) and Agemar (☎0805 211 069, ⓦagemar.it) run car ferries to Durazzo/Durres in **Albania** daily all year round; the journey takes eight hours overnight (from €73 one way, €78 for a reclining seat).

CROATIA

Jadrolinija operates services to Rijeka, Stari Grad, Dubrovnik, Korcula and Split in **Croatia**, departing late evening for a night crossing of the Adriatic. For the full timetable visit ⓦjadrolinija.hr or contact Agenzia P. Lorusso (☎0805 217 619, ⓦagenzialorusso.it) in the Stazione Maríttima (tickets start at €48 for deck passage, €55 for a reclining seat one-way to Dubrovnik).

GREECE

Ferry services to **Greece** are operated by Ventouris (see above), Superfast (ⓦsuperfast.com) and Agoudimos (ⓦagoudimos-lines.com). All three companies offer online booking. Ventouris runs two to four services daily to Corfu and Igoumenitsa; one-way prices start at €45 per person on deck, €46 extra for a car, plus port fees. The service to Igoumenitsa takes about twelve hours and the service to Corfu about ten. Superfast runs a daily overnight sailing to Corfu (9hr), Igoumenitsa (10hr 30min) and Patras (16hr 30min) year-round. Prices start at €56 for deck passage to Corfu in low season, rising to €79 in July and August, while vehicles cost from €547 in low season to €91 in July and August.

INFORMATION

Tourist office Piazza Aldo Moro 33/A, in a small cul-de-sac to the right as you come out of the main train station (summer Mon–Sat 9am–7pm, Sun 9am–1pm; winter Mon–Sat 9.30am–1pm & 4–7pm, Sun 9am–1pm; ☎080 990 9341, ⓦinfopointbari.com).

ACCOMMODATION

Most accommodation is in the modern part of Bari although some small B&Bs are opening up in the old city (see the tourist office or ⓦinfopointbari.com for a comprehensive list). The most affordable hotels are found around the train station, though the area takes a turn for the worse after dark.

Casa dei Venti Via Dante 182 ☎345 740 6687, ⓦcasadeiventi.com. Stylish new B&B in the modern town, about a 10min walk from the train station. Three spacious rooms and a suite, with classic furniture and contemporary decor, all with a/c, fridges and TV. Large breakfasts, in a splendid room wallpapered with Nina Campbell butterflies, include scrambled eggs and other savouries on request. Free wi-fi. €90

Costa Via Crisanzio 12 ☎080 521 9015, ⓦhotel costabari.com. Simple but attractive rooms in an apartment building one block from the station. €90

Giulia Via Crisanzio 12 ☎080 521 6630, ⓦhotel pensionegiulia.it. In the same building as *Costa*, this *pensione* is run by a pleasant couple, has internet access and some en-suite rooms. €80

Hotel Boston Via Piccinni 115 ☎080 521 6633, ⓦbostonbari.it. A stone's throw from the old city, this business traveller's hotel has comfortable, if characterless, rooms and is in a safe area convenient for an evening *passeggiata*. €125

EATING AND DRINKING

There are lots of colourful choices of places to eat in and around the old town of Bari. Most offer traditional Pugliese dishes and seafood, along with the Bari speciality of *orecchiette*, ear-shaped pasta. In the evenings stalls sell *panzarotti* and *sgagliozze* (fried polenta cubes) around Piazza Mercantile and Piazza del Ferrarese.

14

Due Ghiottoni Via Putignani 11 ☎ 080 523 2240. One of the town's top restaurants serves good shellfish and a refined version of Pugliese cuisine in attractive surroundings just outside the old city. Count on €60 for a full meal. 12.30–2.30pm & 8–10.30pm; closed Aug & Mon, except in summer.

La Locanda di Federico Piazza Mercantile 63–64 ☎ 080 522 7705. Lively *osteria* in the old town, attracting a young crowd with dishes such as fish couscous and the Bari classic, *tiella di riso, patate e cozze* (a rice timbale with potato and mussels), which you need to order in advance. Prices are lower than in many fish restaurants – you could eat a full meal for around €30 without wine, a lot less if you just went for a *primo* and a glass of wine. 12.30–2.30pm & 8–10.30pm; closed Mon lunch.

Le Arpie Vico Arco Carmine 1/3 ☎ 080 521 7988. Rustic and moderately priced, serving generous antipasti and classic local specialities like *tiella di riso, patate e cozze* (see above). 12.30–2.30pm & 8–10.30pm; closed Wed

& two weeks in Jan.

Osteria delle Travi Largo Chiurlia 12 ☎ 080 561 7150. This inexpensive old-town trattoria has been serving up authentic local food in pleasing surroundings since 1813. That it's speciality is horse meat shouldn't put you off – there are plenty of other choices as well, and the antipasti buffet is not to be missed. Reservations recommended. Tues–Sat 12.30–2.30pm & 8–10.30pm, Sun 12.30–2.30pm.

Panificio Fiore Strada Palazzo di Città 38. Locals queue for their delicious *focaccia barese*, simply garnished with tomatoes, olives, salt and olive oil (€1.50). 12.30–2.30pm & 8–10.30pm; closed Thurs eve and Sun.

Terranima Via Putignani 213–215 ☎ 080 521 9725. Informal café-restaurant serving a daily changing menu of regional specialities such as *troccoli* with rocket pesto, fava-bean purée and baby squid (€8.50). There's often live music in the evening. Mon–Sat 12.30–2.30pm & 8–10.30pm; closed Aug.

DIRECTORY

Police Via Paolo Aquilino 3 ☎ 080 549 1331.
Post office The main office is near the university in Piazza Umberto I 33/A (Mon–Fri 8am–6.30pm, Sat

8.30am–12.30pm).
Taxis Radio Taxi ☎ 080 554 3333, ⓦ taxibari.it (24hr).

Le Murge

Rising gently from the Adriatic coast, **Le Murge** – a low limestone plateau – dominates the landscape to the south and west of Bari. The towns in the region are not natural holiday destinations: the area is sparsely populated and the small settlements that exist are rural backwaters with a slow pace of life. But they do make an interesting day out or a good stopover if you're heading for the region of Basilicata.

GETTING AROUND   LE MURGE

Andria and Ruvo di Puglia are on the Nord Barese train line from Bari, and Altamura and Gravina on the FAL line. Trains run at least hourly, sometimes half-hourly. Getting to the more out-of-the-way places without a car is more difficult.

Andria and the Low Murge

Easily reached from Barletta or Bari, the main town of the Low Murge is **ANDRIA**, a large agricultural centre at its best during its Monday-morning market – otherwise it has little to entice you to stay, unless you are heading to Castel del Monte on public transport.

Castel del Monte

Via Castel del Monte, Contrada Castel del Monte • Daily: March–Sept 10.15am–7.45pm; Oct–Feb 9.15am–6.45pm; ticket office closes 30min earlier • €3 • A *comune*-sponsored shuttle bus service runs from the train station in Andria 7 times a day

Despite its lack of appeal today, Andria was a favourite haunt of Frederick II, who was responsible for the major local attraction, the **Castel del Monte**, 17km south – the most extraordinary of all Puglia's castles and one of the finest surviving examples of Swabian architecture.

Begun by Frederick in the 1240s, the castle is a high, isolated fortress built around an octagonal courtyard in two storeys of eight rooms. A mystery surrounds its intended

CASTEL DEL MONTE >

14

purpose. Although there was once an iron gate that could be lowered over the main entrance, there are no other visible signs of fortification, and the castle may have served merely as a hunting lodge. Nonetheless, the mathematical precision involved in its construction, and the preoccupation with the number eight, have intrigued writers for centuries. It's argued the castle is in fact an enormous astrological calendar, or that Frederick may have had the octagonal Omar mosque in Jerusalem in mind when he designed it; yet, despite his recorded fascination with the sciences, no one really knows the truth. There is only one record of its use. The defeat of Manfred, Frederick's illegitimate son, at the battle of Benevento in 1266 signalled the end of Swabian power in Puglia; and Manfred's sons and heirs were imprisoned in the castle for over thirty years – a lonely place to be incarcerated.

Ruvo di Puglia

Southeast of Andria, the old centre of **RUVO DI PUGLIA** is an attractive stop, with a quiet, timeless atmosphere. In the autumn, the pavements of the old town are strewn with almonds, spread out to dry in the sun.

The **Museo Jatta** in Piazza Bovio (Mon–Wed 8.30am–1.30pm, Thurs–Sat 8.30am–7.30pm, Sun 8.30am–1.30pm; ⓦpalazzojatta.org; free) houses a dusty collection of local copies of ancient Greek pottery as well as some beautiful originals, including a fifth-century-BC *crater* depicting the death of Talos. Ruvo's thirteenth-century **Duomo**, tucked into the tightly packed streets of the town's old quarter, is also well worth a look. Its beautiful portal is guarded by animated griffins balancing on fragile columns, with a staggering amount of decoration on the outer walls, a fine rose window and arches that taper off into human and animal heads.

ACCOMMODATION AND EATING   THE LOW MURGE

Antichi Sapori Piazza Sant'Isidoro 9, Montegrosso ☏ 0883 569 529. A fine restaurant on the main road from Andria to Montegrosso, where the emphasis is on fine local produce: try *troccoli*, a local pasta, with aubergine, tomato, wild fennel and seasoned ricotta (€8) or *orecchiette* made of *grana arsa* (toasted wheat flour), served with courgette seedlings and salted ricotta. Mon–Fri 12.30–2.30pm & 8–10.30pm, Sat 12.30–2.30pm.

Lama di Luna Localita Montegrosso ☏ 0883 569 50510, ⓦlamadiluna.com. This luxurious and engaging agriturismo, 10km outside town on the road to Canosa di Puglia, may well tempt you to stay put for a good while. Serene, minimalist, but very comfortable rooms occupy an eighteenth-century house on an estate producing organic olive oil and fruit. Sheets are unbleached cotton, soaps are natural olive oil, and you breakfast on jams of organic fruit and wood-baked bread. There is also a good-sized swimming pool, set among a vast olive grove where some of the trees are over a thousand years old, and free use of mountain bikes. There is no restaurant, but there's a weekly party every Wed when owner Pietro makes pizza in a wood-fired oven. €140

Altamura and the High Murge

Around 45km south of Bari (and reachable by FAL train), **ALTAMURA** is the largest town in the High Murge, originally a fifth-century-BC Peucetian settlement – you can still see some parts of the old town. Given its many historical layers, it's perhaps appropriate that Altamura is home to one of southern Italy's best **archeological museums** (Mon–Fri 8.30am–7.30pm, Sat & Sun 8.30am–1.30pm; €2; ☏080 314 6409, ⓦaltamura.cchnet.it) at Via Santeramo 88. The collection here traces the history of the people of the Murge from prehistory to late medieval times, with plenty of exciting finds from all over the peninsula.

Altamura's most striking feature is its **Duomo**, a mixture of styles varying from Apulian-Romanesque to Gothic and Baroque. Take a look, too, at the tiny church of **San Niccolò dei Greci** on Corso Federico di Svevia; built by the Greek colonists in the thirteenth century, it housed their Orthodox religious ceremonies for more than four hundred years.

Down the coast from Bari

The coast south of Bari is a craggy stretch, with rock-hewn villages towering above tiny sandy coves, offering easy escapes from the city. In summer, and on hot weekends, expect beaches to be crowded.

Torre a Mare and Polignano a Mare

Just ten minutes by FS train from Bari (or bus #12 from Piazza Aldo Moro, **TORRE A MARE** is one of the easiest escapes from the city, situated on a rocky ledge high above two large caves. Being so close to Bari, the village can become quite crowded, but there will be fewer people around another twenty minutes on, at **POLIGNANO A MARE**, which remains fairly low-key. It's a small port with a whitewashed medieval centre sprinkled with bars, souvenir and *focacciarie* shops, perched on the edge of the limestone cliffs, and where people head for on a Sunday to watch the waves crashing against the rocks or to sunbathe on the clifftops.

14

ARRIVAL AND DEPARTURE

TORRE A MARE AND POLIGNANO A MARE

By train and bus Both villages are on the FS train line south of Bari, though services to Torre are slightly more frequent. The journey takes around 12min to Torre, 20min to Polignano. Torre is also served by bus #12 from Piazza Aldo Moro.

ACCOMMODATION AND EATING

Covo dei Saraceni Via Conversano 1/A, Polignano ☎ 080 424 1177, ☺ covodeisaraceni.com. An appealing hotel which sits right above the rocks and has comfortable rooms – some with large balconies and private terraces – and a restaurant with panoramic views, which offers residents a 50 percent discount. Excellent deals via the website – even for high season, as long as you book a couple of months in advance. **€230**

Da Tuccino Via S. Caterina 69/F, Polignano ☎ 080 424 1560, ☺ tuccino.it. One of the region's most renowned seafood restaurants, *Da Tuccino* is one of those places middle-aged celebrities like to frequent on holiday, though unless you are a keen follower of 1970s and 80s Italian pop music, you probably won't have heard of any of them. What they come to eat is the magnificent, fresh raw fish. Expect to pay around €100 a head for a full meal. The menu, as you might expect, varies according to the catch of the day and booking is essential. 12.30–2.30pm & 8–10.30pm; closed Mon, plus Sun eve in low season.

Egnazia

Contrada Losciale near Fasano · Daily 8am to 1hr before sunset · €3 including museum · ☺ egnaziaonline.it

Some 8km beyond Polignano a Mare lies the commercial port of **MONOPOLI**, with a nice old town and a charming **Duomo**, but not much else to see. There's more interest south, at the site of the ancient city of **Egnazia**, where an on-site **museum** (same hours and ticket as above) houses an array of artefacts, including a stunning mosaic of the three Graces, an exquisite white-marble head of the Egyptian fertility god, Attis, and examples of the distinctive earthenware for which the ancient town was prized. Right next to the seafront excavations, the water is tempting and clear, so bring swimming stuff and a picnic.

Brief history

Egnazia (also known as Gnathia) was an important Messapian centre during the fifth century BC, fortified with over 2km of walls, large parts of which still stand in the northern corner of the ruined town – up to 7m high. It was later colonized by the Greeks and then the Romans (in 244 BC), who built a forum, amphitheatre, a colonnaded public hall and temples: one was dedicated to Syria, a popular early Roman goddess, who, according to Lucian, was worshipped by men dressed as women. Horace is known to have dropped by here to see the city's famous altar, which ignited wood without a flame.

With the collapse of the Roman Empire, the city fell to subsequent barbarian invasions, and was almost completely destroyed by the Gothic king Totila in 545 AD.

> ### BURRATA – A LUXURY MADE FROM LEFTOVERS
>
> In some of the fancy restaurants around Egnazia, you'll see **burrata** on the menu, a local delicacy in which still-hot mozzarella is formed into a pouch, which is then filled with scraps of leftover mozzarella and fresh cream before closing. It seems to have been invented on a farm in Andria in the early twentieth century, as a way of using up the spare scraps of mozzarella at the end of the day's cheese making. It's at its best when eaten within 24 hours, which has led to its becoming a prestige food, with upmarket delis throughout Italy vying to have the cheese flown in fresh from Puglia.

14

A community struggled on here, seeking refuge in the Messapian tombs, until the tenth century when the settlement was finally abandoned.

ARRIVAL AND DEPARTURE   EGNAZIA

By bus Egnazia can be reached by bus from Fasano train station, 3km or so inland (call or visit Fasano's tourist office for timetable; Piazza Ciaia 10; ☎ 080 441 3086; Mon, Wed & Fri 8am–1pm & 3–6.30pm). Moving on, there are buses almost hourly to Martina Franca (20min).

ACCOMMODATION AND EATING

La Peschiera Contrada Losciale, Località Capitolo, Monopoli ☎ 080 801 066, ⊛ peschierahotel.com. A Bourbon-era fish hatchery converted into a fine resort whose rooms have enchanting sea views and private beaches. **€640**
La Silvana Viale dei Pini 87, Selva di Fasano ☎ 080 433 1161, ⊛ lasilvanahotel.it. An unpretentious hotel with large, simply decorated rooms, balconies and plenty of terrace space. The restaurant serves good, genuine local food, and if you opt for half-board it will cost €65 per person. **€80**
Masseria Torre Maizza, Contrada Coccaro, between Fasano and Savelletri ☎ 080 482 7838, ⊛ masseria torremaizza.com. Stylish resort hotel with spacious rooms in outbuildings once used to house passing pilgrims. There's an Aveda spa, a chic heated pool, a Moroccan-influenced roof terrace and a restaurant that serves sophisticated Pugliese food. Facilities also include a golf course within the grounds, cooking classes, a beach club 4km away, and the chance to sail on the hotel's 14m yacht. **€442**
Pescheria Due Mari Piazza Amati, Savelletri ☎ 080 482 9161. Don't miss the chance to sample spanking-fresh fish in a stylish glass cube on the seafront in the little resort of Savelletri, where the local fishmonger serves raw seafood and deftly cut slivers of fish, accompanied by a glass of chilled white or sparkling wine. A set menu, based around seven types of fish, costs €25. 12.30–2.30pm & 8–10.30pm; closed Sun in winter.

The FSE line: Castellana Grotte to Martina Franca

Meandering lazily down towards the **Valle d'Itria**, the Ferrovia Sud-Est (FSE) train passes through some of the prettiest of Puglia's landscapes. Olives gradually lose ground to vineyards and cherry and peach orchards, neatly partitioned by dry-stone walls. The barren limestone terrain of Le Murge swallows rivers whole producing a landscape cut by deep ravines and pitted with caverns and grottoes.

Grotte di Castellana

Piazzale Anelli, Castellana Grotte • Daily hourly tours: April–20 July & Sept tours 9am–7pm; 21 July to end Aug 9am–8pm; mid-March to early Nov, Dec 26–Jan 6 & carnival time 9am–1pm & 2.30–7pm; rest of year 9.30am–12.30pm • €15 for a full 3km/2hr tour, €10 for 1km/50min tour excluding Grotta Bianca • ☎ 0804 998 211, ⊛ grottedicastellana.it

About 40km out of Bari are the **Grotte di Castellana**, a spectacular set of underground caves. A lift takes you down to the largest of the caverns, La Grave, 60m below ground. From here, there's over 1km of strangely formed caves to explore, ending in the most impressive, the Grotta Bianca – a shimmering sea of white stalagmites and stalactites. To **get to the caves**, simply follow the signs from the Castellana-Grotte station, from where it's about 500m to the grotto.

TRULLI

Curious-looking **trulli** are dotted throughout the Murge area of Puglia. Cylindrical, whitewashed buildings with grey conical roofs tapering out to a point or sphere, they are often adorned with painted symbols. Unique to Puglia, their ancient origins are obscure, but are probably connected to feudal lords who made people working their land build their houses without mortar so they could easily be pulled down if tax inspectors came round. The thick walls insulate equally against the cold in winter and the summer heat, while local limestone is used to make the two-layered roofs water-tight. Most *trulli* have just one room but when more space was needed, a hole was simply knocked in the wall and an identical structure built next door. Although originally they were both dwellings and storehouses, these days they're being snapped up as holiday homes, and some are rented out as self-catering or B&B accommodation. An organization called Trullidea (☎080 432 3860, ⓦtrullidea.it), based in Alberobello, rents basic *trulli* in town and in the countryside for short- and long-term stays (from around €95 per night) and can also arrange excursions and cooking courses.

14

Alberobello

Beyond Putignano, traditional *trulli* (see box above) dominate the landscape. If you want to take a closer look, head for **ALBEROBELLO**. Around 1500 *trulli* pack the narrow streets; most are south of Largo Martellotta in the Rione Monti zone, the rest to the north in Rione Aia Piccola. You can pick up a town map from the tourist office. Inevitably, a rampant tourist industry has grown up around the cute, conical stone huts, and the proprietors of *trulli* given over to displays of woolly shawls, liqueurs and other souvenirs practically drag in passers-by and don't let them go until they've bought something.

INFORMATION

ALBEROBELLO

Tourist office Piazza Sacramento (Easter to Oct Mon–Sat 10am–8pm, Sun 10am–1.30pm & 2–8pm; Oct to Easter Mon–Sat 10am–1.30 & 3.30–6pm, Sun 10am–1.30pm & 2–6pm; ☎080 432 6030).

ACCOMMODATION AND EATING

B&B Pietradimora Via Monte S. Marco 28 ☎349 565 0106, ⓦpietradimora.it. Complete your *trulli* experience by staying in one of the three rooms in this beautifully restored set of *trulli* – it's a bit like sleeping in a giant stone igloo. Breakfast is served on a panoramic terrace. **€140**

L'Aratro Via Monte San Michele 25–29 ☎080 432 2789. Set inside a *trullo*, this is a stellar option, rigorously sourcing all its ingredients locally, and serving a dizzying number of vegetable and cheese antipasti and local specialities including that Pugliese staple, *purè di fave e cicoria* (puréed broad bean and wild chicory; €8) and *cavatelli con cime di rapa* (pasta with turnip tops and fried breadcrumbs; €9). Daily 12.30–2.30pm & 8–10.30pm.

Locorotondo and Cisternino

Just a few kilometres south of Alberobello, **LOCOROTONDO**, which owes its name to its circular layout, has good views over the whole area, speckled with red- and grey-roofed *trulli* in a sea of vines and olive and almond trees. It's a great place to wander for an hour or so.

Beyond, on the road between Locorotondo and Ostuni, **CISTERNINO** rejoices in the nickname "La Vera" (the Real Thing) and is a marvellous antidote to touristy Alberobello: it's a pleasure to wander around the tiny, whitewashed alleyways of its old town. A series of **open-air concerts** is held in the main square, Piazza Vittorio Emanuele, between late June and September: among them is Pietre che Cantano ("The Stones that Sing"; ⓦpietrechecantano.com).

Martina Franca

Trulli are still plentiful by the time you reach **MARTINA FRANCA**, a surprising town with a jubilant Baroque sensibility and a lively *passeggiata* at weekends. It is reputed

> ## THE FESTIVAL DELLA VALLE D'ITRIA
>
> Southern Italy's top performing-arts festival, the **Festival della Valle d'Itria** (☎080 480 5100, ⓦfestivaldellavalleditria.it), takes place in Martina Franca in late July/early August every year. On a par with the Maggio Musicale in Florence (see p.546), the festival is mainly operatic, with performances – often of rarely performed works – in the appropriately grand Palazzo Ducale. But there are classical concerts, and film screenings as well. It's a congenial and unpretentious event, though tickets aren't cheap; they're available from the festival office in the Palazzo Ducale.

to have been founded by settlers from Taranto fed up with constant Saracen attacks during the tenth century, but it was the Angevin prince of Taranto who bolstered the community in the early fourteenth century by granting it certain tax privileges. The town derives its name from this – *franca* meaning duty or stamp. Today its medieval core is adorned with some of the most subtle and least overbearing examples of architecture from the Baroque period you'll find.

Through the **Porta di Santo Stefano**, which marks the entrance to the old town, Piazza Roma is dominated by the hulking **Palazzo Ducale**, which dates from 1688, and is now the town hall. A handful of rooms are open to the public most mornings (Mon–Fri) – most of them smothered in classical eighteenth-century Arcadian murals. Just across the square, the narrow Via Vittorio Emanuele leads right into the old town and Piazza Plebiscito, fronted by the undulating Baroque facade of the **Chiesa di San Martino**, an eighteenth-century church built on the site of an earlier Romanesque structure, of which only the campanile survives. From adjacent Piazza Immacolata you can either bear left down Via Cavour, with its Baroque *palazzi* and balconied streets, or wander further into the old town; the roads running around the edge of the surviving fourteenth-century town walls offer an excellent panorama of the Valle d'Itria, with its neatly ordered fields dotted with *trulli*.

ARRIVAL AND INFORMATION MARTINA FRANCA

By train There's a spasmodic bus service from the FSE train station up to the centre of town; if there is no bus waiting, you may as well walk, as it will only take around 15min – go left out of the station and up Viale della Libertà to Corso Italia, which leads to the old town centre.

Tourist office Piazza XX Settembre 3 (June–Sept Mon–Sat 9am–1pm & 3.30–7pm; Oct–May Mon–Sat 9am–1pm, Tues & Thurs also 4–7pm; ☎080 480 5702).

ACCOMMODATION AND EATING

La Cantina Vico 1 Lanucara 12 ☎080 480 8031. Excellent, moderately priced restaurant signposted off Piazza XX Settembre, the main gate to the old town – try the *bucatini con fagioli* (pasta with beans) for €7, or *agnello con fave e cicoria* (lamb with broad beans and wild greens) for €12. Tues–Sun 12.30–2.30pm & 8–10.30pm.

Lisi Via Verdi 57 ☎080 480 1547. It is a summer tradition – with its origin in festival time – in the Murge for butchers to light a stove in the back of their shops, set a few tables outside, and serve a limited selection of hot dishes – along with some of the excellent local cured meats. *Lisi* is one such place – expect to find the likes of grilled lamb kebabs, beef *tagliata* (a steak grilled rare, and cut into thin slices), home-made sausages or *gnumarielli* – made with lamb intestines. 8–10.30pm; closed Tues Sept–June.

Villagio In Via Arco Grassi 8 ☎080 480 5911, ⓦvillaggioin.it. The most atmospheric accommodation in Martina Franca is in these traditional apartments in the old town, run like bed and breakfasts. Studios include breakfast and daily cleaning (no minimum stay). €75

Taranto

Straddling two harbours and set beside the deep blue waters of the Ionian, **TARANTO** is an unpretentious city with a thriving fish market, fabulous restaurants and a top-notch archeological museum.

The city divides neatly into three distinct parts: the northern spur is the industrial area, home of the steel works and train station. Cross the Ponte di Porta Napoli and you're on the central island containing the old town. The southern spur holds the modern city centre (Borgo Nuovo), the administrative and commercial hub of Taranto, linked to the old town by a swing-bridge.

Brief history

Known as **Taras** to the ancient Greeks, the port became the first city of Magna Graecia (the area of southern Italy colonized by the Greeks) and was renowned for its oysters,

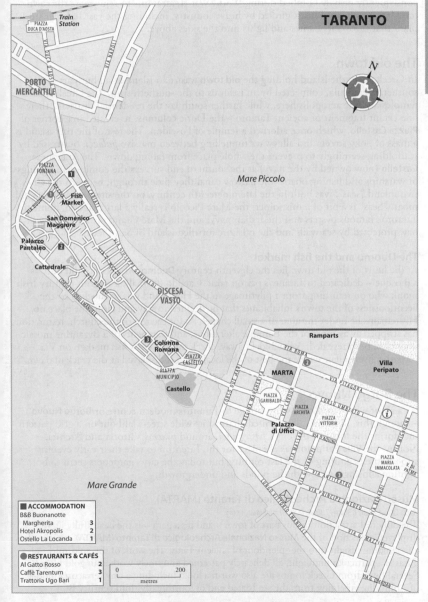

TARANTO

PIAZZA
DUCA D'AOSTA
Train Station

PORTO
MERCANTILE

Mare Piccolo

PIAZZA
FONTANA

Fish
Market

San Domenico
Maggiore

Palazzo
Pantaleo

Cattedrale

DISCESA
VASTO

CORSO VITTORIO EMANUELE

Colonna
Romana

PIAZZA
CASTELLO

PIAZZA
MUNICIPIO

Castello

Ramparts

VIA ROMA

MARTA

Villa
Peripato

VIA PITAGORA

PIAZZA
GARIBALDI

PIAZZA
ARCHITA

CORSO UMBERTO I

PIAZZA
VITTORIA

Palazzo
di Uffici

VIA D'AQUINO

PIAZZA
MARIA
IMMACOLATA

V. DI PALMA

Mare Grande

VIA ANTIFEATRO

VIA PRINCIPE AMEDEO

VIA G. MAZZINI

VIA C. OBERDAN

■ ACCOMMODATION	
B&B Buonanotte Margherita	3
Hotel Akropolis	2
Ostello La Locanda	1

● RESTAURANTS & CAFÉS	
Al Gatto Rosso	2
Caffè Tarentum	3
Trattoria Ugo Bari	1

0   200
metres

14

14

mussels and dyes – the imperial purple was the product of decayed Tarentine molluscs. Resplendent with temples, its acropolis harboured a vast bronze of Poseidon that was one of the wonders of the ancient world. Sadly, little remains of ancient Taras or even of later Roman Tarentum, although their monuments and relics are on display in the city's magnificent museum. After being destroyed by the Romans, Taranto was for years little more than a small fishing port, its strategic position on the sea only being recognized in Napoleonic times. It was home to the Italian fleet after Unification, and consequently heavily bombed during World War II; attempts to rejuvenate the town have left its medieval heart girdled by heavy industry, including the vast Italsider steel plant that throws its flames and lights into the skies above.

The old town

In Greek times the island holding the **old town** wasn't an island at all but part of the southern peninsula, connected by an isthmus to the southern spur. The Greeks raised temples and the acropolis here, while further south lay the residential districts. There's one extant fragment of ancient Taranto – the Doric **columns**, re-erected in a corner of **Piazza Castello**, which once adorned a temple of Poseidon. The rest of the tiny island is a mass of poky streets and alleyways tunnelling between massive *palazzi*, buttressed by scaffolding seemingly to prevent the whole place from falling down. The Aragonese **Castello** (now owned by the navy) at the southern end surveys the comings and goings of warships and fishing boats. The narrow canal they slide through, between the city's two inland "seas", was built in the late nineteenth century, on the site of the castle's old moat. "Seas" is a bit of a misnomer: the Mare Piccolo is really a large lagoon, home to Taranto's famous oysters and the Italian navy; and the Mare Grande is actually a vast bay, protected by sea walls and the offshore fortified island of San Pietro.

The Duomo and the fish market

At the heart of the old town lies the eleventh-century **Duomo**, which once did duty as a mosque – dedicated to Taranto's patron saint, Cataldo (Cathal), a seventh-century Irish monk who on returning from a pilgrimage to the Holy Land was so shocked by the licentiousness of the town's inhabitants that he decided to stay and clean the place up. His remains lie under the altar of a small chapel. As for the rest of the church, restoration has stripped away most of the Baroque alterations, and fragments of a Byzantine mosaic floor have been revealed. A few blocks away, check out the city's **fish market**, on Via Cariati, a lively affair where the best of the local catch is displayed at the crack of dawn.

The Borgo Nuovo

It's a short walk across the swing-bridge to Taranto's modern centre or **Borgo Nuovo** – though this, like Bari's, has limited charms, its wide streets laid out on a grid pattern that forms the focus of the city's *passeggiata*, around piazzas Vittoria and Archita. Nearby, the **Villa Peripato** was *the* place for the Tarentini to take their early evening stroll at the beginning of the last century, but today the city's gardeners seem to be fighting a losing battle with the ponds and undergrowth.

Museo Nazionale Archeologico di Taranto (MARTA)

Piazza Cavour • Daily 8.30am–7.30pm • €5 • ⓦ museotaranto.org

The only real attraction in this part of town – and it's a gem – is the beautifully lit and displayed collection of the **Museo Nazionale Archeologico di Taranto (MARTA)**, which offers a fascinating insight into the splendour of ancient Taras. The work of the goldsmiths of Taras is a particular highlight, all delicately patterned and finely worked in gold filigree. Several finds from Greek tombs are also worth a look, including a tiny terracotta model of Aphrodite emerging from the sea (dated end of fourth/early third century BC).

ARRIVAL AND INFORMATION

By train The train station is on Piazza Duca d'Aosta, and the old town is a 400m walk across the bridge. If you are heading straight for the archeological museum, note that most buses from the station run to Corso Umberto I.

By bus Buses generally arrive at and depart from Porto Mercantile, except FS connections with Metaponto and Potenza, which arrive at Piazza Duca d'Aosta, just outside the train station. Timetables for city buses can be found at ⓦ amat.taranto.it.

Tourist office Corso Umberto I 113 (Mon–Fri 9am–1pm & 4.30–6.30pm, Sat 9am–noon; ☎ 0994 532 392, ⓦ viaggiareinpuglia.it).

ACCOMMODATION

14

Taranto isn't really geared up for tourism, and it is only recently that accommodation options have opened in the old town, and even these are mostly aimed at business people, teachers and students.

B&B Buonanotte Margherita Piazzetta S. Francesco ☎ 349 295 8959, ⓦ buonanottemargherita.it. One of the very few B&Bs in the old town, this little place has two spick-and-span rooms with balconies and a living room with tea-making facilities and a small fridge. €65

Hotel Akropolis Vico I Seminario 3 ☎ 099 470 4110, ⓦ hotelakropolis.it. A modern-style hotel with 14 rooms in an old building: it's aimed more at business travellers than tourists, though it has a picturesque wine bar in an ancient corn-store underground. €150

Ostello La Locanda Piazza Fontana ☎ 099 476 0033, ⓦ ostellolalocanda.it. Directly across the bridge at the entrance to the old city, this hostel has beds in single and triple rooms and dorms. Facilities include internet access, a sun terrace and a laundry for guest use. There is also an Indian restaurant downstairs. Beds €35

EATING AND DRINKING

Al Gatto Rosso Via Cavour 2 ☎ 099 452 9875. Refined, long-established fish restaurant in the new town that delivers friendly service, excellent antipasti and inventive pasta dishes – try *gnocchetti* with prawns, basil and crispy aubergine (€11) – along with classics such as *linguine* with local clams (€13). For a main course, go for deep-fried catch of the day (*frittura mista di paranza*; €13). Tues–Sun 12.30–2.30pm & 8–10.30pm.

Caffè Tarentum Via Anfiteatro 97 ☎ 099 453 3956. Come here for excellent coffee, lovely *cornetti*, wicked *krapfen* (pastries filled with home-made jam) and typical almond-based sweets like *mustazzueli* as well as savoury snacks. 12.30–2.30pm & 8–10.30pm; closed Tues.

Trattoria Ugi Bari Largo S. Nicola ☎ 099 460 8736. Don't leave Taranto without eating at the trattoria known universally as "Da Ugo al Orologio", serving fish at rock-bottom prices for over 70 years. Just look for the clock tower off Piazza Fontana, and you'll be there. Wine costs €2 a litre, antipasti and *primi* cost €3, *secondi* €5, and a four-course meal including wine, fruit and *amaro* (a digestive liqueur), €15. There's not much choice, with no written menu, and you sit at long shared tables with families, fishermen and bank clerks, but the fish is straight from the sea and freshly cooked. 12.30–2.30pm & 8–10.30pm; closed Sat eve & Sun.

Northwest of Taranto

Inland and **northwest** of Taranto, the scenery changes dramatically, with gorges and ravines marking a landscape that's closer to that of Basilicata than Puglia. At first glance, **MASSAFRA**, about 15km from Taranto (regular trains and FSE buses from Porto Mercantile), appears the kind of unprepossessing, shabby dust-blown town you drive through as quickly as possible. However, it's split in two by a ravine, the Gravina di San Marco, that is lined with grottoes dating mainly from the ninth to the fourteenth centuries. Many contain cave-churches, hewn out of the rock by Greek monks and decorated with lavish frescoes. The **Santuario della Madonna della Scala** is built onto an earlier cave-church; a Baroque staircase runs down to the eighteenth-century church, which features a beautiful fresco of a Madonna and Child, dating from the twelfth to the thirteenth centuries; more steps lead down to an eighth-century crypt.

The nearby **Cripta della Buona Nuova** houses a thirteenth-century fresco of the Madonna and a striking painting of Christ Pantocrator. About 200m away, at the bottom of the ravine, is a mass of interconnected caves known as the **Farmacia del Mago Greguro**, now in a pretty pitiful state but once used by the medieval monks as a herbalist's workshop.

Sites in Massafra are visitable only by guided tours arranged with the tourist office at Piazza Garibaldi (Mon–Fri 10am–12.30 & 3.30–5.30pm; ☎ 099 880 4695).

Brindisi and around

14

Across the peninsula, 60km east of Taranto on the opposite coast, lies **BRINDISI**, once a bridging point for crusading knights and still a town that makes its living from people passing through. The natural harbour here, the safest on the Adriatic coast, made Brindisi an ideal choice for early settlers. In Roman times, the port became the main crossing point between the eastern and western empires, and later, under the Normans, there came a steady stream of pilgrims heading east towards the Holy Land. The route is still open, and now Brindisi – primarily – is where you come if you're **heading for Greece**

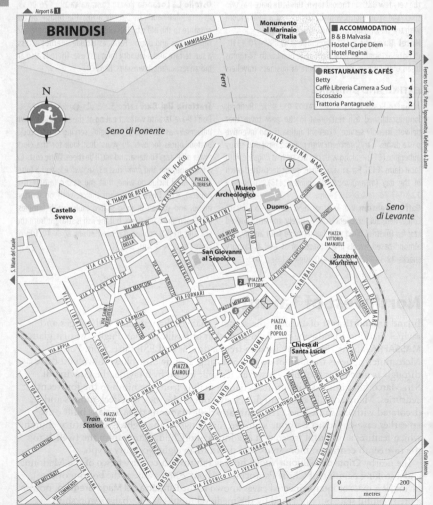

from Italy. On arrival, you may well think that the entire town is full of shipping agents: this, when all is said and done, is the town's main business. But even if you're leaving the same night you'll almost certainly end up with time on your hands. You could just while away time in a bar or restaurant in the old town – it is pretty compact and, although it isn't brimming with ancient monuments, has a pleasant, almost oriental flavour about it, and a few hidden gems tucked down its narrow streets. If you decide to stay, Brindisi's youth hostel is a fun place to base yourself for day-trips to the beach, Ostuni or the **Torre Guaceto**, a lovely nature reserve for biking and swimming.

14

Scalinata Virgiliana

The top of **Scalinata Virgiliana** (Virgil's Steps) marks the end of the ancient Via Appia, which ran all the way from the Porta Capena in Rome. Two columns stood here for years – useful navigation points for ships coming into harbour. The single column that remains has been restored, as has the area around it; the other column was carried off to Lecce.

The Duomo and Museo Archeologico Provinciale

Via Colonne, with its seventeenth- and eighteenth-century *palazzi*, runs up to the **Duomo** (daily 8am–9pm; free) – a remarkable building, if only for the fact that it's survived seven earthquakes since its construction in the eleventh century. Just outside is the **Museo Archeologico Provinciale** (Tues–Sat 9am–1.30pm, Tues also 3.30–6.30pm; free). In addition to ornaments and statues from the necropolises that lined the Via Appia in Roman times, several rooms accommodate bronzes recovered in underwater exploration nearby, as well as finds from the excavations at Egnazia (see p.819).

San Giovanni al Sepolcro

Piazza San Giovanni al Sepolcro • Always open except at lunchtime • Free

Follow Via Tarentini from the Duomo and bear left for the tiny, round church of **San Giovanni al Sepolcro**, an eleventh-century baptistry. It's a little dark and decrepit inside, but you can just make out some of the original thirteenth-century frescoes. And there are more frescoes, this time a century older, in the **Chiesa di Santa Lucia**, just off Piazza del Popolo.

Chiesa di Santa Maria del Casale

Via Ruggero de Simone • Ring bell for entrance at the gate • Free • Take bus #4, from the train station, and ask the driver when to get off

Brindisi's most important medieval monument is further afield: the **Chiesa di Santa Maria del Casale** – a 3km bus ride towards the airport from town. Built by Philip of Anjou at the end of the thirteenth century, it's an odd mixture of styles: the facade is adorned with an Arabic mass of geometric patterns, worked in two shades of sandstone, and the portal has an almost Art Deco touch to it. The stark interior is rescued from gloom by some fourteenth-century frescoes depicting frightening allegorical scenes relating to the Last Judgement, a vision of hell designed to scare the living daylights out of the less devout.

ARRIVAL AND DEPARTURE

BRINDISI

By plane Brindisi's airport (☏ 080 580 0200, ⓦ aeroportidpuglia.it), served by Ryanair from Stansted, is 7km from the city centre. A regular urban bus runs to the Stazione Centrale every 30min (€0.90), taking 10min. There are also buses from the airport direct to Lecce's City Terminal (see p.833); the service is run by COTRAP – tickets cost €5 (sold on board) and the journey takes 40min. If you want to rent a car, all major operators have booths at the airport.

By train The train station is on Piazza Crispi, at the foot of Corso Umberto, a 10- to 15min walk from the port. Destinations Lecce (25 daily; 30min); Ostuni (24 daily; 25min); Taranto (15 daily; 1hr).

By bus Marozzi buses link the town with Rome and Miccolis buses connect it with Naples; these buses arrive at, and depart from, Viale P. Togliatti, a continuation of Viale A. Moro in the new part of town. There are other daily

14

departures to Siena, Florence and Pisa.

By ferry Arriving by ferry from Greece leaves you at Costa Morena, a couple of kilometres southeast of town; a shuttle bus run by the port authority links this with the town centre, dropping off and picking up at the intersection of Corso Garibaldi and Lungomare Regina Margherita, in front of the maritime station.

Destinations Corfu (6 weekly; from 7hr); Igoumenitsa (6 weekly; 8hr); Cephallonia (13 sailings through July & Aug; 16hr); Patras (at least 1 daily in summer; 13hr).

INFORMATION AND GETTING AROUND

By bus Central Brindisi is small enough to walk around, but for transport around town, lots of buses run down Corso Umberto and Corso Garibaldi.

By taxi If you need a taxi call ☎0831 597 901 or ☎0831 597 503.

Tourist office Lungomare Regina Margherita 44 (Mon–Fri 9am–1pm & 3.30–7.30pm, Sat 9am–1.30pm; ☎0831 523 072, ⓦinterradibrindisi.it). Its website is excellent, with lists of B&Bs, villas and hotels, places to eat and things to do.

ACCOMMODATION

B&B Malvasia Vico Scalese, behind Piazza della Vittoria ☎349 380 0689, ⓦmalvasiabrindisi.altervista.org. Two comfy rooms with shared bathrooms above a cultural association with a bar, where you can listen to blues and browse the bookshelves as you drink. It's particularly good for families or a group of friends (you can even bring a pet) and they offer an airport shuttle service for €5. **€60**

Hostel Carpe Diem 2km out of town in Casale at Via Brandi 2 ☎338 323 5545, ⓦhostelcarpediem.it.

A friendly youth hostel with no lock-out, a lively atmosphere, and free shuttles to the port and airport. You can rent a bed for the day (€5.50) if you've got a night departure, with full use of the facilities, including hot power-showers, laundry, bike rental, book exchange, bar and pool table. Dorms **€15**

Hotel Regina Via Cavour 5 ☎0831 562 001, ⓦhotelreginabrindisi.it. A decent three-star with conventional, plain a/c rooms down a quiet side-street 150m from the station. **€80**

FERRIES TO ALBANIA AND GREECE

A staggering array of **agents** sell **ferry tickets** to Albania and Greece, and you should take care to avoid getting ripped off. Ignore the touts clustered around the train station in high season, who specialize in selling imaginary places on nonexistent boats, and always buy your ticket direct from the company's office or an approved agent. Discovery, Via Provinciale per Lecce 27 (☎0831 573 800, ⓦdiscoveryto.it), is a reliable **general agent** which also sells onward ferry tickets to the Cyclades and Crete.

ROUTES

A variety of **routes** operate most of the year, although frequency is reduced outside the peak season – roughly defined as between mid-July and mid-August. **Services** – including some high-speed catamarans – sail to Vlore in Albania and Corfu, Igoumenitsa, Patras, Cephallonia and Zante in Greece. Visit ⓦaferry.it for **timetables** and **prices**. As a rule, nearly all the reliable companies sail in the evening.

PRICES AND BOARDING

Prices vary considerably according to season but there's not much difference between the companies: you'll be looking at a one-way, high-season fare to Corfu/Igoumenitsa for around €64 per person on deck or €94 for a reclining seat (cabins are available for a higher charge), from €76 extra for a car; in low season prices almost halve. High-speed links are more expensive. There are reductions of around 10–20 percent on the return fare if you book with the same company you travel out with and discounts if you have an InterRail, EuroRail, or Italian rail pass (although high-season supplements apply). Check on purchase whether your ticket includes **embarkation tax** – €5 per person or per car.

   Leaving Italy, you should arrive at least one hour – preferably two in high season – before your ship's departure. Allow enough time to get there by the free shuttle bus from Stazione Maríttima (the journey takes around 20min but find out beforehand when the shuttles depart) and make sure that any stopover you are making on the way to Patras is clearly marked on your ticket. It's advisable to **stock up on food and drink** in Brindisi's supermarkets, as there are the inevitable mark-ups once on board.

EATING AND DRINKING

Betty Viale Regina Margherita 6 ☎ 0831 563 465. Great café close to the port with good pastries and ice cream. A good choice for an evening *aperitivo*, as it has a tempting spread of nibbles. Open till the early hours too, so the perfect place to sit and while away the time till your ferry leaves. Daily 6.30am–3am.

Caffè Libreria Camera a Sud Largo Otranto 1 ☎ 0831 529733. This bookshop café makes a nice place to while away a few hours, good place for a lazy breakfast or civilized *aperitivo* – and look out for the regular gastronomic evenings. Daily until late; closed Sun in summer.

Trattoria Pantagruele Via Salita di Ripalta 1 ☎ 0831 560 605. Popular and highly regarded restaurant which serves excellent Pugliese dishes and local seafood: they do a great version of puréed fava beans with tender wild chicory (€7) and the *orecchiette* with a *ragù* made of octopus (€10) is delicious. Look out for local specialities such as the purple prawns from Gallipoli. 12.30–2.30pm & 8–10.30pm; closed Sat lunch & Sun.

14

Around Brindisi: Torre Guaceto

Just 15km northwest of Brindisi is a beautiful nature reserve and protected marine area known as **Torre Guaceto**. You'll need a car to get here, but it's a lovely spot for biking through maquis and olive groves, scuba diving over small reefs of coral and sea grass, or chilling out on the sandy beach; to visit, book at the Serranova visitor centre (☎0831 989 885, ⟨w⟩riservaditorreguaceto.it).

Ostuni

OSTUNI, 40km northwest of Brindisi (35min by train), is known as "the white city" and is one of southern Italy's most stunning small towns. Situated on three hills at the southernmost edge of Le Murge, it was an important Greco-Roman city in the first century AD. The old centre spreads across the highest of the hills, a gleaming white splash of sun-bleached streets and cobbled alleyways, dominating the plains below. Seven kilometres away, the popular sandy coastline has Blue Flag beaches.

The maze of well-preserved winding streets provides a fascinating amble, and there are some exceptional views – particularly from Largo Castello over the woods to the north. Bits of cavorting Baroque twist out of unexpected places, including an ornamented eighteenth-century obelisk, 21m high, dedicated to St Oronzo, which stands in Piazza della Libertà (or Piazza Sant'Oronzo) on the southern edge of the old town. This is the focal point on summer Saturday nights for hordes of people who drive in from the countryside, meet their friends and pack out the bars and cafés. From there, follow the Via Cattedrale uphill towards the Duomo, taking note of the monumental palaces and churches that trim the ascent. One of these, the **Chiesa di San Vito**, houses an ethnography museum, which has been closed for a long restoration. When it eventually reopens, check out the highlight, "Delia", the skeleton of a young pregnant woman found in a crouched position, her bones decorated before burial. At the top of the hill, the fifteenth-century church is nestled into a charming piazza dominated by the Palazzo Vescovile and the Palazzo del Seminario.

ARRIVAL AND INFORMATION

OSTUNI

By train Trains from Brindisi arrive at a station that's some way out of town though there's a connecting bus service to Piazza della Libertà at the foot of the old town.

By bus Buses stop outside the centre, by the basketball stadium, a bus ride or 20min walk into town.

Tourist office Corso Mazzini 8 just off Piazza della Libertà (daily: July & Aug 8am–2pm & 4.30–10.30pm; Sept–June 8am–2pm & 3.30–8pm; ☎ 0831 301 268).

InfoPoint Corso Mazzini 27 (daily Oct–Easter 10am–1pm & 3–7pm; April–May 10am–2pm & 5–9pm; June, July & Sept 10am–1pm & 2–10pm; Aug 10am–midnight; ☎ 339 508 8036, ⟨w⟩borgostuni.it). A very helpful information service run by an association of local owners of hotels, B&Bs and restaurants, advising on accommodation, eating and excursions. It runs a 24hr phone assistance service – in English, French and Italian – helping in emergencies, making hotel and restaurant reservations on your behalf, and so on (☎ 0831 342 332; €5/week).

14

ACCOMMODATION

B&B Nonna Isa Via V. Alfieri 9 ☎347 616 0297, ⓦnonnaisa.it. Three very nice rooms in a small B&B 5min from the *centro storico* in the ninteenth-century part of town. Two of the rooms have balconies with views over the rooftops as far as Marina di Ostuni. €100

Bienbi Via G. Pinto 11 ☎393 930 4223, ⓦbienbi.it. Five serene rooms, in a boutique B&B, fittingly furnished in white, and a roof terrace with views over the old town to the coast. Meals featuring local produce can be arranged on request. €140

Il Frantoio SS16 km 874 ☎0831 330 276, ⓦmasseriailfrantoio.it. A traditional white farmhouse in 72 hectares of olive grove, a 5min drive from Ostuni, with eight rooms furnished with family furniture and heirlooms. The estate produces organic olive oil, fruits and vegetables, and they make delicious meals. Rates include access to selected lidos on nearby beaches. €230

EATING AND DRINKING

Osteria Via B. Cairoli 1, just off the main Corso. This tiny *osteria* looks way older than its 60 years, like a corner of a Novecento film set. Wine (€1.20 a litre) is doled out with old zinc measures and served in ceramic jugs, and you can eat traditional dishes such as broth (€2.50), tripe (€3) or mixed fried fish (€6). Open Mon–Sat mid-morning to early evening, but a bit erratic.

Osteria del Tempo Perso Via G. Tanzarella Vitale 47 ☎0831 304 819. Antipasti include lightly battered zucchini flowers stuffed with ricotta and mint, while among the *primi*, the adventurous could opt for *orecchiette con sugo di asino* (ear-shaped pasta with donkey sauce; €14). Closed all day Mon. 12.30–2.30pm & 8–10.30pm in low season, but for dinner-only in June, July and Aug.

Osteria Piazzetta Cattedrale Largo Arcidiacono ☎0831 335 026, ⓦosteriapiazzettacattedrale.it.

Elegant restaurant opposite the cathedral, which uses locally sourced ingredients to great creative effect – try the stunning *cestino di crepe con crema di cavolfiori, pancetta croccante e vincotto di Primitivo*, a crêpe basket filled with cauliflour purée and crisp bacon and drizzled with sweet wine must – in a constantly evolving seasonal menu, and has *degustazione* menus at €25 and €40 per head excluding wine. If that's beyond your budget, you can lunch on a selection of seven antipasti for €14 per head. 12.30–2.30pm & 8–10.30pm; closed Tues in low season.

Porta Nova Via G. Petrarolo 38 ☎0831 338 983. Set in a fifteenth-century stone city gate overlooking olive groves and the sea, this is a fine place for fish and shellfish, with a following for its raw fish, as well as marvellous dishes such as black *trofie* served with turnip tops, baby squid, anchovy and toasted breadcrumbs (€12). 12.30–2.30pm & 8–10.30pm; closed Wed in winter.

Lecce and Salento

Some 40km south from Brindisi, Baroque **Lecce** is a place to linger, with a few diverting Roman remains and a wealth of fine architecture scattered about an appealing old town. It's also a good starting-point for excursions around **Salento**, the name given to the very tip of Italy's heel extending from just south of Ostuni to Santa Maria di Leuca. Here the landscape begins to take on a distinctive Greek flavour, a mildly undulating region planted with carob, prickly pear and tobacco. The Adriatic coast is pitted with cliffs topped with ruined watchtowers, and rugged coves and caves trail right the way down to the **southern cape**. The hinterland, by comparison, is more barren, although again there's a Greek feel to it, with tiny, sun-blasted villages growing out of the dry, stony, red earth and flat-roofed houses painted in bright pastel colours.

Lecce

The exuberant building styles on display in **LECCE** are the legacy of religious orders (Jesuits, the Teatini and Franciscans) who came to the region at the end of the sixteenth century, bringing an influx of wealth which paid for the opulent churches and *palazzi* that still pervade today's city. The flowery style of "Leccese Baroque" owed as much to the materials to hand as to the skills of the architects: the soft local sandstone could be intricately carved and then became hard with age.

Piazza Sant'Oronzo

Start at **Piazza Sant'Oronzo**, the hub of the old town, named after the first-century bishop of Lecce who went to the lions under Nero. His bronze statue lurches unsteadily from the top of the **Colonna di Sant'Oronzo** that once stood at the end of the Via Appia in Brindisi. It reappeared here in 1666 to honour Oronzo, who was credited with having spared the town from plague ten years earlier. The south side of the piazza is taken up by the **Anfiteatro Romano**, which probably dates from the time

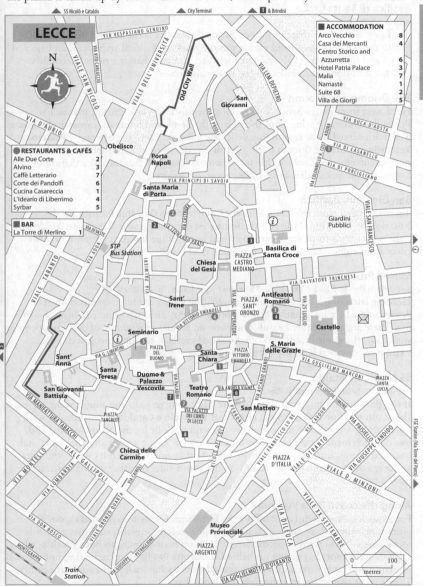

14

LECCE

■ ACCOMMODATION
Arco Vecchio	8
Casa dei Mercanti	4
Centro Storico and Azzurretta	6
Hotel Patria Palace	3
Malia	7
Namastè	1
Suite 68	2
Villa de Giorgi	5

● RESTAURANTS & CAFÉS
Alle Due Corte	2
Alvino	3
Caffè Letterario	7
Corte dei Pandolfi	6
Cucina Casareccia	1
L'Ideario di Liberrimo	4
Syrbar	5

■ BAR
| La Torre di Merlino | 1 |

of Hadrian. In its heyday it seated 20,000 spectators; today it's used for the Christmas nativity scene. Sadly, most of its decorative bas-reliefs of fighting gladiators and wild beasts have been removed for safekeeping, and nowadays it looks rather depleted. Just behind the piazza is another relic of Roman Lecce, the well-preserved **Teatro Romano**, the only one of its kind to be found in Puglia, with rows of seats and orchestra floor still remarkably intact.

Basilica di Santa Croce
Piazzetta Gabriele Riccardi • Free

The finest and most ornate of Lecce's Baroque churches is the **Basilica di Santa Croce**, just to the north, whose florid facade was the work of the local architects Zimbalo and Penna and took around 150 years to complete; its upper half is a riot of decorative garlands and flowers around a central rose window.

The Duomo and around

Head west from Piazza Sant'Oronzo along the bustling Via Vittorio Emanuele to Piazza del Duomo. Facing onto the square, the **Seminario** holds an impressively ornate well, with carved stone resembling delicately wrought iron. The balconied **Palazzo Vescovile** adjoins the **Duomo** itself, twelfth century in origin but rebuilt entirely in the mid-seventeenth by Zimbalo. He tacked on two complex facades and an enormous five-storey campanile that towers 70m above the square.

San Giovanni Battista

There is further work by Zimbalo in the **Church of San Giovanni Battista** (or del Rosario), by the Porta Rudiae in the southwest corner of town. The ornate facade and twisting columns front some extremely odd altars, while dumpy cherubim dive for cover amid scenes resembling an exploding fruit bowl.

Museo Provinciale
Viale Gallipoli • Mon–Sat 8.30am–1.30pm & 2.30–7.30pm, Sun 9.30am–1.30pm • Free • ☏ 0832 307415

Heading left along Viale Gallipoli you reach the town's recently revamped **Museo Provinciale** where imaginative displays bring the city's history – and pre-history – to life. There are also frequent exhibitions, and an annual programme of evening openings with concerts, guided tours and other cultural events – see the Provincia di Lecce website (ⓦprovincia.le.it) for details.

SS Nicolò e Cataldo
Viale San Nicola • Generally open mornings • Free

If the Baroque trappings of the town are beginning to pall, you might want to check out the fine Romanesque church of **SS Nicolò e Cataldo**, a ten-minute walk north along Viale San Nicola from Porta Napoli. Built by the Normans in 1190, its cool interior reveals a generous hint of Saracen in the arches and the octagonal rounded dome. Little remains of the frescoes that once covered its walls, though an image of St Nicolò can be found on the south side, together with a delicately carved portal.

Along the coast: Roca Vecchia

For a quick escape from Lecce follow the Littoranea Otranto coast road through pinewoods where there are several paths leading to long stretches of dunes and little rocky coves. If you want a specific target, carry on further south to **Roca Vecchia**, where a 1960s-style resort has grown up behind the **Grotte Basiliane**, a fascinating honeycomb of man-made caves carved into the soft sandstone dating back to the seventh century. There's great swimming in a sheltered turquoise bay.

ARRIVAL AND DEPARTURE

LECCE

By bus Regional buses arrive at the City Terminal (north of Porta Napoli), and the train station. Between mid-June and late Sept, Salento in Treno e Bus (☎ 0833 541 025, ⓦ salento intrenoebus.it) services depart from several places in town – including the City Terminal, Viale dell'Università and the FS station – and head to Otranto, Santa Maria di Leuca (via Gallipoli) and the seaside resort of Porto Cesareo, among other destinations. For transfers from Brindisi airport, see p.827.

Destinations Gallipoli (approx hourly; 1–2hr); Otranto (8 daily; 1hr); Porto Cesareo (6 daily; 1hr); San Cataldo (8 daily; 30min); Santa Maria di Leuca (summer only, approx hourly; 1hr 45min).

By train FSE and FS trains use the same station, 1km south of the centre at the end of Via Oronzo Quarta. As well as the FSE services to Bari and Taranto via Martina Franca, there are regular FS trains to Gallipoli and around 5 trains a day to Rome

14

INFORMATION

Tourist office Corso Vittorio Emanuele 24 (Sept–June Mon–Sat 8am–2pm & 4–6pm; July & Aug daily 9am–1.30pm & 4.30–8pm; subject to alteration from year to year; ☎ 0832 332 463, ⓦ viaggiareinpuglia.it).
InfoLecce Piazza del Duomo 2 (Mon–Fri 9.30am–1.30pm & 3.30–7.30pm, Sat & Sun 10am–1.30pm & 3.30–7pm;

☎ 347 889 9871) and Via G. Palmieri 47–49 (same hours; ☎ 389 903 0107). Two very well organized private information offices, offering bikes to rent, several guided tours of the city and Salento, and a well-researched website (ⓦ infolecce.it) full of suggested places to eat, stay and explore.

ACCOMMODATION

There is accommodation for all budgets in Lecce, including an appealing selection of boutique hotels and B&Bs. Otherwise, the tourist office can help you find a reasonably priced private room in a historic building in the old town and on the outskirts (from around €60 per night); you could also search ⓦ abitalecce.it or ⓦ caffelletto.it.

Arco Vecchio Via Quinto Fabio Balbo 5 ☎ 339 578 9621, ⓦ arcovecchio.com. Sprucely restored *palazzo* just off the very pleasant Via Paladini, with nine neat, contemporary, minimalist rooms, and, ideal for families or extended stays, a suite with a fully equipped kitchen and its own terrace. Flat-screen TVs, satellite and wi-fi. **€80**
Casa dei Mercanti Piazza Sant'Oronzo 44 ☎ 0832 277 299, ⓦ casadeimercanti.it. Nine newly renovated serviced apartments, smart and international in style, with glossy parquet floors and modern furniture overlooking Piazza Sant'Oronzo. All apartments have flat-screen TVs and full kitchens, and there's a daily cleaning service. **€80**
Centro Storico and Azzurretta Via Vignes 2/B ☎ 0832 242 727, ⓦ bedandbreakfast.lecce.it. Two appealing B&Bs, run by the same family, in a sixteenth-century building with vaulted ceilings, balconies, a reading room and a huge sun terrace looking out over the city's monuments. Rooms in *Centro Storico* are more upmarket and expensive, with tea-making facilities, and breakfast including local pastries is served on the premises. Guests at *Azzurretta* breakfast at the fine *Cin Cin* bar on Piazza Sant'Oronzo. In summer, the owner organizes occasional concerts and tastings of wine and local produce. *Azzurretta* **€85**, *Centro Storico* **€100**
Hotel Patria Palace Piazza Riccardi ☎ 0832 245 111, ⓦ patriapalacelecce.com. A smart, conventional hotel in an eighteenth-century palace near Santa Croce, aimed at business travellers and tourists wanting the security of four-star service and facilities such as minibars, Sky and a fitness room. Rooms are all blue and gold, and give little sense of the historic building, the main concession to design being a Liberty-style lily motif. The five best rooms

have private terraces, 17 rooms look onto Santa Croce, and guests have access to the roof terrace. Substantial discounts on website. **€230**
★ **Malia** Via Paladini 33 ☎ 329 571 663, ⓦ maliabb .com. Fabulous TV-free boutique B&B designed by owner-architect Laura Aguglia, and featured recently in UK style magazine *Wallpaper*. Heart of the B&B is a huge, elegant sitting room with a star-vaulted ceiling, parquet floor, a vast calico sofa, and an ample choice of art and design books and magazines to leaf through. Breakfast – fresh and dried fruit, bread from a wood-fired oven, home-made jams and fresh pastries – is also served here. There are four rooms, each gorgeous, each different, each imaginatively lit, especially the romantic double with a four-poster bed designed by Laura. **€110**
Suite 68 Via Leonardo Prato 7 ☎ 335 716 4922, ⓦ kalekora.it/suite68/home.asp. Six boho-chic rooms in a Baroque *palazzo*, featuring bold rugs and vivid silks, contemporary art by local artists, fabulous glass chandeliers by Lecce glassmaker Massimo Maci, and a blend of distressed and modern furniture, most striking of which is the maze bookshelf in the hall. All rooms have TV, minibar and wi-fi (€2/hr). Reception is open Mon–Fri 9am–1pm & 4–8pm; if you're arriving outside those times, call in advance. **€90**
Villa de Giorgi Via S. Fili 110, Monteroni di Lecce ☎ 0832 327 065, ⓦ villadegiorgi.it. Set in an old turreted manor house surrounded by gardens dotted with fountains and sculptures, this charming B&B is just 7km southwest of the city in a quiet suburb. Breakfast is served in the garden in the summertime. **€70**

14

CAMPING

Namastè Via Novoli km 4.5 ☎0832 329 647, ⓦostellolecce.it; #26 bus from Lecce train station. A centre for yoga and alternative therapies, this campsite has tent pitches, dorms and bungalows of various sizes with cooking facilities. There is a yoga hall, and the fruit grown in the grounds is certified organic. Open year round. Pitches from €21, dorms €18, bungalows €70

EATING AND DRINKING

CAFÉS

Alvino Piazza Sant'Oronzo 30 ☎0832 246 748. *Alvino* serves some of the city's most astonishingly jewel-like sweet confections and savoury snacks. Sample their vast array of *paste di mandorla* (almond-paste cookies). Open all day; closed Tues.

Caffè Letterario Via G. Paladini 46 ☎832 242 351, ⓦcaffeletterario.org. An arty little bookshop-café perfect for an *aperitivo* or after-dinner drinks, with a DJ on Thurs and Sun, and live music or theatre on Wed; check the website for a full programme of events. Tues–Sat 7pm till late, Sun 5pm till late; open Mon eve in summer.

L'Ideario di Liberrimo Via Vittorio Emanuele/Corte dei Cicala ☎0832 245 524, ⓦliberrima.it. Cool – if expensive – wine bar and café linked to the Liberrimo bookshop next door. Salads, antipasti, an abundant and elegantly presented *aperitivo* with nibbles including fresh ricotta, tiny *pizze*, crostini with artichokes and roast almonds. Eat inside to an accompaniment of jazz, or outside on the piazzetta. Open all day, daily.

Syrbar Via Giuseppe Libertini 67/A, Piazza del Duomo. A laidback café-restaurant open from breakfast till late evening, with windows looking onto Piazza del Duomo, though no outdoor tables, as the bishop won't allow it. A fine place for breakfast, lunch or a light dinner nevertheless, with a daily vegetable soup, and a large choice of crostini served with inspired combinations of local cheeses, hams and salamis. Breakfast winners include a *crostino* with ricotta, orange marmalade, raisins and walnuts, and yogurt with honey and nuts. There's a huge range of teas, and on winter evenings you can warm up with a hot grog of cognac infused with cinnamon and orange peel. 12.30–2.30pm & 8–10.30pm; closed Mon in winter.

RESTAURANTS

Alle Due Corte Corte dei Giugni 1 ☎0832 242 223.

Simple traditional Salentino dishes and mouthwatering antipasti draw locals and tourists alike. Try the *taieddha* (oven-baked potatoes, rice, tomatoes, onions and mussels €8.50) in summer or *cocule de maranjana allu sugu* year round (€8). Mon–Sat 12.30–2.30pm & 8–10.30pm.

Corte dei Pandolfi Piazzetta Orsini ☎0832 332 309, ⓦcortedeipandolfi.com. Intimate place in a charming little piazza off Via Paladini, gaining a fine reputation for creative twists on traditional dishes, and using only the freshest ingredients, shown off to perfection in several raw fish dishes. Other dishes worth trying are the plate of mixed seasonal vegetables (€10) and the handmade spaghetti with fresh anchovies, capers and tomato (€12). Mon–Sat 8–10.30pm, Sun 12.30–2.30pm & 8–10.30pm; closed Mon in summer and Tues in winter.

Cucina Casareccia Via Col. A. Costadura 19 ☎0832 245 178. Be sure to call ahead for one of the dozen tables at this Leccese favourite known for its home-style cooking and atmosphere. The pasta is made on site and the accompanying sauces change according to the season – a rib-warming winter dish is *ciceri e tria* (pasta with chickpeas; €8). The *pezzetti di cavallo* (horse stew; €9), a Leccese speciality, is one of the city's best. 12.30–2.30pm & 8–10.30pm; closed Mon & Sun eve.

BAR

La Torre di Merlino Vico del Tufo 10 ☎0832 242 091, ⓦtorredimerlino.it. A well-stocked wine bar offering a spectacular selection of wines and cheese, as well as inventive full meals, near Santa Croce. Go for a glass of wine, and to sample local cheeses and hams, or stay to dine on dishes such as the wonderful *burrata* in *kaitafi* pastry (€10), tuna in a sesame crust (€16) or a tempura of *baccalà* (€12). Daily 8–10.30pm, Tues–Fri & Sun also 12.30–2.30pm.

Otranto

OTRANTO, a kasbah-like town nestling around a harbour, is only an hour by train from Lecce, set in an arid, rocky and windblown landscape, with translucent seas to swim in. The port overflows with tourists in August, when Otranto's nightlife is at its peak, and the town is most entertaining, but the picturesque location and slow pace will reward visitors year-round, even if the number of gaudy souvenir shops detracts a little from the charm of its winding whitewashed lanes.

A variety of musical and theatrical events are held in Otranto throughout the summer, usually centred around the castle, along with an annual festival commemorating the "800 Martyrs" on August 13–15.

Brief history

Otranto's **history** is decidedly grim. One of the last Byzantine towns to fall to the Normans in 1070, it remained a thriving port for Crusaders, pilgrims and traders. But in 1480 a Turkish fleet laid siege to the town, which held out for fifteen days before capitulating. It's said that as a punishment the archbishop, on capture, suffered the indignity of being sawn in half, a popular Turkish spectacle at that time. Nearly 12,000 people lost their lives and the 800 survivors, refusing to convert, were taken up a nearby hill and beheaded. Otranto never really recovered, though the town does feature one glorious survivor of the Turkish attack inside its cathedral: an extraordinary **mosaic floor**.

14

Cattedrale di Santa Maria Annunziata

Piazza Basilica • Daily 7.30am–noon & 3–5pm • Free

The town's Romanesque **Cattedrale di Santa Maria Annunziata** is well worth a visit, its marble-columned nave adorned by an incredible multicoloured mosaic in stone. The central theme is the "Tree of Life". Historical and animal figures are shown as a mix of myth and reality – Alexander the Great, King Arthur, the Queen of Sheba, crabs, fish, serpents and mermaids. The work of a twelfth-century monk, its rough simplicity provides a captivating picture, empowered by a delightful child-like innocence. The rose window was added in the fifteenth century.

The Castello

Via Nicola d'Otranto • Daily: 10am–1pm & 3–7pm; July & Aug 10am–midnight • €2

Not far from the cathedral, the town's Aragonese **Castello** juts out into the bay, defending the harbour. Its walls incorporate fragments of Roman and medieval inscriptions, while Charles V's coat of arms looms from its portal.

Chiesa di San Francesco di Paola

Out on the southern edge of town is the cypress-tree-covered hill, where the survivors of the Turkish siege were beheaded. At the top of the hill, the sixteenth-century **Chiesa di San Francesco di Paola** holds the names of the victims, together with a vivid description of the terrible events of July 1480.

Basilica di San Pietro e Paolo

Daily 7.30am–noon & 3–5pm • Free

On the Bastione dei Pelasgi, the newly restored **Basilica di San Pietro e Paolo** is one of the most important Byzantine monuments in the Salento. This tiny chapel has frescoes, some with Greek inscriptions dating from the tenth to the thirteenth centuries, including a *Last Supper*.

ARRIVAL AND INFORMATION OTRANTO

By train If you are arriving in Otranto by train note that the station is a 15min walk north of the centre, so you may want to arrange a pick-up with your hotel.

Tourist office Piazza Castello (Mon–Sat 9am–1pm & 4–6pm; ☎ 0836 801 436, ⓦ viaggiareinpuglia.it).

ACCOMMODATION

B&B Palazzo d' Mori Bastione dei Pelasgi ☎ 0836 801 088, ⓦ palazzodemori.it. Ten pleasant whitewashed rooms, with white beds, white linen and romantic white mosquito nets overlooking the bay in the historical centre. There is also a lovely roof terrace for breakfast or drinks. €150

Bellavista Via Vittorio Emanuele 18 ☎ 0836 801 058, ⓦ hotelbellavistaotranto.it. Conventional rooms in a light, modern hotel right in the centre of things near the

beach and just outside the old town. The nicest rooms have balconies with sea views. €110

Masseria Bandino On the road to Uggiano La Chiesa ☎ 0836 804 647, ⓦ masseriabandino.it. A charming rural hotel with a great swimming pool set in an eighteenth-century farmhouse where you can dine on typical Salentino fare. The owners can organize horseriding, sailing, or a tour in a classic Ape pick-up. Half-board is €80 per person. €110

14

EATING AND DRINKING

Boomerang Via Vittorio Emanuele II 13/14 ☎0836 802 619. Self-service restaurant with a/c by the park next to the beach; serves delicious, low-priced, simple meals, as well as fresh antipasti and pasta. Open daily all day; closed in winter.

Da Sergio Corso Garibaldi 9 ☎0836 801 408. Unlike many Otranto restaurants, *Da Sergio* focuses on honest, reasonably priced local cuisine, with the average four-course meal costing around €30. 12.30–2.30pm & 8–10.30pm; closed Wed in low season, and from mid-Nov to mid-Dec & mid-Jan to Feb.

To the southern cape

From Otranto, all the way down to the cape at Santa Maria di Leuca, the coastline is steep and rugged. The unmissable journey along the winding road takes you past one spectacular view of sheer cliffs and blue sea after another.

Capo d'Otranto

CAPO D'OTRANTO, 5km south of Otranto, is the easternmost point on the Italian peninsula, topped by a lighthouse and the rather desolate ruins of a seventh-century abbey. This is the first place in Italy to see the sun rise, and is a popular spot to welcome in the New Year. On clear mornings there's a commanding view across the straits – the mountains of Albania are visible about 80km away – and on seriously clear days they say you can even see Corfu, 100km away. If you want to stop and swim, there are a couple of inlets at Porto Badiso and La Fraula, though the first place of any size is **Santa Cesarea Terme**, a spa-town boasting some extraordinarily opulent Moorish-style villas and the reek of sulphur. Old-fashioned **Castro**, perched high above the sea, is a cluster of white- and pastel-washed houses around an Aragonese castle. Continuing, you pass **Marittima**, despite its name, located a little inland, and dominated by a splendid Baroque palace. If you have come this far, you may as well continue along the coast road down to Puglia's southernmost point, Santa Maria di Leuca.

ARRIVAL AND DEPARTURE   THE SOUTHERN CAPE

You can get down as far as Gagliano del Capo, by train: it's at the end of the FSE rail line, just 5km from the cape; the Salento in Treno e Bus service (see p.833) runs to the cape from Otranto (and from Lecce via Gallipoli or inland via Maglie).

ACCOMMODATION

Camping Porto Miggiano 16km from Otranto, just south of Santa Cesarea Terme ☎0836 944 303, ⓦcampingportomiggiano.it. A small, simple but beautiful campsite set among olive trees with steps leading down to a beach. Small bungalows are also available, and there's a restaurant on site. March–Oct. Pitches **€24**, bungalows **€80**

Hotel degli Ulivi Via Litoranea per S. Cesarea Terme, Castro Marina ☎0836 943 037, ⓦhoteldegliulivi.net. Located in Castro's seaside satellite, this has pleasant rooms with big balconies, and a restaurant with a view over the sea. Half-board (obligatory only in mid-Aug) €100 per person. **€100**

Il Giardino Via Sant'Antonio 207, Castro ☎340 603 5400, ⓦilgiardinonelsalento.it. A lovely B&B which has a large garden for breakfast or relaxing, and cooking facilities for guests. **€110**

Palazzo Vecchio Via B. Cellini 38, Marittima ☎0836 920 0369, ⓦbebpalazzovecchio.it. Six simple rooms furnished with antique furniture, along with a more luxurious suite featuring gilded mirrors and a hydromassage bath, in the *palazzo* that dominates Marittima. There is a fabulous garden of palms and orange trees with a swimming pool, and a romantic stone gazebo. There are also rooms with the use of kitchen in an annexe. Rooms **€180**, suite **€220**

The western peninsula: Galatina

GALATINA, 30km south of Lecce, is an intriguing Salentine town on the edge of an area known as Grecia Salentina, a key Greek colony in medieval times that has retained Greek customs and language up until the present. It's an important centre of the Italian tobacco industry today, with much of the weed grown in the fields around. It's also famed for being the centre of the *tarantella* (see box opposite) and for its excellent local

THE DANCE OF THE SPIDER

The small town of Galatina has long been a pilgrimage centre for *tarantate* – women (mostly) who have been "possessed" by the mythical spider of Puglia. **Tarantism** dates back centuries in this region, with the earliest known accounts of it appearing in manuscripts from the fifteenth century. Victims believed that they had been bitten by the Italian tarantula, or the European black widow spider. After descending into a funk of symptoms that included vomiting and sweating, fear and delirium, depression and paranoia, the only cure was the rite of the tarantula, which involved trance-dancing to the local *tarantella*, or *pizzica*, for days on end. The *pizzica* musicians – typically a violinist, guitarist, accordion and tambourine player – would perform fast and feverishly, engaging the victim in a call-and-response ritual, until eventually they were released from their misery.

The cult has continued to fascinate Salentines and others into this century, with the myth and music being both preserved and reinvented. St Paul, patron saint of the *tarantate*, is revered and celebrated to this day in Galatina and surrounding villages. On June 29, the feast day of Sts Peter and Paul, musicians, dancers, *tarantate* and tourists gather at the chapel of St Paul near Galatina's cathedral in the early hours (around 4.30 or 5am) to pay their respects before the crowds arrive for the official early morning Mass. Today, *pizzica* music is enjoying a boom in the Salento and elsewhere. It's worth timing your visit to coincide with the all-night music festival The Night of the Tarantula (La Notte della Taranta; ⓦ lanottedellataranta.it), held in late August at Melpignano, between Galatina and Otranto. *Dances with Spiders* by social anthropologist Karen Lüdtke (Berghahn Books, 2009) is a very readable account of the history of the ritual, and the resurgence of *pizzica* in recent years.

wine. In the old part of town, the church of **Santa Caterina di Alessandria** (daily 9am–noon & 4.30–7pm; free) is also well worth a look for the stunning fourteenth-century frescoes that cover its interior.

ARRIVAL AND INFORMATION
GALATINA

By train Galatina is about half an hour down the FSE rail line from Lecce. Trains run approximately hourly.

Tourist office Via V. Emanuele II (Mon–Fri 10am–2pm;

ⓣ 0836 569 984, ⓦ comune.galatina.le.it); has the lowdown on events surrounding the town's *festa* and offers free bike rental (you'll need to leave ID).

ACCOMMODATION AND EATING

Il Covo della Taranta Corso Garibaldi 13 ⓣ 0836 210 265. Four doors down from the church of San Paolo, this is a reasonably priced and lively pub/pizzeria/trattoria in an eighteenth-century building that serves lunch and dinner accompanied by occasional world-music jam sessions. Tues–Sat 12.30–2.30pm & 8–10.30pm.

Palazzo Baldi Corte Baldi ⓣ 0836 568 345, ⓦ hotel palazzobaldi. Plush, elegant hotel with its own little courtyard for a quiet *aperitivo*. Rooms are romantic, with

exposed stone walls and antique furniture giving a medieval feel, but some – rather more practically – have cooking facilities. Good deals on the website. **€150**

Safi Via Ottavio Scalfo 70/74 ⓣ 349 863 6027, ⓦ safibedbreakfast.it. Huge B&B rooms furnished with a mixture of family heirlooms and IKEA standards in the faded splendour of a Baroque *palazzo* in the historic centre of town. **€100**

Basilicata and Calabria

MATERA

Basilicata and Calabria

More than any other Italian regions, Basilicata and Calabria represent the quintessence of the *mezzogiorno*, the historically under-developed southern tracts of the peninsula. After Unification in 1861, the area was largely neglected and sank into abject poverty that was worsened by emigration. Conditions here were immortalized in Carlo Levi's *Christ Stopped at Eboli* – a vivid account of his time in exile during the Fascist era in which he describes a South characterized by apathy, where malaria is endemic and the peasants' way of life is deeply rooted in superstition. Things have improved, particularly in Basilicata, although tourism is yet to bring the riches found in neighbouring Puglia and Campania.

15

In Basilicata, the greatest draw is **Matera**, whose distinctive Sassi – cave-like dwellings in the heart of the town – give it a uniquely dramatic setting. In the northern part of the region, **Melfi** and **Venosa** are bastions of medieval charm with important relics from the Byzantine and Norman eras. Of the region's two coasts, the **Tyrrhenian** is most engaging, with spots like **Maratea** offering crystal-clear water, a bustling harbour, and opportunities to discover remote sea grottoes. The **Ionian** coast is less charming, though worth a visit for its ancient sites in **Metaponto** and **Policoro** – ruins of the once mighty states that comprised Magna Graecia.

While conditions in Basilicata have improved, **Calabria** remains arguably more marginalized than it was before Unification. Since the war, a massive channelling of funds to finance huge irrigation and land-reclamation schemes, industrial development

---

REGIONAL FOOD AND WINE

The cuisine of **Basilicata**, also known as the **cucina lucana** (Lucanian cuisine), derives from a poor tradition that depended heavily on preserving food, especially pork and fruit, which are dried, and vegetables, which are preserved in oil. **Arab influence** still pervades in the form of aubergines and desserts incorporating figs, almonds and honey. Basilicata is an important producer of durum wheat, which is used to make fresh pasta, rustic breads prepared in wood-fired ovens, and *friselle*, stale bread softened with water, oil and tomatoes. **Strong cheeses**, like matured or smoked ricotta and aged *caciocavallo* are favoured. A rare breed of cow, the *mucca podolica*, grazes around Matera, and the milk and meat they produce are wonderfully flavourful.

Calabria shares many culinary traditions with its neighbour. The trademark of Calabrian cuisine, however, is *peperoncino*, spicy chilli pepper, used liberally in many dishes, and thought to ward off illness and misfortune. Try the spicy *sorpressata* salami, '**Nduia**, a hot *peperoncino* and pork fat spread. As in all southern cuisine, cheeses such as *caciocavallo*, mature *provola* and *pecorino* are ubiquitous. The *cipolla rossa* from Tropea is a sweet red onion used in rustic pies, meat dishes, and in sweet preserves called **composte**. For desserts, try *mostazzolo*, an almond cookie sweetened with honey or wine must, or anything containing *bergamotto*, a citrus fruit that grows along the south coast. Dried figs are a staple and can be found stuffed, dipped in chocolate, or simply arranged in braids or wheels.

Cirò is the success story of Calabrian **wine-making**. Made from the ancient **gaglioppo** grape, it has been given some modern touches and now shifts bottles outside its home territory. Not surprisingly, given its far-south position, Calabria also turns out sweet whites such as Greco di Bianco. The **aglianico** grape makes a star appearance in Basilicata: Aglianico del Vulture is the region's only DOC; it's been dubbed "the Barolo of the south" for its complexity, late ripening and long maturation. Other wines worth trying are the sweet, sparkling Malvasia and Moscato.

BRONZI DI RIACE

Highlights

❶ Matera Sliced by a ravine containing thousands of Sassi – cave dwellings gouged out of rock – Matera's unique landscape never ceases to astonish. **See p.845**

❷ Cripta del Peccato Originale, Contrada Petrapenta The best example of the region's distinctive rock-hewn churches, with vibrant eighth-century frescoes inside. **See p.849**

❸ Tropea promontory This region has it all – white sandy beaches, turquoise water, hills tumbling down to the coast and – in Tropea Town and Pizzo – two of the most beautiful old centres in Calabria. **See p.855**

❹ Bronzi di Riace Two extraordinary, 7ft-high, bronze statues of Greek athletes fished out of the sea and displayed in Reggio Calabria. **See p.857**

❺ Purple Codex, Rossano An illustrated manuscript from the sixth century with fascinating early depictions of the life of Christ. **See p.863**

❻ Capo Colonna A solitary Doric column marks the spot of what was the most important Greek temple on the Ionian coast. **See p.866**

HIGHLIGHTS ARE MARKED ON THE MAP ON P.842

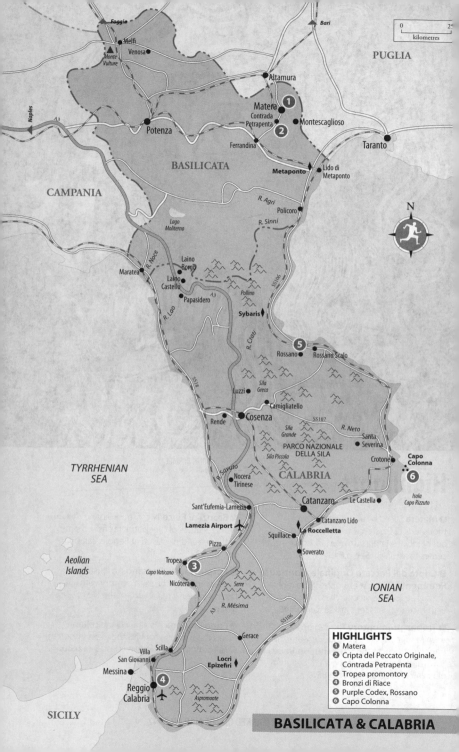

BASILICATA & CALABRIA

HIGHLIGHTS

1. Matera
2. Cripta del Peccato Originale, Contrada Petrapenta
3. Tropea promontory
4. Bronzi di Riace
5. Purple Codex, Rossano
6. Capo Colonna

PUGLIA

Foggia
Melfi
Venosa
Monte Vulture
Altamura
Matera
Contrada Petrapenta
Montescaglioso
Potenza
Ferrandina
Taranto
BASILICATA
Metaponto
Lido di Metaponto

CAMPANIA

Naples
A3
Lago Moliterno
R. Agri
Policoro
R. Sinni

Maratea
T. Noce
Laino Borgo
Laino Castello
Papasidero
R. Lao
A3
Pollino
Sybaris
SS106
R. Crati

Rossano
Rossano Scalo

Luzzi
Sila Greca
SS18
Camigliatello
Rende
Cosenza
SS107
R. Neto
Sila Grande
Santa Severina
PARCO NAZIONALE DELLA SILA
Sila Piccola
Crotone
Capo Colonna

TYRRHENIAN SEA

CALABRIA
R. Savuto
Nocera Tirinese
Le Castella
Isola Capo Rizzuto

Sant'Eufemia-Lamezia
Catanzaro
Lamezia Airport
Catanzaro Lido
La Roccelletta
Pizzo
Squillace
Tropea
Capo Vaticano
Nicótera
Serre
Soverato
R. Mèsima
A3

Aeolian Islands

IONIAN SEA

Gerace
SS106

Villa San Giovanni
Scilla
Locri Epizefiri
Messina
Reggio Calabria
Aspromonte

SICILY

N

0   2
kilometres

and a modern system of communications has brought built-up sprawl to previously isolated towns such as **Crotone** – often hand in hand with the forces of organized crime. The **'Ndrangheta** Mafia – reckoned to be far more powerful and dangerous than the Neapolitan Camorra – continues to maintain a stranglehold across much of the region.

Although unchecked development financed by the 'Ndrangheta has marred parts of the coastline, resorts such as **Scilla**, **Tropea** and **Capo Vaticano** are still charming, and have become favourite hideaway resorts for discerning Italian and foreign visitors.

The interior of the region is dominated by the mountain grandeur of the **Pollino**, **Sila** and **Aspromonte** ranges, offering excellent hiking and rustic local cuisine. The website ⓦaptbasilicata.it is a mine of information for the Basilicata region.

15

GETTING AROUND   BASILICATA AND CALABRIA

Good transport services exist in **Basilicata**, but in hilly and coastal areas, a car is useful. Be warned that if you're planning on driving, the roads tend to be narrow and provincial and you should allow more time than you think you'll need. You'll find plenty of information on transport at ⓦaptbasilicata.it. In **Calabria** there are reliable train services connecting the coastal towns, supplemented by regular buses. Again, your own transport is necessary for reaching remoter spots in the mountainous interior. Most trains are run by the national operator, FS (ⓦtrenitalia.com), though much of Basilicata is served by FAL (Ferrovia Appulo Lucane; ⓦferrovieappulolucane.com). Different bus companies operate in different parts of the region; the main one is SITA (☎0835 385 007, ⓦsitasudtrasporti.it); others are detailed in the text.

Melfi

Way up in the northernmost reaches of Basilicata, on the far side of the imposing **Monte Vulture** (1326m), the hill-town of **MELFI** was long a centre of strategic importance, taken by the Normans in 1041 and their first capital in the south of Italy. Repeatedly damaged by earthquakes, the town preserves an attractive historic centre with a formidable Norman castle that now holds a good museum.

Museo Archeologico

Via Castello • Mon 2–8pm, Tues–Sun 9am–8pm, July to mid-Sept Sat & Sun closes 10pm • €2.50 • ☎0972 238 726

Melfi's hilltop castle now contains an **archeological museum** with prehistoric finds and objects from the Greek, Roman and Byzantine eras. The museum's most celebrated item is an exquisitely carved Roman sarcophagus from the second century, showing the image of the dead girl for whom it was made, reclining on cushions, with five statuettes of gods and heroes on the sides. Look out for the paws carved on the left-hand side of the top of the sarcophagus – all that's left of the girl's pet puppy.

The Duomo

Piazza del Duomo • Daily: summer 9am–1pm & 4–8pm; winter 9am–12.30pm & 3.30–7.30pm • Free, belltower €1

In the centre of town off Via Vittorio Emanuele II, the **Duomo** was originally twelfth-century but was almost entirely rebuilt in 1700. After the 1930 earthquake, a Byzantine-style thirteenth-century *Madonna and Child* fresco was brought to light, which you can see to the left of the altar; to the left of this is another Madonna, in her role as protector of the city – a copy of the original statue stolen from here in 1982. Opposite the fresco, a door provides access to the cathedral's campanile, which has miraculously survived the various cataclysms: the two black stone griffins near the top symbolized the Norman hegemony in the region and are visible everywhere in Melfi, having been adopted as the town's emblem.

ARRIVAL AND DEPARTURE

MELFI

Trains Melfi is on the line between Potenza and Foggia. The station lies a little way west of the centre, connected by local buses. For connections to Matera, change at Potenza.
Destinations Foggia (8 daily; 55min); Potenza (hourly; 1hr 15min).

Buses SITA is the main bus company serving this area (☎ 0971 506 811). There are stops at the station and on Valle Verde.
Destinations Potenza (Mon–Sat 4–5 daily; 1hr 30min–2hr); Venosa (Mon–Sat 4 daily; 45min).

ACCOMMODATION AND EATING

★ **Delle Rose** Via Vittorio Emanuele 29 ☎ 0972 21 682. You'll find this friendly, family-run restaurant with garden seating a little way down from the cathedral, where you can try such local dishes as *baccalà alla trainera* – salt cod with dried pepperoni. First courses cost €6–10, mains are €10–13, and pizzas are served in the evening. Noon–4pm & 6pm–

midnight; closed Thurs except in July & Aug.

Il Tetto Piazza IV Novembre ☎ 0972 236 837, ⓦ albergoiltetto.com. Behind the Duomo, this former seminary retains its plain character, offering clean and spacious en-suite rooms (including family rooms) and a restaurant. €55

Venosa

If Melfi preserves the appearance of a dark medieval town, **VENOSA**, 25km east, has an attractive airiness: a harmonious place surrounded by green rolling hills and neatly divided parcels of farmland. Known in antiquity as Venusia, it was in its time the largest colony in the Roman world, and much is made of the fact that it was the birthplace of the poet Quintus Horatius Flaccus, known to English speakers as **Horace** (65–8 BC). His supposed house lies off Corso Vittorio Emanuele in the *centro storico* (by appointment ☎ 333 915 9547; free), where one large room shows a reconstruction of his living quarters, with a bed and kitchen utensils.

Parco Archeologico

Daily except Tues 9am–1.30pm • €2.50 • ☎ 329 260 7541

Venosa's chief attraction is the **Parco Archeologico**, located just outside the old centre at the bottom of the Corso. The complex consists of ruins from the Roman era including housing, shops and mosaics. Much of the stone here was recycled to build the next-door abbey.

Abbazia della Trinità

Daily 9–11.30am & 3.30–7pm • Free

Adjacent to the archeological park, the sprawling **Abbazia della Trinità** is a rich treasury of remains from different historical periods. An eleventh-century Benedictine abbey was superimposed upon a sixth-century construction – of which substantial traces remain – and this was in turn extended to create a much larger building begun in 1135 but never completed (the perimeter walls and some decorations survive). The eleventh-century church includes a mosaic floor, murals and the tombs of various Norman bigwigs including the great Robert Guiscard.

Castello Ducale

Piazza Umberto • Mon & Wed–Sun 8am–8pm, Tues 2–8pm • €2.50 • ☎ 329 260 7541

The old town's main piazza at the top of Corso Vittorio Emanuele is dominated by the **Castello Ducale**, a moated castle dating from 1470 with four stout towers at each corner. Finds from Venosa's archeological park and abbey can be seen within, and there's a sixteenth-century loggia.

ACCOMMODATION AND EATING   **VENOSA**

★ **Al Baliaggio** Corso Vittorio Emanuele 136 ☎ 0972 35 081. Sharing a courtyard with the *Orazio* hotel, this is easily Venosa's best restaurant, specializing in delicious grilled meat (€10–13) and fish (€13–18) dishes. Mon–Sat noon–2.30pm & 8–11pm.

★ **Orazio** Corso Vittorio Emanuele 142 ☎ 0972 31 135, ⓦ hotelorazio.it. Elegant small hotel in the heart of the old town, once a *palazzo* belonging to the Knights of Malta and still preserving old frescoes and vaulted ceilings. Some rooms have balconies with great views. **€65**

Matera and around

The town of **MATERA**, situated on the edge of a ravine at the eastern end of Basilicata, dates from the Middle Ages when Byzantine and Benedictine monks built rock-hewn churches and monasteries into what are now called the **Sassi** – literally "stones" – an intricate series of terraced caves. Later, farmers, seeking safety from invasions, also settled in the Sassi, fashioning their homes, stables and shops out of the rock, creating one of Italy's oddest townscapes and its most significant troglodyte settlement. During the Spanish Bourbon era, wealthy Sassi dwellers were able to move out of the cave dwellings to the plain above, while the masses were left in squalor below. The area was graphically described in Carlo Levi's 1945 memoir *Christ Stopped at Eboli*, in which the Sassi were compared to Dante's Inferno, with their impoverished, malaria-ridden inhabitants. During the 1950s twenty thousand people were forcibly removed from the Sassi and rehoused in modern districts in the new town.

Nowadays it's hard to picture the conditions that previously existed here; EU funds and private investment have poured in, and the area has been cleaned up and repopulated with homes, B&Bs, hotels, restaurants and workshops. In 1993, the city and its grotto-filled outskirts were declared a UNESCO World Heritage Site, and in 2003 Mel Gibson filmed his controversial *The Passion of the Christ* here.

The Sassi

Divided into two sections – Sasso Caveoso and Sasso Barisano – the **Sassi** district can be entered from a number of different points around the centre of town, some signposted, some not. Via Buozzi weaves through both zones and is a useful reference point, although you will need to leave it in order to penetrate the warren of *chiese rupestri*, or **cave churches** (all open daily, roughly 10am–6pm; free). Note that there's no sun cover, flights of steps are unavoidable, and you'd do well to take some water. To get the most out of the whole area equip yourself with an *itinerario turistico* and a map, both available from the various tourist offices, or take a tour (see p.848).

Santa Maria de Idris and the Convicinio di Sant'Antonio

Santa Maria de Idris April–Oct Mon 2.30–7pm, Tues–Sun 10am–7pm; Nov–March Tues–Sun 10.30am–1.30pm • Free
Convicinio di Sant'Antonio Daily 9am–1.30pm & 3.30–8pm • €1

The most spectacularly sited church, **Santa Maria de Idris**, is perched on the conical Monte Errone that rises in the midst of the Sassi. Inside are frescoes dating from the fourteenth century. Behind and below it, the **Convicinio di Sant'Antonio** holds the most interesting interior. This former monastery complex of four interlinking thirteenth-century churches was turned into wine cellars in 1700 – look for the spouts for wine emerging from what appears to be an altar – and later into houses. Of particular interest are tombs in the floor converted into water tanks that demonstrate considerable ingenuity: the porous stone had to be waterproofed, and rainwater channelled into the tanks.

The Duomo

Daily 7.30am–noon & 4–7pm • Free

Built on a rocky spur rising above the Sassi, Matera's thirteenth-century **Duomo** retains a strong Apulian-Romanesque flavour. Between the figures of saints Peter and Paul on the cathedral's facade is a sculpture of the patron of Matera, the Madonna della Bruna. Every July 2, a painting of the saint is carried through the streets on a papier-mâché float which, at the end of the day-long festivities, is stormed by onlookers and torn apart, in the belief that the pieces offer protection and blessings.

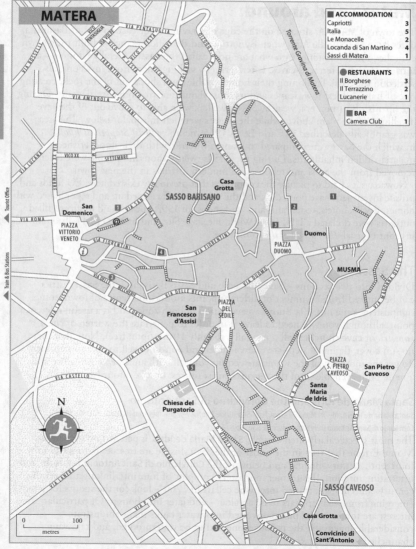

MATERA

ACCOMMODATION	
Capriotti	3
Italia	5
Le Monacelle	2
Locanda di San Martino	4
Sassi di Matera	1

RESTAURANTS	
Il Borghese	3
Il Terrazzino	2
Lucanerie	1

BAR	
Camera Club	1

MUSMA

Via San Giacomo • Tues–Sun: April–Oct 10am–2pm & 4–8pm; Nov–March 10am–2pm • €5 • ☎ 366 935 7768, ⓦ musma.it

Housed in the seventeenth-century Palazzo Pomarici, **MUSMA** is a museum of contemporary sculpture appropriately and strikingly set in rooms carved from the rock. Its permanent collection features works by Picasso, Pomodoro and Gio' and there are regular temporary exhibitions.

The Case Grotte

For a glimpse of what life was like for the Sassi-dwellers, head for one of the four **Case Grotte** in various parts of the Sassi, including one near the Convicinio di Sant'Antonio, another on Via Fiorentini (usually open daily 9.30am–8.30pm in summer, 10am–5pm in winter; around €2). Reconstructed inside a *grotta* and using original furniture, utensils and clothes, these give insights into how families with several children and livestock managed to live together in one-room cave dwellings.

Parco della Murgia

☎ 0835 336 166, ⓦ parcomurgia.it

If you want to explore the **caves** and more *chiese rupestri* in the **Parco della Murgia** on the far side of the ravine, there are several entrances from SS7 northwest of Matera. The park is best seen with a guide – Ferula Viaggi (see p.848) organizes excursions – who can lead you to some of the hundreds of hypogeums and rock-hewn churches in its eight thousand hectares.

The new town: Matera Piano

Most visitors to Matera head straight for the atmospheric Sassi, and understandably so, but **Matera Piano** – the "new" town above begun in the seventeenth century – is worthy of exploration, too, with a host of churches and a livelier feel.

The centre of Matera Piano is **Piazza Vittorio Veneto**, a large and stately square, which in the evening is given over to a long procession of shuffling promenaders. The *materani* take their evening stroll seriously, and the din of the crowds rising up out of this square can be like the noise from a stadium. Matera's modern quarters stretch out to the north and west of here, but most of the things worth seeing are along Via Ridola and its extension Via del Corso, winding off from the bottom end of the piazza.

San Francesco d'Assisi

Piazza San Francesco • Daily: summer 8.30am–12.30pm & 5.30–8pm; winter 7.30am–noon & 4–7pm • Free

Off Via del Corso, the seventeenth-century church of **San Francesco d'Assisi** has an ornate Baroque style that was superimposed on two older churches, traces of which, including some eleventh-century frescoes, can be visited through a passage in the fourth chapel on the left. Set above the altar in the main church are eight panels of a polyptych by Lorenzo Bastiani, a fifteenth-century follower of Bartolomeo Vivarini.

From San Francesco, you can head to the bar-strewn Piazza del Sedile just above the Sassi, or on to Via Ridola to admire the **Chiesa del Purgatorio** (daily 8.30am–12.30pm & 4–7pm), its elliptical facade gruesomely decorated with skulls and with a tall, domed interior.

ARRIVAL AND DEPARTURE

MATERA

By train Matera's central train station is on Piazza Matteotti and is served by the FAL line, linked to Altamura (roughly hourly; 30min) and Bari (11 daily; 1hr 20min) in Puglia, both Mon–Sat only; for Potenza change at Altamura on the FAL line, or take a bus to Ferrandina to pick up the FS line Metaponto–Potenza.

By bus SITA buses stop on Piazza Matteotti, connecting Matera to Montescaglioso, Metaponto and Policoro. The ticket office is below the piazza off Via Don Minzoni. Grassani buses (☎ 0835 721 443, ⓦ grassani.it) for Potenza also stop here (tickets on board). Marino buses (☎ 080 311 2335, ⓦ marinobus.it), running two or three times daily

15

from Naples, stop on the edge of town near the Matera Nord station, Villa Longo, connected to the centre by local buses (every 20–30min).

Destinations Metaponto (Mon–Sat 6 daily; 50min); Montescaglioso (Mon–Sat hourly, Sun 3 daily; 35min); Policoro (Mon–Sat 5 daily; 1hr 25min); Potenza (Mon–Sat 5 daily; 1hr 40min).

INFORMATION, TOURS AND ACTIVITIES

Tourist information Matera has no main tourist office – the task has been devolved to autonomous "info points" scattered around the centre, all primarily promoting their own services. There's one on Piazza Vittorio Veneto (daily 8.30am–1pm & 2.30–9pm; ☎0835 314 359 or ☎346 094 7270), but any can help you with basic information and provide maps. Otherwise head for the APT on Via De Vitti De Marco 9 (Mon & Thurs 9am–1pm & 4–6.30pm, Tues, Wed & Fri 9am–1pm; ☎0835 331 983, ☞aptbasilicata.it); it's primarily an administrative office but it can provide information and material on Matera and Matera province.

Tours For access to parts of the Sassi you might miss on your own, you can join a 2hr guided tour with the excellent Ferula Viaggi, on Via Cappelluti 34 in the new town (☎0835 336 572, ☞www.ferulaviaggi.it), which charges around €52 for groups of up to four with English-speaking guides. Alternatively, you can arrange tours in English or Italian of three of the *chiese rupestri* through Sassi Tourism at Via Lucana 236 (☎338 237 0498) for €15 per person. La Scaletta, a local cultural association, also arranges tours at various prices (☎0835 236 233, ☞lascaletta.net).

Bike rental Ferula Viaggi (see above) rents out bikes for €15/day, and arranges self-guided cycle tours.

ACCOMMODATION

Apart from Maratea, Matera is the only place in Basilicata where you might have difficulty finding a room for the night – booking a week or so in advance is highly recommended. A lot of new B&Bs and some beautiful hotels have recently opened in the Sassi themselves, which are probably the most atmospheric places to stay – although of course the swish furniture, modern plumbing and decor would be unrecognizable to any former *sasso* dweller.

Capriotti Piazza del Duomo 75 ☎0835 333 997, ☞capriotti-bed-breakfast.it. Three tastefully decorated, light-flooded rooms, each with its private entrance and own outdoor space (and one with a terrace), in the vaulted rooms of a restored sixteenth-century *sasso* close to the Duomo. No credit cards. **€70**

Italia Via Ridola 5 ☎0835 333 561, ☞albergoitalia.com. Matera Piano's most convenient hotel, catering mostly to business travellers, where Mel Gibson and his cast stayed, and the best option if you don't fancy sleeping in a cave. **€90**

★ **Le Monacelle** Via Riscatto 9/10 ☎0835 344 097, ☞lemonacelle.it. Built into a former convent and conservatory, this small hotel near the Duomo has spacious rooms, a large panoramic terrace and a garden, as well as

dormitory accommodation. Dorms **€18**, doubles **€86**

Locanda di San Martino Via Fiorentini 71 ☎0835 256 600, ☞www.locandadisanmartino.it. A lovely hotel in the Sassi built into a former carpenter's workshop and a deconsecrated chapel. The rooms are beautifully furnished, fragrant and cool. **€89**

★ **Sassi di Matera** Via Civita 28, Sasso Barisano ☎0835 332 744, ☞sextantio.it. This place is really extraordinary: a beautifully styled hotel in the Sassi incorporating a honeycomb of cave-like, underfloor-heated rooms with state-of-the-art showers, Philippe Starck baths, and furnishings reclaimed from abandoned rural buildings. Breakfast and aperitifs are served in a former cave-church, or on the terrace overlooking the gorge. It costs a fortune, but you'll never forget it. **€200**

EATING AND DRINKING

Thanks to the surge in tourism, there's plenty of choice for eating in Matera. In spite of its close proximity to the sea, traditional Materan food is dominated by meat dishes. You'll find lots of cafés and bars around Piazza San Pietro Caveoso and along Via Buozzi in the Sassi, or in and around Piazza Vittorio and Piazza Sedile in Piano.

Camera Club Via S. Biagio 13 ☎335 109 9603. In a set of caves on the edge of the Sassi near Piazza Vittorio, this watering hole prepares delicious panini and light meals, accompanied by cold beer. There's an outdoor seating area in the evening. Tues–Sun 9pm–late.

Il Borghese Via Lucana 198 ☎0835 314 223. Frequented by locals, this restaurant with a garden has great antipasti and typical *lucana* dishes such as *cavatelli*

con peperoni cruschi (pasta with sundried peppers) and *agnello grigliato* (grilled lamb). Pasta dishes are around €8, mains €10–18. 12.30–3pm & 7.30pm–midnight; closed Wed lunch.

Il Terrazzino Vico San Giuseppe 7 ☎0835 334 119. Enjoy the view over the Sassi at this atmospheric spot, over a meal of oven-baked *orecchiette al tegamino* (with local sausage, tomatoes and mozzarella), or *la pignata*, a dish

of oven-roasted lamb with vegetables and cheese. There's a tourist menu priced at €16; eating à la carte should cost €20–25, less if you have pizza. Noon–3pm & 7.30–11.30pm; closed Tues & two weeks in July.
★ **Lucanerie** Via S. Stefano 61 ☎ 0835 332 133. This

traditionally vaulted trattoria offers some of the best and most abundant *antipasti misti* in town, but save room for specialities like *tortina di formaggio di capra* (a creamy goat's cheese dessert). Meals from around €25. Tues–Sat 12.30–3pm & 7.30pm–midnight, Sun 12.30–3pm.

The Cripta del Peccato Originale

Tues–Sun tours at 9.30am, 11am, 12.30pm & 3.30pm, April–Sept also 5pm & 6.30pm • €8 • ☎ 320 535 0910, ⓦ criptadelpeccatooriginale.it

Some 14km south of Matera in **CONTRADA PETRAPENTA**, the **Cripta del Peccato Originale** (Crypt of Original Sin) is lauded as the "Sistine Chapel of cave churches". Inside, late eighth-century frescoes depict surprisingly dynamic Old Testament scenes, saints and angels on a white background embellished with tendrils of red flowers. Note that you need to **book** by phone in order to visit; tours last around an hour.

Montescaglioso

San Michele Piazza del Popolo • April–Oct Mon 10am–1pm, Tues–Sun 10am–1pm & 3–7pm; Nov–March Tues–Sun 10am–1pm & 3–5pm • Tours €4 • ☎ 334 836 0098 • Buses from Matera Mon–Sat hourly, Sun 3 daily; 35min

Twenty kilometres southeast of Matera, the hilltop village of **MONTESCAGLIOSO** was once a Greek settlement and is now the site of the magnificent eleventh-century Benedictine abbey of **San Michele**, where tours take in sixteenth- and seventeenth-century frescoes. You could easily spend a few hours here exploring the town's winding backstreets, and there are great views over the Bradano valley.

ACCOMMODATION AND EATING

Caveosus Via Chiesa Maggiore 1 ☎ 0835 201 912. Simple backstreet trattoria for a delicious home-cooked lunch that will cost around €15. 12.30–3pm & 7.30–11.30pm; mid-Sept to June closed Tues eve.
L'Orto di Lucania Contrada Dogana ☎ 0835 202 195,

ⓦ ortodilucania.it. This agriturismo on the SP175 3km west of Montescaglioso has a renowned restaurant that focuses on local and seasonal food (booking essential). Should you want to stay, you'll find well-kitted-out rooms and apartments and there's a pool and lovely grounds with fruit trees. €90

Basilicata's Ionian coast

A leisurely thirty-minute drive from Matera, **Basilicata's Ionian coast** from **Metaponto** to **Policoro** consists of a mountainous interior backing onto a seaboard punctuated only by holiday resorts, a plethora of campsites – overflowing in the summer months – and some notable historical sites. Of these, the most significant are connected with the periods of Greek occupation, the most recent of which was that of the Byzantines, who administered the area on and off for five hundred years.

Metaponto

The most extensively excavated of Baslicata's Greek sites, **METAPONTO** was settled in the eighth century BC and owed its subsequent prosperity to the fertility of the surrounding land – perfect for cereal production (symbolized by the ear of corn stamped on its coinage). In about 510 BC, Pythagoras, banished from Kroton, established a school here that contributed to an enduring philosophical tradition. Metapontum's downfall came as a result of a series of catastrophes: absorbed by Rome, embroiled in the Punic Wars, sacked by the slave-rebel Spartacus, and later desolated by a combination of malaria and Saracen raids.

Metaponto today is a straggling, amorphous place, lacking much charm but with sandy beaches at **Metaponto Lido** that attract holiday-makers in summer. There's a train station at **Metaponto Scalo**, and **Metaponto Borgo**, some 800m from Scalo and 3km northwest of Lido, has an important archeological museum, otherwise the place mostly consists of the huge archeological park and modern villas, apartments and hotels.

Museo Archeologico Nazionale

Via Aristea 21 • Mon 2–8pm, Tues–Sun 9am–8pm; early July to mid-Sept Sat & Sun closes 10pm • €2.50 • ☎ 0835 745 327

A short walk north of the train station, the **Museo Archeologico Nazionale** has mainly fifth- and fourth-century-BC exhibits, consisting of statuary, ceramics and jewellery dug up from the archeological park. There's a small but fascinating section on the new insights revealed by the study of fingerprints on shards found in the artisans' quarter.

Parco Archeologico and Tavole Palatine

Daily 9am–1hr before sunset (phone ahead to confirm opening times) • Free • ☎ 0835 745 327

From Metaponto Borgo, follow Via di Apollo 500m east to the entrance of the **Parco Archeologico**, which has the remains of a theatre and a Temple of Apollo Licius. The latter is a sixth-century-BC construction that once possessed 32 columns, but you need some imagination to picture its original appearance.

In a better state of preservation, the **Tavole Palatine**, or Temple of Hera, is around 5km northwest where the main SS106 crosses the River Bradano. With fifteen of its columns remaining, the fifth-century-BC temple is the most evocative remnant of this once mighty state.

15

ARRIVAL AND INFORMATION   METAPONTO

Although you can walk to Metaponto Borgo from the train station, to reach the archeological park you're best off driving or taking a taxi (☎ 338 865 9918).

By train Matera's train station is at Metaponto Borgo, served by FS trains. For Bari change at Taranto.
Destinations Policoro (6 daily; 20min); Sibari (6 daily; 1hr 15min); Taranto (4 daily; 30–50min).
By bus SITA buses stop at the train station and at Piazza Giovanni XXIII.

Destinations Matera (Mon–Sat 4 daily; 50min); Policoro (Mon–Sat 5 daily; 45min); Taranto (Mon–Sat 5 daily; 1hr 40min).
Tourist office The Pro Loco on Piazza Giovanni XXIII keeps flexible hours (☎ 0835 748 903 or ☎ 328 421 3933).

ACCOMMODATION

Kennedy Via Ionio 1 ☎ 0835 741 960, ⊚ www .hrkennedy.it. About 1km from the station and 200m from the sea, off the Lido road, this modern holiday hotel offers excellent value. It has some apartments as well as rooms, and may be half-board-only in high season. **€72**

Camping Internazionale Viale delle Nereidi Grecia ☎ 0835 741 916, ⊚ villageinternazionale.com. This campsite is small but clean, right opposite the beach, and has bungalows (€100) as well as pitches for tents and camper vans. There's a bar and pizzeria. Pitches **€23**

Policoro

Twenty kilometres south of Metaponto, the area between the Sinni and Agri rivers was in its time one of the richest areas on this coast and site of the two Greek colonies of **Siris** and **Heraclea**. The latter was where Pyrrhus, king of Epirus, first introduced elephants to the Romans, and, although winning the first of two battles in 280 BC, suffered such high losses that he declared another such victory would cost him the war – so bequeathing to posterity the term "Pyrrhic victory". Artefacts unearthed from the area can be seen in **POLICORO**, where the **Museo Nazionale della Siritide** at Via Colombo 8 (Mon & Wed–Sun 9am–8pm, Tues 2–8pm; €2.50; ☎ 0835 972 154) has a fabulous collection of clay figurines and jewel-bedecked skeletons, among other items. The ruins of Heraclea are just behind the museum and although in a poor state, they're worth a wander. It's a fifteen-minute walk from the centre of Policoro, or a five-minute walk from the nearest local bus stop.

★ **Pitty** Piazza della Pace ☎ 0835 981 203. For quality seafood, try this terrific restaurant in Policoro's centre, near the bus terminal. Try the *spaghetti con le vongole* (with clams). A full meal will cost you less than €30. 12.30–4pm & 7–11pm; closed Mon Oct–June.

Parco Nazionale Pollino

Straddling Basilicata and Calabria, the **Parco Nazionale Pollino** is one of Italy's largest national parks, covering an area of nearly two thousand square kilometres. It is named for the **Massiccio del Pollino**, a massif in the southern Apennines that reaches a height of 2248m, offering spectacular views over pine forests, plains, limestone slopes, and beyond, to both the Tyrrhenian and Ionian seas. That, and its other major peaks such as the **Serra Dolcedorme** (2267m), are best explored on organized hiking excursions (see box below) aimed at seeking out the park's rare flora and fauna which include the cuirassed pine (the park's symbol), the roe deer and the golden eagle.

The park's lower slopes are home to nearly sixty villages, best seen by car, as public transport connections are irregular. Near the park's eastern boundary are several settlements – Acquaformosa, Civita, San Basile, San Costantino Albanese and San Paolo Albanese among them – founded between 1470 and 1540 by **Albanian refugees** fleeing persecution by the Turks. Here language, costume and religious customs have a decidedly eastern flavour.

From the western side, one logical gateway is **LAINO BORGO**, just off the A3 autostrada, known for its **Santuario delle Cappelle**, fifteen chapels frescoed with scenes from the life of Christ. From here, it is a short drive to **Laino Castello**, an eerie medieval hamlet abandoned after an earthquake in the 1980s that holds commanding views over the Lao river valley.

The park's limestone terrain is particularly susceptible to erosion, which gives rise to its many grottoes, including the **Grotta del Romito** in **PAPASIDERO**. Many guided excursions depart to the Pollino massif from Papasidero, though the town itself is worth a stroll for its elaborately carved portals that precede churches and *palazzi nobili*.

Maratea

The brief stretch of Basilicata's **Tyrrhenian coast** is the most visually ravishing part of the entire region, its tall, sheer cliffs rising dramatically above rocky coves and some first-rate **beaches**. Though these get overcrowded in summer, the encircling mountains mean that there has been minimal development by the holiday industry.

ACTIVITIES IN THE PARCO NAZIONALE POLLINO

From **horseriding** to **hiking**, there are plenty of activities on offer in the park. Try the following operators:

CAI (Club Alpino Italiano) Via C. Pepe 74, Castrovillari ☎ 334 100 5054, ⓦ caicastrovillari.it. The Italian Alpine Club can arrange hikes and nature trails with English-speaking guides.

Ente Parco Complesso Monumentale Santa Maria della Consolazione, Rotonda ☎ 0973 669 311, ⓦ parcopollino.it. The official national park office, with information on activities and hiking maps.

Ferula Viaggi Via Cappelluti 34, Matera ☎ 0835 336 572, ⓦ www.ferulaviaggi.it. Multi-day hiking or biking excursions with guides and lodging.

Viaggiare nel Pollino ☎ 347 263 1462, ⓦ viaggiarenelpollino.com. Thematic tours, hiking, biking and rafting excursions. The website has a mine of information on the park.

The obvious stop here is **MARATEA**, a dispersed settlement stretching for some 20km along the beautiful rocky coastline, including the hamlets of Castrocucco, Marina, Porto, Fiumicello, Cersuta and Acquafredda. Most of the action – and accommodation – is in or around the little seaside area of **Fiumicello**, 5km north of **Maratea Paese** (the inland centre), though the chic elite who have colonized much of the area prefer to be seen in the bars and restaurants of **Marina di Maratea**, directly south of Maratea Paese – if nothing else, a pleasant place to stroll around and gawp at the yachts.

The whole area is well endowed with sandy **beaches**, including those at Fiumicello and Acquafredda; most are well signposted, but don't hesitate to explore the less obvious ones. The coast is also home to fifty or so **grottoes**, most accessible only by boat; enquire at the tourist office (see below) for boat rental agencies.

If you fancy some exercise, try climbing up to **Monte San Biagio** (624m), the highest point above Maratea. The peak is dominated by the **Redentore**, an enormous marble Christ symbolically positioned with its back to the sea, looking towards the mountains of the interior. Opposite the statue, and looking as if it were about to be crushed under the giant's feet, is an eighteenth-century church, the **Santuario di San Biagio**, dedicated to the town's patron saint. On the second Sunday of May, a statue of the saint is carried up the hill in a large procession.

15

ARRIVAL AND INFORMATION   MARATEA

By train Most trains between Salerno and Paola stop at the main Maratea station (Maratea Scalo), below Maratea Paese, from where it's a 5min minibus or taxi ride (or a 20min walk) to Fiumicello. There are also stations at Acquafredda and Marina di Maratea.

By bus or minibus SITA (ⓦsitasudtrasporti.it) runs buses along the coast and to other towns in Basilicata year-round, and also operates a minibus service between late

June and August that connects Marina di Maratea, Fiumicello, Maratea Scalo and Maratea Paese (roughly hourly; buy tickets on board).

Tourist office Piazza del Gesù, Fiumicello (July to mid-Sept daily 9am–1pm & 5–9pm; mid-Sept to June Mon & Thurs 8am–2pm & 3–6pm, Tues, Wed & Fri 8am–2pm; ⓣ0973 876 908, ⓦaptbasilicata.it).

ACCOMMODATION

Accommodation can be sparse and expensive in high season, with many hotels requiring half-board during the peak period. To avoid this, you may do better to rent a room – ask for a list from the tourist office.

B&B Laino Via Rasi 4/C ⓣ0973 876 506 or ⓣ328 975 7216, ⓦbeblaino.it. A short walk up from Fiumicello, this peaceful spot has six rooms, an apartment, a garden with a small pool and sea views. €110

Fiorella Via Santa Venere 21 ⓣ0973 876 921. At the top of Fiumicello's main road on the SS18, this is a functional hotel – clean and spacious but basic – and open all year

round. €73

★ **La Locanda delle Donne Monache** Via C. Mazzei 4, Maratea Paese ⓣ0973 876 139, ⓦlocandamonache .com. Maratea's most distinctive hotel is sited in an elegantly renovated eighteenth-century convent in the old town, with stunning views – just the place for a romantic splurge. Closed Nov–March. €130

EATING

There are dozens of restaurants in the area; most along the coast serve fish and/or pizza and are open May to October and weekends-only the rest of the year.

El Sol Via Santa Venere 151, Fiumicello ⓣ0973 876 928. This casual place signposted off the main road generally pulls in a big local crowd for its pizzas and seafood dishes, such as mussels and swordfish. You'll pay around €6 for a pizza, €12.50 for grilled fish. Daily noon–3pm & 6.30–11.30pm.

Il Sacello La Locanda delle Donne Monache (see

above). This hotel's chic restaurant prepares modern interpretations of the region's cuisine, both land- and sea-based – try the *linguine con baccalà e peperoni cruschi* (linguini with cod and fried pepper flakes). It's expensive though – expect to pay around €150 for two including wine. Daily 12.30–2.30pm & 7.30–10.30pm; closed Nov–March.

Calabria's Tyrrhenian coast

The northern stretch of the Tyrrhenian coast in Calabria is peppered with holiday complexes that crowd the flat littoral. There are some attractive places to break the journey, notably the towns of **Diamante**, **Belvedere** and, further south, **Paola**.

South of the Savuto River the **Piana di Sant'Eufemia** plain is the narrowest part of the Calabrian peninsula, much of it reclaimed only in the last hundred years from malarial swamp: the mosquitoes remain but they no longer carry the disease. Heading south on the highway, past the high tableland of the Tropea promontory, the views grow ever more inspiring as the Autostrada del Sole winds round and through the mountains with the Aeolian islands visible to the west and Sicily to the south.

GETTING AROUND   **CALABRIA'S TYRRHENIAN COAST**

The towns dotted along Calabria's long Tyrrhenian coast are connected by the SS18, the Naples–Reggio train line (though the frequent trains don't always stop at smaller places) and by local independent bus companies. From the Savuto River down to Reggio, the SS18, autostrada and main rail line all run parallel along the coast, apart from the stretch of the Tropea promontory. Just north of here, **Lamezia** has Calabria's main **airport** (☎ 0968 414 333, ⊚ sacal.it), mainly used for domestic and seasonal flights, while nearby **Sant'Eufemia-Lamezia** is the **rail and road junction** for Catanzaro and the Ionian coast.

Pizzo

Following the railway or the SS18 southward, you can make a rewarding stop at the picturesque little town of **PIZZO**, overlooking the sea.

Castello Murat

Piazza del Castello · Mon–Fri 8.30am–8pm, Sat & Sun flexible opening · €2.50 · ☎ 0963 532 523

Off the main Piazza della Repubblica, the small, well-preserved **Castello Murat** is worth a look. The castle was built in 1486 by Ferdinand I of Aragon, and is now named after **Joachim Murat**, Napoleon's brother-in-law and one of his ablest generals. Murat met his ignominious end here after attempting to rouse the people against the Bourbons to reclaim the throne of Naples given to him by Napoleon; the people of Pizzo ignored his haughty entreaties, and he was arrested and court-martialled. In the castle you can see the room in which the French general was imprisoned, with some of his personal effects and copies of the last letters he wrote, and the terrace where he was shot in October 1815.

Chiesetta di Piedigrotta

Daily 9am–1pm & 3–7.30pm, closes 5pm in winter · €3 (tickets from *Bar Aquarium* near the entrance) · ☎ 347 347 2615

A couple of kilometres north of the centre, signposted off the main road into town, the **Chiesetta di Piedigrotta** is a curious rock-hewn church next to a sandy beach. Created in the seventeenth century by Neapolitan sailors rescued from a shipwreck, the church was later enlarged and its interior festooned with eccentric statuary depicting episodes from the Bible. Most of this was the work of a local father-and-son team, and it was augmented by another scion of the family in 1969, who restored the works and contributed a scene of his own, a double portrait of Pope John XXIII and President Kennedy.

INFORMATION   **PIZZO**

Tourist office Pro Loco, Piazza della Repubblica (Tues–Sun 10am–12.30pm & 4–6.30pm; ☎ 0963 531 310, ⊚ prolocopizzo.it).

ACCOMMODATION AND EATING

Casa Armonia Via Armonia 9 ☎ 339 374 3731, ⊚ casaarmonia.com. Central B&B very close to the castle, with a friendly owner, clean, modern rooms and a terrace overlooking the sea. No credit cards. **€65**

★ **Casa Janca** Riviera Prangi, Contrada Marinella

☎0963 264 364 or ☎349 574 7135. This agriturismo signposted off the main road north of town makes a good option for eating and sleeping. Furnished in traditional rustic style, the place is locally renowned for its restaurant, where non-guests can also dine for around €30 on local specialities such as *zuppa di cipolla* (onion soup). Leave space for sampling *tartufo di Pizzo* – the famous local ice cream, a portion of which is a bit like eating a whole box of chocolate truffles. Half-board costs €110 for two. Restaurant March–Oct 12.30–2.30pm & 8–11pm; closed Wed except July–Sept. **€65**

Il Porticato Piazza della Repubblica 57 ☏ 333 138 0766. Most of the action in Pizzo takes place in the main piazza, where you'll find this pizzeria under the portico with outdoor

seating in summer. As well as pizzas (€5–6), there are decent pastas (€6–10), meat (€6–10) and fish (€9–15) dishes. 1–3.30pm & 6.45–11.30pm, closed Tues Oct–June.

La Nave Lungomare Colombo ☏ 333 404 5142. Right by the sea, this seafood restaurant is disguised as a ship. Between April and July you can sample the local tuna or swordfish, for which Pizzo is a fishing centre; mains are mostly €10–15. Noon–3pm & 7.30–midnight; mid–Sept to June closed Wed.

Tropea

Southwest of Pizzo, **TROPEA** can claim to be the prettiest town on the whole of the southern Tyrrhenian coast, built right on the edge of steep cliffs, towering high over its beach. It is also (after Maratea in Basilicata) the most fashionable, with a seaside charm missing from many of the other Calabrian resorts, though the charm can wear pretty thin in the face of the tourist influx during the summer months.

There are numerous **beaches** around the town, all within walking distance of the centre, and the buildings have character without being twee – see particularly the lovely Norman **cathedral** at the bottom of Via Roma, whose interior harbours a couple of unexploded American bombs from the last war (one accompanied by a grateful prayer to the Madonna), a Renaissance ciborium and a statue of the Madonna and Child from the same period. The views from the upper town over the sea and the church of **Santa Maria dell'Isola** on its rock (closed for restoration) are superb, and on a clear day you can see the cone of Stromboli, and sometimes other Aeolian islands looming on the horizon.

15

ARRIVAL AND INFORMATION   TROPEA

By taxi With the often inadequate public transport services, local taxis are often the only means to get around; call ☏ 0963 603 438 or ☏ 331 613 3200. A ride from Tropea to Capo Vaticano will cost around €15.

By train Local trains from Lamezia, Reggio Calabria and Pizzo arrive at Tropea's station located on the outskirts of the *centro storico*, 1km from the beach. There are more frequent connections to and from main towns changing at Pizzo or Rosarno.

Destinations Lamezia Terme (9–13 daily; 40min–1hr 10min); Pizzo (7–12 daily; 35min); Reggio Calabria (2–4 daily; 1hr 40min–2hr).

By bus In summer, regular bus services link Tropea with the local coastal resorts, but transport is more infrequent out of season.

Tourist information Pro Loco, Piazza Ercole (April–Sept daily 9.30am–1pm & 4.30–9pm ☏ 0963 61 475, ⓦ prolocotropea.eu).

ACCOMMODATION

Camping Marina del Convento Via Marina del Convento ☏ 0963 62 501 (summer), ☏ 0963 61 320 (winter), ⓦ marinadelconvento.it. One of two campsites right on the beach at the base of the cliff below Tropea's centre, both with very similar facilities, though *Marina del Convento* also has small, simple bungalows and apartments for around €350 a week in mid-season, more in Aug. May–Oct. Pitches **€19**

Porta del Mare Via Libertà 52 ☏ 0963 607 041, ⓦ valentour.it. An old, remodelled *palazzo* provides modern comforts near the centre, with a large terrace overlooking the sea where breakfast is served in summer

(otherwise it's in your room). Rooms are small and simple, three with balconies. Closed Nov–Feb. **€130**

Villa Antica Via Ruffo 37 ☏ 0963 607 176, ⓦ villa anticatropea.it. Right in the centre of Tropea, this villa from 1906 has quiet grounds and antique pieces. Rooms are all different, accessed from a courtyard or the garden, and some have murals. **€138**

★ **Villa Italia** Via della Vittoria 7 ☏ 0963 666 194, ⓦ bbvillaitalia.it. This bright, modern B&B in an old building near the centre (behind the post office) provides spacious rooms with a/c, TV, free wi-fi and private bathrooms. Breakfast is served in the garden in summer. **€120**

EATING AND DRINKING

Tropea has more trattorias per square metre than any other town in Calabria, often with budget tourist menus. Nightlife, meanwhile, is tranquil, with good wine bars and ice-cream parlours in which to while away the evening. Most places are closed from around October to Easter.

La Cantina del Principe Largo Galluppi 18 ☎0963 61 400. Authentic, moderately priced Calabrese dishes – including stuffed aubergines or peppers and onion fritters – served in a converted cellar or at tables outside; mains from about €12. Daily 6pm–late, also Aug noon–2.30pm.

La Munizione Largo Duomo 12 ☎346 382 7594. Chic cocktail bar behind the cathedral, with a roof terrace boasting excellent views. It serves around 130 wines, cocktails from €5 and meals for around €25, with the accent on tuna and raw fish. Daily 6.30pm–2am.

Le Volpi e L'Uva Via Pelliccia 2/4, signed off Corso Vittorio Emanuele II ☎0963 61 900. Intimate *enoteca*

and restaurant, run by a chef who teaches cookery courses. Seafood dishes are around the €12 mark, and there are some sixty different Southern Italian wines to choose from. Daily noon–2.30pm & 6.30pm–midnight.

Osteria del Pescatore Via del Monte 7 ☎0963 603 018. Excellent, good-value fish is served up in this vaulted cellar near the cathedral; a big plate of *filea alla tropeana* local pasta is €9. Daily 12.30–2.30pm & 7.30–11pm.

Vecchio Forno Via Caivano, off Corso Vittorio Emanuele II ☎347 311 2416. The most historic place to eat in town, serving crisp, freshly baked pizza for around €5 – the smell of *peperoncino* is heavenly. Daily 7pm–late.

Capo Vaticano

Further around the promontory, **Capo Vaticano** holds some of the area's most popular beaches, including **Grotticelle** and **Tonicello**, both spacious enough to allow you to get away from the bustle.

ACCOMMODATION   **GROTTICELLE**

Quattro Scogli ☎0963 663 126 (summer), ☎0963 663 115 (winter), ⓦquattroscogli.it. Immediately above the beach, this campsite is well equipped but can get crowded. You can also rent caravans (€60), cabins with kitchenettes

(€80) and self-contained apartments (€800/week in high season for a two-room place), and there's a hotel run by the same management a few minutes' walk up the road. April–Oct. Pitches **€27**

Scilla

Heading south along the coast, the proximity of Sicily becomes the dominant feature. This stretch of the autostrada can claim to be one of the most panoramic in Italy, burrowing high up through mountains with the Straits of Messina glittering below. Travelling by train or following the old coastal road, you pass through **SCILLA**, with a fine sandy **beach** and lots of action in the summer. Known as Scylla in classical times, this was the legendary location of a six-headed cave monster, one of two hazards to mariners mentioned in the **Odyssey**, the other being the whirlpool Charybdis, corresponding to the modern Cariddi located 6km away on the other side of the strait. Crowning a hefty rock, a **castle** separates the main beach from the fishing village of Chianalea to the north.

Castello Ruffo

Piazza del Castello · Daily 8.30am–7.30pm · €1.50 · ☎0965 704 207

Standing sentinel over Scilla, the **Castello Ruffo** has existed in one form or another for at least eight centuries, while the rock on which it stands has revealed fortifications

---

FERRIES TO SICILY FROM VILLA SAN GIOVANNI

Some 9km southwest of Scilla, **Villa San Giovanni** is the main embarkation point for **Sicily**. State-run FS **ferries** (ⓦtrenitalia.com) leave from directly behind the train station about fifteen times a day and arrive at Messina's train station; the ticket office is in front of Villa's train station. There are more frequent services on the private Caronte ferries (☎800 627 414, ⓦcarontetourist.it), which leave approximately every twenty minutes and pull in closer to the entrance of the autostrada; the ticket office is across from the station. **Crossing-time** for each is about forty minutes. For a car with two people, Caronte charges €36 one way, FS charges €40, and both operators charge around €2.50 for foot passengers. There's also a hydrofoil service for foot passengers operated by Metromare (☎0923 873 813, ⓦmetromaredellostretto.it), leaving roughly hourly on weekdays until 7.30pm (Sat & Sun 5 daily until 8pm), taking twenty minutes (€2.50).

dating back to the fifth century BC. Today, the castle offers the best views in town, and has an exhibition on fishing inside, specifically the rituals of swordfishing.

ACCOMMODATION AND EATING

SCILLA

Bleu de Toi Via Grotte 40 ☎ 0965 790 585. Scilla's best fish restaurants are in Chianalea, and this is the top choice, where you can sample grilled swordfish, tuna and grilled prawns. Pasta dishes are around €10, mains about €15. 1–3.30pm & 8pm–midnight, closed Tues Sept–June and all Jan.

Le Sirene Via Nazionale 57 ☎ 0965 754 019, ⓦ hotel lesirenescilla.com. Try this small, airy hotel if you want to stay centrally in Scilla, right opposite the station and with a wide panoramic terrace overlooking the beach. Four of the rooms are sea-facing. The owners also run a B&B in Chianalea. **€90**

Reggio Calabria and around

REGGIO CALABRIA was one of the first ancient Greek settlements on the Italian mainland; today, it's Calabria's biggest town by some distance, with a population of over 180,000 – but also one that's been synonymous for years with urban decline and the influence of the local mafia, or **'Ndrangheta**. The most attractive areas are the long, mainly pedestrianized **Corso Garibaldi** – the venue for Calabria's liveliest *passeggiata* – and the **lungomare**, the seafront esplanade that affords wonderful views of the Sicilian coastline and, occasionally, Mount Etna. At the southern end of the Corso, you can see remains of sixth-century-BC **city walls** and a **Roman bathing complex**. Just off the Corso lies Reggio's **Duomo**, an airy building heavily restored after the 1908 earthquake.

15

Museo Nazionale

Piazza De Nava • ☎ 0965 812 255, ⓦ archeocalabria.beniculturali.it

The **Museo Nazionale** at the northern end of Corso Garibaldi (closed for restoration at the time of writing) is Reggio's main draw. It holds the most important collection of archeological finds in Calabria, full of items dating from the Hellenic period, with examples from all the major Greek sites in Calabria, including the famous *pinakes* or carved tablets from the sanctuary of Persephone at Locri. The most renowned exhibits in the museum are the **Bronzi di Riace**: two bronze statues dragged out of the Ionian Sea in 1972 near the village of Riace. They are shapely examples of the highest period of Greek art (fifth century BC), and especially prized because there are so few finds from this period in such a good state of repair. While the Museo Nazionale is closed, the *Bronzi* are displayed at the Palazzo del Consiglio nearby at Via Portanova (daily 9am–7.30pm; free). When it reopens, you will also be able to view examples of Byzantine and Renaissance art, including two works by Antonello da Messina.

Piccolo Museo di San Paolo

Via Reggio Campi 4 (Sorgona crossroads) • Daily except Fri 9.30am–1pm • Free • ☎ 0965 892 426

After the Museo Nazionale, Reggio's other must-see attraction is the **Piccolo Museo di San Paolo**, an impressive private collection of religious art including some 160 Russian icons and a *St Michael* attributed to Antonello da Messina.

ARRIVAL AND DEPARTURE

REGGIO CALABRIA

By plane There is a small airport (☎ 0965 642 232, ⓦ aero portodellostretto.it) south of Reggio, serving primarily Italian destinations, with frequent bus connections to the centre.
By train If you're arriving by train, get off at Reggio Lido for the port or museum.

Destinations Cosenza (6 daily; 2hr 40min); Naples (8 daily; 3hr 40min–6hr 30min); Scilla (1–3 hourly; 25min–1hr).
By bus Buses end up at Reggio Centrale station, 1km or so down the long Corso Garibaldi. The local company for trips to Aspromonte is ATAM (☎ 0965 620 121, ⓦ atam-rc.it).
Destinations Gambarie (Mon–Sat 6 daily, Sun 2–3 daily;

15

1hr 35min); Santo Stefano (Mon–Sat 6 daily, Sun 3 daily; 1hr 15min).

By ferry From Reggio's port, Metromare (☏ 0923 873 813, ⊚ metromaredellostretto.it) runs hydrofoils to Messina (Mon–Sat 15 daily, Sun 8 daily; 35min; €3.50).

GETTING AROUND AND INFORMATION

By bus You may want to make use of city buses for getting from one end of town to the other (almost all buses stop at both the museum and the station); tickets cost €1 from kiosks and *tabacchi*.

Tourist offices There are tourist offices at the train station (Mon–Fri 8am–2pm, also Mon & Wed 5.30–8pm; ☏ 0965 894 518, ⊚ prolocoreggiocalabria.it) and the airport (daily 8am–8pm; ☏ 0965 630 301).

ACCOMMODATION

Delfina Via Crocefisso 58 ☏ 334 161 3905, ⊚ bb-delfina.com. This clean, central B&B, near the Duomo, has a friendly, English-speaking owner with plenty of local advice. Rooms have small balconies, fridges, a/c and wi-fi, and there's a computer for guests' use. €65

Hotel Lido Via Tre Settembre 6 ☏ 0965 25 001, ⊚ albergolido.com. It's not exactly bursting with character, but this three-star near the museum and Lido station has reasonable rates, cheerful rooms and good, modern facilities. €90

EATING AND DRINKING

D&P Via Cairoli ☏ 0965 890 420. This is the town's top choice for excellent fresh seafood, including grilled prawns, squid and whatever else has been freshly caught. They also do a memorable spicy spaghetti with swordfish, capers and olives, and all for €30–35 for a full meal without drinks. Mon–Sat noon–3pm & 7.30–10.30pm, Sun noon–3pm.

La Cantina del Macellaio Via Arcovito 26 ☏ 0965 23 932. This traditional-looking place specializes in grilled meat dishes, from steaks to *involtini di vitello* (rolled and stuffed veal) and *salsiccia e fagioli* (local sausage and beans). Expect to pay around €30. Mon–Sat 12.30–2.30pm & 8–11pm.

Spaccanapoli Via Fata Morgana 3 ☏ 0965 312 276.

Just off Corso Garibaldi, this easy-going place offers great value for its self-service lunches and convivial dinners, with pastas and pizzas going for €4–9. Noon–3pm & 7.30–midnight, closed lunchtime in Aug.

Map legend:

■ **ACCOMMODATION**
Delfina — 2
Hotel Lido — 1

● **RESTAURANTS**
D&P — 3
La Cantina del Macellaio — 2
Spaccanapoli — 1

REGGIO CALABRIA

Aspromonte

Most visitors to Reggio leave without having ventured into the great massif of **Aspromonte**, the last spur of the Apennines on the tip of Italy's boot. Here you can be on a beach and a ski slope within the same hour, passing from the brilliant, almost tropical vegetation of the coast to dense forests of beech and pine that rise to nearly 2000m. Although it recently became a national park, the thickly forested mountain has not yet shown any sign of becoming a tourist destination. This is mostly due to its

> ## THE SANTUARIO DELLA MADONNA DI POLSI
>
> If you're in the region in late summer it's worth timing your visit to attend the boisterous **fair** that takes place every year in Aspromonte on the first two days of September at the **Santuario della Madonna di Polsi**, a 10km hike from the park entrance. It's an unashamedly pagan event that involves the sale and slaughter of large numbers of goats – the fair is also known to provide a convenient cover for the meeting of 'Ndrangheta cells from all over the world.

reputation as the stronghold of the **'Ndrangheta**, the Calabrian Mafia, and as such most Italians would think you mad for going there. On top of this, the area remains virtually unsigned, and the oppressive tree cover rarely breaks to provide views. If you're in a car take notice of the *Strada Interotta* ("Road interrupted") signs you'll find at the entrances: don't even think about attempting the rocky dirt tracks across the range unless you are driving an off-road vehicle.

Santo Stefano

You'll find access to the Aspromonte range is easiest from the Tyrrhenian side, with several buses a day leaving Reggio's Piazza Garibaldi for Gambarie and winding their way up the highly scenic SS184 from Gallico, through profusely terraced groves of vine and citrus. The road passes through the village of **SANTO STEFANO**, famous as the birthplace and final resting place of the last of the great brigands who roamed these parts, **Giuseppe Musolino** (1875–1956). Occupying a sort of Robin Hood role in the popular imagination, Musolino was a legend in his own lifetime, the last thirty years of which he spent in jail and, finally, a lunatic asylum – the penalty for having led the *carabinieri* on a long and humiliating dance up and down the slopes of Aspromonte during his profitable career. Just above the village, in the cemetery, you can see Musolino's grave, now renovated but until recently daubed with the signatures of people come to pay their respects.

Cosenza and around

In Calabria's interior, **COSENZA** is a burgeoning city with a small and atmospheric historic centre surrounded by rings of featureless modern construction. Tradition has it that **Alaric the Goth**, the barbarian who gave the Western world a jolt when he prised open the gates of Rome in 410 AD, is buried under the Busento River. Struck down for his sins by malaria while journeying south, he was interred here along with his booty, and the course of the river deviated to cover the traces, lending Cosenza a place in history and giving rise to countless, fruitless projects to discover the tomb's whereabouts.

In the new town, you might take a stroll around the pedestrianized main axis, Corso Mazzini, and Piazza Bilotti to see half a dozen open-air sculptures by the likes of Dalí, De Chirico and Pietro Consagra, part of a bequest that makes up the **Museo all'Aperto Bilotti**, or **MAB**.

Duomo

Piazza del Duomo • Daily 8.30am–noon & 4–7pm • Free

Cosenza's chief sight is the stately **Duomo** in the historic town centre off the main Corso Telesio. Consecrated on the occasion of Frederick II's visit to the city in 1222, it contains the lovely tomb of Isabella of Aragon, who died in Cosenza in 1271 while returning with her husband Philip III – seen kneeling beside her – from an abortive Crusade in Tunisia, as well as a copy of a thirteenth-century Byzantine icon, the *Madonna del Pilerio*, which was once carried around the country during times of plague.

15

15

ARRIVAL AND DEPARTURE
COSENZA

By train Arriving by train, you have to take a bus (every 20min) from the train station a little way outside town – buy tickets from the bar inside the station. For onward journeys, change at Paola for more frequent services to coastal towns.

Destinations Diamante (8 daily; 1hr); Naples (3 daily; 3hr 40min); Paola (25 daily; 25min); Reggio Calabria (4 daily; 2hr 45min).

By bus The bus station is below Piazza Fera, from where it's a 20min walk along the length of Corso Mazzini to the hotels and the *centro storico*. Ferrovie Calabro Lucane (Ⓦferrovie dellacalabria.it) and Scura (Ⓣ0983 565 635, Ⓦiasautolinee .com) operate services to Camigliatello and Lorica, FCL also connects Cosenza and Luzzi, and Consorzio Autolinee (Ⓣ0984 837 133, Ⓦiasautolinee.com) goes to Rende.

Destinations Camigliatello (Mon–Sat 1–2 hourly; 45min); Lorica (Mon–Sat 2 daily; 1hr 15min); Luzzi (Mon–Sat 10 daily; 30min); Rende (Mon–Sat 11 daily; 30min).

ACCOMMODATION

Ostello Re Alarico Vico Serra 10 Ⓣ328 114 9430, Ⓦostellorealarico.com. Just above the River Crati, this hostel occupies an eighteenth-century *palazzo* with antique furnishings, accommodation in double rooms or dormitories and the use of a kitchen and internet. There's a garden for summer barbecues. Dorms €̅1̅8̅, doubles €̅5̅0̅

Via dell'Astrologo Via R. Benincasa 16 Ⓣ338 920 5394, Ⓦviadellastrologo.com. Elegant B&B in a tastefully restored *palazzo* in the heart of the old town, with two spacious en-suite rooms and wi-fi. No credit cards. €̅8̅0̅

EATING AND DRINKING

Calabria Bella Piazza del Duomo Ⓣ0984 793 531. Old-town trattoria next to the Duomo, which serves traditional local dishes and has outside seating in summer. A generous mixed plate of antipasti can be had for about €8; mains are around €12, and there are pizzas. Daily noon–3pm & 5pm–midnight.

Gran Caffè Renzelli Corso Umberto Ⓣ0984 26 814. The *centro storico* has numerous cafés and pubs, but the best aperitif is to be found at this old-fashioned coffee house above the Duomo, with marble-top tables and local pastries. 7am–9pm; July & Aug closed Sat eve & Sun.

Around Cosenza

If you're spending any time in Cosenza, you'll probably be mostly interested in excursions into the **Sila highlands** (see below), but some of the villages dotted around the surrounding hills shouldn't be ignored. In summer, the streets are lively until late, and at night the views over the bowl of the valley are magnificent, with glittering threads and clusters of light. It's also in the summer that the village **festas** normally take place, with each *comune* vying to outdo the others in terms of spectacle and expense.

The hilltop village of **RENDE** holds the prize for the tidiest village in the region: it has good views and an absorbing little **museum** (Mon, Wed & Fri 9am–1pm, Tues & Thurs 9am–1pm & 3–6pm; free) in the Palazzo Zagarese, on Via de Bártolo, devoted to local folk art, costumes, cuisine, music, the Albanian community and emigration.

Northeast of Cosenza, above the village of **Luzzi**, stands the **Abbazia di Sambucina**. A Cistercian abbey founded in the twelfth century and long the centre of this order of monks throughout the south, it has a beautiful, lightly pointed portal (rebuilt in the fifteenth century) and the original presbytery.

EATING
RENDE

Hostaria de Mendoza Piazza degli Eroi 3 Ⓣ0984 444 022. Rustic-looking place that offers a range of authentically Calabrese meat dishes, several of them with fresh truffles. First courses are €8–10, mains €15–20. 1–2.30pm & 8–10.30pm; closed Tues, plus Sun in July, and all Aug.

The Sila

Covering the widest part of the Calabrian peninsula, the **Sila** massif, east of Cosenza, is more of an extensive plateau than a mountain range, though the peaks on its western flank reach heights of nearly 2000m. Protected by the Parco Nazionale della Sila

(Ⓦparcosila.it), it's divided into three main groups: the Sila Greca, Sila Grande and Sila Piccola, of which the Sila Grande is of most interest to tourists.

At one time the Sila was one huge forest and was exploited from earliest times to provide fuel and material for the construction of fleets, fortresses and even for church-building in Rome, resulting in a deforestation that helped bring about the malarial conditions that for centuries blighted much of Calabria. The cutting of trees is now strictly controlled, and **ancient pines** (the so-called **Giganti della Sila**), which can live for several hundred years, are among the region's chief attractions. There's plenty here, too, for the outdoors enthusiast: in summer the area provides relief from the heat of the towns, and in winter there's downhill and cross-country skiing.

The Sila Grande

Densely forested, and the highest, most extensive part of the Sila range, the **Sila Grande** is home to Calabria's main **ski slopes** as well as the region's three principal **lakes** – all artificial (for hydroelectric purposes) and much loved by fishing enthusiasts, who come out in force at weekends. If you want to spend any time up here, the **campsites** enjoy good lakeside locations, while the hotels are mainly in the towns and villages, and many close out of season.

Camigliatello

The town of **CAMIGLIATELLO** is the best known of the resorts, a functional place that's well connected by bus with Cosenza, though it lacks any intrinsic charm. Centred on Via Roma, the town has three ski slopes of its own, and another in Contrada Moccone (a satellite of Camigliatello 3km west), plus a confusion of hotels, restaurants and souvenir shops. If you fancy **skiing**, day-passes are available from around €15 on the slopes and there are facilities for renting equipment (from €20/day) and tuition (group lessons from €20 per person per hour) from the various ski clubs. The Sila terrain also makes ideal **riding** country, though most stables are open in summer only.

INFORMATION	CAMIGLIATELLO
Tourist office The volunteer-run Pro Loco at the top of Via Roma keeps erratic opening hours (roughly 10am–12.30pm &	4–8pm, reduced hours in winter; ☏ 0984 578 159); it has maps of the area and suggestions for walking routes in the park.

ACCOMMODATION

Lo Sciatore Via Roma 126 ☏ 0984 578 105, Ⓦ hotel losciatore.it. Centrally located hotel with clean and comfortable rooms and a good pizzeria/*ristorante*. **€75**
San Lorenzo Si Alberga Campo San Lorenzo 14 ☏ 0984 570 809, Ⓦ sanlorenzosialberga.it. Some 4km

northeast of Camigliatello on the SS177 towards Lago Cecita, this sleek, modern hotel makes the best of its great views. Rooms are spacious and elegant, and there's a top-notch restaurant (see p.862). **€110**

EATING

Da Fulvio Contrada Moccone ☏ 0984 578 790. This great-value trattoria is known for simple, good-value local cooking,

using wild mushrooms and wild boar. You'll pay around €15 for a full meal. 12.15–2.30pm; closed Mon except Aug.

THE STRADA DELLE VETTE

Camigliatello is a useful starting-point for a tough hike that takes in the area's highest peaks, following the **Strada delle Vette** ("road of the peaks") for 13km through pine and beech woods before forking off and up to the three **peaks** of Monte Scuro, Monte Curcio and, highest of all, Monte Botte Donato (1928m). The trail, which is often snowbound between December and May, continues on down to **Lago Arvo** and the resort of **Lorica**, from where it's a shorter distance than following the Strada delle Vette to reach Botte Donato. Or you can save the sweat and take the chair lift from Località Cavaliere, just outside town.

15

★ **La Tavernetta** Campo San Lorenzo 14 ☎ 0984 579 026, ⊛ latavernetta.info. It's well worth making a detour to find this snazzy, modern restaurant attached to the *San Lorenzo* hotel (see p.861), which boasts a well-deserved reputation for its gourmet reinterpretations of regional specialities using local ingredients. Reckon on spending around €40 per person excluding drinks – and book ahead. 12.30–3.30pm & 8–11pm; closed Mon except Aug, and two weeks March & Nov.

Lorica

Like Camigliatello, **LORICA**, 26km southeast, is dedicated to tourism in the height of the winter and summer seasons, but its lakeside location makes it a more relaxed spot, with lots of places for picnicking under the pines and observing the antics of the black squirrels that inhabit them.

ACCOMMODATION   LORICA

Park 108 Via Nazionale 86 ☎ 0984 537 077, ⊛ hotel park108.it. Comfortable four-star hotel, which has a garden with lake views, a sauna and a fitness centre. Look out for special deals. **€110**

15

Calabria's Ionian coast

Calabria's Ionian coast is a mainly flat sandy strip, sometimes monotonous but less developed than the Tyrrhenian side of the peninsula, and generally with cleaner seawater. At the border with Basilicata, mountainous slopes soon give way to the wide **Piana di Sibari**, the most extensive of the Calabrian coastal plains, bounded by Pollino to the north, the Sila Greca to the west and the Sila Grande in the south. The rivers flowing off these mountains, which for centuries kept the land well watered and rich, also helped to transform it into a stagnant, malarial mire, and although land reclamation has restored the area's fertility, without visiting the museum and excavations at **Sybaris** you could pass through the area with no inkling of the civilization that once flourished on these shores. Southeast of here, the old Byzantine centre of **Rossano** and **Crotone**, another ancient Greek city, provide further interest as you travel along the coastline.

The southern part of Calabria's Ionian seaboard is less developed than the rest of the region and less scenic, with a string of mostly unappealing seaside towns and villages. If you like sandy **beaches**, though, this is where to find them – either wild and unpopulated or, if you prefer, glitzy and brochure-style, as at **Soverato**. At **Locri** there's the region's best collection of Greek ruins and, overlooking the coast a short way inland, the craggy medieval strongholds of **Squillace** and **Gerace**.

GETTING AROUND CALABRIA'S IONIAN COAST

The SS106 runs along the whole length of the Ionian coast, passing through every coastal town, and consequently often very slow. Trains run along the coastal line between Taranto and Reggio Calabria every 1–2hr, with frequent local buses connecting the stations to inland towns. Various independent bus companies also operate frequent services between the towns.

Sybaris

Tues–Sun 9am to 1hr before sunset • Free

Long one of the great archeological mysteries tantalizing generations of scholars, the site of ancient **SYBARIS** (Sibari) was only definitely identified in the late 1960s, when aerial and X-ray photography confirmed that the site previously known to be that of Roman Thurium was also that of Sybaris. There are in fact three separate levels of construction that have been unearthed here, one Greek and two Roman, one on top of the other. Together these make up one of the world's largest archeological sites, covering a thousand hectares (compared with Pompeii's fifty), though only ten hectares have so far been dug up.

The **excavations** lie signposted off the SS106, on the right-hand side. Most of them belong to the Roman period, but something of the earlier site might still be turned up – the

A LIFE OF LUXURY

The wealth of Sybaris was only one factor in its fame. The inhabitants of the city – said to number 100,000 – were so fond of luxury and their excesses so legendary that we derive the modern word **sybaritic** from their reputation. The city's laws and institutions were apparently made to ensure the greatest comfort and wellbeing of its citizens, including the banning from the city of all noisy traders, such as metalworkers, and the planting of trees along every street for shade. Cooks were so highly prized that they were apparently bought and sold in the marketplace for great sums and were allowed to patent their recipes, while inventions ascribed to the Sybarites include pasta and the chamberpot. This was all too much for the Crotonians, who under their general Milo destroyed the city in 510 BC, diverting the waters of the river over the site to complete the job.

silt and sand of the river bed have yet to be explored properly, work having been effectively halted for much of the last twenty years owing to shortage of funds. Of the Roman city, the remains are at least impressively displayed and maintained, including baths, a patrician's house with mosaics, and a *decumanus* – main street – claimed to be the widest in existence.

There's plenty more to be seen, from here and other local sites, at the **Museo della Sibaritide** (Tues–Sun 9am–7.30pm, closes 6.30pm in winter; €2; ☏0981 79 392), about 2km before the excavations on the banks of the River Crati, where five large rooms hold an assortment of coins, statuettes, amphorae and mosaic floors.

Rossano

Thirty kilometres down the coast from Sibari, **ROSSANO** was the foremost Byzantine centre in the south, and the focus of a veritable renaissance of literature, theology and art between the eighth and eleventh centuries, a period to which the town's greatest treasures belong. These days, its coastal offshoot of **Rossano Scalo** (site of the train station) has far outstripped its inland parent in terms of size and bustle, and most of the holiday-makers who frequent its beaches never even get round to visiting the hilltop town, 7km up an awkward winding road – something that has helped to preserve the old centre from excessive development.

The Duomo
Piazza del Duomo • 8am–noon & 5–8pm • Free

Rossano's majolica-tiled **Duomo** is an Angevin construction largely rebuilt after an 1836 earthquake, but it does have a much-venerated ninth-century **Byzantine fresco** encased in an elaborate marble setting in the nave. Its Greek epithet, *Madonna Achiropita*, meaning "not painted by hand", refers to its divine authorship.

The Museo Diocesano
Via Arcivescovado • July to mid-Sept daily 9.30am–1pm & 4.30–8pm; mid-Sept to June Tues–Sat 9.30am–12.30pm & 3–6pm, Sun 10am–noon & 4–6pm • €3 • ☏ 0983 525 263

Behind the cathedral, the **Museo Diocesano** contains the famed **codex purpureus Rossanensis**, or Purple Codex, a unique sixth-century manuscript on reddish-purple parchment illustrating the life of Christ. The book, which was brought from Palestine by monks fleeing the Muslim invasions, is open at one page, but you can leaf through a copy and see, among other things, how the Last Supper was originally depicted, with Christ and his disciples not seated but reclining on cushions round the table, and all eating from the same plate.

San Marco
Corso Garibaldi • Daily 9am to 1hr before sunset • Free

In contrast to the cathedral's grandiosity, the diminutive church of **San Marco**, above a gorge on the edge of town, retains a primitive spirituality. Fronted by palms, the five cupolas of the tenth- or eleventh-century construction and the cool white interior impart an almost Middle Eastern flavour.

INFORMATION

ROSSANO

Tourist office Pro Loco, Piazza Matteotti, *centro storico* (daily: June–Sept 10am–1pm & 5–8pm; Oct–May 10am– noon & 4–6pm; ☎ 349 252 1291, ⓦ prolocorossano.it).

ACCOMMODATION

★ **Casa Mazzei** Via T. Mandatoriccio 31 ☎ 347 581 0142, ⓦ bbcasamazzei.it. A short walk from both the Duomo and San Marco in the old town, this B&B is in an antique *palazzo* filled with thoughtfully chosen furniture and ancestral portraits. No credit cards. **€60**

La Terrazza Via Salita Ospedale 11 ☎ 338 774 6255, ⓦ laterrazzabeb.com. At the top of a flight of steps in the old town, this B&B has two rooms with large bathrooms, a/c and free wi-fi. There are great views from the terrace after which it's named. **€75**

Oriental Park Lungomare Sant'Angelo ☎ 0983 290 266, ⓦ orientalpark.altervista.org. By the sea 3km north of Rossano Scalo, this shady campsite has good facilities and chalets and bungalows for rent (€30). Easter–Oct. Pitches **€30**

EATING

La Bizantina Corso Garibaldi 246 ☎ 0983 525 340. Right next to San Marco, this trattoria with tables outside has a rustic, almost medieval-looking interior. There are abundant and delicious antipasti (try the *peperoni e patate* – roast red peppers and potatoes) and pizzas. A full meal should cost around €25 a head. 8pm–midnight; closed Mon except July & Aug.

★ **La Villa** Via San Bartolomeo ☎ 0983 522 214. Just off Piazza SS. Anargiri in the old town, you can enjoy alfresco eating on a panoramic veranda in summer here. It serves typical Calabrese food, with fresh pasta and lots of local sausage, mushrooms and tomatoes (mains €7–12), though most come for the pizzas (€3–6). No credit cards. 8pm–midnight; closed Tues except July & Aug.

Crotone

South of Rossano lies an empty stretch of beach, with, inland, the vineyards of Ciro, the source of Calabria's best-known **wine**. Crossing the River Neto into the fertile **Marchesato** region, you'll have your approach to **CROTONE** (the ancient Greek city of Kroton) blighted by a smoky industrial zone – not the most alluring entry into a city, but a rare thing in Calabria, and a reminder of the false hopes once vested in the industrialization of the region. In spite of this, Crotone today has an agreeable, unspoiled old centre, and makes a good base for the **beaches** that spread to the south and for the Greek ruins at **Capo Colonna**.

Brief history

The site of ancient **Kroton** has been entirely lost, but in its day this was among the most important colonial settlements of Magna Graecia, overshadowed by its more powerful neighbour Sybaris, but with a school of medicine famous throughout the classical world and closely linked with the prowess of the city's athletes, who regularly scooped all the honours at the Olympic Games back in Greece. In 530 BC the mathematician and metaphysician **Pythagoras** took up residence in Kroton and it went on to be the foremost of the Greek cities in Calabria. However, increasingly destabilized by internal conflicts, the city was eventually destroyed by the Romans. A resurgence of sorts occurred in the thirteenth century when it was made the main town of the Marchesato region, a vast feudal domain held by the powerful Ruffo family of Catanzaro. But its prosperity was always hindered by the scourge of malaria, provoking the author George Gissing – himself a victim of malaria during his visit in 1897 – to condemn Crotone as "a squalid little town".

Museo Archeologico Nazionale

Via Risorgimento • Tues–Sun 9am–8pm • €2 • ☎ 0962 23 082

The town's **Museo Archeologico Nazionale** holds the best collection of finds from Magna Graecia on the Ionian coast. Most noteworthy is the so-called **Treasure of Hera**

Lacinia, a beautifully restored group of bronze statuettes – including a sphinx, a gorgon, a horse, a winged siren and a very rare nuraghic boat from Sardinia dating from the seventh to the fifth centuries BC. The most dazzling item is a gold diadem, expertly worked with garlands of leaves and sprigs of myrtle.

INFORMATION

Tourist office Via Molo Sanità, near the port (daily 10am–12.30pm & 5.30–8pm, closed Sun Sept–May; ☎ 329 815 4963).

ACCOMMODATION

Concordia Via Messinetti 12 ☎ 0962 23 910. Round the corner from Piazza della Vittoria in the old town, this hotel has rather a dingy entrance but the rooms are clean and functional. **€90**

Mediterraneo Viale Gallucci 49 ☎ 392 266 8766,

ⓦ bbcrotone.it. A modern apartment close to the beaches south of the centre offers B&B in attic rooms with attached bathrooms and a terrace. There's free wi-fi and a free pick-up from the station. No credit cards. **€70**

EATING AND DRINKING

⭐ **Da Ercole** Viale Gramsci 122 ☎ 0962 901 425, ⓦ ristorantedaercole.eu. This refined seafront restaurant run by Ercole Villirillo, who runs cookery classes all over the world, is one of the few places where you can sample such dishes as *linguine a pitagora* (which feature *prine*, a kind of sea anemone) or *ricciola* with wild artichokes (*ricciola con carciofi selvatici*). A meal will probably weigh in at around €50. 12.30–

2.30pm & 8–11.30pm; closed Sun except July & Aug.

Vinny's Via di Bártolo 22 ☎ 0962 902 243. Located behind *Da Ercole*, this restaurant concentrates on seasonal dishes – so more seafood in the summer, more meat in winter – and has some excellent risottos. Set-price menus are €25 and €35. Tues–Sun 12.30–2.30pm & 8–11pm; closed Sun July & Aug.

Santa Severina

Thirty-five kilometres inland of Crotone, off the road to San Giovanni in Fiore, **SANTA SEVERINA** lies on the eastern fringes of the Sila Piccola. A Byzantine fortified town built on a hilltop, it's a pretty place with great views, but is chiefly worth a detour for the Norman castle that dominates it.

The castle

Piazza Campo • April to mid-Sept daily 9.30am–12.30pm & 3.30–7pm, closes 7.30pm in summer; mid-Sept to March Tues–Sun 9.30am–12.30pm & 3–6pm • €4 • ☎ 0962 51 069

Rebuilt by Robert Guiscard on the ruins of a Byzantine stronghold and remodelled by the Swabians and Angevins, the renovated castle holds a first-rate **museum**, taking in all parts of the construction from the foundations to the first-floor rooms, holding weaponry, costumes and temporary exhibitions. From the stout battlemented walls long views extend over the hilly surroundings towards the mountains of the Sila.

The Duomo and baptistry

Piazza Campo • 8am–noon & 5–8pm • Free

From the castle, cross the piazza – whose flagstones are studded with symbols of the zodiac – to the spacious **Duomo**. Adjacent to it, the eighth-century Byzantine **baptistry** preserves traces of frescoes of the saints, Greek inscriptions on the capitals and its original font. If it's closed, ask in the cathedral for access.

Museo Diocesano

Piazza Campo • April to mid-Sept daily 9.30am–12.30pm & 3.30–7pm, closes 7.30pm in summer; mid-Sept to March Tues–Sun 9.30am–12.30pm & 3–6pm • €2.50 • ☎ 339 405 1632

Next to the Duomo, the **Museo Diocesano** repays a visit for a painfully graphic Christ on the Cross from the fifteenth century, an early printed edition of the Bible, and – its greatest treasure – the *Spilla Angioina*, a brooch from about 1300, studded with gold, pearls and rubies.

★ **Agriturismo Il Querceto** Cerzeto ☎ 0962 51 467 or ☎ 328 262 0680, ⓦ agriturismoilquerceto.kr.it. This 50-hectare organic farm 4km outside town (signposted from the road to Santa Severina) grows olives and citrus fruit and has comfortable rooms. Guests can use the swimming pool, and there are mountain bikes to rent. You can stay on a B&B basis or half-board (€41 per person). No credit cards. €50

Locanda del Re Via Orsi 6 ☎ 0962 51 662. On the steps below the castle, this trattoria focuses on food rooted in the medieval traditions of the area, so expect handmade pasta, lots of wild mushroom, boar, ricotta and pecorino on the fixed-price menus (€10–25). Pizzas are also available. Daily noon–2.45pm & 7–10.30pm.

Capo Colonna and around

On Calabria's extreme eastern point, 11km south of Crotone, the famed column at **CAPO COLONNA** is a solitary remnant of a vast structure that served as the temple for all the Greeks in Calabria. Dedicated to Hera Lacinia, the temple originally possessed 48 of these Doric columns and was the repository of immense wealth before being repeatedly sacked as Magna Graecia and Hellenism itself declined.

There are some excellent **bathing spots** not far south of here. The **Isola Capo Rizzuto** is a spit of land, not an island, with a choice of sandy or rocky inlets to swim from. During the winter the resort is dead, but it can get quite congested in the height of summer and difficult to find a place to stay.

Le Castella

West of Capo Rizzuto, **LE CASTELLA** gets very busy in summer, but it would be hard to spoil the beautifully sited Aragonese **fortress** (June–Sept daily 9am–midnight; Oct–May Tues–Sun 9am–6pm; €3; ☎ 0962 795 160) on an islet just off the main town. There's not much to see inside, but you could wander round the outside of the castle and swim off the rocks, though you'll probably be more tempted by the arc of beach to the south.

La Roccelletta and the ruins of Scolacium

South of Catanzaro Lido, the ruined basilica of Santa Maria della Roccella, or **La Roccelletta**, stands amid an olive grove 100m down the road signposted towards San Floro and Borgia, branching off the SS106. The partly restored redbrick shell is all that remains of what was once the second-largest church in Calabria (after Gerace). Of uncertain date, though probably Norman in origin and founded by Basilian monks, it still has a mighty impact on the unsuspecting viewer. In summer the site is used for open-air contemporary art exhibitions and for concerts.

The church lies adjacent to a large **Zona Archeologica** (daily 8am–1hr before sunset; free) holding the ruins of the Roman town of Scolacium, built over the Greek town of Skylletion. The best-preserved item here is a **teatro**, once able to hold some 3500 spectators, and thought to have been abandoned following a fire some time after 350 AD. A **museum** (Tues–Sun: June–Sept 3.30–7.30pm; Oct–May 9am–1.30pm; free; ☎ 0961 391 356) shows finds from the site.

Squillace

Some 5km south of La Roccelletta, at Lido di Squillace, turn right off SS106 for the old town of **SQUILLACE**, 8km up in the hills. Now a rather isolated mountain village, this was once an important centre, probably most renowned for its associations with the scholar **Cassiodorus** (480–570), who used his position as secretary to the Ostrogoth, Theodoric, to preserve much of Italy's classical heritage against the onset of the Dark Ages and the book-burning propensities of the Christians. Retiring to spend the last thirty years of his life in seclusion in a monastery located in the vicinity – all trace of it has long since disappeared – Cassiodorus composed histories and collections of documents that have been of invaluable use to historians.

On its high crag, Squillace affords lofty views over the Golfo di Squillace and beyond Catanzaro as far as the Sila Píccola mountain range, best enjoyed from its **castle** (May–Sept daily 10am–12.30pm & 5–8.30pm; Oct–April call first; €2; ☎327 658 2692) – a candidate for one of Calabria's most romantic collections of ruins.

Locri Epizefiri

Site Tues–Sun 9am–1hr before sunset, open Mon Aug & Sept • **Museum** Tues–Sun 10am–1pm & 3.30–7.30pm, open Mon Aug & Sept • €4 for museum and site • ☎0964 390 023

Continuing south on the SS106, you'll come to the most famous classical site on this coast, **Locri Epizefiri**, some 5km beyond the resort town of Locri. Founded sometime in the seventh century BC, the city of Locri was responsible for the first written code of law throughout the Hellenic world. Its moment of glory came in the second half of the sixth century when, supposedly assisted by Castor and Pollux, ten thousand Locrians defeated 130,000 Crotonians on the banks of the River Sagra, 25km north. The walls of the city, traces of which can still be seen, measured some 8km in circumference, and the excavations within are now interspersed over a wide area among farms and orchards. A car would be useful to reach some of the more far-flung features, though the most interesting can be visited on foot without too much effort, including a fifth-century-BC Ionic **temple**, a Roman **necropolis** and a well-preserved Greco-Roman **theatre**. In any case make a stop at the **museum** to consult the plan of the site, and examine the most recent finds, including a good collection of **pinakes**, or votive ceramics – though most of the best items are displayed at the Museo Nazionale in Reggio.

15

Gerace

After the Saracens devastated Locri in the seventh century AD, the survivors fled inland to found **GERACE**, on an impregnable site that was later occupied and strengthened by the Normans. At the end of a steep and tortuous road 10km up from modern Locri, its ruined **castle** stands at one end of the town on a sheer cliff; it's usually accessible, though officially out of bounds due to the very precarious state of the paths and walls.

The Duomo

Daily 9.30am–1pm & 3–6.30pm • €2 • ☎0964 356 323

Gerace's **Duomo** was founded in 1045 by Robert Guiscard, enlarged by Frederick II in 1222 and is still the biggest church in Calabria. Its simple and well-preserved interior has twenty columns of granite and marble, each different and with various capitals: the one on the right nearest the altar in *verde antico* marble that changes tone according to the weather.

ACCOMMODATION AND EATING   **GERACE**

Casa di Gianna Via Paolo Frascà 4 ☎0964 355 024, ⓦlacasadigianna.it. Classy backstreet hotel-restaurant with just ten rooms and a superb terrace restaurant that offers a fixed-price menu for €15. 12.30–2.30pm & 7.30–11pm. **€130**

Sicily

VALLEY OF THE TEMPLES, AGRIGENTO

Sicily

I like Sicily extremely – a good on-the-brink feeling – one hop and you're out of Europe…

D.H. Lawrence in a letter to Lady Cynthia Asquith, 1920

Most Sicilians consider themselves, and their island, a separate entity. Coming from the Italian mainland, it's very noticeable that Sicily (Sicilia) has a different feel, that socially and culturally you are all but out of Europe. The largest island in the Mediterranean, and with a strategically vital position, Sicily has a history and outlook derived not from its modern parent but from its erstwhile foreign rulers – from the Greeks who first settled the east coast in the eighth century BC, through a dazzling array of Phoenicians, Carthaginians, Romans, Arabs, Normans, French and Spanish, to the Bourbons seen off by Garibaldi in 1860.

Substantial **relics** of these ages remain, with temples, theatres and churches scattered about the whole island. But there are other, more immediate hints of Sicily's unique past. Sicilian dialect, for example, is still widely spoken in both cities and countryside, varying from place to place; and the food is noticeably different from elsewhere in Italy, spicier and with more emphasis on fish and vegetables; even the flora echoes the change of temperament – oranges, lemons (introduced by the Arabs), prickly pears and palms are ubiquitous.

16

REGIONAL FOOD AND WINE

Sicily's food has been influenced by the island's endless list of invaders, including Greeks, Arabs, Normans and Spanish, even the English, each of them leaving behind them traces of their gastronomy. Dishes such as orange salads, unguent sweet-sour aubergine and, of course, couscous evoke North Africa, while Sicily's most distinctive pasta dish, *spaghetti con le sarde* – with sardines, pine nuts, wild fennel and raisins – is thought to date back to the first foray into Sicily, at Mazara, by an Arab force in 827. The story goes that the army cooks were ordered to forage around for food, and found sardines at the port, wild fennel growing in the fields, and raisins drying in the vineyards. Religious festivals too, are often associated with foods: for example at San Giuseppe, on March 19, altars are made of bread, and at Easter you will find *pasticcerie* full of sacrificial lambs made of marzipan, and Gardens of Adonis (trays of sprouting lentils, chickpeas and other pulses) placed before church altars to symbolize the rebirth of Christ. The last has its roots in fertility rites that predate even the arrival of the Greeks to the island.

Sicily is famous for its **sweets** too, like rich *cassata*, sponge cake filled with sweet ricotta cream and covered with pistachio marzipan, and *cannoli* – crunchy tubes of deep-fried pastry stuffed with sweet ricotta. **Street food** is ubiquitous in cities such as Palermo, dating back to the eighteenth century when wood was rationed, and few people were able to cook at home: deep-fried rice balls, potato croquettes and chickpea-flour fritters compete with dinky-sized pizzas. Naturally, **fish** such as anchovies, sardines, tuna and swordfish are abundant – indeed, it was in Sicily that the technique of canning tuna was invented. **Cheeses** are pecorino, *provolone*, *caciocavallo* and, of course, the sheep's-milk ricotta which goes into so many of the sweet dishes.

Traditionally **wine-making** in Sicily was associated mainly with sweet wines such as Malvasia and the fortified Marsala – in the nineteenth century many a fortune was made providing Malvasia to the Napoleonic army – but the island has also made a name for itself as a producer of quality everyday wines found in supermarkets throughout Italy, such as Corvo, Regaleali, Nicosia, Settesoli and Tria. There are superb wines too – notably Andrea Franchetti's prize-winning Passopisciaro, from the north slopes of Etna – as well as wines across a wide price range from producers such as Tasca d'Almerita, Baglio Hopps, Planeta, Morgante and Murgo.

MODICA, VAL DI NOTO

Highlights

❶ Monreale The magnificently mosaiced cathedral is a testament to Sicily's eclectic Arab, Norman and Byzantine heritage. **See p.886**

❷ The Aeolian Islands An archipelago of seven islands with active volanoes, lava beaches, fractured coastlines and whitewashed villages. **See p.890**

❸ Mount Etna It's an eerie climb up the blackened lunar landscape of this smoking volcano, dominating the landscape of eastern Sicily. **See p.906**

❹ Siracusa Classical dramas are staged every summer in the city's spectacular ancient Greek theatre, while Ortigia, surrounded by sea, has year-round appeal. **See p.912**

❺ Coastal nature reserves Nature reserves such as Zingaro and Vendicari provide respite from the overdevelopment of much of the island's coast. **See p.920 & p.935**

❻ Val di Noto This valley, stretching from Noto to Ragusa, is full of splendid Baroque towns, built after an earthquake, and now enjoying a renaissance, spurred on by UNESCO. **See p.920 & p.923**

❼ Valley of the Temples, Agrigento A spectacular sight, especially at night when the towering Doric columns are artfully floodlit. **See p.925**

HIGHLIGHTS ARE MARKED ON THE MAP ON P.872

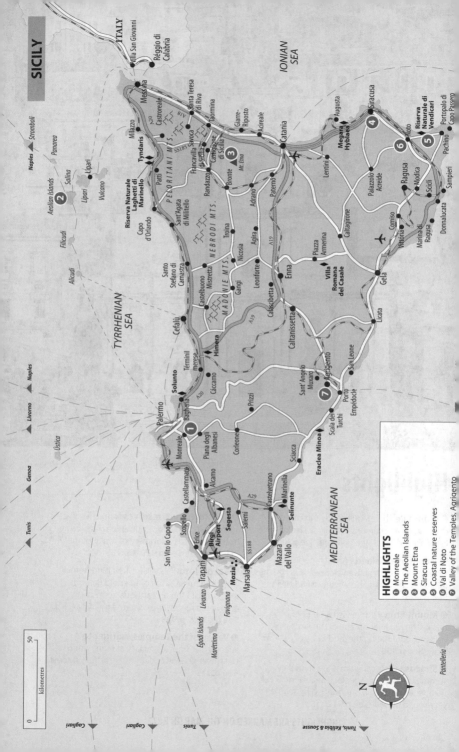

A visit here still induces a real sense of **arrival**. The standard approach for those heading south from the mainland is to cross the Straits of Messina, from Villa San Giovanni or Reggio di Calabria: this way, the train-ferry pilots a course between Scylla and Charybdis, the twin hazards of rock and whirlpool that were a legendary threat to sailors. Coming in by plane, too, there are spectacular approaches to the coastal airports at Palermo, Trapani and Catania.

Once you're on land, deciding **where to go** is largely a matter of time. Inevitably, most points of interest are on the coast: the interior of the island is mountainous, sparsely populated and relatively inaccessible, though in parts extremely beautiful. The capital, **Palermo**, is a filthy, bustling, noisy city with an unrivalled display of Norman art and architecture and Baroque churches, combined with a warren of medieval streets and markets. Heading east, there's no better place in Sicily for a traditional family sea, sun and sand holiday than **Cefalù**, with a magnificent golden sandy beach and a mellow medieval core overlooked by a beetling castle-topped crag. An hour or so further east is the workaday port of Milazzo, departure point for the **Aeolian Islands**, an archipelago of seven islands. Here you can climb two active volcanoes, laze on lava beaches, snorkel over bubbling underwater fumaroles, and wallow in warm, reeking, sulphurous mud baths.

The islands are also linked by hydrofoil with the major port of **Messina**, separated from mainland Italy by the Straits of Messina. If you are travelling to Sicily overland from Italy, Messina will unavoidably be your point of arrival. Devastated by an earthquake and tidal wave in 1908, it is a modern city of little charm and unlikely to hold your interest for long. The most obvious target from here is the almost too charming hill-town of **Taormina**, spectacularly located on a rocky bluff between the Ionian Sea and the soaring peak of Mount Etna. For a gutsier taste of Sicily, head to **Catania**, the island's second city, intellectual and cultured, with a compact Baroque core of black lava and white limestone, and two exuberant markets. From Taormina or Catania, a skirt around the foothills, and even better, up to the craters of **Mount Etna**, is a must.

In the south of the island is **Siracusa**, once the most important city of the Greek world, and beyond it, the Val di Noto, with an alluring group of Baroque towns centring on **Ragusa**. The south coast's greatest draw are the Greek temples at **Agrigento**, while inland, **Enna** is typical of the mountain towns that provided defence for a succession of the island's rulers. Close by is **Piazza Armerina** and its Roman mosaics, while to the west, most of Sicily's fishing industry – and much of the continuing Mafia activity (see box, p.874) – focuses on the area around **Trapani**, itself a salty old port with connections to the rough, sunblasted islands of the Egadi archipelago and Pantelleria.

To see all these places, you'll need at least a couple of weeks – more like a month if you want to travel extensively inland or to the minor islands.

GETTING AROUND   SICILY

Getting around Sicily can be a protracted business. **Trains** along the northern and eastern coasts (Messina–Palermo and Messina–Siracusa) are extensions of – or connect with – trains from Rome and Naples, and delays of over an hour are frequent. **Buses** are generally quicker, though you should expect little (if any) service anywhere on a Sunday.

Bus operators AST ☎ 091 620 8111, ⓦ aziendasiciliana trasporti.it; Cuffaro ☎ 091 616 1510, ⓦ cuffaro.info; Interbus ☎ 091 304 0900, ⓦ interbus.it; SAIS ☎ 091 616 6028, ⓦ saisautolinee.it; SAISTrasporti ☎ 091 617 1141, ⓦ sais trasporti.it; Salemi ☎ 091 617 5411, ⓦ autoservizisalemi .it; Segesta ☎ 091 616 9039, ⓦ segesta.it.

Palermo and around

Palermo is fast, brash, filthy and – at times – insane. Exotic Arabic cupolas float above exuberant Baroque facades, high-fashion shops compete with raffish street-markets, and walls of graffitied municipal cement abut the crumbling shells of collapsing *palazzi* sprouting clusters of prickly pear. Add to this a constant soundtrack of sputtering, swirling traffic, and some of the most anarchic driving in Europe, and you'll quickly see that this is not a city for the faint-hearted. With Sicily's greatest concentration of sights, and the biggest historic centre in Italy bar Rome, Palermo is a complex, multilayered city that can easily feel overwhelming if you try to do or see too much. The best thing to do here is just to wander as the fancy takes you, sifting through the city's jumbled layers of crumbling architecture, along deserted back-alleys, then suddenly emerging in the midst of an ebullient street-market. If you only have a day, select an area (La Kalsa, with its two museums, for example, or the sprawling markets of Ballarò or Capo), and explore: have a couple of target sights in mind by all means, but don't neglect to wander up any particular alley or street that takes your interest. If, on the other hand, you want to see all the major sights and leave time to explore the labyrinthine historical centre at random, allow at least four days in cool weather. In summer, Palermo is far too hot to be comfortable between noon and around 5pm, so avoid it or schedule in a leisurely lunch and siesta.

The essential sights are pretty central and easy to cover on foot. Paramount are the hybrid **Cattedrale** and nearby **Palazzo dei Normanni** (Royal Palace); the glorious Norman churches of **La Martorana** and **San Giovanni degli Eremiti**; the Baroque **San Giuseppe dei Teatini** and **Santa Caterina**; and first-class **museums** of art and archeology.

If the urban grit and grime become overwhelming, head to the famous medieval cathedral of **Monreale** (see p.886), or take a ferry or hydrofoil to the tiny volcanic island of **Ustica** (see p.887), 60km northwest.

Brief history

Occupying a superb position in a wide bay beneath the limestone bulk of Monte Pellegrino, Palermo was originally a Phoenician, then a Carthaginian colony. Its mercantile and strategic attractions were obvious, and under Saracen and Norman rule

---

THE MAFIA

Whatever else the **Mafia** is, it isn't an organization that impinges upon the lives of tourists. For most Sicilians, mafia with a small *m* is so much a way of life and habit of mind that they don't even think about it. If a Sicilian lends a neighbour a bag of sugar, for example, both will immediately be aware of a favour owed, and the debtor uncomfortable until the favour has been returned, and balance restored. As for allegiance to friends, it would be very rare indeed for a Sicilian, asked to recommend a hotel or restaurant, to suggest that you go to one that does not belong to a friend, relative, or someone who forms part of his personal network of favours.

The Mafia, with a capital M, began life as an **early medieval conspiracy**, created to protect the family from oppressive intrusions of the state. Existing to this day, Sicily continues to endure this system of allegiance, preferment and patronage of massive self-perpetuating proportions, from which few local people profit. In many parts of the region, owners of shops and businesses are expected to give **pizzo** (protection money) to the local Mafia. Though efforts to resist the Mafia continue, with local businesses in Palermo and Siracusa, for example, banding together to refuse to pay *pizzo*, it is not uncommon for the Mafia to have the power to close down the enterprises of refuseniks.

in the ninth to twelfth centuries it became the greatest city in Europe, famed both for the wealth of its court, and as an intellectual and cultural melting-pot that brought together the best of Western and Arabic thought. There are plenty of relics from this era, but it's the rebuilding of the sixteenth and seventeenth centuries that really shaped the city centre. In the nineteenth century, wealthy Palermitani began to shun the centre for the elegant suburbs of new "European" boulevards and avenues to the north of Piazza Politeama, which still retain some fine Art Nouveau buildings.

During World War II Allied bombs destroyed much of the port area and the medieval centre (including seventy churches), and for decades much of central Palermo remained a ramshackle bombsite. It is only recently that funds from Rome and the EU have united with political willpower to kickstart the regeneration of the historic centre, though as hundreds of abandoned buildings still testify, there is still a way to go.

Around the Quattro Canti

Historic Palermo sits around the **Quattro Canti**, a gleaming Baroque crossroads that divides it into quadrants. On the southwest corner (entrance on Corso Vittorio Emanuele), **San Giuseppe dei Teatini** (summer Mon–Sat 7.30–11am & 6–8pm, Sun 8.30am–12.30pm & 6–8pm; winter Mon–Sat 7.30am–noon & 5.30–8pm), begun in 1612, is the most harmonious of the city's Baroque churches. Outside, across Via Maqueda, is **Piazza Pretoria**, floodlit at night to highlight the nude figures of its great central fountain, a racy sixteenth-century Florentine design. The piazza also holds the restored **Municipio**, while towering above both square and fountain is the massive flank of **Santa Caterina** (April–Oct Mon–Sat 9.30am–1.30pm & 3–7pm, Sun 9.30am–1.30pm; Nov Mon–Sat 9.30am–1pm & 3–5.30pm, Sun 9.30am–1pm; Dec–March daily 9.30am–1pm), Sicilian Baroque at its most exuberant, every inch of the enormous interior covered in a wildly decorative relief-work.

Piazza Bellini, just around the corner, is the site of two more wildly contrasting churches. The little Saracenic red domes belong to **San Cataldo**, a perfectly proportioned twelfth-century Byzantine chapel flooded with light (March–Oct Mon–Sat 9am–2pm & 3.30–7pm, Sun 9am–2pm; Nov–Feb daily 9am–2pm, 22 Dec–6 Jan daily 9am–5pm; €1). Never decorated, it retains a good mosaic floor.

La Martorana

Piazza Bellini 3 • Mon–Sat 9.30am–1pm & 3.30–5.30pm (6.30pm in summer), Sun 8.30am–9.45am & noon–1pm • Free • ☎ 091 616 1692
San Cataldo's understatement is more than offset by the splendid intricacy of the adjacent **La Martorana** – one of the finest survivors of the medieval city. With a Norman foundation, the church received a Baroque going-over in 1588. Happily, the alterations don't detract from the power of the interior, entered through the slim twelfth-century campanile, which retains its ribbed arches and slender columns. A series of spectacular **mosaics**, animated twelfth-century Greek works, is laid on and around the columns supporting the main cupola. Two original mosaic panels have been set in frames on the walls just inside the entrance to the church: a kneeling George of Antioch (the church's founder) dedicating La Martorana to the Virgin, and King Roger being crowned by Christ.

The Albergheria

The **Albergheria** district just to the northwest of the train station hasn't changed substantially for several hundred years. A maze of tiny streets and tall leaning buildings, it's an engaging place to wander, much of the central area taken up by a street market that all but conceals several fine churches. Via Ponticello leads down past the Baroque church of **Il Gesù**, or **Casa Professa** (daily 7am–noon & 4–6.30pm), the first Jesuit foundation in Sicily and gloriously decorated inside, to **Piazza Ballarò** – along with adjacent **Piazza del Carmine**

16

16

CENTRAL PALERMO

Ferries to Cagliari, Genoa, Livorno, Ustica & Naples, hydrofoils to Ustica, Cefalù & Aeolian Islands ▲

● RESTAURANTS, CAFÉS & PASTICCERIE

Antica Focacceria San Francesco	14
Casa Obatola	16
Cibus	4
Franco 'U Vastiddaru	13
Friggitoria Chiluzzo	17
I Cuochini	8
Il Mirto e la Rosa	5
Ima Sushi	11
Mazzara	9
Michele alla Brace	1
Obika	11
Osteria dei Vespri	20
Osteria lo Bianco	3
Osteria Paradiso	6
Palazzo Riso	18
Pizzeria Italia	10
Primavera	19
Rosciglione	21
Santandrea	12
Spinnato	7
Trattoria Piccolo Napoli	2
Trattoria Torrenuzza	15

▌ BARS

Cana Enoteca	3
Kursaal Kalhesa	2
Kursaal Tonnara	1
Nuovo Montevergini	4

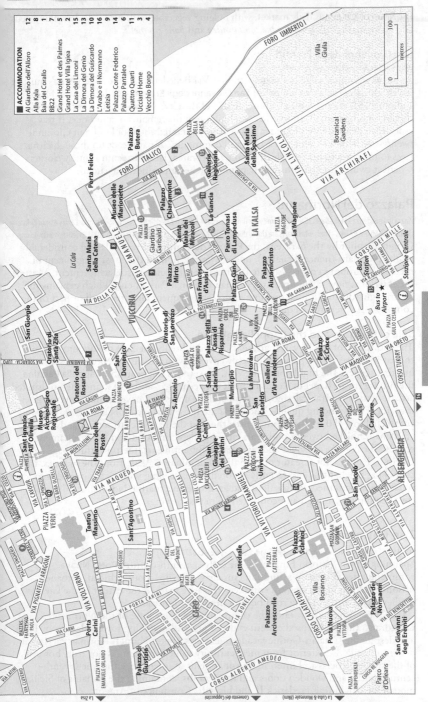

■ ACCOMMODATION

Al Giardino dell'Alloro	12
Alla Kala	8
Baia del Corallo	1
BB22	7
Grand Hotel et des Palmes	5
Grand Hotel Villa Igiea	2
La Casa dei Limoni	15
La Dimora del Genio	13
La Dimora del Guiscardo	10
L'Arabo e il Normanno	16
Letizia	9
Palazzo Conte Federico	14
Palazzo Pantaleo	6
Quattro Quarti	11
Ucciard Home	3
Vecchio Borgo	4

16

the focus of a raucous daily **market**, with bulging vegetable stalls, unmarked drinking dens and gutsy snack-stalls selling *pane con la milza* and *pane e panelle*.

San Giovanni degli Eremiti

Daily: summer 9am–6.30pm; winter 9am–5pm • €6

At the westernmost edge of the quarter, over Via Benedettini, is the Albergheria's quietest haven, the deconsecrated church of **San Giovanni degli Eremiti** – St John of the Hermits. Built in 1132, it's the most obviously Arabic of the city's Norman relics, with five ochre domes topping a small church that was built upon the remains of a mosque. It was especially favoured by its founder, Roger II, who granted the monks of San Giovanni twenty-one barrels of tuna a year, a prized commodity. A path leads up through citrus trees to the church, behind which lie some celebrated, late thirteenth-century cloisters – perfect twin columns with slightly pointed arches surrounding a garden.

Palazzo dei Normanni

Piazza Indipendenza • Mon–Sat 8.15am–5.45pm (sometimes closes at 4.15pm for weddings), Sun 8.15–1pm; last entry 45min before closing • €8.50 but €7 Tues–Thurs when parts are closed during Sicilian parliament sessions • ☎ 091 626 2833, ⊕ federicosecondo.org

Originally built by the Saracens, the **Palazzo dei Normanni** was enlarged considerably by the Normans (hence its name), under whom it housed the most magnificent of medieval European courts – a noted centre of poetic and artistic achievement. Most of the interior is now taken up by the Sicilian Regional Parliament (which explains the security guards, the limited opening hours, and frequent closures of all or part of the complex). Be prepared to queue.

Sala di Ruggero and the Cappella Palatina

The showpiece of the Royal Apartments is undoubtedly the **Sala di Ruggero**, one of the earliest parts of the palace and richly covered with a twelfth-century mosaic of hunting scenes. The highlight of the visit, however, is the beautiful **Cappella Palatina**, the private royal chapel of Roger II, built between 1132 and 1143, and the undisputed artistic gem of central Palermo, its cupola, three apses and nave entirely covered in mosaics of outstanding quality. The oldest are those in the cupola and apses, probably completed in 1150 by Byzantine artists; those in the nave are from the hands of local craftsmen, finished twenty-odd years later and depicting Old and New Testament scenes. The colours are vivid and, as usual in Byzantine art, the powerful image of Christ as Pantocrator (creator of everything) dominates. Aside from the mosaics, the chapel has a delightful and recently restored Arabic ceiling with richly carved wooden stalactites, a patterned marble floor and an impressive marble Norman candlestick (by the pulpit), 4m high and contorted by manic carvings.

The Cattedrale

Via Vittorio Emanuele • Mon–Sat 8.30am–6pm, Sun 4.30–6pm • Free • ☎ 327 817 2381

Spanning Corso Vittorio Emanuele, the early sixteenth-century **Porta Nuova** commemorates Charles V's Tunisian crusade with grim, moustachioed, turbaned prisoners adorning the western entrance. This gate marked the extent of the late medieval city, and the long road beyond heads to Monreale.

The Corso runs back towards the centre, past the huge bulk of the Norman **Cattedrale**. The triple-apsed eastern end and graceful matching towers date from 1185, and despite the Catalan-Gothic facade and arches, there's enough Norman carving and detail to rescue the exterior from mere curiosity value. The same is not true, however, of the sterile Neoclassical interior. The only items of interest are the fine fifteenth-century portal and wooden doors and **royal tombs**, containing the remains of Sicilian monarchs – including Frederick II and his wife, Constance of Aragon.

There's also a **treasury** (Nov–Feb Mon–Sat 9.30am–1.30pm; March–Oct Mon–Sat 9.30am–5.30pm; €3) to the right of the choir, the highlights of which are a jewel-and-pearl-encrusted skullcap and three simple, precious rings, all enterprisingly removed from the tomb of Constance in the eighteenth century.

The Capo

From the cathedral you can bear left, around the apses, and up into the **Capo** quarter, whose tight web of impoverished streets is home to yet another market. Just around the corner from Piazza del Monte is the fine church of **Sant'Agostino** (Mon–Sat 7am–noon & 4–6pm, Sun 7am–noon; free), built in the thirteenth century. Above its main door (on Via Raimondo) there's a latticework rose window, and inside, a tranquil sixteenth-century cloister. The stalls of the **clothes market** (daily 8am to around 8pm) along **Via Sant'Agostino** run all the way down to Via Maqueda and beyond, the streets off to the left gradually becoming wider and more nondescript as they broach the area around the monumental Neoclassic **Teatro Massimo**, supposedly the largest theatre in Italy. To appreciate the interior fully, take a **tour** (☎091 605 3267, ⊕teatromassimo.it; Tues–Sun every 30min 10.10am–2.30pm, except during rehearsals; €8), or attend one of the classical concerts or operas held here between October and June.

The theatre marks the dividing line between old and new Palermo. Via Maqueda becomes the far smarter **Via Ruggero Settimo**, which cuts up through the gridded shopping streets to the huge double square made up of **Piazza Castelnuovo** and **Piazza Ruggero Settimo** (commonly referred to as Piazza Politeama). Dominating the whole lot is Palermo's other massive theatre, the **Politeama Garibaldi**, topped by a flamboyant statue group of sword-brandishing figures on leaping horses.

16

The Vucciria

Tucked into the wedge of streets between Via Roma and Corso Vittorio Emanuele, the morning **Vucciria market**, once the most famous market in Palermo, is now a shadow of its former self, though it still has several basic bars and fish trattorias.

The northern limit of the market is marked by the distinctive church of **San Domenico** (Tues–Sun 8.15am–noon, Sat & Sun also 5–7pm; free), with a fine eighteenth-century facade and tombs inside containing a host of famous Sicilians. The **oratory** behind the church (Oratorio del Rosario; Mon–Sat 9am–1pm; free but tipping is usual) contains fluid exuberant decor by the seventeenth-century maestro of stucco, Giacomo Serpotta, and a masterful Van Dyck altarpiece, painted in 1628 before the artist fled Palermo for Genoa to escape the plague.

Museo Archeologico Regionale

Piazza Olivella 24 • Closed for restoration • ☎091 611 6806

From Piazza San Domenico, Via Roma continues north, passing (on the left) Palermo's main post office. Behind this surreal Fascist-era bulk is a sixteenth-century convent housing the **Museo Archeologico Regionale**, a magnificent collection of finds, mainly from western Sicily. The museum is currently closed for restoration but when it reopens, its displays will almost certainly include Egyptian and Punic remains – notably immense Punic tombs bearing the sculptured forms of their occupants – and Roman sculpture including a giant enthroned Zeus. The highlights of the collection, however, are finds from the temples of Selinunte (see p.937), notably the vivid fifth-century-BC sculpted panels from Temples C and F, such as Perseus beheading the Medusa with a short sword. Look out as well for a glistening, muscular study of Hercules subduing a stag, found at Pompeii, the exquisitely restored bronze ram from Siracusa's Castello Maniace (see p.915) and beautifully preserved Roman mosaics from Marsala.

Santa Zita and the old harbour

Heading towards the water from Via Roma, you'll come to the church of **Santa Zita** (also known as Santa Cita or San Mamiliano), on quiet Via Squarcialupo, whose marvellous **oratory** (Mon–Fri 9am–1pm; ring the bell if closed, or ask in the church in front; €2) holds one of Serpotta's finest stucco extravaganzas – the *Battle of Lepanto*. From here streets spread back to the thumb-shaped inlet of **La Cala**, Palermo's **old harbour**. This was once the main port of Palermo, stretching as far inland as Via Roma, but during the sixteenth century silting caused the water to recede to its current position, and La Cala now does duty as a yachting marina.

La Kalsa

Via Roma, running parallel to Via Maqueda and Via Ruggero Settimo, is a broad, fairly modern addition to the city, all clothes and shoe shops, but there are discoveries aplenty to be made exploring the areas to its east. This southeastern quarter of old Palermo was worst hit during the war, but, after years of decay, it's sloughing off its desolate image. It's here in the **La Kalsa** district that you'll find some of Palermo's most remarkable buildings and churches, as well as its only central park, **Villa Giulia**, just a few minutes' walk along Via Lincoln from the train station and home to an extensive **botanical garden** (daily 9am to 1hr before sunset; €5; ⓦortobotanico.unipa.it).

La Magione and Santa Maria dello Spasimo

Piazza Magione 44 • Mon–Sat 9.30am–noon & 3–6.15pm • Donation requested • ☎ 091 617 0596

Built in 1151, the simple, sparse Norman church of **La Magione** has beautiful cloisters and a chapel, a rare plaster preparation of a crucifixion fresco and a lovely small Arab-Norman column carved with a Koranic inscription. The church backs onto the desolate square of **La Kalsa** (its name is from the Arabic *khalisa*, meaning "pure"), at the centre of the eponymous area. La Kalsa was subjected to saturation bombing during World War II, because of its proximity to the port, with the area now occupied by the square taking the brunt of it.

Across the square, set back off Via Spasimo, is the atmospheric complex of **Santa Maria dello Spasimo** (closed for restoration), a former church, now roofless except for its Gothic apse, that – once it reopens– will hold night-time jazz concerts outside in the courtyard.

Galleria Regionale

Via Alloro 4 • Tues–Fri 9am–6pm, Sat & Sun 9am–1pm • €8, €10 with Palazzo Mirto • ☎ 091 623 0011, ⓦ regione.sicilia.it/beniculturali /palazzoabatellis

A block north of the square, Via Alloro is home to the Palazzo Abatellis, a fifteenth-century palace housing Sicily's **Galleria Regionale**, a stunning medieval-art collection. Inside, there's a simple split: sculpture downstairs, and paintings upstairs, the one exception being a magnificent fifteenth-century fresco, the *Triumph of Death*, which covers an entire wall of the former chapel. The other masterpiece on the ground floor is a calm, perfectly studied, white marble bust of *Eleanora of Aragon* by the fifteenth-century artist Francesco Laurana. Upstairs, there are thirteenth- and fourteenth-century Sicilian works, Byzantine in style, and a fine collection of works by Antonello da Messina (1430–79), including three small portraits of *Sts Gregory, Jerome* and *Augustine* and a celebrated *Annunciation*.

Galleria d'Arte Moderna

Via Sant'Anna 21 • Tues–Sun 9.30am–6.30pm • €7 • ☎ 091 843 1605, ⓦ galleriadartemodernapalermo.it

At the far end of Via Alloro, Piazza Sant'Anna is home to the Convento di Sant'Anna, which has been stunningly restored and opened as the seat of the **Galleria d'Arte Moderna**. The collection of nineteenth- and twentieth-century Sicilian works here is

16

displayed thematically (portraits, nudes, mythology, seascapes, landscapes etc) to great effect. Its **café**, spilling into the courtyard in summer, is one of the loveliest places in the city for lunch or an aperitif.

North of Via Alloro

North of Via Alloro, on Via Merlo, the late eighteenth-century **Palazzo Mirto** (Tues–Fri 9am–6pm, Sat & Sun 9am–1pm; €4 or €10 with Palazzo Abatellis) is one of the few *palazzi* in the city to have retained its imposing original fixtures and fittings. Continue along Via Merlo and you'll reach Piazza Marina, a hectic square dominated by the liana-slung banyan trees of the Giardini Garibaldi. Overlooking the square is the vast **Palazzo Chiaramonte**, one-time headquarters of the Inquisition, and the more intimate and engaging **Museo delle Marionette** off Via Butera at Vicolo Niscemi 5 (Mon–Sat 9am–1pm & 2.30–6.30pm, Sun 10am–1pm; ☎091 328 060, ⊕museomarionettepalermo .it; €5), a definitive collection of traditional Sicilian puppets, screens and painted scenery. From October to June the museum puts on shows on Tuesday and Friday at 5.30pm (€6). Beyond the museum, Via Vittorio Emanuele runs down to the water and ends in the Baroque **Porta Felice**. The whole area around the gate was flattened in 1943, and has since been rebuilt as the ugly **Foro Italico** promenade.

The outskirts

If you are interested in seeing more of Palermo's **Norman relics**, bus #124 runs west from the Politeama to **La Zisa** (from the Arabic, *el aziz*, "magnificent") on Piazza Guglielmo il Buono, a huge palace begun by William I in 1160, with a fine exterior and a rich, well-crafted Islamic interior, housing a collection of Islamic art and artefacts (Mon & Sun 9am–1pm, Tues–Sat 9am–6.30pm; €6; ☎091 652 0269). Closer to the centre, about 1km beyond Porta Nuova at Corso Calatafimi 100, is **La Cuba**, the remains of a slightly later Norman pavilion that formed part of the same royal park as La Zisa: it's now tucked inside an army barracks, but has been well restored and includes access to a Punic necropolis (Tues–Sat 9am–6.30pm, Sun 9am–1pm; €2; ☎091 590 299).

16

Catacombe dei Cappuccini

Piazza dei Cappuccini • April–Oct daily 9am–noon & 3–6pm; Nov–March daily 9am–12.30pm & 3–5.30pm • €3 • ☎091 652 4156 • Take bus #327 from Piazza Indipendenza southwest along Via dei Cappuccini as far as Via Pindemonte

For real horror-movie stuff, head for the catacombs of the **Catacombe dei Cappuccini**, home to some eight thousand mummified bodies. Preserved by various chemical and drying processes – including the use of vinegar and arsenic baths – the mummies were dressed in suits of clothes, then placed in niches along rough-cut stone corridors. Descending into the catacombs is quite unnerving, especially if you arrive in a lull between coach parties. Different caverns are reserved for men, women, the clergy, doctors, lawyers and surgeons. Suspended in individual niches, hand-written notes about their necks, the bodies have become vile, contorted, grinning figures – some decomposed beyond recognition, others complete with skin, hair and eyes.

ARRIVAL AND DEPARTURE | **PALERMO**

BY PLANE

Palermo's Falcone Borsellino airport (☎800 541 880, ⊕gesap.it) is at Punta Raisi, 31km west of the city. Buses (Prestia & Comandè; ☎091 580 457, ⊕prestiaecomande.it) run into the city (every 30min; 5am–midnight; 45min), and stop outside Politeama theatre, Stazione Maríttima, and at Stazione Centrale; tickets (€6.10) on board. For the return, departures are at 4am, 5am and then every 30min until 11pm. Trains (€5.80) run from the airport to Stazione Centrale at 5.54am, 7.20am, and then on the hour and at 20 past the hour until 9.20pm, with the final departure at 10.05pm. From Stazione Centrale they leave at 4.45am, 5.09am, 6.07am and then every 30min between 7.09am and 8.09pm. The airport ticket office number is ☎091 704 4007.

BY TRAIN

All trains arrive at the Stazione Centrale at the southern end of Via Roma. Bus #101 runs from the station along Via Roma to Via della Libertà. It has its own priority lane, so is much faster than most of the city's other services.

Destinations Agrigento (11 daily; 2hr 15min); Catania (3 daily; 3hr 45min); Cefalù (hourly; 45min–1hr); Enna via Caltanisetta (3 daily; 2hr 10min–3hr 15min); Messina (13 daily; 3hr–4hr); Milazzo (13 daily; 2hr 30min–3hr); Trapani (5 daily; 2hr 15min–3hr 45min).

BY BUS

The majority of country- and island-wide buses (see p.874 for details) operate from the recently opened Piazza Cairoli bus station alongside the train station.

Destinations Agrigento (Cuffaro; 5 daily; 2hr 30min); Catania (SAIS Autolinee; 2hr 30min/2hr 40min); Cefalù (SAIS Trasporti; 5 daily; 1hr); Messina (SAIS Autolinee; 5 daily Mon–Sat; 2hr 40min); Piazza Armerina (SAIS Autolinee; hourly; 2hr 15min); Siracusa (Interbus; 3 daily; 3hr 15min); Trapani (Segesta; 1–2 hourly; 2hr).

BY FERRY OR HYDROFOIL

All ferry and hydrofoil services dock at the Stazione Maríttima, just off Via Francesco Crispi. A free *navetta* bus meets arrivals and will take you to the port entrance, from where it's a 10min walk up Via E. Amari to Piazza Castelnuovo. Bus #139 connects the port with Stazione Centrale, though it is rather infrequent, so it is better to walk up Via E. Amari to Piazza Politeama from where buses #101 or #102, and the *linea rossa*, run regularly to the train station. The services detailed here refer to the period from June to Sept; expect frequencies to be greatly reduced or suspended outside these months. Ferry details are available on ⓦ aferries.it, while all hydrofoils are run by Ustica Lines (ⓦ usticalines.it).

Destinations Ferries: Cagliari (1 or less weekly; 14hr 30min); Civitavecchia (1–3 weekly; 17hr); Genoa (1 daily; 20hr); Naples (1–2 daily; 11hr); Tunis (1–2 weekly; 10hr); Ustica (1 daily; 2hr 20min. Hydrofoils: Aeolian Islands (all 1 daily) – Alicudi (2hr), Filicudi (2hr 30min), Lipari (4hr), Panarea (4hr 40 min), Rinella (3hr 15min), Santa Marina Salina (3hr 30min), Stromboli (5hr 15min); Ustica (2 daily; 90min), Vulcano (4hr 25min).

16 GETTING AROUND

BY BUS

City buses (AMAT; ☎ 091 350 111, infoline ☎ 848 800 817 or from a mobile ☎ 199 240 800, ⓦ www.amat.pa.it) cover every corner of Palermo as well as Monreale and Mondello. There's a flat fare of €1.30 valid for 90min, or you can buy an all-day ticket for €3.50, while tickets for the *linea gialla*, *linea rossa* and *linea verde*, and the *circolare* (which all weave in and out and over the *centro storico*) minibus services, cost just €0.52 for a day's use. Buy them from AMAT booths outside Stazione Centrale, at the southern end of Viale della Libertà, in *tabacchi* and anywhere else you see the AMAT sign, or, if you forget, from the driver for a supplement of €0.40. Validate tickets in the machine at the back of the bus as you board – there has recently been a clampdown on people travelling without tickets, with spot checks carried out by plainclothes inspectors. The main city bus rank is outside Stazione Centrale and buses run until midnight (11.30pm on Sun).

BY CAR

Driving in the city is best avoided. Overtaking on both sides is the norm, and indicating virtually unheard of. Blackmarket parking attendants will guide you to a space and charge you a small amount (around €0.50/hr), while meters are installed in some parts of the centre.

Car rental Avis, Via Francesco Crispi 115 ☎ 091 586 940; Hertz, Via Messina 7/E ☎ 091 323 439; Maggiore, Stazione Notarbartolo 79 ☎ 091 681 0801; Sicily By Car, Via Mariano Stabile 6/A ☎ 091 581 045. All of these also have desks at the airport.

BY TAXI

Palermo's three taxi companies – Auto Radio Taxi (☎ 091 513 311, ⓦ autoradiotaxi.it), Radio Taxi Trinacria (☎ 255 455 or ☎ 091 68 78, ⓦ radiotaxitrinacria.it) and Sicilia Uno (☎ 339 408 5713, ⓦ siciliaunotaxipalermo.com) – all charge the same rates. The minimum fare is €4.50; if the driver doesn't want to switch the meter on, agree a fare you are prepared to pay first – not a bad strategy if there is more than one taxi driver about, as they may well bid for custom. For a good reliable official taxi driver who charges less than most call Pino ☎ 328 374 5341, who will do the airport run for €40, and Stazione Centrale to the port for €10. There are ranks at the airport, train and bus stations, and all the main squares.

BY HORSE-DRAWN CARRIAGE

Taking a horse-drawn carriage, a *carrozza*, is a suitably kitsch way to see the city. They tout for business alongside Piazza Pretoria or by the cathedral: there is no fixed rate, so agree a price first.

BY BIKE OR SCOOTER

If you're adept on two wheels, biking is not a bad option: as long as you realize the rules of the road – he who hesitates is lost, and go for the gap – weaving your way in and out of the traffic can be an exhilarating way to save time and legwork. For the more adventurous, scooter rental is also available.

Bike rental Rent Bike, Via Giardinaccio 66 (off Via Maqueda), ☎ 331 750 7886 (€10/day).

INFORMATION

Main tourist office Palermo's provincial tourist office, Piazza Castelnuovo 34 (Mon–Fri 8.30am–2pm & 2.30–6pm; 📞 091 605 8531, 🌐 palermotourism.com), has free maps and booklets on events and transport, as well as lists of accommodation.

Airport tourist office (Mon–Sat 8.30am–7.30pm; 📞 091 591 698).

Information points Run by the *comune*, these handy, and often very well informed, little information points are scattered through the city centre in small kiosks, at Politeama, Via Cavour opposite Feltrinelli, the port, Piazza Bellini, and at the Stazione Centrale, with branches too in Mondello and Sferracavallo. (All are open Sat–Wed 9am–1pm & 3–7pm, Thurs & Fri 9am–1pm & 3–6pm.)

Newspapers For city listings pick up a copy of the local *Il Giornale di Sicilia* or *La Sicilia* or look out for the more youth-oriented *Lapis* (free).

ACCOMMODATION

If you arrive late and need a place on spec, most of Palermo's budget hotels lie on and around the southern ends of Via Maqueda and Via Roma, close to Stazione Centrale. However, you will get far more for your money staying in one of the new wave of B&Bs. Orizzonte Rosso (📞 333 663 8666, 🌐 orizzonterosso.com) is a well-organized outfit with a range of centrally located apartments, which also organizes upmarket boat trips and tailormade excursions all over Sicily.

★ **Al Giardino dell'Alloro** Vicolo S. Carlo 8 📞 338 224 3541, 🌐 giardinodellalloro.it; bus #139 from Stazione Centrale. Lovely B&B in the heart of La Kalsa with books for guests to borrow, a courtyard where breakfast is served, and a living room used as an exhibition space for contemporary Sicilian artists. The five rooms each feature original works of art, and all have kettles and mugs. There is a small kitchen for guests' use, and more rooms in the recently opened annexe. **€85**

Alla Kala Via Vittorio Emanuele 71 📞 091 743 4763, 🌐 allakala.it; bus #139 from Stazione Centrale. An excellent, centrally located choice, this spick-and-span B&B has five stylish designer rooms and a suite with magnificent views of the sailing marina. It has a keen following among those in the know, so book in advance. **€120**

Baia del Corallo Via Plauto 27 📞 091 679 7807, 🌐 ostellopalermo.it; bus #101 from the train station to Piazza de Gaspari, and then bus #628 to Punta Matese. Palermo's youth hostel is by the sea 12km northwest of the city – not the most convenient choice for sightseeing, but handy for the airport and a good cheap option for a first or last night. There's accommodation in double and family rooms as well as in dorms. Dorms **€18**, doubles/family rooms **€56**

★ **BB22** Palazzo Pantelleria, Largo Cavalieri di Malta 22 📞 091 611 1610 or 📞 335 790 8733, 🌐 bb22 .it; bus #107 from Stazione Centrale. Faultless Milanese designer-chic (resinated cement floors, perspex chairs, walls painted in matt hues of stone) blended with a feeling of being at home (free wi-fi, coffee and water) in a historic *palazzo* a few steps from the Vucciria market. Breakfast is served on a small roof terrace. The owners also organize food and wine tours, in both Palermo and further afield, and boat trips to the beach at Mondello. **€140**

Grand Hotel et Des Palmes Via Roma 398 📞 091 602 811, 🌐 grandhoteletdespalmes.com; bus #107 from Stazione Centrale. Although it may no longer have the cachet it had in the days when guests included Wagner, the *Des Palmes* remains an extremely comfortable four-star chain hotel conveniently located on the main Via Roma. What's more, discounts via the hotel website can result in room rates that compete with those of many B&Bs. **€130**

★ **Grand Hotel Villa Igiea** Via Belmonte 43 📞 091 631 2111, 🌐 villaigiea.com. This classic Art Nouveau building, originally a villa of the Florio family (the people who pioneered tuna canning), was designed by Ernesto Basile in 1900, and stands outside the city centre above the marina of Acquasanta. It has a swimming pool overlooking the port, shady terraced gardens, a tennis court and sweeping terraces for the most stylish aperitif in town. Give up all notions of sightseeing in favour of long lazy days by the pool, take a private boat trip to the Zingaro reserve or Ustica, or explore Palermo with a historian or food expert. **€180**

La Casa dei Limoni Piazza Giulio Cesare 9 📞 334 834 3888, 🌐 lacasadeilimoni.it. Clean, friendly B&B right opposite the train station, though it is best to call ahead as the owner doesn't live on the premises. Reasonably priced, and the perfect place to stay if you arrive late or have to leave early. **€64**

★ **La Dimora del Genio** Via Garibaldi 58 📞 347 658 7664, 🌐 ladimoradelgenio.it; 5min walk from Stazione Centrale. Three cosy rooms in a centrally heated seventeenth-century *palazzetto*, furnished with a tasteful blend of antiques, modern furniture and original paintings by the owner's artist husband. The friendly owner is a talented cook, and offers cooking courses for guests, as well as a splendid Sunday dinner for €30 a head. **€90**

La Dimora del Guiscardo Via Vetriera 83–5 📞 328 662 6074, 🌐 ladimoradelguiscardo.it. Little B&B in the heart of La Kalsa, close to the area's bars and restaurants. Clean, simple rooms, and a sole shared bathroom. The owner offers free pick-up from the port, station or airport bus stop, and organizes wine tastings at the nearby *Cana Enoteca* (see p.886). **€60**

16

Letizia Via dei Bottai 30 ☎091 589 110, ⊛hotelletizia .com; bus #139 from Stazione Centrale. Each room in this delightful hotel, just off Piazza Marina, has its own colour scheme and furnishings. There's an enclosed courtyard for breakfast, free wi-fi, and the loan of a mobile phone for the duration of your stay. €115

Palazzo Conte Federico Via dei Biscottari 4 ☎091 651 1881, ⊛contefederico.com; bus #107 from Stazione Centrale. A magnificent (if chilly) Arabic-Norman palace close to Ballarò market, built over the Punic city walls, retaining fourteenth-century frescoed ceilings and an impressive armoury. The aristocratic owners have several comfortable and practical apartments for rent, a very decorous suite, and can offer cooking lessons – followed by a torchlit dinner in the defensive tower. Apartments €120, suite €360

★ **Palazzo Pantaleo** Via Ruggero Settimo 74/H ☎091 325 471 or ☎335 700 6091, ⊛palazzopantaleo .it; bus #107 or #101 from Stazione Centrale. Outstanding, this shipshape B&B has seven huge, light, airy rooms in an eighteenth-century *palazzo* on a quiet *piazzetta* off a major shopping street, a short walk from Piazza Politeama. Great attention to the kind of details that matter if you are on business – instant access in all rooms, and sockets supplied with adapters so that you can charge your mobile phone. On top of that, is respect for the privacy

and independence of guests. On the upper storey is an apartment, and there is also a small kitchen where you can make drinks or snacks. €100

Quattro Quarti Palazzo Arone di Valentino, Via Vittorio Emanuele 376 ☎347 854 7209, ⊛quattroquarti.it. A superior B&B with four smart, elegant rooms in part of a huge *palazzo* owned by the Arone di Valentino family. Guests are very well looked after, making this a great place to consider if you are a little nervous about finding your feet in Palermo. In the main part of the palace, there is a plush suite of rooms furnished with antiques. €130

★ **Ucciard Home** Via Enrico Albanese 34–36 ☎091 348 426, ⊛hotelucciardhome.com. Trendy designer hotel opposite the prison, with sixteen comfortable, stylish rooms and lovely, luxurious bathrooms. Staff are excellent, breakfasts good and deals via the website can be fantastic. €154

Vecchio Borgo Via Quintino Sella 1–7 ☎091 611 8330, ⊛hotelvecchioborgo.eul; bus #107 from Stazione Centrale. A smart and appealing hotel between the Piazza Politeama and one of Palermo's best weekend markets. Comfortable rooms with bold printed fabrics and all amenities (including internet points). Excellent breakfast, including home-made cakes. Garage €10 a night, outdoor car-park free, but spaces limited. Worth checking the website for offers that can make it cheaper than many B&Bs. €119

EATING AND DRINKING

Vendors in the markets and on numerous street corners sell classic Palermitani street food such as *pane e panelli* (chickpea-flour fritters served in bread), *crocchè* (potato croquettes with anchovy and *caciocavallo* cheese), and *pane con la milza* (bread with spleen).

CAFÉS AND STREET FOOD

Casa Obatola Via Alloro 16 ☎091 982 4442. Relaxing little bar with seats outside on a *piazzetta* below Via Alloro, good for a rest before or after visiting the nearby Galleria Regionale. Delicious sandwiches (from €3) and salads, and good pastries. Mon–Sat all day till 9pm.

Cibus Via E. Amari 64 ☎091 612 2651, ⊛cibus.pa.it. High-class grocery store with a great deli counter, and a wood-fired oven where you can get light blistered pizzas and other savoury pastries to eat in or take away. It is 5min walk from the hydrofoil port, so an ideal place to stock up if you are sailing to Ustica or the Aeolian Islands. Mon–Sat 8.30am–11pm, Sun 8.30am–2pm & 6–11pm.

Franco 'U Vastiddaru Piazza Marina. Palermitani street food such as *pane e panelli*, *arancini*, *crocchè* and *pane con la milza* (*pane ca meusa* in Sicilian) – which you can eat at plastic tables on plastic plates with plastic knives and forks on the busy corner of Piazza Marina and Via Vittorio Emanuele. Open daily.

Friggitoria Chiluzzo Piazza Kalsa. Stand under a canopy, drink beer from a bottle, eat *pane e panelli* in paper. Daily 7.30am–8.30pm.

I Cuochini Via Ruggero Settimo 68 ☎091 581 158. Diminutive, spick-and-span *frigittoria* – all gleaming white tiles and zinc – founded in 1826, and concealed within an arched gateway along Via Ruggero Settimo (the only sign is a small ceramic plaque). *Panzerotti* (deep-fried pastries, stuffed with tomato, mozzarella and anchovy, or aubergine, courgette and cheese), *arancini* (with *ragù*, or with cheese and ham), *pasticcino* (a sweet pastry with minced meat), *timballini di pasta* (deep-fried pasta), and *besciamelle fritte* (breadcrumbed and deep-fried *béchamel*) and the like – all at 70c a portion. Mon–Sat 8.30am–2.30pm.

Ima Sushi Fourth floor Rinascente, Via Roma/Piazza S.Domenico ☎091 610 7811, ⊛rinascente.it. If you want to pretend you're not in Palermo for a while (and it happens) head up to this sushi bar on the fourth floor of the Rinascente department store. Colour-coded plates of sushi, California rolls and sashimi on the obligatory conveyor belt, priced at between €2.50 and €7.50. Daily until 11pm.

Mazzara Via Magliocco 15 (off Via Ruggero Settimo ☎091 321 443. Long-established bar-*pasticceria* where Tomasi di Lampedusa is reputed to have penned some of *The Leopard*. These days it serves light brunch and lunches

16

alongside a dangerous selection of pastries and ice creams. try the rare roast beef with rocket and shaved parmesan. Tues–Sun 7.30am–8.30pm.

Michele alla Brace Piazza Borgo Vecchio. At the tiny market of Piazza Borgo Vecchio, you can't miss this huge grill with a couple of plastic tables and a steaming cauldron of vegetables. Buy your fish from one of the nearby stalls and bring it to Michele, who will grill it, and provide you with veg, drinks and a table. Closed Wed.

Obika Fourth floor Rinascente, Via Roma/Piazza S. Domenico ☎091 601 7861, ⓦobika.it. On the top floor of the revamped Rinascente department store, this is the Palermo branch of an exclusive chain of bars specializing in meticulously sourced *mozzarella di bufala*, which appears in exquisitely presented salads and other light dishes. A great lunchtime escape from the heat and chaos of Palermo, and a good place for an aperitif (daily 6.30–9pm), the drinks accompanied by a selection of mouthwatering mozzarella tasters. Daily until 11pm.

Palazzo Riso Via Vittorio Emanuele 365 ☎091 320 532, ⓦpalazzoriso.it. Cool, white, minimalist bar belonging to Palermo's new contemporary art museum. Hazelnut- and chocolate-flavoured coffees, tisanes, *cornetti* with forest fruits, light lunches and *aperitivi*. Eat in the bar, or outside in the shady courtyard. Free wi-fi and use of computers. Daily until 11pm.

Rosciglione Via Gian Luca Barbieri 5 ☎091 651 2959. Watch *cannoli* being made as you eat them at this bakery (which exports worldwide) on the edge of the Ballarò market. Mon–Sat 7am–2pm & 1.30–6pm.

Spinnato Via Principe di Belmonte 107–115 ☎091 749 5104, ⓦspinnato.it. With tables outside on a pedestrianized street, this is the perfect place for breakfast, delicious cakes and ice creams, or an *aperitivo* served with an aesthetic cascade of roast almonds, shelled pistachios and crisps. Nearby are several other members of the Spinnato Empire including *Il Golosone*, Piazza Castelnuovo 22, which serves up its pastries and ice creams fast-food style; and *Al Pinguino*, Via Ruggero Settimo 86, a popular and highly rated shrine to ice cream. Daily 7.30am–8.30pm.

RESTAURANTS

Antica Focacceria San Francesco Via A. Paternostro 58 ☎091 320 264, ⓦafsf.it. This old-fashioned place has been in the same family for five generations. Downstairs they serve traditional Palermitani street food, such as *focaccia schietta* (focaccia with offal and *caciocavallo* cheese), *sfincione* (pizza with onion, tomato, *caciocavallo* and breadcrumbs), *crocchè* (potato croquettes) and *panelli* (chickpea-flour fritters). Upstairs you can eat full meals (try the *pasta con le sarde*, pasta with sardines). There are also several fixed-price menus (*panelli*, *crocchè*, an *arancina* or slice of pizza, *cannolo* and a drink for €7; or the same, with

pasta instead of the *arancina* or pizza for €8.50). In summer you can eat outside. 12.30–2.30pm & 8–10.30pm; closed Tues.

★ **Il Mirto e la Rosa** Via Principe di Granitello 30 ☎091 324 353. This began life as a vegetarian restaurant, and although carefully sourced local fish and meat have now joined the menu, the emphasis on vegetables remains. It is also one of several businesses in Palermo to have publicly refused to pay *pizzo* (see box, p.874). Signature dishes include *caponata* with pistachio-spiked couscous, and home-made *tagliolini* with a sweet, sticky tomato sauce, grilled aubergine and cheese from the Nebrodi mountains. Finish up with a voluptuous dessert followed by home-made cinnamon liqueur. Eating à la carte you'll spend around €25 for three courses without wine, €30 if you have a dessert, but there are various menu deals (€10 for a *primo*, *secondo* and salad, €15 for antipasto, *primo*, *secondo*, salad and dessert). Mon–Sat 12.30–2.30pm & 8–10.30pm.

★ **Osteria dei Vespri** Piazza Croce dei Vespri ☎091 617 1631, ⓦosteriadeivespri.it. Palermo's best restaurant was begun as a hobby a decade ago and continues to be run with passion by brothers Andrea and Alberto Rizzo, who cook complex meals, with a loyal and intelligent use of local Sicilian ingredients. Dishes might include rabbit terrine with pistachios from Bronte, black *tagliolini* served with red mullet, ginger, red onion and fresh fava beans, or quail stuffed with prunes served on a purée of cannellini beans and celeriac. À la carte you'll pay at least €20 per course, while there are *degustazione* menus at €60 and €85 per person, excluding wine. Mon–Sat 12.30–2.30pm & 8–10.30pm.

★ **Osteria lo Bianco** Via E. Amari 104 ☎091 251 4906. Decorated with Juventus souvenirs and religious bric-a-brac, this is one of the cheapest places to eat in town. Traditional Palermitano food, such as *pasta con sarde*, *polpette* (meatballs) in tomato sauce, *ricciola* in a spicy tomato sauce, or a stew of beef, peas and carrots. Two courses with wine and fruit for under €15. Mon–Sat 12.30–2.30pm & 8–10.30pm, Sun 12.30–2.30pm.

Osteria Paradiso Via Serradifalco 23. Typical family-run trattoria, to the north of La Zisa, open only at lunchtime and specializing in fish. There is no written menu – the owner just tells you what's available that day. Specialities include fish cooked in seawater, raw prawns dressed with olive oil and lemon juice, and deep-fried *cicirello*, a long skinny silver fish. Arrive early to get a table. Mon–Sat 12.30–2.30pm.

Pizzeria Italia Via Orologio 54 (opposite Teatro Massimo) ☎091 589 885. Attracting large queues, this is the best place in town for light, oven-blistered pizzas (€4–10). Try the "Palermitana" with tomato, anchovies, onion, artichokes, *caciocavallo* cheese and breadcrumbs. 8–10.30pm; closed Mon.

16

Primavera Piazza Bologni 4 ☎091 329 408. Not far from the cathedral, off Via Vittorio Emanuele, with outdoor seating in a lovely little piazza across from the Palazzo Riso, this popular, reasonably priced trattoria serves home-style cooking such as *pasta con le sarde* and *bucatini con broccoli* (both €10). Bottles of good, inexpensive local wine as well. Tues–Sun 12.30–2.30pm & 8–10.30pm.

★ **Santandrea** Piazza Sant'Andrea ☎091 334 999 or ☎328 131 4595. Chic, but relaxed family-run place a stone's throw from Piazza San Domenico and the Vucciria market, this is definitely one of Palermo's best restaurants, and is known for its key role in Peter Robb's *Midnight in Sicily*. Dishes are seasonal and inventive, with a strong emphasis on local ingredients. Mon–Sat 8–10.30pm.

Trattoria Piccolo Napoli Piazzetta Mulino di Vento 4 ☎091 320 431. Lively trattoria off the Vecchio Borgo market founded in 1951 and run by three generations of the same family. They have two boats at Terrasini: fish is brought in daily, and anything not eaten that day is sold on to the local market stalls. Try raw prawns (€60/kilo), pasta with *neonati* (newborn fish) when it's in season (€12) or what may prove to be the best *caponata* you will ever taste (€4). Mon–Sat 12.30–2.30pm.

★ **Trattoria Torrenuzza** Via Torrenuzza 17 ☎091 252 5532. Bustling, no-frills trattoria where fish is grilled on an outside brazier. Eat at streetside tables in summer, inside in winter. Antipasti (mussel soup, seafood salad, etc) and *primi* (pasta with broccoli, with mussels and clams, or with swordfish and aubergine) are all priced at €5, except for a couple of special dishes such as spaghetti with *ricci di mare* (sea urchin) which ring in at €10. Meat *secondi* (*involtini*, charcoal-grilled sausage and the like) are also €5, while fish dishes (mixed fried or grilled fish, grilled prawns, grilled sea bream or sea bass) cost from €7–10. Calamari and swordfish are frozen (but none the worse for it), the rest of the fish is fresh. Wine is a dangerous €3 a litre, so lunch here could well write off your afternoon. Daily 12.30–2.30pm & 8–10.30pm.

NIGHTLIFE

The most appealing area for nightlife is La Kalsa, in particular the streets between Piazza Garibaldi and Piazza Magione, which are packed with bars and pubs.

Cana Enoteca Via Alloro 105 ☎338 697 5950, ⊚canaenoteca.it. This cosy candle-lit wine bar has an excellent choice of wines and nibbles. The bar staff are welcoming and knowledgeable, and the variety of wines almost overwhelming. 7pm–2am; closed Mon & summer.

Kursaal Kalhesa Foro Italico 21 ☎091 616 2282, ⊚kursaalkalhesa.it. Set deep in the echoing stone vaults of the ancient fortifications of Arabic Palermo, this impressive café and wine bar is furnished with traditional Sicilian furniture, has a huge fire in winter and is a great place for a Sunday brunch. In summer, the Palermo address closes and the bar shifts to an atmospheric ex-tuna-fishing station at the foot of Monte Pellegrino in the seaside town of Vergine Maria. Tues–Sat noon–3pm & 7pm–1.30am, Sun noon–1.30am.

Kursaal Tonnara Tonnara di Bordonaro, Via Bordonaro 9, Vergine Maria ☎091 637 2267, ⊚kursaaltonnara.it; bus #731 to the suburb of Vergine Maria. Evocative place in the remains of a nineteenth-century *tonnara*. Come for an aperitif in its jasmine-scented courtyard, alongside abandoned skeletons of broad wooden tuna-fishing boats, or for one of the frequent concerts, all of which kick off at 10.30pm. There are also indoor and outdoor bars, and an atmospheric sea-facing restaurant, serving light, inventive dishes such as *tagliata* of swordfish in a sesame crust, and a heavenly pistachio mousse. Summer only from around 7pm.

Nuovo Montevergini Piazzetta Montevergini ☎320 234 6796. Alternative venue in a monumental deconsecrated convent with a year-round bar and an autumn-to-spring season of exhibitions, live music, book readings, theatre and film. Opening times vary according to events.

DIRECTORY

Hospital Policlinica, Via Carmelo Lazzaro ☎091 655 1111. For an ambulance call ☎118.

Left luggage Stazione Centrale by track 8 ☎091 603 3040 (daily 7am–11pm); Stazione Marittima ☎091 611 3257 (daily 7am–8pm, but you might have to seek out the custodian).

Pharmacist All-night service at Via Roma 1, Via Roma 207, and Via Mariano Stabile 177.

Police Central city station at Piazza della Vittoria ☎112.

Post office Main post office is the Palazzo delle Poste on Via Roma (Mon–Sat 8am–6.30pm).

Monreale

The Norman cathedral at **MONREALE** (Royal Mountain) holds the most impressive and extensive area of Christian medieval mosaic-work in the world, the undisputed apex of

Sicilian-Norman art. This small hill-town, 8km southwest of Palermo, commands unsurpassed views down the Conca d'Oro valley, to the capital in the distant bay.

The Duomo

Daily 8am–6.30pm, Sun 8am–12.30pm & 3–7pm • Free **Terraces** Daily 9.30am–5.30pm, Sun 8am–12.30pm & 3.30–7pm • €2 **Cloisters** Daily 8am–6.30pm, Sun 8am–12.30pm & 3–7pm • €6

The severe, square-towered exterior of the **Duomo** is no preparation for what's inside. The **mosaics** were almost certainly executed by Greek and Byzantine craftsmen, and they reveal a unitary plan and inspiration. What immediately draws your attention is the all-embracing half-figure of Christ in the central apse, the head and shoulders alone almost twenty metres high. Beneath sit an enthroned Madonna and Child, attendant angels and, below, ranks of saints, each individually and subtly coloured and identified by name. Worth singling out here is the figure of **Thomas à Becket** (marked *SCS Thomas Cantb*), canonized in 1173, just before the mosaics were begun. The nave mosaics are no less remarkable, an animated series that starts with the Creation (to the right of the altar) and runs around the whole church. Most scenes are instantly recognizable: Adam and Eve, Abraham on the point of sacrificing his son, a jaunty Noah's Ark; even the Creation, shown in a set of glorious, simplistic panels portraying God filling his world with animals, water, light … and people. Ask at the desk by the entrance to climb the **terraces** in the southwest corner of the cathedral. The steps give access to the roof and leave you standing right above the central apse – an unusual and precarious vantage-point.

The cloisters

It's also worth visiting the **cloisters**, part of the original Benedictine monastery established here in 1174. The formal garden is surrounded by an elegant arcaded quadrangle, 216 twin columns supporting slightly pointed arches – a legacy of the Arab influence. No two capitals are the same, each a riot of detail and imagination: armed hunters doing battle with winged beasts, flowers, birds, snakes and foliage. Entrance to the cloisters is from Piazza Guglielmo, in the corner by the right-hand tower of the cathedral.

ARRIVAL AND DEPARTURE   **MONREALE**

By bus Bus #389 runs frequently from Piazza dell'Indipendenza, outside the Palazzo dei Normanni (20min).

Ustica

A volcanic, turtle-shaped island 60km northwest of Palermo, **USTICA** is somewhere you could spend an entire holiday, though it is close enough to Palermo for a day-trip. However, travel doesn't come cheap, so make a weekend of it at least if you can. Ustica's fertile uplands are just right for a day's ambling, and there's a path running round the entire rocky coastline, with just a brief stretch where you have to follow the road. The main reason people come here, however, is to dive, for its waters are a diver's paradise, the clear water bursting with fish, sponges, weed and coral. Less adventurous types can easily take a boat trip through Ustica's rugged grottoes and lava outcrops.

The small, rather dishevelled port of **Ustica Town**, where the boats dock, has a few bars, a bank, several restaurants and a handful of places to stay. All these sit around a sloping double piazza, just five minutes' walk uphill from the harbour.

ARRIVAL AND DEPARTURE   **USTICA**

Siremar operates one ferry daily from Palermo to Ustica, while both Siremar and Ustica Lines run 2–5 hydrofoils daily between Easter and Oct (fewer in winter). Travel doesn't come cheap; expect to pay around €30 return by ferry, more than €40 by hydrofoil.

16

> ### DIVING ON USTICA
>
> The island is well set up for divers, and facilities include a decompression chamber, though medical facilities are limited to the pharmacy and the *guardia medica*. The waters are protected by a natural marine reserve, divided into several zones with restrictions on where you can swim, dive and fish. The excellent **Profondo Blu** (☎ 091 844 9609 or ☎ 349 672 6529, ⓦ ustica-diving.it), run by an Italo-Belgian couple, is the island's most organized and experienced dive operator, arranging guided dives and packages – a single dive costs €40, a ten-dive package €330 and a five-day Open Water Diver Padi course €420. It also offers accommodation in a resort of self-catering apartments ouside town (May–Oct; from €450/week), with meals available too (breakfast €5, dinner €35).

ACCOMMODATION

Da Umberto Piazza della Vittoria ☎ 091 844 9542, ⓦ usticatour.it. As well as running the *Da Umberto* restaurant, Gigi Tranchina rents out rooms in over twenty apartments and houses around Ustica, some with great sea views, others more rustic in the middle of the island. Prices depend on size and quality of the accommodation. From €60

Giulia Via S. Francesco 16 ☎ 091 844 9007, ⓦ giulia hotel.com. Open year-round, with ten perfectly acceptable two-star rooms right off the main piazza (single rooms also available), above a lovely restaurant. See the website for weekend packages including certain meals and excursions. No credit cards. €90

Stella Marina Residence Via Cristoforo Colombo 35 ☎ 091 844 8121, ⓦ stellamarinaustica.it. Seventeen smart, self-catering mini-apartments in a small complex right above the port. There's also a nice big terrace for sun-soaking, and a small spa. Rentals are €490–990 per week for a two-person apartment, including breakfast, but they're available on a two-nightly basis May–July & Sept–Oct. €95

EATING

Da Umberto Piazza della Vittoria ☎ 091 844 9542. Tables on the terrace and a menu chiefly consisting of spaghetti dishes (around €8) and seafood main courses that depend on the day's catch (€12–16). Daily 12.30–2.30pm & 8–10.30pm; closed winter.

Giulia Via S. Francesco 13 ☎ 091 844 9007. This simple trattoria (with a few simple rooms above) is the best bet on the island for genuine home-cooking. Try *pennette al usticese* (with herbs, chilli, garlic, pine nuts, raisins, anchovies, capers and olives), *polpettine* (fish balls) with local capers and olives, or *totano* (a big squid) stuffed with shrimp, tomatoes, cheese and breadcrumbs. Fish couscous is available for a minimum of two people. Expect to spend around €35–40 per person. No credit cards. Daily 12.30–2.30pm & 8–10.30pm; closed winter.

The Tyrrhenian coast

From Palermo, the whole of the rugged **Tyrrhenian coast** is hugged by rail, road and motorway, and for the most part, pretty built up. The first attraction is **Cefalù**, a beach resort and cathedral town. Beyond Cefalù, there are several resorts tucked along the narrow strip of land between the Nebrodi mountains and the sea, most of them not worth going out of your way for. Most people tend to head straight for the port of **Milazzo** – Sicily's second-largest port – the main departure point for ferries and hydrofoils to the seven fascinating islands of the **Aeolian archipelago**.

Cefalù

Despite being one of Sicily's busiest international beach resorts, **CEFALÙ** has a parallel life as a small-scale fishing port, tucked onto every available inch of a shelf of land beneath a fearsome crag, **La Rocca**. Roger II founded a mighty cathedral here in 1131 and his church dominates the skyline, the great twin towers of the facade rearing up above the flat roofs of the medieval quarter. Naturally, the fine curving sands are the major attraction but Cefalù is a pleasant town, and nothing like as developed as Sicily's other package resort, Taormina.

The Duomo

Daily: summer 8am–7pm; winter 8am–5.30pm • Free

Halfway along **Corso Ruggero**, the main pedestrianized road through the old town, stands the **Duomo** built – partly at least – as Roger's gratitude for fetching up at Cefalù's safe beach in a violent storm. Inside, covering the apse and presbytery, are the earliest and best preserved of the church **mosaics** in Sicily, dating from 1148. Forty years earlier than those in the cathedral at Monreale, they are thoroughly Byzantine in concept. In high season, when Cefalù's tangibly Arabic central grid of streets is crowded with tourists, you'd do best to visit the cathedral early in the morning, before succumbing to the lure of the long sandy **beach** beyond the harbour.

Museo Mandralisca and La Rocca

There are a couple of other places also worth visiting: the **Museo Mandralisca** (daily 9am–1pm & 3–7pm; €5), at Via Mandralisca 13 (across from Piazza del Duomo), has a wry *Portrait of an Unknown Man* by Antonello da Messina, and a huge shell collection; and **La Rocca** (daily 8am–1hr before sunset; free), which holds the megalithic Tempio di Diana, from where paths continue right around the crag, inside medieval walls, to the sketchy fortifications at the very top.

ARRIVAL AND DEPARTURE   CEFALÙ

By train and bus All trains between Palermo and Messina pull into the station to the south of the town centre a 10min walk from the main drag, Corso Ruggero. Buses also arrive and leave from here.

By ferry In summer there is a once or twice daily hydrofoil service to the Aeolian Islands and Palermo, leaving from the tourist port 20min walk to the east of town.

Tourist office Corso Ruggero 77 (Mon–Sat 8am–8pm; summer usually also Sun 9am–1pm; ☏ 0921 421 050, ⓦ cefalu-tour.pa.it). There is more information on ⓦ palermotourism.com.

ACCOMMODATION

B&B delle Rose Via Gibilmanna ☏ 0921 421 885, ⓦ dellerosebb.it. A pleasant B&B in a quiet location a 20min walk out of town along Via Umberto I. There is a garden and the rooms have private terraces. **€100**

Locanda Cangelosi Via Umberto I 26 ☏ 0921 421 591, ⓦ locandacangelosi.it. This centrally placed little hotel is clean and basic with friendly owners who also have a handful of 2-, 3- and 4-bed apartments with kitchens to rent. **€80**

Villa Cerniglia Lungomare G. Giardina ☏ 320 306 4275, ⓦ villacerniglia.com. A selection of B&B rooms and apartments right on the sea front. Facilities include access to a lido for those seeking the full Sicilian beach experience. **€140**

EATING AND DRINKING

Al Porticciolo Via Carlo Ortolani Bordonaro 66 and 92 ☏ 0921 921 981, ⓦ alporticciolristorante.com. A nice choice for fish or pizza with tables on a terrace built right onto the rocky shore. Try the handmade pasta with zucchini, fresh tuna and wild fennel (€18). 12.30–2.30pm & 8–10.30pm; closed Wed in winter.

Caffè di Noto Via Bagno Cicerone 3 ☏ 0921 42 26 54. This *gelateria* is right at the edge of the *centro storico* and the beginning of the Lungomare, and has fabulous ice creams in flavours including mango, raspberry, prickly pear, and chocolate with chilli. Daily 12.30–2.30pm & 8–10.30pm; closed winter.

16

Milazzo

At the foot of a hilly sickle-shaped castle-topped cape, and dominated by a giant oil refinery, **MILAZZO** is the main port of departure for the **Aeolian Islands** (see box, p.891), which means, at best, a couple of hours in town waiting for a ferry or hydrofoil – at worst, a night in one of the hotels.

The castle

Tues–Sun: summer 9.30am–12.30pm & 4.30–6.30pm; winter 9.30am –12.30pm & 3.30–5.30pm • Free • ☎ 368 387 4010

If there's time to kill, you might like to poke around the streets of the **Borgo**, the old town on the top of the hill, where the magnificently preserved Spanish **castle** sits inside a much larger and older walled city, complete with its own cathedral. Built by Frederick II in the thirteenth century, over Arab foundations on the site of the ancient Greek acropolis, it's one of Sicily's best castles, with views stretching to the Aeolian Islands and beyond.

The steps that run down the far side of the castle walls lead to the Spiaggia di Ponente, a long **beach** of grey gravel with crystal-clear waters.

ARRIVAL AND DEPARTURE   MILAZZO

By bus Buses – including the Giuntabus service from Messina (approx hourly; 50min), whose timings are pretty much organized to tie in with hydrofoil arrivals and departures) stop on the port-side car park (turn right as you disembark from the hydrofoil).

By train The train station is 3km south of the centre, but local buses run into town every 30min during the day, dropping you on the quayside or further up in Piazza della Repubblica.

By boat See box opposite, for details of boat services from Milazzo.

INFORMATION

Tourist office Piazza Duilio 20, just back from the harbour, at the beginning of the main shopping zone (Mon–Fri 9am–1.30pm & 3–6pm, Sat 9am–1pm; ☎ 090 922 2865, ⓦ aastmilazzo.it).

ACCOMMODATION

★ **Cassisi** Via Cassisi 5 ☎ 090 922 9099, ⓦ cassisihotel .com. Elegant, minimalist, family-run hotel, with a deft touch of contemporary oriental style. The buffet breakfast is abundant, with local cheese and salamis, typical pastries and biscuits, and lots of fresh fruit. A 5min walk from the port, and close to the main shopping area. **€130**

★ **Petit Hotel** Via dei Mille 37 ☎ 090 928 6784, ⓦ www.petithotel.it. Ground-breaking eco-hotel in a nineteenth-century building on the seafront overlooking the hydrofoil dock. Staff go out of their way to be helpful, and breakfasts include local salamis and cheeses, organic yogurt, eggs and jams, and home-made cakes. **€110**

Solaris Via Colonello Berte 70 ☎ 333 605 0091, ⓦ bedandbreakfast.milazzo.info. Bright and welcoming B&B a block from the port, with five cheerfully decorated rooms with a/c and fridges. All the rooms have balconies and one has a small covered terrace. **€90**

EATING AND DRINKING

Al Bagatto Via M. Regis 11 ☎ 090 922 4212. A wine bar with a few tables outside where you can sample local salami and cheeses, as well as more substantial dishes – try the *tagliata* of beef (€16). 12.30–2.30pm & 8–10.30pm; closed Wed.

Albatros Via dei Mille 38 ☎ 090 928 3666. The classic café to hang out in while waiting for your ferry or hydrofoil, directly opposite the dock. A great range of pastries, good savouries and ice cream, and skilled bar staff. Try the *nastrino* – a raisin twist – or the *cornetti* with apple and *crema*. Or make the waiting easier with a deftly mixed martini. 7.30am–8.30pm; closed Tues in winter.

Il Spizzico Via dei Mille s/n. Right next to the Ustica Lines office, this takeaway does the best *arancini* hereabouts, including versions filled with spinach and mozzarella or aubergine. Daily 7.30am–8.30pm.

The Aeolian Islands

Volcanic in origin, the **Aeolian Islands** are named after Aeolus, the Greek god who kept the winds he controlled shut tight in one of the islands' many caves. According to Homer, Odysseus put into the Aeolians and was given a bag of wind to help him home, but his sailors opened it too soon and the ship was blown straight back to port. More verifiably, the islands were coveted for their mineral wealth, the mining of obsidian (hard, glass-like lava) providing the basis for early prosperity, because it was the sharpest material available until people learned the art of smelting metals. Later their strategic importance attracted the Greeks, who settled on Lipari in 580 BC, but they later

AEOLIAN ISLANDS INFORMATION

GETTING TO THE ISLANDS

Sailings **from Milazzo** operate daily and are frequent enough to make it unnecessary to book ahead (for which there is a surcharge) except in the high season (unless you're taking a car), although bear in mind that there is a severely reduced service between October and May – and that even moderately rough weather can disrupt the schedules. The **shipping agencies** are down by the harbour and open usual working hours in summer and open just before departures in the low season – Siremar (Via dei Mille 19 ☎090 928 3242, ⊛siremar.it) for **ferries and hydrofoils**, UsticaLines (Via dei Mille 32 ☎090 928 7821, ⊛usticalines.it) for hydrofoils only, and NGI (Via dei Mille 26 ☎090 928 3415, ⊛ngi-spa.it) for ferries only. Hydrofoils are more frequent and twice as quick, but almost twice the price of the ferries. The islands can also be reached from Palermo, Naples, Cefalù and Messina.

GETTING AROUND THE ISLANDS

Getting around in summer is easy, as ferries (*traghetti*) and hydrofoils (*aliscafi*) link all the islands. In winter, services are reduced and in rough weather cancelled altogether, particularly on the routes out to Stromboli, Alicudi and Filicudi. A car might be worth taking to Lipari and Salina, or you can **rent bikes and scooters** when you get there: the islands are very popular with cyclists, though you need to enjoy hills.

ACCOMMODATION AND FACILITIES

In high season (Easter & July–Aug), accommodation is scarce and many places insist on half-board, so you'd be wise to book in advance. From October to March prices can drop by up to fifty percent. There are **campsites** on Vulcano, Salina and Lipari – but camping rough is illegal.

There are **ATMs** on all the islands except Alicudi. Power cuts are commonplace, caused by storms in winter, and in August by over-demand, so a torch is a good idea, especially in winter. Don't be surprised if hotels ask you to be sparing with the **water**, as it is imported by tanker.

16

became a haven for pirates and a place of exile, a state of affairs that continued right into the twentieth century with the Fascists exiling their political opponents to Lipari.

The twentieth century saw mass emigration, mostly to Australia, and even now islands such as Panarea and Alicudi have just a hundred or so year-round inhabitants. It's only recently that the islanders stopped scratching a subsistence living and started welcoming tourists, and these days during the summer months the population of the islands can leap from 10,000 to 200,000. Every island is **expensive**, with prices in shops as well as restaurants reflecting the fact that most food is imported. But get out to the minor isles or come in blustery winter for a taste of what life was like on the islands twenty – or a hundred – years ago: unsophisticated, rough and beautiful.

Vulcano

Closest to the Sicilian mainland, **VULCANO** is the first port of call for ferries and hydrofoils – 45 minutes by hydrofoil, around an hour and a half by ferry – and you know when you are approaching it from the rotten-egg reek of sulphur. The novelty value of its smouldering volcano, and the chance to wallow in warm mud baths and swim above bubbling mid-sea fumaroles, make it a popular destination. Consequently Vulcano has been carelessly developed, its little town ugly, and the promontory of Vulcanello studded with bland mass-market hotels. High prices and mass tourism make Vulcano best seen on a day-trip and as the cost of food on the island is exorbitant, and the restaurants are unexceptional, you're better off bringing a picnic with you.

The crater

The path up to the **crater** (access €3 in summer) begins about 1km out of town on the road to Gelso, marked by a sign warning of the dangers of inhaling volcanic gases. The ascent should take less than an hour. Wear hiking boots, as the ashy track is slithery, and follow the crater in an anticlockwise direction, so you are going downhill rather than up through the clouds of sulphurous emissions on the northern rim. Alternatively, there is an easier hike to **Vulcanello**, the volcanic pimple just to the north of the port, spewed out of the sea in 183 BC: start at the port and head past the Fanghi de Vulcano.

Mud baths, the beach and spa treatments

If you are feeling lazy, the **Fanghi di Vulcano**, or mud baths, and offshore fumaroles are a couple of minutes' walk from the port. In season there's a small entrance fee. Don't wear contact lenses, and be prepared to stink of sulphur for a couple of days. Carry on, and you'll reach a black sand beach. Alternatively, there is a rather nouveau-riche spa, the *Oasi della Salute*, at Via Lentia 1, with three thermal hydromassage pools and a beauty centre (May–Sept; ☎090 985 2093).

Lipari

LIPARI is the biggest and most heavily populated of the islands. Development has not been carefully controlled, and although parts of the island are beautiful and unspoilt, getting there inevitably means passing through villages cluttered with brassy holiday houses. The main port and capital, **Lipari Town** is a busy little place bunched between two harbours.

Lipari Town

The upper town within the fortress walls, the **Castello**, has been continuously occupied since Neolithic times. Alongside the well-marked **excavations**, there's a tangle of churches flanking the main cobbled street, and several buildings that make up the separate sections of the **Museo Archeologico Eoliano** (daily 9am–1.30pm & 3.30–7pm; €6; ☎090 9880174) – a lavish collection of Neolithic pottery, late Bronze Age artefacts, and decorated Greek and Roman vases and statues. Highlights are the towering pyramids of amphorae rescued from ancient shipwrecks, a stunning array of miniature Greek theatrical masks found in tombs, and unique polychrome painted pottery ascribed to an artist known as the Lipari Painter, the colours tinted with volcanic clays such as those found at the Cave Caolina (see box below).

Valle Muria

If you're after beaches and a walk, take the bus west out of Lipari Town (direction Pianoconte) and ask to get down at Località Monte, from where it's a thirty-minute walk to the pebbly beach at **Valle Muria** (if you don't want to walk you can get there and back by boat from Marina Corta in summer: look out for Barney in the green-and-yellow boat; €5 each way).

Quattrocchi and San Calogero

Continuing beyond Località Monte, the road climbs up to **Quattrocchi** ("Four Eyes"), with much-photographed views over spiky *faraglioni* rocks to Vulcano. Just after the village of **Pianoconte**, a side road slinks off down to the ancient thermal baths at **San Calogero** hidden behind a long-disused spa hotel: there's usually an unofficial guide to show you around and allow you a dip if you dare in the scummy 57°C Roman pool.

HIKING FROM CAVE CAOLINA TO SAN CALOGERO

For a great coastal hike, stay on the bus from Lipari asking the driver to drop you at the **Cave Caolina**, a quarry of multicoloured clays used as pigments by the Lipari Painter (whose work can be seen in the Museo Archeologico) from where an easy-to-follow path leads down through the quarry, and back to San Calogero, passing sulphurous fumaroles, a hot spring, and a couple of places where you can scramble down the cliffs for a swim. If you feel happier with a map, there are large-scale Isole Eolie maps on sale in many shops along the main *corso*.

BOAT TRIPS

Tour operators all over town offer year-round **boat trips**, both around Lipari and to all the other islands. The boats mostly run from Marina Corta, but agencies are prominent at the main port too. Universally recommended is Da Massimo, Via Maurolico 2 (☎090 981 3086, ⓦdamassimo.it), with clean, well-maintained boats with freshwater showers and sun shades; English is spoken. They also offer a boat trip to Stromboli with the excellent Magmatrek (see p.900), including a night ascent of the volcano (from €80).

Prices for boat trips are roughly the same everywhere, from €15 for a Lipari and Vulcano tour, Lipari and Salina €30, and from €45 to Panarea and Stromboli. If you want to rent a *gommone* (rubber boat) and putter around yourself, expect to pay €80 per day in low season, and up to €200 in August for a 50m boat with shower and canopy and space for six people. Most operators also run **beach shuttles** in summer to good beaches on Lipari that are otherwise tricky to reach, like Praia Vinci.

ARRIVAL AND DEPARTURE   LIPARI

By ferry or hydrofoil Hydrofoils and ferries dock at the Marina Lunga, while the smaller Marina Corta, formed by a church-topped pier and dwarfed by the castle that crowns the hill above, is used by excursion boats. To get to Marina Corta walk straight along the main *corso* and turn right near the end at Via Maurolico. Most of the services listed are greatly reduced or suspended outside the summer season.

INFORMATION AND GETTING AROUND

By bus From Lipari Town, the rest of the island is easy to reach on a network of buses, which leave regularly from a stop by Marina Lunga, opposite the Esso service station. Buses run in two directions around the island, clockwise to Quattropani, and anticlockwise to Canneto, Porticello and Acquacalda. There are enough departures (up to 10 daily in summer) to be able to get around the whole island easily in a day.

Tourist office Corso Vittorio Emanuele 202 (Mon–Fri 8.30am–1.30pm & 4–7.30pm; July & Aug also Sat 8.30am–1.30pm; ☎090 988 0095, ⓦaasteolie.191.it) has a list of hotels and information – not all of it up to date – for all the Aeolian Islands.

16

ACCOMMODATION

In July and August it's a good idea to listen to the offers of rooms as you step off the boat. Expect to pay around €25–40 per person in August, €20 at other times of the year, for something with a shower, kitchen, and balcony or terrace. The nearest campsite is in Canneto, a 10min bus ride from the port. Unless otherwise stated, all the places below are in Lipari Town.

Baia Unci Via Marina Garibaldi, Canneto ☎090 981 1909, ⓦcampingbaiaunci.it. At the busy resort of Canneto 3km from the port, this campsite has bungalows and tents to rent (€10–19) as well as pitches. There are communal cooking facilities (including fridges) and a restaurant. The bus from Lipari stops outside. Mid-March to mid-Oct. Pitches around €26, bungalows €90

Carasco Porto delle Genti ☎090 981 1605, ⓦcarasco .it. Best choice in town if you have children, as this big 1960s hotel, fused to a cliff on the edge of town, has a vast pool. All the rooms have terraces, and virtually all have sea views. Facilities include a decent restaurant and a poolside bar. €220

★ **Diana Brown** Vico Himera 3 ☎090 981 2584, ⓦdianabrown.it. Spotless place on a quiet alley off the main *corso*, run by a charming South African lady who has lived on the island for thirty years, and so can give good advice on anything you need to know. Rooms come with fridges and kettles; breakfast is served in a sunny roof garden; and there is a wonderfully well stocked book exchange. €100

Enza Marturano Via Maurolico 35 ☎368 322 4997, ⓦenzamarturano.it. Four a/c rooms, with fridges, kitchens and private terraces close to the Marina Corta; breakfast included. It is worth checking the website for special off-season deals. No credit cards. €120

Hotel Tritone Via Mendolita ☎090 981 1595, ⓦbernardigroup.it. Comfortable hotel in a quiet part of town, but just a 5min walk from the centre, built around a swimming pool with thermally heated spring water. There is also a well-equipped spa centre, with a wide range of massage therapies and beauty treatments. It is owned by the same people as the excellent *Filippino* restaurant (see p.894). €360

Villa Meligunis Via Marte 7 ☎090 981 2426, ⓦvillameligunis.it. If you fancy staying in the lap of luxury, push the boat out at this gorgeous converted *palazzo* with excellent views of the citadel and sea from its rooftop restaurant, and a pool alongside; it offers great discounts off-season. €250

EATING AND DRINKING

★ **Al Kasbah** Vico Selinunte 16 ☎ 090 981 1075. Stylish but unpretentious restaurant, with a beautiful long garden, where the Anglo-Aeolian owner will advise on the best ways to sample the spanking-fresh fish. Antipasti (€7–9) and *primi* (€9–11) make creative use of local ingredients, and although the menu changes every year, constant is the handmade ravioli stuffed with fish. They also make their own bread – and the island's best pizza (€6–9), using stone-ground flour. 8–10.30pm; closed Wed Easter–31 Oct & all Nov–March.

★ **Il Filippino** Piazza Municipio ☎ 090 981 1002, ⊕ filippino.it. This stupendous fish restaurant – Lipari's best, in business since 1910 – really knows its stuff. It's in the upper town and has a shaded outdoor terrace where you can eat classy Aeolian specialities like borlotti bean, sardine and fennel soup (€13), *risotto nero* (coloured with squid ink; €13), grouper-stuffed *ravioloni* and local fish in a *ghiotta* sauce (tomatoes, onions, celery, capers and olives; €14). Choose carefully and you might get away with €35 a head, though you could easily spend €60 – and more if you give any serious thought to the massive wine list. 12.30–2.30pm & 8–10.30pm; closed Mon in Oct/Nov & Jan to March, & closed mid-Nov to Dec.

Subba Corso Vittorio Emanuele 92 ☎ 090 981 1352. The island's best and most traditional café, since 1930, has a nice shaded terrace at the rear in the square. Try Lulus, clouds of *crema*-filled choux pastry, or the pistachio- and almond-studded *eoliana* ice cream. Daily 7.30am–8.30pm.

Trattoria d'Oro Via Umberto I 32 ☎ 090 981 1304. A cut above the town's cheaper trattorias, this shady, rustic place is a cool haven on a hot day, and it's very welcoming to families. *Pasta con le sarde* (with sardines and wild fennel) and stuffed squid are typical dishes, with pasta from €7 and fish mains from €10. Daily 12.30–2.30pm & 8–10.30pm.

Salina

North of Lipari, **SALINA**'s two extinct volcanic cones rise out of a fertile land that produces capers and white Malvasia. It's excellent **walking** country with marvellous vantage points over the other islands. Tourism came to Salina far later than Lipari and Vulcano, with the happy result that development and building have always been strictly controlled. Although you could bring a car, there is really little need, as there are bus services between all the main villages.

Santa Marina di Salina

The principal island port is **SANTA MARINA DI SALINA** on the east coast – a relaxed village ranged along Via Risorgimento, a single, pedestrianized main street where chic boutiques and down-to-earth food shops occupy the ground floors of substantial nineteenth-century houses built by those who made their fortune selling sweet wine (*malvasia*) to the British. Most lost their fortunes in 1890 when phylloxera arrived, destroying ninety percent of the vines, and prompting a mass exodus to Australia. When you reach the end of Via Risorgimento, cut down to the Lungomare – where steps lead down to Punta Barone, a little beach with swimming in front of the perplexing remains of an ancient Roman fish farm. Heading back to the port along the Lungomare, there are more swimming spots in waters protected by the sea defences, and another beach in front of the main piazza, close enough to the port to let you have a last swim as you wait for your ferry or hydrofoil.

ACTIVITIES ON SALINA

Walking trails cut right across Salina. Most accessible are the several tracks from the main port, Santa Marina and the nearby hamlet of Lingua with the peak of **Monte Fossa delle Felci** (962m). Look out for trailheads signed from the road between Santa Marina and Lingua, and also from the Circonvalazione that cuts behind Santa Marina. Paths are not very well used, and tend to get overgrown, so cover your legs if you don't want to get scratched by prickly scrub.

If you want an easier time of it, take a **bus** to the sanctuary of **Madonna del Terzito** at Valdichiesa – in the saddle between the two mountains – from where there's a broad, easy-to-follow jeep track; this is about 10km to the top, and should take a couple of hours.

ORTIGIA, SIRACUSA (P.914) >

Lingua

LINGUA, sitting by a pretty lagoon 3km south, makes a pleasant alternative base to Santa Marina. It has two small **museums** in exquisitely restored Aeolian houses overlooking the lagoon with its skew-whiff lighthouse: a small **ethnographic museum** (May–Oct Tues–Sun 9am–1pm & 3–6pm; free) displays examples of rustic art and island culture – mainly kitchen utensils and mill equipment, much of it fashioned from lavic rock, while the **archeological museum** (May–Oct Tues–Sun 9am–6pm; free) has finds from Bronze Age and Roman Salina. Head through the alleyway at the side of the ethnographic museum and you'll be bang in the centre of Lingua's seafront piazza, hub of Salina summer-life, with several little flights of steps leading down to a pebble beach.

Capo Faro and Malfa

Salina's only road climbs from the harbour at Santa Marina and traces the coast north, turning west at **Capo Faro**, with its vineyards and a lighthouse. A couple of kilometres beyond here, the road winds in to **MALFA**, Salina's largest village, set back from the sea. Though quite busy with traffic in the centre, it has an appealing little fishing port tucked away at the foot of cliffs, reached by either a devilishly twisting road or paved stepped footpaths. Its stony beach, backed by dramatic cliffs, is officially closed because of the danger of falling rocks. If this is still the case, do as the locals do and swim instead from the harbour. If you're around in late afternoon, don't miss watching the sunset from the chic cliff-top bar of the *Santa Isabel* hotel (Easter–Oct).

Pollara

Just out of Malfa, a minor road (served by several buses a day) snakes off west to secluded **POLLARA**, raised on a cliff above the sea and occupying a crescent-shaped crater from which Salina's last eruption took place some 13,000 years ago. Scenes from the 1994 film *Il Postino* were shot in a house here which you can occasionally rent: call Pippo Cafarella (☏ 339 425 3684). Pollara's beach, which also featured in *Il Postino*, diminishes every year, and it has now been closed because of the danger of falling rocks. Swim instead from the ancient fishing-boat ramps reached by a cobbled stepped footpath from below the *Postino* house. *Bar L'Oasis* has lilos, kayaks, sun umbrellas and masks to rent, and will bring sandwiches and drinks down from the bar.

Rinella

Most ferries and hydrofoils also call at the little port of **RINELLA**, on the island's south coast. It's a sleepy place with something of a Greek island feel, its higgledy-piggledly fishermen's houses clustered above a black-sand beach. A couple of good bars make it a tempting destination for an aperitif watching the sun set over Filicudi. Buses meet most boat arrivals on the quayside (and call here several times a day). The little village of **Leni** above is less affected by tourism than the rest of the island, and has a good playground.

ACCOMMODATION   SALINA

SANTA MARINA DI SALINA

Da Sabina Via Risorgimento 5/C ☏ 090 984 3134 or ☏ 332 272 6025, �🌐 bbsalina.it. Friendly B&B run by an island family, at the far end of the village from the port (10min walk). Three en-suite rooms open onto a big sea-view terrace, where breakfast is served. No credit cards. **€140**

I Cinque Balconi Via Risorgimento 38 ☏ 090 094 3517, 🌐 icinquebalconi.it. Simple rooms in an eighteenth-century townhouse on Santa Marina's pedestrianized main street, with striking floors of subtle, carefully preserved

original tiles. Behind the hotel, you can while away afternoons in an enchanting secluded garden, shaded by citrus and fig trees. There are eight rooms, and a romantic suite, the latter set alone overlooking the garden, with its own terrace and access. August prices are relatively reasonable. Several rooms have sea views. **€160**

★ **Mamma Santina** Via Sanità ☏ 090 984 3054, 🌐 mammasantina.it. The affable Mario presides over a relaxed boutique-style hotel, set on wide terraces around a swimming pool high above the town with views stretching out to Stromboli and Panarea. The sixteen rooms are in bright seaside colours, with Mediterranean ceramic tile floors and big bathrooms, and there are hammocks on the covered terraces. Call to be picked up from the port, or find the hotel signposted to the left off Via Risorgimento (after no. 66). Closed mid-Dec to mid-March, with excellent deals negotiable in low season. **€230**

Mercanti di Mare Piazza Santa Marina 7 ☎ 090 984 3536, ⊚ hotelmercantidimare.it. Harbourfront three-star hotel with nine, white, airy rooms and an attractive terrace that overlooks the water. **€180**

LINGUA

A Cannata Via Umberto I ☎ 090 984 3161 or ☎ 339 575 4240, ⊚ acannata.it. Simple rooms above a restaurant a few metres back from the sea near the church, plus various apartments of various sizes just across the road and around the village (€500/week). There's a decent restaurant too. **€170**

Il Delfino Via Marina Garibaldi ☎ 090 984 3024, ⊚ ildelfinosalina.it. Smart new rooms with marvelous terraces and views, set back from Lingua's *lungomare*, and older rooms opening directly onto it that are a good bet if you have children. The restaurant is lovely, with tables on the *lungomare*. Half-board-only in Aug. **€240**

Il Gambero Piazza Marina Garibaldi ☎ 090 984 3049, ⊚ ilgamberosalina.it. Above the eponymous restaurant are three rooms with a fabulous shared terrace boasting 360-degree views. The family live half the year in Australia, so speak perfect English. **€100**

La Salina Borgo di Mare Via Manzoni ☎ 090 984 3441, ⊚ lasalinahotel.com. This impressive four-star hotel is set in the restored buildings of the old salt-works, by Lingua's lagoon. The rooms are lovely, individually furnished, most with sea views and private terraces, while traditional tile- and stonework enhances public areas. There's no restaurant, but you can eat at nearby *Il Gambero* on a half-board basis. **€200**

CAPO FARO AND MALFA

Capo Faro Halfway between Santa Marina Salina and Malfa on the main road ☎ 090 984 4330, ⊚ capofaro.it. At the five-star Tasca d'Almerita Malvasia wine estate a series of stunning, contemporary rooms occupy seven Aeolian-style houses that look down across the vineyards. Facilities are top-notch, from magnificent pool to classy bar and restaurant, and you can tour the vineyards on request. No children under 12. **€380**

★ **Signum** Via Scalo 15, Malfa ☎ 090 984 4222, ⊚ hotelsignum.it. Island hotels don't come much better than this, deftly balancing style and luxury with friendly and relaxed service. Thirty comfortable rooms (some classed as superior and deluxe) display a seamless blend of antique furniture and contemporary style and have either terraces or balconies, sea or garden views. There are sea views too, from the splendid infinity pool – indeed swimming here at night and catching sight of Stromboli erupting is an experience that takes some beating. An exquisite spa, tapping into a hot volcanic spring, and offering treatments such as an anti-cellulite caper-rub, is definitely not to be missed. There's also what is probably the island's best restaurant (reservations recommended for non-guests), serving Aeolian specialities. **€280**

16

EATING AND DRINKING

SANTA MARINA DI SALINA

Batana Via Rinascente 17 ☎ 090 984 3311. A peaceful location above the port, sweeping views from its airy roofed terrace and engaging owners make this Santa Marina's top choice for a relaxing meal or extended *aperitivo*. The food is excellent too – the *fritto misto* (€10) of calamari, tiny *ciciarelli* and locally netted prawns is faultless, and the gently spiced and succulent kebab of swordfish (€16) literally melts in the mouth. Deserts are all home-made, and include an apple crumble which may challenge your mum's. Pizza too, from €4.50. Daily 8–10.30pm.

★ **Mamma Santina** Via Sanità ☎ 090 984 3054. This lovely hotel restaurant serves genuine island dishes, using recipes passed down through the generations such as *linguine* with flakes of fish, wine, chilli, garlic and parsley and pasta with a pesto of fourteen herbs. They also do a delicious pasta with melted cheese and courgettes (two people or more). *Secondi* are mostly fish. Pasta dishes from €10, fish from €14. Be sure to try the hot chocolate pudding and the pistacchio *semifreddo*. Daily 12.30–2.30pm & 8–10.30pm; closed mid-Dec to mid-March.

'nni Lausta Via Risorgimento 188 ☎ 090 984 3486. Cool bar-restaurant whose New York-trained owner-chef gives an adventurous twist to local dishes – like raw tuna dressed with wild fennel and capers, or crispy fish cakes made from the day's catch. That said, quality and service can be a bit erratic, and a full meal will cost at least €40 without wine, though you can just have a drink at the bar (until 2am); €5 will buy you a glass of decent Salina wine, with crostini and home-made dips, pestos and salsas. Daily 12.30–2.30pm & 8–10.30pm; closed Nov to March.

Porto Bello Via Bianchi 1 ☎ 090 984 3125. Right above the harbour, and with a terrace looking out to Lipari, this is a reliable and longstanding restaurant owned by a local writer. It serves excellent local antipasti, and is famous (on the island at least) for inventing *pasta al fuoco* – pasta with chopped cherry tomatoes, chilli and grated ricotta – and for serving raw prawns with a yogurt salsa. Both should be tried. Main courses depend on the catch of the day. A four-course meal will cost around €50 or so without wine. A good choice for a splash-out. Daily 12.30–2.30pm & 8–10.30pm; closed winter.

LINGUA

⭐ **Da Alfredo** Piazza Marina Garibaldi ☎ 090 984 3075. Right on the seafront piazza, this little café is famous throughout Italy for its fresh fruit granitas – the summer yachties and boat-trippers queue up for a taste, while Dolce and Gabbana have on occasion brought Naomi Campbell along. The other speciality is *pane cunzato* (from €10), a huge round of grilled bread piled with various combinations of home-cured tuna, capers, tomatoes, baked ricotta and olives. Daily 7.30am–late; closed early Nov to Easter.

RINELLA

Bar Papero Piazzetta Anna Magnani. Run with verve and passion by three siblings, this friendly bar does a great *tavola calda* of home-cooked food (and yummy cakes for afterwards) ideal for lunch or an after-beach *aperitivo*. The same guys also run a fine bar on the terrace below the (otherwise very average) *Hotel Ariana*, a 3min walk away up Via Rotabile. Daily till late.

MALFA

⭐ **Signum** Via Scalo 15 ☎ 090 984 4222, ⊕ hotel signum.it. Young, enthusiastic and attentive staff and great cooking make dinner at the *Signum* special. Signature dishes include an unguent *sformata* of raw prawns with pistachios, light and succulent fish *polpette*, and home-made ravioli stuffed with ricotta, orange and lemon zest, sprinkled with finely chopped lemon leaves. Hotel guests have priority until 4pm, after which bookings are taken from non-residents. Daily 12.30–2.30pm & 8–10.30pm in season.

POLLARA

Al Cappero ☎ 090 984 3968. Simple, family-run place, with something of a Greek taverna feel – make sure you arrive in time to watch the sun set over the islands of Filicudi and Alicudi. *Frittelle di zucchine* (deep-fried courgette fritters) come free, after which there will be two or three pasta dishes (€8–10) of the day, invariably including one dressed with a pesto of their own capers. Fish (€10–12) comes grilled or fried, but the signature dish is a tasty *coniglio in agrodolce*, rabbit stewed in a typical Sicilian sweet–sour sauce. Daily 8–10.30pm; closed Nov–Easter.

Panerea

Only 3km by 1.5km, **PANAREA** is the smallest, loveliest, most painfully stylish and ridiculously expensive of the Aeolians, and in summer its harbours, hotels and villas overflow with an international crowd of designers, models, pop stars, film stars, royalty and their lackeys. In low season, however, the island is an utter delight, accommodation prices relatively sane, and the three-hour walk, up the peak of Pizzo Corvo, and hugging the fractured coastline, one of the most stunning anywhere in Italy.

Cars are banned, and the only transport is by Vespa or electric golf cart. Panarea's couple of hundred year-round inhabitants live in three linked hamlets on the eastern side of the island, Ditella, San Pietro and Drauto, with the boats docking at **San Pietro**. Thirty minutes' walk south of San Pietro, clearly signposted, Zimmari is the island's one sandy **beach**. From here, a steep path leads up to **Punta Milazzese**, where you can see the foundations of 23 Bronze Age huts, with the glorious cove of Cala Junco below. Just before you reach the Bronze Age village is the beginning of the well-marked track up Pizzo Corvo, circling the entire island and ending up at **Calcara** to the north of town, where there are steaming fumaroles on the beach.

ACCOMMODATION   PANAREA

Albergo Girasole Via Drauto ☎ 090 983 018 or ☎ 328 861 8595, ⊕ hotelgirasole-panarea.it. Family-run hotel at Drauto, out on the way to the sandy beach at Zimmari. Great place to stay in low season, but even this part of the island is busy in August. **€240**

Lisca Bianca Via Lani ☎ 090 983 004, ⊕ liscabianca.it. This typical Aeolian building – covered wide terraces, blue shutters, white walls – has some gorgeous views, with stylish rooms overlooking either the sea or the bougainvillea-clad gardens and port. You can see Stromboli from the breakfast terrace, and the bar is one of the best on the island. The *Casa Nonna* annexe has a few cheaper rooms in the village on Via Iditella, and if you can avoid August,

prices aren't too bad at all (website has promotions). Closed Nov–March. **€240**

Pippo and Maria Soldini Via Iditella ☎ 090 983 061 or ☎ 334 703 5010. Up the hill behind the port in Iditella beyond the Carabinieri barracks, these spotlessly clean rooms are among the least expensive places to stay on Panarea. They have their own terraces and are set in a garden and, out of season, owners Pippo and Maria will cook for you. **€120**

Quartara Via S. Pietro ☎ 090 983 027, ⊕ quartarahotel .com. Very classy four-star boutique hotel run by a cheerful family, whose thirteen fashionable rooms have elegant wood furniture and stone floors. A terrace jacuzzi out the

DIVING THE AEOLIANS

There's plenty of fun to be had in Aeolian waters. At **Panarea** you can snorkel over the submerged foundations of a Roman port, and columns of pulsing bubbles around the majestically sculpted islets, or take an easy dive (12–20m) to see what appears to be a submarine snow-storm – the water is full of blobs of a weird white bacteria that grows on sulphur and has the consistency of eggwhite. Also off Panarea are the remains of a British cargo ship deliberately sunk during the Depression as an insurance scam – for the past fifteen years it has been inhabited by a giant fish (about 80kg).

Alternatively, head to the Salinan village of **Pollara**, where a giant offshore crater offers easy diving with lots to see, or explore the wreck of a Roman ship off **Filicudi**; a rope guides you down to the archeological area – a true underwater museum. It is also a beautiful dive, with lots of fish and fascinating rock formations.

The islands' most professional diving outfit is Amphibia, with bases at the ports of Panarea and Salina (☎ 335 613 8529, ⌨ amphibia.it).

back overlooks the port and there's a well-regarded restaurant. Closed Nov–March. **€320**

Raya Via S. Pietro ☎ 090 983 013, ⌨ hotelraya.it. The hotel that put Panarea on the party map. Opened in the 1960s, it remains the hippest, sexiest and most expensive hotel in Sicily, even though owner Myriam Beltrami's refusal to install TVs and telephones means that it has only two stars. The place is built entirely of natural materials, food is organic, though the hotel's claim to be a simple retreat for nature lovers seems a little disingenuous when the place is crawling with party animals. Bar, club and restaurant are down above the harbour, rooms (whitewashed walls, teak furniture, hand-batiked textiles, citronella candles) are built into the hillside above the village, with great views to the sea over groves of olives, hibiscus and bougainvillea. **€540**

EATING AND DRINKING

Da Adelina Via Comunale Mare 28 ☎ 090 983 246, ⌨ adelinapanarea. Intimate candlelit restaurant, with a romantic roof terrace overlooking Panarea's port. Relaxing and unpretentious, with a simple menu of seasonal dishes, such as *moscardini*, tiny octopus, cooked with tomato, capers, wild fennel and chilli (€14) appearing alongside year-round dishes like *pennette adelina*, dressed with anchovies, aubergine, capers, olives, mint and basil (€10). For the main course opt for the mixed fish of the day, either fried or grilled (€18). Daily 12.30–2.30pm & 8–10.30pm; closed Nov–Feb.

Da Francesco Via S. Pietro ☎ 090 983 023, ⌨ dafrancescopanarea.com. Overlooking the harbour, and pretty good value for meals of pasta (around €10–12), including the signature dish "disgraziata" with peppers, chilli, capers, olives, aubergine, tomatoes and baked ricotta, and fish (from €14). It also has rooms to rent in summer, and a smart clothes boutique. Daily 12.30–2.30pm & 8–10.30pm; closed Dec–Feb.

Da Paolino Via Iditella 75 ☎ 090 983 008. Walking north towards Ditella, after 10min or so you'll reach this family-run restaurant whose terrace has fine views of Stromboli. You can spend quite a bit here, but an unpretentious meal of pasta and salad and a glass of wine will cost you around €20 – try the rich *mille baci* pasta with greens (€10) – and the fish is whatever the family have caught that day. Daily 12.30–2.30pm & 8–10.30pm; closed Nov–March.

Stromboli

Despite the regularity of the volcanic explosions, people have always lived on **STROMBOLI**. It is in a constant state of activity, throwing up fountains of fire and glowing rock every twenty minutes or so. A full eruption happens on average every ten years. A flow of lava is often visible from afar, slowly sliding down the northwest side of the volcano into the sea. In January 2003 there was a colossal landslide, triggering a 10m-high tsunami that inundated the coasts of Sicily and Calabria.

Most of the many hotels and rooms to let on the island are on the eastern side, in the adjacent parishes of San Vincenzo, San Bartolo and Piscità, often grouped together as **Stromboli Town** and something of a chic resort since Rossellini and Ingrid Bergman immortalized the place in the 1949 film *Stromboli*. From the quayside, the lower coastal road runs around to the beach of **Ficogrande** and, further on, **Piscità**, where there's a series of tiny lava coves with ashy sand. It's around 25 minutes on foot from

16

the port to here. The other road from the dock cuts up to the **Piazza di San Vincenzo**, which offers glorious views of the offshore islet of Strombolicchio.

On the other side of the island, accessible by hydrofoil, the hamlet of **Ginostra** is a laidback place of steeply terraced, white Aeolian houses, where the only way of getting about is on foot or donkey. **Hydrofoils** run back to Stromboli Town twice a day in summer (once daily in winter), but these are susceptible to cancellation because of rough waters.

GETTING AROUND AND TOURS   STROMBOLI

Taxis and lapas The only transport on the island is three-wheeler pick-up (the Ape, or bee, known as a *lapa*, hereabouts), motorbike or electric car – so if your hotel is any distance from the port you may need a taxi. The only official taxis are the electric golf carts, though unofficial *lapas* may offer their services. Despite this, as the electric cars take 10hr to charge for every 2hr driving, demand quite often simply outstrips supply. It is to be hoped that some solution is found, but as a precaution, ask your hotel at the time of booking if it can organize transport for you.

Of the official taxis, Sabbia Nera (☎ 090 986 399), based near the port, are reliable and friendly.

Boat trips The best boat trips are the tours around the island, calling at Ginostra and Strombolicchio (around 2hr 30min; €30), and trips out at night to see the Sciara del Fuoco (around 1hr 20min; €25. Try Pippo (☎ 338 985 7883), who has a stand in front of the *Beach Bar*, or Paola and Giovanni (☎ 338 431 2803), who work from opposite the *Sirenetta* hotel in Ficogrande.

ACCOMMODATION

In summer, the quayside is thick with three-wheelers and touts offering rooms; prices start at around €25 per person. If you have a booking and are arriving in summer, ask your hotel to arrange a pick-up if you are far from the port or have baggage.

Casa del Mulino Piscità ☎ 338 540 8931, ✉ michele .wegner@gmail.com. Friendly laidback scruffy-bohemian place with four simple rooms (including two adjacent triples with their own terrace and kitchen) in an old windmill perched right on the lava-cliff edge above a black sandy cove. **€75**

Casa del Sole Via Soldato Cincotta, Piscità ☎ 090 986 300. A cheapie in an old building within metres of the sea. Simple 4- to 6-bed apartments are available all year, and accommodation is pretty flexible, whether you want a single or multi-bed room. Kitchen facilities are available, and there's a sun terrace. No credit cards. **€60**

La Sirenetta Park Via Marina 33, Ficogrande ☎ 090 986 025, 🌐 lasirenettahotel.it. Four-star hotel set opposite the black sands of Ficogrande. It's also got a decent-sized outdoor pool, a summer nightclub and access

to watersports facilities. The room rates drop considerably outside summer and at the beginning or end of the season you can stay for around €120. Closed Nov to March. **€240**

★ **Locanda del Barbablù** Via Vittorio Emanuele 17 ☎ 090 986 118, 🌐 barbablu.it. An old Aeolian house, with antique rooms with four-poster beds and original tile floors, provides the most relaxed accommodation on Stromboli. It's combined with a restaurant where you can dine under the stars. Closed Nov–Feb. **€290**

Petrusa Ginostra ☎ 090 981 2305. Ginostra's only official accommodation (though you may find rooms if you ask around) has three large rooms with their own terraces, sharing a bathroom. Half-board is obligatory in July and Aug; you can eat at their bar-restaurant, *L'Incontro*, which has fairly high prices (everything has to be shipped in) but is pretty good. No credit cards. Closed Oct–April. **€110**

CLIMBING STROMBOLI

Guides for the **ascent of the volcano** cost around €28 per person, though if eruptions are thought to be dangerous, the mountain is closed; try Magmatrek on Via Vittorio Emanuele (☎ 090 986 5768, 🌐 magmatrek.it), where the staff are well informed and in constant radio contact with the volcanologists at the control centre. The climb up takes three hours, and you are expected to go at a fair whack; at first, it is no different from climbing any mountain, then suddenly all vegetation stops, giving way to black ash strewn with small jagged boulders spewed out by the volcano. Once on the top, all you can see at first are clouds of white steam – then suddenly there will be a resounding clash, the clouds glow red, and spouts of fire shoot up into the air, the glowing boulders drawing tracks of red light across the night sky. You should not attempt the climb alone. Be equipped for a tough-ish hike, and for a night climb bring warm clothes and a torch.

16

Vilaggio Stromboli Via Regina Elena ☎090 986 018, ⓦvillaggiostromboli.it. With simple rooms jutting up against the breaking waves, this pleasant, quiet place is one of the nicest seaside stays; it also has a good terrace restaurant where you can gaze out over the water. €190

EATING AND DRINKING

La Lampara Via Vittorio Emanuele ☎090 986 009. Dine on the large raised terrace under a pergola of climbing vines among huge pots of basil and rosemary on pizza, pasta and grilled meat and fish. Pizza from €6. Daily 12.30–2.30pm & 8–10.30pm; closed Nov–March.

Locanda del Barbablù Via Vittorio Emanuele 17 ☎090 986 118, ⓦbarbablu.it. Stylish restaurant, specializing in fresh fish and vegetables which keeps things simple by offering just two menus that change every day. A full *degustazione* menu costs €50 with wine extra. Mid-June to mid-Sept daily 12.30–2.30pm & 8–10.30pm; other times of the year open on request.

Zurro Via Marina s/n ☎090 986 283. Not exactly romantic, with its startlingly bright lights, but you eat well at *Zurro*, named for its bearded, piratical-looking chef, a one-time fisherman. Razor-thin slices of raw aubergine, flecked with chilli flakes served with balsamic-dressed rocket and parmesan, *spaghetti alla strombolana*, with cherry tomatoes, anchovies, mint, chilli and garlic (€14) or *pietre di mare* – black ravioli stuffed with *ricciola* (amberjack) and dressed with capers, cherry tomatoes and basil (€14). The chocolate cake is a must. Daily 12.30–2.30pm & 8–10.30pm; closed Nov–March.

Filicudi

FILICUDI, the larger of the two most westerly islands, is a fascinating place, the contours of its sheer slopes traced with steep stone terraces and crisscrossed by stone mule tracks. It is an island best explored by foot, which is just as well, as there is no public transport. The tarmac road that connects the several small settlements gives a false impression of the island, making villages seem far apart when they are, in fact, just a few minutes' walk away, at least if you are fit: most of the tracks are pretty steep, occasionally following, but mostly cutting between, the ancient terraces carved into the slopes of maquis and prickly pear.

The main settlement is **Filicudi Porto**, which has a couple of shops, bars, hotels and a pharmacy. Inland, accessible by road or mule track, are three whitewashed villages, **Valdichiesa**, **Rocche Ciauli** and **Pecorini**. And down on the west coast, about 3km by road from the port, is the lovely little seaside village of **Pecorini Mare**.

GETTING AROUND   FILICUDI

There is no public transport. If you are not up to walking, a red minivan-taxi meets most boat arrivals (€12 to Pecorini Mare). If it's not there, or if you want to book him in advance call D&G Servizio Navetta (☎347 757 5916). Although distances by road can seem considerable, the islands is crisscrossed with a series of mule tracks, which – as long as you don't mind a steepish climb – can get you from one village to another far more quickly than you might imagine.

ACCOMMODATION AND EATING

★ **La Canna** Via Rosa 43, Rocche Ciauli ☎090 988 9956, ⓦlacannahotel.it. The best choice near the port, though it's a stiff climb up the steps to Rocche Ciauli; call ahead and they'll pick you up from the dock. Ten lovely bright rooms

> ## ZUCCO GRANDE: THE ABANDONED VILLAGE
> There are plenty of good **walks** along the ancient mule tracks of Filicudi: one of the nicest is out to the abandoned village of **Zucco Grande**. Walk up to *La Canna* hotel (see above) from the port – follow the well-kept stone mule track that begins from a point almost opposite the hydrofoil and ferry dock – then continue until you meet the tarmacked road. The path continues on the other side of the road, heading towards the settlement of Valdichiesa. After about twenty minutes, the path forks, and you'll see the first of several signs to Zucco Grande. The path is well marked, following the contours through a prickly terrain of gorse, lentisk, prickly pear and euphorbia. Another twenty minutes brings you to the village, abandoned forty years ago when its last inhabitants left for Australia. A couple of pioneering souls have bought ruins here, which are being renovated, but at the moment there is just one inhabitant, Giovanni, who has a couple of **rooms** and can provide a basic dinner (☎347 813 2579).

16

with tiled bathrooms open onto a spacious terrace with a magnificent view over the bay below. There's a small pool (summer only), and the food here is excellent – home-made pasta, fresh fish, local caper salads and plenty of home-produced wine and fruit. Half-board obligatory in Aug. **€200**

★ **La Sirena** Pecorini Mare ☎090 988 9997, ⓦpensionelasirena.it. An oasis you won't want to leave, this cosy inn sits right on the Pecorini Mare seafront, with the fishing boats drawn up alongside. A varied selection of

rooms is available, some with antique furniture and little waterfront balconies, others in self-contained houses not far away. Out on the shaded terrace is the island's most relaxed restaurant (lunch & dinner, non-guests welcome). It gets very busy in Aug, but at most times of year all you can hear is the sound of lapping water as you tuck into the likes of spaghetti with almond sauce and fresh grilled tuna. Half-board-only July & Aug (€110–120 per person). Closed Oct–May. **€140**

Alicudi

End-of-the-line Europe doesn't come much more remote than **ALICUDI**, a stark cone rising from the sea two and a half hours from Milazzo by hydrofoil. Electricity arrived only in the 1990s, and the sole way of getting about is on foot, though the six donkeys are used to carry heavy loads. There are just eighty year-round inhabitants, while superstitions and sightings of ghosts abound – as does the conviction that some Alicudari are blessed with the power to control the weather and divert cyclones. Up the sheer slope behind the tiny port, terraced smallholdings and whitewashed flat-roofed houses linked by lava-paved paths cling on for dear life, among bursts of bougainvillea.

Hiking on Alicudi

Most of the **hiking** here is up stepped tracks that seem to have been designed with giants in mind, so be prepared for a good deal of calf-work. If you don't fancy hauling yourself to the top (675m; 2hr), you'll still get plenty of exercise climbing up to the church of San Bartolomeo, where controversy rages over the removal of the statue of the saint to a more easily accessible church lower down the hill (it is said that since the statue was moved, the island has had bad luck). Otherwise, follow the path north out of the port behind the church of the Carmine, from where it's an easy walk to the narrow stony beach of Bazzina, with a couple of smallholdings behind it.

ACCOMMODATION AND EATING | ALICUDI

Silvio Taranto Via Regina Elena ☎090 988 9922. Although there is a modern hotel in the port, the most interesting option is to call Silvio, a local who speaks English and can put you in touch with people who have rooms to rent. For twenty years he and his wife have been

cooking dinner at their house above the port for whoever needs a place to eat. There's no menu and no choice, and everyone eats the same, sitting at long tables on the family's terrace, drinking locally produced red wine. Expect to pay around €25 per person for dinner. **€50**

The Ionian coast

Sicily's eastern **Ionian coast** draws the largest number of visitors, attracted by **Taormina**, most chic of the island's resorts and famed for its remarkable Greco-Roman theatre, and **Mount Etna**, Europe's highest volcano. Further south, out of the lee of Etna, **Siracusa** was formerly the most important and beautiful city in the Hellenistic world, its enchanting *centro storico* surrounded by water.

Messina and south

MESSINA may well be your first sight of Sicily, and – from the ferry – it's a fine one, the glittering town spread up the hillside beyond the sickle-shaped harbour. Sadly, the image is shattered almost as soon as you step into the city, bombed and shaken to a shadow of its former self by plague, cholera and earthquakes. The great earthquake of 1908 killed 84,000 people, levelled the city and made the shore sink by half a metre overnight. Allied bombing raids in 1943 didn't help, undoing much of the post-earthquake restoration.

Today, the remodelled city guards against future natural disasters, with wide streets and low, reinforced concrete buildings marching off in all directions. Not surprisingly, it's a pretty dull spectacle, and there's little point in hanging around for longer than you need to.

Indeed, poor old Messina is the place to be only on the feast of the Assumption, or **Ferragosto** (Aug 15), when a towering carriage, the Vara – an elaborate column supporting dozens of papier-mâché putti and angels, topped by the figure of Christ – is hauled through the city centre, followed by a firework display on the seafront.

ARRIVAL AND DEPARTURE

MESSINA

By train Messina is connected by direct train with Milazzo, Catania, Taormina, Siracusa, Cefalù and Palermo. It is also the last station in Sicily for trains heading to Italy across the Straits – the trains shunt onto ferries, which carry them over to Villa San Giovanni. All trains pass through the Stazione Centrale, adjacent to the Stazione Maríttima by the harbour, where train-ferries from Calabria dock.

By bus If you are going to the Aeolian Islands it is usually better to take the bus, which stops right at Milazzo's port. Destinations Catania (approx hourly; 1hr 35min); Catania airport (approx hourly; 1hr 50min); Milazzo (approx hourly; 50min); Palermo (6 daily; 2hr 40min); Randazzo (2 daily; 1hr 50min); Taormina (9 daily; 1hr–1hr 50min).

By ferry or hydrofoil To get to the hydrofoil dock (for the Aeolian Islands and Reggio di Calabria) from Messina Centrale walk straight along platform 1, which brings you to the Stazione Maríttima. The hydrofoil dock is straight across the road. Allow 10min on foot if you have luggage. On no account take a taxi from outside the station – they will attempt to charge €15. There is one hydrofoil daily to Reggio di Calabria and the Aeolian Islands throughout the year, and four daily in summer (mid-June to mid-Sept). Car ferries: Car ferries (to and from Villa San Giovanni and Reggio di Calabria) dock and depart several times an hour at quays further to the north, on Via della Libertà, and are well signposted.

INFORMATION

Tourist offices There are two tourist offices just outside the train station: one on Piazza della Repubblica (Mon–Thurs 9am–1.30pm & 3–5pm, Fri 9am–1.30pm; sometimes also open Sat mornings; ☎090 672 944), where good English is spoken, the other just beyond on Via Calabria (Mon–Sat 8am–6.30pm; ☎090 674 236, ⓦaziendaturismomessina .it); both can supply you with Aeolian Islands ferry timetables and accommodation lists.

ACCOMMODATION

Grand Hotel Liberty Via I Settembre 15 ☎090 640 9436, ⓦnh-hotels.it. International-style comfort in a grandish hotel kitted out in vague Liberty style (Art Nouveau motifs on doors, bedheads, wallpaper). Best feature is the roof-top terrace where breakfast is served in good weather. Good deals online. **€120**

Mirage Via N. Scotto 3 ☎090 293 8844, ⓦhotel miragemessina.it. A 1960s period piece, on a narrow alley behind the station with lots of formica, abundant plaster Madonnas and curling posters of Padre Pio and obscure local beauty spots. Friendly owners, and all rooms have phones and bathrooms. **€50**

EATING AND DRINKING

Messina has some good restaurants, many serving freshly caught swordfish from the straits – particularly in May and June, at the height of the swordfish season.

Billé Piazza Cairoli 7 ☎090 781 311. One of Piazza Cairoli's two long-established cafés – both of them Messina institutions. Good range of *cornetti* and other pastries for breakfast, savouries for lunch and cakes for tempting afternoon teas. There are seats outside across the road in the piazza – though service is not always up to scratch. 7.30am–late; closed Tues.

Fratelli La Bufala Corso Vittorio Emanuele 1 ☎090 662 513, ⓦfratellilabufala.eu. A branch of the superior Neapolitan pizza chain committed to using no hydrogenated fats, glutamates or genetically modified ingredients: it is handy for the hydrofoil dock and serves up great pizza (with buffalo mozzarella, of course) along with buffalo-meat *secondi* and Campanian wines. Two could eat a pizza and have a glass of wine for less than €20. Daily 12.30–2.30pm & 8–10.30pm.

Irrera Piazza Cairoli 12 ☎090 673 823, ⓦirrera.it. Founded in 1910, this historic *pasticceria* makes typical Sicilian biscuits, cakes, pastries, *cornetti* and *cannoli* that are if anything even better than at *Billé*, while slick service during lunch (good sandwiches) and the *aperitivo* hour make this a popular spot throughout the day. Daily 7.30am–late.

16

Taormina

TAORMINA, perched high on Monte Tauro, with Mount Etna as backdrop, looks down on two grand, sweeping bays and is Sicily's best-known resort. D.H. Lawrence was so enraptured that he lived here from 1920–23, in a house at the top of the valley cleft, behind the remains of the Greek theatre. Although international tourism has taken its toll, Taormina is still a very charming town, peppered with small, intimate piazzas. The single traffic-free main street is an unbroken line of fifteenth- to nineteenth-century *palazzi* decked out with flower-filled balconies, and there is an agreeably crumbly castle. The downside is that between June and August it's virtually impossible to find anywhere to stay, and the narrow alleys are shoulder-to-shoulder with tourists. April, May or September are slightly better, but to avoid the crowds completely come between October and March, when it's often still warm enough to swim in the sea.

As well as the Greek theatre, there are several vestiges of Roman Taormina around town, including a small **Odeon** (used for musical recitations) next to the tourist office. Really, though, Taormina's attractions are all to do with strolling and window-shopping along the Corso. Centre of town is **Piazza IX Aprile**, with its restored twelfth-century **Torre dell'Orologio** and fabulous views of Etna and the bay from the terraces of its pricey cafés.

The Teatre Greco

Daily 9am–1hr before sunset • €8

The views from the **Teatro Greco** are arguably more stunning than the ruins themselves, encompassing southern Calabria, the Sicilian coastline down to Siracusa and the smouldering heights of Etna. The theatre was founded by Greeks in the third century BC but the visible remains are almost entirely Roman, dating from the end of the first century AD, when Taormina thrived under imperial Roman rule. The theatre was converted to stage gladiatorial combat and a deep trench was dug in the orchestra to accommodate animals and fighters. Between July and August the theatre hosts an international **arts festival** including film, theatre and music (tickets and information from the tourist office).

16

Taormina's beaches

The huge resort of **Giardini-Naxos**, just to the south of Taormina, is a favourite with international package companies, and best avoided: **Mazzarò**, the closest beach to town is lovelier by far. With a much-photographed offshore islet, several fish trattorias and a **cable car** that runs every fifteen minutes from Via Pirandello (the road that encircles old Taormina), it's an ideal place to relax after sightseeing or shopping.

ARRIVAL AND DEPARTURE — TAORMINA

By train Trains pull up at the handsome Taormina-Giardini station on the water's edge, below town. It's a very steep 30min walk up to Taormina (turn right out of the station and then, after 200m, left through a gap in the buildings, marked "Centro") and the road is extremely busy. Much better to take one of the Interbus buses (every 30min to an hour) that pick up outside the train station.

By bus Buses arrive at the terminal on Via Luigi Pirandello in town.

Destinations Catania (16 daily; 1hr 40min); Catania airport (6 daily Mon–Sat; 1hr 25min).

By car If you're arriving by car, make for the Porta Catania multistorey car park, situated below Piazza S. Antonio.

Tourist office Palazzo Corvaja, off Piazza Vittorio Emanuele (Mon–Thurs 8.30am–2pm & 4–7pm, Fri 8.30am–2pm; ⊕0942 23 243, ⊛gate2taormina.com).

ACCOMMODATION

El Jebel Salita Palazzo Ciampoli ⊕0942 625 494, ⊛hoteleljebel.com. Taormina's shrine to conspicuous consumption, its nine suites occupying three floors of a dandified fifteenth-century *palazzo* up a flight of steps from the main *corso*. There's no trace of anything medieval inside, instead it's all very Hollywood-Dubai: lavish bathrooms caked in treacly, liquorice-veined marble, gold taps, claw-foot baths, and enough mirrors to make narcissists feel they've died and gone to heaven. The rooms themselves are more subdued, spacious and very comfortable. Service is excellent, and waiter-served breakfasts are exceptional. Expect to feel discreetly pampered, especially at the spa. Suites only from €430

Pensione Svizzera Via Pirandello 26 ⊕0942 23 790,

ⓦhotelpensionesvizzera.com. Just up from the bus terminal and cable-car station this comfortable hotel has excellent views from its spacious rooms (with prices increasing by €5–10 for a sea view), 24hr bar service, free wi-fi throughout and a shuttle to a private beach. Excellent value for money. €115

San Domenico Palace Piazza S. Domenico 5 ⓣ0942 613 111, ⓦthi.it. The last word in luxury. One of the most celebrated hotels in Italy, housed in a fifteenth-century convent, with gorgeous formal gardens, unsurpassable views, a Michelin-starred restaurant, and stratospheric prices. Staff are refreshingly both relaxed and gracious. Luxuriate in one of the €3000-per-night suites, and you feel you've died and gone to heaven, but do check the website as there are deals on rooms for a fraction of that. €500

Taormina's Odyssey Via Paterno di Biscaria 13, near Porta Catania ⓣ0942 24 533 ⓦtaorminaodyssey.com. Homely and comfortable, with four double rooms and two dorms, this is more of a B&B than a hostel. There is a kitchen, rooms have a/c and TV, and there's even a terrace. It is understandably popular, so book well ahead. Dorms €20, doubles €45

Villa Belvedere Via Bagnoli Croce 79 ⓣ0942 23 791, ⓦvillabelvedere.it. Decent, if unexciting rooms; there's a great pool in a lavish garden, and fantastic views. Look out for good deals €90–195

Villa Carlotta Via Pirandello 81 ⓣ0942 626 058, ⓦhotel villacarlottataormina.com. Splendidly sited above the sea among abundant subtropical vegetation, this hotel could not be anywhere other than Taormina. There's a roof garden with spectacular views of Mount Etna and the sea (very romantic and candle-lit at night), and a terraced garden with a small pool set among citrus and olive trees, bougainvillea and mint, lying between the walls of an old chapel and remains of a Romano-Byzantine cemetery. There's a comfortable, homely sitting room with books, games and snooze-inducing sofas, and all the stylish rooms but one have bathtubs. Good deals on website. €299

Villa Floresta Via Damiano Rosso 1 ⓣ0942 620 184, ⓦvillafloresta.it. Pleasant, family-run B&B in a nineteenth-century *palazzo* tucked into a courtyard with a crumbling fifteenth-century staircase behind Piazza del Duomo. Most rooms have balconies, with views of the sea or the Duomo. €90

Villa Greta Via Leonardo da Vinci 41 ⓣ0942 28 286, ⓦvillagreta.it. Family-run place 15min walk out of town on the road up to Castelmola, with superb balcony views, as well as a dining room with good home-cooking. In winter, there's tea with complimentary home-made cakes and biscuits. €108

★ **Villa Sara** Via Leonardo da Vinci 55 ⓣ0942 28 138, ⓦvillasara.net. Exceptional B&B a 15min walk (or a brief bus ride) up the road to Castelmola. It doesn't look much from the outside, but behind the bare walls is a gracious two-storey apartment where a friendly family rent out three spacious rooms, each with its own bathroom and its own large terrace commanding great views over Taormina, Etna and the sea. €90

Villa Schuler Piazzetta Bastione ⓣ0942 23 481, ⓦvillaschuler.com. This lovely old hotel has been in the same family of German émigrés for a century, and retains the feel of an elegant family-run *pensione* (they take no tour groups). There are great views from its rooms and terrace, and a beautiful garden behind. Worth checking the website for special offers. €180

16

EATING, DRINKING AND NIGHTLIFE

Eating in Taormina can be an expensive business. For snacks or picnic ingredients, head for the indoor market off Via Cappuccini (mornings only, Mon–Sat). Nightlife in Taormina is none too exciting, with most of the action focused on the gay bars around gorgeous Piazza Paladini, just off the Corso.

A'Zammara Via Fratelli Bandiera 15 ⓣ0942 24 408, ⓦazammara.it. Romantic place where you sit in a garden of orange trees eating the likes of home-made *tagliolini* with prawns and pistachios – the latter from nearby Bronte (€12.50), or *involtini di pesce spada*, swordfish wrapped around cheese and breadcrumbs (€16). Expect to pay around €40 for a full meal including wine. Daily 12.30–2.30pm & 8–10.30pm.

Al Grappola d'Uva Via Bagnoli Croce 6–8 ⓣ0942 625 874, ⓦalgrappoladuva.net. Friendly, unpretentious wine bar – a good place to sample Etna wines with olives and local cheeses (€4 including nibbles). They can also organize tours of Etna's vineyards. Open daily all day.

Re di Bastoni Corso Umberto I ⓣ0942 23 037. For unpretentious after-dinner boozing head for the boho *Re di Bastoni*, quite alternative for Taormina and attracting a lively crowd. Around 6pm–late; closed Mon in winter.

Trattoria da Nino Via Luigi Pirandello 37 ⓣ0942 21 265. Welcoming place that, despite its touristy appearance, is popular with locals for its fresh food: the moderately priced mixed vegetable (€12) or mixed fish antipasti (€15) are particularly good. Servings are ample, so you should be able to eat well for around €25. Daily 12.30–2.30pm & 8–10.30pm.

Vecchia Taormina Vico Ebrei 3 ⓣ0942 625 589. Popular pizzeria in an alley across from the Duomo serving light, blistered pizzas (from €6.90) from its wood-fired oven. Daily 12.30pm–late.

Wunderbar Café Piazza IX Aprile ⓣ0942 625 302. Once the haunt of Garbo and Fassbinder, this is the place to splash out on an aperitif or after-dinner drink – go for an Aperol spritz. Open daily all day.

Mount Etna and the Gole di Alcantara

The bleak lava wilderness around the summit of **Etna** is one of the most memorable landscapes Italy has to offer. The volcano's height is constantly shifting, depending on whether eruptions are constructive or destructive, and over the last century it has ranged from 3263m to the present estimate of 3340m. Whatever its exact height, Etna is a substantial mountain, one of the world's biggest active volcanoes, and on a clear day it can be seen from well over half of Sicily. Some of its eruptions have been disastrous: in 1169, 1329 and 1381 the lava reached the sea and in 1669 Catania was wrecked and its castle surrounded by molten rock. The Circumetnea railway line has been repeatedly ruptured by lava flows: nine people were killed on the edge of the main crater in 1979 and in 2001 military helicopters were called in to water-bomb blazing fires. This unpredictability means that it is no longer possible to get close to the main crater. An eruption in 1971 destroyed the observatory supposed to give warning of just such an event, and the volcano has been in an almost continual **state of eruption** since 1998, the most recent being in late 2002 when the resort of Piano Provenzana on the northern side was engulfed with lava. If you do attempt the summit, be sure to heed the warnings.

While in the area, try to make time, too, for the dramatic riverscapes of the **Gole di Alcantara**, between the northern slopes of Etna and the foothills of the Peloritani mountains.

Mount Etna: the ascent

There are several **approaches** to the volcano. If you have a car, you can enjoy some of the best scenery on the north side of the volcano by taking the circular road that leads up from **Linguaglossa** to Piano Provenzana, a good place to bring the kids to learn to ski or toboggan. Note that the ski season on Etna lasts from around November to March.

16

TOURING ETNA'S FOOTHILLS: THE CIRCUMETNEA RAILWAY

A private line, 114km long, the **Circumetnea railway** (☎095 541 250, ⊛circumetnea.it) runs around the base of the volcano passing lava-strewn slopes. The line runs between Catania and Giarre-Riposto, taking about three hours and thirty minutes, and you could start either at Catania (Borgo Stazione, see p.910) or, if approaching from Taormina, at Giarre. There are usually about five services daily in winter and four in summer. Returning to Catania by regular train from Giarre will take twenty minutes, and the journey between Giarre and Taormina also twenty minutes.

Getting off the train to visit some of the towns en route is possible, but not always easy: at **Bronte** for example, which produces eighty percent of Italy's pistachios, the town centre is a long, steep climb up from the station, though the pistachio ice creams and other sweet goodies on offer in its cafés might persuade you it is worth it. You might want to make a beeline for the little village of **Maletto** in June, when it hosts a strawberry festival, the Sagra di Fragola, while for anyone interested in wine, a stop at **Passopisciaro** and **Solicchiata** is a must: a rare chance to visit pre-phylloxera vineyards, and avant-garde producers such as Frank Cornellisen (☎0942 986 315), who shuns the use of sulphates, and Andrea Franchetti (☎338 130 0778), producer of the internationally renowned and prize-winning Passopisciaro.

Most people, however, choose to break the journey at dark, medieval **Randazzo**, the town closest to the summit of Etna, and built entirely of lava. Dangerously near Etna, Randazzo has never actually been engulfed, although the lava flow came so close in 1981 that the town was evacuated: you can see the lava fields clearly on the fringes of town. Poke around the dour streets – meticulously restored after being bombed to bits in 1943, when it figured as the last Sicilian stronghold of the Axis forces – and stop for lunch at *San Giorgio e Il Drago*, Piazza San Giorgio 28 (☎095 923 972; lunch & dinner closed Tues & most of Jan), a trattoria in a nineteenth-century wine cellar. If you decide you want to stay close to Etna, the nicest place, especially if you have children, is the *Turismo Rurale Parco Statella* (☎095 924 036, ⊛parcostatella.com; €74), an eighteenth-century villa with a vast park, horseriding, and its own restaurant, 2km outside town on the way to Linguaglossa.

ETNA AND ALCANTARA ACTIVITIES

The **visitor centre** (8am to 1hr before sunset; ☎0942 985 010, ⊛terralcantara.it; €8 entry, plus extra for excursions) at Motta Camastra (see below) arranges excursions in the Etna region. You can go on guided walks, take on whitewater rafting, or rent waders and salopettes to waddle and splash down the river when the water level is deemed low enough to be safe. There are also guided quad excursions in the Alcantara valley or up Mount Etna (☎339 879 2940, ⊛siciliaquad.com).

On public transport, you'll just see Etna from the southern side, though this does at least get you pretty near the summit. Although there are frequent **buses** to Nicolosi from Catania, only one (around 8am from outside Catania train station) continues to the **Hotel/Rifugio Sapienza** at the end of the negotiable road up the south side of Etna.

There are two ways **up the volcano** from the refuge, by foot or cable car. Now open again after being destroyed in the last eruption, **cable cars** run between 9am and sunset, weather permitting (€60.50 return). The price includes a minibus from the top cable-car station to just below the main crater, though many people prefer to walk. **Walking up** from *Rifugio Sapienza* will take around four hours. Arriving on the early-morning bus, you should have enough time to make it to the top and get back for the return bus to Catania – it leaves around 4.30pm from the hotel.

However you go, at whatever time of year, take warm clothes, good shoes or boots and glasses to keep the flying grit out of your eyes. You can rent boots and jackets cheaply from the cable-car station. Food up the mountain is poor and overpriced.

16

ACCOMMODATION AND EATING · MOUNT ETNA

Hotel/Rifugio Sapienza Piazzale Rifugio Sapienza, Nicolosi Nord, Etna Sud ☎095 915 321, ⊛rifugiosapienza.com. Simple, but comfortable (with central heating in winter) this *rifugio* right by the cable-car station is more like a little Alpine hotel than a refuge. It doesn't have the "away from it all" feel of *Ragabo* or *Citelli*, but is the only refuge accessible on public transport. There are 25 rooms, all with TV and private bathroom, and a decent restaurant too. Half-board is €75 per person. Doubles **€110**

Rifugio Citelli Clearly signposted and marked on all maps ☎095 930 000, ⊛rifugiocitelli.com. A tiny, spartan *rifugio* dating back to the 1930s, from which the views on a clear day stretch to the Aspromonte mountains

of Calabria. When it is open, there is basic accommodation – and occasional mountain-sausage dinners – and an annual programme of excursions ranging from trekking to snow-shoeing. Doubles **€70**

Rifugio Ragabo Strada Mareneve, Pineta Bosco Ragabo, Linguaglossa ☎095 647 841, ⊛ragabo.it. Cosy and warm, this Alpine-style *rifugio*, 1450m above sea level, is the perfect place to get away from it all. It has little pine bedrooms and a restaurant where you can keep the cold at bay with hearty mountain fare. There are excursions and treks available, and they can help you organize skiing. Half-board is €50 per person. Doubles **€70**

The Alcantara valley

Around 2400 BC, the volcano of Monte Moia, at the head of the Alcantara valley, erupted, smothering the river and filling the valley with lava. Over four millennia, the river has carved its way through the deposits of slick grey basalt, scooping it into all manner of strange, sculptural rock formations. Heading along the SS185 from the coast just south of Taormina, the most theatrical (and touristy) part of the gorge is at **Motta Camastra**. There's a **visitor centre** (see box above), a restaurant and souvenir shops. A couple of hundred metres after the visitor centre, there is free public access to the gorge, down a flight of steps.

Francavilla di Sicilia

If you want to escape the crowds, continue another 4km to the largely modern town of **Francavilla di Sicilia**. Here, following brown signs to *Le Gurne*, you twist up to the ancient, and largely abandoned, centre of town, from where a well-marked path winds down to the river, through groves of citrus and nut trees overlooked by a toothy old castle. Here you'll find a series of waterfalls and natural round ponds where you can swim.

Castiglione di Sicilia

The nicest place to stay in the Alcantara valley is **Castiglione di Sicilia**. Fused to a hilltop high above the valley, the town's lovely weather-eroded houses with pantiled roofs cluster below the remains of a castle founded in the fifth century BC by Greek exiles from nearby Naxos. There are plenty of old churches to poke around, though the most remarkable of these is a perfectly restored Byzantine chapel in the valley below, known as "La Cuba" for its perfect symmetry. Behind "La Cuba" a path leads to the river, where there are more little waterfalls and pools.

ACCOMMODATION AND EATING   **CASTIGLIONE DI SICILIA**

Hotel Federico II Via Maggiore Baracca 2 ☎ 0942 980 368, ⓦ hotelfedericosecondo.com. A chic yet reasonably priced little hotel just off the main piazza with an excellent restaurant, *Sine Tempore* (open to non-residents as well) serving local produce to great effect in simple, tasty dishes. The mixed antipasto (€10) is a great way of trying lots of local goodies, while to follow there is *tagliatelle Federico Secondo* (with porcini mushrooms, courgettes and pancetta; €9) or handmade ravioli dressed with pistachios from Bronte (€10). If you're lucky there'll be fresh ricotta warm from the factory at lunchtime and breakfast. Restaurant sometimes closed Wed if there are no guests in the hotel. **€100**

Catania

Bang in the middle of the Ionian coast, **CATANIA** is Sicily's second-largest city, a major transport hub, a thriving commercial centre, and a lively, energetic place with a more international outlook than Palermo. Defined by Etna – even the city's main street is named after the volcano – and the ubiquitous black-grey volcanic stone in pavements and buildings, there's more openness and space than in Palermo, but far less to see, as the ancient and medieval city was engulfed by lava in 1669, and then devastated by an earthquake in 1693. Spearheaded by architect Giovanni Vaccarini, Catania was rebuilt swiftly and on a grand scale, making full use of the lava that had been the old city's nemesis.

Piazza del Duomo

Catania's main square, **Piazza del Duomo**, is a handy orientation point and a stop for most city buses: **Via Etnea** heads north, lined with the city's most fashionable shops and cafés; the fish market and port lie behind to the south; the train station to the east; and the best of the Baroque quarter to the west. It's also one of Sicily's most attractive city squares, rebuilt completely in the first half of the eighteenth century by Vaccarini. Most striking of the buildings is the **Municipio** on the northern side, best seen from the central reserve of the piazza beside the **elephant fountain**, the city's symbol, an eighteenth-century lava elephant supporting an Egyptian obelisk on its back.

The Duomo

Daily 9am–noon & 4–6pm • Free

The **Duomo**, on the piazza's eastern flank, retains marvellous volcanic-rock medieval apses (seen through the gate at Via Vittorio Emanuele 159), though the rest was remodelled by Vaccarini, who incorporated granite columns from Catania's Roman amphitheatre (see p.910) onto the facade. The interior has a series of richly adorned chapels, notably the Cappella di Sant'Agata to the right of the choir, which holds the relics of the saint paraded through the city on her feast day.

From the market to the Castello Ursino

Near the Duomo is Catania's **market**, with slabs and buckets full of twitching fish, endless lanes of vegetable and fruit stalls, and a couple of excellent lunchtime trattorias. From here you can wind through an atmospheric, if dilapidated, neighbourhood to an open space punctured by the **Castello Ursino** (Mon–Fri 9am–1pm & 2.30–7pm,

Sat 9am–8pm; €6; ☎095 345 830), once the proud fortress of Frederick II. Originally the castle stood on a rocky cliff, over the beach, but following the 1669 eruption, which reclaimed this entire area from the sea, all that remains is the blackened keep. The **Museo Civico** within, with a collection that spans almost the entire history of the city, from its ancient Greek origins onwards, is open again after a lengthy restoration, though not all rooms are always accessible.

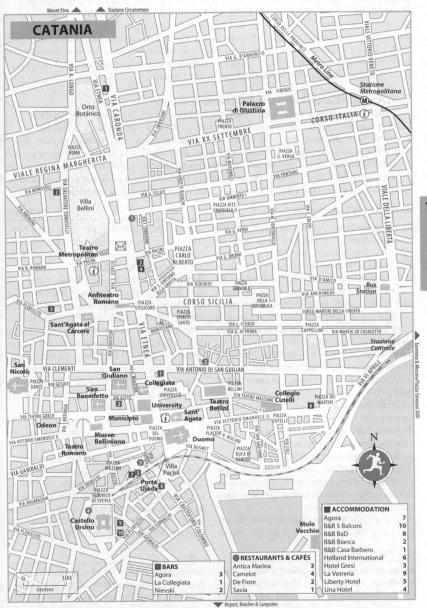

CATANIA

16

■ ACCOMMODATION	
Agora	7
B&B 5 Balconi	10
B&B BaD	8
B&B Bianca	2
B&B Casa Barbero	1
Holland International	6
Hotel Gresi	3
La Vetreria	9
Liberty Hotel	5
Una Hotel	4

■ BARS	
Agora	3
La Collegiata	1
Nievski	2

● RESTAURANTS & CAFÉS	
Antica Marina	3
Camelot	4
De Fiore	2
Savia	1

Via Crociferi

Just above Piazza del Duomo, **Via Crociferi** is lined with some of the most arresting religious and secular Baroque buildings in the city, best seen on a slow amble, peering in the eighteenth-century courtyards and churches. At the bottom of the street, the house where composer Vincenzo Bellini was born in 1801 now houses the **Museo Belliniano** (Mon–Sat 9am–1pm; free; ☎095 715 0535), a collection of photographs, original scores, his death mask and other memorabilia. West from here, the **Teatro Romano** (daily 9am–6.30pm; free) was built of lava in the second century AD on the site of an earlier Greek theatre, and much of the seating and the underground passageways are preserved. Further west, down Via Teatro Greco, the pretty crescent of Piazza Dante stares out over the unfinished facade of **San Nicolò** (Mon–Sat 9am–1pm; free), the biggest church in Sicily, stark and empty of detail both outside and in – save for a meridian line drawn across the floor of the transept.

Sant'Agata al Carcere and the Anfiteatro Romano

Nearby, a few minutes' walk north, the little twelfth-century church of **Sant'Agata al Carcere** was built on the site of the prison where St Agatha was confined before her martyrdom. From here, you drop down into **Piazza Stesicoro**, the enormous square that marks the modern centre of Catania, one half of which is almost entirely occupied by the closed-off, sunken, black remains of the **Anfiteatro Romano**, dating back to the second or third century AD. In its heyday, the amphitheatre could hold around sixteen thousand spectators, and from the church steps above you can see the seating quite clearly.

ARRIVAL AND DEPARTURE
CATANIA

By plane The airport, Fontanarossa (☎095 340 505, ⊛aeroporto.catania.it), is 5km south of the centre. The Alibus #457 (5am–midnight; every 20min; €1) runs from right outside to the central Piazza Stesicoro (on Via Etnea) and to Stazione Centrale in around 20min. A taxi from the rank outside the airport costs around €15 for the same. If you're heading straight to the Aeolian Islands, there are two direct buses run daily (April–Sept) from the airport to the port of Milazzo. Times vary from year to year, so check (☎090 673 782, ⊛giuntabus.com).

By train The Stazione Centrale (☎892 021), where all mainline trains arrive, is in Piazza Giovanni XXIII, northeast of the centre. To get into the centre, take one of the AMT (☎095 751 9111, ⊛amt.ct.it) city buses from the ranks outside the station: #1/4 (not Sun), #4/7, #432 and #448 run along Via VI Aprile and Via Vittorio Emanuele to Piazza del Duomo. Tickets cost €1 for a single journey, €2.50 for a day-pass (*giornaliero*). For the round-Etna train, head to the Stazione Circumetnea (☎095 541 250, ⊛circumetnea .it; see box, p.906) at Via Caronda, at the northern end of Via Etnea, by the Borgo metro station. Train connections are fairly speedy – though not particularly frequent – so it is often quicker to take the bus.

Destinations Enna (Mon–Sat 7 daily; 1hr 20min); Messina (1–2 hourly; 1hr 30min); Palermo (3 daily; 3hr 45min);

Siracusa (hourly; 1hr 30min); Taormina (at least 1 hourly; 40min). Circumetnea to: Paternò/Adrano/Bronte/Maletto/ Randazzo (9 daily in summer, 16 daily in winter; 35min/ 1hr/1hr 35min/1hr 50min/2hr).

By bus The bus station is on Via Archimede, a grotty 5min walk from the train station, up Viale della Libertà, and the ticket offices are currently inconveniently located on the other side of the street, so buy them before going in. Virtually all long-distance services stop at the airport as well – a far easier place to change buses. Local operators include AST (☎095 723 0535; Rifugio Sapienza, Nicolosi, Modica, Piazza Armerina and Siracusa); Interbus/Etna Trasporti (☎095 532 716; Enna, Noto, Piazza Armerina, Ragusa, Siracusa and Taormina); and SAIS (☎095 536 201; Agrigento, Enna, Messina, Palermo).

Destinations Agrigento (approx hourly; 2hr 50min); Enna (12 daily; 1hr 30min–2hr 25min); Messina (1–2 hourly; 1hr 35min); Nicolosi (hourly; 40min); Noto (7 daily; 2hr 25min– 2hr 15min); Palermo (hourly; 2hr 40min); Piazza Armerina (3–6 daily; 1hr 50min); Ragusa (12 daily; 2hr); Rifugio Sapienza (1 daily; 2hr); Rome (2–3 daily; 11hr); Siracusa (approx hourly; 1hr 20min); Taormina (16 daily; 1hr 40min).

By boat There are hydrofoils (3–6 weekly; 3hr; ⊛virtu ferries.com) and fast ferries (1–2 weekly; 10hr; ⊛grimaldi -lines.com) between Catania and Malta in summer.

GETTING AROUND

By bus Catania is served by a network of AMT city buses (⊛amt.ct.it), whose main ranks are outside the Stazione Centrale. Other central pick-up points are Piazza del

Duomo, Piazza Stesicoro, and Piazza Borsellino (below Piazza del Duomo), where there's a stop for the airport. Tickets (€1) are valid for any number of journeys within ninety minutes and are available from *tabacchi*, the newsagents inside Stazione Centrale or the booth outside the station. The same outlets also sell a *biglietto giornaliero* (€2.50), valid for one day's unlimited travel on all local AMT bus routes.

By metro The city has a metro system which operates every 15min (7am–8.30pm) on a limited route running from the main Stazione Centrale (beyond Platform 11) south to Catania Porto and north and northwest to Catania Borgo, the terminal for the Stazione Circumetnea on Via Caronda. Bus tickets are valid on metros as well and must be punched at machines before boarding the train.

By taxi Ranks at Stazione Centrale, Piazza del Duomo and Via Etnea (Piazza Stesicoro); call ☎095 330 966 or ☎095 338 282 for 24hr service.

By car Driving and parking in Catania is a stressful experience: ask at your hotel where to park. Rental outlets include: Avis, Via V. Cagliari 1 (☎0645 210 8391, ⓦavisautonoleggio.it); Sixt, Via Umberto 294/B (☎095 538 831, ⓦsixt.it); Hertz, Via Toselli (☎095 322 560, ⓦhertz.it); Maggiore, Piazza G. Verga (☎095 536 927, ⓦmaggiore.it). All have banches at the airport, where you'll also find Holiday Car Rental (☎095 346 769, ⓦholidaycarrental.it).

INFORMATION

Tourist offices Catania's provincial tourist office (Mon–Fri 9am–1pm, Wed also 3–7pm; ☎095 747 7415) is at Via Beato Bernardo 5 (near Via Cimerosa). There's also a useful office run by the city council at Via Vittorio Emanuele 172, close to the Duomo (Mon–Sat 8.15am–7pm; ☎800 841 042, ⓦcomune.catania.it/turismo). The information office

at Catania airport (Mon–Sat 8am–8am, Sun 10am–4pm; ☎095 093 7023) provides information only on Siracusa.

Newspapers and magazines For what's on check out the Catania editions of daily newspapers *Giornale di Sicilia*, *La Sicilia* and the *Gazzetta del Sud*, and the free fortnightly arts and entertainment guide, *Lapis*.

ACCOMMODATION

Agora Piazza Currò ☎095 723 3010, ⓦagorahostel .com. Catania's youth hostel has dorm bunks and a couple of doubles, and offers internet access and laundry facilities. In the same building is one of Catania's most popular and atmospheric pubs, the *Agora*, where you can eat and drink from morning till the early hours outside or in an underground grotto, which has a river running through it. Dorms **€20**, doubles **€55**

B&B 5 Balconi Via del Plebiscito 133 ☎338 727 2701, ⓦ5balconi.it. Stylish B&B run by a friendly young Italo-English couple in an old-fashioned, neighbourly quarter behind Castello Ursino. The three rooms are furnished with elegant flea-market finds. As the name implies, it has five balconies. Breakfast includes traditional Catanese pastries. **€55**

B&B BaD Via C. Colombo 24 ☎095 346 903, ⓦbad catania.it. Four rooms and an apartment in a self-styled designer B&B owned by a couple of graphic designers, conveniently located behind the Pescheria and Piazza del Duomo. **€80**

B&B Bianca Via S. Tomaselli 43 ☎095 989 0989, ⓦbiancabb.com. Young, friendly B&B behind the Giardino Bellini, where the owners will make sure you are well-informed about what's going on in Catania. There are two rooms, at present with shared bathroom. The communal area is a cheerful place to hang out and chat, with white walls and fittings, scarlet chairs, and a tangerine sofa where you can flop and watch a DVD. **€70**

★ **B&B Casa Barbero** Via Caronda 209 ☎095 820 6301, ⓦcasabarbero.it. Deft use of contemporary colours and design in a beautifully restored Liberty-era *palazzo* with six quiet rooms set around a courtyard. Breakfast is

served either in the courtyard, or in the elaborately stuccoed and frescoed dining room, at tables elegantly laid with Japanese-style ceramics and modern pewter. Bikes for guest use (free but €100 deposit). **€90**

Holland International Via Vittorio Emanuele 8 ☎095 533 605, ⓦhollandintrooms.it. Old-fashioned *pensione*, convenient for the station, and competitive prices for rooms on the first floor of an old *palazzo* with vaulted frescoed ceilings. The air-conditioned rooms come with and without bathroom and all have satellite TV and tea- and coffee-making facilities. There is free wi-fi, and the friendly Dutch owner speaks good English. **€60**

Hotel Gresi Via Pacini 28 ☎095 322 709, ⓦgresi hotel.com. Newly refurbished traditional hotel, with a pleasantly old-fashioned atmosphere, where the spacious rooms have frescoed ceilings. Good location between Via Etnea and the bustling Piazza Carlo Alberto market. **€70**

La Vetreria Via Grimaldi 8 ☎095 281 537, ⓦresidence lavetreria.com. The breakfast room with toy cupboard and little table and chairs signals straight away that this is a place where kids are genuinely welcomed. Occupying a 1920s mirror factory, this popular hotel has tastefully furnished, spacious rooms, and apartments with cooking facilities. **€70**

Liberty Hotel Via S. Vito 40 ☎095 311 651, ⓦliberty hotel.it. Intimate and romantic hotel in an early twentieth-century *palazzo*, a 10min walk from Via Etnea. Wonderfully refurbished in carefully researched Liberty style, the hotel has a calm atmosphere and a trellis-shaded courtyard, making this an ideal place to recuperate after a long journey. There are good-value discounts and packages including trips to Etna, available on the website. There's no restaurant, but a local pizzeria will deliver to the hotel. **€180**

Una Hotel Via Etnea 218 ☎ 095 250 5111, ✺ unahotels .it. Chic designer hotel belonging to a national chain, whose decor reflects the dominant black and cream tones of the city's Baroque architecture: floors of Etna lava and Comiso limestone; beds laid with cream cotton and black velvet; and Baroque-style chairs sprayed gold and upholstered in black velvet. Facilities include roof terrace and restaurant-bar with spectacular views of Etna, and a gym with steam bath. Check website for offers, and packages especially for weekend stays. **€160**

EATING

They take food seriously in Catania, as the city centre's bustling markets testify. For the best snacks, try the markets in Piazza Carlo Alberto and the stall-heavy streets through the Porta Uzeda, to the south of the Duomo. Another popular area for food is lively Piazza Federico di Svevia outside the Castello Ursino. Don't miss the chance to sample the Catanese speciality *selz* – fruit and nut syrups with soda water – served at kiosks throughout the city, most famously on Piazza Vittorio Emanuele (corner of Corso Umberto and Via Oberdan).

Antica Marina Via Pardo 29 ☎ 095 348 197. Trattoria bang in the heart of the fish market where you can eat reasonably priced, fresh fish on tables laid with paper cloths. Go for one of the set menus – a mixed antipasto plus two kinds of pasta or an antipasto plus mixed fried fish for €25 including a lemon sorbet and coffee. Mon–Sat 12.30–2.30pm & 8–10.30pm.

Camelot Piazza Federico di Svevia 75 ☎ 095 723 2103. Lively place where you can feast for a song on Sicilian antipasti (€5) and barbecued sausages and meat (from €3) and drink local wine from plastic cups. 8–10.30pm; closed Mon.

De Fiore Via Coppola 24 ☎ 095 316 283. Cosy, family-run trattoria, serving good, traditional Sicilian food at moderate prices. The Norma with handmade pasta (€6) is wonderful. 12.30–2.30pm & 8–10.30pm; closed Mon in winter.

Savia Via Etnea 302 ☎ 095 322 355. Located opposite the main entrance to the Villa Bellini, this is one of the town's finest stand-up café-bars, and has a fine choice of sweet pastries and savouries. Tues–Sun 7.30am–late.

DRINKING AND NIGHTLIFE

Catania's city council operates *café-concerto* periods during the summer, when the streets and squares of the old town, between Piazza Università and Piazza Bellini, are closed to traffic between 9pm and 2am. The bars here all spill tables out onto the squares and alleys, and live bands keep things swinging until late. Catania's student population ensures a fair choice of youthful bars and pubs – some with live music – that stay open late.

Agora Piazza Currò ☎ 095 723 3010. Lively pub that attracts a mix of locals and travellers from the youth hostel above. They make nice bruschette too, to soak up the booze. Daily noon–late.

La Collegiata Via Collegiata 3 ☎ 095 321 230. A laidback studenty place with a pleasant terrace for a night-time drink or day-time snack. Daily noon–late.

Nievski Via Alessi 15 ☎ 095 313 792. Occupying several floors of a labyrinthine, ramshackle building, this bar-restaurant hosts cultural events, book readings, art exhibitions and live music as well as being a popular meeting place for Catania's alternative set. Noon–late; closed Sun lunch & Mon.

DIRECTORY

Hospital Ospedale Garibaldi, Piazza Maria di Gesù 7, Pronto Soccorso ☎ 095 759 4368.

Internet access Internetteria, Via Penninello 44, just off Via Etnea ☎ 095 310 139. Open Mon–Sat 9am–1am, Sun (winter only) 5–10pm.

Pharmacies Croce Rossa, Via Etnea 274 ☎ 095 317 053; Cutelli, Via Vittorio Emanuele II 54 ☎ 095 531 400; Europa, Corso Italia 111 ☎ 095 383 536. Open all night.

Police Emergencies ☎ 112; Carabinieri, Piazza Giovanni Verga 8, or Vigili Urbani, Via Veniero 7 ☎ 095 531 333. The Questura (police station) is in Piazza S. Nicolella 8 (☎ 095 736 7111).

Post office Main post office and poste restante at Via Etnea 215, close to the Villa Bellini (Mon–Sat 8.15am–6.30pm).

Siracusa

Under ancient Greek rule, **Siracusa** was the most important city in the Western world. Today it is one of Sicily's main draws, thanks to its extensive archeological park, a Greek theatre where plays are still performed and a charming historic centre occupying an

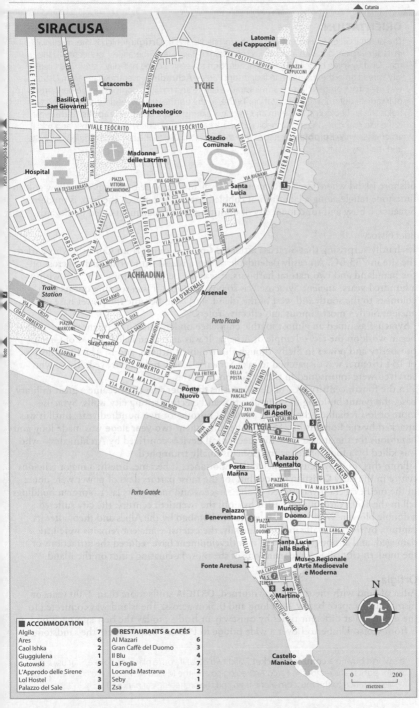

▲ Catania

SIRACUSA

Latomia dei Cappuccini

VIA SAN SEBASTIANO

VIALE TERACATI

VIA AUGUSTO VON PLATEN

PIAZZA CAPPUCCINI

VIA POLITI LAUDIEN

Catacombs

TYCHE

Basilica di San Giovanni

Museo Archeologico

Porto Archeologico & Epipolae ◀

VIALE TEÓCRITO VIALE TEÓCRITO

VIA DEL SANTUARIO

RIVIERA DIONISIO IL GRANDE

VIA TOLLINO

Madonna delle Lacrime

Stadio Comunale

Hospital

VIA TESTAFERRATA

PIAZZA VITTORIA (EXCAVATIONS)

VIA GORIZIA

VIA BIGAMI

◀ 1

VIA DI NATALE

CORSO GELONE

VIA M. CARABELLI

VIALE LUIGI CADORNA

VIA ENNA

VIA RAGUSA

VIA AGRIGENTO

VIA TRAPANI

VIA STATELLO

CORSO TIMOLEONTE

VIA MONTE GRAPPA

VIA FLORIDIA

Santa Lucia

PIAZZA S. LUCIA

VIA MOSCO

ACHRADINA

V. EPICARMO

VIA D'ARSENALE

Arsenale

Train Station

Noto ◀

VIA F. CRISPI

◀ 3

CORSO UMBERTO I

PIAZZA MARCONI

VIALE A. DIAZ

VIA R. MARGHERITA

VIA DANTE

Porto Piccolo

Foro Siracusano

VIA ELORINA

CORSO UMBERTO I

VIA PALERMO

VIA MALTA

VIA BENGASI

VIA RODI

VIA ERITREA

Ponte Nuovo

PIAZZA DELLA POSTA

PIAZZA PANCALI

VIA TRIESTE

VIA TRENTO

LUNGOMARE DI LEVANTE

RIVA GARIBALDI

VIA DI MILLE

VIA XX SETTEMBRE

LARGO XXV LUGLIO

Tempio di Apollo

VIA RESALIBERA

ORTYGIA

◀ 1

◀ 6

4 ▶

VIALE MAZZINI

VIA SAVOIA

VIA CAVOUR

VIA MONTESANTO

VIA MIRABELLA

VITTORIO VENETO

VIA T. GARGALLO

7 ◀

2 ◀

Porta Marina

Palazzo Montalto

VIA LAMPOLINA

PIAZZA ARCHIMEDE

VIA MAESTRANZA

Porto Grande

Palazzo Beneventano

FORO ITALICO

VIA DEL DUOMO

3 ◀

Municipio

Duomo

PIAZZA DEL DUOMO

6 ◀

5 ◀

VIA GIUDECCA

VIA LARGA

VIA ALEA

Santa Lucia alla Badia

Fonte Aretusa ⊺

VIA PICHERALE

VIA CAPODIECI

VIA S. TERESA

7 ◀

8 ◀

San Martino

LUNGOMARE ORTYGIA

Museo Regionale d'Arte Medioevale e Moderna

VIA CASTELLO MANIACE

N

Castello Maniace

0   200

metres

16

■ ACCOMMODATION	
Algila	7
Ares	6
Caol Ishka	2
Giuggiulena	1
Gutowski	5
L'Approdo delle Sirene	4
Lol Hostel	3
Palazzo del Sale	8

● RESTAURANTS & CAFÉS	
Al Mazari	6
Gran Caffè del Duomo	3
Il Blu	4
La Foglia	7
Locanda Mastrarua	2
Seby	1
Zsa	5

> ## ORIENTATION
>
> The original Greek settlement was on the fortified island of **Ortigia**, which is late-medieval in its street plan, but with a generous sprinkling of Baroque exuberance. Connected to the mainland by three bridges, it's compact enough to see in a good half-day's stroll. The Greek city spread onto the mainland in four distinct areas: **Achradina**, over the water from Ortigia, was the city's commercial and administrative centre and today encompasses the new streets that radiate out from the train station; **Tyche**, to the northeast, was residential and now holds the archeological museum and the city's extensive catacombs; **Neapolis**, to the west, is the site of the fascinating archeological park based on ancient Syracuse's public and social amenities; while **Epipolae** stretches way to the northwest, to the city's outer defensive walls and the Euryalus fort.

offshore island where Greek, Roman, medieval and Baroque buildings of mellow golden limestone tangle along a labyrinth of cobbled streets. In between the two, is modern Siracusa, a busy and functional city of undistinguished apartment-lined boulevards.

Brief history

It's hardly surprising that Siracusa attracted **Greek** colonists from Corinth, who settled the site in 733 BC. An easily defendable offshore island with fertile plains across on the mainland and two natural harbours, it was the perfect site for a city, and within a hundred years, ancient Syracuse was so powerful that it was sending out its own colonists to the south and west of the island, and soon became the power base of ancient Sicily's most famous and effective rulers.

Syracuse assumed an almost mythic eminence under **Gelon**, the tyrant of Gela, who began work on the city's Temple of Athena. It was an unparalleled period of Greek prosperity and power in Sicily, though this troubled Athens, and in 415 BC a fleet of 134 triremes was dispatched to take Syracuse – only to be destroyed. Those who survived were imprisoned in the city's stone quarries.

In the fourth century BC, under **Dionysius the Elder**, the city became a great military base, the tyrant building the Euryalus fort and erecting strong city walls. Syracuse more or less remained the leading power in Europe for two hundred years until it was attacked by the **Romans** in 215 BC. The subsequent **two-year siege** was made long and hazardous for the attackers by the mechanical devices contrived by Archimedes – who was killed by a foot soldier as the Romans finally triumphed.

From this time, Syracuse withered in importance. It became, briefly, a major religious centre in the early **Christian period**, but for the most part its days of power were done: in the medieval era it was sacked by the Saracens and most of its later Norman buildings fell in the 1693 earthquake. Passed by until the twentieth century, the city suffered a double blow in World War II when it was **bombed** by the Allies and then, after its capture, by the Luftwaffe in 1943. Luckily, the extensive ancient remains were little damaged, and although decay and new development have reduced the attractions of the modern city, Siracusa remains one of the most fascinating cities on the island.

Ortigia

A fist of land with the thumb downturned, **ORTIGIA** stuffs more than 2700 years of history into a space barely 1km long and 0.5km across. The island was connected to the mainland at different times by causeway or bridge: today the best approach on foot is from Corso Umberto I over a wide **bridge** to Piazza Pancali, where the sandstone

> It's worth buying a **combined ticket** (valid two days) if you're planning to see Siracusa's major sights: a ticket for the Parco Archeologico and the Museo Archeologico costs €13, while entrance to the museum alone is €6 and the archeological park €10.

remnants of the **Tempio di Apollo** sit in a little green park surrounded by railings. Erected around 570 BC in the colony's early years, it was the first grand Doric temple to be built in Sicily, though there's not much left: a few column stumps, part of the inner sanctuary wall and the stereobate.

Porta Marina and Fonte Aretusa

Follow Via Savoia towards the water and you come to the main harbour, Porto Grande. Set back from the water, a curlicued fifteenth-century limestone gateway, the **Porta Marina**, provides one entrance into the webbed streets of the **old town**. The walk uphill ends on a terrace looking over the harbour, from where you slip down to a piazza encircling the **Fonte Aretusa**. The freshwater spring – which bubbles up through the sea bed just offshore – fuelled an attractive Greek myth: the nymph Arethusa, chased by the river god Alpheus, was changed into a spring by the goddess Artemis and, jumping into the sea off the Peloponnese, reappeared as a fountain in Siracusa. The landscaped, papyrus-covered fountain – complete with fish and ducks – is undeniably pretty, and a favourite place to lean and watch the sun set over the Porto Grande. Admiral Nelson took on water supplies here before the Battle of the Nile.

The old town's roads lead on, down the "thumb" of Ortigia, as far as the **Castello Maniace** on the island's southern tip. Built by Frederick II in 1239, the solid, square keep is now a barracks and usually off-limits, although occasionally concerts are held here, publicized by notices around town.

Palazzo Bellomo: Museo Regionale d'Arte Medioevale e Moderna

Via Capodieci 14–16 • Tues–Sat 9am–7pm, Sun 9am–1pm • €8 • ☏ 0931 69 511

Back on the main chunk of Ortigia, the **Museo Regionale d'Arte Medioevale e Moderna** on Via Capodieci is housed in the austere thirteenth-century **Palazzo Bellomo**. Inside is a marvellous collection of gilded Byzantine and Gothic altarpieces, though the highlight is an exquisite, fifteenth-century *Annunciation* by Antonello da Messina, brought back to life by a deft restoration, and occupying a room on its own on the upper floor. Antonello created the painting in Siracusa – the outline of the Cava Grande mountain, which you can see rising behind the Porto Grande, is clearly visible in the background.

Piazza del Duomo

Ortigia's most impressive architecture is Baroque, best displayed in the splendid **Piazza del Duomo**, Sicily's greatest square. A theatrical, elongated space, it is flanked by magnificent buildings, including the seventeenth-century **Municipio** with the remains of an early Ionic temple in its basement. This was abandoned in the fifth century BC, when work began on the **Tempio di Atena**, possibly the most extravagant temple of its time, with doors of ivory and gold, walls painted with war scenes and portraits of tyrants, and its roof crowned with a statue of Athena bearing a golden shield designed to catch the sun and serve as a beacon for sailors.

The ivory, paintings and gold have long gone, yet much of the rest survives, preserved within the **Duomo** (daily 8am–noon & 4–8pm; free), which incorporated the temple in its structure. Twelve of the temple's fluted columns and their architrave are embedded in the Duomo's battlemented Norman wall, while inside, the nave was formed by hacking eight arches in the *cella* walls. Along the north aisle, columns distorted by the 1693 earthquake show how close the entire structure came to toppling then. Indeed, the Norman facade was completely destroyed, and replaced with the rhythmic Baroque that dominates the piazza today.

At the far end of the square, behind the barley-sugar Baroque facade of **Santa Lucia alla Badia** (Tues–Sun 11am–2pm & 3–7pm; free) is one of Caravaggio's most ground-breaking masterpieces, the bleak *Burial of St Lucy*, an astonishingly pared down, almost monochromatic work in which all the action is limited to the bottom third of the canvas.

16

SWIMMING IN THE CITY

In summer, as a break from sightseeing, check out Ortigia's seasonal **solarium** reached by flights of metal steps from the Lungomare di Levante, where you can swim and sunbathe on rocks and wooden decks. *Il Blu* bar (see p.919) will bring you granitas and sandwiches. Alternatively, there's a small (if not always very clean) paying **beach** with sunloungers and umbrellas at the Lido Marea Punta Est, below the Talete car park. Across on the mainland, the lido-bar *Zen*, on Via Dionosio Grande, in the upcoming area known as Borgata, is the in-place to swim by day or hang out at night. Those who prefer long sandy beaches can take bus #22 from Via Rubino to Fontane Bianche (30min), or bus #23 to Arenella (40 min). Both routes run throughout the year, leaving every ninety minutes.

Achradina: Corso Umberto I and the Foro Siracusano

Directly across the bridge from Ortigia's Piazza Pancali is the area known in ancient times as **ACHRADINA**, the commercial centre of old Syracuse. Nineteenth-century **Corso Umberto I** leads up to **Foro Siracusano**, site of the Greek city's marketplace and forum, a few mysterious remains of which are scattered about the garden and playground in its centre. From here, you could either head up the main shopping street, Corso Gelone, towards the archeological park and museum, or cross over to Via Rubino, behind the station, where buses will take you out to the beaches of Arenella and Fontane Bianche.

Tyche: the modern town

The district of **TYCHE**, north of the train station, is of little interest in itself – come to see the archeological park, archeological museum and catacombs, and then head back to the beauties of Ortigia. Though it is not a long walk – about thirty minutes from Ortigia – you may prefer to take a bus. Get off at Viale Teocrito and follow signs east for the archeological museum and west for Neapolis.

Museo Archeologico Paolo Orsi

Via Teocrito 66 • Tues–Sat 9am–6pm, Sun 9am–1pm; last entry 1hr before closing • €6 or combined ticket with Parco Archeologico €13 • ☏ 0931 464 022 • Bus #1, #3, #4 or #12

The well-organized **Museo Archeologico** starts with geological and prehistoric finds, then moves through rooms devoted to the colonies of Naxos, Lentini, Zancle and Megara Hyblaea, and to the main body of the collection: an immensely detailed catalogue of life in ancient Syracuse. The most famous exhibit is a headless **Venus** arising from the sea, the clear white marble almost palpably dripping. Look out, too, for the section dealing with the temples of Syracuse; fragments from each (like the seven lion-gargoyles from the Tempio di Atena) are displayed alongside model and video reconstructions.

Catacombi di San Giovanni

Piazza San Giovanni • Daily 9.30am–12.30pm & 2.30–5pm • Tour of catacombs €6 • ☏ 0931 64 694 • Bus #1, #3, #4 or #12

Tyche is riddled with **catacombs**, since the Romans forbade burial within the walls of a city. All are now inaccessible apart from those beneath the **Basilica di San Giovanni**, a stone's throw from the archeological museum off Viale Teocrito, built over the burial site of Roman martyr St Marcian. The presence of the saint made this a hugely popular burial place, and there are thousands of niches hollowed into the walls to contain the remains of Roman Syracuse's Christians.

Santuario della Madonna delle Lacrime

Daily 7am–12.30pm & 4–7pm • Free • Bus #1, #3, #4 or #12

Opposite the museum, across Viale Teocrito, the monolithic **Santuario della Madonna delle Lacrime** is the newest and least harmonious addition to the city's skyline. Completed in 1994 to house a statue of the Madonna that allegedly wept for five days in 1953, it was designed to resemble a giant teardrop.

Parco Archeologico di Neapolis

Viale Paradiso • Daily 9am–1hr before sunset • €10, or €13 with Museo Archeologico • ☎ 0931 66 206

To the west of Tyche, **NEAPOLIS** is an extensive area that's worth at least half a day, so bring water and a picnic (though you'll need to eat fairly discreetly). The **Ara di Ierone II**, an enormous third-century-BC altar on a solid white plinth, is the first thing you see, across the way from which is the entrance to the theatre and quarries. The **Teatro Greco** is prettily sited, cut out of the rock and looking down into trees below. It's much bigger than the one at Taormina, capable of holding around fifteen thousand people. Around the top of the middle gangway is a set of carved names which marked the various seat blocks occupied by the royal family. Greek dramas are still played here in May and June.

Walk back through the theatre and another path leads down into a leafy **quarry**, the **Latomia del Paradiso**, best known for an unusually shaped cavern that the tyrant Dionysius is supposed to have used as a prison. This, the **Orecchio di Dionisio** (or "Ear of Dionysius"), is a high, S-shaped cave 65m long: Caravaggio, a visitor in 1586, coined the name after the shape of the entrance, but the acoustic properties are such that it's thought that Dionysius may have used it to eavesdrop on his prisoners from above.

The ticket for the theatre and Latomia del Paradiso also gives access to the elliptical **Anfiteatro Romano**. A late building, dating from the third century AD, it's a substantial relic with the tunnels for animals and gladiators clearly visible. Again, some of the seats are inscribed with the owners' names.

Castello Eurialo

Frazione Belvedere • Daily 9am until 1hr before sunset • €4 • ☎ 0931 711 773 • Bus #25 makes the 15min ride from Ortigia passing by the archeological park, to the village of Belvedere; the site is just before the village, on the right. To come back, take bus #26

For terrific views over the city head a few kilometres west of Siracusa to the military and defensive works begun under Dionysius the Elder to defend the port from land attack. They basically consisted of a **great wall**, which defended the ridge of Epipolae (the city's western limit), and the massive **Castello Eurialo** – the most important surviving Greek fortification in the Mediterranean. There are three defensive trenches, the innermost leading off into a system of tunnels and passages. Climb up to the castle proper for hearty **views** down to the oil refineries and tankers of the coast north of the city, and over Siracusa itself.

Bars and **pizzerias** share the view, and make this a great place for an evening out.

ARRIVAL AND DEPARTURE

SIRACUSA

By train The train station is on the mainland, a 20min walk from both Ortigia and the archeological park. Cross over the piazza outside the station to Via Rubino, where every 15min a free minibus runs down to Ortigia.

Destinations Catania (10 daily; 1hr 30min); Messina (9 daily; 3hr); Noto (9 daily; 30min); Ragusa (4 daily; 2hr 10min); Taormina (10 daily; 2hr).

By bus All regional buses – run by AST and Interbus – stop across the road from the train station, on Via Rubino. Most city buses – run by AST – depart from Piazza Pancali in Ortigia, except for those running out to the beaches which leave from Via Rubino. All buses run on circular routes. Tickets cost €1.20 for 120min, and €1.80 for 2 days, and are available at *tabacchi* and newsstands displaying an

AST sticker. Ticket inspections are frequent.

Destinations Catania (via Catania airport; hourly; 1hr 20min); Noto (12 daily; 55 min); Palermo (3 daily; 3hr 15min), Ragusa (5 daily; 2hr 15min–3hr).

By car Siracusa's drivers are as undisciplined as any in Sicily, but nevertheless drivers will find the city a breeze after Palermo and Catania. Parking on the street in Ortigia is almost impossible, so leave your car at the Talete car park to the east of the island. Parking is free during the day and costs €1 overnight. Ortigia is completely closed to traffic (except for residents) on Sundays – and on certain other occasions – a traffic signal at the foot of Corso Matteotti indicates whether access is permitted or not.

INFORMATION

InfoPoint For maps, accommodation, details of performances in the Greek theatre, and other information, the extremely helpful and well-informed InfoPoint is inside the provincial offices at Via Roma 30 (daily 9am–7pm & 2.30–5.30pm, Sat 9am–1pm; ☎ 0931 462 946, ✉ infoturistico@provsr.it).

16

ACCOMMODATION

There's a good choice of accommodation, but in high summer and during the theatre season (May–June) it's wise to book in advance. If you prefer to rent an apartment, ⓦ kasette.it and ⓦ ilsoleazzurro.com have a good choice of quality places both in Ortigia, and outside Siracusa by the sea, while ⓦ lacasadellefate.it has well-appointed mini-apartments on Via Santa Teresa that start at €60 per night.

Algila Via Vittorio Veneto 93 ☎ 0931 465 186, ⓦ algila .it. Recently opened hotel on the eastern seafront of Ortigia, which has all the comforts of a four-star hotel, plus friendly, helpful staff. Styled by Siracusa-born theatre director, Manuel Giliberti, the design has a Maghreb feel, with Tunisian tiles in the bathrooms, kilims on the floors, watercolours of sun-scorched palms and North African piazzas, and a tiny decorative courtyard with fountain. €300
Ares Via Mirabella 49 ☎ 0931 461 145, ⓦ aresbed andbreakfast.it. Comfortable B&B on a quiet street, a skip and a jump from the sea, on the less-touristy east side of Ortigia. Rooms are smart and spotless, there's a lovely roof terrace, and owner Enzo will go out of his way to make sure guests have all the information they need on Ortigia. Breakfast is by voucher at the fabulous Bar del Duomo opposite the cathedral, just a few minutes' walk away. €80
★ **Caol Ishka** Via Elorina, Contrada Pantanelli ☎ 0931 69 057, ⓦ caolishka.it. Minimalist chic in a cluster of traditional stone farm buildings painted the same lavender-mink grey as the sky at dusk, about 2km west of Siracusa. The rooms have cement floors, and spacious bathrooms, with shower-heads the size of soup plates. The grounds are ample, with a good-sized pool, and there is a superb restaurant. A series of little beaches at nearby Isola and boat excursions along the River Ciane make this an ideal choice for anyone who wants to alternate days of sightseeing with lazy days by the beach or pool. In summer there is a ferry direct from the village of Isola across the bay to Ortigia. €230
★ **Giuggiulena** Via Pitagora da Reggio 35 ☎ 0931 468 142, ⓦ giuggiulena.it. Belonging to the same owners as Palazzo del Sale, Giuggiulena is a chic, but friendly and relaxed B&B in a cliff-top villa, along the eastern seafront of Siracusa, and ideal for families. The main living/eating area has floor-to-ceiling windows, and is flooded with light, with a glass cube suspended above the ocean, and a bookcase stuffed with a tempting selection of English paperbacks. All six rooms have balconies overlooking the sea, and you can swim off rocks or forage in rock pools (the hotel has

a supply of chairs, mats and beach shoes), yet Ortigia is just a 15min walk away. Breakfasts are abundant and delicious, and eaten on a balcony overhanging the sea. €80
★ **Gutowski** Lungomare Vittorini 26 ☎ 0931 465 861, ⓦ guthotel.it. Chic simplicity and intelligent design make this hotel overlooking the sea on the eastern edge of Ortigia a good restful choice in the centro storico. It's worth booking in advance to secure one of the rooms with private terrace. Great breakfasts, with freshly squeezed orange juice and, in summer, home-made almond granita. There is also a little wine bar, and private dinners can be arranged for four or more guests. €110
★ **L'Approdo delle Sirene** Riva Garibaldi 15 ☎ 0931 24 857, ⓦ apprododellesirene.com. Family-run B&B in a tastefully renovated waterfront palazzo overlooking the channel between Ortigia and the mainland. Facilities include mini-laptops in rooms, and free wi-fi. Owned and run by a charming mother-and-son team: Fiora runs cooking courses in her apartment next door and Friedrich, who has trained as a pizza chef, is opening a pizzeria. Great home-made breakfasts with abundant fresh fruit are served on a terrace overlooking the sea. You can also borrow bikes, free of charge. €125
Lol Hostel Via Francesco Crispi 92 ☎ 0931 465 088, ⓦ lolhostel.com. Stylish modern hostel with a/c en-suite four-bed dorms, plus private singles and doubles. There is 24hr reception, internet access and the cheapest bike rental in town. It also has a kitchen for guest use. Dorms €22, doubles €50
★ **Palazzo del Sale** Via S. Teresa 25 ☎ 0931 69 558, ⓦ palazzodelsale.it. Stylish, relaxed B&B in a nineteenth-century salt-merchant's home and warehouse on a quiet street behind Piazza del Duomo. Six spacious rooms with wooden floors, architect-designed beds, and intriguing touches such as mirrors framed with driftwood, and lamps with palm-bark shades. Breakfasts are superb, and service is unfussy and friendly. Free wi-fi – though the hefty stone walls mean that the signal can be weak in some rooms – and a PC for guests' use. €110

EATING, DRINKING AND NIGHTLIFE

Al Mazari Via G. Torres 7 ☎ 0931 483 690. Sophisticated, yet cosy restaurant, run by a family from Mazara del Vallo – the place to come for a romantic meal for two, or on your own, if you feel you need a treat. Carefully sourced ingredients, and dishes such as an excellent fish couscous (€20), handmade pasta with prawns and cherry tomatoes (€12), or casarecce pasta with swordfish, aubergine, wild

mint and breadcrumbs (€12) that are typical of western Sicily. 12.30–2.30pm & 8–10.30pm; sometimes closed Sun in winter.
Gran Caffè del Duomo Piazza del Duomo 18 ☎ 0931 21 584. Right in front of the cathedral, this is the place to sit and watch life pass by over a lazy breakfast or aperitif – staff are friendly and attentive and prices are so

reasonable that even street-sweepers and dustmen stop by for a coffee on their morning rounds. Try the *cornetti* filled to order with fresh ricotta. 8am–late; closed Mon except in summer.

Il Blu Via Nizza 50 ☎0931 445 052. Charismatic and unpretentious, *Il Blu* is a great restaurant-bar that does a roaring trade in summer serving fresh fruit *gremolatas* (€3; try white peach, or black fig with chilli) and superior sandwiches to the sun-soaking folk down at the nearby solarium, plus light lunches in the shade of their terrace. Come *aperitivo*-time, there are prosecco cocktails made with fresh fruit (try pineapple, strawberry, peach or black mulberry) and top-notch daiquiris and mojitos. But *Il Blu* is also a restaurant, buying fish daily to create two fish *primi* and *secondi* every evening, such as tuna in a sesame crust stuffed with ricotta (€15). There's also sushi and sashimi. Easter–Nov daily from 6pm, May to late Sept also 12.30–2.30pm.

La Foglia Via Capodieci 29 ☎0931 66 233. Intimate bohemian chic, with Venetian chandeliers, classical music, and tables dressed with rich brocades and antique tablecloths. The sculptor-owner is vegetarian, and local legumes and vegetables feature prominently, though the menu also includes fish and meat. There's a good range of rustic soups (including nettle; €10.50) or try mussels grilled inside lemon leaves (€15), and, if they have it, the *girella* (handmade pasta) filled with wild greens (€12). Daily 12.30–2.30pm & 8–10.30pm.

Locanda Mastrarua Via Vittorio Veneto 11 ☎0931 62 084. Simple contemporary elegance, and a cuisine that focuses on the freshest seasonal vegetables and fish, as well as tasty meat from the Nebrodi mountains. The signature dish is *rua* (€8.50), a generous antipasto platter of crunchy, deep-fried breadcrumbed vegetables, including fennel, sage leaves, mushrooms, zucchini and, in season, *mazzoluto* (think wild-asparagus-meets-onion greens). Fish dishes vary according to the market, but might include a fillet of white fish baked in a crust of zucchini and potato, or sea bass in a crust of spinach and crushed almonds (both at €12). Desserts are light and exceptional – try the ricotta mousse with dark chocolate sauce and a dusting of crushed pistachio. From €30 per head, excluding wine. 12.30–2.30pm & 8–10.30pm; closed Wed.

★ **Seby** Via Mirabello 21. This exceptional *tavola calda* has become an Ortigia institution. Fabulous selection of grilled vegetables, oven-baked pasta, fish and meat dishes, and home-made cakes at very reasonable prices. By day it is self-service, you eat on trays at formica tables with plastic knives and forks and can get an antipasto, pasta and a glass of wine for around €10. In the evening, they get out the tablecloths, crockery and cutlery, and operate as a trattoria – at prices that are still hard to beat. 12.30–2.30pm & 8–10.30pm; closed Wed in winter.

Zsa Via Roma 73 ☎0931 22 204. Good pizza – the dough is made with a light touch, and comes blistered from the wood oven, and the ingredients on top are good quality and abundant. They kick off at €4, but for a bit more you can feast on a *vegetariana*, laden with succulent grilled vegetables laced with radicchio, or a *stufata*, scattered with chilli, and fennel-seed-scented sausages and potatoes. They do a takeaway service as well – just show up and order. Tues–Sat 12.30–2.30pm & 8–10.30pm.

The southern coast and the interior

The **southern coast** and hinterland mark a welcome break from the volcanic fixation of the blacker lands to the north: here the towns are largely spacious and bright, strung across a gentler, unscarred landscape that rolls down to endless long sandy beaches and the sea. Sicily's southeastern bulge was devastated by a calamitous seventeenth-century earthquake and the inland rebuilding, over the next century, was almost entirely Baroque in concept and execution. **Noto**, closest to Siracusa, is the undisputed gem, but there are Baroque treasures aplenty both at **Modica** and **Ragusa**. The coast, too, has some jewels: 10km south of Noto is the magical **Riserva Naturale di Vendicari**, and though certain stretches of the coast are marred by industrial development and pollution, there are some magnificent sands further west. Further west still, is **Agrigento**, sitting on a rise overlooking the sea above its famed series of Greek temples.

Slow cross-country trains and limited-exit motorways do little to encourage stopping in the island's **interior**, but it's only here that you really begin to get off the tourist trail. Much of the land is burned dry during the long summer months, sometimes a dreary picture, but in compensation the region boasts some of Sicily's most curious towns. **Enna** is the obvious target, as central as you can get, the blustery mountain town a pace apart from the dry hills below. There are easy trips to be made from here, north into the hills and south to **Piazza Armerina** and the fabulous Roman mosaics.

Riserva Naturale di Vendicari

Daily: summer 7am–8pm; winter 7am–6.30pm • Free entry (parking €2.50, campers €12)

A line of small-town resorts stretches from Siracusa to Vittoria, and in between there are several sweeps of pristine sands: most notably at the **Riserva Naturale di Vendicari**, 10km south of Noto, a lovely coastal nature reserve. Paths lead to unspoilt beaches of white-gold sand and salt lakes, that, between October and March, attract flamingoes, herons, cranes, black storks and pelicans. Until recently turtles would nest on the beaches, but local appetite for turtle soup led to their disappearance. There are now projects under way to encourage the turtles back to Vendicari.

ACCOMMODATION AND EATING	RISERVA NATURALE DI VENDICARI
Agriturismo Calamosche Oasi di Vendicari ☏ 347 858 7319, ⍟ agriturismocalamosche.it. This little agriturismo is just inside the reserve at the Cala Mosche entrance: look out for a hand-painted sign off the main road. They have seven simple rooms and produce their own	vegetables, almonds, lemons and oil, which are served along with local hams and cheeses, fish and game in the reasonably priced restaurant (around €16 for an antipasto and pasta, with a glass of wine). Closed Nov–March. **€55**

The Baroque towns

The **earthquake of 1693**, which destroyed utterly the towns and villages of southeastern Sicily, had one positive and lasting effect. Where there were ruins, a new generation of confident architects raised new planned towns in an opulent Baroque style. All were harmonious creations, and in 2001 eight of them were selected by UNESCO as World Heritage Sites. Funding has poured into the area, and in recent years there has been an explosion of new hotels and B&Bs. **Noto**, recently restored to perfection, is the most eagerly promoted by the tourist board, while **Ragusa Ibla**, a Baroque town built on a medieval plan, has become a destination for the stylish international set, with a handful of bijou B&Bs and a couple of Michelin-starred restaurants. Liveliest of the lot is **Modica**, a vibrant town famous for the production of chocolate.

Noto

NOTO, half an hour by train or bus from Siracusa, is easily the most harmonious town of those rebuilt after the earthquake, and during the mid-nineteenth century, it replaced Siracusa as provincial capital. Planned and laid out by Giovanni Battista Landolina and adorned by Gagliardi, there's not a town to touch Noto for uniform excellence in design and execution. Each year more monuments are restored, regaining their original apricot- and honey-hued limestone facades, and each year more tour groups visit.

The pedestrianized main Corso is lined with some of Sicily's most captivating buildings, from the flat-fronted church of **San Francesco**, on the right, along as far as Piazza XVI Maggio and the graceful, curving church of **San Domenico**. And **Piazza Municipio** is one of Sicily's finest piazzas, with its perfectly proportioned, tree-planted expanses. The **Duomo**, a striking example of Baroque at its most muscular, has reopened following the collapse of its dome in 1996. Its refreshingly unadorned interior is a striking example of how well the best of Baroque architects knew how to articulate space. Opposite, the **Municipio**, Palazzo Ducezio, is flanked by its own green spaces, the arcaded building presenting a lovely, simple facade of columns and long stone balconies. Head up the steep Via Corrado Nicolaci, an eighteenth-century street that contains the extraordinary **Palazzo Villadorata** at no. 18, its six balconies supported by a panoply of griffins, galloping horses and fat-cheeked cherubs.

ARRIVAL AND INFORMATION	NOTO
By train Although it is fun to take the single-coach train from Siracusa, the train station is a good 10–15min walk away from Noto town centre down Via Principe di Piemonte,	and has no facilities – not even a bench – and is often unmanned, so don't show up early. If you have luggage, you may need a taxi (☏ 338 945 8206 or ☏ 0931 838 713).

By bus Buses stop at the Giardino Pubblico at the eastern end of the historic centre, close to the Porta Reale.

By car Traffic through town is all one-way and while it's easy enough to drive in (follow "centro" signs) or out (destinations are all well signposted), finding a particular spot in a car can be difficult.

Tourist office Piazza XVI Maggio just off the main Corso Vittorio Emanuele in the centre of the old town (winter Mon–Sat and most Sun 9am–1.30pm & 3–7pm; summer daily 9am–1pm & 4–8pm; ☎ 0931 573 779, ⊛ comune.noto.sr.it).

ACCOMMODATION

Fattoria Villa Rosa Casale dei Mori, Corso da Falconara, Noto Marina ☎ 0931 812 909, ⊛ alcasale deimori.com. Comfortable agriturismo with 21 rooms (two with cooking facilities) in an enchanting, creeper-covered, eighteenth-century farmhouse with beautiful grounds. There is a swimming pool suitable for children, a playground and excellent home-cooking in its restaurant. The farm's rabbits, chickens and goats (as well as cats and dogs) can all be visited. Half-board-only July & Aug. €130

Il Castello Via Fratelli Bandiera 2 ⊛ ostellodinoto.it. Youth hostel housed in a converted *palazzo* in the upper part of town with wonderful views, large dorms, excellent showers and laundry service. It's accessible from the centre in a few minutes up signposted steps from Via Cavour, behind the Duomo. Dorms €16, family rooms €19.50 per person

Liberty Rooms Via Francesco Ferruccio/Corso Vittorio Emanuele ☎ 338 230 4042, ⊛ villacatera.com. An exceptionally beautiful Art Nouveau "palazzetto" on Noto's central Corso. Rooms are gracious and furnished with antiques, while a kitchen and a huge roof terrace on which to eat mean there's no need to go out at night. €100

Macrina Vico Grillo ☎ 0931 837 202, ⊛ b-bmacrina .com. Family-run B&B, in a neighbourly street, with a huge walled garden and a couple of swings, so a good choice if you have kids. There's also use of a barbecue, and a little terrace for breakfast. Each of the three rooms is big and airy and has its own terrace. €75

★ **Montandon** Via A. Sofia 50 ☎ 0931 836 389 or ☎ 339 524 4607, ⊛ b-bmontandon.com. Three lovely, huge rooms, each with its own terrace, in a gracious *palazzo* with an enchanting garden (with swings) in Noto Alta. The owner is a marvellous host, and her breakfasts are superb – with home-made jams, and eggs, local ricotta, salami, ham, pastries and fruit. A real gem. €80

EATING AND DRINKING

Caffè Sicilia Corso Vittorio Emanuele 125 ☎ 0931 837 582. You really shouldn't leave Noto without sampling the ice creams at its two (amicably) rival prize-winning *gelaterie*. The *Sicilia* is the more radical, with flavours such as lemon and saffron, and even basil. Tues–Sun 7.30am–8.30pm.

Costanzo Via Silvio Spaventa 7–11 ☎ 0931 835 243. A well-known *pasticceria* and *gelateria*, producing what may be the best ice cream in Italy (the other contender is *Sicilia*) in flavours such as mandarin, ricotta, jasmine and rose (depending on the season), as well as sweets and pastries, including dreamy cassata. 7.30am–8.30pm; closed Wed.

Emily's Wine Via Cavour 34 ☎ 0931 838 028, ⊛ enotecanoto.com. A nice place for a glass of good wine (€6) and tasty snacks such as crostini with ricotta and honey, an unctuous *caponata* (€9), *foccace* (€2–3), local cheeses and hams (€3 per portion). They also have several pasta dishes daily (€5.50–6.50) and a range of lentil and pulse soups to eat in or take away and heat up at home – useful if you have an apartment. Summer daily 11am–3pm & 4pm–late; closed Wed in winter and shorter hours.

Trattoria Baglieri Il Crocifisso Via Principe Umberto 46 ☎ 0931 571 151. Nationally recognized trattoria using seasonal local ingredients in ways that make the taste buds zing: spaghetti with prawns and wild asparagus (€12), rabbit in *agrodolce*, with orange blossom honey, wild greens, celery, carrot and peppers (€12), tuna in a pistachio-and-sesame crust (€14). 12.30–2.30pm & 8–10.30pm; closed Wed.

Modica

A dynamic little town, with solid left-wing allegiances, **MODICA** was the provincial capital until Mussolini shifted base to the more conservative Ragusa. Linked by both train and bus with Siracusa and Ragusa, this Baroque town is well worth a visit, with some great places to stay and eat, and to taste the local speciality, **chocolate**.

Arriving by car you have to negotiate your way through the confusing and badly signposted streets of the modern town, known as Sordo, before winding down to the old town, cascading down the sides of a narrow gorge. A powerful medieval base of the Chiaramonte, Baroque Modica is watched over by the magnificent eighteenth-century facade of **San Giorgio**, at the head of a vast flight of steps. It's thought that Gagliardi was responsible for this: the elliptical facade is topped by a belfry, the church approached by a symmetrical double staircase which switchbacks up across the upper roads of the town.

16

MODICAN CHOCOLATE

Modican chocolate is powerful, gritty stuff, made as the Mayans did, a technique introduced to Sicily by the Spanish, without cocoa butter, and without heat, so that the sugar doesn't melt, and the texture remains crunchy. Traditional flavours are vanilla and cinnamon; innovations include sea salt and chilli. Chocolate fans should not miss the annual festival, **Chocobarocco**, held in late October. At other times of the year sample at *Caffè dell'Arte*, Corso Umberto I 114, or *Bonajuto*, in a little alleyway across the street.

ARRIVAL AND DEPARTURE

MODICA

By train and bus Regional buses drop you right in the centre on Corso Umberto I; the train station is a good 10min walk away at the other end of town – walk up to the ornamental fountain at Piazza Rizone and bear left for the Corso.

By car Drivers can park on the street, but in most central areas you need to buy a parking voucher (from *tabacchi*) to put in your window (€0.30 for 30min, free at lunchtime and evenings, and all day Sun).

ACCOMMODATION

Casa Talia Via Exaudinos 1 ☎ 0932 752 075, ⊚ casa talia.it. Occupying a cluster of restored houses in what was once the Jewish ghetto of Modica, *Casa Talia* is far removed from the bustle of the city centre (there is access by car, but no passing traffic) yet just 5min walk down steps and alleyways to the main Corso. A garden planted with fruit trees adds to the feeling of getting away from it all. Rooms, designed by their architect owners, who live on site, are stylish and practical. Breakfasts are excellent (freshly squeezed juices, home-made cakes, jams and breads), and served in a fascinating whitewashed room occupying what were once caves used as a cistern and stables. **€130**

I Tetti di Siciliando Via Cannata 24 ☎ 0932 942 843, ⊚ siciliando.it. Simple, friendly and unpretentious hotel popular with budget travellers in the tangle of historic streets above Corso Umberto. Rooms are pretty basic, but it's reasonably priced and sociable and the helpful owners have rental bikes (€15/day) and can organize bike tours of the surrounding area. Look for the sign opposite the Agip petrol station towards the top of the Corso (where you'll have to park), and follow the steps

up around the passageway for the signposted "bed, bike and breakfast". **€35**

L'Orangerie Vico de Naro 5 ☎ 0932 754 703, ⊚ lorangerie.it. Tranquil, refined B&B with three huge suites (with kitchens) and four spacious rooms in a *palazzo* with frescoed ceilings and private flower-filled terraces. Doubles **€88**, suites from **€126**

Palazzo Failla Via Blandini 5 ☎ 0932 941 059, ⊚ palazzofailla.it. A handsome upper-town palace, by the Santa Teresa church, reborn as a comfortable four-star hotel, but, with just seven rooms, it retains the intimate feel of a gracious aristocratic *palazzo*. Rooms are elegant and traditional, with tiled floors, high frescoed ceilings and antique beds. There are also three contemporary minimalist rooms in an annexe. The website has some great last-minute deals. **€109**

Palazzo Il Cavaliere Corso Umberto I 259 ☎ 0932 947 219, ⊚ palazzoilcavaliere.it. A down-to-earth aristocratic family run their eighteenth-century palace as a B&B. The setting is splendid and authentic: original Caltagirone tiled floors, frescoed ceilings and antique furniture. There are eight rooms, three of which open on to a courtyard. **€85**

EATING AND DRINKING

Fattoria delle Torri Vico Napolitano 14 ☎ 0932 751 286. This is the one everyone talks about in town – a highly regarded restaurant for choice local dishes and an extensive Sicilian wine list. While not exactly economical, it's a memorable gastronomic experience for which booking is advised. Tues–Sat 12.30–2.30pm & 8–10.30pm, Sun lunch.

La Gazza Ladra Via Blandini 5 ☎ 0932 755 655, ⊚ ristorantelagazzaladra.it. Top-class restaurant that's part of the *Palazzo Failla* hotel, offering creative and exquisitely presented Sicilian cuisine (spaghetti with anchovies, candied orange, wild fennel flowers, chilli and wild onion greens; a fillet of Nebrodi mountain pork, with a cream of pine nuts and asparagus). *Degustazione* menus

at €65 and €80 a head plus drinks. Daily 12.30–2.30pm & 8–10.30pm.

La Locanda del Colonnello Vico Biscari 6 ☎ 0932 752 423. Done-up like a traditional *locanda*, with chequered tiled walls and a *pietra pece* (local limestone, naturally impregnated with petroleum) floor below cantilevered white vaults, with evocative photos of old Modica on its walls. Heavy napery and good service, however, remind you that this is a *Palazzo Failla* enterprise. The mixed antipasto (€9) is highly recommended: sardine *polpettine* with wild fennel, a crisp *scacce* (savoury pastry) with a reduced tomato filling, pepper- and fennel-seed studded salami, a *sformatino* of asparagus, and a miniature *arancino*. *Primi* are all €9, and make great use of legumes,

16

in dishes such as *maccu*, a traditional fava bean purée/soup, or pasta with chickpeas. *Secondi* (€10) include sausages and pancetta in a stickily reduced tomato sauce. 12.30–2.30pm & 8–10.30pm; closed Wed.

Osteria dei Sapori Perduti Corso Umberto I 228–30 ☎0932 944 247. Marvellous value, right on the Corso, where you can eat reasonably priced, traditional rustic dishes with a strong emphasis on beans and pulses, inside or out. The abundant mixed antipasto (€7.50) is a good way to start, and enough for two people, followed by *lolli con le fave* (handmade pasta with fava bean purée) or pasta with broth and meatballs. *Primi* are around €6. The menu is in Sicilian, but translations are available, and you can walk away with a full stomach for €10–15. 12.30–2.30pm & 8–10.30pm; closed Tues.

Taverna Nicastro Via S. Antonino 30 ☎0932 945 884. For traditional meat (and especially pork) dishes, try this delightfully old-fashioned and very reasonably priced trattoria with tables outside on a flight of steps in the upper part of the old town. Specialities include sausages and salamis made on the premises, ravioli stuffed with ricotta and dressed in a sauce of tomato, pancetta, sausage and pork (classic Modican fare, this). If pork's not your thing, there are some good hearty legume dishes. You could eat a four-course meal (including a *cannolo* or a lemon, cinnamon or almond jelly) for under €20, while house wine is €4 per litre. *Nicastro* is signposted from outside San Giorgio, but it's quite a walk, and you will probably still have to stop several people to ask the way before you find it. Tues–Sat 8–10.30pm.

Ragusa

RAGUSA is a town with two identities, literally split in two by the earthquake: the old town of **Ragusa Ibla**, on a jut of land above its valley, was flattened, and within a few years a new town, **Ragusa Superiore**, was built on a grand, planned grid, on a higher ridge to the west. Meanwhile, Ibla was rebuilt – in Baroque style – along its old medieval street-plan.

In the second half of the last century people began to move out of Ibla for the modern comforts of life in the apartment buildings rapidly sprouting up in Ragusa Superiore. All commercial and social activity shifted here, and until fifteen years ago Ibla was all but abandoned. Since then, thanks to generous European and government funding, Ibla has been painstakingly restored, and scores of B&Bs and stylish second homes now occupy its lovely limestone Baroque houses and palaces. However, with a population of just 2000 (out of a total of 70,000), and little in the way of ordinary shops or bars, Ibla is very much a museum town, virtually pedestrianized and dedicated only to tourism. Ragusa Superiore, on the other hand, is a busy and likeable provincial capital, mostly modern, but with a good slice of Baroque on the edge of the cleft between the two cities, where you may well want to spend a little time.

Ragusa Superiore

Ragusa Superiore is essentially a gridded Baroque town, slipping off to right and left on either side of the steeply sloping **Corso Italia**. To the right, down the Corso on a wide terrace above Piazza San Giovanni, stands the **Duomo**, conceived on a grand, symmetrical scale. Finished in 1774, its tapered columns and fine doorways are a fairly sombre background to the vigorous small-town atmosphere around. Back towards the train station, underneath the Ponte Nuovo, there's a **Museo Archeologico** (daily 9am–1.30pm & 3.30–7pm; €4; ☎0932 622 963) dealing mainly with finds from the archeological site of Kamarina (sixth century BC) on the coast to the southwest.

Ragusa Ibla

It's Ragusa Ibla, the original **lower town**, where most people head, its weather-beaten roofs straddling the outcrop of rock about twenty minutes' walk away. The main attraction, situated in the gleaming central core of the town, is Ibla's Duomo, **San Giorgio**. Stridently placed at the top of Piazza del Duomo, it's a masterpiece of Sicilian Baroque, built by Rosario Gagliardi and finished in 1784. The glorious three-tiered facade, sets of triple columns climbing up the wedding-cake exterior to a balconied belfry, is an imaginative work, though typically not much enhanced by venturing inside. As with Gagliardi's other important church in Modica (see p.921), all the beauty is in the immediacy of the powerful exterior.

16

The whole town – often deathly quiet – is ripe for aimless wandering. Gagliardi gets another credit for the elegant rounded facade of the church of San Giuseppe in Piazza Pola, a few steps below the Duomo, while Corso XXV Aprile continues down past abandoned *palazzi* to the Giardino Iblei (daily 8am–8pm), gardens occupying the very edge of the spur on which the town is built.

ARRIVAL AND INFORMATION RAGUSA

By train The train station is in Ragusa Superiore: from here, a left turn takes you along the main road and over the exposed Ponte Nuovo, one of three bridges spanning a huge gully in the ridge.
Destinations Modica (8 daily; 20min); Noto (5 daily; 1hr 30min).
By bus The bus terminus is also in Ragusa Superiore at Via Zama. From here buses #11 and #33, among others, will

take you to Ibla, running around every 30min and stopping at Largo Kamerina and the Giardini Iblei.
Tourist office In Ragusa Superiore on Piazza San Giovanni, corner with Corso Italia (Mon–Fri 9am–7pm, Sat 9am–2pm; ☏ 0932 684 780, ✆ comune.ragusa.gov.it). There is also an information point (hours erratic) in the Giardini Iblei.

ACCOMMODATION

Alla Corte di Morfeo Salita Specula 7, Ragusa Ibla ☏ 0932 245 841, ✆ allacortedimorfeo.com. Wonderful roof terrace and five rooms furnished with a stylish mix of antique and contemporary furniture, including hand-painted wardrobes, Philippe Starck chairs, and mirrors that reproduce the shapes of the columns in the Duomo. The friendly owner is an English teacher, so communication is no problem. If you'd rather stay by the sea, the same family have a B&B with an apartment and three rooms in a villa with garden at Marina di Ragusa. **€80**
Eremo della Giubiliana 7.5km out of Ragusa, along the road to Marina di Ragusa ☏ 0932 669 119, ✆ eremo dellagiubiliana.com. An upmarket agriturismo (with its own 700m private airstrip no less) housed in the restored buildings of a feudal estate dating back to the twelfth century. The grounds are gorgeous, and you can dine on their own organically grown food. **€211**
Locanda Don Serafino Via XI Febbraio 15, Ragusa

Ibla ☏ 0932 22 0065, ✆ locandadonserafino.it. A small, excusive hotel, beautifully set within the hefty stone walls of a nineteenth-century mansion. Two of the rooms, occupying the former stables, are carved straight into the bare rock, and one of them (room 8) has a bathroom inside a cave. **€148**
L'Orto sul Tetto Via Ten. Distefano 56, Ragusa Ibla ☏ 0932 247 785 or ☏ 338 478 0484, ✆ lortosultetto.it. A warm, friendly place a short walk from the Duomo with three serene bedrooms, run by a mother and son. Breakfasts are served on a roof terrace full of plants and include pastries fresh from the bakery. **€110**
Villa Lauro Via Ecce Homo, Ragusa Superiore ☏ 0932 655 177, ✆ villadellauro.it. Minimalist style within the exposed limestone walls of an eighteenth-century *palazzo* in the historic part of Ragusa Superiore. Excellent choice in summer, when you can while away afternoons in the serene, stylish garden with swimming pool. **€170**

EATING AND DRINKING

Ibla has two internationally renowned rival restaurants, each of them well worth splashing out on. However, if you are on a budget, a good alternative is a picnic; wander down narrow, curving Corso 25 Aprile, lined with fancy shops selling local produce.

Pasticceria di Pasquale Corso Vittorio Veneto 104, Ragusa Superiore ☏ 0932 624 635, ✆ pasticceriadi pasquale.com. The best ice cream and utterly divine pastries and cakes in town. Just downhill from the Duomo of San Giovanni. Tues–Sun 7am–9pm.
Ristorante Duomo Via Capitano Bocchieri 31, Ragusa Ibla ☏ 0932 651 265. Meticulously sourced Sicilian ingredients reworked to stunning effect, in what is arguably Sicily's greatest restaurant. Put yourself in the hands of chef Ciccio Sultano, and opt for one of the tasting menus (€150) with wines, selected from the copious cellar, to match each course. At lunchtime there is a simpler three-course tasting menu (€45 without wine, €59 with) – a very good deal. 12.30–2.30pm & 8–10.30pm; closed Sun &

Mon lunch in summer, Sun eve & Mon in winter.
Ristorante Locanda Don Serafino Via Orfanotrofio 39, Ragusa Ibla ☏ 0932 248 778. In a vaulted medieval wine-cellar, lit by candles, this is a place to feast on artisan cheeses, Ragusana beef and lamb, Nebrodi mountain pork and fresh fish. The tasting menu costs €68 without wine. 12.30–2.30pm & 8–10.30pm; closed Tues.
Trattoria la Bettola Largo Kamerina, Ragusa Ibla ☏ 0932 653 377. A rarity in Ibla: a simple, inexpensive family-run trattoria with red-and-white tablecloths that has been around for 30 years. Antipasti cost €4 and include deep-fried and breadcrumbed morsels of local cheeses, aubergine *polpette* and a lemon-scented *tortino* of courgettes. *Primi* (all €7) include *tagliatelle* with cream and

16

saffron, *secondi* (€7—9) feature *maiale ubriaco*, pork braised in wine and wild herbs, in winter, and pork chops with citrus in summer. There is horsemeat as well, if you feel like going totally local. Tues–Sun 12.30–2.30pm & 8–10.30pm.

Agrigento

Though handsome, well sited and awash with medieval atmosphere, **AGRIGENTO** is rarely visited for the town itself. The interest instead focuses on the substantial **remains** of Pindar's "most beautiful city of mortals", a couple of kilometres below. Here, strung out along a ridge facing the sea, is a series of **Doric temples** – the most captivating of Sicilian Greek remains and a grouping unique outside Greece.

In 581 BC colonists from nearby Gela and from Rhodes founded the city of **Akragas** between the rivers of Hypsas and Akragas. They surrounded it with a mighty wall, formed in part by a higher ridge on which stood the acropolis (today occupied by the modern town). The southern limit of the ancient city was a second, lower ridge and it was here, in the "**Valle dei Templi**", that the city architects erected their sacred buildings during the fifth century BC.

Valley of the Temples

Via dei Templi • Daily 8.30am–7pm; July–Sept, the temples of Juno, Concord and Hercules also open Mon–Fri 7.30–10 pm, Sat & Sun 7.30pm–midnight • €10 • ⊕ valleyofthetemples.com • Buses #1, #2 and #3 run to the main entrance from outside Agrigento train station; tickets from bar inside the station. Open entry on summer nights is at the Temple of Juno entrance, accessible from the main entrance by taxi (€2 per person)

A road winds down from the modern city to the **Valle dei Templi**, which is divided into two zones. The more spectacular remains are in the eastern zone – to avoid crowds come in the early morning or (in summer) for the night openings. The western zone may be less architecturally impressive, but gives more of a sense of discovery – and holds the lovely gardens of Kolymbetra.

The eastern zone

The **eastern zone** is unenclosed and is at its crowd-free best in early morning or late evening. A path climbs up to the oldest of Akragas's temples, the **Tempio di Ercole** (Hercules). Probably begun in the last decades of the sixth century BC, nine of the original 38 columns have been re-erected, everything else is scattered around like the pieces of a jigsaw puzzle. Retrace your steps back to the path that leads to the glorious **Tempio della Concordia**, dated to around 430 BC: perfectly preserved and beautifully sited, with fine views to the city and the sea, the tawny stone lends the structure warmth and strength. That it's still so complete is explained by its conversion in the sixth century AD to a Christian church. Restored to its (more or less) original layout in the eighteenth century, it has kept its lines and slightly tapering columns, although it's fenced off to keep the crowds at bay. The path continues, following the line of the ancient city walls, to the **Tempio di Giunone** (Juno or Hera), an engaging half-ruin standing at the very edge of the ridge. The patches of red visible here and there on the masonry denote fire damage, probably from the sack of Akragas by the Carthaginians in 406 BC.

The western zone

The **western zone**, back along the path and beyond the car park, is less impressive, a vast tangle of stone and fallen masonry from a variety of temples. Most notable is the mammoth construction that was the **Tempio di Giove**, or Temple of Olympian Zeus. The largest Doric temple ever known, it was never completed, left in ruins by the Carthaginians and further damaged by earthquakes. Still, the stereobate remains, while on the ground, face to the sky, lies an eight-metre-high *telamone*: a supporting column sculpted as a male figure, arms raised and bent to bear the temple's weight. Other scattered remains litter the area, including the so-called **Tempio dei Dioscuri**

16

(Castor and Pollux), rebuilt in 1832 and actually made up of unrelated pieces from the confused rubble on the ground. When you've had your fill of the ruins, make for the **Giardino Kolymbetra**, an enchanting sunken garden of shady citrus, almond and olive groves, with a stream running through it, set between cave-pocked tufa cliffs that once formed part of the city's irrigation system.

Museo Nazionale Archeologico

Tues–Sat 9am–1pm & 2–7pm, Mon & Sun 9am–1pm • €8

Via dei Templi leads back to the town from the car park via the excellent **Museo Nazionale Archeologico**. The extraordinarily rich collection is devoted to finds from the city and the surrounding area; the best displays are the cases of vases (sixth to third century BC) and a reassembled *telamone* stacked against one wall. Nip over the road on the way out for the **Hellenistic-Roman quarter** (daily 9am until 1hr before sunset; free), which contains lines of houses, inhabited intermittently until the fifth century AD, many with mosaic designs still discernible.

Agrigento Town

It would be a mistake not to scout round the town of **Agrigento**. Thoroughly medieval at its heart, its tiny stepped streets and fine churches look down over the Valle dei Templi (dramatically floodlit at night) and beyond to the sea. The main street, **Via Atenea**, starts at the eastern edge of the old town, above the train station, the streets off to the right harbouring ramshackle *palazzi* and the church of **Santa Maria dei Greci**. It was built over a fifth-century-BC Greek temple, whose flattened columns are visible in the nave, while an underground tunnel reveals the stylobate and column stumps, all part of the church's foundations.

ARRIVAL AND INFORMATION

AGRIGENTO

By train Trains arrive at Agrigento Centrale station at the edge of the old town; don't get out at Agrigento Bassa 3km north of town. There are good connections with Palermo (12 daily; 2hr 15min), but for other destinations the bus is usually faster.

By bus Regional buses use the terminal in Piazza Rosselli, near the post office. City buses to the temples and the beach at San Leone can be picked up here or at the train station. Buy city bus tickets (€1) from kiosks or *tabacchi*.

Destinations Catania and Catania airport (hourly; 2hr 50min); Palermo (5 daily; 2hr 30min); Trapani (3 daily; 3hr).

Tourist office Via Atene 272 (Mon–Fri 9.30am–1.30pm plus Tues & Thurs 3.30–7.30pm; ☎ 0922 596 168).

ACCOMMODATION

BB Locanda di Terra Via F. Crispi 34 ☎ 0922 22 275, ⓦ locandaditerra.it. A seductive, family-run B&B in a nineteenth-century villa where the dramatist Luigi Pirandello spent his summers. Five spacious rooms, a shady garden, a sunny terrace and a common room with facilities for making hot chocolate, tea and coffee. The *La Terra* restaurant is in its garden. €75

Mille e Una Notte Via Garibaldi 46 ☎ 320 483 5856, ⓦ milleeunanottebeb.it. Sensitively run B&B with spick-and-span rooms including two sleeping four and five and a small apartment with cooking facilities. €88

Scala dei Turchi Via Grande 171, Realmonte ☎ 0922 816 238, ⓦ scaladeiturchi.net. A sweet little B&B in the village of Realmonte – the main attraction being that it is close to the stunning white cliffs of Scala dei Turchi and some unspoilt beaches. €50

Enna and the interior

From a bulging V-shaped ridge almost 1000m above sea level, **ENNA** lords it over the surrounding hills of central Sicily. The approach to this doughty mountain stronghold is formidable, the road climbing slowly out of the valley and looping across the solid crag to the summit and town. For obvious strategic reasons, Enna was a magnet for successive hostile armies, who in turn besieged and fortified the town, each doing their damnedest to disprove Livy's description of Enna as *inexpugnabilis*.

FROM TOP CLOISTERS, MONREALE (P.886); TOUR GROUP CLIMBING MOUNT ETNA (P.906) >

Castello di Lombardia

Daily: summer 8am–8pm; winter 9am–5pm • Free

Despite the destructive attention, most of Enna's remains are medieval and in good shape, with the prize exhibit the thirteenth-century **Castello di Lombardia**, dominating the easternmost spur of town. A mighty construction with its strong walls complete, it guards the steep slopes on either side of Enna, its six surviving towers (out of an original twenty) providing lookouts. From the tallest, the **Torre Pisana**, the magnificent **views** take in Enna itself, some rugged countryside in all directions and, if you're lucky, Mount Etna.

Via Roma and the Duomo

In the centre of town virtually all the accredited sights lie stretched out along and around **Via Roma**, which descends from the castle. It's a narrow street, broken by small piazzas – one of which fronts the hemmed-in **Duomo** (daily 9am–noon & 4–7pm; free), dating in part from 1307. The spacious sixteenth-century interior features huge supporting alabaster columns, the bases of which are covered with an amorphous writhing mass of carved figures.

Piazza Vittorio Emanuele and the Chiesa di San Francesco

Via Roma slopes down to the rectangular **Piazza Vittorio Emanuele**, focal point of the evening *passeggiata*. Off here, there's a long cliff-edge belvedere, while the bottom of the piazza is marked by the plain, high wall of the **Chiesa di San Francesco**, whose massive sixteenth-century tower previously formed part of the town's system of watchtowers.

Torre di Federico

This linked the castle with the **Torre di Federico**, which stands in isolation in its little park in the largely modern south of the town. An octagonal tower, 24m high, it's a survivor of the alterations to the city made by Frederick of Aragon who added a (now hidden) underground passage linking it to the *castello*.

16

ARRIVAL AND INFORMATION	ENNA

By bus There are around six buses daily to and from Piazza Armerina, a 30min ride away.

Tourist office Piazza Colaianni, off Via Roma next to the Grande Albergo Sicilia (Mon–Fri 8am–2pm, plus Wed 2.45–6.15pm; ☎ 0935 500 875); has a good town map and accommodation details.

ACCOMMODATION AND EATING

Bianko & Bianko Via Longo 15 ☎ 331 329 4288 or ☎ 327 159 8426, ⓦ biankoebianko.it. The nicest B&B in town with three spacious, light-filled rooms in stylish white. It's handy for the old town, just to the right of the steps of San Cataldo church (bottom of Via Vittorio Emanuele). **€55**

Grotta Azzurra Via Colaianni 1 ☎ 0935 24 328. This place can't be beaten – a no-frills, basement trattoria with *primi* for €3 and *secondi* for €5 or €6. It's at the very bottom of Via Roma, past Piazza Vittorio Emanuele and down an alley. 12.30–2.30pm & 8–10.30pm; closed Sat in winter.

La Casa del Poeta Contrada Parasporino ☎ 329 627 4918, ⓦ lacasadelpoeta.it. Out of town, the most original accommodation is this artistically inclined, nineteenth-century villa, about 1km from Lago di Pergusa, where the rooms are serene and minimalist, and the grounds include a swimming pool. **€100**

Piazza Armerina and around

A thirty-minute drive to the south of Enna, **PIAZZA ARMERINA** lies amid densely planted hills; it's a quiet, unassuming place mainly seventeenth and eighteenth century in appearance, with a skyline pierced by towers and houses huddled together under the joint protection of castle and cathedral. All in all, it's a thoroughly pleasant place to idle around, though the real local draw is an imperial **Roman villa** that stands in rugged countryside at Casale, 5km southwest of Piazza Armerina. It was hidden under mud for seven hundred years, until excavations in the 1950s revealed a lavish villa, probably a hunting lodge and summer home, decorated with polychromatic mosaic floors that are unique in the Roman world for their quality and extent.

ARRIVAL AND INFORMATION   PIAZZA ARMERINA

By bus Buses drop you in Piazza Senatore Marescalchi, a large square on the main road in the lower, modern town, 15min walk from the old centre.
Destinations Enna (6 daily; 30min); Palermo (5 daily

Mon–Sat; 2hr 15min).
Tourist office Via Cavour (Mon–Fri 9am–1pm & 3.30–7.30pm; ☏ 0935 683 049, ⊛ piazza-armerina.it).

ACCOMMODATION AND EATING

Amici Miei Largo Capodarso 5 ☏ 0935 683 541. Despite the distance from the sea, the fish is excellent here, ranging from baked bream to sautéed mussels (dishes €6–14). There are also excellent pizzas in the evening, which you can eat outside on a charming terrace. 12.30–2.30pm & 8–10.30pm; closed Thurs.

Suite d'Autore Piazza Duomo ☏ 0935 688 553, ⊛ suitedautore.it. Top choice in town is the fabulously quirky "art-hotel" opposite the cathedral whose fun-filled

rooms mix contemporary design, stylish artefacts, retro objects, original art and photography. **€140**

Trattoria del Goloso Via Garao 4, just off Piazza Garibaldi ☏ 0935 685 693. An excellent choice for good-value seasonal regional dishes such as handmade pasta with cherry tomatoes, aubergine and basil served with a dollop of fresh ricotta (€6.50). 12.30–2.30pm & 8–10.30pm; closed Wed in winter.

Villa Romana del Casale

Strada Provinciale 15 • Daily 9am–6pm, closes 5pm in winter • €10 • ☏ 0935 680 036, ⊛ villaromanadelcasale.org

16

The **Villa Romana del Casale** dates from the early fourth century BC and was used right up until the twelfth century when a mudslide left it largely covered until the 1950s. The **mosaics** themselves are identifiable as fourth-century Roman-African school, which explains many of the more exotic scenes and animals portrayed; they also point to the villa having had an important owner, possibly Maximianus Herculeus, one of four co-emperors with Diocletian, who divided the Roman world up between them.

The **main entrance** leads into a wide courtyard with fountains, where the **thermae** (baths) group around an octagonal *frigidarium* and a central mosaic showing a lively marine scene. A walkway leads out of the baths and into the villa proper, to the massive central court or **peristyle**, whose surrounding corridors are decorated with animal-head mosaics. From here, a balcony looks down on one of the villa's most interesting pictures, a boisterous circus scene showing a chariot race. Small rooms beyond, on either side of the peristyle, reveal only fragmentary geometric patterns, although one contains probably the villa's most famous image, a two-tiered scene of ten realistically muscular **Roman girls in "bikinis"**, taking part in various gymnastic and athletic activities.

Beyond the peristyle, a long, covered corridor contains the most extraordinary of the mosaics: the **great hunting scene**, which sets armed and shield-bearing hunters against a panoply of wild animals. Along the entire sixty-metre length of the mosaic are tigers, ostriches, elephants, even a rhino, being trapped, bundled up and down gangplanks and into cages, destined for the Games back in Rome. The square-hatted figure overseeing the operation is probably Maximianus himself: his personal area of responsibility in the imperial Tetrarchy was North Africa, where much of the scene is set.

Other rooms beyond are nearly all on a grand scale. The **triclinium**, a dining room with three apses, features the labours of Hercules, and a path leads around the back to the **private apartments**, based around a large basilica. The best mosaics here are a children's circus, where tiny chariots are drawn by colourful birds, and a children's hunt, the kids chased and pecked by the hares and peacocks they're supposed to snare.

By bus From Piazza Armerina, a bus (May–Sept only) leaves Piazza Senatore Marescalchi for the Villa Romana on the hour between 9am and noon, and between 3pm and 6pm, with a stop at Piazza Generale Cascino; it's a half-hour ride, and the return service is on the half-hour, starting at 9.30am.

By taxi A taxi from Piazza Generale Cascino in Piazza Armerina costs around €10 one way.

Trapani and the west

The **west** of Sicily is a land apart. Skirting around the coast from **Trapani** – the provincial capital – the cubic whitewashed houses, palm trees, active fishing harbours and sunburned lowlands seem more akin to Africa than Europe, and historically, the west of the island has always looked south. The earliest of all Sicilian sites, the mountain haunt of **Erice** was dominated by Punic influence; the Carthaginians themselves entrenched themselves in **Marsala**, at Sicily's westernmost point, for several hundred years; while in medieval times the Saracen invaders took their first steps onto the island at **Mazara del Vallo**, a town still strongly Arabic at heart. The Greeks never secured the same foothold in Sicily's west as elsewhere, although the remains at **Segesta** and **Selinunte** count among the island's best. Also worth seeing are the three islands of the **Egadi** archipelago, and the stunning stretch of coastline protected by the **Riserva Naturale dello Zingaro**.

16 Trapani and around

Out on a limb, and with more than a little North African atmosphere about it, **TRAPANI** is an attractive old port town, rediscovering its charms after years of neglect. Halfway point between Europe and Tunis, it was a rich trading centre throughout the early Middle Ages, then flourished again in the nineteenth and early twentieth centuries as a stronghold of the tuna-canning industry. After that, it went into decline, and became a salty old port with a crumbling, sun-scorched historic centre high on atmosphere, but with few creature comforts. Then, it was selected to host the 2004 Americas Cup and received a massive injection of cash – buildings were restored, streets in the historic centre pedestrianized – giving the town and its people a new confidence. These days Trapani is a thoroughly pleasant and authentic place to hang out for a couple of days. Adding to its reviving fortunes, the nearby airport of Birgi is undergoing a renaissance too, and on the way to becoming Sicily's main low-cost airport. Trapani's **Easter celebrations** are justly famous, involving dramatic processions around town, particularly poignant on Good Friday.

The centro storico

The nicest way to approach the **centro storico** is along pedestrianized **Via Garibaldi**, which begins opposite the northwest corner of the Villa Margherita gardens across from the train station. Lined with palaces, churches and little pavement cafés, it leads to Via Torrearsa, a pedestrianized shopping street, which neatly splits the old town in two. West of here Trapani's layout becomes more regularly planned, while the main drag and shopping street, the elegant, pedestrianized **Corso Vittorio Emanuele**, changes its name to Via Carolina and then Via Torre di Ligny as it runs towards the **Torre di Ligny** – utmost point of the scimitar of land that holds the old town.

Back on Via Torrearsa, Corso Italia leads back towards the station via a trio of little piazzas, enlivened by their surrounding churches: the sixteenth-century **Chiesa di Santa Maria di Gesù** (Via San Pietro) is defiantly Renaissance in execution, while the fourteenth-century church of **Sant'Agostino** retains a Gothic portal and delicate rose window.

Chiesa del Purgatorio

Via Francesco d'Assisi • In theory open daily 9am to noon, though it's often closed; ask at the tourist office for current information • Free

South of the Corso, Via Francesco d'Assisi holds the exuberantly sculpted **Chiesa del Purgatorio**, at the junction with Via Domenico Giglio, where the **Misteri**, a group of life-sized eighteenth-century wooden figures representing scenes from the Passion, are displayed when they're not being wheeled around town during Trapani's Easter commemorations.

ARRIVAL AND DEPARTURE TRAPANI

By plane Trapani's airport, 15km south of the centre at Birgi, has flights from Italian cities and Pantelleria (1–3 daily; 40min), as well as several Ryanair services from mainland Europe, Britain and Ireland. Buses (run by Terravision, but usually with Segesta written on the side) call at Trapani port, Trapani station and Palermo's Piazza Politeama and Stazione Centrale and are timed to coincide with Ryanair flights: seats are available only to Ryanair customers (you have to show your boarding card to buy a ticket: €8). Journey time to Palermo is about two hours. AST also has a regular (hourly) service to Trapani port and station.

By train Trains stop at the Stazione Centrale just around the corner from the bus station.

Destinations Marsala (13 daily; 30min); Mazara del Vallo (13 daily; 40min–1hr); Palermo (6 daily; 2hr 15min–4hr);

Segesta Tempio (4 daily; 20min).

By bus Most buses (including those to and from Erice) pull up at the terminal in Piazza Malta. If you're heading straight off to the Egadi Islands, note that the fast buses from the airport, Palermo, Palermo airport and Agrigento stop at the ferry and hydrofoil terminals, as well as the bus station.

Destinations Agrigento (3 daily; 3hr 10min–3hr 40min); Erice (8 daily; 45min); San Vito lo Capo (8 daily; 1hr 20min).

By boat Ferries for the Egadi Islands, Pantelleria, Cagliari and Tunis dock at the Molo di Sanità, while hydrofoils for the Egadi Islands and Ustica dock to the east of the Molo, on Via A. Stati.

Destinations Favignana (hourly; 15–40min); Levanzo (hourly; 20–40min); Marettimo (5 daily; 1hr); Naples (3–4 weekly; 6hr 45min); Ustica (3–4 weekly; 2hr 30min).

INFORMATION

Tourist office Via Torrearsa, near the port (summer Mon–Sat 9am–1pm & 3.30–8pm, Sun 9am–1pm; reduced

times in other periods; ☎0923 544 533, ⓦ comune.trapani .it/turismo).

ACCOMMODATION

Ai Lumi Corso Vittorio Emanuele 71 ☎0923 540 922, ⓦ ailumi.it. Five small, but pristine rooms entered through a flower-filled courtyard. They also own the trattoria of the same name at street-level. **€90**

Lido Valderice Località Lido Valderice ☎0923 573 477 or ☎349 854 2190, ⓦ campinglidovalderice.it; around 5 buses daily (except Sun in winter) from Trapani bus station (direction San Vito via Sciare) to the turn-off, from where it's a 10min walk. Appealing campsite near the beach at Lido Valderice, a 25min bus-ride away, with bungalows and caravans to rent as well as tent pitches. **€5.90** per person, Pitches **€9.90**

Maccotta Via degli Argentieri 4 ☎0923 28 418, ⓦ albergomaccotta.it. Smart and friendly place with spacious, modern rooms with comfortable beds but small

bathrooms; a/c and wi-fi available **€75**

Moderno Via Ten. Genovese 20 ☎0923 21 247, ⓦ hotel moderno.trapani.it. Housed in an old *palazzo* with a courtyard, this has simple, clean rooms with a/c, some with little balconies over the street. **€55**

Tonnara di Bonagia Piazza Tonnara di Bonagia ☎0923 431 111, ⓦ tonnaradibonagia.it. Excellent choice for families, this hotel occupies the buildings of an old tuna fishery (complete with beached tuna-boats and Saracen watchtower) and has accommodation in apartments with a kitchen, as well as conventional rooms. There is a huge pool, a tennis court, laidback activities for kids, local produce for sale, and little paths leading straight out of the grounds to the shore, where you can swim off rocks or a wooden jetty. **€250**

EATING AND DRINKING

Le Baccante Via Garibaldi 56. This recently opened little restaurant bar has appealing candlelit tables on atmospheric Via Garibaldi and in the stepped alleyway above. It is especially good in summer, as the cooking is light and fresh, with inventive salads, along with tasty pasta (€6) and fish (from €10). Summer daily 12.30–2.30pm & 8–10.30pm.

Le Mura Viale delle Sirene 15/19 ☎ 0923 872 622. On the

seafront below the Bastione della Conca, this is a lovely place to eat seafood – there's no better place to try the famed prawns of Mazara del Vallo. It serves exquisite fish dishes, with plenty of simple options as well as more elaborate dishes. Tues–Sat 12.30–2.30pm & 8–10.30pm.

Pizzeria Calvino Via N. Nasi 77 ☎0923 21 464. A Trapani institution, this bustling bakery has been making pizza since

16

1946. Try the local speciality, *rianata* with tomato, pecorino and oregano, or a hearty plate of sausages and potatoes roasted with onions in the pizza oven. 9am–1pm & 5–8pm; closed Tues.

Erice

The nearest and most exhilarating ride from Trapani is to **ERICE**, fifteen minutes away by **cable car** (*funivia*). It's a mountain town with creeping hillside alleys, stone buildings, silent charm and powerful associations. Founded by Elymnians, who claimed descent from the Trojans, the original city was known to the ancient world as Eryx, and a magnificent temple, dedicated to Venus Erycina, Mediterranean goddess of fertility, once topped the mountain. Though the city was considered impregnable, Carthaginian, Roman, Arab and Norman invaders all forced entry over the centuries. But all respected the sanctity of Erice: the Romans rebuilt the temple and set two hundred soldiers to serve as guardians of the shrine, while the Arabs renamed the town Gebel-Hamed, or "Mohammed's mountain".

Scout around the town at random: the most convoluted of routes is only going to take you a couple of hours and every street and piazza is a delight. You enter through the Norman **Porta Trapani**, just inside which is the **Duomo** (daily: March 10am–4pm; April–June & Oct 10am–6pm; July & Aug 10am–8pm; Sept 10am–7pm; Nov–Feb 10am–12.30pm; €2.50) and its battlemented fourteenth-century campanile, the **Torre di Re Federico**, which did service as a lookout tower for Frederick III of Aragon (€2.50). From here there's no set route, though passing through pretty **Piazza Umberto** with its outdoor bars is a good idea.

Castello di Venere

April–Oct daily 10am–1hr before sunset; Nov–March Sat & Sun 10am–4pm • €3.50

A natural start or finish is the ivy-clad **Castello di Venere** at the far end of town; the Norman castle was built on the site of the famed ancient temple, chunks of which are incorporated in the walls. When it's fine, the **views** from the terraces of Erice are phenomenal – over Trapani and the slumbering whales of the Egadi Islands.

ARRIVAL AND INFORMATION

ERICE

By bus To get to Erice from Trapani, take bus #21 or #23 (direction Ospedale S. Antonio Abbate) and get off at the stop before the hospital, from where it's a short walk to the *funivia* station (the cable car operates Mon 2–8.30pm, Tues–Fri 7.30am–8.30pm, Sat & Sun 9.30am–midnight,

though the service may be cancelled if it's windy). The trip costs €3.50 one way, €6 return and you arrive at the Porta Trapani in Erice.

Tourist office Near Porta Trapani at Via Guarrasi 1 (Mon–Fri 8am–2pm; ☎ 0923 869 388).

ACCOMMODATION

Elimo Via Vittorio Emanuele 75 ☎ 0923 869 377, ⍟ hotelelimo.it. Luxurious rooms in a beautifully restored hotel with a small courtyard garden. €130

Il Carmine Piazza del Carmine 23 ☎ 0923 869 089 or ☎ 0923 194 1532, ⍟ ilcarmine.com. Spacious, bright rooms in a former Carmelite convent in the heart of town, with separate private bathrooms. €80

San Domenico Via Tommaso Guerrasi 26 ☎ 0923 860 128, ⍟ hotel-sandomenico.it. Engaging, recently opened, family-run hotel in a medieval house in the heart

of Erice – with the owners' children's toys in evidence in the sitting room along with some robust rustic antiques. Two sets of connecting rooms, and a triple. Breakfast is in a tiny courtyard. €115

Ulisse Camere Via S. Lucia 2 ☎ 0923 860 155 or ☎ 389 985 6089, ⍟ sitodiulisse.it. Nicely furnished rooms dispersed over two buildings, with private bathrooms. The best are grouped around a tranquil central courtyard. They also have a restaurant in Via Chiaramonte serving local dishes. €65

EATING AND DRINKING

If you're coming for the day you may want to bring a picnic since restaurant prices in Erice are vastly inflated – the gardens below the Castello di Venere make a lovely picnic spot, with great views of the Egadi Islands, especially at sunset.

Caffè Maria Via Vittorio Emanuele 4. Don't leave town without a visit to the café or its sister *pasticceria* a few doors

down, for marzipan goodies and exquisite *cannoli*. The café's founder, Maria Grammatico, learned her trade as a girl in a convent, and has co-written a recipe book with writer Mary Taylor Simeti. 7.30am–8.30pm; closed Tues in winter.

La Pentolaccia Via Guarnotti 17 ☎0923 869 099. Atmospherically housed in an old monastery, this moderately priced place serves excellent, home-made pasta and couscous. Try the ravioli stuffed with *cernia* (grouper) in a sauce of cherry tomato, swordfish, mint and prawns (€10) or the *pasta nostromo*, dressed with the roe of

a John Dory, Mazzara prawns, tomatoes and garlic (€15). 12.30–2.30pm & 8–10.30pm; closed Tues.

La Vetta Via G. Fontana. Standard trattoria serving pizza as well in the evenings, with tables outside in summer. 12.30–2.30pm & 8–10.30pm; closed Thurs in winter.

Monte San Giuliano Vicolo S. Rocco 7 ☎0923 869 595. Really excellent food in a restaurant entered through a medieval stone archway. 12.30–2.30pm & 8–10.30pm; closed Mon & three weeks in Nov & Jan.

The Temple of Segesta

Daily 9am to 1hr before sunset • €6

One of the most evocative Doric temples anywhere, the temple at **SEGESTA** lies 35km southeast of Trapani. Although unfinished, this Greek construction of 424 BC is virtually the only relic of an ancient city whose roots – like those of Erice – go back to the twelfth century BC. Unlike Erice, though, ancient Segesta was eventually Hellenized and spent most of the later period disputing its borders with Selinus to the south. The temple dates from a time of prosperous alliance with Athens, the building abandoned when a new dispute broke out with Selinus in 416 BC.

The **temple** itself crowns a low hill, beyond a café and car park. From a distance you could be forgiven for thinking that it's complete: the 36 regular white stone columns, entablature and pediment are all intact, and all it lacks is a roof. However, get closer and you see just how unfinished the building is: stone studs, always removed on completion, still line the stylobate, the tall columns are unfluted and the *cella* walls are missing. Below the car park, a road winds up through slopes of wild fennel to the small **theatre** on a higher hill beyond; there's a **minibus** service every thirty minutes if you don't fancy the twenty-minute climb. The view from the top is justly lauded, across green slopes and the plain to the sea, the deep blue of the bay a lovely contrast to the theatre's white stone – not much damaged by the stilted motorway snaking away below.

16

| ARRIVAL AND DEPARTURE | THE TEMPLE OF SEGESTA |

By bus Using public transport to get to Segesta, you'd do best to catch one of the two direct Tarantola buses from Piazza Malta in Trapani, leaving at 8am, 10am, noon and 2pm (Sun 10am only), returning at 12.50pm, 1.05pm,

4.05pm and 6.30pm (Sun 1.05pm only). There are also bus services from Castellammare del Golfo and Palermo.
By train There are four trains daily from Trapani to Segesta-Calatafimi, from where it's a 20min uphill walk to the site.

The Egadi Islands

Of the various islands, islets and rock stacks that fan out from the west coast of Sicily, the three **Egadi Islands** (Isole Egadi) are best for a quick jaunt – connected by ferry and hydrofoil with Trapani. Saved from depopulation by tourism, in season at least you're not going to be alone, certainly on the main island, **Favignana**, where in August every scrap of flat rock and sand is filled. But a tour of the islands is worthwhile, not least for the caves that perforate the splintered coastlines. Out of season things are noticeably quieter, and in May or June you may witness the bloody **Mattanza**, an age-old slaughter in this noted centre of tuna fishing, though its future is uncertain.

| ARRIVAL | THE EGADI ISLANDS |

Ferries to the islands depart from Trapani's Molo di Sanità; **hydrofoils** from further east along Via Ammiraglio Staiti. Though less frequent, ferries are, as always, much cheaper.

Favignana

FAVIGNANA, island and port town, is first stop for the boats from Trapani, and makes a good base since it has virtually all the accommodation and the Egadis' only campsites.

Only 25 minutes by hydrofoil from the mainland, the island attracts a lot of day-trippers, keen to get onto its few rocky beaches. But get out of the main port and it's easy enough to escape the crowds, even easier with a bike (which can be rented from dozens of outlets in the centre of town). **Caves** all over the island bear prehistoric traces and many are accessible if you're determined enough. Otherwise, the two wings of the island invite separate **walks**; best is the circuit around the eastern part, past the bizarre ancient quarries at Cala Rossa, over the cliffs to Cala Azzurra and then following the coast past the ugly tourist village at Punta Fanfalo to Lido Burrone, one of the island's best beaches, only 1km from the port. Other beaches worth checking out are **Cala Rossa** and **Cala Azzurra**, on the eastern end of the island.

ACCOMMODATION

FAVIGNANA

Aegusa Via Garibaldi 11 ☎ 0923 922 430, ⓦ aegusa hotel.it. A central but quiet choice in town, with 28 cheerful rooms and a well-regarded restaurant. **€90**

Cave Bianche Cala Azzurra ☎ 0923 925 451, ⓦ cave bianchehotel.it. Another hotel inside a quarry, this also has chic, minimalist rooms, plus the added draws of a swimming pool and restaurant. **€305**

Hotel delle Cave Contrada Torretta, Str Vic. della Madonna (but known locally as Zona Cavallo) ☎ 0923 925 423, ⓦ hoteldellecave.it. One of the island's two most striking places to stay – a designer hotel with just

fourteen rooms built on the lip of an abandoned quarry, with two mini-hydromassage pools and gardens inside the quarry itself. **€230**

Villa Antonella Via Punta Marsala ☎ 0923 921 073, ⓦ egadi.com/villaantonella. A family-run B&B a couple of kilometres outside town which also has self-catering mini-apartments sleeping 2–4 people. A good choice for families or those on a budget who want to be able to cook for themselves. It is walkable to town, but you might prefer to have your own transport. **€100**

Levanzo

LEVANZO, to the north, looks immediately inviting, its white houses against the turquoise sea reminiscent of the Greek islands. The steep coast is full of inlets and is riddled with caves. One, the **Grotta del Genovese** (ⓦ grottadelgenovese.it), was discovered in 1949 and contains some remarkable Paleolithic incised drawings, six thousand years old, as well as later Neolithic pictures. To visit the cave, book at least one day in advance, either in person at Via Calvario 11, above the quay, or on ☎ 339 741 8800; departures are twice daily in summer by boat, less frequent in winter by jeep (€20 per person). The island's **interior** has some great **walks** along old cart tracks, and there's a paved (and virtually traffic-free) cornice road leading to a lovely white-pebble **beach** by the jagged rocks of the Faraglioni.

ACCOMMODATION

LEVANZO

Lisola Residence Contrada Case ☎ 0923 194 1530 or ☎ 320 180 9090, ⓦ lisola.eu. Seven apartments (sleeping 2–4) in simple tufa cottages originally built by nineteenth-century tuna-canning magnate Florio for his workers,

400m outside the port. Extras include a large pool, canvas sun umbrellas and loungers, and free transport to the port whenever you need it. Minimum stay three nights or a week in summer. Closed Nov–March. **€85**

Marettimo

MARETTIMO, furthest out of the Egadi Islands, is the place to come for solitude. Very much off the beaten track, it's reached by only a few tourists. White houses are scattered across the rocky island, and there's a bar in the main piazza, along with two restaurants. The spectacular fragmented coastline is pitted with rocky coves sheltering hideaway **beaches**, and there are numerous gentle **walks**, which will take you all over the island.

ACCOMMODATION

MARETTIMO

Marettimo Residence ☎ 0923 923 202, ⓦ marettimo residence.it. An appealing little cluster of resort cottages available for weekly rental above a stony beach south of the main port, or ask at the café in the main square. From **€360/week**

Rosa dei Venti Punta S. Simone ☎ 0923 923 249, ⓦ isoladimarettimo.it. Half a dozen rooms with bathrooms, as well as apartments with cooking facilities, and friendly owners who can arrange boat trips. **€60**

16

Northeast of Trapani

The main reason for heading out northeast of Trapani is to get away from it all in the beguiling surroundings of what is probably Sicily's most beautiful coastal nature reserve.

Scopello and the Riserva Naturale dello Zingaro

The road to Scopello from Castellammare forks just before arriving at the village, with one strand running the few hundred metres down to the **Tonnara do Scopello**, set in its own tiny cove, an old tuna fishery where the writer Gavin Maxwell lived and worked in the 1950s, basing his *Ten Pains of Death* on his experiences here. It's almost too picturesque to be true – not least the row of abandoned buildings on the quayside and the ruined old watchtowers tottering on jagged pinnacles of rock above the sea. The actual village of **SCOPELLO** perches on a ridge a couple of hundred metres above the coastline, comprising little more than a paved square and a fountain, off which run a couple of alleys. Just a stone's throw away is the lovely bay of **Cala Bianca**, where there's good swimming.

Just 2km from Scopello is the southern entrance to the **Riserva Naturale dello Zingaro**, Sicily's first nature reserve, comprising a completely unspoiled 7km stretch of **coastline** backed by steep mountains. At the entrance, there's an **information hut**, where you can pick up a plan showing the **trails** through the reserve. It's less than twenty minutes to the first beach, Punta della Capreria, and 3km to the successive coves of Disa, Berretta and Marinella, which should be a little more secluded.

ARRIVAL AND DEPARTURE   SCOPELLO AND ZINGARO

As Castellammare's train station is 4km east of town, it is far easier to arrive by bus from Trapani. If not, a bus meets train arrivals and shuttles you into Piazza della Repubblica in Castellammare, from where buses run to Scopello (4 daily except on Sun mid-Sept to mid-June). From Scopello it's an easy 2km walk to the reserve's nearest entrance, though there is a bus in summer.

ACCOMMODATION AND EATING

Baia di Guidaloca 3km south of Scopello ☎0924 541 262, ⓦcampinguidaloca.com; the bus from Castellammare passes right by. A lovely campsite, a stone's throw from the bay of Cala Bianca. Easter to mid-Sept. Pitches **€27**

La Tavernetta Via A. Diaz 3 ☎0924 541 129, ⓦalbergolatavernetta.it. Twelve very pleasant, freshly refurbished rooms, all with balconies, sea views and pretty stencilled furniture, and a restaurant in a huge garden of olives, prickly pear and citrus trees. Friendly, accommodating owners and a restaurant specializing in local dishes like couscous (€10) and *spaghetti con e sarde* (€8). Half-board in Aug. **€85**

★ **La Tranchina** Via A. Diaz 7 ☎0924 541 099, ⓦpensione.tranchina.com. Simple rooms with a friendly English-speaking owner; you'll eat well here too – fresh fish, and interesting pasta dishes such as pasta with peppers and home-cured *bottarga* (tuna-fish egg roe). **€86**

South of Trapani

The coast south of Trapani may lack the drama of that to the north, but there are nevertheless several places you may wish to visit. The major attraction is the **ancient Greek site Selinunte**, with its massive ruined temples, though anyone at all interested in Sicily's past should take care not to miss the Phoenician island colony of **Mozia**. There are also two historic port towns you might want to see: **Marsala**, famous for sweet wine, and **Mazara del Vallo**, the most Arabic town in Sicily.

There's little else to stop for around the western coast; even less inland, which is crossed by one major road, the SS188, running from Marsala to **Salemi**, centre of a prosperous wine-making region.

Mozia

Around 15km south of Trapani, the unique Phoenician settlement of **MOZIA** (also known as Mothia or Motya) lies just offshore from the crystalline patchwork of saltpans, which line this part of the coast. Situated on one of the islands in the shallow **Stagnone lagoon**, it was excavated in the late nineteenth century by an Englishman, Joseph Whitaker. You can explore the **ruins** (daily 9.15am–6.15pm; €9) and visit the **museum** he established, worth doing for its magnificent and sensual sculpture alone, *Il Giovinetto di Mozia*.

ARRIVAL AND DEPARTURE   MOZIA

By bus If you're reliant on public transport, the island is more easily reached from Marsala: regular buses run from

Piazza del Popolo to the ferry landing.

ACCOMMODATION AND EATING

Baglio Vajarassa Contrada Spagnola 176 ☎0923 968 628, ⓦbagliovajarassa.com. This peaceful agriturismo lies a couple of kilometres south of the ferry landing, and

has rooms furnished with antiques, and typical local dishes for dinner around a communal table. Half-board only. **€60**

Marsala

Bypassing Mozia, and pretty much keeping within sight of the sea all the way, the western rail loop runs down the coast from Trapani to **MARSALA**, a distance of around 25km. The city, which takes its name from the Arabic Marsah-el-Allah, the port of Allah, was once the main Saracenic base in Sicily, but since the late eighteenth century it has been better known for the dessert wine that carries its name, something every bar and restaurant will sell you.

The centre of Marsala is extremely attractive, a clean sixteenth-century layout that's free of traffic and littered with high, ageing buildings and arcaded courtyards. The town also has two excellent museums.

Museo degli Arazzi Fiamminghi

Via Garraffa 57 • Tues–Sat 9.30am–1pm & 4–6pm, Sun 9.30am–1pm • €4 • ☎0923 711 327

The most central museum, behind the cathedral, is the **Museo degli Arazzi**, whose sole display is a series of eight enormous hand-stitched Flemish wool-and-silk **tapestries** depicting the capture of Jerusalem – sixteenth-century and beautifully rich, in burnished red, gold and green.

Museo Archeologico e della Nave Punica

Via Capo Lilibeo • Mon 9am–1.30pm, Tues–Sun 9am–6pm • €4 • ☎0923 952 535

Housed in one of the stone-vaulted warehouses that line the seafront, the impressive **Museo Archeologico e della Nave Punica** is Marsala's star attraction. Its major exhibit is a reconstructed Punic war ship once rowed by 68 oarsmen, probably sunk during the First Punic War, and rediscovered in 1971. Other bits and pieces on display are from the excavated site (mostly Roman) of Lilybaeum.

EATING   MARSALA

Il Gallo e l'Innamorata Via S. Bilardello 18 ☎0923 195 4446, ⓦilgallo. A small *osteria* with great food, including bruschetta with *bottarga* and *busiati con ragù di*

tonno. All dishes cost €6. Try the spectacular fresh pasta with local prawns, pistaccio pesto and sea-urchin pulp. 12.30–2.30pm & 8–10.30pm; closed Tues.

Mazara del Vallo

Half an hour's drive beyond Marsala, **MAZARA DEL VALLO** is Sicily's most important fishing port and a place of equal distinction for the Arabs and Normans who dominated the island a thousand years ago. The first Saracen gain in Sicily, Mazara was Arabic for 250 years until captured by Count Roger in 1075: the island's first Norman parliament met in the town 22 years later, and a relic of that period is the tiny pink-domed Norman chapel of **San Nicolò**, on the edge of the harbour. North Africans crew the colourful fishing boats that block the harbour and river, the old city kasbah once more houses a Tunisian community. Wandering around the **harbour** area is the most rewarding thing to do in Mazara, although you can also spend an enjoyable hour or so pottering around the town. There's a remodelled Norman **Duomo**, which shelters some Roman and Byzantine remains, and in nearby Piazza del Plebiscito, the fifteenth-century church of Sant'Egido has recently been transformed into the **Museo del Satiro** (daily 9am–6pm; €6), home of a somewhat risqué fourth-century-BC bronze satyr captured in the ecstatic throes of an orgiastic Dionysian dance. It was hauled up by a Mazara fishing boat, the *Captain Ciccio*, in the waters between Pantelleria and Cape Bon, Tunisia, in 1998. Sadly, as the fishermen brought the catch aboard, one of the arms broke off and has so far not been recovered. More archeological finds can be seen at two ex-churches, now both housing **museums** (both Mon–Fri 8am–2pm; free): San Bartolomeo off Via Porta Palermo, is home to the **Mirabilia Urbis**, while San Carlo on Via San Giovanni houses the **Amphoreus**.

Selinunte (Selinus)

Daily 9am to 1hr before sunset • €6 • ☎ 0924 46 277 • Bus from Castelvetrano train station (2–8 daily; 25min), itself 30min by bus from Mazara del Vallo

The westernmost of the Hellenic colonies, the Greek city of Selinus – **Selinunte** in modern Italian – reached its peak in the fifth century BC when a series of mighty temples was erected. A bitter rival of Segesta, whose lands lay adjacent to the north, the powerful city and its fertile plain attracted enemies hand over fist, and it was only a matter of time before Selinus caught the eye of Segesta's ally, Carthage. Geographically vulnerable, the city was sacked by Carthaginians, any recovery forestalled by earthquakes that later razed the city. Despite the destruction, which left the site completely abandoned until it was rediscovered in the sixteenth century, the ruins of Selinus have exerted a romantic hold ever since.

The site

The **site of Selinus** is set back behind the village of Marinella (see below). It's split into two parts with **temples** in each, known only as Temples A–G. The two parts are enclosed within the same site, with the car park and entrance lying through the landscaped earthbanks that preclude views of the east group of temples from the road. The first stop is at the **East Group**. Shrouded in the wild celery which gave the ancient city its name, the temples are in various stages of ruin: the most complete is the one nearest the sea (Temple E), while the northernmost (Temple G) is a tangle of columned wreckage 6m high in places. The road leads down from here, across the (now buried) site of the old harbour to the second part of excavated Selinus, the **acropolis** (where there is another car park), a site containing what remains of the other temples (five in all), as well as the well-preserved city streets and massive, stepped walls which rise above the duned beach below. Temple C stands on the highest point of the acropolis, and there are glorious views from its stones out over the sparkling sea: from this temple were removed some of the best metopes, now on show in Palermo's archeological museum.

Marinella

Marinella, right next to the Greek ruins of Selinunte, is no longer the isolated place it once was, with new buildings in the centre and the seafront slightly top-heavy with trattorias and *pensioni* these days. But it remains an attractive place, certainly if you're planning to make use of the fine sand **beach** that stretches west from the village to the ruins. Regular local buses pull up on the road that leads down to the seafront.

ACCOMMODATION AND EATING	**MARINELLA**

Baffo Lido Azzurro, Via Marco Polo ☎ 0924 46 256. Worth a visit for its pizzas, *fettuccine* dishes, friendly atmosphere and sea views from the terrace of its huge dining room. 12.30–2.30pm & 8–10.30pm; closed Nov–March.

Il Pescatore Via Castore e Polluce 31 ☎ 0924 46 303, ⓦ affittacamereilpescatore.it. A pretty B&B with a genial host, fruit breakfasts on the terrace and rooftop camping. No credit cards. **€50**

La Pineta On the east beach, Mare Pineta ☎0924 46 820. It's a lovely 3km walk along the beach to this trattoria, well worth the effort for its great location, fish dishes and speciality bread, though prices are fairly steep. Bring a torch for the return trek home at night. Summer daily 12.30–2.30pm & 8–10.30pm.

Sicilia Cuore Mio Via della Cittadella 44 ☎0924 46 077 or ☎336 612 769, ⓦsiciliacuoremio.it. This lovely little B&B, in an early twentieth-century farm with garden, faces the archeological site at the back and with a long terrace overlooking the sea in front. Parking free. €80

Pantelleria

Forty kilometres nearer to Tunisia than to Sicily, **PANTELLERIA** is the most singular of Sicily's outlying volcanic islands. Madly trendy (Armani has a *dammuso* here, Madonna rents one), its strategic position kept it in the mainstream of Sicilian history for years. Nowadays the most visible sign of its past is the gloomy black **Castello Barabacane**, whose origins are Roman, but whose present appearance owes most to the Spanish. The island was used as one of the main Mediterranean bases by the Fascists during World War II, and was bombed without mercy by the Allies in May 1943 as they advanced from North Africa. In part, this explains the morose appearance of the island's main town (also called Pantelleria) – thrown up in unedifying concrete.

There are no beaches of any kind in Pantelleria, its rough **black coastline** mainly jagged rocks, but the **swimming** is still pretty good in some exceptionally scenic spots. Inland, the largely mountainous country offers plenty of rambling opportunities, all an easy moped- or bus-ride from the port. If you're spending any length of time on Pantelleria, you may want to stay in one of the local **dammuso** houses: a throwback to the buildings of Neolithic times, their strong walls and domed roofs keep the temperature down indoors. The island's main drawback is the cost of living: there are only a few hotels, where there may be a minimum three-day stay in July and August, while food (and water) is mostly imported and therefore relatively expensive. The best times to visit are May/June or September/October, to avoid the summer's ferocious heat.

Pantelleria Town

PANTELLERIA TOWN is the site of most of the island's accommodation and facilities. It is no one's idea of the perfect island town, as most of it was flattened by Allied bombing in World War II and, save for the glowering silhouette of the castle on the far side of the harbour, consists mostly of simple low-rise, whitewashed concrete cubes. But that is hardly the point: long a stop on the ferry route to Africa, the port is a lively place in which you could easily spend lazy hours watching island life unfold before you.

Scauri and the pool of Sataria

There are seven daily buses along the **southwest coast** to the village of **Scauri**, passing on the way the first of the island's strange **sesi**, massive black Neolithic funeral mounds of piled rock, with low passages leading inside. On foot, it's just over an hour from the *sesi* to **Sataria**, where concrete steps lead down to a tiny square-cut **sea pool**. In the cave behind are more pools where warm water bubbles through, reputed to be good for curing rheumatism and skin diseases.

Gadir and the walk to Cala Levante

Along the **northeast coast** to the villages of Kamma and Tracino (4 daily buses), get the bus to drop you at the top of the route down into **Gadir**, a small anchorage with just a few houses hemmed in by volcanic pricks of rock. From here it's an easy, fairly flat hour's stroll to the charming **Cala Levante**, a huddle of houses around another tiny fishing harbour. Where the road peters out, bear right along the path at the second anchorage and keep along the coast for another five minutes until the **Arco dell'Elefante**, or "Elephant Arch", hoves into view, named after the hooped formation of rock that resembles an elephant stooping to drink.

The Montagna Grande

The principal inland destination is Pantelleria's main volcano, the **Montagna Grande**, whose summit is the island's most distinctive feature seen from out at sea. To reach the trailhead, take a bus to the crumbly old village of **Siba**, perched on a ridge below the volcano. To find the beginning of the track, keep left at the telephone sign by the *tabacchi* here, and strike off the main road.

The Sauna Naturale

From Siba, another (signposted) path – on the left as you follow the road through the village – brings you in around twenty minutes to the **Sauna Naturale** (or Bagno Asciutto). It's little more than a slit in the rock-face, where you can crouch in absolute darkness, breaking out into a heavy sweat as soon as you enter.

ARRIVAL AND DEPARTURE

PANTELLERIA

By plane Pantelleria is a 40min flight from Trapani (1–3 daily), and a 50min flight from Palermo (1–2 daily); the normal one-way fare from either is around €85, but with special offers on the web, you can end up paying less than half that. The airport is 5km southeast of town; a bus connects with flight arrivals and drops you in the central Piazza Cavour in Pantelleria Town.

By boat Arriving by sea, you'll disembark right at the port in the centre of town, unless bad weather forces a landing at Scauri on the island's southwestern side, from where a bus takes foot passengers into town. Siremar runs ferries and Ustica Lines hydrofoils to Pantelleria from Trapani (Oct–May 1 each daily); the ferry takes 6hr (€30) and leaves at midnight, the hydrofoil 2hr 30min (€34) and leaves around 1pm.

INFORMATION AND GETTING AROUND

By bus Local buses leave from Pantelleria Town's Piazza Cavour, with regular departures to all the main villages on the island – but note that there are no services on Sundays.

Information There is no tourist office on Pantelleria; instead check out ⓦ prolocopantelleria.it.

16

ACCOMMODATION

The few hotels in town are mostly characterless and pricey – the following are rather better. One very nice option is to rent a villa or apartment. For upmarket properties look at ⓦ www.travelsicilia.com; for more modest accommodation try the locally based ⓦ agenziarizzo.com or ⓦ pantelleriatravel.com.

La Rosamarina Via Sicania 10, off Via Villa ☏ 328 924 0159. A lovely little B&B in a restored *dammuso*, a 10min walk from the port. Both its two rooms have a/c and one has a kitchen, and there is a courtyard garden with furniture. A perfect place for a quiet island stay. **€110**

Mediterraneo Hotel Via Borgo Italia 5 ☏ 0923 911 299, ⓦ pantelleriahotel.it. A modern hotel on four storeys whose best feature is that most of the rooms overlook the harbour. All rooms have a/c and it has its own restaurant. **€130**

EATING

Donne Fugate Corso Umberto I 10 ☏ 0923 912 688. Charming little restaurant, full of atmosphere, a short walk from the port. The menu, recited by the waiters, is mercifully short, relying on local produce and local *cucina povera* – try the chickpea soup, aromatic with island herbs or – on Thurs – the fish couscous. Desserts are delicious and go down a treat with a glass of *passito di Pantelleria*. Daily 12.30–2.30pm & 8–10.30pm.

La Pergola Via Contrada Suvaki, on the way to Scauri

☏ 0923 918 420. This is a great place to sample extremely good, fresh fish and other local food. Top marks to the pasta with a *ragù* of fish with wild fennel, pine nuts and capers (€9), and the ravioli stuffed with ricotta and mint (€8). *Secondi* include the catch of the day baked in a wood-fired oven – in white wine, with potatoes, or with cherry tomatoes, capers, olives and oregano – for €13–14. 8–10.30pm; closed Tues in winter.

Sardinia

CAGLIARI'S OLD TOWN

17 Sardinia

Closer to the North African coast at Tunisia than the Italian mainland and with a fierce sense of independence, Sardinia (Sardegna) can feel distinctly un-Italian. D.H. Lawrence found it exotically different when he passed through here in 1921 – "lost", as he put it, "between Europe and Africa and belonging to nowhere". The island may seem less remote nowadays – and it's certainly more accessible, with frequent flights serving Cagliari, Olbia and Alghero – but large tracts remain remarkably untouched by tourism, particularly the interior. The island's main draw, however, is its dazzling coastline, with some of the cleanest beaches in Italy, which can be packed in peak season (particularly August), when ferries bring in a steady stream of sun-worshippers from what the islanders call *il continente*, or mainland Italy. The weather is generally warm enough for a swim as early as May, however, and October is bright and sunny – reason enough to avoid the summer crowds.

Although not famed for its cultural riches, the island does hold some surprises, not least the remains of the various civilizations that passed through here. Its central Mediterranean position ensured that it was never left alone for long, and from the Carthaginians onwards the island was ravaged by a succession of invaders, each of them leaving some imprint behind: Roman and Carthaginian ruins, Genoan fortresses and a string of elegant Pisan churches, not to mention some impressive Gothic and Spanish Baroque architecture. Perhaps most striking of all, however, are the remnants of Sardinia's only significant native culture, known as the **nuraghic** civilization after the 7000-odd *nuraghi* (ancient stone towers) that litter the landscape.

On the whole, Sardinia's smaller centres are the most attractive, but the lively capital, **Cagliari** – for many the arrival point – shouldn't be written off. With good accommodation and restaurants, it makes a useful base for exploring the southern third of the island.

REGIONAL FOOD AND WINE

Sardinian cooking revolves around the freshest of ingredients simply prepared: seafood – especially **lobster** – is grilled over open fires scented with myrtle and juniper, as is meltingly tender **suckling pig**. A few wild boar escape the fire long enough to be made into *prosciutto di cinghiale*, a ham with a strong flavour of game. Being surrounded by sparkling seas, Sardinians also make rich, Spanish-inspired **fish stews** and produce **bottarga**, a version of caviar made with mullet eggs. **Pasta** is substantial here, taking the form of *culurgiones* (massive ravioli filled with cheese and egg) or *malloreddus* (saffron-flavoured, gnocchi-like shapes), while cheeses tend to be made from ewe's milk and are either fresh and herby or pungent and salty – like the famous **pecorino sardo**. The island is also famous for the quality and variety of its bread, ranging from parchment-thin *pane carasau* to chunky rustic loaves intended to sustain shepherds on the hills. As in Sicily, there is an abundance of light and airy **pastries**, frequently flavoured with lemon, almonds or orange-flower water.

Vernaccia is the most famous Sardinian **wine**: a hefty drink reminiscent of sherry and treated in a similar way – the bone-dry version as an aperitif and the sweet variant as a dessert wine. The stand-out red is the Cannonau di Sardegna, a heady number much favoured by locals. Among the whites, look out for dry Torbato or the full-flavoured Trebbiano Sardo, both perfect accompaniments to local fish and seafood.

SU NURAXI

Highlights

❶ Cagliari's old town Cagliari's Castello quarter is the most atmospheric part of town, a dense warren of alleys girded by thick walls. **See p.947**

❷ Nora Although much of this Carthaginian and Roman archeological site is submerged under the sea, what remains – including mosaics, a theatre and baths – gives a good indication of the town's former importance. See p.952

❸ Su Nuraxi Sardinia's mysterious prehistoric *nuraghi* are strewn throughout the island, and this is one of the most impressive. See p.956

❹ Sa Sartiglia, Oristano One of the island's most spectacular festivals, involving brilliant feats of equestrian prowess, fabulous costumes and lashings of medieval pageantry. **See p.958**

❺ Tiscali A vast mountain cave housing the remains of a prehistoric village. **See p.963**

❻ Beaches Sardinia has secluded beaches along every coast; among the finest is that at La Pelosa, near Stintino. See p.975

HIGHLIGHTS ARE MARKED ON THE MAP ON P.944

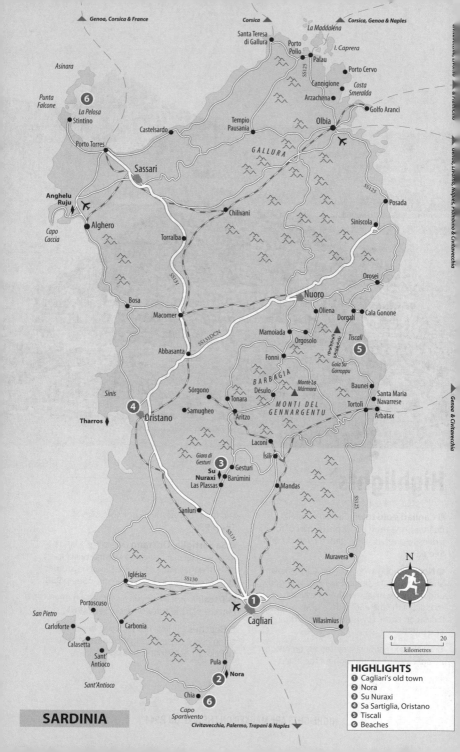

The other main ferry port is **Olbia** in the north, little more than a transit town but conveniently close to the pristine beaches of the jagged northern coast. The Costa Smeralda, a few kilometres distant, is Sardinia's best-known resort area and lives up to its reputation for glitzy opulence.

Both Olbia and Cagliari have airports, as does the vibrant resort of **Alghero** – a fishing port with a distinctive Catalan flavour in the northwest of the island that retains a friendly, unspoiled air despite its healthy tourist industry. Sardinia's biggest interior town, **Nuoro**, makes a useful stopover for visiting some of the remoter mountain areas. Of these, the **Gennargentu** range, covering the heart of the island, holds the highest peaks and provides rich evidence of the island's traditional culture, in particular the numerous village **festivals**.

Brief history

Of all the phases in Sardinia's chequered history, the prehistoric **Nuraghic era** is perhaps the most intriguing. Although little is known about the society, plenty of traces survive, most conspicuous of which are the mysterious, stone-built constructions known as *nuraghi*, mainly built between 1500 and 500 BC both for defensive purposes and as dwellings, and unique to Sardinia. The Nuraghic culture peaked between the tenth and eighth centuries BC, trading with the **Phoenicians**, among others, from the eastern Mediterranean. But from the sixth century BC, the more warlike **Carthaginians** settled on the island, with their capital less than 200km away near present-day Tunis, and their occupation continued gradually until it was challenged by the emergence of **Rome**. Caught in the middle, the Sards fought on both sides until their decisive defeat by the Romans in 177–6 BC. A core of survivors fled into the impenetrable central and eastern mountains, where they retained their independence in an area called Barbaria by the Romans, known today as the **Barbagia**.

The most impressive remains left by the Romans can be seen in **Cagliari**, at nearby **Nora**, and at **Tharros**, west of Oristano – all Carthaginian sites later enlarged by Roman settlers – and strong Latin traces still survive in the Sard dialect today. After the Roman withdrawal around the fifth century, the destructive effects of malaria and corsair raids from North Africa prompted the abandonment of the island's coasts in favour of more secure inland settlements. The numerous coastal watchtowers still surviving testify to the constant threat of piracy and invasion.

In the eleventh century ecclesiastical rights over Sardinia were granted to the rising city-state of **Pisa**, with its influence mainly concentrated in the south, based in **Cagliari**, and Pisan churches can be found throughout Sardinia. By the end of the thirteenth century, however, Pisa's rival **Genoa** had established itself in the north of the island, with power-bases in Sassari and on the coast. The situation was further complicated in 1297, when Pope Boniface VIII gave James II of Aragon exclusive rights over both Sardinia and Corsica in exchange for surrendering his claims to Sicily. Local resistance to the Aragonese was led by **Arborea**, the area around present-day Oristano, and championed in particular by **Eleanor of Arborea**, whose forces succeeded in stemming the Spanish advance. Following her death in 1404, however, Sardinian opposition crumbled, beginning three centuries of **Spanish occupation**. Traces of Spain's long dominion survive in Sardinia's dialects and in the sprinkling of Gothic and Baroque churches and palaces, with **Alghero**, in particular, still retaining a strong Catalan dialect.

17

In the wake of the War of the Spanish Succession (1701–20), Victor Amadeus, Duke of Savoy, took possession of the island, which became the new **Kingdom of Sardinia**. **Garibaldi** embarked on both his major expeditions from his farm on one of Sardinia's outlying islands, **Caprera**, and the Kingdom of Sardinia ended with the **Unification of Italy** in 1861. Since then, Sardinia's integration into the modern nation-state has not always been easy. Outbreaks of **banditry**, for example, associated with the Gennargentu mountains in particular, were ruthlessly suppressed, but there was little money available to address the root causes of the problem, nor much interest in doing so. The island benefited from the **land reforms** of Mussolini, however, which included the harnessing and damming of rivers, the draining of land, and the introduction of agricultural colonies from the mainland.

After **World War II**, Sardinia was granted semi-autonomous status, and the island was saturated with enough DDT to rid it of malaria forever. Such improvements, together with the increasing revenues from tourism, have helped marginalize local opposition towards the central government, at the same time creating a bolthole for wealthy mainlanders and holiday-makers, including at least two prime ministers – Blair and Berlusconi.

ARRIVAL AND DEPARTURE — SARDINIA

By plane If you're coming from the UK, you'll find the regular flights operated by Ryanair, Thomson, bmibaby and easyJet to Alghero, Olbia and Cagliari hard to beat for price. From the Italian mainland there are frequent daily flights to the island's airports from Rome, Milan and Bologna, with less frequent connections from smaller centres. Most routes are served by Alitalia, Air One, easyJet and Ryanair; prices start at around €35 for a one-way Milan–Alghero ticket.

FERRIES TO SARDINIA

From	To	Line	No. per week	Duration
Ajaccio	Porto Torres	SNCM	0–2	4hr
Bonifacio	S. Teresa di Gallura	Saremar & Moby	2–49	1hr
Civitavecchia	Arbatax	Tirrenia	2	10hr 30min
Civitavecchia	Cagliari	Tirrenia	7	15–17hr
Civitavecchia	Olbia	Tirrenia, Moby & Saremar	7–49	5–8hr
Genoa	Arbatax	Tirrenia	2	16hr 30min–20hr 30min
Genoa	Olbia	Tirrenia & Moby	3–14	11–14hr
Genoa	Porto Torres	Tirrenia & Moby	7–14	11hr 30min–13hr
Livorno	Golfo Aranci	Sardinia	7–13	6hr 30min–10hr
Livorno	Olbia	Moby	7–14	6hr–8hr 30min
Marseille	Porto Torres	SNCM & La Meridionale	3–4	9hr 30min–17hr
Naples	Cagliari	Tirrenia	2	16hr 15min
Palermo	Cagliari	Tirrenia	1	13hr 30min
Piombino	Olbia	Moby	3–6 (late May to early Sept)	4hr 30min
Propriano	Porto Torres	SNCM & La Meridionale	2–4	3hr 30min
Trapani	Cagliari	Tirrenia	1	10hr
Vado Ligure (Savona)	Porto Torres	Saremar	3–4	10hr–11hr 15min (June to mid-Sept)

17

By ferry Regular, year-round ferries ply to Sardinia from mainland Italy, Sicily, Corsica and France (see box opposite). You should make bookings well in advance for summer crossings, especially if you have a car or bike; August sailings can be fully booked by May. Basic prices start from about €45 per person, in high season depending on the route taken; the cheapest tickets ("*Ponte*") involve sleeping on deck, pricier tickets include use of a reclining armchair. A berth provides a better night's sleep, but adds another €20 or so. The charge for a vehicle will be around €100 for a medium car in high season. Look out for discounts applying to return tickets bought in advance within certain periods, and for special deals for a car plus two or three passengers.

GETTING AROUND

By car Much the most convenient way of getting around the island is by car; there are rental offices in all the major towns (see p.951 for those in Cagliari).

By bus The island-wide bus service is run by ARST (☎ 800 865 042, ⓦ arst.sardegna.it), supplemented by smaller independent operators covering specific long-distance routes, for example Turmo (☎ 0789 21 487, ⓦ gruppoturmo travel.com) between Cagliari and Olbia.

By train Trains connect the major towns of Cagliari, Oristano, Sassari and Olbia, operated by FS (☎ 892 021 or ☎ 06 3000, ⓦ trenitalia.com). Smaller narrow-gauge lines linking Nuoro and Alghero with the main network are run by ARST (see above). From mid-June to mid-Sept, the Trenino Verde steam and diesel trains (ⓦ treninoverde .com) take scenic routes to various destinations around the island, including Bosa, Palau and Arbatax.

Cagliari and around

Viewing **CAGLIARI**, Sardinia's capital, from the sea at the start of his Sardinian sojourn in 1921, D.H. Lawrence compared it to Jerusalem: "strange and rather wonderful, not a bit like Italy", and the city still makes a striking impression today. Crowned by its historic nucleus squeezed within a protective ring of Pisan fortifications, its setting is enhanced by the calm lagoons (*stagni*) west of the city and along the airport road, a habitat for cranes, cormorants and flamingos. In the centre, the evening promenades along Via Manno are the smartest you'll see in Sardinia, dropping down to the noisier Piazza Yenne and Largo Carlo Felice, around which most of the shops, restaurants, banks and hotels are located. At the bottom of the town, the porticos of portside Via Roma shelter more shops and bars.

Cagliari's main attractions are the **archeological museum** with its captivating collection of nuraghic statuettes, the city walls with their two **Pisan towers** looking down over the port, and the **cathedral** – all within easy distance of each other. There is also a sprinkling of Roman remains, including an impressive **amphitheatre**, while nearby excursions include **Nora**, the most complete ancient site on Sardinia, and the **islands** of Sant'Antioco and San Pietro.

Bastione San Remy

Almost all the sightseeing you will want to do in Cagliari is encompassed within the old **Castello** quarter, on the hill overlooking the port. The most evocative entry to this is from the monumental **Bastione San Remy** on Piazza Costituzione, whose nineteenth-century imperialist tone is tempered by the graffiti and weeds sprouting out of its walls. It's worth the haul up the grandiose flight of steps inside for Cagliari's best views over the port and the lagoons beyond. Sunset is a good time to be here, and there are some chic bars at the top for whiling away an evening.

The Cattedrale

Piazza Palazzo • Mon–Sat 7.30am–8pm, Sun 8am–1pm & 4.30–8.30pm • Free • ☎ 070 663 837, ⓦ duomodicagliari.it

From the Bastione, you can wander off in any direction to explore the intricate maze of Cagliari's citadel, traditionally the seat of the administration, aristocracy and highest ecclesiastical offices, and for the most part little altered since the Middle Ages. Its greatest monument, the **Cattedrale**, has undergone numerous changes since its original

17

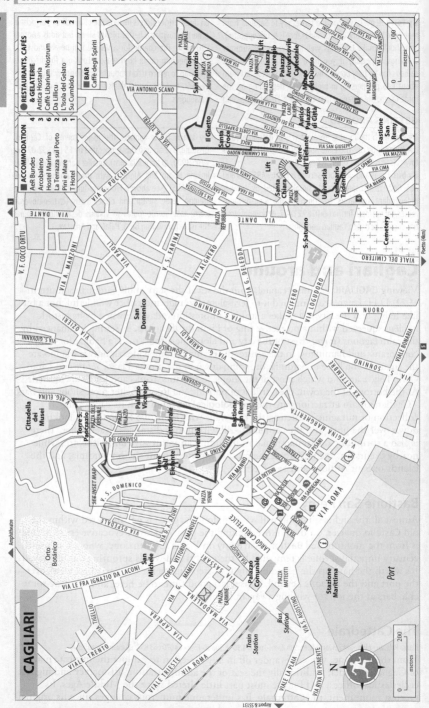

CAGLIARI

● **RESTAURANTS, CAFES & GELATERIE**

Antica Hostaria	4
Caffè Libarium Nostrum	3
Da Lillicu	6
L'Isola del Gelato	2
Su Cumbidu	5
	1

■ **BAR**

Caffè degli Spiriti	1

■ **ACCOMMODATION**

AeR Bundes	4
Arcobaleno	3
Hostel Marina	6
La Terrazza sul Porto	2
Pini e Mare	5
T Hotel	1

construction, however, with its tidy Romanesque facade added in the twentieth century **17** in the old Pisan style.

Inside, a pair of massive stone **pulpits** flank the main doors: they were crafted as a single piece in around 1160 to grace Pisa's cathedral, but were later presented to Cagliari along with the same sculptor's set of lions, which now adorns the outside of the building. Other features of the cathedral include the ornate seventeenth-century **tomb** of Martin II of Aragon (in the left transept), the **aula capitolare** (off the right transept), containing some good religious art, and, under the altar, a densely adorned **crypt** with carvings by Sicilian artists of the Sardinian saints.

Museo del Duomo

Via del Fossario 5 • Sat & Sun 10am–1pm & 4.30–7.30pm • €4 • ☎ 070 652 498, ⓦ museoduomodicagliari.it

Behind the cathedral, the **Museo del Duomo** is primarily worth seeing for two items: the fifteenth-century *Tríttico di Clemente VII*, a painting of unknown authorship, but possibly a copy of a lost painting by Rogier van der Weyden, and the powerful *Retablo della Crocefissione*, a six-panelled polyptych attributed to Michele Cavaro (1517–84).

Antico Palazzo di Città

Piazza Palazzo • Tues–Sun 10am–9pm, mid-Sept to June closes 6pm • €4 • ☎ 070 677 6482

Cagliari's old town hall, the **Antico Palazzo di Città**, has been restored to house an excellent gallery of local and regional art and crafts. You'll see lacework, embroidered fabrics, ceramics and paintings on the first floor, sacred art on the top floor, and temporary exhibitions in the basement, which also reveals traces of the building's original fourteenth-century construction.

Torre di San Pancrazio and Torre dell'Elefante

Piazza dell'Indipendenza (S. Pancrazio) and Via S. Croce (Elefante) • Both towers Tues–Sun: mid-June to Oct 10.30am–7pm; Nov to mid-June 10am–5pm • €4 each • No under-7s • ☎ 320 052 2083

At the far end of Piazza Palazzo a road leads into the smaller Piazza dell' Indipendenza, location of the **Torre di San Pancrazio**, one of the main bulwarks of the city's defences erected by Pisa after it had wrested the city from the Genoans in 1305 (though these did not prevent the Aragonese from walking in just fifteen years later). It's worth ascending the tower for the magnificent views seawards over the old town and port.

From here it's a short walk southwest to the city's second watchtower, the **Torre dell'Elefante**, named after a small carving of an elephant on one side. Like the other tower, it has a half-finished look, with the side facing the old town completely open.

The Cittadella dei Musei

Through the arch at the top of Piazza dell' Indipendenza, Piazza dell'Arsenale leads to **Cittadella dei Musei** museum complex, on the site of the former royal arsenal.

Museo Archeologico

Cittadella dei Musei • Tues–Sun 9am–8pm • €3 • ☎ 070 605 181

Cagliari's most important collection is its **Museo Archeologico**, a must for anyone interested in Sardinia's past. The island's most significant Phoenician, Carthaginian and Roman finds are gathered here, including busts and statues of muses and gods, jewellery and coins, and funerary items from the sites of Nora and Tharros. But the museum's greatest pieces are from Sardinia's **nuraghic** culture, including a series of bronze statuettes, ranging from about thirty to ninety centimetres in height, spindly and highly stylized but packed with invention and quirky humour.

17

Pinacoteca

Cittadella dei Musei • Tues–Sun 9am–8pm • €2 • ☎ 070 662 496

The excellent **Pinacoteca** contains mostly Catalan and Italian religious art from the fifteenth and sixteenth centuries. Look out in particular for the trio of panel paintings next to each other on the top level: the *Retablo di San Bernardino* by Joan Figuera and Rafael Thomas, *Annunciation* by Joan Mates, and *Visitation* by Joan Barcelo.

Museo d'Arte Siamese

Cittadella dei Musei • Tues–Sun: June–Sept 9am–8pm; Oct–May 9am–6pm • €2 • ☎ 070 675 7624

The **Museo d'Arte Siamese** offers the opportunity to make a complete cultural leap, with its fascinating array of items from Southeast Asia originally collected by a Cagliari engineer who spent twenty years in the region. Exhibits include Siamese paintings of Hindu and Buddhist legends, Chinese bowls and boxes, Japanese statuettes and a fearsome array of weaponry.

Mostra di Cere Anatomiche

Cittadella dei Musei • Tues–Sun 9am–1.30pm & 4–7pm • €1.50 • ☎ 070 675 7627

The smallest and most offbeat of the Cittadella's museums is the **Mostra di Cere Anatomiche**, which displays 23 gruesome wax models of anatomical sections crafted by the Florentine Clemente Susini in the nineteenth century.

The Roman amphitheatre

Viale Fra Ignazio • Currently closed for restoration

Cut out of solid rock in the second century AD, the city's **Anfiteatro Romano** could at one time hold Cagliari's entire population of about ten thousand. Much of the site was cannibalized to build churches in the Middle Ages, but you can still see the trenches for the animals, the underground passages and several rows of seats. While the site remains inaccessible, you can appreciate its scale and structure from the outside.

The Orto Botanico

Viale Fra Ignazio • April–Oct Mon–Fri 8.30am–6pm, Sat & Sun 8.30am–1.30pm; Nov–March daily 8.30am–1.30pm • €3 • ☎ 070 675 3522

Below Cagliari's amphitheatre, you can find shady relief on a sizzling afternoon in the **Orto Botanico**, one of Italy's most famous botanical gardens, with around two thousand species of Mediterranean and tropical plants. Also here are Carthaginian and Roman remains, including four cisterns and a spring.

San Saturno

Piazza San Cosimo • Tues–Sat 9am–1pm • Free • ☎ 070 659 869

East of the centre, the main reason to venture into Cagliari's traffic-thronged new town is to see the fifth-century remains of **San Saturno**, Sardinia's oldest church and one of the most important surviving examples of early Christian architecture in the Mediterranean. Set in its own piazza off busy Via Dante, looking Middle Eastern with its palm trees and cupola, the basilica was erected on the spot where the Christian

---

THE BEACHES AT POETTO

Cagliari may not be a beach-lover's paradise, but a break on the beach and a swim are never far away. From the marina at the western end of **Poetto**, a 15min bus ride (#PF and #PQ) from Piazza Matteotti, the fine sandy **beach** extends for some 6km, dotted with bars and public showers. Some sections are lidos charging a standard daily rate for entry (about €5), with deckchairs and parasols available for rent, along with pedalos and windsurfing equipment.

martyr Saturninus met his fate during the reign of Diocletian. Around the sturdy walls, which suffered severe bombardment during World War II, lie various pieces of flotsam from the past: four cannonballs, fragments of Roman sarcophagi and slabs of stone carved with Latin inscriptions. The interior is bare of decoration, though it does hold an excavated necropolis.

ARRIVAL AND DEPARTURE
CAGLIARI

By plane Cagliari's airport (ⓦsogaer.it), where facilities include banks and an information desk (daily 8am–10pm in summer, 9am–9pm in winter), is linked to town at least every 30min from 7.25am until the last flight arrival – about 12.30pm – and takes 10min (tickets €4 from the ticket machine inside the airport); otherwise a taxi ride costs €15–20.

By ferry Cagliari's Stazione Maríttima is a short walk from Via Roma and the train and bus stations. Tirrenia's ticket office is at Via Riva di Ponente (ⓣ892 123 or ⓣ02 2630 2803 from a mobile, ⓦtirrenia.it).

Destinations Civitavecchia (1 daily; 15–17hr); Naples (2 weekly; 16hr 15min); Palermo (1 weekly; 14hr 30min); Trapani (1 weekly; 10hr).

By train Cagliari's main station is centrally located on Piazza Matteotti, used by FS trains. Gottardo station for trains to Mandas and Arbatax (see p.964), operated by

ARST, is in Monserrato, north of the centre, reachable by tram from Piazza della Repubblica (bus #30 or #31 from Piazza Matteotti).

Destinations Arbatax (mid-June to mid-Sept Wed–Mon 2 daily via Mandas; 6hr 45min–7hr 20min); Macomer (7–8 daily, some with change; 1hr 40min–3hr); Olbia (5 daily, some with change; 3hr 30min–4hr 20min); Oristano (11–16 daily; 1hr–1hr 45 min); Sassari (4 daily; 3hr 25min–4hr 25min).

By bus The bus station is next to the train station on Piazza Matteotti; the ARST ticket desk is in the *McDonald's* restaurant, Turmo tickets for Olbia and Santa Teresa di Gallura are sold at a kiosk.

Destinations Barumini (Mon–Sat 2 daily; 1hr 30min); Nuoro (2 daily; 2hr 35min); Olbia (1–2 daily; 4hr 15min– 5hr); Oristano (Mon–Sat 2 daily; 2hr); Sant'Antioco (1–3 daily; 1hr 50min); Sassari (2–3 daily; 3hr 20min).

INFORMATION AND GETTING AROUND

By bus or tram Piazza Matteotti is the terminus for most local buses, operated by CTM (ⓣ800 078 870, ⓦctmcagliari.it). Tickets are sold at a booth in the piazza (€1.20 for 1hr 30min, €2 for 2hr or €3 for a day's travel); useful routes include #7 running up to the museums and cathedral, and #58 and #8N for the Roman amphitheatre.

Car rental Hertz, Piazza Matteotti 8 ⓣ070 651 078 and airport ⓣ070 240 037, ⓦhertz.it; Ruvioli, airport ⓣ070

240 323, ⓦruvioli.it; Sixt, airport ⓣ06 652 111, ⓦsixt.it.

Taxis Rank at Piazza Matteotti; Radiotaxi 4 Mori (ⓣ070 400 101) operates 24hr.

Tourist office There are kiosks outside the Stazione Maríttima; Piazza Ingrao (at the bottom of Viale Regina Margherita), Piazza Costituzione, and Piazza Indipendenza (all daily 8am–8pm; ⓣ329 831 2033, ⓦvisit-cagliari.it).

ACCOMMODATION

★ **AeR Bundes Jack** Via Roma 75 ⓣ070 657 970, ⓦhotelbjvittoria.it. Right across from the port, on the third floor (there's a lift), this *pensione* has spotless, a/c rooms, mostly en suite, with solid wood furnishings and antique tiled floors. The host family is friendly, and there's a ten-percent discount on presentation of this book. **€90**

★ **Arcobaleno** Via Sardegna 38 ⓣ070 684 8325, ⓦaffittacamerearcobalenocagliari.com. Clean and modern en-suite rooms with a/c and wi-fi in a renovated apartment with exposed brickwork. Breakfast is at the nearby *Bar Roma*. **€70**

Hostel Marina Piazza San Sepolcro ⓣ070 450 9709, ⓦhostelmarinacagliari.com. Modern hostel in the heart of the Marina quarter, with dorms sleeping 3–6, family rooms and doubles. Non-members must pay for temporary membership (€3), but all prices include breakfast. Dorms **€22**, doubles **€60**

La Terrazza sul Porto Largo Carlo Felice 36 ⓣ070

658 997 or ⓣ339 876 0155, ⓦlaterrazzasulporto.com. Funky, brightly coloured rooms with TVs, wi-fi and CD players in this easy-going B&B, with shared or private bathrooms, self-service breakfasts and a communal roof terrace. No credit cards. **€50**

T Hotel Via dei Giudicati ⓣ070 47 400, ⓦthotel.it. Large, very swish and contemporary hotel that's geared chiefly towards a well-heeled, business clientele, with fully equipped rooms, a fitness centre and a good courtyard restaurant. It's some distance from the old centre, but well connected by bus #29 from Piazza Matteotti. **€130**

CAMPING

Pini e Mare Capitana ⓣ070 803 103, ⓦpiniemare .com. The nearest campsite to Cagliari is beyond Quartu Sant'Elena, a 45min bus ride east along the coast, in woods close to the sea. Bungalows are available for €75. Closed Oct–Easter. Pitches **€26**

17

EATING, DRINKING AND NIGHTLIFE

Antica Hostaria Via Cavour 60 ☎070 665 870. Upmarket though not over-formal restaurant, with antique trimmings. Meat and fish are given equal billing, and are usually good. You'll spend around €40 a head, excluding drinks. Mon–Sat 12.45–3pm & 8–11pm.

Caffè degli Spiriti Bastione San Remy ☎339 882 2146. This chic, loungey bar with great views over the city is a popular hangout on summer evenings, and there are DJs and live music until late at weekends. April–Oct Mon–Thurs & Sun 9am–2am, Fri & Sat 9am–3am; March, Nov & Dec daily 9am–6pm.

Caffè Libarium Nostrum Via Santa Croce 33. With tables outside right on the old city walls, affording marvellous views, this is a great place for a snack and a drink from early morning to late at night. Daily 7.30am–2am;

closed Mon Nov–May.

★ **Da Lillicu** Via Sardegna 78 ☎070 652 970. This Cagliari institution with plain marble tables serves sensational antipasti, spaghetti and mainly fishy Sard specialities, most €12–25. Booking advised. Daily 1–3pm & 8.30–11pm; closed Sun lunch in winter.

★ **L'Isola del Gelato** Piazza Yenne 35 ☎070 659 824. Cagliari's top *gelateria* offers a staggering variety of ice cream flavours, as well as yoghurt with fresh fruit, making this a great breakfast stop too. March–Oct daily 7am–midnight.

Su Cumbidu Via Napoli 11 ☎070 660 017. This casual wood-beamed restaurant serves heaving plates of antipasti and mainly meaty Sardinian specialities. Set-price menus range €13–25. Daily noon–3pm & 7–11.30pm.

DIRECTORY

Consulates UK, Viale Colombo 160, Quartu Sant'Elena ☎070 828 628; Denmark and Norway, Via Roma 121 ☎070 668 208; Germany, Via R. Garzia 9 ☎070 307 229; Netherlands and Sweden, Via Roma 101 ☎070 670 830.

Festivals Sant'Efisio: May 1–4, including a procession to the saint's church at Nora.

Hospital San Giovanni di Dio, Via Ospedale 54 ☎070 6091.

Internet access Bips, Via Sicilia 23 (daily 9am–9pm), has internet access and phones with reasonable long-distance rates; Lamarì, Via Napoli 43 (Mon–Sat 8.30am–9pm), is a more relaxed internet café.

Laundry Coin-operated *lavanderia* at Via Sicilia 20/A (daily 8am–10pm, last wash at 9pm; €4 for 6kg).

Left luggage *Tabacchi* inside the bus station (Mon–Sat 7am–8pm, also Sun June–Sept; €0.50–1.50 per bag per hr).

Pharmacy Farmacia Popolare, Largo Carlo Felice 39 (summer Mon–Fri 8.30am–1.30pm & 5–8.30pm, Sat 9am–1pm & 5–8.30pm; winter Mon–Fri 9am–1pm & 4.30–7.50pm, Sat 9am–1pm). Night-opening pharmacies are listed on the door.

Post office Piazza del Carmine (Mon–Fri 8.25am–7pm, Sat 8.25am–1pm).

Nora and around

Daily: June–Sept 9.30am–7.30pm; Oct –May 9.30am–dusk • €7 including museum • ☎070 920 9138, ⊛ coptur.net

Forty kilometres south of Cagliari, 3km outside the small town of **PULA**, the ancient remains of **Nora** constitute one of Sardinia's most important archeological sites. Founded by the Phoenicians and settled later by Carthaginians and Romans, Nora was abandoned around the third century AD, possibly as a result of a natural disaster. Now partly submerged under the sea, the remains on land include houses, Carthaginian warehouses, a temple, baths with some well-preserved mosaics, and a theatre which hosts summer performances. The rest is rubble, though its waterside position gives it plenty of atmosphere. The archeological **museum** at Corso Vittorio Emanuele 69 in Pula (daily: April–Oct 9am–8pm; Nov–March 10am–1pm & 3–6.30pm; €5; ☎070 920 9610) gives background and displays some of the finds.

Beside the site is a lovely sandy bay lapped by crystal-clear water, but packed with day-trippers in season. Behind the beach stands the rather ordinary looking eleventh-century church of **Sant'Efisio**, site of the martyrdom of Cagliari's patron saint and the ultimate destination of the annual four-day procession from Cagliari around May 1.

ARRIVAL AND DEPARTURE

NORA AND AROUND

By bus ARST buses connect Pula with Cagliari roughly every hour, less frequent on Sun (50min). From Pula, a local minibus

runs to Nora and the campsites at Santa Margherita di Pula 5–9 times daily (4 daily on Sun in summer only).

ACCOMMODATION

Cala d'Ostia Santa Margherita di Pula ☎ 070 921 470, ⓦ www.campingcaladostia.com. The coast 2km south of Pula holds two campsites sheltered by pine woods and right by the sea. They're very similar; this one has access to a slightly wilder beach, *Flumendosa* (☎ 070 920 8364, ⓦ campingflumendosa.it) is a bit closer to town. Local buses run to both. April–Oct. Pitches €30

Quattro Mori Via Cagliari 10, Pula ☎ 070 920 9124. Flower-bedecked *pensione* near the centre of Pula with good-value, very simple rooms with shared facilities (some singles have private bathrooms). No credit cards. €40

Su Gunventeddu Località Su Gunventeddu ☎ 070 920 9092, ⓦ sugunventeddu.com. At just 100m from the beach, surrounded by greenery, this modern *pensione* has spacious and quiet rooms and a good restaurant. It's 1km from Nora; local buses stop outside. €85

Villa Madau Via Nora 84, Pula ☎ 070 924 9033, ⓦ villamadau.it. Chic hotel with colourful modern decor, a courtyard and a relaxed, indoor/outdoor café-restaurant. €120

EATING

Su Furriadroxu Via XXIV Maggio 11, Pula ☎ 070 924 6148. With an arcaded courtyard, this place specializes in dishes from the Campidano area. Try the ravioli stuffed with ricotta and saffron, cooked in butter and orange, or a mixed meat grill. Pastas and soups are €7, mains €9–13. 8–10.45pm; closed Wed.

Sant'Antioco

Joined to the mainland by a road causeway and bridge, **Sant'Antioco** is the larger of Sardinia's southwest islands, measuring about 15km by 10km at its longest and widest. The main town – also called **SANT'ANTIOCO** – has a sheltered harbour that made this an important base for the Phoenicians, Carthaginians and the Romans, allowing them to command the whole of Sardinia's southwest coast. The second town, **CALASETTA**, on the island's northern tip, lies close to some good beaches and is the port for the island of San Pietro.

The catacombs

Piazza Parrochia • Tours Mon–Sat 9am–noon & 5–8pm (3–6pm in winter), Sun 10.30–11.15am & 5–8pm (3–6pm in winter) • €2.50 • ☎ 0781 83 044

In the upper part of town, the twelfth-century **Basilica of Sant'Antioco** was built over Christian **catacombs**, which were in turn enlarged from an existing Carthaginian burial place. You can join a guided tour round these dingy corridors, with authentic skeletons and reproductions of ceramic objects unearthed during excavation.

The archeological zone and around

Various combinations of ticket are available; one that includes all the sites below costs €13, available from any of the sites • ☎ 0781 82 105, ⓦ archeotur.it

The earliest traces of Sulki – as Sant'Antioco was then known – dating from the eighth century BC, are visible in the extensive **archeological zone**, occupying a hillside at the top of the town. Signposted up a side road outside the basilica, it's less than a 1km walk from the sea.

Punic tofet

Daily 9am–7pm • Museum and tofet €7

The most impressive part of the archeological zone is an extensive **Punic tofet**, or burial site, dedicated to the Carthaginian goddess Tanit and once covering the entire hill where the old city now stands. The numerous urns scattered about here (mostly modern reproductions) contained the ashes of children (dead from natural causes). Finds from here and from the Phoenician, Carthaginian and Roman cities are collected in the **Museo Archeologico**, at the bottom of the hill.

17

Museo Etnografico

Via Necrópoli • Daily: April–Sept 9am–8pm; early Oct 9am–1pm & 3.30–7pm; late Oct to March 9am–1pm & 3–6pm • €3

Just outside the archeological zone, the small but engrossing **Museo Etnografico** consists of one capacious room crammed to the rafters with examples of rural culture – tools, agricultural implements, crafts, bread- and pasta-making equipment – all enthusiastically explained (in Italian) by a guide.

Villaggio ipogeo and Forte Su Pisu

Via Necrópoli • Same hours as Museo Etnografico • €2.50 each

The **villaggio ipogeo**, or Punic necropolis, is worth a glance for its restored *hypogea* (underground chambers) that once held Carthaginian tombs and were later converted into plain dwellings by the local people.

Nearby, the **Forte Su Pisu**, built in 1812, was stormed by corsairs three years later, resulting in the massacre of the entire garrison. There's not much to see here, but it's been tidily restored and is a panoramic spot.

ARRIVAL AND INFORMATION

SANT'ANTIOCO

By bus ARST buses stop in Piazza della Repubblica and in Calasetta. For Cagliari, it's best to catch a bus to Carbonia or Iglesias and take a train from there.
Destinations Cagliari (Mon–Sat 1 daily; 2hr 20min); Carbonia (11–14 daily; 1hr); Iglesias (4–5 daily; 1hr 20min).

Tourist office Porticciolo, Lungomare Caduti di Nassirya (mid-June to mid-Sept daily 9am–1pm & 4–8pm; mid-Sept to mid-June Tues–Sun 9am–1pm & 3–7pm; ☎0781 828 205, ⌨sulcisiglesiente.eu).
Bike and scooter rental Euromoto, Via Nazionale 57 (☎0781 840 907).

ACCOMMODATION

Hotel del Corso Corso Vittorio Emanuele 32 ☎0781 800 265, ⌨hoteldelcorso.it. On the town's main promenading route, this modern place above a bar has a panoramic roof terrace and fairly standard but spacious rooms. **€92**
La Jacaranda Via Risorgimento 22 ☎0781 82 008, ⌨lajacaranda.it. In a quiet lane a short walk from Piazza Garibaldi and the port, this B&B has spacious modern

rooms and a garden where breakfast and other meals are served in summer. **€80**
Tonnara Cala Sapone ☎0781 189 6210, ⌨camping tonnara.it. On the western side of the island, with a pool and direct access to the beach in a sheltered inlet. There's a restaurant and shop, and caravans and bungalows are available to rent. Late April to late Oct. Pitches **€32**

EATING AND DRINKING

La Compagnia del Moro Lungomare Colombo 85 ☎0781 82 040. This bar with outdoor tables facing the seafront makes an agreeable place for a daytime snack or to end up at the evening's end. Panini, *pizzette*, salads and other light meals are served. 7am–midnight; closed Wed in winter.
La Fenicia Viale Trieste 41 ☎329 355 0967. Intimate trattoria where you can sample traditional Sard dishes and local wines at reasonable prices – antipasti at €8–10, pastas

€10–12 and mains €12–16. The *spaghetti con vongole* (with clams) and steamed tuna are recommended. 12.30–2.30pm & 7.30–11.30pm; closed Wed except Aug.
★**Rubiu** Viale Trento 22 ☎0781 196 4107. This modern place specializes in *birre artigianali* – "artisan beers" – brewed here or elsewhere in Italy, and served with *taglieri* (wooden boards) of cold meats and seafood, salads, *foccacce* (€3–7) and the island's best pizzas (€6–10). 7pm–1am; closed Tues.

San Pietro

A 5km ferry ride from Calasetta – and also accessible from the small industrial port of Portoscuso, on the mainland – the island of **SAN PIETRO** has a history and culture distinct from that of Sant'Antioco. The largely Ligurian local dialect is due to the island's settlement two and a half centuries ago by a colony of Genoans after they were evicted from the island of Tabarca, near Tunisia. The only town, **CARLOFORTE**, is both prettier and more elegant than Sant'Antioco, with pastel seafront houses overlooking a palm-fringed port, and narrow balconied alleys beyond. It's lively in summer, particularly during May

17

VISITING SU NURAXI

If you only have time to see one of Sardinia's *nuraghi* (ancient stone dwellings) you should make it the biggest and most famous: **Su Nuraxi**, between Cagliari and Oristano. The majestic UNESCO-protected complex (daily 9am–dusk; €9) is a compelling sight, surrounded by the brown hills of the interior, and a good taste of the primitive grandeur of the island's only indigenous civilization.

Su Nuraxi's dialect name means simply "the nuragh", and not only is it the largest nuraghic complex on the island, but it's also thought to be the oldest, dating probably from around 1500 BC. Comprising a bulky fortress surrounded by the remains of a village, Su Nuraxi was a palace complex at the very least – possibly even a capital city. The central tower once reached 21m (now shrunk to less than 15m), and its outer defences and inner chambers are connected by passageways and stairs. The whole complex is thought to have been covered with earth by Sards and Carthaginians at the time of the Roman conquest, which may account for its excellent state of preservation: if it weren't for a torrential rainstorm that washed away the slopes in 1949, the site may never have been revealed at all.

The site lies fifteen minutes' walk west of the village of **Barumini**, 50km north of Cagliari, to which there are only 2 daily ARST buses (not Sun) taking around 1hr 30min. A day-trip from Cagliari for bus travellers is not feasible, but there are good **accommodation** possibilities, including *Sa Lolla* (☏070 936 8419; €70), a rustic-style hotel on Via Cavour with a basic **restaurant** attached.

---

and June's **La Mattanza** festival, celebrating the local speciality found in all restaurants, tuna. The island's secluded coves and beauty spots are within easy reach.

ARRIVAL AND INFORMATION

SAN PIETRO

By ferry Saremar (☏0781 854 005, ⓦsaremar.it) operates a ferry service with Calasetta roughly every 90min (30min; around €21 for two people in an average-sized car) and hourly with Portovesme on the mainland (around €24). In summer, drivers should join the queue in good

time – and be sure to get a return ticket.
Tourist office Piazza Carlo Emanuele III, opposite the port (April–Sept Mon 10am–1pm, Tues–Sat 10am–1pm & 5–8pm; Oct–March Mon–Sat 10am–noon; ☏0781 854 009, ⓦwww.prolococarloforte.it).

ACCOMMODATION

Hieracon Corso Cavour 62 ☏0781 854 028, ⓦhotel hieracon.com. At the quiet end of the seafront, this hotel has a stylish, old-world ambience, with period furnishings and an internal garden. Some rooms have harbour views, cheaper ones in the loft are viewless. **€100**

Il Ghiro Piazza della Repubblica 7 ☏338 205 0553, ⓦcarlofortebedandbreakfast.it. Ecofriendly B&B overlooking the town's liveliest square, with two wood-beamed rooms, arty decor and organic breakfasts. No credit cards. **€55**

EATING

★ **Al Tonno di Corsa** Via Marconi 47 ☏0781 855 106. This excellent seafood restaurant with sea views is dedicated to the local *cucina tabarkina* in general, and tuna dishes in particular. You'll pay €40–50 for a full meal excluding drinks. 12.30–2.30pm & 8–10.30pm; closed Mon Sept–May.
Da Nicolo Corso Cavour 32 ☏0781 854 048. Highly

esteemed seafront restaurant, where the menu features such local dishes as *cuscus carlofortino, maccheroni con pesto* and, of course, tuna. There's a good-value two-course lunch menu for €20, otherwise starters are €15–18, mains around €20. Noon–3pm & 8–11pm; closed Mon except July & Aug, and mid-Sept to mid-May.

Oristano

The province of Oristano roughly corresponds to the much older entity of **Arborea**, the medieval *giudicato* which championed the Sardinian cause in the struggle against the Spaniards. Then as now, **ORISTANO** was the region's main town, and today it retains more than a hint of medieval atmosphere. The historic centre has a relaxed and elegant

ELEONORA DI ARBOREA

Oristano's finest hour is recalled in the marble statue of **Eleonora d'Arborea** that presides over the piazza named after her in the old centre. Eleonora was the *giudice* of the Arborea region from 1384 to 1404 and is the best loved of Sardinia's medieval rulers, having been the only one who enjoyed any success against the Aragonese invaders. She died from plague in 1404, though her most enduring legacy survived her by several centuries: the formulation of a **Code of Laws**, which was eventually extended throughout the island. Eleonora's statue, carved in 1881, shows her bearing the scroll on which the laws were written, while inset panels depict her various victories.

feel, and although it is 4km from the sea, the town is attractively surrounded by water, its lagoons and irrigation canals helping to make this a richly productive agricultural zone (the southern lagoon, the Stagno di Santa Giusta, is home to a local colony of Sardinia's flamingo population). Many people, however, come to Oristano simply to visit the nearby Sinis peninsula, home to the impressive Punic and Roman ruins of **Tharros** and a string of wild beaches.

Antiquarium Arborense

Piazzetta Corrias • Mon–Fri 9am–8pm, Sat & Sun 9am–2pm & 3–8pm • €5 • ☎ 0783 791 262

One of Sardinia's most absorbing museums, Oristano's **Antiquarium Arborense** is housed in a sixteenth-century merchant's house. As well as rotating exhibitions of its extensive collection of nuraghic, Phoenician, Roman and Greek artefacts, there are scaled-down reconstructions of Roman Tharros and Oristano in 1290, and an absorbing collection of medieval and Renaissance art.

The Duomo

Piazza del Duomo • Daily 8.30am–6.30pm • Free • ☎ 0783 78 684

Oristano's **Duomo** stands in a spacious square up a short walk from Piazza Eleonora. Though started in the thirteenth century, most of the present building is a Baroque reworking, retaining only parts of the apses from its original construction. With the fourteenth-century belltower topped by a multicoloured tiled cupola and a seminary next door, it forms an atmospheric ensemble.

ARRIVAL AND DEPARTURE

ORISTANO

By train Oristano's train station is at the eastern end of town, a 20min walk from the centre, also linked by local buses running every 20–35min – buy tickets from the bar outside the station.
Destinations Cagliari (11–15 daily; 1hr–1hr 30min); Macomer (7–9 daily; 45min–1hr 10min); Olbia (5 daily,

some with change; 2hr 30min–3hr); Sassari (4 daily, some with change; 2hr–2hr 40min).
By bus The bus station is on Via Cagliari, near the Duomo. Destinations Bosa (Mon–Sat 4 daily; 2hr); Cagliari (Mon–Sat 2 daily; 2hr); Nuoro (1 daily; 1hr 45min); Sassari (1–3 daily; 1hr 45min).

INFORMATION

Tourist offices The tourist office, Piazza Eleonora 19 (Mon–Fri 8.30am–1pm & 3–6pm, Sat 9.30am–1.30pm & 4–8pm, Sun 9.30am–1.30pm; ☎0783 368 3210, ⌨ gooristano.com), covers the whole province; Pro Loco,

Via Ciutadella de Menorca 14 (June–Oct Mon–Fri 8.30am–1.30pm & 3.30–8.30pm, Sat 8.30am–1.30pm; Nov–May Mon–Fri 9am–1pm & 3.30–7.30pm; ☎0783 70 621), has information on the city.

ACCOMMODATION

Duomo Via Vittorio Emanuele 34 ☎0783 778 061, ⌨ jostoalduomo.net. Just across from the Duomo, this hotel is a modern refurbishment of a seventeenth-century building, with comfortable rooms set around a central courtyard. **€108**
Hostel Rodia Viale della Repubblica ☎ 0783 251 881, ⌨ hostelrodia.it. Around a 15min walk from the old

centre, this modern complex houses both a hostel and a hotel, though as hostel accommodation is in en-suite doubles, twins and family suites, there's little to distinguish these from the hotel rooms, except the latter have minibars and TVs. Breakfast costs €2–7, meals are €15, and there's internet access and bikes to rent (book ahead). Beds in

17

SA SARTIGLIA

The rituals of Oristano's flamboyant **Sa Sartiglia** festival perhaps originated with knights on the Second Crusade, who in the eleventh century may well have imported the trappings of Saracen tournaments to Sardinia. In the period of the Spanish domination, similarly lavish feasts were held for the ruling knights. In time, these celebrations took on a more theatrical aspect and merged with the annual Carnival – the Sa Sartiglia is now a three-day festival that closes the Carnival period, ending on **Shrove Tuesday**. With all the participants masked and costumed, the whole affair exudes a drama unrivalled by Sardinia's other festivals. The climax of proceedings, in Piazza Eleonora, is the joust after which the festival is named, when the mounted contestants attempt to lance a ring, or *sartiglia*, suspended in the air, charging towards it at full gallop.

shared rooms **€25**, doubles **€80**

L'Arco Vico Ammirato 12 ☎0783 72 849, ⓦarco bedandbreakfast.it. Centrally located off Piazza Martiri, this spotless, wood-beamed and relaxed B&B has two good-size rooms with a/c and a shared bathroom. There's a small terrace, too. No credit cards. **€65**

Spinnaker Marina di Torre Grande ☎0783 22 074, ⓦspinnakervacanze.com. The nearest campsite lies 6km away at Oristano's seaside resort, accessible on frequent buses from the bus and train stations. This is well equipped, with its own private beach, a pool and bungalows (€79). April–Sept. Pitches **€25**

EATING AND DRINKING

Cocco & Dessi Via Tirso 31 ☎0783 252 648. This stylish restaurant has quality meat and seafood dishes, with mains at €11–15 and pizzas. You might finish your meal with a glass of Oristano's celebrated Vernaccia dessert wine. Daily 12.30–2.30pm & 7.30–11.30pm.

La Torre Piazza Roma ☎0783 301 494. For down-to-earth pizza and pasta at low prices head for *La Torre*; their speciality is *pizza ai funghi porcini*. Pizzas are around €7, mains €10–17. Noon–3pm & 7–11pm, closed Mon except Aug.

Lolamundo Piazzetta Corrias ☎0783 301 284. For daytime snacks or an evening drink, this contemporary café in a quiet piazza next to the Antiquarium has a cool vibe and tables outside in summer. Mon–Sat 7am–midnight.

Trattoria Gino Via Tirso 13 ☎0783 71 428. This reliable little place features traditional Sardinian dishes such as *ravioli sardi* (made with butter and sage) and *sebadas* (warm, cheese-filled pastries topped with honey). Pastas are €8–10, mains €9–13. Booking advised. Mon–Sat 12.30–3pm & 8–11pm.

Tharros

Daily 9am to 1hr before sunset • €7 • ☎0783 370 019 • Five buses daily from Oristano (July & Aug only; 50min)

About 20km west of Oristano, the Punic and Roman ruins at **Tharros** are spread across an isthmus that forms the northern tip of the mouth of the Golfo di Oristano. Now overlooked by a sturdy Spanish watchtower, the site was settled by Phoenicians as early as 800 BC, and now consists mostly of Punic and Roman houses arranged on a grid of streets, of which the broad-slabbed Decumanus Maximus is the most impressive. The two solitary Corinthian columns marking the site of a first-century-BC Roman temple are in fact a modern reconstruction. Like Nora (see p.952), there is much more submerged underwater, the result of subsidence.

Near the site stands the fifth-century church of **San Giovanni di Sinis**, which vies with Cagliari's San Saturno for the title of oldest Christian church in Sardinia.

Bosa

Some 60km north of Oristano, **BOSA** presents an appealing picture of pastel houses huddled around a hilltop castle on the banks of the Temo River. Its attractions are low-key – wandering the mazy cobbled lanes of the medieval **Sa Costa** district up to the **castle** is probably the best way to spend your time – but it makes a pleasant, if sleepy place to hole up for a few days. Most of the tourist activity is concentrated in **Bosa Marina**, 2km west, where a crescent of sandy beach is backed by hotels, restaurants and bars.

Bosa's old town centres on the cobbled Corso Vittorio Emanuele, the main street running parallel to the river and cutting through **Sa Piana**, the lower town. The **cathedral** sits at the Corso's eastern end, by the old bridge, while to the north, the medieval lanes of **Sa Costa**, or upper town, straggle up the hill towards the castle.

Castello Malaspina

April–June daily 10am–1pm & 3.30–6.30pm; July daily 10am–1pm & 4–7.30pm; Aug daily 10am–8pm; Sept to mid-Oct daily 10am–1pm & 3.30–6pm; mid- to late Oct 10am–1pm & 3–5pm; Nov–March Sat & Sun 10am–1pm · €3 · ☎ 348 154 4724, ⓦ castellodibosa.it

Erected by the Malaspina family in 1122, the **Castello Malaspina** offers stunning views over the town, river and sea. Inside, the church of **Nostra Signora di Regnos Altos** contains some rare Catalan frescoes dating from around 1300. Take any alley leading up from the Corso to get here, a steep twenty-minute climb, otherwise take the road skirting the back of town that winds round to the castle gate.

San Pietro

April–June Tues–Fri 9.30am–12.30pm, Sat 9.30am–12.30pm & 3.30–6.30pm, Sun 3.30–6.30pm; July & Aug Tues–Fri 9.30am–12.30pm, Sat 9.30am–12.30pm & 4–7pm, Sun 4–7pm; Sept & Oct Tues–Fri 9.30am–12.30pm, Sat 9.30am–12.30pm & 3–5pm, Sun 3–5pm; call for winter visits · €2 · ☎ 333 544 5675

Following the south bank of the river from the old bridge eastwards for about 2km will bring you to **San Pietro**, Bosa's former cathedral and Sardinia's oldest Romanesque church. Built in the eleventh century, it has a Gothic facade added by Cistercian monks a couple of hundred years later and a mainly bare interior.

Bosa Marina

Before Bosa's inhabitants shifted to a more defensible position inland, the town's original site was at what is now **BOSA MARINA**, a conventional minor resort at the mouth of the Temo, with a small choice of hotels and bars and a broad swathe of sandy **beach**. You can also swim from the rocks on the north side of the river-mouth, while the beautiful rocky coast further up has numerous sandy coves, accessible from the spectacular Alghero road. Protected from development, this highly panoramic stretch is one of the last habitats in Sardinia of the griffon vulture.

ARRIVAL AND DEPARTURE
BOSA

By bus Buses stop at Piazza Zanetti, a short walk from Bosa's centre. Tickets are sold at *Gold Bar*, Via Azuni.
Destinations Alghero (2–5 daily; 1hr); Oristano (Mon–Sat 4–5 daily; 2hr).

Trenino Verde Bosa Marina is a terminal for this narrow-track tourist train to Macomer, 30km inland (mid-June to mid-Sept Fri & Sun at 4.30pm; 2hr; ☎ 070 580 246, ⓦ treninoverde.com).

ACCOMMODATION

★ **Bainas** Via San Pietro ☎ 339 209 0967 or ☎ 333 396 7819, ⓦ agriturismobainasbosa.com. A 10min walk from Bosa, this peaceful agriturismo is surrounded by fields and orchards, with rooms giving onto a veranda. Guests can eat in the excellent restaurant (see p.960) for €20. No credit cards. **€70**
Ostello Malaspina Via Sardegna 1, Bosa Marina ☎ 0785 850 681, ⓦ valevacanze.com. One of Sardinia's rare youth hostels, this is a quiet, modern place near the beach, which also serves cheap meals. No credit cards.

Dorms **€16**, doubles **€40**
S'Ammentu Via del Carmine 55 ☎ 348 721 8492, ⓦ sammentu.com. Old-town lodging on four floors (there's a lift), with small but comfortable en-suite rooms, full of character, with a/c, wi-fi and TVs. **€70**
Sa Pischedda Via Roma 8 ☎ 0785 373 065, ⓦ hotel sapischedda.it. Just across the river from the centre, this fine old *palazzo* has a grand staircase leading up to attractive, a/c rooms, some with balcony. There's a classy restaurant and pizzeria, too. **€90**

17

EATING AND DRINKING

Bainas Via San Pietro ☎ 339 209 0967 or ☎ 333 396 7819. This agriturismo outside town (see p.959) serves delicious and wholesome organic dishes using its own home-grown produce, but you'll need to call ahead. Meals cost €27–35 including drinks. No credit cards. Daily 8.30pm–late.

Bar Mouse Piazza Zanetti ☎ 339 117 4216. For snacks and refreshments, avoid the pricey bars on the main Corso in favour of this wine bar and café with terrace seating. Mon–Sat 6am–2pm & 4–10pm, Sun 6am–2pm.

Borgo Sant'Ignazio Via Sant'Ignazio 33 ☎ 0785 374 129. Rustic but elegant restaurant in an alley above the Corso offering local specialities, mainly meat, with main courses costing €12–16. 12.30–3pm & 7.30–11pm; closed Mon & eves in winter.

Verde Fiume Via Lungotemo De Gasperi 51 ☎ 0785 373 482. This place on the river specializes in fresh, local and seasonal produce. You can also bring your own fish which they'll cook for you with an antipasto and coffee for €15. Otherwise starters are around €10, mains €10–15. 12.30–3pm & 7.30pm–midnight; closed Mon in winter.

Nuoro and around

"There is nothing to see in Nuoro: which to tell the truth, is always a relief. Sights are an irritating bore," wrote D.H. Lawrence of the town he visited in 1921, though he was impressed by its appearance – "as if at the end of the world, mountains rising sombre behind". **NUORO**'s superb backdrop – beneath the soaring peak of Monte Ortobene and opposite the sheer and stark heights of Monte Corrasi – is still a major part of its appeal. Some absorbing museums and a vibrant old centre bisected by the pedestrianized **Corso Garibaldi** are added reasons to spend time here.

Evident everywhere are reminders of Nuoro's distinguished literary and artistic heritage, notably in connection with the locally born **Sebastiano Satta** (1867–1914), Sardinia's best-known poet; **Grazia Deledda** (1871–1936), who won the Nobel Prize for Literature in 1926 in recognition of a writing career devoted to recounting the day-to-day trials and passions of local life; and the modernist sculptor **Francesco Ciusa** (1883–1949). With its transport connections, Nuoro also makes a useful gateway to Sardinia's mountainous interior.

MAN (Museo d'Arte Nuoro)

Via Satta 27 • Tues–Sun 10am–1pm & 4–8pm • €3 • ☎ 0784 252 110, ⓦ museoman.it

Housed in a modern building off Corso Garibaldi, **MAN (Museo d'Arte Nuoro)** displays mainly twentieth-century art from the whole island, with a preponderance of Nuorese artists. The works are refreshingly diverse, though mainly focusing on rural and village life, and there are also regular exhibitions of contemporary Italian art.

Museo Tribu (Museo Ciusa)

Piazza Santa Maria della Neve • Tues–Sun 10am–1pm & 4.30–8.30pm • €3 • ☎ 0784 253 052, ⓦ tribunuoro.it

Next to Nuoro's Duomo at the top of the Corso, the **Museo Tribu** is mainly devoted to the work of Nuoro's most celebrated artist, Francesco Ciusa, whose early twentieth-century sculptures invest lowly peasant figures with heroic stature. His most famous work, *La Madre dell'Ucciso* ("The Mother of the Murdered Man"), is a moving study of grief. The rest of the gallery holds temporary exhibitions of pieces by other local figures in the fields of graphic art, ceramics, embroidery and jewellery.

FESTA DEL REDENTORE

Nuoro's biggest annual festival, the **Festa del Redentore**, is one of the most spectacular events on the island's calendar, taking place over the last ten days of August. Enthusiastic dancing and singing in dialect culminate in a costumed procession to Monte Ortobene (see opposite).

Museo della Vita e delle Tradizioni Popolari Sarde

Via Mereu • Tues–Sun 10am–1pm & 4.30–8.30pm • €1 • ☎ 0784 257 035

Nuoro's impressive **Museo della Vita e delle Tradizioni Popolari Sarde** holds Sardinia's most comprehensive range of local costumes, jewellery, masks, carpets and other handicrafts, as well as an array of traditional musical instruments from around the island, including *launeddas* (Sardinian pipes).

Casa di Grazia Deledda and Museo Archeologico

Fans of the author and anyone interested in how local people lived a century ago should drop into the **Casa di Grazia Deledda at** Via Deledda 42 (mid-March to mid-June Tues–Sun 9am–1pm & 3–6pm; mid-June to Sept daily 9am–7pm; Oct to mid-March Tues–Sun 10am–1pm & 3–5pm; free; ☎0784 258 088), the restored home of Nuoro's literary star, displaying various photos and mementoes. From here, it's a brief walk to Piazza Asproni and the **Museo Archeologico** (Tues & Thurs 9am–1pm & 3–5pm, Wed, Fri & Sat 9am–1pm; €2; ☎0784 31 688), which takes in everything from rocks and skulls to carved vases, neolithic jewellery and nuraghic art.

ARRIVAL AND INFORMATION

By train You can reach Nuoro in an hour and a quarter on a narrow-gauge line from Macomer (a stop on the main train line), operated by ARST (Mon–Sat 6 daily; 1hr 10min). The station is on Via Lamarmora, a city bus ride or 15min walk from the old centre.

By bus The bus station is on Via Sardegna, a 10min walk south of the station, where frequent city buses stop. Destinations Aritzo (1 daily; 2hr); Cagliari (3 daily; 2hr 40min–3hr); Fonni (11–12 daily, Sun 3 daily; 40min–1hr 30min); Macomer (Mon–Sat 6 daily; 1hr 10min); Olbia & Olbia airport (9–10 daily; 1hr 45min–3hr 25min); Orgosolo (Mon–Sat 9 daily, Sun 3 daily; 35min); Oristano (1 daily; 1hr 35min); Sassari (4–5 daily; 1hr 40min–2hr 10min); Tonara (1 daily; 1hr 30min).

Tourist office Piazza Italia 19, on the edge of the old quarter (Mon & Wed–Fri 8.30am–2pm, Tues 8.30am–2pm & 3.30–7pm; ☎0784 238 878).

ACCOMMODATION

Nughe 'e' Oro Via Matteotti 14 ☎340 805 2769, ⓦnugheoro.it. On the sixth floor of a modern block near the Duomo, this B&B has bright, airy, wi-fi-enabled rooms with or without private facilities. Photos by the host adorn the walls, and there's a panoramic terrace. No credit cards. **€50**

Silvia e Paolo Corso Garibaldi 58 ☎0784 31 280 or ☎328 921 2199, ⓦsilviaepaolo.it. In the heart of the old centre, this B&B has three modern, spotless rooms with shared or en-suite bathrooms, all overlooking the Corso and with wi-fi. There's a pleasant terrace. **€50**

EATING AND DRINKING

Caffè Tettamanzi Corso Garibaldi 71. Nuoro's oldest bar (from 1875) has the usual tables outside, but the mirrored interior is more unique, with a painted ceiling and cherubs flitting about. 6am–2am; closed Sun in winter.

Il Rifugio Via Mereu 28 ☎0784 232 355. Nuoro's best choice for regional specialities, such as *filindeu nel brodo di pecora* (stringy pasta in a mutton broth), as well as delicious pizzas. Main courses cost €8–18. Service is brisk but friendly, and it's usually packed. 12.45–3pm & 7.45–11.30pm; closed Tues.

La Locanda Via Brofferio 31 ☎0784 31 032. There are no airs or graces in this traditional *osteria* in a large, plain room, which offers Sard dishes at rock-bottom prices. You won't spend more than €20 including drinks, and the €9.20 fixed-price lunchtime menu draws in local workers. Mon–Sat 12.30–3pm & 8.30–10.30pm.

Su Nugoresu Piazza San Giovanni 9 ☎0784 258 017. A pleasant trattoria in a pretty piazza with tables outside in summer. Mon–Fri 12.30–3pm & 8–11pm, Sat & Sun 8–11pm; closed Oct–May.

Monte Ortobene

Signposted west of town, a lane climbs through the forested slopes of **Monte Ortobene** to its summit (955m), 8km away, presided over by a bronze **statue** of the Redeemer. From here there are majestic views over the gorge separating Nuoro from the

17

Supramonte massif, while the woods are perfect for walks, picnics or a dip in the open-air pool at Farcana (summer only). The mountain is the venue for Nuoro's **Festa del Redentore** at the end of August, when a procession from town weaves up the mountain (see box, p.960).

ARRIVAL AND DEPARTURE   MONTE ORTOBENE

By bus Between mid-June and mid-Sept bus #8 runs once or twice hourly from Nuoro's Via Manzoni and the Duomo up to the summit of Monte Ortobene (not Sun). In winter the service operates just twice daily.

ACCOMMODATION

★ **Casa Solotti** ☎0784 33 954, ⓦcasasolotti.it. Monte Ortobene has an excellent, friendly B&B, offering wonderful mountain views and great breakfasts. It's just after the Farcana turn-off, near the bus stop – ring ahead for directions or a pick-up from Nuoro. No credit cards. **€60**

The interior and the east coast

Though little travelled by tourists, Sardinia's **interior** is in many ways the most interesting part of the island, dominated by thick forests and rugged peaks. The local inhabitants have retained a fierce sense of independence and loyalty to their traditions, and this is especially true in the ring of the once almost impenetrable **Monti del Gennargentu**, centred on the island's highest peak, La Mármora (1834m). The range forms the core of the **Barbagia** region, called Barbaria by the Romans who, like their successors, were never able to subdue it, foiled by the guerrilla warfare for which its hidden recesses proved ideal. More recently, the isolation and economic difficulties of the Barbagia's villages led to widescale emigration and, among those who stayed behind, a wave of sheep-rustling, internecine feuding and the kidnapping of wealthy industrialists or their families that continued until the last decades of the twentieth century. Nowadays the Barbagia has huge appeal to **outdoors enthusiasts**, particularly mountain hikers – if you're interested, ask at Oliena's tourist office for routes and lists of guides (see below).

Sardinia's long **eastern seaboard** is highly developed around the resorts of Siniscola and Posada, but further south it preserves its desolate beauty, virtually untouched apart from a couple of isolated spots around **Cala Gonone**, and, further down, around the port of **Arbatax**, in Ogliastra province.

Oliena and around

Though famed as the haunt of bandits until relatively recent times, **OLIENA**, 12km southeast of Nuoro, prefers its reputation as the producer of one of the island's best **wines**, Nepente – a variety of the prized Cannonau – a dry, almost black concoction that turns lighter and stronger over time. The best place to sample it is the **Cantina Oliena** winery, at Via Nuoro 112 (☎0784 287 509).

Oliena lies on the slopes of **Monte Corrasi**, a dramatically rugged limestone elevation which forms part of the Supramonte massif and rises to 1363m. There are numerous organized **excursions** you can make around its various caves and crags, the most famous of which is to the remote Valle Lanaittu and the nuraghic village of Tiscali (see box opposite).

ARRIVAL AND INFORMATION   OLIENA

By bus Buses depart roughly hourly from Nuoro (5–7 on Sun), taking 20min.
Tourist office Corso Deledda 32 (Mon–Sat 9am–1pm & 4–7pm, closed Sat Nov–Easter; ☎0784 286 078, ⓦolienaturismo.com).

ACCOMMODATION AND EATING

CiKappa Via M. Luther King ☎0784 288 024, ⓦ cikappa.it. Functional hotel much favoured by outdoors enthusiasts. In the lively *ristorante*/pizzeria, you can have a full meal of traditional rural cuisine incorporating wild mushroms and boar for around €25. Daily 12.30–3pm & 7.30pm–midnight.

★ **Cooperativa Turistica Enis** Località Maccione ☎0784 288 363, ⓦ coopenis.it. Up a steep hill 3km south of Oliena, this hotel, campsite and restaurant complex is perfectly situated for mountain walks. The clean rooms, basic pitches and terrace restaurant all have lofty views over the valley. Pizzas are available alongside such dishes as rabbit stew and roast suckling pig on fixed-price menus costing €18.50–35. Daily 12.30–3pm & 8–10.30pm. **€80**, pitches **€17**

Santa Maria Corso Deledda 76 ☎328 117 8551, ⓦ bbsantamaria.it. Modern, central B&B with spacious rooms including a traditionally styled suite with its own balcony. All rooms have private bathrooms, a/c and wi-fi, and there's a large, panoramic roof terrace. No credit cards. **€50**

Orgosolo

Some 18km south of Oliena, connected by frequent buses from Nuoro, **ORGOSOLO** is stuck with its label of erstwhile bandit capital of the island. The village's most infamous son, Graziano Mesina – the so-called "Scarlet Rose" – won local hearts in the 1960s by robbing from the rich to give to the poor. Roaming at will through the mountains, even granting interviews to reporters and television journalists, he was eventually captured; after forty years behind bars, he was freed in 2004 and returned to live in Orgosolo.

Today, the only traces of Orgosolo's violent past are in its vivid, graffiti-style **murals**, some covering whole buildings. Portraying village culture and history, many of the paintings are peopled with gun-toting locals and illustrate the oppression of the landless by the landowners.

Cala Gonone

East of Oliena on the coast, the small resort of **CALA GONONE** was until recently accessible only by boat – it's now reached via a tunnel through the 900m-high rock wall off the SS125, from which the road zigzags steeply down to the bay. The rapid development of the settlement has not spoilt the sense of isolation, and it is worth a stay if only to take advantage of the numerous boat tours to the secluded beaches and grottoes along the coast.

HIKES FROM OLIENA, DORGALI AND CALA GONONE

South of Oliena and Dorgali, the Supramonte massif provides lots of opportunities for mountain **hikes**, which should be accompanied by a guide – lists of available guides are available from the tourist offices at Oliena (see opposite) and Dorgali (Via Lamármora 108; Mon–Fri 10am–1pm & 4–8pm; ☎0784 96 243, ⓦ dorgali.it). The most popular excursion is to the nuraghic village of **Tiscali** (daily: May–Sept 9am–7pm; Oct–April 9am–5pm; €5), spectacularly sited within a vast mountain-top cavern, for which you should allow 3–5 hours. One of Sardinia's most dramatic mountain landscapes lies further south, cut through by the Flumineddu valley and the **Gola di Gorroppu**, one of southern Europe's deepest canyons. You'll get some stunning views of the valley from the SS125, running high above it, but you should hook up with a guide to experience it more directly. Even for shorter hikes, you'll need hardy footwear with a secure grip and ankle support, and preferably some head protection against bumps and falls: the boulders can be extremely slippery, especially when wet.

Along the coast, you can make half- or full-day hikes **from Cala Gonone** to the beaches at Cala Luna and Cala Sisine. From Cala Sisine, the route wanders inland up the Sisine canyon, as far as the solitary church of San Pietro, from where a track leads down to the village of Baunei. Again, guides are advised for any but the most straightforward coastal routes.

17

BOAT TOURS FROM CALA GONONE

Tickets for a range of **boat trips** from Cala Gonone to the beaches and deep grottoes that pit the shore are sold at the port. Most famous of the grottoes is the **Grotta del Bue Marino**, formerly home to a colony of Mediterranean monk seals, or "sea ox". It's among Sardinia's most spectacular caves, a luminescent gallery filled with remarkable natural sculptures, resembling organ pipes, wedding cakes and even human heads – one of them is known as Dante, after a fondly imagined resemblance to the poet. Trips here cost around €20 including entry to the grotto. Other sea excursions provide access to various beaches along the coast, the most popular of which are **Cala Luna** and **Cala Sisine** – for more solitude, opt for one of the remoter swimming and snorkeling stops.

ARRIVAL AND INFORMATION

CALA GONONE

By bus ARST buses and Deplano services to and from Olbia airport stop on Viale Bue Marino.
Destinations Dorgali (4–10 daily; 20min); Nuoro (3–7 daily; 1hr 10min); Olbia airport (June–Sept 4 daily; 2hr 15min).

Tourist office Viale Bue Marino (daily: April & Oct 9am–3pm; May, June & Sept 9am–1pm & 3–7pm; July & Aug 9.30am–7pm; ☎0784 93 696, ⓦ dorgali.it).

ACCOMMODATION

Cala Luna Lungomare Palmasera ☎0784 93 133, ⓦ calaluna.net. Bougainvillea-covered hotel with direct access to the beach, modern art on the walls and a great roof terrace, where the restaurant is located. It's worth spending extra on a sea-facing room with balcony. Closed late Nov to March. €110

Camping Cala Gonone Via Collodi ☎0784 93 165, ⓦ www.campingcalagonone.it. Shady but often crowded campsite a brief walk from the bus stop and tourist office,

and 300m up from the seafront. Caravans and chalets can be rented, and a pool and tennis court are available in summer. April–Oct. Pitches €34

Pop Piazza del Porto ☎0784 93 185, ⓦ hotelpop.it. Right by the harbour, all the rooms at this modern hotel have small balconies, though not all have sea views. Staff are friendly, there's a great restaurant and the hotel's speedboat can whisk you to secluded sandy coves. €98

EATING

Il Pescatore Via Acquadolce 7 ☎0784 93 174. Gourmet seafood parlour on the seafront, a bit pricey but worth it for the lobster pasta, linguini and clams and grilled fish platters. You can eat alfresco in summer. Tourist menus are €25 and €30, otherwise reckon on around €40 for a full meal. Daily noon–3pm & 7.30–11pm; closed Nov–March.

Roadhouse Blues Lungomare Palmasera ☎0784 93 187. Overlooking the sea, this bar-restaurant has a buzzy rock'n'roll theme, with "Led Zeppelin" and "Hendrix" among

the pizzas named on the menu (around €8). You can also order tasty but pricey fish dishes, and cocktails and beers are served until late. Daily 7am–midnight; closed mid-Nov to mid-Dec.

Su Recreu Piazza Andrea Doria ☎0784 93 135. Up from the port, this café-bar serves the town's best ice cream as well as healthy breakfasts, sandwiches and snacks till late (tourist menus are €15–20). There's live salsa music on summer evenings. Daily 8am–late; closed early Nov to mid-March.

Arbatax and around

South of Cala Gonone and the majestic Gorroppu gorge, the SS125 descends steeply to **TORTOLI**, the fairly nondescript provincial capital of Ogliastra. The ferry port of **ARBATAX** lies around 5km west, with a small beach that's famous for its red rocks, but there are much better **beaches** outside town – 6km north at **Santa Maria Navarrese**, 2km south at **Porto Frailis** and 5km south at **Lido Orrì**.

ARRIVAL AND DEPARTURE

ARBATAX AND AROUND

By train Arbatax station, by the port, is a terminus of the narrow-gauge Trenino Verde railway (ⓦ treninoverde .com), which follows a scenic inland route to Mandas from where you can change for a faster train to Cagliari; the full journey from the coast to Cagliari takes around 7hr (mid-June to mid-Sept Wed–Mon).

Destinations Cagliari (mid-June to mid-Sept Wed–Mon 2 daily via Mandas; 6hr 50min–7hr 15min).
By bus Buses to Santa Maria Navarrese, Cagliari and Nuoro leave from Tortoli. An hourly local bus service links Arbatax and Tortoli, also taking in Lido Orri and Porto Frailis between mid-June and mid-Sept.

By ferry Ferry tickets are available from the Tirrenia office near the port, on your right as you head towards the station (☎0782 667 067).

Destinations Civitavecchia (2 weekly; 11hr); Genoa (2 weekly; 17hr–22hr 30min).

ACCOMMODATION

Entula Via Sindaco Lorrai 2, Porto Frailis ☎329 348 1855, ⓦentula.com. Comfortable B&B 5min from the beach and good restaurants, with spacious rooms with a/c and a garden where breakfast is served. No credit cards. Closed Dec & Jan. **€60**

Ostello Bellavista Via Pedra Longa, Santa Maria Navarrese ☎0782 614 039, ⓦostelloinogliastra.com. Independent hostel in a great position on a height above

Santa Maria, though it's actually more like an informal lodge, where each of the plain white doubles has private bathroom and a sea view. Doubles **€74**

Telis Porto Frailis ☎0782 667 140, ⓦwww .campingtelis.com. Close to the beach, this campsite has good facilities (including two pools), bungalows to rent (€106/night for two) and caravans (€96/night). Pitches **€32**

EATING

Il Faro Porto Frailis ☎0782 667 499. There are a few restaurants in Arbatax, but you're better off heading to this place overlooking the beach, which has a good choice

of grilled fish and a lively atmosphere. Mains are €12–15. Easter–Sept daily 12.30–2.30pm & 5.30–10.30pm; Oct–March 12.30–2.30pm.

The Gennargentu massif

The central region of the Barbagia holds the **Gennargentu** chain of mountains – the name means "silver gate", referring to the snow that covers them every winter. Here, you'll find the island's only skiing facilities on **Monte Bruncu Spina**, Sardinia's second-highest peak (1829m). In spring and summer, you can explore this and other areas on **mountain treks**, best undertaken in the company of guides for which the tourist office at Nuoro can supply a list.

Buried within chestnut forests, the isolated villages of the region make useful bases for both skiers and trekkers, for example **FONNI**, 36km south of Nuoro and at 1000m the island's highest village. Try to coincide your visit with one of Fonni's costumed **festivals**, principally the Madonna dei Mártiri, on the Monday following the first Sunday in June, and on San Giovanni's day on June 24. Other centres for excursions and to get a flavour of the moutain culture include **TONARA**, a quiet, traditional village some 30km southwest of Fonni, famed for its chestnuts and *torrone* (a sticky, sweet nougat confection), and **ARITZO**, 15km further south.

ACCOMMODATION

THE GENNARGENTU MASSIF

La Capannina Via Maxia 36, Aritzo ☎0784 629 121, ⓦhotelcapannina.net. Old-fashioned, chalet-style hotel with a garden and restaurant. Rooms are on the small side, but clean and tidy, and some have balconies with valley views. **€80**

Sa Orte Via Roma 14, Fonni ☎0784 58 020, ⓦhotel saorte.it. Elegantly restored, granite hotel with period

trappings and its own restaurant. Rooms are spacious with modern bathrooms. **€80**

Tia Zicca Via Galusè 2, Tonara ☎346 012 3114, ⓦtiazicca.it. In the older part of the villlage, this simple B&B has two en-suite rooms, a garden and a panoramic terrace where breakfast can be served. Closed Nov & Jan. No credit cards. **€55**

Olbia

The largest town in Sardinia's northeastern wedge, **OLBIA** owes its recent phenomenal growth to the huge influx of tourists bound for one of the Mediterranean's loveliest stretches of coast, the **Costa Smeralda** (see p.968). Awash with traffic and ugly apartment blocks, Olbia is the least Sardinian of all the island's towns. Its port and airport, however, make it an inevitable stop for some, and there's a first-class museum, plus numerous bars and restaurants, usually abuzz with tourists.

17

Museo Archeologico

Molo Brin • Mon, Tues & Fri–Sun: mid-June to mid-Sept 10am–1pm & 8–11pm; mid-Sept to mid-June 10am–1pm & 5–8pm • Free • ☏ 0789 28 290

Olbia's chief attraction is the **Museo Archeologico**, a fortress-like construction on a miniature island by the port. The currently limited displays range from Proto-Sard prehistory through to the Carthaginian, Greek and Roman eras, and include a magnificent terracotta head of Hercules wearing a lion's mane – a Roman copy of a Greek original.

San Simplicio

Via S. Simplicio • Daily 6.30am–1pm & 3.30–8pm • Free

Part of the great Pisan reconstruction programme of the eleventh and twelfth centuries, the basilica of **San Simplicio** has three aisles separated by pillars and columns recycled from Roman constructions – even the stoup for the holy water was formerly an urn that held cremated ashes. The church is the venue for Olbia's biggest **festa**, six days of processions, costumed dancing and fireworks around May 15, commemorating San Simplicio's martyrdom in the fourth century.

OLBIA

ACCOMMODATION
Cavour	4
Gallura	3
Janas	2
Porto Romano	1

RESTAURANTS & CAFÉS
Antica Trattoria	1
Gallura	2
Il Gámbero	3
La Tasca	4

ARRIVAL AND DEPARTURE

By plane Olbia's airport (W olbiairport.it) is connected by buses #2 and #10 every 20–30min until 11.40pm, which take just 10min to reach the central Piazza Regina Margherita (tickets €1 from the ticket machine in the terminal, €1.50 on board). Taxis cost about €20. There are summer-only bus services from the airport to the resorts of Porto Cervo and Cannigione (4 daily) and Cala Gonone (4 daily), and year-round to Nuoro (3–6 daily); other destinations can be reached from Olbia city.

By ferry Ferries (see box, p.946) dock at the Stazione Maríttima, Isola Bianca, 2km from the centre, connected by city bus #9 twice hourly (€1 from the information office, or €1.50 on board), or you can take one of the infrequent trains to Olbia's main station. The Stazione Maríttima holds the ticket offices for Tirrenia and Moby Lines. Sardinia Ferries to Livorno leave from Golfo Aranci, 15km up the coast (5–8 buses daily summer only; or see below for trains). Book early for all departures.

Destinations Civitavecchia (1–4 daily; 4hr 45min–8hr); Genoa (3–12 weekly; 10hr–15hr 30min); Livorno (1–2

daily; 5hr 45min–8hr 30min); Piombino (June to early Sept 3–6 weekly; 4hr 30min).

By train Trains for Sassari and Cagliari run several times daily from the station just off Corso Umberto.

Destinations Cagliari (5–6 daily, some with change; 3hr 30min–5hr 30min); Golfo Aranci (5–7 daily; 30min); Oristano (4–5 daily, some with change; 2hr 35min); Sassari (5–6 daily, some with change; 1hr 50min).

By bus The stop for ARST buses is on Corso Vittorio Veneto, just past the level crossing at the bottom of Corso Umberto. Tickets are sold at *Adela Café*, by the stop. Summer-only Sun Lines buses for Porto Cervo leave from Piazza Crispi, on the seafront.

Destinations Arzachena (11–19 daily; 30–50min); Cagliari (Mon–Sat 1 daily; 4hr 20min); Golfo Aranci (mid-June to mid-Sept 5–8 daily; 25min); Nuoro (4–9 daily; 2hr 35min); Palau (6–17 daily; 1hr 10min); Porto Cervo (June–Sept 4–5 daily; Oct–May Mon–Sat 1 daily; 1hr 35min); Santa Teresa di Gallura (4–14 daily; 1hr 30min–2hr 15min); Sassari (1–2 daily; 1hr 20min–1hr 45min).

INFORMATION

Tourist offices Tourist information for the city is dispensed at the Muncipio at the bottom of Corso Umberto (Mon–Sat 9am–2pm, Aug also Thurs–Sat 5–8pm; T 0789 52 206, W olbiaturismo.it). The office covering the whole province is at Via Nanni 39 (July & Aug Mon–Fri 9am–1pm & 3–6pm, Sat 9am–1pm; Sept–June Mon–Fri 8am–2pm;

T 0789 557 732, W olbiatempioturismo.it), and there's an information desk at the airport (daily 8am–11.30pm; T 0789 563 444).

Internet access InterSmeraldo, Via Porto Romano 6/B, off the Corso.

Left luggage Stazione Maríttima (daily 6am–10pm).

ACCOMMODATION

Cavour Via Cavour 22 T 0789 204 033, W cavourhotel .it. This tasteful renovation of a traditional building on a central alley has smart, simply furnished rooms, free parking and wi-fi. **€90**

Gallura Corso Umberto 145 T 0789 24 648. This old-fashioned hotel has plain, en-suite rooms and rustic trimmings. Breakfasts are superb, and there's a first-class restaurant. **€80**

★ **Janas** Via Lamármora 61 T 349 872 8140,

W janasaffittacamere.com. This B&B in a renovated old house has three spacious ground-floor rooms, all with private bathrooms, and one giving on to the shady garden where breakfast is taken. **€70**

Porto Romano Via Nanni 2 T 349 192 7996, W bed andbreakfastportoromano.it. Central but quiet B&B, offering doubles with private or en-suite bathrooms, use of cooking facilities, and a terrace with a barbecue. No credit cards. **€70**

EATING AND DRINKING

Antica Trattoria Via delle Terme 1 T 0789 24 053. Popular place with a buzzing atmosphere, a tasty array of antipasti, and pizzas. There are good-value tourist menus (€15–25), and a small garden for eating alfresco. Mon–Sat 12.30–2.45pm & 7.30–11.30pm.

★ **Gallura** Corso Umberto 145 T 0789 24 648. One of the top spots in the region to sample delicious, authentic *gallurese* dishes, with a huge menu and fairly high prices (most meat dishes around €18). The soups and antipasti are a joy, and there's an excellent wine list too. Tues–Sun 1–2.30pm & 8–10.30pm.

Il Gámbero Via Lamármora 6 T 0789 23 874. Locals

and tourists alike appreciate the rustic trimmings and hangings at this centrally located restaurant. The fare is mainly seafood, with good antipasti including *affumicati di mare* (smoked tuna and swordfish). Count on €50–60 for a full meal for two including drinks. Tues–Sun 12.30–2.30pm & 7.30–10pm; July & Aug open daily.

La Tasca Via Cavour 3 T 347 853 6185. Handy spot for a daytime sit-down and snack, or to while away the evening, when it offers cocktails and regular DJs and live music. Salads and pizzas are €6–8. June–Sept daily 10am–2am; Oct–May Mon–Sat 10am–midnight.

17 The Costa Smeralda and around

Long a magnet for Italy's glitziest celebrities, the five-star development of the **Costa Smeralda** in the 1960s helped to transform the economy of the entire island. A coastline this beautiful inevitably comes at a price, however: budget accommodation is virtually nonexistent, while the high-end hotels are mostly devoid of much character. **Arzachena** and **Cannigione** are cheaper bases from which to explore the area.

The Costa Smeralda begins about 12km north of Olbia and is defined as the 10km strip between the gulfs of Cugnana and Arzachena. Although strict rules were imposed to prevent overzealous development – you won't see any multistorey hotels, advertising hoardings or fast-food restaurants – the area has little in common with the rest of Sardinia, and the luxurious holiday villages have a bland, almost suburban feel. This hasn't stopped the mega-rich from coming in droves – Silvio Berlusconi owns six properties here.

Porto Cervo and around

The "local"-style rustic-red architecture of **PORTO CERVO**, the main centre of the Costa Smeralda, embodies the dream of an idyllic Mediterranean village without any of the irritations of real life. Graffiti- and litter-free, Porto Cervo exults in its exclusivity, with a glittering yachting marina as its centrepiece.

You'll need your own transport to reach the sandy **beaches** dotted down the coast south of Porto Cervo. None is clearly marked; just follow any dirt track down to the sea – the rougher it is, the more promising. Try **Capriccioli** and **Liscia Ruia**, 6km south of Porto Cervo.

ARRIVAL AND DEPARTURE
PORTO CERVO

By bus Porto Cervo is connected to Olbia and Arzachena by ARST and (in summer) Sun Lines buses. For other destinations, change at Arzachena.

Destinations Arzachena (Mon–Sat 5–7 daily; 25–40min); Olbia (Mon–Sat 5–11 daily, June–Sept Sun 4 daily; 25min–1hr 10min).

ACCOMMODATION

Camping Cugnana Località Cugnana ☎0789 33 184, ⓦwww.campingcugnana.it. Just south of the Costa Smeralda, 12km north of Olbia, this campsite has a pool, bungalows (€500/week), and a shuttle service to nearby beaches. In summer, Sun Lines buses stop right outside. April–Sept. Pitches **€23.60**

Arzachena and around

Inland **ARZACHENA** is the nearest "normal" town to the Costa Smeralda, not particularly inspiring in itself but well equipped with banks, shops and restaurants. It's a transport hub for local bus services, and close to **CANNIGIONE**, a small yachting resort on the **Golfo di Arzachena**. This deep, narrow bay shares many of the Costa Smeralda's natural features, but without the air of exclusivity.

ARRIVAL AND INFORMATION
ARZACHENA AND AROUND

By bus ARST services run to most places along the coast, and there are daily Turmo connections to Olbia, Palau and Santa Teresa. Sun Lines buses also connect Olbia and Porto Cervo with Cannigione in summer.
Destinations Cannigione (3–13 daily; 10min); Olbia (8–19 daily; 45min); Palau (5–14 daily; 20min); Santa Teresa di Gallura (6–12 daily; 1hr).

Tourist offices There are information offices at Malchittu, between Arzachena and Cannigione (Mon–Sat 9am–2pm & 3–6pm; ☎0789 83 306), and at Via Orecchioni, Cannigione (Mon & Tues 9am–2pm & 4–7pm, Wed–Sun 9am–2pm & 3–8pm; ☎0789 88 229).

ACCOMMODATION AND EATING

Centro Vacanze Isuledda La Conia ☎0789 86 003, ⓦisuledda.it. A couple of kilometres north of Cannigione, this campsite is right on the shore and has caravans and bungalows to rent. It gets a bit overwhelmed in August, and there's not much shade. Sun Lines buses stop outside in summer. April–Oct. Pitches €37

Hotel del Porto Via Nazionale 94, Cannigione ☎0789 88 011, ⍟hoteldelporto.com. The best-value of Cannigione's hotels is this place, with balconied rooms overlooking the marina and a good café and restaurant below. €140

Santa Lucia Via Cagliari 11, Arzachena ☎0789 83 012 or ☎338 269 3640, ⍟bbslucia.it. This B&B lies in a quiet backstreet in the centre of town, with a peaceful walled garden, five comfortable rooms and freshly baked cakes for breakfast. No credit cards. €80

★ **Tavola Azzurra** Via Vasco da Gama 12, Cannigione ☎347 121 5328. Below the church, this *rosticceria* has a brisk, authentic feel, offering delicious portions of fresh seafood and other hot snacks for €3.50–6 each (pastas are around €10). Daily 9am–3pm & 5–11pm; closed Oct–March.

The Maddalena islands

The profusion of minor **islands** off Sardinia's northeastern coast, more than sixty in all, form part of **La Maddalena national park**, which can be explored on various boat tours from the mainland or from the archipelago's only port, **La Maddalena**, reachable on ferries from **Palau** (10km up the coast from Cannigione).

The island invites aimless wandering and offers a variety of sandy and rocky beaches in mostly undeveloped coves. The **beaches** on the northern and western coasts are most attractive, particularly those around the tiny port of Madonetta, 5km west of La Maddalena, and at Cala Lunga, 5km north of town. Attached to the main island by a causeway is neighbouring **Caprera**, the island on which Garibaldi spent his last years.

La Maddalena

The attractive, upbeat town of **LA MADDALENA** gets very busy in July and August but you'll find little open here in winter. Most of the action takes place in the narrow lanes between Piazza Umberto I and Cala Gavetta (the marina for small boats), a five-minute walk from the ferry port heading left. Behind the seafront stretches a warren of backstreets dotted with bars and trattorias. It's worth noting that prices are usually higher than those on the Sardinian mainland.

ARRIVAL AND DEPARTURE   LA MADDALENA

By ferry Various operators run ferries from Palau to the archipelago's only port, La Maddalena (every 15min in peak season, 1–2 hourly in winter). Tickets are sold at Palau's Stazione Maríttima and cost around €9 return per person, €40 return for two people in a medium-sized car, but there are significant discounts when bought on the preceding day.

INFORMATION AND GETTING AROUND

By bus Local buses run to various parts of the island and to Caprera from Piazza Umberto I near the port (roughly every hour in summer, less frequent in winter). Tickets are €1 from vendors or €1.50 on board.

By bike or moped Bikes and mopeds can be rented from any of the outlets on the seafront towards Cala Gavetta for about €15 a day for a bike, or €60 for a scooter (prices drop outside peak season).

Tourist office Piazza Barone des Geneys (Mon & Wed 8am–2pm & 3–6pm, Aug 3–7pm, Tues, Thurs & Fri 8am–2pm, Aug & Sept also Sat & Sun 8am–2pm; Oct–July Mon–Fri 8am–2pm; ☎0789 736 321, ⍟comune.lamaddalena.ot.it).

ACCOMMODATION

La Piccola Parigi Via Italia 8 ☎347 058 8615, ⍟lapiccolaparigibedandbreakfast.it. Central B&B on two floors of an apartment block, with airy, modern rooms, private bathrooms and internet access. No credit cards. €80

Maddalena Località Moneta ☎0789 728 051, ⍟campingmaddalena.it. The best equipped of the island's campsites lies close to town and Caprera, and has caravans and bungalows to rent (from €60). June–Sept. Pitches €22

Residenza Mordini Via Principe Amedeo 3 ☎0789 737 325, ⍟residenzamordini.it. In a renovated 1930s building close to the ferry port, this swish hotel offers well-equipped rooms with a blend of antique and modern furnishings, spa facilities and free parking. €150

17

EATING

Osteria da Liò Via Vittorio Emanuele 4 ☎0789 737 507. Simple, family-run *osteria* in the centre, with some outdoor tables. The *spaghetti bottarga e vongole* (with fish roe and clams) is exceptional. Fixed-price menus are €15 and €18, alternatively you'll pay around €40 each without drinks. April–Oct Mon–Sat noon–3pm & 7.30–10.30pm, Sun 7.30–10.30pm; Nov–March Tues–Sun noon–3pm & 7.30–10.30pm.

Ristorante Pizzeria 48 Corso Garibaldi 48 ☎320 938 8860. This place in the centre is ideal for pizzas (€6–13) and straightforward island dishes, including *trofie casarecce mari e monti* (home-made pasta with meat and seafood) and *tagliatelle con cozze e menta* (pasta with mussels and mint). The tourist menu is €20, otherwise mains are €12–20. Daily noon–3pm & 7–midnight; closed Nov & Feb.

Caprera

Though partly used for military purposes, **CAPRERA**'s protected wooded parkland is open to all, and is little developed apart from Garibaldi's house in the centre and a couple of secluded, self-contained tourist complexes.

Giuseppe Garibaldi (1807–82) came to live in Caprera in 1855, after a twenty-year exile from Italy. It was from here that he embarked on his spectacular conquest of Sicily and Naples in 1861, accompanied by his thousand Red Shirts, and it was here that he returned after his campaigns to resume a simple farming life. Having bought the northern part of the island for £360, he spent much of his time writing his memoirs and some bad novels. In 1864 a group of English admirers provided the money for Garibaldi to buy the rest of Caprera from local landowners.

Compendio Garibaldino

Tues–Sun 9am–1.30pm & 2–7.15pm • €5 • ☎0789 727 162, ⓦ compendiogaribaldino.it

Garibaldi's old house, the elegant South American-style Casa Bianca, has been preserved pretty much as he left it, though it now displays the **Compendio Garibaldino** museum. Visitors are escorted past the bed where he slept, a smaller one where he died, various scrolls, manifestoes and pronouncements, as well as an array of personal memorabilia. A stopped clock and a wall calendar indicate the precise time and date of his death. The tour ends with Garibaldi's **tomb** in the garden, its rough granite contrasting with the more pompous tombs of his last wife and five of his children. Garibaldi had requested to be cremated, but following the wishes of his son Menotti, his corpse was embalmed. In 1932, fifty years after his death, his tomb was opened to reveal the body perfectly intact.

Santa Teresa di Gallura and around

The road northwest from Arzachena passes a succession of lovely bays, some dramatic rocky coastline, and a handful of campsites. Six kilometres west of Palau, the slender isthmus of **Porto Pollo** is Sardinia's busiest watersports centre, with ideal conditions for **windsurfing** and **kitesurfing**. There are numerous surf schools and rental outfits, while the sheltered, dune-backed beaches will equally appeal to non-surfers.

Some 15km further west, **SANTA TERESA DI GALLURA** is Sardinia's northernmost port. The town gets extremely lively in summer, with a buzzing nightlife, but the main draw is the **beaches**, many enjoying superb views over to Corsica, just 11km away. There's one stretch of sand right at the edge of town, but some of the finest beaches on the whole island are a short bus-ride away, with **Punta Falcone** and **La Marmorata** to the east, and **Capo Testa**, with its wind-sculpted granite rock formations, 3km west of Santa Teresa.

ARRIVAL AND INFORMATION

SANTA TERESA DI GALLURA

By bus Santa Teresa is served by buses from Arzachena and Palau (6–12 daily).

By ferry From the port on the eastern side of town,

Moby Lines and Saremar operate sailings to Bonifacio in Corsica (2–7 daily; 50min; €16.50–23 one way, plus €26–35 per car).

Tourist office Piazza Vittorio Emanuele (mid-July to mid-Sept Mon–Fri 9am–1pm & 5–10pm, Sat & Sun 9am–1pm & 5–9pm; mid-Sept to mid-July Mon–Fri 9am–1pm; ☎0789 754 127, ✆comunestg.it).

GETTING AROUND

By bus Between mid-June to mid-Sept, eight local buses daily link Santa Teresa with the beaches of Marmorata and Capo Testa; tickets on board, €1.50).

By bike, scooter or car Global Rent, at Piazza San Vittorio 7 (☎0789 755 080), has bikes (€25/day), scooters (from €30/day) and cars (from €65/day) to rent.

ACCOMMODATION

Comfort Scano Inn Via Lazio 4 ☎0789 754 447, ✆albergoscano.it. Small and functional, family-run hotel off the Capo Testa road, with standard rooms with a/c and a decent restaurant. **€80**

★ **La Chicca di Francesca** Via Basilicata 4 ☎347 335 0779, ✆lachiccadifrancesca.com. Set in lush gardens a 5min walk from the centre, this B&B has three rooms with wood furnishings, balconies, private bathrooms and a/c. No credit cards. **€70**

La Liccia SP90 ☎0789 755 190, ✆campinglaliccia

.com. The nearest campsite to Santa Teresa lies 6km south, signposted off the Castelsardo road and a 10min walk from a good beach. Pitches are large, terraced and shady, and there are caravans and bungalows (from €42). Mid-May to Aug. Pitches **€21**

★ **Moderno** Via Umberto 39 ☎0789 754 233, ✆modernohotel.eu. This friendly, centrally located hotel has airy rooms in pale blues and greens with Sardinian touches and spacious bathrooms. **€90**

EATING AND DRINKING

Marlin Via Garibaldi 4 ☎0789 754 557. Seafood is the main event here – the mixed grill is a massive feast – but they also serve delicious fresh pastas and meat dishes as well as pizzas in the evening. First courses are €11–14, mains are €12–18. Daily noon–2.30pm & 7–10.30pm; closed Wed Oct–Dec, plus all Jan & Feb.

Papè Satan Via Lamármora 20 ☎0789 755 048. This *ristorante*/pizzeria with a garden and courtyard specializes in Neapolitan-style pizzas (served all day; €7–12), and other Neapolitan specialities such as spaghetti with octopus (€14). Daily noon–3pm & 7–11.30pm; closed Nov–March.

Castelsardo

On Sardinia's north coast, 70km southwest from Santa Teresa di Gallura, **CASTELSARDO** lies picturesquely draped over a promontory overlooking the **Golfo dell'Asinara**. The town was the Sardinian power-base of the Genoan Doria family for nearly 250 years, and the historic centre preserves a pungent medieval flavour, crowned by a **castle** that now holds a museum of basketwork. This local speciality, combined with the town's photogenic setting, has helped to transform Castelsardo into a fully fledged holiday resort, with numerous hotels, restaurants and handicrafts shops.

Museo dell'Intreccio Mediterraneo

Castello di Castelsardo • July to mid-Sept daily 9am–midnight; late Sept daily 9.30am–1pm & 3–6.30pm; Oct–June Tues–Sun 9.30am–1pm & 3pm–1hr before sunset • €2 • ☎079 471 380

Artfully incorporated into the small chambers of Castelsardo's castle, the **Museo dell'Intreccio Mediterraneo** showcases the local mastery in the craft of basketweaving. There's much to admire in this assortment of bowls, bottles, lobster traps and even boats, often skilfully patterned. Some of the most prized items are woven from the leaves of the local dwarf-palm, others use rushes and asphodel. Elsewhere in the castle you'll come across replicas of medieval **weaponry** and some marvellous coastal views.

ARRIVAL AND DEPARTURE   CASTELSARDO

By bus Castelsardo has bus connections with Sassari (5–11 daily; 1hr) and Santa Teresa di Gallura (3–6 daily; 1hr 40min).

17 Sassari

Sardinia's second city, **SASSARI** combines an insular, traditional feel, as embodied in its well-preserved old quarter, with a forward-looking, confident air that is most evident in its modern centre. Here, leading off from the grandiose Piazza Italia, the café-lined Via Roma holds the city's principal sight, the **Museo Sanna**, displaying some of the island's most important archeological finds.

Brief history

While Cagliari was Pisa's base of operations in Sardinia during the Middle Ages, Sassari was the Genoan capital, ruled by the Doria family, whose power reached throughout the Mediterranean. Under the Aragonese it became an important centre of Spanish hegemony, and the Spanish stamp is still strong, not least in its churches. In the sixteenth century the Jesuits founded Sardinia's first **university** here, which continues to excel in the spheres of law, medicine and politics.

The Duomo

Mon–Sat 8.30am–noon & 4–6.45pm, Sun 8.30–11.30am & 5–6.45pm • Free

Sassari's **old quarter**, a network of alleys and piazzas bisected by the main Corso Vittorio Emanuele, is a good area for strolling around. At the heart of it is the **Duomo**, whose florid facade is Sardinia's most imposing example of Baroque architecture, added to a simpler Aragonese-Gothic base from the fifteenth and sixteenth centuries.

Behind it, the eighteenth-century **Palazzo Ducale** now houses the town hall. On the other side of the Corso, **Piazza Tola** retains its medieval feel and is the venue of a daily market.

Museo Sanna

Via Roma 64 • Tues–Sun 9am–8pm • €4 • ☎ 079 272 203, ⓦ museosannasassari.it

Organized chronologically from prehistoric through nuraghic to Phoenician, Carthaginian and Roman items, the **Museo Sanna** offers a fascinating review of

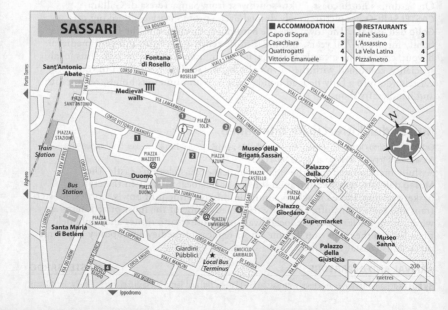

LA CAVALCATA

One of Sardinia's showiest festivals – **La Cavalcata** – takes place in Sassari on the penultimate Sunday of May, the highlight of a month of cultural activities. Northern Sardinia's equivalent to Cagliari's Sant'Efisio festival and originally staged for the benefit of visiting Spanish kings or other dignitaries, it attracts hundreds of richly costumed participants from villages throughout the province and beyond. The festival is divided into three stages: the morning features a horseback parade and a display of the embroidered and decorated costumes unique to each village, after which there is a show of stirring feats of horsemanship at the local race-course. The day ends with traditional songs and dances back in Piazza Italia.

Sardinia's distant past. Alongside the coins, jewellery and amphorae from the classical period, the most impressive displays are connected with the nuraghic period, notably a collection of **bronze statuettes**, including warriors with boldly stylized ox-head helmets, boats with equally extravagant prows, and a shepherd holding either a dog or goat on the end of a lead.

Fontana di Rosello

Corso Trinità • Tues–Sun: March–Sept 10am–8pm; Oct–Feb 10am–5pm • Free

On the edge of the old quarter outside Porta Rosello, it's worth seeking out the **Fontana di Rosello**, now somewhat stranded at the bottom of a flight of grassy steps. Built in 1606 in late Renaissance style by Genoan stonemasons, the fountain is elaborately carved with dolphins and four statues representing the seasons. The city's old **wash-house** stands adjacent.

ARRIVAL AND DEPARTURE

SASSARI

By train Coming to Sassari by train, you'll usually have to change at Ozieri-Chilivani, though journeys from Alghero are direct. The station lies at the bottom of the old town's Corso Vittorio Emanuele.

Destinations Alghero (9–12 daily; 35min); Cagliari (5 daily, some with change; 2hr 50min–3hr 45min); Macomer (6 daily, some with change; 1hr 10min–1hr 45min); Olbia (6 daily, some with change; 1hr 450min); Oristano (5 daily; 2hr–2hr 40min).

By bus The bus station is on Via XXV Aprile, a right turn out

of the train station, for all long-distance buses as well as the regular service linking the city with Alghero airport (ⓦ aeroportodialghero.it).

Destinations Alghero (4–10 daily; 45min–1hr); Bosa (Mon–Sat 3 daily; 2hr 10min); Cagliari (2–3 daily; 1hr 45min–2hr); Nuoro (4–6 daily; 1hr 50min–2hr 25min); Olbia (1–2 daily; 1hr 25min–1hr 45min); Oristano (1–3 daily; 1hr 45min–2hr); Santa Teresa di Gallura (2–5 daily; 2hr 15min–2hr 40min); Stintino (1–6 daily; 45min–1hr 15min).

INFORMATION

Tourist office Sassari Via Sebastiano Satta 13 (Tues–Fri 9am–1.30pm & 3–6pm, Sat 9am–1.30pm; ☏ 079 200

8072, ⓦ comune.sassari.it).

Internet access Internet Point, Piazza Mazzotti 4.

ACCOMMODATION

Capo di Sopra Corso Vittorio Emanuele 24 ☏ 079 202 8095 or ☏ 339 119 2757, ⓦ capodisopra.com. Central B&B run by an ex-DJ, offering three spacious rooms with private bathrooms in an old apartment with antique traces. **€65**

Casachiara Vicolo Bertolinis 7 ☏ 079 200 5052 or ☏ 333 695 7118, ⓦ casachiara.net. This relaxed B&B on the second floor of an eighteenth-century *palazzo* in the old quarter has rather dark but colourfully painted rooms with private bathrooms. No credit cards. **€65**

★ **Quattrogatti** Via Sant'Eligio 5 ☏ 079 237 819 or ☏ 349 406 0481, ⓦ quattrogattibnb.it. Modern, bright and colourful B&B with three spacious, individually decorated rooms, which come with DVD players, wi-fi and private bathrooms. **€70**

Vittorio Emanuele Corso Vittorio Emanuele 100 ☏ 079 235 538, ⓦ hotelvesassari.it. An old-town *palazzo* flashily renovated to appeal to business folk. Comfortable and good value, though bedrooms are a bit bland and there's no car park. **€80**

17

EATING AND DRINKING

★ **Fainè Sassu** Via Usai 17 ☎079 236 402. The menu here is confined to a Ligurian and *sassarese* speciality: *fainè*, a sort of pancake made of chickpea flour, either plain or cooked with onions, sausage or anchovies. It's ideal for a snack, costing €5–8. Mon, Tues & Thurs–Sun 7–11pm; closed June–Sept.

L'Assassino Vícolo Pettenadu 19 ☎079 233 463. With tables in a lovely courtyard or in a vaulted room inside, this place offers local dishes such as *salsiccia con i fagioli* (sausage with green beans) with good fixed-price menus (€24 & €28). 12.30–3pm & 7.30pm–late; closed Sun in

summer, Mon in winter.

La Vela Latina Largo Sisini 3 ☎079 233 737. A smart, modern trattoria hidden away in the old town, specializing in Sard dishes and island wines. Mains €10–15 and fixed-price menus are €25 and €35. Tables outside in summer. Mon–Sat 1–2.30pm & 8–10.30pm.

Pizzalmetro Via Usai 10 ☎079 492 0837. Sizzling pizzas are served by the metre to eat in or take away – just point out how much you want. Half a metre will cost €6.50–11. 7–11pm; closed Sun in summer, Mon in winter.

Stintino and around

The coast north of Sassari is lined with beaches, the most alluring of them lying around the port and resort of **STINTINO**, on Sardinia's northwestern tip. Until recently nothing more than a remote jumble of fishermen's cottages jammed between two narrow harbours, Stintino remains a small, laidback village for most of the year, but is transformed into a busy holiday centre in the tourist season. With no beaches to speak of in the resort itself, most of the sunning and swimming takes place to either side – 4km south at the beach of **Le Saline** or the same distance north at La Pelosa (see opposite) – though most of the area's bars, restaurants and reasonably priced **accommodation** lie in Stintino.

ARRIVAL AND INFORMATION

By bus Stintino and La Pelosa are linked to Sassari by ARST buses 5–6 times daily in summer, 1–5 times in winter.

Tourist office Via Sassari 123 (June, July & Sept daily 9.30am–12.30pm & 3–8pm; Aug daily 9.30am–12.30pm,

3–8pm & 10pm–midnight; Oct Mon–Sat 9.30am–12.30pm; Nov–May Mon–Sat 11am–12.30pm; ☎079 520 081, ⊛infostintino.it).

ACCOMMODATION AND EATING

Geranio Rosso Via XXI Aprile 8 ☎079 523 292, ⊛hotelgeraniorosso.it. Small, central hotel with friendly staff and tastefully decorated rooms (including family rooms) with a/c and modern bathrooms. **€92**

Il Porto Vecchio Via Tonnara 69 ☎339 435 3582, ⊛bbstintino.com. This simple B&B has some rooms facing the port, Sardinian decoration and abundant buffet breakfasts. Closed Jan & Feb. No credit cards. **€70**

Lina Via Lépanto 30 ☎079 523 505. The best thing about this trattoria (next to a hotel of the same name) is its location, with a terrace overlooking the fishing boats

moored in Portu Minori. The food is decent local fare, with tourist menus at €14 and €17. Daily 10am–3pm & 7.30–11pm; closed Nov–Easter.

★ **Silvestrino** Via Sassari 14 ☎079 523 007, ⊛silvestrino.it. On the town's main street, this hotel has a touch of luxury in its rooms, some of which have their own terrace and terrific views. The restaurant (open to all) is one of Stintino's best, renowned for its seafood (try the lobster soup). Restaurant daily 12.30–2.30pm & 7.30–10.30pm; closed mid-Oct to Feb. Hotel closed Dec & Jan. **€100**

TRIPS TO ASINARA

Previously a prison island, the elongated offshore isle of **Asinara** is now a national park and nature reserve. Boat excursions from Stintino leave daily between Easter and October at around 9am, returning at 5/6pm. A simple return ticket to the island is €18, otherwise a package that includes bike rental or other transport on the island, swimming stops, lunch and a guide costs €40–70. Book tickets at least one day before from the kiosk by the port or an agency in town such as La Nassa, Via Tonnara 35 (☎0789 520 060, ⊛escursioniasinara.it).

La Pelosa

Some 4km up the road from Stintino a clutter of tourist villages backs the otherwise idyllic promontory of **La Pelosa**, location of one of Sardinia's most deluxe **beaches**. With its fine sand, turquoise water and views out to the isles of Piana and Asinara, it can get horribly crowded in the peak tourist season, but nothing can spoil its setting. The beach can be reached by hourly bus from Stintino (June–Sept 8am–midnight; €1).

Alghero

ALGHERO, 40km southwest of Sassari, is one of Sardinia's most charming towns, and one of its busiest resorts. The predominant flavour here is Catalan, owing to a wholesale Hispanicization that followed the overthrow of the Doria family by Pedro IV of Aragon in 1354, a process so thorough that it became known as "Barcelonetta". The traces are still strong in the old town today, with its flamboyant churches and narrow cobbled lanes named in both Italian and Catalan, all sheltered within a stout girdle of walls that now hold bars and restaurants – a fine venue for watching the sunset.

The Cattedrale

Piazza del Duomo • Daily 7am–noon & 5–7.30pm • Free • **Campanile** June–Aug Mon & Fri 10.30am–12.30pm & 7–9pm, Tues–Thurs 10.30am–12.30pm; Sept & Oct Mon & Fri 10.30am–12.30pm & 4–6pm, Tues & Thurs 10.30am–12.30pm; Nov–May by arrangement • €2 • ☎ 079 973 3041

In the heart of the old quarter, Alghero's predominantly sixteenth-century **Cattedrale** sports an incongruously Neoclassical entrance. In the lofty nave, alternating pillars and columns rise to an impressive octagonal dome. To get the full picture, take a look at the Gothic doorway at the back of the building on Via Umberto, from where you can join a tour of the campanile.

Palazzo d'Albis and the Palazzo Carcassona

Two of the best examples of the Catalan-Gothic style that characterizes some of Alghero's finest architecture are the **Palazzo d'Albis** on Piazza Civica and the elegantly austere Jewish palace **Palazzo Carcassona** in Via Sant'Erasmo (now a restaurant), both from the sixteenth century.

The towers

A walk around the old town should take in the circuit of seven defensive **towers** which dominate Alghero's centre and its surrounding walls. At the top of the **Giardini Pubblici** stands the first of these massive bulwarks – the **Porta Terra**, also known as the Jewish Tower, erected at the expense of the prosperous Jewish community before their expulsion in 1492 and now holding a bookshop. In between the towers on the walled seafront are displayed replicas of medieval catapults and other defensive machinery.

The port and beaches

Below the walls, the wide quay of the **port** is nudged by rows of colourful fishing boats, bordered by bars and busy with kiosks and trinket-sellers. The town's **beaches** begin further north, backed by hotels, but you'll find more tranquillity at **Le Bombarde** and **Lazzaretto**, two beaches around 8km west of town beyond the town of Fertilia.

17

ARRIVAL AND DEPARTURE

ALGHERO

By plane Visitors arriving at Alghero airport (w aeroporto dialghero.it) can catch hourly local buses into the centre of town (tickets €1 from machines in the terminal, €1.50 on board), or direct services to Cagliari, Nuoro, Sassari and, in summer, Cagliari, Stintino and Santa Teresa di Gallura. Taxis into Alghero cost €20–25.

By train The station lies some way out of the centre,

connected by regular city buses #AP and Alfa.
Destinations Sassari (9–12 daily; 35min).

By bus Buses from the airport and from out of town arrive at the Giardini Pubblici, by the port and old centre.
Destinations Bosa (2–7 daily; 55min); Sassari (4–10 daily; 1hr).

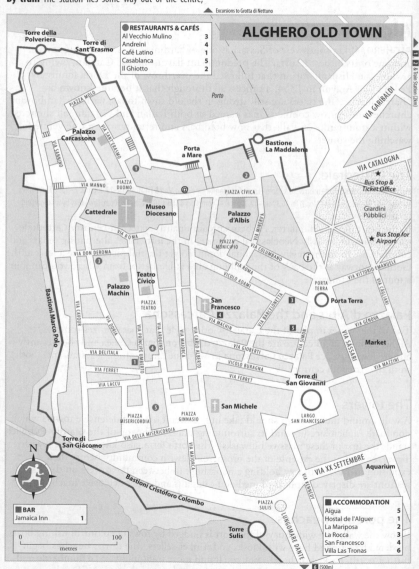

ALGHERO OLD TOWN

RESTAURANTS & CAFÉS
Al Vecchio Mulino	3
Andreini	4
Café Latino	1
Casablanca	5
Il Ghiotto	2

BAR
Jamaica Inn	1

ACCOMMODATION
Aigua	5
Hostal de l'Alguer	1
La Mariposa	2
La Rocca	3
San Francesco	4
Villa Las Tronas	6

17

NEPTUNE'S GROTTO

One of the best excursions you can make is to **Neptune's Grotto** (daily: April & Oct 9am–7pm; May–Sept 9am–8pm; Nov–March 10am–4pm; last tour 1hr before closing; €13), a marine cave dramatically lit with stalagmites and stalactites. The grotto is reachable on **boat excursions** from Alghero's port between March and October (€15 excluding the entry charge). Before buying tickets, check with the operator that you'll be able to visit the grotto on that day, as you can't enter if the sea is too rough – and if the winds are up, be prepared for a choppy ride (40min). Alternatively there are one to three **local buses** daily from Alghero departing from the Giardini Pubblici (€4.50 return), leaving you at the top of a long and steep flight of steps that corkscrews down to the cave mouth.

INFORMATION AND GETTING AROUND

Tourist office Piazza Porta Terra (April–Oct Mon–Sat 9am–8pm, Sun 9am–noon; Nov–March Mon–Sat 9am–7pm; ☎ 079 979 054, ⊛ alghero-turismo.it); airport (daily 8.30am–1pm & 3.30–10pm; ☎ 079 935 150).

Internet access Fotoclub, Piazza Civica (daily: summer 9.30am–9pm; winter 9.30am–1.30pm & 4.30–8.30pm).
By bike Raggi di Sardegna, Via Maiorca 119, rents bikes (☎ 334 305 2480; €7–12/day).

ACCOMMODATION

Aigua Via Machin 22 ☎ 340 077 7688, ⊛ aigua.it. Five mini-apartments in the same building, with vaulted wood ceilings, exposed brickwork and tiled floors; some are equipped with kitchen facilities. **€75**
Hostal de l'Alguer Via Parenzo, off Via Zara ☎ 079 930 478, ⊛ algherohostel.com. Reachable from Alghero by local bus, this hostel 6km along the coast at Fertilia is modern and clean with some private rooms. Dorms **€18**, doubles **€52**
La Mariposa Via Lido 22 ☎ 079 950 480, ⊛ lamariposa .it. A couple of kilometres north of Alghero, this busy campsite has shady pitches and offers private rooms and bungalows (from €32). There's a shop, bar-restaurant and private beach. April to mid-Oct. Pitches **€30**
La Rocca Via Roma 75 ☎ 328 481 5988, ⊛ bblarocca

.com. In a restored sixteenth-century *palazzo* in the heart of the old town, this B&B has just one room, but it's spacious and charmingly old-fashioned. An apartment is also available. No credit cards. **€85**
★ **San Francesco** Via Machin 2 ☎ 079 980 330, ⊛ sanfrancescohotel.com. The only hotel in the old town lies just behind the San Francesco church, with clean, simply furnished and quiet en-suite rooms, and breakfast in the cloister. Closed Nov–Feb. **€100**
Villa Las Tronas Lungomare Valencia 1 ☎ 079 981 818, ⊛ hotelvillalastronas.it. Grandly sited on a promontory a 10min walk south of the centre, this castellated five-star from 1884 is full of character, still retaining a baronial air with its old-fashioned furnishings. There's also an excellent restaurant, a spa, and a saltwater pool carved out of the rock. **€330**

EATING AND DRINKING

Al Vecchio Mulino Via Don Deroma 3 ☎ 079 977 254. In the heart of the old town, this serves up tasty, well-priced sea- and land-based dishes (around €15) and pizzas in low-vaulted cellars and has a good selection of white wines. Daily 7pm–midnight; closed Tues in winter, all Nov & two weeks in Jan.
Andreini Via Ardoino 45 ☎ 079 982 098. The place to come for a first-rate – if pricey – fishy feast (though they also offer creative meat dishes), in an atmospheric, grotto-like dining room, or outside in summer. Mains are €20–25, and there are tasting menus for €60–70. Daily 12.30–2.30pm & 7.30–11pm; closed Mon Nov–March.
Café Latino Piazza del Duomo 6 ☎ 079 976 541. A great place for an evening aperitif, with parasols on the walls overlooking the port. Snacks and ice creams are also served. Daily 9am–2am; closed Tues Oct–May.

Casablanca Via Principe Umberto 72 ☎ 079 983 353. With vaulted rooms, this is the best place in town for a straightforward pizza or pasta dish in a convivial atmosphere; mains are €10–15. Daily 12.30–2.30pm & 7.30–11.30pm; closed Mon & Thurs lunchtime June–Sept, all Wed Oct–May.
Il Ghiotto Piazza Civica 23 ☎ 079 974 820. Shop selling local specialities and fine Sardinian wines, with a restaurant offering a great range of takeaway snacks as well as hot meals to eat inside or at outdoor tables – pastas, seafood and meat (mostly under €10). Daily 12.30–2.30pm & 7–11.30pm; closed Mon in winter.
Jamaica Inn Via Principe Umberto 57 ☎ 079 973 3050. This pub – right in the thick of things – is a lively spot for cocktails, and it serves meals too, with main courses €12–16. Daily 1–3pm & 7.30pm–2am; closed Mon Oct–June.

RAPHAEL'S *GALATEA*, VILLA FARNESINA, ROME

Contexts

History

A smattering of remains exist from the Neanderthals who occupied the Italian peninsula half a million years ago, but the main period of colonization began after the last Ice Age, with evidence of Paleolithic and Neolithic settlements dating from around 20,000 BC and 4000 BC respectively. More sophisticated tribes developed towards the end of the prehistoric period, between 2400 and 1800 BC; those who left the most visible traces were the Ligurians (who inhabited a much greater area than modern Liguria), the Siculi of southern Italy and Latium, and the Sards, who farmed and raised livestock on Sardinia. More advanced still were migrant groups from the eastern Mediterranean, who introduced the techniques of working copper. Later, various Bronze Age societies (1600–1000 BC) built a network of farms and villages in the Apennines, and on the Sicilian and southern coasts, the latter population trading with Mycenaeans in Greece.

Other tribes brought Indo-European languages into Italy. The Veneti, Latins and Umbrii moved down the peninsula from the north, while the Piceni and the Messapians in Puglia crossed the Adriatic from what is now Croatia. The artificial line between prehistory and history is drawn around the eighth century BC with the arrival of the **Phoenicians** and their trade links between Carthage and southern Italy. This soon encouraged the arrival of the **Carthaginians** in Sicily, Sardinia and the Latium coast – just when **Greeks** and **Etruscans** were gaining influence.

Etruscans and Greeks

Greek settlers colonized parts of the Tuscan coast and the Bay of Naples in the eighth century BC, moving on to **Naxos** on Sicily's Ionian coast, and founding the city of Syracuse in the year 736 BC. The colonies they established in Sicily and southern Italy came to be known as **Magna Graecia**. Along with Etruscan cities to the north they were the earliest Italian civilizations to leave substantial buildings and written records.

The Greek settlements were hugely successful, introducing the vine and the olive to Italy, and establishing a high-yielding agricultural system. Cities like **Syracuse** and **Tarentum** were wealthier and more sophisticated than those on mainland Greece, dominating trade in the central Mediterranean, despite competition from Carthage. Ruins such as the temples of **Agrigento** and **Selinunte**, the fortified walls around Gela, and the theatres at Syracuse and Taormina on Sicily attest to a great prosperity, and Magna Graecia became an enriching influence on the culture of the Greek homeland – Archimedes, Aeschylus and Empedocles were all from Sicily. Yet these colonies suffered from the same factionalism as the Greek states, and the cities of Tarentum,

2000 BC	Eighth century BC	736 BC	44 BC
Bronze Age societies established across the peninsula.	Etruscans establish sophisticated civilizations in various centres, notably around the Arno and Tiber rivers.	The city of Syracuse is founded by Greek settlers.	Julius Caesar is assassinated.

Metapontum, Sybaris and Croton were united only when faced with the threat of outside invasion. From 400 BC, after Sybaris was razed to the ground, the other colonies went into irreversible economic decline, to become satellite states of Rome.

The **Etruscans** were the other major civilization of the period, mostly living in the area between the **Tiber** and **Arno** rivers. Their language, known mostly from funerary texts, is one of the last relics of an ancient language common to the Mediterranean. Some say they arrived in Italy around the ninth century BC from western Anatolia, others that they came from the north, and a third hypothesis places their origins in Etruria. Whatever the case, they set up a cluster of **twelve city-states** in northern Italy, traded with Greek colonies to the south and were the most powerful people in northern Italy by the sixth century BC, edging out the indigenous population of Ligurians, Latins and Sabines. Tomb frescoes in Umbria and Lazio depict a refined and luxurious culture with highly developed systems of divination, based on the reading of animal entrails and the flight of birds. Herodotus wrote that the Etruscans recorded their ancestry along the female line, and tomb excavations in the nineteenth century revealed that women were buried in special sarcophagi carved with their names. Well-preserved chamber tombs with wall paintings exist at **Cerveteri** and **Tarquinia**, the two major sites in Italy. The Etruscans were technically advanced, creating new agricultural land through irrigation and building their cities on ramparted hilltops – a pattern of settlement that has left a permanent mark on central Italy. Their kingdom contracted, however, after invasions by the **Cumans**, **Syracusans** and **Gauls**, and was eventually forced into alliance with the embryonic Roman state. Almost none of their towns have survived the archeological record – the only exception being modern-day Marzabotto or Misa, a fine example of Etruscan urban planning.

Roman Italy

The growth of **Rome**, a border town between the Etruscans and the Latins, gained impetus around 600 BC from a coalition of Latin and Sabine communities. The **Tarquins**, an Etruscan dynasty, oversaw the early expansion, but in 509 BC the Romans ejected the Etruscan royal family and became a **republic**, with power shared jointly between two consuls, both elected for one year. Further changes came half a century later, after a protracted class struggle that resulted in the **Law of the Twelve Tables**, which made patricians and plebeians equal. Thus stabilized, the Romans set out to systematically conquer the northern peninsula and, after the fall of Veii in 396 BC, succeeded in capturing **Sutri** and **Nepi**, towns which Livy considered the "barriers and gateways of Etruria". Various wars and truces with other cities brought about agreements to pay harsh tributes.

The **Gauls** captured Rome in 390, refusing to leave until they had received a vast payment, but this proved a temporary reversal. The Romans took **Campania** and the fertile land of Puglia after defeating the **Samnites** in battles over a period of 35 years. They then set their sights on the wealthy Greek colonies to the south, including Tarentum, whose inhabitants turned to the Greek king, **Pyrrhus of Epirus**, for military support. He initially repelled the Roman invaders, but lost his advantage and was defeated at **Beneventum** in 275 BC. The Romans had by then established their rule in most of southern Italy, and now became a threat to Carthage. In 264 they had the

79 AD	First to second century AD	313 AD
Vesuvius erupts, covering Pompeii and Herculaneum.	Peace and prosperity under Roman rule sees agriculture and cities flourish across much of Europe.	Christianity is declared the state religion by Constantine in the Edict of Milan.

chance of obtaining **Sicily**, when the Mamertines, a mercenary army in control of Messina, appealed to them for help against the Carthaginians. The Romans obliged – sparking off the **First Punic War** – and took most of the island, together with Sardinia and Corsica. With their victory in 222 BC over the Gauls in the Po Valley, all Italy was now under Roman control.

They also turned a subsequent military threat to their advantage, in what came to be known as the **Second Punic War**. The Carthaginians had watched the spread of Roman power across the Mediterranean with some alarm, and at the end of the third century BC they allowed **Hannibal** to make an Alpine crossing into Italy with his army of infantry, horsemen and elephants. Hannibal crushed the Roman legions at Lago Trasimeno and Cannae (216 BC), and then halted at Capua. With remarkable cool, considering Hannibal's proximity, **Scipio** set sail on a retaliatory mission to the Carthaginian territory of **Spain**, taking Cartagena, and continuing his journey into **Africa**. It was another fifty years before Carthage was taken, closely followed by all of Spain, but the Romans were busy in the meantime adding **Macedonian Greece** to their territory.

These conquests gave Roman citizens a tax-free existence subsidized by captured treasure, but society was sharply divided between those enjoying the benefits, and those who were not. The former belonged mostly to the **senatorial party**, who ignored demands for reform by their opposition, the popular party. The radical reforms sponsored by the tribune **Gaius Gracchus** came too close to democracy for the senatorial party, whose declaration of martial law was followed by the assassination of Gracchus. The majority of people realized that the only hope of gaining influence was through the army, but **General Gaius Marius**, when put into power, was ineffective against the senatorial clique, who systematically picked off the new regime.

The first century BC saw civil strife on an unprecedented scale. Although Marius was still in power, another general, **Sulla**, was in the ascendancy, leading military campaigns against northern invaders and rebellious subjects in the south. Sulla subsequently took power and established his dictatorship in Rome, throwing out a populist government which had formed while he was away on a campaign in the east. Murder and exile were common, and cities which had sided with Marius during their struggle for power were punished with massacres and destruction. Thousands of Sulla's war veterans were given confiscated land, but much of it was laid to waste. In 73 BC a gladiator named **Spartacus** led 70,000 dispossessed farmers and escaped slaves in a revolt, which lasted for two years before they were defeated by the legions.

Julius Caesar and Augustus

Rome became calmer only after Sulla's death, when **Pompey**, another general, and **Licinus Crassus**, a rich builder, became masters of Rome. Pompey's interest lay in lucrative wars elsewhere, so his absence from the capital gave **Julius Caesar** the chance to make a name for himself as an orator and raiser of finance. When Pompey returned in 60 BC, he made himself, Crassus and Caesar rulers of the **first Triumvirate**.

Caesar bought himself the post of consul in 59 BC, then spent the next eight years on campaigns against the **Gauls**. His military success needled Pompey, and he eventually turned against his colleague, giving Caesar the chance to hit back. In 49 BC he crossed the river **Rubicon**, committing the offence of entering Roman territory with an army

410 AD	754 AD	800 AD
The decline of the Roman Empire leads to the Sack of Rome.	Pepin the Short removes the Lombards from Rome and lays the foundation for the Papal States.	Charlemagne is crowned Holy Roman Emperor. By his death the empire stretches from below Rome to the Italian Lakes.

without first informing the Senate, but when he reached the city there was no resistance – everyone had fled, and Caesar became absolute ruler of Rome. He spent the next four years on civil reforms, writing his history of the Gallic wars, and chasing Pompey and his followers through Spain, Greece and Egypt. A group of enemies within the Senate, including his adopted son **Brutus**, conspired to murder him in 44 BC, a few months after he had been appointed ruler for life. **Octavian**, Caesar's nephew and heir, Lepidus and Marcus Antonius (**Mark Antony**) formed the **second Triumvirate** the following year. Again, the arrangement was fraught with tensions, the battle for power this time being between Antony and Octavian. While Antony was with **Cleopatra**, Octavian spent his time developing his military strength and the final, decisive battle took place at **Actium** in 31 BC, where Antony committed suicide.

As sole ruler of the new regime, Octavian, renaming himself **Augustus Caesar**, embarked on a series of reforms and public works, giving himself complete powers despite his unassuming official title of "First Citizen".

The emperors

Tiberius (14–37 AD), the successor to Augustus, ruled wisely, but thereafter began a period of decadence. During the psychopathic reign of **Caligula** (37–41) the civil service kept the empire running; **Claudius** (41–54) conquered southern Britain, and was succeeded by his stepson **Nero** (54–68), who violently persecuted the **Christians**. Nero committed suicide when threatened by a coup, leading to a rapid succession of four emperors in the year 68. The period of prosperity during the rule of the **Flavian** emperors (Vespasian and his sons Titus and Domitian) was a forerunner for the **Century of the Antonines**, a period named after the successful reigns of Nerva, Trajan, Hadrian, Antonius and **Marcus Aurelius**. These generals consolidated the empire's infrastructure, and created an encouraging environment for artistic achievement. A prime example is the formidable bronze equestrian statue of Marcus Aurelius in Rome – a work not equalled in sophistication until the Renaissance.

A troubled period followed under the rule of Marcus Aurelius's son **Commodus** (180–193) and his successors, none of whom were wholly in control of the legions. Artistic, intellectual and religious life stagnated, and the balance of economic development tilted in favour of the north, while the agricultural south grew ever more impoverished.

Barbarians and Byzantines

In the middle of the third century, incursions by **Goths** in Greece, the Balkans and Asia, and the **Franks** and **Alamanni** in Gaul foreshadowed the collapse of the empire. **Aurelian** (270–275) re-established some order after terrible civil wars, to be followed by **Diocletian** (284–305), whose persecution of Christians produced many of the Church's present-day saints. **Plagues** had decimated the population, but problems of a huge but static economy were compounded by the doubling in size of the army at this time to about half a million men. To ease administration, Diocletian **divided the empire** into two halves, east and west, basing himself as ruler of the western empire in Mediolanum (Milan). This measure brought about a relative recovery, coinciding with the rise of **Christianity**, which was declared the state religion during the reign of **Constantine** (306–337). **Constantinople**, capital of the eastern empire, became a thriving trading

1176	1200–1550	1346
Battle of Legnano. An affiliation of northern cities defeats Barbarossa, making way for a string of independent city-states.	Powerful city-states keep relative peace, which enables the flourishing of the arts known as the Renaissance.	The Black Death decimates the population of Europe; Florence's population is cut by half.

and manufacturing city, while Rome itself went into decline, as the enlargement of the senatorial estates and the impoverishment of the lower classes gave rise to something comparable to a primitive feudal system.

Barbarians (meaning outsiders, or foreigners) had been crossing the border into the empire since 376 AD, when the **Ostrogoths** were driven from their kingdom in southern Russia by the **Huns**, a tribe of ferocious horsemen. The Huns went on to attack the **Visigoths**, 70,000 of whom crossed the border and settled inside the empire. When the Roman aristocracy saw that the empire was no longer a shield against barbarian raids, they were less inclined to pay for its support, seeing that a more comfortable future lay in being on good terms with the barbarian successor states.

By the fifth century, many legions were made up of troops from conquered territories, and several posts of high command were held by outsiders. With little will or loyalty behind it, the **empire floundered**, and on New Year's Eve of 406, Vandals, Alans and Sueves crossed the frozen Rhine into Gaul, chased by the Huns from their kingdoms in what are now Hungary and Austria. By 408, the imperial government in Ravenna could no longer hold off **Alaric** (commander of Illyricum – now Croatia) who went on to **sack Rome** in 410, causing a crisis of morale in the West. "When the whole world perished in one city," wrote Saint Jerome, "then I was dumb with silence."

The bitter **end of the Roman Empire** in the west came after **Valentinian III**'s assassination in 455. His eight successors over the next twenty years were finally ignored by the Germanic troops in the army, who elected their general **Odoacer** as king. The remaining Roman aristocracy hated him, and the eastern emperor, **Zeno**, who in theory now ruled the whole empire, refused to recognize him. In 487, Zeno rid himself of the Ostrogoth leader **Theodoric** by persuading him to march on Odoacer in Italy. By 493, Theodoric had succeeded, becoming ruler of the western territories.

A lull followed. The Senate in Rome and the civil service continued to function, and the remains of the empire were still administered under Roman law. Ostrogothic rule of the west continued after Theodoric's death, but in the 530s the eastern emperor, **Justinian**, began to plan the reunification of the Roman Empire "up to the two oceans". In 536 his general **Belisarius** landed in Sicily and moved north through Rome to Ravenna; complete reconquest of the Italian peninsula was achieved in 552, after which the Byzantines retained a presence in the south and in Sardinia for five hundred years.

During this time the **Christian Church** developed as a more or less independent authority, since the emperor was at a safe distance in Constantinople. Continual invasions had led to an uncertain political scene in which the **bishops of Rome** emerged with the strongest voice – justification of their primacy having already been given by Pope Leo I (440–461), who spoke of his right to "rule all who are ruled in the first instance by Christ". A confused period of rule followed, as armies from northern Europe tried to take more territory from the old empire.

Lombards and Franks

During the chaotic sixth century, the **Lombards**, a Germanic tribe, were driven southwest into Italy, and by the eighth century, when the **Franks** arrived from Gaul, they were extending their power throughout the peninsula. The Franks were orthodox Christians, and therefore acceptable to Gallo-Roman nobility, integrating quickly

1380	1498	1508	1559
Venice defeats Genoa in the War of Chioggia and is established as Italy's supreme maritime trading nation.	Leonardo da Vinci paints *The Last Supper* in Milan.	Pope Julius II commissions Michelangelo to paint the ceiling frescoes of the Sistine Chapel in Rome.	Sicily, Sardinia, Naples, the Duchy of Milan and parts of Tuscany come under Spanish rule.

and taking over much of the provincial administration. They were ruled by the Merovingian royal family, but the mayors of the palace – the Carolingians – began to take power in real terms. Led by **Pepin the Short**, they saw an advantage in supporting the papacy, giving Rome large endowments and forcibly converting pagans in areas they conquered. When Pepin wanted to oust the Merovingians, and become King of the Franks, he appealed to the pope in Rome for his blessing, who was happy to agree, anointing the new Frankish king with holy oil.

This alliance was useful to both parties. In 755 the pope called on the Frankish army to confront the Lombards. The Franks forced them to hand over treasure and 22 cities and castles, which then became the northern part of the **Papal States**. Pepin died in 768, with the Church indebted to him. According to custom, he divided the kingdom between his two sons, one of whom died within three years. The other was Charles the Great, or **Charlemagne**.

An intelligent and innovative leader, Charlemagne was proclaimed King of the Franks and of the Lombards, and patrician of the Romans, after a decisive war against the Lombards in 774. On Christmas Day of the year 800, Pope Leo III expressed his gratitude for Charlemagne's political support by crowning him **Emperor of the Holy Roman Empire**, an investiture that forged an enduring link between the fortunes of Italy and those of northern Europe. By the time Charlemagne died, all of Italy from south of Rome to Lombardy, including Sardinia, was part of the huge **Carolingian Empire**. The parts that didn't come under his domain were Sicily and the southern coast, which were gradually being reconquered by Arabs from Tunisia; and Puglia and Calabria, colonized by Byzantines and Greeks.

The task of holding these gains was beyond Charlemagne's successors, and by the beginning of the tenth century the family was extinct and the rival Italian states had become prizes for which the western (French) and eastern (German) Frankish kingdoms competed. Power switched in 936 to **Otto**, king of the eastern Franks. Political disunity in Italy invited him to intervene, and in 962 he was crowned emperor; Otto's son and grandson (Ottos II and III) set the seal on the renewal of the Holy Roman Empire.

Popes and emperors

On the death of **Otto III** in 1002, Italy was again without a recognized ruler. In the north, noblemen jockeyed for power, and the papacy was manipulated by rival Roman families. The most decisive events were in the south, where Sicily, Calabria and Puglia were captured by the **Normans**, who proved effective administrators and synthesized their own culture with the existing half-Arabic, half-Italian south. In **Palermo** in the eleventh century they created the most dynamic culture of the Mediterranean world.

Meanwhile in Rome, a series of reforming popes began to strengthen the Church. **Gregory VII**, elected in 1073, was the most radical, demanding the right to depose emperors if he so wished. **Emperor Henry IV** was equally determined for this not to happen. The inevitable quarrel broke out, over a key appointment to the archbishopric of Milan. Henry denounced Gregory as "now not pope, but false monk"; the pope responded by excommunicating him, thereby freeing his subjects from their

1633	**1693**	**1740–96**
Galileo is sentenced to house arrest for the rest of his life for maintaining that the Earth moves around the Sun.	A powerful earthquake and subsequent tsunami destroys much of Sicily and kills around 60,000.	Austrian rule over northern Italy, Naples and Sardinia introduces wide-ranging administrative, judicial and educational reforms.

allegiance. By 1077 Henry was aware of his tactical error and tried to make amends by visiting the pope at **Canossa**, where the emperor, barefoot and penitent, was kept waiting outside for three days. The formal reconciliation did nothing to heal the rift, and Henry's son, **Henry V**, continued the feud, eventually coming to a compromise in which the emperor kept control of bishops' land ownership, while giving up rights over their investiture.

After this symbolic victory, the papacy developed into the most comprehensive and advanced centralized government in Europe in the realms of law and finance, but it wasn't long before unity again came under attack. This time, the threat came from **Emperor Frederick I** (Barbarossa), who besieged many northern Italian cities from his base in Germany from 1154. **Pope Alexander III** responded with ambiguous pronouncements about the imperial crown being a "benefice" which the pope conferred, implying that the emperor was the pope's vassal. The issue of papal or imperial supremacy was to polarize the country for the next two hundred years, almost every part of Italy being torn by struggles between **Guelphs** (supporting the pope) and **Ghibellines** (supporting the emperor).

Henry VI's son, **Frederick II**, assumed the imperial throne at the age of three and a half, inheriting the Norman **Kingdom of Sicily**. Later linked by marriage to the great **Hohenstaufen** dynasty in Germany, he inevitably turned his attentions to northern Italy. However, his power base was small, and opposition from the Italian commune and the papacy snowballed into civil war. His sudden death in 1250 marked a major downturn in imperial fortunes.

The emergence of city-states

Charles of Anjou, brother of King Louis IX of France, defeated Frederick II's heirs in southern Italy, and received **Naples and Sicily** as a reward from the pope. His oppressive government finally provoked an uprising on Easter Monday 1282, a revolt that came to be known as the **Sicilian Vespers**, as some two thousand occupying soldiers were murdered in Palermo at the sound of the bell for vespers. For the next twenty years the French were at war with **Peter of Aragon**, who took Sicily and then tried for the southern mainland.

If imperial power was on the defensive, the papacy was in even worse shape. Knowing that the pontiff had little military backing or financial strength left, **Philip of France** sent his men to the pope's summer residence in 1303, subjecting the old man to a degrading attack. Boniface died within a few weeks; his French successor, Clement V, promptly moved the papacy to **Avignon** in southern France.

The declining political power of the major rulers was countered by the growing autonomy of the cities. By 1300, a broad belt of some three hundred virtually **independent city-states** stretched from central Italy to the northernmost edge of the peninsula. In the middle of the century the population of Europe was savagely depleted by the **Black Death** – brought into Europe by a Genoese ship returning from the Black Sea – but the city-states survived, developing a concept of citizenship quite different from the feudal lord-and-vassal relationship. By the end of the fourteenth century the richer and more influential states had swallowed up the smaller *comune*, leaving four as clear political front-runners. These were **Genoa** (controlling the Ligurian coast),

1796	1805	1815	1849
Napoleon invades northern Italy.	Napoleon is crowned King of Italy in Milan's Duomo.	Settlement of Vienna. With Napoleon's decline the Austrians rule again, but unrest is rife.	Revolutions throughout Italy are crushed.

Florence (ruling Tuscany), **Milan**, whose sphere of influence included Lombardy and much of central Italy, and **Venice**. Smaller principalities, such as Mantua and Ferrara, supported armies of mercenaries, ensuring their security by building impregnable fortress-palaces.

Perpetual vendettas between the propertied classes often induced the citizens to accept the overall rule of one **signore** in preference to the bloodshed of warring clans. A despotic form of government evolved, sanctioned by official titles from the emperor or pope, and by the fifteenth century most city-states were under princely rather than republican rule. In the south of the fragmented peninsula was the **Kingdom of Naples**; the **States of the Church** stretched up from Rome through modern-day Le Marche, Umbria and the Romagna; **Siena**, **Florence**, **Modena**, **Mantua** and **Ferrara** were independent states, as were the **Duchy of Milan**, and the maritime republics of **Venice** and **Genoa**, with a few odd pockets of independence like Lucca, for example, and Rimini.

The commercial and secular city-states of late medieval times were the seedbed for the **Renaissance**, when urban entrepreneurs (such as the Medici) and autocratic rulers (such as Federico da Montefeltro) enhanced their status through the financing of architectural projects, paintings and sculpture. It was also at this time that the Tuscan dialect – the language of Dante, Petrarch and Boccaccio – became established as Italy's literary language; it later became the nation's official spoken language.

By the mid-fifteenth century the five most powerful states – Naples, the papacy, Milan, and the republics of Venice and Florence – reached a tacit agreement to maintain the new balance of power. Yet though there was a balance of power at home, the history of each of the independent Italian states became inextricably bound up with the power politics of other European countries.

French and Spanish intervention

The inevitable finally happened when an Italian state invited a larger power in to defeat one of its rivals. In 1494, at the request of the Duke of Milan, **Charles VIII** of France marched south to renew the Angevin claim to the Kingdom of Naples. After the accomplishment of his mission, Charles stayed for three months in Naples, before heading back to France; the kingdom was then acquired by **Ferdinand II of Aragon**, subsequently ruler of all Spain.

The person who really established the Spanish in Italy was the Habsburg **Charles V** (1500–58), who within three years of inheriting both the Austrian and Spanish thrones bribed his way to being elected Holy Roman Emperor. In 1527 the imperial troops sacked **Rome**, a calamity widely interpreted at the time as God's punishment of the disorganized and dissolute Italians. The French remained troublesome opposition, but they were defeated at Pavia in 1526 and Naples in 1529. With the treaty of Cateau-Cambrésis in 1559, Spain held Sicily, Naples, Sardinia, the Duchy of Milan and some Tuscan fortresses, and they were to exert a stranglehold on Italian political life for the next 150 years. The remaining smaller states became satellites of either Spanish or French rule; only the papacy and Venice remained independent.

Social and economic troubles were as severe as the political upheavals. While the papacy combated the spread of the **Reformation** in northern Europe, the major

1861	1908	1915	1922
Italy is declared a unified nation under King Vittorio Emanuele II; Venice and Rome are added ten years later.	An earthquake destroys Messina in Sicily.	Italy enters World War I on the side of Britain, France and Russia.	Mussolini becomes Prime Minister and within three years has declared himself Il Duce, dictator of Italy.

manufacturing and trading centres were coming to terms with the opening up of the Atlantic and Indian Ocean trade routes – discoveries which meant that northern Italy would increasingly be bypassed. Mid-sixteenth-century **economic recession** prompted wealthy Venetian and Florentine merchants to invest in land rather than business, while in the south high taxes and repressive feudal regimes produced an upsurge of banditry and even the raising of peasant militias – resistance that was ultimately suppressed brutally by the Spanish.

The seventeenth century was a low point in Italian political life, with little room for manoeuvre between the papacy and colonial powers. The Spanish eventually lost control of Italy at the start of the eighteenth century when, as a result of the War of the Spanish Succession, Lombardy, Mantua, Naples and Sardinia all came under Austrian control. The machinations of the major powers led to **frequent realignments** in the first half of the century. Piemonte, ruled by the Duke of Savoy, Victor Amadeus II, was forced in 1720 to surrender Sicily to the Austrians in return for Sardinia. In 1734 Naples and Sicily passed to the Spanish Bourbons, and three years later the House of Lorraine acquired Tuscany on the extinction of the Medici.

Relatively enlightened Bourbon rule in the south did little to arrest the economic polarization of society, but the northern states advanced under the intelligent if autocratic rule of Austria's **Maria Theresa** (1740–80) and her son **Joseph II** (1780–90), who prepared the way for early industrialization. Lightning changes came in April 1796, when the French armies of **Napoleon** invaded northern Italy. Within a few years the French had been driven out again, but by 1810 Napoleon was in command of the whole peninsula, and his puppet regimes remained in charge until Waterloo. Napoleonic rule had profound effects, reducing the power of the papacy, reforming feudal land rights and introducing representative government to Italy. Elected assemblies were provided on the French model, giving the emerging middle class a chance for political discussion and action.

Unification

The fall of Napoleon led to the Vienna Settlement of 1815, by which the Austrians effectively restored the old ruling class. **Metternich**, the Austrian Chancellor, did all he could to foster any local loyalties that might weaken the appeal of unity, yet the years between 1820 and 1849 became years of revolution. Uprisings began in Sicily, Naples and Piemonte, when **King Ferdinand** introduced measures that restricted personal freedom and destroyed many farmers' livelihoods. A makeshift army quickly gained popular support in Sicily, and forced some concessions, before Ferdinand invited the Austrians in to help him crush the revolution. In the north, the oppressive laws enacted by **Vittorio Emanuele I** in the Kingdom of Piemonte sparked off student protests and army mutinies in Turin. Vittorio Emanuele abdicated in favour of his brother, Carlo Felice, and his son, **Carlo Alberto**; the latter initially gave some support to the radicals, but Carlo Felice then called in the Austrians, and thousands of revolutionaries were forced into exile. Carlo Alberto became King of Sardinia in 1831. A secretive, excessively devout and devious character, he did a major volte-face when he assumed the throne by forming an alliance with the Austrians.

1929	1930s	1940
The Lateran Pact recognizes the Vatican as an autonomous Church state within the Kingdom of Italy.	Italy invades Ethiopia and sends aircraft and weapons to aid Franco's nationalist side in the Spanish Civil War.	Italy declares war on France and Britain, announces a Tripartite Pact with Japan and Germany and invades France, Albania and Greece.

In 1831 further uprisings occurred in Parma, Modena, the Papal States, Sicily and Naples. Their lack of coordination, and the readiness with which Austrian and papal troops intervened, ensured that revolution was short-lived. But even if these actions were unsustained, their influence grew.

One person profoundly influenced by these insurgencies was **Giuseppe Mazzini**. Arrested as Secretary of the Genoese branch of the Carbonari (a secret radical society) in 1827 and jailed for three months in 1830, he formulated his political ideology and set up "**Young Italy**" on his release. Among the many to whom the ideals of "Young Italy" appealed was **Giuseppe Garibaldi**, soon to play a central role in the **Risorgimento**, as the movement to reform and unite the country was known.

Crop failures in 1846 and 1847 produced widespread **famine and cholera outbreaks**. In Sicily an army of peasants marched on the capital, burning debt collection records, destroying property and freeing prisoners. Middle- and upper-class moderates were worried, and formed a government to control the uprising, but Sicilian **separatist** aims were realized in 1848. Fighting spread to Naples, where **Ferdinand II** made some temporary concessions, but nonetheless he retook Sicily the following year. At the same time as the southern revolution, serious disturbances took place in Tuscany, Piemonte and the Papal States. Rulers fled their duchies, and Carlo Alberto altered course again, prompted by Metternich's fall from power in Vienna: he granted his subjects a constitution and declared war on Austria. In Rome, the pope fled from rioting and Mazzini became a member of the city's republican triumvirate in 1849, with Garibaldi organizing the defences.

None of the uprisings lasted long. Twenty thousand revolutionaries were expelled from Rome, Carlo Alberto abdicated in favour of his son Vittorio Emanuele II after military defeats at the hands of the Austrians, and the dukes returned to Tuscany, Modena and Parma. One thing that survived was Piemonte's constitution, which throughout the 1850s attracted political refugees to the cosmopolitan state.

Cavour and Garibaldi

Nine years of radical change began when **Count Camillo Cavour** became Prime Minister of Piemonte in 1852. The involvement of Piemontese troops in the Crimean War brought Cavour into contact with Napoleon III at the Congress of Paris, at which the hostilities were ended, and in July 1858 the two men had secret talks on the "Italian question". Napoleon III had decided to support Italy in its fight against the Austrians – the only realistic way of achieving unification – as long as resistance was non-revolutionary. Having bargained over the division of territory, they waited for a chance to provoke Austria into war. This came in 1859, when Cavour wrote an emotive anti-Austrian speech for Vittorio Emanuele at the opening of parliament. His battle cry for an end to the **grido di dolore** (cry of pain) was taken up all over Italy. The Austrians ordered demobilization by the Piemontese, who did the reverse.

The war was disastrous from the start, and thousands died at Magenta and Solferino. In July 1859, Napoleon III made a truce with the Austrians without consulting Cavour, who resigned in fury. Provisional governments remained in power in Tuscany, Modena and the Romagna. Cavour returned to government in 1860, and soon France, Piemonte and the papacy agreed to a series of plebiscites, a move that ensured that by mid-March of 1860, **Tuscany** and the new state of **Emilia** (duchies of Modena and

1943		1944
US and UK troops land in Sicily. Italy declares an armistice with the Allied forces.	Mussolini is rescued from Italian captivity by German forces and establishes a puppet government on Lake Garda.	Rome is liberated but bloody hand-to-hand fighting continues throughout the rest of northern Italy. Around 50,000 Allied soldiers and 45,000 Italian partisans die.

Parma plus the Romagna) had voted for **union with Piemonte**. A secret treaty between Vittorio Emanuele and Napoleon III ceded Savoy and Nice to France, subject to plebiscites. The result was as planned, no doubt due in part to the presence of the French Army during voting.

Garibaldi promptly set off for Nice with the aim of blowing up the ballot boxes, only to be diverted when he reached Genoa, where he heard of an **uprising in Sicily**. Commandeering two old paddle-steamers and obtaining just enough rifles for his thousand Red Shirts, he headed south. More support came when they landed in Sicily, and Garibaldi's army outflanked the 12,000 Neapolitan troops to take the island. After that, they crossed to the mainland, easily occupied Naples, then struck out for Rome. Cavour, anxious that he might lose the initiative, hastily dispatched a Piemontese army to **annex the Papal States**, except for the Patrimony around Rome. Worried by the possibility that the anti-Church revolutionaries who made up the Red Shirt army might stir up trouble, Cavour and Vittorio Emanuele travelled south to Rome, accompanied by their army, and arranged plebiscites in Sicily, Naples, Umbria and the Papal Marches that offered little alternative but to vote for annexation by Piemonte. After their triumphal parade through Naples, they thanked Garibaldi for his trouble, took command of all territories and held elections to a new parliament. In February 1861, the members formally announced the **Kingdom of Italy**.

Cavour died the same year, before the country was completely unified, since Rome and Venice were still outside the kingdom. Garibaldi marched unsuccessfully on Rome in 1862, and again five years later, by which time Venice had been subsumed. It wasn't until Napoleon III was defeated by Prussia in 1870 that the French troops were ousted from Rome. Thus by 1871 **Unification** was complete.

The world wars

After the Risorgimento, some things still hadn't changed. The ruling class were slow to move towards a broader-based political system, while living standards actually worsened in some areas, particularly in Sicily. When Sicilian peasant farmers organized into **fasci** – forerunners of trade unions – the prime minister sent in 30,000 soldiers, closed down newspapers and interned suspected troublemakers without trial. In the 1890s capitalist methods and modern machinery in the Po Valley created a new social structure, with rich **agrari** at the top of the pile, a mass of farm labourers at the bottom, and an intervening layer of estate managers.

In the 1880s Italy's **colonial expansion** began, initially concentrated in bloody – and ultimately disastrous – campaigns in Abyssinia and Eritrea in 1886. In 1912 Italy wrested the Dodecanese islands and Libya from Turkey, a development deplored by many, including **Benito Mussolini**, who during this war was the radical secretary of the PSI (Partito Socialista Italiano) in Forlì.

World War I and the rise of Mussolini

Italy entered **World War I** in 1915 with the chief aims of settling old scores with Austria and furthering its colonial ambitions through French and British support. A badly equipped, poorly commanded army took three years to force Austria into defeat, finally achieved in the last month of the war at Vittorio Veneto. Some territory was gained

1945		1946
Mussolini is captured on Lake Como trying to escape to Switzerland with his mistress, executed and strung up from a petrol station in Milan the following day.	German armies in Italy sign their surrender. Roberto Rossellini films *Rome, Open City* in war-torn Rome and kickstarts Italian Neorealism.	Italians vote for a republic and an end to the monarchy.

– Trieste, Gorizia, and what became Trentino-Alto Adige – but at the cost of over half a million dead, many more wounded, and a mountainous war debt.

The middle classes, disillusioned with the war's outcome and alarmed by inflation and social unrest, turned to Mussolini, now a figurehead of the Right. In 1921, recently elected to parliament, Mussolini formed the Partito Nazionale Fascista, whose **squadre** terrorized their opponents by direct personal attacks and the destruction of newspaper offices, printing shops, and socialist and trade union premises. By 1922 the party was in a position to carry out an insurrectionary "**March on Rome**". Plans for the march were leaked to Prime Minister Facta, who needed the king's signature on a martial law decree if the army were to meet the march. Fears of civil war led to the king's refusal. Facta resigned, Mussolini made it clear that he would not join any government he did not lead, and on October 29 was awarded **the premiership**. Only then did the march take place.

Zealous **squadristi** now urged Mussolini towards **dictatorship**, which he announced early in 1925. Political opposition and trade unions were outlawed, the free press disintegrated under censorship and Fascist takeovers, elected local governments were replaced by appointed officials, powers of arrest and detention were increased, and special courts were established for political crimes. In 1929, Mussolini ended a sixty-year feud between Church and State by reorganizing the **Vatican** as an autonomous Church state within the Kingdom of Italy. (As late as 1904, anyone involved in the new regime, even as a voter, had been automatically excommunicated.) By 1939, the motto "Everything within the State; nothing outside the State; nothing against the State" had become fact, with the government controlling the larger part of Italy's steel, iron and ship-building industries, as well as every aspect of political life.

World War II

Mussolini's involvement in the **Spanish Civil War** in 1936 brought about the formation of the "**Axis**" with Nazi Germany. Italy entered **World War II** totally unprepared and with outdated equipment, but in 1941 invaded Yugoslavia to gain control of the Adriatic coast. Before long, though, Mussolini was on the defensive. Tens of thousands of Italian troops were killed on the Russian front in the winter of 1942, and in July 1943 the Allied forces gained a first foothold in Europe, when Patton's American Seventh Army and the British Eighth Army under Montgomery landed in Sicily. A month later they controlled the island.

In the face of these and other reversals Mussolini was overthrown by his own Grand Council, who bundled him away to the isolated mountain resort of Gran Sasso, and replaced him with the perplexed **Marshal Badoglio**. The Allies wanted Italy's surrender, for which they secretly offered amnesty to the king, Vittorio Emanuele III, who had coexisted with the Fascist regime for 21 years. On September 8 a radio broadcast announced that an **armistice** had been signed, and on the following day the Allies crossed onto the mainland. As the Anglo-American army moved up through the peninsula, German divisions moved south to meet them, springing Mussolini from jail to set up the **republic of Salò** on Lago di Garda. It was a total failure, and increasing numbers of men and women from Communist, Socialist or Catholic parties swelled the opposing partisan forces to 450,000. In April 1945 Mussolini fled for his life, but was caught by partisans before reaching Switzerland. He and his

1958	1969
Italy is a founder member of the European Economic Community (EEC) which is renamed the European Community (EC) in 1992 and becomes part of the European Union (EU) in 2009.	Bomb in Milan's Piazza Fontana kills 17 people and marks the beginning of ten years during which a toxic mix of the Italian secret service, far-right and -left terrorist groups attempt to destabilize the country.

lover, Claretta Petacci, were shot and strung upside down from a filling-station roof in Milan's Piazzale Loreto.

The postwar years

A popular mandate declared Italy a republic in 1946, and Alcide de Gasperi's **Democrazia Cristiana (DC)** party formed a government. During the 1950s Italy became a front-rank industrial nation, massive firms such as Fiat and Olivetti helping to double the GDP and triple industrial production. American financial aid – the Marshall Plan – was an important factor in this expansion, as was the availability of a large and compliant workforce, a substantial proportion of which was drawn from the villages of the south.

The DC at first operated in alliance with other right-wing parties, but in 1963, in a move precipitated by the increased politicization of the blue-collar workers, they were obliged to share power for the first time with the **Partito Socialista Italiano (PSI)**. The DC politician who was largely responsible for sounding out the socialists was **Aldo Moro**, the dominant figure of Italian politics in the 1960s. Moro was prime minister from 1963 to 1968, a period in which the economy was disturbed by inflation and the removal of vast sums of money by wealthy citizens alarmed by the arrival in power of the PSI. The decade ended with the "**autunno caldo**" ("hot autumn") of 1969, when strikes, occupations and demonstrations paralyzed the country.

The 1970s and 1980s

In the 1970s the situation continued to worsen. More extreme forms of unrest broke out, instigated in the first instance by the far right, who were almost certainly behind a bomb which killed sixteen people in Piazza Fontana, Milan, in 1969, and the Piazza della Loggia bombing in Brescia five years later. **Neo-fascist terrorism** continued throughout the next decade, reaching its hideous climax in 1980, when 84 people were killed and 200 wounded in a bomb blast at Bologna train station. At the same time, a plethora of left-wing terrorist groups sprang up, many of them led by disaffected intellectuals at the northern universities. The most active of these were the **Brigate Rosse** (Red Brigades). They reached the peak of their notoriety in 1978, when a Red Brigade group kidnapped and killed Aldo Moro himself. A major police offensive in the early 1980s nullified most of the Brigate Rosse, but a number of hardline splinter groups from the various terrorist organizations are still in existence.

Inconsistencies and secrecy beset those trying to discover who was really responsible for the terrorist activity of the 1970s. One Red Brigade member who served eighteen years in jail for his part in the assassination of Aldo Moro recently asserted that it was spies working for the **Italian secret services** who masterminded the operation. A report prepared by the PDS (Italy's party of the democratic left) in 2000 stirred up further controversy: it alleged that in the 1970s and 1980s the Establishment pursued a "**strategy of tension**" and that indiscriminate bombing of the public and the threat of a right-wing coup were devices to stabilize centre-right political control of the country. The perpetrators of bombing campaigns were rarely caught, said the report, because "those massacres, those bombs, those military actions had been organized or promoted

1978	1980	1992
Aldo Moro, leader of the Christian Democrats and ex-prime minister, is kidnapped and murdered by Red Brigade terrorists after 55 days of imprisonment.	Bomb in Bologna train station kills 85 people.	Anti-Mafia judges Giovanni Falcone and Paolo Borsellino murdered.

or supported by men inside Italian state institutions and, as has been discovered more recently, by men linked to the structures of United States intelligence". "Other bombing campaigns were attributed to the left to prevent the Communist Party from achieving power by democratic means," said Valter Bielli, PDS MP, and one of the report's authors. The report drew furious rebuttals from centre-right groups and the US embassy in Rome.

By whatever means, the DC government certainly clung to power. It was partly sustained by the so-called "historic compromise" negotiated in 1976 with **Enrico Berlinguer**, leader of the **Partito Comunista Italiano (PCI)**. By this arrangement the PCI – polling 34 percent of the national vote, just three points less than the DC – agreed to abstain from voting in parliament in order to maintain a government of national unity. The pact was rescinded in 1979, and after Berlinguer's death in 1984 the PCI's share of the vote dropped to around 27 percent. The combination of this withdrawal of popular support and the collapse of the Communist bloc led to a realignment of the PCI under the leadership of **Achille Occhetto**, who turned the party into a democratic socialist grouping along the lines of left-leaning parties in Germany or Sweden – a transformation encapsulated by the party's new name – the **Partito Democratico della Sinistra** ("Democratic Party of the Left").

In its efforts to exclude the left wing from power, the DC had been obliged to accede to demands from minor parties such as the **Radical Party**, which gained eighteen seats in the 1987 election, one of them going to the porn star Ilona Staller, better known as **La Cicciolina**. Furthermore, the DC's reputation was severely damaged in the early 1980s by a series of scandals, notably the furore surrounding the activities of the P2 Masonic Lodge, when links were discovered between corrupt bankers, senior DC members, and fanatical right-wing groups. As its popularity fell, the DC was forced to offer the premiership to politicians from other parties. In 1981 Giovanni Spadolini of the Republicans became the first non-DC prime minister since the war, and in 1983 **Bettino Craxi** was installed as the first premier from the PSI, a position he held for four years.

Even through the upheavals of the 1970s the national income of Italy continued to grow, and there developed a national obsession with **Il Sorpasso**, a term signifying the country's overtaking of France and Britain in the economic league table. Experts disagreed as to whether Il Sorpasso actually happened (most thought it hadn't), and calculations were complicated by the huge scale of tax evasion and other illicit financial dealings in Italy. All strata of society were involved in the withholding of money from central government, but the ruling power in this **economia sommersa** (submerged economy) was, and to a certain extent still is, the **Mafia**, whose contacts penetrate to the highest levels in Rome. The most traumatic proof of the Mafia's infiltration of the political hierarchy came in May 1992, with the murders of anti-Mafia judges **Giovanni Falcone** and **Paolo Borsellino**, whose killers could only have penetrated the judges' security with the help of inside information.

Mani Pulite

The murders of the immensely respected Falcone and Borsellino marked a fault-line in the political history of modern Italy, and the late 1980s and early 1990s saw the rise of

1994	2001–06	2002
Silvio Berlusconi's centre-right Forza Italia party wins the general election with the National Alliance and the Lega Nord. It falls after eight months when the Lega withdraws support for the coalition.	A second government headed by Silvio Berlusconi becomes the longest post-war government.	The euro replaces the lira as Italy's currency.

a number of new political parties, as people became disillusioned with the old DC-led consensus. One was the right-wing Lega Nord (Northern League), whose autocratic leader, Umberto Bossi, capitalized on concerns that the hard-working, law-abiding North was supporting the corrupt South, while the Fascist MSI, renamed the Alleanza Nazionale (AN), or National Alliance, and now a wide coalition of right-wingers led by the persuasive Gianfranco Fini, has gained ground in recent years.

In 1992 the new government of Giuliano Amato – a politician untainted by any hint of corruption – instigated the biggest round-up of Mafia members in nearly a decade, leading to the arrest of Salvatore "Toto" Riina, the Mafia *capo di tutti capi* (boss of bosses) and the man widely believed to have been behind the Falcone and Borsellino killings. The arrest of Riina followed the testimony of numerous supergrasses, who also implicated key members of the establishment in Mafia activities, including the former prime minister Giulio Andreotti, who was brought to trial.

Bettino Craxi once called Andreotti a fox, adding "sooner or later all foxes end up as fur coats", but it was Craxi himself who was one of the first to fall from grace. Craxi was at the centre of the powerful Socialist establishment that ran the key city of Milan, when in February 1992 a minor party official was arrested on corruption charges. This represented just the tip of a long-established culture of kickbacks and bribes that went right to the top of the Italian political establishment, not just in Milan but across the entire country, and was nicknamed Tangentopoli ("Bribesville"). By the end of that year thousands were under arrest and what came to be known as the Mani Pulite or "Clean Hands" investigation, led by the crusading Milan judge, Antonio di Pietro, was under way. In January 1999, Craxi was convicted with twenty others of corruption and sentenced to five years in prison, dying a year later in exile in Tunisia.

Italy today and the Berlusconi effect

The established Italian parties, most notably the Christian Democrats and the Socialists, were almost entirely wiped out in the municipal elections of 1993, and the national elections of 1994 saw yet another political force emerge to fill the power vacuum: the centre-right **Forza Italia** or "Come on Italy", led by the media mogul **Silvio Berlusconi**, who used the power of his TV stations to build support, and swept to power as prime minister in a populist alliance with Bossi's Lega Nord and the fascist National Alliance. The fact that Berlusconi was not a politician was perhaps his greatest asset, and most Italians, albeit briefly, saw this as a new beginning – the end of the old, corrupt regime, and the birth of a truly modern Italian state. However, as one of the country's top northern industrialists, and a former crony of Craxi, Berlusconi was as bound up with the old ways as anyone.

Although he went on to win three more elections in the following eight years and was head of Italy's **longest-lasting postwar government**, Berlusconi proved to be no more successful at ruling the country than any of his predecessors. On a personal front not only did he resist all attempts to reduce the scope of his media business and its conflict of interest with his premiership (see p.994), but his time in the public eye was also accompanied by a constantly evolving charge-sheet covering money-laundering, corruption, sex scandals, gerrymandering and forcing through backdated legislation to get himself out of sticky court cases.

2006	2008	
Italy wins the football World Cup for the fourth time (previously in 1934, 1938 and 1982).	Roberto Saviano's book and subsequent film *Gomorrrah* document the influence of the Camorra on every aspect of Neapolitan life.	In general elections, as leader of the People of Freedom political coalition, Berlusconi is returned for his fourth term as prime minister.

FROM CRUISESHIP TO PREMIERSHIP: SILVIO BERLUSCONI

Perhaps the one thing the Italians aren't very good at is politics. They've had 63 different governments since World War II, and the country was embroiled in a series of corruption scandals in the early 1990s that led to a shake-up of the entire system. Nonetheless Italians still don't trust politicians, which perhaps explains how they chose the cruiseship crooner and self-made media tycoon Silvio Berlusconi, as prime minister for four terms. The gaffes, scandals and sleaze that characterized his time in power are now the things for which contemporary Italy is most famous. A notorious and shameless womanizer, Berlusconi was almost brought down in 2009 when a series of prostitutes went public on their relationships with him. He survived as prime minister (Italians are relatively tolerant of sexual dalliances) but not as a husband – his wife Veronica Lario announced she was leaving him shortly after. His social life continued to dominate headlines when a 17-year-old prostitute was released from arrest after a phone call from the premier and details of wild "bunga bunga" parties titillated the country.

Berlusconi also got into trouble when representing Italy abroad, famously accusing a German MEP of acting like a Nazi camp guard; and at home his battle with the Italian judiciary ("a cancerous growth" in his view) combined with, mostly successful, attempts to change laws to protect him from being tried for corruption, arguably occupied more of his political time than any other issues. Unlike most modern politicians he just doesn't seem to care what people think, which in Italy – a country of notorious naysayers – helped to make him a popular leader. As for the fact that as head of a media business and prime minister he virtually controlled all mainstream television (and clearly used this to his own advantage), he simply says: "If I, taking care of everyone's interests, also take care of my own, you can't talk about a conflict of interest."

After being ingloriously pushed aside as Italy teetered on the edge of bankruptcy, Berlusconi continues his various personal battles with the country's judicial system while his influence over Italian politics endures.

But perhaps more worrying still was his effect on the state of the nation: the media-mogul-turned-politician's promises of freedom and prosperity were shown to be empty. Economic decline, social stagnation and stifling bureaucracy continue to have modern-day Italy in a stranglehold. Both Berlusconi's governments and the various shortlived left-wing coalitions that have also been in power in the last decade have been too preoccupied with self-promotion, scandal and in-fighting to begin to resolve the malaise of the country. When faced with global financial crises and their country on the verge of bankruptcy, Berlusconi was finally forced to quit in November 2011, and an emergency government of technocrats was put together under the economist **Mario Monti** who has been left to try and steer Italy out of yet another crisis, one that affects the rest of the world.

2009	2011	2012
An earthquake strikes L'Aquila in Abruzzo killing over 300 people.	In the dock again, after years of trials for fiscal impropriety, Silvio Berlusconi resigns as Italy teeters on the edge of bankruptcy. Mario Monti is invited to steer Italy through the financial crisis.	Earthquakes strike in northern Italy causing significant damage and loss of life in Modena, Parma and Mantua.

Italian art

Pick up any history of Western art and you'll find the biggest chapter by far will be on Italy. The country's contribution to the pantheon of creativity through the past three thousand years is immense, whether it's the legacy of the Romans and the early Christian era or the enormous and unprecedented achievements of the Renaissance in Florence and Rome. It's the reason many people visit Italy in the first place, and this short history is designed to give you the most basic of backgrounds to enhance your trip.

The Etruscans

A sensible way to begin any account of Italian art is with the **Etruscans**, who lived in central Italy – in Etruria – from around 900 BC until their incorporation into the Roman world in 88 BC. The Romans borrowed heavily from their civilization, and thus in many ways the influence of the Etruscans is still felt today: our alphabet, for example, is based on the Etruscan system; and bishops' crooks and the "fasces" symbol, of a bundle of rods with an axe – found, among other places, behind the speaker's rostrum in the US House of Representatives – are just two other Etruscan symbols that endure. The Etruscans were also master craftsmen, working in terracotta, gold and bronze, and accomplished carvers in stone, and it is these skills – together with their obvious sensuality and the ease with which they enjoyed life – that make their civilization so beguiling. A lot of Etruscan objects have survived from tombs, particularly those found in the sites of Tarquinia and Cerveteri – terracotta sculptures such as the sculpture of the married couple or *Apollo* and *Hercules* in the Villa Giulia museum in Rome, or bronzes like the *Orator* and the *Chimera* in the archeological museum in Florence.

The Romans

The militaristic **Romans**, who wrested control of the region from the Etruscans, are not usually known as great artists. There were great builders, certainly, and the wall paintings and mosaics of Pompeii and Herculaneum demonstrate that there were gifted artists around. But the fact is that a great deal of Roman art and sculpture is in fact copied from ancient Greek originals – most famously the *Laocoön* and *Apollo Belvedere* in the Vatican or any number of sculptures in the Palazzo Nuovo of the Capitoline Museums in Rome. There's no doubting the skill of Roman sculptors who re-created these works, though, and the Romans as a whole were prolific creators of sculptural art. Above all they were good portraitists, and there are lots of likenesses of both ordinary people and most of the great emperors still with us today, including a huge hoard in the Vatican Museums, as well as fantastic sarcophagi portraying battle scenes in relief – a medium which was also used to adorn triumphal arches and other architectural features.

Early Christian and Byzantine art

The **early Christians** borrowed the tendency to decorate sarcophagi with relief sculptures from the Romans, though by now these depicted fundamental Christian themes like the shepherd and the lamb, Christ enthroned or the alpha and omega symbols. Early Christian paintings were done in the catacombs and other burial places, mainly depictions of saints but again often borrowing colour and other styles from the

Romans. However, mosaics were the more commonly used medium as the decoration in churches, especially during the reign of the Emperor Justinian, whose period in power during the middle of the sixth century marks the high point of early **Byzantine** art. These usually depicted a group of saints lined up with the church's donor, centring on a figure of Christ enthroned in glory, for example in the basilica of Santa Maria Maggiore in Rome, whose mosaics are a fifth-century comic strip of the Old Testament, or, a little later, in the new Christian Roman capital of Ravenna, where the sixth-century basilicas of San Vitale and Sant'Apollinaire Nuovo hold stupendous cycles of mosaics.

The Middle Ages

The medium of mosaic stayed in use for hundreds of years, and indeed was the principal method used to decorate the basilica of San Marco in Venice (see p.351) in the thirteenth century. However, mosaic was an inevitably monumental and static medium, and before long frescoes became preferred in churches, albeit following the rather stiff and formal styles of the mosaicists, along with panel paintings depicting Christ or the Madonna and a group of saints.

Nicola Pisano (1220–1285) was the first great sculptor of the Middle Ages in what we now call Italy, a native of Pisa and famous for his work on the pulpit in Pisa's baptistry, whose sculptural complexity bears comparison with the best pre-Christian sarcophagi. He passed on his talent to his son, **Giovanni Pisano** (1250–1315), who continued to work in the same Gothic tradition but with more fluidity and skill, creating pulpits in both Pistoia and Pisa cathedrals as well as a series of statues for the facade of Siena's cathedral and another pulpit inside. One of Nicola Pisano's assistants on this, **Arnolfo di Cambio** (1240–1310) was also very active at this time. He produced the famous statue of *St Peter* in St Peter's in Rome, whose foot is worn smooth by worshippers, and developed the design for funerary tombs which was followed for the next couple of centuries, but he's perhaps best-known as the architect responsible for the construction of the cathedral in Florence in the late 1200s.

At about the same time, **Pietro Cavallini** (1250–1330) introduced a new level of realism into the mosaics he designed and the frescoes he painted, moving away somewhat from the stiff Byzantine figures people were used to – as evidenced by the frescoes in the basilica of St Francis in Assisi, in the church of Santa Cecilia in Rome, and some fragmentary frescoes in Naples. **Cimabue**, too (1240–1302), was a pioneer of his time, name-checked by Dante in his *Purgatorio* as being eclipsed in talent only by his pupil, **Giotto di Bondone** (1267–1337) – no disgrace as Giotto, as he is now known, was certainly the greatest artist of this time, widely regarded as the link between Gothic art and everything else that followed. This is due to the fact that he was the first to truly break away from the heavily stylized forms of the Byzantine and Gothic era and give his figures proper, human form. His frescoes in the Scrovegni Chapel in Padua are justifiably famous, and have a humane power that makes them one of the great unmissable sights of Italy, although most other works by him are lost or disputed – apart from his frescoes in the basilica of St Francis in Assisi, an altarpiece in the Uffizi, a crucifix in Rimini and one or two other small-scale works.

Despite the influence of Giotto, the dominant school of painting at the time was in fact in Siena, headed up by **Duccio di Buoninsegna** (1255–1318) and **Simone Martini** (1284–1344), both of whom followed a more traditional path, engaging with the more formal Byzantine style to some extent but making it into a more refined and elegant style of their own. Duccio's masterpiece is probably his *Maestà*, currently in the museum of Siena's cathedral, which was so admired on its completion that it was carried around the town in a procession. Simone Martini was a pupil of Duccio and painted the same subject in the town hall of Siena; he is also known for his frescoes in the church of St Francis in Assisi and his *Annunciation* in the Uffizi.

The Renaissance

The fifteenth century in Italy really belongs to what we now call the **Renaissance**, a remarkable time, centred on Florence and Tuscany in particular. In architecture this involved an attempt to get back to classical ideas coupled with ingenious new building methods and techniques, while in the visual arts there was a move away from a more iconic style of painting towards an approach that placed man centre-stage in as realistic a fashion as possible, with perspective, elements of portraiture and landscape. At the same time artists in general began to gain a new respect, moving gradually away from being considered as mere artisans to take their place as members of the professional classes.

If the Renaissance begins anywhere it's with **Lorenzo Ghiberti** (1378–1455), whose victory in a competition sponsored by the Florentine authorities to design the doors of the city's baptistry arguably kickstarted the movement, and occupied the artist for the best part of the next fifty years, with a design that exhibited more drama, naturalism and perspective than had been previously seen, and spawning a legacy of Florentine sculptors who would blaze a trail through the rest of the fifteenth century. The runner-up in the competition, **Filippo Brunelleschi** (1377–1446), went on to specialize in architecture, and added a dome to the city's cathedral that would prove to be one of the engineering wonders of the century (see p.518), while Ghiberti's pupil **Donatello** (1386–1466) became arguably the greatest sculptor of his age, with an appreciation of nature and an ability to render it in marble that upstaged everyone who had gone before. His skill is manifest in numerous examples around the country, but most notably in his early sculptures of the *Evangelists* in Orsanmichele in Florence, now split between the church and the Bargello, where his iconic figure of *David* also resides. In 1425 Donatello began to work with another sculptor, **Michelozzo** (1396–1472), producing the tomb of Cardinal Brancacci in Naples, among other things; Michelozzo also worked on Ghiberti's bronze doors. Another sculptor who went in for the baptistry doors competition was **Jacopo della Quercia** (1374–1438), a Sienese artist who was influenced by the work of Nicola Pisano and Arnolfo di Cambio. He is responsible for the Fonte Gaia in Siena's main square, and work in the churches of San Frediano and San Petronio, in Lucca and Bologna respectively.

The invention of perspective is sometimes credited to **Paolo Uccello** (1397–1475), whose most famous work, in the National Gallery in London, shows the foreshortened body of the "soldier who died for perspective" in his *Battle Scene* there. But Uccello was more interested in perspective for its own sake (hence a painting like this) rather than using it to create more realistic pictures, and it was **Masaccio** (1401–1428) who in fact developed it properly – most potently in his fresco of the *Trinity* in the church of Santa Maria Novella, whose extraordinary depth and realism were revolutionary at the time. His contemporary **Masolino da Panicale** (1383–1447) was another veteran of Ghiberti's doors, but he painted in a more traditional style that harkened back to his Gothic predecessors.

Masaccio's only pupil, **Fra Filippo Lippi** (1406–1469), was a clear follower of his master, but he was influenced by the Flemish masters too, as we can see in his dramatic and naturalistic frescoes in Prato's cathedral. At the same time, **Fra Angelico** (1395–1455) painted more monumental and in some ways more staid creations, though with a greater emphasis on colour – as you can see if you visit the home of his greatest works, painted in the monastery at which he was a Dominican monk – San Marco in Florence. Meanwhile, in Verona, Fra Angelico's contemporary **Antonio Pisanello** (1395–1455) was decorating some of the principal churches of his home town in a well-developed Gothic style, along with a series of frescoes in the Palazzo Ducale in Mantua.

One of the painters closest in style to Masaccio was **Domenico Ghirlandaio** (1449–94), whose frescoes adorn the church of Santa Maria Novella among other churches in Florence. However, perhaps the greatest of the next generation of Renaissance artists was **Luca Signorelli** (1445–1523), who in fact painted Fra Angelico's portrait (as well as his own) into his amazing *Last Judgement*, in a chapel in Orvieto cathedral – a work which is said to have influenced Michelangelo's later work on the same subject in the Sistine Chapel.

To the south of Florence, in Arezzo, another contemporary of Mantegna, **Piero della Francesca** (1410–1492), was experimenting with perspective in the same way, but his work today looks less archaic, almost modern, in its outlook compared to others of the time, with calm, understated colours and cool sense of form – best seen in his series of paintings depicting the *Legend of the True Cross* in Arezzo's church of San Francesco.

Piero della Francesca was a big influence on the Umbrian painter, **Melozzo da Forlì** (1438–1494), who worked in Rome in the last two decades of the fifteenth century, decorating a number of churches, including Santi Apostoli and San Marco – the latter including a famous picture showing his patron Pope Sixtus IV that's now in the Vatican Pinacoteca. Among fellow Umbrians, **Pietro Perugino** (1446–1524) was known for his harmoniously composed paintings – less full of drama than some of his contemporaries, but theatrically staged nonetheless, as serene, beautifully coloured tableaux, that almost epitomize the symmetrical beauty of much of Renaissance art. His assistant, **Pinturicchio** (1454–1513), also produced beautifully composed works of great form and colour, but made no attempt at any sort of profound vision; some of his best-known and most accessible work is in the church of Santa Maria del Popolo in Rome.

Andrea Mantegna (1431–1506), who worked in the north of Italy, in Padua and then Mantua, was one of the most inventive practitioners of the new Renaissance techniques, peopling his paintings with living, breathing human beings and setting them against backdrops that had realism and perspective – much more so, say, than his contemporary **Benozzo Gozzoli** (1421–1497), whose frescoes in the chapel in Florence's Palazzo Medici-Ricciardi are more decorative than naturalistic. Some of Mantegna's best work is in the Palazzo Ducale in Mantua, where he painted a series of marvellous family frescoes for the Gonzagas.

Towards the end of the fifteenth century, **Sandro Botticelli** (1445–1510), too, developed a style of his own, apprenticed at a young age to Fra Filippo Lippi but increasingly creating pictures which married naturalism with elegance. He also worked as much for wealthy merchants as the Church, painting canvases rather than frescoes, and as such his work is smaller-scale and less concerned with monumental religious themes than others, and overall more decorative, using ancient Greek and Roman stories as his subject matter instead.

Botticelli's best-known contemporary was **Leonardo da Vinci** (1452–1519), a Florentine who died in France and is now known as the ultimate "Renaissance Man", as comfortable designing weaponry or writing a learned thesis as with drawing or painting. Precious little work has survived from Leonardo, partly because he was so busy with other projects, and partly because he insisted on deciding when something was completed himself, and so works were often left unfinished or never delivered. *The Last Supper* in Milan's Santa Maria delle Grazie is probably his most famous piece of work in Italy, and is incredibly naturalistic for its time, not only realistically depicting the characters in the story, but actually telling the story, too.

The sixteenth century

At the end of the fifteenth century the emphasis shifted from Florence, to Rome and to Venice. The **High Renaissance** is generally used to describe a period of time during the first half of the sixteenth century, when all the ideas of the Renaissance were in tune, and there was a group of artists – led by Michelangelo and Raphael in Rome, and Titian in Venice – who were at the height of their powers, interpreting the humanist principles of the time with an almost divine virtuosity and skill, until the mid-century backlash started with the more empty showiness of **Mannerism**.

At the turn of the sixteenth century Ghirlandaio's studio took on a young and hungry Florentine painter called **Michelangelo Buonarotti** (1475–1564), who from the outset was something special, studying anatomy so as to get the draughtsmanship of his figures exactly right, as can be seen in his early – and renowned – figure of *David* in the Uffizi.

Michelangelo preferred sculpture to painting, but his fame quickly spread, and he was still a relatively young man when he was called to Rome to decorate the Sistine Chapel for Pope Julius II in 1506 – a feat which took four years, and to this day is perhaps the most heroic and accomplished single piece of work that any painter has achieved. He was an artist who never let up, and it's possible to follow the development of his style around Italy, taking in early works like the figure of *Bacchus* in Florence's Bargello and his pietà in St Peter's in Rome right up to the Sistine Chapel's dark *Last Judgement*, which he painted over thirty years after the ceiling. It's perhaps testament to Michelangelo's originality and uncompromising approach that both Sistine Chapel works caused an equal level of outcry at the time.

His contemporary **Raphael** (1483–1520), a native of Perugia, with Michelangelo represents the high point of the Renaissance, the point at which the era's ideas and inventions with regards to form, light, naturalism and composition all converged. Unlike Michelangelo, Raphael was an out-and-out painter, and naturally he was called to work for the pope as well, his best work probably being the suite of rooms he decorated for the same Pope Julius II in the Vatican Palace. It seems almost incredible that these two great artists were for a period working in the same building at the same time, creating arguably the two greatest pieces of Renaissance painting ever within a few yards of each other. Yet that is what happened, although Raphael enjoyed a much shorter life than Michelangelo, and works by him are scarce by comparison. However, his later work in the nearby Villa Farnesina in Rome is also among his best, and there are paintings by him in a number of different Italian galleries.

Venice was a booming city at this time, and it first embraced the Renaissance in the elderly figure of **Giovanni Bellini** (1430–1516). He had been influenced by Andrea Mantegna, who had married his sister, and became known for introducing naturalistic details into his religious paintings. He also headed up a large workshop, one that was responsible for turning out the next generation of Venetian painters, including Sebastiano del Piombo, Giorgione and Titian. **Giorgione** (1476–1510) died young and there's hardly any work by him in existence now, but what there is marks him out as one of the greatest Venetian painters, in particular a mysterious painting that has been named *The Tempest* due to the fact that no one really knows what it depicts or what it is about. It was a revolutionary painting for its time, principally in the way it incorporates nature into the composition, almost as a character in its own right. The second great Venetian painter of this time was **Titian** (1487–1576), a talent so revered that it was said that even the Holy Roman Emperor Charles V had stopped to pick up one of his brushes – a story which perhaps says as much about the evolving status of artists during the Renaissance as it does about Titian. Titian was a colourist, and brilliant, too, at composition, and he rewrote the rules of both in his great painting of *The Assumption* in the Frari church in Venice. He was also a great portraitist, as can be seen in his depiction of the Farnese pope Paul III, which hangs in the Capodimonte Museum in Naples, as well as many other great portraits he painted during his long careeer. **Sebastian del Piombo** (1485–1547) is thought to have finished some of Giorgione's paintings after he died, and he also worked with Raphael on the Villa Farnesina, but he became closest of all to Michelangelo, whose influence can be seen in his later works, for example the two that hang in the Trinità dei Monti church in Rome.

Of the Venetians that followed this group, **Lorenzo Lotto** (1480–1556) followed in the footsteps of Giorgione, as did his friend **Palma il Vecchio** (1480–1528), although it's **Tintoretto** who stands out. His distinctive, dramatic style prefigured the Baroque with its theatrical lighting and dashing, almost unfinished style – all a far cry from the cool delivery of Titian, but typical of the time in his determination to break free of the dominant Renaissance approach and forge a style of his own. A prolific artist, his work can be found everywhere, all over Italy, but the four paintings he did for the Scuola di San Marco in Venice are among his best, as are those in the Scuola di San Rocco, also in Venice.

The third great sixteenth-century Venetian painter was arguably **Paolo Veronese**, who was also a great stylist, painting big narrative works that decorated the Palladian Villa Barbaro in Maser and the church of San Giovanni e Paolo in Venice. Meanwhile in Parma, **Correggio** (1489–1534) was busily decorating the churches and the cathedral in a soft flowing style in which he perfected his *sotto in su* technique, in which figures are depicted on domes and ceiling as if floating in the sky – an effect which was to be taken up with a vengeance in the decades to come.

Mannerism

Veronese and Correggio worked towards the end of the sixteenth century, and in some way their styles anticipate what has become known as **Mannerism**, a somewhat derogatory term derived from the Italian word *maniera* or "style". This alluded to the fact that the artists who followed on from the Renaissance greats had to find a way of distinguishing themselves, which they did by using increasingly flashy techniques of perspective and draughtsmanship – all style and no substance, if you like. Mannerist paintings tended to go for cheap and immediate effects – in colour, subject matter and delivery – and as such they prefigure the equally dramatic Baroque era that was to follow. Perhaps the ultimate Mannerist painter is **Giulio Romano** (1499–1546), whose frescoes in Mantua's Palazzo del Te are still quite shocking today. But other painters fall into this post-Renaissance category, for example **Francesco Parmigianino** (1503–1540), who worked alongside Correggio in Parma and is probably best-known for a painting that has become known as the *Madonna with the Long Neck*, in the Uffizi in Florence, a very elegant painting that typifies the Mannerist approach to the human form.

Other so-called Mannerist painters include **Giorgio Vasari** (1511–1574), whose work is common in Italy – he was quite prolific – although he is probably best-known for his biographies of the various Renaissance artists, from which we know a great deal about these men and their time. **Agnolo Bronzino** (1503–72) was another gifted Mannerist painter who worked mainly in Florence and concentrated on portraiture. His contemporary, **Benvenuto Cellini** (1500–71) was an artist turned writer who made beautiful pieces in bronze and gold that still survive today but who is more renowned for his racy autobiography which describes his life in Rome during the sixteenth century. Giovanni da Bologna or **Giambologna** (1529–1608), as he's better known, was a Florentine sculptor who also worked in bronze and marble, and whose aim to produce a piece that could be viewed from all angles was Mannerist to its core, and can be seen at its best in Florence's Bargello.

The Baroque

The end of the sixteenth century saw upheaval in Europe, with the Reformation gaining pace in northern Europe and the Catholic Church forced to retrench in its southern heartlands, giving way to another new style that got stuck with a derogatory name: the **Baroque**, a term which literally meant grotesque, and was coined to describe the grand and theatrical style in painting and architecture that swept Europe at the beginning of the seventeenth century.

The first artist of the Baroque age was perhaps **Annibale Carracci** (1560–1609), of Bologna, whose work in the Palazzo Farnese, depicting a series of mythological scenes, prefigures the style with its overtones of fantasy, illusion and mild titillation. **Guido Reni** (1575–1642), also from Bologna, focused more on religious themes, but with a sentimentality that made his pictures popular everywhere and his work much in demand. Less sentimental but equally dramatic, the works of **Michelangelo Merisi da Caravaggio** (d.1610) have stood the test of time better, as has his reputation, perhaps because his story fits the archetype of artist-as-outlaw that's very much in tune with modern tastes. Nonetheless his pictures were strikingly original at the time, using models from the streets for religious figures and making street life, clothes, and the nitty-gritty of the human form, warts and all, a fit subject for religious art – as can be seen in his paintings in the church of Santa Maria del Popolo and other churches in Rome, where he worked for much of his life. Caravaggio was a great dramatist, composing his pictures in a theatrical manner that was increasingly typical of the times. He was also a superb technician, particularly with regard to light, and perhaps the greatest exponent of a technique known as chiaroscuro – basically the interplay of light and dark on the canvas. This style was taken up with relish by the artists of the Baroque era, and done to death by some of them, not least a group of painters from Naples – **Luca Giordano** (1632–1705), **Massimo Stanzione** (1585–1656) and **Battistello Caracciolo** (d.1637) – who raised the city's status in the art world at a time when it was becoming one of the most populous and important cities in Europe. Giordano in particular was a massively prolific painter, and you can't move for his work in Naples, though perhaps the best place to see it is the Cappella del Pio Monte della Misericordia, where one of his finest paintings hangs alongside a great work by Caravaggio, both done for the same church. Hot on the heels of these artists in Naples was **Francesco Solimena** (1657–1747), a Neapolitan late-Baroque painter who was hugely successful, and whose work is also ubiquitous, but at its best in the city's Gesù Nuovo.

A pupil of Carracci, **Domenichino** (1581–1641) also worked on the Farnese Palace, and decorated the church of Sant'Andrea delle Valle in Rome with another student of Carracci, **Giovanni Lanfranco** (1582–1647), though the two fell out shortly after this, after which Domenichino went to Naples and relative obscurity. Lanfranco meanwhile went on to bigger and better things, becoming an expert in *sotto in su* technique and as such landing commissions for all kinds of domes and ceilings, both in Rome and in Naples. Another follower of Carracci, and also from Bologna, Giovanni Francesco Barbieri, known as **Guercino** or "the squinter" because he was cross-eyed (1591–1666), fell out with Reni, who accused him of stealing all his ideas, but who still managed to produce a fair body of work, most famous of which is his *St Petronilla* altarpiece which he painted for St Peter's but which now hangs in Rome's Capitoline Museums.

Working alongside Lanfranco in Rome, **Pietro da Cortona** (1596–1669) was another great illusionist, whose ceiling in the Palazzo Barberini in Rome is perhaps the ultimate in Baroque *sotto in su* trickery – a mass of writhing figures, clouds and drapery that are at once in the room with you and at the same time escaping into the sky beyond. The Barberini pope, Urban VIII, was the greatest pope of the Baroque age, not least because he was the patron of **Gianlorenzo Bernini** (1598–1680), who was without question the greatest Baroque artist of all, producing a lifetime's work of sculpture and architecture that more than any other defines what Baroque really means. The best of his small-scale statues – in Rome's Galleria Borghese – are virtuosic pieces of dynamic sculpture, intensely theatrical, that invite you to study them from all angles, while Bernini's work for Rome's church of Santa Maria in Vitorria, depicting the *Ecstasy of St Theresa*, is the very essence of Baroque drama.

All those who came into contact with Bernini were influenced by him, and **Giovanni Baciccia** (1639–1709) was no exception, taking on the illusionistic challenge of the age and decorating the Gesù church in Rome with a vigour and invention that rivalled even Cortona's Palazzo Barberini work. **Andrea Pozzo** (1642–1709), too, took the style's illusionism to an extreme, decorating another Jesuit Rome church, Sant'Ignazio, with one of the biggest fakes of the era – painting in a trompe l'oeil dome which from one point in the nave looks exactly like the real thing.

The eighteenth century

The late Baroque style became what is known as the **Rococo** in the early eighteenth century – basically an ornate style of interior decoration that is a toned-down and more domestic version of the Baroque. By comparison to what had gone before, the period, and indeed the eighteenth century in general, was not a great era for Italian art, partly because interior decoration was indeed what artists increasingly came to specialize in, working for the aristocracy and the wealthy merchant classes rather than their traditional patron, the Church. Landscape painting became popular, as seen in the Venetian scenes of **Francesco Guardi** (1712–93) and **Antonio Canaletto** (1697–1768), the latter of whom churned out views of Venice that were extremely popular, though he never reproduced the same quality when painting other cities. Guardi, too, painted only Venice, though with a more impressionistic style that may be more suited to modern tastes. Perhaps the greatest Italian Rococo artist, however, was **Giambattista Tiepolo** (1696–1770), whose flamboyant frescoes were sought after in palaces and castles all over Italy, although they were essentially fantasy works, used as decoration rather than for any deeper meaning – an approach that was ably continued by his son **Giandomenico Tiepolo** (1727–1804).

Later eighteenth-century Italian art took many forms – the architectural fantasies and complex etchings of **Giambattista Piranesi** (1720–78), for example, or the Venetian genre scenes of **Pietro Longhi** (1702–85). But ultimately the style that caught on was the one that prevailed over the rest of Europe, **Neoclassicism** – a movement inspired by the art and architecture of the ancient world, which at the time was being excavated in sites around Rome and in Pompeii and Herculaneum, and for which for most people meant a return to truly civilized artistic ideals. **Antonio Canova** (1757–1822) was the best-known and most prolific Italian Neoclassical artist; he produced a huge body of work, although he is perhaps most famous for his renderings of Napoleon at the beginning of the nineteenth century, and in particular of Napoleon's famously sluttish sister, Pauline, in the Galleria Borghese.

The nineteenth century to the modern day

The nineteenth century, too, was not an especially auspicious time for Italian art, and the international focus was by now firmly in France and elsewhere. After Canova, the mantle of Neoclassical sculpture had been taken up by **Pietro Canonica** (1869–1959), a Rome-based sculptor who specialized in civic and public sculpture as well as busts of the rich and famous, and **Vincenzo Gemito** (1859–1929), known for his genre studies of Naples lowlife. Another Neapolitan artist, **Domenico Morelli** (1823–1901), also specialized in historical and religious themes, passing on his penchant for drama to his student **Antonio Mancini** (1852–1930). Mancini quickly developed a style of his own which had more in common with the realist movement that by this time was sweeping through France and other parts of Europe. Shortly after, around the middle of the nineteenth century, a group of painters based in Tuscany, the **Macchiaioli** movement, also tried to get away from a more traditional approach, prefiguring to some extent the French Impressionists, though they were much less influential. They saw their brief as loosening the chains of figurative painting while also depicting real-life themes, and one of their best-known figures, **Giovannia Fattori** (1825–1908), while initially concentrating on historical scenes and portraits, eventually became a painter of landscapes in a style that was influenced by the French Barbizon school.

Giovanni Fattori taught the young **Amedeo Modigliani** (1884–1920), a painter from Livorno who lived fast and died young after he decided to ditch the relatively wholesome landscapes of the Macchiaioli to concentrate on idiosyncratic depictions of the lowlife of Paris, where he died at the age of 35. The big homegrown Italian movement of the twentieth century, however, was the **Futurists**, a quasi-fascist group of abstract painters led by the poet Filippo Marinetti, who believed in the purity of the modern world and all that went with it, including war, weaponry and in particular World War I, which unfortunately claimed their most talented painter Umberto Boccioni (1882–1916) as a victim. Other Futurists included **Giacomo Balla** (1871–1958) and **Carlo Carra** (1881–1966), and you can see much of their work in Rome's Galleria Nazionale d'Arte Moderna, along with selected works by perhaps the greatest and most influential Italian artist of the twentieth century, **Giorgio de Chirico** (1888–1978), who with Carra set up the **Metafisica movement** after World War I – a reaction against Cubism and abstraction and a precursor of Dadaism and the Surrealist movement and work of Magritte. De Chirico is known for his strange dreamlike landscapes – figurative and yet unreal – which display an almost dysfunctional vision of the modern world.

Italian architecture

The architecture of Italy perhaps doesn't dominate the Western world in the same way the country's art does, but the fact remains that tracing the history of Italy's buildings is akin to tracing that of Europe in general. The Renaissance and Baroque periods are the most distinctive, but buildings and architecture from all eras make up the fabric of the Italian landscape – more, perhaps, than any other European country.

The Greeks and the Etruscans

The first great Italian builders were the **Greeks**, who, during the Hellenistic age – between the third and first century BC – left an indelible mark on the Italian regions they occupied. Greek architecture followed a very rigid system, one that has been subsequently followed on and off by just about every architectural era at some point, so it's hard to overstate their importance, which was based on the three classical orders: the Doric, the oldest and lowest, Ionic, the middle order, and Corinthian, the highest and most florid. You can find examples of each in the various **temples** the Greeks left in the south – at Paestum, just south of Naples, and at Agrigento and Siracusa in Sicily, the latter of which has been incorporated into the city's cathedral. The Greeks built small **theatres** too, two examples of which remain in Sicily, in Taormina and Siracusa.

At the same time as the Greeks were leaving their mark on the south, the **Etruscans** occupied parts of central Italy, though they didn't leave much in the way of architecture apart from a series of necropolises, at Cerveteri and Tarquinia in Lazio, and a third-century-BC gateway in Volterra in Tuscany, part of a set of walls that once encircled this ancient Etruscan city.

The Romans

The **Romans** were great and ingenious builders, and they moved architectural forms on from the Greeks, still using columns and pediments but often making these more decorative than supportive. That they could do this was down to the invention of concrete, which allowed the Romans more flexibility in what they built, and their use of the arch, the innate strength of which allowed them to build more solid yet more diverse structures. As with everything else, the Romans were less interested in aesthetics than the Greeks, and favoured function above form at all times; they also liked to build on a large scale, preferring big, grandiose, imperial structures that showed off the power of their system and empire. The Pantheon and Colosseum in Rome are just two examples of this love of size for its own sake, but really any Roman site demonstrates it.

The Roman love of order is also evident in the planned nature of their **towns**, which had their random, poor quarters but whose commercial heart, around the main forum, had a uniform style across the empire. You can see this in Rome itself, and in the ruins at nearby Ostia Antica; while settlements like Pompeii and Herculaneum demonstrate how rigid the Roman street grid could be, with three horizontal main streets – the *decumanus inferior, major* and *superior* – crossed at right angles by other main streets or *cardos*. The forums were surrounded by shops and businesses, law courts usually in the form of a basilica – a long building with aisles either side and at least one temple – usually a rectangular colonnaded building topped with a triangular pediment with steps leading up to the main entrance.

The Romans also built for their leisure time, constructing theatres and more usually **amphitheatres** for the staging of gladiatorial games and other spectacles. The Colosseum in Rome is the best-known and largest example of this kind of building, but there are other impressive amphitheatres dotted all over Italy – in Pompeii and Pozzuoli near Naples, and in Verona, to name just the most intact examples.

Roman militarism led to the building of some structures that had no more purpose than to celebrate a famous victory or conquest of a new territory, the **triumphal arch** – a form which interestingly stayed with us right up to the nineteenth century (for example in Paris and New York). Usually they would be decorated with frieze sculptures illustrating the heroic battles. There are three intact triumphal arches in and around the Forum in Rome, and others in Benevento near Naples, in Aosta, and in Rimini and Ancona on the Adriatic coast. Another way of celebrating imperial triumphs was to decorate a **column** with sculpted friezes, but far fewer of these survive – only two in fact, in Rome, dedicated by and to the emperors Trajan and Marcus Aurelius.

Finally there are the **mausoleums** that were raised by emperors to hold the remains of themselves and their families – planned as large and fitting tributes to their imperial dynasties. As you might expect the best of these are in Rome, and most impressive is probably the mausoleum of Hadrian, which has been adapted as the Castel Sant'Angelo and is as much a medieval and Renaissance monument as a Roman one.

The early Christian and Byzantine era

The first Christian structures in Italy were probably the **catacombs**. A series of artificial underground tunnels and caverns, they're not strictly architecture as such, but some of the features – altars, arches etc, used in underground places of worship – were later adopted when Christianity became the dominant religion and Christian buildings were erected above ground, too.

The first Christian buildings adopted the Roman **basilica** as their model, for example in Santa Sabina or Santa Maria Maggiore in Rome, with one main and two side aisles, and were often built on the site of a saint's martyrdom or final resting-place, for example St Peter's on the Vatican Hill. Often they incorporated ancient columns from previous Roman buildings, and were quite bare. Later, the capital of the Church moved to Ravenna and early Christian architecture moved to a **Byzantine** style, with round churches, mosaics rather than paintings, and often a dome – a style which caught on quickly, and, as you can tell from looking at the skyline of Rome today, never really went away.

The Middle Ages

The first style of the Middle Ages, predominant during the tenth and eleventh centuries, was the **Romanesque**, identifiable by its round arches and a return to the basic basilical plan, often with transepts added – not only to add extra space but also so that the footprint of the church made the shape of a cross. There was also a tendency to build campaniles or belltowers separate from the church, and sometimes a separate baptistry too – as can be seen in Pisa, where the Duomo, Baptistry and famous leaning belltower form a perfect Romanesque ensemble. There are other superb examples of the Romanesque style in Parma and Modena, and in the south at Monreale in Sicily, whose Norman cathedral still bears a large Byzantine strain in its impressive mosaics – a bit like another Romanesque-Byzantine hybrid, the basilica of San Marco in Venice. Another fine Romanesque Italian church, and one which formed something of a blueprint for many that followed, is the church of Sant'Ambrogio in Milan.

By the twelfth century, the **Gothic** style began to dominate across Europe, characterized by its use of pointed arches, vaulting, and an emphasis on verticality, space and light. However, it never took hold in Italy to the extent it did in France or

DOMESTIC ARCHITECTURE

Italian architecture isn't just about palaces and churches: **domestic architecture** is also a source of interest and the layout of small towns and farming settlements have had as much impact on Italy's landscape as the country's better-known monuments and buildings.

HILL-TOWNS

Throughout the Middle Ages, the countryside was unsafe, unhealthy and, in many places, uncultivated, but its topography, with an abundance of hills and mountains rising steeply from fertile plains, provided natural sites for **fortified settlements** which could both remove the population from malarial swamps and bandits, and preserve the limited fertile land for cultivation.

In the period of their greatest expansion – between the twelfth and fourteenth centuries – **hill-towns** sprang up all over the peninsula. Many were superimposed on early Etruscan cities – Chiusi and Cortona – or were cave dwellings, such as Matera, in Basilicata. Most hill-towns were built within high and sometimes battlemented walls, the sheer drop afforded by these sites (often extended by the use of towers) enabling inhabitants to make good use of gravity by dropping a crushing blow onto the heads of enemies attempting to scale the walls. It was also a good way of dispatching the dead, as well as a simple form of rubbish disposal. Houses were densely packed together and constructed with materials found on or near their site, which adds to the impression that they arise naturally from their geological foundations. Most day-to-day activities were carried out in the streets, traces of which are still visible in the surviving evidence of public fountains and washhouses, wells and communal ovens. Although many hill-towns were genuinely self-contained communities, they were often under the political and economic control of the cities, particularly in north and central Italy. Each city-state set up **satellite towns** of its own, to protect trade routes or to operate as garrisons for soldiers, weaponry and food in case of war. For example, Siena established the fortified hill-town of Monteriggioni in the early thirteenth century along an important route from Rome into France, which also passed through **San Gimignano**. At roughly the same time, Florence founded similar frontier outposts, including San Giovanni Valdarno, Scarperia and Firenzuola.

VILLAS AND FARMHOUSES

If you're travelling through Tuscany, Umbria or Le Marche, you're likely to see another classic Italian structure – the **country villa** or *Casa della Mezzadria*, which became widespread during the Renaissance. Usually square in plan, it was built using a combination of brick, stone and terracotta under a tent-like roof with a dove tower (*la torre colombaia*) at its apex – doves and pigeons were adept at killing snakes and consuming weeds and also provided valuable meat to the table. The house derives its name from the system of sharecropping or *mezzadria* (based on the word *mezza* – "half"), under which the peasant farmer yielded up half his produce to the landowner. Used only occasionally by the landlord, these houses were the primary residence of the estate manager (*il fattore*), who oversaw the landlord's interests.

In contrast, the architecture of the **farming complex** (*la cascina*) was stark, with high rectangular porticoes supported by square columns. The estate accommodated four architecturally distinct elements: the owner-manager's house, which was more elaborate in design and often taller than the other buildings; housing for workers, tenement-like in character, with external balconies running along the upper floors used to dry and store crops; cow barns; and stables for horses with hay lofts above. Today, many farmhouses have been converted into tourist accommodation or *agriturismi*. In southern Italy the **masseria** is a more common type of farming settlement – massive, complex structures that dominate vast tracts of countryside. Consisting of a dense cluster of separate buildings, *masserie* were sometimes enclosed by a high-perimeter wall with defence towers built into it. At its largest a *masseria* virtually operated as a self-contained village incorporating church, school, medical clinic and shop, in addition to accommodating the full range of agricultural requirements for stabling, housing (of day-labourers called *braccianti*) and storage. In their purest, least-altered form, village *masserie* are still visible in parts of Sicily. **Trulli**, found along the coast of Puglia and inland, form one of the most remote, curious and ancient types of farm settlement in Italy. Of uncertain origin, they consist of clusters of single circular rooms, each covered by a conical roof (see p.821).

England, and as a result there are relatively few Gothic buildings here, and those that exist have often been dulled by the heavier lines of the Renaissance style that succeeded it. The style was adopted most successfully in Venice, where a particular form of florid Gothic architecture took root and is in evidence throughout the city – in the Palazzo Ducale most prominently, but also in some of the buildings on the Grand Canal, the Ca' Foscari and Palazzo Giustinian for example. Otherwise there are isolated examples of the Gothic style throughout the country: Cistercian abbeys like that of Fossanova in Lazio; some of the French-looking churches of the Angevin monarchs of Naples, in particular the monastic complex of Santa Chiara; and the cathedral in Siena, which exhibits a peculiarly Italian form of the Gothic style – very ornate on the outside, much like the nearby cathedral of Orvieto in Umbria. Perhaps the most impressive Gothic building in Italy, at least from a purists' point of view, is the cathedral of Milan, a vast building which took five hundred years to build but exhibits all the classic features of the style, with a facade and roof that is a forest of pinnacles.

The Renaissance

Spreading through Italy from the fifteenth century onwards, the Renaissance was perhaps the high point of Italian architecture, as it was in the arts and most other disciplines, and its influence on building methods and styles remains to this day. Essentially, the Renaissance ushered in the period of the professional architect rather than a collection of masons, whose vision of a building was paramount; it also led to a spread of architectural ideas and techniques to domestic as well as religious and royal buildings.

Florence was at the heart of the Renaissance and the architect who led its revival was **Filippo Brunelleschi** (1377–1446), who became famous for designing an elegant dome to top the city's Gothic cathedral – a dome which was not only a magnificent engineering feat at the time but today is still the most enduring symbol of the city. Brunelleschi was familiar with and keen to emulate the building methods and feats of ancient Rome and Greece but was also successful in creating his own style, which incorporated the methods of the past but in an increasingly modern way. As such, he more than anyone is responsible for the fact that so many modern buildings still incorporate the columns and capitals, pediments and frames of ancient Greece and Rome.

Another Florentine, **Michelozzo di Bartolomeo** (1396–1471), succeeded Brunelleschi as chief architect of the cathedral, and built the seminal Medici-Ricciardi palace – a prototype for the classic Renaissance palace, with its rustic basement and more refined first floor. He worked on a number of other Florentine buildings at the time including the "tribune" of the Annunziata church, which he designed as an ancient Roman temple – a design which was finished off by **Leone Battista Alberti** (1404–72). Alberti was like Leonardo da Vinci in that he was the complete Renaissance man, skilled in all disciplines but perhaps excelling at architecture, although unlike his contemporaries he had nothing to do with the actual building of any of his designs. His focus was on the aesthetic of a building rather than what made it stand up, and as such he could let his imagination run riot, which he did in buildings like the Palazzo Rucellai in Florence, the Tempio Malatestiano in Rimini and the church of Sant'Andrea in Mantua.

The building of the Palazzo Rucellai was overseen by **Bernardo Rossellino** (1409–64), another architect who had a big influence both in Florence and beyond. He also completed the work on Brunelleschi's cathedral dome and is perhaps best known for the design and creation of the Renaissance "new town" of Pienza for Pope Pius II.

The High Renaissance

Arguably the greatest architect of the High Renaissance was **Donato Bramante** (1443–1514), who learned a lot from his Florentine predecessors but spun it into a style of his own, in the ingenious rebuildings of the churches of San Satiro and

Santa Marie delle Grazie in Milan, and most famously in his little Tempietto in Rome, which faithfully turned back to the classical orders of the past but with a small-scale sensibility that was very much of its time. Bramante's best years were in Rome, and he was commissioned to develop the buildings of the Vatican Palace as well as rebuilding St Peter's itself. The Greek-cross plan he came up with for the latter never saw the light of day, but the building was started while he was alive and as such he must take credit for at least part of it.

The St Peter's project spanned more than a century, and Bramante's place was taken by **Michelangelo** (1475–1564), who added the dome but died before he could achieve very much. In Rome, the other great artist of the High Renaissance, **Raphael** (1483–1520), undertook architectural commissions too, designing the Chigi chapel in the church of Santa Maria del Popolo and encouraging his pupil **Giulio Romano** (1499–1546) to take on vast projects such as the Palazzo del Te in Mantua. Raphael decorated another building for the Chigi family in Rome, the Villa Farnesina, which was built to the designs of **Baldassare Peruzzi** (1481–1536), an important architect who designed much in his native Siena, and who worked on the Villa Farnese in Caprarola in Lazio with **Antonio Sangallo the Younger** (1483–1546) – the most talented member of a family of architects. Sangallo was very much the successor of Bramante and Raphael in Rome, and was responsible – again along with a very aged Michelangelo – for perhaps the city's finest Renaissance palace, the supremely elegant and dignified Palazzo Farnese, in 1514.

Meanwhile **Jacopo Sansovino** (1486–1570) was the principal architect at the time in Venice, and was responsible for many of the large public buildings around Piazza San Marco, most notably the Library and Loggetta, as well as several churches, all of which display an inventiveness that plays well with the fripperies of the existing Venetian-Gothic buildings there. Not far from Venice, in Vicenza, **Andrea Palladio** (1508–80) achieved an influence that stretched far and wide, with his refined take on Renaissance principles, building a number of palaces and villas between 1540 and 1580 that became the apotheosis of the refined country house – a symmetrical central block, with a columned portico and a central dome. Palladio rigorously followed classical rules and while this means his buildings sometimes appear dull, it is also perhaps the reason why his principles are still alive today.

In Rome, **Giacomo Vignola** (1507–73) took over as the latest architect to oversee the progress of St Peter's and at the same time built the influential church of the Gesù in the city, to a striking new design that dispensed with aisles and focused everything on the enormous cupola and the high altar. The church, or at least its facade, was finished by **Giacomo della Porta** (1533–1602), who unwittingly came up with a design that more or less every Roman church would follow for a century or more – one which used all the columns and pediments of the classical orders, but mixed them up in a new and freer way than before, with scrollwork and other features that heralded the new, flashier age of the Baroque.

The Baroque era

As in painting and sculpture, the **Baroque era** was one of massive change, with the Church defiant in the face of the Reformation sweeping across the rest of Europe, and looking for new ways to keep the faithful on message. The theatrical and dramatic nature of the painting and sculpture at the time seeped into architecture, too, and nowhere more so than in Rome, where the Baroque became the dominant architectural style – and the one that most defines the city today (much as Florence is above all defined by the Renaissance).

The chief architect of this time was **Carlo Maderno** (1556–1629), and it was he who took over and at long last finished St Peter's, some would say by ruining its original design and converting it to a Latin cross, which undermined the original dome-focused plan. It's the St Peter's of Maderno that you see today, and the church is in many ways a Baroque church inside and out – much like the piazza outside, whose columned arms are the brainchild of the greatest sculptor and architect of the Baroque age, **Gianlorenzo Bernini** (1598–1680). Bernini was a prodigy of the most amazing kind, the son of a sculptor and extremely successful – as a sculptor – while still very young. He was enormously talented and incredibly prolific, which means that he more than anyone else may have shaped the Rome you see today. Patronized as he was by the pope at the time, Urban VIII, it's Bernini's features that define the interior of St Peter's, not least his vast and flashy baldachino under the dome, and although he only gravitated towards architecture later in life he is responsible for a variety of buildings and architectural features around the rest of the city. He restored Piazza Navona and added the massive Fountain of the Four Rivers as its centrepiece; he built the small oval church of Sant'Andrea delle Quirinale, and he worked on the enormous Palazzo Barberini, the seat of his benefactor Urban VIII, as well as the Montecitorio and Chigi palaces.

It's said that the figure in Bernini's Fountain of the Four Rivers in Rome is shielding its eyes from the horrors of the nearby church of Sant'Agnese in Agone, because it was built by **Francesco Borromini** (1599–1667), his greatest rival, and the only one who came close to Bernini in talent at the time. As well as being more of an architect, Borromini was a very different sort of man to Bernini: more troubled, and much less of a man about town, but he, too, left his mark on Rome, becoming known as an architect who could come up with ingenious solutions to thorny architectural problems, often shoehorning grand buildings into sites for which they were ill-suited – for example the churches of San Carlo alle Quattro Fontane and Sant'Ivo alla Sapienza, both of which are clever and unique designs. He also worked with Bernini on the Palazzo Barberini, adding a lovely circular staircase as a counterpart to Bernini's more traditional rectangular one.

The other great Baroque architect active in Rome was **Pietro da Cortona** (1596–1669), whose contribution to the Palazzo Barberini is mentioned on p.81, but who also designed the clever and very theatrical church of Santa Maria della Pace and its small piazza.Outside of Rome, the big centres for the Baroque were in southern Italy – in **Naples**, where architects like **Cosimo Fanzago** (1591–1678) and **Fernando Sanfelice** (1675–1748) were active, and in **Lecce**, whose central core is a Baroque extravaganza, with an array of exuberant buildings fashioned from the soft local sandstone.

Neoclassicism

Like much of the rest of Europe, Italy entered a relatively bland era after the Baroque – deliberately so, for the spirit of the **Neoclassical** movement that followed was essentially a revolt against the excesses of the Baroque style, and at heart a return to the solid principles of Classicism. **Luigi Vanvitelli** (1700–73) was probably the foremost eighteenth-century Italian architect. The son of a Dutch landscape painter living in Naples, he worked with **Nicola Salvi** (1697–1751) on the Rococo fantasy, Rome's Trevi Fountain, and later, after a handful of small commissions in Rome, designed and built the enormous Royal Palace at Caserta in 1752, a massive Versailles-like blend of both perfect symmetry and ludicrous grandiloquence, as well as remodelling the more restrained Palazzo Reale in nearby Naples. His successor as most prominent Italian architect was **Giuseppe Valadier** (1762–1839), a purer exponent of Neoclassical principles, who taught architecture at Rome's Accademia San Luca and laid out many key parts of the city centre, including the great open space of the Piazza del Popolo, the Pincio and the streets leading off it.

The nineteenth century saw the construction of a series of **shopping arcades** in the big Italian cities – the Galleria Umberto in Naples, what is now the Galleria Sordi in Rome and perhaps most successfully the Galleria Vittorio Emanuele II in Milan, built in 1865 by **Giuseppe Mengoni** (1829–77), who unfortunately died when he fell from the roof a few days before it opened. Around this time, the era of the Unification of Italy, Rome was remodelled as a capital fit for the new country, and it saw a huge amount of construction, most of it a mixture of the functional nineteenth-century apartment buildings that you find in most European capitals and the odd piece of faux-grandeur like the semicircular Piazza della Repubblica at the top of Via Nazionale, or, most strikingly, the hideous Vittoriano monument overlooking Piazza Venezia, the work of one **Giuseppe Sacconi** (1854–1905) in 1895 – though even this monstrosity has become accepted over the years.

The modern era

The early **twentieth century** saw several international styles touch Italy in some way, for example Art Nouveau, but none really caught on and there wasn't a new indigenous architectural movement until the **Futurists**. Chief architect of the Futurists was **Antonio Sant'Elia** (1888–1916), who never really built anything but had far-reaching ideas about the modern city that at the time were more science fiction than anything else. **Giuseppe Terragni** (1904–43) was his true heir, an arch-rationalist who built the Casa del Fascio in Como in 1936, and was the designer of an unrealized project in Rome based on Dante's *Divine Comedy* as a tribute to the Italian poet. Terragni worked under Mussolini but died young, after which Mussolini's preferred architect became **Marcello Piacentini** (1881–1960), who was responsible for some of the most celebrated of the Duce's architecture – the Stadio dei Marmi, the housing complex of Garbatella and EUR, all in Rome, as well as the chilling open space of Brescia's Piazza della Vittoria. Piacentini worked on EUR's Palazzo dello Sport with **Pier Luigi Nervi** (1891–1979), a celebrated Italian architect who specialized in buildings based around prefabricated and reinforced concrete and who later became known for enormous works such as aircraft hangars, the trade-fair halls in Turin, and the Olympic Stadium and the Papal Audience Chamber in Rome. Nervi worked with another Italian architect, **Gio Ponti** (1891–1979), on the prestigious and at the time – 1950 – audacious Pirelli Tower in Milan, until recently still the tallest building in Italy. Ponti was a great Italian designer as well as architect and set up the bilingual design magazine *Domus*, which is still in circulation today.

Perhaps the best-known Italian architect of the current era is **Renzo Piano** (b.1937), though more for his work outside Italy than in his home country. Famous initially for his Paris Beaubourg collaboration with Richard Rogers, he has since worked on numerous prestige projects around the world – Hong Kong's airport, the redesign of Potsdamer Platz in Berlin, and many big museum projects and extensions. But he recently returned to his roots, designing the hugely successful Auditorium Parco della Musica in Rome in 2002.

An A–Z of Italian film

From the earliest days of cinema, the Italians have always been passionate movie-lovers and movie-makers. But Italy's films really came to the forefront of world cinema in the postwar period; this was partly due to the location shift from studio-based films to the country's towns and landscape. Their style and technique were ground-breaking, and the use of real sites added a dimension, a mood, which made Italian cinema linger in the memory.

8 1/2 (1963). Fellini's most autobiographical film, about a "blocked" film director recalling his past life, loves and successes. It's also perhaps his most revered movie, though you could at a pinch call it self-indulgent. The title refers to the number of films Fellini had directed up to that point.

Amarcord (1973). One of several Fellini films that uses the director's home town of Rimini as a location, this time under Fascism. Also very autobiographical, it's a tale of youth and a satire of the Church and Mussolini all rolled into one.

Aprile (1998). Nanni Moretti appears to be continually questioning the worth of everything, including his own work and in fact went too far for some critics in this movie, which focuses on his inability to decide how to finish his films – or even whether to finish them. Although poorly received, it's still a very funny film.

Bicycle Thieves (1948). A young boy is the witness to his father's humiliation in De Sica's classic movie, set in the poorer quarters of Rome, when he sees him steal a bicycle out of desperation (to get his job back) and immediately get caught. The child's illusions are dashed, and the blame is laid on society for not providing the basic human requirements, although in retrospect its message seems politically ambiguous – the masses are seen as hostile, and the only hope seems to lie in the family unit, which the hero falls thankfully back on at the end.

The Brownnose (1991). Daniele Luchetti's film satirizes the favoured Italian way of outwitting the system and getting things done – and the oiling of the wheels of bureaucracy by means of gifts and bribery involves the anti-hero in all manner of scrapes.

Cabiria (1914). The Italians were once famous for their silent costume epics, often set in the period of the Roman Empire, anticipating the Fascist nostalgia for ancient Rome by at least a decade. This film by Giovanni Pastrone, set in ancient Carthage, was the most sophisticated and innovative of the genre, with spectacular sets and lighting effects that were imitated by the American director D.W. Griffith.

Casanova (1976). Fellini's take on the notorious womanizer is an oddly (and deliberately) artificial-looking film. It wasn't actually shot in Venice, and the water in the lagoon is, in fact, a shaken plastic sheet – an odd backlash against the real landscapes of the Neorealists.

Christ Stopped at Eboli (1979). A surprisingly unincisive critique of "the problem of the south", set in a poverty-stricken mountain village in Basilicata.

Cinema Paradiso (1988). Giuseppe Tornatore's Oscar-winning movie was shot in the director's native village near Palermo, and tells its story through a series of flashbacks. The central figure, a successful film director named Salvatore, returns to the village for the funeral of the projectionist of the magical Cinema Paradiso of his childhood, only to find that it is about to be razed to make way for a car park.

The City of Women (1980). This dream-like, late Fellini film explores the great Italian director's own sexual fantasies, using Marcello Mastroianni to act them out.

Come Te Nessuno Mai (1999). This coming-of-age story by Gabriele Muccino is an interesting take on the US high-school comedy genre; his very Italian students are highly politicized youngsters, planning strikes and taking part in a 24-hour sit-in, both of which provide a backdrop for the inevitable angst and first love.

The Conformist (1970). One of Bertolucci's early films, adapted from the novel by Alberto Moravia, with a spiritually empty hero searching for father-substitutes in Fascist Rome in a dream-like jumble of flashbacks. *The Conformist* was Bertolucci's first step on the path to world recognition.

Dear Diary (1993). Director, actor and screenwriter Nanni Moretti achieved great acclaim with this film in three parts, covering such diverse subjects as twentieth-century architecture, children and telephones, Pasolini's unsolved murder, the myth of rural idyll, as well as Moretti's own fight against cancer. Much of the film is spent following Moretti on his scooter through Rome, or travelling by ferry from one island to another.

Death in Venice (1971). Style constantly threatened to overtake content in Visconti's work, and this film version of Thomas Mann's novella about a washed-up writer obsessed by a young boy is perhaps the best example, dripping with emotion and visual set-pieces. Mann's writer is a composer in Visconti's film, enabling the director to lay on the strings of Mahler with a trowel.

Decameron (1971). Pasolini's film of the Italian literary classic was a record hit at the box office because of its explicit sex scenes, although the director's intention had been political rather than salacious, with Boccaccio's fourteenth-century tales transposed from their original middle-class Florentine setting to the dispossessed of Naples.

The Earth Trembles (1948). This version of the nineteenth-century Sicilian author Giovanni Verga's novel *The House by the Medlar Tree* is about a family of fishermen destroyed by circumstance, and was shot on location on the stark Sicilian coast, using an entire village as cast, speaking in their native Sicilian (with an Italian voice-over and subtitles). There's a pervading atmosphere of stoic fatalism and a truly sophisticated visual style incorporating stunning tableaux.

The Eclipse (1962). Antonioni used the impersonal Stock Exchange building in Rome as the background to this slow-moving tale of doomed love. Short on plot, but with a memorable visual subtlety.

The Garden of the Finzi-Continis (1970). Vittorio De Sica's film about a Jewish family living in prewar Ferrara captures perfectly the elegiac, dreamy quality of Giorgio Bassani's great novel.

Germany, Year Zero (1947). The final, desolate film of Rossellini's "*War Trilogy*", set in the ruins of postwar Berlin, and telling the story of a child whom circumstances push to suicide.

Gold of Naples (1955). A film about Naples basically, directed by Vittorio De Sica, following six different Neapolitan characters whose lives are ultimately interconnected. It stars two of the most successful Neapolitan actors of all time – Sophia Loren and Toto.

Gomorrah (2008). The most notorious Italian film to emerge in recent years, based on Roberto Saviano's best-selling book about the Neapolitan Camorra. It's a tough affair, portraying a Naples you're not likely to see on any visit – it's shot in the housing projects north of the city and uses locals as actors.

Good Morning Babylon (1987). Perhaps the Taviani brothers' best film, tracking the life journeys of two brothers who make their fortune in Hollywood during the silent-movie era but end up fighting on opposite sides in World War I. A big, epic film, beautifully made.

The Gospel According to Matthew (1964). Pasolini's film is a radical interpretation of a familiar story – the life of Christ as detailed in the gospel of St Matthew. As you might expect in a Pasolini film, Christ is a radical, intent on changing the world, and not necessarily by peaceful means either.

Hands Over the City (1963). This docudrama by Francesco Rosi and starring Rod Steiger is a brutal critique of the mob-dominated construction industry in Naples. Perhaps the most shocking thing about it is that it could still be made today.

Ignorant Fairies (2001). Themes of love, loss and deception wrapped up in a soundtrack of Middle Eastern and Latin music. Commenting on the current changes in Italian film, the director Ozpetek says, "The public is more demanding now. At the same time, people have become

more willing to experiment. Before they would have looked to foreign films for that type of cinema."

Il Divo (2008). Paolo Sorrentino's biopic of the power-addicted and most influential figure of postwar Italian politics, Giulio Andreotti. which pulled no punches and perhaps should be judged by the reaction of its subject, who walked out halfway through.

Il Postino (1994). Michael Radford's film is a humorous tale set in 1930s Italy, which follows the artistic and political awakening of the central character, played by Italian comic Massimo Troisi (who sadly died soon after the film's completion).

I Vitelloni (1953). All through his long career Fellini used films as a kind of personal notebook in which to hark back to his youth. This is set in an unrecognizable Rimini, his birthplace, before the days of mass tourism.

Jesus of Nazareth (1977). Jesus is not a man of peace but the champion of the sub-proletariat and the enemy of hypocrisy in Franco Zefferelli's syrupy TV movie, filmed in the surprisingly biblical-looking landscape of the poorer regions of southern Italy and using the peasants of the area in the cast.

Journey to Italy (1953). A well-to-do couple visit Italy – specifically Naples – and inherit an estate, running into problems in their relationship. A powerful film, much of which was scripted on location or improvised, it's full of brooding atmosphere and is perhaps Rossellini's best work.

Kaos (1984). An adapation of Pirandello stories shot in scenic Sicily, both loving of the Italian landscape and redolent of a time past.

La Dolce Vita (1960). Marcello Mastroianni is the now-iconic paparazzo in Fellini's stylish 1960s classic about celebrity, style – and ultimately emptiness.

La Luna (1979). Jill Clayburgh stars in this tale of the tortured son of a tortured opera singer, directed by Bertolucci at the beginning of his career. It's hard to care about the characters, but it's undeniably beautifully put together.

La Notte (1961). The bleak townscape of industrial Milan is the backdrop for this Francesco Rosi film. Not a lot happens, but it's deftly done, with slow, lingering scenes and dialogue.

La Sconosciuta (2006). Tornatore's film involves an East European prostitute forced to abandon her children as she tries to earn a living in an Italian town.

The Last Kiss (2001). Muccino's romantic comedy dealing with panic at parenthood and the chasing of vanishing youth, won a flurry of awards and universal approval.

La Strada (1954). One of Fellini's early films, and following a recognizably realistic storyline (unlike his later movies). Also, his characters are motivated by human values rather than social ones – searching for love instead of solidarity.

L'Avventura (1960). The volcanic landscape of Sicily is the sensuous backdrop for this typically bleak yet perceptive Antonioni tale of middle-class relationships and ultimately amoral choices.

Life is Beautiful (1997). Roberto Benigni's film addresses the Holocaust and dares to combine comedy with genocide. Parents' desire to protect the innocence of their child, rather than the Holocaust itself, is the theme of the film, and Benigni (who also plays the lead role with his wife, Nicoletta Braschi, as his co-star) incorporates visual gags and a poignancy that's almost unbearable at times.

Light of My Eyes (2001). Set in Rome, this is a haunting exploration of the alienation that many feel in their lives and their romantic relationships. The story is particularly strong thanks to the character of Maria, the female lead, free of the usual stereotypes and beautifully acted and directed by Giuseppe Piccioni.

Luna Rossa (2001). Neapolitan director Antonio Capuano's mesmerizing portrayal of a Camorra family from the inside, borrowing from Greek tragedy for its structure and with a soundtrack by indie-rockers Almamegretta. Visually rich, brooding, confusing and violent, the film is artistically assured in a way that few others have been in recent years.

Many Wars Ago (1970). Rosi's film about the inhumanity of war depicts a mutiny among Italian troops on the Austrian front during World War I.

Mario's War (2005). Capuano's gritty film looks at a well-to-do Neapolitan family who foster a disturbed boy.

Marrakech Express (1989). Not the Crosby, Stills & Nash song, but a Salvatores' road movie telling the story of a group of seven young Italians setting off for Morocco in search of their friend.

Mediterraneo (1991). This Gabriele Salvatores film shows eight reluctant Italian sailors stranded on a Greek island in 1941, and recounts their gradual integration into local life. It won an Oscar for Best Foreign Language Film the year of its release.

Mery per Sempre (1989). Marco Risi films deal with specific social problems, and this follows the lives of half a dozen youngsters in prison. Its sequel, *Ragazzi Fuori* (1990), shows them fresh out of jail.

Mid-August Lunch (2008). The directorial debut of *Gomorrah* scriptwriter Gianni di Gregorio, and it couldn't be more different: a gentle comedy about a hapless middle-aged man who cares for his mother in a Trastevere flat and ends up making lunch for a group of elderly ladies. For once, a movie that celebrates being old.

Miracle in Milan (1951). Vittorio De Sica's fantastic fable, about a young man who is given a white dove which possesses the power to grant the wishes of everyone living in his slummy suburb. Surreal special effects are used to create a startling impact, for example in a shot of the hero and heroine flying high above the pinnacles of Milan cathedral on a broomstick.

Novecento (1976). Bertolucci's historical masterpiece spans the first half of the twentieth century and is deliberately epic in scale, following the fates of two brothers as they make their way through World War I, the rise of Fascism and

beyond. It's six hours long (though split into two parts), but the story is well told with a compelling narrative.

Obsession (1943). Luchino Visconti's adaptation of the American novel *The Postman Always Rings Twice* – a lowlife story of adultery and murder transposed to northern Italy – was something new in the Italian cinema: it had an honesty and intensity, a lack of glamour, that pointed the way to the Neorealist films of the immediate postwar period.

Open Doors (1990). Gianni Amelio's political drama is set in Fascist Palermo just before World War II, but its subject matter – a liberal judge being obstructed in his investigations of all-pervasive corruption – was particularly apposite at the time.

Padre Padrone (1977). The Taviani brothers' mini-epic set in Sardinia details the showdown between an overbearing father and his rebellious son.

Paisà (1946). The second film of Rossellini's "*War Trilogy*" traces the Allied Occupation north from Sicily to the Po Valley, in six self-contained episodes.

Pinocchio (2002). Adapted from the Italian writer Carlo Collodi's 1880 fable, this Roberto Benigni film grossed US$7m in its first weekend, a new record at the Italian box office. Benigni doubles as star and director, playing opposite his wife, Braschi, who is the blue-haired fairy.

Puerto Escondido (1992). A slightly far-fetched plot, in which an ordinary man is shot by bank robbers and ends up living in a commune in Mexico. But, as in all Salvatores' movies, the story is well told and ultimately meaningful.

Red Desert (1964). The alienating oil refineries and power plants at Ravenna make a perfect setting for this movie in what is the cinematic equivalent of an existential novel.

Rehearsal for War (1998). Mario Martone's film examines the Yugoslav conflict and the power of the imagination in our perception of evil.

Roma (1972). Religion is a major theme in Fellini's work, and he's at his best when satirizing the Roman Catholic Church, as in the grotesque clerical fashion parade in this, one of his best-known movies.

Rome, Open City (1945). As the tanks were rolling out of Rome in 1945, Roberto Rossellini cobbled together the bare minimum of finances, crew and equipment and started shooting this movie, using real locations, documentary footage, and low-grade film, and coming up with a grainy, idiosyncratic style that influenced not only his Italian contemporaries, but also the American film noir of the late 1940s.

Sailing Home (2001). Vincenzo Marra's movie was made on a shoestring budget: it uses fishermen rather than professional actors, is spoken in Neapolitan dialect (at home it was released with Italian subtitles) and was shot in semi-documentary style.

Salvatore Giuliano (1962). Francesco Rosi's film traces the story of a bandit from Sicily's mountains who became a hero on the island after his violent death in the 1950s. One of the best films about Sicily and the Mafia you'll ever see, and perhaps the only one that never mentions the M-word.

Senso (1954). This adaptation of a nineteenth-century novel opens to the strains of Verdi in the Venice opera house, La Fenice, one night in 1866, and is Visconti's view of the politically controversial Unification, portrayed through the lives of a few aristocrats. It was the first major Italian film to be made in colour.

Shoeshine (1946). An anatomy of a friendship between two Roman boys, destroyed first by black-marketeers, then by the police. Like many Neorealist films, children are seen as the innocent victims of adult corruption.

The Son's Room (2001). Nanni Moretti's latest film is a much darker work than the more famous *Dear Diary*, exploring a family's grief; it won a Palme d'Or at Cannes.

The Spider's Strategem (1970). Filmed in the strange, star-shaped Renaissance town of Sabbioneta near Mantua, this was the first of many feature films sponsored by RAI, the Italian state TV network, and is about a destructive father–son relationship with flashbacks to the Fascist era.

Splendor (1989). The owner of the cinema in a small provincial town is forced to sell up to a property developer in Ettore Scola's nostalgic film.

Stolen Children (1992). One of Gianni Amelio's best-known films outside Italy deals with corrupt society as seen through the eyes of a child.

Theorem (1968). Pasolini's film intercuts shots of a spiritually empty middle-class Milanese family, into which a mysterious young stranger insinuates himself, with desolate scenes of a volcanic wasteland.

Three Brothers (1981). Three different political attitudes, as the brothers of the title, reunited for their mother's funeral back home in Puglia, argue, reminisce and dream.

Toto Che Visse Due Volte (1998). Daniele Ciprì and Franco Maresco's film, set in Sicily, ruffled a few feathers with its violation of religious and sexual taboos, but this iconoclastic work didn't trouble the establishment. When the film censors banned its release, the deputy prime minister – a film buff – stepped in and disbanded their board.

Totò Looks for a Home (1949). The Neapolitan comic actor Totò had a colossal career spanning several decades. Here, he and his family search for somewhere to live in the postwar ruins of Rome, in a comic variation on a Neorealist theme.

The Tree of Wooden Clogs (1978). Ermanno Olmi's film has a cast from Bergamo speaking dialect with Italian subtitles, and was a worldwide hit.

Vento di Terra (2004). Vincenzo Marra's follow-up to *Sailing Home* was shot in Naples, and depicts life in the city as hard and unrewarding.

The Way We Laughed (1998). One of Amelio's most successful recent films, this is the story of two brothers leaving rural Sicily for Turin in the late 1950s – a nostalgic film that suggests the present-day malaises Italy is experiencing have their roots in the late 1950s and early 1960s.

We Have a Pope (2011). Nanni Moretti is seen by some as Rome's Woody Allen, chronicling the lives and neuroses of the city's inhabitants with a series of gentle, well-acted and sophisticated human comedies. His latest follows a man elected against his will as the new pope, and how he deals with the panic that ensues.

The White Sheikh (1952). The heroine of this film falls in love with the Valentino-type actor playing the romantic lead for "photo romance" comics (being shot on the coast outside Rome), and has her illusions dashed when reality intervenes and he makes a bungling attempt to seduce her.

Yesterday, Today, Tomorrow (1965). This Vittorio De Sica comedy tells the stories of three Italian women: a cigarette seller in Naples, a prostitute in Rome and the wife of an industrialist in Milan. Marcello Mastroianni is superb, as is Sophia Loren, who also gets her kit off (well, almost).

REALISM AND NEOREALISM IN ITALIAN CINEMA

The Fascist regime was surprisingly slow to recognize the potential of the cinema, but in 1937 Mussolini inaugurated "**Cinecittà**", the film studio complex just outside Rome that is still the nerve centre of the Italian movie industry, to produce a stream of propagandist films.

The late 1930s and early 1940s saw an element of documentary-style **realism** creep into film-making: contemporary social themes were addressed; non-professional actors were sometimes used; and directors – even those with the official stamp of approval – made the occasional realistic documentary, with none of the bombast or gloss of the typical Fascist film. It was on films such as these that future Neorealist directors such as Luchino Visconti, Roberto Rossellini and Vittorio De Sica worked their apprenticeships, learning techniques that they would draw on a few years later when they were allowed to unleash their creative imaginations.

In 1945, Rossellini's groundbreaking *Rome, Open City* ushered in a new wave of **Neorealism**. This movement had no manifesto, but its main exponents – again, Rossellini, De Sica and Visconti – intended their films to present the everyday stuff of life and not romantic dreams. They developed specific aims (even if they didn't always stick to them), to show real people rather than conventional heroes, real time, real light and real places – using non-actors and shooting on location, not in studios.

Books

TRAVEL CLASSICS

Henry James *Italian Hours*. Urbane travel pieces from the young James; perceptive about particular monuments and works of art, superb on the different atmospheres of Italy.

D.H. Lawrence *D.H. Lawrence and Italy*. Lawrence's three Italian travelogues collected into one volume. *Sea and Sardinia* and *Twilight in Italy* combine the author's seemingly natural ill-temper when travelling with a genuine sense of regret for a way of life almost visibly passing away. *Etruscan Places*, published posthumously, consists of his more philosophical musings on Etruscan art and civilization.

Norman Lewis *Naples '44*. Lewis was among the first Allied troops to move into Naples following the Italian surrender in World War II, and this is his diary of his experiences there – it is without question the finest thing you can read on World War II

in Italy. Lewis's more recent *In Sicily* is a broad contemporary portrait of the island he has married into and returns to frequently.

Mary McCarthy *The Stones of Florence/Venice Observed*. Published now in a single volume, this mixture of high-class reporting on the contemporary cities and anecdotal detail on their histories is one of the few accounts of these two cities that doesn't read as if it's been written in a library.

Jan Morris *Venice* (titled *The World of Venice* in US). Some people think this is the most acute modern book written about any Italian city, while others find it unbearably fey. At least give it a look. The author has more recently published what she claims is her final book, *Trieste and the Meaning of Nowhere*, an aptly elegiac salute to this curious frontier city.

CONTEMPORARY TRAVEL AND IMPRESSIONS

Matthew Fort *Eating Up Italy*. Food writer Fort's voyage around Italy on a Vespa, discovering the mainland by eating its food from region to region, and painting an eloquent picture of the contemporary country. See also his more recent *Sweet Honey, Bitter Lemons*, which focuses on Sicily.

Annie Hawes *Extra Virgin*. Belonging to the Mayes/Mayle school of expats abroad, but superior to most of the genre, this relates how two sisters overcome various adversities and much local incomprehension to find their idyll on a Ligurian mountain. It's funny and smart, interspersed with plenty of culinary culture and peasant lore.

Frances Mayes *Under the Tuscan Sun; Bella Tuscany*. The

trials and triumphs of American author and boyfriend as they renovate a farmhouse near Cortona, interspersed with recipes.

Peter Moore *Vroom with a View*. Moore is an entertaining and honest travel companion on this Bryson-like tour of Italy on a battered scooter, sharing all the highs and lows along the way. A fun and light-hearted holiday read.

★**Tim Parks** *Italian Neighbours*; *An Italian Education*; *A Season with Verona*. Novelist Tim Parks has lived in Italy since 1981. The first two of these deftly told tales of family life examine what it means to be Italian, and how national identity is absorbed. *A Season with Verona* relates his passion for his local football team, but draws in much more besides.

HISTORY

Jérôme Carcopino *Daily Life in Ancient Rome*. Detailed but never dull, this is a seminal work of Roman social history, with background on everything from education and religion to domestic daily rituals.

Edward Gibbon *The History of the Decline and Fall of the Roman Empire*. Awe inspiring in its erudition, Gibbon's masterpiece is one of the greatest histories ever written, and one of the finest compositions of English prose. Penguin publish an abridged version for those without the time to tackle the entire work.

David Gilmour *The Pursuit of Italy*. This newly published one-volume paperback is easily the most digestible history of Italy you can buy. It's full of interesting contemporary insights, and what it lacks in detail it more than makes up for in readability.

★**Paul Ginsborg** *A History of Contemporary Italy*. A scholarly but readable account of postwar Italian history, illustrating the complexity of contending economic, social and political currents. Bringing the story up to date, Ginsborg's

Italy and Its Discontents unravels the knotty background to Berlusconi's rise to power.

Robert Hughes *Rome*. The Australian art historian's stab at writing a definitive, chronological guide to the city's art and architecture, and not a bad effort – a big book, but beautifully written and very engaging, with lots of cultural and historical background, anecdote and opinion.

Valerio Lintner *A Traveller's History of Italy*. A brief history of the country, from the Etruscans right up to the present day. Well written and sensibly concise, it's just the thing for the dilettante historian of the country.

★**Mark Thompson** *The White War*. Italy's role in World War I is just a sideshow in many non-Italian histories of the conflict, and is often misrepresented within the country. Thompson's book is a magisterial account of the catastrophes and triumphs of the Italian campaign, and a brilliant explication of the part the war has played in forming the nation's self-image.

CRIME AND SOCIETY

★ **Tobias Jones** *The Dark Heart of Italy*. Written during a three-year period in Parma, this is an interconnected sequence of essays dealing with various aspects of modern Italian society. Bewildered and fascinated at every turn, Jones reveals a culture in which evasiveness and ethical malleability are as significant as the much-celebrated virtues of vivacity, charm and sophistication.

Norman Lewis *The Honoured Society*. Lewis's classic account of the Mafia, originally written in the 1960s, is still the most enjoyable introduction to the subject available.

★ **Peter Robb** *Midnight in Sicily*. The Australian Robb spent fifteen years in the Italian South and this book focuses on the structure of the Mafia, the trials of the bosses in the 1980s and the high-profile assassinations that ensued. It's a thorough, fast-paced study, providing deep insights into the dynamics of Sicilian society.

★ **Robert Saviano** *Gomorrah*. Saviano's exposé of the Neapolitan Camorra is the first to have dished the dirt on the most violent grouping of Italy's various organized criminal gangs, and he is currently in hiding because of it. At heart it's a passionate protest against a problem which only seems to get worse, and has been made into a well-received movie.

Alexander Stille *Excellent Cadavers*. Stille traces the rise, successes, failures and eventual assassinations of anti-Mafia magistrates Giovanni Falcone and Paolo Borsellino, as well as blowing the cover of Andreotti and Craxi.

ART, ARCHITECTURE AND ARCHEOLOGY

★ **Frederick Hartt** *History of Italian Renaissance Art: Painting, Sculpture and Architecture* (o/p). If one book on this vast subject can be said to be indispensable, this is it – due to both the comprehensiveness of its coverage and the range of its illustrations.

Anthony Hughes *Michelangelo*. An ideal single-volume introduction to arguably the greatest artist of the Renaissance, which sets Michelangelo within his historical and political context.

Ross King *Brunelleschi's Dome*. An intriguing account of the architectural innovations and intense rivalries behind the construction of Florence's Duomo. It also paints an engaging picture of life in the medieval city.

Peter Murray *The Architecture of the Italian Renaissance*. Begins with Romanesque buildings and finishes with Palladio – valuable both as a gazetteer of the main monuments and as a synopsis of the underlying concepts.

Catherine Puglisi *Caravaggio*. An intelligent and engaging study of one of the most innovative artists of the Renaissance, enhanced with sumptuous colour plates throughout.

ITALIAN CRIME FICTION

Andrea Camilleri *The Shape of Water*; *The Terracotta Dog*; *The Snack Thief*; and others. Camillieri is perhaps the best known and most translated of the current wave of Italian crime writers, and his Inspector Montalbano series, set in Sicily, has achieved worldwide popularity. Rightly so – the plots, characterization (Montelbano is a classic maverick cop with a complicated personal life), and contemporary Sicilian background make for an absorbing and entertaining read.

Michael Dibdin *Cabal*; *Ratking*; and others. Not all of the late Michael Dibdin's novels are set in Rome, but the author was as interested in Italy as in his characters, with the result that his Aurelio Zen novels tell us plenty about the way Italian society operates – and they're well-plotted whodunnits to boot, with Zen as a classically eccentric, loner detective.

Michele Giuttari *A Florentine Death*; *A Death in Tuscany*; *The Death of a Mafia Don*. Giuttari is the former police chief of Florence, and he uses all his knowledge and experience to put together these tightly plotted police procedurals, with lots of local colour.

Donna Leon *Death at La Fenice*; *A Venetian Reckoning*; *Fatal Remedies*; and others. Venice-based crime thrillers featuring Guido Brunetti, the honest police *commissario* in a world of high-level intrigue and corruption.

Iain Pears *The Raphael Affair*; *The Bernini Bust*; *The Titian Committee*; *Death and Restoration*; and others. Recently reissued, and rightly so, Pears' successful series of thrillers with an art historical theme are all set in Rome and make great holiday reading. There are plenty of local settings and descriptions, not to mention fast-paced art-world intrigue, with robbery, forgery and general skulduggery.

Douglas Preston with Mario Spezi *The Monster of Florence*. Between 1974 and 1985 the area around Florence was terrorized by Italy's most notorious serial killer. The crimes were truly monstrous, but Preston describes them without undue prurience, in a gripping book which develops into a hard-hitting indictment of the still unfinished investigation. Essentially a modern Italian tale of incompetent officials, deranged conspiracy theorists and unbelievable witnesses.

Nigel Spivey *Etruscan Art*. An in-depth look at the art of the elusive Etruscans, whose history and lives are told through their tomb art. Sumptuously illustrated throughout, this is an intriguing story of a long-lost race.

Giorgio Vasari *Lives of the Artists*. The sixteenth-century artist's classic work on his predecessors and contemporaries, with essays on Giotto, Brunelleschi, Mantegna, Leonardo, Michelangelo, Raphael and more. The first real work of art history and still among the most penetrating books you can read on Italian Renaissance art.

FOOD AND DRINK

★ **Accademia Italiana della Cucina** *La Cucina*. Perhaps the widest selection of authentic Italian recipes you can find in one volume, and certainly the best available introduction to the regional variations in Italian cuisine. A lovely lesson in the simplicity and diversity of Italian food, though perhaps not quite as practical as Marcella Hazan's book.

Elizabeth David *Italian Food*. The writer who introduced Italian cuisine – and ingredients – to Britain. Ahead of its time when it was published in the 1950s, and imbued with all the enthusiasm and diversity of Italian cookery. An inspirational book.

★ **Marcella Hazan** *The Classic Italian Cookbook*. A step-by-step guide that never compromises the spirit or authenticity of the recipes, Hazan draws her recipes from all over the peninsula, emphasizing the intrinsically regional nature of Italian food. The best Italian cookbook for the novice in the kitchen.

Fred Plotkin *Italy for the Gourmet Traveller*. Comprehensive, region-by-region guide to the best of Italian cuisine, with a foodie's guide to major towns and cities, a gazetteer of restaurants and specialist food and wine shops, and descriptions of local dishes, with recipes.

Claudia Roden *The Food of Italy*. A culinary classic, this regional guide takes in local recipes from the people for whom they are second nature. Authentic and accessible.

Michèle Shah *Wines of Italy*. An excellent pocket guide to the regional wines and winemaking techniques of Italy, with up-to-date information on the best current producers and labels.

ANCIENT AND ITALIAN CLASSICS

Dante Alighieri *The Divine Comedy*. No work in any other language bears comparison with Dante's poetic exegesis of the moral scheme of God's Creation; in late medieval Italy it was venerated both as a book of almost scriptural authority and as the ultimate refinement of the vernacular Tuscan language.

Giovanni Boccaccio *The Decameron*. Set in the plague-racked Florence of 1348, this assembly of one hundred short stories is a fascinating social record as well as a constantly diverting comic sequence.

Benvenuto Cellini *Autobiography*. The shamelessly egocentric record of the travails and triumphs of the sculptor and goldsmith's career – one of the freshest literary productions of its time.

Livy *The Early History of Rome*. Lively chronicle of the city's evolution from the days of Romulus and Remus.

Alessandro Manzoni *The Betrothed*. No poolside thriller, but a skilful melding of the romance of two young lovers and a sweeping historical drama, all suffused with an almost religious sense of human destiny. First published in 1823, but reissued in 1840 after Manzoni had improved the novel's diction through study of the Tuscan dialect – a landmark in the transition towards linguistic nationalism.

Suetonius *The Twelve Caesars*. The inside story of Caligula, Nero, Domitian and others, elegantly written and very enjoyable, by the private secretary to Hadrian, who made the most of his unique access to the annals of recent imperial history.

Virgil *The Aeneid*. The central work of Latin literature, depicting the adventures of Aeneas after the fall of Troy, and thus celebrating Rome's heroic lineage.

MODERN ITALIAN LITERATURE

Niccolò Ammaniti *I'm Not Scared*; *Steal You Away*; *The Crossroads*; *Me & You*. One of the bright young lights of contemporary Italian literature, the Roman Ammaniti is a bit of a star in his own country, and becoming increasingly popular overseas, with all four of his shortish novels available in translation. His style is haunting, usually in the first-person, and full of suspense, as it deals with the secret, distasteful and frequently horrifying side of life, often through the eyes of children.

Giorgio Bassani *The Garden of the Finzi-Continis*. Gentle, elegiac novel, set in the Jewish community of Ferrara during the Fascist period, on the eve of the mass deportations to Germany. Infused with a sense of regret for a Europe that died with the war.

Italo Calvino *If on a Winter's Night a Traveller*. Calvino's fiction became increasingly concerned with the nature of fiction itself, and this witty novel marks the culmination of the process. Other titles include *The Castle of Crossed Destinies*, *Invisible Cities*, *Difficult Loves* and *Mr Palomar*.

Umberto Eco *The Name of the Rose*. An allusive, tightly plotted, monastic detective story. Check out also his equally hyped, though rather more impenetrable, *Foucault's Pendulum* and *Baudolino*, another medieval fable, this time interspersed with reflections on the postmodern age.

Carlo Emilio Gadda *That Awful Mess on Via Merulana.* Superficially a detective story, this celebrated modernist novel is so dense a weave of physical reality and literary diversions that the reader is led away from a solution rather than towards it; it enjoys the sort of status in Italian fiction that *Ulysses* has in English.

Natalia Ginzburg *The Things We Used to Say.* The constraints of family life are a dominant theme in Ginzburg's writing, and her own upbringing is the source material for this characteristically rigorous yet lyrical work.

Giuseppe di Lampedusa *The Leopard.* Perhaps the most famous Sicilian novel, recounting the dramatic nineteenth-century transition from Bourbon to Piemontese rule from an aristocrat's point of view. A good character-study and rich with incidental detail.

Carlo Levi *Christ Stopped at Eboli.* First published in 1945, this memoir, describing Levi's exile to a remote region of Basilicata by the Fascists, was the first to awaken modern Italy to the plight of its southern regions.

★ **Primo Levi** *If This is a Man/The Truce; The Periodic Table.* Levi's experiences in Auschwitz are the main subject of *If This is a Man,* while *The Truce* records his journey back to Turin after his liberation. Levi's training as a chemist forms the background of *The Periodic Table,* a mixture of autobiographical reflection and practical observation. All show an unwavering exactitude of recollection and judgement.

Margaret Mazzantini *Don't Move.* Intense psychological novel of midlife crisis, sex and obsession in Rome that was a massive bestseller in Italy and made into a movie directed by the author's husband. The city and its outskirts form a bleak, rain-soaked backdrop.

Elsa Morante *History.* Capturing daily Roman life during the last war, this is probably the most vivid fictional picture of the conflict as seen from the city.

★ **Alberto Moravia** *The Conformist.* A psychological novel about a man sucked into the abyss of Fascism by his desperation to conform; *The Woman of Rome* is an earlier work, a teeming and sensual novel, centred on the activities of a Roman prostitute.

Pier Paolo Pasolini *A Violent Life.* This super-naturalistic evocation of life in the slum areas of Rome caused a scandal when it was published in 1959, but is now considered one of the classics of Italian postwar fiction.

Cesare Pavese *Moon and the Bonfire* (o/p); *Devil in the Hills.* Exploring the difficulties of achieving an acceptance of one's past, *Moon and the Bonfire* was written shortly before Pavese's suicide at the age of 42; *Devil in the Hills* is an early collection of tales of adolescence in and around Turin.

★ **Leonardo Sciascia** *Sicilian Uncles; The Wine Dark Sea; The Day of the Owl* (o/p). Writing again and again about his native Sicily, Sciascia has made of that island "a metaphor of the modern world". Economically written, Sciascia's short stories are packed with incisive insights, and infused with the author's humane and sympathetic views of its people. *The Moro Affair* is an illuminating account of the kidnapping of the ex-prime minister Aldo Moro by the Brigate Rosse in 1978.

Ignazio Silone *Fontamara; Bread and Wine; The Seed Beneath the Snow.* From his exile in Switzerland, Silone wrote about his native Abruzzo, and these three novels have now been published in one volume by Steerforth Press, titled *The Abruzzo Trilogy. Fontamara* tells the tale of a small village driven to revolt against its landlords and the Fascist thugs sent to enforce their rule, while *Bread and Wine* is a more introspective work, examining Silone's political commitment and religious beliefs.

Italo Svevo *Zeno's Conscience.* Complete critical indifference to his early efforts so discouraged Svevo that he gave up writing altogether, until encouraged by James Joyce, who taught him English in Trieste. The resultant novel is a unique creation, a comic portrait of a character at once wistful, helpless and irrepressible.

ANCIENT ROME IN FICTION

Robert Graves *I Claudius; Claudius the God.* Having translated Suetonius' *Twelve Caesars,* Graves used the madness and corruption of the Imperial Age to create a gripping, if not necessarily historically accurate, tale.

Robert Harris *Imperium; Lustrum.* No one brings to life the Roman Republic quite as vividly as Harris, viewing the power struggles and intrigues of the main protagonists through the eyes of Cicero's faithful secretary, the freed slave Tiro.

Conn Iggulden *The Gates of Rome; The Death of Kings; The Field of Swords; The Gods of War.* Iggulden's engaging four-book series, *Emperor,* is a historical romp documenting the rise and fall of Julius Caesar, from the rites of passage of the young man during the turmoil of the last decades of the Republic to his eventual murder in Pompey's theatre.

Allan Massie *Augustus; Tiberius; Caesar; Caligula.* Massie's series of novels aspires to re-create the Roman Empire at its height through the imagined memoirs of its key figures, and does so with great success, in a series of novels that offers a well-researched but palatable way into the minutiae of the era.

Thornton Wilder *The Ides of March.* A suppositional reconstruction of the last year of the life of Julius Caesar through his letters, writings and reports.

Giovanni Verga *Cavalleria Rusticana; Sparrow; The House by the Medlar Tree*. Verga, born in the nineteenth century in Catania, spent several years in various European salons before coming home to write his best work. Much of it is a reaction against the pseudo-sophistication of society circles, stressing the simple lives of ordinary people, accompanied by a heavy smattering of emotion, wounded honour and feuds to the death.

Elio Vittorini *Conversations in Sicily*. A Sicilian emigrant returns from the north of Italy after fifteen years to see his mother on her birthday. The conversations of the title are with the people he meets on the way, and reveal a poverty- and disease-ridden Sicily.

William Weaver (ed) *Open City: Seven Writers in Postwar Rome* (o/p). A nicely produced anthology of pieces by the cream of Italy's twentieth-century novelists – Bassani, Silone, Ginzburg, Moravia, among others – selected and with an introduction by one of the most eminent Italian translators of recent years.

LITERATURE SET IN ITALY

E.M. Forster *A Room with a View*. Set in and around Florence, this is the ultimate novel about how the nature of the Italian light, temperament and soul can make the English upper classes lose their heads.

James Hamilton-Paterson *Cooking with Fernet-Branca*. An excellent comic novel which is packed full of laughs at everyone's expense – sad middle-aged writers, foodies, and most of all the middle-class English expat community in Tuscany.

Nathaniel Hawthorne *The Marble Faun*. A nineteenth-century take on the lives of Anglo-American expats in the Eternal City: sculptors, passionate lovers – the usual mad mix and excessive goings-on that you'll still find today.

Ernest Hemingway *A Farewell to Arms*. Hemingway's first novel is partly based on his experiences as a teenage ambulance-driver on Italy's northeast front during World War I – a terse account of the futility of this particular corner of the conflict.

Patricia Highsmith *The Talented Mr Ripley*. The novel follows the fortunes of the eponymous hero through Italy as he exchanges his own identity for that of the man he has murdered. Good locations in the film of the book, starring Matt Damon and directed by Anthony Minghella.

Thomas Mann *Death in Venice*. Irascible and ultra-traditional old novelist visits Venice to recover after a breakdown and becomes obsessed with a beautiful young boy, awakening an internal debate about the nature of beauty and art to which the city is a fitting and resonant backdrop.

Ian McEwan *The Comfort of Strangers*. An ordinary young English couple fall foul of a sexually ambiguous predator in a Venice which is never named, but evoked by means of arch little devices such as quotes from Ruskin.

Stendhal *The Charterhouse of Parma*. A panoramic nineteenth-century French novel that dramatizes the struggles and intrigues of the Italian Papal States before Unification. A wonderful read, and a good insight into the era to boot.

Irving Stone *The Agony and the Ecstasy*. Stone's dramatized life of Michelangelo, popular "faction" that is entertaining even if it doesn't exactly get to the root of the artist's work and times.

Barry Unsworth *After Hannibal; Stone Virgin* (o/p). *After Hannibal* is a black comedy of expat life, set in Umbria, where the author lives. The earlier *Stone Virgin*, set in Venice, is about a conservation expert who falls under the spell of a statue of the Madonna he is working on.

Salley Vickers *Miss Garnet's Angel*. The unique atmosphere of Venice is captured in this tale of a desiccated spinster awakened by the city to the finer things in life. The author's sound knowledge of the place and its art triumphs over a potentially hackneyed tale.

Italian

The ability to speak English confers prestige in Italy, and there's often no shortage of people willing to show off their knowledge. But using at least some Italian, however tentatively, can mark you out from the masses in a country used to hordes of tourists. The words and phrases below should help you master the basics, and the *Rough Guide Italian Phrasebook* – which packs a huge amount of vocabulary into a handy dictionary format – is a useful back-up. There are lots of good pocket dictionaries – the Collins range represents the best all-round choice.

Pronunciation

Italian is one of the easiest European languages to learn, especially if you already have a smattering of French or Spanish. **Pronunciation** is straightforward: Italian words are generally stressed on the penultimate syllable unless an accent (´ or `) denotes otherwise, and words are usually enunciated with exaggerated, open-mouthed clarity.

The only difficulties you're likely to encounter are the few consonants that are different from English:

c before e or i is pronounced as in **ch**urch, while **ch** before the same vowels is hard, as in **c**at.

sci or **sce** are pronounced as in **sh**eet and **sh**elter respectively.

g is soft before e or i, as in **g**eranium; hard before h, as in **g**arlic.

gn has the ni sound of o**ni**on.

gl in Italian is softened to something like li in English, as in sta**ll**ion.

h is not aspirated, as in **h**onour.

When speaking to strangers, the third person is the polite form (ie *lei* instead of *tu* for "you"). It's also worth remembering that Italians don't use "please" and "thank you" half as much as English speakers: it's all implied in the tone, though if in doubt, err on the polite side.

WORDS AND PHRASES

BASICS

good morning	buongiorno
good afternoon/evening	buonasera
goodnight	buonanotte
hello/goodbye	ciao (informal; to strangers use phrases above)
goodbye	arrivederci
yes	sì
no	no
please	per favore
thank you (very much)	(molte/mille) grazie
you're welcome	prego
all right/that's ok	va bene
how are you?	come stai/sta? (informal/formal)
I'm fine	bene
do you speak English?	parla Inglese?

I don't understand	non ho capito
I don't know	non lo so
excuse me	mi scusi
excuse me (in a crowd)	permesso
I'm sorry	mi dispiace
I'm here on holiday	Sono qui in vacanza
I'm English/Irish/ Welsh/Scottish/ American/ Australian/ Canadian/ a New Zealander	Sono Inglese/Irlandese/ Gallese/Scozzese/ Americano/a (m/f)/ Australiano/a (m/f)/ Canadese/ Neozelandese
What's your name?	Come ti chiami/si chiama? (informal/formal)
wait a minute!	aspetta!
let's go!	andiamo!
here/there	qui/là

good/bad	buono/cattivo	when?	quando?
big/small	grande/píccolo	what?	cosa?
cheap/expensive	economico/caro	what is it?	cos'è?
early/late	presto/tardi	how much/many?	quanto/quanti?
hot/cold	caldo/freddo	why?	perché?
near/far	vicino/lontano	is it/is there…?	c'è…?
quickly/slowly	velocemente/lentamente	What time does it open/close?	A che ora apre/chiude?
		What's it called in Italian?	Come si chiama in Italiano?

QUESTIONS

where?	dove?
where is/are…?	dov'è/dove sono…?

Travel and directions

Where is…?	Dov'è…?	ferry	il traghetto
How do I get to…?	Per arrivare a…?	hydrofoil	l'aliscafo
the centre	il centro	plane	l'aereo
the (main) square	la piazza (principale)	train	il treno
the station	la stazione	Do I have to change?	Devo cambiare?
the bus station	l'autostazione	Which platform does it leave from?	Da quale binario parte?
the port	il porto		
Turn left/right	Giri a sinistra/destra	How long does it take?	Quanto ci vuole?
Go straight on	Vai sempre diritto	Can you tell me when to get off?	Mi può dire dove scendere?
How far is it to…?	Quant'è lontano a…?		
What time does the… arrive/leave?	A che ora arriva/parte…?	I'd like a ticket to…	Vorrei un biglietto per…
		one-way	solo andata
bus	l'autobus	return	andata e ritorno
coach	il pullman		

SIGNS

entrance/exit	entrata/uscita	open/closed	aperto/chiuso
arrivals/departures	arrivi/partenze	closed for restoration	chiuso per restauro
free entrance	ingresso líbero	closed for holidays	chiuso per ferie
gentlemen/ladies	signori/signore	pull/push	tirare/spingere
wc	gabinetto/bagno	cash desk	cassa
vacant/engaged	libero/occupato	out of order	guasto
no smoking	vietato fumare	ring the bell	suonare il campanello

ACCOMMODATION

I'd like to book a room	Vorrei prenotare una cámera	hot/cold water	acqua calda/fredda
		How much is it?	Quanto costa?
I have a booking	Ho una prenotazione	Is breakfast included?	È compresa la prima colazione?
Is there a hotel nearby?	C'è un albergo qui vicino?		
Do you have…?	Ha…?	Do you have anything cheaper?	Ha qualcosa che costa di meno?
a single/ double/triple	una cámera singola/ doppia/tripla	Can I see the room?	Posso vedere la cámera?
a bed	un letto	I'll take it	Lo/La prendo (m/f)
for one/two/three night/s	per una/due/tre notti	hotel	albergo
for one/two week/s	per una/due settimana/e	hostel	ostello
with a double bed	con un letto matrimoniale	campsite	campeggio
		lift	ascensore
with twin beds	con due letti	key	chiave
with a shower/bath	con doccia/bagno	full/half board	pensione completa/ mezza pensione
with a balcony	con balcone		

RESTAURANTS

I'd like to reserve a table (for two)	Vorrei riservare una távola (per due)	Is service included?	Il servizio è incluso?
Can we sit outside?	Possiamo sederci fuori?	(set) menu	menù (fisso)
Can I order?	Posso ordinare?	waiter/waitress	cameriere/a
I'm a vegetarian	Sono vegetariano/a (m/f)	knife	coltello
Does it contain meat?	C'è carne dentro?	fork	forchetta
It's good	È buono	spoon	cucchiaio
The bill, please	Il conto, per favore	plate	piatto
		bicchiere	glass

SHOPPING AND SERVICES

I'd like to buy…	Vorrei comprare…	bank	banca
How much does it cost/ do they cost?	Quanto costa/cóstano?	money exchange	cambio
		post office	posta
It's too expensive	È troppo caro	tourist office	ufficio turistico
with/without	con/senza	shop	negozio
more/less	più/meno	supermarket	supermercato
enough, no more	basta	market	mercato
I'll take it	Lo/la prendo (m/f)	ATM	Bancomat
Do you take credit cards?	Accettate carte di credito?		

DAYS, TIMES AND MONTHS

What time is it?	Che ore sono?	Friday	venerdì
It's nine o'clock	Sono le nove	Saturday	sabato
today	oggi	Sunday	domenica
tomorrow	domani	January	gennaio
day after tomorrow	dopodomani	February	febbraio
yesterday	ieri	March	marzo
now	adesso	April	aprile
later	più tardi	May	maggio
in the morning	di mattina	June	giugno
in the afternoon	nel pomeriggio	July	luglio
in the evening	di sera	August	agosto
Monday	lunedì	September	settembre
Tuesday	martedì	October	ottobre
Wednesday	mercoledì	November	novembre
Thursday	giovedì	December	dicembre

NUMBERS

1	uno	16	sedici
2	due	17	diciassette
3	tre	18	diciotto
4	quattro	19	diciannove
5	cinque	20	venti
6	sei	21	ventuno
7	sette	22	ventidue
8	otto	30	trenta
9	nove	40	quaranta
10	dieci	50	cinquanta
11	undici	60	sessanta
12	dodici	70	settanta
13	tredici	80	ottanta
14	quattordici	90	novanta
15	quindici	100	cento

101	centuno	500	cinquecento
110	centodieci	1000	mille
200	duecento	5000	cinquemila

Italian menu reader

BASICS AND SNACKS

aceto	vinegar
aglio	garlic
biscotti	biscuits
burro	butter
caramelle	sweets
cioccolato	chocolate
formaggio	cheese
frittata	omelette
marmellata	jam
olio	oil
olive	olives
pane	bread
pepe	pepper
riso	rice
sale	salt
uova	eggs
yogurt	yogurt
zucchero	sugar
zuppa	soup

THE FIRST COURSE (IL PRIMO)

brodo	clear broth
minestrina	clear broth with small pasta shapes
minestrone	thick vegetable soup
pasta al forno	baked pasta, usually with minced meat, tomato and cheese
pasta e fagioli	soup with pasta and beans
pastina in brodo	pasta in clear broth
stracciatella	broth with egg

PASTA

bucatini	thick, hollow spaghetti-type pasta common in Rome and Lazio
cannelloni	thick pasta tubes usually filled with veal
capellini	thin noodles of pasta, thicker than *capelli d'angeli*
conchiglie	seashell-shaped pasta shapes, good for capturing thick sauces
farfalle	literally "butterflies", or bow ties

fettuccine	flat, ribbon-like egg noodles
fusilli	tight spirals of pasta
gnocchi	potato and pasta dumplings, often served *"alla sorrentina"*, or with tomato and basil sauce
lasagne	big squares of egg noodles, most commonly baked in the oven with white sauce and beef *ragù*
linguini	thin, flat noodles, often served with seafood
macaroni	small tubes of pasta
maltagliati	flat triangles of pasta, often used in soup
orecchiette	small ear-shaped pieces of pasta
paccheri	large tubes of pasta
panzarotti	filled pasta shapes from Puglia
pappardelle	thick, flat egg noodles
penne	the most common tubes of pasta
pici	thick Tuscan spaghetti
ravioli	literally "little turnips" – flat, square parcels of filled pasta
rigatoni	large, curved and ridged tubes of pasta – larger than *penne* but smaller than *paccheri*
spaghetti	the most common pasta shape of all – long, thin, non-egg noodles
tagliatelle	flat ribbon egg noodles, slightly thinner than *fettuccine*
tonnarelli	another name for *bucatini*
tortellini/tortolloni	triangles of filled pasta folded into rounded shapes
tortiglioni	narrow *rigatoni*

PASTA SAUCE (SALSA)

amatriciana	cubed bacon and tomato
arrabbiata	("angry") spicy tomato with chillies
bolognese	meat
burro	butter
carbonara	cream, ham and beaten egg
funghi	mushroom
panna	cream
parmigiano	parmesan cheese
peperoncino	olive oil, garlic and fresh chillies
pesto	ground basil, garlic and pine nuts
pomodoro	tomato
puttanesca	"whorish", with tomato, anchovy, olive oil and oregano
ragù	meat
vongole	clams

THE SECOND COURSE (IL SECONDO)

MEAT (CARNE)

agnello	lamb
bistecca	steak
carpaccio	slices of raw beef
cervello	brain, usually calves'
cinghiale	wild boar
coniglio	rabbit
costolette	cutlet, chop
fegato	liver
maiale	pork
manzo	beef
ossobuco	shin of veal
pancetta	bacon
pollo	chicken
polpette	meatballs
rognoni	kidneys
salsiccia	sausage
saltimbocca	veal with ham
spezzatino	stew
trippa	tripe
vitello	veal

FISH (PESCE) AND SHELLFISH (CROSTACEI)

acciughe	anchovies
anguilla	eel
aragosta	lobster
baccalà	dried salted cod
calamari	squid
cefalo	grey mullet
cozze	mussels
dentice	sea bream
gamberetti	shrimps
gamberi	prawns
granchio	crab
merluzzo	cod
ostriche	oysters
pesce spada	swordfish
polpo	octopus
rospo	monkfish
sampiero	John Dory
sarde	sardines
sogliola	sole
tonno	tuna
trota	trout
vongole	clams

VEGETABLES (CONTORNI) AND SALAD (INSALATA)

asparagi	asparagus	funghi	mushrooms
carciofi	artichokes	insalata verde/mista	green salad/mixed salad
carciofini	artichoke hearts	lenticchie	lentils
cavolfiori	cauliflower	melanzane	aubergine
cavolo	cabbage	patate	potatoes
cipolla	onion	peperoni	peppers
erbe aromatiche	herbs	piselli	peas
fagioli	beans	pomodori	tomatoes
fagiolini	green beans	radicchio	red salad leaves
finocchio	fennel	spinaci	spinach

COOKING TERMS

al dente	firm, not overcooked	alla milanese	fried in egg and breadcrumbs
al ferri	grilled without oil		
al forno	baked	alla pizzaiola	cooked with tomato sauce
al sangue	rare	allo spiedo	on the spit
alla brace	barbecued	arrosto	roast
alla griglia	grilled	ben cotto	well done

bollito/lesso	boiled	in umido	stewed
cotto	cooked	ripieno	stuffed
crudo	raw	stracotto	braised, stewed
fritto	fried		

CHEESE (FORMAGGIO)

dolcelatte	creamy blue cheese	pecorino	strong, hard sheep's cheese
fontina	northern Italian cheese, often used in cooking	provola/provolone	smooth, round mild cheese, made from buffalo or sheep's milk; sometimes smoked
gorgonzola	soft, strong, blue-veined cheese		
mozzarella	soft white cheese, traditionally made from buffalo's milk	ricotta	soft, white sheep's cheese

DESSERTS (DOLCI), FRUIT (FRUTTA) AND NUTS (NOCI)

amaretti	macaroons	limone	lemon
ananas	pineapple	macedonia	fruit salad
anguria	watermelon	mandorle	almonds
arachidi	peanuts	mele	apples
arance	oranges	melone	melon
banane	bananas	pere	pears
cacchi	persimmons	pesche	peaches
ciliegie	cherries	pinoli	pine nuts
coccomero	watermelon	pistacchio	pistachio nut
crostata	pastry tart with jam or chocolate topping	sorbetto	sorbet
		torta	cake, tart
fichi	figs	uva	grapes
fichi d'india	prickly pears	zabaglione	dessert made with eggs, sugar and Marsala wine
frágole	strawberries		
gelato	ice cream	zuppa inglese	trifle

DRINKS

acqua minerale (con gas/senza gas)	mineral water (fizzy/still)	succo	concentrated fruit juice with sugar
aranciata	orangeade	tè	tea
birra	beer	tonica	tonic water
bottiglia	bottle	vino	wine
caffè	coffee	rosso	red
cioccolato caldo	hot chocolate	bianco	white
ghiaccio	ice	rosato	rosé
granita	iced drink with coffee or fruit	secco	dry
		dolce	sweet
latte	milk	litro	litre
limonata	lemonade	mezzo	half
spremuta	fresh fruit juice	quarto	quarter
spumante	sparkling wine	caraffa	carafe
		salute!	cheers!

Glossary of artistic and architectural terms

agora square or marketplace in an ancient Greek city

ambo a kind of simple pulpit, popular in Italian medieval churches

apse semicircular recess at the altar (usually eastern) end of a church

architrave the lowest part of the entablature

atrium inner courtyard

baldacchino a canopy on columns, usually placed over the altar in a church

basilica originally a Roman administrative building, adapted for early churches; distinguished by lack of transepts

belvedere a terrace or lookout point

caldarium the steam room of a Roman bath

campanile belltower, sometimes detached, usually of a church

capital top of a column

Catalan-Gothic hybrid form of architecture, mixing elements of fifteenth-century Spanish and northern European styles

cella sanctuary of a temple

chancel part of a church containing the altar

chiaroscuro the balance of light and shade in a painting, and the skill of the artist in depicting the contrast between the two

ciborium another word for baldacchino, see above

cornice the top section of a classical facade

cortile galleried courtyard or cloisters

cosmati work decorative mosaic-work on marble, usually highly coloured, found in early Christian Italian churches, especially in Rome; derives from the name Cosma, a common name among families of marble workers at the time

cryptoporticus underground passageway

cyclopean walls fortifications built of huge, rough stone blocks, common in the pre-Roman settlements of Lazio

Decumanus Maximus the main street of a Roman town – the second cross-street was known as the Decumanus Inferiore

entablature the section above the capital on a classical building, below the cornice

ex voto artefact designed in thanksgiving to a saint

fresco wall-painting technique in which the artist applies paint to wet plaster for a more permanent finish

loggia roofed gallery or balcony

metope a panel on the frieze of a Greek temple

Mithraism pre-Christian cult associated with the Persian god of light, who slew a bull and fertilized the world with its blood

nave central space in a church, usually flanked by aisles

Pantocrator usually refers to an image of Christ, portrayed with outstretched arms

piano nobile main floor of a palazzo, usually the first

polyptych painting on several joined wooden panels

portico covered entrance to a building, or porch

presepio/presepe Christmas crib

putti cherubs

reliquary receptacle for a saint's relics, usually bones; often highly decorated

sgraffito decorative technique whereby one layer of plaster is scratched to form a pattern

stereobate visible base of any building, usually a Greek temple

stucco plaster made from water, lime, sand and powdered marble, used for decorative work

thermae baths, usually elaborate buildings in Roman villas

triptych painting on three joined wooden panels

trompe l'oeil work of art that deceives the viewer by means of tricks with perspective

Small print and index

A ROUGH GUIDE TO ROUGH GUIDES

Published in 1982, the first Rough Guide – to Greece – was a student scheme that became a publishing phenomenon. Mark Ellingham, a recent graduate in English from Bristol University, had been travelling in Greece the previous summer and couldn't find the right guidebook. With a small group of friends he wrote his own guide, combining a highly contemporary, journalistic style with a thoroughly practical approach to travellers' needs.

The immediate success of the book spawned a series that rapidly covered dozens of destinations. And, in addition to impecunious backpackers, Rough Guides soon acquired a much broader readership that relished the guides' wit and inquisitiveness as much as their enthusiastic, critical approach and value-for-money ethos.

These days, Rough Guides include recommendations from budget to luxury and cover more than 200 destinations around the globe, as well as producing an ever-growing range of eBooks and apps.

Visit **roughguides.com** to see our latest publications.

Rough Guide credits

Editor: Ann-Marie Shaw
Layout: Nikhil Agarwal and Pradeep Thapliyal
Cartography: Animesh Pathak
Picture editor: Tim Draper
Proofreader: Diane Margolis
Managing editor: Monica Woods
Assistant editor: Jalpreen Kaur Chhatwal
Production: Charlotte Cade
Cover design: Nicole Newman, Dan May, Nikhil Agarwal
Editorial assistant: Olivia Rawes

Senior pre-press designer: Dan May
Design director: Scott Stickland
Travel publisher: Joanna Kirby
Digital travel publisher: Peter Buckley
Reference director: Andrew Lockett
Operations coordinator: Becky Doyle
Publishing director (Travel): Clare Currie
Commercial manager: Gino Magnotta
Managing director: John Duhigg

Publishing information

This eleventh edition published March 2013 by
Rough Guides Ltd,
80 Strand, London WC2R 0RL
11, Community Centre, Panchsheel Park,
New Delhi 110017, India
Distributed by the Penguin Group
Penguin Books Ltd,
80 Strand, London WC2R 0RL
Penguin Group (USA)
375 Hudson Street, NY 10014, USA
Penguin Group (Australia)
250 Camberwell Road, Camberwell,
Victoria 3124, Australia
Penguin Group (NZ)
67 Apollo Drive, Mairangi Bay, Auckland 1310,
New Zealand
Penguin Group (South Africa)
Block D, Rosebank Office Park, 181 Jan Smuts Avenue,
Parktown North, Gauteng, South Africa 2193
Rough Guides is represented in Canada by Tourmaline
Editions Inc. 662 King Street West, Suite 304, Toronto,
Ontario M5V 1M7
Printed in Singapore by Toppan Security Printing Pte. Ltd.
© Robert Andrews, Ros Belford, Jonathan Buckley, Martin
Dunford, Tim Jepson, Lucy Ratcliffe and Celia Woolfrey, 2013

MIX
Paper from
responsible sources
FSC™ C018179

Help us update

We've gone to a lot of effort to ensure that the eleventh
edition of **The Rough Guide to Italy** is accurate and
up-to-date. However, things change – places get
"discovered", opening hours are notoriously fickle,
restaurants and rooms raise prices or lower standards.
If you feel we've got it wrong or left something out,
we'd like to know, and if you can remember the address,
the price, the hours, the phone number, so much the better.

Please send your comments with the subject line
"**Rough Guide Italy Update**" to ✉ mail@uk.roughguides
.com. We'll credit all contributions and send a copy of
the next edition (or any other Rough Guide if you prefer)
for the very best emails.

Find more travel information, connect with fellow
travellers and book your trip on ⓦ roughguides.com

ABOUT THE AUTHORS

Robert Andrews visits southern Italy two or three times a year and has worked on Rough Guides to Sicily and Sardinia, as well as various UK titles.

Ros Belford co-authored the first edition of this guide, and has since written and broadcast extensively about Italy and the Mediterranean. She has two daughters and spends as much time as she can on the Aeolian Island of Salina.

Jonathan Buckley has written and contributed to several Rough Guides and has published eight novels. He is a fellow of the Royal Literary Fund.

Martin Dunford is one of the founders of Rough Guides and has worked in travel publishing for three decades. He travels to Italy at least once every year and is the author of more than ten guidebooks; he was publisher of Rough Guides for many years before leaving to pursue freelance and other travel interests and now works as a freelance writer and as a publishing and digital consultant to the travel industry. He is an investor and entrepreneur, with two digital travel start-up businesses – ⓦtripbod.com and ⓦcoolplaces.co.uk. When not on the road, he lives in Blackheath, London, with his wife and two daughters, and in Norfolk, where he and his family go to canoe, sail and mess around on the beach.

Natasha Foges was born and brought up in North London, studied English and Latin Literature at university and worked as a teacher for several years. She moved to Italy for a year in 2003 and ended up staying for four, during which time she took on an array of jobs, from paparazzo's assistant to Latin teacher, before trying her hand at travel journalism. Now back in London and a Senior Editor at Rough Guides, she returns as often as she can, both for research purposes and to get her fix of proper Italian ice cream.

Lucy Ratcliffe is a freelance travel writer and editor. She has been visiting and writing about the Lakes region of northern Italy for over twelve years and is the author of several guides to the area. She now shares her time between Bergamo and Barcelona.

Celia Woolfrey co-wrote the first edition of the guide and has enjoyed many journeys around Italy since. Based in London, she is a journalist and web consultant (@towerofturtles, ⓦcardie.co.uk).

Acknowledgements

Robert Andrews I would like to give loads of thanks to QBC for invaluable insights and great company, and to Eveline and Carlo in Calabria and Mario Zizi on Mount Ortobene, Sardinia, for generous hospitality.

Ros Belford Thanks to Izzy and Juno for everything. To Emma, Gaetano, Max, Ilana, Chiara, Alex, Corallina and Ondina Zangari for moral support, welcome distraction and a corkscrew. To Seby and Silvia at Il Blu in Ortigia for fuelling the book with apricot proseccos, and to all at La Cambusa on Salina for letting me use the terrace as my office. Above all thanks to Andrea for making everything alright again.

Marc Di Duca *Grazie* to all who helped me along the way in Italy, especially the dedicated staff at tourist offices in Ancona, Macerata, Merano, Bolzano, Trento and Rovereto. Thanks to Andy and Monica at Rough Guides and to my editor Ann-Marie, as well as to my fellow authors for their input. Huge thanks also to my Kiev in-laws for looking after son Taras while I was travelling, and to my wife Tanya.

Martin Dunford I would like to thank everyone in Italy who helped me along the way; my family – Caroline, Daisy and Lucy – who were there in spirit; and Annie Shaw – a real pleasure to be working together again after all this time.

Natasha Foges I would like to thank editor Annie Shaw for being a pleasure to work with; Ed Wright, cartographer *per eccellenza*, for his advice on maps; Kate Zagorski for her invaluable help with Emilia-Romagna; Harriet Foges for her company in Abruzzo, and for her calm in the face of various brushes with the *carabinieri*; Rudy for coming along for the ride, and not complaining once; and Will Widén for giving up his holidays yet again, and for approaching everything (from hire-car mishaps to earthquakes) with cheerful good humour.

Charles Hebbert I would like to thank Diamante and Vittorio, Maria Teresa and Leonardo, Bob and Jenny in Vicenza, and Caroline for all her help.

Lucy Ratcliffe I would once again like to thank Stefania Gatta from the Italian State Tourism, Roberto Ricca from Brescia Tourism and Irene Lilla from Distretto dei Laghi for all their help and Luca, Charlotte and Nico for their dedication to ice cream tasting.

Jo-Ann Titmarsh I'd like to thank Erika Carpeneto at the Turismo Torino office for her huge contribution to the update, and Maurizio Distasi at the Aosta Tourist Office for his help and advice. Thanks to Battista Cornaglia of Casa Scaparone and the staff of Grand Hotel Sitea for their kind hospitality.

Readers' letters

Thanks to all the readers who have taken the time to write in with comments and suggestions (and apologies if we've inadvertently omitted or misspelt anyone's name):

John Bensley, Eric Dunkerley, Christopher Hamilton, Norma McCann, B.R. Shepherd, Janet Young.

Photo credits

All photos © Rough Guides except the following:
(Key: t-top; c-centre; b-bottom; l-left; r-right)

p.1 Martin Rietze/Barcroft Media/Getty Images
p.4 Danita Delimont/Getty Images
p.5 Nadia Isakova/Corbis
p.9 Image Source/Getty Images (t); Travel Ink/Getty Images (b)
p.11 Slow Images/Getty Images
p.12 Giuseppe Bellini/Getty Images)
p.13 Antonio Moreno/Getty Images
p.14 William Cho/Getty Images
p.15 Matz Sjoeberg/Getty Images (t)
p.16 Valentino Grassi (Ideas in Motion)/Getty Images (t); Byzantine School/Getty Images (b)
p.17 David Madison/Getty Images (br)
p.18 Adam Jones/Getty Images (tl); Giovanni Guarino/Getty Images (tr); Matteo Colombo/Getty Images (b)
p.19 Luca Da Ros/Corbis (t); Getty Images (c); Sylvain Sonnet/Corbis (b)
p.20 SuperStock)/Getty Images (t); Anna Henly/Getty Images (b)
p.21 Richard Broadwell/Alamy (t); DEA/G.Carfagna/Getty Images (b)
p.22 Mario Cipriani/Atlantide Phototravel/Corbis (t); Carlo Morucchio/Getty Images (b)
p.24 Cornelia Doerr/Getty Images (tl); Chris Parker/Getty Images (tr)
p.26 Vittorio Zunino Celotto/Getty Images
p.50 Gavin Hellier/Getty Images
p.79 isphotoart/Getty Images
p.117 VisionsofAmerica/Joe Sohm/Getty Images (tl)
p.136 Yvan Travert/Getty Images
p.139 Damiano Levati/Getty Images
p.155 Alessandro Rizzi/Getty Images (t); Gege Gatt/Getty Images (b)
p.174 Alan Copson/Getty Images
p.177 Vincenzo Lombardo/Getty Images
p.199 Blend Images/PBNJ Productions/Getty Images
p.302 Peter Adams/Getty Images
p.305 Maremagnum/Getty Images

p.321 Matteo Colombo/Getty Images
p.432 Guy Vanderelst/Getty Images
p.435 DEA/E. Lessing/Getty Images
p.445 Slow Images/Getty Images
p.460 Travel Pictures/Alamy
p.463 DEA/G. Sosio/Getty Images
p.481 Getty Images
p.674 Miles Ertman/Getty Images
p.677 Peter Adams/Getty Images
p.693 DEA/Getty Images (t); Jon Arnold Images/Getty Images (b)
p.710 peetjohn/Getty Images
p.713 DEA/A. De Gregorio/DeAgostini/Getty Images
p.729 Rino Savastano/Getty Images (t); Paul Oomen/Getty Images (b)
p.736 Mark Thomas/Getty Images
p.739 Slow Images/Getty Images
p.765 Panoramic Images/Getty Images (t); Jon Spaull/Getty Images (c); Samuel Magal/Getty Images (b)
p.797 Slow Images/Getty Images
p.801 Rocielma/Getty Images
p.817 Rudi Sebastian/Getty Images
p.838 Peter Adams/Getty Images
p.841 DEA/G. Nimatallah/Getty Images
p.851 LatitudeStock/Ron Badkin/Getty Images (t); Vincenzo Lombardo/Getty Images (b)
p.871 Slow Images/Getty Images
p.927 Design Pics/Patrick Swan/Getty Images (b)
p.940 Vladimir Pcholkin/Getty Images
p.943 Doug Pearson/Getty Images
p.955 Danita Delimont/Getty Images (t); Franz Pritz/Getty Images

Front cover Blue Vespa © David Sutherland/Corbis
Back cover Canal Grande, Venice © Visions Of Our Land/Getty Images (t); Countryside, Tuscany © Slow Images/Getty Images; Palazzo Altemps, Rome © Rough Guides

Index

Maps are marked in grey

Map symbols

The symbols below are used on maps throughout the book

✈	Airport	♦	Place of interest	⊠	Gate	∩	Arc
★	Bus/taxi	∴	Ruin	🍇	Vineyard/winery	☥	Church (regional maps)
Ⓜ	Metro station	✡	Synagogue	⌣	Bridge	▮	Building
@	Internet café/access	⊙	Statue	≈	Swimming pool/area	⊡	Church
ⓘ	Information office	⛪	Monastery	▲	Mountain peak	⬭	Stadium
☎	Telephone office	ⵣ	Gardens	⋀⋀	Mountain range	⊡	Christian cemetery
Ⓟ	Parking	☡	Lighthouse	⌒	Cave	▯	Beach
✛	Hospital	♜	Castle	☇	Viewpoint	⬭	Park
✉	Post office	⋀	Campsite	⛴	Boat	●–●●	Cable car
⌂	Abbey	�🏛	Archeological site	⚓	Ferry/boat stop	⋯⋯	Funicular

Listings key

- ■ Accommodation
- ● Restaurant/café
- ■ Bar/pub/club
- ● Shop

ROUGH
GUIDES

WE GET AROUND

ONLINE start your journey at roughguides.com

EBOOKS & MOBILE APPS

GUIDEBOOKS from Amsterdam to Zanzibar

PHRASEBOOKS learn the lingo

MAPS so you don't get lost

GIFTBOOKS inspiration is our middle name

LIFESTYLE from iPads to climate change

...SO
YOU
CAN
TOO

BOOKS | EBOOKS | APPS
Start your journey at **roughguides.com**

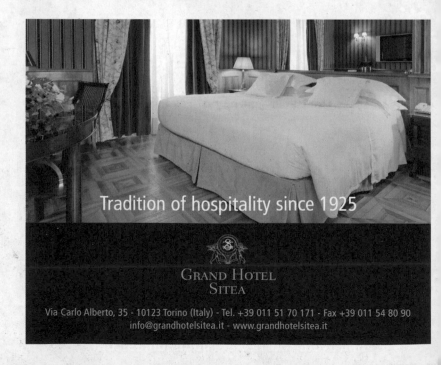